Historical Common Names

of Great Plains Plants,

with Scientific Names Index

Volume I: Common Names

Compiled by Elaine Nowick

Zea Books
Lincoln, Nebraska
2015

Title page: *Tripsacum dactyloides* (Gamagrass) by Frank Lamson-Scribner, 1897.

Historical Common Names of Great Plains Plants, with Scientific Names Index:
Volume I: Common Names

Copyright © 2015 Elaine Nowick.

ISBN 978-1-60962-062-2   hardcover
ISBN 978-1-60962-058-5   paperback
ISBN 978-1-60962-059-2   e-book

Set in Times New Roman types.
Design and composition by Paul Royster.
Illustrations are based on published originals
found online at www.plantillustrations.org

Zea Books are published by the
University of Nebraska–Lincoln Libraries.

Electronic edition (pdf) available online at http://digitalcommons.unl.edu/zeabook/
Print edition can be ordered from http://www.lulu.com/spotlight/unllib

Contents

Eupatorium perfoliatum (Joe Pye weed)
[C.F. Millspaugh, 1892]

Preface

Although the term "common names" occurs in the title of this book, there are relatively few plants known to the majority of people. Many individuals today suffer from "plant blindness" and don't really notice the plant life around them. Some environmentalists look to a past golden age when people were more in tune with the natural world. In the millennia before agriculture, our species and our hominid ancestors survived by hunting and gathering. Being able to recognize edible and poisonous plants would have been a vital skill for them, as it is for all animal species except strict carnivores. It is not known when speech first evolved, but plant names were most likely among the earliest words. As Gilmore (1932) states, "Indigenous peoples always have names for the plants they use and even the ones they don't use but are aware of." Most of these ancient names have been lost in the sands of time.

From the onset of agriculture about 10,000 years ago until the mid-twentieth century, most of the human species survived by farming. Survival came to depend on the few cultivated species, and humankind's attention shifted to those species and their weedy pests. The exceptions were often the herbal practitioners. Among Europeans up until the Middle Ages, and among other peoples around the world, healers were often the most knowledgeable about botany. Even among formally trained medical doctors until quite recently, botany was an integral part of their training. Writers of herbals and pharmacopeias were very concerned that herbal practitioners and herb gatherers be able to identify accurately the correct plant species to be used to treat a specific ailment, and modern editors of ancient herbals can often reliably assign a contemporary scientific name to plants from their descriptions.

The age of exploration greatly accelerated the movement of plant species around the world. The earliest Europeans to arrive in the New World were very interested in the plant species used by the indigenous peoples. Plant species from the Americas began appearing in herbals around the 1600's. Early European settlers often adopted the native names, sometimes in garbled form. The Joe Pye weed (*Eupatorium perfoliatum* L. or *Eupatorium purpureum* L.) is an example. The original Native American name was said to be "jopi." Homesickness may have led some Europeans to give names familiar to them to similar but unrelated plants, such as the Evening-primrose (*Oenothera*) which is not related to the European primrose (*Primula*). Europeans also invented names for the new plants they observed. Some of the earliest botanical explorers in the Americas were sponsored by wealthy Europeans wanting the distinction of owning rare or unusual plants for their gardens and conservatories. Collectors such as John Banister, John and William Bartram, Frederick Pursh, André and François Michaux, and Peer Kalm sent herbarium samples, plants, seeds, and cuttings to nurseries, gardens, and institutions throughout Europe. The proliferation of known types of plants and also of names for them created an awareness of the need for proper identification and a uniform terminology. Common names were often confusing. The same name could be used for several different species and several names could be used for the same species. Plant names for the same species often differed by locality or dialect. Educated people of the time used Latin as their common language and in communicating about plants they used lengthy Latin descriptions. Tournefort, the Bauhins, and others provided detailed but cumbersome descriptions of the new plants species they were cataloging. Linnaeus is generally credited with creating the Latin binomial system. His "Genera Plantarum" published in 1737 and "Species Plantarum" in 1753 serve as the basis for scientific plant names now in use. One of the beauties of the Latin binomial system is that it not only simplifies the Latin descriptions, but also reflects relationships among plant species. All species in the given genus have a close morphological similarity and later research has often revealed genetic similarities that for the most part support these relationships. Often, Linnaeus' scientific names were adapted from the classical Greek or Latin name for the species or a closely related plant, but often were quite arbitrary and may have said little about the named species itself.

For many Great Plains and Western species, scientific names predate common names, at least in European languages, unlike plant species from Europe and eastern North America. The first Europeans to arrive in the Great Plains and the West were the Spanish in the southern range and the French trappers arriving from the north. But even before the Europeans arrived, their influence on the region was being felt. The arrival of the first horses, the descendants of horses escaped from the early Spanish explorers, brought huge cultural changes. Displacements of indigenous people from the East caused waves of war and social disruption to radiate into the Plains and Rocky Mountains. European diseases preceded movement of people and devastated the native tribes. These changes surely would have been accompanied by changes in language referring to plants, disruptions in the passing of knowledge about the uses of plants, and unfortunately loss of knowledge of plant life as long-term residents of the environment were pushed out. Works on ethnobotany and journals of early botanical explorers often recorded native names when they were aware of them. The explorers' journals also sometimes provided Spanish, French, or German names for Great Plains and Western flora. The spelling and tribal designations in this book are as reported in the original work. Later works by anthropologists and ethnobotanists were also consulted for current plant names of Native Americans.

The Lewis and Clark Expedition to explore the northern limits of the Louisiana Purchase ushered in a fifty-year period of government-sponsored scientific surveys of botany, geology, zoology and general natural history in the western territories, inspired by the visionary Thomas Jefferson. Lewis, Clark, and the other journal keepers of the Corps of Discovery recorded native plant names and noted plants they recognized on the way. Closely following Lewis and Clark, were collectors such as Thomas Nuttall, Constantine Rafinesque, and John Bradbury. Travelers such as Josiah Gregg, Henry Marie Brackenridge, and Prince Maximilian were broadly educated and took great interest in natural history and anthropology, noting the plant species they observed and their native uses. Many of Lewis and Clark's species were described after much delay by Frederich Pursh, who also collected botanical samples in the eastern United States. The Lewis and Clark expedition was succeeded by a series of military-led scientific explorations following the courses of the major rivers in the Great Plains and then by the railroad surveys attempting to find the best route to the Pacific by rail. These surveys included botanists, zoologists, and geologists, as well as surveyors.

The Civil War put an end to these surveys, but the Hatch Act passed by Congress in 1862 set in motion an entirely new phase in plant research. The founding of the "People's Universities" put science at the service of the common person. The land grant universities were given a mission not only to perform serious scientific research, but also to translate that research into a form that ordinary farmers could use to improve their lives. The publications of the land grant universities and the cooperative extension services in the Plains states were rich sources of information for this dictionary. The extension agents and university professors were anxious both to identify accurately the species mentioned and to enable the common people to recognize them by using local names for the species.

In the 1800's a number of periodicals dealing with botany were published in the United States, and these were also used as sources of names. In the late 1800's quite a few popular guides to wildflowers were published. As settlers became established in the western United States, some of them became better educated and had more time to spend on activities beyond the basics of life. The appearance of these botanical guides may also reflect an increasing alienation from the natural world—there is an underlying assumption in these works that the readers would not be familiar with the wildflowers and not have either common or scientific names for them.

It is a myth that each species has one and only one, permanent and unique scientific name. For example, the USDA Plants Database (http://plants.usda.gov/) lists 21 scientific synonyms for *Calamagrostis stricta* subsp. *inexpansa* (northern reedgrass). Linnaeus and his contemporaries believed that species were static and permanently distinct, although the differences might be subtle. Darwin's *On the Origin of Species* was published in 1859; his revolutionary idea was that species changed through time. We now know that species do evolve, and that populations within a species can diverge, and that there are degrees of plant-to-plant variation within a species arising from genetic differences and environmental effects. During the 1700s, when new plants were arriving in Europe at a very fast rate, communications were slow and unreliable, so it is not surprising that some species designations have needed revision. New techniques such as chromosome karyotyping, biochemical analysis, and DNA sequencing have shed further light on taxonomic relations.

One of the great strengths of the binomial system is that there is a mechanism for determining the "correct" name for each species and publishing the accepted name as well as its Latin synonyms. The *International Code of Botanical Nomenclature* as adopted by the International Botanical Congress is updated periodically. Names of new or revised species are created and disseminated in accord with the code. For this work the references used for contemporary Latin names and synonyms unless otherwise noted were: The Plants Database (http://plants.usda.gov) published by the USDA; W3Tropicos (http://www.tropicos.org/) from the Missouri Botanic Gardens; and the International Plant Names Index (http://www.ipni.org/), a joint project of the Royal Botanic Gardens, Kew Gardens, the Harvard University Herbaria, and the Australian National Herbarium.

While scientists were adopting the system of Latin binomials, common names continued to be created and are still invented even today. Latin binomials are the best way for scientists to communicate with one another about plant species, but common names have both interest and value, and there is a great deal of information embedded within common names. They record the relation of humans to a particular plant species, and they are accessible to people who are not formally trained in botany. Some academic researchers had mixed feelings or even hostility towards common names. John Torrey and Asa Gray are considered to be the joint parents of American botany. In one of his botanical reports attached to the railroad surveys, Torrey condescendingly states, "There is, however, little dependence to be placed on the common names of plants, especially among rude and ignorant people." Nathaniel Britton and Addison Brown, on the other hand, saw no antagonism between common and scientific names and felt that, "they [popular names] are invaluable; not for science, but for the common intelligence, and the appreciation and enjoyment of the plant world."

There have been occasional efforts to standardize common names. The Pharmacopeias and Dispensatories used conventionalized vocabularies usually in English for the plant species used as medicinals. Several associations representing the nursery industry, landscape architects, florists and other horticulturists formed the American Joint Committee on Horticultural Nomenclature. This committee issued several editions of standardized plant names. In the second edition of *Standardized Plant Names*, Harlan Kelsey, Secretary of the American Joint Committee on Horticultural Nomenclature recognizes the value of common names while acknowledging their limitations.

> "In this 1942 edition of STANDARDIZED PLANT NAMES the editors have adopted what seemed the best common names for plants and plant products so far as was feasible at this time. Many thousands of new names were supplied for plants that had no common names, or with common names wholly unsuitable or more properly belonging to other plants.
>
> "In thousands of other cases, especially of plants new or little known, common names are missing, for an appropriate name suggests itself usually only on intimate acquaintance with the particular plant or with its history."

Some botanists have included English names in their works, more rightly called vernacular names than common names, since they are often direct translations of the Latin scientific name. Britton and Brown, Thomas Meehan, and others admit that they made up likely common names for species when they didn't know of one. As Liberty Hyde Bailey states, "One cannot 'make' common names, although one may coin an English name. A name is not common until it comes into general use. Most plants do not possess true common names."[1] Nevertheless, in this work there has been no attempt to distinguish between vernacular and true common names.

What's in a common name? Why bother with names that may be confusing or misleading and in some cases racist,

sexist, or otherwise insensitive? As John Smith (1882) says "With regard to the adoption of common, or what are termed popular, names, it is unfortunate that many of them are vulgar and undignified, and derogatory to the useful, pretty, and curious plants which they designate…" In their defense, common names often reflect knowledge of a plant species' ecology. Common names may also refer to the appearance of the plant, its taste, or its use. While common names may refer to the function of a plant in relation to humans, rather than to anything about the plant itself, this still may be more telling than a scientific name given as a tribute to a person who may have had no relation either to the named species or the region. Scientific names have also rather arbitrarily been given for a species' resemblance to another species more familiar to the namer. Yet other scientific names are based on classical names for either different plant species or unknown species. No one would argue for a preference for common names in the scientific literature, but in a time when humans are becoming increasingly "plant-blind" and detached from the natural world, encouraging the use of current common names and even creation of new ones may encourage humans to look again at the ultimate source of all their nourishment and of even the air they breathe.

It is hoped that this reference work will be of use to historians, writers of historical fiction or natural history, restorationists, and the general public. This dictionary was compiled from first person accounts of early explorers and plant collectors. When they were available or when the original writer did not include a scientific name, later editions with appropriate footnotes were used. Other sources include floras, extension publications, government reports, botanical periodicals, earlier common name compilations, wildflower guides, and other publications. Dates and locations are included when appropriate. The dates are the reporting dates since it would not be possible to accurately determine when a name came into existence or became archaic. Explanations for the common names are included if they are known. Common name spellings are according to Kartesz and Thieret.[2] Alternate spelling are enclosed in parentheses. Readers are encouraged to send additions to these names if they are aware of them to the author for inclusion in later editions. Please include as much information as possible.

Elaine Nowick
Cañon City, Colorado
April 2014

1. Bailey, L. H. 1933. *How plants get their names.* New York: MacMillan Co.
2. Kartesz, John T. and John W. Thieret. 1991. Common names for vascular plants: Guidelines for use and application. *Sida* 14(3):421–434.

Echinacea purpurea [Rudbeckia purpurea] (Purple coneflower, Red sunflower)
[W.P.C. Barton, 1823]

Acknowledgments

This work would not have been possible without the online availability of many sources consulted, including the Biological Heritage Library and several taxonomic databases among others. In the past, consulting many of these sources would have involved traveling to archives where they are housed. Now they are available to everyone. I also am especially grateful to the Wyoming Heritage Center and the University of Nebraska Library Archives for access to their materials.

Sue Ann Gardner, Linnea Fredrickson, and Paul Royster of University of Nebraska Libraries Office of Scholarly Communications have provided patient editing and generous preparation of the online and print editions. This work was begun as a sabbatical project funded by the University of Nebraska and I am grateful for continuing support in hosting the electronic version.

Taraxacum officinale (Aphaka, Blow-ball, Cankerwort, Caput monach, Couronne de moine, Dandelion, Doonhead, Grunsel, Irish daisy, Lion's tooth, Milk gowan, Monk's head, One-o'clock, Papencruitz, Pissabed, Puffball, Swine's snout, Wild endive, Witch gowan)
[Martin Cilenšek, 1892]

References

1. Rydberg, Per Axel. 1932. *Flora of the Prairie and Plains of Central North America*. Lancaster, Pa: Science Press Printing Co.

2. Gray, Asa, revised and extended by L.H. Bailey. 1895. *Field, Forest, and Garden Botany: A Simple introduction to the common plants of the United States East of the 100th Meridian, both wild and cultivated*. New York: American Book Company.

3. Great Plains Flora Association. 1977. *Atlas of the Flora of the Great Plains*. Coordinator, R.L. McGregor; Editor, T.M. Barkley. Ames: Iowa State University Press.

4. Macgregor, Ronald L., T.M. Barkley, and the Great Plains Flora Association. 1986. *Flora of the Great Plains*. University Press of Kansas.

5. Britton, N., and Addison Brown. 1913. *An Illustrated Flora of the Northern United States and Canada from Newfoundland to the Parallel of the Southern Boundary of Virginia and from the Atlantic Ocean Westward to the 102d Meridian*. New York: Dover Publications, 1970.

6. Millspaugh, Charles F. 1974. *American Medicinal Plants; An Illustrated and Descriptive Guide to Plants Indigenous to and Naturalized in the United States which are Used in Medicine*. New York: Dover Publ. reprint of 1892 ed.

7. Rafinesque, C.S. 1828. *Medical Flora or Manual of the Medical Botany of the United States of North America. Containing a selection of above 100 figures and descriptions of medical plants, with their names, qualities, properties, history, &c.: and notes or remarks on nearly 500 equivalent substitutes*. Philadelphia: Atkinson & Alexander.

8. Marshall, Humphry. 1785. *Arbustum Americanum: The American Grove or, and Alphabetical Catalogue of Forest Trees and Shrubs, Native of the American United States, Arranged According to the Linnaean System*. Containing, the particular distinguishing Characters of each Genus, with plain simple and familiar Descriptions of the Manner of Growth, Appearance, etc. of their several Species and Varieties. Also some hints of their uses in Medicine, Dyes, and Domestic Oeconomy (Facsimile of the edition of 1785), and *Catalogue Alphabetique des Arbres et Arbrisseaux* (Facsimile of the edition of 1788). New York: Hafner Publishing Co. 1967.

9. Charles E. Bessey. Papers (1865-1915). University of Nebraska-Lincoln.

10. Nuttall, Thomas. 1818. *The Genera of North American Plants and a Catalogue of the Species to the Year 1817*. Philadelphia: D. Heart.

11. Bessey, Charles E. 1888. *The Grasses and Forage Plants of Nebraska*. Annual Report of the State Board of Agriculture for the year 1887, pages 140-172. Prepared by Robert W. Furnas, Secretary Nebraska State Board of Agriculture Lincoln Neb: State Journal Company Printers.

12. Nuttall, Thomas. 1821. *Journal of the Travels into the Arkansa Territory during the Year 1819 with Occasional Observations on the Manners of the Aborigines*. Philadelphia: Thos. H. Palmer.

13. Gray, Asa. 1849. *The Genera of the Plants of the United States*, illustrated by figures and analyses from nature by Isaac Sprague. New York: George P. Putnam.

14. Smith, John. 1882. *Dictionary of Popular Names of the Plants which Furnish the Natural and Acquired Wants of Man, in All Matters of Domestic and General Economy: Their History, Products, & Uses*. London: Macmillan and Co.

15. Gray, Asa, Sereno Watson continued, and edited by Benjamin Lincoln Robinson. 1895. *Synoptical Flora of North America*. New York: American Book Co.

16. Nuttall, Thomas. 1837. Collections towards a Flora of the Territory of Arkansas. *Transactions of the American Philosophical Society*, new series. Volume 5, part 6, pages 139-203.

17. *Journal of André Michaux, 1793-1796*. 1889. Source: Englished from the original French, appearing in American Philosophical Society, *Proceedings*, 1889, pages 91-101, 114-140, from Reuben Gold Thwaites. 1904. Early Western Travels 1748-1846.

18. Michaux, François André. 1904. *Travels to the West of the Alleghany Mountains*. Reprint from London edition 1805 from Reuben Gold Thwaites. Early Western Travels 1748-1846.

19. Eaton, Amos, and John Wright. 1840. *North American Botany Comprising the Native and Common Cultivated Plants North of Mexico: Genera Arranged According*

to the Artificial and Natural Methods. Troy, New York: Elias Gates.

20. Michaux, François André. 1857. *North American Sylva or a Description of the Forest Trees of the United States, Canada, and Nova Scotia Considered Particularly with Respect to Their Use in the Arts and Their Introduction to Commerce to which is Added a Description of the Most Useful of the European Forest Trees.* Translated from the French of François André Michaux. Philadelphia: D. Rice & A. N. Hart.

21. Edith S. and Frederic E. Clements papers, 1893-1967. Accession Number 1678, Box Number 36, Folder Number 13, American Heritage Center, University of Wyoming Laramie, Wyoming.

22. Edith S. and Frederic E. Clements papers, 1893-1967. Accession Number 1678, Box Number 48, Folder Number 1, American Heritage Center, University of Wyoming Laramie, Wyoming.

23. Graustein, Jeannette E. (editor). 1950/51. Nuttall's travels into the Old Northwest: An unpublished 1810 diary. *Cronica Botanic*, Volume 14(1/2).

24. Nuttall, Thomas. 1817. Observation on the genus Eriogonum, and the natural order Polygonae of Jussieu. *Journal of the Academy of Natural Sciences of Philadelphia*, Volume 1, number 3: 24-37.

25. Nuttall, Thomas, and Nathaniel J. Wyeth. 1834. A catalogue of a collection of plants made chiefly in the valleys of the Rocky Mountains or Northern Andes, towards the sources of the Columbia River, by Mr. Nathaniel B. Wyeth. *Journal of the Academy of Natural Sciences Philadelphia*, Volume 7: [5]-60, 8 leaves of plates.

26. Torrey, John. 1826. *A compendium of the Flora of the Northern and Middle States.* New York: S.B. Collins, Selected Americana from Sabin.

27. Bradbury, John. 1986. *Travels in the Interior of America in the Years 1809, 1810, and 1811.* Bison book reprint. Originally published London: Sherwood, Neely, and Jones, 1819.

28. Fremont, J.C. Brevet, Col. 1850. *The Exploring Expedition to the Rocky Mountains, Oregon, and California to which is Added a Description of the Physical Geography of California with Recent Notices of the Gold Region from the Latest and most Authentic Sources.*

29. Pursh, Frederick. 1869. *Journal of a Botanical Excursion in the Northeastern Parts of the States of Pennsylvania and New York during the Year 1807.* Reprinted in 1969 by Ira J. Friedman, Inc. Port Washington, Long Island, New York, Empire State Historical Publications Series, number 73.

30. Josiah, Gregg. 1954. *Commerce of the Prairies*, edited by Max L. Moorhead. Norman, Oklahoma: University of Oklahoma Press. Originally published in 1844.

31. *Diary & Letters of Josiah Gregg: Southwestern Enterprises, 1840-1847.* Edited by Maurice Garland Fulton. Norman, Oklahoma: University of Oklahoma Press, 1941.

32. Rydberg, Per Axel. 1895. *Botanical Exploration of Central Nebraska.* Thesis presented by Per Axel Rydberg for the degree of Master of Arts, University of Nebraska, 1895.

33. Royal Horticultural Society. 1914. *Journal Kept by David Douglas during his Travels in North America, 1823-1827, Together with a Particular Description of Thirty-Three Species of American Oaks and Eighteen Species of* Pinus. London: William Wesley & Son.

34. Maximilian, Alexander Philipp, Prince. 1843. *Travels in the Interior of North America in the Years 1832, 1833, and 1834.* London: [s.n.], 1844.

35. Moulton, Gary E. (editor). 1986. *The Journals of the Lewis & Clark Expedition.* Lincoln: University of Nebraska Press.

36. Wislizenus, F.A. 1912. *A Journey to the Rocky Mountains in the Year 1830.* St. Louis: Missouri Historical Society.

37. Gilmore, Melvin R. *Uses of Plants by the Indians of the Missouri River Region.* Reprint of the 1919 edition. Lincoln: University of Nebraska Press.

38. James, Edwin (compiler). 1823. *Account of an Expedition from Pittsburgh to the Rocky Mountains Performed in the Years 1819 and '20* by order of the Hon. J.C. Calhoun, Sec'y of War, under the command of Major Stephen H. Long, from the notes of Major Long, Mr. T. Say, and other gentlemen of the exploring party. Philadelphia: H.C. Carey and I. Lea.

39. Brackenridge, Henri Marie. 1814. *Views of Louisiana, Together with a Journal of a Voyage up the Missouri River in 1811.* Chicago: Quadrangle Books, [1962].

40. Densmore, Frances. 1928. *Uses of Plants by the Chippewa*, pages 275-397 in *Forty-fourth Annual Report of the Bureau of Ethnology to the Secretary of the Smithsonian Institution*, 1926-1927. Washington: U.S. Government Printing Office.

41. *The America of 1750: Peters Kalm's Travels in North America*, the English edition of 1770. New York: Dover Publications, Inc. 1937, 1964.

42. Green, Jacob. 1814. *An Address on the Botany of the United States*, delivered before the Society for the Promotion of Useful Arts. To which is added *A Catalogue of Plants Indigenous to the State of New York.* Albany: Websters and Skinners.

43. Williams, Mentor L. (editor). 1992. *Schoolcraft's Narrative Journal of Travels through the Northwestern Regions of the United States extending from Detroit through the Great Chain of American Lakes to the Sources of the Mississippi River in the Year 1820.* East Lansing: Michigan State University Press.

44. Carroll, H. Bailey (editor). 1941. *Gúadal p'a: The Journal of J.W. Abert, from Bent's Fort to St. Louis in 1845.* Canyon, Texas: The Panhandle-Plains Historical Society.

45. Beal, W.J. 1896. *Grasses of North America.* New York: Henry Holt and Co.

46. Pickering, Charles. 1879. *Chronological History of Plants: Man's Record of his Own Existence Illustrated through their Names, Uses, and Companionship.* Boston: Little, Brown & Co.

47. Owen, Daid Dale, et al. 1852. *Report of a Geological Survey of Wisconsin, Iowa, and Minnesota; and Incidentally of a Portion of Nebraska Territory.* Philadelphia: Lippincott, Grambo & Co.

48. Welch, J. Milton. 1882/92. The Medical Flora of Kansas or, the Medical Plants Indigenous in That State. *Transactions of the National Eclectic Medical Association.* http://www.henriettesherbal.com/eclectic/journals/net-1882-kansas.html (Mar. 10, 2006).

49. Felter, Harvey Wickes, and John Uri Lloyd. 1898. *King's American Dispensatory.* Scanned version, 1999-2005. Henriette Kress, copyright. http://www.ibiblio.org/herbmed/eclectic/kings/main.html (August 9, 2005).

50. USDA, NRCS. 2014. The PLANTS Database. http://plants.usda.gov (March 31, 2014). Greensboro, North Carolina: National Plant Data Team.

51. *Selected North Dakota and Minnesota Range Plants.* http://www.ext.nodak.edu/extpubs/ansci/range/eb69-1.htm#North (January 16, 2004).

52. Ellingwood, Finley. 1919. *American Materia Medica.* Scanned version copyright 2001-2004, Michael Moore. http://www.ibiblio.org/herbmed/eclectic/ellingwood/main.html (June 2, 2004).

53. Felter, Harvey Wickes. 1922. *The Eclectic Materia Medica, Pharmacology and Therapeutics.* http://www.ibiblio.org/herbmed/eclectic/felter/main.html (June 7, 2004).

54. Petersen, Fred J. 1905. *Materia Medica and Clinical Therapeutics.* http://www.ibiblio.org/herbmed/eclectic/petersen/main.html (June 9, 2004).

55. Council of the Pharmaceutical Society of Great Britain. 1911. *British Pharmaceutical Codex.* http://www.ibiblio.org/herbmed/eclectic/bpc1911/main.html (June 10, 2004).

56. Pammel, L.H., and J.B. Weems. 1901. *Grasses of Iowa.* Ames, Iowa: Iowa Geological Survey, *Bulletin* No. 1.

57. Sayre, Lucius E. 1917. *A Manual of Organic Materia Medica and Pharmacognosy.* http://www.ibiblio.org/herbmed/eclectic/sayre/main.html (June 22, 2004).

58. Cook, William, 1869. *Physiomedical Dispensatory.* http://www.ibiblio.org/herbmed/eclectic/cook/cook.htm (June 23, 2004).

59. Lloyd, John Uri. 1911. *History of the Vegetable Drugs of the Pharmacopoeia of the United States.* http://www.ibiblio.org/herbmed/eclectic/lloyd-hist/main.html (June 27, 2004).

60. Potter, Samuel O.L. 1902. *Compendium of Materia Medica, Therapeutics, and Prescription Writing.* Scanned version, copyright 2000-2004, Henriette Kress. http://www.ibiblio.org/herbmed/eclectic/potter-comp/main.html (June 29, 2004).

61. Scudder, John M. 1870. *Specific Medication and Specific Medicines.* Scanned version copyright, 1999-2004, Henriette Kress. http://www.ibiblio.org/herbmed/eclectic/spec-med/main.html (June 30, 2004).

62. Blatchley, W.S. 1912. *Indiana Weed Book.* Indianapolis, Indiana: Nature Publishing Co.

63. Fitzpatrick, T.J. 1899. *Manual of the Flowering Plants of Iowa.* Privately published.

64. Harding, A.R. 1908. *Ginseng and Other Medicinal Plants: A Book of Valuable Information for Growers as well as Collectors of Medicinal Roots, Barks, Leaves, etc.* Columbus, Ohio: A. R. Harding.

65. Bruner, W.E. 1931. Vegetation of Oklahoma. *Ecological Monographs,* Volume 1, number 2: 98-188.

66. Flint, Charles L. 1903. *Grasses and Forage Plants: A Practical Treatise.* Revised edition. Boston: Lee and Shepard Publishers.

67. Hackel, Eduard. 1890. *The True Grasses.* Translated from *Die naturlichen pflanzenfamilies* by F. Lamson-Scribner and Effie A. Southworth. New York: Henry Holt and Co.

68. Clarke, Geo. H., and M. Oscar Malte. 1913. *Fodder and Pasture Plants.* Published by direction of The Honourable Martin Burrell, Minister of Agriculture. Ottawa: Government Printing Bureau.

69. Henkel, Alice. 1904. *Weeds Used in Medicine. Farmers' Bulletin,* number 188. U.S. Department of Agriculture. Washington: Government Printing Office.

70. Dewey, Lyster H. 1895. *Weeds, and How to Kill Them. Farmers' Bulletin,* number 28. U.S. Department of Agriculture. Washington: Government Printing Office.

71. Chesnut, V.K. 1898. *Thirty Poisonous Plants of the United States. Farmers' Bulletin*, number 86. U.S. Department of Agriculture. Washington: Government Printing Office.

72. Greene, Wesley. 1907. Plants of Iowa: A Preliminary List of the Native and Introduced Plants of the State, Not under Cultivation. *Bulletin of the State Horticultural Society*. Des Moines: Bishard Brothers Printers.

73. Bergen, Francis D. 1892. Popular American Plant Names. *Botanical Gazette*, Volume 17, number 6: 361-380.

74. Bergen, Francis D. 1893. Popular American Plant Names II. *Botanical Gazette*, Volume 18, number 11: 20-427.

75. Bergen, Fannie D. 1894. Popular American Plant Names III. *Botanical Gazette*, Volume 19, number 11: 429-444. Informant for grass is Charles Bessey.

76. Bergen, Fannie D. 1896. Popular American Plant Names IV. *Botanical Gazette*, Volume 22, number 6: 473-487. Names marked with (W) come from Williamson's *History of Maine*.

77. Bergen, Fannie D. 1898. Popular American plant names V. *Botanical Gazette*, Volume 26, number 4: 247-252.

78. Bergen, Fannie D. 1898. Popular American Plant Names VI. *Botanical Gazette*, Volume 26, number 4: 253-258.

79. Hayward, Sylvanus. 1891. Popular Names of American Plants. *Journal of American Folklore*, Volume 4, number 13: 147-150.

80. Kay, George F., and James H. Lees. 1913. *The Weed Flora of Iowa*. Iowa Geologic Survey, *Bulletin*, number 4. Des Moines: Iowa Geological Survey.

81. Hitchcock, A.S. 1951. *Manual of the grasses of the United States*. Second edition, revised by Agnes Chase. New York: Dover, reprinted in 1971. Originally published as USDA *Miscellaneous Publication*, number 200.

82. Pammel, L.H., and Charlotte M. King. 1930. *Honey plants of Iowa*. Iowa Geological Survey, *Bulletin*, number 7. Des Moines: Iowa Geological Survey.

83. Kurz, Rudolph Freidrich. 1937. *Journal of Rudolph Friedrich Kurz: An Account of His Experiences among Fur Traders and American Indians on the Mississippi and the Upper Missouri Rivers during the Years 1846-1852*. Translated by Myrtis Jarrell, edited by J.N.B. Hewitt. Lincoln, Nebraska: Bison Books, University of Nebraska.

84. Meehan, Thomas. 1880. *Native Ferns and Flowers of the United States*. Philadelphia: American Natural History Publications Co. Ltd.

85. Over, William H. 1932. *Flora of South Dakota: An Illustrated Check-List of Flowering Plants, Shrubs, and Trees of South Dakota*. Vermillion, South Dakota: University of South Dakota.

86. Meehan, Thomas. 1878. *Native Flowers and Ferns of the United States in Their Botanical, Horticultural, and Popular Aspects*. Boston: L. Prang and Co.

87. Vasey, George. 1884. *Agricultural Grasses of the United States*. Washington: Government Printing Office.

88. Vasey, George. 1885. *A Descriptive Catalogue of the Grasses of the United States, including Especially the Grass Collections at the New Orleans Exposition Made by the U.S. Department of Agriculture, and the State Exhibit of Grasses*, with notes on such species as are more or less employed in agriculture, or deserving of trial for cultivation. Washington: Gibson Bros., Printers and Bookbinders.

89. Tabeau, Pierre Antoine, 1755-1820. 1939. *Tabeau's Narrative of Loisel's Expedition to the Upper Missouri*, edited by Annie Heloise Abel, translated from the French by Rose Abel Wright. Norman: University of Oklahoma Press.

90. Fernald, C.H. 1885. *Grasses of Maine*. Augusta: Sprague & Son, Printer to the State.

91. Pammel, L.H. 1911. *A Manual of Poisonous Plant: Chiefly of Eastern North America*, with brief notes on economic and medicinal plants, and numerous illustrations. Cedar Rapids, Iowa: Torch Press.

92. Hobbs, Charles E. 1876. *C.E. Hobbs' Botanical Hand-Book of Common Local, English, Botanical and Pharmacopoeial Names Arranged in Alphabetical Order, of Most of the Crude Vegetable Drugs, etc. in Common Use*. Boston: Chas. C. Roberts.

93. Winter, John Mack. 1936. *An Analysis of the Flowering Plants of Nebraska with Keys to the Families, Genera, and Species, and with Notes Concerning Their Occurrence, Range, and Frequency within the State*. Conservation and Survey Division, University of Nebraska, contribution from the Botanical Survey of Nebraska, New Series, number X. Printed by the authority of the State of Nebraska.

94. Lamson-Scribner, F. 1897-1901. *American Grasses*. Washington: U.S. Government Printing Office.

95. Petersen, N.F. 1911. *Flora of Nebraska: A List of the Conifers and Flowering Plants of the State with Keys for their Determination*. 2nd edition. Plainview, Nebraska: Published by the author.

96. Carleton, M.A. 1891. Observations on the Native Plants of Oklahoma Territory and Adjacent Districts. *Contributions from the U.S. National Herbarium*, Volume 1: 220-232.

97. Stemen, Thomas R., and W. Stanley Myers. 1937. *Oklahoma Flora*. Oklahoma City, Oklahoma: Harlow Publishing Co. 706 pgs.

98. Sandoz, Flora. 1926. Flora Sandoz collection. Manuscript & archival materials. Chadron State University Herbarium.

99. Prier, C.W. 1923. Systematic List of the Grasses Collected near Norman in the Fall of 1922. *Proceedings of the Oklahoma Academy of Science* Volume 3: 85-87.

100. Goyne, Minetta Altgelt. 1991. *A Life among the Texas Flora: Ferdinand Lindheimer's Letters to George Engelmann*. College Station: Texas A&M University Press, 236 pages.

101. Blankenship, J. W. 1905. *Native Economic Plants of Montana*. Montana Agricultural College Experiment Station, *Bulletin*, Volume 56, 38 pages.

102. Mooney, James. 1981. *Sacred Formulas of the Cherokees*. Smithsonian Institution, Bureau of American Ethnology, *Seventh Annual Report for 1885-1886*, pages 301-397.

103. Palmer, Edward. 1871. *Food Products of the North American Indians*. U.S. Department of Agriculture, *Report of the Commission for 1870*, pages 404-428.

104. Havard, V. 1896. Drink Plants of the North American Indians. *Bulletin of the Torrey Botanical Club*, Volume 23, number 2: 33-46.

105. Gilmore, Melvin R. 1932. Some Chippewa Uses of Plants. *Papers of the Michigan Academy of Science, Arts, and Letters*, Volume 17: 119-143.

106. Pellet, Frank C. 1930. *American Honey Plants: Together with Those which Are of Special Value to the Beekeeper as Sources of Pollen*. 3rd edition. Hamilton, Illinois: *American Bee Journal*, 419 pages.

107. Hedrick, U.P. 1919. *Sturtevant's Notes on Edible Plants*. Report of the New York Agricultural Experiment Station for the Year 1919, Part 2. Albany: J.B. Lyon, State Printers.

108. Havard, V. 1878. *Botanical Outlines of the Country Marched over by the Seventh United States Cavalry, during the Summer of 1877*. Report of the chief of Engineers App. QQ, pages 1,681-1,687.

109. Bailey, L.H. 1949. *Manual of Cultivated Plants, Most Commonly Grown in the Continental United States and Canada*. New York: MacMillan Co.

110. De Candolle, Alphonse. 1964. *Origin of Cultivated Plants*. Reprint of 2nd edition, 1886. New York: Hafner Publishing Co.

111. Wilcox, E. Mead, George K.K. Link, and Venus W. Pool. 1915. *Handbook of Nebraska Grasses, with Illustrated Keys for Their Identification, Together with a General Account of Their Structure and Economic Importance. Bulletin of the Agricultural Experiment Station of Nebraska* V, XXVII, Article V.

112. McComb, H.A. 1937. *Trees, Shrubs, and Vines at the North Platte Experimental Substation. Bulletin of the Agricultural Experiment Station of Nebraska*, number 310, *Bulletin*, number 42 of the North Platte Experimental Substation.

113. Bessey, Charles E. 1890. *Preliminary Report on the Native Trees and Shrubs of Nebraska. Bulletin of the Agricultural Experiment Station of Nebraska*, number 18, Volume IV, article 4. Lincoln, Nebraska: University of Nebraska.

114. Bessey, Charles E. 1894. *Preliminary List of the Honey-Producing Plants of Nebraska. Bulletin of the Agricultural Experiment Station of Nebraska*, number 40, Volume VII, article IV. Lincoln, Nebraska: State Journal Company Printers.

115. Keim, F.D., G.W. Beadle, and A.L. Frolik. 1932. *Identification of the More Important Prairie Hay Grasses of Nebraska by Their Vegetative Characters*. Agricultural Experiment Station, *Research Bulletin*, number 65.

116. Frolik, A.L., and F.D. Keim. 1958. *Common Native Grasses of Nebraska*. Nebraska Agricultural Experiment Station, *Circular*, number 59.

117. Sanborn, C.E., and E.E. Scholl. 1908. *Texas Honey Plants*. Texas Agricultural Experiment Stations, *Bulletin* number 102.

118. Pittuck, B.C. 1898. *Grasses and Forage Plants*. Texas Agricultural Experiment Station *Bulletin*, number 46.

119. Featherly, Henry Ira. 1938. *Grasses of Oklahoma. Technical Bulletin*, Oklahoma Agricultural Experiment Station, number 3.

120. Gruchy, James H. B. 1938. *A preliminary Study of the Larger Aquatic Plants of Oklahoma with Special Reference to Their Value in Fish Culture*. Oklahoma Agricultural and Mechanical College, *Technical Bulletin*, number 4.

121. Munson, Patrick J. 1981. Contributions to Osage and Lakota Ethnobotany. *Plains Anthropologist*, Volume 93: 229-240.

122. Cory, V.L., and H.B. Parks. 1937. *Catalogue of the Flora of the State of Texas*. Texas Agricultural Experiment Station, *Bulletin*, number 550.

123. Torrey, John. 1856. Botanical Report. *Explorations and Surveys for a Railroad Route from the Mississippi River to the Pacific Ocean*. War Department. Routes in California to connect with the route near the thirty-fifth and thirty-second parallels, and route near the thirty-second parallel, between the Rio Grande and Pimas villages,

explored by Lieutenant John G. Parke, Corps of Topographical engineers in 1854 and 1855. Reports of Explorations and to aecertain the most practicable and economical route for a railroad from the Mississippi River to the Pacific Ocean made under the direction of the secretary of War in 1852-1856, according to the Acts of Congress of March 3, 1853, May 31, 1854, and August 6, 1854. Volume VII.

124. Conner, A.B. 1937. *Valuable Plants Native to Texas.* Texas Agricultural Experiment Station, *Bulletin*, number 551.

125. Gates, Frank. 1930. *Principal Poisonous Plants in Kansas.* Kansas State Agricultural Experiment Station, *Technical Bulletin*, number 25.

126. Stevens, O.A. 1933. *Poisonous Plants and Plant Products.* North Dakota Agricultural Experiment Station, *Bulletin*, number 265.

127. Steven, O.A. 1933. *Wild Flowers of North Dakota.* North Dakota Agricultural Experiment Station, *Bulletin*, number 269.

128. Barnett, H.L. 1933. *Some Edible and Poisonous Mushrooms of North Dakota.* North Dakota Agricultural Experiment Station, *Bulletin*, number 270.

129. Departments of Chemistry and Botany. 1894. *Native and Introduced Forage Plants.* South Dakota Agricultural College and Experiment Station, *Bulletin*, number 40.

130. Williams, Thomas A. 1895. *Native Trees and Shrubs of South Dakota.* South Dakota Agricultural College and Experiment Station, *Bulletin*, number 43.

131. Saunders, D.A. 1899. *Ferns and Flowering Plants of South Dakota.* South Dakota Agricultural Experiment Station, *Bulletin*, number 64.

132. Whipple, Lieut. A.W., Thomas Eubank, and Prof. William W. Turner. 1855. Report upon the Indian Tribes. *Explorations and Surveys for a Railroad Route from the Mississippi River to the Pacific Ocean Route Near the Thirty-Fifth Parallel*, under the command of Lieut. A.W. Whipple Topographical Engineers in 1853 and 1854, Volume 3.

133. Van Es, L., and L.R. Waldron. 1903. *Some Stock Poisoning Plants of North Dakota.* North Dakota Agricultural Experiment Station, *Bulletin*, number 58.

134. Copple, R.F., and A.E. Aldous. 1932. *Identification of Certain Native and Naturalized Grasses by Their Vegetative Characters.* Kansas State Agricultural Experiment Station, *Technical Bulletin*, number 32.

135. Fisher, R.W. 1910. *Ornamental Trees and Shrubs for Montana.* Montana Agricultural Experiment Station, *Bulletin*, number 80.

136. Hansen, N.E. 1930. *Evergreens in South Dakota.* South Dakota Agricultural Experiment Station, *Bulletin*, number 254.

137. Hansen, N.E. 1931. *Ornamental Trees of South Dakota.* South Dakota State Agricultural Experiment Station, *Bulletin*, number 260.

138. Olmsted, Frederick Law, Frederick V. Coville, and Harlan P. Kelsey. 1923. *Standardized Plant Names.* Salem, Massachusetts: American Joint Committee on Horticultural Nomenclature.

139. Smith, E.C., and L.W. Durrell. 1944. *Sedges and Rushes of Colorado (Grass-Like Plants).* Colorado Agricultural Experiment Station, *Technical Bulletin*, number 32.

140. Harrington, H.D., and L.W. Durrell. 1944. *Key to Some Colorado Grasses in Vegetative Condition.* Colorado Agricultural Experiment Station, *Technical Bulletin*, number 33.

141. Nelson, Aven. 1899. *Some Native Forage Plants for Alkali Soils.* Wyoming Agricultural Experiment Station, *Bulletin*, number 42.

142. Nelson, Aven. 1902. *Native Vines in Wyoming Homes.* Wyoming Agricultural Experiment Station, *Bulletin*, number 50.

143. Nowosad, F.S., D.E. Newton Swales, and W.G. Dore. 1936. *Identification of Certain Native and Naturalized Hay and Pasture Grasses by Their Vegetative Characters.* MacDonald College, *Technical Bulletin*, number 16.

144. Hitchcock, A.S., and G.L. Clothier. 1899. *Native Agricultural Grasses of Kansas.* Kansas State Agricultural Experiment Station, *Bulletin*, number 87.

145. Hitchcock, A.S., and Geo. L. Clothier. 1897. *Kansas Weeds. IV. Fruits and Seeds.* Kansas State Agricultural Experiment Station, *Bulletin*, number 66.

146. Reitz, Louis P., and H.E. Morris. 1939. *Important Grasses and Other Common Plants on Montana Ranges.* Montana State Agricultural Experiment Station, *Bulletin*, number 375.

147. Bigelow, J.M. 1856. Report on the botany of the expedition. *Explorations and Surveys for a Railroad Route from the Mississippi River to the Pacific Ocean.* War Department. Route near the thirty-fifth parallel explored by Lieutenant A. W. Whipple, topographical engineers in 1853 and 1854, Volume 4.

148. Durrell, L.W., and I.E. Newsom. 1939. *Colorado's Poisonous and Injurious plants.* Colorado State Experiment Station, *Bulletin*, number 455.

149. Wooton, E.O. 1904. *Native Ornamental Plants of New Mexico*. New Mexico Agricultural Experiment Station, *Bulletin*, number 51.

150. Wooton, E.O. 1894. *New Mexico Weeds*. New Mexico Agricultural Experiment Station, *Bulletin*, number 13.

151. Wooton, E.O. 1896. *Some New Mexico Forage Plants*. New Mexico Agricultural Experiment Station, *Bulletin*, number 18.

152. Wooton, E.O., and Paul C. Standley. 1912. *Grasses and Grass-Like plants of New Mexico*. New Mexico Agricultural Experiment Station, *Bulletin*, number 81.

153. Wooton, E.O. 1913. *Trees and Shrubs of New Mexico*. New Mexico Agricultural Experiment Station, *Bulletin*, number 87.

154. Torrey, John. 1857. *Descriptions of Plants Collected along the Route, by W.P. Blake, and at the Mouth of the Gila*. Article VII in Lieutenant R.S. Williamson. Report of Explorations in California for Railroad Routes to connect with the routes near the 35th and 32d parallels of north latitude. Volume 5 in *Explorations and Surveys for a Railroad Route from the Mississippi River to the Pacific Ocean*.

155. American Joint Committee on Horticultural Nomenclature. 1942. *Standardized Plant Names*. Second edition. Harlan P. Kelsey and William A. Dayton (editors). Harrisburg, Pennsylvania: J. Horace McFarland Co.

156. Clute, Willard N. 1923. *American Plant Names*. Second edition. Joliet, Illinois: Willard N. Clute & Co.

157. Stuhr, Ernst T. 1929. *Native Drug Plants of Nebraska*. Corvallis, Oregon: School of Pharmacy, Oregon State University.

158. Lyons, A.B. 1900. *Plant Names, Scientific and Popular*. Detroit: Nelson, Baker & Co.

159. *The International Plant Names Index* (2012). Published on the Internet, http://www.ipni.org [accessed April 5, 2014].

160. Cooper, J.G. 1860. *Botanical Report*. In: *Explorations and Surveys for a Railroad Route from the Mississippi River to the Pacific Ocean*. Volume 12, part 2. Route near the forty-seventh and forty-ninth parallels, explored by I.I. Stevens, Governor of Washington Territory in 1853-55. Washington: A.O.P. Nicholson, Printer.

161. Newberry, J.S. 1857. *Botanical Report*. In: *Explorations and Surveys for a Railroad Route from the Mississippi River to the Pacific Ocean*. Volume 6. Routes in California and Oregon explored by Lieut. R.S. Williamson, Corps of Topographical Engineers and Lieut. Henry L. Abbot, Corps of Topographical Engineers in 1855. Washington: A.O.P. Nicholson, Printer.

162. Woodward, Marcus. 1969. *Leaves from Gerard's Herball*. New York: Dover Publications, 305 pages.

163. Silveus, W.A. 1933. *Texas Grasses: Classification and Description of Grasses*. San Antonio, Texas: Clegg Co.

164. Marcy, Randolph B. 1854. *Exploration of the Red River of Louisiana in the Year 1852*. Washington: A.O.P. Nicholson, Public Printer. Including App. G. Botany: Description of the plants collected during the expedition by Dr. John Torrey.

165. Miller, Philip. 1768. *The Gardeners' Dictionary*. Eighth edition. Printed for the author; and sold by John and Francis Rivington.

166. Merrill, Elmer Drew. 1949. *Index Rafinesquianus; the Plant Names Published by C. S. Rafinesque with Reductions, and a Consideration of His Methods, Objectives, and Attainments*. Jamaica Plain, Massachusetts, Arnold Arboretum of Harvard University.

167. Rich, Oliver O. 1814. *A Synopsis of the Genera of American Plants*. Georgetown, District of Columbia: Printed by J.M. Carter.

168. Michaux, André. 1803. *Flora Boreali-Americana*. Facsimile of the 1803 edition with introduction by Joseph Ewan. New York: Hafner Press.

169. Index Fungorum Partnership. 2004. *Index Fungorum*. CABI Bioscience. http://www.indexfungorum.org/Names/Names.asp (October 28, 2005).

170. Lincoff, Gary H. 1995. *National Audubon Society Field Guide to North American Mushrooms*. Alfred A. Knopf: New York.

171. Missouri Botanical Garden. 2005. W3 Most nomenclature. http://mobot.mobot.org/W3T/Search/most.html (November 1, 2005).

172. Goodale, George L. 1882. *Wild Flowers of America*, with fifty-colored plates, from original drawings, by Isaac Sprague. Boston: S.E. Cassino, 1882, c1879.

173. Clarke, Charles Baron. 1909. *Illustrations of Cyperaceae*. London: Williams & Norgate.

174. Linnaeus, Carl. 1753. *Species Plantarum*. A facsimile of the first edition 1753. London: the Ray Society reprinted 1957.

175. Miller, Orson K., Jr. 1972. *Mushrooms of North America*. New York: E. P. Dutton & Co.

176. Huffamn, D.M., L.H. Tiffany, G. Knaphus, and R.A. Healy. 2008. *Mushrooms and Other Fungi of the Midcontinental United States*. Second edition. Iowa City: University of Iowa Press.

177. Gronovius, J.F., and John Clayton. 1762. *Flora virginica. Lugduni Batavorum.* Photolithographed by Murray Printing Co. Cambridge, Massachusetts, for the Arnold Arboretum, 1946.

178. *John Gerard's Grete Herball Catalogue Horti – Modern Scientific Names by Benjamin Daydon Jackson – Cultivated in His Garden, 1596-1599.* 1876, privately printed.

179. Ryden, Mats. 1984. *English Plant Names in the Great Herball* (1526).

180. Gerarde, John. 1633. **The herball or Generall historie of plantes.** Gathered by Iohn Gerarde of London Master in Chirurgerie very much enlarged and amended by Thomas Iohnson citizen and apothecarye of London.

181. Ewan, Joseph, and Nesta Ewan. 1970. *John Banister and His Natural History of Virginia, 1678-1692.* Urbana, Chicago, London: University of Illinois Press.

182. Harper, Francis. 1791. *The Travels of William Bartram.* Francis Harpers Naturalist edition. Athens and London: University of Georgia Press, 1998.

183. Bartram, William. 1968. *Botanical and Zoological Drawings, 1756-1788*; reproduced from the Fothergill album in the British Museum (Natural History). Edited, with an introduction and commentary, by Joseph Ewan.

184. Muhlenberg, Henry. 1793. Index Lancastriensis, Auctore Henrico Muhlenberg, D. D. *Transactions of the American Philosophical Society*, Volume 3: 157-184.

185. Pechanec, Joseph F. 1936. The Identification of Grasses on the Upper Snake River Plains by their Vegetative Characters. *Ecology*, Volume 17, number 3: 479-490.

186. Barton, William. 1814. *Vegetable Materia Medica of the United States, or, Medical Botany: Containing a Botanical, General, and Medical History of Medicinal Plants Indigenous to the United States.* Illustrated by coloured engravings, made after drawings from nature, done by the author. Philadelphia: H.C. Carey and I. Lea, 1825. Biodiversity Heritage Library, http://www.biodiversitylibrary.org/Default.aspx.

187. Barton, William. 1818. *Compendium Florae Philadelphicae: Containing a Description of the Indigenous and Naturalized Plants Found within a Circuit of Ten Miles around Philadelphia.* V, II only. Philadelphia: Carey & Sons. Biodiversity Heritage Library, http://www.biodiversitylibrary.org/item/84268#7 (accessed January 22, 2010).

188. Hooker, William Jackson. 1829. *Flora Boreali-Americana Atlas; or the Botany of the Northern Parts of British America.* London: Henry G. Bohn.

189. Catesby, Mark. 1767. *Hortus Europae americanus, or, A collection of 85 Curious Trees and Shrubs: The Produce of North America, Adapted to the Climates and Soils of Great-Britain, Ireland, and Most Parts of Europe, &c Together with Their Blossoms, Fruits and Seeds, Observations on Their Culture, Growth, Constitution and Virtues, with Directions How to Collect, Pack Up and Secure Them in Their Passage.* London: Printed for J. Millan.

190. Rickett, H.W. 1963. *Jane Colden: Botanic Manuscript.* New York: Chanticleer Press.

Historical Common Names
of Great Plains Plants

Volume I:

Common Names

Aconitum napellus (Aconite monkshood, Adam-and-Eve)
[J.E. Sowerby, 1863]

A

Aaron's-beard [Aaron's beard, Aaronsbeard] - *Cotinus coggygria* Scop. (19, 92) (1840-1876), *Cymbalaria muralis* P.G. Gaertn., B. Mey. & Scherb. (5, 155) (1913-1942), *Opuntia leucotricha* DC. (155) (1942)

Aaron's-beard cactus [Aaronsbeard cactus] - *Opuntia leucotricha* DC. (138) (1923)

Aaron's-beard prickly-pear [Aaronsbeard pricklypear] - *Opuntia leucotricha* DC. (155) (1942)

Aaron's-flannel [Aaron's flannel] - *Verbascum thapsus* L. (5, 158) (1900-1913)

Aaron's-rod [Aaron's rod] - *Aralia spinosa* L. (156) (1923), *Hylotelephium telephium* (L.) H. Ohba. subsp. *telephium* (5, 73, 76, 79, 156) (1891-1923)

Ababai - *Carica papaya* L. (110) (1886) Caribbean

Abata cola - *Cola acuminata* (P. Beauv.) Schott & Endl. (50) (present)

Abavo - *Adansonia digitata* L. (165) (1768)

Abbatitchim (Hebrew) - *Citrullus lanatus* (Thunb.) Matsumura & Nakai (110) (1886)

Abbey - *Populus alba* L. (158) (1900)

Abcess root [Abscess-root] - *Polemonium reptans* L. (57, 92, 158) (1876-1917)

Abel - *Populus alba* L. (5, 158) (1900-1913)

Abele or Abele tree [Abele-tree] - *Populus alba* L. (5, 72, 92, 109, 156, 158) (1876-1923)

Abelia - *Abelia* R. Br. (138, 155) (1923-1942)

Abellana - *Musa* ×*paradisiaca* L. [*acuminata* × *balbisiana*] (107) (1570)

Abeti - *Picea mariana* (Mill.) Britton, Sterns & Poggenb. (46) (1879)

Abies - *Picea abies* (L.) H. Karst. (178) (1596), *Tsuga canadensis* (L.) Carr. (53) (1922)

Abo'djigûn (Chippewa, something turned out or over) - *Phragmites australis* (Cav.) Trin. ex Steud. (40) (1928)

Abortive-flower crowfoot [Abortive-flowered crow-foot] - *Ranunculus abortivus* L. (187) (1818)

Abraham's-cabbage [Abraham's cabbage] - *Amaranthus retroflexus* L. (79) (1891) NH

Abre de Judée - *Cercis* L. (8) (1785)

Abrecocke - *Prunus armeniaca* L. (178) (1526)

Abronia - *Abronia* Juss. (158) (1900), *Abronia umbellata* Lam. (92) (1876)

Abrotano - *Artemisia abrotanum* L. (158) (1900)

Abrotanum - *Artemisia abrotanum* L. (158) (1900)

Abrus - *Abrus* Adans. (50, 158) (1900–present)

Absconda - *Ilex mucronata* (L.) M. Powell, Savol. & S. Andrews (46) (1879)

Absinthe [Absinth] - *Artemisia ludoviciana* Nutt. (28) (1850), *Artemisia tridentata* Nutt. (28) (1850), *Artemisia absinthium* L. (5, 6, 85, 107, 138, 156) (1892-1932)

Absinthe Grande - *Artemisia absinthium* L. (158) (1900)

Absinthium - *Artemisia absinthium* L. (50, 53, 55, 57, 92, 109, 157, 158) (1876–present)

Abutilon - *Abutilon* Mill. (138, 155, 158) (1900-1942), *Abutilon theophrasti* Medik (177) (1762)

Acacia - *Acacia mearnsii* De Wild. (106, 107) (1919-1930), *Acacia* Mill. (1, 50, 138, 155, 158) (1900–present), *Mimosa* L. (7) (1828)

Acacia à large silique (French) - *Lysiloma latisiliquum* (L.) Benth. (20) (1857)

Acacia blanc (French) - *Robinia pseudoacacia* L. (8) (1785)

Acacia with rose-coloured flowers - *Robinia pseudoacacia* L. (189) (1767)

Acaena - *Acaena* Mutis ex L. (50, 138) (1923–present)

Acaja - *Spondias* L. (174) (1753)

Acanthopanax - *Eleutherococcus Maxim.* (155) (1942)

Acanthus - *Acanthus* L. (50, 138, 155) (1923–present)

Acanthus bristle-thistle [Acanthus bristlethistle] - *Carduus acanthoides* L. (155) (1942)

Accippitrina - *Hieracium* L. (180) (1633)

Accomodation plant - *Physalis virginiana* Mill. (156) (1923)

Acelga - *Beta* L. (107) (1919) Spain & Portugal

Ache - *Apium graveolens* L. (107, 174) (1623-1753), *Petroselinum crispum* (P. Mill.) Nyman ex A.W. Hill (156, 158) (1900-1923)

Ache parsley - *Apium graveolens* L. var. *dulce* (P. Mill.) DC. (5, 156, 158) (1900-1923)

Achiote - *Bixa orellana* L. (92, 177) (1762-1876)

Acid lettuce - *Lactuca virosa* L. (60) (1902)

Acid mulberry - *Morus australis* Poir. (138) (1923)

Acimine - *Annona montana* Macfad. (41) (1770), *Annona muricata* L. (41) (1770)

Ackerklee (German) - *Trifolium pratense* L. (6) (1892)

Ackers wibel (High Dutch) - *Ornithogalum* L. (180) (1633)

Ackerspergel (German) - *Spergula arvensis* L. (158) (1900)

Ack-root [Ackroot] - *Juglans* L. (92) (1876) from Indian name for walnut 92

Acnida - *Amaranthus cannabinus* (L.) Sauer (174, 177) (1753-1762), *Amaranthus rudis* Sauer (125) (1930) KS

Aconite - *Aconitum* L. (1, 109) (1932-1949), *Aconitum columbianum* Nutt. (148) (1939), *Aconitum napellus* L. (53, 54, 55, 57, 59, 60, 61, 92, 107, 138, 156) (1870-1923)

Aconite monkshood - *Aconitum napellus* L. (155) (1942)

Aconite saxifrage - *Boykinia aconitifolia* Nutt. (5) (1913)

Aconitum - *Aconitum napellus* L. (60) (1902)

Acore odorant (French) - *Acorus calamus* L. (7, 186) (1814)

Acore vrai (French) - *Acorus calamus* L. (158) (1900)

Acoro (Italian) - *Acorus calamus* L. (186) (1814)

Acoro calamo (Spanish, Portuguese) - *Acorus calamus* L. (186) (1814)

Acorum - *Acorus calamus* L. (186) (1814)

Acorus des Indes ou Asiatique (French) - *Acorus calamus* L. (186) (1814)

Acoumack-pea - *Chamaecrista fasciculata* (Michx.) Greene var. *fasciculata* (187) (1818)

Acrid buttercups - *Ranunculus acris* L. (6) (1892)

Acrid crowfoot - *Ranunculus acris* L. (7) (1828)

Acrid lettuce - *Lactuca virosa* L. (92, 157, 158) (1876-1900)

Acrocomia - *Acrocomia* Mart. (155) (1942)

Acrostichum - *Acrostichum* L. (158) (1900)

Actee a grappe (French) - *Cimicifuga racemosa* (L.) Nutt. (6) (1892)

Actinella - *Tetraneuris herbacea* Greene (156) (1923)

Actinidia - *Actinidia* Lindl. (138, 155) (1931-1942)

Actinomeris - *Verbena urticifolia* L. (174) (1753), *Verbesina alternifolia* (L.) Britton ex Kearney (62, 72, 158) (1900-1907)

Acuminate-leaf cottonwood [Acuminate leaved cottonwood] - *Populus* ×*acuminata* Rydb. [*angustifolia* × *deltoides*] (149, 153) (1904)

Acuminatus aster - *Oclemena acuminata* (Michx.) Greene (155) (1942)

Acute-leaf arrowhead [Acute-leaved arrow-head] - *Sagittaria lancifolia* L. subsp. *lancifolia* (187) (1818)

Adam-and-Eve [Adam and Eve] - *Aconitum napellus* L. (74) (1893) Washington Co. ME, *Aplectrum hyemale* (Muhl. ex Willd.) Torr.

3

(50, 92, 97, 109, 156, 158) (1876–present), *Aplectrum* Nutt. (1, 19, 158) (1840-1932)

Adam-and-Eve-in-the-bower - *Aconitum napellus* L. (76) (1896) Deering ME

Adam's-apple [Adams' apple] - *Citrus limetta* Risso (92) (1876)

Adam's-cup [Adam's cup] - *Sarracenia purpurea* L. (5, 73, 156) (1892-1923) Dudley MA

Adam's-fig [Adam's fig] - *Musa* ×*paradisiaca* L. [*acuminata* × *balbisiana*] (107) (1919)

Adam's-flannel [Adam's flannel] - *Verbascum thapsus* L. (5, 14, 69, 156) (1882-1923)

Adam's-needle [Adam's needle] - *Scandix pecten-veneris* L. (5, 156) (1913-1923), *Yucca filamentosa* L. (2, 50, 107, 109, 158) (1900–present), *Yucca glauca* Nutt. (5, 93) (1913-1936), *Yucca glauca* Nutt. var. *glauca* (38, 108) (1820-1878), *Yucca gloriosa* L. (92, 182) (1791-1876), *Yucca* L. (10, 158, 167) (1814-1900)

Adam's-needle yucca [Adamsneedle yucca] - *Yucca filamentosa* L. (155) (1942)

Adam's-needle-and-thread [Adam's needle and thread] - *Yucca filamentosa* L. (78, 158) (1898-1900)

Adam's-rod [Adam's rod] - *Verbascum thapsus* L. (5, 14) (1882-1913)

Adanson's acacia [Adanson acacia] - *Acacia nilotica* (L.) Willd. ex Delile (155) (1942)

Adder's pogonia - *Pogonia ophioglossoides* (L.) Ker-Gawl. (158) (1900)

Adder's-fern [Adder's fern] - *Ophioglossum* L. (158) (1900), *Ophioglossum vulgatum* L. (5) (1913)

Adder's-flower [Adder's flower] - *Silene dioica* (L.) Clairville (156) (1923) no longer in use by 1923

Adder's-grass - *Ophioglossum* L. (158) (1900)

Adder's-leaf [Adder leaf, Adder's leaf] - *Erythronium americanum* Ker. (7, 92, 157) (1828-1900)

Adder's-meat [Adder's meat] - *Malaxis unifolia* Michx. (92) (1876), *Stellaria holostea* L. (5, 156) (1913-1923) no longer in use by 1923

Adder's-mouth [Adder mouth, Adder's mouth] - *Malaxis* Soland. ex Sw. (1) (1932), *Malaxis unifolia* Michx. (19) (1840), *Stellaria media* (L.) Vill. (92) (1876)

Adder's-mouth orchid [Adder's mouth orchid] - *Malaxis* Soland. ex Sw. (50) (present)

Adder's-mouth orchis - *Pogonia ophioglossoides* (L.) Ker-Gawl. (158) (1900)

Adder's-mouth pogonia [Adder's mouth pogonia] - *Pogonia ophioglossoides* (L.) Ker-Gawl. (5, 156, 158) (1900-1923)

Adder's-spear [Adder's spear] - *Canna indica* L. (73) (1892) MA, *Ophioglossum* L. (158) (1900), *Ophioglossum vulgatum* L. (5) (1913)

Adder's-tongue [Adder tongue, Adders tongue, Adder's tongue, Adders toong, Adderstongue] - *Erythronium americanum* Ker. (2, 19, 49, 57, 58, 92) (1840-1917), *Erythronium* L. (1, 93, 156, 158) (1900-1936), *Goodyera repens* (L.) R. Br. ex Ait. f. (78) (1898) ME, *Hieracium venosum* L. (5, 156) (1913-1923), *Maianthemum* G.H. Weber ex Wiggers (7) (1828), *Ophioglossum engelmannii* Prantl. (3, 5, 97) (1913-1977), *Ophioglossum* L. (1, 4, 10, 50, 138, 155, 158) (1818–present), *Ophioglossum vulgatum* L. (3, 5, 14, 46, 122, 178) (1596-1977) accidentally introduced by 1671

Adder's-tongue fern [Adder-tongue fern, Adder's tongue fern] - *Ophioglossum engelmannii* Prantl. (124) (1937) TX, *Ophioglossum vulgatum* L. (19, 92) (1840-1876)

Adder's-tongue malaxis [Adder-tongue malaxis] - *Malaxis unifolia* Michx. (187) (1818)

Adder's-tongue-leaf arethusa [Adder's tongue leaved arethusa] - *Pogonia ophioglossoides* (L.) Ker-Gawl. (42) (1814)

Adder's-violet [Adder's violet, Adders' violet] - *Erythronium americanum* Ker. (157) (1929), *Goodyera pubescens* (Willd.) R. Br. ex Ait. f. (5, 19, 49, 82, 156) (1840-1930)

Adder's-wort, [Adder's wort, Adderswort] - *Echium vulgare* L. (5, 92, 156, 157, 158) (1876-1929?) obsolete (1923) 156

Addison Brown's leather flower - *Clematis addisonii* Britt. (5) (1913)

Addison's rosette grass - *Dichanthelium ovale* (Ell.) Gould & C.A. Clark var. *addisonii* (Nash) Gould & C.A. Clark (50) (present)

Adelia - *Adelia* L. (155, 158) (1900-1942), *Forestiera acuminata* (Michx.) Poir. (5, 97) (1913-1937), *Forestiera* Poir. (138) (1923)

Adenocaulon - *Adenocaulon bicolor* Hook. (5) (1913), *Adenocaulon* Hook. (155, 158) (1900-1942)

Adhotathny - *Sassafras albidum* (Nutt.) Nees (46) (1879)

Adiantum - *Adiantum pedatum* L. (57) (1917)

A'djidamo'wano (Chippewa, squirrel tail) - *Achillea millefolium* L. (40, 155, 165) (1768-1942), *Hordeum jubatum* L. (40) (1928), *Oligoneuron rigidum* (L.) Small var. *rigidum* (40) (1928), *Solidago canadensis* L. var. *scabra* Torr. & Gray (40) (1928), *Solidago flexicaulis* L. (40) (1928), *Solidago juncea* Aiton (40) (1928)

Adluma - *Adlumia fungosa* (Aiton) Greene ex B. S. P. (2) (1895) Madison WI

Adlumia - *Adlumia* Raf. ex DC. (50) (present)

Ado - *Colocasia esculenta* (L.) Schott (182) (1791)

Adolphia - *Adolphia* Meisn. (155) (1942)

Adonis - *Adonis* L. (138, 155) (1923-1942)

Adonis blazing star [Adonis blazingstar] - *Mentzelia multiflora* (Nutt.) Gray (50) (present)

Adonis with red floures - *Adonis annua* L. (180) (1633)

Adonis'-flower [Adonis' flower, Adonis flower, Adonis floure] - *Adonis annua* L. (5, 178, 180) (1526-1913)

Ador - *Triticum spelta* L. (180) (1633)

Adoreum - *Triticum spelta* L. (180) (1633)

Adoxa - *Adoxa* L. (50) (present)

Adzuki bean - *Vigna angularis* (Willd.) Ohwi & Ohashi (109, 138) (1923-1949)

Aegilops - *Aegilops cylindrica* Host (119) (1938)

Aeonium - *Aeonium* Webb & Berth. (155) (1942)

Aethiopian apple - *Solanum lycopersicum* L. var. *lycopersicum* (180) (1633)

Aethiopian mulleine - *Salvia aethiops* L. (178) (1526)

Aethiopis - *Salvia aethiops* L. (178) (1526)

Aethl - *Tamarix aphylla* (L.) H. Karst. (122) (1937) TX

Aethusa - *Aethusa cynapium* L. (174) (1753), *Aethusa* L. (155) (1942)

Aethyl - *Tamarix aphylla* (L.) H. Karst. (124) (1937) TX

Aetna broom - *Genista aetnensis* (Biv.) DC. (138) (1923)

Afghan blistercress - *Erysimum perofskianum* Fisch. & C.A. Mey. (138) (1923)

Afican millet - *Sorghum bicolor* (L.) Moench (19) (1840)

African arctotis - *Arctotis stoechadifolia* Berg. (155) (1942)

African cane - *Pennisetum glaucum* (L.) R. Br. (87) (1884)

African chillies - *Capsicum annuum* L. var. *annuum* (53) (1922)

African daisy - *Arctotis stoechadifolia* Berg. (109) (1949)

African dogstooth grass - *Cynodon transvaalensis* Burtt-Davy (50) (present)

African lilac - *Melia azedarach* L. (49) (1898)

African lily - *Agapanthus* L'Hér. (92) (1876)

African marygold - *Tagetes erecta* L. (19, 109) (1840-1949)

African millet - *Eleusine coracana* (L.) Gaertn. (109, 138) (1923-1949), *Pennisetum glaucum* (L.) R. Br. (109) (1949), *Sorghum bicolor* (L.) Moench subsp. *bicolor* (87) (1884)

African oil palm - *Elaeis guineensis* Jacq. (138) (1923)

African rose - *Papaver rhoeas* L. (5, 156, 158) (1913-1923)

African saffron - *Carthamus tinctorius* L. (49, 158) (1898)

African tamarix - *Tamarix africana* Poir. (138) (1923)

African turmeric - *Canna indica* L. (92) (1876)

Afterbirth-weed - *Stylosanthes biflora* (L.) Britton, Sterns & Poggenb. (158) (1900)

Afternoon ladies - *Mirabilis longiflora* L. (92) (1876)

Afzelia - *Seymeria* Pursh (155, 158) (1900–1942)

Agabwen - *Asarum canadense* L. (105) (1932)

Agalboche luisant (French) - *Gymnanthes lucida* Sw. (20) (1857)

Agapanthus - *Agapanthus* L'Hér. (138, 155) (1923-1942) Greek for love flower

Agar agar - *Hydropuntia edulis* (S.G.Gmelin) Gurgel & Fredericq (92, 107) (1876-1919)

Agaricus - *Agaricus campestris* L. (42) (1814), *Agaricus* L. (155) (1942)

Agaricus albus - *Fomitopsis officinalis* (Batsch) Bondartsev & Singer (53, 92) (1876-1922)

Agarita (Spanish) - *Mahonia trifoliolata* (Moric.) Fedde (106, 124) (1930-1937) TX, Mexico

Agarroba - *Robinia neomexicana* Gray (153) (1913) NM

Agarrobo (Spanish) - *Ceratonia siliqua* L. (110) (1886)

Agaryk - *Polyporus officinalis* (Batsch) Fr. (178, 179) (1526-1596)

Agastache - *Agastache scrophulariifolia* (Willd.) Kuntze (187) (1818)

Agave - *Agave* L. (138, 155) (1923-1942), *Manfreda virginica* (L.) Salisb. ex Rose (19) (1840)

Agawak-minš (Chippewa, prickly tree) - *Zanthoxylum americanum* Mill. (105) (1932)

Age - *Capsicum annuum* L. var. *annuum* (107) (1919)

Ageratum - *Ageratum conyzoides* L. (174) (1753), *Ageratum houstonianum* Mill. (92) (1876), *Ageratum* L. (82, 138, 155) (1930-1942)

Aggouria (Modern Greek) - *Cucumis sativus* L. (110) (1886)

A'gimak' (Chippewa, snowshoe wood) - *Fraxinus* L. (40) (1928)

Aglet-head rush [Aglet-headed rush] - *Eleocharis palustris* (L.) Roemer & J.A. Schultes (5) (1913)

Aglet-head spike-rush [Aglet-headed spike-rush] - *Eleocharis palustris* (L.) Roemer & J.A. Schultes (156) (1923)

Agno casto (Portuguese) - *Ricinus communis* L. (110) (1886) usually refers to Vitex agnus castus

Agnus castus - *Vitex agnus-castus* L. (92) (1876)

Ago'biso'wĭn (Chippewa, refers to sewing) - *Cypripedium reginae* Walt. (40) (1928)

Agoŋg'osimĭnûn' (Chippewa) - *Maianthemum racemosum* (L.) Link subsp. *racemosum* (40) (1928)

Agoseris - *Agoseris* Raf. (50, 155) (1942–present)

Agouman (French) - *Phytolacca americana* L. var. *americana* (158) (1900)

Agreeto (Italian) - *Mahonia trifoliolata* (Moric.) Fedde (180) (1633)

Agria skilla - *Pancratium maritimum* L. (46) (1879)

Agrimonia - *Agrimonia eupatoria* L. (57) (1917)

Agrimony - *Agrimonia eupatoria* L. (14, 19, 46, 49, 52, 53, 57, 58, 92, 107, 156) (1649-1923), *Agrimonia gryposepala* Wallr. (3, 48) (1882-1977), *Agrimonia* L. (1, 2, 4, 10, 50, 93, 155, 156, 157, 158, 167, 184) (1793–present), *Agrimonia pubescens* Wallr. (5, 50) (1913–present), *Agrimonia striata* Michx. (3) (1977), *Bidens tripartita* L. (158) (1900)

Agrioriganum - *Origanum vulgare* L. (178) (1526)

Agripaume - *Leonurus cardiaca* L. (158) (1900)

Agrito - *Mahonia trifoliolata* (Moric.) Fedde (122) (1937) TX

Agrostis-like panic grass - *Panicum rigidulum* Bosc ex Nees var. *elongatum* (Pursh) Lelong (66) (1903)

Agryote - *Prunus* L. (179) (1526)

Agthamungi - *Rubus idaeus* L. subsp. *strigosus* (Michx.) Focke (37) (1919), *Rubus occidentalis* L. (37) (1919)

Ague root (ague-root) - *Aletris farinosa* L. (5, 6, 7, 64, 92, 156) (1828-1923)

Ague tree [Ague-tree] - *Sassafras albidum* (Nutt.) Nees (5, 92, 156, 158) (1876-1923), *Sassafras* Nees. & Eberm. (1) (1932)

Aguebark [Ague bark, Ague-bark] - *Ptelea trifoliata* L. (5, 92, 156, 157, 158) (1876-1923)

Ague-grass [Ague grass] - *Aletris farinosa* L. (7, 64, 92, 156) (1828-1923)

Agueweed [Ague weed, Ague-weed] - *Eupatorium perfoliatum* L. (5, 6, 7, 52, 53, 69, 92, 156, 157, 158) (1814-1923), *Gentianella quinquefolia* (L.) Small subsp. *quinquefolia* (5, 156) (1913-1923), *Grindelia squarrosa* (Pursh) Dunal (54) (1905)

Aguja (Portuguese) - *Geranium maculatum* L. (186) (1814)

Agulha - *Geranium maculatum* L. (186) (1814)

Agur-grass [Agur grass] - *Aletris farinosa* L. (5, 6) (1892-1913)

Agurka (Bohemian) - *Cucumis sativus* L. (110) (1886)

Agutiguepo-obi - *Orobanche uniflora* L. (174) (1753)

Agwĭn'gûsibûg (Chippewa, ground squirrel leaf) - *Streptopus lanceolatus* (Ait.) Reveal var. *roseus* (Michx.) Reveal (40) (1928)

Aha (Crow) - *Pediomelum esculentum* (Pursh) Rydb. (101) (1905) MT

Ahate di Panucho (Mexico) - *Annona squamosa* L. (110) (1886)

Ahawĭ akǎ'tǎ' - *Ratibida columnifera* (Nutt.) Wood & Standl. (102) (1886)

Ahawĭ akǎ'tǎ' (Cherokee, deer eye) - *Rudbeckia fulgida* Aiton (102) (1886)

Ahite Franckincense, Olibanum or Thus - *Liquidambar styraciflua* L. (181) (~1678)

Ah'-o-ly (Pima) - *Lophophora lewinii* (Hennings ex Lewin) C.H. Thomps. (132) (1855)

Aie green - *Aloe vera* (L.) Burm. f. (178) (1596)

Aigremoine Commune (French) - *Agrimonia eupatoria* L. (7) (1828)

Aiguilletes d'armes (French) - *Phalaris arundinacea* L. (180) (1633)

Ail (French) - *Allium sativum* L. (158) (1900)

Ailante - *Ailanthus altissima* (Mill) Swingle (6) (1892)

Ailanthus - *Ailanthus altissima* (Mill) Swingle (5, 52, 85, 92, 137, 138, 158) (1876-1932), *Ailanthus* Desf. (50, 138, 155) (1923–present)

Ailanto - *Ailanthus altissima* (Mill) Swingle (49) (1898)

Ailantus tree - *Ailanthus* Desf. (15) (1895)

Aipi - *Manihot esculenta* Crantz (109) (1949)

Aipo (Potugual) - *Apium graveolens* L. (107) (1919)

Air-bell - *Campanula rotundifolia* L. (158) (1900)

Airelle (French) - *Vaccinium* L. (8) (1785)

Airelle à étamines longues (French) - *Vaccinium stamineum* L. (8) (1785)

Airelle à feuilles de troëne (French) - *Arsenococcus ligustrinus* (L.) Small (8) (1785)

Airelle à fleurs accompagnées de feuilles (French) - *Gaylussacia frondosa* (L.) Torr. & Gray (8) (1785)

Airelle à fleurs en corymbe (French) - *Vaccinium corymbosum* L. (8) (1785), *Vaccinium* L. (73) (1892)

Airelle blanche (French) - *Symphoricarpos albus* (L.) Blake (8) (1785)

Airelle de marais (French) - *Gaultheria hispidula* (L.) Muhl. ex Bigelow (possibly) (8) (1785)

Airelle de Pensylvanie (French) - *Vaccinium pallidum* Aiton (8) (1785)

Airif - *Galium aparine* L. (5, 156, 158) (1900-1923) no longer in use by 1923

Airplant [Air-plant] - *Kalanchoe pinnata* (Lam.) Pers. (109) (1949), *Tillandsia* L. (50) (present)

Air-potato [Airpotato] - *Dioscorea bulbifera* L. (109, 138) (1923-1949)

Aiseweed [Aise weed, Aise-weed] - *Aegopodium podagraria* L. (5, 156) (1913-1923)

Aiten - *Juniperus communis* L. (5, 157, 158) (1900-1913)

Aitnach - *Juniperus communis* L. (157, 158) (1900-1929)

Aits (Scotland) - *Avena sativa* L. (158) (1900)

Aiva (Russian) - *Cydonia oblonga* Mill. (110) (1886)

Aiwina (Finnish) - *Linum usitatissimum* L. (110) (1886)

Aizoon saxifrage - *Saxifraga paniculata* Mill. subsp. *neogaea* (Butters) D. Löve (138) (1923)

Aizoon stonecrop - *Sedum aizoon* L. (138, 155) (1931-1942)

Ajava seed - *Trachyspermum copticum* (L.) Link (92) (1876)

Ajenjos (Spanish) - *Artemisia absinthium* L. (158) (1900)

Ajes - *Ipomoea batatas* (L.) Lam. (110) (1886)

Aji (Peru) - *Capsicum annuum* L. var. *annuum* (107) (1532)

Akasgia - *Trachyspermum copticum* (L.) Link (92) (1876)

Akebia - *Akebia* Dcne. (138, 155) (1931-1942)

Akee - *Blighia sapida* Koenig (109, 138) (1923-1949)

Akeley - *Aquilegia vulgaris* L. (156) (1923)

Aker-when (Swedish) - *Apera spica-venti* (L.) Beauv. (46) (1879)

Akiwasas (Pawnee, naming names) - *Viburnum lentago* L. (37) (1919)

Akûn'damo (Chippewa, watcher or spy) - *Silphium perfoliatum* L. (40) (1928)

Alabama fothergilla - *Fothergilla major* (Sims) Lodd. (138) (1923)

Alabama lip-fern [Alabama lipfern] - *Cheilanthes alabamensis* (Buckl.) Kunze (4, 5, 50, 97, 122, 155) (1913–present)

Alabama snow-wreath - *Neviusia alabamensis* Gray (86) (1878)

Alabama supplejack - *Berchemia scandens* (Hill.) Trelease (138) (1923) TX

Alamo - *Populus deltoides* Bartr. ex Marsh. (5, 156) (1913-1923)

Alamo (Spanish) - *Populus deltoides* Bartr. ex Marsh. subsp. *monilifera* (Aiton) Eckenwalder (147) (1856), *Populus* L. (147) (1856)

Alamo-vine [Alamo vine] - *Merremia dissecta* (Jacq.) Hallier f. (122, 124) (1937) TX

Alant (German) - *Inula helenium* L. (6) (1892)

Alaska cedar - *Chamaecyparis nootkatensis* (D. Don) Spach (75) (1894) WA

Alaska club-moss [Alaskan club-moss] - *Lycopodium sitchense* Rupr. (5) (1913)

Alaska draba - *Draba stenoloba* Ledeb. (50) (present)

Alaska piperia - *Piperia unalascensis* (Spreng.) Rydb. (5) (1913)

Alaskan orchis - *Piperia unalascensis* (Spreng.) Rydb. (3) (1977)

Alaunwurzel (German) - *Heuchera villosa* Michx. (possibly) (7) (1828)

Alazor (Spanish) - *Carthamus tinctorius* L. (158) (1900)

Albany beechdrops [Albany beech drops] - *Pterospora andromedea* Nutt. (5, 7, 19, 92, 156, 158) (1828-1923)

Albany hemp - *Laportea canadensis* (L.) Weddell (5, 19, 92, 156, 157, 158) (1840-1929)

Alberta saxifrage - *Saxifraga occidentalis* S. Wats. (50, 155) (1942–present)

Alberta spruce - *Picea glauca* (Moench) Voss (109, 112, 136, 138) (1923-1968)

Albino elder - *Sambucus racemosa* L. var. *racemosa* (138) (1923)

Albizzia - *Albizia* Durazz. (138, 155) (1931-1942)

Alcamet - *Lawsonia inermis* L. (179) (1526)

Alcanna - *Lawsonia inermis* L. (92) (1876)

Alchornea - *Alchornea* Sw. (50) (present)

Alcoleaz (Portugal) - *Colocasia esculenta* (L.) Schott (110) (1886)

Alconet - *Lithospermum canescens* (Michx.) Lehm. (92) (1876)

Alcornoque of Spain - *Byrsonima crassifolia* (L.) Kunth (92) (1876)

Alder buckthorn [Alder-buckthorn] - *Frangula alnus* Mill. (5, 49, 53, 55, 82, 109, 156, 158) (1898–1949), *Frangula* Mill. (13) (1849), *Rhamnus alnifolia* L'Her. (3, 4, 138, 155) (1923-1986)

Alder dogwood - *Cornus rugosa* Lam. (6, 7) (1828-1932), *Frangula alnus* Mill. (158) (1900)

Alder or Alder tree [Alder-tree] - *Alnus glutinosa* (L.) Gaertn. (5, 41, 187) (1770-1913), *Alnus incana* (L.) Moench (40, 95) (1911-1928), *Alnus incana* (L.) Moench subsp. *rugosa* (DuRoi) Clausen (101, 122, 124) (1905-1937), *Alnus* P. Mill. (1, 4, 8, 10, 50, 82, 106, 109, 138, 155, 158, 167) (1785–present), *Alnus serrulata* (Aiton) Willd. (19) (1840)

Alder-leaf buckthorn [Alderleaf buckthorn, Alder-leaved buckthorn] - *Frangula caroliniana* (Walt.) Gray (5, 156) (1913-1923), *Rhamnus alnifolia* L'Her. (5, 50, 82, 93, 156, 158) (1900–present)

Alder-leaf clethra [Alder-leaved clethra] - *Clethra alnifolia* L. (8, 187) (1785-1818)

Alder-leaf dogwood [Alder-leaved dogwood] - *Cornus rugosa* Lam. (5, 92, 156) (1898-1923)

Alder-leaf mountain-mahogany [Alderleaf mountain mahogany] - *Cercocarpus montanus* Raf. (50) (present)

Alderne - *Sambucus nigra* L. (158) (1900)

Ale gill - *Glechoma hederacea* L. (156) (1923) no longer in use by 1923 (156) formerly used in brewing

Alecoast - *Balsamita major* Desf. (5, 158) (1900-1913)

Alecost [Ale-cost] - *Balsamita major* Desf. (5, 107, 156, 158) (1900-1923) no longer in use by 1923

Alectoria - *Alectoria* Ach. (155) (1942)

Alectryon - *Alectryon* Gaertn. (155) (1942)

Alehoof [Ale hoof, Ale-hoof] - *Glechoma hederacea* L. (5, 7, 10, 46, 92, 107, 156, 157, 158, 187) (1671-1929) no longer in use by 1923

Alehoue - *Glechoma hederacea* L. (178) (1526)

Aleppo grass [Aleppo-grass] - *Sorghum halepense* (L.) Pers. (109) (1949)

Aleppo pine - *Pinus halepensis* Mill. (109, 138) (1923-1949)

Aletris - *Aletris farinosa* L. (52, 54, 64) (1905-1919)

Alétris Farineux (French) - *Aletris farinosa* L. (6) (1892)

Aletris Meunier (French) - *Aletris farinosa* L. (7) (1828)

Aletris radix (Official name of Materia Medica) - *Aletris farinosa* L. (7) (1828)

Aleurites - *Aleurites* J.R. Forst. & G. Forst. (50) (present)

Alexanders [Alexander] - *Thaspium trifoliatum* (L.) Gray var. *aureum* Britt. (19, 92) (1840-1876), *Zinnia* L. (92) (1876), *Zizia aptera* (Gray) Fern. (19) (1840), *Zizia trifoliata* (Michx.) Fern. (5) (1913), *Zizia* W.D.J. Koch (1, 93, 158) (1900-1936)

Alexandra palm - *Archontophoenix alexandrae* (F. Muell.) H. Wendl. & Drude (109) (1949) for Princess Alexandra of Denmark

Alexandrine clover - *Trifolium alexandrinum* L. (110) (1886)

Alface (Spanish) - *Lactuca sativa* L. (180) (1633)

Alfafa (Spanish from Arabic) - *Medicago sativa* L. (45, 110) (1886-1896)

Alfalfa - *Medicago* L. (1, 4, 50, 93) (1932–present), *Medicago sativa* L. (3, 4, 5, 32, 45, 50, 52, 63, 66, 68, 72, 82, 85, 87, 93, 95, 97, 106, 107, 109, 114, 118, 122, 124, 125, 129, 138, 151, 155, 156, 157, 158) (1884–present) from alfacfacah meaning best sort of fodder in Arabian or from Al-chelfa that which grows after something else

Alfalfa dodder - *Cuscuta approximata* Bab. (50, 82) (1930–present), *Cuscuta epithymum* (L.) L. (68) (1913) Ottawa

Alfasafat (Spanish from Arabic) - *Medicago sativa* L. (110) (1886)

Alfilaria - *Erodium cicutarium* (L.) L'Hér. ex Aiton (5, 45, 87, 122, 138, 157) (1884-1937) among Spanish, *Erodium* L'Her. ex Aiton (1, 106) (1930-1932)

Alfilerilla [Alfillarilla, Alfilarilla] - *Erodium cicutarium* (L.) L'Hér. ex Aiton (5, 76, 109, 155, 156, 158) (1896), *Erodium* L'Her. ex Aiton (45) (1896), *Erodium moschatum* (L.) L'Hér. ex Aiton (76) (1896) Berkeley CA

Alforfon (Spanish) - *Fagopyrum esculentum* Moench (46) (1879)

Alga (Millanois) - *Triticum spelta* L. (180) (1633)

Alga-like pondweed - *Potamogeton confervoides* Reichb. (5) (1913)

Algaroba [Algarroba] - *Ceratonia siliqua* L. (92) (1876), *Prosopis juliflora* (Sw.) DC. (107, 158) (1900-1919), *Prosopis laevigata* (Willd.) M.C.Johnst. (107) (1919)

Algaroba bean - *Ceratonia siliqua* L. (92) (1876)

Algarola (Spanish) - *Prosopis juliflora* (Sw.) DC. (76) (1896) AZ

Algerian ivy - Hedera helix L. subsp. canariensis (Willd.) Cout. (109, 138) (1923-1949)

Algerita [Algeritas] - *Mahonia trifoliolata* (Moric.) Fedde (15, 50, 155) (1895–present)

Algodon (Southern Europe) - *Gossypium herbaceum* L. (110) (1886)

Alhuzama - *Vitex agnus-castus* L. (106) (1930)

Aliso - *Platanus wrightii* S. Wats. (153) (1913) NM

Alixier arborescent (French) - *Crataegus viridis* L. (20) (1857)

Alkakengie - *Physalis alkekengi* L. (180) (1633)

Alkali aster - *Xylorhiza glabriuscula* Nutt. (155) (1942)

Alkali blite - *Chenopodium rubrum* L. (1, 3, 4) (1932-1986)

Alkali bluegrass - *Poa secunda* J. Presl (155) (1942)

Alkali bulrush - *Schoenoplectus maritimus* (L.) Lye (139, 155) (1942-1944)

Alkali buttercup - *Ranunculus cymbalaria* Pursh (50) (present)

Alkali cordgrass - *Spartina gracilis* Trin. (3, 50, 146, 155) (1939–present)

Alkali dropseed - *Sporobolus airoides* (Torr.) Torr. (116, 140) (1944-1958)

Alkali grass [Alkali-grass, Alkaligrass] - *Distichlis* Raf. (1, 93) (1932-1936), *Distichlis spicata* (L.) Greene (5, 94, 116, 119, 144, 146) (1899-1958), *Pascopyrum smithii* (Rydb.) A. Löve (68) (1890), *Puccinellia distans* (Jacq.) Parl. (140) (1944) CO, *Puccinellia nuttalliana* (J.A. Schultes) A.S. Hitchc. (3) (1977), *Puccinellia* Parl. (50) (present), *Sporobolus airoides* (Torr.) Torr. (129) (1894) SD

Alkali lyme grass [Alkali lyme-grass] - *Leymus salinus* (M.E. Jones) A. Löve subsp. *salinus* (94) (1901)

Alkali mallow - *Malvella leprosa* (Ortega) Krapov (50) (present)

Alkali marsh aster - *Almutaster pauciflorus* (Nutt.) A.& D. Löve (50) (present)

Alkali milkvetch [Alkali milk-vetch] - *Astragalus racemosus* Pursh (4) (1986)

Alkali mountain grass - *Puccinellia nuttalliana* (J.A. Schultes) A.S. Hitchc. (141) (1899)

Alkali muhly - *Muhlenbergia asperifolia* (Nees & Meyen ex Trin.) Parodi (140, 155) (1942-1944)

Alkali plantain - *Plantago eriopoda* Torr. (3, 4) (1977-1986)

Alkali sacaton - *Sporobolus airoides* (Torr.) Torr. (3, 50, 119, 122, 140, 146, 155) (1937–present)

Alkali saccatone - *Panicum bulbosum* Kunth (94) (1901) TX

Alkali sagebrush - *Artemisia longifolia* Nutt. (155) (1942)

Alkali seepweed - *Suaeda* Forsk. ex J.F. Gmel. (155) (1942), *Suaeda moquinii* (Torr.) Greene (155) (1942)

Alkali sida - *Malvella leprosa* (Ortega) Krapov (155) (1942)

Alkali swainsonpea - *Sphaerophysa* DC. (50) (present), *Sphaerophysa salsula* (Pallas) DC. (50) (present)

Alkali wildrye - *Leymus simplex* (Scribn. & Williams) D.R. Dewey (50) (present)

Alkali yellowtops - *Flaveria campestris* Johnst. (50) (present)

Alkali-grass [Alkali-grass] - *Zigadenus elegans* Pursh (75, 157, 158) (1894-1900) MN, *Zigadenus venenosus* S. Wats. var. *gramineus* (Rydb.) Walsh ex M.E. Peck (148) (1939) CO

Alkaline grass - *Distichlis spicata* (L.) Greene (88, 151) (1885-1896)

Alkali-weed [Alkaliweed, Alkali weed] - *Cressa* L. (4, 50) (1986–present)

Alkanet - *Anchusa* L. (1, 82, 85, 109, 158) (1900-1949), possibly *Lithospermum caroliniense* (Walter ex J.F. Gmel.) MacMill. var. *caroliniense* (184) (1793)

Alkegnegi berries - *Physalis alkekengi* L. (92) (1876)

Alkegneki - *Physalis alkekengi* L. (109) (1949)

Alkékenge coqueret (French) - *Physalis alkekengi* L. (158) (1900)

Alkekengi - *Physalis alkekengi* L. (158) (1900), *Physalis peruviana* L. (107) (1919)

Alkekengi (of shops) - *Physalis alkekengi* L. (180) (1633)

Allamanda - *Allamanda* L. (138, 155) (1931-1942)

All-bone [Allbone, All bones, All-bones] - *Lichen roccella* L. (92) (1876), *Stellaria holostea* L. (5, 156, 180) (1633-1923)

Allegheny barberry - *Berberis canadensis* P. Mill. (138) (1923)

Allegheny blackberry - *Rubus alleghaniensis* Porter (50, 138, 155) (1923–present)

Allegheny foamflower - *Tiarella cordifolia* L. (138) (1923)

Allegheny fringe [Alleghany fringe] - *Adlumia fungosa* (Aiton) Greene ex B. S. P. (5, 92, 156) (1876-1923)

Allegheny goatsbread [Alleghany goatsbread] - *Aruncus dioicus* (Walt.) Fern. var. *dioicus* (155) (1942)

Allegheny menziesia [Alleghany menziesia] - *Menziesia pilosa* (Michx. ex Lam.) Juss. ex Pers. (5, 138) (1913-1923)

Allegheny monkey-flower [Allegheny monkeyflower, Alleghany monkey-flower, Alleghany monkeyflower] - *Mimulus ringens* L. (3, 4, 50, 109, 138, 155) (1923–present)

Allegheny mountain spurge [Alleghany mountain spurge] - *Pachysandra procumbens* Michx. (5, 156) (1913-1923)

Allegheny nailwort - *Paronychia argyrocoma* (Michx.) Nutt. (138) (1923)

Allegheny onion [Alleghany onion] - *Allium allegheniense* Small (5, 155) (1913-1942)

Allegheny pachysandra [Allegany pachysandra] - *Pachysandra procumbens* Michx. (109) (1949)

Allegheny plum - *Prunus alleghaniensis* Porter (138) (1923)

Allegheny sandmyrtle - *Leiophyllum buxifolium* (Berg.) Ell. (138) (1923)

Allegheny service-berry [Allegany serviceberry] - *Amelanchier arborea* (Michx. f.) Fern. (155) (1942)

Allegheny shadblow - *Amelanchier arborea* (Michx. f.) Fern. (138) (1923)

Allegheny sloe [Alleghany sloe] - *Prunus alleghaniensis* Porter (5, 156) (1913-1923)

Allegheny thermopsis [Alleghany thermopsis] - *Thermopsis mollis* (Michx.) M. A. Curtis (5) (1913)

Allegheny thorn [Alleghany thorn] - *Crataegus intricata* Lange (5, 97) (1913-1937)

Allegheny vine [Alleghany vine, Alleghany-vine] - *Adlumia fungosa* (Aiton) Greene ex B. S. P. (5, 50, 73, 109, 156) (1892–present), *Adlumia* Raf. ex DC. (1) (1932)

Alleluia - *Genista tinctoria* L. (5) (1913), *Oxalis montana* Raf. (possibly) (5, 156, 178) (1526-1923)

Allemand - *Chenopodium ambrosioides* L. (107) (1745)

Allen's buttercup - *Ranunculus allenii* B.L. Rob. (5, 50) (1913–present)

Allen's eriogonum - *Eriogonum alleni* S. Wats. (5) (1913)

Allen's sundrops - *Oenothera fruticosa* L. subsp. *fruticosa* (5) (1913)

All-good [All good] - *Chenopodium bonus-henricus* L. (5, 107, 156) (1913-1923)

All-heal [All heal] - *Prunella vulgaris* L. (5, 158) (1900-1913), *Stachys byzantina* K. Koch ex Scheele (107, 156) (1919-1923), *Stachys palustris* L. (107, 156) (1919-1923), *Valeriana officinalis* L. (5, 92, 156) (1876-1923)

Allia - *Allium canadense* L. (46) (1879)

Alliaire Commune (French) - *Alliaria petiolata* (Bieb.) Cavara & Grande (158) (1900)

Alliaria - *Alliaria* Heister ex Fabr. (50) (present), *Alliaria petiolata* (Bieb.) Cavara & Grande (178) (1526)

Alligator alternathera - *Alternanthera philoxeroides* (Mart.) Griseb. (155) (1942)

Alligator bark juniper - *Juniperus deppeana* Steud. (153) (1913)

Alligator bonnets - *Nuphar lutea* (L.) Sm. subsp. *sagittifolia* (Walt.) E.O. Beal (5, 156) (1913-1923), *Nymphaea odorata* Aiton subsp. *odorata* (156) (1923)

Alligator buttons - *Nelumbo lutea* Willd. (156) (1923)

Alligator juniper - *Juniperus deppeana* Steud. (109, 122, 124, 138) (1923-1949)

Alligator tree [Alligator-tree] - *Liquidambar styraciflua* L. (5, 156) (1913-1923)

Alligator wampee - *Pontederia cordata* L. (158) (1900)

Alligator wood - *Liquidambar styraciflua* L. (74) (1893) WV

Alligator-apple [Alligator apple] - *Annona glabra* L. (92, 165) (1807-1876), *Annona muricata* L. (92, 165) (1807-1876)

Alligator-pear [Alligator pear] - *Persea* Mill. (106) (1930)

Allium - *Allium sativum* L. (52) (1919)

Allocarya - *Plagiobothrys* Fisch. & C.A. Mey. (158) (1900)

All-seed [All seed] - *Amaranthus blitum* L. (92) (1876), *Chenopodium polyspermum* L. (156) (1923), *Polygonum aviculare* L. (158) (1900), *Radiola linoides* Roth (156) (1923)

Allspice - *Lindera benzoin* Blume. (7) (1828), *Pimenta dioica* (L.) Merr. (92, 107, 109, 138) (1876-1949)

Allspice bush - *Lindera benzoin* Blume. (6, 186) (1814-1892)

Allspice of Carolina - *Calycanthus floridus* L. (183) (~1756)

Allthorn - *Koeberlinia spinosa* Zucc. (122, 124) (1937)

Allum root - *Heuchera* L. (10) (1818)

All-yellow sedge [All yellow sedge] - *Carex folliculata* L. (66) (1903)

Almicigo (Spanish) - *Bursera simaruba* (L.) Sargent (20) (1857)

Almond - *Prunus* L. (158) (1900)

Almond cherry - *Prunus caroliniana* (P. Mill.) Aiton (possibly) (20) (1857)

Almond eucalyptus - *Eucalyptus amygdalina* Labill. (138) (1923)

Almond or Almond tree - *Prunus dulcis* (Mill.) D.A. Webber (7, 59, 82, 106, 107, 110, 138, 165) (1526-1923)

Almond willow - *Salix amygdaloides* Anderss. (113, 130) (1890-1895)

Almond-leaf willow [Almond-leaved willow] - *Salix amygdaloides* Anderss. (5, 156) (1913-1923)

Alnus - *Alnus rubra* Bong. (52) (1919)

Alocasia - *Alocasia* (Schott) G. Don (138, 155) (1923-1942)

Aloe - *Aloe* L. (109, 178, 179) (1526-1949), *Aloe vera* (L.) Burm. f. (178) (1596)

Aloe root [Aloe-root] - *Aletris farinosa* L. (5, 6, 7, 64, 92, 156) (1828-1908)

Aloe yucca - *Yucca aloifolia* L. (50) (present)

Aloe-leaf yucca [Aloe-leafed yucca] - *Yucca aloifolia* L. (124) (1937)

Alouseme (Mexican) - *Purshia stansburiana* (Torr.) Henrickson (147) (1856)

Alpine aster - *Aster alpinus* L. (155) (1942)

Alpine azalea - *Loiseleuria* Desv. (156) (1923), *Loiseleuria procumbens* (L.) Desv. (5) (1913)

Alpine bartsia - *Bartsia alpina* L. (5) (1913)

Alpine bearberry - *Arctostaphylos* Adans. (1) (1932), *Arctostaphylos alpina* (L.) Spreng. (5) (1913)

Alpine birch - *Betula nana* L. (5) (1913)

Alpine bistort - *Polygonum viviparum* L. (3, 5, 131) (1899-1977)

Alpine bladderpod - *Lesquerella alpina* (Nutt.) S. Wats. (50) (present)

Alpine bluegras - *Poa alpina* L. (140) (1944)

Alpine bog kalmia - *Kalmia microphylla* (Hook.) Heller (138) (1923)

Alpine brook saxifrage - *Saxifraga rivularis* L. (5, 156) (1913-1923)

Alpine brown bent - *Agrostis canina* L. (66) (1903)

Alpine bulrush - *Trichophorum alpinum* (L.) Pers. (50) (present)

Alpine cat-tail [Alpine cat's tail] - *Phleum alpinum* L. (5) (1913)

Alpine chickweed - *Cerastium beeringianum* Cham. & Schlecht. subsp. *earlei* (Rydb.) Hultén (5) (1913)

Alpine circaea - *Circaea alpina* L. (155) (1942)

Alpine clematis - *Clematis columbiana* (Nutt.) Torr. & Gray var. *tenuiloba* (Gray) J. Pringle (131) (1899) SD

Alpine club-moss - *Lycopodium alpinum* L. (5, 50) (1913–present)

Alpine cotton-grass [Alpine cotton grass] - *Trichophorum* Pers. (1) (1932), *Trichophorum alpinum* (L.) Pers. (5) (1913)

Alpine cress - *Cardamine bellidifolia* L. (5, 156) (1913-1923)

Alpine currant - *Ribes alpinum* L. (107, 109) (1919-1949)

Alpine enchanter's nightshade - *Circaea alpina* L. (131) (1899) SD

Alpine everlasting - *Antennaria alpina* (L.) Gaertn. (5) (1913)

Alpine fescue - *Festuca brachyphylla* J.A. Schultes ex J.A. & J.H. Schultes (50) (present)

Alpine fir - *Abies lasiocarpa* (Hook.) Nutt. (101, 109, 138, 155) (1905-1942) MT

Alpine fleabane - *Erigeron elatus* (Hook.) Greene (138) (1923)

Alpine forget-me-not [Alpine forgetmenot] - *Myosotis sylvatica* Ehrh. ex Hoffmann (138, 155) (1923-1942)

Alpine foxtail - *Alopecurus alpinus* Sm. (5, 45, 94) (1896-1913)

Alpine golden buckwheat - *Eriogonum flavum* Nutt. (50) (present)

Alpine holy grass [Alpine holygrass] - *Hierochloe alpina* (Sw. ex Willd.) Roemer & J.A. Schultes (66, 90) (1885-1903), *Hierochloe alpina* (Sw. ex Willd.) Roemer & J.A. Schultes subsp. *alpina* (5, 45, 94) (1896-1913)

Alpine ladies'-mantle [Alpine ladies mantle] - *Alchemilla alpina* L. (165) (1768)

Alpine leafy-bract aster [Alpine leafybract aster] - *Symphyotrichum foliaceum* (DC.) Nesom (50) (present), *Symphyotrichum foliaceum* (DC.) Nesom var. *apricum* (Gray) Nesom (155) (1942)

Alpine milfoil - *Achillea alpina* L. (165) (1768)

Alpine milkvetch [Alpine milk vetch] - *Astragalus alpinus* L. (4, 5, 85, 131, 155) (1899-1986)

Alpine monkey-flower [Alpine monkeyflower] - *Mimulus tilingii* Regel var. *caespitosus* (Greene) A.L. Grant (138) (1923)

Alpine oat - *Helictotrichon mortonianum* (Scribn.) Henrard (140) (1944) CO

Alpine phacelia - *Phacelia hastata* Dougl. ex Lehm. var. *hastata* (155) (1942)

Alpine pine - *Pinus albicaulis* Engelm. (101) (1905) MT

Alpine pondweed - *Potamogeton alpinus* Balbis (50) (present)

Alpine poppy - *Papaver alpinum* L. (109, 138) (1923-1949)

Alpine ptarmigan-berry [Alpine ptarmiganberry] - *Arctostaphylos alpina* (L.) Spreng. (155) (1942)

Alpine pussytoes - *Antennaria alpina* (L.) Gaertn. (155) (1942)

Alpine pyrola - *Pyrola asarifolia* Michx. (155) (1942)

Alpine reed bent - *Calamagrostis pickeringii* Gray (66) (1903)

Alpine rockcress [Alpine rock cress] - *Arabis alpina* L. (5, 138, 155) (1913-1942)

Alpine rush - *Juncus alpinoarticulatus* Chaix subsp. *nodulosus* (Wahlenb.) Hämet-Ahti (155) (1942)

Alpine sagebrush - *Artemisia scopulorum* Gray (155) (1942)

Alpine sedge - *Carex hallii* Olney (5) (1913), *Carex scirpoidea* Michx. (66) (1903)

Alpine spear grass - *Poa laxa* Haenke (5) (1913)

Alpine speedwell - *Vernonia noveboracensis* (L.) Michx. (1, 93) (1932-1936), *Veronica wormskjoldii* Roemer & J.A. Schultes (138) (1923)

Alpine strawberry - *Fragaria vesca* L. (49, 107, 138) (1919-1932)

Alpine sweet grass [Alpine sweetgrass] - *Hierochloe alpina* (Sw. ex Willd.) Roemer & J.A. Schultes subsp. *alpina* (50) (present)

Alpine sweet-vetch [Alpine sweetvetch] - *Hedysarum alpinum* L. (50) (present)

Alpine timothy - *Phleum alpinum* L. (45, 50, 94, 146, 152, 155) (1896–present)

Alpine vanilla grass - *Hierochloe alpina* (Sw. ex Willd.) Roemer & J.A. Schultes subsp. *alpina* (45) (1896)

Alpine violet - *Viola labradorica* Schrank. (5) (1913)

Alpine whitlow grass - *Draba alpina* L. (5) (1913)

Alpine willow herb - *Epilobium anagallidifolium* Lam. (5) (1913)

Alpine woodsia - *Woodsia alpina* (Bolton) S.F. Gray (5, 50) (1913–present)

Alpine yarrow - *Achillea alpina* L. (155) (1942)

Alpine-azalea [Alpine azalea] - *Loiseleuria* Desv. (138) (1923), *Loiseleuria procumbens* (L.) Desv. (109, 138, 156) (1923-1949)

Alpinia - *Alpinia* Roxb. (138) (1923)

Alpist - *Phalaris canariensis* L. (158) (1900) Europe and Canary Islands, *Phalaris caroliniana* Walt. (158) (1900)

Alpisti - *Phalaris canariensis* L. (178) (1596), *Phalaris canariensis* L. (178, 180) (1596-1633)

Alsatian clover - *Trifolium hybridum* L. (5, 93, 156, 158) (1900-1936)

Alsei (German) - *Artemisia absinthium* L. (158) (1900)

Alsike - *Trifolium hybridum* L. (129, 158) (1894-1900)

Alsike clover - *Trifolium hybridum* L. (3, 4, 5, 45, 50, 68, 76, 82, 85, 93, 106, 109, 110, 129, 138, 155, 156, 158) (1894–present)

Alstonia - *Alstonia* R. Br. (155) (1942)

Alstroemeria - *Alstroemeria* L. (138, 155) (1923-1942)

Altai fescue - *Festuca altaica* Trin. (50) (present)

Altea (Spanish) - *Althaea officinalis* L. (158) (1900)

Alteris - *Aletris farinosa* L. (57) (1917)

Alternate-branch dogwood [Alternate branched dogwood] - *Cornus alternifolia* L. f. (8) (1785)

Alternate-leaf cornel [Alternate-leaved cornel] - *Cornus alternifolia* L. f. (5, 156) (1913-1923)

Alternate-leaf dogwood [Alternate-leaved dogwood, Alternate leaved dog wood] - *Cornus alternifolia* L. f. (5, 42, 72) (1814-1913)

Alternathera - *Alternanthera* Forsk. (155) (1942)

Althea rose - *Alcea rosea* L. (46) (1879)

Althee (German) - *Althaea officinalis* L. (158) (1900)

Altsa'sti (Cherokee, wreath for the head) - *Vicia caroliniana* Walt. (102) (1886)

Alubia (Spanish) - *Phaseolus vulgaris* L. (107) (1919)

Alumbloom [Alum-bloom, Alum bloom] - *Geranium maculatum* L. (5, 64, 76, 156, 157, 158) (1896-1929)

Alumroot [Alum-root, Alum root] - *Geranium maculatum* L. (5, 6, 7, 49, 52, 55, 64, 76, 92, 156, 157, 158, 186) (1814-1923), *Heuchera americana* L. (5, 14, 49, 57, 92, 158, 186, 187) (1814-1882), *Heuchera* L. (2, 4, 50, 40, 82, 93, 109, 138, 155, 156, 158) (1895–present), *Heuchera richardsonii* R. Br. (3, 121) (1918?-1977), possibly *Heuchera villosa* Michx. (7) (1828)

Aluyne (French) - *Artemisia absinthium* L. (158) (1900)

Alvaradoa - *Alvaradoa* Liebm. (155) (1942)

Alyssum - *Alyssum minus* (L.) Rothm. (50) (present), *Alyssum desertorum* Stapf (4) (1986), *Alyssum* L. (1, 4, 138, 155, 158) (1900-1986), *Lobularia maritima* (L.) Desv. (possibly) (92) (1876)

Alyssum-leaf phlox [Alyssumleaf phlox] - *Phlox alyssifolia* Greene (50) (present)

Alyxia - *Alyxia* Banks ex R. Br. (155) (1942)

Ămădita'tĭ (Cherokee, water dipper) - *Eupatorium purpureum* L. (102) (1886) stem was used as straw for sucking water

Amadou - *Boletus fomentarius* L. (92) (1876)

Amandalarios - *Prunus dulcis* (Mill.) D.A. Webber (107) (1919)

Amandes de terre (French) - *Cyperus esculentus* L. (158) (1900)

Amanita - *Amanita muscaria* (L.) Lam., (14, 148) (1882-1939), *Amanita* Pers. (155) (1942)

Amanitopsis - *Amanitopsis* Roze (155) (1942)

Amara-dulcis [Amara dulcis] - *Solanum dulcamara* L. (158, 178) (1599-1900)

Amaranth - *Amaranthus hybridus* L. (157, 158) (1900-1929), *Amaranthus hypochondriacus* L. (49, 58, 92) (1869-1898), *Amaranthus* L. (1, 10, 109, 138, 155) (1818-1949), *Amaranthus tricolor* L. (110) (1886)

Amaryllis - *Amaryllis* L. (155) (1942) Greek for splendor, name of sheperdess in Virgil

Amazon-lily [Amazonlily] - *Eucharis grandiflora* Planch. & Linden (109) (1949), *Eucharis* Planch. & Linden (138) (1923)

Amazon-vine [Amazonvine] - *Stigmaphyllon* A. Juss. (50, 138) (1923–present)

Ambarella - *Spondias dulcis* Parkinson (109) (1949)

Ambel - *Nymphaea lotus* L. (174) (1753)

Amber - *Hypericum perforatum* L. (5, 156, 158) (1900-1923)

Amber seed - *Abelmoschus esculentus* (L.) Moench (92) (1876)

Amber tree - *Acanthospermum* Schrank (92) (1876), *Gentianopsis virgata* (Raf.) Holub (92) (1876)

Amberboa - *Amberboa* (Pers.) Less. (155) (1942)

Ambiguous sunflower - *Helianthus ×ambiguus* (Gray) Britt. [*divaricatus × giganteus*] (72) (1907)

Ambrette - *Abelmoschus esculentus* (L.) Moench (92) (1876)

Ambroise de Mexique (French) - *Chenopodium ambrosioides* L. (158) (1900)

Ambrose - *Chenopodium botrys* L. (5, 156, 157, 158) (1900-1929), *Teucrium scorodonia* L. (156) (1923)

Ambrosia - *Ambrosia artemisiifolia* L. (57, 92) (1876-1917), *Ambrosia artemisiifolia* L. var. *elatior* (L.) Descourtils (92) (1876), *Chenopodium ambrosioides* L. (69, 156, 158) (1900-1904), *Chenopodium botrys* L. (75) (1894) Concord MA

Ambrosie - *Ambrosia artemisiifolia* L. (6) (1892)

Ameda - *Pinus strobus* L. (46) (1879)

American panic grass [American panic-grass] - *Dichanthelium sabulorum* (Lam.) Gould & C.A. Clark var. *thinium* (A.S. Hitchc. & Chase) Gould & C.A. Clark (94) (1901)

American abscess-root [American abscess root] - *Polemonium reptans* L. (5, 156) (1913-1923)

American adenocaulon - *Adenocaulon bicolor* Hook. (155) (1942)

American agave - *Agave americana* L. (92) (1876)

American alder - *Alnus incana* (L.) Moench subsp. *rugosa* (DuRoi)

Clausen (5, 156, 158) (1900-1923), *Alnus serrulata* (Aiton) Willd. (92) (1876)

American aletris - *Aletris farinosa* L. (165) (1768)

American alkanet - *Lithospermum canescens* (Michx.) Lehm. (156, 157, 158) (1900-1923)

American allspice - *Calycanthus floridus* L. (156) (1923)

American aloe - *Agave americana* L. (2, 92, 103, 110) (1871-1895), *Agave* L. (2, 156, 167) (1814-1895), *Manfreda virginica* (L.) Salisb. ex Rose (58) (1869)

American alumroot - *Heuchera americana* L. (50, 138, 155) (1923–present)

American anchusa - *Lithospermum canescens* (Michx.) Lehm. (92, 157, 158) (1876-1929)

American angelica - *Angelica atropurpurea* L. (64) (1907)

American arbor-vitae [American arbor vitae, American arborvitae] - *Thuja occidentalis* L. (2, 8, 107, 109, 112, 136, 138) (1785-1949)

American archangel - *Angelica atropurpurea* L. (57) (1917)

American arrow-head - *Sagittaria latifolia* Willd. (46) (1879) NY

American asarabacca - *Asarum canadense* L. (186, 187) (1814-1818)

American asp - *Populus tremuloides* Michx. (158) (1900)

American aspen or American aspen tree - *Populus tremuloides* Michx. (5, 6, 8, 20, 19, 49, 53, 57, 72, 82, 92, 93, 108, 109, 131, 156, 157, 158, 160) (1785-1949)

American atragene - *Clematis occidentalis* (Hornem.) DC. var. *occidentalis* (42) (1814)

American bald cypress - *Taxodium distichum* (L.) L.C. Rich. (2) (1895)

American balm Gilead - *Populus balsamifera* L. subsp. *balsamifera* (92) (1876)

American baneberry [American bane berry] - *Actaea rubra* (Aiton) Willd. (42) (1814) SD

American barberry - *Berberis canadensis* P. Mill. (5, 107, 156) (1913-1923), *Berberis vulgaris* L. (92) (1876)

American barberry bush - *Berberis canadensis* P. Mill. (7) (1828)

American basswood - *Tilia americana* L. (50, 109) (1949–present)

American bastard-sanicle - *Mitella diphylla* L. (187) (1818)

American beakgrain - *Diarrhena americana* Beauv. (50) (present), *Diarrhena obovata* (Gleason) Brandenburg (3, 50) (1977–present)

American beans - *Phaseolus vulgaris* L. (107) (1670)

American beauty-berry [American beautyberry] - *Callicarpa americana* L. (4, 50, 155) (1942–present)

American beebalm [American bee balm] - *Monarda didyma* L. (5) (1913)

American beech - *Fagus grandifolia* Ehrh. (2, 5, 57, 65, 97, 107, 109, 112, 138, 158) (1895-1949), *Fagus* L. (112, 138) (1923-1937)

American beech tree - *Fagus sylvatica* L. (8) (1785)

American bellflower - *Campanulastrum americanum* (L.) Small (4, 50, 155) (1942–present)

American bennet - *Geum virginianum* L. (157, 158) (1900-1929)

American bird's-foot trefoil - *Lotus unifoliolatus* (Hook.) Benth. (50) (present)

American bittersweet [American bitter-sweet] - *Celastrus scandens* L. (50, 109 122, 124, 138, 155) (1923–present)

American black cherry - *Padus serotina* (Ehrh.) Borkh. (46) (1879)

American black currant - *Ribes americanum* Mill. (50, 109 138, 155) (1923–present)

American black larch - *Larix laricina* (Du Roi.) Koch. (58) (1869)

American black lime - *Tilia americana* L. (8) (1785)

American black poplar - *Populus nigra* L. var. *hudsonica* C.K.Schneid. (20) (1857)

American black-berried elder - *Sambucus nigra* L. (8) (1785)

American blackberry bush - *Rubus occidentalis* L. (41) (1770)

American bladdernut [American bladder-nut, American bladder nut] - *Staphylea trifolia* L. (2, 4, 50, 5, 65, 72, 97, 107, 109, 138, 155, 156) (1895–present)

American blue vervain - *Verbena hastata* L. (57, 157, 158) (1900-1929)

American bluehearts - *Buchnera americana* L. (3, 50) (1977-present)

American bog asphodel - *Narthecium americanum* Ker-Gawl. (5, 158) (1900-1913)

American bog gale - *Myrica gale* L. (8) (1785)

American box - *Ostrya virginiana* (Mill.) K. Koch var. *virginiana* (38) (1820)

American boxwood [American box-wood] - *Cornus florida* L. (158) (1900)

American bramble - *Rubus occidentalis* L. (41) (1770)

American brooklime - *Veronica americana* Schwein. ex Benth. (5, 82, 93, 131, 156, 158) (1899-1936)

American broomrape - *Conopholis americana* (L. f.) Wallr. (92, 156) (1876-1923)

American buchnera - *Buchnera americana* L. (42) (1814)

American buckbean - *Menyanthes trifoliata* L. (7) (1828)

American bugbane - *Cimicifuga americana* Michx. (2, 5, 156) (1895-1923)

American bugleweed - *Lycopus americanus* Muhl. ex W. Bart. (4, 138, 155) (1923-1986)

American bugseed - *Corispermum americanum* (Nutt.) Nutt. (50) (present)

American bulrush - *Schoenoplectus americanus* (Pers.) Volk. ex Schinz & R. Keller (139, 155) (1942-1944)

American burnet - *Sanguisorba canadensis* L. (138) (1923)

American burnweed - *Erechtites hieraciifolia* (L.) Raf. ex DC. (50, 155) (1942–present)

American bur-reed [American burreed] - *Sparganium americanum* Nutt. (50, 155) (1942–present)

American button-wood, American button wood - *Cephalanthus occidentalis* L. (42, 187) (1814-1818)

American callicarpa - *Callicarpa americana* L. (42) (1814)

American calumba - *Frasera caroliniensis* Walt. (14) (1882), *Frasera* Walt. (2, 158) (1895–1900)

American carrot - *Daucus pusillus* Michx. (72, 97, 122) (1907-1937)

American ceanothus - *Ceanothus americanus* L. (8) (1785)

American cembra pine - *Pinus flexilis* James (4, 20) (1857-1986)

American centaury - *Centaurea americana* Nutt. (86) (1878), *Sabatia* Adans. (2, 5, 19, 156) (1840-1923), *Sabatia angularis* (L.) Pursh (57, 58, 92, 156, 158, 186) (1814-1923), *Sabatia campestris* Nutt. (48) (1882) KS

American century plant - *Agave americana* L. (50) (present)

American chamaerhodos - *Chamaerhodos erecta* (L.) Bunge subsp. *nuttallii* (Pickering ex Rydb.) Hultén (5) (1913)

American cherry-laurel - *Prunus caroliniana* (P. Mill.) Aiton (109) (1949)

American chestnut or American chestnut tree - *Castanea dentata* (Marsh.) Borkh. (2, 5, 8, 46, 82, 107, 109, 137, 138, 187 (possibly)) (1785-1949), *Castanea sativa* Mill. (20) (1857)

American chickweed wintergreen - *Trientalis borealis* Raf. subsp. *borealis* (2) (1895)

American chinaroot [American china root] - *Smilax pseudochina* L. (5, 49, 92) (1876-1913)

American climbing buckwheat - *Polygonum scandens* L. (187) (1818)

American climbing fern - *Lygodium palmatum* (Bernh.) Sw. (50) (present)

American climbing staff-tree - *Celastrus scandens* L. (8) (1785)

American cocklebur - *Xanthium spinosum* L. (50) (present), *Xanthium strumarium* L. var. *canadense* (Mill.) Torr. & Gray (5, 62, 72, 93, 97, 131, 158) (1899-1937)

American cock's foot - *Dactylis glomerata* L. (56, 66) (1901-1903)

American coffee bean [American coffee-bean] or American coffeebean tree - *Gymnocladus dioicus* (L.) K. Koch (5, 6, 49, 92, 156, 157) (1892-1929)

American coffee tree - *Gymnocladus dioicus* (L.) K. Koch (61, 157, 158) (1870-1929)

American columbine - *Aquilegia canadensis* L. (138, 155, 187) (1818-1942)

American columbo - *Frasera caroliniensis* Walt. (possibly) (5, 7, 49, 57, 61, 64, 92, 186) (1814-1923), *Frasera* Walt. (156) (1923)

American colycinth - *Cucurbita foetidissima* Kunth (38) (1820)

American common hazle nut - *Corylus americana* Walt. (42) (1814)

American common holly - *Ilex aquifolium* L. (8) (1785)

American cornelian tree - *Cornus florida* L. (158) (1900)

American cow-parsnip [American cow parsnip] - *Heracleum maximum* Bartr. (107) (1919)

American cowslip [American cowslips] - *Caltha palustris* L. (5, 6, 19) (1840-1913), *Dodecatheon* L. (1, 10, 82, 156) (1818-1932), *Dodecatheon meadia* L. (2, 5, 14, 82, 97, 131, 156) (1882–1937)

American crab - *Malus angustifolia* (Aiton) Michx. var. *angustifolia* (107) (1919)

American crab apple - *Malus coronaria* (L.) Mill. (72, 106) (1907-1930), *Malus coronaria* (L.) Mill. var. *coronaria* (2, 107) (1895-1919), *Malus glaucescens* Rehdr. (5) (1913)

American cranberry - *Gaultheria hispidula* (L.) Muhl. ex Bigelow (possibly) (41) (1770), *Vaccinium* L. (1, 7, 41, 73) (1770-1932), *Vaccinium macrocarpon* Aiton (2, 5, 46, 47, 86, 109, 156, 158) (1852-1949), *Viburnum opulus* L. var. *americanum* Aiton (50, 138, 155) (1923–present)

American cress - *Barbarea verna* (P. Mill.) Aschers. (5, 156, 107) (1913-1923)

American cupscale - *Sacciolepis striata* (L.) Nash (50) (present)

American custard-apple - *Asimina triloba* (L.) Dunal (6, 49) (1892)

American cypress - *Taxodium distichum* (L.) L.C. Rich. (possibly) (189) (1767)

American daisy - *Houstonia caerulea* L. (86) (1878)

American date-plum [American date plum] - *Diospyros virginiana* L. (14) (1882)

American dewberry bush - *Rubus hispidus* L. (8) (1785)

American dianthera - *Justicia americana* (L.) Vahl (3, 4) (1977-1986)

American dittany - *Cunila origanoides* (L.) Britton (5, 7, 49, 92, 122, 158) (1828-1937)

American dodder - *Cuscuta americana* L. (42) (1814), *Cuscuta glomerata* Choisy (5, 82, 85, 93) (1913-1936)

American dog violet - *Viola canina* L. (174, 177) (1753-1762), *Viola conspersa* Reichenb. (3, 5, 156) (1913-1977)

American dogbane - *Apocynum androsaemifolium* L. (46) (1879), *Apocynum cannabinum* L. (46) (1879)

American dog's-tooth-violet [American dog's-tooth violet] - *Erythronium americanum* Ker. (187) (1818)

American dogwood - *Cornus florida* L. (158) (1900)

American dragonhead [American dragon head, American dragonhead] - *Dracocephalum parviflorum* Nutt. (5, 50, 72, 93, 131, 155) (1899–present)

American dune grass [American dunegrass] - *Leymus mollis* (Trin.) Pilger subsp. *mollis* (138) (1923)

American eel-grass [American eelgrass] - *Vallisneria americana* Michx. (50) (present)

American elder or American elder tree - *Sambucus nigra* L. subsp. *canadensis* (L.) R. Bolli (5, 41, 49, 53, 72, 93, 97, 109, 122, 124, 138, 155, 156, 157, 158) (1770-1942)

American elm - *Ulmus americana* L. (1, 3, 4, 5, 14, 37, 41, 46, 50, 82, 85, 97, 108, 109, 112, 122, 124, 138, 153, 155, 156, 157, 158) (1770–present), *Ulmus rubra* Muhl. (157) (1929)

American espen - *Populus tremuloides* Michx. (158) (1900)

American eurotia - *Krascheninnikovia lanata* (Pursh) A.D.J. Meeuse & Smit (5, 93) (1913-1936)

American false hellebore [American falsehellebore, American false-hellebore] - *Veratrum viride* Ait. (71, 139, 155) (1898-1944)

American false penny-royal [American false pennyroyal, American falsepennyroyal] - *Hedeoma pulegioides* (L.) Pers. (50, 155) (1942–present)

American featherfoil [American feather foil] - *Hottonia inflata* Ell. (5, 97, 122, 124) (1913-1937)

American feverfew [American fever-few, American fever few] - *Parthenium integrifolium* L. (5, 72, 97, 156, 158) (1900–1937)

American figwort - *Scrophularia marilandica* L. (157, 158) (1900-1929)

American filbert - *Corylus americana* Walt. (155) (1942)

American fleur-de-lis - *Iris versicolor* L. (64, 158) (1900-1908)

American flote grass - *Glyceria septentrionalis* A.S. Hitchc. (5) (1913)

American flower-de-luce - *Iris versicolor* L. (64, 158) (1900-1908)

American fly honeysuckle (American fly-honeysuckle) - *Lonicera canadensis* Bartr. ex Marsh. (5, 138, 156) (1913-1923)

American foxglove - *Aureolaria pedicularia* (L.) Raf. ex Farw. (49, 92) (1876-1898), *Digitalis pupurea* L. (92) (1876)

American fringe - *Chionanthus virginicus* L. (5, 156) (1913-1923)

American frog's-bit [American frog's bit] - *Limnobium spongia* (Bosc) L.C. Rich. ex Steud. (156) (1923)

American garlic - *Allium canadense* L. (46) (1879)

American gentian - *Gentiana catesbaei* Walt. (92) (1876)

American germander - *Teucrium canadense* L. (4, 5, 62, 80, 82, 93, 95, 138, 155, 156, 158) (1900–present)

American ginseng - *Panax quinquefolius* L. (7, 50, 64, 92, 109, 138, 155, 157, 158) (1828–present)

American globeflower - *Trollius laxus* Salisb. (5) (1913)

American great bulrush - *Schoenoplectus tabernaemontani* (K.C. Gmel.) Palla (5) (1913)

American great burnet - *Sanguisorba canadensis* L. (5) (1913)

American great valerian - *Polemonium reptans* L. (5, 156) (1913-1923)

American Greek valerian - *Polemonium reptans* L. (49, 92, 158) (1876-1900)

American green alder - *Alnus viridis* (Vill.) Lam. & DC. (138, 155) (1923-1942)

American gromwell - *Lithospermum latifolium* Michx. (3, 5, 72, 155, 156) (1907-1977)

American gum tree - *Bursera simaruba* (L.) Sargent (107, 174) (1753-1919)

American hackberry - *Celtis occidentalis* L. (2) (1895)

American halfchaff sedge - *Lipocarpha maculata* (Michx.) Torr. (50) (present)

American harebell - *Campanula rotundifolia* L. (155) (1942)

American haspen - *Populus tremuloides* Michx. (158) (1900)

American hawthorne - *Crataegus succulenta* Schrad. ex Link (85) (1932)

American hazel - *Corydalis micrantha* (Engelm. ex Gray) Gray subsp. *micrantha* (46) (1879)

American hazelnut [American hazel-nut] - *Corylus americana* Walt. (1, 2, 8, 50, 82, 109, 138, 157, 187) (1818–present)

American heath - *Hudsonia ericoides* L. (5, 156) (1913-1923), *Physostegia virginiana* (L.) Benth. (5, 156) (1913-1923)

American heather - *Physostegia virginiana* (L.) Benth. (156) (1923)

American hellebore - *Veratrum viride* Ait. (49, 52, 53, 54, 55, 59, 60, 92) (1876-1922)

American hemlock - *Cicuta maculata* L. (7, 92) (1828-1876)

American hemp - *Abutilon theophrasti* Medik (5, 156, 158) (1900-1923), *Apocynum cannabinum* L. (6, 64, 157, 158) (1892–1929)

American herb Christopher - *Actaea pachypoda* Ell. (6) (1892)

American herb Christopher with red berries - *Actaea rubra* (Aiton) Willd. (165) (1768)

American herb Christopher with white berries - *Actaea pachypoda* Ell. (165) (1768)

American herb Paris - *Trillium* L. (10) (1818)

American hogpeanut - *Amphicarpaea bracteata* (L.) Fern. (50) (present)

American holly - *Ilex opaca* Aiton (2, 5, 7, 15, 20, 38, 49, 92, 97, 107, 108, 109, 122, 124, 138, 147, 156) (1828-1937)

American honeysuckle - *Lonicera caprifolium* L. (156) (1923)

American hop - *Humulus lupulus* L. var. *lupuloides* E. Small (109) (1949)

American hop tree - *Ostrya virginiana* (Mill.) K. Koch (82) (1930)

American hop-hornbeam [American hop hornbeam, American hophornbeam] - *Ostrya virginiana* (Mill.) K. Koch var. *virginiana* (2, 6, 109, 138, 155) (1892-1949)

American hornbeam [American horn-beam] - *Carpinus caroliniana* Walt (2, 5, 41, 72, 93, 97, 109, 138, 156) (1770-1949), *Carpinus caroliniana* Walt. subsp. *caroliniana* (20, 42, 187) (1814-1857), *Carpinus caroliniana* Walt. subsp. *virginiana* (Marsh.) Furlow (8) (1785)

American horse-chestnut [American horse chestnut] - *Aesculus glabra* Willd. (5, 20, 156, 157, 158) (1857-1929)

American iceplant [American ice-plant] - *Monotropa uniflora* L. (5, 157, 158) (1900–1929)

American Indian-hemp [American Indian hemp] - *Apocynum cannabinum* L. (6, 59) (1892–1911)

American indigo - *Baptisia tinctoria* (L.) R. Br. ex Aiton f. (64, 92, 157) (1876-1908)

American ipecac - *Apocynum androsaemifolium* L. (6) (1892), *Euphorbia ipecacuanhae* L. (6, 49, 53, 92) (1892-1922), *Gillenia* Moench (2) (1895), *Gillenia trifoliata* (L.) Moench (156, 186) (1825-1923), *Porteranthus* Britt. ex Small (1) (1932), *Porteranthus stipulatus* (Muhl. ex Willd.) Britt. (2, 3, 5, 64, 49, 57, 92, 97, 109, 122, 156, 158) (1895-1977)

American ipecacuanha - *Euphorbia ipecacuanhae* L. (53, 186, 187) (1814-1922)

American ironwood [American iron-wood] - *Carpinus caroliniana* Walt. subsp. *caroliniana* (6) (1892)

American ivy - *Hedera* L. (1) (1932), *Parthenocissus quinquefolia* (L.) Planch. (5, 6, 8, 13, 49, 57, 58, 92, 106, 142, 156, 157, 158) (1785-1929)

American Jacob's-ladder [American Jacob's ladder] - *Polemonium vanbruntiae* Britton (5) (1913), *Smilax herbacea* L. (158) (1900)

American jasmine - *Ipomoea coccinea* L. (5, 156, 158) (1900-1923)

American jointvetch - *Aeschynomene americana* L. (155) (1942)

American joy [American-joy] - *Ampelopsis* Michx. (42) (1814), *Parthenocissus quinquefolia* (L.) Planch. (74, 157, 158) (1893-1929)

American Judas-tree [American Judas tree] - *Cercis canadensis* L. (5, 42, 93, 157, 158) (1814--1936)

American jute - *Abutilon theophrasti* Medik (5, 62, 74, 156, 157, 158) (1895-1929)

American kino root - *Geranium maculatum* L. (5, 92, 156) (1876-1923)

American knapweed - *Centaurea americana* Nutt. (106) (1930)

American korycarpus - *Diarrhena americana* Beauv. (5, 72) (1907-1913)

American larch - *Larix laricina* (Du Roi.) Koch (1, 5, 10, 20, 41, 46, 49, 57, 61, 92, 109, 138) (1770-1949)

American large aspen - *Populus grandidentata* Michx. (20) (1857)

American laurel - *Kalmia* L. (1, 2, 8, 10) (1818-1932), *Kalmia latifolia* L. (5, 6, 14, 71, 156, 187) (1818-1923), *Kalmia polifolia* Wangenh. (1, 2, 8, 10) (1818-1932)

American lettuce - *Lactuca canadensis* L. (157) (1929)

American licorice - *Amphicarpaea bracteata* (L.) Fern. var. *comosa* (L.) Fern. (5) (1913), *Glycyrrhiza lepidota* Pursh (5, 50, 92, 93, 97, 155, 156, 157, 158) (1876–present)

American lime or American lime tree [American lime-tree] - *Tilia americana* L. (20, 157, 158) (1857-1929)

American linden or American linden tree - *Tilia americana* L. (3, 5, 8, 85, 93, 95, 97, 109, 112, 131, 138, 155, 156, 157, 158) (1785-1977), *Osmanthus americanus* (L.) Benth. & Hook. f. ex Gray var. *americanus* (8, 19, 92, 107) (1785-1876)

American lin-tree - *Tilia americana* L. (157, 158) (1900-1929)

American lipocarpha - *Lipocarpha maculata* (Michx.) Torr. (5) (1913)

American liverleaf - *Hepatica nobilis* Schreb. var. *obtusa* (Pursh) Steyermark (49) (1898)

American liverwort - *Hepatica nobilis* Schreb. (53) (1922)

American locust - *Robinia pseudoacacia* L. (46, 187) (1818–1879)

American long-leaf sundew [American long leaved sun dew] - *Drosera intermedia* Hayne (42) (1814)

American lopseed - *Phryma leptostachya* L. (50, 155) (1942–present)

American lotus - *Nelumbo lutea* Willd. (3, 5, 50, 72, 82, 97, 106, 109, 120, 121, 138, 158, 183) (~1756–present)

American lotus-lily [American lotus lily] - *Nelumbo lutea* Willd. (157, 158) (1900-1929)

American lungwort - *Mertensia virginica* (L.) Pers. ex Link (46) (1879)

American maidenhair - *Adiantum pedatum* L. (7, 109, 138, 155, 157, 158) (1828-1949)

American mandrake - *Podophyllum peltatum* L. (64, 92, 158) (1876-1908)

American mangle - *Rhizophora mangle* L. (20) (1857)

American manna grass [American mannagrass] - *Glyceria grandis* S. Wats. (50, 140, 143, 155) (1936–present)

American marsh pennywort [American marsh penny wort] - *Hydrocotyle americana* L. (5, 156) (1913-1923)

American meadowsweet [American meadow sweet] - *Spiraea alba* Du Roi var. *latifolia* (Aiton) Dippel (5) (1913), *Spiraea* L. (5) (1913), *Spiraea salicifolia* L. (72) (1907)

American mezereon - *Dirca palustris* L. (5, 6, 19, 49, 92, 156) (1840-1923)

American milfoil - *Myriophyllum sibiricum* Komarov (4) (1986)

American milkvetch [American milk vetch] - *Astragalus americanus* (Hook.) M.E.Jones (4, 50) (1986–present)

American millet grass [American milletgrass] - *Milium effusum* L. (50) (present)

American mint - *Mentha arvensis* L. (156) (1923)

American mistletoe - *Phoradendron leucarpum* (Raf.) Reveal & M.C. Johnston (2, 5, 49, 53, 97, 122, 124, 138, 156, 174) (1753-1937)

American mitella - *Mitella diphylla* L. (190) (~1759)

American monk's-hood - *Aconitum uncinatum* L. (165) (1768)

American moss - *Tillandsia usneoides* (L.) L. (14) (1882)

American mountain-ash [American mountain ash] - *Sorbus americana* Marsh. (2, 5, 6, 82, 135, 138) (1892-1930)

American mulberry - *Morus rubra* L. (109, 156, 158) (1900-1949)

American nelumbo - *Nelumbo lutea* Willd. (5, 111, 157, 158) (1900-1929)

American nettle tree [American nettle-tree] - *Celtis occidentalis* L. (6, 20, 158, 187) (1818-1900)

American nightshade - *Phytolacca americana* L. (5, 69, 181) (~1678-1913), *Phytolacca americana* L. var. *americana* (6, 41, 49, 64, 71, 156, 157, 158, 186) (1770-1923)

American oat - *Helictotrichon hookeri* (Scribn.) Henr. (94) (1901)

American oil nut - *Pyrularia oleifera* (Muhl. ex Willd.) A. Gray (19) (1840)

American olive *Osmanthus americanus* (L.) Benth. & Hook. f. ex Gray var. *americanus* (8, 19, 92, 107) (1785-1876)

American onion garlick - *Allium canadense* L. (42) (1814)

American panicum - *Dichanthelium sabulorum* (Lam.) Gould & C.A. Clark var. *thinium* (A.S. Hitchc. & Chase) Gould & C.A. Clark (5) (1913)

American pansy - *Viola pedata* L. (156, 158) (1900-1923)

American parsley-fern - *Cryptogramma acrostichoides* R. Br. (109) (1949)

American pasqueflower [American pasque-flower] - *Anemone* L. (155) (1942), *Pulsatilla patens* (L.) Mill. (50) (present), *Pulsatilla patens* (L.) Mill. subsp. *multifida* (Pritz.) Zamels (138, 157, 158) (1900-1929)

American pawpaw - *Asimina triloba* (L.) Dunal (95, 157) (1911-1929)

American pellitory - *Parietaria pensylvanica* Muhl. ex Willd. (157) (1929)

American pennyroyal - *Hedeoma* Pers. (156) (1923), *Hedeoma pulegioides* (L.) Pers. (1, 2, 5, 6, 7, 46, 49, 53, 55, 57, 59, 63, 72, 82, 85, 93, 95, 156, 157, 158) (1879–1937)

American pennywort [American penny-wort] - *Hydrocotyle americana* L. (187) (1818)

American penthorum - *Penthorum sedoides* L. (187) (1818)

American pepper - *Capsicum annuum* L. (92) (1876)

American pillwort - *Pilularia americana* A. Braun (4, 50) (1986–present)

American plane or American plane tree [American planetree] - *Platanus occidentalis* L. (2, 8, 19, 38, 92, 109, 138, 155, 158) (1785-1949)

American planer tree - *Planera aquatica* J.F. Gmel. (2) (1895)

American plum - *Prunus americana* Marsh. (50, 82, 107, 137, 138, 155) (1919–present)

American pokeweed - *Phytolacca americana* L. (50) (present)

American poplar - *Liriodendron tulipifera* L. (186, 187) (1814-1818), *Populus tremuloides* Michx. (5, 6, 49, 52, 53, 156, 157, 158) (1892-1929)

American pulsatilla - *Pulsatilla patens* (L.) Mill. (5) (1913), *Pulsatilla patens* (L.) Mill.subsp. *multifida* (Pritz.) Zamels (6, 49, 157, 158) (1892-1929)

American pyrola - *Pyrola americana* Sweet (155) (1942)

American raspberry - *Rubus idaeus* L. subsp. *strigosus* (Michx.) Focke (46) (1879), *Rubus occidentalis* L. (8, 12) (1785-1820)

American red bellflower [American red bell flower, American red bell-flower] - *Ipomoea quamoclit* L. (5, 156, 158) (1900-1923)

American red centaury - *Sabatia angularis* (L.) Pursh (158) (1900)

American red currant - *Ribes triste* Pallas (5, 155) (1913-1942)

American red elder - *Sambucus racemosa* L. var. *racemosa* (109) (1949)

American red raspberry - *Rubus idaeus* L. (50) (present), *Rubus idaeus* L. subsp. *strigosus* (Michx.) Focke (1, 93, 155, 156, 158) (1900-1942)

American redbud [American red bud] - *Cercis canadensis* L. (2, 42, 137, 138) (1814-1895)

American red-rod cornel - *Cornus sericea* L. (186) (1814)

American red-rod cornus - *Cornus sanguinea* L. (8) (1785)

American rice - *Zizania* L. (10) (1818)

American rockbrake [American rock-brake, American rock brake] - *Cryptogramma acrostichoides* R. Br. (5, 50, 138) (1913–present), *Cryptogramma* R. Br. (50) (present)

American rosebay - *Rhododendron maximum* L. (71) (1898)

American rough-leaf elm tree [American rough leaved elm-tree] - *Ulmus americana* L. (8) (1785)

American rowan tree - *Sorbus scopulina* Greene (5) (1913)

American rown tree - *Sorbus americana* Marsh. (5) (1913)

American saffron - *Carthamus tinctorius* L. (49, 53, 57, 92, 158) (1876-1922)

American saltwort - *Batis maritima* L. (14) (1882)

American sanicle - *Heuchera americana* L. (5, 49, 92, 156, 158, 186) (1814-1923), *Heuchera villosa* Michx. (possibly) (5, 92, 156) (1876-1923), *Sanicula marilandica* L. (157, 158) (1900-1929)

American sapota - *Manilkara zapota* (L.) van Royen (165) (1768)

American sarsaparilla - *Aralia nudicaulis* L. (49, 58, 64, 92, 157, 158) (1869-1908)

American sassafras tree - *Sassafras albidum* (Nutt.) Nees (14) (1882)

American savin - *Juniperus virginiana* L. (46) (1879)

American savine - *Juniperus virginiana* L. (57) (1917)

American scarlet rose-mallow - *Hibiscus coccineus* Walt (86) (1878)

American sea rocket - *Cakile edentula* (Bigelow) Hook. (5, 156) (1913-1923), *Cakile edentula* (Bigelow) Hook. subsp. *edentula* var. *edentula* (2) (1895)

American seepweed - *Suaeda calceoliformis* (Hook.) Moq. (155) (1942)

American senna - *Cassia* L. (93) (1936), *Senna marilandica* (L.) Link (5, 7, 49, 53, 57, 92, 156, 157, 158, 186, 187) (1818-1923)

American service tree - *Sorbus americana* Marsh. (5, 6, 8) (1785-1913)

American shieldfern [American shield-fern] - *Dryopteris intermedia* (Muhl. ex Willd.) Gray (5, 122) (1913-1937)

American shrub yellow-root [American shrub yellow root] - *Xanthorhiza simplicissima* Marsh. (49) (1898)

American shrubby cinquefoil - *Dasiphora floribunda* (Pursh) Kartesz (8) (1785)

American silver fir - *Abies balsamea* (L.) Mill. (5, 58, 92, 158) (1869-1913), *Abies balsamea* (L.) Mill. var. *balsamea* (20) (1857)

American skullcap - *Scutellaria lateriflora* L. (157, 158) (1900-1929)

American slough grass [American sloughgrass] - *Beckmannia syzigachne* (Steud.) Fern. (possibly) (3, 50, 140, 155) (1942–present)

American smartweed - *Polygonum punctatum* Ell. (157, 158) (1900-1929)

American smoke tree [American smoketree, American smoke-tree] - *Cotinus coggygria* Scop. (112) (1937), *Cotinus obovatus* Raf. (5, 15, 65, 138, 156) (1895-1931)

American sneezewort - *Helenium* L. (10) (1818)

American snowball - *Styrax americanus* Lam. (156) (1923), *Styrax grandifolius* Aiton (156) (1923)

American snowbell - *Styrax americanus* Lam. (138) (1923)

American snowdrop tree - *Styrax americanus* Lam. (122) (1937) TX

American spearmint [America spear mint] - *Mentha spicata* L. (19) (1840)

American speedwell - *Valeriana dioica* L. (50, 95, 155) (1911–present), *Veronica americana* Schwein. ex Benth. (50, 95, 155) (1911–present)

American spikehead - *Aralia racemosa* L. (5, 6, 64, 72) (1892–1913)

American spikenard - *Aralia racemosa* L. subsp. *racemosa* (50) (present)

American spindle tree [American spindle-tree] - *Euonymus atropurpurea* Jacq. (157, 158) (1900-1929)

American spongeplant - *Limnobium spongia* (Bosc) L.C. Rich. ex Steud. (50) (present)

American spotted cowbane [American spotted cow bane] - *Cicuta maculata* L. (42) (1814)

American spur-gentian [American spurgentian] - *Halenia deflexa* (Sm.) Griseb. (155) (1942)

American spurred gentian - *Halenia deflexa* (Sm.) Griseb. (50) (present)

American star thistle [American star-thistle] - *Centaurea americana* Nutt. (5, 50, 97, 158) (1913–present)

American starflower - *Trientalis borealis* Raf. subsp. *borealis* (138) (1923)

American stickseed - *Hackelia deflexa* (Wahlenb.) Opiz var. *americana* (Gray) Fern. & I.M. Johnston (50) (present)

American stoneseed - *Lithospermum latifolium* Michx. (50) (present)

American strawberry - *Fragaria vesca* L. (7) (1828), *Fragaria vesca* L. subsp. *americana* (Porter) Staudt (138, 155) (1923-1942)

American strawberry bush - *Euonymus americanus* L. (2, 82) (1895-1930)

American striped maple - *Acer pensylvanicum* L. (8) (1785)

American sugar maple - *Acer rubrum* L. (165) (1768)

American sumac - *Rhus hirta* (L.) Sudworth (5) (1913)

American sweet cicely - *Osmorhiza longistylis* (Torr.) DC. (46) (1879)

American sweet violet - *Viola canadensis* L. (5, 156, 158) (1900-1923)

American sweet-scented arborvitae [American sweet-scented arbor vitae] - *Thuja occidentalis* L. (8) (1785)

American sycamore - *Platanus occidentalis* L. (46, 50) (1879–present)

American thick-stamen - *Pachysandra procumbens* Michx. (86) (1878) Meehan knew no common name and made this up

American thrift - *Limonium carolinianum* (Walt.) Britt. (5, 92, 156) (1876-1923)

American tiger lily - *Lilium philadelphicum* L. (158) (1900)

American tomentil - *Geranium maculatum* L. (92) (1876)

American trail plant [American trailplant] - *Adenocaulon bicolor* Hook. (50) (present)

American tulip-tree [American tuliptree, American tulip tree] - *Liriodendron tulipifera* L. (186) (1814)

American Turk's-cap lily [American Turk's cap lily, American Turkscap lily, American Turks-cap lily] - *Lilium superbum* L. (2, 109, 138) (1895-1949)

American twin-flower [American twinflower] - *Linnaea borealis* L. subsp. *americana* (Forbes) Hultén ex Clausen (138, 155) (1923-1942)

American upright honeysuckle - *Rhododendron calendulaceum* (Michx.) Torr. (41) (1770)

American valerian - *Cypripedium arietinum* R.Br. (5, 156) (1913-1923), *Cypripedium parviflorum* Salisb. var. *parviflorum* (5, 7, 55, 156) (1828-1923), *Cypripedium parviflorum* Salisb. var. *pubescens* (Willd.) Knight (6, 49, 53, 58) (1869-1922), *Cypripedium reginae* Walt. (55, 64, 158) (1900-1911), *Valeriana pauciflora* Michx. (7) (1828)

American vallisneria - *Vallisneria americana* Michx. (possibly) (187) (1818)

American veratrum - *Veratrum viride* Ait. (possibly) (55) (1911)

American vervain - *Verbena hastata* L. (5, 156, 157, 158) (1900-1929)

American vetch - *Viburnum sieboldii* Miq. (4, 5, 50, 72, 93, 95, 97, 131, 155, 156, 158, 187) (1818–present), *Vicia americana* Muhl. ex Willd. subsp. *americana* (3, 50) (1977–present), *Vicia americana* Muhl. ex Willd. subsp. *minor* (Hook.) C.R. Gunn (3) (1977)

American water cress [American water-cress] - *Cardamine pensylvanica* Muhl. ex Willd. (42, 46) (1814-1879), *Cardamine rotundifolia* Michx. (5, 131, 156) (1899-1923)

American water hemlock [American water-hemlock] - *Cicuta maculata* L. (6, 57, 71, 92, 158) (1876-1917)

American water-horehound [American water-hoarhound, American water horehound] - *Lycopus americanus* Muhl. ex W. Bart. (50) (present)

American water-horehound [American water-hoarhound, American water horehound] - *Lycopus virginicus* L. (157, 158) (1900-1929)

American water-lily [American water lily, American waterlily] - *Nymphaea odorata* Aiton (3, 138, 155) (1932-1977)

American water-lotus [American water lotus] - *Nelumbo lutea* Willd. (possibly) (46, 107) (1879-1919)

American water-parsnip [American water parsnip] - *Sium suave* Walt. (157, 158) (1900-1929)

American water-pepper - *Polygonum punctatum* Ell. var. *punctatum* (46) (1879)

American water-plantain [American waterplantain] - *Alisma plantago-aquatica* L. (155, 156) (1923-1942), *Alisma subcordatum* Raf. (5, 50, 93, 97) (1913–present)

American waterweed [American water-weed] - *Elodea canadensis* Michx. (156, 158) (1900-1923) England

American water-willow [American water willow] - *Justicia americana* (L.) Vahl (50) (present)

American waterwort - *Elatine rubella* Rydb. (155) (1942)

American wayfaring tree [American wayfaring tree, American wayfaring-tree] - *Viburnum lantanoides* Michx. (5, 109, 156) (1913-1949)

American white ash - *Fraxinus americana* L. (6, 8, 157, 158) (1785-1929)

American white avens - *Geum canadense* Jacq. (156, 158) (1900-1923)

American white birch - *Betula papyrifera* Marsh (2, 3, 157, 158) (1895-1929)

American white elm - *Ulmus americana* L. (93) (1936)

American white hellebore - *Veratrum viride* Ait. (2, 7, 156) (1895-1923)

American white ipecac - *Euphorbia ipecacuanhae* L. (5, 156) (1913-1923)

American white water-lily [American white waterlily] - *Nymphaea odorata* Aiton (50) (present)

American wild carrot - *Daucus pusillus* Michx. (50) (present)

American wild celery [American wildcelery] - *Vallisneria americana* Michx. (155) (1942)

American wild lettuce - *Lactuca canadensis* L. (158) (1900)

American wild mint - *Mentha arvensis* L. (5, 72, 82, 93, 131, 138, 157, 158) (1899–1936)

American wild valerian - *Valeriana dioica* L. (158) (1900), *Valeriana pauciflora* Michx. (5, 156) (1913-1923), *Valeriana uliginosa* (Torr. & Gray) Rydb. (5) (1913)

American wintergreen - *Pyrola americana* Sweet (50) (present)

American wisteria - *Wisteria frutescens* (L.) Poir. (2, 5, 138) (1895-1923)

American wolf's-bane - *Aconitum uncinatum* L. (165) (1768)

American wood anemony - *Anemone quinquefolia* L. (109, 138) (1923-1949)

American wood strawberry - *Fragaria vesca* L. subsp. *americana* (Porter) Staudt (5, 93, 97, 157, 158) (1900-1937)

American woodbine - *Lonicera caprifolium* L. (5, 156) (1913-1923), *Parthenocissus quinquefolia* (L.) Planch. (92, 158) (1876-1900)

American wood-sage [American wood sage, American woodsage] - *Teucrium canadense* L. (97, 158) (1900-1937)

American woolly-fruit sedge [American woollyfruit sedge] - *Carex lasiocarpa* Ehrh. var. *americana* Fern. (50) (present)

American wormroot - *Spigelia marilandica* (L.) L. (64) (1907)

American wormseed - *Chenopodium ambrosioides* L. (49, 52, 55, 57, 60, 62, 69, 109) (1902-1949), *Chenopodium ambrosioides* L. var. *ambrosioides* (6, 53, 54, 92, 158) (1892-1922)

American yam - *Dioscorea villosa* L. (42) (1814)

American yellow lily - *Lilium canadense* L. (86) (1878)

American yellow-fruit nettle-tree [American yellow-fruited nettle-tree] - *Celtis occidentalis* L. (8) (1785)

American yellow-rocket [American yellowrocket] - *Barbarea orthoceras* Ledeb. (50) (present)

American yellow-wood - *Cladrastis kentukea* (Dum.-Cours.) Rudd . (5, 14, 97, 156) (1882-1937)

American yew - *Taxus canadensis* Willd. (2, 72, 92) (1876-1907)

Americanische Cunile (German) - *Cunila origanoides* (L.) Britton (7) (1828)

Americanische Schierling (German) - *Cicuta maculata* L. (7) (1828)

Americanische Wormsaamen (German) - *Chenopodium ambrosioides* L. var. *ambrosioides* (6) (1892–1900)

Americanischer Polei [Amerikanischer Poley] (German) - *Hedeoma pulegioides* (L.) Pers. (6, 158) (1892)

Americanisher Nachteschatten (German) - *Phytolacca americana* L. var. *americana* (186) (1814)

Americansiche Weissball (German) - *Cephalanthus occidentalis* L. (6, 7) (1828-1932)

Amerikanische Dattellpflaume (German) - *Diospyros virginiana* L. (158) (1900)

Amerikanische Kermesbeere (German) - *Phytolacca americana* L. var. *americana* (6) (1892)

Amerikanische Kraftwurzel (German) - *Panax quinquefolius* L. (158) (1900)

Amerikanische Nard (German) - *Aralia racemosa* L. (158) (1900)

Amerikanische Rermesbeere (German) - *Phytolacca americana* L. var. *americana* (186) (1814)

Amerikanische Scharlachbeere (German) - *Phytolacca americana* L. var. *americana* (6, 186) (1814-1892)

Amerikanischer Aralie (German) - *Aralia racemosa* L. (6) (1892)

Amerikanischer Epheu (German) - *Parthenocissus quinquefolia* (L.) Planch. (158) (1900)

Amerikanischer Schwertel (German) - *Iris versicolor* L. (158) (1900)

Amerikanischer Wasserschierling (German) - *Cicuta maculata* L. (6) (1892)

Amerikanischer Ziersrauch (German) - *Prunus serotina* Ehrh. (158) (1900)

Amethyst aster - *Symphyotrichum ×amethystinum* (Nutt.) Nesom [*ericoides × novae-angliae*] (5, 72, 93, 138, 155) (1907-1942)

Amethyst eryngo - *Eryngium amethystinum* L. (138) (1923)

Amil - *Indigofera caroliniana* Mill. (10) (1818)

Ammania - *Ammannia* L. (155, 158) (1900-1942)

Ammi - *Ammi* L. (155) (1942)

Ammole - *Yucca glauca* Nutt. (28) (1850)

Amoena phlox - *Phlox amoena* Sims. (138) (1923)

Amole - *Chlorogalum pomeridianum* (DC.) Kunth (78) (1898) CA, *Yucca elata* (Engelm.) Engelm. (149, 153) (1904-1913) NM, *Yucca glauca* Nutt. (156) (1923)

Amorous apples - *Solanum lycopersicum* L. var. *lycopersicum* (107) (1588)

Amorpha - *Amorpha canescens* Pursh (28) (1850), *Amorpha fruticosa* L. (174) (1753), *Amorpha* L. (8, 155) (1785-1942)

Amorpha d'Amerique (French) - *Amorpha fruticosa* L. (8) (1785)

Amote - *Ipomoea batatas* (L.) Lam. (110) (1886)

Ampelopsis - *Ampelopsis* Michx. (155, 158) (1900-1942)

Amphiachyris - *Amphiachyris dracunculoides* (DC.) Nutt. (5, 158) (1900-1913)

Ampimecan (Chippeways) - *Vaccinium macrocarpon* Aiton (7) (1828)

Ampola - *Papaver rhoeas* L. (158) (1900)

Amsinckia - *Amsinckia* Lehm. (158) (1900), *Amsinckia lycopsoides* Lehm. (5) (1913)

Amsonia - *Amsonia tabernaemontana* Walt. (82) (1930), *Amsonia tabernaemontana* Walt. var. *tabernaemontana* (5, 97) (1913-1937), *Amsonia* Walt. (4, 82, 155, 158) (1900-1986)

Amugdalai - *Prunus dulcis* (Mill.) D.A. Webber (110) (1886)

Amur ampelopsis - *Ampelopsis brevipedunculata* (Maxim.) Trautv. (155) (1942)

Amur corktree - *Phellodendron amurense* Rupr. (137, 138) (1923-1931)

Amur honeysuckle - *Lonicera maackii* (Rupr.) Herder (50, 138, 155) (1923–present)

Amur maple - *Acer ginnala* Maxim. (50, 109, 112, 137, 138, 155) (1923–present)

Amur privet - *Ligustrum amurense* Carr. (112, 138) (1923-1937)

Amur silver grass [Amur silvergrass] - *Miscanthus sacchariflorus* (Maxim.) Franch. (50) (present)

Amy root [Amy-root] - *Apocynum cannabinum* L. (5, 62, 64, 156, 157, 158) (1900–1929)

Amygdala amara - *Prunus dulcis* (Mill.) D.A. Webber (55, 57, 59) (1911-1917)

Amygdala dulcis - *Prunus dulcis* (Mill.) D.A. Webber (possily) (55, 57, 59) (1911-1917)

Amygdalus - *Prunus dulcis* (Mill.) D.A. Webber (110) (1886), *Prunus persica* (L.) Batsch (52, 54) (1905-1919)

Amyris - *Amyris* P. Br. (155) (1942)

Anacardium - *Anacardium occidentale* L. (52, 57) (1917-1919)

Anachuite wood - *Cordia boissieri* A. DC. (92) (1876)

Ana'kun (Chippewa) - *Schoenoplectus tabernaemontani* (K.C. Gmel.) Palla (40) (1928)

Anamita - *Amanita muscaria* var. *muscaria* (L.) Pers. (92) (1876)

Ananas (Spanish) - *Ananas comosus* (L.) Merr.var. *comosus* (110) (1886)

Anaphalis pussy-toes - *Antennaria anaphaloides* Rydb. (3, 4) (1977-1986), *Antennaria parlinii* Fern. subsp. *fallax* (Greene) Bayer & Stebbins (3, 4) (1977-1986)

Anaqua - *Ehretia anacua* (Teran & Berl.) I.M. Johnston (106, 122) (1930-1937)

Anatto or Anatto tree [Anatto-tree] - *Bixa* L. (138) (1923), *Bixa orellana* L. (possibly) (110) (1886)

Anchic - *Arachis hypogaea* L. (107) (1625) Peru

Anchor tree - *Malus coronaria* (L.) Mill. var. *coronaria* (41) (1770)

Anchu - *Anchusa officinalis* L. (107) (1919)

Anda'nkalagi'skĭ (Cherokee, it removes things from the gums) - *Geranium maculatum* L. (102) (1886)

Andean prairie clover - *Dalea cylindriceps* Barneby (50) (present)

Ande'gobûg (Chippewa, crow leaf) - *Stachys palustris* L. (40) (1928)

Ande'gopĭn (Chippewa, crow plant) - *Lycopus asper* Greene (40) (1928)

Andornkraut (German) - *Marrubium vulgare* L. (158) (1900)

Andorra juniper - *Juniperus communis* L. var. *depressa* Pursh (112) (1937), *Juniperus horizontalis* Moench (109) (1949)

Andrache (Greek) - *Portulaca oleracea* L. (110) (1886)

Andrachen - *Portulaca oleracea* L. (107) (1919)

Andrew's cross - *Hypericum* L. (42) (1814)

Andrew's gentian [Andrews gentian] - *Gentiana andrewsii* Griseb. (155) (1942)

Andromeda - *Andromeda* L. (8, 14, 155) (1785-1942), *Leucothoe axillaris* (Lam.) D. Don. (183) (~1756)

Andromeda lignum (Official name of herbal medicine) - *Oxydendrum arboreum* (L.) DC. (possibly) (7) (1828)

Andromede (French) - *Andromeda* L. (8) (1785)

Andromede à grappe (French) - *Leucothoe racemosa* (L.) Gray (possibly) (8) (1785)

Andromede Caliculée (French) - *Chamaedaphne calyculata* (L.) Moench (8) (1785)

Andromede de Maryland (French) - *Lyonia mariana* (L.) D. Don (8) (1785)

Andromede en arbre (French) - *Oxydendrum arboreum* (L.) DC. (possibly) (8) (1785)

Andromede luisante (French) - *Lyonia lucida* (Lam.) K. Koch (8) (1785)

Andromede paniculée (French) - *Leucothoe racemosa* (L.) Gray (possibly) (8) (1785)

Andromedier (French) - *Oxydendrum arboreum* (L.) DC. (possibly) (7) (1828)

Androstephium - *Androstephium caeruleum* (Scheele) Greene (3, 5, 97) (1913-1977), *Androstephium* Torr. (158) (1900) Greek for 'man's crown', the filaments forming a crown

Anemone - *Anemone berlandieri* Pritz. (97) (1937), *Anemone* L. (1, 2, 15, 50, 63, 82, 109, 138, 155, 156, 158, 165) (1807–present), *Anemone quinquefolia* L. (82) (1930), *Thalictrum thalictroides* (L.) Eames & Boivin (76) (1896) Sulphur Grove OH

Anemone rue - *Thalictrum thalictroides* (L.) Eames & Boivin (49) (1898)

Anemonella - *Thalictrum* **L.** (138, 155) (1923-1942), *Thalictrum thalictroides* (L.) Eames & Boivin (138, 155) (1923-1942)

Anemoy - *Anemone* L. (15) (1895)

Anet - *Anethum graveolens* L. (158, 179) (1526-1900)

Anethon - *Anethum graveolens* L. (107) (1919)

Angelica or Angelica tree [Angelica-tree] - *Angelica archangelica* L. (58) (1869), *Angelica atropurpurea* L. (7, 64) (1828-1907), *Angelica grayi* (Coult. & Rose) Coult. & Rose (64) (1907), *Angelica* L. (1, 50, 138, 155) (1923–present), *Aralia* L. (8) (1785), *Aralia spinosa* L. (2, 5, 7, 14, 19, 38, 46, 49, 58, 106, 109, 156) (1617-1949)

Angelica tree [Angelica-tree] - *Zanthoxylum americanum* Mill. (5, 6, 49, 157, 158) (1892-1929), *Zanthoxylum clava-herculis* L. (49, 156) (1898-1923)

Angelico - *Ligusticum canadense* (L.) Britton (5, 156) (1913-1923)

Angelic-root [Angelic root] - *Angelica lucida* L. (7, 124) (1828-1937)

Angelin - *Andira* Juss. (138) (1923)

Angelin tree [Angelintree] - *Andira* Juss. (155) (1942)

Angélique en arbre (French) - *Aralia spinosa* L. (8) (1785)

Angelonia - *Angelonia* Humb. & Bonpl. (138, 155) (1931-1942)

Angel's trumpet-flower [Angel's trumpet flower] - *Datura stramonium* L. (106) (1930)

Angel's-eye [Angeleyes, Angel eyes, angel-eyes] - *Houstonia caerulea* L. (5, 73, 156) (1892-1923) no longer in use by 1923

Angel's-eye [Angel's eye, Angel-eye] - *Veronica chamaedrys* L. (5, 156) (1913-1923)

Angel's-hair [Angel's hair] - *Cuscuta gronovii* Willd. ex J.A. Schultes (77) (1898) LA

Angel's-trumpets [Angel trumpets, Angel-trumpets] - *Acleisanthes longiflora* Gray (5, 73, 122, 124, 156) (1892-1937), *Brugmansia suaveolens* (Humb. & Bonpl. ex Willd.) Bercht. & K. Presl (138) (1923)

Angel's-wings [Angel wings, Angelwings] - *Polygala alba* Nutt. (122, 124) (1937) TX

Angiopteris - *Onoclea sensibilis* L. (174, 177) (1753-1762)

Angle-berries [Angleberries] - *Lathyrus pratensis* L. (5, 156) (1913-1923)

Angled cottonwood - *Populus deltoides* Bartr. ex Marsh. subsp. *deltoides* (108) (1878)

Angled spike-rush - *Eleocharis quadrangulata* (Michx.) Roemer & J.A. Schultes (120) (1938)

Angled spurge - *Euphorbia hexagona* Nutt. ex Spreng. (5, 93, 97, 131) (1899-1937)

Angled-fruit stewartia [Angled-fruited stewartia] - *Stewartia ovata* (Cav.) Weatherby (5) (1913)

Angle-fruit milkvine [Anglefruit milkvine] - *Matelea gonocarpos* (Walt.) Shinners (50) (present)

Anglepod [Angle pod, Angle-pod] - *Cynanchum* L. (1) (1932), *Cynanchum laeve* (Michx.) Pers. (82, 106, 156) (1923-1930), *Gonolobus* Michx. (82, 92, 156) (1876-1930), *Matelea* Aubl. (4) (1986), *Matelea gonocarpos* (Walt.) Shinners (4) (1986)

Angle-pod milkvetch [Anglepod milkvetch] - *Matelea gonocarpos* (Walt.) Shinners (155) (1942)

Anglestem [Angle stem] - *Silphium perfoliatum* L. (37) (1919)

Angle-twig poplar [Angletwig poplar] - *Populus deltoides* Bartr. ex Marsh. subsp. *deltoides* (155) (1942)

Angola pea - *Cajanus cajan* (L.) Millsp. (92) (1876)

Angola weed - *Roccella fuciformis* (L.) DC. (92) (1876)

Angular centaury - *Sabatia angularis* (L.) Pursh (7, 49, 61) (1828-1898)

Angular luffa - *Luffa acutangula* (L.) Roxb. (110) (1886)

Angular-stalk sabbatia [Angular-stalked sabbatia] - *Sabatia angularis* (L.) Pursh (186) (1814)

Angular-stem American centaury [Angular stemmed American centaury] - *Sabatia angularis* (L.) Pursh (possibly) (42) (1814)

Anib' (Chippewa) - *Viburnum acerifolium* L. (40) (1928)

A'nibimĭn (Chippewa) - *Vaccinium macrocarpon* Aiton (40) (1928)

Anil - *Indigofera suffruticosa* Mill. (92) (1876)

Animated oats [Animated oat] - *Avena sterilis* L. (19, 45, 50, 109, 119, 138) (1840–present)

Anime - *Hymenaea courbaril* L. (92) (1876)

Animu'sĭd (Chippewa) - *Hepatica nobilis* Schreb. (40) (1928)

A'nina'tĭg (Chippewa) - *Acer saccharum* Marsh. (40) (1928)

Anise - *Pimpinella anisum* L. (53, 55, 57, 107, 138) (1911–1923), *Pimpinella* L. (138) (1923)

Anise (of scripture) - *Anethum graveolens* L. (158) (1900)

Anise hyssop - *Agastache foeniculum* (Pursh) Kuntze (5, 157, 158) (1900–1929)

Anise tree [Anisetree] - *Illicium* L. (138) (1923)

Aniseroot [Anise root, Anise-root] - *Collinsonia canadensis* L. (7) (1828), *Osmorhiza longistylis* (Torr.) DC. (3, 4, 5, 92, 93, 157, 158) (1876-1986)

Anise-scented goldenrod [Anise-scented golden-rod] - *Solidago odora* Aiton (5, 97, 156) (1913-1937)

Anise-seed [Anise seed, Anniseede] - *Pimpinella anisum* L. (92, 178) (1526-1876)

Anise-seed tree [Anise seed tree] - *Illicium* L. (10) (1818)

Anisum - *Pimpinella anisum* L. (57, 59, 178) (1596-1917)

Anit-fat - *Fucus vesiculosus* L. (60) (1902) commercial name

Ankee millet - *Echinochloa crus-galli* (L.) Beauv. (56) (1901)

Annatto or Annatto tree - *Bixa orellana* L. (92, 109, 138) (1876-1949)

Anne Arundel's spurge [Anne Arundel spurge] - *Euphorbia ipecacuanhae* L. (5) (1913)

Annotto tree - *Bixa orellana* L. (92) (1876)

Annual agoseris - *Agoseris heterophylla* (Nutt.) Greene (155) (1942)

Annual astragalus - *Astragalus nuttallianus* DC. (97) (1937)

Annual beard grass [Annual beard-grass, Annual beardgrass] - *Polypogon monspeliensis* (L.) Desf. (5, 45, 66, 119, 140, 163) (1852-1944)

Annual blue grass [Annual bluegrass, Annual blue-grass] - *Poa annua* L. (3, 50, 119, 122, 140, 143, 155, 163) (1852–present)

Annual brome grass - *Bromus hordeaceus* L. (80) (1913)

Annual buckwheat - *Eriogonum annuum* Nutt. (50) (present)

Annual burnet - *Sanguisorba annua* (Nutt. ex Hook.) Torr. & Gray (122) (1937)

Annual bursage - *Ambrosia acanthicarpa* Hook. (3, 4) (1977-1986)

Annual canary grass [Annual canarygrass] - *Phalaris canariensis* L. (50) (present)

Annual candytuft - *Iberis amara* L. (50) (present)

Annual capsicum - *Capsicum annuum* L. (110) (1886)

Annual chrysanthemum - *Chrysanthemum carinatum* Schousboe (138) (1923)

Annual eriogonum - *Eriogonum annuum* Nutt. (3, 4, 5, 93, 97, 98, 131, 155) (1899-1986)

Annual fimbry - *Fimbristylis annua* (All.) R. & S. (50) (present)

Annual fleabane [Annual flea bane] - *Erigeron annuus* (L.) Pers. (3, 4, 155) (1942-1986)

Annual gentian - *Gentianella amarella* (L.) Boerner subsp. *acuta* (Michx.) J. Gillett (155) (1942)

Annual knawel - *Scleranthus annuus* L. (4, 155) (1942-1986)

Annual marjoram - *Origanum majorana* L. (109) (1949)

Annual marsh-elder [Annual marshelder] - *Iva annua* L. (50) (present)

Annual meadow grass [Annual meadow-grass] - *Poa annua* L. (5, 56, 72, 143, 187) (1818-1936)

Annual mercury - *Mercurialis annua* L. (107) (1919)

Annual morning-glory [Annual morning glory] - *Ipomoea purpurea* (L.) Roth (80) (1913)

Annual muhly - *Muhlenbergia minutissima* (Steud.) Swall. (50) (present)

Annual pearlwort [Annual pearl-wort] - *Sagina apetala* Ard. (19) (1840)

Annual phlox - *Phlox drummondii* Hook. (109) (1949)

Annual poa - *Poa annua* L. (45) (1896)

Annual quamoclit - *Ipomoea quamoclit* L. (124) (1937)

Annual rabbit's-foot grass [Annual rabbitsfoot grass] - *Polypogon monspeliensis* (L.) Desf. (50) (present)

Annual ragweed - *Ambrosia artemisiifolia* L. (50) (present)

Annual sage - *Salvia carduacea* Benth. (106) (1930), *Salvia columbariae* Benth. (106) (1930)

Annual salt-marsh aster [Annual saltmarsh aster] - *Symphyotrichum subulatum* (Michx.) Nesom (5, 155) (1913-1942)

Annual sea blite - *Suaeda maritima* (L.) Dumort. subsp. *maritima* (5) (1913)

Annual skeleton-weed - *Shinnersoseris rostrata* (Gray) S. Tomb (3) (1977)

Annual sow-thistle [Annual sow thistle] - *Sonchus oleraceus* L. (5, 72, 80, 122, 156, 157, 158) (1900–1937)

Annual spear grass - *Poa annua* L. (66, 87, 90) (1885-1903)

Annual sweet vernal grass - *Anthoxanthum aristatum* Boiss. (163) (1852)

Annual tickle grass [Annual ticklegrass] - *Agrostis elliottiana* Schultes (155) (1942)

Annual vernal grass - *Anthoxanthum aristatum* Boiss. (50, 56) (1901–present)

Annual wallrocket - *Diplotaxis muralis* (L.) DC. (50) (present)

Annual wild rice [Annual wildrice] - *Zizania aquatica* L. (155) (1942), *Zizania palustris* L. var. *interior* (Fassett) Dore (122) (1937)

Annual winecup [Annual wine cup] - *Callirhoe digitata* Nutt. (124) (1937)

Annual wormwood - *Artemisia annua* L. (5, 72, 93) (1907-1936)

Anoda - *Anoda cristata* (L.) Schlecht. (50, 155, 158) (1900–present)

Anomalos - *Malaxis unifolia* Michx. (46) (1783)

Anonymos yellow sandbind - *Hudsonia tomentosa* Nutt. (46) (1783)

Another sort of great Knapweede - *Centaurea solstitialis* L. (178) (1526)

Anserine (French) - *Argentina anserina* (L.) Rydb. (158) (1900)

Anserine anthelmintique (French) - *Chenopodium ambrosioides* L. var. *ambrosioides* (186) (1814)

Ansérine sauvage (French) - *Chenopodium album* L. (158) (1900)

Anserine vermifuge - *Chenopodium ambrosioides* L. var. *ambrosioides* (6, 7, 186) (1814-1892)

Antelope-brush [Antelope brush] - *Purshia* DC. ex Poir. (138) (1923), *Purshia tridentata* (Pursh) DC. (106, 138) (1923-1930)

Antelope-horns [Antelope horns, Antelopehorns, Antelopehorn] - *Asclepias asperula* (Dcne.) Woods. (4) (1986), *Asclepias asperula* (Dcne.) Woods. subsp. *capricornu* (Woods.) Woods. (50, 122, 124) (1937–present), *Asclepias* L. (155) (1942)

Antennaria - *Antennaria parviflora* Nutt. (157) (1929)

Anthemis - *Chamaemelum nobile* (L.) All. (52, 57, 59) (1911-1919)

Anthericum - *Echeandia* Ortega (155) (1942)

Anthurium - *Anthurium* Schott (138, 155) (1923-1942)

Anthyllis - *Anthyllis* L. (155) (1942)

Antigopher plant - *Euphorbia lathyris* L. (71) (1898)

Antonskraut (German) - *Epilobium palustre* L. (6) (1892)

Anumguah - *Packera aurea* (L.) A.& D. Löve (possibly) (7) (1828)

Anys - *Pimpinella anisum* L. (179) (1526)

Aontashe (Omaha-Ponca) - *Liatris scariosa* (L.) Willd. var. *scariosa* (37) (1919)

Aonyeyapi (Dakota) - *Prunus pumila* L. var. *besseyi* (Bailey) Gleason (37) (1919)

A-óobe (Cuchan Yuma) - *Nicotiana* L. (132) (1855)

Apache-plume [Apache plume, Apacheplume] - *Fallugia paradoxa* (D. Don) Endl. (4, 50, 122, 124, 153, 155) (1913–present), *Geum triflorum* Pursh var. *ciliatum* (Pursh) Fassett (156) (1923)

Apahnostephus - *Aphanes arvensis* L. (158) (1900)

Apalachine à Feuilles de Prunier (French) - *Ilex verticillata* (L.) Gray (6) (1892)

Apalachine tea - *Ilex glabra* (L.) Gray (92) (1876)

Apalanche (French) - *Ilex* L. (8) (1785)

Apalanche a feuilles de prunier (French) - *Ilex verticillata* (L.) Gray (186) (1814)

Apalanche glabre (French) - *Ilex glabra* (L.) Gray (8) (1785)

Apalanche verticillée (French) - *Ilex verticillata* (L.) Gray (8) (1785)

Aparejo grass - *Muhlenbergia utilis* (Torr.) A.S. Hitchc. (94, 152, 163) (1852-1912)

Aparu (Pawnee, berry) - *Rubus idaeus* L. subsp. *strigosus* (Michx.) Focke (37) (1919), *Rubus occidentalis* L. (37) (1919)

Aparu-huradu (Pawnee, ground berry) - *Fragaria vesca* L. subsp. *americana* (Porter) Staudt (37) (1919), *Fragaria virginiana* Duchesne (37) (1919)

Apé (Otahiti) - *Alocasia macrorrhizos* (L.) Schott (110) (1886)

Apfelsine (German) - *Citrus ×aurantium* L. [*maxima × reticulata*] (110) (1886)

Aphaka - *Taraxacum officinale* G.H. Weber ex Wiggers (177, 180) (1633-1762)

Aphake - *Taraxacum officinale* G.H. Weber ex Wiggers (107) (1919)

Aphanostephus - *Aphanostephus* DC. (158) (1900), *Aphanostephus skirrobasis* (DC.) Trelease (5, 97) (1913-1937)

Aphion - *Papaver orientale* L. (107) (1919) Turks & Armenians

Apini - *Humulus lupulus* L. (110) (1886)

Apio (Spain) - *Apium graveolens* L. (107) (1919)

Apios (Greek) - *Pyrus communis* L. (110) (1886)

Apium - *Apium graveolens* L. (57) (1917), *Petroselinum crispum* (P. Mill.) Nyman ex A.W. Hill (107) (1919)

Apium risus (Laughing parsley) - *Pulsatilla patens* (L.) Mill. subsp. *multifida* (Pritz.) Zamels (86) (1878) old name, said to cause laughing and foolishness and convulsions by poisonous qualities

Apli (Scandinavian) - *Malus sylvestris* Mill. (110) (1886)

Apocyn Amer. - *Apocynum androsaemifolium* L. (7) (1828)

Apocynum - *Apocynum cannabinum* L. (52, 54, 57, 59) (1905-1917)

Apocynum radix (Official name of Materia Medica) - *Apocynum androsaemifolium* L. (7) (1828)

Appalachian bristle fern - *Trichomanes boschianum* Sturm. (50) (present)

Appalachian bunchflower - *Melanthium parviflorum* (Michx.) S. Wats. (50) (present)

Appalachian cherry - *Prunus pumila* L. var. *susquehanae* (hort. ex Willd.) Jaeger (5) (1913)

Appalachian hemlock-parsley [Appalachian hemlockparsley] - *Conioselinum chinense* (L.) Britton, Sterns & Poggenb. (155) (1942)

Appalachian penstemon - *Penstemon pallidus* Small (155) (1942)

Appalachian quillwort - *Isoetes engelmanni* A. Br. (50) (present)

Appalachian tea - *Ilex cassine* L. (156) (1923), *Ilex glabra* (L.) Gray (5, 107, 156) (1913-1923), *Ilex vomitoria* Aiton (5, 156) (1913-1923), *Viburnum nudum* L. var. *cassinoides* (L.) Torr. & Gray (5, 156) (1913-1923)

Appendaged water-leaf - *Hydrophyllum appendiculatum* Michx. (5, 72) (1907-1913)

Apple or Apple tree - *Cydonia oblonga* Mill. (179) (1526), *Malus* Mill. (1, 8, 50, 109, 138, 155, 158, 179) (1526–present), *Malus sylvestris* Mill. (57, 61, 92) (1870-1917), *Pyrus* L. (10, 82, 256) (1818-1930)

Apple geranium - *Pelargonium odoratissimum* (L.) L'Hér. ex Aiton (109) (1949)

Apple guava - *Psidium guajava* L. (107) (1919)

Apple haw - *Crataegus aestivalis* Torr. & Gray. (20, 74) (1857-1893)

Apple pine - *Pinus strobus* L. (5, 10, 20, 19) (1818-1857)

Apple root [Apple-root] - *Euphorbia corollata* L. (5, 7, 49, 92, 156, 157, 158) (1828-1923) no longer in use by 1923

Apple serviceberry - *Amelanchier sanguinea* (Pursh) DC. var. *grandiflora* (Wieg.) Rehd. (155) (1942)

Apple shadblow - *Amelanchier sanguinea* (Pursh) DC. var. *grandiflora* (Wieg.) Rehd. (138) (1923)

Apple-leaf willow [Apple-leaved willow] - *Salix discolor* Muhl. (85) (1932)

Apple-mint [Apple mint] - *Mentha ×rotundifolia* (L.) Huds. [*longifolia × suaveolens*] (5, 109, 138, 156) (1913-1949)

Apple-of-paradice [Apple of paradice] - *Musa ×paradisiaca* L. [*acuminata × balbisiana*] (178, 179) (1526-1596)

Apple-of-Peru [Apple of Peru, Appleofperu] - *Datura inoxia* P. Mill. (180) (1633), *Datura stramonium* L. (6, 49, 69, 71, 157, 158) (1892–1929), *Nicandra* Adans. (138, 155, 158) (1900-1942), *Nicandra physalodes* (L.) Gaertn. (1, 4, 5, 50, 63, 109, 138, 155, 156, 158) (1899–present)

Apple-of-Sodom [Apple of Sodom] - *Solanum carolinense* L. (5, 156, 157, 158) (1900-1929)

Apple-pie [Apple pie] - *Artemisia vulgaris* L. (156, 157) (1923-1929), *Epilobium hirsutum* L. (5, 156) (1913-1923)

Apple-riennie - *Artemisia abrotanum* L. (158) (1900), *Matricaria recutita* L. (158) (1900)

Apples-of-love [Apples of loue] - *Solanum melongena* L. (46, 107) (1879-1919), *Solanum lycopersicum* L. var. *lycopersicum* (180) (1633)

Apricocke tree - *Prunus armeniaca* L. (178) (1526)

Apricot - *Prunus armeniaca* L. (7, 19, 92, 106, 107) (1828-1937), *Prunus* L. (138, 155) (1923-1942)

Apricot-vine - *Passiflora incarnata* L. (156) (1923)

April-fools [April fools, April-fool] - *Pulsatilla patens* (L.) Mill. (5) (1913), *Pulsatilla patens* (L.) Mill. subsp. *multifida* (Pritz.) Zamels (74, 157, 158) (1893-1929) Rockford IL, possibly becuase it flowers around April 1 and often is snowed under

Apûk'we (Chippewa) - *Typha latifolia* L. (40) (1928)

Apwynis (Lithuanian) - *Humulus lupulus* L. (110) (1886)

Aquatic knot-weed - *Polygonum amphibium* L. var. *emersum* Michx. (187) (1818)

Aquatic oak - *Quercus nigra* L. (18) (1805)

Aquinas - *Solanum tuberosum* L. (107) (1919)

Arabian coffee - *Coffea arabica* L. (109, 138) (1923-1949)

Arabian jasmine - *Jasminum sambac* (L.) Aiton (109, 138) (1923-1949)

Arabian lavender - *Lavandula stoechas* L. (92) (1876)

Arabian manna - *Tamarix gallica* L. (92) (1876)

Arabian millet grass - *Sorghum halepense* (L.) Pers. (88) (1885)

Arabian millett - *Sorghum halepense* (L.) Pers. (45, 87) (1884-1896)

Arabian sticadoue - *Lavandula stoechas* L. (178) (1526)

Arabis - *Iberis umbellata* L. (178) (1526)

Aracus - *Vicia cracca* L. (110) (1886)

Aralia - *Aralia hispida* Vent. (52) (1919), *Aralia* L. (138, 155, 158) (1900-1942), *Aralia racemosa* L. (52) (1919)

Aralia radix (Official name of Materia Medica) - *Aralia nudicaulis* L. (7) (1828)

Aralie (French) - *Aralia* L. (8) (1785)

Aralie á tige nue (French) - *Aralia nudicaulis* L. (158) (1900)

Aralie épineuse (French) - *Aralia spinosa* L. (8) (1785)

Arancio dolce (Italian) - *Citrus ×aurantium* L. [*maxima × reticulata*] (110) (1886)

Arange - *Citrus ×aurantium* L. [*maxima × reticulata*] (178) (1526)

Arapahoe sedge - *Carex arapahoensis* Clokey (139) (1944)

Araticu porche - *Annona muricata* L. (177) (1762)

Araticu-ponhe - *Annona muricata* L. (165) (1648)

Arbell - *Populus alba* L. (158) (1900)

Arbol de Hierro (Mexican) - *Olneya tesota* Gray (106, 123) (1856-1930)

Arborvitae or Arborvitae tree [Arbor vita, Arbor vitae, Arborvita] - *Thuja* L. (1, 8, 50, 10, 14, 109, 138, 167) (1785–present), *Thuja occidentalis* L. (5, 6, 7, 20, 49, 50, 52, 53, 54, 57, 61, 92, 136, 174, 177, 178, 184) (1596–present), *Thuja plicata* Donn ex D. Don (5, 6, 10, 35, 38, 40, 41) (1806-1928)

Arbousier (French) - *Arbutus* L. (8) (1785)

Arbousier menzies (French) - *Arbutus menziesii* Pursh (20) (1857)

Arbre à la puce (French) - *Toxicodendron toxicarium* (Salisb.) Gillis (8) (1785)

Arbre à la puce grimpant (French) - *Toxicodendron radicans* (L.) Kuntze subsp. *radicans* (8) (1785)

Arbre a poison (French) - *Toxicodendron toxicarium* (Salisb.) Gillis (6) (1892)

Arbre à Suif (French) - *Morella cerifera* (L.) Small (6) (1892)

Arbre de Cire (French) - *Morella cerifera* (L.) Small (8) (1785), *Myrica* L. (8) (1785)

Arbre de cire nain (French) - *Morella cerifera* (L.) Small (possibly) (8) (1785)

Arbre de niege (French) - *Chionanthus virginicus* L. (8) (1785)

Arbre de vie (French) - *Thuja* L. (8) (1785)

Arbus (Russian) - *Citrullus lanatus* (Thunb.) Matsumura & Nakai (110) (1886)

Arbute tree - *Arbutus menziesii* Pursh (106) (1930)

Arbutus - *Epigaea repens* L. (106) (1930)

Arbutus-leaved aronia - *Photinia pyrifolia* (Lam.) Robertson & Phipps (187) (1818)

Archangel - *Anethum* L. (5, 92, 156) (1876-1923), *Angelica archangelica* L. (19) (1840), *Angelica atropurpurea* L. (5, 92, 156) (1876-1923), *Asclepias tuberosa* L. (75) (1894) near Providence RI, *Collinsonia canadensis* L. (19) (1840), *Lamium album* L. (107) (1919), *Lamium* L. (10, 184) (1793-1818), *Lycopus virginicus* L. (77) (1898) Dixfield ME

Archaungell - *Lamium* L. (179) (1526)

Archer's earthstar - *Geastrum archeri* Berk. (128) (1933) ND

Archil - *Roccella tinctoria* DC. (92) (1876)

Arctic anemone - *Anemone parviflora* Michx. (155) (1942)

Arctic arnica - *Arnica angustifolia* Vahl. (possibly) (5, 131, 155, 156) (1899-1942)

Arctic aster - *Eurybia merita* (A. Nels.) Nesom (4) (1986)

Arctic bladderpod [Arctic bladder pod] - *Lesquerella arctica* (DC.) S. Wats. (5, 50) (1913–present)

Arctic bluegrass - *Poa arctica* R. Br. (140) (1944)

Arctic bramble - *Rubus ostryifolius* Rydb. (5, 107, 155) (1913-1942)

Arctic brome - *Bromus kalmii* Gray (50) (present)

Arctic buttercup - *Ranunculus hyperboreus* Rottb. (5) (1913)

Arctic camomile [Arctic chamomile] - *Tripleurospermum maritima* (L.) W.D.J. Koch subsp. *maritima* (5, 93, 156) (1913-1936), *Tripleurospermum perforata* (Merat) M. Lainz (156) (1923)

Arctic campion - *Silene suecica* (Lodd.) Greuter & Burdet (109, 138) (1923-1949)

Arctic chrysanthemum - *Dendranthema arcticum* (L.) Tzvelev subsp. *arcticum* (138) (1923)

Arctic cinquefoil - *Potentilla nana* Willd. ex Schlecht. (5) (1913)

Arctic cottongrass - *Eriophorum callitrix* Cham. ex C.A. Mey. (50) (present)

Arctic daisy - *Dendranthema arcticum* (L.) Tzvelev subsp. *arcticum* (5) (1913)

Arctic erigeron - *Erigeron uniflorus* L. (5) (1913)

Arctic harebell - *Campanula uniflora* L. (5) (1913)

Arctic hare's foot sedge - *Carex lachenalii* Schk. (5) (1913)

Arctic holy grass - *Hierochloe pauciflora* R. Br. (5) (1913)

Arctic iris - *Iris setosa* Pallas ex Link (138) (1923)

Arctic kobresia - *Kobresia simpliciuscula* (Wahlenb.) Mackenzie (5) (1913)

Arctic leopard's-bane [Arctic leopard's bane] - *Arnica angustifolia* Vahl. (possibly) (5, 156) (1913-1923)

Arctic lychnis - *Silene involucrata* (Cham. & Schlecht.) Bocquet subsp. *involucrata* (5) (1913)

Arctic meadow grass - *Puccinellia angustata* (R. Br.) Rand & Redf. (5) (1913)

Arctic meadow rue - *Thalictrum alpinum* L. (5) (1913)

Arctic milkvetch [Arctic milk vetch] - *Astragalus americanus* (Hook.) M.E.Jones (5, 131) (1899-1913)

Arctic oxytrope - *Oxytropis arctica* R. Br. (5) (1913)

Arctic pearlwort - *Sagina saginoides* (L.) H. Karst. (5) (1913)

Arctic poppy - *Papaver nudicaule* L. (5, 107) (1913-1919)

Arctic reedgrass - *Calamagrostis coarctata* (Torr.) Eat. (50) (present)

Arctic rockcress [Arctic rock cress] - *Arabis media* N. Busch (5) (1913)

Arctic sandwort - *Minuartia arctica* (Stev. ex Ser.) Graebn. (5) (1913)

Arctic senecio - *Tephroseris atropurpurea* (Ledeb.) Holub (5) (1913)

Arctic spear grass - *Poa arctica* R. Br. subsp. *arctica* (5) (1913)

Arctic sweet grass [Arctic sweetgrass] - *Hierochloe pauciflora* R. Br. (50) (present)

Arctic sweet-colt's-foot [Arctic sweet colts foot, Arctic sweet colts-foot] - *Petasites* ×*vitifolius* Greene [*frigidus* × *sagittatus*] (5) (1913), *Petasites fragrans* C. Presl (50) (present), *Petasites frigidus* (L.) Fries var. *palmatus* (Aiton) Cronq. (50) (present), *Petasites hybridus* (L.) G. Gaertn., B. Mey. & Scherb. (5) (1913), *Petasites* Mill. (50) (present)

Arctic whitlowgrass - *Draba fladnizensis* Wulf. (138) (1923)

Arctic willow - *Salix arctica* Pallas (5) (1913)

Arctic woodrush [Arctic wood rush] - *Luzula arctica* Blytt subsp. *arctica* (5, 50) (1913–present)

Arctium - *Arctium lappa* L. (174, 177) (1753-1762)

Arctogrostis - *Arctagrostis latifolia* (R. Br.) Griseb. (5, 19) (1840-1913)

Arctotis - *Arctotis* L. (138, 155) (1931-1942)

Ardisia - *Ardisia* Sw. (138) (1923)

Areche - *Atriplex hortensis* L. (107, 158) (1538-1900) England

Arequipa - *Echinocactus* Link & Otto (possibly) (155) (1942)

Arethusa - *Arethusa bulbosa* L. (5, 48, 138, 156, 174) (1753-1923), *Arethusa* L. (138, 155) (1923-1942)

Argemone - *Argemone mexicana* L. (6, 174, 180) (1633-1892)

Argemone (French) - *Argemone mexicana* L. (6) (1892)

Argentill - *Aphanes arvensis* L. (5) (1913)

Argentina - *Argentina anserina* (L.) Rydb. (158) (1900)

Argentine - *Argentina anserina* (L.) Rydb. (158) (1900)

Argentine anemone - *Anemone multifida* Poir. (155) (1942)

Argentine thistle - *Onopordum acanthium* L. (158) (1900)

Argosier argenté (French) - *Shepherdia argentea* (Pursh) Nutt. (20) (1857)

Argutus - *Rubus ostryifolius* Rydb. (82) (1930) IA

Arianocoe - *Nicotiana tabacum* L. (181) (~1678)

Arid-land goosefoot [Aridland goosefoot] - *Chenopodium desiccatum* A. Nels. (50) (present)

Arikury-palm [Arikurypalm] - *Syagrus* C. Martius (155) (1942)

Arisarum trifolium (Official name of Materia Medica) - *Arisaema triphyllum* (L.) Schott (7) (1828)

Aristea - *Aristea* Aiton (155) (1942)

Aristoloche - *Aristolochia* L. (8, 50) (1785-present)

Aristoloche en arbre (French) - *Aristolochia macrophylla* Lam. (8) (1785)

Aristoloche serpentaire (French) - *Aristolochia serpentaria* L. (186) (1814)

Aristolochia clematitis - *Aristolochia clematitis* L. (178) (1526)

Aristolochia root - *Aristolochia serpentaria* L. (92) (1876)

Arizona agoseris - *Agoseris glauca* (Pursh) Raf. (155) (1942)

Arizona ash - *Fraxinus velutina* Torr. (112) (1937)

Arizona boxelder - *Acer negundo* L. var. *arizonicum* Sarg. (50, 155) (1942–present)

Arizona buckthorn - *Sideroxylon lanuginosum* Michx. (106) (1930)

Arizona cotton grass [Arizona cotton-grass] - *Digitaria californica* (Benth.) Henr. (94) (1901)

Arizona cottontop - *Digitaria californica* (Benth.) Henr. (3, 50, 155) (1942–present)

Arizona cypress - *Cupressus arizonica* Greene (122, 124, 138, 153) (1913-1923)

Arizona fescue - *Festuca arizonica* Vasey (152) (1912) NM

Arizona goldenrod - *Solidago velutina* DC. (155) (1942)

Arizona gourd - *Cucurbita foetidissima* Kunth (156) (1923)

Arizona loco - *Astragalus arizonicus* Gray (155) (1942)

Arizona madrone - *Arbutus arizonica* (Gray) Sargent (155) (1942)

Arizona pine - *Pinus arizonica* Engelm. (138) (1923)

Arizona planetree - *Platanus wrightii* S. Wats. (138) (1923)

Arizona poppy - *Kallstroemia grandiflora* Torr. ex Gray (possibly) (106) (1930)

Arizona rush - *Juncus interior* Wieg. var. *arizonicus* (Wieg.) F.J. Herm. (139) (1944)

Arizona stemless actinea - *Tetraneuris acaulis* (Pursh) Greene var. *arizonica* (Greene) Parker (155) (1942)

Arizona threeawn [Arizona three awn] - *Aristida arizonica* Vasey (3, 122, 155) (1937-1977)

Arizona water cactus - *Ferocactus wislizeni* (Engelm.) Britt. & Rose (138) (1923)

Arizona wheat grass [Arizona wheat-grass] - *Elymus arizonicus* (Scribn. & J.G. Sm.) Gould (94) (1901)

Arizona wyethia [Arizonian wyethia] - *Wyethia arizonica* Gray (86) (1878)

Arkansas bedstraw - *Galium arkansanum* Gray (5, 97) (1913-1937)

Arkansas bittercress - *Erysimum capitatum* (Dougl. ex Hook.) Greene var. *capitatum* (138) (1923)

Arkansas buckeye - *Aesculus* ×*bushii* Schneid. [*glabra* × *pavia*] (138) (1923)

Arkansas cabbage - *Streptanthus maculatus* Nutt. subsp. *obtusifolius* (Hook.) Rollins (19) (1840)

Arkansas calamint - *Clinopodium arkansanum* (Nutt.) House (4) (1986)

Arkansas doze-daisy [Arkansas dozedaisy] - *Aphanostephus skirrobasis* (DC.) Trelease (50) (present)

Arkansas erysimum - *Erysimum capitatum* (Dougl. ex Hook.) Greene var. *capitatum* (155) (1942)

Arkansas hawthorn - *Crataegus mollis* Scheele (138, 155) (1923-1942)

Arkansas ironweed - *Vernonia arkansana* DC. (50) (present)

Arkansas least-daisy [Arkansas leastdaisy] - *Chaetopappa asteroides* (Nutt.) DC. (50) (present)

Arkansas oak - *Quercus arkansana* Sargent (138) (1923)

Arkansas post oak - *Quercus stellata* Wangenh. (155) (1942)

Arkansas rose [Arkansa rose] - *Rosa arkansana* Porter (72, 85, 138, 155) (1923-1942), *Rosa arkansana* Porter var. *suffulta* (Greene) Cockerell (5, 93) (1913-1936), *Rosa arkansana* Porter (72) (1907)

Arkansas sedge - *Carex arkansana* Bailey (50) (present)

Arkansas spurge - *Euphorbia spathulata* Lam (5, 93, 97) (1913-1937)

Arkansas wild rye - *Elymus villosus* Muhl. ex Willd. (56, 72) (1901-1907)

Arkansas yucca - *Yucca arkansana* Trel. (50, 124, 155) (1937–present)

Armagosa - *Castela erecta* Turpin. (possibly) (57) (1917)

Armillaria - *Armillaria* (Fr.) Staude (155) (1942)

Armoracia - *Armoracia* P.G. Gaertn., B. Mey. & Scherb. (50) (present), *Armoracia rusticana* P.G. Gaertn., B. Mey. & Scherb. (50, 57, 107) (1917–present)

Armoratia - *Armoracia rusticana* P.G. Gaertn., B. Mey. & Scherb. (possibly) (180) (1633)

Armstrong - *Polygonum aviculare* L. (158) (1900)

Armuda (Armenian) - *Cydonia oblonga* Mill. (110) (1886)

Arnberry - *Rubus idaeus* L. (158) (1900)

Arnica - *Arnica fulgens* Pursh (3) (1977), *Arnica* L. (1, 50, 93, 138, 148, 155, 158) (1900–present), *Leontodon autumnalis* L. (73, 156) (1892-1923), *Taraxacum officinale* G.H. Weber ex Wiggers (5, 157, 158) (1900-1929)

Arnica bud [Arnica-bud] - *Leontodon autumnalis* L. (5, 75, 156) (1894-1923) Allston MA

Arnica weed - *Amblyolepis setigera* DC. (106) (1930)

Arnold's hawthorn [Arnold hawthorn] - *Crataegus ×anomala* Sargent [*intricata* × *mollis*] (138) (1923), *Crataegus mollis* Scheele (50) (present)

Arnold's thorn - *Crataegus ×anomala* Sargent [*intricata* × *mollis*] (5) (1913)

Arnotta - *Bixa orellana* L. (92) (1876)

Arnotto - *Bixa orellana* L. (109, 110) (1886-1949)

Aro (Spanish) - *Arisaema triphyllum* (L.) Schott (158) (1900)

Aro di Egitto (Italian) - *Colocasia esculenta* (L.) Schott (110) (1886)

Aromatic aster - *Symphyotrichum oblongifolium* (Nutt.) Nesom (3, 4, 5, 50, 72, 82, 93, 97, 122, 131, 155) (1899–present)

Aromatic calamus - *Acorus calamus* L. (42) (1814)

Aromatic sumac [Aromatic sumach] - *Rhus aromatica* Aiton var. *aromatica* (3) (1977), *Rhus aromatica* Aiton var. *pilosissima* (Engelm.) Shinners (3) (1977), *Rhus aromatica* Aiton var. *serotina* (Greene) Rehd. (3) (1977), *Rhus trilobata* Nutt. var. *trilobata* (3) (1977)

Aromatic sweet-flag [Aromatic sweet flag] - *Acorus calamus* L. (42) (1814)

Aromatic wintergreen - *Gaultheria* L. (156) (1923)

Arona - *Calla palustris* L. (46) (1879)

Aronia - *Orontium aquaticum* L. (177) (1762)

Aroostook sedge - *Carex sterilis* Willd. (5) (1913)

Arous (Arabic) - *Oryza sativa* L. (110) (1886)

Arracacha - *Arracacia xanthorrhiza* E.N. Bancroft (110) (1886)

Arracacia - *Arracacia* E.N. Bancroft (155) (1942)

Arrach [Arache] - *Atriplex hortensis* L. (92, 158, 179) (1526-1900)

Arrise - *Anethum graveolens* L. (107) (1919) of New Testament

Arroche (French) - *Atriplex hortensis* L. (158) (1900)

Arrow aster - *Symphyotrichum urophyllum* (Lindl.) Nesom (138, 155) (1923-1942)

Arrow bamboo - *Pseudosasa japonica* (Sieb. & Zucc. ex Steud.) Makino ex Nakai (138) (1923)

Arrow crotolaria - *Crotalaria sagittalis* L. (155) (1942)

Arrow grass [Arrow-grass] - *Aristida purpurascens* Poir. (5, 119, 163) (1852-1938)

Arrow podgrass - *Triglochin palustre* L. (155) (1942)

Arrow rattle-box - *Crotalaria sagittalis* L. (187) (1818)

Arrow-arum [Arrow arum] - *Peltandra* Raf. (2, 50, 109, 138, 156) (1895–present), *Peltandra virginica* (L.) Schott. (107, 156) (1919-1923)

Arrowbeam [Arrow beam, Arrow-beam] - *Euonymus europaea* L. (5, 156) (1913-1923)

Arrow-feather [Arrowfeather] - *Aristida purpurascens* Poir. var. *purpurascens* (122) (1937)

Arrow-feather threeawn [Arrowfeather threeawn] - *Aristida purpurascens* Poir. (3, 50, 155) (1942–present)

Arrowgrass [Arrow grass, Arrow-grass] - *Triglochin* L. (1, 50, 92, 148, 158, 167) (1814–present), *Triglochin maritimum* L. (3, 19, 49, 92, 126, 138, 156) (1840-1977)

Arrowhead [Arrow-head, Arrow head] - *Sagittaria ambigua* J.G.Sm. (3) (1977), *Sagittaria graminea* Michx. (85) (1932), *Sagittaria* L. (1, 93, 109, 120, 138, 155, 156, 167, 184) (1793-1942), *Sagittaria latifolia* Willd. (14, 40, 78, 92, 103, 107, 121, 156) (1871-1928)

Arrow-head rattlebox [Arrowhead rattlebox] - *Crotalaria sagittalis* L. (50) (present)

Arrow-head violet [Arrow-head violet] - *Viola sagittata* Aiton (4) (1986)

Arrow-head-grass [Arrow-headed grass] - *Triglochin* L. (10, 41) (1770-1818)

Arrowleaf [Arrow-leaf, Arrow leaf] - *Balsamorhiza sagittata* (Pursh) Nutt. (101) (1905), *Sagittaria engelmanniana* J.G. Sm. (5) (1913), *Sagittaria* L. (122) (1937), *Sagittaria lancifolia* L. subsp. *media* (Micheli) Bogin (124) (1937), *Sagittaria latifolia* Willd. (37, 75, 156) (1830-1923), *Symphyotrichum cordifolium* (L.) Nesom (106) (1930)

Arrow-leaf arrowhead [Arrow-leaved Arrow-head] - *Sagittaria latifolia* Willd. (187) (1818)

Arrow-leaf aster [Arrow-leaved aster] - *Symphyotrichum cordifolium* (L.) Nesom (3, 4, 5, 72, 82, 93, 97, 106, 131) (1899-1986)

Arrow-leaf balsamroot [Arrowleaf balsamroot] - *Balsamorhiza sagittata* (Pursh) Nutt. (50, 155) (1942–present)

Arrow-leaf bindweed [Arrow leaved bind weed] - *Ipomoea sagittata* Poir. (42) (1814)

Arrow-leaf crotolaria [Arrow leaved crotolaria] - *Crotalaria sagittalis* L. (42) (1814)

Arrow-leaf lettuce [Arrow-leaved lettuce] - *Lactuca canadensis* L. (5, 62, 72, 97, 158) (1899-1913)

Arrow-leaf mallow [Arrowleaf mallow] - *Malvella sagittifolia* (Gray) Fraxell. (50) (present)

Arrow-leaf pondlily [Arrow-leaved pond lily] - *Nuphar lutea* (L.) Sm. subsp. *sagittifolia* (Walt.) E.O. Beal (5) (1913)

Arrow-leaf spoonflower [Arrow-leaved spoonflower] - *Xanthosoma sagittifolium* (L.) Schott (86) (1878)

Arrow-leaf sweet-colt's-foot [Arrowleaf sweet coltsfoot] - *Petasites sagittatus* (Pursh) Gray (5, 50) (1913–present)

Arrow-leaf tearthumb [Arrowleaf tearthumb, Arrow-leaved tearthumb, Arrow-leaved tear thumb] - *Polygonum sagittatum* L. (5, 50, 62, 72, 82, 93, 155, 156, 158) (1899–present)

Arrow-leaf violet [Arrowleaf violet, Arrow leaf violet] - *Viola sagittata* Aiton (50, 3, 5, 72, 86, 97, 124, 138, 155, 156) (1878–present)

Arrowplant [Arrow-plant] - *Maranta arundinacea* L. (92) (1876)

Arrowroot - *Maranta arundinacea* L. (49, 50, 107, 109, 110) (1886–present), *Maranta* L. (7, 138) (1828-1923)

Arrow-wood [Arrow wood] - *Cornus florida* L. (5, 156) (1913-1923), *Cornus sericea* L. (35) (1806) William Clark, *Euonymus atropurpurea* Jacq. (5, 7, 92, 156) (1828-1923), *Frangula alnus* Mill. (5, 156, 158) (1900-1923), *Pluchea sericea* (Nutt.) Coville (106) (1930), *Viburnum acerifolium* L. (40) (1928), *Viburnum dentatum*

L. (2, 5, 7, 46, 92, 109, 112, 138, 156) (1828-1937), *Viburnum ellipticum* Hook. (19) (1840), *Viburnum* L. (1, 2, 4, 38, 82, 93, 156) (1820-1986)

Arroyo twinevine [Arroyo twine vine] - *Funastrum cynanchoides* (Dcne.) Schlechter subsp. *cynanchoides* (4) (1986)

Arroz (Spanish) - *Oryza sativa* L. (110) (1886)

Arsenick - *Polygonum hydropiper* L. (158) (1900)

Arsmart [Arsesmart, Aarse-smart, Arssmert] - *Polygonum amphibium* L. var. *emersum* Michx. (181) (~1678), *Polygonum hydropiper* L. (46, 157, 158, 179) (1526-1929) deliberately introduced by colonists by 1671, Josselyn, *Polygonum hydropiperoides* Michx. (46, 92) (1671-1876), *Polygonum persicaria* L. (46) (1671) deliberately introduced by colonists by 1671, Josselyn, *Polygonum punctatum* Ell. (157, 158) (1900-1929), *Polygonum punctatum* Ell. var. *punctatum* (46) (1671)

Artetyke - *Primula veris* L. (179) (1526)

Artichoke - *Cynara cardunculus* L. (107) (1919), *Cynara* L. (10) (1818), *Cynara scolymus* L. (92, 109, 110, 138) (1876-1949), *Helianthus tuberosus* L. (35, 80, 85) (1806-1923) Lewis & Clark

Artichoke-leaf milkweed [Artichoke leaved milk weed] - *Asclepias cinerea* Walt. (42) (1814)

Artichoke-leaf swallow-wort [Artichoke leaved swallow wort] - *Asclepias cinerea* Walt. (42) (1814)

Artificial grass - Fodder legumes in general (92) (1876)

Artillery - *Pilea microphylla* (L.) Liebm. (109) (1949)

Artillery plant - *Pilea trianthemoides* (Sw.) Lindl. (92) (1876)

Arum - *Arisaema triphyllum* (L.) Schott (57, 64) (1908-1917), *Arum* L. (138, 155) (1923-1942) the ancient Latin name

Arum radix (Official name of Materia Medica) - *Arisaema triphyllum* (L.) Schott (7) (1828)

Arum wild ginger [Arum wildginger] - *Hexastylis arifolia* (Michx.) Small var. *arifolia* (138, 155) (1931-1942)

Arum-leaf arrowhead [Arumleaf arrowhead, Arum-leaved arrowhead] - *Sagittaria cuneata* Sheld. (5, 50, 72, 93, 97, 131) (1894–present)

Aruncus - *Aruncus dioicus* (Walt.) Fern. var. *vulgaris* (Maxim.) Hara (174, 177) (1753-1762)

Arzeneykräftige Osterluzey (German) - *Helianthus tuberosus L.* (186) (1814)

Asa Gray's lily - *Lilium grayi* S. Wats. (5) (1913)

Asa Gray's thorn - *Crataegus flabellata* (Spach) Kirchn. (5) (1913)

A-sáblal - *Lomatium cous* (S. Wats.) Coult. & Rose (35) (1806)

Asa'dĭ (Chippewa) - *Populus tremuloides* Michx. (37) (1919)

Asa'kûmĭg (Chippewa) - *Sphagnum* L. (40) (1928)

Asaŋpi ijatke (Lakota) - *Ratibida pinnata* (Vent.) Barnh. (121) (1918?-1970?)

Asarabacca - *Asarum canadense* L. (5, 64, 92, 156) (1876-1923), *Asarum* L. (2, 10, 158, 167) (1814-1900)

Asarabica - *Asarum canadense* L. (156) (1923)

Asaret (French) - *Asarum canadense* L. (158) (1900)

Asaret du Canada (French) - *Asarum canadense* L. (7) (1828)

Asari Canadensis herba (Official name of Materia Medica) - *Asarum canadense* L. (7) (1828)

Asarum - *Asarum canadense* L. (52, 181) (~1678-1919)

Asasment - *Phaseolus* L. (181) (~1678)

A'sawan (Chippewa) - *Athyrium filix-femina* (L.) Roth (40) (1928)

Ascending milkvetch [Ascending milk vetch] - *Astragalus laxmannii* Jacq. (5, 82, 131) (1899–1930)

Asclepiade a la Soie (French) - *Asclepias syriaca* L. (6, 158) (1892-1900)

Asclépiade incarnate (French) - *Asclepias incarnata* L. (158) (1900)

Asclepiade tubereuse (French) - *Asclepias tuberosa* L. (6, 158) (1892-1900)

Asclepias - *Asclepias tuberosa* L. (52, 54) (1905-1919)

Asclepias tuberosa radix (Official name of Materia Medica) - *Asclepias tuberosa* L. (7) (1828)

Ascopo (Natives of Roanoke) - *Persea carolinensis* (Raf.) Nees (46) (1879)

Ascyre (French) - *Hypericum* L. (8) (1785)

Ascyre à feuilles de mille pertuis (French) - *Hypericum hypericoides* (L.) Crantz subsp. *hypericoides* (8) (1785)

Ascyre perforée (French) - *Hypericum hypericoides* (L.) Crantz subsp. *hypericoides* (8) (1785)

Ascyre velue (French) - *Hypericum setosum* L. (possibly) (8) (1785)

Ash maple - *Acer negundo* L. (92, 57) (1876-1900), *Acer negundo* L. var. *negundo* (19) (1840)

Ash or Ash tree [Asshe tre] - *Fraxinus americana* L. (157, 158) (1900-1929), *Fraxinus excelsior* L. (41, 107, 179) (1526-1919), *Fraxinus* L. (1, 3, 4, 7, 8, 10, 35, 40, 50, 82, 93, 106, 109, 138, 155, 156, 158) (1785–present), *Fraxinus pennsylvanica* Marsh. (37) (1919), *Fraxinus profunda* (Bush) Bush (187) (1818)

Ash-colored Grapeflower [Ash coloured Grape flower, Ash-coloured Grape-floure] - *Muscari neglectum* Guss. ex Ten. (178, 180) (1596-1633)

A'-she-ki (Zuñi) - *Pinus* L. (132) (1855)

Ashe's panicum - *Dichanthelium commutatum* (J.A. Schultes) Gould (5) (1913)

Ash-leaf maple [Ash-leaved maple] - *Acer* L. (1, 13, 108) (1849-1932), *Acer negundo* L. (5, 8, 20, 28, 41, 42, 43, 93, 106, 130, 131, 156, 158, 165, 187, 189)(1767-1936), *Acer negundo* L. var. *negundo* (2, 107, 108) (1878-1919)

Ash-leaf shagbark hickory [Ashleaf shagbark hickory] - *Carya ovata* (Mill.) K. Koch (155) (1942)

Ash-leaf toothache tree [Ash-leaved tooth-ach tree] - *Zanthoxylum americanum* Mill. (8) (1785)

Ash-loving bracket fungus - *Fomes fraxinophilus* (Peck) Sacc. (128) (1933)

Ash-of-Jerusalem - *Reseda luteola* L. (156) (1923)

Ashweed [Ash-weed, Ash weed, Ashe weed, Ashe-weed] - *Aegopodium podagraria* L. (5, 107, 156, 165) (1768-1923), *Packera tomentosa* (Michx.) C. Jeffrey (156) (1923)

Ashwort [Ash wort] - *Packera tomentosa* (Michx.) C. Jeffrey (5, 19, 92) (1840-1913)

Ashy grape - *Vitis cinerea* (Engelm.) Millard (5) (1913)

Ashy hydrangea - *Hydrangea cinerea* Small (5, 138) (1913-1923)

Ashy sunflower - *Helianthus mollis* Lam. (3, 4, 50, 109, 138, 155) (1923–present)

Asia-glory [Asiaglory] - *Argyreia* Lour. (155) (1942)

Asiatic dayflower [Asiatic day flower] - *Commelina communis* L. (5, 50, 57) (1913–present), *Commelina communis* L. var. *communis* (50) (present)

Asiatic horse chestnut - *Aesculus hippocastanum* L. (6) (1892)

Asiatic plantain - *Plantago major* L. (155) (1942)

Asiatic poison bulb - *Crinum asiaticum* L. (92) (1876)

Asiatic sweetleaf - *Symplocos paniculata* (Thunb.) Miq. (138) (1923)

Asiatic tamarisk - *Tamarix chinensis* Lour. (82) (1930)

A'sĭsûwe'mĭnaga'wûnj (Chippewa) - *Prunus virginiana* L. (40) (1928)

A'skibwan' (Chippewa, raw thing) - *Helianthus tuberosus* L. (40) (1928)

Askirawiyu (Pawnee) - *Oxalis stricta* L. (37) (1919), *Oxalis violacea* L. (37) (1919)

Askutasquash (Northeastern Indians) - *Cucurbita pepo* L. (107) (1919) source of English name "squash"

Askutstat (Pawnee) - *Dyssodia papposa* (Vent.) A.S. Hitchc. (37) (1919)

Aslimtka (Sioux) - *Grindelia squarrosa* (Pursh) Dunal (101) (1905)

Asmart [Ass-smart] - *Polygonum persicaria* L. (7) (1828), *Polygonum punctatum* Ell. var. *punctatum* (6) (1892)

Asparagus - *Asparagus* L. (50, 138, 155, 158) (1900–present) ancient Greek name of Persian origin, *Asparagus officinalis* L. (3, 5, 19, 49, 57, 72, 85, 92, 97, 107, 114, 117, 124, 157, 158, 178) (1596-1977)

Asparagus lettuce - *Lactuca sativa* L. (109) (1949)

Asparagus pea - *Psophocarpus tetragonolobus* (L.) DC. (109) (1949)

Asparagus-fern - *Asparagus setaceus* (Kunth) Jessop (109) (1949)

Aspe - *Populus tremuloides* Michx. (46) (1617)

Aspen [Aspin] or Aspen tree [Aspen-tree] - *Populus alba* L. (5, 156) (1913-1923), *Populus* L. (1, 2, 4, 109, 155, 158, 167) (1814-1986), *Populus tremula* L. (177) (1762), *Populus tremuloides* Michx. (28, 35, 40, 47, 92, 108, 112) (1806-1937)

Aspen fleabane - *Erigeron speciosus* (Lindl.) DC. (50) (present), *Erigeron speciosus* (Lindl.) DC. var. *macranthus* (Nutt.) Cronq. (50, 155) (1942–present)

Aspen of Europe - *Populus tremula* L. (158) (1900)

Aspen poplar - *Populus alba* L. (158) (1900), *Populus tremuloides* Michx. (38) (1820)

Aspen popple - *Populus tremuloides* Michx. (122, 124) (1937) TX

Aspen-leaf birch [Aspen-leaved birch] - *Betula populifolia* Marshall (8) (1785)

Asperge (French) - *Asparagus officinalis* L. (158) (1900)

Asphodel - *Asphodelus* L. (138, 155) (1923-1942), *Narthecium americanum* Ker-Gawl. (92) (1876)

Aspic - *Lavandula angustifolia* Mill. (92) (1876)

Aspidium - *Dryopteris filix-mas* (L.) Schott (53, 57, 59) (1911-1922), *Dryopteris marginalis* (L.) A. Gray (64) (1908)

Asplenium lady's-fern [Asplenium ladyfern] - *Athyrium filix-femina* (L.) Roth var. *asplenoides* (Michx.) Farw. (50) (present)

Assiminier [Asiminier] (French) - *Asimina* Adans. (8, 13) (1785-1849), *Asimina triloba* (L.) Dunal (6, 7, 20, 49, 158) (1828-1900)

Assimnier à trois lobes (French) - *Annona squamosa* L. (8) (1785)

Assimnier glabre (French) - *Annona glabra* L. (8) (1785)

Assiniboia sedge - *Carex assiniboinensis* W. Boott. (5, 50) (1913–present)

Ass's-ear [Ass-ear] - *Symphytum officinale* L. (64, 156) (1908-1923)

Ass's-eyes [Asses' eyes] - *Mucuna pruriens* (L.) DC. (92) (1876)

Ass's-foot [Ass's foot] - *Tussilago farfara* L. (5, 156) (1913-1923)

Ass's-thistle [Ass's thistle, Asse's thistle] - *Onopordum acanthium* L. (5, 156) (1913-1923)

Assyrian Clauer - *Trigonella corniculata* (L.) L. (178) (1770)

Aster - *Aster* L. (1, 2, 50, 63, 109, 138, 155, 158) (1899–present), *Ionactis* Greene (50) (present), *Machaeranthera* Nees (158) (1900), *Symphyotrichum* Nees (50) (present)

Aster boltonia - *Boltonia asteroides* (L.) L'Hér. (122) (1937)

Aster-like boltonia - *Boltonia asteroides* (L.) L'Hér. (5, 72, 131) (1899-1913)

Asthmaweed [Asthma weed, Asthma-weed] - *Lobelia inflata* L. (5, 6, 7, 62, 69, 92, 156, 157, 158) (1828-1923)

Astilbe - *Astilbe biternata* (Vent.) Britt. (5) (1913), *Astilbe* Buch.-Ham. ex D. Don (138, 155) (1931-1942)

Astragalus - *Astragalus australis* (L.) Lam. (107) (1919)

Astrantia - *Peucedanum ostruthium* (L.) W.D.J. Koch (178) (1526)

Astringent root - *Comptonia peregrina* (L.) Coult. (7) (1828), *Geranium maculatum* L. (92, 156) (1876-1923)

Â'talĭ kûlĭ (Cherokee, it climbs the mountain) - *Panax quinquefolius* L. (possibly) (102) (1886) addressed in Cherokee rituals as "great man" or "little man"

Atamaran - *Annona squamosa* L. (165) (1678)

Atamasco lily [Atamasco-lily] - *Amaryllis* L. (167) (1814), *Zephyranthes atamasca* (L.) Herbert (2, 5, 107, 109, 138, 156) (1895-1949)

Atamosco - *Zephyranthes atamasca* (L.) Herbert (181) (~1678)

Atasi - *Linum usitatissimum* L. (110) (1886)

Ate (Mexico) - *Annona squamosa* L. (110) (1886)

A'teba'kwe (Abenaki) - *Phaseolus vulgaris* L. (107) (1919)

Athel tamarisk - *Tamarix aphylla* (L.) H. Karst. (109) (1949)

Athenian poplar - *Populus balsamifera* L. (possibly) (19) (1840)

Atikatsatsiks (Pawnee, spider bean) - *Desmanthus illinoensis* (Michx.) MacM. ex B.L. Robins. & Fern. (37) (1919)

Ati-kuraru (Pawnee) - *Amphicarpaea bracteata* (L.) Fern. var. *comosa* (L.) Fern. (37) (1919)

Atit (Pawnee) - *Phaseolus vulgaris* L. (37) (1919)

Atlantic azolla - *Azolla caroliniana* Willd. (155) (1942)

Atlantic camas - *Camassia scilloides* (Raf.) Cory (50, 155) (1942–present)

Atlantic coast knotweed - *Polygonum ramosissimum* Michx. var. *ramosissimum* (5) (1913)

Atlantic coreopsis - *Coreopsis tripteris* L. (155) (1942)

Atlantic isopyrum - *Enemion biternatum* Raf. (155) (1942)

Atlantic manna grass [Atlantic mannagrass] - *Glyceria obtusa* (Muhl.) Trin. (50) (present)

Atlantic ninebark - *Physocarpus opulifolius* (L.) Maxim. var. *intermedius* (Rydb.) B.L. Robins. (50) (present)

Atlantic panic grass - *Dichanthelium acuminatum* (Sw.) Gould & C.A. Clark var. *acuminatum* (56) (1901)

Atlantic panicum - *Dichanthelium acuminatum* (Sw.) Gould & C.A. Clark var. *acuminatum* (72) (1907)

Atlantic pigeonwings - *Clitoria mariana* L. (50, 155) (1942–present)

Atlantic poison ivy - *Toxicodendron toxicarium* (Salisb.) Gillis (50) (present)

Atlantic poison oak - *Toxicodendron pubescens* Mill. (50) (present)

Atlantic St. Peter's-wort [Atlantic St. Peterswort] - *Hypericum crux-andreae* (L.) Crantz (155) (1942)

Atlantic white cedar - *Chamaecyparis thyoides* (L.) Britton, Sterns & Poggenb. (50) (present)

Atlantic wild indigo [Atlantic wildindigo] - *Baptisia alba* (L.) Vent. var. *macrophylla* (Larisey) Isely (155) (1942)

Atlantic yam - *Dioscorea villosa* L. (155) (1942)

Atlee galls - *Tamarix aphylla* (L.) H. Karst. (92) (1876) abnormal parasitic growth on this species

Atoca - *Vaccinium macrocarpon* Aiton (7) (1828)

Atopa (Canada) - *Vaccinium macrocarpon* Aiton (7) (1828)

Atopa or atocas (French Canadians) - *Gaultheria hispidula* (L.) Muhl. ex Bigelow (possibly) (41) (1770)

Attar of roses - *Rosa* ×*damascena* Mill. [*gallica* × *moschata*] (57) (1917) source

Attitaash - *Adenorachis arbutifolia* (L.) Nieuwl. (46) (1879)

Attitaash (Narrangansett) - *Gaylussacia baccata* (Wang.) K. Koch (46) (1879)

Attitaash (New England Indians) - *Vaccinium pallidum* Aiton (107) (1919)

Attoa - *Annona squamosa* L. (110) (1886)

Attoto yam - *Dioscorea cayenensis* Lam. (109) (1949)

At-tung-a-wi-at (Eskimo) - *Arctostaphylos uva-ursi* (L.) Spreng. (107) (1919)

A-ú-ba (Diegeño Yuma) - *Nicotiana* L. (132) (1855)

Aubergine - *Solanum melongena* L. (110, 156) (1886-1923)

Aublet's verbena - *Glandularia canadensis* (L.) Nutt. (possibly) (86) (1878)

Aubrieta - *Aubrieta* Adans. (138) (1923)

Aucuba - *Aucuba* Thunb. (138) (1923)

Audubon's yellow water-lily - *Nymphaea mexicana* Zucc. (86) (1878)

Aufgeblasene Lobelie (German) - *Lobelia inflata* L. (186) (1814)

Augentrost (German) - *Euphrasia stricta* D. Wolff ex J.F. Lehm. (6) (1892)

August lily - *Hosta plantaginea* (Lam.) Aschers. (156) (1923)

August plum - *Prunus americana* Marsh. (107) (1919)

Auld-wive's-tongues - *Populus tremuloides* Michx. (37, 158) (1900-1919)

Aune (French) - *Alnus* P. Mill. (possibly) (8) (1785)

Aune à feuilles argentées (French) - *Alnus incana* (L.) Moench subsp. *rugosa* (DuRoi) Clausen (8) (1785)

Aune commun (French) - *Alnus rubra* Bong. (possibly) (8) (1785)

Aune de l'Oregon (French) - *Alnus rubra* Bong. (20) (1857)

Aune maritime - *Alnus maritima* (Marsh.) Muhl. ex Nutt. (8, 20) (1785-1857)

Aune menu feuillé (French) - *Alnus incana* (L.) Moench subsp. *rugosa* (DuRoi) Clausen (20) (1857)

Aunee (French) - *Inula helenium* L. (6) (1892)

Aunt Jerichos - *Angelica atropurpurea* L. (5, 156) (1913-1923), *Angelica* L. (75) (1894) Northeastern US

Aunt Lucy - *Ellisia nyctelea* (L.) L. (50) (present)

Auricled bladderpod [Auricled bladder-pod] - *Lesquerella auriculata* (Engelm. & Gray) S. Wats. (97) (1937)

Auricled gerardia - *Agalinis auriculata* (Michx.) Blake (5, 72, 97) (1907-1937)

Auricled milkweed - *Asclepias engelmanniana* Woods. (5, 93, 97) (1913-1937)

Auricled parthenium - *Parthenium integrifolium* L. var. *auriculatum* (Britt.) Cornelius ex Cronq. (5) (1913)

Auricled twayblade - *Listera auriculata* Wieg. (5, 50) (1913–present)

Aurone Mâle (French) - *Artemisia abrotanum* L. (158) (1900)

Ausas (Lettonian) - *Avena sativa* L. (110) (1886)

Ausier - *Salix viminalis* L. (5, 156) (1913-1923)

Austin grass - *Urochloa texana* (Buckl.) R. Webster (118) (1898) TX

Australian bluebell-creeper [Australian bluebell creeper] - *Sollya heterophylla* Lindl. (109, 138) (1923-1949)

Australian brake - *Pteris tremula* R.Br. (138) (1923)

Australian dammar-pine - *Agathis robusta* (C. Moore ex F. Muell.) Bailey (138) (1923)

Australian geranium - *Geranium dissectum* L. (107) (1919)

Australian grass - *Sorghum halepense* (L.) Pers. (158) (1900)

Australian maidenhair fern - *Adiantum capillus-veneris* L. (138) (1923)

Australian millet - *Panicum decompositum* R. Br. (107) (1919)

Australian oats - *Bromus catharticus* Vahl (88) (1885)

Australian pea [Australian-pea] - *Dipogon lignosus* (L.) Verdc. (109, 138) (1923-1949)

Australian pepper - *Schinus molle* L. (107) (1919)

Australian rye grass [Australian rye-grass] - *Lolium perenne* L. subsp. *multiflorum* (Lam.) Husnot (119) (1938)

Australian saltbush - *Atriplex semibaccata* R. Br. (118) (1898)

Australian tea-tree - *Leptospermum laevigatum* (Gaertner) F. Muell. (109, 138) (1923-1949)

Australian-beech - *Eucalyptus polyanthemos* Schauer (109) (1949)

Australian-pine - *Casuarina* Rumph. ex L. (109) (1949)

Austrian brome grass - *Bromus inermis* Leyss. (68) (1890)

Austrian brome hay - *Bromus inermis* Leyss. (68) (1890)

Austrian fieldcress - *Rorippa austriaca* (Crantz) Bess. (4, 155) (1942-1986)

Austrian flax - *Linum austriacum* L. (138) (1923)

Austrian pine - *Picea mariana* (Mill.) Britton, Sterns & Poggenb. (112) (1937), *Pinus nigra* Arnold (109, 112, 136, 138) (1923-1949)

Austrian turkey oak - *Quercus cerris* L. (138) (1923)

Austrian yellowcress - *Rorippa austriaca* (Crantz) Bess. (50) (present)

Automobile-weed - *Tribulus terrestris* L. (156) (1923)

Autumn adonis - *Adonis annua* L. (109) (1949)

Autumn bell-flower - *Gentiana linearis* Froel. (46) (1671)

Autumn bent grass [Autumn bentgrass] - *Agrostis perennans* (Walt.) Tuckerman (3, 122, 155) (1937-1977)

Autumn blue grass [Autumn bluegrass] - *Poa autumnalis* Muhl. ex Ell. (50) (present)

Autumn coralroot - *Corallorrhiza odontorhiza* (Willd.) Poir. (50) (present)

Autumn crocus - *Colchicum autumnale* L. (50) (present)

Autumn dwarf gentian - *Gentianella amarella* (L.) Boerner subsp. *acuta* (Michx.) J. Gillett (50) (present)

Autumn elaeagnus - *Elaeagnus umbellata* Thunb. (155) (1942)

Autumn olive - *Elaeagnus umbellata* Thunb. (50, 138) (1923–present)

Autumn onion - *Allium stellatum* Ker (50) (present)

Autumn panic - *Digitaria cognata* (J.A. Schultes) Pilger var. *pubiflora* Vasey ex L.H. Dewey (66) (1903)

Autumn sage - *Salvia greggii* Gray (138) (1923)

Autumn sneezeweed - *Helenium autumnale* L. (71) (1898)

Autumn sneezewort - *Helenium autumnale* L. (71, 86) (1878-1898) used as snuff to cause sneezing

Autumn squash - *Cucurbita maxima* Dcne. (109) (1949)

Autumn Virginia ladies'-traces [Autum Virginia ladies Traces] - *Corallorrhiza odontorhiza* (Willd.) Poir. (181) (~1678)

Autumn water-starwort [Autumn waterstarwort] - *Callitriche hermaphroditica* L. (155) (1942)

Autumn willow - *Salix serissima* (Bailey) Fern. (1, 3, 4, 5, 50, 85, 138, 155) (1913–present)

Autumn willowherb - *Epilobium brachycarpum* K. Presl (155) (1942)

Autumn zephyr-lily [Autumn zephyrlily] - *Zephyranthes candida* (Lindl.) Herbert (138) (1923)

Autumnal adonis - *Adonis annua* L. (42) (1814)

Autumnal gentian - *Gentianella amarella* (L.) Boerner subsp. *acuta* (Michx.) J. Gillett (92) (1876)

Autumnal hawkbit - *Leontodon autumnalis* L. (5, 156) (1913-1923)

Autumnal peranual gentian - *Gentiana autumnalis* L. (183) (~1756)

Autumnal scirpus - *Fimbristylis autumnalis* (L.) Roemer & J.A. Schultes (187) (1818)

Autumnal starwort - *Callitriche hermaphroditica* L. (131) (1899)

Autumn-crocus - *Colchicum autumnale* L. (109) (1949), *Colchicum* L. (138) (1923)

Avellane - *Corylus americana* Walt. (46) (1879)

Avens - *Geum aleppicum* Jacq. (40) (1928), *Geum* L. (1, 2, 4, 10, 50, 92, 93, 109, 138, 155, 156, 158, 167) (1814–present), *Geum macrophyllum* Willd. (157) (1929), *Geum urbanum* L. (57, 107) (1917-1919), *Geum virginianum* L. (7, 19) (1828-1840)

Averoyne - *Artemisia abrotanum* L. (158) (1900)

Avicenne cotonneux (French) - *Avicennia germinans* (L.) L. (20) (1857)

Avocado - *Persea americana* Mill. (109, 138) (1923-1949), *Persea borbonia* (L.) Spreng. (109, 138) (1923-1949), *Persea* Mill. (106) (1930)

Avocat (Louisiana) - *Persea americana* Mill. (7) (1828)

Avogado pear - *Persea americana* Mill. (7) (1828)

Avoine (French) - *Avena sativa* L. (158) (1900)

Awbel - *Populus alba* L. (158) (1900)

Awiza (Lithuanian) - *Avena sativa* L. (110) (1886)

Awl tree - *Morinda citrifolia* L. (92, 107) (1876-1919)

Awl-fruit sedge [Awl-fruited sedge] – possibly *Carex collinsii* Nutt. (66) (1903), *Carex stipata* Muhl. ex Willd. (5, 66, 72) (1903-1893)

Awl-leaf arrowhead - *Sagittaria subulata* (L.) Buch. (50, 138) (1923–present)

Awl-leaf rush [Awl-leaved rush] - *Juncus coriaceus* Mackenzie (5) (1913)

Awlwort [Awl wort] - *Subularia aquatica* L. (13, 15, 19, 92, 156) (1840-1923), *Subularia* L. (13, 15) (1849-1895) from subula (awl)

Awned brachyelytrum - *Brachyelytrum erectum* (Schreb. ex Spreng.) Beauv. (66, 90) (1885-1903)

Awned brome grass - *Bromus tectorum* L. (80) (1913)

Awned cyperus - *Cyperus squarrosus* L. (5, 72) (1907-1913)

Awned darnel - *Lolium perenne* L. subsp. *multiflorum* (Lam.) Husnot (85) (1932)

Awned hair grass - *Muhlenbergia capillaris* (Lam.) Trin. (92) (1876)

Awned half-chaff sedge [Awned halfchaff sedge] - *Lipocarpha aristulata* (Coville) G. Tucker (50) (present)

Awned hemicarpha - *Lipocarpha aristulata* (Coville) G. Tucker (5) (1913)

Awned mountain mint - *Pycnanthemum setosum* Nutt. (5) (1913)

Awned ray grass [Awned ray-grass] - *Lolium perenne* L. subsp. *multiflorum* (Lam.) Husnot (72) (1907)

Awned rye grass [Awned rye-grass] - *Lolium perenne* L. subsp. *multiflorum* (Lam.) Husnot (5, 119) (1913-1938)

Awned sedge - *Carex atherodes* Spreng. (5, 66, 72) (1903-1913)

Awned wheat grass [Awned wheat-grass] - *Elymus caninus* (L.) L. (5, 56, 72, 90, 93, 111) (1885-1936), *Elymus trachycaulus* (Link) Gould ex Shinners subsp. *subsecundus* (Link) A.& D. Löve (68)

(1890), *Elymus trachycaulus* (Link) Gould ex Shinners subsp. *trachycaulus* (5) (1913)

Awnless barnyard grass - *Echinochloa muricata* (Beauv.) Fern. var. *microstachya* Wieg. (56) (1901)

Awnless brome grass [Awnless brome-grass] - *Bromus briziformis* Fisch. & C. A. Mey. (5) (1913)

Awnless brome grass [Awnless brome-grass] - *Bromus inermis* Leyss. (5, 56, 68, 109, 111, 118, 119, 143, 146, 163) (1852-1949)

Awnless muhlenbergia - *Muhlenbergia sobolifera* (Muhl. ex Willd.) Trin. (66) (1903)

Awnless terrell grass - *Elymus submuticus* (Hook.) Smyth & Smyth (56) (1901)

Awn-petal meadow-beauty [Awn-petaled meadow beauty] - *Rhexia aristosa* Britton (5) (1913)

Awn-petal rush [Awn-petaled rush] - *Juncus marginatus* Rostk. (5) (1913)

Awts - *Avena sativa* L. (158) (1900)

Axil goldenrod [Axil golden-rod] - *Solidago caesia* var. *caesia* L. (19) (1840)

Axil-flower [Axilflower] - *Mecardonia acuminata* (Walt.) Small (50) (present)

Axillary gentian - *Enicostema verticillatum* (L.) Engl. ex Gilg (7) (1828)

Axseed - *Coronilla* L. (158) (1900), *Coronilla varia* L. (5, 156, 158) (1900-1923) no longer in use by 1923

Axweed [Ax weed] - *Aegopodium podagraria* L. (5, 92) (1876-1913)

Axwort - *Coronilla varia* L. (5, 156, 158) (1900-1923) no longer in use by 1923

Aya'bĭdji'bikûgi'sĭn (Chippewa) - *Aralia racemosa* L. (40) (1928)

Ayac - *Maclura pomifera* (Raf.) Schneid. (7) (1828)

Ayacotle (Mexico) - *Phaseolus vulgaris* L. (107) (1919)

Ayapana - *Eupatorium triplinerve* Vahl (92) (1876)

Ayegreen [Aye-green] - *Sempervivum tectorum* L. (156, 180) (1633-1923)

Aza (Basque) - *Brassica oleracea* L. (110) (1886)

Azafrancillo - *Carthamus tinctorius* L. (158) (1900)

Azalea - *Rhododendron* L. (2, 106, 138) (1895-1930), *Rhododendron viscosum* (L.) Torr. (possibly) (92) (1876)

Azalée (French) - *Rhododendron* L. (8) (1785)

Azalée à fleurs rouge (French) - *Rhododendron periclymenoides* (Michx.) Shinners (8) (1785)

Azalée visqueuse (French) - *Rhododendron viscosum* (L.) Torr. (8) (1785)

Azalée visqueuse des marais (French) - *Rhododendron viscosum* (L.) Torr. (possibly) (8) (1785)

Azaro - *Asarum canadense* L. (158) (1900)

Azebuche (Andalusian) - *Olea europaea* L. (110) (1886)

Azedarach - *Melia azedarach* L. (57) (1917)

Azedarach bark - *Melia azedarach* L. (92) (1876)

Azolla - *Azolla* Lam. (155) (1942)

Azores forget-me-not - *Myosotis azorica* H.C. Wats. ex Hook. (138) (1923)

Azores jasmine - *Jasminum fluminense* Vell. (138) (1923)

Azorian fennel - *Foeniculum vulgare* Mill. (165) (1807)

Aztec dahlia - *Dahlia pinnata* Cav. (138) (1923)

Aztec marigold - *Tagetes erecta* L. (109, 138) (1923-1949)

Aztec tobacco - *Nicotiana rustica* L. (75, 138) (1894-1923) NY

Azuŋtka jazaŋpi onpijapi (Lakota, kidney pain treatment) - *Lactuca tatarica* (L.) C.A. Mey. var. *pulchella* (Pursh) Breitung (121) (1918?-1970?)

Azure aster - *Symphyotrichum oolentangiense* (Riddell) Nesom var. *oolentangiense* (4) (1986)

Azure blue sage - *Salvia azurea* Michx. ex Lam. (50) (present)

Azure ceanothus - *Ceanothus caeruleus* Lag. (possibly) (138) (1923)

Azure fir - *Abies magnifica* A. Murr. (138) (1923)

Azure larkspur - *Delphinium carolinianum* Walt. (5, 158) (1900-1913), *Delphinium carolinianum* Walt. subsp. *carolinianum* (2) (1895)

Azure red fir - *Abies magnifica* A. Murr. (155) (1942)

Azure sage - *Salvia azurea* Michx. ex Lam. (138, 155) (1923-1942)

B

Baba (Baque) - *Vicia faba* L. (110) (1886)
Babaraune - *Berberis vulgaris* L. (157, 158) (1900-1929)
Babington's curse [Babington's-curse] - *Elodea canadensis* Michx. (156, 158) (1900-1923) introduced into England by botanist of that name
Bab's root [Bab's-root] - *Orbexilum pedunculatum* (P. Mill.) Rydb. var. *pedunculatum* (158) (1900)
Babul acacia - *Acacia nilotica* (L.) Willd. ex Delile (155) (1942)
Babur - *Acacia nilotica* (L.) Willd. ex Delile (158) (1900)
Baby bonnets - *Coursetia axillaris* Coult. & Rose (122, 124) (1937) TX
Baby pondweed - *Potamogeton pusillus* L. (155) (1942), *Potamogeton pusillus* L. subsp. *pusillus* (3) (1977), *Potamogeton pusillus* L. subsp. *tenuissimus* (Mert. & Koch) Haynes & C.B. Hellquist (3) (1977)
Baby's-breath gypsophila [Babysbreath gypsophila] - *Gypsophila paniculata* L. (50) (present)
Baby-blue eyes [Baby blue-eyes] - *Nemophila menziesii* Hook. & Arn. (75, 77, 109, 138) (1894-1949), *Nemophila phacelioides* Nutt. (3, 97) (1937-1977)
Baby's-breath [Babies' breath, Baby's breath, Babies'-breath, Babysbreath] - *Galium mollugo* L. (75, 156) (1894-1923) Eastern MA, *Galium sylvaticum* L. (156) (1923), *Gayophytum diffusum* Torr. & Gray subsp. *parviflorum* Lewis & Szweykowski (3) (1977), *Gayophytum* Juss. (1) (1932), *Gayophytum ramosissimum* Torr. & Gray (85) (1932), *Gypsophila* L. (50, 93, 156, 158) (1900–present), *Gypsophila muralis* L. (3, 85) (1932-1977), *Gypsophila paniculata* L. (4, 5, 76, 85, 109, 138, 155, 156, 158) (1896-1986), *Hedyotis nigricans* (Lam.) Fosberg var. *nigricans* (156) (1923), *Muscari botryoides* (L.) Mills (5, 73) (1892-1913), *Androstephium caeruleum* (Scheele) Greene (158) (1900)
Baby's-feet [Baby's feet, Babies' feet] - *Polygala paucifolia* Willd. (5, 73, 79, 156) (1891-1923) NH
Baby's-slippers [Baby's slippers, Babysslippers] - *Hybanthus verticillatus* (Ort.) Baill. (50) (present), *Polygala paucifolia* Willd. (5, 74, 156) (1893-1923) Western MA
Baby's-tears [Babys-tears] - *Soleirolia soleirolii* (Req.) Dandy (109) (1949)
Baby's-toes [Baby's toes, Babies' toes] - *Polygala paucifolia* Willd. (5, 73, 156) (1892-1923) Hubbardston MA
Baby-white aster [Babywhite aster] - *Chaetopappa ericoides* (Torr.) Nesom (155) (1942)
Bacchante - *Baccharis* L. (8) (1785)
Bacchante de Virginie - *Baccharis halimifolia* L. (8) (1785)
Baccharis - *Baccharis* L. (50, 155, 158) (1900–present)
Bachelor's-button [Bachelor's button, Bachelor's buttons, Batchelor's buttons] - *Achillea ptarmica* L. (165) (1768) England, *Arctium lappa* L. (158) (1900), *Centaurea cyanus* L. (3, 4, 5, 106, 109, 114, 156, 157, 158) (1894-1986), *Centaurea* L. (1) (1932), *Centaurea nigra* L. (5, 156) (1913-1923) no longer in use by 1923, *Cichorium intybus* L. (5, 75, 106, 156, 158) (1894-1930), *Dicentra cucullaria* (L.) Bernh. (5, 156) (1913-1923), *Gomphrena globosa* L. (19, 77, 92) (1840-1898), *Lychnis flos-cuculi* L. (92) (1876), *Ranunculus acris* L. (5, 76, 92) (1876-1913) Bethlehem PA, *Silene dioica* (L.) Clairville (156) (1923)
Bachsbohne - *Menyanthes trifoliata* L. (6) (1892)
Backache brake - *Athyrium filix-femina* (L.) Roth (5, 92, 157) (1876-1929)
Backache root [Backache-root] - *Liatris aspera* Michx. (48) (1828) KS, *Liatris* Gaertn. ex Schreber. (7) (1828), *Liatris spicata* (L.)

Willd. (92, 156) (1876-1923), *Liatris spicata* (L.) Willd. var. *spicata* (5, 157) (1913-1929)
Back's sedge - *Carex backii* Boott (5, 50, 66) (1903–present)
Backwort [Back wort] - *Symphytum officinale* L. (5, 64, 156) (1907-1923)
Baclin - *Bidens cernua* L. (158) (1900)
Baconweed [Bacon-weed] - *Chenopodium album* L. (5, 156, 157, 158) (1900-1929)
Badamier de Malabar - *Terminalia catappa* L. (20) (1857)
Badderlock - Alaria esculenta (L.) Greville (107) (1919)
Badderlocks wingkelp - Alaria esculenta (L.) Greville (155) (1942)
Badger [Badgers] - *Pulsatilla patens* (L.) Mill. (5) (1913), *Pulsatilla patens* (L.) Mill.subsp. *multifida* (Pritz.) Zamels (76) (1896) WI
Badgerbrush [Badger-brush] - *Symphoricarpos* Duham. (possibly) (156) (1923)
Badgerweed [Badger-weed] - *Pulsatilla patens* (L.) Mill. subsp. *multifida* (Pritz.) Zamels (157, 158) (1900-1929)
Badiane - *Illicium parviflorum* Michx. (92) (1876)
Badiane de al Floride (French) - *Illicium floridanum* Ellis (7) (1828)
Bad-man's-oatmeal [Bad-man's oatmeal] - *Conium maculatum* L. (69, 158) (1900-1904)
Baffaloe clover - *Trifolium reflexum* L. (187) (1818)
Bagan' (Chippewa) - *Corylus americana* Walt. (40) (1928), *Corylus cornuta* Marsh (40) (1928)
Bag-leaves - *Hylotelephium telephium* (L.) H. Ohba. subsp. *telephium* (156) (1923)
Bahama grass [Bahama-grass] - *Cynodon dactylon* (L.) Pers. (5, 109, 158) (1900-1949)
Bahama tea - *Lantana camara* L. (7) (1828)
Bahia - *Bahia* Lag. (50, 155) (1942–present), *Picradeniopsis oppositifolia* (Nutt.) Rydb. ex Britton (131, 148) (1899-1948), *Picradeniopsis* Rydb. ex Britton (50) (present)
Bahia grass - *Paspalum notatum* Flueggé (122, 163) (1852-1937)
Bailey's ballmoss [Bailey ball moss] - *Tillandsia baileyi* Rose ex Small (122, 124) (1937) TX
Bailey's blackberry - *Rubus flagellaris* Willd. (5, 97) (1913-1937)
Bailey's cornel - *Cornus sericea* L. subsp. *sericea* (5, 130) (1895-1913)
Bailey's dogwood [Bailey dogwood] - *Cornus sericea* L. subsp. *sericea* (5, 131, 138, 155) (1899–1942)
Bailey's echinocereus [Bailey echinocereus] - *Echinocereus reichenbachii* (Terscheck ex Walp.) Haage f. var. *baileyi* (Rose) N.P. Taylor (155) (1942)
Bailey's hedgehog cactus - *Echinocereus reichenbachii* (Terscheck ex Walp.) Haage f. var. *baileyi* (Rose) N.P. Taylor (50) (present)
Bailey's rabbitbrush - *Chrysothamnus baileyi* Woot. & Standl. (50) (present)
Bailey's sedge - *Carex baileyi* Britton (5, 50) (1913–present)
Bairnwort [Bairn wort] - *Bellis perennis* L. (5, 92, 158) (1876-1913)
Baka hi (Osage) - *Populus deltoides* Bartr. ex Marsh. subsp. *monilifera* (Aiton) Eckenwalder (121) (1918?-1970?)
Baked-apple berry [Baked-apple-berry] - *Rubus chamaemorus* L. (5, 73, 156) (1892-1923) Grand Mana ID
Bakerblom - *Anthemis cotula* L. (186) (1814)
Baker's monkshood [Baker monkshood] - *Aconitum columbianum* Nutt. (155) (1942)
Bakskitits (Pawnee, stick head) - *Grindelia squarrosa* (Pursh) Dunal (37) (1919)
Balam-pulli - *Tamarindus indica* L. (174) (1753)
Balcones Escarpment maple - *Acer grandidentatum* Nutt. (124) (1937)

Bald brome - *Bromus racemosus* L. (3, 50, 155) (1942–present)

Bald cypress [Baldcypress] - *Taxodium distichum* (L.) L.C. Rich. (5, 20, 46, 50, 65, 97, 109) (1857–present), *Taxodium* L.C. Rich. (138) (1923)

Bald rush [Bald-rush] - *Rhynchospora scirpoides* (Torr.) Gray (66, 156) (1903-1923)

Bald rye grass - *Elymus virginicus* L. (68) (1890)

Bald spikerush - *Eleocharis erythropoda* Steud. (50) (present)

Bald wheat grass - *Elymus trachycaulus* (Link) Gould ex Shinners subsp. *trachycaulus* (68) (1890)

Balderbrae - *Anthemis cotula* L. (158) (1900)

Balderbraw - *Anthemis cotula* L. (157) (1929)

Balderherb [Balder-herb] - *Amaranthus hybridus* L. (156, 158) (1900-1923)

Balders - *Anthemis cotula* L. (5, 76, 156, 157, 158) (1896-1923) no longer in use by 1923

Baldersbraa - *Anthemis cotula* L. (186) (1814)

Bald-eyebrow [Bald-eye-brow] - *Anthemis cotula* L. (157, 158) (1900-1929)

Bald-hip rose - *Rosa gymnocarpa* Nutt. (138) (1923)

Baldmoney [Bald-money] - *Gentianella amarella* (L.) Boerner subsp. *acuta* (Michx.) J. Gillett (5, 156) (1913-1923), *Penstemon cobaea* Nutt. (156) (1923)

Baldwin's cyperus - *Cyperus croceus* Vahl (5) (1913), *Cyperus entrerianus* Boeckl. (5) (1913)

Baldwin's flatsedge - *Cyperus croceus* Vahl (50) (present)

Baldwin's hoptree [Baldwin hoptree] - *Ptelea trifoliata* L. subsp. *trifoliata* var. *trifoliata* (155) (1942)

Baldwin's ironweed - *Vernonia baldwinii* Torr. (50) (present)

Baldwin's milkvine - *Matelea baldwyniana* (Sweet) Woods. (50) (present)

Baldwin's vincetoxicum - *Matelea baldwyniana* (Sweet) Woods. (5, 97) (1913-1937)

Baldymony - *Gentianella* Moench (179) (1526)

Balewort - *Papaver somniferum* L. (5, 156) (1913-1923) no longer in use by 1923

Balfour polyscias - *Polyscias scutellaria* (Burm. f.) Fosberg (138) (1923)

Balisier - *Heliconia caribaea* Lam. (109) (1949)

Balkan catchfly - *Silene cserei* Baumg. (50) (present)

Ball cactus - *Coryphantha* (Engelm.) Lem. (93) (1936), *Escobaria missouriensis* (Sweet) D.R. Hunt var. *missouriensis* (156) (1923), *Escobaria vivipara* (Nutt.) Buxbaum var. *vivipara* (127) (1933)

Ball sage - *Salvia mellifera* Greene (106) (1930)

Ballensbro - *Anthemis cotula* L. (186) (1814)

Ballhead [Ball-head] - *Ipomopsis congesta* (Hook.) V. Grant (3, 4) (1977-1986)

Ballhead gilia - *Ipomopsis congesta* (Hook.) V. Grant subsp. *congesta* (155) (1942)

Ballhead ipomopsis - *Ipomopsis congesta* (Hook.) V. Grant (50) (present)

Ballhead sandwort - *Arenaria congesta* Nutt. (155) (1942)

Ballmoss [Ball moss] - *Hechtia* Klotzsch (122) (1937) TX

Ballmustard [Ball mustard] - *Neslia paniculata* (L.) Desv. (3, 4, 5, 50, 80, 155, 156) (1913–present)

Ballogan - *Lapsana communis* L. (5) (1913)

Balloon vine [Balloonvine, Balloon-vine] - *Cardiospermum halicacabum* L. (1, 2, 5, 13, 15, 76, 92, 97, 106, 107, 122, 124, 138, 156, 158) (1895–1937), *Cardiospermum* L. (4, 50) (1986–present)

Balloon-flower [Balloonflower] - *Platycodon* A. DC. (138) (1923), *Platycodon grandiflorum* (Jacq.) A. DC. (109) (1949) from the inflated buds

Balloonpod milkvetch - *Astragalus whitneyi* var. *sonneanus* (Greene) Jeps. (155) (1942)

Balloonvine heartseed - *Cardiospermum halicacabum* L. (155) (1942)

Ballota - *Ballota* L. (155) (1942)

Ballota oak - *Quercus ilex* L. (107) (1919)

Ball's slender lyme grass - *Elymus villosus* Muhl. ex Willd. (56) (1901)

Balm - *Melissa* L. (7, 10, 138, 156, 167) (1814-1923)

Balm - *Melissa officinalis* L. (10, 19, 49, 57, 107, 156) (1818-1923)

Balm mint [Balm-mint] - *Melissa officinalis* L. (5, 156) (1913-1923), *Mentha* ×*piperita* L. [*aquatica* × *spicata*] (5, 158) (1900-1913)

Balmleaf [Balm leaf, Balm-leaf] - *Melissa officinalis* L. (5, 156) (1913-1923)

Balm-leaf hempweed [Balm-leaved hemp-weed] - *Ageratina aromatica* (L.) Spach (187) (1818)

Balm-of-Gilead [Balm of Gilead] or Balm-of-Gilead tree [Balm of Gilead tree] - *Abies balsamea* (L.) Mill. (5, 60, 92) (1876-1913), *Abies balsamea* (L.) Mill. var. *balsamea* (20) (1857), *Populus* ×*jackii* Sargent [*balsamifera* × *deltoides*] (4, 50) (1986–present), *Populus balsamifera* L. (57) (1917), *Populus balsamifera* L. subsp. *balsamifera* (1, 5, 72, 85, 91, 92, 108, 109, 156, 158) (1876-1949), *Populus deltoides* Bartr. ex Marsh. subsp. *deltoides* (19) (1840), *Populus heterophylla* L. (5, 156) (1913-1923)

Balm-of-Gilead fir [Balm of Gilead Fir] or Balm-of-Gilead fir tree [Balm of Gilead fir-tree] - *Abies balsamea* (L.) Mill. (8, 14, 58, 75, 92, 158) (1785-1914)

Balm-of-Gilead herb [Balm of Gilead herb] - *Cedronella canariensis* (L.) Willd. ex Webb & Berth. (19, 92) (1840-1876)

Balm-of-Gilead poplar - *Populus balsamifera* L. subsp. *balsamifera* (138, 155) (1923-1942)

Balm-of-heaven [Balm of heaven] - *Umbellularia californica* (Hook. & Arn.) Nutt. (14, 107, 154) (1857-1919)

Balm-of-warrior's-wound [Balm of warrior's wound] - *Hypericum perforatum* L. (156, 157, 158) (1900-1929)

Balmony - *Chelone glabra* L. (5, 6, 49, 53, 57, 58, 61, 86, 92, 156) (1869-1923), *Chelone* L. (2) (1895), *Monarda* L. (2) (1895)

Balsam - *Euphorbia cyparissias* L. (5, 75, 156) (1894-1923), *Impatiens capensis* Meerb. (5, 156) (1913-1923), *Impatiens* L. (2, 10, 13, 15, 85) (1818-1930), *Impatiens pallida* Nutt. (5, 156) (1913-1923), *Pseudognaphalium obtusifolium* (L.) Hilliard & Burtt subsp. *obtusifolium* (75) (1894)

Balsam amyris - *Amyris balsamifera* L. (155) (1942)

Balsam balm - *Monarda clinopodia* L. (5) (1913)

Balsam groundsel - *Packera paupercula* (Michx.) A.& D. Löve (3, 4, 5, 19, 50, 72, 93, 93, 122, 131, 155, 158) (1840–present)

Balsam hickery - *Carya glabra* (Mill.) Sweet (8) (1785)

Balsam jewelweed [Balsam jewel weed] - *Impatiens pallida* Nutt. (49, 53) (1898)

Balsam of fir - *Abies balsamea* (L.) Mill. (57) (1917)

Balsam of Gilead [Balsam-of-Gilead] - *Abies balsamea* (L.) Mill. (58) (1869)

Balsam opfel - *Momordica balsamina* L. (180) (1633)

Balsam poplar - *Populus angustifolia* James (160) (1860), *Populus balsamifera* L. (1, 3, 4, 5, 10, 14, 20, 19, 40, 50, 57, 85, 91, 92, 93, 105, 108, 109, 112, 130, 131, 135, 138, 156, 157, 158) (1818-1986), *Populus balsamifera* L. subsp. *balsamifera* (113) (1890)

Balsam spruce - *Abies balsamea* (L.) Mill. (58) (1869)

Balsam spurge - *Euphorbia cyparissias* L. (156, 158) (1900-1923)

Balsam tree [Balsam-tree] - *Clusia* L. (167) (1814), *Populus balsamifera* L. (8) (1785)

Balsam vine - *Momordica balsamina* L. (possibly) (7, 92) (1828-1876)

Balsam willow - *Salix pyrifolia* Anderss. (1, 5, 131, 138) (1899-1932)

Balsam, Balsam fir, or Balsam tree [Balsam-tree] - *Abies balsamea* (L.) Mill. (1, 5, 10, 19, 46, 55, 57, 72, 109, 112, 135, 136, 138, 147, 155, 158) (1818-1949), *Abies concolor* (Gord. & Glend.) Lindl. ex Hildebr. (possibly) (149, 153) (1904-1913) NM, *Abies fraseri* (Pursh) Poir. (158) (1900), *Abies lasiocarpa* (Hook.) Nutt. (101) (1905) MT, *Abies* Mill. (1) (1932)

Balsam-apple [Balsam apple, Balsamapple] - *Echinocystis lobata* (Michx.) Torr. & Gray (157) (1929), *Echinocystis* Torr. & Gray (1, 82) (1930-1932), *Echinopepon wrightii* (Gray) S. Watson (122) (1937) TX, *Mimosa microphylla* Dry. (167) (1814), *Momordica*

balsamina L. (19, 61, 92, 107, 109, 138) (1840-1949), *Momordica* L. (138) (1923)

Balsam-flowers [Balsam flowers] - *Melilotus officinalis* (L.) Lam. (5, 156) (1913-1923)

Balsamier des Florides (French) - *Amyris elemifera* L. (20) (1857)

Balsamina - *Momordica balsamina* L. (92) (1876)

Balsamio - *Hemizonia fasciculata* (DC.) Torr. & Gray (76) (1896) CA

Balsamite odorante (French) - *Balsamita major* Desf. (158) (1900)

Balsamkraut (German) - *Balsamita major* Desf. (158) (1900)

Balsam-pear - *Momordica charantia* L. (109, 138) (1923-1949)

Balsamroot [Balsam root, Balsam-root] - *Balsamorhiza hookeri* Nutt. (107) (1919), *Balsamorhiza* Nutt. (1, 4, 155, 158) (1900-1986), *Balsamorhiza sagittata* (Pursh) Nutt. (3, 85, 131, 146) (1899-1977)

Balsamweed [Balsam weed, Balsam-weed] - *Impatiens balsamina* L. (19) (1840), *Impatiens capensis* Meerb. (73, 158) (1892-1900), *Impatiens pallida* Nutt. (49, 53, 92) (1876-1922), *Pseudognaphalium macounii* (Greene) Kartesz (5, 156) (1913-1923), *Pseudognaphalium obtusifolium* (L.) Hilliard & Burtt subsp. *obtusifolium* (5, 92, 156) (1876-1923)

Baltic rush - *Juncus balticus* Willd. (3, 5, 50, 66, 72, 93, 155) (1907–present)

Bamboo brier [Bamboo-brier] - *Smilax glauca* Walt. (92) (1876), *Smilax rotundifolia* L. (5, 156) (1913-1923)

Bamboo greenbrier - *Smilax tamnoides* L. (155) (1942)

Bamboo vine - *Smilax bona-nox* L. (78) (1898) TX, *Smilax laurifolia* L. (5) (1913), *Smilax pseudochina* L. (50) (present)

Bamia - *Hibiscus moscheutos* L. subsp. *moscheutos* (178) (1526)

Bamira - *Acorus calamus* L. (186) (1814)

Bammony - *Chelone glabra* L. (73) (1892) Belleisle NB

Banana - *Musa ×paradisiaca* L. [*acuminata × balbisiana*] (92, 109, 110) (1876-1949), *Musa* L. (7, 50, 138) (1828–present), *Yucca baccata* Torr. (103) (1871)

Banana yucca - *Yucca baccata* Torr. (50, 138) (1923–present)

Baneberry [Bane berry, Bane-berry, Bane berries] - *Actaea* L. (1, 4, 42, 50, 13, 15, 63, 93, 109, 138, 155, 156, 158) (1814–present), *Actaea pachypoda* Ell. (156) (1923), *Actaea rubra* (Aiton) Willd. (3, 10, 19, 127, 156) (1818-1977), *Actaea spicata* L. (14, 92) (1876-1882)

Banewort [Bane-wort] - *Atropa bella-donna* L. (156) (1923)

Bang - *Cannabis sativa* L. (7, 110) (1828-1886), *Cannabis sativa* L. subsp. *indica* (Lam.) E. Small & Cronq. (92) (1876)

Bangalay - *Eucalyptus botryoides* Sm. (138) (1923)

Banister's naked waterweed [Banister's naked water-weed] - *Podostemum ceratophyllum* Michx. (181) (~1678)

Bank cress - *Barbarea verna* (P. Mill.) Aschers. (5, 156) (1913-1923), *Sisymbrium officinale* (L.) Scop (107, 157, 158) (1919-1923)

Bank thistle [Bank-thistle] - *Carduus nutans* L. (5, 156, 158) (1900-1923), *Cirsium vulgare* (Savi) Ten. (5, 156, 158) (1900-1923)

Bankberry - *Vaccinium macrocarpon* Aiton (72, 105) (1932) Fortune Bay Newfoundland

Bank's pine - *Pinus banksiana* Lamb. (5) (1913)

Banksia pine [Banksian pine] - *Pinus banksiana* Lamb. (1, 20) (1857-1932)

Bankweed [Bank-weed] - *Sisymbrium officinale* (L.) Scop (156) (1923)

Bannal - *Cytisus scoparius* (L.) Link (5) (1913)

Banner oats - *Avena sativa* L. (67) (1890)

Banner sorghum - *Sorghastrum secundum* (Ell.) Nash (94) (1901)

Banwort [Ban wort] - *Bellis perennis* L. (5, 158) (1900–1913)

Banyan - *Ficus benghalensis* L. (107, 109) (1919-1949)

Baobab - *Adansonia digitata* L. (50, 92, 107, 109, 155, 165) (1768–present)

Bapoki hi (Osage, popping blackhaw plant) - *Sambucus nigra* L. subsp. *canadensis* (L.) R. Bolli (121) (1918?-1970?)

Baptisia - *Baptisia tinctoria* (L.) R. Br. ex Aiton f. (52, 54, 57, 60, 61, 64, 157) (1870-1919)

Baptisia (German) - *Baptisia tinctoria* (L.) R. Br. ex Aiton f. (6) (1892)

Baptisia tinctoria herba (Official name of Materia Medica) - *Baptisia tinctoria* (L.) R. Br. ex Aiton f. (7) (1828)

Baptisia tinctoria radix (Official name of Materia Medica) - *Baptisia tinctoria* (L.) R. Br. ex Aiton f. (7) (1828)

Bar Harbor juniper - *Juniperus horizontalis* Moench (112) (1937)

Barbados aloe [Barbadoes aloe, Barbadoes alloe] - *Aloe vera* (L.) Burm. f. (92, 109, 165) (1768-1949)

Barbados cedar [Barbadoes cedar] - *Cedrela odorata* L. (92) (1876), *Juniperus virginiana* L. var. *silicicola* (Small) J. Silba (20) (1857)

Barbados cotton - *Gossypium herbaceum* L. (110) (1886)

Barbados flowerfence [Barbadoes flower fence] - *Caesalpinia pulcherrima* (L.) Sw. (92, 109) (1876-1949)

Barbados ground cherry [Barbadoes ground cherry, Barbadoes ground-cherry] - *Physalis pubescens* L. var. *pubescens* (5, 97, 122) (1913-1937)

Barbados nuts [Barbadoes nuts] - *Jatropha curcas* L. (92) (1876)

Barbados pride [Barbadoes pride] - *Adenanthera pavonina* L. (107) (1919), *Caesalpinia pulcherrima* (L.) Sw. (92, 109) (1876-1949)

Barbados-cherry [Barbadoes-cherry, Barbadoes cherry] - *Malpighia glabra* L. (92, 107, 109) (1876-1949)

Barbados-gooseberry [Barbadoes gooseberry, Barbadoes-gooseberry] - *Pereskia aculeata* Mill. (14, 107, 109, 155) (1882-1949), *Pereskia* Mill. (14) (1882), *Physalis peruviana* L. (107) (1919)

Barbara's buttons - *Marshallia* Schreb. (50) (present)

Barbary corn (Provence) - *Zea mays* L. (110) (1886)

Barbary fig - *Opuntia ficus-indica* (L.) Mill. (156) (1923), *Opuntia humifusa* (Raf.) Raf. var. *humifusa* (158) (1900)

Barbary matrimony-vine - *Lycium barbarum* L. (138) (1923)

Barbary wolfberry - *Lycium barbarum* L. (155) (1942)

Barbe de capuchin (French) - *Cichorium intybus* L. (107) (1919)

Barbeau (French) - *Centaurea cyanus* L. (5, 76, 156, 158) (1896-1923) LA, for M. Barbeau who brought it from France

Barbed beard grass [Barbed beard-grass] - *Bothriochloa barbinodis* (Lag.) Herter (119) (1938)

Barbed foxtail grass - *Setaria verticillata* (L.) Beauv. (85) (1932)

Barbed panic grass [Barbed panic-grass] - *Dichanthelium dichotomum* (L.) Gould var. *dichotomum* (119, 163) (1852-1938)

Barbed panicum - *Dichanthelium dichotomum* (L.) Gould var. *dichotomum* (5) (1913), *Dichanthelium sphaerocarpon* (Ell.) Gould var. *isophyllum* (Scribn.) Gould & C.A. Clark (5) (1913)

Barbed witch grass [Barbed witch-grass] - *Panicum capillare* L. (5, 85, 163) (1852-1932), *Panicum hillmani* Chase (119) (1938) SD

Barberry - *Berberis canadensis* P. Mill. (2, 7) (1828-1932), *Berberis* L. (1, 4, 50, 10, 13, 14, 15, 82, 93, 106, 109, 138, 155, 156, 158, 167) (1814–present), *Berberis vulgaris* L. (6, 19, 49, 53, 55, 57, 58, 61, 85, 92, 107, 157, 158, 184) (1793-1932), *Mahonia aquifolium* (Pursh) Nutt. (59, 60, 103, 148) (1870-1939), *Mahonia haematocarpa* (Woot.) Fedde (149) (1904), *Mahonia* Nutt. (50) (present), *Mahonia pinnata* (Lag.) Fedde subsp. *pinnata* (76) (1896), *Opuntia ficus-indica* (L.) Mill. (156) (1923), *Opuntia humifusa* (Raf.) Raf. var. *humifusa* (5) (1913)

Barberry bush - *Berberis canadensis* P. Mill. (7) (1828), *Berberis* L. (8, 190) (~1759-1785)

Barberry fig - *Opuntia ficus-indica* (L.) Mill. (107) (1919)

Barberry tree [Barberry-trees] - *Berberis vulgaris* L. (46) (1671)

Barberry-leaf haw [Barberry-leaved haw] - *Crataegus crus-galli* L. (5, 97) (1913-1937)

Barberry-leaf hawthorn [Barberryleaf hawthorn] - *Crataegus crus-galli* L. (155) (1942)

Barberton daisy - *Gerbera jamesonii* Bolus ex Hooker f. (109) (1949)

Barcelona nuts - *Corylus avellana* L. (107) (1919)

Barclay's maurandia [Barclay maurandia] - *Maurandya barclaiana* Lindl. (138) (1923)

Barclay's willow - *Salix barclayi* Anderss. (5) (1913)

Bardana - *Arctium lappa* L. (174, 177) (1753-1762)

Bardana (Spanish) - *Arctium lappa* L. (92, 158) (1876-1900)

Bardane (French) - *Arctium lappa* L. (5, 6, 64, 158) (1876-1913)

Barentraube - *Arctostaphylos uva-ursi* (L.) Spreng. (6) (1892)

Bare-stem loco [Barestem loco] - *Astragalus calycosus* Torr. ex S. Watson (155) (1942)

Bare-stem paspalum [Barestem paspalum] - *Paspalum setaceum* Michx. (155) (1942)

Bare-stem tickclover [Barestem tickclover] - *Desmodium nudiflorum* (L.) DC. (155) (1942)

Baretta - *Helietta parvifolia* (Gray ex Hemsl.) Benth. (122) (1937)

Bargeman's cabbage - *Brassica rapa* L. var. *rapa* (158) (1900)

Barilla - *Salsola kali* L. (182) (1791), *Salsola* L. (7) (1828)

Bark maple - *Acer glabrum* Torr. (5) (1913)

Barley - *Elyhordeum* Mansf. ex Zizin & Petrowa (50) (present), *Hordeum jubatum* L. (108) (1878), *Hordeum* L (10, 45, 50, 155, 184) (1793–present), *Hordeum secalinum* Schreb. (108, 161) (1857-1878), *Hordeum vulgare* L. (7, 19, 49, 53, 85, 92, 107, 109, 119, 138, 140, 155, 178, 179, 180) (1526-1944)

Barley big - *Hordeum vulgare* L. (180) (1633)

Barley grass [Barley-grass] - *Hordeum bulbosum* L. (87) (1884), *Hordeum* L (66, 92) (1876-1903), *Hordeum murinum* L. (163) (1852), *Hordeum pusillum* Nutt. (66) (1903)

Barn grass [Barngrass, Barn-grass] - *Echinochloa crus-galli* (L.) Beauv. (5, 66, 90, 92, 119) (1885-1938), *Pennisetum glaucum* (L.) R. Br. (7, 78) (1828-1898) ME, *Setaria viridis* (L.) Beauv. (78) (1898) ME

Barnaby's thistle - *Centaurea* L. (106) (1930), *Centaurea solstitialis* L. (3, 5, 19, 93, 156) (1840-1977)

Barnacle grass [Barnacle-grass] - *Zostera marina* L. (5, 156) (1913-1923), *Echinochloa* Beauv. (1, 93) (1932-1936), *Echinochloa crus-galli* (L.) Beauv. (3, 11, 21, 19, 45, 50, 56, 62, 66, 68, 72, 80, 85, 87, 88, 90, 92, 94, 109, 111, 118, 119, 122, 129, 131, 138, 140, 143, 144, 145, 151, 152, 155) (1840–present)

Barnyard millet - *Echinochloa crus-galli* (L.) Beauv. (68) (1890)

Barras - *Abies alba* Mill. (92) (1876)

Barratt's sedge - *Carex barrattii* Schw. & Torr. (5, 50) (1913–present)

Barrel cactus [Barrelcactus] - *Echinocactus* Link & Otto (104) (1896), *Echinocactus texensis* Hopffer. (4) (1986), *Ferocactus* Britt. & Rose (109, 155) (1942-1949), *Ferocactus wislizeni* (Engelm.) Britt. & Rose (76, 149) (1896-1904)

Barrel gentian - *Gentiana andrewsii* Griseb. (5, 75, 156, 157) (1894-1913) MA

Barrelier's alkanet - *Anchusa barrelieri* (All.) Vitman (165) (1807)

Barrelier's bugloss - *Anchusa barrelieri* (All.) Vitman (50) (present)

Barren bilberry - *Arctostaphylos uva-ursi* (L.) Spreng. (156) (1923)

Barren brome grass - *Bromus sterilis* L. (5) (1913)

Barren chickweed - *Cerastium arvense* L. (5) (1913)

Barren hemp - *Cannabis sativa* L. (157) (1929)

Barren myrtle - *Arctostaphylos uva-ursi* (L.) Spreng. (156, 157) (1900-1923)

Barren oak - *Quercus ilicifolia* Wangenh. (5, 10) (1818-1913), *Quercus marilandica* Muench (156, 158) (1900-1923), *Quercus nigra* L. (2, 5, 19, 33, 58, 106, 187) (1818-1930)

Barren oats [Barren otes] - *Bromus sterilis* L. (180) (1633)

Barren scrub oak - *Quercus laevis* Walt. (10, 19, 33) (1818-1840)

Barren sedge - *Carex sterilis* Willd. (19, 187) (1818-1840)

Barren spleenwort [Barren spleenewort] - *Asplenium scolopendrium* L. var. *americanum* (Fern.) Kartesz & Gandhi (possibly) (178) (1596)

Barren white oak - *Quercus stellata* Wangenh. (8, 187) (1785-1818)

Barrens scrub oak - *Quercus laevis* Walt. (2, 20) (1857-1895)

Barren-strawberry [Barren strawberry] - *Duchesnea indica* (Andr.) Focke (156) (1923), *Potentilla canadensis* L. (5, 156) (1913-1923), *Potentilla* L. (158) (1900), *Potentilla norvegica* (76) (1896) Hartford ME; Medford MA, *Potentilla norvegica* L. subsp. *monspeliensis* (L.) Aschers. & Graebn. (5, 156, 158) (1900–1923), *Waldsteinia fragarioides* (Michx.) Tratt. (1, 2, 5, 109, 138, 156) (1895-1949), *Waldsteinia* Willd. (156) (1923)

Barr's milkvetch - *Astragalus barrii* Barneby (50) (present)

Barr's orphaca [Barr orphaca] - *Astragalus barrii* Barneby (4) (1986)

Bartel parent - *Rubus invisus* (Bailey) Britt. (2) (1895)

Bartonia - *Bartonia* Muhl. ex Willd. (155) (1942)

Bartramia moss - *Bartramia pomiformis* Hedw. (50) (present)

Bartram's ixia - *Calydorea coelestina* (Bartr.) Goldblatt & Henrich (50) (present)

Bartram's oak [Bartram oak] - *Quercus* ×*heterophylla* Michx. f. [*phellos* × *rubra*] (10, 20, 33, 97, 187) (1818-1937)

Bartram's serviceberry [Bartram serviceberry] - *Amelanchier bartramiana* (Tausch) M. Roem. (155) (1942)

Bartram's shadblow [Bartram shadblow] - *Amelanchier bartramiana* (Tausch) M. Roem. (138) (1923)

Bartram's tree-orchis - *Epidendrum conopseum* Ait.f. (86) (1878)

Base broom - *Genista tinctoria* L. (5, 156) (1913-1923)

Base vervain - *Veronica chamaedrys* L. (5, 156) (1913-1923)

Base-horehound [Base hoarhound, Base-hoarhound] - *Stachys aspera* Michx. (5) (1913)

Basel [Basyll] - *Ocimum basilicum* L. (179) (1526)

Base-mustard [Base mustard] - *Cleome* L. (42) (1814)

Bashful bulrush - *Trichophorum planifolium* (Spreng.) Palla (50) (present)

Bashte (Omaha-Ponca) - *Fragaria vesca* L. subsp. *americana* (Porter) Staudt (37) (1919), *Fragaria virginiana* Duchesne (37) (1919), Bashte-hi (Strawberry vine)

Ba'sibûgûk' (Chippewa, small leaf) - *Artemisia dracunculus* L. (40) (1928)

Ba'sibûgûk' (Chippewa, small leaves) - *Dalea purpurea* Vent. var. *purpurea* (40) (1928)

Basil - *Acinos arvensis* (Lam.) Dandy (156) (1923), *Clinopodium vulgare* L. (1, 2) (1895-1932), *Cunila origanoides* (L.) Britton (156) (1923), *Ocimum basilicum* L. (19, 109) (1840-1949), *Ocimum* L. (138) (1923), *Pycnanthemum* Michx. (4) (1986), *Pycnanthemum virginianum* (L.) T. Dur. & B.D. Jackson ex B.L. Robins. & Fern. (5, 106) (1913-1930)

Basil beebalm - *Monarda clinopodioides* Gray (3, 4, 50) (1977–present)

Basil mountain mint - *Pycnanthemum clinopodioides* Torr. & Gray (5) (1913)

Basil-balm [Basil balm] - *Acinos arvensis* (Lam.) Dandy (5, 156) (1913-1923), *Monarda clinopodia* L. (156) (1923)

Basil-pennyroyal [Basil pennyroyal] - *Pycnanthemum virginianum* (L.) T. Dur. & B.D. Jackson ex B.L. Robins. & Fern. (156) (1923)

Basil-thyme [Basil thyme] - *Acinos arvensis* (Lam.) Dandy (5) (1913), *Calamintha nepeta* (L.) Savi subsp. *nepeta* (156) (1923), *Clinopodium vulgare* L. (156) (1923)

Basilweed [Basil-weed, Basil weed] - *Clinopodium* L. (184) (1793), *Clinopodium vulgare* L. (5, 156) (1913-1923)

Basin fleabane - *Erigeron pulcherrimus* Heller (50) (present)

Basin wild rye [Basin wildrye] - *Leymus cinereus* (Scribn. & Merr.) A.Löve (50) (present)

Basket ash - *Fraxinus nigra* Marsh (5, 156, 158) (1900)

Basket fern - *Dryopteris filix-mas* (L.) Schott (5, 158) (1900-1913)

Basket grass - *Oplismenus compositus* (L.) Beauv. (138) (1923)

Basket oak - *Quercus michauxii* Nutt. (2, 5, 97, 107, 156) (1895-1937), *Quercus prinus* L. (109) (1949)

Basket selaginella - *Selaginella apoda* (L.) Spring (possibly) (109, 138) (1923-1949)

Basket willow - *Salix discolor* Muhl. (19) (1840), *Salix purpurea* L. (85) (1932), *Salix viminalis* L. (5, 19, 92, 109, 156) (1840-1949)

Basket-flower [Basketflower] - *Centaurea americana* Nutt. (3, 4, 109, 138) (1923-1986)

Basket-flower centaurea [Basketflower centaurea] - *Centaurea americana* Nutt. (155) (1942)

Basket-ivy [Basketivy] - *Cymbalaria* Hill (155) (1942)

Basket-of-gold - *Aurinia saxatilis* (L.) Desv. (109) (1949)

Bass - *Schoenoplectus tabernaemontani* (C.C. Gmel.) Palla (possibly) (158) (1900)

Bass tree [Bass-tree] - *Tilia americana* L. (156) (1923)

Bassia - *Bassia* All. (155) (1942)

Bassombe - *Acorus calamus* L. (186) (1814)

Basswood [Bass wood, Bass-wood] - *Liriodendron tulipifera* L. (5, 156) (1913-1923), *Tilia americana* L. (4, 5, 9, 20, 35, 40, 72, 82, 85, 49, 93, 97, 105, 106, 112, 113, 114, 121, 130, 131, 135, 156, 157, 158) (1806-1986), *Tilia americana* L. var. *americana* (19, 92, 187) (1818-1876), *Tilia* L. (1, 2, 4, 7, 13, 15, 50, 107, 109, 122, 124, 155) (1895–present)

Basswood lime tree - *Tilia americana* L. (57) (1917)

Basswood of the Southeastern United States - *Tilia americana* L. var. *caroliniana* (P. Mill.) Castigl. (124) (1937)

Bast tree [Bast-tree] - *Tilia americana* L. (5, 92, 157, 158) (1876-1913)

Bašta (Osage) - *Ratibida pinnata* (Vent.) Barnh. (121) (1918?-1970?)

Bastard acacia - *Robinia pseudoacacia* L. (5, 157, 158) (1900-1929)

Bastard alkanet - *Buglossoides arvensis* (L.) I.M. Johnston (5, 92, 157, 158) (1876-1913)

Bastard anemones - *Pulsatilla patens* (L.) Mill. subsp. *multifida* (Pritz.) Zamels (poss) (180) (1633)

Bastard asphodel - *Narthecium americanum* Ker-Gawl. (158) (1900)

Bastard bearsfoot - *Helleborus foetidus* L. (92) (1876)

Bastard boneset - *Eupatorium sessilifolium* L. (5, 7) (1828-1932)

Bastard box [Bastardbox] - *Eucalyptus goniocalyx* F. Muell. ex Miq. (138) (1923)

Bastard bunium - *Barbarea vulgaris* W.T. Aiton (possibly) (180) (1633)

Bastard calamus - *Acorus calamus* L. (178) (1596)

Bastard calamus aromaticus - *Acorus calamus* L. (46) (1671)

Bastard cedar - *Guazuma ulmifolia* Lam. (92, 107) (1876-1919)

Bastard china - *Smilax pseudochina* L. (8) (1785)

Bastard china root - *Smilax pseudochina* L. (92) (1876)

Bastard crane's-bill [Bastard Cranes bill] - *Erodium malacoides* (L.) L'Hér. ex Aiton (possibly) (178) (1526)

Bastard cress - *Lepidium campestre* (L.) Aiton f. (5, 92, 158) (1876-1913), *Thlaspi arvense* L. (5, 158) (1900-1913)

Bastard dittany [Bastard dittanie] - *Dictamnus albus* L. (92, 178) (1526-1876)

Bastard dog's-bane [Bastard Dogs-bane] - *Matelea gonocarpos* (Walter) Shinners (possibly) (184) (1793)

Bastard elm - *Celtis occidentalis* L. (5, 158) (1900-1913)

Bastard feverfew - *Parthenium hysterophorus* L. (158) (1900)

Bastard fig - *Opuntia phaeacantha* Engelm. var. *camanchica* (Engelm. & Bigelow) L. Benson (107) (1919)

Bastard fiorin grass [Bastard fiorin-grass] - *Agrostis stolonifera* L. (187) (1818)

Bastard floure-de-luce - *Iris pseudacorus* L. (180) (1633)

Bastard French physic nut - *Jatropha gossypiifolia* L. (92) (1876)

Bastard gentian - *Gentianella amarella* (L.) Boerner subsp. *acuta* (Michx.) J. Gillett (5, 92) (1876-1913)

Bastard ginnie pepper - *Solanum pseudocapsicum* L. (178) (1526)

Bastard hedgehysop - *Justicia americana* (L.) Vahl (184) (1793)

Bastard hellebore - *Epipactis helleborine* (L.) Crantz (5, 92) (1876-1913)

Bastard hemp [Bastard-hemp] - *Datisca* L. (167) (1814), *Galeopsis bifida* Boenn. (5, 92, 158) (1876-1913), *Rhus hirta* (L.) Sudworth (10) (1818)

Bastard horehound [Bastard hoarhound] - *Ballota nigra* L. (5, 92, 158) (1876-1913)

Bastard indigo - *Amorpha fruticosa* L. (5, 106, 109, 157, 158, 165) (1768-1949), *Amorpha* L. (8) (1785)

Bastard ipecac - *Asclepias curassavica* L. (92) (1876), *Triosteum perfoliatum* L. (6, 49, 57, 58, 157, 158) (1869-1917)

Bastard ipecacuanha - *Triosteum perfoliatum* L. (186) (1814)

Bastard iron wood - *Zanthoxylum fagara* (L.) Sargent (15, 20) (1857-1895)

Bastard jasmine - *Lycium barbarum* L. (75, 158) (1894) IA

Bastard jesssamine - *Lycium barbarum* L. (5) (1913)

Bastard Jesuit bark - *Iva frutescens* L. (7) (1828)

Bastard knot grass - *Corrigiola litoralis* L. (92) (1876)

Bastard loosestrife - *Ludwigia palustris* (L.) Ell. (5) (1913)

Bastard millet grass - *Paspalum* L. (92) (1876)

Bastard mustard - *Cleome viscosa* L. (92) (1876)

Bastard nigelle - *Agrostemma githago* L. (71) (1898)

Bastard parsley - *Caucalis platycarpos* L. (92) (1876)

Bastard pellitory - *Achillea ptarmica* L. (5, 92, 165) (1768-1913) England

Bastard pennyroyal - *Trichostema dichotomum* L. (2, 5, 106) (1895-1930)

Bastard pimpernel - *Anagallis* L. (10) (1818), *Anagallis minima* (L.) Krause (5, 19, 92) (1840-1913)

Bastard pine - *Pinus taeda* L. (5) (1913)

Bastard poppy [Bastard poppie] - *Papaver hybridum* L. (178) (1526)

Bastard potatoes - *Solanum tuberosum* L. (178) (1526)

Bastard rhubarb [Bastard rubarbe] - *Rumex alpinus* L. (178) (1526)

Bastard rocket - *Sinapis arvensis* L. (5, 157) (1900–1929)

Bastard saffron - *Carthamus tinctorius* L. (7, 49, 53, 92, 158, 178) (1526-1922)

Bastard sarsaparilla - *Carex hirta* L. (possibly) (92) (1876)

Bastard sena - *Colutea arborescens* L. (178) (1526)

Bastard sensitive plant - *Aeschynomene virginica* (L.) Britton, Sterns & Poggenb. (5) (1913)

Bastard speedwell - *Veronica spuria* L. (138) (1923)

Bastard toadflax [Bastard toad flax, Bastard toad-flax] - *Comandra* Nutt. (1, 50, 93, 158) (1900–present), *Comandra umbellata* (L.) Nutt. (5, 50, 72, 93, 131, 158, 187) (1818–present), *Comandra umbellata* (L.) Nutt. subsp. *pallida* (A. DC.) Piehl (3) (1977), *Comandra umbellata* (L.) Nutt. subsp. *umbellata* (3, 50) (1977–present), *Thesium linophyllon* L. (92) (1876)

Bastard turnip - *Bryonia alba* L. (53) (1922)

Bastard vervain - *Verbena rigida* Spreng. (187) (1818)

Bastard vetch - *Oxytropis* DC. (10) (1818)

Bastard wormwood - *Ambrosia artemisiifolia* L. (6, 158) (1892), *Ambrosia artemisiifolia* L. var. *elatior* (L.) Descourtils (7, 92, 157) (1828-1900)

Ba'sûnûkûk' (Chippewa) - *Artemisia dracunculus* L. (40) (1928)

Batatas - *Ipomoea batatas* (L.) Lam. (110, 182) (1791-1886), *Solanum tuberosum* L. (107) (1919)

Bathflower [Bath flower, Bath-flower] - *Trillium erectum* L. (5, 64) (1908-1913), *Trillium grandiflorum* (Michx.) Salisb. (5, 75) (1894-1913) Franklin Center Quebec, corruption of beth flower which is corruption of birth flower

Bathroot [Bath-root, Bath root] - *Trillium erectum* L. (64, 156) (1908-1923), *Trillium undulatum* Willd. (29) (1869)

Batoko-plum - *Flacourtia indica* (Burm. f.) Merr. (109) (1949)

Battatas de Canada - *Helianthus tuberosus* L. (107) (1629)

Batter-dock [Batter dock] - *Petasites hybridus* (L.) G. Gaertn., B. Mey. & Scherb. (5, 156) (1913-1923), *Petasites sagittatus* (Pursh) Gray (5) (1913), *Potamogeton natans* L. (5, 156, 158) (1900-1923)

Battledoe - *Nyssa sylvatica* Marsh. (46) (1758)

Battledore barley - *Hordeum vulgare* L. (107) (1919)

Battlefield flower [Battle-field flower] - *Viola tricolor* L. (74, 158) (1893-1900) Gordonsville, VA, often found on old Civil War battlefields

Batweed [Bat weed] - *Arctium lappa* L. (6) (1892)

Bauhinia - *Bauhinia* L. (138) (1923)

Baume de Cheval (French) - *Collinsonia canadensis* L. (6) (1892)

Baume des sauvages (French) - *Pluchea foetida* (L.) DC. (7) (1828)

Baume vert (French) - *Mentha spicata* L. (158) (1900)

Baume-coq (French) - *Balsamita major* Desf. (158) (1900)

Baumweischel (German) - *Prunus cerasus* L. (110) (1886)

Bawme - *Melissa officinalis* L. (179) (1526)

Bawme tre - *Melissa officinalis* L. (179) (1526)

Bay [Baye] or Bay tree [Bay-tree] - *Magnolia virginiana* L. (106) (1930), *Laurus* L. (7, 8, 184) (1785-1828), *Laurus nobilis* L. (46, 107, 92) (1671-1876), *Gordonia lasianthus* L. (46) (1610), *Pimenta racemosa* (P. Mill.) J.W. Moore (109) (1949), *Umbellularia californica* (Hook. & Arn.) Nutt. (54, 106) (1905-1930)

Bay bush [Bay-bush] - *Myrica gale* L. (5, 92, 156) (1876-1923)

Bay forget-me-not [Bay forgetmenot] - *Myosotis laxa* Lehm. (50, 138, 155) (1923–present)

Bay galls [Bay-galls] - *Persea borbonia* (L.) Spreng. (5, 156) (1913-1923)

Bay laurel - *Laurus nobilis* L. (55) (1911), *Umbellularia californica* (Hook. & Arn.) Nutt. (106) (1930)

Bay willow - *Salix pentandra* L. (109, 112) (1937-1949)

Bay willowherb [Bay willow-herb] - *Chamerion angustifolium* (L.) Holub subsp. *angustifolium* (5, 156) (1913-1923)

Bayberry [Bay berry] - *Morella caroliniensis* (P. Mill.) Small (5, 156) (1913-1923), *Morella cerifera* (L.) Small (2, 6, 19, 46, 49, 52, 53, 57, 61, 92, 156) (1840-1923), *Morella pensylvanica* (Mirbel) Kartesz (109) (1949), *Myrica gale* L. (47) (1852), *Myrica* L. (2, 7, 138, 167) (1814-1923)

Bayberry bush - *Morella cerifera* (L.) Small (41) (1770)

Baybush [Bay-bush] - *Comptonia peregrina* (L.) Coult. (possibly) (156) (1923)

Bayes - *Laurus* L. (179) (1526)

Bay-leaf rough bindweed [Bay leaved rough bindweed] - *Smilax laurifolia* L. (8) (1785)

Bay-leaf willow [Bay-leaved willow] - *Salix pentandra* L. (156) (1923)

Bayonet rush - *Juncus militaris* Bigel. (5, 50, 156) (1913–present)

Bayonet-grass - *Eleocharis palustris* (L.) Roemer & J.A. Schultes (156) (1923)

Bayou violet - *Viola affinis* Le Conte (155) (1942)

Bay-rum tree [Bay-rum-tree] - *Pimenta racemosa* (P. Mill.) J.W. Moore (109) (1949)

Bay-willow [Bay willow] - *Chamerion angustifolium* (L.) Holub subsp. *angustifolium* (5, 156, 157, 158) (1900-1929)

Bazu-hi (Omaha-Ponca) - *Lithospermum canescens* (Michx.) Lehm. (37) (1919)

Bazzies - *Arctium lappa* L. (158) (1900)

BaΘoŋ (Osage) - *Pinus* L. (121) (1918-1970)

Beach aster - *Erigeron glaucus* Ker-Gawl. (109) (1949)

Beach clotbur - *Xanthium strumarium* L. (5, 72) (1907-1913)

Beach cocklebur - *Xanthium strumarium* L. var. *canadense* (Mill.) Torr. & Gray (93, 155) (1936-1942)

Beach false foxglove - *Agalinis fasciculata* (Ell.) Raf. (50) (present)

Beach fleabane - *Erigeron glaucus* Ker-Gawl. (138) (1923)

Beach goldenrod [Beach golden-rod] - *Solidago sempervirens* L. (5, 156) (1913-1923)

Beach grass [Beachgrass, Beach-grass] - *Ammophila arenaria* (L.) Link (45, 56, 66, 87, 88, 90, 94, 138) (1885-1923), *Ammophila* Host (109, 138) (1923-1949) ME, *Uniola paniculata* L. (5, 163) (1852-1913)

Beach pea - *Lathyrus japonicus* Willd. var. *maritimus* (L.) Kartesz & Gandhi (2, 5, 19, 41, 46, 47, 92, 109, 156) (1770-1949)

Beach pinweed [Beach pin-weed] - *Lechea maritima* Leggett ex B.S.P. (5) (1913)

Beach plum - *Prunus pumila* L. (5, 76, 156, 158) (1896-1913) Aroostock Co. & Somerset Co. ME (76)

Beach sandwort - *Minuartia dawsonensis* (Britt.) House (5) (1913)

Beach sedge - *Carex silicea* Olney (50) (present)

Beach wormwood - *Artemisia stelleriana* Bess. (5, 109, 138, 155 156) (1913-1949)

Beach-drops - *Epifagus virginiana* (L.) W. Bart. (122) (1937)

Beach-heather [Beachheather, Beach heather] - *Hudsonia* L. (1, 155) (1932-1942), *Hudsonia tomentosa* Nutt. (4, 5, 156, 158) (1900-1986)

Beach-woods threeawn [Beachwoods threeawn] - *Aristida tuberculosa* Nutt. (155) (1942)

Bead grass [Bead-grass] - *Paspalum setaceum* Michx. (115, 157) (1900-1932)

Bead plant [Bead-plant, Bead-plant] - *Nertera granadensis* (L. f.) Druce (109, 138) (1923-1949)

Bead tree [Beade tree] - *Adelia vaseyi* (Coult.) Pax & K. Hoffmann (109, 137, 155) (1923-1949), *Azadirachta indica* Adr. Juss. (possibly) (7) (1828), *Melia azedarach* L. (19, 49, 92, 178) (1526-1898), *Melia* L. (109) (1949)

Beaded lipfern - *Cheilanthes wootonii* Maxon (4, 50) (1986–present)

Beadle's mock orange [Beadle mockorange] - *Philadelphus floridus* Beadle (138) (1923)

Beadle's yellow-fruit thorn [Beadle's yellow-fruited thorn] - *Crataegus intricata* Lange (5) (1913)

Beadruby [Bead ruby, Bead-ruby] - *Maianthemum canadense* Desf. (5, 75, 155, 158) (1894-1942) NY, *Maianthemum* G.H. Weber ex Wiggers (155) (1942)

Beak willow [Beak-willow] - *Salix bebbiana* Sargent (138, 156) (1923)

Beakchervil - *Acanthospermum* Schrank (155) (1942), *Anthriscus* Pers. (155) (1942)

Beaked agrimony - *Agrimonia pubescens* Wallr. (50) (present)

Beaked corn salad [Beaked cornsalad] - *Valerianella radiata* (L.) Dufr. (5, 50, 97, 122, 156, 158) (1900–present)

Beaked dodder - *Cuscuta rostrata* Shuttlw. ex Engelm. & Gray (5) (1913)

Beaked filbert - *Corylus cornuta* Marsh (155) (1942)

Beaked hazel - *Corylus cornuta* Marsh (19, 92, 158) (1840-1900)

Beaked hazelnut [Beaked hazel-nut] - *Corylus cornuta* Marsh (1, 2, 4, 5, 50, 82, 85, 107, 109, 130, 131, 138) (1895–present)

Beaked lygodesmia - *Shinnersoseris rostrata* (Gray) S. Tomb (5, 93) (1913-1936)

Beaked nightshade - *Solanum rostratum* Dunal (5, 131, 156, 158) (1899-1923)

Beaked panic grass [Beaked panicgrass, Beaked panic-grass] - *Panicum anceps* Michx. (50, 99, 119, 163) (1852–present)

Beaked panicum - *Panicum anceps* Michx. (3, 5, 155) (1913-1977)

Beaked parsley - *Anthriscus cerefolium* (L.) Hoffmann (5) (1913)

Beaked rush - *Rhynchospora capillacea* Torr. (85) (1932), *Rhynchospora* Vahl (1, 156) (1923-1932)

Beaked sedge - *Carex rostrata* Stokes (5, 50, 139, 155, 187) (1814–present)

Beaked seg - *Carex rostrata* Stokes (42) (1818)

Beaked skeleton-weed [Beaked skeletonweed] - *Shinnersoseris rostrata* (Gray) S. Tomb (50) (present), *Shinnersoseris* S. Tomb (50) (present)

Beaked spike rush [Beaked spikerush] - *Eleocharis rostellata* (Torr.) Torr. (5, 50) (1913–present)

Beaked violet - *Viola rostrata* Pursh (19, 92, 156) (1840-1923)

Beaked willow - *Salix bebbiana* Sargent (1, 4, 5, 93, 138, 156) (1890-1930)

Beakgrain - *Diarrhena* Beauv. (50, 155) (1942–present)

Beak-pod evening primrose [Beakpod evening primrose] - *Oenothera canescens* Torr. & Frem. (3) (1977)

Beakrush [Beak rush] - *Rhynchospora capillacea* Torr. (3) (1977), *Rhynchospora* Vahl (155) (1942), *Rhynchospora corniculata* (Lam.) A. Gray (156) (1923)

Bean tree [Beantree, Bean-tree] - *Catalpa bignonioides* Walt. (5, 6, 49, 53, 156) (1892-1923), *Ceratonia siliqua* L. (92) (1876), *Laburnum anagyroides* Medik. (109) (1949), *Melia azedarach* L. (107) (1919)

Bean trefoil - *Menyanthes trifoliata* L. (5, 92, 156, 158) (1876-1923)

Bean vine - *Phaseolus polystachys* (L.) B.S.P. (5) (1913)

Beane [Beane] - *Phaseolus* L. (1, 7, 106, 109, 138) (1828-1949), *Phaseolus vulgaris* L. (82) (1930), *Vicia faba* L. (110) (1886)

Beanweed [Bean-weed] - *Pinguicula vulgaris* L. (5, 156) (1913-1923)

Bear - *Hordeum* L (158) (1900)

Bear barley [Beare barley] - *Hordeum vulgare* L. (158, 180) (1633-1900)

Bear bush [Bear-bush] - *Ilex glabra* (L.) Gray (156) (1923)

Bear clover - *Chamaebatia foliolosa* Benth. (106) (1930)

Bear corn - *Veratrum viride* Ait. (5, 6, 64, 71, 156) (1874-1913)

Bear grass - *Cenchrus tribuloides* L. (5, 75) (1894-1913), *Nassella neesiana* (Trin. & Rupr.) Barkworth (87) (1884)

Bear huckleberry [Bear-huckleberry] - *Gaylussacia ursina* (M.A. Curtis) Torr. & Gray ex Gray (77, 156) (1898-1923) Mountains of New England, *Vaccinium hirsutum* Buckl. (75) (1894) NC

Bear oak [Bear's Oak] - *Quercus ilicifolia* Wangenh. (2, 5, 20, 33, 46, 156, 181, 187) (~1678-1923)

Bear plum - *Clintonia borealis* (Ait.) Raf. (75) (1894) Franconia NH

Bear poppy [Bearpoppy] - *Arctomecon* Torr. & Frém. (155) (1942)

Bear sedge - *Carex ursina* Dewey (5) (1913)

Bear whortleberry [Bear's whortleberry] - *Arctostaphylos uva-ursi* (L.) Spreng. (5, 157) (1913-1929)

Bearbed [Bear's bed] - *Polytrichum juniperinum* Hedw. (50, 58, 92) (1869–present)

Bearberry [Bear berry, Bear-berry] - *Arbutus* L. (8, 167) (1785-1814), *Arctostaphylos* Adans. (1, 2, 4, 106, 156) (1895-1986), *Arctostaphylos uva-ursi* (L.) Spreng. (3, 4, 5, 6, 7, 8, 10, 14, 19, 34, 38, 40, 41, 42, 49, 52, 53, 55, 57, 58, 59, 85, 86, 92, 103, 106, 107, 108, 109, 112, 113, 130, 138, 153, 155, 156, 157) (1770-1986), *Cornus canadensis* L. (156) (1923), *Frangula californica* (Eschsch.) Gray (74) (1893) Santa Barbara CA, *Frangula purshiana* (DC.) Cooper (52, 107) (1919), *Ilex crenata* Thunb. (5, 156, 158) (1900–1923), *Lonicera involucrata* Banks ex Spreng. (101, 112, 160) (1860-1937), *Lonicera* L. (possibly) (1) (1932), *Rubus canadensis* L. (156) (1923), *Shepherdia canadensis* Nutt. (156) (1923), *Sophora affinis* Torr. & Gray (124) (1937) TX, *Vaccinium macrocarpon* Aiton (5, 7, 73, 156) (1828-1923) Fortune Bay Newfoundland

Bearberry honeysuckle - *Lonicera involucrata* Banks ex Spreng. (103, 138) (1870-1923)

Bearberry willow - *Salix uva-ursi* Pursh (5, 138) (1913-1923)

Bear-bilberry [Bear's bilberry] - *Arctostaphylos uva-ursi* (L.) Spreng. (157) (1929)

Bearbind [Bear-bind] - *Convolvulus arvensis* L. (92, 156, 157, 158) (1898-1923), *Polygonum convolvulus* L. (5, 156, 158) (1900-1923)

Bear-bine - *Calystegia sepium* (L.) R. Br. subsp. *sepium* (156) (1923)

Bearbough [Beares bough] - *Acanthus mollis* L. (179) (1526)

Bearbreeches [Bear's breeches, Bear's breech] - *Acanthus* L. (109) (1949), *Acanthus mollis* L. (50) (present)

Beard grass [Beard-grass, Beardgrass] - *Achnatherum eminens* (Cav.) Barkworth (87) (1884), *Agropogon littoralis* (Sm.) C.E. Hubbard [*Agrostis stolonifera × Polypogon monospeliensis*] (94) (1901), *Andropogon gerardii* Vitman (108, 119) (1878-1938), *Andropogon* L. (1, 10, 56, 138, 155, 158, 184) (1793-1942), *Aristida basiramea* Engelm. ex Vasey (119) (1938), *Aristida dichotoma* Michx. (19) (1840), *Aristida purpurascens* Poir. (87) (1884), *Aristida purpurea* Nutt. (3, 11, 50) (1888–present), *Bothriochloa* Kuntze (1, 50) (1932–present), *Gymnopogon* P. Beauv. (66) (1903), *Paspalum setaceum* Michx. (5, 111) (1913-1915), *Polypogon* Desf. (1, 66, 93, 152) (1903-1932), *Polypogon monspeliensis* (L.) Desf. (87) (1884), *Saccharum brevibarbe* (Michx.) Pers. var. *contortum* (Ell.) R. Webster (163) (1852), *Schizachyrium scoparium* (Michx.) Nash var. *scoparium* (45, 108) (1878-1896), *Sorghastrum nutans* (L.) Nash (19, 92) (1840-1876)

Bearded beggarticks - *Bidens aristosa* (Michx.) Britton (50, 155) (1942–present)

Bearded blue-bunch wheat grass [Bearded bluebunch wheatgrass] - *Pseudoroegneria spicata* (Pursh) A. Löve subsp. *spicata* (140, 155) (1942-1944)

Bearded darnel - *Lolium temulentum* L. (5, 66, 111, 157, 158) (1903-1915)

Bearded day-flower - *Commelina virginica* L. (97) (1937)

Bearded fescue - *Festuca subulata* Trin. (50, 155) (1942–present)

Bearded flatsedge - *Cyperus squarrosus* L. (50, 155) (1942–present)

Bearded fox-tail grass - *Polypogon monspeliensis* (L.) Desf. (165) (1768)

Bearded hair grass [Bearded hair-grass] - *Muhlenbergia capillaris* (Lam.) Trin. (94) (1901)

Bearded joint [Bearded-joint] - *Dichanthelium dichotomum* (L.) Gould var. *dichotomum* (94) (1901)

Bearded joint grass - *Dichanthelium dichotomum* (L.) Gould var. *dichotomum* (5) (1913), *Dichanthelium sphaerocarpon* (Ell.) Gould var. *isophyllum* (Scribn.) Gould & C.A. Clark (5) (1913)

Bearded knot-weed - *Polygonum bellardii* All. (187) (1818)

Bearded leafy muhly - *Muhlenbergia mexicana* (L.) Trin. (155) (1942)

Bearded lichen - *Usnea xanthopoga* Nyl. (50) (present)

Bearded maple - *Acer barbatum* Michx. (20) (1857)

Bearded melic grass [Bearded melic-grass] - *Melica aristata* Thurb. ex Boland. (94) (1901)

Bearded moss - *Parmelia jubata* (L.) Ach. (possibly) (103) (1871)

Bearded pink - *Calopogon tuberosus* (L.) B.S.P. var. *tuberosus* (5, 156) (1913-1923)

Bearded rock muhly - *Muhlenbergia sobolifera* (Muhl. ex Willd.) Trin. (155) (1942)

Bearded sand-verbena [Bearded sandverbena] - *Abronia pogonantha* Heimerl (155) (1942)

Bearded shorthusk [Bearded short husk, Bearded short-husk] - *Brachyelytrum erectum* (Schreb. ex Spreng.) Beauv. (5, 50, 94, 111, 119, 155) (1901–present)

Bearded skeleton grass [Bearded skeletongrass] - *Gymnopogon ambiguus* (Michx.) Britton, Sterns & Poggenb. (3, 50, 155) (1942–present)

Bearded sprangletop - *Leptochloa fusca* (L.) Kunth subsp. *fascicularis* (Lam.) N. Snow (3, 50, 155) (1942–present)

Bearded wheat - *Triticum aestivum* L. (158, 180) (1633-1900)

Bearded wheat grass - *Elymus caninus* (L.) L. (5, 56, 66, 129) (1894-1913), *Elymus trachycaulus* (Link) Gould ex Shinners subsp. *subsecundus* (Link) A.& D. Löve (56, 85) (1901-1932), *Elymus trachycaulus* (Link) Gould ex Shinners subsp. *trachycaulus* (5) (1913), *Thinopyrum intermedium* (Host) Barkworth & D.R. Dewey (129) (1894)

Beardless barley - *Hordeum vulgare* L. (155, 163) (1942-1952)

Beardless barnyard grass [Beardless barnyardgrass] - *Echinochloa muricata* (Beauv.) Fern. var. *microstachya* Wieg. (155) (1942)

Beardless blue-bunch wheat grass [Beardless bluebunch wheatgrass] - *Pseudoroegneria spicata* (Pursh) A. Löve subsp. *inermis* (Scribn. & J.G. Sm.) A. Löve (155) (1942)

Beardless broom sedge - *Schizachyrium tenerum* Nees (94) (1901)

Beardless darnel rye grass [Beardless darnel ryegrass] - *Lolium temulentum* L. (155) (1942)

Beardless false oat - *Trisetum wolfii* Vasey (94) (1901)

Beardless rabbit's-foot grass [Beardless rabbitsfoot grass] - *Polypogon viridis* (Gouan) Breistr. (50) (present)

Beardless Virginia wild rye [Beardless Virginia wildrye] - *Elymus submuticus* (Hook.) Smyth & Smyth (155) (1942)

Beardless wheat grass - *Pseudoroegneria spicata* (Pursh) A. Löve subsp. *inermis* (Scribn. & J.G. Sm.) A. Löve (50) (present)

Beardless wild rye [Beardless wild-rye, Beardless wildrye] - *Leymus triticoides* (Buckl.) Pilger (50, 163) (1852–present)

Beardtongue [Beard-tongue, Beard tongue] - *Penstemon acuminatus* Dougl. ex Lindl. (156) (1923), *Penstemon gracilis* Nutt. (77) (1898), *Penstemon laevigatus* Aiton (106) (1930), *Penstemon* Schmidel (1, 4, 50, 63, 93, 127, 158) (1899–present)

Bearefore - *Acanthus mollis* L. (179) (1526)

Beargrape [Bears' grape, Bear's grape] - *Arctostaphylos uva-ursi* (L.) Spreng. (6, 92, 106, 107, 156) (1876–1930)

Bear-grass [Bear grass, Bear's grass, Bears' grass] - *Camassia quamash* (Pursh) Greene subsp. *quamash* (7) (1828), *Dasylirion wheeleri* S. Wats. (78, 151) (1896-1898) AZ NM, *Hudsonia tomentosa* Nutt. (5, 156, 158) (1900), *Nolina* Michx. (149) (1904), *No-*

lina microcarpa S. Wats. (153) (1913) NM, *Polytrichum commune* Hedw. (78) (1898) ME, *Xerophyllum tenax* (Pursh) Nutt. (35, 101, 138) (1806-1923), *Yucca filamentosa* L. (5, 7, 92, 156, 158) (1828-1913), *Yucca glauca* Nutt. (5, 72, 93, 97, 153, 156) (1907-1937), *Yucca* L. (2) (1895)

Bearmat [Bear-mat] - *Chamaebatia foliolosa* Benth. (106) (1930)

Bearpaw root [Bears' paw root, Bear's-paw root] - *Dryopteris filix-mas* (L.) Schott (5, 92, 158) (1876-1913)

Bear's-bread [Bears' bread] - *Polytrichum commune* Hedw. (73) (1892) Dennysville ME

Bear's-ear [Bears' ear] - *Platanthera orbiculata* (Pursh) Lindl. (156) (1923)

Bear's-foot [Bear's foot, Bearsfoot] - *Aconitum napellus* L. (107, 156) (1919-1923), *Alchemilla monticola* Opiz (possibly) (156, 165) (1768-1923), *Helleborus foetidus* L. (7, 92) (1828-1876), *Smallanthus uvedalius* (L.) Mackenzie ex Small (4, 49, 52, 53, 54, 57, 158) (1898-1986)

Bear's-fright [Bearfright] - *Croton capitatus* Michx. (7, 92) (1828–1876)

Bear's-grape bilberry [Bear's grape bilberry] - *Arctostaphylos uva-ursi* (L.) Spreng. (5) (1913)

Bear's-paw [Bear's paw] - *Thelypteris noveboracensis* (L.) Nieuwl. (78) (1898) Plattsburg NY

Bear's-tongue [Bear tongue, Bear-tongue] - *Clintonia borealis* (Ait.) Raf. (5, 156) (1913-1923)

Bear-thread [Bear's thread, Bear's-thread] - *Yucca filamentosa* L. (5, 7, 19, 156, 158) (1828-1923)

Beartwig [Beares twygge] - *Acanthus mollis* L. (179) (1526)

Bearweed [Bear weed] - *Symplocarpus foetidus* (L.) Salisb. ex Nutt. (86) (1878)

Bearwood [Bear-wood] - *Frangula purshiana* (DC.) Cooper (52, 160) (1860-1919)

Beaumont's root [Beaumont root] - *Gillenia trifoliata* (L.) Moench (186) (1814), *Porteranthus stipulatus* (Muhl. ex Willd.) Britt. (7) (1828), *Veronicastrum* Heister ex Fabr. (5, 7, 49, 53, 61, 92, 157, 158) (1828-1923), *Veronicastrum virginicum* (L.) Farw. (5, 64, 92, 156, 157, 158) (1876-1923) no longer in use by 1923

Beautiful cinquefoil - *Potentilla pulcherrima* Lehm. (50) (present)

Beautiful fleabane - *Erigeron formosissimus* Greene (50) (present)

Beautiful sandwort - *Minuartia rubella* (Wahlenb.) Hiern. (50) (present)

Beautiful sedum - *Sedum pulchellum* Michx. (2) (1895)

Beautiful tuberous cymbidium - *Calopogon tuberosus* (L.) B.S.P. var. *tuberosus* (possibly) (42) (1814)

Beautiful-for-a-day [Beautiful for a day] - *Hemerocallis fulva* (L.) L. (180) (1633)

Beauty-berry [Beautyberry] - *Callicarpa americana* L. (156) (1923), *Callicarpa* L. (109, 155) (1942-1949)

Beauty-bush [Beauty bush] - *Kolkwitzia amabilis* Graebn. (109, 112) (1937-1949)

Beauty-fruit - *Callicarpa americana* L. (156) (1923), *Callicarpa* L. (156) (1923)

Beauty-of-the-night [Beauty of the night] - *Mirabilis jalapa* L. (92) (1876)

Beaver tree [Beavertree] - *Magnolia macrophylla* Michx. (7) (1828), *Magnolia virginiana* L. (5, 6, 19, 41, 49, 52, 92, 106, 156, 186) (1770-1930)

Beaver wood [Beaver-wood] - *Celtis occidentalis* L. (5, 6, 75, 156, 158) (1892–1923), *Magnolia virginiana* L. (6, 20, 186, 187) (1818-1892)

Beaver-lily - *Nuphar lutea* (L.) Sm. subsp. *advena* (Aiton) Kartesz & Gandhi (156, 158) (1900-1923)

Beaver-poison [Beaver poison] - *Cicuta maculata* L. (2, 6, 71, 92, 156, 158) (1876-1923)

Beaver-root [Beaver root] - *Heracleum maximum* Bartr. (37) (1919), *Nuphar lutea* (L.) Sm. subsp. *advena* (Aiton) Kartesz & Gandhi (92, 156, 158) (1876-1923)

Beaver-tail cactus [Beavertail cactus] - *Opuntia basilaris* Engelm. & Bigelow (109, 138) (1923-1949)

Beaver-tail prickly-pear [Beavertail pricklypear] - *Opuntia basilaris* Engelm. & Bigelow (155) (1942)

Bebb's sedge [Bebb sedge] - *Carex bebbii* Olney ex Fern. (5, 50, 139) (1913–present)

Bebb's willow [Bebb willow] - *Salix bebbiana* Sargent (5, 50, 72, 85, 131, 155) (1899–present)

Bebb's zizia - *Zizia trifoliata* (Michx.) Fern. (5) (1913)

Beberitze (German) - *Berberis vulgaris* L. (158) (1900)

Bec de Grue (French) - *Geranium maculatum* L. (6, 186) (1814-1892)

Beccabunga - *Veronica beccabunga* L. (92) (1876)

Becco di gru (Italian) - *Geranium maculatum* L. (186) (1814)

Bec-de-grue tacheté (French) - *Geranium maculatum* L. (158) (1900)

Becengenes - *Solanum melongena* L. (46) (1879)

Bechords - *Typha* L. (180) (1633)

Bechtel's crab [Bechtel crab] - *Malus ioensis* (Wood) Britton var. *ioensis* (4, 112, 137) (1931-1986)

Be'cigodji'bigûk (Chippewa) - *Caulophyllum thalictroides* (L.) Michx. (40) (1928)

Be'cigodji'bigûk (Chippewa, one root) - *Geranium maculatum* L. (40) (1928)

Beckenweidt - *Fagopyrum esculentum* Moench (180) (1633)

Beckmannia - *Beckmannia syzigachne* (Steud.) Fern. (possibly) (72) (1907)

Beckmann's grass - *Beckmannia syzigachne* (Steud.) Fern. (possibly) (5) (1913)

Beckwith's clover [Beckwith clover] - *Trifolium beckwithii* Brewer ex S. Wats. (4, 5, 50, 129, 131, 155) (1894–present)

Beckwith's milkvetch [Beckwith milkvetch] - *Astragalus beckwithii* Torr. & Gray (155) (1942)

Bed sandwort [Bedsandwort] - *Spergula arvensis* L. (76) (1896) Western US, *Spergularia canadensis* (Pers.) G. Don var. *canadensis* (5) (1913), *Spergularia rubra* (L.) J.& K. Presl (5) (1913)

Bedeguar - *Rosa canina* L. (5, 92) (1876-1913), *Rosa eglanteria* L. (5) (1913)

Bedengiam - *Solanum melongena* L. (110) (16th century)

Bede-sedge - *Sparganium* L. (158) (1900)

Bede-segg - *Sparganium* L. (158) (1900)

Bede-seggin - *Sparganium* L. (158) (1900)

Bedflower [Bed-flower] - *Galium verum* L. (156, 158) (1900-1923) no longer in use by 1923

Bed's-foot [Bed's foot] - *Clinopodium arkansanum* (Nutt.) House (5) (1913), *Clinopodium vulgare* L. (5, 156) (1913-1923)

Bedstraw [Bed straw] - *Galium aparine* L. (49, 53, 85, 92, 93, 107) (1876-1936), *Galium* L. (1, 2, 4, 10, 50, 82, 93, 109, 138, 155, 156, 158) (1818–present), *Galium mollugo* L. (82) (1930), *Galium trifidum* L. (19) (1840), *Galium triflorum* Michx. (19) (1840), *Galium verum* L. (5, 7) (1828-1913)

Bedstraw asperula - *Galium glaucum* L. (5, 156) (1913-1923)

Bedstraw bellflower - *Campanula aparinoides* Pursh (5, 93, 155, 156) (1913-1942)

Bedstraw milkweed - *Asclepias verticillata* L. (5, 97, 122) (1913-1937)

Bedstraw St. John's-wort [Bedstraw St. John's wort] - *Hypericum galioides* Lam. (5, 138) (1913-1923)

Bedstraw woodruff - *Galium glaucum* L. (155) (1942)

Be'dukadak'igisĭn (Chippewa, it sticks up) - *Agastache foeniculum* (Pursh) Kuntze (40) (1928)

Bee larkspur - *Delphinium elatum* L. (2, 138) (1895-1923)

Bee laurel - *Rhododendron maximum* L. (5, 156) (1913-1923) no longer in use by 1923

Bee nettle [Bee-nettle] - *Galeopsis bifida* Boenn. (5, 156, 158) (1900-1923), *Lamium album* L. (5, 156) (1913-1923)

Bee plant [Beeplant] - *Cleome* L. (4) (1986), *Cleome serrulata* Pursh (85) (1932)

Bee spiderflower - *Cleome serrulata* Pursh (155) (1942)

Bee tree [Bee-tree] - *Tilia americana* L. (5, 156, 157, 158) (1900-

1929), *Tilia americana* L. var. *heterophylla* (Vent.) Loud. (5, 156) (1913-1923), *Tilia* L. (2) (1895)

Beebalm [Bee balm, Bee-balm] - *Melissa* L. (1) (1932), *Melissa officinalis* L. (1, 5, 106, 109, 156) (1913-1949), *Monarda didyma* L. (2, 86, 92, 107, 109, 156) (1878-1949), *Monarda* L. (4, 50, 106, 138, 155, 156) (1923–present)

Bee-blossom [Bee blossom] - *Gaura coccinea* Nutt. ex Pursh (124) (1937), *Gaura* L. (50) (present)

Beebread [Bee-bread] - *Borago officinalis* L. (156) (1923), *Trifolium pratense* L. (157, 158) (1900-1929)

Beech [Beach] or Beech tree [Beech-tree] - *Fagus grandifolia* Ehrh. (35, 43, 65, 105, 106, 122, 124, 182, 184) (1791-1932), *Fagus grandifolia* Ehrh. subsp. *grandifolia* (41, 187) (1770-1818), *Fagus* L. (1, 7, 8, 10, 109, 137, 138, 156, 167, 190) (~1759-1949), *Fagus sylvatica* L. (18) (1805)

Beech fern - *Phegopteris hexagonoptera* (Michx.) Fee (97) (1937), *Thelypteris* Schmidel (4) (1986), *Thelypteris* Schmidel (possibly) (1) (1932)

Beechdrops [Beech drops, Beech-drops] - *Conopholis americana* (L. f.) Wallr. (156) (1923), *Epifagus* Nutt. (1, 2, 10, 50) (1818–present) parasitic on beeches, *Epifagus virginiana* (L.) W. Bart. (5, 7, 19, 49, 57, 61, 86, 92, 157, 186, 187) (1814-1923), *Orobanche uniflora* L. (157) (1929)

Beech-wheat [Beech wheat] - *Fagopyrum esculentum* Moench (5, 6, 156, 180) (1633-1923)

Beech-woods violet [Beechwoods violet] - *Viola sororia* Willd. (155) (1942)

Bee-flower [Beeflower, Bee flower] - *Cleome* L. (1, 93) (1932-1936), *Cleome serrulata* Pursh (98) (1926)

Beefsteak [Beef steak] - *Saxifraga stolonifera* Meerb. (19) (1840), *Trillium sessile* L. (156) (1840)

Beefsteak plant [Beefsteak-plant, Beefsteakplant] - *Pedicularis canadensis* L. (5, 156) (1913-1923), *Perilla frutescens* (L.) Britton (4, 5, 50, 156, 158) (1900–present), *Perilla frutescens* (L.) Britton var. *frutescens* (50) (present), *Saxifraga stolonifera* Meerb. (92) (1876), *Trillium recurvatum* Beck (possibly) (156) (1923), *Trillium sessile* L. (156) (1923)

Beef-suet tree [Beef suet tree] - *Shepherdia argentea* (Pursh) Nutt. (5, 156, 158) (1900-1923) no longer in use by 1923

Beefwood - *Casuarina* Rumph. ex L. (109, 138) (1923-1949)

Beehive [Bee-hive] - *Medicago scutellata* (L.) Mill. (19, 92) (1840-1876)

Beerenwortel (German) - *Symplocarpus foetidus* (L.) Salisb. ex Nutt. (186) (1814)

Bee's-nest [Bee's nest] - *Daucus carota* L. (157) (1929)

Bee's-nest plant [Beesnest plant] - *Daucus carota* L. (92, 158) (1876-1900)

Beet - *Beta* L. (109, 138) (1923-1949)

Beet [Bete] - *Beta vulgaris* L. (19, 107, 109, 179) (1526-1949)

Beetlebung [Beetle-bung, Beetle bung] - *Nyssa sylvatica* Marsh. (5, 156) (1913-1923) no longer in use by 1923

Beetleweed [Beetle weed, beetle-weed] - *Nemophila aphylla* (L.) Brummitt (5, 10, 156) (1818-1923)

Bee-tree linden [Beetree linden] - *Tilia americana* L. var. *heterophylla* (Vent.) Loud. (138) (1923)

Beetroot [Beet-root] - *Amaranthus retroflexus* L. (157, 158) (1900-1929), *Beta vulgaris* L. (109, 110) (1949-1886)

Beets (French) - *Beta vulgaris* L. (180) (1633)

Beeweed [Bee weed, Bee-weed] - *Symphyotrichum cordifolium* (L.) Nesom (5, 156, 158) (1900-1923), *Symphyotrichum lowrieanum* (Porter) Nesom (5, 75) (1894-1913) WV

Beewort - *Acorus calamus* L. (5, 64, 156, 157, 158) (1900-1929)

Beggar's-button [Beggar's buttons] - *Arctium lappa* L. (5, 64, 69, 156, 158) (1900–1923)

Beggar's-lice [Beggar lice, Beggar-lice, Beggarlice, Beggarslice] - *Agrimonia eupatoria* L. (156) (1923), *Bidens cernua* L. (156) (1923), *Bidens frondosa* L. (5, 156, 158) (1900–1923), *Cynoglossum* L. (77)

(1898) Sulphur Grove OH, *Cynoglossum officinale* L. (156) (1923), *Desmodium canadense* (L.) DC. (74, 156, 158) (1893-1923) MA, *Galium aparine* L. (5, 93, 156, 157, 158) (1900–1936), *Galium* L. (76) (1896) Southwest MO, *Hackelia virginiana* (L.) I.M. Johnston (2, 5, 50, 62, 63, 80, 145, 156, 157, 158) (1895–present)

Beggar's-needles [Beggar's needles] - *Scandix pecten-veneris* L. (5, 156) (1913-1923)

Beggarticks [Beggar ticks, Beggar's ticks, Beggars' ticks, Beggars-ticks, Beggar-ticks] - *Agrimonia eupatoria* L. (74, 156) (1893-1923) WV, *Agrimonia gryposepala* Wallr. (5) (1913), *Bidens bipinnata* L. (58) (1869), *Bidens cernua* L. (76) (1896) Paris ME, *Bidens connata* Muhl. ex Willd. (62, 76) (1896-1912), *Bidens frondosa* L. (3, 4, 5, 63, 76, 80, 85, 92, 93, 145) (1896-1986), *Bidens* L. (1, 2, 4, 50, 93, 106, 155, 158) (1895–present), *Bidens tripartita* L. (3) (1977), *Bidens vulgata* Greene (3, 4, 82) (1930-1986), *Cynoglossum officinale* L. (156) (1923), *Desmodium canadense* (L.) DC. (156, 158) (1900-1923), *Desmodium cuspidatum* (Muhl. ex Willd.) DC. ex Loud. var. *cuspidatum* (5, 85, 93) (1913-1936), *Desmodium* Desv. (1, 93) (1932-1936), *Hackelia virginiana* (L.) I.M. Johnston (5, 77, 156, 157, 158) (1898-1929), *Lappula* Moench (1, 93) (1932-1936)

Beggarweed [Beggar weed, Beggar-weed] - *Cuscuta epilinum* Weihe. (156) (1923), *Desmodium tortuosum* (Sw.) DC. (109, 118) (1898-1949), *Polygonum aviculare* L. (5, 156, 158) (1900-1923), *Spergula arvensis* L. (158) (1900)

Beggary - *Fumaria officinalis* L. (156, 158) (1900-1923)

Begonia - *Begonia* L. (138) (1923)

Behen - *Podophyllum peltatum* L. (156) (1923), *Silene vulgaris* (Moench) Garcke (5, 156) (1913-1923) no longer in use by 1923

Belamcanda - *Belamcanda* Adans. (50) (present) from native Asian name

Belene - *Hyoscyamus niger* L. (5, 156) (1913-1923) no longer in use by 1923

Belene chenile - *Hyoscyamus niger* L. (158) (1900)

Beleño negro (Spanish) - *Hyoscyamus niger* L. (158) (1900)

Belingela - *Solanum melongena* L. (107) (1658)

Bell pepper - *Capsicum annuum* L. (92, 109) (1876-1949)

Bell thistle [Bell-thistle] - *Cirsium vulgare* (Savi) Ten. (5, 158, 156) (1913-1923)

Belladonna - *Atropa bella-donna* L. (52, 53, 54, 55, 57, 59, 60, 61, 92, 109, 138, 180) (1633-1949), *Atropa* L. (138) (1923)

Belladonna lily [Belladonnalily] - *Amaryllis belladonna* L. (138, 155, 165) (1768-1942)

Bellardi's bog-sedge [Bellardi bog sedge] - *Kobresia myosuroides* (Vill.) Fiori (50) (present)

Bellard's kobresia - *Kobresia myosuroides* (Vill.) Fiori (5) (1913)

Bellbind [Bell bind, Bell-bind] - *Calystegia sepium* (L.) R. Br. subsp. *sepium* (5, 156, 158) (1900–1923), *Convolvulus arvensis* L. (156, 157, 158) (1900-1923) no longer in use by 1923

Belle Isle cress [Belleisle cress] - *Barbarea verna* (P. Mill.) Aschers. (46, 107, 109, 156) (1879-1949)

Bellflower [Bell-flower] - *Campanula* L. (1, 2, 4, 10, 50, 82, 93, 109, 122, 155, 156, 158, 184) (1793–present), *Campanula rotundifolia* L. (92) (1876), *Campanula uniflora* L. (5) (1913), *Campanulastrum* Small (50) (present)

Bell-flower chironia [Bell flowered chironia] - *Sabatia campanulata* (L.) Torr. (42) (1814)

Bellis - *Bellis* L. (50) (present)

Bell-olive tree [Bell olive tree, bell olive-tree] - *Halesia carolina* L. (5, 156) (1913-1923)

Bellon-patsia - *Lycopodiella cernua* var. *cernua* (L.) Pichi Sermolli (174) (1753)

Belloot oak - *Quercus ilex* L. (107) (1919)

Bell-ragges - *Rorippa palustris* (L.) Bess. (157, 158) (1900-1929)

Bell-rue [Bell rue] - *Clematis* L. (1) (1932)

Bells - *Aquilegia canadensis* L. (5, 76, 157, 158) (1896-1929) Sulphur Grove OH

Bell's oxytropis - *Oxytropis bellii* (Britton ex Macoun) Palib. (5) (1913)

Bellware [Bell ware] - *Zostera marina* L. (5, 156) (1913-1923)

Bellwood [Bell-wood] - *Halesia carolina* L. (156) (1923)

Bellwort [Bell-wort] - *Uvularia grandiflora* Smith. (85) (1932), *Uvularia* L. (1, 7, 109, 158, 184) (1793-1949), *Uvularia perfoliata* L. (19, 49, 92, 107) (1840-1919), *Uvularia sessilifolia* L. (107) (1919)

Belly-ache root [Bellyache root] - *Angelica lucida* L. (7, 92, 177) (1726-1876)

Belly-ache weed [Belly-ache-weed, Bellyache weed] - *Solidago bicolor* L. (5, 76, 156) (1896-1923) Paris ME

Belmony - *Gentiana andrewsii* Griseb. (79) (1891) NH

Belote oak - *Quercus ilex* L. (107) (1919)

Beloved tree - *Ilex vomitoria* Aiton (possibly) (182) (1791)

Belvedere [Belvidere] - *Kochia scoparia* (L.) Schrad. (4, 5, 109, 138, 158, 180) (1633-1986)

Belvedere cypress [Belvidere cypress] - *Kochia scoparia* (L.) Schrad. (156, 157) (1923-1929)

Belvedere summer-cypress [Belvedere summercypress] - *Kochia scoparia* (L.) Schrad. (155) (1942)

Bembi - *Acorus calamus* L. (186) (1814)

Ben nuts - *Moringa oleifera* Lam. (92) (1876)

Ben oil - *Moringa oleifera* Lam. (92) (1876)

Bendee - *Abelmoschus esculentus* (L.) Moench (58, 92) (1869-1876)

Bene-benni - *Sesamum orientale* L. (19) (1840)

Bengal clockvine - *Thunbergia grandiflora* Roxb. (138) (1923)

Bengal grass - *Setaria italica* (L.) Beauv. (45, 66, 92, 107) (1896-1919)

Bengal root - *Zingiber purpureum* Roscoe (92) (1876), *Zinnia grandiflora* Nutt. (138) (1923)

Bengal rose - *Rosa chinensis* Jacq. (109) (1949)

Benincasa - *Benincasa hispida* (Thunb.) Cogn. (110) (1886)

Benjamin bush [Benjamin-bush] - *Lindera benzoin* Blume. (2, 5, 6, 49, 58, 92, 107, 156) (1869-1923)

Benjamin fig - *Ficus benjamina* L. (138) (1923)

Benjamin tree [Benjamin-tree] - *Lindera benzoin* Blume. (8) (1785)

Benjamins [Benjamin] - *Lindera benzoin* Blume. (46) (1879), *Trillium cernuum* L. (156) (1923), *Trillium erectum* L. (73, 79) (1891-1892), *Trillium* L. (73) (1892), *Trillium undulatum* Willd. (73, 156) (1892-1923)

Benne - *Sesamum orientale* L. (49, 57, 92) (1876-1917)

Bennels - *Phragmites australis* (Cav.) Trin. ex Steud. (5, 107) (1913-1919)

Benner - *Geum virginianum* L. (5) (1913)

Bennert - *Bellis perennis* L. (5, 158) (1900-1913)

Bennet - *Geum* L. (184) (1793), *Geum virginianum* L. (7, 92) (1828-1876), *Pimpinella saxifraga* L. (5, 156) (1913-1923)

Bennet (German) - *Geum virginianum* L. (7) (1828)

Bennet weed - *Alopecurus myosuroides* Huds (5) (1913)

Benny - *Sesamum* L. (7) (1828)

Benoite aquatique (French) - *Geum rivale* L (6, 158) (1892-1900)

Benoite de Virginie (French) - *Geum virginianum* L. (7) (1828)

Bensoin officinarum - *Lindera benzoin* Blume. (177) (1762)

Bent - *Schoenoplectus tabernaemontani* (K.C. Gmel.) Palla (156, 158) (1900-1923)

Bent grass [Bentgrass, Bent-grass] - *Agrostis capillaris* L. (56, 87, 88, 90) (1885-1901), *Agrostis gigantea* Roth (56, 92) (1876-1901), *Agrostis* L. (1, 10, 41, 66, 87, 92, 93, 109, 138, 155, 184) (1770-1949), *Agrostis vinealis* Schreb. (19) (1840), *Andropogon virginicus* L. (19) (1840), *Apera spica-venti* (L.) Beauv. (19) (1840)

Bent milkvetch [Bent milk vetch] - *Astragalus distortus* Torr. & Gray (5, 72, 82, 97) (1907-1937)

Bent sedge - *Carex styloflexa* Buckley (5, 50) (1913–present)

Bent-awn plume grass [Bent awn plume grass] - *Saccharum brevibarbe* (Michx.) Pers. var. *contortum* (Ell.) R. Webster (122) (1937)

Bent-flower milkvetch [Bent-flowered milk vetch] - *Astragalus vexilliflexus* Sheldon (4, 50) (1986–present)

Benwarksgras (Swedish) - *Linnaea borealis* L. (46) (1879)

Benzoelorbeer (German) - *Lindera benzoin* Blume. (6) (1892)

Benzoin - *Lindera benzoin* Blume. (6) (1892)

Benzoin Lorbeer (German) - *Lindera benzoin* Blume. (186) (1814)

Bepadji' ckanakĭz'ĭt Ma'zana'tĭg (Chippewa, prickly nettle) - *Urtica dioica* L. subsp. *gracilis* (Aiton) Seland. (40) (1928)

Bequilla - *Sesbania herbacea* (P. Mill.) McVaugh (4) (1986)

Berberis - *Mahonia aquifolium* (Pursh) Nutt. (54, 59, 60, 64) (1902-1911)

Berberis (French) - *Berberis vulgaris* L. (158) (1900)

Berberis baccae (Official name of Materia Medica) - *Berberis canadensis* P. Mill. (7) (1828)

Berberitze (German) - *Berberis canadensis* P. Mill. (7) (1828)

Berberos (Spanish) - *Berberis vulgaris* L. (158) (1900)

Berberry [Berberies without stones] - *Berberis vulgaris* L. (178) (1526)

Berberry [Berberies] - *Berberis canadensis* P. Mill. (156) (1923), *Berberis* L. (15) (1895), *Berberis vulgaris* L. (6, 58, 179) (1526-1892)

Berbine - *Verbena officinalis* L. (5) (1913)

Bere - *Hordeum vulgare* L. (107) (1919)

Berengenas - *Solanum melongena* L. (107) (1919)

Bergamont - *Citrus ×aurantium* L. [*maxima × reticulata*] (107) (1919)

Bergamot - *Monarda fistulosa* L. (85) (1932)

Bergamot herb - *Mentha aquatica* L. (92) (1876)

Bergamot mint - *Mentha aquatica* L. (1, 5, 109, 138, 155, 156, 158) (1900–1949)

Bergbeere (German) - *Gaultheria procumbens* L. (7) (1828)

Bergia - *Bergia* L. (50, 155, 158) (1900–present)

Bergman's cabbage - *Brassica rapa* L. var. *rapa* (5) (1913)

Bergthee (German) - *Gaultheria procumbens* L. (6) (1892)

Berlandier's abutilon [Berlandier abutilon] - *Abutilon berlandieri* Gray ex S. Wats. (155) (1942)

Berlandier's daisy [Berlandier daisy] - *Berlandiera texana* DC. (122, 124) (1937)

Berlandier's evening primrose [Berlandier evening primrose] - *Calylophus berlandieri* Spach. (4) (1986)

Berlandier's flax - *Linum berlandieri* Hook. var. *berlandieri* (4) (1986)

Berlandier's golden aster - *Heterotheca canescens* (DC.) Shinners & Gray (97) (1937)

Berlandier's Indian mallow - *Abutilon berlandieri* Gray ex S. Wats. (50) (present)

Berlandier's sundrops - *Calylophus berlandieri* Spach. (50) (present)

Berlandier's wolfberry - *Lycium berlandieri* Dunal (50) (present)

Berlandier's yellow flax - *Linum berlandieri* Hook. (50, 122, 155) (1937–present), *Linum berlandieri* Hook. var. *berlandieri* (5, 50, 97, 155) (1913–present)

Bermud grass - *Cynodon dactylon* (L.) Pers. (45) (1896)

Bermuda arrowroot [Bermuda arrow-root] - *Maranta arundinacea* L. (49, 138) (1898-1923)

Bermuda cress - *Barbarea verna* (P. Mill.) Aschers. (5, 156) (1913-1923)

Bermuda grass [Bermudagrass, Bermuda-grass] - *Cynodon dactylon* (L.) Pers. (3, 5, 7, 10, 45, 50, 56, 66, 67, 87, 88, 90, 92, 94, 99, 109, 111, 119, 122, 138, 144, 152, 155, 158, 163) (1818–present), *Cynodon* L.C. Rich. (50, 66, 158) (1900–present)

Bermuda mulberry - *Callicarpa americana* L. (5, 65, 156, 158) (1900-1931), *Callicarpa* L. (10) (1818)

Bermuda potatos [Bermudas-Potatos] - *Ipomoea batatas* (L.) Lam. (177) (1762)

Bermuda-buttercup - *Oxalis pes-caprae* L. (109) (1949)

Bernhardi's aster - *Eurybia schreberi* (Nees) Nees (5) (1913)

Bernuda blue-eyed-grass [Bernuda blue-eyedgrass] - *Sisyrinchium angustifolium* Mill. (155) (1942)

Berrelia - *Salicornia maritima* Wolff & Jefferies (46) (1671)

Berried-tea - *Gaultheria procumbens* L. (186) (1814)

Berro - *Rorippa nasturtium-aquaticum* (L.) Hayek (158) (1900)

Berry alder [Berry-alder] - *Frangula alnus* Mill. (5, 156, 158) (1900–1923)

Berry bladder fern [Berry bladder-fern, Berry bladderfern] - *Cystopteris bulbifera* (L.) Bernh. (109, 138, 155) (1923-1949)

Berry tree [Berry-tree] - *Ribes uva-crispa* L. var. *sativum* DC. (5, 156) (1913-1923)

Berry-bearing aralia - *Aralia racemosa* L. (42, 187) (1814-1818)

Berry-bearing poplar - *Populus deltoides* Bartr. ex Marsh. (5, 158) (1900-1913)

Berseem - *Trifolium alexandrinum* L. (109) (1949)

Bertram - *Tanacetum parthenium* (L.) Schultz-Bip. (158) (1900)

Berula - *Berula* Bess. ex W.D.J. Koch (155) (1942)

Berza (Spanish) - *Brassica oleracea* L. (110) (1886)

Beschreikraut (German) - *Conyza canadensis* (L.) Cronq. var. *canadensis* (158) (1900)

Be-shamed-Mary [Be shamed Mary] - *Mimosa microphylla* Dry. (156) (1923)

Besom - *Calluna vulgaris* (L.) Hull (5) (1913), *Cytisus scoparius* (L.) Link (5, 156) (1913-1923)

Bessey's agalinis - *Agalinis tenuifolia* (Vahl) Raf. (5, 93) (1913-1936)

Bessey's cherry [Bessey cherry] - *Prunus pumila* L. var. *besseyi* (Bailey) Gleason (5, 125, 138, 155) (1913-1942)

Bessey's gerardia - *Agalinis tenuifolia* (Vahl) Raf. (72, 97, 131) (1899-1907)

Bessey's locoweed - *Oxytropis besseyi* (Rydb.) Blank. (4, 50) (1986–present)

Bessey's point vetch [Bessey pointvetch] - *Oxytropis besseyi* (Rydb.) Blank. (155) (1942)

Bessey's sunflower - *Helianthus tuberosus* L. (possibly) (97) (1937) OK

Bethflower [Beth-flower] - *Trillium erectum* L. (5) (1913), *Trillium sessile* L. (48) (1882) KS

Bethlehem lungwort - *Pulmonaria saccharata* Mill. (138) (1923)

Bethlehem-sage - *Pulmonaria saccharata* Mill. (109) (1949)

Bethlehem-star [Bethlehemstar] - *Ornithogalum* L. (7) (1828)

Bethony - *Stachys officinalis* (L.) Trev. (179) (1526)

Bethroot [Beth-root, Beth root] - *Trillium cernuum* L. (7) (1828), *Trillium erectum* L. (5, 52, 64, 92, 156) (1876-1919), *Trillium sessile* L. (58) (1869)

Betonica - *Stachys officinalis* (L.) Trev. (57) (1917)

Betonie with white flowers - *Stachys officinalis* (L.) Trev. (178) (1526)

Betony - *Lycopus virginicus* L. (92) (1876), *Stachys* L. (109, 138, 155) (1923-1949), *Stachys officinalis* (L.) Trev. (5) (1913), *Teucrium canadense* L. (77) (1898) Western US

Betony arnica - *Arnica lonchophylla* Greene subsp. *lonchophylla* (155) (1942)

Betony-leaf noseburn [Betonyleaf noseburn] - *Tragia betonicifolia* Nutt. (50) (present)

Betteraves (French) - *Beta vulgaris* L. (107) (1612)

Bettie grass - *Aletris farinosa* L. (6) (1892)

Betula - *Betula pubescens* Ehrh. (52) (1919)

Beyrich's love grass [Beyrich's love-grass] - *Eragrostis secundiflora* J. Presl subsp. *oxylepis* (Torr.) S.D. Koch (119) (1938)

Bhang - *Cannabis sativa* L. (14, 59) (1882) mentioned in Arabian nights, *Cannabis sativa* L. subsp. *indica* (Lam.) E. Small & Cronq. (92) (1876)

Biada (Tuscan) - *Triticum spelta* L. (180) (1633)

Biannual lettuce - *Lactuca ludoviciana* (Nutt.) Riddell (50) (present)

Biaškagemesek (Chippewa) - *Eupatorium purpureum* L. (105) (1932)

Biberbaum (German) - *Magnolia virginiana* L. (186) (1814)

Bibernel - *Sanguisorba minor* Scop. subsp. *muricata* (Spach) Nordborg (92) (1876)

Bibernell (German) - *Sanguisorba minor* Scop. subsp. *muricata* (Spach) Nordborg (158) (1900)

Bi'bigwe'wûnûck (Chippewa, flute-reed) - *Heracleum maximum* Bartr. (40) (1928)

Bibigwûnûkûk' (Chippewa, resembling a flute) - *Monarda fistulosa* L. subsp. *fistulosa* var. *mollis* (L.) Benth. (40) (1928)

Bible-leaf - *Balsamita major* Desf. (156) (1923) no longer in use by 1923

Bicknell's cranesbill - *Geranium bicknellii* Britton (50) (present)

Bicknell's gentian [Bicknell gentian] - *Geranium bicknellii* Britton (155) (1942)

Bicknell's panic grass - *Dichanthelium boreale* (Nash) Freckmann (5) (1913)

Bicknell's sedge - *Carex bicknellii* Britt. (3, 5, 50, 72) (1893–present)

Bicknell's thorn - *Crataegus succulenta* Schrad. ex Link (5) (1913)

Bico de cegonha (Portuguese) - *Geranium maculatum* L. (186) (1814)

Bico de grou (Portuguese) - *Geranium maculatum* L. (186) (1814)

Biddy-biddy - *Acaena novae-zelandiae* Kirk (50) (present)

Biddy's-eyes - *Viola tricolor* L. (158) (1900)

Bieberklee - *Menyanthes trifoliata* L. (158) (1900)

Biennial cinquefoil - *Potentilla biennis* Greene (50, 155) (1942–present)

Biennial gaura - *Gaura biennis* L. (5, 72, 82, 93, 97, 156) (1907-1937)

Biennial oenothera - *Oenothera biennis* L. (41) (1770)

Biennial wormwood - *Artemisia biennis* Willd. (3, 4, 5, 50, 72, 93, 131, 155) (1899–present)

Biesloack (Dutch) - *Allium schoenoprasum* L. (180) (1633)

Bifuss (German) - *Artemisia vulgaris* L. (6) (1892)

Big barley - *Hordeum vulgare* L. (107, 180) (1633-1919)

Big bean - *Vicia faba* L. (7, 179) (1526-1828)

Big betony - *Stachys grandiflora* (Willd.) Benth. (138) (1923), *Stachys tenuifolia* Willd. (138) (1923)

Big blue grass [Big bluegrass] - *Poa secunda* J. Presl (146, 155) (1939-1944)

Big blue huckleberry - *Vaccinium arboreum* Marsh. (50) (present), *Vaccinium corymbosum* L. (156) (1923)

Big blue lobelia [Bigblue lobelia] - *Lobelia siphilitica* L. (155) (1942)

Big bluejoint [Big blue joint] - *Schizachyrium scoparium* (Michx.) Nash var. *scoparium* (75) (1894)

Big bluestem [Big blue-stem Big blue stem] - *Andropogon gerardii* Vitman (3, 5, 11, 50, 56, 65, 85, 93, 94, 111, 115, 119, 122, 124, 129, 134, 140, 144, 155, 163) (1852–present), *Poa secunda* J. Presl (146, 155) (1939-1942), *Schizachyrium scoparium* (Michx.) Nash var. *scoparium* (75) (1894)

Big buckeye - *Aesculus flava* Aiton (5, 156) (1913-1923)

Big cerastium - *Cerastium fontanum* Baumg. subsp. *vulgare* (Hartman) Greuter & Burdet (155) (1942)

Big chickasaw plum - *Prunus angustifolia* Marsh. var. *angustifolia* (138, 155) (1923-1942)

Big chickweed - *Cerastium fontanum* Baumg. subsp. *vulgare* (Hartman) Greuter & Burdet (50) (present)

Big cordgrass - *Spartina cynosuroides* (L.) Roth (122) (1937)

Big coreopsis - *Coreopsis grandiflora* Hogg ex Sweet (138) (1923)

Big cottonwood - *Populus deltoides* Bartr. ex Marsh. (5, 156, 158) (1900–1923)

Big crow's-foot [Big crow's foot] - *Eleusine coracana* (L.) Gaertn. (129) (1894)

Big daisy - *Leucanthemum vulgare* Lam. (5, 156) (1913-1923)

Big dammarpine - *Agathis robusta* (C. Moore ex F. Muell.) Bailey (155) (1942)

Big devil's-beggarticks [Big devils beggartick] - *Bidens vulgata* Greene (50) (present)

Big goldenrod - *Solidago squarrosa* Muhl. (156) (1923)

Big heliotrope - *Heliotropium arborescens* L. (138) (1923)

Big hellebore - *Veratrum viride* Ait. (5, 64) (1908-1913)

Big hickory - *Carya laciniosa* (Michx. f.) G. Don (158) (1900)

Big hickory-nut - *Carya laciniosa* (Michx. f.) G. Don (possibly) (113) (1890)

Big ivy - *Kalmia latifolia* L. (6, 7, 71) (1828-1898)

Big Key plane-tree maple [Bigkey planetree maple] - *Acer pseudoplatanus* L. (155) (1942)

Big laurel - *Magnolia grandiflora* L. (19, 20) (1840-1857), *Rhododendron maximum* L. (71, 156) (1898-1923)

Big lotus - *Lotus unifoliolatus* (Hook.) Benth. (114) (1894) Neb

Big marigold - *Tagetes erecta* L. (109) (1949)

Big merrybells - *Uvularia grandiflora* Smith. (138, 155) (1923-1942)

Big plantain-lily [Big plantainlily] - *Hosta plantaginea* (Lam.) Aschers. (138) (1923)

Big quaking grass - *Briza maxima* L. (50, 138) (1923–present)

Big sage - *Artemisia tridentata* Nutt. (146) (1939)

Big sagebrush - *Artemisia tridentata* Nutt. (3, 4, 50, 146, 155) (1939–present)

Big sand grass - *Calamovilfa longifolia* (Hook.) Scribn. (5, 56, 129) (1901-1894)

Big sandreed [Big sand-reed] - *Calamovilfa gigantea* (Nutt.) Scribn, & Merr. (3, 119, 155) (1938-1977)

Big sarsaparilla - *Aristolochia macrophylla* Lam. (5, 156) (1913-1923)

Big scentless mockorange - *Philadelphus inodorus* L. (138) (1923)

Big shagbark [Big shag bark, Big shag-bark] - *Carya laciniosa* (Michx. f.) G. Don (5, 72, 93, 97, 156, 158) (1900-1937)

Big shellbark - *Carya laciniosa* (Michx. f.) G. Don (107, 156) (1919-1923)

Big shell-bark hickory [Big shellbark hickory] - *Carya laciniosa* (Michx. f.) G. Don (2, 4, 109) (1895-1986)

Big smooth crabgrass - *Digitaria ischaemum* (Schreb.) Schreb. ex Muhl. (155) (1942)

Big tooth maple - *Acer saccharum* subsp. *grandidentatum* (Torr. & A.Gray) Desmarais (124) (1937)

Big tupelo - *Nyssa aquatica* L. (122, 124, 138) (1923-1937)

Big wandflower - *Sparaxis fragrans* (Jacq.) Ker-Gawl. subsp. *grandiflora* (D. Delar.) Goldbl. (138) (1923)

Big whortleberry - *Vaccinium membranaceum* Dougl. (138, 155) (1923-1942)

Big yellow waterlily [Big yellow water-lily] - *Nelumbo* Adans. (93) (1936), *Nelumbo lutea* Willd. (5) (1913)

Bigarade - *Citrus ×aurantium* L. [*maxima × reticulata*] (92) (1876)

Big-berry manzanita [Big-berried manzanita] - *Arctostaphylos glauca* Lindl. (106) (1930)

Bigbloom [Big-bloom, Bigbloom] - *Magnolia macrophylla* Michx. (5, 7, 92, 156) (1828-1923)

Big-bud hickory - *Carya laciniosa* (Michx. f.) G. Don (109) (1949)

Big-cone pine - *Pinus coulteri* D. Don (109) (1949)

Bigelow's aster [Bigelow aster] - *Machaeranthera bigelovii* (Gray) Greene var. *bigelovii* (138, 155) (1931-1942)

Bigelow's beggarticks - *Bidens bigelovii* Gray (50) (present)

Bigelow's blue grass [Bigelow's blue-grass, Bigelow's bluegrass] - *Poa bigelovii* Vasey & Scribn. (94, 122) (1901-1937)

Bigelow's gentian [Bigelow gentian] - *Gentiana affinis* Griesb. (155) (1942)

Bigelow's glasswort - *Salicornia bigelovii* Torr. (5) (1913)

Bigelow's milkvetch [Bigelow milkvetch] - *Astragalus mollissimus* Torr. var. *bigelovii* (Gray) Barneby (155) (1942)

Bigelow's sage [Bigelow sage] - *Artemisia bigelovii* Gray (50) (present)

Bigelow's sagebrush [Bigelow sagebrush] - *Artemisia bigelovii* Gray (122, 155) (1937-1942)

Bigelow's sage-bush - *Artemisia bigelovii* Gray (5) (1913)

Bigelow's sneezeweed [Bigelow sneezeweed] - *Helenium bigelovii* Gray (138) (1923)

Big-flower cinquefoil [Bigflower cinquefoil] - *Potentilla fissa* Nutt. (50, 155) (1942–present)

Big-flower common allamanda [Bigflower common allamanda] - *Allamanda cathartica* L. (155) (1942)

Big-flower coreopsis [Bigflower coreopsis] - *Coreopsis grandiflora* Hogg ex Sweet (3, 4, 155) (1942-1986)

Big-flower gerardia [Bigflower gerardia] - *Aureolaria grandiflora* (Benth.) Pennell var. *serrata* (Torr. ex Benth.) Pennell (3) (1977)

Big-flower gilia [Bigflower gilia] - *Collomia grandiflora* Douglas (138) (1923)

Big-flower pawpaw [Bigflower pawpaw] - *Asimina obovata* (Willd.) Nash (155) (1942)

Big-flower prickly-pear [Bigflower pricklypear] - *Opuntia macrorhiza* Engelm. var. *macrorhiza* (155) (1942)

Big-fruit dodder [Bigfruit dodder] - *Cuscuta megalocarpa* Rydb. (50) (present)

Big-fruit evening-primrose [Bigfruit evening-primrose] - *Oenothera macrocarpa* Nutt. (50) (present)

Bigg [Big] - *Hordeum* L (158) (1900), *Hordeum vulgare* L. (180) (1633)

Big-head bog rush [Big-headed bog-rush] - *Juncus nodosus* L. (129) (1894)

Big-head pygmy cudweed [Bighead pygmycudweed] - *Evax prolifera* Nutt. ex DC. (50) (present)

Bigleaf - *Magnolia macrophylla* Michx. (7) (1828)

Big-leaf aster [Bigleaf aster] - *Eurybia macrophylla* (L.) Cass. (138, 155) (1931-1942)

Big-leaf cotoneaster [Bigleaf cotoneaster] - *Cotoneaster bullatus* var. *macrophyllus* Rehder & E.H. Wilson (138) (1923)

Big-leaf cow-parsnip [Bigleaf cow-parsnip] - *Heracleum mantegazzianum* Sommier & Levier (138) (1923)

Big-leaf European linden [Bigleaf European linden] - *Tilia platyphyllos* Scop. (138) (1923)

Big-leaf hackberry [Bigleaf hackberry] - *Celtis occidentalis* L. var. *occidentalis* (138, 155) (1923-1942)

Big-leaf honeybush [Bigleaf honeybush] - *Melianthus major* L. (138) (1923)

Big-leaf ivy [Big leaved ivy] - *Kalmia latifolia* L. (5, 49, 92, 156) (1876-1923)

Big-leaf laurel - *Rhododendron maximum* L. (5, 71, 156) (1898-1923)

Big-leaf magnolia [Bigleaf magnolia] - *Magnolia macrophylla* Michx. (7, 138) (1828-1923)

Big-leaf maple [Bigleaf maple] - *Acer macrophyllum* Pursh (50, 106, 155) (1930–present)

Big-leaf periwinkle [Bigleaf periwinkle] - *Vinca major* L. (138) (1923)

Big-leaf white violet [Bigleaf white violet] - *Viola macloskeyi* Lloyd (155) (1942)

Big-leaf winter-creeper [Bigleaf wintercreeper] - *Euonymus fortunei* (Turcz.) Hand.-Maz. var. *fortunei* (138) (1923)

Big-leaf witch hazel [Bigleaf witch hazel] - *Hamamelis virginiana* L. (7) (1828)

Big-leaf woodland sunflower [Bigleaf woodland sunflower] - *Helianthus hirsutus* Raf. (138) (1923)

Bignone (French) - *Bignonia* L. (8) (1785)

Bignone de Virginie (French) - *Campsis radicans* (L.) Seem. ex Bureau (8, 20) (1785-1857)

Bignone porte-croix (French) - *Pithecoctenium crucigerum* (L.) A.H. Gentry (8) (1785)

Bignone toujours verte (French) - *Gelsemium sempervirens* (L.) J. St.-Hil. (8) (1785)

Bignonia - *Bignonia* L. (155, 158) (1900-1942), *Campsis radicans* (L.) Seem. ex Bureau (158) (1900)

Big-pod sesbania [Bigpod sesbania] - *Sesbania herbacea* (P. Mill.) McVaugh (50) (present)

Bigroot [Big-root, Big root] - *Balsamorhiza sagittata* (Pursh) Nutt. (101) (1905), *Ipomoea leptophylla* Torr. (101) (1905), *Marah macrocarpus* (Greene) Greene var. *macrocarpus* (14, 123) (1856-1882)

Big-root heuchera - *Heuchera villosa* Michx. var. *villosa* (5) (1913)

Big-root lady's-thumb [Bigroot ladysthumb] - *Polygonum amphibium* L. var. *emersum* Michx. (155) (1942)

Big-root morning-glory [Bigroot morning glory, Bigroot morning-glory] - *Ipomoea pandurata* (L.) G.F.W. Mey. (3, 4, 155) (1942-1986)

Big-root spring-parsley [Bigroot springparsley] - *Cymopterus macrorhizus* Buckl. (50) (present)

Big-seed alfalfa dodder [Bigseed alfalfa dodder] - *Cuscuta indecora* Choisy (50, 155) (1942–present)

Big-seed biscuitroot [Bigseed biscuitroot] - *Lomatium macrocarpum* (Nutt. ex Torr. & Gray) Coult. & Rose (50) (present)

Big-seed dodder [Bigseed dodder] - *Cuscuta indecora* Choisy var. *neuropetala* (Engelm.) A.S. Hitchc. (50) (present)

Big-seed false flax [Bigseed falseflax] - *Camelina sativa* (L.) Crantz (155) (1942)

Big-seed lomatium [Bigseed lomatium] - *Lomatium macrocarpum* (Nutt. ex Torr. & Gray) Coult. & Rose (155) (1942)

Big-sting nettle [Bigsting nettle] - *Urtica dioica* L. (155) (1942)

Big-tooth aspen [Bigtooth aspen] - *Populus grandidentata* Michx. (4, 50, 155) (1942–present)

Big-tooth maple [Bigtooth maple] - *Acer grandidentatum* Nutt. (50, 138, 155) (1923–present)

Big-top love grass [Bigtop lovegrass] - *Eragrostis hirsuta* (Michx.) Nees (50) (present)

Big-tree plum - *Prunus mexicana* S. Wats. (3, 4) (1977-1986)

Bi'jikiwi'bûgesan (Chippewa, cattle plum) - *Astragalus crassicarpus* Nutt. (40) (1928)

Bi'jikiwi'gini̇g (Chippewa, cattle rose) - *Rosa arkansana* Porter (40) (1928)

Bi'jikiwi̇n'gûck (Chippewa, cattle herb) - *Artemisia frigida* Willd. (40) (1928)

Bi'jikiwûck' (Chippewa, cattle medicine) - *Polygala senega* L. (40) (1928)

Bilbernel - *Sanguisorba minor* Scop. subsp. *muricata* (Spach) Nordborg (5) (1913)

Bilberry [Bill berry] - *Amelanchier canadensis* (L.) Medik. (5, 156, 158) (1900-1923), *Vaccinium* L. (1, 41, 73) (1770-1932), *Vaccinium myrtillus* L. (14, 107) (1882-1919), *Vaccinium scoparium* Leiberg (131) (1899), *Vaccinium uliginosum* L. (73) (1892), *Vaccinium vitis-idaea* L. (19, 92) (1840-1876), *Viburnum nudum* L. (5, 73, 156) (1892-1923)

Billion-dollar grass [Billion dollar grass, Billion-dollar-grass] - *Echinochloa frumentacea* Link (1, 50, 109) (1932–present)

Billy-buttons - *Arctium lappa* L. (158) (1900)

Biloxi violet - *Viola affinis* Le Conte (155) (1942)

Bilsenkraut (German) - *Hyoscyamus niger* L. (6, 158, 180) (1633-1900)

Bilsted - *Liquidambar* L. (2) (1895), *Liquidambar styraciflua* L. (5, 49, 156) (1898-1923)

Biltmore ash - *Fraxinus americana* L. (5, 138, 155) (1913-1942)

Biltmore thorn - *Crataegus intricata* Lange (5) (1913)

Bima'kwûd (Chippewa, twisting around) - *Celastrus scandens* L. (40) (1928)

Bi-na-quat (Chippewa) - *Celastrus scandens* L. (47) (1852)

Bind knotweed - *Polygonum convolvulus* L. (19) (1840)

Bindweed [Bind weed, Bind-weed] - *Calystegia sepium* (L.) R. Br. (47, 107) (1852-1919), *Calystegia sepium* (L.) R. Br. subsp. *sepium* (178) (1526), *Convolvulus arvensis* L. (6, 19, 106, 122, 145, 178) (1596-1937), *Convolvulus* L. (1, 2, 10, 14, 50, 63, 82, 93, 109, 125, 156, 158, 184) (1793–present), *Ipomoea* L. (10) (1818), *Ipomoea pandurata* (L.) G.F.W. Mey. (92) (1876), *Ipomoea purpurea* (L.) Roth (92) (1876), *Polygonum convolvulus* L. (95, 106) (1911-1930), *Polygonum convolvulus* L. var. *convolvulus* (85) (1932), *Polygonum* L. (1, 93) (1932-1936), *Polygonum scandens* L. (62) (1912)

Bindweed euploca - *Heliotropium convolvulaceum* (Nutt.) Gray (possibly) (155) (1942)

Bindweed heliotrope - *Heliotropium convolvulaceum* (Nutt.) Gray (5, 97) (1913-1937)

Bindweed polygonum [Bind-weed polygonum] - *Polygonum convolvulus* L. (187) (1818)

Bindweed-nightshade [Bindweed nightshade, Binde-weed nightshade] - *Circaea lutetiana* L. (156, 158, 180) (1633-1923) no longer in use by 1923

Bine - *Humulus lupulus* L. (107, 157, 158) (1919-1923)

Bi̇ne'bûg (Chippewa, prairie chicken or grouse leaf) - *Comarum palustre* L. (40) (1928)

Binken (High Dutch) - *Juncus* L. (180) (1633)

Bipinnate phacelia - *Phacelia bipinnatifida* Michx. (86) (1878)

Birch or Birch tree - *Betula* L. (1, 4, 7, 8, 10, 35, 50, 93, 106, 109, 112, 138, 155, 167, 184) (1785–present)

Birch-leaf meadowsweet [Birchleaf meadowsweet, Birch-leaved meadow sweet] - *Spiraea betulifolia* Pallas (155) (1942), *Spiraea betulifolia* Pallas var. *corymbosa* (Raf.) Maxim. (5) (1913), *Spiraea chamaedryfolia* L. var. *ulmifolia* (Scop.) Maxim. (155) (1942), *Aruncus dioicus* (Walt.) Fern. var. *vulgaris* (Maxim.) Hara (155) (1942)

Birch-leaf poplar - *Populus nigra* L. var. *betulifolia* (Pursh) Torr. (19) (1840)

Bird brier - *Rosa canina* L. (5) (1913)

Bird cherry [Bird-cherry, Birdcherry, Birds cherries] - *Ampelopsis arborea* (L.) Koehne (possibly) (156) (1923), *Prunus avium* (L.) L. (92, 107, 110, 178) (1526-1919), *Prunus padus* L. (19, 82, 107) (1840-1930), *Prunus pensylvanica* L. f. (3, 4, 5, 74, 107, 137, 156, 158) (1893-1986), *Prunus pensylvanica* L. f. var. *pensylvanica* (3, 4, 5, 47, 74, 107, 137, 156, 158) (1852-1986)

Bird grape - *Vitis rotundifolia* Michx. var. *munsoniana* (Simpson ex Munson) M.O. Moore (15) (1895)

Bird grass - *Poa pratensis* L. (68) (1890), *Poa trivialis* L. (5) (1913)

Bird knotgrass [Bird knot-grass] - *Polygonum aviculare* L. (156) (1923)

Bird lime - *Viscum album* L. (92) (1876)

Bird pepper [Bird's pepper, Birds' pepper] - *Capsicum annuum* L. var. *annuum* (53) (1922), *Lepidium virginicum* L. (5, 73, 156, 157, 158) (1892–1929)

Bird rape - *Brassica rapa* L. var. *rapa* (155) (1942)

Bird rock-brake - *Pellaea mucronata* (D.C. Eat.) D.C. Eat. (86) (1878)

Bird thistle [Bird-thistle] - *Cirsium vulgare* (Savi) Ten. (5, 156, 158) (1913-1923)

Bird vetch [Bird-vetch] - *Vicia cracca* L. (4, 5, 50, 155, 156) (1923–present)

Bird wheat [Bird's wheat] - *Polytrichum commune* Hedw. (78) (1898) Kennebec Valley ME

Birdbell [Bird-bell, Bird bell] - *Prenanthes altissima* L. (5, 75, 156) (1894-1923) NY

Birdeine - *Primula laurentiana* Fern. (178) (1526)

Birdgrass [Bird's grass, Bird-grass, Bird grass] - *Polygonum aviculare* L. (5, 158) (1900-1913)

Bird-in-the-bush [Birds-in-the-bush] - *Argemone mexicana* L. (5, 73, 156) (1892-1923) Arlington MA, no longer in use by 1923

Bird-lime [Bird lime] - *Galium aparine* L. (156) (1923), *Ilex opaca* Aiton (92) (1876)

Bird-lime wort [Birdlime woort] - *Lychnis viscaria* L. (178) (1526)

Bird-of-paradise flower [Bird of paradise flower] - *Caesalpinia gilliesii* (Hook.) Wallich ex D. Dietr. (106, 124, 153) (1913-1937)

Bird-on-the-wing [Bird on the wing] - *Polygala paucifolia* Willd. (5, 76, 156) (1896-1923) ME

Bird's-bill [Birds' bill, Birds'-bill] - *Dodecatheon* L. (1) (1932)

Bird's-bread [Bird's bread] - *Sedum acre* L. (5, 156) (1913-1923)

Birdseed [Bird-seed, Bird seed] - *Brassica rapa* L. var. *rapa* (158) (1900), *Lepidium* L. (1) (1932), *Lepidium virginicum* L. (156) (1923), *Senecio vulgaris* L. (5, 156, 158) (1900–1923)

Bird-seed grass [Bird-seed-grass] - *Phalaris canariensis* L. (5, 93, 119) (1913-1938)

Bird-seed plantain - *Plantago major* L. (157, 158) (1900-1929)

Bird's-egg astragalus [Bird egg astragalus] - *Astragalus ceramicus* Sheldon (98) (1926)

Bird's-egg pea [Bird-egg pea] - *Astragalus ceramicus* Sheldon var. *filifolius* (Gray) F. J. Herm. (158) (1900)

Bird's-eggs [Bird's eggs] - *Silene vulgaris* (Moench) Garcke (5, 156) (1913-1923) no longer in use by 1923

Bird's-eye [Bird's eye, Bird's-eyes, Birds-eyes, Birds eies] - *Primula laurentiana* Fern. (178) (1526), *Adonis annua* L. (5, 156, 165) (1768-1923), *Adonis vernalis* L. (92) (1876), *Anagallis arvensis* L. (5, 156, 157, 158) (1900-1929), *Gilia tricolor* Benth. (109) (1949), *Lotus corniculatus* L. (5, 156, 158) (1900-1923), *Sagina procumbens* L. (5, 156) (1913-1923), *Veronica biloba* L. (5, 156) (1913-1923), *Veronica chamaedrys* L. (5, 156) (1913-1923), *Veronica officinalis* L. var. *tournefortii* (Vill.) Reichenb. (5, 156) (1913-1923)

Bird's-eye gilia [Birdseye gilia] - *Gilia tricolor* Benth. (138) (1923)

Bird's-eye primrose [Bird's eye primrose, Birdseye primrose] - *Primula laurentiana* Fern. (5, 72, 109, 138, 156) (1907-1949), *Primula mistassinica* Michx. (19) (1840)

Bird's-eye speedwell [Birdeye speedwell] - *Veronica chamaedrys* L. (158) (1900), *Veronica persica* Poir. (3, 4, 50) (1977–present)

Bird's-foot [Bird's foot, Birdes foote] - *Ornithopus perpusillus* L. (178) (1526), *Ornithopus sativus* Brot. (110) (1886)

Bird's-foot cliffbreak [Birdfoot cliffbreak] - *Pellaea mucronata* (D.C. Eat.) D.C. Eat. (50, 155) (1942–present)

Bird's-foot deervetch [Birdfoot deervetch] - *Lotus corniculatus* L. (50, 155) (1942–present)

Bird's-foot sagebrush [Birdfoot sagebrush] - *Artemisia pedatifida* Nutt. (50, 155) (1942–present)

Bird's-foot trefoil [Birds-foot trefoil, Birdsfoot trefoil] - *Lotus corniculatus* L. (3, 4, 5, 45, 85, 109, 138) (1896-1986), *Lotus* L. (156, 158) (1900-1923), *Lotus unifoliolatus* (Hook.) Benth. (156) (1923)

Bird's-foot violet [Bird foot violet, Birdfoot violet, Bird-foot violet, Birdsfoot violet, Bird's foot violet] - *Viola pedata* L. (2, 4, 5, 49, 50, 72, 82, 86, 92, 97, 109, 122, 124, 131, 155, 156, 158) (1876–present)

Bird's-nest [Bird's nest, Birds-nest, Birds nest, Birds' nest, Birdsnest] - *Daucus carota* L. (62, 75, 76, 156) (1896-1912), *Monotropa* L. (7, 167, 184) (1793-1828), *Monotropa uniflora* L. (6, 19, 49, 156) (1840-1923), *Pastinaca sativa* L. (5, 156) (1913-1923)

Bird's-nest cactus [Bird's nest cactus] - *Escobaria missouriensis* (Sweet) D.R. Hunt var. *missouriensis* (145) (1897)

Bird's-nest fern [Birdsnest fern, Birds-nest-fern] - *Asplenium nidus* L. (109, 138) (1923-1949)

Bird's-nest fungus [Birds' nest fungus] - *Cyathus vernicosus* (Bull.) DC. (128) (1933) ND

Bird's-nest plant [Bird's nest plant, Birds' nest plant] - *Daucus carota* L. (106, 156, 157, 158) (1900-1930), *Monotropa uniflora* L. (5, 92, 158) (1876-1913)

Bird's-nest root [Birds' nest root] - *Daucus carota* L. (92) (1876)

Bird's-tongue [Birds tongue] - *Anagallis arvensis* L. (5, 156, 157, 158) (1900–1929), *Fraxinus excelsior* L. (92) (1876), *Polygonum aviculare* L. (5, 156, 158) (1900–1923)

Birdweed [Bird weed, Bird-weed] - *Polygonum aviculare* L. (5, 7, 92, 156, 158) (1828-1923)

Birke (German) - *Betula pubescens* Ehrh. (158) (1900)

Birn (German) - *Pyrus communis* L. (110) (1886)

Birthroot [Birth-root, Birth root] - *Trillium erectum* L. (2, 6, 49, 57, 64, 75, 79, 92, 156) (1869-1917), *Trillium* L. (1, 106, 158) (1900-1930)

Birthroot [Birth-root, Birth root] - *Trillium sessile* L. (58) (1869)

Birthwort [Birth wort, Birth-wort] - *Aristolochia clematitis* L. (5, 10) (1818-1913), *Aristolochia* L. (2, 8, 10, 109, 158, 167) (1785-1949), *Aristolochia macrophylla* Lam. (19) (1840), *Aristolochia serpentaria* L. (6, 58, 64, 92, 156, 184) (1793-1923), *Trillium erectum* L. (64) (1908)

Birthwort Dutchman's-pipe [Birthwort Dutchmanspipe] - *Aristolochia clematitis* L. (155) (1942)

Bisbee weed - *Galeopsis bifida* Boenn. (77) (1898) Paris ME

Biscuit plant - *Smilax rotundifolia* L. (75) (1894) Allston MA, children eat tendrils and new leaves

Biscuitleaves [Biscuit leaves, Biscuit-leaves] - *Smilax rotundifolia* L. (5, 73, 156) (1892-1923) Allston MA, children eat tendrils and new leaves

Biscuitroot [Biscuit root, Biscuit-root] - *Camassia scilloides* (Raf.) Cory (101) (1905) MT, *Lomatium ambiguum* (Nutt.) Coult. & Rose (101, 103, 107) (1870-1919), *Lomatium cous* (S. Wats.) Coult. & Rose (101, 146) (1905-1939) CA, *Lomatium* Raf. (1) (1932), *Lomatium simplex* (Nutt.) J.F. Macbr. var. *simplex* (101) (1905), *Lomatium triternatum* (Pursh) Coult. & Rose (101) (1905) MT

Biscuits - *Sarracenia flava* L. (5, 156) (1913-1923) no longer in use by 1923

Bishop's goutweed [Bishops goutweed] - *Aegopodium podagraria* L. (155) (1942)

Bishop's pine [Bishop pine] - *Pinus muricata* D. Don (50, 109, 138) (1923–present)

Bishop's-cap [Bishop's cap, Bishops-cap, Bishopscap] - *Euonymus americanus* L. (156) (1923), *Mitella diphylla* L. (63, 92, 156) (1876-1923), *Mitella* L. (1, 2, 109, 138) (1895-1949), *Mitella nuda* L. (3, 4, 156) (1923-1986)

Bishop's-elder [Bishop's elder] - *Aegopodium podagraria* L. (5, 156) (1913-1923)

Bishop's-leaves [Bishop's leaves] - *Scrophularia umbrosa* Dumort. (92, 107) (1876-1919)

Bishop's-weed [Bishop's weed, Bishop weed, Bishopsweede] - *Aegopodium podagraria* L. (5, 107, 109) (1913-1949), *Ammi* L. (10) (1818), *Mentha aquatica* L. (158) (1900), *Trachyspermum copticum* (L.) Link (92) (1876), *Ammi majus* L. (178) (1526)

Bishop's-wig [Bishop's wig] - *Arabis alpina* L. (5) (1913)

Bishop's-wort [Bishop's wort, Bishopswort] - *Nigella sativa* L. (92) (1876), *Stachys officinalis* (L.) Trev. (5) (1913)

Bisnaga - *Ferocactus wislizeni* (Engelm.) Britt. & Rose (9, 149) (1873-1910) NM

Bissum - *Hydrangea arborescens* L. (156, 158) (1900-1923), *Hydrangea* L. (7) (1828)

Bistort - *Polygonum bistorta* L. (57, 92, 107) (1876-1919), *Polygonum* L. (1) (1932), *Polygonum viviparum* L. (4) (1986)

Bistorta - *Polygonum bistorta* L. (57) (1917)

Bistorte - *Polygonum bistorta* L. (179) (1526)

Bite-tongue [Bite tongue] - *Polygonum hydropiper* L. (5, 156, 157, 158) (1900-1929)

Biting crowfoot - *Ranunculus acris* L. (156) (1923), *Ranunculus bulbosus* L. (156) (1923), *Ranunculus sceleratus* L. (5, 156, 158) (1900–1923)

Biting dragon [Biting-dragon] - *Artemisia dracunculus* L. (157, 158) (1900-1929)

Biting knotweed [Biting knot-weed, Biting knot weed] - *Polygonum hydropiper* L. (5, 92, 156, 157, 158) (1876-1923), *Polygonum punctatum* Ell. (19) (1840), *Polygonum punctatum* Ell. var. *punctatum* (6) (1892)

Biting persicaria - *Polygonum hydropiper* L. (5, 156, 157, 158) (1900-1929)

Biting radish - *Raphanus sativus* L. (178) (1526)

Biting stonecrop [Biting stone crop] - *Sedum acre* L. (5, 49, 57, 92, 156) (1876–1923)

Bit-leaf American vetch [Bitleaf American vetch] - *Vicia americana* Muhl. ex Willd. subsp. *americana* (155) (1942)

Bitter almond [Bytter almonde] - *Prunus dulcis* (Mill.) D.A. Webber (55, 57, 59, 92, 179) (1526-1911)

Bitter aloe - *Aloe vera* (L.) Burm. f. (92) (1876)

Bitter apple - *Citrullus colocynthis* (L.) Schrad. (19, 38, 55, 57, 92) (1820-1917)

Bitter balsam - *Populus angustifolia* James (160) (1860)

Bitter bugle - *Lycopus americanus* Muhl. ex W. Bart. (5, 156, 158) (1900-1923), *Lycopus europaeus* L. (156) (1923)

Bitter bugleweed - *Lycopus europaeus* L. (5) (1913)

Bitter bush - *Quercus ilicifolia* Wangenh. (5) (1913)

Bitter candy-tuft [Bitter candy tuft] - *Iberis amara* L. (52, 92) (1876-1919)

Bitter cassava - *Manihot esculenta* Crantz (92, 109) (1876-1949)

Bitter cottonwood - *Populus angustifolia* James (30) (1844)

Bitter cucumber - *Citrullus colocynthis* (L.) Schrad. (92) (1876)

Bitter dock - *Rumex acetosella* L. (40) (1928), *Rumex obtusifolius* L. (3, 4, 5, 6, 50, 58, 62, 64, 69, 80, 93, 97, 122, 145, 155, 156, 157, 158) (1869–present)

Bitter dogbane [Bitter dog-bane] - *Apocynum androsaemifolium* L. (7, 92, 156, 157, 158) (1828-1929), *Apocynum cannabinum* L. (158) (1900)

Bitter fennel - *Foeniculum vulgare* Mill. (107) (1919)

Bitter fleabane - *Erigeron acris* L. (5, 50, 155, 156) (1913–present)

Bitter gourd - *Citrullus colocynthis* (L.) Schrad. (92, 107) (1876-1919)

Bitter grape - *Vitis rotundifolia* Michx. (possibly) (7) (1828)

Bitter grass [Bittergrass] - *Panicum amarum* Ell. (50) (present)

Bitter herb - *Centaurium erythraea* Raf. (5) (1913), *Chelone glabra* L. (5, 92) (1876-1913)

Bitter hickory - *Carya cordiformis* (Wangenh.) K. Koch (5, 9, 113, 156) (1890-1923)

Bitter lettuce - *Lactuca virosa* L. (155) (1942)

Bitter milkwort - *Polygala polygama* Walt. (5, 156) (1913-1923)

Bitter nightshade - *Solanum dulcamara* L. (155, 156) (1923-1942)

Bitter oak - *Quercus cerris* L. (92) (1876), *Quercus ilicifolia* Wangenh. (5) (1913)

Bitter orange - *Citrus* ×*aurantium* L. [*maxima* × *reticulata*] (107) (1919), *Poncirus trifoliata* (L.) Raf. (122, 124) (1937) TX

Bitter panic - *Panicum amarum* Ell. var. *amarulum* (A.S. Hitchc. & Chase) P.G. Palmer (5, 66) (1903-1913)

Bitter panic grass [Bitter panic-grass, Bitter panicgrass] - *Panicum amarum* Ell. (50, 94) (1901–present)

Bitter pecan - *Carya aquatica* (Michx. f.) Nutt. (5, 156) (1913-1923)

Bitter pignut - *Carya cordiformis* (Wangenh.) K. Koch (5) (1913)

Bitter purple willow - *Salix purpurea* L. (6) (1892)

Bitter redberry - *Cornus florida* L. (6, 7) (1828-1932)

Bitter rubberweed - *Hymenoxys odorata* DC. (50) (present)

Bitter smartweed - *Polygonum punctatum* Ell. var. *punctatum* (155) (1942)

Bitter sneezeweed - *Helenium amarum* (Raf.) H. Rock (4) (1986), *Helenium amarum* (Raf.) H. Rock var. *amarum* (4, 155) (1942-1986)

Bitter thistle - *Cnicus benedictus* L. (5, 69, 156) (1903-1923)

Bitter trefoil - *Menyanthes trifoliata* L. (5, 92, 158) (1876-1913)

Bitter vetch - *Lathyrus* L. (10) (1818)

Bitter willow - *Salix purpurea* L. (5, 156) (1913-1923)

Bitter wintercress - *Barbarea vulgaris* W.T. Aiton (138, 155) (1923-1942)

Bitter wintergreen - *Chimaphila umbellata* (L.) Bart. (5, 6, 19, 92, 158) (1840-1913)

Bitter-ash [Bitter ash] - *Euonymus atropurpurea* Jacq. (92, 156, 158) (1876-1923), *Picrasma excelsa* (Sw.) Planch. (92) (1876)

Bitter-bark [Bitter bark] - *Picrasma excelsa* (Sw.) Planch. (92) (1876), *Pinckneya bracteata* (Bartr.) Raf. (7, 92) (1828-1876)

Bitter-blain [Bitter blain] - *Lindernia diffusa* (L.) Wettst. (92) (1876), *Vancouveria hexandra* (Hook.) C. Morren & Decne. (possibly) (93) (1936)

Bitter-bloom [Bitter bloom] - *Sabatia angularis* (L.) Pursh (5, 7, 92, 156, 158) (1828-1923)

Bitter-buttons [Bitter buttons] - *Tanacetum vulgare* L. (5, 69, 156, 158) (1900-1923)

Bitter-clover [Bitter clover] - *Sabatia angularis* (L.) Pursh (5, 92, 156, 158) (1876-1923)

Bittercress [Bitter cress, Bitter-cress] - *Barbarea vulgaris* W.T. Aiton (5, 107, 156, 157) (1919-1986), *Cardamine* L. (1, 2, 4, 13, 50, 93, 109, 138, 155, 156, 158) (1895–present), *Cardamine pensylvanica* Muhl. ex Willd. (3, 4, 85) (1932-1986), *Cardamine pratensis* L. (156) (1923)

Bitter-grass [Bitter grass] - *Aletris farinosa* L. (5, 6, 7, 92, 156) (1828-1913)

Bitter-herb - *Centaurium erythraea* Raf. (156) (1923)

Bitterklee (German) - *Menyanthes trifoliata* L. (6, 158) (1892)

Bitternut [Bitter-nut, Bitter nut] - *Carya cordiformis* (Wangenh.) K. Koch (2, 5, 10, 19, 72, 92, 95, 109, 155, 156, 187) (1818-1949)

Bitternut hickory [Bitter-nut hickory, Bitter nut hickory] - *Carya cordiformis* (Wangenh.) K. Koch (1, 3, 4, 20, 46, 50, 82, 93, 97, 138, 155) (1857–present)

Bitter-plant [Bitter plant] - *Aletris farinosa* L. (5, 156) (1913-1923)

Bitter-root [Bitter root, Bitterroot] - *Apocynum androsaemifolium* L. (6, 7, 92, 101, 109, 148, 156) (1828-1949), *Apocynum cannabinum* L. (49, 53, 54, 64, 156, 157, 158) (1898–1929), *Erysimum capitatum* (Dougl. ex Hook.) Greene var. *capitatum* (7) (1828), *Gentiana catesbaei* Walt. (7) (1828), *Lewisia* Pursh (15) (1895), *Lewisia rediviva* Pursh (15, 101, 109, 138) (1895-1949), *Menyanthes trifoliata* L. (6, 7) (1828-1892)

Bittersüss (German) - *Solanum dulcamara* L. (6, 158) (1892)

Bittersweet [Bitter sweet, Bitter-sweet] - *Celastrus* L. (50, 93, 138, 155, 156) (1923–present), *Celastrus scandens* L. (9, 22, 37, 40, 65, 85, 103, 105, 106, 107, 112, 130, 131, 156, 158) (1870-1937), *Chimaphila umbellata* (L.) Bart. (5, 73, 156, 158) (1892-1923) NH, *Lonicera dioica* L. (156) (1923), *Menispermum canadense* L. (23) (1810) NY, *Solanum dulcamara* L. (1, 3, 4, 5, 6, 14, 19, 49, 52, 53, 55, 57, 61, 62, 71, 92, 93, 4, 156, 158, 187) (1818-1986), *Solanum* L. (1, 93) (1932-1936)

Bitterweed [Bitter weed, Bitter-weed] - *Ambrosia artemisiifolia* L. (6, 58, 75, 76, 156, 158) (1869-1923) from effect on milk when eaten by cattle, *Ambrosia artemisiifolia* L. var. *elatior* (L.) Descourtils (5) (1913), *Ambrosia* L. (1, 10, 12, 93) (1818-1936), *Ambrosia trifida* L. (5, 49, 92, 131, 156, 157, 158) (1876–1929), *Chelone glabra* L. (156) (1923), *Conyza canadensis* (L.) Cronq. var. *canadensis* (5, 69, 156, 157, 158) (1900-1929), *Helenium amarum* (Raf.) H. Rock var. *amarum* (106, 138, 156) (1923-1930), *Hymenoxys* Cass. (4) (1986), *Hymenoxys odorata* DC. (3, 4) (1977-1986), *Solidago rugosa* Mill. (5, 156) (1913-1923)

Bitterweed actinea - *Actinella odorata* (DC.) A.Gray (155) (1942)

Bitterwood [Bitter-wood, Bitter wood] - *Picrasma excelsa* (Sw.) Planch. (15, 92) (1876-1895), *Simarouba* Aubl. (15) (1895), *Simmondsia chinensis* (Link) C.K. Schneid. (92) (1876)

Bitterworm [Bitter worm, Bitter-worm] - *Menyanthes trifoliata* L. (5, 92, 158) (1876-1913)

Bitterwort [Bitter wort] - *Menyanthes trifoliata* L. (156) (1923)

Bixa - *Bixa orellana* L. (174) (1753)

Biznacha (Spanish, Mexican) - *Ferocactus wislizeni* (Engelm.) Britt. & Rose (103, 107) (1870-1919)

Björnblad (Swedish, bear's leaf) - *Symplocarpus foetidus* (L.) Salisb. ex Nutt. (41) (1770)

Björnrötter (Swedish, bear's root) - *Symplocarpus foetidus* (L.) Salisb. ex Nutt. (41) (1770)

Blåblomster (Swedish, blue flower) - *Hepatica nobilis* Schreb. var. *obtusa* (Pursh) Steyermark (41) (1770)

Blachnum - *Woodwardia virginica* (L.) Sm. (92) (1876)

Black alder [Blacke aller] or Black alder tree - *Alnus glutinosa* (L.) Gaertn. (5, 109, 156) (1913-1949), *Alnus incana* (L.) Moench (5, 35, 156) (1806-1923), *Alnus incana* (L.) Moench subsp. *rugosa* (DuRoi) Clausen (20) (1857), *Alnus serrulata* (Aiton) Willd. (7, 49, 53) (1828-1898), *Frangula alnus* Mill. (5, 92, 156, 158, 178) (1526-1923)

Black alpine sedge - *Carex nigricans* C.A. Mey. (139) (1944)

Black American larch-tree - *Larix laricina* (Du Roi) K.Koch (possibly) (8) (1785)

Black American oak - *Quercus nigra* L. (14) (1882)

Black angelica - *Ballota nigra* L. (156) (1923)

Black archangel - *Ballota nigra* L. (5, 158) (1900–1913)

Black ash - *Acer negundo* L. (5, 156, 158) (1900), *Fraxinus americana* L. (52) (1919), *Fraxinus nigra* Marsh. (2, 3, 20, 19, 53, 57, 63, 72, 80, 92, 138, 155, 156, 158) (1840-1977), *Fraxinus pennsylvanica* Marsh. (5, 93, 156) (1913-1936)

Black ballota - *Ballota nigra* L. (155) (1942)

Black bamboo - *Phyllostachys nigra* (Lodd.) Munro (109) (1949)

Black baneberry - *Actaea spicata* L. (138, 155) (1931-1942)

Black bark - *Quercus velutina* Lam. (46) (1649)

Black barley - *Hordeum vulgare* L. (158) (1900) variety

Black bean - *Lablab purpureus* (L.) Sweet (183) (~1756)

Black bearberry [Black bear-berry] - *Arctostaphylos alpina* (L.) Spreng. (5, 92, 156) (1876-1923)

Black beech - *Fagus grandifolia* Ehrh. (78) (1898) Western US

Black beet [Blacke beete] - *Beta vulgaris* L. (178) (1526)

Black beggarticks [Black beggar-ticks] - *Bidens frondosa* L. (97) (1937)

Black bent - *Panicum virgatum* L. (129) (1894) SD

Black bent grass [Black bentgrass, Black-bent grass] - *Agrostis gigantea* Roth (155) (1942), *Alopecurus myosuroides* Huds (5) (1913), *Panicum virgatum* L. (5) (1913)

Black bindweed [Black bind-weed, Blacke bindeweed] - *Polygonum convolvulus* L. (5, 50, 62, 72, 80, 82, 93, 131, 156, 178, 187) (1526–present), *Convolvulus arvensis* L. (80) (1913), *Polygonum cilinode* Michx. (2) (1895)

Black birch or Black birch tree - *Betula lenta* L. (1, 5, 7, 20, 19, 46, 49, 58, 92, 105, 107, 109, 156, 190) (~1759-1949), *Betula nigra* L. (5, 8, 14, 40, 124, 156, 158) (1785-1937), *Betula occidentalis* Hook. (1, 5, 95, 113, 130, 137, 158) (1890-1913)

Black birdweed - *Polygonum convolvulus* L. (92, 106, 158) (1876-1930)

Black blueberry - *Vaccinium fuscatum* Aiton (5, 156) (1913-1923)

Black borehound - *Ballota nigra* L. (92) (1876)

Black bunch grass [Black bunch-grass] - *Pleuraphis jamesii* Torr. (94) (1901)

Black caco - *Colocasia esculenta* (L.) Schott (92) (1876)

Black caraway - *Nigella sativa* L. (92) (1876)

Black cherry - *Prunus serotina* Ehrh. (3, 7, 50, 82, 92, 125, 131, 138, 155, 157) (1882–present)

Black chokeberry [Black choak-berry] - *Photinia melanocarpa* (Michx.) Robertson & Phipps (5, 19, 72, 138) (1840-1923)

Black chokecherry - *Prunus virginiana* L. var. *melanocarpa* (A. Nels.) Sargent (50, 155) (1942–present)

Black clover - *Medicago lupulina* L. (85) (1932)

Black club-rush - *Eleocharis melanocarpa* Torr. (66) (1903)

Black cohosh - *Actaea* L. (93) (1936), *Actaea racemosa* L. (5, 6, 7, 15, 49, 52, 53, 54, 55, 57, 58, 92, 156) (1828-1923), *Actaea rubra* (Aiton) Willd. (5, 156) (1913-1923), *Actaea rubra* (Aiton) Willd. (76) (1896), *Cimicifuga* Wernischeck (13) (1849)

Black corrans [Blacke corrans] - *Ribes nigrum* L. (178) (1526)

Black cottonwood - *Populus ×acuminata* Rydb. [*angustifolia × deltoides*] (5, 93, 112, 130, 131, 157) (1895–1936), *Populus angustifolia* James (1, 5, 113, 156) (1890–1923), *Populus heterophylla* L. (156) (1923)

Black couch grass - *Alopecurus myosuroides* Huds (5) (1913)

Black crowberry - *Empetrum nigrum* L. (5, 19, 156) (1840-1923)

Black cumin - *Nigella sativa* L. (107) (1919)

Black cummin - *Nigella sativa* L. (92) (1876)

Black currant [Black currants] - *Ribes americanum* Mill. (46, 107) (1649-1919), *Ribes hudsonianum* Richards. (85) (1932), *Ribes nigrum* L. (14, 19, 41, 46, 49, 92, 107, 110) (1770-1919)

Black cypress (Georgia & Carolinas) - *Taxodium distichum* (L.) L.C. Rich. (20) (1857)

Black cypress wood - *Taxodium distichum* (L.) L.C. Rich. (92) (1876)

Black dalea - *Dalea frutescens* Gray (4, 155) (1942-1986)

Black drink - *Ilex cassine* L. (7) (1828)

Black elder - *Sambucus nigra* L. subsp. *canadensis* (L.) R. Bolli (7) (1828)

Black flatsedge - *Cyperus niger* Ruiz & Pavón (50) (present)

Black garden currant - *Ribes nigrum* L. (156) (1923)

Black gentian - *Seseli libanotis* (L.) W.D.J. Koch (92) (1876)

Black ginger - *Zingiber officinale* Roscoe (92) (1876)

Black gram - *Vigna angularis* (Willd.) Ohwi & Ohashi (110) (1886), *Vigna mungo* (L.) Hepper (109) (1949)

Black grama [Black gramma] - *Bouteloua eriopoda* (Torr.) Torr. (3, 50, 119, 122, 151, 152, 155, 163) (1852–present), *Bouteloua hirsuta* Lag. (5, 56, 65, 93, 111, 116, 129, 144, 152, 163) (1852-1936),

Pleuraphis mutica Buckl. (45, 94, 151) (1896-1901)

Black grama grass - *Bouteloua hirsuta* Lag. (75) (1894)

Black grass [Blac-grass] - *Alopecurus myosuroides* Huds (92) (1876), *Bromus sterilis* L. (5) (1913), *Alopecurus geniculatus* L. (165) (1768)

Black greasewood - *Sarcobatus vermiculatus* (Hook.) Torr. (155) (1942)

Black green-wattle acacia [Blackgreen-wattle acacia] - *Acacia mearnsii* De Wild. (155) (1942)

Black gum or Black gum tree - *Nyssa aquatica* L. (5) (1913), *Nyssa* L. (1) (1828), *Nyssa ogeche* Bartr. ex Marsh. (17) (1796), *Nyssa sylvatica* Marsh. (5, 20, 46, 65, 106, 107, 109, 122, 156) (1857-1949)

Black haw [Black-haw, Blackhaw] - *Crataegus chrysocarpa* Ashe (101) (1905) MT, *Crataegus douglasii* Lindl. (35, 106, 135) (1806-1930), *Nyssa biflora* Walt. (181) (~1678), *Sideroxylon lanuginosum* Michx. (5, 156) (1913-1923), *Viburnum* L. (158) (1900), *Viburnum lentago* L. (5, 35, 37, 57, 156, 158) (1806-1923) Meriwether Lewis, *Viburnum opulus* L. var. *opulus* (124) (1937), *Viburnum prunifolium* L. (3, 4, 5, 8, 19, 48, 49, 50, 52, 53, 54, 57, 58, 59, 60, 61, 63, 72, 82, 92, 97, 106, 107, 109, 121, 138, 156, 158, 177, 181) (~1678–present)

Black hawthorn - *Crataegus douglasii* Lindl. (50, 138) (1923–present)

Black hazel - *Ostrya virginiana* (Mill.) K. Koch (156, 157, 158) (1900-1929)

Black hellebore [Blacke elebore] - *Helleborus niger* L. (2, 15, 49, 52, 53, 55, 57, 61, 92, 179) (1526-1922)

Black henbane [Blacke henbane] - *Hyoscyamus niger* L. (5, 6, 7, 46, 50, 92, 148, 155, 156, 158, 178, 180) (1526–present) accidently introduced by 1671

Black hickory - *Carya alba* (L.) Nutt. ex Ell. (5, 78, 156, 158) (1898-1923), *Carya glabra* (Mill.) Sweet (156) (1923), *Carya glabra* (Mill.) Sweet var. *glabra* (5, 78) (1898-1913) Sulphur Grove MO, *Carya texana* Buckl. (3, 4, 50, 155) (1942–present)

Black Hills meadow-rue - *Thalictrum nigromontanum* Boivin (50) (present)

Black Hills pine - *Pinus ponderosa* P.& C. Lawson var. *scopulorum* Engelm. (136) (1930) SD

Black Hills spruce - *Picea glauca* (Moench) Voss (4, 40, 109, 112, 136) (1928-1986), *Tsuga canadensis* (L.) Carr. (136) (1930) SD

Black horehound [Black hoarhound] - *Ballota* L. (158) (1900), *Ballota nigra* L. (5, 50, 92, 156, 158) (1876–present)

Black huckleberry - *Gaylussacia baccata* (Wang.) K. Koch (2, 5, 47, 49, 63, 72, 82, 106, 107, 109, 138, 156) (1852-1949)

Black hurts - *Gaylussacia* Kunth (73) (1892) Newfoundland, short for whortleberries

Black Indian hemp - *Apocynum androsaemifolium* L. (6, 58) (1869-1892), *Apocynum cannabinum* L. (64, 92, 157, 158) (1876-1908)

Black ironwood - *Krugiodendron ferreum* (Vahl) Urb. (15) (1895)

Black Italian poplar - *Populus deltoides* Bartr. ex Marsh. (5) (1913)

Black jack [Black-jack, Black-jacks] - *Quercus nigra* L. (19, 27, 58, 187) (1811-1869)

Black jack oak [Black jack oak, Black-jack oak] - *Quercus nigra* L. (2, 5, 14, 20, 33, 44, 46, 92, 97) (1827-1937)

Black knapweed - *Centaurea nigra* L. (5, 14, 19, 156) (1840-1923)

Black larch - *Larix laricina* (Du Roi.) Koch. (5, 7, 19, 49, 92) (1828-1913)

Black laurel - *Gordonia lasianthus* L. (5, 156) (1913-1923)

Black lime tree [Black lime-tree] - *Tilia americana* L. (5, 156, 157, 158) (1900-1929)

Black linn - *Magnolia acuminata* (L.) L. (5, 156) (1913-1923)

Black liquorice - *Glycyrrhiza glabra* L. (92) (1876)

Black locust - *Gleditsia triacanthos* L. (5, 157, 158) (1900-1929), *Robinia* L. (93) (1936), *Robinia pseudoacacia* L. (3, 4, 5, 6, 27, 44, 49, 50, 61, 65, 72, 82, 85, 92, 93, 97, 106, 109, 112, 114, 122, 124, 125, 135, 148, 155, 156, 157, 158) (1894-1986)

Black maidenhair [Black maiden's hair, Blacke maiden haire] -

Adiantum capillus-veneris L. (5, 109, 158) (1900-1949), *Asplenium adiantum-nigrum* L. (178) (1596)

Black mangrove or Black mangrove tree - *Avicennia germinans* (L.) L. (106) (1930)

Black maple - *Acer palmatum* Thunb. (3, 4, 5, 15, 19, 50, 82, 138, 155, 158) (1840–present), *Acer saccharum* Marsh. (5, 156, 158) (1900–1923)

Black masterwort - *Astrantia major* L. (92) (1876)

Black medic [Black medick] - *Medicago lupulina* L. (3, 4, 5, 45, 50, 62, 68, 80, 82, 92, 97, 106, 107, 109, 155, 156, 158) (1896–present)

Black mercury - *Toxicodendron radicans* (L.) Kuntze subsp. *radicans* (71, 158) (1898-1900) ME, *Toxicodendron toxicarium* (Salisb.) Gillis (73) (1892) Harmony ME

Black mercury vine [Black mercury-vine] - *Toxicodendron radicans* (L.) Kuntze (5) (1913), *Toxicodendron toxicarium* (Salisb.) Gillis (156) (1923)

Black mercyrt - *Toxicodendron radicans* (L.) Kuntze subsp. *radicans* (157) (1929)

Black merry - *Prunus avium* (L.) L. (5) (1913)

Black millet - *Sorghum bicolor* (L.) Moench (67) (1890), *Sorghum bicolor* (L.) Moench subsp. *bicolor* (158) (1900)

Black moss - *Bryoria fremontii* (Tuck.) Brodo & D. Hawksw. (101) (1905) MT, *Tillandsia usneoides* (L.) L. (2, 5, 92) (1876-1913)

Black mould - *Rhizopus nigricans* Ehrenb. (56) (1901)

Black mountain rice - *Patis racemosa* (Sm.) Romasch., P.M. Peterson & R. J. Soreng (66, 94, 129) (1894-1903)

Black mulberry - *Morus nigra* L. (1, 19, 92, 93, 97, 107, 109, 110, 122, 124, 138) (1840-1937)

Black mullein [Blacke mulleine] - *Verbascum* L. (180) (1633), *Verbascum nigrum* L. (92, 138) (1876-1923)

Black mustard - *Brassica* L. (1, 93) (1932-1936), *Brassica nigra* (L.) W.D.J. Koch (3, 4, 5, 15, 6, 45, 50, 52, 57, 58, 59, 62, 63, 69, 72, 80, 82, 85, 92, 97, 106, 107, 109, 114, 131, 145, 155, 156, 157, 158) (1869–present), *Raphanus raphanistrum* L. (5, 156) (1913-1923), *Raphanus sativus* L. (76) (1896)

Black nightshade [Black night-shade] - *Atropa bella-donna* L. (156) (1923), *Solanum americanum* Mill. (3) (1977), *Solanum nigrum* L. (2, 5, 62, 71, 72, 80, 92, 93, 107, 124, 125, 126, 131, 138, 155, 156, 157, 158) (1895-1936), *Solanum ptychanthum* Dunal (4) (1986)

Black nonesuch - *Medicago lupulina* L. (5, 156, 158) (1900-1923)

Black oak [Blacke oak, Black-Oak, Black Oake] - *Quercus* ×*benderi* Baenitz [*coccinea* × *rubra*] (5, 156) (1913-1923), *Quercus ellipsoidalis* E.J. Hill (82, 156) (1923-1930), *Quercus emoryi* Torr. (149, 153) (1904-1919) NM, *Quercus nigra* L. (8, 9, 18, 41, 113, 177, 181) (~1678-1910), *Quercus robur* L. (107) (1919), *Quercus rubra* L. (156, 158) (1900-1923), *Quercus velutina* Lam. (1, 2, 3, 4, 5, 14, 18, 19, 20, 33, 46, 50, 65, 78, 82, 92, 93, 95, 97, 109, 124, 138, 155, 156, 157, 158, 182, 187) (1629–present)

Black oat grass [Black oat-grass] - *Piptochaetium avenaceum* (L.) Parodi (5, 45, 66, 92, 94, 163) (1852-1913)

Black onion - *Allium nigrum* L. (155, 165) (1768-1942)

Black oyster plant - *Scolymus hispanicus* L. (107) (1919)

Black pepillary - *Populus nigra* L. (158) (1900)

Black persimmon - *Diospyros texana* Scheele (107, 122, 124) (1919-1937)

Black pine - *Pinus banksiana* Lamb. (5) (1913), *Pinus jeffreyi* Grev. & Balf. (109) (1949), *Pinus rigida* Mill. (10, 38, 43, 187) (1818-1820)

Black pipple - *Populus nigra* L. (158) (1900)

Black plums - *Prunus maritima* Marsh. (possibly) (46) (1879)

Black popillary - *Populus nigra* L. (158) (1900)

Black poplar - *Populus nigra* L. (4, 5, 8, 14, 92, 109, 138, 155, 156, 158) (1882-1986)

Black poppy [Blacke poppy] - *Papaver somniferum* L. (92, 179) (1526-1876)

Black prairie clover - *Dalea frutescens* Gray (50) (present)

Black pursely - *Chamaesyce hypericifolia* (L.) Millsp. (7) (1828)

Black purslane - *Chamaesyce maculata* (L.) Small (158) (1900)

Black pursley - *Chamaesyce maculata* (L.) Small (92) (1876)

Black puslane - *Chamaesyce hypericifolia* (L.) Millsp. (6, 49) (1892-1898)

Black pusley - *Chamaesyce maculata* (L.) Small (5, 156) (1913-1923)

Black quick-grass - *Agrostis gigantea* Roth (119) (1938)

Black quitch - *Agrostis gigantea* Roth (5) (1913)

Black radish [Blacke radish] - *Raphanus sativus* L. (178, 180) (1526-1633) John Gerarde

Black raspberry [Black-raspberry] - *Rubus occidentalis* L. (1, 3, 4, 5, 9, 19, 40, 46, 47, 50, 63, 72, 82, 85, 93, 97, 107, 113, 130, 131, 156, 157, 158, 187) (1818–present)

Black rattlepod [Black rattle pod] - *Baptisia bracteata* Muhl. ex Ell. (37) (1919)

Black rush [Black-rush] - *Juncus balticus* Willd. var. *montanus* Engelm. (139) (1944), *Juncus bulbosus* L. (19) (1840), *Schoenoplectus tabernaemontani* (K.C. Gmel.) Palla (5, 75, 156, 158) (1894-1923)

Black sage - *Artemisia tridentata* Nutt. (156) (1923), *Salvia mellifera* Greene (106) (1930)

Black sagebrush - *Artemisia nova* A. Nels. (155) (1942)

Black salsify - *Scolymus hispanicus* L. (107) (1919)

Black saltwort - *Glaux* L. (1, 10) (1818-1932), *Glaux maritima* L. (5, 92, 156, 158) (1876-1923)

Black Sampson - *Echinacea angustifolia* DC. (47, 49, 52, 54) (1852-1919), *Echinacea purpurea* (L.) Moench (5, 92, 156) (1876-1923)

Black Samson echinacea [Black-samson echinacea, Blacksamson echinacea] - *Echinacea angustifolia* DC. (50, 155) (1942–present)

Black sanicle - *Sanicula marilandica* L. (5, 92, 155, 157, 158) (1876-1942)

Black scrub oak - *Quercus ilicifolia* Wangenh. (2, 5, 33, 156, 187) (1818-1923)

Black sedge - *Carex atratiformis* Britt. (5, 139) (1913-1944)

Black snakeroot [Black snake-root, Black-snake root] - *Aristolochia serpentaria* L. (5, 102, 156) (1886–1923), *Asarum canadense* L. (156, 158) (1900-1923), *Cimicifuga racemosa* (L.) Nutt. (2, 5, 6, 7, 14, 15, 19, 42, 49, 55, 57, 60, 64, 92, 109, 156, 177) (1814-1949), *Cimicifuga* Wernischeck (10, 13) (1818-1849), *Sanicula canadensis* L. (157, 158) (1900-1929), *Sanicula* L. (2) (1895), *Sanicula marilandica* L. (3, 5, 49, 58, 85, 92, 93, 97, 131, 156, 157, 158) (1869-1977)

Black snakeweed [Black snake-weed] - *Asarum canadense* L. (64) (1907), *Hexastylis virginica* (L.) Small (5, 92, 156) (1876-1923)

Black spleenwort - *Asplenium adiantum-nigrum* L. (92) (1876)

Black spruce - *Picea glauca* (Moench) Voss (5, 158) (1900-1913), *Picea mariana* (Mill.) Britton, Sterns & Poggenb. (5, 6, 10, 20, 19, 46, 49, 50, 92, 109, 136, 138, 158) (1818-1949)

Black spurge - *Chamaesyce hypericifolia* (L.) Millsp. (7) (1828), *Chamaesyce maculata* (L.) Small (5, 92, 156) (1876-1923), *Euphorbia ipecacuanhae* L. (156) (1923)

Black St. John's-wort - *Hypericum punctatum* Lam. (187) (1818)

Black sugar maple - *Acer palmatum* Thunb. (2, 5, 20, 72, 82, 85, 97, 158) (1857-1937)

Black sumac [Black shumack, Black sumach] - *Rhus copallinum* L. (76, 93, 95, 156, 157) (1896-1936)

Black swallow-wort [Blacke swallowwoort] - *Cynanchum louiseae* Kartesz & Gandhi (4, 5, 156, 178) (1526-1986)

Black swamp cypress - *Taxodium distichum* (L.) L.C. Rich. (5, 20) (1857-1913)

Black tamarind - *Tamarindus indica* L. (92) (1876)

Black tang - *Fucus vesiculosus* L. (53) (1922)

Black thorn [Black-thorn] - *Acacia farnesiana* (L.) Willd. (19) (1840), *Crataegus calpodendron* (Ehrh.) Medik. (5, 157) (1913-1929), *Prunus spinosa* L. (92, 107, 109, 137, 138) (1876-1949), *Viburnum lentago* L. (5, 92, 156, 158) (1876-1923)

Black three-leaf grass [Blacke three leafed grasse] - *Trifolium reflexum* L. (178) (1526)

Black ti-ti [Black titi] - *Cliftonia monophylla* (Lam.) Britton (possibly) (106) (1930), *Cyrilla racemiflora* L. (106, 156) (1923-1930)

Black tree - *Avicennia germinans* (L.) L. (106) (1930)
Black trefoil - *Medicago lupulina* L. (5, 158) (1900–1913)
Black truffle - *Tuber griseum* Borch ex Pers. (92) (1876)
Black urn - *Urnula craterium* (Schwein.) Fr. (128) (1933) ND
Black walnut [Black wallnut, Black walnutt] - *Carya laciniosa* (Michx. f.) G. Don (190) (~1759), *Juglans nigra* L. (1, 4, 5, 7, 9, 12, 14, 20, 19, 27, 35, 37, 41, 44, 46, 50, 57, 65, 72, 82, 85, 91, 92, 93, 95, 97, 105, 107, 109, 112, 113, 121, 122, 124, 125, 130, 131, 135, 138, 153, 156, 157, 158, 181, 182, 187, 189) (~1678–present)
Black wattle or Black wattle tree - *Acacia mearnsii* De Wild. (106, 107, 109, 138, 158) (1900-1949)
Black western chokecherry - *Padus virginiana* subsp. *melanocarpa* (A. Nelson) W.A. Weber (138) (1923)
Black whortleberry [Black whortle-berry] - *Gaylussacia baccata* (Wang.) K. Koch (19, 49) (1840-1898), *Vaccinium myrtilloides* Michx. (131) (1899), *Vaccinium myrtillus* L. (92) (1876), *Vaccinium pallidum* Aiton (19) (1840)
Black willow - *Baccharis salicifolia* (Ruiz & Pavón) Pers. (75) (1894) Santa Barbara Co. CA, *Salix amygdaloides* Anderss. (5, 156) (1913-1923) often mistaken for Salix nigra, *Salix caroliniana* Michx. (158) (1900), *Salix discolor* Muhl. (55) (1911), *Salix nigra* Marsh. (1, 3, 4, 5, 9, 20, 19, 49, 50, 52, 53, 54, 58, 61, 65, 72, 80, 92, 93, 95, 97, 108, 112, 113, 131, 138, 149, 153, 155, 156, 157, 158) (1840–present)
Black yew [Blacke yuy] - *Hedera helix* L. (179) (1526)
Black-alder [Black alder] - *Ilex* L. (7) (1828), *Ilex verticillata* (L.) Gray (2, 5, 6, 15, 49, 53, 57, 61, 72, 92, 106, 107, 109, 156, 186, 187) (1814-1949), *Viburnum molle* Michx (156) (1923), *Viburnum nudum* L. (156) (1923)
Blackamoor - *Typha latifolia* L. (5, 156, 157, 158) (1900-1923)
Black-apple [Black apple] - *Rubus chamaemorus* L. (73, 107) (1892-1919) NB, Grand Mana ID
Black-base quillwort [Black-based quillwort] - *Isoetes melanopoda* Gay & Durieu ex Durieu (5) (1913)
Black-bead elder [Blackbead elder] - *Sambucus racemosa* L. var. *melanocarpa* (Gray) McMinn (138) (1923)
Blackberry [Black-berry] - *Ribes nigrum* L. (156) (1923), *Rubus allegheniensis* Porter (82, 93, 156) (1923-1936), *Rubus allegheniensis* Porter var. *allegheniensis* (72, 95, 157) (1900-1907), *Rubus flagellaris* Willd. (46, 52, 53, 59, 82, 92, 107, 113, 114) (1671-1930) IA, *Rubus frondosus* Bigelow (40) (1928), *Rubus* L. (1, 4, 50, 106, 138, 155, 158, 181) (1814–present), *Rubus occidentalis* L. (5, 74, 157, 158) (1893–1929), *Rubus trivialis* Michx. (46) (1879), *Vaccinium myrtillus* L. (14, 178) (1526-1882)
Black-berry elder [Black-berried elder] - *Sambucus nigra* L. (158) (1900), *Sambucus nigra* L. subsp. *canadensis* (L.) R. Bolli (19, 85, 156) (1840-1942)
Blackberry lily [Black berry lily, Blackberry-lily] - *Belamcanda* Adans (138, 158) (1900-1923), *Belamcanda chinensis* (L.) DC. (3, 5, 19, 50, 72, 92, 93, 109, 138, 155, 158) (1840–present)
Black-berry-bearing gum [Black-berry-bearing-gum] - *Nyssa aquatica* L. (177) (1762)
Blackberry-heath [Black-berry heath, Black berried heath] - *Empetrum nigrum* L. (5, 156) (1913-1923)
Black-bird bindweed - *Polygonum convolvulus* L. (5, 156, 158) (1900-1923)
Black-blue whortleberry - *Vaccinium pallidum* Aiton (19) (1840)
Blackbrush [Black brush] - *Acacia rigidula* Benth. (106, 122, 124) (1930-1937) TX, *Flourensia* DC. (153) (1913) NM
Black-brush acacia [Blackbrush acacia] - *Acacia rigidula* Benth. (50) (present)
Blackbur [Black bur, Black-bur] - *Geum aleppicum* Jacq. (5, 156, 158) (1900–1923)
Blackburn's palmetto [Blackburn palmetto] - *Sabal palmetto* (Walt.) Lodd. ex J. A. & J. H. Schultes (138) (1923)
Blackbutt - *Eucalyptus pilularis* Sm. (138) (1923)

Blackcap [Black cap, Black-cap] - *Rubus occidentalis* L. (1, 2, 5, 74, 93, 107, 156, 157, 158) (1893-1937), *Typha latifolia* L. (5, 156, 157, 158) (1900-1929)
Blackcap raspberry - *Rubus occidentalis* L. (155) (1942)
Black-cherry [Black cherry] - *Atropa bella-donna* L. (49) (1898)
Black-choke - *Prunus serotina* Ehrh. (157, 158) (1900-1929)
Black-dogwood [Black dogwood] - *Frangula alnus* Mill. (5, 92, 156, 158) (1876-1923)
Black-edge sedge [Black-edged sedge] - *Carex albicans* Willd. ex Spreng. var. *albicans* (5) (1913)
Black-eyed bean - *Vigna mungo* (L.) Hepper (138) (1923), *Vigna sinensis* (L.) Endl. (5, 156) (1913-1923)
Black-eyed clockvine - *Thunbergia alata* Bojer ex Sims (138) (1923)
Black-eyed Susan [Blackeyed Susan] - *Hibiscus trionum* L. (5, 73, 156, 158) (1892–1923) NH, New Brunswick, *Rudbeckia hirta* L. (3, 4, 5, 50, 62, 63, 72, 73, 76, 80, 82, 85, 93, 95, 97, 105, 122, 127, 131, 138, 155, 156, 157, 158) (1892–present), *Rudbeckia hirta* L. var. *pulcherrima* Farw. (50, 109) (1949–present), *Rudbeckia triloba* L. (82) (1930) IA, *Thunbergia alata* Bojer ex Sims (109) (1949)
Blackflower [Black flower, Black-flower] - *Melanthium* L. (167) (1814), *Melanthium virginicum* L (5, 19, 92, 156, 158) (1840-1923)
Black-foot daisy - *Melampodium leucanthum* Torr. & Gray (4) (1986)
Black-foot quillwort [Blackfoot quillwort] - *Isoetes melanopoda* Gay & Durieu ex Durieu (50) (present)
Black-fruit medlar [Black-fruited medlar] - *Photinia melanocarpa* (Michx.) Robertson & Phipps (187) (1818)
Black-fruit mountain-rice [Black-fruited mountain rice] - *Patis racemosa* (Sm.) Romasch., P.M. Peterson & R. J. Soreng (5, 50, 56) (1901–present)
Black-fruit spike rush [Blackfruit spikerush, Black-fruit spikerush] - *Eleocharis melanocarpa* Torr. (5, 50) (1913–present)
Black-fruit swamp-service [Black-fruited swamp-service] - *Photinia melanocarpa* (Michx.) Robertson & Phipps (187) (1818)
Black-girdle bulrush [Blackgirdle bulrush] - *Scirpus atrocinctus* Fern. (50) (present)
Black-grass [Black grass, Blackgrass] - *Juncus bulbosus* L. (66) (1903), *Juncus gerardi* Lois. (3, 5, 46, 156) (1879-1977)
Black-grass [Black grass, Blackgrass] - *Medicago lupulina* L. (5, 156, 158) (1900-1923)
Black-haw viburnum [Blackhaw viburnum] - *Viburnum prunifolium* L. (155) (1942)
Blackheart [Black-heart, Black heart] - *Persicaria maculosa* Gray (5, 75, 77, 156, 158) (1894-1923), from the shape of dark spots on the leaves
Black-jack [Black jack, Black-jacks] - *Pinus banksiana* Lamb. (32) (1895) Neb, *Plantago lanceolata* L. (5, 156, 158) (1900-1923) no longer in use by 1923, *Quercus marilandica* Muench (95, 122, 158, 164) (1854-1937)
Black-jack oak [Black jack oak] - *Quercus imbricaria* Michx. (18, 33) (1805-1828), *Quercus marilandica* Muench (1, 3, 4, 5, 20, 44, 50, 65, 72, 82, 93, 97, 138, 155, 156) (1845–present)
Black-joint bamboo [Blackjoint bamboo] - *Phyllostachys nigra* (Lodd.) Munro (138) (1923)
Black-lady [Black lady] - *Populus nigra* L. (156, 158) (1900-1923)
Black-parsley [Black parsley] - *Chamaesyce hypericifolia* (L.) Millsp. (6) (1892)
Blackroot [Black-root, Black root] - *Aletris farinosa* L. (6, 7) (1828-1892), *Pterocaulon* Ell. (7) (1828), *Pterocaulon virgatum* (L.) DC. (10, 19, 57) (1818-1917), *Veronicastrum virginicum* (L.) Farw. (5, 6, 7, 48, 49, 53, 61, 64, 77, 92, 93, 156, 157, 158) (1828-1936)
Black-salsify - *Scolymus hispanicus* L. (138) (1923)
Blackseed [Black seed] - *Medicago lupulina* L. (5, 156, 158) (1900-1923), *Sporobolus indicus* (L.) R. Br. var. *indicus* (5) (1913)

Black-seed groundsel [Black-seeded groundsel] - *Senecio integerrimus* Nutt. var. *exaltatus* (Nutt.) Cronq. (72) (1907)

Black-seed hop clover [Blackseed hop clover] - *Medicago lupulina* L. (72) (1907)

Black-seed millet grass [Black seed millet grass] - *Patis racemosa* (Sm.) Romasch., P.M. Peterson & R. J. Soreng (19) (1840)

Black-seed needlegrass [Blackseed needlegrass] - *Piptochaetium avenaceum* (L.) Parodi (92, 122) (1876-1937)

Black-seed plantain [Blackseed plantain] - *Plantago rugelii* Dcne. (50, 155) (1942–present)

Black-seed ricegrass [Blackseed ricegrass] - *Patis racemosa* (Sm.) Romasch., P.M. Peterson & R. J. Soreng (50, 155) (1942–present)

Black-seed spear grass [Blackseed speargrass] - *Piptochaetium avenaceum* (L.) Parodi (50) (present)

Blacksnap [Black snap, Black snaps] - *Gaylussacia baccata* (Wang.) K. Koch (5, 75, 156) (1894-1923)

Black-spot horn-poppy [Blackspot hornpoppy] - *Glaucium corniculatum* (L.) J. H. Rudolph (50, 155) (1942–present)

Black-stem spleenwort [Blackstem spleenwort] - *Asplenium resiliens* Kunze. (3, 4, 5, 50) (1913–present)

Black-stikweet - *Ageratina altissima* (L.) King & H.E. Robins. (177) (1762)

Black-tip groundsel [Black tipped groundsel] - *Senecio lugens* Richards. (131) (1899)

Blackweed [Black weed] - *Ambrosia artemisiifolia* L. (76, 156, 158) (1896-1923) Long Island NY, no longer in use by 1923, *Ambrosia artemisiifolia* L. var. *elatior* (L.) Descourtils (5) (1913), *Chenopodium album* L. (77) (1898) Eastern Long Island, stains fingers black, *Sparganium erectum* L. subsp. *stoloniferum* (Graebn.) Hara (156) (1923)

Blackwood [Black wood] - *Avicennia germinans* (L.) L. (77, 106) (1898-1930) Florida Keys

Blackwood [Black wood] or Black-wood tree - *Acacia melanoxylon* R. Br. ex Aiton f. (50, 158) (1900–present)

Black-wood acacia [Blackwood acacia] - *Acacia melanoxylon* R. Br. ex Aiton f. (109, 138, 155) (1923-1949)

Blackwort [Black wort] - *Symphytum officinale* L. (5, 64, 156) (1907-1923)

Bladder campion - *Silene latifolia* Poir. (50) (present), *Silene vulgaris* (Moench) Garcke (5, 15, 92, 93, 107, 109, 156) (1876-1949)

Bladder champion - *Silene vulgaris* (Moench) Garcke (45) (1896)

Bladder cucumber - *Echinocystis lobata* (Michx.) Torr. & Gray (114) (1894)

Bladder fern [Bladderfern, Bladder-fern] - *Cystopteris* Bernh. (1, 50, 78, 109, 138, 155) (1898–present), *Cystopteris bulbifera* (L.) Bernh. (72, 97) (1907-1937), *Cystopteris fragilis* (L.) Bernh. (5, 46, 92) (1876-1913)

Bladder fucus - *Fucus vesiculosus* L. (92) (1876)

Bladder herb [Bladder-herb] - *Physalis alkekengi* L. (158) (1900)

Bladder ketmia - *Hibiscus trionum* L. (5, 72, 80, 92, 145, 156, 158) (1876–1923)

Bladder nut [Bladder-nut, Bladdernut] or Bladder nut tree - *Staphylea bolanderi* Gray (8) (1785), *Staphylea* L. (4, 13, 15, 50, 93, 109, 138, 158) (1849–present), *Staphylea trifolia* L. (58, 61, 82, 92, 95, 177, 184, 187) (1793-1930)

Bladder sedge - *Carex intumescens* Rudge (5, 72) (1907-1913)

Bladder senna [Bladder-senna] - *Colutea arborescens* L. (19, 92) (1840-1876), *Colutea* L. (7, 138) (1828-1923)

Bladder silene - *Silene vulgaris* (Moench) Garcke (155) (1942)

Bladder wrack - *Fucus vesiculosus* L. (52, 53, 55, 57, 60, 92) (1876-1922)

Bladder-flower [Bladderflower] - *Araujia* Brot. (155) (1942)

Bladder-fruit sedge [Bladder-fruited sedge] - *Carex utriculata* Boott (66) (1903)

Bladderpod [Bladder pod, Bladder-pod] - *Lesquerella globosa* (Desv.) S. Wats. (156) (1923), *Lesquerella gordonii* (Gray) S. Wats. (106) (1930), *Lesquerella grandiflora* (Hook.) S. Wats. (124) (1937), *Lesquerella ludoviciana* (Nutt.) S. Wats. (3, 4, 98) (1926-

1986), *Lesquerella* S. Wats. (1, 4, 50, 93, 122, 127, 155, 156, 158) (1900–present), *Lobelia inflata* L. (6, 69, 157, 158) (1892–1929), *Physaria* (Nutt. ex Torr. & Gray) Gray (158) (1900)

Bladder-pod lobelia [Bladder-podded lobelia, Bladder podded lobelia] - *Lobelia inflata* L. (5, 92, 156, 186) (1814-1923)

Bladder-snout - *Utricularia macrorhiza* Le Conte (156, 158) (1900-1923)

Bladderwort - *Utricularia gibba* L. (3) (1977), *Utricularia* L. (1, 2, 4, 10, 26, 50, 93, 138, 156, 158) (1826–present), *Utricularia macrorhiza* Le Conte (3, 19, 85, 92) (1840-1977), *Utricularia minor* L. (3) (1977)

Blade-apple [Bladeapple] - *Pereskia aculeata* Mill. (138) (1923)

Blaeberry - *Vaccinium myrtillus* L. (107) (1919), *Vaccinium stamineum* L. (187) (1818), *Vaccinium uliginosum* L. (5, 156) (1913-1923) no longer in use by 1923

Blaewort - *Campanula rotundifolia* L. (158) (1900)

Blaje zitkatačaŋ hu stola (Lakota, little wild tea of the plains) - *Dalea villosa* (Nutt.) Spreng (121) (1918?-1970?)

Blake's milkvetch [Blake's milk vetch] - *Astragalus robbinsii* (Oakes) Gray var. *minor* (Hook.) Barneby (5) (1913)

Blanchard's thorn - *Crataegus irrasa* Sarg. (5) (1913)

Bland's grape [Blands' grape, Bland grape] - *Vitis labrusca* L. (possibly) (7) (1828)

Blanket-flower [Basketflower, Blanket flower] - *Gaillardia aristata* Pursh (3, 4, 85, 156) (1923-1986), *Gaillardia* Foug. (1, 4, 50, 93, 158) (1900–present)

Blanket-leaf [Blanket leaf] - *Verbascum thapsus* L. (5, 69, 156, 158) (1900-1923)

Blasenkirschen (German) - *Physalis alkekengi* L. (158) (1900)

Blau cohosch (German) - *Caulophyllum thalictroides* (L.) Michx. (6, 7) (1828-1932)

Blaue Kardinals blume (German) - *Lobelia siphilitica* L. (186) (1814)

Blaver - *Campanula rotundifolia* L. (158) (1900), *Centaurea cyanus* L. (5, 156, 157, 158) (1900–1929), *Papaver dubium* L. (5, 156, 158) (1900–1923)

Blawort - *Centaurea cyanus* L. (157, 158) (1900-1929)

Blazing star [Blazing-star, Blazingstar] - *Aletris farinosa* L. (5, 6, 7, 49, 53, 64, 92, 156) (1828-1922), *Chamaelirium luteum* (L.) A. Gray (2, 5, 6, 7, 19, 52, 53, 58, 64, 156, 187) (1818-1922), *Chamaelirium* Willd. (1, 2, 109) (1895-1949), *Liatris cylindracea* Michx (82) (1930), *Liatris* Gaertn. ex Schreber. (1, 2, 4, 7, 50, 63, 82, 86, 93, 106, 109, 114, 127, 158) (1878–present), *Liatris punctata* Hook (3, 98, 148) (1926-1977), *Liatris scariosa* (L.) Willd. var. *scariosa* (37, 40, 131, 157) (1899-1929), *Liatris squarrosa* (L.) Michx. (49, 53, 82, 92, 156) (1876-1930), *Liatris squarrosa* (L.) Michx. var. *squarrosa* (85, 95) (1911-1932), *Mentzelia* L. (1, 4, 50, 138) (1923–present), *Mentzelia laevicaulis* (Dougl. ex Hook.) Torr. & Gray (157) (1929)

Blé de Turquie (French "Turkish wheat") - *Zea mays* L. (110) (1886) possibly from resemblance of ear to beards of Turkish men rather than to place of origin

Blé Noir (French) - *Fagopyrum esculentum* Moench (158) (1900)

Blé sarrasin (French "Saracen wheat") - *Fagopyrum esculentum* Moench (110) (1886)

Bleaberry - *Vaccinium myrtillus* L. (92) (1876)

Blechnum - *Blechnum* L. (138) (1923)

Bled - *Zea mays* L. (46) (1879)

Bled ou Fourment (French) - *Triticum aestivum* L. (180) (1633)

Bleeding-heart [Bleeding heart, Bleeding hearts, Bleedingheart] - *Cypripedium parviflorum* Salisb. var. *parviflorum* (7) (1828), *Cypripedium parviflorum* Salisb. var. *pubescens* (Willd.) Knight (92) (1876), *Dicentra* Bernh. (1, 4, 50, 13, 155) (1849–present), *Lamprocapnos spectabilis* (L.) Fukuhara (76, 92, 109, 138) (1876-1949)

Blek-starr (Swedish) - *Carex pallescens* L. (46) (1879)

Blessed herb - *Geum urbanum* L. (92) (1876)

Blessed milk-thistle [Blessed milkthistle] - *Silybum marianum* (L.) Gaertn. (IT, 155) (1949–present)

42

Blessed thistle - *Cnicus benedictus* L. (5, 7, 19, 49, 57, 58, 69, 92, 156) (1828-1923), *Cnicus* L. (2, 7, 63) (1828-1899), *Silybum marianum* (L.) Gaertn. (46, 50, 109) (1649–present)
Bletilla - *Bletilla* Reichenb. f. (138) (1923)
Blette (French) - *Chenopodium capitatum* (L.) Asch. (46) (1879)
Blighia - *Blighia* Koenig (50) (present)
Blight - *Rubigo alnea* (Pers.) Link (92) (1876)
Blind gentian - *Gentiana andrewsii* Griseb. (5, 73, 75, 156, 157) (1892-1929) Northeast US
Blind nettle [Blind-nettle] - *Galeopsis bifida* Boenn. (5, 156, 158) (1900–1923), *Lamium album* L. (5, 92, 156) (1876-1923), *Lamium* L. (179) (1526)
Blind prickly-pear [Blind pricklypear] - *Opuntia rufida* Engelm. (155) (1942)
Blind starwort - *Stellaria lanceolata* (Michx.) Torr. (19) (1840)
Blindeyes [Blind-eyes, Blind eyes] - *Papaver dubium* L. (4, 5, 50, 156) (1913–present), *Papaver rhoeas* L. (158) (1900)
Blind-pear - *Opuntia rufida* Engelm. (109) (1949)
Blindweed [Blind-weed, Blind weed] - *Capsella bursa-pastoris* (L.) Medik. (157, 158) (1900-1929), *Polygonum* L. (77) (1898) Sulphur Grove OH, twining species
Blinking chickweed [Blinking-chickweed] - *Montia fontana* L. (5, 156) (1913-1923)
Blinks - *Montia fontana* L. (5, 156) (1913-1923)
Blister buttercup - *Ranunculus sceleratus* L. (155) (1942)
Blister pine - *Abies balsamea* (L.) Mill. (5, 75, 158) (1894-1923) WV
Blister plant - *Ranunculus acris* L. (5) (1913), *Ranunculus recurvatus* Poir. (156) (1923)
Blister sedge - *Carex vesicaria* L. (50, 139, 155) (1942–present)
Blistercress [Blistercress] - *Erysimum* L. (109, 138) (1923-1949)
Blister-flower [Blister flower] - *Ranunculus acris* L. (156, 157, 158) (1900-1929), *Ranunculus bulbosus* L. (5, 156) (1913-1923), *Ranunculus recurvatus* Poir. (156) (1923)
Blisterweed [Blister-weed] - *Ranunculus acris* L. (6, 7, 92, 157, 158) (1828-1929)
Blisterwort [Blister wort, Blister-wort] - *Ranunculus acris* L. (156) (1923), *Ranunculus recurvatus* Poir. (50) (present), *Ranunculus sceleratus* L. (5, 156, 158) (1900–1923)
Blite - *Amaranthus blitum* L. (165) (1768), *Chenopodium bonus-henricus* L. (5, 156) (1913-1923), *Chenopodium capitatum* (L.) Asch. (46, 92, 184) (1793-1879), *Chenopodium* L. (7) (1828), *Suaeda* Forsk. ex J.F. Gmel. (158) (1900)
Blite goosefoot - *Chenopodium capitatum* (L.) Asch. (50, 155) (1942–present)
Blo (Dakota Teton) - *Apios americana* Medik. (37) (1919)
Blo (Lakota) - *Apios americana* Medik. (121) (1918?-1970?)
Block-head cactus [Blockhead cactus] - *Cylindropuntia leptocaulis* (DC.) F.M.Knuth (100) (1850) TX
Blockwood - *Haematoxylum campechianum* L. (92) (1876)
Blodworte - *Achillea millefolium* L. (179) (1526), *Polygala sanguinea* L. (179) (1526)
Blood elder - *Sambucus ebulus* L. (92) (1876)
Blood geranium - *Geranium sanguineum* L. (92) (1876)
Blood marigold - *Zinnia violacea* Cav. (92) (1876)
Blood panic grass [Blood panicgrass] - *Dichanthelium consanguineum* (Kunth) Gould & C.A. Clark (50) (present)
Blood polygala - *Polygala sanguinea* L. (3, 4, 155) (1942-1986)
Blood ragweed - *Ambrosia trifida* L. var. *texana* Scheele (155) (1942)
Blood-flower [Bloodflower, Blood flower] - *Asclepias curassavica* L. (57, 109, 138) (1917-1949)
Blood-flower milkweed [Bloodflower milkweed] - *Asclepias curassavica* L. (155) (1942)
Bloodleaf [Blood leaf, Blood-leaf] - *Iresine diffusa* Humb. & Bonpl. ex Willd. (5, 97, 156) (1913-1937), *Iresine* P. Br. (109, 138, 155) (1923-1949), *Iresine rhizomatosa* Standl. (4) (1986)
Blood-red cranesbill [Bloodred cranesbill] - *Geranium sanguineum* L. (138) (1923)

Blood-red dogwood [Blood red dogwood] - *Cornus sanguinea* L. (82) (1930)
Blood-red lily [Blood Red Lillie] - *Lilium bulbiferum* L. (178) (1596)
Bloodroot [Blood-root, Blood root] - *Lachnanthes caroliana* (Lam.) Dandy (86) (1878), *Lithospermum canescens* (Michx.) Lehm. (77) (1898) Southwest MO, *Sanguinaria canadensis* L. (1, 2, 4, 5, 6, 13, 14, 15, 19, 37, 40, 41, 46, 47, 49, 50, 52, 53, 54, 55, 57, 58, 59, 60, 61, 63, 64, 65, 72, 82, 85, 92, 97, 105, 106, 109, 127, 131, 138, 155, 156, 157, 158, 177, 184, 186, 187) (1770–present), *Sanguinaria* L. (50, 82, 93, 138, 155, 156, 190) (~1759–present)
Bloodstaunch [Blood staunch, Blood-staunch] - *Conyza canadensis* (L.) Cronq. var. *canadensis* (5, 69, 92, 157, 158) (1876-1923) no longer in use by 1923
Bloodstrange [Blood strange, Blood-strange] - *Myosurus minimus* L. (5, 156, 158, 180) (1633-1923)
Blood-tunic onion [Bloodtunic onion] - *Allium haematochiton* S. Wats. (155) (1942)
Bloodtwig [Blood twig] - *Cornus florida* L. (92) (1876)
Blood-twig dogwood [Bloodtwig dogwood] - *Cornus sanguinea* L. (109, 138) (1923-1949)
Bloodweed [Blood weed, Blood-weed] - *Ambrosia trifida* L. (82) (1930), *Ambrosia trifida* L. var. *texana* Scheele (122) (1937), *Asclepias curassavica* L. (92) (1876)
Bloodwood [Blood wood] - *Corymbia citriodora* (Hook.) K.D.Hill & L.A.S.Johnson (92) (1876)
Bloodwort [Blood wort, Blood-wort] - *Achillea millefolium* L. (69, 157, 158) (1526-1900), *Centaurium erythraea* Raf. (5, 156) (1913-1923), *Hieracium venosum* L. (7, 92, 157) (1828-1900), *Lachnanthes caroliana* (Lam.) Dandy (86) (1878), *Rumex sanguineus* L. (5, 46, 107) (1671-1919), *Sanguinaria canadensis* L. (7, 10, 184) (1793-1828), *Sanguisorba minor* Scop. subsp. *muricata* (Spach) Nordborg (5, 156, 157, 158) (1900-1929)
Bloody amaranth - *Amaranthus caudatus* L. (165) (1768)
Bloody choakberry - *Amelanchier canadensis* (L.) Medik. (19) (1840)
Bloody dock - *Rumex sanguineus* L. (5, 10) (1818-1913)
Bloody dogwood [Bloody dog wood] - *Cornus sanguinea* L. (42) (1814)
Bloody geranium - *Geranium sanguineum* L. (19) (1840)
Bloody marigold [Bloody marygold] - *Zinnia violacea* Cav. (19) (1840)
Bloody-butcher [Bloody butcher, Bloody-butchers, Bloody butchers] - *Trillium recurvatum* Beck (50, 156) (1923–present), *Trillium sessile* L. (156) (1923)
Bloody-noses [Bloody noses] - *Trillium recurvatum* Beck (possibly) (156) (1923)
Bloody-vein dock [Bloody-veined dock] - *Rumex sanguineus* L. (107) (1919)
Bloody-warrior [Bloody warrior] - *Castilleja coccinea* (L.) Spreng. (5, 75, 156, 158) (1894-1923) no longer in use by 1923
Bloom grass - *Bromus pubescens* Muhl. ex Willd. (92) (1876)
Bloomer's ricegrass [Bloomers ricegrass] - *Achnatherum* ×*bloomeri* (Boland.) Barkworth [*hymenoides* × *occidentale*] (155) (1942)
Bloomer's stipa - *Achnatherum* ×*bloomeri* (Boland.) Barkworth [*hymenoides* × *occidentale*] (94) (1901)
Bloomfell [Bloom fell, Bloom-fell] - *Lotus corniculatus* L. (5, 156, 158) (1900–1923)
Blooming Sally - *Chamerion angustifolium* (L.) Holub subsp. *angustifolium* (5, 138, 156, 157, 158) (1900-1929)
Blooming spurge - *Euphorbia corollata* L. (5, 6, 7, 49, 53, 92, 93, 156, 157, 158) (1828-1936)
Blooming-down - *Dianthus barbatus* L. (158) (1900)
Blooming-willow [Blooming willow] - *Chamerion angustifolium* (L.) Holub subsp. *angustifolium* (5, 156, 157, 158) (1900-1929)
Bloomy down - *Dianthus barbatus* L. (5, 156) (1913-1923) no longer in use by 1923
Blotched spurge - *Chamaesyce maculata* (L.) Small (5, 156, 158) (1900-1923)

Blow-ball [Blowball] - *Taraxacum officinale* G.H. Weber ex Wiggers (5, 62, 64, 69, 156, 157, 158) (1900-1929)

Blowleaf [Blow leaf] - *Hylotelephium telephium* (L.) H. Ohba. subsp. *telephium* (79) (1891) NH

Blowout beardtongue - *Penstemon haydenii* S. Wats. (50) (present)

Blowout grass [Blow-out grass, Blowoutgrass] - *Eragrostis capillaris* (L.) Nees (75) (1894) Neb, *Eragrostis trichodes* (Nutt.) Wood (5, 93, 111, 116, 119) (1913-1958), *Hesperostipa comata* (Trin. & Rupr.) Barkworth subsp. *comata* (5) (1913), *Muhlenbergia pungens* Thurb. (93, 111) (1915-1936), *Redfieldia flexuosa* (Thurb.) Vasey (3, 50, 111, 119, 140, 155) (1915–present), *Redfieldia* Vasey. (1, 50, 93, 155) (1932–present)

Blow-wives [Blowwives] - *Achyrachaena mollis* Schauer (50, 155) (1942–present)

Blubber grass - *Bromus hordeaceus* L. (5) (1913)

Blue agarita - *Mahonia swaseyi* (Buckl. ex Young) Fedde (124) (1937) TX

Blue anemone - *Hepatica nobilis* Schreb. (156) (1923)

Blue ash - *Fraxinus pennsylvanica* Marsh. (5, 156, 157) (1913-1929), *Fraxinus quadrangulata* Michx. (3, 4, 5, 10, 19, 20, 35, 63, 72, 82, 92, 97, 109, 138, 155, 158) (1818-1986)

Blue aster - *Symphyotrichum laeve* (L.) A.& D. Löve var. *laeve* (82, 85) (1930-1932), *Symphyotrichum oolentangiense* (Riddell) Nesom var. *oolentangiense* (106) (1930)

Blue balm - *Monarda didyma* L. (92) (1876)

Blue barberry - *Mahonia pinnata* (Lag.) Fedde subsp. *pinnata* (107) (1919)

Blue bean - *Lupinus argenteus* Pursh (148) (1939)

Blue beech - *Carpinus caroliniana* Walt. (2, 5, 82, 93, 95, 156) (1895-1936), *Carpinus caroliniana* Walt. subsp. *caroliniana* (19, 92) (1840-1876), *Carpinus caroliniana* Walt. subsp. *virginiana* (Marsh.) Furlow (109) (1949), *Carpinus* L. (1) (1932), *Ostrya virginiana* (Mill.) K. Koch var. *virginiana* (38) (1820)

Blue Bellflower of China [Blew Belflower of China] - *Platycodon grandiflorum* (Jacq.) A. DC. (178) (1526)

Blue bilberry - *Vaccinium corymbosum* L. (19, 156) (1840-1923)

Blue bindweed [Blew Bindweed] - *Solanum dulcamara* L. (5, 156, 158) (1900–1923), *Ipomoea nil* (L.) Roth (178) (1526)

Blue birch - *Betula ×caerulea* Blanch. [*papyrifera* × *populifolia*] (1, 5) (1913–1932), *Betula pendula* Roth (156) (1923)

Blue blazing-star [Blue blazing star] - *Liatris aspera* Michx. (86, 156) (1878-1923), *Liatris pilosa* (Aiton) Willd. (possibly) (186) (1814), *Liatris scariosa* (L.) Willd. var. *scariosa* (157, 158) (1900-1929), *Liatris spicata* (L.) Willd. (187) (1818)

Blue boneset - *Conoclinium coelestinum* (L.) DC. (5, 75, 122, 124, 156, 158) (1900-1937)

Blue bunch grass [Blue bunchgrass] - *Festuca idahoensis* Elmer (3) (1977)

Blue bunch wheat grass [Bluebunch wheatgrass] - *Pseudoroegneria spicata* (Pursh) A. Löve subsp. *spicata* (3, 50, 146, 185) (1936–present)

Blue bur - *Lappula squarrosa* (Retz.) Dumort. (62) (1912) IN

Blue camas - *Camassia* Lindl. (1) (1932)

Blue camomile [Blue chamomile] - *Symphyotrichum tradescantii* (L.) Nesom (92, 156) (1898-1923)

Blue cardinal - *Lobelia siphilitica* L. (92) (1876)

Blue cardinal plant - *Lobelia siphilitica* L. (186) (1814)

Blue cardinal-flower [Blue cardinal flower, Blue cardinal's flower] - *Lobelia siphilitica* L. (3, 4, 5, 6, 7, 93, 97, 98, 131, 156, 157, 158, 186, 187) (1814-1986)

Blue catalpa - *Paulownia tomentosa* (Thunb.) Sieb. & Zucc. ex Steud. (possibly) (156) (1923)

Blue cat-tail [Blue cat's-tail] - *Echium vulgare* L. (156, 157, 158) (1900-1929)

Blue centaury - *Centaurea cyanus* L. (92) (1876)

Blue chicory [Blue chiccory] - *Cichorium intybus* L. (6) (1892)

Blue clematis - *Clematis occidentalis* (Hornem.) DC. (possibly) (156) (1923)

Blue cohosh - *Actaea pachypoda* Ell. (76) (1896) Paris ME, *Actaea rubra* (Aiton) Willd. (158) (1900), *Caulophyllum* Michx. (13, 93, 155, 158) (1849-1942), *Caulophyllum thalictroides* (L.) Michx. (3, 4, 5, 6, 15, 37, 40, 49, 50, 52, 53, 54, 55, 57, 58, 63, 72, 85, 92, 109, 131, 138, 155, 156, 157, 158) (1869–present)

Blue Cupid's-daisy [Blue Cupids-daisy] - *Catananche caerulea* L. (138) (1923)

Blue currant [Blue current] - *Ribes americanum* Mill. (35) (1806)

Blue cypress - *Cupressus forbesii* Jepson (75) (1894) CA

Blue daisy [Blue daisies] - *Symphyotrichum tradescantii* (L.) Nesom (156) (1923)

Blue dangleberry - *Gaylussacia frondosa* (L.) Torr. & Gray (49) (1898)

Blue dawnflower [Blue dawn-flower] - *Ipomoea indica* (Burm. f.) Merr. (109, 138) (1923-1949)

Blue dogwood - *Cornus alternifolia* L. f. (5, 156) (1913-1923)

Blue Douglas fir [Blue Douglas-fir] - *Pseudotsuga menziesii* (Mirbel) Franco var. *glauca* (Beissn.) Franco (138) (1923)

Blue Egyptian lotus - *Nymphaea caerulea* Savigny (138) (1923)

Blue elder - *Sambucus nigra* L. subsp. *cerulea* (Raf.) R. Bolli (109) (1949)

Blue elderberry - *Sambucus nigra* L. subsp. *cerulea* (Raf.) R. Bolli (106, 122) (1930-1937), *Stapelia* L. (106) (1930)

Blue false indigo - *Baptisia australis* (L.) R. Br. ex Aiton f. (3, 4, 5, 97, 156) (1913-1937), *Baptisia australis* (L.) R. Br. ex Aiton f. var. *minor* (Lehm.) Fern. (3, 4) (1977-1986)

Blue fescue - *Festuca arvernensis* Auquier, Kerguélen & Markgr.-Dannenb. (109, 138) (1923-1949)

Blue field madder - *Sherardia arvensis* L. (5, 50, 156) (1913–present)

Blue field morning-glory - *Ipomoea hederacea* Jacq. (80) (1913)

Blue flag - *Iris* L. (1, 93, 158) (1900-1936), *Iris missouriensis* Nutt. (3, 85, 101) (1905-1977)

Blue flag iris [Blueflag iris] - *Iris versicolor* L. (3, 6, 7, 19, 37, 40, 46, 49, 52, 53, 54, 55, 57, 58, 61, 64, 86, 92, 138, 155, 157, 158) (1649-1977)

Blue flax - *Linum* L. (1) (1932), *Linum lewisii* Pursh (101, 122) (1905-1937), *Linum lewisii* Pursh var. *lewisii* (3, 4) (1977-1986), *Linum perenne* L. (50) (present)

Blue fleabane - *Erigeron acris* L. (5, 156) (1913-1923)

Blue flower-de-luce [Blew flower-deluce] - *Iris versicolor* L. (46) (1671)

Blue flower-de-lyce [Blewe flourdelyce] - *Iris germanica* L. (178, 179) (1526-1596)

Blue fly honeysuckle [Blue fly-honeysuckle] - *Lonicera caerulea* L. (5, 156) (1913-1923)

Blue fringed gentian - *Gentianopsis crinita* (Froel) Ma. (92, 156) (1876-1923)

Blue funnel-lily [Blue funnel lily, Blue funnellily] - *Androstephium caeruleum* (Scheele) Greene (50, 155) (1942–present)

Blue gentian [Blue-gentian] - *Gentiana catesbaei* Walt. (7, 92) (1828-1876), *Gentiana saponaria* L. (156) (1923), *Gentiana andrewsii* Griseb. (85, 156) (1923-1932), *Gentiana saponaria* L. var. *saponaria* (5) (1913)

Blue giant hyssop - *Agastache foeniculum* (Pursh) Kuntze (50) (present)

Blue ginseng - *Caulophyllum thalictroides* (L.) Michx. (5, 6, 7, 64, 92, 156, 157, 158) (1828-1929)

Blue grama - *Bouteloua gracilis* (Willd. ex Kunth) Lag. ex Griffiths (3, 5, 50, 56, 75, 93, 94, 98, 111, 115, 116, 119, 122, 129, 134, 140, 151, 152, 155, 163) (1852–present)

Blue grama grass - *Bouteloua gracilis* (Willd. ex Kunth) Lag. ex Griffiths (75) (1894)

Blue grape - *Vitis aestivalis* Michx. (5, 107, 156) (1913-1923)

Blue grape-flower [Blew grape-floure] - *Muscari botryoides* (L.) Mills (180) (1633)

Blue grass [Bluegrass, Blue-grass] - *Poa compressa* L. (3, 19, 45, 66,

87, 90, 92, 187) (1818-1977), *Poa* L. (1, 50, 93, 119, 138, 146, 152, 155) (1912–present), *Poa pratensis* L. (45, 56, 68, 125, 152) (1896-1930), *Thinopyrum intermedium* (Host) Barkworth & D.R. Dewey (75) (1894) Neb

Blue gum or Blue gum tree - *Eucalyptus globulus* Labill. (60, 92, 106, 138) (1876-1930)

Blue harebells [Blew hare-bels] - *Hyacinthoides nonscripta* (L.) Chouard ex Rothm. (180) (1633)

Blue hedge-hyssop - *Bacopa caroliniana* (Walt.) B.L. Robins. (5) (1913)

Blue huckleberry - *Gaylussacia frondosa* (L.) Torr. & Gray (46, 49, 156) (1879-1923), *Vaccinium pallidum* Aiton (5, 63, 97) (1899-1913)

Blue hyssop - *Bacopa caroliniana* (Walt.) B.L. Robins. (122) (1937) TX

Blue indigo - *Baptisia australis* (L.) R. Br. ex Aiton f. (48, 156, 158) (1882-1923)

Blue jack - *Quercus incana* Bartr. (75) (1894) SC

Blue jessamine - *Clematis crispa* L. (5, 156) (1913-1923)

Blue lady's-bower [Blew Ladies Bowre] - *Clematis viticella* L. (178) (1526)

Blue larkspur - *Delphinium bicolor* Nutt. (127) (1933), *Delphinium carolinianum* Walt. (5, 122, 124, 158) (1900), *Delphinium decorum* Fisch. & C.A. Mey. (76) (1896), *Delphinium nuttallianum* Pritz ex. Walp. (4) (1986)

Blue lettuce - *Lactuca biennis* (Moench) Fern. (155) (1942), *Lactuca floridana* (L.) Gaertn. (82) (1930), *Lactuca floridana* (L.) Gaertn. var. *villosa* (Jacq.) Cronq. (82, 85) (1930-1932), *Lactuca tatarica* (L.) C.A. Mey. (50) (present), *Lactuca tatarica* (L.) C.A. Mey. var. *pulchella* (Pursh) Breitung (3, 4, 50, 80, 95, 148, 156) (1911–present)

Blue lily - *Iris versicolor* L. (78) (1898) Madison WI

Blue lobelia - *Lobelia siphilitica* L. (6, 92, 125, 127, 157, 158, 186) (1814-1892)

Blue loco - *Astragalus lentiginosus* Dougl. ex Hook. var. *diphysus* (Gray) M.E. Jones (155) (1942)

Blue lotus (of Egypt) - *Nymphaea caerulea* Savigny (109) (1949)

Blue lucy - *Prunella vulgaris* L. (156) (1923)

Blue lungwort - *Pulmonaria officinalis* L. (109) (1949)

Blue lupine - *Lupinus argenteus* Pursh (127) (1933), *Lupinus subcarnosus* Hook. (106) (1930)

Blue lupine [Blew Lupines] - *Lupinus angustifolius* L. (178) (1526)

Blue magnolia - *Magnolia acuminata* (L.) L. (49, 156) (1898-1923)

Blue mallow - *Malva rotundifolia* L. (5, 92, 106, 156, 157, 158) (1876-1930)

Blue marsh bellflower - *Campanula aparinoides* Pursh (5, 93) (1913-1936)

Blue marsh violet - *Viola conspersa* Reichenb. (174, 177) (1753-1762), *Viola cucullata* Aiton (138) (1923)

Blue melilot - *Trigonella caerulea* (L.) Ser. (41) (1770)

Blue milkwort [Blew Milke woort] - *Polygala vulgaris* L. (178, 180) (1526-1633)

Blue mistflower - *Conoclinium coelestinum* (L.) DC. (50) (present)

Blue monkey-flower - *Mimulus ringens* L. (85) (1932)

Blue morning-glory [Blue morning glory] - *Ipomoea hederacea* Jacq. (77, 157, 158) (1898–1929) Southwest MO

Blue Mountain onion [BlueMountain onion] - *Allium fibrillum* M.E. Jones (155) (1942)

Blue mountain tea - *Solidago odora* Aiton (5, 49, 52, 156) (1898-1923), *Solidago rugosa* Mill. (156) (1923)

Blue mud-plantain [Blue mud plantain] - *Heteranthera limosa* (Sw.) Vahl. (50) (present), *Heteranthera peduncularis* Benth. (5) (1913)

Blue mustard - *Chorispora tenella* (Pallas) DC. (3, 4, 97) (1937-1986)

Blue myrtle - *Vinca minor* L. (62, 156) (1912-1923)

Blue nodding locoweed - *Oxytropis deflexa* (Pallas) DC. var. *sericea* Torr. & Gray (50) (present)

Blue oak - *Quercus douglasii* Hook. & Arn. (138) (1923), *Quercus*

macrocarpa Michx. (5, 156, 158) (1900–1923)

Blue Oriental Iacint [Blew Orientall Iacint, Blue Oriental Iacinth, Blew Orientall Iacinth] - *Hyacinthus orientalis* L. (178, 180) (1596-1633)

Blue palmetto - *Rhapidophyllum hystrix* (Pursh) H. Wendl. & Drude ex Drude (2, 106) (1895-1930)

Blue passion-flower [Blue passion flower, Blue passionflower] - *Passiflora caerulea* L. (19, 107) (1840-1919)

Blue pearl grass - *Molinia caerulea* (L.) Moench (56) (1901)

Blue penstemon - *Penstemon glaber* Pursh (138) (1923)

Blue phlox - *Phlox divaricata* L. (138, 156) (1923), *Phlox divaricata* L. subsp. *laphamii* (Wood) Wherry (3, 4) (1977-1986)

Blue pimpernel [Blew pimpernell] - *Scutellaria lateriflora* L. (5, 6, 156, 157, 158) (1892–1929), *Anagallis arvensis* L. subsp. *foemina* (Mill.) Schinz & Thellung (178) (1526)

Blue pipe [Blew pipe] - *Syringa vulgaris* L. (5, 178) (1526-1913)

Blue plantain-lily [Blue plantainlily] - *Hosta ventricosa* (Salisb.) Stearn (109, 138) (1923–1949)

Blue poplar - *Liriodendron tulipifera* L. (5) (1913)

Blue poppy - *Centaurea cyanus* L. (5, 156, 158) (1900–1923)

Blue prairie aster - *Symphyotrichum oblongifolium* (Nutt.) Nesom (127) (1933) ND

Blue prairie violet - *Viola nephrophylla* Greene (4) (1986)

Blue rattlebush [Blue rattle-bush] - *Baptisia australis* (L.) R. Br. ex Aiton f. (158) (1900)

Blue Ridge basswood [Blueridge basswood] - *Tilia americana* L. var. *americana* (155) (1942)

Blue Ridge blueberry [Blueridge blueberry] - *Vaccinium pallidum* Aiton (50, 138, 155) (1923–present)

Blue Ridge carrionflower [Blueridge carrionflower, Blue Ridge carrionflower] - *Smilax lasioneura* Hook. (50) (present)

Blue Ridge linden [Blueridge linden] - *Tilia americana* L. var. *americana* (155) (1942)

Blue rocket - *Aconitum napellus* L. (156) (1923)

Blue ruin - *Muhlenbergia uniflora* (Muhl.) Fern. (78) (1898) ME

Blue sage - *Artemisia cana* Pursh (101) (1905), *Artemisia tridentata* Nutt. (156) (1923), *Salvia* ×*superba* Stapf [*sylvestris* × *villicaulis*] (82) (1930) IA, *Salvia azurea* Michx. ex Lam. (4) (1986), *Salvia reflexa* Hornem. (80) (1913)

Blue scarlet-pimpernel [Blue scarlet pimpernel] - *Anagallis arvensis* L. subsp. *foemina* (Mill.) Schinz & Thellung (92) (1876)

Blue scorpion-grass - *Myosotis stricta* Link ex Roemer & J.A. Schultes (156) (1923), *Myosotis versicolor* (Pers.) J.E. Smith (156) (1923)

Blue seal [Blew seal] - *Polygonatum pubescens* (Willd.) Pursh (46) (1671)

Blue sedge - *Carex glaucodea* Tuckerm. ex Olney (50) (present)

Blue selaginella - *Selaginella uncinata* (Desv. ex Poir.) Spring (138) (1923)

Blue skullcap [Blue skull-cap, Blue scullcap] - *Scutellaria lateriflora* L. (3, 5, 50, 58, 85, 92, 93, 97, 156) (1869–present)

Blue Spanish fir - *Abies procera* Rehd. (138, 155) (1923-1942)

Blue speedwell - *Pseudolysimachion longifolium* (L.) Opiz (82) (1930) IA

Blue spring daisy [Blue spring-daisy] - *Erigeron pulchellus* Michx. (5, 156, 158) (1900–1923)

Blue spruce - *Picea mariana* (Mill.) Britton, Sterns & Poggenb. (5) (1913), *Picea pungens* Engelm. (50, 136, 149) (1904–present)

Blue stickseed - *Lappula squarrosa* (Retz.) Dumort. (3, 4) (1977-1986)

Blue stokesia - *Stokesia laevis* (Hill) Greene (86) (1878)

Blue succory - *Cichorium intybus* L. (6) (1892)

Blue Texas star - *Amsonia ciliata* Walt. var. *texana* (Gray) Coult. (124) (1937), *Amsonia* Walt. (122) (1937)

Blue thistle [Blue-thistle] - *Cirsium vulgare* (Savi) Ten. (5, 156) (1913-1923), *Echium vulgare* L. (5, 7, 19, 75, 92, 106, 156, 157, 158) (1828-1930), *Eryngium articulatum* Hook. (106) (1930)

Blue thornapple [Blue thorn apple] - *Datura stramonium* L. (42) (1814)

Blue threeawn - *Aristida purpurea* Nutt. var. *nealleyi* (Vasey) Allred (50, 155) (1942–present)

Blue toadflax [Blue toad flax, Blue toad-flax] - *Nuttallanthus canadensis* (L.) D.A. Sutton (5, 72, 93, 95, 97, 122, 131) (1899–1937), *Nuttallanthus texanus* (Scheele) D.A. Sutton (124) (1937)

Blue torenia - *Torenia fournieri* Linden ex E. Fourn. (138) (1923)

Blue valerian - *Polemonium reptans* L. (77) (1898) Parke Co. IN

Blue verbena - *Verbena hastata* L. (155) (1942)

Blue vervain - *Verbena hastata* L. (3, 4, 46, 58, 62, 63, 72, 80, 82, 85, 93, 97, 106, 122, 127, 131, 138, 156, 157, 158) (1869-1986), *Verbena officinalis* L. (156) (1923), *Verbena stricta* Vent. (92, 145) (1876-1897)

Blue vetch - *Vicia cracca* L. (5, 156, 158) (1900-1923)

Blue vine-snapdragon [Blue vine snapdragon] - *Maurandella antirrhiniflora* (Humb. & Bonpl. ex Willd.) Rothm. (124) (1937) TX

Blue violet - *Viola lanceolata* L. (124) (1937), *Viola nephrophylla* Greene (82, 127) (1930-1933), *Viola palmata* L. (85) (1932), *Viola pedata* L. (48, 49, 92) (1876-1898)

Blue waxweed [Blue wax weed] - *Cuphea* P. Br. (1) (1932), *Cuphea viscosissima* Jacq (3, 4, 5, 50, 86, 97, 156) (1878–present)

Blue whortleberry - *Gaylussacia frondosa* (L.) Torr. & Gray (5, 19, 49, 92) (1840-1913)

Blue wild indigo [Blue wild-indigo, Blue wildindigo] - *Baptisia australis* (L.) R. Br. ex Aiton f. (5, 50, 138, 155) (1913–present)

Blue wild rye [Blue wildrye] - *Elymus glaucus* Buckl. (3, 50, 109, 155) (1942–present)

Blue wood-aster [Blue wood aster] - *Symphyotrichum cordifolium* (L.) Nesom (62, 95, 109, 138) (1911-1949)

Blue wood-lettuce [Blue wood lettuce] - *Lactuca biennis* (Moench) Fern. (3, 4) (1977-1986)

Blue woodruff [Blew woodroofe] - *Asperula arvensis* L. (50, 178) (1526–present)

Blue-ash [Blue ash] - *Syringa vulgaris* L. (5, 156) (1913-1923)

Bluebanners [Blue-banners] - *Campanula rotundifolia* L. (158) (1900)

Bluebead [Blue bead] - *Caryopteris* Bunge (109, 138) (1923-1949), *Clintonia borealis* (Ait.) Raf. (50, 156) (1923–present), *Lupinus argenteus* Pursh (148) (1939)

Bluebell [Blue-bell, Blue bell, Blue bells, Blue-bells] - *Aquilegia vulgaris* L. (5, 76, 156) (1896-1923) Northern OH, *Campanula* L. (1, 93) (1932-1936), *Campanula rotundifolia* L. (95, 105, 109, 127, 155, 156, 158) (1900-1932), *Clematis crispa* L. (5, 156) (1913-1923), *Gentiana catesbaei* Walt. (7, 92) (1828-1876), *Glechoma hederacea* L. (77) (1898) Cambridge MA, *Mertensia paniculata* (Aiton) G. Don. (35, 85) (1806-1923), *Mertensia* Roth (1, 50, 93, 109 138, 155) (1923–present), *Mertensia virginica* (L.) Pers. ex Link (possibly) (5, 63, 156) (1899–1923), *Muscari botryoides* (L.) Mills (5, 73, 156, 158) (1892-1923) Chestertown MD, *Nemophila menziesii* Hook. & Arn. var. *menziesii* (75) (1894) Santa Barbara CA, *Polemonium reptans* L. (5, 49, 73, 92, 156, 158) (1879-1923) Mansfield O, *Polemonium vanbruntiae* Britton (156) (1923), *Veronica americana* Schwein. ex Benth. (75, 156, 158) (1894-1923) Fort Fairfield ME

Bluebell bellflower - *Campanula rotundifolia* L. (50) (present)

Bluebell creeper [Bluebell-creeper] - *Sollya* Lindl. (138) (1923)

Bluebell of Scotland [Blue bells of Scotland, Bluebells-of-Scotland] - *Campanula rotundifolia* L. (5, 46, 86, 93, 156) (1878-1936)

Bluebell phacelia - *Phacelia minor* (Harvey) Thellung ex F. Zimmerman (138) (1923)

Blueberry [Blueberries, Blue berries, Blue berry] - *Caulophyllum thalictroides* (L.) Michx. (5, 6, 7, 58, 92, 156) (1828-1923), *Gaylussacia frondosa* (L.) Torr. & Gray (92, 187) (1818-1876), *Lantana* L. (7) (1828), *Vaccinium angustifolium* Aiton (40) (1928), *Vaccinium* L. (1, 4, 50, 105, 106, 138, 155, 156) (1923–present), *Vaccinium myrtilloides* Michx. (156) (1923), *Vaccinium ovalifolium* J.E. Smith (106) (1930), *Vaccinium pallidum* Aiton (103) (1870), *Vaccinium uliginosum* L. (106) (1930), *Vaccinium vitis-idaea* L. (106) (1930)

Blue-berry cohosh [Blueberry cohosh] - *Caulophyllum thalictroides* (L.) Michx. (7) (1828)

Blue-berry cornel [Blueberry cornel, Blue berry cornel, Blue-berried cornel, Blueberry cornell] - *Cornus amomum* Mill. (5, 156, 157, 158) (1900–1929), *Cornus sericea* L. (6, 7, 92, 187) (1818-1932)

Blue-berry cornus [Blue-berried cornus] - *Cornus sericea* L. (186) (1814)

Blue-berry dogwood [Blue berry dog wood, Blueberry dogwood, Blue-berried dogwood] - *Cornus sericea* L. (42, 186) (1814)

Blue-berry elder [Blueberry elder] - *Sambucus nigra* L. subsp. *cerulea* (Raf.) R. Bolli (138) (1923)

Blue-berry root [Blueberry-root] - *Caulophyllum thalictroides* (L.) Michx. (5, 64, 156, 157, 158) (1900–1929)

Bluebill - *Clematis pitcheri* Torr. & Gray (50) (present)

Blueblossom [Blue-blossom] - *Ceanothus thyrsiflorus* Esch. (109, 138) (1923-1949)

Blueblow [Blue-blow] - *Centaurea cyanus* L. (157, 158) (1900-1929)

Bluebonnet [Blue bonnets, Blue-bonnets, Bluebonnets] - *Centaurea cyanus* L. (5, 92, 157, 158) (1876-1913), *Lupinus* L. (1, 93) (1932-1936), *Lupinus subcarnosus* Hook. (106, 122) (1930-1937)

Blue-bonnet-white-apron - *Collinsia verna* Nutt. (156) (1923)

Bluebottle [Blue-bottle, Blue bottle, Blue bottles] - *Campanula rotundifolia* L. (158) (1900), *Centaurea cyanus* L. (5, 7, 10, 14, 19, 42, 92, 93, 106, 109, 114, 131, 156, 157, 158) (1814-1949), *Centaurea* L. (1, 158, 167) (1814-1900), *Muscari botryoides* (L.) Mills (5, 73, 156) (1892-1923) Mansfield O

Bluebowls - *Gilia rigidula* Benth. (50) (present)

Bluebuttons [Blue-buttons, Blue buttons] - *Knautia arvensis* (L.) Duby (3, 4, 5, 156, 158) (1900-1986)

Bluecaps [Blue caps, Blue-caps] - *Centaurea cyanus* L. (5, 156, 157, 158) (1900-1929), *Knautia arvensis* (L.) Duby (4, 5, 156, 158) (1900-1986)

Blue-crown passion-flower [Bluecrown passionflower] - *Passiflora caerulea* L. (138) (1923)

Bluecurls [Blue curls, Blue-curl, Blue-curls] - *Phacelia congesta* Hook. (122) (1937), *Prunella* L. (75) (1894), *Prunella vulgaris* L. (5, 156, 158) (1900–1923), *Trichostema dichotomum* L. (5, 19, 92, 106, 124, 158) (1840-1937), *Trichostema* L. (2, 4, 50, 138, 155, 158) (1894-present), *Trichostema lanceolatum* Benth. (106) (1930)

Blue-daisy [Blue daisy, Blue daisies] - *Cichorium intybus* L. (5, 76, 106, 157, 158) (1896-1929) Southold Long Island

Blue-dandelion [Blue dandelion] - *Cichorium intybus* L. (5, 73, 79, 106, 156, 157) (1891–1930) IA

Blue-devil [Blue devil, Blue devils, Blue-devils] - *Echium vulgare* L. (5, 75, 109, 156, 157, 158) (1894-1949), *Symphyotrichum lowrieanum* (Porter) Nesom (5, 75) (1894-1913) WV, *Symphyotrichum oolentangiense* (Riddell) Nesom var. *oolentangiense* (156) (1923)

Blue-eye [Blue eye, Blue eyes] - *Collinsia verna* Nutt. (156) (1923), *Papaver rhoeas* L. (5, 156) (1913-1923), *Veronica chamaedrys* L. (5, 156) (1913-1923)

Blue-eyed babies - *Houstonia caerulea* L. (5, 73, 156) (1892-1923) Springfield MA, no longer in use by 1923

Blue-eyed cape-marigold - *Dimorphotheca sinuata* DC. (138) (1923)

Blue-eyed Mary [Blue eyed Mary, Blue eyed Marys] - *Collinsia* Nutt. (1, 4, 50) (1932–present), *Collinsia parviflora* Lindl. (85) (1932) SD, *Collinsia verna* Nutt. (3, 4, 5, 72, 75, 97, 138, 156, 158) (1894-1986), *Sisyrinchium angustifolium* Mill. (5, 156, 157, 158) (1900-1929)

Blue-eyed-grass [Blue-eyed grass] - *Houstonia caerulea* L. (5, 76, 156) (1896-1923) Brodhead WI, *Sisyrinchium angustifolium* Mill. (3, 19, 46, 65, 85, 156, 157) (1840-1977), *Sisyrinchium* L. (1, 50, 92, 93, 109, 122, 124, 138, 156, 158) (1900–present), *Sisyrinchium septentrionale* Bickn. (85) (1932)

Blue-eyed-lily [Blue-eyed lily, Blue-eyed lilly] - *Sisyrinchium angustifolium* Mill. (5, 156, 157, 158) (1900-1929)

Blue-eyed-Mary collinsia - *Collinsia verna* Nutt. (155) (1942) Concord MA

Blue-flower lettuce [Blue flowered lettuce] - *Lactuca tatarica* (L.) C.A. Mey. var. *pulchella* (Pursh) Breitung (80) (1913)

Blue-flower pimpernel [Blew-flowered pimpernel] - *Veronica anagallis-aquatica* L. (46) (1671)

Blue-flower sowthistle [Blue-flowered sow-thistle] - *Lactuca floridana* (L.) Gaertn. (187) (1818)

Blue-gentian [Blue gentian] - *Isanthus brachiatus* (L.) Britton, Sterns & Poggenb. (5, 156, 158) (1900–1923), *Trichostema brachiatum* L. (19) (1840)

Blue-grass [Blue grass, Bluegrass] - *Carex panicea* L. (5, 156) (1913-1923), *Sisyrinchium angustifolium* Mill. (5, 75, 156, 158) (1894-1923) Concord MA

Bluehearts [Blue hearts, Blue-hearts] - *Buchnera americana* L. (5, 19, 97, 122, 156) (1840-1937), *Buchnera* L. (1, 2, 4, 158) (1895-1986)

Blue-iris [Blue iris] - *Mertensia virginica* (L.) Pers. ex Link (possibly) (156) (1923)

Bluejacket - *Tradescantia ohiensis* Raf. (50) (present)

Bluejoint [Blue-joint, Blue joint] - *Andropogon gerardii* Vitman (5, 45, 75, 119) (1894-1938), *Calamagrostis canadensis* (Michx.) Beauv. (3, 11, 45, 50, 56, 75, 87, 88, 115, 116, 129) (1884–present), *Elymus repens* (L.) Gould (5) (1913), *Pascopyrum smithii* (Rydb.) A. Löve (68, 134) (1890-1932), *Schizachyrium scoparium* (Michx.) Nash var. *scoparium* (5, 45) (1896-1913), *Thinopyrum intermedium* (Host) Barkworth & D.R. Dewey (45, 87, 88) (1884-1896)

Blue-joint grass [Blue joint grass] - *Andropogon gerardii* Vitman (56) (1901) IA, *Calamagrostis canadensis* (Michx.) Beauv. (56, 66, 68, 90, 92, 93) (1885-1936)

Blue-joint reed grass [Bluejoint reedgrass] - *Calamagrostis canadensis* (Michx.) Beauv. (140, 155) (1942-1944)

Blue-leaf acacia [Blueleaf acacia] - *Acacia salicina* Lindl. (138, 155) (1923-1942), *Rhododendron viscosum* (L.) Torr. (138) (1923)

Blue-leaf cinquefoil [Blueleaf cinquefoil] - *Potentilla diversifolia* Lehm. var. *diversifolia* (155) (1942)

Blue-leaf grape [Blueleaf grape] - *Vitis aestivalis* Michx. (138) (1923)

Blue-leaf honeysuckle [Blueleaf honeysuckle] - *Lonicera korolkowii* Stapf (138) (1923)

Blue-leaf noble fir [Blueleaf noble fir] - *Abies procera* Rehd. (138, 155) (1923-1942)

Blue-leaf strawberry [Blueleaf strawberry] - *Fragaria virginiana* Duchesne subsp. *glauca* (S. Wats.) Staudt (155) (1942)

Blue-leaf sundrops [Blueleaf sundrops] - *Oenothera fruticosa* L. subsp. *glauca* (Michx.) Straley (138) (1923)

Blue-leaf willow [Blueleaf willow] - *Salix myricoides* Muhl. var. *myricoides* (138, 156) (1923)

Bluelips [Blue lips] - *Collinsia grandiflora* Lindl. (138) (1923), *Collinsia* Nutt. (1) (1932), *Collinsia parviflora* Lindl. (3, 4) (1977-1986)

Bluepoint [Blue-point] - *Pascopyrum smithii* (Rydb.) A. Löve (93) (1936) SD

Blue-sailors [Blue sailors, Bluesailors] - *Cichorium intybus* L. (5, 73, 82, 93, 106, 122, 124, 156, 157, 158) (1892-1937)

Bluestar [Blue star] - *Amsonia* Walt. (4, 50) (1986–present)

Bluestem [Blue-stem, Blue stem] - *Andropogon gerardii* Vitman (40, 45, 56, 78, 87, 90, 144) (1885-1928), *Andropogon* L. (1, 50, 93, 155) (1932–present), *Echium vulgare* L. (5, 75, 156, 157, 158) (1900-1929) WV, *Pascopyrum smithii* (Rydb.) A. Löve (93, 163) (1852-1936), *Sabal minor* (Jacq.) Pers. (106) (1930), *Thinopyrum intermedium* (Host) Barkworth & D.R. Dewey (45, 67, 87, 88) (1885-1896)

Blue-stem goldenrod [Blue-stem golden-rod, Blue-stemmed goldenrod, Blue-stemmed goldenrod] - *Solidago caesia* L. (5, 19, 72, 97, 156) (1840-1937)

Blue-stem grass [Bluestem grass] - *Pascopyrum smithii* (Rydb.) A. Löve (101, 122) (1905-1937), *Schizachyrium scoparium* (Michx.) Nash (5) (1913)

Blue-stem joepye weed [Bluestem joepyeweed] - *Eupatorium purpureum* L. (155) (1942)

Blue-stem palmetto [Bluestem palmetto] - *Sabal minor* (Jacq.) Pers. (138) (1923)

Blue-stem wheat grass [Bluestem wheatgrass] - *Pascopyrum smithii* (Rydb.) A. Löve (140, 155) (1942-1944)

Blue-stem willow [Bluestem willow] - *Salix irrorata* Anderss. (138) (1923)

Bluet (French) - *Centaurea cyanus* L. (158) (1900)

Bluetangle [Blue-tangle, Blue tangle, Blue tangles, Blue-tangles] - *Gaylussacia frondosa* (L.) Torr. & Gray (2, 5, 92, 107, 156, 187) (1818-1923)

Blue-thistle - *Cirsium vulgare* (Savi) Ten. (158) (1900)

Bluetops [Blue tops, Blue-tops] - *Centaurea nigra* L. (5, 156) (1913-1923) no longer in use by 1923

Bluets [Bluet] - *Centaurea cyanus* L. (106) (1930), *Gaylussacia frondosa* (L.) Torr. & Gray (92) (1876), *Hedyotis* L. (4) (1986), *Hedyotis nigricans* (Lam.) Fosberg var. *nigricans* (156) (1923), *Houstonia caerulea* L. (2, 5, 86, 109, 138, 156, 187) (1818-1949), *Houstonia* L. (1, 50, 155, 156, 158) (1900–present), *Houstonia longifolia* Gaertn. (3) (1977), *Oldenlandia* L. (158) (1900), *Vaccinium* L. (73) (1892) New Brunswick, French Canadians

Blue-tulip [Bluetulip, Blue tulip] - *Pulsatilla* Mill. (1) (1932)

Bluevine [Blue-vine] - *Cynanchum laeve* (Michx.) Pers. (106, 156) (1923-1930)

Blueweed [Blue-weed, Blue weed] - *Echium* L. (1, 4) (1932-1986), *Echium vulgare* L. (3, 5, 62, 63, 75, 77, 92, 106, 109, 156, 157, 158) (1876-1977), *Helianthus ciliaris* DC. (150) (1894) NM

Bluewood [Blue-wood] - *Condalia hookeri* M.C. Johnston var. *hookeri* (107) (1919), *Symphoricarpos albus* (L.) Blake var. *albus* (38) (1820), *Symphoricarpos* Duham. (possibly) (7) (1828)

Bluff pine - *Pinus ponderosa* P.& C. Lawson (108) (1878)

Bluish Cherry [Blewish Cherrie] - *Prunus cerasus* L. (178) (1526)

Blum Wolfsmilch (German) - *Euphorbia corollata* L. (7) (1828)

Blunt broom sedge - *Carex tribuloides* Wahl. (5, 50) (1913–present), *Carex tribuloides* Wahl. var. *tribuloides* (50, 72) (1907–present)

Blunt hair grass - *Sphenopholis obtusata* (Michx.) Scribn. (42) (1814)

Blunt manna grass - *Glyceria obtusa* (Muhl.) Trin. (5) (1913)

Blunt panic grass [Blunt panic-grass] - *Panicum obtusum* H.B.K. (5, 99, 119) (1913-1938)

Blunt spike-rush [Blunt spike rush] - *Eleocharis engelmanni* Steud. (5, 50) (1913–present), *Eleocharis obtusa* (Willd.) J.A. Schultes (120) (1938)

Blunt spike-sedge [Blunt spikesedge] - *Eleocharis ovata* (Roth) Roemer & J.A. Schultes (3) (1977)

Blunted spurge - *Euphorbia spathulata* Lam (122) (1937)

Blunt-flower meadow grass [Blunt-flowered meadow-grass] - *Glyceria obtusa* (Muhl.) Trin. (187) (1818)

Blunt-fruit sweet cicely [Blunt-fruited sweet cicely] - *Osmorhiza depauperata* Phil. (5) (1913)

Blunt-leaf bedstraw [Bluntleaf bedstraw] - *Galium obtusum* Bigelow (3, 4, 50) (1977–present)

Blunt-leaf cress [Blunt leaved cress] - *Rorippa teres* (Michx.) R. Stuckey (72) (1907)

Blunt-leaf dock [Blunt leaf dock, Blunt leaved dock, Blunt-leaved dock] - *Rumex obtusifolius* L. (5, 6, 49, 58, 64, 69, 92, 156, 157, 158) (1869-1929)

Blunt-leaf inga [Blunt leaved inga] - *Pithecellobium unguis-cati* (L.) Benth. (20) (1857)

Blunt-leaf milkweed [Blunt leaf milkweed] - *Asclepias amplexicaulis* Sm. (3, 4, 5, 72, 82, 93, 97, 122, 124) (1907-1986)

Blunt-leaf moerhingia [Blunt-leaved moerhingia] - *Moehringia lateriflora* (L.) Fenzl (5) (1913)

Blunt-leaf orchid [Bluntleaved orchid] - *Platanthera obtusata* (Banks ex Pursh) Lindl. (50) (present)

Blunt-leaf pondweed [Bluntleaf pondweed] - *Potamogeton obtusifolius* Mert. & Koch (3, 5, 50, 155) (1913–present)

Blunt-leaf sandwort [Bluntleaf sandwort] - *Moehringia lateriflora* (L.) Fenzl (50, 5, 72, 131, 155) (1899–present)

Blunt-leaf spurge [Blunt-leaved spurge] - *Euphorbia spathulata* Lam (5, 72, 93, 97) (1907-1937)

Blunt-leaf willow [Blunt-leaved willow] - *Salix ×obtusata* Fernald [*myricoides × pyrifolia*] (5) (1913), *Salix scouleriana* Barr. (20) (1857)

Blunt-leaf yellow cress [Blunt-leaved yellow cress, Blunt-leaf yellowcress, Bluntleaf yellowcress] - *Rorippa curvipes* Greene (50) (present), *Rorippa teres* (Michx.) R. Stuckey (5, 97) (1913-1937)

Blunt-lobe cliff fern [Bluntlobe cliff fern] - *Woodsia obtusa* (Spreng.) Torr. (50) (present)

Blunt-lobe fern [Blunt-lobed fern] - *Woodsia obtusa* (Spreng.) Torr. (97) (1937)

Blunt-lobe woodsia [Blunt-lobed woodsia] - *Woodsia obtusa* (Spreng.) Torr. (3, 4, 72, 109) (1907-1986)

Blunt-scale bahia [Bluntscale bahia] - *Bahia pedata* Gray (50) (present)

Blunt-scale eatonia [Blunt scaled eatonia] - *Sphenopholis obtusata* (Michx.) Scribn. (56, 72) (1901-1907)

Blunt-scale grass [Blunt scaled grass] - *Sphenopholis obtusata* (Michx.) Scribn. (134, 140) (1932-1944)

Blunt-scale sphenopholis [Blunt-scaled sphenopholis] - *Sphenopholis obtusata* (Michx.) Scribn. (119) (1938)

Blunt-seed sweetroot [Bluntseed sweetroot] - *Osmorhiza depauperata* Phil. (50, 155) (1942–present)

Blunt-tooth blanket-flower [Blunt-toothed blanketflower] - *Gaillardia amblyodon* J. Gay (86) (1878)

Blur grape - *Vitis aestivalis* Michx. (97) (1937)

Blush stonecrop - *Hylotelephium erythrostictum* (Miq.) H. Ohba. (138) (1923)

Blust - *Humulus lupulus* L. (110) (1886)

Blutfennich (Bohemian) - *Digitaria sanguinalis* (L.) Scop. (67) (1890)

Blutkraut (German) - *Sanguinaria canadensis* L. (158) (1900)

Blutwurzel (German) - *Sanguinaria canadensis* L. (6, 158) (1892-1900)

Bo (Osage) - *Viburnum prunifolium* L. (121) (1918?-1970?)

Bo tree [Bo-tree] - *Ficus religiosa* L. (109) (1949)

Boar thistle [Boar-thistle] - *Cirsium arvense* (L.) Scop. (157, 158) (1900-1929), *Cirsium vulgare* (Savi) Ten. (5, 75, 156, 158) (1894-1923) WV

Board pine - *Pinus strobus* L. (possibly) (46) (1879)

Bobartia - *Echinacea purpurea* (L.) Moench (174) (1753)

Bob's root - *Orbexilum pedunculatum* (P. Mill.) Rydb. (5, 49, 156) (1898-1923)

Bocconia - *Macleaya cordata* (Willd.) R. Br. (92, 114) (1876-1894)

Bockstorchschnabel (German) - *Geranium robertianum* L. (158) (1900)

Bodark - *Maclura pomifera* (Raf.) Schneid. (158) (1900)

Bodin's milkvetch [Bodin milk vetch] - *Astragalus bodinii* Sheldon (4, 50) (1986–present)

Bodmon sok (Kalmuck) - *Phlomis tuberosa* L. (107) (1919)

Boebera - *Dyssodia papposa* (Vent.) A.S. Hitchc. (125) (1930) KS

Bofareira - *Ricinus communis* L. (92) (1876)

Bog arum - *Calla palustris* L. (86) (1878)

Bog asphodel - *Abama* Adans. (158) (1900), *Narthecium americanum* Ker-Gawl. (156) (1923)

Bog aster - *Oclemena nemoralis* (Aiton) Greene (5, 155) (1913–1942), *Symphyotrichum ×longulum* (Sheldon) Nesom [*boreale × puniceum*] (85) (1932), *Symphyotrichum puniceum* (L.) A. & D. Löve var. *puniceum* (4) (1986)

Bog bedstraw - *Galium labradoricum* Wiegand (155) (1942)

Bog bilberry - *Vaccinium tenellum* Aiton (174, 177) (1753-1762), *Vaccinium uliginosum* L. (5, 107, 156) (1913-1923)

Bog birch - *Betula nana* L. (1) (1932), *Betula pumila* L. (50) (present), *Betula pumila* L. var. *glandulifera* Regel (4, 50) (1986–present), *Frangula caroliniana* (Walt.) Gray (5, 156) (1913-1923)

Bog blueberry [Bog blue-berry] - *Vaccinium uliginosum* L. (5, 156) (1913-1923)

Bog bulrush - *Schoenoplectus mucronatus* (L.) Palla (156) (1923)

Bog club-moss - *Lycopodiella inundata* (L.) Holub (5) (1913)

Bog cord grass [Bog cordgrass] - *Spartina cynosuroides* (L.) Roth (50) (present)

Bog cotton - *Eriophorum* L. (156) (1923)

Bog fern - *Thelypteris simulata* (Davenport) Nieuwl. (50) (present)

Bog fleabane - *Erigeron lonchophyllus* Hook. (85) (1932)

Bog goldenrod [Bog goldenrod] - *Solidago uliginosa* Nutt. (5, 72) (1907-1913)

Bog hemp - *Boehmeria cylindrica* (L.) Sw. (3) (1977)

Bog hop - *Menyanthes trifoliata* L. (156, 158) (1900-1923)

Bog kalmia - *Kalmia polifolia* Wangenh. (109, 138) (1923-1949)

Bog Labrador tea - *Ledum groenlandicum* Oeder (50) (present)

Bog marsh cress [Bog marshcress] - *Rorippa palustris* (L.) Bess. (155) (1942)

Bog moss [Bog-moss] - *Sphagnum palustre* L. (107, 184) (1793-1919)

Bog muhly - *Muhlenbergia uniflora* (Muhl.) Fern. (50) (present)

Bog myrtle - *Myrica gale* L. (5, 14, 19, 156) (1840-1923)

Bog orchid - *Habenaria* Willd. (50) (present), *Platanthera hyperborea* (L.) Lindl. var. *viridiflora* (Cham.) Luer (85) (1932), *Platanthera* L.C. Rich (1, 93) (1932-1936)

Bog panic grass [Bog panic-grass] - *Dichanthelium dichotomum* (L.) Gould var. *dichotomum* (163) (1852)

Bog panicum - *Dichanthelium dichotomum* (L.) Gould var. *dichotomum* (5) (1913)

Bog reed [Bog-reed] - *Phragmites australis* (Cav.) Trin. ex Steud. (5, 119) (1913-1938)

Bog reed grass [Bog reed-grass] - *Calamagrostis stricta* (Timm) Koel. subsp. *inexpansa* (Gray) C.W. Greene (5, 56, 85, 93, 94, 116) (1901-1958)

Bog rhubarb - *Petasites hybridus* (L.) G. Gaertn., B. Mey. & Scherb. (5) (1913)

Bog rose - *Arethusa bulbosa* L. (156) (1923)

Bog rosemary - *Andromeda* L. (138) (1923), *Andromeda polifolia* L. var. *glaucophylla* (Link) DC. (156) (1923)

Bog rush [Bogrush] - *Juncus bufonius* L. (85) (1932) SD, *Juncus effusus* L. (5, 28, 120, 156) (1850-1938), *Juncus effusus* L. var. *solutus* Fern. & Wieg. (3) (1977), *Juncus* L. (41, 158) (1770-1900), *Kyllinga brevifolia* Rottb. (possibly) (92) (1876), *Schoenus* L. (10, 50) (1818–present)

Bog sedge - *Carex magellanica* Lam. subsp. *irrigua* (Wahlenb.) Hultén (5) (1913), *Carex nigra* (L.) Reichard (66) (1903)

Bog star - *Parnassia palustris* L. (127) (1933) ND

Bog starwort [Bog-starwort] - *Stellaria alsine* Grimm (5, 19, 187) (1818-1913)

Bog stitchwort - *Stellaria alsine* Grimm (5, 156, 187) (1818-1923)

Bog violet - *Viola nephrophylla* Greene (85) (1932) SD

Bog white violet - *Viola lanceolata* L. (50) (present)

Bog whortle-berry [Bog whortleberry] - *Vaccinium uliginosum* L. (5, 156) (1913-1923)

Bog willow [Bog-willow] - *Salix candida* Flueggé ex Willd. (85) (1932), *Salix discolor* Muhl. (5, 19, 156, 158) (1840-1923), *Salix pedicellaris* Pursh (1, 4, 5, 50, 72, 131, 155, 156) (1899–present)

Bog willowherb - *Epilobium leptophyllum* Raf. (50) (present)

Bog wintergreen - *Pyrola asarifolia* Michx. (5, 85, 156) (1913-1932)

Bog yellow cress - *Rorippa palustris* (L.) Bess. (4, 50) (1986–present)

Bogbean [Bog-bean, Bog bean] - *Menyanthes* L. (1, 138, 155) (1923-1942), *Menyanthes trifoliata* L. (5, 6, 49, 92, 109, 131, 156, 158) (1892-1949)

Bogberry [Bog berry] - *Vaccinium oxycoccos* L. (5) (1913), *Rubus pubescens* Raf. var. *pubescens* (156) (1923)

Bogleaves [Bog leaves] - *Hylotelephium telephium* (L.) H. Ohba. subsp. *telephium* (5) (1913)

Bog-myrtle [Bog myrtle] - *Menyanthes trifoliata* L. (5, 92, 156, 158) (1876-1923) ME

Bognut [Bog-nut, Bog nut] - *Menyanthes trifoliata* L. (5, 156, 158) (1900–1923)

Bog-onion [Bog onion] - *Arisaema triphyllum* (L.) Schott (64, 73, 78, 92, 157) (1876-1908), *Osmunda regalis* L. (158) (1900)

Bog-rhubarb - *Petasites hybridus* (L.) G. Gaertn., B. Mey. & Scherb. (156) (1923)

Bog-rosemary [Bog rosemary] - *Andromeda polifolia* L. (138, 156) (1923)

Bog-rosemary andromeda [Bogrosemary andromeda] - *Andromeda polifolia* L. (155) (1942)

Bog-rush - *Cladium mariscoides* (Muhl.) Torr. (156) (1923)

Bog-strawberry [Bog strawberry] - *Comarum palustre* L. (5, 156) (1913-1923)

Bog-violet [Bog violet] - *Pinguicula vulgaris* L. (5, 156) (1913-1923)

Bogwort [Bog wort] - *Vaccinium oxycoccos* L. (5) (1913)

Bohea tea - *Smilax herbacea* L. (19) (1840)

Bois à perdix (French, shrub for partridges) - *Shepherdia argentea* (Pursh) Nutt. (41) (1770)

Bois blanc (French) - *Liriodendron tulipifera* L. (43) (1820)

Bois blanc (French, white wood) - *Tilia americana* L. (41) (1770)

Bois bouton (French) - *Cephalanthus* L. (8) (1785), *Cephalanthus occidentalis* L. (8) (1785), *Cornus florida* L. (7) (1828)

Bois connu (Illinois French) - *Celtis occidentalis* L. (17) (1796)

Bois d'arc (French) - *Maclura pomifera* (Raf.) Schneid. (2, 20, 30, 37, 44, 78, 121, 124, 156, 158, 164) (1844-1937)

Bois de couleuvre (French) - *Colubrina arborescens* (P. Mill.) Sargent (20) (1857)

Bois de cuir (French) - *Dirca palustris* L. (8) (1785)

Bois de diable (French) - *Acer circinatum* Pursh (33) (1827)

Bois de fleche (French, Louisiana Purchase) - *Cornus florida* L. (7) (1828)

Bois de Marais (French, Louisiana Purchase) - *Cephalanthus occidentalis* L. (7) (1828)

Bois de marque (French) - *Ilex* L. (41) (1770)

Bois de plomb (French Canadian lead wood) - *Dirca palustris* L. (6, 7, 41) (1770-1892)

Bois de plomb (French) - *Cephalanthus occidentalis* L. (6) (1892)

Bois d'orignal (French, elk wood) - *Acer spicatum* Lam. (41) (1770)

Bois dur (French) - *Carpinus* L. (41) (1770), *Ostrya carpinifolia* Scop. (20) (1857), *Ulmus americana* L. (8) (1785)

Bois inconnu (Illinois French, New Orleans, Illinois) - *Celtis occidentalis* L. (17, 20) (1796) Illinois French

Bois jaune (French, yellow wood) - *Liriodendron tulipifera* L. (17, 186) (1796-1814), *Maclura pomifera* (Raf.) Schneid. (39) (1814)

Bois noir (French, black wood) - *Acer spicatum* Lam. (41) (1770), *Cercis canadensis* L. (17) (1796)

Bois retors (French) - *Celastrus scandens* L. (103) (1870)

Bois rouge (French) - *Cornus sericea* L. (35) (1806) Meriwether Lewis, *Cornus sericea* L. subsp. *sericea* (35, 101) (1806-1905)

Bois shavanon (French Creole) - *Catalpa ovata* G. Don (17, 20) (1796-1857)

Boisduvalia - *Epilobium* L. (158) (1900)

Boisivrant de la Jamaique (French) - *Piscidia piscipula* (L.) Sargent (20) (1857)

Boispuant (French, Louisiana Purchase) - *Ptelea* L. (7) (1828) Louisiana Purchase

Bokara clover - *Melilotus officinalis* (L.) Lam. (possibly) (129) (1894)

Bokhara clover - *Melilotus officinalis* (L.) Lam. (possibly) (5, 45, 68, 82, 156, 157, 158) (1896-1929)

Bolander's bladdernut [Bolander bladdernut] - *Staphylea bolanderi* Gray (138) (1923)

Bolander's onion [Bolander onion] - *Allium bolanderi* S. Wats. (155) (1942)

Bolander's sagebrush [Bolander sagebrush] - *Artemisia cana* Pursh subsp. *bolanderi* (Gray) G.H. Ward (155) (1942)

Bolander's spear-grass - *Poa bolanderi* Vasey (94) (1901)

Bolander's water hemlock [Bolander waterhemlock] - *Cicuta maculata* L. var. *bolanderi* (S. Wats.) Mulligan (155) (1942)

Bolays - *Prunus domestica* L. var. *insititia* (L.) Fiori & Paoletti (179) (1526)

Bolbonac - *Lunaria annua* L. (107, 180) (1633-1919)

Bolder - *Schoenoplectus tabernaemontani* (K.C. Gmel.) Palla (156, 158) (1900-1923)

Bolean birch - *Betula papyrifera* Marsh (5, 157, 158) (1900-1929)

Boletus - *Fomitopsis officinalis* (Batsch) Bondartsev & Singer (52) (1919)

Boletus (of the oak) - *Phellinus igniarius* (L.) Quél. (92) (1876)

Boleweed [Bole weed] - *Centaurea nigra* L. (5) (1913)

Bolewort [Bole wort] - *Ptilimnium capillaceum* (Michx.) Raf. (5, 156) (1913-1923)

Bolgan leaves - *Lapsana communis* L. (5) (1913)

Bolle (German) - *Allium cepa* L. (158) (1900)

Bolleana poplar - *Populus alba var. pyramidalis* Bunge (112, 138) (1923-1937)

Bolle's poplar [Bolles poplar] - *Populus alba* L. (135) (1910)

Bolo-root - *Sanguinaria canadensis* L. (156) (1923)

Boltonia - *Boltonia* L'Hér. (82, 138, 155, 158) (1900-1930)

Bolton's aster - *Boltonia diffusa* Ell. (124) (1937)

Bombast - *Gossypium herbaceum* L. (178) (1526)

Bonaparte's crown [Bonaparte's-crown] - *Euphorbia cyparissias* L. (5, 156, 158) (1900-1923) no longer in use by 1923

Bonavist - *Lablab purpureus* (L.) Sweet (109, 183) (~1756-1949)

Bonavista bean - *Lablab purpureus* (L.) Sweet (107) (1919)

Bonduc - *Caesalpinia bonduc* (L.) Roxb. (52) (1919), *Caesalpinia* L. (8) (1785), *Gymnocladus dioicus* (L.) K. Koch (38) (1820)

Bonduc nuts - *Caesalpinia bonduc* (L.) Roxb. (92) (1876)

Bondue - *Gymnocladus dioicus* (L.) K. Koch (6, 7) (1828-1932)

Boneflower [Bone flower, Bone-flower] - *Bellis perennis* L. (5, 158) (1900-1913)

Boneset - *Ageratina altissima* (L.) King & H.E. Robins. (80) (1913) IA, *Eupatorium* L. (1, 2, 93, 106, 109, 122, 156) (1895-1936), *Eupatorium perfoliatum* L. (3, 4, 5, 6, 7, 12, 19, 40, 49, 52, 53, 55, 57, 58, 59, 61, 62, 63, 69, 72, 92, 93, 105, 114, 122, 124, 131, 138, 155, 156, 157, 158, 186, 187) (1814-1986), *Eupatorium rotundifolium* L. (80) (1913), *Symphytum officinale* L. (5, 107, 156) (1913-1923)

Bone-tree - *Sambucus nigra* L. (158) (1900)

Bonewort [Bone wort] - *Bellis perennis* L. (5, 158, 179) (1526-1913), *Solanum nigrum* L. (77) (1898) Western US

Bongay - *Aesculus hippocastanum* L. (5, 156) (1913-1923)

Bonjean's dicranum moss - *Dicranum bonjeanii* De Not in Lisa (50) (present)

Bonnet grass - *Agrostis capillaris* L. (45) (1896), *Agrostis gigantea* Roth (5, 19, 66, 92) (1840-1912)

Bonnet pepper - *Capsicum annuum* L. (92, 107) (1876-1919)

Bonneted hazel - *Corylus americana* Walt. (95, 97, 113, 130, 156) (1890–1937)

Bonnets - *Nuphar lutea* (L.) Sm. subsp. *advena* (Aiton) Kartesz & Gandhi (74, 158) (1893-1900)

Bonny-dame [Bonny-dame] - *Atriplex hortensis* L. (92, 158) (1876-1900)

Bonny-rabbits [Bonny rabbits] - *Antirrhinum majus* L. (5) (1913)

Bonseet - *Eupatorium perfoliatum* L. (7) (1828)

Bonsenkraut (German) - *Symplocarpus foetidus* (L.) Salisb. ex Nutt. (186) (1814)

Boor tree [Boor-tree] - *Sambucus nigra* L. (92, 158) (1876-1900), *Sambucus racemosa* L. (5, 156) (1913-1923)

Bootjack [Boot-jack, Bootjacks, Boot jacks] - *Bidens aristosa* (Michx.) Britton (124) (1937), *Bidens discoidea* (Torr. & Gray) Britton (80) (1913), *Bidens frondosa* L. (80) (1913), *Bidens* L. (106) (1930)

Boots - *Caltha palustris* L. (5) (1913), *Viburnum prunifolium* L. (158) (1900)

Boott's goldenrod [Boott's golden-rod, Boott goldenrod] - *Solidago arguta var. boottii* (Hook.) Palmer & Steyermark (5, 97, 122, 138) (1913-1937)

Boott's rattlesnake-root [Boott's rattlesnakeroot] - *Prenanthes boottii* (DC.) Gray (5) (1913)

Boott's sedge - *Carex picta* Steud. (5, 50) (1913–present)

Boott's shield-fern - *Dryopteris ×boottii* (Tuckerman) Underwood [*cristata × intermedia*] (5, 50) (1913–present)

Boott's woodfern [Boott woodfern] - *Dryopteris ×boottii* (Tuckerman) Underwood (pro sp.) [*cristata × intermedia*] (138) (1923)

Borage - *Borago* L. (1, 50, 82, 109, 138) (1923–present), *Borago officinalis* L. (5, 19, 57, 92, 106, 107, 156, 184) (1793-1930)

Borden's grass - *Agrostis capillaris* L. (87) (1884)

Bore tree [Bore-tree] - *Sambucus nigra* L. (158) (1900), *Sambucus nigra* L. subsp. *canadensis* (L.) R. Bolli (156) (1923), *Sambucus racemosa* L. (5, 35, 156) (1806-1923) no longer in use by 1923

Boreal bog sedge - *Carex magellanica* Lam. subsp. *irrigua* (Wahlenb.) Hultén (50) (present)

Boreal sourdock [Boreal sour dock] - *Oxyria digyna* (L.) Hill (7, 92) (1828-1876)

Boreal sweetvetch - *Hedysarum boreale* Nutt. (50) (present)

Borecole - *Brassica* L. (107) (1919), *Brassica oleracea* L. (14) (1882)

Bosc's goosefoot - *Chenopodium standleyanum* Aellen (72, 93, 97, 131) (1899-1907)

Bosc's panic grass [Bosc's panicgrass] - *Dichanthelium boscii* (Poir.) Gould & C.A. Clark (50) (present)

Bosc's panicum - *Dichanthelium boscii* (Poir.) Gould & C.A. Clark (5) (1913)

Bosc's paspalum - *Paspalum boscianum* Flueggé (5) (1913)

Bosc's thorn - *Crataegus flabellata* (Spach) Kirchn. (5) (1913)

Boston ivy - *Parthenocissus tricuspidata* (Sieb. & Zucc.) Planch. (106, 109) (1930-1949)

Boston pink - *Saponaria officinalis* L. (5, 64, 74, 156, 157, 158) (1893-1929)

Boston smilax - *Asparagus asparagoides* (L.) Druce (92) (1876)

Botany baybkino - *Eucalyptus resinifera* Sm. (92) (1876)

Bottery tree [Bottery-tree] - *Sambucus nigra* L. subsp. *canadensis* (L.) R. Bolli (156) (1923) no longer in use by 1923

Bottle fern - *Cystopteris fragilis* (L.) Bernh. (5, 158) (1900-1913)

Bottle gentian - *Gentiana andrewsii* Griseb. (4, 5, 75, 93, 156, 157) (1894-1986)

Bottle gourd - *Lagenaria* Ser. (109) (1949), *Lagenaria siceraria* (Molina) Standl. (10, 50, 107, 121) (1818–present)

Bottle grass [Bottle-grass] - *Pennisetum glaucum* (L.) R. Br. (87, 90, 92) (1876-1903), *Setaria viridis* (L.) Beauv. (50, 56, 66, 90, 92, 129, 143) (1885-1936)

Bottlebrush [Bottle brush, Bottle-brush] - *Callistemon* R. Br. (109) (1949), *Elymus hystrix* L. (94) (1901), *Elymus hystrix* L. var. *hystrix* (111) (1915), *Equisetum arvense* L. (5, 157, 158) (1900-1929), *Equisetum sylvaticum* L. (5) (1913), *Hippuris vulgaris* L. (5, 93, 131, 156, 158) (1899–1936), *Melaleuca* L. (109) (1949)

Bottle-brush buckeye [Bottlebrush buckeye] - *Aesculus parviflora* Walt. (109, 138, 155) (1923-1949)

Bottle-brush grass [Bottlebrush grass, Bottlebrushgrass] - *Elymus hystrix* L. (possibly) (45, 56, 66, 90) (1885-1903), *Elymus hystrix* L. var. *hystrix* (3, 5, 72, 92, 119, 155) (1876-1977), *Elymus* L. (93, 155) (1936-1942)

Bottle-brush sedge [Bottlebrush sedge] - *Carex hystericina* Muhl. ex Willd. (3, 50, 139, 155) (1942–present)

Bottle-brush squirreltail [Bottlebrush squirreltail] - *Elymus elymoides* (Raf.) Swezey subsp. *elymoides* (140, 155) (1942-1944)

Bottle-grass [Bottle grass] - *Trifolium arvense* L. (5, 76, 156, 158) (1896-1923) MA, no longer in use by 1923

Bottle-rush [Bottle rush] - *Elymus hystrix* L. var. *hystrix* (5) (1913)

Bottle-rush Indian wheat [Bottlerush Indianwheat] - *Plantago aristata* Michx. (155) (1942)

Bottletree [Bottle-tree] - *Brachychiton* Schott & Endl. (109) (1949), *Sterculia* L. (138) (1923), *Streptanthus maculatus* Nutt. subsp. *obtusifolius* (Hook.) Rollins (138) (1923)

Bottom shellbark hickory - *Carya laciniosa* (Michx. f.) G. Don (109) (1949)

Bottom-land aster [Bottomland aster] - *Symphyotrichum ontarione* (Wiegand) Nesom (50) (present)

Bottonweed [Botton weed] - *Dipsacus fullonum* L. (5) (1913)

Boufferole - *Arctostaphylos uva-ursi* (L.) Spreng. (7, 8) (1785)

Bougainvillea - *Bougainvillea* Comm. ex Juss. (138) (1923)

Bouillon blanc [Bouillon-blanc] (French) - *Verbascum thapsus* L. (6, 158) (1892–1900)

Boulder bast [Boulder-bast] - *Schoenoplectus tabernaemontani* (K.C. Gmel.) Palla (5, 156) (1913-1923)

Boulder fern - *Dennstaedtia punctilobula* (Michx.) T. Moore (5) (1913)

Boulder raspberry - *Rubus deliciosus* Torr. (4, 112, 138, 155) (1923-1986)

Bouleau (French) - *Betula* L. (8) (1785), *Betula pubescens* Ehrh. (158) (1900)

Bouleau à canot (French) - *Betula nigra* L. (8) (1785), *Betula papyrifera* Marsh (20) (1857)

Bouleau à feuilles de tremble (French) - *Betula populifolia* Marshall (8) (1785)

Bouleau à papier (French) - *Betula papyrifera* Marsh (8) (1785)

Bouleau bâtard (French) - *Betula nigra* L. (17) (1796)

Bouleau blanc (French) - *Betula papyrifera* Marsh (20) (1857)

Bouleau mérisier (French) - *Betula lenta* L. (8) (1785)

Bouleau nain (French) - *Betula lenta* L. (8) (1785)

Bouleau noir (French) - *Betula nigra* L. (8) (1785)

Bouleau occidental (French) - *Betula occidentalis* Hook. (20) (1857)

Bouncing Bess - *Saponaria officinalis* L. (156) (1923)

Bouncing Bet [Bouncing-Bet, Bouncingbet] - *Dianthus barbatus* L. (74) (1893) Ferrisburgh VT, *Saponaria* L. (1, 93) (1932-1936), *Saponaria officinalis* L. (1, 4, 50, 5, 19, 49, 62, 64, 80, 85, 92, 95, 97, 109, 114, 131, 138, 148, 155, 156, 157, 158, 187) (1818–present)

Bountry - *Sambucus nigra* L. (92, 158) (1876-1900)

Bouquet larkspur - *Delphinium grandiflorum* L. (82, 109) (1930-1949)

Bouquet mud-plantain [Bouquet mudplantain] - *Heteranthera multiflora* (Griseb.) Horn (50) (present)

Bourdaine (French) - *Frangula alnus* Mill. (158) (1900)

Bourgeau prickly rose - *Rosa acicularis* Lindl. subsp. *sayi* (Schwein.) W.H. Lewis (155) (1942)

Bourgeau rose - *Rosa acicularis* Lindl. subsp. *sayi* (Schwein.) W.H. Lewis (138) (1923)

Bourgène (French) - *Arctium lappa* L. (158) (1900)

Bourholm (French) - *Arctium lappa* L. (158) (1900)

Bourquepine (French) - *Rhamnus cathartica* L. (6) (1892)

Bourse à pasteur (French) - *Capsella bursa-pastoris* (L.) Medik. (158) (1900)

Bourse de Pasteur (French) - *Capsella bursa-pastoris* (L.) Medik. (6) (1892)

Bourse de pasteur on Cure (French) - *Capsella bursa-pastoris* (L.) Medik. (180) (1633)

Bouton rouge (French) - *Cercis canadensis* L. (158) (1900)

Boutry - *Sambucus nigra* L. (158) (1900), *Sambucus racemosa* L. (5, 156) (1913-1923) no longer in use by 1923

Bouvardia - *Bouvardia* Salisb. (138) (1923)

Bowdark - *Maclura pomifera* (Raf.) Schneid. (30, 156, 158) (1844-1923)

Bowel hivegrass - *Aphanes arvensis* L. (5) (1913)

Bower actinidia - *Actinidia arguta* (Sieb. & Zucc.) Planch. ex Miq. (109, 137, 155) (1923-1949)

Bowie's oxalis [Bowie oxalis] - *Oxalis bowiei* Lindl. (138) (1923)

Bowlweed [Bowl-weed] - *Centaurea nigra* L. (156) (1923)

Bowman's root [Bowman's-root, Bowman root, Bowmanroot] - *Apocynum cannabinum* L. (64, 158) (1900-1907), *Euphorbia corollata* L. (5, 6, 7, 49, 61, 92, 156, 157, 158) (1828-1929), *Gillenia trifoliata* (L.) Moench (2, 5, 19, 49, 64, 138, 156, 186) (1840-1923),

Ludwigia alternifolia L. (158) (1900), *Porteranthus stipulatus* (Muhl. ex Willd.) Britt. (7, 49, 92) (1828-1898), *Veronicastrum virginicum* (L.) Farw. (5, 7, 49, 53, 64, 92, 93, 156, 157, 158, 178) (1526-1936)

Bowstring-hemp [Bowstring hemp] - *Sansevieria hyacinthoides* (L.) Druce (92) (1876), *Sansevieria* Thunb. (109) (1949)

Bow-wood [Bow wood] - *Maclura* Nutt. (12) (1821), *Maclura pomifera* (Raf.) Schneid. (2, 5, 7, 10, 12, 30, 34, 38, 92, 156) (1818–1923)

Bow-wood [Bow wood] - *Toxicodendron vernix* (L.) Kuntze (5) (1913), *Lepidium ruderale* L. (178, 180) (1526-1633)

Box - *Cephalanthus occidentalis* L. (5, 156, 158) (1900–1923)

Box blueberry - *Vaccinium ovatum* Pursh (138) (1923), *Vaccinium oxycoccos* L. (107) (1919)

Box elder [Box-elder, Box elder] - *Acer* L. (1, 13) (1849-1932), *Acer negundo* L. (3, 4, 5, 9, 12, 15, 20, 28, 35, 37, 38, 42, 43, 50, 65, 72, 82, 92, 93, 95, 97, 106, 109, 112, 114, 122, 124, 130, 131, 135, 138, 153, 155, 156, 157, 95, 138, 155, 158, 187) (1814–present), *Acer negundo* L. var. *negundo* (2, 20, 19, 50, 101, 107, 149) (1840–present), *Acer negundo* L. var. *violaceum* (Kirchn.) Jaeger (50, 85) (1932–present)

Box huckleberry - *Gaylussacia brachycera* (Michx.) Gray (5, 138, 156) (1913-1923)

Box knotweed - *Polygonum buxiforme* Small (50, 155) (1942–present)

Box or Box tree [Box-tree, Box tre] - *Buxus* L. (179) (1526), *Buxus sempervirens* L. (19, 49, 92, 107) (1840-1919), *Cornus florida* L. (6, 7, 14, 186) (1825-1892)

Box sandmyrtle - *Leiophyllum buxifolium* (Berg.) Ell. (138) (1923)

Box white oak - *Quercus stellata* Wangenh. (2, 5, 156) (1895-1923)

Boxberry [Box berry, Box-berry] - *Gaultheria procumbens* L. (2, 5, 6, 7, 14, 49, 53, 79, 92) (1828-1922), *Mitchella repens* L. (73, 156) (1892-1923) Bedford MA

Box-leaf andromeda [Box-leaved andromeda] - *Chamaedaphne calyculata* (L.) Moench (42, 187) (1814-1818)

Box-leaf eugenia [Box-leaved eugenia] - *Eugenia foetida* Pers. (20) (1857)

Box-leaf wintergreen [Box-leaved wintergreen] - *Arctostaphylos uva-ursi* (L.) Spreng. (156) (1923)

Boxthorn [Box-thorn, Box thorn] - *Lycium barbarum* L. (5, 75, 92, 156, 158) (1876-1923), *Lycium* L. (10, 109) (1818-1949)

Boxwood [Box wood] - *Amelanchier canadensis* (L.) Medik. (5, 76, 156, 158) (1896-1923) Western US, *Buxus sempervirens* L. (7) (1828), *Cornus florida* L. (5, 49, 58, 92, 156, 158) (1869-1923)

Bo-yak (Chippewa, straight-grained ash) - *Fraxinus americana* L. (105) (1932)

Boynton's hawthorn [Boynton hawthorn] - *Crataegus intricata* Lange (138) (1923)

Boynton's thorn - *Crataegus intricata* Lange (5) (1913)

Boys-and-girls [Boys and girls] - *Dicentra cucullaria* (L.) Bernh. (5, 74, 156, 158) (1893-1923) NY, no longer in use by 1923

Boy's-love [Boy's-love] - *Artemisia abrotanum* L. (5, 73, 92, 156, 157, 158) (1892–1929) Wellfleet MA, *Artemisia absinthium* L. (5, 75, 156) (1894-1923) New England, for aphrodisiac qualities or use in love divinations

Bozsekens eruyt - *Capsella bursa-pastoris* (L.) Medik. (180) (1633)

Bozzleweed - *Iva* L. (1) (1932)

Brachyelytrum - *Brachyelytrum* Beauv. (66) (1903), *Brachyelytrum septentrionale* (Babel) G. Tucker (56) (1901)

Bracken - *Osmunda regalis* L. (5) (1913), *Pteridium aquilinum* (L.) Kuhn (4, 103, 107, 109, 138) (1871-1986), *Pteridium* Gleditsch ex Scop. (4, 138, 155) (1923-1986)

Bracken fern [Brackenfern] - *Pteridium aquilinum* (L.) Kuhn var. *latiusculum* (Desv.) Underwood ex Heller (3) (1977), *Pteridium* Gleditsch ex Scop. (50) (present)

Bract milkweed - *Asclepias brachystephana* Engelm. ex Torr. (50) (present)

Bracted balsam fir - *Abies balsamea* (L.) Mill. var. *phanerolepis* Fernald (155) (1942)

Bracted bindweed - *Calystegia sepium* (L.) R. Br. subsp. *sepium* (5, 62, 156, 158) (1900–1923), *Calystegia spithamaea* (L.) Pursh (5, 156) (1913-1923)

Bracted bur-marigold - *Bidens aristosa* (Michx.) Britton (82) (1930)

Bracted false indigo - *Baptisia bracteata* Muhl. ex Ell. (82) (1930)

Bracted green orchis - *Coeloglossum viride* (L.) Hartman var. *virescens* (Muhl. ex Willd.) Luer (5, 156) (1913-1923)

Bracted iris - *Iris bracteata* S. Wats. (138) (1923)

Bracted plantain - *Plantago aristata* Michx. (3, 4, 62, 70, 80, 145) (1895-1986)

Bracted spiderwort - *Tradescantia bracteata* Small ex Britt. (138, 155) (1923-1942)

Bracted vervain - *Verbena bracteata* Lag. & Rodr. (3, 82, 85, 127) (1930-1977)

Bracted viburnum - *Viburnum bracteatum* Rehd. (138) (1923)

Bractless blazing star [Bractless blazingstar] - *Mentzelia nuda* (Pursh) Torr. & Gray (50, 155) (1942–present)

Bractless mentzelia - *Mentzelia nuda* (Pursh) Torr. & Gray (3, 131, 155) (1899-1977)

Bradbury's monarda [Bradbury monarda] - *Monarda bradburiana* Beck (4, 5, 97) (1913-1986)

Bradley's spleenwort - *Asplenium bradleyi* D.C. Eaton (5, 50, 97) (1913–present)

Bragge - *Lolium temulentum* L. (157, 158) (1900-1929)

Brainerd's thorn - *Crataegus brainerdii* Sarg. (5) (1913)

Brake - *Pteridium aquilinum* (L.) Kuhn (1, 4, 5, 72, 103, 107, 109, 131) (1871-1986), *Pteridium* Gleditsch ex Scop. (1) (1932), *Pteris* L. (2, 109, 138, 184) (1793-1949)

Brake aspidium - *Athyrium filix-femina* (L.) Roth (42) (1814)

Brake fern - *Pteridium aquilinum* (L.) Kuhn (101, 148) (1905-1939), *Pteris* L. (50) (present)

Brake spike-rush - *Eleocharis rostellata* (Torr.) Torr. (66) (1903)

Braken - *Pteridium aquilinum* (L.) Kuhn (148) (1939)

Braken fern - *Pteridium aquilinum* (L.) Kuhn (97) (1937)

Brakeroot [Brake root] - *Polypodium virginianum* L. (7, 49, 58, 92) (1828-1869)

Braknagras (Swedish) - *Isoetes lacustris* L. (46) (1879)

Bralins - *Arctostaphylos uva-ursi* (L.) Spreng. (156) (1923) no longer in use by 1923

Bramble - *Rubus* L. (7, 8, 10, 82, 156, 184) (1785-1930), *Rubus pensilvanicus* Poir. (3) (1977)

Bramble brier - *Rosa canina* L. (5) (1913)

Brampton stock - *Matthiola incana* (L.) Aiton f. (109) (1949)

Branca ursina - *Acanthus mollis* L. (165) (1768) medicinal name

Branch eliber - *Veratrum album* L. (75) (1894)

Branch ivy - *Leucothoe axillaris* (Lam.) D. Don. (71) (1898)

Branched aristida - *Aristida oligantha* Michx (5, 119) (1913-1938)

Branched bartonia - *Bartonia paniculata* (Michx.) Muhl. (5, 97) (1913-1937)

Branched broom-rape - *Orobanche ramosa* L. (5) (1913)

Branched bur-reed - *Sparganium androcladum* (Engelm.) Morong (50) (present)

Branched centaury - *Centaurium pulchellum* (Sw.) Druce (50) (present)

Branched cinquefoil - *Potentilla hippiana* Lehm. (5) (1913)

Branched eriogonum - *Eriogonum pauciflorum* Pursh var. *pauciflorum* (5, 93, 131) (1899-1936)

Branched false goldenweed - *Oonopsis multicaulis* (Nutt.) Greene (50) (present)

Branched foldwing - *Dicliptera brachiata* (Pursh) Spreng. (50) (present)

Branched Harts toong - *Asplenium scolopendrium* L. var. *americanum* (Fern.) Kartesz & Gandhi (possibly) (178) (1596)

Branched noseburn - *Tragia ramosa* Torr. (50) (present)

Branched nuttallia - *Mentzelia nuda* (Pursh) Torr. & Gray var. *nuda* (5, 93, 97) (1913–1937)

Branching andromeda - *Leucothoe racemosa* (L.) Gray (possibly) (165) (1807)

Branching aristida - *Aristida dichotoma* Michx. (187) (1818)

Branching bur-reed - *Sparganium androcladum* (Engelm.) Morong (5, 72) (1907-1913)

Branching centaury - *Centaurium pulchellum* (Sw.) Druce (5) (1913)

Branching foxtail - *Chloris verticillata* Nutt. (5, 163) (1852-1913), *Setaria vulpiseta* (Lam.) Roemer & J.A. Schultes (94) (1901)

Branching phytolacca - *Phytolacca americana* L. (186) (1814)

Branching sabbatia - *Sabatia brevifolia* Raf. (5) (1913)

Branching spear grass - *Eragrostis capillaris* (L.) Nees (66) (1903), *Eragrostis trichodes* (Nutt.) Wood (94) (1901)

Branching tragia - *Tragia ramosa* Torr. (5, 97) (1913-1937)

Branching whitlow-grass [Branching whitlow grass] - *Draba ramosissima* Desv. (5) (1913)

Branchy St. John's-wort [Branchy St. John's wort] - *Hypericum denticulatum* Walt. (2) (1895)

Brandegee's Jacob's-ladder [Brandegee's Jacob's ladder] - *Polemonium brandegeei* (Gray) Greene (50) (present)

Brandegee's onion [Brandegee onion] - *Allium brandegeei* S. Wats. (155) (1942)

Brand's phacelia - *Phacelia gilioides* Brand. (50) (present)

Brandy mint [Brandy-mint] - *Mentha ×piperita* L. (pro sp.) [*aquatica × spicata*] (5, 156, 157) (1900–1929)

Brandy-bottle [Brandy bottles] - *Nuphar lutea* (L.) Sm. subsp. *advena* (Aiton) Kartesz & Gandhi (92, 156) (1876-1923)

Brank - *Fagopyrum esculentum* Moench (5, 14, 107, 156, 158) (1882-1923)

Brasenia - *Brasenia* Schreber (50) (present)

Brasenia (Official name of Materia Medica) - *Brasenia schreberi* Gmel. (7) (1828)

Brash oak - *Quercus stellata* Wangenh. (5, 156) (1913-1923)

Brasil - *Condalia hookeri* M.C. Johnston var. *hookeri* (122, 124) (1937) TX

Brasiletto - *Caesalpinia* L. (167) (1814) tropical species

Brassic - *Brassica oleracea* L. (110) (1886)

Braunelle - *Prunella vulgaris* L. (158) (1900)

Braun-heil (German) - *Prunella vulgaris* L. (158) (1900)

Braun's holly fern [Braun hollyfern, Braun's holly-fern] - *Polystichum braunii* (Spenner) Fee (4, 5, 19, 50, 138) (1840–present)

Braun's quillwort [Braun quillwort] - *Isoetes tenella* Léman (5) (1913)

Brawlines - *Arctostaphylos uva-ursi* (L.) Spreng. (157) (1929)

Brawlins - *Arctostaphylos uva-ursi* (L.) Spreng. (107) (1919)

Bray's oak [Brays oak] - *Quercus muehlenbergii* Engelm. (122) (1937) TX

Brazil - *Condalia hookeri* M.C. Johnston var. *hookeri* (106) (1930)

Braziletto - *Lonchocarpus punctatus* Kunth (92) (1876)

Brazilian blady-grass - *Imperata brasiliensis* Trin. (94) (1901)

Brazilian clover - *Medicago sativa* L. (5, 118, 157, 158) (1898–1929)

Brazilian Dutchman's-pipe [Brazil Dutchmanspipe] - *Aristolochia labiata* Willd. (155) (1942)

Brazilian flat-sedge - *Cyperus haspan* L. (138) (1923)

Brazilian morning-glory - *Ipomoea setosa* Ker-Gawl. (109) (1949)

Brazilian nightshade - *Solanum seaforthianum* Andr. (138) (1923)

Brazilian parrotfeather - *Myriophyllum aquaticum* (Vell.) Verdc. (138) (1923)

Brazilian peppertree [Brazilian pepper-tree] - *Schinus terebinthifolius* Raddi (109, 138) (1923-1949)

Brazilian primrose-willow - *Ludwigia longifolia* (DC.) H. Hara (138) (1923)

Brazilian tea [Brazil tea] - *Ilex paraguensis* St.Hilaire (92) (1876)

Brazilian watermeal - *Wolffia brasiliensis* Weddell (50) (present)

Brazilian waterweed - *Egeria densa* Planch. (50) (present)

Brazilwood [Brazil wood] - *Lonchocarpus punctatus* Kunth (7) (1828)

Bread of St. John - *Ceratonia siliqua* L. (110) (1886)

Bread-and-biscuit [Bread and biscuit] - *Linaria vulgaris* Mill. (73)

(1892), *Lomatium ambiguum* (Nutt.) Coult. & Rose (76) (1896) CA, from Indian use of plant

Bread-and-butter - *Linaria vulgaris* Mill. (5, 157, 158) (1900–1929) Ipswich MA, *Smilax rotundifolia* L. (5, 73, 156) (1892-1923) Cape Ann MA, young leaves are eaten by children

Bread-and-butter toadflax - *Linaria vulgaris* Mill. (155) (1942)

Breadfruit [Bread fruit, Bread-fruit] - *Artocarpus altilis* (Parkinson) Fosberg (92, 109, 110, 138, 155) (1876-1949), *Artocarpus* J.R. & G. Forst. (138) (1923), *Pandanus tectorius* Parkinson ex Zucc. (107) (1919)

Breadroot [Bread root, Bread-root] - *Lomatium ambiguum* (Nutt.) Coult. & Rose (101, 103, 107) (1870-1919) MT, *Lomatium cous* (S. Wats.) Coult. & Rose (101) (1905) MT, *Lomatium simplex* (Nutt.) J.F. Macbr. var. *simplex* (101) (1905) MT, *Lomatium triternatum* (Pursh) Coult. & Rose (101) (1905) MT, *Osmunda cinnamomea* L. (5) (1913), *Pediomelum esculentum* (Pursh) Rydb. (14, 19, 28, 49, 92, 101, 103, 107, 127) (1811-1933), *Pediomelum* Rydb. (1) (1932)

Breadroot scurf pea - *Pediomelum esculentum* (Pursh) Rydb. (3, 4) (1977-1986)

Breakstone - *Aphanes arvensis* L. (5) (1913), *Sagina procumbens* L. (5, 156) (1913-1923)

Break-your-spectacles - *Centaurea cyanus* L. (157, 158) (1900-1929)

Breastweed [Breast weed, Breast-weed] - *Saururus cernuus* L. (5, 19, 92, 106, 156, 158) (1840-1930)

Brechenmachende Wolfsmilch (German) - *Euphorbia ipecacuanhae* L. (156) (1923)

Brechwolfsmilch (German) - *Euphorbia ipecacuanhae* L. (6) (1892)

Brède de Malabar - *Amaranthus tricolor* L. (110) (1886)

Breeches-flower [Breechesflower, Breeches flowers] - *Dicentra* Bernh. (13) (1849), *Dicentra cucullaria* (L.) Bernh. (5, 74, 156, 158) (1893-1923) NY

Brei - *Panicum miliaceum* L. (67) (1890) possibly for porridge from this species

Breittblättriger Dreistein (German) - *Triosteum* L. (186) (1814)

Brelles (French) - *Allium schoenoprasum* L. (180) (1633)

Brennessel [Brenn-Nessel] (German) - *Urtica dioica* L. (158) (1900), *Urtica urens* L. (6) (1892)

Brere - *Rosa* L. (179) (1526)

Brere rose - *Rosa canina* L. (5) (1913)

Bresic (Celtic) - *Brassica oleracea* L. (107, 110) (1886-1919)

Bresych - *Brassica oleracea* L. (110) (1886)

Bresych yr yd (Welsh) - *Brassica napus* L. (110) (1886)

Breweria - *Bonamia* Thouars (155, 158) (1900-1942)

Brewer's angelica [Brewer angelica] - *Angelica atropurpurea* L. (155) (1942), *Angelica breweri* Gray (155) (1942)

Brewer's cliff-brake - *Pellaea breweri* D.C. Eat. (131) (1899)

Brewer's onion [Brewer onion] - *Allium falcifolium* Hook. & Arn. (155) (1942)

Brewer's reed-grass - *Calamagrostis breweri* Thurb. (94) (1901)

Brewer's rockcress [Brewer rockcress] - *Arabis breweri* S. Wats. (155) (1942)

Brewster - *Magnolia virginiana* L. (6) (1892)

Brick globemallow - *Sphaeralcea angustifolia* (Cav.) G. Don (138) (1923), *Sphaeralcea bonariensis* (Cav.) Griseb. (138) (1923)

Brick timber - *Ilex mucronata* (L.) M. Powell, Savol. & S. Andrews (5, 73) (1892-1913) Fortune Bay, Newfoudland

Brickellbush - *Brickellia* Ell. (50) (present)

Brickellia - *Brickellia* Ell. (155) (1942), *Brickellia grandiflora* (Hook.) Nutt. (3) (1977)

Brickell's goldenweed [Brickell goldenweed] - *Hazardia brickellioides* (Blake) W.D. Clark (155) (1942)

Bridal canyon-poppy - *Romneya trichocalyx* Eastw. (138) (1923)

Bridal-roses [Bridal roses] - *Tanacetum parthenium* (L.) Schultz-Bip. (75) (1894)

Bridal-veil broom - *Retama monosperma* (L.) Boiss. (138) (1923)

Bridalwreath [Bridal-wreath, Bridal wreath] - *Spiraea prunifolia* Sieb. & Zucc. (109, 135, 138) (1910-1949)

Bride's-laces [Brides' laces] - *Phalaris arundinacea* L. (5, 158) (1900-1913) Neb

Brideweed [Bride-weed] - *Linaria vulgaris* Mill. (5, 156, 157, 158) (1900-1929)

Bridewort [Bride wort, Bride-wort] - *Filipendula ulmaria* (L.) Maxim. (5, 156) (1913-1923), *Linaria vulgaris* Mill. (156) (1923) no longer in use by 1923, *Spiraea salicifolia* L. (156) (1923)

Brier - *Smilax rotundifolia* L. (92) (1876)

Brier herb - *Rubus saxatilis* L. (19, 92) (1840-1876)

Brier rose - *Rosa canina* L. (107) (1919), *Rubus rosifolius* Sm. (92) (1876)

Brierberry [Brier berry, Brier-berry] - *Rubus cuneifolius* Pursh (5, 156) (1913-1923)

Briery-thistle [Briery thistle] - *Eryngium* L. (158) (1900), *Eryngium leavenworthii* Torr. & Gray (5, 76, 156) (1896-1923) Waco TX

Bright wheat - *Triticum aestivum* L. (180) (1633) John Gerarde

Bright-eyes [Bright eyes] - *Houstonia caerulea* L. (5, 73, 156) (1892-1923) Baltimore MD, no longer in use by 1923

Bright-green spike-rush [Bright green spike rush] - *Eleocharis olivacea* Torr. (5, 50) (1913–present)

Bright-green spleenwort [Brightgreen spleenwort] - *Asplenium trichomanes-ramosum* L. (50) (present)

Brilliant campion - *Lychnis fulgens* Fisch. ex Sims (138) (1923)

Brilliant coneflower [Brilliant cone-flower] - *Rudbeckia fulgida* Aiton (5, 86) (1878-1913)

Brinjal - *Solanum melongena* L. (156) (1923)

Brinton's root [Brinton root, Brinton-root] - *Veronicastrum virginicum* (L.) Farw. (5, 7, 19, 49, 53, 64, 92, 156, 157, 158) (1828-1923) no longer in use by 1923

Brisbane box [Brisbane-box, Brisbanebox] - *Lophostemon confertus* (R. Br.) P.G. Wilson & Waterhouse (109, 138) (1923-1949)

Bristle fern - *Trichomanes boschianum* Sturm. (5) (1913)

Bristle flax - *Linum aristatum* Engelm. (50) (present)

Bristle grass [Bristlegrass] - *Setaria* Beauv (50, 155) (1942–present), *Setaria setosa* (Sw.) Beauv. (87) (1884)

Bristle persicaria - *Polygonum setaceum* Baldw. (122) (1937)

Bristle-bract sedge [Bristlebract sedge] - *Carex tribuloides* Wahl. (155) (1942)

Bristle-cone fir [Bristlecone fir] - *Abies bracteata* (D. Don) D. Don ex Poit. (50, 138, 155) (1923–present)

Bristle-cone pine [Bristle cone pine, Bristlecone pine] - *Pinus aristata* Engelm. (109, 138, 153) (1923-1949)

Bristle-leaf sedge [Bristleleaf sedge, Bristleleaved sedge] - *Carex eburnea* Boott. (50, 72) (1907–present)

Bristle-leaf white sedge [Bristle-leaved white sedge] - *Carex eburnea* Boott. (66) (1903)

Bristle-point oat [Bristle-pointed oat] - *Avena strigosa* Schreb. (107) (1919)

Bristle-spike galingale [Bristle-spiked galingale] - *Cyperus strigosus* L. (66) (1903)

Bristle-stalk sedge [Bristle-stalked sedge] - *Carex leptalea* Wahl (5) (1913), Carex leptalea Wahlenb. subsp. leptalea (66) (1903)

Bristle-stem elder [Bristlestem elder] - *Aralia hispida* Vent. (19, 49, 53, 58, 92) (1840-1922)

Bristle-stem sarsaparilla [Bristle stem sarsaparilla] - *Aralia hispida* Vent. (19, 49, 53, 58, 92) (1840-1922)

Bristle-tail grass [Bristle tailed grass] - *Chaiturus* Willd. (possibly) (92) (1876)

Bristle-thistle [Bristlethistle] - *Carduus* L. (155) (1942)

Bristly acacia - *Robinia hispida* L. (5) (1913)

Bristly aralia - *Aralia hispida* Vent. (42, 138, 155) (1814-1942)

Bristly blackberry - *Rubus setosus* Bigelow (5) (1913)

Bristly buckhorn - *Plantago aristata* Michx. (62) (1912) IN

Bristly buttercup - *Ranunculus hispidus* Michx. (3, 4, 50, 138, 155) (1923–present), *Ranunculus pensylvanicus* L. f. (5, 93, 131) (1899-1913), *Ranunculus sceleratus* L. (85) (1932)

Bristly clubmoss - *Lycopodium annotinum* L. (3) (1977)

Bristly copperleaf - *Acalypha hispida* Burm. f. (50) (present)

Bristly crowfoot - *Ranunculus pensylvanicus* L. f. (3, 4, 5, 63, 72, 156) (1899-1986)

Bristly cyperus - *Cyperus hystricinus* Fernald. (5) (1913)

Bristly flatsedge - *Cyperus hystricinus* Fernald. (50) (present)

Bristly foxtail [Bristly fox tail, Bristly fox-tail] - *Pennisetum glaucum* (L.) R. Br. (92) (1876), *Setaria verticillata* (L.) Beauv. (3, 5, 66, 80, 93, 94, 111, 129) (1903-1977)

Bristly gooseberry - *Ribes oxyacanthoides* L. subsp. *setosum* (Lindl.) Sinnott (3, 4, 5, 85, 107) (1913-1986)

Bristly greenbrier [Bristly greenbriar] - *Smilax bona-nox* L. (5, 97) (1913-1937), *Smilax tamnoides* L. (3, 50, 138, 155) (1923–present)

Bristly hawkbit - *Leontodon hispidus* L. (50) (present)

Bristly locust or Bristly locust tree - *Robinia hispida* L. (2, 50, 82, 156, 158) (1895–present)

Bristly mesquite [Bristly mesquit] - *Bouteloua hirsuta* Lag. (5, 87, 94) (1884-1913)

Bristly muskit - *Bouteloua hirsuta* Lag. (66) (1903)

Bristly nama - *Nama hispidum* Gray (50) (present)

Bristly Nutka rose - *Rosa nutkana* K. Presl var. *hispida* Fern. (138) (1923)

Bristly ox-tongue [Bristly oxtongue] - *Picris echioides* L. (5, 50, 155, 50, 156, 158) (1900–present)

Bristly panick grass - *Pennisetum* L.C. Rich. ex Pers. (10) (1818)

Bristly persicaria - *Polygonum hydropiperoides Michx.* (5) (1913)

Bristly raspberry - *Rubus setosus* Bigelow (19) (1840)

Bristly rose - *Rosa nitida* Willd. (138) (1923)

Bristly rose-acacia [Bristly rose acacia] - *Robinia hispida* L. (92) (1876)

Bristly rush - *Juncus coriaceus* Mackenzie (66) (1903)

Bristly sarsaparilla - *Aralia hispida* Vent. (2, 5, 46, 109, 156) (1879-1949), *Smilax tamnoides* L. (5) (1913)

Bristly scaleseed - *Spermolepis echinata* (Nutt. ex DC.) Heller (50) (present)

Bristly sedge - *Carex comosa* Boott. (5, 72) (1907-1913)

Bristly-fruit mallow [Bristly fruited mallow] - *Modiola caroliniana* (L.) G. Don (5, 156) (1913-1923)

Bristly-fruit spermolepis [Bristly-fruited spermolepis] - *Spermolepis echinata* (Nutt. ex DC.) Heller (5, 97) (1913-1937)

Bristly-spike sedge [Bristly-spiked sedge] - *Carex vulpinoidea* Michx. var. *vulpinoidea* (5, 66) (1903-1913)

Bristly-stalk sedge [Bristlystalk sedge] - *Carex leptalea* Wahl (50) (present)

Bristol three-leaf grass [Bristoll Three leafed grasse] - *Trifolium pratense* L. (178) (1526)

British Columbia wild ginger [British Columbia wildginger, BritishColumbia wildginger] - *Asarum caudatum* Lindl. (50, 155) (1942–present)

British inula - *Inula britannica* L. (138) (1923)

British oak - *Quercus robur* L. (55) (1911)

British tea - *Ulmus* L. (92) (1876)

British tobacco - *Turnera ulmifolia* L. (187) (1818), *Tussilago farfara* L. (92) (1876)

Brittle bladderfern - *Cystopteris fragilis* (L.) Bernh. (50, 138, 155) (1923–present)

Brittle fern [Brittle-fern] - *Cystopteris* Bernh. (158) (1900), *Cystopteris fragilis* (L.) Bernh. (5, 72, 97, 109, 131, 158) (1899-1949)

Brittle maidenhair - *Adiantum tenerum* Sw. (109) (1949)

Brittle opuntia - *Opuntia fragilis* (Nutt.) Haw. (5, 93, 131) (1899-1936)

Brittle prickly-pear [Brittle pricklypear] - *Opuntia fragilis* (Nutt.) Haw. (50, 155) (1942–present), *Opuntia fragilis* (Nutt.) Haw. var. *fragilis* (50) (present)

Brittle thatch palm - *Thrinax morrisii* H. Wendl. (138) (1923)

Brittle willow - *Salix fragilis* L. (5, 72, 109, 138, 155, 156, 158) (1900-1942)

Brittle-joint willow [Brittle joint willow] - *Salix nigra* Marsh. (19) (1840)

Brittle-leaf manzanita [Brittleleaf manzanita] - *Arctostaphylos tomentosa* (Pursh) Lindl. (155) (1942)

Brittle-stem hemp nettle [Brittlestem hempnettle] - *Galeopsis bifida* Boenn. (155) (1942)

Britton's agrimony - *Agrimonia striata* Michx. (5) (1913)

Britton's bush clover - *Lespedeza ×brittonii* Bickn. [*procumbens × virginica*] (5) (1913)

Britton's coneflower [Britton's cone flower] - *Rudbeckia hirta* L. var. *hirta* (5) (1913)

Britton's panic grass [Britton's panic-grass] - *Dichanthelium dichotomum* (L.) Gould var. *ensifolium* (Baldw. ex Ell.) Gould & C.A. Clark (94) (1901)

Britton's phlox - *Phlox subulata* L. subsp. *brittonii* (Small) Wherry (5) (1913)

Britton's sedge - *Carex tetrastachya* Scheele (50) (present)

Britton's skullcap [Brittons skullcap] - *Scutellaria brittonii* Porter (4, 5, 50, 155) (1913–present)

Britton's wood sorrel - *Oxalis stricta* L. (5) (1913)

Briza-like brome grass [Briza-like brome-grass] - *Bromus briziformis* Fisch. & C. A. Mey. (94) (1901)

Broad bean [Broadbean] - *Vicia faba* L. (107, 109, 110, 138, 155) (1886-1949)

Broad beech fern [Broad beech-fern, Broad beechfern] - *Phegopteris hexagonoptera* (Michx.) Fee (5, 50, 109, 155) (1913–present)

Broad burweed [Broad bur-weed] - *Xanthium strumarium* L. (53) (1922)

Broad cocklebur - *Xanthium strumarium* L. (1900) (158)

Broad cotton-grass [Broad cotton grass] - *Eriophorum angustifolium* Honckeny subsp. *subarcticum* (Vassiljev) Hultén ex Kartesz & Gandhi (66) (1903)

Broad loose-flower sedge [Broad looseflower sedge] - *Carex laxiflora* Lam. (50) (present)

Broad plantain - *Plantago major* L. (41) (1770)

Broad prickly-tooth wood fern [Broad prickly-toothed wood fern] - *Dryopteris campyloptera* (Kunze) Clarkson (5) (1913), *Dryopteris expansa* (K. Presl) Fraser-Jenkins & Jermy (5) (1913)

Broad willow-leaf oak [Broad willow-leaved oak] - *Quercus incana* Bartr. (8) (1785)

Broad-beard beard tongue [Broadbeard beardtongue] - *Penstemon angustifolius* Nutt. ex Pursh (50) (present)

Broad-blade Dutchman's-pipe [Broadblade Dutchmanspipe] - *Aristolochia labiata* Willd. (155) (1942)

Broader mouse-ear chickweed - *Cerastium fontanum* Baumg. subsp. *vulgare* (Hartman) Greuter & Burdet (187) (1818)

Broader-leaf spring-beauty [Broader-leaved spring beauty] - *Claytonia caroliniana* Michx. (2) (1895)

Broad-flower fescue grass [Broad-flowered fescue grass] - *Chasmanthium latifolium* (Michx.) Yates (87) (1884)

Broad-fruit bur-reed [Broad fruited bur-reed, Broad-fruited bur-reed] - *Sparganium eurycarpum* Engelm. ex Gray (5, 50, 93, 131) (1899–present), *Sparganium* L. (93) (1936)

Broad-glume brome grass [Broad glumed brome grass] - *Bromus latiglumis* (Shear) A.S. Hitchc. (56) (1901)

Broad-leaf acacia [Broadleaf acacia] - *Acacia longifolia* (Andr.) Willd. (138, 155) (1931-1942)

Broad-leaf andromeda [Broad-leaved andromeda] - *Lyonia mariana* (L.) D. Don (8) (1785)

Broad-leaf arctic bent [Broad-leaved arctic bent] - *Arctagrostis latifolia* (R. Br.) Griseb. (94) (1901)

Broad-leaf arnica [Broadleaf arnica] - *Arnica latifolia* Bong. (155) (1942)

Broad-leaf arrowhead [Broad-leaved arrow-head, Broad-leaved arrowhead] - *Sagittaria latifolia* Willd. (5, 50, 72, 85, 93, 97, 120, 131, 156) (1899–present)

Broad-leaf asarabacca [Broadleaved asarabacca, Broad-leaved asabaraca] - *Asarum canadense* L. (7, 64, 158) (1828-1907)

Broad-leaf beard grass [Broad-leaved beard grass, Broad-leaved beard-grass] - *Gymnopogon ambiguus* (Michx.) Britton, Sterns & Poggenb. (5, 119, 163) (1852-1938)

Broad-leaf bethroot [Broadleaf bethroot] - *Trillium cernuum* L. (7) (1828)

Broad-leaf birthwort [Broad leaved birth wort] - *Aristolochia macrophylla* Lam. (42) (1814)

Broad-leaf bitternut hickory [Broadleaf bitternut hickory] - *Carya cordiformis* (Wangenh.) K. Koch (155) (1942)

Broad-leaf cactus [Broadleaf cactus] - *Epiphyllum oxypetalum* (DC.) Haw. (138) (1923)

Broad-leaf cactus [Broad-leafed cactus] - *Opuntia ficus-indica* (L.) Mill. (44) (1845)

Broad-leaf cat-tail [Broad-leaved cat-tail] - *Typha latifolia* L. (5, 50, 72, 93, 97, 120, 131, 156, 157, 158) (1907-1938)

Broad-leaf chickweed [Broad-leaved chickweed] - *Moehringia lateriflora* (L.) Fenzl (127) (1933)

Broad-leaf circaea [Broadleaf circaea] - *Circaea lutetiana* L. subsp. *canadensis* (L.) Asch. & Magnus (155) (1942)

Broad-leaf clover [Broad-leaved clover] - *Trifolium pratense* L. (5, 45, 156, 157, 158) (1896-1929)

Broad-leaf collinsia [Broadleaf collinsia, Broad-leaved collinsia] - *Collinsonia canadensis* L. (7) (1828), *Collinsia verna* Nutt. (5, 158) (1900–1913)

Broad-leaf cow-wheat [Broad-leaved cow-wheat] - *Melampyrum lineare* Desr. var. *latifolium* Bart. (5) (1913)

Broad-leaf creeping bent [Broad-leaved creeping bent] - *Agrostis stolonifera* L. (66) (1903)

Broad-leaf dichronema [Broad-leaved dichronema] - *Rhynchospora latifolia* (Baldw. ex Ell.) Thomas (5) (1913)

Broad-leaf dock [Broad-leaved dock] - *Rumex obtusifolius* L. (5, 62, 64, 69, 72, 92, 93, 97, 156, 157, 158) (1872-1937)

Broad-leaf dogwood [Broad-leaved dogwood] - *Cornus rugosa* Lam. (possibly) (92) (1876)

Broad-leaf dwarf flower-de-luce [Broad leafed Dwarfe Flowerde-luce] - *Iris pumila* L. (178) (1596)

Broad-leaf enchanter's-nightshade [Broadleaf enchanter's nightshade] - *Circaea lutetiana* L. (50) (present)

Broad-leaf epiphyllum [Broadlaef epiphyllum] - *Epiphyllum oxypetalum* (DC.) Haw. (155) (1942)

Broad-leaf flat-top white aster [Broad-leaved flat-top white aster] - *Doellingeria infirma* (Michx.) Greene (5, 72) (1907-1913)

Broad-leaf fly-poison [Broad-leaved fly poison] - *Amianthium muscitoxicum* (Walt.) Gray (2) (1895)

Broad-leaf goldenrod [Broadleaf goldenrod, Broad-leaf golden-rod] - *Solidago flexicaulis* L. (3, 4, 5, 19, 82, 85, 131, 138) (1840-1986)

Broad-leaf grape fern [Broad-leaf grapefern, Broadleaf grapefern] - *Botrychium multifidum* (Gmel.) Trev. (138, 155) (1923-1942)

Broad-leaf gumplant [Broad-leaved gum-plant, Broad-leaved gum plant] - *Grindelia squarrosa* (Pursh) Dunal (5, 72, 97, 122, 131, 157, 158) (1899-1937)

Broad-leaf helleborine [Broadleaf helleborine] - *Epipactis helleborine* (L.) Crantz (50) (present)

Broad-leaf hog's-fennel [Broad-leaved hog's fennel] - *Peucedanum ostruthium* (L.) W.D.J. Koch (5) (1913)

Broad-leaf hyssopus [Broad leafed hyssopus] - *Hyssopus officinalis* L. (178) (1526)

Broad-leaf ironweed [Broad-leaved ironweed] - *Vernonia glauca* (L.) Willd. (possibly) (5) (1913)

Broad-leaf kalmia [Broad-leaved kalmia] - *Kalmia latifolia* L. (5, 7, 8, 20, 92) (1785-1913)

Broad-leaf laurel [Broad-leaved laurel] - *Kalmia latifolia* L. (19, 71, 92) (1840-1898)

Broad-leaf marshallia [Broad-leaved marshallia] - *Marshallia trinervia* (Walt.) Trel. (5) (1913)

Broad-leaf milkweed [Broadleaf milkweed] - *Asclepias latifolia* (Torr.) Raf. (3, 4, 5, 50, 97, 122, 155) (1913–present)

Broad-leaf mustard [Broad-leaved mustard] - *Brassica juncea* (L.) Czern. (109) (1949)

Broad-leaf onion garlick [Broad-leaved onion garlick] - *Allium tricoccum* Ait. (42) (1814)

Broad-leaf panic grass [Broad-leaved panic grass] - *Dichanthelium latifolium* (L.) Gould & C.A. Clark (66, 90) (1885-1903)

Broad-leaf panicum [Broad-leaved panicum] - *Dichanthelium latifolium* (L.) Gould & C.A. Clark (3, 5) (1913-1977)

Broad-leaf pepperweed [Broadleaved pepperweed] - *Lepidium latifolium* L. (50) (present)

Broad-leaf plantain [Broad-leaved plantain] - *Plantago major* L. (6, 156, 157, 158) (1892-1929)

Broad-leaf reed-mace [Broad-leaved reed-mace] - *Typha latifolia* L. (41) (1770)

Broad-leaf rosette grass [Broadleaf rosette grass] - *Dichanthelium latifolium* (L.) Gould & C.A. Clark (50) (present)

Broad-leaf sedge [Broad leaved sedge] - *Carex platyphylla* Carey (5, 50) (1913–present)

Broad-leaf snakeroot [Broad leaved snake root] - *Aristolochia macrophylla* Lam. (42) (1814)

Broad-leaf spike grass [Broad-leaved spike grass, Broad-leaved spike-grass] - *Chasmanthium latifolium* (Michx.) Yates (5, 56, 66, 72, 94, 99, 119, 163) (1852-1938)

Broad-leaf spurge [Broad-leaved spurge] - *Euphorbia platyphyllos* L. (5) (1913)

Broad-leaf starwort [Broad leaved star wort] - *Eurybia macrophylla* (L.) Cass. (42) (1814)

Broad-leaf tick-trefoil [Broad-leaved tick-trefoil] - *Desmodium cuspidatum* (Muhl. ex Willd.) DC. ex Loud. var. *cuspidatum* (131) (1899)

Broad-leaf twayblade [Broad-leaved tway-blade] - *Listera convallarioides* (Sw.) Nutt. ex Ell. (5) (1913)

Broad-leaf uniola [Broadleaf uniola] - *Chasmanthium latifolium* (Michx.) Yates (122, 138, 155) (1923-1942)

Broad-leaf Virginia knapweed [Broad-leaved Virginia Knapweed, with a knobbed root] - *Liatris aspera* Michx. (181) (~1678)

Broad-leaf water-leaf [Broad-leaved water-leaf] - *Hydrophyllum canadense* L. (5) (1913)

Broad-leaf wattle [Broad-leaved wattle] - *Acacia pycnantha* Benth. (109) (1949)

Broad-leaf willow [Broad-leaved willow] - *Salix myricoides* Muhl. var. *myricoides* (5) (1913)

Broad-leaf willowherb [Broad-leaved willow-herb] - *Chamerion latifolium* (L.) Holub (5) (1913)

Broad-leaf wood violet [Broad-leaved wood violet] - *Viola sororia* Willd. (5) (1913)

Broad-leaf wormwood [Broad leafed wormwood] - *Artemisia rupestris* L. (179) (1526)

Broad-lip twayblade [Broad-lipped twayblade] - *Listera convallarioides* (Sw.) Nutt. ex Ell. (50) (present)

Broad-pod acacia [Broad-podded acacia] - *Lysiloma latisiliquum* (L.) Benth. (20) (1857)

Broad-scale boltonia [Broad-scaled boltonia] - *Boltonia asteroides* (L.) L'Her. var. *latisquama* (Gray) Cronq. (5, 97) (1913-1937)

Broad-tooth hedge-nettle [Broad-toothed hedge nettle] - *Stachys* L. (5) (1913), *Stachys latidens* Small ex Britt. (5) (1913)

Broad-wing sedge [Broadwing sedge, Broad-winged sedge] - *Carex alata* Torr. (5, 50, 72) (1907–present)

Broadwort [Broad wort] - *Matthiola incana* (L.) Aiton f. (92) (1876)

Broccoli - *Brassica* L. (107) (1919), *Brassica oleracea* L. (156) (1923)

Brome - *Bromus* L. (50, 155) (1942–present), *Cytisus scoparius* (L.) Link (179) (1526)

Brome grass [Bromegrass, Brome-grass] - *Bromus catharticus* Vahl (152) (1912), *Bromus ciliatus* L. (58) (1869), *Bromus inermis* Leyss. (85) (1932), *Bromus kalmii* Gray (56, 72) (1901-1907), *Bromus* L. (1, 10, 41, 92, 93, 109, 138, 152, 158, 184) (1770-1949), *Bromus pubescens* Muhl. ex Willd. (92) (1876)

Brome-like sedge - *Carex bromoides* Schk. Ex Willd. (5, 50, 66) (1912–present)

Brompton queens - *Matthiola incana* (L.) Aiton f. (19, 92) (1840-1876)

Brompton stocks [Brompton stock] - *Matthiola incana* (L.) Aiton f. (19, 92) (1840-1876)

Bronze iris - *Iris fulva* Ker.-Gawl. (124) (1937) TX

Brook alder - *Ilex verticillata* (L.) Gray (92) (1876)

Brook celandine - *Impatiens capensis* Meerb. (5, 156, 157, 158) (1900-1929)

Brook cinquefoil - *Potentilla rivalis* Nutt. (3, 4, 50, 155) (1942–present)

Brook euonymus - *Euonymus americanus* L. (122, 138, 156) (1923-1937)

Brook flatsedge - *Cyperus bipartitus* Torr. (3, 155) (1942-1977)

Brook grass [Brook-grass, Brookgrass] - *Andropogon glomeratus* (Walt.) B.S.P. (5, 94) (1901-1913), *Catabrosa aquatica* (L.) Beauv. (3, 85, 140, 155) (1932-1977), *Catabrosa* Beauv. (1, 93) (1932-1936)

Brook liverwort - *Marchantia polymorpha* L. (92) (1876)

Brook lobelia - *Lobelia kalmii* L. (5, 131) (1899-1913)

Brook mint [Brook-mint] - *Mentha spicata* L. (5, 156, 158) (1900-1923)

Brook parnassia - *Parnassia asarifolia* Vent. (138) (1923)

Brook pimpernel - *Veronica anagallis-aquatica* L. (19) (1671)

Brook solentine - *Impatiens capensis* Meerb. (158) (1900)

Brook sunflower - *Bidens laevis* (L.) Britton, Sterns & Poggenb. (5, 62, 156) (1912-1923)

Brook thorn - *Crataegus douglasii* Lindl. (108) (1878)

Brookbean [Brook-bean] - *Menyanthes trifoliata* L. (5, 92, 156, 158) (1876-1923)

Brookflower [Brook-flower, Brook flower] - *Hydrophyllum virginianum* L. (5, 156, 158) (1900-1923)

Brookfoam - *Telesonix* Raf. (50) (present)

Brooklime [Brook-lime, Brook lime] - *Nasturtium officinale* W.T. Aiton (possibly) (5, 156, 157, 158) (1900-1929), *Veronica americana* Schwein. ex Benth. (3, 4, 46, 48) (1629-1986), *Veronica beccabunga* L. (19, 92, 107) (1840-1919), *Veronica* L. (1, 77, 93, 158) (1898-1936)

Brookweed [Brook-weed, Brook weed] - *Samolus* L. (4, 50, 138) (1900–present), *Samolus valerandi* L. (19, 92, 184) (1793-1876), *Samolus valerandi* L. subsp. *parviflorus* (Raf.) Hultén (5, 10, 156) (1818-1923)

Broom - *Baptisia tinctoria* (L.) R. Br. ex Aiton f. (186) (1814), *Cytisus* Desf. (106, 138, 156) (1923-1930), *Cytisus scoparius* (L.) Link (5, 49, 52, 53, 57, 59, 60, 107) (1898-1919), *Genista* L. (138) (1923), *Sorghum bicolor* (L.) Moench (184) (1793)

Broom beard grass [Broom beard-grass, Broom beardgrass, Broom bearded grass] - *Schizachyrium scoparium* (Michx.) Nash var. *scoparium* (5, 42, 72, 99, 131) (1814-1923)

Broom beard-sedge [Broom beard sedge] - *Schizachyrium scoparium* (Michx.) Nash var. *scoparium* (62) (1912)

Broom birch - *Betula pubescens* Ehrh. subsp. *pubescens* (5, 156) (1913-1923)

Broom brush - *Hypericum prolificum* L. (5, 74) (1893-1913) WV

Broom clover - *Baptisia tinctoria* (L.) R. Br. ex Aiton f. (64, 157) (1908-1929)

Broom crowberry [Broom-crowberry] - *Corema conradii* (Torr.) Torr. ex Loud. (138, 156) (1923)

Broom cypress - *Kochia scoparia* (L.) Schrad. (5, 156, 157, 158) (1913-1929)

Broom flax - *Linum aristatum* Engelm. (4) (1986)

Broom grass [Broom-grass] - *Andropogon gerardii* Vitman (5) (1913), *Andropogon* L. (1) (1932), *Andropogon virginicus* L. (87) (1884), *Bothriochloa saccharoides* (Sw.) Rydb. (11) (1888), *Bromus kalmii* Gray (7, 92) (1828-1876), *Bromus pubescens* Muhl. ex Willd. (19) (1840), *Schizachyrium scoparium* (Michx.) Nash (5) (1913), *Schizachyrium scoparium* (Michx.) Nash var.

scoparium (19, 45, 66, 87, 90) (1840-1912), *Sorghum* Moench (10) (1818)

Broom groundsel - *Senecio spartioides* Torr. & Gray (155) (1942)

Broom herb - *Cytisus scoparius* (L.) Link (92) (1876)

Broom hickory - *Carya glabra* (Mill.) Sweet (82, 156) (1923-1930), *Carya glabra* (Mill.) Sweet var. *glabra* (2, 5, 19, 107, 187) (1818-1919)

Broom lupine - *Lupinus latifolius* Lindl. ex J.G. Agardh subsp. *latifolius* (138) (1923)

Broom pine - *Pinus palustris* Mill. (20, 92, 182) (1791-1876)

Broom reed grass [Broom reed-grass] - *Calamagrostis scopulorum* M.E. Jones (94) (1901)

Broom sedge - *Carex scoparia* Schkuhr ex Willd. (50, 139, 155) (1942–present)

Broom snakeweed - *Gutierrezia sarothrae* (Pursh) Britton & Rusby (3, 50, 155) (1942–present)

Broomcorn [Broom-corn, Broom corn] - *Sorghum bicolor* (L.) Moench subsp. *bicolor* (14, 56, 66, 87, 92, 107, 109, 119, 155, 158) (1882-1949), *Sorghum* Moench (7) (1828)

Broom-corn grass [Broom corn grass] - *Sorghum bicolor* (L.) Moench subsp. *bicolor* (92) (1876)

Broom-corn millet [Broomcorn millet] - *Panicum miliaceum* L. (3, 5, 50, 56, 109, 119, 122, 138, 140, 155, 158, 163) (1852–present)

Broomflower [Broom flowers] - *Cytisus scoparius* (L.) Link (92) (1876)

Broom-like ragwort [Broomlike ragwort] - *Kochia scoparia* (L.) Schrad. (50) (present), *Senecio spartioides* Torr. & Gray (50) (present)

Broom-like sedge - *Carex scoparia* Schkuhr ex Willd. (66) (1903)

Broom-like senecio - *Senecio spartioides* Torr. & Gray (5, 93, 122) (1913-1937)

Broomrape [Broom-rape, Broom rape] - *Conopholis americana* (L. f.) Wallr. (7) (1828), *Monotropa uniflora* L. (177) (1762), *Orobanche* L. (1, 4, 10, 14, 50, 155, 158, 184) (1793–present), *Orobanche ludoviciana* Nutt. (3, 4, 93, 157) (1900-1986), *Orobanche ludoviciana* Nutt. subsp. *ludoviciana* (85) (1932), *Orobanche uniflora* L. (19) (1840)

Broom-sedge [Broom sedge, Broomsedge] - *Andropogon* L. (155) (1942), *Andropogon virginicus* L. (3, 5, 62, 67, 87, 94, 119, 122, 124, 163) (1852-1977), *Aristida purpurascens* Poir. (5, 119, 163) (1852-1938), *Schizachyrium scoparium* (Michx.) Nash (5) (1913), *Schizachyrium scoparium* (Michx.) Nash var. *scoparium* (45, 75, 128, 134, 163) (1852-1933)

Broom-sedge bluestem [Broom sedge bluestem] - *Andropogon virginicus* L. (5, 50) (1913–present)

Broomtops [Broom tops] - *Cytisus scoparius* (L.) Link (49, 53, 55, 58) (1911-1922)

Broomweed [Broom-weed, Broom weed] - *Amphiachyris* (A. DC.) Nutt. (50) (present), *Amphiachyris dracunculoides* (DC.) Nutt. (3, 4, 106, 155, 156) (1923-1986), *Bigelowia nudata* (Michx.) DC. (156) (1923), *Gutierrezia* Lag. (93, 122) (1936-1937), *Gutierrezia sarothrae* (Pursh) Britton & Rusby (5, 37, 76, 93, 97, 121, 122, 127, 148, 156) (1896-1939), *Gutierrezia texana* (DC.) Torr. & Gray (106) (1930)

Brotherwort - *Origanum vulgare* L. (179) (1526), *Thymus praecox* Opiz subsp. *arcticus* (Dur.) Jalas (possibly) (5) (1913)

Broussonetia - *Broussonetia* L'Hér. ex Vent. (50) (present)

Brown ash - *Fraxinus nigra* Marsh (5, 156) (1913-1923)

Brown beaked-rush [Brown beaked rush] - *Rhynchospora fusca* (L.) Ait. f. (5) (1913)

Brown beak-rush [Brown beak rush] - *Rhynchospora fusca* (L.) Ait. f. (66) (1903)

Brown bent grass [Brown bent-grass] - *Agrostis canina* L. (2, 5, 19, 66, 90, 165) (1768-1913)

Brown bog-rush - *Rhynchospora glomerata* (L.) Vahl (187) (1818)

Brown bugle - *Ajuga reptans* L. (5, 158) (1900-1913)

Brown cedar - *Juniperus monosperma* (Engelm.) Sarg. (113) (1890)

Brown cotton-grass - *Scirpus cyperinus* (L.) Kunth (187) (1818)

Brown cress - *Nasturtium officinale* W.T. Aiton (possibly) (5, 156, 157, 158) (1900-1929)

Brown crowberry - *Corema conradii* (Torr.) Torr. ex Loud. (5, 156) (1913-1923)

Brown cyperus - *Cyperus fuscus* L. (5) (1913)

Brown cypress - *Kochia scoparia* (L.) Schrad. (156, 157, 158) (1900-1929)

Brown daisy [Brown-daisy] - *Rudbeckia hirta* L. (5, 75, 156, 157, 158) (1894-1929) Concord MA

Brown dragon [Brown-dragon] - *Arisaema triphyllum* (L.) Schott (5, 156, 158) (1896-1923), *Arisaema triphyllum* (L.) Schott subsp. *triphyllum* (19) (1840)

Brown durra - *Sorghum bicolor* (L.) Moench subsp. *bicolor* (155) (1942)

Brown flatsedge - *Cyperus fuscus* L. (50) (present)

Brown foxtail - *Setaria verticillata* (L.) Beauv. (5) (1913)

Brown gum - *Eucalyptus robusta* Sm. (138) (1923)

Brown hickory - *Carya glabra* (Mill.) Sweet (156) (1923), *Carya glabra* (Mill.) Sweet var. *glabra* (5) (1913)

Brown knapweed - *Centaurea jacea* L. (5) (1913)

Brown lily - *Hemerocallis fulva* (L.) L. (187) (1818)

Brown millet - *Panicum miliaceum* L. (5, 119) (1913-1938)

Brown mint - *Mentha spicata* L. (5, 158) (1900–1913)

Brown mustard - *Brassica nigra* (L.) W.D.J. Koch (6, 69, 157) (1892-1904)

Brown rush - *Luzula spicata* (L.) DC. (66) (1903)

Brown sedge - *Carex buxbaumii* Wahlenb. (5) (1913), *Carex nigra* (L.) Reichard (72) (1907), *Cyperus flavicomus* Michx. (66) (1903)

Brown wide-lip orchid [Brown widelip orchid] - *Liparis liliifolia* (L.) L.C. Rich. ex Ker-Gawl. (50) (present)

Brown-Betty [Brown Betty] - *Rudbeckia hirta* L. (5, 75, 156, 158) (1900-1923) Passaic, NJ, no longer in use by 1923

Brown-brush - *Hypericum prolificum* L. (156) (1923)

Brown-bush - *Parthenium hysterophorus* L. (158) (1900)

Browned sedge - *Carex adusta* Boott. (5) (1913)

Brown-eyed Susan [Browneyed Susan, Brown-eyed-Susan, Browneyedsusan] - *Rudbeckia hirta* L. (5, 76, 156, 157, 158) (1896–1929), *Rudbeckia triloba* L. (3, 4, 5, 50, 63, 109, 138, 155, 156, 158) (1899–present)

Brown-fruit rush [Brownfruit rush, Brown-fruited rush] - *Juncus pelocarpus* E. Meyer. (5, 50) (1913–present)

Brownie lady-slipper [Brownie ladyslipper] - *Cypripedium fasciculatum* Kellogg ex S. Wats. (138) (1923)

Brownish beak-fern [Brownish beakfern] - *Rhynchospora capitellata* (Michx.) Vahl (50) (present)

Brownish sedge - *Carex brunnescens* (Pers.) Poir. (5, 50) (1913–present)

Brownish-fruit rush [Brownish-fruited rush] - *Juncus articulatus* L. (66) (1903)

Brown-plume ptiloria [Brown-plumed ptiloria] - *Stephanomeria pauciflora* (Torr.) A. Nels. (5, 93, 97) (1913-1937)

Brown-plume wire-lettuce [Brownplume wirelettuce] - *Stephanomeria pauciflora* (Torr.) A. Nels. (50) (present)

Brown's thorn - *Crataegus margarettiae* Ashe (5, 82) (1913-1930)

Brown's wild rye - *Leymus innovatus* (Beal) Pilger (94) (1901)

Brown's willow - *Salix phlebophylla* Anderss. (5) (1913)

Browntop [Brown-top, Brown top] - *Agrostis capillaris* L. (143) (1936) Quebec, *Poa pratensis* L. (90) (1885) ME

Brown-top millet [Brown top millet] - *Urochloa fasciculata* (Sw.) R. Webster (122) (1937) TX

Brown-top panicum [Browntop panicum] - *Urochloa fasciculata* (Sw.) R. Webster (155) (1942)

Brown-top signal grass [Browntop signalgrass] - *Urochloa fasciculata* (Sw.) R. Webster (50) (present)

Brownweed [Brown-weed] - *Bigelowia nudata* (Michx.) DC. (156) (1923), *Gutierrezia* Lag. (158) (1900), *Gutierrezia sarothrae*

(Pursh) Britton & Rusby (156) (1923)

Brown-wood post oak [Brownwood post oak] - *Quercus stellata* Wangenh. (155) (1942)

Brownwort [Brown wort] - *Prunella vulgaris* L. (5, 157, 158) (1900-1929), *Scrophularia umbrosa* Dumort. (107) (1919)

Bruiseroot [Bruise root] - *Glaucium flavum* Crantz (92, 156) (1876-1923), *Glaucium flavum* Crantz (possibly) (7) (1828), *Glaucium flavum* Crantz (possibly) (7) (1828), *Symphytum officinale* L. (5, 64, 156) (1907-1923)

Bruisewort [Bruise wort, Bruise-wort, Bruse-wort] - *Bellis perennis* L. (5, 158, 179) (1526-1913), *Saponaria officinalis* L. (5, 64, 92, 156, 157, 158, 180, 187) (1633-1929)

Brum - *Galium verum* L. (158) (1900)

Brunella - *Prunella vulgaris* L. (174, 177) (1753-1762)

Bruner's joe-pye weed [Bruner joepyeweed] - *Eupatorium maculatum* L. var. *bruneri* (Gray) Breitung (155) (1942)

Bruner's trumpetweed [Bruner's trumpet weed] - *Eupatorium maculatum* L. var. *bruneri* (Gray) Breitung (5) (1913)

Brun-hwen (Swedish) - *Agrostis canina* L. (46) (1879)

Brunnenkresse (German) - *Rorippa nasturtium-aquaticum* (L.) Hayek (158) (1900)

Brunnichia - *Brunnichia ovata* (Walt.) Shinners (5, 97) (1913-1937)

Brush - *Ratibida columnifera* (Nutt.) Wood & Standl. (5, 76, 158) (1896-1913)

Brushes - *Centaurea cyanus* L. (5, 64, 73, 78, 92, 156, 157, 158) (1900-1929)

Brussel sprouts - *Brassica* L. (107) (1919)

Bryght - *Ranunculus ficaria* L. (179) (1526)

Bryonia - *Bryonia alba* L. (52, 54, 57, 60) (1902-1919), *Bryonia cretica* L. subsp. *dioica* (Jacq.) Tutin (57, 60) (1902-1917)

Bryony [Briony] - *Bryonia alba* L. (52, 53, 57, 60, 92) (1876-1922), *Bryonia cretica* L. subsp. *dioica* (Jacq.) Tutin (55, 57, 60, 92, 179) (1526–1917), *Bryonia* L. (109) (1949) from Greek for "to sprout" referring to the shoots that come annually from the tuber, *Sicyos angulatus* L. (7) (1828)

Bryony-leaf rough-bindweed [Bryony leaved rough bindweed] - *Smilax tamnoides* L. (8) (1785)

Bubby-blossoms - *Calycanthus floridus* L. (156) (1923)

Bubby-bush [Bubbybush, Bubby bush] - *Calycanthus floridus* L. var. *glaucus* (Willd.) Torr. & Gray (5, 74, 156) (1913-1923) Banner Elk NC

Buchweizen [Buchweitzen] (German) - *Fagopyrum esculentum* Moench (6, 110, 158) (1886-1900) corrupted into buckwheat in English

Buck plantain [Buck-plantain] - *Plantago lanceolata* L. (5, 75, 156) (1894-1923) WV

Buck thistle [Buck-thistle] - *Carduus nutans* L. (5, 156, 158) (1900-1923), *Cirsium vulgare* (Savi) Ten. (158) (1900)

Buckbean [Buck bean, Buck-bean] - *Menyanthes* L. (2, 4, 50, 85, 92, 156, 158) (1895–present), *Menyanthes trifoliata* L. (1, 3, 5, 6, 10, 19, 49, 50, 57, 63, 72, 93, 109, 131, 148, 156, 158, 184) (1793–present), *Thermopsis* R. Br. ex Aiton f. (4) (1986)

Buckberry [Buck-berry] - *Gaylussacia ursina* (M.A. Curtis) Torr. & Gray ex Gray (138) (1923), *Vaccinium* L. (1) (1932), *Vaccinium scoparium* Leiberg (92, 97) (1876-1937), *Vaccinium stamineum* L. (5, 97, 156, 158) (1900-1937)

Buckbrush [Buck brush, Buck-brush] - *Apocynum androsaemifolium* L. (156) (1923), *Ceanothus cuneatus* (Hook.) Nutt. (106) (1930) CA, *Ceanothus sanguineus* Pursh (106) (1930) CA, *Cephalanthus occidentalis* L. (156) (1923), *Cornus racemosa* Lam. (106) (1930) Arkansas, *Elaeagnus commutata* Bernh. ex Rydb. (156) (1923), *Purshia tridentata* (Pursh) DC. (106) (1930) Northeast Oregon, *Symphoricarpos albus* (L.) Blake var. *albus* (106) (1930), *Symphoricarpos* Duham. (112) (1937), *Symphoricarpos occidentalis* Hook. (5, 9, 37, 98, 101, 106, 113, 114, 127, 130, 156, 158) (1873-1933), *Symphoricarpos symphoricarpos* (L.) MacMill. (5, 9, 37, 98, 101, 106, 113, 114, 127, 130, 156, 158) (1894-1986)

Bucke - *Fagopyrum esculentum* Moench (180) (1633)

Buckesshorne - *Coronopus squamatus* (Forsk.) Aschers. (179) (1526)

Buck-eye [Buckeye, Buck's Eyes] - *Aesculus pavia* L. (71, 177) (1762-1898), *Aesculus flava* Aiton (23, 35) (1806-1810), *Aesculus glabra* Willd. (23, 52, 61, 92, 148) (1810-1939), *Aesculus hippocastanum* L. (6) (1892), *Aesculus* L. (1, 10, 13, 15, 18, 50, 82, 106, 109, 155) (1805–present), *Aesculus parviflora* Walt. (107) (1919)

Buckhorn [Buck horn, Buck-horn, Buck's horn, Buckshorn, Buck's-horn, Bucks-horne, Bucks horne] - *Carara coronopus* (L.) Medik. (5) (1913), *Coronopus squamatus* (Forsk.) Aschers. (156, 178) (1526-1923) no longer in use by 1923, *Lycopodium clavatum* L. (5) (1913), *Osmunda regalis* L. (73) (1892), *Plantago aristata* Michx. (4) (1986), *Plantago lanceolata* L. (4, 21, 62, 80, 82, 156) (1893-1986), *Plantago maritima* L. (5) (1913), *Plantago maritima* L. var. *juncoides* (Lam.) Gray (156) (1923), *Plantago patagonica* Jacq. (3) (1977)

Buckhorn brake - *Osmunda regalis* L. (5, 49, 92, 157) (1876-1913)

Buckhorn male fern [Buckhorn male-fern] - *Osmunda regalis* L. (157) (1929)

Buckhorn plantain [Buck-horn plantain, Buck-horne plantaines, Buckshorn plantain] - *Plantago lanceolata* L. (75, 155, 156, 180) (1633-1942), *Plantago coronopus* L. (92, 107) (1876-1919)

Buckley's beardtongue - *Penstemon buckleyi* Pennell (50) (present)

Buckley's centaury - *Centaurium calycosum* (Buckley) Fernald (5, 122) (1913-1937)

Buckley's hickory - *Carya texana* Buckl. (97) (1937)

Buckley's penstemon - *Penstemon buckleyi* Pennell (3, 4) (1977-1986)

Buckley's rush grass [Buckley's rush-grass] - *Sporobolus buckleyi* Vasey (94) (1901)

Buckley's spear grass - *Poa secunda* J. Presl (5) (1913)

Buck's-grass [Buck's grass] - *Lycopodium clavatum* L. (5) (1913)

Buckthorn [Bucke thorne] - *Frangula alnus* Mill. (53, 57, 59) (1911-1922), *Frangula caroliniana* (Walt.) Gray (107) (1919), *Frangula* Mill. (50) (present), *Rhamnus alnifolia* L'Her. (184) (1793), *Rhamnus cathartica* L. (5, 6, 7, 19, 57, 61, 58, 59, 82, 92, 112, 126, 135, 158, 178) (1526-1937), *Rhamnus crocea* Nutt. (103) (1870), *Rhamnus* L. (5, 6, 7, 19, 57, 61, 58, 59, 82, 92, 112, 126, 135, 158) (1818–present), *Rhamnus lanceolata* Pursh (85, 95, 113) (1890-1932), *Sideroxylon* L. (1, 153, 158) (1900-1932) NM

Buckthorn brake [Buck thorn brake] - *Osmunda regalis* L. (52, 57) (1917-1919)

Buckthorn plantain - *Plantago lanceolata* L. (5, 93) (1913-1936)

Buckthorn-weed - *Amsinckia* Lehm. (1) (1932)

Buckwheat [Buck-wheat] - *Eriogonum* Michx. (50) (present), *Fagopyrum esculentum* Moench (3, 4, 5, 6, 19, 50, 72, 85, 92, 93, 95, 106, 107, 110, 114, 156, 158, 180) (1633–present), *Fagopyrum* Mill. (1, 14, 50, 82, 109, 138, 155, 158) (1882–1949), *Polygonum* L. (10, 167) (1814-1818)

Buckwheat tree [Buckwheat-tree] - *Cliftonia* Banks ex Gaertn. f. (15) (1895), *Cliftonia monophylla (Lam.) Britton* (20, 106) (1857-1930)

Buckwheat vine - *Brunnichia ovata* (Walt.) Shinners (156) (1923)

Bud sagebrush - *Picrothamnus desertorum* Nutt. (155) (1942)

Buddhist bauhinia - *Bauhinia variegata* L. (138) (1923)

Budwood - *Cornus florida* L. (92) (1876)

Büdöskey ar - *Anthemis cotula* L. (186) (1814)

Buff fleabane - *Erigeron ochroleucus* Nutt. (50) (present)

Buffalo bean [Buffalo bean, Buffalo-bean, Buffalo beans] - *Astragalus crassicarpus* Nutt. (158) (1900), *Astragalus crassicarpus* Nutt. var. *crassicarpus* (5, 76, 85, 156) (1896-1932), *Astragalus* L. (1, 93, 106) (1930-1936)

Buffalo bunch grass [Buffalo bunch-grass] - *Festuca altaica* Trin. (45, 87) (1884-1896)

Buffalo bur [Buffalo-bur, Buffalo burr] - *Glycyrrhiza lepidota* Pursh (131) (1899) SD, *Solanum* L. (1) (1932), *Solanum rostratum* Dunal (3, 4, 5, 56, 62, 70, 75, 80, 85, 93, 95, 97, 114, 122, 125, 156, 158) (1894-1986)

Buffalo clover [Buffalo-clover] - *Melilotus officinalis* (L.) Lam.

(187), *Trifolium reflexum* L. (3, 4, 5, 47, 50, 63, 72, 82, 85, 92, 93, 97, 122, 155, 156, 158) (1852–present), *Trifolium stoloniferum* Muhl. ex Eat. (7, 19) (1828-1840)

Buffalo currant [Buffalo currants] - *Ribes aureum* Pursh (2, 63, 72, 92, 93, 106, 107, 108, 131, 135, 149, 156, 158) (1878-1936), *Ribes aureum* Pursh var. *villosum* DC. (3, 4, 5, 109) (1913-1986)

Buffalo gourd [Buffalogourd] - *Cucurbita foetidissima* Kunth (3, 4, 121, 138, 155) (1923-1986)

Buffalo grass [Buffalo-grass, Buffalograss] - *Bouteloua gracilis* (Willd. ex Kunth) Lag. ex Griffiths (5, 30, 75, 87, 88, 101, 108, 146) (1844-1939), *Bouteloua hirsuta* Lag. (5, 75, 129) (1894–1913), *Bouteloua* Lag. (1) (1932), *Buchloe dactyloides* (Nutt.) Engelm. (3, 5, 11, 22, 28, 30, 45, 50, 56, 67, 72, 75, 85, 87, 88, 94, 111, 119, 122, 129, 134, 140, 144, 146, 152, 155, 163, 164) (1844–present), *Buchloe* Engelm. (1, 45, 50, 93) (1896–present), *Hesperostipa spartea* (Trin.) Barkworth (56) (1901) IA, *Heteranthera dubia* (Jacq.) MacM. (156) (1923), *Tripsacum dactyloides* (L.) L. (5, 14, 107) (1882-1919)

Buffalo nut [Buffalo-nut] - *Pyrularia pubera* Michx. (2, 5, 107, 156) (1895-1923), *Trapa natans* L. (156) (1923)

Buffalo rye - *Leymus condensatus* (J. Presl) A. Löve (101) (1905) MT

Buffalo-apple [Buffalo apple] - *Astragalus crassicarpus* Nutt. (158) (1900), *Astragalus crassicarpus* Nutt. var. *crassicarpus* (5, 76, 156) (1896-1923) ND

Buffalo-berry [Buffalo berry, Buffaloberry] - *Shepherdia argentea* (Pursh) Nutt. (3, 4, 5, 14, 22, 33, 37, 72, 75, 78, 85, 92, 93, 95, 101, 103, 107, 108, 109, 112, 113, 120, 131, 135, 153, 156, 158) (1827-1986), *Shepherdia* Nutt. (1, 50, 82, 93, 108, 138, 158) (1878–present)

Buffalo-bur nightshade [Buffalobur nightshade] - *Solanum rostratum* Dunal (50, 155) (1942–present)

Buffalo-fat [Buffalo fat] - *Shepherdia argentea* (Pursh) Nutt. (20) (1857)

Buffalo-grease [Buffalo grease] - *Shepherdia argentea* (Pursh) Nutt. (35) (1806) William Clark

Buffalo-pea [Buffalo pea, Buffalo peas] - *Astragalus crassicarpus* Nutt. (131, 158) (1899-1900), *Astragalus crassicarpus* Nutt. var. *crassicarpus* (5, 37, 114) (1894-1919), *Astragalus* L. (1) (1932), *Vicia americana* Muhl. ex Willd. (5, 76, 93, 156, 158) (1896-1923)

Buffalo-weed [Buffalo weed] - *Ambrosia trifida* L. (5, 156, 157, 158) (1900–1929), *Astragalus crassicarpus* Nutt. var. *berlandieri* Barneby (156) (1923)

Buffpetal - *Rhynchosida physocalyx* (Gray) Fryxell (50) (present)

Bugbane [Bug-bane, Bug bane] - *Cimicifuga racemosa* (L.) Nutt. (6, 19, 58, 64, 92, 156) (1840-1923), *Cimicifuga* Wernischeck (13, 15, 109, 156, 167) (1814-1949), *Veratrum viride* Ait. (64, 71, 156) (1898-1923)

Bû'giso'wĭn (Chippewa, swimming or bath) - *Artemisia dracunculus* L. (40) (1928), *Asclepias incarnata* L. (40) (1928)

Bugle - *Ajuga chamaepitys* (L.) Schreb. (19, 92) (1840-1876), *Ajuga* L. (10, 50, 138, 155, 158, 167) (1814–present), *Ajuga reptans* L. (5, 156, 158) (1900-1923), *Lycopus americanus* Muhl. ex W. Bart. (57) (1917), *Lycopus virginicus* L. (57) (1917)

Bugle (French) - *Ajuga reptans* L. (158) (1900)

Bugle-lily [Buglelily] - *Watsonia* Mill. (138) (1923)

Bugleweed [Bugle weed, Bugle-weed] - *Ajuga* L. (109, 156) (1923-1949), *Ajuga reptans* L. (156) (1923), *Baptisia tinctoria* (L.) R. Br. ex Aiton f. (106) (1930), *Lycopus asper* Greene (40) (1928), *Lycopus* L. (1, 4, 93, 106, 138, 155, 158) (1900-1986), *Lycopus uniflorus* Michx. (3, 156) (1923-1977), *Lycopus virginicus* L. (2, 5, 6, 7, 19, 47, 49, 52, 53, 54, 61, 63, 92, 93, 95, 122, 156, 157, 158) (1840-1937)

Buglewort [Bugle wort, Bugle-wort] - *Lycopus virginicus* L. (5, 7, 92, 156, 158) (1828-1923)

Bugloss [Buglos, Buglosse] - *Anchusa arvensis* (L.) Bieb. (93) (1936), *Anchusa* L. (1, 50, 82, 109, 138, 155, 156, 179) (1526–present) SD, *Anchusa officinalis* L. (19, 46, 107) (1617-1919), *Picris echioides* L. (5, 156, 158) (1900-1923), *Symphytum asperum* Lepechin (77) (1898) Paris ME

Bugloss picris [Bugloss-picris] - *Picris echioides* L. (5, 156, 158) (1900–1923)

Buglossoides - *Buglossoides* Moench (50) (present)

Buglossum - *Anchusa azurea* Mill. (165) (1768)

Bugseed [Bug seed, Bug-seed] - *Corispermum americanum* (Nutt.) Nutt. var. *rydbergii* Mosyakin (3, 93, 97, 131, 145, 156) (1897-1977), *Corispermum* L. (1, 2, 50, 93, 158) (1900–present), *Corispermum nitidum* Kit. ex J.A. Schultes (3, 4) (1977-1986)

Bugweed [Bug-weed] - *Corispermum americanum* (Nutt.) Nutt. var. *rydbergii* Mosyakin (5, 156, 158) (1900–1923)

Bugwort - *Cimicifuga racemosa* (L.) Nutt. (64, 92, 156) (1898-1923), *Veratrum viride* Ait. (64) (1908)

Bûgwûdj'mĭskodi'simĭn (Chippewa, unusual reddish bean) - *Amphicarpaea bracteata* (L.) Fern. var. *comosa* (L.) Fern. (40) (1928)

Buissonn à plumes (French) - *Cercocarpus ledifolius* Nutt. (20) (1857)

Bulb bittercress - *Cardamine bulbosa* (Schreber. ex Muhl.) B.S.P. (138, 155) (1923-1942)

Bulb buttercup - *Ranunculus bulbosus* L. (155) (1942)

Bulb cloak fern [Bulb cloakfern] - *Astrolepis sinuata* (Lag. ex Sw.) Benham & Windham subsp. *sinuata* (155) (1942)

Bulb panicum - *Panicum bulbosum* Kunth (122) (1937)

Bulb water hemlock [Bulb waterhemlock] - *Cicuta bulbifera* L. (155) (1942)

Bulb-bearing cowbane [Bulb bearing cow bane] - *Cicuta bulbifera* L. (42) (1814)

Bulb-bearing lily - *Lilium bulbiferum* L. (107) (1919)

Bulb-bearing loosestrife [Bulb-bearing loose-strife] - *Lysimachia terrestris* (L.) Britton, Sterns & Poggenb. (5, 72, 156, 187) (1818-1923)

Bulb-bearing water hemlock [Bulb-bearing water-hemlock] - *Cicuta bulbifera* L. (5, 72, 93, 131, 156, 158) (1899–1936)

Bulbed asphodill - *Ornithogalum pyrenaicum* L. (180) (1633)

Bulbed red lillie - *Lilium bulbiferum* L. (178) (1596)

Bulbed-violet [Bulbed violet] - *Leucojum vernum* L. (180) (1633)

Bulblet bladder fern [Bulbet bladderfern] - *Cystopteris bulbifera* (L.) Bernh. (3, 4, 50) (1977–present)

Bulblet cystopteris - *Cystopteris bulbifera* (L.) Bernh. (4, 5) (1913-1986)

Bulblet-bearing water hemlock - *Cicuta bulbifera* L. (50) (present)

Bulbous amanita - *Amanita phalloides* (Fr.) Link (71) (1898)

Bulbous arethusa - *Arethusa bulbosa* L. (42) (1814)

Bulbous asphodill - *Ornithogalum pyrenaicum* L. (178) (1596)

Bulbous bittercress - *Cardamine bulbosa* (Schreber. ex Muhl.) B.S.P. (50) (present)

Bulbous blue grass [Bulbous bluegrass] - *Poa bulbosa* L. (3, 50, 155) (1942–present)

Bulbous buttercup - *Ranunculus bulbosus* L. (2, 3, 4, 5, 6, 93, 158) (1895–1986)

Bulbous cress - *Cardamine bulbosa* (Schreber. ex Muhl.) B.S.P. (5, 93, 131) (1899–1936)

Bulbous crowfoot [Bulbous crowfoote] - *Ranunculus bulbosus* L. (6, 45, 49, 63, 156, 178) (1526-1923)

Bulbous flower-de-luce [Bulbous flowerdeluce] - *Iris xiphium* L. (178) (1596)

Bulbous fumitory - *Adoxa moschatellina* L. (5, 156, 158, 165) (1768-1923)

Bulbous melic grass - *Melica bulbosa* Geyer ex Porter & Coult. (87) (1884)

Bulbous panic grass [Bulbous panic-grass] - *Panicum bulbosum* Kunth (163) (1852)

Bulbous rush - *Juncus bulbosus* L. (5) (1913)

Bulbous water hemlock - *Cicuta bulbifera* L. (3, 4) (1977-1986)

Bulbous woodrush - *Luzula bulbosa* (Wood) Smyth & Smyth (50) (present)

Bulbous-rooted arethusa - *Arethusa bulbosa* L. (187) (1818)

Bulbous-rooted turkey-pod - *Cardamine bulbosa* (Schreber. ex Muhl.) B.S.P. (187) (1818)

Bulbous-rooted wall-cress - *Cardamine bulbosa* (Schreber. ex Muhl.) B.S.P. (187) (1818)

Bulbous-violet [Bulbous violets] - *Leucojum* L. (180) (1633)

Bull bay or Bull bay tree - *Magnolia grandiflora* L. (106, 109) (1930-1949)

Bull brier [Bull-brier] - *Smilax pseudochina* L. (5, 156) (1913-1923), *Smilax rotundifolia* L. (109) (1949)

Bull crown grass [Bull crowngrass] - *Paspalum boscianum* Flueggé (50) (present)

Bull daisy [Bull-daisy] - *Leucanthemum vulgare* Lam. (5, 156, 158) (1900-1923)

Bull grape - *Vitis labrusca* L. (possibly) (7) (1828), *Vitis rotundifolia* Michx. (15) (1895), *Vitis vulpina* L. (5, 74, 156, 158) (1893-1923) Alabama

Bull grass [Bull-grass, Bull grass] - *Bromus hordeaceus* L. (5) (1913), *Muhlenbergia emersleyi* Vasey (122) (1937) TX, *Paspalum plicatulum* Michx. (75) (1894) Alabama, *Spartina pectinata* Bosc ex Link (5, 119) (1913-1938), *Tripsacum dactyloides* (L.) L. (5, 119) (1913-1938), *Tripsacum* L. (93) (1936)

Bull nettle [Bull-nettle] - *Cnidoscolus* J. Pohl (4) (1986), *Cnidoscolus stimulosus* (Michx.) Engelm. & Gray (78) (1898) Southern US, *Cnidoscolus texanus* (Muell.-Arg.) Small (4, 122) (1937-1986), *Solanum carolinense* L. (5, 49, 52, 53, 62, 75, 77, 156, 157, 158) (1898), *Solanum elaeagnifolium* Cav. (150) (1894)

Bull nut [Bull-nut, Bullnut] - *Carya alba* (L.) Nutt. ex Ell. (5, 73, 156, 158) (1892-1923) Peoria IL

Bull pine - *Pinus aristata* Engelm. (153) (1913) NM, *Pinus echinata* Mill. (5) (1913), *Pinus ponderosa* P.& C. Lawson (32, 135, 158) (1895-1910), *Pinus ponderosa* P.& C. Lawson var. *ponderosa* (153) (1913), *Pinus ponderosa* P.& C. Lawson var. *scopulorum* Engelm. (1, 75, 136, 149) (1894-1932)

Bull thistle [Bull-thistle] - *Cirsium pumilum* (Nutt.) Spreng. (73, 156) (1892-1923), *Cirsium vulgare* (Savi) Ten. (3, 4, 5, 50, 56, 62, 80, 82, 155, 156, 158) (1900-present)

Bullac grape - *Vitis rotundifolia* Michx. (5) (1913)

Bullace - *Prunus domestica* L. var. *insititia* (L.) Fiori & Paoletti (5, 107, 110) (1886-1919), *Prunus dulcis* (Mill.) D.A. Webber (92) (1876), *Vitis rotundifolia* Michx. (2, 107) (1895-1919)

Bullace grape [Bullace-grape] - *Vitis* L. (possibly) (1) (1932), *Vitis rotundifolia* Michx. (15, 156) (1895-1923)

Bullace plum - *Prunus domestica* L. var. *insititia* (L.) Fiori & Paoletti (156) (1923)

Bullberry [Bull-berry, Bull berry] - *Shepherdia argentea* (Pursh) Nutt. (5, 36, 101, 104, 108, 156, 158) (1830-1923) no longer in use by 1923, *Shepherdia* Nutt. (1) (1932), *Vaccinium uliginosum* L. (156) (1923)

Bulldogs [Bull-dogs, Bull-dog] - *Antirrhinum majus* L. (5, 92, 156, 158) (1898-1923)

Bullet grape - *Vitis labrusca* L. (possibly) (7) (1828), *Vitis vulpina* L. (7) (1828)

Bullflower [Bull-flower] - *Caltha palustris* L. (5, 156, 157, 158) (1900-1929)

Bull-grip - *Smilax rotundifolia* L. (156) (1923)

Bull-head lily [Bullhead lily] - *Nuphar lutea* (L.) Sm. subsp. *advena* (Aiton) Kartesz & Gandhi (79, 158) (1891-1900) NH

Bull-horn acacia [Bullhorn acacia] - *Acacia cornigera* (L.) Willd. (138, 155) (1931-1942)

Bull-horn wattle [Bullhorn wattle] - *Acacia cornigera* (L.) Willd. (50) (present)

Bullimong - *Fagopyrum esculentum* Moench (180) (1633)

Bullit grape - *Vitis rotundifolia* Michx. (15) (1895)

Bullock-heart custard-apple [Bullockheart custardapple] - *Annona reticulata* L. (155) (1942)

Bullock's lungwort [Bullock's-lungwort, Bullock lungwort] - *Verbascum thapsus* L. (5, 14, 69, 92, 156, 158) (1876-1923)

Bullock's-eye [Bullocks eie, Bullock's eye] - *Sempervivum tectorum* L. (92, 156) (1876-1923), *Sempervivum tectorum* L. (possibly) (180) (1633)

Bullock's-heart [Bullocks-heart] - *Annona reticulata* L. (109, 110) (1886-1949), *Annona glabra* L. (110) (1886)

Bullpates - *Deschampsia caespitosa* (L.) Beauv. (5) (1913), *Deschampsia caespitosa* (L.) Beauv. (5) (1913)

Bull-poll [Bull poll] - *Deschampsia caespitosa* (L.) Beauv. (5) (1913)

Bullrattle [Bull-rattle] - *Silene latifolia* Poir. subsp. *alba* (Mill.) Greuter & Burdet (5, 156, 158) (1900-1923) no longer in use by 1923, *Silene vulgaris* (Moench) Garcke (5, 156) (1913-1923) no longer in use by 1923

Bull's coraldrops - *Besseya bullii* (Eat.) Rydb. (50) (present)

Bull's synthyris - *Besseya bullii* (Eat.) Rydb. (5, 72) (1907-1913)

Bull-segg - *Typha latifolia* L. (5, 156, 158) (1900-1923)

Bull's-eye daisy [Bull's eye daisy, Bullseye daisy] - *Leucanthemum vulgare* Lam. (5, 156, 158) (1900-1923), *Rudbeckia hirta* L. (156) (1923)

Bull's-eyes [Bull's eyes, Bullseye, Bulls-eyes] - *Caltha palustris* L. (156) (1923), *Rudbeckia hirta* L. (76) (1896) Paris ME

Bull's-eyes [Bull's eyes, Bullseye] - *Leucanthemum vulgare* Lam. (73, 75) (1892)

Bull's-foot [Bull's foot, Bulls-foot, Bullsfoot] - *Tussilago farfara* L. (5, 58, 92, 156) (1869-1923)

Bull-tongue arrowhead [Bulltongue arrowhead] - *Sagittaria lancifolia* L. (50) (present)

Bullweed [Bull-weed] - *Centaurea nigra* L. (5, 156) (1913-1923)

Bullwort [Bull wort, Bull-wort] - *Ptilimnium capillaceum* (Michx.) Raf. (5, 156) (1913-1923)

Bully - *Sideroxylon* L. (50) (present)

Bulrush [Bull rush, Bullrush, Bul-Rush, Bulrushes] - *Cyperus* L. (7) (1828), *Juncus effusus* L. (19, 92) (1840-1876), *Schoenoplectus* (Reichenb.) Palla (50) (present), *Schoenoplectus acutus* (Muhl. ex Bigelow) A.& D. Löve var. *acutus* (35, 101, 152) (1806-1912), *Schoenoplectus americanus* (Pers.) Volk. ex Schinz & R. Keller (85) (1932), *Schoenoplectus tabernaemontani* (C.C. Gmel.) Palla (possibly) (37, 66, 107, 158) (1830-1919), *Scirpus* L. (1, 50, 93, 109, 138, 139, 156) (1923-present), *Scirpus pallidus* (Britt.) Fern. (41) (1770), *Typha latifolia* L. (5, 107, 156, 157, 158) (1900-1929)

Bulwand - *Artemisia vulgaris* L. (156, 157) (1923-1929)

Bumble - *Schoenoplectus tabernaemontani* (C.C. Gmel.) Palla (possibly) (158) (1900)

Bumblebee root [Bumble bee root, Bumblebee-root] - *Trillium erectum* L. (5, 6, 64, 73, 156) (1874-1923) New England, no longer in use by 1923

Bumelia - *Sideroxylon* L. (155) (1942), *Sideroxylon lycioides* L. (5) (1913)

Bumelia-ironwood - *Sideroxylon lycioides* L. (156) (1923)

Bunch cut grass [Bunch cutgrass] - *Leersia monandra* Sw. (50) (present)

Bunch evergreen - *Lycopodium dendroideum* Michx. (73) (1892) NH, *Lycopodium obscurum* L. (5, 158) (1900-1913)

Bunch grape - *Vitis aestivalis* Michx. (15, 107) (1895), *Vitis cinerea* (Engelm.) Millard (156) (1923)

Bunch grass [Bunchgrass, Bunch-grass] - *Achnatherum hymenoides* (Roemer & J.A. Schultes) Barkworth (45, 87, 129) (1884-1896), *Aristida purpurea* Nutt. (129) (1894), *Calamagrostis stricta* (Timm) Koel. (87) (1884), *Deschampsia caespitosa* (L.) Beauv. (88) (1885), *Eragrostis tenuifolia* (A. Rich.) Hochst. ex Steud. (45, 87, 88) (1885-1896), *Festuca altaica* Trin. (75, 87, 88, 161) (1857-1894), *Festuca ovina* L. (45) (1896), *Hesperostipa comata* (Trin. & Rupr.) Barkworth subsp. *comata* (5, 45) (1896-1913), *Nassella neesiana* (Trin. & Rupr.) Barkworth (87) (1884), *Nassella viridula* (Trin.) Barkworth (87) (1884), *Nolina texana* S. Wats. (122, 124) (1937) TX, *Poa arida* Vasey (163) (1852), *Poa* L. (45) (1896), *Pseudoroegneria spicata* (Pursh) A. Löve subsp. *spicata* (163) (1852), *Schizachyrium scoparium* (Michx.) Nash (5) (1913), *Schizachyrium scoparium* (Michx.) Nash var. *scoparium* (65, 75, 128) (1894-1931), *Sphenopholis* Scribn. (93) (1936), *Sporobolus airoides* (Torr.) Torr. (116, 129, 149, 151, 152) (1894-1958), *Sporobolus* *heterolepis* (Gray) Gray (5, 119, 129) (1894-1938), *Sporobolus wrightii* Munro ex Scribn. (163) (1852)

Bunch hair grass [Bunch hair-grass] - *Muhlenbergia capillaris* (Lam.) Trin. var. *trichopodes* (Ell.) Vasey (94) (1901)

Bunch hawthorn - *Crataegus dodgei* Ashe (138) (1923)

Bunch pink - *Dianthus barbatus* L. (5, 73, 92, 156, 158) (1876–1923), *Silene armeria* L. (156) (1923)

Bunch redtop [Bunch red-top] - *Poa secunda* J. Presl (5, 94) (1901-1913)

Bunch spear grass - *Poa arida* Vasey (5, 129) (1894-1913)

Bunchberry [Bunch berry] - *Cornus* L. (1, 85) (1932) SD, *Cornus canadensis* L. (3, 4, 5, 40, 92, 107, 109, 138, 156, 158) (1876-1986)

Bunchberry dogwood - *Cornus canadensis* L. (50, 155) (1942–present)

Bunchberry elder - *Sambucus racemosa* L. var. *racemosa* (155) (1942)

Bunchflower [Bunch-flower, Bunch flower] - *Melanthium* L. (1, 50, 138, 155) (1923–present), *Melanthium latifolium* Desr. (19, 92) (1840-1876), *Melanthium virginicum* L (3, 5, 72, 122, 124, 155, 156, 158) (1900-1977), *Mertensia virginica* (L.) Pers. ex Link (possibly) (156) (1923)

Bunch-plum [Bunch plums, Bunch plum] - *Cornus canadensis* L. (5, 73, 156, 158) (1892-1923) NH

Bundled cassia - *Chamaecrista fasciculata* (Michx.) Greene var. *fasciculata* (42) (1814)

Bundle-flower [Bundleflower] - *Desmanthus cooleyi* (Eat.) Trel. (3) (1977), *Desmanthus illinoensis* (Michx.) MacM. ex B.L. Robins. & Fern. (3) (1977), *Desmanthus leptolobus* Torr. & Gray (3) (1977), *Desmanthus* Willd. (50, 155) (1942–present)

Bundle-root buttercup [Bundle-rooted buttercup] - *Ranunculus fascicularis* Muhl. ex Bigelow (5) (1913)

Bunk - *Cichorium intybus* L. (5, 156, 157, 158) (1900-1929) no longer in use by 1923 156, *Conium maculatum* L. (5, 69, 156, 158) (1900-1923)

Bunny-ears - *Opuntia microdasys* (Lehm.) Lehm. Ex Pfeiff. (109) (1949)

Bunny-mouth - *Antirrhinum majus* L. (158) (1900)

Bunny-rabbit [Bunny rabbits] - *Antirrhinum majus* L. (156, 158) (1900-1923)

Bunweed - *Senecio jacobea* L. (92) (1876)

Bupleurum - *Bupleurum* L. (50) (present)

Bur - *Humulus lupulus* L. (157, 158) (1900-1929)

Bur beakchervil - *Anthriscus sylvestris* (L.) Hoffmann (155) (1942), *Torilis japonica* (Houtt.) DC. (155) (1942)

Bur beggarticks - *Bidens tripartita* L. (155) (1942)

Bur bristle grass [Bur bristlegrass] - *Setaria verticillata* (L.) Beauv. (140) (1944)

Bur clover [Burr clover] - *Medicago arabica* (L.) Huds. (45) (1896), *Medicago lupulina* L. (103) (1870), *Medicago minima* L. (3) (1977), *Medicago polymorpha* L. (5, 45, 50, 76, 87, 93, 97, 106, 107, 122, 124, 156) (1884–present)

Bur cucumber [Bur-cucumber, Burcucumber, Burr cucumber] - *Cyclanthera dissecta* (Torr. & Gray) Arn. (122) (1937) TX, *Sicyos angulatus* L. (3, 4, 82, 107, 131, 157, 158) (1899-1986), *Sicyos* L. (1, 4, 50, 155) (1932–present), *Trichosanthes anguina* L. (107) (1919)

Bur grass [Bur-grass, Burr grass] - *Cenchrus echinatus* L. (19) (1840), *Cenchrus* L. (1, 10, 92, 93) (1818-1936), *Cenchrus spinifex* Cav. (119) (1938), *Cenchrus tribuloides* L. (2, 5, 46, 62, 66, 150) (1894-1912)

Bur ironweed - *Vernonia arkansana* DC. (138, 155) (1923-1942)

Bur nut [Bur-nut] - *Tribulus* L. (1, 174) (1753-1932), *Tribulus terrestris* L. (85, 156) (1923-1932)

Bur oak [Burr oak, Burr-oak] - *Quercus macrocarpa* Michx. (1, 3, 4, 5, 9, 37, 40, 44, 50, 65, 72, 85, 93, 95, 97, 109, 112, 113, 122, 124, 155, 156, 158) (1845–present), *Quercus macrocarpa* Michx. (108, 130, 131, 135) (1878-1910)

Bur ragweed [Bur-ragweed] - *Ambrosia acanthicarpa* Hook. (93) (1936), *Ambrosia grayi* (A. Nels.) Shinners (3, 4) (1977-1986)

Bur snakeroot - *Sanicula canadensis* L. (40) (1928)

Bur thistle [Bur-thistle, Burr thistle, Burthistle] - *Cirsium vulgare* (Savi) Ten. (156, 158) (1900-1923), *Xanthium* L. (7) (1828), *Xanthium strumarium* L. (92, 158) (1876-1900)

Bur tree [Bur-tree] - *Sambucus nigra* L. (158) (1900)

Bur vine - *Verbena simplex* Lehm. (77) (1898) Southwest MO, *Verbena stricta* Vent. (77) (1898) Southwest MO, *Verbena urticifolia* L. (77) (1898) Southwest MO.

Burburr [Burr-bur] - *Arctium lappa* L. (69) (1904)

Burden's dew grass - *Agrostis gigantea* Roth (5) (1913)

Burden's grass - *Agrostis capillaris* L. (66, 90) (1885-1903) ME, *Agrostis gigantea* Roth (45) (1896)

Burdock - *Arctium* L. (1, 4, 50, 69, 82, 93, 109, 155, 156, 158) (1900–present), *Arctium lappa* L. (7, 10, 14, 19. 49, 52, 53, 55, 57, 58, 59, 64, 80, 85, 92, 106, 114, 145, 158, 184, 187) (1793-1930), *Arctium minus* Bernh. (37, 40, 63, 82, 122, 124, 125) (1899–1937), *Xanthium strumarium* L. (34) (1834)

Burdock grass - *Tragus racemosus* (L.) All. (5) (1913)

Burdockbur - *Arctium lappa* L. (148) (1939)

Burdock-grass [Burdock grass] - *Arctium lappa* L. (92) (1876)

Bur-flag - *Sparganium* L. (158) (1900)

Burflower [Burr flower, Burr-flower, Bur flower] - *Hydrophyllum virginianum* L. (6, 19, 92, 156, 158) (1840-1923)

Burgundy clover - *Medicago sativa* L. (5, 157, 158) (1900–1929)

Burgundy hay [Burgundy-hay, Burgundie hay] - *Medicago sativa* L. (157, 158, 178) (1526-1929)

Burgundy pitch - *Abies alba* Mill. (57, 92) (1876-1917), *Picea abies* (L.) H. Karst. (92) (1876)

Burgundy trefoil - *Medicago sativa* L. (156) (1923)

Burhead [Bur-head, Burrhead] - *Echinodorus berteroi* (Spreng.) Fassett (3, 158) (1900-1977), *Echinodorus cordifolius* (L.) Griseb. (85, 156) (1923-1932), *Echinodorus* L.C. Rich. ex Engelm. (1, 50, 122, 155) (1932–present), *Galium aparine* L. (5, 156, 157, 158) (1900-1929)

Bur-heart clover [Bur heart clover] - *Medicago arabica* (L.) Huds. (5) (1913)

Burit - *Saponaria officinalis* L. (179) (1526)

Burke's leafy-bract aster [Burke leafybract aster] - *Symphyotrichum foliaceum* (DC.) Nesom var. *canbyi* (Gray) Nesom (50) (present)

Burke's sandwort [Burke sandwort] - *Arenaria congesta* Nutt. var. *subcongesta* (S. Wats.) S. Wats. (155) (1942)

Burk's grama - *Bouteloua trifida* Thurb. (94) (1901)

Bur-marigold [Bur marigold, Bur-marigolds, Burr marigold, Burr marygold] - *Bidens cernua* L. (46, 62, 98) (1879–1926), *Bidens connata* Muhl. ex Willd. (62, 92, 114) (1894-1912), *Bidens frondosa* L. (19, 187) (1818-1840), *Bidens* L. (1, 2, 10, 82, 93, 109, 156) (1818-1949), *Bidens laevis* (L.) Britton, Sterns & Poggenb. (114) (1894)

Burmedick [Burr medick] - *Medicago minima* L. (50) (present)

Burnet - *Sanguisorba* L. (1, 2, 4, 50, 138, 155, 156, 158) (1895–present), *Sanguisorba minor* Scop. subsp. *muricata* (Spach) Nordborg (19, 45, 46, 107, 109, 157, 158, 178) (1526-1949), *Sanguisorba officinalis* L. (14) (1882)

Burnet clover - *Sanguisorba minor* Scop. subsp. *muricata* (Spach) Nordborg (129) (1894)

Burnet rose - *Rosa spinosissima* L. (19, 107) (1840-1919)

Burnet saxifrage [Burnet-saxifrage] - *Pimpinella saxifraga* L. (5, 156) (1913-1923), *Sanguisorba canadensis* L. (19) (1840)

Burnet sheepbur - *Acaena novae-zelandiae* Kirk (155) (1942)

Burnet-rose [Burnet rose] - *Anagallis arvensis* L. (5, 156, 157, 158) (1900–1929)

Burning nettle - *Urtica urens* L. (5, 156) (1913-1923)

Burningbush [Burning bush, Burning-bush] - *Cotinus coggygria* Scop. (156) (1923), *Dictamnus albus* L. (109) (1949), *Euonymus americanus* L. (5, 19, 92, 156) (1840-1923), *Euonymus atropur-*

purea Jacq. (2, 5, 6, 15, 37, 49, 53, 72, 85, 93, 95 109, 121, 130, 131, 135, 157, 158) (1892-1949), *Euonymus* L. (1, 13, 93, 156) (1932-1936), *Kochia scoparia* (L.) Schrad. (93) (1936)

Burning-heart [Burning heart] - *Euonymus americanus* L. (5, 156) (1913-1923)

Burntweed [Burnt weed, Burnt-weed] - *Chamerion angustifolium* (L.) Holub subsp. *angustifolium* (5, 74, 156, 157, 158) (1893-1929) Penobscot River ME, lumberman

Burnweed - *Erechtites hieraciifolia* (L.) Raf. ex DC. (50) (present), *Erechtites* Raf. (50, 155) (1942–present)

Burnwood bark [Burnwood bark] - *Cyrilla racemiflora* L. (5, 156) (1913-1923)

Burrage - *Borago officinalis* L. (92) (1876)

Bur-reed [Burr reed, Burr-reed, Bur-reed, Burreed, Burre-Reed] - *Sparganium erectum* L. (19, 92, 187) (1818-1876), *Sparganium erectum* L. subsp. *stoloniferum* (Graebn.) Hara (3, 156) (1923-1977), *Sparganium eurycarpum* Engelm. ex Gray (85, 129) (1894-1932), *Sparganium* L. (1, 50, 155, 158, 167, 180) (1633–present)

Bur-reed sedge - *Carex sparganioides* Muhl. ex Willd. (5, 50, 66, 72) (1893–present)

Burrier's oak - *Quercus ×heterophylla* Michx. f. [*phellos × rubra*] (19, 187) (1818-1840)

Burro brush - *Hymenoclea monogyra* Torr. & Gray ex Gray (122) (1937) TX

Burro grass [Burrograss, Burro-grass] - *Scleropogon brevifolius* Phil. (3, 50, 122, 155, 163) (1852–present), *Scleropogon* Phil. (50) (present)

Burro weed [Burroweed] - *Allenrolfea* Kuntze (153) (1913) NM, *Isocoma tenuisecta* Greene (155) (1942), *Oonopsis foliosa* (Gray) Greene var. *foliosa* (155) (1942)

Burrow brush - *Hymenoclea monogyra* Torr. & Gray ex Gray (124) (1937) TX

Bursage - *Ambrosia* L. (155) (1942)

Burseed [Burr seed, Bur-seed] - *Arctium lappa* L. (92) (1876), *Lappula* Moench (1, 93) (1932-1936), *Lappula squarrosa* (Retz.) Dumort. (5, 62, 72, 80, 93, 131, 156, 158) (1899-1923)

Bursting-heart [Bursting heart] - *Euonymus atropurpurea* Jacq. (156, 157, 158) (1900-1929)

Burstwort [Burstwoort] - *Herniaria glabra* L. (138) (1923), *Herniaria* L. (138, 180) (1633-1923)

Burton's myrtle [Burton myrtle, Burton-myrtle] - *Myrica gale* L. (5, 156) (1913-1923)

Burweed [Bur weed, Bur-weed, Burr weed, Burrweed, Burr-weed] - *Galeopsis bifida* Boenn. (77) (1898) Paris ME, *Galium aparine* L. (107) (1919), *Iva xanthifolia* Nutt. (131) (1899) SD, *Sparganium erectum* L. (184) (1793), *Sparganium erectum* L. subsp. *stoloniferum* (Graebn.) Hara (156) (1923), *Xanthium* L. (7) (1828), *Xanthium spinosum* L. (14, 46, 62, 92, 156) (1878-1923), *Xanthium strumarium* L. (58, 107, 158) (1869-1919), *Xanthium strumarium* L. var. *canadense* (Mill.) Torr. & Gray (156) (1923), *Xanthium strumarium* L. var. *glabratum* (DC.) Cronq. (72) (1907)

Burweed marsh-elder [Burweed marsh elder] - *Iva xanthifolia* Nutt. (5, 21, 72, 93, 97, 122) (1893–1937)

Burwort [Burr wort, Bur-wort] - *Ranunculus acris* L. (6, 7, 92) (1828-1932)

Buryt - *Saponaria officinalis* L. (157, 158) (1900-1929)

Busei (Japanese) - *Brassica rapa* L. var. *rapa* (110) (1886)

Bush bean - *Phaseolus vulgaris* L. (107, 109) (1919-1949)

Bush broom - *Hypericum prolificum* L. (156) (1923)

Bush cherry - *Prunus fruticosa* Pallas (138) (1923)

Bush chinquapin - *Chrysolepis sempervirens* (Kellogg) Hjelmqvist (106) (1930)

Bush cinquefoil - *Dasiphora floribunda* (Pursh) Kartesz (155) (1942)

Bush clover [Bush-clover, Bushclover] - *Lespedeza ×neglecta* Mackenzie & Bush [*stuevei × virginica*] (97) (1937), *Lespedeza capitata* Michx. (3, 85, 114, 156) (1894-1977), *Lespedeza* Michx. (1, 2, 4, 63, 93, 109, 138, 156, 158) (1895-1986), *Lespedeza violacea* (L.)

Pers. (5, 72, 97) (1907-1937), *Lespedeza virginica* (L.) Britton (19, 92) (18401876)

Bush dogwood [Bush dog-wood] - *Cornus racemosa* Lam. (19) (1840)

Bush glasswort - *Sarcocornia perennis* (P. Mill.) A.J. Scott (122) (1937)

Bush grape - *Vitis acerifolia* Raf. (3, 4) (1977-1986), *Vitis rupestris* Scheele (15, 107) (1895-1919)

Bush grass [Bush-grass] - *Muhlenbergia porteri* Scribn. ex Beal (163) (1852)

Bush honeysuckle [Bush honey suckle, Bush-honeysuckle] - *Diervilla lonicera* Mill. (5, 19, 40, 49, 58, 61, 72, 92, 105, 106, 156) (1840-1876), *Diervilla* Mill. (1, 2, 82, 109, 138, 156) (1895-1949), *Diervilla sessilifolia* Buckley (82) (1930), *Lonicera* L. (1) (1932), *Lonicera morrowii* Gray (82) (1930), *Lonicera tatarica* L. (63, 93, 112, 156) (1899–1937)

Bush huckleberry - *Gaylussacia dumosa* (Andr.) Torr. & Gray (5, 156) (1913-1923)

Bush knotweed - *Polygonum ramosissimum* Michx. (122) (1937) TX

Bush lady's-bower [Bush Ladies Bowre] - *Clematis integrifolia* L. (178) (1526)

Bush maple - *Acer pensylvanicum* L. (156) (1923), *Acer spicatum* Lam. (82, 156) (1923–1930)

Bush monkeyflower [Bush monkey-flower] - *Diplacus aurantiacus* (W. Curtis) Jepson subsp. *aurantiacus* (138) (1923)

Bush morning-glory [Bush morning glory, Bush morningglory] - *Ipomoea leptophylla* Torr. (4, 5, 37, 50, 85, 93, 95, 97, 121, 122, 124, 131, 155, 158) (1899–present)

Bush muhly - *Muhlenbergia porteri* Scribn. ex Beal (50, 122, 155) (1937–present)

Bush palmetto - *Sabal minor* (Jacq.) Pers. (109) (1949)

Bush pawpaw - *Asimina parviflora* (Michx.) Dunal (124) (1937) TX

Bush pea - *Thermopsis mollis* (Michx.) M. A. Curtis (5, 156) (1913-1923), *Thermopsis rhombifolia* (Nutt. ex Pursh) Nutt. ex Richards. (5) (1913)

Bush pereskia - *Pereskia grandifolia* Haw. (138) (1923)

Bush poppy [Bush-poppy] - *Dendromecon rigida* Benth. (109) (1949)

Bush red pepper [Bush redpepper] - *Capsicum annuum* L. var. *annuum* (138) (1923)

Bush seepweed - *Suaeda moquinii* (Torr.) Greene (155) (1942)

Bush squash [Bush squashes] - *Cucurbita pepo* L. var. *melopepo* (L.) Alef. (109) (1949)

Bush trefoil - *Desmodium canadense* (L.) DC. (19, 156) (1840-1923)

Bush vetch - *Vicia sepium* L. (5, 107) (1913-1919)

Bush whoitle-berry [Bush-whoitle-berry] - *Gaylussacia dumosa* (Andr.) Torr. & Gray (possibly) (177) (1762)

Bush whorleberry - *Gaylussacia dumosa* (Andr.) Torr. & Gray (19, 92, 187) (1818-1876)

Bush willow - *Salix humilis* Marsh. (5, 93, 156) (1913-1936)

Bush-clover dodder [Bushclover dodder] - *Cuscuta pentagona* Engelm. var. *glabrior* (Engelm.) Gandhi, Thomas & Hatch (50) (present)

Bushel bean - *Phaseolus lunatus* L. (107) (1814)

Bush's cone flower - *Echinacea paradoxa* (J.B.S. Norton) Britt. (5) (1913)

Bush's cyperus - *Cyperus lupulinus* (Spreng.) Marcks subsp. *macilentus* (Fern.) Marcks (5) (1913)

Bush's flatsedge - *Cyperus lupulinus* (Spreng.) Marcks subsp. *macilentus* (Fern.) Marcks (139) (1944)

Bush's goosefoot - *Chenopodium berlandieri* Moq. var. *bushianum* (Aellen) Cronq. (50) (present)

Bush's panicum - *Dichanthelium boreale* (Nash) Freckmann (5) (1913)

Bush's paspalum - *Paspalum setaceum* Michx. (5) (1913)

Bush's poppy-mallow [Bush's poppymallow] - *Callirhoe bushii* Fern. (50) (present)

Bush's sedge [Bush sedge] - *Carex bushii* Mackenzie (3, 5, 50) (1913–present)

Bush's skullcap - *Scutellaria bushii* Britt. (5) (1913)
Bush's thorn - *Crataegus dispessa* Ashe (5) (1913)
Bush's yellow wood sorrell - *Oxalis stricta* L. (5) (1913)
Bushy arctotis - *Arctotis stoechadifolia* Berg. (138) (1923)
Bushy aster - *Symphyotrichum dumosum* (L.) Nesom var. *dumosum* (5, 72, 97, 131, 155, 156) (1899-1937)
Bushy atriplex - *Atriplex canescens* (Pursh) Nutt. (5, 93, 131, 158) (1899-1936)
Bushy beard grass [Bushy beard-grass, Bushy beardgrass] - *Andropogon glomeratus* (Walt.) B.S.P. var. *glomeratus* (3, 5, 119, 122, 155, 163) (1852-1977)
Bushy blazing star [Bushy blazingstar] - *Mentzelia dispersa* S. Wats. (50) (present)
Bushy bluestem [Bushy blue-stem, Bushy blue stem] - *Andropogon glomeratus* (Walt.) B.S.P. var. *glomeratus* (119) (1938), *Sorghastrum nutans* (L.) Nash (5, 11, 56, 99, 119, 129, 131) (1888-1938)
Bushy cinquefoil - *Potentilla paradoxa* Nutt. (4, 5, 72, 85, 93, 131) (1899-1986)
Bushy gayophyton - *Gayophytum ramosissimum* Torr. & Gray (131) (1899)
Bushy gerardia - *Aureolaria pedicularia* (L.) Raf. var. *pedicularia* (5, 49, 92, 156) (1898-1923)
Bushy goldenrod [Bushy golden-rod] - *Euthamia graminifolia* (L.) Nutt. var. *graminifolia* (5, 62, 72, 82, 85, 93, 106, 156, 158) (1923-1930), *Euthamia* Nutt. ex Cass. (1, 93) (1932-1936)
Bushy knotweed [Bushy knot-weed] - *Polygonum ramosissimum* Michx. (3, 5, 50, 72, 80, 93, 97, 98, 131, 155) (1899–present)
Bushy peppergrass - *Lepidium ramosissimum* A. Nels. (3, 4) (1977-1986)
Bushy pinweed [Bushy pin-weed] - *Lechea stricta* Leggett ex Britton (5, 93) (1913-1936)
Bushy salt-sage - *Atriplex canescens* (Pursh) Nutt. (141) (1899) WY
Bushy seedbox - *Ludwigia alternifolia* L. (3, 4) (1977-1986)
Bushy St. John's-wort [Bushy St. John's wort] - *Hypericum densiflorum* Pursh (5) (1913)
Bushy vetch - *Lathyrus venosus* Muhl. (3, 127, 156) (1923-1977)
Bushy vetchling - *Lathyrus venosus* Muhl. (4) (1986)
Bushy wallflower - *Erysimum repandum* L. (3, 4) (1977-1986)
Bûsidji'bĭkûgûk (Chippewa, plump root) - *Thaspium barbinode* (Michx.) Nutt. (40) (1928)
Busserolle - *Arctostaphylos uva-ursi* (L.) Spreng. (6) (1892)
Butcher's prick tree [Bitcher's prick-tree] - *Euonymus europaea* L. (5, 156) (1913-1923), *Frangula alnus* Mill. (156, 158) (1900-1923)
Butler's quillwort - *Isoetes butleri* Engelman (4, 5) (1913-1986)
Butler's sand-parsley [Butler's sandparsley] - *Ammoselinum butleri* (Engelm. ex S. Wats.) Coult. & Rose (50, 97) (1937–present)
Butomus - *Sparganium* L. (180) (1633)
Butte candle [Buttecandle] - *Cryptantha celosioides* (Eastw.) Payson (50) (present)
Butte marigold - *Tetraneuris acaulis* (Pursh) Greene (127) (1933) ND
Butte primrose - *Oenothera caespitosa* Nutt. (possibly) (127) (1933) ND
Butter daisy [Butter-daisy] - *Leucanthemum vulgare* Lam. (5, 156, 158) (1900-1923)
Butter dock [Butter-dock] - *Rumex obtusifolius* L. (5, 64, 156, 157, 158) (1900-1929) leaves used for wrapping butter
Butter leaves [Butter-leaves] - *Atriplex hortensis* L. (107, 158) (1900-1919)
Butter oak - *Quercus rubra* L. (46) (1649)
Butter twitch - *Arrhenatherum elatius* (L.) Beauv. ex J. Presl & C. Presl (5) (1913)
Butter-and-eggs [Butter & eggs, Butter and eggs] - *Linaria* Mill. (1, 93) (1932-1936), *Linaria vulgaris* Mill. (3, 5, 6, 45, 48, 49, 50, 62, 63, 72, 77, 80, 82, 85, 93, 95, 97, 109, 122, 124, 127, 131, 148, 155, 156, 157, 158) (1882–present), *Narcissus* ×*incomparabilis* Mill. [*poeticus* × *pseudonarcissus*] (92) (1876), *Narcissus pseudonarcissus* L. (75) (1894)

Butterbur [Butter bur, Butter-bur] - *Petasites frigidus* (L.) Fries var. *palmatus* (Aiton) Cronq. (5, 85, 156) (1913-1932), *Petasites hybridus* (L.) G. Gaertn., B. Mey. & Scherb. (5, 156) (1913-1923), *Petasites* Mill. (possibly) (1, 50, 138, 155) (1923–present), *Tussilago farfara* L. (5, 156) (1913-1923), *Tussilago* L. (10) (1818)
Buttercress [Butter cress, Butter-cress, Butter cresses] - *Ranunculus acris* L. (5, 156, 157, 158) (1900–1929), *Ranunculus bulbosus* L. (156) (1923), *Ranunculus repens* L. (156) (1923)
Buttercup [Butter cup, Buttercups] - *Argentina anserina* (L.) Rydb. (158) (1900), *Caltha palustris* L. (14) (1882), *Ranunculus acris* L. (7, 19, 157, 158) (1828-1929), *Ranunculus bulbosus* L. (46, 49, 57, 92, 107, 156) (1876-1917), *Ranunculus ficaria* L. (107) (1919), *Ranunculus* L. (1, 2, 4, 13, 15, 50, 63, 93, 106, 109, 127, 138, 155, 156, 158) (1849–present)
Buttercup oxalis - *Oxalis pes-caprae* L. (138) (1923)
Butter-daisy [Butter daisy] - *Ranunculus acris* L. (156, 157, 158) (1900-1923), *Ranunculus bulbosus* L. (156) (1923), *Ranunculus repens* L. (5, 107, 156) (1913-1923)
Butter-flower [Butter flower] - *Ranunculus acris* L. (156) (1923), *Ranunculus bulbosus* L. (5, 6, 156) (1892), *Ranunculus repens* L. (156) (1923)
Butterfly bauhinia - *Bauhinia monandra* Kurz (138) (1923)
Butterfly bush - *Buddleja davidii* Franch. (112) (1937)
Butterfly flower [Butterfly-flower, Butterflyflower] - *Asclepias tuberosa* L. (5, 156) (1913-1923), *Baptisia tinctoria* (L.) R. Br. ex Aiton f. (190) (~1759), *Bauhinia monandra* Kurz (109) (1949), *Lupinus perennis* L. (190) (~1759), *Schizanthus* Ruiz & Pavón (109, 138) (1923-1949)
Butterfly lily [Butterfly-lily] - *Calochortus gunnisonii* S. Wats. (5) (1913), *Calochortus* Pursh. (1, 93, 109) (1932-1949)
Butterfly milkweed - *Asclepias tuberosa* L. (4, 50, 122, 155) (1942–present), *Asclepias tuberosa* L. subsp. *interior* Woods. (3, 50) (1977–present)
Butterfly pea [Butterfly-pea] - *Centrosema* (DC.) Benth. (138, 158) (1900-1923), *Clitoria* L. (1, 2, 4, 109, 138, 156, 158) (1895-1986), *Clitoria mariana* L. (4, 5, 97, 122, 124, 156) (1913-1986)
Butterfly tulip [Butter-fly tulip] - *Calochortus luteus* Dougl. ex Lindl. (107) (1919), *Calochortus venustus* Dougl. ex Benth. (86) (1878)
Butterfly violet - *Viola nephrophylla* Greene (122, 138, 155) (1923-1942)
Butterfly weed [Butter-fly weed, Butterflyweed, Butterfly-weed] - *Asclepias* L. (1, 106) (1930-1932), *Asclepias speciosa* Torr. (101) (1905), *Asclepias tuberosa* L. (5, 6, 7, 19, 37, 42, 47, 49, 53, 54, 58, 62, 63, 64, 82, 85, 92, 95, 97, 106, 107, 109, 131, 138, 156, 157, 158, 186, 187)(1814-1949), *Calochortus luteus* Dougl. ex Lindl. (86) (1878) CA, *Gaura coccinea* Nutt. ex Pursh (156) (1923), *Gaura* L. (1, 4, 93) (1932-1986)
Butterfly-banners [Butterfly banners] - *Dicentra cucullaria* (L.) Bernh. (5, 156) (1913-1923)
Butterfly-dock [Butterfly dock] - *Petasites hybridus* (L.) G. Gaertn., B. Mey. & Scherb. (5, 156) (1913-1923)
Butterjags [Butter-jags, Butter jags] - *Lotus corniculatus* L. (92, 158) (1876-1900)
Buttermilk lily [Buttermilk-lily] - *Trillium grandiflorum* (Michx.) Salisb. (156) (1923)
Butternut [Butter nuts, Butter nut] - *Euphorbia cyparissias* L. (73) (1892) Harmony ME, *Juglans cinerea* L. (1, 2, 3, 4, 5, 6, 7, 9, 10, 19, 20, 40, 46, 49, 50, 52, 53, 54, 57, 61, 72, 82, 85, 92, 93, 95, 105, 107, 109, 113, 138, 155, 156, 157, 158) (1857–present), *Juglans* L. (156, 190) (~1759-1923)
Butternutsträ (Swedish) - *Juglans cinerea* L. (41) (1770)
Butter-print [Butter print] - *Abutilon theophrasti* Medik (5, 62, 76, 80, 156, 158) (1896-1923)
Butter-root - *Lewisia rediviva* Pursh (107) (1919)
Butter-rose [Butter rose] - *Ranunculus acris* L. (5, 156) (1913-1923), *Ranunculus bulbosus* L. (156) (1923), *Ranunculus repens* L. (156) (1923)

Butterweed [Butter weed, Butter-weed] - *Abutilon theophrasti* Medik (5, 73, 156, 157, 158) (1892-1923) Peoria IL, *Conyza canadensis* (L.) Cronq. var. *canadensis* (2, 5, 6, 49, 58, 62, 69, 92, 156, 157, 158) (1869-1923), *Erechtites hieraciifolia* (L.) Raf. ex DC. (156) (1923), *Lactuca canadensis* L. (5, 76, 156, 157, 158) (1896-1929) Sulphur Grove OH, *Packera glabella* (Poir) C. Jeffrey (2, 3, 4, 5, 7, 50, 92, 156) (1828–present), *Senecio* L. (106) (1930)

Butterwort [Butter wort, Butter woorts] - *Isoloba elatior* (Michx.) Raf. (19, 92, 183) (~1756-1840), *Pinguicula* L. (1, 2, 10, 156) (1818-1932), *Pinguicula vulgaris* L. (156, 178) (1526-1923)

Button aster - *Symphyotrichum ericoides* (L.) Nesom var. *ericoides* (156) (1923)

Button cactus - *Epithelantha micromeris* (Engelm.) A. Weber ex Britt. & Rose var. *micromeris* (138) (1923)

Button eryngo - *Eryngium yuccifolium* Michx. (50) (present)

Button grass - *Arrhenatherum elatius* (L.) Beauv. ex J. Presl & C. Presl (5) (1913)

Button rush - *Juncus saximontanus* A. Nels. (139) (1944)

Button sage - *Salvia mellifera* Greene (106) (1930)

Button sedge - *Carex bullata* Schk. (5, 50, 156) (1913–present)

Button snakeroot [Button-snakeroot, Button snake root] - *Eryngium* L. (7) (1828), *Eryngium yuccifolium* Michx. (2, 3, 4, 5, 6, 19, 49, 52, 53, 54, 58, 63, 64, 72, 85, 92, 97, 104, 109, 122, 124, 131, 138, 156, 157, 158) (1840-1937), *Liatris aspera* Michx. (14, 156) (1882–1923), *Liatris* Gaertn. ex Schreber. (1, 2, 7, 63, 93, 106, 109, 156) (1828-1949), *Liatris pilosa* (Aiton) Willd. (possibly) (186) (1814), *Liatris spicata* (L.) Willd. (19, 49, 53, 57, 61, 156) (1840-1923), *Liatris spicata* (L.) Willd. var. *spicata* (157) (1929), *Liatris squarrosa* (L.) Michx. (14) (1882)

Button snakeweed - *Eryngium leavenworthii* Torr. & Gray (156) (1923)

Button thistle [Button-thistle] - *Cirsium vulgare* (Savi) Ten. (5, 156, 158) (1900-1923)

Button tree [Button-tree] - *Cephalanthus* L. (8) (1785), *Cephalanthus occidentalis* L. (5, 6, 7, 8, 156, 157, 158) (1828-1923), *Conocarpus erectus* L. (20) (1857) Jamaica

Button twitch - *Arrhenatherum elatius* (L.) Beauv. ex J. Presl & C. Presl (5) (1913)

Buttonball [Button balls, Button ball, Button-ball] or Buttonball tree - *Platanus occidentalis* L. (5, 75, 95, 106, 156, 157) (1900-1930)

Buttonbur [Button-bur, Button bur] - *Xanthium strumarium* L. (158) (1900), *Xanthium strumarium* L. var. *canadense* (Mill.) Torr. & Gray (156) (1923), *Xanthium strumarium* L. var. *glabratum* (DC.) Cronq. (5) (1913)

Buttonbush [Button bush, Button-bush] - *Cephalanthus* L. (1, 2, 4, 41, 50, 82, 109, 138, 155, 156, 158) (1770–present), *Cephalanthus occidentalis* L. (19, 72, 92, 114, 127, 131, 156) (1828-1937), *Conocarpus erectus* L. (7) (1828)

Buttonbush dodder [Button-bush dodder] - *Cuscuta cephalanthi* Engelm. (3, 4, 5, 50, 72, 122) (1907–present)

Button-snakeroot eryngo [Buttonsnakeroot eryngo] - *Eryngium yuccifolium* Michx. (155) (1942)

Buttonweed [Button-weed, Button weed] - *Abutilon theophrasti* Medik (5, 73, 156, 157, 158) (1892-1929) Chesterton MD, *Centaurea nigra* L. (5, 156) (1913-1923), *Diodia* L. (1, 4, 155, 156) (1923-1986), *Diodia teres* Walt. (3, 106, 145, 156) (1897–1977), *Diodia virginiana* L. (92, 156) (1876-1923), *Dipsacus fullonum* L. (5, 156) (1913-1923), *Lactuca canadensis* L. (possibly) (29) (1869), *Malva rotundifolia* L. (156) (1923), *Oldenlandia* L. (156) (1923), *Spermacoce glabra* Michx. (3) (1977), *Spermacoce* L. (1, 4, 158) (1900-1986)

Button-willow [Button willow] - *Cephalanthus occidentalis* L. (5, 106, 156) (1913-1930)

Buttonwood [Button wood, Button-wood] - *Cephalanthus* L. (42) (1814), *Cephalanthus occidentalis* L. (6, 10, 14, 41, 49, 177) (1762-1898), *Laguncularia racemosa* (L.) Gaertn. f. (106) (1930), *Platanus* L. (12) (1821), *Platanus occidentalis* L. (5, 10, 14, 20, 19, 38, 41, 44, 97, 106, 109, 113, 158, 187) (1770-1949)

Buttonwood dodder - *Cuscuta cephalanthi* Engelm. (124) (1937)

Buttonwood shrub [Button-wood shrub] - *Cephalanthus occidentalis* L. (5, 7, 92, 156, 158) (1828-1923)

Buude-hi - *Quercus rubra* L. (37) (1919)

Buxbaum's sedge [Buxbaum sedge] - *Carex buxbaumii* Wahlenb. (50, 66, 139, 187) (1818–present)

Buzzard's-berry [Buzzard's berry] - *Ilex crenata* Thunb. (106) (1930) Arkansas

Buzzies - *Arctium lappa* L. (76) (1896) Southold Long Island

Byl steel (Belgis Noveboracensibus) - *Liquidambar styraciflua* L. (177) (1762)

Byorn-blad (Bear's leaf) - *Symplocarpus foetidus* (L.) Salisb. ex Nutt. (186) (1814)

Byorn-retter (Bear's foot) - *Symplocarpus foetidus* (L.) Salisb. ex Nutt. (186) (1814)

Byzantine speedwell - *Veronica officinalis* L. var. *tournefortii* (Vill.) Reichenb. (5, 156) (1913-1923)

C

Caballine aloes - *Sansevieria hyacinthoides (L.) Druce* (92) (1876)

Cabanis beard-grass - *Andropogon ternarius* Michx. var. *cabanisii* (Hack.) Fern. & Grisc. (5) (1913)

Cabbage - *Brassica* L. (1, 107, 184) (1793-1932), *Brassica oleracea* L. (7, 50, 82, 85, 92, 97, 106, 156, 107, 109) (1828–present)

Cabbage angelin or Cabbage angelin tree [Cabbage angelintree] - *Andira inermis* (W. Wright) Kunth ex DC. (138, 155) (1923-1942)

Cabbage lettuce - *Lactuca sativa* L. (180) (1633)

Cabbage palm - *Sabal palmetto* (Walt.) Lodd. ex J.A. & J.H. Schultes (182) (1791)

Cabbage palmetto - *Sabal palmetto* (Walt.) Lodd. ex J.A. & J.H. Schultes (2, 106) (1895-1930)

Cabbage rose - *Rosa centifolia* L. (55, 57, 92, 107, 109, 138) (1876-1949)

Cabbage tree - *Sabal palmetto* (Walt.) Lodd. ex J.A. & J.H. Schultes (182) (1791), *Serenoa repens* (Bartr.) Small (20) (1857)

Cabbage-bark tree [Cabbagebark tree] - *Andira inermis* (W. Wright) Kunth ex DC. (50) (present)

Cabbage-wood - *Ceiba pentandra* (L.) Gaertn. (107) (1919)

Cabinet cherry - *Prunus serotina* Ehrh. (156, 157, 158) (1900-1929), *Prunus virginiana* L. (19) (1840), *Prunus virginiana* L. var. *virginiana* (5) (1913)

Cabomba - *Cabomba caroliniana* Gray (5, 106) (1913-1930)

Cabo'mĭnaga'wûnj (Chippewa, smooth berry) - *Ribes oxyacanthoides* L. subsp. *oxyacanthoides* (40) (1928)

Cabul clover - *Melilotus officinalis* (L.) Lam. (possibly) (5, 156, 157, 158) (1900-1929)

Cabus (French) - *Brassica oleracea* L. (107, 110) (1886-1919)

Cabutos - *Brassica oleracea* L. (107) (1536)

Caca'gomĭn (Chippewa) - *Cornus canadensis* L. (40) (1928)

Cacanon - *Raphanus sativus* L. (180) (1633)

Cacao - *Theobroma cacao* L. (107, 109, 110, 138) (1886-1949)

Cacao beans - *Theobroma cacao* L. (92) (1876)

Cacao butter - *Theobroma cacao* L. (92) (1876) the fixed oil

Caçapililol xochitl - *Lonicera sempervirens* L. (177) (1762)

Cacautl (Mexico) - *Theobroma cacao* L. (107) (1919)

Cachanilla (Spanish) - *Pluchea sericea* (Nutt.) Coville (106) (1930) NM

Cachew nut [Cachew nut] - *Anacardium occidentale* L. (7, 91) (1828-1911)

Cacia rose - *Robinia hispida* L. (8) (1785)

Cacida - *Scutellaria integrifolia* L. (183) (~1756)

Cactus - *Opuntia polyacantha* Haw. (101) (1905), *Selenicereus grandiflorus* (L.) Britt. & Rose (55) (1911)

Cactus-apple [Cactus apple] - *Opuntia engelmannii* Salm-Dyck (50) (present)

Cadio - *Xanthium strumarium* L. var. *canadense* (Mill.) Torr. & Gray (150) (1894) NM

Cadlock - *Brassica nigra* (L.) W.D.J. Koch (5, 157, 158) (1900-1929), *Raphanus raphanistrum* L. (5, 76) (1896-1913) Nova Scotia

Caesalpinia - *Caesalpinia* L. (155) (1942)

Caesar's amanita [Caesars amanita] - *Amanita caesarea* (Scop.) Pers. (155) (1942)

Cahinca - *Chiococca alba* (L.) A.S. Hitchc. (49) (1898)

Cahinca root - *Chiococca alba* (L.) A.S. Hitchc. (92) (1876)

Cahohamo - *Glycyrrhiza* L. (7) (1828)

Cailleau - *Lantana camara* L. (92) (1876)

Cailleau (Louisiana) - *Lantana* L. (7) (1828)

Caillelait commune (French) - *Galium verum* L. (7) (1828)

Caille-lait jaune (French) - *Galium verum* L. (158) (1900)

Cain - *Arundinaria gigantea* (Walter) Muhl. (possibly) (35) (1806)

Cainca - *Chiococca alba* (L.) A.S. Hitchc. (49) (1898)

Cainito - *Chrysophyllum cainito* L. (174) (1753)

Cajan - *Cajanus cajan* (L.) Millsp. (109) (1949)

Cajeput or Cajeput tree [Cajeput-tree] - *Umbellularia californica* (Hook. & Arn.) Nutt. (14, 75, 107) (1882-1919)

Cal - *Brassica oleracea* L. (110) (1886)

Calabash - *Lagenaria siceraria* (Molina) Standl. (7, 10, 19, 110) (1818-1886)

Calabash gourd - *Lagenaria siceraria* (Molina) Standl. (92, 138, 155) (1876-1942)

Calabash tree [Calabash-tree] - *Crescentia cujete* L. (109, 138) (1923-1949), *Crescentia* L. (138) (1923)

Calabassa (Spanish) - *Cucurbita pepo* L. (107) (1561)

Calabassier cujete - *Crescentia cujete* L. (20) (1857)

Calabazilla - *Cucurbita foetidissima* Kunth (5, 74, 156, 157, 158) (1893-1929) Southern CA

Calami Radix (Official name of Materia Medica) - *Acorus calamus* L. (7) (1828)

Calamint [Calamynt] - *Calamintha* Mill. (1, 2, 179) (1895-1932 from ancient name), *Calamintha nepeta* (L.) Savi subsp. *nepeta* (156) (1923), *Calamintha sylvatica* Bromf. subsp. *ascendens* (Jord.) P.W. Ball (92) (1876), *Pycnanthemum incanum* (L.) Michx. var. *incanum* (5) (1913), *Pycnanthemum muticum* (Michx.) Pers. (5) (1913), *Pycnanthemum pycnanthemoides* (Leavenworth) Fern. var. *pycnanthemoides* (5) (1913)

Calamint of the mountain [Calamynt of the mountayne] - *Calamintha sylvatica* Bromf. subsp. *ascendens* (Jord.) P.W. Ball (179) (1526) Neb Gn is ancient name

Calaminth - *Calamintha nepeta* (L.) Savi subsp. *nepeta* (156) (1923)

Calamo aromatico (Spanish, Italian) - *Acorus calamus* L. (158) (1900)

Calamo odoranto (Italian) - *Acorus calamus* L. (186) (1814)

Calamus - *Acorus calamus* L. (5, 10, 19, 49, 50, 53, 57, 58, 59, 64, 92, 93, 97, 121, 155, 156, 158, 186, 187) (1814–present)

Calamus Aromaticus (Official name of Materia Medica) - *Acorus calamus* L. (7, 165, 180) (1633-1828)

Calamus-root [Calamus root] - *Acorus calamus* L. (72, 85, 101, 122, 138, 156, 157) (1886-1937), *Acorus* L. (1) (1932)

Calathian violet - *Gentiana saponaria* L. (156) (1923), *Gentiana saponaria* L. var. *saponaria* (5) (1913)

Calavances - *Vigna unguiculata* (L.) Walp. (107) (1919)

Calcareous cryptantha - *Cryptantha thyrsiflora* (Greene) Payson (50) (present)

Calceolaria - *Hybanthus* Jacq. (155, 158) (1900-1942)

Calendula - *Calendula officinalis* L. (49, 52, 54, 55, 92) (1876-1919)

Calf clover [Calf-clover] - *Trifolium arvense* L. (5, 76, 156, 158) (1896-1923) Southold Long Island, no longer in use by 1923

Calf corn - *Clintonia borealis* (Ait.) Raf. (78) (1898) Hartford ME

Calf-kill [Calf kill] - *Holcus lanatus* L. (5) (1913), *Kalmia angustifolia* L. (5, 156) (1913-1923), *Leucothoe axillaris* (Lam.) D. Don. (71) (1898)

Calf's-mouth [Calf's mouth] - *Antirrhinum majus* L. (156) (1923)

Calf-snout [Calf snout] - *Antirrhinum majus* L. (5, 158) (1900-1913)

Calico aster - *Symphyotrichum lateriflorum* (L.) A.& D. Löve (50) (present), *Symphyotrichum lateriflorum* (L.) A.& D. Löve var. *lateriflorum* (50, 85, 155, 156) (1923–present)

Calico bush [Calico-bush] - *Kalmia* L. (10) (1818), *Kalmia latifolia* L. (2, 5, 6, 7, 49, 71, 92, 106, 109, 138, 156) (1892-1949)

Calico Dutchman's-pipe [Calico Dutchmanspipe] - *Aristolochia elegans* Mast. (138) (1923)

Calico flower [Calico-flower, Calicoflower] - *Aristolochia elegans* Mast. (109, 138) (1923-1949)

Calico tree - *Kalmia latifolia* L. (18, 187) (1805-1818)

Calico wood [Calico-wood] - *Halesia carolina* L. (5, 156) (1913-1923)

California adolphia - *Adolphia californica* S. Watson (155) (1942)

California amaranth - *Amaranthus californicus* (Moq.) S. Wats. (50) (present)

California amorpha - *Amorpha californica* Nutt. (155) (1942)

California aralia - *Aralia californica* S. Wats. (155) (1942)

California barberry - *Mahonia aquifolium* (Pursh) Nutt. (64, 157) (1908-1929), *Mahonia pinnata* (Lag.) Fedde subsp. *pinnata* (106) (1930)

California bay or California bay tree [Californian bay tree] - *Umbellularia californica* (Hook. & Arn.) Nutt. (20, 109, 138) (1857-1949)

California big tree [California big-tree] - *Sequoiadendron giganteum* (Lindl.) Buchh. (109) (1949)

California bitter-root [Californian bitter root] - *Marah fabaceus* (Naud.) Naud. ex Greene (14) (1882)

California black currant [Californian black currant] - *Ribes bracteosum* Dougl. ex Hook. (107) (1919)

California black walnut - *Juglans californica* S. Wats. (138) (1923)

California bluebell - *Phacelia minor* (Harvey) Thellung ex F. Zimmerman (109) (1949)

California bottle-brush - *Elymus californicus* (Bol. ex Thurb.) Gould (94) (1901)

California boxelder [California box-elder, Californian box elder] - *Acer negundo* L. var. *californicum* (Torr. & Gray) Sarg. (20) (1857) IA

California brickellbush - *Brickellia californica* (Torr. & Gray) Gray (50) (present)

California brickellia - *Brickellia californica* (Torr. & Gray) Gray (155) (1942)

California brome - *Bromus carinatus* H. & A. (3, 50) (1977–present)

California buckeye - *Aesculus californica* (Spach) Nutt. (71, 106, 109, 138, 155) (1898-1949)

California buckthorn - *Frangula californica* (Eschsch.) Gray (53, 138) (1922-1923)

California buttonwood - *Platanus racemosa* Nutt. (20) (1857)

California chestnut oak - *Lithocarpus densiflorus* (Hook. & Arn.) Rehd. (161) (1857)

California chia - *Salvia columbariae* Benth. (104) (1896)

California chinquapin - *Chrysolepis sempervirens* (Kellogg) Hjelmqvist (138) (1923)

California clover - *Medicago arabica* (L.) Huds. (45) (1896-1913), *Medicago polymorpha* L. (87) (1884) Southern states, *Medicago sativa* L. (52) (1919)

California coffee tree - *Frangula californica* (Eschsch.) Gray (53) (1922)

California columbine - *Aquilegia formosa* Fisch. ex DC. (138, 155) (1931-1942)

California coneflower - *Rudbeckia californica* Gray (138) (1923), *Rudbeckia hirta* L. var. *hirta* (5) (1913)

California copperleaf - *Acalypha californica* Benth. (50, 155) (1942–present)

California cress - *Sisymbrium officinale* (L.) Scop (156) (1923)

California dandelion - *Hypochaeris radicata* L. (106, 156) (1923-1930)

California daylily - *Hesperocallis undulata* Gray (78) (1898)

California dewberry - *Rubus vitifolius* Cham. & Schlecht. (138) (1923)

California Dutchman's-pipe [California Dutchmanspipe] - *Aristolochia californica* Torr. (155) (1942)

California false indigo - *Amorpha californica* Nutt. (106) (1930)

California feverbush [California fever bush] - *Garrya fremontii* Torr. (57) (1917)

California field oak - *Quercus agrifolia* Née (107) (1919)

California flowering ash [Californian flowering ash] - *Fraxinus dipetala* Hook. & Arn. (20) (1857)

California foothill pine - *Pinus sabiniana* Dougl. ex Dougl. (50) (present)

California fuchsia [California-fuchsia] - *Epilobium canum* (Greene) Raven subsp. *angustifolium* (Keck) Raven (109) (1949)

California gold fern [California goldfern] - *Pentagramma triangularis* (Kaulfuss) Yatskievych, Windham & Wollenweber (86, 138) (1878-1923)

California grape - *Vitis californica* Benth. (138) (1923)

California hair grass [Californian hair-grass] - *Deschampsia holciformis* J. Presl (94) (1901)

California holly - *Heteromeles arbutifolia* (Lindl.) M. Roemer (74, 106) (1893-1930) Santa Barbara CA

California hop tree [California hop-tree] - *Ptelea crenulata* Greene (106) (1930)

California horse-chestnut [Californian horse chestnut] - *Aesculus californica* (Spach) Nutt. (2, 20, 103, 107) (1857-1919)

California huckleberry - *Vaccinium ovatum* Pursh (77) (1898) CA, *Vaccinium oxycoccos* L. (5) (1913)

California hyacinth [Californian hyacinth] - *Triteleia grandiflora* Lindl. var. *grandiflora* (107) (1919)

California incense-cedar - *Calocedrus decurrens* (Torr.) Florin (138) (1923)

California Indian pink - *Silene californica* Dur. (109) (1949)

California juniper - *Juniperus californica* Carr. (138) (1923), *Juniperus occidentalis* Hook. (107) (1919)

California lady-slipper [California ladyslipper] - *Cypripedium californicum* Gray (138) (1923)

California laurel [California-laurel] - *Umbellularia* (Nees) Nutt. (138) (1923), *Umbellularia californica* (Hook. & Arn.) Nutt. (14, 54, 57, 75, 106, 109, 138, 154, 161) (1857-1949)

California lilac - *Ceanothus* L. (15) (1895), *Ceanothus thyrsiflorus* Esch. (52, 76) (1896-1919) CA

California lip fern [Californian lip-fern] - *Aspidotis californica* (Hook.) Nutt. ex Copeland (86) (1878)

California live oak [Californian live oak] - *Quercus agrifolia* Née (138) (1923), *Quercus chrysolepis* Liebm. (75) (1894) CA

California loosestrife - *Lythrum californicum* Torr. & Gray (50) (present)

California magnificent fir - *Abies magnifica* A. Murr. (158) (1900)

California maple - *Acer macrophyllum* Pursh (106) (1930)

California melic grass [California melic-grass] - *Melica californica* Scribn. (94) (1901)

California mustard - *Sisymbrium officinale* (L.) Scop (76, 157, 158) (1896-1929) Rumford ME

California nettle - *Urtica dioica* L. subsp. *gracilis* (Aiton) Seland. (50) (present)

California nutmeg [California-nutmeg] or California nutmeg tree - *Torreya californica* Torr. (19, 78, 92, 138, 161) (1840-1898)

California oat grass - *Danthonia californica* Boland. (87) (1884)

California olive [Californian olive] - *Umbellularia californica* (Hook. & Arn.) Nutt. (75, 107) (1894-1919)

California parnassia - *Parnassia caroliniana* Michx. (138) (1923)

California pepper tree [California pepper-tree, California pepper-tree] - *Schinus molle* L. (109, 138) (1923-1949)

California pitcher plant [Californian pitcher plant, Californian pitcherplant] - *Darlingtonia californica* Torr. (14, 138) (1882-1923)

California planetree - *Platanus racemosa* Nutt. (138) (1923)

California pleuropogon - *Pleuropogon californicus* (Nees) Benth. ex Vasey (94) (1901)

California poison sumac - *Toxicodendron diversilobum* (Torr. & Gray) Greene (71) (1898)

California polypody [Californian polypody] - *Polypodium californicum* Kaulfuss (86) (1878)

California poppy [California-poppy, Californiapoppy] - *Eschscholzia californica* Cham. (2, 50, 82, 106, 109, 155) (1895–present), *Eschscholzia californica* Cham. subsp. *californica* (28, 50) (1850–present), *Eschscholzia* Cham. (50, 73, 122, 123, 138, 158) (1856–present)

California privet - *Ligustrum ovalifolium* Hassk. (109, 122, 124, 135, 138) (1910-1949)

California rape - *Sinapis arvensis* L. (109) (1949)

California redbud - *Cercis canadensis* L. var. texensis (S. Wats.) M. Hopkins (138) (1923)

California reed grass [Californian reed-grass] - *Cinna bolanderi* Scribn. (94) (1901)

California rose [California-rose] - *Calystegia pellita* (Ledeb.) G. Don (109) (1949)

California rose-mallow [California rosemallow] - *Hibiscus moscheutos* L. subsp. *lasiocarpos* (Cav.) O.J. Blanchard (155) (1942)

California sagebrush - *Artemisia californica* Less. (155) (1942)

California sassafras [Californian sassafras] - *Umbellularia californica* (Hook. & Arn.) Nutt. (14) (1882)

California shrub ash - *Fraxinus dipetala* Hook. & Arn. (138) (1923)

California silver fir - *Abies magnifica* A. Murr. (158) (1900)

California silverbush - *Argythamnia californica* Brandeg. (155) (1942)

California spikenard - *Aralia californica* S. Wats. (64) (1907)

California spotted clover - *Medicago arabica* (L.) Huds. (5) (1913)

California strawberry - *Fragaria vesca* L. subsp. *californica* (Cham. & Schlecht.) Staudt (138) (1923)

California sunflower - *Helianthus californicus* DC. (138) (1923)

California sycamore - *Platanus racemosa* Nutt. (106, 147) (1856-1930)

California thistle - *Cirsium arvense* (L.) Scop. (156) (1923)

California timothy - *Phalaris angusta* Nees ex Trin. (94) (1901), *Phalaris caroliniana* Walt. (5, 11, 19, 45) (1840-1888)

California timothy grass - *Phalaris caroliniana* Walt. (87, 88) (1884-1885)

California toothwort - *Cardamine californica* (Nutt.) Greene var. *californica* (138) (1923)

California tree-mallow [California treemallow] - *Lavatera assurgentiflora* Kellogg (138) (1923)

California trillium - *Trillium chloropetalum* var. *giganteum* (Hook. & Arn.) Munz (138) (1923)

California trout lily [California troutlily] - *Erythronium californicum* Purdy (138) (1923)

California umbellularia [Californian umbellularia] - *Umbellularia californica* (Hook. & Arn.) Nutt. (20) (1857)

California vetch - *Vicia americana* Muhl. ex Willd. subsp. *americana* (155) (1942)

California Washington palm - *Washingtonia filifera* (L. Linden) H. Wendl. (138) (1923)

California waterweed - *Ludwigia peploides* (Kunth) Raven subsp. *peploides* (106) (1930)

California wax myrtle - *Morella californica* (Cham. & Schlecht.) Wilbur (106) (1930)

California white cedar - *Calocedrus decurrens* (Torr.) Florin (161) (1857)

California white oak [Californian white oak] - *Quercus lobata* Née (107, 138, 161) (1857-1923)

California wild rose - *Rosa californica* Cham. & Schlecht. (138) (1923)

California wood - *Caesalpinia mexicana* Gray (92) (1876)

California yellow mustard - *Sinapis alba* L. (109) (1949)

California yerba santa - *Eriodictyon californicum* (Hook. & Arn.) Torr. (50) (present)

Calite - *Chenopodium album* L. (150) (1894) NM

Calite de agua (Spanish) - *Amaranthus blitoides* S. Wats. (150) (1894) NM, *Amaranthus retroflexus* L. (150) (1894) NM

Calla - *Calla* L. (1, 155, 158) (1900-1942) ancient name, calla or calla lily of florists is Zantedeschia, *Zantedeschia aethiopica* (L.) Spreng. (109) (1949) this is calla or calla lily of florists, *Zantedeschia* Spreng. (138) (1923)

Calla lily - *Zantedeschia aethiopica* (L.) Spreng. (5, 50, 92) (1876–present)

Callahuala root - *Campyloneurum angustifolium* (Sw.) Fée (92) (1876)

Callery pear - *Pyrus calleryana* Dcne. (138) (1923)

Callicarpa - *Callicarpa americana* L. (174, 177) (1753-1762), *Callicarpa* L. (8, 158) (1785-1900)

Callicarpa d'Amerique (French) - *Callicarpa americana* L. (8) (1785)

Calliopsis - *Coreopsis tinctoria* Nutt. (138) (1923)

Callirhoe - *Callirhoe alcaeoides* (Michx.) Gray (114) (1894)

Callitriche - *Callitriche palustris* L. (174, 177) (1753-1762)

Calloosa grape - *Vitis shuttleworthii* House (15) (1895)

Calmint hyssop - *Agastache nepetoides* (L.) Kuntze (187) (1818)

Calmus - *Acorus calamus* L. (75, 158, 186) (1814-1900)

Calophanes - *Dyschoriste* Nees (158) (1900)

Calopogon -, *Calopogon tuberosus* (L.) B.S.P. var. *tuberosus* (5, 48, 156) (1913-1923)

Caltrappe - *Centaurea calcitrapa* L. (179) (1526)

Caltrop [Caltrops] - *Centaurea calcitrapa* L. (5, 107, 156) (1913-1923), *Kallstroemia maxima* (L.) Hook. & Arn. (10) (1818), *Kallstroemia* Scop. (50, 155, 158) (1900–present), *Tribulus* L. (1, 13, 14, 15, 93, 158) (1849-1932), *Tribulus terrestris* L. (80, 156, 178) (1526-1923)

Calvel de la India - *Tabernaemontana divaricata* (L.) R. Br. ex Roemer & J.A. Schultes (109) (1949)

Calycant - *Calycanthus* L. (8) (1785)

Calycant de Caroline - *Calycanthus floridus* L. (8) (1785)

Calycine madwort - *Alyssum alyssoides* (L.) L. (165) (1768)

Calycled andromeda - *Chamaedaphne calyculata* (L.) Moench (165) (1807)

Calycocarpum - *Calycocarpum* Nutt. (50) (present)

Calycose houstonia - *Houstonia purpurea* L. var. *calycosa* Gray (5, 97) (1913-1937)

Calypso - *Calypso bulbosa* (L.) Oakes (86, 138, 156, 158) (1878-1923), *Calypso bulbosa* (L.) Oakes var. *americana* (R. Br. ex Ait. f.) Luer (5) (1913), *Calypso* Salisb. (1, 138, 158) (1900-1932) for Calypso of Greek mythology

Camaru - *Physalis pubescens* L. (107) (1648)

Camas [Camass, Kamas, Kmass] - *Camassia* Lindl. (2, 109, 155) (1895-1949) from camass or quamash the Indian name, *Camassia scilloides* (Raf.) Cory (14, 35, 101, 106, 156) (1803-1930) William Clark, from Nootka 'chamash' (sweet), *Zigadenus elegans* Pursh subsp. *glaucus* (Nutt.) Hultén (126) (1933), *Zigadenus venenosus* S. Wats. var. *gramineus* (Rydb.) Walsh ex M.E. Peck (148) (1939)

Camash - *Camassia* Lindl. (1) (1932)

Camelia - *Camellia japonica* L. (92) (1876)

Camelina - *Camelina sativa* (L.) Crantz. (possibly) (180) (1633)

Camel's-foot [Camel's foot] - *Cypripedium acaule* Ait. (5, 156) (1913-1923) no longer in use by 1923

Camel's-thorn [Camel's thorn, Camelsthorn] - *Alhagi maurorum* Medik. (92, 107, 155) (1876-1942)

Camil - *Achillea millefolium* L. (158) (1900)

Camline - *Camelina sativa* (L.) Crantz (156, 157, 158) (1900-1929), *Camelina sativa* (L.) Crantz subsp. *sativa* (184) (1793)

Cammock - *Achillea millefolium* L. (158) (1900), *Hypericum perforatum* L. (5, 156, 157, 158) (1900–1929), *Ononis campestris* G. Koch & Ziz (92) (1876)

Camomile [Chamomile, Camomylle] - *Adonis annua* L. (5, 156) (1913-1923), *Anthemis cotula* L. (138, 155, 158, 167) (1814-1942), *Anthemis* L. (4, 10, 50, 156, 184) (1793–present), *Chamaemelum nobile* (L.) All. (19, 49, 52, 53, 54, 58, 92, 107, 109, 179) (1526-1949), *Matricaria discoidea* DC. (85) (1932), *Matricaria* L. (1, 93, 158) (1900-1936), *Polygonum virginianum* L. (82) (1930)

Camomile puante (French) - *Anthemis cotula* L. (7, 186) (1814-1828)

Camomilla fetida (Italian) - *Anthemis cotula* L. (186) (1814)

Camomille commune on d'Allemagne (French) - *Matricaria recutita* L. (158) (1900)

Camoroche - *Argentina anserina* (L.) Rydb. (157, 158) (1900-1929)

Camote - *Ipomoea batatas* (L.) Lam. (110) (1886)

Camp root - *Geum aleppicum* Jacq. (5) (1913)

Campanilla - *Ipomoea* L. (106) (1930)

Campanule (French) - *Campanula rotundifolia* L. (158) (1900)

Campeachy wood - *Haematoxylum campechianum* L. (92) (1876)

Campernelle jonquil - *Narcissus* ×*odorus* L. [*jonquilla* × *pseudonarcissus*] (109) (1949)

Camphor geranium - *Tanacetum parthenium* (L.) Schultz-Bip. (75) (1894) Western MA

Camphor pluchea - *Pluchea camphorata* (L.) DC. (50) (present)

Camphor tree [Camphor-tree] - *Cinnamomum camphora* (L.) J. Presl (19, 20, 92, 109) (1840-1949)

Camphorweed [Camphor-weed, Camphor weed] - *Heterotheca* Cass. (4) (1986), *Heterotheca subaxillaris* (Lam.) Britton & Rusby (50, 122, 124) (1937–present), *Pluchea* Cass. (50) (present), *Trichostema lanceolatum* Benth. (156) (1923)

Campion - *Lychnis* L. (50, 138, 155, 156) (1923–present), *Silene* L. (1, 4, 10, 13, 15, 93, 109, 138, 156) (1818-1986), *Silene stellata* (L.) Aiton f. (possibly) (184) (1793)

Campion of Constantinople - *Lychnis chalcedonica* L. (178) (1526)

Campion pink - *Silene vulgaris* (Moench) Garcke (7, 92) (1828-1876)

Campsis - *Campsis* Lour. (50) (present)

Can wíyape (Dakota Teton, tree-twiner) - *Vitis cinerea* (Engelm.) Millard (37) (1919)

Canada-pest [Canada pest] - *Eustoma exaltatum* (L.) Salisb. ex G. Don subsp. *russellianum* (Hook) Kartesz (75, 158) (1894-1900) Deer Lodge MT, *Eustoma* Salisb. ex G. Don (158) (1900)

Canadian anemone [Canada anemone] - *Anemone canadensis* L. (5, 50, 72, 82, 85, 93, 127, 131, 158) (1899–present)

Canadian arbor-vitae - *Thuja occidentalis* L. (46) (1879)

Canadian balsam [Canada balsam] - *Abies balsamea* (L.) Mill. (14, 58, 92) (1869-1882)

Canadian barberry - *Berberis canadensis* P. Mill. (8) (1785)

Canadian beach-head iris [Canada beachhead iris] - *Iris setosa* Pallas ex Link var. *canadensis* M. Foster ex B.L. Robins. & Fern. (50) (present)

Canadian beedruby [Canada beedruby] - *Maianthemum canadense* Desf. (155) (1942)

Canadian bent grass [Canada bent grass] - *Calamagrostis canadensis* (Michx.) Beauv. var. *macouniana* (Vasey) Stebbins (68) (1890)

Canadian berberry - *Berberis canadensis* P. Mill. (42) (1814)

Canadian bitter-root [Canadian bitter root] - *Lewisia rediviva* Pursh (14) (1882)

Canadian black snakeroot [Canadian blacksnakeroot] - *Sanicula canadensis* L. var. *canadensis* (50) (present)

Canadian blue grass [Canadian bluegrass, Canadian blue-grass, Canada bluegrass, Canada blue grass, Canada blue-grass] - *Poa compressa* L. (3, 27, 50, 56, 68, 85, 94, 109, 111, 119, 122, 138, 140, 143, 155, 163) (1819–present)

Canadian blueberry [Canada blueberry] - *Vaccinium myrtilloides* Michx. (5, 138) (1913-1923)

Canadian brome [Canada brome] - *Bromus kalmii* Gray (155) (1942), *Bromus pubescens* Muhl. ex Willd. (3) (1977)

Canadian brome grass [Canada brome grass] - *Bromus ciliatus* L. var. *ciliatus* (42) (1814), *Bromus kalmii* Gray (122) (1937)

Canadian buffaloberry [Canadian buffalo berry, Canadian buffalo-berry] - *Shepherdia canadensis* Nutt. (5, 85, 93, 131, 156, 158) (1899-1932)

Canadian bullberry [Canadian bull berry] - *Shepherdia canadensis* Nutt. (108) (1878)

Canadian bur - *Cynoglossum officinale* L. (92, 156, 157, 158) (1876-1929), *Xanthium strumarium* L. var. *canadense* (Mill.) Torr. & Gray (158) (1900)

Canadian burnet - *Sanguisorba canadensis* L. (2, 156) (1895-1923)

Canadian cat's-foot [Canadian cat's foot] - *Antennaria howellii* Greene subsp. *canadensis* (Greene) Bayer (5) (1913)

Canadian cat's-foot [Canadian cat's foot] - *Antennaria neglecta* Greene (5) (1913)

Canadian cistus [Canada cistus] - *Helianthemum canadense* (L.) Michx. (42) (1814)

Canadian clearweed [Canada clearweed] - *Pilea pumila* (L.) Gray (50, 155) (1942–present)

Canadian cocklebur [Canada cocklebur] - *Xanthium strumarium* L. (50) (present)

Canadian columbine - *Aquilegia canadensis* L. (46) (1879)

Canadian crookneck [Canada crookneck, Canada crook-neck] - *Cucurbita maxima* Dcne. (158) (1900), *Cucurbita moschata* (Duchesne ex Lam.) Duchesne ex Poir. (107) (1919)

Canadian dioiceous bonduc - *Gymnocladus dioicus* (L.) K. Koch (8) (1785)

Canadian dogwood [Canadian dog wood] - *Cornus canadensis* L. (42) (1814)

Canadian Dutchman's-breeches [Canadian Dutchman's breeches] - *Dicentra canadensis* (Goldie) Walp. (2) (1895)

Canadian dwarf-cherry honeysuckle - *Lonicera canadensis* Bartr. ex Marsh. (8) (1785)

Canadian elderberry - *Sambucus nigra* L. subsp. *canadensis* (L.) R. Bolli (107) (1919)

Canadian erigeron [Canada erigeron] - *Conyza canadensis* (L.) Cronq. var. *canadensis* (157, 158) (1900-1929)

Canadian fleabane [Canada fleabane] - *Conyza canadensis* (L.) Cronq. var. *canadensis* (5, 6, 7, 49, 53, 55, 57, 58, 61, 85, 92, 93, 122, 156, 157, 158) (1828-1937), *Conyza* Less. (1, 93) (1932-1936)

Canadian garlic [Canada garlic] - *Allium canadense* L. (155) (1942)

Canadian gaultheria - *Gaultheria procumbens* L. (8) (1785)

Canadian germander [Canada germander] - *Teucrium canadense* L. (50) (present)

Canadian ginger [Canada ginger] - *Asarum canadense* L. (49, 156) (1898-1923)

Canadian goldenrod [Canadian golden-rod, Canada goldenrod, Canada golden-rod] - *Solidago canadensis* L. (4, 5, 19, 50, 62, 72, 80, 82, 85, 95, 97, 122, 127, 131, 138, 155, 156, 158) (1840-present), *Solidago canadensis* L. var. *canadensis* (3, 50) (1977–present), *Solidago canadensis* L. var. *gilvocanescens* Rydb. (3) (1977), *Solidago canadensis* L. var. *hargeri* Fern. (3) (1977), *Solidago canadensis* L. var. *salibrosa* (Piper) M.E.Jones (3) (1977), *Solidago canadensis* L. var. *scabra* Torr. & Gray (3, 50) (1977–present)

Canadian gooseberry [Canada gooseberry] - *Ribes oxyacanthoides* L. (50, 155) (1942–present)

Canadian hawkweed [Canada hawkweed] - *Hieracium canadense* Michx. (5, 50, 72, 85, 131, 155, 156, 158) (1899–present)

Canadian hemlock [Canada hemlock] - *Tsuga canadensis* (L.) Carr. (109, 112, 136, 138) (1923-1949)

Canadian hemp [Canada hemp] - *Apocynum cannabinum* L. (6, 14, 49, 52, 53, 54, 55, 57, 64, 106, 156, 157, 158) (1882-1929)

Canadian holly - *Ilex mucronata* (L.) M. Powell, Savol. & S. Andrews (8) (1785)

Canadian honewort - *Cryptotaenia canadensis* (L.) DC. (50) (present)

Canadian honeywort [Canadian honey-wort] - *Cryptotaenia canadensis (L.) DC.* (187) (1818)

Canadian horseweed - *Conyza canadensis* (L.) Cronq. (50) (present)

Canadian lettuce [Canada lettuce] - *Lactuca canadensis* L. (50, 80, 155, 157) (1900–present)

Canadian lily [Canada lily] - *Lilium canadense* L. (2, 5, 50, 138, 155, 156, 157, 158) (1895–present)

Canadian lousewort - *Pedicularis canadensis* L. (50) (present)

Canadian lyme grass [Canada lyme grass, Canada lyme-grass, Canadian lime grass] - *Elymus canadensis* L. (5, 42, 56, 66, 90, 119) (1814-1938)

Canadian maidenhair, Canadian maiden hair - *Adiantum pedatum* L. (42, 46, 165) (1768-1879)

Canadian mayflower [Canada mayflower] - *Maianthemum canadense* Desf. (50) (present)

Canadian milkvetch [Canada milkvetch, Canada milk vetch, Canadian milk vetch] - *Astragalus canadensis* L. (3, 4, 42, 50, 85, 155) (1814–present), *Astragalus canadensis* L. var. *canadensis* (5, 50, 93) (1913–present)

Canadian mint [Canada mint] - *Mentha arvensis* L. (155) (1942)

Canadian moonseed [Canada moonseed] - *Menispermum canadense* L. (5, 6, 8, 49, 53, 64, 97, 131, 156, 158) (1892–1937)

Canadian mountain tea - *Gaultheria procumbens* L. (8) (1785)

Canadian nettle [Canada nettle] - *Laportea canadensis* (L.) Weddell (5, 19, 92, 93, 156, 157, 158) (1840-1923)

Canadian parrot-feather [Canada parrotfeather] - *Myriophyllum verticillatum* L. (138, 155) (1923-1942)

Canadian parsley-leaf vine [Canadian parsley-leaved vine] - *Vitis vinifera* L. (possibly) (8) (1785)

Canadian pea [Canada pea] - *Vicia cracca* L. (5, 76, 156, 158) (1896-1923) Paris ME

Canadian pine - *Pinus resinosa* Aiton (5) (1913)

Canadian pitch [Canada pitch] - *Tsuga canadensis* (L.) Carr. (57, 92) (1876-1917) source

Canadian plum [Canada plum] - *Prunus americana* Marsh. (46, 156) (1879–1923), *Prunus nigra* Aiton (3, 5, 137, 138, 156) (1913-1977)

Canadian poplar - *Populus ×canadensis* Moench (pro sp.) [*deltoides × nigra*] (20) (1857), *Populus balsamifera* L. (135) (1910) MT

Canadian potato [Canada potato] - *Helianthus tuberosus* L. (5, 156, 158) (1900–1923)

Canadian pussytoes - *Antennaria howellii* Greene subsp. *canadensis* (Greene) Bayer (155) (1942)

Canadian raspberry - *Rubus odoratus* L. (5) (1913)

Canadian rattleweed [Canadian rattle weed] - *Astragalus canadensis* L. var. *canadensis* (5) (1913)

Canadian red-berry elder [Canadian red-berried elder] - *Sambucus nigra* L. subsp. *canadensis* (L.) R. Bolli (8) (1785)

Canadian rice [Canada rice] - *Piptatherum canadense* (Poir) Barkworth (66, 90) (1885-1903), *Zizania aquatica* L. (5, 14, 157, 158) (1882-1929)

Canadian rice grass [Canadian ricegrass] - *Piptatherum canadense* (Poir) Barkworth (50) (present)

Canadian rockrose [Canada rock rose] - *Helianthemum canadense* (L.) Michx. (5, 42, 156) (1814-1923)

Canadian root [Canada root, Canada-root] - *Asclepias tuberosa* L. (5, 7, 64, 92, 156, 158) (1828-1923)

Canadian round-leaf smilax [Canadian round leaved smilax] - *Smilax rotundifolia* L. (8) (1785)

Canadian rush [Canada rush] - *Juncus canadensis* J. Gay ex Laharpe (5, 50, 72, 155) (1907–present)

Canadian sagebrush [Canada sagebrush] - *Artemisia campestris* L. subsp. *borealis* (Pallas) Hall & Clements (155) (1942)

Canadian sanicle [Canada sanicle] - *Sanicula canadensis* L. (3, 155) (1942-1977)

Canadian sea-buckthorn - *Shepherdia canadensis* Nutt. (8) (1785)

Canadian shepherdia - *Shepherdia canadensis* Nutt. (20) (1857)

Canadian small-reed - *Calamagrostis canadensis* (Michx.) Beauv. (90) (1885)

Canadian snakeroot [Canada snakeroot, Canada snake root, Canada snake-root] - *Asarum canadense* L. (7, 53, 57, 58, 64, 92, 109, 156, 158, 186) (1814-1949)

Canadian snapdragon [Canadian snap dragon] - *Nuttallanthus canadensis* (L.) D.A. Sutton (42) (1814)

Canadian spike-sedge [Canada spikesedge] - *Eleocharis geniculata* (L.) Roemer & J.A. Schultes (50) (present)

Canadian spiraea - *Spiraea hypericifolia* L. (8) (1785)

Canadian spiraea - *Spiraea japonica* L. f. var. *fortunei* (Planch.) Rehd. (8) (1785)

Canadian St. John's-wort [Canadian St. John's wort] - *Hypericum canadense* L. (5, 72, 93, 131) (1899-1936)

Canadian sweet gale [Canada sweet gale] - *Comptonia peregrina* (L.) Coult. (5, 156) (1913-1923)

Canadian tea [Canada tea] - *Gaultheria procumbens* L. (5, 92, 156) (1876-1923)

Canadian thistle [Canada thistle] - *Cirsium arvense* (L.) Scop. (3, 4, 5, 19, 45, 49, 50, 56, 57, 58, 62, 63, 72, 75, 80, 82, 85, 93, 95, 106, 131, 145, 155, 156, 157, 158, 187, 195) (1814–present), *Cirsium undulatum* (Nutt.) Spreng (3, 160) (1860-1977)

Canadian tickclover [Canada tickclover, Canadian tick-trefoil] - *Desmodium canadense* (L.) DC. (3, 4, 5, 72, 93, 155, 158) (1907-1986)

Canadian tick-trefoil [Canada tick-trefoil] - *Desmodium canadense* (L.) DC. (5, 72, 93, 158) (1900-1936)

Canadian toadflax [Canada toadflax] - *Nuttallanthus canadensis* (L.) D.A. Sutton (50) (present)

Canadian tree onion [Canada tree onion] - *Allium canadense* L. (165) (1768)

Canadian turpentine [Canada turpentine] - *Abies balsamea* (L.) Mill. (57, 60, 92) (1876-1917) source

Canadian viburnum - *Viburnum lentago* L. (8) (1785)

Canadian violet [Canada violet] - *Viola canadensis* L. (2, 5, 41, 72, 85, 93, 131, 138, 155, 156, 158) (1770-1942), *Viola canadensis* L. var. *rugulosa* (Greene) A.S. Hitchc. (3) (1977)

Canadian wall cress - *Arabis canadensis* L. (42) (1814)

Canadian waterleaf - *Hydrophyllum canadense* L. (156) (1923)

Canadian waterweed [Canada waterweed] - *Elodea canadensis* Michx. (50, 155) (1942–present)

Canadian weed - *Elodea canadensis* Michx. (156) (1923)

Canadian white violet - *Viola canadensis* L. (50) (present)

Canadian wild ginger [Canada wild ginger, Canada wildginger] - *Asarum canadense* L. (2, 50, 138, 155) (1895–present)

Canadian wild lettuce [Canada wild lettuce] - *Lactuca canadensis* L. (158) (1900)

Canadian wild rye [Canada wildrye, Canada wild rye, Canada wild-rye] - *Elymus canadensis* L. (3, 11, 50, 116, 140, 143, 146, 155) (1888–present)

Canadian woodnettle - *Laportea canadensis* (L.) Weddell (50, 155) (1942–present)

Canadian wormwood [Canada wormwood] - *Artemisia campestris* L. subsp. *borealis* (Pallas) Hall & Clements (5, 72, 93, 95, 131, 156) (1899-1936)

Canadian yew [Canada yew] or Canadian yew tree [Canadian yew-tree] - *Taxus canadensis* Willd. (5, 8, 50, 138) (1785–present)

Canadische Collinsonie (German) - *Collinsonia canadensis* L. (6, 7) (1828-1932)

Canadische Edeltanne (German) - *Tsuga canadensis* (L.) Carr. (6) (1892)

Canadische Gelbwurzel (German) - *Hydrastis canadensis* L. (6) (1892)

Canadische Hanf (German) - *Apocynum cannabinum* L. (6) (1892)

Canadische Haselwurz (German) - *Asarum canadense* L. (7) (1828)

Canadische Hollunder (German) - *Sambucus nigra* L. subsp. *canadensis* (L.) R. Bolli (6) (1892)

Canadische Hydrastis (German) - *Hydrastis canadensis* L. (186) (1814)

Canadische Lattich (German) - *Lactuca canadensis* L. (6) (1892)

Canadische Schlagenwurz (German) - *Asarum canadense* L. (158) (1900)

Canadischer Hanf (German) - *Apocynum cannabinum* L. (158) (1900)

Canadisches Berufkraut (German) - *Conyza canadensis* (L.) Cronq. var. *canadensis* (6, 158) (1892-1900)

Canadisches Bludkraut (German) - *Sanguinaria canadensis* L. (186) (1814)

Canadisches Mondkorn (German) - *Menispermum canadense* L. (158) (1900)

Canadisches Sonnenroschen (German) - *Helianthemum canadense* (L.) Michx. (6) (1892)

Canaigre - *Rumex hymenosepalus* Torr. (37, 57, 107, 109, 122, 124, 138, 155, 158) (1900–1949)

Canaigre dock - *Rumex hymenosepalus* Torr. (50) (present)

Canary - *Phalaris* L. (184) (1793)

Canary archil - *Roccella tinctoria* DC. (92) (1876)

Canary bird seed - *Phalaris canariensis* L. (12) (1819)

Canary broom - *Genista canariensis* L. (138) (1923)

Canary corn [Canarie corne] - *Phalaris canariensis* L. (180) (1633)

Canary date palm - *Phoenix canariensis* hort. ex Chabaud (138) (1923)

Canary grass [Canary-grass, Canary grass, Canarie grasse] - *Phalaris arundinacea* L. (158) (1900), *Phalaris canariensis* L. (3, 56, 67, 85, 86, 90, 92, 107, 109, 111, 119, 122, 131, 155, 157, 158, 163, 180) (1633-1977), *Phalaris caroliniana* Walt. (45, 88, 158) (1885-1900), *Phalaris* L. (1, 45, 50, 66, 93, 152, 155, 158) (1896–present)

Canary monkey-flower [Canary monkeyflower] - *Mimulus brevipes* Benth. (138) (1923)

Canary seed [Canarie seed, Canarie seede] - *Phalaris canariensis* L. (92, 178, 180) (1596-1876), *Phalaris* L. (7, 10) (1818-1828)

Canary vine [Canary-vine] - *Adlumia fungosa* (Aiton) Greene ex B. S. P. (5, 76, 156) (1896-1923) Madison WI

Canary weed - *Roccella tinctoria* DC. (92) (1876)

Canary-balm [Canarybalm] - *Cedronella canariensis* (L.) Willd. ex Webb & Berth. (138) (1923)

Canary-grass [Canary grass] - *Lepidium* L. (1) (1932), *Lepidium virginicum* L. (62) (1912)

Canatillo - *Ephedra* L. (153) (1913) NM

Canby's aster [Canby aster] - *Pyrrocoma integrifolia* (Porter ex A.Gray) Greene (155) (1942), *Symphyotrichum foliaceum* (DC.) Nesom var. *canbyi* (Gray) Nesom (50) (present)

Canby's blue grass [Canby's bluegrass, Canby bluegrass] - *Poa secunda* J. Presl (3, 155) (1942-1977)

Canby's bulrush - *Schoenoplectus etuberculatus* (Steud.) Soják (5, 50) (1913–present)

Canby's lobelia - *Lobelia canbyi* Gray (5) (1913)

Canby's marsh pennywort [Canby's marsh penny wort] - *Hydrocotyle prolifera* Kellogg (5) (1913)

Canby's mountain-lover [Canby's mountain-lover] - *Paxistima canbyi* Gray (5, 86, 156) (1878-1923)

Canby's pachistima [Canby pachistima] - *Paxistima canbyi* Gray (138) (1923)

Canby's thorn - *Crataegus crus-galli* L. (5) (1913)

Cancer jalap [Cancer-jalap] - *Phytolacca americana* L. (5, 69) (1903-1913), *Phytolacca americana* L. var. *americana* (64, 156, 158) (1900-1907)

Cancer wintergreen - *Gaultheria hispidula* (L.) Muhl. ex Bigelow (92) (1876)

Cancer-drops [Cancer drops] - *Epifagus virginiana* (L.) W. Bart. (5, 92, 156) (1876-1923), *Orobanche uniflora* L. (7) (1828)

Cancer-root [Cancer root] - *Orobanche* L. (1, 158) (1900-1932), *Conopholis americana* (L. f.) Wallr. (5, 156) (1913-1923), *Conopholis* Wallr. (2) (1895), *Epifagus* Nutt. (2, 10) (1818-1895), *Epifagus virginiana* (L.) W. Bart. (5, 7, 19, 49, 57, 92, 156, 186, 187) (1814-1917) thought to be cure for cancer, *Gelsemium sempervirens* (L.) J. St.-Hil. (1) (1932), *Knautia arvensis* (L.) Duby (156) (1923), *Orobanche fasciculata* Nutt. (101) (1905), *Orobanche uniflora* L. (5, 19, 93, 157, 158) (1840-1936), *Phytolacca americana* L. var. *americana* (6, 49, 71) (1892-1898)

Cancerweed [Cancer weed, Cancer-weed] - Orobanche L. (35) (1806) Meriwether Lewis, *Prenanthes alba* L. (5, 49, 156, 158) (1898-1923), *Prenanthes aspera* Michx. (157) (1929), *Salvia lyrata* L. (3, 4, 5, 19, 92, 156) (1840-1986)

Cancerwort - *Kickxia elatine* (L.) Dumort. (5) (1913)

Candelabrum cactus - *Opuntia imbricata* (Haw.) DC. var. *imbricata* (149) (1904) NM

Candelilla - *Euphorbia antisyphilitica* Zucc. (122) (1937) TX

Candle alder - *Alnus serrulata* (Aiton) Willd. (187) (1818)

Candle anemone [Candle anemony] - *Anemone cylindrica* Gray (3, 4, 50, 109, 138, 155, 156) (1923–present)

Candle larkspur - *Delphinium elatum* L. (109) (1949)

Candle rush - *Juncus effusus* L. (5, 156) (1913-1923)

Candle tree [Candle-tree, Candletree] - *Catalpa bignonioides* Walt. (5, 156) (1913-1923) IA, *Catalpa speciosa* (Warder) Warder ex Engelm. (156) (1923), *Parmentiera cereifera* Seem. (138) (1923)

Candleberry [Candle berry, Candle-berry] or Candleberry tree [Candel berry tree, Candle-berry-tree] - *Morella cerifera* (L.) Small (5, 6, 41, 49, 52, 53, 73, 92, 156) (1770-1923)

Candleberry myrtle [Candelberry myrtle, Candle-berry myrtle] - *Morella cerifera* (L.) Small (5, 8, 14, 92, 156, 177, 189) (1762-1923), *Myrica* L. (8, 10, 14) (1785-1882)

Candleberry tree [Candel berry tree, Candle-berry-tree] - *Aleurites moluccana* (L.) Willd. (92, 109) (1876-1949)

Candlenut tree [Candelnut tree, Candle-nut tree, Candlenuttree] - *Aleurites moluccana* (L.) Willd. (107, 109, 138, 155) (1919-1949)

Candlewick [Candle-wick] - *Typha latifolia* L. (5, 14, 156, 157, 158) (1882-1923), *Verbascum thapsus* L. (5, 69, 158) (1900-1913)

Candle-wick mullein - *Verbascum thapsus* L. (156) (1923)

Candlewood [Candelwood, Candle wood] - *Amyris balsamifera* L. (92) (1876), *Fouquieria* Kunth (15) (1895), *Fouquieria splendens* Engelm. (149, 153) (1904-1913)

Candy crane's-bill [Candie Cranes bill] - *Erodium gruinum* (L.) L'Hér. ex Aiton (possibly) (178) (1526)

Candy grass [Candy-grass] - *Eragrostis cilianensis* (All.) Vign. ex Janchen (94, 119, 129) (1894-1938)

Candy mustard [Candie mustard] - *Iberis umbellata* L. (178) (1526)

Candytuft [Candy-tuft, Candy tuft] - *Iberis amara* L. (92) (1876), *Iberis* L. (109, 138, 155, 158, 190) (~1759-1949), *Iberis umbellata* L. (19) (1840)

Candytuft gilia - *Ipomopsis congesta* (Hook.) V. Grant (155) (1942)

Candy-weed - *Polygala lutea* L. (156) (1923)

Cane [Canes] - *Arundinaria gigantea* (Walt.) Muhl. subsp. *gigantea* (7, 12, 19, 38, 45, 66, 94, 182) (1791-1912), *Arundinaria* Michx. (10, 66, 155) (1818-1942), *Sorghum* Moench (78) (1898) OH

Cane ash - *Fraxinus americana* L. (5, 156, 157, 158) (1900–1929)

Cane bluestem - *Bothriochloa barbinodis* (Lag.) Herter (3, 50, 155) (1942–present)

Cane brake - *Arundinaria* Michx. (92) (1876)

Cane grass - *Cynodon dactylon* (L.) Pers. (5) (1913), *Phragmites* Adans. (1) (1932), *Phragmites australis* (Cav.) Trin. ex Steud. (101) (1905) MT

Cane withy - *Salix alba* L. (158) (1900) SD

Cane-like panicum - *Lasiacis divaricata* (L.) A.S. Hitchc. (87) (1884)

Canell - *Cinnamomum* Schaeffer (possibly) (179) (1526)

Canella - *Canella winterana* (L.) Gaertn. (57, 58, 92) (1869-1917)

Canescent primrose - *Oenothera macrocarpa* Nutt. subsp. *incana* (Gray) Reveal (97) (1937)

Canescent whitlow-grass [Canescent whitlow grass] - *Draba breweri* S. Wats. var. *cana* (Rydb.) Rollins (5) (1913)

Can-hoop [Can hoop] - *Ilex laevigata* (Pursh) Gray (5, 156) (1913-1923)

Canistel - *Pouteria campechiana* (Kunth) Baehni (109, 138) (1923-1949)

Canker - *Papaver rhoeas* L. (158) (1900)

Canker blooms (Shakespeare) - *Rosa canina* L. (5) (1913)

Canker rose - *Rosa canina* L. (5) (1913)

Canker violet - *Viola rostrata* Pursh (92, 156) (1898-1923)

Canker-leaf [Canker leaf] - *Pyrola americana* Sweet (49) (1898)

Canker-lettuce [Canker lettuce] - *Pyrola americana* Sweet (5, 53, 58, 92, 156) (1869-1923)

Canker-root [Cankerroot, Canker root] - *Coptis trifolia* (L.) Salisb. (5, 49, 53, 64, 76, 92, 156) (1896-1923) Oxford Co. ME, *Kickxia*

elatine (L.) Dumort. (3, 4, 5) (1913-1986), *Limonium carolinianum* (Walt.) Britt. (92) (1876), *Prenanthes alba* L. (92) (1876)

Canker-rose [Canker rose] - *Papaver rhoeas* L. (5, 156, 158) (1900–1923)

Cankerweed [Canker-weed, Canker weed] - *Prenanthes alba* L. (92) (1876), *Prenanthes serpentaria* Pursh (5, 156) (1913-1923), *Senecio jacobea* L. (5, 156) (1913-1923)

Cankerwort - *Taraxacum officinale* G.H. Weber ex Wiggers (5, 62, 64, 69, 156, 157, 158) (1900-1929)

Canna - *Canna indica* L. (92) (1876)

Canna down - *Eriophorum callitrix* Cham. ex C.A. Mey. (5, 156) (1913-1923)

Canneberge d'Amerique (French) - *Vaccinium macrocarpon* Aiton (7) (1828)

Cannon-ball tree [Cannon ball tree] - *Couroupita guianensis* Aubl. (92, 109) (1876-1949)

Canoe birch - *Betula papyrifera* Marsh (1, 2, 4, 5, 10, 20, 19, 37, 47, 72, 92, 93, 95, 109, 112, 113, 130, 131, 137, 138, 157, 158, 187) (1818-1986), *Betula pendula* Roth (156) (1923), *Betula pubescens* Ehrh. (107, 156) (1919-1923)

Canoe tree - *Liriodendron tulipifera* L. (41) (1770)

Canoe wood [Canoe-wood] - *Liriodendron tulipifera* L. (20, 49, 92, 156) (1649-1857), *Magnolia acuminata* (L.) L. (2, 5) (1895-1913)

Canonotha - *Lindera benzoin* Blume. (46) (1879)

Cantaloupe - *Cucumis melo* L. (50, 82, 107, 138) (1919–present)

Cantaurea - *Centaurea montana* L. (82) (1930)

Canterbury - *Symphoricarpos albus* (L.) Blake var. *laevigatus* (Fern.) Blake (156) (1923) no longer in use by 1923

Canterbury bells - *Campanula glomerata* L. (5, 156) (1913-1923), *Campanula medium* L. (19, 82, 109) (1840-1930), *Campanula trachelium* L. (5, 156) (1913-1923)

Čanxlogan inkpa gmigmela (Lakota, small end rounded weed) - *Chenopodium album* L. (121) (1918?-1970?)

Canyon cup grass [Canyon cupgrass] - *Eriochloa lemmonii* Vasey & Scribn. (50, 155) (1942–present)

Canyon grape - *Vitis arizonica* Engelm. (15, 107, 138) (1895-1923)

Canyon poppy - *Romneya* Harvey (138) (1923)

Canyon shrub - *Rhus trilobata* Nutt. (112) (1937) Neb

Čaŋ pežuta čikala (Lakota, little wood medicine) - *Mentha arvensis* L. (121) (1918?-1970?)

Čaŋčjaxu (Lakota, chewing wood) - *Populus deltoides* Bartr. ex Marsh. subsp. *monilifera* (Aiton) Eckenwalder (121) (1918?-1970?)

Čaŋičaxpe hu (Lakota, woody whip) - *Urtica dioica* L. subsp. *gracilis* (Aiton) Seland. (121) (1918?-1970?)

Čaŋijuwi skaska naxča (Lakota, possibly meaning loose white vine) - *Clematis ligusticifolia* Nutt. (121) (1918?-1970?)

Čaŋpa (Lakota) - *Prunus virginiana* L. (121) (1918?-1970?)

Čaŋte jazaŋpi ičuwa (Lakota, heart pain treatment) - *Astragalus* L. (121) (1918?-1970?)

Čaŋxlogaŋ hu pteptečela (Lakota, short buffalo-weed) - *Erigeron pumilus* Nutt. (121) (1918?-1970?)

Čaŋxlogaŋ makatola (Lakota, green earth weed) - *Fritillaria atropurpurea* Nutt. (121) (1918?-1970?)

Čaŋxlogaŋ paŋpaŋla (Lakota, soft weed) - *Tradescantia ohiensis* Raf. (121) (1918?-1970?)

Čaŋxlogaŋ škiškita (Lakota, rough weed) - *Solanum triflorum* Nutt. (121) (1918?-1970?)

Čaŋxlogaŋ wakaljapi (Lakota, boiling weed) - *Coreopsis tinctoria* Nutt. (121) (1918?-1970?)

Čaŋxlogaŋ wapoštaŋ (Lakota, hat weed) - *Chamaesyce geyeri* (Engelm.) Small var. *geyeri* (121) (1918?-1970?)

Čaŋxlogaŋ waštemna (Lakota, odorous weed) - *Ambrosia artemisiifolia* L. (121) (1918?-1970?), *Artemisia campestris* L. (121) (1918?-1970?)

Čaŋzi (Lakota, yellow wood) - *Rhus glabra* L. (121) (1918?-1970?)

Cape blue water-lily - *Nymphaea capensis* Thunb. (109) (1949)

Cape bugloss - *Anchusa capensis* Thunb. (82, 138, 155) (1923-1942)

Cape Cod waterlily [Capecod waterlily] - *Nymphaea odorata* Aiton subsp. *odorata* (138, 155) (1923-1942)

Cape gooseberry [Cape-gooseberry] - *Physalis alkekengi* L. (92) (1876), *Physalis heterophylla* Nees (5) (1913), *Physalis peruviana* L. (109, 138) (1923-1949), *Physalis pubescens* L. (156) (1923)

Cape oxalis - *Oxalis purpurea* L. (138) (1923)

Cape pittosporum - *Pittosporum viridiflorum* Sims (138) (1923)

Cape plumbago - *Plumbago auriculata* Lam. (138) (1923)

Cape pond-weed [Cape-pondweed] - *Aponogeton distachyos* L. f. (109, 138) (1923-1949)

Cape water-hawthorn [Cape water hawthorn] - *Aponogeton distachyos* L. f. (155) (1942)

Cape waterlily - *Nymphaea capensis* Thunb. (138, 155) (1931-1942)

Cape-honeysuckle - *Tecoma capensis* (Thunb.) Lindl. (109, 138) (1923-1949)

Cape-jasmine [Cape jasmine] - *Gardenia jasminoides* J.Ellis (92, 109, 138) (1876-1949)

Cape-marigold [Cape marigold] - *Castalis tragus* (Aiton) Norl. (82) (1930) IA, *Dimorphotheca* Moench (82, 109, 138) (1923-1949)

Caper bush [Caper-bush] - *Euphorbia lathyris* L. (5, 71, 156) (1898-1923) OK

Caper euphorbia - *Euphorbia lathyris* L. (155) (1942)

Caper spurge - *Euphorbia lathyris* L. (5, 6, 71, 92, 107, 109, 156) (1876-1949)

Capers - *Caltha palustris* L. (5, 76, 157, 158) (1896–1929) Berwick ME

Cape-smilax [Cape smilax] - *Asparagus asparagoides* (L.) Druce (92) (1876) name better applied to other plant 158

Capeweed [Cape weed] - *Roccella tinctoria* DC. (92) (1876)

Capil Veneris (Official name of Materia Medica) - *Adiantum pedatum* L. (7) (1828)

Capillaire - *Gaultheria hispidula* (L.) Muhl. ex Bigelow (73, 156) (1892-1923)

Capillaire - *Gaultheria* L. (1) (1932)

Capillaire de Montpelier (French) - *Adiantum capillus-veneris* L. (97) (1937)

Capillaire du Canada (French) - *Adiantum pedatum* L. (7, 158) (1828–1900)

Capillary beaked-rush [Capillary beaked rush] - *Rhynchospora capillacea* Torr. (5) (1913)

Capillary eragrostis - *Eragrostis capillaris* (L.) Nees (56, 72) (1901-1907)

Capillary panic grass [Capillary panic-grass] - *Panicum capillare* L. (143) (1852-1936)

Capitate beaked-rush [Capitate beaked rush] - *Rhynchospora cephalantha* Gray (5) (1913)

Capitate croton - *Croton capitatus* Michx. (5, 97) (1913-1937)

Capitate gilia - *Ipomopsis spicata* (Nutt.) V. Grant subsp. *capitata* (Gray) V. Grant (131) (1899)

Capitate pedicularis - *Pedicularis capitata* Adams. (5) (1913)

Capitate sedge - *Carex capitata* L. (5, 50) (1913–present)

Capitate spike-rush [Capitate spike rush] - *Eleocharis geniculata* (L.) Roemer & J.A. Schultes (5) (1913)

Capjnusek (Bohemian) - *Geranium maculatum* L. (186) (1814)

Capon's-tail [Capon's tail] - *Aquilegia vulgaris* L. (5, 156) (1913-1923)

Capon's-tail grass [Capon's tail grass] - *Vulpia myuros* (L.) K.C. Gmel. (5, 92) (1876-1913)

Capper plant - *Euphorbia lathyris* L. (7) (1828)

Caprock fern - *Pleopeltis polypodioides* (L.) Andrews & Windham subsp. *polypodioides* (97) (1937) OK

Capsella - *Capsella bursa-pastoris* (L.) Medik. (52) (1919), *Capsella* Medik. (50, 180) (present)

Capucos coles - *Brassica oleracea* L. (107) (1536)

Capul - *Schaefferia cuneifolia* Gray (122) (1937) TX

Capuli (Mexico) - *Prunus serotina* Ehrh. (107) (1919)

Capulinos (Mexico) - *Prunus serotina* Ehrh. (107) (1919)

Caput monach - *Taraxacum officinale* G.H. Weber ex Wiggers (180) (1633)

Caraccas kino - *Coccoloba uvifera* (L.) L. (92) (1876)

Caragana - *Caragana arborescens* Lam. (106, 112) (1930-1937)

Carageenan - *Chondrus crispus* (L.) J. Stackhouse (57, 58) (1917-1869)

Carambola - *Averrhoa carambola* L. (109, 138) (1923-1949) from Oriental vernacular name

Caranna - *Dacryodes excelsa* Vahl (92) (1876)

Caranna gum - *Bursera simaruba* (L.) Sargent (92) (1876)

Caraway [Carawaies] - *Arnoglossum* Raf. (7) (1828), *Carum carvi* L. (1, 3, 4, 5, 19, 50, 53, 55, 57, 58, 59, 63, 72, 80, 85, 107, 109, 131, 138, 155, 156, 158, 178, 186) (1526–present)

Caraway seed - *Carum carvi* L. (92) (1876)

Carberry [Car-berry] - *Ribes uva-crispa* L. var. *sativum* DC. (5, 156) (1913-1923)

Card teasel [Card-teasel] - *Dipsacus fullonum* L. (5, 122, 124, 156, 158) (1900–1937)

Card thistle - *Dipsacus fullonum* L. (5, 156) (1913-1923)

Cardamine coreopsis - *Coreopsis tinctoria* Nutt. var. *tinctoria* (155) (1942)

Cardealina - *Lobelia cardinalis* L. (186) (1814)

Cardiacke - *Alliaria petiolata* (Bieb.) Cavara & Grande (158) (1900)

Cardiaire (French) - *Leonurus cardiaca* L. (158) (1900)

Cardinal larkspur - *Delphinium cardinale* Hook. (138) (1923)

Cardinal plant - *Lobelia cardinalis* L. (186, 187) (1814-1818)

Cardinale (French) - *Lobelia cardinalis* L. (186) (1814)

Cardinale bleue (French) - *Lobelia siphilitica* L. (186) (1814)

Cardinal-feather [Cardinal feather, Cardinal's feather, Cardinal's feather] - *Acalypha phleoides* Cav. (124) (1937) TX, *Acalypha radians* Torr. (50, 124) (1937–present)

Cardinal-flower [Cardinal flower, Cardinalflower, Cardinal's flower, Cardinals' flower] - *Lobelia cardinalis* L. (1, 3, 4, 6, 5, 7, 19, 34, 37, 44, 46, 50, 63, 72, 82, 86, 92, 95, 97, 109, 122, 124, 125, 138, 148, 155, 157, 158, 184, 186) (1793–present)

Cardinalizia - *Lobelia cardinalis* L. (186) (1814)

Cardoon - *Cynara cardunculus* L. (19, 92, 107, 109, 110, 138) (1840-1949)

Careless - *Amaranthus hybridus* L. (5, 156, 157, 158) (1900–1929)

Carelessweed [Careless-weed, Careless weed] - *Amaranthus* L. (106) (1930), *Amaranthus palmeri* S. Wats. (50) (present), *Amaranthus retroflexus* L. (122) (1937), *Iva* L. (1) (1932), *Iva xanthifolia* Nutt. (156) (1923)

Carey's persicaria - *Polygonum careyi* Olney (5) (1913)

Carey's sedge - *Carex careyana* Torr. ex Dewey (5, 50, 66) (1912–present)

Carib heliconia - *Heliconia bihai* (L.) L. (138) (1923)

Carib tea - *Capraria biflora* L. (7, 92) (1828-1876)

Caribbean spider lily [Caribbean spiderlily] - *Hymenocallis caribaea* (L.) Herbert (138) (1923)

Caribean grape - *Vitis tiliifolia* Humb. & Bonpl. ex Roem. & Schult. (107) (1919)

Carissa - *Carissa* L. (138) (1923), *Carissa macrocarpa* (Ecklon) A. DC. (138) (1923)

Carleton's four-o'clock [Carleton four-o'clock] - *Mirabilis glabra* (S. Wats.) Standl. (4) (1986)

Carleton's umbrella wort [Carleton's umbrella-wort] - *Mirabilis glabra* (S. Wats.) Standl. (5, 97) (1913-1937)

Carlick - *Moricandia arvensis* (L.) DC. (158) (1900)

Carlock - *Moricandia arvensis* (L.) DC. (158) (1900)

Carnation - *Dianthus caryophyllus* L. (19, 109, 138) (1840-1949), *Dianthus* L. (1, 7, 15, 138, 155, 156, 158) (1828-1942)

Carnation clover [Carnation-clover] - *Trifolium incarnatum* L. (5, 93, 156, 158) (1900-1936)

Carnation-grass [Carnation grass] - *Carex flacca* Schreb. (5, 92, 156) (1913-1923), *Carex hirta* L. (5, 156) (1913-1923), *Carex panicea* L. (5, 156) (1913-1923)

Carob or Carob tree - *Ceratonia* L. (138) (1923), *Ceratonia siliqua* L. (92, 110, 138) (1876-1923)

Carolina allspice [Carolinian allspice] - *Calycanthus floridus* L. (8, 19, 92, 107, 109, 156) (1785-1949), *Calycanthus* L. (2, 8, 10, 82, 167) (1785-1930)

Carolina anemone - *Anemone caroliniana* Walt. (3, 4, 5, 50, 72, 85, 86, 93, 97, 131, 155) (1878–present)

Carolina ash [Carolinian ash] - *Fraxinus americana* L. (8) (1785), *Fraxinus caroliniana* Mill. (5, 20, 156) (1857-1923)

Carolina aster - *Ampelaster carolinianus* (Walt.) Nesom (155) (1942)

Carolina azolla - *Azolla caroliniana* Willd. (5, 72) (1907-1913)

Carolina bark - *Pinckneya bracteata* (Bartr.) Raf. (92) (1876)

Carolina basswood - *Tilia americana* L. var. *caroliniana* (P. Mill.) Castigl. (109) (1949)

Carolina bean - *Phaseolus lunatus* L. (109) (1949)

Carolina beechdrops [Carolina beech-drops] - *Monotropsis odorata* Schwein. ex Ell. (5, 156) (1913-1923)

Carolina blue flag - *Iris hexagona* Walt. var. *hexagona* (5) (1913)

Carolina buckthorn - *Frangula caroliniana* (Walt.) Gray (5, 20, 93, 97, 138, 156) (1857-1937), *Sideroxylon lycioides* L. (5, 156) (1913-1923)

Carolina canary grass [Carolina canarygrass, Carolina canary-grass] - *Phalaris caroliniana* Walt. (5, 50, 119, 155) (1913–present)

Carolina cedar - *Juniperus virginiana* L. (5, 92, 157, 158) (1876-1913)

Carolina cherry-laurel - *Prunus caroliniana* (P. Mill.) Aiton (138) (1923)

Carolina clover - *Trifolium carolinianum* Michx. (2, 3, 4, 5, 50, 97, 122, 155) (1895–present)

Carolina clubmoss [Carolina club-moss] - *Lycopodiella caroliniana* (L.) Pichi Sermolli var. *caroliniana* (5, 122) (1913-1937)

Carolina cocculus - *Cocculus carolinus* (L.) DC. (2, 4) (1895-1986)

Carolina coralseed - *Cocculus carolinus* (L.) DC. (50) (present)

Carolina cottonwood - *Populus deltoides* Bartr. ex Marsh. subsp. *deltoides* (138) (1923)

Carolina crabgrass - *Digitaria cognata* (J.A. Schultes) Pilger var. *cognata* (50) (present)

Carolina cranebill [Carolina cranesbill, Carolina crane-bill, Carolina crane's bill, Carolina crane's-bill] - *Geranium carolinianum* L. (3, 4, 5, 72, 85, 97, 131, 157) (1899-1986)

Carolina cyrilla - *Cyrilla racemiflora* L. (20) (1857)

Carolina desert-chicory - *Pyrrhopappus carolinianus* (Walt.) DC. (50) (present)

Carolina draba - *Draba reptans* (Lam.) Fern. (50) (present)

Carolina dwarf dandelion - *Krigia virginica* (L.) Willd. (5, 97, 122) (1913-1937)

Carolina elephant's-foot (Carolina elephant's foot or Carolina elephantsfoot, Carolina elephantfoot Carolina elephant foot) - *Elephantopus carolinianus* Willd. (5, 50, 97, 122, 124, 156) (1913–present)

Carolina fanwort - *Cabomba caroliniana* Gray (50) (present)

Carolina fimbry - *Fimbristylis caroliniana* (Lam.) Fern. (50) (present)

Carolina fothergilla [Carolinian fothergilla] - *Fothergilla gardenii* L. (8) (1785)

Carolina foxtail - *Alopecurus carolinianus* Walt. (3, 50, 155) (1942–present)

Carolina garlick - *Nothoscordum borbonicum* Kunth (possibly) (165) (1768)

Carolina geranium - *Geranium carolinianum* L. (50, 155, 157) (1929–present)

Carolina globe tree - *Cephalanthus occidentalis* L. (177) (1762)

Carolina grass-of-Parnassus - *Parnassia caroliniana* Michx. (5, 156) (1913-1923)

Carolina gromwell - *Lithospermum caroliniense* (Walt. ex J.F. Gmel.) MacM. (138, 155) (1923-1942)

Carolina hemlock - *Tsuga caroliniana* Engelm. (5, 50, 109, 138) (1913–present)

Carolina hippo - *Euphorbia ipecacuanhae* L. (6) (1892)
Carolina holly [Carolinian holly] - *Ilex ambigua* (Michx.) Torr. (97) (1937) OK, *Ilex cassine* L. (8) (1785)
Carolina horsenettle [Carolina horse nettle] - *Solanum carolinense* L. (4, 50) (1986–present), *Solanum carolinense* L. var. *carolinense* (50) (present)
Carolina ipecac - *Euphorbia ipecacuanhae* L. (6, 49, 156) (1892-1923)
Carolina jasmine [Carolina jasmin] - *Gelsemium sempervirens* (L.) J. St.-Hil. (49, 53, 64, 86, 156) (1878-1923)
Carolina jessamine [Carolina-jessamine] - *Gelsemium sempervirens* (L.) J. St.-Hil. (5, 10, 49, 59, 64, 92, 138) (1876-1923)
Carolina joint-tail [Carolina jointtail] - *Coelorachis cylindrica* (Michx.) Nash (155) (1942)
Carolina kidney-bean tree [Carolina kidney bean tree] - *Wisteria frutescens* (L.) Poir. (possibly) (10, 12) (1818-1820)
Carolina larkspur - *Delphinium carolinianum* Walt. (5, 50, 97, 131, 133, 155, 158) (1899–present)
Carolina laurel cherry - *Prunus caroliniana* (P. Mill.) Aiton (2, 92) (1876-1895)
Carolina leaf-flower - *Phyllanthus carolinensis* Walt. (50) (present)
Carolina lily - *Lilium michauxii* Poir. (5, 50, 122, 138) (1913–present)
Carolina love grass [Carolina lovegrass] - *Eragrostis pectinacea* (Michx.) Nees ex Steud. (3, 155) (1942-1977)
Carolina maple - *Acer rubrum* L. (5, 97) (1913-1937)
Carolina milkvetch [Carolina milk vetch] - *Astragalus canadensis* L. var. *canadensis* (5, 42, 93, 97, 131) (1814-1937)
Carolina moonseed [Carolinian moonseed] - *Cocculus carolinus* (L.) DC. (5, 8, 97, 109) (1785-1949)
Carolina mosquito-fern [Carolina mosquitofern] - *Azolla caroliniana* Willd. (50) (present)
Carolina nutsedge - *Scleria pauciflora* Muhl. ex Willd. var. *caroliniana* (Willd.) Wood (50) (present)
Carolina oat grass [Carolina oatgrass] - *Danthonia epilis* Scribn. (50) (present)
Carolina oblique-leaf lime tree [Carolinian oblique-leaved lime-tree] - *Tilia americana* L. var. *caroliniana* (P. Mill.) Castigl. (8) (1785)
Carolina parnassia - *Parnassia caroliniana* Michx. (138) (1923)
Carolina phlox - *Phlox carolina* L. (64) (1907)
Carolina phyllanthus - *Phyllanthus carolinensis* Walt. (5, 97) (1913-1937)
Carolina pine - *Pinus echinata* Mill. (5) (1913)
Carolina pinkroot [Carolina pink root, Carolina pink-root] - *Spigelia marilandica* (L.) L. (5, 6, 10, 49, 53, 55, 57, 64, 92, 156, 184, 186) (1793-1923)
Carolina poplar [Carolinian poplar] - *Populus ×canadensis* Moench [*deltoides × nigra*] (4, 50, 82, 109, 135, 155) (1910–present), *Populus balsamifera* L. (5, 85, 92, 156) (1876-1932), *Populus deltoides* Bartr. ex Marsh. (5, 156, 158) (1900–1923), *Populus deltoides* Bartr. ex Marsh. subsp. *deltoides* (20, 112) (1857-1937), *Populus deltoides* Bartr. ex Marsh. subsp. *monilifera* (Aiton) Eckenwalder (2) (1895)
Carolina potato [Carolina potatoe] - *Ipomoea batatas* (L.) Lam. (19, 92) (1840-1876)
Carolina prickly-ash [Carolina prickly ash] - *Zanthoxylum clavaherculis* L. (20) (1857)
Carolina prickly-leaf smilax [Carolinian prickly leaved smilax] - *Smilax bona-nox* L. (8) (1785)
Carolina puccoon - *Lithospermum caroliniense* (Walt. ex J.F. Gmel.) MacM. (50) (present)
Carolina red bay - *Persea carolinensis* (Raf.) Nees (2) (1895)
Carolina redbud [Carolinian red-buds] - *Lyonia lucida* (Lam.) K. Koch (8) (1785)
Carolina redroot [Carolina red-root, Carolina red root] - *Lachnanthes caroliana* (Lam.) Dandy (5, 50, 156) (1913–present)
Carolina rhododendron - *Rhododendron carolinianum* Rehd. (5, 138) (1913-1923)

Carolina rockrose [Carolina rock rose] - *Helianthemum carolinianum* (Walt.) Michx. (86) (1878)
Carolina rose - *Rosa carolina* L. (50, 155, 156) (1923–present)
Carolina rose-bay - *Rhododendron catawbiense* Michx. (156) (1923)
Carolina rose-leaf spiraea [Carolinian rose-leaved spiraea] - *Spiraea betulifolia* Pallas var. *lucida* (Dougl. ex Greene) C.L. Hitchc. (8) (1785)
Carolina rush - *Juncus megacephalus* M.A. Curtis (72) (1907) IA
Carolina sandwort - *Minuartia caroliniana* (Walt.) Mattf. (155) (1942)
Carolina scentless syringa [Carolinian scentless syringa] - *Philadelphus inodorus* L. (8) (1785)
Carolina sedge - *Carex caroliniana* Schwein. (5, 50) (1913–present)
Carolina shrubby callicarpa [Carolinian shrubby callicarpa] - *Callicarpa americana* L. (8) (1785)
Carolina shrubby kidney-bean [Carolinian shrubby kidney bean] - *Wisteria frutescens* (L.) Poir. (8, 106) (1785-1930)
Carolina shrub-trefoil - *Ptelea trifoliata* L. (8) (1785)
Carolina smooth-bark annona [Caroliniana smooth-barked annona] - *Annona glabra* L. (8) (1785)
Carolina snailseed - *Cocculus carolinus* (L.) DC. (138, 155) (1923-1942)
Carolina spicewood tree [Carolinian spice wood tree] - *Litsea aestivalis* (L.) Fern. (8) (1785)
Carolina spider-lily [Carolina spiderlily] - *Hymenocallis caroliniana* (L.) Herbert (50) (present)
Carolina spindle tree [Carolinian spindle tree] - *Euonymus atropurpureus* Jacq. (possibly) (8) (1785)
Carolina spring-beauty [Carolina spring beauty, Carolina spring-beauty] - *Claytonia caroliniana* Michx. (5, 138, 156) (1913-1923)
Carolina storax tree [Carolinian storax tree] - *Styrax americanus* Lam. (8) (1785)
Carolina sun rockrose [Carolina sun rock-rose] - *Helianthemum carolinianum* (Walt.) Michx. (86) (1878)
Carolina tea - *Abutilon* Mill. (190) (~1759), *Ilex vomitoria* Aiton (5, 156) (1913-1923)
Carolina thermopsis - *Thermopsis villosa* (Walt.) Fern. & Schub. (138) (1923)
Carolina tillandsia [Carolinian tillandsia] - *Tillandsia usneoides* (L.) L. (8) (1785)
Carolina vanilla [Carolina-vanilla] - *Carphephorus odoratissimus* (J.F. Gmel.) Herbert (5, 92, 107, 138, 156) (1876-1923)
Carolina vetch - *Vicia caroliniana* Walt. (5, 72, 97) (1907-1937)
Carolina vincetoxicum - *Matelea carolinensis* (Jacq.) Woods. (5, 97) (1913-1937)
Carolina vine [Carolinian vine] - *Ampelopsis arborea* (L.) Koehne (8) (1785)
Carolina watershield [Carolina water shield, Carolina watershield] - *Cabomba caroliniana* Gray (5, 156) (1913-1923)
Carolina whitlow-grass [Carolina whitlow grass] - *Draba reptans* (Lam.) Fern. (5, 72, 97, 131) (1907-1937)
Carolina wild woodbine - *Gelsemium sempervirens* (L.) J. St.-Hil. (5, 64, 156) (1907-1923)
Carolina willow - *Salix caroliniana* Michx. (3, 4) (1977-1986)
Carolina woodrush - *Luzula acuminata* Raf. var. *carolinae* (S. Wats.) Fern. (50) (present)
Carolina woolly-white [Carolina woollywhite] - *Hymenopappus scabiosaeus* L'Hér. (50) (present)
Carolina yellow buckeye - *Aesculus flava* Aiton (155) (1942)
Carolina yellow jessamine - *Gelsemium sempervirens* (L.) J. St.-Hil. (109) (1949)
Carolina yellow-eyed grass - *Xyris caroliniana* Walt. (5, 50) (1913–present)
Caroliniana shrub-trefoil - *Ptelea trifoliata* L. (8) (1785)
Carota - *Daucus carota* L. (57) (1917)
Carotte (French) - *Daucus carota* L. (158) (1900)
Caroubier (French) - *Ceratonia siliqua* L. (92, 110) (1876-1886)

Cassie-oil plant

Carpathian balsam - *Pinus cembra* L. (92) (1876)

Carpenteria - *Carpenteria californica* Torr. (138) (1923), *Carpenteria* Torr. (138) (1923)

Carpenter's-grass [Carpenter's grass, Carpenters grasse] - *Achillea millefolium* L. (69, 158, 179) (1526-1904)

Carpenter's-herb [Carpenter's herb, Carpenter-herb] - *Ajuga reptans* L. (5, 156, 158) (1900-1923) no longer in use by 1923, *Lycopus virginicus* L. (92, 157, 158) (1876-1929), *Prunella vulgaris* L. (5, 156, 157, 158) (1900–1929)

Carpenter's-leaf [Carpenters' leaf] - *Galax urceolata* (Poir.) Brummitt (7, 92) (1828-1876) Banner Elk NC

Carpenter's-square [Carpenter's square] - *Prunella vulgaris* L. (156) (1923), *Scrophularia marilandica* L. (5, 50, 92, 156) (1876–present), *Scrophularia nodosa* L. (6, 52, 58) (1869-1919), *Scrophularia nodosa* var. *marilandica* Gray. (77) (1898) Southwestern MO

Carpenter's-weed [Carpenter weed, Carpenter-weed, Carpenter's weed] - *Prunella vulgaris* L. (1, 5, 73, 79, 80, 106) (1891-1932)

Carpet bent - *Agrostis stolonifera* L. (138) (1923)

Carpet bent grass [Carpet bent-grass] - *Agrostis stolonifera* L. (143) (1852-1936)

Carpet bugle - *Ajuga reptans* L. (138, 155) (1923-1942)

Carpet cress [Carpet-cress] - *Coronopus squamatus* (Forsk.) Aschers. (156) (1923)

Carpet grass [Carpet-grass] - *Axonopus compressus* (Sw.) Beauv. (5, 94, 119, 122, 138, 163) (1852-1938), *Axonopus fissifolius* (Raddi) Kuhlm. (109) (1949)

Carpet phlox - *Phlox hoodii* Richards. subsp. *glabrata* (E. Nels.) Wherry (50) (present)

Carpet-grass [Carpet grass] - *Lippia* L. (106) (1930), *Phyla nodiflora* (L.) Greene (106) (1930)

Carpetweed [Carpet weed, Carpet-weed] - *Chamaesyce geyeri* (Engelm.) Small (85) (1932) SD, *Chamaesyce* S.F. Gray (1) (1932), *Mollugo* L. (1, 13, 50, 93, 155, 158, 184) (1793–present), *Mollugo verticillata* L. (4, 5, 15, 19, 62, 63, 72, 85, 92, 93, 97, 122, 145, 155, 156, 158, 187) (1818-1986), *Phyla lanceolata* (Michx.) Greene (124) (1937) TX, *Phyla nodiflora* (L.) Greene (124) (1937) TX

Carpousia or carpousea (Modern Greek) - *Citrullus lanatus* (Thunb.) Matsumura & Nakai (110) (1886)

Carrageen moss [Carragheen moss] - *Chondrus crispus* (L.) J. Stackhouse (92) (1876)

Carrion-flower [Carrionflower, Carrion flower] - *Glechoma hederacea* L. (92) (1876), *Phallus* Junius ex L. (78) (1898) MA, *Smilax ecirrata* (Engelm. ex Kunth) S. Wats. (156) (1923), *Smilax herbacea* L. (3, 72, 85, 97, 109, 156, 157, 158) (1900-1977), *Smilax* L. (1) (1932), *Smilax lasioneura* Hook. (3) (1977), *Smilax pulverulenta* Michx. (3) (1977), *Stapelia* L. (109, 155) (1942-1949)

Carrion-flower greenbrier [Carrionflower greenbrier] - *Smilax herbacea* L. (155) (1942)

Carriuela - *Ipomoea purpurea* (L.) Roth (150) (1894) NM

Carrizo [Carizo, Carizzo] - *Calamovilfa gigantea* (Nutt.) Scribn. & Merr. (119) (1938) OK, *Calamovilfa longifolia* (Hook.) Scribn. (5) (1913), *Phragmites* Adans. (152) (1912) NM, *Phragmites australis* (Cav.) Trin. ex Steud. (149, 152) (1904-1912) NM

Carrot [Carot] - *Daucus carota* L. (62, 106, 107, 184) (1793-1930), *Daucus* L. (1, 4, 10, 138, 155, 156, 158) (1818-1986)

Carrot-leaf parsley [Carrot-leaved parsley] - *Lomatium foeniculaceum* (Nutt.) Coult. & Rose subsp. *foeniculaceum* (5, 93, 97, 122) (1913-1937)

Carrotweed [Carrot-weed, Carrot weed] - *Ambrosia artemisiifolia* L. (6, 156, 158) (1892-1923) no longer in use by 1923, *Ambrosia artemisiifolia* L. var. *elatior* (L.) Descourtils (5, 7, 92) (1828-1913)

Carrubo, currabio, or carubio (Italian) - *Ceratonia siliqua* L. (110) (1886)

Carruth's sagebrush [Carruth sagebrush] - *Artemisia carruthii* Wood ex Carruth. (155) (1942)

Carruth's sagewort - *Artemisia carruthii* Wood ex Carruth. (50) (present)

Carson's water parsnip - *Sium carsonii* Dur. ex Gray (5) (1913)

Carsous - *Rorippa nasturtium-aquaticum* (L.) Hayek (158) (1900)

Cartamo (Spanish) - *Carthamus tinctorius* L. (158) (1900)

Carthaginian apple - *Punica granatum* L. (92) (1876)

Carthame (French) - *Carthamus tinctorius* L. (158) (1900)

Carthamine - *Carthamus tinctorius* L. (110) (1886)

Carthusian pink - *Dianthus carthusianorum* L. (138) (1923)

Cart-track plant - *Plantago major* L. (107, 156) (1919-1923)

Carui - *Carum carvi* L. (179) (1526)

Carum - *Carum carvi* L. (57, 174, 178) (1523-1917), *Carum* L. (50) (present)

Carved puffball - *Calvatia caelata* (Bull.) Morgan (128) (1933) ND

Carved Virginia Puffball - *Morchella* Dill. ex Pers (181) (~1678)

Carvell - *Osmorhiza longistylis* (Torr.) DC. (46) (1879)

Carvies - *Carum carvi* L. (5, 156, 158) (1900–1923)

Caryota - *Caryota* L. (138) (1923)

Casabanana - *Sicana odorifera* (Vell.) Naud. (109, 138) (1923-1949)

Cascade fir - *Abies amabilis* (Dougl. ex Loud.) Dougl. ex Forbes (138, 155) (1923-1942)

Cascade toothwort - *Cardamine nuttallii* Greene (138) (1923)

Cascara buckthorn - *Frangula purshiana* (DC.) Cooper (138) (1923)

Cascara sagrada - *Frangula purshiana* (DC.) Cooper (52, 53, 54, 55, 57, 59, 101, 106, 109) (1905-1949)

Cascara tree - *Frangula purshiana* (DC.) Cooper (101) (1905)

Cascarilla bark - *Croton linearis* Jacq. (92) (1876)

Caschou - *Anacardium occidentale* L. (165) (1807)

Case lale - *Tulipa* L. (180) (1633)

Case-weed (Northen England) - *Capsella bursa-pastoris* (L.) Medik. (180) (1633) John Gerarde

Caseweed [Case weed, Case-weed] - *Capsella bursa-pastoris* (L.) Medik. (5, 156, 157, 158) (1900-1929)

Cashau - *Prosopis laevigata* (Willd.) M.C.Johnst. (107) (1919)

Cashaw - *Cucurbita maxima* Dcne. (110) (1886), *Prosopis juliflora* (Sw.) DC. (158) (1900)

Cashes - *Conium maculatum* L. (5, 69, 71, 156, 158) (1898–1923)

Cashew - *Anacardium* L. (155) (1942), *Anacardium occidentale* L. (107, 109, 110, 138) (1886-1923)

Cashew nut [Cashew-nut] - *Anacardium occidentale* L. (52, 57, 92, 165) (1807-1917)

Cassaba melon - *Cucumis melo* L. (109) (1949)

Cassabel - *Acorus calamus* L. (186) (1814)

Cassabully - *Barbarea vulgaris* W.T. Aiton (157) (1929)

Cassandra - *Chamaedaphne calyculata* (L.) Moench (86, 156) (1878-1923)

Cassava - *Manihot esculenta* Crantz (138) (1923)

Cassava plant - *Manihot esculenta* Crantz (92) (1876)

Casse - *Senna marilandica* (L.) Link (186) (1814)

Casse Diable (French) - *Hypericum perforatum* L. (158) (1900)

Casse-lunette (French) - *Centaurea cyanus* L. (158) (1900)

Cassena - *Ilex cassine* L. (2, 7) (1828-1932), *Ilex vomitoria* Aiton (5, 15, 109, 156) (1895-1949)

Cassena bush [Cassena-bush] - *Ilex cassine* L. (156) (1923), *Ilex vomitoria* Aiton (156) (1923)

Casseweed [Casse-weed] - *Capsella bursa-pastoris* (L.) Medik. (157, 158, 179) (1526-1929)

Cassia - *Cassia* L. (50, 158) (1900–present), *Chamaecrista fasciculata* (Michx.) Greene var. *fasciculata* (19) (1840), *Senna marilandica* (L.) Link (157, 186) (1814-1929)

Cassia buds - *Cinnamomum verum* J. Presl (92) (1876)

Cassia flower [Cassia-flower] - *Acacia farnesiana* (L.) Willd. (158) (1900)

Cassia stick tree - *Cassia fistula* L. (92) (1876)

Cassia-flower tree [Cassiaflower-tree] - *Cinnamomum verum* J. Presl (138) (1923)

Cassie - *Acacia farnesiana* (L.) Willd. (92, 109, 156, 158) (1876-1949), *Senna marilandica* (L.) Link (186) (1814)

Cassie-oil plant - *Acacia farnesiana* (L.) Willd. (107) (1919)

Cassier - *Senna marilandica* (L.) Link (186) (1814)

Cassina - *Ilex cassine* L. (107) (1919)

Cassine - *Cassine* L. (8) (1785), *Ilex cassine* L. (174, 177) (1753-1762), *Ilex vomitoria* Aiton (104, 182) (1791-1896)

Cassine (French) - *Cassine* L. (8) (1785)

Cassine de Caroline - *Ilex cassine* L. (8) (1785)

Cassu - *Anacardium occidentale* L. (165) (1807)

Cassumuniar - *Zingiber purpureum* Roscoe (92) (1876)

Cassuvium - *Anacardium occidentale* L. (165) (1807)

Castanea - *Castanea sativa* Mill. (178) (1526)

Castilles (French) - *Ribes rubrum* L. (46, 110) (1879-1886)

Castor - *Ricinus communis* L. (7) (1828)

Castor bean [Castor-bean] - *Ricinus communis* L. (5, 21, 78, 85, 92, 97, 106, 109, 122, 124, 125, 148, 156) (1876-1949), *Ricinus* L. (138) (1923)

Castor wood [Castor-wood] - *Magnolia virginiana* L. (6, 186) (1825-1892)

Castor-oil plant [Castor]oil plant, Castor-oil-plant) - *Ricinus communis* L. (5, 10, 19, 85, 92, 107, 109, 110, 125, 156) (1818-1949), *Ricinus* L. (156) (1923)

Cat clover [Cat's clover, Catclover, Cat-clover] - *Lotus corniculatus* L. (5, 156) (1913-1923)

Cat grape - *Vitis palmata* Vahl (15, 138. 156) (1895-1923)

Cat grass [Catgrass] - *Pennisetum glaucum* (L.) R. Br. (7) (1828)

Cat greenbrier - *Smilax glauca* Walt. (50, 155) (1942–present)

Cat pine - *Picea glauca* (Moench) Voss (5, 75, 158) (1894-1913) Buckfield ME

Cat spruce - *Abies alba* Mill. (possibly) (78) (1898), *Picea glauca* (Moench) Voss (5, 158) (1900-1913), *Picea mariana* (Mill.) Britton, Sterns & Poggenb. (5, 75) (1894-1913)

Cat tree [Cat-tree] - *Euonymus europaea* L. (5, 156) (1913-1923)

Cat valerian [Cat's valerian] - *Valeriana officinalis* L. (5, 156) (1913-1923)

Cat whin - *Rosa canina* L. (5) (1913)

Cataire (French) - *Nepeta cataria* L. (158) (1900)

Catalina ceanothus - *Ceanothus arboreus* Greene (109) (1949)

Catalina cherry - *Prunus ilicifolia* (Nutt. ex Hook. & Arn.) D. Dietr. subsp. *lyonii* (Eastw.) Raven (109, 138) (1923-1949)

Catalina lyon shrub [Catalina lyonshrub] - *Lyonothamnus floribundus* Gray (138) (1923)

Catalina nightshade - *Solanum wallacei* (Gray) Parish (138) (1923)

Catalpa (French) - *Catalpa ovata* G. Don (8, 20) (1785-1857)

Catalpa or Catalpa tree [Catalpa-tree] - *Catalpa bignonioides* Walt. (5, 6, 12, 14, 20, 38, 49, 58, 63, 97, 122, 124, 156) (1820-1937), *Catalpa ovata* G. Don (8, 92, 189) (1767-1876), *Catalpa* Scop. (1, 10, 26, 50, 82, 138, 155, 158) (1818–present), *Catalpa speciosa* (Warder) Warder ex Engelm. (3, 82, 106, 114, 156) (1894-1977)

Catalpa willow - *Chilopsis linearis* (Cav.) Sweet (77) (1898) TX

Catanance - *Lathyrus nissolia* L. (178) (1526)

Cataria - *Nepeta cataria* L. (57) (1917)

Catawba or Catawba tree - *Catalpa bignonioides* Walt. (5, 75, 156) (1894-1923) WV, *Catalpa ovata* G. Don (20, 92) (1857-1876) for Indian tribe, *Catalpa speciosa* (Warder) Warder ex Engelm. (4, 5, 63, 82, 158) (1899-1986)

Catawba rhododendron - *Rhododendron catawbiense* Michx. (5, 138) (1913-1923)

Catawba rose-bay - *Rhododendron catawbiense* Michx. (156) (1923)

Catberry [Cat berry, Cat-berry] - *Ilex mucronata* (L.) M. Powell, Savol. & S. Andrews (5, 73, 156) (1892-1923) Fortune Bay, Newfoudland, *Nemopanthus* Raf. (1) (1932)

Catbird grape - *Vitis palmata* Vahl (156) (1923)

Catbrier [Cat briar, Cat-brier] - *Smilax bona-nox* L. (117, 156) (1908-1923), *Smilax* L. (1, 92, 93) (1876-1936), *Smilax rotundifolia* L. (156) (1923)

Catchfly [Catch fly] - *Antirrhinum majus* L. (158) (1900), *Apocynum androsaemifolium* L. (6, 7, 92, 156, 157, 158) (1828-1929), *Silene dichotoma* Ehrh. (80) (1913), *Silene* L. (1, 4, 10, 13, 15, 50, 93,

109, 138, 156, 158, 167, 184) (1793–present) insects often caught in sticky exudate, *Silene virginica* L. (15, 92) (1876-1895)

Catchfly gentian [Catchfly-gentian] - *Eustoma exaltatum (L.) Salisb.* (138) (1923), *Eustoma* Salisb. ex G. Don (4) (1986)

Catchfly grass [Catch-fly-grass, Catchfly-grass, Catchflygrass, Catch-fly grass] - *Leersia lenticularis* Michx. (3, 5, 19, 45, 56, 66, 94, 122, 155, 163) (1840-1977)

Catchfly prairie gentian - *Eustoma exaltatum* (L.) Salisb. ex G. Don (50) (present)

Catchu tree - *Acacia polyacantha* Willd. (50) (present)

Catchweed [Catch-weed, Catch weed] - *Asperugo* L. (1) (1932), *Asperugo procumbens* L. (5, 156, 158) (1900–1923), *Galium aparine* L. (5, 19, 49, 53, 92, 107, 156, 158, 187) (1818-1923), *Galium asprellum* Michx. (156) (1923)

Catchweed bedstraw - *Galium aparine* L. (3, 4, 155) (1942-1986)

Cat-claw acacia [Catclaw acacia] - *Acacia greggii* Gray (50, 155) (1942–present)

Cat-claw mimosa [Catsclaw mimosa, Catclaw mimosa] - *Mimosa aculeaticarpa* Ortega var. *biuncifera* (Benth.) Barneby (4, 50, 155) (1942–present)

Cat-claw sensitive brier [Catclaw sensitive brier, Catclaw sensitive brier] - *Mimosa microphylla* Dry. (155) (1942), *Mimosa nuttallii* (DC.) B.L. Turner (4) (1986)

Cat-claw trumpet [Catclaw trumpet] - *Macfadyena unguis-cati* (L.) A.H. Gentry (138) (1923)

Catepuce - *Euphorbia lathyris* L. (156) (1923)

Caterpillar fern - *Asplenium scolopendrium* L. (92) (1876)

Caterpillar phacelia - *Phacelia patuliflora* (Engelm. & Gray) Gray (106) (1930)

Caterpillar scorpion-grass [Caterpillar Scorpion grasse] - *Ornithopus perpusillus* L. (178) (1526)

Caterpillars - *Myosotis scorpioides* L. (156, 158) (1900-1923), *Phacelia congesta* Hook. (50) (present)

Catesby's gentian [Catesbian gentian] - *Gentiana catesbaei* Walt. (7) (1828)

Catesby's leucothoe - *Leucothoe axillaris* (Lam.) D. Don. (5) (1913)

Catesby's pitcherplant [Catesby pitcherplant] - *Sarracenia* ×*catesbaei* Ell. [*flava* × *purpurea*] (138) (1923)

Cat-foot poplar [Cat foot poplar] - *Populus nigra* L. (5, 156, 158) (1900–1923)

Catgut [Cat gut, Cat-gut] - *Coursetia* DC. (1) (1932), *Tephrosia* Pers. (7) (1828), *Tephrosia virginiana* (L.) Pers (2, 4, 5, 49, 63, 92, 102, 156, 158) (1886-1986) from long wiry roots

Cat-gut weed [Catgut weed] - *Tephrosia virginiana* (L.) Pers (157) (1929)

Cathartic broom grass [Cathartic broom-grass] - *Bromus kalmii* Gray (187) (1818)

Cathartic buckthorn - *Rhamnus cathartica* L. (20) (1857)

Cathartic flax - *Linum catharticum* L. (5, 156) (1913-1923)

Cathay rose - *Rosa multiflora* Thunb. ex Murray (138) (1923)

Cat-in-clover - *Lotus corniculatus* L. (158) (1900)

Catlocks [Cat-locks] - *Eriophorum callitrix* Cham. ex C.A. Mey. (5, 156) (1913-1923)

Catmint [Cat mint, Cat-mint] - *Agastache nepetoides* (L.) Kuntze (156) (1923), *Nepeta cataria* L. (1, 5, 7, 10, 19, 46, 49, 53, 62, 63, 69, 85, 92, 93, 95, 109, 156, 157, 187) (1671-1949), *Nepeta* L. (167, 190) (~1759-1814)

Catnep - *Nepeta cataria* L. (5, 49, 53, 63, 109, 157, 158, 187) (1818-1949), *Nepeta* L. (158) (1900)

Catnep tragia - *Tragia betonicifolia* Nutt. (97, 156) (1923-1937)

Catnip - *Agastache nepetoides* (L.) Kuntze (131) (1899) SD, *Nepeta cataria* L. (1, 3, 4, 7, 19, 37, 40, 47, 49, 50, 53, 57, 61, 62, 69, 72, 80, 82, 85, 92, 93, 95, 97, 106, 107, 109, 114, 131, 138, 145, 155, 156, 157, 158) (1852–present), *Nepeta* L. (50, 82, 156) (1923–present)

Catnip giant hyssop [Catnep giant-hyssop] - *Agastache nepetoides* (L.) Kuntze (3, 4, 5, 72, 93, 97, 155) (1907-1986)

Cat-o'-nine-tails - *Typha latifolia* L. (5, 92, 156, 158) (1876-1923)

Cat-paw ragwort [Cat's paw ragwort] - *Packera antennariifolia* (Britt.) W.A. Weber & A. Löve (5) (1913)

Cat-pea [Cat-peas, Cat pea] - *Vicia cracca* L. (5, 156, 158) (1900-1923)

Catposy [Cat-posy] - *Bellis perennis* L. (158) (1900) archaic

Catrup - *Nepeta cataria* L. (158) (1900)

Cat's heal-all - *Nepeta cataria* L. (156) (1923)

Cat's-claw [Catclaw, Cat-claw, Catsclaw, Cats-claw, Cat's-claws, Cat's claws] - *Acacia greggii* Gray (76, 106) (1896-1930), *Acacia* Mill. (106) (1930), *Macfadyena unguis-cati* (L.) A.H. Gentry (109) (1949), *Mimosa aculeaticarpa* Ortega var. *biuncifera* (Benth.) Barneby (124) (1937) . - *Mimosa borealis* Gray (97) (1937), *Mimosa* L. (4, 152) (1913-1986)

Cat's-cradles [Cat's cradles] - *Plantago lanceolata* L. (5, 156) (1913-1923) no longer in use by 1923

Cat's-ear [Cat's ear, Cats-ear] - *Antennaria plantaginifolia* (L.) Richards (156) (1923), *Hieracium gronovii* L. (5, 156) (1913-1923), *Hypochaeris* L. (1, 138) (1923-1932), *Hypochaeris radicata* L. (106, 156) (1923-1930)

Cat's-eye [Cats eye, Cats' eye, Cat's eye] - *Scabiosa stellata* L. (19, 92) (1840-1876), *Veronica chamaedrys* L. (5, 156) (1913-1923), *Veronica officinalis* L. var. *tournefortii* (Vill.) Reichenb. (5, 156) (1913-1923)

Cat's-faces - *Viola striata* Aiton (158) (1900)

Cat's-foot [Cats foot, Cat's foot, Cat foot] - *Antennaria dimorpha* (Nutt.) Torr. & Gray (46) (1879), *Antennaria dioica* (L.) Gaertn. (46) (1879), *Antennaria howellii* Greene subsp. *canadensis* (Greene) Bayer (156) (1923), *Antennaria parlinii* Fern. subsp. *fallax* (Greene) Bayer & Stebbins (127) (1933), *Antennaria plantaginifolia* (L.) Richards (156) (1923), *Asarum canadense* L. (64, 92, 156, 158) (1898-1923), *Filago pyramidata* L. (184) (1793), *Glechoma hederacea* L. (5, 49, 92, 157, 158) (1876-1929), *Pseudognaphalium obtusifolium* (L.) Hilliard & Burtt subsp. *obtusifolium* (6) (1892)

Cat's-hair [Cat's hair] - *Chamaesyce hirta* (L.) Millsp. (53) (1922)

Cat's-milk, [Cats milk, Cat's milk, Cat-milk] - *Euphorbia helioscopia* L. (5, 92, 156) (1876-1923)

Cat's-paw [Cat's paws, Cat's-paws] - *Antennaria* Gaertner (1, 50, 98) (1926–present), *Antennaria plantaginifolia* (L.) Richards (156) (1923), *Glechoma hederacea* L. (157, 158) (1900-1929)

Cat-tail [Cat's tail, Cats Taile, Cat's-tail, Cats tails] - *Echium vulgare* L. (5, 156) (1913-1923) no longer in use by 1923, *Elodea canadensis* Michx. (158) (1900), *Equisetum arvense* L. (5, 157, 158) (1900-1929), *Hippuris vulgaris* L. (5, 156, 158) (1900–1923), *Phleum* L. (66) (1903), *Schoenoplectus tabernaemontani* (C.C. Gmel.) Palla (possibly) (103) (1871), *Typha* L. (1, 7, 10, 50, 14, 93, 138, 148, 155, 158, 167, 180) (1633–present), *Typha latifolia* L. (5, 19, 21, 40, 41, 46, 49, 85, 92, 101, 107, 121, 156, 157, 158, 184, 187) (1671-1970)

Cat-tail gayfeather [Cattail gayfeather] - *Liatris pycnostachya* Michx. (138) (1923)

Cat-tail grass [Cat's tail grass, Cats-tail grass] - *Pennisetum glaucum* (L.) R. Br. (56) (1901), *Phleum* L. (10) (1818), *Phleum pratense* L. (19, 92, 108) (1840-1876)

Cat-tail millet [Cattailmillet, Cat-tails millet] - *Pennisetum glaucum* (L.) R. Br. (45, 87, 151, 155) (1884-1942), *Setaria italica* (L.) Beauv. (5, 45) (1896-1913)

Cat-tail reed [Cattail reed] - *Typha* L. (122) (1937)

Cat-tail rush [Cattail rush] - *Typha latifolia* L. (49) (1898)

Cat-tail sedge - *Carex squarrosa* L. (72) (1907), *Carex typhina* Michx. (5, 50) (1913-present)

Cat-whistle [Cat whistle, Cat-whistles] - *Equisetum palustre* L. (5, 158) (1900-1913)

Catwort [Cat's wort, Cats wort, Cat's-wort] - *Nepeta cataria* L. (69, 92, 157, 158) (1876-1929)

Caucasian bluestem - *Bothriochloa bladhii* (Retz.) S.T. Blake (3, 50) (1977–present)

Caucasian insect powder - *Chrysanthemum coccineum* Willd. (92) (1876)

Caucasian inula - *Chrysopsis mariana* (L.) Ell. (138) (1923)

Caucasian yellow mustard - *Sinapis alba* L. (109) (1949)

Caughuawaga thorn - *Crataegus suborbiculata* Sarg. (5) (1913)

Caule wort - *Brassica oleracea* L. (179) (1526)

Caulifiore - *Brassica oleracea* L. (180) (1633)

Cauliflora - *Brassica oleracea* L. (180) (1633)

Cauliflower - *Brassica* L. (107) (1919), *Brassica oleracea* L. (156) (1923)

Caulophyllum radix (Official name of Materia Medica) - *Caulophyllum thalictroides* (L.) Michx. (7) (1828)

Caulx - *Brassica oleracea* L. (107) (1919)

Causeway grass - *Poa annua* L. (5) (1913)

Cauwoord (Belgium, gourd) - *Cucurbita pepo* L. (107) (1586)

Cavendish banana - *Musa acuminata* Colla (138) (1923)

Cavolo - *Brassica oleracea* L. (107) (1919)

Cayenne - *Capsicum annuum* L. (59, 92) (1876-1911)

Cayenne cyperus - *Cyperus aggregatus* (Willd.) Endl. (5) (1913), *Capsicum annuum* L. (19, 58, 82, 92, 107) (1840-1930), *Capsicum annuum* L. var. *annuum* (50, 52, 53, 57, 110) (1917–present), *Capsicum annuum* L. var. *glabriusculum* (Dunal) Heiser & Pickersgill (107) (1919), *Capsicum* L. (7) (1828)

Céanote (French) - *Ceanothus* L. (8) (1785)

Céanote d"Amérique (French) - *Ceanothus americanus* L. (8) (1785)

Céanothe (French) - *Ceanothus americanus* L. (158) (1900)

Ceanothe thyrsiflore (French) - *Ceanothus thyrsiflorus* Esch. (20) (1857)

Ceanothus - *Ceanothus americanus* L. (52, 54, 57, 174) (1753-1917), *Ceanothus* L. (50, 138, 155) (1923–present), *Ceanothus thyrsiflorus* Esch. (52) (1919)

Ceba (Spanish) - *Allium* L. (180) (1633)

Cebola (Spanish) - *Allium* L. (180) (1633)

Cebolla (Spanish) - *Allium* L. (180) (1633)

Cedar acacia - *Acacia elata* A. Cunningham ex Benth. (155) (1942)

Cedar elm - *Ulmus crassifolia* Nutt. (122, 124) (1937)

Cedar mistletoe - *Phoradendron juniperinum* Engelm. ex Gray (122, 124) (1937)

Cedar of Lebanon - *Cedrus libani A.Rich.* (20) (1857)

Cedar of North America - *Juniperus virginiana* L. (189) (1767)

Cedar or Cedar tree - *Cedrus* Trew (109, 138) (1923-1949) from Kedrus the ancient Greek name, *Chamaecyparis* Spach. (50) (present), *Juniperus* L. (121, 148, 167) (1814-1970), *Juniperus monosperma* (Engelm.) Sarg. (153) (1913), *Juniperus occidentalis* Hook. (149) (1904), *Juniperus virginiana* L. (37, 39, 46, 65) (1830-1931), *Thuja occidentalis* L. (75) (1894) ME, *Thuja plicata* Donn ex D. Don (101) (1905) MT

Cedar pine - *Pinus virginiana* Mill. (5) (1913) **Cedar wattle** - *Acacia elata* A. Cunningham ex Benth. (50) (present)

Cedar-apple [Cedar apple, Cedar-apples, Cedar apples] - *Juniperus virginiana* L. (92) (1876) insect galls, *Yucca filamentosa* L. (100) (1850) the fruit

Cedar-like club-moss - *Lycopodium sabinifolium* Willd. (5) (1913)

Cedar-moss [Cedar moss] - *Ceratophyllum demersum* L. (156) (1923)

Cedrat - *Citrus medica* L. (92) (1876) oil from fruit rind

Cédre blanc (French) - *Thuja occidentalis* L. (19, 40, 41) (1770-1928), *Chamaecyparis thyoides* (L.) Britton, Sterns & Poggenb. (8) (1785)

Cédre de Virginie (French) - *Juniperus virginiana* L. (6) (1892)

Cédre rouge (French) - *Juniperus virginiana* L. (41) (1770)

Cèdre rouge de Caroline (French) - *Juniperus virginiana* L. (8) (1785)

Cedrela - *Cedrela* P. Br. (138) (1923)

Cedro - *Juniperus scopulorum* Sarg. (153) (1913) NM

Cedronella - *Cedronella* Moench (138) (1923)

Ceiba - *Ceiba* Mill. (138) (1923) from aboriginal name

Ceiba - *Ceiba pentandra* (L.) Gaertn. (107, 138) (1919-1923)

Čejaka or šejaka (Lakota, mint) - *Mentha arvensis* L. (121) (1918?-1970?)

Cekela or zekhalea (Basque) - *Secale cereale* L. (110) (1886)

Celandine - *Chelidonium* L. (1, 15, 50, 57, 109, 155, 156, 158, 167) (1814–present), *Chelidonium majus* L. (5, 7, 10, 19, 46 (1671), 49, 50, 53, 54, 82, 92, 156, 158, 184, 187) (1671–present), *Impatiens capensis* Meerb. (74, 76) (1893), *Impatiens* L. (7) (1828), *Thalictrum pubescens* Pursh (5, 76, 156) (1896-1913) Oxford Co. ME

Celandine tree - *Macleaya cordata* (Willd.) R. Br. (92) (1876)

Celandine-poppy [Celandine poppy] - *Stylophorum diphyllum* (Michx.) Nutt. (2, 5, 13, 15, 92, 109, 138, 156) (1849-1949)

Celaster (German) - *Celastrus scandens* L. (158) (1900)

Celastre (French) - *Celastrus scandens* L. (158) (1900), *Celastrus* L. (8) (1785)

Celendyne - *Ranunculus ficaria* L. (179) (1526)

Celeri (French) - *Apium graveolens* L. (107) (1919)

Celery [Cellery] - *Apium graveolens* L. var. *dulce* (P. Mill.) DC. (5, 85, 50, 109, 155) (1913-1949), *Apium* L. (50, 155) (1942–present), *Apium graveolens* L. (7, 14, 57, 92, 106, 107, 109, 122, 138, 184) (1793-1949)

Celery cabbage - *Brassica rapa* L. var. *amplexicaulis* Tanaka & Ono (109) (1949)

Celery crowfoot - *Ranunculus sceleratus* L. (19) (1840)

Celery-grass - *Vallisneria americana* Michx. (156) (1923)

Celery-leaf crowfoot [Celery-leaved crowfoot, Scelery-leaved Crow-foot] - *Ranunculus sceleratus* L. (5, 6, 93, 97, 125, 131, 158, 187) (1818-1936)

Celery-seed [Celery seed] - *Rumex obtusifolius* L. (5, 156, 157, 158) (1900-1929)

Celestial - *Calydorea coelestina* (Bartr.) Goldblatt & Henrich (124) (1937) TX, *Nemastylis geminiflora* Nutt. (124) (1937) TX

Celidonia mayor (Spanish) - *Chelidonium majus* L. (158) (1900)

Cellydony - *Chelidonium majus* L. (179) (1526)

Cembra pine - *Pinus cembra* L. (92) (1876), *Pinus* L. (50) (present)

Cenada (Spanish) - *Hordeum vulgare* L. (180) (1633)

Cenhinnen (Welsh) - *Allium sativum* L. (110) (1886)

Ceniglo antelmintico - *Chenopodium ambrosioides* L. var. *ambrosioides* (186) (1814)

Ceniza - *Leucophyllum frutescens* (Berl.) I.M. Johnston (124) (1937) TX

Cenizo - *Atriplex canescens* (Pursh) Nutt. (5, 158) (1900–1913), *Leucophyllum frutescens* (Berl.) I.M. Johnston (109) (1949)

Centaurea - *Centaurea* L. (138, 155) (1923-1942)

Centaurée americaine (French) - *Sabatia angularis* (L.) Pursh (158) (1900)

Centaurée anguleuse (French) - *Sabatia angularis* (L.) Pursh (7) (1828)

Centaurium - *Centaurium* Hill (155) (1942)

Centaury - *Centaurea* L. (4, 184) (1793-1986), *Centaurea nigra* L. (5, 156) (1913-1923), *Centaurium beyrichii* (Torr. & Gray ex Torr.) B.L. Robins. (97) (1937), *Centaurium* Hill (1, 50, 82, 93, 109, 156) (1923–present), *Centaurium spicatum* (L.) Fernald. (82) (1930), *Polygala polygama* Walt. (156) (1923), *Sabatia angularis* (L.) Pursh (186, 187) (1814-1818)

Centeno (French) - *Secale cereale* L. (158) (1900)

Centeno (Spanish) - *Secale cereale* L. (180) (1633)

Centinode - *Polygonum aviculare* L. (158) (1900)

Centipede grass [Centipede-grass] - *Eremochloa ophiuroides* (Munro) Hack. (109) (1949)

Centipede-plant - *Homalocladium platycladum* (F.J. Muell.) Bailey (109) (1949) needs little mowing

Centory - *Centaurium erythraea* Raf. (179) (1526), *Sabatia angularis* (L.) Pursh (186) (1814)

Centranth - *Centranthus* Neck. ex Lam. & DC. (109) (1949) from Greek for spurred flower

Centry - *Sabatia angularis* (L.) Pursh (186, 187) (1814-1818)

Century plant [Centuryplant] - *Agave americana* L. (61, 92, 109, 122, 124, 138, 147) (1870-1949), *Agave* L. (149) (1904), *Agave parryi* Engelm. (78) (1898) AZ

Cepe - *Allium* L. (180) (1633)

Céphalante (French) - *Cephalanthus* L. (8) (1785)

Céphalante d'Occident (French) - *Cephalanthus occidentalis* L. (8) (1785)

Cephalanthe d'Amerique (French) - *Cephalanthus occidentalis* L. (6, 7) (1828-1932)

Cephalanthus Cortex (Official name of Materia Medica) - *Cephalanthus occidentalis* L. (7) (1828)

Cephalaria - *Cephalaria* Schrad. ex Roemer & J.A. Schultes (138) (1923)

Cerastium - *Cerastium* L. (138, 155) (1923-1942)

Cereal rye - *Secale cereale* L. (50) (present)

Cereus - *Cereus* Mill. (14, 155) (1882-1942), *Selenicereus grandiflorus* (L.) Britt. & Rose (60) (1902)

Cerfeuil sauvage (French Canadians) - *Cryptotaenia canadensis* (L.) DC. (41) (1770)

Ceriman - *Monstera deliciosa* Liebm. (109, 138) (1923-1949)

Cerisier á feuilles de houx (French) - *Prunus ilicifolia* (Nutt. ex Hook. & Arn.) D. Dietr. (20) (1857)

Cerisier á feuilles molles (French) - *Prunus emarginata* (Dougl. ex Hook.) D. Dietr. var. *mollis* (Dougl. ex Hook.) Brewer (20) (1857)

Cerisier de Virginie (French) - *Prunus serotina* Ehrh. (158) (1900)

Ceroline - *Impatiens capensis* Meerb. (157, 158) (1900-1929), *Impatiens pallida* Nutt. (157) (1929)

Cerulean indigo-bush amorpha [Cerulean indigobush amorpha] - *Amorpha fruticosa* L. (155) (1942)

Češlošlo pežuta (Lakota, diarrhea medicine) - *Asclepias pumila* (Gray) Vail (121) (1918?-1970?)

Cestrum - *Cestrum* L. (138) (1923)

Cevallia - *Cevallia* Lag. (158) (1900)

Ceylon cinnamom - *Cinnamomum verum* J. Presl (92) (1876)

Ceylon moss - *Hydropuntia edulis* (S.G.Gmelin) Gurgel & Fredericq (92) (1876)

Ceylon-gooseberry - *Dovyalis hebecarpa* (G. Gardn.) Warb. (109) (1949)

Chadlock [Chadlocke] - *Moricandia arvensis* (L.) DC. (158) (1900), *Sinapis arvensis* L. (5, 157, 180) (1633-1929)

Chaenactis - *Chaenactis* DC. (155, 158) (1900-1942)

Chaetopappa - *Chaetopappa asteroides* (Nutt.) DC. (5, 97) (1913-1937), *Chaetopappa* DC. (158) (1900)

Chafeweed [Chafe-weed, Chafe weed, Chafweed] - *Omalotheca sylvatica* (L.) Schultz-Bip. & F.W. Schultz (5) (1913), *Filago vulgaris* Lam. (5, 156) (1913-1923), *Omalotheca sylvatica* (L.) Schultz-Bip. & F.W. Schultz (156) (1923), *Pseudognaphalium obtusifolium* (L.) Hilliard & Burtt subsp. *obtusifolium* (5, 92) (1876-1913)

Chaffseed [Chaff-seed, Chaff seed] - *Schwalbea americana* L. (5, 19, 156) (1840-1923), *Schwalbea* L. (2) (1895)

Chaffweed [Chaff weed] - *Anagallis* L. (1, 10, 156) (1818-1932), *Anagallis minima* (L.) Krause (4, 5, 50, 85, 92, 93, 131, 156) (1899–present)

Chaffy sedge - *Carex crinita* Lam. (42, 187) (1814-1818)

Chaffy seg - *Carex crinita* Lam. (42) (1814)

Chaha san (Dakota Teton, pale bark) - *Betula papyrifera* Marsh (37) (1919)

Chain fern [Chainfern, Chain-fern] - *Woodwardia areolata* (L.) T. Moore (138) (1923), *Woodwardia* Sm. (2, 4, 5, 50, 78, 109, 138, 155, 158) (1895–present)

Chair-bottom rush - *Schoenoplectus pungens* (Vahl) Palla var. *pungens* (66) (1903)

Chairman's bulrush - *Schoenoplectus americanus* (Pers.) Volk. ex Schinz & R. Keller (50) (present)

Chairmaker's rush [Chairmakers rush, Chair-makers rush] - *Schoenoplectus americanus* (Pers.) Volk. ex Schinz & R. Keller (156) (1923-1977), *Schoenoplectus pungens* (Vahl) Palla var. *pungens* (129) (1894), *Scirpus lineatus* Michx. (120) (1938) OK

Chak (Winnebago) - *Juglans nigra* L. (37) (1919)

Chakida-kahtsu (Pawnee) - *Yucca glauca* Nutt. (35, 37) (1806-1830)

Chalice vine [Chalice-vine] - *Solandra* Sw. (109, 138) (1923-1949)

Chalk Hill hymenopappus - *Hymenopappus tenuifolius* Pursh (50) (present)

Chalk maple - *Acer leucoderme* Small (50, 138, 155) (1923–present)

Chalk plant [Chalk-plant] - *Gypsophila paniculata* L. (156) (1923)

Chamaepitys - *Ajuga chamaepitys (L.) Schreb.* (178) (1526)

Chamaerhodos - *Chamaerhodos* Bunge (158) (1900)

Chamaesaracha - *Chamaesaracha coniodes* (Moric. ex Dunal) Britton (3, 4) (1977-1986)

Chamisal - *Adenostoma fasciculatum* Hook. & Arn. (106) (1930)

Chamise - *Adenostoma fasciculatum* Hook. & Arn. (74, 106) (1893-1930) Santa Barbara CA, *Adenostoma* Hook. & Arn. (155) (1942)

Chamise brush - *Adenostoma fasciculatum* Hook. & Arn. (74) (1893) Santa Barbara CA

Chamiso - *Adenostoma fasciculatum* Hook. & Arn. (138) (1923), *Adenostoma* Hook. & Arn. (138) (1923)

Chamiso (Mexican) - *Atriplex canescens* (Pursh) Nutt. (147) (1856)

Chamisso's arnica [Chamisso arnica] - *Arnica chamissonis* Less. (155) (1942)

Chamisso's cottongrass - *Eriophorum chamissonis* C.A. Mey. (50) (present)

Chamisso's lupine [Chamisso lupine] - *Lupinus chamissonis* Eschsch. (138) (1923)

Chamisso's shield fern - *Polystichum munitum* (Kaulfuss) K. Presl (86) (1878) for botanist on Vancouver's voyage

Chamiza - *Atriplex canescens* (Pursh) Nutt. (124) (1937) TX

Chamœ-cerasus de Canada - *Lonicera canadensis* Bartr. ex Marsh. (8) (1785)

Chamomile Romaine (French) - *Anthemis altissima* L. (6) (1892)

Champignon - *Agaricus campestris* L. (165) (1768)

Champin's grape [Champin grape] - *Vitis ×champinii* Planch. [*mustangensis × rupestris*] (138) (1923)

Champion - *Quercus rubra* L. (156) (1923)

Champion oak - *Quercus rubra* L. (14, 158) (1882)

Champlain willow - *Salix nigra* Marsh. (20) (1857)

Chan iyuwe (Dakota, twining on a tree) - *Humulus lupulus* L. var. *lupuloides* E. Small (37) (1919)

Chan wiziye (Dakota) - *Punctelia borreri* (Sm.) Krog (37) (1830)

Chan wiziye (Dakota) - *Usnea barbata* (L.) Weber ex F.H. Wigg. (37) (1830)

Chan-di (Dakota) - *Nicotiana quadrivalvis* Pursh (37) (1919)

Chandler's grass [Chandler grass] - *Elymus repens* (L.) Gould (45, 64, 66, 69, 90) (1885-1908)

Changeable flowerdeluce [Changeable floure de-luce] - *Iris pumila* L. (178) (1596), *Iris xiphium* L. (180) (1633)

Changma abutilon - *Abutilon theophrasti* Medik (155) (1942)

Chan-ha san (Dakota, pale bark) - *Acer saccharum* Marsh. (37) (1919)

Chanhaloga pezhuta (Dakota) - *Verbena hastata* L. (37) (42)

Chan-li (Dakota Teton) - *Nicotiana quadrivalvis* Pursh (37) (1919)

Channankpa (Dakota, tree ears) - *Polystictus versicolor* (L.) Fr. (37) (1830)

Channel-leaf helonias [Channelled-leaved helonias] - *Amianthium muscitoxicum* (Walt.) Gray (187) (1818)

Channelweed [Channel-weed] - *Vallisneria americana* Michx. (possibly) (187) (1818)

Chanpa (Dakota) - *Prunus virginiana* L. var. *virginiana* (37) (1919)

Chan-pezhuta (Dakota, wood-medicine) - *Osmorhiza longistylis* (Torr.) DC. (37) (1919)

Chan-sapa (Dakota Teton, black wood) - *Juglans nigra* L. (37) (1919)

Chan-shasha (Dakota, red wood) - *Cornus amomum* Mill. (37) (1919)

Chan-shasha-hinchake (Dakota) - *Cornus sericea* L. subsp. *sericea* (37) (1919)

Chanshilshila (Dakota Teton) - *Silphium laciniatum* L. (37) (1919)

Chanshinshinla (Dakota) - *Silphium laciniatum* L. (37) (1919)

Chan-shushka (Dakota-Teton) - *Acer negundo* L. (37) (1919)

Chansu (Dakota) - *Carya ovata* (Mill.) K. Koch (37) (1919) Chansu-hu (Hickory tree)

Chanure - *Apocynum cannabinum* L. (46) (1879)

Chanvre (French) - *Cannabis sativa* L. (6, 110) (1886)

Chanvre aquatique (French) - *Bidens tripartita* L. (158) (1900)

Chanvre bâtard (French) - *Galeopsis bifida* Boenn. (158) (1900)

Chanvre du Canada (French) - *Apocynum cannabinum* L. (6, 158) (1892-1900)

Chan-zi (Dakota, yellow-wood) - *Rhus glabra* L. (37) (1919)

Chaparral broom - *Baccharis pilularis* DC. (106) (1930)

Chaparral goldenweed - *Ericameria brachylepis* (Gray) Hall (155) (1942), *Ericameria pinifolia* (Gray) Hall (155) (1942)

Chaparral lily - *Lilium rubescens* S. Wats. (109, 138) (1923-1949)

Chaparral snapdragon - *Nuttallanthus canadensis* (L.) D.A. Sutton (138, 155) (1923-1942), *Sairocarpus coulterianus* (Benth. ex A. DC.) D.A. Sutton (138, 155) (1931-1942)

Chaparral tea - *Croton pottsii* (Klotzsch) Muell.-Arg. var. *pottsii* (104, 107) (1896-1919)

Chaparral yucca - *Yucca whipplei* Torr. var. *whipplei* (138) (1923)

Chaparro armagoso - *Castela erecta* Turpin. (possibly) (57) (1917)

Chapman's bluegrass [Chapman bluegrass] - *Poa chapmaniana* Scribn. (3, 50, 155) (1942–present)

Chapman's club-moss - *Lycopodiella appressa* (Chapman) Cranfill (5) (1913)

Chapman's hill thorn - *Crataegus punctata* Jacq. (5) (1913)

Chapman's honey plant [Chapman honey plant] - *Echinops sphaerocephalus* L. (106) (1930)

Chapman's spear grass [Chapman's spear-grass] - *Poa chapmaniana* Scribn. (5, 56, 72, 119, 163) (1852-1938)

Chapparal - *Phyla cuneifolia* (Torr.) Greene (77) (1898)

Chap-ta-haza (Dakota, beaver berries) - *Ribes americanum* Mill. (37) (1919)

Chaputa (Dakota) - *Sambucus nigra* L. subsp. *canadensis* (L.) R. Bolli (37) (1919) Chaputa-hu (elder bush)

Charas - *Cannabis sativa* L. subsp. *indica* (Lam.) E. Small & Cronq. (92) (1876)

Chard - *Beta vulgaris* L. (107) (1919)

Chardon Marie (French) - *Silybum marianum* (L.) Gaertn. (158) (1900)

Charity - *Polemonium caeruleum* L. (109) (1949)

Charlock - *Brassica* L. (107) (1919), *Brassica nigra* (L.) W.D.J. Koch (156) (1923), *Moricandia arvensis* (L.) DC. (62, 138, 156, 158) (1900-1923) IN, *Raphanus raphanistrum* L. (6, 19, 156) (1840-1923), *Sinapis alba* L. (5, 157, 158) (1900–1929), *Sinapis arvensis* L. (3, 4, 5, 14, 15, 14, 41, 85, 92, 97, 107, 109, 155, 180) (1170-1986), *Sinapis* L. (1, 93) (1932-1936)

Charlock mustard - *Sinapis arvensis* L. (50) (present)

Charme - *Carpinus* L. (8) (1785)

Charme (Upper Louisiana) - *Carpinus caroliniana* Walt. subsp. *caroliniana* (20) (1857)

Charme à fruit d'houblon (French) - *Ostrya carpinifolia* Scop. (8) (1785)

Charme de Virginie (French) - *Carpinus caroliniana* Walt. subsp. *virginiana* (Marsh.) Furlow (8) (1785)

Chasbowl - *Papaver rhoeas* L. (158) (1900)

Chashke-hu (Winnebago) - *Quercus macrocarpa* Michx. (37) (1919)

Chasse diable (French) - *Hypericum perforatum* L. (6) (1892)

Chaste shrub - *Itea virginica* L. (156) (1923)

Chaste tree [Chaste-tree, Chastetree] - *Vitex agnus-castus* L. (7, 82, 92, 109, 158, 178) (1596-1949), *Vitex* L. (50, 82, 138) (1923–present), *Vitex negundo* L. (182) (1791), *Vitex negundo* var. *heterophylla* (Franch.) Rehder (82) (1930)

Chatagnier (French) - *Castanea sativa* Mill. (6, 8) (1785-1892)

Chataignier à feuilles d'aune (French) - *Castanea pumila* (L.) Mill. var. *pumila* (20) (1857)

Chataignier d'Amérique (French) - *Castanea dentata* (Marshall) Borkh. (possibly) (8) (1785)

Chataignier nain (French) - *Castanea pumila* (L.) Mill. (possibly) (8) (1785)

Chataire (French) - *Nepeta cataria* L. (158) (1900)

Chaw-stick [Chaw stick] - *Gouania lupuloides* (L.) Urban (92, 107) (1876-1919)

Chayote - *Sechium edule* (Jacq.) Sw. (106, 107, 109, 110, 138) (1919-1949), *Sechium* P. Browne (138) (1923)

Chayot (Aztec) - *Sechium edule* (Jacq.) Sw. (110) (1886)

Chayotli (Mexico) - *Sechium edule* (Jacq.) Sw. (107) (1919)

Cheat - *Bromus* L. (93) (1936), *Bromus secalinus* L. (1, 3, 5, 46, 56, 62, 66, 72, 75, 80, 85, 87, 88, 90, 93, 94, 119, 145, 158, 163, 187) (1818-1977), *Camelina sativa* (L.) Crantz (5, 156, 157, 158) (1900-1929), *Coelorachis cylindrica* (Michx.) Nash (3) (1977), *Lolium temulentum* L. (75, 119, 157, 158) (1894-1938)

Cheat grass [Cheatgrass] - *Bromus secalinus* L. (92, 158) (1876-1900), *Bromus tectorum* L. (50, 146) (1939–present)

Cheatgrass brome - *Bromus tectorum* L. (140, 155) (1942-1944)

Chechniquamins - *Castanea pumila* (L.) Mill. (46) (1879)

Checker-berry [Checker berry, Checkerberry, Chequer-berry, Chequer berry] - *Arctostaphylos uva-ursi* (L.) Spreng. (7) (1828), *Gaultheria procumbens* L. (1, 2, 5, 6, 7, 49, 57, 79, 92, 107, 109, 156) (1828-1949), *Mitchella repens* L. (18, 49, 53, 92, 156) (1805-1923)

Checker-bloom [Checkerbloom] - *Sidalcea* Gray (50) (present), *Sidalcea malviflora* (DC.) Gray ex Benth. (106, 109, 138) (1923-1949)

Checkered rattlesnake-plantain [Checkered rattlesnake plantain] - *Goodyera tesselata* Lodd. (50, 138) (1923–present)

Checkered-lily [Chequered lily] - *Fritillaria* L. (10) (1818)

Checker-mallow [Checkermallow] - *Sidalcea* Gray (155) (1942)

Cheddar pink - *Dianthus gratianopolitanus* Vill. (109, 138) (1923-1949)

Cheekweed [Cheek weed] - *Stellaria longipes* Goldie subsp. *longipes* (46) (1671)

Cheerful sunflower - *Helianthus ×laetiflorus* Pers. [*pauciflorus × tuberosus*] (50) (present)

Cheese plant - *Malva rotundifolia* L. (73) (1892)

Cheese rennet-herb [Cheese rennet herb] - *Galium aparine* L. (92) (1876)

Cheese-bowl [Cheese bowl, Cheesebowl, Cheesebowls] - *Papaver* L. (180) (1633), *Papaver rhoeas* L. (5, 92, 156, 158) (1876-1923) no longer in use by 1923, *Papaver somniferum* L. (5, 156) (1913-1923) no longer in use by 1923

Cheesecake [Cheese-cake, Cheese cake] - *Malva sylvestris* L. (5, 156) (1913-1923)

Cheese-cake plant - *Malva sylvestris* L. (157, 158) (1900-1929)

Cheeseflower [Cheese flower, Cheese-flower] - *Malva rotundifolia* L. (156) (1923), *Malva sylvestris* L. (5, 156, 157, 158) (1900–1929)

Cheese-rennet [Cheese-rennet] - *Galium verum* L. (107, 156, 158) (1919-1923)

Cheeses - *Malva rotundifolia* L. (5, 62, 73, 80, 92, 97, 156) (1892–1937), *Malva sylvestris* L. (107) (1919)

Cheeses (Fruit) - *Malva* L. (1) (1932)

Cheese's running mallow - *Malva rotundifolia* L. (131) (1899)

Cheesetts - *Malva rotundifolia* L. (76) (1896) Oxford Co., ME

Cheeseweed [Cheese weed] - *Sphaeralcea angustifolia* (Cav.) G. Don (76) (1896), *Sphaeralcea emoryi* Torr. ex Gray (76) (1896) CA

Cheeseweed mallow - *Malva parviflora* L. (50) (present)

Chelandine - *Chelidonium majus* L. (49) (1898)

Chélidoine (French) - *Chelidonium majus* L. (158) (1900)

Chelidonium - *Chelidonium majus* L. (54, 57) (1905-1917)

Chelone (French) - *Chelone glabra* L. (6) (1892)

Chelone (German) - *Chelone glabra* L. (6) (1892)

Chelonide glabre (French) - *Chelone glabra* L. (7) (1828)

Ché-m t-toh (Cuchan Yuma) - *Citrullus lanatus* (Thunb.) Matsumura & Nakai (132) (1855)

Ché-mĕt-a-qúis (Cuchan Yuam) - *Cucumis melo* L. (132) (1855)

Ché-mĕt-on-ya (Cuchan Yuma) - *Citrullus lanatus* (Thunb.) Matsumura & Nakai (132) (1855)

Chêne (French) - *Quercus* L. (8) (1785)

Chêne à feuilles chataignier (French) - *Quercus prinus* L. (8) (1785)

Chêne à feuilles houx (French) - *Quercus agrifolia* Née (20) (1857)

Chêne à fleurs denses (French) - *Lithocarpus densiflorus* (Hook. & Arn.) Rehd. (20) (1857)

Chêne à lattes (French) - *Quercus imbricaria* Michx. (17, 33) (1796–1827)

Chêne blanc (French) - *Quercus alba* L. (8) (1785)

Chêne blanc de marais (French) - *Quercus bicolor* Willd (8) (1785)

Chêne blanc de moyenne grandeur (French) - *Quercus stellata* Wangenh. (8) (1785)

Chene de Banister (French) - *Quercus ilicifolia* Wangenh. (181) (~1678)

Chêne de Douglas (French) - *Quercus douglasii* Hook. & Arn. (20) (1857)

Chêne de Lea (French) - *Quercus ×leana* Nutt. [*imbricaria × velutina*] (20) (1857)

Chêne faule à larges feuilles (French) - *Quercus incana* Bartr. (8) (1785)

Chêne faule toujours vert (French) - *Quercus virginiana* Mill. (8) (1785)

Chêne nain à feuilles chataignier (French) - *Quercus prinoides* Willd. (8) (1785)

Chêne noir (French) - *Quercus nigra* L. (8) (1785)

Chêne noir à feuilles digitées (French) - *Quercus falcata* Michx. (8) (1785)

Chêne noir à feuilles entier (French) - *Quercus marilandica* Muenchh. (8) (1785)

Chêne noir nain (French) - *Quercus ilicifolia* Wangenh. (8) (1785)

Chêne occidental (French) - *Quercus garryana* Dougl. ex Hook. (20) (1857)

Chêne ondule (French) - *Quercus ×pauciloba* Rydb. [*gambelii × turbinella*] (20) (1857)

Chêne rouge à grande espéce (French) - *Quercus rubra* L. (8) (1785)

Chêne rouge aquatique (French) - *Quercus rubra* L. (6) (1892)

Chêne rouge de montagne (French) - *Quercus falcata* Michx. (8) (1785)

Chêne rouge nain (French) - *Quercus ilicifolia* Wangenh. (8) (1785)

Chenile - *Hyoscyamus niger* L. (156) (1923) no longer in use by 1923

Chenille copperleaf - *Acalypha hispida* Burm. f. (138, 155) (1931-1942)

Chenille-plant - *Acalypha hispida* Burm. f. (109) (1949)

Chenipodium - *Chenopodium ambrosioides* L. (52) (1919)

Chénopode à grappes (French) - *Chenopodium botrys* L. (158) (1900)

Chénopode Anthelmintique (French) - *Chenopodium ambrosioides* L. var. *ambrosioides* (6) (1892)

Chenopodio vermifugo - *Chenopodium ambrosioides* L. var. *ambrosioides* (186) (1814)

Cherimoya - *Annona cherimola* Miller (109, 137, 155) (1923-1949)

Cherokee rose - *Rosa laevigata* Michx. (19, 106, 109, 122, 138, 156) (1840-1949)

Cherokee sedge - *Carex cherokeensis* Schwein. (5, 50) (1913–present)

Cherry [Cherries, Cherye] or Cherry tree [Cherry trees] - *Prunus cerasus* L. (106, 107, 114) (1894-1930), *Prunus* L. (1, 4, 7, 10, 63, 138, 148, 155, 158, 167, 179) (1526-1986)

Cherry birch - *Betula lenta* L. (1, 5, 7, 19, 46, 49, 72, 75, 92, 107, 109, 156) (1828-1949), *Betula occidentalis* Hook. (5, 93, 158) (1900-1936)

Cherry elaeagnus - *Elaeagnus multiflora* Thunb. (138) (1923)

Cherry fig tree - *Ficus citrifolia* Mill. (20) (1857)

Cherry plum - *Prunus cerasifera* Ehrh. (107, 109) (1919-1949)

Cherry tomato [Cherry tomatoes] - *Physalis* L. (77) (1898) Eastern end of Long Island, *Physalis peruviana* L. (107) (1919), *Solanum lycopersicum* L. var. *cerasiforme* (Dunal) Spooner, J. Anderson &

R.K. Jansen (122) (1937) TX, *Solanum lycopersicum* L. var. *lycopersicum* (5) (1913)

Cherry wood [Cherry-wood] - *Viburnum opulus* L. (5, 156, 158) (1900-1923) no longer in use by 1923

Cherry-laurel [Cherry laurel] - *Prunus caroliniana* (P. Mill.) Aiton (74) (1893) Southern states, *Prunus* L. (138) (1923), *Prunus laurocerasus* L. (49, 57, 92, 107) (1876-1919)

Cherry-pie [Cherry pie] - *Epilobium hirsutum* L. (5, 156) (1913-1923)

Cherry-stone juniper [Cherrystone juniper] - *Juniperus monosperma* (Engelm.) Sarg. (112, 138) (1923-1937)

Chervil [Cheruell] - *Anthriscus cerefolium* (L.) Hoffmann (7, 110, 138, 156) (1828-1923), *Anthriscus* Pers. (92, 179) (1526-1876), *Chaerophyllum* L. (1, 4, 50, 155, 158) (1900–present), *Chaerophyllum procumbens* (L.) Crantz (3) (1977), *Chaerophyllum tainturieri* Hook. (4) (1986), *Cryptotaenia canadensis (L.) DC.* (187) (1818), *Lonicera periclymenum* L. (179) (1526), *Myrrhis* Mill. (possibly) (10) (1818)

Chesnut - *Castanea dentata* (Marsh.) Borkh. (19) (1840), *Castanea sativa* Mill. (182, 184) (1791-1793)

Chesnut-colored sedge - *Cyperus erythrorhizos* Muhl. (129) (1894)

Chess - *Bromus arvensis* L. (19) (1840), *Bromus* L. (1, 93, 158) (1932-1936), *Bromus secalinus* L. (5, 45, 56, 62, 66, 67, 75, 80, 87, 88, 90, 94, 111, 119, 122, 158, 163) (1852-1938)

Chess brome - *Bromus secalinus* L. (155) (1942)

Chess grass - *Bromus secalinus* L. (92) (1876)

Chestayne - *Castanea sativa* Mill. (179) (1526)

Chestnut [Chestnuts, Chestnutte] or Chestnut tree - *Fagus grandifolia* Ehrh. (190) (~1759), *Castanea dentata* (Marsh.) Borkh. (20, 46, 53, 57, 82, 106, 156, 182) (1791-1930), *Castanea* Mill. (10, 109, 112, 138, 156, 167) (1814-1949), *Castanea mollissima* Blume (112) (1937), *Castanea pumila* (L.) Mill. (156) (1923), *Castanea pumila* (L.) Mill.var. *ozarkensis* (Ashe) Tucker (65) (1931), *Castanea sativa* Mill. (6, 7, 8, 18, 41, 52, 58, 110, 178, 179) (1526-1919)

Chestnut oak [Chestnut-Oak, Chestnut Oake] - *Quercus muehlenbergii* Engelm. (1, 2, 5, 65, 72, 82, 93, 97, 153, 156, 157, 158) (1895-1929), *Quercus prinus* L. (2, 19, 41, 107, 122, 138, 156, 177, 181, 189) (~1678-1937)

Chestnut rush - *Juncus castaneus* Smith. (5, 50) (1913–present)

Chestnut sedge - *Carex castanea* Wahlenb. (5) (1913), *Cyperus erythrorhizos* Muhl. (66) (1903)

Chestnut white oak - *Quercus prinus* L. (10, 33, 187) (1818-1826)

Chestnut-leaf oak [Chestnut-leaved oak] - *Quercus prinus* L. (8) (1785)

Chevre-feuille (French) - *Lonicera* L. (8) (1785)

Chevre-feuille de Virginie (French) - *Lonicera sempervirens* L. var. *virginiana* (Marshall) Castigl. (8) (1785)

Chevre-feuille toujours vert (French) - *Lonicera sempervirens* L. (possibly) (8) (1785)

Chewing's fescue [Chewings fescue] - *Festuca rubra* L. (109, 155) (1942-1949)

Cheyenne violet - *Viola canadensis* L. var. *rugulosa* (Greene) A.S. Hitchc. (155) (1942)

Chia - *Salvia columbariae* Benth. (77, 106, 107) (1898-1930) CA

Chia seed - *Salvia hispanica* L. (92) (1876)

Chiaka (Dakota) - *Mentha arvensis* L. (37) (1919)

Chialota (Spanish) - *Argemone hispida* Gray (76) (1896)

Chiballs - *Allium schoenoprasum* L. (46) (1607)

Chicalota - *Argemone mexicana* L. (6) (1892)

Chichasaw plum - *Prunus angustifolia* Marsh. (156) (1923)

Chick pea - *Cicer arietinum* L. (19, 50, 92, 107, 109) (1840–present)

Chick vetch - *Lathyrus odoratus* L. (92) (1876)

Chick wintergreen - *Trientalis borealis* Raf. subsp. *borealis* (19, 92) (1840-1876)

Chickaberry - *Gaultheria procumbens* L. (75) (1894) Stonington CT

Chickasaw - *Apocynum androsaemifolium* L. (77) (1898) ME

Chickasaw plum [Chicasaw plum, Chickasaw plumb] - *Prunus angustifolia* Marsh. (1, 2, 3, 4, 5, 8, 50, 63, 72, 82, 93, 96, 97, 107, 109, 113, 122, 138, 155, 158, 164, 182) (1785–present)

Chicken corn [Chicken-corn, Chickencorn] - *Sorghum bicolor* (L.) Moench (56) (1901) IA, *Sorghum bicolor* (L.) Moench subsp. *drummondii* (Nees ex Steud.) de Wet & Harlan (109, 155) (1942-1949)

Chicken grape [Chicken-grape] - *Vitis aestivalis* Michx. (46) (1879), *Vitis vulpina* L. (2, 7, 15, 73, 95, 107, 156, 158) (1828-1923)

Chicken-berry [Chicken berry] - *Gaultheria procumbens* L. (5, 73, 156) (1892-1923) NH, no longer in use by 1923, *Mitchella repens* L. (76, 156) (1896-1923) Western US, no longer in use by 1923

Chicken-fighters [Chicken fighters] - *Viola palmata* L. (5, 76, 156) (1896-1923) Newton NC, among children who play games with the flowers

Chicken-pepper [Chicken pepper] - *Ranunculus abortivus* L. (156, 158) (1900-1923)

Chicken's-heads [Chicken's heads] - *Pedicularis canadensis* L. (77) (1898) Southold Long Island

Chicken's-toes [Chicken toe, Chickens'-toes, Chickens' toes, Chicken's toes] - *Corallorrhiza odontorhiza* (Willd.) Poir. (49, 53, 64, 158) (1900-1922), *Salicornia maritima* Wolff & Jefferies (73) (1892) Kittery ME

Chicken-thief [Chickenthief] - *Mentzelia oligosperma* Nutt. ex Sims (50) (present)

Chickenweed [Chicken weed, Chicken-weed] - *Roccella tinctoria* DC. (92) (1876), *Senecio vulgaris* L. (5, 156, 158) (1900–1923) no longer in use by 1923, *Stellaria media* (L.) Vill. (156) (1923) no longer in use by 1923, *Stellaria media* (L.) Vill. subsp. *media* (5, 157, 158) (1900-1929)

Chickling vetch - *Lathyrus sativus* L. (107, 110) (1886-1919)

Chickpea [Chick-pea] - *Cicer arietinum* L. (107, 110, 138) (1886-1923), *Cicer* L. (138) (1923)

Chickweed [Chick-weed, Chick weed] - *Anagallis arvensis* L. (42, 157) (1814-1929), *Cerastium fontanum* Baumg. subsp. *vulgare* (Hartman) Greuter & Burdet (19, 80, 102) (1840-1913), *Cerastium* L. (42, 158) (1814-1900), *Cerastium nutans* Raf. (145) (1897), *Holosteum umbellatum* L. (184) (1793), *Lepidium virginicum* L. (156) (1923), *Spergularia* (Pers.) J.& K. Presl (93, 158, 165) (1768-1936), *Stellaria* L. (1, 4, 13, 15, 156, 167) (1814-1986), *Stellaria longipes* Goldie subsp. *longipes* (1, 4, 13, 15, 156, 167) (1814-1986), *Stellaria media* (L.) Vill. (19, 40, 49, 57, 80, 92, 106, 107, 122, 155) (1840-1942), *Stellaria media* (L.) Vill. subsp. *media* (7, 42, 85, 95, 131) (1814-1932), *Trientalis* L. (50, 167) (1814–present)

Chickweed nailwort [Chickweede naile woort] - *Draba verna* L. (178) (1526)

Chickweed phlox - *Phlox bifida* Beck subsp. *stellaria* (Gray) Wherry (5, 156) (1913-1923)

Chickweed wintergreen - *Trientalis borealis* Raf. subsp. *borealis* (5, 156, 179) (1526-1923), *Trientalis* L. (2, 156) (1895-1942)

Chickweed with leaves like germander [Chickweede with leaues like germander] - *Veronica agrestis* L. (178) (1526)

Chico - *Sarcobatus* Nees (1, 93) (1932-1936), *Sarcobatus vermiculatus* (Hook.) Torr. (148, 153) (1913-1939)

Chico grass - *Tuctoria greenei* (Vasey) J. Reeder (94) (1901)

Chicoreé sauvage (French) - *Cichorium intybus* L. (6, 158) (1892–1900)

Chicorium - *Cichorium intybus* L. (57) (1917)

Chicory [Chycory] - *Cichorium intybus* L. (5, 45, 49, 50, 57, 62, 63, 72, 80, 82, 85, 92, 93, 95, 97, 98, 106, 107, 109, 122, 124, 148, 156, 157, 158, 179) (1526–present), *Cichorium* L. (1, 4, 50, 82, 155, 156, 158) (1900–present)

Chicory lettuce - *Lactuca tatarica* (L.) C.A. Mey. var. *pulchella* (Pursh) Breitung (155) (1942)

Chicot - *Gymnocladus dioicus* (L.) K. Koch (5, 38, 156, 157, 158) (1820-1929)

Chicot (French) - *Gymnocladus dioicus* (L.) K. Koch (6, 20, 107) (1857-1919)

Chiendent - *Elymus repens* (L.) Gould (92) (1876)
Chien-dent (French) - *Elymus caninus* (L.) L. (46) (1879)
Chiendent officinal (French) - *Elymus repens* (L.) Gould (158) (1900)
Chigger-flower [Chigger flower] - *Asclepias tuberosa* L. (77) (1898) Southwest MO, said to harbor chigger mites
Chiggerweed [Chigger-weed, Chigger weed] - *Anthemis cotula* L. (5, 76, 156, 157, 158) (1896–1929) said to harbor chigger mites
Chihuahua sagebrush - *Artemisia ludoviciana* Nutt. subsp. *redolens* (Gray) Keck (155) (1942)
Childing cudweed - *Filago vulgaris* Lam. (5, 156) (1913-1923)
Childing daisy - *Bellis perennis* L. (5, 158) (1900–1913)
Childing pink - *Petrorhagia prolifera* (L.) P.W. Ball & Heywood (5, 156) (1913-1923)
Childing sweet william - *Petrorhagia prolifera* (L.) P.W. Ball & Heywood (5, 156) (1913-1923)
Children's-bane [Children's bane] - *Cicuta maculata* L. (6, 7, 71, 92, 133, 156, 158) (1828-1923) no longer in use by 1923
Chile (Mexico) - *Capsicum annuum* L. (possibly) (7) (1828)
Chile dodder - *Cuscuta suaveolens* Ser. (155) (1942)
Chilean beet [Chilian beet] - *Beta vulgaris* L. (107) (1919)
Chilean clover [Chilian clover] - *Medicago sativa* L. (5, 45, 118, 157, 158) (1896–1929)
Chilean gunnera - *Gunnera tinctoria* (Molina) Mirbel (138) (1923)
Chilean parqui - *Cestrum parqui* L'Hér. (138) (1923)
Chilean water milfoil - *Myriophyllum aquaticum* (Vell.) Verdc. (120) (1938) OK
Chilean winterberry - *Aristotelia chilensis* (Molina) Stuntz (155) (1942)
Chili cojote - *Cucurbita foetidissima* Kunth (74, 157, 158) (1893-1929) Southern CA
Chili strawberry - *Fragaria chiloensis* (L.) Mill. (110) (1886)
Chillies - *Capsicum annuum* L. (92, 107) (1876-1919)
Chilly pepper - *Capsicum annuum* L. (92) (1876)
Chiloe strawberry - *Fragaria chiloensis* (L.) Mill. (138) (1923)
Chimalati - *Helianthus annuus* L. (107) (1919)
Chimaphila - *Chimaphila umbellata* (L.) Bart. (52, 54) (1905-1919)
Chimico (Albanian) - *Citrullus lanatus* (Thunb.) Matsumura & Nakai (110) (1886)
Chimney pink [Chimney pinks] - *Saponaria officinalis* L. (5, 64, 74, 157, 158) (1893–1929)
Chimney-sweeps [Chimney sweeps] - *Plantago lanceolata* L. (5, 156, 157, 158) (1900-1929)
Chimneyweed [Chimney weed] - *Roccella tinctoria* DC. (92) (1876)
China aster - *Callistephus chinensis* (L.) Nees (19, 92, 109) (1840-1949)
China bean - *Vigna sinensis* (L.) Endl. (5) (1913)
China brier - *Smilax* L. (2) (1895), *Smilax pseudochina* L. (2, 49) (1895-1898)
China cockle - *Vaccaria hispanica* (Mill.) Rauschert (157) (1929)
China crook-neck - *Cucurbita maxima* Dcne. (158) (1900)
China fleecevine [China fleece-vine] - *Polygonum aubertii* Henry (109, 138) (1923-1949)
China pink - *Dianthus chinensis* L. (19, 92, 114) (1840-1894)
China root [China-root] - *Dioscorea villosa* L. (58, 92) (1869-1876)
China root of Mexico - *Smilax pseudochina* L. (49) (1898)
China rose - *Rosa chinensis* Jacq. (109) (1949)
China tree [China-tree] - *Melia azedarach* L. (15, 106, 107, 109) (1895-1949)
China wood-oil tree [China wood-oil-tree] - *Vernicia fordii* (Hemsl.) Airy Shaw (109) (1949)
Chinaberry [China-berry, China berry] or Chinaberry tree - *Melia azedarach* L. (37, 106, 109, 122, 138, 153) (1913-1949), *Sapindus saponaria* L. var. *drummondii* (Hook. & Arn.) Bensons (106) (1930)
China-fir - *Cunninghamia* R. Br. (109, 138) (1923-1949)
China-grass [China grass] - *Boehmeria nivea* (L.) Gaud. (92, 110) (1876-1886)

China-laurel [Chinalaurel] - *Anthyllis vulneraria* L. (155) (1942), *Antidesma* L. (155) (1942)
Chincone - *Senecio vulgaris* L. (156, 158) (1900-1923)
Chinese ailanthus - *Ailanthus altissima* (Mill) Swingle (6) (1892)
Chinese angelica tree [Chinese angelica-tree] - *Aralia chinensis* L. (109) (1949), *Aralia elata* (Miq.) Seem. (135) (1910)
Chinese aralia - *Aralia chinensis* L. (138, 155) (1931-1942)
Chinese arborvitae - *Platycladus orientalis* (L.) Franco (112) (1937)
Chinese bittersweet - *Celastrus orbiculatus* Thunb. ex Murray (82) (1930) IA
Chinese box - *Euonymus japonicus* Thunb. (92) (1876), *Murraya exotica* L. (107) (1919)
Chinese bush clover - *Lespedeza cuneata* (Dumort.-Cours.) G. Don (4) (1986)
Chinese cabbage - *Brassica* L. (107) (1919), *Brassica rapa* L. var. *amplexicaulis* Tanaka & Ono (109) (1949)
Chinese catalpa - *Catalpa ovata* G. Don (50, 155) (1942–present)
Chinese chestnut - *Castanea mollissima* Blume (109) (1949)
Chinese chives - *Allium tuberosum* Rottl. ex Spreng. (50) (present)
Chinese cork tree [Chinese corktree] - *Phellodendron amurense* Rupr. (137) (1931)
Chinese date - *Ziziphus zizyphus* (L.) Karst. (107) (1919)
Chinese elaeagnus - *Elaeagnus umbellata* Thunb. var. *parvifolia* (Royle) Schneid. (138) (1923)
Chinese elm - *Ulmus parvifolia* Jacq. (82, 109, 138) (1923-1949), *Ulmus pumila* L. (93, 112) (1936-1937)
Chinese evergreen - *Aglaonema modestum* Schott ex Engl. (109) (1949)
Chinese fan palm [Chinese fan-palm] - *Livistona chinensis* (Jacq.) R. Br. ex Mart. (109, 138) (1923-1949)
Chinese fir [Chinese-fir] - *Cunninghamia lanceolata* (Lamb.) Hook. (138) (1923)
Chinese flowering crab - *Malus spectabilis* (Aiton) Borkh. (138) (1923)
Chinese forget-me-not - *Cynoglossum amabile* Stapf & Drummond (109) (1949)
Chinese foxtail - *Setaria faberi* Herrm. (3) (1977)
Chinese hat plant [Chinese-hat-plant] - *Holmskioldia sanguinea* Retz. (109) (1949)
Chinese hemlock-parsley [Chinese hemlockparsley] - *Conioselinum chinense* (L.) Britton, Sterns & Poggenb. (50) (present)
Chinese hibiscus - *Hibiscus rosa-sinensis* L. (107, 109, 138) (1919-1949)
Chinese holly - *Ilex cornuta* Lindl. & Paxton (138) (1923)
Chinese honeysuckle - *Lonicera japonica* Thunb. (5, 156) (1913-1923)
Chinese houses - *Collinsia heterophylla* Graham (138) (1923)
Chinese indigo - *Indigofera decora* Lindl. (138) (1923)
Chinese katsura tree [Chinese katsura-tree] - *Cercidiphyllum japonicum* Sieb. & Zucc. ex J. Hoffmann & H. Schult. (138) (1923)
Chinese lantern [Chineselantern] - *Quincula lobata* (Torr.) Raf. (3, 50) (1977–present), *Quincula* Raf. (155) (1942)
Chinese lantern plant [Chinese lantern-plant] - *Physalis alkekengi* L. (109, 156) (1923-1949)
Chinese lespedeza - *Lespedeza cuneata* (Dumort.-Cours.) G. Don (50, 155) (1942–present)
Chinese matrimony-vine - *Lycium chinense* Mill. (138) (1923)
Chinese mustard - *Brassica juncea* (L.) Czern. (107) (1919)
Chinese parasol tree [Chinese parasoltree, Chinese parasol-tree] - *Firmiana simplex* (L.) W. Wight (109, 138) (1923-1949), *Sterculia* L. (138) (1923)
Chinese peony - *Paeonia lactiflora* Pallas (138) (1923)
Chinese pink - *Dianthus chinensis* L. (138) (1923)
Chinese pistache - *Pistacia chinensis* Bunge (138) (1923)
Chinese preserving melon - *Benincasa hispida* (Thunb.) Cogn. (109) (1949)
Chinese privet - *Ligustrum amurense* Carr. (82) (1930), *Ligustrum sinense* Lour. (138) (1923)

Chinese quince - *Pseudocydonia sinensis* (Dum.-Cours.) Schneid. (109, 138) (1923-1949)

Chinese rose - *Rosa chinensis* Jacq. (138) (1923)

Chinese scholar tree [Chinese scholartree, Chinese scholartree] - *Sophora japonica* L. (109, 138) (1923-1949)

Chinese silk plant [Chinese silk-plant] - *Boehmeria nivea* (L.) Gaud. (109) (1949)

Chinese silver grass [Chinese silvergrass] - *Miscanthus sinensis* Anderss. (50) (present)

Chinese smilax - *Smilax pseudochina* L. (124) (1937) TX

Chinese soapberry - *Sapindus saponaria* L. (138) (1923)

Chinese sugarcane [Chinese sugar-cane, Chinese sugar cane] - *Sorghum bicolor* (L.) Moench (56) (1901) IA, *Sorghum bicolor* (L.) Moench subsp. *bicolor* (66, 87, 158) (1884-1903), *Sorghum halepense* (L.) Pers. (45) (1896)

Chinese sumac [Chinese sumach] - *Ailanthus altissima* (Mill) Swingle (5, 6, 49, 52, 57, 92, 106, 156, 158) (1876-1930), *Ailanthus* Desf. (15) (1895)

Chinese tallow or Chinese tallow tree [Chinese tallowtree, Chinese tallow-tree] - *Triadica sebifera* (L.) Small (50, 109, 138) (1923–present)

Chinese tamarix - *Tamarix chinensis* Lour. (109, 138) (1923-1949)

Chinese thorn-apple [Chinese thornapple] - *Datura quercifolia* Kunth (50) (present)

Chinese tree - *Syringa* L. (112) (1937)

Chinese velvetbean - *Mucuna pruriens* (L.) DC. var. *pruriens* (138) (1923)

Chinese white poplar - *Populus tomentosa* Carr. (138) (1923)

Chinese wild peach - *Prunus persica* (L.) Batsch (137, 138) (1923-1931)

Chinese wingnut - *Pterocarya stenoptera* C. DC. (138) (1923)

Chinese wisteria - *Wisteria sinensis* (Sims) DC. (109, 138) (1923-1949)

Chinese yam - *Dioscorea oppositifolia* L. (50, 109) (1949–present)

Chink [Chinks] - *Gaultheria procumbens* L. (5, 73, 92, 156) (1876-1923)

Chinkapin [Chincapin] - *Castanea pumila* (L.) Mill. (20, 181, 189) (~1678-1857), *Quercus prinoides* Willd. (5) (1913)

Chinkapin oak - *Quercus muehlenbergii* Engelm. (4, 5, 50, 155, 157, 158) (1900–present), *Quercus prinoides* Willd. (158) (1900)

Chino or Chino grass - *Bouteloua breviseta* Vasey (122, 163) (1852-1937) TX

Chinook licorice [Chinook liquorice] - *Lupinus littoralis* Dougl. (74) (1893) Washington, DC

Chinquapin (French) - *Castanea pumila* (L.) Mill. (possibly) (8) (1785)

Chinquapin [Chinquepin] - *Castanea pumila* (L.) Mill. (5, 8, 19, 38, 41, 46, 65, 92, 97, 106, 107, 109, 122, 137, 138, 156, 181, 1884) (~1678-1937), *Castanea pumila* (L.) Mill.var. *ozarkensis* (Ashe) Tucker (97) (1937), *Castanea pumila* (L.) Mill.var. *pumila* (124) (1937), *Chrysolepis chrysophylla* (Douglas ex Hook.) Hjelmq. (161) (1857), *Quercus prinoides* Willd. (10, 19) (1818-1840)

Chinquapin bush [Chinquapin-bush] - *Castanea pumila* (L.) Mill. (177, 181) (~1678-1762)

Chinquapin oak [Chinquepin oak] - *Quercus muehlenbergii* Engelm. (3, 138, 156, 158) (1900-1977), *Quercus prinoides* Willd. (1, 2, 8, 18, 33, 156, 187) (1785-1932)

Chinwood [Chin wood] - *Taxus baccata* L. (92) (1876), *Taxus* L. (7) (1828)

Chionanthe (French) - *Chionanthus* L. (8) (1785), *Chionanthus virginicus* L. (6) (1892)

Chionanthe de Virginie (French) - *Chionanthus virginicus* L. (8, 20) (1785-1857)

Chionanthus - *Chionanthus virginicus* L. (52, 54) (1905-1919)

Chiquebi (Native Americans) - *Helianthus tuberosus* L. (110) (1618)

Chirimoya - *Annona cherimola* Miller (possibly) (110) (1886)

Chisos bluebonnet - *Lupinus havardii* S. Wats. (122) (1937) TX

Chisos Mountain bluebonnet - *Lupinus havardii* S. Wats. (124) (1937) TX

Chisos red oak - *Quercus gravesii* Sudworth (122) (1937) TX

Chisos wild cherry - *Prunus serotina* Ehrh. var. *virens* (Woot. & Standl.) McVaugh (122) (1937) TX

Chistmas berry - *Heteromeles arbutifolia* (Lindl.) M. Roemer (106) (1930)

Chittam - *Frangula purshiana* (DC.) Cooper (106) (1930)

Chittam wood [Chittam-wood, Chittem wood, Chittim wood, Chittim-wood] - *Cotinus obovatus* Raf. (15, 97, 135, 156) (1895-1937), *Frangula purshiana* (DC.) Cooper (59) (1911), *Sideroxylon lycioides* L. (5) (1913)

Chittem bark - *Frangula purshiana* (DC.) Cooper (49, 52, 53, 57, 59) (1911-1922)

Chives [Chiues] - *Allium schoenoprasum* L. (2, 92, 109, 110, 138, 155, 156, 165, 180) (1633-1949)

Chizahaw (Osage) - *Polygonum convolvulus* L. (7) (1828)

Chlora-like chironia [Chlora like chironia] - *Sabatia chloroides* Pursh (42) (1814)

Chloris - *Chloris* Sw. (155) (1942), *Chloris verticillata* Nutt. (144) (1899)

Chmeli (Slavic) - *Humulus lupulus* L. (110) (1886)

Chocho (Jamaica) - *Sechium edule* (Jacq.) Sw. (106, 107, 110) (1886-1930)

Cho-cho vine - *Sicyos angulatus* L. (86) (1878)

Chock-cheese - *Malva sylvestris* L. (157, 158) (1900-1929)

Choco [Choko] - *Sechium edule* (Jacq.) Sw. (107, 110) (1886-1919)

Chocolate - *Geum rivale* L (74, 76) (1893–1896) NH ME, root used in beverage, *Theobroma cacao* L. (92) (1876)

Chocolate corn - *Sorghum bicolor* (L.) Moench subsp. *bicolor* (87) (1884)

Chocolate flower [Chocolate-flower] - *Geranium maculatum* L. (5, 64, 73, 156, 157, 158) (1892–1929) Stratham NH

Chocolate lily - *Fritillaria atropurpurea* Nutt. (127) (1933) ND

Chocolate nuts - *Theobroma cacao* L. (92) (1876)

Chocolate plant - *Geum virginianum* L. (156) (1923)

Chocolate root [Chocolate-root] - *Geum canadense* Jacq. (156) (1923), *Geum rivale* L (5, 6, 92, 156, 158) (1876–1923), *Geum virginianum* L. (5, 7, 49, 157, 158) (1828-1913)

Choctaw root [Choctaw-root] - *Apocynum cannabinum* L. (64, 106, 156) (1900-1907)

Choice dielytra - *Dicentra canadensis* (Goldie) Walp. (92) (1876)

Choke pondweed [Choke pond-weed] - *Elodea canadensis* Michx. (5, 14, 93, 156) (1882-1936)

Chokeberry [Choke-berry, Choke berry] - *Adenorachis arbutifolia* (L.) Nieuwl. (46, 47, 76, 82, 92, 107, 156) (1876-1930), *Photinia* Lindl. (1, 50, 138, 155) (1923–present)

Chokecherry [Choke cherry, Choke-cherry, Choke cherries, Choke-cherries, Choak cherry] - *Amelanchier canadensis* (L.) Medik. (92) (1876), *Padus serotina* (Ehrh.) Borkh. (19) (1840), *Padus virginiana* subsp. *melanocarpa* (A. Nelson) W.A. Weber (112) (1937), *Prunus* L. (93, 108, 153, 155) (1878-1942), *Prunus serotina* Ehrh. (156, 158) (1900-1923), *Prunus virginiana* L. (1, 3, 4, 9, 35, 40, 46, 47, 50, 57, 63, 72, 82, 92, 95, 103, 106, 107, 108, 109, 112, 113, 114, 121, 125, 126, 130, 131, 135, 137, 156, 157, 158, 187) (1806–present), *Prunus virginiana* L. var. *demissa* (Nutt.) Torr. (22, 74, 101, 112, 113, 137) (1890-1937), *Prunus virginiana* L. var. *melanocarpa* (A. Nels.) Sargent (85) (1932), *Prunus virginiana* L. var. *virginiana* (5, 50, 37, 97) (1913–present)

Choke-dog [Choke dog] - *Gonolobus* Michx. (92) (1876)

Chokepear [Choke-pear, Choke pear] - *Photinia melanocarpa* (Michx.) Robertson & Phipps (5) (1913), *Photinia pyrifolia* (Lam.) Robertson & Phipps (5, 73, 156) (1892-1923), *Pyrus communis* L. (5) (1913)

Chokeweed [Choak weed] - *Polygonum scandens* L. var. *dumetorum* (L.) Gleason (46) (1610)

Chôli (Old German) - *Brassica oleracea* L. (110) (1886)

Cholla - *Opuntia imbricata* (Haw.) DC. var. *imbricata* (149) (1904), *Opuntia* Mill. (1, 4, 93, 155) (1932-1986) flat-stemmed species are pricklypear, cylindrical-stemmed species are cholla, *Opuntia tunicata* (Lehm.) Link & Otto var. *davisii* (Engelm. & Bigelow) L. Benson (97) (1937)

Cholza (Persian) - *Portulaca oleracea* L. (110) (1886)

Chondrilla - *Chondrilla juncea* L. (70) (1895)

Chondrus - *Chondrus crispus* (L.) J. Stackhouse (57) (1917)

Chongras (Louisiana) - *Phytolacca americana* L. var. *americana* (6, 7, 71) (1828-1898)

Chopped-eggs - *Linaria vulgaris* Mill. (157, 158) (1900-1929)

Chorispora - *Chorispora* R. Br. ex DC. (50) (present)

Chorogi - *Stachys affinis* Bunge (138) (1923)

Chosanwa (Winnebago) - *Crataegus chrysocarpa* Ashe (37) (1919)

Chottam wood - *Cotinus obovatus* Raf. (5) (1913)

Chou oléifère (French) - *Brassica rapa* L. var. *rapa* (107) (1919)

Chou-gras - *Phytolacca americana* L. var. *americana* (107) (1817)

Chowley - *Vigna sinensis* (L.) Endl. (5) (1913)

Chren (Russia) - *Armoracia rusticana* P.G. Gaertn., B. Mey. & Scherb. (110) (1886)

Chris root - *Helleborus viridis* L. (5, 76) (1896-1913) Sulphur Grove OH, probably short for Christmas root

Christmas American mistletoe [Christmas American-mistletoe] - *Phoradendron leucarpum* (Raf.) Reveal & M.C. Johnston (155) (1942)

Christmas bells - *Ipomoea* L. (106) (1930)

Christmas berry [Christmasberry, Christmas-berry] - *Heteromeles arbutifolia* (Lindl.) M. Roemer var. *arbutifolia* (109, 138) (1923-1949)

Christmas berry tree [Christmas-berry-tree] - *Schinus terebinthifolius* Raddi (109) (1949)

Christmas bush [Christmasbush] - *Alchornea* Sw. (155) (1942)

Christmas cactus - *Opuntia leptocaulis* DC. (50) (present), *Schlumbergera truncata* (Haw.) Moran (109, 138) (1923-1949)

Christmas daisy - *Callistephus chinensis* (L.) Nees (92) (1876)

Christmas evergreen - *Selaginella rupestris* (L.) Spring (5, 92, 158) (1876-1913)

Christmas fern [Christmasfern, Christmas-fern] - *Polystichum acrostichoides* (Michx.) Schott (3, 50, 72, 97, 109, 122, 138, 155) (1907–present), *Polystichum munitum* (Kaulfuss) K. Presl (3) (1977), *Polystichum* Roth. (4) (1986)

Christmas flower - *Eranthis hyemalis* (L.) Salisb. (5, 156) (1913-1923), *Helleborus viridis* L. (106) (1930)

Christmas hawthorn - *Crataegus suborbiculata* Sarg. (138) (1923)

Christmas holly - *Ilex opaca* Aiton (65) (1931) OK

Christmas mistletoe - *Phoradendron tomentosum* (DC.) Engelmann. ex Gray (50) (present)

Christmas rose [Christmas-rose] - *Helleborus niger* L. (2, 15, 49, 53, 55, 92, 109, 138) (1876-1949) for time of flowering under mild climates, *Helleborus viridis* L. (5, 76, 156) (1896-1923) Sulphur Grove OH

Christophine - *Sechium edule* (Jacq.) Sw. (109) (1949)

Christ's eye - *Salvia verbenaca* L. (92) (1876)

Christ's ladder - *Centaurium erythraea* Raf. (156) (1923)

Christ's tears - *Coix lacryma-jobi* L. (163) (1852)

Christ's thorn [Christ-thorn] - *Paliurus spina-christi* Mill. (92, 109, 138) (1876-1949), *Pyracantha coccinea* M. Roemer (5, 156) (1913-1923)

Chrysanthemum - *Chrysanthemum* L. (4, 138, 155, 158) (1900-1986), *Tanacetum vulgare* L. (82) (1930) IA

Chrysis - *Helianthus annuus* L. (174) (1753)

Chrysodium - *Acrostichum* L. (2) (1895)

Chrysogonum - *Chrysogonum virginianum* L. (5, 174, 181) (~1678-1913)

Chrysothamnus - *Chrysothamnus* Nutt. (158) (1900)

Chuckles - *Aquilegia canadensis* L. (157) (1929)

Chufa - *Cyperus esculentus* L. (2, 109, 138, 155, 158) (1895-1949)

Chufa flatsedge - *Cyperus esculentus* L. (50, 155) (1942–present)

Churchbrooms [Church brooms, Church broom] - *Dipsacus fullonum* L. (5, 156, 158) (1900–1923)

Church-mouse threeawn [Churchmouse threeawn] - *Aristida dichotoma* Michx. (50, 155) (1942–present), *Aristida dichotoma* Michx. var. *curtissii* Gray ex S. Wats. & Coult. (3) (1977), *Aristida dichotoma* Michx. var. *dichotoma* (5) (1913)

Churchsteeples - *Agrimonia eupatoria* L. (50) (present)

Churl's treacle [Churles tryacle] - *Allium sativum* L. (178, 179) (1526-1596)

Churnstaff [Churn-staff] - *Euphorbia helioscopia* L. (5, 92, 156) (1876-1923) no longer in use by 1923

Churrus - *Cannabis sativa* L. subsp. *indica* (Lam.) E. Small & Cronq. (92) (1876) resinous substance

Chyches - *Cicer arietinum* L. (179) (1526)

Chyna roots - *Smilax pseudochina* L. (46) (1879)

Čibagup (Chippewa) - *Dirca palustris* L. (105) (1932)

Cibotium - *Cibotium* Kaulfuss (138) (1923)

Ciboule - *Allium fistulosum* L. (165) (1768)

Cicely root [Cicely-root] - *Osmorhiza longistylis* (Torr.) DC. (156, 157, 158) (1900-1929)

Cicer milkvetch - *Astragalus cicer* L. (50) (present)

Cicera - *Lathyrus cicera* L. (110) (1886)

Cichorea iaulne (French) - *Hieracium* L. (180) (1633)

Cichorie (German) - *Cichorium intybus* L. (6, 158) (1892-1900)

Cicuta - *Cicuta douglasii* (DC.) J.M.Coult. & Rose (71) (1898), *Cicuta maculata* L. (92, 125) (1876-1930)

Cicuta Americana (Official name of Materia Medica) - *Cicuta maculata* L. (7) (1828)

Cicuta mayor - *Conium maculatum* L. (158) (1900)

Cicuta officinalis (Official name of Materia Medica) - *Conium maculatum* L. (7) (1828)

Ciderage - *Polygonum hydropiper* L. (157, 158) (1900-1929)

Cigagwa'tĭgon (Chippewa, skunk-like) - *Ribes triste* Pallas (40) (1928)

Cigar flower [Cigar-flower] - *Cuphea ignea* A. DC. (possibly) (86, 109) (1878-1949)

Cigar tree [Cigar-tree] - *Catalpa bignonioides* Walt. (5, 49, 53, 156) (1898-1923), *Catalpa* Scop. (1) (1932), *Catalpa speciosa* (Warder) Warder ex Engelm. (4, 5, 156, 158) (1900-1986)

Cigarbox cedar [Cigarbox-cedar] - *Cedrela odorata* L. (138) (1923)

Ciguë officinale (French) - *Conium maculatum* L. (158) (1900)

Či-kadak (Chippewa) - *Aralia racemosa* L. (105) (1932)

Ciliate meadow beauty - *Rhexia petiolata* Walt. (5) (1913)

Ciliate-leaf aster [Ciliate-leaved aster] - *Symphyotrichum ericoides* (L.) Nesom var. *prostratum* (Kuntze) Nesom (72) (1907)

Ciliate-leaf paspalum [Ciliate-leaved paspalum] - *Paspalum setaceum* Michx. (5, 56, 72) (1893-1901)

Cimicifuga - *Cimicifuga racemosa* (L.) Nutt. (54, 55, 57, 59, 60, 64) (1902-1917)

Cimnel [Cimnell] (summer squash) - *Cucurbita pepo* L. (107, 181) (~1678-1675)

Cinchweed - *Pectis* L. (50) (present)

Cindria (Spanish) - *Citrullus lanatus* (Thunb.) Matsumura & Nakai (110) (1886)

Cineraria - *Pericallis cuneata* (L'Hér.) Bolle (138) (1923)

Cĭngob' (Chippewa) - *Picea rubens* Sarg. (40) (1928)

Cinnamon - *Cinnamomum verum* J. Presl (110, 138) (1886-1923)

Cinnamon clethra - *Clethra acuminata* Michx. (138, 156) (1923)

Cinnamon fern [Cinnamon-fern] - *Osmunda cinnamomea* L. (1, 5, 50, 72, 92, 97, 109, 122, 124, 138, 187) (1818–present)

Cinnamon honeysuckle - *Rhododendron viscosum* (L.) Torr. (75, 156) (1894–1923) WV

Cinnamon rose - *Rosa cinnamomea* L. (19, 82, 107, 109, 138, 178) (1526-1949)

Cinnamon sedge - *Acorus calamus* L. (64, 158) (1900-1908)

Cinnamon tree [Cinnamon-tree] - *Cinnamomum verum* J. Presl (109) (1949)

Cinnamon vine [Cinnamon-vine, Cinnamonvine] - *Dioscorea oppositifolia* L. (109, 138, 155) (1923-1949), *Linnaea borealis* L. (156) (1923)

Cinnamon wood [Cinnamon-wood] - *Sassafras albidum* (Nutt.) Nees (5, 92, 156, 158) (1876-1923)

Cinque - *Triosteum perfoliatum* L. (6, 177, 186) (1762-1892)

Cinquefoil [Cink-foil, Cinque-foil] - *Alchemilla alpina* L. (165) (1768), *Argentina anserina* (L.) Rydb. (35) (1806), *Dasiphora floribunda* (Pursh) Kartesz (112) (1937), *Onobrychis viciifolia* Scop. (158) (1900), *Potentilla canadensis* L. (46, 48, 57, 92, 156) (1671-1923), *Potentilla hippiana* Lehm. (4) (1986), *Potentilla* L. (1, 2, 4, 7, 10, 50, 109, 138, 155, 156, 167, 184) (1793–present) five-leaved in French), *Potentilla norvegica* L. (19) (1840), *Potentilla norvegica* L. subsp. *monspeliensis* (L.) Aschers. & Graebn. (40, 80, 82) (1928), *Potentilla pensylvanica* L. (4) (1986), *Potentilla plattensis* Nutt. (4) (1986)

Cinquefoil [Synkefoyle] - *Potentilla reptans* L. (179) (1526)

Cinquefoil herb - *Potentilla canadensis* L. (92) (1876)

Cinquefoil root - *Potentilla canadensis* L. (92) (1876)

Cintli (Mexico) - *Zea mays* L. (110) (1886) goddess Cinteutl was similar to Greek goddess Ceres

Cipolla (Italian) - *Allium* L. (180) (1633)

Cipres - *Chamaecyparis thyoides* (L.) Britton, Sterns & Poggenb. (46) (1879)

Cipressi - *Chamaecyparis thyoides* (L.) Britton, Sterns & Poggenb. (46) (1879)

Cique commune (French) - *Conium maculatum* L. (7) (1828)

Cique d'Amerique (French) - *Cicuta maculata* L. (6, 7) (1828-1932)

Cique ordinaire (French) - *Conium maculatum* L. (6) (1892)

Circaea - *Circaea* L. (155) (1942)

Circinate white water crowfoot - *Ranunculus trichophyllus* Chaix var. *trichophyllus* (72) (1907)

Cirier (French) - *Morella cerifera* (L.) Small (8) (1785), *Myrica* L. (8) (1785)

Cirier inodore (French) - *Morella inodora* (Bartr.) Small (20) (1857)

Cirier nain (French) - *Morella cerifera* (L.) Small (possibly) (8) (1785)

Cistus-leaf St. John's-wort [Cistus-leaved St. John's wort] - *Hypericum sphaerocarpum* Michx. (2) (1895)

Citron (French) - *Podophyllum peltatum* L. (43) (1820)

Citron [Cytron] - *Citrus medica* L. (107, 109, 110, 138, 179) (1526-1949)

Citron melon - *Citrullus lanatus* (Thunb.) Matsumura & Nakai (92) (1876)

Citron paintbrush - *Castilleja purpurea* (Nutt.) G. Don var. *citrina* (Pennell) Shinners (3) (1977)

Citronella - *Collinsonia canadensis* L. (5, 64, 156) (1907-1923)

Citronella grass [Citronella-grass] - *Cymbopogon nardus* (L.) Rendle (109) (1949)

Citronella horsebalm - *Collinsonia canadensis* L. (138) (1923)

Citronelle - *Melissa officinalis* L. (92) (1876)

Citronelle (French) - *Artemisia abrotanum* L. (158) (1900)

Citronelle oil - *Cymbopogon nardus* (L.) Rendle (92) (1876)

Citronnier (French) - *Citrus medica* L. (possibly) (110) (1886)

Citrouilles - *Cucurbita pepo* L. (107) (1703)

Citruels - *Citrullus lanatus* (Thunb.) Matsumura & Nakai (182) (1791)

Citrulle [Cytrulle] - *Citrullus lanatus* (Thunb.) Matsumura & Nakai (179) (1526), *Cucurbita pepo* L. (179) (1526)

Citruls - *Citrullus lanatus* (Thunb.) Matsumura & Nakai (182) (1791)

City goosefoot - *Chenopodium urbicum* L. (50, 62, 155) (1912–present)

Ciuet - *Allium schoenoprasum* L. (180) (1633)

Cives [Ciues] - *Allium schoenoprasum* L. (19, 92, 156, 165, 178, 180) (1596-1876)

Civet bean - *Phaseolus lunatus* L. (107, 109, 138) (1919-1949)

Ciwade'imīnaga'wûnj (Chippewa, sour fruit) - *Heuchera americana* L. var. *hirsuticaulis* (Wheelock) Rosendahl, Butters & Lakela (40) (1928)

Ciwade'imīn'ībûg (Chippewa, sour leaf) - *Heuchera* L. (40) (1928)

Clabber-grass [Clabbergrass] - *Galium aparine* L. (92) (1876), *Galium verum* L. (7) (1828)

Clabber-spoon [Clabber spoon] - *Clitoria mariana* L. (5) (1913)

Cladothrix - *Tidestromia lanuginosa* (Nutt.) Standl. (5, 97) (1913-1937), *Tidestromia* Standl. (158) (1900)

Clambering monkshood - *Aconitum uncinatum* L. (138, 155) (1931-1942)

Clammy azalea - *Rhododendron viscosum* (L.) Torr. (5, 156) (1913-1923)

Clammy base mustard - *Polanisia dodecandra* (L.) DC. (42) (1814)

Clammy campion - *Lychnis viscaria* L. (138) (1923)

Clammy chickweed [Clammy chick-weed, Clammy chick weed] - *Cerastium glomeratum* Thuill. (42) (1814), *Cerastium nutans* Raf. (5, 156) (1913-1923)

Clammy cudweed - *Pseudognaphalium viscosum* (Kunth) W.A. Weber (4) (1986)

Clammy cuphea - *Cuphea hyssopifolia* Kunth (187) (1818), *Cuphea viscosissima* Jacq (5, 155, 156, 158) (1900-1942)

Clammy everlasting - *Pseudognaphalium macounii* (Greene) Kartesz (5, 156) (1913-1923)

Clammy groundcherry [Clammy ground cherry, Clammy ground cherry, Clammy ground-cherry] - *Physalis heterophylla* Nees (3, 4, 5, 50, 62, 72, 85, 93, 97, 122, 131, 155) (1899–present)

Clammy hedge - *Gratiola virginiana* L. (5) (1913)

Clammy hedge-hyssop [Clammy hedge hyssop, Clammy hedgehyssop] - *Gratiola neglecta* Torr. (50) (present), *Gratiola virginiana* L. (72, 97, 120, 122, 156) (1907-1938)

Clammy honeysuckle - *Rhododendron viscosum* (L.) Torr. (5) (1913)

Clammy lichnia - *Lychnis viscaria* L. (19) (1840)

Clammy locust or Clammy locust tree - *Robinia viscosa* Vent. (2, 5, 19, 46, 92, 109, 138, 156) (1840-1949)

Clammy mouse-ear chickweed - *Cerastium glomeratum* Thuill. (156, 187) (1818-1923), *Cerastium nutans* Raf. (187) (1818)

Clammy mustard - *Cleome viscosa* L. (92) (1876), *Polanisia dodecandra* (L.) DC. subsp. *dodecandra* (7) (1828)

Clammy sage - *Salvia sclarea* L. (92) (1876)

Clammy whortle-berry - *Gaylussacia baccata* (Wang.) K. Koch (42) (1814)

Clammyweed [Clammy-weed, Clammy weed] - *Cleome viscosa* L. (92) (1876), *Polanisia dodecandra* (L.) DC. subsp. *dodecandra* (5, 72, 80, 85, 95, 97, 156, 157, 158) (1900–1937), *Polanisia dodecandra* (L.) DC. subsp. *trachysperma* (Torr. & Gray) Iltis (3, 4, 82, 131) (1899-1986), *Polanisia* Raf. (1, 4, 50, 93, 155, 158) (1900–present)

Clamoun - *Kalmia latifolia* L. (5, 156) (1913-1923) no longer in use by 1923

Clappedepouch - *Capsella bursa-pastoris* (L.) Medik. (157, 158) (1900-1929) archaic

Clapweed - *Ephedra antisyphilitica* Berl. ex C.A. Mey. (4, 50) (1986–present)

Clapwort [Clap-wort] - *Conopholis americana* (L. f.) Wallr. (5, 7, 92) (1828-1913)

Claret-cup cactus - *Echinocereus triglochidiatus* Engelm. (109) (1949)

Claret-cup echinocereus [Claretcup echinocereus] - *Echinocereus triglochidiatus* Engelm. (155) (1942)

Clarkia - *Clarkia* Pursh (138) (1923)

Clary [Clarey, Clarry] - *Salvia sclarea* L. (5, 19, 46, 92, 107, 109, 156, 179) (1526-1949)

Clasping bellflower - *Triodanis perfoliata* (L.) Nieuwl. (19) (1840), *Triodanis perfoliata (L.) Nieuwl. var. perfoliata* (5, 62, 156) (1912-1923)

Clasping coneflower - *Dracopis amplexicaulis* (Vahl.) Cass. (50, 124) (1937–present)

Clasping milkweed - *Asclepias amplexicaulis* Sm. (50) (present)
Clasping peppergrass - *Lepidium perfoliatum* L. (3, 4) (1977-1986)
Clasping pepperweed - *Lepidium perfoliatum* L. (50, 155) (1942–present)
Clasping pondweed - *Potamogeton perfoliatus* L. (72) (1907)
Clasping Venus' looking-glass - *Triodanis perfoliata* (L.) Nieuwl. (50) (present), *Triodanis perfoliata* (L.) Nieuwl. var. *perfoliata* (50, 155) (1942–present)
Clasping-leaf boltonia [Clasping-leaved boltonia] - *Boltonia decurrens* (Torr. & Gray) Wood. (5) (1913)
Clasping-leaf brown-eyed Susan [Clasping leaf brown-eyed-Susan] - *Rudbeckia grandiflora* (D. Don) J.F. Gmel. ex DC. var. *alismifolia* (Torr. & Gray) Cronq. (97) (1937), *Dracopis amplexicaulis* (Vahl.) Cass. (5, 97, 122) (1913-1937)
Clasping-leaf coneflower [Claspingleaf coneflower] - *Dracopis amplexicaulis* (Vahl.) Cass. (5, 97, 138, 155) (1913-1942)
Clasping-leaf dogbane [Claspingleaf dogbane, Clasping-leaved dogbane] - *Apocynum androsaemifolium* L. (122) (1937), *Apocynum cannabinum* L. (5, 72, 93, 97, 157, 158) (1900-1937)
Clasping-leaf mullen [Clasping-leaved mullen] - *Verbascum phlomoides* L. (5) (1913)
Clasping-leaf pondweed [Clasping-leaved pondweed] - *Potamogeton perfoliatus* L. (5, 50, 93, 156) (1913–present)
Clasping-leaf potamogeton [Clasping-leaved potamogeton] - *Potamogeton richardsonii* (Benn.) Rydb. (131) (1899)
Clasping-leaf St. John's-wort [Clasping leaved St. John's wort] - *Hypericum gymnanthum* Engelm. & Gray (5, 72, 97) (1907-1937)
Clasping-leaf twistedstalk [Clasping-leaved twisted stalk, Clasping-leaved twisted-stalk, Clasingleaf twistedstalk] - *Streptopus amplexifolius* (L.) DC. (5, 97, 155) (1913-1942)
Clasp-leaf pennycress [Claspleaf pennycress] - *Microthlaspi perfoliatum* (L.) F.K. Mey. (50) (present)
Clasp-leaf twistedstalk [Claspleaf twistedstalk] - *Streptopus amplexifolius* (L.) DC. (50) (present)
Clavalier (French) - *Zanthoxylum americanum* Mill. (158) (1900)
Clavalier aite (French) - *Zanthoxylum fagara* (L.) Sargent (20) (1857)
Clavalier de la Caroline (French) - *Zanthoxylum clava-herculis* L. (20) (1857)
Claver - *Lotus corniculatus* L. (5, 158) (1900-1913)
Claver-grass [Claver grass, Clayver-grass] - *Galium aparine* L. (5, 156, 158) (1900-1923)
Clayton's aster - *Eurybia divaricata* (L.) Nesom (5) (1913)
Clayton's bedstraw [Claytons bedstraw] - *Galium tinctorium* L. (5, 155) (1913-1942)
Clayton's cliff-brake - *Aspidotis densa* (Brack.) Lellinger (5) (1913), *Pellaea atropurpurea* (L.) Link (5, 158) (1900-1913)
Clayton's fern - *Osmunda claytoniana* L. (1, 5, 72) (1893-1932)
Clayton's flowering fern - *Osmunda claytoniana* L. (5) (1913)
Clayton's lobelia - *Lobelia spicata* Lam. (187) (1818)
Clayton's sweetroot [Clayton sweetroot] - *Osmorhiza claytonii* (Michx.) C.B. Clarke (50, 155) (1942–present)
Clayweed [Clay-weed] - *Tussilago farfara* L. (5, 156) (1913-1923)
Clear-eye - *Salvia sclarea* L. (5, 156) (1913-1923), *Salvia sclarea* L. (5, 156) (1913-1923), *Salvia verbenaca* L. (92) (1876)
Clearweed [Clear weed] - *Pilea* Lindl. (1, 4, 50, 155, 158) (1900–present), *Pilea pumila* (L.) Gray (3, 5, 97, 156) (1913-1977), *Pilea pumila* (L.) Gray var. *pumila* (19, 92, 95, 131, 158) (1840-1899)
Cleats [Cleets] - *Tussilago farfara* L. (5, 156) (1913-1923) no longer in use by 1923
Cleaver-grass [Cleaver grass] - *Trifolium pratense* L. (92) (1876) archaic
Cleavers [Cleaver] - *Galium aparine* L. (1, 2, 5, 49, 52, 53, 57, 61, 72, 92, 93, 107, 131, 156, 157, 158) (1870-1936), *Galium* L. (2, 4, 10, 76, 93, 156, 158) (1818-1986)
Cleavers' goose-grass - *Galium aparine* L. (187) (1818)
Cleaverwort [Cleaver-wort, Cleaver wort] - *Galium aparine* L. (5, 92, 156, 157, 158) (1876-1923), *Galium verum* L. (7) (1828)

Cleft phlox - *Phlox bifida* Beck (5) (1913)
Clematis - *Clematis ×jackmanii* T. Moore [*lanuginosa × viticella*] (112) (1937), *Clematis crispa* L. (156) (1923), *Clematis* L. (109, 112, 155, 156) (1923-1949), *Clematis virginiana* L. (112) (1937)
Clematis pipe vine - *Clematis texensis* Buckl. (124) (1937) TX
Cleome - *Cleome hassleriana* Chod. (92) (1876), *Cleome* L. (93, 158) (1900-1936), *Cleome serrulata* Pursh (106) (1930)
Cleomella - *Cleomella angustifolia* Torr. (3, 106) (1930-1977), *Cleomella* DC. (158) (1900)
Clethra - *Clethra* L. (8) (1785)
Clethra (French) - *Clethra* L. (8) (1785)
Clethra à feuilles d'aune (French) - *Clethra alnifolia* L. (8) (1785)
Clethra loosestrife - *Lysimachia clethroides* Duby (138) (1923)
Cleveland shootingstar - *Dodecatheon clevelandii* Greene (138) (1923)
Cliff dogbane - *Apocynum androsaemifolium* L. (155) (1942)
Cliff elm - *Ulmus thomasii* Sarg. (5, 156, 157, 158) (1900-1929)
Cliff fern - *Woodsia* R. Br. (50) (present)
Cliff stonecress - *Aurinia saxatilis* (L.) Desv. (155) (1942)
Cliffbrake [Cliff-brake] - *Pellaea atropurpurea* (L.) Link (97) (1937), *Pellaea* Link (4, 50, 109, 138, 155, 158) (1900–present), *Pellaea wrightiana* Hook. (97) (1937)
Cliff-rose [Cliff rose] - *Armeria maritima* (P. Mill.) Willd (156) (1923), *Purshia mexicana* (D. Don) Henrickson (106) (1930), *Purshia stansburiana* (Torr.) Henrickson (106) (1930)
Cliffweed [Cliff-weed] - *Heuchera americana* L. (156, 158) (1900-1923), *Heuchera villosa* Michx. (possibly) (7, 92) (1828-1876)
Cliftonie á feuilles de troene (French) - *Cliftonia monophylla (Lam.) Britton* (20) (1857)
Climath - *Toxicodendron radicans* (L.) Kuntze subsp. *radicans* (157, 158) (1900-1929), *Toxicodendron toxicarium* (Salisb.) Gillis (156) (1923)
Climbing bindweed - *Polygonum convolvulus* L. (5, 156, 158) (1900-1923)
Climbing birthwort [Climbing Birthwoort] - *Aristolochia clematitis* L. (178) (1526)
Climbing bittersweet [Climbing bitter-sweet] - *Celastrus scandens* L. (3, 5, 15, 42, 47, 49, 72, 82, 92, 95, 97, 106, 108, 125, 126, 156, 157, 158) (1814-1977)
Climbing boneset - *Mikania scandens* (L.) Willd. (5, 97, 106, 122, 124, 156) (1913-1937)
Climbing buckwheat - *Polygonum convolvulus* L. (4, 92, 156, 158, 187) (1818-1986), *Polygonum scandens* L. (19, 82) (1840-1930), *Polygonum scandens* L. var. *dumetorum* (L.) Gleason (46) (1879)
Climbing celastrus - *Celastrus scandens* L. (187) (1818)
Climbing colicweed [Climbing colic weed] - *Adlumia fungosa* (Aiton) Greene ex B. S. P. (19) (1840)
Climbing dayflower - *Commelina diffusa* Burm. f. (50) (present)
Climbing dogbane [Climbing dog's-bane, Climing dogs bane] - *Periploca graeca* L. (158, 178) (1526-1900), *Periploca* L. (158) (1900), *Trachelospermum difforme* (Walt.) Gray (97, 156) (1923-1937), *Periploca graeca* L. (178) (1526)
Climbing false buckwheat - *Polygonum scandens* L. (3, 50, 62, 72, 131, 156) (1899–present), *Polygonum scandens* L. var. *dumetorum* (L.) Gleason (2) (1895), *Polygonum scandens* L. var. *scandens* (5, 50, 93, 97) (1913–present)
Climbing fern [Climbing-fern] - *Lygodium palmatum* (Bernh.) Sw. (5, 19) (1840-1913), *Lygodium* Swartz (2, 50, 108, 138, 161) (1857–present)
Climbing fig - *Ficus pumila* L. (138) (1923)
Climbing fumitory - *Adlumia fungosa* (Aiton) Greene ex B. S. P. (2, 72, 92, 109, 138, 156) (1876-1949), *Adlumia* Raf. ex DC. (1, 138, 156) (1923932)
Climbing groundsel - *Delairea odorata* Lem. (138) (1923)
Climbing hempweed - *Mikania scandens* (L.) Willd. (5, 92, 106, 109, 156) (1876-1949), *Mikania* Willd. (2) (1895)

Climbing ivy - *Toxicodendron radicans* (L.) Kuntze (5) (1913), *Toxicodendron radicans* (L.) Kuntze subsp. *radicans* (157, 158) (1900-1929) Neb SD, *Toxicodendron toxicarium* (Salisb.) Gillis (156) (1923)

Climbing jointfir - *Ephedra altissima* Desf. (138) (1923)

Climbing lily [Climbing-lily] - *Gloriosa* L. (109) (1949)

Climbing mikania - *Mikania scandens* (L.) Willd. (187) (1818)

Climbing milkweed - *Cynanchum laeve* (Michx.) Pers. (4, 80, 82, 106, 156) (1923-1986), *Enemion biternatum* Raf. (145) (1897) KS, *Matelea* Aubl. (4) (1986), *Matelea baldwyniana* (Sweet) Woods. (4) (1986), *Matelea decipiens* (Alex.) Woods. (4) (1986)

Climbing nightshade - *Solanum dulcamara* L. (4, 5, 50, 62, 93, 97, 156, 158) (1900–present)

Climbing orangeroot [Climbing orange root, Climbing orange-root] - *Celastrus scandens* L. (5, 92, 156, 157, 158) (1876-1923)

Climbing philodendron - *Philodendron giganteum* Schott (138) (1923)

Climbing poison ivy - *Toxicodendron radicans* (L.) Kuntze (85, 93) (1932–1936)

Climbing prairie rose - *Rosa setigera* Michx. (3, 113) (1890–1977)

Climbing rose - *Rosa setigera* Michx. (4, 5, 50, 72, 82, 93, 156) (1907–present)

Climbing sailor - *Cymbalaria muralis* P.G. Gaertn., B. Mey. & Scherb. (5, 156) (1913-1923) no longer in use by 1923

Climbing staff-tree - *Celastrus scandens* L. (49, 57, 92) (1876-1917)

Climbing sumac - *Toxicodendron radicans* (L.) Kuntze (5) (1913), *Toxicodendron radicans* (L.) Kuntze subsp. *radicans* (157, 158) (1900-1929)

Climbing sumach - *Toxicodendron radicans* (L.) Kuntze (19, 92) (1840-1876) KS, *Toxicodendron toxicarium* (Salisb.) Gillis (156) (1923)

Climbing thorough-wort - *Mikania scandens* (L.) Willd. (19) (1840)

Climbing trumpet-flower [Climbing trumpet flower] - *Campsis radicans* (L.) Seem. ex Bureau (8) (1785)

Climbing wild rose - *Rosa setigera* Michx. (2) (1895)

Climbing ylang-ylang - *Artabotrys hexapetalus* (L.f.) Bhandari (109) (1949)

Cling-rascal [Cling rascal] - *Galium aparine* L. (5, 156, 158) (1900-1923) no longer in use by 1923

Clinopodium - *Clinopodium* L. (50) (present)

Clintonia - *Clintonia borealis* (Ait.) Raf. (5, 40, 156) (1913-1928)

Clinton's bulrush - *Trichophorum clintonii* (Gray) S.G. Sm. (50) (present)

Clinton's club rush - *Trichophorum clintonii* (Gray) S.G. Sm. (5) (1913)

Clinton's fern - *Dryopteris clintoniana* (D.C. Eaton) Dowell. (5) (1913)

Clinton's lily - *Clintonia borealis* (Ait.) Raf. (5) (1913)

Clinton's woodfern [Clinton woodfern] - *Dryopteris clintoniana* (D.C. Eaton) Dowell. (50, 138) (1923–present)

Clit-bur - *Arctium lappa* L. (158) (1900)

Clive - *Arctium lappa* L. (158) (1900)

Clivers - *Galium aparine* L. (46, 92, 158) (1671-1900), *Galium asprellum* Michx. (156) (1923), *Galium* L. (2) (1895)

Cloak fern [Cloakfern] - *Argyrochosma dealbata* (Pursh) Windham (3, 97) (1937-1977), *Argyrochosma fendleri* (Kunze) Windham (4) (1986), *Notholaena* R. Br. (50, 155) (1942–present)

Cloaked bulrush - *Scirpus pallidus* (Britt.) Fern. (50) (present)

Clock - *Plantago lanceolata* L. (5, 158) (1900), *Taraxacum officinale* G.H. Weber ex Wiggers (64) (1907)

Clockvine [Clock-vine] - *Thunbergia* Retz. (109, 138) (1923-1949)

Cloistered-heart [Cloistered heart] - *Gentiana andrewsii* Griseb. (5, 156, 157) (1913-1923) no longer in use by 1923

Closed bladderwort - *Utricularia purpurea* Walt. (95) (1911), *Utricularia subulata* L. (5) (1913)

Closed blue gentian - *Gentiana andrewsii* Griseb. (5) (1913)

Closed bottle gentian - *Gentiana andrewsii* Griseb. (50) (present)

Closed gentian - *Gentiana andrewsii* Griseb. (3, 63, 72, 86, 93, 109, 127, 131, 138, 156, 157) (1878-1977), *Gentiana clausa* Raf. (7) (1828)

Close-flower dropseed [Close-flowered drop seed] - *Muhlenbergia torreyana* (J.A. Schultes) A.S. Hitchc. (66) (1903)

Close-flower small reed [Close-flowered small reed] - *Calamagrostis stricta* (Timm) Koel. subsp. *inexpansa* (Gray) C.W. Greene (66) (1903)

Close-sheath cotton grass [Close-sheathed cotton grass] - *Eriophorum brachyantherum* Trautv. & C.A. Mey. (5) (1913)

Close-spike sedge [Close-spiked sedge] - *Carex stipata* Muhl. ex Willd. (187) (1818)

Clotbur [Clot-bur, Clotburr, Clote-bur, Clot Burre] - *Arctium lappa* L. (6, 92, 93, 156, 158) (1892–1936), *Xanthium* L. (1, 2, 7, 10, 156, 158) (1818-1923), *Xanthium spinosum* L. (52, 148) (1919-1939), *Xanthium strumarium* L. var. *canadense* (Mill.) Torr. & Gray (5, 150, 156) (1894-1923), *Xanthium strumarium* L. var. *glabratum* (DC.) Cronq. (5, 62) (1912-1913)

Clote - *Arctium* L. (179) (1526)

Clotebur [Clote-bur] - *Arctium lappa* L. (158) (1900), *Xanthium strumarium* L. (178) (1526)

Clothed lip fern - *Cheilanthes lanosa* (Michx.) D.C.Eat. (5, 19) (1840-1913)

Clothier's-brush [Clothier's brush] - *Dipsacus fullonum* L. (5, 156, 158) (1900-1923)

Cloth-of-gold crocus - *Crocus angustifolia* Weston (109, 138) (1923-1949)

Clotweed [Clot-weed, Clott-weed] - *Xanthium spinosum* L. (156) (1923), *Xanthium strumarium* L. (184, 187) (1793-1818)

Cloud grass [Cloudgrass, Cloud-grass] - *Agrostis nebulosa* Boiss. & Reut. (109, 138) (1923-1949)

Cloud sedge - *Carex haydeniana* Olney (139) (1944) CO

Cloudberry [Cloud berry, Cloud-berry, Clowde-berry] - *Rubus allegheniensis* Porter (156) (1923), *Rubus chamaemorus* L. (5, 7, 14, 46, 106, 107, 156) (1671-1930), *Rubus flagellaris* Willd. (92) (1876), *Rubus* L. (1) (1932), *Rubus ostryifolius* Rydb. (5) (1913)

Cloud-berry root [Cloud berry root] - *Rubus flagellaris* Willd. (92) (1876)

Clove currant - *Ribes aureum* Pursh (73, 156, 158) (1892-1923), *Ribes aureum* Pursh var. *villosum* DC. (5, 155) (1913-1942)

Clove garlic - *Allium sativum* L. (92) (1876)

Clove pepper - *Pimenta dioica* (L.) Merr. (92) (1876)

Clove pink - *Dianthus caryophyllus* L. (92, 109, 138) (1876-1949), *Dianthus* L. (7) (1828)

Clove tree [Clovetree] - *Myrcianthes fragrans* (Sw.) McVaugh (138) (1923)

Cloven-lip toadflax - *Linaria bipartita* (Vent.) Willd. (138) (1923)

Clover - *Desmodium canadense* (L.) DC. (158) (1900), *Trifolium* L. (1, 4, 7, 35, 45, 50, 63, 82, 93, 138, 155, 156, 158) (1896–present)

Clover broom - *Baptisia tinctoria* (L.) R. Br. ex Aiton f. (5, 6, 7, 64, 106, 156, 157) (1828-1930)

Clover broom-rape - *Orobanche minor* J.E. Smith (5, 156) (1913-1923)

Clover dodder - *Cuscuta epithymum* (L.) L. (3, 5, 50, 62, 80, 85, 131, 155, 156, 158) (1900–present)

Clove-root - *Geum urbanum* L. (107) (1919)

Clove-strip [Clove strip] - *Ludwigia peploides* (Kunth) Raven (5, 156, 158) (1900–1923), *Ludwigia peploides* (Kunth) Raven subsp. *glabrescens* (Kuntze) Raven (158) (1900)

Clown's all-heal [Claownes All-heale] - *Stachys palustris* L. (5, 178) (1526-1913)

Clown's all-heal of New England [Clowne's all-heal of New England] - *Verbena hastata* L. (46) (1671)

Clown's lungwort [Clown's-lungwort] - *Verbascum thapsus* L. (69, 158) (1900-1904)

Clown's treacle - *Allium sativum* L. (158) (1900)

Clown's woundwort - *Stachys palustris* L. (5, 156) (1913-1923)

Clown's-heal [Clown heal, Clown's heal] - *Stachys palustris* L. (5, 92, 156) (1876-1923)

Club mushroom [Club mushrooms] - *Clavaria* L. (7, 184) (1793-1828)

Club rush [Club-rush] - *Eleocharis tenuis* (Willd.) J.A. Schultes (19) (1840), *Fimbristylis* Vahl. (10) (1818), *Schoenoplectus tabernaemontani* (C.C. Gmel.) Palla (possibly) (158) (1900), *Scirpus* L. (1, 92) (1876-1932)

Club spike moss - *Selaginella selaginoides* (L.) Beauv. ex Mart. & Schrank (50) (present)

Club squash - *Cucurbita pepo* L. (19) (1840)

Club-grass - *Scirpus* L. (184) (1793)

Club-leaf vetch [Clubleaf vetch] - *Vicia americana* Muhl. ex Willd. subsp. *minor* (Hook.) C.R. Gunn (155) (1942)

Clubmoss [Club-moss, Club moss] - *Lycopodiella inundata* (L.) Holub (46) (1879), *Lycopodium clavatum* L. (6, 14, 19, 46, 49, 52, 53, 55, 59, 92) (1840-1922), *Lycopodium* L. (1, 4, 10, 50, 138, 155, 158, 184) (1793–present), *Selaginella densa* Rydb. (146) (1939) MT, *Selaginella selaginoides* (L.) Beauv. ex Mart. & Schrank (46) (1879)

Clubweed [Club-weed] - *Centaurea nigra* L. (156) (1923)

Cluckies - *Aquilegia canadensis* L. (5, 156) (1913-1923) no longer in use by 1923

Clump verbena - *Glandularia canadensis* (L.) Nutt. (109) (1949)

Clump-foot cabbage [Clumpfoot cabbage] - *Symplocarpus foetidus* (L.) Salisb. ex Nutt. (5) (1913)

Clunweed [Clun weed] - *Centaurea nigra* L. (5) (1913)

Cluster cherry - *Prunus padus* L. (92) (1876)

Cluster dodder - *Cuscuta glomerata* Choisy (3) (1977)

Cluster goldenrod - *Solidago glomerata* Michx. (138) (1923)

Cluster hollygrape - *Mahonia pinnata* (Lag.) Fedde (138) (1923)

Cluster mallow [Clustered mallow] - *Malva verticillata* L. (3, 4, 50, 155) (1942–present)

Cluster pine - *Pinus pinaster* Aiton (92, 109, 138) (1923-1949)

Cluster sanicle - *Sanicula odorata* (Raf.) K.M. Pryer & L.R. Phillippe (3) (1977)

Cluster serviceberry - *Amelanchier pumila* (Torr. & Gray) Nutt. ex M. Roemer (155) (1942)

Cluster St. Johns-wort [Cluster St. Johnswort] - *Hypericum densiflorum* Pursh (138) (1923)

Cluster tarweed - *Madia glomerata* Hook. (155) (1942)

Cluster-amaryllis - *Lycoris* Herbert (138) (1923)

Clusterberry [Cluster berries] - *Vaccinium vitis-idaea* L. (possibly) (5) (1913)

Clustered alpine rush - *Juncus castaneus* Smith. (5) (1913)

Clustered alpine saxifrage - *Saxifraga nivalis* L. (5) (1913)

Clustered amaranth - *Amaranthus hybridus* L. (165) (1768)

Clustered aster - *Eurybia divaricata* (L.) Nesom (42) (1814)

Clustered beaked rush - *Rhynchospora glomerata* (L.) Vahl (5) (1913)

Clustered beaksedge - *Rhynchospora glomerata* (L.) Vahl (50) (present)

Clustered bellflower - *Campanula glomerata* L. (5, 156) (1913-1923)

Clustered black cherry - *Prunus virginiana* L. (189) (1767)

Clustered black snakeroot [Clustered blacksnakeroot] - *Sanicula odorata* (Raf.) K.M. Pryer & L.R. Phillippe (50) (present)

Clustered blue morning-glory - *Jacquemontia tamnifolia* (L.) Griseb. (122, 124) (1937)

Clustered bluets - *Oldenlandia uniflora* L. (5, 156) (1913-1923)

Clustered broomrape - *Orobanche fasciculata* Nutt. (50) (present)

Clustered cancer root [Clustered cancer-root] - *Orobanche fasciculata* Nutt. (5, 93, 158) (1900-1936)

Clustered dock - *Rumex conglomeratus* Murr. (5) (1913)

Clustered fescue [Cluster fescue] - *Festuca paradoxa* Desv. (3, 50, 155) (1942–present)

Clustered field sedge [Clustered-field sedge] - *Carex praegracilis* W.

Boott (3, 5, 50) (1913–present)

Clustered love grass [Clustered love-grass] - *Eragrostis secundiflora* J. Presl (5, 99, 119) (1913-1938), *Leptochloa fusca* (L.) Kunth subsp. *fascicularis* (Lam.) N. Snow (99) (1923)

Clustered millet grass - *Patis racemosa* (Sm.) Romasch., P.M. Peterson & R. J. Soreng (19) (1840)

Clustered oreocarya - *Cryptantha celosioides* (Eastw.) Payson (5, 93, 131) (1899–1936)

Clustered poppy mallow - *Callirhoe involucrata* (Torr. & Gray) Gray (156) (1923), *Callirhoe triangulata* (Leavenworth) Gray (5, 72, 97, 122) (1907-1937)

Clustered rush - *Rhynchospora macrostachya* Torr. ex Gray (66) (1903)

Clustered salt grass [Clustered salt-grass] - *Leptochloa fusca* (L.) Kunth subsp. *fascicularis* (Lam.) N. Snow (5, 94) (1901-1913)

Clustered snakeroot [Clustered snake root, Clustered snake-root] - *Sanicula odorata* (Raf.) K.M. Pryer & L.R. Phillippe (5, 72, 93, 97) (1907-1937)

Clustered Solomon's-seal [Clustered Solomon's seal, Clustered Solomon seal] - *Maianthemum racemosum* (L.) Link subsp. *racemosum* (92, 156) (1876-1923)

Clustered spear grass - *Puccinellia distans* (Jacq.) Parl. (66) (1903)

Cluster-flower amaranth [Cluster-flowered amaranth] - *Amaranthus hybridus* (187) (1818)

Cluster-flower beard grass [Cluster-flowered beard grass] - *Andropogon glomeratus* (Walt.) B.S.P. (66, 187) (1818-1903)

Cluster-flower convallary [Cluster-flowered convallary] - *Maianthemum racemosum* (L.) Link subsp. *racemosum* (187) (1818)

Cluster-flower loose-strife [Cluster-flowered loose-strife] - *Lysimachia terrestris* (L.) Britton, Sterns & Poggenb. (possibly) (187) (1818)

Cluster-flower snowberry [Cluster-flowered snowberry] - *Chiococca alba* (L.) A.S. Hitchc. (49) (1898)

Cluster-flower Solomon's-seal [Cluster flowered Solomon's seal] - *Maianthemum racemosum* (L.) Link subsp. *racemosum* (42) (1814)

Cluster-flower vaccinium [Cluster-flowered vaccinium] - *Vaccinium corymbosum* L. (8) (1785)

Cluster-head rush - *Scirpus polyphyllus* Vahl (66) (1903)

Clustering muhlenbergia - *Muhlenbergia glomerata* (Willd.) Trin. (66, 90) (1885-1903)

Clustering slender grass - *Leptochloa fusca* (L.) Kunth subsp. *fascicularis* (Lam.) N. Snow (66) (1903)

Cluster-leaf oak [Cluster-leaved oak] - *Quercus hypoleucoides* A.Camus (possibly) (20) (1857)

Cluster-like Solomon's-Seal of America [Cluster like Salomons Seale of America] - *Uvularia sessilifolia* L. (181) (~1678)

Cluster-spike amorpha [Clusterspike amorpha] - *Amorpha herbacea* Walt. (155) (1942)

Cluster-spike muhlenbergia [Cluster-spiked muhlenbergia] - *Muhlenbergia glomerata* (Willd.) Trin. (90) (1885)

Cluster-spike sedge [Cluster-spiked sedge] - *Carex tenuiflora* Wahl. (66) (1903)

Clute's panicum - *Dichanthelium dichotomum* (L.) Gould var. *dichotomum* (5) (1913)

Cluverwort - *Aquilegia vulgaris* L. (5, 156) (1913-1923)

Clyver [Clyuer] - *Arctium* L. (179) (1526)

Clyvers [Clyuers] - *Galium aparine* L. (179) (1526)

Cnidoscolus - *Cnidoscolus* J. Pohl (50) (present)

Cniquier (French) - *Caesalpinia* L. (8) (1785)

Cniquier dioïque (French) - *Gymnocladus dioicus* (L.) K. Koch (8) (1785)

Coach-whip [Coach whip] - *Fouquieria splendens* Engelm. (15) (1895)

Coach-whip cactus [Coach whip cactus] - *Fouquieria splendens* Engelm. (153) (1913)

Coakum [Coacum] - *Phytolacca americana* L. (5) (1913), *Phytolacca americana* L. var. *americana* (7, 49, 64, 69, 92, 156, 158, 186) (1814-1923)

Coan - *Brassica oleracea* L. (107) (1919)

Co-ap'-e (Chemehuevi Shoshone) - *Nicotiana* L. (132) (1855)

Coarse armillaria - *Armillaria ventricosa* (Peck) Peck (155) (1942)

Coarse cyperus - *Cyperus odoratus* L. (5) (1913)

Coast amaranth - *Amaranthus pumilus* Raf. (5) (1913)

Coast azalea - *Rhododendron atlanticum* (Ashe) Rehd. (138) (1923)

Coast bedstraw - *Galium circaezans* Michx. var. *circaezans* (5) (1913)

Coast blistercress - *Erysimum capitatum* (Dougl. ex Hook.) Greene (138) (1923)

Coast blite - *Chenopodium rubrum* L. (1, 156) (1923-1932)

Coast cinquefoil - *Potentilla pensylvanica* L. var. *litoralis* (Rydb.) Boivin (5) (1913)

Coast cockspur grass - *Echinochloa walteri* (Pursh) Nash (50) (present)

Coast cyperus - *Cyperus polystachyos* Rottb. var. *texensis* (Torr.) Fern. (5) (1913)

Coast erysimum - *Erysimum capitatum* (Dougl. ex Hook.) Greene (155) (1942)

Coast fiddleneck - *Amsinckia spectabilis* Fisch. & C.A. Mey. (155) (1942)

Coast germander - *Teucrium cubense* Jacq. (124) (1937) TX

Coast goldenweed - *Isocoma menziesii* (Hook. & Arn.) Nesom var. *vernonioides* (Nutt.) Nesom (155) (1942)

Coast hedge nettle - *Stachys hyssopifolia* Michx. (5) (1913), *Stachys pilosa* Nutt. var. *pilosa* (5) (1913)

Coast iris - *Iris missouriensis* Nutt. (138, 155) (1923-1942)

Coast jointweed [Coast joint weed, Coast joint-weed] - *Polygonella articulata* (L.) Meisn. (5, 50, 122, 124, 156) (1913–present)

Coast juniper - *Juniperus barbadensis* var. *australis* (Endl.) ined. (122) (1937)

Coast knotgrass - *Polygonum maritimum* L. (5) (1913)

Coast lily - *Lilium maritimum* Kellogg (138) (1923)

Coast rhododendron - *Rhododendron macrophyllum* D. Don ex G. Don (138) (1923)

Coast sabbatia - *Sabatia calycina* (Lam.) Heller (5, 122) (1913-1937)

Coast sandbur - *Cenchrus spinifex* Cav. (122) (1937)

Coast sedge - *Carex exilis* Dewey (5) (1913)

Coast vincetoxicum - *Matelea gonocarpos* (Walt.) Shinners (5) (1913)

Coast violet - *Viola brittoniana* Pollard (5) (1913)

Coast wheat grass - *Thinopyrum pycnanthum* (Godr.) Barkworth (5) (1913)

Coastal blue-eyed grass - *Sisyrinchium fuscatum* Bickn. (50) (present)

Coastal false asphodel - *Tofieldia racemosa* (Walt.) Britton, Sterns & Poggenb. (50) (present)

Coastal plain willow - *Salix caroliniana* Michx. (50) (present)

Coastal sandbur - *Cenchrus spinifex* Cav. (50) (present)

Coastal sand-verbena [Coastal sand verbena] - *Abronia latifolia* Eschsch. (50) (present)

Coastal sedge - *Carex exilis* Dewey (50) (present)

Coat-flower - *Petrorhagia saxifraga* (L.) Link (109) (1949)

Cob cactus - *Echinocereus reichenbachii* (Terscheck ex Walp.) Haage f. (109) (1949)

Cobaea beardtongue [Cobaea beard-tongue] - *Penstemon cobaea* Nutt. (5, 50, 93, 97) (1913–present)

Cobaea penstemon - *Penstemon cobaea* Nutt. (3, 4, 122, 138, 155) (1923-1986)

Cobnut [Cob nut] - *Corylus avellana* L. (107) (1919)

Cocash - *Erigeron philadelphicus* L. (7) (1828), *Symphyotrichum puniceum* (L.) A.& D. Löve var. *puniceum* (5, 49, 156, 158) (1898-1923) no longer in use by 1923

Cocash root - *Symphyotrichum puniceum* (L.) A.& D. Löve var. *puniceum* (92) (1876)

Cocash weed [Cocash-weed] - *Packera aurea* (L.) A.& D. Löve (92, 156, 158) (1898-1923)

Cochineal cactus - *Opuntia cochenillifera* (L.) Mill. (109, 138) (1923-1949)

Cochineal fig - *Opuntia cochenillifera* (L.) Mill. (92) (1876)

Cochineal nopalaea - *Opuntia cochenillifera* (L.) Mill. (155) (1942)

Cock grass - *Bromus secalinus* L. (5) (1913)

Cock sorrel - *Rumex acetosa* L. (5, 156) (1913-1923)

Cockeno - *Papaver rhoeas* L. (158) (1900)

Cockhead [Cock head] - *Stachys palustris* L. (5) (1913)

Cockiloorie - *Bellis perennis* L. (158) (1900) archiac

Cockle [Cockel, Cockles, Cokyll] - *Agrostemma githago* L. (6) (1892), *Agrostemma* L. (190) (~1759), *Lychnis* L. (15) (1895), *Utricularia subulata* L. (5) (1913), *Vaccaria hispanica* (Mill.) Rauschert (5, 76, 156, 157, 158) (1896-1923), *Agrostemma githago* L. (6, 19, 71, 148, 165, 179, 184, 187) (1768-1939), *Bidens frondosa* L. (156) (1923)

Cocklebur [Cockle bur, Cockle-bur, Cockle-burr, Cockle burr, Cockleburr] - *Agrimonia eupatoria* L. (7, 49, 52, 53, 58, 92, 107, 156) (1828-1923), *Agrimonia gryposepala* Wallr. (5) (1913), *Arctium lappa* L. (5, 156, 158) (1900–1923), *Xanthium* L. (1, 2, 4, 50, 93, 125, 155, 158) (1895–present), *Xanthium spinosum* L. (5, 52, 156, 158) (1900-1923), *Xanthium strumarium* L. (3, 4, 57, 58, 145, 187) (1818-1986), *Xanthium strumarium* L. var. *canadense* (Mill.) Torr. & Gray (5, 21, 63, 80, 85, 95, 97, 106, 145, 148, 150) (1893-1939), *Xanthium strumarium* L. var. *glabratum* (DC.) Cronq. (1, 2, 7, 156, 158) (1828-1923)

Cockle-button [Cockle button] - *Arctium lappa* L. (5, 64, 69, 156) (1903–1923)

Cockle-corn [Cockle corn] - *Agrostemma githago* L. (92) (1876)

Cockly-bur - *Arctium lappa* L. (158) (1900)

Cockmint [Cock mint] - *Balsamita major* Desf. (92, 158) (1876-1900)

Cockoo flower - *Cardamine pratensis* L. (5, 107, 156) (1913-1923)

Cockoo spit - *Cardamine pratensis* L. (5) (1913)

Cocks - *Plantago lanceolata* L. (5, 156, 158) (1900–1923)

Cockscomb [Cock's comb, Cocks-comb, Cock's-comb] - *Amaranthus hybridus* L. (156) (1923), *Amaranthus tricolor* L. (58) (1869), *Celosia argentea* L. (184) (1793), *Celosia cristata* L. (19, 92, 109) (1840-1949), *Celosia* L. (138) (1923), *Cynosurus echinatus* L. (92) (1876), *Erythrina crista-galli* L. (92) (1876), *Onobrychis viciifolia* Scop. (158) (1900)

Cockscomb-yam - *Rajania cordata* L. (138) (1923)

Cock's-eggs [Cocks-eggs] - *Salpichroa origanifolia* (Lam.) Baill. (109, 138) (1923-1949)

Cock's-foot [Cocksfoot, Cocks-foot, Cock's foot, Cock-foot] - *Aquilegia vulgaris* L. (5, 156) (1913-1923) no longer in use by 1923, *Chelidonium majus* L. (158) (1900), *Dactylis glomerata* L. (5, 45, 46, 68, 109, 143) (1896-1949), *Dactylis* L. (66, 155) (1903-1942), *Echinochloa crus-galli* (L.) Beauv. (151) (1896)

Cock's-foot grass [Cocksfoot grass, Cocks' foot grass, Cock's-foot-grass, Cock's foot-grass] - *Dactylis glomerata* L. (19, 87, 90, 92, 119, 184) (1793-1938), *Echinochloa crus-galli* (L.) Beauv. (92) (1876)

Cocks'-foot panicum - *Echinochloa crus-galli* (L.) Beauv. (187) (1818)

Cock's-head [Cock's head] - *Astragalus agrestis* Dougl. ex G. Don (5, 131, 156) (1899-1923)

Cock's-head plant - *Onobrychis viciifolia* Scop. (158) (1900)

Cockspur - *Echinochloa* Beauv. (155) (1942)

Cockspur coral-tree - *Erythrina crista-galli* L. (109) (1949)

Cockspur grass [Cockspur-grass] - *Cenchrus echinatus* L. (187) (1818), *Echinochloa* Beauv. (50) (present), *Echinochloa crus-galli* (L.) Beauv. (5, 62, 99, 119) (1912-1938)

Cockspur hawthorn [Cock-spur hawthorn, Cockspur-hawthorn] - *Crataegus crus-galli* L. (3, 4, 50, 63, 155, 187) (1818–present), *Crataegus pedicellata* Sarg. (181) (~1678)

Cockspur rye - *Sclerotium clavus* DC. (92) (1876)

Cockspur thorn [Cock-spur thorn] - *Crataegus crus-galli* L. (2, 5, 19, 41, 72, 97, 109, 132, 137, 138, 156, 158) (1770-1949)

Cock-up-hat [Cockup-hat] - *Stillingia sylvatica* Garden ex L. (6, 7, 92, 158) (1828-1900)

Cocoa - *Theobroma cacao* L. (107) (1919)

Cocoa plum [Coco-plum, Coco plum] - *Chrysobalanus icaco* L. (92, 106, 107, 138) (1876-1930), *Chrysobalanus* L. (10) (1818)

Cocoanut palm [Cocoa-nut palm] - *Cocos nucifera* L. (106, 110) (1886-1930)

Coco-grass [Coco grass] - *Cyperus rotundus* L. (2, 5, 156) (1895-1923)

Coconut [Cocoanuts] - *Cocos* L. (109) (1949), *Saxifraga mertensiana* Bong. (74) (1893) Southern CA, bulbs

Cocowort - *Capsella bursa-pastoris* (L.) Medik. (92, 157, 158) (1876-1929)

Cocum - *Phytolacca americana* L. (77) (1898) Sulphur Grove OH, *Phytolacca americana* L. var. *americana* (6, 71, 186) (1814-1892) Northern tribes

Cocushaw - *Xanthosoma sagittifolium* (L.) Schott (46) (1879)

Codagam - *Centella asiatica* (L.) Urban (174) (1753)

Codded loose-strife of Virginia - *Oenothera biennis* L. (181) (~1678)

Codded willow herbe [Codded Willow-herbe] - *Epilobium hirsutum* L. (178, 180) (1526-1633)

Cod-head [Cod head] - *Chelone glabra* L. (5, 156) (1913-1923) no longer in use by 1923

Codlins-and-cream - *Epilobium hirsutum* L. (5, 92, 156) (1876-1923)

Codogno (Italian) - *Cydonia oblonga* Mill. (110) (1886)

Coe bell - *Silene vulgaris* (Moench) Garcke (5) (1913)

Coe plant - *Rhododendron maximum* L. (5) (1913)

Coe-grass [Coe grass] - *Juncus bufonius* L. (5, 156) (1913-1923)

Coenuillier a Grandes Fleurs (French) - *Cornus florida* L. (6) (1892)

Coffee - *Coffea arabica* L. (110) (1886), *Coffea* L. (138) (1923)

Coffee bean - *Glycine soja* Sieb. & Zucc. (107) (1919)

Coffee bean tree - *Gymnocladus dioicus* (L.) K. Koch (10, 12) (1818-1820)

Coffee corn - *Sorghum bicolor* (L.) Moench subsp. *bicolor* (19, 92) (1840–1876)

Coffee leaf [Coffee-leaf] - *Pyrola americana* Sweet (156) (1923)

Coffee nut [Coffee-nuts, Coffee-nut] or Coffee nut tree - *Gymnocladus dioicus* (L.) K. Koch (5, 35, 44, 156, 157, 158) (1806-1929)

Coffee pea - *Cicer arietinum* L. (92) (1876)

Coffee plant [Coffee-plant] - *Oenothera biennis* L. (5, 74, 156) (1893–1923) Eastern states, used to make beverage in harvest fields

Coffee senna - *Senna occidentalis* (L.) Link (5, 97, 122, 124) (1913-1937)

Coffee tree [Coffee-tree, Coffeetree] - *Gymnocladus dioicus* (L.) K. Koch (7, 8, 18, 20, 27, 38, 49, 82, 112, 125, 156) (1785-1937), *Gymnocladus* Lam. (50, 155) (1942–present)

Coffee weed [Coffee-weed] - *Cichorium intybus* L. (5, 106, 158) (1900–1930), *Senna occidentalis* (L.) Link (5, 156) (1913-1923), *Senna tora* (L.) Roxb. (5, 156) (1913-1923)

Coffee-berry [Coffee berry] - *Frangula californica* (Eschsch.) Gray (106, 109) (1930-1949)

Coffe-weed - *Rumex crispus* L. (156) (1923)

Coffin plant [Coffin-plant] - *Anaphalis margaritacea* (L.) Benth. & Hook (187) (1818)

Cohiba (Haiti) - *Nicotiana tabacum* L. (6, 7) (1828-1932)

Cohoche bleu (French) - *Caulophyllum thalictroides* (L.) Michx. (6, 7) (1828-1932)

Cohosh [Co-hosh] - *Actaea* L. (63, 109, 158) (1899–1949), *Actaea rubra* (Aiton) Willd. (187) (1818), *Caulophyllum* Michx. (50) (present), *Caulophyllum thalictroides* (L.) Michx. (7, 29, 187) (1818-1869), *Cimicifuga racemosa* (L.) Nutt. (possibly) (19) (1840)

Cohosh bugbane - *Cimicifuga racemosa* (L.) Nutt. (138) (1923)

Cohosh meadow rue - *Thalictrum coriaceum* (Britt.) Small (5) (1913)

Cohurden (French, gourd) - *Cucurbita pepo* L. (107) (1536)

Cohush - *Actaea pachypoda* Ell. (79) (1891), *Caulophyllum thalictroides* (L.) Michx. (7) (1828)

Coirce, cuirce, or corca (Irish) - *Avena sativa* L. (110) (1886)

Cokan (Virginian tribes) - *Phytolacca americana* L. var. *americana* (6) (1892)

Cokyll - *Lolium temulentum* L. (178, 179) (1526-1596), *Nigella sativa* L. (179) (1526)

Col (Irish) - *Brassica oleracea* L. (107) (1919)

Cola - *Cola acuminata* (P. Beauv.) Schott & Endl. (57, 107) (1917-1919)

Colanut [Cola nut] - *Cola acuminata* (P. Beauv.) Schott & Endl. (107, 109) (1919-1949)

Colchicum - *Colchicum autumnale* L. (52, 54, 57, 59, 60, 92) (1876-1919)

Colchis ivy - *Hedera colchica* (K. Koch) K. Koch (109, 138) (1923-1949)

Cold-water root [Cold water root] - *Symphyotrichum puniceum* (L.) A.& D. Löve var. *puniceum* (92) (1876)

Cole [Coles] - *Brassica* L. (109) (1949), *Brassica napus* L. (7, 19) (1828-1840)

Cole-florey [Cole-Florie] - *Brassica oleracea* L. (180) (1633)

Coleosanthus - *Brickellia* Ell. (158) (1900)

Coleseed [Cole seed, Cole-seed] - *Brassica rapa* L. var. *rapa* (5, 92, 158) (1876-1913)

Coleus - *Coleus* Lour. (138) (1923)

Colewort [Cole wort, Colewoorts] - *Brassica oleracea* L. (92, 180) (1633-1876)

Coley-flowers [Coley flowers] - *Brassica oleracea* L. (178) (1526)

Coliander - *Coriandrum sativum* L. (92) (1876)

Colic root [Colic-root, Colicroot] - *Aletris farinosa* L. (5, 6, 14, 55, 57, 64, 92, 156) (1871-1917), *Aletris* L. (1, 109) (1932-1949), *Apocynum androsaemifolium* L. (156, 157, 158) (1900-1929), *Asarum canadense* L. (5, 75, 158) (1900-1913) WV, *Asclepias tuberosa* L. (6, 19) (1840-1892), *Chamaelirium luteum* (L.) A. Gray (6) (1892), *Dioscorea villosa* L. (5, 6, 49, 53, 57, 58, 64, 75, 92, 93, 156, 158) (1892-1936), *Liatris spicata* (L.) Willd. (52, 156) (1919-1923), *Liatris spicata* (L.) Willd. var. *spicata* (5) (1913), *Liatris squarrosa* (L.) Michx. (156) (1923), *Liatris squarrosa* (L.) Michx. var. *squarrosa* (131, 157) (1899-1929)

Colic weed [Colic-weed, Colicweed] - *Corydalis flavula* (Raf.) DC. (5, 156, 158) (1900-1923), *Dicentra* Bernh. (possibly) (7) (1828), *Dicentra canadensis* (Goldie) Walp. (5, 156, 157) (1913-1929), *Dicentra cucullaria* (L.) Bernh. (5, 19, 92, 156, 158) (1840-1923)

Colicwort - *Aphanes arvensis* L. (5) (1913)

Colima - *Zanthoxylum clava-herculis* L. (158) (1900), *Zanthoxylum fagara* (L.) Sargent (106, 122, 124) (1930-1937)

Coliseum - *Cymbalaria muralis* P.G. Gaertn., B. Mey. & Scherb. (156) (1923)

Coliseum ivy - *Cymbalaria muralis* P.G. Gaertn., B. Mey. & Scherb. (5) (1913)

Colla - *Cola acuminata* (P. Beauv.) Schott & Endl. (107) (1919)

Collar earthstar - *Geastrum triplex* Jungh. (128) (1933) ND

Collard [Collards] - *Brassica* L. (107) (1919), *Symplocarpus foetidus* (L.) Salisb. ex Nutt. (5, 64, 156) (1908-1923), *Symplocarpus* Salisb. ex Nutt. (92) (1876)

College-flower [Collegeflower] - *Hymenopappus flavescens* Gray (50) (present)

Collieflore - *Brassica oleracea* L. (180) (1633)

Collins' rock cress [Collin's rockcress] - *Arabis holboellii* Hornem. var. *collinsii* (Fern.) Rollins (5, 50) (1913–present)

Collins' sedge [Collins sedge] - *Carex collinsii* Nutt. (5, 50) (1913–present)

Collinsia - *Collinsia* Nutt. (138, 155, 158) (1923-1942), *Collinsia verna* Nutt. (19, 92) (1840-1876), *Collinsia violacea* Nutt. (3, 4) (1977-1986)

Collinsia (Official name of Materia Medica) - *Collinsonia canadensis* L. (7, 52, 54, 57, 64) (1828-1919)

Collinsian gentian - *Gentiana saponaria* L. (7) (1828)

Collinsone du Canada (French) - *Collinsonia canadensis* L. (7) (1828)

Collinson's flower - *Collinsonia canadensis* L. (5, 86) (1878-1913)

Collmarkraut - *Anagallis arvensis* L. (158) (1900)

Collomia - *Collomia linearis* Nutt. (157) (1929), *Collomia* Nutt. (4, 158) (1900-1986)

Colloquintide [Colloquintida] - *Citrullus colocynthis* (L.) Schrad. (179) (1526)

Colocasia - *Colocasia esculenta* (L.) Schott (110) (1886) colocasia of Diosorides is actually nelumbo according to Alfonse DeCandolle, *Nelumbo lutea* Willd. (183) (~1756)

Colocynth - *Citrullus colocynthis* (L.) Schrad. (50, 52, 57, 92, 107) (1876–present)

Colocynth-apple [Colocynth apple] - *Citrullus colocynthis* (L.) Schrad. (92) (1876)

Colocynthis - *Citrullus colocynthis* (L.) Schrad. (54) (1905)

Cologne-plant - *Balsamita major* Desf. (156) (1923)

Colombo (Official name of Materia Medica) - *Frasera caroliniensis* Walt. (possibly) (7) (1828)

Colombo root - *Frasera caroliniensis* Walt. (possibly) (7) (1828)

Colombo Wurzel (German) - *Frasera caroliniensis* Walt. (possibly) (7) (1828)

Colonial bent - *Muhlenbergia tenuiflora* (Willd.) Britton, Sterns & Poggenb. (109) (1949)

Colonial bent grass [Colonial bent-grass, Colonial bentgrass] - *Agrostis capillaris* L. (50, 143) (1936–present)

Colophony - *Pinus palustris* Mill. (92) (1876) source

Colorado barberry - *Berberis fendleri* Gray (138) (1923)

Colorado beardtongue - *Penstemon auriberbis* Pennell (50) (present) NM

Colorado beeblossom - *Gaura neomexicana* Woot. subsp. *coloradensis* (Rydb.) Raven & Gregory (50) (present)

Colorado blue grass - *Elymus repens* (L.) Gould (5) (1913), *Thinopyrum intermedium* (Host) Barkworth & D.R. Dewey (75) (1894)

Colorado blue spruce - *Picea pungens* Engelm. (135, 136, 153) (1910-1930)

Colorado bluestem [Colorado blue-stem, Colorado blue stem] - *Pascopyrum smithii* (Rydb.) A. Löve (56, 68, 152) (1901-1913), *Pseudoroegneria spicata* (Pursh) A. Löve subsp. *spicata* (94) (1901), *Thinopyrum intermedium* (Host) Barkworth & D.R. Dewey (144) (1899)

Colorado bottom grass - *Urochloa texana* (Buckl.) R. Webster (118) (1898) TX

Colorado bulrush - *Eleocharis parvula* (Roem. & Schult.) Link ex Bluff, Nees & Schauer (139) (1944)

Colorado columbine - *Aquilegia caerulea* James. (138, 155) (1923-1942)

Colorado desert aster - *Ximenia* Plum. (155) (1942), *Xylorhiza cognata* (Hall) T.J. Wats. (155) (1942)

Colorado fir - *Abies concolor* (Gord. & Glend.) Lindl. ex Hildebr. (possibly) (109) (1949)

Colorado grass [Colorado-grass] - *Urochloa texana* (Buckl.) R. Webster (56, 109, 119, 163) (1852-1949)

Colorado greenthread - *Thelesperma ambiguum* Gray (50, 155) (1942–present)

Colorado gumweed - *Grindelia inornata* Greene (50) (present)

Colorado hemp - *Sesbania herbacea* (P. Mill.) McVaugh (158) (1900)

Colorado juniper - *Juniperus scopulorum* Sarg. (112, 136, 138) (1923-1937)

Colorado loco-vetch [Colorado loco vetch] - *Oxytropis lambertii* Pursh (86, 156) (1878-1923)

Colorado locoweed [Colorado loco weed] - *Oxytropis lambertii* Pursh (5, 71) (1898-1913)

Colorado man root - *Ipomoea leptophylla* Torr. (86) (1878)

Colorado mountain sage - *Artemisia frigida* Willd. (157) (1929)

Colorado pinyon pine - *Pinus flexilis* James (155) (1942)

Colorado red cedar - *Juniperus scopulorum* Sarg. (112) (1937) Neb

Colorado rubber plant - *Hymenoxys* Cass. (1) (1932), *Hymenoxys richardsonii* (Hook.) Cockerell var. *floribunda* (Gray) Parker (3, 4, 148) (1939-1986), *Hymenoxys richardsonii* (Hook.) Cockll. (3, 4) (1977-1986)

Colorado sand grass - *Andropogon hallii* Hack. (56, 94, 111) (1901-1915)

Colorado spruce - *Picea pungens* Engelm. (109, 112, 136, 138) (1923-1949)

Colorado wild rye [Colorado wildrye] - *Leymus ambiguus* (Vasey & Scribn.) D.R. Dewey (140) (1944)

Coloured calamagrostis - *Phalaris arundinacea* L. (187) (1818)

Coloured reed-grass - *Phalaris arundinacea* L. (187) (1818)

Coloured willow herb - *Epilobium coloratum* Biehler (42) (1814)

Colsa - *Brassica rapa* L. var. *rapa* (107) (1919)

Colsat - *Brassica rapa* L. var. *rapa* (107) (1919)

Colt herb [Colt-herb] - *Tussilago farfara* L. (5, 156) (1913-1923)

Colton's loco [Colton loco] - *Astragalus coltonii* M.E. Jones (155) (1942)

Coltsfoot [Colt's foot, Colt's-foot, Colt foot] - *Arnoglossum plantagineum* Raf. (124) (1937) TX, *Asarum canadense* L. (7, 49, 58, 64, 75, 77, 177, 186, 190) (~1759-1908), *Caltha palustris* L. (5, 76) (1896–1913) ME, *Nemophila aphylla* (L.) Brummitt (5, 75, 156) (1894-1923), *Petasites sagittatus* (Pursh) Gray (possibly) (35) (1806) Meriwether Lewis, *Tussilago farfara* L. (5, 14, 19, 49, 53, 55, 57, 58, 92, 156) (1840-1923), *Tussilago* L. (1, 10, 138, 167) (1814-1932)

Coltsfoot snakeroot [Coltsfoot snakeroot, Colt's-foot snakeroot, Colt's-foot-snakeroot] - *Asarum canadense* L. (79, 92, 156, 158) (1876-1923) NH

Coltsroot - *Caltha palustris* L. (76) (1896) Sulphur Grove OH

Colt's-tail [Colt's tail, Coltstail] - *Conyza canadensis* (L.) Cronq. var. *canadensis* (5, 6, 19, 49, 53, 58, 69, 92, 156, 157, 158) (1840-1929)

Colubrina - *Polygonum amphibium* L. (46) (1879)

Columbia - *Frasera caroliniensis* Walt. (possibly) (7, 186) (1814-1828)

Columbia kino - *Coccoloba uvifera* (L.) L. (92) (1876)

Columbia lily - *Lilium columbianum* Leichtlin (138) (1923)

Columbia monkshood - *Aconitum columbianum* Nutt. (155) (1942)

Columbia needle grass [Columbia needlegrass] - *Achnatherum lemmonii* (Vasey) Barkworth (122, 185) (1936-1937), *Achnatherum occidentale* (Thurb. ex S. Watson) Barkworth (3) (1977)

Columbia wolffia - *Wolffia columbiana* Karst. (5, 72, 97, 120) (1907-1938)

Columbian monkshood - *Aconitum columbianum* Nutt. (50, 155) (1942–present)

Columbian watermeal - *Wolffia columbiana* Karst. (50) (present)

Columbine [Collombines, Colombines] - *Aquilegia canadensis* L. (82, 124, 127, 157) (1900-1930), *Aquilegia formosa* Fisch. ex DC. (35) (1806), *Aquilegia* L. (1, 2, 4, 10, 13, 15, 50, 82, 93, 138, 155, 156, 158, 167, 184) (1793–present), *Aquilegia vulgaris* L. (46, 92, 114, 178) (1526-1894)

Columbine meadowrue - *Thalictrum aquilegifolium* L. (138) (1923)

Columbo - *Frasera caroliniensis* Walt. (156, 186) (1814-1923), *Frasera speciosa* Dougl. ex Griseb. (106) (1930)

Columbo-root - *Frasera caroliniensis* Walt. (186) (1814)

Columbus grass - *Sorghum almum* Parodi (50) (present)

Colza - *Brassica napus* L. (109) (1949), *Brassica rapa* L. var. *rapa* (92, 107, 158) (1876-1919)

Coma (Mexican) - *Sideroxylon lycioides* L. (5, 106, 156) (1913-1930)

Comanche cactus - *Opuntia phaeacantha* Engelm. var. *camanchica* (Engelm. & Bigelow) L. Benson (5) (1913)

Comandra - *Comandra* Nutt. (155) (1942)

Comarona (Spanish) - *Sphaeralcea emoryi* Torr. ex Gray (76) (1896) CA

Comb - *Echinacea angustifolia* DC. (76) (1896) Burnside SD, *Echinacea angustifolia* DC. var. *angustifolia* (156) (1923)

Comb (Dakota) - *Echinacea pallida* (Nutt.) Nutt. (158) (1900)

Comb flower [Comb-flower] - *Echinacea purpurea* (L.) Moench (156) (1923), *Helianthus annuus* L. (5, 92, 156, 157, 148) (1876-1939)

Comb fringe grass - *Dactyloctenium radulans* (R. Br.) Beauv. (possibly) (92) (1876)

Comb grass - *Eragrostis pectinacea* (Michx.) Nees ex Steud. (111) (1915)

Comb plant - *Echinacea angustifolia* DC. (37) (1919)

Comb-leaf evening primrose [Combleaf evening primrose] - *Oenothera coronopifolia* Torr. & Gray (3, 4) (1977-1986)

Combs' paspalum [Combs paspalum] - *Paspalum almum* Chase (122, 163) (1852-1937)

Comfrey - *Symphytum* L. (1, 109, 138, 155, 156, 158) (1900-1949), *Symphytum officinale* L. (5, 19, 46, 49, 52, 53, 57, 58, 64, 92, 107) (1649-1922)

Comfrey with the white flowers [Compherie with the white flower] - *Symphytum officinale* L. (46) (1671) accidentally introduced by 1671

Commass - *Camassia quamash* (Pursh) Greene (35) (1806)

Commo apple - *Malus sylvestris* Mill. (63) (1899)

Common adder's-tongue [Common adderstongue] - *Erythronium americanum* Ker. (157) (1929), *Ophioglossum vulgatum* L. (138, 155, 187) (1818-1942)

Common adonis - *Adonis annua* L. (165) (1768)

Common agrimony - *Agrimonia eupatoria* L. (2, 7, 155, 165) (1768-1942)

Common alder - *Alnus incana* (L.) Moench subsp. *rugosa* (DuRoi) Clausen (5, 156, 158) (1900–1923), *Alnus rubra* Bong. (8, 92) (1785-1876), *Alnus serrulata* (Aiton) Willd. (3, 20, 49, 53, 187) (1818-1977)

Common allamanda - *Allamanda cathartica* L. (138, 155) (1931-1942)

Common alumroot [Common alum root, Common alum-root] - *Heuchera americana* L. (2, 5, 156, 158) (1895–1923)

Common American agave - *Agave americana* L. (165) (1768)

Common American alder - *Alnus serrulata* (Aiton) Willd. (42) (1814)

Common American berberry - *Berberis canadensis* P. Mill. (42) (1814)

Common American chestnut - *Castanea sativa* Mill. (42) (1814)

Common American dodder - *Cuscuta gronovii* Willd. ex J.A. Schultes (86) (1878)

Common American hemp - *Cannabis sativa* L. (92) (1876)

Common American nettle tree - *Celtis occidentalis* L. (42) (1814)

Common American white oak - *Quercus alba* L. (8) (1785)

Common Andrew's cross - *Hypericum crux-andreae* (L.) Crantz (42) (1814)

Common angelica - *Angelica atropurpurea* L. (6) (1892)

Common apple or Common apple tree - *Malus sylvestris* Mill. (1, 49, 63, 137) (1898-1932)

Common apricot - *Prunus armeniaca* L. (109, 137) (1931-1949)

Common arborvitae - *Thuja occidentalis* L. (135) (1910)

Common arrowhead - *Sagittaria latifolia* Willd. (3, 138, 155, 157) (1923-1977)

Common artichoke - *Cynara* L. (10) (1818), *Helianthus tuberosus* L. (47) (1852)

Common asparagus - *Asparagus officinalis* L. (42, 109) (1814-1949)

Common autumn-crocus - *Colchicum autumnale* L. (138) (1923)

Common baldcypress - *Taxodium distichum* (L.) L.C. Rich. (138) (1923)

Common balloonvine [Common balloon vine] - *Cardiospermum halicacabum* L. (4) (1986)

Common balm [Common balme] - *Melissa officinalis* L. (3, 75, 138, 178) (1526-1977)

Common banana - *Musa ×paradisiaca* L. [*acuminata × balbisiana*] (138) (1923)

Common baneberry [Common bane berry] - *Actaea spicata* L. (42) (1814)

Common barberry - *Berberis vulgaris* L. (6, 50, 53, 72, 82, 109, 112, 157) (1900–present)

Common barley - *Hordeum vulgare* L. (50, 110, 119, 180) (1633–present)

Common basil - *Ocimum basilicum* L. (138) (1923)

Common beak rush - *Rhynchospora glomerata* (L.) Vahl (66) (1903)

Common bean - *Phaseolus vulgaris* L. (107, 138) (1919-1923)

Common bear grass [Common beargrass] - *Sclerochloa dura* (L.) Beauv. (50) (present), *Xerophyllum tenax* (Pursh) Nutt. (50) (present), *Yucca filamentosa* L. (2) (1895)

Common beech - *Fagus grandifolia* Ehrh. (46) (1649)

Common beech fern - *Phegopteris connectilis* (Michx.) Watt (5) (1913)

Common beet - *Beta vulgaris* L. (138) (1923)

Common beggarticks [Common beggar's ticks, Common beggar-ticks] - *Bidens frondosa* L. (2, 49, 62, 158) (1895–1912)

Common betony - *Stachys nuttallii* Shuttlw. ex Benth. (138) (1923), *Stachys officinalis* (L.) Trev. (138) (1923)

Common bindweed [Common bind weed] - *Calystegia sepium* (L.) R. Br. subsp. *sepium* (56) (1901)

Common birch - *Betula pubescens* Ehrh. (41) (1770)

Common bishop's-cap [Common bishopscap] - *Mitella diphylla* L. (138) (1923)

Common black currant - *Ribes americanum* Mill. (22, 47) (1852-1893)

Common black raspberry - *Rubus occidentalis* L. (135) (1910)

Common blackberry - *Rubus allegheniensis* Porter (4) (1986), *Rubus flagellaris* Willd. (63, 96, 103) (1870-1899), *Rubus ostryifolius* Rydb. (135) (1910)

Common blackberry bush [Common blackberry-bush] - *Rubus flagellaris* Willd. (186, 187) (1814-1818)

Common blackcap - *Rubus occidentalis* L. (138) (1923)

Common bladder fern - *Cystopteris fragilis* (L.) Bernh. (3) (1977)

Common bladder-senna - *Colutea arborescens* L. (138) (1923)

Common bladderwort - *Utricularia macrorhiza* Le Conte (4, 50, 156, 158) (1900–present)

Common blazing star - *Liatris squarrosa* (L.) Michx. (2) (1895)

Common bloodroot - *Sanguinaria canadensis* L. (7) (1828)

Common blue aster - *Symphyotrichum cordifolium* (L.) Nesom (93) (1936)

Common blue flag - *Iris versicolor* L. (156) (1923), *Iris virginica* L. (187) (1818)

Common blue mould - *Penicillium glaucum* Link (56) (1901)

Common blue squill - *Hyacinthoides nonscripta* (L.) Chouard ex Rothm. (138) (1923)

Common blue violet - *Viola cucullata* Aiton (19, 86, 156) (1840-1923), *Viola nephrophylla* Greene (5, 72, 82, 97) (1907-1937), *Viola palmata* L. (2) (1895)

Common blue wood aster - *Symphyotrichum cordifolium* (L.) Nesom (5, 50, 72, 82, 97, 156) (1907–present)

Common bluecurls [Common blue-curls, Common blue curls] - *Trichostema dichotomum* L. (2) (1895)

Common blue-eyed-grass [Common blue eyed grass] - *Sisyrinchium angustifolium* Mill. (72, 138, 155, 157) (1923-1942)

Common bluets - *Hedyotis nigricans* (Lam.) Fosberg var. *nigricans* (155) (1942)

Common bogbean - *Menyanthes trifoliata* L. (138, 155) (1923-1942)

Common boneset - *Eupatorium perfoliatum* L. (50) (present)

Common borage - *Borago officinalis* L. (50, 82, 138) (1923–present)

Common bottle gourd - *Lagenaria siceraria* (Molina) Standl. (92) (1876)

Common box - *Buxus sempervirens* L. (109) (1949)

Common bracken - *Pteridium aquilinum* (L.) Kuhn var. *latiusculum* (Desv.) Underwood ex Heller (3) (1977)

Common brake - *Pteridium aquilinum* (L.) Kuhn (2, 14, 97, 187) (1818-1937)

Common brome grass [Common bromegrass] - *Bromus inermis* Leyss. (138) (1923)

Common broom - *Cytisus scoparius* (L.) Link (59) (1911)

Common broom grass [Common broom-grass] - *Andropogon virginicus* L. (187) (1818)

Common buckthorn - *Rhamnus cathartica* L. (3, 4, 50, 55, 106, 109, 138, 155, 156) (1923–present)

Common buckwheat - *Fagopyrum esculentum* Moench (109, 138, 155) (1923-1949)

Common bugle - *Ajuga reptans* L. (50, 92, 165) (1768–present)

Common bugloss - *Anchusa officinalis* L. (138, 155) (1931-1942), *Borago officinalis* L. (92) (1876), *Echium vulgare* L. (42) (1814)

Common bulbous crow-foot - *Ranunculus bulbosus* L. (187) (1818)

Common bulrush - *Schoenoplectus tabernaemontani* (C.C. Gmel.) Palla (possibly) (1, 14, 40, 139) (1882-1944), *Scirpus atrovirens* Willd. (156) (1923)

Common bunch flower - *Melanthium virginicum* L (80) (1913)

Common bur - *Cirsium vulgare* (Savi) Ten. (5) (1913)

Common bur clover - *Medicago polymorpha* L. (124) (1937)

Common bur thistle - *Cirsium vulgare* (Savi) Ten. (93, 95) (1911-1936)

Common burdock - *Arctium lappa* L. (6, 42) (1814-1892), *Arctium minus* Bernh. (3, 4, 5, 62, 72, 82, 93, 95, 97, 109, 131, 157, 158) (1899-1986)

Common bur-marigold - *Bidens frondosa* L. (5, 156, 158) (1900–1923)

Common burnet - *Sanguisorba minor* Scop. subsp. *muricata* (Spach) Nordborg (157, 158) (1900-1929)

Common bur-reed - *Sparganium eurycarpum* Engelm. ex Gray (72) (1907)

Common buttercup - *Ranunculus abortivus* L. (85) (1932), *Ranunculus acris* L. (156) (1923), *Ranunculus hispidus* Michx. var. *nitidus* (Chapman) T. Duncan (82) (1930)

Common butterwort - *Pinguicula vulgaris* L. (5) (1913)

Common buttonbush - *Cephalanthus occidentalis* L. (4, 50, 138, 155) (1923–present)

Common cabbage - *Brassica oleracea* L. (19, 110) (1840-1886)

Common calamus aromaticus - *Acorus calamus* L. (165) (1768)

Common California poppy [Common California-poppy] - *Eschscholzia californica* Cham. (138) (1923)

Common calla - *Zantedeschia aethiopica* (L.) Spreng. (138) (1923)

Common camass - *Camassia scilloides* (Raf.) Cory (107) (1919)

Common camomile [Common chamomile] - *Chamaemelum nobile* (L.) All. (10, 138, 165) (1807-1923)

Common canary grass - *Phalaris canariensis* L. (66) (1903)

Common candy tuft - *Iberis umbellata* L. (92) (1876)

Common carrot - *Daucus carota* L. (138) (1923)

Common cashew - *Anacardium occidentale* L. (155) (1942)

Common castor-bean - *Ricinus communis* L. (138) (1923)

Common catalpa - *Catalpa bignonioides* Walt. (2, 109, 138) (1895-1949)

Common cat-tail [Common cattail] - *Typha latifolia* L. (3, 35, 109, 138, 155, 156, 157, 158) (1806-1977)

Common celandine - *Chelidonium majus* L. (6, 42) (1814-1892)

Common centaury - *Centaurium erythraea* Raf. (possibly) (14) (1882)

Common centorie - *Centaurium erythraea* Raf. (possibly) (180) (1633)

Common century plant - *Agave americana* L. (2) (1895)

Common cerastium - *Cerastium arvense* L. subsp. *strictum* (L.) Ugborogho (155) (1942)

Common chain fern [Common chain-fern] - *Woodwardia virginica* (L.) Sm. (86) (1878)

Common chaste tree - *Vitex agnus-castus* L. (4) (1986)

Common cherry-laurel - *Prunus laurocerasus* L. (109) (1949)

Common chess - *Bromus secalinus* L. (56) (1901)

Common chestnut - *Castanea sativa* Mill. (10) (1818)

Common chickweed - *Stellaria media* (L.) Vill. (3, 4, 50, 15, 156, 187) (1818–present), *Stellaria media* (L.) Vill. subsp. *media* (5, 62, 72, 93, 97, 157, 158, 165) (1768-1937)

Common chicory - *Cichorium intybus* L. (3, 156) (1923-1977)

Common chokeberry - *Photinia pyrifolia* (Lam.) Robertson & Phipps (2) (1895)

Common chokecherry - *Prunus virginiana* L. (112, 137, 138, 155) (1923-1942)

Common chrysanthemum - Chrysanthemum ×morifolium Ramat. (possibly) (138) (1923)

Common cinquefoil - *Potentilla canadensis* L. (5, 62, 138) (1912-1923), *Potentilla simplex* Michx. (50) (present)

Common clammy weed - *Polanisia dodecandra* (L.) DC. subsp. *dodecandra* (7) (1828)

Common clary - *Salvia sclarea* L. (138) (1923)

Common cleavers - *Galium aparine* L. (187) (1818), *Galium verum* L. (7) (1828)

Common clover - *Trifolium pratense* L. (45) (1896)

Common club moss - *Lycopodium clavatum* L. (6) (1892)

Common cocklebur [Common cockle-bur] - *Xanthium strumarium* L. (158) (1900), *Xanthium strumarium* L. var. *canadense* (Mill.) Torr. & Gray (93, 95, 156) (1911-1936), *Xanthium strumarium* L. var. *glabratum* (DC.) Cronq. (62) (1912)

Common cockscomb - *Celosia cristata* L. (138) (1923)

Common coffee - *Coffea arabica* L. (109) (1949)

Common coleus - *Coleus scutellarioides* (L.) Benth. (138) (1923)

Common coltsfoot - *Tussilago farfara* L. (138) (1923)

Common columbine - *Aquilegia canadensis* L. (122) (1937)

Common comandra - *Comandra umbellata* (L.) Nutt. (155) (1942)

Common comfrey - *Symphytum officinale* L. (109, 138, 156) (1923-1949)

Common corncockle - *Agrostemma githago* L. (50, 155) (1942-present)

Common cornflower - *Centaurea cyanus* L. (106) (1930)

Common cosmos - *Cosmos bipinnatus* Cav. (138) (1923)

Common cottonwood - *Populus deltoides* Bartr. ex Marsh. (112) (1937), *Populus deltoides* Bartr. ex Marsh. subsp. *monilifera* (Aiton) Eckenwalder (130) (1895)

Common couch grass - *Elymus repens* (L.) Gould (45) (1896)

Common cowparsnip [Common cow-parsnip] - *Heracleum maximum* Bartr. (50, 138, 155) (1923–present)

Common cowpea - *Vigna sinensis* (L.) Endl. (109) (1949)

Common crab grass - *Digitaria sanguinalis* (L.) Scop. (66) (1903)

Common cranberry - *Vaccinium macrocarpon* Aiton (7) (1828)

Common crane's-bill - *Geranium maculatum* L. (186, 187) (1814-1818)

Common crapemyrtle - *Lagerstroemia indica* L. (138) (1923)

Common creeper - *Parthenocissus quinquefolia* (L.) Planch. (187) (1818)

Common crocus - *Crocus angustifolia* Weston (138) (1923)

Common crupina - *Crupina vulgaris* Cass. (50) (present)

Common cryptomeria - *Cryptomeria japonica* (L. f.) D. Don (138) (1923)

Common cupfern - *Dennstaedtia cicutaria* (Sw.) T. Moore (138) (1923)

Common currant - *Ribes rubrum* L. (109) (1949)

Common custard-apple - *Annona reticulata* L. (109) (1949)

Common daffodil - *Narcissus pseudonarcissus* L. (138) (1923)

Common dahlia - *Dahlia pinnata* Cav. (82, 109) (1930-1949)

Common daisy-fleabane - *Erigeron strigosus* Muhl. ex Willd. var. *strigosus* (158) (1900)

Common dandelion - *Taraxacum officinale* G.H. Weber ex Wiggers (4, 7, 50, 63, 80, 82, 95, 109, 127, 155, 156) (1828–present), *Taraxacum officinale* G.H. Weber ex Wiggers subsp. *officinale* (50, 55) (–present)

Common darnel - *Lolium perenne* L. (68, 90, 143) (1890-1936)

Common dayflower [Common day-flower] - *Commelina communis* L. (155) (1942), *Commelina virginica* L. (86) (1878)

Common deerberry - *Vaccinium stamineum* L. (155) (1942)

Common devil's-claws [Common devilsclaws] - *Proboscidea louisianica* (P. Mill.) Thellung (155) (1942)

Common dill - *Anethum graveolens* L. (165) (1807)

Common dittany - *Cunila origanoides* (L.) Britton (50) (present)

Common dock - *Rumex* ×*acutus* L. [*crispus* × *obtusifolius*] (187) (1818), *Rumex obtusifolius* L. (64, 69, 157, 158) (1900-1907)

Common dodder - *Cuscuta gronovii* Willd. ex J. A. Schultes (47, 62, 156) (1852-1912, 1923)

Common dog-fennel [Common dog fennel] - *Anthemis cotula* L. (62) (1912)

Common dog-mustard [Common dogmustard] - *Erucastrum gallicum* (Willd.) O. E. Schulz (50) (present)

Common dog's-bane - *Apocynum androsaemifolium* L. (187) (1818)

Common dogwood [Common dog-wood, Common dog wood] - *Cornus florida* L. (7, 42) (1814-1828), *Cornus sanguinea* L. (19) (1840)

Common dooryard plantain - *Plantago major* L. (62) (1912)

Common dracena - *Cordyline fruticosa* (L.) Chev. (138) (1923)

Common dragon - *Dracunculus vulgaris* Schott (138) (1923)

Common duckmeat - *Spirodela polyrhiza* (L.) Schleid. (50) (present)

Common duckweed - *Lemna minor* L. (50, 155) (1942–present)

Common Dutchman's-pipe [Common Dutchmanspipe] - *Aristolochia macrophylla* Lam. (155) (1942)

Common dwarf Juneberry [Common dwarf June berry] - *Amelanchier canadensis* (L.) Medik. (135) (1910)

Common dwarf lupine - *Lupinus nanus* Douglas ex Benth. (138) (1923)

Common dwarf-dandelion [Common dwarf dandelion] - *Krigia caespitosa* (Raf.) Chambers (3) (1977)

Common eggplant - *Solanum melongena* L. (138) (1923)

Common elder - *Sambucus nigra* L. (55, 158) (1900-1911), *Sambucus nigra* L. subsp. *canadensis* (L.) R. Bolli (2, 5, 38, 47, 63, 82, 92, 106, 156, 157) (1852-1930)

Common elderberry - *Sambucus nigra* L. subsp. *canadensis* (L.) R. Bolli (4, 50) (1986–present)

Common ellisia - *Ellisia nyctelea* (L.) L. (80) (1913)

Common elm - *Ulmus americana* L. (157, 158) (1919), *Ulmus glabra* Huds. (55) (1911)

Common enchanter's-nightshade [Common enchanter's nightshade] - *Circaea lutetiana* L. (158) (1900)

Common English barley - *Hordeum vulgare* L. (158) (1900)

Common English cherry [Common English cherrie] - *Prunus cerasus* L. (178) (1526)

Common European alder - *Alnus glutinosa* (L.) Gaertn. (20) (1857)

Common European ash - *Fraxinus excelsior* L. (20) (1857)

Common European barberry - *Berberis vulgaris* L. (158) (1900)

Common European elm - *Ulmus glabra* Huds. (20) (1857)

Common European oak - *Quercus robur* L. (20) (1857)

Common European walnut - *Juglans regia* L. (20) (1857)

Common European white birch - *Betula pubescens* Ehrh. (20) (1857)

Common European willow - *Salix alba* L. (93, 158) (1900-1936)

Common evening-primrose [Common evening primrose, Common eveningprimrose] - *Oenothera biennis* L. (2, 3, 4, 5, 6, 50, 62, 72, 93, 97, 109, 127, 138, 155, 156, 157, 158) (1892–present), *Oenothera villosa* Thunb. (4) (1986), *Oenothera villosa* Thunb. subsp. *strigosa* (Rydb.) W. Dietr. & P.H. Raven (3) (1977), *Oenothera villosa* Thunb. subsp. *strigosa* (Rydb.) W. Dietr. & P.H. Raven (95) (1911)

Common everlasting - *Antennaria dioica* (L.) Gaertn. (156) (1923), *Pseudognaphalium obtusifolium* (L.) Hilliard & Burtt subsp. *obtusifolium* (62, 156, 157) (1900-1929)

Common fennel - *Foeniculum vulgare* Mill. (92, 138, 155, 165) (1807-1942)

Common fennel flower - *Nigella damascena* L. (2) (1895)

Common feverfew - *Tanacetum parthenium* (L.) Schultz-Bip. (5, 156) (1913-1923)

Common fiddleneck - *Amsinckia menziesii* (Lehm.) A. Nels. & J.F. Macbr. (50) (present)

Common field daisy - *Leucanthemum vulgare* Lam. (158) (1900)

Common field sorrel - *Rumex acetosella* L. (41) (1770)

Common field strawberry - *Fragaria virginiana* Duchesne (157, 158) (1900-1929)

Common field thistle - *Cirsium vulgare* (Savi) Ten. (72) (1907)

Common fig - *Ficus carica* L. (109, 138) (1923-1949)

Common filbert - *Corylus avellana* L. (109) (1949)

Common fir - *Picea abies* (L.) H. Karst. (92) (1876)

Common five-finger - *Potentilla canadensis* L. (19) (1840)

Common flax - *Linum usitatissimum* L. (3, 4, 50, 82, 155, 156) (1923–present)

Common fleabane - *Erigeron annuus* (L.) Pers. (156) (1923), *Erigeron philadelphicus* L. (63) (1899)

Common floating pondweed - *Potamogeton natans* L. (5, 72, 93, 158) (1900-1936)

Common fool's-parsley - *Aethusa cynapium* L. (165) (1768)

Common four-o'-clock - *Mirabilis jalapa* L. (138) (1923)

Common foxglove - *Digitalis pupurea* L. (109, 138) (1923-1949)

Common foxtail grass - *Alopecurus pratensis* L. (90) (1885)

Common freesia - *Freesia corymbosa* (Burm. f.) N.E. Br. (138) (1923)

Common fringe tree - *Chionanthus virginicus* L. (20) (1857)

Common gaillardia - *Gaillardia aristata* Pursh (50) (present)

Common garden columbine - *Aquilegia vulgaris* L. (2) (1895)

Common garden petunia - *Petunia ×atkinsiana* D. Don ex Loud. [*axillaris × integrifolia*] (109) (1949)

Common garden poppy - *Papaver somniferum* L. (148) (1939)

Common garden radish - *Raphanus sativus* L. (92) (1876)

Common garden sage - *Salvia officinalis* L. (106) (1930)

Common garden verbena - *Glandularia ×hybrida* (Grönland & Rümpler) Nesom & Pruski [*peruviana × phlogiflora* or *platensis*] (109) (1949)

Common garlic - *Allium sativum* L. (50, 165) (1768–present)

Common gaura - *Gaura biennis* L. (156) (1923)

Common ginger - *Zingiber officinale* Roscoe (109, 138) (1923-1949)

Common ginger-lily [Common gingerlily] - *Hedychium coronarium* Koenig (138) (1923)

Common globe-amaranth - *Gomphrena globosa* L. (138) (1923)

Common globeflower - *Trollius europaeus* L. (138) (1923)

Common globe-hyacinth [Common globe hyacinth] - *Muscari botryoides* (L.) Mills (158) (1900)

Common globethistle - *Echinops sphaerocephalus* L. (138) (1923)

Common goatbeard - *Aruncus dioicus* (Walt.) Fern. var. *vulgaris* (Maxim.) Hara (138) (1923)

Common goat's-rue [Common goatsrue] - *Galega officinalis* L. (138, 155) (1923-1942)

Common goldenrod [Common golden rod] - *Solidago canadensis* L. var. *scabra* Torr. & Gray (58) (1869), *Solidago* L. (92) (1876), *Solidago virgaurea* L. (41) (1770)

Common goldstar - *Hypoxis hirsuta* (L.) Cov. (50) (present)

Common goldstar-grass [Common goldstargrass] - *Hypoxis hirsuta* (L.) Cov. (155) (1942)

Common goldthread - *Coptis trifolia* (L.) Salisb. (7) (1828)

Common gorse - *Ulex europaeus* L. (138) (1923)

Common grama - *Bouteloua gracilis* (Willd. ex Kunth) Lag. ex Griffiths (5) (1913)

Common grape fern [Common grapefern] - *Botrychium dissectum* Spreng. (155) (1942)

Common grape-hyacinth [Common grape hyacinth, Common grapehyacinth] - *Muscari botryoides* (L.) Mills (50, 138, 155) (1923–present)

Common great plantain [Common great-plantane] - *Plantago major* L. (187) (1818)

Common green barberry - *Berberis vulgaris* L. (135) (1910)

Common greenbrier [Common green brier, Common green-briar] - *Smilax rotundifolia* L. (2, 130) (1895)

Common gromwell - *Lithospermum officinale* L. (49, 156) (1898-1923)

Common ground ivy - *Glechoma hederacea* L. (93) (1936)

Common groundcherry [Common ground-cherry, Common ground cherry] - *Physalis longifolia* Nutt. (4) (1986), *Physalis pubescens* L. (138) (1923)

Common groundsel - *Senecio vulgaris* L. (3, 5, 122, 131, 155, 156, 158, 187) (1818-1977)

Common gypsophila - *Gypsophila elegans* Bieb. (138, 155) (1923-1942)

Common gypsyweed - *Veronica officinalis* L. (50) (present)

Common hackberry - *Celtis occidentalis* L. (50, 155) (1942–present)

Common hair grass - *Deschampsia flexuosa* (L.) Trin. (90) (1885), *Deschampsia flexuosa* (L.) Trin. var *flexuosa* (66) (1903)

Common hairy rockcress - *Arabis hirsuta* (L.) Scop. var. *pycnocarpa* (M. Hopkins) Rollins (155) (1942)

Common harebell - *Campanula rotundifolia* L. (2) (1895)

Common haricot - *Phaseolus vulgaris* L. (possibly) (110) (1886)

Common hawkbit - *Leontodon autumnalis* L. (5) (1913), *Leontodon hispidus* L. subsp. *hispidus* (5) (1913)

Common healall - *Prunella vulgaris* L. (47) (1852)

Common heath grass [Common heathgrass] - *Danthonia decumbens* (L.) DC. (50) (present)

Common hedge nettle - *Stachys palustris* L. (62) (1912)

Common heliotrope - *Heliotropium arborescens* L. (82, 109, 138) (1923-1949)

Common hemicarpha - *Lipocarpha micrantha* (Vahl) G. Tucker (3, 5) (1913-1977)

Common hemlock - *Conium maculatum* L. (7, 42) (1814-1828) IA, *Tsuga canadensis* (L.) Carr. (109) (1949)

Common hemp - *Cannabis sativa* L. (7, 138, 157, 158) (1828-1929)

Common hemp nettle - *Galeopsis bifida* Boenn. (4) (1986)

Common heronbill - *Erodium moschatum* (L.) L'Hér. ex Aiton (138) (1923)

Common hickory - *Carya alba* (L.) Nutt. ex Ell. (20, 43, 177, 187) (1762-1857)

Common holly - *Ilex opaca* Aiton (106) (1930)

Common hollyhock - *Alcea rosea* L. (165) (1768)

Common honey-locust [Common honeylocust] - *Gleditsia triacanthos* L. (138, 155) (1923-1942)

Common honeysuckle - *Lonicera caprifolium* L. (156) (1923)

Common hop [Common hops] - *Humulus lupulus* L. (3, 4, 6, 7, 38, 47, 50, 93, 106, 108, 138, 155, 156, 187) (1818–present)

Common hoptree - *Ptelea trifoliata* L. (50, 137, 138, 155) (1923–present)

Common horehound [Common hoarhound] - *Marrubium vulgare* L. (3, 4, 5, 82, 93, 97, 109, 138, 155, 157, 158) (1913-1986)

Common hornbeam - *Carpinus betulus* L. (14) (1882)

Common horsebalm [Common horse balm] - *Collinsonia canadensis* L. (42) (1814)

Common horsechestnut [Common horse-chestnut, Common horse chestnut] - *Aesculus hippocastanum* L. (6, 71, 82, 109, 155, 165) (1768-1942)

Common horse-gentian [Common horsegentian] - *Triosteum perfoliatum* L. (138, 155) (1923-1942)

Common horsetail - *Equisetum arvense* L. (80) (1913)

Common hound's-tongue [Common houndstongue, Common hound's tongue] - *Cynoglossum officinale* L. (42, 138, 155, 156) (1814-1923), *Cynoglossum virginianum* L. (187) (1818)

Common houseleek - *Sempervivum tectorum* L. (109) (1949)

Common houstonia - *Houstonia caerulea* L. (2) (1895)

Common huckleberry - *Gaylussacia baccata* (Wang.) K. Koch (2) (1895), *Vaccinium pallidum* Aiton (47) (1852)

Common husk-tomato [Common husk tomato] - *Physalis pubescens* L. (2) (1895)

Common hyacinth - *Hyacinthus orientalis* L. (109, 138) (1923-1949)

Common Indian fig - *Opuntia ficus-indica* (L.) Mill. (42) (1814), *Opuntia* Mill. (10) (1818)

Common Indian hemp - *Apocynum cannabinum* L. (2) (1895)

Common Indian physic - *Gillenia trifoliata* (L.) Moench (2) (1895)

Common Indian pipe - *Monotropa uniflora* L. (2) (1895)

Common Indian turnip - *Arisaema triphyllum* (L.) Schott (2, 5) (1895-1913)

Common ironweed - *Vernonia baldwinii* Torr. (124) (1937), *Vernonia fasciculata* Michx. (80) (1913), *Vernonia noveboracensis* (L.) Michx. (2, 138) (1895-1923)

Common ivy - *Hedera helix* L. (49) (1898)

Common jack-in-the-pulpit [Common jackinthepulpit] - *Arisaema triphyllum* (L.) Schott subsp. *triphyllum* (155) (1942)

Common jointfir - *Ephedra distachya* L. (138) (1923)

Common jujube - *Ziziphus zizyphus* (L.) Karst. (109, 110, 138) (1886-1949)

Common juniper - *Juniperus communis* L. (2, 4, 7, 10, 20, 41, 50, 85, 109, 130, 136, 138, 155) (1770–present)

Common kale - *Brassica oleracea* L. (109) (1949)

Common knot-grass - *Polygonum aviculare* L. (187) (1818)

Common knotweed - *Polygonum arenastrum* Jord. ex Boreau (3) (1977), *Polygonum aviculare* L. (2, 7) (1828-1932)

Common lady fern [Common ladyfern] - *Athyrium filix-femina* (L.) Roth (50) (present)

Common lady's-mantle [Common ladysmantle, Common ladies mantle] - *Alchemilla monticola* Opiz (155, 165) (1768-1942)

Common lady's-slipper [Common ladies' slipper] - *Cypripedium parviflorum* Salisb. (19) (1840)

Common lamb's-quarter [Common lamb's quarter] - *Chenopodium album* L. (42) (1814)

Common lantana - *Lantana camara* L. (138) (1923)

Common larch - *Larix decidua* Mill. (19) (1840)

Common larkspur - *Consolida ajacis* (L.) Schur (158) (1900)

Common laurel - *Kalmia latifolia* L. (177) (1762)

Common leek - *Allium porrum* L. (165) (1768)

Common lespedeza - *Kummerowia striata* (Thunb.) Schindl. (4, 155) (1942-1986)

Common lettuce - *Lactuca sativa* L. (92) (1876)

Common licorice - *Glycyrrhiza glabra* L. (138, 178) (1526-1923)

Common lilac - *Syringa vulgaris* L. (82, 109, 112, 138, 156) (1923-1949)

Common lily-of-the-valley [Common lily of the valley] - *Convallaria majalis* L. (42) (1814)

Common linden - *Tilia ×vulgaris* Hayne [*cordata* × *platyphyllos*] (138) (1923)

Common liverwort - *Hepatica nobilis* Schreb. (7) (1828)

Common lizardtail - *Saururus cernuus* L. (138, 155) (1923-1942)

Common lobelia - *Lobelia inflata* L. (7) (1828)

Common locust or Common locust tree - *Robinia pseudoacacia* L. (2, 6, 82, 138, 157, 158) (1892-1929)

Common lousewort [Common louse-wort] - *Pedicularis canadensis* L. (4, 63, 72, 187) (1818-1986)

Common lovage [Common Louage] - *Levisticum officinale* W.D.J. Koch (178) (1526)

Common lungwort - *Pulmonaria officinalis* L. (138) (1923)

Common lupines - *Lupinus albus* L. (178) (1526)

Common maidenhair - *Adiantum capillus-veneris* L. (50) (present)

Common mallow - *Malva neglecta* Wallr. (3, 4, 50) (1977–present), *Malva rotundifolia* L. (3, 4, 5, 15, 80, 145, 156, 157, 158) (1895-1986), *Malva sylvestris* L. (92, 158) (1876-1900)

Common manna grass - *Glyceria fluitans* (L.) R. Br. (66, 90) (1885-1903) **Common manzanita** - *Arctostaphylos manzanita* Parry (104, 106, 155) (1896-1942)

Common maple - *Acer campestre* L. (165) (1768)

Common mare's-tail - *Hippuris vulgaris* L. (50) (present)

Common marjoram - *Origanum vulgare* L. (92, 187) (1818-1876)

Common marshmallow - *Althaea officinalis* L. (50, 165) (1768-present)

Common marsh-marigold [Common marshmarigold, Common marsh marygold] - *Caltha palustris* L. (42, 155) (1814-1942)

Common matrimony-vine - *Lycium barbarum* L. (138) (1923)

Common maul - *Malva rotundifolia* L. (158) (1900)

Common maws - *Malva rotundifolia* L. (158) (1900)

Common mayapple - *Podophyllum peltatum* L. (138, 155) (1923-1942)

Common mayweed - *Anthemis cotula* L. (38) (1820)

Common meadow grass [Common Medow Grasse] - *Poa pratensis* L. (5, 68, 90, 178, 180) (1596-1913)

Common meadow-beauty [Common meadowbeauty] - *Rhexia virginica* L. (122, 138) (1923-1937)

Common meadowsweet - *Spiraea salicifolia* L. (possibly) (2, 63) (1895-1899)

Common melon tree - *Carica papaya* L. (20) (1857)

Common mignonette - *Reseda odorata* L. (109, 138) (1923-1949)

Common milfoil [Common millfoil] - *Achillea millefolium* L. (41, 63, 165) (1768-1899)

Common milk tare [Common milke tare] - *Astragalus glycyphyllos* L. (178) (1526)

Common milkweed [Common milk weed] - *Asclepias speciosa* Torr. (148) (1939), *Asclepias syriaca* L. (2, 4, 3, 5, 6, 19, 40, 50, 59, 53, 57, 62, 63, 64, 72, 80, 82, 85, 93, 95, 109, 114, 127, 131, 138, 155, 156, 157, 158) (1892–present), *Polygala incarnata* L. (92) (1876)

Common millet - *Panicum miliaceum* L. (7, 66, 68, 110) (1828-1913), *Setaria italica* (L.) Beauv. (32, 45, 56, 119, 140) (1895-1944)

Common mint - *Mentha spicata* L. (5, 62, 156) (1912-1923)

Common miterwort - *Mitella diphylla* L. (2) (1895)

Common mock orange - *Philadelphus coronarius* L. (135) (1910)

Common monkey-flower [Common monkeyflower] - *Mimulus guttatus* DC. (155) (1942)

Common monkshood [Common monk's-hood] - *Aconitum napellus* L. (165) (1768)

Common montbretia - *Crocosmia* ×*crocosmiiflora* (V. Lemoine) N.E. Br. [aurea × pottsii] (109) (1949)

Common moonseed - *Menispermum canadense* L. (50, 109 138, 155) (1923–present)

Common moonwort - *Botrychium lunaria* (L.) Sw. (50) (present)

Common morning-glory [Common morning glory, Common morningglory] - *Ipomoea purpurea* (L.) Roth (3, 4, 19, 92, 93, 109, 138, 145, 155, 156) (1840-1986)

Common motherwort - *Leonurus cardiaca* L. (3, 50, 82, 138, 155) (1923–present)

Common mouse-ear chickweed [Common mouse ear chickweed] - *Cerastium fontanum* Baumg. (50) (present), *Cerastium fontanum* Baumg. subsp. *vulgare* (Hartman) Greuter & Burdet (4, 15, 156) (1895-1986)

Common mugwort - *Artemisia vulgaris* L. (5, 95, 156, 157) (1911-1929)

Common mullein - *Verbascum thapsus* L. (3, 4, 6, 45, 50, 63, 109, 145, 156, 158) (1892–present)

Common mushroom - *Agaricus campestris* L. (128, 165) (1768-1933)

Common mushroom agaricus - *Agaricus campestris* L. (155) (1942)

Common mustard - *Brassica nigra* (L.) W.D.J. Koch (19) (1840), *Moricandia arvensis* (L.) DC. (82) (1930)

Common nard - *Nardus stricta* L. (92) (1876)

Common nasturtium - *Tropaeolum majus* L. (138) (1923)

Common navew - *Brassica rapa* L. var. *rapa* (158) (1900)

Common nettle - *Urtica dioica* L. (14, 19, 61, 92, 157, 158, 187) (1818-1929)

Common New Jersey tea tree - *Ceanothus americanus* L. (42) (1814)

Common nightshade [Common night shade, Common night-shade] - *Circaea lutetiana* L. (42) (1814), *Solanum nigrum* L. (2, 71, 80, 85, 92, 95, 107, 156, 157, 158) (1895-1937)

Common ninebark - *Physocarpus opulifolius* (L.) Maxim. (50, 109 138, 155) (1923–present)

Common nipplewort - *Lapsana communis* L. (50, 155) (1942–present)

Common nutmeg - *Myristica fragrans* Houtt. (138) (1923)

Common oats [Common oat, Common Otes] - *Avena sativa* L. (7, 45, 49, 50, 53, 56, 66, 110, 140, 155, 158, 180) (1633–present)

Common occident frogbit [Common occident-frogbit] - *Limnobium spongia* (Bosc) L.C. Rich. ex Steud. (155) (1942)

Common oleander - *Nerium oleander* L. (138) (1923)

Common olive - *Olea europaea* L. (138) (1923)

Common onion - *Allium cepa* L. (165) (1768)

Common orange day-lily - *Hemerocallis fulva* (L.) L. (109) (1949)

Common osier - *Salix viminalis* L. (5, 138, 156) (1913-1923)

Common palmetto - *Sabal palmetto* (Walt.) Lodd. ex J.A. & J.H. Schultes (109) (1949)

Common pampas grass [Common pampasgrass] - *Cortaderia selloana* (J.A. & J.H. Schultes) Aschers. & Graebn. (138) (1923)

Common pansy - *Viola tricolor* L. (138) (1923)

Common papaw [Common pawpaw] - *Asimina triloba* (L.) Dunal (2, 63, 82, 155, 156) (1895-1942)

Common paper-mulberry [Common papermulberry] - *Broussonetia papyrifera* (L.) L'Hér. ex Vent. (155) (1942)

Common parsley - *Petroselinum crispum* (P. Mill.) Nyman ex A.W. Hill (5, 7, 49, 92, 93, 156, 158) (1828-1936)

Common parsnip - *Pastinaca sativa* L. (45) (1896)

Common pea - *Pisum sativum* L. (92, 138) (1876-1923)

Common pear - *Pyrus communis* L. (82, 137, 138) (1923–1931)

Common pearlbush - *Exochorda racemosa* (Lindl.) Rehd. (138) (1923)

Common pearl-everlasting [Common pearleverlasting] - *Anaphalis margaritacea* (L.) Benth. & Hook (155) (1942)

Common Pennsylvania black oak [Common Pennsylvanian black oak] - *Quercus nigra* L. (8) (1785)

Common penstemon - *Penstemon campanulatus* (Cav.) Willd. (138) (1923)

Common peony - *Paeonia officinalis* L. (92, 138) (1876-1923)

Common pepperweed - *Lepidium densiflorum* Schrad. (50) (present)

Common perennial gaillardia - *Gaillardia aristata* Pursh (138, 155) (1923-1942)

Common perilla - *Perilla frutescens* (L.) Britton (3, 4, 155) (1942-1986)

Common periwinkle - *Vinca minor* L. (3, 50, 109, 138, 155) (1923–present)

Common persicary - *Persicaria maculosa* Gray (5) (1913)

Common persimmon - *Diospyros virginiana* L. (2, 50, 109, 138, 155, 158) (1900–present)

Common petunia - *Petunia* ×*atkinsiana* D. Don ex Loud. [axillaris × integrifolia] (138) (1923)

Common pickerel weed - *Pontederia cordata* L. (2) (1895)

Common pigweed - *Amaranthus retroflexus* L. (93, 150, 157, 158) (1894-1936)

Common pimpernel - *Anagallis arvensis* L. (42, 165) (1807-1814), *Anagallis minima* (L.) Krause (3) (1977)

Common pipsissewa - *Chimaphila umbellata* (L.) Bart. (138, 155) (1923-1942)

Common pitcherplant [Common pitcherplant] - *Sarracenia purpurea* L. (109, 138) (1923-1949)

Common plantain - *Plantago major* L. (3, 4, 5, 43, 45, 47, 50, 63, 72, 80, 85, 93, 92, 97, 131, 145, 156, 157, 158) (1820–present)

Common plum - *Prunus domestica* L. (109, 110, 137, 138) (1886-1949)

Common poinsettia - *Euphorbia pulcherrima* Willd. ex Klotzsch (155) (1942)

Common poison ivy [Common poisonivy] - *Toxicodendron radicans* (L.) Kuntze subsp. *pubens* (Engelm.) Gillis (Scheele) Gillis (155) (1942)

Common poke - *Phytolacca americana* L. var. *americana* (157) (1929)

Common pokeberry - *Phytolacca americana* L. (138, 155) (1923-1942)

Common pokeweed - *Phytolacca americana* L. var. *americana* (2) (1895)

Common pole bean - *Phaseolus vulgaris* L. (19) (1840)

Common polypody - *Polypodium virginianum* L. (3, 4, 49, 86, 109, 122, 131, 138, 155, 158, 187) (1818-1986)

Common pomegranate - *Punica granatum* L. (138) (1923)

Common pondweed - *Potamogeton natans* L. (156) (1923)

Common poolmat - *Zannichellia palustris* L. (155) (1942)

Common poppy - *Papaver rhoeas* L. (82) (1930), *Papaver somniferum* L. (156) (1923)

Common portulaca - *Portulaca grandiflora* Hook. (138, 155) (1923-1942)

Common prickly-ash [Common prickly ash] - *Zanthoxylum americanum* Mill. (50, 137, 138, 155) (1923–present)

Common prickly-pear [Common prickly pear, Common pricklypear] - *Opuntia ficus-indica* (L.) Mill. (2, 138, 155) (1895-1942)

Common privet - *Ligustrum vulgare* L. (41, 109) (1770-1949)

Common purple lilac - *Syringa vulgaris* L. (112) (1937)

Common purslane - *Portulaca oleracea* L. (3, 4, 15, 38, 103, 4, 138, 155) (1870-1986)

Common pussytoes - *Antennaria dioica* (L.) Gaertn. (138, 155) (1931-1942)

Common pyrethrum - *Chrysanthemum coccineum* Willd. (109) (1949)

Common quack grass - *Elymus repens* (L.) Gould (56) (1901)

Common quickset - *Crataegus monogyna* Jacq. (187) (1818)

Common quince - *Cydonia oblonga* Mill. (137, 138) (1923-1931)

Common radish - *Raphanus sativus* L. (158) (1900)

Common ragweed - *Ambrosia artemisiifolia* L. (3, 4, 92, 155, 156, 158) (1898-1986)

Common raspberry - *Rubus occidentalis* L. (96) (1891)

Common red cedar - *Juniperus virginiana* L. (7, 112) (1828-1937)

Common red clover - *Trifolium pratense* L. (6) (1892)

Common red currant - *Ribes rubrum* L. (47, 138) (1852-1923)

Common red haw - *Crataegus mollis* Scheele (82) (1930)

Common red oak - *Quercus rubra* L. (138) (1923)

Common red pepper [Common redpepper] - *Capsicum annuum* L. (138) (1923)

Common red raspberry - *Rubus idaeus* L. subsp. *strigosus* (Michx.) Focke (138) (1923)

Common reed - *Phragmites australis* (Cav.) Trin. ex Steud. (3, 50, 94, 140, 155) (1977–present)

Common reed grass [Common reed-grass] - *Cinna arundinacea* L. (56) (1901), *Phragmites* Adans. (93) (1936), *Phragmites australis* (Cav.) Trin. ex Steud. (2, 5, 66, 99, 107, 119, 152) (1895-1938)

Common rhubarb - *Rheum rhabarbarum* L. (138) (1923)

Common river grass [Common rivergrass] - *Scolochloa festucacea* (Willd.) Link (14, 50) (1882–present)

Common rose - *Rosa gallica* L. (19) (1840)

Common rose-mallow [Common rosemallow] - *Hibiscus moscheutos* L. (138) (1923), *Hibiscus moscheutos* L. subsp. *moscheutos* (155) (1942)

Common rue - *Ruta graveolens* L. (7, 109, 138) (1828-1949)

Common rush - *Equisetum hyemale* L. (4, 5) (1913-1986), *Juncus effusus* L. (5, 50, 72, 138, 155, 156) (1907–present), *Juncus effusus* L. var. *conglomeratus* (L.) Engelm. (50) (present)

Common Russian thistle [Common Russianthistle] - *Salsola kali* L. (155) (1942)

Common rye - *Secale cereale* L. (119, 163) (1852-1938)

Common sagebrush [Common sage-brush] - *Artemisia tridentata* Nutt. (95, 108, 158) (1878-1911)

Common sagebush [Common sage-bush] - *Artemisia tridentata* Nutt. (5) (1913)

Common sainfoin - *Onobrychis viciifolia* Scop. (155) (1942)

Common saltwort - *Salsola kali* L. (156) (1923)

Common sanvitalia - *Sanvitalia procumbens* Lam. (138) (1923)

Common sapota - *Manilkara zapota* (L.) van Royen (165) (1768)

Common sarsaparilla - *Aralia nudicaulis* L. (38) (1820)

Common sassafras - *Sassafras albidum* (Nutt.) Nees (138, 155) (1923-1942)

Common savin [Common sauin] - *Juniperus sabina* L. (178) (1596)

Common scouring rush [Common scouring-rush] - *Equisetum hyemale* L. (38, 97) (1820-1937)

Common screwpine - *Pandanus utilis* Bory (138) (1923)

Common sea reed - *Ammophila arenaria* (L.) Link (90) (1885) ME

Common sea-buckthorn - *Hippophae rhamnoides* L. (138) (1923)

Common seakale - *Crambe maritima* L. (138) (1923)

Common sedge - *Carex nigra* (L.) Reichard (5) (1913)

Common selaginella - *Selaginella arenicola* Underwood subsp. *riddellii* (Van Eselt.) R. Tryon (122) (1937)

Common selfheal - *Prunella vulgaris* L. (41, 50, 155) (1770–present)

Common serinia - *Krigia caespitosa* (Raf.) Chambers (155) (1942)

Common serviceberry - *Amelanchier arborea* (Michx. f.) Fern. (50) (present)

Common sheep sorrel - *Rumex acetosella* L. (50) (present)

Common shooting-star [Common shootingstar] - *Dodecatheon meadia* L. (138) (1923)

Common silk plant - *Asclepias syriaca* L. (42) (1814)

Common silkweed [Common silk weed] - *Asclepias syriaca* L. (57, 58, 02, 157, 158) (1869-1917)

Common skullcap [Common Skull-cap] - *Scutellaria galericulata* L. (187) (1818)

Common small blue flag - *Iris missouriensis* Nutt. (35) (1806)

Common smartweed - *Polygonum hydropiper* L. (2, 62, 80, 156) (1895–1923)

Common smoketree - *Cotinus coggygria* Scop. (138) (1923)

Common snakehead - *Chelone glabra* L. (7) (1828)

Common snapdragon - *Antirrhinum majus* L. (109, 138, 155) (1923-1949)

Common sneezeweed - *Helenium autumnale* L. (7, 50, 138, 155) (1828–present)

Common snowberry - *Symphoricarpos albus* (L.) Blake (50) (present), *Symphoricarpos albus* (L.) Blake var. *albus* (138) (1923), *Symphoricarpos* Duham. (50, 155) (1942–present)

Common snowdrop - *Galanthus nivalis* L. (109, 138) (1923-1949)

Common soapwort - *Saponaria officinalis* L. (64, 157, 158) (1900-1929)

Common sorghum - *Sorghum bicolor* (L.) Moench subsp. *bicolor* (110) (1886)

Common sorrel [Common-sorrel] - *Oxalis corniculata* L. (187) (1818), *Rumex acetosa* L. (92) (1876), *Rumex acetosella* L. (157, 158) (1900-1929)

Common sow thistle [Common sowthistle, Common sow-thistle] - *Sonchus oleraceus* L. (3, 4, 50, 19, 62, 80, 82, 155, 157, 158, 187) (1818–present)

Common spatterdock - *Nuphar lutea* (L.) Sm. subsp. *advena* (Aiton) Kartesz & Gandhi (109) (1949)

Common spear grass [Common spear-grass] - *Poa pratensis* L. (66, 92, 187) (1818-1903)

Common speedwell - *Veronica arvensis* L. (85) (1932), *Veronica officinalis* L. (2, 3, 4, 5, 62, 131, 156, 158) (1895-1986)

Common spicebush - *Lindera benzoin* Blume. (2, 6, 155) (1895–1942)

Common spiderwort - *Tradescantia virginiana* L. (109) (1949)

Common spikerush [Common spike-rush] - *Eleocharis palustris* (L.) Roemer & J.A. Schultes (50, 66, 129) (1894–present)

Common spikesedge - *Eleocharis palustris* (L.) Roemer & J.A. Schultes (139) (1944)

Common spinach - *Spinacia oleracea* L. (138) (1923)

Common spleenwort - *Asplenium trichomanes* L. (92) (1876)

Common spurge - *Chamaesyce hypericifolia* (L.) Millsp. (6) (1892)

Common squash - *Cucurbita pepo* L. (92) (1876)

Common St John's-wort [Common St. John's wort, Common St. Johnswort] - *Hypericum perforatum* L. (3, 4, 5, 50, 62, 72, 93, 155, 156, 157, 158, 187) (1818–present)

Common St. Peter's-wort [Common St. Peter's wort] - *Hypericum crux-andreae* (L.) Crantz (2) (1895)

Common staghorn fern - *Platycerium bifurcatum* (Cav.) C. Chr. (138) (1923)

Common star lily [Common starlily] - *Leucocrinum montanum* Nutt. ex Gray (50, 155) (1942–present)

Common star-of-Bethlehem - *Ornithogalum umbellatum* L. (138, 155) (1923-1942)

Common stock - *Matthiola incana* (L.) Aiton f. (82, 138) (1923–1930)

Common stonecrop - *Sedum acre* L. (109) (1949)

Common stork's-bill - *Erodium cicutarium* (L.) L'Hér. ex Aiton (157, 158) (1900-1929)

Common stramonium - *Datura stramonium* L. (71) (1898)

Common strawberry - *Fragaria vesca* L. (7, 92) (1828-1876), *Fragaria virginiana* Duchesne (possibly) (47) (1852)

Common strawberry blite - *Chenopodium capitatum* (L.) Asch. (42) (1814)

Common sumac [Common sumach] - *Rhus copallinum* L. (5, 156) (1913-1923), *Rhus hirta* (L.) Sudworth (15) (1895)

Common summer-cypress - *Kochia scoparia* (L.) Schrad. (138) (1923)

Common sundew - *Drosera rotundifolia* L. (158) (1900)

Common sundrops - *Oenothera fruticosa* L. (138) (1923), *Oenothera fruticosa* L. subsp. *fruticosa* (5, 72) (1907-1913) IA

Common sunflower - *Helianthus annuus* L. (2, 3, 4, 5, 19, 41, 50, 57, 62, 63, 72, 80, 82, 92, 93, 95, 97, 105, 109, 122, 127, 131, 138, 145, 155, 157, 158) (1770–present)

Common swamp blueberry - *Vaccinium corymbosum* L. (2) (1895)

Common sweetbrier [Common Sweete brier] - *Rosa eglanteria* L. (178) (1526)

Common sweetflag [Common sweet flag] - *Acorus calamus* L. (2, 42) (1814-1895)

Common sweetleaf - *Symplocos tinctoria* (L.) L'Her. (50, 138) (1923–present)

Common sweet-rush - *Acorus calamus* L. (165) (1768)

Common switchwort - *Stellaria graminea* L. (3) (1977)

Common sword fern [Common swordfern] - *Nephrolepis exaltata* (L.) Schott (138) (1923)

Common tansy [Common tansey] - *Artemisia vulgaris* L. (19) (1840), *Tanacetum vulgare* L. (3, 4, 50, 63, 109, 138, 155, 156) (1899–present)

Common tare - *Vicia sativa* L. (5, 156, 158) (1900-1923)

Common teasel - *Dipsacus fullonum* L. (4, 5, 62, 156, 158) (1900-1986)

Common thistle - *Cirsium vulgare* (Savi) Ten. (19, 62, 63, 92, 158, 187) (1818-1900)

Common thorn - *Crataegus calpodendron* (Ehrh.) Medik. (5, 157) (1900–1929)

Common thorn tree - *Crataegus punctata* Jacq. (19) (1840)

Common thorn-apple [Common thorn apple] - *Datura stramonium* L. (7, 42, 80) (1814-1913)

Common thoroughwort - *Eupatorium perfoliatum* L. (5, 62, 95, 97, 157, 158) (1900–1937)

Common three-leaf Virginia pine [Common three leaved Virginian pine] - *Pinus rigida* Mill. (8, 20) (1785-1857)

Common threesqaure - *Schoenoplectus pungens* (Vahl) Palla var. *pungens* (50) (present), *Schoenoplectus pungens* (Vahl) Palla (50) (present)

Common thrift - *Armeria maritima* (P. Mill.) Willd (138, 155) (1923-1942)

Common thyme - *Thymus vulgaris* L. (92, 109, 138) (1876-1949)

Common timothy - *Phleum pratense* L. (45, 87) (1884-1896)

Common toadflax [Common toad-flax, Common toad flax] - *Linaria vulgaris* Mill. (42, 138, 157, 158) (1814-1929)

Common tobacco - *Nicotiana rustica* L. (19) (1840), *Nicotiana tabacum* L. (43, 138) (1820-1923)

Common tomato - *Solanum lycopersicum* L. var. *lycopersicum* (155) (1942)

Common trout lily [Common troutlily] - *Erythronium americanum* Ker. (138) (1923)

Common trumpet-creeper [Common trumpetcreeper] - *Campsis radicans* (L.) Seem. ex Bureau (20, 155) (1857-1942)

Common trumpet-flower [Common flower, Common trumpet flower] - *Campsis radicans* (L.) Seem. ex Bureau (20, 155) (1857-1942)

Common tulip - *Tulipa gesneriana* L. (19, 138) (1840-1923)

Common tupelo - *Nyssa sylvatica* Marsh. (2) (1895)

Common twinleaf - *Jeffersonia diphylla* (L.) Pers. (7) (1828)

Common twinpod - *Physaria brassicoides* Rydb. (155) (1942)

Common unicorn plant [Common unicornplant, Common unicorn-plant] - *Proboscidea louisianica* (P. Mill.) Thellung (2, 109, 138) (1895-1949)

Common valerian - *Valeriana officinalis* L. (5, 109, 138, 156) (1913-1949)

Common vanilla - *Vanilla planifolia* B.D. Jackson (109) (1949)

Common velvet grass [Common velvetgrass] - *Holcus lanatus* L. (50, 155) (1942–present)

Common verbain - *Verbena hastata* L. var. *hastata* (37) (1919)

Common vervain - *Verbena hastata* L. (49, 53, 156, 157, 158) (1900-1929), *Verbena* L. (80) (1913), *Verbena officinalis* L. (41) (1770), *Verbena stricta* Vent. (93, 95) (1911-1936)

Common vetch - *Vicia sativa* L. (4, 5, 68, 72, 80, 85, 109, 110, 138, 155, 158) (1886-1986)

Common viper's-bugloss [Common vipersbugloss] - *Echium vulgare* L. (50, 155) (1942–present)

Common virgin's-bower [Common virgin's bower] - *Clematis virginiana* L. (13, 38, 63, 158) (1820-1899)

Common wall cress - *Arabidopsis thaliana* (L.) Britton (42) (1814)

Common wallflower - *Erysimum cheiri* (L.) Crantz (138) (1923)

Common walnut - *Juglans regia* L. (92) (1876)

Common water flags [Common Waterflags] - *Iris pseudacorus* L. (178) (1596)

Common water hemlock - *Cicuta maculata* L. (4) (1986)

Common water plantain - *Alisma plantago-aquatica* L. (42) (1814)

Common water starwort [Common waterstarwort, Common water-starwort] - *Callitriche palustris* L. (155) (1942)

Common watercress [Common water-cress] - *Rorippa nasturtium-aquaticum* (L.) Hayek (157, 158) (1900-1929)

Common water-hyacinth - *Eichhornia crassipes* (Mart.) Solms (138) (1923)

Common waxplant - *Hoya carnosa* (L. f.) R. Br. (138) (1923)

Common wheat - *Triticum aestivum* L. (50, 109, 119) (1938–present)

Common white candytuft - *Iberis amara* L. (138) (1923)

Common white daffodil - *Narcissus* ×*medioluteus* Mill. [*poeticus* × *tazetta*] (180) (1633)

Common white jasmine - *Jasminum officinale* L. (138) (1923)

Common white lettuce - *Prenanthes alba* L. (2) (1895)

Common white lilac - *Syringa vulgaris* L. (112) (1937)

Common white poplar - *Populus* ×*canescens* (Aiton) Sm. [*alba* × *tremula*] (20) (1857)

Common white violet - *Viola blanda* Willd. (156) (1923)

Common white water crowfoot [Common white water-crowfoot] - *Ranunculus aquatilis* L. (120) (1938), *Ranunculus trichophyllus* Chaix var. *trichophyllus* (72) (1907)

Common white waterlily [Common white water lily] - *Nymphaea odorata* Aiton subsp. *tuberosa* (Paine) Wiersma & Hellquist (82) (1930)

Common wild basil - *Clinopodium vulgare* L. (187) (1818)

Common wild bird cherry - *Prunus pensylvanica* L. f. (135) (1910)

Common wild cinquefoil - *Potentilla canadensis* L. (2) (1895)

Common wild clematis - *Clematis ligusticifolia* Nutt. (135) (1910)

Common wild gooseberry - *Ribes niveum* Lindl. (63, 95) (1899-1911)

Common wild hydrangea - *Bacopa rotundifolia* (Michx.) Wettst. (187) (1818)

Common wild oat grass - *Danthonia spicata* (L.) Beauv. ex Roemer & J.A. Schultes (5, 72) (1907-1913)

Common wild onion - *Allium canadense* L. var. *mobilense* (Regal) Ownbey (93) (1936)

Common wild plum - *Prunus americana* Marsh. (2) (1895)

Common wild potato - *Apios americana* Medik. (35) (1806)

Common wild rice [Common wildrice] - *Zizania palustris* L. (138) (1923)

Common wild sarsaparilla - *Aralia nudicaulis* L. (2) (1895)

Common wild virgin's-bower [Common wild virgin's bower] - *Clematis virginiana* L. (2) (1895)

Common willow - *Salix alba* L. (5, 156) (1913-1923)

Common winter cress - *Barbarea vulgaris* W.T. Aiton (15, 156) (1895–1923)

Common winterberry [Common winter berry] - *Ilex verticillata* (L.) Gray (2, 138) (1895-1923)

Common winter-cherry [Common winter cherry] - *Physalis alkekengi* L. (19) (1840)

Common winterfat - *Krascheninnikovia lanata* (Pursh) A.D.J. Meeuse & Smit (155) (1942)

Common wintergreen - *Gaultheria procumbens* L. (47) (1852), *Pyrola americana* Sweet (43) (1820)

Common witch grass [Common witchgrass] - *Elymus repens* (L.) Gould (45) (1896), *Panicum capillare* L. (140, 155) (1942-1944)

Common witch-hazel - *Hamamelis virginiana* L. (138) (1923)

Common wolf's-bane - *Aconitum napellus* L. (165) (1768)

Common wolf's-tail [Common wolfstail] - *Lycurus phleoides* H.B.K. (50) (present)

Common wood betony - *Pedicularis canadensis* L. (86) (1878)

Common wood fern [Common wood-fern, Common woodfern] - *Dryopteris carthusiana* (Vill.) H.P. Fuchs (possibly) (158) (1900), *Dryopteris intermedia* (Muhl. ex Willd.) Gray (5, 138) (1913-1923)

Common wood rush [Common woodrush] - *Luzula campestris* (L.) DC. (5, 66) (1903-1913)

Common wood sorrel [Common woodsorrel, Common wood-sorrel] - *Oxalis montana* Raf. (possibly) (7, 138, 156) (1828-1923)

Common woodbine - *Parthenocissus quinquefolia* (L.) Planch. (38) (1820)

Common woodrush - *Luzula multiflora* (Ehrh.) Lej. (50) (present)

Common woodsia - *Woodsia obtusa* (Spreng.) Torr. (86, 109, 138, 155) (1878-1949)

Common woody aster - *Xylorhiza glabriuscula* Nutt. (155) (1942)

Common wormwood - *Artemisia absinthium* L. (possibly) (5, 7, 63, 72, 85, 93, 95, 109, 138, 155, 156) (1828-1942), *Artemisia dracunculus* L. (131) (1899)

Common yam - *Dioscorea villosa* L. (possibly) (138) (1923)

Common yarrow - *Achillea millefolium* L. (2, 6, 45, 50, 63, 109, 138, 155, 156, 165, 178) (1596–present)

Common yellow daffodil - *Narcissus pseudonarcissus* L. (178, 180) (1596-1633)

Common yellow day-lily - *Hemerocallis lilioasphodelus* L. (109) (1949)

Common yellow monkey-flower Common yellow monkey flower - *Mimulus guttatus* DC. (4) (1986)

Common yellow mustard - *Brassica rapa* L. var. *rapa* (106) (1930)

Common yellow oxalis - *Oxalis stricta* L. (50, 138, 155) (1923–present)

Common yellow pondlily [Common yellow pond lily] - *Nuphar lutea* (L.) Sm. subsp. *advena* (Aiton) Kartesz & Gandhi (158) (1900)

Common yellow-eyed grass - *Xyris caroliniana* Walt. (66) (1903)

Common yucca - *Yucca filamentosa* L. (138) (1923)

Common zinnia - *Zinnia violacea* Cav. (138) (1923)

Commons' panicum - *Dichanthelium ovale* (Ell.) Gould & C.A. Clark var. *addisonii* (Nash) Gould & C.A. Clark (5) (1913)

Commyn - *Pimpinella anisum* L. (179) (1526)

Comosandalos (Hermonians) - *Lilium bulbiferum* L. (180) (1633)

Compact brome - *Bromus madritensis* L. (50) (present)

Compact chess - *Bromus madritensis* L. (5) (1913)

Compact dodder - *Cuscuta compacta* Juss. ex Choisy (5, 50, 97) (1913–present), *Cuscuta compacta* Juss. ex Choisy var. *compacta* (50) (present)

Compact onion - *Allium vineale* L. subsp. *compactum* (Thuill.) Coss. & Germ. (50) (present)

Compact prairie clover - *Dalea compacta* Spreng. (50) (present)

Compact prairie clover - *Dalea cylindriceps* Barneby (3) (1977)

Compact sandwort - *Arenaria kingii* (S. Wats.) M.E. Jones (155) (1942)

Compact stiff-stem flax [Compact stiffstem flax] - *Linum compactum* A. Nels. (4) (1986)

Compass plant [Compass-plant, Compassplant] - *Lactuca serriola* L. (70, 156, 158) (1895-1923), *Silphium* L. (1, 93) (1932-1936), *Silphium laciniatum* L. (3, 4, 5, 14, 37, 47, 50, 58, 63, 72, 82, 86, 93, 95, 97, 109, 131, 138, 155, 156, 157, 158) (1852–present), *Silphium perfoliatum* L. (85) (1932) SD, *Silphium terebinthinaceum* Jacq. (156) (1923)

Compassweed [Compass weed] - *Silphium laciniatum* L. (92, 122) (1876-1937)

Composite dropseed - *Sporobolus compositus* (Poir.) Merr. (50) (present), *Sporobolus compositus* (Poir.) Merr. var. *compositus* (50) (present)

Comptonia (Official name of Materia Medica) - *Comptonia peregrina* (L.) Coult. (7) (1828)

Comptonier odorant (French) - *Comptonia peregrina* (L.) Coult. (7) (1828)

Comyn - *Cuminum cyminum* L. (179) (1526)

Conch grass - *Agrostis gigantea* Roth (5) (1913)

Conch nut - *Passiflora maliformis* L. (107) (1919)

Conchalagua - *Zeltnera muehlenbergii* (Griseb.) G.Mans. (75) (1894) CA

Conch-apple [Conch apple] - *Passiflora maliformis* L. (107) (1919)

Concho grass - *Urochloa texana* (Buckl.) R. Webster (118) (1898) TX

Concolor fir - *Abies concolor* (Gord. & Glend.) Lindl. ex Hildebr. (possibly) (112, 136) (1930-1937)

Cone fuchsia - *Fuchsia magellanica* Lam. (138) (1923)

Cone pepper - *Capsicum annuum* L. (109) (1949)

Cone-bearing willow - *Salix humilis* Marsh. var. *tristis* (Aiton) Griggs (187) (1818)

Conecup spikerush - *Eleocharis tuberculosa* (Michx.) Roemer & J.A. Schultes (50) (present)

Conedisk [Cone disk, Cone-disk] - *Rudbeckia laciniata* L. (92, 57) (1876-1900)

Cone-disk sunflower - *Rudbeckia laciniata* L. (156, 158) (1900-1923)

Coneflower [Cone-flower, Cone flower] - *Dracopis amplexicaulis* (Vahl.) Cass. (4) (1986), *Echinacea angustifolia* DC. (49, 52, 53, 54) (1905-1922), *Ratibida columnifera* (Nutt.) Wood & Standl. (38, 106) (1820-1930), *Ratibida pinnata* (Vent.) Barnh. (85, 95, 114) (1894-1932), *Ratibida* Raf (1, 50, 82, 93, 109, 158) (1900–present), *Rudbeckia californica* Gray (138) (1923), *Rudbeckia fulgida* Aiton (102) (1886), *Rudbeckia grandiflora* (D. Don) J.F. Gmel. ex DC. var. *alismifolia* (Torr. & Gray) Cronq. (97) (1937), *Rudbeckia hirta* L. (45, 80, 148) (1896-1939), *Rudbeckia* L. (1, 2, 4, 50, 82, 93, 109, 138, 155, 156, 158) (1895–present), *Rudbeckia laciniata* L. (40, 46, 57, 58, 82, 95, 157) (1869-1930), *Rudbeckia triloba* L. (82) (1930)

Cone-fruit catch-fly - *Silene conica* L. (19) (1840)

Cone-gall willow - *Salix ×conifera* Wangenh. *[discolor × humilis]* (19) (1840)

Cone-spur bladderwort [Conespur bladderwort] - *Utricularia gibba* L. (4) (1986)

Confederate vine [Confederate-vine] - *Antigonon leptopus* Hook. & Arn. (109) (1949)

Confederate violet - *Viola sororia* Willd. (109) (1949)

Confederate-jasmine - *Trachelospermum jasminoides* (Lindl.) Lem. (138) (1923)

Confederate-rose - *Hibiscus mutabilis* L. (109) (1949)

Congdon's yellow-eyed grass - *Xyris smalliana* Nash (5) (1913)

Congho grass - *Urochloa texana* (Buckl.) R. Webster (163) (1852)

Congo root [Congo-root] - *Orbexilum pedunculatum* (P. Mill.) Rydb. var. *pedunculatum* (5, 49, 156, 158) (1898-1923)

Conical-fruit sedge [Conical-fruited sedge] - *Carex conoidea* Schk. ex Willd. (66) (1903)

Conium (Official name of Materia Medica) - *Conium maculatum* L. (7, 57, 60, 92) (1828-1917)

Conjurer's nut - *Nestronia umbellula* Raf. (183) (~1756)

Conobea - *Leucospora multifida* (Michx.) Nutt. (5, 72, 97) (1907-1937)

Conocarpe droit - *Conocarpus erectus* L. (20) (1857)
Conotweed [Conot weed] - *Ambrosia artemisiifolia* L. (6) (1892), *Ambrosia artemisiifolia* L. var. *elatior* (L.) Descourtils (7) (1828)
Conquer-John [Conquer John] - *Polygonatum biflorum* (Walt.) Ell. (5, 10, 75, 157, 158) (1818-1929)
Conqueror John - *Polygonatum biflorum* (Walt.) Ell. (156) (1923)
Conquerors - *Aesculus hippocastanum* L. (156) (1923)
Conrad's broom crowberry - *Corema conradii* (Torr.) Torr. ex Loud. (5) (1913)
Conrad's rush - *Juncus conradi* Tuckerm. ex Torr. (66) (1903)
Consound - *Bellis perennis* L. (158) (1900), *Symphytum officinale* L. (5, 156) (1913-1923)
Consumption brake - *Botrychium biternatum* (Sav.) Underwood (possibly) (92) (1876)
Consumption-weed [Consumption weed] - *Moneses uniflora* (L.) Gray (7) (1828), *Pyrola americana* Sweet (5, 58, 92, 156, 158) (1869-1923)
Consumptive's-weed [Consumptive's weed] - *Eriodictyon californicum* (Hook. & Arn.) Torr. (57) (1917)
Continental weed - *Linaria vulgaris* Mill. (5, 6) (1892-1913)
Conval lily [Conval-lily] - *Convallaria majalis* L. (5, 156, 158, 178) (1596-1923) no longer in use by 1923
Convallaria - *Convallaria majalis* L. (52, 54, 59, 60) (1905-1919)
Convovulus - *Convolvulus* L. (138) (1923)
Convulsion root [Convulsion-root] - *Monotropa uniflora* L. (5, 6, 73, 79, 157, 158) (1891–1929)
Convulsion weed [Convulsion-weed] - *Monotropa uniflora* L. (5, 92, 156, 158) (1876-1923)
Conyzella - *Conyza canadensis* (L.) Cronq. var. *canadensis* (177) (1762)
Cooch grass [Cooch-grass] - *Elymus repens* (L.) Gould (158) (1900)
Coo-grape - *Ampelopsis cordata* Michx. (156) (1923)
Cook grass [Cook-grass] - *Bromus secalinus* L. (119) (1938) OK
Cooley's bundle-flower [Cooley's bundleflower] - *Desmanthus cooleyi* (Eat.) Trel. (50) (present)
Cool-tankard [Cool tankard] - *Borago officinalis* L. (107, 156) (1919-1923)
Coolweed [Cool weed] - *Pilea* Lindl. (158) (1900), *Pilea pumila* (L.) Gray (5, 155, 156) (1913-1942), *Pilea pumila* (L.) Gray var. *pumila* (7, 92, 158) (1828-1900)
Coolwort - *Mitella diphylla* L. (79) (1891) NH, *Mitella nuda* L. (57) (1917), *Tiarella cordifolia* L. (5, 156) (1913-1923)
Coonroot [Coon-root, Coon root] - *Sanguinaria canadensis* L. (64, 74, 157, 158) (1893-1929)
Coon's-tail [Coon's tail, Coontail, Coon-tail] - *Ceratophyllum demersum* L. (50, 97, 156) (1923–present), *Ceratophyllum* L. (4, 109) (1949-1986)
Coontie - *Zamia pumila* L. (2, 50) (1895–present)
Coontie - *Zamia pumila* L. subsp. *pumila* (138) (1923)
Cooper's flag - *Typha latifolia* L. (35) (1806)
Cooper's goldenweed [Cooper goldenweed] - *Ericameria cooperi* (Gray) Hall (155) (1942)
Cooper's milkvetch [Cooper's milk vetch, Cooper milk vetch] - *Astragalus neglectus* (Torr. & Gray) Sheldon (3, 4, 5, 50, 72) (1907–present)
Cooper's reed - *Typha latifolia* L. (187) (1818)
Cootamundra wattle - *Acacia baileyana* F. Muell. (50, 138) (1923–present)
Cootamundra-wattle acacia - *Acacia baileyana* F. Muell. (155) (1942)
Cootnwood - *Paulownia tomentosa* (Thunb.) Sieb. & Zucc. ex Steud. (possibly) (156) (1923)
Copalm - *Liquidambar styraciflua* L. (156) (1923), *Pyrola americana* Sweet (156) (1923) no longer in use by 1923
Copalm (French) - *Liquidambar styraciflua* L. (17, 20, 49, 92) (1796-1898)

Copper alternathera - *Alternanthera bettzichiana* (Regel) Voss (155) (1942)
Copper beech - *Fagus sylvatica* L. (109) (1949)
Copper iris - *Iris fulva* Ker.-Gawl. (50, 138, 156) (1923–present)
Copper zephyr-lily [Copper zephyrlily] - *Zephyranthes longifolia* Hemsl. (50, 155) (1942–present)
Copper-colored St. John's-wort [Copper-colored St. John's wort] - *Hypericum denticulatum* Walt. (5) (1913)
Copper-flower daylily [Copper-flowered day lily] - *Hemerocallis fulva* (L.) L. (187) (1818)
Copperleaf [Copper-leaf, Copper leaf] - *Acalypha* L. (50, 109, 138, 155) (1923–present), *Acalypha virginica* L. (62, 156) (1912-1923), *Pyrola americana* Sweet (5, 158) (1900-1913)
Copper-rose [Copper rose] - *Papaver rhoeas* L. (158) (1900)
Coppertip - *Crocosmia* Planch. (138) (1923)
Coprosma - *Coprosma* J.R. & G. Forst. (138) (1923)
Copse buckwheat - *Polygonum scandens* L. var. *dumetorum* (L.) Gleason (5) (1913)
Coptide - *Coptis trifolia* (L.) Salisb. (156) (1923) no longer in use by 1923
Coptis (Official name of Materia Medica) - *Coptis trifolia* (L.) Salisb. (7, 57, 64) (1828-1917)
Coptis triphylle (French) - *Coptis trifolia* (L.) Salisb. (7) (1828)
Coq des jardin (French) - *Balsamita major* Desf. (158) (1900)
Coquelicot (French) - *Papaver rhoeas* L. (158) (1900)
Coquelourdes (French) - *Pulsatilla patens* (L.) Mill. subsp. *multifida* (Pritz.) Zamels (poss) (180) (1633)
Coracan - *Eleusine coracana* (L.) Gaertn. (110) (1886)
Coral ardisia - *Parathesis crenulata* (Vent.) Hook. f. (138) (1923)
Coral baneberry [Coral bane berry] - *Actaea spicata* L. (42) (1814)
Coral bean [Coralbean] - *Erythrina herbacea* L. (122, 124, 138) (1923-1937), *Sophora secundiflora* (Ortega) Lag. ex DC. (106, 153) (1913-1930)
Coral evergreen - *Lycopodium clavatum* L. (5, 73) (1892-1913)
Coral greenbrier [Coral green-brier, Coral green-briar] - *Smilax walteri* Pursh. (50, 138, 156) (1923–present)
Coral honeysuckle - *Lonicera* L. (possibly) (10) (1818)
Coral honeysuckle - *Lonicera sempervirens* L. (5, 46, 97, 112, 156, 158) (1879-1937)
Coral mushrooms - *Clavaria* L. (7) (1828)
Coral pea - *Adenanthera pavonina* L. (107) (1919)
Coral plant [Coral-plant] - *Russelia equisetiformis* Schlecht. & Cham. (109) (1949)
Coral tree [Coral-tree, Coraltree] - *Erythrina corallodendron* L. (138) (1923), *Erythrina crista-galli* L. (92) (1876), *Erythrina herbacea* L. (10) (1818), *Erythrina* L. (109, 138) (1923-1949)
Coral vine [Coral-vine, Coralvine] - *Antigonon* Endl. (106, 155) (1930-1942), *Antigonon leptopus* Hook. & Arn. (106, 109) (1930-1949), *Cuscuta* L. (1, 93) (1932-1936)
Coral-and-pearl - *Actaea rubra* (Aiton) Willd. (157, 158) (1900-1929)
Coralbead [Coral bead] - *Cocculus* DC. (1, 50) (1932)
Coral-bead plant - *Abrus precatorius* L. (107) (1919)
Coralbells [Coral bells] - *Heuchera sanguinea* Engelm. (82, 109, 138) (1923-1949)
Coralberry [Coral-berry, Coral berry] - *Actaea rubra* (Aiton) Willd. (5, 156) (1913-1923), *Cocculus carolinus* (L.) DC. (122, 124) (1937) TX, *Symphoricarpos albus* (L.) Blake var. *laevigatus* (Fern.) Blake (37, 72, 93, 95, 97, 125, 131, 158) (1899-1936), *Symphoricarpos* Duham. (1, 4, 82, 93, 112) (1930-1986), *Symphoricarpos occidentalis* Hook. (4, 50, 80, 82, 106, 109, 121, 122, 124, 156) (1923–present), *Symphoricarpos symphoricarpos* (L.) MacMill. (2, 63, 92, 108, 112, 138) (1878-1937)
Coralbloom [Coral bloom] - *Erythrina herbacea* L. (7, 92) (1828-1876)
Coralblow [Coral-blow] - *Russelia* Jacq. (109, 138) (1923-1949)
Coral-like clavaria [Coral like clavaria] - *Clavaria coralloides* L. (42) (1814)

Coralline honeysuckle - *Lonicera chrysantha* Turcz. ex Ledeb. (138) (1923)

Corallita - *Antigonon leptopus* Hook. & Arn. (106, 109) (1930-1949)

Corallorhiza - *Corallorrhiza odontorhiza* (Willd.) Poir. (52, 64) (1908-1919)

Coralroot [Coral-root, Coral root] - *Corallorrhiza* Gagnebin (1, 50, 93, 156, 158) (1900–present), *Corallorrhiza odontorhiza* (Willd.) Poir. (49, 53, 57, 64, 92) (1876-1922), *Corallorrhiza trifida* Chat. (19, 85) (1840-1932)

Coral-teeth [Coral teeth] - *Corallorrhiza odontorhiza* (Willd.) Poir. (19) (1840)

Coralwort [Coral wort] - *Cardamine concatenata* (Michx.) Sw. (184) (1793), *Cardamine diphylla* (Michx.) Wood (42) (1814)

Cord grass [Cord-grass, Cordgrass] - *Spartina cynosuroides* (L.) Roth (11, 129) (1888-1894), *Spartina gracilis* Trin. (93) (1936), *Spartina maritima* (M.A. Curtis) Fern. (92) (1876), *Spartina pectinata* Bosc ex Link (119) (1938), *Spartina* Schreber (45, 50, 155) (1896–present)

Cordate cissus - *Ampelopsis cordata* Michx. (106) (1930)

Cordia - *Cordia* L. (138) (1923)

Coreopsis - *Bidens coronata* (L.) Britton (106) (1930) Delaware River valley, *Coreopsis* L. (138, 155) (1923-1942), *Coreopsis lanceolata* L. (174) (1753), *Coreopsis tinctoria* Nutt. (114, 127) (1894–1933)

Coreopsis beggarticks - *Bidens aristosa* (Michx.) Britton (3, 4, 155) (1942-1986)

Coriander [Coryandre] - *Coriandrum* L. (138) (1923) from Latin and Greek connected with word for bug, *Coriandrum sativum* L. (1, 5, 19, 46, 49, 50, 53, 55, 57, 58, 59, 85, 92, 97, 107, 109, 122, 138, 156, 179) (1526–present) cultivated by English colonists by 1671

Coriandrum - *Coriandrum sativum* L. (57, 59) (1911-1917)

Cork elm - *Ulmus alata* Michx. (5, 158) (1900-1913), *Ulmus thomasii* Sarg. (1, 5, 72, 82, 85, 93, 95, 109, 135, 156, 157, 158) (1900-1949)

Cork fir - *Abies lasiocarpa* (Hook.) Nutt. var. *arizonica* (Merriam) Lemmon (109, 138) (1923-1949)

Cork oak - *Quercus suber* L. (20, 107, 138) (1857-1932)

Cork or Cork tree [Cork-tree, Corktree] - *Adansonia digitata* L. (107) (1919) Florida Keys, *Byrsonima crassifolia* (L.) Kunth (92) (1876), *Phellodendron* Rupr. (109, 138) (1923-1949), *Quercus suber* L. (92) (1876)

Cork passion-flower [Cork passionflower] - *Passiflora suberosa* L. (138) (1923)

Cork wood [Cork-wood, Corkwood] - *Annona glabra* L. (165) (1807) Jamaica, *Leitneria floridana* Chapman (5, 122, 156) (1913-1937), *Quercus suber* L. (92) (1876)

Cork-bark fir [Corkbark fir, Cork bark fir] - *Abies lasiocarpa* (Hook.) Nutt. var. *arizonica* (Merriam) Lemmon (153, 155) (1913-1942) NM

Cork-pod milkvine [Corkpod milkvine] - *Matelea gonocarpos* (Walt.) Shinners (155) (1942)

Corkscrew plant - *Spiranthes lacera* (Raf.) Raf. var. *gracilis* (Bigelow) Luer (5, 156) (1913-1923)

Corkwing - *Cymopterus* Raf. (155) (1942)

Corky white elm - *Ulmus thomasii* Sarg. (2, 5, 156, 157, 158) (1895-1929)

Corn - *Zea* L. (45, 50) (1896–present), *Zea mays* L. (21, 50, 68, 92, 107, 182) (1791–present)

Corn (in England) - *Triticum* L. (45) (1896)

Corn [Corne] - *Triticum aestivum* L. (180) (1633)

Corn bindweed - *Polygonum convolvulus* L. (5, 93, 97, 122, 156, 158) (1900-1937)

Corn bluebottle [Corn blue-bottle] - *Centaurea cyanus* L. (5, 156, 157, 158) (1900–1929)

Corn brome - *Bromus squarrosus* L. (5, 50, 56, 72) (1893–present)

Corn buttercup - *Ranunculus arvensis* L. (50, 155) (1942–present)

Corn camomile [Corn chamomile] - *Anthemis arvensis* L. (3, 4, 5, 19, 50, 63, 92, 156, 158, 165) (1807–present), *Anthemis* L. (1) (1932)

Corn campion - *Agrostemma githago* L. (1, 5, 85, 156, 157, 158, 165) (1768-1932), *Agrostemma* L. (1, 93) (1932-1936)

Corn catchfly - *Silene conica* L. (5, 156) (1913-1923)

Corn centaury - *Centaurea cyanus* L. (5, 156, 157, 158) (1900–1929)

Corn chrysanthemum - *Chrysanthemum segetum* L. (107, 109, 156) (1919-1949)

Corn crowfoot - *Ranunculus arvensis* L. (5, 158) (1900–1913)

Corn daisy [Corne daisie] - *Chrysanthemum segetum* L. (178) (1526)

Corn ergot [Corn-ergot] - *Erysibe vera* Wallroth (possibly) (49, 52, 53) (1919-1922), *Ustilago maydis* (DC.) Corda (48, 52) (1882-1919)

Corn feverfew - *Anthemis arvensis* L. (6) (1892), *Matricaria recutita* L. (158) (1900)

Corn flag [Corn-flag, Corne-flag] - *Gladiolus communis* L. (92) (1876), *Gladiolus* L. (180) (1633), *Iris pseudacorus* L. (5, 156, 158) (1900-1923)

Corn gladin [Corne gladin] - *Gladiolus* L. (180) (1633)

Corn grass [Corn-grass, Corngrass] - *Apera spica-venti* (L.) Beauv. (5) (1913), *Dichanthelium clandestinum* (L.) Gould (5, 119) (1913-1938), *Leymus cinereus* (Scribn. & Merr.) A.Löve (35) (1806)

Corn gromwell - *Buglossoides arvensis* (L.) I.M. Johnston (3, 5, 50, 62, 72, 80, 93, 97, 155, 156, 157, 158) (1900–present), *Onosmodium virginianum* (L.) A. DC. (92) (1876)

Corn heath - *Fagopyrum esculentum* Moench (5) (1913)

Corn kale [Corn-kale] - *Moricandia arvensis* (L.) DC. (156, 158) (1900-1923), *Sinapis arvensis* L. (5, 157) (1913–1929)

Corn lily [Corn-lily] - *Clintonia borealis* (Ait.) Raf. (156) (1923)

Corn marigold [Corn-marigold] - *Chrysanthemum* L. (92) (1876), *Chrysanthemum segetum* L. (5, 107, 109, 138, 156) (1913-1949)

Corn mayweed - *Tripleurospermum perforata* (Merat) M. Lainz (5, 156) (1913-1923)

Corn mint - *Mentha arvensis* L. (5, 156, 158) (1900–1923)

Corn mustard - *Moricandia arvensis* (L.) DC. (156, 158) (1900-1923), *Sinapis arvensis* L. (5, 92, 157) (1876-1929)

Corn of Asia [Corne of Asia] - *Zea mays* L. (180) (1633)

Corn pink - *Agrostemma githago* L. (5, 156, 157, 158) (1900–1929), *Cerastium arvense* L. (42) (1814)

Corn pope - *Papaver rhoeas* L. (158) (1900)

Corn popple - *Papaver rhoeas* L. (158) (1900)

Corn poppy - *Papaver rhoeas* L. (3, 5, 50, 15, 49, 92, 107, 109, 138, 155, 156, 158) (1895–present)

Corn puppy - *Papaver rhoeas* L. (158) (1900)

Corn pusley - *Chamaesyce hypericifolia* (L.) Millsp. (78) (1898) Southold LI, *Chamaesyce maculata* (L.) Small (78) (1898) Southold Long Island

Corn salad [Corn-salad, Cornsalad, Corn sallad, Corne Sallad, Corne sallade] - *Valerianella amarella* (Lindheimer ex Engelm.) Krok (124) (1937), *Valerianella locusta* (L.) Lat. (107, 109, 110, 138) (1886-1949), *Valerianella* Mill. (1, 4, 50, 155, 156, 158) (1900–present), *Valerianella radiata* (L.) Dufr. (1, 3, 4, 7, 19, 92, 158, 178) (1526-1986)

Corn smut - *Erysibe vera* Wallroth (possibly) (49, 53) (1922), *Ustilago maydis* (DC.) Corda (37, 57, 157) (1830-1929)

Corn snakeroot [Corn snake root] - *Eryngium yuccifolium* Michx. (5, 6, 7, 49, 53, 58, 64, 92, 156, 157, 158) (1828-1929), *Liatris spicata* (L.) Willd. (156) (1923), *Liatris spicata* (L.) Willd. var. *spicata* (157) (1929)

Corn snapdragon - *Misopates orontium* (L.) Raf. (5, 155) (1913-1942), *Sairocarpus coulterianus* (Benth. ex A. DC.) D.A. Sutton (5, 155) (1913-1942)

Corn sow-thistle [Corn sow thistle] - *Sonchus arvensis* L. (5, 19, 122, 157, 158) (1840-1929)

Corn speedwell - *Veronica arvensis* L. (3, 4, 5, 50, 63, 72, 82, 97, 122, 156) (1899–present)

Corn spurry [Corn spurrey, Corn-spurrey] - *Legousia speculum-veneris* (L.) Fisch. ex A. DC. (1) (1932), *Sagina decumbens* (Ell.) Torr. & Gray (possibly) (167) (1814), *Spergula arvensis* L. (1, 3, 4, 5, 19, 50, 85, 107, 110, 155, 156, 158, 187) (1840–present)

Corn thistle [Corn-thistle] - *Cirsium arvense* (L.) Scop. (5, 156, 157, 158) (1900-1929)

Corn woundwort - *Stachys arvensis* L. (5, 156) (1913-1923), *Stachys pilosa* Nutt. var. *arenicola* (Britton) G. Mulligan & D. Munro (5, 156) (1913-1923)

Cornbind [Corn-bind, Corn bind] - *Convolvulus arvensis* L. (62, 156, 157, 158) (1900-1929), *Polygonum convolvulus* L. (5, 156, 158) (1900-1923)

Cornbinks [Corn binks, Corn-binks] - *Centaurea cyanus* L. (5, 156, 157, 158) (1900–1929)

Cornbottles [Corn bottles, Corn-bottle] - *Centaurea cyanus* L. (5, 156, 157, 158) (1900–1929)

Cornbrand [Corn brand] - *Erysibe vera* Wallroth (possibly) (49, 53) (1898–1922)

Corncockle [Corn-cockle, Corn cockle] - *Agrostemma githago* L. (1, 5, 6, 10, 42, 62, 71, 72, 80, 85, 97, 131, 148, 156, 157, 158) (1814-1939), *Agrostemma* L. (1, 4, 15, 50, 93, 155, 156, 158, 167) (1814–present)

Cornel [Cornels] or Cornel tree [Cornell tree] - *Cornus florida* L. (6, 92) (1876-1892), *Cornus* L. (1, 2, 8, 10, 82, 158, 184) (1785-1932), *Cornus mas* L. (92, 178) (1526-1876)

Cornel cherry - *Cornus mas* L. (20) (1857)

Cornel dogwood - *Cornus sanguinea* L. (107) (1919)

Cornelian cherry [Cornelian-cherry] - *Cornus florida* L. (41) (1770), *Cornus mas* L. (19, 92, 109, 138) (1840-1949), *Cornus sanguinea* L. (41) (1770)

Cornelian tree [Cornelian-tree] - *Cornus florida* L. (5, 156) (1913-1923)

Cornel-leaf aster [Cornel-leaved aster] - *Doellingeria infirma* (Michx.) Greene (5, 156) (1913-1923)

Corn-field camomile [Cornfield camomile] - *Anthemis arvensis* L. (155) (1942)

Corn-field horsetail [Cornfield horsetail] - *Equisetum arvense* L. (5) (1913)

Cornflower [Corn-flower, Corn flower] - *Centaurea cyanus* L. (4, 5, 82, 85, 93, 97, 109, 131, 138, 155, 156, 157, 158, 178) (1526-1986), *Centaurea* L. (1, 93) (1932-1936), *Erythronium americanum* Ker. (78) (1898) ME, *Uvularia grandiflora* Smith. (156) (1923), *Uvularia sessilifolia* L. (78) (1898) ME

Corn-heath - *Fagopyrum esculentum* Moench (156) (1923)

Cornish heath - *Erica vagans* L. (109, 138) (1923-1949)

Corn-lily [Corn-lilly] - *Convolvulus arvensis* L. (157, 158) (1900-1929)

Cornouiller (French) - *Cornus* L. (8) (1785)

Cornouiller à feuilles alternes (French) - *Cornus alternifolia* L. f. (8) (1785)

Cornouiller a feuilles glauques (French) - *Cornus foemina* Mill. (8) (1785)

Cornouiller à grandes fleurs (French) - *Cornus florida* L. (158) (1900)

Cornouiller de Nuttall (French) - *Cornus nuttallii* Audubon ex Torr. & Gray (20) (1857)

Cornouiller fleuri (French) - *Cornus florida* L. (7) (1828)

Cornouiller sanguin (French) - *Cornus sanguinea* L. (8) (1785)

Cornouiller soyeaux (French) - *Cornus amomum* Mill. (158) (1900)

Cornouilles de la Floride (French) - *Cornus florida* L. (8) (1785)

Cornroot [Corn-root, Corn root] - *Sanguinaria canadensis* L. (156) (1923)

Corn-rose [Corn Rose] - *Agrostemma githago* L. (5, 156, 157, 158) (1900–1929), *Papaver rhoeas* L. (5, 49, 92, 156, 158) (1876–1923)

Corn-sedge [Corne-Sedge] - *Gladiolus* L. (180) (1633)

Cornsilk [Corn silk] - *Cuscuta* L. (77) (1898) Southold Long Island

Corn-stalk weed [Cornstalk weed, Cornstalk-weed] - *Potamogeton illinoensis* Morong (possibly) (5, 156, 158) (1900-1923)

Cornucopia floripondio - *Datura inoxia* P. Mill. (138) (1923)

Cornuile a Feuilles Rondie (French) - *Cornus rugosa* Lam. (6) (1892)

Cornuille Soyeux (French) - *Cornus sericea* L. (6) (1892)

Cornus - *Cornus florida* L. (52, 54, 60) (1902–1919)

Cornus florida (Official name of Materia Medica) - *Cornus florida* L. (7) (1828)

Corombile (Albanian) - *Prunus domestica* L. var. *insititia* (L.) Fiori & Paoletti (110) (1886)

Coromeleia (Modern Greek) - *Prunus domestica* L. var. *insititia* (L.) Fiori & Paoletti (110) (1886)

Coronilla - *Coronilla* L. (138, 155) (1923-1942), *Coronilla varia* L. (5, 85, 156) (1913-1932)

Corpse plant [Corpse-plant] - *Monotropa uniflora* L. (2, 5, 6, 63, 92, 156, 157, 158) (1895-1929)

Correlated spurge - *Euphorbia corollata* L. (187) (1818)

Correll's buckwheat - *Eriogonum correllii* Reveal (50) (present)

Correll's eriogonum - *Eriogonum correllii* Reveal (4) (1986)

Corsican moss - *Alsidium helminthochorton* (Schwendimann) Kützing (92) (1876), *Laurencia obtusa* (Hudson) Lamouroux (107) (1919)

Corsican pine - *Pinus nigra* Arnold (138) (1923)

Corydalis - *Corydalis* DC. (1, 138, 155, 158) (1900-1942), *Dicentra canadensis* (Goldie) Walp. (52, 53, 54, 57) (1905-1922)

Corylus - *Corylus americana* Walt. (46) (1879)

Corymbed aster - *Doellingeria umbellata* (P. Mill.) Nees var. *umbellata* (82) (1930), *Eurybia divaricata* (L.) Nesom (156) (1923)

Corymbed hymenopappus - *Hymenopappus scabiosaeus* L'Her. var. *corymbosus* (Torr. & Gray) B.L. Turner (5) (1913)

Corymbed rattlesnake root - *Prenanthes crepidinea* Michx. (5) (1913)

Corymbed spiraea - *Spiraea betulifolia* Pallas var. *corymbosa* (Raf.) Maxim. (5) (1913), *Spiraea betulifolia* Pallas var. *lucida* (Dougl. ex Greene) C.L. Hitchc. (131) (1899)

Corymbed St. John's-wort [Corymbed St. John's wort] - *Hypericum punctatum* Lam. (5) (1913)

Coryphantha - *Coryphantha* (Engelm.) Lem. (155) (1942)

Cory's columbine - *Aquilegia canadensis* L. (122, 124) (1937)

Cory's jointreed - *Ephedra coryi* E.L. Reed (50) (present)

Cory's onion [Cory onion] - *Allium coryi* M.E. Jones (155) (1942)

Cosmopolitan bulrush - *Schoenoplectus maritimus* (L.) Lye (50) (present)

Cosmos - *Cosmos bipinnatus* Cav. (82) (1930) IA, *Cosmos* Cav. (138) (1923)

Cossack asparagus - *Typha latifolia* L. (107) (1919)

Cost - *Balsamita major* Desf. (5, 156, 158, 179) (1526-1923) no longer in use by 1923 (156) from Latin costus

Costa Rican nightshade [Costa Rica nightshade] - *Solanum wendlandii* Hook. f. (138) (1923)

Costmary - *Balsamita major* Desf. (4, 5, 50, 107, 109, 138, 156, 158, 179) (1526-1986), *Balsamita* Mill. (1) (1932)

Cotoneaster - *Cotoneaster* Medik. (138) (1923)

Cotonier (French Canadian) - *Asclepias syriaca* L. (41) (1770)

Cotonier (French, cotton tree) - *Platanus occidentalis* L. (17, 41) (1770-1796)

Cotta grass [Cotta-grass] - *Cottea pappophoroides* Kunth (94) (1901)

Cottage pink - *Dianthus plumarius* L. (109) (1949)

Cottagers - *Digitalis pupurea* L. (5, 69) (1903-1913)

Cotton - *Gossypium barbadense* L. (55) (1911), *Gossypium herbaceum* L. (19, 52, 54, 55, 61, 92, 106, 107, 110, 114, 125) (1840-1930), *Gossypium* L. (7, 15, 109, 138) (1828-1949)

Cotton burdock - *Arctium tomentosum* P. Mill. (155) (1942)

Cotton grass[Cotton-grass] - *Digitaria insularis* (L.) Mez ex Ekman (94) (1901)

Cotton gum [Cotton-gum] - *Nyssa aquatica* L. (5, 106, 109) (1913-1949)

Cotton rosemallow - *Hibiscus mutabilis* L. (138) (1923)

Cotton rush - *Eriophorum callitrix* Cham. ex C.A. Mey. (5, 156) (1913-1923)

Cotton thistle [Cottonthistle] - *Onopordum acanthium* L. (5, 19, 92, 107, 156, 158) (1840-1923), *Onopordum* L. (1, 50, 138, 155, 158) (1900–present)

Cotton tree [Cotton-tree] - *Asclepias syriaca* L. (107) (1760), *Gossypium herbaceum* L. (178) (1526), *Platanus occidentalis* L. (20, 187) (1818-1857) Canada & upper Louisiana (Louisiana Purchase), *Populus ×canadensis* Moench [*deltoides × nigra*] (17) (1796), *Populus deltoides* Bartr. ex Marsh. (5, 156, 158) (1900-1923), *Populus deltoides* Bartr. ex Marsh. subsp. *deltoides* (10) (1818), *Populus heterophylla* L. (20) (1857), *Populus* L. (17) (1796), *Populus nigra* L. (158) (1900)

Cotton tree of Carolina - *Populus deltoides* Bartr. ex Marsh. (8) (1785)

Cotton-batting [Cotton batting] - *Pseudognaphalium stramineum* (Kunth) W.A. Weber (4) (1986)

Cotton-batting cudweed [Cottonbatting cudweed] - *Pseudognaphalium stramineum* (Kunth) W.A. Weber (155) (1942)

Cotton-batting plant [Cottonbatting plant] - *Pseudognaphalium stramineum* (Kunth) W.A. Weber (50) (present)

Cotton-flower [Cottonflower] - *Gossypianthus lanuginosus* (Poir.) Moq. var. *lanuginosus* (4) (1986)

Cottongrass [Cotton-grass, Cotton grass] - *Eriophorum angustifolium* Honckeny subsp. *subarcticum* (Vassiljev) Hultén ex Kartesz & Gandhi (3, 19, 50, 92, 156) (1840–present), *Eriophorum callitrix* Cham. ex C.A. Mey. (5, 156) (1913-1923), *Eriophorum gracile* W.D.J. Koch (85) (1932), *Eriophorum* L. (1, 7, 10, 50, 93, 156, 158) (1818–present), *Eriophorum viridicarinatum* (Engelm.) Fern. (3) (1977), *Scirpus cyperinus* (L.) Kunth (156, 184) (1793-1923), *Trichophorum alpinum* (L.) Pers. (66) (1903)

Cotton-rose [Cotton rose, Cottonrose] - *Filago* L. (156) (1923), *Filago pyramidata* L. (92) (1876), *Filago vulgaris* Lam. (5, 156) (1913-1923), *Hibiscus mutabilis* L. (109) (1949), *Logfia* Cass. (50) (present)

Cottonsedge [Cotton sedge] - *Eriophorum* L. (139, 155) (1942-1944)

Cottonseed tree [Cotton seed tree, Cottonseed-tree] - *Baccharis halimifolia* L. (5, 156) (1913-1923)

Cottontop [Cotton top] - *Digitaria californica* (Benth.) Henr. (122) (1937) TX

Cottontop echinocactus - *Echinocactus polycephalus* Engelm. & Bigelow (155) (1942)

Cottonweed [Cotton-weed, Cotton weed] - *Abutilon theophrasti* Medik (5, 156, 157, 158) (1900-1929), *Anaphalis margaritacea* (L.) Benth. & Hook (5, 92, 156, 158) (1876-1923), *Anemone cylindrica* Gray (127, 156) (1923-1933), *Antennaria plantaginifolia* (L.) Richards (156) (1923), *Epilobium* L. (1) (1932), *Froelichia gracilis* (Hook.) Moq. (3) (1977)

Cottonwood [Cotton wood, Cotton-wood] or Cottonwood tree [Cotton wood tree] - *Populus ×canadensis* Moench [*deltoides × nigra*] (12, 20) (1820-1857), *Populus deltoides* Bartr. ex Marsh. (5, 35, 72, 82, 97, 109, 131, 156, 158) (1806-1949), *Populus deltoides* Bartr. ex Marsh. subsp. *deltoides* (1, 3, 23, 27, 19, 92, 164) (1810-1977), *Populus deltoides* Bartr. ex Marsh. subsp. *monilifera* (Aiton) Eckenwalder (2, 3, 4, 9, 20, 32, 37, 46, 92, 108, 113, 114, 147, 160, 161) (1852-1986), *Populus heterophylla* L. (20) (1857), *Populus* L. (1, 4, 50, 35, 93, 109, 122, 125, 155) (1806–present), *Tilia americana* L. var. *heterophylla* (Vent.) Loud. (156) (1923)

Cottonwood poplar - *Populus deltoides* Bartr. ex Marsh. subsp. *deltoides* (12) (1821)

Cottony burdock - *Arctium tomentosum* P. Mill. (5) (1913)

Cottony golden aster - *Chrysopsis gossypina* (Michx.) Ell. (5) (1913)

Cottony jujube - *Colubrina elliptica* (Sw.) Brizicky & W.L. Stern (109) (1949)

Cotula - *Anthemis cotula* L. (7, 57) (1828-1917)

Cotula bastarda (Portuguese) - *Anthemis cotula* L. (186) (1814)

Cotula fetida (Spanish, Italian) - *Anthemis cotula* L. (186) (1814)

Cotyledon - *Cotyledon* L. (138) (1923)

Couch bent grass [Couch bent-grass] - *Calamagrostis rubescens* Buckley (possibly) (94) (1901)

Couch grass [Couch-grass] - *Agropyron* Gaertner (93) (1936), *Elymus repens* (L.) Gould (5, 19, 45, 49, 52, 53, 54, 55, 59, 56. 62, 64, 66, 67, 69, 87, 88, 90, 92, 94, 111, 118, 119, 129, 143, 157, 158, 163) (1840-1938), *Holcus lanatus* L. (46) (1671) accidentally introducedby 1671 Josselyn

Coucommer - *Cucumis sativus* L. (179) (1526)

Coucourde (gourd) - *Cucurbita pepo* L. (107) (1587)

Coudougner or coing (French) - *Cydonia oblonga* Mill. (110) (1886)

Coughroot [Cough-root, Cough root] - *Trillium cernuum* L. (5, 92, 156, 158) (1876-1923)

Coughweed [Cough weed, Cough-weed] - *Packera aurea* (L.) A.& D. Löve (92, 156, 158) (1898-1923)

Coughwort - *Tussilago farfara* L. (5, 156) (1913-1923)

Coulter's canyon-poppy [Coulter canyon-poppy] - *Romneya coulteri* Harvey (138) (1923)

Coulter's pine [Coulter pine] - *Pinus coulteri* D. Don (20, 50, 109, 138) (1857–present) for Thomas Coulter, 1793-1843, Irish botanist

Country mallow - *Malva rotundifolia* L. (5, 106, 156, 157, 158) (1900–1930), *Malva sylvestris* L. (5, 156, 158) (1900–1923)

Country walnut - *Aleurites moluccana* (L.) Willd. (107) (1919)

Countryman's-treacle [Countrymans' treacle, Country-man's treacle] - *Ruta graveolens* L. (92, 156) (1898-1923)

Courbaril - *Hymenaea courbaril* L. (138) (1923)

Courge de la Florida (French) - *Cucurbita moschata* (Duchesne ex Lam.) Duchesne ex Poir. (107) (1919)

Courgen (France, gourd) - *Cucurbita pepo* L. (107) (1536)

Couronne de moine (French) - *Taraxacum officinale* G.H. Weber ex Wiggers (158) (1900)

Couronne de St. Jean (French) - *Artemisia vulgaris* L. (6) (1892)

Cous - *Lomatium ambiguum* (Nutt.) Coult. & Rose (101) (1905) MT, *Lomatium cous* (S. Wats.) Coult. & Rose (101) (1905) MT, *Lomatium* Raf. (1) (1932), *Lomatium simplex* (Nutt.) J.F. Macbr. var. *simplex* (101) (1905) MT, *Lomatium triternatum* (Pursh) Coult. & Rose (101) (1905) MT

Cous root - *Lomatium ambiguum* (Nutt.) Coult. & Rose (101) (1905) MT, *Lomatium cous* (S. Wats.) Coult. & Rose (101) (1905) MT, *Lomatium simplex* (Nutt.) J.F. Macbr. var. *simplex* (101) (1905) MT, *Lomatium triternatum* (Pursh) Coult. & Rose (101) (1905) MT

Couve (Portuguese) - *Brassica* L. (107) (1919)

Coventry bells [Couentrie bels] - *Campanula medium* L. (92, 178) (1526-1876), *Pulsatilla patens* (L.) Mill. subsp. *multifida* (Pritz.) Zamels (possibly) (180) (1633) Cambridgeshire, England

Coville's lipfern [Coville lipfern] - *Cheilanthes covillei* Maxon (138) (1923)

Coville's phacelia - *Phacelia covillei* S. Wats. (5) (1913)

Cow basil [Cow basill] - *Mentha arvensis* L. (178) (1526), *Vaccaria hispanica* (Mill.) Rauschert (178) (1526)

Cow clover [Cow-clover] - *Trifolium pratense* L. (5, 109, 157, 158) (1900-1940), *Trifolium willdenovii* Spreng. (possibly) (106) (1930)

Cow cockle [Cowcockle] - *Saponaria* L. (1, 93) (1932-1936), *Vaccaria hispanica* (Mill.) Rauschert (1, 4, 85, 148) (1932-1986)

Cow cress [Cow-cress] - *Lepidium campestre* (L.) Aiton f. (5, 15, 156, 158) (1895–1923)

Cow garlic [Cow-garlic] - *Allium vineale* L. (156, 158) (1900-1923)

Cow herb [Cow-herb, Cowherb] - *Vaccaria hispanica* (Mill.) Rauschert (1, 3, 4, 5, 19, 72, 80, 92, 95, 109, 156, 157, 158) (1840-1986)

Cow mushroom - *Boletus* L. (78) (1898) NH

Cow oak - *Quercus michauxii* Nutt. (2, 5, 107, 156) (1895-1923)

Cow parsley - *Heracleum sphondylium* L. (92) (1876)

Cow pea [Cow-pea, Cowpea] - *Vigna* Savi (50, 82, 138, 156) (1923–present), *Vigna sinensis* (L.) Endl. (5, 82, 106, 109, 156) (1913-1949)

Cow plant [Cowplant] - *Rhododendron maximum* L. (71, 75, 156) (1898-1923) no longer in use by 1923

Cow poison - *Delphinium trolliifolium* Gray (71) (1898)

Cow soapwort - *Vaccaria hispanica* (Mill.) Rauschert (50, 138, 155) (1923–present)

Cow sorrel - *Rumex acetosella* L. (5, 73, 156, 157, 158) (1892-1929) Miramichi NB, pronounced cow-serls

Cow tree - Clusia minor L. (92) (1876)

Cow vetch [Cow-vetch] - *Astragalus canadensis* L. (82) (1930) IA, *Vicia cracca* L. (72, 138, 155, 156, 158) (1900-1923), *Vicia villosa* Roth (85) (1932) SD

Cowage - *Mucuna pruriens* (L.) DC. var. *pruriens* (19, 138) (1840-1923)

Cowaw-esuck (Narragansett) - *Pinus strobus* L. (46) (1879)

Cowbane - *Cicuta* L. (1, 93) (1932-1936), *Cicuta maculata* L. (56, 71, 80, 125, 133, 184) (1793-1898), *Cicuta virosa* L. (92) (1876), *Oxypolis* Raf. (1) (1932), *Oxypolis rigidior* (L.) Raf. (possibly) (5, 72, 97, 156) (1907-1937)

Cow-basil [Cow basil, Cow-Basill, Cow basill] - *Mentha arvensis* L. (178) (1526), *Vaccaria hispanica* (Mill.) Rauschert (5, 156, 157, 158, 178, 180) (1526-1929)

Cowbell [Cow-bell] - *Silene vulgaris* (Moench) Garcke (156) (1923) no longer in use by 1923

Cowbell silene - *Silene latifolia* Poir. (155) (1942), *Silene latifolia* Poir. subsp. *alba* (Mill.) Greuter & Burdet (155) (1942), *Silene vulgaris* (Moench) Garcke (155) (1942)

Cowberry [Cow-berry, Cow berry] - *Comarum palustre* L. (5, 156) (1913-1923), *Mitchella repens* L. (73, 156) (1892-1923) Ulster Co NY, *Potentilla* L. (1) (1932), *Vaccinium vitis-idaea* L. (5, 14, 19, 92, 107, 109, 138, 156, 178) (1526-1949)

Cowboy's delight - *Sphaeralcea coccinea* (Nutt.) Rydb. subsp. *coccinea* (98) (1926) Neb

Cow-cabbage [Cow cabbage] - *Heracleum* L. (1) (1932), *Nymphaea odorata* Aiton (7, 92) (1828-1876)

Cow-collard - *Symplocarpus foetidus* (L.) Salisb. ex Nutt. (186) (1814)

Cowgourde - *Cucumis sativus* L. (179) (1526)

Cow-grass [Cow grass] - *Polygonum aviculare* L. (5, 156, 158) (1900-1923) no longer in use by 1923, *Trifolium pratense* L. (5, 45, 66, 68, 92, 156, 158) (1896-1923) Ottawa, no longer in use by 1923

Cowhage - *Mucuna pruriens* (L.) DC. (92, 107) (1876-1919)

Cow-herb - *Saponaria* L. (1, 158) (1900-1932), *Vaccaria hispanica* (Mill.) Rauschert (131) (1899)

Cowhitch - *Mucuna pruriens* (L.) DC. var. *pruriens* (19) (1840)

Cowitch [Cow-itch, Cow itch] - *Ampelopsis arborea* (L.) Koehne (106) (1930), *Campsis radicans* (L.) Seem. ex Bureau (5, 156) (1913-1923), *Cissus trifoliata* (L.) L. (106, 124) (1930-1937), *Mucuna pruriens* (L.) DC. (92, 107) (1876-1919), *Parthenocissus heptaphylla* (Buckl.) Britt. ex Small (106) (1930)

Cowlice [Cow-lice] - *Bidens frondosa* L. (156, 158) (1900-1923)

Cowlily [Cow-lily, Cow lily] - *Caltha palustris* L. (5, 74, 156, 157, 158) (1893-1929), *Nuphar lutea* (L.) Sm. subsp. *advena* (Aiton) Kartesz & Gandhi (92, 97, 156, 157, 158) (1876-1937), *Nuphar* Sm. (1, 109, 155) (1932-1949)

Cowlips [Cow lips] - *Caltha palustris* L. (6) (1892)

Cow-paps - *Silene vulgaris* (Moench) Garcke (156) (1923) no longer in use by 1923

Cowparsnep [Cow parsnep] - *Heracleum maximum* Bartr. (7, 19) (1828-1840), *Heracleum sphondylium* L. (48) (1527-1793)

Cowparsnip [Cow parsnip, Cow-parsnip] - *Heracleum* L. (1, 2, 4, 10, 40, 50, 82, 93, 101, 138, 155, 156, 158) (1818–present), *Heracleum maximum* Bartr. (4, 5, 37, 49, 52, 62, 63, 72, 80, 82, 85, 92, 95, 106, 127, 131, 146, 156, 157, 158, 187) (1818-1986), *Heracleum sphondylium* L. (14, 107) (1882-1919)

Cowquake [Cow-quake, Cow quake] - *Briza media* L. (5) (1913), *Spergula arvensis* L. (5, 156, 158) (1900-1923) no longer in use by 1923

Cow-rattle [Cow rattle, Cow-rattle] - *Silene latifolia* Poir. subsp. *alba* (Mill.) Greuter & Burdet (5, 156, 158) (1900–1923) no longer in use by 1923

Cowslip [Cowslips, Cowslyp] - *Caltha* L. (7) (1828), *Caltha palustris* L. (2, 5, 6, 12, 5, 40, 92, 107, 156, 157, 158) (1892–1929), *Do-*

decatheon L. (93) (1936), *Dodecatheon pulchellum* (Raf.) Merr. subsp. *pulchellum* (127) (1933), *Impatiens capensis* Meerb. (5, 76, 156, 158) (1896-1923) OH, *Maianthemum canadense* Desf. (5, 73, 156, 158) (1892-1923), *Mertensia platyphylla* Heller (35) (1806), *Mertensia virginica* (L.) Pers. ex Link (35, 92) (1806-1876) William Clark, *Primula* L. (1) (1932), *Primula veris* L. (109, 179) (1526-1949), *Ranunculus fascicularis* Muhl. ex Bigelow (5, 156, 158) (1900–1923), *Trillium recurvatum* Beck (78) (1898) IN

Cowslip primrose - *Primula veris* L. (92, 138) (1876-1923) England

Cowslips of Jerusalem - *Pulmonaria officinalis* L. (178) (1526)

Cowslop [Cowslops] - *Caltha palustris* L. (74, 157, 158) (1893–1929) Ferrisburgh VT

Cow's-lungwort [Cow's lungwort] - *Verbascum thapsus* L. (5, 6, 69, 156, 158) (1892-1923) no longer in use by 1923

Cow's-tail [Cows' tail] - *Conyza canadensis* (L.) Cronq. var. *canadensis* (5, 69, 73, 92, 156, 157, 158) (1876-1929) Normal, IL

Cowthwort - *Leonurus cardiaca* L. (5, 156, 157, 158) (1900–1929)

Cowtongue [Cow tongue, Cow-tongue] - *Clintonia borealis* (Ait.) Raf. (5, 73, 156) (1892-1923) Aroostock Co ME; NB, *Polygonum sagittatum* L. (177) (1762)

Cow-wheat [Cow wheat] - *Melampyrum* (Tourn.) L. (1, 2, 10, 180) (1633-1932), *Melampyrum lineare* Desr. (possibly) (156, 187) (1818–1923), *Melampyrum lineare* Desr. var. *lineare* (19, 46, 63) (1783-1899), *Rhinanthus minor* L. subsp. *minor* (156) (1923)

Cow-wort [Cow's wort, Cow's-wort] - *Pedicularis palustris* L. (5, 156) (1913-1923)

Coxscomb evergreen - *Erythrina crista-galli* L. (19) (1840)

Coyolli (Mexico) - *Cocos nucifera* L. (110) (16th century) Mexico

Coyote weed - *Croton setigerus* Hook. (106) (1930)

Coyote willow - *Salix exigua* Nutt. (3, 4, 155) (1942-1986), *Salix interior* Rowlee (3) (1977)

Coyotillo - *Karwinskia humboldtiana* (J.A. Schultes) Zucc. (122, 124) (1937) TX

Crab - *Malus* Mill. (138) (1923)

Crab apple [Crab-apple, Crabapple] - *Malus coronaria* (L.) Mill. (5, 20) (1857-1913), *Malus coronaria* (L.) Mill. var. *coronaria* (19, 41, 47, 92, 103) (1770-1876), *Malus fusca* (Raf.) Schneid. (106) (1930), *Malus ioensis* (Wood) Britton (37) (1919), *Malus* Mill. (106, 155) (1930-1942), *Pyrus* L. (4) (1986)

Crab cactus [Crabcactus] - *Schlumbergera* Lem. (138, 155) (1923-1942), *Schlumbergera truncata* (Haw.) Moran (109) (1949)

Crab cherry - *Prunus avium* (L.) L. (5) (1913)

Crab stock - *Malus sylvestris* Mill. (5) (1913)

Crab thistle [Crab-thistle] - *Onopordum acanthium* L. (158) (1900)

Crab tree [Crab-tree] - *Malus coronaria* (L.) Mill. (5) (1913), *Malus coronaria* (L.) Mill. var. *coronaria* (41) (1770), *Malus* Mill. (158) (1900), *Malus sylvestris* Mill. (5) (1913), *Pyrus* L. (167) (1814)

Crabgrass [Crab-grass, Crab grass] - *Dactyloctenium aegyptium* (L.) Willd. (5) (1913), *Digitaria* Haller (1, 7, 10, 50, 93, 110) (1818–present), *Digitaria ischaemum* (Schreb.) Schreb. ex Muhl. (119, 145) (1897-1938), *Digitaria sanguinalis* (L.) Scop. (3, 11, 19, 45, 56, 62, 67, 87, 88, 92, 94, 107, 111, 119, 122, 134, 145, 152) (1840-1977), *Eleusine* Gaertn. (93) (1936), *Eleusine indica* (L.) Gaertn. (5, 66, 72, 87, 88, 92, 119, 145, 187) (1818-1938), *Eragrostis mexicana* (Hornem.) Link subsp. *mexicana* (94, 152) (1901-1912), *Eragrostis tef* (Zuccagni) Trotter (56) (1901), *Polygonum aviculare* L. (5) (1913)

Crab's-claw - *Polygonum persicaria* L. (158) (1900)

Crab's-eye [Crab's eye] - *Abrus precatorius* L. (92) (1876), *Lecanora affinis* Eversm. (107) (1919)

Crabweed [Crab-weed] - *Polygonum aviculare* L. (158) (1900)

Crack willow - *Salix fragilis* L. (3, 4, 5, 50, 85, 107, 109, 156, 158) (1900–present)

Cracker-berry - *Cornus canadensis* L. (156, 158) (1900-1923)

Crackers - *Gaylussacia baccata* (Wang.) K. Koch (5, 156) (1913-1923)

Craf (Welsh) - *Allium sativum* L. (110) (1886)

Crag aster - *Ionactis alpina* (Nutt.) Greene (155) (1942)

Crain - *Ranunculus ficaria* L. (5, 156) (1913-1923)

Crakeberry [Crake berry, Crake-berry] - *Empetrum nigrum* L. (5, 10, 107, 156) (1818-1923) no longer in use by 1923

Crake-needles [Crake needles] - *Scandix pecten-veneris* L. (5) (1913)

Cramberry [Cram berry] - *Vaccinium oxycoccos* L. (5, 156) (1913-1923)

Crambling rocket - *Reseda alba* L. (180) (1633), *Reseda lutea* L. (5, 156, 178) (1596-1923), *Sisymbrium officinale* (L.) Scop (107) (1919)

Cramp bark [Cramp-bark] or Cramp-bark tree - *Viburnum opulus* L. (5, 49, 52, 53, 54, 57, 58, 59, 92, 156, 158) (1869-1923)

Cramp-root - *Geum aleppicum* Jacq. (156) (1923)

Cran (French) - *Armoracia rusticana* P.G. Gaertn., B. Mey. & Scherb. (110) (1886)

Cran de Bretagne (French) - *Armoracia rusticana* P.G. Mey. & Scherb. (158) (1900)

Cranberry [Cran berry] - *Vaccinium* L. (1, 10, 156, 167) (1814-1932), *Vaccinium macrocarpon* Aiton (2, 14, 19, 40, 43, 47, 86, 92, 103, 106, 107, 109) (1820-1949), *Vaccinium oxycoccos* L. (5, 107) (1913-1919), *Vaccinium vitis-idaea* L. (107) (1919)

Cranberry bush - *Viburnum* L. (1) (1932), *Viburnum opulus* L. (47) (1852), *Viburnum opulus* L. var. *americanum* Aiton (105, 106, 109) (1930-1949)

Cranberry tree - *Viburnum* L. (1) (1932), *Viburnum opulus* L. (2, 63, 72, 107, 130, 131, 156, 158) (1895-1923)

Crandall currant - *Ribes aureum* Pursh (2) (1895)

Craneberry [Crane-berry, Crane berry, Cranesberry] - *Vaccinium macrocarpon* Aiton (7, 19) (1828-1840), *Vaccinium oxycoccos* L. (5, 92, 156) (1876-1923)

Cranebill [Cranesbill, Cranesbill, Crane's-bill, Crane's bill] - *Erodium* L'Her. ex Aiton (45) (1896), *Geranium* L. (1, 2, 4, 13, 15, 82, 93, 106, 109, 138, 156, 158, 184) (~1759-1986), *Geranium maculatum* L. (19, 46, 49, 52, 53, 54, 55, 57, 59, 61, 64, 92, 102, 156, 157, 158, 186) (1649-1929), *Geranium molle* L. (5) (1913) from shape of root (76) name better applied to another plant (158), *Geranium oreganum* Howell (76) (1896), *Geranium robertianum* L. (41) (1770)

Crane-fly orchis [Cranefly orchis] - *Tipularia discolor* (Pursh) Nutt. (5, 122, 156) (1913-1937)

Crane-neck - *Cucurbita moschata* (Duchesne ex Lam.) Duchesne ex Poir. (107) (1776)

Crane-willow [Crane willow] - *Cephalanthus occidentalis* L. (5, 6, 49, 156, 157, 158) (1892–1929)

Cranjero (Mexico) - *Celtis pallida* Torr. (107) (1919)

Cranson de Bretagne (French) - *Armoracia rusticana* P.G. Gaertn., B. Mey. & Scherb. (110) (1886)

Cranxero (Mexico) - *Celtis pallida* Torr. (107) (1919)

Crap - *Fagopyrum esculentum* Moench (5, 156, 158) (1900-1923), *Lolium perenne* L. (5) (1913)

Crapeberry [Crape-berry] - *Corema conradii* (Torr.) Torr. ex Loud. (156) (1923)

Crape-jasmine - *Tabernaemontana divaricata* (L.) R. Br. ex Roemer & J.A. Schultes (109, 138) (1923-1949)

Crape-myrtle [Crapemyrtle, Crape myrtle] - *Lagerstroemia indica* L. (109, 122, 124) (1937-1949), *Lagerstroemia* L. (138) (1923)

Crape-needle - *Scandix pecten-veneris* L. (156) (1923) no longer in use by 1923

Crashed - *Rorippa nasturtium-aquaticum* (L.) Hayek (5) (1913)

Crashes - *Nasturtium officinale* W.T. Aiton (possibly) (156, 158) (1900-1923) no longer in use by 1923

Crassula - *Crassula* L. (155) (1942)

Crataegus - *Crataegus aestivalis* Torr. & Gray. (107) (1919), *Crataegus monogyna* Jacq. (54) (1905)

Craw peas [Craw-peas] - *Lathyrus pratensis* L. (5) (1913)

Crawberry [Craw-berry, Craw berry] - *Vaccinium oxycoccos* L. (5, 156) (1913-1923)

Crawe's sedge - *Carex crawei* Dewey (5, 50, 66, 72) (1893–present)

Crawford's sedge - *Carex crawfordii* Fernald (5, 50) (1913–present)

Crawford's squaw-weed [Crawford's squaw weed] - *Packera paupercula* (Michx.) A.& D. Löve (5) (1913)

Crawley - *Corallorrhiza* Gagnebin (75) (1894) NC, *Corallorrhiza odontorhiza* (Willd.) Poir. (158) (1900), *Pterospora andromedea* Nutt. (61) (1870)

Crawley root [Crawley-root] - *Corallorrhiza maculata* (Raf.) Raf. (157) (1929), *Corallorrhiza odontorhiza* (Willd.) Poir. (5, 49, 52, 53, 57, 64, 92, 156, 158) (1900-1923)

Crawling phlox - *Phlox bifida* Beck (72) (1907) IA, *Phlox stolonifera* Sims. (5) (1913)

Crawly grass - *Sporobolus buckleyi* Vasey (78) (1898) TX

Crazy - *Ranunculus acris* L. (157, 158) (1900-1929)

Crazy bet [Crazy-bet] - *Caltha palustris* L. (5, 157) (1913-1929)

Crazyweed [Crazy-weed, Crazy weed] - *Astragalus mollissimus* Torr (5, 71, 97, 156, 157, 158) (1898–1937), *Crotalaria sagittalis* L. (156) (1923), *Oxytropis* DC. (155) (1942), *Oxytropis lambertii* Pursh (71, 133, 146, 156) (1898-1939), *Oxytropis splendens* Dougl. ex Hook (133) (1903)

Cream clematis - *Clematis florida* Thunb. (138) (1923)

Cream milkvetch - *Astragalus racemosus* Pursh (50) (present), *Astragalus racemosus* Pursh var. *longisetus* M.E. Jones (50) (present), *Astragalus racemosus* Pursh var. *racemosus* (50) (present)

Cream naricissus - *Narcissus tazetta* L. (50) (present)

Cream pea - *Lathyrus ochroleucus* Hook. (50) (present)

Cream peavine - *Lathyrus ochroleucus* Hook. (155) (1942)

Cream violet - *Viola striata* Aiton (138, 156) (1923)

Cream wild indigo [Cream wild-indigo, Cream wildindigo] - *Baptisia bracteata* Muhl. ex Ell. (138, 155) (1923-1942)

Cream-colored avens - *Geum virginianum* L. (5) (1913)

Cream-colored goldenrod - *Solidago bicolor* L. (106) (1930)

Cream-colored indigo - *Baptisia bracteata* var. *glabrescens* (Larisey) Isely (48) (1882)

Cream-colored jewelweed [Cream-colored jewel-weed] - *Impatiens pallida* Nutt. (156) (1923)

Cream-colored pea - *Lathyrus ochroleucus* Hook. (85) (1932)

Cream-colored vetchling - *Lathyrus ochroleucus* Hook. (5, 72, 93, 131) (1899–1936)

Creamcups [Cream-cups, Cream cups] - *Platystemon* Benth. (15) (1895), *Platystemon californicus* Benth. (74, 106, 109, 138) (1893-1949) Santa Barbara Co, CA, *Platystigma linearis* Benth. (74) (1893) Santa Barbara Co, CA

Cream-flower rockcress [Creamflower rockcress] - *Arabis hirsuta* (L.) Scop. var. *pycnocarpa* (M. Hopkins) Rollins (50) (present)

Cream-flower ticktrefoil [Cream-flowered tick trefoil] - *Desmodium ochroleucum* M.A. Curtis ex Canby (5) (1913)

Creamy poisonvetch - *Astragalus racemosus* Pursh (3, 4) (1977-1986)

Creamy-bell honeysuckle - *Lonicera chrysantha* Turcz. ex Ledeb. (112) (1937)

Creashak [Creashaks] - *Arctostaphylos uva-ursi* (L.) Spreng. (107, 156, 157) (1919-1929)

Cree potato - *Pediomelum esculentum* (Pursh) Rydb. (5, 156, 158) (1900–1923)

Cree turnip - *Pediomelum esculentum* (Pursh) Rydb. (158) (1900)

Creek goldenrod - *Solidago canadensis* L. var. *salibrosa* (Piper) M.E.Jones (155) (1942)

Creek gum - *Eucalyptus camaldulensis* Dehnhardt (57, 138) (1917-1923)

Creek maple - *Acer rubrum* L. (5, 156, 157, 158) (1900–1929)

Creek plum - *Prunus rivularis* Scheele (4, 50, 107, 155) (1919–present)

Creek stuff - *Spartina cynosuroides* (L.) Roth (5) (1913)

Creek thatch - *Spartina cynosuroides* (L.) Roth (5) (1913), *Spartina maritima* (M.A. Curtis) Fern. (5) (1913)

Creek-grass [Creek grass] - *Potamogeton epihydrus* Raf. (5) (1913)

Creek-sedge [Creek sedge] - *Spartina alterniflora* Loisel. (94) (1901), *Spartina maritima* (M.A. Curtis) Fern. (5) (1913)

Creeper [Creepers] - *Calystegia sepium* (L.) R. Br. subsp. *sepium* (5, 73, 156, 158) (1892–1923), *Echinocystis lobata* (Michx.) Torr. & Gray (5, 76, 158) (1896-1913) ME, *Parthenocissus* Planch. (7, 50, 155) (1828–present), *Parthenocissus quinquefolia* (L.) Planch. (19, 92) (1840–1876)

Creeping aster - *Eurybia surculosa* (Michx.) Nesom (5) (1913)

Creeping barberry - *Mahonia repens* (Lindl.) G. Don (2, 4 50, 113, 130) (1890–present)

Creeping beard grass [Creeping beard-grass] - *Oplismenus hirtellus* (L.) Beauv. (94) (1901)

Creeping bellflower - *Campanula rapunculoides* L. (3, 4, 5, 107, 155, 156) (1913-1986)

Creeping bent - *Agrostis capillaris* L. (45) (1896), *Agrostis gigantea* Roth (45) (1896), *Agrostis stolonifera* L. (109, 138, 163) (1852-1949)

Creeping bent grass [Creeping bent-grass, Creeping brentgrass] - *Agrostis gigantea* Roth (5, 119) (1913-1938), *Agrostis stolonifera* L. (42, 50, 56, 68, 122, 143, 155, 165) (1768–present)

Creeping bindweed [Creeping bind weed] - *Calystegia sepium* (L.) R. Br. subsp. *angulata* Brummitt (42) (1814)

Creeping blackberry - *Rubus canadensis* L. (49) (1898), *Rubus pubescens* Raf. (4) (1986), *Rubus trivialis* Michx. (19, 92) (1840–1876)

Creeping bluets - *Houstonia serpyllifolia* Michx. (109, 138) (1923-1949)

Creeping bur - *Lycopodium clavatum* L. (5) (1913)

Creeping burhead [Creeping bur-head, Creeping burrhead] - *Echinodorus cordifolius* (L.) Griseb. (5, 50, 97, 120) (1913–present)

Creeping bush-clover [Creeping bush clover] - *Lespedeza repens* (L.) Bart. (5, 97) (1913-1937)

Creeping buttercup - *Ranunculus hispidus* Michx. var. *nitidus* (Chapman) T. Duncan (2, 80) (1895–1913), *Ranunculus repens* L. (5, 6, 50, 72, 138, 155, 156, 158) (1892–present)

Creeping charlie [Creeping-charlie, Creeping charley] - *Glechoma hederacea* L. (5, 73, 80, 82, 156, 157, 158) (1892-1930), *Lysimachia nummularia* L. (109) (1949), *Malva rotundifolia* L. (62) (1912) IN, *Sedum acre* L. (5, 156) (1913-1923)

Creeping checker-berry [Creeping checker berry] - *Mitchella repens* L. (6) (1892)

Creeping Cherley - *Pilea nummulariifolia* (Sw.) Weddell (109) (1949)

Creeping cinquefoil - *Potentilla reptans* L. (92) (1876)

Creeping cotoneaster - *Cotoneaster adpressus* Boiss. (138) (1923)

Creeping cranebill [Creeping Cranes bill] - *Erodium cicutarium* (L.) L'Hér. ex Aiton (possibly) (178) (1526)

Creeping crowfoot [Creeping crow-foot] - *Ranunculus repens* L. (6, 107, 187) (1818-1919)

Creeping cucumber - *Melothria* L. (4, 158) (1900-1986), *Melothria pendula* L. (3, 4, 5, 19, 92, 97, 122, 124, 156) (1840-1986)

Creeping dayflower [Creeping day-flower] - *Commelina communis* L. (98) (1926), *Commelina diffusa* Burm. f. (3) (1977), *Murdannia nudiflora* (L.) Brenan (5, 97, 138) (1913-1937)

Creeping dogwood [Creeping dog wood] - *Cornus sericea* L. subsp. *sericea* (42) (1814)

Creeping epigaea - *Epigaea repens* L. (187) (1818)

Creeping eragrostis - *Eragrostis hypnoides* (Lam.) Britton, Sterns & Poggenb. (56, 72) (1901-1907)

Creeping eryngo - *Eryngium prostratum* Nutt. ex DC. (50) (present)

Creeping evergreen mitchella - *Mitchella repens* L. (8) (1785)

Creeping fern - *Lygodium palmatum* (Bernh.) Sw. (5) (1913)

Creeping fescue - *Festuca rubra* L. (68) (1890)

Creeping fig - *Ficus pumila* L. (109) (1949)

Creeping forget-me-not - *Omphalodes verna* Moench (109) (1949)

Creeping foxtail - *Alopecurus arundinaceus* Poir (3, 155) (1942-1977)

Creeping great valerian - *Polemonium reptans* L. (5, 156) (1913-1923)

Creeping Greek valerian - *Polemonium reptans* L. (86, 158) (1878-1900)

Creeping greenhead [Creeping green head] - *Oldenlandia uniflora* L. (19, 156) (1840-1923)

Creeping ground laurel - *Epigaea repens* L. (41, 187) (1770-1818)

Creeping gypsophila - *Gypsophila repens* L. (138) (1923)

Creeping hedgehyssop [Creeping hedge hyssop] - *Gratiola virginiana* L. (19) (1840)

Creeping hemlock - *Taxus canadensis* Willd. (5, 75) (1894-1913)

Creeping hollygrape - *Mahonia repens* (Lindl.) G. Don (138) (1923)

Creeping Jack - *Sedum acre* L. (5, 156) (1913-1923) no longer in use by 1923

Creeping Jenny [Creeping Jennie, Creeping-Jennie, Creeping-jenny] - *Convolvulus arvensis* L. (85) (1932) SD, *Echinocystis lobata* (Michx.) Torr. & Gray (5, 76, 156, 158) (1896-1923), *Glechoma hederacea* L. (156) (1923), *Lycopodium clavatum* L. (5, 73) (1892-1913), *Lycopodium complanatum* L. (5, 73, 158) (1892-1913) Bedford MA, *Lysimachia nummularia* L. (5, 50, 109, 158) (1900–present), *Sedum reflexum* L. (156) (1923)

Creeping juniper - *Juniperus horizontalis* Moench (3, 4, 50, 109, 130, 136, 138, 155) (1895–present)

Creeping knotweed - *Polygonum amphibium* L. var. *emersum* Michx. (19) (1840)

Creeping lady's-sorrel [Creeping ladies sorrel] - *Oxalis corniculata* L. (4) (1986)

Creeping lespedeza - *Lespedeza repens* (L.) Bart. (3, 4, 155) (1942-1986)

Creeping lichnidia - *Phlox pilosa* L. (19) (1840)

Creeping lippia - *Phyla nodiflora* (L.) Greene (138) (1923)

Creeping loosestrife - *Lysimachia nummularia* L. (156, 158) (1900-1923)

Creeping love grass [Creeping lovegrass] - *Neeragrostis* Bush (50) (present), *Neeragrostis reptans* (Michx.) Nicora (50, 155) (1942–present)

Creeping mahonia - *Mahonia repens* (Lindl.) G. Don (155) (1942)

Creeping manna grass [Creeping mannagrass] - *Glyceria acutiflora* Torr. (50) (present)

Creeping meadow foxtail - *Alopecurus arundinaceus* Poir (50) (present)

Creeping meadow grass [Creeping meadow-grass] - *Eragrostis hypnoides* (Lam.) Britton, Sterns & Poggenb. (111) (1915), *Neeragrostis reptans* (Michx.) Nicora (66, 163, 187) (1818-1903)

Creeping mesquite - *Hilaria belangeri* (Steud.) Nash (163) (1852)

Creeping milkweed - *Asclepias asperula* (Dcne.) Woods. subsp. *capricornu* (Woods.) Woods. (5) (1913)

Creeping mitchella - *Mitchella repens* L. (187) (1818)

Creeping muhly - *Muhlenbergia repens* (J. Presl) A.S. Hitchc. (122) (1937)

Creeping nailwort - *Paronychia sessiliflora* Nutt. (50) (present)

Creeping oxalis - *Oxalis corniculata* L. (138, 155) (1923-1942)

Creeping panic - *Panicum repens* L. (94) (1901)

Creeping parthenium - *Parthenium integrifolium* L. var. *hispidum* (Raf.) Mears (5) (1913)

Creeping pearlwort - *Sagina procumbens* L. (156) (1923)

Creeping phlox - *Phlox andicola* E. Nels. (98) (1926), *Phlox stolonifera* Sims. (109, 138) (1923-1949), *Phlox subulata* L. (77) (1898) Sulphur Grove OH

Creeping pigeon-berry [Creeping pigeon berry] - *Epigaea repens* L. (42) (1814)

Creeping poa - *Poa compressa* L. (68) (1890)

Creeping polemonium - *Polemonium reptans* L. (3, 4, 138, 155) (1923-1986)

Creeping primrose-willow [Creeping primrose willow] - *Ludwigia peploides* (Kunth) Raven (5, 156, 158) (1900–1923), *Ludwigia peploides* (Kunth) Raven subsp. *glabrescens* (Kuntze) Raven (158) (1900), *Ludwigia repens* Forst. (50) (present)

Creeping rattlesnake-plantain - *Goodyera repens* (L.) R. Br. ex Ait. f. (138) (1923)

Creeping red cedar - *Juniperus horizontalis* Moench (131, 136) (1899-1930)

Creeping reimaria - *Reimarochloa oligostachya* (Munro ex Benth.) (94) (1901)

Creeping root plant - *Goodyera repens* (L.) R. Br. ex Ait. f. (5) (1913)

Creeping rush - *Juncus repens* Michx. (5) (1913), *Juncus subtilis* E. Meyer (5) (1913)

Creeping sage - *Salvia sonomensis* Greene (106) (1930)

Creeping Sally - *Lysimachia nummularia* L. (5, 156) (1913-1923)

Creeping saxifrage - *Saxifraga stolonifera* Meerb. (19) (1840)

Creeping sea meadow grass - *Puccinellia maritima* (Huds.) Parl. (66) (1903)

Creeping sedge - *Carex chordorrhiza* Ehrh. Ex L. f. (5, 50, 72) (1893–present)

Creeping selaginella - *Selaginella apoda* (L.) Spring (5) (1913)

Creeping snapdragon - *Knautia arvensis* (L.) Duby (19) (1840)

Creeping snowberry [Creeping snow-berry] - *Gaultheria hispidula* (L.) Muhl. ex Bigelow (2, 5, 40, 41, 107, 109, 156) (1770-1949), *Gaultheria* L. (1, 156) (1923-1932)

Creeping soft grass - *Holcus mollis* L. (45, 66) (1896-1903)

Creeping spear grass [Creeping spear-grass] - *Poa compressa* L. (129) (1894)

Creeping spearwort - *Ranunculus flammula* L. (5, 156) (1913-1923), *Ranunculus flammula* L. var. *filiformis* (Michx.) Hook. (2) (1895)

Creeping spike rush [Creeping spike-rush] - *Eleocharis palustris* (L.) Roemer & J.A. Schultes (5, 72, 120, 156) (1907-1938)

Creeping spurge - *Chamaesyce maculata* (L.) Small (80) (1913)

Creeping St. John's-wort [Creeping St. John's wort, Creeping St. Johnswort] - *Hypericum adpressum* Raf. ex W. Bart. (5, 156) (1913-1923)

Creeping strawberry - *Dalibarda repens* L. (156) (1923)

Creeping thistle [Creeping-thistle] - *Cirsium arvense* (L.) Scop. (5, 62, 156, 157, 158) (1900-1929)

Creeping velvet grass [Creeping velvetgrass] - *Holcus mollis* L. (50) (present)

Creeping vetch - *Vicia faba* L. (7) (1828), *Vicia hirsuta* (L.) Gray (19) (1840)

Creeping vine - *Lycopodium complanatum* L. (78) (1898) Ferrisburgh VT

Creeping water rocket - *Rorippa sylvestris* (L.) Besser (possibly) (10) (1818)

Creeping water-parsley - *Berula erecta* (Huds.) Coville (156) (1923)

Creeping water-parsnip [Creeping water parsnip] - *Berula erecta* (Huds.) Coville (5, 158) (1900–1913)

Creeping water-primrose [Creeping waterprimrose] - *Ludwigia peploides* (Kunth) Raven subsp. *glabrescens* (Kuntze) Raven (155) (1942)

Creeping wheat - *Elymus repens* (L.) Gould (45) (1896)

Creeping wheat grass [Creeping wheat-grass] - *Elymus repens* (L.) Gould (64, 69) (1904-1908)

Creeping whorled mint - *Mentha arvensis* L. (5, 93) (1913-1936)

Creeping wild rye [Creeping wildrye] - *Leymus triticoides* (Buckl.) Pilger (155) (1942)

Creeping wild white hellebore [Creeping wilde white Hellebore] - *Epipactis helleborine* (L.) Crantz (178) (1596)

Creeping wintergreen - *Gaultheria hispidula* (L.) Muhl. ex Bigelow (19, 92) (1840-1876), *Gaultheria procumbens* L. (1, 2, 5, 6, 156) (1892-1932)

Creeping wood sorrel [Creeping woodsorrel] - *Oxalis corniculata* L. (50) (present)

Creeping yellow cress [Creeping yellowcress] - *Rorippa sinuata* (Nutt.) A.S. Hitchc. (3, 4) (1977-1986), *Rorippa sylvestris* (L.) Bess. (50) (present)

Creeping yellow water cress - *Rorippa sylvestris* (L.) Bess. (5) (1913)

Creeping-root burning-bush [Creeping-rooted burning-bush] - *Euonymus americanus* L. (187) (1818)

Creeping-root Jacob's-ladder [Creeping-rooted Jacob's-ladder] - *Polemonium reptans* L. (187) (1818)

Creeping-root plant - *Goodyera repens* (L.) R. Br. ex Ait. f. (156) (1923)

Creeping-root spindle-tree [Creeping-rooted spindle-tree] - *Euonymus americanus* L. (187) (1818)

Creeping-root violet [Creepingroot violet] - *Viola canadensis* L. var. *rugulosa* (Greene) A.S. Hitchc. (50) (present)

Crenate-leaf phacelia [Crenateleaf phacelia, Crenate-leaved phacelia] - *Phacelia integrifolia* Torr. (5, 97, 122) (1913-1937)

Creosote bush - *Larrea tridentata* (Sessé & Moc. ex DC.) Coville var. *tridentata* (106, 149, 153) (1904-1930)

Creosote bush [Creasote bush] - *Larrea tridentata* (Sessé & Moc. ex DC.) Coville (14, 124) (1882-1937)

Creosote plant - *Larrea* Ort. (13) (1849), *Larrea tridentata* (Sessé & Moc. ex DC.) Coville (15, 107, 147) (1856-1919)

Cress - *Lepidium* L. (2, 10) (1818-1895), *Lepidium sativum* L. (5, 92, 107, 179) (1526–1919)

Cressa - *Cressa* L. (158) (1900)

Cresses of India - *Trollius laxus* Salisb. (180) (1633)

Cress-leaf coreopsis [Cressleaf coreopsis, Cress leaf coreopsis] - *Coreopsis tinctoria* Nutt. var. *tinctoria* (122, 124) (1937)

Cress-leaf groundsel [Cressleaf groundsel, Cress-leaved groundsel] - *Packera glabella* (Poir) C. Jeffrey (5, 97, 155, 156) (1913-1942)

Cress-leaf tickseed [Cress-leaved tickseed] - *Coreopsis tinctoria* Nutt. var. *tinctoria* (5, 97) (1913-1937)

Cresson de fontaine (French) - *Rorippa nasturtium-aquaticum* (L.) Hayek (158) (1900)

Cresson jaune (French) - *Rorippa palustris* (L.) Bess. (17) (1796)

Crested agave - *Agave univittata* Haw. (138) (1923)

Crested anoda - *Anoda* Cav. (50) (present), *Anoda cristata* (L.) Schlecht. (50) (present)

Crested arrowhead - *Sagittaria cristata* Engelm. (50, 72) (1907–present)

Crested beardtongue [Crested beard-tongue] - *Penstemon eriantherus* Pursh (3, 4, 5, 85, 93, 127, 131) (1899-1986)

Crested coral - *Clavulina cristata* (Fr.) Schroer. (170) (1995)

Crested coral fungus - *Clavulina cristata* (Fr.) Schroer. (128) (1933) ND

Crested coralroot [Crested coral root] - *Hexalectris spicata* (Walt.) Barnh (3, 5, 122, 156) (1913-1977)

Crested dog's-tail [Crested dogtail] - *Cynosurus cristatus* L. (45, 56, 66, 68, 109, 138) (1896-1949) IA NM

Crested dog's-tail grass [Crested dog's tail grass] - *Cynosurus cristatus* L. (5, 50, 92) (1876–present)

Crested dwarf iris - *Iris cristata* Ait. (5, 97) (1913-1937)

Crested false buckwheat - *Polygonum cuspidatum* Sieb. & Zucc. (72) (1907)

Crested false buckwheat - *Polygonum scandens* L. var. *cristatum* (Engelm. & Gray) Gleason (5) (1913)

Crested feather grass [Crested feather-grass] - *Achnatherum coronatum* (Thurb.) Barkworth (94) (1901)

Crested fern - *Dryopteris cristata* (L.) A. Gray (5, 86) (1878-1913)

Crested hair grass - *Koeleria macrantha* (Ledeb.) J.A. Schultes (5, 92) (1876-1913)

Crested iris - *Iris cristata* Ait. (107, 138) (1919-1923)

Crested koeleria - *Koeleria macrantha* (Ledeb.) J.A. Schultes (66, 87) (1884-1903)

Crested prickly-poppy [Crested pricklypoppy] - *Argemone pleiacantha* Greene (possibly) (138, 155) (1923-1942), *Argemone polyanthemos* (Fedde) G. Ownbey (50) (present)

Crested rye grass [Crested ryegrass] - *Lolium perenne* L. var. *perenne* (155) (1942)

Crested sagittaria - *Sagittaria cristata* Engelm. (5) (1913)

Crested sedge - *Carex cristatella* Britt. (5, 50, 72) (1893–present)

Crested shield fern [Crested shield-fern] - *Dryopteris cristata* (L.) A. Gray (4, 5, 72, 86) (1878-1986)

Crested wheat grass [Crested wheatgrass, Crested wheat-grass] - *Agropyron cristatum* (L.) Gaertn. (3, 50, 140, 143, 146, 155, 185) (1852–present)

Crested wood fern [Crested woodfern] - *Dryopteris cristata* (L.) A. Gray (3, 5, 50, 138, 155) (1911–present)

Cretan brake - *Pteris cretica* L. (50, 138) (1923–present)

Cretan bryony - *Bryonia cretica* L. subsp. *dioica* (Jacq.) Tutin (55) (1911)

Cretan mullein [Cretan-mullein] - *Verbascum blattaria* L. (174) (1753)

Cretan rye - *Secale cereale* L. (66) (1903)

Cretan sandwort [Crete sandwort] - *Arenaria cretica* Spreng. (155) (1942)

Cricket-bat willow [Cricketbat willow] - *Salix alba* L. (138) (1923)

Crimean linden - *Tilia euchlora* K. Koch (109, 138) (1923-1949)

Crimmon - *Hordeum vulgare* L. (180) (1633)

Crimson bramble - *Rubus ostryifolius* Rydb. (107) (1919)

Crimson catchfly - *Silene virginica* L. (187) (1818)

Crimson clover - *Trifolium incarnatum* L. (3, 4, 5, 45, 50, 63, 66, 68, 72, 82, 85, 93, 95, 97, 106, 109, 114, 138, 146, 155, 156) (1894–present)

Crimson fountain grass - *Pennisetum alopecuroides* (L.) Spreng. (138) (1923)

Crimson hibiscus - *Hibiscus coccineus* Walt (183) (~1756)

Crimson monkey-flower [Crimson monkeyflower] - *Mimulus cardinalis* Dougl. ex Benth. (138) (1923)

Crimson rambler - *Rosa multiflora* Thunb. ex Murray (82) (1930)

Crimson weigela - *Weigela floribunda* (Sieb. & Zucc.) K. Koch (138) (1923)

Crimson-disk aster - *Eurybia divaricata* (L.) Nesom (5) (1913)

Crimson-eye rosemallow [Crimson-eyed rose mallow, Crimsoneyed rosemallow] - *Hibiscus moscheutos* L. (50) (present), *Hibiscus moscheutos* L. subsp. *moscheutos* (5, 50, 138, 156) (1913–present)

Crimson-sedge copperleaf [Crimsonsedge copperleaf] - *Acalypha armentacea* Roxb. (138) (1923)

Crinkle awn - *Trachypogon spicatus* (L.) Kuntze (122) (1937) TX

Crinkled hair-grass - *Deschampsia flexuosa* (L.) Trin. (119) (1938)

Crinkled passionflower - *Passiflora gracilis* Jacq. ex Link (138) (1923)

Crinkleroot [Crinkle-root, Crinkle root] - *Cardamine diphylla* (Michx.) Wood (2, 5, 74, 92, 138, 156) (1876-1923)

Crinum - *Crinum* L. (138) (1923) Greek for lily, *Crinum americanum* L. (174) (1753)

Crinum lily - *Crinum* L. (109) (1949)

Crisp parsley [Crispe parsley] - *Petroselinum crispum* (P. Mill.) Nyman ex A.W. Hill (possibly) (178) (1526)

Crisp tansy [Crispe tansie] - *Tanacetum vulgare* L. (178) (1526)

Crisped bunchflower [Crisped bunch flower] - *Melanthium latifolium* Desr. (5) (1913)

Crisped thistle - *Carduus crispus* L. (41) (1770)

Crisp-leaf amaranth [Crisp-leaved amaranth] - *Amaranthus crispus* (Lesp. & Thev.) N. Terracc (5) (1913)

Crisp-leaf eriogonum [Crisp-leaved eriogonum] - *Eriogonum corymbosum* Benth. (5) (1913)

Crisp-leaf mint [Crisped-leaved mint, Crispleaf mint] - *Mentha ×piperita* L. [*aquatica × spicata*] (5, 155, 158) (1900-1942)

Cristatella - *Polanisia jamesii* (Torr. & Gray) Iltis (3, 4) (1977-1986), *Polanisia* Raf. (158) (1900)

Critical meadowrue - *Thalictrum venulosum* Trel. (155) (1942)

Crocklety-bur - *Arctium lappa* L. (158) (1900)

Crocus [Crocuses] - *Anemone parviflora* Michx. (106) (1930), *Crocus* L. (138) (1923), *Epigaea repens* L. (5, 156) (1913-1923), *Iris pumila* L. (73) (1892) NH, *Pulsatilla patens* (L.) Mill.subsp. *multifida* (Pritz.) Zamels (6, 74, 126, 127) (1892-1933)

Crompled lettuce - *Lactuca sativa* L. (180) (1633)

Croneberry [Crone-berry, Crone berry] - *Vaccinium oxycoccos* L. (5, 156) (1913-1923)

Crooked andryala - *Andryala integrifolia* L. (42) (1814)

Crooked stonecrop - *Sedum reflexum* L. (156) (1923)

Crooked yellow stonecrop - *Sedum reflexum* L. (5) (1913)

Crooked-neck [Crooked neck] - *Cucurbita moschata* (Duchesne ex Lam.) Duchesne ex Poir. (107) (1772)

Crooked-neck sedge [Crooked-necked sedge] - *Carex tetanica* Schkuhr (66) (1903)

Crooked-stem aster - *Symphyotrichum prenanthoides* (Muhl. ex Willd.) Nesom (5, 72, 82, 156) (1907-1930)

Crooked-wood - *Cephalanthus occidentalis* L. (156) (1923)

Crook-neck squash - *Cucurbita maxima* Dcne. (158) (1900)

Crop grass [Crop-grass] - *Digitaria* Haller (7) (1828), *Eleusine indica* (L.) Gaertn. (5, 66, 187) (1818-1913)

Crop-ear bass wood - *Tilia americana* L. var. *caroliniana* (P. Mill.) Castigl. (19) (1840)

Cropweed [Crop weed, Crop-weed] - *Centaurea nigra* L. (5, 156) (1913-1923)

Cross cleavers [Crosscleavers, Cross-cleavers] - *Galium circaezans* Michx. (5, 19, 72, 92, 93, 97, 122, 156, 158) (1840-1937)

Cross gentian - *Gentiana cruciata* L. (138) (1923)

Cross mint - *Mentha ×piperita* L. [*aquatica × spicata*] (5, 158) (1900–1913)

Crossbluthige Cornel (German) - *Cornus florida* L. (6) (1892)

Cross-branch goose-grass [Cross-branched goose-grass] - *Galium circaezans* Michx. (187) (1818)

Crossflower - *Chorispora tenella* (Pallas) DC. (50) (present)

Cross-leaf heath [Crossleaf heath] - *Erica tetralix* L. (138) (1923)

Cross-leaf milkwort [Cross-leaved milkwort] - *Polygala cruciata* L. (5, 72) (1907-1913)

Cross-of-Jerusalem [Cross of Jerusalem] - *Lychnis chalcedonica* L. (5, 156, 158) (1900–1923)

Cross-toes [Cross-toes, Crosstoes] - *Lotus corniculatus* L. (5, 92, 156, 158) (1876-1923)

Crossvine [Cross vine, Cross-vine] - *Ampelopsis arborea* (L.) Koehne (106) (1930) GA, *Bignonia capreolata* L. (5, 109, 122, 124, 138, 156) (1913-1949), *Campsis radicans* (L.) Seem. ex Bureau (5, 92, 106, 156, 158) (1876-1930), *Lophophora lewinii* (Hennings ex Lewin) C.H. Thomps. (5) (1913), *Pithecoctenium crucigerum* (L.) A.H. Gentry (8) (1785), *Tecoma* Juss. (7) (1828)

Crossweed [Cross weed, Cross-weed] - *Diplotaxis* DC. (158) (1900), *Diplotaxis muralis* (L.) DC. (5, 158) (1900–1913), *Diplotaxis tenuifolia* (L.) DC. (5, 156) (1913-1923)

Crosswort [Cross wort, Cross-wort, Crosse woort] - *Crucianella* L. (109, 138) (1923-1949), *Cruciata laevipes* Opiz (178) (1526), *Eupatorium perfoliatum* L. (5, 6, 7, 53, 69, 92, 156, 158, 186, 187) (1814-1923), *Lysimachia quadrifolia* L. (5, 7, 92, 156, 158) (1828-1923)

Crosswort gentian [Crossewoort gentian, Crosse woort gentian] - *Gentiana cruciata* L. (178, 180) (1526-1633)

Crotalaria - *Crotalaria* L. (155) (1942)

Croton - *Codiaeum* Juss. (109) (1949), *Codiaeum variegatum* (L.) Juss. (138) (1923), *Croton* L. (1, 4, 50, 93, 106, 158) (1900–present), *Croton texensis* (Klotzsch) Muell.-Arg. (85, 148) (1932-1939)

Crotonopsis - *Croton michauxii* G.L. Webster (5, 97) (1913-1937), *Croton willdenowii* G.L. Webster (3) (1977)

Crouper bush [Crouper-bush] - *Cephalanthus occidentalis* L. (5, 75, 156, 158) (1900-1923) Ferrisbrugh VT

Crow cress [Crow-cress] - *Lepidium virginicum* L. (157) (1929)

Crow garlic [Crow garlick] - *Allium vineale* L. (5, 155, 156, 158, 165) (1768-1942)

Crow onion - *Allium vineale* L. (156, 158) (1900-1923)

Crow peas [Crow-peas] - *Lathyrus pratensis* L. (156) (1923), *Vicia sepium* L. (5, 156) (1913-1923)

Crow silk - *Conferva* L. (92) (1876)

Crow vetch - *Vicia cracca* L. (155) (1942)

Crow victuals [Crow-victuals] - *Glechoma hederacea* L. (5, 73, 158) (1892-1900) Chestertown MD, name used by Negroes

Crowberry [Crow-berry, Crow berry] - *Arctostaphylos uva-ursi* (L.) Spreng. (73, 156, 157, 158) (1892-1929) Barnstable MA, *Empetrum* L. (1, 138, 167) (1814-1932), *Empetrum nigrum* L. (5, 10, 92, 103, 107, 109, 138) (1870-1949), *Phytolacca americana* L. var. *americana* (6, 71) (1892), *Vaccinium oxycoccos* L. (5, 156) (1913-1923)

Crow-corn [Crow corn] - *Aletris farinosa* L. (5, 6, 64, 156) (1892-1913)

Crow-corn root [Crow corn root] - *Aletris farinosa* L. (92) (1876)

Crowded calamagrostis - *Calamagrostis coarctata* (Torr.) Eat. (66) (1903)

Crowd-grass - *Moricandia arvensis* (L.) DC. (156) (1923)

Crowdweed [Crowd-weed, Crowd weed] - *Lepidium campestre* (L.) Aiton f. (5, 74, 156, 158) (1893-1923) WV, *Moricandia arvensis* (L.) DC. (158) (1900), *Sinapis arvensis* L. (5, 74) (1893-1913) WV

Crow-flower [Crow flower] - *Lychnis flos-cuculi* L. (5, 156) (1913-1923) no longer in use by 1923

Crowfoot [Crow-foot, Crow foot, Crowfote, Crow's foot] - *Anemone canadensis* L. (5) (1913) Burnside SD, *Caltha palustris* L. (5, 76, 156, 157, 158) (1896–1929) South Berwick ME, *Cardamine concatenata* (Michx.) Sw. (5, 74, 156) (1913-1923) IN, no longer in use by 1923, *Dactyloctenium aegyptium* (L.) Willd. (5) (1913), *Digitaria sanguinalis* (L.) Scop. (5) (1913), *Eleusine indica* (L.) Gaertn. (66, 87, 88) (1884-1903), *Geranium maculatum* L. (5, 6, 7, 52, 53, 64, 76, 92, 156, 158, 186) (1814-1923) from shape of root, *Lycopodium complanatum* L. (5, 158) (1900-1913), *Lycopodium dendroideum* Michx. (73) (1892) Chestertown MD, *Lycopodium obscurum* L. (5, 155, 158) (1900-1942), *Pulsatilla patens* (L.) Mill. subsp. *multifida* (Pritz.) Zamels (76) (1896), *Ranunculus abortivus* L. (80) (1913) IA, *Ranunculus acris* L. (19, 46) (1649-1840), *Ranunculus bulbosus* L. (46, 49, 57, 61) (1870-1917), *Ranunculus* L. (93) (1936), *Ranunculus* L. (1, 2, 4, 10, 13, 15, 63, 109, 155, 156, 158, 167, 184) (1793-1986), *Ranunculus repens* L. (46) (1649), *Ranunculus sceleratus* L. (179) (1526)

Crowfoot cranebill [Crowefoote Cranes bill] - *Geranium sylvaticum* L. (178) (1526)

Crowfoot garlic [Crow foot garlic] - *Allium vineale* L. (92) (1876)

Crowfoot geranium - *Geranium maculatum* L. (19) (1840)

Crowfoot grama - *Bouteloua gracilis* (Willd. ex Kunth) Lag. ex Griffiths (152) (1912) NM

Crowfoot grass [Crow-foot-grass, Crowfoot-grass] - *Dactyloctenium aegyptium* (L.) Willd. (94, 163) (1852-1901), *Eleusine indica* (L.) Gaertn. (80, 187) (1818-1913)

Crowfoot sedge - *Carex crus-corvi* Shuttlew. ex Kunz. (155) (1942)

Crowfoot violet [Crow-foot violet] - *Viola pedata* L. (5, 73, 156, 158) (1892-1923) New England

Crown beggarticks - *Bidens coronata* (L.) Britton (155) (1942)

Crown coreopsis - *Bidens alba* var. *radiata* (Sch. Bip.) R.E. Ballard (138) (1923)

Crown daisy [Crowndaisy] - *Chrysanthemum coronarium* L. (109, 138) (1923-1949)

Crown grass [Crowngrass] - *Paspalum* L. (50) (present)

Crownbeard [Crown beard] - *Verbesina* L. (1, 2, 4, 50, 93, 106, 155, 158) (1895–present), *Verbesina occidentalis* (L.) Walt. (possibly) (19) (1840), *Verbesina virginica* L. (49) (1898)

Crowned beggarticks - *Bidens coronata* (L.) Britton (50) (present)

Crowned lily - *Androstephium caeruleum* (Scheele) Greene (86) (1878)

Crow-needles [Crow-needle, Crow needles] - *Scandix pecten-veneris* L. (5, 156) (1913-1923) obsolete by 1956

Crown-leaf evening-primrose [Crownleaf evening-primrose] - *Oenothera coronopifolia* Torr. & Gray (50) (present)

Crown-of-the-field [Crown of the field] - *Agrostemma githago* L. (5, 156, 157, 158) (1900–1929), *Lychnis coronaria* (L.) Desr. (92) (1876)

Crown-of-thorn euphorbia [Crownofthorneuphorbia] - *Euphorbia milii* Des Moulins (155) (1942)

Crown-of-thorns - *Euphorbia milii* Des Moulins (109) (1949)

Crown-tipped coral - *Clavicorona pyxidata* (Fr.) Doty (170) (1995)

Crownvetch [Crown vetch] - *Coronilla* L. (4, 50, 156) (1923–present), *Coronilla varia* L. (3, 4, 109, 138, 156) (1923-1986)

Crownvetch coronilla - *Coronilla varia* L. (155) (1942)

Crow-peas [Crow pea] - *Empetrum nigrum* L. (5, 156) (1913-1923)

Crow-poison [Crow poison, Crowpoison] - *Amianthium* A. Gray (155) (1942), *Amianthium muscitoxicum* (Walt.) Gray (5, 75, 138, 155) (1894–1942) Banner Elk NC, *Nothoscordum bivalve* (L.) Britt. (50, 122) (1937–present), *Veratrum viride* Ait. (6, 71) (1892–1898)

Crow's-nest - *Daucus carota* L. (57, 156) (1917–1923) obsolete by 1923

Crow-soap [Crow soap] - *Saponaria officinalis* L. (64, 156, 157, 158, 179) (1526-1929)

Crow's-toes [Crow toes, Crow's toes, Crow-toes] - *Cardamine concatenata* (Michx.) Sw. (5, 76, 156) (1896-1923) Sulphur Grove OH, no longer in use by 1923, *Lotus corniculatus* L. (5, 156, 158) (1900–1923)

Cruel plant - *Euphorbia cyathophora* Murray (82) (1930)

Crunchweed [Crunch-weed] - *Moricandia arvensis* (L.) DC. (156) (1923)

Crunocallis - *Montia chamissoi* (Ledeb. ex Spreng.) Greene (5) (1913)

Crux Saint Andraeae - *Hypericum setosum* L. (181) (~1678)

Crux Sancti Andraeae - *Hypericum hypericoides* (L.) Crantz subsp. *hypericoides* (181) (~1678)

Cryptantha - *Cryptantha* Lehm. ex G. Don (50, 155) (1942–present)

Cryptanthe - *Cryptantha* Lehm. ex G. Don (158) (1900)

Cryptomeria - *Cryptomeria* D. Don (138) (1923)

Crystal flower - *Mitella nuda* L. (156) (1923)

Crystal tea [Crystal-tea] - *Ledum palustre* L. (138) (1923)

Crystalwort [Crystal wort, Crystal-wort] - *Hepatica* Mill. (92) (1876), *Hepatica nobilis* Schreb. (92, 156) (1876-1923), *Hepatica nobilis* Schreb. var. *obtusa* (Pursh) Steyermark (5) (1913)

Cuajaloche (Spanish) - *Galium verum* L. (158) (1900)

Cuba grass - *Sorghum halepense* (L.) Pers. (5, 45, 87, 158) (1885-1913)

Cuban royal palm - *Roystonea elata* (Bartr.) F. Harper (109) (1949)

Cuban spinach - *Claytonia perfoliata* Donn ex Willd. (107) (1919)

Cube-seed iris [Cubeseed iris] - *Iris prismatica* Pursh ex Ker-Gawl. (138) (1923)

Cucklebur [Cuckle bur] - *Xanthium strumarium* L. (35) (1806), *Xanthium strumarium* L. var. *canadense* (Mill.) Torr. & Gray (76) (1896) Sulphur Grove OH

Cucklemoors - *Arctium lappa* L. (158) (1900)

Cuckles [Cuckle] - *Bidens frondosa* L. (5, 75, 79, 156, 158) (1891-1923) Concord MA

Cuckold [Cuckolds] - *Bidens bipinnata* L. (5, 156, 157) (1900-1929), *Bidens connata* Muhl. ex Willd. (156) (1923), *Bidens coronata* (L.) Britton (92) (1876), *Bidens frondosa* L. (19, 158) (1840-1900)

Cuckold burs - *Xanthium strumarium* L. (12) (1821)

Cuckold hazel nut [Cuckold hazle nut] - *Corylus cornuta* Marsh (42) (1814)

Cuckold-dock [Cuckold dock] - *Arctium lappa* L. (5, 64, 69, 156, 158) (1900–1923)

Cuckold-nut - *Corylus americana* Walt. (8) (1785), *Corylus cornuta* Marsh (8) (1785)

Cuckold's-horns [Cuckold's horns] - *Proboscidea louisianica* (P. Mill.) Thellung (38) (1820)

Cuckoldy-bur - *Arctium lappa* L. (158) (1900)

Cuckoo-bread [Cuckoo bread, Cuckow-bread] - *Oxalis* L. (184) (1793), *Oxalis montana* Raf. (possibly) (7, 92) (1828-1876)

Cuckoo-buds [Cuckoo buds] - *Ranunculus acris* L. (157, 158) (1900-1929), *Ranunculus bulbosus* L. (5, 92) (1876-1913), *Ranunculus* L. (14) (1882)

Cuckoo-button [Cuckoo button, Cuckoo-buttons] - *Arctium lappa* L. (158) (1900), *Arctium minus* Bernh. (5) (1913)

Cuckoo-flower [Cuckooflower, Cuckoo flower, Cuckow flower] - *Cardamine pratensis* L. (2, 92, 109, 131) (1876-1949), *Lychnis flos-cuculi* L. (5, 92, 156, 178) (1526-1923), *Oxalis montana* Raf. (possibly) (5, 156) (1913-1923), *Silene latifolia* Poir. subsp. *alba* (Mill.) Greuter & Burdet (5, 156) (1913-1923)

Cuckoo-grass [Cuckoo grass] - *Luzula campestris* (L.) DC. (92) (1876)

Cuckoo-point [Cuckow-point] - *Arum* L. (184) (1793)

Cuckoos [Cuckoo] - *Lychnis flos-cuculi* L. (5, 156) (1913-1923) no longer in use by 1923

Cuckoo's-cap [Cuckoo's cap] - *Aconitum napellus* L. (156) (1923)

Cuckoo's-meat [Cuckoo's meat, Cuckoo-meat, Cuckoo meat] - *Oxalis montana* Raf. (possibly) (5, 156) (1913-1923)

Cucumber - *Cucumis* L. (138) (1923), *Cucumis sativus* L. (7, 19, 57, 82, 92, 106, 107, 109, 110, 114, 138, 184) (1793-1949)

Cucumber root [Cucumber-root] - *Medeola* (138) (1923), *Medeola virginiana* L. (7, 138, 186) (1814-1923)

Cucumber sunflower - *Helianthus debilis* Nutt. (138) (1923)

Cucumber tree [Cucumber-tree, Cucumbertree] - *Liriodendron tulipifera* L. (5, 74, 156) (1893-1923), *Magnolia acuminata* (L.) L. (8, 10, 13, 14, 15, 18, 20, 19, 49, 82, 92, 106, 109, 137, 138, 156, 182, 184) (1785-1949), *Magnolia ashei* Weatherby (122, 124) (1937), *Magnolia fraseri* Walt. (5, 156) (1913-1923), *Magnolia macrophylla* Michx. (5, 156) (1913-1923), *Magnolia tripetala* L. (5, 156) (1913-1923)

Cucumber-leaf sunflower - *Helianthus debilis* Nutt. subsp. *cucumerifolius* (Torr. & Gray) Heiser (109) (1949)

Cucurma - *Frasera caroliniensis* Walt. (possibly) (7) (1828)

Cudbear - *Lecanora tartarea* (L.) Ach. (92) (1876)

Cudweed [Cud-weed, Cud weed] - *Antennaria parviflora* Nutt. (157) (1929), *Antennaria plantaginifolia* (L.) Richards (92) (1876), *Artemisia* L. (1) (1932), *Artemisia ludoviciana* Nutt. (156) (1923), *Artemisia ludoviciana* Nutt. subsp. *ludoviciana* (5) (1913), *Evax prolifera* Nutt. ex DC. (124) (1937) TX, *Filago vulgaris* Lam. (5, 156) (1913-1923), *Gnaphalium* L. (1, 2, 4, 7, 10, 50, 93, 155, 156, 158, 167, 184) (1793–present), *Gnaphalium uliginosum* L. (19, 92) (1840-1876), *Pseudognaphalium* Kirp. (50) (present)

Cudweed everlasting - *Helichrysum petiolare* Hilliard & Burtt (138) (1923)

Cudweed mugwort - *Artemisia ludoviciana* Nutt. subsp. *ludoviciana* (157, 158) (1900-1929)

Cudweed of America [Cudweede of America] - *Anaphalis margaritacea* (L.) Benth. & Hook (178) (1526)

Cudweed sagebrush - *Artemisia ludoviciana* Nutt. subsp. *ludoviciana* (155) (1942)

Cudweed wormwood - *Artemisia ludoviciana* Nutt. subsp. *ludoviciana* (138) (1923)

Cuechiliz (Mexico) - *Phytolacca americana* L. var. *americana* (7) (1828)

Culantrillo (Spanish) - *Adiantum capillus-veneris* L. (158) (1900)

Culcas (Egypt) - *Colocasia esculenta* (L.) Schott (110) (16th century)

Culen (Chile) - *Chenopodium ambrosioides* L. (14) (1882)

Culrage - *Polygonum hydropiper* L. (157, 158, 179) (1526-1929)

Culrage (French) - *Polygonum hydropiper* L. (possibly) (180) (1633)

Cultivated apple - *Malus sylvestris* Mill. (137) (1931)

Cultivated barley - *Hordeum vulgare* L. (56, 163) (1852-1901)

Cultivated carrot - Daucus carota L. (109) (1949)

Cultivated celery - *Apium graveolens* L. var. *dulce* (P. Mill.) DC. (93) (1936)

Cultivated fennel - *Foeniculum vulgare* Mill. (106) (1930)

Cultivated flax - *Linum usitatissimum* L. (5, 93) (1913-1936)

Cultivated garlic - *Allium sativum* L. (50) (present)

Cultivated gooseberry - *Ribes uva-crispa* L. var. *sativum* DC. (82) (1930)

Cultivated larkspur - *Delphinium grandiflorum* L. (82) (1930)

Cultivated licorice - *Glycyrrhiza glabra* L. (50) (present)

Cultivated oats [Cultivated oat] - *Avena sativa* L. (93, 163) (1852-1936)

Cultivated onion - *Allium cepa* L. (106) (1930)

Cultivated parsnip - *Pastinaca sativa* L. (109) (1949)

Cultivated plum - *Prunus domestica* L. (82) (1930)

Cultivated radish - *Raphanus sativus* L. (50) (present)

Cultivated rape - *Brassica rapa* L. (93) (1936)

Cultivated red raspberry - *Rubus idaeus* L. subsp. *strigosus* (Michx.) Focke (135) (1910)

Cultivated rice - *Oryza sativa* L. (56, 163) (1852-1901)

Cultivated rye - *Secale cereale* L. (56, 93, 163) (1852-1936)

Cultivated strawberry - *Fragaria chiloensis* (L.) Mill. (82) (1930)

Cultivated verbena - *Glandularia peruviana* (L.) Druce (possibly) (114) (1894) Neb

Cultivated wheat - *Triticum aestivum* L. (56) (1901)

Culverfoot [Culver-foot] - *Geranium molle* L. (5, 156) (1913-1923)

Culver's physic [Culver's-physic, Culvers-physic, Culversphysic] - *Veronicastrum virginicum* (L.) Farw. (5, 6, 19, 48, 49, 53, 57, 92, 156, 157, 158) (1840-1929)

Culver's root [Culver's-root, Culvers-root, Culvert root] - *Veronicastrum* Heister ex Fabr. (158) (1900), *Veronicastrum virginicum* (L.) Farw. (1, 2, 3, 4, 5, 6, 7, 40, 47, 49, 50, 52, 53, 54, 55, 57, 59, 63, 64, 72, 82, 92, 93, 106, 109, 131, 138, 155, 157, 158) (1828–present)

Culverwort - *Aquilegia canadensis* L. (156) (1923)

Cul-wha-mo (Chinook) - *Lupinus littoralis* Dougl. (35) (1806)

Cuman ragweed - *Ambrosia psilostachya* DC. (50) (present)

Cumar (Quichuen) - *Ipomoea batatas* (L.) Lam. (110) (1886)

Cumaro - *Celtis laevigata* Willd. var. *reticulata* (Torr.) L. Benson (153) (1913) NM

Cumbalam - *Benincasa hispida* (Thunb.) Cogn. (110) (1886)

Cumich (German) - *Carum carvi* L. (59, 107) (1911-1919)

Cumin - *Cuminum cyminum* L. (92, 107, 109, 122, 138) (1876-1949)

Cumin seede - *Cuminum cyminum* L. (178) (1526)

Cummin - *Cuminum cyminum* L. (92) (1876)

Cummin seed - *Cuminum cyminum* L. (92) (1876)

Cunila - *Cunila* L. (50) (present)

Cunila herba (Official name of Materia Medica) - *Cunila origanoides* (L.) Britton (7) (1828)

Cunile d'Amerique (French) - *Cunila origanoides* (L.) Britton (7) (1828)

Cunningham beefwood's [Cunningham beefwood] - *Casuarina cunninghamiana* Miq. (138) (1923)

Cup fern [Cup-fern, Cupfern] - *Cystopteris fragilis* (L.) Bernh. (92) (1876), *Dennstaedtia* Bernh. (109, 138) (1923-1949)

Cup grass [Cupgrass] - *Eriochloa* Kunth (50, 155) (1942–present)

Cup moss - *Lecanora esculenta* (Pall.) Eversm. (107) (1919)

Cup plant [Cup-plant] - *Silphium compositum* var. *reniforme* (Raf. ex Nutt.) Torr. & Gray (50) (present), *Silphium* L. (1, 93) (1932-1936), *Silphium perfoliatum* L. (3, 4, 5, 37, 40, 47, 49, 50, 58, 62, 63, 72, 82, 92, 93, 97, 106, 109, 127, 131, 156, 158) (1852–present)

Cup rosinweed - *Silphium perfoliatum* L. (138, 155) (1923-1942)

Cupflower [Cup flower] - *Nierembergia* Ruiz & Pavón (109, 138) (1923-1949)

Cuphea - *Cuphea* P. Br. (138, 155) (1923-1942)

Cupid's-daisy [Cupids-daisy] - *Catananche* L. (109, 138) (1923-1949)

Cupid's-delight [Cupid's delight] - *Viola tricolor* L. (73, 158) (1892-1899) Salem MA

Cupid's-flower [Cupid's flower] - *Ipomoea quamoclit* L. (5, 156) (1913-1923)

Cup-leaf penstemon [Cupleaf penstemon] - *Penstemon murrayanus* Hook. (138) (1923)

Cup-mushroom - *Peziza* Fr. (184) (1793)

Cuprose-rose [Cuprose rose] - *Papaver rhoeas* L. (158) (1900)

Cupseed [Cup-seed, Cup seed] - *Calycocarpum lyoni* (Pursh) Nutt. (2, 4, 50, 5, 97, 156) (1895–present), *Calycocarpum* Nutt. (1, 158) (1900-1932)

Cup-seed stickseed [Cupseed stickseed] - *Lappula occidentalis* (S. Wats.) Greene var. *cupulata* (Gray) Higgins (3, 4) (1977-1986)

Cups-of-flame [Cups of flame] - *Eschscholzia californica* Cham. (76) (1896), *Eschscholzia* Cham. (73) (1892) CA

Cups-of-gold [Cups of gold] - *Eschscholzia californica* Cham. (76) (1896) CA

Cup-tip coral fungus - *Clavicorona pyxidata* (Fr.) Doty (128) (1933) ND

Curage (French, Louisiana) - *Polygonum persicaria* L. (7, 180) (1633-1828) Louisiana Purchase

Curcuma - *Curcuma longa* L. (92) (1876), *Hydrastis canadensis* L. (49, 64) (1907-1908)

Curcume - *Hydrastis canadensis* L. (29) (1869)

Curdwort [Cud-wort] - *Galium verum* L. (156, 158) (1900-1923)

Cure-all [Cure all, Cureall] - *Geum rivale* L (5, 156, 158) (1900–1923), *Geum virginianum* L. (7, 92) (1828-1876), *Melissa officinalis* L. (92) (1876), *Oenothera biennis* L. (6) (1892), *Prunella vulgaris* L. (77) (1898) Western US

Curled Cresses - *Lepidium sativum* L. (178) (1526)

Curled dock - *Rumex crispus* L. (1, 5, 6, 56, 62, 64, 69, 72, 77, 80, 92, 93, 97, 107, 125. 131, 145, 156, 157, 158, 187) (1818-1892)

Curled garden cole - *Brassica oleracea* L. (180) (1633)

Curled hyssop [Curlde hyssope] - *Hyssopus officinalis* L. (178) (1526)

Curled kitchen kale - *Brassica oleracea* L. (109) (1949)

Curled lettuce - *Lactuca sativa* L. (180) (1633)

Curled mallow [Curled mallows, Curled Mallowes] - *Malva crispa* (L.) L. (19, 72, 109, 178) (1526-1949), *Malva verticillata* L. (5, 107, 156) (1913-1923)

Curled maple - *Acer rubrum* L. (12) (1821)

Curled Mexicali onion - *Allium crispum* Greene (155) (1942)

Curled mint - *Mentha × piperita* L. [*aquatica × spicata*] (5, 92, 158) (1876-1913)

Curled mustard - *Brassica juncea* (L.) Czern. (156) (1923)

Curled parsley - *Petroselinum crispum* (P. Mill.) Nyman ex A.W. Hill (possibly) (178) (1526)

Curled sage - *Salvia officinalis* L. (178) (1526)

Curled savoy cole [Curled sauoy cole] - *Brassica oleracea* L. (180) (1633)

Curled tansy [Curled Tansie] - *Tanacetum vulgare* L. (178) (1526)

Curled thistle - *Carduus crispus* L. (5, 93, 156) (1913-1936)

Curlew-berry [Curlew berry] - *Empetrum nigrum* L. (5, 156) (1913-1923)

Curl-flower - *Clematis crispa* L. (156) (1923)

Curl-flower clematis [Curl-flowered clematis] - *Clematis crispa* L. (5) (1913)

Curlock - *Moricandia arvensis* (L.) DC. (158) (1900), *Raphanus raphanistrum* L. (5) (1913), *Sinapis arvensis* L. (5) (1913)

Curls - *Amaranthus retroflexus* L. (77) (1898) Sulphur Grove OH

Curly abutilon - *Herissantia crispa* (L.) Briz. (155) (1942)

Curly clematis - *Clematis crispa* L. (138) (1923)

Curly dock - *Rumex crispus* L. (3, 4, 50, 58, 98, 155) (1869–present)

Curly grass - *Schizaea pusilla* Pursh (5, 11, 22) (1888-1913)

Curly hard grass [Curly hard-grass] - *Parapholis incurva* (L.) C.E. Hubb. (94) (1901)

Curly heads - *Clematis ochroleuca* Aiton (5) (1913)

Curly mallow - *Malva crispa* (L.) L. (50, 138, 155) (1923–present)

Curly mesquit - *Prosopis pubescens* Benth. (76) (1896) NM

Curly mesquite - *Hilaria belangeri* (Steud.) Nash (65, 163) (1852-1931), *Hilaria cenchroides* Kunth (94) (1901)

Curly mesquite grass - *Hilaria belangeri* (Steud.) Nash (122) (1937) NM

Curly mezquite - *Prosopis pubescens* Benth. (147) (1856)

Curly muckweed [Curly muck-weed] - *Potamogeton crispus* L. (5, 120, 156) (1913-1938)

Curly pondweed - *Potamogeton crispus* L. (50, 155, 158) (1900–present)

Curly sedge - *Carex rupestris* All. (50) (present)

Curly three-awn [Curly threeawn] - *Aristida desmantha* Trin. & Rupr. (19, 155) (1840-1942)

Curly wild ginger [Curly wildginger] - *Asarum canadense* L. (138, 155) (1923-1942)

Curlycup gumweed - *Grindelia squarrosa* (Pursh) Dunal (50, 155)

(1942–present), *Grindelia squarrosa* (Pursh) Dunal var. *quasiperennis* Lunell (3, 50) (1977–present), *Grindelia squarrosa* (Pursh) Dunal var. *serrulata* (Rydb.) Steyermark (50) (present), *Grindelia squarrosa* (Pursh) Dunal var. *squarrosa* (3, 50) (1977–present)

Curly-heads - *Clematis ochroleuca* Aiton (156) (1923)

Curly-leaf dayflower [Curly-leaved dayflower, Curly-leaved dayflower] - *Commelina erecta* L. var. *angustifolia* (Michx.) Fern. (5, 97, 155) (1913-1942)

Curly-leaf dock [Curly-leaved dock] - *Rumex crispus* L. (85, 122) (1932-1937)

Curly-top gumweed [Curlytop gumweed] - *Grindelia nuda* Wood var. *nuda* (3, 50) (1977–present), *Grindelia squarrosa* (Pursh) Dunal (4, 98) (1926-1986)

Curly-top knotweed [Curlytop knotweed] - *Polygonum lapathifolium* L. (50) (present)

Curly-top ladysthumb [Curlytop ladysthumb] - *Polygonum lapathifolium* L. (155) (1942)

Currant [Currants] - *Mahonia trifoliolata* (Moric.) Fedde (15) (1895) TX, *Ribes* L. (2, 4, 7, 10, 50, 82, 93, 106, 109, 138, 155, 156, 158, 184) (1793–present)

Currant bush [Currant-bush] - *Ribes* L. (8) (1785)

Currant tomato - *Solanum pimpinellifolium* Jusl. (138) (1923)

Currant tree [Currant-tree] - *Amelanchier ×intermedia* Spach [*arborea × canadensis*] (5) (1913), *Amelanchier canadensis* (L.) Medik. (106, 156) (1923-1930) Southeastern US, no longer in use by 1923, *Ribes nigrum* L. (41) (1770)

Currant-leaf [Currant leaf] - *Mitella diphylla* L. (5, 19, 92, 156) (1840-1923)

Currant-leaf maple [Currant leaved maple] - *Acer glabrum* Torr. (20) (1857)

Cursed buttercup - *Ranunculus sceleratus* L. (50) (present), *Ranunculus sceleratus* L. var. *multifidus* Nutt. (50) (present), *Ranunculus sceleratus* L. var. *sceleratus* (50) (present)

Cursed crowfoot - *Ranunculus repens* L. (148) (1939) CO, *Ranunculus sceleratus* L. (3, 4, 5, 6, 63, 125, 156, 158) (1892–1986)

Cursed thistle [Cursed-thistle] - *Cirsium arvense* (L.) Scop. (5, 49, 62, 92, 156, 157, 158) (1898-1912)

Curtis' angelica [Curtis angelica] - *Angelica triquinata* Michx. (5) (1913)

Curtis' aster [Curtis aster] - *Symphyotrichum retroflexum* (Lindl. ex DC.) Nesom (138, 155) (1931-1942)

Curtis' goldenrod [Curtis' golden-rod] - *Solidago caesia* L. var. *curtisii* (Torr. & Gray) Wood (5) (1913)

Curtis' heuchera - *Heuchera americana* L. var. *americana* (5) (1913)

Curtiss' milkwort - *Polygala curtissii* Gray (5) (1913)

Curtiss' paspalum - *Paspalum praecox* Walt. (94) (1901)

Curtiss' possum-haw [Curtiss possumhaw] - *Ilex crenata* Thunb. (155) (1942)

Curtiss' three-awn [Curtiss threeawn, Curtis threeawn] - *Aristida dichotoma* Michx. var. *curtissii* Gray ex S. Wats. & Coult. (3, 155) (1942-1977)

Curtiss' triple-awn grass [Curtiss' triple-awned grass, Curtiss's triple-awned grass] - *Aristida dichotoma* Michx. var. *curtissii* Gray ex S. Wats. & Coult. (5, 99, 119) (1913-1938)

Curtiss' water hemlock [Curtiss waterhemlock] - *Cicuta maculata* L. var. *maculata* (155) (1942)

Curuba - *Sicana odorifera* (Vell.) Naud. (109) (1949)

Curved sedge - *Carex maritima* Gunn (5, 50) (1913–present)

Curve-fruit corydalis [Curved-fruited corydalis] - *Corydalis crystallina* Engelm. (97, 131) (1899-1937)

Curve-leaf yucca [Curveleaf yucca] - *Yucca filamentosa* L. (138, 155) (1923-1942)

Curve-pod fumewort [Curvepod fumewort] - *Corydalis crystallina* Engelm. (50) (present), *Corydalis curvisiliqua* Engelm. subsp. *grandibracteata* (Fedde) G.B. Ownbey (50) (present), *Corydalis curvisiliqua* Engelm. subsp. *occidentalis* (Engelm. ex Gray) W.A. Weber (50) (present)

Curve-pod locoweed [Curvepod locoweed] - *Astragalus curvicarpus* (E. Sheld.) J.F. Macbr. (155) (1942)

Curve-seed butterwort [Curveseed butterwort] - *Ceratocephala* Moench (50) (present), *Ceratocephala testiculata* (Crantz) Bess. (50) (present)

Curve-tip flatsedge - *Cyperus squarrosus* L. (139) (1944)

Cuscus - Vetiveria zizaniodes (L.) Nash (92) (1876)

Cushaw - *Cucurbita maxima* Dcne. (110) (1886), *Cucurbita moschata* (Duchesne ex Lam.) Duchesne ex Poir. (107, 109, 138) (1919-1949) Indian name

Cushaw crook-neck - *Cucurbita maxima* Dcne. (158) (1900)

Cush-cush - *Dioscorea trifida* L. f. (109) (1949)

Cushion cactus - *Escobaria missouriensis* (Sweet) D.R. Hunt var. *missouriensis* (101) (1905) MT

Cushion draba - *Draba breweri* S. Wats. var. *cana* (Rydb.) Rollins (50) (present)

Cushion euphorbia - *Euphorbia epithymoides* L. (155) (1942)

Cushion gypsophila - *Gypsophila muralis* L. (138, 155) (1923-1942)

Cushion pink - *Silene acaulis* L. (5, 109, 156) (1913-1949)

Cushion spurge - *Euphorbia epithymoides* L. (138) (1923)

Cushion witch grass [Cushion witchgrass] - *Panicum capillare* L. (155) (1942)

Cusick's bluegrass [Cusick bluegrass] - *Poa cusickii* Vasey (50, 155) (1942–present)

Cusick's serviceberry [Cusick serviceberry] - *Amelanchier alnifolia* (Nutt.) Nutt. ex M. Roemer var. *cusickii* (Fern.) C.L. Hitchc. (155) (1942)

Cusp blazing star - *Liatris mucronata* DC. (50) (present)

Cusp dodder - *Cuscuta cuspidata* Engelm. (3, 4, 50) (1977–present)

Cuspidate dodder - *Cuscuta cuspidata* Engelm. (5, 72, 93, 97) (1907-1937)

Cuspidate sedge - *Carex recta* Boott. (5) (1913)

Custard-apple [Custardapple, Custard apple] - *Annona* L. (15, 109) (1895-1949), *Asimina obovata* (Willd.) Nash (183) (~1756), *Asimina triloba (L.) Dunal* (5, 7, 8, 19, 35, 92, 156, 157, 158, 187) (1785-1929), *Annona muricata* L. (41, 110) (1770-1886) America, *Annona squamosa* L. (110, 155) (1886-1942) British India, *Annona reticulata* L. (110, 138) (1886-1923) West Indies

Cut grass [Cut-grass, Cutgrass] - *Leersia oryzoides* (L.) Sw. (19, 66, 81, 80, 187) (1818-1951), *Leersia* Sw. (50, 155) (1942–present), *Leersia virginica* Willd. (88) (1885)

Cut toothwort - *Cardamine concatenata* (Michx.) Sw. (138) (1923)

Cutch grass [Cutch-grass] - *Elymus repens* (L.) Gould (158) (1900)

Cut-heal - *Valeriana officinalis* L. (5, 156) (1913-1923)

Cut-leaf anemone [Cutleaf anemone, Cut-leaved anemone] - *Anemone multifida* Poir. (156, 158) (1900-1923), *Anemone multifida Poir. var. hudsoniana* DC. (5, 93) (1913-1936), *Pulsatilla patens* (L.) Mill.subsp. *multifida* (Pritz.) Zamels (50) (present)

Cut-leaf annual germander [Cut-leaved annual germander] - *Teucrium botrys* L. (5) (1913)

Cut-leaf aplopappus [Cutleaf aplopappus] - *Machaeranthera pinnatifida* (Hook.) Shinners subsp. *pinnatifida* (122) (1937)

Cut-leaf beech [Cutleaf beech] - *Fagus sylvatica* L. (109) (1949)

Cut-leaf chaste-tree [Cutleaf chaste-tree] - *Vitex negundo* L. var. *negundo* (138) (1923)

Cut-leaf cinquefoil [Cut-leaved cinquefoil] - *Potentilla bimundorum* Soják (5) (1913)

Cut-leaf cissus [Cut-leaved cissus] - *Cissus trifoliata* (L.) L. (5, 97) (1913-1937)

Cut-leaf coneflower [Cutleaf coneflower] - *Rudbeckia laciniata* L. (50, 138, 155) (1923–present), *Rudbeckia laciniata* L. var. *laciniata* (50) (present)

Cut-leaf cranebill [Cut-leaved crane's bill] - *Geranium dissectum* L. (5, 131) (1899-1913)

Cut-leaf cyclanthera [Cutleaf cyclanthera] - *Cyclanthera dissecta* (Torr. & Gray) Arn. (5, 50) (1913–present)

Cut-leaf daisy [Cutleaf daisy] - *Erigeron compositus* Pursh (50) (present)

Cut-leaf Engelmann's flower [Cut-leaved Engelmann flower] - *Engelmannia peristenia* (Raf.) Goodman & Lawson (84, 86) (1878-1880)

Cut-leaf eriocarpum [Cut-leaved eriocarpum] - *Machaeranthera pinnatifida* (Hook.) Shinners subsp. *pinnatifida* (131) (1899)

Cut-leaf evening-primrose [Cut-leaved evening primrose] - *Oenothera coronopifolia* Torr. & Gray (5, 131) (1899-1913), *Oenothera laciniata* Hill (4, 5, 50, 85, 93, 97, 155) (1899–present)

Cut-leaf gerardia [Cutleaf gerardia, Cut-leaved gerardia] - *Agalinis auriculata* (Michx.) Blake (5, 97, 122) (1913-1937)

Cut-leaf germander [Cutleaf germander, Cut-leaved germander] - *Teucrium laciniatum* Torr. (3, 4, 6, 97) (1892-1986)

Cut-leaf goldenrod [Cutleaf goldenrod, Cut-leaved golden-rod, Cut-leaved goldenrod] - *Solidago arguta* Aiton (5, 131, 122) (1899-1937)

Cut-leaf goosefoot [Cut-leaved goosefoot] - *Chenopodium multifidum* L. (5) (1913)

Cut-leaf grape fern [Cutleaf grape fern, Cutleaf grapefern, Cut-leaved grape-fern] - *Botrychium biternatum* (Sav.) Underwood (122) (1937), *Botrychium dissectum* Spreng. (4, 5, 50, 138, 155) (1913–present)

Cut-leaf ground-cherry [Cutleaf ground cherry, Cut-leaved ground cherry] - *Physalis angulata* L. (3, 4, 5, 50, 72, 97, 122, 124) (1907–present)

Cut-leaf horehound [Cutleaf hoarhound - *Lycopus americanus* Muhl. ex W. Bart. (122) (1937)

Cut-leaf ironplant [Cutleaf ironplant] - *Machaeranthera pinnatifida* (Hook.) Shinners subsp. *pinnatifida* (3, 4, 98) (1926-1986)

Cut-leaf maple [Cut-leaved maple] - *Acer negundo* L. (156, 157, 158) (1900-1929)

Cut-leaf meadow parsley [Cut-leaved meadow parsley] - *Thaspium pinnatifidum* (Buckl.) Gray (5) (1913)

Cut-leaf mermaid-weed [Cut-leaved mermaid-weed] - *Proserpinaca pectinata* Lam. (5) (1913)

Cut-leaf nightshade [Cut-leaved nightshade] - *Solanum triflorum* Nutt. (3, 4, 5, 50, 72, 85, 93, 97, 121, 126, 131, 148, 155, 156) (1899–present)

Cut-leaf pepper root [Cut-leaved pepper root] - *Cardamine concatenata* (Michx.) Sw. (5) (1913)

Cut-leaf ragweed [Cut-leaved ragweed] - *Ambrosia artemisiifolia* L. var. *elatior* (L.) Descourtils (93) (1936)

Cut-leaf red alder [Cutleaf red alder] - *Alnus rubra* Bong. (155) (1942)

Cut-leaf selfheal [Cutleaf selfheal] - *Prunella laciniata (L.) L.* (50) ()

Cut-leaf sideranthus [Cut-leaved sideranthus] - *Machaeranthera pinnatifida* (Hook.) Shinners subsp. *pinnatifida* (5, 93, 97) (1913-1937)

Cut-leaf stephanandra [Cutleaf stephanandra] - *Stephanandra incisa* (Thunb.) Zabel (138) (1923)

Cut-leaf sumac - *Rhus hirta* (L.) Sudworth (112) (1937)

Cut-leaf teasel [Cutleaf teasel, Cut-leaved teasel] - *Dipsacus laciniatus* L. (3, 4, 50, 155) (1942–present)

Cut-leaf toothwort [Cutleaf toothwort, Cut-leaved toothwort, Cut-leaved tooth-wort] - *Cardamine concatenata* (Michx.) Sw. (5, 50, 86, 155) (1878–present)

Cut-leaf violet [Cut-leaved violet] - *Viola brittoniana* Pollard var. *pectinata* (Bickn.) Alexander (5) (1913)

Cut-leaf vipergrass [Cutleaf vipergrass] - *Scorzonera laciniata* L. (50) (present)

Cut-leaf water milfoil [Cutleaf watermilfoil] - *Myriophyllum pinnatum* (Walt.) Britton, Sterns & Poggenb. (50) (present)

Cut-leaf water-horehound [Cut-leaved water horehound, Cut-leaved water hoarhound] - *Lycopus americanus* Muhl. ex W. Bart. (5, 72, 93, 97, 131, 158) (1907-1937)

Cut-leaf water-parsley [Cut-leaved water-parsley (sic)] - *Berula erecta* (Huds.) Coville (156) (1923)

Cut-leaf water-parsnip [Cutleaf waterparsnip, Cut-leaf water parsnip, Cut-leaved water parsnip, Cut-leaved water-parsnip] - *Berula erecta* (Huds.) Coville (5, 50, 93, 95, 131, 158) (1899–present)

Cutler's alpine goldenrod [Cutler's alpine golden-rod] - *Solidago cutleri* Fern. (5) (1913)

Cut-paper [Cut paper] - *Broussonetia papyrifera* (L.) L'Hér. ex Vent. (5, 75, 156, 158) (1894-1923) WV

Cuttanimmons - *Peltandra virginica* (L.) Schott. (181) (~1678)

Cutting-almond [Cutting almond] - *Parthenium integrifolium* L. (92, 156, 158) (1898-1923)

Cyclamen - *Dodecatheon meadia* L. (77) (1898) Alabama

Cyclanthera - *Cyclanthera dissecta* (Torr. & Gray) Arn. (3, 4) (1977-1986), *Cyclanthera* Schrad. (4, 50, 155) (1942–present)

Cycloloma - *Cycloloma atriplicifolium* (Spreng.) Coult. (21, 72, 131) (1893-1899), *Cycloloma* Moq. (50) (present)

Cyclops acacia - *Acacia cyclops* G. Don (50, 138, 155) (1923–present)

Cydonia (Greek) - *Cydonia oblonga* Mill. (110) (1886)

Cydonium - *Cydonia oblonga* Mill. (57) (1917)

Cylinder flatsedge - *Cyperus retrorsus* Chapman var. *retrorsus* (155) (1942)

Cylinder joint grass - *Coelorachis cylindrica* (Michx.) Nash (50) (present)

Cylindrical blazing star [Cylindric blazing star] - *Liatris cylindracea* Michx (5, 72) (1907-1913)

Cylindrical boehmeria - *Boehmeria cylindrica* (L.) Sw. (42) (1814)

Cylindrical-spike sedge [Cylindrical-spiked sedge] - *Carex bullata* Schk. (possibly) (66) (1903)

Cylindric-fruit ludwigia [Cylindric-fruited ludwigia] - *Ludwigia glandulosa* Walt. (4, 5, 97) (1913-1986)

Cylindric-fruit primrose-willow [Cylindricfruit primrose-willow] - *Ludwigia glandulosa* Walt. (50) (present)

Cymbalaria - *Cymbalaria* Hill (50) (present)

Cymling (summer squash) - *Cucurbita pepo* L. (107) (1803) Thomas Jefferson

Cynamome - *Cinnamomum* Schaeffer (possibly) (179) (1526)

Cynosbata - *Rosa canina* L. (49) (1898)

Cynthia - *Krigia biflora* (Walt.) Blake (156) (1923), *Krigia biflora* (Walt.) Blake var. *biflora* (5) (1913), *Krigia virginica* (L.) Willd. (72) (1907)

Cyperus-like sedge - *Carex pseudocyperus* L. (5, 50, 66, 72) (1893–present)

Cypre (Louisiana) - *Taxodium distichum* (L.) L.C. Rich. (20) (1857)

Cyprès (French) - *Cupressus* L. (8) (1785), *Taxodium distichum* (L.) L.C. Rich. (20) (1857)

Cyprès à feuilles d'Acacia (French) - *Taxodium distichum* (L.) L.C. Rich. (8) (1785)

Cyprès à feuilles d'Thuya (French) - *Chamaecyparis thyoides* (L.) Britton, Sterns & Poggenb. (8) (1785)

Cypress - *Euphorbia cyparissias* L. (5, 73, 156, 158) (1892-1923)

Cypress euphorbia - *Euphorbia cyparissias* L. (155) (1942)

Cypress gilia - *Ipomopsis rubra* (L.) Wherry (156) (1923)

Cypress herb - *Santolina chamaecyparissus* L. (92) (1876)

Cypress moss - *Lycopodium alpinum* L. (5) (1913)

Cypress of America - *Taxodium distichum* (L.) L.C. Rich. (189) (1767)

Cypress or Cypress tree [Cypress-tree, Cypresse tree] - Cupressus L. (8, 10, 20, 50, 109, 138, 167) (1785–present) from ancient Latin name, *Larix laricina* (Du Roi.) Koch. (75, 78) (1894-1898), *Liriodendron tulipifera* L. (186) (1814), *Taxodium distichum* (L.) L.C. Rich. (7, 65) (1828-1931)

Cypress panic grass [Cypress panicgrass] - *Dichanthelium dichotomum* (L.) Gould (50) (present)

Cypress spurge - *Euphorbia cyparissias* L. (3, 4, 50, 62, 72, 80, 92, 109, 122, 138, 156, 158) (1876–present)

Cypress swamp sedge - *Carex joorii* Bailey (5, 50) (1913–present)

Cypress vine [Cypress-vine, Cypressvine, Cyprus vine - *Adlumia fungosa* (Aiton) Greene ex B. S. P. (5, 156) (1913-1923), *Ipomoea* L. (1, 158) (1900-1932), *Ipomoea quamoclit* L. (4, 5, 7, 50, 92, 97, 109, 138, 156, 158) (1828–present)

Cypresse spurge - *Euphorbia cyparissias* L. (178, 180) (1526-1633)

Cypress-grass [Cypress grass, Cyprus grass] - *Cyperus diandrus* Torr. (5, 156) (1913-1923), *Cyperus* L. (10, 158) (1818-1900)

Cypress-knee sedge [Cypressknee sedge] - *Carex decomposita* Muhl. (50) (present)

Cypress-leaf savin [Cypress-leav'd savin] - *Juniperus virginiana* L. (181) (~1678)

Cyprian iris - *Iris germanica* L. (138) (1923)

Cypripede jaune (French) - *Cypripedium parviflorum* Salisb. var. *pubescens* (Willd.) Knight (6) (1892), *Cypripedium reginae* Walt. (158) (1900)

Cypripedium - *Cypripedium* L. (57) (1917), *Cypripedium parviflorum* Salisb. var. *pubescens* (Willd.) Knight (54) (1905)

Cyprus - *Taxodium distichum* (L.) L.C. Rich. (12) (1819)

Cyrille de Caroline (French) - *Cyrilla racemiflora* L. (20) (1857)

Cyuers - *Allium schoenoprasum* L. (178, 179) (1526-1596)

D

Dackretter - *Veratrum viride* Ait. (possibly) (7) (1828)

Daddy-nut [Daddy-nuts] or Daddy-nut tree - *Tilia americana* L. (156, 157, 158) (1900-1929), *Tilia* L. (74) (1893) Madison WI

Dado - *Prenanthes alba* L. (40) (1928)

Dado'cabodji'bĭk (Chippewa, milk root) - *Prenanthes alba* L. (40) (1928), *Taraxacum officinale* G.H. Weber ex Wiggers (40) (1928)

Daffodil - *Narcissus pseudonarcissus* L. (5, 19, 49, 50, 92, 109, 156) (1840–present)

Daffodill with the yellow circle - *Narcissus ×medioluteus* Mill. *[poeticus × tazetta]* (178) (1596)

Daffodilly - *Narcissus* L. (180) (1633), *Narcissus pseudonarcissus* L. (5, 180) (1633-1913)

Daffodowndilly - *Narcissus* L. (180) (1633), *Narcissus pseudonarcissus* L. (5, 180) (1633-1913)

Daffy - *Narcissus pseudonarcissus* L. (5, 73) (1892-1913) NH

Daffy-down-dilly [Daffy down dilly] - *Trillium erectum* L. (5, 64, 75) (1894-1913) Bradford VT

Daftberry [Daft-berry] - *Atropa bella-donna* L. (156) (1923)

Dagger cocklebur [Dagger cockle-bur] - *Xanthium spinosum* L. (5, 62, 70, 156) (1895-1923)

Dagger fern [Dagger-fern] - *Polystichum acrostichoides* (Michx.) Schott (109) (1949)

Dagger-flower - *Machaeranthera tanacetifolia* (Kunth) Nees (5) (1913)

Dagger-flower plant [Dagger flower plant] - *Yucca gloriosa* L. (92) (1876)

Dagger-leaf spikerush [Daggerleaf spikerush] - *Eleocharis lanceolata* Fern. (50) (present)

Daggers - *Iris pseudacorus* L. (5, 156, 158) (1900-1923) no longer in use by 1923, *Phalaris arundinacea* L. (158) (1900)

Daggerweed [Dagger weed] - *Yucca glauca* Nutt. (37) (1830)

Daheya - *Juglans cinerea* L. (46) (1879)

Dahlia - *Dahlia* Cav. (82, 138) (1923-930), *Dahlia pinnata* Cav. (92, 107) (1876-1919)

Dahlia sunflower - *Helianthus ×multiflorus* L. *[annuus × decapetalus]* (76) (1896) Sulphur Grove OH

Dahoon - *Ilex cassine* L. (8, 109, 138) (1785-1949)

Dahoon holly - *Ilex aquifolium* L. (189) (176), *Ilex cassine* L. (2, 5, 15, 107, 156) (1895-1923), *Ilex vomitoria* Aiton (92) (1876)

Dahurian buckthorn - *Rhamnus davurica* Pallas (50, 138, 155) (1923–present), *Rhamnus davurica* Pallas subsp. *davurica* (50) (present)

Daisy [Daisies, Daysy] - *Aster* L. (76, 158) (1896), *Bellis* L. (1, 2, 10, 109, 155, 156, 158, 167) (1814-1949) cultivated varieties, *Bellis perennis* L. (19, 92, 179) (1526-1876), *Chrysanthemum* L. (50) (present), *Erigeron philadelphicus* L. (7, 76, 156, 158) (1828-1923), *Erigeron pumilus* Nutt. (5, 76, 158) (1896–1913), *Leucanthemum* Mill. (50) (present), *Leucanthemum vulgare* Lam. (7) (1828)

Daisy beggarticks - *Bidens laevis* (L.) Britton, Sterns & Poggenb. (19) (1840)

Daisy fleabane [Daisy-fleabane] - *Erigeron annuus* (L.) Pers. (5, 62, 63, 80, 82, 97, 121, 122, 145, 156, 158) (1897–1937), *Erigeron* L. (57) (1917), *Erigeron philadelphicus* L. (5, 156, 158) (1900-1923), *Erigeron pulchellus* Michx. (7, 86) (1828-1878), *Erigeron pumilus* Nutt. (121) (1918?-1970?), *Erigeron strigosus* Muhl. ex Willd. (3, 4, 145) (1897-1986), *Erigeron strigosus* Muhl. ex Willd. var. *strigosus* (5, 72, 80, 93, 97, 131, 156) (1899–1937)

Daisy of America - *Astranthium integrifolium* (Michx.) Nutt. (12) (1821)

Daisy-leaf aster [Daisyleaf aster] - *Machaeranthera canescens* (Pursh) A. Gray subsp. *canescens* var. *canescens* (155) (1942)

Daisy-leaf fleabane [Daisy-leaved flea-bane] - *Erigeron pulchellus* Michx. (86) (1878)

Daisy-leaf water cress [Daisy leaved water cress] - *Cardamine bellidifolia* L. (19) (1840)

Dakota gentian - *Gentiana andrewsii* Griseb. var. *dakotica* A. Nels. (50) (present)

Dakota mock vervain - *Glandularia bipinnatifida* (Nutt.) Nutt. (50) (present), *Glandularia bipinnatifida* (Nutt.) Nutt. var. *bipinnatifida* (50) (present)

Dakota potato - *Apios americana* Medik. (76) (1896) MN

Dakota tipsinna - *Pediomelum esculentum* (Pursh) Rydb. (76) (1896) Burnside SD, from Indian name

Dakota turnip - *Pediomelum esculentum* (Pursh) Rydb. (76, 158) (1896–1900) MN

Dakota vervain - *Glandularia bipinnatifida* (Nutt.) Nutt. var. *bipinnatifida* (4, 138, 155) (1923-1986)

Dakota vetch - *Lotus unifoliolatus* (Hook.) Benth. var. *unifoliolatus* (131) (1899) SD

Dalea - *Dalea* L. (106, 155) (1930-1942)

Dalibarda - *Dalibarda* L. (138) (1923), *Dalibarda repens* L. (5, 138) (1913-1923)

Dallis grass [Dallisgrass, Dallis-grass] - *Paspalum dilatatum* Poir. (3, 50, 109, 119, 138, 155, 163) (1852–present)

Dalmatian toadflax - *Linaria dalmatica* (L.) Mill.subsp. *dalmatica* (50, 155) (1942–present), *Linaria dalmatica* (L.) P. Mill. (50, 138, 155) (1923–present)

Dalmation cap - *Tulipa gesneriana* L. (178) (1596), *Tulipa* L. (180) (1633)

Damacene - *Prunus* L. (179) (1526)

Damask nigella [Damaske nigella] - *Nigella damascena* L. (178) (1526)

Damask plum [Damaske plomme] - *Prunus domestica* L. (179) (1526)

Damask rose [Damaske rose] - *Rosa ×damascena* Mill. *[gallica × moschata]* (19, 109, 138) (1840-1949), *Rosa blanda* Aiton (46) (1617)

Damask-violet [Damask violet] - *Hesperis matronalis* L. (5, 156, 158) (1900-1923)

Damasson - *Prunus domestica* L. (179) (1526)

Dame's-gilliflower [Dame's gilliflower] - *Hesperis matronalis* L. (5, 158) (1900-1913)

Dame's-rocket [Dame's rocket, Dames rocket] - *Hesperis* L. (4) (1986), *Hesperis matronalis* L. (1, 3, 4, 5, 50, 72, 85, 138, 155, 156, 158) (1900–present)

Dame's-violet [Dame's violet, Dames-violet, Dames Violets] - *Hesperis* L. (156) (1923), *Hesperis matronalis* L. (1, 5, 15, 74, 92, 109, 156, 158, 178, 180) (1526-1893)

Damewort [Dame-wort] - *Hesperis matronalis* L. (156) (1923)

Damiana - *Turnera diffusa* Willd. ex J.A. Schultes (50, 52, 54, 55, 57, 60) (1902–present)

Damiana (Spanish) - *Isocoma veneta* (Kunth) Greene (76) (1896)

Damiana goldenweed - *Isocoma veneta* (Kunth) Greene (155) (1942), *Pyrrocoma uniflora* (Hook.) Greene var. *uniflora* (155) (1942)

Dammar-pine [Dammarpine] - *Agathis* Salisb. (109, 138, 155) (1923-1949)

Damson - *Prunus domestica* L. var. *insititia* (L.) Fiori & Paoletti (107) (1919)

Dandelion - *Nothocalais cuspidata* (Pursh) Greene (76) (1896) Burnside SD, *Taraxacum* G.H. Weber ex Wiggers (1, 4, 50, 82, 109, 138,

155, 156) (1923–present), *Taraxacum officinale* G.H. Weber ex Wiggers (3, 5, 10, 19, 37, 41, 52, 53, 57, 59, 62, 64, 69, 72, 80, 85, 93, 97, 106, 107, 114, 131, 138, 145, 157, 158, 180, 184, 187) (1633-1977), *Taraxacum officinale* G.H. Weber ex Wiggers subsp. *officinale* (6, 46, 47, 58, 61, 92) (1671-1892)

Dandelion cynthia - *Krigia dandelion* (L.) Nutt. (86) (1878)

Dandelion hawk's-beard [Dandelion hawksbeard] - *Crepis runcinata* (James) Torr. & Gray (155) (1942), *Crepis runcinata* (James) Torr. & Gray subsp. *runcinata* (155) (1942)

Dane's blood - *Campanula glomerata* L. (5, 92, 156) (1876-1923)

Danewort [Danewoort] - *Sambucus ebulus* L. (92, 107, 178) (1526-1919)

Dangleberry [Dangle-berry] - *Gaylussacia frondosa* (L.) Torr. & Gray (2, 5, 46, 107, 138, 156) (1879-1932), *Vaccinium stamineum* L. (5, 92, 156, 158) (1898-1923)

Danthonia - *Danthonia* DC. (155) (1942)

Daphne - *Daphne* L. (138) (1923) Greek name for Laurus nobilis

Daphne willow - *Salix daphnoides* Vill. (138) (1923)

Dark long-leaf willow [Dark long-leaved willow] - *Salix petiolaris* Sm. (5) (1913)

Dark shield fern - *Athyrium filix-femina* (L.) Roth var. *asplenoides* (Michx.) Farw. (187) (1818)

Dark-brown sedge - *Carex atrofusca* Schk. (5, 50) (1913–present)

Dark-eye sunflower [Darkeye sunflower] - *Helianthus atrorubens* L. (109, 138) (1923-1949)

Darkey-head [Darkey head] - *Rudbeckia hirta* L. (5, 62) (1912-1913)

Dark-green bulrush [Darkgreen bulrush, Dark green bulrush] - *Scirpus atrovirens* Willd. (3, 5, 72) (1907-1977), *Scirpus georgianus* Harper (3) (1977), *Scirpus pallidus* (Britt.) Fern. (3) (1977)

Dark-green sedge - *Carex venusta* Dewey var. *minor* Boeckl. (5, 50) (1913–present)

Dark-leaf mugwort [Darkleaf mugwort, Dark-leaved mugwort] - *Artemisia ludoviciana* Nutt. (5, 93, 97, 122) (1913-1937)

Dark-purple rockbrake [Dark purple rock brake] - *Pellaea atropurpurea* (L.) Link (86) (1878)

Dark-throat shootingstar [Darkthroat shootingstar] - *Dodecatheon pulchellum* (Raf.) Merr. (50) (present), *Dodecatheon pulchellum* (Raf.) Merr. subsp. *pulchellum* (50, 155) (1942–present)

Darlington's ash - *Fraxinus pennsylvanica* Marsh. (5) (1913)

Darlington's spurge - *Euphorbia purpurea* (Raf.) Fern. (5) (1913)

Darnel - *Lolium* L. (1, 7, 10, 66) (1818-1932), *Lolium perenne* L. (19, 45, 85, 92, 184, 187) (1793-1932), *Lolium temulentum* L. (5, 14, 56, 67, 72, 88, 92, 94, 119, 155, 157, 158, 163, 178, 179) (1526-1942)

Darnel grass - *Lolium perenne* L. (92) (1876), *Lolium temulentum* L. (92) (1876)

Darnel rye grass [Darnel ryegrass] - *Lolium temulentum* L. (50, 155) (1942–present)

Darnell - *Agrostemma githago* L. (179) (1526)

Darning-needle [Darning needle] - *Hesperostipa spartea* (Trin.) Barkworth (56) (1901) IA

Darru oru fu (Hungarian) - *Geranium maculatum* L. (186) (1814)

Dart grass - *Holcus lanatus* L. (5) (1913)

Darwin's barbarry [Darwin barbarry] - *Berberis darwinii* Hook. (138) (1923)

Dasheen - *Colocasia esculenta* (L.) Schott (109, 138) (1923-1949)

Dashel - *Cirsium arvense* (L.) Scop. (157, 158) (1900-1929), *Sonchus oleraceus* L. (157, 158) (1900-1929)

Dasistoma - *Dasistoma* Raf. (50) (present)

Date [Dates] or Date tree - *Phoenix canariensis* hort. ex Chabaud (178, 179) (1526-1596), *Phoenix dactylifera* L. (92) (1876)

Date palm - *Phoenix dactylifera* L. (107, 110, 138) (1886-1923), *Phoenix* L. (138) (1923)

Date yucca - *Yucca* L. (138) (1923)

Date-plum [Dateplum, Date plum] - *Celtis australis* L. (178) (1526), *Diospyros* L. (1, 2, 8, 10, 158) (1818-1932), *Diospyros texana* Scheele (106) (1930), *Diospyros virginiana* L. (5, 49, 92, 156)

(1876–1923), *Phoenix dactylifera* L. (92) (1876)

Datil - *Yucca baccata* Torr. (153) (1913) NM

Datil palm - *Syagrus romanzoffiana* (Cham.) Glassman (138) (1923)

Datil yucca - *Yucca baccata* Torr. (155) (1942)

Datura - *Datura* L. (138, 155) (1923-1942), *Datura stramonium* L. (57) (1917)

Davallia - *Dennstaedtia* Bernh. (138) (1923)

David root - *Chiococca alba* (L.) A.S. Hitchc. (7, 49, 92) (1828-1898)

David's spurge - *Euphorbia davidii* Subils (50) (present)

Davis Mountain mock vervain - *Glandularia wrightii* (Gray) Umber (50) (present)

Davis' sedge - *Carex davisii* Schwein. & Torr. (3, 5, 50, 66, 72) (1893–present)

Dawke - *Daucus carota* L. (157, 158, 179) (1526-1929)

Dawson's crab [Dawson crab] - *Malus* ×*dawsoniana* Rehd. [*fusca* × *pumila*] (138) (1923)

Day cestrum - *Cestrum diurnum* L. (138) (1923)

Day jessamine - *Cestrum diurnum* L. (109) (1949)

Day nettle - *Lamium album* L. (5) (1913), *Lamium purpureum* L. (5, 158) (1900–1913)

Dayberry [Day-berry] - *Ribes uva-crispa* L. var. *sativum* DC. (5, 156) (1913-1923)

Da'yewû (Cherokee, it sews itself up) - *Arnoglossum atriplicifolium* (L.) H.E. Robins. (102) (1886) leaves are said to grow together again when torn

Dayflower [Day flower, Day-flower] - *Commelina communis* L. (3, 98) (1926-1977), *Commelina erecta* L. var. *angustifolia* (Michx.) Fern. (19, 85, 92) (1840-1932), *Commelina* L. (1, 7, 50, 93, 109, 122, 124, 138, 155, 156, 158) (1828–present), *Commelina virginica* L. (65) (1931), *Hemerocallis lilioasphodelus* L. (92) (1876)

Daylily [Day lily, Day-lily, Day-Lillie] - *Hemerocallis fulva* (L.) L. (3, 10, 72, 93) (1818-1977), *Hemerocallis* L. (50, 107, 109, 138, 156, 158) (1900–present), *Hemerocallis lilioasphodelus* L. (92, 180) (1633-1876), *Hosta plantaginea* (Lam.) Aschers. (156) (1923), *Hosta* Tratt. (156) (1923)

Dazeg - *Bellis perennis* L. (158) (1900)

Dead Sea apple - *Quercus infectoria* Olivier (insect galls infecting oaks) (92) (1876) not a species of oak, but an abnormal growths caused by parasites

Deadly amanita - *Amanita muscaria* var. *muscaria* (L.) Pers. (71) (1898)

Deadly meade saffron - *Colchicum autumnale* L. (178) (1596)

Deadly nightshade - *Atropa bella-donna* L. (19, 52, 53, 54, 55, 57, 60, 92, 156, 178, 180) (1596-1923), *Solanum americanum* Mill. (187) (1818), *Solanum interius* Rydb. (50) (present), *Solanum nigrum* L. (5, 19, 62, 71, 92, 93, 97, 124, 156) (1840-1937)

Dead-man's flower - *Anaphalis margaritacea* (L.) Benth. & Hook (187) (1818)

Dead-man's-fingers [Dead man's fingers] - *Platanthera grandiflora* (Bigelow) Lindl. (156) (1923) no longer in use by 1923

Dead-men's-bellows - *Ajuga reptans* L. (158) (1900)

Dead-men's-bells [Dead men's bells] - *Digitalis pupurea* L. (92) (1876), *Penstemon digitalis* Nutt. ex Sims (77) (1898) Western US, from growing on graves

Dead-men's-bones [Dead men's bones] - *Linaria vulgaris* Mill. (5, 73, 157, 158) (1892-1929) Troy NY

Deadnettle [Dead-nettle, Dead nettle, Deed nettel] - *Lamium* L. (1, 4, 50, 7, 10, 93, 106, 109, 138, 155, 156, 158, 167, 179) (1526–present), *Angelica atropurpurea* L. (92) (1876), *Lamium album* L. (6, 57, 107) (1892-1919), *Lamium amplexicaule* L. (19, 62, 63, 85, 92, 122, 124, 187) (1818-1937), *Pilea pumila* (L.) Gray (156) (1923), *Stachys palustris* L. (5, 156) (1913-1923)

Deaf-nettle [Deaf nettle] - *Lamium purpureum* L. (5, 158) (1900-1913)

Deal pine - *Pinus strobus* L. (5, 92) (1876-1913)

Dear's-eye [Dear's eye] - *Aesculus pavia* L. (177) (1762)

Death baby - *Phallus* Junius ex L. (76) (1896) MA, appearance near house supposedly foretold a death in the family

Death camas [Deathcamas, Death camass] - *Stenanthium gramineum* (Ker-Gawl.) Morong (156) (1923), *Zigadenus elegans* Pursh (157) (1929), *Zigadenus* Michx. (1, 50, 93, 155) (1932–present), *Zigadenus nuttallii* (Gray) S. Wats. (3) (1977), *Zigadenus venenosus* S. Wats. (101) (1905), *Zigadenus venenosus* S. Wats. var. *gramineus* (Rydb.) Walsh ex M.E. Peck (3, 5, 85, 93, 133, 146, 148, 157, 158) (1903-1977)

Death cup - *Amanita phalloides* (Fr.) Link (71) (1898)

Death-come-quickly - *Geranium robertianum* L. (156, 157, 158) (1900-1929)

Death-cup amanita [Deathcup amanita] - *Amanita phalloides* (Fr.) Link (155) (1942)

Death-head moss [Death head moss] - *Usnea hirta* (L.) F. H. Wigg. (92) (1876)

Death-of-man [Death of man] - *Cicuta maculata* L. (6, 7, 71, 92, 156, 158) (1828-1923)

Death-root - *Trillium erectum* L. (156) (1923)

Death's flower - *Vinca major* L. (92) (1876)

Death's herb - *Atropa bella-donna* L. (156) (1923)

Deb's apron strings - *Saccharina longicruris* (Bachelot de la Pylaie) Kuntze (73) (1892) ME

Deciduous cypress - *Taxodium distichum* (L.) L.C. Rich. (14) (1882)

Deciduous holly - *Ilex crenata* Thunb. (3, 4, 5, 97, 106, 122, 124, 156) (1913-1986)

Deciduous rough bindweed [Deciduous rough bind-weed] - *Smilax rotundifolia* L. (187) (1818)

Deciduous service-bush - *Ilex verticillata* (L.) Gray (186) (1814)

Deciduous winter-berry - *Ilex verticillata* (L.) Gray (186) (1814)

Decorated silver fir - *Abies procera* Rehd. (20) (1857)

Decumaria - *Decumaria barbara* L. (5) (1913)

Decumary - *Decumaria barbara* L. (19) (1840)

Decumbent butterfly-weed [Decumbent butterfly weed] - *Asclepias asperula* (Dcne.) Woods. subsp. *capricornu* (Woods.) Woods. (5, 72, 122) (1907-1937)

Decumbent five-finger - *Potentilla simplex* Michx. (5) (1913)

Decumbent milkvetch - *Astragalus miser* Dougl. var. *decumbens* (Nutt. ex Torr. & Gray) Cronq. (155) (1942)

Decumbent milkweed - *Asclepias asperula* (Dcne.) Woods. subsp. *capricornu* (Woods.) Woods. (5, 97) (1913-1937)

Decumbent pearlwort - *Sagina decumbens* (Ell.) Torr. & Gray (5, 97) (1913-1937)

Decumbent pencil flower - *Stylosanthes biflora* (L.) Britton, Sterns & Poggenb. (5) (1913)

Deep-green sedge - *Carex tonsa* (Fernald) Bicknell (5) (1913)

Deep-root clubmoss [Deeproot clubmoss] - *Lycopodium tristachyum* Pursh (50) (present)

Deer brush - *Ceanothus* L. (1) (1932)

Deer bush - *Ceanothus thyrsiflorus* Esch. (52) (1919)

Deer fern [Deerfern] - *Blechnum spicant* (L.) Sm. (86, 138) (1878-1923)

Deer laurel - *Rhododendron maximum* L. (5, 156) (1913-1923)

Deer plum - *Licania michauxii* Prance (106) (1930) Alabama

Deer sedge - *Carex hallii* Olney (5) (1913)

Deer vine [Deer-vine] - *Linnaea borealis* L. (5, 75, 156, 158) (1894-1923) ME

Deer wood [Deer-wood] - *Ostrya virginiana* (Mill.) K. Koch (156, 157, 158) (1900-1929)

Deer-balls [Deer balls] - *Elaphomyces granulatus* Fr. (92) (1876)

Deerberry [Deer-berry, Deer berry] - *Gaultheria procumbens* L. (5, 7, 49, 73, 92, 156, 186) (1814-1892), *Ilex vomitoria* Aiton (156) (1923), *Mitchella repens* L. (6, 49, 53, 92, 156) (1892-1923) no longer in use by 1923, *Vaccinium* L. (1, 3, 4, 5, 27, 109, 156, 158) (1900-1986), *Vaccinium stamineum* L. (1, 2, 3, 4, 5, 19, 46, 50, 65, 92, 97, 107, 109, 138, 156, 158) (1879–present)

Deer-clover [Deer clover] - *Lotus glaber* Mill. (106) (1930)

Deerfood [Deer-food, Deer food] - *Brasenia schreberi* Gmel. (5, 7, 92, 156) (1828-1923)

Deer-foot vanilla-leaf [Deerfoot vanillaleaf] - *Achlys triphylla* (Sm.) DC. (155) (1942)

Deer-grass [Deergrass, Deer grass] - *Muhlenbergia rigens* (Benth.) A.S. Hitchc. (94, 122, 163) (1852-1937), *Rhexia* L. (2) (1895), *Rhexia virginica* L. (5, 19, 86, 92, 156) (1840-1923), *Trichophorum caespitosum* (L.) Hartman (46) (1879)

Deer-horn cactus [Deerhorn cactus, Deerhorncactus] - *Peniocereus greggii* (Engelm.) Britt. & Rose (138, 155) (1931-1942)

Deering's velvetbean [Deering velvetbean] - *Mucuna pruriens* (L.) DC. var. *utilis* (Wallich ex Wight) Baker ex Burck (138) (1923)

Deer-pea vetch [Deer pea vetch] - *Vicia ludociciana* Nutt. (4) (1986)

Deer's-ears [Deer's ears] - *Frasera caroliniensis* Walt. (156) (1923), *Frasera speciosa* Dougl. ex Griseb. (106) (1930) translation of Navaho name

Deer's-foot [Deer-foot] - *Brasenia schreberi* Gmel. (156) (1923)

Deer's-hair [Deer's hair, Deer hair] - *Trichophorum caespitosum* (L.) Hartman (5, 46, 156) (1879-1923)

Deer's-tongue [Deer's tongue, Deer tongue, Deer-tongue] - *Carphephorus odoratissimus* (J.F. Gmel.) Herbert (5, 49, 53, 57, 92, 106, 107, 156) (1876-1930), *Erythronium albidum* Nutt. (5, 75) (1894-1913) Anderson IN, *Erythronium americanum* Ker. (5, 75, 92, 157) (1876-1923) Anderson IN, *Rhododendron maximum* L. (71) (1898), *Erythronium* L. (7) (1828)

Deer-tongue dicanthelium [Deertongue dicanthelium] - *Dichanthelium clandestinum* (L.) Gould (4) (1986)

Deer-tongue grass [Deer-tongue-grass] - *Dichanthelium clandestinum* (L.) Gould (5, 50, 75, 119) (1894–present)

Deervetch [Deer vetch] - *Lotus* L. (155) (1942), *Lotus unifoliolatus* (Hook.) Benth. var. *unifoliolatus* (4, 98) (1926-1986)

Deerweed - *Lotus glaber* Mill. (106) (1930)

Deerwort boneset [Deerwort-boneset] - *Ageratina altissima* (L.) King & H.E. Robins. (5, 7, 92, 156) (1828-1923)

Deil's spoons - *Alisma plantago-aquatica* L. (156) (1923), *Alisma subcordatum* Raf. (5) (1913), *Potamogeton natans* L. (5, 156, 158) (1900-1923)

Delicious raspberry - *Rubus deliciosus* Torr. (50) (present)

Delnorte manzanita - *Arctostaphylos ×cinerea* T.J. Howell [*canescens × viscida*] (155) (1942)

Delta arrowhead - *Sagittaria platyphylla* (Engelm.) J.G. Smith (50, 155) (1942–present)

Delta bulrush [Delta bullrush] - *Schoenoplectus deltarum* (Schuyler) Soják (50) (present)

Delta maidenhair fern - *Adiantum raddianum* K. Presl (138) (1923)

Demágene-minš (Chippewa, Pipestem wood) - *Spiraea salicifolia* L. (105) (1932)

De-min (Chippewa, heart berry) - *Fragaria* L. (105) (1932)

Dende lyon - *Taraxacum officinale* G.H. Weber ex Wiggers subsp. *vulgare* (Lam.) Schinz & R. Keller (190) (~1759)

Dennett grass - *Elymus virginicus* L. var. *virginicus* (5, 87, 111, 129) (1885-1915)

Dens leon - *Taraxacum officinale* G.H. Weber ex Wiggers subsp. *vulgare* (Lam.) Schinz & R. Keller (59) (1488)

Dens leonis - *Taraxacum officinale* G.H. Weber ex Wiggers (177, 180) (1633-1762)

Dense bladderpod - *Lesquerella condensata* A. Nels. (50) (present)

Dense button-snakeroot [Dense button snakeroot] - *Liatris spicata* (L.) Willd. (156) (1923), *Liatris spicata* (L.) Willd. var. *spicata* (5, 131, 157) (1899-1923)

Dense cotton-flower [Dense cottonflower] - *Guilleminea densa* (Willd.) Moq. (4) (1986)

Dense long-beak sedge [Dense long-beaked sedge] - *Carex sychnocephala* Carey (5, 72) (1907-1913)

Dense panic grass [Dense panic-grass] - *Panicum rigidulum* Bosc ex Nees var. *elongatum* (Pursh) Lelong (5, 99) (1913-1923)

Dense rush grass - *Sporobolus indicus* (L.) R. Br. var. *indicus* (5) (1913)

Dense-flower aster [Dense-flowered aster] - *Symphyotrichum ericoides* (L.) Nesom var. *ericoides* (5, 72, 82, 93, 97, 131) (1899-1937)

Devil's-apple

Dense-flower bent grass [Dense flowered bent grass] - *Agrostis stolonifera* L. (5) (1913)

Dense-flower hedge-nettle [Dense-flowered hedge nettle] - *Stachys tenuifolia* Willd. (5, 72) (1907-1913)

Dense-flower oak [Dense flowered oak] - *Lithocarpus densiflorus* (Hook. & Arn.) Rehd. (20) (1857)

Dense-flower persicaria [Dense-flowered persicaria] - *Polygonum amphibium* L. var. *emersum* Michx. (5) (1913)

Dense-flower prairie clover [Dense-flowered prairie clover] - *Dalea compacta* Spreng. (131) (1899), *Dalea cylindriceps* Barneby (5, 93) (1913-1936)

Dense-flower St. John's-wort [Dense-flowered St. John's wort] - *Hypericum densiflorum* Pursh (5) (1913)

Dense-flower water-willow [Dense-flowered water willow, Dense-flowered waterwillow, Denseflowered water willow] - *Justicia americana* (L.) Vahl (5, 72, 97, 122) (1907-1937)

Dense-flower wreath aster [Dense-flowered wreath-aster] - *Symphyotrichum ericoides* (L.) Nesom var. *ericoides* (158) (1900)

Dense-leaf elodea [Denseleaved elodea] - *Egeria densa* Planch. (155) (1942)

Densely-flowered bent - *Agrostis densiflora* Vasey (94) (1901)

Densely-flowered manna grass [Densely flowered manna-grass] - *Glyceria obtusa* (Muhl.) Trin. (94) (1901)

Densely-flowered plume grass [Densely-flowered plume-grass] - *Saccharum giganteum* (Walt.) Pers. (56, 94) (1901)

Dense-spike blazing star [Densespike blazing star] - *Liatris densispicata* (Bush) Gaiser (50) (present), *Liatris densispicata* (Bush) Gaiser var. *interrupta* Gaiser (50) (present)

Dense-tuft hairsedge [Densetuft hairsedge] - *Bulbostylis capillaris* (L.) Kunth ex C.B. Clarke (50) (present), *Bulbostylis capillaris* (L.) Kunth ex C.B. Clarke subsp. *capillaris* (50) (present)

Dent corn - *Zea mays* L. subsp. *mays* (109, 119) (1938-1949)

Dent de chiene jaune (French) - *Erythronium americanum* Ker. (7) (1828)

Dent de lion (French) - *Taraxacum officinale* G.H. Weber ex Wiggers (158) (1900), *Taraxacum officinale* G.H. Weber ex Wiggers subsp. *officinale* (6) (1892)

Dent de lyon (French) - *Taraxacum officinale* G.H. Weber ex Wiggers (180) (1633)

Deodar - *Cedrus deodara* (Roxb. ex D. Don) G. Don f. (138) (1923) deodar is native name in Himalayas

Deodar cedar - *Cedrus deodara* (Roxb. ex D. Don) G. Don f. (109) (1949) deodar is native name in Himalayas

Depressed whitlow wort - *Paronychia depressa* (Torr. & Gray) Nutt. ex A. Nels. (5, 93) (1913-1936)

Deptford pink - *Dianthus armeria* L. (4, 5, 50, 15, 46, 72, 155, 156) (1879-present)

Des choux (French) - *Brassica oleracea* L. (180) (1633)

Descurea - *Descurainia sophia* (L.) Webb ex Prantl (174) (1753)

Deseret-weed - *Glycyrrhiza lepidota* Pursh (156) (1923)

Desert bear-poppy [Desert bearpoppy] - *Arctomecon merriamii* Coville (155) (1942)

Desert biscuitroot - *Lomatium foeniculaceum* (Nutt.) Coult. & Rose (50) (present), *Lomatium foeniculaceum* (Nutt.) Coult. & Rose subsp. *daucifolium* (Torr. & Gray) Theobald (50) (present), *Lomatium foeniculaceum* (Nutt.) Coult. & Rose subsp. *foeniculaceum* (50) (present)

Desert blazing star [Desert blazingstar] - *Mentzelia multiflora* (Nutt.) Gray (155) (1942)

Desert broom - *Baccharis sarothroides* Gray (106) (1930)

Desert bush - *Parkinsonia microphylla* Torr. (106) (1930)

Desert centaury - *Centaurium exaltatum* (Griseb.) W. Wight ex Piper (50) (present)

Desert dandelion - *Malacothrix* DC. (1) (1932)

Desert false indigo - *Amorpha fruticosa* L. (50) (present)

Desert goldenweed - *Ericameria linearifolia* (DC.) Urbatsch & Wussow (155) (1942)

Desert goosefoot - *Chenopodium pratericola* Rydb. (50) (present)

Desert groundsel - *Senecio eremophilus* Richards (155) (1942)

Desert gum - *Eucalyptus rudis* Sm. (109, 138) (1923-1949)

Desert horse-purslane [Desert horsepurslane] - *Trianthema portulacastrum* L. (50) (present)

Desert love grass [Desert lovegrass] - *Eragrostis pectinacea* (Michx.) Nees ex Steud. (155) (1942)

Desert madwort - *Alyssum desertorum* Stapf (50) (present), *Alyssum desertorum* Stapf var. *desertorum* (50) (present)

Desert matrimony - *Lycium fremontii* Gray (106) (1930)

Desert mentzelia - *Mentzelia multiflora* (Nutt.) Gray (155) (1942)

Desert milkweed - *Asclepias erosa* Torr. (155) (1942)

Desert oak - *Quercus wislizeni* A. DC. var. *frutescens* Engelm. (75) (1894) Southern CA

Desert parsley [Desert-parsley, Desertparsley] - *Lomatium* Raf. (50) (present)

Desert prince's-plume [Desert princesplume] - *Stanleya* Nutt. (50, 155) (1942–present), *Stanleya pinnata* (Pursh) Britton var. *integrifolia* (James ex Torr.) Rollins (50) (present)

Desert ragwort - *Senecio eremophilus* Richards (50) (present)

Desert rue [Desertrue] - *Thamnosma* Torr. & Frem. (50, 155) (1942–present)

Desert salt grass [Desert saltgrass] - *Distichlis spicata* (L.) Greene (140) (1944)

Desert sand-verbena [Desert sand verbena, Desert sandverbena] - *Abronia villosa* S. Wats. (50, 155) (1942–present)

Desert seepweed - *Suaeda suffrutescens* S. Wats. (3, 4, 50, 155) (1942–present)

Desert sumac - *Rhus microphylla* Engelm. (4) (1986)

Desert thorn [Desert-thorn, Desertthorn] - *Lycium* L. (50, 155) (1942–present)

Desert willow - *Salix glauca* L. subsp. *glauca* var. *acutifolia* (Hook.) C.K. Schneid. (5) (1913)

Desert wire-lettuce [Desert wirelettuce] - *Stephanomeria runcinata* Nutt. (50, 155) (1942–present)

Desert yaupon - *Schaefferia cuneifolia* Gray (122, 124) (1937) TX

Desert-chicory - *Pyrrhopappus* DC. (50) (present)

Desert-marigold - *Baileya* Harvey & Gray ex Gray (109) (1949)

Desert-willow [Desertwillow, Desert willow] - *Chilopsis* D. Don (138) (1923), *Chilopsis linearis* (Cav.) Sweet (4, 50, 77, 109, 122, 124, 138, 149, 153, 155) (1898–present)

Des-shean (Monomonie) - *Elodea* Michx. (23) (1810)

Deutscher safran (German) - *Carthamus tinctorius* L. (158) (1900)

Deutzia - *Deutzia gracilis* Sieb. & Zucc. (92) (1876), *Deutzia scabra* Thunb. (82) (1930), *Deutzia* Thunb. (82, 138) (1923-930)

Devil wood [Devilwood, Devil-wood, Devil's wood] - *Osmanthus americanus* (L.) Benth. & Hook. f. ex Gray var. *americanus* (19, 20, 92) (1840-1876), *Osmanthus americanus* Benth. & Hook. (2, 75, 107) (1894-1919), *Osmanthus* Lour. (possibly) (109) (1949)

Devil-in-the-bush (Devil in the bush) - *Nigella damascena* L. (79, 156) (1891-1923)

Devil's beggartick [Devils beggarticks] - *Bidens frondosa* L. (50, 155) (1942–present)

Devil's daisy [Devil's-daisy] - *Leucanthemum vulgare* Lam. (158) (1900)

Devil's flower - *Linaria vulgaris* Mill. (5) (1913), *Silene dioica* (L.) Clairville (156) (1923) no longer in use by 1923

Devil's grass - *Elymus repens* (L.) Gould (62, 64, 69) (1904-1912) IN, *Paspalum distichum* L. (5) (1913)

Devil's hop-vine [Devil's hop vine] - *Smilax rotundifolia* L. (5, 156) (1913-1923)

Devil's vine - *Calystegia sepium* (L.) R. Br. subsp. *sepium* (5, 62, 156) (1912-1923) no longer in use by 1923

Devil's weed [Devil's-weed] - *Lactuca canadensis* L. (5, 75, 156, 158) (1900-1923) WV

Devil's-apple [Devil's apple] - *Datura stramonium* L. (5, 6, 62, 69, 71, 92, 156, 157, 158) (1892–1929), *Podophyllum peltatum* L. (5, 64, 156, 158) (1900–1923)

Devil's-apron [Devil's apron] - *Laminaria saccharina* (Linnaeus) J.V.Lamouroux (92) (1876), *Saccharina longicruris* (Bachelot de la Pylaie) Kuntze (73) (1892) Northeastern US

Devil's-apronstrings [Devil's apron strings] - *Saccharina longicruris* (Bachelot de la Pylaie) Kuntze (73) (1892) NE coast

Devil's-bit [Devil's bit, Devilbit] - *Aletris farinosa* L. (6, 7, 64, 156, 191) (1814-1908), *Arisaema triphyllum* (L.) Schott (7) (1828), *Chamaelirium luteum* (L.) A. Gray (5, 6, 7, 53, 58, 64, 92, 156, 187) (1818-1923), *Chamaelirium* Willd. (1, 2, 156) (1895-1932), *Liatris aspera* Michx. (49, 156) (1898–1923), *Liatris scariosa* (L.) Willd. var. *scariosa* (157, 158) (1900-1929), *Liatris spicata* (L.) Willd. var. *spicata* (5, 92, 131, 157) (1876-1929), *Succisa pratensis* Moench (50) (present), *Veratrum viride* Ait. (possibly) (7) (1828)

Devil's-bit herb [Devil's bit herb] - *Succisa pratensis* Moench (92) (1876)

Devil's-bit root [Devil's bit root] - *Succisa pratensis* Moench (92) (1876)

Devil's-bite [Devil's bite, Devilsbite] - *Liatris aspera* Michx. (75, 156) (1894–1923), *Liatris spicata* (L.) Willd. (156) (1923), *Veratrum viride* Ait. (5, 64, 71, 92, 156) (1876-1923), *Succisa pratensis* Moench (179) (1526)

Devil's-bones [Devil's bones] - *Dioscorea villosa* L. (6, 64, 92, 156, 158) (1892-1923)

Devil's-bootjacks [Devil's bootjacks] - *Bidens connata* Muhl. ex Willd. (62) (1912) IN

Devil's-bouquet [Devil's bouquet] - *Nyctaginia capitata* Choisy (124) (1937)

Devil's-claw [Devil's claw, Devil's claws, Devilsclaws] - *Acacia greggii* Gray (106) (1930), *Proboscidea louisianica* (P. Mill.) Thellung (1, 3, 4, 145, 156, 158) (1897-1986), *Proboscidea* Schmidel (155) (1942), *Ranunculus arvensis* L. (5, 156, 158) (1900-1923)

Devil's-club [Devil's club, Devilsclub] - *Aralia spinosa* L. (106) (1930), *Oplopanax horridus* Miq. (5, 138, 156) (1913-1923)

Devil's-darning-needle [Devil's darning needle] - *Clematis virginiana* L. (5, 50, 156, 158) (1900–present), *Scandix pecten-veneris* L. (5, 156) (1913-1923) no longer in use by 1923

Devil's-dye [Devil's dye] - *Indigofera* L. (92) (1876)

Devil's-ear [Devil's ear] - *Arisaema triphyllum* (L.) Schott (156, 157, 158) (1900-1929)

Devil's-fig [Devil's fig] - *Argemone mexicana* L. (5, 6, 92, 156) (1876-1923)

Devil's-fingers [Devil's fingers] - *Lotus corniculatus* L. (5, 158) (1900-1913), *Populus nigra* L. (5, 156) (1913-1923)

Devil's-flax [Devil's flax] - *Linaria vulgaris* Mill. (5, 75, 156, 157, 158) (18994-1929) WV

Devil's-grandmother [Devil's grandmother] - *Elephantopus tomentosus* L. (5, 75, 156) (1894-1923)

Devil's-grass [Devil's grass] - *Chondrilla juncea* L. (5, 75, 156) (1894-1923) WV

Devil's-grip [Devil's grip] - *Mollugo verticillata* L. (5, 76, 156, 158) (1896-1923) North Berwick ME, name given by section hands along railroad because the plant is so hard to eradicate

Devil's-gut [Devil's gut, Devil's-guts, Devil's guts, Devil's-guts] - *Cuscuta americana* L. (7, 92) (1828-1876), *Cuscuta epilinum* Weihe. (156) (1923), *Cuscuta epithymum* (L.) L. (62) (1912) IN, *Cuscuta gronovii* Willd. ex J.A. Schultes (5, 156) (1913-1923), *Equisetum arvense* L. (79) (1891) NH, *Ranunculus repens* L. (158) (1900), *Spergula arvensis* L. (76, 158) (1896-1900) Paris ME

Devil's-hair [Devil's hair] - *Clematis virginiana* L. (5, 74, 156, 158) (1893-1923) VA

Devil's-head [Devil's head] - *Echinocactus texensis* Hopffer. (4) (1986)

Devils-head echinocactus - *Echinocactus texensis* Hopffer. (155) (1942)

Devil's-head-in-a-bush [Devil's head-in-a-bush] - *Hibiscus trionum* L. (5, 73, 156, 158) (1892-1923) NH, New Brunswick; no longer in use by 1923

Devil's-horns [Devil's horns] - *Proboscidea louisianica* (P. Mill.) Thellung (156) (1923)

Devil's-in-a-bush [Devil's in a bush] - *Nigella damascena* L. (92) (1876)

Devil's-ironweed [Devil's iron weed, Devil's ironweed] - *Lactuca canadensis* L. (5, 75, 156, 157, 158) (1894-1929) WV, *Liatris* Gaertn. ex Schreber. (7) (1828) Concord MA, because the corm or tuber is thought to look as if bitten off

Devil's-milk [Devil's milk] - *Chelidonium majus* L. (156, 158) (1900-1923), *Euphorbia helioscopia* L. (5, 92, 156) (1876-1923), *Euphorbia peplus* L. (5, 156) (1913-1923)

Devil's-paintbrush [Devil's paint-brush] - *Hieracium aurantiacum* L. (5, 62, 106, 109, 156) (1912-1949)

Devil's-pitchfork [Devil's pitchfork] - *Bidens frondosa* L. (5, 75, 156, 158) (1900-1923) Ferrisburgh VT, Concord MA

Devil's-plague [Devil's plague] - *Daucus carota* L. (62, 75, 106, 156, 157, 158) (1900-1930) IN

Devil's-pumpkin [Devil's pumpkin] - *Passiflora suberosa* L. (76) (1896) Florida Keys

Devil's-rattlebox [Devil's rattle box, Devil's rattle-box] - *Silene vulgaris* (Moench) Garcke (5, 76, 156) (1896-1923) Stockbridge MA, no longer in use by 1923

Devil's-root [Devil's root] - *Chamaelirium luteum* (L.) A. Gray (7) (1828), *Orobanche minor* J.E. Smith (5, 156) (1913-1923)

Devil's-scourge [Devil's scourge] - *Hypericum perforatum* L. (6) (1892)

Devil's-shoestring [Devil's shoe-string, Devil's shoe string, Devil's-shoestrings, Devil's shoe-strings, Devil's shoestrings, Devil's shoe strings] - *Cynanchum laeve* (Michx.) Pers. (106, 156) (1923-1930), *Polygonum amphibium* L. var. *emersum* Michx. (80) (1913) IA, *Tephrosia* Pers. (7) (1828), *Tephrosia virginiana* (L.) Pers (5, 49, 92, 102, 156, 157, 158) (1876-1929), *Viburnum lantanoides* Michx. (156) (1923)

Devil's-snuffbox [Devil's snuff box] - *Lycoperdon* Pers. (14) (1882), *Ustilago maydis* (DC.) Corda (73) (1892) Chestertown MD

Devil's-spoons - *Alisma subcordatum* Raf. (157) (1929)

Devil's-tether [Devil's tether] - *Polygonum convolvulus* L. (5, 156, 158) (1900-1923)

Devil's-thread [Devil's thread] - *Clematis virginiana* L. (156) (1923)

Devil's-tongue [Devil's tongue, Devilstongue] - *Opuntia ficus-indica* (L.) Mill. (73, 156) (1892-1923) Northern OH, *Opuntia humifusa* (Raf.) Raf. (5, 50) (1913–present), *Opuntia humifusa* (Raf.) Raf. var. *humifusa* (50, 73, 158) (1892–present) Northern OH

Devil's-trumpet [Devil's trumpet] - *Datura stramonium* L. (5, 69, 156, 158) (1900-1929)

Devil's-turnip [Devil's turnip] - *Bryonia alba* L. (53) (1922), *Bryonia cretica* L. subsp. *dioica* (Jacq.) Tutin (92) (1876)

Devil's-umbrellas [Devil's umbrellas] - *Hymenomyces* Fr. (73) (1892) Baltimore MD

Devil's-walkingstick [Devil's walking-stick, Devil's walking stick, Devil's-walking-stick] - *Ailanthus altissima* (Mill) Swingle (5, 76, 156, 158) (1896-1923) Sulphur Grove OH, *Aralia spinosa* L. (138, 155, 156) (1923-1942), *Oplopanax horridus* Miq. (101, 160) (1860-1905)

Devil-tree alstonia [Deviltree alstonia] - *Alstonia macrophylla* Wallich ex G. Don (155) (1942)

Devilweed aster - *Chloracantha spinosa* (Benth.) Nesom (155) (1942)

Devioweed [Devio-weed] - *Symphyotrichum lateriflorum* (L.) A.& D. Löve (75) (1894) WV

Dew cup [Dewcup] - *Alchemilla monticola* Opiz (possibly) (5) (1913)

Dew flower [Dew-flowers] - *Commelina* L. (1) (1932), *Penstemon cobaea* Nutt. (156) (1923)

Dew grass - *Agrostis gigantea* Roth (66) (1903), *Dactylis glomerata* L. (5, 92) (1876-1913)

Dew plant [Dew-plant] - *Aptenia cordifolia* (L. f.) Schwant. (109) (1949), *Drosera rotundifolia* L. (92, 156, 158) (1898-1923), *Mesembryanthemum* L. (73) (1892) Northern OH

Dewberry [Dew-berry, Dew berry] - *Gaultheria procumbens* L. (6)

(1892), *Rubus baileyanus* Britton (82) (1930), *Rubus caesius* L. (14) (1882), *Rubus canadensis* L. (2, 46, 58, 63, 92, 103, 105, 107) (1671-1932), *Rubus flagellaris* Willd. (3, 5, 62, 72, 97, 107, 156, 187) (1818-1977), *Rubus* L. (4, 138, 155) (1923-1986), *Rubus pubescens* Raf. var. *pubescens* (5, 73) (1892–1913), *Rubus trivialis* Michx. (19, 124) (1840-1937)

Dewdrop [Dew drop] - *Dalibarda repens* L. (5, 74, 156) (1893-1923) NY

Dewey's sedge [Dewey sedge] - *Carex deweyana* Schwein. (5, 50, 66, 72, 139) (1903–present)

Dew-grass [Dew grass] - *Drosera anglica* Huds. (46) (1671), *Drosera rotundifolia* L. (46) (1671)

Dewitt's snakeroot [Dewitt snakeroot] - *Prenanthes autumnalis* Walt. (5, 156) (1913-1923), *Prenanthes* L. (7) (1828)

Dewtry - *Datura stramonium* L. (5, 69, 156, 158) (1900-1923) no longer in use by 1923

Dewy-leaf aster - *Eurybia macrophylla* (L.) Cass. (5) (1913)

Dhood wort - *Scutellaria lateriflora* L. (19) (1840)

Diabetes-weed [Diabetes weed] - *Verbesina helianthoides* Michx. (156) (1923)

Diamond flower [Diamondflower, Diamond-flower, Diamondflowers] - *Hedyotis nigricans* (Lam.) Fosberg (50) (present), *Hedyotis nigricans* (Lam.) Fosberg var. *nigricans* (50) (present), *Ionopsidium acaule* (Desf.) Reichenb. (138) (1923), *Ionopsidium* Reichenb. (109, 138) (1923-1949)

Diamond maidenhair fern - *Adiantum trapeziforme* L. (138) (1923)

Diamond plant - *Mesembryanthemum crystallinum* L. (92) (1876)

Diamond willow - *Salix eriocephala* Michx. (3, 4, 5, 9, 22, 78, 85, 113, 130, 155) (1873-1986), *Salix lutea* Nutt. (3) (1977), *Salix prolixa* Anderss. (1, 101) (1905-1932) younger stem form diamond-shaped excrescences about the "knots", *Salix vestita* Pursh (135) (1910) MT

Diamond-leaf willow [Diamondleaf willow] - *Salix planifolia* Pursh (50) (present)

Diandrus sedge - *Cyperus diandrus* Torr. (66) (1903)

Dianthera - *Justicia americana* (L.) Vahl (174, 177) (1753-1762), *Justicia* L. (155) (1942)

Dianthus - *Dianthus armeria* L. (92) (1876)

Diapedium - *Dicliptera brachiata* (Pursh) Spreng. (5, 97) (1913-1937), *Dicliptera* Juss. (158) (1900)

Diapensia - *Diapensia lapponica* L. (5, 174) (1753-1913)

Dichondra - *Dichondra carolinensis* Michx. (5) (1913)

Dichonema - *Rhynchospora colorata* (L.) H. Pfeiffer (66) (1903)

Dichotoma silene - *Silene dichotoma* Ehrh. (50) (present)

Dicky daisy - *Bellis perennis* L. (158) (1900)

Dicliptera - *Dicliptera brachiata* (Pursh) Spreng. (3) (1977)

Diclytra - *Dicentra canadensis* (Goldie) Walp. (157) (1929)

Dididplis - *Didiplis* Raf. (50) (present)

Didier's tulip - *Tulipa gesneriana* L. (50) (present)

Die Winde (German) - *Convolvulus arvensis* L. (6) (1892)

Diéges (Albanian) - *Lepidium sativum* L. (110) (1886)

Diel's cotoneaster [Diels cotoneaster] - *Cotoneaster dielsianus* E. Pritz. (138) (1923)

Dielytra - *Dicentra canadensis* (Goldie) Walp. (92) (1876), *Lamprocapnos spectabilis* (L.) Fukuhara (92) (1876)

Diente de leon (Spanish) - *Taraxacum officinale* G.H. Weber ex Wiggers (158) (1900) MA

Diervilla - *Diervilla florida* (Bunge) Siebold & Zucc. (possibly) (112) (1937), *Diervilla lonicera* Mill. (174) (1753)

Dierville (French) - *Diervilla lonicera* Mill. (8) (1785)

Diethra - *Lamprocapnos spectabilis* (L.) Fukuhara (73) (1892) MA

Different-leaved pond-weed - *Potamogeton spirillus* Tuck. (187) (1818)

Diffuse cinquefoil - *Potentilla rivalis* Nutt. var. *millegrana* (Engelm. ex Lehm.) S. Wats. (5, 93, 72, 131) (1899-1936)

Diffuse crabgrass [Diffuse crab-grass] - *Digitaria cognata* (J.A. Schultes) Pilger var. *cognata* (5, 119, 163) (1852-1938)

Diffuse eryngo - *Eryngium diffusum* Torr. (4, 97) (1937-1986)

Diffuse knapweed - *Centaurea diffusa* Lam. (4) (1986)

Diffuse panicum - *Digitaria cognata* (J.A. Schultes) Pilger (72) (1907)

Diffuse purple panicum - *Digitaria cognata* (J.A. Schultes) Pilger (56) (1901)

Diffuse rush - *Juncus diffusissimus* Buckl. (5) (1913)

Digger pine - *Pinus sabiniana* Dougl. ex Dougl. (107, 109, 138) (1919-1949)

Digitalis - *Digitalis pupurea* L. (54, 55, 59, 60) (1902-1905)

Dike-but - *Xanthium strumarium* L. (158) (1900)

Dill (German) - *Anethum graveolens* L. (158) (1900)

Dill [Dyll] - *Anethum graveolens* L. (1, 3, 4, 5, 19, 50, 58, 82, 85, 107, 109, 138, 155, 156, 158, 165, 179, 184) (1538–present), *Anethum* L. (50, 82, 158) (1900–present), *Anthemis tinctoria* L. (46, 57, 103) (1671-1917), *Foeniculum vulgare* Mill. (5, 93, 156, 158) (1900-1923)

Dillenia - *Dillenia* L. (138) (1923)

Dillenius' ticktrefoil - *Desmodium glabellum* (Michx.) DC. (50) (present)

Dillen's tickclover [Dillen tickclover] - *Desmodium perplexum* Schub. (155) (1942)

Dillen's ticktrefoil [Dillen's tick trefoil, Dillen's tick-trefoil] - *Desmodium perplexum* Schub. (5, 72, 93, 97) (1907-1937)

Dillisk - *Palmaria palmata* (L.) Weber & Mohr (92, 107) (1876-1919)

Dillweed [Dilweed] - *Anthemis cotula* L. (5, 7, 156, 157, 158) (1828-1929)

Dilly - *Anethum graveolens* L. (158) (1900), *Anthemis cotula* L. (7) (1828)

Dillydilweed [Dillidillweed] - *Anthemis cotula* L. (92, 157, 158) (1876-1929)

Diluvim ladies'-tresses - *Spiranthes diluvialis* Sheviak (50) (present)

Dindle - *Sonchus arvensis* L. (5, 157, 158) (1900-1929) no longer in use by 1929, *Taraxacum officinale* G.H. Weber ex Wiggers (157, 158) (1900-1929)

Dingleberry - *Vaccinium erythrocarpum* Michx. (138, 156) (1923)

Dinkel barley - *Hordeum vulgare* L. (158) (1900) variety

Dioecious sedge - *Carex sterilis* Willd. (50) (present)

Dioecous meadow-rue - *Thalictrum dioicum* L. (187) (1818)

Dioscorea - *Dioscorea villosa* L. (52, 54, 57, 64) (1905-1919)

Diospiros - *Coix lacryma-jobi* L. (180) (1633)

Diospyros - *Diospyros* L. (50) (present)

Diospyros (Official name of Materia Medica) - *Diospyros virginiana* L. (7, 57) (1828-1917)

Dipelta - *Astragalus* L. (138) (1923)

Dipper gourd - *Lagenaria siceraria* (Molina) Standl. (37) (1919)

Dirca (French) - *Dirca* L. (8) (1785)

Dirca des marais (French) - *Dirca palustris* L. (8) (1785)

Dircier triflore (French) - *Dirca palustris* L. (7) (1828)

Dirty Dick [Dirty-Dick] - *Chenopodium album* L. (156, 157, 158) (1900-1929)

Dirty John - *Chenopodium vulvaria* L. (156) (1923)

Disc mayweed - *Matricaria discoidea* DC. (50) (present)

Dish mustard - *Thlaspi arvense* L. (5, 156, 158) (1900-1923), *Thlaspi arvense* L. (possibly) (180) (1633)

Dishcloth [Dish cloth] - *Trillium erectum* L. (64, 73) (1892-1908) Franklin Center Quebec

Disk water-hyssop [Disk waterhyssop] - *Bacopa rotundifolia* (Michx.) Wettst. (50, 155) (1942–present)

Distaff thistle - *Carthamus* L. (50) (present)

Distai'yĭ (Cherokee, the roots are tough) - *Tephrosia virginiana* (L.) Pers (102) (1886)

Ditaxis - *Argythamnia* P. Br. (155, 158) (1900-1942)

Ditch buttercup - *Ranunculus sceleratus* L. (126, 127) (1933)

Ditch crowfoot - *Ranunculus sceleratus* L. (5, 156) (1913-1923)

Ditch fern - *Osmunda regalis* L. (5, 157) (1900-1913)

Ditch millet - *Paspalum scrobiculatum* L. (94) (1901)

Ditch polypogon - *Agropogon littoralis* (Sm.) C. E. Hubbard [*Agrostis stolonifera* × *Polypogon monospeliensis*] (122, 155) (1937–1942)

Ditch rabbits-foot grass [Ditch rabbitsfoot grass] - *Polypogon interruptus* Kunth (50) (present)

Ditch stonecrop [Ditch stone crop] - *Penthorum* L. (1, 2, 4, 156, 158) (1895-1986), *Penthorum sedoides* L. (4, 5, 49, 50, 53, 63, 72, 97, 120, 155, 156, 157, 158) (1898–present)

Ditch sunflower [Ditch sunflower] - *Bidens coronata* (L.) Britton (138, 155, 156) (1923-1942)

Ditchbur [Ditch-bur] - *Xanthium strumarium* L. (158) (1900)

Ditch-grass [Ditch grass, Ditchgrass] - *Ruppia cirrhosa* (Petag.) Grande (157) (1929), *Ruppia* L. (1, 158) (1900-1932), *Ruppia maritima* L. (3, 92, 97, 156, 158) (1900-1977)

Ditch-moss [Ditch moss, Ditchmoss] - *Elodea canadensis* Michx. (19, 72, 109, 131, 156, 158) (1840-1949)

Dithering grass - *Briza media* L. (5) (1913)

Dittander - *Lepidium* L. (184) (1793), *Lepidium latifolium* L. (46, 92, 107, 180) (1633-1919)

Dittany - *Cunila* L. (2, 4) (1895-1986), *Cunila origanoides* (L.) Britton (4, 19, 57, 58, 57, 58, 156, 177, 181, 184, 186) (~1678-1986), *Dictamnus* L. (109) (1949)

Diuers sorts of beanes - *Phaseolus* L. (178) (1526)

Diuers sorts of double Stocke gilloflowers - *Matthiola incana* (L.) Aiton f. (178) (1526)

Diuers sorts of Gooseberries - *Ribes uva-crispa* L. var. *sativum* DC. (178) (1526)

Diuers sorts of Gourds - *Cucurbita* L. (178) (1526)

Diuers sorts of Vines - *Vitis tiliifolia* Humb. & Bonpl. ex Roem. & Schult. (57) (1917)

Diuerse sorts of Marigoldes - *Calendula officinalis* L. (178) (1526)

Diverging lespedeza - *Lespedeza violacea* (L.) Pers. (187) (1818)

Diverse-glume wild rye [Diverseglume wildrye] - *Elymus diversiglumis* Scribn. & Ball (50) (present)

Diverse-leaf kidney bean [Diverse-leaved kidney-bean] - *Vicia villosa* Roth subsp. *villosa* (47) (1852)

Divinum remedium - *Peucedanum ostruthium* (L.) W.D.J. Koch (92) (1876)

Dixie iris - *Iris hexagona* Walt. var. *hexagona* (50) (present), *Iris virginica* L. (50, 138) (1923–present)

Djibe'gûb (Chippewa) - *Dirca palustris* L. (40) (1928)

Do (Osage) - *Apios americana* Medik. (121) (1918?-1970?)

Doan grape - *Vitis ×doaniana* Munson ex Viala [*acerifolia* × *mustangensis*] (138) (1923)

Docchan (Arabic, "smoke") - *Nicotiana tabacum* L. (110) (1886)

Dock (Swedish, dolls) - *Veratrum album* L. (41) (1770)

Dock [Docke] - *Rumex altissimus* Wood (21) (1893), *Rumex crispus* L. (19, 56) (1840-1901), *Rumex* L. (1, 2, 4, 7, 10, 50, 93, 101, 103, 109, 138, 155, 156, 158, 167, 179, 184) (1526–present)

Dock cress [Docke Cresses, Dock Cresses] - *Lapsana communis* L. (5, 178, 180) (1526-1913)

Dock rosinweed - *Silphium terebinthinaceum* Jacq. (138) (1923)

Dock-leaf persicaria [Dock-leaved persicaria] - *Polygonum lapathifolium* L. (5, 93, 131, 156) (1899-1936)

Dockmackie - *Viburnum acerifolium* L. (19, 92, 109, 156) (1840-1949)

Dockmakie - *Viburnum acerifolium* L. (5) (1913)

Dock-mockie maple - *Acer spicatum* Lam. (58) (1869)

Dockor (Swedish, dolls) - *Veratrum album* L. (41) (1770)

Dockrötter (Swedish, dolls) - *Veratrum album* L. (41) (1770)

Doconangia - *Itea virginica* L. (174, 177) (1753-1762)

Dodder [Dodyr] - *Cuscuta americana* L. (7, 19, 92, 187) (1818-1876), *Cuscuta glomerata* Choisy (37, 46) (1610-1879), *Cuscuta indecora* Choisy (85) (1932), *Cuscuta pentagona* Engelm. var. *pentagona* (145) (1897), *Cuscuta* L. (1, 2, 4, 14, 50, 82, 93, 106, 158, 179, 184) (1526–present)

Dodder grass - *Briza media* L. (5) (1913)

Dodder-cake [Dodder cake] - *Camelina sativa* (L.) Crantz (92) (1876) oil cakes made from refuse

Dodger - *Cirsium arvense* (L.) Scop. (157, 158) (1900-1929)

Dodge's quillwort - *Isoetes ×dodgei* A. A. Eat. [*riparia* × *tenella*] (5, 50) (1913–present)

Dodge's shield fern [Dodge's shield-fern] - *Thelypteris simulata* (Davenport) Nieuwl. (5) (1913)

Dog bent [Dog's bent] - *Agrostis canina* L. (66) (1903)

Dog bent grass [Dog's bent grass] - *Agrostis canina* L. (5, 87, 90, 92) (1876-1913)

Dog blow [Dog-blow] - *Leucanthemum vulgare* Lam. (5, 158) (1900-1913)

Dog bramble - *Ribes cynosbati* L. (5, 107, 156) (1913-1923)

Dog brier [Dogbrier, Dog-brier] - *Rosa canina* L. (107, 138) (1919-1923), *Smilax rotundifolia* L. (78) (1898) MA

Dog bur [Dog-bur] - *Cynoglossum* L. (75) (1894) WV, *Cynoglossum officinale* L. (62, 75, 156, 157, 158) (1900-1929), *Cynoglossum virginianum* L. (5, 156) (1913-1923)

Dog camomile [Dog-chamomile, Dog's camomile] - *Anthemis cotula* L. (5, 49, 93, 156, 157, 158) (1898-1936), *Anthemis* L. (1) (1932)

Dog camovyne [Dog's camovyne] - *Anthemis cotula* L. (157, 158) (1900-1929), *Matricaria recutita* L. (158) (1900)

Dog couch grass - *Elymus trachycaulus* (Link) Gould ex Shinners subsp. *trachycaulus* (143) (1936) Quebec

Dog daisy [Dog-daisy] - *Achillea millefolium* L. (157, 158) (1900-1929), *Anthemis cotula* L. (5, 156, 157, 158) (1900-1929), *Bellis perennis* L. (158) (1900) North England, *Leucanthemum vulgare* Lam. (5, 156, 158) (1900-1923)

Dog dandelion [Dog-dandelion] - *Leontodon autumnalis* L. (5, 75, 156) (1894-1923) Allston MA

Dog flower [Dog-flower] - *Trillium erectum* L. (156) (1923)

Dog grape [Dogs grape] - *Vitis labrusca* L. (possibly) (7) (1828)

Dog grass [Dog's grass, Dogs-grasse] - *Cynodon dactylon* (L.) Pers. (7) (1828), *Elymus caninus* (L.) L. (46, 92) (1876-1879), *Elymus repens* (L.) Gould (5, 45, 49, 53, 62, 64, 66, 69, 78, 87, 90, 92) (1876-1922) dog's eat it for medicinal qualities in exciting vomit

Dog parsley [Dog's parsley] - *Aethusa cynapium* L. (6) (1892)

Dog poison [Dog-poison] - *Aethusa cynapium* L. (5, 6, 92, 156) (1876-1923)

Dog rose - *Rosa canina* L. (5, 19, 49, 55, 57, 58, 92, 109, 156) (1840-1949)

Dog rowan tree [Dog-rowan tree] - *Viburnum opulus* L. (5, 156, 158) (1900-1923) no longer in use by 1923

Dog tansy [Dog's tansy] - *Argentina anserina* (L.) Rydb. (156, 157, 158) (1900-1929) Scotland

Dog thistle [Dog-thistle] - *Cirsium arvense* (L.) Scop. (157, 158) (1900-1929)

Dog thorn - *Rosa canina* L. (5) (1913)

Dog tree [Dog-tree] - *Cornus florida* L. (6, 7, 92, 186) (1825-1892)

Dog violet - *Viola canina* L. (2) (1895)

Dogachamus - *Cornus rugosa* Lam. (possibly) (92) (1876)

Dogbane [Dog-bane, Dog bane, Dog's bane, Dogs' bane, Dogsbane] - *Apocynum androsaemifolium* L. (6, 19, 40, 49, 58, 63, 85, 92, 157, 158) (1840-1932), *Apocynum cannabinum* L. (6, 41, 105, 124, 125, 127, 148, 157) (1770-1937), *Apocynum* L. (2, 4, 50, 40, 93, 138, 155, 156, 158, 184, 190) (~1759–present), *Cynanchum* L. (10) (1818), *Isocoma menziesii* (Hook. & Arn.) Nesom var. *vernonioides* (Nutt.) Nesom (82) (1930)

Dog-banner - *Anthemis cotula* L. (157, 158) (1900-1929)

Dogberry [Dog-berry, Dog berry] - *Clintonia borealis* (Ait.) Raf. (5, 75, 156) (1894-1923) Bath ME, *Ilex verticillata* (L.) Gray (156) (1923), *Photinia pyrifolia* (Lam.) Robertson & Phipps (5, 73) (1892-1913) Northeastern US, *Ribes cynosbati* L. (3, 4, 5, 156, 158) (1900-1986), *Sorbus americana* Marsh. (5, 156) (1913-1923) no longer in use by 1923, *Viburnum lantanoides* Michx. (5, 156) (1913-1923)

Dogberry [Dog-berry, Dog berry] or Dogberry tree [Dogberrie tree] - *Cornus* L. (8) (1785), *Cornus sanguinea* L. (92, 107, 178) (1526-1919), *Cornus sericea* L. subsp. *sericea* (5, 156, 158) (1900-1923)

Dog-binder - *Anthemis cotula* L. (157, 158) (1900-1929)

Dog-elder [Dog elder] - *Aegopodium podagraria* L. (5, 156) (1913-1923), *Viburnum opulus* L. (156) (1923) no longer in use by 1923

Dog-fennel [Dog fennel, Dog's fennel, Dog's fennel] - *Anthemis cotula* L. (3, 4, 5, 7, 49, 58, 62, 63, 72, 73, 80, 85, 92, 122, 145, 156, 157, 158, 186, 187) (1814-1986), *Anthemis* L. (1, 4, 93) (1932-1986), *Eupatorium capillifolium* (Lam.) Small (5, 156) (1913-1923), *Helenium autumnale* L. (156) (1923), *Symphyotrichum ericoides* (L.) Nesom var. *ericoides* (5, 156, 158) (1900-1923)

Dog-finkle [Dog finkle] - *Anthemis cotula* L. (5, 157, 158) (1900-1929)

Doggers - *Phalaris arundinacea* L. (5) (1913)

Dog-grass [Dog grass] - *Carex straminea* Willd. ex Schkuhr (5, 156) (1913-1923)

Dog-hobble [Dog hobble] - *Leucothoe axillaris* (Lam.) D. Don. (5, 156) (1913-1923), *Viburnum lantanoides* Michx. (156) (1923)

Dog-laurel [Dog laurel] - *Leucothoe axillaris* (Lam.) D. Don. (5, 71, 156) (1898-1923)

Dog-lily [Dog lily] - *Nuphar lutea* (L.) Sm. subsp. *advena* (Aiton) Kartesz & Gandhi (158) (1900)

Dogmint [Dog mint, Dog-mint] - *Clinopodium* L. (7) (1828), *Clinopodium vulgare* L. (5, 92, 156) (1876-1923)

Dogmoss - *Lichen caninus* L. (7) (1828)

Dog-mustard [Dog mustard] - *Erucastrum gallicum* (Willd.) O. E. Schulz (3, 4) (1977-1986)

Dog-nettle [Dog-nettle] - *Galeopsis bifida* Boenn. (5, 156, 158) (1900-1923), *Galeopsis ladanum* L. (5, 156) (1913-1923), *Lamium album* L. (156) (1923), *Lamium purpureum* L. (156, 158) (1900-1923)

Dog-parsley [Dog parsley, Dogparsley] - *Aethusa cynapium* L. (5, 156) (1913-1923), *Lomatium nuttallii* (Gray) J.F. Macbr. (4, 93) (1936-1986), *Lomatium* Raf. (155) (1942)

Dog-plum [Dog plum] - *Clintonia umbellulata* (Michx.) Morong (5, 50, 156) (1913–present)

Dog-prick mushroom [Dog's prick mushroom] - *Mutinus caninus* (Huds.) Fr. (181) (~1678)

Dogs-and-cats [Dogs and cats] - *Trifolium arvense* L. (5, 156, 158) (1913-1923) no longer in use by 1923

Dog's-dinner [Dog's dinner] - *Hudsonia tomentosa* Nutt. (5, 76, 156, 158) (1896-1923) Wellfleet MA

Dog's-finger [Dog's finger] - *Digitalis pupurea* L. (5, 69, 92) (1876-1913)

Dog's-mouth [Dogs' mouth, Dog's mouth] - *Antirrhinum majus* L. (5, 92, 156, 158) (1876-1923)

Dog's-rib [Dogs rib, Dog-ribs] - *Plantago lanceolata* L. (5, 156, 158, 180) (1633-1923) no longer in use by 1923

Dog's-snout [Dogs-snout] - *Mimulus* L. (184) (1793)

Dog's-stones [Dogstones] - *Platanthera flava* (L.) Lindl. var. *flava* (46) (1671), *Platanthera lacera* (Michx.) G. Don (46) (1671)

Dog's-tail [Dog's tail, Dog's-tails, Dog-tails] - *Eleusine indica* (L.) Gaertn. (5) (1913), *Polygonum aviculare* L. (77) (1898)

Dog's-toes [Dog toes, Dog-toes, Dog's toes] - *Antennaria plantaginifolia* (L.) Richards (5, 73, 75, 76, 156, 158) (1892-1923)

Dog's-tongue [Dog's tongue] - *Carphephorus odoratissimus* (J.F. Gmel.) Herbert (5, 156) (1913-1923), *Cynoglossum officinale* L. (156, 157, 158) (1900-1929)

Dog-tail grass [Dog's tail grass, Dogs' tail grass, Dog's-tail grass, Dog's-tail-grass] - *Cynosurus cristatus* L. (5, 68, 92, 94) (1876-1913), *Eleusine indica* (L.) Gaertn. (19) (1840), *Eleusine indica* (L.) Gaertn. (75, 92, 145, 184) (1793-1897)

Dogthe (Osage) - *Pediomelum esculentum* (Pursh) Rydb. (121) (1918?-1970?)

Dogtooth [Dogs tooth, Dog's tooth, Dogs-tooth] - *Cynodon dactylon* (L.) Pers. (67) (1890), *Erythronium* L. (184, 190) (~1759-1793)

Dogtooth grass [Dog's tooth grass, Dog's-tooth grass, Dogtooth-grass] - *Cynodon dactylon* (L.) Pers. (5, 158) (1900-1913), *Cynodon* L.C. Rich. (155) (1942), *Elymus caninus* (L.) L. (5, 46) (1892-1913), *Elymus trachycaulus* (Link) Gould ex Shinners subsp. *trachycaulus* (5) (1913)

Dogtooth-violet [Dog's tooth violet, Dog's-tooth violet, Dog-tooth violet, Dog-toothed violet] - *Erythronium albidum* Nutt. (85, 122, 124, 156) (1923-1937), *Erythronium americanum* Ker. (5, 19, 49, 50, 57, 58, 92, 156, 157) (1840–present), *Erythronium grandiflorum* Pursh (35, 101, 107) (1806-1919), *Erythronium* L. (1, 10, 93, 167) (1814-1936), *Erythronium oregonum* Applegate (35) (1806)

Dog-town grass [Dog town grass, Dogtown-grass] - *Aristida adscensionis* L. (94) (1901), *Aristida purpurea* Nutt. var. *longiseta* (Steud.) Vasey (111, 163) (1852-1915)

Dog-violet [Dog violet] - *Erythronium americanum* Ker. (7) (1828)

Dogweed [Dog weed] - *Elymus repens* (L.) Gould (92) (1876), *Dyssodia* Cav. (155) (1942), *Verbesina encelioides* (Cav.) Benth. & Hook. f. ex Gray (145) (1897) KS

Dogwood [Dog-wood, Dog wood] or Dogwood tree [Dogwood-tree, Dogwood trees] - *Amelanchier canadensis* (L.) Medik. (76, 158) (1896-1900) Western US, *Cornus racemosa* Lam. (63, 82) (1899–1930), *Cornus sanguinea* L. (14, 107) (1882-1919) bark once used for washing mangy dogs, *Cornus sericea* L. subsp. *sericea* (105, 112) (1932-1937), *Euonymus atropurpurea* Jacq. (156) (1923), *Prunus pensylvanica* L. f. (5, 156) (1913-1923), *Rhamnus alnifolia* L'Her. (5, 156) (1913-1923), *Solanum dulcamara* L. (5, 156) (1913-1923), *Toxicodendron radicans* (L.) Kuntze subsp. *radicans* (48) (1882) KS, *Toxicodendron vernix* (L.) Kuntze (71) (1898) MA, *Viburnum lantanoides* Michx. (5, 76, 156) (1896-1923) Bath ME, *Cornus alternifolia* L. f. (47) (1852), *Cornus amomum* Mill. (85) (1932), *Cornus asperifolia* Michx. (22) (1893), *Cornus florida* L. (7, 12, 19, 20, 38, 41, 49, 52, 53, 54, 57, 58, 60, 92, 158, 177, 182, 184, 186, 187, 189, 190) (~1759-1922), *Cornus foemina* Mill. (9, 19, 113) (1840-1910), *Cornus* L. (1, 2, 10, 50, 82, 93, 106, 109, 138, 155, 158) (1818–present)

Dogwood-leaf aster [Dogwood-leaved aster] - *Doellingeria infirma* (Michx.) Greene (187) (1818)

Doldenblüthiges Harnkraut (German) - *Chimaphila umbellata* (L.) Bart. (6, 158) (1892-1900)

Doldentragendes Wintergrün - *Chimaphila umbellata* (L.) Bart. (186) (1814)

Dolichos - *Phaseolus vulgaris* L. (possibly) (110) (1886) Theophrastus, probably this species

Doll - *Cajanus cajan* (L.) Millsp. (4, 110, 156) (1886-1986)

Dollarleaf [Dollar-leaf, Dollar leaf] - *Desmodium rotundifolium* DC. (156) (1923), *Pyrola americana* Sweet (5, 92, 156, 158) (1876-1923)

Doll-cheese [Doll cheeses] - *Malva rotundifolia* L. (5, 106, 156, 157, 158) (1900–1930)

Doll's-daisy [Doll's daisy] - *Boltonia* L'Hér. (50) (present)

Doll's-eyes - *Actaea pachypoda* Ell. (156) (1923)

Dolma (Turkey) - *Lagenaria siceraria* (Molina) Standl. (107) (1919)

Dome-top aster [Dome-topped aster] - *Eurybia schreberi* (Nees) Nees (5) (1913)

Donald's honeysuckle [Donald honeysuckle] - *Lonicera dioica* L. (155) (1942)

Donkey's-eyes [Donkeys' eyes] - *Mucuna pruriens* (L.) DC. (92) (1876)

Donsen - *Typha* L. (180) (1633)

Doonhead - *Taraxacum officinale* G.H. Weber ex Wiggers (64) (1907) 1913-1923

Doon-head-clock - *Taraxacum officinale* G.H. Weber ex Wiggers (69, 157, 158) (1900-1929)

Door-grass [Door grass] - *Polygonum aviculare* L. (5, 73, 156, 158) (1892–1923) Southern IN

Doorweed [Door-weed, Door weed] - *Polygonum aviculare* L. (2, 47, 62, 72, 145, 156, 158) (1852-1923), *Polygonum hydropiper* L. (92) (1876), *Polygonum* L. (1, 93, 106) (1930-1936), *Polygonum persicaria* L. (92) (1876), *Polygonum tenue* Michx. (93) (1936)

Dooryard dock - *Rumex longifolius* DC. (50) (present)

Dooryard grass [Door-yard grass] - *Polygonum aviculare* L. (129, 156) (1894-1923) SD, *Polygonum erectum* L. (129) (1894) SD

Dooryard knotweed - *Polygonum aviculare* L. (80) (1913) IA

Dooryard plantain [Door-yard plantain] - *Plantago major* L. (5, 93, 122, 156, 157, 158) (1900-1937)

Doranapfel (German) - *Datura stramonium* L. (158) (1900)

Dotted beebalm - *Monarda punctata* L. subsp. *punctata* var. *occidentalis* (Epling) Palmer & Steyermark (4) (1986)

Dotted blazing star - *Liatris punctata* Hook (50, 121) (1918–present), *Liatris punctata* Hook. var. *punctata* (50) (present)

Dotted borya - *Forestiera segregata* (Jacq.) Krug & Urban var. *segregata* (19) (1840)

Dotted button-snakeroot [Dotted button snake root, Dotted button snakeroot] - *Liatris punctata* Hook (82, 122) (1930-1937), *Liatris punctata* Hook. var. *punctata* (5, 72, 97, 131) (1899-1937)

Dotted gayfeather - *Liatris punctata* Hook (138, 155) (1923-1942) Neb

Dotted haw - *Crataegus punctata* Jacq. (5) (1913)

Dotted hawthorn - *Crataegus punctata* Jacq. (50, 137, 138, 155) (1923–present)

Dotted millet - *Eriochloa contracta* Hitchc. (119) (1938), *Eriochloa* Kunth (93) (1936), *Eriochloa punctata* (L.) Desv. ex Hamilton (5, 99) (1913-1923)

Dotted smartweed [Dotted smart-weed] - *Polygonum punctatum* Ell. (5, 50, 93, 97, 155, 157, 158) (1900–present), *Polygonum punctatum* Ell. var. *confertiflorum* (Meisn.) Fassett (50) (present), *Polygonum punctatum* Ell. var. *punctatum* (50, 156) (1923–present)

Dotted wolffia - *Wolffia brasiliensis* Weddell (5) (1913)

Dotted-fruit thorn [Dotted-fruited thorn] - *Crataegus punctata* Jacq. (156) (1923)

Doubke's spruce [Doubke spruce] - *Abies fraseri* (Pursh) Poir. (158) (1900)

Double bladderpod [Double bladder pod, Double bladder-pod] - *Physaria* (Nutt. ex Torr. & Gray) Gray (1, 4, 93) (1932-1986), *Physaria brassicoides* Rydb. (3, 4, 5, 131) (1913-1986)

Double bridalwreath [Double bridal wreath] - *Physocarpus opulifolius* (L.) Maxim. var. *opulifolius* (112) (1937), *Spiraea prunifolia* Sieb. & Zucc. (112) (1937)

Double camomile [Double Cammomill] - *Chamaemelum nobile* (L.) All. (178) (1526)

Double cinnamon rose - *Rosa cinnamomea* L. (178) (1526)

Double colewort - *Brassica oleracea* L. (180) (1633)

Double crispe Colewort - *Brassica oleracea* L. (180) (1633)

Double curled Colewort - *Brassica oleracea* L. (180) (1633)

Double feverfew [Double feuerfew] - *Tanacetum parthenium* (L.) Schultz-Bip. (75, 178) (1526-1894) Western MA

Double field campion - *Silene latifolia* Poir. subsp. *alba* (Mill.) Greuter & Burdet (178) (1526)

Double goldenrod [Double golden-rod] - *Solidago canadensis* L. (158) (1900), *Solidago canadensis* L. var. *scabra* Torr. & Gray (5, 156) (1913-1923)

Double honeysuckles [Double honisuckles] - *Lonicera caprifolium* L. (178) (1526)

Double musk rose - *Rosa moschata* J. Herrm. (possibly) (178) (1526)

Double nigella - *Nigella sativa* L. (178) (1526)

Double peony [Double pionie] - *Paeonia officinalis* L. (178) (1526)

Double ptarmica - *Achillea ptarmica* L. (165) (1768) England

Double red campions - *Lychnis coronaria* (L.) Desr. (178) (1526)

Double red hollyhock [Double red hollyhocke] - *Alcea rosea* L. (178) (1526)

Double red Johns [Double red Iohns] - *Dianthus carthusianorum* L. (178) (1526)

Double red poppy [Double red poppie] - *Papaver rhoeas* L. (178) (1526)

Double sneezewort [Double Sneeze woort] - *Achillea ptarmica* L. (178) (1526)

Double spruce - *Abies fraseri* (Pursh) Poir. (5, 19) (1840-1913)

Double spruce - *Picea mariana* (Mill.) Britton, Sterns & Poggenb. (2, 5, 6, 20, 49, 107) (1895-1919)

Double Sweet Williams [Double Sweete Williams] - *Dianthus barbatus* L. (178) (1526)

Double sweetbrier [Double sweete brier] - *Rosa eglanteria* L. (178) (1526)

Double tansy - *Tanacetum vulgare* L. (92, 158) (1876-1900)

Double twinpod - *Physaria brassicoides* Rydb. (50) (present)

Double white daffodill - *Narcissus poeticus* L. (178) (1596)

Double white poppy [Double white poppie] - *Papaver somniferum* L. (178) (1526)

Double yellow crowfoot [Double yellow crowfoote] - *Ranunculus acris* L. (178) (1526)

Double yellow daffodill - *Narcissus pseudonarcissus* L. (180) (1633)

Double yellow narcissus - *Narcissus pseudonarcissus* L. (180) (1633)

Double yellow wallflower [Double yellow wall flowers] - *Erysimum cheiri* (L.) Crantz (178) (1526)

Double-bristle aster [Double-bristled aster] - *Ionactis linariifolius* (L.) Greene (156) (1923)

Double-claw [Double claw] - *Proboscidea louisianica* (P. Mill.) Thellung (5, 7, 92, 156, 158) (1828-1923)

Double-ear wheat [Double eared Wheat] - *Triticum aestivum* L. (180) (1633)

Double-file viburnum [Doublefile viburnum] - *Viburnum plicatum* Thunb. (138) (1923)

Double-flower cherry [Double floured Cherrie] - *Prunus cerasus* L. (178) (1526)

Double-flower cherry bearing fruit [Double flowred Cherrie bearing fruit] - *Prunus cerasus* L. (178) (1526)

Double-flower crab [Double flowering crab] - *Malus ioensis* (Wood) Britton var. *ioensis* (112) (1937)

Double-flower creeping buttercup [Double-flowered creeping buttercup] - *Ranunculus repens* L. (109) (1949)

Double-head panic [Double-headed panic] - *Panicum anceps* Michx. (66) (1903)

Double-leaf - *Listera cordata* (L.) R. Br. ex Ait. f. (5, 156) (1913-1923)

Double-tooth - *Bidens cernua* L. (5, 156, 158) (1900-1923), *Bidens* L. (184) (1793)

Doubtful knight's spur - *Consolida ajacis* (L.) Schur (50) (present)

Doubtful larkspur - *Consolida ajacis* (L.) Schur (155) (1942)

Douce-Amere (French) - *Solanum dulcamara* L. (6) (1892)

Douglas' California poppy [Douglas California-poppy] - *Eschscholzia californica* Cham. subsp. *californica* (138) (1923)

Douglas' chanaectis [Douglas chanaectis] - *Chaenactis douglasii* (Hook.) Hook. & Arn. (155) (1942)

Douglas' clematis [Douglas clematis] - *Clematis hirsutissima* Pursh (138) (1923)

Douglas' coreopsis [Douglas coreopsis] - *Coreopsis douglasii* (DC.) Hall (138) (1923)

Douglas' dusty-maiden [Douglas' dustymaiden] - *Chaenactis douglasii* (Hook.) Hook. & Arn. (50) (present), *Chaenactis douglasii* (Hook.) Hook. & Arn. var. *douglasii* (50) (present)

Douglas' fiddleneck [Douglas fiddleneck] - *Amsinckia douglasiana* A. DC. (155) (1942)

Douglas fir [Douglas' fir] - *Pseudotsuga menziesii* (Mirb.) Franco (20, 101, 108, 112, 123, 136, 138) (1857-1937), *Pseudotsuga menziesii* (Mirbel) Franco var. *menziesii* (109, 149) (1904-1949)

Douglas' golden arborvitae [Douglas golden arborvitae] - *Thuja occidentalis* L. (136) (1930)

Douglas' hackberry [Douglas hackberry] - *Celtis laevigata* Willd. var. *reticulata* (Torr.) L. Benson (155) (1942)

Douglas' honeysuckle - *Lonicera dioica* L. (5, 72, 97, 131, 158) (1899-1937)

Douglas' iris [Douglas iris] - *Iris douglasiana* Herb. (138) (1923)

Douglas' knotweed [Douglas knot-weed, Douglas knotweed] - *Polygonum douglasii* Greene (5, 50, 72, 97, 131, 155) (1899–present), *Polygonum douglasii* Greene subsp. *douglasii* (50) (present)

Douglas' maple [Douglas maple] - *Acer glabrum* Torr. var. *douglasii* (Hook.) Dippel (50) (present)

Douglas' meadowsweet [Douglas meadow sweet] - *Spiraea douglasii* Hook. (135) (1910)

Douglas' oak [Douglas's oak] - *Quercus douglasii* Hook. & Arn. (20) (1857)

Douglas' phlox - *Phlox caespitosa* Nutt. (5, 93, 131) (1899-1936)

Douglas' rabbitbrush [Douglas rabbitbrush] - *Chrysothamnus viscidiflorus* (Hook.) Nutt. (155) (1942)

Douglas' ragwort - *Senecio flaccidus* Less. var. *douglasii* (DC.) B.L. Turner & T.M. Barkl. (131) (1899)

Douglas' rayless goldenrod [Douglas's rayless goldenrod] - *Chrysothamnus viscidiflorus* (Hook.) Nutt. (131) (1899)

Douglas' Rocky Mountain maple [Douglas Rocky Mountain maple] - *Acer glabrum* Torr. var. *douglasii* (Hook.) Dippel (155) (1942)

Douglas' sand grass [Douglas' sand-grass] - *Poa douglasii* Nees (94) (1901)

Douglas' sedge [Douglas sedge] - *Carex douglasii* Boott. (5, 50, 139, 155) (1913–present)

Douglas' spiraea [Douglas spiraea] - *Spiraea douglasii* Hook. (138) (1923)

Douglas' spruce [Douglas spruce] - *Pseudotsuga menziesii* (Mirb.) Franco (2, 108, 135, 136, 147, 153, 161) (1857-1930) MT

Douglas' spruce fir [Douglas spruce fir, Douglas's spruce fir] - *Pseudotsuga menziesii* (Mirb.) Franco (14, 20) (1857-1882)

Douglas' thorn - *Crataegus douglasii* Lindl. (5) (1913)

Douglas' water hemlock [Douglas waterhemlock] - *Cicuta douglasii* (DC.) J.M.Coult. & Rose (155) (1942)

Doura - *Sorghum bicolor* (L.) Moench subsp. *bicolor* (158) (1900), *Sorghum halepense* (L.) Pers. (45) (1896)

Doura corn - *Sorghum bicolor* (L.) Moench subsp. *bicolor* (87) (1884)

Dourra (Modern Egypt) - *Sorghum bicolor* (L.) Moench subsp. *bicolor* (110) (1886)

Dove-dock [Dove dock] - *Tussilago farfara* L. (5) (1913)

Dove-foot crane's-bill [Dove's foot crane's bill, Dove's-foot crane's-bill] - *Geranium molle* L. (72, 156) (1907-1923) obsolete by 1923

Dover catchfly - *Silene nutans* L. (5, 156) (1913-1923)

Dover grass - *Lolium pratense* (Huds.) S.J. Darbyshire (5) (1913)

Dove's-dung [Dove's dung] - *Ornithogalum umbellatum* L. (107) (1919)

Dove's-foot [Dove's foot, Doues foote, Doues fote, Dovefoot, Dovefoot] - *Geranium carolinianum* L. (35, 46) (1671-1806), *Geranium* L. (179) (1526), *Geranium maculatum* L. (64, 157, 158) (1900-1929), *Geranium molle* L. (5, 178) (1526-1913), *Geranium sylvaticum* L. (92) (1876)

Down thistle [Down-thistle] - *Onopordum acanthium* L. (5, 156, 158) (1900-1923)

Down-hill-of-life - *Lysimachia nummularia* L. (5, 75, 156, 158) (1900-1923) Lincolnton NC

Downweed [Down-weed] - *Filago vulgaris* Lam. (5, 156) (1913-1923)

Downy agrimony - *Agrimonia pubescens* Wallr. (3, 4) (1977-1986)

Downy alder - *Alnus viridis* (Vill.) Lam. & DC. (1) (1932)

Downy andromeda - *Andromeda polifolia* L. var. *glaucophylla* (Link) DC. (155) (1942)

Downy archangel - *Angelica triquinata* Michx. possibly (42) (1814)

Downy arrowhead - *Sagittaria latifolia* Willd. (155) (1942)

Downy arrow-wood [Downy arrowwood] - *Viburnum dentatum* L. var. *dentatum* (156) (1923), *Viburnum rafinesquianum* Schult. (3, 4, 50) (1977–present)

Downy black oak - *Quercus falcata* Michx. (19, 33) (1827-1840)

Downy blephilia - *Blephilia ciliata* (L.) Benth. (5, 72, 82) (1907-1930)

Downy blue violet - *Viola sororia* Willd. (3, 4) (1977-1986)

Downy bog-rosemary - *Andromeda polifolia* L. var. *glaucophylla* (Link) DC. (138) (1923)

Downy brome - *Bromus tectorum* L. (3, 146, 155) (1939-1977)

Downy brome grass [Downy brome-grass, Downy bromegrass] - *Bromus tectorum* L. (5, 56, 62, 72, 80, 85, 94, 119, 140, 143, 148, 185) (1901-1944)

Downy carrion-flower [Downy carrionflower] - *Smilax pulverulenta* Michx. (50) (present)

Downy chess - *Bromus tectorum* L. (122, 140, 143, 146) (1936-1944)

Downy cinquefoil - *Potentilla intermedia* L. (5) (1913) MT

Downy danthonia - *Danthonia sericea* Nutt. (50) (present)

Downy false foxglove [Downy false fox glove] - *Aureolaria flava* (L.) Farw. var. *flava* (5, 72, 156) (1907-1923)

Downy forestiera - *Forestiera pubescens* Nutt. (155) (1942)

Downy gentian - *Gentiana puberulenta* J. Pringle (4, 5, 50, 85, 93, 131, 138, 155, 157) (1899–present)

Downy goldenrod [Downy golden-rod] - *Solidago petiolaris* Aiton (3) (1977), *Solidago petiolaris* Aiton var. *angusta* (Torr. & Gray) Gray (4) (1986), *Solidago puberula* Nutt. (5) (1913)

Downy grape - *Vitis cinerea* (Engelm.) Millard (2, 5, 72, 97, 122, 156) (1895-1937)

Downy green alder - *Alnus viridis* (Vill.) Lam. & DC. (156) (1923)

Downy ground-cherry [Downy ground cherry] - *Physalis missouriensis* Mackenzie & Bush (3) (1977), *Physalis pubescens* L. (4) (1986), *Physalis pubescens* L. var. *integrifolia* (Dunal) Waterfall (3) (1977)

Downy haw - *Crataegus mollis* Scheele (93) (1936)

Downy hawthorn - *Crataegus mollis* Scheele (3, 4, 137, 138, 155) (1923-1986)

Downy heuchera - *Heuchera pubescens* Pursh (5, 97) (1913-1937)

Downy Indian paintbrush - *Castilleja purpurea* (Nutt.) G. Don var. *purpurea* (50) (present), *Castilleja purpurea* (Nutt.) G. Don. (50) (present)

Downy lady's-slipper [Downy ladies' slipper, Downy ladies'-slipper, Downy lady's slipper] - *Cypripedium parviflorum* Salisb. (5, 97, 156) (1913-1937)

Downy leucothoe - *Leucothoe axillaris* (Lam.) D. Don. (5) (1913)

Downy lime tree - *Tilia americana* L. var. *caroliniana* (P. Mill.) Castigl. (20) (1857)

Downy lobelia - *Lobelia puberula* Michx. (5, 65, 72, 97) (1907-1937)

Downy Lyme grass - *Leymus arenarius* (L.) Hochst. (5) (1913)

Downy milk-pea [Downy milk pea] - *Galactia regularis* (L.) Britton, Sterns & Poggenb. (4) (1986), *Galactia volubilis* (L.) Britt. (5, 72, 97) (1907-1937)

Downy mint - *Pycnanthemum verticillatum* (Michx.) Pers. var. *pilosum* (Nutt.) Cooperrider (82) (1930) IA

Downy oat grass [Downy oat-grass] - *Avenula pubescens* (Huds.) Dumort. (66) (1903), *Trisetum spicatum* (L.) Richter (5, 94) (1901-1913)

Downy pagoda-plant - *Blephilia ciliata* (L.) Benth. (50) (present)

Downy paintbrush [Downy paint-brush] - *Castilleja sessiliflora* Pursh (3, 4) (1977-1986), *Castilleja sulphurea* Rydb. (85) (1932) SD

Downy paintedcup [Downy painted-cup, Downy painted cup] - *Castilleja sessiliflora* Pursh (5, 50, 72, 93, 97, 122) (1907–present)

Downy persoon - *Trisetum spicatum* (L.) Richter (66) (1903)

Downy phlox - *Phlox pilosa* L. (5, 50, 93, 97, 131, 138, 155, 156) (1899–present), *Phlox pilosa* L. subsp. *fulgida* (Wherry) Wherry (50) (present), *Phlox pilosa* L. subsp. *pilosa* (50) (present)

Downy poplar - *Populus heterophylla* L. (2, 5, 156) (1895-1923)

Downy ragged goldenrod [Downy ragged golden-rod] - *Solidago petiolaris* Aiton (5, 50, 97, 122) (1913–present), *Solidago petiolaris* Aiton var. *angusta* (Torr. & Gray) Gray (50) (present)

Downy rattlesnake-plantain [Downy rattlesnake plantain] - *Goodyera pubescens* (Willd.) R. Br. ex Ait. f. (5, 50, 72, 109, 138, 156) (1907–present)

Downy red oak [Downy-red oak] - *Quercus falcata* Michx. (187) (1818)

Downy redroot [Downy red-root] - *Ceanothus herbaceus* Raf. (72) (1907) IA

Downy rosemyrtle - *Rhodomyrtus tomentosus* (Aiton) Hassk. (138) (1923)

Downy rye grass [Downy ryegrass] - *Leymus innovatus* (Beal) Pilger (50) (present)

Downy saskatoon - *Amelanchier canadensis* (L.) Medik. (137) (1931) SD

Downy serviceberry - *Amelanchier canadensis* (L.) Medik. (155) (1942)

Downy shadblow - *Amelanchier canadensis* (L.) Medik. (138) (1923)

Downy skullcap [Downy skull cap] - *Scutellaria incana* Biehler (5, 72) (1907-1913)

Downy storax - *Styrax americanus* Lam. (5, 122) (1913-1937)

Downy sumac - *Rhus copallinum* L. (145) (1897) KS

Downy thorn - *Crataegus mollis* Scheele (5) (1913)

Downy thornapple - *Datura metel* L. (107) (1919)

Downy triple-awn [Downy triple awn] - *Aristida stricta* Michx. (66) (1903)

Downy viburnum - *Viburnum dentatum* L. var. *dentatum* (138) (1923)

Downy violet - *Viola pubescens* Aiton (155) (1942)

Downy whorled mint - *Mentha arvensis* L. (5, 93) (1913-1936)

Downy willow herb - *Epilobium strictum* Muhl. ex Spreng. (5) (1913)

Downy wood fern [Downy woodfern] - *Thelypteris dentata* (Forsk.) E. St. John (138) (1923)

Downy woundwort - *Stachys drummondii* Benth. (5) (1913), *Stachys germanica* L. (5) (1913)

Downy yellow violet - *Viola pubescens* Aiton (3, 4, 5, 50, 85, 138, 156) (1913–present)

Downy-cone silver fir [Downy-coned silver fir] - *Abies lasiocarpa* (Hook.) Nutt. (20) (1857)

Downy-leaf arrow-wood [Downy-leaved arrow-wood] - *Viburnum dentatum* L. var. *dentatum* (5, 63, 72) (1899-1913)

Downy-leaf violet [Downy-leaved violet] - *Viola pubescens* Aiton (2) (1895)

Dozedaisy - *Aphanostephus* DC. (50) (present)

Dr. Feay's lobelia - *Lobelia feayana* Gray (86) (1878)

Dr. Tinker's weed - *Triosteum perfoliatum* L. (6, 49, 58) (1869-1892)

Dr. Witt's rattlesnake root - *Prenanthes alba* L. (46) (1879) VA

Dr. Witt's snakeroot [Dr. Witts snake-root] - *Prenanthes alba* L. (177) (1762), *Prenanthes serpentaria* Pursh (187) (1818)

Draba - *Armoracia rusticana* P.G. Gaertn., B. Mey. & Scherb. (107) (100 AD), *Draba* L. (1, 50, 155) (1932–present)

Draba milkvetch [Draba milk vetch] - *Astragalus spatulatus* Sheldon (4) (1986)

Dracaena - *Dracaena* L. (109, 138) (1923-1949) Greek 'female dragon', juice when thickened said to resemble dragon's blood

Dracena - *Cordyline* Comm. ex R. Br. (138) (1923)

Drachen Aron (German) - *Arisaema dracontium* (L.) Schott (6) (1892)

Draco - *Artemisia dracunculus* L. (180) (1633)

Dracontium - *Symplocarpus foetidus* (L.) Salisb. ex Nutt. (64) (1908)

Dragee aux cheueaux (French) - *Fagopyrum esculentum* Moench (180) (1633)

Dragge - *Lolium temulentum* L. (5, 157, 158) (1900-1929)

Dragon (French) - *Artemisia dracunculus* L. (180) (1633)

Dragon [Dragons] - *Arisaema triphyllum* (L.) Schott (46) (1879), *Artemisia dracunculus* L. (158) (1900), *Dracunculus* Mill. (possibly) (138) (1923), *Dracunculus vulgaris* Schott (178) (1596)

Dragon arum - *Arisaema dracontium* (L.) Schott (2) (1895), *Arisaema* Martens (156) (1923)

Dragon-bridges - *Onoclea sensibilis* L. (177, 181) (~1678-1762)

Dragoncellum - *Artemisia dracunculus* L. (180) (1633)

Dragoness plant - *Clintonia borealis* (Ait.) Raf. (19, 92) (1840-1876)

Dragonhead [Dragon-head, Dragon head, Dragon's head] - *Arisaema dracontium* (L.) Schott (122, 124) (1937) TX, *Calydorea coelestina* (Bartr.) Goldblatt & Henrich (124) (1937) TX, *Dracocephalum* L. (1, 4, 10, 50, 93, 109, 138, 155, 156, 158, 184) (1793–present), *Dracocephalum moldavica* L. (114) (1894), *Dracocephalum parviflorum* Nutt. (3, 85, 156) (1923-1977), *Nemastylis geminiflora* Nutt. (124) (1937) TX, *Physostegia virginiana* (L.) Benth. (5, 19, 85, 92, 93, 97, 124) (1840-1937), *Prunella vulgaris* L. (5, 75, 85, 156) (1894-1932)

Dragonroot [Dragon root, Dragon-root, Dragon's root] - *Arisaema dracontium* (L.) Schott (3, 5, 6, 72, 93, 97, 109, 138, 156, 157, 187)

(1818-1977), *Arisaema* Martens (1) (1932), *Arisaema triphyllum* (L.) Schott (7, 49, 53, 58, 79, 92, 107) (1828-1922), *Pterospora andromedea* Nutt. (7) (1828)

Dragonroot jack-in-the-pulpit [Dragonroot jackinthepulpit] - *Arisaema dracontium* (L.) Schott (155) (1942)

Dragon's-blood [Dragon's blood] - *Geranium robertianum* L. (5, 156, 158) (1900-1923), *Sanguinaria canadensis* L. (46) (1649)

Dragon's-claws [Dragon's claws] - *Corallorrhiza maculata* (Raf.) Raf. (5, 156, 158) (1900-1923), *Corallorrhiza maculata* (Raf.) Raf. var. *maculata* (75) (1894), *Corallorrhiza odontorhiza* (Willd.) Poir. (5, 19, 49, 53, 64, 92, 156, 158) (1840-1922)

Dragon's-mouth [Dragon's mouth] - *Antirrhinum majus* L. (5, 156, 158) (1900-1923), *Arethusa bulbosa* L. (50, 73, 156) (1892–present)

Dragon's-tail [Dragon-tail] - *Arisaema dracontium* (L.) Schott (156) (1923)

Dragon's-tongue [Dragon's tongue] - *Chimaphila maculata* (L.) Pursh (5, 156) (1913-1923) no longer in use by 1923

Dragon-turnip [Dragon turnip] - *Arisaema triphyllum* (L.) Schott (6, 7, 64, 92, 157, 158) (1828-1929)

Dragonwort [Dragon wort] - *Polygonum bistorta* L. (92) (1876)

Dragunbeifuss (German) - *Artemisia dracunculus* L. (158) (1900)

Drake - *Avena fatua* L. (5, 107) (1913-1919), *Lolium temulentum* L. (157, 158) (1900-1929)

Drank - *Lolium temulentum* L. (158) (1900)

Draper's teasel - *Dipsacus fullonum* L. (5, 156, 158) (1900-1923)

Dravick - *Lolium temulentum* L. (157, 158) (1900-1929)

Drawke - *Agrostemma githago* L. (179) (1526), *Lolium temulentum* L. (5) (1913)

Dreiblatt (German) - *Menyanthes trifoliata* L. (158) (1900)

Dreiblattrige Lederbaum [Driblattrige Lederbaum] (German) - *Ptelea trifoliata* L. (6) (1892)

Dreiblättriger Aron [Dreyblattrige Aron] (German) - *Arisaema triphyllum* (L.) Schott (7, 158) (1828-1900)

Dreifaltigkeitskraut (German) - *Viola tricolor* L. (158) (1900)

Dreilappige (German) - *Asimina triloba* (L.) Dunal (6) (1892)

Dreistein (German) - *Triosteum perfoliatum* L. (6) (1892)

Drew - *Zostera marina* L. (5, 156) (1913-1923)

Dreyblättrige Spierstaude (German) - *Gillenia trifoliata* (L.) Moench (186) (1814)

Drimophylle pauciflore - *Umbellularia californica* (Hook. & Arn.) Nutt. (20, 107) (1857-1919)

Droke - *Lolium temulentum* L. (157, 158) (1900-1929)

Drooping aster - *Symphyotrichum lateriflorum* (L.) A.& D. Löve (possibly) (187) (1818)

Drooping avens - *Geum rivale* L (5, 158) (1900-1913)

Drooping beak rush - *Rhynchospora inexpansa* (Michx.) Vahl (66) (1903)

Drooping bulbous saxifrage - *Saxifraga cernua* L. (5) (1913)

Drooping bulrush - *Scirpus lineatus* Michx. (50) (present)

Drooping catchfly - *Silene caroliniana* subsp. *pensylvanica* (Michx.) Clausen (138) (1923), *Silene pendula* L. (138) (1923)

Drooping indigobush amorpha - *Amorpha fruticosa* L. (155) (1942)

Drooping juniper - *Juniperus flaccida* Schlecht. (122) (1937)

Drooping lady's-tresses [Drooping ladies' tresses] - *Spiranthes cernua* (L.) L.C. Rich. (5) (1913)

Drooping leucothoe - *Leucothoe axillaris* (Lam.) D. Don. (138) (1923)

Drooping reed grass - *Cinna latifolia* (Trev. ex Goepp.) Griseb. (66) (1903)

Drooping sedge - *Carex crinita* Lam. (156) (1923), *Carex prasina* Wahl. (5, 50) (1913–present)

Drooping star-of-Bethlehem - *Ornithogalum nutans* L. (5, 50) (1913–present)

Drooping starwort [Drooping star-wort] - *Chamaelirium luteum* (L.) A. Gray (5, 6, 53, 58, 64, 92, 156, 187) (1818-1922)

Drooping three-leaf nightshade [Drooping three-leaved nightshade] - *Trillium cernuum* L. (187) (1818)

Dryland blueberry

Drooping trillium - *Trillium cernuum* L. (156) (1923)

Drooping wakerobin [Drooping wake robin] - *Trillium flexipes* Raf. (5) (1913)

Drooping wood sedge - *Carex arctata* Boott. Ex Hook. (5, 50) (1913–present)

Drooping woodreed - *Cinna latifolia* (Trev. ex Goepp.) Griseb. (3, 50, 155) (1942–present)

Drooping-flower lady's-traces [Drooping-flowered ladies' traces] - *Spiranthes cernua* (L.) L.C. Rich. (86) (1878)

Dropberry [Drop-berry, Drop berry] - *Polygonatum biflorum* (Walt.) Ell. (92) (1876), *Polygonatum biflorum* (Walt.) Ell. var. *commutatum* (J.A. & J.H. Schultes) Morong (156, 157, 158) (1900-1929)

Dropseed [Drop-seed, Drop seed] - *Muhlenbergia minutissima* (Steud.) Swall. (93) (1936), *Muhlenbergia schreberi* J.F. Gmel. (45, 87, 92) (1876-1896), *Sporobolus compositus* (Poir.) Merr. var. *compositus* (116) (1958), *Sporobolus neglectus* Nash (80) (1913), *Sporobolus* R. Br. (1, 50, 93) (1932–present), *Sporobolus vaginiflorus* (Torr. ex Gray) Wood (80) (1913)

Dropseed grass [Drop seed grass, Drop-seed grass, Drop-seed-grass] - *Apera spica-venti* (L.) Beauv. (92) (1876), *Muhlenbergia glomerata* (Willd.) Trin. (45) (1896), *Muhlenbergia racemosa* (Michx.) Britton, Sterns & Poggenb. (80) (1913), *Muhlenbergia* Schreb. (66, 87) (1884-1903), *Muhlenbergia schreberi* J.F. Gmel. (19, 119) (1840-1938), *Sporobolus* R. Br. (45, 66, 152) (1896-1912), *Sporobolus vaginiflorus* (Torr. ex Gray) Wood (145) (1897), *Sporobolus cryptandrus* (Torr.) Gray (56, 144, 145) (1897-1901)

Dropsy plant - *Melissa officinalis* L. (5, 92) (1876-1913)

Dropsy-wort - *Melissa officinalis* L. (156) (1923)

Dropwort - *Filipendula vulgaris* Moench (109, 138, 179) (1526-1949), *Gillenia trifoliata* (L.) Moench (156, 186) (1825, 1923)

Drosera - *Drosera rotundifolia* L. (52, 54, 57) (1905-1917)

Drosere a Feuilles Rondes (French) - *Drosera rotundifolia* L. (6) (1892)

Drug fumitory - *Fumaria officinalis* L. (50, 155) (1942–present), *Fumaria officinalis* L. subsp. *wirtgenii* (W.D.J. Koch) Arcang. (50) (present)

Drug rockweep - *Ascophyllum nodosum* (Linnaeus) Le Jolis (155) (1942)

Drug speedwell - *Veronica officinalis* L. (155) (1942)

Drug sweetflag - *Acorus calamus* L. (155) (1942)

Drug wormseed goosefoot - *Chenopodium ambrosioides* L. var. *ambrosioides* (155) (1942)

Drumheads - *Polygala cruciata* L. (5, 156) (1913-1923)

Drummond's anemone [Drummond anemone] - *Anemone canadensis* L. (155) (1942), *Anemone drummondii* S. Wats. (155) (1942)

Drummond's aster [Drummond aster] - *Symphyotrichum drummondii* (Lindl.) Nesom (50) (present), *Symphyotrichum drummondii* (Lindl.) Nesom var. *drummondii* (3, 4, 5, 50, 72, 82, 93, 97, 122, 155) (1907–present)

Drummond's campion [Drummond campion] - *Silene drummondii* Hook. var. *drummondii* (50, 155) (1942–present)

Drummond's clematis [Drummond clematis] - *Clematis drummondii* Torr. & Gray (155) (1942)

Drummond's cooperia - *Cooperia drummondii* Herb. (5, 97) (1913-1937)

Drummond's dropseed - *Sporobolus compositus* (Poir.) Merr. var. *drummondii* (Trin.) Kartesz & Gandhi (50) (present)

Drummond's evening-primrose [Drummond evening-primrose] - *Oenothera drummondii* Hook. (138) (1923)

Drummond's false pennyroyal [Drummond false pennyroyal, Drummond falsepennyroyal] - *Hedeoma drummondii* Benth. (3, 4, 50, 155) (1942–present)

Drummond's goldenrod [Drummond's golden-rod] - *Solidago rugosa* Mill. subsp. *aspera* (Aiton) Cronq. (5) (1913)

Drummond's halfchaff sedge - *Lipocarpha drummondii* (Nees) G. Tucker (50) (present)

Drummond's hemicarpha [Drummond hemicarpha] - *Lipocarpha drummondii* (Nees) G. Tucker (3) (1977)

Drummond's ironweed [Drummond's iron-weed] - *Vernonia missurica* Raf. (5) (1913)

Drummond's leaf-flower - *Phyllanthus abnormis* Baill. (50) (present)

Drummond's maple - *Acer rubrum* L. (5, 20, 50) (1857–present)

Drummond's milkvetch [Drummond milk vetch, Drummond milkvetch] - *Astragalus drummondii* Dougl. ex Hook. (4, 5, 93, 131, 155) (1899-1986)

Drummond's mountain avens - *Dryas drummondii* Richards. ex Hook. (5) (1913)

Drummond's onion - *Allium drummondii* Regel (50) (present)

Drummond's pennyroyal - *Hedeoma drummondii* Benth. (131) (1899)

Drummond's phlox [Drummond phlox] - *Phlox drummondii* Hook. (82, 109, 122, 138) (1923-1949)

Drummond's pineweed [Drummond pineweed] - *Hypericum drummondii* (Grev. & Hook.) Torr. & Gray (155) (1942)

Drummond's pink - *Silene drummondii* Hook. var. *drummondii* (5, 131) (1899-1913)

Drummond's pitcherplant [Drummond's pitcher plant, Drummond pitcherplant] - *Sarracenia leucophylla* Raf. (84, 86, 138) (1878-1923)

Drummond's post oak - *Quercus margarettiae* (Ashe) Small (122) (1937) IA

Drummond's red maple [Drummond red maple] - *Acer rubrum* L. (155) (1942)

Drummond's rockcress, Drummond's rock cress - *Arabis drummondii* Gray (5, 50, 155) (1913–present)

Drummond's rush [Drummond rush] - *Juncus drummondii* E. Mey. (139) (1944)

Drummond's rush grass - *Sporobolus compositus* (Poir.) Merr. var. *drummondii* (Trin.) Kartesz & Gandhi (5) (1913)

Drummond's sedge [Drummond sedge] - *Carex rupestris* All. var. *drummondiana* (Dewey) Bailey (139) (1944)

Drummond's sidesaddle flower - *Sarracenia leucophylla* Raf. (84) (1880)

Drummond's skullcap - *Scutellaria drummondii* Benth. (4, 50, 97) (1937–present)

Drummond's sleepy-daisy [Drummond's sleepydaisy] - *Xanthisma texanum* DC. subsp. *drummondii* (Torr. & Gray) Semple (50) (present)

Drummond's soapberry - *Sapindus saponaria* L. var. *drummondii* (Hook. & Arn.) Bensons (5, 97) (1913-1937)

Drummond's St. John's-wort [Drummond's St. John's wort] - *Hypericum drummondii* (Grev. & Hook.) Torr. & Gray (5, 72, 97) (1907-1937)

Drummond's stitchwort - *Minuartia drummondii* (Shinners) McNeill (50) (present)

Drummond's thistle [Drummond thistle] - *Cirsium drummondii* Torr. & Gray (4, 155) (1942-1986)

Drummond's willowherb [Drummond's willow herb] - *Epilobium saximontanum* Hausskn. (131) (1899)

Drunk - *Lolium temulentum* L. (5, 157, 158) (1900-1929)

Drunkards - *Caltha palustris* L. (5, 157) (1900-1929), *Gaultheria procumbens* L. (5, 73, 156) (1892-1923) Barnstable MA, young children believed plant caused intoxication, no longer in use by 1923

Drunkwort - *Nicotiana tabacum* L. (92) (1876) obsolete by 1923

Dry plains milkvetch [Dryplains milkvetch] - *Astragalus lentiginosus* Dougl. ex Hook. var. *diphysus* (Gray) M.E. Jones (155) (1942)

Dry strawberry - *Waldsteinia fragarioides* (Michx.) Tratt. (5, 156) (1913-1923)

Dry whiskey - *Ariocarpus fissuratus* (Engelm.) K. Schum. (107) (1919)

Dryad - *Dryas* L. (1) (1932)

Dryas - *Dryas octopetala* L. (174) (1753)

Dryland blueberry - *Vaccinium pallidum* Aiton (109, 138, 156) (1923-1949)

Dryskens (Dutch) - *Leucojum vernum* L. (180) (1633)
Dry-spike sedge [Dryspike sedge, [Dry-spiked sedge] - *Carex foenea* Willd. (50) (present), *Carex siccata* Dewey (50) (present)
Dsindsom - *Panax quinquefolius* L. (186) (1814)
Dubock (German) - *Equisetum arvense* L. (158) (1900)
Duchesnea - *Duchesnea* Sm. (50) (present)
Duck grass - *Poa palustris* L. (5, 56, 90) (1885-1913)
Duck oak - *Quercus nigra* L. (5) (1913)
Duck retten - *Veratrum viride* Ait. (5) (1913)
Duck willow - *Salix alba* L. (5, 156, 158) (1900-1923)
Duck-acorn [Duck acorn] - *Nelumbo* Adans. (1) (1932), *Nelumbo lutea* Willd. (106, 156, 158) (1900-1930)
Duckblind - *Mikania scandens* (L.) Willd. (106) (1930) Kankakee IL
Duck-grass - *Stuckenia pectinatus* (L.) Boerner (156) (1923), *Vallisneria americana* Michx. (possibly) (187) (1818)
Duckmeat [Duck-meat, Duck-meat, Ducke meate, Duck's meat, Ducks' meat, Duck'smeat, Duck's-meat] - *Lemna* L. (122, 158, 167, 184) (1793-1937), *Lemna minor* L. (5, 92, 178, 179) (1526-1913), *Lemna trisulca* L. (19, 156) (1840-1923), *Spirodela polyrhiza* (L.) Schleid. (3, 156) (1923-1977), *Spirodela* Scheilen (50) (present), *Wolffia* Horkel ex Schleid. (158) (1900)
Duck-moss - *Stuckenia pectinatus* (L.) Boerner (156) (1923)
Duck-potato - *Sagittaria* L. (109) (1949)
Duck-potato arrowhead [Duck potato arrowhead, Duckpotato arrowhead] - *Sagittaria cuneata* Sheld. (3, 155) (1942-1977)
Duckretter [Duck retter] - *Veratrum viride* Ait. (possibly) (71, 64, 92) (1876-1908)
Ducks - *Cypripedium candidum* Muhl. ex Willd. (5, 156) (1913-1923), *Cypripedium* L. (75) (1894) PA, *Cypripedium parviflorum* Salisb. (5, 156) (1913-1923), *Cypripedium reginae* Walt. (5, 156) (1913-1923)
Duck's-bill [Duck-bill] - *Pedicularis* L. (1) (1932)
Duck's-foot [Duck foot, Duck's foot, Ducks foot, Ducks' foot] - *Alchemilla monticola* Opiz (possibly) (156) (1923), *Podophyllum peltatum* L. (6, 7, 14, 64, 92, 156, 158, 186) (1814-1923) no longer in use by 1923
Duckweed - *Lemna* L. (1, 10, 50, 93, 155, 158) (1818–present), *Lemna minor* L. (3, 92) (1876-1977), *Lemna trisulca* L. (85) (1932), *Spirodela polyrhiza* (L.) Schleid. (156) (1923)
Dudaim melon - *Cucumis melo* L. (109, 138) (1923-1949)
Dudder-grass [Dudder grass] - *Adiantum capillus-veneris* L. (5, 158) (1900-1913)
Dudleya - *Dudleya* Britt. & Rose (138) (1923)
Dudley's rush [Dudley rush] - *Juncus dudleyi* Wieg. (3, 5, 50, 93, 139) (1913–present)
Duke of Argyll's tea-tree - *Lycium barbarum* L. (158) (1900)
Dulcamara - *Solanum dulcamara* L. (53, 55, 57, 187) (1818-1917)
Dulcamara (Spanish) - *Solanum dulcamara* L. (158) (1900)
Dulcifilix folia (Official name of Materia Medica) - *Comptonia peregrina* (L.) Coult. (7) (1828)
Dulichium - *Dulichium arundinaceum* (L.) Britt. var. *arundinaceum* (5, 66, 72) (1903-1913), *Dulichium* Rich. (50) (present)
Dull-seed knotweed [Dullseed knotweed] - *Polygonum convolvulus* L. (155) (1942)
Dulse - *Palmaria palmata* (L.) Weber & Mohr (92, 107) (1876-1919)
Dumb cane - *Dieffenbachia seguine* (Jacq.) Schott (92, 109) (1876-1949) West Indies, those who chew it said to lose power of speech
Dumb foxglove - *Gentiana andrewsii* Griseb. (156) (1923)
Dumb-nettle [Dumb nettle] - *Lamium album* L. (5, 107, 156) (1913-1923), *Lamium amplexicaule* L. (92) (1876)
Dumb-watch [Dumb watch, Dumb watches] - *Sarracenia purpurea* L. (74, 156) (1893-1923) Cape May Co. NJ
Dummy-weed [Dummy weed] - *Tussilago farfara* L. (5, 156) (1913-1923) no longer in use by 1923
Dunbar's crab [Dunbar crab] - *Malus glaucescens* Rehdr. (138) (1923)
Dunbar's thorn - *Crataegus beata* Sarg. (5) (1913)

Dunche-down - *Typha latifolia* L. (158) (1900)
Dune manzanita - *Arctostaphylos pumila* Nutt. (155) (1942)
Dune paspalum - *Paspalum setaceum* Michx. (155) (1942)
Dunhead sedge - *Carex phaeocephala* Piper (139) (1944)
Dunny-nettle [Dunny nettle] - *Ballota nigra* L. (158) (1900)
Dupontia grass - *Trisetum melicoides* (Michx.) Vasey ex Scribn. (66) (1903)
Durand's white oak - *Quercus sinuata* Walt. var. *sinuata* (122, 124) (1937)
Durchwachsener Wasserdost (German) - *Eupatorium perfoliatum* L. (158, 186) (1814-1900)
Durchwachsener Wasserhanf (German) - *Eupatorium perfoliatum* L. (6, 158) (1892–1900)
Durchwasser Wasserdost (German) - *Eupatorium perfoliatum* L. (7) (1828)
Durchwasserdost (German) - *Eupatorium perfoliatum* L. (7) (1828)
Durfa grass [Durfa-grass] - *Elymus repens* (L.) Gould (64, 69) (1904-1908)
Durfee grass - *Elymus repens* (L.) Gould (45, 64, 69) (1896-1904)
Durra - *Sorghum bicolor* (L.) Moench subsp. *bicolor* (107, 119, 155, 158) (1900-1942), *Sorghum halepense* (L.) Pers. (45) (1896)
Duscle - *Solanum nigrum* L. (5, 156, 157, 158) (1900-1929)
Dusky willow - *Salix melanopsis* Nutt. (20) (1857)
Dusty clover - *Lespedeza capitata* Michx. (5, 156, 158) (1900-1923)
Dusty husband - *Arabis alpina* L. (5) (1913)
Dusty zenobia - *Zenobia pulverulenta* (W. Bartram ex Willd.) Pollard (138) (1923)
Dusty-miller [Dustymiller, Dusty miller] - *Artemisia stelleriana* Bess. (109, 155, 156) (1923-1949), *Centaurea cineraria* L. (109, 138) (1923-1949), *Centaurea* L. (75) (1894) Boston Florists' catalogue, *Lychnis coronaria* (L.) Desr. (109, 156) (1923-1949), *Senecio bicolor* (Willd.) Todaro subsp. *cineraria* (DC.) Chater (92, 109) (1876-1949)
Dutch amphor - *Cinnamomum camphora* (L.) J. Presl (92) (1876)
Dutch beech - *Populus alba* L. (5, 156, 158) (1900-1923)
Dutch caseknife bean - *Phaseolus coccineus* L. (107) (1919)
Dutch clover - *Medicago lupulina* L. (19, 92) (1840-1876), *Medicago sativa* L. (157, 158) (1900-1929), *Trifolium repens* L. (5, 45, 68, 156, 157, 158) (1896–1929)
Dutch cock's-head [Dutch Cocks Head] - *Onobrychis viciifolia* Scop. (178) (1526)
Dutch curse - *Leucanthemum vulgare* Lam. (156) (1923)
Dutch flax - *Camelina sativa* (L.) Crantz (5, 156, 157, 158) (1900-1929)
Dutch grass - *Elymus repens* (L.) Gould (64, 69) (1904-1908)
Dutch mice - *Lathyrus tuberosus* L. (107) (1919)
Dutch morgan - *Leucanthemum vulgare* Lam. (5, 156, 158) (1900-1923)
Dutch myrtle - *Myrica gale* L. (5, 92, 156) (1876-1923)
Dutch pink - *Reseda luteola* L. (5, 92, 156) (1876-1923)
Dutch reed [Dutch-reed] - *Phragmites australis* (Cav.) Trin. ex Steud. (5, 119) (1913-1938)
Dutch rush - *Equisetum hyemale* L. (5, 6, 14, 92, 107, 158) (1871-1919)
Dutch stonecrop - *Penthorum sedoides* L. (157) (1929)
Dutch white clover - *Trifolium repens* L. (122, 124) (1937)
Dutch yellow mustard - *Sinapis alba* L. (109) (1949)
Dutch-cheese [Dutch cheese] - *Malva rotundifolia* L. (5, 106, 156, 157, 158) (1900-1929) from shape of seed pods
Dutchman's-breeches [Dutchman's breeches, Dutchmans' breeches, Dutch-mans' breeches, Dutchmans-breeches] - *Dicentra* Bernh. (1, 7, 93) (1828-1936), *Dicentra canadensis* (Goldie) Walp. (58, 92) (1869-1876), *Dicentra cucullaria* (L.) Bernh. (3, 4, 5, 15, 50, 63, 72, 85, 93, 109, 125, 131, 138, 155, 156, 158, 187) (1818–present), *Thamnosma* Torr. & Frem. (4) (1986)
Dutchman's-laudunum [Dutchmans' laudunum] - *Passiflora rubra* L. (92) (1876)

Dutchman's-pipe [Dutchman's pipe, Dutchmanspipe, Dutchmans-pipe] - *Aristolochia* L. (1, 50, 155) (1932–present), *Aristolochia macrophylla* Lam. (2, 5, 7, 10, 92, 97, 109, 138, 156) (1818-1949), *Monotropa uniflora* L. (5, 75, 156, 158) (1900-1923)

Dutchman's-pipe plant [Dutchmans' pipe plant] - *Paronychia* Mill. (92) (1876)

Duwaduwa-hi (Omaha-Ponca) - *Yucca glauca* Nutt. (37) (1830)

Dwale - *Atropa bella-donna* L. (49, 53, 92, 156) (1898-1923), *Solanum dulcamara* L. (158) (1900)

Dwarf alder - *Fothergilla gardenii* L. (possibly) (5, 156) (1913-1923), *Rhamnus alnifolia* L'Her. (5, 19, 76, 156, 158) (1840-1923) Western US

Dwarf amaranth - *Amaranthus pumilus* Raf. (19) (1840)

Dwarf ash - *Aegopodium podagraria* L. (156) (1923)

Dwarf Asiatic elm - *Ulmus pumila* L. (138) (1923)

Dwarf banana - *Musa acuminata* Colla (109) (1949)

Dwarf barberry - *Berberis thunbergii* DC. (135) (1910)

Dwarf barren oak - *Quercus ilicifolia* Wangenh. (8) (1785)

Dwarf bastard senna [Dwarfe Bastard Sena] - *Coronilla valentina* L. (178) (1526)

Dwarf bay [Dwarfe Bay] or Dwarf bay tree [Dwarfe Bay tree] - *Daphne mezereum* L. (5, 156, 178) (1526-1923)

Dwarf bilberry - *Vaccinium caespitosum* Michx. (5, 107, 156) (1913-1923)

Dwarf bindweed [Dwarf bind weed] - *Calystegia spithamaea* (L.) Pursh (42) (1814)

Dwarf birch - *Betula lenta* L. (8) (1785), *Betula nana* L. (3, 5, 19, 85, 130, 137, 156) (1840-1977), *Betula pumila* L. (2, 5, 19, 156) (1840-1923)

Dwarf black oak - *Quercus ilicifolia* Wangenh. (5, 8) (1785-1913)

Dwarf black sumac - *Rhus copallinum* L. (5) (1913)

Dwarf blackberry - *Rubus pubescens* Raf. (4, 85) (1932-1986)

Dwarf blueberry - *Vaccinium angustifolium* Aiton (5) (1913), *Vaccinium pallidum* Aiton (46, 86, 106, 156) (1878-1930)

Dwarf burningbush - *Euonymus nanus* M. Bieb. (138) (1923)

Dwarf bush-honeysuckle - *Diervilla lonicera* Mill. (138) (1923)

Dwarf buttercup - *Ranunculus fascicularis* Muhl. ex Bigelow (156, 158) (1900-1923), *Ranunculus rhomboideus* Goldie (85) (1932)

Dwarf Canadian primrose - *Primula mistassinica* Michx. (5, 156) (1913-1923)

Dwarf candleberry myrtle - *Morella cerifera* (L.) Small (possibly) (8) (1785)

Dwarf cape-gooseberry [Dwarf cape gooseberry] - *Physalis pubescens* L. (2, 5, 158) (1895–1913)

Dwarf cape-jasmine - *Gardenia jasminoides* J. Ellis (138) (1923)

Dwarf cassandra - *Chamaedaphne calyculata* (L.) Moench (5) (1913)

Dwarf cassia - *Chamaecrista fasciculata* (Michx.) Greene (5) (1913), *Chamaecrista fasciculata* (Michx.) Greene var. *fasciculata* (92, 187) (1818-1876)

Dwarf cedar - *Juniperus horizontalis* Moench (7, 35) (1806-1828)

Dwarf cherry - *Prunus pumila* L. (5, 72, 103, 107, 158) (1870-1919), *Prunus pumila* L. var. *besseyi* (Bailey) Gleason (4) (1986), *Prunus pumila* L. var. *susquehanae* (hort. ex Willd.) Jaeger (1) (1932)

Dwarf chestnut - *Castanea pumila* (L.) Mill. (possibly) (8) (1785), *Castanea pumila* (L.) Mill.var. *pumila* (20) (1857)

Dwarf chestnut oak - *Quercus prinoides* Willd. (2, 5, 8, 10, 33, 93, 97, 156, 187) (1785-1937)

Dwarf chinkapin oak - *Quercus prinoides* Willd. (4, 50, 155) (1942–present)

Dwarf chinquapin oak - *Quercus prinoides* Willd. (3, 138) (1923-1977)

Dwarf chironia - *Centaurium pulchellum* (Sw.) Druce (42) (1814)

Dwarf clematis - *Clematis ochroleuca* Aiton (5) (1913)

Dwarf cliff brake [Dwarf cliffbrake] - *Pellaea glabella* Mett. ex Kuhn subsp. *occidentalis* (E. Nels.) Windham (4, 155) (1942-1986)

Dwarf club rush - *Eleocharis quinqueflora* (F.X. Hartmann) Schwarz (5) (1913)

Dwarf club-moss - *Selaginella rupestris* (L.) Spring (5, 158) (1900-1913)

Dwarf common snowberry - *Symphoricarpos albus* (L.) Blake (155) (1942)

Dwarf convolvulus - *Convolvulus tricolor* L. (138) (1923)

Dwarf coral plant - *Erythrina herbacea* L. (86) (1878)

Dwarf cornel - *Cornus canadensis* L. (2, 5, 19, 46, 92, 107, 131, 156, 158) (1840-1923)

Dwarf crab - *Malus sieboldii* (Regel) Rehd. (137) (1931)

Dwarf crabgrass - *Digitaria serotina* (Walt.) Michx. (50) (present)

Dwarf crested iris - *Iris cristata* Ait. (50) (present)

Dwarf crowfoot - *Ranunculus pusillus* Poir. (5) (1913)

Dwarf cudweed - *Omalotheca supina* (L.) DC. (5, 156) (1913-1923)

Dwarf dalea - *Dalea nana* Torr. ex Gray (3, 4, 155) (1942-1986)

Dwarf daylily - *Hemerocallis minor* Mill. (138) (1923)

Dwarf diervilla - *Diervilla lonicera* Mill. (42) (1814)

Dwarf dock - *Rumex hastatulus* Baldw. (97) (1937)

Dwarf early blueberry - *Vaccinium pallidum* Aiton (2) (1895)

Dwarf elder - *Aegopodium podagraria* L. (5, 156) (1913-1923), *Aralia hispida* Vent. (5, 49, 52, 53, 57, 58, 61, 79, 92, 156) (1869-1923), *Sambucus ebulus* L. (107) (1919)

Dwarf elderberry [Dwarf elder berries] - *Sambucus ebulus* L. (92) (1876)

Dwarf elm - *Ulmus pumila* L. (109) (1949)

Dwarf false indigo - *Amorpha fruticosa* L. (possibly) (112) (1937), *Amorpha nana* Nutt. ex Fraser (5, 50, 85, 93, 106, 112, 130) (1895-1937)

Dwarf fig tree [Dwarfe Fig tree] - *Ficus carica* L. (178) (1526)

Dwarf filbert - *Corylus americana* Walt. (8) (1785), *Corylus cornuta* Marsh (8) (1785)

Dwarf five-finger - *Potentilla canadensis* L. (possibly) (5) (1913)

Dwarf flameflower [Dwarf flame flower] - *Talinum parviflorum* Nutt. (122, 124) (1937)

Dwarf flax [Dwarfe flaxe] - *Linum catharticum* L. (5, 156, 178) (1526-1923)

Dwarf fleabane [Dwarfe Fleabane] - *Conyza ramosissima* Cronq. (5, 85, 122, 156) (1913-1937), *Erigeron compositus* Pursh (131) (1899), *Plantago psyllium* L. (178) (1526)

Dwarf flower-de-luce - *Iris pumila* L. (19) (1840)

Dwarf flower-de-luce with reddish flowers [Dwarfe Flowerdeluce with reddish flowers] - *Iris pumila* L. (178) (1596)

Dwarf flowering plum - *Prunus glandulosa* Thunb. (109) (1949)

Dwarf fothergilla - *Fothergilla gardenii* L. (138) (1923)

Dwarf French pink [Dwarf French pinks] - *Silene armeria* L. (5, 74, 156) (1893-1923)

Dwarf ginseng - *Panax trifolius* L. (2, 5, 138, 156) (1895-1923)

Dwarf goat's-beard [Dwarf goatsbeard] - *Krigia dandelion* (L.) Nutt. (5, 156) (1913-1923)

Dwarf goldenrod [Dwarf golden-rod] - *Solidago nemoralis* Aiton (5, 93, 122, 156, 158) (1900-1937), *Solidago nemoralis* Aiton var. *longipetiolata* (Mackenzie & Bush) Palmer & Steyermark (85) (1932)

Dwarf goldenweed - *Ericameria nana* Nutt. (155) (1942)

Dwarf grass poley - *Lythrum hyssopifolia* L. (19) (1840)

Dwarf gray willow - *Salix humilis* Marsh. var. *tristis* (Aiton) Griggs (5, 72, 82, 156) (1907-1930)

Dwarf groundcherry - *Physalis pumila* Nutt. (50) (present)

Dwarf groundnut [Dwarf ground-nut] - *Panax trifolius* L. (19, 92) (1840-1876)

Dwarf hackberry - *Celtis tenuifolia* Nutt. (3, 4, 50) (1977–present)

Dwarf hairy birch - *Betula pumila* L. (42) (1814)

Dwarf hazel nut [Dwarf hazle nut] - *Corylus americana* Walt. (42) (1814)

Dwarf hemicarpha - *Lipocarpha micrantha* (Vahl) G. Tucker (66) (1903)

Dwarf hog's succory - *Arnoseris minima* (L.) Schweig. & Koerte (possibly) (5) (1913)

Dwarf hollyrose [Dwarfe hollyrose] - *Helianthemum salicifolium* (L.) Mill. (178) (1526)

Dwarf honeysuckle - *Cornus suecica* L. (156) (1923)

Dwarf Hood's phlox [Dwarf Hoods phlox] - *Phlox hoodii* Richards. subsp. *muscoides* (Nutt.) Wherry (155) (1942)

Dwarf hop clover [Dwarf hop-clover] - *Trifolium campestre* Schreber. (156) (1923)

Dwarf horse-chestnut - *Aesculus parviflora* Walt. (109) (1949)

Dwarf horseweed - *Conyza ramosissima* Cronq. (50) (present)

Dwarf houseleek [Dwarf house-leek, Dwarf house leek] - *Sedum reflexum* L. (5, 156) (1913-1923)

Dwarf huckleberry - *Gaylussacia dumosa* (Andr.) Torr. & Gray (2, 5, 156) (1895-1923), *Gaylussacia frondosa* (L.) Torr. & Gray (107) (1919)

Dwarf Indian mallow [Dwarf Indian-mallow] - *Abutilon parvulum* Gray (50) (present)

Dwarf indigo [Dwarf-indigo] - *Amorpha nana* Nutt. ex Fraser (138) (1923)

Dwarf indigo amorpha [Dwarfindigo amorpha] - *Amorpha nana* Nutt. ex Fraser (155) (1942)

Dwarf ipomopsis - *Ipomopsis pumila* (Nutt.) V. Grant (50) (present)

Dwarf iris - *Iris pumila* L. (50) (present), *Iris verna* L. (5, 156) (1913-1923)

Dwarf Japanese quince - *Chaenomeles japonica* (Thunb.) Lindl. ex Spach (109) (1949)

Dwarf juniper - *Juniperus communis* L. (3, 4, 136) (1930-1986)

Dwarf lake iris - *Iris lacustris* Nutt. (5, 50) (1913–present)

Dwarf larkspur - *Delphinium tricorne* Michx. (4, 5, 50, 63, 71, 72, 93, 97, 125) (1898–present)

Dwarf laurel - *Kalmia angustifolia* L. (5, 19, 41, 71, 86, 156) (1770-1923), *Kalmia* L. (167) (1814)

Dwarf lawn grass - *Poa annua* L. (85) (1932) SD

Dwarf locoweed - *Oxytropis multiceps* Nutt. (4) (1986), *Oxytropis nana* Nutt. (4) (1986)

Dwarf mallow - *Malva rotundifolia* L. (5, 15, 85, 92, 156, 157, 158) (1895–1932)

Dwarf manzanita - *Arctostaphylos nummularia* Gray (106) (1930)

Dwarf maple - *Acer glabrum* Torr. (20, 93) (1857-1936)

Dwarf masterwort - *Astrantia minor* L. (155) (1942)

Dwarf meadow grass [Dwarf meadow-grass] - *Poa annua* L. (5, 119, 163) (1852-1938)

Dwarf meadow rue - *Thalictrum alpinum* L. (5) (1913)

Dwarf milkweed - *Asclepias involucrata* Engelm. ex Torr. (4, 50, 155) (1942–present), *Asclepias ovalifolia* Dcne. (5, 85) (1913-1932), *Asclepias pumila* (Gray) Vail (3) (1977), *Asclepias uncialis* Greene (4) (1986), *Asclepias verticillata* L. (19) (1840)

Dwarf milkwort - *Polygala paucifolia* Willd. (5, 7, 92, 156) (1828-1923)

Dwarf millet grass - *Piptatherum pungens* (Torr.) Barkworth (19) (1840)

Dwarf mistletoe [Dwarfmistletoe] - *Arceuthobium* Bieb. (50, 155) (1942–present)

Dwarf morning-glory [Dwarf morning glory] - *Calystegia spithamaea* (L.) Pursh (5, 19, 156) (1840-1923), *Convolvulus tricolor* L. (109) (1949), *Evolvulus* L. (50) (present)

Dwarf mountain maple - *Acer glabrum* Torr. (5) (1913)

Dwarf mountain pine - *Pinus mugo* Turra (136) (1930)

Dwarf mulberry [Dwarfe Mulberries] - *Rubus chamaemorus* L. (178) (1526)

Dwarf nettle - *Urtica urens* L. (5, 6, 92, 156) (1876-1923)

Dwarf Nikko fir - *Abies homolepis* Sieb. and Zucc. (155) (1942)

Dwarf ninebark - *Physocarpus monogynus* (Torr.) Coult. (112) (1937)

Dwarf nipplewort - *Arnoseris minima* (L.) Schweig. & Koerte (possibly) (5, 156) (1913-1923)

Dwarf nut rush - *Scleria verticillata* Muhl. ex Willd. (66) (1903)

Dwarf oak [Dwarfe Oak] - *Quercus ilicifolia* Wangenh. (181) (~1678), *Quercus intricata* Trel. (122) (1937), *Quercus prinoides* Willd. (29) (1869)

Dwarf oats - *Atriplex nudicaulis* Boguslaw (19) (1840)

Dwarf odorous galingale - *Cyperus squarrosus* L. (66) (1903)

Dwarf orchis - *Platanthera obtusata* (Banks ex Pursh) Lindl. (5) (1913)

Dwarf oriental rye - *Eremopyrum orientale* (L.) Jaubert & Spach (66) (1903)

Dwarf palmetto - *Sabal minor* (Jacq.) Pers. (2, 50, 97) (1895–present)

Dwarf panicum - *Dichanthelium strigosum* (Muhl. ex Ell.) Freckmann var. *leucoblepharis* (Trin.) Freckmann (5, 50) (1913–present)

Dwarf partridge pea - *Chamaecrista fasciculata* (Michx.) Greene var. *fasciculata* (42) (1814)

Dwarf pear - *Malus coronaria* (L.) Mill. var. *coronaria* (19) (1840)

Dwarf pine - *Pinus mugo* Turra (57) (1917)

Dwarf pink - *Houstonia caerulea* L. (19, 86, 156) (1840-1923)

Dwarf plantain - *Plantago virginica* L. (5, 19, 72, 93, 97) (1840-1937)

Dwarf poinciana - *Caesalpinia pulcherrima* (L.) Sw. (109) (1949)

Dwarf poison milkweed - *Asclepias pumila* (Gray) Vail (148) (1939)

Dwarf polemonium - *Polemonium pulcherrimum* Hook. subsp. *lindleyi* (Wherry) V. Grant (138) (1923)

Dwarf prairie willow - *Salix humilis* Marsh. (3) (1977)

Dwarf prickly fan-leaf palmetto [Dwarf prickly fan-leaved palmetto] - *Serenoa repens* (Bartr.) Small (182) (1791)

Dwarf pussy willow - *Salix humilis* Marsh. var. *tristis* (Aiton) Griggs (138, 155) (1923-1942)

Dwarf pussy-toes - *Antennaria plantaginifolia* (L.) Richards (3, 4) (1977-1986)

Dwarf ragweed - *Ambrosia pumila* (Nutt.) Gray (155) (1942)

Dwarf raspberry - *Rubus pubescens* Raf. (3) (1977), *Rubus pubescens* Raf. var. *pubescens* (2, 63, 72, 107, 131, 156) (1895-1923)

Dwarf rattlesnake-plantain [Dwarf rattlesnake plantain] - *Goodyera repens* (L.) R. Br. ex Ait. f. (3) (1977)

Dwarf red blackberry - *Rubus pubescens* Raf. (50, 155) (1942–present), *Rubus pubescens* Raf. var. *pubescens* (5, 50) (1913–present)

Dwarf red cedar - *Juniperus horizontalis* Moench (92) (1876)

Dwarf red oak [Dwarfe red oak] - *Quercus ilicifolia* Wangenh. (33, 187) (1818-1827)

Dwarf red-fruit medlar [Dwarf red fruited medlar] - *Amelanchier canadensis* (L.) Medik. (8) (1785)

Dwarf rockjasmine - *Androsace occidentalis* Pursh (155) (1942)

Dwarf Rocky Mountain maple - *Acer glabrum* Torr. (112) (1937)

Dwarf rose bay [Dwarf rose-bay] - *Rhododendron* L. (8) (1785), *Rhododendron maximum* L. (5, 20) (1857-1913)

Dwarf sagebrush - *Artemisia cana* Pursh (3) (1977)

Dwarf samphire - *Salicornia bigelovii* Torr. (19) (1840)

Dwarf saskatoon - *Amelanchier pumila* (Torr. & Gray) Nutt. ex M. Roemer (138) (1923)

Dwarf saskatoon service-berry [Dwarf saskatoon serviceberry] - *Amelanchier pumila* (Torr. & Gray) Nutt. ex M. Roemer (155) (1942)

Dwarf scouring rush - *Equisetum scirpoides* Michx. (3, 4, 50) (1977–present)

Dwarf sealwort - *Polygonatum biflorum* (Walt.) Ell. (158) (1900)

Dwarf senna - *Chamaecrista fasciculata* (Michx.) Greene var. *fasciculata* (156, 158) (1900-1923)

Dwarf sheep laurel - *Kalmia angustifolia* L. (71) (1898)

Dwarf Siberian kale - *Brassica oleracea* L. (109) (1949)

Dwarf sieva bean - *Phaseolus lunatus* L. (109) (1949)

Dwarf snakeroot - *Polygala verticillata* L. (19) (1840)

Dwarf snapdragon - *Chaenorhinum* (DC.) Reichenb. (50) (present), *Chaenorhinum minus* (L.) Lange (4, 50) (1986–present)

Dwarf snowberry - *Symphoricarpos albus* (L.) Blake var. *pauciflorus* (J.W. Robbins) S.F. Blake (138) (1923)

Dwarf Solomon's-seal [Dwarf Solomon's-seal, Dwarf Solomon seal] - *Maianthemum dilatatum* (Wood) A. Nels. & J.F. Macbr. (19, 92) (1840–1876), *Polygonatum biflorum* (Walt.) Ell. (5, 157, 158) (1900-1929)

Dwarf spike rush [Dwarf spike-rush, Dwarf spikerush] - *Eleocharis parvula* (Roem. & Schult.) Link ex Bluff, Nees & Schauer (50, 66) (1903–present)

Dwarf spleenwort - *Asplenium ruta-muraria* L. (19, 92) (1840-1876), *Asplenium trichomanes* L. (5, 86) (1878-1913)

Dwarf spurge [Dwarfe Spurge] - *Euphorbia exigua* L. (50, 178) (1526–present)

Dwarf St. John's-wort [Dwarf St. John's wort] - *Hypericum mutilum* L. (3, 4, 5, 50, 72, 156) (1907–present)

Dwarf stinger - *Urtica urens* L. (19, 92) (1840-1876)

Dwarf strawberry-tomato [Dwarf strawberry tomato] - *Physalis pubescens* L. (158) (1900)

Dwarf succory - *Arnoseris minima* (L.) Schweig. & Koerte (possibly) (156) (1923)

Dwarf sumac [Dwarf sumach] - *Rhus copallinum* L. (3, 4, 15, 95, 106, 107, 113, 156, 157) (1890-1986), *Rhus lanceolata* (Gray) Britt. (124) (1937) TX

Dwarf sundew - *Drosera brevifolia* Pursh (50) (present)

Dwarf sunflower [Dwarf sun-flower] - *Rudbeckia* L. (167) (1814)

Dwarf sweet bay - *Persea borbonia* (L.) Spreng. (182) (1791)

Dwarf swine's-succory [Dwarf swine's succory] - *Arnoseris minima* (L.) Schweig. & Koerte (possibly) (5) (1913)

Dwarf thorn - *Crataegus uniflora* Muench. (5) (1913)

Dwarf tiger-lily [Dwarf tiger lily] - *Belamcanda chinensis* (L.) DC. (5, 73, 156, 158) (1892-1923) Mansfield OH

Dwarf trillium - *Trillium nivale* Riddell (138, 155, 156) (1923-1942)

Dwarf umbil - *Cypripedium acaule* Ait. (7, 86) (1828-1878), *Cypripedium* L. (92) (1876)

Dwarf upland willow - *Salix humilis* Marsh. var. *tristis* (Aiton) Griggs (156) (1923)

Dwarf violet iris - *Iris verna* L. (50) (present)

Dwarf wakerobin [Dwarf wake robin] - *Trillium pusillum* Michx. (19, 50) (1840–present)

Dwarf waterlily [Dwarf water-lily, Dwarf water lily] - *Nymphoides peltata* (Gmel.) Kuntze (92, 156) (1876-1923)

Dwarf water-plantain [Dwarf water plantain] - *Echinodorus tenellus* (Mart.) Buch. (72) (1907) IA

Dwarf white trillium - *Trillium nivale* Riddell (3, 85) (1932-1977)

Dwarf white wakerobin [Dwarf white wake-robin, Dwarf white wake robin] - *Trillium nivale* Riddell (2, 5, 50, 157, 158) (1895–present)

Dwarf whorleberry - *Vaccinium oxycoccos* L. (5) (1913), *Vaccinium tenellum* Aiton (19) (1840)

Dwarf wild cherry - *Prunus virginiana* L. var. *demissa* (Nutt.) Torr. (113, 114) (1890-1894)

Dwarf wild flax - *Linum catharticum* L. (92) (1876)

Dwarf wild indigo - *Amorpha nana* Nutt. ex Fraser (3, 4) (1977-1986)

Dwarf wild larkspur - *Delphinium tricorne* Michx. (2, 156) (1895)

Dwarf wild rose - *Rosa virginiana* Mill. (5) (1913)

Dwarf willow - *Salix herbacea* L. (5) (1913), *Salix humilis* Marsh. (8) (1785), *Salix humilis* Marsh. var. *tristis* (Aiton) Griggs (46, 113, 156) (1879-1923)

Dwarf willow-leaf oak [Dwarf Willow leaved Oak] - *Quercus geminata* Small (183) (~1756)

Dwarf yellow daylily [Dwarf yellow day-lily] - *Hemerocallis minor* Mill. (109) (1949)

Dwarf yew - *Taxus canadensis* Willd. (5, 92) (1876-1913)

Dwarf-dandelion [Dwarfdandelion, Dwarf dandelion] - *Krigia dandelion* (L.) Nutt. (5, 65, 72, 97, 156) (1907-1937), *Krigia* Schreb. (2, 50, 156) (1895–present) *Krigia virginica* (L.) Willd. (19, 138, 156) (1840-1923)

Dwarf-indigo amorpha [Dwarfindigo amorpha] - *Amorpha nana* Nutt. ex Fraser (155) (1942)

Dwayberry - *Atropa bella-donna* L. (156) (1923)

Dye bedstraw - *Galium tinctorium* L. (155) (1942)

Dye flowers - *Coreopsis* L. (75) (1894) Banner Elk NC

Dyeberry [Dye berry] - *Vaccinium myrtillus* L. (92) (1876)

Dye-leaves [Dye leaves] - *Symplocos tinctoria* (L.) L'Her. (5, 75, 156) (1894-1923) Banner Elk NC

Dyer's baptisia - *Baptisia tinctoria* (L.) R. Br. ex Aiton f. (6) (1892)

Dyer's broom [Dyers' broom, Dyers-broom] - *Genista tinctoria* L. (5, 6, 7, 19, 49, 92, 107, 156) (1828-1923)

Dyer's cleavers [Dyers' cleavers] - *Galium tinctorium* L. (19, 92, 156, 157, 158) (1840-1923)

Dyer's dilatris [Dyers' dilatris] - *Lachnanthes caroliana* (Lam.) Dandy (6) (1892)

Dyer's goosegrass [Dyers' goose-grass] - *Galium tinctorium* L. (187) (1818)

Dyer's greenweed [Dyer's green weed] - *Genista tinctoria* L. (5, 6, 49, 92, 109) (1876-1949)

Dyer's indigo - *Indigofera tinctoria* L. (110) (1886)

Dyer's lichen [Dyers' lichen] - *Roccella tinctoria* DC. (92) (1876)

Dyer's madder - *Rubia tinctoria* L. (49, 92) (1876-1898)

Dyer's mignonette - *Reseda luteola* L. (5, 156) (1913-1923)

Dyer's oak - *Quercus velutina* Lam. (5, 14, 92, 156, 157, 158, 187) (1818-1929)

Dyers' oak [Dyer's oak] - *Quercus infectoria* Olivier (55, 58, 92) (1869-1911)

Dyer's rocket - *Reseda luteola* L. (5, 15, 72) (1895-1913)

Dyer's saffron [Dyers' saffron] - *Carthamus tinctorius* L. (49, 53, 58, 92, 158) (1869-1922)

Dyer's weed [Dyers' weed, Dyer's-weed] - *Genista tinctoria* L. (49, 92, 156) (1876-1923), *Isatis tinctoria* L. (92) (1876), *Reseda luteola* L. (5, 15, 19, 92, 156) (1840-1923), *Solidago nemoralis* Aiton (5, 131, 156, 158) (1899), *Solidago rugosa* Mill. (5, 156) (1913-1923)

Dyer's weld - *Reseda luteola* L. (156) (1923)

Dyer's whin - *Genista tinctoria* L. (5) (1913)

Dyer's woad [Dyers woad] - *Isatis tinctoria* L. (109) (1949)

Dyers woodruff - *Galium tinctorium* L. (109, 155) (1942-1949)

Dyer's-weed goldenrod [Dyersweed goldenrod] - *Solidago nemoralis* Aiton (155) (1942)

Dyeweed [Dye-weed] - *Genista tinctoria* L. (5, 156) (1913-1923)

Dyschoriste - *Dyschoriste oblongifolia* (Michx.) Kuntze (5) (1913)

Dysentery root [Dysentery-root] - *Hackelia virginiana* (L.) I.M. Johnston (5, 156, 157, 158) (1900–1929)

Dysentery weed [Dysentery-weed] - *Gnaphalium uliginosum* L. (158) (1900), *Hackelia virginiana* (L.) I.M. Johnston (5, 156, 157, 158) (1900-1929)

Dyssodia - *Dyssodia* Cav. (50) (present)

E

Eardrop [Ear drop, Ear-drops] - *Fuchsia magellanica* Lam. (19, 92) (1840-1876), *Impatiens capensis* Meerb. (5) (1913), *Lamprocapnos spectabilis* (L.) Fukuhara (76) (1896) Sulphur Grove OH

Eardrop vine [Ear-drop vine] - *Brunnichia ovata* (Walt.) Shinners (122, 124) (1937) TX

Eared coreopsis - *Coreopsis auriculata* L. (138) (1923)

Eared redstem - *Ammannia auriculata* Willd. (50) (present)

Eared watermoss - *Salvinia auriculata* Aubl. (50) (present)

Earjewel [Ear jewel, Ear-jewel] - *Impatiens capensis* Meerb. (5, 74, 156, 157, 158) (1893-1929) VT

Earl loco - *Astragalus mollissimus* Torr. var. *earlei* (Greene ex Rydb.) Tidestrom (155) (1942)

Ear-leaf acacia [Earleaf acacia] - *Acacia auriculiformis* A. Cunningham ex Benth. (155) (1942)

Ear-leaf ammannia [Earleaf ammannia] - *Ammannia auriculata* Willd. (3, 155) (1942-1977)

Ear-leaf bladderpod [Earleaf bladderpod] - *Lesquerella auriculata* (Engelm. & Gray) S. Wats. (50) (present)

Ear-leaf brome [Earleaf brome] - *Bromus latiglumis* (Shear) A.S. Hitchc. (155) (1942)

Ear-leaf false foxglove [Earleaf false foxglove] - *Agalinis auriculata* (Michx.) Blake (50) (present)

Ear-leaf gerardia [Earleaf gerardia] - *Agalinis auriculata* (Michx.) Blake (3, 4) (1977-1986)

Ear-leaf magnolia [Ear-leaved magnolia] - *Magnolia macrophylla* Michx. (20) (1857)

Ear-leaf umbrella tree [Ear-leaved umbrella tree, Ear-leaved umbrella-tree] - *Magnolia fraseri* Walt. (2, 5, 109, 156) (1895-1949)

Early aira grass [Early aira-grass] - *Aira praecox* L. (165) (1768)

Early aster - *Eurybia divaricata* (L.) Nesom (156) (1923)

Early blue violet - *Viola conspersa* Reichenb. (5, 156) (1913-1923), *Viola palmata* L. (5, 50, 72, 93, 156) (1907–present), *Viola sagittata* Aiton (5, 156) (1913-1923)

Early blueberry - *Vaccinium pallidum* Aiton (107, 156) (1919-1923)

Early bluegrass - *Poa cuspidata* Nutt. (50) (present)

Early bluetop fleabane - *Erigeron vetensis* Rydb. (50) (present)

Early branching panic grass [Early-branching panic-grass] - *Dichanthelium villosissimum* (Nash) Freckmann var. *praecocius* (A.S. Hitchc. & Chase) Freckmann (163) (1852)

Early branching panicum - *Dichanthelium villosissimum* (Nash) Freckmann var. *praecocius* (A.S. Hitchc. & Chase) Freckmann (5) (1913)

Early bugloss - *Anchusa barrelieri* (All.) Vitman (138, 155) (1931-1942)

Early bulbous stock gilloflower [Early bulbous stocke gilloflower] - *Leucojum vernum* L. (178) (1596)

Early bunch grass [Early bunchgrass, Early bunch-grass] - *Sphenopholis obtusata* (Michx.) Scribn. (5, 56, 94, 111, 119, 129, 140) (1894-1944)

Early buttercup - *Ranunculus fascicularis* Muhl. ex Bigelow (3, 4, 5, 50, 97) (1913–present), *Ranunculus hispidus* Michx. (72) (1907), *Ranunculus hispidus* Michx. var. *nitidus* (Chapman) T. Duncan (158) (1900)

Early cestrum - *Cestrum fasciculatum* (Schlecht.) Miers (138) (1923)

Early coral root [Early coral-root] - *Corallorrhiza trifida* Chat. (5, 93, 156, 157) (1900-1936)

Early cress - *Barbarea verna* (P. Mill.) Aschers. (109, 156) (1923-1949)

Early crocus - *Crocus imperati* Ten. (138) (1923)

Early crowfoot - *Ranunculus fascicularis* Muhl. ex Bigelow (82, 156) (1923-1930), *Ranunculus hispidus* Michx. var. *nitidus* (Chapman) T. Duncan (156) (1923)

Early dwarf pea - *Pisum sativum* L. (109) (1949)

Early everlasting - *Antennaria neglecta* Greene (5) (1913), *Antennaria plantaginifolia* (L.) Richards (5, 156, 158) (1900-1923)

Early fleabane - *Erigeron vernus* (L.) Torr. & Gray (5) (1913)

Early goldenrod [Early goldenrod] - *Solidago juncea* Aiton (5, 106, 156) (1913-1930)

Early hair grass - *Aira praecox* L. (5) (1913)

Early hawkweed [Early hawk-weed] - *Hieracium venosum* L. (5, 156, 157) (1913-1929)

Early honeysuckle - *Rhododendron periclymenoides* (Michx.) Shinners (5) (1913)

Early larkspur - *Delphinium carolinianum* Walt. subsp. *virescens* (Nutt.) Brooks (98) (1926)

Early lupine - *Lupinus affinis* J.G. Agardh (138) (1923)

Early marigold - *Tetraneuris herbacea* Greene (156) (1923)

Early meadow-parsnip [Early meadow parsnip] - *Zizia aurea* (L.) W.D.J. Koch (5, 156, 158) (1900-1923)

Early meadow-rue [Early meadow rue, Early meadowrue] - *Thalictrum dioicum* L. (2, 5, 50, 63, 72, 82, 85, 86, 127, 131, 138, 155, 156, 158) (1878–present), *Thalictrum venulosum* Trel. (3, 4) (1977-1986)

Early mesquite - *Buchloe dactyloides* (Nutt.) Engelm. (119) (1938)

Early milkweed - *Asclepias ovalifolia* Dcne. (127) (1933)

Early mushroom - *Pholiota praecox* (Pers.) P. Kumm. (128) (1933) ND

Early panicum - *Dichanthelium villosissimum* (Nash) Freckmann var. *praecocius* (A.S. Hitchc. & Chase) Freckmann (3) (1977)

Early pedicularis - *Pedicularis canadensis* L. (155) (1942)

Early purple aster - *Symphyotrichum puniceum* (L.) A.& D. Löve var. *puniceum* (5, 156, 158) (1900-1923)

Early purple-circle daffolill [Early purple circle daffolill] - *Narcissus poeticus* L. (178, 180) (1526-1633)

Early purple-fringe orchis [Early purple-fringed orchis, Early purple fringed orchis] - *Platanthera grandiflora* (Bigelow) Lindl. (5) (1913)

Early red clover - *Trifolium pratense* L. (45) (1896)

Early saxifrage - *Saxifraga virginiensis* Michx. (2, 86, 156, 187) (1818-1923), *Saxifraga virginiensis* Michx. var. *virginiensis* (5) (1913)

Early scorpion-grass [Early scorpion grass] - *Myosotis verna* Nutt. (5, 97, 122, 156) (1913-1937)

Early summer fools [Early Sommer fooles] - *Leucojum aestivum* L. (178) (1596)

Early sweet blueberry - *Vaccinium pallidum* Aiton (106) (1930)

Early trillium - *Trillium nivale* Riddell (156) (1923)

Early violet - *Viola cucullata* Aiton (156) (1923)

Early wake-robin [Early wake robin] - *Trillium nivale* Riddell (5, 72, 93, 157, 158) (1900-1936)

Early water avens - *Geum vernum* (Raf.) Torr. & Gray (5) (1913)

Early white rose - *Rosa blanda* Aiton (108) (1878)

Early white saxifrage - *Saxifraga virginiensis* Michx. (86) (1878)

Early wild grape - *Vitis riparia* Michx. (9, 113) (1873-1890), *Vitis vulpina* L. (95, 130) (1895-1911)

Early wild oat - *Aira praecox* L. (66) (1903)

Early wild oat grass [Early wild oat-grass] - *Aira praecox* L. (94) (1901)

Early wild rose - *Rosa blanda* Aiton (2, 5) (1895–1913)

Early winter Belle Isle cress - *Barbarea verna* (P. Mill.) Aschers. (5) (1913)

Early wintercress [Early winter-cress. Early winter cress] - *Barbarea verna* (P. Mill.) Aschers. (15, 46, 107, 138) (1879-1923)

Early wood buttercup - *Ranunculus abortivus* L. (3, 4) (1977-1986)

Early wood-betony [Early woodbetony] - *Pedicularis canadensis* L. (138) (1923)

Early yellow violet - *Viola rotundifolia* Michx. (156) (1923)

Early yucca - *Yucca louisianensis* Trel. (122, 124) (1937) TX

Early-flowering fleabane [Early-flowering flea-bane] - *Erigeron pulchellus* Michx. (86) (1878)

Early-flowering hair grass [Early flowering hair-grass] - *Aira praecox* L. (187) (1818)

Early-flowering red lychnis [Early flowering Red Lychnis] - *Silene virginica* L. (183) (~1756)

Early-leaf brome [Earlyleaf brome] - *Bromus latiglumis* (Shear) A.S. Hitchc. (50) (present)

Earning grass [Earning-grass] - *Pinguicula vulgaris* L. (5, 156) (1913-1923)

Earth caltrops - *Tribulus terrestris* L. (177) (1762)

Earth-almond [Earth almond] - *Arachis hypogaea* L. (107) (1919), *Cyperus esculentus* L. (5, 156, 158) (1900-1923)

Earth-apple [Earth apple] - *Helianthus tuberosus* L. (5, 62, 92, 156, 158) (1876-1923)

Earthclub [Earth club, Earth-club] - *Conopholis americana* (L. f.) Wallr. (5, 7, 92, 156) (1876-1923)

Earthgall [Earth-gall, Earth gall, Erthe galle] - *Centaurium erythraea* Raf. (5, 156, 179) (1526-1923), *Prenanthes serpentaria* Pursh (156) (1923), *Veratrum viride* Ait. (5, 7, 64, 71, 92, 156) (1828-1923)

Earthnut [Earth-nut, Earth nut] - *Arachis hypogaea* L. (55, 92, 107) (1876-1919), *Cyperus esculentus* L. (158) (1900)

Earthnut pea - *Lathyrus tuberosus* L. (107) (1919)

Earthpea [Earth pea] - *Arachis hypogaea* L. (14) (1882)

Earthplum [Earth-plum] - *Astragalus crassicarpus* Nutt. var. *berlandieri* Barneby (156) (1923), *Astragalus crassicarpus* Nutt. var. *crassicarpus* (156) (1923)

Earthsmoke [Earth-smoke, Earth smoke] - *Fumaria officinalis* L. (92, 156) (1876-1923), *Fumaria vaillantii* Loisel. (50, 158) (1900–present)

East Indian balm [East Indian balme] - *Moluccella laevis* L. (178) (1526)

East Indian lotus - *Nelumbo nucifera* Gaertn. (109) (1949)

East Indian millet [East India millet] - *Pennisetum glaucum* (L.) R. Br. (87) (1884)

East Indian polypody - *Phymatosorus scolopendria* (Burm. f.) Pic. Serm. (138) (1923)

East Tennessee pinkroot [East Tennessee pink-root] - *Ruellia humilis* Nutt. (157) (1929)

Eastening-wort [Easteningwort] - *Knautia arvensis* (L.) Duby (158) (1900)

Easter bell [Easter-bell, Easterbell, Easter bells, Easterbells] - *Stellaria holostea* L. (5, 109, 138, 156) (1923-1949)

Easter broom - *Genista canariensis* L. (138) (1923)

Easter cactus [Eastercactus] - *Schlumbergera* Lem. (138) (1923)

Easter daisy - *Townsendia* Hook. (4) (1986)

Easter flower [Easter-flower, Easter flowers] - *Narcissus* L. (78) (1898) OH, *Narcissus pseudonarcissus* L. (73) (1892), *Pulsatilla patens* (L.) Mill. (5) (1913), *Pulsatilla patens* (L.) Mill.subsp. *multifida* (Pritz.) Zamels (157, 158) (1900-1929), *Trillium grandiflorum* (Michx.) Salisb. (156) (1923)

Easter giant - *Polygonum bistorta* L. (92) (1876)

Easter lily - *Erythronium albidum* Nutt. (156) (1923), *Lilium longiflorum* Thunb. (138) (1923)

Eastern beebalm - *Monarda bradburiana* Beck (50) (present)

Eastern black walnut - *Juglans nigra* L. (155) (1942)

Eastern blue-eyed grass - *Sisyrinchium atlanticum* Bicknell (5, 50) (1913–present)

Eastern bluestar - *Amsonia tabernaemontana* Walt. (50) (present)

Eastern bottle-brush grass [Eastern bottlebrush grass] - *Elymus hystrix* L. (50) (present), *Elymus hystrix* L. var. *bigeloviana* (Fern.) Bowden (50) (present), *Elymus hystrix* L. var. *hystrix* (50) (present)

Eastern bracken - *Pteridium aquilinum* (L.) Kuhn var. *latiusculum* (Desv.) Underwood ex Heller (155) (1942)

Eastern burningbush - *Euonymus atropurpurea* Jacq. (155) (1942)

Eastern camass - *Camassia quamash* (Pursh) Greene subsp. *quamash* (158) (1900), *Camassia scilloides* (Raf.) Cory (3, 5) (1913-1977)

Eastern cedar - *Juniperus virginiana* L. (149) (1904) NM

Eastern chokecherry [Eastern choke cherry] - *Prunus virginiana* L. var. *virginiana* (93) (1936) Neb

Eastern cleomella - *Cleomella angustifolia* Torr. (4) (1986)

Eastern cottonwood - *Populus deltoides* Bartr. ex Marsh. (50) (present), *Populus deltoides* Bartr. ex Marsh. subsp. *deltoides* (50) (present)

Eastern daisy fleabane - *Erigeron annuus* (L.) Pers. (50) (present)

Eastern downy phlox - *Phlox pilosa* L. subsp. *pilosa* (155) (1942)

Eastern eulophus - *Perideridia americana* (Nutt. ex DC.) Reichenb. (5) (1913)

Eastern false rue-anemone [Eastern false rue anemone] - *Enemion biternatum* Raf. (50) (present)

Eastern featherbells - *Stenanthium gramineum* (Ker-Gawl.) Morong (50) (present), *Stenanthium gramineum* (Ker-Gawl.) Morong var. *robustum* (S. Wats.) Fern. (50) (present)

Eastern fireberry hawthorn - *Crataegus chrysocarpa* Ashe (155) (1942)

Eastern flat-top agaricus [Eastern flat-topped agaricus] - *Agaricus placomyces* Peck (170) (1995)

Eastern fox sedge - *Carex triangularis* Boeckl. (50) (present)

Eastern gama grass [Eastern gamagrass, Eastern gama-grass] - *Tripsacum dactyloides* (L.) L. (50, 155, 163) (1852–present)

Eastern green violet - *Hybanthus concolor* (T.F.Forst) Spreng. (50) (present)

Eastern hay-scented fern - *Dennstaedtia punctilobula* (Michx.) T. Moore (50) (present)

Eastern hemlock - *Tsuga canadensis* (L.) Carr. (50) (present)

Eastern ironweed [Eastern iron-weed] - *Vernonia noveboracensis* (L.) Michx. (62) (1912)

Eastern manna grass [Eastern mannagrass] - *Glyceria septentrionalis* A.S. Hitchc. (122) (1937)

Eastern marsh fern [Eastern marshfern] - *Thelypteris palustris* Schott (50) (present), *Thelypteris palustris* Schott var. *pubescens* (Lawson) Fern. (4, 50) (1986–present)

Eastern milkpea - *Galactia regularis* (L.) Britton, Sterns & Poggenb. (50) (present)

Eastern mistletoe - *Phoradendron leucarpum* (Raf.) Reveal & M.C. Johnston (4) (1986)

Eastern mountain ash - *Sorbus americana* Marsh. (85) (1932)

Eastern narrow-leaf sedge [Eastern narrowleaf sedge] - *Carex amphibola* Steud. (50) (present)

Eastern ninebark [Eastern nine bark] - *Physocarpus opulifolius* (L.) Maxim. var. *opulifolius* (72) (1907)

Eastern oats - *Avena sativa* L. (110) (1886)

Eastern ox-eye daisy - *Leucanthemum vulgare* Lam. (56) (1901) IA

Eastern penstemon - *Penstemon hirsutus* (L.) Willd. (138) (1923)

Eastern persimmon - *Diospyros virginiana* L. (122, 124) (1937) TX

Eastern poison ivy - *Toxicodendron radicans* (L.) Kuntze (50) (present), *Toxicodendron radicans* (L.) Kuntze subsp. *negundo* (Greene) Gillis (50) (present), *Toxicodendron radicans* (L.) Kuntze subsp. *pubens* (Engelm.) Gillis (Scheele) Gillis (50) (present), *Toxicodendron radicans* (L.) Kuntze subsp. *verrucosum* (Scheele) Gillis (50) (present), *Toxicodendron toxicarium* (Salisb.) Gillis (4) (1986)

Eastern poplar - *Populus deltoides* Bartr. ex Marsh. (155) (1942)

Eastern prickly gooseberry - *Ribes cynosbati* L. (50) (present)

Eastern prickly-pear [Eastern prickly pear] - *Opuntia humifusa* (Raf.) Raf. (4) (1986), *Opuntia humifusa* (Raf.) Raf. var. *humifusa* (5, 158) (1900-1913)

Eastern purple coneflower - *Echinacea purpurea* (L.) Moench (50) (present)

Eastern quamash - *Camassia quamash* (Pursh) Greene subsp. *quamash* (158) (1900)

Eastern red cedar [Eastern redcedar] - *Juniperus virginiana* L. (50, 155) (1942–present), *Juniperus virginiana* L. var. *virginiana* (50) (present)

Eastern red oak - *Quercus rubra* L. var. *rubra* (155) (1942)

Eastern redbud - *Cercis canadensis* L. (5, 50, 95, 50, 97, 106, 112, 122, 124, 131, 155, 156, 158) (1899–present), *Cercis canadensis* L. var. *canadensis* (50) (present)

Eastern rough sedge - *Carex scabrata* Schwein (50) (present)

Eastern sedge - *Carex atlantica* Bailey (5) (1913)

Eastern sensitive brier [Eastern sensitive briar] - *Mimosa rupertiana* B.L. Turner (50) (present)

Eastern showy aster - *Eurybia conspicua* (Lindl.) Nesom (50) (present)

Eastern silvery aster - *Symphyotrichum concolor* (L.) Nesom (5) (1913)

Eastern star sedge - *Carex radiata* (Wahlenb.) Small (50) (present)

Eastern straw sedge - *Carex straminea* Willd. ex Schkuhr (50) (present)

Eastern swamp saxifrage - *Saxifraga pensylvanica* L. (50) (present)

Eastern swamp-privet [Eastern swampprivet] - *Forestiera acuminata* (Michx.) Poir. (50) (present)

Eastern tetraneuris - *Tetraneuris herbacea* Greene (5) (1913)

Eastern tragis - *Tragia urens* L. (5) (1913)

Eastern turkeybeard - *Xerophyllum asphodeloides* (L.) Nutt. (50) (present)

Eastern wahoo - *Euonymus atropurpurea* Jacq. (50, 155) (1942–present), *Euonymus atropurpurea* Jacq. var. *atropurpurea* (50) (present)

Eastern white pine - *Pinus strobus* L. (50) (present)

Eastern wild crab apple - *Malus coronaria* (L.) Mill. (112) (1937)

Eastern wild gooseberry - *Ribes rotundifolium* Michx. (5) (1913)

Eastern wild plum - *Prunus americana* Marsh. (153) (1913) NM

Eastern woodland sedge - *Carex blanda* Dewey (50) (present)

Eastern yampah - *Perideridia americana* (Nutt. ex DC.) Reichenb. (50) (present)

Eastwood manzanita's [Eastwood manzanita] - *Arctostaphylos glandulosa* Eastw. (155) (1942)

Eastwood's amsonia [Eastwood amsonia] - *Amsonia tomentosa* Torr. & Frém. var. *stenophylla* Kearney & Peebles (155) (1942)

Eaton's aster [Eatons aster] - *Symphyotrichum eatonii* (Gray) Nesom (4, 50, 97, 155) (1937–present)

Eaton's grape fern [Eaton's grape-fern] - *Botrychium multifidum* (Gmel.) Trev. (5) (1913)

Eaton's grass [Eaton's-grass] - *Sphenopholis* ×*pallens* (Biehler) Scribn. [*obtusata* × *pensylvanica*] (111) (1915), *Sphenopholis nitida* (Biehler) Scribn. (56, 94, 129) (1894-1901)

Eaton's lip fern [Eaton lipfern, Eaton's lip-fern] - *Cheilanthes eatonii* Baker (155) (1942)

Eaton's panic grass [Eaton's panic-grass] - *Dichanthelium spretum* (J.A. Schultes) Freckmann (163) (1852)

Eaton's panicum - *Dichanthelium spretum* (J.A. Schultes) Freckmann (5) (1913)

Eaton's quillwort - *Isoetes* ×*eatonii* Dodge [*engelmannii* × *tenella*] (5) (1913)

Eaton's rosette grass - *Dichanthelium spretum* (J.A. Schultes) Freckmann (50) (present)

Eaton's sagittaria - *Sagittaria graminea* Michx. var. *graminea* (5) (1913)

Eaton's shield fern [Eaton's shield-fern] - *Polystichum scopulinum* (D.C. Eaton) Maxon. (1, 5) (1913-1932)

Eaver - *Lolium temulentum* L. (158) (1900)

Eb kapor (Hungarian) - *Anthemis cotula* L. (186) (1814)

Ebanach (Arabic) - *Spinacia oleracea* L. (110) (1886)

Eberraute (German) - *Artemisia abrotanum* L. (158) (1900)

Ebony - *Diospyros* L. (109, 156) (1900-1949), *Ebenopsis ebano* (Berland.) Barneby & J.W. Grimes (124) (1937) TX

Ebony sedge - *Carex ebenea* Rydb. (139) (1944)

Ebony spleenwort [Ebony spleen-wort, Ebony spleen wort] - *Asplenium platyneuron* (L.) B.S.P. (3, 4, 5, 19, 42, 50, 86, 122, 138, 155, 187) (1814–present), *Asplenium platyneuron* (L.) B.S.P. var. *platyneuron* (50, 72) (1907–present)

Ebulus - *Sambucus ebulus* L. (174, 178) (1523-1753)

Echeveria - *Echeveria* DC. (138, 155) (1931-1942), *Echinacea angustifolia* DC. (52, 54, 57) (1905-1917), *Echinacea angustifolia* DC. var. *angustifolia* (64) (1907), *Echinacea* Moench (155) (1942), *Echinacea pallida* (Nutt.) Nutt. (158) (1900)

Echinocactus - *Echinocactus* Link & Otto (155, 158) (1900-1942)

Echinocereus - *Echinocereus* Engelm. (155, 158) (1900-1942)

Echinocystis - *Echinocystis* Torr. & Gray (50) (present)

Eckige Chironie (German) - *Sabatia angularis* (L.) Pursh (186) (1814)

Eclipta - *Eclipta* L. (50, 158) (1900–present), *Eclipta prostrata* (L.) L. (72) (1907)

Ecopa (Crow) - *Leucocrinum montanum* Nutt. ex Gray (101) (1905) MT

Écorce noire (French) - *Scolymus hispanicus* L. (110) (1886)

Ecushaw - *Cucurbita moschata* (Duchesne ex Lam.) Duchesne ex Poir. (107) (1586)

Edder's-tongue - *Ophioglossum* L. (158) (1900)

Eddo - *Colocasia esculenta* (L.) Schott (109) (1949)

Ed-du (Breton "black wheat") - *Fagopyrum esculentum* Moench (110) (1886)

Edel leberkraut (German) - *Hepatica nobilis* Schreb. (46) (1879)

Edellebere (German) - *Hepatica nobilis* Schreb. var. *obtusa* (Pursh) Steyermark (6) (1892)

Edeltanne (German) - *Abies alba* Mill. (possibly) (158) (1900)

Edging candytuft - *Iberis sempervirens* L. (109) (1949)

Edging lobelia - *Lobelia erinus* L. (138) (1923)

Edible galingale - *Cyperus esculentus* L. (5, 156) (1913-1923)

Edible pine - *Pinus edulis* Engelm. (103) (1871)

Edible thistle - *Cirsium edule* Nutt. (50) (present)

Edible valerian - *Valeriana edulis* Nutt. (63, 72, 155, 156, 158) (1899-1942)

Edible-pod pea [Edible-podded pea] - *Pisum sativum* L. (109) (1949)

Edible-rooted caraway - *Perideridia gairdneri* (Hook. & Arn.) Mathias subsp. *gairdneri* (107) (1919)

Edler Wiederthon (German) - *Drosera rotundifolia* L. (158) (1900)

Edson's thorn - *Crataegus schuettei* Ashe (5) (1913)

E-eesse (Cuchan Yuma) - *Prosopis pubescens* Benth. (132) (1855)

Eel-grass [Eel grass, Eelgrass] - *Vallisneria americana* Michx. (5, 72, 92, 122, 131, 156, 158) (1899-1937), *Vallisneria* L. (2, 50, 109, 158) (1895–present), *Zostera marina* L. (107, 156) (1913-1919)

Eel-grass pondweed [Eel-grass pond-weed] - *Potamogeton zosteriformis* Fern. (72, 85, 131, 156) (1894-1932)

Eendenpoot - *Podophyllum peltatum* L. (186) (1814)

Eenhorn - *Chamaelirium luteum* (L.) A. Gray (7, 92) (1828-1876)

Eestrige - *Salsola kali* L. (158) (1900)

Ee'-yah (Pinal Leño Apache) - *Prosopis* L. (132) (1855)

Efflorescent lichen - *Spiloma melaleucum* Ach. (19) (1840)

Effuse eriogonum - *Eriogonum effusum* Nutt. (5, 93) (1913-1936)

Egeria - *Egeria* Planch. (50) (present)

Egg squash - *Cucurbita pepo* L. var. *ovifera* (L.) Alef. (19, 92) (1840-1876)

Egg-apple [Egg apple] - *Solanum melongena* L. (92, 156) (1876-1923)

Egg-bonnet - *Brasenia schreberi* Gmel. (156) (1923)

Egg-bract sedge [Eggbract sedge] - *Carex ovalis* Goodenough (50) (present)

Eggert's thorn - *Crataegus coccinioides* Ashe (5, 97) (1913-1937)

Egg-fruit - *Pouteria campechiana* (Kunth) Baehni (109) (1949)

Egg-leaf penstemon [Eggleaf penstemon] - *Penstemon ovatus* Dougl. ex Hook. (138) (1923)

Egg-leaf silktassel [Eggleaf silktassel] - *Garrya ovata* Benth. (50) (present)

Egg-leaf skullcap [Eggleaf skullcap] - *Scutellaria ovata* Hill (3, 4) (1977-1986)

Eggleston's sedge [Eggleston sedge] - *Carex egglestonii* Mackenzie (139) (1944)

Eggplant [Egg-plant, Egg plant] - *Solanum melongena* L. (19, 82, 85, 92, 107, 156) (1840-1932), *Symphoricarpos albus* (L.) Blake var. *albus* (5, 158) (1900-1913), *Symphoricarpos albus* (L.) Blake var. *laevigatus* (Fern.) Blake (156) (1923)

Egg-pod loco [Eggpod loco] - *Astragalus oocarpus* Gray (155) (1942)

Eggs-and-bacon - *Linaria vulgaris* Mill. (5, 156) (1913-1923), *Lotus corniculatus* L. (158) (1900)

Eglantere - *Rosa eglanteria* L. (158) (1900)

Eglantine [Eglentyne] - *Linnaea borealis* L. (156) (1923), *Rosa eglanteria* L. (19, 46, 63, 92, 107, 109, 156, 158, 179) (1526-1949) Shakespeare and Spenser

Eglantine gall - *Rosa canina* L. (92) (1876)

Eglantine rose - *Rosa eglanteria* L. (5, 92, 158) (1876-1913)

Egret mudplantian - *Heteranthera peduncularis* Benth. (50) (present)

Egrimony - *Agrimonia eupatoria* L. (46, 179) (1526-1671)

Egriot - *Prunus cerasus* L. (5) (1913)

Egyptian bean hibiscus [Egyptian bean hybiscus] - *Nelumbo lutea* Willd. (183) (~1756)

Egyptian clover - *Trifolium alexandrinum* L. (109) (1949) Clark

Egyptian corn - *Sorghum bicolor* (L.) Moench subsp. *bicolor* (107) (1919)

Egyptian corn (Turkey) - *Zea mays* L. (110) (1886)

Egyptian grass [Egyptian-grass] - *Dactyloctenium aegyptium* (L.) Willd. (5, 50, 66, 92, 163) (1852–present), *Sorghum halepense* (L.) Pers. (45, 158) (1896-1900)

Egyptian gum Arabic tree - *Acacia nilotica* (L.) Willd. ex Delile (158) (1900)

Egyptian lily - *Zantedeschia aethiopica* (L.) Spreng. (19) (1840)

Egyptian lupin - *Lupinus albus* L. (110) (1886)

Egyptian millet - *Pennisetum glaucum* (L.) R. Br. (87) (1884), *Pennisetum* L.C. Rich. ex Pers. (158) (1900), *Sorghum halepense* (L.) Pers. (5, 45, 158) (1896-1913)

Egyptian pea - *Cicer arietinum* L. (107) (1919)

Egyptian rice-corn - *Sorghum bicolor* (L.) Moench (56) (1901) IA, *Sorghum halepense* (L.) Pers. (45) (1896)

Egyptian rose - *Knautia arvensis* (L.) Duby (5, 156, 158) (1900-1923)

Egyptian senna - *Senna alexandrina* Mill. (19) (1840)

Egyptian thorn - *Acacia nilotica* (L.) Willd. ex Delile (158) (1900), *Pyracantha coccinea* M. Roemer (5) (1913)

Egyptian waterlily [Egyptian water lily] - *Nymphaea lotus* L. (107) (1919)

Egyptian wheat - *Triticum turgidum* L. (19, 66, 67) (1840-1903)

Eherreiskraut (German) - *Artemisia abrotanum* L. (158) (1900)

Ehrenpreis - *Veronica serpyllifolia* L. (158) (1900)

Eibisch (German) - *Althaea officinalis* L. (158) (1900)

Eight-joint panicum [Eight-jointed panicum] - *Dichanthelium spretum* (J.A. Schultes) Freckmann (5, 50) (1913–present)

Einblüthige Monotropa (German) - *Monotropa uniflora* L. (6) (1892)

Einblumige Sommerwurz (German) - *Orobanche uniflora* L. (186) (1814)

Eisengraue Magnolie (German) - *Magnolia virginiana* L. (186) (1814)

Eker Tengtongues (German) - *Rorippa nasturtium-aquaticum* (L.) Hayek (158) (1900)

Elaeagnus - *Elaeagnus* L. (50, 138, 155) (1923–present)

Elaeis - *Elaeis guineensis* Jacq. (110) (1886)

Elaia (Greek) - *Olea europaea* L. (110) (1886)

Elaphoboscon - *Pastinaca sativa* L. (107) (1919)

Elastic gum - *Sideroxylon lanuginosum* Michx. (65) (1931) OK

Elaterium - *Ecballium elaterium* (L.) A. Rich. (92) (1876)

Elaterium cucumber - *Ecballium elaterium* (L.) A. Rich. (92) (1876)

Elatine - *Knautia arvensis* (L.) Duby (177, 178) (1526-1762)

Elbowbush [Elbow-bush, Elbow bush] - *Cephalanthus occidentalis* L. (156) (1923), *Forestiera pubescens* Nutt. (4, 124) (1937-1986)

Elder [Eldre] or Elder tree - *Sambucus* L. (1, 2, 8, 10, 82, 93, 109, 112, 138, 155, 156, 158, 184) (1785-1936), *Sambucus nigra* L. subsp. *canadensis* (L.) R. Bolli (9, 49, 52, 53, 57, 58, 61, 95, 112, 113, 114, 125, 130, 148, 157, 158, 187, 190) (~1759-1939), *Sambucus racemosa* L. (106) (1930), *Sambucus racemosa* L. var. *racemosa* (112) (1937)

Elder bush - *Sambucus nigra* L. subsp. *canadensis* (L.) R. Bolli (6) (1892)

Elder flowers [Elder-flowers] - *Sambucus nigra* L. subsp. *canadensis* (L.) R. Bolli (92, 158) (1876-1900)

Elder rob - *Sambucus nigra* L. subsp. *canadensis* (L.) R. Bolli (92) (1876) juice of elderberries

Elder rose - *Viburnum opulus* L. (178) (1526)

Elderberry [Elder-berry, Elder berry] - *Sambucus* L. (4, 50) (1986–present), *Sambucus nigra* L. (107) (1919), *Sambucus nigra* L. subsp. *canadensis* (L.) R. Bolli (3, 6, 22, 37, 105, 121, 125, 145, 156, 157) (1892-1977), *Sambucus nigra* L. subsp. *cerulea* (Raf.) R. Bolli (101) (1905)

Elder-blow [Elder-blows] - *Sambucus nigra* L. subsp. *canadensis* (L.) R. Bolli (156, 158) (1900-1923)

Elder-leaf ash [Elder-leaved ash] - *Fraxinus americana* L. (52, 53) (1919-1922), *Fraxinus nigra* Marsh. (53) (1922)

Elder-leaf mountain-ash [Elder-leaved mountain ash, Elder leaved-mountain ash] - *Sorbus americana* Marsh. (5, 156) (1913-1923), *Sorbus sambucifolia* (Cham. & Schlecht.) M. Roemer (2) (1895)

Elder-leaf rowan tree [Elder-leaved rowan tree] - *Sorbus sambucifolia* (Cham. & Schlecht.) M. Roemer (2) (1895)

Elder-leaf sumach [Elder-leaved sumach] - *Sorbus americana* Marsh. (156) (1923) no longer in use by 1929

Elder-scented iris - *Iris germanica* L. (19) (1840)

Eldin - *Petasites hybridus* (L.) G. Gaertn., B. Mey. & Scherb. (5, 156) (1913-1923) no longer in use by 1923

Eldoes - *Colocasia esculenta* (L.) Schott (7) (1828)

Eldorado manzanita - *Arctostaphylos nissenana* Merriam (155) (1942)

Eldorado onion - *Allium hyalinum* Curran (155) (1942)

Eldre - *Sambucus nigra* L. (179) (1526)

Elebore - *Helleborus niger* L. (179) (1526)

Elebore Vert (French) - *Helleborus viridis* L. (6) (1892)

Elecampane - *Inula helenium* L. (57, 61, 62, 63, 64, 72, 92, 109, 138, 156) (1870-1949), *Inula* L. (167) (1814)

Elecampine - *Inula helenium* L. (5, 6, 7, 19, 49, 52, 53, 54, 55) (1828-1922), *Inula* L. (1, 158) (1900-1932)

Election pink - *Rhododendron periclymenoides* (Michx.) Shinners (5, 73, 79, 156) (1891-1923) NH, bloomed at election time, no longer in use by 1923

Election posies [Election-posies] - *Castilleja coccinea* (L.) Spreng. (5, 73, 158) (1892-1913) Dudley MA

Electric-light plant [Electric light plant] - *Cleome hassleriana* Chod. (156) (1923)

Elegant cinquefoil - *Potentilla concinna* Richards (50, 131, 155) (1899–present)

Elegant cyperus - *Cyperus flavicomus* Michx. (5) (1913)

Elephant flower - *Pedicularis* L. (1) (1932)

Elephant grass [Elephants grass, Elephant's grass] - *Pennisetum purpureum* Schumacher (138, 163) (1852-1923)

Elephant's-ear [Elephants' ear, Elephant's ears, Elephants-ear] - *Begonia* L. (92) (1876), *Colocasia esculenta* (L.) Schott (138) (1923), *Platanthera orbiculata* (Pursh) Lindl. (156) (1923)

Elephant's-foot [Elephant's foo, Elephantsfoot] - *Elephantopus carolinianus* Willd. (3, 19) (1840-1977), *Elephantopus* L. (1, 4, 10) (1818-1986), *Elephantopus tomentosus* L. (57) (1917)

Elephant's-head [Elephant's head] - *Pedicularis* L. (1) (1932)

Elephant's-trunk [Elephant's trunk] - *Proboscidea louisianica* (P. Mill.) Thellung (5, 156, 158) (1900-1923)

Eleven-o'-clock-lady [Eleven o'clock lady] - *Ornithogalum umbellatum* L. (5, 158) (1900-1913)

Elfdock [Elf-dock, Elfe docke] - *Inula helenium* L. (5, 64, 156, 179) (1526-1923)

Elfwort - *Inula helenium* L. (5, 64, 156) (1907-1923)

Elk River wild crab - *Malus ioensis* (Wood) Britton (137) (1931) SD

Elk sedge - *Carex garberi* Fern. (50) (present), *Carex geyeri* Boott (139) (1944) CO

Elk thistle - *Cirsium foliosum* (Hook.) DC. (155) (1942)

Elk tree [Elk-tree] - *Oxydendrum arboreum* (L.) DC. (possibly) (5, 7, 52, 92, 156) (1828-1923)

Elkbark [Elk-bark, Elk bark] - *Magnolia macrophylla* Michx. (5, 7, 92, 156) (1828-1923), *Magnolia virginiana* L. (6, 186) (1825-1892), *Magnolia virginiana* L. (possibly) (156) (1923)

Elknut [Elk nut, Elk-nut] - *Pyrularia pubera* Michx. (5, 156) (1913-1923)

Elkton grape - *Vitis labrusca* L. (possibly) (7) (1828)

Elkweed - *Frasera speciosa* Dougl. ex Griseb. (50) (present), *Frasera* Walt. (155) (1942)

Elkwood [Elk-wood, Elk wood] - *Acer spicatum* Lam. (29) (1869), *Magnolia macrophylla* Michx. (7) (1828), *Magnolia tripetala* L. (5, 156) (1913-1923), *Oxydendrum arboreum* (L.) DC. (possibly) (7, 92) (1828-1876)

Ellan wood [Ellanwood] - *Sambucus nigra* L. (92, 158) (1876-1900)

Ellar - *Sambucus nigra* L. (158) (1900)

Ellarne - *Sambucus nigra* L. (158) (1900)

Ellebore - *Symplocarpus foetidus* (L.) Salisb. ex Nutt. (186) (1814)

Elleborine - *Epipactis helleborine* (L.) Crantz (178) (1596)

Ellen - *Sambucus nigra* L. (158) (1900)

Eller - *Alnus glutinosa* (L.) Gaertn. (5, 156) (1913-1923), *Alnus incana* (L.) Moench (46) (1879)

Ellet - *Sambucus nigra* L. (158) (1900)

Ellhorn - *Sambucus nigra* L. (92, 158) (1876-1900)

Elliot's beard grass [Elliot's beard-grass, Elliotts beardgrass] - *Andropogon gyrans* Ashe var. *gyrans* (5, 122, 163) (1852-1937)

Elliot's bent grass [Elliot's bent-grass, Elliott bentgrass] - *Agrostis elliottiana* Schultes (5, 50, 119, 155) (1913-present)

Elliot's bluestem - *Andropogon gyrans* Ashe var. *gyrans* (50) (present)

Elliot's broom-sedge [Elliot's broom sedge] - *Andropogon gyrans* Ashe var. *gyrans* (94) (1901)

Elliot's gentian - *Gentiana catesbaei* Walt. (5) (1913)

Elliot's oak - *Quercus pagoda* Raf. (5) (1913)

Elliot's sabbatia - *Sabatia brevifolia* Raf. (5) (1913)

Elliot's sida - *Sida elliottii* Torr & Gray. (5) (1913)

Elliottian gentian - *Gentiana saponaria* L. (7) (1828)

Elliott's black blueberry - *Vaccinium elliottii* Chapman (5) (1913)

Elliott's goldenrod [Elliott's golden-rod] - *Solidago latissimifolia* Mill. (5) (1913)

Elliott's paspalum - *Paspalum distichum* L. (94) (1901)

Elliptical buttercup - *Ranunculus glaberrimus* Hook. var. *ellipticus* (Greene) Greene (50) (present)

Elliptical-leaf St. John's-wort [Elliptical-leaved St. John's wort] - *Hypericum ellipticum* Hook. (2) (1895)

Elliptic-leaf St. John's-wort [Elliptic-leaved St. John's wort] - *Hypericum ellipticum* Hook. (5) (1913)

Ellis' stinking milkvetch - *Astragalus praelongus* Sheldon var. *ellisiae* (Rydb.) Barneby (50) (present)

Ellisia - *Ellisia* L. (50, 155) (1942-present), *Ellisia nyctelea* (L.) L. (80) (1913)

Ellwanger's hawthorn [Ellwanger hawthorn] - *Crataegus pedicellata* Sarg. (138) (1923)

Elm bark - *Ulmus rubra* Muhl. (157) (1929)

Elm cap - *Hypsizygus ulmarius* (Bull.) Redhead (3, 37) (1830-1977)

Elm goldenrod [Elm golden-rod] - *Solidago ulmifolia* Muhl. ex Willd. (19) (1840)

Elm mushroom - *Hypsizygus ulmarius* (Bull.) Redhead (128) (1933)

Elm or elm tree - *Ulmus americana* L. (19, 35, 12, 101, 164) (1806-1905), *Ulmus* L. (1, 4, 8, 10, 50, 82, 93, 106, 109, 138, 158) (1785-present), *Ulmus rubra* Muhl. (157) (1929)

Elmer's wheatgrass [Elmer wheatgrass] - *Elymus lanceolatus* (Scribn. & J.G. Sm.) Gould (155) (1942)

Elm-leaf blackberry [Elmleaf blackberry] - *Rubus ulmifolius* Schott (138) (1923)

Elm-leaf goldenrod [Elmleaf goldenrod, Elm-leaved golden-rod, Elm-leaved goldenrod] - *Solidago ulmifolia* Muhl. ex Willd. (3, 4, 5, 50, 72, 82, 86, 97, 122, 187) (1818-present), *Solidago ulmifolia* Muhl. ex Willd. var. *ulmifolia* (50) (present)

Elm-leaf spiraea [Elmleaf spiraea] - *Spiraea chamaedryfolia* L. (138) (1923), *Spiraea chamaedryfolia* L. var. *ulmifolia* (Scop.) Maxim. (138) (1923)

Elnorne - *Sambucus nigra* L. (158) (1900)

Elodea - *Elodea canadensis* Michx. (109) (1949), *Elodea* Michx. (155) (1942)

Elongate panicum [Elongated panicum] - *Dichanthelium linearifolium* (Scribn. ex Nash) Gould (3, 72) (1907-1977)

Elren - *Sambucus nigra* L. (158) (1900)

Elsholtzia - *Elsholtzia ciliata* (Thunb.) Hyl. (5) (1913)

Eltrot - *Heracleum maximum* Bartr. (3) (1977)

Elymus - *Zizania aquatica* L. (177) (1762)

Emblic - *Phyllanthus emblica* L. (107, 109) (1919-1949) Arabic

Emerson's thorn - *Crataegus submollis* Sarg. (5) (1913)

Emetic herb - *Lobelia inflata* L. (53, 92) (1876-1922)

Emetic holly - *Ilex vomitoria* Aiton (5, 156) (1913-1923)

Emetic root [Emetic-root] - *Euphorbia corollata* L. (7, 49, 92, 157, 158) (1828-1929), *Lobelia inflata* L. (6) (1892)

Emeticweed [Emetic weed, Emetic-weed] - *Lobelia inflata* L. (5, 6, 7, 46, 53, 59, 92, 156, 186, 187) (1814-1923)

Emmer - *Triticum turgidum* L. (107, 109) (1919-1949)

Emmon's sedge - *Carex albicans* Willd. ex Spreng. var. *albicans* (5, 72) (1907-1913)

Emory's black oak - *Quercus emoryi* Torr. (122) (1937) TX

Emory's sedge [Emory sedge] - *Carex emoryi* Dewey (3, 50, 139, 155) (1942-present)

Empress tree - *Paulownia tomentosa* (Thunb.) Sieb. & Zucc. ex Steud. (possibly) (156) (1923)

Encemilla - *Croton pottsii* (Klotzsch) Muell.-Arg. var. *pottsii* (104, 107) (1896-1919)

Enchanter's herb [Enchanters' herb] - *Verbena officinalis* L. (92) (1876)

Enchanter's nightshade [Inchanters night-shade] - *Circaea ×intermedia* Ehrh. [*alpina × lutetiana*] (92) (1876), *Circaea* L. (1, 2, 4, 10, 50, 158, 190) (~1759-present), *Circaea lutetiana* L. (5, 19, 72, 93, 97, 131, 156, 178) (1526-1937), *Circaea lutetiana* L. subsp. *canadensis* (L.) Asch. & Magnus (3) (1977)

Enchanter's plant - *Verbena officinalis* L. (5, 156) (1913-1923)

Enchanter's-wort [Entchanters-wort] - *Circaea lutetiana* L. (184) (1793)

Enchanting vetch [Inchaunting vetch] - *Lathyrus nissolia* L. (178) (1526)

Encino (Spanish) - *Quercus agrifolia* Née (75) (1894) CA

Endive [Endyue] - *Cichorium intybus* L. (10, 19) (1818-1840), *Cichorium* L. (184) (1793), *Cichorium endivia* L. (92, 107, 109, 110, 179) (1526-1949)

Endivie (German) - *Cichorium intybus* L. (158) (1900)

Endolepis - *Endolepis* Torr. (50) (present)

Enebro (Spanish) - *Juniperus communis* L. (158) (1900)

Eneldo (Spanish) - *Anethum graveolens* L. (158) (1900)

Enequen - *Apocynum cannabinum* L. (46) (1879)

Engelmannia - *Engelmannia peristenia* (Raf.) Goodman & Lawson (5) (1913)

Engelmann's adder's-tongue [Engelmann's addertongue, Engelmann adderstongue] - *Ophioglossum engelmannii* Prantl. (122, 155) (1937-1942)

Engelmann's arrowhead [Engelmann arrowhead, Engelmann's arrow-head] - *Sagittaria engelmanniana* J.G. Sm. (5, 50, 72, 155) (1893–present)

Engelmann's aster [Engelmann aster] - *Eucephalus engelmannii* (D.C. Eat.) Greene (155) (1942)

Engelmann's cyperus - *Cyperus odoratus* L. (5) (1913)

Engelmann's daisy [Engelmanns daisy] - *Engelmannia peristenia* (Raf.) Goodman & Lawson (3, 4, 50, 122, 124) (1937–present)

Engelmann's dock - *Rumex hastatulus* Baldw. (122) (1937)

Engelmann's evening-primrose [Engelmann's evening primrose] - *Oenothera engelamanii* (Small) Munz (4, 50) (1986–present)

Engelmann's false goldenweed - *Oonopsis engelmannii* (Gray) Greene (50) (present)

Engelmann's flatsedge [Engelmann flatsedge] - *Cyperus odoratus* L. (155) (1942)

Engelmann's goldenweed - *Oonopsis engelmannii* (Gray) Greene (3, 4, 5) (1913-1986)

Engelmann's hawthorn [Engelmann hawthorn] - *Crataegus engelmannii* Sarg. (155) (1942)

Engelmann's milkweed - *Asclepias engelmanniana* Woods. (4, 50) (1986–present)

Engelmann's oonopsis [Engelman's oonopsis] - *Oonopsis engelmannii* (Gray) Greene (5) (1913)

Engelmann's prickly-pear [Engelmann pricklypear] - *Opuntia engelmannii* Salm-Dyck (155) (1942)

Engelmann's quillwort [Engelman's quillwort] - *Isoetes engelmanni* A. Br. (5) (1913)

Engelmann's sedge [Engelman sedge] - *Carex engelmannii* Bailey (139) (1944), *Cyperus odoratus* L. (66) (1903)

Engelmann's sorrel - *Rumex hastatulus* Baldw. (5) (1913)

Engelmann's spikerush [Engelmann's spike-rush, Engelmann's spike rush] - *Eleocharis engelmanni* Steud. (5, 50) (1913–present)

Engelmann's spruce [Engelman spruce] - *Picea engelmannii* Parry ex Engelm. (135, 136, 138, 153) (1910-1930)

English batata (Brazil) - *Solanum tuberosum* L. (110) (1886)

English bean - *Vicia faba* L. (107) (1919)

English bent - *Agrostis gigantea* Roth (66) (1903)

English blue hyacinth [English blew iacint] - *Hyacinthoides nonscripta* (L.) Chouard ex Rothm. (178) (1596)

English bluebell - *Hyacinthoides nonscripta* (L.) Chouard ex Rothm. (109) (1949)

English bluegrass [English blue-grass, English blue grass] - *Lolium perenne* L. (5, 75) (1894-1913) WV, *Lolium pratense* (Huds.) S.J. Darbyshire (68) (1890), *Poa compressa* L. (5, 56, 68, 88, 119, 129) (1885-1938)

English buckhorn plantain - *Plantago lanceolata* L. (85) (1932) SD

English bull's-eye [English bull's eye, English bullseye] - *Rudbeckia hirta* L. (5, 76, 157, 156, 158) (1896-1929) York Co. ME

English camomile [English chamomile] - *Chamaemelum nobile* (L.) All. (46, 49, 57, 155) (1649-1942)

English catchfly - *Silene gallica* L. (5) (1913)

English charlock - *Moricandia arvensis* (L.) DC. (80) (1913) IA, *Sinapis arvensis* L. (145) (1897) KS

English cherry-laurel - *Prunus laurocerasus* L. (138) (1923)

English cost - *Tanacetum vulgare* L. (158) (1900)

English cudweed [English cudweede] - *Omalotheca sylvatica* (L.) Schultz-Bip. & F.W. Schultz (178) (1526)

English daisy - *Bellis* L. (4) (1986), *Bellis perennis* L. (4, 107, 109, 138, 155, 158) (1900-1986)

English elm - *Ulmus glabra* Huds. (82, 93, 107, 109, 112, 135, 138, 156) (1910-1949)

English gooseberry - *Ribes uva-crispa* L. var. *sativum* DC. (possibly) (19, 109) (1840-1949)

English grass - *Agrostis capillaris* L. (66) (1903), *Agrostis gigantea* Roth (56) (1901) IA, *Poa pratensis* L. (19, 68) (1840-1913) Ottawa

English harebell [English hare-bels] - *Hyacinthoides nonscripta* (L.) Chouard ex Rothm. (180) (1633)

English holly - *Ilex aquifolium* L. (109, 138) (1923-1949)

English hyacinth [English iacinth] - *Hyacinthoides nonscripta* (L.) Chouard ex Rothm. (180) (1633)

English ivy - *Hedera helix* L. (19, 106, 109, 138) (1840-1949)

English maidenhair [English maiden hair] - *Asplenium trichomanes* L. (5, 86, 158) (1878-1923)

English masterwort - *Aegopodium podagraria* L. (5) (1913)

English mercury - *Chenopodium bonus-henricus* L. (5, 19, 92, 156) (1840-1923)

English moss - *Sedum acre* L. (57) (1917)

English oak - *Quercus robur* L. (93, 138) (1923-1936)

English pepper-grass [English pepper grass] - *Lepidium campestre* (L.) Aiton f. (5, 156, 158) (1900–1923)

English plantain - *Plantago lanceolata* L. (3, 4, 5, 62, 63, 75, 82, 97, 145, 156, 157, 158) (1894-1986)

English ray grass - *Lolium perenne* L. (67, 68) (1890-1913) Ottawa

English reddish hyacinth [English reddish iacint] - *Hyacinthoides nonscripta* (L.) Chouard ex Rothm. (178) (1596)

English rye - *Lolium perenne* L. (56) (1901) IA

English rye grass [English rye-grass] - *Lolium perenne* L. (68, 109, 119, 163) (1890-1949)

English sea colewort [English sea colewoorts] - *Brassica oleracea* L. (180) (1633)

English sloe - *Prunus spinosa* L. (19) (1840)

English sorrel - *Rumex acetosa* L. (5, 156) (1913-1923)

English strawberry - *Fragaria vesca* L. (19, 49) (1840-1898)

English thistle - *Cirsium vulgare* (Savi) Ten. (145) (1897) KS, *Dipsacus fullonum* L. (62, 75) (1894-1912), *Lactuca serriola* L. (70) (1895)

English treacle - *Alliaria petiolata* (Bieb.) Cavara & Grande (158) (1900)

English violet - *Viola odorata* L. (5, 55) (1911-1922)

English walnut or English walnut tree - *Juglans regia* L. (41, 92, 107) (1770-1919)

English water cress - *Sisymbrium officinale* (L.) Scop (92) (1876)

English wheat - *Triticum turgidum* L. (67, 109) (1890-1949)

English white hyacinth [English white iacint] - *Hyacinthoides nonscripta* (L.) Chouard ex Rothm. (178) (1596)

English white hyssop [English white hyssope] - *Hyssopus officinalis* L. (178) (1526)

English yellow mustard - *Sinapis alba* L. (109) (1949)

English yew - *Taxus baccata* L. (50, 109, 138) (1923–present)

Englishman's foot - *Plantago major* L. (41, 92) (1770-1876)

Enslen's vine - *Cynanchum laeve* (Michx.) Pers. (5, 156) (1913-1923)

Entenfuss - *Podophyllum peltatum* L. (186) (1814)

Entire-leaf black oak [Entire-leaved black oak] - *Quercus marilandica* Muenchh. (8) (1785)

Entire-leaf foxglove [Entire-leaved foxglove] - *Aureolaria laevigata* (Raf.) Raf. (5) (1913)

Entire-leaf groundsel [Entireleaf groundsel, Entire-leaved groundsel] - *Senecio integerrimus* Nutt. (5, 122, 131) (1899-1937)

Entire-leaf mountain avens [Entire-leaved mountain avens] - *Dryas integrifolia* Vahl. (5) (1913)

Entire-leaf nettle tree [Entire-leaved nettle tree] - *Celtis tenuifolia* Nutt. (12) (1821)

Entire-leaf painted-cup [Entire-leaved painted-cup] - *Castilleja indivisa* Engelm. (5, 97, 122) (1913-1937)

Entire-leaf prickly lettuce [Entire-leaved prickly lettuce] - *Lactuca sativa* L. (82) (1930)

Entire-leaf ragweed [Entire-leaved ragweed] - *Ambrosia trifida* L. var. *trifida* (72) (1907)

Entire-leaf rosinweed [Entire-leaved rosin-weed] - *Silphium integrifolium* Michx. (93, 97) (1936-1937)

Entire-leaf rosinwood [Entire-leaved rosin wood] - *Silphium integrifolium* Michx. (5, 72) (1907-1913)

Entire-leaf skullcap [Entire-leaved Skull-cap] - *Scutellaria integrifolia* L. (187) (1818)

Entire-leaf thelypodium [Entire-leaved thelypodium] - *Thelypodium integrifolium* (Nutt.) Endl. ex Walp. (5, 72) (1907-1913)

Entire-leaf thelypody [Entireleaved thelypody] - *Thelypodium integrifolium* (Nutt.) Endl. ex Walp. (50) (present), *Thelypodium integrifolium* (Nutt.) Endl. ex Walp. subsp. *integrifolium* (50) (present)

Entire-leaf thorn-apple [Entire leaf thorn apple, Entire-leaved thorn apple, Entire-leaved thorn-apple] - *Datura inoxia* P. Mill. (5) (1913), *Datura metel* L. (97, 124) (1937)

Entire-leaf western daisy [Entireleaf western daisy] - *Astranthium integrifolium* (Michx.) Nutt. (50) (present)

Epazotl (Mexico) - *Chenopodium ambrosioides* L. (107) (1919)

Eperviére (French) - *Hieracium* L. (158) (1900)

Ephedra - *Ephedra antisyphilitica* Berl. ex C.A. Mey. (3, 57) (1917-1977), *Ephedra* L. (155) (1942)

Ephemerine de Virginie (French) - *Tradescantia virginiana* L. (86) (1878) because flowers remain open only one day

Épiaire (French) - *Stachys* L. (158) (1900)

Épicéa (French) - *Picea abies* (L.) H. Karst. (158) (1900)

Epidendron - *Epidendrum* L. (86) (1878) meaning 'upon a tree'

Epidendrum tree-grass - Epidendrum magnoliae Muhl. (183) (1756)

Epigaea - *Epigaea repens* L. (52, 54) (1905-1919)

Épigée (French) - *Epigaea* L. (8) (1785)

Épigée rampante (French) - *Epigaea repens* L. (8) (1785)

Epilobium - *Chamerion angustifolium* (L.) Holub subsp. *angustifolium* (52, 57) (1917)

Epimedium - *Epimedium* L. (138) (1923) Dioscorides name for this species

Epine - *Mespilus* L. (8) (1785)

Épine à feuilles de perfil (French) - *Crataegus marshallii* Eggl. (8) (1785)

Épine à feuilles de prunier (French) - *Photinia floribunda* (Lindl.) Robertson & Phipps (8) (1785)

Épine à feuilles en coin (French) - *Crataegus cuneiformis* (Marshall) Eggl. (8) (1785)

Epine à feuilles luisantes (French) - *Crataegus crus-galli* L. (possibly) (8) (1785)

Épine de Canada (French) - *Amelanchier canadensis* (L.) Medik. (8) (1785)

Épine vinette (French) - *Berberis canadensis* P. Mill. (7) (1828), *Berberis* L. (8) (1785), *Berberis vulgaris* L. (6, 158) (1892)

Epine vinette du Canada (French) - *Berberis canadensis* P. Mill. (8) (1785)

Épinette à la bière (Canada) - *Picea mariana* (Mill.) Britton, Sterns & Poggenb. (20) (1857)

Épinette blanche du Canada (French) - *Picea glauca* (Moench) Voss (8) (1785)

Epinette noire (Canada) - *Picea mariana* (Mill.) Britton, Sterns & Poggenb. (20) (1857)

Épinette rouge (French Canada) - *Larix laricina* (Du Roi.) Koch. (20, 41, 168) (1770-1857)

Epinettes des prairies - *Grindelia squarrosa* (Pursh) Dunal (28) (1850)

Equisteum - *Equisetum hyemale* L. (52, 57) (1917-1919)

Erable (French) - *Acer* L. (8, 20) (1785-1857)

Erable à feuilles argentées (French) - *Acer rubrum* L. (8) (1785)

Erable à feuilles de frêne (French) - *Acer negundo* L. (8) (1785)

Erable à grandes feuilles (French) - *Acer macrophyllum* Pursh (20) (1857)

Erable circiné (French) - *Acer circinatum* Pursh (20) (1857)

Erable de Californie (French) - *Acer negundo* L. var. *californicum* (Torr. & Gray) Sarg. (20) (1857)

Erable de Canada (French) - *Acer pensylvanicum* L. (8) (1785)

Erable de Drummond (French) - *Acer rubrum* L. (20) (1857)

Erable de montagne (French) - *Acer grandidentatum* Nutt. (20) (1857)

Erable de Pensylvanie (French) - *Acer pensylvanicum* L. (8) (1785)

Erable jaspé (French) - *Acer pensylvanicum* L. (168) (1803)

Erable rouge (French) - *Acer rubrum* L. (8) (1785)

Erable sucre (French) - *Acer rubrum* L. (8) (1785)

Erable triparti (French) - *Acer glabrum* Torr. (20) (1857)

Erangelia - *Galanthus nivalis* L. (174) (1753)

Erba renaiola (Italian, from rena "sand" - *Spergula arvensis* L. (110) (1886)

Erdapfel (German) - *Helianthus tuberosus* L. (158) (1900)

Erdartischocke (German) - *Helianthus tuberosus* L. (158) (1900)

Erdbeartege Sandbeere (German) - *Arctostaphylos uva-ursi* (L.) Spreng. (7) (1828)

Erdbeere (German) - *Fragaria vesca* L. (6, 158) (1892–1900)

Erdrauch (German) - *Fumaria officinalis* L. (158) (1900)

Erebinthus - *Tephrosia virginiana* (L.) Pers (177) (1762)

Erect blackberry - *Rubus andrewsianus* Blanch. (82) (1930)

Erect brome - *Bromus erectus* Huds. (50) (present)

Erect brome grass - *Bromus erectus* Huds. (87) (1884)

Erect bugle - *Ajuga genevensis* L. (5) (1913)

Erect cinquefoil - *Potentilla erecta* (L.) Raeusch. (50) (present)

Erect dayflower - *Commelina erecta* L. (155) (1942), *Commelina erecta* L. var. *angustifolia* (Michx.) Fern. (3) (1977), *Commelina erecta* L. var. *erecta* (3) (1977)

Erect digitaria - *Digitaria filiformis* (L.) Koel. (187) (1818)

Erect hedge-parsley - *Torilis arvensis* (Huds.) Link (5, 97, 122, 156) (1913-1937)

Erect knotweed [Erect knot-weed] - *Polygonum achoreum* Blake (3) (1977), *Polygonum erectum* L. (4, 5, 50, 62, 72, 80, 93, 97, 131, 155) (1899–present), *Polygonum ramosissimum* Michx. (80) (1913)

Erect mountain leather-flower [Erect mountain leather flower] - *Clematis ochroleuca* Aiton (5) (1913)

Erect muhlenbergia - *Brachyelytrum erectum* (Schreb. ex Spreng.) Beauv. (66, 187) (1818-1903)

Erect rhynchosia - *Rhynchosia tomentosa* (L.) Hook. & Arn. var. *tomentosa* (5) (1913)

Erect silky leather-flower [Erect silky leather flower] - *Clematis ochroleuca* Aiton (5) (1913)

Erect spiderling - *Boerhavia erecta* L. (50, 155) (1942–present)

Erect-fruit wintercress [Erect-fruited winter cress] - *Barbarea stricta* Andrz. ex Besser (5) (1913), *Barbarea orthoceras* Ledeb. (155) (1942)

Eresimo (Spanish) - *Sisymbrium officinale* (L.) Scop (158) (1900)

Erfinen (Welsh) - *Brassica rapa* L. (110) (1886)

Ergot - *Claviceps purpurea* (Fr.) Tul. (7, 49, 52, 55, 57, 59, 60, 61, 92, 148) (1828-1939)

Ergot of corn - *Ustilago maydis* (DC.) Corda (92) (1876)

Ergot of rye - *Claviceps purpurea* (Fr.) Tul. (54, 55, 57, 60) (1902-1917)

Ergota - *Claviceps purpurea* (Fr.) Tul. (55, 57, 59, 60) (1902-1917)

Ericameria - *Ericameria* Nutt. (158) (1900)

Erigeron - *Conyza canadensis* (L.) Cronq. var. *canadensis* (52, 54) (1905-1919), *Erigeron* L. (158) (1900)

Erigeron de Canada (French) - *Conyza canadensis* (L.) Cronq. var. *canadensis* (6) (1892)

Erigeron de Philadelphie (French) - *Erigeron philadelphicus* L. (7) (1828)

Erineos (Greek) - *Ficus carica* L. (110) (1886)

Eriocarpum - *Xanthisma* DC. (158) (1900)

Eriodictyon - *Eriodictyon californicum* (Hook. & Arn.) Torr. (52, 54) (1905-1919)

Eriogonum - *Eriogonum flavum* Nutt. (127) (1933), *Eriogonum* Michx. (155, 158) (1900-1942)

Erithraea - *Centaurium erythraea* Raf. (174) (1753)

Erth-thought [Erththought] - *Asplenium* L. (178, 179) (1526-1596)

Erurye (Spanish, old name) - *Medicago sativa* L. (110) (1886)

Erva de capitaon - *Hydrocotyle umbellata* L. (174, 177) (1753-1762)

Ervilia - *Lathyrus cicera* L. (110) (1886)

Eryngium - *Eryngium yuccifolium* Michx. (52, 64) (1907-1919)

Eryngo - *Eryngium* L. (1, 4, 10, 50, 109, 138, 155, 156, 158) (1818–present), *Eryngium yuccifolium* Michx. (6, 53, 64) (1892)

Erysimum - *Erysimum* L. (155) (1942)

Erysimum (French) - *Sisymbrium officinale* (L.) Scop (158) (1900)

Erythronium - *Erythronium americanum* Ker. (92) (1876)

Erythronium (Official name of Materia Medica) - *Erythronium americanum* Ker. (7) (1828)

Escallonia - *Escallonia* Mutis ex L. f. (138) (1923)

Escarpment cherry - *Prunus serotina* Ehrh. var. *eximia* (Small) Little (122) (1937) TX

Eschalote d'Espagne (French) - *Allium scorodoprasum* L. (110) (1886)

Eschscholtzia - *Eschscholzia californica* Cham. (92) (1876)

Escurripa - *Lobelia cardinalis* L. (186) (1814)

Eseldistel (German) - *Onopordum acanthium* L. (3) (1977)

Esharusha (Crow) - *Pediomelum esculentum* (Pursh) Rydb. (101) (1905) MT

Esparcet - *Onobrychis viciifolia* Scop. (106, 109) (1930-1949)

Esparcette (French) - *Onobrychis viciifolia* Scop. (28, 46, 68, 158) (1850-1913)

Espargata (Portuguese) - *Spergula arvensis* L. (110) (1886)

Esparicllas (Spanish) - *Spergula arvensis* L. (110) (1886)

Esparraguera (Spanish) - *Asparagus officinalis* L. (158) (1900)

Esparsette - *Onobrychis viciifolia* Scop. (129) (1894)

Espeautre (French) - *Triticum spelta* L. (180) (1633)

Espetonga (Osage) - *Liriodendron tulipifera* L. (7) (1828)

Espina cerval (Spanish) - *Rhamnus cathartica* L. (158) (1900)

Estragon (French) (Spanish) - *Artemisia dracunculus* L. (158) (1900)

Estramonio (Spanish) - *Datura stramonium* L. (158) (1900)

Estuary pipewort - *Eriocaulon parkeri* B. L. Robinson (50) (present)

Esturary sedge - *Carex recta* Boott. (50) (present)

E'-tahl (Kioway) - *Zea mays* L. (132) (1855)

Eternal flower - *Pseudognaphalium obtusifolium* (L.) Hilliard & Burtt subsp. *obtusifolium* (92) (1876)

Ethiopian madflower - *Chasmanthe aethiopica* (L.) N.E. Br. (155) (1942)

Ethiopian sour-gourd - *Adansonia digitata* L. (165) (1768)

Etl (Aztec) - *Phaseolus vulgaris* L. (107) (1919)

Etnach - *Juniperus communis* L. (157, 158) (1900-1929)

Eto-mico (King's tree) - *Persea borbonia* (L.) Spreng. (182) (1791)

Etruscan honeysuckle - *Lonicera etrusca* Santi (138) (1923)

Etwoi (Flathead) - *Camassia scilloides* (Raf.) Cory (101) (1905) MT

Eucalyptus - *Eucalyptus globulus* Labill. (57) (1917), *Eucalyptus* L'Hér. (106, 138) (1923-1930)

Eufrace - *Euphrasia* L. (179) (1526)

Eugene poplar - *Populus ×canadensis* Moench [*deltoides* × *nigra*] (109) (1949)

Eugenia - *Eugenia* L. (138) (1923)

Eulalia - *Miscanthus sinensis* Anderss. (56, 94, 109, 138, 163) (1852-1949)

Eulophus - *Perideridia americana* (Nutt. ex DC.) Reichenb. (3) (1977), *Perideridia* Reichnb. (158) (1900)

Eunanus - *Mimulus* L. (possibly) (158) (1900)

Euonymous - *Euonymus atropurpurea* Jacq. (52, 55, 57) (1911-1917)

Euonymus - *Euonymus* L. (138, 155) (1923-1942)

Eupatoire percefeuille (French) - *Eupatorium perfoliatum* L. (7) (1828)

Eupatorie perfoliée (French) - *Eupatorium perfoliatum* L. (6, 158) (1892–1900)

Eupatorio (Spanish) - *Eupatorium perfoliatum* L. (158) (1900)

Eupatorium - *Agrimonia eupatoria* L. (174, 177) (1753-1762), *Eupatorium* L. (138, 155) (1923-1942), *Eupatorium perfoliatum* L. (52, 57) (1917), *Eupatorium purpureum* L. (52) (1919)

Eupatory - *Teucrium scorodonia* L. (179) (1526)

Euphorbe à grandes fleurs (French) - *Euphorbia corollata* L. (6) (1892)

Euphorbe vomitive (French) - *Euphorbia ipecacuanhae* L. (6) (1892)

Euphorbia - *Euphorbia corollata* L. (52) (1919), *Euphorbia cyparissias* L. (45) (1896), *Euphorbia ipecacuanhae* L. (92) (1876), *Euphorbia* L. (155) (1942)

Euphorbia radix (Official name of Materia Medica) - *Euphorbia corollata* L. (7) (1828)

Euphraise (French) - *Euphrasia stricta* D. Wolff ex J.F. Lehm. (6) (1892)

Euphrasia - *Euphrasia stricta* D. Wolff ex J.F. Lehm. (52, 54) (1905-1919)

Euphrasy - *Euphrasia stricta* D. Wolff ex J.F. Lehm. (6) (1892)

Eurasian chestnut - *Castanea sativa* Mill. (109) (1949)

Eureka lily - *Lilium occidentale* Purdy (138) (1923)

Eureka Springs hawthorn - *Crataegus crus-galli* L. (155) (1942)

European alder - *Alnus glutinosa* (L.) Gaertn. (5, 92, 137, 138, 155, 156) (1876-1942), *Alnus incana* (L.) Moench (109) (1949)

European angelica - *Angelica archangelica* L. (57, 64) (1908-1917)

European ash - *Fraxinus excelsior* L. (109, 112, 138) (1923-1949)

European aspen - *Populus tremula* L. (92, 109, 137, 155) (1876-1949)

European avens - *Geum urbanum* L. (57, 92) (1876-1917)

European barberry - *Berberis vulgaris* L. (5, 15, 93, 138, 155, 156, 157) (1895-1936)

European basswood - *Tilia ×vulgaris* Hayne [*cordata* × *platyphyllos*] (112) (1937)

European beach grass [European beach-grass] - *Ammophila arenaria* (L.) Link (109) (1949)

European bean - *Vicia faba* L. (107, 109) (1919-1949)

European beech - *Fagus sylvatica* L. (107, 109, 135, 138) (1910-1949)

European bellflower - *Campanula rapunculoides* L. (5, 156) (1913-1923)

European bindweed [European bind-weed] - *Convolvulus arvensis* L. (56, 80) (1901-1913)

European birch - *Betula pubescens* Ehrh. (112) (1937)

European bird cherry - *Prunus padus* L. (109, 137, 138) (1923-1949)

European bittersweet [European bitter-sweet] - *Solanum dulcamara* L. (109) (1949)

European black alder - *Frangula alnus* Mill. (158) (1900)

European black currant - *Ribes nigrum* L. (109, 138) (1923-1949)

European black elderberry - *Sambucus nigra* L. (50) (present)

European black hawthorn - *Crataegus nigra* Waldst. & Kit. (137, 138) (1923-1931)

European brooklime - *Veronica beccabunga* L. (156) (1923)

European buckthorn - *Frangula alnus* Mill. (156) (1923)

European bugleweed - *Lycopus europaeus* L. (138) (1923)

European burningbush - *Euonymus europaea* L. (138) (1923)

European centaury - *Centaurium erythraea* Raf. (156) (1923), *Centaurium erythraea* Raf. (5, 156) (1913-1923)

European chain fern [European chainfern] - *Woodwardia radicans* (L.) J. Sm. (138) (1923)

European chestnut - *Castanea sativa* Mill. (107) (1919)

European columbine - *Aquilegia vulgaris* L. (5, 15, 155, 156) (1895-1942)

European common hazel nut [European common hazle nut] - *Corylus avellana* L. (42) (1814)

European corn salad - *Valerianella locusta* (L.) Lat. (5, 156) (1913-1923)

European cowlily - *Nuphar lutea* (L.) Sm. (155) (1942)

European cranberry - *Vaccinium oxycoccos* L. (5, 92, 109, 156) (1876-1949)

European cranberry bush [European cranberrybush, European cranberry-bush] - *Viburnum opulus* L. (50, 109 138) (1923–present)

European cranberry viburnum - *Viburnum opulus* L. (155) (1942)

European daisy - *Bellis perennis* L. (5, 158) (1900–1913)

European dogwood [European dog-wood] - *Euonymus europaea* L. (5, 156) (1913-1923)

European dune grass [European dunegrass] - *Leymus arenarius* (L.) Hochst. (138) (1923)

European dwarf cherry - *Prunus fruticosa* Pallas (109) (1949)

European elder - *Sambucus nigra* L. (82, 107, 109, 138, 155, 158) (1919-1949)

European field pansy - *Viola arvensis* Murray (5, 50) (1913–present)

European filbert - *Corylus avellana* L. (109) (1949)

European fly honeysuckle (European fly-honeysuckle) - *Lonicera xylosteum* L. (109, 138, 156) (1923-1949)

European globeflower - *Trollius europaeus* L. (2) (1895)

European glorybind - *Convolvulus arvensis* L. (155) (1942)

European goldenrod [European golden-rod] - *Solidago virgaurea* L. (19, 92, 138) (1840-1923)

European gooseberry - *Ribes uva-crispa* L. var. *sativum* DC. (82, 156) (1923-1930)

European grape - *Vitis vinifera* L. (107, 138) (1919-1923)

European green alder - *Alnus viridis* (Vill.) Lam. & DC. (138, 155) (1931-1942)

European hackberry - *Celtis australis* L. (138) (1923)

European hedge strawberry - *Fragaria vesca* L. (5) (1913)

European heliotrope - *Heliotropium europaeum* L. (5, 122) (1913-1937)

European hellebore - *Veratrum album* L. (60) (1902)

European hemlock - *Conium maculatum* L. (148) (1939) CO

European holly - *Ilex aquifolium* L. (92) (1876)

European hop - *Humulus lupulus* L. (109) (1949)

European hornbeam - *Carpinus betulus* L. (109, 138) (1923-1949)

European horse mint [European horsemint] - *Mentha spicata* L. (5, 158) (1900)

European larch - *Larix decidua* Mill. (28) (1850), *Larix decidua* Mill. (107, 109, 112, 138) (1919-1949)

European lily-of-the-valley [European lily of the valley] - *Convallaria majalis* L. (50) (present)

European linden - *Tilia* ×*vulgaris* Hayne [*cordata* × *platyphyllos*] (106, 109, 112) (1930-1949)

European maidenhair - *Adiantum capillus-veneris* L. (158) (1900)

European mallow - *Malva alcea* L. (5, 156) (1913-1923)

European marsilea - *Marsilea quadrifolia* L. (5) (1913)

European May Day tree - *Prunus padus* L. (82) (1930) IA

European meadowsweet - *Filipendula ulmaria* (L.) Maxim. (138) (1923)

European millet - *Panicum miliaceum* L. (111) (1915) Neb

European mistletoe - *Viscum album* L. (50, 138) (1923–present)

European morning glory - *Convolvulus arvensis* L. (80, 82) (1913-1930) IA

European mountain ash - *Sorbus aucuparia* L. (82, 135, 137, 138) (1910-1931)

European mulberry trees - *Morus alba* L. (182) (1791)

European pellitory - *Achillea ptarmica* L. (5, 156) (1913-1923)

European plum - *Prunus domestica* L. (82, 107, 109) (1919-1949)

European privet - *Ligustrum vulgare* L. (50, 122, 138, 155) (1923–present)

European pyrola - *Pyrola americana* Sweet (138, 155) (1923-1942)

European raspberry - *Rubus idaeus* L. (107, 138, 158) (1900-1919)

European red elder - *Sambucus racemosa* L. (109, 138) (1923-1949)

European red raspberry - *Rubus idaeus* L. (1) (1932)

European sage - *Salvia nemorosa* L. (85) (1932), *Salvia officinalis* L. (82) (1930) IA

European shadblow - *Amelanchier canadensis* (L.) Medik. (possibly) (138) (1923)

European silver fir - *Abies alba* Mill. (possibly) (158) (1900)

European skullcap - *Scutellaria galericulata* L. (5, 157, 158) (1900-1929)

European Solomon's-seal [European Solomonseal] - *Polygonatum multiflorum* (L.) All. (138) (1923)

European spindle-tree [European spindle tree] - *Euonymus europaea* L. (82) (1930) IA

European St. John's-wort - *Hypericum perforatum* L. (156) (1923)

European stickseed - *Lappula squarrosa* (Retz.) Dumort. (5, 50, 93, 155, 156, 158) (1900–present)

European strawberry - *Fragaria vesca* L. (155) (1942)

European thrift - *Armeria maritima* (P. Mill.) Willd (5, 156) (1913-1923)

European turkey oak - *Quercus cerris* L. (138) (1923)

European vervain - *Verbena officinalis* L. (5, 62, 97, 122, 156) (1912-1937)

European water horehound [European water hoarhound] - *Lycopus europaeus* L. (156) (1923)

European water-clover [European waterclover] - *Marsilea quadrifolia* L. (50) (present)

European waterlily [European water lily] - *Nymphaea alba* L. (92) (1876)

European wayfaring tree - *Viburnum lantana* L. (156) (1923)

European weeping birch - *Betula pendula* Roth (112, 138) (1923-1937)

European white birch - *Betula pendula* Roth (109) (1949), *Betula pubescens* Ehrh. (135, 137, 138, 158) (1900-1931)

European white oak - *Quercus robur* L. (20) (1857)

European white waterlily [European white water-lily] - *Nymphaea alba* L. (109, 138, 155) (1923-1949)

European whortleberry - *Vaccinium myrtillus* L. (138) (1923)

European willow - *Salix alba* L. (5, 49, 156) (1898)

European wood anemone - *Anemone nemorosa* L. (109, 137, 155) (1923-1949)

European wood betony [European woodbetony] - *Pedicularis palustris* L. (138) (1923)

European wood strawberry - *Fragaria vesca* L. (5, 72, 158) (1900)

European yellow lupine - *Lupinus luteus* L. (138) (1923)

European yellow oxalis - *Oxalis stricta* L. (155) (1942)

Eurotia - *Krascheninnikovia* Guldenstaedt (158) (1900)

Evan's root [Evans-root, Evan root] - *Geum rivale* L (5, 92, 156, 158) (1876-1923), *Geum virginianum* L. (7) (1828)

Evening beauty - *Mirabilis longiflora* L. (92) (1876)

Evening campion - *Silene latifolia* Poir. subsp. *alba* (Mill.) Greuter & Burdet (109, 138, 155, 156) (1923-1949), *Silene nivea* (Nutt.) Muhl. ex Otth (50) (present)

Evening lychnis - *Silene latifolia* Poir. subsp. *alba* (Mill.) Greuter & Burdet (5, 15, 156) (1895)

Evening rain lily - *Cooperia drummondii* Herb. (50) (present)

Evening star [Evening-star] - *Cooperia drummondii* Herb. (138) (1923), *Mentzelia decapetala* (Pursh ex Sims) Urban & Gilg ex Gilg (127) (1933) ND

Evening stock - *Matthiola longipetala* (Vent.) DC. (109) (1949)

Evening tree-primrose - *Oenothera biennis* L. (187) (1818)

Evening trumpet-flower [Evening trumpet flower] - *Gelsemium sempervirens* (L.) J. St.-Hil. (5, 64, 156) (1907-1923)

Evening-blooming lychnis - *Silene latifolia* Poir. subsp. *alba* (Mill.) Greuter & Burdet (158) (1900)

Evening-primrose [Evening primrose, Eveningprimrose] - *Calylophus serrulatus* (Nutt.) Raven (96, 98) (1891-1926), *Oenothera albicaulis* Pursh (158) (1900), *Oenothera biennis* L. (14, 46, 49, 53, 57, 80, 85, 92, 107, 114, 122, 124, 131, 145, 157) (1879-1937), *Oenothera* L. (1, 2, 50, 63, 93, 109, 138, 155, 156, 158) (1895–present)

Evening-star rainlily [Eveningstar rainlily] - *Cooperia drummondii* Herb. (155) (1942)

Ever grass [Ever-grass] - *Lolium perenne* L. (5, 119) (1913-1938)

Ever-bearing grape [Everbearing grape] - *Vitis rotundifolia* Michx. var. *munsoniana* (Simpson ex Munson) M.O. Moore (15) (1895)

Evergreeen - *Hylotelephium telephium* (L.) H. Ohba. subsp. *telephium* (5, 73, 156) (1892-1923) Chesterton MD, *Lycopodium complanatum* L. (78) (1898), *Prunus caroliniana* (P. Mill.) Aiton (74) (1893) GA, *Selaginella rupestris* (L.) Spring (92) (1876)

Evergreen alkanet - *Pentaglottis sempervirens* (L.) Tausch ex Bailey (165) (1807)

Evergreen andromeda - *Chamaedaphne calyculata* (L.) Moench (187) (1818), *Lyonia lucida* (Lam.) K. Koch (183) (~1756)

Evergreen bignonia [Ever-green bignonia] - *Campsis radicans* (L.) Seem. ex Bureau (8) (1785), *Gelsemium sempervirens* (L.) J. St.-Hil. (8) (1785)

Evergreen blueberry - *Vaccinium myrsinites* Lam. (156) (1923)

Evergreen bugloss - *Pentaglottis sempervirens* (L.) Tausch ex Bailey (138, 155) (1931-1942)

Evergreen burningbush - *Euonymus japonicus* Thunb. (138) (1923)

Evergreen candytuft - *Iberis sempervirens* L. (138) (1923)

Evergreen cassena - *Ilex vomitoria* Aiton (5, 156) (1913-1923)

Evergreen cassine [Ever-green cassine] - *Ilex cassine* L. (8) (1785)

Evergreen cherry - *Prunus caroliniana* (P. Mill.) Aiton (106) (1930), *Prunus ilicifolia* (Nutt. ex Hook. & Arn.) D. Dietr. (107) (1919)

Evergreen coral honeysuckle - *Lonicera sempervirens* L. (122, 124) (1937)

Evergreen dwarf andromeda [Ever-green dwarf andromeda] - *Chamaedaphne calyculata* (L.) Moench (8) (1785)

Evergreen fern - *Polypodium virginianum* L. (86) (1878)

Evergreen grass - *Arrhenatherum elatius* (L.) Beauv. ex J. Presl & C. Presl (5, 45, 67, 87, 88) (1884-1913), *Lolium pratense* (Huds.) S.J. Darbyshire (5, 45, 66, 68, 87) (1884-1913)

Evergreen holly - *Ilex opaca* Aiton (19) (1840), *Ilex vomitoria* Aiton (122, 124) (1937) TX

Evergreen honeysuckle [Ever-green honeysuckle] - *Lonicera sempervirens* L. (8) (1785)

Evergreen laurel-leaf tuliptree [Ever-green laurel-leaved tulip-tree] - *Magnolia grandiflora* L. (8) (1785)

Evergreen millet - *Sorghum halepense* (L.) Pers. (5, 87, 88) (1884-1913)

Evergreen oak - *Quercus agrifolia* Née (75, 161) (1857-1894) CA, *Quercus ilex* L. (92) (1876), *Quercus oblongifolia* Torr. (107) (1919)

Evergreen rose - *Rosa bracteata* Wendl. (5) (1913)

Evergreen shining-leaf andromeda [Ever-green shining-leaved andromeda] - *Lyonia lucida* (Lam.) K. Koch (8) (1785)

Evergreen snakeroot [Evergreen snake root, Evergreen snake-root] - *Polygala paucifolia* Willd. (5, 7, 92, 156) (1828-1923)

Evergreen spindletree [Ever-greenspindle tree] - *Euonymus americanus* L. (possibly) (8) (1785)

Evergreen stonecrop - *Sedum hybridum* L. (155) (1942)

Evergreen sumac - *Rhus virens* Lindheimer ex Gray (122, 124) (1937) TX

Evergreen tamarix - *Tamarix aphylla* (L.) H. Karst. (124) (1937) TX

Evergreen taxodium - *Sequoia sempervirens* (Lamb. ex D. Don) Endl. (20) (1857)

Evergreen thorn - *Pyracantha coccinea* M. Roemer (5, 156) (1913-1923)

Evergreen white oak - *Quercus oblongifolia* Torr. (75) (1894)

Evergreen wild cherry - *Prunus caroliniana* (P. Mill.) Aiton (possibly) (106) (1930)

Evergreen willow-leaf oak [Evergreen willow-leaved oak] - *Quercus virginiana* Mill. (8) (1785)

Evergreen winterberry [Evergreen winter-berry] - *Ilex glabra* (L.) Gray (5, 8, 156) (1785-1923)

Evergreen wood fern, Evergreen wood-fern - *Dryopteris marginalis* (L.) A. Gray (3, 5, 64, 158) (1900-1977)

Everlasting - *Anaphalis margaritacea* (L.) Benth. & Hook (2, 106, 190) (~1759-1930), *Antennaria* Gaertner (1, 2, 4, 109, 127, 158) (1895-1986), *Filago* L. (158) (1900), *Gnaphalium* L. (1, 2, 4, 10, 92, 93, 158) (1818-1986), *Gnaphalium palustre* Nutt. (3) (1977), *Helichrysum bracteatum* (Vent.) Andr. (109) (1949), *Helichrysum* Mill. (138) (1923), *Hylotelephium telephium* (L.) H. Ohba. subsp. *telephium* (5, 73, 156) (1892-1923) Hemmingford Quebec, *Pseudognaphalium macounii* (Greene) Kartesz (85, 156) (1923-1932), *Saxifraga virginiensis* Michx. var. *virginiensis* (5) (1913), *Saxifraga virginiensis* Michx. (76, 156) (1896-1923) Lynn MA

Everlasting flower - *Anaphalis margaritacea* (L.) Benth. & Hook (46) (1879)

Everlasting grass [Everlasting-grass] - *Eriochloa punctata* (L.) Desv. ex Hamilton (5, 94, 155, 163) (1852-1942)

Everlasting pea [Euerlasting Pease] - *Lathyrus* L. (10, 82, 156) (1818-1930), *Lathyrus latifolius* L. (3, 4, 5, 19, 46, 109, 156, 158) (1879-1986), *Lathyrus polymorphus* Nutt. subsp. *polymorphus* (5, 158) (1900–1913), *Lathyrus sylvestris* L. (178) (1526)

Everlasting-grass - *Onobrychis viciifolia* Scop. (158) (1900)

Ever-living borage [Euerliuing Borage] - *Pentaglottis sempervirens* (L.) Tausch ex Bailey (178) (1526)

Ever-trembling asp - *Populus tremuloides* Michx. (46) (1629)

Everwhite [Ever-white] - *Anaphalis margaritacea* (L.) Benth. & Hook (156, 158) (1900-1923)

Eve's-cups [Eve's cup, Eve's cups] - *Sarracenia flava* L. (92) (1876), *Sarracenia purpurea* L. (6) (1892)

Eve's-darning-needle [Eve's darning needle, Eve's darning-needle] - *Yucca filamentosa* L. (5, 73, 156, 158) (1892-1923) Fort Worth TX

Eve's-necklace [Eve's necklace] - *Sophora affinis* Torr. & Gray (97) (1937) OK

Eve's-thread [Eve's thread] - *Hemerocallis fulva* (L.) L. (75, 156) (1894-1923) WV, *Yucca filamentosa* L. (158) (1900)

Eveweed [Eve-weed] - *Hesperis matronalis* L. (156) (1923)

Evi or hevi (Polynesia) - *Spondias dulcis* Parkinson (110) (1886)

Evodia - *Tetradium* Lour. (138) (1923)

Evolvulus - *Evolvulus* L. (155, 158) (1900-1942), *Evolvulus nuttallianus* J.A. Schultes (5, 93, 97, 131) (1899-1937)

Ewe - *Taxus baccata* L. (178, 179) (1526-1596)

Ewe tree - *Tsuga canadensis* (L.) Carr. (46) (1609)

Ewe-gown [Ewe gown] - *Bellis perennis* L. (5, 158) (1900–1913)

Exciter-of-Desire [Exciter of Desire] (India) - *Cannabis sativa* L. (6) (1892)

Eyebalm [Eye-balm, Eye balm] - *Hydrastis canadensis* L. (5, 7, 49, 64, 92, 156) (1828-1923)

Eyebane - *Chamaesyce nutans* (Lag.) Small (4, 50) (1986–present)

Eyeberry [Eye-berry] - *Gaultheria procumbens* L. (156) (1923), *Mitchella repens* L. (156) (1923), *Rubus pubescens* Raf. var. *pubescens* (105) (1932)

Eyebright [Eye-bright, Eye bright] - *Anagallis arvensis* L. (5, 156, 158) (1900-1923), *Chamaesyce hypericifolia* (L.) Millsp. (6, 19, 49, 82) (1840-1930), *Drosera rotundifolia* L. (5, 73, 156, 158) (1892-1923) NH, *Euphrasia* L. (1, 10, 156, 167) (1814-1932), *Euphrasia nemorosa* (Pers.) Wallr. (5, 156) (1913-1923), *Euphrasia stricta* D. Wolff ex J.F. Lehm. (6, 7, 10, 19, 49, 52, 53, 54, 57, 58, 92) (1818-1922), *Houstonia caerulea* L. (5, 73, 75, 156) (1892-1923) Isles of Shoals ME, *Lobelia inflata* L. (5, 6, 69, 92, 156, 157, 158, 186) (1814-1929), *Mimulus moschatus* Dougl. ex Lindl. (156) (1923), *Mimulus ringens* L. (156) (1923), *Monotropa uniflora* L. (5, 156, 158) (1900–1923), *Pedicularis labradorica* Wirsing (5) (1913), *Sabatia angularis* (L.) Pursh (92) (1876), *Veronica chamaedrys* L. (5, 156) (1913-1923)

Eye-grass [Eyegrass] - *Xyris* L. (7, 10) (1818-1828)

Eyeroot [Eye-root, Eye root] - *Hydrastis canadensis* L. (5, 49, 64, 92, 156) (1876-1923)

Eyeseed [Eye seed] - *Salvia verbenaca* L. (5, 156) (1913-1923)

Ezhon zhide (Omaha-Ponca, red elm) - *Ulmus rubra* Muhl. (37) (1919)

Ezhon zhide gthigthide (Omaha-Ponca, slippery red elm) - *Ulmus rubra* Muhl. (37) (1919)

Ezhon zhon (Omaha-Ponca) - *Ulmus americana* L. (37) (1919)

Ezhon zhon ska (White elm) (Omaha-Ponca) - *Ulmus americana* L. (37) (1919)

Ezhon zhon zi (Omaha-Ponca, yellow elm) - *Ulmus thomasii* Sarg. (37) (1919)

F

Fabes - *Ribes uva-crispa* L. var. *sativum* DC. (5, 156) (1913-1923) no longer in use by 1923

Fagara (French) - *Zanthoxylum americanum* Mill. (8) (1785), *Zanthoxylum* L. (8) (1785)

Faggina (Italian) - *Fagopyrum esculentum* Moench (46, 110) (1879-1886)

Fagiolo (Italian) - *Phaseolus vulgaris* L. (possibly) (110) (1886)

Fagiuolo (Italian) - *Phaseolus vulgaris* L. (107) (1919)

Fair fescue - *Festuca filiformis* Pourret (138) (1923)

Fair-hair hyacinth [Faire-haired Iacinth] - *Muscari comosum* (L.) Mill. (180) (1633)

Fair-hair hyacinth of Turkey [Faire haired Iacint of Turkie] - *Muscari comosum* (L.) Mill. (178) (1596)

Fairies - *Aquilegia formosa* Fisch. ex DC. (76) (1896) Norridgewock ME, white varieties

Fair-maid-of-France [Fair maids of France] - *Achillea ptarmica* L. (5, 156) (1913-1923)

Fairy bells [Fairybells, Fairy bells] - *Digitalis pupurea* L. (5, 69, 156) (1903–1923), *Disporum lanuginosum* (Michx.) Nichols (156) (1923), *Disporum* Salisb. ex D. Don (50, 138, 155, 156) (1923–present), *Disporum trachycarpum* (S. Wats.) Benth. & Hook. f. (3) (1977)

Fairy candles - *Cimicifuga racemosa* (L.) Nutt. (156) (1923)

Fairy cap - *Digitalis pupurea* L. (5, 69, 156) (1903–1923)

Fairy cheeses [Fairy-cheese, Fairy-cheeses] - *Malva rotundifolia* L. (5, 106, 156, 157, 158) (1900-1930)

Fairy circle [Fairy circles, Fairy-circle] - *Juniperus communis* L. (73, 157, 158) (1892-1929) Eastern MA, *Juniperus communis* L. var. *montana* Ait. (5) (1913)

Fairy creeper - *Adlumia fungosa* (Aiton) Greene ex B. S. P. (5, 73, 156) (1892-1923) Fredericton, NB

Fairy cup - *Mitella diphylla* L. (5, 74, 156) (1893-1923) NY

Fairy fingers - *Digitalis pupurea* L. (5, 69, 92) (1876-1913)

Fairy flax - *Linum catharticum* L. (5, 156) (1913-1923)

Fairy gloves [Fairy glove, Fairy's glove] - *Digitalis pupurea* L. (5, 92, 156) (1876-1923)

Fairy grass - *Briza media* L. (5) (1913)

Fairy horse [Fairies' horse] - *Senecio jacobea* L. (5, 156) (1913-1923)

Fairy lantern - *Calochortus albus* Dougl. ex Benth. (109) (1949)

Fairy lily - *Zephyranthes atamasca* (L.) Herbert (5, 156) (1913-1923), *Zephyranthes* Herbert (156) (1923)

Fairy lint - *Linum catharticum* L. (5, 156) (1913-1923)

Fairy paintbrush [Fairy's paint-brush] - *Hieracium aurantiacum* L. (156) (1923)

Fairy slipper - *Calypso bulbosa* (L.) Oakes (50) (present), *Calypso bulbosa* (L.) Oakes var. *americana* (R. Br. ex Ait. f.) Luer (50) (present), *Calypso* Salisb. (50) (present)

Fairy smoke [Fairy-smoke] - *Monotropa uniflora* L. (5, 75, 156, 157, 158) (1900-1929) Deering ME

Fairy sword [Fairyswords] - *Cheilanthes lindheimeri* (Sm.) Hook. (50) (present)

Fairy table [Fairy-table] - *Hydrocotyle* L. (158) (1900)

Fairy thimbles - *Digitalis pupurea* L. (5, 69) (1903-1913)

Fairy wand [Fairywand] - *Chamaelirium luteum* (L.) A. Gray (50, 138, 156) (1923–present), *Chamaelirium* Willd. (109) (1949)

Fairy weed - *Digitalis pupurea* L. (5) (1913)

Fairy-wand bladderwort - *Utricularia juncea* Vahl (5) (1913)

Faitour's grass [Faitour's-grass] - *Euphorbia esula* L. (156, 158) (1900-1923), *Euphorbia esula* L. var. *esula* (5) (1913)

Fajol (Spanish) - *Fagopyrum esculentum* Moench (46) (1879)

Fakos or fakai (Greek) - *Lens culinaris* Medik. (110) (1886)

Falcaria - *Falcaria* Fabr. (50) (present)

Falkland Island sedge - *Carex macloviana* d'Urv. (5) (1913)

Fall aster - *Symphyotrichum lowrieanum* (Porter) Nesom (5) (1913)

Fall dandelion - *Leontodon autumnalis* L. (5, 46, 156) (1879-1923)

Fall gramma grass - *Bouteloua curtipendula* (Michx.) Torr. var. *curtipendula* (99) (1923)

Fall grape - *Vitis cinerea* (Engelm.) Millard var. *cinerea* (177) (1762), *Vitis cinerea* (Engelm.) Millard var. *helleri* (Bailey) M.O. Moore (15) (1895)

Fall lettuce - *Lactuca canadensis* L. (156) (1923)

Fall marsh grass - *Spartina cynosuroides* (L.) Roth (87) (1884), *Spartina pectinata* Bosc ex Link (99) (1923)

Fall meadow rue - *Thalictrum pubescens* Pursh (5) (1913)

Fall panic grass [Fall panicgrass] - *Panicum dichotomiflorum* Michx. (50) (present), *Panicum dichotomiflorum* Michx. var. *dichotomiflorum* (50) (present)

Fall panicum - *Panicum dichotomiflorum* Michx. (3, 122, 155) (1937-1977)

Fall phlox - *Phlox paniculata* L. (3, 4, 50) (1977–present)

Fall poison - *Amianthium muscitoxicum* (Walt.) Gray (92) (1876)

Fall prairie thistle - *Cirsium altissimum* (L.) Hill (47) (1852)

Fall redtop [Fall red-top] - *Tridens flavus* (L.) A.S. Hitchc. (99) (1923)

Fall rosette grass - *Dichanthelium wilcoxianum* (Vasey) Freckmann (50) (present)

Fall witch grass [Fall witchgrass, Fall witch-grass] - *Digitaria cognata* (J.A. Schultes) Pilger (94) (1901), *Digitaria cognata* (J.A. Schultes) Pilger var. *cognata* (3, 122, 155, 163) (1852-1977), *Digitaria* Haller (1) (1932)

Fallflower [Fall flower, Fall-flower] - *Symphyotrichum ericoides* (L.) Nesom var. *ericoides* (5, 156, 158) (1900–1923)

Fall-roses [Fall roses] - *Aster* L. (76) (1896), *Callistephus chinensis* (L.) Nees (73) (1892) Mansfield OH

Falsche Acazie (German) - *Robinia pseudoacacia* L. (158) (1900)

Falsche Acazie [Falsche Acacien] (German) - *Robinia pseudoacacia* L. (6, 158) (1892-1900)

False acacia [False acasia] - *Robinia pseudoacacia* L. (2, 5, 6, 14, 19, 49, 63, 82, 93, 106, 107, 156, 157, 158, 187) (1818-1936), *Senna marilandica* (L.) Link (42) (1814)

False agave - *Hechtia texensis* S. Wats. (122, 124) (1937) TX

False alder - *Ilex verticillata* (L.) Gray (5, 92, 156) (1876-1923)

False alkanet - *Buglossoides arvensis* (L.) I.M. Johnston (156) (1923)

False aloe [False-aloe] - *Aletris farinosa* L. (19) (1840), *Aletris* L. (167) (1814), *Manfreda virginica* (L.) Salisb. ex Rose (5, 49, 50, 58, 92, 97, 156) (1869–present)

False anemone - *Enemion biternatum* Raf. (156) (1923), *Enemion* Raf. (156) (1923)

False anise - *Agastache foeniculum* (Pursh) Kuntze (127) (1933) ND

False asphodel - *Tofieldia glutinosa* (Michx.) Pers. subsp. *glutinosa* (5) (1913), *Tofieldia* Huds. (2) (1895), *Tofieldia racemosa* (Walt.) Britton, Sterns & Poggenb. (5) (1913)

False asphodel - *Triantha glutinosa* (Michx.) Baker (possibly) (156) (1923)

False aster - *Boltonia asteroides* (L.) L'Hér. (19, 127) (1840-1933)

False baby's-breath [False babys-breath] - *Galium aristatum* L. (109) (1949), *Galium mollugo* L. (109) (1949)

False balm - *Monarda clinopodioides* Gray (97) (1937) OK

False banana - *Asimina triloba* (L.) Dunal (5, 156, 157, 158) (1900-1929)

False bark-tree - *Iva* L. (167) (1814)

False beechdrops [False beech-drops, False beech drops] - *Monotropa hypopithys* L. (2, 5, 92, 156) (1840-1923)

138

False berry - *Ilex verticillata* (L.) Gray (19) (1840)
False bindweed - *Calystegia* R. Br. (50) (present)
False bittersweet [False bitter-sweet or false bitter sweet] - *Celastrus scandens* L. (5, 19, 49, 57, 58, 61, 92, 109, 135, 156, 157) (1840-1949)
False bog rush - *Kyllinga brevifolia* Rottb. (19) (1840), *Rhynchospora glomerata* (L.) Vahl (5, 156) (1913-1923)
False boneset - *Brickellia* Ell. (1, 4, 93, 158) (1900-1986), *Brickellia eupatorioides* (L.) Shinners (50) (present), *Brickellia eupatorioides* (L.) Shinners var. *chlorolepis* (Woot. & Standl.) B.L. Turner (50) (present), *Brickellia eupatorioides* (L.) Shinners var. *corymbulosa* (Torr. & Gray) Shinners (3, 50, 98) (1926–present), *Brickellia eupatorioides* (L.) Shinners var. *eupatorioides* (5, 19, 50, 72, 82, 85, 92, 93, 95, 97, 122, 124, 156) (1840–present), *Brickellia eupatorioides* (L.) Shinners var. *texana* (Shinners) Shinners (50) (present)
False box - *Cornus florida* L. (5, 19, 92) (1840-1913)
False boxwood [False box-wood, False box wood] - *Cornus florida* L. (5, 156) (1913-1923)
False broomweed - *Haploesthes* Gray (4, 50) (1986–present), *Haploesthes greggii* Gray (50) (present)
False buckthorn - *Sideroxylon lanuginosum* Michx. (107, 156) (1919-1923)
False buckwheat - *Polygonum* L. (5) (1913), *Polygonum scandens* L. (4, 158) (1900-1986), *Polygonum scandens* L. var. *dumetorum* (L.) Gleason (5) (1913), *Polygonum scandens* L. var. *scandens* (1, 85) (1932)
False buffalo grass [False buffalograss, False buffalo-grass] - *Monroa squarrosa* (Nutt.) Torr. (3, 5, 11, 50, 75, 85, 94, 122, 129, 140, 145, 152, 155, 163) (1852–present), *Monroa* Torr. (1, 50, 93) (1932–present), *Muhlenbergia richardsonis* (Trin.) Rydb. (111) (1915) Neb
False bugbane - *Trautvetteria caroliniensis* (Walt.) Vail (5, 156) (1913-1923), *Trautvetteria* F. & M. (2, 156) (1895-1923)
False bugloss - *Lithospermum canescens* (Michx.) Lehm. (19) (1840)
False bunium - *Barbarea vulgaris* W.T. Aiton (possibly) (180) (1633)
False buttonweed - *Spermacoce* L. (50) (present)
False calais - *Nothocalais* (Gray) Greene (158) (1900), *Nothocalais cuspidata* (Pursh) Greene (72, 131) (1899-1907)
False camomile [False chamomile, False-chamomile] - *Boltonia asteroides* (L.) L'Hér. (19, 156) (1840-1923), *Matricaria* L. (138) (1923), *Matricaria recutita* L. (4) (1986)
False chinaroot [False china root, False china-root] - *Smilax pseudochina* L. (5, 49, 156) (1913-1923)
False choak-dog - *Matelea obliqua* (Jacq.) Woods. (19) (1840)
False cloak fern - *Argyrochosma* (Sm.) Windham (50) (present)
False cloak fern - *Argyrochosma dealbata* (Pursh) Windham (4) (1986)
False cohosh - *Caulophyllum thalictroides* (L.) Michx. (19) (1840)
False coltsfoot [False colt's foot] - *Asarum canadense* L. (5, 19, 64, 92, 156, 158) (1840-1923)
False couch grass - *Elymus ×pseudorepens* (Scribn. & J.G. Sm.) Barkworth & D.R. Dewey [*lanceolatus × trachycaulus*] (5, 56, 94) (1901-1913)
False cowslip - *Dodecatheon meadia* L. (19) (1840)
False crawley - *Pterospora andromedea* Nutt. (92, 156, 158) (1876-1923)
False cress - *Thlaspi arvense* L. (156) (1923)
False crowfoot - *Asarum canadense* L. (156) (1923)
False cypress [False-cypress] - *Chamaecyparis* Spach. (2, 109) (1895-1949)
False daffodil [False-daffodil] - *Sternbergia lutea* (L.) Ker-Gawl. ex Spreng. (138) (1923)
False daisy - *Eclipta prostrata* (L.) L. (50) (present)
False damiana - *Chrysactinia mexicana* Gray (122) (1937) TX
False dandelion - *Agoseris glauca* (Pursh) Raf. (3, 127, 156) (1923-1977), *Agoseris glauca* (Pursh) Raf. (5) (1913), *Agoseris* Raf. (4, 156) (1923-1986), *Krigia biflora* (Walt.) Blake (75, 156) (1894-

1923), *Krigia biflora* (Walt.) Blake var. *biflora* (5) (1913), *Nothocalais* (Gray) Greene (158) (1900), *Nothocalais cuspidata* (Pursh) Greene (3, 5, 85, 93, 95, 98) (1911-1936), *Pyrrhopappus carolinianus* (Walt.) DC. (3, 157) (1929–1977), *Pyrrhopappus* DC. (1, 2, 158) (1900-1932)
False dogfennel [False dog-fennel, False dog fennel] - *Dyssodia papposa* (Vent.) A.S. Hitchc. (5, 97, 122, 156, 158) (1900-1937)
False dogfennel [False dog-fennel, False dog fennel] - *Dyssodia tagetoides* Torr. & Gray (50) (present)
False dogwood - *Acer pensylvanicum* L. (92, 156) (1898-1923), *Acer spicatum* Lam. (19) (1840)
False dragonhead [False dragon-head, False-dragonhead, False dragon's headFalse dragonshead] - *Dracocephalum* L. (1) (1932), *Physostegia angustifolia* Fern. (4) (1986), *Physostegia* Benth. (2, 4, 138) (1895-1986), *Physostegia virginiana* (L.) Benth. (3, 63, 72, 82, 131, 156, 158) (1899-1977)
False dropseed - *Brachyelytrum septentrionale* (Babel) G. Tucker (19) (1840)
False eglantine (possibly) - *Rosa carolina* L. (46) (1649)
False elm - *Celtis occidentalis* L. (5, 156, 158) (1900–1923)
False feverfew [False fever-few] - *Parthenium* L. (167) (1814)
False flax [Falseflax] - *Camelina* Crantz (1, 4, 50, 93, 155, 156, 158) (1900–present), *Camelina sativa* (L.) Crantz (5, 15, 70, 72, 80, 85, 97, 107, 131, 145, 156, 157, 158) (1895-1937), *Gilia incisa* Benth. (122, 124) (1937), *Lepidium campestre* (L.) Aiton f. (5, 92, 156, 158) (1876-1932), *Linaria vulgaris* Mill. (6) (1892)
False foxglove - *Agalinis* Raf. (50) (present), *Aureolaria flava* (L.) Farw. var. *flava* (19) (1840), *Aureolaria pedicularia* (L.) Raf. var. *pedicularia* (156) (1923), *Aureolaria* Raf. (1, 4, 50) (1932–present), *Aureolaria virginica* (L.) Pennell (92) (1876), *Dasistoma* Raf. (158) (1900)
False fringe tree - *Cotinus coggygria* Scop. (19, 92) (1840-1876)
False garlic [Falsegarlic] - *Nothoscordum* Kunth. (1, 50, 155) (1932–present)
False gaura - *Stenosiphon linifolius* (Nutt. ex James) Heynh. (50) (present)
False gentian - *Gentianella amarella* (L.) Boerner subsp. *acuta* (Michx.) J. Gillett (156) (1923)
False goat's-beard [False goat's-beard] - *Astilbe biternata* (Vent.) Britt. (5, 156) (1913-1923)
False goats-beard astilbe [False goatsbeard astilbe] - *Astilbe biternata* (Vent.) Britt. (155) (1942)
False golden-aster [False goldenaster] - *Heterotheca* Cass. (50) (present)
False goldenrod [False goldenrod] - *Solidago sphacelata* Raf. (5, 156) (1913-1923)
False goldenweed - *Oonopsis* Nutt. (50) (present)
False grape [False grapes] - *Ampelopsis* Michx. (42) (1814), *Parthenocissus quinquefolia* (L.) Planch. (3, 6, 19, 37, 49, 58, 92, 156, 157, 158) (1840-1929)
False grass - *Leersia oryzoides* (L.) Sw. (5) (1913)
False gromwell - *Onosmodium* Michx. (1, 2, 4, 82, 156, 158) (1895-1986), *Onosmodium molle* Michx. (82) (1930), *Onosmodium molle* Michx. subsp. *hispidissimum* (Mackenzie) Boivin (3) (1977), *Onosmodium molle* Michx. subsp. *occidentale* (Mackenzie) Cochrane (3, 85) (1932-1977), *Onosmodium virginianum* (L.) A. DC. (19, 40, 48, 49, 58, 92) (1840-1928)
False groundnut [False ground nut] - *Arachis hypogaea* L. (19) (1840)
False Guinea grass - *Sorghum halepense* (L.) Pers. (87) (1884)
False heath - *Hudsonia ericoides* L. (19) (1840)
False heather - *Hudsonia* L. (158) (1900), *Hudsonia tomentosa* Nutt. (5, 156, 158) (1900-1923)
False hedgehyssop [False hedge hyssop] - *Lindernia dubia* (L.) Pennell var. *dubia* (19) (1840)
False hellebore [False-hellebore] - *Adonis vernalis* L. (49, 57, 92) (1876-1917), *Veratrum californicum* Dur. var. *californicum* (148)

(1939), *Veratrum* L. (1, 50, 109, 138, 156) (1923–present), *Veratrum viride* Ait. (5, 6, 64, 71, 156) (1892-1923)

False helleborine - *Epipactis helleborine* (L.) Crantz (156) (1923)

False hemp - *Galeopsis bifida* Boenn. (156) (1923), *Rhus hirta* (L.) Sudworth (19, 92) (1840-1876)

False honeysuckle [False-honeysuckle] - *Rhododendron canadense* (L.) Torr. (19) (1840), *Rhododendron periclymenoides* (Michx.) Shinners (156) (1923)

False horehound [False hoarhound] - *Ballota nigra* L. (19, 156) (1840-1923)

False hyacinth - *Camassia scilloides* (Raf.) Cory (156) (1923)

False ice plant - *Sedum ternatum* Michx. (19) (1840)

False indigo [False-indigo] - *Amorpha canescens* Pursh (22) (1893), *Amorpha fruticosa* L. (3, 4, 5, 9, 37, 63, 72, 82, 85, 93, 95, 97, 106, 112, 113, 114, 130, 131, 156, 157, 158) (1873-1986), *Amorpha* L. (1, 2, 50, 93, 106, 138, 158) (1895–present), *Baptisia australis* (L.) R. Br. ex Aiton f. (92, 156, 158) (1876-1923), *Baptisia tinctoria* (L.) R. Br. ex Aiton f. (6, 156) (1892-1923), *Baptisia* Vent. (2, 4, 63, 82, 125) (1899-1986)

False ipecac - *Gillenia trifoliata* (L.) Moench (64, 156) (1907-1923), *Triosteum perfoliatum* L. (6) (1892)

False ipecacuanha - *Triosteum perfoliatum* L. (186) (1814)

False jalap - *Mirabilis jalapa* L. (92) (1876), *Mirabilis* L. (7) (1828)

False jasmine - *Gelsemium sempervirens* (L.) J. St.-Hil. (6) (1892)

False Jerusalem cherry [False Jerusalem-cherry] - *Solanum capsicastrum* Link ex Schauer (109, 138) (1923-1949)

False jessamine - *Lycium barbarum* L. (156) (1923)

False Jesuit's bark [False Jesuit's-bark] - *Iva frutescens* L. (5) (1913), *Iva frutescens* L. subsp. *oraria* (Bartlett) R.C. Jackson (156) (1923)

False John's-wort [False John's wort, False johnswort] - *Hypericum gentianoides* (L.) Britton, Sterns & Poggenb. (5, 19, 92, 157) (1840-1929)

False lettuce - *Lactuca floridana* (L.) Gaertn. (5, 85) (1913-1932), *Lactuca floridana* (L.) Gaertn. var. *villosa* (Jacq.) Cronq. (5) (1913)

False lily-of-the-valley - *Maianthemum canadense* Desf. (5, 127, 158) (1900-1933), *Maianthemum* G.H. Weber ex Wiggers (109) (1949)

False loosestrife [False loose-strife] - *Ludwigia* L. (1, 2, 4, 93, 106, 156, 158) (1895-1986), *Ludwigia palustris* (L.) Ell. (5, 156, 157, 158) (1900-1929), *Ludwigia polycarpa* Short & Peter (5, 156) (1913-1923)

False lupine - *Thermopsis mollis* (Michx.) M. A. Curtis (156) (1923), *Thermopsis* R. Br. ex Aiton f. (158) (1900), *Thermopsis rhombifolia* (Nutt. ex Pursh) Nutt. ex Richards. (5, 37, 126) (1913-1933)

False madwort - *Berteroa* DC. (50) (present)

False mahogany - *Persea borbonia* (L.) Spreng. (5) (1913)

False mallow [False-mallow, Falsemallow, False mallows] - *Malvastrum* Gray (2, 15, 50, 93, 109, 155, 158) (1895–present), *Napaea dioica* L. (possibly) (19) (1840), *Sida spinosa* L. (5, 92, 156) (1876-1923), *Sphaeralcea coccinea* (Nutt.) Rydb. subsp. *coccinea* (127, 157) (1900-1933)

False manna - *Alhagi maurorum* Medik. (92) (1876), *Larix decidua* Mill. (92) (1876), *Pinus lambertiana* Dougl. (92) (1876), *Tamarix gallica* L. (92) (1876)

False mayweed - *Tripleurospermum maritima* (L.) W.D.J. Koch subsp. *maritima* (50) (present)

False meadowrue [False meadow rue] - *Enemion biternatum* Raf. (82) (1930) IA

False melic [Falsemelic] - *Schizachne* Hack. (50) (present), *Schizachne purpurascens* (Torr.) Swall. (3, 50, 140, 155) (1942–present)

False mercury [False mercurie] - *Chenopodium bonus-henricus* L. (178) (1526)

False mermaid - *Floerkea proserpinacoides* Willd. (5, 13, 15, 19, 156) (1840-1923), *Floerkea* Willd. (1, 2) (1895-1932)

False mesquite grass - *Buchloe dactyloides* (Nutt.) Engelm. (87) (1884)

False mistletoe - *Phoradendron leucarpum* (Raf.) Reveal & M.C. Johnston (2, 156) (1895–1923)

False miterwort [False mitrewort, False mitre wort] - *Tiarella cordifolia* L. (5, 92, 156) (1876-1923), *Tiarella* L. (1, 2, 109) (1895-1949)

False motherwort - *Ballota nigra* L. (19) (1840)

False mountain mint - *Pycnanthemum pycnanthemoides* (Leavenworth) Fern. var. *pycnanthemoides* (19) (1840)

False mustard - *Polanisia dodecandra* (L.) DC. subsp. *dodecandra* (5, 7, 19, 92, 156, 157, 158) (1828-1929)

False needle grass [False needle-grass] - *Aristida* L. (152) (1912) NM, *Scleropogon* Phil. (152, 163) (1852-1912) NM

False nettle [Falsenettle] - *Boehmeria cylindrica* (L.) Sw. (4, 5, 72, 93, 95, 122, 156) (1907-1986), *Boehmeria* Jacq. (1, 2, 50, 93, 155, 156) (1895–present), *Laportea canadensis* (L.) Weddell (40) (1928), *Pilea pumila* (L.) Gray (156) (1923)

False nutgrass - *Cyperus strigosus* L. (3) (1977)

False oat [False oats] - *Trisetum* Pers. (1, 93, 152) (1932-1936)

False oat grass [False oat-grass] - *Arrhenatherum elatius* (L.) Beauv. ex J. Presl & C. Presl (5, 45, 56, 68) (1896-1913)

False orange amanita - *Amanita muscaria* var. *muscaria* (L.) Pers. (71) (1898)

False Oregon grape - *Mahonia aquifolium* (Pursh) Nutt. (103) (1870)

False Paraguay tea - *Viburnum nudum* L. var. *cassinoides* (L.) Torr. & Gray (5, 156) (1913-1923)

False parsley - *Aethusa cynapium* L. (5, 156) (1913-1923)

False pempernel - *Lindernia dubia* (L.) Pennell (131) (1899)

False pennyroyal [Falsepennyroyal] - *Hedeoma drummondii* Benth. (124) (1937), *Hedeoma* Pers. (50, 155) (1942–present), *Isanthus brachiatus* (L.) Britton, Sterns & Poggenb. (3, 5, 72, 85, 93, 97, 122, 156, 158) (1900-1977), *Isanthus* Michx. (2, 155, 156, 158) (1895–1942), *Trichostema brachiatum* L. (19, 63) (1840-1899), *Trichostema dichotomum* L. (156) (1923), *Trichostema lanceolatum* Benth. (156) (1923)

False pimpernel [Falsepimpernel] - *Anagallis* L. (1) (1932), *Anagallis minima* (L.) Krause (5, 97, 122, 156) (1913-1937), *Lindernia* All. (1, 2, 50, 155, 158) (1895–present), *Lindernia dubia* (L.) Pennell (3, 4) (1977-1986), *Lindernia dubia* (L.) Pennell var. *anagallidea* (Michx.) Cooperrider (3) (1977), *Lindernia dubia* (L.) Pennell var. *dubia* (93, 95, 156) (1911-1936), *Pimpinella saxifraga* L. subsp. *nigra* (Mill.) Gaudin (92) (1876)

False pondweed [False pond-weed] - *Zannichellia palustris* L. (19) (1840)

False quackgrass - *Elymus* ×*pseudorepens* (Scribn. & J.G. Sm.) Barkworth & D.R. Dewey [*lanceolatus* × *trachycaulus*] (140, 155) (1942-1944)

False red mallow - *Sphaeralcea bonariensis* (Cav.) Griseb. (85) (1932) IA

False red oak - *Quercus velutina* Lam. (19) (1840)

False red sandal - *Adenanthera pavonina* L. (92) (1876)

False redtop [False red-top, False red top] - *Eragrostis pectinacea* (Michx.) Nees ex Steud. (5) (1913), *Eragrostis spectabilis* (Pursh) Steud. (119) (1938), *Panicum virgatum* L. (129) (1894) SD, *Poa palustris* L. (2, 5, 45, 66, 68, 72, 90, 92, 129) (1876-1913), *Tridens flavus* (L.) A.S. Hitchc. var. *flavus* (134) (1932)

False rice - *Leersia oryzoides* (L.) Sw. (66, 87, 88, 90) (1885-1903)

False rocket - *Iodanthus pinnatifidus* (Michx.) Steud. (5, 156) (1913-1923), *Iodanthus* Torr. & Gray (13, 158) (1849-1900)

False rue-anemone [False rue anemone] - *Enemion biternatum* Raf. (1, 4, 5, 72, 97) (1907-1986), *Enemion* Raf. (50, 158) (1900–present)

False saffron - *Carthamus* L. (1) (1932), *Carthamus tinctorius* L. (19, 49, 92, 107, 109, 158) (1840-1949)

False salsify - *Scorzonera* L. (4) (1986)

False sanicle - *Mitella diphylla* L. (5, 74, 156) (1893-1923) NY

False sarsaparilla - *Aralia nudicaulis* L. (5, 49, 57, 58, 92, 156, 157, 158) (1869-1929), *Smilax glauca* Walt. (156) (1923), *Smilax pseudochina* L. (156) (1923), *Smilax walteri* Pursh. (156) (1923)

False scabish - *Marshallia obovata* (Walt.) Beadle & F.E. Boynt. (156) (1923)

False semaphore grass [False semaphoregrass] - *Pleuropogon sabinei* R. Br. (50) (present)

False senna - *Senna alexandrina* Mill. (19) (1840)

False sensitive plant - *Aeschynomene virginica* (L.) Britton, Sterns & Poggenb. (19) (1840)

False snowdrop [False snow drop] - *Nothoscordum borbonicum* Kunth (19) (1840)

False Solomon's-seal [False Solomon's seal, False Solomonseal, False Solomons-seal] - *Maianthemum* G.H. Weber ex Wiggers (2, 109, 138, 155, 156) (1895-1949), *Maianthemum racemosum* (L.) Link subsp. *racemosum* (40, 121, 138, 156, 157, 158) (1918-1970), *Maianthemum stellatum* (L.) Link (5, 85, 156) (1913-1932)

False spikenard - *Maianthemum racemosum* (L.) Link subsp. *racemosum* (3, 5, 46, 65, 85, 93, 97, 107, 158) (1900-1977)

False spiraea [False-spiraea] - *Sorbaria* (Ser. ex DC.) A. Braun (109, 138) (1923-1949)

False springbeauty [False spring beauty] - *Montia fontana* L. (19) (1840)

False St. John's-wort - *Hypericum gentianoides* (L.) Britton, Sterns & Poggenb. (156) (1923)

False star-grass [False star grass] - *Aletris farinosa* L. (19, 92) (1840-1876)

False starwort - *Boltonia asteroides* (L.) L'Hér. (156) (1923)

False strawberry - *Potentilla norvegica* L. subsp. *monspeliensis* (L.) Aschers. & Graebn. (80) (1913) IA

False summer sedge - *Carex ×aestivaliformis* Mackenzie [*aestivalis × gracillima*] (5) (1913)

False sunflower [False sun-flower] - *Bidens laevis* (L.) Britton, Sterns & Poggenb. (86) (1878), *Helenium autumnale* L. (5, 7, 19, 71, 86, 92, 93, 156, 157, 158) (1828-1936), *Helenium* L. (167) (1814), *Helianthella quinquenervis* (Hook.) Gray (3, 4) (1977-1986), *Heliopsis helianthoides* (L.) Sweet (4, 5, 156) (1923-1986), *Heliopsis helianthoides* (L.) Sweet var. *scabra* (Dunal) Fern. (4, 5, 62, 93, 95, 156) (1911-1986), *Heliopsis* Pers. (158) (1900), *Silphium* L. (167) (1814)

False sweet flag [False sweet-flag] - *Iris pseudacorus* L. (5, 156, 158) (1900-1923)

False sycamore - *Melia azedarach* L. (107) (1919), *Platanus occidentalis* L. (5, 19, 92, 156, 158) (1840-1923)

False syringa - *Philadelphus coronarius* L. (19, 92, 156) (1840-1923)

False toadflax [False toad-flax, False toad flax] - *Comandra* Nutt. (156) (1923), *Comandra umbellata* (L.) Nutt. (possibly) (19, 156) (1840-1923)

False uncinia - *Carex microglochin* Wahl. (5) (1913)

False unicorn - *Chamaelirium luteum* (L.) A. Gray (58, 92) (1869-1876)

False unicorn plant - *Chamaelirium luteum* (L.) A. Gray (5, 6) (1892-1913)

False unicornroot [False unicorn root] - *Aletris farinosa* L. (6, 49, 52, 53) (1892-1922), *Chamaelirium luteum* (L.) A. Gray (19, 57, 64) (1840-1917)

False unicornwort [False unicorn wort] - *Aletris farinosa* L. (49) (1898)

False valerian - *Packera aurea* (L.) A.& D. Löve (5, 6, 19, 49, 92, 156, 158) (1840-1923)

False varnish tree [False varnish-tree] - *Ailanthus altissima* (Mill) Swingle (5, 156, 158) (1900-1923)

False vervain - *Verbena hastata* L. (5, 93, 156, 157, 158) (1900-1937)

False violet - *Dalibarda* L. (156) (1923), *Dalibarda repens* L. (19, 156) (1840-1923)

False Virginia creeper - *Parthenocissus quinquefolia* (L.) Planch. (131) (1899)

False virgin's-bower [False virgin bower] - *Clematis occidentalis* (Hornem.) DC. var. *occidentalis* (19) (1840)

False wakerobin [False wake robin] - *Trillium erectum* L. (19) (1840)

False wallflower [False wall flower] - *Erysimum capitatum* (Dougl. ex Hook.) Greene var. *capitatum* (156) (1923), *Erysimum* L. (13) (1849)

False wheat - *Elymus repens* (L.) Gould (5) (1913)

False white cedar - *Thuja occidentalis* L. (5, 49, 53, 92) (1876-1922)

False white heather - *Cassiope* D. Don. (106) (1930), *Cassiope mertensiana* (Bong.) D. Don (106) (1930)

False wintergreen - *Pyrola americana* Sweet (5, 49, 53, 58, 61, 156, 158) (1869-1923), *Pyrola chlorantha* Sw. (156) (1923)

False Winter's bark - *Canella winteriana* (L.) Gaertn. (92) (1876)

False wormwood - *Ambrosia artemisiifolia* L. (156) (1923)

False yarrow [Falseyarrow] - *Chaenactis* DC. (155) (1942)

False-gold groundsel [Falsegold groundsel] - *Packera pseudaurea* (Rydb.) W.A. Weber & A. Löve (50) (present)

False-hop sedge [False hop sedge] - *Carex lupuliformis* Sartwell ex Dewey (50) (present)

False-tarragon sagebrush [Falsetarragon sagebrush] - *Artemisia dracunculus* L. (155) (1942)

Fameflower [Fame flower, Fame-flower] - *Phemeranthus teretifolius* (Pursh) Raf. (5, 72, 86, 97, 131) (1878-1937), *Talinum* Adans. (1, 4, 50, 155) (1932–present), *Talinum calycinum* Engelm. (3, 4) (1977-1986)

Fan maidenhair fern - *Adiantum tenerum* Sw. (138) (1923)

Fan selaginella - *Selaginella flabellata* (L.) Spring (138) (1923)

Fancy - *Agrostis capillaris* L. (56) (1901) IA, *Viola tricolor* L. (158) (1900)

Fancy geranium - *Pelargonium ×domesticum* Bailey [*angulosum × cucullatum*] (109) (1949)

Fancy pelargonium - *Pelargonium ×domesticum* Bailey [*angulosum × cucullatum*] (109) (1949)

Fan-leaf cinquefoil [Fanleaf cinquefoil] - *Potentilla gracilis* Dougl. ex Hook. var. *flabelliformis* (Lehm.) Nutt. ex Torr. & Gray (155) (1942)

Fan-leaf thorn [Fan-leaved thorn] - *Crataegus flabellata* (Spach) Kirchn. (72) (1907)

Fan-leaf vervain [Fanleaf vervain] - *Verbena plicata* Greene (4, 50) (1986–present)

Fan-palmetto - *Sabal* Adans. (possibly) (167) (1814)

Fan-petals [Fanpetals] - *Sida* L. (50) (present)

Fan-shaped barley - *Hordeum vulgare* L. (110) (1886)

Fanweed [Fan-weed] - *Thlaspi arvense* L. (156) (1923)

Fanwort - *Cabomba* Aubl. (50, 109) (1949–present)

Fanwort - *Cabomba caroliniana* Gray (3, 4, 156) (1923-1986)

Farbeginster (German) - *Genista tinctoria* L. (6) (1892)

Farbende Baptisia (German) - *Baptisia tinctoria* (L.) R. Br. ex Aiton f. (7) (1828)

Färbende Podolyria (German) - *Baptisia tinctoria* (L.) R. Br. ex Aiton f. (186) (1814)

Farbersaflor (German) - *Carthamus tinctorius* L. (158) (1900)

Fareweel summer - *Symphyotrichum lateriflorum* (L.) A.& D. Löve (75) (1894) WV

Farewell-summer [Farewell summer] - *Symphyotrichum ericoides* (L.) Nesom var. *ericoides* (5, 156) (1913-1923), *Symphyotrichum lateriflorum* (L.) A.& D. Löve var. *lateriflorum* (5, 156) (1913-1923), *Symphyotrichum novae-angliae* (L.) G.L.Nesom (156) (1923)

Farewell-to-spring - *Clarkia amoena* (Lehm.) A. Nels. & J. F. Macbr. subsp. *amoena* (109, 138) (1923–1949)

Farkleberry [Farkle-berry] - *Vaccinium arboreum* Marsh. (2, 5, 7, 19, 50, 92, 106, 155, 156, 158) (1828–present), *Vaccinium* L. (1) (1932)

Farmer's-ruin - *Spergula arvensis* L. (158) (1900)

Farouch (French) - *Trifolium incarnatum* L. (110) (1886)

Farra (Italian) - *Triticum spelta* L. (180) (1633)

Farradje (French, Roussillon) - *Trifolium incarnatum* L. (110) (1886)

Farratage (French, Languedoc) - *Trifolium incarnatum* L. (110) (1886)

Farwell's water milfoil - *Myriophyllum farwellii* Morong (5) (1913)

Fascicled agalinis - *Agalinis fasciculata* (Ell.) Raf. (5) (1913)

Fascinating nut - *Nestronia umbellula* Raf. (183) (~1756)

Faselen (German) - *Phaseolus* L. (107) (1919)

Faséole or fazéole (French) - *Phaseolus vulgaris* L. (possibly) (110) (until end of 17th century)

Fasiolos - *Phaseolus vulgaris* L. (possibly) (110) (1886) Dioscorides, probably this species)

Fasiolum - *Phaseolus vulgaris* L. (possibly) (110) (1886) Charlemagne

Fasoler (Spanish) - *Phaseolus vulgaris* L. (possibly) (110) (1886)

Fasoulia (Modern Greek) - *Phaseolus vulgaris* L. (possibly) (110) (1886)

Fasulé (Albanian) - *Phaseolus vulgaris* L. (possibly) (110) (1886)

Fat pine - *Pinus palustris* Mill. (5, 19) (1840-1913)

Fat-hen [Fat hen] - *Atriplex prostrata* subsp. *calotheca* (Rafn) M.A.Gust. (156, 158) (1900-1923), *Capsella bursa-pastoris* (L.) Medik. (158) (1900), *Chenopodium album* L. (5, 156, 157, 158) (1900-1929), *Chenopodium bonus-henricus* L. (5, 107, 156) (1913-1923), *Chenopodium rubrum* L. (158) (1900)

Fat-hen saltbush - *Atriplex patula* L. (156) (1923)

Faulbaum (German) - *Frangula alnus* Mill. (158) (1900)

Faux acacia (French) - *Robinia* L. (8) (1785)

Faux acacia (French) - *Robinia pseudoacacia* L. (8) (1785)

Faux sapin (French) - *Picea abies* (L.) H. Karst. (158) (1900)

Faverole - *Calla palustris* L. (158) (1900)

Fawn lily [Fawn-lily, Fawnlily] - *Erythronium albidum* Nutt. (156) (1923), *Erythronium americanum* Ker. (156) (1923), *Erythronium* L. (50, 109, 155) (1942–present)

Fawn-colored mushroom - *Pluteus cervinus* (Schaeff.) P. Kumm. (128) (1933)

Faxon's aster - *Symphyotrichum pilosum* (Willd.) Nesom var. *pringlei* (Gray) Nesom (5) (1913)

Faxon's pondweed - *Potamogeton* ×*faxonii* Morong [*illinoensis* × *nodosus*] (5) (1913)

Fayal myrtle - *Morella faya* (Aiton) Wilbur (20) (1857)

Fayberry [Fay berry, Fay-berry] - *Ribes uva-crispa* L. var. *sativum* DC. (5, 156) (1913-1923)

Fé (Catalan) - *Trifolium incarnatum* L. (110) (1886)

Feaberry [Fea berry, Fea-berry] - *Ribes uva-crispa* L. var. *sativum* DC. (5, 110, 156) (1886-1923)

Fearh grass - *Agrostis capillaris* L. (46) (1879)

Feather bamboo - *Bambusa vulgaris* Schrad. ex J.C. Wendl. (138) (1923)

Feather beds - *Chara vulgaris* L. (19, 187) (1818-1840)

Feather bunch grass [Feather bunch-grass] - *Nassella viridula* (Trin.) Barkworth (5, 56, 93, 94, 111, 129) (1901-1936)

Feather bush - *Cercocarpus ledifolius* Nutt. (20) (1857)

Feather cockscomb - *Celosia argentea* L. (138) (1923)

Feather columbine - *Thalictrum pubescens* Pursh (156) (1923)

Feather dalea - *Dalea formosa* Torr. (155) (1942)

Feather elm - *Ulmus americana* L. (124) (1937) TX

Feather finger grass [Feather finger-grass] - *Chloris virgata* Sw. (50, 138, 163) (1852–present)

Feather grass [Feather-grass, Feathergrass] - *Leptochloa panicea* (Retz.) Ohwi subsp. *mucronata* (Michx.) Nowack (94) (1901), *Achnatherum eminens* (Cav.) Barkworth (87) (1884), *Holcus lanatus* L. (5, 75) (1894–1913) WV, *Leptochloa panicea* (Retz.) Ohwi subsp. *brachiata* (Steudl.) N. Snow (5, 87, 119) (1884–1938), *Piptochaetium avenaceum* (L.) Parodi (5, 92, 184) (1793–1913), *Piptochaetium avenacioides* (Nash) Valencia & Costas (94) (1901)

Feather pappus grass [Feather pappusgrass] - *Enneapogon desvauxii* Desv. ex Beauv. (155) (1942)

Feather sedge grass [Feather sedge-grass] - *Bothriochloa saccharoides* (Sw.) Rydb. (5) (1913)

Feather Solomon's-plume [Feather Solomonplume] - *Maianthemum racemosum* (L.) Link subsp. *racemosum* (155) (1942)

Feather tree [Feather-tree] - *Cotinus coggygria* Scop. (7, 92) (1828-1876), *Cotinus obovatus* Raf. (possibly) (156) (1923)

Feathered columbine - *Thalictrum dioicum* L. (5, 156, 158) (1900-1923)

Featherfen - *Matricaria* L. (7) (1828)

Featherfew [Feather few, Feather-few, Fetherfew] - *Tanacetum parthenium* (L.) Schultz-Bip. (5, 19, 46, 49, 76, 92, 156, 158) (1671-1923)

Feather-finger [Featherfinger] - *Chloris virgata* Sw. (122) (1937) TX

Featherfleece [Feather-fleece] - *Stenanthium gramineum* (Ker-Gawl.) Morong var. *robustum* (S. Wats.) Fern. (109, 138) (1923-1949)

Featherfoil [Feather foil] - *Hottonia inflata* Ell. (156) (1923), *Hottonia* L. (2) (1895)

Feather-geranium [Feather geranium] - *Chenopodium botrys* L. (5, 92, 93, 95, 109, 156, 157, 158) (1876-1949)

Feather-leaf cedar - *Thuja occidentalis* L. (5, 19) (1840-1913)

Feather-leaf orchis [Feather-leaved orchis] - *Platanthera blephariglottis* (Willd.) Lindl. var. *blephariglottis* (5) (1913)

Feather-leaf sheepbur [Featherleaf sheepbur] - *Acaena pinnatifida* Ruiz & Pavón (155) (1942)

Feather-plume [Featherplume, Feather plume] - *Dalea formosa* Torr. (4, 50) (1986–present)

Feathertop - *Pennisetum villosum* R. Br. ex Fresen. (138) (1923)

Feather-vein willow [Feathervein willow] - *Salix planifolia* Pursh (155) (1942)

Featherweed [Feather weed, Feather-weed] - *Pseudognaphalium obtusifolium* (L.) Hilliard & Burtt subsp. *obtusifolium* (5, 73, 156, 157) (1892-1923) Northern NY, seed heads used for bed filling, no longer in use by 1923

Feathery bamboo - *Bambusa vulgaris* Schrad. ex J.C. Wendl. (109) (1949)

Feathery bunch grass [Feathery bunch-grass] - *Nassella viridula* (Trin.) Barkworth (157) (1929)

Feathery climbing fern - *Lygodium microphyllum* (Cav.) R. Br. (138) (1923)

Feathery false lily-of-the-valley [Feathery false lily of the valley] - *Maianthemum racemosum* (L.) Link (50) (present), *Maianthemum racemosum* (L.) Link subsp. *racemosum* (50) (present)

Febrifuge plant - *Tanacetum parthenium* (L.) Schultz-Bip. (92, 158) (1876-1900)

February daphne - *Daphne mezereum* L. (138) (1923)

Febues du Bresil (Brazilian beans) - *Phaseolus vulgaris* L. (107) (1605)

Fee's lip fern [Fee lipfern] - *Cheilanthes feei* T. Moore (155) (1942)

Feetches - *Lathyrus japonicus* Willd. var. *maritimus* (L.) Kartesz & Gandhi (46) (1617)

Fe'i banana - *Musa troglodytarum* L. (109) (1949)

Feldgarbe (German) - *Achillea millefolium* L. (158) (1900)

Feldkamille (German) - *Matricaria recutita* L. (158) (1900)

Feldminze (German) - *Mentha arvensis* L. (158) (1900)

Feldraute (German) - *Fumaria officinalis* L. (158) (1900)

Feldrose (German) - *Papaver rhoeas* L. (158) (1900)

Feldz Wibel (High Dutch) - *Ornithogalum* L. (180) (1633)

Felix mas - *Dryopteris filix-mas* (L.) Schott (54) (1905)

Fellen - *Solanum dulcamara* L. (156) (1923)

Fellow snowdrop - *Erythronium americanum* Ker. (49) (1898)

Felon herb [Fellon-herb, Felon-herb] - *Artemisia vulgaris* L. (107, 156, 157) (1919-1923), *Hieracium pilosella* L. (5, 156) (1913-1923)

Felon-grass [Felon grass] - *Peucedanum ostruthium* (L.) W.D.J. Koch (5, 156) (1913-1923)

Felonweed [Felon weed, Felon-weed] - *Senecio jacobea* L. (5, 156) (1913-1923)

Felonwort [Fellenwort] - *Chelidonium majus* L. (156, 158) (1900-1923), *Peucedanum ostruthium* (L.) W.D.J. Koch (5, 156) (1913-1923), *Solanum dulcamara* L. (5, 92, 156, 158) (1876-1923)

Felt-leaf ceanothus [Feltleaf ceanothus] - *Ceanothus arboreus* Greene (109) (1949)

Feltwort - *Verbascum thapsus* L. (5, 69, 156, 158) (1900-1923)

Felwort [Fellwort] - *Gentianella amarella* (L.) Boerner subsp. *acuta* (Michx.) J. Gillett (5, 156) (1913-1923), *Gentianella* Moench (179) (1526), *Sabatia difformis* (L.) Druce (10) (1818)

Female agaric - *Boletus agaricum* Pollini (possibly) (92) (1876)

Female balsam-apple [Female balsam apple] - *Momordica balsamina* L. (178, 180) (1526-1633)

Female dogwood - *Cornus amomum* Mill. (157, 158) (1900-1929), *Cornus sericea* L. (6, 186) (1825-1892)

Female dragon [Female-dragon] - *Calla palustris* L. (5, 158) (1900-1913)

Female fern [Female Ferne] - *Athyrium filix-femina* (L.) Roth (5, 92, 157) (1876-1929), *Polypodium virginianum* L. (2, 5, 7, 49, 58, 92) (1828-1895), *Pteridium aquilinum* (L.) Kuhn (178) (1596), *Thelypteris palustris* Schott var. *pubescens* (Lawson) Fern. (158) (1900)

Female fluellin - *Kickxia elatine* (L.) Dumort. (5) (1913), *Knautia arvensis* (L.) Duby (156) (1923)

Female knot-grass - *Hippuris vulgaris* L. (158) (1900)

Female mercury [Female mercurie] - *Mercurialis annua* L. (178, 180) (1526-1633)

Female mullein [Female mulleine] - *Verbascum lychnitis* L. (178) (1526)

Female nervine - *Cypripedium reginae* Walt. (7, 92, 156, 158) (1828-1923)

Female oak - *Quercus velutina* Lam. (157, 158) (1900-1929)

Female peony [Female Pionie] - *Paeonia officinalis* L. (178) (1526)

Female Virginia dogwood [Female virginian dogwood] - *Cornus alternifolia* L. f. (8) (1785)

Female water-dragon - *Calla palustris* L. (156) (1923)

Female-regulator [Female regulator] - *Packera aurea* (L.) A.& D. Löve (6, 49, 53, 58, 92, 158) (1869-1922)

Fen grape - *Vaccinium macrocarpon* Aiton (92) (1876)

Fen grass-of-Parnassus [Fen grass of Parnassus] - *Parnassia glauca* Raf. (50) (present)

Fen orchis - *Liparis loeselii* (L.) L.C. Rich (72, 93) (1907-1936)

Fenberry [Fen berry] - *Vaccinium macrocarpon* Aiton (5, 92, 156) (1876-1923), *Vaccinium oxycoccos* L. (5) (1913)

Fench (Catalan) - *Trifolium incarnatum* L. (110) (1886)

Fench pursley - *Chamaesyce maculata* (L.) Small (78) (1898)

Fenchel (German) - *Foeniculum vulgare* Mill. (158) (1900)

Fenchelholz (German) - *Sassafras albidum* (Nutt.) Nees (158) (1900)

Fendler's aster [Fendler aster] - *Symphyotrichum fendleri* (Gray) Nesom (3, 4, 5, 50, 93, 97, 122) (1913–present)

Fendler's barberry - *Berberis fendleri* Gray (153) (1913)

Fendler's bladderpod - *Lesquerella fendleri* (Gray) Wats (50) (present)

Fendler's blue grass [Fendler's blue-grass, Fendler bluegrass] - *Poa fendleriana* (Steud.) Vasey (94, 155) (1901-1942)

Fendler's ceanothus [Fendler ceanothus] - *Ceanothus fendleri* Gray (50, 130, 138, 155) (1895–present)

Fendler's cloak fern [Fendler cloak fern] - *Argyrochosma fendleri* (Kunze) Windham (4) (1986)

Fendler's cryptanthe - *Cryptantha fendleri* (Gray) Greene (5) (1913)

Fendler's euphorbia [Fendler euphorbia] - *Chamaesyce fendleri* (Torr. & Gray) Small (3, 4, 155) (1942-1986)

Fendler's false cloak fern - *Argyrochosma fendleri* (Kunze) Windham (50) (present)

Fendler's flatsedge - *Cyperus fendlerianus* Boeckl. (139) (1944)

Fendler's globe-mallow [Fendler's globemallow] - *Sphaeralcea angustifolia* (Cav.) G. Don (50) (present)

Fendler's hawkweed - *Hieracium fendleri* Schultz-Bip. (131) (1899)

Fendler's lip fern [Fendler lipfern, Fendler's lip-fern] - *Cheilanthes fendleri* Hook. (4, 50, 97, 138, 155) (1923–present)

Fendler's oak [Fendler oak] - *Quercus ×pauciloba* Rydb. [*gambelii* × *turbinella*] (155) (1942)

Fendler's penstemon [Fendler penstemon] - *Penstemon fendleri* Torr. & Gray (50, 155) (1942–present)

Fendler's redroot - *Ceanothus fendleri* Gray (131) (1899)

Fendler's rockcress - *Arabis fendleri* (S. Wats.) Greene (50) (present)

Fendler's rose [Fendler rose] - *Rosa woodsii* Lindl. var. *woodsii* (130, 138) (1895-1923)

Fendler's sandmat - *Chamaesyce fendleri* (Torr. & Gray) Small (50) (present)

Fendler's sandwort [Fendler sandwort] - *Arenaria fendleri* Gray (5, 50, 155) (1913–present)

Fendler's spurge - *Chamaesyce fendleri* (Torr. & Gray) Small (5, 93, 97) (1913-1937)

Fendler's threeawn [Fendler three awn, Fendler threeawn] - *Aristida purpurea* Nutt. var. *fendleriana* (Steud.) Vasey (5, 50, 119, 122, 155) (1913–present), *Aristida purpurea* Nutt. var. *longiseta* (Steud.) Vasey (50) (present)

Fendler's triple-awn grass [Fendler's triple-awned grass] - *Aristida purpurea* Nutt. var. *fendleriana* (Steud.) Vasey (5, 50, 119) (1913–present)

Fennel [Fenell] - *Anethum* L. (7, 19, 165, 184) (1793-1840), *Foeniculum* P. Mill. (50, 155, 156, 158) (1900–present), *Foeniculum vulgare* Mill. (1, 5, 7, 19, 46, 49, 53, 55, 57, 59, 72, 95, 107, 109, 122, 156, 157, 158, 165) (1671-1949)

Fennel giant-hyssop [Fennel gianthyssop] - *Agastache foeniculum* (Pursh) Kuntze (155) (1942)

Fennel-flower [Fennel flower] - *Nigella damascena* L. (19, 156) (1840-1923), *Nigella* L. (1, 109, 156) (1923-1949), *Nigella sativa* L. (107) (1919)

Fennel-leaf parsley [Fennel-leaved parsley] - *Lomatium graveolens* (S. Watson) Dorn & R.L. Hartm. (131) (1899)

Fennel-leaf pondweed [Fennel-leaved pondweed, Fennel-leaved pond-weed, Fennelleaf pondweed] - *Stuckenia pectinatus* (L.) Boerner (5, 72, 93, 97, 120, 131, 155, 156, 158) (1899-1942)

Fenouil (French) - *Foeniculum vulgare* Mill. (158) (1900)

Fenouil puant (French) - *Anethum graveolens* L. (158) (1900)

Fenugreek [Fenegreke] - *Trigonella foenum-graecum* L. (19, 57, 92, 107, 109, 110, 129, 179) (1526-1949)

Fern - *Cystopteris* Bernh. (7) (1828)

Fern [Ferne] - *Pteridium aquilinum* (L.) Kuhn (178, 179) (1526-1596)

Fern asparagus - *Asparagus setaceus* (Kunth) Jessop (138, 155) (1923-1942)

Fern brake - *Osmunda regalis* L. (92) (1876)

Fern bush [Fern-bush] - *Comptonia peregrina* (L.) Coult. (7) (1828)

Fern flatsedge - *Cyperus filicinus* Vahl. (50) (present), *Cyperus lupulinus* (Spreng.) Marcks subsp. *lupulinus* (3) (1977)

Fern grass [Ferngrass] - *Desmazeria rigida* (L.) Tutin (50) (present)

Fern meadow-burs - *Comptonia peregrina* (L.) Coult. (possibly) (156) (1923)

Fern rattlesnake-root [Fern rattle-snake-root, Fern rattle S\snake root] - *Botrychium virginianum (L.) Sw.* (177, 181) (~1678-1762)

Fernald's bulrush - *Schoenoplectus maritimus* (L.) Lye (5) (1913)

Fernald's hay sedge - *Carex siccata* Dewey (50) (present)

Fernald's thorn - *Crataegus jonesiae* Sarg. (5) (1913)

Fernald's yellow-cress [Fernald's yellowcress] - *Rorippa palustris* (L.) Bess. subsp. *fernaldiana* (Butters & Abbe) Jonsell (50) (present)

Fernando's holly-grape [Fernando hollygrape] - *Mahonia nevinii* (Gray) Fedde (138) (1923)

Ferngale [Fern gale, Fern-gale] - *Comptonia peregrina* (L.) Coult. (5, 7, 92, 156) (1828-1923)

Fern-leaf acacia [Fernleaf acacia] - *Acacia angustissima* (Mill.) Kuntze (155) (1942)

Fern-leaf beech [Fernleaf beech] - *Fagus sylvatica* L. (109) (1949)

Fern-leaf false foxglove [Fern-leaved false foxglove, Fern-leaved false foxglove] - *Aureolaria pedicularia* (L.) Raf. ex Farw. (5, 86, 97, 156) (1878-1937)

Fern-leaf fleabane [Fernleaf fleabane] - *Erigeron compositus* Pursh (155) (1942)

Fern-leaf foxglove [Fern-leaved foxglove] - *Aureolaria pedicularia* (L.) Raf. var. *pedicularia* (97) (1937)

Fern-leaf gale [Fern-leaved gale] - *Comptonia peregrina* (L.) Coult. (187) (1818)

Fern-leaf lyonshrub [Fernleaf lyonshrub] - *Lyonothamnus floribundus* Gray subsp. *aspleniifolius* (Greene) Raven (138) (1923)

Fern-leaf maple [Fernleaf maple] - *Acer japonicum* Thunb. (109) (1949)

Fern-leaf polyscias [Fernleaf polyscias] - *Polyscias cumingiana* (K. Presl) (138) (1923)

Fern-leaf yarrow [Fernleaf yarrow] - *Achillea filipendulina* Lam. (109, 137, 155) (1923-1949)

Fernroot [Fern-root, Fern root] - *Polypodium virginianum* L. (7, 49, 92) (1828)

Fernwort bush [Fern wort bush] - *Comptonia peregrina* (L.) Coult. (5) (1913)

Feroutgé (French, Gascony) - *Trifolium incarnatum* L. (110) (1886)

Ferrago - *Secale cereale* L. (180) (1633)

Ferruginous andromeda - *Lyonia ferruginea* (Walt.) Nutt. (possibly) (42) (1814)

Fescue - *Festuca* L. (50, 109, 138, 155, 184) (1793–present), *Vulpia* K.C. Gmel. (50) (present)

Fescue grass [Fescue-grass] - *Festuca* L. (1, 10, 66, 93, 152, 163) (1818-1936), *Lolium pratense* (Huds.) S.J. Darbyshire (19, 92) (1840-1876), *Vulpia octoflora* (Walt.) Rydb. var. *octoflora* (85) (1932)

Fescue sandwort - *Arenaria capillaris* Poir. subsp. *americana* Maguire (155) (1942)

Fescue scolochloa - *Scolochloa festucacea* (Willd.) Link (56, 72) (1901-1907)

Fescue sedge - *Carex brevior* (Dewey) Mackenzie (3) (1977), *Carex festucacea* Schkuhr (5, 50, 72) (1893–present)

Fescue-like sedge [Fescue-like-sedge] - *Carex festucacea* Schkuhr (187) (1818)

Festid shrub [Festid-shrub] - *Asimina triloba* (L.) Dunal (157) (1929)

Festoon-pine [Festoon pine] - *Lycopodium complanatum* L. (5) (1913), *Selaginella rupestris* (L.) Spring (5, 19, 92, 158) (1840-1913)

Feterita - *Sorghum bicolor* (L.) Moench (109, 119) (1938-1949)

Fetid buckeye - *Aesculus glabra* Willd. (2, 5, 13, 15, 49, 53, 93, 156, 157, 158) (1849-1936)

Fetid camomile - *Anthemis cotula* L. (5, 93, 95, 97, 157, 158) (1900-1937)

Fetid currant - *Ribes glandulosum* Grauer (2, 5, 107, 156) (1895-1923)

Fetid gourd - *Cucurbita foetidissima* Kunth (121) (1918?-1970?)

Fetid groundsel - *Senecio viscosus* L. (5) (1913)

Fetid hellebone - *Symplocarpus foetidus* (L.) Salisb. ex Nutt. (64) (1908)

Fetid hellebore - *Helleborus foetidus* L. (15, 92) (1876-1895), *Symplocarpus foetidus* (L.) Salisb. ex Nutt. (156) (1923)

Fetid horehound [Fetid hoarhound] - *Ballota* L. (156) (1923), *Ballota nigra* L. (5, 156, 158) (1900-1923)

Fetid marigold [Foetid marigold] - *Dyssodia* Cav. (1, 2, 158) (1895-1932), *Dyssodia papposa* (Vent.) A.S. Hitchc. (3, 4, 5, 37, 50, 63, 62, 72, 80, 85, 93, 95, 121, 131, 148, 156, 158) (1899–present)

Fetid marsh-fleabane [Fetid marsh fleabane] - *Pluchea foetida* (L.) DC. (5, 156) (1913-1923)

Fetid mayweed [Fetid may-weed] - *Anthemis cotula* L. (157, 158) (1900-1929)

Fetid nightshade - *Hyoscyamus niger* L. (5, 156, 158) (1900-1923)

Fetid pothos - *Symplocarpus foetidus* (L.) Salisb. ex Nutt. (23) (1810)

Fetid rayless goldenrod [Fetid rayless golden-rod] - *Ericameria nauseosa* (Pallas ex Pursh) Nesom & Baird subsp. *nauseosa* var. *glabrata* (Gray) Nesom & Baird (5, 93, 112, 158) (1900-1937)

Fetid shrub [Fetid-shrub] - *Asimina triloba* (L.) Dunal (5, 156, 157, 158) (1900-1929)

Fetid sumac - *Rhus trilobata* Nutt. var. *trilobata* (93) (1936)

Fetid wild pumpkin - *Cucurbita foetidissima* Kunth (156) (1923)

Fetter bush [Fetterbush, Fetter-bush] - *Leucothoe axillaris* (Lam.) D. Don. (5, 71) (1898-1913), *Leucothoe* D. Don (156) (1923), *Lyonia lucida* (Lam.) K. Koch (5, 109, 156) (1913-1949)

Fetter-foe - *Tanacetum parthenium* (L.) Schultz-Bip. (158) (1900)

Fetticus - *Valerianella locusta* (L.) Lat. (5, 156) (1913-1923)

Feuerkraut (German) - *Erechtites hieraciifolia* (L.) Raf. ex DC. (6) (1892)

Feve commune (French) - *Vicia faba* L. (7, 68) (1828-1913)

Fever bush [Feverbush, Fever-bush] - *Ilex* L. (7) (1828), *Ilex verticillata* (L.) Gray (5, 6, 106, 156) (1892-1930), *Lindera benzoin* Blume. (5, 6, 7, 19, 46, 58, 92, 156, 157, 186, 187) (1814-1929)

Fever bush [Feverbush, Fever-bush] - *Lindera* Thunb. (2) (1895)

Fever plant [Fever-plant] - *Oenothera biennis* L. (5, 74, 156, 157, 158) (1893-1929) Eastern states, used as diaphoretic, archaic

Fever tree - *Eucalyptus globulus* Labill. (92) (1876), *Pinckneya bracteata* (Bartr.) Raf. (7, 92) (1828-1876), *Pinckneya* Michx. (2) (1895)

Fevercup [Fever cup, Fever-cup] - *Sarracenia purpurea* L. (5, 74, 156) (1893-1923)

Feverfew [Fever few, fever-few] - *Agrimonia gryposepala* Wallr. (5) (1913), *Centaurium erythraea* Raf. (156) (1923), *Matricaria* L. (184) (1793), *Parthenium hysterophorus* L. (124) (1937), *Parthenium* L. (1) (1932), Tanacetum L. (possibly) (10) (1818), *Tanacetum parthenium* (L.) Schultz-Bip. (4, 49, 50, 57, 58, 61, 76, 92, 109, 138, 158) (1869–present)

Feverfew chrysanthemum - *Tanacetum parthenium* (L.) Schultz-Bip. (155) (1942)

Feverfew-camomile [Feverfew-chamomile] - *Tanacetum parthenium* (L.) Schultz-Bip. (138) (1923)

Feverolles - *Vicia faba* L. (7, 34, 92, 107) (1828-1919)

Fever-root [Fever root, Feverroot] - *Corallorrhiza odontorhiza* (Willd.) Poir. (64, 92, 158) (1876-1923), *Corallorrhiza trifida* Chat. (157) (1929), *Pterospora andromedea* Nutt. (7, 58) (1828-1869), *Triosteum* L. (158) (1900), *Triosteum perfoliatum* L. (5, 6, 7, 19, 57, 58, 92, 107, 156, 158, 177, 184, 186, 187) (1793-1923)

Fever-twig [Fever-twig] - *Celastrus scandens* L. (5, 7, 49, 92, 156, 157, 158) (1828-1929), *Lycium barbarum* L. (156) (1923), *Solanum dulcamara* L. (71, 158) (1898–1900)

Fever-twitch [Fever twitch] - *Celastrus scandens* L. (92) (1876)

Feverweed [Fever weed, Fever-weed] - *Agalinis* Raf. (48) (1882) IA, *Aureolaria pedicularia* (L.) Raf. var. *pedicularia* (5, 49, 92, 156) (1898-1923), *Verbena stricta* Vent. (73, 156, 158) (1892–1923) Peoria IL, thought to be specific for fever and ague

Feverwood [Fever wood, Fever-wood] - *Lindera benzoin* Blume. (49, 92, 186) (1814-1898)

Feverwort [Fever wort, Fever-wort] - *Eupatorium perfoliatum* L. (6, 7, 69, 92, 156, 157, 158) (1828-1923), *Triosteum* L. (2, 4, 10, 156) (1818-1986), *Triosteum perfoliatum* L. (5, 6, 48, 49, 50, 63, 92, 97, 155, 156, 158, 186) (1825–present)

Fevier (French) - *Robinia pseudoacacia* L. (17) (1796), *Gleditsia* L. (8) (1785)

Févier à épines à trois pointes (French) - *Gleditsia triacanthos* L. (8) (1785)

Févier aquatique (French) - *Gleditsia aquatica* Marsh. (8) (1785)

Fevier épineux (French) - *Gleditsia triacanthos* L. (17) (1796)

Few-flower alpine meadow grass [Few-flowered alpine meadow grass] - *Poa laxa* Haenke (90) (1885)

Few-flower aristida [Few flowered aristida, Few-flowered aristida] - *Aristida oligantha* Michx (99, 119, 163) (1852-1938)

Few-flower aster [Fewflower aster, Few-flowered aster] - *Almutaster pauciflorus* (Nutt.) A.& D. Löve (3, 4) (1977-1986), *Canadanthus modestus* (Lindl.) Nesom (155) (1942)

Few-flower beakrush [Few-flowered beaked rush] - *Rhynchospora oligantha* A. Gray (5) (1913)

Few-flower buckwheat [Fewflower buckwheat] - *Eriogonum pauciflorum* Pursh (50) (present), *Eriogonum pauciflorum* Pursh var. *gnaphalodes* (Benth.) Reveal (50) (present), *Eriogonum pauciflo-*

rum Pursh var. *pauciflorum* (50) (present)

Few-flower clubrush [Few-flowered club rush] - *Eleocharis quinqueflora* (F.X. Hartmann) Schwarz (5) (1913)

Few-flower cranberry tree [Few-flowered cranberry tree, Few-flowered cranberr-tree] - *Viburnum edule* (Michx.) Raf. (5, 158) (1900-1923)

Few-flower croomia [Few-flowered croomia] - *Croomia pauciflora* (Nutt.) Torr. (86) (1878)

Few-flower eriogonum [Few-flowered eriogonum] - *Eriogonum pauciflorum* Pursh (5, 131) (1899-1913)

Few-flower goat's rue [Few-flowered goat's rue] - *Tephrosia hispidula* (Michx.) Pers. (5, 97) (1913-1937)

Few-flower lion's-heart [Few-flowered lion's heart] - *Physostegia virginiana* (L.) Benth. subsp. *virginiana* (5) (1913)

Few-flower milkweed [Few flowered milkweed] - *Asclepias lanceolata* Walt. (5, 122) (1913-1937)

Few-flower nutrush [Few-flowered nut rush] - *Scleria oligantha* Michx. (5, 66) (1903-1913)

Few-flower nutsedge [Fewflower nutsedge] - *Scleria pauciflora* Muhl. ex Willd. (50) (present), *Scleria pauciflora* Muhl. ex Willd. var. *pauciflora* (50) (present)

Few-flower panic grass [Few-flowered panic grass] - *Dichanthelium depauperatum* (Muhl.) Gould (90) (1885), *Dichanthelium oligosanthes* (J.A. Schultes) Gould var. *oligosanthes* (119) (1938)

Few-flower panicum [Few-flowered panicum] - *Dichanthelium oligosanthes* (J.A. Schultes) Gould var. *oligosanthes* (5) (1913)

Few-flower psoralea [Few-flowered psoralea] - *Psoralidium tenuiflorum* (Pursh) Rydb. (5, 72, 93, 97, 121, 131) (1899–1937)

Few-flower razor-sedge [Fewflower razor-sedge, Fewflower razorsedge] - *Scleria pauciflora* Muhl. ex Willd. (3, 155) (1942-1977)

Few-flower sedge [Fewflower sedge, Few-flowered sedge] - *Carex pauciflora* Lightf. (5, 50, 66) (1903–present)

Few-flower sorghum [Few-flowered sorghum] - *Chrysopogon pauciflorus* (Chapm.) Benth. ex Vasey (94) (1901)

Few-flower spikerush [Fewflower spikerush] - *Eleocharis quinqueflora* (F.X. Hartmann) Schwarz (50) (present)

Few-flower threeawn [Few-flowered threeawn] - *Aristida oligantha* Michx (3, 5) (1913-1977)

Few-flower tickclover [Few-flowered tickclover] - *Desmodium pauciflorum* (Nutt.) DC. (4) (1986)

Few-flower ticktrefoil [Few-flowered tick-trefoil, Few-flowered tick trefoil] - *Desmodium pauciflorum* (Nutt.) DC. (5, 50, 72, 97) (1907–present)

Few-fruit sedge [Few-fruited sedge] - *Carex oligocarpa* Schkuhr ex Willd. (5, 72) (1907-1913), *Carex oligosperma* Michx. (66) (1903)

Few-hair beard grass [Few-haired beard-grass] - *Andropogon hallii* Hack. (5) (1913)

Few-leaf sunflower [Few leaved sunflower, Few-leaved sunflower] - *Helianthus occidentalis* Riddell (5, 72, 122) (1907-1937)

Few-nerve cottongrass [Fewnerved cottongrass] - *Eriophorum tenellum* Nutt. (50) (present)

Few-ray goldenrod [Few-rayed golden-rod] - *Solidago uliginosa* Nutt. var. *uliginosa* (5) (1913)

Few-seed bog sedge [Fewseeded bog sedge] - *Carex microglochin* Wahl. (50) (present)

Few-seed mentzelia [Few-seeded mentzelia] - *Mentzelia oligosperma* Nutt. ex Sims (5, 97, 131) (1913-1937)

Few-seed sedge [Fewseed sedge] - *Carex oligocarpa* Schkuhr ex Willd. (155) (1942), *Carex oligosperma* Michx. (5, 50) (1913-present)

Fiall-groe (Swedish) - *Poa alpina* L. (46) (1879)

Fiall-kampe - *Phleum alpinum* L. (46) (1879)

Fiare-for-a-day [Fiare for a day] - *Hemerocallis fulva* (L.) L. (180) (1633)

Fibraurea (Official name of Materia Medica) - *Coptis trifolia* (L.) Salisb. (7) (1828)

Fibrous bladderwort - *Utricularia gibba* L. (5, 122) (1913-1937)

Fibrous-root sedge [Fibrousroot sedge, Fibrous-rooted sedge] - *Carex communis* Bailey (5, 50) (1913–present), *Carex decidua* Boott (72) (1907)

Fibrous-root wheat grass [Fibrous-rooted wheat grass] - *Elymus caninus* (L.) L. (5, 90) (1885-1913), *Elymus trachycaulus* (Link) Gould ex Shinners subsp. *trachycaulus* (5) (1913)

Ficaria - *Ranunculus ficaria* L. (55) (1911)

Fichte (German) - *Picea abies* (L.) H. Karst. (158) (1900)

Ficus de Algarua - *Ficus carica* L. (178) (1526)

Ficus indica - *Opuntia ficus-indica* (L.) Mill. (177, 178) (1526-1762)

Fiddle - *Daucus carota* L. (157, 158) (1900-1929)

Fiddle dock - *Rumex obtusifolius* L. (157) (1929), *Rumex pulcher* L. (5, 122, 156) (1913-1937)

Fiddle-grass [Fiddle-grass] - *Epilobium hirsutum* L. (5, 156) (1913-1923)

Fiddleheads [Fiddle heads] - *Osmunda cinnamomea* L. (5, 73) (1892-1913), *Osmunda* L. (73) (1892)

Fiddleleaf - *Nama jamaicense* L. (122) (1937)

Fiddleleaf - *Nama* L. (50) (present)

Fiddle-leaf bindweed [Fiddle-leaved bind-weed, Fiddle-leaved bind weed] - *Ipomoea pandurata* (L.) G.F.W. Mey. (42, 186, 187) (1814-1818)

Fiddle-leaf hawksbeard [Fiddleleaf hawksbeard] - *Crepis runcinata* (James) Torr. & Gray (50) (present), *Crepis runcinata* (James) Torr. & Gray subsp. *runcinata* (50) (present)

Fiddleneck [Fiddle neck] - *Amsinckia* Lehm. (1, 4, 50, 155) (1932–present), *Amsinckia menziesii* (Lehm.) A. Nels. & J.F. Macbr. (3) (1977), *Amsinckia tessellata* Gray (97) (1937) OK, *Phacelia tanacetifolia* Benth. (106) (1930)

Fiddleneck acacia - *Acacia nilotica* (L.) Willd. ex Delile (155) (1942)

Fiddle-shaped greenbrier - *Smilax bona-nox* L. (5) (1913)

Fieberklee (German) - *Menyanthes trifoliata* L. (6, 158) (1892–1900)

Field ash - *Fraxinus pennsylvanica* Marsh. (95) (1911) Neb

Field avens - *Geum aleppicum* Jacq. (2) (1895)

Field balm [Field-balm] - *Calamintha nepeta* (L.) Savi subsp. *nepeta* (5, 156) (1913-1923), *Clinopodium* L. (5) (1913), *Glechoma hederacea* L. (5, 109, 157, 158) (1900-1949)

Field balsam - *Pseudognaphalium obtusifolium* (L.) Hilliard & Burtt subsp. *obtusifolium* (157) (1929)

Field basil - *Clinopodium vulgare* L. (5, 156) (1913-1923)

Field bindweed - *Calystegia sepium* (L.) R. Br. subsp. *angulata* Brummitt (19) (1840), *Convolvulus arvensis* L. (3, 4, 50, 62, 82, 107) (1912–present), *Convolvulus* L. (4) (1986)

Field brome - *Bromus arvensis* L. (3, 5, 50, 56, 155) (1901–present)

Field brome grass - *Bromus arvensis* L. (68) (1890)

Field buttercup - *Ranunculus acris* L. (157, 158) (1900-1929)

Field calamint - *Calamintha nepeta* (L.) Savi subsp. *nepeta* (5) (1913)

Field camomile - *Anthemis arvensis* L. (5, 72, 155, 156, 158) (1900-1942)

Field chess - *Bromus arvensis* L. (5, 72) (1907-1913) IA

Field chickweed - *Cerastium arvense* L. (5, 50, 72, 131, 156) (1899–present), *Cerastium arvense* L. subsp. *strictum* (L.) Ugborogho (50) (present)

Field clover - *Trifolium arvense* L. (19, 158) (1840-1900), *Trifolium campestre* Schreber. (50) (present)

Field corn - *Zea mays* L. (119) (1938)

Field cottonrose - *Logfia arvensis* (L.) Holub (50) (present)

Field cress - *Lepidium campestre* (L.) Aiton f. (5, 156, 158) (1900-1923), *Lepidium virginicum* L. (157) (1929), *Thlaspi arvense* L. (85) (1932) SD

Field cypress - *Ajuga chamaepitys* (L.) Schreb. (92) (1876)

Field daisy [Field-daisy] - *Leucanthemum vulgare* Lam. (5, 49, 53, 82, 93, 106, 156) (1898-1936)

Field dodder - *Cuscuta pentagona* Engelm. (3, 4) (1977-1986), *Cuscuta pentagona* Engelm. var. *pentagona* (5, 62, 72, 80, 82, 93, 95, 97, 131, 156) (1899–1937)

Field evening-primrose [Field evening primrose] - *Oenothera biennis* L. (157, 158) (1900-1929)

Field foxtail grass [Field fox-tail grass] - *Alopecurus myosuroides* Huds (165) (1768)

Field garlic - *Allium oleraceum* L. (50) (present), *Allium vineale* L. (5, 19, 62, 85, 155, 156, 158) (1840-1942)

Field goldenrod [Field golden-rod] - *Solidago nemoralis* Aiton (5, 62, 72, 93, 131, 156, 158) (1899–1936)

Field gromwell - *Buglossoides arvensis* (L.) I.M. Johnston (187) (1818)

Field ground-cherry [Field groundcherry] - *Physalis mollis* Nutt. (50) (present)

Field hawkweed - *Hieracium caespitosum* Dumort. (5) (1913)

Field horsetail [Field horse-tail] - *Equisetum arvense* L. (3, 4, 5, 50, 72, 131, 155, 157, 158, 187) (1818–present)

Field kale [Field-kale] - *Moricandia arvensis* (L.) DC. (156, 158) (1900-1923), *Sinapis arvensis* L. (5, 157) (1900-1929)

Field lady's-mantle [Field lady's mantle, Field ladysmantle] - *Aphanes arvensis* L. (5, 155) (1913-1942)

Field larkspur - *Consolida regalis* S.F. Gray (2, 63, 72, 82, 138, 156) (1895-1930)

Field lily - *Lilium canadense* L. (156, 157, 158) (1900-1929)

Field locoweed - *Oxytropis campestris* (L.) DC. (50) (present)

Field lupine - *Lupinus albus* L. (107) (1919)

Field madder - *Sherardia* L. (156) (1923)

Field milkvetch [Field milk vetch] - *Astragalus agrestis* Dougl. ex G. Don (4) (1986)

Field milkwort - *Polygala sanguinea* L. (5, 72, 93, 156, 157) (1900-1929)

Field mint - *Mentha arvensis* L. (3, 4, 5, 19, 93, 98, 138, 155, 156, 158) (1840-1986), *Nepeta cataria* L. (69, 156, 158) (1900-1904)

Field mouse ear [Field mouse-ear] - *Cerastium arvense* L. (156) (1923), *Myosotis arvensis* (L.) Hill (5, 156) (1913-1923)

Field mouse-ear chickweed - *Cerastium arvense* L. (86) (1878)

Field mustard - *Brassica rapa* L. (50) (present), *Brassica rapa* L. var. *rapa* (50, 109) (1949–present), *Sinapis arvensis* L. (107) (1919)

Field oak - *Quercus agrifolia* Née (106) (1930)

Field organie - *Origanum vulgare* L. (178) (1526)

Field ox-eye daisy [Field oxeyedaisy] - *Leucanthemum vulgare* Lam. (155) (1942)

Field oxytropis - *Oxytropis campestris* (L.) DC. (5) (1913)

Field pansy - *Viola bicolor* Pursh (5, 50, 93, 97) (1913–present), *Viola tricolor* L. (6) (1892)

Field paspalum - *Paspalum laeve* Michx. (3, 5, 50, 99, 155) (1913–present)

Field pea [Field-pea] - *Pisum sativum* L. (107, 109, 110) (1886-1949)

Field pellitory - *Achillea ptarmica* L. (165) (1768) England

Field pennycress [Field penny cress, Field penny-cress] - *Thlaspi arvense* L. (4, 5, 50, 63, 72, 80, 97, 155, 156, 158) (1899–present)

Field peppergrass [Field pepper-grass, Field pepper grass] - *Lepidium campestre* (L.) Aiton f. (3, 4, 62) (1912-1986), *Thlaspi arvense* L. (131) (1899) SD

Field pepperweed - *Lepidium campestre* (L.) Aiton f. (50, 155) (1942–present)

Field pine - *Hudsonia ericoides* L. (5, 156) (1913-1923)

Field poppy - *Papaver rhoeas* L. (4, 5, 107, 156, 158) (1900-1986)

Field pumpkin - *Cucurbita pepo* L. (50, 82, 109) (1930–present)

Field pussytoes - *Antennaria neglecta* Greene (3, 4, 50, 155) (1942–present)

Field restharrow - *Ononis campestris* G. Koch & Ziz (178) (1526)

Field rush [Field-rush] - *Luzula multiflora* (Ehrh.) Lej. subsp. *multiflora* var. *multiflora* (187) (1818)

Field sagewort - *Artemisia campestris* L. (50) (present), *Artemisia campestris* L. subsp. *borealis* (Pallas) Hall & Clements (50) (present), *Artemisia campestris* L. subsp. *caudata* (Michx.) Hall & Clem. (50) (present)

Field sandbur - *Cenchrus longispinus* (Hack.) Fern. (3, 140) (1944-1977), *Cenchrus spinifex* Cav. (122) (1937)

Field sandwort - *Spergularia rubra* (L.) J.& K. Presl (42) (1814)

Field scabiosa - *Knautia arvensis* (L.) Duby (50) (present)

Field scabious - *Knautia arvensis* (L.) Duby (4, 5, 92, 155, 156, 158) (1876-1986)

Field scorpion-grass [Field scorpion grass] - *Myosotis arvensis* (L.) Hill (5, 156) (1913-1923)

Field sedge - *Carex conoidea* Schk. ex Willd. (5, 72) (1907-1913)

Field snakecotton [Field snake cotton] - *Froelichia floridana* (Nutt.) Moq. (4) (1986)

Field soapwort - *Vaccaria hispanica* (Mill.) Rauschert (19, 156, 157, 158) (1840-1929)

Field sorrel - *Oxalis corniculata* L. (80) (1913) IA, *Oxalis stricta* L. (80) (1913) IA, *Rumex acetosella* L. (5, 19, 62, 156, 157, 158) (1840-1929)

Field sowthistle [Field sow thistle, Field sow-thistle] - *Sonchus arvensis* L. (3, 4, 50, 82, 155, 157) (1900–present)

Field speedwell - *Veronica agrestis* L. (3, 4, 5, 19, 155, 158) (1840-1986)

Field spurry - *Sagina saginoides* (L.) H. Karst. (155) (1942)

Field thistle - *Cirsium arvense* (L.) Scop. (4) (1986), *Cirsium discolor* (Muhl. ex Willd.) Spreng. (3, 5, 62, 72, 93, 95, 97, 122, 131, 156) (1899-1977)

Field thyme - *Calamintha nepeta* (L.) Savi subsp. *nepeta* (156) (1923), *Clinopodium vulgare* L. (5, 19, 92, 156) (1840-1923)

Field violet - *Viola arvensis* Murray (5, 156) (1913-1923), *Viola bicolor* Pursh (155) (1942)

Field watercress [Field water cress] - *Cardamine pratensis* L. (19) (1840)

Field woodrush - *Luzula campestris* (L.) DC. (50, 155) (1942–present), *Luzula multiflora* (Ehrh.) Lej. subsp. *frigida* (Buch.) Krecz. (139) (1944)

Field wormwood - *Artemisia campestris* L. (19) (1840)

Field woundwort - *Stachys arvensis* L. (5, 156) (1913-1923)

Field yam-root - *Smilax herbacea* L. (156) (1923)

Field-corn [Field corn] - *Convolvulus arvensis* L. (42) (1814)

Field-of-the-cloth-of-gold [Field of the cloth of gold] - *Lesquerella grandiflora* (Hook.) S. Wats. (124) (1937) TX

Field's cat's-foot [Field's cat's foot] - *Antennaria neglecta* Greene (5) (1913)

Fieldweed [Field weed] - *Anthemis cotula* L. (7, 92) (1828-1876)

Fieldweed [Field weed] - *Erigeron philadelphicus* L. (7) (1828)

Fieldwort [Field wort] - *Anthemis cotula* L. (92, 157, 158) (1876-1929)

Fiery azalea - *Rhododendron calendulaceum* (Michx.) Torr. (156) (1923)

Fiery cuphea - *Cuphea ignea* A. DC. (138) (1923)

Fiery red lily [Fierie red lilly] - *Lilium bulbiferum* L. (180) (1633)

Fig of India - *Opuntia ficus-indica* (L.) Mill. (178) (1526)

Fig of the Christians (Moors) - *Opuntia ficus-indica* (L.) Mill. (110) (1886)

Fig or Fig tree - *Ficus carica* L. (7, 19, 53, 55, 57, 92, 107, 110, 178) (1526-1922), *Ficus* L. (109, 138) (1923-1949)

Fighting-cocks [Fighting cocks] - *Viola cucullata* Aiton (76, 156) (1896-1923), *Viola nephrophylla* Greene (5) (1913)

Fig-leaf gourd [Figleaf gourd] - *Cucurbita ficifolia* Bouche (109) (1949)

Fig-leaf grape [Figleaf grape] - *Vitis aestivalis* Michx. var. *aestivalis* (155) (1942)

Fig-leaf pumpkin [Fig-leafed pumpkin] - *Cucurbita ficifolia* Bouche (110) (1886)

Fig-marigold [Figmarigold, Figmarigold] - *Mesembryanthemum* L. (138, 155) (1931-1942)

Figuero inferno (Portuguese) - *Ricinus communis* L. (110) (1886)

Figuier à feuilles courtes (French) - *Ficus citrifolia* Mill. (20) (1857)

Figuier doré (French) - *Ficus aurea* Nutt. (20) (1857)

Figuier peduncule (French) - *Ficus citrifolia* Mill. (20) (1857)

Figwort [Fig-wort, Figwoort] - *Ranunculus ficaria* L. (156) (1923), *Scrophularia* L. (1, 2, 4, 7, 10, 50, 82, 93, 155, 156, 158) (1818–

present), *Scrophularia lanceolata* Pursh (3, 82) (1930-1977), *Scrophularia marilandica* L. (19, 61, 62, 63, 85, 92, 93, 106, 156, 184, 187) (1793-1936), *Scrophularia nodosa* L. (6, 52, 57, 58, 178) (1526-1917)

Figwort buttercup - *Ranunculus ficaria* L. (5) (1913)

Figwort giant-hyssop - *Agastache scrophulariifolia* (Willd.) Kuntze (5) (1913)

Figwort herb - *Scrophularia marilandica* L. (92) (1876)

Figwort root - *Scrophularia nodosa* L. (92) (1876)

Filago - *Evax prolifera* Nutt. ex DC. (5, 97, 131) (1899–1937), *Filago* L. (158) (1900)

Filaree [Filerie, Fileree] - *Erodium cicutarium* (L.) L'Hér. ex Aiton (3, 76, 5, 156, 158) (1896-1977), *Erodium* L'Her. ex Aiton (1, 106) (1930-1932), *Erodium moschatum* (L.) L'Hér. ex Aiton (76) (1896) Berkeley CA

Filaria - *Erodium cicutarium* (L.) L'Hér. ex Aiton (4) (1986)

Filbert [Philburt, Filberts, Filberds, or Philberds] - *Corylus americana* Walt. (5, 42, 46, 97, 156, 177) (1762-1937), *Corylus avellana* L. (19, 107, 138) (1840-1932) for Philibert King of France, *Corylus cornuta* Marsh (35, 46) (1617-1806), *Corylus* L. (2, 7, 14, 92, 109, 138, 155) (1828-1942)

File lily - *Lilium canadense* L. (5) (1913)

File-blade aster - *Eurybia radula* (Aiton) Nesom (5) (1913)

Filiform dropseed - *Muhlenbergia torreyi* (Kunth) A.S. Hitchc. ex Bush (5) (1913)

Filiform fescue grass - *Festuca filiformis* Pourret (5) (1913)

Filiform pondweed - *Stuckenia filiformis* (Pers) Boerner subsp. *filiformis* (5) (1913)

Filipendula - *Oenanthe* L. (10) (1818)

Filix mas - *Dryopteris filix-mas* (L.) Schott (55, 178) (1596-1911)

Filix Veneris (Official name of Materia Medica) - *Adiantum pedatum* L. (7) (1828)

Filmy angelica - *Angelica breweri* Gray (155) (1942), *Angelica triquinata* Michx. (138, 155) (1923-1942)

Filmy-fern - *Trichomanes boschianum* Sturm. (5) (1913)

Fimble - *Cannabis sativa* L. (107, 156) (1919-1923)

Fimbry - *Fimbristylis* Vahl. (50) (present)

Finberry [Finberries] - *Vaccinium macrocarpon* Aiton (86, 92) (1876-1884)

Finckle - *Foeniculum vulgare* Mill. (107, 165) (1686-1807)

Fine bent - *Agrostis capillaris* L. (66) (1903) England

Fine bent grass [Fine bent-grass] - *Agrostis capillaris* L. (165) (1768)

Fine prairie grass - *Muhlenbergia glomerata* (Willd.) Trin. (45) (1896)

Fine slough grass - *Muhlenbergia glomerata* (Willd.) Trin. (45) (1896)

Fine-haired fern [Fine haired fern] - *Dennstaedtia punctilobula* (Michx.) T. Moore (5) (1913)

Fine-John [Fine John] - *Agrostis gigantea* Roth (5) (1913)

Fine-leaf actinea [Fineleaf actinea] - *Tetraneuris linearifolia* (Hook.) Greene var. *linearifolia* (155) (1942)

Fine-leaf bitterweed [Fineleaf bitterweed] - *Tetraneuris linearifolia* (Hook.) Greene var. *linearifolia* (122) (1937)

Fine-leaf blazingstar [Fine-leaved blazing-star] - *Liatris pilosa* (Aiton) Willd. var. *pilosa* (156) (1923)

Fine-leaf blue grass [Fine-leaf bluegrass, Fine-leafed blue-grass] - *Poa secunda* J. Presl (94) (1901)

Fine-leaf four-nerve daisy [Fineleaf fournerved daisy] - *Tetraneuris linearifolia* (Hook.) Greene (50) (present)

Fine-leaf gerardia [Fineleaf gerardia] - *Agalinis auriculata* (Michx.) Blake (3, 4) (1977-1986)

Fine-leaf hedge-mustard [Fine-leaved hedge mustard, Fine-leaved hedge-mustard] - *Descurainia sophia* (L.) Webb ex Prantl (5, 157, 158) (1900-1929)

Fine-leaf hymenopappus [Fineleaf hymenopappus] - *Hymenopappus filifolius* Hook. (50, 155) (1942–present)

Fine-leaf pondweed [Fineleaf pondweed] - *Stuckenia filiformis* (Pers) Boerner (50) (present)

Fine-leaf sheep fescue [Fineleaf sheep fescue, Fine-leaf sheep's fescue, Fine-leaved sheep's fescue] - *Festuca filiformis* Pourret (50, 68) (1890–present)

Fine-leaf sneezeweed [Fine-leaved sneezeweed] - *Helenium amarum* (Raf.) H. Rock var. *amarum* (5, 72, 97, 158) (1900-1937)

Fine-leaf tetraneuris [Fine-leaved tetraneuris] - *Tetraneuris linearifolia* (Hook.) Greene (5, 97) (1913-1937)

Fine-leaf thelesperma [Fine-leaved thelesperma] - *Thelesperma filifolium* (Hook.) Gray var. *filifolium* (5, 97) (1913-1937)

Fine's bent [Fines bent] - *Agrostis gigantea* Roth (56) (1901) IA

Finetop [Fine-top, Fine top] - *Agrostis canina* L. (5) (1913), *Agrostis capillaris* L. (66, 87, 88, 90) (1885-1903), *Sporobolus airoides* (Torr.) Torr. (144) (1899)

Fine-top grass [Fine top grass] - *Sporobolus airoides* (Torr.) Torr. (151) (1896)

Fine-top salt grass [Fine-top salt-grass] - *Sporobolus airoides* (Torr.) Torr. (5, 94) (1901-1913)

Fingel - *Foeniculum vulgare* Mill. (158) (1900)

Finger coreopsis - *Coreopsis palmata* Nutt. (3, 4, 138, 155) (1923-1986)

Finger fern [Finger Ferne] - *Asplenium scolopendrium* L. var. *americanum* (Fern.) Kartesz & Gandhi (possibly) (178) (1596)

Finger flower - *Digitalis pupurea* L. (69, 92) (1876-1904)

Finger grass [Fingergrass, Finger-grass] - *Andropogon gerardii* Vitman (45) (1896), *Chloris* Sw. (138) (1923), *Digitaria* Haller (155) (1942), *Digitaria ischaemum* (Schreb.) Schreb. ex Muhl. (119) (1938), *Digitaria sanguinalis* (L.) Scop. (5, 19, 45, 56, 62, 66, 80, 92, 107, 119, 143, 155) (1840-1938)

Finger poppy-mallow [Finger poppymallow, Finger poppy mallow] - *Callirhoe digitata* Nutt. (3, 4, 155) (1942-1986)

Finger speedwell - *Veronica triphyllos* L. (50) (present)

Finger-berry [Finger berry] - *Rubus allegheniensis* Porter (156) (1923), *Rubus flagellaris* Willd. (74) (1893) Ann Arbor MI **Finger-comb grass** - *Dactyloctenium aegyptium* (L.) Willd. (5) (1913)

Fingerleaf [Finger leaf] - *Lupinus* L. (7) (1828), *Potentilla canadensis* L. (92) (1876)

Finger-leaf black oak [Finger-leaved black oak] - *Quercus falcata* Michx. (8) (1785)

Finger-shaped paspalum - *Paspalum distichum* L. (66) (1903)

Finger-spike broom grass [Finger-spiked broom grass] - *Andropogon gerardii* Vitman (87, 88) (1884-1885)

Finger-spike Indian grass [Finger-spiked Indian grass] - *Andropogon gerardii* Vitman (144) (1899)

Finger-spike wood grass [Finger-spiked wood grass] - *Andropogon gerardii* Vitman (66, 90) (1885-1903)

Fingrigo - *Pisonia aculeata* L. (20) (1857)

Finkel - *Foeniculum vulgare* Mill. (5, 156, 158) (1900-1923)

Finochio - *Foeniculum vulgare* Mill. (107, 165) (1807-1919)

Fin's grass - *Elymus repens* (L.) Gould (45, 64, 69) (1896-1904)

Finzach - *Polygonum aviculare* L. (158) (1900)

Fior cardinale (Italian) - *Lobelia cardinalis* L. (186) (1814)

Fiorin - *Agrostis capillaris* L. (45, 46) (1879-1896), *Agrostis gigantea* Roth (5, 45, 56, 109, 119) (1896-1949), *Agrostis stolonifera* L. (66) (1903)

Fiorin grass - *Agrostis gigantea* Roth (67, 88, 92) (1885-1890) from Irish name, *Agrostis stolonifera* L. (42, 68, 92) (1814-1890)

Fir balsam [Fir-balsam] or Fir balsam tree - *Abies balsamea* (L.) Mill. (46, 138) (1879-1923), *Abies balsamea* (L.) Mill. var. *balsamea* (20) (1857)

Fir club-moss - *Huperzia selago* (L.) Bernh. ex Mart. & Schrank var. *selago* (5, 50, 92) (1876–present)

Fir moss - *Huperzia selago* (L.) Bernh. ex Mart. & Schrank var. *selago* (5) (1913)

Fir or Fir tree [Firre tree] - *Abies balsamea* (L.) Mill. (5, 92) (1876-1913), *Abies* Mill. (1, 50, 109, 138, 158) (1900–present), *Picea abies* (L.) H. Karst. (178, 180) (1596-1633)

Fir pine - *Abies balsamea* (L.) Mill. (5, 158) (1900-1913)

Fir rape [Fir-rape] - *Epifagus virginiana* (L.) W. Bart. (92) (1876), *Monotropa hypopithys* L. (156) (1923), *Monotropa uniflora* L. (92) (1876)

Fir rope - *Monotropa hypopithys* L. (5, 156) (1913-1923) no longer in use by 1923

Fir-cone amanita [Fircone amanita] - *Amanita strobiliformis* (Paulet ex Vittad.) Bertill. (155) (1942)

Fire cherry - *Prunus pensylvanica* L. f. (5, 76, 156, 158) (1896-1923) Franklin Co. ME, appering on newly burnt lands

Fire lily - *Lilium philadelphicum* L. (156) (1923)

Fire manzanita - *Arctostaphylos nummularia* Gray (155) (1942)

Fireballs [Fire balls, Fire-balls] - *Lychnis chalcedonica* L. (5, 73, 156, 158) (1892–1923) Mansfield OH, no longer in use by 1923

Fire-berry hawthorn [Fireberry hawthorn] - *Crataegus chrysocarpa* Ashe (50, 155) (1942–present)

Firebush [Fire bush] - *Kochia scoparia* (L.) Schrad. (21) (1893)

Fire-cracker flower [Fire cracker flower] - *Dichelostemma ida-maia* (Alph.Wood) Greene (86, 109) (1878-1949)

Firegrass - *Aphanes arvensis* L. (5) (1913)

Fireleaves [Fire leaves, fire-leaves] - *Plantago media* L. (5, 156) (1913-1923)

Fire-lily - *Hemerocallis fulva* (L.) L. (156) (1923)

Fire-on-the-mountain [Fire on the mountain] - *Euphorbia cyathophora* Murray (3, 4, 50, 156) (1923–present)

Firepink [Fire pink] - *Silene virginica* L. (2, 5, 15, 92, 97, 109, 138, 156) (1895-1949)

Firethorn [Fire thorn] - *Cotoneaster* Medik. (156) (1923), *Pyracantha coccinea* M. Roemer (5, 156) (1913-1923), *Pyracantha* M. Roemer (138) (1923)

Firetop [Fire top, Fire-top] - *Chamerion angustifolium* (L.) Holub subsp. *angustifolium* (5, 74, 156, 157, 158) (1893-1929) Penobscot River ME, lumberman

Fireweed [Fire weed, Fire-weed] - *Amsinckia lycopsoides* Lehm. (106) (1930) CA, a skin irritant, *Chamerion angustifolium* (L.) Holub subsp. *circumvagum* (Mosquin) Kartesz (50) (present), *Chamerion angustifolium* (L.) Holub subsp. *angustifolium* (3, 40, 50, 63, 82, 85, 92, 106, 107, 109, 137, 131, 156, 157, 158) (1876–present), *Chamerion* Raf. ex Holub (1, 4, 50, 93) (1932–present), *Conyza canadensis* (L.) Cronq. var. *canadensis* (5, 69, 92, 156, 157, 158) (1876-1929), *Datura stramonium* L. (5, 69, 156, 158) (1900-1923), *Erechtites hieraciifolia* (L.) Raf. ex DC. (5, 6, 19, 48, 49, 53, 57, 58, 61, 62, 63, 72, 80, 92, 93, 122, 156, 157, 158, 187) (1818-1936), *Erechtites hieraciifolia* (L.) Raf. ex DC. var. *hieraciifolia* (19, 187) (1818-1840), *Erechtites* Raf. (1, 3, 4, 158) (1900-1986), *Lactuca canadensis* L. (5, 6, 156, 158, 187) (1818-1923), *Packera aurea* (L.) A.& D. Löve (6, 92, 156, 158) (1876-1923), *Plantago media* L. (5, 156) (1913-1923), *Senecio* L. (7) (1828)

Fireweed fiddleneck - *Amsinckia menziesii* (Lehm.) A. Nels. & J.F. Macbr. (155) (1942)

Firewheel - *Gaillardia pulchella* Foug. (50) (present), *Gaillardia pulchella* Foug. var. *pulchella* (50) (present)

First broad-leaf mountain moly [First broad leaued mountaine moly] - *Allium victorialis* L. (180) (1633)

First-flower-of-the-spring [First flower of the spring] - *Primula* L. (10) (1818)

Fisfisat (Arabic) - *Medicago sativa* L. (110) (1886)

Fish geranium - *Pelargonium ×hortorum* Bailey [*inquinans × zonale*] (109, 138) (1923-1949)

Fish mint [Fish-mint] - *Mentha aquatica* L. (5, 156, 158) (1900-1923), *Mentha spicata* L. (5, 156, 158) (1900–1923)

Fish poison - *Aesculus pavia* L. (5, 156) (1913-1923), *Lepidium bidentatum* Montin (92, 107) (1876-1919)

Fish-blankets - *Ceratophyllum demersum* L. (156) (1923)

Fisher's dupontia - *Dupontia fisheri* R. Br. (5, 94) (1901-1913)

Fisher's tundra grass [Fisher's tundragrass] - *Dupontia fisheri* R. Br. (50) (present)

Fish-grass - *Cabomba caroliniana* Gray (109) (1949)

Fish-hawk cactus - *Ferocactus wislizeni* (Engelm.) Britt. & Rose (76) (1896) AZ

Fishhook [Fish-hooks] - *Erythronium americanum* Ker. (156) (1923), *Ferocactus hamatacanthus* (Muehlenpfordt) Britt. & Rose var. *hamatacanthus* (122) (1937) TX

Fishhook cactus - *Sclerocactus uncinatus* (Galeotti) N.P. Taylor var. *wrightii* (Engelm.) N.P. Taylor (138) (1923) AZ NM

Fish-leaves - *Potamogeton natans* L. (158) (1900)

Fish-mouth [Fish mouth] - *Chelone glabra* L. (5, 92, 156) (1876-1923) no longer in use by 1923

Fish-tail palm - *Caryota* L. (109) (1949)

Fishweed [Fish-weed] - *Chenopodium ambrosioides* L. var. *ambrosioides* (156) (1923), *Potamogeton* L. (1) (1932)

Fishwood [Fish wood, Fish-wood] - *Euonymus americanus* L. (5, 156) (1913-1923)

Fit plant - *Monotropa uniflora* L. (5, 49) (1898-1913)

Fit root [Fit-root, Fitroot] - *Monotropa uniflora* L. (5, 6, 7, 158) (1828-1892)

Fitch - *Vicia sativa* L. (92) (1876)

Fit-root plant [Fit root plant] - *Monotropa uniflora* L. (92, 156) (1876-1923)

Five-angle dodder [Fiveangled dodder] - *Cuscuta pentagona* Engelm. (50) (present)

Five-finger [Fivefinger, Five finger] - *Panax quinquefolius* L. (6, 7, 64, 156, 157, 158) (1828-1929), *Parthenocissus quinquefolia* (L.) Planch. (76, 157, 158) (1896-1929), *Potentilla arguta* Pursh subsp. *arguta* (40) (1928), *Potentilla canadensis* L. (2, 5, 62, 72, 92, 97, 156) (1876-1937), *Potentilla* L. (1, 2, 82, 93, 109) (1895-1949), *Potentilla norvegica* L. subsp. *monspeliensis* (L.) Aschers. & Graebn. (80, 82) (1913-1930)

Five-finger creeper [Five-fingered creeper] - *Parthenocissus quinquefolia* (L.) Planch. (156) (1923)

Five-finger ivy [Five-fingered ivy] - *Parthenocissus quinquefolia* (L.) Planch. (74, 156, 158) (1893-1923)

Fivefinger-grass [Five-fingered grass] - *Potentilla* L. (190) (~1759)

Five-fingers root [Fivefingers root] - *Panax quinquefolius* L. (92) (1876)

Five-flower gentian [Five-flowered gentian] - *Gentianella quinquefolia* (L.) Small subsp. *quinquefolia* (5, 7, 49, 156) (1828-1923)

Five-hook bassia [Fivehook bassia] - *Bassia hyssopifolia* (Pallas) Kuntze (4, 155) (1942-1986)

Five-horn smotherweed [Fivehorn smotherweed] - *Bassia hyssopifolia* (Pallas) Kuntze (50) (present)

Five-leaf akebia [Fiveleaf akebia] - *Akebia quinata* (Houtt.) Dcne. (138, 155) (1931-1942)

Five-leaf anemone [Five leaved anemone] - *Anemone quinquefolia* L. (42) (1814)

Five-leaf creeper [Five-leaved creeper] - *Parthenocissus quinquefolia* (L.) Planch. (46) (1879)

Five-leaf ivy [Five-leaved ivy] - *Parthenocissus quinquefolia* (L.) Planch. (130, 156, 158) (1895-1923)

Five-leaf wild ivy [Five leaved wild ivy] - *Parthenocissus quinquefolia* (L.) Planch. (42) (1814)

Fiveleaf-grass [Five leaved grass, Fiue leued grasse] - *Potentilla reptans* L. (92, 179) (1526-1876)

Five-leaves - *Parthenocissus quinquefolia* (L.) Planch. (6, 49, 92) (1876–1892)

Five-nerve false sunflower [Five-nerved false sunflower] - *Helianthella quinquenervis* (Hook.) Gray (131) (1899)

Five-nerve helianthella [Fivenerve helianthella] - *Helianthella quinquenervis* (Hook.) Gray (50) (present)

Five-sisters [Five-sisters] - *Lysimachia quadrifolia* L. (5, 156, 158) (1900-1923)

Five-spike blue grama [Fivespike blue grama] - *Bouteloua gracilis* (Willd. ex Kunth) Lag. ex Griffiths (155) (1942)

Five-spot - *Nemophila maculata* Benth. ex Lindl. (109) (1949)

Five-stamen chickweed [Fivestamen chickweed] - *Cerastium semidecandrum* L. (50) (present)

Five-stamen cinquefoil [Five stamened cinquefoil] - *Potentilla rivalis* Nutt. var. *pentandra* (Engelm.) S. Wats. (5, 72, 93) (1907-1936)

Five-stamen mouse-ear chickweed [Five-stamened mouse-ear chickweed] - *Cerastium semidecandrum* L. (5) (1913)

Five-stamen tamarisk [Fivestamen tamarisk] or Fivestamen tamarix - *Tamarix chinensis* Lour. (50, 138, 155) (1923–present)

Flachskraut (German) - *Linaria vulgaris* Mill. (158) (1900)

Flack (Swedish) - *Phalaris arundinacea* L. (46) (1879)

Flag - *Iris* L. (10, 184) (1793-1818), *Iris missouriensis* Nutt. (148) (1939), *Typha latifolia* L. (27, 35) (1806-1811)

Flag root [Flag-root] - *Acorus calamus* L. (5, 7, 93, 156, 157) (1828-1936)

Flag-lily [Flag-lilly, Flag lily] - *Iris* L. (7, 156) (1828, 1923), *Iris versicolor* L. (5, 6, 49, 64, 92, 156, 157, 158) (1892-1913)

Flagons - *Iris pseudacorus* L. (5, 156, 158) (1900-1923) no longer in use by 1923

Flag-tule - *Typha latifolia* L. (157) (1929)

Flambe (French) - *Iris* L. (180) (1633)

Flambe varié (French) - *Iris versicolor* L. (158) (1900)

Flambe variée (French) - *Iris versicolor* L. (158) (1900)

Flame azalea - *Rhododendron calendulaceum* (Michx.) Torr. (5, 109, 138, 156) (1913-1949)

Flame buckeye - *Aesculus pavia* L. (155) (1942)

Flame lily - *Lilium philadelphicum* L. (5, 156, 158) (1900-1923)

Flame-colored azalea - *Rhododendron calendulaceum* (Michx.) Torr. (156) (1923)

Flameflower [Flame flower, Flame-flower] - *Phemeranthus teretifolius* (Pursh) Raf. (72, 156) (1907-1923), *Talinum* Adans. (93, 109) (1936-1949), *Talinum aurantiacum* Engelm. (122) (1937)

Flame-leaf sumac [Flameleaf sumac] - *Rhus copallinum* L. (50, 155) (1942–present)

Flame-poppy [Flamepoppy] - *Stylomecon heterophylla* (Benth.) G. Taylor (138) (1923)

Flame-ray gerbera - *Gerbera jamesonii* Bolus ex Hooker f. (138) (1923)

Flaming azalea - *Rhododendron flammeum* (Michx.) Sarg. (possibly) (182) (1791)

Flaming orchis - *Platanthera psycodes* (L.) Lindl. (5, 156) (1913-1923)

Flaming pinkster - *Rhododendron calendulaceum* (Michx.) Torr. (156) (1923)

Flaming trumpet - *Pyrostegia venusta* (Ker-Gawl.) Miers (138) (1923)

Flamy - *Viola tricolor* L. (158) (1900)

Flanders cherry [Flaunders cherrie] - *Prunus cerasus* L. (178) (1526)

Flank starwort [Flanke starwoort] - *Symphyotrichum novi-belgii* (L.) Nesom var. *novi-belgii* (178) (1526)

Flannel bush [Flannel-bush] - *Fremontodendron californicum* (Torr.) Coville (109) (1949)

Flannel flower - *Verbascum thapsus* L. (92) (1876)

Flannel mullein - *Verbascum thapsus* L. (155) (1942)

Flannel plant [Flannel-plant] - *Verbascum thapsus* L. (6, 156) (1892-1923)

Flannel-leaf [Flannel leaf] - *Verbascum thapsus* L. (5, 69, 156, 158) (1900-1923)

Flapdock - *Digitalis pupurea* L. (69) (1904)

Flat blites - *Atriplex hortensis* L. (178) (1526)

Flat club-moss - *Lycopodium complanatum* L. (possibky) (187) (1818)

Flat club-rush - *Trichophorum planifolium* (Spreng.) Palla (66) (1903)

Flat crab grass [Flat crab-grass] - *Axonopus compressus* (Sw.) Beauv. (5) (1913), *Axonopus furcatus* (Flueggé) A.S. Hitchc. (163) (1852)

Flat cyperus - *Cyperus compressus* L. (5) (1913)

Flat joint grass [Flat joint-grass] - *Axonopus compressus* (Sw.) Beauv. (5, 163) (1852-1913)

Flat pea - *Lathyrus sylvestris* L. (68, 109, 118) (1898-1949)

Flat peach - *Prunus persica* (L.) Batsch (109) (1949)

Flat squash - *Cucurbita pepo* L. var. *melopepo* (L.) Alef. (possibly) (19) (1840)

Flat stemrush [Flat stem-rush] - *Eleocharis tricostata* Torr. (66) (1903)

Flat walnut - *Juglans ailanthifolia* Carr. (possibly) (138) (1923)

Flat wheat - *Triticum aestivum* L. (180) (1633)

Flat-cup agaricus [Flatcup agaricus] - *Agaricus placomyces* Peck (155) (1942)

Flat-globe dodder [Flatglobe dodder] - *Cuscuta umbellata* Kunth (50) (present)

Flat-leaf bladderwort [Flatleaf bladderwort, Flat-leaved bladderwort] - *Utricularia intermedia* Hayne (5, 50, 72) (1907–present)

Flat-leaf panic-grass [Flat-leaved panic-grass] - *Urochloa platyphylla* (Munro ex C. Wright) R.D. Webster (94) (1901)

Flat-pod pea [Flat-podded pea] - *Lathyrus cicera* L. (110) (1886)

Flatsedge [Flat-sedge] - *Cyperus* L. (50, 138, 139) (1923–present)

Flat-spine burr ragweed [Flatspine burr ragweed] - *Ambrosia acanthicarpa* Hook. (50) (present)

Flat-spine stickseed [Flatspine stickseed] - *Lappula occidentalis* (S. Wats.) Greene (50) (present)

Flat-stalk grass [Flat stalked grass] - *Poa compressa* L. (90) (1885)

Flat-stalk meadow grass [Flat-stalked meadow grass] - *Poa compressa* L. (45) (1896)

Flat-stem dropseed [Flat-stemmed dropseed] - *Muhlenbergia torreyana* (J.A. Schultes) A.S. Hitchc. (5) (1913)

Flat-stem meadow grass [Flat-stemmed meadow grass, Flat-stemmed meadow-grass] - *Poa compressa* L. (5, 119, 143) (1913-1938)

Flat-stem panic [Flat-stemmed panic] - *Panicum anceps* Michx. (5, 94, 119, 163) (1852-1938)

Flat-stem poa [Flat-stemmed poa] - *Poa compressa* L. (45) (1896)

Flat-stem pondweed [Flatstem pondweed] - *Potamogeton zosteriformis* Fern. (3, 50, 155) (1942–present)

Flat-stem sedge [Flat stemmed sedge] - *Cyperus compressus* L. (42) (1814)

Flat-stem spikerush [Flatstem spikerush, Flat-stemmed spike rush] - *Eleocharis compressa* Sull. var. *compressa* (5, 50) (1913–present)

Flat-stem spikesedge [Flatstem spikesedge] - *Eleocharis compressa* Sullivant (3) (1977)

Flat-stem sporobolus [Flat-stemmed sporobolus] - *Muhlenbergia torreyana* (J.A. Schultes) A.S. Hitchc. (94) (1901)

Flat-stem tufted spikerush [Flat stemmed tufted spike-rush] - *Eleocharis compressa* Sullivant (129) (1894)

Flattened oat grass [Flattened oatgrass] - *Danthonia compressa* Austin ex Peck (50) (present)

Flattened pipewort - *Eriocaulon compressum* Lam. (5, 50) (1913–present)

Flattened wild oat grass - *Danthonia compressa* Austin ex Peck (5) (1913)

Flatterdock [Flatter-dock, Flatter dock] - *Nuphar lutea* (L.) Sm. subsp. *advena* (Aiton) Kartesz & Gandhi (156) (1923), *Nymphaea alba* L. (107) (1919), *Potamogeton natans* L. (158) (1900)

Flat-top [Flat top] - *Eriogonum* Michx. (106) (1930), *Vernonia noveboracensis* (L.) Michx. (19, 72, 86, 156) (1840-1923)

Flat-top aster [Flattop aster] - *Doellingeria umbellata* (P. Mill.) Nees var. *umbellata* (138, 155) (1931-1942)

Flat-top goldenrod [Flat-top golden-rod, Flat-topped golden-rod, Flat-topped goldenrod] - *Euthamia graminifolia* (L.) Nutt. var. *graminifolia* (5, 50, 93, 156, 158) (1900–present)

Flat-top goldentop - *Euthamia graminifolia* (L.) Nutt. (50) (present)

Flat-top goldentop - *Euthamia graminifolia* (L.) Nutt. var. *graminifolia* (50) (present)

Flat-top mille graines - *Oldenlandia corymbosa* L. (50) (present)

Flat-top white aster [Flat-topped white aster] - *Doellingeria umbellata* (P. Mill.) Nees (131) (1899)

Flaver - *Avena fatua* L. (107) (1919)

Flaveria - *Flaveria campestris* Johnst. (3) (1977), *Flaveria* Juss. (158) (1900)

Flaw floure - *Pulsatilla patens* (L.) Mill. subsp. *multifida* (Pritz.) Zamels (possibly) (180) (1633)

Flax - *Linum* L. (1, 4, 10, 13, 15, 50, 82, 93, 109, 138, 155, 158, 184) (1793–present), *Linum perenne* L. (35) (1806), *Linum rigidum* Pursh (148) (1939), *Linum usitatissimum* L. (5, 19, 72, 85, 95, 97, 107, 109, 110, 114, 138, 158, 179, 180) (1526-1949)

Flax bellflower [Flax bell-flower] - *Campanula rotundifolia* L. (19) (1840)

Flax dodder - *Cuscuta epilinum* Weihe. (5, 14, 80, 82, 156) (1882-1937)

Flax drop - *Cuscuta europaea* L. (92) (1876)

Flax snapdragon [Flax snap dragon] - *Linaria vulgaris* Mill. (19) (1840)

Flax vine [Flax-vine] - *Cuscuta epilinum* Weihe. (156) (1923), *Cuscuta europaea* L. (19, 92) (1840-1876)

Flaxen wheat - *Triticum aestivum* L. (180) (1633)

Flax-flower ipomopsis [Flaxflowered ipomopsis] - *Ipomopsis longiflora* (Torr.) V. Grant (50) (present)

Flaxleaf - *Thesium linophyllon* L. (50) (present)

Flax-leaf agalinis [Flax-leaved agalinis] - *Agalinis linifolia* (Nutt.) Britt. (5) (1913)

Flax-leaf basil [Flax-leaved basil] - *Pycnanthemum flexuosum* (Walt.) Britton, Sterns & Poggenb. (187) (1818)

Flax-leaf brachystemum [Flax leaved brachystemum] - *Pycnanthemum flexuosum* (Walt.) Britton, Sterns & Poggenb. (42) (1914)

Flax-leaf gerardia [Flax-leaved gerardia] - *Agalinis linifolia* (Nutt.) Britt. (72) (1907)

Flax-leaf navelseed [Flaxleaf navelseed] - *Omphalodes linifolia* (L.) Moench (138) (1923)

Flax-leaf pimpernel [Flaxleaf pimpernel, Flax-leaved pimpernel] - *Anagallis monelli* L. (138, 155, 165) (1807-1942)

Flax-leaf starwort [Flax-leaved star wort] - *Symphyotrichum subulatum* (Michx.) Nesom (19) (1840)

Flax-leaf stenosiphon [Flax-leaved stenosiphon] - *Stenosiphon linifolius* (Nutt. ex James) Heynh. (5, 97) (1913-1937)

Flax-leaf whitetop aster [Flaxleaf whitetop aster] - *Ionactis linariifolius* (L.) Greene (50) (present)

Flax-lily [Flaxlily] - *Phormium* J.R. & G. Forst. (138) (1923)

Flax-olive - *Daphne mezereum* L. (156) (1923)

Flaxseed [Flax seed] - *Linum usitatissimum* L. (53, 57, 59, 92, 157) (1876-1929)

Flax-seed plantain [Flaxseed plantain] - *Plantago psyllium* L. (155) (1942)

Flax-tail [Flax tail, Flax-tail] - *Typha latifolia* L. (5, 156, 157, 158) (1900-1929)

Flaxweed [Flax weed] - *Cuscuta europaea* L. (92) (1876), *Comandra umbellata* (L.) Nutt. (184) (1793), *Descurainia sophia* (L.) Webb ex Prantl (5, 93, 156) (1913-1936), *Linaria vulgaris* Mill. (5, 156, 157, 158) (1900-1929)

Fleabane [Flea-bane, Flea bane] - *Conyza canadensis* (L.) Cronq. var. *canadensis* (19, 45, 52, 54) (1840-1919), *Conyza* Less. (10, 42, 167) (1814-1818), *Erigeron annuus* (L.) Pers. (80, 82) (1913-1930), *Erigeron glabellus* Nutt. (85) (1932), *Erigeron* L. (1, 2, 4, 10, 50, 57, 63, 93, 109, 138, 155, 156, 184) (1793-present), *Erigeron philadelphicus* L. (127) (1933), *Erigeron pulchellus* Michx. (86) (1878), *Inula* L. (10) (1818), *Plantago psyllium* L. (178) (1526), *Sericocarpus asteroides* (L.) B.S.P. (42) (1814)

Fleadock [Flea-dock, Flea dock] - *Petasites hybridus* (L.) G. Gaertn., B. Mey. & Scherb. (5, 156) (1913-1923) no longer in use by 1923

Fleaseed [Flea seed] - *Plantago psyllium* L. (92) (1876)

Fleaweed [Flea-weed] - *Trichostema lanceolatum* Benth. (156) (1923)

Fleawort [Fleawort, Flea wort] - *Galium verum* L. (156, 158) (1900-1923) no longer in use by 1923, *Plantago psyllium* L. (92) (1876), *Senecio vulgaris* L. (92, 156, 158) (1876-1923)

Fleckstorchschnabel (German) - *Geranium maculatum* L. (158) (1900)

Fleece goldenweed - *Ericameria arborescens* (Gray) Greene (155) (1942), *Isocoma acradenia* (Greene) Greene var. *acradenia* (155) (1942)

Fleischfarbige Schwalbenwurzel (German) - *Asclepias incarnata* L. (158) (1900)

Flenort (Swedish) - *Parnassia palustris* L. (46) (1879)

Flesh-colored asclepias - *Asclepias incarnata* L. (49, 52, 53, 92, 158) (1876-1922)

Flesh-colored milkweed [Flesh-coloured milk-weed, Flesh-coloured milk weed] - *Asclepias incarnata* L. (42, 187) (1814-1818)

Flesh-colored swallowwort, Flesh-coloured swallow wort - *Asclepias incarnata* L. (42, 158) (1814-1900)

Fleshy hawthorn - *Crataegus succulenta* Schrad. ex Link (50, 138, 155) (1923–present)

Fleshy starwort - *Stellaria crassifolia* Ehrh. var. *crassifolia* (50) (present), *Stellaria crassifolia* Ehrh. (50) (present)

Fleshy stitchwort - *Stellaria crassifolia* Ehrh. (4, 122) (1937-1986), *Stellaria crassifolia* Ehrh. var. *crassifolia* (5) (1913)

Fleshy-leaf thorn [Fleshy-leaved thorn] - *Sarcobatus vermiculatus* (Hook.) Torr. (35) (1806)

Fleur-de-lis [Fleur de lis] - *Iris germanica* L. (5) (1913), *Iris* L. (1, 7, 93, 109, 156, 158) (1828-1949), *Iris missouriensis* Nutt. (85) (1932) SD

Fleur-de-luce [Fleur de luce] - *Iris versicolor* L. (53) (1922), *Iris virginica* L. (187) (1818)

Flexible pine - *Pinus flexilis* James (108) (1878)

Flexile milkvetch [Flexile milk vetch] - *Astragalus flexuosus* (Hook.) Dougl. ex G. Don (5, 50, 131, 155) (1899–present), *Astragalus flexuosus* (Hook.) Dougl. ex G. Don var. *elongatus* (Hook.) M.E. Jones (50) (present)

Flexuose hair-grass - *Deschampsia flexuosa* (L.) Trin. var *flexuosa* (187) (1818)

Flexuous spear grass [Flexuous spear-grass] - *Poa autumnalis* Muhl. ex Ell. (5, 163) (1852-1913)

Flieder (German) - *Sambucus nigra* L. (158) (1900)

Fliegen Fangemdes (German) - *Apocynum androsaemifolium* L. (7) (1828)

Flint corn - *Zea mays* L. subsp. *mays* (109, 119) (1938-1949)

Flix - *Linum usitatissimum* L. (5, 156, 158) (1900-1923)

Flixweed [Flix-weed, Flix weed, Flixe weede] - *Descurainia sophia* (L.) Webb ex Prantl (3, 4, 5, 72, 92, 156, 157, 158, 178) (1526-1986) from German for thread or hair

Flixweed [Flix-weed, Flix weed, Flixe weede] - *Diplotaxis muralis* (L.) DC. (5, 156, 158) (1900-1923)

Float foxtail grass [Flote fox-tail grass] - *Alopecurus geniculatus* L. (165) (1768)

Float grass [Flote grass] - *Alopecurus geniculatus* L. (5, 46) (1879-1913), *Catabrosa aquatica* (L.) Beauv. (46) (1879), *Glyceria fluitans* (L.) R. Br. (5, 92, 107) (1876-1919)

Floating arum [Floating-arum] - *Orontium aquaticum* L. (5, 156) (1913-1923), *Orontium* L. (167) (1814)

Floating bur-reed - *Sparganium angustifolium* Michx. (19) (1840), *Sparganium fluctuans* (Morong) B.L. Robins. (5, 50) (1913–present)

Floating chainfern - *Azolla caroliniana* Willd. (122) (1937) TX

Floating clubrush [Floating club-rush] - *Schoenoplectus subterminalis* (Torr.) Soják (66) (1903)

Floating evening-primrose [Floating evening primrose] - *Ludwigia peploides* (Kunth) Raven (4, 50) (1986–present), *Ludwigia peploides* (Kunth) Raven subsp. *glabrescens* (Kuntze) Raven (4) (1986)

Floating fern [Floating-fern] - *Ceratopteris* Brongn. (109) (1949)

Floating foxtail - *Alopecurus geniculatus* L. (5, 19, 45, 66, 90, 94) (1840-1912)

Floating lady's-thumb [Floating ladysthumb] - *Polygonum amphibium* L. var. *stipulaceum* Coleman (155) (1942)

Floating liverwort - *Ricciocarpos natans* (L.) Corda (19) (1840)

Floating manna grass [Floating manna-grass] - *Catabrosa aquatica* (L.) Beauv. (56, 67) (1890-1901), *Glyceria fluitans* (L.) R. Br. (5,

150

56, 72, 87, 88, 90, 94) (1885-1913), *Glyceria septentrionalis* A.S. Hitchc. (5, 163) (1852-1913)

Floating marsh pennywort [Floating marsh penny wort, Floating marsh-penny-wort] - *Hydrocotyle ranunculoides* L. f. (5, 50, 97, 158) (1913–present)

Floating marsh-marigold [Floating marsh marigold] - *Caltha natans* Pallas ex Georgi (5) (1913)

Floating meadow grass [Floating meadow-grass] - *Glyceria fluitans* (L.) R. Br. (45, 66, 129) (1894-1903)

Floating moss - *Salvinia natans* (L.) All. (5) (1913)

Floating paspalum - *Paspalum fluitans* (Ell.) Kunth (66) (1903)

Floating pennywort - *Hydrocotyle ranunculoides* L. f. (155) (1942)

Floating pondweed - *Potamogeton natans* L. (50, 85, 156) (1923–present)

Floating primrose-willow [Floating primrose willow] - *Ludwigia peploides* (Kunth) Raven (5, 97, 156, 158) (1900-1937), *Ludwigia peploides* (Kunth) Raven subsp. *glabrescens* (Kuntze) Raven (50, 158) (1900–present)

Floating water grass [Floating water-grass] - *Paspalum fluitans* (Ell.) Kunth (94) (1901)

Floating watermoss - *Salvinia natans* (L.) All. (50) (present)

Floating water-primrose [Floating waterprimrose] - *Ludwigia peploides* (Kunth) Raven (155) (1942)

Floatingheart [Floating-heart, Floating heart] - *Nymphoides aquatica* (J.F. Gmel.) Kuntze (122, 124) (1937) TX, *Nymphoides cordata* (Ell.) Fern. (5, 19, 86, 156) (1840-1923), *Nymphoides* Hill (1, 2, 109, 138) (1895-1949), *Nymphoides peltata* (Gmel.) Kuntze (5, 138, 156) (1913-1923)

Floating-leaf pondweed [Floating-leaved pondweed, Floatingleaf pondweed] - *Potamogeton natans* L. (3, 155) (1942-1977)

Flodman's thistle - *Cirsium flodmanii* (Rydb.) Arthur (4, 5, 50) (1913–present)

Floppers - *Kalanchoe pinnata* (Lam.) Pers. (109) (1949)

Floptop [Flop-top] - *Saponaria officinalis* L. (156) (1923)

Floramor [Floramour] - *Amaranthus hybridus* L. (5, 156, 158, 165) (1768-1923)

Flora's-paintbrush [Flora's paint brush, Flora's paint-brush, Floras-paintbrush] - *Emilia coccinea* (Sims) G. Don (109) (1949), *Hieracium aurantiacum* L. (5, 75, 156) (1894-1923) Oxford Co. & Penobscot Co. ME

Florentine tulip - *Tulipa sylvestris* L. (138) (1923)

Florid cornel - *Cornus florida* L. (7, 186) (1825-1828)

Florida allspice - *Calycanthus floridus* L. (57) (1917)

Florida amphicarpon - *Amphicarpum muehlenbergianum* (J.A. Schultes) A.S. Hitchc. (94) (1901)

Florida anise - *Illicium floridanum* Ellis (92) (1876)

Florida anise tree - *Illicium floridanum* Ellis (7) (1828)

Florida arrowroot - *Zamia pumila* L. (92) (1876)

Florida balsam - *Amyris elemifera* L. (92) (1876)

Florida balsam tree - *Amyris elemifera* L. (7) (1828)

Florida bark - *Pinckneya bracteata* (Bartr.) Raf. (7, 92) (1828-1876)

Florida cornel - *Cornus florida* L. (92, 156, 158) (1898-1923)

Florida crinum - *Crinum americanum* L. (138) (1923)

Florida curly-head [Florida curly head] - *Aristida floridana* (Chapman) Vasey (94) (1901)

Florida dogwood - *Cornus florida* L. (5, 92, 156, 158) (1898-1923)

Florida elder - *Sambucus nigra* L. subsp. *canadensis* (L.) R. Bolli (155) (1942)

Florida froelichia - *Froelichia floridana* (Nutt.) Moq. (72) (1907)

Florida laurel - *Symplocos tinctoria* (L.) L'Her. (5, 156) (1913-1923)

Florida lettuce - *Lactuca floridana* (L.) Gaertn. (3, 4, 5, 72, 97) (1907-1986)

Florida mahogany - *Persea borbonia* (L.) Spreng. (106, 156) (1923-1930)

Florida maple - *Acer barbatum* Michx. (155) (1942)

Florida milkweed - *Asclepias longifolia* Michx. (5, 72, 93, 97) (1907-1937)

Florida moss - *Tillandsia usneoides* (L.) L. (5, 156) (1913-1923)

Florida mudmidget - *Wolffiella gladiata* (Hegelm.) Hegelm. (50) (present)

Florida nutmeg - *Torreya taxifolia* Arnot. (50) (present)

Florida paspalum - *Paspalum floridanum* Michx. (3, 5, 50, 94, 99, 119, 155) (1901–present)

Florida pepper - *Peperomia humilis* A. Dietr. (19) (1840)

Florida pine - *Pinus palustris* Mill. (5) (1913)

Florida royal palm [Floridian royal palm] - *Roystonea elata* (Bartr.) F. Harper (109) (1949)

Florida soap berry - *Sapindus saponaria* L. var. *saponaria* (20) (1857)

Florida strangler fig - *Ficus aurea* Nutt. (138) (1923)

Florida thatch palm - *Thrinax radiata* Lodd. ex J.A. & J.H. Schultes (138) (1923)

Florida torch wood [Florida torch wood - *Amyris elemifera* L. (20) (1857)

Florida torreya - *Torreya taxifolia* Arnot. (138) (1923)

Florida trumpetbush - *Tecoma stans* (L.) Juss. ex Kunth (138) (1923)

Florida waterhemp - *Acnida floridana* S. Watson (155) (1942)

Florida wolffiella - *Wolffiella gladiata* (Hegelm.) Hegelm. (5) (1913)

Florida yellow flax - *Linum floridanum* (Planch.) Trel. var. *floridanum* (5) (1913)

Florida yew tree - *Torreya taxifolia* Arnot. (19) (1840)

Floripondio - *Brugmansia candida* Pers. (138) (1923)

Florist's chrysanthemum [Florists chrysanthemum] - *Dendranthema* ×*grandiflorum* Kitam. [*indicum* × *japonicum*] (109) (1949)

Florist's cineraria [Florsits cineraria] - *Pericallis cuneata* (L'Hér.) Bolle (109) (1949)

Florist's violet [Florists violet] - *Viola odorata* L. (109) (1949)

Flos Adonis - *Adonis annua* L. (178) (1526)

Floss-silk tree [Floss-silk-tree] - *Chorisia speciosa* St.Hil. (138) (1923)

Flowan - *Anthemis cotula* L. (157, 158) (1900-1929)

Flower-cup fern - *Woodsia alpina* (Bolton) S.F. Gray (5, 19, 92) (1840-1913)

Flower-de-luce [Flower de luce, Floure-de-luce] - *Iris* L. (2, 10, 180, 190) (1633-1895), *Iris pseudacorus* L. (180) (1633), *Iris versicolor* L. (6, 49, 92, 157) (1876–1929)

Flower-de-luce of Dalmatia [Flowerdeluce of Dalmatia] - *Iris pallida* Lam. (178) (1596)

Flower-fence - *Senna ligustrina* (L.) Irwin & Barneby (177) (1762)

Flower-gentle [Flower gentle] - *Amaranthus hybridus* L. (5, 156, 158) (1900–1923)

Flowering almond - *Prunus* L. (112) (1937), *Prunus triloba* Lindl. (109) (1949)

Flowering aloe [Flowering aloes] - *Agave americana* L. (7, 92) (1828-1876)

Flowering ash - *Fraxinus* L. (possibly) (10) (1818)

Flowering box - *Vaccinium vitis-idaea* L. (possibly) (5) (1913)

Flowering boxberry [Flowering box-berry] - *Vaccinium vitis-idaea* L. (156) (1923)

Flowering brake - *Osmunda regalis* L. (92, 157) (1876-1900)

Flowering bramble - *Rubus rosifolius* Sm. (92) (1876)

Flowering cornel - *Cornus florida* L. (49, 53, 58, 92, 156, 158) (1869-1923)

Flowering currant - *Ribes americanum* Mill. (156) (1923), *Ribes aureum* Pursh (73, 112, 135, 156, 158) (1892–1937), *Ribes aureum* Pursh var. *villosum* DC. (5) (1913)

Flowering dogwood - *Cornus florida* L. (2, 3, 4, 5, 6, 49, 53, 82, 97, 105, 122, 124, 138, 155, 156, 158) (1892-1986), *Cornus* L. (1) (1932)

Flowering fern [Flowering-fern] - *Osmunda cinnamomea* L. (19) (1840), *Osmunda* L. (10, 158, 184) (1793-1900), *Osmunda regalis* L. (5, 92, 157, 187) (1818-1929)

Flowering flag - *Iris versicolor* L. (156) (1923), *Linum grandiflorum* Desf. (50, 109 138, 155) (1923–present), *Linum perenne* L. (44) (1845)

Flowering maple - *Abutilon* Mill. (109) (1949)

Flowering nettle [Flowering-nettle] - *Galeopsis bifida* Boenn. (5, 19, 92, 156, 158) (1840-1923)

Flowering plum - *Prunus triloba* Lindl. (135, 138) (1910-1923) MT

Flowering quince - *Chaenomeles japonica* (Thunb.) Lindl. ex Spach (73, 138) (1892-1923), *Chaenomeles* Lindl. (109) (1949)

Flowering raspberry - *Rubus idaeus* L. subsp. *strigosus* (Michx.) Focke (47) (1852), *Rubus* L. (1) (1932), *Rubus odoratus* L. (19, 47, 107, 138, 156) (1840-1923), *Rubus parviflorus* Nutt. (106) (1930)

Flowering reed - *Canna* L. (10) (1818)

Flowering spurge - *Euphorbia corollata* L. (3, 4, 5, 6, 47, 50, 62, 72, 80, 82, 85, 86, 93, 97, 109, 122, 125, 138, 156, 157, 158) (1852–present)

Flowering straw - *Lygodesmia texana* (Torr. & Gray) Greene (97) (1937) OK

Flowering thistle - *Argemone mexicana* L. (5, 73, 156) (1892-1923) Mansfield OH

Flowering wintergreen - *Polygala paucifolia* Willd. (5, 15, 19, 92, 109, 156) (1840-1949)

Flowering-ash [Flowering ash] - *Chionanthus virginicus* L. (5, 156) (1913-1923)

Flowering-dogwood [Flowering dogwood] - *Amelanchier ×intermedia* Spach [*arborea × canadensis*] (5) (1913)

Flowering-fern - *Osmunda regalis* L. (109) (1949)

Flowering-moss [Flowering moss] - *Phlox subulata* L. (5, 73, 156) (1892-1923) Northern OH, *Pyxidanthera barbulata* Michx. (2, 5, 156) (1895-1923), *Sedum pulchellum* Michx. (5, 156, 158) (1900-1923)

Flowering-mulberry [Flowering mulberry] - *Rubus odoratus* L. (46) (1879)

Flowering-plantain [Flowering plantain] - *Parnassia glauca* Raf. (19) (1840)

Flowering-rush [Flowering rush] - *Butomus* L. (109) (1949), *Butomus umbellatus* L. (3, 50) (1977–present)

Flowering-spurge euphorbia [Floweringspurge euphorbia] - *Euphorbia corollata* L. (155) (1942)

Flowering-willow [Flowering willow] - *Chamerion angustifolium* (L.) Holub subsp. *angustifolium* (5, 92, 156, 157, 158) (1876-1929)

Flower-of-an-hour [Flower of an hour, Flowerofanhour] - *Hibiscus trionum* L. (3, 4, 5, 15, 50, 92, 93, 97, 109, 114, 127, 131, 138, 155, 156, 158) (1894–present)

Flower-of-gold [Flower of gold] - *Solidago* L. (76) (1896) CA

Flower-of-stone [Flower of stone] - *Selaginella lepidophylla* (Hook. & Grev.) Spring (50) (present)

Flower-of-the-sun [Flower of the sunne, many on one stalk] - *Helianthus ×multiflorus* L. [*annuus × decapetalus*] (178) (1526)

Flower-of-the-sun [Flower of the sunne] - *Helianthus annuus* L. (178) (1526)

Flower-sup fern - *Woodsia* R. Br. (158) (1900)

Flower-velure - *Amaranthus hybridus* L. (165) (1768) obsolete by this time

Flowerwheel [Flower wheel] - *Gaillardia pulchella* Foug. (124) (1937) TX

Flowery senna - *Senna corymbosa* (Lam.) Irwin & Barneby (138) (1923)

Flowery syringa - *Philadelphus inodorus* L. (19) (1840)

Fluellin - *Veronica officinalis* L. (5, 92, 156, 158) (1876-1923)

Fluff grass - *Dasyochloa pulchella* (Kunth) Willd. ex Rydb. (122) (1937) TX

Fluffweed - *Filago* L. (155) (1942)

Fluss Blatt (German) - *Podophyllum peltatum* L. (186) (1814)

Fluxroot [Flux-root, Flux root] - *Asclepias tuberosa* L. (5, 7, 92, 156, 186) (1814-1923) no longer in use by 1923, *Gentiana catesbaei* Walt. (92) (1876), *Gentiana villosa* L. (7) (1828)

Fluxweed [Flux weed, Flux-weed] - *Chamaesyce hypericifolia* (L.) Millsp. (49) (1898), *Isanthus brachiatus* (L.) Britton, Sterns & Poggenb. (5, 50, 155, 50, 156, 158) (1900–present), *Isanthus* Michx. (50, 155) (1942–present), *Trichostema brachiatum L.* (75) (1894)

Fly agaric - *Amanita muscaria* var. *muscaria* (L.) Pers. (52, 53, 60, 71, 92, 170) (1876-1995)

Fly amanita - *Amanita muscaria* var. *muscaria* (L.) Pers. (71, 155) (1898-1942)

Fly blossom - *Lonicera involucrata* Banks ex Spreng. (160) (1860)

Fly flower [Fly-flower] - *Dicentra cucullaria* (L.) Bernh. (156) (1923)

Fly fungus - *Amanita muscaria* var. *muscaria* (L.) Pers. (71) (1898)

Fly honeysuckle [Fly honey-suckle, Fly-honeysuckle] - *Lonicera* L. (1) (1932), *Lonicera xylosteum* L. (5) (1913)

Fly poison [Fly-poison, Flypoison, Fly Pison] - *Amianthium* A. Gray (156) (1923), *Amianthium muscitoxicum* (Walt.) Gray (2, 5, 50, 92, 97, 183) (1756–present)

Fly-away - *Agrostis hyemalis* (Walt.) Britton, Sterns & Poggenb. (5) (1913)

Fly-away grass [Fly away grass, Fly-away-grass] - *Agrostis hyemalis* (Walt.) Britton, Sterns & Poggenb. (119, 143, 163) (1852-1938), *Agrostis scabra* Willd. (56, 66, 90) (1885-1903)

Fly-catcher [Fly catcher] - *Sarracenia purpurea* L. (6) (1892)

Fly-killer [Fly killer] - *Amanita muscaria* var. *muscaria* (L.) Pers. (71) (1898)

Flytrap [Fly-trap, Fly trap] - *Apocynum androsaemifolium* L. (6, 7, 92, 156, 157, 158) (1898-1929), *Sarracenia purpurea* L. (5, 49, 52, 57, 92, 156) (1898-1923)

Fo no ki - *Magnolia virginiana* L. (186) (1814)

Foalfoot [Foal foot, Foal-foot, Foles foot] - *Tussilago farfara* L. (5, 92, 156) (1876-1923)

Foamflower [Foam flower] - *Tiarella cordifolia* L. (5, 156) (1913-1923), *Tiarella* L. (138) (1923)

Foeniculum - *Foeniculum vulgare* Mill. (57, 107) (1586-1917)

Foennel - *Foeniculum vulgare* Mill. (107) (1538)

Foenugreek seed - *Trigonella foenum-graecum* L. (92) (1876)

Foenum graecum - *Trigonella foenum-graecum* L. (57) (1917)

Foetid bumelia - *Sideroxylon foetidissimum* Jacq. subsp. *foetidissimum* (20) (1857)

Foetid hellebore - *Symplocarpus foetidus* (L.) Salisb. ex Nutt. (6) (1892)

Fogfruit [Fog-fruit, Fog fruit] - *Lippia* L. (82, 158) (1900-1930), *Phyla lanceolata* (Michx.) Greene (2, 3, 5, 63, 72, 82, 97, 120, 122, 133, 156) (1857-1977), *Phyla* Lour. (50) (present), *Phyla nodiflora* (L.) Greene (106) (1930)

Foin francais (French) - *Onobrychis viciifolia* Scop. (46) (1879)

Foldwing - *Dicliptera* Juss. (50) (present)

Foliose saxifrage - *Saxifraga foliolosa* R. Br. (5) (1913)

Folk's-glove [Folk's glove] - *Digitalis pupurea* L. (5, 92, 156) (1876-1923)

Folle avoine (French) - *Zizania aquatica* L. (41, 66) (1770-1903)

Fontanesia - *Fontanesia* Labill. (138) (1923)

Fool hay [Fool-hay] - *Agrostis hyemalis* (Walt.) Britton, Sterns & Poggenb. (5, 119) (1913-1938), *Panicum capillare* L. (5, 94, 119) (1901-1938)

Fool's-cicely [Fool's cicely] - *Aethusa cynapium* L. (5, 156) (1913-1923)

Fool's-parsley [Fool's parsley, Fools' parsley] - *Aethusa cynapium* L. (5, 6, 14, 72, 156) (1882-1923), *Aethusa* L. (1, 10) (1818-1932), *Apium divaricatum* Benth. & Hook.f. ex S.Wats. (19, 92) (1840-1876)

Fools-parsley aethusa - *Aethusa cynapium* L. (155) (1942)

Fool's-stones [Fools' stones, Fooles stone, Fool-stone] - *Dactylorhiza* Neck. ex Nevski (possibly) (184) (1793)

Foothill bladderpod - *Lesquerella ludoviciana* (Nutt.) S. Wats. (50) (present)

Foothill iris - *Iris hartwegii* Baker (138) (1923)

Foothills arnica - *Arnica fulgens* Pursh (50) (present)

Forefather's-cup [Forefather's cup, Forefathers' cup] - *Sarracenia purpurea* L. (5, 74, 92, 156) (1876-1923) New England

Forefather's-pitcher [Forefather's pitcher] - *Sarracenia purpurea* L. (5, 76) (1896-1913) ME

Forest agaricus - *Agaricus silvicola* (Vittad.) Peck (155) (1942)

Forest muhly - *Muhlenbergia sylvatica* Torr. ex Gray (3, 155) (1942-1977)

Forest red gum - *Eucalyptus tereticornis* Sm. (109) (1949)

Forest wood rush - *Luzula luzuloides* (Lam.) Dandy & Wilmott (5) (1913)

Forgat mig ei (Swedish) - *Myosotis arvensis* (L.) Hill (46) (1879)

Forget-me-not [Forget me not, For-get-me-not, For-get-me-nots, Forgetmenot] - *Houstonia caerulea* L. (73, 76, 156) (1892-1923), *Myosotis arvensis* (L.) Hill (19) (1840), *Myosotis* L. (1, 2, 4, 50, 82, 109, 138, 155, 158) (1895–present), *Myosotis laxa* Lehm. (156) (1923), *Myosotis scorpioides* L. (5, 92, 158) (1876-1913), *Myosotis sylvatica* Ehrh. ex Hoffmann (85) (1932), *Myosotis verna* Nutt. (5, 156) (1913-1923), *Polemonium reptans* L. (86, 156, 158) (1878-1923), *Sisyrinchium angustifolium* Mill. (78) (1898) Hartford ME, *Veronica chamaedrys* L. (5, 156) (1913-1923)

Fork chickweed - *Paronychia canadensis* (L.) Wood (19) (1840)

Fork fern [Fork-fern, Forkfern] - *Acrostichum aureum* L. (19) (1840), *Acrostichum* L. (167) (1814)

Forked aristida - *Aristida dichotoma* Michx. (187) (1818)

Forked beard grass [Forked beard-grass, Forked beardgrass] - *Andropogon gerardii* Vitman (5, 99, 131) (1899-1923)

Forked blue-curls [Forked bluecurls] - *Trichostema dichotomum* L. (50) (present)

Forked catchfly - *Silene dichotoma* Ehrh. (4, 5, 19, 93) (1840-1986)

Forked chickweed - *Paronychia canadensis* (L.) Wood (1, 2, 4, 13, 158) (1849-1986), *Paronychia fastigiata* (Raf.) Fern. (4) (1986), *Paronychia* Mill. (1, 2, 5, 13, 97, 156, 158) (1849-1937)

Forked fern - *Acrostichum aureum* L. (92) (1876)

Forked fimbry - *Fimbristylis dichotoma* (L.) Vahl (50) (present)

Forked panic grass [Forked panic-grass] - *Dichanthelium dichotomum* (L.) Gould var. *dichotomum* (119, 163) (1852-1938)

Forked panicum - *Dichanthelium dichotomum* (L.) Gould var. *dichotomum* (5, 72, 131) (1899-1907)

Forked rush - *Juncus dichotomus* Ell. (5, 50) (1913–present)

Forked scale-seed - *Spermolepis divaricata* (Walt.) Britton (4) (1986)

Forked silene - *Silene dichotoma* Ehrh. (155) (1942)

Forked spermolepis - *Spermolepis divaricata* (Walt.) Britton (3) (1977)

Forked spike - *Andropogon gerardii* Vitman (19, 92) (1840–1876)

Forked spleenwort - *Asplenium septentrionale* (L.) Huds. (4, 50) (1986–present)

Forked stem - *Riccia fluitans* L. (92) (1876)

Forked threeawn - *Aristida basiramea* Engelm. ex Vasey (3) (1977)

Forked triple-awn grass [Forked triple-awned grass] - *Aristida basiramea* Engelm. ex Vasey (119) (1938)

Forked whitlow wort [Forked whitlow-wort] - *Paronychia canadensis* (L.) Wood (5, 97, 156) (1913-1937)

Forked-leaf blackjack [Forked-leaved black jack] - *Quercus laevis* Walt. (75) (1894)

Forking aster - *Eurybia furcata* (Burgess) Nesom (5) (1913)

Forking larkspur - *Consolida regalis* S.F. Gray (109) (1949)

Forking nailwort - *Paronychia canadensis* (L.) Wood (155) (1942)

Forking whitlow-wort [Forking whitlowwort] - *Paronychia canadensis* (L.) Wood (5, 97, 156) (1913-1937)

Forkstems - *Riccia fluitans* L. (19) (1840)

Fork-tip threeawn [Forktip threeawn] - *Aristida basiramea* Engelm. ex Vasey (155) (1942)

Fork-tip three-awn grass [Forktip threeawn grass] - *Aristida basiramea* Engelm. ex Vasey (5) (1913)

Fork-tip three-awn grass [Forktip threeawn grass] - *Aristida dichotoma* Michx. var. *curtissii* Gray ex S. Wats. & Coult. (50) (present)

Forsythia - *Forsythia* Vahl (138) (1923)

Fort Thompson grass [Ft. Thompsongrass] - *Paspalum distichum* L. (155) (1942)

Fortune's fontanesia [Fortune fontanesia] - *Fontanesia phillyreoides* Labill. subsp. *fortunei* (Carr.) Yaltirik (138) (1923)

Fortune's forsythia [Fortune forsythia] - *Forsythia suspensa* (Thunb.) Vahl (138) (1923)

Fortune's spiraea [Fortune spiraea] - *Spiraea douglasii* Hook. (138) (1923), *Spiraea japonica* L. f. var. *fortunei* (Planch.) Rehd. (138) (1923)

Fortune-teller - *Taraxacum officinale* G.H. Weber ex Wiggers (64, 69, 156, 157, 158) (1900-1929)

Fothergilla - *Fothergilla gardenii* L. (possibly) (5, 156) (1913-1923), *Fothergilla* L. (8, 138) (1785-1923)

Fothergilla (French) - *Fothergilla* L. (8) (1785)

Fothergilla de Caroline (French) - *Fothergilla gardenii* L. (8) (1785)

Fougère male (French) - *Dryopteris filix-mas* (L.) Schott (158) (1900)

Fountain chickweed - *Stellaria alsine* Grimm (187) (1818)

Fountain grass - *Pennisetum* L.C. Rich. ex Pers. (50) (present)

Fountain palm - *Livistona chinensis* (Jacq.) R. Br. ex Mart. (109) (1949), *Livistona* R. Br. (109) (1949)

Fountain plant [Fountain-plant] - *Amaranthus tricolor* L. (75) (1894), *Russelia equisetiformis* Schlecht. & Cham. (109) (1949)

Fountain tree - *Cedrus deodara* (Roxb. ex D. Don) G. Don f. (92) (1876)

Four-angled cassiope - *Cassiope tetragona* (L.) D. Don (5) (1913)

Four-leaf campion [Four-leaved campion, Four leaved campion] - *Silene stellata* (L.) Aiton f. (possibly) (42, 187) (1814-1818)

Four-leaf clover fern [Four-leafed clover fern] - *Marsilea vestita* Hook. & Grev. subsp. *vestita* (122) (1937) TX

Four-leaf loosestrife [Fourleaf loosestrife] - *Lysimachia quadrifolia* L. (86, 155) (1878-1942)

Four-leaf mare's-tail [Four-leaved mare's tail] - *Hippuris tetraphylla* L. f. (5) (1913)

Four-leaf marsilia [Four-leaved marsilia] - *Marsilea quadrifolia* L. (3) (1977)

Four-leaf milkweed [Four-leaved milkweed, Four leaved milk weed] - *Asclepias quadrifolia* Jacq. (4, 5, 42, 50, 72, 97, 156) (1814–present)

Four-leaf nightshade [Four-leaved night-shade] - *Trillium erectum* L. (46) (1671)

Four-leaf swallow-wort [Four leaved swallow wort] - *Asclepias quadrifolia* Jacq. (42) (1814)

Four-leaf-grass [Fower leafed grasse] - *Trifolium repens* L. (178) (1526)

Four-nerve daisy - *Tetraneuris* Greene (50) (present)

Four-o'-clock [Four-o'clock, Four-o-clock, Four-o'-clocks] - *Mirabilis jalapa* L. (3, 92, 109) (1876-1977), *Mirabilis* L. (4, 7, 50, 122, 138, 155) (1828–present), *Mirabilis nyctaginea* (Michx.) MacM. (80) (1913), *Oenothera biennis* L. (5, 156, 158) (1900-1923)

Four-part gentian [Four-parted gentian] - *Gentianella propinqua* (Richards.) J. Gillett subsp. *propinqua* (5) (1913)

Four-point evening-primrose [Fourpoint evening primrose] - *Oenothera rhombipetala* Nutt. ex Torr. & Gray (3, 4, 50) (1977–present)

Four-row barley [Four rowed barley] - *Hordeum vulgare* L. (56, 66) (1901-1903)

Four-stamen chickweed [Fourstamen chickweed] - *Cerastium diffusum* Pers. (50) (present)

Four-stamen tamarisk [Fourstamen tamarisk] or Four-stamen tamarix [Fourstamen tamarix] - *Tamarix parviflora* DC. (138, 155) (1923-1942)

Four-toes [Four toes] - *Antennaria plantaginifolia* (L.) Richards (5, 76, 156, 158) (1896-1923) Salem MA

Four-wing fruited halesia [Four-winged fruited halesia] - *Halesia tetraptera* L. (8) (1785)

Four-wing halesia [Four-winged halesia] - *Halesia tetraptera* L. (2) (1895)

Four-wing poison milkvetch [Fourwing poisonmilkvetch] - *Astragalus tetrapterus* Gray (155) (1942)

Four-wing saltbush [Fourwing saltbush] - *Atriplex canescens* (Pursh) Nutt. (4, 50, 155) (1942–present)

Fowl bluegrass [Fowl blue-grass] - *Poa palustris* L. (3, 50, 143, 155) (1936–present)

Fowl grass [Fowl-grass] - *Glyceria striata* (Lam.) A.S. Hitchc. (5, 119) (1913-1938)

Fowl manna grass [Fowl mannagrass] - *Glyceria striata* (Lam.) A.S. Hitchc. (3, 50, 122, 140, 143, 155) (1936–present)

Fowl meadow grass [Fowl meadow-grass] - *Glyceria striata* (Lam.) A.S. Hitchc. (94, 111, 119, 129, 143, 163) (1894-1938), *Poa palustris* L. (2, 5, 45, 56, 66, 68, 87, 88, 90, 92, 109, 129, 143) (1884-1949), *Poa trivialis* L. (5) (1913)

Fowler's knotweed - *Polygonum fowleri* Robinson (5) (1913)

Fox geranium - *Geranium robertianum* L. (5, 156, 157, 158) (1900-1929)

Fox grape [Foxgrape] - *Vitis labrusca* L. (7, 15, 46, 107, 109, 138) (1828-1949), *Vitis vulpina* L. (5, 7, 8, 74, 156, 158) (1894–present), *Spartina patens* (Ait.) Muhl. (5, 94) (1901–1913)

Fox sedge - *Carex vulpinoidea* Michx. (3, 5, 50, 66, 72, 129, 139, 155) (1894–present)

Foxberry [Fox berry, Fox-berry] - *Arctostaphylos uva-ursi* (L.) Spreng. (7) (1828), *Mitchella repens* L. (76, 156) (1896-1923) Lynn MA, no longer in use by 1923, *Vaccinium vitis-idaea* L. (107, 156) (1919-1923) no longer in use by 1923, *Vitis vulpina* L. (92) (1876)

Foxfeet [Fox feet] - *Huperzia selago* (L.) Bernh. ex Mart. & Schrank var. *selago* (5) (1913)

Foxglove (of Texas school childern) - *Penstemon cobaea* Nutt. (124) (1937)

Foxglove [Fox glove, Fox-glove, Foxgloves] - *Agalinis* Raf. (48) (1882) KS, *Campsis radicans* (L.) Seem. ex Bureau (5, 73, 158) (1892-1913) Chesterton MD, *Digitalis* L. (50, 82, 109, 138, 155, 156, 158, 184) (1793–present), *Digitalis pupurea* L. (4, 19, 49, 52, 53, 54, 55, 57, 60, 61, 69, 82, 92, 106, 148, 156) (1840-1939), *Penstemon* Schmidel (77) (1898) TX, *Phytolacca americana* L. var. *americana* (158) (1900), *Sarracenia purpurea* L. (5, 73, 76, 156) (1892-1923) NH

Foxglove beardtongue [Foxglove beard-tongue] - *Penstemon digitalis* Nutt. ex Sims (5, 72, 97) (1907-1937)

Foxglove penstemon - *Penstemon digitalis* Nutt. ex Sims (122, 138) (1923-1937)

Fox-plum [Fox plum] - *Arctostaphylos uva-ursi* (L.) Spreng. (5, 156) (1913-1923)

Foxtail [Fox tail, Fox-tail, Fox tails, Foxetaile, Fox-taile] - *Alopecurus carolinianus* Walt. (122) (1937), *Alopecurus* L. (1, 45, 50, 155) (1896–present), *Alopecurus pratensis* L. (19, 184) (1793-1840), *Hordeum* L (1, 93) (1932-1936), *Hordeum murinum* L. (88) (1885), *Lagurus ovatus* L. (178, 180) (1596-1633), *Lycopodium clavatum* L. (5, 92) (1876-1913), *Lycopodium* L. (78) (1898) St. Andrews NB, *Pennisetum glaucum* (L.) R. Br. (45, 66, 80, 90, 131, 152) (1896-1913), *Setaria* Beauv (56) (1901), *Setaria setosa* (Sw.) Beauv. (87) (1884), *Setaria viridis* (L.) Beauv. var. *viridis* (152) (1912) NM

Foxtail barley - *Hordeum jubatum* L. (3, 50, 122, 140, 143, 155, 163) (1852–present), *Hordeum murinum* L. (155) (1942)

Foxtail bristle grass [Foxtail bristlegrass] - *Setaria italica* (L.) Beauv. (50) (present)

Foxtail cactus - *Escobaria* Britt. & Rose (50) (present)

Foxtail clubmoss [Fox-tail club-moss] - *Lycopodiella alopecuroides* (L.) Cranfill (5, 50) (1913–present)

Foxtail dalea - *Dalea leporina* (Aiton) Bullock (4, 155) (1942-1986)

Foxtail fescue - *Vulpia myuros* (L.) K.C. Gmel. (122, 155) (1937-1942)

Foxtail grass [Fox tail grass, Fox-tail grass, Foxtail-grass] - *Alopecurus* L. (10, 66, 93) (1818-1936), *Alopecurus pratensis* L. (46) (1879), *Hordeum jubatum* L. (45, 87) (1884-1896), *Pennisetum glaucum* (L.) R. Br. (85, 92) (1876-1932), *Phalaris caroliniana* Walt. (5) (1913), *Setaria* Beauv (1, 93) (1932-1936), *Setaria verticillata* (L.) Beauv. (5, 163) (1852-1913), *Andropogon bicornis* L. (165) (1807)

Foxtail millet - *Setaria italica* (L.) Beauv. (3, 68, 109, 119, 122, 140, 155) (1913-1977)

Foxtail muhly - *Muhlenbergia andina* (Nutt.) A.S. Hitchc. (50) (present)

Foxtail panic [Fox-tail panic] - *Pennisetum glaucum* (L.) R. Br. (19) (1840)

Foxtail pine - *Pinus aristata* Engelm. (153) (1913) NM, *Pinus balfouriana* Grev. & Balf. (138) (1923), *Pinus taeda* L. (5) (1913)

Foxtail prairie clover - *Dalea leporina* (Aiton) Bullock (50) (present)

Foxtail sedge - *Carex alopecoidea* Tuckerman (5, 50, 66, 72) (1893–present)

Fragalo (Italian) - *Fragaria* L. (107) (1571)

Fraghe (Italian) - *Fragaria* L. (107) (1571)

Fragile fern - *Cystopteris* Bernh. (4) (1986), *Cystopteris fragilis* (L.) Bernh. (4) (1986)

Fragile rock brake - *Cryptogramma stelleri* (S. G. Gmel.) Prantl. (50) (present)

Fragile sedge - *Carex membranacea* Hook. (5, 50) (1913–present) IA

Fragrant amorpha - *Amorpha fruticosa* L. (155) (1942)

Fragrant ash - *Fraxinus cuspidata* Torr. (122, 138) (1923-1937)

Fragrant balm - *Monarda didyma* L. (2, 5, 109, 156) (1895-1949)

Fragrant bedstraw [Fragrant bed-straw] - *Galium triflorum* Michx. (5, 37, 50, 72, 97, 122, 131, 156, 157, 158) (1899–present)

Fragrant bellwort - *Uvularia perfoliata* L. (156) (1923)

Fragrant clethra - *Clethra alnifolia* L. (187) (1818)

Fragrant crab or Fragrant crab tree [Fragrant crab-tree] - *Malus coronaria* (L.) Mill. var. *coronaria* (156) (1923), *Malus glaucescens* Rehdr. (5) (1913)

Fragrant cudweed - *Pseudognaphalium obtusifolium* (L.) Hilliard & Burtt subsp. *obtusifolium* (4, 155) (1942-1986)

Fragrant cyperus galingale - *Cyperus squarrosus* L. (42) (1814)

Fragrant Dutchman's-pipe [Fragrant Dutchmanspipe] - *Aristolochia odoratissima* L. (155) (1942)

Fragrant everlasting - *Pseudognaphalium obtusifolium* (L.) Hilliard & Burtt subsp. *obtusifolium* (3, 4, 6, 62) (1892-1986)

Fragrant false garlic - *Nothoscordum borbonicum* Kunth (50) (present)

Fragrant false indigo - *Amorpha nana* Nutt. ex Fraser (5, 72, 93, 97, 131) (1899-1937)

Fragrant flatsedge - *Cyperus odoratus* L. (50) (present)

Fragrant giant hyssop - *Agastache foeniculum* (Pursh) Kuntze (5, 37, 72, 93, 106, 131, 157, 158) (1899–1936)

Fragrant goldenrod [Fragrant golden-rod] - *Euthamia graminifolia* (L.) Nutt. var. *graminifolia* (5, 62, 82, 93, 95, 131, 156) (1899-1930), *Euthamia* Nutt. ex Cass. (158) (1900), *Solidago odora* Aiton (138, 187) (1818-1923)

Fragrant hickory - *Carya alba* (L.) Nutt. ex Ell. (5, 158) (1900–1913)

Fragrant Jerusalem-oak [Fragrant Jerusalem oak] - *Chenopodium ambrosioides* L. (7) (1828)

Fragrant laurel - *Ceanothus velutinus* Dougl. ex Hook. (106) (1930) Western Washington

Fragrant life-everlasting [Fragrant life everlasting] - *Pseudognaphalium obtusifolium* (L.) Hilliard & Burtt subsp. *obtusifolium* (5, 156) (1913-1923)

Fragrant lilac - *Syringa villosa* Vahl (112) (1937)

Fragrant meadow fern [Fragrant meadow-fern] - *Thelypteris palustris* Schott var. *pubescens* (Lawson) Fern. (158) (1900)

Fragrant mimosa - *Mimosa borealis* Gray (50, 155) (1942–present)

Fragrant orchid - *Gymnadenia conopsea* (L.) R. Br. (50) (present)

Fragrant picradenia - *Hymenoxys odorata* DC. (158) (1900)

Fragrant plantain-lily - *Hosta plantaginea* (Lam.) Aschers. (109) (1949)

Fragrant shield fern [Fragrant shield-fern] - *Dryopteris fragrans* (L.) Schott (5) (1913)

Fragrant sumac [Fragrant sumach] - *Rhus aromatica* Aiton (4, 6, 12, 49, 50, 52, 53, 54, 107, 155, 158) (1820–present), *Rhus aromatica* Aiton var. *aromatica* (5) (1913), *Rhus aromatica* Aiton var. *serotina* (Greene) Rehd. (50) (present), *Rhus trilobata* Nutt. var. *trilobata* (108) (1878)

Fragrant tailgrape - *Artabotrys hexapetalus* (L.f.) Bhandari (138, 155) (1923-1942)

Fragrant thistle - *Cirsium pumilum* (Nutt.) Spreng. (5, 156) (1913-1923)

Fragrant unicorn plant [Fragrant unicorn-plant] - *Proboscidea louisianica* (Mill.) Thell. subsp. *fragrans* (Lindl.) Bretting (97) (1937)

Fragrant waterlily [Fragrant water-lily] - *Nymphaea odorata* Aiton (109, 187) (1818-1949)

Fragrant white waterlily [Fragrant white water lily] - *Nymphaea odorata* Aiton (4) (1986)

Fragrant wood fern - *Dryopteris fragrans* (L.) Schott (5, 50) (1913–present)

Fragrant woodbine - *Lonicera caprifolium* L. (5, 156) (1913-1923)

Fragrant woodsia - *Woodsia ilvensis* (L.) R. Br. (3) (1977)

Fragrant-leaf goldenrod [Fragrant-leaved goldenrod] - *Solidago odora* Aiton (49, 52) (1898-1919)

Fragraria baccae (Official name of Materia Medica) - *Fragaria vesca* L. (7) (1828)

Frail-rush [Frail rush] - *Schoenoplectus tabernaemontani* (C.C. Gmel.) Palla (possibly) (158) (1900)

Fraises - *Fragaria* L. (107) (1542)

Fraisier Sauvage (French) - *Fragaria vesca* L. (7) (1828)

Frajol (Spanish) - *Phaseolus vulgaris* L. (possibly) (110) (1886)

Framboise (French) - *Rubus idaeus* L. (107, 158) (1900-1919)

Framboisier odorant de Virginie (French) - *Rubus odoratus* L. (8) (1785)

Framboysses - *Rubus idaeus* L. subsp. *strigosus* (Michx.) Focke (46) (1879)

Frambuesa (Spanish) - *Rubus idaeus* L. (158) (1900)

Franchet's cotoneaster [Franchet cotoneaster] - *Cotoneaster franchetii* Boiss. (138) (1923)

Frangipani - *Plumeria* L. (109, 138) (1923-1949)

Frangula - *Frangula alnus* Mill. (55, 57, 59, 174) (1753-1917)

Frank spurry [Franke spurrie] - *Spergula arvensis* L. (178) (1526)

Frankincense tree - *Pinus taeda* L. (181) (~1678)

Frankinsence pine - *Pinus taeda* L. (5) (1913)

Franklinia - *Franklinia alatamaha* Bartr. ex Marsh. (2, 8, 13, 20) (1785-1895), *Franklinia* Bartr. ex Marsh. (8, 138) (1785-1923)

Franklinia (French) - *Franklinia* Bartr. ex Marsh. (8) (1785)

Franklin's phacelia [Franklin phacelia] - *Phacelia linearis* (Pursh) Holz. (5, 155) (1913-1942)

Franklin's plant [Franklin plant] - *Dalibarda repens* L. (76) (1896) Oxford Co ME

Frank's eragrostis - *Eragrostis frankii* C.A. Mey. ex Steud. (72) (1907)

Frank's love grass [Frank's love-grass] - *Eragrostis frankii* C.A. Mey. ex Steud. (5, 99, 163) (1852-1923)

Frank's sedge [Franks sedge, Frank sedge] - *Carex frankii* Kunth (3, 5, 50, 120, 155) (1913–present)

Frasera - *Frasera caroliniensis* Walt. (57, 64) (1907-1917), *Frasera speciosa* Dougl. ex Griseb. (106) (1930), *Frasera* Walt. (155) (1942)

Frasera officinalis - *Frasera caroliniensis* Walt. (186) (1814)

Frasera radix (Official name of Materia Medica) - *Frasera caroliniensis* Walt. (possibly) (7) (1828)

Frasere colombo (French) - *Frasera caroliniensis* Walt. (possibly) (7) (1828)

Fraser's balsam fir [Fraser balsam fir] - *Abies fraseri* (Pursh) Poir. (5, 20, 155, 158) (1857-1942)

Fraser's cymophyllus - *Cymophyllus fraserianus* (Ker-Gawl.) Kartesz & Gandhi (50) (present)

Fraser's fir - *Abies fraseri* (Pursh) Poir. (2) (1895)

Fraser's magnolia [Fraser magnolia] - *Magnolia fraseri* Walt. (5, 138) (1913-1923)

Fraser's marsh St. John's-wort [Fraser's marsh St. Johnswort] - *Triadenum fraseri* (Spach) Gleason (50) (present)

Fraser's meadow garlic [Fraser meadow garlic] - *Allium canadense* L. var. *fraseri* M. Ownbey (50) (present)

Fraser's sedge [Fraser sedge] - *Cymophyllus fraserianus* (Ker-Gawl.) Kartesz & Gandhi (5, 66, 138) (1903-1923)

Fraser's sundrops [Fraser sundrops] - *Oenothera fruticosa* L. subsp. *glauca* (Michx.) Straley (138) (1923)

Fraser's wild onion - *Allium canadense* L. var. *fraseri* M. Ownbey (50) (present), *Allium textile* A. Nels. & Macbr. (93, 97) (1936-1937)

Frauendistel (German) - *Silybum marianum* (L.) Gaertn. (158) (1900)

Frauenflachs (German) - *Linaria vulgaris* Mill. (6) (1892)

Frauenhaar [Frauen-haar] (German) - *Adiantum capillus-veneris* L. (158) (1900), *Adiantum pedatum* L. (7) (1828)

Frauenminze (German) - *Balsamita major* Desf. (158) (1900)

Fraxinella - *Dictamnus albus* L. (178) (1526), *Dictamnus* L. (109) (1949)

Fraxinus - *Fraxinus americana* L. (52) (1919)

Fraysas - *Fragaria* L. (107) (1554)

Freckled lily - *Lilium philadelphicum* L. (78) (1898) ME

Freesia - *Freesia* Ecklon ex Klatt (138) (1923)

Freisamkraut (German) - *Viola tricolor* L. (6, 158) (1892–1900)

Fremontia - *Fremontodendron californicum* (Torr.) Coville (138) (1923), *Fremontodendron* Coville (138) (1923)

Fremont's aster [Fremont aster] - *Symphyotrichum spathulatum* (Lindl.) Nesom var. *spathulatum* (155) (1942)

Fremont's clematis [Fremont clematis] - *Clematis fremontii* S. Wats. (4, 125, 138, 155) (1923-1986)

Fremont's cottonwood [Fremont cottonwood] - *Populus fremontii* S. Wats. (138) (1923)

Fremont's evening-primrose [Fremont's evening primrose] - *Oenothera macrocarpa* Nutt. subsp. *fremontii* (S. Wats.) W.L. Wagner (3, 4, 50) (1977–present)

Fremont's goldenweed [Fremont goldenweed] - *Oonopsis foliosa* (Gray) Greene var. *foliosa* (155) (1942)

Fremont's goosefoot [Fremont goosefoot] - *Chenopodium fremontii* S. Wats. (3, 4, 50, 93, 131, 155) (1899–present)

Fremont's leather flower - *Clematis fremontii* S. Wats. (5, 50) (1913–present)

Fremont's monkey-flower [Fremont monkeyflower] - *Mimulus fremontii* (Benth.) Gray (50) (present)

Fremont's primrose - *Oenothera* L. (5) (1913)

French barley - *Hordeum vulgare* L. (158) (1900) variety

French bean (Anglo-Indians) - *Phaseolus lunatus* L. (110) (1886)

French beans (diuers sorts) - *Phaseolus* L. (178) (1526)

French clover - *Gomphrena globosa* L. (73) (1892) Northern OH, *Medicago sativa* L. (45, 118) (1896–1898), *Trifolium incarnatum* L. (5, 45, 93, 158) (1896–1936)

French corne glaaden - *Gladiolus communis* L. (178) (1596)

French cress - *Barbarea vulgaris* W.T. Aiton (157) (1929)

French daffodill - *Narcissus ×medioluteus* Mill. [*poeticus × tazetta*] (180) (1633)

French leek - *Allium porrum* L. (158) (1900)

French lungwort - *Hieracium murorum* L. (5, 156) (1913-1923)

French mallow - *Lavatera olbia* L. (178) (1526)

French mallowes - *Althaea officinalis* L. (46) (1617), *Malva crispa* (L.) L. (178) (1526)

French marigold [French marygold] - *Tagetes patula* L. (19, 109, 138) (1840-1949)

French nettle - *Lamium purpureum* L. (5, 158) (1900-1913)

French pink [French pinks] - *Centaurea cyanus* L. (5, 76, 156, 157, 158) (1896-1929), *Dianthus barbatus* L. (5, 74, 156, 158) (1893–1923) Brunswick, NY

French plums - *Prunus domestica* L. (55) (1911)

French purslane - *Portulaca grandiflora* Hook. (158) (1900)

French pursley - *Chamaesyce maculata* (L.) Small (78) (1898) Sulphur Grove OH, *Portulaca grandiflora* Hook. (156) (1923)

French pussley [French pusley] - *Portulaca grandiflora* Hook. (5, 73) (1892–1913) Southern VT

French rhubarb - *Rheum rhabarbarum* L. (92) (1876)

French rose - *Rosa gallica* L. (19, 49, 58, 109, 138) (1840-1949)

French rye grass [French rye-grass] - *Arrhenatherum elatius* (L.) Beauv. ex J. Presl & C. Presl (45) (1896)

French sage - *Phlomis fruticosa* L. (178) (1526)

French scorzonera - *Reichardia picroides* (L.) Roth (107) (1919)

French sparrow-grass [French sparrow grass] - *Ornithogalum pyrenaicum* L. (92) (1876)

French spinach - *Chenopodium rubrum* L. (156, 158) (1900-1923)

French sword-flag - *Gladiolus communis* L. (180) (1633)

French tamarisk - *Tamarix gallica* L. (82, 109, 135) (1910-1949)

French tamarix - *Tamarix gallica* L. (138) (1923)

French wheat - *Fagopyrum esculentum* Moench (180) (1633)

French willow - *Chamerion angustifolium* (L.) Holub subsp. *angustifolium* (5, 156, 157, 158) (1900-1929)

French willowherb [French willow herb, French willow-herb] - *Chamerion angustifolium* (L.) Holub subsp. *angustifolium* (5, 156, 157, 158) (1900-1929)

French-grass [French grass] - *Orbexilum onobrychis* (Nutt.) Rydb. (5, 156) (1913-1923), *Onobrychis viciifolia* Scop. (46, 92) (1876-1879)

Frenchman's-buttons [Frenchman's buttons] - *Phlox pilosa* L. (156) (1923)

French-mulberry [French mulberry] - *Callicarpa americana* L. (2, 5, 58, 77, 97, 106, 109, 122, 124, 156, 158) (1895–1949)

Frenchweed [French weed, French weed] - *Galinsoga parviflora* Cav. (106) (1930), *Thlaspi arvense* L. (5, 126, 156) (1913-1933)

Frêne (French) - *Fraxinus* L. (8) (1785)

Frêne à petites fleurs (French) - *Fraxinus caroliniana* Mill. (20) (1857)

Frêne blanc (French) - *Fraxinus americana* L. (8) (1785)

Frêne d'Amérique (French) - *Fraxinus americana* L. (8) (1785)

Fréne de l'Oregon (French) - *Fraxinus latifolia* Benth. (20) (1857)

Fréne de Pensylvanie (French) - *Fraxinus pennsylvanica* Marsh. (8) (1785)

Frêne Épineux (French) - *Zanthoxylum americanum* Mill. (6, 8, 158) (1785-1900), *Zanthoxylum* L. (8) (1785)

Fréne noir (French) - *Fraxinus nigra* Marsh (8) (1785)

Fresa (Spanish) - *Fragaria* L. (107) (1919)

Fresas (French) - *Fragaria* L. (107) (1536)

Fresera (Spanish) - *Fragaria* L. (107) (1919)

Freshwater cord grass [Fresh-water cord-grass, Fresh-water cord-grass, Freshwater cord-grass] - *Spartina cynosuroides* (L.) Roth (45, 56, 66, 87, 90, 94) (1884-1912), *Spartina pectinata* Bosc ex Link (5) (1913)

Fresno - *Fraxinus velutina* Torr. (153) (1913) NM

Fretz's thorn - *Crataegus pruinosa* (Wendl.) K. Koch (5) (1913)

Friar's-cap [Friar's cap, Friars' cap] - *Aconitum napellus* L. (92, 107, 156) (1876-1923)

Friar's-cowl [Friar's cowl] - *Aconitum napellus* L. (92, 156) (1876–1923)

Fries' pondweed [Fries pondweed, Fries's pondweed] - *Potamogeton friesii* Rupr. (5, 50, 72, 155) (1907–present)

Frijolillo (Spanish) - *Sophora secundiflora* (Ortega) Lag. ex DC. (104, 106, 107, 122) (1896-1937)

Fringe cup [Fringe-cup] - *Mitella diphylla* L. (5, 74, 156) (1893-1923) NY

Fringe flower - *Chionanthus virginicus* L. (14, 52) (1882-1919)

Fringe tree [Fringetree, Fringe-tree] - *Chionanthus* L. (2, 7, 8, 10, 26, 82, 109, 138, 156, 189) (1767-1949), *Chionanthus virginicus* L. (5, 6, 19, 20, 49, 53, 54, 57, 58, 61, 65, 92, 97, 135, 156, 174, 184) (1753-1937), *Oemleria cerasiformis* (Torr. & Gray ex Hook. & Arn.) Landon (35) (1806)

Fringed bear grass [Fringed bear-grass] - *Sorghastrum nutans* (L.) Nash (187) (1818)

Fringed black bindweed - *Polygonum cilinode* Michx. (5) (1913)

Fringed bleeding-heart [Fringed bleedingheart] - *Dicentra eximia* (Ker-Gawl.) Torr. (138) (1923)

Fringed bog-bean [Fringed bog bean] - *Nymphoides peltata* (Gmel.) Kuntze (92, 156) (1876-1923)

Fringed brome - *Bromus ciliatus* L. (3, 50, 122, 140, 155) (1937–present), *Bromus ciliatus* L. var. *ciliatus* (50) (present)

Fringed brome grass [Fringed brome-grass] - *Bromus ciliatus* L. (5, 56, 66, 68, 72, 90, 143, 163) (1852-1936)

Fringed crabgrass [Fringed crab-grass] - *Digitaria ciliaris* (Retz.) Koel. (5, 99) (1913-1923)

Fringed dodder - *Cuscuta suaveolens* Ser. (50) (present)

Fringed gentian - *Gentianopsis crinita* (Froel) Ma. (1, 2, 5, 7, 19, 47, 63, 72, 85, 109, 138, 155, 156) (1828-1949), *Gentianopsis detonsa* (Rottb.) Ma subsp. *detonsa* (1, 2, 5, 7, 19, 47, 63, 72, 85, 109, 133, 138, 155, 156) (1899-1949), *Gentianopsis* Ma. (4) (1986)

Fringed goldenrod [Fringed golden-rod] - *Solidago juncea* Aiton (19) (1840)

Fringed greenbrier [Fringed green-briar] - *Smilax bona-nox* L. (156) (1923)

Fringed hibiscus - *Hibiscus schizopetalus* (Dyer) Hook. f. (138) (1923)

Fringed houstonia - *Houstonia canadensis* Willd. ex Roemer & J.A. Schultes (5, 97) (1913-1937)

Fringed loosestrife - *Lysimachia ciliata* L. (3, 4, 5, 50, 72, 82, 85, 93, 97, 122, 127, 131, 138, 156) (1899–present), *Lysimachia radicans* Hook. (1) (1932)

Fringed milkwort - *Polygala paucifolia* Willd. (5, 156) (1913-1923)

Fringed nutrush - *Scleria ciliata* Michx. (50) (present)

Fringed orchid - *Platanthera* L.C. Rich (1, 50) (1932–present)

Fringed orchis - *Habenaria* Willd. (156) (1923)

Fringed phacelia - *Phacelia fimbriata* Michx. (5) (1913)

Fringed polygala - *Polygala paucifolia* Willd. (2, 15, 92, 109, 138, 156) (1895-1949)

Fringed poppy-mallow [Fringed poppy mallow] - *Callirhoe digitata* Nutt. (5, 97, 122, 156) (1913-1937)

Fringed pore fungus - *Polyporus arcularius* (Batsch) Fr. (128) (1933)

Fringed puccoon - *Lithospermum incisum* Lehm. (85) (1932)

Fringed quickweed - *Galinsoga quadriradiata* Cav. (3, 4, 155) (1942-1986)

Fringed razor-sedge [Fringed razorsedge] - *Scleria ciliata* Michx. (155) (1942)

Fringed sage - *Artemisia frigida* Willd. (146) (1939)

Fringed sagebrush - *Artemisia frigida* Willd. (155) (1942)

Fringed sedge - *Carex castanea* Wahlenb. (66) (1903), *Carex crinita* Lam. (5, 50, 66, 155, 156) (1912–present), *Carex crinita* Lam. var. *brevicrinis* Fern. (50) (present)

Fringed signal grass [Fringed signalgrass] - *Urochloa ciliatissima* (Buckl.) R. Webster (50) (present)

Fringed steironema - *Lysimachia ciliata* L. (155) (1942)

Fringed twinevine - *Funastrum cynanchoides* (Dcne.) Schlechter subsp. *cynanchoides* (50) (present)

Fringed violet - *Viola sagittata* Aiton var. *ovata* (Nutt.) Torr. & Gray (5, 156) (1913-1923)

Fringed waterlily [Fringed water-lily] - *Nymphoides peltata* (Gmel.) Kuntze (156) (1923)

Fringed willowherb - *Epilobium ciliatum* Raf. (50) (present), *Epilobium ciliatum* Raf. subsp. *ciliatum* (50) (present)

Fringed wormwood - *Artemisia frigida* Willd. (138) (1923)

Fringed yellow-eyed grass - *Xyris fimbriata* Ell. (5, 50, 124) (1913–present)

Fringe-leaf aster [Fringed-leaved aster] - *Symphyotrichum ericoides* (L.) Nesom var. *ericoides* (187) (1818)

Fringe-leaf paspalum [Fringeleaf paspalum] - *Paspalum setaceum* Michx. (155) (1942)

Fringe-leaf ruellia [Fringeleaf ruellia] - *Ruellia humilis* Nutt. (3, 4) (1977-1986)

Fringe-leaf wild petunia [Fringeleaf wild petunia] - *Ruellia humilis* Nutt. (50) (present)

Fringeless purple orchis - *Platanthera peramoena* (Gray) Gray (5) (1913)

Fringepod [Fringe pod] - *Ulex europaeus* L. (19, 106) (1840-1930)

Frisky grass - *Lolium pratense* (Huds.) S.J. Darbyshire (5) (1913)

Frisky meadow grass - *Lolium pratense* (Huds.) S.J. Darbyshire (5) (1913)

Frisoles (Peru) - *Phaseolus vulgaris* L. (possibly) (110) (1886)

Frisoles (Spanish) - *Phaseolus vulgaris* L. (possibly) (110) (1886)

Frittillary - *Fritillaria* L. (50, 109, 138, 155) (1923–present)

Froelichia - *Froelichia* Moench (93, 158) (1900-1936)

Frog cheese - *Lycoperdon proteus* Bull. (92) (1876)

Frog orchid - *Coeloglossum* Hartm. (50) (present)

Frog plant [Frog-plant, Frog plants] - *Hylotelephium telephium* (L.) H. Ohba. subsp. *telephium* (5, 73, 156) (1892-1923) NH

Frog slime - *Spirogyra* Link In C. G. Nees (78) (1898) NH

Frog spawn - *Spirogyra* Link In C. G. Nees (73) (1892) Parts of NB

Frog spit - *Spirogyra* Link In C. G. Nees (73) (1892)

Frogbit [Frog bit, Frogs-bit, Frog's bit, Frogs-bit] - *Hydrocharis* L. (138, 155, 167) (1814-1942), *Hydrocharis morsus-ranae* L. (109, 138) (1923-1949), *Limnobium* Rich. (1, 2, 158) (1895-1932), *Limnobium spongia* (Bosc) L.C. Rich. ex Steud. (5, 10, 122) (1818-1937)

Frog-fruit [Frog fruit] - *Phyla lanceolata* (Michx.) Greene (93, 124, 156) (1923-1937), *Phyla nodiflora* (L.) Greene (124) (1937)

Frog-grass [Frog grass, Frog grasse, Frogge-grasse] - *Juncus bufonius* L. (156) (1923)

Frog-grass [Frog grass, Frog grasse, Frogge-grasse] - *Suaeda maritima* (L.) Dumort. (178) (1526)

Frogleaf [Frog-leaf] - *Brasenia schreberi* Gmel. (5, 7, 92, 156) (1828-1923)

Froglily [Frog-lilly, Frog lily] - *Nuphar lutea* (L.) Sm. subsp. *advena* (Aiton) Kartesz & Gandhi (92, 156, 157, 158) (1876-1929)

Frog's-bladder [Frog's bladder] - *Hylotelephium telephium* (L.) H. Ohba. subsp. *telephium* (5, 73, 156) (1892-1923) NY

Frog's-foot [Frogges Fote] - *Lemna minor* L. (178, 179) (1526-1596)

Frog's-mouth [Frog-mouth, Frog's mouth] - *Hylotelephium telephium* (L.) H. Ohba. subsp. *telephium* (5, 73, 156) (1892-1923) NY

Frog's-throats [Frogs' throats] - *Hylotelephium telephium* (L.) H. Ohba. subsp. *telephium* (73) (1892) Bedford MA

Frogweed [Frog weed] - *Juncus bufonius* L. (5) (1913)

Frogwort [Frog wort] - *Ranunculus bulbosus* L. (5, 92, 158) (1876-1913)

Front Range beardtongue - *Penstemon virens* Pennell (50) (present)

Frost aster - *Symphyotrichum ericoides* (L.) Nesom var. *ericoides* (82, 106) (1930)

Frost flower [Frost flower, Frost-flower] - *Aster* L. (73, 76, 156, 158) (1892-1923), *Symphyotrichum lateriflorum* (L.) A.& D. Löve var. *lateriflorum* (106, 156) (1923-1930)

Frost grape - *Vitis labrusca* L. (possibly) (7) (1828), *Vitis riparia* Michx. (82, 107, 109) (1919-1949), *Vitis vulpina* L. (2, 5, 7, 15, 19, 50, 72, 82, 92, 95, 97, 107, 108, 113, 122, 138, 155, 156, 158) (1828–present)

Frost plant [Frostplant] - *Helianthemum canadense* (L.) Michx. (6, 19, 49, 92) (1840-1898)

Frostblite [Frost-blite, Frost blite] - *Chenopodium album* L. (5, 156, 157, 158) (1900-1929)

Frost-blow - *Symphyotrichum ericoides* (L.) Nesom var. *ericoides* (156) (1923)

Frosted hawthorn - *Crataegus pruinosa* (Wendl.) K. Koch (138, 155) (1923-1942)

Frost-flower - *Helianthemum canadense* (L.) Michx. (156) (1923)

Frostweed [Frost weed, Frost-weed] - *Cunila origanoides* (L.) Britton (156) (1923), *Erigeron philadelphicus* L. (7) (1828), *Helianthemum bicknellii* Fern. (3, 4, 157) (1929-1986), *Helianthemum canadense* (L.) Michx. (2, 5, 6, 15, 49, 92, 156) (1876-1923), *Helianthemum* Mill. (1, 4, 13, 50, 93) (1849–present), *Symphyotrichum ericoides* (L.) Nesom var. *ericoides* (5, 156) (1913-1923), *Verbesina virginica* L. (4) (1986)

Frostweed aster [Frost-weed aster] - *Symphyotrichum ericoides* (L.) Nesom var. *ericoides* (156) (1923)

Frostwort [Frost wort] - *Helianthemum canadense* (L.) Michx. (5, 6, 7, 49, 57, 72, 92) (1828-1917), *Helianthemum* Mill. (155) (1942), *Ranunculus bulbosus* L. (158) (1900)

Frosty hawthorn - *Crataegus pruinosa* (Wendl.) K. Koch (4) (1986)

Frothy poppy - *Silene vulgaris* (Moench) Garcke (5, 156) (1913-1923) no longer in use by 1923

Fruitful thorn - *Crataegus crus-galli* L. (5) (1913)

Fryle (Swedish) - *Spergula arvensis* L. (110) (1886)

Ft. Thompson grass [Ft. Thompsongrass] - *Paspalum distichum* L. (155) (1942)

Fuchsia - *Fuchsia* L. (138) (1923), *Fuchsia magellanica* Lam. (92) (1876)

Fuchsia-flower gooseberry [Fuchsia-flowered gooseberry] - *Ribes speciosum* Pursh (109) (1949)

Fünfblättrige Kraftwurzel (German) - *Panax quinquefolius* L. (186) (1814)

Fugi - *Wisteria sinensis* (Sims) DC. (106) (1930)

Fuirena - *Fuirena simplex* Vahl (3) (1977)

Fuller's grass [Fullers grasse] - *Saponaria officinalis* L. (179) (1526)

Fuller's herb [Fuller's-herb] - *Saponaria officinalis* L. (5, 49, 64, 92, 156, 157, 158) (1898–1929)

Fuller's teasel [Fullers teasel] - *Dipsacus fullonum* L. (5, 50, 62, 106, 138, 155, 156, 158) (1898–present), *Dipsacus fullonum* L. subsp. *fullonum* (50) (present)

Fuller's thistle [Fullers thistle] - *Dipsacus fullonum* L. (5, 109, 156) (1913-1949)

Fuller's weed [Fuller's-weed] - *Dipsacus fullonum* L. (158) (1900)

Fullmoon maple - *Acer japonicum* Thunb. (109, 137, 155) (1923-1949)

Fulton's Mexican plum [Fulton Mexican plum] - *Prunus mexicana* S. Wats. (155) (1942)

Fulvous oak - *Quercus chrysolepis* Liebm. (161) (1857)

Fulvous-flower touch-me-not [Fulvous-flowered touch-me-not] - *Impatiens capensis* Meerb. (187) (1818)

Fume-of-the-earth [Fume of the erthe] - *Fumaria officinalis* L. (179) (1526)

Fumeroots [Fume-roots] - *Corydalis* DC. (156) (1923)

Fumeterre (French) - *Fumaria officinalis* L. (158) (1900)

Fumewort - *Corydalis* DC. (4, 50) (1896–present), *Corydalis solida* (L.) Clairv. (107) (1919)

Fumitory - *Dicentra canadensis* (Goldie) Walp. (157) (1929), *Fumaria* L. (50, 155, 158, 184) (1793–present), *Fumaria officinalis* L. (1, 5, 7, 10, 19, 49, 92, 156, 158) (1818-1932)

Fumyterry - *Fumaria officinalis* L. (179) (1526)

Funaria moss - *Funaria hygrometrica* Hedw. (50) (present)

Fungus agaric - *Fomitopsis officinalis* (Batsch) Bondartsev & Singer (52) (1919)

Funnel-form beardtongue [Funnel-form beard-tongue] - *Penstemon tubiflorus* Nutt. (5, 97) (1913-1937)

Funnel-lily [Funnellily] - *Androstephium* Torr. (155) (1942)

Funnelvine - *Arrabidaea* DC. (155) (1942)

Furrowed grass [Furrowed grasse] - *Phalaris arundinacea* L. (180) (1633)

Furrow-leaf pondweed [Furrow-leaved pond-weed] - *Potamogeton diversifolius* Raf. (187) (1818)

Furry goldenrod - *Solidago caesia* L. var. *curtisii* (Torr. & Gray) Wood (138) (1923)

Furry jasmine - *Jasminum multiflorum* (Burm. f.) Andr. (138) (1923)

Furry willow - *Salix cordata* Michx. (5, 131) (1899-1913)

Furse - *Ulex* L. (45, 109) (1896-1949)

Furze - *Genista tinctoria* L. (92) (1876), *Ulex europaeus* L. (5, 19, 106, 156) (1840-1930)

Furzetop [Furze top] - *Agrostis canina* L. (5) (1913)

Fusain (French) - *Euonymus atropurpurea* Jacq. (6) (1892), *Euonymus* L. (8) (1785)

Fusain de Caroline à fleurs noires (French) - *Euonymus atropurpureus* Jacq. (possibly) (8) (1785)

Fusain toujours vert (French) - *Euonymus americanus* L. (possibly) (8) (1785)

Fuss-balls - *Lycoperdon* Pers. (46) (1671)

Fussblatt - *Podophyllum peltatum* L. (6) (1892)

Fussy-gussy [Fussy gussy] - *Pseudognaphalium obtusifolium* (L.) Hilliard & Burtt subsp. *obtusifolium* (5) (1913)

Fustic - *Maclura tinctoria* (L.) D. Don ex Steud. (92) (1876)

Fustic tree [Fustic-tree] - *Cladrastis kentukea* (Dum.-Cours.) Rudd . (5, 7, 92, 156) (1828-1923)

Fustic wood - *Maclura tinctoria* (L.) D. Don ex Steud. (92) (1876)

Fuzzy common persimmon - *Diospyros virginiana* L. (155) (1942)

Fuzzy deutzia - *Deutzia scabra* Thunb. (138) (1923)

Fuzzy phacelia - *Phacelia hirsuta* Nutt. (50) (present)

Fuzzy prairie rose - *Rosa setigera* Michx. var. *tomentosa* Torr. & Gray (155) (1942)

Fuzzybean - *Strophostyles* Ell. (50) (present)

Fuzzy-guzzy - *Pseudognaphalium obtusifolium* (L.) Hilliard & Burtt subsp. *obtusifolium* (73, 156) (1892-1923) Mansfiled OH, no longer in use by 1923

Fuzzy-spike wildrye [Fuzzyspike wildrye] - *Leymus innovatus* (Beal) Pilger (155) (1942)

Fuzzy-tongue penstemon [Fuzzytongue penstemon] - *Penstemon eriantherus* Pursh (50, 155) (1942–present)

Fuzzyweed [Fuzzy weed] - *Artemisia dracunculus* L. (37) (1919)

Fuzzy-wuzzy sedge [Fuzzy wuzzy sedge] - *Carex hirsutella* Mack (50) (present)

Fygge - *Ficus* L. (179) (1526)

Fyncle - *Foeniculum vulgare* Mill. (107) (1538)

Fyncle, *Foeniculum vulgare* Mill.
(W. Woodville et al. 1832)

G

Gaasedild - *Anthemis cotula* L. (186) (1814)

Gabisan'ikeäg' (Chippewa, it is silent) - *Hepatica nobilis* Schreb. var. *obtusa* (Pursh) Steyermark (40) (1928)

Gachelkraut (German) - *Achillea millefolium* L. (158) (1900)

Gach-hach-gik - *Magnolia virginiana* L. (186) (1814)

Gadelier sauvage (French) - *Ribes aureum* Pursh (89) (1820)

Gadrise - *Viburnum opulus* L. (5, 156, 158) (1900-1923) no longer in use by 1923

Gaga'mimĭc (Chippewa) - *Tsuga canadensis* (L.) Carr. (40) (1928)

Ga'gawan'dagisĭd (Chippewa, deceptive) - *Juniperus communis* L. (40) (1928)

Gaged marsh marigold [Gaged marsh marygold] - *Caltha palustris* L. (42) (1814)

Ga'gige'bûg (Chippewa, everlasting leaf) - *Chimaphila umbellata* (L.) Bart. (40) (1928)

Gagroot [Gag-root, Gag root] - *Lobelia inflata* L. (5, 69, 92, 156, 157, 158) (1876-1923)

Gaillardia - *Gaillardia* Foug. (138, 155) (1923-1942)

Gainier (French) - *Cercis canadensis* L. (158) (1900), *Cercis* L. (8) (1785)

Gaint cape water-hawthorn [Gaint cape waterhawthorn] - *Aponogeton distachyos* L.f. (possibly) (155) (1942)

Gairdner's caraway - *Perideridia gairdneri* (Hook. & Arn.) Mathias subsp. *gairdneri* (131) (1899)

Gairdner's yampah - *Perideridia gairdneri* (Hook. & Arn.) Mathias (50) (present)

Gaiter tree [Gaiter-tree] - *Euonymus europaea* L. (5, 156) (1913-1923), *Viburnum opulus* L. (5, 156, 158) (1900-1923) no longer in use by 1923

Gajugĕns'ĭbûg (Chippewa, little cat leaf) - *Nepeta cataria* L. (40) (1928)

Galangal - *Alpinia* Roxb. (155) (1942)

Galanthus - *Galanthus nivalis* L. (174) (1753)

Galaticum - *Hordeum vulgare* L. (180) (1633)

Galax - *Galax* Sims (138) (1923)

Galax - *Nemophila aphylla* (L.) Brummitt (5, 138, 156) (1913-1923)

Galaxy - *Nemophila aphylla* (L.) Brummitt (5, 156) (1913-1923)

Galbanum mechoacan - *Ipomoea pandurata* (L.) G.F.W. Mey. (46) (1879)

Gale - *Morella cerifera* (L.) Small (184) (1793), *Myrica gale* L. (41) (1770), *Myrica* L. (10) (1818)

Galé d'Amérique (French) - *Myrica gale* L. (8) (1785)

Gale leaf willow - *Salix myricoides* Muhl. (19) (1840)

Galearis - *Galearis* Raf. (50) (present)

Galingal - *Cyperus diandrus* Torr. (5, 156) (1913-1923)

Galingale - *Cyperus diandrus* Torr. (5, 156) (1913-1923), *Cyperus esculentus* L. (62) (1912) IN, *Cyperus flavescens* L. (5, 156) (1913-1923), *Cyperus* L. (1, 109, 158, 184) (1793–1949), *Dulichium arundinaceum* (L.) Britt. var. *arundinaceum* (19) (1840)

Galinsoga - *Galinsoga parviflora* Cav. (5, 72, 97, 106) (1907-1937), *Galinsoga* Ruiz & Pavón (158) (1900)

Galipot tree - *Picea abies* (L.) H. Karst. (158) (1900)

Galium - *Galium aparine* L. (57) (1917)

Gall - *Quercus infectoria* Olivier (55, 57) (1911-1917) not a species of oak, but an abnormal growths caused by insects

Gall bush [Gall-bush] - *Myrica gale* L. (156) (1923)

Gall flower [Gall-flower] - *Gentianella quinquefolia* (L.) Small subsp. *quinquefolia* (156) (1923)

Gall oak - *Quercus infectoria* Olivier (92) (1876) not a species of oak, but an abnormal growths caused by parasites

Galla - *Quercus infectoria* Olivier (55, 57, 59) (1911-1917) not a species of oak, but an abnormal growths caused by insects

Gallant-soldier - *Galinsoga parviflora* Cav. (50) (present), *Galinsoga* Ruiz & Pavón (50) (present)

Gallberry [Gall berry] - *Ilex glabra* (L.) Gray (5, 106, 156) (1913-1930)

Galleta - *Pleuraphis jamesii* Torr. (3, 119, 140, 151, 155) (1896-1977)

Galleta [Guyetta, Gietta, Gieta] - *Pleuraphis rigida* Thurb. (94) (1901), *Pleuraphis mutica* Buckl. (151) (1896)

Galleta grass [Galleta-grass] - *Pleuraphis jamesii* Torr. (122, 151, 152, 163) (1852-1937), *Pleuraphis mutica* Buckl. (151) (1896)

Gallicam - *Daucus carota* L. (107) (27 AD)

Gall-of-the-earth [Gall of the earth] - *Aureolaria flava* (L.) Farw. var. *flava* (18) (1805), *Gentianella quinquefolia* (L.) Small subsp. *quinquefolia* (5, 156) (1913-1923), *Lactuca floridana* (L.) Gaertn. (187) (1818), *Platanthera orbiculata* (Pursh) Lindl. (156) (1923), *Prenanthes alba* L. (49) (1898), *Prenanthes* L. (7, 76) (1828-1896), *Prenanthes serpentaria* Pursh (2, 5, 92, 156) (1876-1942), *Prenanthes trifoliolata* (Cass.) Fern. (156) (1923), *Pterospora andromedea* Nutt. (92, 156, 158) (1898-1923)

Gallon - *Petasites hybridus* (L.) G. Gaertn., B. Mey. & Scherb. (5, 156) (1913-1923) no longer in use by 1923

Gallow-grass [Gallow grass, Gallows-grass] - *Cannabis sativa* L. (5, 92, 107, 156, 157, 158) (1876-1929)

Gallpot - *Abies alba* Mill. (92) (1876), *Picea abies* (L.) H. Karst. (92) (1876)

Gallweed [Gall-weed] - *Gentianella quinquefolia* (L.) Small subsp. *quinquefolia* (5, 49, 92, 156) (1876-1923), *Linaria vulgaris* Mill. (156) (1923) no longer in use by 1923

Gallwort [Gall-wort, Gall wort] - *Linaria vulgaris* Mill. (5, 92, 157, 158) (1876-1929)

Galpinsia - *Calylophus hartwegii* (Benth.) Raven subsp. *hartwegii* (97) (1937) OK, *Calylophus* Spach (158) (1900)

Gamagrass [Gama-grass, Gama grass] - *Saccharum giganteum* (Walt.) Pers. (5) (1913), *Tripsacum dactyloides* (L.) L. (2, 45, 46, 66, 67, 72, 87, 88, 92, 94, 111, 119, 144) (1884-1938), *Tripsacum* L. (3, 45, 50, 93, 155) (1896–present)

Gambel's oak [Gambel oak] - *Quercus gambelii* Nutt. (4, 50, 155) (1942–present)

Gambel's snapdragon [Gambel's snap-dragon] - *Antirrhinum speciosum* (Nutt.) Gray (86) (1878) NM

Gambier Parry's pine - *Pinus ponderosa* P.& C. Lawson (158) (1900), *Pinus ponderosa* P.& C. Lawson var. *scopulorum* Engelm. (5) (1913)

Gamote (Mexican) - *Cymopterus montanus* Nutt. ex Torr. & Gray (14, 107) (1882)

Gander's-teeth [Gander teeth] - *Mimosa microphylla* Dry. (156) (1923)

Gang flower - *Polygala vulgaris* L. (92) (1876)

Ganges amaranth - *Amaranthus tricolor* L. (138) (1923)

Ganja [Ganjah] - *Cannabis sativa* L. (6, 53, 92) (1876-1922)

Gänsedistel (German) - *Sonchus oleraceus* L. (158) (1900)

Gänsekopf (German) - *Sonchus oleraceus* L. (186) (1814)

Gänserich (German) - *Argentina anserina* (L.) Rydb. (158) (1900)

Gaping Dutchman's-pipe [Gaping Dutchmanspipe] - *Aristolochia ringens* Vahl (155) (1942)

Gaping grass - *Steinchisma hians* (Ell.) Nash (50) (present)

Gaping monkey flower [Gaping monkey-flower] - *Mimulus ringens* L. (187) (1818)

Gaping panic grass - *Steinchisma hians* (Ell.) Nash (5) (1913)

Garangtoging (Iroquois, a child) - *Panax quinquefolius* L. (41, 177) (1750–1770)

Garantogen - *Panax quinquefolius* L. (7, 92) (1828-1876)

Garantoquen [Garant-oquen] - *Panax quinquefolius* L. (6, 158, 186) (1814-1900)

Garantquen - *Panax quinquefolius* L. (157) (1929)

Garbantzua (Basque) - *Cicer arietinum* L. (110) (1886)

Garbanzo - *Cicer arietinum* L. (109) (1949)

Garbanzo (Castilean) - *Cicer arietinum* L. (110) (1886)

Garden ageratum - *Ageratum conyzoides* L. (82) (1930) IA

Garden alkanet - *Anchusa officinalis* L. (165) (1807)

Garden alternthera - *Alternanthera bettzichiana* (Regel) Voss (138) (1923)

Garden angelica - *Angelica archangelica* L. (49, 57, 58, 64, 92, 165) (1807-1917)

Garden artichoke - *Cynara scolymus* L. (19, 92) (1840-1876)

Garden asparagus - *Asparagus officinalis* L. (50, 109, 138, 155) (1923–present)

Garden baby's-breath [Garden babysbreath] - *Gypsophila scorzonerifolia* Ser. (50) (present)

Garden balm - *Melissa officinalis* L. (5) (1913)

Garden balsam - *Impatiens balsamina* L. (14, 82, 92, 109, 138) (1882-1949)

Garden barberry - *Berberis vulgaris* L. (157, 158) (1900-1929)

Garden bean [Garden beans] - *Phaseolus vulgaris* L. (37, 121) (1918-1919), *Vicia faba* L. (19, 46) (1671-1840)

Garden bear's-britches [Garden Beares breech] - *Acanthus mollis* L. (178) (1526)

Garden bee balm - *Melissa officinalis* L. (93) (1936)

Garden beet - *Beta vulgaris* L. (7) (1828)

Garden bugloss - *Anchusa officinalis* L. (165) (1807)

Garden burnet - *Sanguisorba minor* Scop. subsp. *muricata* (Spach) Nordborg (5, 156, 157, 158) (1900-1929)

Garden camomile [Garden chamomile] - *Anthemis arvensis* L. (6) (1892), *Chamaemelum nobile* (L.) All. (5, 58, 92, 156) (1869-1923)

Garden carrot - *Daucus carota* L. (92) (1876)

Garden catchfly - *Silene armeria* L. (5, 19, 156) (1840-1923)

Garden celandine - *Chelidonium majus* L. (52, 92, 158) (1876-1919)

Garden celery - *Apium graveolens* L. (110) (1886), *Apium graveolens* L. var. *dulce* (P. Mill.) DC. (92, 155) (1876-1942)

Garden cherry - *Prunus cerasus* L. (19) (1840)

Garden chervil - *Anthriscus cerefolium* (L.) Hoffmann (5, 156) (1913-1923)

Garden chicory - *Cichorium endivia* L. (92) (1876)

Garden chrysanthemum - *Chrysanthemum coronarium* L. (19) (1840)

Garden clary [Garden clarie] - *Salvia sclarea* L. (178) (1526)

Garden colewort - *Brassica oleracea* L. (180) (1633)

Garden columbine - *Aquilegia vulgaris* L. (19, 92, 156) (1840-1923)

Garden coreopsis - *Coreopsis tinctoria* Nutt. (93) (1936)

Garden cornflower - *Centaurea cyanus* L. (50) (present)

Garden cress [Garden-cress, Gardyne cress] - *Lepidium sativum* L. (3, 4, 15, 109, 110, 138, 155, 156, 158, 179) (1526-1986)

Garden currant - *Ribes rubrum* L. (85, 109) (1932-1949)

Garden dahlia - *Dahlia pinnata* Cav. (109) (1949)

Garden daisy - *Bellis perennis* L. (5, 158) (1900–1913)

Garden dewberry - *Rubus aboriginum* Rydb. (50) (present)

Garden dill - *Anethum graveolens* L. (158) (1900)

Garden dock - *Rumex patientia* L. (19) (1840)

Garden egg - *Solanum melongena* L. (156) (1923)

Garden endive - *Cichorium endivia* L. (19, 92) (1840-1876)

Garden fly-honeysuckle - *Lonicera tatarica* L. (5, 156) (1913-1923)

Garden forget-me-not - *Myosotis sylvatica* Ehrh. ex Hoffmann (3, 4) (1977-1986)

Garden garth - *Lepidium sativum* L. (158) (1900)

Garden geranium - *Pelargonium odoratissimum* (L.) L'Hér. ex Aiton (92) (1876)

Garden gooseberry - *Ribes uva-crispa* L. (72) (1907), *Ribes uva-crispa* L. var. *sativum* DC. (156) (1923)

Garden heliotrope [Garden-heliotrope] - *Valeriana officinalis* L. (5, 76, 109, 156) (1896-1949)

Garden hemlock - *Aethusa cynapium* L. (6) (1892)

Garden huckleberry - *Solanum nigrum* L. (156) (1923)

Garden hyacinth - *Hyacinthus orientalis* L. (19) (1840)

Garden iris - *Iris germanica* L. (19) (1840)

Garden karse - *Lepidium sativum* L. (158) (1900)

Garden larkspur - *Consolida ajacis* (L.) Schur (97, 114) (1894–1937)

Garden lavender - *Lavandula angustifolia* Mill. (57) (1917)

Garden leek - *Allium porrum* L. (50) (present)

Garden lettuce - *Lactuca sativa* L. (50, 92, 138, 180) (1633–present)

Garden loosestrife - *Lysimachia punctata* L. (3) (1977)

Garden malowe - *Alcea rosea* L. (179) (1526)

Garden marigold - *Calendula officinalis* L. (49, 53, 58) (1898-1922)

Garden mint [Gardyn mynte] - *Mentha spicata* L. (5, 156, 158, 179) (1526-1923)

Garden nasturtium - *Tropaeolum majus* L. (82, 109, 138) (1923-1949)

Garden nightshade - *Solanum nigrum* L. (5, 71, 92, 93, 125, 156, 157, 158) (1876-1936)

Garden onion - *Allium cepa* L. (19, 50, 155) (1840–present)

Garden orach [Garden orache] - *Atriplex hortensis* L. (3, 7, 19, 46, 50, 92, 138, 155, 158) (1649–present)

Garden orpine - *Hylotelephium telephium* (L.) H. Ohba. subsp. *telephium* (5, 156) (1913-1923)

Garden parsley - *Petroselinum crispum* (P. Mill.) Nyman ex A.W. Hill (5, 58, 93, 158) (1869-1936)

Garden parsnip - *Pastinaca sativa* L. (6, 155) (1892)

Garden patience - *Rumex crispus* L. (6) (1892), *Rumex patientia* L. (5, 92, 107, 156, 158) (1876-1923)

Garden pea [Garden-pea] - *Pisum sativum* L. (3, 109, 110) (1886-1977)

Garden pepper-cress - *Lepidium sativum* L. (158) (1900)

Garden pepper-grass [Garden pepper grass, Garden peppergrass] - *Lepidium sativum* L. (5, 72, 158) (1900–1913)

Garden persicary - *Polygonum orientale* L. (156, 158) (1900-1923)

Garden petunia - *Petunia* ×*atkinsiana* D. Don ex Loud. [*axillaris* × *integrifolia*] (82) (1930)

Garden phlox - *Phlox paniculata* L. (5, 72, 85, 93, 95, 97, 138, 156) (1907-1937)

Garden pink - *Dianthus plumarius* L. (138) (1923)

Garden plague - *Aegopodium podagraria* L. (5, 156) (1913-1923)

Garden poppy - *Papaver somniferum* L. (5, 15, 106, 156) (1895-1930)

Garden portulaca - *Portulaca grandiflora* Hook. (5, 97, 156, 158) (1900-1937)

Garden purslane - *Portulaca grandiflora* Hook. (5, 156, 158) (1900-1923), *Portulaca oleracea* L. (57, 92) (1876-1917)

Garden radish - *Raphanus sativus* L. (5, 19, 72, 155, 158, 180) (1633-1942)

Garden ranunculus - *Ranunculus repens* L. (2) (1895)

Garden raspberry - *Rubus idaeus* L. (19) (1840)

Garden rhubarb - *Rheum rhabarbarum* L. (50, 109, 155) (1942–present)

Garden rocket - *Eruca* Mill. (1) (1932), *Eruca vesicaria* (L.) Cav. subsp. *sativa* (Mill.) Thellung (5, 85, 156) (1913-1932), *Hesperis matronalis* L. (92, 158) (1876-1900)

Garden rue - *Ruta graveolens* L. (49, 53) (1898-1922)

Garden sage - *Salvia officinalis* L. (49, 53, 58, 92, 138, 156) (1869-1923)

Garden silkweed - *Asclepias curassavica* L. (58) (1869)

Garden snapdragon - *Antirrhinum majus* L. (50) (present)

Garden snowberry - *Symphoricarpos albus* (L.) Blake var. *laevigatus* (Fern.) Blake (138) (1923)

Garden sorrel - *Rumex acetosa* L. (19, 92, 109, 156) (1840-1949)

Garden speedwell - *Veronica agrestis* L. (5, 156, 158) (1900-1923)

Garden spurge - *Chamaesyce hypericifolia* (L.) Millsp. (49, 53)

(1898-1922), *Euphorbia cyparissias* L. (5, 156) (1913-1923), *Euphorbia lathyris* L. (6, 71, 92) (1876-1898)

Garden strawberry - *Chenopodium capitatum* (L.) Asch. (possibly) (77) (1898) Paris ME, *Fragaria chiloensis* (L.) Mill. (82, 107) (1919-1930)

Garden sunflower - *Helianthus annuus* L. (92, 156, 157, 158) (1898-1929)

Garden syringa - *Philadelphus coronarius* L. (5, 156) (1913-1923)

Garden thyme - *Thymus vulgaris* L. (92) (1876)

Garden tickseed - *Coreopsis tinctoria* Nutt. (5, 72, 131, 156) (1899–1923)

Garden tomato - *Solanum lycopersicum* L. (50) (present), *Solanum lycopersicum* L. var. *lycopersicum* (50) (present)

Garden valerian - *Valeriana officinalis* L. (5, 156) (1913-1923)

Garden vetch - *Vicia sativa* L. (50) (present)

Garden violet - *Viola odorata* L. (109) (1949), *Viola tricolor* L. (19, 158) (1840-1900)

Garden wild plum - *Prunus hortulana* Bailey (5) (1913)

Garden yellow-rocket [Garden yellowrocket] - *Barbarea vulgaris* W.T. Aiton (50) (present)

Garden-cress pepperweed [Gardencress pepperweed] - *Lepidium sativum* L. (50, 155) (1942–present)

Gardener's-delight [Gardener's delight] - *Lychnis coronaria* (L.) Desr. (5, 156) (1913-1923) no longer in use by 1923

Gardener's-eye [Gardener's eye] - *Lychnis coronaria* (L.) Desr. (5, 156) (1913-1923) no longer in use by 1923

Gardener's-garters [Gardener's garters] - *Phalaris arundinacea* L. (163) (1852) *Phalaris canariensis* L. (92) (1876)

Garden-gate - *Viola tricolor* L. (158) (1900)

Gardes (France) - *Ribes rubrum* L. (110) (1886) possibly from gardis "rough, harsh, pungent, or sour"

Garent-Oguen (Iroquois, a child) - *Panax quinquefolius* L. (41, 177) (1770)

Garget - *Phytolacca americana* L. (5, 69) (1903-1913), *Phytolacca americana* L. var. *americana* (2, 6, 7, 49, 53, 64, 71, 92, 107, 152, 6, 157, 158, 186) (1814-1923)

Garget plant - *Phytolacca americana* L. var. *americana* (59) (1911)

Gargetweed [Garget weed] - *Phytolacca americana* L. var. *americana* (49) (1898)

Garland chrysanthemum - *Chrysanthemum coronarium* L. (109) (1949)

Garland crab - *Malus coronaria* (L.) Mill. var. *coronaria* (107, 156) (1919-1923)

Garland crab apple - *Malus coronaria* (L.) Mill. var. *coronaria* (2) (1895)

Garland flower [Garland-flower] - *Hedychium coronarium* Koenig (109) (1949), *Hedychium* Koenig (92) (1876)

Garland spiraea - *Spiraea alba* Du Roi (112) (1937)

Garland tree - *Malus coronaria* (L.) Mill. var. *coronaria* (156) (1923)

Garlic [Garlick, Garlicke, Garlyke] - *Allium* L. (101, 156, 184) (1793-1923), *Allium sativum* L. (3, 19, 49, 52, 53, 57, 58, 92, 109, 110, 138, 155, 158, 165, 178, 179) (1526-1977), *Allium vineale* L. (56) (1901)

Garlic leek [Garlicke leke] - *Allium ampeloprasum* L. (178) (1596)

Garlic mustard [Garlicmustard, Garlicke mustard] - *Alliaria* Heister ex Fabr.(possibly) (1, 4) (1932-1986), *Alliaria petiolata* (Bieb.) Cavara & Grande (3, 4, 5, 50, 155, 158) (1900–present), *Lepidium campestre* (L.) Aiton f. (178) (1526)

Garlic root [Garlic-root] - *Alliaria petiolata* (Bieb.) Cavara & Grande (5, 156) (1913-1923)

Garlic sage - *Teucrium scorodonia* L. (92, 156) (1898-1923)

Garlic shrub - *Mansoa alliacea* (Lam.) A.H. Gentry (92) (1876)

Garlicwort [Garlic wort] - *Alliaria petiolata* (Bieb.) Cavara & Grande (107, 158) (1900-1919)

Garlleg (Welsh) - *Allium sativum* L. (110) (1886)

Garnetberry [Garnet-berry, Garnet berry - *Ribes rubrum* L. (92, 156) (1876-1923)

Garnier du Canada (French) - *Cercis canadensis* L. (8) (1785)

Garrambullo - *Lycium torreyi* Gray (149, 153) (1904-1919) NM

Gartenlauch (German) - *Allium sativum* L. (158) (1900)

Garvance (French) - *Cicer arietinum* L. (110) (1886)

Gasantho (Omaha-Ponca, rattle) - *Astragalus canadensis* L. var. *canadensis* (37) (1919)

Gasatho (Omaha-Ponca, rattle) - *Baptisia bracteata* Muhl. ex Ell. (37) (1919)

Gascoine Cherrie - *Prunus cerasus* L. (178) (1526)

Gäsekresse (German) - *Capsella bursa-pastoris* (L.) Medik. (158) (1900)

Gaskins - *Prunus avium* (L.) L. (5, 92) (1876-1913), *Ribes uva-crispa* L. var. *sativum* DC. (156) (1923) no longer in use by 1923

Gaspe's groundsel [Gaspe groundsel] - *Packera paupercula* (Michx.) A.& D. Löve (155) (1942)

Gaspe's paper birch [Gaspe paper birch] - *Betula papyrifera* Marsh. var. *papyrifera* (155) (1942)

Gasplant [Gas-plant] - *Dictamnus albus* L. (109, 138) (1923-1949) will often give a flash of light when a burning match is held under the flower cluster, *Dictamnus* L. (138) (1923)

Gassedill (Norwegian) - *Anthemis cotula* L. (186) (1814)

Gasseguld (Norwegian) - *Anthemis cotula* L. (186) (1814)

Gattan tree - *Viburnum opulus* L. (156) (1923) no longer in use by 1923

Gatten or Gatten tree [Gatten-tree] - *Euonymus europaea* L. (5, 156) (1913-1923), *Viburnum opulus* L. (5, 158) (1900-1913)

Gatteridge - *Euonymus europaea* L. (5, 156) (1913-1923)

Gattinger's agalinis - *Agalinis gattingeri* (Small) Small (5) (1913)

Gattinger's goldenrod [Gattinger's goldenrod] - *Solidago gattengeri* Chapman (5, 72) (1907-1913)

Gattinger's hypericum [Gattinger hypericum] - *Hypericum lobocarpum* Gattinger (138) (1923)

Gattinger's panic grass [Gattinger's panicgrass] - *Panicum gattingeri* Nash (50) (present)

Gattinger's thorn - *Crataegus pruinosa* (Wendl.) K. Koch (5) (1913)

Gattinger's witch grass - *Panicum gattingeri* Nash (5) (1913)

Gatunas - *Mimosa* L. (153) (1913) NM

Gauchheil (German) - *Anagallis arvensis* L. (158) (1900)

Gaul - *Myrica gale* L. (46) (1671)

Gaule - *Myrica gale* L. (178) (1526)

Gaulther (French) - *Gaultheria* L. (8) (1785)

Gaulther rampant (French) - *Gaultheria procumbens* L. (8) (1785)

Gaultheria - *Gaultheria* L. (8) (1785), *Gaultheria procumbens* L. (52) (1919)

Gaultheria (Official name of Materia Medica) - *Gaultheria procumbens* L. (7) (1828)

Gaura - *Gaura biennis* L. (82, 145) (1897-1930), *Gaura coccinea* Nutt. ex Pursh (127) (1933), *Gaura* L. (82, 138, 155) (1930-1942), *Gaura suffulta* Engelm. ex Gray (4) (1986)

Gautiere rampante (French) - *Gaultheria procumbens* L. (7) (1828) TX

Gawa'komĭc (Chippewa) - *Ulmus rubra* Muhl. (40) (1919), *Zanthoxylum americanum* Mill. (37) (1919)

Gay lady's-slipper [Gay ladies' slipper] - *Cypripedium reginae* Walt. (19) (1840)

Gay mallows - *Lavatera thuringiaca* L. (19) (1840)

Gay orchis - *Galearis spectabilis* (L.) Raf. (5, 19, 156, 158) (1840-1923)

Gayac bois saint - *Guaiacum sanctum* L. (20) (1857)

Gaybine - *Convolvulus* L. (92) (1876), *Ipomoea nil* (L.) Roth (92) (1876)

Gayfeather [Gay-feather, Gay feather] - *Liatris aspera* Michx. (5, 49, 106, 156) (1923-1977), *Liatris* Gaertn. ex Schreber. (4, 7, 86, 98, 109, 138, 155) (1828-1986), *Liatris lancifolia* (Greene) Kittell (3) (1977), *Liatris ligulistylis* (A. Nels.) K. Schum. (3) (1977), *Liatris mucronata* DC. (3) (1977), *Liatris punctata* Hook (98) (1926), *Liatris scariosa* (L.) Willd. var. *scariosa* (158) (1900), *Liatris spicata* (L.) Willd. (19, 49, 52, 92, 156) (1840-1923), *Liatris spicata*

(L.) Willd. var. *spicata* (5, 93, 157) (1913-1936), *Liatris squarrosa* (L.) Michx. var. *glabrata* (Rydb.) Gaiser (3, 98) (1926-1977), *Liatris squarrosa* (L.) Michx. var. *hirsuta* (Rydb.) Gaiser (3, 4) (1977-1986)

Gayophytum - *Gayophytum* Juss. (158) (1900)

Gaywings [Gay wings] - *Polygala paucifolia* Willd. (5, 74, 156) (1893-1923) VT NY

Gazania - *Gazania* Gaertn. (138) (1923) for Theodore of Gaza, 1398-1478, translator of Aristotle and Theophrastus

Gean - *Prunus avium* (L.) L. (5, 107) (1913-1919)

Geel Spozckel bloemen (Dutch) - *Narcissus pseudonarcissus* L. (180) (1633)

Gefleckter Schierling (German) - *Conium maculatum* L. (158) (1900)

Gefleckter Storchsnabel (German) - *Geranium maculatum* L. (6, 7, 186) (1814-1932)

Geigenblättrige Winde (German) - *Ipomoea pandurata* (L.) G.F.W. Mey. (7, 186) (1814-1828)

Geiger tree [Geiger-tree] - *Cordia sebestena* L. (109, 138) (1923-1949)

Geisraute (German) - *Galega officinalis* L. (158) (1900)

Gelatina aquatica (Official name of Materia Medica) - *Brasenia schreberi* Gmel. (7) (1828)

Gelb Frauenshuh (German) - *Cypripedium parviflorum* Salisb. var. *parviflorum* (7) (1828)

Gelb Frauenshuh (German) - *Cypripedium parviflorum* Salisb. var. *pubescens* (Willd.) Knight (6) (1892)

Gelb Hundzahn (German) - *Erythronium americanum* Ker. (7) (1828)

Gelb Puckuhn (German) - *Hydrastis canadensis* L. (7) (1828)

Gelbe Rübe (German) - *Daucus carota* L. (158) (1900)

Gelber Jasmin (German) - *Gelsemium sempervirens* (L.) J. St.-Hil. (6) (1892)

Gelber Senf (German) - *Sinapis alba* L. (158) (1900)

Gelbfrauenshuhwurz (German) - *Cypripedium reginae* Walt. (158) (1900)

Gelsemium - *Gelsemium sempervirens* (L.) J. St.-Hil. (54, 57, 60, 64) (1902-1917)

Gelsiminum - *Jasminum officinale* L. (178) (1526)

Gem fruit [Gem-fruit] - *Tiarella cordifolia* L. (5, 19, 92, 156) (1840-1923)

Gemeine Ballote (German) - *Ballota nigra* L. (158) (1900)

Gemeine Calamus (German) - *Acorus calamus* L. (186) (1814)

Gemeine Lobelie (German) - *Lobelia siphilitica* L. (6, 186) (1814-1892)

Gemeine Oderminig (German) - *Agrimonia eupatoria* L. (7) (1828)

Gemeine Rade (German) - *Agrostemma githago* L. (6) (1892)

Gemeine Rermesbeere (German) - *Phytolacca americana* L. var. *americana* (186) (1814)

Gemeine Schierling (German) - *Conium maculatum* L. (7) (1828)

Gemeine Stechappel (German) - *Datura stramonium* L. (7) (1828)

Gemeines Bürlapp (German) - *Lycopodium clavatum* L. (6) (1892)

General Marion's weed - *Apocynum cannabinum* L. (6) (1892)

Genesta (Italian & German) - *Cytisus scoparius* (L.) Link (59) (1911)

Genet des Teintuiers (French) - *Genista tinctoria* L. (6) (1892)

Geneva bugle - *Ajuga genevensis* L. (138, 155, 165) (1768-1942)

Genevrier (French) - *Juniperus* L. (8) (1785)

Genévrier commun (French) - *Juniperus communis* L. (158) (1900)

Genevrier de Virginie (French) - *Juniperus virginiana* L. (8) (1785)

Genevrier des Andes (French) - *Juniperus virginiana* L. (20) (1857)

Geniev commun (French) - *Juniperus communis* L. (7) (1828)

Genip - *Melicoccus bijugatus* Jacq. (109) (1949)

Genip tree - *Exothea paniculata* (Juss.) Radlk. (20) (1857)

Gensang - *Panax quinquefolius* L. (7) (1828)

Genson - *Triosteum perfoliatum* L. (5, 156, 158) (1900-1923) no longer in use by 1923

Gentian - *Gentiana affinis* Griesb. (85) (1932), *Gentiana* L. (1, 93) (1932-1936), *Gentiana puberulenta* J. Pringle (37) (1919), *Triosteum perfoliatum* L. (186) (1814)

Gentian rockbell - *Wahlenbergia marginata* (Thunb.) A. DC. (138) (1923)

Gentiane de Catesby (French) - *Gentiana catesbaei* Walt. (7) (1828)

Gentleman's sorrrel - *Rumex acetosella* L. (5, 73, 156, 158) (1892-1923) Cambridge MA

Gentleman's-cane [Gentleman's cane] - *Polygonum orientale* L. (5, 75, 77, 156, 158) (1894-1923) OH, stems cut by children into canes

Gentleman's-hats [Gentleman's hats] - *Silene noctiflora* L. (73) (1892) Gilsum NH

Gentlemen-and-ladies [Gentlemen and ladies] - *Dodecatheon meadia* L. (156) (1923)

Georgia amorpha - *Amorpha nitens* Boynt. (155) (1942)

Georgia aster - *Symphyotrichum shortii* (Lindl.) Nesom (138, 155) (1931-1942)

Georgia bark - *Pinckneya bracteata* (Bartr.) Raf. (7, 20, 92) (1828-1876), *Pinckneya* Michx. (2) (1895)

Georgia buckeye - *Aesculus sylvatica* Bartr. (138) (1923)

Georgia bulrush - *Scirpus georgianus* Harper (50) (present)

Georgia bush-honeysuckle - *Diervilla rivularis* Gattinger (138) (1923)

Georgia farkleberry - *Vaccinium stamineum* L. (155) (1942)

Georgia gooseberry - *Ribes curvatum* Small (138) (1923)

Georgia hackberry - *Celtis tenuifolia* Nutt. (5, 97, 155) (1913-1942)

Georgia oak - *Quercus georgiana* M.A. Curtis (138) (1923)

Georgia pine - *Pinus palustris* Mill. (5, 52) (1913-1919)

Georgia pitch pine - *Pinus palustris* Mill. (20) (1857)

Geraine (French) - *Geranium maculatum* L. (186) (1814)

Geranio (Spanish, Portuguese) - *Geranium maculatum* L. (158, 186) (1814-1900)

Geranion - *Geranium maculatum* L. (186) (1814)

Geranium - *Geranium maculatum* L. (52, 54, 57, 59, 114) (1894-1917), *Geranium texanum* (Trel.) Heller (122) (1937), *Pelargonium* L'Hér. ex Aiton (138) (1923), *Pelargonium odoratissimum* (L.) L'Hér. ex Aiton (92) (1876)

Geranium maculé (French) - *Geranium maculatum* L. (7, 158) (1828-1900)

Geranium radix - *Geranium maculatum* L. (7) (1828)

Gerarde - *Morchella* Dill. ex Pers (181) (~1678)

Gerardia - *Agalinis aspera* (Dougl. ex Benth.) Britton (85) (1932), *Agalinis* Raf. (1, 4) (1932-1986), *Agalinis tenuifolia* (Vahl) Raf. (98) (1926)

Gerbera - *Gerbera* Gmel. (138) (1923)

German basswood - *Tilia × vulgaris* Hayne [*cordata × platyphyllos*] (112) (1937)

German camomile [German-camomile, German chamomile] - *Matricaria recutita* L. (5, 49, 50, 52, 53, 55, 57, 58, 59, 92, 122, 155, 156, 158) (1869–present)

German catchfly - *Lychnis viscaria* L. (109) (1949)

German clover [Germaine Clauer] - *Melilotus officinalis* (L.) Lam. (178) (1526) John Gerarde, *Trifolium incarnatum* L. (68) (1913) Ottawa

German contrayerva - *Cynanchum vincetoxicum* (L.) Pers. (92) (1876)

German elder - *Sambucus nigra* L. (158) (1900)

German insect powder - *Chrysanthemum coccineum* Willd. (92) (1876)

German iris - *Iris germanica* L. (50, 109, 138) (1923–present)

German ivy [German-ivy] - *Delairea odorata* Lem. (92, 109) (1876-1949)

German knotgrass [German knot grass, German knot-grass] - *Scleranthus annuus* L. (5, 50, 92, 156, 158) (1876–present), *Scleranthus* L. (50, 187) (1818–present)

German lactucarium - *Lactuca virosa* L. (92) (1876)

German madwort [German-madwort] - *Asperugo* L. (1, 50, 158) (1900–present), *Asperugo procumbens* L. (5, 50, 156, 158) (1900–present)

German medic fodder [Germaine Medicke Fodder] - *Medicago arabica* (L.) Huds. (178) (1526)

German millet - *Setaria italica* (L.) Beauv. (5, 45, 56, 68, 87, 88, 90, 109, 119, 151, 156) (1884-1949)

German millet-grass [German millet grass] - *Scleranthus annuus* L. (92) (1876)

German pellitory - *Achillea ptarmica* L. (92) (1876)

German rampion - *Oenothera biennis* L. (107, 156) (1919-1923)

German sarsaparilla - *Carex arenaria* L. (92) (1876)

German scammony - *Calystegia sepium* (L.) R. Br. subsp. *sepium* (5, 156, 158) (1900-1923)

German tinder - *Boletus fomentarius* L. (92) (1876)

German valerian - *Valeriana officinalis* L. (92) (1876)

German wheat - *Triticum turgidum* L. (107) (1919)

Germander - *Teucrium canadense* L. (19, 57, 80, 82, 92, 106, 131, 184) (1793-1930), *Teucrium canadense* L. var. *occidentale* (Gray) McClintock & Epling (127, 158) (1900-1933), *Teucrium* L. (1, 2, 4, 7, 10, 50, 82, 109, 138, 155, 156) (1818–present)

Germander sage - *Teucrium scorodonia* L. (156) (1923)

Germander speedwell - *Veronica chamaedrys* L. (5, 109, 156) (1913-1949)

Germander spiraea - *Spiraea chamaedryfolia* L. (138) (1923)

Germander-chickweed [Germander chickweed] - *Veronica agrestis* L. (5, 156, 158) (1900-1923)

Gerste (German) - *Hordeum vulgare* L. (158) (1900)

Gersten (High Dutch) - *Hordeum vulgare* L. (180) (1633)

Gersten (Low Dutch) - *Hordeum vulgare* L. (180) (1633)

Gertwurz (German) - *Artemisia abrotanum* L. (158) (1900)

Geschwürwurzel (German) - *Polemonium reptans* L. (158) (1900)

Geslings - *Salix discolor* Muhl. (158) (1900) England, catkins

Gesneria - *Gesneria* L. (138) (1923)

Geum radix (Official name of Materia Medica) - *Geum virginianum* L. (7) (1828)

Geyer's aster - *Symphyotrichum laeve* (L.) A.& D. Löve var. *geyeri* (Gray) Nesom (50) (present)

Geyer's euphorbia [Geyer euphorbia] - *Chamaesyce geyeri* (Engelm.) Small var. *geyeri* (155) (1942)

Geyer's larkspur [Geyer larkspur] - *Delphinium geyeri* Greene (50, 155) (1942–present)

Geyer's monkey-flower - *Mimulus glabratus* Kunth var. *jamesii* (Torr. & Gray ex Benth.) Gray (97) (1937)

Geyer's onion [Geyer onion] - *Allium geyeri* Wats. (50, 155) (1942–present)

Geyer's sandmat - *Chamaesyce geyeri* (Engelm.) Small (50) (present), *Chamaesyce geyeri* (Engelm.) Small var. *geyeri* (50) (present)

Geyer's spurge - *Chamaesyce geyeri* (Engelm.) Small (5, 93, 97) (1913-1937)

Geyer's spurge - *Chamaesyce geyeri* (Engelm.) Small var. *geyeri* (3, 4, 72, 121, 131) (1899-1986)

Geyer's water-plantain [Geyer waterplantain, Geyer's water plantain] - *Alisma gramineum* Lej. (5, 93, 155) (1913-1942)

Geyer's yellow monkey-flower [Geyer's yellow monkey flower] - *Mimulus glabratus* Kunth var. *jamesii* (Torr. & Gray ex Benth.) Gray (5) (1913)

Ghohona - *Paspalum scrobiculatum* L. (92) (1876)

Ghost-flower - *Monotropa uniflora* L. (5, 73, 77, 156, 157, 158) (1892-1929) NB, S. Berick ME

Ghost-pipe [Ghostpipe] - *Orobanche* L. (155) (1942), *Orobanche uniflora* L. (155) (1942)

Ghostweed [Ghost-weed] - *Euphorbia marginata* Pursh (78) (1898) Waco TX

Giant alocasia - *Alocasia macrorrhizos* (L.) Schott (155) (1942)

Giant arborvitae [Giant arbor-vitae] - *Thuja plicata* Donn ex D. Don (103, 109, 138) (1871-1949)

Giant arrowhead - *Sagittaria calycina* Engelm. var. *calycina* (3, 138, 155) (1923-1977)

Giant bird's-nest [Giant bird's nest] - *Pterospora andromedea* Nutt. (5, 93, 156, 158) (1900-1923), *Pterospora* Nutt. (1) (1932)

Giant blue sage - *Salvia azurea* Michx. ex Lam. (124) (1937) TX

Giant bristle grass [Giant bristlegrass] - *Setaria magna* Griseb. (50, 122) (1937–present)

Giant bulrush - *Schoenoplectus californicus* (C.A. Mey.) Palla (124) (1937), *Schoenoplectus tabernaemontani* (K.C. Gmel.) Palla (85) (1932)

Giant bur-reed [Giant burreed] - *Sparganium eurycarpum* Engelm. ex Gray (155) (1942)

Giant cactus [Giantcactus] - *Carnegia gigantea* (Engelm.) Britt. & Rose (76, 103, 104, 106, 109, 138, 155) (1870-1949), *Carnegiea* Britt. & Rose (138) (1923)

Giant cane - *Arundinaria gigantea* (Walter) Muhl. (5, 50, 119, 163) (1913–present)

Giant chain fern [Giant chainfern] - *Woodwardia fimbriata* Sm. (138) (1923)

Giant chickweed [Giantchickweed] - *Myosoton aquaticum* (L.) Moench (50) (present)

Giant chinquapin - *Chrysolepis chrysophylla* (Douglas ex Hook.) Hjelmq. (106) (1930), *Chrysolepis chrysophylla* (Douglas ex Hook.) Hjelmqvist var. *chrysophylla* (138) (1923)

Giant clover - *Trifolium pratense* L. (5, 45, 158) (1896-1913)

Giant cut grass [Giant cutgrass] - *Zizaniopsis miliacea* (Michx.) Doell & Aschers. (50) (present)

Giant daisy [Giant-daisy, Giantdaisy] - *Tanacetum vulgare* L. (138, 155) (1923-1942)

Giant dropseed - *Sporobolus giganteus* Nash (3, 50, 155) (1942–present)

Giant duckweed - *Spirodela polyrhiza* (L.) Schleid. (50) (present)

Giant fennel [Giantfennel] - *Foeniculum vulgare* Mill. (157, 158) (1900-1929)

Giant fescue - *Lolium giganteum* (L.) S.J. Darbyshire (50) (present)

Giant foxtail grass [Giant foxtail-grass] - *Setaria magna* Griseb. (5, 163) (1852-1913)

Giant garlic - *Allium scorodoprasum* L. (155) (1942)

Giant gaura - *Stenosiphon linifolius* (Nutt. ex James) Heynh. (124) (1937) TX

Giant goldenrod [Giant golden-rod] - *Solidago gigantea* Aiton (19, 50, 72, 138, 155) (1840–present)

Giant granadilla - *Passiflora quadrangularis* L. (109, 138) (1923-1949)

Giant holly fern [Giant hollyfern] - *Polystichum munitum* (Kaulfuss) K. Presl (138) (1923)

Giant hyssop [Gianthyssop] - *Agastache* Clayton ex Gronov. (1, 50, 82, 93, 109, 155, 156, 158) (1900–present), *Agastache nepetoides* (L.) Kuntze (19, 82, 85, 106, 114, 131, 156) (1840-1930), *Agastache scrophulariifolia* (Willd.) Kuntze (63, 72, 93) (1899-1936), *Waltheria* L. (2) (1895)

Giant ironweed - *Vernonia gigantea* (Walter) Trel. ex Branner & Coville (50) (present)

Giant lousewort - *Pedicularis procera* Gray (50) (present)

Giant millet - *Setaria magna* Griseb. (56, 94) (1901)

Giant orchis - *Platanthera dilatata* (Pursh) Lindl. ex Beck (19) (1840)

Giant paspalum - *Paspalum floridanum* Michx. (155) (1942)

Giant pine - *Pinus lambertiana* Dougl. (107) (1919)

Giant puff-ball - *Calvatia gigantea* (Batsch) Lloyd (72) (1907)

Giant ragweed - *Ambrosia trifida* L. (3, 4, 21, 62, 82, 97, 125, 155, 157, 158) (1893-1929)

Giant red Indian paintbrush - *Castilleja miniata* Dougl. ex Hook. (50) (present)

Giant reed [Giantreed] - *Arundo donax* L. (109, 119, 122, 138, 163) (1852-1949), *Arundo* L. (41, 155) (1770-1942)

Giant reed grass [Giant reed-grass] - *Arundo donax* L. (88) (1885), *Calamovilfa gigantea* (Nutt.) Scribn, & Merr. (5, 163) (1852-1913)

Giant root - *Marah macrocarpus* (Greene) Greene var. *macrocarpus* (123) (1856)

Giant rye grass [Giant rye-grass] - *Leymus condensatus* (J. Presl) A. Löve (45, 56, 87, 88, 94, 111, 157) (1885-1915)

Giant sandreed - *Calamovilfa gigantea* (Nutt.) Scribn, & Merr. (50) (present)

Giant sedge - *Carex atherodes* Spreng. (129) (1894) SD, *Carex gigantea* Rudge (50) (present)

Giant sequoia - *Sequoiadendron giganteum* (Lindl.) Buchh. (50, 138) (1923–present)

Giant snowdrop - *Galanthus elwesii* Hook. f. (109) (1949)

Giant Solomon's-seal [Giant Solomon's seal, Giant Solomon seal] - *Polygonatum biflorum* (Walt.) Ell. (19, 58, 92) (1840-1869), *Polygonatum biflorum* (Walt.) Ell. var. *commutatum* (J.A. & J.H. Schultes) Morong (5, 157, 158) (1900-1929)

Giant spider-flower - *Cleome hassleriana* Chod. (109) (1949)

Giant spurrey - *Spergula arvensis* L. (129) (1894) SD

Giant St. John's-wort [Giant St. John's wort, Giant St. Johnswort] - *Hypericum ascyron* L. (5, 93, 124, 155, 156, 158) (1900–1937)

Giant sumpweed - *Iva xanthifolia* Nutt. (50) (present)

Giant sunflower - *Helianthus giganteus* L. (5, 72, 107, 109, 138) (1907-1949)

Giant taro - *Alocasia macrorrhizos* (L.) Schott (138) (1923)

Giant tarweed [Giant tar weed] - *Grindelia grandiflora* Hook. (124) (1937)

Giant torchlily - *Kniphofia uvaria* (L.) Oken (138) (1923)

Giant water grass [Giant water-grass] - *Paspalum floridanum* Michx. (94) (1901)

Giant white fawnlily - *Erythronium oregonum* Applegate (50) (present)

Giant whortleberry - *Vaccinium corymbosum* L. (19, 92, 156) (1840-1923)

Giant wild rye [Giant wild-rye, Giant wildrye] - *Leymus condensatus* (J. Presl) A. Löve (140, 50, 146, 155) (1939–present)

Giant's-throatwort [Giants Throatwoort, Giants Throate woort] - *Campanula latifolia* L. (178) (1526)

Gibbals - *Plantago maritima* L. (5) (1913), *Plantago maritima* L. var. *juncoides* (Lam.) Gray (156) (1923)

Gibbous duckweed - *Lemna gibba* L. (93) (1936)

Gibbous panic grass [Gibbous panic-grass] - *Sacciolepis striata* (L.) Nash (5, 94, 119, 163) (1852-1938)

Gibraltar candytuft - *Iberis gibraltarica* L. (109, 138) (1923-1949)

Giftbaum (German) - *Toxicodendron radicans* (L.) Kuntze subsp. *radicans* (158) (1900)

Gift-Lattich (German) - *Lactuca virosa* L. (158) (1900)

Giftsumach (German) - *Toxicodendron radicans* (L.) Kuntze subsp. *radicans* (158) (1900), *Toxicodendron toxicarium* (Salisb.) Gillis (6) (1892)

Gigantic arborvitae [Gigantic arbor vitae] - *Thuja plicata* Donn ex D. Don (20) (1857)

Gigantic black oak - *Quercus velutina* Lam. (182) (1791)

Gigantic pine - *Pinus lambertiana* Dougl. (10, 20) (1818-1857)

Giglio - *Lilium candidum* L. (180) (1633)

Giglio azurro (Italian) - *Iris* L. (180) (1633)

Gijib'inûskon' (Chippewa, it is round) - *Equisetum hyemale* L. (40) (1928)

Gi'jikan'dûg (Chippewa, cedar-like) - *Thuja occidentalis* L. (40) (1928)

Gilbert's relief grass - *Phalaris caroliniana* Walt. (45, 87, 88) (1885-1896)

Gilead buds - *Populus balsamifera* L. (157) (1929)

Gilenia - *Porteranthus trifoliatus* (L.) Britton (64) (1907)

Gilgen Schwertel (German) - *Iris* L. (180) (1633)

Gilia - *Gilia capitata* Sims (82) (1930), *Ipomopsis aggregata* (Pursh) V. Grant subsp. *aggregata* (157) (1929), *Ipomopsis rubra* (L.) Wherry (92) (1876)

Gilia beardtongue - *Penstemon ambiguus* Torr. (50) (present)

Gilia penstemon - *Penstemon ambiguus* Torr. (3, 4, 155) (1942-1986)

Gill - *Glechoma hederacea* L. (106) (1930)

Gill-cup - *Ranunculus bulbosus* L. (158) (1900)

Gillenia - *Gillenia trifoliata* (L.) Moench (156) (1923), *Porteranthus stipulatus* (Muhl. ex Willd.) Britt. (57) (1917)

Gillenia occidentale (French) - *Porteranthus stipulatus* (Muhl. ex Willd.) Britt. (7) (1828)

Gillenia radix - *Porteranthus stipulatus* (Muhl. ex Willd.) Britt. (7) (1828)

Gillenwurzel (German) - *Porteranthus stipulatus* (Muhl. ex Willd.) Britt. (7) (1828)

Gill-go-by-the-ground - *Glechoma hederacea* L. (92, 156) (1876-1923)

Gill-go-over-the-ground - *Glechoma hederacea* L. (49) (1898)

Gilliflower - *Dianthus caryophyllus* L. (92) (1876)

Gilliflower-grass [Gilliflower grass] - *Carex flacca* Schreb. (5, 156) (1913-1923), *Carex panicea* L. (5, 156) (1913-1923)

Gillman's goldenrod [Gillman's golden-rod] - *Solidago simplex* var. *gillmanii* (Gray) Ringius (5) (1913)

Gilloflowers of diuers sort and colours - *Dianthus caryophyllus* L. (178) (1526)

Gill-over-the-ground - *Glechoma hederacea* L. (1, 63, 73, 75, 106, 109, 156) (1892-1949), *Glechoma* L. (1) (1932)

Gillrun - *Glechoma hederacea* L. (92) (1876)

Gill-run-over - *Glechoma hederacea* L. (156) (1923)

Gill-run-over-grass - *Glechoma hederacea* L. (77) (1898) Cambridge MA

Gilly flower [Gilly flowers, Gillyflowers] - *Erysimum cheiri* (L.) Crantz (46) (1671) cultivated by English colonists by 1671, *Matthiola incana* (L.) Aiton f. (46, 92) (1671-1876)

Gine'biwûck (Chippewa, snake-like) - *Plantago major* L. (40) (1928)

Gingembre (French) - *Asarum canadense* L. (41) (1770), *Zingiber officinale* Roscoe (180) (1633)

Ginger [Gynger] - *Sedum acre* L. (5, 156) (1913-1923) no longer in use by 1923, *Tussilago farfara* L. (5, 156) (1913-1923), *Zingiber* Mill. (138) (1923), *Zingiber officinale* Roscoe (92, 107, 178, 179) (1526-1919)

Ginger mint [Gingermint] - *Mentha ×gracilis* Sole [*arvensis × spicata*] (50) (present)

Ginger plant [Ginger-plant] - *Tanacetum vulgare* L. (5, 69, 156, 158) (1900-1923)

Ginger root - *Tussilago farfara* L. (75) (1894) MN

Gingerberry [Ginger berry, Ginger-berry] - *Gaultheria* L. (167) (1814), *Gaultheria procumbens* L. (5, 156) (1913-1923)

Ginger-lily [Gingerlily] - *Hedychium* Koenig (109, 138) (1923-1949)

Ginger-pine [Ginger pine] - *Chamaecyparis lawsoniana* (A. Murr.) Parl. (75) (1894)

Gingiber - *Zingiber officinale* Roscoe (180) (1633)

Gingo tree - *Ginkgo biloba* L. (92) (1876)

Ginkgo or Gingko tree - *Ginkgo biloba* L. (92, 107, 109, 137) (1876-1949) from Chinese name Gink-go

Ginnie Pepper - *Capsicum annuum* L. (178) (1526)

Ginoje'wûkûn (Chippewa, pike plant) - *Rumex crispus* L. (40) (1928)

Ginsano - *Panax quinquefolius* L. (186) (1814)

Ginsem [Gin-sem] - *Panax quinquefolius* L. (177, 186) (1762-1814)

Ginseng - *Aralia nudicaulis* L. (101) (1905) MT, true ginseng is Panax quinquefolia, *Oplopanax horridus* Miq. (103) (1870), *Panax* L. (1, 10, 50, 93, 138, 155, 158) (1818–present), *Panax quinquefolius* L. (2, 3, 4, 5, 6, 14, 19, 37, 41, 47, 49, 52, 53, 57, 61, 63, 64, 72, 92, 95, 97, 102, 105, 107, 156, 158, 182, 184, 186, 187) (1770-1986)

Ginseng d'Amerique (French) - *Panax quinquefolius* L. (possibly) (6) (1892)

Ginseng root - *Panax quinquefolius* L. (7) (1828)

Ginshang - *Panax quinquefolius* L. (75, 156) (1894-1923) VT

Ginsing - *Panax quinquefolius* L. (92, 57) (1876-1900)

Ginster - *Cytisus scoparius* (L.) Link (156) (1923)

Gin-zeng - *Panax quinquefolius* L. (177) (1762)

Gin-zing - *Panax quinquefolius* L. (177) (1762)

Gipsy flower [Gypsy flower, Gipsy-flower, Gypsyflower, Gypsyflower] - *Cynoglossum officinale* L. (5, 50, 62, 85, 156, 157, 158) (1900–present)

Gipsy herb [Gypsy herb] - *Lycopus europaeus* L. (5) (1913)

Gipsy plant [Gipsy-plant, Gypsy-plant] - *Lycopus europaeus* L. (156) (1923) no longer in use by 1923

Gipsy-combs [Gypsy combs] - *Dipsacus fullonum* L. (5, 156, 158) (1900-1923)

Gipsy-rose [Gypsy rose] - *Knautia arvensis* (L.) Duby (5, 156, 158) (1900-1923)

Gipsyweed [Gypsy weed, Gipsy weed, Gypsy-weed, Gypsyweed - *Lycopus americanus* Muhl. ex W. Bart. (5, 156, 158) (1900-1923), *Lycopus europaeus* L. (5, 156) (1913-1923) no longer in use by 1923, *Lycopus* L. (158) (1900), *Lycopus rubellus* Moench (5, 156) (1913-1923), *Lycopus virginicus* L. (6, 7, 49, 92, 157, 158) (1828-1929), *Veronica officinalis* L. (5, 75, 156) (1894-1923) WV

Gipsywort [Gypsywort, Gypsy-wort, Gypsiewort] - *Lycopus americanus* Muhl. ex W. Bart. (5, 156, 158) (1900-1923), *Lycopus* L. (158, 180, 184) (1793-1900), *Lycopus rubellus Moench* (5, 156) (1913-1923), *Lycopus virginicus L.* (6, 92) (1876-1892)

Girald's actinidia [Girald actinidia] - *Actinidia arguta* (Sieb. & Zucc.) Planch. ex Miq. (155) (1942)

Girald's ailanthus [Girald ailanthus] - *Ailanthus altissima* (Mill) Swingle (155) (1942)

Girasol - *Heliotropium arborescens* L. (92) (1876)

Girasole - *Helianthus tuberosus* L. (5, 92, 109, 156) (1876-1949)

Girasole (Italian) - *Ricinus communis* L. (110) (1886)

Girello (Italian) - *Cynara cardunculus* L. (110) (1886)

Girls-and-boys [Girls and boys] - *Dicentra cucullaria* (L.) Bernh. (74) (1893) VT

Girr or Kirr (Danish) - *Spergula arvensis* L. (110) (1886)

Gĭ'tciöde'imĭnĭdji'bĭk (Chippewa, big heart-berry root) - *Potentilla arguta* Pursh subsp. *arguta* (40) (1928)

Gith - *Nigella sativa* L. (179) (1526)

Giugiolena (Itlay) - *Sesamum* L. (7) (1828)

Giunco (Italian) - *Juncus* L. (180) (1633)

Gi'zĭso'bûgons' (Chippewa, sun small leaf) - *Heliopsis helianthoides* (L.) Sweet var. *scabra* (Dunal) Fern. (40) (1928), *Pediomelum argophyllum* (Pursh) J. Grimes (40) (1928), *Rudbeckia laciniata* L. (40) (1928)

Gi'zĭso'mûki'ki (Chippewa, sun medicine) - *Solidago* L. (40) (1928)

Gi'zûswe'bigwa'ĭs (Chippewa, it is scattering) - *Rudbeckia laciniata* L. (40) (1928)

Glabrous sideranthus - *Machaeranthera pinnatifida* (Hook.) Shinners subsp. *pinnatifida* (97) (1937)

Glacier lily [Glacierlily] - *Erythronium grandiflorum* Pursh (138) (1923)

Glade fern - *Diplazium pycnocarpon* (Spreng.) Broun (3, 4) (1977-1986)

Glade lily [Glade-lily] - *Lilium philadelphicum* L. (5, 75, 156, 158) (1894-1923) WV

Glade mallow - *Napaea dioica* L. (5, 72, 156) (1907-1923), *Napaea* L. (1, 2, 13, 15) (1849-1932)

Gladecress - *Leavenworthia* Torr. (50) (present)

Gladiolus - *Gladiolus communis* L. (92) (1876), *Gladiolus* L. (138, 180) (1633-1923)

Gladon - *Iris pseudacorus* L. (178, 179) (1526-1596)

Gladwine - *Iris foetidissima* L. (92) (1876)

Gladwin's iris [Gladwin iris] - *Iris foetidissima* L. (138) (1923)

Glaieul bleu (French) - *Iris versicolor* L. (6, 158) (1892-1900)

Glais (French) - *Gladiolus* L. (180) (1633)

Gland cinquefoil - *Potentilla glandulosa* Lindl. (155) (1942)

Glandular birch - *Betula nana* L. (5) (1913)

Glandular chinquefoil - *Potentilla arguta* Pursh (63) (1899)

Glandular cinquefoil - *Potentilla arguta* Pursh subsp. *arguta* (5, 93) (1913-1936), *Potentilla glandulosa* Lindl. (131) (1899)

Glandular clotbur - *Xanthium strumarium* L. var. *canadense* (Mill.) Torr. & Gray (5, 95) (1911-1913)

Glandular cocklebur - *Xanthium strumarium* L. var. *canadense* (Mill.) Torr. & Gray (93) (1936)

Glandular croton - *Croton glandulosus* L. (5, 72, 97) (1907-1937)

Glandular lobelia - *Lobelia glandulosa* Walt. (5) (1913)

Glandular persicary - *Polygonum pensylvanicum* L. (62) (1912)

Glandular sideranthus - *Machaeranthera pinnatifida* (Hook.) Shinners subsp. *pinnatifida* (97) (1937)

Glandular thorn - *Crataegus chrysocarpa* Ashe (72) (1907)

Glandular willowherb - *Epilobium halleanum Hausskn* (50) (present)

Glandulous birch - *Betula nana* L. (42) (1814)

Glasswort [Glass-wort, Glassewoort] - *Salicornia bigelovii* Torr. (122) (1937), *Salicornia* L. (1, 2, 10, 26, 41, 93, 155, 158) (1770-1942), *Salicornia maritima* Wolff & Jefferies (19, 46, 92, 95, 156, 157, 178) (1526-1929), *Salsola* L. (158) (1900)

Glastum - *Isatis tinctoria* L. (178) (1526)

Glatte (German) - *Chelone glabra* L. (6) (1892)

Glatter Wegedorn (German) - *Frangula alnus* Mill. (158) (1900)

Glauce (French) - *Glaux maritima* L. (158) (1900)

Glaucescent sedge - *Carex glaucodea* Tuckerm. ex Olney (5) (1913)

Glaucium - *Solanum lycopersicum* L. var. *lycopersicum* (180) (1633)

Glaucous alder - *Alnus incana* (L.) Moench (42) (1814)

Glaucous anticlea - *Zigadenus elegans* Pursh subsp. *elegans* (5, 97) (1913-1937)

Glaucous blue grass [Glaucous bluegrass] - *Poa glauca* Vahl. (50) (present)

Glaucous bristly foxtail - *Pennisetum glaucum* (L.) R. Br. (5) (1913)

Glaucous drypetes - *Drypetes glauca* Vahl (20) (1857)

Glaucous goosefoot [Glaucous goose foot] - *Chenopodium glaucum* L. (42) (1814)

Glaucous hawksbeard - *Crepis runcinata* (James) Torr. & Gray (5) (1913)

Glaucous honeysuckle - *Lonicera dioica* L. (5, 72, 156, 158) (1900-1923)

Glaucous leather flower - *Clematis glaucophylla* Small (5) (1913)

Glaucous small reed - *Calamagrostis coarctata* (Torr.) Eat. (66) (1903)

Glaucous spear grass - *Poa glauca* Vahl. (5) (1913)

Glaucous starwort [Glaucous star wort] - *Stellaria palustris* (Murr.) Retz. (5) (1913), *Symphyotrichum novi-belgii* (L.) Nesom var. *novi-belgii* (42) (1814)

Glaucous sundrops - *Oenothera fruticosa* L. subsp. *glauca* (Michx.) Straley (5) (1913)

Glaucous white lettuce - *Prenanthes racemosa* Michx. subsp. *multiflora* Cronq. (5, 72, 131) (1899–1913)

Glaucous willow - *Salix discolor* Muhl. (5, 72, 82, 108, 130, 131, 156, 158) (1878-1930)

Glaucous zygadenus - *Zigadenus elegans* Pursh (72, 133) (1903-1907)

Glaucous-leaf greenbrier [Glaucous-leaved greenbrier] - *Smilax glauca* Walt. (5, 93, 97) (1913-1937)

Glaucous-leaf laurel [Glaucous-leaved laurel] - *Kalmia polifolia* Wangenh. (187) (1818)

Glechoma - *Glechoma* L. (50) (present), *Glechoma hederacea* L. (57) (1917)

Glen pepper [Glen-pepper, Glenn pepper] - *Lepidium campestre* (L.) Aiton f. (5, 74, 156, 158) (1893–1923) WV

Glen weed [Glenn-weed] - *Lepidium campestre* (L.) Aiton f. (5, 74, 158) (1893–1913) WV, first noticed on Glenn farm

Glidewort [Glide woort] - *Lycopus europaeus* L. (178) (1526)

Globe [Globes] - *Gomphrena globosa* L. (73) (1892) Southern VT, *Nicandra physalodes* (L.) Gaertn. (77) (1898) Sulphur Grove OH

Globe beaksedge - *Rhynchospora recognita* (Gale) Kral (50) (present)

Globe bladderpod - *Lesquerella globosa* (Desv.) S. Wats. (50, 155) (1942–present)

Globe cactus - *Escobaria vivipara* (Nutt.) Buxbaum var. *vivipara* (145) (1897) KS, *Mammillaria* Haw. (50) (present)

Globe candytuft - *Iberis umbellata* L. (109) (1949)

Globe centaurea - *Centaurea macrocephala* Puschk. ex Willd. (138) (1923)

Globe crowfoot - *Trollius europaeus* L. (92) (1876)

Globe flatsedge - *Cyperus echinatus* (L.) Wood (3, 4, 50) (1977–present)

Globe gilia - *Gilia capitata* Sims (138) (1923)

Globe hyancinth - *Muscari botryoides* (L.) Mills (92) (1876)

Globe-amaranth [Globe amaranth] - *Gomphrena globosa* L. (19, 77, 92, 156) (1840-1923), *Gomphrena* L. (138) (1923), *Ranunculus acris* L. (92) (1876)

Globeberry [Globe berry, Globe berries] - *Ibervillea* Greene (4, 50) (1986–present), *Ibervillea lindheimeri* (Gray) Greene (4) (1986), *Taxus baccata* L. (92) (1876)

Globeflower [Globe-flower, Globe flower] - *Cephalanthus occidentalis* L. (5, 6, 7, 49, 58, 92, 156) (1828-1923), *Trollius europaeus* L. (109) (1949), *Trollius* L. (138, 156) (1923), *Trollius laxus* Salisb. (19, 92) (1840-1876)

Globe-flower shrub [Globe-flower-shrub, Globe-flowered-shrub] - *Cephalanthus occidentalis* L. (184, 187) (1793-1818)

Globe-fruit ludwigia [Globe-fruited ludwigia] - *Ludwigia sphaerocarpa* Ell. (5) (1913)

Globe-lily - *Nuphar lutea* (L.) Sm. subsp. *advena* (Aiton) Kartesz & Gandhi (156) (1923)

Globemallow [Globe-mallow, Globe mallow] - *Iliamna rivularis* (Dougl. ex Hook.) Greene var. *rivularis* (156) (1923), *Sidalcea* Gray (158) (1900), *Sphaeralcea fendleri* Gray (156) (1923), *Sphaeralcea* St. Hill. (4, 50, 109, 138, 155, 158) (1900–present)

Globepea - *Sphaeralcea* St.-Hil. (155) (1942), *Sphaerophysa* DC. (155) (1942)

Globethistle [Globe thistle] - *Echinops* L. (1, 82, 109, 138) (1923-1949), *Echinops ritro* L. (82) (1930), *Echinops sphaerocephalus* L. (19, 106, 156) (1840-1930)

Globe-tulip - *Calochortus* Pursh. (109) (1949)

Globose cyperus - *Cyperus echinatus* (L.) Wood (5, 156) (1913-1923)

Globose sedge - *Carex perglobosa* Mackenzie (139) (1944)

Globose-fruit thorn [Globose-fruited thorn] - *Crataegus calpodendron* (Ehrh.) Medik. (5) (1913)

Glockenblume (German) - *Campanula rotundifolia* L. (158) (1900)

Glomerate dodder - *Cuscuta glomerata* Choisy (5, 72, 95, 97, 122, 131) (1899-1937)

Glomerate rush - *Juncus effusus* L. var. *conglomeratus* (L.) Engelm. (5) (1913)

Glomerate sedge - *Carex aggregata* Mackenzie (3, 5, 50) (1913–present)

Gloria (Spanish) - *Solanum dulcamara* L. (158) (1900)

Glorybind - *Convolvulus* L. (155) (1942)

Glorybower - *Clerodendrum* L. (109, 138) (1923-1949)

Glorybush - *Tibouchina* Aubl. (138) (1923)

Gloryless [Glory-less] - *Adoxa moschatellina* L. (5, 158) (1900–1913)

Glorylily [Glory lily] - *Gloriosa* L. (109, 138) (1923-1949)

Glory-of-the-snow - *Chionodoxa* Boiss. (109, 138) (1923-1949), *Chionodoxa luciliae* Boiss. (138) (1923)

Glossy abelia - *Abelia ×grandiflora* (André) Rehd. [*chinensis × uniflora*] (138) (1923)

Glossy buckthorn - *Frangula alnus* Mill. (138, 155) (1923-1942)

Glossy cordia - *Cordia laevigata* Lam. (138) (1923)

Glossy cupfern - *Dennstaedtia bipinnata* (Cav.) Maxon (138) (1923)

Glossy hawthorn - *Crataegus nitida* (Englem.) Sargent (138) (1923)

Glossy privet - *Ligustrum lucidum* Aiton f. (138) (1923)

Glossy willow - *Salix lucida* Muhl. (5, 93, 95, 156) (1911-1936)

Gloucester-nut - *Carya laciniosa* (Michx. f.) G. Don (187) (118)

Glouteron (French) - *Arctium lappa* L. (6, 158) (1892–1900)

Glutinous triantha - *Tofieldia glutinosa* (Michx.) Pers. subsp. *glutinosa* (5) (1913)

Glycine - *Wisteria frutescens* (L.) Poir. (2, 138) (1895), *Wisteria sinensis* (Sims) DC. (92) (1876)

Glycine (French) - *Glycine* Willd. (8) (1785)

Glycine ligneuse (French) - *Wisteria frutescens* (L.) Poir. (8) (1785)

Glycyrrhiza - *Glycyrrhiza glabra* L. (52, 57) (1917-1919)

Gmelin's buttercup - *Ranunculus gmelinii* DC. (50) (present)

Gmelin's puccoon - *Lithospermum caroliniense* (Walt. ex J.F. Gmel.) MacM. (5, 93) (1913-1936)

Gnavelle (French) - *Scleranthus annuus* L. (158) (1900)

Goat bush [Goatbush, Goat's bush] - *Castela erecta* Turpin. (possibly) (92) (1876), *Castela* Turpin (13) (1849)

Goat grass [Goatgrass] - *Aegilops cylindrica* Host (3) (1977), *Aegilops* L. (50, 155) (1942–present)

Goat pepper - *Capsicum annuum* L. var. *annuum* (107) (1919)

Goat willow - *Salix caprea* L. (109, 138) (1923-1949)

Goatbeard [Goat beard] - *Tragopogon porrifolius* L. (19) (1840)

Goat-chicory [Goat chicory] - *Agoseris monticola* Greene (85) (1932), *Agoseris* Raf. (1) (1932)

Goat-foot morning-glory [Goat foot morning-glory, Goatfoot morning-glory] - *Ipomoea pes-caprae* (L.) R. Br. (122, 124) (1937) TX

Goat's head [Goat head] - *Tribulus terrestris* L. (4) (1986)

Goat's leaf [Goat's leaves, Gotes leues] - *Lonicera periclymenum* L. (92, 179) (1526-1876)

Goat's rice - *Tephrosia virginiana* (L.) Pers (157) (1929)

Goat's-beard [Goat's beard, Goats-beard, Goatsbeard] - *Aruncus dioicus* (Walt.) Fern. var. *pubescens* (Rydb.) Fern. (97) (1937), *Aruncus dioicus* (Walt.) Fern. var. *vulgaris* (Maxim.) Hara (2, 5, 63, 156) (1895-1923), *Aruncus* L. (1, 72, 109, 138, 155, 156) (1907-1942), *Tragopogon dubius* Scop. (3, 4, 98) (1926-1986), *Tragopogon* L. (4, 50, 109) (1949–present), *Tragopogon porrifolius* L. (19, 92, 184) (1526-1939), *Tragopogon pratensis* L. (63, 107, 146, 156, 178) (1526-1939)

Goat's-beard grass [Goats' beard grass] - *Aegopogon cenchroides* Humb. & Bonpl. ex Willd. (92) (1876), *Aegopogon* Humb. & Bonpl. ex Willd. (45) (1896)

Goat's-foot [Goat's foot] - *Aegopodium podagraria* L. (92, 156) (1876-1923)

Goat's-rue [Goatsrue, Goat's rue, Goats-rue] - *Coursetia* DC. (1, 158) (1900-1932), *Galega* L. (138, 155, 158) (1923-1942), *Galega officinalis* L. (49, 57, 82, 92, 107, 109, 129, 158, 178) (1526-1949), *Tephrosia virginiana* (L.) Pers (2, 4, 5, 19, 49, 63, 72, 92, 97, 102, 156, 157, 158, 187) (1818-1986)

Goat's-wheat [Goats wheat] - *Fagopyrum esculentum* Moench (180) (1633)

Goatweed [Goat's weed] - *Capraria biflora* L. (92) (1876), *Croton capitatus* Michx. (106) (1930)

Gobernadora - *Larrea tridentata* (Sessé & Moc. ex DC.) Coville (15) (1895)

Gobernadora (Spanish) - *Larrea* Ort. (13) (1849) Mexico

Gobo - *Abelmoschus esculentus* (L.) Moench (107) (1919)

Gobo (of Japanese) - *Arctium lappa* L. (109) (1949)

God tree - *Ceiba pentandra* (L.) Gaertn. (92) (1876)

Godetia - *Clarkia* Pursh (138) (1923)

God's wonder plant - *Hypericum perforatum* L. (6) (1892)

God's-eye [God's eye] - *Veronica chamaedrys* L. (5, 156) (1913-1923)

Gogeda'djibûg (Chippewa) - *Pulsatilla patens* (L.) Mill.subsp. *multifida* (Pritz.) Zamels (40) (1928)

Goggles - *Ribes uva-crispa* L. var. *sativum* DC. (156) (1923) no longer in use by 1923

Gold - *Helianthus annuus* L. (5, 156, 158) (1900–1923)

Gold coast jasmine - *Jasminum dichotomum* Vahl (109) (1949)

Gold fern [Gold-fern, Goldfern] - *Pentagramma triangularis* (Kaulfuss) Yatskievych, Windham & Wollenweber (109) (1949), *Pityrogramma austroamericana* Domin (109) (1949), *Pityrogramma* Link (109, 138) (1923-1949)

Gold thrum crowfoote double - *Ranunculus auricomus* L. (178) (1526)

Gold-and-silver plant [Gold and silver plant, Gold-and-silver plants, Gold and silver plants, Gold-and-silver-plants] - *Lunaria annua* subsp. *annua* L. (possibly) (74, 156) (1893-1923) NJ

Gold-apple [Gold apple] - *Solanum lycopersicum* L. var. *lycopersicum* (107) (1919)

Goldaster - *Chrysopsis* Nutt. (155) (1942)

Goldballs [Gold balls, Gold-balls] - *Ranunculus acris* L. (156) (1923) no longer in use by 1923, *Ranunculus bulbosus* L. (156) (1923) no longer in use by 1923, *Ranunculus repens* L. (5, 156) (1913-1923)

Gold-band lily [Goldband lily] - *Lilium auratum* L. (109, 138) (1923-1949)

Goldbrier [Goldbriar] - *Acacia farnesiana* (L.) Willd. (7) (1828)

Gold-chain [Gold chain] - *Sedum acre* L. (5, 156) (1913-1923)

Goldcup [Gold cup, Gold cups, Goldcups] - *Ranunculus acris* L. (92) (1876), *Ranunculus bulbosus* L. (5, 6) (1892-1913), *Ranunculus* L. (14) (1882)

Gold-dust [Gold dust] - *Aurinia saxatilis* (L.) Desv. (156) (1923) no longer in use by 1923

Golden - *Helianthus annuus* L. (5, 156, 157, 158) (1900–1929)

Golden alexanders - *Taenidia integerrima* (L.) Drude (5, 156) (1913-1923), *Thaspium trifoliatum* (L.) Gray var. *aureum* Britt. (8) (1785), *Zizia aurea* (L.) W.D.J. Koch (3, 5, 156, 158) (1900-1977), *Zizia trifoliata* (Michx.) Fern. (5, 156) (1913-1923), *Zizia* W.D.J. Koch (4) (1986)

Golden apples - *Solanum lycopersicum* L. var. *lycopersicum* (180) (1633)

Golden aster [Golden-aster] - *Chrysopsis* Nutt. (1, 2, 4, 82, 106, 109, 138, 156, 158) (1895-1986), *Chrysopsis pilosa* Nutt. (124) (1937), *Heterotheca canescens* (DC.) Shinners & Gray (4, 50) (1986–present), *Heterotheca stenophylla* (Gray) Shinners var. *angustifolia* (Rydb.) Semple (3) (1977), *Heterotheca villosa* (Pursh) Shinners var. *foliosa* (Nutt.) Harms (3, 85) (1932-1977), *Heterotheca villosa* (Pursh) Shinners var. *minor* (Hook.) Semple (3) (1977), *Heterotheca villosa* (Pursh) Shinners var. *villosa* (3, 82, 127, 156) (1923-1977), *Pityopsis falcata* (Pursh) Nutt. (156) (1923), *Pityopsis graminifolia* (Michx.) Nutt. var. *graminifolia* (156) (1923)

Golden barley - *Hordeum vulgare* L. (158) (1900) variety

Golden camomile [Golden chamomile] - *Acmella oppositifolia* (Lam.) R.K. Jansen (155) (1942), *Anthemis tinctoria* L. (50) (present)

Golden chinquapin - *Chrysolepis chrysophylla* (Douglas ex Hook.) Hjelmq. (106) (1930)

Golden clematis - *Clematis tangutica* (Maxim.) Korsh. (109) (1949)

Golden clover - *Wislizenia refracta* Engelm. (106) (1930)

Golden columbine - *Aquilegia chrysantha* Gray (50, 86, 138, 155) (1878–present)

Golden coreopsis - *Coreopsis tinctoria* Nutt. (5, 85, 92, 93, 97, 122, 156, 158) (1876-1937)

Golden corydalis - *Corydalis aurea* Willd. (2, 3, 4, 5, 72, 85, 97, 122, 127, 131, 145, 155, 156) (1897–1986), *Corydalis curvisiliqua* Engelm. subsp. *occidentalis* (Engelm. ex Gray) W. A. Weber (3) (1977), *Corydalis micrantha* (Engelm. ex Gray) Gray subsp. *australis* (Chapman) G. B. Ownbey (5) (1913)

Golden cress - *Lepidium sativum* L. (156, 158) (1900–1923)

Golden crocus - *Crocus angustifolia* Weston (92) (1876)

Golden crownbeard [Golden crown-beard] - *Verbesina encelioides* (Cav.) Benth. & Hook. f. ex Gray (50, 155, 156) (1923–present), *Verbesina encelioides* (Cav.) Benth. & Hook. f. ex Gray subsp. *exauriculata* (Robins. & Greenm.) J. R. Coleman (4, 5, 50, 97) (1986–present)

Golden currant [Golden currants] - *Ribes aureum* Pursh (2, 50, 63, 82, 93, 107, 109, 113, 114, 130, 131, 135, 149, 155, 156, 158) (1890–present), *Ribes aureum* Pursh var. *villosum* DC. (5, 50, 85, 122, 138) (1913–present)

Golden daisy [Golden-daisy] - *Leucanthemum vulgare* Lam. (92, 158) (1876-1900)

Golden dewdrop - *Duranta erecta* L. (106, 109) (1930-1949)

Golden dock - *Rumex maritimus* L. (1, 3, 4, 5, 50, 72, 85, 93, 98, 131, 155, 156) (1899–present)

Golden draba - *Draba aurea* Vahl ex Hornem. (50, 155) (1942–present)

Golden eardrops - *Ehrendorferia chrysantha* (Hook. & Arn.) Rylander (138) (1923)

Golden fairy-lantern [Golden fairy lantern] - *Calochortus amabilis* Purdy (109) (1949)

Golden gladecress - *Leavenworthia aurea* Torr. (50) (present)

Golden groundsel - *Packera aurea* (L.) A.& D. Löve (138, 155) (1931-1942)

Golden guineas - *Ranunculus ficaria* L. (5) (1913)

Golden hawkweed - *Hieracium aurantiacum* L. (62) (1912) IN

Golden hedge-hyssop [Golden hedgehyssop] - *Gratiola aurea* Muhl. (5, 50, 155, 158) (1900–present)

Golden honey plant [Golden honey-plant] - *Verbesina alternifolia* (L.) Britton ex Kearney (106, 156) (1923-1930)

Golden ironweed - *Verbesina alternifolia* (L.) Britton ex Kearney (156) (1923)

Golden Jerusalem - *Rudbeckia hirta* L. (5, 73, 156, 158) (1892-1923) NH, no longer in use by 1923

Golden jewelweed - *Impatiens pallida* Nutt. (157) (1929)

Golden knops - *Ranunculus bulbosus* L. (5) (1913)

Golden leatherfern - *Acrostichum aureum* L. (50) (present)

Golden loosestrife - *Lysimachia vulgaris* L. (5, 138, 156) (1913-1923)

Golden lungwort - *Hieracium murorum* L. (5, 156) (1913-1923)

Golden maidenhair [Golden-maidenhair, Golden-maiden-hair] - *Pontederia* L. (184) (1793)

Golden marguerite - *Anthemis tinctoria* L. (109, 156) (1923-1949)

Golden meadow-parsnip [Golden meadow parsnip] - *Thaspium trifoliatum* (L.) Gray var. *aureum* Britt. (8) (1785), *Zizia aurea* (L.) W.D.J. Koch (5, 72, 93, 95, 97, 122, 131, 156, 158) (1899-1937)

Golden millet - *Setaria italica* (L.) Beauv. (5, 45, 56, 151, 158) (1896-1931)

Golden moss - *Sedum acre* L. (5, 156) (1913-1923)

Golden motherwort - *Omalotheca sylvatica* (L.) Schultz-Bip. & F.W. Schultz (5, 92, 156) (1876-1923)

Golden mouse-ear hawkweed [Golden mouse-ear hawk-weed] - *Hieracium aurantiacum* L. (5, 156) (1913-1923)

Golden oat grass [Golden oat-grass] - *Trisetum flavescens* (L.) Beauv. (5, 45, 68) (1896-1913)

Golden oats - *Trisetum flavescens* (L.) Beauv. (67) (1890)

Golden oenothera - *Oenothera grandiflora* L'Hér. ex Aiton (183) (~1756)

Golden osier - *Myrica gale* L. (5, 156) (1913-1923), *Salix alba* L. (72, 158) (1900-1907) IA

Golden papertree - *Edgeworthia papyrifera* Sieb. & Zucc. (138) (1923)

Golden parosela - *Dalea aurea* Nutt. ex Pursh (5, 85, 93, 97, 131) (1899–1937)

Golden Pastinake (German) - *Thaspium trifoliatum* (L.) Gray var. *aureum* Britt. (8) (1785)

Golden pea - *Thermopsis rhombifolia* (Nutt. ex Pursh) Nutt. ex Richards. (3) (1977)

Golden peppergrass [Golden pepper-grass, Golden pepper grass] - *Lepidium sativum* L. (5, 156, 158) (1900-1923)

Golden polypody - *Phlebodium* (R. Br.) J. Sm. (50) (present), *Phlebodium aureum* (L.) J. Sm. (50, 138) (1923–present)

Golden prairie-clover [Golden prairie clover] - *Dalea aurea* Nutt. ex Pursh (4, 50) (1986–present)

Golden prince's-plume [Golden princesplume] - *Stanleya pinnata* (Pursh) Britton (50) (present)

Golden qualing aspen - *Populus tremuloides* Michx. (155) (1942)

Golden ragwort - *Packera aurea* (L.) A.& D. Löve (2, 5, 6, 58, 63, 97, 109, 131, 156, 158) (1869-1949)

Golden saxifrage - *Chrysosplenium iowense* Rydb. (107) (1919), *Chrysosplenium* L. (1, 10, 167) (1814-1932), *Chrysosplenium oppositifolium* L. (5, 19, 63, 156) (1840-1923)

Golden sedge - *Carex aurea* Nutt. (5, 50, 139, 155) (1913–present)

Golden selenia - *Selenia aurea* Nutt. (3, 4, 50) (1977–present)

Golden senecio - *Packera aurea* (L.) A.& D. Löve (6, 48, 49, 53, 92, 158) (1876-1922)

Golden St. John's-wort [Golden St. John's wort, Golden St. John-swort] - *Hypericum frondosum* Michx. (2, 5, 97, 138) (1895-1937)

Golden summer daylily [Golden summer day-lily] - *Hemerocallis fulva* var. *aurantiaca* (Baker) M. Hotta (109) (1949)

Golden thickseed sunflower [Golden thickseed Sun-flower] - *Bidens aurea* (Aiton) Sherff (187) (1818)

Golden thistle - *Sclerolepis uniflora* (Walt.) Porter (92) (1876), *Scolymus hispanicus* L. (107, 109) (1919-1949), *Scolymus* L. (92) (1876)

Golden tickseed - *Coreopsis tinctoria* Nutt. (50, 121) (1918–present), *Coreopsis tinctoria* Nutt. var. *tinctoria* (50) (present)

Golden trefoil - *Hepatica nobilis* Schreb. var. *obtusa* (Pursh) Steyermark (5) (1913)

Golden waterlily [Golden water-lily] - *Nymphaea mexicana* Zucc. (86) (1878)

Golden wattle - *Acacia longifolia* (Andr.) Willd. (106) (1930), *Acacia pycnantha* Benth. (50, 109, 138, 158) (1900–present)

Golden whitlow-grass [Golden whitlow grass] - *Draba aurea* Vahl ex Hornem. (5, 133) (1899-1913)

Golden willow - *Salix alba* L. (112, 138) (1923-1937)

Golden willowherb [Golden willow-herb] - *Lysimachia vulgaris* L. (5, 156) (1913-1923)

Golden withy - *Myrica gale* L. (156) (1923)

Golden zizia - *Zizia aurea* (L.) W.D.J. Koch (50, 155) (1942–present)

Golden-apple [Golden apple] - *Citrus* ×*aurantium* L. [*maxima* × *reticulata*] (92) (1876), *Cydonia oblonga* Mill. (92) (1876)

Golden-band lily [Golden-banded lily] - *Lilium auratum* L. (107) (1919)

Golden-banner [Goldenbanner] - *Thermopsis* R. Br. ex Aiton f. (50) (present)

Goldenbell [Golden-bell, Golden bell, Golden bells, Golden-bells, Goldenbells] - *Forsythia* ×*intermedia* Zabel [*suspensa* × *viridissima*] (112) (1937), *Forsythia suspensa* (Thunb.) Vahl (112) (1937), *Forsythia* Vahl (82, 109) (1930-1949)

Goldenbough [Golden bough] - *Phoradendron leucarpum* (Raf.) Reveal & M.C. Johnston (92) (1876)

Goldenbush - *Ericameria* Nutt. (50) (present)

Goldenchain [Golden-chain, Golden chain] - *Laburnum anagyroides* Medik. (92, 109, 138) (1876-1949)

Goldenclub [Golden club, Golden-club] - *Orontium aquaticum* L. (5, 19, 41, 46, 50, 86, 92, 107, 138, 156, 187) (1770–present), *Orontium* L. (2, 10, 50, 109, 138, 156) (1818–present)

Goldencrest [Golden crest] - *Lophiola aurea* Ker-Gawl. (50, 156) (1923–present)

Goldencup [Golden-cup, Golden cup] - *Hunnemannia fumariifolia* Sweet (109, 138) (1923-1949), *Hunnemannia* Sweet (138) (1923), *Ranunculus ficaria* L. (5) (1913)

Goldenes Kreuzkraut (German) - *Packera aurea* (L.) A.& D. Löve (6) (1892)

Goldeneye [Golden eye, Golden-eye] - *Heterotheca villosa* (Pursh) Shinners var. *villosa* (156) (1923), *Viguiera* Kunth (4, 50, 155) (1942–present)

Golden-feather [Golden feather] - *Tanacetum parthenium* (L.) Schultz-Bip. (109) (1949)

Golden-flower corydalis [Golden-flowered corydalis] - *Corydalis aurea* Willd. (187) (1818)

Golden-flower groundsel [Golden-flowered groundsel] - *Packera aurea* (L.) A.& D. Löve (187) (1818)

Golden-fruit sedge [Golden fruited sedge] - *Carex aurea* Nutt. (5, 66) (1903-1913)

Goldenglow [Golden glow, Golden-glow] - *Rudbeckia* L. (1) (1932), *Rudbeckia laciniata* L. (3, 4, 5, 125, 148, 156, 157, 158) (1900-1986)

Goldenhead - *Acamptopappus* (Gray) Gray (50, 155) (1942–present)

Golden-heather [Goldenheather, Golden heather] - *Hudsonia* L. (50) (present)

Goldenknops [Golden-knops] - *Ranunculus acris* L. (157, 158) (1900-1929)

Golden-leaf chestnut [Golden-leaved chestnut] - *Chrysolepis chrysophylla* (Douglas ex Hook.) Hjelmq. (20) (1857)

Golden-moss [Golden moss] - *Sedum acre* L. (5, 156) (1913-1923)

Goldenoak [Golden oak] - *Aureolaria virginica* (L.) Pennell (5, 7, 92, 156) (1828-1923)

Goldenpert [Golden pert] - *Gratiola aurea* Muhl. (4, 5, 46, 158) (1783-1986), *Gratiola virginiana* L. (156) (1923)

Goldenrain tree [Goldenrain-tree, Golden-rain tree] - *Koelreuteria* Laxm. (109, 138) (1923-1949), *Koelreuteria paniculata* Laxm. (112, 138) (1923-1937)

Goldenrod [Golden-rod, Golden rod] - *Euthamia graminifolia* (L.) Nutt. (40) (1928), *Euthamia graminifolia* (L.) Nutt. var. *graminifolia* (4) (1986), *Oligoneuron rigidum* (L.) Small var. *rigidum* (56, 145, 148) (1897-1901), *Oligoneuron* Small (1, 50) (1932–present), *Solidago canadensis* L. (56, 80, 145) (1897-1901), *Solidago canadensis* L. var. *scabra* Torr. & Gray (40) (1928), *Solidago gigantea* Aiton (80, 145) (1897-1913), *Solidago* L. (1, 2, 4, 10, 14, 21, 37, 40, 50, 63, 82, 93, 98, 106, 109, 114, 138, 155, 156, 158, 167, 184, 190) (~1759–present), *Solidago missouriensis* Nutt. (148) (1939), *Solidago mollis* Bartl. (148) (1939), *Solidago odora* Aiton (57) (1917), *Solidago speciosa* Nutt. var. *pallida* Porter (85) (1932)

Goldenrod aster [Golden-rod Aster] - *Sericocarpus linifolius* (L.) B.S.P. (187) (1818)

Goldenrod starwort [Golden rod star wort] - *Sericocarpus linifolius* (L.) B.S.P. (possibly) (42) (1814)

Goldenroot [Golden root] - *Hydrastis canadensis* L. (49, 64) (1907-1908)

Goldens - *Leucanthemum vulgare* Lam. (7, 49) (1828-1898)

Goldenseal [Golden-seal, Golden seal] - *Frasera caroliniensis* Walt. (possibly) (7) (1828), *Hydrastis canadensis* L. (1, 2, 5, 6, 7, 15, 49, 52, 53, 54, 55, 57, 59, 60, 61, 63, 64, 72, 92, 97, 138, 156) (1870-1937), *Hydrastis* L. (109, 156) (1923-1949), *Maianthemum racemosum* (L.) Link subsp. *racemosum* (5, 75, 156, 157, 158) (1894-1929) Banner Elk NC

Golden-shower - *Cassia fistula* L. (109, 138) (1923-1949)

Goldenstar [Golden-star, Golden stars] - *Bloomeria crocea* (Torr.) Coville var. *aurea* (Kellogg) Ingram (138) (1923), *Chrysogonum virginianum* L. (109, 138) (1923-1949), *Chrysopsis mariana* (L.) Ell. (5, 156) (1913-1923), *Pityopsis graminifolia* (Michx.) Nutt. var. *graminifolia* (156) (1923)

Goldenthread [Golden thread] - *Coptis trifolia* (L.) Salisb. (10) (1818)

Goldentop [Golden-top, Golden top] - *Euthamia* Nutt. ex Cass. (50) (present), *Lamarckia aurea* (L.) Moench (94, 109, 122, 163) (1852-1949)

Goldentop grass - *Lamarckia aurea* (L.) Moench (138) (1923)

Golden-trefoil - *Hepatica nobilis* Schreb. (156) (1923) no longer in use by 1923

Goldentuft [Golden-tuft] - *Aurinia saxatilis* (L.) Desv. (109, 138, 156) (1923-1949)

Golden-tuft alyssum [Goldentuft alyssum] - *Aurinia saxatilis* (L.) Desv. (155) (1942)

Golden-twig dogwood [Goldentwig dogwood] - *Cornus sericea* L. subsp. *sericea* (109) (1949)

Golden-wattle acacia [Goldenwattle acacia] - *Acacia pycnantha* Benth. (138) (1923)

Goldenwave [Golden-wave] - *Coreopsis basalis* (A. Dietr.) Blake (109, 138) (1923-1949)

Goldenweed - *Grindelia papposa* Nesom & Suh (4) (1986), *Haplopappus* Cass. (4) (1986), *Machaeranthera grindelioides* (Nutt.) Shinners (3, 4) (1977-1986), *Petroselinum crispum* (P. Mill.) Nyman ex A.W. Hill (155) (1942)

Golden-wonder millet [Golden wonder millet] - *Setaria italica* (L.) Beauv. (56, 109, 119) (1901-1949)

Golden-yarrow [Goldenyarrow] - *Eriophyllum confertiflorum* (DC.) Gray (138) (1923)

Gold-eye - *Hypoxis hirsuta* (L.) Cov. (156) (1923)

Goldeye-grass [Gold-eye-grass] - *Hypoxis hirsuta* (L.) Cov. (138) (1923), *Hypoxis* L. (138) (1923)

Goldfields - Lasthenia Cass. (138) (1923)

Goldflower [Gold flower] - *Caltha palustris* L. (86) (1878), *Hypericum ×moserianum* Luquet ex André [*calycinum × patulum*] (109, 138) (1923-1949)

Gold-hair paspalum [Goldhair paspalum] - *Paspalum setaceum* Michx. (155) (1942)

Goldheather [Gold heather] - *Hudsonia ericoides* L. (156) (1923)

Goldicup [Goldicups] - *Ranunculus acris* L. (92, 157, 158) (1876-1929)

Goldie's fern [Goldie fern, Goldie's-fern] - *Dryopteris goldiana* (Hook. ex Goldie) Gray (5, 72, 109, 138) (1907-1949)

Goldie's wood fern [Goldie woodfern] - *Dryopteris goldiana* (Hook. ex Goldie) Gray (4, 5, 50, 155) (1913–present)

Goldilocks [Goldylocks, Goldy-locks] - *Bigelowia nudata* (Michx.) DC. subsp. *nudata* (19) (1840)

Goldins - *Leucanthemum vulgare* Lam. (184) (1793)

Goldins gold - *Calendula officinalis* L. (107) (1919)

Gold-joint - *Chrysogonum* L. (167) (1814)

Goldknops [Gold-knops, Gold knops] - *Ranunculus acris* L. (5, 157, 158) (1900–1929), *Ranunculus repens* L. (5) (1913)

Goldmoss [Gold moss] - *Sedum acre* L. (138, 156) (1923)

Gold-moss stonecrop [Goldmoss stonecrop] - *Sedum acre* L. (155) (1942)

Goldner Günsel (German) - *Ajuga reptans* L. (158) (1900)

Gold-of-Pleasure [Gold of Pleasure] - *Alyssum* L. (10) (1818), *Camelina sativa* (L.) Crantz (3, 4, 5, 50, 107, 156, 157, 158) (1876–present), *Camelina sativa* (L.) Crantz subsp. *sativa* (50) (present)

Gold-plush prickly-pear [Goldplush picklypear] - *Opuntia microdasys* (Lehm.) Lehm. Ex Pfeiff. (155) (1942)

Gold-star-grass [Goldstargrass] - *Hypoxis* L. (155) (1942)

Goldstem [Gold stem] - *Sorghastrum* Nash (93) (1936) Neb

Goldthread [Gold-thread, Gold thread] - *Coptis* Salisb. (1, 13, 53, 109, 138, 156) (1849-1949), *Coptis trifolia* (L.) Salisb. (5, 7, 14, 19, 40, 49. 53, 57, 58, 64, 92, 105, 138, 156, 186) (1814-1932), *Cuscuta gronovii* Willd. ex J.A. Schultes (156) (1923), *Cuscuta pentagona* Engelm. var. *pentagona* (156) (1923)

Goldwatch [Gold watch] - *Nuphar lutea* (L.) Sm. subsp. *advena* (Aiton) Kartesz & Gandhi (74) (1893) Mauch Chunk PA

Goldweed [Gold weed, Gold-weed] - *Ranunculus acris* L. (156) (1923), *Ranunculus arvensis* L. (5, 158) (1900–1913), *Ranunculus bulbosus* L. (156) (1923), *Ranunculus repens* L. (156) (1923)

Goldwerz (High Dutch) - *Lilium martagon* L. (180) (1633)

Gold-wreath acacia [Goldwreath acacia] - *Acacia salicina* Lindl. (155) (1942)

Gollindrinera - *Chamaesyce prostrata (Aiton) Small* (92) (1876)

Gomart d'Amerique (French) - *Bursera simaruba* (L.) Sargent (20) (1857)

Gombo - *Abelmoschus esculentus* (L.) Moench (58, 92, 107, 110) (1869-1919)

Gombo sassafras - *Sassafras albidum* (Nutt.) Nees (107) (1919)

Goɲe (Osage) - *Celtis occidentalis* L. (121) (1918?-1970?)

Gooba nut - *Cola acuminata* (P. Beauv.) Schott & Endl. (109) (1949)

Goobers [Goober] - *Arachis hypogaea* L. (73, 109) (1892-1949) Southern US

Good King Henry [Good-King-Henry] - *Chenopodium bonus-henricus* L. (5, 72, 92, 107, 109, 138, 156) (1876-1949)

Goodby-summer [Good-by summer] - *Aster* L. (75, 158) (1894–1900) Lincolnton NC

Goodenough's sedge - *Carex nigra* (L.) Reichard (5) (1913)

Gooding's willow [Goodings willow] - *Salix gooddingii* Ball (50, 155) (1942–present)

Good-morning-spring [Good morning spring] - *Claytonia virginica* L. (5, 73, 158) (1892–1913) Hemmingford Quebec

Goodyera - *Goodyera* R. Br. (158) (1900)

Gools - *Caltha palustris* L. (5, 156, 157) (1900-1929)

Gooranut - *Cola acuminata* (P. Beauv.) Schott & Endl. (107) (1919)

Goose grass [Goosegrass, Goose-grass] - *Eleusine* Gaertn. (50) (present), *Eleusine indica* (L.) Gaertn. (3, 5, 85, 94, 111, 119, 122, 134, 140, 163) (1852-1977), *Poa annua* L. (87) (1884), *Puccinellia maritima* (Huds.) Parl. (5, 45, 66) (1896-1913)

Goose plum [Goose-plum] - *Prunus americana* Marsh. (5, 107, 156, 158) (1900–1923)

Gooseberry [Goose berry, Gooseberries] - *Ribes hirtellum* Michx. (103) (1870), *Ribes* L. (2, 4, 7, 10, 35, 82, 95, 106, 109, 138, 155, 156) (1828-1986), *Ribes niveum* Lindl. (22, 82) (1893-1930), *Ribes oxyacanthoides* L. subsp. *oxyacanthoides* (40) (1928), *Ribes uva-crispa* L. (110) (1886), *Ribes uva-crispa* L. var. *sativum* DC. (92, 107, 110, 114) (1876-1919), *Vaccinium arboreum* Marsh. (5, 156, 158) (1900-1923), *Vaccinium stamineum* L. (5, 156, 158, 177) (1762-1923)

Gooseberry tree [Gooseberry-tree] - *Phyllanthus acidus* (L.) Skeels (109) (1949)

Gooseberry-pie [Gooseberry pie] - *Epilobium hirsutum* L. (5, 156) (1913-1923)

Goosebill [Goosbyll] - *Stellaria graminea* L. (179) (1526)

Goosefoot [Goose-foot, Goose foot] - *Chenopodium album* L. (41, 150) (1770-1894), *Chenopodium ambrosioides* L. var. *ambrosioides* (92) (1876), *Chenopodium bonus-henricus* L. (107) (1919), *Chenopodium glaucum* L. (85) (1932), *Chenopodium* L. (1, 4, 42, 50, 2, 10, 93, 109, 138, 155, 158) (1814–present), *Chenopodium vulvaria* L. (92) (1876)

Goose-foot corn salad - *Valerianella chenopodiifolia* (Pursh) DC. (5, 72) (1907-1913)

Goose-foot maple [Goose foot maple] - *Acer pensylvanicum* L. (5, 156) (1913-1923), *Acer spicatum* Lam. (156) (1923)

Goose-grass [Goose grass, Goosegrass] - *Carex hirta* L. (5, 156) (1913-1923), *Galium aparine* L. (2, 5, 19, 46, 49, 53, 92, 105, 122, 131, 156, 157, 158) (1671-1929), *Galium* L. (184) (1793), *Galium verum* L. (7) (1828), *Polygonum aviculare* L. (5, 62, 92, 129, 156, 158) (1894–1923), *Polygonum erectum* L. (77, 129) (1894-1898), *Argentina anserina* (L.) Rydb. (92, 107, 156, 157, 158) (1898-1929), *Triglochin* L. (148) (1939) CO

Goose's-hare [Gooses hare] - *Galium aparine* L. (92) (1876)

Goose-tansy [Goose tansy] - *Argentina anserina* (L.) Rydb. (5, 107, 156, 157, 158) (1913-1929), *Argentina* Hill (possibly) (1) (1932)

Goose-tongue [Goose tongue] - *Achillea ptarmica* L. (5, 92, 156, 165) (1768-1923) England, *Melissa officinalis* L. (5, 75) (1894-1913) Concord MA, *Plantago maritima* L. var. *juncoides* (Lam.) Gray (156) (1923)

Gooseweed [Goose-weeds] - *Atriplex* L. (156) (1923)

Gopher plant [Gopher-plant] - *Euphorbia lathyris* L. (71, 156) (1898-1923)

Gopher wood [Gopher-wood] - *Cladrastis kentukea* (Dum.-Cours.) Rudd . (5, 156) (1913-1923), *Lawsonia inermis* L. (92) (1876)

Gopher-apple [Gopher apple] - *Licania michauxii* Prance (106) (1930)

Gopherberry [Gopher-berry, Gopher berry] - *Gaylussacia dumosa* (Andr.) Torr. & Gray (5, 156) (1913-1923)

Gopher-plum [Gopher plum] - *Chrysobalanus icaco* L. (106) (1930)

Gopherweed [Gopher weed] - *Baptisia lanceolata* (Walt.) Ell. (74) (1893)

Gordaldo - *Achillea millefolium* L. (156) (1923)

Gordoloba - *Achillea millefolium* L. (69, 76, 158) (1896-1904)

Gordoloba (Spanish) - *Verbascum thapsus* L. (158) (1900)

Gordolobo - *Achillea millefolium* L. (69, 76, 158) (1896-1904) CA

Gordonia - *Gordonia* Ell. (138) (1923)

Gordon's bladderpod [Gordon's bladder-pod] - *Lesquerella gordonii* (Gray) S. Wats. (50, 97) (1937–present)

Gordon's buckwheat - *Eriogonum gordonii* Benth. (50) (present)

Gordon's eriogonum - *Eriogonum gordonii* Benth. (4) (1986)

Gordon's mockorange [Gordon mockorange] - *Philadelphus lewisii* Pursh (138) (1923)

Goroffle - *Lindera benzoin* Blume. (46) (1879)

Gorse - *Ulex europaeus* L. (5, 106, 156) (1913-1930), *Ulex* L. (45, 138) (1896-1923)

Gorst - *Juniperus communis* L. (157, 158) (1900-1929)

Goslin weed - *Pulsatilla patens* (L.) Mill.subsp. *multifida* (Pritz.) Zamels (6) (1892)

Gosling [Goslings] - *Pulsatilla patens* (L.) Mill. (5) (1913), *Pulsatilla patens* (L.) Mill. subsp. *multifida* (Pritz.) Zamels (74, 157, 158) (1893-1929) MN, *Salix* L. (75) (1894) Frankin Centre PQ

Gosling-weed [Gosling weed] - *Galium aparine* L. (5, 156, 157, 158) (1900-1929)

Gosmore - *Hypochaeris* L. (1) (1932), *Hypochaeris radicata* L. (5, 156) (1913-1923)

Gossypium - *Gossypium herbaceum* L. (52, 54) (1905-1919)

Go-to-bed-at-noon [Go to bed at noone] - *Tragopogon pratensis* L. (5, 156, 158, 178) (1526-1923)

Götterbaum (German) - *Ailanthus altissima* (Mill) Swingle (6, 158) (1892-1900)

Gouet à Dragon (French) - *Arisaema dracontium* (L.) Schott (6, 19) (1840-1892)

Gouet à Trois Feuilles (French) - *Arisaema triphyllum* (L.) Schott (6, 10, 19, 158) (1818-1982)

Gourd [Gourde, Gowrde] - *Cucurbita foetidissima* Kunth (157) (1929), *Cucurbita* L. (1, 50, 93, 138, 167) (1814–present), *Cucurbita maxima* Dcne. (110) (1886), *Cucurbita pepo* L. (107, 179) (1526-1919), *Cucurbita pepo* L. var. *ovifera* (L.) Alef. (138) (1923), *Lagenaria* Ser. (138) (1923), *Lagenaria siceraria* (Molina) Standl. (7, 19, 92, 110, 182) (1791-1886)

Gourd of Alexandry [Gowrde of Alexandry] - *Citrullus colocynthis* (L.) Schrad. (179) (1526)

Gourganes (French) - *Gymnocladus dioicus* (L.) K. Koch (20) (1857)

Gousailiers blans - *Ribes cynosbati* L. (46) (1879)

Goutweed [Gout-weed, Gout weed] - *Aegopodium* L. (50, 138, 155, 156, 165) (1768–present), *Aegopodium podagraria* L. (5, 92, 107, 109, 138, 156, 165) (1768-1949) used in Germany for pain of gout, *Angelica sylvestris* L. (92) (1876), *Sonchus arvensis* L. (157) (1929)

Goutwort [Gout-wort, Goutwoort] - *Aegopodium podagraria* L. (5, 156, 178) (1526-1923)

Governor's-plum [Governors-plum] - *Flacourtia indica* (Burm. f.) Merr. (109) (1949)

Gowan [Gowans] - *Bellis perennis* L. (92) (1876) Scotland, *Ranunculus bulbosus* L. (5) (1913)

Gowen's cypress [Gowen cypress] - *Cupressus goveniana* Gord. (109, 138) (1923-1949) for James Robert Gowen, Secr. Royal Hort Soc. 1845-1850

Gowiddie - *Ledum groenlandicum* Oeder (possibly) (77) (1898) Newfoundland

Gowins - *Chaptalia tomentosa* Vent. (183) (~1756)

Gowk's-thumbs - *Campanula rotundifolia* L. (158) (1900)

Gowlan - *Bellis perennis* L. (158) (1900)

Graceful buttercup - *Ranunculus inamoenus* Greene (50) (present), *Ranunculus inamoenus* Greene var. *alpeophilus* (A. Nels.) L. Benson (50) (present)

Graceful sedge - *Carex gracillima* Schwein. (5, 50) (1913–present)

Grades (France) - *Ribes rubrum* L. (110) (1886)

Gradilles (France) - *Ribes rubrum* L. (110) (1886)

Grain sorghum - *Sorghum bicolor* (L.) Moench subsp. *bicolor* (50) (present)

Grains de boeuf (French) - *Shepherdia argentea* (Pursh) Nutt. (28) (1850)

Grains de perdix (French, partridge grains) - *Gaultheria hispidula* (L.) Muhl. ex Bigelow (41) (1770)

Grains de volaille (French) - *Nelumbo lutea* Willd. (35) (1806) William Clark

Graisse du boeuf (French) - *Shepherdia argentea* (Pursh) Nutt. (20, 89, 101) (1820-1905)

Grama [Gramma] - *Bouteloua curtipendula* (Michx) Torr. (119) (1938), *Bouteloua gracilis* (Willd. ex Kunth) Lag. ex Griffiths (11, 30, 45, 88) (1844-1896), *Bouteloua* Lag. (1, 50, 155) (1932–present)

Grama grass [Grama-grass, Gramma grass] - *Bouteloua curtipendula* (Michx) Torr. (116) (1958), *Bouteloua gracilis* (Willd. ex Kunth) Lag. ex Griffiths (5, 22, 72, 85, 87, 101, 118, 119, 152, 164) (1853-1938), *Bouteloua hirsuta* Lag. (87, 164) (1852-1884), *Bouteloua* Lag. (1, 45, 66, 67, 87, 93, 152, 164) (1852-1936), *Muhlenbergia texana* Buckl. (151) (1896) NM

Granadilla - *Passiflora edulis* Sims (92) (1876), *Passiflora incarnata* L. (181, 182) (~1678-1791), *Passiflora quadrangularis* L. (107) (1919)

Granatum - *Punica granatum* L. (54, 57, 59, 60) (1902-1917)

Grand ciguë (French) - *Conium maculatum* L. (6, 158) (1892-1900)

Grand fir - *Abies grandis* (Dougl. ex D. Don) Lindl. (50, 155) (1942–present)

Grand magnolia - *Magnolia grandiflora* L. (8) (1785)

Grand redstem - *Ammannia robusta* Heer & Regel (50) (present)

Grand vine - *Linnaea borealis* L. (72) (1907) IA

Grande kalmie (French) - *Kalmia latifolia* L. (6, 7) (1828-1932)

Grande marguarite (French) - *Leucanthemum vulgare* Lam. (49) (1898)

Grande mauve (French) - *Malva sylvestris* L. (158) (1900)

Grande morelle des Indes (French) - *Phytolacca americana* L. var. *americana* (186) (1814)

Grandfather graybeard - *Chionanthus virginicus* L. (156) (1923)

Granejo - *Celtis pallida* Torr. (106) (1930)

Grangas (Swedish) - *Equisetum sylvaticum* L. (46) (1879)

Granite gilia - *Leptodactylon pungens* (Torr.) Torr. ex Nutt. (155) (1942)

Granite prickly-phlox [Granite prickly phlox] - *Leptodactylon pungens* (Torr.) Torr. ex Nutt. (50) (present)

Granjeno - *Celtis pallida* Torr. (122, 124) (1937) TX

Granny-threads - *Ranunculus repens* L. (156, 158) (1900-1923)

Grano (Italian) - *Triticum aestivum* L. (180) (1633)

Grantogen - *Panax quinquefolius* L. (157, 158) (1900-1929)

Granular-spike sedge [Granular-spiked sedge] - *Carex granularis* Muhl. ex Willd. (66) (1903)

Grape - *Vitis* L. (1, 4, 50, 106, 109, 138, 155, 158) (1900–present)

Grape cherry [Grape Cherrie] - *Prunus cerasus* L. (178) (1526)

Grape fern [Grape-fern, Grapefern] - *Botrychium biternatum* (Sav.) Underwood (possibly) (19) (1840), *Botrychium dissectum* Spreng. (97) (1937), *Botrychium multifidum* (Gmel.) Trev. (45, 50) (1896–present), *Botrychium* Sw. (1, 4, 50, 138, 155, 156) (1923–present)

Grape flower - *Muscari botryoides* (L.) Mills (5, 178) (1596-1913), *Muscari neglectum* Guss. ex Ten. (5) (1913)

Grape honeysuckle - *Lonicera reticulata* Raf. (3, 4, 50, 138, 155) (1923–present)

Grape of history - *Vitis vinifera* L. (109, 178) (1526-1949)

Grape vine - *Vitis* L. (13, 15) (1849-1895)

Grapefruit [Grape fruit] - *Citrus* ×*limonia* Osbeck [limon × reticulata] (109) (1949), *Citrus maxima* (Burm. f.) Merr. (106, 107, 138) (1919-1930)

Grape-hyacinth [Grapehyacinth, Grape hyacinth] - *Muscari botryoides* (L.) Mills (5, 156) (1913-1923), *Muscari* Mill. (109, 138, 155, 156) (1923-1949), *Muscari neglectum* Guss. ex Ten. (92, 107) (1876-1919)

Grape-pear - *Amelanchier canadensis* (L.) Medik. (107) (1919)

Graperoot [Grape root] - *Mahonia aquifolium* (Pursh) Nutt. (5, 76, 157) (1896-1929) Northern UT

Grape-vine grass [Grape vine grass, Grapevine-grass] - *Panicum obtusum* H.B.K. (5, 119) (1913-1938)

Grape-vine mesquite - *Panicum obtusum* H.B.K. (151, 163) (1852-1896)

Grapewort [Grape wort] - *Actaea rubra* (Aiton) Willd. (5, 156) (1913-1923)

Graphephorum - *Trisetum melicoides* (Michx.) Vasey ex Scribn. (5) (1913)

Gray moss

Grass - *Asparagus officinalis* L. (158) (1900)

Grass pea - *Lathyrus nissolia* L. (50) (present), *Lathyrus sativus* L. (68, 109) (1913-1949)

Grass pondweed [Grass pond-weed] - *Potamogeton gramineus* L. (19) (1840)

Grass water-plantain [Grass waterplantain] - *Alisma plantago-aquatica* L. (155) (1942)

Grass-cactus [Grass cactus] - *Yucca glauca* Nutt. var. *glauca* (101) (1905), *Yucca* L. (1, 93) (1932-1936)

Grass-cloth plant [Grass cloth plant] - *Boehmeria nivea* (L.) Gaud. (92) (1876)

Grassflower [Grass-flower, Grass flower] - *Claytonia virginica* L. (5, 158) (1900–1913), *Sisyrinchium angustifolium* Mill. (5, 75, 156, 157, 158) (1894-1929) Concord MA, children

Grassland croton - *Croton dioicus* Cav. (50) (present)

Grass-leaf arrowhead [Grass-leaved arrowhead] - *Sagittaria graminea* Michx. (72) (1907)

Grass-leaf gayfeather [Grassleaf gayfeather] - *Liatris pilosa* (Aiton) Willd. var. *pilosa* (138) (1923)

Grass-leaf golden aster [Grassleaf golden aster] - *Pityopsis graminifolia* (Michx.) Nutt. var. *graminifolia* (5, 97, 122) (1913-1937)

Grass-leaf goldenrod [Grass-leaf golden-rod, Grassleaf goldenrod] - *Euthamia graminifolia* (L.) Nutt. var. *graminifolia* (19, 155) (1840-1942)

Grass-leaf lady's-tresses [Grassleaf ladiestresses, Grass-leaved ladies' tresses] - *Spiranthes praecox* (Walt.) S. Wats. (5, 122) (1913-1937)

Grass-leaf mudplantain [Grassleaf mudplantain] - *Heteranthera dubia* (Jacq.) MacM. (50) (present)

Grass-leaf roseling [Grassleaf roseling] - *Callisia graminea* (Small) G. Tucker (50) (present)

Grass-leaf rush [Grassleaf rush, Grass-leaved rush] - *Juncus marginatus* Rostk. (3, 5, 50, 66, 72, 93) (1903–present)

Grass-leaf sagittaria [Grass-leaved sagittaria] - *Sagittaria graminea* Michx. (5, 93, 97, 120, 131) (1899-1938)

Grass-leaf schollera [Grass-leaved schollera] - *Heteranthera dubia* (Jacq.) MacM. (187) (1818)

Grass-leaf sotol [Grassleaf sotol] - *Yucca whipplei* Torr. var. *whipplei* (138) (1923)

Grass-leaf starwort [Grass-leaved star-wort] - *Arenaria lanuginosa* (Michx.) Rohrb. (187) (1818)

Grass-leaf stenanthium [Grass-leaved stenanthium] - *Stenanthium gramineum* (Ker-Gawl.) Morong (5) (1913)

Grass-leaf stitchwort [Grass-leaved stitch-wort] - *Stellaria longipes* Goldie subsp. *longipes* (187) (1818)

Grass-like beaked rush - *Rhynchospora glomerata* (L.) Vahl (5) (1913)

Grass-like sedge [Grasslike sedge] - *Carex panicea* L. (5, 50, 156) (1913–present)

Grass-like spiderwort - *Callisia graminea* (Small) G. Tucker (5, 97) (1913-1937)

Grass-like starwort [Grasslike starwort] - *Stellaria graminea* L. (50) (present)

Grass-nut - *Triteleia laxa* Benth. (109) (1949)

Grass-of-fakirs [Grass of Fakirs] (India) - *Cannabis sativa* L. (6) (1892)

Grass-of-Parnassus [Grass of Parnassus] - *Parnassia caroliniana* Michx. (72, 92, 131, 156) (1876-1923), *Parnassia glauca* Raf. (3, 4) (1977-1986), *Parnassia* L. (1, 2, 10, 13, 109, 158) (1818-1949) plant called Grass-of-Parnassus by Dioscorides from Mt. Parnassus, *Parnassia palustris* L. (46, 127) (1879–1933), *Parnassia palustris* L. var. *parviflora* (DC.) Boivin (3, 85) (1932-1977)

Grass-of-the-Andes [Grass of the Andes] - *Arrhenatherum elatius* (L.) Beauv. ex J. Presl & C. Presl (5) (1913), *Avena sativa* L. (92) (1876)

Grass-pink [Grass pink] - *Calopogon* R. Br. ex Ait. f. (1, 75, 156) (1894-1932), *Calopogon tuberosus* (L.) B.S.P. var. *tuberosus* (5,

72, 86, 122, 156) (1878-1937), *Calopogon tuberosus* (L.) Britton, Sterns & Poggenb. var. *tuberosus* (19) (1840), *Dianthus armeria* L. (76, 156) (1896–1923) Paris ME, *Dianthus plumarius* L. (138) (1923)

Grass-pink orchid - *Calopogon* R. Br. ex Ait. f. (109) (1949), *Calopogon tuberosus* (L.) B.S.P. var. *tuberosus* (138) (1923)

Grass-poly [Grass poly, Grass-poley, Grass poley, Grase-poley, Grass-polley, Grasspoly] - *Cuphea viscosissima* Jacq (184) (1793), *Decodon verticillatus* (L.) Ell. (5, 7, 19, 106, 156) (1828-1930), *Lythrum hyssopifolia* L. (5, 46, 156) (1879-1923)

Grassweed [Grass-weed] - *Zostera marina* L. (5, 10, 19, 156) (1818-1840)

Grass-wrack [Grass wrack] - *Potamogeton zosteriformis* Fern. (5, 156) (1913-1923), *Zostera marina* L. (5, 107, 156) (1913-1919)

Grassy arrowhead - *Sagittaria graminea* Michx. (50, 155) (1942–present), *Sagittaria graminea* Michx. var. *graminea* (50) (present)

Grassy deathcamas - *Zigadenus venenosus* S. Wats. var. *gramineus* (Rydb.) Walsh ex M.E. Peck (50, 155) (1942–present)

Grassy rush - *Butomus umbellatus* L. (107) (1919)

Graswurzel (German) - *Elymus repens* (L.) Gould (158) (1900)

Graue Magnolia (German) - *Magnolia virginiana* L. (186) (1814)

Gravel chickweed - *Scleranthus annuus* L. (5, 19, 92, 156, 158) (1840-1923)

Gravel plant [Gravel-plant] - *Epigaea repens* L. (5, 6, 53, 57, 92, 156) (1876-1923)

Gravelroot [Gravel root, Gravel-root] - *Collinsonia canadensis* L. (6) (1892), *Eupatorium purpureum* L. (5, 6, 7, 49, 53, 54, 58, 64, 75, 92, 102, 157, 158) (1828-1929) said to be a remedy for calculi, *Diervilla lonicera* Mill. (5, 49, 58, 92, 156) (1869-1923), *Epigaea repens* L. (6, 49, 53, 58, 92) (1869-1922), *Eupatorium purpureum* L. (49, 52, 53) (1919-1922), *Onosmodium virginianum* (L.) A. DC. (58, 92, 156) (1869-1923), *Verbesina helianthoides* Michx. (48, 50, 52, 53, 156) (1882–present), *Verbesina virginica* L. (49) (1898)

Gravelweed crownbeard - *Verbesina helianthoides* Michx. (155) (1942)

Graves' beach plum - *Prunus maritima* Marsh. var. *gravesii* (Small) G.J. Anderson (5) (1913)

Grave's quillwort - *Isoetes ×eatonii* Dodge [*engelmannii* × *tenella*] (5) (1913)

Graveyard moss - *Euphorbia cyparissias* L. (78) (1898) IN

Graveyard spurge - *Euphorbia cyparissias* L. (62, 156) (1912-1923) IN

Graveyard weed - *Euphorbia cyparissias* L. (5, 75, 156, 158) (1894-1923) WV

Gray beardtongue [Gray beard-tongue] - *Penstemon canescens* (Britt.) Britt. (5, 72) (1907-1913)

Gray birch - *Betula alleghaniensis* Britt. var. *alleghaniensis* (1, 2, 5, 72, 109, 156) (1895-1949), *Betula occidentalis* Hook. (5, 158) (1900-1913), *Betula pubescens* Ehrh. subsp. *pubescens* (2, 5, 109, 112, 138, 156) (1895-1923)

Gray chickweed - *Cerastium brachypetalum* Desportes ex Pers. (50) (present)

Gray dogwood - *Cornus foemina* Mill. (4) (1986), *Cornus racemosa* Lam. (3, 50, 121, 138, 155, 156) (1918–present)

Gray downy rosebay [Grey downy rose bay] - *Rhododendron canescens* (Michx.) Sweet (42) (1814)

Gray field speedwell - *Veronica polita* Fries (50) (present)

Gray five-eyes [Gray fiveeyes] - *Chamaesaracha coniodes* (Moric. ex Dunal) Britton (50) (present)

Gray gentian [Grey gentian] - *Gentiana villosa* L. (7) (1828)

Gray goldenrod [Gray golden-rod] - *Solidago nemoralis* Aiton (3, 5, 50, 82, 93, 97, 127, 156, 158) (1900–present), *Solidago nemoralis* Aiton var. *longipetiolata* (Mackenzie & Bush) Palmer & Steyermark (50) (present)

Gray linden - *Tilia americana* L. var. *americana* (138) (1923)

Gray moss - *Tillandsia usneoides* (L.) L. (156) (1923)

Gray oak [Grey oak] - *Quercus incana* Bartr. (33) (1827), *Quercus rubra* L. (156) (1923), *Quercus rubra* L. var. *ambigua* (Gray) Fern. (5, 19, 20, 33) (1827-1913)

Gray pea [Grey pea] - *Pisum sativum* L. (107) (1919)

Gray pine [Grey pine] - *Pinus banksiana* Lamb. (1, 20, 5, 10, 136) (1818-1932)

Gray polypody - *Pleopeltis polypodioides* (L.) Andrews & Windham subsp. *polypodioides* (5, 122) (1913-1937)

Gray poplar - *Populus ×canescens* (Aiton) Sm. [*alba × tremula*] (4, 50, 20, 138) (1857–present)

Gray ragwort - *Packera cana* (Hook.) W.A. Weber & A. Löve (3, 4) (1977-1986)

Gray sedge - *Carex amphibola* Steud. (5, 72) (1907-1913)

Gray willow [Grey willow] - *Salix cinerea* L. (138) (1923), *Salix humilis* Marsh. var. *tristis* (Aiton) Griggs (156) (1923), *Salix sericea* Marsh. (19) (1840)

Graybark [Grey bark] possibly - *Quercus prinus* L. (46) (1649)

Gray-bark dogwood [Gray-barked dogwood] - *Cornus foemina* Mill. (85) (1932)

Gray-bark grape [Graybark grape] - *Vitis cinerea* (Engelm.) Millard (3, 50) (1977–present)

Gray-beard tree [Gray beard tree, Graybeard-tree] - *Chionanthus virginicus* L. (5, 92, 156) (1876-1923)

Gray-feather - *Liatris scariosa* (L.) Willd. var. *scariosa* (157) (1929)

Gray-green reindeer lichen [Greygreen reindeer lichen] - *Cladina rangiferina* (L.) Nyl. (50) (present)

Gray-green rush grass [Grey-green rush grass] - *Sporobolus clandestinus* (Biehler) A.S. Hitchc. (5) (1913)

Gray-green wood sorrel - *Oxalis stricta* L. (4) (1986)

Gray-head coneflower [Gray-headed coneflower, Gray-headed coneflower, Gray-headed cone-flower] - *Ratibida columnifera* (Nutt.) Wood & Standl. (122, 156) (1923-1937), *Ratibida pinnata* (Vent.) Barnh. (5, 72, 93, 97, 131) (1899-1937)

Gray-head prairie coneflower [Grayhead prairie coneflower] - *Ratibida pinnata* (Vent.) Barnh. (3) (1977)

Gray-leaf evening-primrose [Gray-leaved evening primrose] - *Oenothera coronopifolia* Torr. & Gray (5) (1913), *Oenothera latifolia* (Rydb.) Munz (97) (1937)

Gray-leaf red raspberry [Grayleaf red raspberry] - *Rubus idaeus* L. subsp. *strigosus* (Michx.) Focke (50) (present)

Gray-lock actinea [Graylock actinea] - *Tetraneuris grandiflora* (Torr. & Gray ex Gray) Parker (155) (1942)

Graymile - *Lithospermum officinale* L. (5, 156) (1913-1923)

Gray's angelica [Grays angelica] - *Angelica grayi* (Coult. & Rose) Coult. & Rose (155) (1942), *Angelica triquinata* Michx. (155) (1942)

Gray's cyperus - *Cyperus grayi* Torr. (5) (1913)

Gray's flatsedge - *Cyperus grayi* Torr. (50) (present)

Gray's galingale - *Cyperus grayi* Torr. (66) (1903)

Gray's gentian - *Gentiana rubricaulis* Schwein. (5) (1913)

Gray's lily [Grays lily] - *Lilium grayi* S. Wats. (50, 138) (1923–present)

Gray's lousewort - *Pedicularis procera* Gray (4) (1986)

Gray's pedicularis [Grays pedicularis] - *Pedicularis procera* Gray (155) (1942)

Gray's saxifrage - *Saxifraga caroliniana* Gray (5) (1913)

Gray's sedge - *Carex grayi* Carey (5, 50, 66, 72) (1903–present)

Gray's strawberry - *Fragaria virginiana* Duchesne subsp. *grayana* (Vilm. ex J. Gay) Staudt (5, 97) (1913-1937)

Greasebush [Grease-bush, Grease bush] - *Glossopetalon planitierum* (Ensign) St. John (3, 4) (1977-1986), *Sarcobatus* Nees (108) (1878), *Sarcobatus vermiculatus* (Hook.) Torr. (108) (1878)

Greasewood [Grease-wood] - *Adenostoma fasciculatum* Hook. & Arn. (106) (1930) CA, *Atriplex canescens* (Pursh) Nutt. (147) (1856), *Larrea tridentata* (Sessé & Moc. ex DC.) Coville var. *tridentata* (106, 153) (1913-1930), *Salvia apiana* Jepson (75) (1894), *Sarcobatus* Nees (1, 50, 93, 155, 158) (1900–present), *Sarcobatus ver-*

miculatus (Hook.) Torr. (3, 4, 5, 50, 75, 85, 93, 101, 113, 130, 146, 148, 153) (1890–present)

Greasewood chamise - *Adenostoma fasciculatum* Hook. & Arn. (155) (1942)

Great African marigold - *Tagetes erecta* L. (178) (1526)

Great Amazon lily [Great Amazonlily] - *Eucharis grandiflora* Planch. & Linden (138) (1923)

Great American aloe - *Agave americana* L. (165) (1768)

Great angelica - *Angelica atropurpurea* L. (46, 49, 64, 107, 156) (1629-1923)

Great arborvitae [Great arbor vitae] - *Thuja plicata* Donn ex D. Don (161) (1857)

Great aspen - *Populus alba* L. (5, 156, 158) (1900–1923), *Populus grandidentata* Michx. (158) (1900)

Great aster - *Symphyotrichum grandiflorum* (L.) Nesom (138, 155) (1931-1942)

Great azure sage - *Salvia azurea* Michx. ex Lam. var. *grandiflora* Benth. (138) (1923)

Great basil [Great basill] - *Ocimum basilicum* L. (178) (1526)

Great Basin lupine - *Lupinus ×alpestris* A. Nels. (50) (present)

Great bearbind - *Calystegia sepium* (L.) R. Br. subsp. *sepium* (42) (1814)

Great berberry [Great berberries] - *Berberis vulgaris* L. (178) (1526)

Great bilberry - *Vaccinium uliginosum* L. (5) (1913)

Great bindweed [Great bind weed] - *Calystegia sepium* (L.) R. Br. subsp. *sepium* (5, 85, 93, 97, 122, 156, 158) (1900-1937), *Ipomoea nil* (L.) Roth (190) (~1759)

Great bitter-flower [Great bitter flower] - *Caltha palustris* L. (5) (1913)

Great bitterweed [Great bitter-weed] - *Ambrosia trifida* L. (19) (1840)

Great black cherry [Great blacke cherrie] - *Prunus cerasus* L. (178) (1526)

Great black oak - *Quercus velutina* Lam. (182) (1791)

Great bladder sedge - *Carex intumescens* Rudge (50) (present)

Great bladderwort - *Utricularia macrorhiza* Le Conte (93) (1936)

Great blue lobelia - *Lobelia flaccidifolia* Small (124) (1937) TX, *Lobelia siphilitica* L. (6, 50, 82, 156) (1892–present), *Lobelia siphilitica* L. var. *ludoviciana* A. DC. (50) (present)

Great bougainvillea - *Bougainvillea spectabilis* Willd. (138) (1923)

Great bulrush - *Schoenoplectus acutus* (Muhl. ex Bigelow) A.& D. Löve var. *acutus* (121) (1918-1970), *Schoenoplectus tabernaemontani* (C.C. Gmel.) Palla (possibly) (72, 93, 138, 155, 156, 158) (1900-1942)

Great bunch grass [Great bunch-grass] - *Festuca altaica* Trin. (45, 56, 87) (1884-1901)

Great bur [Grete burr, Grete burr, Grete burre] - *Arctium* L. (179) (1526), *Arctium lappa* L. (5, 156) (1913-1923)

Great burdock - *Arctium lappa* L. (3, 5, 72, 82, 93, 109, 155, 158) (1900-1977)

Great burnet - *Sanguisorba* L. (10) (1818), *Sanguisorba officinalis* L. (156, 158) (1900-1923)

Great bur-reed - *Sparganium eurycarpum* Engelm. ex Gray (3) (1977)

Great butter-flower [Great butter flower] - *Caltha palustris* L. (157, 158) (1900-1929) IA

Great cabbage palm - *Sabal palmetto* (Walt.) Lodd. ex J.A. & J.H. Schultes (182) (1791)

Great celandine - *Chelidonium majus* L. (49, 52, 53) (1919-1922)

Great chickweed - *Stellaria palustris* (Murr.) Retz. (15, 156) (1895–1923), *Stellaria pubera* Michx. (5, 158) (1900–1913)

Great cinquefoile - *Potentilla recta* L. (178) (1526)

Great clotbur - *Arctium lappa* L. (5, 46) (1671-1913) accidentally introduced by 1671, Josselyn, *Xanthium strumarium* L. var. *canadense* (Mill.) Torr. & Gray (5, 97) (1913-1937)

Great cocklebur - *Xanthium strumarium* L. var. *canadense* (Mill.) Torr. & Gray (93) (1936) Neb

Great comfrey - *Symphytum officinale* L. (178) (1526)
Great common sedge - *Carex lacustris* Willd. (5) (1913)
Great coneflower [Great cone-flower] - *Rudbeckia maxima* Nutt. (5, 97, 122, 124, 138) (1913-1937), *Centaurea montana* L. (178) (1526)
Great crambling rocket - *Reseda alba* L. (178) (1526)
Great daisy [Great-daisy] - *Leucanthemum vulgare* Lam. (158) (1900)
Great double Affrican Marigold - *Tagetes erecta* L. (178) (1526)
Great duckwood - *Spirodela polyrhiza* (L.) Schleid. (72) (1907)
Great fescue grass - *Lolium giganteum* (L.) S.J. Darbyshire (5) (1913)
Great field daisy [Great field daisie] - *Leucanthemum vulgare* Lam. (178) (1526)
Great fir - *Abies grandis* (Dougl. ex D. Don) Lindl. (109) (1949)
Great fleabane - *Pulicaria dysenterica* (L.) Bernh. (178) (1526)
Great flower-de-luce of Dalmatia [Great floure-de-luce of Dalmatia] - *Iris pallida* Lam. (180) (1633)
Great flower-gentle [Great flower gentle] - *Amaranthus caudatus* L. (178) (1526)
Great flower-of-the-sun [Great flower of the sunne] - *Helianthus annuus* L. (178) (1526)
Great fox sedge - *Carex conjuncta* Boott (42) (1814)
Great fox seg - *Carex conjuncta* Boott (42) (1814)
Great goldenrod [Great golden-rod] - *Solidago canadensis* L. var. *scabra* Torr. & Gray (19, 187) (1818-1840)
Great goose-grass [Great goose grass] - *Asperugo procumbens* L. (5, 92, 156, 158) (1876-1923)
Great grape-flower [Great grape-floure] - *Muscari botryoides* (L.) Mills (180) (1633)
Great green orchis - *Platanthera orbiculata* (Pursh) Lindl. (2, 156) (1895-1923)
Great hairy willowherb [Great hairy willow-herb, Great hairy willow herb] - *Epilobium hirsutum* L. (5, 156) (1913-1923)
Great hare's-foot [Great Hares foote] - *Trifolium incarnatum* L. (178) (1526)
Great hart cherry [Great hart cherrie] - *Prunus cerasus* L. (178) (1526)
Great hedge bedstraw [Great hedge-bedstraw] - *Galium mollugo* L. (5, 156) (1913-1923)
Great helleborine - *Epipactis gigantea* Dougl. Ex Hook. (109) (1949)
Great henbit - *Lamium amplexicaule* L. (187) (1818)
Great high angelica - *Angelica atropurpurea* L. (5) (1913)
Great Holand Rose - *Rosa centifolia* L. (178) (1526)
Great honeywort [Great honie woort] - Cerinthe major L. (178) (1526)
Great houseleek [Great houseleeke] - *Sempervivum tectorum* L. (178) (1526)
Great Indian plantain - *Arnoglossum muehlenbergii* (Schultz-Bip.) H.E. Robins. (5, 72, 82, 156) (1907-1930)
Great ironweed [Great iron-weed] - *Vernonia arkansana* DC. (5, 97, 122) (1913-1937)
Great Lakes sand cherry [Great Lakes sandcherry] - *Prunus pumila* L. var. *pumila* (50) (present)
Great laurel - *Rhododendron* L. (156) (1923), *Rhododendron maximum* L. (5, 57, 71, 156) (1898-1923)
Great laurel tree - *Magnolia grandiflora* L. (182) (1791)
Great leopard's-bane [Great leopardsbane] - *Doronicum pardalianches* L. (92) (1876)
Great lobelia - *Lobelia siphilitica* L. (4, 5, 6, 62, 63, 72, 82, 93, 98, 106, 114, 156, 157, 158) (1882-1986)
Great long-lived pine - *Pinus palustris* Mill. (182) (1791)
Great lyme grass [Great lyme-grass] - *Elymus canadensis* L. (94) (1901)
Great manzanita - *Arctostaphylos glauca* Lindl. (138) (1923)
Great maple - *Acer pseudoplatanus* L. (165, 178) (1526-1768)
Great masterwort - *Astrantia major* L. (138) (1923)
Great medicine - *Salix humilis* Marsh. var. *tristis* (Aiton) Griggs (46) (1879)

Great millet - *Sorghum halepense* (L.) Pers. (45) (1896)
Great morel - *Atropa bella-donna* L. (156) (1923)
Great mountain garlic [Great mountaine Garlicke] - *Allium ampeloprasum* L. (180) (1633)
Great mountain lily [Great mountaine lilly] - *Lilium martagon* L. (180) (1633)
Great mullein - *Verbascum thapsus* L. (174) (1753)
Great mullen - *Verbascum thapsus* L. (5, 14, 34, 41, 69, 72, 93, 97, 157, 158) (1834-1936)
Great nettle - *Urtica dioica* L. (5, 58, 93, 156) (1869-1936), *Urtica dioica* L. subsp. *gracilis* (Aiton) Seland. (19) (1840)
Great northern aster - *Canadanthus modestus* (Lindl.) Nesom (5, 82) (1913-1930)
Great orange daylily - *Hemerocallis fulva* var. *aurantiaca* (Baker) M. Hotta (138) (1923)
Great orange-colored Virginia jasmine [Great orange coloured Virginia jasmine] - *Campsis radicans* (L.) Seem. ex Bureau (181) (~1678)
Great orpin - *Hylotelephium telephium* (L.) H. Ohba. subsp. *telephium* (178) (1526)
Great oxeye [Great ox-eye] - *Leucanthemum vulgare* Lam. (49) (1898)
Great pennyroyal [Great penniroyall] - *Mentha pulegium* L. (178) (1526)
Great periwinkle [Great peruinkle] - *Vinca minor* L. (174) (1753)
Great Plains bladderpod - *Lesquerella arenosa* (Richards.) Rydb. (50) (present)
Great Plains cottonwood - *Populus deltoides* Bartr. ex Marsh. subsp. *monilifera* (Aiton) Eckenwalder (109) (1949)
Great Plains false willow - *Baccharis salicina* Torr. & Gray (50) (present)
Great Plains flatsedge - *Cyperus lupulinus* (Spreng) Marcks (50) (present)
Great Plains lady's-tresses [Great Plains ladies'-tresses] - *Spiranthes magnicamporum* Sheviak (50) (present)
Great Plains sedge - *Carex melanostachya* Bieb. ex Willd. (50) (present)
Great Plains stickseed - *Lappula cenchrusoides* A. Nels. (50) (present)
Great Plains white fringed orchid - *Platanthera praeclara* Sheviak & Bowles (50) (present)
Great plantain [Grete plantayne] - *Plantago major* L. (5, 7, 62, 179) (1526-1913)
Great pondlily [Great pond lily] - *Nelumbo lutea* Willd. (possibly) (12) (1821)
Great purple bind weed - *Ipomoea purpurea* (L.) Roth (42) (1814)
Great purple knapweed [Great purple knapweede] - *Centaurea scabiosa* L. (178) (1526)
Great purple orchis - *Platanthera peramoena* (Gray) Gray (5) (1913)
Great ragweed - *Ambrosia trifida* L. (5, 49, 50, 62, 63, 80, 92, 93, 106, 131, 156, 157, 158) (1898–present), *Ambrosia trifida* L. var. *trifida* (50) (present)
Great rainlily - *Cooperia pedunculata* Herbert (138) (1923)
Great red hibiscus - *Hibiscus coccineus* Walt (2) (1895)
Great red rose - *Rosa centifolia* L. (178) (1526)
Great red rosemallow [Great red rose mallow] - *Hibiscus coccineus* Walt (2) (1895)
Great reed-mace - *Typha latifolia* L. (5, 41, 156, 157, 158) (1770-1929)
Great rosebay [Great rose-bay] - *Rhododendron maximum* L. (2, 156) (1895-1942)
Great rosemallow - *Hibiscus grandiflorus* Michx. (138) (1923)
Great round-head garlic [Great round-headed garlick] - *Allium ampeloprasum* L. (165) (1768)
Great sanicle - *Alchemilla monticola* Opiz (possibly) (156) (1923)
Great scouring-rush [Great scouring rush] - *Equisetum fluviatile* L. (6) (1892), *Equisetum hyemale* L. var. *affine* (Engelm.) A.A. Eat. (72) (1907)

Great sea starwort [Great sea star woort] - *Tripleurospermum perforata* (Merat) M. Lainz (155) (1942)

Great silver fir - *Abies fraseri* (Pursh) Poir. (138) (1923)

Great silverbell - *Halesia tetraptera* L. (138) (1923)

Great snakeroot - *Hexastylis virginica* (L.) Small (181) (~1678)

Great snakeweed [Great snake weede] - *Polygonum bistorta* L. (178) (1526)

Great snapdragon - *Antirrhinum majus* L. (5, 158) (1900–1913)

Great Solomon's-seal [Great solomonseal, Great Solomon's seal] - *Polygonatum biflorum* (Walt.) Ell. var. *commutatum* (J.A. & J.H. Schultes) Morong (138, 155, 156, 157, 158) (1900-1942)

Great Spanish orpin - *Hylotelephium telephium* (L.) H. Ohba. subsp. *telephium* (178) (1526)

Great spurred violet - *Viola selkirkii* Pursh ex Goldie (3, 4, 5, 156) (1913-1986)

Great St. John's-wort [Great St. Johnswort, Great St. John's wort] - *Hypericum ascyron* L. (2, 4, 5, 50, 72, 156, 158) (1900–present)

Great starwort - *Stellaria pubera* Michx. (155) (1942)

Great stinging nettle - *Urtica dioica* L. (49, 92) (1876-1898)

Great sunflower - *Helianthus giganteus* L. (38) (1820)

Great throatwort [Great throate woort] - *Campanula trachelium* L. (178) (1526)

Great thrumwort - *Alisma subcordatum* Raf. (5, 157) (1900-1929)

Great thumb-wort - *Alisma plantago-aquatica* L. (156) (1923)

Great trefoil - *Medicago sativa* L. (5, 157, 158) (1900-1929)

Great trumpetleaf [Great trumpet leaf] - *Sarracenia leucophylla* Raf. (2) (1895)

Great turnip - *Brassica rapa* L. var. *rapa* (180) (1633)

Great upright-branch Virginia bastard spiderwort [Great upright brancht Virginia bastard spiderwort] - *Commelina erecta* L. (181) (~1678)

Great Valley gumweed - *Grindelia camporum* Greene var. *camporum* (50) (present)

Great water dock [Great water-dock, Great-water dock] - *Rumex orbiculatus* Gray (3, 4, 49, 92) (1876-1986)

Great water plantain - *Alisma plantago-aquatica* L. (165) (1768)

Great waterleaf - *Hydrophyllum appendiculatum* Michx. (50) (present)

Great waterlily [Great water-lily] - *Nelumbo lutea* Willd. (157, 158) (1900-1929)

Great western brome - *Bromus carinatus* H. & A. (94) (1901)

Great white mullein - *Verbascum thapsus* L. (41) (1770)

Great white oxeye [Great white ox-eye] - *Leucanthemum vulgare* Lam. (5, 158) (1900–1913)

Great white trillium - *Trillium grandiflorum* (Michx.) Salisb. (156) (1923)

Great whortleberry - *Vaccinium corymbosum* L. (5) (1913)

Great wild valerian - *Valeriana officinalis* L. (5, 49, 53, 92, 156) (1898-1923)

Great willowherb [Great willow herb, Great willow-herb] - *Chamerion angustifolium* (L.) Holub subsp. *angustifolium* (2, 5, 49, 53, 63, 72, 93, 109, 131, 156, 157, 158) (1895-1949)

Great yellow lily - *Nelumbo lutea* Willd. (157, 158) (1900-1929)

Great yellow monk's-hood - *Aconitum lycoctonum* L. (165) (1768)

Great yellow waterlily [Great yellow water lily, Great yellow water-lily] - *Nelumbo lutea* Willd. (74, 156) (1893-1923) NY

Great yellow wolf's-bane - *Aconitum lycoctonum* L. (165) (1768)

Great yellow wood sorrel - *Oxalis stricta* L. (5) (1913)

Great-berry manzanita [Great-berried manzanita] - *Arctostaphylos glauca* Lindl. (109) (1949)

Greater & Lesser thorough leafed yellow Salomons Seale of America - *Uvularia perfoliata* L. (181) (~1678)

Greater ammi - *Ammi majus* L. (155) (1942)

Greater bearbind [Greater bear-bind] - *Calystegia sepium* (L.) R. Br. subsp. *sepium* (158) (1900)

Greater bladderwort [Greater bladder-wort] - *Utricularia macrorhiza* Le Conte (5, 63, 72, 95, 97, 131, 156, 158) (1899-1937)

Greater burdock [Greater burrdock] - *Arctium lappa* L. (50) (present)

Greater caltrop - *Kallstroemia maxima* (L.) Hook. & Arn. (156) (1923), *Kallstroemia parviflora* J.B.S. Norton (5, 97) (1913-1937)

Greater celandine - *Chelidonium majus* L. (42, 155, 156, 158) (1814-1942)

Greater centaury - *Centaurea scabiosa* L. (4, 5, 156) (1923-1986)

Greater creeping rush - *Juncus subtilis* E. Meyer (50) (present)

Greater creeping spearwort - *Ranunculus flammula* L. (50) (present), *Ranunculus flammula* L. var. *filiformis* (Michx.) Hook. (50) (present)

Greater duckweed - *Spirodela polyrhiza* (L.) Schleid. (5, 93, 97, 120) (1913-1938)

Greater fair-hair hyacinth [Greater faire haired Iacint] - *Muscari comosum* (L.) Mill. (178) (1596)

Greater fringed gentian - *Gentianopsis crinita* (Froel.) Ma. (50) (present)

Greater henbit - *Lamium amplexicaule* L. (5, 158) (1900–1913)

Greater knapweed - *Centaurea scabiosa* L. (14, 50) (1882–present)

Greater nettle - *Urtica dioica* L. (157, 158) (1900-1929)

Greater pinweed [Greater pin-weed] - *Lechea mucronata* Raf. (157, 158) (1900-1929)

Greater plantain - *Plantago major* L. (156, 157, 158) (1900-1929)

Greater prickly sedge - *Carex muricata* L. (5) (1913)

Greater purple fringed orchid - *Platanthera grandiflora* (Bigelow) Lindl. (50) (present)

Greater ragweed - *Ambrosia trifida* L. (80, 82) (1913-1930)

Greater St. John's wort [Greater St. John's-wort] - *Hypericum ascyron* L. (3) (1977), *Hypericum majus* (Gray) Britton (3, 4) (1977-1986)

Greater starwort - *Stellaria holostea* L. (5, 156) (1913-1923)

Greater stichwort - *Stellaria holostea* L. (5, 156) (1913-1923)

Greater straw sedge - *Carex normalis* Mackenzie (50) (present)

Greater tickseed - *Coreopsis major* Walt. (5) (1913)

Greater water dock - *Rumex orbiculatus* Gray (50) (present), *Rumex orbiculatus* Gray var. *borealis* Rech. f. (50) (present)

Greater water dock - *Rumex orbiculatus* Gray var. *orbiculatus* (50) (present)

Greater yellow lady's-slipper [Greater yellow lady's slipper] - *Cypripedium parviflorum* Salisb. var. *pubescens* (Willd.) Knight (50) (present), *Cypripedium parviflorum* Salisb. var. *pubescens* (Willd.) Knight (50) (present)

Greatest blush bear's-ears [Greatest blush Bears' ears] - *Dodecatheon meadia* L. (181) (~1678)

Great-flower dogwood [Great-flowered dogwood] - *Cornus florida* L. (186) (1814)

Great-flower gaillardia [Great-flowered gaillardia, Great flowered gaillardia] - *Gaillardia aristata* Pursh (5, 131) (1899-1913)

Great-flower magnolia [Great-flowered magnolia] - *Magnolia grandiflora* L. (2) (1895)

Great-flower St. John's-wort [Great flowered St. John's-wort] - *Hypericum ascyron* L. (156) (1923)

Great-flower white trillium [Great-flowered white trillium] - *Trillium grandiflorum* (Michx.) Salisb. (2) (1895)

Great-leaf larkspur [Great leaved larkspur] - *Delphinium grandiflorum* L. (2) (1895)

Great-leaf magnolia [Great-leaved magnolia] - *Magnolia macrophylla* Michx. (2, 156) (1895-1942)

Grecian foxglove - *Digitalis lanata* Ehrh. (50, 109 138, 155) (1923–present)

Grecian laurel - *Laurus nobilis* L. (138) (1923)

Grecian silkvine - *Periploca graeca* L. (138, 155) (1923-1942)

Greek anemone - *Anemone berlandieri* Pritz. (155) (1942), *Anemone blanda* Schott & Kotschy (155) (1942)

Greek beans [Greeke beanes] - *Vicia americana* Muhl. ex Willd. subsp. *americana* (5, 107) (1913-1919)

Greek broom - *Cytisus villosus* Pourret (138) (1923)

Greek honeywort - *Cerinthe retorta* Sm. (138) (1923)

Greek nuts - *Prunus dulcis* (Mill.) D.A. Webber (92) (1876)

Greek stock - *Matthiola longipetala* (Vent.) DC. (138) (1923)

Greek valerian [Greeke valerian, Greek-valerian] - *Polemonium caeruleum* L. (92, 109, 138, 178) (1526-1949), *Polemonium* L. (2, 19, 82, 156, 158) (1840-1930), *Polemonium reptans* L. (5, 50, 72, 82, 156) (1907–present)

Green acacia - *Parkinsonia florida* (Benth. ex Gray) S. Wats. (154) (1857)

Green acerates - *Asclepias viridiflora* Raf. (155) (1942)

Green adder's-mouth [Green adder's mouth] - *Malaxis unifolia* Michx. (5, 72) (1907-1913)

Green adder's-mouth orchid [Green adder's mouth orchid] - *Malaxis unifolia* Michx. (50) (present)

Green alder - *Alnus incana* (L.) Moench subsp. *rugosa* (DuRoi) Clausen (5, 156, 158) (1900–1923), *Alnus viridis* (Vill.) Lam. & DC. (2, 5, 156) (1895-1923), *Rhamnus alnifolia* L'Her. (156) (1923)

Green amaranth - *Amaranthus hybridus* L. (156, 157, 158) (1900-1929), *Amaranthus* L. (92) (1876), *Amaranthus retroflexus* L. (5, 93, 107, 148, 156) (1913-1939)

Green antelope-horn [Green antelopehorn] - *Asclepias viridis* Walt. (50) (present)

Green archangel - *Lycopus europaeus* L. (5, 92, 156) (1876-1923) no longer in use by 1923, *Lycopus virginicus* L. (158) (1900)

Green arrow-arum [Green arrow arum, Green arrowarum] - *Peltandra virginica* (L.) Schott. (5, 50, 97, 109, 156) (1913–present)

Green ash - *Fraxinus pennsylvanica* Marsh. (2, 4, 5, 9, 20, 46, 50, 63, 72, 82, 85, 93, 97, 101, 112, 113. 124, 130, 131, 135, 138, 156) (1857–present)

Green baneberry - *Actaea rubra* (Aiton) Willd. (155) (1942)

Green bark acacia - *Parkinsonia florida* (Benth. ex Gray) S. Wats. (106) (1930)

Green bottle grass [Green bottle-grass] - *Setaria viridis* (L.) Beauv. (119) (1938), *Setaria viridis* (L.) Beauv. var. *viridis* (5) (1913)

Green bristle grass [Green bristle-grass, Green bristlegrass] - *Setaria viridis* (L.) Beauv. (50, 122, 140, 143, 155) (1936–present), *Setaria viridis* (L.) Beauv. var. *viridis* (50) (present)

Green broom - *Cytisus scoparius* (L.) Link (5, 156) (1913-1923), *Genista tinctoria* L. (92) (1876)

Green bulrush - *Scirpus atrovirens* Willd. (50, 138, 139, 155) (1923–present)

Green carpetweed - *Mollugo verticillata* L. (50) (present)

Green cliffbrake - *Pellaea viridis* (Forsk.) Prantl (138) (1923)

Green comet milkweed - *Asclepias viridiflora* Raf. (50) (present)

Green coneflower [Green cone-flower] - *Ratibida columnifera* (Nutt.) Wood & Standl. (82) (1930)

Green dogfennel [Green dog-fennel, Green dog fennel] - *Matricaria discoidea* DC. (101) (1905), *Matricaria* L. (1, 93) (1932-1936)

Green dracena - *Cordyline australis* (G. Forst.) Endl. (138) (1923)

Green dragon - *Arisaema dracontium* (L.) Schott (6, 50, 57, 92, 93, 109, 125, 156, 157, 158, 187) (1818–present), *Arisaema* Martens (1) (1932)

Green duckmeat [Green duck meat] - *Lemna minor* L. (19) (1840)

Green eelgrass [Green eel grass] - *Ranunculus trichophyllus* Chaix var. *trichophyllus* (5) (1913)

Green endive - *Lactuca virosa* L. (157, 158) (1900-1929)

Green false foxglove - *Agalinis viridis* (Small) Pennell (50) (present)

Green false hellebore - *Veratrum viride* Ait. (50) (present)

Green false nightshade - *Chamaesaracha coronopus* (Dunal) Gray (3, 4) (1977-1986)

Green flatsedge - *Cyperus virens* Michx. (4, 155) (1942-1986)

Green fly orchid - *Epidendrum conopseum* Ait.f. (50) (present)

Green foxtail [Green fox tail] - *Setaria viridis* (L.) Beauv. (3, 11, 50, 56, 66, 80, 87, 90, 111, 115, 119, 129, 131, 134, 140, 143, 145) (1884–present), *Setaria viridis* (L.) Beauv. var. *viridis* (93, 94) (1901-1936)

Green foxtail grass - *Setaria viridis* (L.) Beauv. (92) (1876)

Green foxtail grass - *Setaria viridis* (L.) Beauv. var. *viridis* (5) (1913)

Green fringed orchid - *Platanthera lacera* (Michx.) G. Don (5, 50, 109, 156) (1913–present)

Green gages - *Prunus domestica* L. (92) (1876)

Green gentian - *Frasera* Walt. (50) (present), *Swertia* L. (4) (1986)

Green gerardia - *Agalinis viridis* (Small) Pennell (4) (1986)

Green ginger - *Artemisia vulgaris* L. (156, 157) (1923-1929)

Green gram - *Glycine max* (L.) Merr. (158) (1900), *Vigna mungo* (L.) Hepper (110) (1886)

Green grass [Green-grass] - *Poa glauca* Vahl. (187) (1818), *Poa pratensis* L. (5, 45, 68) (1896-1913)

Green greasewood - *Gutierrezia sarothrae* (Pursh) Britton & Rusby (113, 130) (1890-1895)

Green gypsophila - *Gypsophila acutifolia* Stev. ex Spreng. (138) (1923)

Green haw - *Crataegus viridis* L. (4, 122) (1937-1986)

Green hawthorn - *Crataegus viridis* L. (50, 155) (1942–present)

Green hellebore - *Helleborus viridis* L. (2, 5, 6, 15, 57, 106, 156) (1892-1930), *Veratrum viride* Ait. (49, 53, 55, 57, 64, 92, 156) (1876-1922)

Green hollowroot [Greene hollow roote] - *Adoxa moschatellina* L. (178) (1526)

Green lily - *Schoenocaulon drummondii* Gray (122, 124) (1937)

Green locust - *Robinia pseudoacacia* L. (5, 156) (1913-1923)

Green mangle - *Iva frutescens* L. subsp. *oraria* (Bartlett) R.C. Jackson (156) (1923)

Green meadow grass [Green meadow-grass] - *Poa glauca* Vahl. (187) (1818), *Poa pratensis* L. (66, 90) (1885-1903)

Green milkweed - *Asclepias engelmanniana* Woods. (124) (1937), *Asclepias hirtella* (Pennell) Woods (50) (present), *Asclepias* L. (1, 2, 63, 93) (1895), *Asclepias viridiflora* Raf. (3, 4, 5, 19, 72, 85, 92, 93, 97, 131, 156) (1840-1986)

Green mint - *Mentha spicata* L. (156) (1923)

Green mould - *Eurotium glabrum* Blaser (possibly) (56) (1901)

Green mountain spinnery - *Carya ovata* (Mill.) K. Koch (109) (1949)

Green muhly - *Muhlenbergia racemosa* (Michx.) Britton, Sterns & Poggenb. (140, 155) (1942-1944)

Green needle grass [Green needlegrass] - *Nassella viridula* (Trin.) Barkworth (3, 50, 140, 155) (1942–present)

Green orchis - *Platanthera flava* (L.) Lindl. var. *flava* (85) (1932)

Green osier [Green-osier] - *Cornus alternifolia* L. f. (5, 29, 76, 156) (1869-1923), *Cornus rugosa* Lam. (5, 6, 156) (1892-1923)

Green ozier - *Cornus rugosa* Lam. (92) (1876)

Green parrot's-feather [Green parrot's feather, Green parrot-feather] - *Myriophyllum pinnatum* (Walt.) Britton, Sterns & Poggenb. (4, 155) (1942-1986)

Green penstemon - *Penstemon virens* Pennell (155) (1942)

Green perilla - *Perilla frutescens* (L.) Britton (138) (1923)

Green pigeon - *Setaria viridis* (L.) Beauv. (87) (1884)

Green pigeon grass - *Setaria viridis* (L.) Beauv. (88) (1885)

Green pigweed [Green pig-weed] - *Amaranthus hybridus* L. (4) (1986), *Chenopodium album* L. (19) (1840)

Green prairie coneflower - *Ratibida tagetes* (James) Barnhart (50) (present)

Green pyrola - *Pyrola chlorantha* Sw. (155) (1942)

Green rein orchis - *Platanthera flava* (L.) Lindl. var. *flava* (5, 156) (1913-1923)

Green River grass - *Urochloa texana* (Buckl.) R. Webster (87) (1884)

Green rush - *Juncus acuminatus* Michx. (66) (1903)

Green sedge - *Carex virescens* Muhl. ex Willd. (19, 187) (1818-1840), *Carex viridula* Michx. (139, 155) (1942-1944), *Carex viridula* Michx. subsp. *viridula* (5) (1913), *Cyperus virens* Michx. (66) (1903)

Green sorrel - *Rumex acetosa* L. (5, 156) (1913-1923)

Green spleenwort - *Asplenium trichomanes-ramosum* L. (3, 4, 5, 155) (1913-1986)

Green sprangletop - *Leptochloa dubia* (H.B.K.) Nees (3, 50, 122, 155) (1937–present)

Green starwort [Green star wort] - *Symphyotrichum novi-belgii* (L.) Nesom var. *novi-belgii* (42) (1814)

Green stipa - *Nassella viridula* (Trin.) Barkworth (56) (1901)

Green strawberry - *Fragaria chiloensis* (L.) Mill. (107) (1919)

Green sumac - *Rhus virens* Lindheimer ex Gray (106) (1930)

Green thorn - *Smilax laurifolia* L. (41) (1770)

Green thorn-apple [Green thorn apple] - *Datura stramonium* L. (19) (1840)

Green trillium - *Trillium viride* Beck (155) (1942)

Green valerian - *Polemonium reptans* L. (92) (1876)

Green Valley grass - *Sorghum halepense* (L.) Pers. (45) (1896)

Green veratrum - *Veratrum viride* Ait. (49, 64) (1898–1908)

Green violet [Greenviolet] - *Hybanthus concolor* (T.F.Forst.) Spreng. (2, 3, 4, 5, 19, 156) (1840-1986), *Hybanthus* Jacq. (1, 4, 50, 122, 158) (1937–present)

Green wakerobin [Green wake robin, Green wake-robin] - *Trillium viride* Beck (5, 97) (1913-1937)

Green wattle - *Acacia decurrens* Willd. (50, 109, 138) (1923–present), *Acacia mearnsii* De Wild. (107) (1919) naturalized in CA

Green wood orchis - *Platanthera clavellata* (Michx.) Luer (156) (1923)

Green woodland orchis - *Platanthera clavellata* (Michx.) Luer (3) (1977)

Green-and-white hellebore [Green and whitte hellebore] - *Veratrum* L. (10) (1818)

Green-arrow [Greenarrow, Green arrow] - *Achillea millefolium* L. (69, 156, 158) (1900-1923)

Green-bark blueberry - *Vaccinium pallidum* Aiton (46) (1879)

Greenbark ceanothus - *Ceanothus spinosus* Nutt. (109) (1949)

Greenberry [Green berry] - *Gaultheria procumbens* L. (5) (1913)

Greenbrier [Green brier, Greenbriar, Green briar, Green bryar] - *Smilax bona-nox* L. (3, 117, 156) (1908-1977), *Smilax ecirrata* (Engelm. ex Kunth) S. Wats. (3) (1977), *Smilax* L. (1, 8, 12, 50, 93, 106, 109, 122, 138, 155, 156) (1785–present), *Smilax rotundifolia* L. (5, 19, 72, 92, 97, 107, 156, 187) (1818-1937), *Smilax tamnoides* L. (9, 35, 85, 113, 130) (1806-1932)

Green-ebony - *Jacaranda mimosifolia* D. Don (138) (1923)

Greene's goldenweed [Greenes goldenweed] - *Ericameria greenei* (Gray) Nesom (155) (1942)

Greene's mountain ash, Greenes mountainash - *Sorbus scopulina* Greene (50, 155) (1942–present)

Greene's rush - *Juncus greenei* Oakes & Tuckerm. (5, 50, 66) (1912–present)

Greene's slender agoseris [Greenes slender agoseris] - *Agoseris aurantiaca* (Hook.) Greene (155) (1942)

Greeneyes [Green eyes] - *Berlandiera* DC. (4, 50) (1986–present)

Green-field speedwell [Green field speedwell] - *Veronica agrestis* L. (50) (present)

Green-flower amaranth [Green-flowered amaranth] - *Amaranthus viridis* L. (187) (1818)

Green-flower hedgehog cactus [Green-flowered hedgehog cactus] - *Echinocereus viridiflorus* Engelm. (5) (1913)

Green-flower wintergreen [Greenflowered wintergreen, Green flowered wintergreen, Green-flowered wintergreen] - *Pyrola chlorantha* Sw. (50, 95, 157) (1911–present)

Green-flowered hellebore - *Veratrum viride* Ait. (187) (1818)

Green-fruit bur-reed [Green-fruited bur-reed] - *Sparganium erectum* L. subsp. *stoloniferum* (Graebn.) Hara (5) (1913)

Green-head coneflower [Green-headed cone-flower, Green-headed coneflower, Green-headed cone flower] - *Rudbeckia laciniata* L. (5, 62, 97, 131, 156, 157, 158) (1899–1937)

Greenish fringed orchis [Greenish fringed-orchis] - *Platanthera leucophaea* (Nutt.) Lindl. (158) (1900)

Greenish orchis - *Platanthera flava* (L.) Lindl. var. *flava* (5, 156) (1913-1923)

Greenish strawberry [Greenish strawberrie] - *Fragaria virginiana* Duchesne (178) (1526)

Greenish-flower wintergreen [Greenish-flowered wintergreen] - *Pyrola chlorantha* Sw. (5, 131) (1899-1913?)

Greenish-white sedge - *Carex albolutescens* Schwein (5) (1913)

Green-keel cottonsedge [Green-keeled cottonsedge] - *Eriophorum viridicarinatum* (Engelm.) Fern. (139) (1944)

Greenland bluegrass - *Poa glauca* Vahl. (155) (1942)

Greenland buttercup - *Ranunculus auricomus* L. (50) (present)

Greenland primrose - *Primula egaliksensis* Wormsk. ex Hornem. (5) (1913)

Greenland sandwort - *Minuartia groenlandica* (Retz.) Ostenf. (138, 155) (1931-1942)

Green-leaf bluebells [Greenleaf bluebells] - *Mertensia oblongifolia* (Nutt.) G. Don (155) (1942)

Green-leaf five-eyes [Greenleaf fiveeyes] - *Chamaesaracha coronopus* (Dunal) Gray (50) (present)

Green-leaf hawthorn [Green leaved hawthorn] - *Crataegus viridis* L. (42) (1814)

Green-leaf manzanita [Greenleaf manzanita] - *Arctostaphylos patula* Greene (155) (1942)

Green-pitaya echinocereus [Greenpitaya echinocereus] - *Echinocereus viridiflorus* Engelm. (155) (1942)

Green-plume rabbitbrush [Greenplume rabbitbrush] - *Ericameria nauseosa* (Pallas ex Pursh) Nesom & Baird subsp. *nauseosa* var. *glabrata* (Gray) Nesom & Baird (155) (1942)

Green's hawkweed - *Hieracium greenii* Porter & Britton (5) (1913)

Greensauce [Green-sauce, Green sauce] - *Oxalis acetosella* L. (92, 156) (1876-1923), *Rumex acetosa* L. (5) (1913), *Rumex acetosella* L. (156, 158) (1900-1923)

Green-scale willow [Green-scaled willow] - *Salix chlorolepis* Fernald (5) (1913)

Green-spike sedge [Green-spiked sedge] - *Carex virescens* Muhl. ex Willd. (66) (1903)

Green-stem forsythia [Greenstem forsythia] - *Forsythia viridissima* Lindl. (138) (1923)

Greenthread - *Thelesperma filifolium* (Hook.) Gray (4) (1986), *Thelesperma filifolium* (Hook.) Gray var. *intermedium* (Rydb.) Shinners (3) (1977), *Thelesperma* Less. (50, 155) (1942–present), *Thelesperma megapotamicum* (Spreng.) Kuntze (98) (1926)

Green-vein lady's-tresses [Greenvein ladies' tresses] - *Spiranthes praecox* (Walt.) S. Wats. (50) (present)

Green-wattle acacia [Greenwattle acaica] - *Acacia mearnsii* De Wild. (107, 155) (1919-1942) ND

Greenweed [Green weed, Green-weed] - *Genista tinctoria* L. (6, 49, 92, 156) (1876-1923)

Green-white sedge [Greenwhite sedge] - *Carex albolutescens* Schwein (50) (present)

Greenwood [Green wood, Green-wood] - *Genista tinctoria* L. (5, 6, 7, 92, 156) (1828-1923) IA, *Parkinsonia florida* (Benth. ex Gray) S. Wats. (76) (1896)

Gregg's ash [Gregg ash] - *Fraxinus greggii* Gray (122, 138) (1923-1937)

Gregg's ceanothus - *Ceanothus greggii* Gray (124) (1937)

Gregg's haploesthes - *Haploesthes greggii* Gray (5, 97) (1913-1937)

Grenadier - *Punica granatum* L. (92) (1876)

Grenadine - *Dianthus caryophyllus* L. (109) (1949)

Grenes - *Lemna minor* L. (178, 179) (1526-1596)

Grevillea - *Grevillea* R. Br. ex Knight (138) (1923)

Griffith's slender grama - *Bouteloua repens* (Kunth) Scribn. & Merr. (122) (1937)

Griffith's wheatgrass [Griffiths wheatgrass] - *Elymus albicans* (Scribn. & J.G. Sm.) A. Löve (140, 155) (1942-1944)

Grim-the-collier - *Hieracium aurantiacum* L. (5, 156) (1913-1923)

Grindelia - *Grindelia camporum* Greene (57) (1917), *Grindelia camporum* Greene var. *camporum* (52, 60) (1902-1919), *Grindelia squarrosa* (Pursh) Dunal (possibly) (53, 57, 60, 157) (1900-1929), *Grindelia stricta* DC. var. *angustifolia* (Gray) M.A. Lane (57) (1917)

Grindwurz (German) - *Rumex obtusifolius* L. (6) (1892)

Grinsel - *Senecio vulgaris* L. (5, 156, 158) (1900-1923) no longer in use by 1923

Grip or Grip-grass [Grip grass] - *Galium aparine* L. (5, 92, 156, 158) (1876-1923) no longer in use by 1923

Grise de buff - *Shepherdia argentea* (Pursh) Nutt. (35) (1806) William Clark

Grisebach's bristle grass [Grisebach bristle grass] - *Setaria grise-bachii* Fourn. (122) (1937)

Grisebach's panicum - *Dichanthelium aciculare* (Desv. ex Poir.) Gould & C.A. Clark (5) (1913)

Grizzly-bear cactus - *Opuntia erinacea* Engelm. & Bigelow ex Engelm. (109) (1949)

Grizzly-bear pricklypear [Grizzlybear pricklypear] - *Opuntia erinacea* Engelm. & Bigelow ex Engelm. (155) (1942)

Gromell reed - *Coix lacryma-jobi* L. (180) (1633)

Gromwell - *Buglossoides arvensis* (L.) I.M. Johnston (92) (1876), *Lithospermum caroliniense* (Walt. ex J.F. Gmel.) MacM. (48) (1882), *Lithospermum* L. (1, 2, 7, 10, 93, 109, 138, 155, 156, 158, 184) (1793-1949), *Lithospermum latifolium* Michx. (4) (1986), *Lithospermum officinale* L. (5, 19, 63, 72) (1840-1907)

Gromyll - *Lithospermum officinale* L. (179) (1526)

Gronovius' dodder [Gronovius dodder, Gronvi's dodder] - *Cuscuta gronovii* Willd. ex J.A. Schultes (3, 4, 5, 72, 82, 131, 155) (1899-1986)

Gronovius' hawkweed - *Hieracium gronovii* L. (5) (1913)

Grooved flax - *Linum sulcatum* Riddell (3, 4, 50, 155) (1942–present), *Linum sulcatum* Riddell var. *sulcatum* (50) (present)

Grooved milkvetch [Grooved milk vetch] - *Astragalus bisulcatus* (Hook.) Gray (131) (1899)

Grooved yellow flax - *Linum sulcatum* Riddell (72, 122, 131) (1899-1907), *Linum sulcatum* Riddell var. *sulcatum* (5, 97) (1913-1937)

Groove-stem Indian plaintain [Groovestem Indian plaintain] - *Arnoglossum plantagineum* Raf. (50) (present)

Groseille à maquereaux (French "mackerel currant") - *Ribes uva-crispa* L. var. *sativum* DC. (110) (1886)

Groseille d'outre mer (French) - *Ribes rubrum* L. (46) (1879)

Groseiller (French) - *Ribes* L. (8) (1785)

Groseiller à feuilles d'aube-épine (French) - *Ribes oxyacanthoides* L. (8) (1785)

Groseiller à fruit hérisssé (French) - *Ribes cynosbati* L. (8) (1785)

Groseiller de Pensylvanie à fruit noir (French) - *Ribes americanum* Mill. (8) (1785)

Groseillier d'outremer (French "currant from beyond the seas") - *Ribes rubrum* L. (46) (1879)

Gross blüthige Kornel (German) - *Cornus florida* L. (158) (1900)

Gross Kalmie (German) - *Kalmia latifolia* L. (6) (1892)

Grosser Wegerich (German) - *Plantago major* L. (158) (1900)

Grosser Wegetritt (German) - *Plantago major* L. (6) (1892)

Grosses Löwenmaul (German) - *Antirrhinum majus* L. (158) (1900)

Ground almond - *Cyperus esculentus* L. (158) (1900)

Ground bean - *Amphicarpaea bracteata* (L.) Fern. (105) (1932)

Ground bur-nut [Ground bur nut, Ground burnut] - *Tribulus terrestris* L. (5, 72, 97, 156) (1907-1937)

Ground cedar - *Juniperus horizontalis* Moench (108) (1878)

Ground centaury - *Frasera caroliniensis* Walt. (156) (1923), *Polygala nuttallii* Torr & Gray. (5, 92) (1876-1913)

Ground century - *Frasera caroliniensis* Walt. (64) (1907)

Ground clematis - *Clematis recta* L. (138) (1923)

Ground goldenrod [Ground golden-rod] - *Solidago mollis* Bartl. (5, 93, 156) (1913-1936)

Ground goldflower [Ground gold-flower] - *Pityopsis falcata* (Pursh) Nutt. (156) (1923)

Ground hele [Ground-hele, Ground heel] - *Veronica officinalis* L. (5, 75, 92, 156, 158) (1876-1923)

Ground hemlock - *Taxus baccata* L. (10, 29) (1818-1869), *Taxus brevifolia* Nutt. (101) (1905), *Taxus canadensis* Willd. (2, 19, 92, 109) (1840-1949)

Ground honeysuckle - *Lotus corniculatus* L. (5, 156, 158) (1900–1923)

Ground indigo-bush amorpha [Ground indigobush amorpha] - *Amorpha fruticosa* L. (155) (1942)

Ground ivy [Ground-ivy] - *Gaultheria procumbens* L. (7) (1828), *Glechoma hederacea* L. (49, 63, 80, 82, 92, 106, 107, 109, 138, 156) (1671-1949), *Glechoma* L. (1, 158) (1900-1932), *Nepeta cataria* L. (157) (1929), *Passiflora incarnata* L. (156) (1923)

Ground juniper - *Juniperus horizontalis* Moench (46) (1879)

Ground laurel - *Epigaea repens* L. (1, 2, 5, 6, 49, 53, 58, 92, 106, 156) (1869-1932)

Ground lily - *Trillium cernuum* L. (5, 7, 156, 158) (1828-1923), *Trillium erectum* L. (6, 49, 92) (1876-1892), *Trillium grandiflorum* (Michx.) Salisb. (156) (1923), *Trillium sessile* L. (58) (1869)

Ground moss - *Polytrichum juniperinum* Hedw. (50, 92) (1876–present)

Ground pea [Ground-pea, Ground peas] - *Apios americana* Medik. (38, 74, 156) (1820-1923) Northeastern US, *Arachis hypogaea* L. (73) (1892) KY

Ground thyme - *Thymus praecox* Opiz subsp. *arcticus* (Dur.) Jalas (possibly) (7) (1828)

Ground vine [Ground-vine] - *Linnaea borealis* L. (5, 7, 92, 156, 158) (1828-1923)

Ground willow - *Salix arctica* Pallas (5) (1913)

Ground-apple [Ground apple] - *Anthemis* L. (92) (1876), *Apios americana* Medik. (35) (1806), *Chamaemelum nobile* (L.) All.

Ground-artichoke [Ground artichoke] - *Helianthus* L. (1) (1932)

Ground-ash [Ground ash] - *Aegopodium podagraria* L. (107, 156) (1919-1923), *Angelica sylvestris* L. (107) (1919)

Groundberry [Ground-berry, Ground berry] - *Gaultheria procumbens* L. (5, 7, 92, 156) (1828-1923), *Mitchella repens* L. (34) (1834)

Groundbroom - *Hypericum gentianoides* (L.) Britton, Sterns & Poggenb. (7) (1828)

Ground-burnut [Ground but nut, Ground burnut] - *Tribulus terrestris* L. (5, 72, 97, 156) (1907-1937)

Ground-cedar [Groundcedar, Ground cedar] - *Hudsonia tomentosa* Nutt. (5, 156, 158) (1900-1923), *Lycopodium complanatum* L. (5, 50, 73, 138, 158) (1892–present)

Ground-cherry [Ground cherry, Groundcherry] - *Physalis cinerascens* (Dunal) A.S. Hitchc. var. *cinerascens* (4) (1986), *Physalis lanceolata* Michx. (80, 114) (1894-1932), *Physalis angulata* L. (107) (1919), *Physalis cinerascens* (Dunal) A.S. Hitchc. var. *cinerascens* (4) (1986), *Physalis heterophylla* Nees (37, 98, 121) (1919-1977), *Physalis hispida* (Waterfall) Cronq. (3) (1977), *Physalis* L. (1, 2, 4, 7, 10, 50, 63, 93, 109, 138, 145, 155, 156, 158) (1818–present), *Physalis lanceolata* Michx. (80, 114) (1894-1913), *Physalis longifolia* Nutt. var. *longifolia* (3) (1977), *Physalis longifolia* Nutt. var. *subglabrata* (Mackenzie & Bush) Cronq. (3) (1977), *Physalis peruviana* L. (85, 107) (1919-1932), *Physalis pubescens* L. (19, 107, 156) (1840-1923), *Physalis virginiana* Mill. (156) (1923), *Physalis virginiana* Mill. var. *virginiana* (3) (1977), *Physalis viscosa* L. (19, 49, 92) (1840-1898), *Prunus fruticosa* Pallas (109) (1949)

Ground-festoon - *Lycopodium complanatum* L. (158) (1900)

Ground-holly [Ground holly] - *Arctostaphylos uva-ursi* (L.) Spreng. (156) (1923), *Chimaphila maculata* (L.) Pursh (7) (1828), *Chimaphila umbellata* (L.) Bart. (5, 6, 49, 53, 58, 92, 156, 158) (1869-1923), *Gaultheria procumbens* L. (7) (1828)

Ground-hurts - *Vaccinium* L. (73) (1892) Newfoundland, any low species

Groundie-swallow [Groundie swallow] - *Senecio vulgaris* L. (92, 156, 158) (1898-1923)

Ground-lemon [Ground lemon] - *Podophyllum peltatum* L. (5, 7, 64, 92, 156, 157, 158) (1828-1929)

Ground-maple [Ground maple] - *Heuchera villosa* Michx. (possibly) (7, 92, 156) (1828-1923)

Ground-moss [Ground moss] - *Cyperus strigosus* L. (156) (1923), *Hudsonia tomentosa* Nutt. (5, 156, 158) (1900-1923)

Groundnut [Ground-nut, Ground nut, Ground nutts] - *Apios americana* Medik. (2, 3, 4, 5, 46, 50, 72, 85, 93, 97, 103, 107, 109, 114, 121, 131, 156) (1870–present), *Apios* Fabr. (2, 4, 50, 155) (1895–present), *Arachis hypogaea* L. (7, 14, 55, 73, 92, 109, 155) (1828-1942), *Claytonia* L. (1, 93) (1932-1936), *Claytonia lanceolata* Pall. ex Pursh (101) (1905) MT, *Erigenia bulbosa* (Michx.) Nutt. (156) (1923), *Glycine* Willd. (93, 155) (1936-1942), *Panax trifolius* L. (2, 5, 76, 156) (1895-1923)

Groundnut peavine - *Lathyrus tuberosus* L. (155) (1942)

Ground-oak [Ground oak] - *Licania michauxii* Prance (106) (1930)

Groundpine [Ground-pine, Ground pine] - *Ajuga chamaepitys* (L.) Schreb. (92) (1876), *Ajuga* L. (10, 158) (1818-1900), *Hypericum gentianoides* (L.) Britton, Sterns & Poggenb. (5, 7, 156, 177, 184, 187) (1762-1932), *Lycopodium clavatum* L. (5, 6) (1892-1913), *Lycopodium complanatum* L. (5, 19, 92, 158) (1840-1913), *Lycopodium dendroideum* Michx. (4, 10, 187) (1818-1986), *Lycopodium* L. (1, 7) (1828-1932), *Lycopodium obscurum* L. (3, 5, 40, 131, 138, 155, 158) (1899-1977), *Lycopodium tristachyum* Pursh (5) (1913), *Selaginella arenicola* Underwood subsp. *riddellii* (Van Eselt.) R. Tryon (124) (1937), *Teucrium canadense* L. (5, 158) (1900-1913)

Groundpine bugle - *Ajuga chamaepitys* (L.) Schreb. (155) (1942)

Ground-pink [Ground pink] - *Phlox subulata* L. (2, 5, 63, 86, 108, 109, 156) (1878-1949)

Groundplum [Ground-plum, Ground plum, Ground plums] - *Astragalus crassicarpus* Nutt. (4, 40, 72, 121, 127, 131, 158) (1899-1986), *Astragalus crassicarpus* Nutt. var. *berlandieri* Barneby (156, 158) (1900-1923), *Astragalus crassicarpus* Nutt. var. *crassicarpus* (2, 47, 63, 85, 92, 98, 101, 107, 108, 114, 156) (1852-1932), *Astragalus* L. (103) (1870), *Astragalus plattensis* Nutt. (3) (1977)

Ground-plum milkvetch [Groundplum milkvetch] - *Astragalus crassicarpus* Nutt. (50, 155) (1942–present), *Astragalus crassicarpus* Nutt. var. *berlandieri* Barneby (50) (present), *Astragalus crassicarpus* Nutt. var. *crassicarpus* (50) (present)

Ground-potato [Ground potato] - *Pediomelum esculentum* (Pursh) Rydb. (35) (1806) William Clark

Ground-raspberry [Ground raspberry] - *Hydrastis canadensis* L. (5, 6, 7, 49, 59, 64, 92, 156) (1828-1923)

Groundsel [Groundsell] - *Baccharis* L. (158) (1900), *Baccharis salicina* Torr. & Gray (157) (1929), *Erechtites hieraciifolia* (L.) Raf. ex DC. var. *hieraciifolia* (187) (1818), *Packera aurea* (L.) A.& D. Löve (6, 58) (1869-1892), *Packera plattensis* (Nutt.) W.A. Weber & A. Löve (148) (1939) CO, *Senecio eremophilus* Richards (85) (1932), *Senecio integerrimus* Nutt. (148) (1939), *Senecio integerrimus* Nutt. var. *exaltatus* (Nutt.) Cronq. (85) (1932), *Senecio* L. (1, 2, 4, 7, 93, 106, 109, 138, 155, 156, 158, 162, 184) (1793-1986), *Senecio riddellii* Torr. & Gray (148) (1939), *Senecio vulgaris* L. (4, 19, 46, 92, 158) (1649-1986) accidentally introduced at least by 1671

Groundsel balsam - *Packera paupercula* (Michx.) A.& D. Löve (158) (1900)

Groundsel bush [Groundselbush, Groundsel-bush] - *Baccharis halimifolia* L. (5, 109, 138, 156) (1913-1949)

Groundsel tree [Groundsel-tree] - *Baccharis halimifolia* L. (5, 7, 19, 92, 122, 124, 156) (1828-1937)

Groundsel tree [Groundsel-tree] - *Baccharis* L. (1, 10, 93) (1818-1936)

Groundsmoke - *Gayophytum* Juss. (50, 155) (1942–present)

Ground-squirrel pea [Ground squirrel pea] - *Jeffersonia diphylla* (L.) Pers. (5, 7, 49, 64, 92, 156) (1828-1923)

Groundstar [Ground star] - *Geastrum* Pers. (7) (1828)

Ground-willow [Ground willow] - *Persicaria amphibia* (L.) Delarbre (5) (1913), *Polygonum amphibium* L. (156, 157, 158) (1900-1929)

Grouse whortleberry - *Vaccinium scoparium* Leiberg (50, 155) (1942–present)

Grouseberry [Grouse-berry, Grouse berry] - *Gaultheria procumbens* L. (5, 6, 7, 92, 156) (1828-1923), *Vaccinium scoparium* Leiberg (1, 3, 4, 85) (1932-1986), *Viburnum opulus* L. (156) (1923) no longer in use by 1923

Grove bluegrass - *Poa alsodes* Gray (50, 155) (1942–present)

Grove meadow grass - *Poa alsodes* Gray (5) (1913)

Grove sandwort - *Moehringia lateriflora* (L.) Fenzl (4) (1986)

Grove thorn - *Crataegus lucorum* Sarg. (5) (1913)

Grove woodrush - *Luzula multiflora* (Ehrh.) Lej. (155) (1942)

Grownswell - *Senecio vulgaris* L. (179) (1526)

Gruber's thorn - *Crataegus iracunda* Beadle (5) (1913)

Grub-root - *Chamaelirium luteum* (L.) A. Gray (156) (1923)

Grüne Minze (German) - *Mentha spicata* L. (158) (1900)

Grüner Germer (German) - *Veratrum viride* Ait. (6) (1892)

Grundheil (German) - *Veronica serpyllifolia* L. (158) (1900)

Grundy-swallow [Grundy swallow] - *Packera aurea* (L.) A.& D. Löve (5, 156, 158) (1900-1923)

Grune Niesswurz (German) - *Helleborus viridis* L. (6) (1892)

Grunsel - *Taraxacum officinale* G.H. Weber ex Wiggers (156, 157, 158) (1900-1929)

Gruscha (Russian) - *Pyrus communis* L. (110) (1886)

Gthebe moŋkoŋ (Osage, vomit medicine) - *Phytolacca americana* L. (121) (1918?-1970?)

Gthoŋpa (Osage) - *Prunus virginiana* L. (121) (1918?-1970?)

Guadalupe cucumber [Guadaloupe cucumber] - *Melothria pendula* L. (50) (present)

Guadalupe cypress - *Cupressus forbesii* Jepson (109, 138) (1923-1949) found on Guadalupe Isl. Mex.

Guadalupe inga [Guadaloupe inga] - *Pithecellobium unguis-cati* (L.) Benth. (20) (1857)

Guadalupe naias [Guadaloupe naias] - *Najas guadalupensis* (Spreng.) Magnus (5, 93, 97, 120) (1913-1938)

Guaiac - *Guaiacum officinale* L. (92) (1876)

Guaiacan - *Diospyros virginiana* L. (7) (1828)

Guaiacana - *Diospyros* L. (8) (1785)

Guaiacum - *Guaiacum officinale* L. (92) (1876)

Guajacana - *Diospyros virginiana* L. (174, 177, 189) (1753-1767)

Guajava or Guajavos (Peru & San Domingo) - *Psidium guajava* L. (110) (1886)

Guajillo - *Acacia berlandieri* Benth. (122, 124) (1937) TX

Guama - *Inga laurina* (Sw.) Willd. (138) (1923)

Guamachil - *Pithecellobium dulce* (Roxb.) Benth. (138) (1923)

Guamis (Spanish) - *Larrea* Ort. (13) (1849) Mexico

Guamuchil - *Pithecellobium dulce* (Roxb.) Benth. (107) (1919)

Guanabana - *Annona muricata* L. (109, 155) (1942-1949)

Guatemote (Spanish) - *Baccharis glutinosa* Pers. (106) (1930)

Guava - *Psidium guajava* L. (92, 106, 109, 110, 138) (1876-1949), *Psidium* L. (138) (1923)

Guava (Spanish) - *Prosopis laevigata* (Willd.) M.C.Johnst. (107) (1919)

Guayabos - *Psidium guajava* L. (107) (1740)

Guayac - *Guaiacum officinale* L. (7) (1828)

Guayacan - *Guaiacum angustifolium* Engelm. (124) (1937)

Guaymochil - *Pithecellobium dulce* (Roxb.) Benth. (109) (1949)

Guayule - *Parthenium argentatum* Gray (109, 122) (1937-1949)

Guayva - *Psidium guajava* L. (92) (1876)

Guaza - *Cannabis sativa* L. (6, 53) (1892–1922)

Gube (Omaha-Ponca) - *Celtis occidentalis* L. (37) (1919)

Guelder-maple [Guelder maple] - *Viburnum acerifolium* L. (92) (1876)

Guelder-rose [Guelder rose] - *Viburnum opulus* L. (19, 107, 178) (1596-1919), *Viburnum opulus* L. var. *opulus* (92, 109) (1876-1949)

Guelder-rose-leaf spiraea [Guelder rose-leaved spiraea] - *Physocarpus opulifolius* (L.) Maxim. var. *opulifolius* (8) (1785)

Gueldres-rose - *Viburnum opulus* L. (158) (1900)

Guele de lion (French) - *Antirrhinum majus* L. (158) (1900)

Guele de loup (French) - *Antirrhinum majus* L. (158) (1900)

Gui (French) - *Viscum* L. (8) (1785)

Gui rouge (French) - *Phoradendron rubrum* (L.) Griseb. (8) (1785)

Guiana cashew - *Anacardium excelsum* (Bertero & Balb. ex Kunth) Skeels (155) (1942)

Guiana-chestnut - *Pachira aquatica* Aubl. (138) (1923)

Guild tree [Guild-tree] - *Berberis vulgaris* L. (157, 158) (1900-1929)

Guilfoyle's polyscias [Guilfoyle polyscias] - *Polyscias guilfoylei* (Bull ex Cogn. & E. March.) Bailey (138) (1923)

Guilty-cup [Guilty cup] - *Ranunculus acris* L. (157, 158) (1900-1929)

Guimauve (French) - *Althaea* L. (165) (1768), *Althaea officinalis* L. (55, 158) (1900-1911)

Guinea corn [Guinea-corn] - *Sorghum bicolor* (L.) Moench (56, 92) (1876-1901), *Sorghum bicolor* (L.) Moench subsp. *bicolor* (14, 66, 87, 184) (1793-1903), *Sorghum halepense* (L.) Pers. (45) (1896), *Zea mays L.* (110) (1886)

Guinea grass [Guineagrass, Guinea-grass] - *Sorghum halepense* (L.) Pers. (45, 88, 158) (1885-1900), *Urochloa maxima* (Jacq.) R. Webster (7, 56, 87, 92, 109, 110, 122, 163) (1828-1949)

Guinea pepper - *Capsicum annuum* L. (19, 92, 107) (1840-1919), *Capsicum annuum* L. var. *annuum* (53) (1922)

Guinea sorrel - *Hibiscus sabdariffa* L. (92) (1876)

Guinea squash - *Solanum melongena* L. (156) (1923)

Guinea wheat - *Zea mays* L. (107, 158) (1586–1900)

Guinea-hen flower [Guinea hen flower] - *Fritillaria* L. (158) (1900) no longer in use by 1900

Guirila - *Chrysanthemum coccineum* Willd. (92) (1876)

Gulden klee (German) - *Hepatica nobilis* Schreb. (46) (1879)

Gulden-rod - *Solidago canadensis* L. (177) (1762)

Gulf black willow - *Salix nigra* Marsh. (155) (1942)

Gulf Coast amaranth - *Gomphrena nealleyi* Coult. & Fisher (124) (1937)

Gulf Coast cedar - *Juniperus barbadensis* var. *australis* (Endl.) ined. (124) (1937)

Gulf Coast guajillo - *Havardia pallens* (Benth.) Britt. & Rose (124) (1937) TX

Gulf Coast pea - *Centrosema virginianum* (L.) Benth. (124) (1937) TX

Gulf Coast waterhemp [Gulfcoast waterhemp] - *Amaranthus australis* (Gray) Sauer (155) (1942)

Gulf cockspur - *Echinochloa crus-pavonis* (H.B.K.) Schult. var. *macera* (Wieg.) Gould (155) (1942)

Gulf cockspur grass - *Echinochloa crus-pavonis* (H.B.K.) Schult. var. *macera* (Wieg.) Gould (50) (present)

Gulf guajillo tenaza - *Havardia pallens* (Benth.) Britt. & Rose (122) (1937) TX

Gulf love grass [Gulf lovegrass] - *Eragrostis pectinacea* (Michx.) Nees ex Steud. var. *miserrima* (Fourn.) J. Reeder (155) (1942)

Gulfweed [Gulf weed] - *Sargassum natans* (L.) Gaillon (41, 92, 181) (~1678-1876)

Gullkulla (Swedish) - *Trifolium aureum* Pollich (46) (1879)

Gum anime - *Hymenaea courbaril* L. (92) (1876)

Gum Arabic tree - *Acacia nilotica* (L.) Willd. ex Delile (50) (present)

Gum bully - *Sideroxylon lanuginosum* Michx. subsp. *oblongifolium* (Nutt.) T.D. Pennington (50) (present)

Gum elastic - *Sideroxylon lanuginosum* Michx. (5) (1913)

Gum elemi tree - *Amyris elemifera* L. (165) (1807), *Amyris* P. Br. (167) (1814)

Gum or Gum tree [Gum-tree] - *Eucalyptus* L'Hér. (106, 109) (1930-1949), *Liquidambar styraciflua* L. (27) (1811), *Nyssa aquatica* L. (20) (1857), *Nyssa sylvatica* Marsh. (18, 35) (1805-1806)

Gum plant [Gumplant, Gum-plant] - *Grindelia camporum* Greene var. *camporum* (52, 54, 69, 75) (1903-1919), *Grindelia squarrosa* (Pursh) Dunal (85, 156) (1923-1932), *Grindelia* Willd. (1, 156, 158) (1900-1932), *Silphium laciniatum* L. (156) (1923), *Silphium terebinthinaceum* Jacq. (156) (1923), *Symphytum officinale* L. (5, 64, 156) (1907-1923) no longer in use by 1923

Gum rockrose - *Cistus ladaniferus* L. (138) (1923)

Gum succory - *Chondrilla juncea* L. (5, 156) (1913-1923)

Gum wax - *Liquidambar styraciflua* L. (49) (1898)

Gumara (New Zealand) - *Ipomoea batatas* (L.) Lam. (110) (1886)

Gumbo - *Abelmoschus esculentus* (L.) Moench (15, 107, 109, 138) (1895-1949)

Gumbo evening-primrose [Gumbo evening primrose] - *Oenothera caespitosa* Nutt. (4) (1986), *Oenothera caespitosa* Nutt. subsp. *caespitosa* (4) (1986)

Gumbo limbo - *Bursera simaruba* (L.) Sargent (15) (1895)

Gumbo-lily [Gumbo lily] - *Mentzelia decapetala* (Pursh ex Sims) Urban & Gilg ex Gilg (156) (1923), *Oenothera caespitosa* Nutt. (possibly) (85, 127) (1932-1933) name widely used "much to writer's disapproval" (127), *Oenothera caespitosa* Nutt. subsp. *caespitosa* (3, 4) (1977-1986)

Gum-elastic - *Sideroxylon lanuginosum* Michx. (106, 156) (1923-1930)

Gummi Copal - *Rhus copallinum* L. (177) (1762)

Gummier (French) - *Bursera simaruba* (L.) Sargent (20) (1857)

Gummy love grass [Gummy lovegrass] - *Eragrostis curtipedicellata* Buckl. (3, 50, 155) (1942–present)

Gumweed [Gum weed] - *Grindelia squarrosa* (Pursh) Dunal (95, 98, 106, 114, 145, 148) (1894-1939), *Grindelia* Willd. (4, 50, 93, 146, 155) (1936–present), *Silphium laciniatum* L. (37) (1919)

Gumwood [Gum-wood] - *Eucalyptus* L'Hér. (92) (1876), *Liquidambar styraciflua* L. (177) (1762)

Gunbright [Gun bright, Gun-bright] - *Equisetum hyemale* L. (5, 78, 92, 158) (1876-1913) ME, said to have been used by Indians to polish guns

Gundelreben (German) - *Glechoma hederacea* L. (158) (1900)

Gunebo-lily [Gunebo lily] - *Mentzelia decapetala* (Pursh ex Sims) Urban & Gilg ex Gilg (5, 158) (1900-1913), *Mentzelia laevicaulis* (Dougl. ex Hook.) Torr. & Gray (76) (1896) ND

Gû'nĭgwalĭ'skĭ (Cherokee, it becomes discolored when bruised) - *Scutellaria lateriflora* L. (102) (1886) Red juice comes out of stem when bruised or chewed

Gunjah - *Cannabis sativa* L. (6, 14, 53) (1882–1922), *Cannabis sativa* L. subsp. *indica* (Lam.) E. Small & Cronq. (92) (1876) dried flower branches

Gunnera - *Gunnera* L. (138) (1923)

Gunnison's mariposa [Gunnison mariposa] - *Calochortus gunnisonii* S. Wats. (155) (1942)

Gunnison's mariposa lily - *Calochortus gunnisonii* S. Wats. (5, 50, 93) (1913–present), *Calochortus gunnisonii* S. Wats. var. *gunnisonii* (50) (present)

Gurke (German) - *Cucumis sativus* L. (110) (1886)

Gutter tree [Gutter-tree] - *Cornus sanguinea* L. (92) (1876), *Cornus sericea* L. subsp. *sericea* (5, 156, 158) (1900–1923)

Gutweed [Gut-weed] - *Sonchus arvensis* L. (5, 158) (1900–1913)

Guzigwa'kominaga'wûnj (Chippewa, thorny wood) - *Amelanchier canadensis* (L.) Medik. (possibly) (40) (1928)

Gwinis-du (Breton "black corn") - *Fagopyrum esculentum* Moench (110) (1886)

Gylofre - *Dianthus caryophyllus* L. (179) (1526)

Gyp grass - *Bouteloua breviseta* Vasey (163) (1852)

Gyp phacelia - *Phacelia integrifolia* Torr. (3, 4) (1977-1986)

Gyphill grass [Gyphill-grass] - *Erioneuron pilosum* (Buckl.) Nash (119) (1938) OK

Gypsophill [Gypsophila, Gypsophyll] - *Gypsophila* L. (138, 155, 158) (1900-1942), *Gypsophila paniculata* L. (158) (1900)

Gypsum phacelia - *Phacelia integrifolia* Torr. (50) (present)

Gyromia - *Medeola virginiana* L. (46) (1879)

H

Haar (German near Salzburg) - *Linum usitatissimum* L. (110) (1886) from German for thread or hair

Haarige Himbeere - *Rubus flagellaris* Willd. (186) (1814)

Habascon - *Angelica lucida* L. (46) (1879)

Habichtskraut (German) - *Hieracium* L. (158) (1900)

Hackberry [Hack-berry] or Hackberry tree - *Celtis* L. (1, 4, 50, 7, 10, 82, 93, 106, 109, 138, 155) (1923–present), *Celtis laevigata* Willd. var. *reticulata* (Torr.) L. Benson (35, 65, 149, 153) (1806-1931), *Celtis occidentalis* L. (3, 4, 5, 6, 9, 14, 17, 20, 27, 28, 34, 35, 37, 44, 46, 82, 85, 92, 93, 95, 97, 107, 112, 113, 121, 130, 131, 135, 138, 156, 158) (1796-1986), *Celtis occidentalis* L. var. *occidentalis* (112) (1937), *Celtis tenuifolia* Nutt. (12) (1821)

Hackel's fescue - *Festuca dasyclada* Hack. ex Beal (94) (1901)

Hackmack - *Larix laricina* (Du Roi.) Koch. (5) (1913)

Hackmatack [Hack-matack, Hacmatack] - *Juniperus communis* L. (5, 73, 157, 158) (1892-1929) Ipswich Mass, *Larix laricina* (Du Roi.) Koch. (5, 19, 46, 58, 92, 109) (1840-1949), *Larix* Mill (7) (1828), *Thuja occidentalis* L. (6) (1892)

Hackmetack - *Larix laricina* (Du Roi.) Koch. (49, 92) (1876-1879)

H'ade wathazhinde (Ponca) - *Panicum virgatum* L. (37) (1830)

H'ade-sathe (Omaha-Ponca, sour herb) - *Oxalis stricta* L. (37) (1919), *Oxalis violacea* L. (37) (1919)

H'ade-zhide (Omaha-Ponca, red hay) - *Andropogon gerardii* Vitman (37) (1830)

Hadoga (Osage) - *Urtica dioica* L. subsp. *gracilis* (Aiton) Seland. (121) (1918?-1970?)

Hafer (German) - *Avena sativa* L. (158) (1900)

Hafer corn [Hafer-corn] - *Avena sativa* L. (158) (1900)

Haferschlehen (German) - *Prunus domestica* L. var. *insititia* (L.) Fiori & Paoletti (110) (1886)

Hag taper - *Verbascum thapsus* L. (14, 156) (1882-1923) no longer in use by 1923

Hagberry [Hag-berry] - *Celtis occidentalis* L. (19) (1840), *Prunus padus* L. (92, 107) (1876-1919)

Hagweed - *Cytisus scoparius* (L.) Link (5) (1913)

Hahnenfuss (German) - *Ranunculus repens* L. (6) (1892)

Hah'-ñi (Kiwomi Keres) - *Pinus* L. (132) (1855)

Hah-wib' (Chemehuevi Shoshonee) - *Zea mays* L. (132) (1855)

Hailweed [Hail weed] - *Cuscuta epithymum* (L.) L. (5) (1913)

Hainberry - *Rubus idaeus* L. (158) (1900)

Hair club-rush - *Eleocharis acicularis* (L.) Roemer & J.A. Schultes (66) (1903)

Hair fern - *Adiantum pedatum* L. (157, 158) (1900-1929)

Hair grass [Hairgrass, Hair-grass] - *Agrostis hyemalis* (Walt.) Britton, Sterns & Poggenb. (111, 140, 143) (1915-1944), *Agrostis scabra* Willd. (56, 66, 90, 92) (1885-1903), *Aira elegans* Willd. ex Kunth (122) (1937), *Aira* L. (10, 66, 92, 155, 164) (1793-1942), *Deschampsia* Beauv. (1, 50, 152, 155) (1912–present), *Deschampsia caespitosa* (L.) Beauv. (45, 85, 87, 90) (1884-1932), *Deschampsia flexuosa* (L.) Trin. var *flexuosa* (19, 50) (1840–present), *Muhlenbergia capillaris* (Lam.) Trin. (3, 66) (1903-1977), *Sporobolus airoides* (Torr.) Torr. (93, 94) (1936)

Hair-awn muhly [Hairawn muhly] - *Muhlenbergia capillaris* (Lam.) Trin. (50, 155) (1942–present)

Hairbell [Hair bell, Hair-bell] - *Campanula rotundifolia* L. (19, 92, 158) (1840-1900)

Hairbread [Hair bread] - *Bouteloua curtipendula* (Michx.) Torr. var. *curtipendula* (19) (1840)

Hair-cap moss - *Polytrichum juniperinum* Hedw. (19, 49, 52, 54, 57, 58, 61) (1840-1917)

Hair-cap moss [Hair cap moss] - *Polytrichum juniperinum* Hedw. (92) (1876)

Hair-grass dropseed - *Sporobolus airoides* (Torr.) Torr. (5) (1913)

Hairhound [Hair-hound] - *Ballota nigra* L. (5, 156, 158) (1900-1923)

Hairif - *Galium aparine* L. (5, 156, 158) (1900-1923) no longer in use by 1923

Hair-like eragrostis - *Eragrostis trichodes* (Nutt.) Wood (56, 72) (1901-1907)

Hair-like fimbristylis - *Bulbostylis capillaris* (L.) Kunth ex C.B. Clarke subsp. *capillaris* (66) (1903)

Hair-like love grass [Hair-like love-grass] - *Eragrostis trichodes* (Nutt.) Wood (5, 119) (1913-1938)

Hair-like sedge - *Carex capillaris* L. (5, 50) (1913–present)

Hair-like stenophyllus - *Bulbostylis capillaris* (L.) Kunth ex C.B. Clarke subsp. *capillaris* (5, 72) (1907-1913)

Hair-mouth moss - *Ditrichum pallidum* (Hedw.) Hampe (19) (1840)

Hair-panicle meadow grass [Hair-panicled meadow grass] - *Eragrostis capillaris* (L.) Nees (66, 187) (1818-1903)

Hair-sedge [Hairsedge] - *Bulbostylis* Kunth (50) (present)

Hair-spine prickly-pear [Hairspine pricklypear] - *Opuntia polyacantha* Haw. var. *polyacantha* (50) (present)

Hair-stalk panic grass [Hair-stalked panic grass] - *Panicum capillare* L. (66, 87, 90) (1885-1903)

Hair-stamen - *Trichostema* L. (167) (1900)

Hairweed [Hair weed, Hair-weed] - *Cuscuta epithymum* (L.) L. (5, 156) (1913-1923) no longer in use by 1923

Hairy aeschynomene - *Aeschynomene americana* L. (165) (1768)

Hairy ageratum - *Ageratum conyzoides* L. (165) (1768)

Hairy agrimonia - *Agrimonia eupatoria* L. (131) (1899) SD

Hairy Allegheny goat's-bread [Hairy Alleghany goatsbread] - *Aruncus dioicus* (Walt.) Fern. var. *pubescens* (Rydb.) Fern. (155) (1942)

Hairy alumroot - *Heuchera villosa* Michx. (138) (1923)

Hairy amaranth - *Amaranthus retroflexus* L. (165) (1768)

Hairy American bramble - *Rubus flagellaris* Willd. (186) (1814)

Hairy American yellow lady's slipper - *Cypripedium parviflorum* Salisb. var. *pubescens* (Willd.) Knight (42) (1814)

Hairy angelica - *Angelica venenosa* (Greenway) Fern. (5, 138, 155, 156) (1913-1942)

Hairy arnica - *Arnica mollis* Hook (5, 155) (1913-1942)

Hairy arrowleaf [Hairy arrow-leaf] - *Sagittaria latifolia* Willd. (5) (1913)

Hairy bastard saffron [Hairie bastard saffron] - *Cnicus benedictus* L. (possibly) (178) (1526)

Hairy beardtongue [Hairy beard tongue] - *Penstemon hirsutus* (L.) Willd. (5, 72) (1907-1913)

Hairy bedstraw - *Galium pilosum* Aiton (3, 4, 5, 50, 97, 122, 155) (1913–present), *Galium pilosum* Aiton var. *puncticulosum* (Michx.) Torr. & Gray (50) (present)

Hairy bindweed - *Convolvulus arvensis* L. (93) (1936)

Hairy bittercress [Hairy bitter-cress, Hairy bitter cress] - *Cardamine hirsuta* L. (5, 72, 93, 157) (1900-1936)

Hairy blephilia - *Blephilia hirsuta* (Pursh) Benth. (5, 72, 97) (1907-1937)

Hairy bracken fern [Hairy brackenfern] - *Pteridium aquilinum* (L.) Kuhn var. *pubescens* Underwood (50) (present)

Hairy brome - *Bromus commutatus* Schrad. (155) (1942), *Bromus ramosus* Huds. (50) (present) TX

Hairy brome grass - *Bromus ciliatus* L. (5) (1913), *Bromus racemosus* L. (5) (1913)

Hairy bush-clover [Hairy bush clover] - *Lespedeza hirta* (L.) Hornem. (5, 72, 97) (1907-1937)

Hairy buttercup - *Ranunculus sardous* Crantz. (possibly) (5, 50) (1913–present)

Hairy butterwort - *Pinguicula villosa* L. (5) (1913)

Hairy button snakeroot [Hairy button snake root, Hairy button snake-root] - *Liatris pycnostachya* Michx. (122, 124, 156) (1923-1937), *Liatris pycnostachya* Michx. var. *pycnostachya* (5, 93) (1913-1936)

Hairy chamaesaracha - *Chamaesaracha coniodes* (Moric. ex Dunal) Britton (5, 97) (1913-1937)

Hairy cheat - *Bromus hordeaceus* L. (85) (1932), *Bromus hordeaceus* L. subsp. *hordeaceus* (163) (1852)

Hairy chess - *Bromus commutatus* Schrad. (122) (1937)

Hairy chestnut - *Castanea mollissima* Blume (138) (1923)

Hairy clematis - *Clematis hirsutissima* Pursh (50) (present)

Hairy coreopsis - *Coreopsis pubescens* Ell. (138) (1923) SD

Hairy corn salad [Hairy cornsalad] - *Valerianella amarella* (Lindheimer ex Engelm.) Krok (50) (present)

Hairy crabgrass - *Digitaria sanguinalis* (L.) Scop. (50, 140, 155) (1942–present)

Hairy crazyweed - *Oxytropis monticola* Gray (155) (1942)

Hairy creeper - *Parthenocissus quinquefolia* (L.) Planch. (138) (1923)

Hairy creeping love grass [Hairy creeping love-grass] - *Neeragrostis reptans* (Michx.) Nicora (5, 93, 99, 119) (1913-1938)

Hairy cress - *Cardamine hirsuta* L. (107) (1919)

Hairy cup grass [Hairy cupgrass] - *Eriochloa villosa* (Thunb.) Kunth (50, 155) (1942–present)

Hairy dicksonia - *Dennstaedtia punctilobula* (Michx.) T. Moore (5) (1913)

Hairy disporum - *Disporum lanuginosum* (Michx.) Nichols (3) (1977)

Hairy dogwood [Hairy dog wood] - *Cornus rugosa* Lam. (42) (1814)

Hairy dozedaisy - *Aphanostephus ramosissimus* DC. (50) (present)

Hairy dropseed - *Blepharoneuron tricholepis* (Torr.) Nash (122) (1937), *Muhlenbergia andina* (Nutt.) A.S. Hitchc. (5) (1913)

Hairy evening-primrose - *Oenothera villosa* Thunb. (50) (present)

Hairy eyebright - *Euphrasia nemorosa* (Pers.) Wallr. (5) (1913)

Hairy false golden-aster [Hairy false goldenaster] - *Heterotheca villosa* (Pursh) Shinners (50) (present)

Hairy feverfew - *Parthenium integrifolium* L. var. *hispidum* (Raf.) Mears (122) (1937)

Hairy figwort - *Scrophularia marilandica* L. (97) (1937)

Hairy fimbristylis - *Fimbristylis puberula* (Michx.) Vahl (5) (1913)

Hairy fimbry - *Fimbristylis puberula* (Michx.) Vahl (50) (present)

Hairy finger grass - *Digitaria sanguinalis* (L.) Scop. (5) (1913)

Hairy five-eyes [Hairy five eyes] - *Chamaesaracha sordida* (Dunal) Gray (3) (1977)

Hairy five-finger - *Potentilla villosa* Pallas ex Pursh (19) (1840)

Hairy Florida maple - *Acer barbatum* Michx. (155) (1942)

Hairy forked nailwort - *Paronychia fastigiata* (Raf.) Fern. (50) (present)

Hairy four-o'clock [Hairy four o'clock] - *Mirabilis hirsuta* (Pursh) MacM. (4, 50, 98) (1926–present)

Hairy fuirena - *Fuirena squarrosa* Michx. (5) (1913)

Hairy gaura - *Gaura villosa* Torr. (3, 4) (1977-1986)

Hairy germander - *Teucrium canadense* L. var. *occidentale* (Gray) McClintock & Epling (5, 72, 93, 97, 131, 155) (1899-1907)

Hairy gold-aster [Hairy goldaster] - *Heterotheca villosa* (Pursh) Shinners var. *villosa* (155) (1942)

Hairy golden-aster [Hairy golden aster] - *Heterotheca villosa* (Pursh) Shinners var. *villosa* (5, 72, 93, 97, 122, 131, 138, 158) (1899–1937)

Hairy goldenrod [Hairy golden-rod] - *Solidago nemoralis* Aiton (5, 72, 93, 97, 155) (1907-1942)

Hairy goose-grass - *Galium pilosum* Aiton var. *puncticulosum* (Michx.) Torr. & Gray (187) (1818)

Hairy grama - *Bouteloua hirsuta* Lag. (1, 3, 50, 65, 85, 116, 119, 121, 122, 134, 140, 152, 155, 163) (1912–present), *Bouteloua hirsuta*

Lag. var. *hirsuta* (50) (present), *Bouteloua hirsuta* Lag. var. *pectinata* (Featherly) Cory (122) (1937), *Bouteloua parryi* (Fourn.) Griffiths (94) (1901)

Hairy grass [Hairy-grass] - *Agrostis hyemalis* (Walt.) Britton, Sterns & Poggenb. (93) (1936)

Hairy hawkbit - *Leontodon hirtus* L. (5) (1913), *Leontodon hispidus* L. subsp. *hispidus* (5) (1913)

Hairy hawkweed [Hairy hawk-weed] - *Hieracium gronovii* L. (5, 97, 156, 158) (1900–1937), *Hieracium longipilum* Torr. (50) (present)

Hairy hawthorn - *Crataegus mollis* Scheele (130) (1895)

Hairy hedge-hyssop [Hairy hedge hyssop] - *Gratiola pilosa* Michx. (5, 122) (1913-1937)

Hairy hedge-nettle [Hairy hedgenettle] - *Stachys pilosa* Nutt. (50) (present)

Hairy heuchera - *Heuchera villosa* Michx. (5) (1913)

Hairy honeysuckle - *Lonicera hirsuta* Eaton (2, 5, 130, 138, 156) (1895-1913)

Hairy huckleberry - *Gaylussacia dumosa* (Andr.) Torr. & Gray (46) (1879)

Hairy laurel - *Kalmia hirsuta* Walt. (5) (1913)

Hairy leafcup - *Smallanthus uvedalius* (L.) Mackenzie ex Small (50) (present)

Hairy lespedeza - *Lespedeza hirta* (L.) Hornem. (3, 4, 50, 155) (1942–present)

Hairy lip fern [Hairy lipfern, Hairy lip-fern] - *Cheilanthes lanosa* (Michx.) D.C.Eat. (3, 5, 50, 86, 97, 122, 155) (1878–present)

Hairy love grass [Hairy love-grass] - *Eragrostis pilosa* (L.) Beauv. (99) (1923)

Hairy ludwigia - *Ludwigia hirtella* Raf. (5, 97) (1913-1937)

Hairy lupine - *Lupinus villosus* Willd. (19) (1840)

Hairy lychnidea - *Phlox pilosa* L. (187) (1818)

Hairy manzanita - *Arctostaphylos columbiana* Piper (155) (1942), *Arctostaphylos tomentosa* (Pursh) Lindl. (106) (1930)

Hairy maple - *Acer barbatum* Michx. (19) (1840)

Hairy marsilea - *Marsilea vestita* Hook. & Grev. (131) (1899)

Hairy meadow grass [Hairy meadow-grass] - *Eragrostis pilosa* (L.) Beauv. (187) (1818)

Hairy mesquite - *Bouteloua hirsuta* Lag. (116) (1958)

Hairy mesquite grass [Hairy mesquite-grass] - *Bouteloua curtipendula* (Michx) Torr. (151) (1896)

Hairy mesquite grass [Hairy mesquite-grass] - *Bouteloua hirsuta* Lag. (5, 56, 72, 119) (1893-1938), *Bouteloua hirsuta* Lag. var. *pectinata* (Featherly) Cory (119) (1938)

Hairy milkweed [Hairy milk weed] - *Asclepias incarnata* L. subsp. *pulchra* (Ehrh. ex Willd.) Woods. (5, 42, 138, 156) (1814–1923) Neb

Hairy mistletoe - *Phoradendron tomentosum* (DC.) Engelmann. ex Gray (4) (1986)

Hairy mock orange [Hairy mockorange] - *Philadelphus hirsutus* Nutt. (2, 138) (1895-1923)

Hairy monkey-flower - *Mimetanthe pilosa* (Benth.) Greene (49) (1898)

Hairy moss - *Polytaenia* DC. (50) (present)

Hairy mountain-mint [Hairy mountain mint] - *Pycnanthemum verticillatum* (Michx.) Pers. var. *pilosum* (Nutt.) Cooperrider (4, 5, 97) (1913-1986)

Hairy muskit - *Bouteloua curtipendula* (Michx) Torr. (66) (1903)

Hairy nama - *Hydrolea quadrivalvis* Walt. (5) (1913)

Hairy nightshade - *Solanum physalifolium* Rusby (3) (1977)

Hairy Norwegian cinquefoil - *Potentilla norvegica* L. subsp. *monspeliensis* (L.) Aschers. & Graebn. (155) (1942)

Hairy nut rush - *Scleria ciliata* Michx. (5) (1913)

Hairy oats - *Avena strigosa* Schreb. (67) (1890)

Hairy pagoda-plant - *Blephilia hirsuta* (Pursh) Benth. (50) (present)

Hairy panic grass [Hairy panic-grass] - *Dichanthelium acuminatum* (Sw.) Gould & C.A. Clark var. *fasciculatum* (Torr.) Freckmann (85, 119, 163) (1852-1938)

Hairy panicum - *Dichanthelium acuminatum* (Sw.) Gould & C.A. Clark var. *fasciculatum* (Torr.) Freckmann (5) (1913), *Dichanthelium sabulorum* (Lam.) Gould & C.A. Clark var. *thinium* (A.S. Hitchc. & Chase) Gould & C.A. Clark (72) (1907), *Dichanthelium scabriusculum* (Ell.) Gould & C.A. Clark (56) (1901)

Hairy parsley - *Lomatium foeniculaceum* (Nutt.) Coult. & Rose (131) (1899), *Lomatium foeniculaceum* (Nutt.) Coult. & Rose subsp. *foeniculaceum* (5, 85, 93, 97) (1913-1937)

Hairy parthenium - *Parthenium integrifolium* L. var. *hispidum* (Raf.) Mears (5) (1913)

Hairy pennyroyal - *Hedeoma hispida* Pursh (82) (1930)

Hairy pepperwort - *Marsilea vestita* Hook. & Grev. (5, 97, 122) (1913-1937)

Hairy phacelia - *Phacelia gilioides* Brand. (3, 4) (1977-1986), *Phacelia hirsuta* Nutt. (5, 97, 122) (1937)

Hairy phlox - *Phlox amoena* Sims. (5) (1913), *Phlox pilosa* L. (5, 156) (1913-1923)

Hairy pinesap [Hairy pine sap] - *Monotropa hypopithys* L. (5) (1913)

Hairy pinweed [Hairy pin-weed] - *Lechea mucronata* Raf. (4, 5, 50, 72, 93, 97, 155, 157, 158) (1900–present)

Hairy pipewort - *Lachnocaulon anceps* (Walt.) Morong (possibly) (5, 156) (1913-1923)

Hairy pointed violet - *Viola cucullata* Aiton (76) (1896) New Brunswick

Hairy popcorn-flower [Hairy popcornflower] - *Plagiobothrys scouleri* (Hook. & Arn.) I.M. Johnston var. *hispidulus* (Greene) Dorn (155) (1942)

Hairy portulaca - *Portulaca pilosa* L. (5, 97, 122) (1913-1937)

Hairy prairie clover - *Dalea villosa* (Nutt.) Spreng (5, 93, 95, 97, 121, 131) (1899-1970)

Hairy prickly-poppy [Hairy prickly poppy] - *Argemone hispida* Gray (4) (1986)

Hairy puccoon - *Lithospermum caroliniense* (Walt. ex J.F. Gmel.) MacM. (2, 5, 63, 93, 97, 98, 121, 156) (1895-1937)

Hairy purslane speedwell - *Veronica peregrina* L. subsp. *xalapensis* (Kunth) Pennell (50) (present)

Hairy rockcress [Hairy rock cress, Hairy rock-cress] - *Arabis hirsuta* (L.) Scop. (2, 5, 50, 72, 131, 155) (1895–present)

Hairy ruellia - *Ruellia humilis* Nutt. (5, 72, 93, 97, 122, 124, 157) (1900-1937)

Hairy rush grass - *Sporobolus compositus* (Poir.) Merr. var. *drummondii* (Trin.) Kartesz & Gandhi (5) (1913)

Hairy sedge - *Carex hirta* L. (5, 156) (1913-1923), *Carex lacustris* Willd. (50) (present)

Hairy six-weeks fescue [Hairy sixweeks fescue] - *Vulpia octoflora* (Walt.) Rydb. var. *hirtella* (Piper) Henr. (155) (1942)

Hairy skullcap - *Scutellaria pilosa* Michx. (5, 97) (1913-1937)

Hairy slender paspalum - *Paspalum setaceum* Michx. (66) (1903)

Hairy small-leaf tick-trefoil [Hairy small-leaved tick trefoil, Hairy small-leaved tick-trefoil] - *Desmodium ciliare* (Muhl. ex Willd.) DC. (50) (present), *Desmodium obtusum* (Muhl. ex Willd.) DC. (5, 97) (1913-1937)

Hairy Solomon's-seal [Hairy Solomon's seal] - *Polygonatum biflorum* (Walt.) Ell. (5, 72, 157, 158) (1900-1929), *Polygonatum pubescens* (Willd.) Pursh (42) (1814)

Hairy spicebush [Hairy spice bush, Hairy spice-bush] - *Lindera melissifolia* (Walt.) Blume (5, 156) (1913-1923)

Hairy spreading spurge - *Chamaesyce humistrata* (Engelm.) Small (5, 93, 97, 122) (1913-1937)

Hairy spurge - *Chamaesyce vermiculata* (Raf.) House (5) (1913)

Hairy St. John's-wort [Hairy St. John's wort] - *Hypericum setosum* L. (2) (1895)

Hairy stickseed [Hairy stick seed] - *Hackelia virginiana* (L.) I.M. Johnston (5) (1913), *Lappula occidentalis* (S. Wats.) Greene var. *cupulata* (Gray) Higgins (72, 93, 97, 122) (1907-1937)

Hairy sticktight - *Lappula occidentalis* (S. Wats.) Greene (85) (1932)

Hairy strawberry shrub - *Calycanthus floridus* L. (5) (1913)

Hairy sumac [Hairy sumach] - *Rhus hirta* (L.) Sudworth (5, 156) (1913-1923)

Hairy sundew [Hairy sun dew] - *Drosera filiformis* Raf. (possibly) (42) (1814)

Hairy sunflower - *Helianthus hirsutus* Raf. (3, 4, 50) (1977–present)

Hairy sunflower - *Helianthus mollis* Lam. (5, 65, 72, 97, 122) (1907-1937)

Hairy swallow-wort [Hairy swallow wort] - *Asclepias incarnata* L. subsp. *pulchra* (Ehrh. ex Willd.) Woods. (42) (1814)

Hairy swamp milkweed - *Asclepias incarnata* L. subsp. *pulchra* (Ehrh. ex Willd.) Woods. (155) (1942)

Hairy sweet cicely - *Osmorhiza claytonii* (Michx.) C.B. Clarke (5, 158) (1900-1913)

Hairy tare - *Vicia hirsuta* (L.) Gray (5, 19, 107) (1840-1919)

Hairy thoroughwort - *Eupatorium rotundifolium* L. var. *ovatum* (Bigelow) Torr. (5) (1913)

Hairy tickseed - *Coreopsis lanceolata* L. (5) (1913)

Hairy tick-trefoil - *Desmodium canadense* (L.) DC. (93) (1936)

Hairy toadlily - *Tricyrtis hirta* (Thunb.) Hook. (138) (1923)

Hairy tridens - *Erioneuron pilosum* (Buckl.) Nash (3) (1977)

Hairy trilisa - *Carphephorus paniculatus* (J.F. Gmel.) Herbert (5) (1913)

Hairy triodia - *Erioneuron pilosum* (Buckl.) Nash (122) (1937)

Hairy umbrella-sedge [Hairy umbrella sedge] - *Fuirena squarrosa* Michx. (50) (present)

Hairy umbrella-wort [Hairy umbrellawort, Hairy umbrella-wort] - *Mirabilis hirsuta* (Pursh) MacM. (5, 72, 93, 97, 131, 158) (1899-1937)

Hairy vervain - *Glandularia bipinnatifida* (Nutt.) Nutt. var. *bipinnatifida* (97) (1937)

Hairy vetch - *Vicia hirsuta* (L.) Gray (5, 93, 156) (1913-1936), *Vicia villosa* Roth (3, 4, 68, 82, 93, 95, 97, 109, 118, 138, 155) (1898-1986)

Hairy vincetoxicum - *Matelea carolinensis* (Jacq.) Woods. (5) (1913)

Hairy violet - *Viola hirsutula* Brainerd (5) (1913)

Hairy water-clover [Hairy waterclover] - *Marsilea vestita* Hook. & Grev. (50) (present)

Hairy waterleaf - *Hydrophyllum appendiculatum* Michx. (107) (1919)

Hairy white old-field aster [Hairy white oldfield aster] - *Symphyotrichum pilosum* (Willd.) Nesom (50) (present)

Hairy whitetop - *Cardaria pubescens* (C.A. Mey.) Jarmolenko (50, 155) (1942–present)

Hairy wild bergamot [Hairy wildbergamot] - *Monarda fistulosa* L. subsp. *fistulosa* var. *mollis* (L.) Benth. (138) (1923)

Hairy wild indigo - *Thermopsis villosa* (Walt.) Fern. & Schub. (5, 97) (1913-1937)

Hairy wild rye [Hairy wildrye] - *Elymus villosus* Muhl. ex Willd. (50, 155) (1942–present)

Hairy willow - *Salix glauca* L. subsp. *glauca* var. *villosa* (D. Don ex Hook.) Anderss. (130) (1895), *Salix vestita* Pursh (5) (1913)

Hairy willowherb [Hairy willow-herb] - *Epilobium hirsutum* L. (156) (1923)

Hairy willowweed [Hairy willow-weed] - *Epilobium hirsutum* L. (138) (1923)

Hairy wood chess [Hairy wood-chess] - *Bromus kalmii* Gray (5, 85, 119, 163) (1852-1938)

Hairy wood lettuce [Hairy wood-lettuce] - *Lactuca hirsuta* Muhl. ex Nutt. (5, 72, 97, 122) (1907-1937)

Hairy wood rush - *Luzula acuminata* Raf. var. *acuminata* (66, 72) (1903-1907), *Luzula acuminata* Raf. var. *carolinae* (S. Wats.) Fern. (5) (1913)

Hairy wood sunflower - *Helianthus atrorubens* L. (5, 97, 156) (1913-1937)

Hairy woodland brome - *Bromus pubescens* Muhl. ex Willd. (50) (present)

Hairy woolly grass [Hairy woollygrass] - *Erioneuron pilosum* (Buckl.) Nash (50) (present)

182

Hairy yellow violet - *Viola pubescens* Aiton (5, 72, 131) (1899-1913)

Hairy-beak sedge [Hairy-beaked sedge] - *Carex vestita* Willd. (187) (1818)

Hairy-flower festuca [Hairy-flowered festuca] - *Vulpia myuros* (L.) K.C. Gmel. (187) (1818)

Hairy-flower lyme grass [Hairy flowered lyme grass] - *Elymus virginicus* L. var. *virginicus* (56, 94) (1901)

Hairy-flower paspalum [Hairy-flowered paspalum] - *Paspalum dilatatum* Poir. (87) (1884)

Hairy-fruit chervil [Hairyfruit chervil] - *Chaerophyllum tainturieri* Hook. (50) (present)

Hairy-fruit rosemallow [Hairy fruited rose mallow, Hairy-fruited rose mallow, Hairy-fruited rose-mallow] - *Hibiscus moscheutos* L. subsp. *lasiocarpos* (Cav.) O.J. Blanchard (2, 5, 97, 124) (1895–1937)

Hairy-fruit sedge [Hairyfruit sedge, Hairy-fruited sedge] - *Carex trichocarpa* Muhl. (5, 50, 66, 72) (1903–present)

Hairy-joint meadow-parsnip [Hairy-jointed meadow parsnip, Hairy-jointed meadow-parsnip] - *Thaspium barbinode* (Michx.) Nutt. (5, 50, 72, 97) (1907–present)

Hairy-leaf paspalum [Hairyleaf paspalum] - *Paspalum laeve* Michx. (155) (1942)

Hairy-scale Virginia wild rye [Hairyscale Virginia wildrye] - *Elymus virginicus* L. var. *virginicus* (155) (1942)

Hairy-seed paspalum [Hairyseed paspalum] - *Paspalum pubiflorum* Rupr. ex Fourn. (3, 50, 155) (1942–present)

Hairy-seed sedge [Hairyseed sedge] - *Carex trichocarpa* Muhl. (155) (1942)

Hairy-stem aster [Hairy stemmed aster] - *Symphyotrichum lateriflorum* (L.) A.& D. Löve var. *lateriflorum* (5, 72, 156) (1907-1923), *Symphyotrichum pilosum* (Willd.) Nesom var. *pilosum* (72) (1907)

Hairy-stem gooseberry [Hairystem gooseberry] - *Ribes hirtellum* Michx. (50, 155) (1942–present)

Hairy-vein blue lettuce [Hairy-veined blue lettuce] - *Lactuca floridana* (L.) Gaertn. var. *villosa* (Jacq.) Cronq. (5, 72, 93) (1907-1936)

Hakakut (Pawnee, sore mouth) - *Menispermum canadense* L. (37) (1919)

Hakastahkata (Pawnee, yellow vine) - *Cuscuta glomerata* Choisy (37) (1919)

Hakusits (Pawnee, thorn) - *Zanthoxylum americanum* Mill. (37) (1919)

Halberd hexastylis - *Hexastylis arifolia* (Michx.) Small. (5) (1913)

Halberd knotweed [Halbert knotweed] - *Polygonum arifolium* L. (19) (1840)

Halberd violet [Halbert violet] - *Viola hastata* Michx. (19) (1840)

Halberd willow - *Salix hastata* L. (138) (1923)

Halberd-leaf arache [Halberd-leaved arache] - *Atriplex prostrata* subsp. *calotheca* (Rafn) M.A.Gust. (72) (1907)

Halberd-leaf mallow [Halberd-leaved mallow] - *Hibiscus laevis* All. (156) (1923)

Halberd-leaf orache [Halberd-leaved orache, Halberd-leaved orach, Halbert-leaved orache] - *Atriplex subspicata* (Nutt.) Rydb. (5, 62, 93, 131, 158, 187) (1818-1936)

Halberd-leaf rose-mallow [Halbard leaf rose mallow, Halberdleaf rosemallow, Halberd-leaved rose mallow, Halberd-leaved rose-mallow] - *Hibiscus laevis* All. (2, 4, 5, 50, 72, 93, 92, 97, 124, 156, 158) (1895–present)

Halberd-leaf smilax [Halberd-leaved smilax] - *Smilax pseudochina* L. (5) (1913)

Halberd-leaf tear-thumb [Halbardleaf tear thumb, Halberd-leaved tear thumb, Halberd-leaved tear-thumb] - *Persicaria arifolia* (L.) Haraldson (5, 86, 122, 156) (1878-1937)

Halberd-leaf violet [Halberd-leaved violet] - *Viola hastata* Michx. (2, 5, 156) (1895-1923)

Halberd-leaf yellow violet [Halberdleaf yellow violet] - *Viola hastata* Michx. (50) (present)

Hale's cyperus - *Cyperus erythrorhizos* Muhl. (5) (1913)

Halesia - *Halesia* Ellis ex L. (8) (1785)

Halesia (French) - *Halesia* Ellis ex L. (8) (1785)

Halesia à fruit à deux (French) - *Halesia carolina* L. (8) (1785)

Halesia à fruit à quatre (French) - *Halesia tetraptera* L. (8) (1785)

Half-breed weed [Halfbreed weed] - *Iva xanthifolia* Nutt. (80) (1913)

Half-chaff sedge [Halfchaff sedge] - *Lipocarpha* R. Br. (50) (present)

Half-moon loco [Halfmoon loco] - *Astragalus allochrous* Gray (155) (1942)

Half-moon milkvetch [Halfmoon milkvetch] - *Astragalus allochrous* Gray var. *playanus* Isely (50) (present)

Half-skirt daffodil [Halfskirt daffodil] - Narcissus ×incomparabilis Mill. [poeticus × pseudonarcissus] (138) (1923)

Halicacabum - *Physalis alkekengi* L. (178) (1526)

Halish - *Cannabis sativa* L. subsp. *indica* (Lam.) E. Small & Cronq. (92) (1876)

Hall's beard-grass [Hall's beardgrass] - *Andropogon hallii* Hack. (5, 56, 72, 119, 131, 163) (1852-1938)

Hall's bluestem [Hall's blue-stem] - *Andropogon hallii* Hack. (85) (1932)

Hall's bulrush [Halls bulrush] - *Schoenoplectus hallii* (Gray) S.G. Sm. (50) (present), *Scirpus hallii* Gray (3, 50, 139, 155) (1942–present)

Hall's club rush - *Scirpus hallii* Gray (5, 72) (1907-1913)

Hall's crab [Hall crab] - *Malus halliana* Koehne (138) (1923)

Hall's cyperus - *Cyperus setigerus* Torr. & Hook. (5) (1913)

Hall's milkweed [Halls milkweed] - *Asclepias hallii* Gray (4, 50, 155) (1942–present)

Hall's panic grass [Hall's panicgrass] - *Panicum hallii* Vasey (50) (present)

Hall's panicum [Halls panicum] - *Panicum hallii* Vasey (122, 155) (1937-1942)

Hall's rush [Hall rush] - *Juncus hallii* Engelm. (139) (1944), *Scirpus hallii* Gray (129) (1894)

Hall's sedge [Hall sedge] - *Carex hallii* Olney (139) (1944)

Hamamelier d'Hyver (French) - *Hamamelis virginiana* L. (7) (1828)

Hamamelis - *Hamamelis virginiana* L. (52, 53, 54, 55, 57, 174, 177, 189) (1753-1922)

Hamamelis (French) - *Hamamelis* L. (8) (1785)

Hamamelis Cortex (Official name of Materia Medica) - *Hamamelis virginiana* L. (7) (1828)

Hamamelis de Virginie (French) - *Hamamelis virginiana* L. (8) (1785)

Ha'mi (Kiwomi Keres) - *Nicotiana* L. (132) (1855)

Hammer sedge - *Carex hirta* L. (5, 50, 156) (1913–present)

Hammerwort - *Parietaria pensylvanica* Muhl. ex Willd. (5, 93, 156, 157) (1900–1936)

Hammock sedge - *Carex fissa* Mack. (50) (present)

Hand-leaf maple [Hand-leaved maple] - *Acer palmatum* Thunb. (165) (1768)

Hand-leaf violet - *Viola palmata* L. (5, 19, 156) (1840-1923)

Hand-of-God [Hand of God] - *Ricinus communis* L. (178) (1526)

Handsome blazing star - *Liatris elegans* (Walt.) Michx. (122, 124) (1937), *Liatris elegans* (Walt.) Michx. var. *elegans* (5, 97) (1913-1937)

Handsome Harry - *Rhexia virginica* L. (5, 76) (1896-1913) Eastern MA

Handsome sedge - *Carex formosa* Dewey (5, 50) (1913–present)

Hanf (German) - *Cannabis sativa* L. (6, 110) (1886–1892)

Hanfnessel (German) - *Galeopsis bifida* Boenn. (158) (1900)

Hanging moss - *Tillandsia usneoides* (L.) L. (5, 156) (1913-1923)

Hanke (Oregon tribes) - *Apios americana* Medik. (7) (1828)

Hankee - *Pediomelum esculentum* (Pursh) Rydb. (35) (1806) William Clark

Hankow aster - *Symphyotrichum ciliatum* (Ledeb.) Nesom (155) (1942)

Hankow willow - *Salix matsudana* Koidzumi (138) (1923)

Hank-sintsh (Winnebago, woodchuck tail) - *Achillea millefolium* L. (37) (1919)

Hanna (Persian) - *Lawsonia inermis* L. (110) (1886)

Hanpok-hischasu (Winnebago, owl eyes) - *Physalis lanceolata* Michx. (37) (1919)

Hansen's sitanion - *Elymus ×hansenii* Scribn. [*glaucus × elymoides* or *multisetus*] (94) (1901)

Hante or h'ante sha (Dakota) - *Juniperus virginiana* L. (37) (1830) seeds were hante itika (cedar eggs)

Hantola - *Zanthoxylum americanum* Mill. (6) (1892)

Hanuga-hi (Omaha-Ponca) - *Urtica dioica* L. subsp. *gracilis* (Aiton) Seland. (37) (1919)

Hanwinska (Winnebago, white herb) - *Artemisia ludoviciana* Nutt. subsp. *ludoviciana* (37) (1919)

Hánse (Mandan) - *Shepherdia argentea* (Pursh) Nutt. (35) (1806) Ässáy according to William Clark

Haṇtkaṇ or hiṇtkan (Lakota, hair, fur, or fuzz scraped off) - *Typha latifolia* L. (121) (1918–1970?)

Ha'-o-mi (Kiwomi Keres) - *Nicotiana* L. (132) (1855)

Haploesthes - *Haploesthes* Gray (158) (1900)

Haplopappus - *Haplopappus* Cass. (50) (present)

Håpniss [Hopniss, Hopnis] (Native American, Delaware) - *Apios americana* Medik. (7, 41, 46) (1770-1879)

Hapsintsh (Winnebago) - *Vitis cinerea* (Engelm.) Millard (37) (1919), *Vitis vulpina* L. (37) (1919)

Harbinger-of-spring [Harbinger of spring] - *Erigenia bulbosa* (Michx.) Nutt. (4, 5, 50, 138, 155, 156, 158) (1900–present), *Erigenia* Nutt. (1, 2, 138, 155, 158) (1900-1942)

Harbison's buckeye [Harbison buckeye] - *Aesculus ×mutabilis* (Spach) Scheele [*pavia × sylvatica*] (138) (1923)

Harbison's willow [Harbison willow] - *Salix caroliniana* Michx. (155) (1942)

Hard fescue - *Festuca brevipila* Tracey (45, 50, 56, 68, 109, 129, 138, 155) (1890–present)

Hard fescue grass - *Festuca brevipila* Tracey (19, 50, 66) (1840–present)

Hard grass [Hardgrass] - *Dactylis glomerata* L. (5, 92) (1876-1913), *Sclerochloa* Beauv. (50, 155) (1942–present), *Sclerochloa dura* (L.) Beauv. (155) (1942)

Hard maple - *Acer palmatum* Thunb. (5, 158) (1900–1913), *Acer rubrum* L. (5, 19, 65, 74, 76, 156) (1840-1931), *Acer saccharum* Marsh. (5, 37, 72, 82, 85, 106, 156) (1907-1932)

Hard meadow grass - *Desmazeria rigida* (L.) Tutin (19) (1840)

Hard pine - *Pinus palustris* Mill. (5) (1913), *Pinus resinosa* Aiton (5, 78) (1898-1913) ME

Hard rush - *Juncus effusus* L. (5, 156) (1913-1923)

Hard thistle [Hard-thistle] - *Cirsium arvense* (L.) Scop. (5, 156, 157, 158) (1913-1929)

Hard time - *Thymus vulgaris* L. (178) (1526)

Hardane - *Arctium lappa* L. (156) (1923) no longer in use by 1923

Hard-bark hickory - *Carya alba* (L.) Nutt. ex Ell. (5, 156, 158) (1900-1923)

Hardhack [Hard-hack] - *Collinsonia canadensis* L. (6, 58, 92) (1869-1892), *Dasiphora floribunda* (Pursh) Kartesz (5, 76, 156, 158) (1896-1923) MA, *Ostrya virginiana* (Mill.) K. Koch var. *virginiana* (75, 156, 157, 158) (1894-1929) Franconia NH, *Spiraea salicifolia* L. (156) (1923), *Spiraea tomentosa* L. (2, 5, 48, 49, 57, 58, 92, 109, 138, 156) (1869-1949)

Hardheads [Hard-head] - *Acroptilon* Cass. (50) (present), *Acroptilon repens* (L.) DC. (50) (present), *Centaurea nigra* L. (5, 156) (1913-1923)

Hard-iron - *Atriplex prostrata* subsp. *calotheca* (Rafn) M.A.Gust. (158) (1900)

Hard-leaf goldenrod [Hardleaf golden-rod, Hard-leaved golden-rod, Hard-leaved goldenrod] - *Oligoneuron rigidum* (L.) Small var. *rigidum* (5, 19, 122, 131) (1840-1937)

Hard-nut hickory - *Carya laciniosa* (Michx. f.) G. Don (46) (1879)

Hardock - *Arctium lappa* L. (5, 64, 69, 92, 156, 158) (1876-1923) no longer in use by 1923

Hard-stem bulrush [Hardstem bulrush, Hardstem bulrush] - *Schoenoplectus acutus* (Muhl. ex Bigelow) A.& D. Löve var. *acutus* (3, 50) (1977–present)

Hardweed [Hard weed, Hard-weed] - *Centaurea nigra* L. (5, 156) (1913-1923)

Hardy aster - *Symphyotrichum novae-angliae* (L.) G.L.Nesom (76) (1896)

Hardy bonduc - *Gymnocladus dioicus* (L.) K. Koch (38) (1820)

Hardy catalpa - *Catalpa speciosa* (Warder) Warder ex Engelm. (5, 112, 156, 158) (1900–1923)

Hardy cluster-amaryllis - *Lycoris squamigera* Maxim. (138) (1923)

Hardy crinum - *Crinum bulbispermum* (Burm. f.) Milne-Redhead & Schweickerdt (138) (1923)

Hardy Florida trumpetbush - *Tecoma stans* (L.) Juss. ex Kunth (138) (1923)

Hardy grindelia - *Grindelia camporum* Greene var. *camporum* (49) (1898)

Hardy heliotrope - *Valeriana officinalis* L. (5, 76, 156) (1896-1923)

Hardy pampas grass [Hardy pampas-grass] - *Saccharum ravennae* (L.) L. (163) (1852)

Hardy tuberous-root moonflower [Hardy tuberous-rooted moon-flower] - *Ipomoea pandurata* (L.) G.F.W. Mey. (77) (1898) sold under this name by J. Lewis Childs, Floral Park NY

Hare figwort - *Scrophularia lanceolata* Pursh (5, 72, 93, 97) (1907-1937)

Hare herde - *Verbascum thapsus* L. (14, 156) (1882-1923)

Hare sedge - *Carex ovalis* Goodenough (42) (1814)

Hare seg - *Carex ovalis* Goodenough (42) (1814)

Hare trefle - *Trientalis borealis* Raf. subsp. *borealis* (179) (1526)

Harebell [Hare-bell, Hare bell] - *Campanula divaricata* Michx. (44) (1845), *Campanula* L. (1, 2, 93) (1895-1937), *Campanula rotundifolia* L. (3, 4, 5, 40, 44, 63, 72, 86, 92, 93, 105, 109, 131, 156, 158) (1845-1986) also in England

Harebell hyacinth [Hare bell hyacinth] - *Muscari neglectum* Guss. ex Ten. (19) (1840)

Harebell phacelia - *Phacelia campanularia* Gray (138) (1923)

Harebur [Hareburr, Hare-bur] - *Arctium lappa* L. (92, 158) (1876-1900)

Hare-foot clover [Hare's-foot clover, Hare's foot clover] - *Trifolium arvense* L. (5, 156) (1913-1923)

Hare-foot fern [Hares-foot-fern] - *Phlebodium aureum* (L.) J. Sm. (109) (1949)

Hare-foot locoweed [Haresfoot locoweed] - *Oxytropis lagopus* Nutt. var. *atropupurea* (Rydb.) Barneby (50) (present)

Hare-foot sedge [Hare's-foot sedge, Hare's foot sedge] - *Carex ovalis* Goodenough (5) (1913), *Carex tribuloides* Wahl. var. *tribuloides* (187) (1818)

Hare's colewort - *Sonchus oleraceus* L. (5, 156, 157, 158) (1900-1929)

Hare's grass - *Aristida californica* Thurb. ex S. Wats. (94) (1901)

Hare's lettuce - *Sonchus oleraceus* L. (5, 62, 156, 157, 158) (1900-1929) IN, old English name

Hare's locoweed - *Oxytropis lagopus* Nutt. var. *atropupurea* (Rydb.) Barneby (4) (1986)

Hare's thistle - *Sonchus oleraceus* L. (5, 156, 157, 158) (1900-1929)

Hare's-beard [Hare's beard, Hares beard] - *Verbascum thapsus* L. (5, 69, 92, 156, 158) (1876-1929)

Hare's-ear [Hare's ear, Hares ear, Haresear] - *Bupleurum rotundifolium* L. (5, 50, 85, 92, 97, 156) (1876–present), *Conringia* Heister ex Fabr. (1, 93, 155, 158) (1900-1942), *Conringia orientalis* (L.) Dumort. (5, 158) (1900–1913)

Hare's-ear mustard [Hare's ear mustard] - *Conringia* Heister ex Fabr. (50, 97) (1937–present), *Conringia orientalis* (L.) Dumort. (3, 4, 50, 80, 131, 156) (1899–present)

Hare's-foot [Hares foot, Hares foote, Hairs foot] - *Lagerstroemia* L. (190) (~1759), *Trifolium arvense* L. (92, 158, 178, 187) (1526-1900)

Hare's-palace [Hare's palace] - *Sonchus oleraceus* L. (62, 157, 158) (1900-1929) IN, old English name

Hare's-tail [Hare's tail] - *Eriophorum callitrix* Cham. ex C.A. Mey. (5, 156) (1913-1923), *Eriophorum vaginatum* L. (66) (1903)

Hare-tail grass [Hare's-tail grass, Hares' tail grass, Hare's-tail-grass] - *Lagurus ovatus* L. (45, 92, 109) (1896-1949)

Harewost - *Maianthemum* G.H. Weber ex Wiggers (7) (1828)

Harford's melic grass [Harford's melic-grass] - *Melica harfordii* Boland. (94) (1901)

Harger's goldenrod - *Solidago canadensis* L. var. *hargeri* Fern. (50) (present)

Haricot - *Phaseolus vulgaris* L. (107) (1919) corrpution of Greek arachos used for several legumes

Haricot (French) - *Phaseolus vulgaris* L. (6, 110) (1886-1892) corrpution of Greek arachos used for several legumes

Haricot bean - *Phaseolus vulgaris* L. (138) (1923)

Harison's yellow rose [Harisons yellow rose] - *Rosa ×harisonii* Rivers [*foetida × spinosissima*] (109) (1949) originated in garden of Rev Harison of New York City about 1830

Harlequin blue flag - *Iris versicolor* L. (50) (present)

Harlequin glory-bower [Harlequin glorybower] - *Clerodendrum trichotomum* Thunb. (138) (1923)

Harmal peganum - *Peganum harmala* L. (50) (present)

Harmala - *Peganum harmala* L. (178) (1526)

Harnacker (Swedish) - *Parnassia palustris* L. (46) (1879)

Harping Johnny - *Hylotelephium telephium* (L.) H. Ohba. subsp. *telephium* (156) (1923) no longer in use by 1923

Harriman's yucca [Harriman yucca] - *Yucca harrimaniae* Trel. (155) (1942)

Har'-say (Pima) - *Carnegia gigantea* (Engelm.) Britt. & Rose (132) (1855)

Harsee (Indians) - *Carnegia gigantea* (Engelm.) Britt. & Rose (107, 147) (1856-1919)

Harsh goldenrod [Harsh golden-rod] - *Solidago rugosa* Mill. subsp. *rugosa* var. *rugosa* (19) (1840)

Hart peas [Hart Pease] - *Cardiospermum halicacabum* L. (178) (1526)

Hart Wright's persicaria - *Polygonum amphibium* L. var. *stipulaceum* Coleman (72) (1907)

Hart Wright's sedge - *Carex hyalinolepis* Steud. (5) (1913)

Hartford climbing fern - *Lygodium palmatum* (Bernh.) Sw. (2, 5, 109, 138) (1895-1949)

Hartford fern [Hartford-fern] - *Lygodium palmatum* (Bernh.) Sw. (2, 5) (1895-1913)

Hartheu (German) - *Hypericum perforatum* L. (6, 158) (1892)

Hartleberry [Hartleberries] - *Vaccinium pallidum* Aiton (46) (1617)

Hartmannia - *Oenothera speciosa* Nutt. (124) (1937) TX

Hart's clover - *Melilotus officinalis* (L.) Lam. (5, 156, 157, 158) (1900-1929)

Hart's garlic [Harts garlicke] - *Allium vineale* L. (178) (1596)

Hart's trefoil - *Melilotus officinalis* (L.) Lam. (157, 158) (1900-1929)

Hart's-eye [Hart's eye] - *Pastinaca sativa* L. (5, 157, 158) (1900-1929)

Hartshorn [Harts horne] - *Rhamnus cathartica* L. (6, 59) (Pre 1066-1892), *Plantago coronopus* L. (178) (1526)

Hartshorn bush [Harts horn bush] - *Osmunda regalis* L. (5, 92, 157) (1876-1929)

Hartshorn plant [Hartshorn-plant] - *Pulsatilla patens* (L.) Mill. (5) (1913), *Pulsatilla patens* (L.) Mill. subsp. *multifida* (Pritz.) Zamels (6, 74, 157, 158) (1892-1929)

Hartshorn plantain [Harts horn plantain] - *Plantago coronopus* L. (92) (1876)

Hart's-thorn [Hart's thorn] - *Rhamnus cathartica* L. (156, 158) (1900-1923)

Hart's-tongue [Hart's tongue, Hartstongue, Harts toong, Hertes tongue] - *Asplenium* L. (possibly) (7) (1828), *Asplenium scolopendrium* L. var. *americanum* (Fern.) Kartesz & Gandhi (2, 5, 138, 178, 179) (1526-1923)

Hart's-tongue fern [Hart's tonguefern] - *Asplenium scolopendrium* L. var. *americanum* (Fern.) Kartesz & Gandhi (50) (present)

Hartweg's evening-primrose [Hartweg evening primrose] - *Calylophus hartwegii* (Benth.) Raven (4) (1986)

Hartweg's sundrops - *Calylophus hartwegii* (Benth.) Raven (50) (present)

Hartweg's tansy mustard - *Descurainia incana* (Bernh. ex Fisch. & C.A. Mey.) Dorn subsp. *procera* (Greene) Kartesz & Gandhi (5) (1913)

Hartwright's persicaria - *Polygonum amphibium* L. var. *stipulaceum* Coleman (131) (1899)

Harvest brodlaea - *Brodiaea coronaria* (Salisb.) Engl. (109) (1949)

Harvestbells [Harvest bells] - *Gentiana saponaria* L. (156) (1923), *Gentiana saponaria* L. var. *saponaria* (5) (1913)

Harvestlice [Harvest lice, Harvest-lice] - *Agrimonia eupatoria* L. (156) (1923), *Agrimonia parviflora* Aiton (50) (present), *Bidens connata* Muhl. ex Willd. (92, 156) (1876-1923), *Bidens frondosa* L. (158) (1900), *Galium aparine* L. (156) (1923)

Harvest-lily [Harvest lily] - *Calystegia sepium* (L.) R. Br. subsp. *sepium* (5, 156) (1913-1923) no longer in use by 1923

Harvey's beaksedge - *Rhynchospora harveyi* W. Boott (50) (present)

Harvey's buttercup - *Ranunculus harveyi* (Gray) Britt. (5) (1913)

Harvey's coreopsis - *Coreopsis grandiflora* Hogg ex Sweet var. *harveyana* (Gray) Sherff (97) (1937)

Hasenkraut (German) - *Hypericum perforatum* L. (158) (1900)

Hasenpfatlin (German) - *Antennaria dioica* (L.) Gaertn. (46) (1879)

Hashash - *Cannabis sativa* L. (6) (1892)

Ha-shi (Navajo) - *Pinus* L. (132) (1855)

Hashisch - *Cannabis sativa* L. (6) (1892)

Hashish - *Cannabis sativa* L. (6, 59) (1892-1911), *Cannabis sativa* L. subsp. *indica* (Lam.) E. Small & Cronq. (92) (1876)

Hasill - *Corylus americana* Walt. (46) (1617)

Haskwort - *Campanula latifolia* L. (92) (1876)

Hasse's feather grass [Hasse's feather-grass] - *Nassella lepida* (Hitchc.) Barkworth (94) (1901)

Hasse's sedge - *Carex hassei* Bailey (5) (1913)

Hassock grass - *Deschampsia caespitosa* (L.) Beauv. (5, 92) (1876-1913)

Hastanhanka (Dakota) - *Vitis cinerea* (Engelm.) Millard (37) (1919), *Vitis vulpina* L. (37) (1919)

Hastate knot-grass [Hastate knot grass] - *Polygonum arifolium* L. (92) (1876)

Hastgroning (Swedish) - *Equisetum sylvaticum* L. (46) (1879)

Hastings' tansy mustard - *Descurainia incana* (Bernh. ex Fisch. & C.A. Mey.) Dorn subsp. *procera* (Greene) Kartesz & Gandhi (131) (1899)

Hatchet vetch - *Coronilla varia* L. (178) (1526), *Securigera securidaca* (L.) O. Deg. & Dorf. (178) (1526)

Hathorn - *Crataegus monogyna* Jacq. (5) (1913)

Hatpins - *Eriocaulon decangulare* L. (156) (1923)

Hat-ta-wa-no-min-schi - *Cornus florida* L. (6, 186) (1825-1892)

Hau tree - *Hibiscus tiliaceus* L. (106) (1930)

Haules - *Hordeum* L (158) (1900)

Havard's grama - *Bouteloua chondrosioides* (Kunth) Benth. ex S. Wats. (94) (1901)

Havard's oak [Havard oak] - *Quercus havardii* Rydb. (50, 155) (1942–present)

Havard's poverty grass - *Aristida havardii* Vasey (94) (1901)

Havard's shinnery - *Quercus havardii* Rydb. (122, 124) (1937)

Havard's three-awn [Havard's threeawn, Havard three awn, Havard threeawn] - *Aristida havardii* Vasey (50, 122, 155) (1937–present)

Haver - *Avena sativa* L. (107, 158) (1900-1919)

Haver grass - *Bromus hordeaceus* L. (5) (1913), *Bromus sterilis* L. (5) (1913)

Havercorn - *Avena fatua* L. (5) (1913)

Haw [Haws] - *Avena sativa* L. (158) (1900)

Haw [Haws] or Haw tree - *Crataegus* L. (1, 35, 93, 106) (1806-1936), *Crataegus monogyna* Jacq. (5) (1913)

Hawahawa (Pawnee) - *Typha latifolia* L. (37) (1830)

Hawaii arrowhead - *Sagittaria latifolia* Willd. (possibly) (50) (present)

Hawaiian giant taro - *Alocasia macrorrhizos* (L.) Schott (138) (1923)

Ha-wish (Navajo) - *Quercus* L. (132) (1855)

Hawkberry - *Prunus avium* (L.) L. (5) (1913)

Hawkbit [Hawk bit] - *Hieracium venosum* L. (5, 92, 156) (1876-1923), *Leontodon* L. (4, 155, 156, 158) (1900-1986), *Taraxacum officinale* G.H. Weber ex Wiggers (41) (1770)

Hawk's-beard [Hawk's beard, Hawk beard, Hawksbeard] - *Crepis capillaris* (L.) Wallr. (92) (1876), *Crepis* L. (4, 50, 93, 155, 156, 158) (1900–present), *Crepis runcinata* (James) Torr. & Gray (3, 85, 127) (1932-1977)

Hawkweed [Hawk-weed, Hawk weed, Hawke-weed] - *Erechtites hieraciifolia* (L.) Raf. ex DC. var. *hieraciifolia* (187) (1818), *Hieracium aurantiacum* L. (106) (1930), *Hieracium canadense* Michx. (3) (1977), *Hieracium gronovii* L. (19) (1840), *Hieracium* L. (1, 2, 4, 10, 50, 63, 93, 109, 138, 155, 156, 158, 180, 184, 190) (~1759–present) sap said to sharpen eyesight, *Hieracium lachenalii* K.C. Gmel. (5) (1913), *Hieracium venosum* L. (7, 49, 92) (1828-1898), *Leontodon autumnalis* L. (19) (1840), *Picris hieracioides* L. (156) (1923)

Hawkweed picris - *Picris hieracioides* L. (5) (1913)

Hawthorn - *Crataegus coccinioides* Ashe (4) (1986), *Crataegus crusgalli* L. (5) (1913), *Crataegus* L. (1, 2, 4, 7, 10, 50, 82, 105, 106, 109, 112, 138, 156, 158, 184) (1793–present), *Crataegus mollis* Scheele (82) (1930), *Crataegus monogyna* Jacq. (5, 19, 54, 107) (1840-1919), *Crataegus succulenta* Schrad. ex Link (3, 112) (1937-1977), *Crataegus viridis* L. (3) (1977), *Ribes oxyacanthoides* L. subsp. *oxyacanthoides* (5) (1913)

Hawthorn gooseberry - *Ribes oxyacanthoides* L. (156, 158) (1900-1923)

Hay plant - *Galium odoratum* (L.) Scop. (5) (1913)

Hay sedge - *Carex foenea* Willd. (5, 72) (1907-1913)

Haycocks - *Linaria vulgaris* Mill. (157, 158) (1900-1929)

Hayden's beardtongue [Hayden's beard-tongue] - *Penstemon haydenii* S. Wats. (5, 93) (1913-1936)

Hayden's penstemon [Hayden penstemon] - *Penstemon haydenii* S. Wats. (4, 155) (1942-1986)

Hayden's poison vetch [Hayden poisonvetch] - *Astragalus bisulcatus* (Hook.) Gray var. *haydenianus* (Gray) Barneby (155) (1942)

Hayden's sedge - *Carex haydenii* Dewey (5, 50, 72) (1893–present)

Hay-fever weed [Hay fever weed] - *Ambrosia artemisiifolia* L. (156) (1923), *Ambrosia artemisiifolia* L. var. *elatior* (L.) Descourtils (5) (1913), *Ambrosia trifida* L. (5, 72, 156) (1907-1923)

Hayhofe [Hay hofe] - *Glechoma hederacea* L. (5, 156, 157, 158) (1900-1929), *Glechoma hederacea* L. (156) (1923)

Haymaids [Hay maids, Hay-maids] - *Glechoma hederacea* L. (5, 92, 156, 157, 158) (1876-1929)

Hay-scented cup fern [Hay-scented cupfern] - *Dennstaedtia punctilobula* (Michx.) T. Moore (138) (1923)

Hay-scented fern [Hay-scented-fern] - *Dennstaedtia punctilobula* (Michx.) T. Moore (5, 109) (1913-1949)

Haystack weed - *Phytolacca americana* L. (77) (1898)

Haz shutsh (Winnebago, red fruit) - *Amelanchier alnifolia* (Nutt.) Nutt. ex M. Roemer (37) (1919)

Hazel [Hazle] or Hazel tree - *Corylus americana* Walt. (12, 40, 92) (1821-1928), *Corylus avellana* L. (41, 92) (1770-1876), *Corylus* L. (8, 155, 156, 184) (1785-1942)

Hazel alder - *Alnus incana* (L.) Moench subsp. *rugosa* (DuRoi) Clausen (5, 138, 155, 156) (1913-1942), *Alnus serrulata* (Aiton) Willd. (50, 109, 187) (1818–present)

Hazel brush - *Corylus americana* Walt. (22) (1893)

Hazel crottles - *Sticta pulmonaria* (L.) Biroli (92) (1876)

Hazel dodder - *Cuscuta coryli* Engelm. (3, 5, 50, 72, 82, 85, 93, 95, 97, 122, 124) (1907–present)

Hazelnut [Hazel nut, Hazel-nut, Hasel nuts, Hazle-nut] or Hazelnut tree [Hasel nut tree] - *Corylus americana* Walt. (4, 5, 19, 37, 38, 46, 47, 72, 82, 85, 92, 93, 97, 105, 106, 107, 113, 130, 131, 156) (1820-1986), *Corylus avellana* L. (107, 112) (1919-1937), *Corylus cornuta* Marsh (35) (1806), *Corylus* L. (2, 4, 7, 8, 10, 14, 42, 50, 82, 93, 112, 138, 167) (1785–present)

Hazelwort [Hazel wort] - *Asarum canadense* L. (156) (1923)

Hazi (Omaha-Ponca) - *Vitis cinerea* (Engelm.) Millard var. *cinerea* (37) (1919) Hazi-hi (grape vine), *Vitis vulpina* L. (37) (1919)

Haz-ni-hu (Winnebago, water-fruit bush) - *Rhus glabra* L. (37) (1919)

Haz-ponoponoh' (Winnebago, crunching fruit) - *Ribes missouriense* Nutt. (37) (1919)

Haz-scheck (Winnebgao) - *Fragaria vesca* L. subsp. *americana* (Porter) Staudt (37) (1919), *Fragaria virginiana* Duchesne (37) (1919)

Haz-shutz (Winnebago, red fruit) - *Shepherdia argentea* (Pursh) Nutt. (37) (1919)

He balsam - *Picea mariana* (Mill.) Britton, Sterns & Poggenb. (5) (1913)

He loll - *Clintonia borealis* (Ait.) Raf. (79) (1891) NH

Head lettuce - *Lactuca sativa* L. (109) (1949)

Head sedge - *Carex cephalophora* Muhl. ex Willd. (19, 187) (1818-1840)

Headache [Head-ache] - *Papaver argemone* L. (5, 156) (1913-1923), *Papaver dubium* L. (5, 156, 158) (1900–1923), *Papaver rhoeas* L. (5, 156, 158) (1900–1923)

Headache plant [Head-ache plant, Headache-plant] - *Pulsatilla patens* (L.) Mill. (5) (1913), *Pulsatilla patens* (L.) Mill. subsp. *multifida* (Pritz.) Zamels (74, 157, 158) (1893-1929)

Headache-weed - *Clematis hirsutissima* Pursh (101) (1905), *Clematis viorna* L. (156) (1923)

Head-betony [Head betony] - *Pedicularis canadensis* L. (5, 92, 156) (1876-1923), *Teucrium canadense* L. (77) (1898) Western US

Headgrass - *Xyris* L. (7) (1828)

Headsman [Headsmen] - *Plantago lanceolata* L. (5, 156, 158) (1900–1923)

Headwark - *Papaver rhoeas* L. (158) (1900)

Heal-all [Healall] - *Clintonia borealis* (Ait.) Raf. (2, 73, 79, 156) (1891-1923), *Collinsonia canadensis* L. (6, 7, 55, 58, 86, 92) (1828-1911), *Pedicularis canadensis* L. subsp. *canadensis* (7) (1828), *Platanthera macrophylla* (Goldie) Lindl. (possibly) (7) (1828), *Platanthera orbiculata* (Pursh) Lindl. (5, 7, 156, 158) (1828-1923), *Prunella vulgaris* L. (1, 2, 5, 45, 57, 72, 82, 92, 93, 97, 106, 109, 114, 156, 158) (1876-1937), *Rhodiola rosea* L. (156) (1923), *Scrophularia* L. (7) (1828), *Scrophularia marilandica* L. (92, 93, 131, 156) (1876-1936), *Scrophularia nodosa* L. (6, 52, 58) (1869-1919)

Heal-bite [Heal bite] - *Alyssum alyssoides* (L.) L. (5, 156, 158) (1900–1923)

Heal-dog - *Alyssum alyssoides* (L.) L. (158) (1900)

Healing herb [Healing-herb] - *Plantago media* L. (5, 156) (1913-1923), *Symphytum officinale* L. (5, 64, 92, 156) (1876-1923)

Healing-blade [Healing blade] - *Plantago major* L. (5, 62, 156, 157, 158) (1900–1929) IN, old English name, *Sempervivum tectorum* L. (156) (1923)

Heart liverleaf [Heart liver-leaf, Heart liver leaf] - *Anemone canadensis* L. (49, 53) (1898–1922), *Hepatica nobilis* Schreb. var. *acuta* (Pursh) Steyermark (5, 19, 49, 53, 72, 92) (1840-1922)

Heart liverwort - *Hepatica nobilis* Schreb. (74) (1893), *Hepatica nobilis* Schreb. var. *acuta* (Pursh) Steyermark (5) (1913), *Hepatica nobilis* Schreb. var. *obtusa* (Pursh) Steyermark (5) (1913)

Heart nut [Heartnut] - *Carya cordiformis* (Wangenh.) K. Koch (109) (1949)

Heart pine - *Pinus palustris* Mill. (5) (1913)

Heart snakeroot [Heart snake root, Heart snake-root] - *Asarum canadense* L. (5, 7, 64, 92, 156, 158) (1828-1923), *Hexastylis virginica* (L.) Small (186) (1814)

Heart trefoil - *Medicago arabica* (L.) Huds. (5) (1913)

Heartleaf [Heart leaf] - *Medicago arabica* (L.) Huds. (5) (1913)

Heartleaf [Heart leaves, Heart-leaf] - *Hepatica nobilis* Schreb. var. *acuta* (Pursh) Steyermark (102) (1886), *Hexastylis arifolia* (Michx.) Small var. *arifolia* (75, 156) (1894-1923) GA, *Hexastylis virginica* (L.) Small (5, 75, 156) (1894-1923), *Maianthemum canadense* Desf. (156) (1923)

Heart-leaf alexanders [Heart-leaved alexanders] - *Zizia aptera* (Gray) Fern. (5, 72, 131) (1899-1913)

Heart-leaf ampelopsis [Heartleaf ampelopsis] - *Ampelopsis cordata* Michx. (138, 155) (1923-1942)

Heart-leaf arnica [Heartleaf arnica] - *Arnica cordifolia* Hook. (5, 50, 133, 155) (1899–present)

Heart-leaf aster [Heartleaf aster, Heart-leaved aster] - *Symphyotrichum cordifolium* (L.) Nesom (62, 82, 155, 156, 187) (1818-1942)

Heart-leaf avens [Heartleaf avens] - *Geum vernum* (Raf.) Torr. & Gray (3, 4) (1977-1986)

Heart-leaf balsam poplar [Heart-leaved balsam poplar] - *Populus balsamifera* L. subsp. *balsamifera* (20) (1857)

Heart-leaf buttercup [Heartleaf buttercup, Heart-leaved buttercup] - *Ranunculus cardiophyllus* Hook. (5, 50) (1913–present)

Heart-leaf cucumber tree [Heart-leaved cucumber tree] - *Magnolia acuminata* (L.) L. (20) (1857)

Heart-leaf dalibarda [Heart leaved dalibarda] - *Dalibarda repens* L. (42) (1814)

Heart-leaf fig-marigold [Heartleaf figmarigold] - *Aptenia cordifolia* (L. f.) Schwant. (138) (1923)

Heart-leaf four-o'clock [Heartleaf four o'clock] - *Mirabilis nyctaginea* (Michx.) MacM. (50) (present)

Heart-leaf hexastylis [Heart-leaved hexastylis] - *Hexastylis arifolia* (Michx.) Small. (5) (1913)

Heart-leaf listeria [Heart-leaved listeria] (sic) - *Listera cordata* (L.) R. Br. ex Ait. f. (possibly) (187) (1818)

Heart-leaf liverwort [Heart-leaved liverwort] - *Hepatica nobilis* Schreb. (156) (1923)

Heart-leaf lizard's-tail [Heart leaved lizard's tail] - *Saururus* L. (190) (~1759)

Heart-leaf loosestrife [Heart-leaved loose-strife] - *Lysimachia ciliata* L. (187) (1818)

Heart-leaf mesembryanthemum [Heartleaf mesembryanthemum] - *Aptenia cordifolia* (L. f.) Schwant. (155) (1942)

Heart-leaf nettle [Heartleaf nettle] - *Urtica chamaedryoides* Pursh (50) (present)

Heart-leaf noseburn [Heartleaf noseburn] - *Tragia cordata* Michx. (50) (present)

Heart-leaf penstemon [Heartleaf penstemon] - *Keckiella cordifolia* (Benth.) Straw (138) (1923)

Heart-leaf peppervine [Heartleaf peppervine] - *Ampelopsis cordata* Michx. (50) (present)

Heart-leaf plantain [Heart-leaved plantain] - *Plantago cordata* Lam (5, 156) (1913-1923)

Heart-leaf pontederia [Heart-leaved pontederia] - *Pontederia cordata* L. (187) (1818)

Heart-leaf rattletop [Heart-leaved rattle top] - *Cimicifuga racemosa* (L.) Nutt. (5) (1913)

Heart-leaf rose-mallow [Heartleaf rosemallow] - *Hibiscus martianus* Zucc. (50) (present)

Heart-leaf skullcap [Heartleaf skullcap, Heart-leaved skull-cap, Heart-leaved skullcap, Heart leaved skull cap] - *Scutellaria ovata* Hill (50) (present), *Scutellaria ovata* Hill subsp. *ovata* (5, 72, 82, 97) (1907-1937)

Heart-leaf snakeroot [Heart-leaved snake root] - *Cimicifuga racemosa* (L.) Nutt. (5) (1913)

Heart-leaf starwort [Heart leaved star wort] - *Symphyotrichum cordifolium* (L.) Nesom (42) (1814)

Heart-leaf twayblade [Heartleaf twayblade] - *Listera cordata* (L.) R. Br. ex Ait. f. var. *cordata* (5, 50) (1913–present)

Heart-leaf umbrella-wort [Heart-leaved umbrella-wort, Heart-leaved umbrella wort] - *Mirabilis nyctaginea* (Michx.) MacM. (5, 93, 97, 131) (1899-1936)

Heart-leaf wild ginger [Heartleaf wildginger] - *Hexastylis virginica* (L.) Small (138) (1923)

Heart-leaf willow [Heart-leaved willow] - *Salix eriocephala* Michx. (1, 5, 19, 72, 93, 97, 108, 130, 131, 138, 155) (1840-1942)

Heart-of-the-earth - *Prunella vulgaris* L. (5, 156, 158) (1900–1923)

Heart-pea [Heart pea] - *Cardiospermum halicacabum* L. (5, 107, 156, 158) (1900–1923)

Hearts - *Oxalis montana* Raf. (possibly) (5, 156) (1913-1923)

Heart's-ear - *Polygonum persicaria* L. (158) (1900)

Heart's-ease [Heart's ease, Heartsease, Hearts' ease] - *Persicaria maculosa* Gray (5, 19, 75, 79, 92, 106, 156, 158) (1840-1930) from shape of dark spots on leaves, *Persicaria pensylvanica* (L.) M. Gómez (possibly) (82, 85, 114) (1894-1932), *Polygonum amphibium* L. (77, 156, 158) (1898-1923), *Polygonum amphibium* L. var. *emersum* Michx. (5, 114) (1894-1913), *Polygonum* L. (77, 106) (1898–1930), *Polygonum lapathifolium* L. (82) (1930), *Prunella vulgaris* L. (77) (1898) Cambridge MA, *Viola* L. (1, 82) (1930-1932), *Viola tricolor* L. (5, 6, 15, 19, 57, 92, 97, 109, 158) (1840-1949)

Heartseed [Heart seed, Heart-seed] - *Cardiospermum halicacabum* L. (1, 2, 5, 10, 13, 15, 92, 156, 158) (1818-1932), *Cardiospermum* L. (109, 138, 158, 167) (1814-1949), *Polygonum pensylvanicum* L. (105) (1932)

Heart's-eye - *Pastinaca sativa* L. (156) (1923)

Heart's-pansy - *Viola tricolor* L. (158) (1900)

Heart-spot knotweed - *Polygonum persicaria* L. (19) (1840)

Heartweed [Heart weed, Heart-weed] - *Persicaria maculosa* Gray (5, 62, 75, 77, 156, 158) (1898-1923)

Heart-wing sorrel [Heartwing sorrel] - *Rumex hastatulus* Baldw. (3, 4, 50, 155) (1942–present)

Heartwort [Heart-wort] - *Aristolochia* L. (158) (1900), *Melilotus officinalis* (L.) Lam. (5, 156, 157, 158) (1900–1929)

Heath - *Calluna vulgaris* (L.) Hull (107) (1919), *Empetrum nigrum* L. (5) (1913), *Erica* L. (92, 109, 138) (1876-1949), *Hudsonia tomentosa* Nutt. (76, 156, 158) (1896–1923) Wellfleet MA

Heath aira grass [Heath aira-grass] - *Deschampsia flexuosa* (L.) Trin. var *flexuosa* (165) (1768)

Heath aster - *Chaetopappa* DC. (158) (1900), *Symphyotrichum ericoides* (L.) Nesom var. *ericoides* (109, 138, 155) (1923-1949)

Heath corn - *Fagopyrum esculentum* Moench (92, 158) (1876-1900)

Heath cypress - *Lycopodium alpinum* L. (5) (1913)

Heath grass - *Danthonia decumbens* (L.) DC. (5) (1913)

Heath mulberry - *Rubus chamaemorus* L. (156) (1923)

Heath pea [Heath-pea] - *Lathyrus japonicus* Willd. var. *maritimus* (L.) Kartesz & Gandhi (107, 156) (1919-1923)

Heath sedge - *Carex flacca* Schreb. (5, 50, 156) (1913–present)

Heathbells [Heath bells, Heath-bells, Heath-bell] - *Campanula rotundifolia* L. (5, 156, 158) (1900-1923)

Heathberry [Heath-berry] - *Empetrum nigrum* L. (5, 156) (1913-1923)

Heather - *Calluna* Salisb. (109, 156) (1923-1949), *Calluna vulgaris* (L.) Hull (5, 92, 106, 156) (1876-1930), *Cassiope* D. Don. (106) (1930), *Eriogonum effusum* Nutt. (106) (1930) CO

Heather goldenweed - *Ericameria cuneata* (Gray) McClatchie var. *cuneata* (155) (1942), *Ericameria ericoides* (Less.) Jepson (155) (1942)

Heather grass [Heather-grass] - *Danthonia decumbens* (L.) DC. (5, 94) (1901-1913)

Heatherbells - *Campanula rotundifolia* L. (156) (1923)

Heath-leaf aster [Heath-leaved aster] - *Symphyotrichum ericoides* (L.) Nesom var. *ericoides* (187) (1818)

Heath-like aster - *Symphyotrichum ericoides* (L.) Nesom var. *ericoides* (82, 156) (1923-1930)

Heath-like hudsonia - *Hudsonia ericoides* L. (5) (1913), *Hudsonia tomentosa* Nutt. (5) (1913)

Heavenward tree - *Ailanthus altissima* (Mill) Swingle (5, 156, 158) (1900-1923) no longer in use by 1923

Heavy sedge - *Carex gravida* Bailey (5, 50, 72) (1893–present), *Carex gravida* Bailey var. *gravida* (3) (1977), *Carex gravida* Bailey var. *lunelliana* (Mack.) Herm. (3) (1977)

Heavy-scent clematis [Heavy-scented clematis] - *Clematis orientalis* L. (2) (1895)

Heavy-top broom grass [Heavy-topped broom grass] - *Andropogon glomeratus* (Walt.) B.S.P. (87, 88) (1884-1885)

Heavy-wood pine [Heavy-wooded pine] - *Pinus ponderosa* P.& C. Lawson (1, 20, 136) (1857-1932)

Heck-how - *Conium maculatum* L. (69, 158) (1900-1904)

Hedeoma - *Hedeoma pulegioides* (L.) Pers. (55, 59) (1911-1917)

Hedeoma herba (Official name of Materia Medica) - *Hedeoma pulegioides* (L.) Pers. (7) (1828)

Hedeome pouliot (French) - *Hedeoma pulegioides* (L.) Pers. (7) (1828)

Hederich (German) - *Sisymbrium officinale* (L.) Scop (158) (1900)

Hedge bamboo - *Bambusa multiplex* (Lour.) Raeusch. ex Schult. & Schult. f. (138) (1923)

Hedge beech - *Celtis occidentalis* L. (possibly) (46) (1649)

Hedge bindweed [Hedge bind weed] - *Calystegia* R. Br. (4) (1986), *Calystegia sepium* (L.) R. Br. subsp. *angulata* Brummitt (3, 4, 5, 14, 42, 62, 72, 80, 82, 93, 131, 138, 156, 158) (1814-1986)

Hedge buckwheat - *Polygonum scandens* L. var. *dumetorum* (L.) Gleason (5, 72, 97) (1907-1937)

Hedge cactus - *Cereus repandus* (L.) Mill. (109) (1949)

Hedge cornbind - *Polygonum scandens* L. (155) (1942)

Hedge false bindweed - *Calystegia sepium* (L.) R. Br. (50) (present), *Calystegia sepium* (L.) R. Br. subsp. *angulata* Brummitt (50) (present)

Hedge fumitory - *Fumaria officinalis* L. (5, 156, 158) (1900–1923)

Hedge glorybind - *Calystegia sepium* (L.) R. Br. subsp. *sepium* (155) (1942)

Hedge hyssop [Hedgehyssop] - *Bacopa monnieri* (L.) Pennell (156) (1923), *Gratiola aurea* Muhl. (19, 92) (1840-1876), *Gratiola* L. (1, 2, 4, 10, 26, 50, 155, 156) (1826–present), *Gratiola neglecta* Torr. (3, 4) (1977-1986), *Gratiola virginiana* L. (4, 85, 93) (1932-1986)

Hedge maple - *Acer campestre* L. (50, 109 137, 138, 155) (1923–present)

Hedge mustard [Hedgemustard, Hedge-mustard] - *Barbarea vulgaris* W.T. Aiton (157) (1929), *Erysimum* L. (1, 10, 93) (1818-1936), *Sisymbrium* L. (4, 13, 15, 50, 156) (1849–present), *Sisymbrium officinale* (L.) Scop (3, 4, 5, 7, 13, 15, 49, 50, 62, 63, 72, 76, 80, 85, 92, 97, 107, 131, 145, 156, 157, 158) (1828–present)

Hedge nettle [Hedgenettle, Hedge-nettle] - *Stachys aspera* Michx. (114, 187) (1818-1894), *Stachys germanica* L. (1, 2, 93) (1895-1936), *Stachys* L. (4, 10, 50, 63, 106, 156, 158) (1818–present), *Stachys palustris* L. (5, 40, 72, 82, 85, 92, 93, 127, 131, 156) (1899-1936), *Stachys pilosa* Nutt. var. *pilosa* (3, 4) (1977-1986)

Hedge plant - *Maclura pomifera* (Raf.) Schneid. (5, 156, 158) (1900-1923)

Hedge thorn - *Crataegus monogyna* Jacq. (5) (1913)

Hedge tree - *Maclura pomifera* (Raf.) Schneid. (78) (1898) Southwest MO

Hedge-apple [Hedge apple] - *Maclura pomifera* (Raf.) Schneid. (156) (1923)

Hedgebell [Hedge-bells] - *Calystegia sepium* (L.) R. Br. subsp. *sepium* (158) (1900), *Convolvulus arvensis* L. (92, 156, 157, 158) (1876-1929)

Hedgeberry [Hedge berry] - *Prunus avium* (L.) L. (92) (1876), *Celtis occidentalis* L. (156) (1923)

Hedge-garlic [Hedge garlic] - *Alliaria* Heister ex Fabr.(possibly) (1, 158) (1900-1932), *Alliaria petiolata* (Bieb.) Cavara & Grande (5, 92, 156, 158) (1876-1923)

Hedgehog [Hedge hog, Hedge hogs] - *Scandix pecten-veneris* L. (5, 156) (1913-1923) no longer in use by 1923

Hedgehog burweed [Hedge-hog-bur-weed] - *Xanthium strumarium* L. var. *canadense* (Mill.) Torr. & Gray (62, 158) (1900-1912)

Hedgehog cactus [Hedge hog cactus] - *Echinocactus texensis* Hopffer. (92) (1876), *Echinocereus viridiflorus* Engelm. (4, 85) (1932-1986), *Pediocactus* Britton & Rose (50) (present)

Hedgehog cereus - *Echinocereus* Engelm. (1, 50) (1932–present)

Hedgehog club-rush [Hedge-hog club rush] - *Cyperus echinatus* (L.) Wood (5, 19, 156) (1840-1923)

Hedgehog coneflower [Hedgehog cone-flower] - *Echinacea purpurea* (L.) Moench (156) (1923), *Echinacea* Moench (138) (1923)

Hedgehog gourd - *Cucumis dipsaceus* C.G. Ehrenb. ex Spach (109) (1949)

Hedgehog grass [Hedge hog grass, Hedge-hog grass, Hedge-hog-grass] - *Cenchrus echinatus* L. (19, 92, 163, 184, 187) (1818-1876), *Cenchrus* L. (42) (1814), *Cenchrus tribuloides* L. (2, 5, 62, 66, 75) (1894-192), *Echinochloa crus-galli* (L.) Beauv. (92) (1876), *Elymus hystrix* L. (possibly) (19, 88) (1840-1885)

Hedgehog holly [Hedge-hog holly] - *Ilex mucronata* (L.) M. Powell, Savol. & S. Andrews (8) (1785)

Hedgehog prickly poppy [Hedgehog pricklypoppy, Hedgehog prickly-poppy] - *Argemone hispida* Gray (138, 155) (1923-1942), *Argemone squarrosa* Greene (3, 4, 50) (1977–present)

Hedgehog thistle [Hedge hog thistle] - *Echinocactus* Link & Otto (14) (1882), *Opuntia humifusa* (Raf.) Raf. var. *humifusa* (158) (1900), *Pediocactus simpsonii* (Engelm.) Britton & Rose (5) (1913)

Hedgehog woodrush - *Luzula echinata* (Small.) Hermann (50) (present)

Hedgehog-grass [Hedge hog grass, Hedge-hog grass, Hedge-hog-grass] - *Carex flava* L. (46) (1671)

Hedgehog-thistle - *Opuntia ficus-indica* (L.) Mill. (156) (1923)

Hedge-lily [Hedge lily] - *Calystegia sepium* (L.) R. Br. subsp. *sepium* (5, 156, 158) (1900-1923) no longer in use by 1923

Hedgemaids [Hedge maids, Hedge-maids] - *Glechoma hederacea* L. (5, 92, 156, 157, 158) (1876-1929)

Hedge-oats [Hedge-Otes] - *Bromus sterilis* L. (180) (1633)

Hedge-parsley [Hedge parsley, Hedgeparsley] - *Torilis* Adans. (1, 4, 50) (1932–present), *Torilis japonica* (Houtt.) DC. (4) (1986)

Hedge-peak [Hedge peak] - *Rosa canina* L. (5) (1913)

Hedge-pink [Hedge pink] - *Saponaria officinalis* L. (5, 62, 64, 156, 157, 158) (1900-1929)

Hedge-taper [Hedge-tapers, Hedge taper] - *Verbascum thapsus* L. (5, 69, 156, 157, 158) (1900-1929)

Hedgeweed [Hedge weed, Hedge-weed] - *Sisymbrium officinale* (L.) Scop (5, 156, 158) (1900-1923)

Hediodilla - *Larrea tridentata* (Sessé & Moc. ex DC.) Coville var. *tridentata* (149) (1904) NM

Hediodillo - *Larrea tridentata* (Sessé & Moc. ex DC.) Coville var. *tridentata* (106) (1930)

Hediondillo (Spanish, stinking) - *Larrea tridentata* (Sessé & Moc. ex DC.) Coville var. *tridentata* (153) (1913) NM

Hedte-shutsh (Winnebago) - *Erythronium mesochoreum* Knerr (37) (1830)

Hedysarum - *Coronilla varia* L. (178) (1526), *Hedysarum alpinum* L. (131) (1899), *Hedysarum boreale* Nutt. (5) (1913), *Hedysarum* L. (1, 4, 158) (1900-1986)

H'eh'aka ta pezhuta (Dakota, elk medicine) - *Monarda fistulosa* L. (37) (1919)

He-huckleberry - *Cyrilla racemiflora* L. (5, 156) (1913-1923), *Lyonia ligustrina* (L.) DC. (109, 138, 156) (1923-1949)

Heidekorn (German) - *Fagopyrum esculentum* Moench (6) (1892)

Heil-aller-Schaden (German) - *Veronica serpyllifolia* L. (158) (1900)

Heilege dille (German) - *Anthemis cotula* L. (186) (1814)

Helbeh - *Trigonella foenum-graecum* L. (107) (1919)

Helecho macho (Spanish) - *Dryopteris filix-mas* (L.) Schott (158) (1900)

Helenie d'Automne (French) - *Helenium autumnale* L. (7) (1828)

Helenium (Official name of Materia Medica) - *Helenium autumnale* L. (7) (1828)

Helfringwort - *Ajuga reptans* L. (158) (1900)

Heliantheme du Canada (French) - *Helianthemum canadense* (L.) Michx. (6) (1892)

Helianthemoides - *Turnera ulmifolia L.* (1, 10, 13) (1818-1932)

Heliconia - *Heliconia* L. (138) (1923) for Mt. Helicon, seat of the muses

Heliopsis - *Heliopsis* Pers. (50, 155) (1942–present)

Heliotrope - *Heliotropium curassavicum* L. var. *obovatum* DC. (93, 157) (1929–1936), *Heliotropium europaeum* L. (156) (1923), *Heliotropium* L. (1, 2, 4, 50, 82, 106, 138, 155, 156, 158) (1895–present)

Hell-bind - *Cuscuta epilinum* Weihe. (156) (1923)

Hellebore - *Amianthium muscitoxicum* (Walt.) Gray (5, 156) (1913–1923), *Eranthis hyemalis* (L.) Salisb. (156) (1923), *Helleborus foetidus* L. (19) (1840), *Helleborus* L. (109, 138, 156, 167) (1814-1949), *Helleborus viridis* L. (184) (1793), *Symplocarpus foetidus* (L.) Salisb. ex Nutt. (186) (1814), *Veratrum viride* Ait. (possibly) (7, 23) (1810-1828)

Helleborine - *Epipactis gigantea* Dougl. ex Hook. (3, 85) (1932-1977), *Epipactis helleborine* (L.) Crantz (5, 156) (1913-1923), *Epipactis* Zinn. (possibly) (1, 50, 158) (1900–present)

Helleborus - *Helleborus niger* L. (52) (1919)

Helleborus trifolius (Official name of Materia Medica) - *Coptis trifolia* (L.) Salisb. (7) (1828)

Heller's everlasting - *Pseudognaphalium helleri* (Britt.) A. Anderb. subsp. *helleri* (5) (1913)

Heller's panicum [Heller panicum] - *Dichanthelium oligosanthes* (J.A. Schultes) Gould var. *scribnerianum* (Nash) Gould (155) (1942)

Heller's rosette grass - *Dichanthelium oligosanthes* (J.A. Schultes) Gould var. *oligosanthes* (50) (present)

Heller's wild onion - *Allium drummondii* Regel (97) (1937)

Hellroot [Hell root, hell-root] - *Orobanche minor* J.E. Smith (5, 156) (1913-1923)

Hellvine [Hell-vine] - *Campsis radicans* (L.) Seem. ex Bureau (156) (1923)

Hellweed [Hell-weed, Hell weed] - *Calystegia sepium* (L.) R. Br. subsp. *sepium* (156) (1923), *Cuscuta epithymum* (L.) L. (156) (1923), *Cuscuta europaea* L. (92) (1876), *Ranunculus arvensis* L. (5, 156, 158) (1900-1923)

Helmet flower [Helmet-flower] - *Aconitum napellus* L. (107, 156) (1919-1923), *Scutellaria galericulata* L. (46) (1879), *Scutellaria* L. (158) (1900), *Scutellaria lateriflora* L. (92) (1876)

Helmetpod [Helmet-pod, Helmet pod] - *Jeffersonia diphylla* (L.) Pers. (5, 7, 64, 92, 156) (1828-1923)

Helmkraut (German) - *Scutellaria* L. (158) (1900), *Scutellaria lateriflora* L. (6) (1892)

Helonias - *Chamaelirium luteum* (L.) A. Gray (52, 54) (1905-1919), *Helonias bullata* L. (19, 174) (1753-1840)

Helxine - *Parietaria officinalis* L. (178) (1526), *Parietaria pensylvanica* Muhl. ex Willd. (156, 157) (1923-1929)

Hemicarpha - *Lipocarpha micrantha* (Vahl) G. Tucker (72) (1907) IA

Hemlock [Hemloc, Hemlocke] - *Cicuta maculata* L. var. *angustifolia* Hook. (148) (1939), *Conium maculatum* L. (10, 14, 49, 53, 55, 60, 71, 92, 148, 179, 184, 187) (1526-1939), *Leucothoe axillaris* (Lam.) D. Don. (71) (1898), *Leucothoe* D. Don (75) (1894) NC, *Oxypolis* Raf. (1) (1932), *Oxypolis rigidior* (L.) Raf. (possibly) (156) (1923), *Sium suave* Walt. (156) (1923)

Hemlock [Hemloc, Hemlocke] or Hemlock tree - *Pinus* L. (167) (1814), *Pseudotsuga menziesii* (Mirb.) Franco (147) (1856), *Tsuga canadensis* (L.) Carr. (2, 6, 19, 49, 53, 58, 61, 108, 136, 161) (1840-1930), *Tsuga Carr* (1, 50, 109, 138) (1923–present)

Hemlock bark - *Tsuga canadensis* (L.) Carr. (92) (1876)

Hemlock beggarticks - *Bidens bipinnata* L. (19) (1840)

Hemlock dropwort [Hemlock-dropwort] - *Oxypolis rigidior* (L.) Raf. (possibly) (5, 156) (1913-1923)

Hemlock fir - *Abies balsamea* (L.) Mill. (92) (1876), *Tsuga canadensis* (L.) Carr. (6) (1892)

Hemlock geranium - *Erodium cicutarium* (L.) L'Hér. ex Aiton (19) (1840)

Hemlock gum - *Tsuga canadensis* (L.) Carr. (92) (1876)

Hemlock heron's-bill [Hemlock heron's bill] - *Erodium cicutarium* (L.) L'Hér. ex Aiton (5, 158) (1900)

Hemlock panicum - *Dichanthelium sabulorum* (Lam.) Gould & C.A. Clark var. *patulum* (Scribn. & Merr.) Gould & C.A. Clark (5) (1913)

Hemlock pine - *Tsuga canadensis* (L.) Carr. (5, 40) (1913-1928)

Hemlock pitch - *Tsuga canadensis* (L.) Carr. (57, 92) (1876-1917)

Hemlock rose grass - *Dichanthelium sabulorum* (Lam.) Gould & C.A. Clark var. *thinium* (A.S. Hitchc. & Chase) Gould & C.A. Clark (50) (present)

Hemlock rosette grass - *Dichanthelium sabulorum* (Lam.) Gould & C.A. Clark var. *patulum* (Scribn. & Merr.) Gould & C.A. Clark (50) (present), *Dichanthelium sabulorum* (Lam.) Gould & C.A. Clark var. *thinium* (A.S. Hitchc. & Chase) Gould & C.A. Clark (50) (present)

Hemlock spruce [Hemlockparsley, Hemlock-spruce] - *Tsuga canadensis* (L.) Carr. (6, 8, 10, 20, 46, 52, 53, 54, 55, 57, 58, 92, 182, 187) (1791-1922)

Hemlock spruce fir [Hemlok spruce-firr] or Hemlock spruce fir-tree - *Abies balsamea* (L.) Mill. (177) (1762), *Tsuga canadensis* (L.) Carr. (8, 14, 20) (1785-1882)

Hemlock stork's-bill [Hemlock stork's bill] - *Erodium cicutarium* (L.) L'Hér. ex Aiton (5, 92, 97, 156, 157, 158) (1876-1937)

Hemlock water parsnip - *Sium suave* Walt. (72, 131, 157) (1899-1929)

Hemlock-chervil [Hemlock chervil] - *Torilis japonica* (Houtt.) DC. (5, 156) (1900-1923)

Hemlock-leaf moonwort [Hemlock-leaved moonwort] - *Botrychium virginianum* (L.) Sw. (5, 157, 158) (1900–1929)

Hemlock-parsley [Hemlockparsley, Hemlock parsley] - *Conioselinum chinense* (L.) Britton, Sterns & Poggenb. (1, 5, 92, 93, 95, 156) (1876-1932), *Conioselinum* Hoffmann (50, 155, 158) (1900–present), *Sium suave* Walt. (5, 50, 155) (1913–present)

Hemp - *Cannabis* L. (1, 4, 50, 82, 93, 138, 155, 158) (1900–present), *Cannabis sativa* L. (4, 5, 6, 14, 21, 19, 53, 57, 59, 61, 72, 80, 82, 85, 92, 93, 95, 107, 109, 110, 114, 131, 145, 148, 155, 156, 157, 158, 184) (1793-1986)

Hemp agrimony - *Ageratina altissima* (L.) King & H.E. Robins. (156) (1923), *Eupatorium cannabinum* L. (92) (1876)

Hemp bamboo - *Sinocalamus latiflorus* (Munro) McClure (138) (1923)

Hemp broom-rape - *Orobanche ramosa* L. (5, 156) (1913-1923)

Hemp deadnettle [Hemp dead nettle, Hemp dead-nettle] - *Galeopsis bifida* Boenn. (5, 19, 156, 158) (1840-1923)

Hemp dogbane - *Apocynum cannabinum* L. (3, 122, 138, 155, 156) (1923-1977)

Hemp nettle [Hemp-nettle, Hempnettle] - *Galeopsis bifida* Boenn. (1, 3, 5, 10, 63, 72, 85, 92, 156, 158) (1899-1977), *Galeopsis* L. (4, 50, 155, 156, 158) (1900–present)

Hemp sesbania - *Sesbania herbacea* (P. Mill.) McVaugh (155) (1942)

Hemp tree [Hemp-tree] - *Vitex agnus-castus* L. (82, 109, 158) (1930-1949), *Vitex negundo* var. *heterophylla* (Franch.) Rehder (82) (1930) IA

Hempseed [Hemp seed] - *Cannabis sativa* L. (92) (1876)

Hempweed [Hemp-weed, Hemp weed] - *Cannabis sativa* L. (92, 157, 158, 179) (1526-1929), *Eupatorium hyssopifolium* L. (19) (1840), *Eupatorium* L. (184) (1793)

Hen plant [Hen-plant] - *Plantago lanceolata* L. (5, 156, 157, 158) (1900-1929), *Plantago major* L. (5, 156, 157, 158) (1900-1929)

Hen-and-chickens [Hen and chickens] - *Bellis perennis* L. (5, 92, 158) (1876-1913), *Sempervivum tectorum* L. (73, 109, 155, 156) (1892-1949)

Henbane - *Hyoscyamus* L. (50, 109 138, 155, 158) (1900–present), *Hyoscyamus niger* L. (1, 3, 4, 6, 7, 10, 14, 20, 49, 52, 53, 54, 55, 57, 59, 60, 61, 85, 92, 126, 138, 156, 158, 179, 184) (1793-1986)

Henbane of Peru - *Datura inoxia* P. Mill. (180) (1633), *Nicotiana tabacum* L. (178) (1526)

Henbell - *Hyoscyamus niger* L. (158) (1900)

Henbit [hen-bit, Hen bit] - *Ballota nigra* L. (5, 156, 158) (1900-1923), *Lamium amplexicaule* L. (4, 3, 5, 19, 62, 72, 75, 92, 93, 97, 122, 124, 156, 158, 178) (1596-1986), *Lamium* L. (1, 7, 93) (1828-1936)

Henbit archangel - *Lamium amplexicaule* L. (187) (1818)

Henbit deadnettle [Henbit dead-nettle, Henbit dead nettle] - *Lamium amplexicaule* L. (5, 50, 155, 50, 156, 158) (1900–present)

Henderson troutlily [Henderson troutlily]'s - *Erythronium hendersonii* S. Wats. (138) (1923)

Henderson's allamanda [Henderson allamanda] - *Allamanda cathartica* L. (138) (1923)

Henderson's common allamanda [Henderson common allamanda] - *Allamanda cathartica* L. (155) (1942)

Henderson's shootingstar [Henderson shootingstar] - *Dodecatheon hendersonii* Gray (138) (1923)

Hendon's bent grass [Hendon bent grass] - *Cynosurus cristatus* L. (5) (1913)

Henkam - *Hyoscyamus niger* L. (158) (1900)

Henna - *Lawsonia inermis* L. (109, 110, 138) (1886-1949), *Lawsonia* L. (138) (1923)

Henne - *Lawsonia inermis* L. (92) (1876)

Hen-pepper - *Capsella bursa-pastoris* (L.) Medik. (156) (1923) Ferrisburgh VT

Hens - *Viola canadensis* L. (74, 156, 158) (1893-1923)

Hen's-bill - *Onobrychis viciifolia* Scop. (158) (1900)

Hen's-foot [Hen's foot] - *Caucalis platycarpos* L. (92) (1876)

Hen's-toes [Hens' toes] - *Spiranthes cernua* (L.) L.C. Rich. (78) (1898) ME

Hep tree - *Rosa canina* L. (92) (1876)

Hepatica - *Hepatica* Mill. (1, 2, 138) (1895-1932), *Hepatica nobilis* Schreb. (40, 82, 105, 156) (1923-1932), *Hepatica nobilis* Schreb. var. *acuta* (Pursh) Steyermark (82) (1930), *Hepatica nobilis* Schreb. var. *obtusa* (Pursh) Steyermark (6, 40, 42, 49, 165, 174, 177) (1753-1892)

Hepatica (Official name of Materia Medica) - *Hepatica nobilis* Schreb. (7) (1828)

Hepatique (French) - *Hepatica nobilis* Schreb. (46) (1879), *Hepatica nobilis* Schreb. var. *obtusa* (Pursh) Steyermark (6) (1892)

Hepatique trilobe (French) - *Hepatica nobilis* Schreb. (7) (1828)

Hepburn's sedge - *Carex nardina* Fries var. *hepburnii* (Boott) Kükenth. (139) (1944)

Heraclotic nuts - *Corylus avellana* L. (107) (1919)

Herb ax-weed - *Aegopodium podagraria* L. (156) (1923)

Herb bane [Herb-bane] - *Orobanche minor* J.E. Smith (5, 156) (1913-1923)

Herb Barbara [Herb-Barbara] - *Barbarea vulgaris* W.T. Aiton (5, 92) (1876-1913)

Herb Bennet [Herb Bennett] - *Conium maculatum* L. (6, 71, 107) (1892–1919) *Geum aleppicum* Jacq. (5, 19, 156) (1840-1923), *Geum canadense* Jacq. (5, 156) (1913-1923), *Geum urbanum* L. (107) (1919), *Geum virginianum* L. (5, 92) (1876-1913)

Herb Christopher [Herb-Christopher] - *Actaea pachypoda* Ell. (156, 158) (1900-1923), *Actaea rubra* (Aiton) Willd. (5, 10, 156, 157, 158, 187) (1818-1929), *Actaea spicata* L. (92) (1876), *Filipendula ulmaria* (L.) Maxim. (5) (1913), *Osmunda regalis* L. (5, 92, 157) (1876-1929), *Stachys officinalis* (L.) Trev. (5) (1913)

Herb Dutchman's-pipe [Herb Dutchmanspipe] - *Aristolochia serpentaria* L. (155) (1942)

Herb Gerard [Herb-Gerard, Herbe Gerard] - *Aegopodium podagraria* L. (5, 107, 156, 165, 178) (1526-1923)

Herb grace [Herb-grace] - *Bacopa monnieri* (L.) Pennell (5) (1913),

Verbena officinalis L. (5, 156) (1913-1923)

Herb Impius - *Filago vulgaris* Lam. (5) (1913)

Herb ivy [Herb-ivy] - *Carara coronopus* (L.) Medik. (5) (1913), *Coronopus squamatus* (Forsk.) Aschers. (156) (1923)

Herb John [Herb-John, Herbe John] - *Hypericum perforatum* L. (5, 62, 156, 157, 158, 179) (1526-1929)

Herb Margaret - *Bellis perennis* L. (5) (1913), *Leucanthemum vulgare* Lam. (5, 92, 156, 158) (1876-1923)

Herb mercury - *Mercurialis annua* L. (5, 156) (1913-1923)

Herb of Santa Barbara - *Barbarea* Aiton f. (13) (1849)

Herb Paris - *Trillium erectum* L. (156) (1923)

Herb patience - *Rumex patientia* L. (107, 109) (1919-1949)

Herb Peter - *Primula veris* L. (92) (1876)

Herb Robert [Herb-Robert, Herbe Robert] - *Geranium robertianum* L. (2, 4, 7, 15, 19, 46 (1671), 92, 109, 138, 156, 157, 158, 178) (1526-1986) deliberately introduced by colonists by 1671

Herb Saint Barbara [Herbe Saint Barbara] - *Barbarea vulgaris* W.T. Aiton (possibly) (180) (1633)

Herb sherard - *Sherardia arvensis* L. (5, 156) (1913-1923)

Herb Sophia - *Descurainia sophia* (L.) Webb ex Prantl (5, 50, 92, 97, 156, 157, 158) (1876–present)

Herb treemallow - *Lavatera trimestris* L. (138) (1923)

Herb Trinity [Herb-Trinity] - *Hepatica nobilis* Schreb. (92, 156) (1876-1923), *Hepatica nobilis* Schreb. var. *obtusa* (Pursh) Steyermark (5, 6) (1892-1913), *Viola tricolor* L. (158) (1900)

Herb true love - *Trillium erectum* L. (46) (1671)

Herb tuppence - *Lysimachia nummularia* L. (158) (1900)

Herb twopence [Herb-twopence, Herbe Two pence] - *Lysimachia nummularia* L. (5, 156, 158, 178) (1526-1923)

Herb wickopy [Herb-wicopy, Herb-wickopy] - *Chamerion angustifolium* (L.) Holub subsp. *angustifolium* (5, 156, 157, 158) (1900-1929)

Herb William [herb-William] - *Ptilimnium capillaceum* (Michx.) Raf. (5, 156) (1913-1923)

Herba agrimonia (Official name of Materia Medica) - *Agrimonia eupatoria* L. (7) (1828)

Herba britannica - *Rumex orbiculatus* Gray (174) (1753)

Herba catariae - *Nepeta cataria* L. (49) (1898)

Herba del pasmo - *Ericameria laricifolia* (Gray) Shinners (52, 54) (1905-1919)

Herba impia - *Filago vulgaris* Lam. (156) (1923)

Herba nepetae - *Nepeta cataria* L. (49) (1898)

Herba paris - *Trillium erectum* L. (46) (1671)

Herba salicariae - *Lythrum salicaria* L. (49) (1898)

Herba spagna (Itallian) - *Medicago sativa* L. (110) (1886)

Herba Veneris (Official name of Materia Medica) - *Adiantum pedatum* L. (7) (1828)

Herbaceous carrion-flower - *Smilax herbacea* L. (93) (1936)

Herbaceous periwinkle - *Vinca herbacea* Waldst. & Kit. (50, 138) (1923–present)

Herb-aux-charpentiers [Herbe aux Charpentiers] (French) - *Achillea millefolium* L. (156, 158) (1900-1923)

Herbe a 3 quarts (French, Louisiana) - *Verbesina virginica* L. (7) (1828) Lousiana Purchase

Herbe à beau-père (French) - *Abrus precatorius* L. (158) (1900)

Herbe à fiévre (French) - *Eupatorium perfoliatum* L. (6, 158) (1892-1900)

Herbe a la ouate (French) - *Asclepias syriaca* L. (6, 158) (1892-1900)

Herbe à la puce (Fr. Can.) - *Apocynum androsaemifolium* L. (41) (1770)

Herbe a l'hirondelle (French) - *Chelidonium majus* L. (6) (1892)

Herbe a malo (French) - *Alisma plantago-aquatica* L. (possibly) (166) (1807)

Herbe à quartre feuilles (Four-leaved grass)(French) - *Veronicastrum virginicum* (L.) Farw. (17) (1796)

Herbe à Robert (French) - *Geranium robertianum* L. (158) (1900)

Herbe a serpente a sonnetes (French) - *Podophyllum peltatum* L. (43) (1820)

Herbe aux chantres (French) - *Sisymbrium officinale* (L.) Scop (158) (1900)

Herbe aux chats (French) - *Nepeta cataria* L. (158) (1900)

Herbe aux vers (French) - *Tanacetum vulgare* L. (158) (1900)

Herbe de Feu (French) - *Erechtites hieraciifolia* (L.) Raf. ex DC. (6) (1892)

Herbe de la lache - *Phytolacca americana* L. var. *americana* (186) (1814)

Herbe de la Laque (French) - *Phytolacca americana* L. var. *americana* (6) (1892)

Herbe de Paigne (French) - *Chimaphila umbellata* (L.) Bart. (186) (1814)

Herbe de St. Antoine (French) - *Epilobium palustre* L. (6) (1892)

Herbe de Ste. Christophr blanc (French) - *Actaea pachypoda* Ell. (6) (1892)

Herbe Franckincense - *Seseli libanotis* (L.) W.D.J. Koch (178) (1526)

Herbe paralysy - *Primula veris* L. (179) (1526)

Herbe Parfaite (French) - *Eupatorium perfoliatum* L. (6, 158) (1892–1900)

Herbe phylyp - *Saponaria officinalis* L. (179) (1526)

Herbe St. Jean (French) - *Hypericum perforatum* L. (6) (1892)

Herbilia (Italian) - *Pisum sativum* L. (110) (930 AD)

Herb-like willow - *Salix herbacea* L. (5) (1913)

Herb-of-grace [Herb of grace, Herb-o'-grace] - *Bacopa monnieri* (L.) Pennell (156) (1923), *Ruta graveolens* L. (14, 92, 107, 156) (1876-1923)

Herb-of-the-cross - *Verbena officinalis* L. (5, 50, 62, 156) (1912–present)

Herb-robert geranium [Herbrobert geranium] - *Geranium robertianum* L. (155) (1942)

Hercules pricklyash - *Zanthoxylum americanum* Mill. (158) (1900), *Zanthoxylum clava-herculis* L. (155) (1942)

Hercules'-club [Hercules' club, Hercules club, Herculesclub] - *Aralia spinosa* L. (2, 5, 49, 58, 63, 92, 97, 109, 124, 155, 156) (1869-1942), *Zanthoxylum clava-herculis* L. (5, 14, 93, 124, 138, 156, 158, 181) (~1678-1936)

Herdgehog woodrush - *Luzula echinata* (Small.) Hermann (50) (present)

Herd's grass [Herds-grass, Herd's-grass, Herds-grass, Herd grass] - *Agrostis capillaris* L. (66, 90) (1885-1903), *Agrostis gigantea* Roth (5, 45, 92, 94, 187) (1818-1901), *Phleum pratense* L. (5, 45, 46, 56, 66, 68, 87, 90, 92, 109, 119, 143) (1884-1949), *Poa pratensis* L. (45) (1896)

Herd's grass of New England [Herds grass of New England] - *Phleum pratense* L. (92) (1876)

Herd's grass of Pennsylvania [Herds grass of Pennsylvania] - *Agrostis capillaris* L. (87, 88, 92) (1876-1885)

Here a pisser (Canada) - *Chimaphila maculata* (L.) Pursh (7) (1828)

Herehoune - *Marrubium vulgare* L. (158) (1900)

Herneh - *Pennisetum glaucum* (L.) R. Br. (46) (1879)

Heron's-bill [Heron's bill, Herons-bill, Heronbill, Herons' bill] - *Erodium cicutarium* (L.) L'Hér. ex Aiton (92, 156, 157) (1898-1929), *Erodium* L'Her. ex Aiton (106, 109, 138, 155) (1923-1949) from shape of seed pod

Hervey's aster - *Eurybia ×herveyi* (Gray) Nesom [*macrophylla × spectabilis*] (5) (1913)

Herzgespann (German) - *Leonurus cardiaca* L. (158) (1900)

Hesper palm - *Brahea* Mart. ex Endl. (109) (1949)

Heterotheca - *Heterotheca* Cass. (158) (1900), *Heterotheca subaxillaris* (Lam.) Britton & Rusby (5, 97) (1913-1937)

Heth - *Arctostaphylos uva-ursi* (L.) Spreng. (6) (1892)

Hetich - *Ipomoea batatas* (L.) Lam. (181) (~1678)

He'-to-co-ni (Zuñi) - *Nicotiana* L. (132) (1855)

Hètre - *Fagus* L. (8) (1785)

Hètre des bois à feuilles pourpres (French) - *Fagus sylvatica* L. (8) (1785)

Heuchera - *Heuchera americana* L. (57, 174, 177) (1753–1917)

Heuchera radix (Official name of Materia Medica) - *Heuchera villosa* Michx. (possibly) (7) (1828)

Heuchere Erable (French) - *Heuchera villosa* Michx. (possibly) (7) (1828)

Hever - *Avena fatua* L. (5) (1913)

Hever grass - *Arrhenatherum elatius* (L.) Beauv. ex J. Presl & C. Presl (5) (1913)

Hexagon beech fern - *Phegopteris hexagonoptera* (Michx.) Fee (5) (1913)

Hexagon stonecrop - *Sedum sexangulare* L. (138, 155) (1923-1942)

Hexaka tawote (Lakota, elk food) - *Monarda fistulosa* L. (121) (1918?-1970?)

Hexehasel (German) - *Hamamelis virginiana* L. (7) (1828)

Hexenkraut (German) - *Hypericum perforatum* L. (6, 158) (1892–1900)

Heydencorn - *Fagopyrum esculentum* Moench (180) (1633)

Heydenkorn - *Fagopyrum esculentum* Moench (107) (1552)

Heyder's mammillaria [Heyder mammillaria] - *Mammillaria heyderi* Muehlenpfordt (155) (1942)

Heyoka ta pezhuta (Dakota, medicine of the heyoka) - *Sphaeralcea coccinea* (Nutt.) Rydb. subsp. *coccinea* (37) (1919)

Hiarteblad (Swedish) - *Parnassia palustris* L. (46) (1879)

Hibelia - *Campanulastrum americanum* (L.) Small (77) (1898) Sulphur Grove OH, spikes of flowers resemble *Lobelia syphylitica* (High lobelia) from a distance

Hibiscus - *Hibiscus* L. (138, 155, 158) (1923-1942)

Hickory elm - *Ulmus thomasii* Sarg. (5, 156, 157, 158) (1900-1929)

Hickory nut - *Carya alba* (L.) Nutt. ex Ell. (14) (1882), *Carya ovata* (Mill.) K. Koch (37) (1919)

Hickory or Hickory tree [Hiccory-tree] - *Carya alba* (L.) Nutt. ex Ell. (6, 34, 40, 41, 46, 92, 189) (1767-1928), *Carya laciniosa* (Michx. f.) G. Don (92) (1876), *Carya* Nutt. (7, 10, 35, 50, 82, 93, 106, 112, 138, 155, 156, 158, 167, 182, 190) (1791–present) from aboriginal hicori, *Juglans* L. (167, 190) (~1759-1814)

Hickory pine - *Pinus aristata* Engelm. (109, 153) (1913-1949), *Pinus pungens* Lamb. (5) (1913)

Hickory poplar - *Liriodendron tulipifera* L. (5, 74) (1893-1913) WV

Hidden dropseed - *Sporobolus clandestinus* (Biehler) A.S. Hitchc. (155) (1942)

Hidden-flower panic grass [Hidden-flowered panic grass] - *Dichanthelium clandestinum* (L.) Gould (66, 90) (1885-1903)

Hidden-flower vilfa [Hidden flowered vilfa] - *Sporobolus vaginiflorus* (Torr. ex Gray) Wood (66) (1903)

Hidden-fruit bladderwort [Hidden-fruited bladderwort] - *Utricularia geminiscapa* Benj. (5) (1913)

Hidden-fruit sedge [Hidden-fruited sedge] - *Carex lyngbyei* Hornem. (5) (1913)

Hiel de tierra (Spanish) - *Fumaria officinalis* L. (158) (1900)

Hierba carmin - *Phytolacca americana* L. var. *americana* (186) (1814)

Hierba de pico - *Geranium maculatum* L. (186) (1814)

Hierusalem artichoke - *Helianthus tuberosus* L. (107, 177) (1762–1919)

Hi'-e-tran (Kiwomi Keres) - *Populus* L. (132) (1855)

Higan cherry - *Prunus subhirtella* Miq. (138) (1923)

High angelica - *Angelica atropurpurea* L. (6, 49, 92) (1876-1898)

High angelicam - *Angelica atropurpurea* L. (64) (1907)

High black blueberry - *Vaccinium fuscatum* Aiton (156) (1923)

High blueberry [High blue-berry] - *Gaylussacia frondosa* (L.) Torr. & Gray (49, 156) (1898-1923), *Vaccinium corymbosum* L. (107, 156) (1919-1923)

High cranberry - *Viburnum opulus* L. (49, 52, 53, 54, 58, 59, 61, 92, 156) (1869–1923)

High cranberry bark - *Viburnum opulus* L. (92) (1876)

High daisy - *Tanacetum vulgare* L. (109) (1949)

High dandelion - *Hieracium canadense* Michx. (5, 158) (1900–1913)

High geranium - *Hydrangea arborescens* L. (156) (1923)

High goldenrod [High golden-rod] - *Solidago canadensis* L. (158) (1900), *Solidago canadensis* L. var. *scabra* Torr. & Gray (5) (1913)

High heal-all [High healall] - *Pedicularis canadensis* L. (5, 156) (1913-1923), *Pedicularis canadensis* L. subsp. *canadensis* (92) (1876)

High laurel - *Kalmia latifolia* L. (71) (1898)

High mallow - *Malva sylvestris* L. (3, 4, 5, 15, 50, 72, 92, 93, 107, 114, 122, 131, 155, 156, 157, 158) (1894–present)

High pennyroyal - *Cunila origanoides* (L.) Britton (156, 158) (1900-1923)

High veronica - *Veronicastrum virginicum* (L.) Farw. (6) (1892)

High whortleberry - *Vaccinium corymbosum* L. (156) (1923)

High-belia [Highbelia, High belia] - *Lobelia cardinalis* L. (6) (1892), *Lobelia siphilitica* L. (5, 6, 75, 92, 156, 158) (1876-1923)

High-brush blackberry [Highbrush blackberry] - *Rubus ostryifolius* Rydb. (155) (1942)

High-bush blueberry [Highbush blueberry] - *Vaccinium corymbosum* L. (5, 106, 109, 138, 156) (1923-1949)

High-bush cranberry [Highbush cranberry] - *Viburnum opulus* L. (3, 4, 35, 37, 52, 57, 73, 112, 156, 158) (1806-1986), *Viburnum opulus* L. var. *americanum* Aiton (possibly) (4, 106) (1930-1986)

High-bush huckleberry - *Gaylussacia baccata* (Wang.) K. Koch (5, 156) (1913-1923)

High-daisy [High daisy] - *Tanacetum vulgare* L. (109) (1949)

Highland black-gum - *Nyssa sylvatica* Marsh. (106) (1930)

Highland cranberry - *Viburnum edule* (Michx.) Raf. (40) (1928)

Highland huckleberry - *Gaylussacia baccata* (Wang.) K. Koch (72) (1907)

Highland rush - *Juncus trifidus* L. (5, 50) (1913–present)

Highland willow oak - *Quercus nigra* L. (189) (1767)

High-taper [High taper] - *Verbascum thapsus* L. (5, 6, 14, 92, 158) (1882-1913)

High-water shrub [Highwater-shrub] - *Iva frutescens* L. (5, 19) (1840-1913), *Iva frutescens* L. subsp. *oraria* (Bartlett) R.C. Jackson (156) (1923)

Hig-taper [Hig taper] - *Verbascum thapsus* L. (5, 158) (1900-1913)

Hilaria - *Hilaria* Kunth (155) (1942)

Hilder - *Sambucus nigra* L. (158) (1900)

Hill clematis - *Clematis ligusticifolia* Nutt. (106, 156) (1923-1930)

Hill vervenia - *Phacelia distans* Benth. (106) (1930)

Hillberry [Hill-berry, Hill berry] - *Gaultheria procumbens* L. (5, 6, 7, 92, 156) (1828-1923)

Hillerne - *Sambucus nigra* L. (158) (1900)

Hillman's panic grass [Hillman's panicgrass] - *Panicum hillmani* Chase (50) (present)

Hillman's panicum [Hillman panicum] - *Panicum hillmani* Chase (3, 155) (1942-1977)

Hill's oak - *Quercus ellipsoidalis* E.J. Hill (4, 5, 72, 156) (1907-1986)

Hill's pondweed - *Potamogeton hillii* Morong (5, 50, 131) (1899–present)

Hill's thistle - *Cirsium hillii* (Canby) Fernald (5) (1913), *Cirsium pumilum* (Nutt.) Spreng. (72) (1907)

Hillside blueberry - *Vaccinium pallidum* Aiton (4) (1986)

Hillside ground-cherry [Hillside ground cherry] - *Physalis hederifolia* Gray var. *comata* (Rydb.) Waterfall (5, 72, 97, 122) (1907-1937)

Hillside hawthorn - *Crataegus punctata* Jacq. (4) (1986)

Hillside sedge - *Carex siccata* Dewey (5) (1913)

Hills-of-snow - *Hydrangea arborescens* L. (5, 156) (1913-1923)

Hill-trot - *Daucus carota* L. (157, 158) (1900-1929)

Hillwort - *Mentha pulegium* L. (92) (1876)

Himalayan clematis - *Clematis orientalis* L. (138) (1923)

Himalayan dragonshead - *Physostegia virginiana* (L.) Benth. subsp. *virginiana* (155) (1942)

Himalayan honeysuckle [Himalaya-honeysuckle] - *Leycesteria formosa* Wallich (109, 138) (1923-1949)

Himalayan pine - *Picea abies* (L.) H. Karst. (138) (1923), *Pinus wallichiana* A.B. Jacks. (109) (1949)

Himbaringa - *Apios americana* Medik. (38) (1820)

Himili - *Aletris farinosa* L. (7) (1828)

Himmelbrand (German) - *Verbascum thapsus* L. (158) (1900)

Hinbthi-abe (Omaha-Ponca, beans) - *Amphicarpaea bracteata* (L.) Fern. var. *comosa* (L.) Fern. (37) (1919) Hinbthi-abe-hu (bean vine)

Hinbthinge (Omaha-Ponca) - *Phaseolus vulgaris* L. (37) (1919)

Hinbthi-si-tanga (Omaha-Ponca, large-seeded bean) - *Lathyrus brachycalyx* Rydb. subsp. *brachycalyx* . (37) (1919)

Hindberry [Hind-berries] - *Rubus idaeus* L. (92, 158) (1876-1900), *Rubus occidentalis* L. (46) (1622)

Hinde-hi (Omaha-Ponca) - *Tilia americana* L. (37) (1919)

Hindheal [Hind-heal, Hindheel] - *Chenopodium botrys* L. (5, 156, 157, 158) (1900-1929), *Tanacetum vulgare* L. (92, 156, 158) (1876-1923)

Hindischkraut (German) - *Solanum dulcamara* L. (158) (1900)

Hinds' walnut [Hinds walnut] - *Juglans hindsii* (Jepson) Jepson ex R.E. Sm. (138) (1923)

Hinds' willow [Hinds willow] - *Salix exigua* Nutt. (155) (1942)

Hindu datura - *Datura metel* L. (138, 155) (1931-1942)

Hindu lotus - *Nelumbo nucifera* Gaertn. (possibly) (138, 155) (1923-1942)

Hing-flower - *Physalis virginiana* Mill. (156) (1923)

Hini (Missouri & Osage) - *Veronicastrum virginicum* (L.) Farw. (6, 7, 56, 92, 157, 158) (1828-1929)

Hinih (Western Indians) - *Pterocaulon* Ell. (7) (1828)

Hinshke (Winnebago) - *Tilia americana* L. (37) (1919)

Hinta-chan (Dakota) - *Tilia americana* L. (37) (1919)

Hiɳdse (Osage) - *Tilia americana* L. (121) (1918?-1970?)

Hiɳdse hiu (Osage) - *Asimina triloba* (L.) Dunal (121) (1918?-1970?)

Hiɳdse waxtha (Osage) - *Asimina triloba* (L.) Dunal (121) (1918?-1970?)

Hiɳta (Lakota) - *Tilia americana* L. (121) (1918?-1970?)

Hip brier - *Rosa eglanteria* L. (5, 158) (1900-1913)

Hip fruit - *Rosa canina* L. (92) (1876)

Hip rose - *Rosa canina* L. (5) (1913), *Rosa eglanteria* L. (5) (1913)

Hip tree [Hiptree] - *Rosa canina* L. (5, 49, 58, 92) (1869-1913)

Hippo - *Euphorbia corollata* L. (7, 49, 92) (1828-1898)

Hippocastanum - *Aesculus* L. (165) (1768) used as food for horses & resembles chestnut

Hips - *Rosa canina* L. (92) (1876)

Hipwort [Hip-wort, Hip wort] - *Cotyledon* L. (86) (1878) old European name

Hirschdorn (German) - *Rhamnus cathartica* L. (158) (1900)

Hirschuffor kerschouff (Arabic) - *Cynara cardunculus* L. (110) (1886)

Hirse - *Panicum miliaceum* L. (158) (1900)

Hirse grass - *Panicum miliaceum* L. (5) (1913)

Hirss-starr (Swedish) - *Carex panicea* L. (46) (1879)

Hirsute caltrop - *Kallstroemia hirsutissima* Vail ex Small (5, 97) (1913-1937)

Hirsute sedge - *Carex complanata* Torr. (5, 50) (1913–present)

Hirtentäschel (German) - *Capsella bursa-pastoris* (L.) Medik. (158) (1900)

Hirtentäschlein (German) - *Capsella bursa-pastoris* (L.) Medik. (6, 158) (1892-1900)

Hispaniolan palmetto - *Sabal palmetto* (Walt.) Lodd. ex J.A. & J.H. Schultes (109) (1949)

Hispid blackberry - *Rubus hispidus* L. (5) (1913)

Hispid buttercup - *Ranunculus hispidus* Michx. (5, 63, 97) (1899-1937)

Hispid crow-foot - *Ranunculus hispidus* Michx. (187) (1818)

Hispid false mallow - *Malvastrum hispidum* (Pursh) Hochr. (50) (present)

Hispid golden-aster [Hispid golden aster] - *Heterotheca villosa* (Pursh) Shinners var. *minor* (Hook.) Semple (5, 97) (1913-1937)

Hispid greenbrier [Hispid greenbriar] - *Smilax tamnoides* L. (5, 35, 72, 93, 97) (1806-1937)

Hispid purshia - *Onosmodium virginianum* (L.) A. DC. (187) (1818)

Hispid stylosanthes - *Stylosanthes biflora* (L.) Britton, Sterns & Poggenb. (187) (1818)

OF GREAT PLAINS PLANTS

Hogbed

Hispid yellow-cress [Hispid yellow cress, Hispid yellowcress] - *Rorippa palustris* (L.) Bess. subsp. *hispida* (Desv.) Jonsell (5, 50, 131) (1899–present)

Hitchcock's grape-fern - *Botrychium simplex* E. Hitchcock. (5) (1913)

Hitchcock's sedge - *Carex hitchcockiana* Dewey (5, 50, 66, 72) (1893–present)

Hive vine [Hive-vine, Hivevine] - *Coronilla varia* L. (5, 156, 158) (1900–1923), *Desmodium rotundifolium* DC. (5, 74, 156) (1893-1923) WV, *Mitchella repens* L. (92, 156) (1876-1923) no longer in use by 1923

Hma (Dakota) - *Juglans nigra* L. (37) (1919)

Hoar-dock - *Arctium lappa* L. (158) (1900)

Hoarwort - *Filago vulgaris* Lam. (5, 156) (1913-1923)

Hoary alder - *Alnus incana* (L.) Moench (2, 5, 46, 72, 82, 93, 156) (1879–1936)

Hoary alyssum - *Berteroa* DC. (1, 93) (1932-1936), *Berteroa incana* (L.) DC. (5, 72, 80, 85) (1907-1932)

Hoary andryala - *Andryala integrifolia* L. (165) (1807)

Hoary aster - *Machaeranthera canescens* (Pursh) Gray (4) (1986), *Machaeranthera canescens* (Pursh) Gray subsp. *canescens* var. *canescens* (155) (1942)

Hoary azalea - *Rhododendron canescens* (Michx.) Sweet (5, 122, 124, 156) (1913-1937)

Hoary basil - *Pycnanthemum incanum* (L.) Michx. (187) (1818)

Hoary bindweed - *Convolvulus arvensis* L. (5, 97, 122) (1913-1937)

Hoary cedronella - *Cedronella canariensis* (L.) Willd. ex Webb & Berth. (138) (1923)

Hoary cinquefoil - *Potentilla argentea* L. (5, 156, 158) (1900–1923)

Hoary cress - *Cardaria* Desv. (4) (1986), *Cardaria draba* (L.) Desv. (3, 4, 5, 97, 107) (1913-1986)

Hoary erigeron - *Erigeron canus* Gray (5, 50, 85, 93, 97, 131) (1899–present)

Hoary euphorbia - *Chamaesyce lata* (Engelm.) Small (3, 4, 155) (1942-1986)

Hoary evening-primrose [Hoary evening primrose] - *Oenothera macrocarpa* Nutt. subsp. *incana* (Gray) Reveal (4) (1986)

Hoary false alyssum - *Berteroa* DC. (3, 4) (1977-1986)

Hoary false goldenaster - *Heterotheca canescens* (DC.) Shinners & Gray (50) (present)

Hoary false madwort - *Berteroa incana* (L.) DC. (50) (present)

Hoary fleabane - *Erigeron canus* Gray (155) (1942)

Hoary frostweed [Hoary frost-weed] - *Helianthemum bicknellii* Fern. (5, 50, 72, 85, 97, 131, 156) (1899–present)

Hoary goldenweed - *Hazardia brickellioides* (Blake) W.D. Clark (155) (1942), *Hazardia cana* (Gray) Greene (155) (1942)

Hoary goosefoot [Hoary goose foot] - *Chenopodium incanum* (S. Wats.) Heller (42) (1814)

Hoary gromwell - *Lithospermum canescens* (Michx.) Lehm. (155) (1942)

Hoary hedge mustard - *Descurainia incana* (Bernh. ex Fisch. & C.A. Mey.) Dorn subsp. *incana* (156) (1923)

Hoary madwort - *Berteroa incana* (L.) DC. (165) (1768)

Hoary manzanita - *Arctostaphylos canescens* Eastw. (50, 155) (1942–present)

Hoary milkvetch [Hoary milk vetch] - *Astragalus sericoleucus* Gray (5, 93) (1913-1936)

Hoary mock orange [Hoary mockorange] - *Philadelphus pubescens* Loisel. (138) (1923)

Hoary mountain-mint [Hoary mountain mint] - *Pycnanthemum incanum* (L.) Michx. var. *incanum* (5, 97) (1913-1937)

Hoary pea [Hoarypea, hoary-pea] - *Lathyrus polymorphus* Nutt. subsp. *incanus* (Sm. & Rydb.) A.S. Hitchc (50) (present), *Tephrosia* Pers. (50, 156) (1923–present), *Tephrosia virginiana* (L.) Pers (5, 49, 86, 92, 156, 157, 158) (1878-1929)

Hoary peavine - *Lathyrus polymorphus* Nutt. (3, 98) (1926–1977), *Lathyrus polymorphus* Nutt. subsp. *incanus* (Sm. & Rydb.) A.S. Hitchc (155) (1942)

Hoary phlox - *Phlox hoodii* Richards. subsp. *canescens* (Torr. & Gray) Wherry (85) (1932)

Hoary plantain - *Plantago media* L. (5, 156) (1913-1923)

Hoary puccoon - *Lithospermum canescens* (Michx.) Lehm. (2, 4, 47, 50, 5, 63, 72, 85, 93, 97, 127, 131, 156, 157, 158) (1852–present), *Lithospermum caroliniense* (Walt. ex J.F. Gmel.) MacM. (98) (1926)

Hoary sagebrush [Hoary sage-bush] - *Artemisia cana* Pursh (5, 93, 95, 131) (1899–1936)

Hoary sandmat - *Chamaesyce lata* (Engelm.) Small (50) (present)

Hoary sedge - *Carex canescens* L. (5) (1913)

Hoary skullcap - *Scutellaria incana* Biehler (4) (1986)

Hoary spurge - *Chamaesyce lata* (Engelm.) Small (5, 97, 122) (1913-1937)

Hoary tansyaster - *Machaeranthera canescens* (Pursh) Gray subsp. *canescens* (50) (present), *Machaeranthera canescens* (Pursh) Gray subsp. *canescens* var. *canescens* (50) (present) *Machaeranthera canescens* (Pursh) Gray subsp. *glabra* (Gray) B.L. Turner (50) (present)

Hoary tickclover - *Desmodium canadense* (L.) DC. (3, 4, 138, 155) (1923-1986)

Hoary tick-trefoil [Hoary ticktrefoil, Hoary tick trefoil] - *Desmodium canadense* (L.) DC. (5, 50, 62, 72, 97) (1907–present)

Hoary verbena - *Verbena stricta* Vent. (50) (present)

Hoary vervain - *Verbena stricta* Vent. (3, 4, 5, 62, 63, 72, 80, 82, 85, 97, 106, 131, 156, 158) (1899-1986)

Hoary vetchling - *Lathyrus polymorphus* Nutt. (4) (1986)

Hoary Virginia rattlebroom [Hoary Virginia rattle broom] - *Crotalaria sagittalis* L. (181) (~1678)

Hoary whitlow-grass [Hoary whitlow grass] - *Draba incana* L. (5) (1913)

Hoary willow - *Salix candida* Flueggé ex Willd. (1, 3, 4, 5, 72, 93) (1907-1986)

Hoary-leaf alder [Hoary leaved alder] - *Alnus incana* (L.) Moench (42) (1814)

Hoary-leaf arnica [Hoaryleaf arnica] - *Arnica chamissonis* Less. subsp. *foliosa* (Nutt.) Maguire var. *andina* (Nutt.) Ediger & Barkl. (155) (1942)

Hoary-leaf Virginia mock syringa [Hoary leaved Virginia mock syringa] - *Spiraea tomentosa* L. (181) (~1678)

Hoary-pod Virginia willowherb [Hoary podded Virginia willow herb] - *Oenothera humifusa* Nutt. (181) (~1678)

Hobble bush [Hobblebush, Hobble-bush] - *Viburnum lantanoides* Michx. (2, 5, 19, 29, 75, 92, 109, 138, 156) (1811-1949) branches often take root at ends

Hock [Hocke] - *Alcea rosea* L. (158, 179) (1526–1900)

Hock-cockle [Hock cockle] - *Plantago lanceolata* L. (77) (1898) Southold Long Island

Hockholler - *Alcea rosea* L. (158) (1900)

Hod-the-rake - *Ranunculus repens* L. (156, 158) (1900-1923)

Hoe grass [Hoegrass] - *Muhlenbergia porteri* Scribn. ex Beal (155) (1942)

Hoe nightshade - *Solanum physalifolium* Rusby (50) (present)

Hof potato [Hof potatoe] - *Ipomoea pandurata* (L.) G.F.W. Mey. (186) (1814)

Hog brake - *Pteridium aquilinum* (L.) Kuhn (73, 79) (1891-1892) hogs like roots

Hog crawberry - *Arctostaphylos uva-ursi* (L.) Spreng. (5) (1913)

Hog millet - *Panicum miliaceum* L. (109, 152) (1912-1949)

Hog nut - *Carya glabra* (Mill.) Sweet var. *glabra* (82, 187) (1818-1930)

Hog-apple [Hog-apple] - *Podophyllum peltatum* L. (5, 6, 64, 76, 92, 156, 157, 158) (1892-1929) fruit eaten by pigs and boys (76)

Hog-bane [Hog's-bane] - *Chenopodium simplex* (Torr.) Raf. (158) (1900)

Hogbean [Hog bean, Hog's bean, Hog's-bean] - *Hyoscyamus niger* L. (5, 6, 92, 156, 158) (1876-1923)

Hogbed [Hog bed, Hog-bed, Hog's bed] - *Lycopodium clavatum* L. (6) (1892), *Lycopodium complanatum* L. (5, 92, 158) (1876-1913), *Lycopodium* L. (7) (1828)

193

Hog-bite [Hog bite] - *Chondrilla juncea* L. (5, 75, 156) (1894-1923) WV

Hog-cranberry [Hog cranberry] - *Arctostaphylos uva-ursi* (L.) Spreng. (75, 156) (1894-1923) Provincetown MA, *Empetrum nigrum* L. (5, 75, 156) (1894-1923) Islands of Penobscot Co. ME, no longer in use by 1923

Hog-fennel [Hog fennel, Hogfennel, Hog's fennel] - *Anthemis cotula* L. (5, 156, 157, 158) (1900-1929), *Peucedanum* L. (155, 158) (1900-1942), *Peucedanum ostruthium* (L.) W.D.J. Koch (156) (1923)

Hog-lily [Hog lily] - *Nuphar lutea* (L.) Sm. subsp. *advena* (Aiton) Kartesz & Gandhi (74) (1893) Concord MA

Hog-onion [Hog onion] - *Dichelostemma capitatum* (Benth.) Wood subsp. *capitatum* (75) (1894) CA, corm tastes like elm bark and is eaten by children

Hog-peanut [Hogpeanut, Hog peanut, Hog pea nut, Hog pea-nut] - *Amphicarpaea bracteata* (L.) Fern. (3, 4, 107, 121, 156) (1918?-1986), *Amphicarpaea bracteata* (L.) Fern. var. *comosa* (L.) Fern. (5, 40, 72, 93, 124, 127, 131, 158) (1899-1937), *Amphicarpaea* Ell. ex Nutt. (2, 50, 82, 93, 155, 156, 158) (1900–present)

Hog-physic [Hog physic, Hog's physic] - *Lobelia cardinalis* L. (5, 75, 156, 157, 158) (1894-1929) Plymouth Co. Mass

Hog-plum [Hog plum, Hog's plum] - *Colubrina texensis* (Torr. & Gray) Gray (122, 124) (1937) TX, *Prunus americana* Marsh. (5, 74, 107, 156) (1893-1923) TX, *Prunus hortulana* Bailey (76) (1896) Southwestern MO, *Prunus rivularis* Scheele (4, 155) (1942-1986), *Spondias mombin* L. (107, 109) (1919-1949), *Spondias purpurea* L. (107) (1919), *Ximenia* Plum. (15) (1895)

Hog-potata [Hog potata] - *Zigadenus venenosus* S. Wats. var. *gramineus* (Rydb.) Walsh ex M.E. Peck (158) (1900)

Hog-potato [Hog potato, Hog's potato, Hog-potatoe, Hog's potato] - *Ipomoea pandurata* (L.) G.F.W. Mey. (158, 187) (1818-1900), *Stenanthium gramineum* (Ker-Gawl.) Morong (156) (1923), *Zigadenus venenosus* S. Wats. var. *gramineus* (Rydb.) Walsh ex M.E. Peck (5, 158) (1900-1913)

Hog's haw - *Crataegus brachyacantha* Sarg. & Engelm. (74) (1893)

Hog's-turnip [Hog's turnip] - *Ranunculus bulbosus* L. (158) (1900)

Hog-succory [Hog's succory] - *Arnoseris minima* (L.) Schweig. & Koerte (possibly) (156) (1923)

Hog-taper - *Verbascum thapsus* L. (158) (1900)

Hogweed [Hog-weed, Hog weed] - *Ambrosia artemisiifolia* L. (2, 6, 58, 62, 72, 80, 92, 152, 158) (1869-1923), *Ambrosia artemisiifolia* L. var. *elatior* (L.) Descourtils (5, 19, 92, 157) (1840-1929), *Ambrosia* L. (45) (1896), *Conyza canadensis* (L.) Cronq. var. *canadensis* (5, 156, 157, 158) (1900-1929), *Eupatorium capillifolium* (Lam.) Small (5) (1913), *Polygonum aviculare* L. (158) (1900)

Hogwort [Hog wort] - *Croton capitatus* Michx. (5, 7, 50, 72, 92, 106, 156) (1828–present), *Croton capitatus* Michx. var. *capitatus* (50) (present)

Hohlzahn (German) - *Galeopsis bifida* Boenn. (158) (1900)

Hoils - *Hordeum* L (158) (1900)

Hokshi chekpa (Dakota, baby's navel) - *Lycoperdon perlatum* Pers. (possibly) (37) (1830)

Hokshi-chekpa wah'cha (Dakota, twin flower) - *Pulsatilla patens* (L.) Mill. (37) (1919)

Holboell's rockcress [Holboell's rock cress, Holboell rockcress] - *Arabis holboellii* Hornem. (5, 50, 131, 155) (1899–present)

Holdt's locust [Holdt locust] - *Robinia* ×*holdtii* Beissn. [*neomexicana* × *pseudoacacia*] (138) (1923)

Holewort - *Corydalis solida* (L.) Clairv. (92) (1876)

Hollard - *Alnus glutinosa* (L.) Gaertn. (5, 156) (1913-1923)

Hollek - *Alcea rosea* L. (158) (1900)

Hollihocke - *Alcea rosea* L. (178) (1526)

Hollikocke - *Alcea rosea* L. (158) (1900)

Hollow aphodill - *Asphodelus fistulosus* L. (178) (1596)

Hollow-leaf lavender [Hollow leave'd Lavender] - *Sarracenia purpurea* L. subsp. *purpurea* var. *purpurea* (181) (~1678)

Hollow-leaf sea lavender [Hollow-leaved sea lavender] - *Sarracenia purpurea* L. subsp. *purpurea* var. *purpurea* (181) (~1678)

Hollowroot [Hollow root, Hollow-root] - *Adoxa moschatellina* L. (5, 158, 165) (1768-1913)

Hollow-root musk - *Adoxa moschatellina* L. (156) (1923)

Hollow-stem hempweed [Hollow-stemmed hemp-weed] - *Eupatorium purpureum* L. (187) (1818)

Hollow-wort [Hollow wort] - *Corydalis solida* (L.) Clairv. (92) (1876)

Hollunder (German) - *Sambucus nigra* L. (158) (1900)

Holly barberry - *Mahonia aquifolium* (Pursh) Nutt. (2, 109, 135) (1895-1949)

Holly bay - *Gordonia lasianthus* L. (5, 19, 92, 156) (1840-1923)

Holly fern [Hollyfern, Holly-fern] - *Polystichum lonchitis* (L.) Roth. (4) (1986), *Polystichum* Roth. (1, 4, 50, 109, 138, 155) (1923–present)

Holly mahonia - *Mahonia aquifolium* (Pursh) Nutt. (109) (1949)

Holly malpighia - *Malpighia coccigera* L. (138) (1923)

Holly oak - *Quercus ilex* L. (107, 138) (1919-1923), *Quercus ilicifolia* Wangenh. (5) (1913)

Holly of America - *Ilex coriacea* (Pursh) Chapman (189) (1767)

Holly or Holly tree - *Ilex aquifolium* L. (41) (1770), *Ilex cassine* L. (107) (1919), *Ilex* L. (1, 4, 8, 10, 15, 106, 109, 138, 155, 158) (1785-1986), *Ilex opaca* Aiton (12, 57) (1821-1917)

Holly-bay - *Magnolia virginiana* L. (possibly) (156) (1923)

Holly-grape [Hollygrape] - *Mahonia* Nutt. (138) (1923)

Hollyhock [Hollyhocks, Hollihocke, Holyhocke] - *Alcea* L. (50) (present), *Alcea rosea* L. (3, 4, 46, 50, 57, 58, 82, 85, 92, 106, 107, 109, 114, 138, 155, 156, 158, 179, 184) (1671–present), *Althaea* L. (1, 4, 82) (1930-1986)

Hollyhock mallow - *Malva alcea* L. (138) (1923)

Holly-leaf barberry [Hollyleaved barberry, Holly-leaved barberry] - *Mahonia aquifolium* (Pursh) Nutt. (5, 50, 64, 157, 160) (1860-present)

Holly-leaf cherry [Hollyleaf cherry, Holly-leaved cherry] - *Prunus ilicifolia* (Nutt. ex Hook. & Arn.) D. Dietr. (20, 109, 138) (1857-1949)

Holly-leaf oak [Holly-leaved oak] - *Quercus agrifolia* Née (20) (1857)

Holly-oak [Holly oak] - *Alcea rosea* L. (158) (1900)

Holly-rose [Holly rose] - *Cistus salvifolius* L. (92) (1876), *Helianthemum canadense* (L.) Michx. (6) (1892)

Holmes' weed [Holmes'-weed, Holmes weed, Holmesweed] - *Scrophularia* L. (7) (1828), *Scrophularia marilandica* L. (92, 156, 157, 158) (1876-1929), *Scrophularia nodosa* L. (6) (1892)

Holosteum - *Holosteum* L. (50) (present), *Juncus bufonius* L. (174) (1753)

Holy clover - *Onobrychis viciifolia* Scop. (109) (1949)

Holy grass [Holygrass] - *Angelica archangelica* L. (92) (1876), *Angelica sylvestris* L. (107) (1919), *Hierochloe odorata* (L.) Beauv. (5, 80, 85, 87, 90, 92, 140) (1876-1944) strewn before church doors in N. Europe

Holy hay [Holyhay, Holy-hay] - *Medicago sativa* L. (5, 157, 158) (1900–1929)

Holy herb - *Verbena officinalis* L. (5, 62, 92) (1876-1913)

Holy hoke - *Alcea rosea* L. (158) (1900)

Holy plant - *Verbena officinalis* L. (156) (1923)

Holy rope [Holy-rope] - *Galeopsis bifida* Boenn. (156, 158) (1900-1923) obsolete (1923)

Holy thistle [Holy thystle] - *Cnicus benedictus* L. (5, 49, 58, 69, 92, 156, 179) (1526-1923), *Silybum marianum* (L.) Gaertn. (107, 109, 156, 158) (1900-1949)

Holy wood - *Guaiacum sanctum* L. (20) (1857)

Holz mangolt (German) - *Pyrola americana* Sweet (46) (1879)

Holzinger's eupatorium - *Eupatorium purpureum* L. var. *holzingeri* (Rydb.) E. Lamont (50) (present)

Holzinger's trumpet-weed - *Eupatorium purpureum* L. var. *holzingeri* (Rydb.) E. Lamont (97) (1937)

Holzinger's Venus' looking-glass - *Triodanis holzingeri* McVaugh (50) (present)

Homer's molley - *Allium canadense* L. (46) (1671)

Homestead lily - *Hemerocallis fulva* (L.) L. (156) (1923)

Homewort - *Sempervivum tectorum* L. (156) (1923)

Honduras coralblow - *Russelia equisetiformis* Schlecht. & Cham. (138) (1923)

Honesta - *Prunus americana* Marsh. (46) (1879)

Honesty [Honestie] - *Lunaria annua* subsp. *annua* L. (possibly) (5, 19, 92, 107, 109, 138, 156, 178) (1526-1949), *Lunaria* L. (138, 156) (1923), *Lunaria rediviva* L. (19) (1840)

Honewort [Hone wort] - *Cryptotaenia canadensis* (L.) DC. (1, 3, 5, 72, 85, 95, 97, 107, 131, 184) (1793-1977), *Cryptotaenia* DC. (50, 93, 158) (1900–present)

Honey - *Gleditsia triacanthos* L. (5, 158) (1900–1913), *Melilotus officinalis* (L.) Lam. (possibly) (5) (1913)

Honey clover [Honey-clover] - *Melilotus* Mill. (1) (1932), *Melilotus officinalis* (L.) Lam. (possibly) (5, 76, 156) (1896–1923), *Trifolium hybridum* L. (156) (1923)

Honey locust [Honeylocust, Honey-locust] - *Gleditsia* L. (1, 2, 4, 7, 8, 10, 82, 93, 109, 138, 155, 156, 167) (1814-1986), *Gleditsia triacanthos* L. (3, 4, 5, 8, 9, 10, 18, 19, 27, 35, 38, 41, 50, 63, 72, 82, 85, 92, 95, 97, 106, 107, 109, 112, 113, 114, 122, 124, 130, 135, 156, 157, 158, 177, 184, 187) (1762–present), *Prosopis juliflora* (Sw.) DC. (158) (1900), *Robinia hispida* L. (5, 74, 156) (1893-1923), *Robinia pseudoacacia* L. (5, 157, 158) (1900-1929), *Robinia viscosa* Vent. (5, 156) (1913-1923)

Honey lotus [Honey-lotus] - *Melilotus officinalis* (L.) Lam. (possibly) (5, 92, 156, 157, 158) (1876-1929)

Honey mesquit [Honey-mesquit] - *Prosopis juliflora* (Sw.) DC. (76, 158) (1896-1900) AZ

Honey mesquite - *Prosopis glandulosa* Torr. (4, 50, 155) (1942–present), *Prosopis juliflora* (Sw.) DC. (107) (1919)

Honey mushroom - *Armillaria mellea* (Vahl) P. Kumm. (170) (1995)

Honey plant [Honey-plant] - *Melissa officinalis* L. (5, 156) (1913-1923)

Honey vine [Honeyvine] - *Cynanchum laeve* (Michx.) Pers. (50) (present), *Enemion biternatum* Raf. (77) (1898) TX

Honeyballs [Honey-balls, Honey-ball] - *Cephalanthus occidentalis* L. (5, 156, 157, 158) (1913-1929)

Honey-berry [Honey berries] - *Exothea paniculata* (Juss.) Radlk. (92) (1876)

Honey-blobs [Honey blobs] - *Ribes uva-crispa* L. var. *sativum* DC. (5, 156, 157, 158) (1913-1929)

Honey-bloom [Honey bloom] - *Apocynum androsaemifolium* L. (6, 7, 92, 156, 157, 158) (1828-1929)

Honey-bread [Honey bread] - *Ceratonia siliqua* L. (92) (1876)

Honeybush - *Melianthus* L. (138) (1923)

Honey-cap [Honey cap] - *Armillaria mellea* (Vahl) P. Kumm. (128) (1933) ND

Honey-color armillaria [Honeycolor armillaria] - *Armillaria mellea* (Vahl) P. Kumm. (155) (1942)

Honey-pod - *Prosopis juliflora* (Sw.) DC. (158) (1900)

Honey-shucks [Honey shucks] - *Gleditsia triacanthos* L. (5, 156, 157, 158) (1900-1929)

Honey-stalks [Honey stalks] - *Trifolium repens* L. (5, 156, 157, 158) (1900-1929)

Honeysuckle [Honey suckle, Honey-suckle, Honisuckles] - *Aquilegia canadensis* L. (5, 76, 156, 158) (1896-1923), *Aquilegia* L. (2, 79) (1891–1895) Northeastern US, *Castilleja sessiliflora* Pursh (77) (1898) Burnside SD, *Lonicera caprifolium* L. (19, 92) (1840-1876), *Lonicera ciliosa* (Pursh) Poir. ex DC. (35) (1806), *Lonicera dioica* L. (possibly) (105) (1932), *Lonicera* L. (1, 2, 4, 8, 7, 40, 50, 82, 93, 106, 109, 138, 155, 156, 158, 190) (~1759–present) for nectar at bottom of flower, *Lonicera periclymenum* L. (178) (1526), *Lonicera reticulata* Raf. (63) (1899), *Lonicera sempervirens* L. (possibly) (114) (1894), *Rhododendron calendulaceum* (Michx.) Torr. (177) (1762), *Rhododendron periclymenoides* (Michx.) Shinners (73) (1892) MD, *Symphoricarpos* Duham. (35)

(1806), *Trifolium repens* L. (76) (1896) Oxford Co. ME

Honeysuckle clover [Honey-suckle clover] - *Trifolium pratense* L. (5, 156, 157, 158) (1876-1929) England, *Trifolium repens* L. (5, 156, 158) (1900-1923) no longer in use by 1923

Honeysuckle penstemon - *Penstemon murrayanus* Hook. (124) (1937)

Honeysweet [Honey-sweet, Honey sweet] - *Filipendula ulmaria* (L.) Maxim. (5, 156) (1913-1923), *Tidestromia* Standl. (50) (present)

Honeyweed - *Leonurus sibiricus* L. (50) (present)

Honeywort - *Cerinthe* L. (138) (1923)

Honink (Winnebago) - *Phaseolus vulgaris* L. (37) (1919)

Honink-boije (Winnebago) - *Amphicarpaea bracteata* (L.) Fern. var. *comosa* (L.) Fern. (37) (1919)

Honysocle - *Melilotus* Mill. (179) (1526)

Hoŋbõiŋθu (Osage, cut bean) - *Amphicarpaea bracteata* (L.) Fern. (121) (1918?-1970?)

Hoŋbthiŋ (Osage) - *Phaseolus vulgaris* L. (121) (1918?-1970?) Osage have at least two named varieties

Hooded arrowhead - *Sagittaria calycina* Engelm. (50) (present), *Sagittaria calycina* Engelm. var. *calycina* (50) (present)

Hooded blue violet - *Viola cucullata* Aiton (156) (1923), *Viola nephrophylla* Greene (5, 93) (1913-1936)

Hooded coralroot - *Corallorrhiza striata* Lindl. (50) (present), *Corallorrhiza striata* Lindl. var. *striata* (50) (present)

Hooded grass - *Bromus hordeaceus* L. (5) (1913)

Hooded lady's-tresses [Hooded ladies' tresses] - *Spiranthes romanzoffiana* Cham. (3, 50, 93) (1936–present)

Hooded milfoil - *Utricularia geminiscapa* Benj. (5) (1913), *Utricularia inflata* Walt. (19) (1840), *Utricularia macrorhiza* Le Conte (92) (1876), *Utricularia purpurea* Walt. (5, 156) (1913-1923)

Hooded pitcherplant - *Sarracenia minor* Walt. (138) (1923)

Hooded skullcap - *Scutellaria galericulata* L. (93) (1936)

Hooded water-milfoil [Hooded water milfoil] - *Utricularia macrorhiza* Le Conte (92, 181) (~1678-1876)

Hooded willow-herb [Hooded willow herb, Hooded willow herbe] - *Scutellaria galericulata* L. (5, 92, 156, 157, 158, 178) (1526-1929), *Scutellaria lateriflora* L. (92) (1876)

Hooded windmill grass [Hooded windmillgrass] - *Chloris cucullata* Bisch. (50, 155) (1942–present)

Hood-leaf violet - *Viola cucullata* Aiton (73) (1892)

Hood's phlox [Hoods phlox] - *Phlox hoodii* Richards. (3, 85, 93, 155) (1932-1977)

Hood's sedge [Hood sedge] - *Carex hoodii* Boott (50, 139, 155) (1942–present)

Hoodwort [Hood-wort] - *Scutellaria lateriflora* L. (5, 6, 52, 58, 77, 92, 156, 157, 158) (1869-1929) Western US

Hoofs - *Tussilago farfara* L. (5, 156) (1913-1923) no longer in use by 1923

Hoof-shaped bracket fungus - *Fomes fomentarius* (L.) Fr. (128) (1933)

Hook violet - *Viola adunca* J.E. Sm. (5, 8, 155) (1913-1942)

Hooked agrimony - *Agrimonia gryposepala* Wallr. (4) (1986)

Hooked bristle grass [Hooked bristlegrass] - *Setaria verticillata* (L.) Beauv. (50, 140, 155) (1942–present)

Hooked buttercup - *Ranunculus recurvatus* Poir. (3, 4, 155) (1942-1986)

Hooked crowfoot - *Ranunculus recurvatus* Poir. (5, 63, 72, 93, 156) (1899-1936)

Hooked pepperwort - *Marsilea vestita* Hook. & Grev. subsp. *vestita* (155) (1942)

Hookers - *Viola cucullata* Aiton (156) (1923)

Hooker's blue flag - *Iris setosa* Pallas ex Link var. *canadensis* M. Foster ex B.L. Robins. & Fern. (5) (1913)

Hooker's evening-primrose [Hooker eveningprimrose, Hooker's evening primrose] - *Oenothera elata* Kunth subsp. *hirsutissima* (Gray ex S. Wats.) W. Dietr. (3, 50, 155) (1942–present)

Hooker's gaertneria - *Ambrosia acanthicarpa* Hook. (5) (1913)

Hooker's manzanita [Hooker manzanita] - *Arctostaphylos hookeri* G. Don (155) (1942)

Hooker's oat - *Helictotrichon hookeri* (Scribn.) Henr. (5) (1913)

Hooker's orchid [Hooker orchid] - *Platanthera hookeri* (Torr. ex Gray) Lindl. (50, 138) (1923–present)

Hooker's orchis - *Platanthera hookeri* (Torr. ex Gray) Lindl. (5, 72) (1907-1913) IA

Hooker's othake - *Palafoxia sphacelata* (Nutt. ex Torr.) Cory (5, 97) (1913-1937)

Hooker's pelican Dutchman's-pipe [Hookers pelican Dutchmanspipe] - *Aristolochia grandiflora* Sw. (155) (1942)

Hooker's sandwort [Hooker sandwort] - *Arenaria hookeri* Nutt. (5, 50, 131, 155) (1899–present), *Arenaria hookeri* Nutt. subsp. *hookeri* (50) (present)

Hooker's scratchdaisy - *Croptilon hookerianum* (Torr. & Gray) House var. *validum* (Rydb.) E.B. Sm. (50) (present)

Hooker's sedge [Hooker sedge] - *Carex hookeriana* Dew (139) (1944)

Hooker's townsend daisy - *Townsendia hookeri* Beaman (50) (present)

Hooker's willow - *Salix hookeriana* Barratt ex Hook. (20) (1857)

Hook-heal [Hook heal] - *Prunella vulgaris* L. (5, 92, 156, 158) (1876-1923)

Hook-spur violet [Hookspur violet, Hook-spurred violet] - *Viola adunca* J.E. Sm. (4, 50) (1986–present)

Hook-style crowfoot [Hook styled crowfoot] - *Ranunculus recurvatus Poir.* (2) (1895)

Hookweed [Hook weed, Hook-weed] - *Prunella vulgaris* L. (5, 92, 156, 157, 158) (1876-1929)

Hoop ash - *Celtis occidentalis* L. (5, 19, 20, 27, 75, 156, 158) (1811-1923), *Fraxinus nigra* Marsh (5, 156, 158) (1900–1923), *Prunus padus* L. (92) (1876)

Hoop tree - *Azadirachta indica* Adr. Juss. (possibly) (7) (1828), *Melia azedarach* L. (92) (1876)

Hoopkoop plant - *Kummerowia striata* (Thunb.) Schindl. (5, 158) (1900–1913)

Hoop-petticoat [Hoop petticoat] - *Narcissus bulbocodium* L. (92) (1876)

Hoop-petticoat daffodil - *Narcissus bulbocodium* L. (109) (1949)

Hoop-wood - *Ilex laevigata* (Pursh) Gray (156) (1923)

Hoorletta (Swedish) - *Buglossoides arvensis* (L.) I.M. Johnston (46) (1879)

Hop [Hops, Hoppes] - *Humulus japonicus* Sieb. & Zucc. (21) (1893), *Humulus L.:* (1, 4, 50, 93, 106, 109, 138, 155, 156, 158, 167) (1814–present), *Humulus lupulus* L. (5, 7, 10, 27, 49, 52, 53, 55, 57, 59, 60, 72, 85, 92, 92, 95, 107, 110, 131, 157, 179, 184, 187) (1526-1922), *Humulus lupulus* L. var. *lupuloides* E. Small (37) (1919)

Hop clover [Hop-clover] - *Medicago lupulina* L. (5, 85, 93, 109, 122, 156, 158) (1900–1949), *Trifolium aureum* Pollich (5, 46, 80, 156) (1879-1923), *Trifolium campestre* Schreber. (19, 82, 85, 106) (1840-1932)

Hop hornbeam [Hop-hornbeam, Hophornbeam, Hophorn-bean] or Hop hornbeam tree [Hop horn beam tree] - *Carpinus betulus* L. (14) (1882), *Ostrya carpinifolia* Scop. (8, 10, 38, 42, 49) (1785-1898), *Ostrya knowltonii* Coville (153) (1913), *Ostrya* Scop. (1, 2, 4, 50, 82, 109, 138, 155, 156, 158) (1895–present), *Ostrya virginiana* (Mill.) K. Koch var. *virginiana* (4, 5, 19, 40, 50, 57, 75, 92, 93, 97, 112, 121, 122, 124, 130, 156, 158) (1840–present)

Hop medick [Hop-medick] - *Medicago lupulina* L. (5, 14, 19, 62, 92, 156, 158) (1840-1923)

Hop sedge - *Carex lupulina* Muhl. ex Willd. (3, 5, 50, 66, 72, 155) (1907–present)

Hop tree [Hop-tree, Hoptree] - *Ptelea* L. (1, 4, 50, 15, 82, 109, 138, 155, 158) (1895–present), *Ptelea trifoliata* L. (3, 4, 6, 49, 53, 82, 92, 106, 107, 112, 137, 156) (1892-1986), *Ptelea trifoliata* L. subsp. *angustifolia* (Benth.) V. Bailey var. *angustifolia* (Benth.) M.E. Jones (112) (1937), *Ptelea trifoliata* L. subsp. *trifoliata* var. *mollis* Torr. & Gray (112, 137) (1931-1937)

Hop trefoil [Hop-trefoil] - *Medicago lupulina* L. (92, 158) (1876-1900), *Trifolium aureum* Pollich (156) (1923)

Hop vine [Hop vine] - *Humulus* L. (153) (1913), *Humulus lupulus* L. (7, 44, 60, 92, 157, 158) (1828-1929), *Humulus lupulus* L. var. *neomexicanus* A. Nels. & Cockerell (149) (1904)

Hopbush - *Dodonaea* Mill. (138) (1923)

Hopéa - *Symplocos* Jacq. (8) (1785)

Hopéa des teinturiers (French) - *Symplocos tinctoria* (L.) L'Her. (8) (1785)

Hopfen (German) - *Humulus lupulus* L. (6, 7) (1828-1932)

Hopfenbaum (German) - *Ptelea trifoliata* L. (158) (1900)

Hopfenhausche (German) - *Ostrya virginiana* (Mill.) K. Koch var. *virginiana* (6) (1892)

Hop-horn beans - *Ostrya virginiana* (Mill.) K. Koch (157) (1929)

Hop-hornbeam copperleaf [Hophornbeam copperleaf] - *Acalypha ostryifolia* Riddell (155) (1942)

Hopi tea greenthread - *Thelesperma megapotamicum* (Spreng.) Kuntze (50) (present)

Hop-like sedge - *Carex lupuliformis* Sartwell ex Dewey (5, 72) (1907-1913), *Carex lupulina* Muhl. ex Willd. (187) (1818)

Hopniss (Delaware) - *Apios americana* Medik. (7, 46) (1828-1879)

Hoppner's sedge - *Carex subspathacea* Wormsk. ex Horner (5, 50) (1913–present)

Hor (Danish) - *Linum usitatissimum* L. (110) (1886)

Hor härr (Danish) - *Linum usitatissimum* L. (110) (1886)

Horehound [Hoarhound, Hore-hound, Horehounde] - *Ballota* L. (50) (present), *Eupatorium rotundifolium* L. (156) (1923), *Marrubium* L. (50, 82, 93, 109, 138, 155, 156, 158, 167) (1814–present), *Marrubium vulgare* L. (1, 7, 19, 49, 50, 53, 55, 57, 59, 85, 92, 106, 107, 158, 179, 184, 187) (1526–present)

Horehound lion's-tail [Hoarhound lion's-tail] - *Chaiturus marrubiastrum* (L.) Reichenb. (158) (1900)

Horehound motherwort [Hoar-hound motherwort, Hoarhound motherwort] - *Chaiturus marrubiastrum* (L.) Reichenb. (5, 156, 158) (1900–1923)

Horhowne - *Marrubium vulgare* L. (158) (1900)

Horn grass - *Bromus catharticus* Vahl (92) (1876)

Horn loco - *Astragalus hornii* Gray (155) (1942)

Horn poppy [Hornpoppy] - *Glaucium flavum* Crantz (possibly) (7) (1828), *Glaucium* Mill. (138, 155) (1923-1942)

Hornbaum (German) - *Cornus florida* L. (158) (1900)

Hornbeam [Horn beam] or Hornbeam tree - *Carpinus caroliniana* Walt. (35, 78, 85, 105, 122) (1806-1937), *Carpinus caroliniana* Walt. subsp. *caroliniana* (19, 92) (1840-1876), *Carpinus* L. (1, 2, 8, 10, 42, 109, 138, 167, 184) (1785-1949), *Nyssa sylvatica* Marsh. (5, 73, 156) (1892-1923) NH, no longer in use by 1923, *Ostrya virginiana* (Mill.) K. Koch (82) (1930)

Hornbeam three-seed mercury [Hornbeam three-seeded mercury] - *Acalypha ostryifolia* Riddell (5, 97, 122) (1913-1937)

Hornbine [Horn-bine, Horn bine] - *Nyssa sylvatica* Marsh. (5, 75, 156) (1894-1923) Southern states, no longer in use by 1923

Horne-bound tree [Horne bound tree] - *Nyssa biflora* Walt. (46) (1879)

Horned beakrush - *Rhynchospora corniculata* (Lam.) A. Gray (155) (1942)

Horned bladderwort - *Urtica urens* L. (19, 92, 187) (1818–1876), *Utricularia cornuta* Michx. (5, 156) (1913-1923)

Horned clover - *Medicago lupulina* L. (5, 156, 158) (1900–1923)

Horned fern - *Ceratopteris thalictroides* (L.) Brongn. (86) (1878)

Horned milfoil - *Utricularia geminiscapa* Benj. (5) (1913), *Utricularia purpurea* Walt. (5, 156) (1913-1923)

Horned nightshade - *Solanum angustifolium* Mill. (155) (1942)

Horned pondweed - *Zannichellia* L. (1, 50, 85, 156) (1923–present), *Zannichellia palustris* L. (3, 50, 97, 120) (1937–present)

Horned poppy [Horned-poppy] - *Glaucium flavum* Crantz (10, 15, 23, 19, 92, 156) (1810-1923), *Glaucium* Mill. (4, 109, 156, 158) (1900-1986)

Horned rush - *Rhynchospora corniculata* (Lam.) A. Gray (5, 66, 156) (1903-1923), *Rhynchospora macrostachya* Torr. ex Gray (3) (1977)

Horned sand grass - *Triplasis americana* P. Beauv. (66) (1903)

Horned spurge - *Euphorbia brachycera* Engelm. (50) (present)

Hornemann's willow herb [Hornemann's willowherb, Hornemann willowherb] - *Epilobium hornemannii* Reichenb. (5, 50, 131, 155) (1899–present)

Horn-pine [Hornpipe, Horn pine] - *Nyssa sylvatica* Marsh. (5, 75, 156) (1894-1923) Southern states, no longer in use by 1923

Hornpipe - *Nyssa sylvatica* Marsh. (5, 156) (1913-1923) no longer in use by 1923

Hornseed [Horn seed] - *Sclerotium clavus DC.* (92) (1876)

Hornwort [Horn wort] - *Ceratophyllum demersum* L. (3, 5, 19, 72, 85, 92, 93, 97, 120, 131, 155, 156, 157, 158) (1840-1977), *Ceratophyllum* L. (1, 4, 50, 10, 109, 155, 158, 167) (1814–present)

Horone - *Marrubium vulgare* L. (158) (1900)

Horse agaricus - *Agaricus arvensis* Schaeff. (155) (1942)

Horse aloes - *Sansevieria hyacinthoides (L.) Druce* (92) (1876)

Horse bean [Horse-bean, Horsebean] - *Vicia faba* L. (7, 68, 92, 107) (1828-1919)

Horse beech - *Carpinus caroliniana* Walt. (156) (1923)

Horse bramble - *Rosa canina* L. (5) (1913)

Horse cinquefoil - *Potentilla hippiana* Lehm. (155) (1942)

Horse daisy [Horse-daisy] - *Anthemis cotula* L. (157, 158) (1900–1929), *Leucanthemum vulgare* Lam. (5, 156, 158) (1900–1923)

Horse Dung Mushroom with dewey heads - *Pilobolus* Tode (181) (~1678)

Horse fleaweed - *Baptisia tinctoria* (L.) R. Br. ex Aiton f. (5, 92) (1876-1913)

Horse flower [Horse-floure] - *Melampyrum* (Tourn.) L. (180) (1633)

Horse gowan [Horse-gowan] - *Leucanthemum vulgare* Lam. (49, 158) (1898-1900), *Matricaria recutita* L. (5, 156, 158) (1900–1923), *Taraxacum officinale* G.H. Weber ex Wiggers (64, 69, 156, 157, 158) (1900-1929)

Horse grass [Horse-grass] - *Panicum miliaceum* L. (119) (1938) OK

Horse laurel - *Rhododendron maximum* L. (5, 71, 75, 156) (1894-1923) PA

Horse millet - *Pennisetum glaucum* (L.) R. Br. (45) (1896)

Horse mint [Horse-mint, Horsemint, Horsmynte] - *Mentha ×rotundifolia* (L.) Huds. [*longifolia × suaveolens*] (5, 156) (1913-1923), *Mentha arvensis* L. (19) (1840), *Mentha spicata* L. (5, 155, 156, 179) (1526-1942)

Horse mushroom - *Agaricus arvensis* Schaeff. (92, 170) (1876-1995)

Horse plum [Horse-plum] - *Prunus americana* Marsh. (5, 156, 158) (1900-1923), *Prunus nigra* Aiton (5, 156) (1913-1923)

Horse savin - *Juniperus communis* L. (5, 157, 158) (1900-1929)

Horse thistle [Horse-thistle] - *Cirsium vulgare* (Savi) Ten. (5, 156, 158) (1900-1923), *Lactuca serriola* L. (156, 158) (1900-1923), *Lactuca virosa* L. (5) (1913)

Horse violet [Horse-violet] - *Viola pedata* L. (5, 73, 158) (1892-1913) New England

Horsebalm [Horse-balm, Horse balm] - *Collinsonia canadensis* L. (5, 6, 19, 41, 46, 53, 64, 86, 92, 156) (1770-1923), *Collinsonia* L. (2, 50, 155, 156, 158) (1895–present)

Horsebean [Horse-bean, Horse bean] - *Parkinsonia aculeata* L. (106) (1930), *Parkinsonia* L. (106) (1930)

Horseblob [Horse blobs, Horse blob, Horse-blob] - *Caltha palustris* L. (5, 92, 156, 157) (1876-1929)

Horsebrier [Horse-brier, Horse brier, Horse briar] - *Smilax rotundifolia* L. (5, 19, 44, 75, 109, 156) (1894-1949)

Horsecane [Horse cane, Horse-cane] - *Ambrosia trifida* L. (5, 49, 92, 156, 158) (1898–1923)

Horse-chestnut [Horse chestnut, Horsechestnut] or Horse-chestnut tree - *Aesculus glabra* Willd. (124) (1937), *Aesculus hippocastanum* L. (5, 6, 19, 46, 49, 53, 54, 58, 61, 82, 85, 92, 112, 107, 138, 156) (1840-1937), *Aesculus* L. (1, 8, 10, 13, 15, 82, 109, 138, 155, 156, 158, 167) (1785-1949), *Aesculus pavia* L. (71) (1898)

Horse-crippler [Horse crippler] - *Echinocactus texensis* Hopffer. (50) (present)

Horse-crippler cactus [Horse crippler cactus] - *Echinocactus texensis* Hopffer. (109) (1949)

Horse-elder [Horse elder] - *Inula helenium* L. (5, 64, 156) (1907-1923)

Horsefly-weed [Horse-fly weed, Horsefly weed, Horse fly weed] - *Baptisia tinctoria* (L.) R. Br. ex Aiton f. (5, 6, 7, 58, 64, 92, 106, 107, 156, 157, 186) (1814-1930)

Horsefoot [Horse foot, Horse-foot] - *Tussilago farfara* L. (5, 156) (1913-1923)

Horse-gentian [Horse gentian, Horsegentian] - *Triosteum angustifolium* L. (3) (1977), *Triosteum* L. (1, 2, 4, 50, 138, 155) (1895–present), *Triosteum perfoliatum* L. (3, 4, 5, 6, 49, 58, 63, 72, 92, 93, 95, 105, 156, 157, 158) (1892–1986)

Horse-ginseng [Horse ginseng] - *Triosteum perfoliatum* L. (5, 6, 7, 19, 92, 156, 158) (1828-1923)

Horse-gold [Horse gold] - *Ranunculus acris* L. (5, 156, 157, 158) (1900-1929), *Ranunculus arvensis* L. (5, 156, 158) (1900-1923) IA KS, *Ranunculus repens* L. (5, 156) (1913-1923)

Horseheal [Horse-heal, Horse heal, Horshele] - *Inula helenium* L. (5, 62, 64, 92, 156, 179) (1526-1923)

Horsehoof [Horse hoof, Horse-hoof] - *Tussilago farfara* L. (5, 92, 156) (1876-1923)

Horse-knobs [Horse knobs, Horse knob] - *Centaurea nigra* L. (5, 92) (1876-1913)

Horse-knops [Horse knops] - *Centaurea nigra* L. (5, 156) (1913-1923)

Horselily [Horse-lily, Horse lily] - *Nuphar lutea* (L.) Sm. subsp. *advena* (Aiton) Kartesz & Gandhi (76, 156, 158) (1896-1923) Hartford ME

Horse-mint [Horsemint, Horse mint] - *Arnoglossum atriplicifolium* (L.) H.E. Robins. (38) (1820), *Monarda didyma* L. (5, 7, 156) (1828-1923), *Monarda fistulosa* L. (37, 85, 114, 121, 124, 156) (1894–1937), *Monarda fistulosa* L. subsp. *fistulosa* var. *mollis* (L.) Benth. (40, 101) (1905-1928), *Monarda* L. (1, 2, 4, 93, 106, 109, 156, 158) (1895-1986), *Monarda punctata* L. (1, 2, 5, 49, 52, 53, 57, 63, 72, 82, 97, 124, 156) (1895-1937), *Monarda punctata* L. subsp. *punctata* var. *occidentalis* (Epling) Palmer & Steyermark (3) (1977), *Pycnanthemum incanum* (L.) Michx. (46) (1879), *Pycnanthemum* Michx. (1, 93) (1932-1936)

Horsenettle [Horse nettle] - *Solanum carolinense* L. (1, 3, 5, 19, 49, 52, 53, 56, 57, 62, 63, 70, 72, 80, 85, 92, 95, 97, 122, 145, 156, 157, 158, 187) (1818-1977), *Solanum elaeagnifolium* Cav. (150) (1894), *Solanum* L. (1, 93) (1932-1936)

Horse-pipe [Horse pipe, Horsepipe] - *Equisetum arvense* L. (5, 157, 158) (1900-1929), *Equisetum hyemale* L. (5, 92, 158) (1876-1913)

Horse-purslane [Horse purslane] - *Trianthema portulacastrum* L. (4) (1986)

Horseradish [Horse-radish, Horse radish] - *Armoracia* P. Gaertn. & B. Mey. & Scherb. (93) (1936), *Armoracia rusticana* P.G. Gaertn., B. Mey. & Scherb. (1, 3, 4, 5, 7, 15, 19, 50, 55, 57, 58, 63, 85, 92, 107, 155, 156, 178, 184) (1633–present)

Horseradish tree [Horseradish-tree, Horse-radish-tree] - *Moringa* Adans. (138) (1923), *Moringa oleifera* Lam. (109, 138) (1923-1949)

Horseshoe geranium [Horse-shoe geranium] - *Pelargonium zonale* (L.) L'Hér. ex Aiton (19, 109, 138) (1840-1949)

Horseshoe violet [Horse shoe violet] - *Viola pedata* L. (5, 73, 74, 158) (1898-1913) MA

Horseshoe-vetch - *Hippocrepis* L. (109) (1949)

Horse-sorrel [Horse sorrel] - *Rumex acetosella* L. (5, 6, 62, 73, 75, 80, 156, 157, 158) (1898-1929)

Horse-sugar [Horse sugar] - *Symplocos tinctoria* (L.) L'Her. (2, 7, 93, 156, 183) (~1756-1923)

Horsetail [Horse tail, Horse-tail] - *Conyza canadensis* (L.) Cronq. var. *canadensis* (92, 145) (1876-1897), *Equisetum arvense* L. (19) (1840), *Equisetum fluviatile* L. (107) (1919), *Equisetum hyemale* L. (49, 53, 92, 107) (1919-1922), *Equisetum* L. (1, 4, 10, 14, 37, 50, 126, 138, 148, 155, 158) (1793–present)

Horsetail milkweed - *Asclepias subverticillata* (Gray) Vail (50) (present), *Asclepias verticillata* L. (138) (1923)

Horsetail paspalum - *Paspalum fluitans* (Ell.) Kunth (3, 50) (1977–present), *Paspalum setaceum* Michx. (155) (1942)

Horsetail rush - *Eleocharis equisetoides* (Ell.) Torr. (66) (1903)

Horsetail tree [Horsetail-tree] - *Casuarina equisetifolia* L. (109, 138) (1923-1949)

Horse-thyme [Horse thyme] - *Clinopodium vulgare* L. (5, 156) (1913-1923), *Clinopodium vulgare* L. (possibly) (92) (1876)

Horseweed [Horse-weed, Horse weed] - *Ambrosia trifida* L. (5, 7, 49, 62, 76, 92, 106, 122, 145, 156, 157, 158) (1828-1937), *Bigelowia nudata* (Michx.) DC. (156) (1923), *Collinsia* Nutt. (possibly) (10) (1818), *Collinsonia canadensis* L. (5, 6, 7, 58, 64, 86, 92, 184, 190) (~1759-1913), *Collomia* Nutt. (138) (1923), *Conyza canadensis* (L.) Cronq. (3, 4, 98, 121) (1918-1986), *Conyza canadensis* (L.) Cronq. var. *canadensis* (2, 5, 6, 7, 40, 45, 49, 58, 62, 63, 69, 72, 80, 92, 93, 95, 97, 114, 125, 131, 148, 156, 157, 158) (1828-1939), *Conyza* Less. (1, 50, 93, 158) (1900–present), *Iva* L. (1) (1932), *Iva xanthifolia* Nutt. (85) (1932), *Lactuca canadensis* L. (5, 75, 156) (1894-1923) WV, *Spiraea thunbergii* Sieb. ex Blume (92) (1876), *Spiraea tomentosa* L. (92) (1876)

Horseweed fleabane - *Conyza canadensis* (L.) Cronq. var. *canadensis* (155) (1942)

Horst's beech [Horst beech] - *Carpinus caroliniana* Walt. (156) (1923)

Hortulan plum - *Prunus hortulana* Bailey (50, 109 137, 138, 155) (1923–present)

Hosh-kawn - *Yucca baccata* Torr. (5) (1913)

Hotsprings fimbry - *Fimbristylis thermalis* S. Wats. (50) (present)

Hottentot-fig - *Carpobrotus edulis* (L.) N.E. Br. (109) (1949)

Houatte (Canada) - *Apocynum cannabinum* L. (6) (1892)

Houatte (Canada, Louisiana) - *Apocynum androsaemifolium* L. (7) (1828)

Houatte tubereuse (French) - *Asclepias tuberosa* L. (7) (1828)

Houblon (French) - *Humulus lupulus* L. (6) (1892)

Houblon commune (French) - *Humulus lupulus* L. (7) (1828)

Houghton's cyperus - *Cyperus houghtonii* Torr. (5) (1913)

Houghton's flatsedge [Houghton flatsedge] - *Cyperus houghtonii* Torr. (50) (present), *Cyperus lupulinus* (Spreng) Marcks (3) (1977)

Houghton's goldenrod [Houghton's golden-rod] - *Oligoneuron houghtonii* (Torr. & Gray ex Gray) Nesom (5) (1913)

Houghton's sedge - *Carex houghtoniana* Torr. ex Dewey (5, 50) (1913–present)

Hound grass - *Elymus caninus* (L.) L. (46) (1879)

Houndbene - *Marrubium vulgare* L. (5, 158) (1900–1913)

Hound's tree - *Cornus sanguinea* L. (14) (1882)

Hound's-bane [Hound's bane] - *Marrubium vulgare* L. (156) (1923)

Houndsbene - *Marrubium vulgare* L. (69) (1904)

Hound's-berry [Hound's berry] - *Solanum nigrum* L. (5, 156, 157, 158) (1900-1929)

Hound's-berry tree [Hounds' berry tree] - *Cornus sanguinea* L. (92) (1876)

Hound's-tongue [Hounds-tongue, Hound's tongue, Hounds' tongue, Hondes tonge] - *Carphephorus odoratissimus* (J.F. Gmel.) Herbert (5, 92, 156) (1876-1923), *Clintonia borealis* (Ait.) Raf. (78) (1898) ME, *Cynoglossum* L. (1, 2, 4, 7, 10, 50, 93, 107, 109, 138, 155, 156, 158, 184) (1793–present), *Cynoglossum officinale* L. (3, 4, 5, 19, 45, 47, 49, 62, 63, 72, 80, 92, 106, 145, 157, 158, 178, 179) (1526-1986)

Hound's-tongue with a very small flower [Hounds tongue with a very small flower] - *Hackelia virginiana* (L.) I.M. Johnston (181) (~1678)

House holly fern [House holly-fern, House hollyfern] - *Cyrtomium falcatum* (L. f.) C. Presl (109, 138) (1923-1949)

House leek tree - *Aeonium arboreum* (L.) Webb & Berthel. (92) (1876)

House poplar - *Populus nigra* L. (43) (1820)

House-amaryllis - *Hippeastrum puniceum* (Lam.) Kuntze (138) (1923)

Houseleek [House leek] - *Hylotelephium telephium* (L.) H. Ohba. subsp. *telephium* (79) (1891) NH, *Sempervivum* L. (109, 138, 155, 156) (1923-1949), *Sempervivum tectorum* L. (19, 46, 58, 92, 156, 179) (1526-1923)

Houselily [House lilly (sic)] - *Nuphar lutea* (L.) Sm. subsp. *advena* (Aiton) Kartesz & Gandhi (157) (1929)

Houstonia - *Houstonia* L. (138) (1923)

Houstonia with a small purple Flower - *Houstonia serpyllifolia* Michx. (183) (~1756)

Houx (French) - *Ilex* L. (8) (1785), *Ilex opaca* Aiton (7) (1828)

Houx de Canada (French) - *Ilex mucronata* (L.) M. Powell, Savol. & S. Andrews (8) (1785)

Houx de la Caroline (French) - *Ilex cassine* L. (8) (1785)

Houx ordinaire d'Amérique (French) - *Ilex aquifolium* L. (8) (1785)

Hove - *Glechoma hederacea* L. (5, 92, 157, 158) (1876-1929)

Howard's evening-primrose [Howard's evening primrose] - *Oenothera howardii* (A. Nels.) W. L. Wagner (50) (present)

Howard's rabbitbrush [Howard rabbitbrush] - *Ericameria parryi* (Gray) Nesom & Baird var. *howardii* (Parry ex Gray) Nesom & Baird (155) (1942)

Howard's rayless goldenrod [Howard's rayless golden-rod] - *Ericameria parryi* (Gray) Nesom & Baird var. *howardii* (Parry ex Gray) Nesom & Baird (5) (1913)

Howell's grass - *Calamagrostis howellii* Vasey (87) (1884)

Howell's manzanita [Howell manzanita] - *Arctostaphylos hispidula* T.J. Howell (155) (1942)

Howell's monkshood [Howell monkshood] - *Aconitum columbianum* Nutt. (155) (1942)

Howell's pussytoes - *Antennaria howellii* Greene (50) (present)

Howe's sedge - *Carex atlantica* Bailey subsp. *capillacea* (Bailey) Reznicek (5) (1913)

Hoxwa (Lakota) - *Acorus calamus* L. (121) (1918-1970)

Hrusska (Bohemian) - *Pyrus communis* L. (110) (1886)

H'thi-wathe-hi (Omaha-Ponca, plant that makes sore) - *Toxicodendron toxicarium* (Salisb.) Gillis (37) (1919)

Huachuca panicum - *Dichanthelium acuminatum* (Sw.) Gould & C.A. Clark var. *fasciculatum* (Torr.) Freckmann (155) (1942)

Huajillo - *Acacia berlandieri* Benth. (106) (1930) TX

Huamuchil - *Pithecellobium dulce* (Roxb.) Benth. (109) (1949)

Hubam sweet clover [Hubam sweetclover] - *Melilotus officinalis* (L.) Lam. (155) (1942)

Hubbard squash - *Cucurbita maxima* Dcne. (107) (1919)

Hucińška (Lakota, spoon plant) - *Asclepias viridiflora* Raf. (121) (1918?-1970?)

Huckleberry - *Gaylussacia baccata* (Wang.) K. Koch (2, 46, 58, 92) (1869-1895), *Gaylussacia frondosa* (L.) Torr. & Gray (5) (1913), *Gaylussacia* Kunth (1, 2, 106, 109, 138, 156) (1895-1949), *Vaccinium* L. (1, 7, 10, 41, 158) (1770-1932), *Vaccinium membranaceum* Dougl. (35, 85, 101) (1806-1923), *Vaccinium myrtillus* L. (92, 103) (1870-1876), *Vaccinium myrtillus* L. var. *oreophilum* (Rydb.) Dorn (153) (1913) NM, *Vaccinium pallidum* Aiton (65) (1931)

Huckleberry lily [Huckleberry-lily] - *Lilium philadelphicum* L. (5, 156, 158) (1900-1923)

Hudson Bay currant - *Ribes hudsonianum* Richards. (107) (1919)

Hudson Bay pine - *Pinus banksiana* Lamb. (5, 19) (1840-1913)

Hudson Bay sedge - *Carex heleonastes* Ehrh. (5, 50) (1913–present)

Hudsonia - *Hudsonia ericoides* L. (156) (1923) - *Hudsonia tomentosa* Nutt. (156) (1923)

Hudsonian anemone - *Anemone multifida* Poir. var. *hudsoniana* DC. (155) (1942)

Hudson's anemone - *Anemone multifida* Poir. var. *multifida* () ()

Hudson's balsam fir [Hudson balsam fir] - *Abies balsamea* (L.) Mill. (155) (1942)

Hudson's fir [Hudson fir] - *Abies balsamea* (L.) Mill. (138) (1923)

Hühnerdarn (German) - *Anagallis arvensis* L. (6) (1892)

Hugo rose - *Rosa xanthina* Lindl. (109) (1949)

Hugonis rose - *Rosa xanthina* Lindl. (112, 138) (1923-1937)

Huile de Colza (French) - *Brassica rapa* L. var. *rapa* (158) (1900)

Huile de navette (French) - *Brassica rapa* L. var. *rapa* (1900)

Huisache - *Acacia farnesiana* (L.) Willd. (106, 107, 109, 122, 124) (1919-1949)

Huisachillo - *Acacia tortuosa* (L.) Willd. (124) (1937) TX

Huksik (Winnebago) - *Corylus americana* Walt. (37) (1919)

Hulless barley - *Hordeum vulgare* L. (119) (1938)

Humb or hum (Danish) - *Spergula arvensis* L. (110) (1886)

Humble plant [Humble-plant] - *Mimosa pudica* L. (92, 109, 182) (1791-1949)

Humboldt's lily [Humboldt lily] - *Lilium humboldtii* Roezl & Leichtl. ex Duchartre (138) (1923)

Humle (Scandinavian) - *Humulus lupulus* L. (110) (1886)

Hummingbird tree [Humming bird tree] - *Chelone* L. (42) (1814)

Hummingbird-trumpet - *Epilobium canum* (Greene) Raven subsp. *angustifolium* (Keck) Raven (138) (1923) Santa Barbara Co. CA

Hump-back bladderwort - *Utricularia gibba* L. (124) (1937)

Humped baldderwort - *Utricularia gibba* L. (5, 50, 97) (1913–present)

Humuli strobili (Official name of Materia Medica) - *Humulus lupulus* L. (7) (1828)

Humulus - *Humulus lupulus* L. (59, 60, 174, 177) (1753-1911)

Hundekameelblomst (Danish) - *Anthemis cotula* L. (186) (1814)

Hundeurt (Danish) - *Anthemis cotula* L. (186) (1814)

Hundkamiller (Swedish) - *Anthemis cotula* L. (186) (1814)

Hundredeyes [Hundred eyes, Hundred-eyes] - *Vinca major* L. (92) (1876), *Vinca minor* L. (156, 158) (1900-1923)

Hundred-fold - *Galium verum* L. (108) (1878)

Hundred-leaf rose [Hundred leaf rose, Hundred-leaved rose] - *Rosa centifolia* L. (19, 57, 92) (1840-1917)

Hundredleaf-grass [Hundred-leaf grass, Hundred-leaved grass] - *Achillea millefolium* L. (107, 156) (1919-1923)

Hundsbloom (German) - *Anthemis cotula* L. (186) (1814)

Hundsdill (German) - *Anthemis cotula* L. (186) (1814)

Hundskamille (German) - *Anthemis cotula* L. (186) (1814)

Hundskohl (German) - *Apocynum cannabinum* L. (158) (1900)

Hundspetersilie (German) - *Aethusa cynapium* L. (6) (1892)

Hundsromey (German) - *Anthemis cotula* L. (186) (1814)

Hundszunge (German) - *Cynoglossum officinale* L. (158) (1900)

Hungarian brome - *Bromus inermis* Leyss. (109, 118) (1898-1949)

Hungarian brome grass [Hungarian brome-grass] - *Bromus inermis* Leyss. (5, 56, 68, 72, 94, 119, 143, 163) (1852-1938)

Hungarian fodder grass - *Bromus inermis* Leyss. (68) (1890)

Hungarian grass [Hungarian-grass] - *Setaria italica* (L.) Beauv. (5, 45, 56, 66, 67, 87, 88, 90, 94, 109, 131, 158) (1884-1949)

Hungarian iris - *Iris variegata* L. (138) (1923)

Hungarian lilac - *Syringa josikaea* Jacq. f. ex Reichenb. (109, 112, 138) (1923-1949)

Hungarian millet - *Setaria italica* (L.) Beauv. (5, 56, 66, 68, 92, 119, 158) (1876-1938)

Hungarian speedwell - *Veronica austriaca* L. subsp. *teucrium* (L.) D.A. Webb (138) (1923)

Hungarian wormwood - *Artemisia pontica* L. (5, 156) (1913-1923)

Hungary mead saffron [Hungarie meade saffron] - *Colchicum autumnale* L. (178) (1596)

Hunger flower [Hunger-flower] - *Draba breweri* S. Wats. var. *cana* (Rydb.) Rollins (156) (1923), *Draba incana* L. (92) (1876)

Hunger grass - *Alopecurus myosuroides* Huds (5) (1913)

Hunger-root - *Smilax rotundifolia* L. (156) (1923)

Hungerweed [Hunger weed, Hunger-weed] - *Ranunculus arvensis* L. (5, 92, 156, 158) (1876-1923)

Hungry vine [Hungry-vine] - *Smilax rotundifolia* L. (5, 156) (1913-1923) no longer in use by 1923

Hungry-root - *Aralia racemosa* L. (156) (1923)

Hŭn-i-bist (Comanche Shoshonee) - *Zea mays* L. (132) (1855)

Huntingdon's willow [Huntingdon willow] - *Salix alba* L. (5, 156, 158) (1900-1923)

Huntsman's-cup [Huntsman's cup, Huntsmans' cup] - *Sarracenia purpurea* L. (5, 6, 13, 15, 49, 74, 92, 156) (1849-1923) New England

Hupestola (Lakota, pointed stem) - *Yucca glauca* Nutt. (121) (1918-1970)

Hupestula (Dakota) - *Yucca glauca* Nutt. (37) (1830)

Huron tansy - *Tanacetum bipinnatum* (L.) Schultz-Bip. subsp. *huronense* (Nutt.) Breitung (138) (1923)

Hurrah grass [Hurrahgrass] - *Paspalum setaceum* Michx. (155) (1942)

Hurrbur [Hurr bur, Hurr-bur] - *Arctium lappa* L. (5, 64, 92, 156, 158) (1876-1923)

Hurtleberry [Hurtleberye] - *Gaylussacia baccata* (Wang.) K. Koch (46) (1879), *Vaccinium myrtillus* L. (14) (1882)

Hurt-sickle [Hurtsickle, Hurt sickle] - *Centaurea cyanus* L. (5, 156, 157, 158) (1900-1929), *Centaurea nigra* L. (5, 156) (1913-1923)

Huskroot [Husk root] - *Aletris farinosa* L. (5) (1913)

Husks-of-the-ancient [Husks of the ancient] - *Ceratonia siliqua* L. (92) (1876)

Husk-tomato [Husk tomato] - *Physalis alkekengi* L. (156) (1923), *Physalis* L. (2, 109, 156) (1895–1949), *Physalis peruviana* L. (85) (1932), *Physalis pubescens* L. (50, 107, 156) (1919–present), *Physalis pubescens* L. var. *integrifolia* (Dunal) Waterfall (50) (present), *Physalis virginiana* Mill. (156) (1923)

Huskwort - *Aletris farinosa* L. (64, 156) (1908-1923)

Hŭs'-quim (Delaware) - *Zea mays* L. (132) (1855)

Hutton's cockscomb [Hutton cockscomb] - *Celosia argentea* L. (138) (1923)

Huttonweed [Hutton-weed] - *Dipsacus fullonum* L. (75, 158) (1894-1900) WV, found on Hutton farm

Hvita cedern (Swedish) - *Thuja occidentalis* L. (41) (1770)

Hviteteja - *Anthemis cotula* L. (186) (1814)

Hwen (Swedish) - *Apera spica-venti* (L.) Beauv. (46) (1879)

Hwita klacker (Swedish) - *Linnaea borealis* L. (46) (1879)

Hwit-wisil (Swedish) - *Parnassia palustris* L (46) (1879)

Hyacinth - *Hyacinthus* L. (109, 138, 184) (1793-1949)

Hyacinth meadow garlic - *Allium canaderse* L. var. *hyacinthoides* (Bush) M. Ownbey (50) (present)

Hyacinth-bean [Hyacinth bean] - *Lablab purpureus* (L.) Sweet (109, 138, 156) (1923-1949)

Hybrid balsam poplar - *Populus ×brayshawii* Boivin [*angustifolia* × *balsamifera*] (4, 50) (1986–present)

Hybrid clover - *Trifolium hybridum* L. (106, 156) (1923-1930)

Hybrid crack willow - *Salix ×rubens* Schrank (50) (present)

Hybrid stonecrop - *Sedum hybridum* L. (138) (1923)

Hydrangea (French) - *Hydrangea* L. (8)

Hydrangea [Hydrangia] - *Hydrangea arborescens* L. (19, 54, 57, 60, 64, 92, 158, 174, 177) (1753-1917), *Hydrangea* L. (1, 8, 50, 138, 155, 158) (1785–present)

Hydrangea de Virginie (French) - *Hydrangea arborescens* L. (8) (1785)

Hydraste du Canada [Hydraste de Canada] (French) - *Hydrastis canadensis* L. (7, 186) (1814-1828)

Hydrastis - *Hydrastis canadensis* L. (53, 54, 55, 57, 59) (1905-1922)

Hydrastis (French) - *Hydrastis canadensis* L. (6) (1892)

Hydrastis radix (Official name of Materia Medica) - *Hydrastis canadensis* L. (7) (1828)

Hydrocotyle - Hydrocotyle L. (50) (present)

Hydropelte (French) - *Brasenia schreberi* Gmel. (7) (1828)

Hydropiper - *Elatine hydropiper* L. (174, 177) (1753-1762), *Polygonum punctatum* Ell. (157, 158) (1900-1929)

Hye malowe - *Althaea officinalis* L. (179) (1526)

Hyebele - *Aralia hispida* Vent. (156) (1923)

Hyeble - *Aralia hispida* Vent. (5, 92) (1876-1913)

Hygrometer moss - *Funaria hygrometrica* Hedw. (19) (1840)

Hygtaper - *Verbascum thapsus* L. (179) (1526)

Hylder - *Sambucus nigra* L. (158) (1900)

Hymenocallis - *Hymenocallis caroliniana* (L.) Herbert (5) (1913)

Hymenopappus - *Hymenopappus* L'Hér. (50, 155, 158) (1900–present)

Hyndhele - *Teucrium scorodonia* L. (179) (1526)

Hyosciamus (Official name of Materia Medica) - *Hyoscyamus niger* L. (7) (1828)

Hyoscyamus - *Hyoscyamus niger* L. (54, 57, 59, 60) (1902-1905)

Hypericon (Spanish) - *Hypericum perforatum* L. (158) (1900)

Hypericum - *Hypericum perforatum* L. (57) (1917)

Hypericum-leaf dog's-bane [Hypericum leaved dog's bane] - *Apocynum cannabinum* L. (42) (1814)

Hypericum-like andrew's-cross [Hypericum like andrew's cross] - *Hypericum hypericoides* (L.) Crantz subsp. *hypericoides* (42) (1814)

Hypocrite plant - *Euphorbia cyathophora* Murray (156) (1923)

Hyssop [Hysop, Hysope] - *Agastache nepetoides* (L.) Kuntze (106) (1930), *Artemisia* L. (27) (1811), *Hypericum perforatum* L. (158) (1900)**,** *Hyssopus* L. (10, 109, 138, 167, 184) (1793-1949) possibly ancient hyssop of bible, *Hyssopus officinalis* L. (5, 7, 19, 46, 49, 57, 85, 92, 107, 131, 138, 156) (1617-1932)

Hyssop hedge-nettle [Hyssop hedge nettle] - *Stachys hyssopifolia* Michx. (5) (1913), *Stachys pilosa* Nutt. var. *pilosa* (5) (1913), *Stachys tenuifolia* Willd. (156) (1923)

Hyssop loosestrife - *Lythrum hyssopifolia* L. (5, 156) (1913-1923)

Hyssop mountain-mint [Hyssop mountain mint] - *Pycnanthemum flexuosum* (Walt.) Britton, Sterns & Poggenb. (5) (1913)

Hyssop of Candie [Hyssope of Candie] - *Hyssopus officinalis* L. (178) (1526)

Hyssop skullcap - *Scutellaria integrifolia* L. (5) (1913)

Hyssop spurge [Hyssope spurge] - *Euphorbia peplus* L. (178) (1526)

Hyssop-leaf erigeron [Hyssop-leaved erigeron] - *Erigeron hyssopifolius* Michx. (5) (1913)

Hyssop-leaf eupatorium [Hyssop-leaved eupatorium] - *Eupatorium hyssopifolium* L. (187) (1818)

Hyssop-leaf skullcap [Hyssop-leaved Skull-cap] - *Scutellaria integrifolia* L. (187) (1818)

Hyssop-leaf thoroughwort [Hyssopleaf thoroughwort, Hyssop-leaved thoroughwort] - *Eupatorium hyssopifolium* L. (5, 19, 122) (1840-1937)

Hyssop-leaf tickseed [Hyssopleaf tickseed] - *Corispermum americanum* (Nutt.) Nutt. var. *rydbergii* Mosyakin (4, 155) (1942-1986)

Hyssopus - *Hyssopus officinalis* L. (57) (1917)

HYSSOPE.

Hyssop, *Hyssopus officinalis* L.
(F. P. Chaumeton, 1830)

I

I/lšanáta(n)qi - *Cirsium edule* Nutt. (35) (1806)

Iabloko (Russian) - *Malus sylvestris* Mill. (110) (1886)

Iabluko (Ancient Slavic) - *Malus sylvestris* Mill. (110) (1886)

Iagged elder (Jagged elder) - *Sambucus nigra* L. (178) (1526)

Iagged germander (Jagged germander) - *Teucrium canadense* L. (178) (1526)

Iagged leafed hyssope (Jagged-leaf hyssop) - *Hyssopus officinalis* L. (178) (1526)

Ibamerara - *Spondias mombin* L. (174) (1753)

Iberian centuarea - *Centaurea iberica* Trev. ex Spreng. (155) (1942)

Iberian cranesbill - *Geranium ibericum* Cav. (138) (1923)

Iberian knapweed - *Centaurea iberica* Trev. ex Spreng. (50) (present)

Iberian star-thistle [Iberian star thistle] - *Centaurea iberica* Trev. ex Spreng. (4) (1986)

Iberian violet - *Viola bicolor* Pursh (155) (1942)

Ibervillea - *Ibervillea* Greene (158) (1900)

Ice plant [Ice-plant, Iceplant] - *Euphorbia marginata* Pursh (106) (1930) TX, *Mesembryanthemum crystallinum* L. (15, 19, 107, 109, 138) (1840-1949), *Monotropa uniflora* L. (6, 7, 49, 61, 156) (1828-1923)

Ice vine - *Cissampelos pareira* L. (92) (1876)

Icegrass - *Phippsia algida* (C.J. Phipps) R. Br. (50) (present)

Iceland moss - *Cetraria islandica* (L.) Acharius (49, 55, 57, 58, 92, 107) (1869-1911), *Sedum ternatum* Michx. (156) (1923)

Iceland poppy - *Papaver nudicaule* L. (5, 109, 138) (1913–1949)

Ice-leaf [Ice leaf] - *Verbascum thapsus* L. (5, 69, 156, 158) (1900–1923)

Iceplant mesembryanthemum - *Mesembryanthemum crystallinum* L. (155) (1942)

Ice-root - *Hydrastis canadensis* L. (156) (1923)

Ichah'pe-hu (Dakota, whip plant) - *Echinacea angustifolia* DC. (37) (1919)

Ĭ'ckode'bûg (Chippewa, fire leaf) - *Artemisia dracunculus* L. (40) (1928)

Ĭ'ckode'wadji'bĭk (Chippewa, fire root) - *Capsella bursa-pastoris* (L.) Medik. (40) (1928)

Idaho fescue - *Festuca idahoensis* Elmer (50, 146, 155) (1939–present)

Idaho trillium - *Trillium petiolatum* Pursh (138) (1923)

Idianisch apfel (German) - *Cucurbita pepo* L. (107) (1552)

Ie-länger-ie-lieber (German) - *Viola tricolor* L. (158) (1900)

Iennetten - *Narcissus* L. (180) (1633)

If (French) - *Taxus canadensis* Willd. (5, 8) (1785-1913), *Taxus* L. (8) (1785)

If occidental (French) - *Taxus brevifolia* Nutt. (20) (1857)

Iffs - *Tsuga canadensis* (L.) Carr. (46) (1879)

Igname or inhame (Africa) - *Dioscorea* L. (110) (1886) may refer to several species

I-go-to-sleep [I go to sleep] - *Senna tora* (L.) Roxb. (183) (~1756)

Iguame Indigené (French) - *Dioscorea villosa* L. (6) (1892)

Ihridh (Arabic) - *Carthamus tinctorius* L. (110) (1886)

Ikwe'mĭc (Chippewa) - *Prunus americana* Marsh. (40) (1928)

Illecebra - *Sedum acre* L. (178) (1526)

Illinois acacia - *Desmanthus illinoensis* (Michx.) MacM. ex B.L. Robins. & Fern. (5, 86) (1878-1913)

Illinois bundleflower - *Desmanthus illinoensis* (Michx.) MacM. ex B.L. Robins. & Fern. (4, 155) (1942-1986)

Illinois fragrant sumac - *Rhus aromatica* Aiton var. *aromatica* (155) (1942)

Illinois gooseberry - *Ribes missouriense* Nutt. (5) (1913), *Ribes niveum* Lindl. (76, 156) (1896-1923) KY

Illinois greenbrier - *Smilax illinoensis* Mangaly (50) (present)

Illinois hickory [Illinois hickery] - *Carya illinoinensis* (Wangenh.) K. Koch (8) (1785)

Illinois horse-gentian - *Triosteum aurantiacum* Bickn. var. *illinoense* (Wiegand) Palmer & Steyermark (50) (present)

Illinois mimosa - *Desmanthus illinoensis* (Michx.) MacM. ex B.L. Robins. & Fern. (5, 72, 97, 157) (1900–1937)

Illinois ninebark - *Physocarpus opulifolius* (L.) Maxim. var. *intermedius* (Rydb.) B.L. Robins. (138, 155) (1923-1942)

Illinois nut [Illinois-nut] - *Carya illinoinensis* (Wangenh.) K. Koch (5, 156, 158) (1900-1923)

Illinois pecan - *Carya illinoinensis* (Wangenh.) K. Koch (158) (1900)

Illinois pondweed - *Potamogeton illinoensis* Morong (3, 50, 72, 155) (1942–present)

Illinois strawberry - *Fragaria virginiana* Duchesne subsp. *grayana* (Vilm. ex J. Gay) Staudt (155) (1942)

Illinois tickclover - *Desmodium illinoense* Gray (3, 4) (1977-1986)

Illinois ticktrefoil [Illinois tick-trefoil, Illinois tick trefoil] - *Desmodium illinoense* Gray (5, 50, 72, 93, 97, 131) (1899–present)

Ill-scented sumac [Ill-scented sumach] - *Rhus trilobata* Nutt. (109, 122, 156) (1923-1949), *Rhus trilobata* Nutt. var. *trilobata* (5, 65, 97) (1913-1937)

Ill-scented trillium - *Trillium erectum* L. (64, 156) (1908-1923)

Ill-scented wake robin - *Trillium erectum* L. (5, 64, 72) (1893-1908)

Il-togh (Swedish) - *Luzula acuminata* Raf. var. *acuminata* (46) (1879)

Immerschön Ruhkraut (German) - *Pseudognaphalium obtusifolium* (L.) Hilliard & Burtt subsp. *obtusifolium* (6) (1892)

Immortal flower - *Helichrysum bracteatum* (Vent.) Andr. (92) (1876)

Immortelle (French) - *Pseudognaphalium obtusifolium* (L.) Hilliard & Burtt subsp. *obtusifolium* (6) (1892)

Immortelle [Immortelles] - *Erythrina* L. (109) (1949), *Gomphrena globosa* L. (156) (1923)

Imo (Japan) - *Colocasia esculenta* (L.) Schott (110) (1886)

Imperatoria - *Peucedanum ostruthium* (L.) W.D.J. Koch (57) (1917)

Imperial crown - *Lilium martagon* L. (190) (~1759)

Imperial masterwort - *Astrantia major* L. (92) (1876)

Imperial masterwort - *Peucedanum ostruthium* (L.) W.D.J. Koch (5, 7, 92, 156) (1828-1923)

Imphee - *Sorghum bicolor* (L.) Moench (56, 92) (1876-1901), *Sorghum bicolor* (L.) Moench subsp. *bicolor* (158) (1900), *Sorghum halepense* (L.) Pers. (45) (1896)

Impudent-lawyer [Impudent lawyer] - *Linaria vulgaris* Mill. (5, 75, 156, 157, 158) (1894-1929) WV

I'natû ga'n'ka (Cherokee, snake tongue) - *Asplenium rhizophyllum* L. (102) (1885)

Incense tree [Incense-tree] - *Liquidambar styraciflua* L. (156) (1923)

Inch plant - *Tradescantia crassifolia* Cav. (73) (1892) MA

Inch plum - *Prunus mexicana* S. Wats. (155) (1942)

Increaser-of-Pleasure [Increaser of Pleasure] (India) - *Cannabis sativa* L. (6) (1892)

Indian abutilon [India abutilon] - *Abutilon indicum* (L.) Sweet (155) (1942)

Indian almond [Indian-almond] - *Terminalia catappa* L. (20, 107, 109, 138) (1857-1949)

Indian apple [Indian-apple, Indian-apples] - *Astragalus crassicarpus* Nutt. var. *crassicarpus* (98) (1926) Neb, *Datura inoxia* P. Mill. (4) (1986), *Podophyllum peltatum* L. (5, 6, 49, 64, 92, 156, 157, 158) (1892-1929)

Indian arrow - *Euonymus atropurpurea* Jacq. (73, 92, 156) (1876–1923)

Indian arrowroot [Indian arrow root] - *Maranta arundinacea* L. (92) (1876)

Indian arrow-wood [Indian arrow wood, Indian arrowwood] - *Cor-*

nus florida L. (5, 156, 158) (1900-1923), *Euonymus atropurpurea* Jacq. (5, 6, 49, 53, 58, 92, 157, 158) (1892-1929)

Indian balm - *Trillium cernuum* L. (7) (1828), *Trillium erectum* L. (6, 49, 64, 92) (1876-1908)

Indian bark [Indian-bark] - *Magnolia virginiana* L. (5, 6, 92, 156, 186) (1825-1923)

Indian bay - *Laurus nobilis* L. (92) (1876)

Indian bean [Indian-bean] or Indian bean tree [Indian bean-tree] - *Catalpa bignonioides* Walt. (5, 6, 49, 63, 72, 109, 156) (1892-1949), *Catalpa* Scop. (1, 2) (1895-1932), *Catalpa speciosa* (Warder) Warder ex Engelm. (106, 156) (1923-1930)

Indian beard grass [Indian beard-grass] - *Andropogon glomeratus* (Walt.) B.S.P. (5) (1913), *Sorghastrum nutans* (L.) Nash (56) (1901)

Indian beet - *Lupinus perennis* L. (156) (1923)

Indian bent grass [Indian bent-grass] - *Sporobolus indicus* (L.) R. Br. var. *indicus* (165) (1768)

Indian birch - *Bursera simaruba* (L.) Sargent (107) (1919)

Indian black-drink [Indian black drink] - *Ilex vomitoria* Aiton (5, 92, 156) (1876-1923)

Indian blanket - *Gaillardia pulchella* Foug. (124) (1937) TX

Indian blanket flower - *Gaillardia pulchella* Foug. (4) (1986)

Indian boys-and-girls [Indian boys and girls, Indian-boys-and-girls] - *Dicentra cucullaria* (L.) Bernh. (5, 76, 156, 158) (1896-1923) WI, no longer in use by 1923

Indian breadroot [Indian bread-root, Indian bread root] - *Pediomelum esculentum* (Pursh) Rydb. (5, 93, 122, 138, 156, 158) (1900–1937), *Pediomelum hypogaeum* (Nutt. ex Torr. & Gray) Rydb. var. *hypogaeum* (156) (1923), *Pediomelum* Rydb. (50) (present)

Indian buckwheat - *Fagopyrum tataricum* (L.) Gaertn. (92) (1876)

Indian cannabis - *Cannabis sativa* L. (57) (1917)

Indian caustic barley [Indian causticke barley] - *Setaria* Beauv (181) (~1678)

Indian cedar - *Ostrya virginiana* (Mill.) K. Koch (156, 157, 158) (1900–1929)

Indian cherry [Indian-cherry] - *Amelanchier canadensis* (L.) Medik. (5, 106, 156, 158) (1895–1930) PA, no longer in use by 1923, *Frangula caroliniana* (Walt.) Gray (2, 5, 62, 5, 106, 107, 109, 113, 122, 156) (1890–1949), *Prunus angustifolia* Marsh. (possibly) (107) (1919)

Indian chickweed - *Mollugo* L. (1, 13, 15, 158) (1849–1932), *Mollugo verticillata* L. (5, 62, 156, 187) (1818–1923)

Indian chief - *Dodecatheon meadia* L. (5, 75, 156) (1894-1923) Rockford IL

Indian chocolate - *Geum rivale* L (5, 6, 92, 107, 156, 158) (1876-1923)

Indian cigar tree - *Catalpa bignonioides* Walt. (5, 156) (1913-1923), *Catalpa* Scop. (4) (1986)

Indian clover - *Melilotus indicus* (L.) All. (122) (1937) TX

Indian corn [Indian-corn] - *Zea* L. (45, 155, 158, 163, 167) (1814-1942), *Zea mays* L. (7, 10, 37, 40, 41, 56, 57, 66, 68, 87, 92, 94, 103, 106, 109, 110, 117, 119, 121, 138, 155, 158, 182, 184) (1791-1949)

Indian couch grass [Indian couch-grass] - *Cynodon dactylon* (L.) Pers. (158) (1900)

Indian creeper - *Campsis radicans* (L.) Seem. ex Bureau (156) (1923)

Indian cress [Indian cresses] - *Tropaeolum majus* L. (7, 19, 92, 107, 138) (1828-1923)

Indian cucumber - *Medeola* L. (10, 50, 167) (1814–present), *Medeola virginiana* L. (19, 46, 50, 86, 186, 187) (1814–present) Native Americans ate roots which taste like cucumbers

Indian cucumber-root [Indian cucumber root] - *Medeola* L. (1, 109, 156) (1923-1949), *Medeola virginiana* L. (5) (1913)

Indian cup [Indian-cup] - *Sarracenia purpurea* L. (5, 156) (1913-1923), *Silphium perfoliatum* L. (5, 62, 93, 109, 156, 158) (1900-1949)

Indian cup plant - *Silphium perfoliatum* L. (49, 61, 92) (1870-1898)

Indian currant [Indian-currant, Indian currants] - *Ribes aureum* Pursh (35) (1806), *Symphoricarpos* Duham. (82) (1930), *Symphori-*

carpos occidentalis Hook. (112) (1937), *Symphoricarpos orbiculatus* Moench (2, 8, 63, 80, 92, 106, 109, 113, 114, 130, 156, 158) (1785-1949)

Indian currant snowberry [Indiancurrant snowberry] - *Symphoricarpos orbiculatus* Moench (155) (1942)

Indian datura - *Datura metel* L. (92) (1876)

Indian dillenia - *Dillenia indica* L. (138) (1923)

Indian doob - *Cynodon dactylon* (L.) Pers. (5) (1913)

Indian dream - *Pellaea atropurpurea* (L.) Link (92) (1876)

Indian dye [Indian-dye] - *Hydrastis canadensis* L. (5, 6, 49, 64, 156) (1892-1923)

Indian elm - *Ulmus rubra* Muhl. (5, 92, 156, 157, 158) (1876-1929)

Indian fig [Indian-fig, Indianfig] - *Opuntia engelmannii* Salm-Dyck (107) (1919), *Opuntia ficus-indica* (L.) Mill. (6, 109, 110, 155, 156, 182, 191) (1791-1949) OK, *Opuntia humifusa* (Raf.) Raf. var. *humifusa* (5, 158) (1900-1913), *Opuntia* Mill. (1, 2, 10, 14, 106) (1818-1930)

Indian ginger - *Asarum canadense* L. (5, 7, 49, 53, 58, 64, 92, 156, 158, 186) (1814-1923), *Asarum* L. (10) (1818)

Indian ginger-lily [India ginger-lily, India gingerlily] - *Hedychium gardnerianum* Shepard ex Ker-Gawl. (138) (1923)

Indian goose grass [Indian goosegrass] - *Eleusine indica* (L.) Gaertn. (50) (present)

Indian gooseberry - *Gaylussacia frondosa* (L.) Torr. & Gray (8) (1785)

Indian grass [Indian-grass, Indiangrass] - *Andropogon bicornis* L. (41) (1770), *Andropogon glomeratus* (Walt.) B.S.P. (19) (1840), *Andropogon virginicus* L. (187) (1818), *Molinia caerulea* (L.) Moench (5) (1913), *Sorghastrum* Nash (1, 50, 93, 155) (1932–present), *Sorghastrum nutans* (L.) Nash (3, 5, 45, 50, 56, 66, 72, 85, 87, 92, 94, 115, 119, 122, 131, 134, 140, 144, 163) (1852–present)

Indian gravelroot [Indian gravel-root, Indian gravel root] - *Eupatorium purpureum* L. (5, 64, 156, 158) (1900-1923)

Indian hazel nut - *Caesalpinia bonduc* (L.) Roxb. (92) (1876)

Indian head - *Lycoperdon solidum* L. (103) (1871)

Indian heart [Indian-heart] - *Cardiospermum halicacabum* L. (158) (1900)

Indian heliotrope - *Heliotropium indicum* L. (5, 50, 97, 122) (1913–present)

Indian hemp [Indianhemp] - *Abutilon theophrasti* Medik (5, 76, 156, 158) (1896-1923) OH, *Apocynum androsaemifolium* L. (49, 101, 157, 158) (1900-1929), *Apocynum cannabinum* L. (5, 19, 41, 46, 49, 50, 53, 54, 58, 61, 62, 63, 72, 80, 82, 85, 93, 97, 105, 106, 114, 125, 127, 131, 145, 148, 156, 157, 158, 177, 187, 189) (1762–present), *Apocynum* L. (2, 10, 93, 190) (~1759-1936), *Asclepias incarnata* L. (46) (1879), *Cannabis sativa* L. (6, 57, 60, 125) (1876-1922), *Cannabis sativa* L. subsp. *indica* (Lam.) E. Small & Cronq. (52, 53, 54, 55, 92) (1905-1919), *Linaria vulgaris* Mill. (75, 156) (1894-1923) WV

Indian hemp dogbane - *Apocynum cannabinum* L. (4) (1986)

Indian hippo - *Gillenia trifoliata* (L.) Moench (5, 64, 92, 156, 186) (1814-1923), *Porteranthus stipulatus* (Muhl. ex Willd.) Britt. (7, 49) (1828-1898)

Indian iceroot - *Hydrastis canadensis* L. (5) (1913)

Indian Jack-in-the-pulpit [Indian Jackinthepulpit] - *Arisaema triphyllum* (L.) Schott (155) (1942)

Indian jujube [India jujube] - *Colubrina elliptica* (Sw.) Brizicky & W.L. Stern (109, 138) (1923-1949), *Ziziphus obtusifolia* (Hook. ex Torr. & Gray) Gray var. *obtusifolia* (106) (1930), *Ziziphus zizyphus* (L.) Karst. (110) (1886)

Indian kale - *Colocasia esculenta* (L.) Schott (92) (1876)

Indian lettuce - *Claytonia perfoliata* Donn ex Willd. subsp. *perfoliata* (156) (1942), *Frasera caroliniensis* Walt. (possibly) (7, 64, 92, 156, 182, 186) (1791-1923), *Pyrola americana* Sweet (5, 92, 156, 158) (1900-1923)

Indian licorice [Indian liquorice] - *Abrus* Adans. (158) (1900), *Abrus precatorius* L. (49, 57, 92, 158) (1876-1917)

Indian lilac - *Melia azedarach* L. (49) (1898)

Indian lotus - *Nelumbo nucifera* Gaertn. (possibly) (5) (1913)

Indian love grass [Indian lovegrass, India love grass, India loveg-rass] - *Eragrostis pilosa* (L.) Beauv. (3, 4, 50, 122, 140, 155) (1937–present)

Indian maguey - *Agave* L. (75, 147) (1856-1894)

Indian mallow [Indian-mallow, Indian mallows] - *Abutilon incanum* (Link) Sweet (122) (1937), *Abutilon* Mill. (1, 4, 50, 15, 156) (1895–present), *Abutilon theophrasti* Medik (5, 58, 62, 80, 85, 92, 97, 131, 156, 157, 158) (1840-1932), *Sida* L. (93, 158, 184) (1793-1936), *Sida spinosa* L. (5, 92, 156) (1876-1923), *Abutilon incanum* (Link) Sweet (155) (1942)

Indian manzanita - *Arctostaphylos mewukka* Merriam (155) (1942)

Indian marsh milkweed [Indian marsh milk-weed] - *Eupatorium purpureum* L. (157) (1929)

Indian milkvetch [Indian milk vetch] - *Astragalus australis* (L.) Lam. (4, 5, 131, 155) (1899-1986)

Indian millet - *Achnatherum hymenoides* (Roemer & J.A. Schultes) Barkworth (5, 56, 94, 101, 111, 129, 141) (1886-1915), *Achnatherum* P. Beauv. (1, 93) (1932-1936), *Panicum miliaceum* L. (45, 88) (1885-1896), *Pennisetum glaucum* (L.) R. Br. (45, 109) (1896-1949), *Piptatherum micranthum* (Trin. & Rupr.) Barkworth (94, 129) (1894-1901), *Sorghum bicolor* (L.) Moench (56) (1901), *Sorghum bicolor* (L.) Moench subsp. *bicolor* (19, 66, 87, 92, 158) (1840-1903), *Sorghum halepense* (L.) Pers. (45) (1896), *Sorghum* Moench (7) (1828), *Zea mays* L. (178) (1596)

Indian mocassin - *Cypripedium acaule* Ait. (5, 156) (1913-1923)

Indian mountain rice - *Achnatherum hymenoides* (Roemer & J.A. Schultes) Barkworth (163) (1852)

Indian mozemize - *Sorbus americana* Marsh. (5, 74) (1893-1913) Ferrisburgh VT

Indian mugwort - *Parthenium hysterophorus* L. (158) (1900)

Indian mulberry [Indian-mulberry] - *Morinda citrifolia* L. (92, 107, 138) (1876-1923), *Morinda* L. (138) (1923)

Indian mustard [India mustard] - *Brassica juncea* (L.) Czern. (3, 4, 5, 50, 97, 107, 155, 156, 157, 158) (1900–present)

Indian olive - *Pyrularia pubera* Michx. (182) (1791)

Indian paint [Indian-paint] - *Chenopodium capitatum* (L.) Asch. (5, 75, 156, 158) (1894-1923) from bright color of fruit, *Hydrastis canadensis* L. (7, 49) (1828-1898), *Lithospermum canescens* (Michx.) Lehm. (3, 75, 77, 156, 157, 158) (1898-1977), *Lithospermum incisum* Lehm. (101) (1905), *Lithospermum* L. (1, 93) (1932-1936), *Sanguinaria canadensis* L. (6, 49, 53, 186, 187) (1818-1892), *Tradescantia* L. (78) (1898) Mineral Point WI, juice said to irritate skin and make it red

Indian paintbrush [Indian paint-brush, Indian paint brush] - *Castilleja coccinea* (L.) Spreng. (3, 5, 73, 97, 138, 155, 156, 158) (1892-1977), *Castilleja* Mutis ex L. f. (1, 4, 50, 93) (1932–present), *Castilleja purpurea* (Nutt.) G. Don var. *lindheimeri* (Gray) Shinners (97, 124) (1937), *Castilleja sulphurea* Rydb. (85) (1932)

Indian paper tree [India paper tree, India papertree] - *Perideridia gairdneri* (Hook. & Arn.) Mathias subsp. *gairdneri* (138) (1923)

Indian parsley - *Aletes* J.M. Coult. & Rose (50) (present)

Indian pea - *Astragalus crassicarpus* Nutt. var. *crassicarpus* (101) (1905), *Astragalus* L. (103) (1870)

Indian pear - *Amelanchier canadensis* (L.) Medik. (5, 156, 158) (1900-1923) no longer in use by 1923, *Malus fusca* (Raf.) Schneid. (103) (1870)

Indian Pepper - *Capsicum annuum* L. var. *annuum* (178) (1526)

Indian physic [Indian-physic, Indianphysic, Indian physick] - *Apocynum cannabinum* L. (64, 92, 156) (1898-1923), *Euphorbia corollata* L. (6, 7, 49) (1828-1898), *Gillenia trifoliata* (L.) Moench (5, 19, 49, 61, 64, 92, 109, 156, 181, 184, 186, 187) (~1678-1949), *Magnolia fraseri* Walt. (5, 156) (1913-1923), *Magnolia macrophylla* Michx. (20) (1857), *Porteranthus stipulatus* (Muhl. ex Willd.) Britt. (3, 4, 7, 49, 50, 61, 92, 102, 138, 155, 158)) (1828–present)

Indian pine - *Pinus taeda* L. (5, 8, 14) (1785-1882)

Indian pink - *Castilleja coccinea* (L.) Spreng. (5, 75, 156) (1894-1923) Peoria IL, *Castilleja minor* (Gray) Gray (5) (1913) obsolete by 1923, *Cleome* L. (1, 93) (1932-1936), *Ipomoea quamoclit* L. (5, 156, 158) (1900-1923) no longer in use by 1923, *Lychnis floscuculi* L. (5, 156) (1913-1923) no longer in use by 1923, *Polygala paucifolia* Willd. (5, 74, 156) (1893-1923) Montague MA, *Silene californica* Dur. (76) (1896) CA, *Silene caroliniana* Walt. (76) (1896), *Silene virginica* L. (5, 156) (1913-1923), *Spigelia* L. (92, 186) (1814-1876), *Spigelia marilandica* (L.) L. (5, 6, 55, 64, 92, 97, 122, 124, 156) (1876-1937)

Indian pipe [Indianpipe, Indian-pipe] - *Monotropa* L. (2, 4, 50, 138, 155, 156, 158) (1895–present), *Monotropa uniflora* L. (1, 3, 4, 5, 6, 19, 49, 50, 63, 72, 92, 95, 131, 138, 155, 156, 157, 158) (1892–present)

Indian pitcher - *Sarracenia purpurea* L. (5, 73, 156) (1892-1923) NH

Indian plant - *Hydrastis canadensis* L. (92) (1876)

Indian plantain - *Arnoglossum atriplicifolium* (L.) H.E. Robins. (47) (1852), *Arnoglossum plantagineum* Raf. (4, 95, 124, 157) (1900-1937), *Arnoglossum* Raf. (1, 2, 4, 50, 63, 75, 82, 93, 156, 158) (1894–present), *Hasteola suaveolens* (L.) Pojark. (82) (1930) IA, *Plantago psyllium* L. (4) (1986)

Indian plantroot [Indian plant root] - *Pediomelum esculentum* (Pursh) Rydb. (124) (1937) TX

Indian plume [Indian's plume] - *Monarda didyma* L. (5, 156) (1913-1923)

Indian poke [Indianpoke] - *Veratrum viride* Ait. (2, 7, 53, 59, 64, 71, 78, 92, 107, 156) (1828-1922) ME

Indian pokeweed [Indian poke weed] - *Melanthium woodii* (J.W. Robbins ex Wood) Bodkin (5) (1913)

Indian posy [Indian-posy, Indian posey] - *Anaphalis margaritacea* (L.) Benth. & Hook (5, 156, 158, 190) (~1759-1923), *Asclepias tuberosa* L. (5, 64, 156, 157, 158) (1900-1929), *Pseudognaphalium obtusifolium* (L.) Hilliard & Burtt subsp. *obtusifolium* (5, 6, 49, 75, 76, 92) (1876-1913)

Indian potato - *Apios americana* Medik. (7, 92, 121, 156) (1828-1970), *Helianthus giganteus* L. (5, 156) (1913-1923)

Indian puccoon - *Lithospermum canescens* (Michx.) Lehm. (156, 157, 158) (1900-1929)

Indian redroot [Indian red-root, Indian red root] - *Lachnanthes caroliana* (Lam.) Dandy (5, 92, 156) (1876-1923)

Indian reed - *Cinna arundinacea* L. (19, 66, 92, 94) (1840-1903), *Sorghastrum nutans* (L.) Nash (163) (1852)

Indian reed grass [Indian reed-grass] - *Cinna arundinacea* L. (5, 56, 92, 119, 129) (1894-1938)

Indian rice - *Zizania aquatica* L. (2, 43, 46, 66, 67, 87, 88, 92, 107, 111, 129, 131, 157, 158, 187) (1818-1919), *Zizania* L. (1, 45, 66, 93, 158) (1896-1936), *Zizaniopsis miliacea* (Michx.) Doell & Aschers. (45) (1896)

Indian rice grass [Indian ricegrass] - *Achnatherum hymenoides* (Roemer & J.A. Schultes) Barkworth (3, 50, 98, 140, 146, 155, 185) (1926–present)

Indian root [Indian-root] - *Aralia racemosa* L. (64, 73, 92, 156, 157, 158) (1876-1929)

Indian rubber tree [India rubber tree, India rubbertree] - *Ficus elastica* Roxb. ex Hornem. (138) (1923)

Indian rushpea [Indian rush-pea] - *Hoffmannseggia glauca* (Ortega) Eifert (4, 50, 155) (1942–present)

Indian sage [Indian-sage] - *Eupatorium perfoliatum* L. (5, 6, 7, 49, 53, 69, 93, 156, 157, 158, 186, 187) (1814-1936)

Indian salad - *Hydrophyllum virginianum* L. (107, 156) (1919-1923)

Indian salt - *Rhus glabra* L. (92) (1876), *Saccharum officinarum* L. (92) (1876)

Indian sanicle - *Ageratina altissima* (L.) King & H.E. Robins. (5, 92, 156) (1876-1923)

Indian shamrock - *Trillium cernuum* L. (7) (1828), *Trillium erectum* L. (6, 64, 92) (1876-1908)

Indian shoe - *Cypripedium parviflorum* Salisb. (5, 156) (1913-1923), *Cypripedium parviflorum* Salisb. var. *pubescens* (Willd.) Knight (92) (1876), *Cypripedium reginae* Walt. (64) (1908)

Indian shot - *Canna indica* L. (92, 109) (1876-1949), *Canna* L. (2, 10) (1818-1895)

Indian slipper - *Cypripedium acaule* Ait. (78) (1898) ME

Indian soap plant [Indian soap-plant] - *Sapindus saponaria* L. var. *drummondii* (Hook. & Arn.) Bensons (5, 156) (1913-1923), *Sapindus saponaria* L. var. *saponaria* (92) (1876)

Indian strawberry [India-strawberry] - *Chenopodium capitatum* (L.) Asch. (5, 19, 92, 156, 158) (1840-1923), *Duchesnea indica* (Andr.) Focke (5, 50, 92, 156, 158) (1876–present), *Duchesnea* Sm. (109, 156) (1923-1949), *Fragaria vesca* L. subsp. *americana* (Porter) Staudt (131) (1899)

Indian suicide plant - *Cicuta maculata* L. var. *angustifolia* Hook. (157) (1929)

Indian tartaricum - *Fagopyrum tataricum* (L.) Gaertn. (92) (1876)

Indian tea - *Ceanothus americanus* L. (37, 156) (1919-1923), *Ilex vomitoria* Aiton (156) (1923)

Indian teakettles - *Sarracenia purpurea* L. (156) (1923)

Indian thistle - *Dipsacus fullonum* L. (5, 75, 156, 158) (1900-1923) WV

Indian tobacco [Indian-tobacco] - *Antennaria* Gaertner (93) (1936) Neb, *Antennaria plantaginifolia* (L.) Richards (5, 62, 73, 156, 158) (1892-1923), *Cornus sericea* L. subsp. *sericea* (107) (1919), *Lobelia cardinalis* L. (148) (1939) CO, *Lobelia inflata* L. (3, 4, 5, 6, 7, 46, 47, 49, 50, 52, 53, 55, 57, 59, 60, 61, 62, 63, 69, 72, 92, 97, 101, 109, 125, 138, 156, 157, 158, 186, 187) (1814–present), *Nicotiana rustica* L. (5, 75, 156) (1894-1923) NY, *Verbascum thapsus* L. (41) (1770)

Indian tobacco lobelia [Indiantobacco lobelia] - *Lobelia inflata* L. (155) (1942)

Indian tree spurge - *Euphorbia tirucalli* L. (109) (1949)

Indian turmeric [Indian-turmeric] - *Hydrastis canadensis* L. (5, 6, 49, 64, 156) (1892-1923)

Indian turnip - *Arisaema dracontium* (L.) Schott (156) (1923), *Arisaema* Martens (1, 93, 158) (1932-1936), *Arisaema triphyllum* (L.) Schott (7, 37, 46, 49, 53, 57, 58, 64, 72, 86, 92, 93, 97, 156, 157, 158, 187) (1818-1937), *Arisaema triphyllum* (L.) Schott subsp. *triphyllum* (107, 109) (1919-1949), *Arum* L. (167) (1814), *Pediomelum esculentum* (Pursh) Rydb. (47, 49, 85, 101, 103, 107, 127, 131) (1870-1933), *Pediomelum* Rydb. (1) (1932)

Indian uncus - *Veratrum viride* Ait. (possibly) (71) (1898)

Indian warrior - *Pedicularis* L. (1) (1932)

Indian wheat (Italy) - *Zea mays* L. (107) (1645)

Indian wheat [India-wheat] - *Fagopyrum tataricum* (L.) Gaertn. (109, 156) (1923-1949)

Indian white sage - *Salvia officinalis* L. (178) (1526)

Indian wickape - *Dirca palustris* L. (78) (1898) Western US

Indian wickopy - *Chamerion angustifolium* (L.) Holub subsp. *angustifolium* (157, 158) (1900-1929)

Indian wickup - *Chamerion angustifolium* (L.) Holub subsp. *angustifolium* (5) (1913)

Indian wild plum - *Astragalus crassicarpus* Nutt. var. *crassicarpus* (98) (1926) Neb

Indian woodoats - *Chasmanthium latifolium* (Michx.) Yates (50) (present)

Indian yellow clover - *Melilotus indicus* (L.) All. (124) (1937) TX

Indianische Aronswurz (German) - *Arisaema triphyllum* (L.) Schott (158) (1900)

Indianischer Hanf (German) - *Apocynum cannabinum* L. (158) (1900)

Indian's-dream [Indian's dream] - *Aspidotis densa* (Brack.) Lellinger (50) (present), *Pellaea atropurpurea* (L.) Link (5, 158) (1900-1913)

India-wheat - *Fagopyrum esculentum* Moench (158) (1900), *Plantago patagonica* Jacq. (146) (1939) MT, *Urochloa ciliatissima* (Buckl.) R. Webster (94) (1901), *Zea mays* L. (14, 18, 19, 37) (1805-1919)

Indicator - *Botrychium virginianum* (L.) Sw. (78, 158) (1898-1900) Jackson WV, thought to indicate presence of ginseng

Indigo - *Indigofera* L. (4, 10, 92, 138, 155, 158) (1818-1986), *Indigofera tinctoria* L. (19, 55, 182) (1791-1922), *Tephrosia purpurea* (L.) Pers. (92) (1876)

Indigo broom - *Baptisia tinctoria* (L.) R. Br. ex Aiton f. (5, 7, 58, 64, 92, 157) (1828–1929)

Indigo bush [Indigobush, Indigo-bush] - *Amorpha fruticosa* L. (138, 156) (1923), *Psorothamnus spinosus* (Gray) Barneby (106) (1930)

Indigo leadplant [Indigo lead plant] - *Amorpha* L. (82) (1930) IA

Indigo plant - *Amorpha fruticosa* L. (112) (1937), *Indigofera* L. (1, 92) (1876-1932)

Indigo Sauvage (French) - *Baptisia tinctoria* (L.) R. Br. ex Aiton f. (6, 157) (1892-1929)

Indigo tree [Indigo-tree] - *Amorpha fruticosa* L. (possibly) (189) (1767)

Indigo trefle (French) - *Baptisia tinctoria* (L.) R. Br. ex Aiton f. (6, 7) (1828-1932)

Indigoberry [Indigo berry] - *Randia aculeata* L. (92) (1876)

Indigo-bush amorpha [Indigobush amorpha] - *Amorpha fruticosa* L. (155) (1942)

Indigofera - *Baptisia tinctoria* (L.) R. Br. ex Aiton f. (58) (1869)

Indigoweed [Indigo weed, Indigo-weed] - *Baptisia tinctoria* (L.) R. Br. ex Aiton f. (5, 6, 7, 49, 53, 64, 92, 106, 157, 186) (1814-1930)

Indischer Ingwer (German) - *Asarum canadense* L. (158) (1900)

Indisches Süssholz (German) - *Abrus precatorius* L. (158) (1900)

Indländischer Rhabarber (German) - *Rheum rhabarbarum* L. (158) (1900)

Indo-Malayan alocasia [IndoMalayan alocasia] - *Alocasia macrorrhizos* (L.) Schott (155) (1942)

Infalted melic-grass - *Melica bulbosa* Geyer ex Porter & Coult. (94) (1901)

Infant's-breath [Infant's breath] - *Galium mollugo* L. (156) (1923), *Lysimachia nummularia* L. (77) (1898) Oxford Co. ME

Inflata sedge - *Carex vesicaria* L. (5) (1913)

Inflated melic grass [Inflated melic-grass] - *Melica bulbosa* Geyer ex Porter & Coult. (94) (1901)

Inflated oxytrope - *Oxytropis podocarpa* Gray (5) (1913)

Inflated sedge - *Carex bullata* Schk. (66) (1903)

Inflated-scale flatsedge [Inflatedscale flatsedge] - *Cyperus aggregatus* (Willd.) Endl. (50) (present)

Inga de la Guadaloupe - *Pithecellobium unguis-cati* (L.) Benth. (20) (1857)

Inga ongle de chat - *Pithecellobium unguis-cati* (L.) Benth. (20) (1857)

Ingahawmp (Snakes) - *Shepherdia argentea* (Pursh) Nutt. (101) (1905) MT

Ingathahe-hazi-i-ta (Omaha-Ponca, thunder grapes - *Menispermum canadense* L. (37) (1919)

Ingtha hazi itai (Omaha-Ponca) - *Parthenocissus quinquefolia* (L.) Planch. (37) (1919)

Ini-iže (Osage) - *Lagenaria siceraria* (Molina) Standl. (121) (1918?-1970?)

Inijaŋ pežuta or inijaŋpi (Lakota, sore mouth medicine) - *Erigeron annuus* (L.) Pers. (121) (1918?-1970?)

Inï'nïwïn'dïbïge'gûn (Chippewa) - *Trillium grandiflorum* (Michx.) Salisb. (40) (1928)

Inï'nïwûnj (Chipewwa, man-like) - *Asclepias syriaca* L. (40) (1928)

Injin physic - *Porteranthus stipulatus* (Muhl. ex Willd.) Britt. (74) (1893) Banner Elk NC

Ink bush - *Phytolacca americana* L. (77) (1898) Southold Long Island

Ink-ball oak - *Quercus ×benderi* Baenitz [*coccinea* × *rubra*] (19) (1840)

Inkberry [Ink-berry, Ink berry] - *Ilex glabra* (L.) Gray (2, 5, 12, 19, 48, 92, 106, 107, 109, 122, 156) (1840-1949), *Ilex* L. (41) (1770), *Phytolacca americana* L. (5, 37) (1913-1919), *Phytolacca americana* L. var. *americana* (62, 64, 69, 156) (1903-1912), *Rivina humilis* L. (97) (1937) OK

Ink-berry bush - *Phytolacca americana* L. (77) (1898)

Ink-berry hawthorn [Inkberry hawthorn] - *Crataegus multiflora* Bunge (138) (1923)

Ink-berry roots - *Phytolacca americana* L. var. *americana* (157) (1929)

Inkroot [Ink-root, Ink root] - *Armeria maritima* (P. Mill.) Willd (58, 92) (1869-1876), *Limonium carolinianum* (Walt.) Britt. (5, 49, 58, 92, 156) (1876-1923), *Limonium vulgare* Mill. (49) (1898)

Inky cap - *Coprinus atramentarius* (Bull.) Fr., (128) (1933)

Inland blue grass [Inland bluegrass, Inland blue-grass] - *Poa nemoralis* L. subsp. *interior* (Rydb.) W.A. Weber (3, 50, 122, 155, 163) (1852–present)

Inland boxelder - *Acer negundo* L. var. *interius* (Britton) Sarg. (155) (1942)

Inland ceanothus - *Ceanothus herbaceus* Raf. (155) (1942)

Inland cord grass - *Spartina gracilis* Trin. (5) (1913)

Inland gooseberry - *Ribes oxyacanthoides* L. subsp. *setosum* (Lindl.) Sinnott (50) (present)

Inland Jersey-tea - *Ceanothus herbaceus* Raf. (138) (1923)

Inland marsh fleabane - *Pluchea camphorata* (L.) DC. (5, 97, 122) (1913-1937), *Pluchea odorata* (L.) Cass (124) (1937)

Inland nightshade - *Solanum interius* Rydb. (155) (1942)

Inland pondweed - *Stuckenia filiformis* (Pers) Boerner subsp. *occidentalis* (J.W. Robbins) Haynes, D.H. Les, & M. Kral (5, 85) (1913-1932)

Inland rush - *Juncus interior* Wieg. (3, 5, 50, 93, 139, 155) (1911–present), *Juncus interior* Wieg. var. *interior* (50) (present)

Inland salt grass [Inland saltgrass] - *Distichlis spicata* (L.) Greene (50, 140, 155) (1942–present)

Inland sedge - *Carex interior* Bailey (5, 50, 72, 139, 155) (1907–present)

Innocence - *Collinsia verna* Nutt. (5, 156, 158) (1900-1923), *Hedyotis nigricans* (Lam.) Fosberg var. *nigricans* (156) (1923), *Houstonia caerulea* L. (5, 19, 73, 86, 156) (1840-1923) Boston MA, *Houstonia humifusa* (Gray) Gray (97) (1937) OK

Inodoruous candle tree - *Morella inodora* (Bartr.) Small (20) (1857)

Insaneroot [Insane root, Insane-root] - *Hyoscyamus niger* L. (5, 156, 158) (1900–1923)

Insect flowers - *Tanacetum coccineum* (Willd.) Grierson (57) (1917)

Inshtogah'te-hi (Omaha-Ponca, eye-lotion plant - *Symphoricarpos symphoricarpos* (L.) MacMill. (37) (1919)

Interior iris - *Iris virginica* L. var. *shrevei* (Small) E. Anders. (155) (1942)

Interior ironweed - *Vernonia baldwinii* Torr. subsp. *interior* (Small) Faust (50) (present)

Intermediate aristida - *Aristida longispica* Poir. var. *geniculata* (Raf.) Fern (56) (1901)

Intermediate barley - *Hordeum jubatum* L. subsp. *intermedium* Bowden (50) (present)

Intermediate bush-clover [Intermediate bush clover] - *Lespedeza ×simulata* Mackenzie & Bush [*capitata × virginica*] (5, 97) (1913–1937)

Intermediate dogbane - *Apocynum ×floribundum* Greene (5) (1913)

Intermediate lion's-heart [Intermediate lionsheart] - *Physostegia intermedia* (Nutt.) Engelm. & Gray (3) (1977)

Intermediate milkweed - *Asclepias syriaca* L. (5) (1913)

Intermediate scouring-rush [Intermediate scouring rush] - *Equisetum ×ferrissii* Clute [*hyemale × laevigatum*] (4) (1986)

Intermediate wheatgrass - *Thinopyrum intermedium* (Host) Barkworth & D.R. Dewey (3, 50) (1977–present)

Intermediate wood fern [Intermediate woodfern] - *Dryopteris intermedia* (Muhl. ex Willd.) Gray (50) (present)

Intermedium wheatgrass - *Thinopyrum intermedium* (Host) Barkworth & D.R. Dewey (97) (1937)

Interrupted clubmoss [Interrupted club moss] - *Lycopodium annotinum* L. (5) (1913)

Interrupted fern [Interrupted-fern] - *Osmunda claytoniana* L. (5, 50, 109, 138) (1913–present)

Interrupted pondweed - *Stuckenia vaginatus* (Turcz.) Holub (5) (1913)

Introduced heliotrope - *Heliotropium indicum* L. (124) (1937)

Introduced sage - *Salvia pratensis* L. (50) (present)

Inubthon-kithe-sabe-hi (Omaha-Ponca, black perfume plant) - *Aquilegia canadensis* L. (37) (1919)

Inul - *Inula helenium* L. (64) (1907)

Inula - *Inula helenium* L. (54, 55, 57, 64) (1905-1917), *Inula* L. (138, 155) (1923-1942)

Inundated clubmoss - *Lycopodiella inundata* (L.) Holub (50) (present)

Involucred fly-honeysuckle - *Lonicera involucrata* Banks ex Spreng. (5) (1913)

Involute-leaf sedge [Involute-leaved sedge] - *Carex duriuscula* C.A. Mey. (5, 72) (1907-1913), *Carex sterilis* Willd. (5) (1913)

Iodanthus - *Iodanthus* Torr. & Gray (50) (present)

Ione manzanita - *Arctostaphylos myrtifolia* Parry (155) (1942)

Ioue (French) - *Juncus* L. (180) (1633)

Iowa barley - *Elyhordeum iowense* Pohl (50) (present)

Iowa bunch grass - *Sporobolus heterolepis* (Gray) Gray (56) (1901)

Iowa crab - *Malus ioensis* (Wood) Britton var. *ioensis* (4) (1986)

Iowa golden saxifrage - *Chrysosplenium iowense* Rydb. (5, 72) (1907-1913)

Iowa moonwort - *Botrychium campestre* W.H. Wagner & Farrar (50) (present)

Iowa pigweed - *Amaranthus graecizans* L. (80) (1913) IA

Iowa thistle - *Cirsium ×iowense* (Pammel) Fern.[*altissimum × discolor*] (80, 82, 97) (1930-1937)

Iowa wild crab apple - *Malus ioensis* (Wood) Britton var. *ioensis* (82) (1930) IA

I'-pah (Kiowa) - *Pinus* L. (132) (1855)

Ipecac - *Apocynum androsaemifolium* L. (7) (1828), *Euphorbia corollata* L. (7, 49) (1828-1898), *Porteranthus stipulatus* (Muhl. ex Willd.) Britt. (7) (1828), *Triosteum perfoliatum* L. (7) (1828)

Ipecac euphorbia - *Euphorbia ipecacuanhae* L. (155) (1942)

Ipecac spurge - *Euphorbia ipecacuanhae* L. (2, 5, 53, 92, 156) (1876-1923)

Ipecacuan - *Gillenia trifoliata* (L.) Moench (186) (1814)

Ipecacuana - *Euphorbia corollata* L. (7) (1828), *Podophyllum peltatum* L. (186) (1814)

Ipecacuana (Official name of Materia Medica) - *Euphorbia corollata* L. (7) (1828)

Ipecacuanha - *Podophyllum peltatum* L. (186) (1814)

Ipecacuanha spurge - *Euphorbia ipecacuanhae* L. (6, 7, 49, 57) (1828-1917)

Ipecacuanhua - *Gillenia trifoliata* (L.) Moench (181, 186) (~1678-1825)

Ipedendrum - Epidendrum magnoliae Muhl. (183) (1756)

Ipomoea - *Ipomoea* L. (109) (1949)

Ipomopsis - *Ipomopsis* Michx. (50) (present)

Ir - *Acorus calamus* L. (186) (1814)

Iranian stork's-bill [Iranian stork's bill] - *Erodium gruinum* (L.) L'Hér. ex Aiton (50) (present)

Iris - *Iris* L. (50, 138, 155) (1923–present), *Iris versicolor* L. (57, 64) (1908-1917)

Iris root - *Iris versicolor* L. (157) (1929)

Iris varié (French) - *Iris versicolor* L. (158) (1900)

Irish broom - *Cytisus scoparius* (L.) Link (49, 53, 92) (1876-1922)

Irish cabbage - *Symplocarpus foetidus* (L.) Salisb. ex Nutt. (186) (1814)

Irish daisy - *Taraxacum officinale* G.H. Weber ex Wiggers (5, 64, 69, 156, 157, 158) (1900-1949)

Irish juniper - *Juniperus communis* L. (109) (1949)

Irish mahogany - *Alnus glutinosa* (L.) Gaertn. (5, 156) (1913-1923)

Irish moss - *Chondrus crispus* (L.) J. Stackhouse (55, 57, 58, 59, 92) (1869-1917), *Euphorbia cyparissias* L. (5, 73, 158) (1892-1913) New Brunswick

Irish potato - *Solanum tuberosum* L. (156) (1923)

Iris-leaf bugle-lily [Irisleaf buglelily] - *Watsonia meriana* (L.) Mill. (138) (1923)

Iron ipomopsis - *Ipomopsis laxiflora* (Coult.) V. Grant (50) (present)

Iron oak - *Quercus marilandica* Muench (158) (1900), *Quercus stellata* Wangenh. (2, 5, 19, 72, 156, 187) (1818-1925)

Iron plant - *Machaeranthera* Nees (93) (1936) Neb

Iron tree [Irontree] - *Metrosideros* Banks ex Gaertn. (138) (1923)

Iron-grass [Iron grass] - *Carex caryophyllea* Latourrette (5, 156) (1913-1923), *Polygonum aviculare* L. (156, 158) (1900-1923)

Ironhead [Iron head] - *Centaurea nigra* L. (5) (1913)

Iron-plant goldenweed [Ironplant goldenweed] - *Machaeranthera pinnatifida* (Hook.) Shinners subsp. *pinnatifida* (155) (1942)

Ironweed [Iron weed, Iron weed] - *Ambrosia trifida* L. (157) (1929), *Centaurea nigra* L. (5, 156) (1913-1923), *Verbena hastata* L. (5, 75, 156, 158) (1900-1923), *Verbesina alternifolia* (L.) Britton ex Kearney (4, 80) (1913-1986), *Verbesina* L. (82) (1930), *Vernicia fordii* (Hemsl.) Airy Shaw (97) (1937), *Vernonia angustifolia* Michx. (92) (1876), *Vernonia arkansana* DC. (145) (1897), *Vernonia baldwinii* Torr. (80, 92) (1876-1913), *Vernonia fasciculata* Michx. (47, 48, 58, 82, 114, 127) (1869-1930), *Vernonia noveboracensis* (L.) Michx. (86, 156) (1878-1923), *Vernonia* Schreber (1, 2, 7, 50, 63, 82, 93, 106, 109, 138, 155, 156, 158) (1828-present)

Ironwood [Iron wood, Iron-wood] - *Carpinus caroliniana* Walt. (5, 75, 156) (1894-1923), *Carpinus caroliniana* Walt. subsp. *carolinian* (92) (1876), *Carpinus* L. (1, 82, 156) (1923-1932), *Cliftonia monophylla* (Lam.) Britton (possibly) (106) (1930), *Cyrilla racemiflora* L. (106, 156) (1923-1930), *Eugenia procera* (Sw.) Poir. (107) (1919), *Lyonothamnus floribundus* Gray (74) (1893) CA, *Olneya tesota* Gray (103, 106, 107) (1870-1930), *Ostrya carpinifolia* Scop. (20, 177) (1762-1857), *Ostrya* Scop. (1, 2, 93) (1932-1986), *Ostrya virginiana* (Mill.) K. Koch (4, 5, 9, 40, 57, 65, 72, 85, 93, 97, 109, 113, 130, 156, 157, 158) (1873-1986), *Ostrya virginiana* (Mill.) K. Koch var. *virginiana* (2, 6, 19, 47, 49, 92, 131) (1840-1899), *Sideroxylon celastrinum* (Kunth) T. D. Pennington (124) (1937) TX, *Sideroxylon* L. (7) (1828), *Sideroxylon lycioides* L. (5, 20, 106) (1857-1930)

Ironwort [Iron-wort, Ironwort] - *Anthemis cotula* L. (46) (1671) accidentally introduced by 1671, *Galeopsis bifida* Boenn. (5, 156, 158) (1900-1923), *Galeopsis ladanum* L. (5, 92, 156) (1876-1923)

Irregular polypody - *Polypodium amorphum* Suksdorf (50) (present)

Isabella wood [Isabella-wood] - *Persea borbonia* (L.) Spreng. (5, 156) (1913-1923)

Island manzanita - *Arctostaphylos insularis* Greene ex Parry (155) (1942)

Islay - *Prunus ilicifolia* (Nutt. ex Hook. & Arn.) D. Dietr. (74, 107, 109) (1893-1949) Southern CA and Western AZ

Isopappus - *Croptilon divaricatum* (Nutt.) Raf. (5, 97) (1913-1937)

Isopyrum - *Enemion* Raf. (155) (1942)

Ispaŋapŋheča (Lakota) - *Ostrya virginiana* (Mill.) K. Koch (121) (1918?-1970?)

Iss-salth (Chinook) - *Arctostaphylos uva-ursi* (L.) Spreng. (107) (1919)

Italian alder - *Alnus cordata* (Loisel.) Loisel. Or Desf. (138, 155) (1931-1942)

Italian alkanet - *Anchusa azurea* Mill. (165) (1807)

Italian arum - *Arum italicum* Mill. (138, 155) (1923-1942)

Italian barley - *Hordeum vulgare* L. (158) (1900) variety

Italian black poplar - *Populus deltoides* Bartr. ex Marsh. (158) (1900), *Populus deltoides* Bartr. ex Marsh. subsp. *monilifera* (Aiton) Eckenwalder (14) (1882)

Italian bugloss - *Anchusa azurea* Mill. (50, 138, 155) (1923-present)

Italian clematis - *Clematis viticella* L. (138) (1923)

Italian clover - *Trifolium incarnatum* L. (5, 45, 68, 110, 156, 158) (1886-1923)

Italian cocklebur - *Xanthium strumarium* L. var. *canadense* (Mill.) Torr. & Gray (155) (1942)

Italian daffodil [Italian dafodil] - *Narcissus tazetta* L. (178, 180) (1596-1633)

Italian honeysuckle - *Lonicera caprifolium* L. (5, 156) (1913-1923)

Italian juice - *Glycyrrhiza glabra* L. (92) (1876)

Italian leather flower - *Clematis viticella* L. (50) (present)

Italian millet - *Setaria italica* (L.) Beauv. (5, 45, 56, 85, 87, 90, 92, 93, 94, 107, 110, 140, 151, 152, 158, 163) (1852-1944)

Italian oatmeal [Italian oatemeale] - *Setaria italica* (L.) Beauv. (178) (1596)

Italian poplar - *Populus nigra* L. (19) (1840)

Italian ray grass [Italian ray-grass] - *Lolium perenne* L. subsp. *multiflorum* (Lam.) Husnot (45, 56, 66, 67, 157) (1890-1929)

Italian rocket - *Reseda lutea* L. (180) (1633), *Reseda luteola* L. (5, 156) (1913-1923)

Italian rye - *Lolium perenne* L. subsp. *multiflorum* (Lam.) Husnot (45) (1896)

Italian rye grass [Italian ryegrass, Italian rye-grass] - *Lolium perenne* L. (87, 90, 118) (1884-1898), *Lolium perenne* L. subsp. *multiflorum* (Lam.) Husnot (5, 50, 68, 87, 88, 92, 94, 109, 110, 119, 122, 129, 138, 143, 155, 163) (1852-present)

Italian stone pine - *Pinus pinea* L. (50, 109, 139) (1944-present)

Italian tamarisk [Italian tamariske] - *Tamarix gallica* L. (178) (1526)

Italian woodbine - *Lonicera caprifolium* L. (156) (1923)

It-brings-the-frost (Onondaga Indians) - *Aster* L. (75, 155) (1894-1942) NY

Itchweed [Itch-weed, Itch weed, Ich weed] - *Symplocarpus foetidus* (L.) Salisb. ex Nutt. (186) (1814), *Veratrum album* L. (41) (1770), *Veratrum viride* Ait. (5, 6, 7, 19, 49, 59, 64, 71, 92, 156) (1828-1913)

Itea - *Itea* L. (8) (1785), *Itea virginica* L. (5, 19, 174, 177) (1753-1913)

Itea (French) - *Itea* L. (8) (1785)

Itéa de Virginie (French) - *Itea virginica* L. (8) (1785)

Ithaca dewberry - *Rubus invisus* (Bailey) Britt. (97) (1937)

Itomico - *Magnolia macrophylla* Michx. (7) (1828)

Itopta sapa tapežuta (Lakota, black-footed ferret medicine) - *Euphorbia marginata* Pursh (121) (1918?-1970?)

Its (Pawnee) - *Apios americana* Medik. (37) (1919)

Iunco (Spanish) - *Juncus* L. (180) (1633)

Ivory - *Lolium temulentum* L. (119) (1938) OK

Ivory plum [Ivory plums] - *Gaultheria hispidula* (L.) Muhl. ex Bigelow (5, 73, 156) (1892-1923) no longer in use by 1923, *Gaultheria procumbens* L. (5, 73, 79, 92, 156) (1876-1923)

Ivory-leaves [Ivory leaves] - *Gaultheria procumbens* L. (73) (1892) Ipswich MA

Ivraie (French) - *Lolium temulentum* L. (158) (1900)

Ivray - *Lolium temulentum* L. (157, 158) (1900-1929)

Ivrepeba - *Solanum carolinense* L. (181) (~1678)

Ivy - *Hedera helix* L. (7, 49, 92, 106) (1828-1930), *Hedera* L. (8, 138, 155, 158, 184) (1785-1923), *Kalmia angustifolia* L. (75, 177) (1762-1894) VA, *Kalmia* L. (167) (1814), *Kalmia latifolia* L. (49, 71, 75, 77, 156, 177) (1762-1898), *Parthenocissus quinquefolia* (L.) Planch. (41) (1770)

Ivy bindweed - *Polygonum convolvulus* L. (5, 156, 158) (1900-1923)

Ivy bush [Ivy-bush] - *Kalmia latifolia* L. (5, 71, 156, 187) (1818-1898)

Ivy chickweed - *Veronica hederifolia* L. (5, 156, 158) (1900-1923)

Ivy flower [Ivy-flower] - *Hepatica nobilis* Schreb. (156) (1923), *Hepatica nobilis* Schreb. var. *obtusa* (Pursh) Steyermark (5) (1913)

Ivy geranium - *Pelargonium peltatum* (L.) L'Hér. ex Aiton (109) (1949)

Ivy gourd [Ivy-gourd] - *Coccinia grandis* (L.) Voigt (109, 138) (1923-1949)

Ivy groundsel - *Delairea odorata* Lem. (138) (1923)

Ivy henbit [Iuie hen bit] - *Veronica hederifolia* L. (178) (1526)

Ivy speedwell - *Veronica hederifolia* L. (5, 19) (1840-1913)

Ivy starglory - *Ipomoea hederifolia* L. (138) (1923)

Ivy tree [Ivy-tree] - *Kalmia angustifolia* L. (189) (1767)

Ivy tree of Virginia [Ivy-tree of Virginia] - *Kalmia latifolia* L. (189) (1767)

Ivy treebine - *Cissus trifoliata* (L.) L. (155) (1942)

Ivyberry [Ivy berry, Ivy-berry] - *Gaultheria procumbens* L. (5, 73, 156) (1892-1923) NB

Ivy-leaf - *Prenanthes* L. (184) (1793)

Ivy-leaf crowfoot [Ivy-leaved crowfoot] - *Ranunculus hederaceus* L. (5) (1913)

Ivy-leaf duckweed [Ivy-leaved duckweed] - *Lemna trisulca* L. (5, 72, 93, 156) (1907-1936)

Ivy-leaf geranium [Ivyleaf geranium] - *Pelargonium peltatum* (L.) L'Hér. ex Aiton (138) (1923)

Ivy-leaf ground-cherry [Ivyleaf groundcherry] - *Physalis hederifolia* Gray (50) (present), *Physalis hederifolia* Gray var. *comata* (Rydb.) Waterfall (50) (present)

Ivy-leaf morning-glory [Ivyleaf morning-glory, Ivyleaf morning-glory, Ivy-leaved morning glory, Ivy-leaved morning-glory] - *Ipomoea hederacea* Jacq. (3, 4, 5, 50, 62, 72, 85, 93, 97, 131, 138, 155, 157) (1899–present)

Ivy-leaf rough bindweed [Ivy leaved rough bindweed] - *Smilax glauca* Walt. (8) (1785)

Ivy-leaf speedwell [Ivyleaf speedwell, Ivy-leaved speedwell] - *Veronica hederifolia* L. (3, 4, 5, 50, 155, 156, 158) (1900–present)

Ivy-leaf toadflax [Ivy-leaved toad flax, Ivy-leaved toadflax] - *Cymbalaria muralis* P.G. Gaertn., B. Mey. & Scherb. (5, 92, 156) (1876-1923)

Ivyweed [Ivy weed] - *Cymbalaria muralis* P.G. Gaertn., B. Mey. & Scherb. (5, 156) (1913-1923)

Ivywood [Ivy wood] - *Kalmia latifolia* L. (71) (1898)

Iwarancuse - Vetiveria zizaniodes (L.) Nash (92) (1876)

Ixia - *Ixia* L. (138, 155) (1923-1942) Greek "bird lime" perhaps referring to juice

Ixora - *Ixora* L. (138) (1923)

Izna-kithe-iga hi (Omaha-Ponca) - *Monarda fistulosa* L. (possibly) (37) (1919)

Ivy tree, *Kalmia angustifolia* L.
(G.D. Ehret, 1754)

J

Jabonera (Spanish) - *Phytolacca americana* L. var. *americana* (158) (1900)

Jabon's-ladder [Jabons-ladder] - *Polemonium caeruleum* L. (109) (1949)

Jaburan - *Ophiopogon jaburan* (Sieb.) Lodd. (138) (1923)

Jacaranda - *Jacaranda* Juss. (138) (1923)

Jachendel (German) - *Juniperus communis* L. (158) (1900)

Jacinth - *Hyacinthus orientalis* L. (92) (1876)

Jack bean [Jack-bean] - *Canavalia ensiformis* (L.) DC. (109) (1949), *Lablab purpureus* (L.) Sweet (156) (1923)

Jack fruit [Jack-fruit, Jackfruit] - *Artocarpus heterophyllus* Lam. (109, 155) (1942-1949)

Jack oak - *Quercus imbricaria* Michx. (5, 33, 156, 187) (1818-1923), *Quercus marilandica* Muench (158) (1900), *Quercus nigra* L. (106) (1930)

Jack pine - *Pinus banksiana* Lamb. (5, 50, 75, 109, 112, 136, 138, 155) (1894–present)

Jackass clover - *Wislizenia* Engelm. (106) (1930) so named by C.I. Graham who once lost a team of jackasses in a field of these plants, *Wislizenia refracta* Engelm. (106) (1930)

Jack-by-the-hedge [Iacke by the hedge] - *Alliaria petiolata* (Bieb.) Cavara & Grande (5, 92, 156, 158, 178) (1526-1923) no longer in use by 1923, *Tragopogon pratensis* L. (158) (1900)

Jacket-and-breeches [Jacket and breeches] - *Aquilegia canadensis* L. (76) (1896)

Jack-go-to-bed-at-noon - *Tragopogon pratensis* L. (50) (present)

Jack-in-a-box [Jack in a box] - *Hernandia sonora* L. (92) (1876)

Jack-in-the-bush - *Alliaria petiolata* (Bieb.) Cavara & Grande (5) (1913), *Nigella damascena* L. (76) (1896) Worcester MA

Jack-in-the-pulpit [Jack in the pulpit, Jackinthepulpit] - *Arisaema* Martens (1, 93, 155) (1932-1942), *Arisaema triphyllum* (L.) Schott (3, 5, 6, 35, 40, 49, 50, 53, 57, 58, 64, 73, 85, 86, 92, 93, 97, 122, 124, 125, 127, 138, 156, 157, 158) (1806–present), *Arisaema triphyllum* (L.) Schott subsp. *pusillum* (Peck) Huttleston (50) (present), *Arisaema triphyllum* (L.) Schott subsp. *triphyllum* (50, 107, 109) (1919–present), *Nigella damascena* L. (76) (1896) Rutalnd MA, *Trillium recurvatum* Beck (78) (1898) IL

Jack-in-trousers - *Aquilegia canadensis* L. (5, 76, 156, 157, 158) (1896–1929) Lynn MA, children's name

Jack-jump-about - *Aegopodium podagraria* L. (156) (1923), *Lotus corniculatus* L. (158) (1900)

Jackman's clematis [Jackman clematis] - *Clematis* ×*jackmanii* T. Moore [*lanuginosa* × *viticella*] (138) (1923)

Jacko-bush - *Iva frutescens* L. subsp. *oraria* (Bartlett) R.C. Jackson (156) (1923)

Jack-of-the-buttery [Jack of the buttery] - *Sedum acre* L. (92) (1876)

Jack-over-the-ground - *Glechoma hederacea* L. (73) (1892) Eastern MA

Jack's thorn - *Crataegus chrysocarpa* Ashe (5) (1913)

Jackson vine [Jackson-vine] - *Lycium barbarum* L. (5, 73, 156, 158) (1892-1923) Mansfield OH, *Smilax smallii* Morong (156) (1923)

Jacksonville violet - *Viola affinis* Le Conte (155) (1942)

Jack-straws [Jack straws] - *Plantago lanceolata* L. (5, 156, 158) (1900-1923) no longer in use by 1923

Jacobinia - *Justicia* L. (138) (1923)

Jacob's flower - *Smilax herbacea* L. (5, 14, 22, 40) (1882-1913)

Jacobskraut (German) - *Senecio vulgaris* L. (158) (1900)

Jacob's-ladder [Jacob's ladder, Jacobs-ladder] - *Celastrus scandens* L. (5, 73, 158) (1892-1913) Stratham NH, *Chelidonium majus* L. (156, 158) (1900-1923), *Diodia virginiana* L. (156) (1923), *Gladiolus* L. (75) (1894) Lincolnton NC, *Hyacinthus orientalis* L. (75) (1894) OH, *Linaria vulgaris* Mill. (5, 6, 73, 158) (1892-1913) parts of NE US, *Polemonium caeruleum* L. (2) (1895), *Polemonium* L. (1, 10) (1818-1932), *Polemonium reptans* L. (49, 61, 86, 92, 156, 158, 184) (1793-1923) for ladder-like leaf, *Polemonium vanbruntiae* Britton (156) (1923), *Smilax herbacea* L. (19, 30, 92) (1830-1876), *Streptopus lanceolatus* (Ait.) Reveal var. *roseus* (Michx.) Reveal (78) (1898) ME, *Tradescantia crassifolia* Cav. (73, 78) (1892-1898)

Jacob's-staff [Jacob's staff] - *Verbascum thapsus* L. (5, 69, 156, 158) (1900-1923)

Jacob's-sword [Jacob's sword] - *Iris pseudacorus* L. (5, 156, 158) (1900-1923) no longer in use by 1923

Jaffna moss - *Hydropuntia edulis* (S.G.Gmelin) Gurgel & Fredericq (92) (1876)

Jagged chickweed - *Holosteum* L. (158) (1900), *Holosteum umbellatum* L. (4, 5, 50, 156) (1913–present)

Jagged rose pennywort [Jagged rose-penny wort] - *Hydrocotyle americana* L. (46) (1671)

Jagged-leaf rudbeckia [Jagged-leaved rudbeckia] - *Rudbeckia laciniata* L. (187) (1818)

Jagged-leaf toothwort [Jagged-leaved tooth-wort, Jagged leaved tooth wort] - *Cardamine concatenata* (Michx.) Sw. (181, 191) (1678–1814)

Jagong - *Zea mays* L. (92) (1876)

Jajoba - *Simmondsia chinensis* (Link) C.K. Schneid. (107) (1919), *Sinapis alba* L. (107) (1919)

Jakfruit - *Artocarpus heterophyllus* Lam. (109, 155) (1942-1949)

Jalap - *Phytolacca americana* L. var. *americana* (6, 71) (1892-1898)

Jalap cancer-root [Jalap cancer root] - *Phytolacca americana* L. var. *americana* (49, 186) (1814-1898)

Jalap plant - *Mirabilis jalapa* L. (92) (1876)

Jamaica buckthorn - *Rosa laevigata* Michx. (156) (1923)

Jamaica cotton - *Gossypium hirsutum* L. var. *hirsutum* (109) (1949)

Jamaica crab grass [Jamaica crab-grass] - *Urochloa reptans* (L.) Stapf (94) (1901)

Jamaica dogwood - *Piscidia piscipula* (L.) Sargent (20, 52, 53, 55, 57, 60, 92, 106) (1857-1930)

Jamaica goldfern - *Pityrogramma sulphurea* (Sw.) Maxon (138) (1923)

Jamaica licorice - *Abrus precatorius* L. (58) (1869)

Jamaica samphire - *Borrichia frutescens* (L.) DC. (156) (1923)

Jamaica sorrel - *Hibiscus sabdariffa* L. (109) (1949)

Jamaica swamp sawgrass - *Cladium mariscus* (L.) Pohl subsp. *jamaicense* (Crantz) Kükenth. (50) (present)

Jamaica thatch palm - *Thrinax radiata* Lodd. ex J.A. & J.H. Schultes (138) (1923)

Jamaica thistle - *Argemone mexicana* L. (5, 156) (1913-1923)

Jamaica wild licorice [Jamaica wild liquorice] - *Abrus precatorius* L. (165) (1768)

Jamaica-honeysuckle - *Passiflora laurifolia* L. (109) (1949)

Jambolan - *Syzygium cumini* (L.) Skeels (109) (1949)

Jambolan-plum - *Syzygium cumini* (L.) Skeels (109, 138) (1923-1949)

James' beardtongue [James' beard-tongue] - *Penstemon jamesii* A. Nels. (50, 131) (1899–present)

James' boykinia [James boykinia] - *Telesonix jamesii* (Torr.) Raf. (155) (1942)

James' bundle-flower [James bundleflower] - *Desmanthus cooleyi* (Eat.) Trel. (155) (1942)

James' clammy-weed [James' clammyweed] - *Polanisia jamesii* (Torr. & Gray) Iltis (50) (present)

James' cristatella - *Polanisia jamesii* (Torr. & Gray) Iltis (5, 72, 97) (1907-1937)

James' cryptantha [James cryptantha] - *Cryptantha cinerea* (Greene) Cronq. (50) (present), *Cryptantha cinerea* (Greene) Cronq. var. *jamesii* Cronq. (3, 50, 98, 155) (1926–present)

James' dalea [James dalea] - *Dalea jamesii* (Torr.) Torr. & Gray (3, 4, 155) (1942-1986)

James' eriogonum - *Eriogonum correllii* Reveal (5, 97, 155) (1913-1942)

James' galleta - *Pleuraphis jamesii* Torr. (50) (present)

James' hoffmannseggia [James' hoffmanseggia] - *Caesalpinia jamesii* (Torr. & Gray) Fisher (5, 97) (1913-1937)

James' holdback - *Caesalpinia jamesii* (Torr. & Gray) Fisher (50) (present)

James' ironweed [James' iron-weed] - *Vernonia marginata* (Torr.) Raf. (5, 97) (1913-1937)

James' mimosa - *Desmanthus cooleyi* (Eat.) Trel. (97) (1937)

James' mimulus - *Mimulus glabratus* Kunth var. *jamesii* (Torr. & Gray ex Benth.) Gray (72) (1907)

James' monkey-flower [James' monkeyflower, James' monkey flower] - *Mimulus glabratus* Kunth var. *jamesii* (Torr. & Gray ex Benth.) Gray (50, 86, 131) (1878–present)

James' nailwort [James nailwort] - *Paronychia jamesii* Torr. & Gray (4, 50, 155) (1942–present)

James' parosela - *Dalea jamesii* (Torr.) Torr. & Gray (97) (1937)

James' penstemon [James penstemon] - *Penstemon jamesii* A. Nels. (155) (1942)

James' prairie clover - *Dalea jamesii* (Torr.) Torr. & Gray (50) (present)

James' rushpea [James rush-pea] - *Caesalpinia jamesii* (Torr. & Gray) Fisher (4) (1986)

James' saxifrage - *Telesonix jamesii* (Torr.) Raf. (4) (1986)

James' sedge - *Carex jamesii* Schwein. (5, 50, 72) (1893–present)

James' tea - *Ledum groenlandicum* Oeder (possibly) (49) (1898)

James' telesonix - *Telesonix jamesii* (Torr.) Raf. (50) (present)

James' whitlow-wort [James' whitlow wort] - *Paronychia jamesii* Torr. & Gray (5, 93, 97, 131) (1899–1937)

James' wild buckwheat - *Eriogonum correllii* Reveal (4) (1986)

Jamestown lily - *Datura stramonium* L. (5, 69, 71, 75, 156, 158) (1894-1923)

Jamestown-weed [Jamestown weed] - *Datura inoxia* P. Mill. (77) (1898), *Datura* L. (1, 10) (1818-1932), *Datura stramonium* L. (5, 6, 49, 52, 53, 54, 59, 61, 69, 71, 92, 106, 109, 156, 157, 158, 187, 191) (1814-1949)

James-weed [James weed] - *Datura stramonium* L. (18) (1805)

Jano - *Chilopsis linearis* (Cav.) Sweet (153) (1913) NM

Japanese anemone [Japanese anemony] - *Anemone hupehensis* (Lemoine) Lemoine (109, 138) (1923-1949), *Anemone hupehensis* var. *japonica* (Thunb.) Bowles & Stearn (138) (1923), *Anemone multifida* Poir. var. *hudsoniana* DC. (109) (1949)

Japanese anise-tree [Japanese anisetree] - *Illicium parviflorum* Michx. (138) (1923)

Japanese astilbe - *Astilbe japonica* (Morr. & Dcne.) Gray (138, 155) (1931-1942)

Japanese aucuba - *Aucuba japonica* Thunb. (138) (1923)

Japanese azalea - *Rhododendron japonicum* (Gray) Sur. (138) (1923)

Japanese bamboo - *Polygonum cuspidatum* Sieb. & Zucc. (4) (1986)

Japanese barberry - *Berberis thunbergii* DC. (50, 82, 85, 109, 112, 138, 155) (1923–present)

Japanese barnyard millet - *Echinochloa frumentacea* Link (109, 163) (1852-1949)

Japanese birch - *Betula platyphylla* Suk. (4) (1986)

Japanese black pine - *Pinus thunbergiana* Franco (109, 138) (1923-1949)

Japanese bristle grass [Japanese bristlegrass] - *Setaria faberi* Herrm. (50) (present)

Japanese brome - *Bromus japonicus* Thunb. ex Murr. (3, 50, 140, 155) (1942–present)

Japanese butterbur - *Petasites japonicus* (Sieb. & Zucc.) Maxim.

(138) (1923), *Petasites* Mill. (possibly) (138) (1923)

Japanese catalpa - *Catalpa ovata* G. Don (138) (1923)

Japanese chess - *Bromus japonicus* Thunb. ex Murr. (122, 140, 146) (1937-1944)

Japanese chestnut - *Castanea crenata* Sieb. & Zucc. (109, 138) (1923-1949)

Japanese climbing fern - *Lygodium japonicum* (Thunb. ex Murr.) Sw. (138) (1923)

Japanese clover [Japan clover] - *Kummerowia striata* (Thunb.) Schindl. (3, 5, 45, 50, 66, 87, 97, 109, 158) (1884–present)

Japanese creeper - *Parthenocissus tricuspidata* (Sieb. & Zucc.) Planch. (138) (1923)

Japanese elm - *Ulmus parvifolia* Jacq. (possibly) (112) (1937)

Japanese fleeceflower - *Polygonum cuspidatum* Sieb. & Zucc. (138, 155) (1923-1942) IA

Japanese flowering cherry - *Prunus serrulata* Lindl. (109) (1949)

Japanese flowering crab - *Malus floribunda* Sieb. ex Van Houtte (138) (1923)

Japanese foxtail - *Setaria faberi* Herrm. (50) (present)

Japanese globeflower [Japan globe-flower] - *Kerria japonica* (L.) DC. (156) (1923)

Japanese holly - *Ilex crenata* Thunb. (109, 138) (1923-1949)

Japanese honeysuckle [Japan honeysuckle] - *Lonicera japonica* Thunb. (3, 4, 5, 50, 138, 155, 156) (1913–present)

Japanese hop - *Humulus japonicus* Sieb. & Zucc. (3, 4, 50, 93, 138, 155) (1923–present)

Japanese iris - *Iris ensata* Thunb. (109, 138) (1923-1949), *Iris laevigata* Fisch. (109) (1949)

Japanese ivy - *Parthenocissus tricuspidata* (Sieb. & Zucc.) Planch. (109, 138) (1923-1949)

Japanese knotweed - *Polygonum cuspidatum* Sieb. & Zucc. (3, 5, 50, 109) (1913–present) NM

Japanese larch - *Larix kaempferi* (Lam.) Carr. (109, 138) (1923-1949)

Japanese lawn grass [Japanese lawn-grass, Japanese lawngrass] - *Zoysia japonica* Steud. (109, 138) (1923-1949)

Japanese lespedeza - *Kummerowia striata* (Thunb.) Schindl. (4) (1986)

Japanese lilac - *Syringa reticulata* (Blume) H. Hara subsp. *reticulata* (82) (1930)

Japanese loosestrife - *Lysimachia japonica* Thunb. (138) (1923)

Japanese maple - *Acer japonicum* Thunb. (165) (1768), *Acer palmatum* Thunb. (50, 109 137, 138, 155) (1923–present)

Japanese millet - *Echinochloa frumentacea* Link (1, 138, 155) (1923-1942), *Setaria italica* (L.) Beauv. (107) (1919)

Japanese mustard - *Brassica juncea* (L.) Czern. (155) (1942)

Japanese pachysandra - *Pachysandra terminalis* Sieb. & Zucc. (109, 138) (1923-1949)

Japanese pagoda-tree - *Sophora japonica* L. (109) (1949)

Japanese pittosporum - *Pittosporum tobira* (Thunb.) Aiton f. (109) (1949)

Japanese plum - *Eriobotrya japonica* (Thunb.) Lindl. (107, 109) (1919-1949)

Japanese plume grass - *Miscanthus sinensis* Anderss. (5) (1913)

Japanese primrose - *Primula japonica* Gray (138) (1923)

Japanese privet [Japan privet] - *Ligustrum japonicum* Thunb. (138) (1923), *Ligustrum* L. (106) (1930)

Japanese quince - *Chaenomeles japonica* (Thunb.) Lindl. ex Spach (107, 112) (1919-1937), *Chaenomeles speciosa* (Sweet) Nakai (109) (1949)

Japanese raisin-tree - *Hovenia dulcis* Thunb. (109) (1949)

Japanese raspberry - *Rubus parviflorus* Nutt. (155) (1942)

Japanese rose [Japan rose] - *Rosa multiflora* Thunb. ex Murray (4, 19, 138, 155) (1840-1986), *Rosa rugosa* Thunb. (82, 135) (1910-1930)

Japanese snailseed - *Cocculus orbiculatus* (L.) DC. (138) (1923)

Japanese snowball - *Viburnum plicatum* Thunb. (109) (1949)

Japanese snowbell - *Styrax japonicus* Sieb. & Zucc. (138) (1923)

Japanese spindle-tree [Japanese spindle tree] - *Euonymus japonicus* Thunb. (107) (1919)

Japanese spiraea - *Spiraea japonica* L. f. (5, 138) (1913-1923)

Japanese timber bamboo - *Phyllostachys bambusoides* Sieb. & Zucc. (138) (1923)

Japanese tree lilac - *Syringa reticulata* (Blume) H. Hara subsp. *reticulata* (138) (1923)

Japanese vitex - *Vitex negundo* L. var. *negundo* (124) (1937)

Japanese walnut - *Juglans ailanthifolia* Carr. (138) (1923)

Japanese wisteria - *Wisteria floribunda* (Willd.) DC. (109, 138) (1923-1949), *Wisteria frutescens* (L.) Poir. (174) (1753)

Japanese yew - *Taxus cuspidata* Sieb. & Zucc. (109, 112, 136, 138) (1923-1949)

Japizapi hu (Lakota, mouth organ plant) - *Maianthemum racemosum* (L.) Link subsp. *racemosum* (121) (1918-1970)

Jasmin Jaune (French) - *Gelsemium sempervirens* (L.) J. St.-Hil. (6) (1892)

Jasmine - *Jasminum* L. (109, 138) (1923-1949) from ancient Arabic name, *Jasminum officinale* L. (19, 92) (1840-1876), *Lycium barbarum* L. (5, 73) (1892-1913) Mansfield OH

Jasmine bindweed - *Ipomoea quamoclit* L. (19) (1840)

Jatropha - *Solanum carolinense* L. (52) (1919)

Jaundice-berry [Jaundice berry] - *Berberis vulgaris* L. (5, 92, 107, 156, 157, 158) (1876-1923)

Jaundice-root - *Hydrastis canadensis* L. (49, 64, 92) (1876-1908)

Jaundice-tree [Jaundice tree] - *Berberis vulgaris* L. (5, 156) (1913-1923)

Java fan palm - *Livistona rotundifolia* (Lam.) Mart. (138) (1923)

Java sugar - *Saccharum officinarum* L. (7) (1828)

Java-bean - *Senna obtusifolia* (L.) Irwin & Barneby (50) (present)

Javelina brush - *Condalia ericoides* (Gray) M.C. Johnston (122) (1937) TX

Jayweed [Jay-weed] - *Anthemis cotula* L. (157, 158) (1900-1929)

Jažopi hu (Lakota, whistle stem) - *Sium suave* Walt. (121) (1918?-1970?)

Jeff Davis' cholla [JeffDavis cholla] - *Opuntia tunicata* (Lehm.) Link & Otto (155) (1942)

Jeffersone (French) - *Jeffersonia diphylla* (L.) Pers. (7) (1828)

Jeffersonia - *Jeffersonia diphylla* (L.) Pers. (64) (1907)

Jeffrey's pine [Jeffrey pine] - *Pinus jeffreyi* Grev. & Balf. (109, 138) (1923-1949)

Jeffrey's shootingstar [Jeffrey shootingstar] - *Dodecatheon jeffreyi* Van Houtte (138) (1923)

Jellazoji (Lithuanian) - *Brassica napus* L. (110) (1886)

Jenepre - *Juniperus communis* L. (178, 179) (1526-1596)

Jenny stonecrop - *Sedum reflexum* L. (138, 155) (1931-1942)

Jenny-wren [Jenny wren] - *Geranium robertianum* L. (5, 156, 157, 158) (1900-1929)

Jequirity - *Abrus precatorius* L. (49, 55, 57) (1898-1917)

Jequirity rosary-pea [Jequirity rosarypea] - *Abrus precatorius* L. (155) (1942)

Jerenio (Spanish) - *Geranium maculatum* L. (186) (1814)

Jersey live-long - *Pseudognaphalium luteoalbum* (L.) Hilliard & Burtt (92) (1876)

Jersey pine - *Pinus virginiana* Mill. (5, 10) (1818-1913)

Jersey scrub pine - *Pinus virginiana* Mill. (2, 19) (1840-1895)

Jersey tea [Jersey-tea] - *Ceanothus americanus* L. (7, 92, 138, 157, 158) (1828-1929), *Ceanothus herbaceus* Raf. (50) (present)

Jersey-tea ceanothus [Jerseytea ceanothus] - *Ceanothus americanus* L. (155) (1942)

Jerusalem apple - *Solanum lycopersicum* L. var. *lycopersicum* (107) (1835)

Jerusalem artichoke - *Helianthus tuberosus* L. (3, 5, 50, 7, 14, 19, 37, 40, 62, 63, 72, 82, 92, 93, 95, 97, 105, 107, 110, 122, 124, 127, 131, 138, 145, 155, 156, 158) (1882-present)

Jerusalem cherry [Jerusalem-cherry] - *Solanum pseudocapsicum* L. (19, 92, 109, 138) (1840-1949)

Jerusalem corn - *Sorghum bicolor* (L.) Moench subsp. *bicolor* (119) (1938) OK

Jerusalem cowslip - *Pulmonaria officinalis* L. (92, 107) (1876-1919) OK

Jerusalem cross [Jerusalem-cross] - *Lychnis chalcedonica* L. (92, 158) (1876-1900)

Jerusalem date - *Bauhinia monandra* Kurz (109) (1949)

Jerusalem oak [Jerusalem-oak] - *Chenopodium ambrosioides* L. var. *ambrosioides* (6, 7, 41, 58, 92, 156, 158, 186, 187) (1770-1923), *Chenopodium botrys* L. (1, 3, 4, 72, 85, 122, 138, 156, 157, 158) (1900-1986)

Jerusalem oak leaves - *Chenopodium ambrosioides* L. var. *ambrosioides* (92) (1876)

Jerusalem oak seed - *Chenopodium ambrosioides* L. var. *ambrosioides* (92) (1876)

Jerusalem potato - *Helianthus tuberosus* L. (156) (1923)

Jerusalem sage [Jerusalem-sage] - *Phlomis fruticosa* L. (109) (1949), *Phlomis* L. (138, 156) (1923), *Phlomis tuberosa* L. (5, 92) (1876-1913), *Pulmonaria officinalis* L. (92, 109) (1876-1949)

Jerusalem star [Jerusalem-star] - *Tragopogon porrifolius* L. (5, 92, 156, 158) (1876-1923)

Jerusalem sunflower [Jerusalemsunflower] - *Helianthus tuberosus* L. (3, 5, 50, 7, 14, 19, 37, 40, 62, 63, 72, 82, 92, 93, 95, 97, 105, 107, 110, 122, 124, 127, 131, 138, 145, 155, 156, 158) (1882-present), possibly a corruption of Girasole articocco, Italian for sunflower artichoke, name dates back to at least 1686

Jerusalem tea - *Chenopodium ambrosioides* L. (69, 92, 156, 157, 158) (1898-1923)

Jerusalem thorn [Jerusalem-thorn] - *Parkinsonia aculeata* L. (109) (1949), *Parkinsonia* L. (106) (1930), *Parkinsonia microphylla* Torr. (106) (1930)

Jerusalem-artichoke sunflower [Jerusalemartichoke sunflower] - *Helianthus tuberosus* L. (155) (1942)

Jerusalem-oak goosefoot [Jerusalemoak goosefoot] - *Chenopodium botrys* L. (50, 155) (1942-present)

Jessamine - *Gelsemium sempervirens* (L.) J. St.-Hil. (7, 59) (1828-1911), *Jasminum* L. (109) (1949), *Lycium barbarum* L. (73, 158) (1892-1900) Stratham NH, *Mandevilla brachysiphon* (Torr.) Pichon (75) (1894)

Jesuit tea - *Chenopodium ambrosioides* L. (69, 156, 157, 158) (1900-1929)

Jesuit-berry - *Mitchella repens* L. (156) (1923)

Jesuit's-bark [Jesuit's bark] - *Iva frutescens* L. (5, 75) (1894-1913) NY, *Iva frutescens* L. subsp. *oraria* (Bartlett) R.C. Jackson (156) (1923)

Jesuit's-nut [Jesuit nut, Jesuits-nut, Jesuits' nuts] - *Trapa natans* L. (92, 107, 109) (1876-1949)

Jesuit's-waternut [Jesuit's water-nut] - *Trapa natans* L. (156) (1923)

Jesup's thorn - *Crataegus jesupii* Sarg. (5) (1913)

Jetbead - *Rhodotypos scandens* (Thunb.) Makino (138) (1923), *Rhodotypos* Siebold & Zucc. (138) (1923)

Jewbush [Jewbush] - *Pedilanthus tithymaloides* (L.) Poit. (92, 155) (1876-1942)

Jewelweed [Jewel-weed, Jewel weed] - *Impatiens capensis* Meerb. (5, 50, 53, 86, 156) (1878-present), *Impatiens* L. (1, 2, 7, 13, 15, 106) (1828-1932), *Impatiens pallida* Nutt. (4, 5, 19, 53, 57, 92) (1840-1986)

Jew's-apple [Jew's apple] - *Solanum melongena* L. (107, 156) (1919-1923)

Jew's-ear [Jew's ear, Jews' ear] - *Auricularia auricula-judae* (Bulliard) J. Schröter (92) (1876), *Solanum lycopersicum* L. var. *lycopersicum* (5, 156, 158) (1900-1923)

Jew's-harp [Jews harp] - *Trillium cernuum* L. (7) (1828), *Trillium sessile* L. (58) (1869)

Jew's-harp plant [Jews' harp plant, Jewsharp plant, Jew's-harp plant] - *Trillium cernuum* L. (5, 156, 158) (1900-1923) no longer in use by 1923, *Trillium erectum* L. (92) (1876)

Jew's-mallow [Jew's mallow, Jews-mallow] - *Corchorus olitorius* L. (92, 109) (1876-1949), *Kerria japonica* (L.) DC. (156) (1923)

Jibagup (Chippewa) - *Dirca palustris* L. (105) (1932)

Jiggerweed [Jigger weed] - *Boerhavia erecta* L. (77) (1898) Florida Keys

Jim Hill mustard - *Sisymbrium altissimum* L. (156) (1923)

Jim Hill weed - *Thlaspi arvense* L. (156) (1923)

Jimmyweed - *Oonopsis foliosa* (Gray) Greene var. *foliosa* (155) (1942)

Jimpson seed - *Datura stramonium* L. (92) (1876)

Jimsonweed [Jimson-weed, Jimson weed] - *Datura* L. (1, 50, 156) (1923–present), *Datura stramonium* L. (3, 4, 5, 6, 49, 50, 52, 53, 57, 59, 62, 63, 69, 71, 72, 73, 80, 85, 92, 97, 106, 109, 124, 125, 148, 156, 157) (1892–present)

Jimsonweed datura - *Datura stramonium* L. (155) (1942)

Jin chen [Jin-chen] - *Panax quinquefolius* L. (6, 186) (1814-1892)

Jĭn'gwakwan'dûg (Chippewa, pine) - *Artemisia dracunculus* L. (40) (1928)

Jinks - *Gaultheria procumbens* L. (73, 156) (1892-1923)

Jin-seng - *Panax quinquefolius* L. (186) (1814)

Jinshang - *Panax quinquefolius* L. (158) (1900)

Jĭngwak' (Chippewa) - *Pinus resinosa* Aiton (40) (1928), *Pinus strobus* L. (40) (1928)

Joan silverpin [Joan silver-pin, Joan silver pin] - *Papaver rhoeas* L. (92) (1876), *Papaver somniferum* L. (5, 156) (1913-1923)

Jobarde - *Sempervivum tectorum* L. (179) (1526)

Job's-drops [Iobs drops] - *Coix lacryma-jobi* L. (180) (1633)

Job's-tear [Job's tear, Job's tears, Jobs-tears, Job's tear's, Iobs Teares] - *Coix* L. (138, 167) (1814–1923), *Coix lacryma-jobi* L. (19, 45, 50, 56, 67, 88, 92, 94, 122, 138, 178, 180184) (1596–present), *Maianthemum racemosum* (L.) Link subsp. *racemosum* (5, 75, 156, 157, 158) (1894–1929) NY

Jockey grass - *Briza media* L. (5) (1913)

Joe Pye weed [Joe-Pye-weed, Joe-pye weed, Joe pye's weed] - *Eupatorium* L. (93) (1936), *Eupatorium maculatum* L. (4, 40, 109) (1929-1986), *Eupatorium purpureum* L. (2, 19, 49, 53, 58, 62, 63, 64, 72, 82, 92, 93, 97, 105, 106, 109, 122, 127, 138, 156) (1840-1937)

Joemna (Sweden) - *Lycopodium complanatum* L. (46) (1879)

Joe-Pye [Joe pye, Joe Pie, Joepye] - *Eupatorium perfoliatum* L. (7) (1828), *Eupatorium purpureum* L. (5, 6, 7, 19, 49, 92, 95) (1828-1911)

Joe-the-weed - *Eupatorium purpureum* L. (157) (1929)

Johandel (German) - *Juniperus communis* L. (158) (1900)

Johanneskraut-Blattrige Wolfsmilch (German) - *Chamaesyce hypericifolia* (L.) Millsp. (6) (1892)

Johannis brodbaum (German) - *Ceratonia siliqua* L. (110) (1886)

Johannisblut (German) - *Hypericum perforatum* L. (158) (1900)

Johanniskraut (German) - *Hypericum perforatum* L. (6, 158) (1892–1900)

Johanniswurzel (German) - *Dryopteris filix-mas* (L.) Schott (158) (1900)

John-go-to-bed-at-noon - *Anagallis arvensis* L. (158) (1900), *Ornithogalum umbellatum* L. (158) (1900)

Johnnies - *Viola tricolor* L. (73) (1892) Mansfield OH

Johnny smokers - *Geum triflorum* Pursh var. *ciliatum* (Pursh) Fassett (5, 156) (1913-1923)

Johnny-jump [Johnny jump] - *Dodecatheon meadia* L. (5, 75, 156) (1894-1923) Southern CA

Johnny-jumper [Johnny jumper] - *Viola tricolor* L. (92, 158) (1876-1900)

Johnny-jump-up [Johhnyjumpup, Johnny-jump-ups] - *Viola bicolor* Pursh (3, 4, 155) (1942-1986), *Viola cucullata* Aiton (74, 156) (1893-1923), *Viola palmata* L. (5, 156) (1913-1923), *Viola pedata* L. (156, 158) (1900-1923), *Viola tricolor* L. (50, 73, 74, 158) (1892–present)

Johnny-smokers [Johnny smokers] - *Geum triflorum* Pursh (74) (1893) Rockford IL, fruits have conspicuous plumose styles

John's cabbage - *Hydrophyllum virginianum* L. (6) (1892)

Johnson grass [Johnson-grass, Johnsongrass] - *Bromus catharticus* Vahl (5) (1913), *Holcus* L. (93) (1936) Neb, *Sorghum bicolor* (L.) Moench (75) (1894) Neb, *Sorghum halepense* (L.) Pers. (5, 45, 50, 56, 72, 80, 85, 87, 88, 94, 109, 111, 119, 122, 129, 138, 140, 152, 155, 158, 163) (1852–present)

Johnston's knotweed - *Polygonum douglasii* Greene subsp. *johnstonii* (Munz) Hickman (50) (present)

John's-wort [Johns-wort, Johnswort, John's wort - *Hypericum* L. (184) (1793), *Hypericum perforatum* L. (5, 92, 157, 158) (1876–1929)

John's-wort hardhack [John's-wort hard-hack] - *Spiraea hypericifolia* L. (19) (1840)

Joint grass [Joint-grass] - *Paspalum distichum* L. (5, 66, 119, 151, 163) (1852-1938)

Joint plant - *Tradescantia crassifolia* Cav. (73) (1892) Cambridge MA

Jointed charlock - *Raphanus* L. (1) (1932), *Raphanus raphanistrum* L. (5, 6, 15, 80, 106, 107, 156) (1892–1930)

Jointed goatgrass - *Aegilops cylindrica* Host (50, 119, 155) (1938–present)

Jointed pod fern [Jointed pod-fern] - *Blechnum spicant* (L.) Sm. (86) (1878)

Jointed rush - *Juncus articulatus* L. (5, 156) (1913-1923), *Juncus nodusus* L. (139, 155) (1942-1944)

Jointed-leaf knotweed [Jointed-leaved knot-weed] - *Polygonella articulata* (L.) Meisn. (187) (1818)

Joint-fir [Jointfir, Joint fir] - *Ephedra antisyphilitica* Berl. ex C.A. Mey. (124, 158) (1900-1937), *Ephedra* L. (50, 138, 155, 158) (1900–present)

Joint-grass [Joint grass] - *Equisetum fluviatile* L. (107) (1919)

Joint-leaf rush [Jointleaf rush] - *Juncus articulatus* L. (50) (present)

Joint-rush [Joint rush] - *Equisetum* L. (37) (1830)

Joint-tail [Jointtail] - *Rottboellia* L. f. (155) (1942)

Jointvetch - *Aeschynomene* L. (50, 155) (1942–present)

Jointweed [Joint-weed, Joint weed] - *Hippuris vulgaris* L. (5, 93, 156, 158) (1900-1936), *Polygonella americana* (F & M) Small (4, 124) (1937-1986), *Polygonella articulata* (L.) Meisn. (19, 47, 92) (1840-1876), *Polygonella* Michx. (1) (1932), *Polygonum* L. (2) (1895)

Jojarbe - *Sempervivum tectorum* L. (156) (1923)

Jo'mĭnaga'wûnj (Chippewa) - *Vitis vulpina* L. (40) (1928)

Jones' columbine [Jones columbine] - *Aquilegia jonesii* Parry (155) (1942)

Jones' rush grass [Jones' rush-grass] - *Muhlenbergia jonesii* (Vasey) Hitchc. (94) (1901)

Jones's fescue - *Festuca subulata* Trin. (94) (1901)

Jonquil - *Erythronium americanum* Ker. (78) (1898) ME, *Narcissus jonquilla* L. (19, 50, 92, 109, 138) (1840–present)

Jonquil flower - *Narcissus jonquilla* L. (92) (1876)

Jopi-weed - *Eupatorium purpureum* L. (6) (1892)

Jordhumble (Swedish) - *Trifolium aureum* Pollich (46) (1879)

Joseph's coat amaranth - *Amaranthus tricolor* L. (155) (1942)

Joseph's flower - *Tragopogon pratensis* L. (5, 156, 158) (1900-1923)

Joseph's-coat [Joseph's coat] - *Amaranthus tricolor* L. (92) (1876), *Coleus scutellarioides* (L.) Benth. (75) (1894)

Joshua yucca - *Yucca brevifolia* Engelm. (138) (1923)

Joshua-tree - *Yucca brevifolia* Engelm. (109) (1949)

Jove's-beard [Jove's beard] - *Amorpha fruticosa* L. (possibly) (189) (1767)

Jove's-fruit [Jove's fruit] - *Diospyros virginiana* L. (92, 156, 158) (1876-1923) no longer in use by 1923, *Lindera melissifolia* (Walt.) Blume (5, 156) (1913-1923)

Joy - *Kalmia latifolia* L. (181) (~1678)

Joy-leaf [Joyleaf, Joy leaf] - *Prenanthes alba* L. (5, 156) (1913-1923), *Prenanthes altissima* L. (5, 156) (1913-1923)

Joy-of-the-ground - *Vinca minor* L. (156) (1923)

Joyweed - *Alternanthera* Forsk. (50) (present)

Juba's-bush [Juba's bush, Juba-bush] - *Iresine diffusa* Humb. & Bonpl. ex Willd. (5, 156) (1913-1923), *Iresine rhizomatosa* Standl. (50) (present)

Juba's-bush bloodleaf [Jubasbush bloodleaf] - *Iresine rhizomatosa* Standl. (155) (1942)

Jucato (Jamaica) - *Phytolacca americana* L. var. *americana* (7) (1828)

Judas tree [Judas' tree, Judas-tree] - *Cercis canadensis* L. (8, 10, 19, 58, 92, 95, 106, 107, 156, 187) (1785-1930), *Cercis* L. (1, 8, 93, 158, 167) (1785-1936), *Sambucus nigra* L. (158) (1900)

Judée du Canada (French) - *Cercis canadensis* L. (8) (1785)

Judenkirschen (German) - *Physalis alkekengi* L. (158) (1900)

Judge Daly's sunflower - *Helianthus maximiliani* Schrad. (5) (1913)

Jug plant [Jug-plant] - *Hexastylis arifolia* (Michx.) Small var. *arifolia* (156) (1923)

Jugotine (French) - *Sesamum* L. (7) (1828)

Juice-pear [Juice pear] - *Amelanchier canadensis* (L.) Medik. (5, 73, 158) (1892-1913)

Juice-plum - *Amelanchier canadensis* (L.) Medik. (156) (1923) no longer in use by 1923

Juicy-pear [Juicy pear] - *Amelanchier canadensis* (L.) Medik. (73) (1892) Provincetown MA

Jujube - *Ziziphus zizyphus* (L.) Karst. (76, 92, 107, 110, 158) (1876-1919), *Zizyphus* Mill (13, 50, 109, 138, 155, 158) (1849–present)

Juliana lilac - *Syringa josikaea* Jacq. f. ex Reichenb. (138) (1923)

July flower [July-flower] - *Matthiola annua* (L.) Sweet (19, 92) (1840-1876), *Prosopis juliflora* (Sw.) DC. (158) (1900) Jamaica

Jumble-beads [Jumble beads] - *Abrus precatorius* L. (55, 92) (1876-1911)

Jumping cholla - *Opuntia fulgida* Engelm. (50) (present)

Jumpseed [Jump-seed] - *Polygonum virginianum* L. (possibly) (50, 156) (1923–present)

Jump-up-and-kiss-me-quick - *Portulaca pilosa* L. (155) (1942)

Junco - *Koeberlinia* Zucc. (122, 153) (1913-1937) NM TX

June flower [June-flower] - *Viola canadensis* L. (156, 158) (1900-1923)

June grape - *Vitis riparia* Michx. (15) (1895)

June grass [June-grass, Junegrass] - *Danthonia spicata* (L.) Beauv. ex Roemer & J.A. Schultes (75, 90) (1885-1894), *Koeleria macrantha* (Ledeb.) J.A. Schultes (3, 45, 75, 85, 87, 98, 115, 116, 122, 134, 140, 146, 152, 185) (1884-1977), *Koeleria* Pers. (1, 50, 93, 152) (1912–present), *Poa compressa* L. (56) (1901) IA, *Poa pratensis* L. (2, 45, 56, 66, 67, 87, 88, 90, 92, 109, 125, 134, 143, 163) (1852-1949)

June pink - *Rhododendron viscosum* (L.) Torr. (77) (1898) NH

June plum - *Amelanchier canadensis* (L.) Medik. (5, 76) (1896-1913) Western US

June riverbank grape - *Vitis riparia* Michx. (155) (1942)

Juneberry [June-berry, June berry] - *Amelanchier alnifolia* (Nutt.) Nutt. ex M. Roemer (3, 37, 130) (1895-1977), *Amelanchier arborea* (Michx. f.) Fern. (3, 4, 20) (1857-1986), *Amelanchier canadensis* (L.) Medik. (5, 7, 19, 46, 63, 65, 72, 73, 85, 92, 93, 95, 105, 107, 106, 108, 112, 114, 131, 147, 156, 158) (1828-1937), *Amelanchier* Medik. (1, 2, 4, 93, 106, 109, 138, 155, 156, 158) (1895-1986), *Pyrus canadensis* (L.) Farw. (187) (1818), *Symphoricarpos occidentalis* Hook. (101, 156) (1905-1923)

June-bud [June bud] - *Cercis canadensis* L. (156) (1923) no longer in use by 1923, *Cercis* L. (106) (1930)

Jungle grass - *Echinochloa* Beauv. (1) (1932)

Jungle-plum [Jungleplum] - *Sideroxylon* L. (155) (1942)

Jungle-rice [Jungle rice, Junglerice] - *Echinochloa colona* (L.) Link (5, 50, 56, 94, 119, 122, 155, 163) (1852–present)

Juniper bark - *Juniperus communis* L. (92) (1876)

Juniper bush [Juniper-bush] - *Juniperus communis* L. (92) (1876), *Juniperus virginiana* L. (5) (1913)

Juniper cypress - *Larix laricina* (Du Roi.) Koch. (5) (1913)

Juniper leaves - *Juniperus sabina* L. (92) (1876)

Juniper or Juniper tree [Juniper-tree] - *Celtis occidentalis* L. (5, 156, 158) (1900-1923), *Chamaecyparis thyoides* (L.) Britton, Sterns & Poggenb. (5, 20) (1857-1913), *Juniperus communis* L. (5, 19, 35, 40, 52, 53, 57, 58, 60, 72, 78, 92, 107, 113, 157, 158, 187) (1806-1929), *Juniperus communis* L. var. *montana* Ait. (131) (1899), *Juniperus deppeana* Steud. (149) (1904), *Juniperus* L. (1, 4, 8, 10, 38, 50, 109, 121, 122, 148, 155, 158, 167, 184) (1785–present) from Latin meaning "renewing its youth", *Juniperus sabina* L. (78) (1898) Western US, *Juniperus virginiana* L. (78, 106, 108) (1878-1930), *Larix laricina* (Du Roi.) Koch. (73, 75, 78, 79) (1891-1898), *Picea mariana* (Mill.) Britton, Sterns & Poggenb. (5) (1913), *Taxus canadensis* Willd. (79) (1891) NH

Juniper polytrichum moss - *Polytrichum juniperinum* Hedw. (50) (present)

Juniper tamarix - *Tamarix chinensis* Lour. (138) (1923)

Juniper-berry [Juniper berries] - *Gaylussacia brachycera* (Michx.) Gray (156) (1923), *Juniperus communis* L. (92) (1876)

Juno's-rose [Iuno's rose] - *Lilium candidum* L. (180) (1633)

Juno's-tears [Juno's tears] - *Verbena officinalis* L. (5, 92, 156) (1876-1923) no longer in use by 1923

Junquilia [Iunquilia] - *Narcissus jonquilla* L. (180) (1633)

Junshand - *Panax quinquefolius* L. (157) (1929)

Jupiter's-beard [Jupiter's beard, Jupitersbeard, Jupiters-beard] - *Centranthus ruber* (L.) DC. (109, 138) (1923-1949), *Sempervivum tectorum* L. (92, 156) (1898-1923)

Jupiter's-distaff [Iupiters Distaffe] - *Salvia glutinosa* L. (178) (1526)

Jupiter's-eye [Jupiter's eye] - *Sempervivum tectorum* L. (92) (1876)

Jupiter's-nuts [Jupiter's nuts] - *Juglans regia* L. (92) (1876)

Jupiter's-staff [Jupiter's staff] - *Verbascum thapsus* L. (5, 69, 158) (1900-1913)

Juripeba - *Solanum carolinense* L. (181) (~1678)

Jusquiame noir (French) - *Hyoscyamus niger* L. (6, 7, 158) (1828-1900)

Justiceweed [Justice weed, Justice-weed, Justices' weed] - *Eupatorium hyssopifolium* L. (92) (1876), *Eupatorium leucolepis* (DC.) Torr. & Gray (5, 92, 156) (1876-1923)

K

Kaal (Danish) - *Brassica oleracea* L. (110) (1886)

Kaal (Norwegian) - *Brassica oleracea* L. (107) (1919)

Kaapsit (Pawnee) - *Celtis occidentalis* L. (37) (1919)

Kab (Keltic and Slavic languages) - *Brassica oleracea* L. (110) (1886)

Kactos (Greek) - *Cynara cardunculus* L. (possibly) (110) (1886)

Kada-kuns (Chippewa, little kada) - *Aralia nudicaulis* L. (105) (1932)

Kaddig (German) - *Juniperus communis* L. (158) (1900)

Kadegimnedu (Chippewa) - *Ceanothus americanus* L. (105) (1932)

Kadem-sku-min (Chippewa) - *Rubus occidentalis* L. (105) (1932)

Kade-wigwas (Chippewa) - *Betula lenta* L. (105) (1932)

Kaer (Esthonian) - *Avena sativa* L. (110) (1886)

Kaffir [Kafir] - *Sorghum bicolor* (L.) Moench subsp. *bicolor* (109, 119, 155) (1938-1949)

Kaffir corn [Kafir corn, Kafir-corn] - *Sorghum bicolor* (L.) Moench (56) (1901), *Sorghum bicolor* (L.) Moench subsp. *bicolor* (107, 119, 151) (1896-1938)

Kâ'ga skûntaï (Cherokee, crow shin) - *Adiantum pedatum* L. (102) (1885)

Kaho rahik (Pawnee, old name) - *Lycoperdon perlatum* Pers. (possibly) (37) (1919)

Kahts-kiwahaaru (Pawnee, swamp medicine) - *Mentha arvensis* L. (37) (1919)

Kahts-pidipatski (Pawnee, small medicine) - *Dalea purpurea* Vent. var. *purpurea* (37) (1919)

Kahts-pirakari or kahts-pilakari (Pawnee, medicine with many children) - *Rumex hymenosepalus* Torr. (37) (1919)

Kahtstakat (Pawnee, yellow medicine) - *Mirabilis nyctaginea* (Michx.) MacM. (37) (1919)

Kahtstaraha (Pawnee, buffalo medicine) - *Osmorhiza longistylis* (Torr.) DC. (37) (1919)

Kahts-tawas (Pawnee, rough medicine) - *Silphium laciniatum* L. (37) (1919)

Kahts-tuwiriki (Pawnee, whirlwind medicine) - *Ipomoea leptophylla* Torr. (37) (1919)

Kahtsu-dawidu or Kahtsu-rawidu (Pawnee, round medicine) - *Liatris scariosa* (L.) Willd. var. *scariosa* (37) (1919)

Kaisersalat (German) - *Artemisia dracunculus* L. (158) (1900)

Kaladana - *Ipomoea hederacea* Jacq. (55, 157) (1911–1929)

Kaladana seed - *Ipomoea nil* (L.) Roth (92) (1876)

Kalanchoe - *Kalanchoe* Adans. (138) (1923)

Kalben-Moos (German) - *Lycopodium clavatum* L. (6) (1892)

Kale - *Brassica* L. (107) (1919), *Brassica napus* L. (7, 19) (1828-1840), *Brassica oleracea* L. (107, 138) (1919-1923)

Kalfwerefwor (Swedish) - *Lycopodium clavatum* L. (46) (1879)

Kali - *Salsola soda* L. (174) (1753)

Kalipika tsitsiks (Pawnee) - *Euphorbia marginata* Pursh (37) (1919)

Kalispell - *Heuchera* L. (1) (1932)

Kalmia - *Kalmia* L. (8, 138) (1785-1923), *Kalmia latifolia* L. (52, 57, 71, 138) (1898-1923)

Kalmia (French) - *Kalmia* L. (8) (1785)

Kalm's brome [Kalm brome] - *Bromus kalmii* Gray (155) (1942)

Kalm's brome grass [Kalm's brome-grass] - *Bromus kalmii* Gray (56, 94) (1897-1901)

Kalm's chess - *Bromus kalmii* Gray (5, 72) (1907-1913)

Kalm's lobelia - *Lobelia kalmii* L. (3, 4, 5, 156) (1913-1986)

Kalm's St. John's-wort [Kalm's St. John's wort, Kalm St. John-swort] - *Hypericum kalmianum* L. (2, 5, 138, 156) (1895-1923)

Kalmus (Danish, Dutch, German) - *Acorus calamus* L. (7, 158, 186) (1814-1900)

Kalmusfid - *Acorus calamus* L. (186) (1814)

Kalmuss (Swedish, Hungarian) - *Acorus calamus* L. (186) (1814)

Kalmuss sakkenes - *Acorus calamus* L. (186) (1814)

Kalú - *Acacia farnesiana* (L.) Willd. (158) (1900) HI

Kamas - *Camassia scilloides* (Raf.) Cory (28) (1850)

Kamass root - *Camassia scilloides* (Raf.) Cory (103) (1871)

Kamosh - *Camassia scilloides* (Raf.) Cory (107) (1919)

Kan (Chinese) - *Citrus reticulata* Blanco (110) (1886), *Saccharum officinarum* L. (110) (1886)

Kanas (Keltic and Breton) - *Cannabis sativa* L. (110) (1886)

Kan-chê (Chinese) - *Saccharum officinarum* L. (110) (200 BC)

Kandalla (Ceylon, cultivated plant) - *Colocasia esculenta* (L.) Schott (110) (1886)

Kande (Omaha-Ponca) - *Prunus angustifolia* Marsh. (37) (1919) Kande-hi (Plum tree)

Kangaroo-thorn [Kangaroo thorn] - *Acacia paradoxa* DC. (109, 138) (1923-1949)

Kangaroo-thorn acacia - *Acacia paradoxa* DC. (155) (1942)

Kangra buckwheat - *Fagopyrum tataricum* (L.) Gaertn. (138) (1923)

Kanna perse hein (Estonian) - *Anthemis cotula* L. (186) (1814)

Kannapersed (Estonian) - *Anthemis cotula* L. (186) (1814)

Kanœträd - *Liriodendron tulipifera* L. (186) (1814)

Kansas arrowhead - *Sagittaria ambigua* J.G.Sm. (50) (present)

Kansas gayfeather [Kansas gay feather] - *Liatris pycnostachya* Michx. (155, 156) (1923-1942)

Kansas hawthorn - *Crataegus coccinioides* Ashe (50, 155) (1942–present)

Kansas mugwort - *Artemisia carruthii* Wood ex Carruth. (5, 97) (1913-1937)

Kansas rainlily [Kansas rain lily] - *Cooperia drummondii* Herb. (155) (1942)

Kansas sage - *Salvia azurea* Michx. ex Lam. var. *grandiflora* Benth. (48) (1882)

Kansas sagittaria - *Sagittaria ambigua* J.G.Sm. (5, 97) (1913-1937)

Kansas thistle - *Solanum rostratum* Dunal (4, 77) (1898-1986)

Kansas violet - *Viola nephrophylla* Greene (155) (1942)

Kante (Dakota, plum) - *Prunus angustifolia* Marsh. (37) (1919) Kante-hu (Plum tree)

Kanteen - *Gelidium corneum* (Hudson) J.V.Lamouroux (107) (1919)

Kantsh (Winnebago) - *Prunus angustifolia* Marsh. (37) (1919) Kantsh-hu (Plum tree)

Kaol (Breton) - *Brassica oleracea* L. (107, 110) (1886-1919)

Kao-liang (Chinese "tall millet or great millet" - *Sorghum bicolor* (L.) Moench (110) (1886)

Kap (Keltic and Slavic languages) - *Brassica oleracea* L. (110) (1886)

Kapak-minš (Chippewa, brittle tree) - *Lindera benzoin* Blume. (105) (1932)

Kapa-mava [Kapa mava] - *Anacardium occidentale* L. (110, 165) (1807-1886)

Kaposta - *Brassica oleracea* L. (107) (1919)

Kappes - *Brassica oleracea* L. (107) (1919)

Kapu nos (Bohemian) - *Geranium maculatum* L. (186) (1814)

Kardinaals bloem - *Lobelia cardinalis* L. (186) (1814)

Kari (Georgian) - *Avena sativa* L. (110) (1886)

Karili - *Acorus calamus* L. (186) (1814)

Karipika (Pawnee) - *Euphorbia marginata* Pursh (37) (1919)

Karípiku (Pawnee) - *Asclepias syriaca* L. (37) (1919)

Karo - *Pittosporum crassifolium* Banks & Soland. ex A. Cunningham (109, 138) (1923-1949)

Karolina kalmia - *Kalmia carolina* Small. (138) (1923)

Karoub - *Ceratonia siliqua* L. (92) (1876) tree is takharrout

Karpiele (Polish) - *Brassica napus L.* (110) (1886)

Karpus (Turkey) - *Citrullus lanatus* (Thunb.) Matsumura & Nakai (110) (1886)

Kars - *Rorippa nasturtium-aquaticum* (L.) Hayek (158) (1900)

Karse - *Rorippa nasturtium-aquaticum* (L.) Hayek (158) (1900)

Karvamozenzel (Ukranian) - *Geranium maculatum* L. (186) (1814)

Karweles - *Acorus calamus* L. (186) (1814)

Kâsd'úta (Cherokee, simulating ashes) - *Pseudognaphalium macounii* (Greene) Kartesz (102) (1886) from appearance of leaves

Käsepappel (German) - *Malva sylvestris* L. (158) (1900)

Kasie - *Senna marilandica* (L.) Link (186) (1814)

Kasien - *Senna marilandica* (L.) Link (186) (1814)

Kassader - *Ipomoea pandurata* (L.) G.F.W. Mey. (7) (1828)

Kässekraut (German) - *Malva rotundifolia* L. (158) (1900)

Kassia - *Senna marilandica* (L.) Link (186) (1814)

Kassien - *Senna marilandica* (L.) Link (186) (1814)

Kassod tree [Kassod-tree] - *Senna siamea* (Lam.) Irwin & Barneby (109) (1949)

Kastanie (German) - *Castanea sativa* Mill. (6) (1892)

Kastilez (Brittany) - *Ribes rubrum* L. (110) (1886)

Kataaru (Pawnee) - *Hierochloe odorata* (L.) Beauv. (37) (1830)

Katesbys Enzian (German) - *Gentiana catesbaei* Walt. (7) (1828)

Katjiletti-pullu - *Xyris torta Sm.* (174, 177) (1753-1762)

Katniss - *Sagittaria latifolia* Willd. (41, 46) (1770–1879), *Zizania aquatica* L. (46) (1879)

Katsura tree [Katsura-tree] - *Cercidiphyllum japonicum* Sieb. & Zucc. ex J. Hoffmann & H. Schult. (109, 138) (1923-1949)

Kattanemmons - *Peltandra virginica* (L.) Schott. (181) (~1678)

Katzenkraut (German) - *Nepeta cataria* L. (158) (1900)

Katzenminze (German) - *Nepeta cataria* L. (158) (1900)

Kaulion (Greek) - *Brassica oleracea* L. (107) (1919)

Kauwe-šabu-min (Chippewa, prickly gooseberry) - *Ribes cynosbati* L. (105) (1932)

Kawa subo (Japanese) - *Acorus calamus* L. (186) (1814)

Kba'agne-minš (Chippewa) - *Comptonia peregrina* (L.) Coult. (possibly) (105) (1932)

Kearney's threeawn [Kearney threeawn] - *Aristida longispica* Poir. var. *geniculata* (Raf.) Fern (155) (1942)

Keays' weed [Keays weed] - *Galeopsis bifida* Boenn. (77) (1898) Paris ME

Kedlock - *Moricandia arvensis* (L.) DC. (158) (1900), *Sinapis alba* L. (5, 92, 157, 158) (1876–1929), *Sinapis arvensis* L. (5) (1913)

Keeled brome - *Bromus carinatus* H. & A. (56) (1901)

Keeled bulrush - *Isolepis carinata* Hook. & Arn. ex Torr. (50) (present)

Keermesbeer (German) - *Phytolacca americana* L. var. *americana* (158) (1900)

Keeslip - *Galium verum* L. (158) (1900)

Kegchros (Greek) - *Panicum miliaceum* L. (107, 110) (1886-1919)

Keipe (Sweden) - *Allium scorodoprasum* L. (110) (1886)

Kellerman's sunflower - *Helianthus* ×*kellermanii* Britt. [*grosseserratus* × *salicifolius*] (5) (1913)

Kellock - *Moricandia arvensis* (L.) DC. (158) (1900)

Kellogg's oak - *Quercus kelloggii* Newberry (161) (1857)

Kellogg's sedge [Kellogg sedge] - *Carex lenticularis* Michx. var. *lipocarpa* (Holm) L.A. Standley (139) (1944)

Kellogg's spear-grass - *Poa kelloggii* Vasey (94) (1901)

Kellogg's spurred lupine - *Lupinus caudatus* Kellogg subsp. *argophyllus* (Gray) L. Phillips (50) (present)

Kellogg's thorn - *Crataegus kelloggii* Sarg. (5) (1913)

Kellup's weed [Kellup weed, Kellip-weed] - *Leucanthemum vulgare* Lam. (75, 158) (1894–1900) Montpelier VT

Kelp - *Nuphar lutea* (L.) Sm. subsp. *advena* (Aiton) Kartesz & Gandhi (76, 158) (1896-1900) South Berwick ME

Kelp ware - *Fucus vesiculosus* L. (52, 53) (1919-1922)

Kelpwort [Kelp-wort] - *Salicornia* L. (7) (1828), *Salsola kali* L. (5, 156, 158) (1900-1923)

Kelsey's locust [Kelsey locust] - *Robinia hispida* L. var. *kelseyi* (Cowell ex Hutchinson) Isely (138) (1923)

Kelsey's phlox - *Phlox kelseyi* Britton (5, 85, 93, 131) (1899-1936)

Kemps [Kemp] - *Plantago lanceolata* L. (5, 62, 156, 157, 158) (1900-1929) IN, old English, *Plantago major* L. (158) (1900), *Plantago media* L. (92) (1876)

Kempseed [Kemp-seed] - *Plantago lanceolata* L. (5, 62, 156, 158) (1900-1923) IN, old English

Kengashi - *Ipomoea hederacea* Jacq. (157) (1929)

Kenilworth - *Cymbalaria muralis* P.G. Gaertn., B. Mey. & Scherb. (5) (1913)

Kenilworth ivy [Kenilworthivy] - *Cymbalaria* Hill (158) (1900), *Cymbalaria muralis* P.G. Gaertn., B. Mey. & Scherb. (4, 50, 107, 138, 155, 156) (1919–present)

Kenningwort - *Chelidonium majus* L. (46, 156) (1671-1923)

Kentucky bluegrass [Kentucky blue grass, Kentucky blue-grass] - *Poa pratensis* L. (3, 5, 45, 50, 56, 66, 67, 68, 72, 85, 87, 90, 92, 94, 109, 111, 115, 118, 119, 122, 129, 134, 138, 140, 143, 144, 146, 155, 163, 185) (1852–present), *Poa pratensis* L. subsp. *pratensis* (50) (present)

Kentucky coffee bean - *Gymnocladus dioicus* (L.) K. Koch (76) (1896)

Kentucky coffee tree [Kentucky coffee-tree, Kentucky coffeetree] - *Gymnocladus dioicus* (L.) K. Koch (1, 2, 3, 4, 5, 6, 9, 14, 37, 48, 50, 63, 72, 76, 82, 85, 92, 97, 107, 109, 112, 113, 130, 131, 138, 155, 156, 157, 158) (1873–present), *Gymnocladus* Lam. (93) (1936)

Kentucky hemp - *Laportea canadensis* (L.) Weddell (14) (1882)

Kentucky hunter - *Calystegia sepium* (L.) R. Br. subsp. *sepium* (77) (1898) Sulphur Grove OH; Paris ME

Kentucky mahogany - *Gymnocladus dioicus* (L.) K. Koch (5, 6, 49, 92, 156, 157, 158) (1892-1929)

Kentucky moss - *Portulaca grandiflora* Hook. (5, 76, 156, 158) (1896–1923) Sulphur Grove OH

Kentucky viburnum - *Viburnum molle* Michx (138) (1923)

Kentucky wisteria - *Wisteria frutescens* (L.) Poir. (138) (1923)

Kentucky yellow-wood [Kentucky yellow wood] - *Cladrastis kentukea* (Dum.-Cours.) Rudd . (5, 92, 156) (1876-1923)

Kenukatía-minš (Chippewa) - *Rosa* L. (105) (1932)

Kerasaia (Modern Greek) - *Prunus avium* (L.) L. (110) (1886)

Kerasie (Albanian) - *Prunus avium* (L.) L. (110) (1886)

Keravoulia (Modern Boeotians) - *Physalis alkekengi* L. (107) (1919)

Kerch (Armorican) - *Avena sativa* L. (110) (1886)

Kerlock - *Brassica nigra* (L.) W.D.J. Koch (5, 157, 158) (1900-1929), *Moricandia arvensis* (L.) DC. (158) (1900), *Sinapis arvensis* L. (5) (1913)

Kernelwort - *Scrophularia nodosa* L. (92) (1876)

Kerrato agave - *Agave americana* L. (165) (1768)

Kerria - *Kerria* DC. (138) (1923), *Kerria japonica* (L.) DC. (138) (1923)

Kettle-dock [Kettle dock] - *Senecio jacobea* L. (5, 156) (1913-1923)

Keugthe hi (Osage) - *Baptisia* Vent. (121) (1918?-1970?)

Kewapa (Lakota) - *Nelumbo lutea* Willd. (121) (1918?-1970?)

Key thatch palm - *Thrinax morrisii* H. Wendl. (138) (1923)

Khakiweed - *Alternanthera pungens* Kunth (50) (present)

Khas-khas - Vetiveria zizaniodes (L.) Nash (163) (1852)

Khuskhus [Khus-khus, Khus khus] - Vetiveria zizaniodes (L.) Nash (92, 109, 163) (1852-1949)

Kiarr-kafle (Swedish) - *Alopecurus geniculatus* L. (46) (1879)

Kiarr-tatel (Swedish) - *Catabrosa aquatica* (L.) Beauv. (46) (1879)

Kicking-colt [Kicking colt] - *Impatiens capensis* Meerb. (5, 73, 156, 157, 158) (1892-1929) E. MA

Kicking-horses [Kicking horses] - *Impatiens capensis* Meerb. (5, 76, 156, 157, 158) (1896-1923) Paris ME, because ripe seed vessels burst open when touched

Kiditako (Pawnee) - *Fraxinus pennsylvanica* Marsh. (37) (1919)

Kidney bean [Kidney-bean] - *Phaseolus* L. (82, 103, 178, 184) (1526-1930), *Phaseolus polystachios* (L.) B.S.P. (10) (1818), *Phaseolus*

vulgaris L. (6, 107, 109, 110, 138) (1886-1949), *Vigna sinensis* (L.) Endl. (156) (1923)

Kidney fern - *Woodwardia areolata* (L.) T. Moore (19) (1840)

Kidney liverleaf [Kidney liver-leaf] - *Hepatica nobilis* Schreb. var. *obtusa* (Pursh) Steyermark (5, 19, 49, 53) (1840-1922)

Kidney vetch - *Anthyllis vulneraria* L. (3, 5, 68, 109) (1913-1977)

Kidney-bean root [Kidney bean root] - *Eupatorium purpureum* L. (92) (1876)

Kidney-bean tree [Kidney bean tree] - *Wisteria frutescens* (L.) Poir. (5, 106, 156) (1913-1930)

Kidney-bean vetch [Kidney bean vetch] - *Anthyllis* L. (92) (1876), *Anthyllis vulneraria* L. (92) (1876)

Kidney-leaf asarabacca [Kidney-leaved asarabacca] - *Asarum canadense* L. (186) (1814)

Kidney-leaf buttercup [Kidney-leaved buttercup] - *Ranunculus abortivus* L. (126) (1933)

Kidney-leaf crowfoot [Kidney-leaved crowfoot] - *Ranunculus abortivus* L. (5, 62, 97, 127, 131, 156, 158) (1899–1937)

Kidney-leaf grass-of-parnassus [Kidney-leaved grass-of-parnassus] - *Parnassia asarifolia* Vent. (5) (1913)

Kidney-leaf hemlock fern [Kidney leaved hemlock fern] - *Botrychium lunarioides* (Michx.) Sw. (42) (1814)

Kidney-leaf heteranthera [Kidney-leaved heteranthera] - *Heteranthera reniformis* R. & P. (187) (1818)

Kidney-leaf mudplantain [Kidneyleaf mudplantain] - *Heteranthera reniformis* R. & P. (50) (present)

Kidney-leaf silphium [Kidney-leaved silphium] - *Silphium compositum* var. *reniforme* (Raf. ex Nutt.) Torr. & Gray (5) (1913), *Silphium integrifolium* Michx. var. *laeve* Torr. & Gray (5) (1913)

Kidney-leaf twayblade [Kidneyleaf twayblade] - *Listera smallii* Wieg. (5, 50) (1913–present)

Kidney-leaf violet [Kidneyleaf violet, Kidney-leaved violet] - *Viola renifolia* Gray (3, 4, 5, 155) (1913–1986)

Kidneyroot [Kidney root] - *Eupatorium purpureum* L. (5, 64) (1907-1908)

Kidney-vetch anthyllis [Kidneyvetch anthyllis] - *Anthyllis vulneraria* L. (155) (1942)

Kidneywort [Kidney-wort] - *Baccharis pilularis* DC. (138) (1923), *Cotyledon* L. (86) (1878) old European name, *Eupatorium purpureum* L. (156) (1923), *Hepatica nobilis* Schreb. (156) (1923), *Hepatica nobilis* Schreb. var. *obtusa* (Pursh) Steyermark (6) (1892), *Saxifraga stellaris* L. (5, 156) (1913-1923)

Kiery - *Amaranthus hypochondriacus* L. (110) (1886)

Kiha piliwus hawastat (Pawnee, broom weed) - *Dalea purpurea* Vent. var. *purpurea* (37) (1919)

Kihapiliwus (Pawnee, broom) - *Artemisia dracunculus* L. (37) (1919)

Kikar - *Acacia nilotica* (L.) Willd. ex Delile (158) (1900)

Kiks-bushes - *Baccharis halimifolia* L. (156) (1923) no longer in use by 1923

Kilk - *Moricandia arvensis* (L.) DC. (158) (1900)

Kill-cow [Kill cow] - *Eleocharis tenuis* (Willd.) J.A. Schultes (5, 75, 156) (1894-1923) WV

Killikinic [Killikinick] - *Arctostaphylos uva-ursi* (L.) Spreng. (103) (1870), *Cornus amomum* Mill. (158) (1900), *Cornus sericea* L. subsp. *sericea* (158) (1900)

Kill-kid [Kill-kid] - *Kalmia angustifolia* L. (5, 156) (1913-1923)

Kill-lamb [Kill lamb] - *Kalmia angustifolia* L. (92) (1876), *Lyonia mariana* (L.) D. Don (71) (1898)

Killwart [Kill-wart] - *Chelidonium majus* L. (158) (1900)

Killweed [Kill-weed] - *Lythrum salicaria* L. (156) (1923)

Killwort - *Chelidonium majus* L. (5, 156) (1913-1923)

Kinara (Greek) - *Cynara cardunculus* L. (possibly) (110) (1886)

King devil [King-devil] - *Hieracium caespitosum* Dumort. (156) (1923), *Hieracium piloselloides* Vill. (5, 156) (1913-1923)

King Kunigundus herbe - *Eupatorium cannabinum* L. (178) (1526)

King orange - *Citrus reticulata* Blanco (138) (1923)

King physic - *Salix humilis* Marsh. var. *tristis* (Aiton) Griggs (46) (1879)

King-cob [King cob] - *Ranunculus bulbosus* L. (46) (1879)

Kingcup [King cup, King cups, Kingcups, King's cup, Kings' cup] - *Caltha palustris* L. (5, 156) (1913–1923), *Ranunculus acris* L. (76, 157, 158) (1896–1929) ME, *Ranunculus bulbosus* L. (5, 6, 46, 92) (1879–1918), *Ranunculus* L. (14) (1882)

Kingcure - *Chimaphila maculata* (L.) Pursh (7) (1828)

Kinghead [King-head] - *Ambrosia trifida* L. (62, 156) (1912-1923)

Kingnut [King-nut, King nut] - *Carya alba* (L.) Nutt. ex Ell. (5, 75, 156, 158) (1894-1923), *Carya laciniosa* (Michx. f.) G. Don (2, 5, 82, 93, 109, 156, 158) (1895-1949), *Carya ovata* (Mill.) K. Koch (5, 156) (1913-1923)

Kingnut hickory - *Carya laciniosa* (Michx. f.) G. Don (3) (1977)

King-of-the-meadow [King of the meadow] - *Eupatorium purpureum* L. (5, 64, 76, 156, 158) (1896–1923), *Thalictrum pubescens* Pursh (79) (1891) Northeast US

King's clover [Kings' clover] - *Melilotus officinalis* (L.) Lam. (5, 92, 156, 157, 158) (1876–1929)

King's cure-all [King's-cure-all] - *Oenothera biennis* L. (5, 74, 156, 157, 158) (1893-1923) Southern states, no longer in use by 1923, *Silene stellata* (L.) Aiton f. (156) (1923)

King's desert-grass - *Blepharidachne kingii* (S. Wats.) Hack. (94) (1901)

King's fern [Kings' fern, King fern] - *Osmunda regalis* L. (5, 92, 157) (1876-1913)

King's fescue - *Leucopoa kingii* (S. Wats.) W.A. Weber (94) (1901)

King's sandwort [Kings sandwort] - *Arenaria kingii* (S. Wats.) M.E. Jones (155) (1942)

King's-chalice [King's chalice] - *Narcissus* ×*medioluteus* Mill. *[poeticus × tazetta]* (180) (1633)

King's-crown [King's crown, King's-crown, Kynges crowne] - *Melilotus* Mill. (179) (1526), *Melilotus officinalis* (L.) Lam. (5, 156, 157, 158) (1900-1929)

King's-cure [King's cure, King's-cure, Kings' cure] - *Chimaphila maculata* (L.) Pursh (92) (1876), *Chimaphila umbellata* (L.) Bart. (5, 92, 156, 158, 186) (1825-1923) no longer in use by 1923

King's-evilroot [Kings' evil root] - *Saxifraga pensylvanica* L. (52) (1919)

Ki-ni-ha-nick - *Cornus sericea* L. (186) (1814)

Kinikenich - *Arctostaphylos uva-ursi* (L.) Spreng. (34) (1834)

Kinna (Modern Greek) - *Lawsonia inermis* L. (110) (1886)

Kinnikinnick [Kinnikinik, Kinnikinnick, Kinnikinic, Kinnikinnik] - *Arctostaphylos* Adans. (1) (1932), *Arctostaphylos uva-ursi* (L.) Spreng. (5, 19, 50, 73, 85, 86, 92, 101, 106, 148, 155, 156, 157) (1840–present), *Cornus amomum* Mill. (5, 37, 72, 85, 93, 95, 107, 156, 157, 158) (1900–1932), *Cornus* L. (1) (1932), *Cornus sericea* L. (2, 6, 46, 47, 58, 63, 113, 130) (1852–1899), *Cornus sericea* L. subsp. *sericea* (5, 37, 101, 156, 158) (1900–1923), *Cornus suecica* L. (107) (1919), *Gaultheria procumbens* L. (156) (1923), *Lobelia inflata* L. (156) (1923), *Rhus virens* Lindheimer ex Gray (106) (1930)

Kinnikinnick bark - *Cornus sericea* L. (92) (1876)

Kino - *Coccoloba uvifera* (L.) L. (107) (1919), *Eucalyptus camaldulensis* Dehnhardt (57) (1917)

Kino Americanus (Official name of Materia Medica) - *Geranium maculatum* L. (7) (1828)

Kiosa (Swedish) - *Apera spica-venti* (L.) Beauv. (46) (1879)

Kiplohkos (Lettons) - *Allium sativum* L. (110) (1886)

Kipper nut - *Bunium bulbocastanum* L. (92) (1876)

Kirganeli - *Phyllanthus niruri* L. (174) (1753)

Kirik-tara-kata (Pawnee, yellow eyes) - *Helianthus annuus* L. (37) (1919)

Kirilow's indigo [Kirilow indigo] - *Indigofera kirilowii* Maxim. ex Palibin (138) (1923)

Kirit (Pawnee, cricket) - *Sagittaria latifolia* Willd. (37) (1830)

Kirit-tacharush (Pawnee, eye-itch) - *Typha latifolia* L. (37) (1830) flying down causing eye irritation

Kisaktomas-nut - *Carya* Nutt. (158) (1900)

Kiskatom - *Carya* Nutt. (158) (1900) no longer in use by 1900

Kisky-Thomas-nut - *Carya* Nutt. (158) (1900)

Kiskytom - *Carya alba* (L.) Nutt. ex Ell. (6, 75) (1892) Ostego Co. NY

Kisosit (Pawnee) - *Oxalis stricta* L. (37) (1919), *Oxalis violacea* L. (37) (1919)

Kisses - *Gaura suffulta* Engelm. ex Gray (50) (present), *Viola tricolor* L. (158) (1900)

Kiss-me - *Viola tricolor* L. (158) (1900)

Kiss-me-Dick - *Euphorbia cyparissias* L. (5, 156) (1913-1923)

Kiss-me-over-the-fence - *Polygonum orientale* L. (77) (1898) Sulphur Grove OH

Kiss-me-over-the-garden-gate - *Polygonum orientale* L. (3, 4, 50) (1977–present)

Kiss-me-quick [Kiss me quick] - *Euphorbia cyparissias* L. (156, 158) (1900-1923), *Portulaca pilosa* L. (50) (present)

Kiss-me-quick-and-go - *Artemisia abrotanum* L. (156, 157, 158) (1900–1929)

Kisu-sit (Pawnee, long tapering) - *Helianthus tuberosus* L. (37) (1919)

Kisúts (Pawnee) - *Vitis cinerea* (Engelm.) Millard (37) (1919), *Vitis vulpina* L. (37) (1919)

Kitapato (Pawnee) - *Salix* L. (37) (1919)

Kitchen rose - *Rosa cinnamomea* L. (73) (1892) Boston MA, *Rosa eglanteria* L. (5, 158) (1900-1913)

Kitchen-garden purslane - *Portulaca oleracea* L. (109) (1949)

Kitedzi - *Mucuna pruriens* (L.) DC. (107) (1919)

Kitembilla - *Dovyalis hebecarpa* (G. Gardn.) Warb. (109) (1949)

Kit-of-the-wall - *Sedum acre* L. (156) (1923)

Kitsarius (Pawnee, green juice) - *Chenopodium album* L. (37) (1919)

Kitsitsaris (Pawnee, bad plant) - *Desmanthus illinoensis* (Michx.) MacM. ex B.L. Robins. & Fern. (37) (1919)

Kits-kat (Pawnee, standing in water) - *Sagittaria latifolia* Willd. (37) (1919)

Kitten's-breeches [Kitten breeches, Kitten-breeches] - *Dicentra cucullaria* (L.) Bernh. (5, 76, 158) (1896–1913) Sulphur Grove OH

Kittentail [Kitten-tails] - *Besseya* Rydb. (1, 4, 50) (1932–present), *Besseya wyomingensis* (A. Nels.) Rydb. (3, 85) (1932-1977)

Kiu makan (Omaha-Ponca, wound medicine) - *Asclepias tuberosa* L. (37) (1919)

Kiwaut (Pawnee) - *Artemisia ludoviciana* Nutt. subsp. *ludoviciana* (37) (1919)

Kiwoh'ki (Pawnee) - *Artemisia frigida* Willd. (37) (1919)

Kjo (Japanese) - *Fagopyrum esculentum* Moench (46) (1879)

K'kwĕ ulasu'la (Cherokee, partridge mocassin) - *Cypripedium parviflorum* Salisb. (102) (1885)

Klanglein (German) - *Linum usitatissimum* L. (110) (1886)

Klapperrose (German) - *Papaver rhoeas* L. (158) (1900)

Klasgras (Swedish) - *Linnaea borealis* L. (46) (1879)

Klatschrose (German) - *Papaver rhoeas* L. (158) (1900)

Klebkraut (German) - *Galium aparine* L. (158) (1900)

Kleebaum (German) - *Ptelea trifoliata* L. (158) (1900)

Kleh (Chippewa) - *Arctostaphylos uva-ursi* (L.) Spreng. (107) (1919)

Kleiner Schachtelbalm (German) - *Equisetum arvense* L. (158) (1900)

Kleiner Scheilung (German) - *Aethusa cynapium* L. (6) (1892)

Kleines Sinngrün (German) - *Vinca minor* L. (158) (1900)

Kleinste Christwurz (German) - *Coptis trifolia* (L.) Salisb. (7, 186) (1814-1828)

Klette (German) - *Arctium lappa* L. (6) (1892)

Klettenwurzel (German) - *Arctium lappa* L. (158) (1900)

Klops - *Plantago lanceolata* L. (156) (1923) no longer in use by 1923

Kmass - *Camassia scilloides* (Raf.) Cory (78) (1898) CA

Knap - *Trifolium pratense* L. (5, 157, 158) (1900–1929)

Knap-bottle [Knap bottle] - *Silene vulgaris* (Moench) Garcke (5, 156) (1913-1923) no longer in use by 1923

Knapweed [Knap weed] - *Centaurea calcitrapa* L. (7, 92) (1828-1876), *Centaurea cyanus* L. (157, 158) (1900-1929), *Centaurea ja-* cea L. (19, 42) (1814-1840), *Centaurea* L. (4, 10, 50) (1818–present), *Centaurea nigra* L. (7, 82, 138, 156) (1828-1930), *Centaurea solstitialis* L. (7, 80) (1828-1913)

Knawel - *Scleranthus annuus* L. (1, 5, 10, 92, 156, 158, 187) (1818-1932), *Scleranthus* L. (4, 13, 155, 158) (1900-1986)

Kneckenschell (Dutch) - *Pulsatilla patens* (L.) Mill. subsp. *multifida* (Pritz.) Zamels (poss) (180) (1633)

Knee grass [Knee-grass] - *Panicum dichotomiflorum* Michx. (145) (1897) KS

Knee knotweed - *Polygonum pensylvanicum* L. (19) (1840)

Knee-high blackberry - *Rubus cuneifolius* Pursh (5, 156) (1913-1923)

Kneh-boschem - *Acorus calamus* L. (186) (1814)

Kniepier panicale - *Exothea paniculata* (Juss.) Radlk. (20) (1857)

Knieskern's beaked rush - *Rhynchospora knieskernii* Carey (5) (1913)

Knight's-cross [Knight's cross, Knight-cross] - *Lychnis chalcedonica* L. (5, 156, 158) (1900-1923)

Knight's-spur [Knights' spur] - *Consolida regalis* S.F. Gray (92, 156) (1898-1923), *Consolida* S.F. Gray (50) (present)

Knitback [Knit-back Knit back] - *Symphytum officinale* L. (5, 64, 92, 156) (1876-1923)

Knitweed [Knit-weed] - *Hypericum gentianoides* (L.) Britton, Sterns & Poggenb. (156) (1923)

Knobby comfrey [Knobbie comfrey] - *Symphytum officinale* L. (178) (1526)

Knobby-root Virginia fumitory with twin flowers [Knobby rooted Virginia fumitory with twin flowers] - *Dicentra cucullaria* (L.) Bernh. (181) (~1678)

Knob-cone pine [Knobcone pine] - *Pinus attenuata* Lemmon (109, 138) (1923-1949)

Knob-grass [Knob grass] - *Collinsonia canadensis* L. (5, 64, 92) (1876-1913)

Knoblauch (German) - *Allium sativum* L. (110, 158) (1886-1900)

Knoblauchkraut (German) - *Alliaria petiolata* (Bieb.) Cavara & Grande (158) (1900)

Knobroot [Knob root] - *Collinsonia canadensis* L. (5, 6, 55, 64, 92) (1876-1913)

Knobweed [Knob-weed, Knob weed] - *Centaurea nigra* L. (5, 156) (1913-1923), *Collinsonia canadensis* L. (5, 7, 64, 86, 156) (1828-1923)

Knockaway - *Ehretia anacua* (Teran & Berl.) I.M. Johnston (106) (1930)

Knock-heads - *Plantago lanceolata* L. (156) (1923)

Knollige Schwalbenwurz (German) - *Asclepias tuberosa* L. (7, 6, 158, 186) (1814-1900)

Knollinger Hahnenfuss (German) - *Ranunculus bulbosus* L. (6) (1892)

Knopfbusch (German) - *Cephalanthus occidentalis* L. (6) (1892)

Knop-sedge - *Sparganium* L. (158) (1900)

Knopweed [Knop weed, Knop-weed] - *Centaurea calcitrapa* L. (5, 156) (1913-1923)

Knot bindweed - *Polygonum convolvulus* L. (5, 156, 158) (1900-1923)

Knot grass [Knotgrass] - *Elymus repens* (L.) Gould (5, 92) (1876-1913), *Paspalum distichum* L. (3, 4, 50, 94, 119, 122, 151, 155, 163) (1852–present)

Knotberry [Knot-berry, Knot berry, Knotberries] - *Rubus chamaemorus* L. (5, 6, 46, 92, 178) (1526-1913)

Knöterich (German) - *Polygonum punctatum* Ell. var. *punctatum* (6) (1892)

Knotgrass [Knot grass, Knot-grass, Knotgrasse] - *Collinsonia canadensis* L. (156) (1923) no longer in use by 1923, *Hippuris vulgaris* L. (5, 156) (1913-1923), *Paronychia* Mill. (158) (1900), *Polygonum aviculare* L. (5, 7, 19, 45, 46, 62, 92, 97, 122, 129, 131, 156, 158, 179) (1526-1937) accidentally introduced by 1671, *Polygonum* L. (1, 93, 167) (1814-1936)

Knotgrass spurge - *Chamaesyce polygonifolia* (L.) Small (156) (1923)

Knotroot [Knot-root, Knot root] - *Collinsia* Nutt. (possibly) (10) (1818), *Collinsonia canadensis* L. (6, 7, 64, 86, 92, 156) (1828-1923)

Knotroot bristle grass [Knotroot bristlegrass] - *Setaria parviflora* (Poir.) Kerguélen (3, 122, 155) (1937-1977)

Knot-root grass [Knot root grass] - *Muhlenbergia mexicana* (L.) Trin. (5, 56) (1901-1913), *Muhlenbergia racemosa* (Michx.) Britton, Sterns & Poggenb. (68) (1890)

Knot-sheath sedge [Knotsheath sedge] - *Carex retrorsa* Schwein (50) (present)

Knotted hedge-parsley - *Torilis nodosa* (L.) Gaertn. (5, 97, 122) (1913-1937)

Knotted pearlwort - *Sagina nodosa* (L.) Fenzl (5, 156) (1913-1923)

Knotted rush - *Juncus nodosus* L. var. *nodosus* (50) (present), *Juncus nodosus* L. (3, 5, 50, 72, 93, 156) (1907–present)

Knotted spike-rush [Knotted spike rush] - *Eleocharis interstincta* (Vahl) R. & S. (5, 50, 156) (1913–present)

Knotty brake - *Dryopteris filix-mas* (L.) Schott (5, 92, 158) (1876-1913)

Knotty maple [Knottie maple] - *Acer rubrum* L. (46) (1879)

Knotty-leaf rush [Knotty-leaved rush] - *Juncus acuminatus* Michx. (156) (1923)

Knotty-root dandelion [Knottie rooted Dandelion] - *Taraxacum officinale* G.H. Weber ex Wiggers (possibly) (180) (1633)

Knotty-root figwort [Knotty rooted figwort] - *Scrophularia nodosa* L. (92) (1876)

Knotweed [Knot-weed] - *Polygonum achoreum* Blake (4) (1986), *Polygonum arenastrum* Jord. ex Boreau (4) (1986), *Polygonum aviculare* L. (4, 125, 129) (1894-1986), *Polygonum bellardii* All. (4) (1986), *Polygonum buxiforme* Small (4) (1986), *Polygonum douglasii* Greene (4) (1986), *Polygonum douglasii* Greene subsp. *johnstonii* (Munz) Hickman (4) (1986), *Polygonum* L. (1, 4, 50, 82, 93, 106, 109, 158) (1900–present), *Polygonum ramosissimum* Michx. (4, 85) (1932-1986), *Polygonum ramosissimum* Michx. var. *ramosissimum* (4, 85) (1932-1986), *Polygonum tenue* Michx. (4) (1986), *Polygonum virginianum* L. (122, 184) (1793-1937)

Knotweed leaf-flower [Knotweed leafflower] - *Phyllanthus polygonoides* Nutt. (155) (1942)

Knotweed spurge - *Chamaesyce polygonifolia* (L.) Small (5, 156) (1913-1923)

Knotwort [Knot-wort] - *Polygonum aviculare* L. (158, 179) (1526-1900)

Knuträd - *Liriodendron tulipifera* L. (186) (1814)

Knutræ - *Liriodendron tulipifera* L. (186) (1814)

Knutt (Swedish) - *Spergula arvensis* L. (110) (1886)

Knyl-hafre (Swedish) - *Arrhenatherum elatius* (L.) Beauv. ex J. Presl & C. Presl (46) (1879)

Koa - *Acacia koa* Gray (50) (present)

Koa acacia - *Acacia koa* Gray (155) (1942)

Kobuks - *Magnolia virginiana* L. (186) (1814)

Kobus - *Magnolia virginiana* L. (186) (1814)

Kobus magnolia - *Magnolia kobus* DC. (138) (1923)

Kobusi - *Magnolia virginiana* L. (186) (1814)

Kochia - *Kochia* Roth (93) (1936), *Kochia scoparia* (L.) Schrad. (3, 4, 5, 93, 97) (1913-1986)

Koda millet - *Paspalum scrobiculatum* L. (107) (1919)

Koedild - *Anthemis cotula* L. (186) (1814)

Koehne's ammannia - *Ammannia latifolia* L. (5, 155) (1913-1942)

Koeleria - *Koeleria macrantha* (Ledeb.) J.A. Schultes (56, 72) (1901-1907), *Koeleria* Pers. (155) (1942)

Koeler's grass - *Koeleria macrantha* (Ledeb.) J.A. Schultes (5, 116, 119, 163) (1852-1958)

Koeskatoma nuts - *Carya alba* (L.) Nutt. ex Ell. (33) (1827)

Kohl - *Brassica oleracea* L. (107, 110) (1886-1919)

Kohl (German) - *Brassica oleracea* L. (110) (1886)

Kohl (Swedish) - *Brassica oleracea* L. (107) (1919)

Kohlrabi [Kohl-rabi] - *Brassica* L. (107) (1919)

Kohlsaatsöl (German) - *Brassica rapa* L. var. *rapa* (158) (1900)

Kohuhu - *Pittosporum tenuifolium* Gaertn. (109) (1949)

Kokbenognik keya (Chippewa, willow for making baskets) - *Salix interior* Rowlee (105) (1932)

Kokum - *Phytolacca americana* L. var. *americana* (48) (1882)

Kol (Breton) - *Brassica oleracea* L. (110) (1886)

Kola - *Cola acuminata* (P. Beauv.) Schott & Endl. (52, 53, 57) (1917-1922)

Kolanut [Kola nut] - *Cola acuminata* (P. Beauv.) Schott & Endl. (52, 107) (1919)

Kolicwurzel (German) - *Apocynum androsaemifolium* L. (158) (1900)

Kolla - *Cola acuminata* (P. Beauv.) Schott & Endl. (107) (1919)

Koloquinten (German) - *Citrullus colocynthis* (L.) Schrad. (57) (1917)

Kombu - *Alaria* Grev. (155) (1942), *Euphorbia* L. (155) (1942)

Konah (Snake) - *Lewisia rediviva* Pursh (101) (1905) MT

Königskerze (German) - *Verbascum thapsus* L. (6, 158) (1892–1900)

Konjibik (Chippewa) - *Ceanothus americanus* L. (105) (1932)

Konker tree [Konker-tree] - *Aesculus hippocastanum* L. (156) (1923)

Konouti manzanita - *Arctostaphylos manzanita* Parry subsp. *elegans* (Eastw.) P.V. Wells (155) (1942)

Konse (Indians of Orgeon and Idaho) - *Lomatium ambiguum* (Nutt.) Coult. & Rose (107) (1919)

Konsusi - *Magnolia virginiana* L. (186) (1814)

Konung Salomons ljusstake (Swedish) - *Lepidium campestre* (L.) Aiton f. (46) (1879)

Koole kraut (Germane) - *Brassica oleracea* L. (180) (1633)

Kooyah - *Valeriana edulis* Nutt. (28, 76, 103) (1850-1896) Northwest Indians

Kopper-Lobebliae - *Lobelia siphilitica* L. (186) (1814)

Kops kohl (German) - *Brassica oleracea* L. (107) (1919)

Korean clover - *Kummerowia stipulacea* (Maxim.) Makino (3, 50) (1977–present)

Korean lawn grass [Korean lawn-grass] - *Zoysia japonica* Steud. (109) (1949), *Zoysia matrella* (L.) Merr. (94) (1901)

Korean lespedeza - *Kummerowia stipulacea* (Maxim.) Makino (4, 155) (1942-1986)

Korean rose - *Rosa xanthina* Lindl. (138) (1923)

Korean velvet grass [Korean velvet-grass] - *Zoysia tenuifolia* Willd. ex Thiele (109) (1949)

Koren (Russia) - *Acorus calamus* L. (186) (1814)

Korn Rade (German) - *Agrostemma githago* L. (6) (1892)

Kornblume (German) - *Centaurea cyanus* L. (158) (1900)

Kotolo milkweed - *Asclepias eriocarpa* Benth. (155) (1942)

Kotzebue's grass-of-parnassus - *Parnassia kotzebuei* Cham. ex Spreng. (5) (1913)

Kouril-skoi-tchai (Siberia "Kurile tea") - *Dasiphora floribunda* (Pursh) Kartesz (107) (1919)

Kousa dogwood - *Cornus kousa* Hance (138) (1923)

Kouse root - *Lomatium ambiguum* (Nutt.) Coult. & Rose (76, 103) (1870-1896)

Kraanhals (Dutch) - *Geranium maculatum* L. (186) (1814)

Kraftwurzel (German) - *Panax quinquefolius* L. (6, 186) (1814-1892)

Krambai (Greek) - *Brassica oleracea* L. (110) (1886)

Krameria - *Krameria* L. (155, 158) (1900-1942)

Kranewett (German) - *Juniperus communis* L. (158) (1900)

Krastavak (Slavic) - *Cucumis sativus* L. (110) (1886)

Krauseminze (German) - *Mentha ×piperita* L. [*aquatica × spicata*] (158) (1900)

Krauser Ampfer (German) - *Rumex crispus* L. (6) (1892)

Kraut - *Brassica oleracea* L. (107) (1919)

Kraut curd-herb (Switzerland) - *Trigonella caerulea* (L.) Ser. (107) (1919)

Kraut-grass - *Moricandia arvensis* (L.) DC. (156) (1923)

Krautweed [Kraut-weed, Kraut weed] - *Moricandia arvensis* (L.) DC. (158) (1900), *Raphanus raphanistrum* L. (5, 156) (1913-1923), *Sinapis arvensis* L. (5, 74, 157) (1893–1929)

Kreen - *Armoracia rusticana* P.G. Gaertn., B. Mey. & Scherb. (110) (1886)

Krenai (Lithuania) - *Armoracia rusticana* P.G. Gaertn., B. Mey. & Scherb. (110) (1886)

Kreusel (German) - *Portulaca oleracea* L. (110) (1886)

Kreuzdorn (German) - *Rhamnus cathartica* L. (6, 158) (1892-1900)

Kreuzkraut (German) - *Senecio vulgaris* L. (158) (1900)

Krigia - *Krigia virginica* (L.) Willd. (possibly) (156) (1923)

Krommunda (Modern Greek) - *Allium cepa* L. (110) (1886)

Krommuon - *Allium cepa* L. (110) (1886)

Kropfklette (German) - *Xanthium strumarium* L. (158) (1900)

Kropfwurz (German) - *Scrophularia nodosa* L. (6) (1892)

Krötendill (German) - *Anthemis cotula* L. (186) (1814)

Krug holly - *Ilex krugiana* Loes. (106) (1930)

Krunslauk (Esthonian) - *Allium sativum* L. (110) (1886)

Ksapitahako (Pawnee, to whirl in the hand) - *Echinacea angustifolia* DC. (37) (1919)

Ksho-hin (Winnebago, prairie chicken feather) - *Typha latifolia* L. (37) (1830)

Kudonea - *Cydonia oblonga* Mill. (107) (1919)

Kudzu - *Pueraria* DC. (50) (present), *Pueraria montana* (Lour.) Merr. var. *lobata* (Willd.) Maesen & S. Almeida (50) (present)

Kudzu vine [Kudzu-vine] - *Pueraria* DC. (4) (1986), *Pueraria montana* (Lour.) Merr. var. *lobata* (Willd.) Maesen & S. Almeida (4, 109) (1949-1986)

Kudzubean [Kudzu-bean] - *Pueraria* DC. (155) (1942), *Pueraria montana* (Lour.) Merr. var. *lobata* (Willd.) Maesen & S. Almeida (138) (1923)

Kuei-xu - *Triadica sebifera* (L.) Small (46) (1879) China

Kuhdill - *Anthemis cotula* L. (186) (1814)

Kuhnia - *Brickellia* Ell. (82) (1930)

Kumlien aster - *Symphyotrichum oblongifolium* (Nutt.) Nesom (155) (1942)

Kummel - *Carum carvi* L. (107) (1919)

Kummerowia - *Kummerowia* Schindl. (50) (present)

Kumquat - *Fortunella japonica* (Thunb.) Swingle (107, 138) (1919-1923), *Fortunella* Swingle (109) (1949)

Kunth's panicum - *Dichanthelium consanguineum* (Kunth) Gould & C.A. Clark (5) (1913)

Kurbs (German, gourd) - *Cucurbita pepo* L. (107) (1919)

Kurj-noha (Bohemian) - *Portulaca oleracea* L. (110) (1886)

Kurrajong - *Brachychiton populneum* (Schott) R. Br. (109) (1949)

Kurza noka (Polish) - *Portulaca oleracea* L. (110) (1886)

Kus apaaru kaaruts (Pawnee, cherry-sitting-hiding) - *Prunus pumila* L. var. *besseyi* (Bailey) Gleason (37) (1919)

Kus kus - *Vetiveria zizaniodes* (L.) Nash (92) (1876)

Kuttanemmons - *Peltandra virginica* (L.) Schott. (181) (~1678)

Ku'-we (Delaware) - *Pinus* L. (132) (1855)

Kyum (Burmese) - *Saccharum officinarum* L. (110) (1886)

L

La nielle des bles (French) - *Agrostemma githago* L. (6) (1892)

La palma - *Yucca torreyi* Shafer (149, 153) (1904-1913) NM

La palmilla - *Yucca elata* (Engelm.) Engelm. (149, 153) (1904-1913) NM

La petite cique (French) - *Aethusa cynapium* L. (6) (1892)

Labaria plant - *Dracontium polyphyllum* L. (92) (1876)

Labdanum - *Cistus ladaniferus* L. (92) (1876)

Labkraut - *Galium verum* L. (158) (1900)

Lablab - *Lablab purpureus* (L.) Sweet (110) (1886)

Labrador - *Ledum groenlandicum* Oeder (possibly) (75, 77) (1894-1898) ME

Labrador bedstraw - *Galium labradoricum* Wiegand (4) (1986)

Labrador buttercup - *Ranunculus rhomboideus* Goldie (50, 155) (1942–present)

Labrador marsh bedstraw - *Galium labradoricum* Wiegand (5) (1913)

Labrador pine - *Pinus banksiana* Lamb. (5) (1913)

Labrador reed grass - *Calamagrostis stricta* (Timm) Koel. subsp. *inexpansa* (Gray) C.W. Greene (5) (1913)

Labrador Solomon's-plume [Labrador Solomonplume] - *Maianthemum trifolium* (L.) Sloboda (155) (1942)

Labrador tea [Labrador-tea] - *Ledum glandulosum* Nutt. (148) (1939), *Ledum groenlandicum* Oeder (5, 19, 40, 49, 57, 92, 104, 106, 107, 109, 156) (1840-1949) leaves used as tea substitute during the Revolutionary War, *Ledum* L. (1, 2, 7, 10, 138, 156) (1818-1932), *Ledum palustre* L. (14) (1882)

Labrador tea plant - *Ledum groenlandicum* Oeder (possibly) (43) (1820)

Labrador willow - *Salix argyrocarpa* Anderss. (138) (1923)

Laburnum or Laburnum tree - *Laburnum anagyroides* Medik. (92) (1876), *Laburnum* Medik. (138) (1923) from ancient latin name

Lace cactus - *Echinocereus reichenbachii* (Terscheck ex Walp.) Haage f. (4, 97, 109) (1937-1986)

Lace echinocereus - *Echinocereus reichenbachii* (Terscheck ex Walp.) Haage f. (155) (1942)

Lace fern [Lace-fern] - *Cheilanthes gracillima* D.C. Eat. (109) (1949)

Lace grass [Lace-grass, Lacegrass] - *Eragrostis capillaris* (L.) Nees (3, 5, 50, 93, 94, 119, 122, 155, 163) (1852–present)

Lace hedgehog cactus - *Echinocereus reichenbachii* (Terscheck ex Walp.) Haage f. (50) (present)

Lace lichen - *Ramalina leptocarpha* Tuck. (123) (1856)

Lace-buttons [Lace-button, Lace buttons] - *Erigeron annuus* (L.) Pers. (5, 156, 158) (1900-1949)

Laceflower [Lace flower, Lace-flower] - *Daucus carota* L. (75, 106, 156, 157, 158) (1894–1930) Philadelphia PA, *Ptilimnium nuttallii* (DC.) Britton (50) (present)

Lacepod [Lace pod] - *Thysanocarpus curvipes* Hook. (76) (1896) CA

Lacey's oak - *Quercus laceyi* Small (122, 124) (1937)

Lacmus - *Roccella tinctoria* DC. (92) (1876)

Lactucarium - *Lactuca sativa* L. (92) (1876)

Lacy germander - *Teucrium laciniatum* Torr. (50) (present)

Lacy tansy-aster [Lacy tansyaster] - *Machaeranthera pinnatifida* (Hook.) Shinners (50) (present)

Ladanum - *Cistus incanus* L. subsp. *creticus* (L.) Heywood (92) (1876)

Ladder fern - *Nephrolepis cordifolia* (L.) K. Presl (107) (1919)

Ladies-and-gentleman [Ladies and gentleman] - *Dicentra canadensis* (Goldie) Walp. (74) (1893) Franklin Centre PQ

Ladino clover - *Trifolium repens* L. (4) (1986)

Lad-savour - *Artemisia abrotanum* L. (157, 158) (1900-1929)

Lad's-love [Lad's love] - *Artemisia abrotanum* L. (5, 73, 92, 156)

(1876-1923) New England, for aphrodisiac qualitites or use in love divinations

Lady birch - *Betula pubescens* Ehrh. (107, 158) (1900-1919)

Lady Bird's centaury - *Centaurium texense* (Griseb.) Fernald (50) (present)

Lady brake - *Osmunda regalis* L. (157) (1929)

Lady fern [Ladyfern, Lady-fern] - *Athyrium filix-femina* (L.) Roth (2, 3, 4, 40, 46, 72, 97, 109, 131, 138, 155, 157) (1895-1986), *Athyrium* Roth (1, 4, 50) (1932–present)

Lady grass - *Phalaris arundinacea* L. (5) (1913)

Lady laurel - *Daphne mezereum* L. (5, 156) (1913-1923)

Lady tulip - *Tulipa clusiana* DC. (109) (1949)

Lady Washington's geranium [Lady Washington geranium] - *Pelargonium ×domesticum* Bailey [*angulosum × cucullatum*] (138) (1923)

Lady-by-the-gate [Lady by the gate] - *Saponaria officinalis* L. (5, 64, 76, 156, 157, 158) (1896–1929)

Lady-by-the-lake - *Collinsia verna* Nutt. (156) (1923)

Lady-in-a-boat [Lady in a boat] - *Lamprocapnos spectabilis* (L.) Fukuhara (74) (1893) Fanconia NH

Lady-in-a-chaise [Lady in a chaise] - *Arisaema triphyllum* (L.) Schott (79) (1891) NH

Lady-in-the-green [Lady in the green] - *Nigella damascena* L. (79) (1891) Northeast US

Lady-never-fade - *Anaphalis margaritacea* (L.) Benth. & Hook (5, 156, 158) (1900)

Lady-of-the night - *Brunfelsia americana* L. (109) (1949)

Lady-pea - *Vigna sinensis* (L.) Endl. (156) (1923), *Vigna unguiculata* (L.) Walp. (5) (1913)

Lady's bedstraw [Ladies' bedstraw, Lady's bedstraws, Lady's-bedstraw] - *Galium aparine* L. (57) (1917) from legend that Mother of Jesus rested on hay containing one of the species, *Galium* L. (109) (1949), *Galium trifidum* L. (187) (1818), *Galium verum* L. (5, 92, 156) (1876-1923)

Lady's chewing-tobacco [Ladies chewing tobacco] - *Antennaria plantaginifolia* (L.) Richards (73) (1892) WI

Lady's sorrel [Ladies' sorrel, Lady's-sorrel] - *Oxalis corniculata* L. (2, 5, 156) (1895-1923), *Oxalis stricta* L. (1, 73, 156, 158) (1892-1932)

Lady's sourgrass [Ladies' sour grass, Lady sour grass, Lady's-sourgrass] - *Oxalis stricta* L. (37, 74) (1893-1919) NJ

Lady's wood sorrel - *Oxalis corniculata* L. (19) (1840)

Lady's-bouquet [Lady's bouquet] - *Galium triflorum* Michx. (37) (1919)

Lady's-bower [Ladies' bower] - *Clematis virginiana* L. (49) (1898), *Clematis vitalba* L. (92) (1876), *Clematis* L. (190) (~1759)

Lady's-breastpin [Lady's breast-pin] - *Coreopsis basalis* (A. Dietr.) Blake (76) (1896) Sulphur Grove OH

Lady's-cleavers [Ladies' cleavers] - *Galium verum* L. (158) (1900)

Lady's-clover [Ladies' clover, Lady's clover] - *Oxalis montana* Raf. (possibly) (5, 156) (1913-1923)

Lady's-comb [Lady's comb] - *Scandix pecten-veneris* L. (5, 156) (1913-1923)

Lady's-cushion [Ladies' cushion, Ladies cuchion] - *Armeria maritima* (P. Mill.) Willd (5, 156) (1913-1923), *Centaurea nigra* L. (5, 156) (1913-1923) no longer in use by 1923

Lady's-delight [Lady's delight] - *Viola tricolor* L. (5, 73, 158) (1892-1913) MA

Lady's-dresses [Ladies' dresses] - *Spiranthes* Rich. (75) (1894)

Lady's-eardrop [Ladies' ear drops, Ladies ear-drop, Ladies'-eardrop] - *Brunnichia ovata* (Walt.) Shinners (106, 156) (1923-1930),

Impatiens capensis Meerb. (73, 156, 157, 158) (1892–1929), *Lamprocapnos spectabilis* (L.) Fukuhara (74) (1893) Concord MA

Lady's-fingers [Lady's fingers, Ladies'-fingers, Ladies' fingers] - *Lotus corniculatus* L. (5, 156) (1913-1923), *Digitalis pupurea* L. (5, 69) (1903-1913), *Anthyllis vulneraria* L. (5, 92) (1876-1913), *Lathyrus pratensis* L. (5, 156) (1913-1923)

Lady's-foxglove [Lady's foxglove] - *Verbascum thapsus* L. (69, 158) (1900-1904)

Lady's-glove [Ladies' glove, Lady glove, Lady's glove, Lady's-gloves] - *Digitalis pupurea* L. (5, 69, 92) (1876–1913), *Lotus corniculatus* L. (158) (1900)

Lady's-hair [Lady's hair] - *Adiantum capillus-veneris* L. (5, 158) (1900–1913), *Briza media* L. (5) (1913)

Lady's-laces [Ladies laces [Ladies' laces [Ladies'-laces [Lady-laces] - *Phalaris arundinacea* L. (5, 158, 178, 180) (1526-1913)

Lady's-lint [Lady's lint] - *Stellaria holostea* L. (5, 156) (1913-1923) no longer in use by 1923

Lady's-mantle [Ladies' mantle, Ladies mantle, Ladysmantle, Lady's mantle] - *Alchemilla alpina* L. (7, 10, 19) (1818–1840), *Alchemilla* L. (50, 155, 156) (1923–present), *Alchemilla monticola* Opiz (possibly) (5, 92, 156, 178) (1596–1923) from leaf shape

Lady's-milk [Lady's milk] - *Silybum marianum* (L.) Gaertn. (156, 158) (1900-1923)

Lady's-nightcap [Lady's nightcap, Ladies' nightcap, Ladies'-nightcap] - *Calystegia sepium* (L.) R. Br. subsp. *sepium* (5, 156, 158) (1900–1923) no longer in use by 1923

Lady's-pocket [Ladies'-pocket] - *Impatiens capensis* Meerb. (73, 157, 158) (1892-1929)

Lady's-purse [Lady's purse] - *Capsella bursa-pastoris* (L.) Medik. (5, 156, 157, 158) (1900-1923)

Lady's-rouge [Ladies' rouge] - *Carthamus tinctorius* L. (7) (1828)

Lady's-shoes [Ladies-shoes [Lady's shoes] - *Aquilegia vulgaris* L. (5, 156) (1913-1923)

Lady's-shoes-and-stockings - *Lotus corniculatus* L. (158) (1900)

Lady's-slipper [Lady's slipper, Ladies' slipper, Lady-slipper, Lady-slipper, Ladie-slipper, Lady's slippers] - *Cypripedium* L. (1, 50, 57, 92, 93, 109, 127, 138, 155, 156, 158, 167, 184) (1793–present), *Cypripedium montanum* Dougl. ex Lindl. (35) (1806), *Cypripedium parviflorum* Salisb. (55, 64, 102) (1886-1911), *Cypripedium parviflorum* Salisb. var. *pubescens* (Willd.) Knight (49, 53, 58, 59, 61) (1869-1922), *Cypripedium reginae* Walt. (40, 55, 64) (1908-1928), *Impatiens balsamina* L. (73, 92) (1876-1892), *Impatiens capensis* Meerb. (5, 73, 156) (1892-1923) NY, *Linaria vulgaris* Mill. (77) (1898) MA, *Lotus corniculatus* L. (158) (1900), *Polygala paucifolia* Willd. (5, 76, 156) (1896-1923) Gardiner ME

Lady's-smock [Ladies' smock, Lady's smock, Ladiesmock, Ladiessmock] - *Cardamine* L. (7, 10, 42) (1814–1828), *Cardamine pratensis* L. (2, 5, 92, 107, 109, 156) (1876–1949), *Sibara virginica* (L.) Rollins (184) (1793)

Lady's-thimble [Lady thimble, Lady's thimble, Lady's thimbles] - *Campanula rotundifolia* L. (158) (1900), *Digitalis pupurea* L. (5, 69, 156) (1904-1923)

Lady's-thistle [Lady's thistle] - *Silybum marianum* (L.) Gaertn. (156, 158) (1900-1923)

Lady's-thumb [Ladies' thumb, Lady's thumb] - *Persicaria maculosa* Gray (3, 4, 5, 19, 45, 62, 72, 80, 82, 92, 93, 97, 106, 114, 122, 124, 125, 156) (1818-1986), *Polygonum* L. (1, 106) (1930-1932)

Lady's-tobacco [Ladies' tobacco] - *Anaphalis margaritacea* (L.) Benth. & Hook (5, 76, 106, 156, 158) (1896-1923) Eastern US, *Antennaria* Gaertner (1) (1932), *Antennaria plantaginifolia* (L.) Richards (5, 156, 158) (1900-1923), *Gnaphalium* L. (76) (1896) Madison WI

Lady's-traces [Ladies' traces] - *Spiranthes* Rich. (75) (1894)

Lady's-tresses [Ladies' tresses, Ladies tresses, Ladies'-tresses] - *Spiranthes cernua* (L.) L.C. Rich. (3, 85, 98) (1926-1977), *Spiranthes* Rich. (1, 50, 75, 93, 109, 138, 156) (1923–present), *Spiranthes romanzoffiana* Cham. (127) (1933), *Spiranthes torta* (Thunb.) Garay & H.R. Sweet (187) (1818)

Laelia - *Laelia* Adans. (138) (1923)

Lagonihah (Missouri tribes) - *Angelica lucida* L. (7) (1828)

Lagopus - *Trifolium arvense* L. (174, 177, 178) (1526-1762)

Laictue (French) - *Lactuca sativa* L. (180) (1633)

Laiteron (French) - *Sonchus oleraceus* L. (158) (1900)

Laitue du Canada (French) - *Lactuca canadensis* L. (6) (1892)

Laitue vireuse (French) - *Lactuca virosa* L. (158) (1900)

Lake bank sedge - *Carex lacustris* Willd. (5) (1913)

Lake bur-reed - *Sparganium americanum* Nutt. (19) (1840)

Lake cress - *Nasturtium officinale* W.T. Aiton (possibly) (156) (1923) OK

Lake cress - *Neobeckia aquatica* (Eat.) Greene (2, 63) (1895-1899)

Lake gooseberry - *Ribes lacustre* (Pers.) Poir. (2) (1895)

Lake Huron tansy - *Tanacetum bipinnatum* (L.) Schultz-Bip. subsp. *huronense* (Nutt.) Breitung (5) (1913)

Lake iris - *Iris lacustris* Nutt. (138) (1923)

Lake knotweed - *Polygonum amphibium* L. var. *emersum* Michx. (19) (1840)

Lake quillwort - *Isoetes lacustris* L. (5) (1913)

Lake rush - *Schoenoplectus tabernaemontani* (K.C. Gmel.) Palla (156) (1923)

Lake sedge - *Carex lacustris* Willd. (66) (1903)

Lake shore sedge [Lakeshore sedge] - *Carex lenticularis* Michx. (50) (present)

Lake St. John's-aster [Lake St. John aster] - *Symphyotrichum novi-belgii* (L.) Nesom var. *villicaule* (Gray) J. Labrecque & L. Brouillet (155) (1942)

Lake watercress [Lake water cress, Lake water-cress] - *Nasturtium officinale* W.T. Aiton (possibly) (156) (1923), *Neobeckia aquatica* (Eat.) Greene (5) (1913)

Lakeweed [Lake weed, Lake-weed] - *Polygonum hydropiper* L. (92, 157, 158) (1876–1929)

Lamance iris - *Iris brevicaulis* Raf. (3, 138, 155) (1923-1977)

Lamarck's evening-primrose [Lamarck evening-primrose] - *Oenothera glazioviana* Micheli (138) (1923)

Lambert's crazyweed [Lambert crazyweed] - *Oxytropis lambertii* Pursh (155) (1942)

Lambkill [Lamb-kill, Lamb kill] - *Kalmia angustifolia* L. (2, 5, 71, 92, 106, 109, 138, 156) (1895-1949), *Kalmia latifolia* L. (6, 7, 49, 53) (1828-1932), *Rhododendron canadense* (L.) Torr. (5, 156) (1913-1923)

Lambs - *Aesculus hippocastanum* L. (5, 156) (1913-1923)

Lamb's cress - *Cardamine hirsuta* L. (5, 107, 156, 157) (1913-1929)

Lamb's laurel [Lamb laurel] - *Kalmia angustifolia* L. (71) (1898)

Lamb's mint [Lamb mint] - *Mentha ×piperita* L. [*aquatica × spicata*] (5, 156, 157) (1900–1929), *Mentha spicata* L. (5, 156, 158) (1900-1923)

Lamb's-ears [Lambs-ears] - *Stachys byzantina* K. Koch ex Scheele (109) (1949), *Stachys officinalis* (L.) Trev. (109) (1949)

Lamb's-foot [Lamb's foot] - *Plantago major* L. (5, 156, 157, 158) (1900–1929)

Lamb's-legs - *Plantago media* L. (156) (1923)

Lamb's-lettuce [Lamb's lettuce, Lamb lettuce] - *Plantago media* L. (5, 92) (1876–1913), *Valerianella chenopodiifolia* (Pursh) DC. (19) (1840), *Valerianella locusta* (L.) Lat. (5, 156, 107, 110) (1886–1923), *Valerianella radiata* (L.) Dufr. (1, 4, 5, 7, 92, 156, 158, 187) (1818-1986), *Valerianella* Mill. (1, 4, 158) (1900-1986)

Lamb's-noses [Lamb's noses] - *Dodecatheon meadia* L. (156) (1923)

Lamb's-quarters [Lambs' quarter, Lamb's quarters, Lamb's-quarters, Lambsquarter, Lambsquarters] - *Chenopodium album* L. (3, 4, 5, 35, 37, 45, 50, 62, 72, 80, 85, 92, 93, 95, 97, 103, 107, 121, 122, 125, 131, 145, 150, 156, 157, 158, 187) (1818–present), *Chenopodium album* L. var. *album* (50) (present), *Chenopodium* L. (1, 4, 7, 93, 146, 190) (~1759-1986), *Chenopodium watsonii* A. Nels. (21) (1893), *Trillium cernuum* L. (158) (1900), *Trillium erectum* L. (5, 49, 92, 156) (1876-1923), *Atriplex subspicata* (Nutt.) Rydb. (5, 156, 158) (1900-1923)

Lambs-quarters goosefoot [Lambsquarters goosefoot] - *Chenopodium album* L. (155) (1942)

Lamb's-succory [Lambsuccory, Lamb succory] - *Arnoseris* Gaertn. (155) (1942), *Arnoseris minima* (L.) Schweig. & Koerte (possibly) (5, 156) (1913-1923)

Lamb's-sucklings [Lamb's sucklings, Lamb-sucklings] - *Trifolium repens* L. (5, 156, 157, 158) (1900-1929)

Lamb's-tail [Lamb's tail, Lamb's tails] - *Lycopodium clavatum* L. (5) (1913), *Salix discolor* Muhl. (156, 158) (1900-1923) England, catkins

Lamb's-toes [Lambs' toes] - *Anthyllis vulneraria* L. (92) (1876)

Lamb's-tongue [Lambs tongue, Lambs tongue, Lambs' tongues] - *Erythronium americanum* Ker. (5, 7, 75, 86, 92, 156, 157) (1828-1929) Banner Elk NC, *Mentha arvensis* L. (5, 156, 158) (1900-1923) no longer in use by 1923, *Plantago media* L. (5, 156) (1913-1923)

Lambs-tongue groundsel [Lambstongue groundsel] - *Senecio integerrimus* Nutt. (155) (1942)

Lambs-tongue ragwort [Lambstongue ragwort] - *Senecio integerrimus* Nutt. (50) (present), *Senecio integerrimus* Nutt. var. *integerrimus* (50) (present)

Lammint - *Mentha ×piperita* L. [*aquatica × spicata*] (157) (1929), *Mentha spicata* L. (158) (1900)

Lamourou (West Indies) - *Ricinus communis* L. (110) (1886)

Lamp rush - *Juncus effusus* L. var. *solutus* Fern. & Wieg. (50) (present)

Lampourde (French) - *Xanthium strumarium* L. (12) (1821)

Lampsana - *Lapsana communis* L. (178) (1526), *Sinapis arvensis* L. (possibly) (180) (1633)

Lampuca - *Hieracium* L. (180) (1633)

Lancashire asphodel [Lancashire asphodill] - *Narthecium americanum* Ker-Gawl. (158, 178) (1596-1900)

Lancaster cyperus - *Cyperus lancastriensis* Porter ex Gray (5) (1913)

Lance coreopsis - *Coreopsis lanceolata* L. (138, 155) (1923-1942)

Lance pickerelweed - *Pontederia cordata* L. (155) (1942)

Lance selfheal - *Prunella vulgaris* L. subsp. *lanceolata* (W. Bart.) Hultén (50) (present)

Lance spleenwort - *Asplenium ruta-muraria* L. var. *lanceolum* Christ (50) (present)

Lance-leaf anemone [Lanceleaf anemone] - *Anemone lancifolia* Pursh (155) (1942)

Lance-leaf balsam tree [Lance-leaved balsam tree] - *Populus balsamifera* L. subsp. *balsamifera* (8) (1785)

Lance-leaf basil [Lance-leaved basil] - *Pycnanthemum virginianum* (L.) T. Dur. & B.D. Jackson ex B.L. Robins. & Fern. ? (187) (1818)

Lance-leaf blanket-flower [Lanceleaf blanketflower] - *Gaillardia aestivalis* (Walt.) Rock (50) (present)

Lance-leaf blazing star [Lanceleaf blazing star] - *Liatris lancifolia* (Greene) Kittell (50) (present)

Lance-leaf bluebells [Lanceleaf bluebells] - *Mertensia lanceolata* (Pursh) DC. (155) (1942)

Lance-leaf buckthorn [Lanceleaf buckthorn, Lance-leaved buckthorn] - *Rhamnus lanceolata* Pursh (5, 50, 72, 82, 155) (1907–present), *Rhamnus lanceolata* Pursh subsp. *glabrata* (Gleason) Kartesz & Gandhi (4, 50) (1986–present)

Lance-leaf coreopsis [Lanceleaf coreopsis] - *Coreopsis lanceolata* L. (122) (1937)

Lance-leaf cottonwood [Lanceleaf cottonwood] - *Populus ×acuminata* Rydb. [*angustifolia × deltoides*] (4, 50, 85) (1932–present)

Lance-leaf euonymus [Lanceleaf euonymus] - *Euonymus hamiltonianus* Wall. (138) (1923)

Lance-leaf figwort [Lanceleaf figwort] - *Scrophularia lanceolata* Pursh (50, 155) (1942–present)

Lance-leaf fogfruit [Lanceleaf fogfruit] - *Phyla lanceolata* (Michx.) Greene (50) (present)

Lance-leaf gaillardia [Lance-leaved gaillardia] - *Gaillardia aestivalis* (Walt.) Rock (97) (1937)

Lance-leaf garlic [Lance-leaved garlic] - *Allium tricoccum* Ait. (156) (1923)

Lance-leaf goldenweed [Lanceleaf goldenweed] - *Machaeranthera juncea* (Greene) Shinners (155) (1942), *Pyrrocoma lanceolata* (Hook.) Greene var. *lanceolata* (50, 155) (1942–present)

Lance-leaf grape fern [Lance-leaved grape-fern] - *Botrychium lanceolatum* (S.G. Gmel.) Angs. (5, 50) (1913–present)

Lance-leaf greenbrier [Lance-leaved greenbrier] - *Smilax smallii* Morong (5, 50) (1913–present)

Lance-leaf ground-cherry [Lanceleaf ground cherry] - *Physalis angulata* L. (5, 122) (1913-1937)

Lance-leaf loosestrife [Lanceleaf loosestrife, Lance-leaved loosestrife] - *Lysimachia hybrida* Michx. (122) (1937), *Lysimachia lanceolata* Walt. (5, 50, 72, 82, 85, 97) (1907–present)

Lance-leaf lungwort [Lance-leaved lungwort] - *Mertensia lanceolata* (Pursh) DC. (5, 131) (1899-1913)

Lance-leaf painted-cup [Lance-leaved painted-cup] - *Castilleja septentrionalis* Lindl. (5) (1913)

Lance-leaf plantain [Lance-leaved plantain] - *Plantago lanceolata* L. (5, 45) (1896-1913)

Lance-leaf plantain-lily [Lanceleaf plantainlily] - *Hosta lancifolia* Engl. (138) (1923)

Lance-leaf psoralea [Lance-leaved psoralea] - *Psoralidium lanceolatum* (Pursh) Rydb. (5, 93, 97, 131) (1899–1937)

Lance-leaf ragweed [Lanceleaf ragweed [Lance-leaved ragweed] - *Ambrosia bidentata* Michx. (5, 50, 62, 97, 122, 155) (1912–present)

Lance-leaf sabbatia [Lance-leaved sabbatia] - *Sabatia difformis* (L.) Druce (5) (1913)

Lance-leaf sage [Lanceleaf sage [Lance-leaved sage] - *Salvia reflexa* Hornem. (3, 4, 5, 50, 72, 93, 97, 131, 155) (1899–present)

Lance-leaf salvia [Lance-leaved salvia] - *Salvia reflexa* Hornem. (80) (1913)

Lance-leaf silverbush [Lanceleaf silverbush] - *Argythamnia lanceolata* (Benth.) Muell.-Arg. (155) (1942) IA

Lance-leaf thistle [Lance leaved thistle] - *Cirsium vulgare* (Savi) Ten. (56) (1901)

Lance-leaf tickseed [Lanceleaf tickseed [Lance-leaved tickseed] - *Coreopsis lanceolata* L. (5, 50) (1913–present)

Lance-leaf violet [Lanceleaf violet [Lance-leaved violet] - *Viola lanceolata* L. (2, 5, 72, 93, 122, 138, 155, 156) (1895-1942)

Lanceolate draba - *Draba breweri* S. Wats. var. *cana* (Rydb.) Rollins (155) (1942)

Lancepod - *Lonchocarpus* Kunth (138) (1923)

Land caltrop [Land caltrops] - *Tribulus terrestris* L. (5, 107, 156, 158, 174) (1753-1923)

Land cress [Land-cress] - *Barbarea verna* (P. Mill.) Aschers. (5, 107, 156) (1913-1923), *Barbarea vulgaris* W.T. Aiton (157) (1929), *Cardamine hirsuta* L. (5, 156, 157) (1913-1929)

Landlauch - *Allium* L. (7) (1828)

Lang-de-beef [Langue-de-beef, Langdebefe] - *Anchusa* L. (179) (1526), *Borago officinalis* L. (156) (1923), *Picris hieracioides* L. (5, 156) (1913-1923)

Lange's thorn - *Crataegus intricata* Lange (5) (1913)

Langsdorff's yellow monkey flower - *Mimulus guttatus* DC. (5) (1913)

Langsdorf's reed-bent - *Calamagrostis canadensis* (Michx.) Beauv. var. *langsdorfii* (Link) Inman (94) (1901)

Langue de chien (French) - *Cynoglossum officinale* L. (158) (1900)

Languid lady - *Mertensia* Roth (1) (1932)

Lank galingale - *Cyperus strigosus* L. (156) (1923)

Lantana - *Lantana* L. (138) (1923), *Viburnum lantana* L. (112) (1937)

Lantern plant - *Physalis longifolia* Nutt. var. *subglabrata* (Mackenzie & Bush) Cronq. (124) (1937) TX

Lantern-leaves - *Ranunculus repens* L. (156, 158) (1900-1923)

Laouzerdo (Southern France) - *Medicago sativa* L. (110) (1886) morphed into luzerne, hence source of name

Lapham's phlox - *Phlox divaricata* L. subsp. *laphamii* (Wood) Wherry (50) (present)

Lapland buttercup - *Ranunculus lapponicus* L. (5) (1913)

Lapland cornel - *Cornus suecica* L. (5, 156) (1913-1923)

Lapland pedicularis - *Pedicularis lapponica* L. (5) (1913)

Lapland rhododendron - *Rhododendron lapponicum* (L.) Wahlenb. (138) (1923)

Lapland rose-bay [Lapland rose bay] - *Rhododendron lapponicum* (L.) Wahlenb. (5, 107, 156) (1913-1923)

Lap-love - *Convolvulus arvensis* L. (156, 157, 158) (1900-1929)

Laportea - *Laportea* Gaud. (50) (present)

Lappa - *Arctium lappa* L. (6, 52, 55, 57, 64) (1892–1919)

Larb - *Arctostaphylos uva-ursi* (L.) Spreng. (6, 101, 103) (1870-1905) MT

Larch agaric - *Fomitopsis officinalis* (Batsch) Bondartsev & Singer (49, 52, 53, 57, 92) (1876-1922)

Larch or Larch tree - *Abies procera* Rehd. (158) (1900), *Larix decidua* Mill. (possibly) (8) (1785), *Larix* Mill (1, 7, 50, 109, 138) (1828–present) from ancient Latin name, *Larix occidentalis* Nutt. (35) (1806)

Larch-leaf goldenweed [Larchleaf goldenweed] - *Ericameria laricifolia* (Gray) Shinners (155) (1942)

Larch-leaf sandwort [Larchleaf sandwort] - *Minuartia yukonensis* Hultén (155) (1942)

Larea ball - *Helianthus annuus* L. (5) (1913), *Helianthus annuus* L. (156) (1923)

Laredo mahonia - *Mahonia trifoliolata* (Moric.) Fedde (155) (1942)

Large agrimony - *Agrimonia parviflora* Aiton (48) (1882)

Large alfalfa dodder - *Cuscuta indecora* Choisy (3, 4) (1977-1986)

Large aspen - *Populus grandidentata* Michx. (possibly) (187) (1818)

Large beardtongue [Large beard-tongue] - *Penstemon grandiflorus* Nutt. (3, 4, 50, 127) (1933–present)

Large bellwort - *Uvularia grandiflora* Smith. (127, 156) (1923-1933)

Large bindweed [Large bind-weed] - *Calystegia sepium* (L.) R. Br. subsp. *sepium* (95, 127) (1911-1933)

Large blazing star - *Liatris scariosa* (L.) Willd. var. *scariosa* (72) (1907)

Large blue blazing star - *Liatris scariosa* (L.) Willd. var. *scariosa* (93) (1936)

Large blue flag [Large blue-flag] - *Iris versicolor* L. (93, 156) (1923-1936)

Large blue iris - *Iris versicolor* L. (72) (1907)

Large blue lettuce - *Lactuca tatarica* (L.) C.A. Mey. var. *pulchella* (Pursh) Breitung (122) (1937)

Large blue lobelia - *Lobelia siphilitica* L. (138) (1923)

Large bog sedge - *Carex angustata* Boott (66) (1903)

Large brown cup fungus - *Peziza badia* Pers. (128) (1933)

Large buckeye - *Aesculus flava* Aiton (5, 20, 156) (1857-1923)

Large buttercup - *Ranunculus macranthus* Scheele (122, 124) (1937)

Large button snakeroot [Large button-snakeroot, Large button sanke-root, Large button snakeroot] - *Liatris aspera* Michx. (82, 122) (1930-1937), *Liatris scariosa* (L.) Willd. var. *scariosa* (5, 97, 131, 157, 158) (1899-1937)

Large buttonweed [Large button-weed] - *Diodia virginiana* L. (97) (1937)

Large buttonwood [Large button wood] - *Platanus occidentalis* L. (8) (1785)

Large cane - *Arundinaria gigantea* (Walter) Muhl. (2, 107, 163) (1852-1919)

Large coralroot [Large coral-root, Large coral root] - *Corallorrhiza maculata* (Raf.) Raf. (5, 93, 122, 156, 157) (1900-1937), *Corallorrhiza maculata* (Raf.) Raf. var. *maculata* (72) (1907)

Large crab grass [Large crab-grass] - *Digitaria sanguinalis* (L.) Scop. (5, 72, 99, 131, 143, 163) (1852-1937)

Large cranberry - *Vaccinium macrocarpon* Aiton (2, 5, 7, 109, 156) (1828-1949)

Large crowfoot grass - *Echinochloa crus-galli* (L.) Beauv. (151) (1896)

Large daisy - *Chrysanthemum* L. (190) (~1759)

Large duckweed - *Spirodela* Scheilen (93) (1936)

Large fennel - *Foeniculum vulgare* Mill. (157, 158) (1900-1929)

Large flowering-spurge [Large flowering spurge, Large-flowering spurge] - *Euphorbia corollata* L. (49, 52, 53, 57, 92, 157, 158) (1876–1929)

Large fothergilla - *Fothergilla major* (Sims) Lodd. (138) (1923)

Large fringed orchis - *Platanthera grandiflora* (Bigelow) Lindl. (156) (1923)

Large goldenrod [Large golden-rod] - *Solidago gigantea* Aiton (187) (1818)

Large hop-trefoil - *Trifolium aureum* Pollich (46, 80) (1879–1913)

Large houstonia - *Houstonia purpurea* L. (5, 97) (1913-1937)

Large Indian breadroot - *Pediomelum esculentum* (Pursh) Rydb. (50) (present)

Large jujube - *Ziziphus zizyphus* (L.) Karst. (106, 112) (1930-1937)

Large laurel [Large laurell] - *Kalmia latifolia* L. (190) (~1759)

Large lophotocarpus - *Sagittaria calycina* Engelm. var. *calycina* (93, 97) (1936-1937), *Sagittaria calycina* Engelm. var. *spongiosa* Engelm. (5, 120) (1913-1938)

Large magnolia - *Magnolia grandiflora* L. (20) (1857)

Large marsh pink - *Sabatia dodecandra* (L.) Britton, Sterns & Poggenb. (5) (1913)

Large mesquite - *Bouteloua repens* (Kunth) Scribn. & Merr. (163) (1852)

Large mountain laurel - *Kalmia latifolia* L. (2) (1895)

Large mouse-ear chickweed - *Cerastium fontanum* Baumg. subsp. *vulgare* (Hartman) Greuter & Burdet (72, 93, 156, 187) (1818-1936)

Large naias - *Najas marina* L. (5, 97) (1913-1937)

Large oilnut [Large oil nut] - *Juglans nigra* L. (46) (1649)

Large peppergrass - *Lepidium virginicum* L. (80) (1913)

Large periwinkle - *Vinca major* L. (92) (1876)

Large pinweed [Large pin-weed] - *Lechea mucronata* Raf. (5) (1913)

Large purple agalinis - *Agalinis purpurea* (L.) Pennell (5, 93) (1913-1936)

Large purple aristida - *Aristida purpurea* Nutt. var. *longiseta* (Steud.) Vasey (56) (1901)

Large purple aster - *Symphyotrichum patens* (Aiton) G.L. Nesom var. *patens* (156) (1923)

Large purple fringed orchis - *Platanthera grandiflora* (Bigelow) Lindl. (5) (1913)

Large purple fringe-orchid - *Platanthera grandiflora* (Bigelow) Lindl. (138) (1923)

Large purple gerardia - *Agalinis purpurea* (L.) Pennell (72, 122, 124) (1907-1937)

Large purple poppy - *Callirhoe papaver* (Cav.) Gray (97) (1937)

Large pussy willow - *Salix discolor* Muhl. (3) (1977)

Large quaking grass - *Briza maxima* L. (66, 42) (1814-1903)

Large rampion - *Oenothera biennis* L. (5, 156, 157, 158) (1900-1929)

Large round-leaf orchis [Large round-leaved orchis] - *Platanthera orbiculata* (Pursh) Lindl. (5) (1913)

Large Russian vetch - *Vicia villosa* Roth (107) (1919)

Large sand-bur - *Cenchrus tribuloides* L. (94) (1901)

Large sedge - *Carex gigantea* Rudge (5) (1913)

Large silver bell tree - *Styrax americanus* Lam. (124) (1937) TX

Large smooth beardtongue [Large smooth beard-tongue] - *Penstemon glaber* Pursh (5, 93) (1913-1936)

Large snapdragon - *Antirrhinum majus* L. (109) (1949)

Large spikenard - *Aralia racemosa* L. (7) (1828)

Large spotted spurge [Large spotted-spurge] - *Chamaesyce hypericifolia* (L.) Millsp. (6, 49, 53, 92) (1876-1922), *Chamaesyce nutans* (Lag.) Small (5, 62, 93, 156, 158) (1900-1936)

Large St. John's-wort [Large St. Johnswort] - *Hypericum majus* (Gray) Britton (50) (present)

Large swollen bladderwort - *Utricularia inflata* Walt. (5) (1913)

Large tooth-leaf primrose [Large tooth-leaved primrose] - *Calylophus serrulatus* (Nutt.) Raven (97) (1937)

Large tooth-root cymbidium [Large tooth rooted cymbidium] - *Corallorrhiza odontorhiza* (Willd.) Poir. (42) (1814)
Large toothwort - *Cardamine maxima* (Nutt.) Wood (5) (1913)
Large tupelo - *Nyssa aquatica* L. (2, 5, 20, 107, 156) (1857-1923)
Large turtle liver - *Hexastylis virginica* (L.) Small (46) (1879)
Large twayblade [Large tway-blade] - *Leptorchis liliifolia* (Rich. ex Lindl.) Kuntze (72) (1907), *Liparis liliifolia* (L.) L.C. Rich. ex Ker-Gawl. (5, 156) (1913-1923)
Large two-leaf orchis [Large two-leaved orchis] - *Platanthera orbiculata* (Pursh) Lindl. (5, 156) (1913-1923)
Large water grass [Large water-grass] - *Paspalum dilatatum* Poir. (5, 94) (1901-1913)
Large water-starwort - *Callitriche heterophylla* Pursh (120) (1938)
Large white ground-cherry [Large white ground cherry] - *Leucophysalis grandiflora* (Hook.) Rydb. (5) (1913)
Large white indigo - *Baptisia alba* (L.) Vent. var. *macrophylla* (Larisey) Isely (97) (1937)
Large white petunia - *Petunia axillaris* (Lam.) Britton, Sterns & Poggenb. (109) (1949)
Large white waterlily [Large white water lily] - *Nymphaea odorata* Aiton (6) (1892)
Large white wild indigo - *Baptisia alba* (L.) Vent. var. *macrophylla* (Larisey) Isely (93) (1936)
Large white-grain mountain-rice [Large white-grained mountain-rice] - *Oryzopsis asperifolia* Michx. (90) (1885)
Large yellow carex - *Carex flava* L. (66) (1903)
Large yellow flax - *Linum berlandieri* Hook. (124) (1937)
Large yellow lady's-slipper [Large yellow lady's slipper, Large yellow ladies' slipper] - *Cypripedium parviflorum* Salisb. var. *pubescens* (Willd.) Knight (127, 156, 187) (1818-1933), *Cypripedium reginae* Walt. (64, 72) (1907-1908)
Large yellow loosestrife - *Lysimachia punctata* L. (50) (present)
Large yellow mocassin flower - *Cypripedium parviflorum* Salisb. var. *pubescens* (Willd.) Knight (86) (1878)
Large yellow pondlily [Large yellow pond lily] - *Nuphar lutea* (L.) Sm. subsp. *advena* (Aiton) Kartesz & Gandhi (5, 37, 131, 158) (1899–1919)
Large yellow sweet plumb - *Prunus americana* Marsh. (8) (1785)
Large yellow-flower goldenrod [Large yellow-flowered goldenrod] - *Oligoneuron rigidum* (L.) Small var. *rigidum* (80) (1913)
Large-bladder ground-cherry [Large bladder ground cherry] - *Physalis longifolia* Nutt. var. *subglabrata* (Mackenzie & Bush) Cronq. (5, 122, 124) (1913-1937)
Large-bract aster [Large-bracted aster] - *Symphyotrichum foliaceum* (DC.) Nesom var. *canbyi* (Gray) Nesom (5, 93) (1913-1936)
Large-bract corydalis [Large-bracted corydalis] - *Corydalis curvisiliqua* Engelm. subsp. *grandibracteata* (Fedde) G.B. Ownbey (4) (1986)
Large-bract Indian breadroot [Largebract Indian breadroot] - *Pediomelum cuspidatum* (Pursh) Rydb. (50) (present)
Large-bract plantain [Large-bracted plantain, Largebracted plantain] - *Plantago aristata* Michx. (5, 50, 72, 93, 97, 131, 156) (1899–present), *Plantago patagonica* Jacq. (97) (1937)
Large-bract psoralea [Large-bracted psoralea] - *Pediomelum cuspidatum* (Pursh) Rydb. (5, 93, 97, 131) (1899–1937)
Large-bract tick trefoil [Largebract ticktrefoil, Large-bracted tick trefoil] - *Desmodium cuspidatum* (Muhl. ex Willd.) DC. ex Loud. (5, 50, 97) (1913–present), *Desmodium cuspidatum* (Muhl. ex Willd.) DC. ex Loud. var. *longifolium* (Torr. & Gray) Schub. (50) (present)
Large-bract vervain [Large-bracted vervain] - *Verbena bracteata* Lag. & Rodr. (5, 72, 93, 97, 131, 1564, 138, 155) (1899-1937)
Large-bract wild indigo [Large-bracted wild indigo] - *Baptisia bracteata* Muhl. ex Ell. (5, 72, 93, 97) (1907-1937)
Large-flower agoseris [Large-flowered agoseris] - *Agoseris glauca* (Pursh) Raf. (5) (1913), *Agoseris glauca* (Pursh) Raf. (131) (1899)
Large-flower aplopappus [Large flowered aplopappus] - *Rayjacksonia phyllocephala* (DC.) R.L. Hartman & M.L. Lane (124) (1937)
Large-flower aster [Large-flowered aster] - *Symphyotrichum grandiflorum* (L.) Nesom (5) (1913)
Large-flower baby-blue-eyes [Largeflower baby blue eyes] - *Nemophila phacelioides* Nutt. (50) (present)
Large-flower beardtongue [Large-flowered beard-tongue [Large flowered beard tongue] - *Penstemon grandiflorus* Nutt. (5, 72, 93, 97, 131) (1899–1937)
Large-flower bellwort [Large-flowered bellwort] - *Uvularia grandiflora* Smith. (5, 50, 72, 97) (1907–present)
Large-flower bindweed [Large-flowered bind-weed] - *Calystegia sepium* (L.) R. Br. subsp. *sepium* (187) (1818)
Large-flower blue lettuce [Large-flowered blue lettuce] - *Lactuca tatarica* (L.) C.A. Mey. var. *pulchella* (Pursh) Breitung (5, 72, 93, 97, 131) (1899-1936)
Large-flower bluegrass [Large-flowered blue-grass, Large-flowered blue-grass] - *Poa eminens* Presl. (94) (1901)
Large-flower California hyacinth [Large-flowered California hyacinth] - *Triteleia grandiflora* Lindl. var. *grandiflora* (86) (1878)
Large-flower Carolina rose [Largeflower Carolina rose] - *Rosa carolina* L. var. *carolina* (155) (1942)
Large-flower clammy-weed [Large-flowered clammy weed, Large-flowered clammy-weed] - *Polanisia dodecandra* (L.) DC. subsp. *trachysperma* (Torr. & Gray) Iltis (4, 5, 72, 97) (1907-1986)
Large-flower coneflower [Large-flowered cone-flower] - *Rudbeckia grandiflora* (D. Don) J.F. Gmel. ex DC. (5, 97, 122) (1913-1937)
Large-flower cornel [Large-flowered cornel] - *Cornus florida* L. (186, 187) (1814-1818)
Large-flower dogwood [Large-flowered dogwood] - *Cornus nuttallii* Audubon ex Torr. & Gray (20) (1857)
Large-flower everlasting [Large-flowered everlasting [Large flowered everlasting] - *Anaphalis margaritacea* (L.) Benth. & Hook (5, 72, 97, 156, 158) (1900–1937)
Large-flower fameflower [Largeflower fameflower] - *Talinum calycinum* Engelm. (50) (present)
Large-flower goldenrod [Large-flowered goldenrod] - *Oligoneuron rigidum* (L.) Small var. *rigidum* (80) (1913) 3, *Solidago squarrosa* Muhl. (156) (1923)
Large-flower gray hawk's-beard [Large-flowered gray hawks-beard] - *Crepis occidentalis* Nutt. (5, 50) (1913–present)
Large-flower hexastylis [Large-flowered hexastylis] - *Hexastylis shuttleworthii* (Britten & Baker) Small. (5) (1913)
Large-flower leafcup [Large-flowered leaf-cup] - *Smallanthus uvedalius* (L.) Mackenzie ex Small (5, 97, 158) (1900-1937)
Large-flower magnolia [Large-flowered magnolia] - *Magnolia grandiflora* L. (20) (1857)
Large-flower marigold [Large flowered marygold] - *Bidens laevis* (L.) Britton, Sterns & Poggenb. (42) (1814)
Large-flower marshallia [Large-flowered marshallia] - *Marshallia grandiflora* Beadle & F.E. Boynt. (5) (1913)
Large-flower melica [Large-flowered melica] - *Melica stricta* Boland. (94) (1901)
Large-flower milkweed [Large flowered milk weed] - *Asclepias hallii* Gray (42) (1814)
Large-flower mock orange [Large flowering mock orange] - *Philadelphus inodorus* L. (2, 135) (1895-1910)
Large-flower mouse-ear chickweed [Large-flowered mouse-ear chickweed] - *Cerastium arvense* L. (187) (1818)
Large-flower opuntia [Large-flowered opuntia] - *Opuntia macrorhiza* Engelm. var. *macrorhiza* (97) (1937)
Large-flower penstemon [Large-flowered penstemon] - *Penstemon grandiflorus* Nutt. (122, 124) (1937)
Large-flower sensitive-pea [Large-flowered sensitive pea] - *Chamaecrista fasciculata* (Michx.) Greene (5) (1913), *Chamaecrista fasciculata* (Michx.) Greene var. *fasciculata* (5, 86) (1878-1913)

Large-flower skeleton-plant [Largeflower skeletonplant] - *Lygodesmia grandiflora* (Nutt.) Torr. & Gray (50) (present)

Large-flower skullcap [Large-flowered skullcap] - *Scutellaria integrifolia* L. (5) (1913)

Large-flower spear grass, Large-flowered spear grass, Largeflower speargrass] - *Poa eminens* Presl. (5, 50) (1913–present)

Large-flower spurge [Large flowered spurge [Large-flowered spurge] - *Euphorbia corollata* L. (6, 156) (1892)

Large-flower stickseed [Large-flowered stickseed] - *Hackelia floribunda* (Lehm.) I.M. Johnston (4, 5, 93, 131) (1899-1986)

Large-flower sticktight [Large-flowered sticktight] - *Hackelia floribunda* (Lehm.) I.M. Johnston (85) (1932)

Large-flower stork's-bill [Large flowered stork's bill] - *Erodium texanum* Gray (122, 124) (1937)

Large-flower swallow-wort [Large flowered swallow wort] - *Gomphocarpus grandiflorus* (L. f.) K. Schum. (possibly) (42) (1814)

Large-flower syringa [Large-flowered syringa] - *Philadelphus inodorus* L. (5) (1913)

Large-flower talinum [Large-flowered talinum] - *Talinum calycinum* Engelm. (5, 93, 97) (1913-1937)

Large-flower thoroughwort [Largeflower thoroughwort] - *Brickellia grandiflora* (Hook.) Nutt. (5, 122) (1913-1937)

Large-flower tickclover [Largeflower tickclover] - *Desmodium glutinosum* (Muhl. ex Willd.) Wood (3, 4, 155) (1942-1986)

Large-flower tickseed [Largeflower tickseed] - *Coreopsis grandiflora* Hogg ex Sweet (5, 50, 97) (1913–present)

Large-flower Townsend daisy [Largeflower Townsend daisy] - *Townsendia grandiflora* Nutt. (50) (present)

Large-flower townsendia [Large-flowered townsendia] - *Townsendia grandiflora* Nutt. (5, 97) (1913-1937)

Large-flower valerian [Large-flowered valerian] - *Valeriana pauciflora* Michx. (5, 156) (1913-1923)

Large-flower verbena [Large-flowered verbena] - *Glandularia canadensis* (L.) Nutt. (5, 72, 97, 158) (1900-1937)

Large-flower vincetoxicum [Large-flowered vincetoxicum] - *Matelea obliqua* (Jacq.) Woods. (5) (1913)

Large-flower wakerobin [Large flowered wake robin [Large-flowered wake-robin] - *Trillium grandiflorum* (Michx.) Salisb. (5, 72, 156) (1907-1923)

Large-flower yellow false foxglove [Largeflower yellow false foxglove] - *Aureolaria grandiflora* (Benth.) Pennell var. *serrata* (Torr. ex Benth.) Pennell (50) (present)

Large-flower yellow flax [Large-flowered yellow flax] - *Linum rigidum* Pursh (72, 122, 131) (1899-1937), *Linum rigidum* Pursh var. *rigidum* (5, 97) (1913-1937)

Large-flower zygadenus [Large-flowered zygadenus] - *Zigadenus glaberrimus* Michx. (5) (1913)

Large-foot trefoil [Large foot trefoil] - *Lotus pedunculatus* Cav. (possibly) (45) (1896)

Large-fruit beard grass [Large-fruited beard-grass] - *Heteropogon melanocarpus* (Ell.) Ell. ex Benth. (94) (1901)

Large-fruit evening-primrose [Large-fruited evening primrose] - *Oenothera macrocarpa* Nutt. subsp. *macrocarpa* (86) (1878)

Large-fruit hawthorn [Large fruited hawthorn] - *Crataegus punctata* Jacq. (42) (1814)

Large-fruit matrimony vine [Large-fruited matrimony vine] - *Lycium carolinianum* Walt. var. *quadrifidum* (Dunal) C.L. Hitchc. (124) (1937)

Large-fruit panicum [Large-fruited panicum] - *Dichanthelium dichotomum* (L.) Gould var. *dichotomum* (72) (1907), *Dichanthelium oligosanthes* (J.A. Schultes) Gould var. *scribnerianum* (Nash) Gould (56) (1901)

Large-fruit snakeroot [Large-fruited snake-root] - *Sanicula trifoliata* Bicknell (5, 72) (1907-1913)

Large-fruit thorn [Large-fruited thorn] - *Crataegus punctata* Jacq. (5, 72) (1907-1913)

Large-head clover [Large-headed clover] - *Trifolium macrocephalum* (Pursh) Poir. (76) (1896)

Large-leaf anglepod [Largeleaf angle pod, Large-leaved angle-pod] - *Matelea gonocarpos* (Walt.) Shinners (5, 97, 122, 156) (1913-1937)

Large-leaf aster [Large-leaved aster] - *Eurybia macrophylla* (L.) Cass. (5, 72, 95, 106, 156) (1907-1930)

Large-leaf avens [Largeleaf avens, Large-leaved avens] - *Geum macrophyllum* Willd. (5, 50, 72, 131, 155) (1899–present)

Large-leaf cotinus [Large leaved cotinus] - *Cotinus obovatus* Raf. (20) (1857)

Large-leaf cucumber tree [Large-leaved cucumber-tree] - *Magnolia macrophylla* Michx. (109, 156) (1923-1949)

Large-leaf Dutchman's-pipe [Largeleaf Dutchmanspipe] - *Aristolochia labiata* Willd. (155) (1942)

Large-leaf goldenrod [Largeleaf goldenrod [Large-leaved goldenrod] - *Solidago macrophylla* Pursh (5, 122) (1913-1937)

Large-leaf grass-of-parnassus [Large-leaved grass-of-parnassus] - *Parnassia grandifolia* DC. (5) (1913)

Large-leaf holly [Largeleaf holly, Large-leaved holly] - *Ilex longipes* Chapman ex Trel. (122) (1937), *Ilex montana* (Torr. & Gray) Gray (5, 156) (1913-1923)

Large-leaf lime [Large-leaved lime] - *Tilia platyphyllos* Scop. (109) (1949)

Large-leaf linden [Large-leaved linden] - *Tilia americana* L. var. *heterophylla* (Vent.) Loud. (20) (1857)

Large-leaf maple [Large-leaved maple] - *Acer macrophyllum* Pursh (20, 161) (1857)

Large-leaf moehringia [Large-leaved moehringia] - *Moehringia macrophylla* (Hook.) Fenzl (5) (1913)

Large-leaf phlox [Large-leaved phlox] - *Phlox amplifolia* Britton (5) (1913)

Large-leaf pondweed [Largeleaf pondweed [Large-leaved pondweed] - *Potamogeton amplifolius* Tuckern. (5, 50, 93, 131, 155) (1899–present)

Large-leaf sandwort [Large-leaved sandwort] - *Moehringia macrophylla* (Hook.) Fenzl (5) (1913)

Large-leaf storax [Large-leaved storax] - *Styrax grandifolius* Aiton (5) (1913)

Large-leaf umbrella tree [Large-leaved umbrella tree [Large-leaved umbrella-tree] - *Magnolia macrophylla* Michx. (5, 20, 156) (1857-1923)

Large-leaf Virginia mulberry tree [Large-leaved Virginian mulberry tree] - *Morus rubra* L. (8) (1785)

Large-leaf waterleaf [Large-leaved water-leaf] - *Hydrophyllum macrophyllum* Nutt. (5, 72) (1907-1913)

Large-leaf white violet [Large-leaved white violet] - *Viola macloskeyi* Lloyd (5) (1913)

Large-leaf wild indigo [Largeleaf wild indigo] - *Baptisia alba* (L.) Vent. var. *macrophylla* (Larisey) Isely (50) (present)

Large-panicle sedge [Large-panicled sedge] - *Carex decomposita* Muhl. (5, 66) (1903-1913)

Large-panicle vilfa [Large-panicled vilfa] - *Sporobolus cryptandrus* (Torr.) Gray (66) (1903)

Large-pod pinweed [Largepod pinweed [Largepodded pin-weed] - *Lechea intermedia* Leggett (5, 50) (1913–present)

Larger American abele - *Populus grandidentata* Michx. (2) (1895)

Larger blue flag - *Iris versicolor* L. (2, 5, 6, 53, 157) (1874-1922)

Larger bur-marigold - *Bidens laevis* (L.) Britton, Sterns & Poggenb. (5, 62, 72, 93, 156) (1907-1936)

Larger buttonweed [Larger button weed] - *Diodia virginiana* L. (5, 122, 124) (1913-1937)

Larger Canadian St. John's-wort [Larger Canadian St. John's wort] - *Hypericum majus* (Gray) Britton (5, 93) (1913-1936)

Larger coral-root - *Corallorrhiza maculata* (Raf.) Raf. (157) (1929)

Larger daisy fleabane - *Erigeron annuus* (L.) Pers. (72, 156) (1907-1923)

Larger duckweed - *Spirodela polyrhiza* (L.) Schleid. (156) (1923), *Spirodela* Scheilen (1) (1932)

Larger floating-heart [Larger floating heart] - *Nymphoides aquatica* (J.F. Gmel.) Kuntze (5) (1913)

Larger ground plum - *Astragalus crassicarpus* Nutt. var. *berlandieri* Barneby (5, 93, 97, 131) (1899-1937)

Larger Indian bean - *Catalpa speciosa* (Warder) Warder ex Engelm. (5, 63, 72, 158) (1899–1913)

Larger marsh St. John's-wort [Larger marsh St. John's wort] - *Triadenum walteri* (J.G. Gmel.) Gleason (5) (1913)

Larger mouse-ear - *Cerastium fontanum* Baumg. subsp. *vulgare* (Hartman) Greuter & Burdet (80) (1913)

Larger mouse-ear chickweed - *Cerastium fontanum* Baumg. subsp. *vulgare* (Hartman) Greuter & Burdet (5, 97) (1913-1937)

Larger purple fringed orchis - *Platanthera grandiflora* (Bigelow) Lindl. (2) (1895)

Larger sensitive-pea - *Chamaecrista fasciculata* (Michx.) Greene var. *fasciculata* (158) (1900)

Larger short-awn chess [Larger short-awned chess] - *Bromus marginatus* Nees ex Steud. (56) (1901)

Larger skullcap - *Scutellaria integrifolia* L. (5) (1913)

Larger Solomon's-seal [Larger Solomon's seal] - *Polygonatum biflorum* (Walt.) Ell. (2) (1895)

Larger straw sedge - *Carex normalis* Mackenzie (5) (1913)

Larger water-starwort [Larger waterstarwort] - *Callitriche heterophylla* Pursh (5, 155) (1913-1942)

Larger wintergreen - *Pyrola americana* Sweet (158) (1900)

Larger with-rod [Larger withe rod] - *Viburnum nudum* L. (5) (1913)

Larger yellow lady's-slipper [Larger yellow lady's slipper] - *Cypripedium parviflorum* Salisb. var. *pubescens* (Willd.) Knight (6) (1892)

Large-root alocasia [Large-rooted alocasia] - *Alocasia macrorrhizos* (L.) Schott (110) (1886)

Large-seed forget-me-not [Large-seeded forget-me-not] - *Myosotis macrosperma* Engelm. (50, 131) (1899–present)

Large-spot St. John's-wort [Large-spotted St. John's wort] - *Hypericum punctatum* Lam. (5, 97) (1913-1937)

Largest red oak - *Quercus rubra* L. (8) (1785)

Large-stipule Indian physic [Large stipuled Indian physic] - *Porteranthus stipulatus* (Muhl. ex Willd.) Britt. (2) (1895)

Large-stipule psoralea [Large-stipuled psoralea] - *Orbexilum stipulatum* (Torr. & Gray) Rydb. (5) (1913)

Large-thorn acacia [Large-thorned acacia] - *Gleditsia triacanthos* L. (189) (1767)

Large-tooth aspen [Largetooth aspen] - *Populus grandidentata* Michx. (5, 72, 109, 138, 156, 158) (1900–1949)

Large-tubercle dock [Large-tubercled dock] - *Rumex pallidus* Bigelow (5) (1913)

Large-tubercle spike rush [Large-tubercled spike rush] - *Eleocharis tuberculosa* (Michx.) Roemer & J.A. Schultes (5) (1913)

Laritsits (Pawnee) - *Shepherdia argentea* (Pursh) Nutt. (37) (1919)

Larkheel [Lark heel] - *Consolida regalis* S.F. Gray (92) (1876)

Lark-heel wolf's-bane [Larks heele Wolfesbane] - *Delphinium elatum* L. (possibly) (178) (1526)

Lark's-claw [Larks' claw] - *Consolida regalis* S.F. Gray (92) (1876)

Lark's-heel [Lark's heel] - *Consolida regalis* S.F. Gray (156) (1923)

Larkspur [L'arks S'pur, Lark-spur] - *Delphinium menziesii* DC. (190) (~1759), *Consolida regalis* S.F. Gray (19, 57, 71, 92) (1840-1917), *Delphinium bicolor* Nutt. (126) (1933), *Delphinium* L. (1, 2, 4, 7, 10, 13, 15, 50, 63, 82, 93, 148, 138, 155, 158, 167, 184) (1793-present), *Delphinium nuttallianum* Pritz ex. Walp. (85) (1932), *Linaria vulgaris* Mill. (158) (1900)

Larkspur coreopsis - *Coreopsis delphiniifolia* Lam. (109, 138) (1923-1949)

Larkspur tickseed - *Coreopsis delphiniifolia* Lam. (5) (1913)

Larkspur violet - *Viola pedatifida* G. Don (4, 5, 93, 138, 156) (1923-1986)

Larpente's plumbago [Larpente plumbago] - *Ceratostigma plumbaginoides* Bunge (138) (1923)

Larrabell - *Helianthus annuus* L. (157, 158) (1900-1929)

Lasater's pride - *Abronia fragrans* Nutt. ex Hook. (124) (1937) TX

Last-rose-of-summer - *Symphyotrichum novae-angliae* (L.) G.L.Nesom (156) (1923)

Latanier - *Sabal* Adans. (7) (1828)

Late Carolina poplar - *Populus* ×*canadensis* Moench [*deltoides* × *nigra*] (155) (1942)

Late coralroot [Late coral-root [Late coral root] - *Corallorrhiza odontorhiza* (Willd.) Poir. (3, 64, 122, 156, 158) (1900–1977)

Late dropseed [Late drop-seed [Late drop seed] - *Muhlenbergia uniflora* (Muhl.) Fern. (66, 94) (1901–1903)

Late eupatorium - *Eupatorium serotinum* Michx. (3, 155) (1942–1977)

Late fragrant sumac - *Rhus aromatica* Aiton var. *serotina* (Greene) Rehd. (155) (1942)

Late goldenrod [Late goldenrod] - *Solidago gigantea* Aiton (3, 4, 5, 72, 82, 93, 95, 97, 122, 131) (1899-1986), *Solidago petiolaris* Aiton (19) (1840)

Late lilac - *Syringa villosa* Vahl (138) (1923)

Late low blueberry - *Vaccinium pallidum* Aiton (156) (1923)

Late pear - *Pyrus pyrifolia* (Burm. f.) Nakai (137, 138) (1923-1931)

Late purple aster - *Symphyotrichum patens* (Aiton) G.L. Nesom var. *patens* (5, 50, 72, 97, 156) (1907–present)

Late ripe cherry [Late ripe cherrie] - *Prunus cerasus* L. (178) (1526)

Late thoroughwort - *Eupatorium serotinum* Michx. (138) (1923)

Late white aster - *Oligoneuron album* (Nutt.) Nesom (82) (1930)

Late-flowering dropseed - *Muhlenbergia uniflora* (Muhl.) Fern. (5) (1913)

Late-flowering finger grass [Late-flowering finger-grass] - *Digitaria serotina* (Walt.) Michx. (5) (1913)

Late-flowering goosefoot [Lateflowering goosefoot] - *Chenopodium album* L. var. *striatum* (Krasan) Kartesz, (50) (present)

Late-flowering rush daffodil [Late flouring Rush Daffodill] - *Narcissus jonquilla* L. (180) (1633)

Late-flowering sporobolus [Late flowering sporobolus] - *Muhlenbergia uniflora* (Muhl.) Fern. (90) (1885)

Late-flowering thoroughwort [Lateflowering thoroughwort, Late flowering thoroughwort] - *Eupatorium serotinum* Michx. (5, 50, 72, 82, 97, 122) (1907–present)

Late-fruit sedge [Late-fruited sedge] - *Carex retrorsa* Schwein (66, 129) (1894-1903)

Lateral-flowered sandwort [Lateral flowered sandwort] - *Moehringia lateriflora* (L.) Fenzl (42) (1814)

Latherwort - *Saponaria officinalis* L. (64, 156, 157, 158) (1900–1929)

Latouwe (Low Dutch) - *Lactuca sativa* L. (180) (1633)

Lattich (Germanes) - *Lactuca sativa* L. (180) (1633)

Lauch (German) - *Allium porrum* L. (158, 180) (1633-1900)

Laughing-jackass [Laughing jackass] - *Arethusa bulbosa* L. (75) (1894)

Laurel - *Kalmia* L. (106, 112, 184) (1793-1937), *Kalmia latifolia* L. (7, 18, 46, 49, 53, 71, 187) (1649-1922), *Laurus* L. (7, 109, 138) (1828-1949), *Laurus nobilis* L. (57, 107, 179) (1526-1919), *Magnolia* L. (92) (1876), *Magnolia macrophylla* Michx. (7) (1828), *Rhododendron catawbiense* Michx. (5, 156) (1913-1923), *Rhododendron* L. (12, 75) (1821-1894), *Rhododendron lapponicum* (L.) Wahlenb. (5, 156) (1913-1923), *Rhododendron maximum* L. (18, 71) (1805-1898) PA, *Kalmia angustifolia* L. (190) (~1759)

Laurel clockvine - *Thunbergia laurifolia* Lindl. (138) (1923)

Laurel greenbrier - *Smilax laurifolia* L. (50, 138) (1923–present)

Laurel leaves - *Laurus nobilis* L. (92) (1876)

Laurel magnolia [Laurel-magnolia] - *Magnolia virginiana* L. (2, 5, 6, 106, 156) (1892-1930)

Laurel oak - *Quercus hemisphaerica* Bartr. ex Willd. (109) (1949), *Quercus imbricaria* Michx. (5, 20, 19, 33, 82, 93, 113, 156, 187) (1818-1936), *Quercus laurifolia* Michx. (5, 7, 33, 138) (1827-1923), *Quercus phellos* L. (156) (1923)

Laurel sumac - *Malosma laurina* (Nutt.) Nutt. ex Abrams (106, 109) (1930-1949)

Laurel tree [Laurel-tree] - *Persea borbonia* (L.) Spreng. (106) (1930)

Laurel tree of Carolina [Laurel-tree of Carolina] - *Magnolia virginiana* L. (189) (1767)

Laurel willow - *Salix pentandra* L. (50, 112, 138, 155) (1923–present)

Laurel-berry [Laurel berries] - *Laurus nobilis* L. (92) (1876)

Laurel-cherry - *Prunus caroliniana* (P. Mill.) Aiton (106) (1930), *Prunus* L. (155) (1942)

Laurel-leaf greenbrier [Laurel-leaved greenbrier] - *Smilax laurifolia* L. (5) (1913)

Laurel-leaf oak [Laurelleaf oak] - *Quercus laurifolia* Michx. (122) (1937)

Laurel-leaf smilax [Laurel-leafed smilax] - *Smilax laurifolia* L. (124) (1937)

Laurel-leaf tuliptree [Laurel-leaved tulip-tree] - *Magnolia* L. (8) (1785)

Laurel-leaf tuliptree [Laurel-leaved tulip-tree] - *Magnolia virginiana* L. (41) (1770)

Laurel-leaf willow [Laurel-leaved willow] - *Salix pentandra* L. (3, 4, 85, 109, 135) (1910-1986)

Laurestinus - *Viburnum* L. (82) (1930) IA, *Viburnum tinus* L. (109, 138) (1923-1949)

Laurier (French) - *Laurus* L. (8) (1785), *Myrica gale* L. (41) (1770)

Laurier amande (Louisiana) - *Prunus caroliniana* (P. Mill.) Aiton (possibly) (7) (1828)

Laurier articulé (French) - *Litsea aestivalis* (L.) Fern. (8) (1785)

Laurier benzoin (French) - *Lindera benzoin* Blume. (6) (1892)

Laurier beujoin (French) - *Lindera benzoin* Blume. (8) (1785)

Laurier cerise (French) - *Prunus laurocerasus* L. (8) (1785)

Laurier de Bourbon (French) - *Persea borbonia* (L.) Spreng. (8) (1785)

Laurier rose - *Nerium oleander* L. (49) (1898)

Laurier sassafras (French) - *Sassafras albidum* (Nutt.) Nees (8) (1785)

Laurier tulipier (French) - *Magnolia grandiflora* L. (8, 20) (1785-1857), *Magnolia* L. (8) (1785)

Laurocerasus - *Prunus laurocerasus* L. (57) (1917)

Laurus alexandrina - *Streptopus amplexifolius* (L.) DC. var. *amplexifolius* (174) (1753)

Laurus borbonia - *Persea borbonia* (L.) Spreng. (182) (1791)

Laurus Cerasus - *Prunus caroliniana* (P. Mill.) Aiton (183) (~1756)

Laury-Mundy - *Prunus caroliniana* (P. Mill.) Aiton (106) (1930)

Lauten (Spanish) - *Plantago lanceolata* L. (158) (1900)

Lavender [Lauendre] - *Balsamita major* Desf. (158) (1900), *Lavandula angustifolia* Mill. (19, 53, 61, 107) (1840–1922), *Lavandula* L. (82, 106, 109, 138, 179) (1526-1949) from Latin lavo "to wash" referring to the use of lavender in the bath

Lavender grass - *Molinia caerulea* (L.) Moench (5) (1913)

Lavender hyssop - *Agastache foeniculum* (Pursh) Kuntze (3, 4, 98) (1926-1986)

Lavender thrift [Lavender-thrift] - *Limonium carolinianum* (Walt.) Britt. (5, 92, 156) (1876-1923)

Lavender violet - *Viola pedata* L. (156) (1923)

Lavender-cotton [Lavendercotton, Lavender cotton] - *Lavandula angustifolia* Mill. (46) (1671), *Matricaria discoidea* DC. (10, 19) (1818-1840), *Santolina chamaecyparissus* L. (46, 92, 109, 138) (1671-1949) cultivated by English colonists by 1671, Josselyn, *Santolina* L. (138, 155, 158) (1900-1942)

Lavender-leaf evening-primrose [Lavenderleaf eveningprimrose] - *Calylophus lavandulifolius* (Torr. & Gray) Raven (155) (1942)

Lavender-leaf primrose [Lavender-leaved primrose] - *Calylophus lavandulifolius* (Torr. & Gray) Raven (4, 5, 97) (1913-1986)

Lavender-leaf sundrops [Lavenderleaf sundrops] - *Calylophus lavandulifolius* (Torr. & Gray) Raven (50) (present)

Laver - Callicarpa dichotoma (Lour.) K.Koch (107) (1919), *Sargassum natans* (L.) Gaillon (92) (1876)

Lavose - *Levisticum officinale* W.D.J. Koch (92) (1876)

Lawn daisy [Lawndaisy] - *Bellis perennis* L. (50) (present)

Lawn plant - *Phyla nodiflora* (L.) Greene (106) (1930)

Lawson's cypress [Lawson cypress] - *Chamaecyparis lawsoniana* (A. Murr.) Parl. (109, 138) (1923-1949) for Charles Lawson, 1794-1873, Britain

Lawyers - *Rosa canina* L. (5) (1913)

Lax hornpod - *Mitreola petiolata* (J.F. Gmel.) Torr. & Gray (50) (present)

Lax-flower panicum [Lax-flowered panicum] - *Dichanthelium laxiflorum* (Lam.) Gould (5) (1913)

Laxmann's milkvetch - *Astragalus laxmannii* Jacq. (50) (present)

Laylock - *Syringa vulgaris* L. (156) (1923) no longer in use by 1923

Layreole - *Daphne laureola* L. (179) (1526)

Lazy-daisy [Lazy daisy] - *Aphanostephus* DC. (4) (1986), *Aphanostephus pilosus* Buckl. (3) (1977), *Aphanostephus ramosissimus* DC. (3) (1977), *Aphanostephus skirrobasis* (DC.) Trelease (3) (1977)

Lazy-man's grass [Lazy-mans-grass] - *Eremochloa ophiuroides* (Munro) Hack. (109) (1949) needs little mowing

Le Blé Noir (French) - *Fagopyrum esculentum* Moench (6) (1892)

Le Blé Sarrasin (French) - *Fagopyrum esculentum* Moench (6) (1892)

Le Conte's paspalum - *Paspalum floridanum* Michx. (5) (1913)

Le Conte's violet [LeConte violet] - *Viola affinis* Le Conte (5, 155) (1913-1942)

Le Cotonnière (French) - *Pseudognaphalium obtusifolium* (L.) Hilliard & Burtt subsp. *obtusifolium* (6) (1892)

Le Fraisier (French) - *Fragaria vesca* L. (6, 158) (1892–1900)

Le frêne à fleurs de Californie (French) - *Fraxinus dipetala* Hook. & Arn. (20) (1857)

Le Fréne Blanc (French) - *Fraxinus americana* L. (6) (1892)

Le Liseron (French) - *Convolvulus arvensis* L. (6) (1892)

Le Tournesol (French) - *Helianthus annuus* L. (6) (1892)

Lea oak - *Quercus imbricaria* Michx. (5, 156) (1913-1923)

Lead amaranth - *Amaranthus blitum* L. (19) (1840)

Lead-colored amaranth [Lead coloured amaranth] - *Amaranthus blitum* L. (42) (1814)

Lead-grass [Lead grass] - *Sarcocornia perennis* (P. Mill.) A.J. Scott (77) (1898) Southold Long Island, from weight in salt-meadow hay

Leadplant [Lead plant, Lead plant] - *Amorpha canescens* Pursh (3, 4, 5, 19, 28, 47, 50, 63, 82, 85, 92, 95, 97, 106, 109, 112, 114, 122, 127, 130, 131, 138, 156, 158) (1850–present), *Amorpha fruticosa* L. (131, 156, 157) (1899–1929), *Amorpha* L. (112) (1937)

Leadplant amorpha - *Amorpha canescens* Pursh (155) (1942)

Leadweed [Lead weed] - *Sarcocornia perennis* (P. Mill.) A.J. Scott (77) (1898) Southold Long Island, from weight in salt-meadow hay

Leadwort [Lead wort] - *Amorpha canescens* Pursh (156) (1923), *Plumbago* L. (109) (1949)

Leaf mustard - *Brassica juncea* (L.) Czern. (109) (1949)

Leaf plant - *Kalanchoe pinnata* (Lam.) Pers. (19) (1840)

Leaf-beet - *Beta vulgaris* L. (107) (1919)

Leaf-buds - *Populus balsamifera* L. (157) (1929)

Leafcup [Leaf-cup, Leaf cup] - *Polymnia canadensis* L (82) (1930), *Polymnia* L. (1, 2, 4, 82, 155, 158) (1895-1986), *Smallanthus uvedalius* (L.) Mackenzie ex Small (52, 53, 92, 156) (1876-1923)

Leafless bladderwort [Leafless bladder-wort] - *Utricularia cornuta* Michx. (19) (1840)

Leafless pyrola - *Pyrola picta* Sm. (155) (1942)

Leaf-rooting spleenwort [Leaf-rooting spleen-wort] - *Asplenium rhizophyllum* L. (187) (1818)

Leafy arnica - *Arnica chamissonis* Less. subsp. *foliosa* (Nutt.) Maguire var. *andina* (Nutt.) Ediger & Barkl. (155) (1942)

Leafy aster - *Symphyotrichum frondosum* (Nutt.) Nesom (155) (1942)

Leafy blue flag - *Iris brevicaulis* Raf. (5) (1913)

Leafy bluebells - *Mertensia oblongifolia* (Nutt.) G. Don (155) (1942)

Leafy bulrush - *Scirpus polyphyllus* Vahl (5, 50) (1913–present)

Leafy euphorbia - *Euphorbia esula* L. (155) (1942)

Leafy false goldenweed - *Oonopsis foliosa* (Gray) Greene var. *foliosa* (50) (present)

Leafy gold-aster [Leafy goldaster] - *Heterotheca villosa* (Pursh) Shinners var. *foliosa* (Nutt.) Harms (155) (1942)

Leafy goosefoot - *Chenopodium foliosum* (Moench) Aschers. (50) (present)

Leafy madwort - *Lobularia maritima* (L.) Desv. (165) (1768)

Leafy muhly - *Muhlenbergia mexicana* (L.) Trin. (155) (1942)

Leafy musineon - *Musineon divaricatum* (Pursh) Raf. (5, 131) (1899-1913)

Leafy pondweed - *Potamogeton foliosus* Raf. (3, 50, 72, 93, 97, 120, 131, 155) (1899–present), *Potamogeton foliosus* Raf. subsp. *foliosus* (50) (present)

Leafy prairie clover - *Dalea foliosa* (Gray) Barneby (5, 72) (1907-1913)

Leafy raspberry - *Rubus frondosus* Bigelow (19) (1840)

Leafy rose - *Rosa foliolosa* Nutt. (4, 155) (1942-1986)

Leafy spurge - *Euphorbia agraria* Bieb. (3) (1977), *Euphorbia esula* L. (4, 50, 156, 158) (1900–present), *Euphorbia esula* L. var. *esula* (5, 50, 93) (1913–present)

Leafy stonecrop - *Sedum dasyphyllum* L. (138, 155) (1931-1942)

Leafy vaccinium - *Gaylussacia frondosa* (L.) Torr. & Gray (8) (1785)

Leafy white prickly poppy - *Argemone gracilenta* Greene (5) (1913)

Leafy wild parsley [Leafy wildparsley] - *Musineon divaricatum* (Pursh) Raf. (50) (present), *Musineon divaricatum* (Pursh) Raf. var. *divaricatum* (50) (present)

Leafy-bract aster [Leafybract aster [Leafy-bracted aster] - *Symphyotrichum foliaceum* (DC.) Nesom var. *foliaceum* (5, 155) (1913-1942) MT

Leafy-bract beggarticks [Leafybract beggarticks] - *Bidens tripartita* L. (155) (1942)

Leafy-bract tickseed [Leafy-bracted tickseed] - *Bidens tripartita* L. (5, 72, 93, 97) (1907-1937)

Leafy-coned silver fir - *Abies bracteata* (D. Don) D. Don ex Poit. (20) (1857)

Leafy-flower blackberry [Leafy-flowered blackberry] - *Rubus frondosus* Bigelow (5) (1913)

Leafy-stem false dandelion [Leafy-stemmed false dandelion] - *Pyrrhopappus carolinianus* (Walt.) DC. (5, 97) (1913–1937)

Leamington - *Artemisia abrotanum* L. (73) (1892) Ipswich MA

Lean flatsedge - *Cyperus setigerus* Torr. & Hook. (50) (present)

Lea's oak - *Quercus* ×*leana* Nutt. [*imbricaria* × *velutina*] (20) (1857)

Least amaranth - *Amaranthus blitum* L. (165) (1768)

Least bluet [Least bluets] - *Houstonia pusilla* Schoepf (5, 63, 65, 72, 97) (1899–1937)

Least chickweed [Least chick weed] - *Cerastium semidecandrum* L. (42) (1814)

Least cryptantha - *Cryptantha minima* Rydb. (97) (1937)

Least daisy - *Chaetopappa asteroides* (Nutt.) DC. (122) (1937)

Least duckweed - *Lemna minor* L. (5, 155) (1913-1942), *Lemna minuta* Kunth (50) (present)

Least hop clover [Least hop-clover] - *Trifolium dubium* Sibth. (5, 122) (1913-1937)

Least hop trefoil [Least hop-trefoil] - *Melilotus officinalis* (L.) Lam. (5) (1913), *Trifolium dubium* Sibth. (5, 158) (1900-1913)

Least mouse-ear chickweed - *Cerastium semidecandrum* L. (187) (1818)

Least spike-rush [Least spike rush] - *Eleocharis acicularis* (L.) Roemer & J.A. Schultes (5, 156) (1913-1923)

Least-daisy [Leastdaisy] - *Chaetopappa* DC. (50) (present)

Leather bush [Leather-bush] - *Dirca palustris* L. (5, 92, 156) (1876-1923)

Leather fern [Leatherfern] - *Acrostichum* L. (50) (present), *Rumohra adiantiformis* (G. Forst.) Ching (138) (1923)

Leather flower [Leatherflower, Leather-flower] - *Clematis bigelovii* Torr. (153) (1913) NM

Leather flower [Leatherflower, Leather-flower] - *Clematis* L. (1, 50, 93) (1932–present), *Clematis pitcheri* Torr. & Gray (82) (1930), *Clematis viorna* L. (2, 5, 15, 19, 63, 72, 92, 138, 156) (1840-1923)

Leather wood fern [Leather woodfern] - *Dryopteris marginalis* (L.) A. Gray (138, 155) (1923-1942)

Leather-breeches - *Amsinckia lycopsoides* Lehm. (106) (1930)

Leather-leaf [Leatherleaf, Leather leaf] - *Chamaedaphne calyculata* (L.) Moench (5, 19, 86, 92, 109, 138, 156) (1840-1949), *Chaptalia tomentosa* Vent. (183) (~1756), *Eubotrys* Nutt. (1, 2, 138, 156) (1895-1932), *Maytenus phyllanthoides* Benth. (122) (1937) TX

Leather-leaf grape [Leatherleaf grape] - *Vitis shuttleworthii* House (15) (1895)

Leather-leaf holly-grape [Leatherleaf hollygrape] - *Mahonia bealei* (Fortune) Carr. (138) (1923)

Leather-root - *Orbexilum* Raf. (50) (present)

Leatherweed [Leather-weed, Leather weed] - *Croton pottsii* (Klotzsch) Muell. Arg. (4, 50) (1986–present), *Jatropha dioica* Sessé (124) (1937)

Leatherwood [Leather-wood, Leather wood] - *Cyrilla racemiflora* L. (106, 156) (1923-1930), *Dirca* L. (1, 2, 8, 10, 109, 138, 167) (1814–1949), *Dirca palustris* L. (5, 6, 7, 14, 19, 23, 41, 49, 65, 72, 92, 105, 138, 156) (1770-1932)

Leathery grape fern - *Botrychium multifidum* (Gmel.) Trev. (5) (1913)

Leathery knotweed - *Polygonum achoreum* Blake (50, 155) (1942–present)

Leathery rush - *Juncus coriaceus* Mackenzie (50) (present)

Leavenworth's eryngo [Leavenworth eryngo] - *Eryngium leavenworthii* Torr. & Gray (3, 4, 5, 50, 97, 155) (1913–present)

Leavenworth's sedge - *Carex leavenworthii* Dewey (3, 5, 50, 72) (1893–present)

Leavenworth's vetch - *Vicia faba* L. (93) (1913-1936), *Vicia ludoviciana* Nutt. subsp. *leavenworthii* (Torr. & Gray) Lassetter & Gunn. (72) (1907)

Leaverwood [Leaver wood, Leaver-wood] - *Dirca palustris* L. (5, 92, 156) (1876-1923)

Lebbeck's tree [Lebbeck-tree] - *Albizia lebbeck* (L.) Benth. (109) (1949)

Lebbek - *Albizia lebbeck* (L.) Benth. (138) (1923)

Lebelie syphilitique (French) - *Lobelia siphilitica* L. (6) (1892)

Leberkraut (German) - *Hepatica nobilis* Schreb. (7) (1828)

Lebesbaum (German) - *Thuja occidentalis* L. (6) (1892)

Lechuga (Spanish) - *Lactuca sativa* L. (180) (1633)

Lechuguilla - *Agave lecheguilla* Torr. (122, 138) (1923-1937) TX, *Agave univittata* Haw. (124) (1937) TX

Leder-Holz (German) - *Dirca palustris* L. (6, 7) (1828-1892)

Ledingham's false dragonhead - *Physostegia ledinghamii* (Boivin) Cantino (50) (present)

Ledum - *Ledum groenlandicum* Oeder (possibly) (57) (1917)

Ledum (French) - *Ledum* L. (8) (1785)

Leechwort [Leech-wort] - *Plantago lanceolata* L. (5, 156, 157, 158) (1900–1929)

Leek [Leeks, Leke, Leekes] - *Allium atroviolaceum* Boiss. (110) (1886), *Allium* L. (121) (1918-1970), *Allium porrum* L. (3, 19, 92, 109, 138, 155, 158, 178, 179, 180) (1526-1977), *Hylotelephium telephium* (L.) H. Ohba. subsp. *telephium* (5, 73) (1892-1913) Stowe VT

Leek cress - *Alliaria petiolata* (Bieb.) Cavara & Grande (156, 158) (1900-1923)

Leggett's pinweed [Leggett pin-weed] - *Lechea pulchella* Raf. var. *pulchella* (5) (1913)

Leghorn straw grass - *Cynosurus cristatus* L. (5) (1913)

Leiberg's monkshood [Leiberg monkshood] - *Aconitum columbianum* Nutt. (155) (1942)

Leiberg's panicum [Leiberg panicum] - *Dichanthelium leibergii* (Vasey) Freckmann (3, 50, 155) (1942–present)

Leimonia - *Scolymus hispanicus* L. (107) (322 BC) in American seed catalogs in 1870's

Leindotter (German) - *Camelina sativa* (L.) Crantz (158) (1900)

Leinkraut (German) - *Linaria vulgaris* Mill. (6, 158) (1892-1900)

Leitneria - *Leitneria floridana* Chapman (5) (1913)

Lelache - *Syringa vulgaris* L. (156) (1923)

Lemita - *Rhus trilobata* Nutt. (149) (1904) NM, *Rhus trilobata* Nutt. var. *trilobata* (153) (1913) NM

Lemmon's acacia [Lemmons acacia] - *Acacia angustissima* (Mill.) Kuntze var. *hirta* (Nutt.) B.L. Robins. (155) (1942)

Lemmon's canary grass [Lemmon's canary-grass] - *Phalaris lemmonii* Vasey (94) (1901)

Lemmon's dropseed [Lemmon's drop-seed] - *Muhlenbergia glauca* (Nees) B.D. Jackson (94) (1901)

Lemmon's onion [Lemmons onion] - *Allium lemmonii* S. Wats. (155) (1942)

Lemmon's rockcress [Lemmons rockcress] - *Arabis lemmonii* S. Wats. (155) (1942)

Lemmon's speargrass [Lemmon's spear-grass] - *Puccinellia lemmonii* (Vasey) Scribn. (94) (1901)

Lemmon's wild ginger [Lemmons wildginger] - *Asarum lemmonii* S. Wats. (155) (1942)

Lemmon's wool grass [Lemmon's wool-grass] - *Eriochloa lemmonii* Vasey & Scribn. (94) (1901)

Lemon acacia - *Neptunia lutea* (Leavenworth) Benth. (155) (1942)

Lemon apple - *Podophyllum peltatum* L. (53) (1922)

Lemon balm [Lemon-balm] - *Melissa* L. (1) (1932), *Melissa officinalis* L. (5, 49, 75, 92, 109, 156) (1876-1949)

Lemon beebalm - *Monarda citriodora* Cerv. ex Lag. (3, 4, 50, 155) (1942–present), *Monarda citriodora* Cerv. ex Lag. subsp. *citriodora* var. *citriodora* (50) (present)

Lemon daylily - *Hemerocallis lilioasphodelus* L. (138) (1923)

Lemon grass [Lemon-grass] - *Ctenium aromaticum* (Walt.) Wood (5) (1913)

Lemon grass [Lemon-grass] - *Cymbopogon citratus* (DC. ex Nees) Stapf (92, 109) (1876-1949)

Lemon gum - *Eucalyptus citriodora* Hook. (138) (1923)

Lemon lily - *Hemerocallis lilioasphodelus* L. (78, 156) (1898–1923), *Lilium parryi* S. Wats. (138) (1923)

Lemon lobelia - *Melissa officinalis* L. (5, 75) (1894-1913) Northeastern US

Lemon mint - *Hedeoma drummondii* Benth. (124) (1937) TX, *Monarda citriodora* Cerv. ex Lag. (4, 156) (1923-1986), *Monarda* L. (1) (1932), *Monarda pectinata* Nutt. (1) (1932)

Lemon monarda - *Monarda citriodora* Cerv. ex Lag. (156) (1923), *Monarda pectinata* Nutt. (97, 98) (1926–1937)

Lemon or Lemon tree - *Citrus ×limonia* Osbeck [*limon × reticulata*] (92, 107) (1876-1919), *Citrus limon* (L.) Burm. f. (50, 52, 58, 92, 106, 109) (1869–present), *Citrus medica* L. (7, 19, 110) (1828-1886)

Lemon scurf-pea [Lemon scurfpea, Lemon scurf pea] - *Psoralidium lanceolatum* (Pursh) Rydb. (4, 50, 98) (1923–present)

Lemon trout lily [Lemon troutlily] - *Erythronium citrinum* S. Wats. (138) (1923)

Lemon verbena - *Aloysia triphylla* (L'Hér.) Britt. (92, 109) (1876-1949)

Lemon vine [Lemon-vine] - *Pereskia aculeata* Mill. (109) (1949), *Pereskia grandifolia* Haw. (109) (1949)

Lemon walnut - *Juglans cinerea* L. (5, 92, 156, 157, 158) (1898–1929)

Lemonade sumac - *Rhus trilobata* Nutt. (138) (1923)

Lemonade-and-sugar tree [Lemonade and sugar tree] - *Rhus integrifolia* (Nutt.) Benth. & Hook. f. ex Brewer & S. Wats. (76) (1896) San Diego, CA, *Rhus ovata* S. Wats. (76) (1896) San Diego, CA

Lemonade-berry - *Rhus integrifolia* (Nutt.) Benth. & Hook. f. ex Brewer & S. Wats. (109) (1949)

Lemonis succus - *Citrus limon* (L.) Burm. f. (52) (1919)

Lemon-scent [Lemonscent, Lemon scent] - *Pectis angustifolia* Torr. (50) (present), *Pectis* L. (1) (1932)

Lemon-scent pectis [Lemon scented pectis] - *Pectis angustifolia* Torr. (5, 93, 122, 124) (1913-1937)

Lemon-scent spotted gum [Lemon-scented spotted gum] - *Eucalyptus citriodora* Hook. (109) (1949)

Lemon-verbena - *Aloysia triphylla* (L'Hér.) Britt. (138) (1923)

Lemonweed [Lemon weed] - *Psoralidium lanceolatum* (Pursh) Rydb. (106) (1930)

Leña amarilla (Spanish) - *Mahonia pinnata* (Lag.) Fedde subsp. *pinnata* (74, 76, 107) (1893-1919) CA Mexico

L'endormie (French) - *Datura stramonium* L. (6) (1892)

Lens pepperweed - *Cardaria chalapensis* (L.) Hand.-Maz. (155) (1942)

Lens-pod hoary cress [Lens-podded hoary cress] - *Cardaria chalapensis* (L.) Hand.-Maz. (4) (1986)

Lens-pod whitetop [Lenspod whitetop] - *Cardaria chalapensis* (L.) Hand.-Maz. (50) (present)

Lenszic (Lithuanian) - *Lens culinaris* Medik. (110) (1886)

Lenticular sedge - *Carex lenticularis* Michx. (5) (1913)

Lentil [Lentils, Lentyle] - *Lens culinaris* Medik. (107, 109, 92, 110, 178, 179) (1526-1949) from ancient Latin 'lens' for the shape of seed

Lentil tare - *Vicia tetrasperma* (L.) Moench (5, 156) (1913-1923)

Lentils of the water [Lentylles of the water] - *Lemna minor* L. (178, 179) (1526-1596)

Lentisco - *Rhus integrifolia* (Nutt.) Benth. & Hook. f. ex Brewer & S. Wats. (76) (1896) San Diego, CA, *Rhus ovata* S. Wats. (76) (1896) San Diego, CA

Lentiscus-leaf sumach [Lentiscus-leaved sumach] - *Rhus copallinum* L. (8) (1785)

Leonard's skullcap - *Scutellaria parvula* Michx. var. *missouriensis* (Torr.) Goodman & Lawson (50) (present)

Leonard's small skullcap [Leonard small skullcap] - *Scutellaria parvula* Michx. var. *missouriensis* (Torr.) Goodman & Lawson (3) (1977)

Leonurus - *Leonurus cardiaca* L. (57) (1917)

Leopard flower [Leopard-flower] - *Belamcanda chinensis* (L.) DC. (156) (1923)

Leopard flower [Leopard-flower] - *Belamcanda chinensis* (L.) DC. (5, 158) (1900-1913)

Leopard lily - *Belamcanda chinensis* (L.) DC. (5, 158) (1900-1913), *Fritillaria atropurpurea* Nutt. (3, 85, 121, 127) (1918-1977), *Fritillaria* L. (1, 93) (1932-1936), *Lilium pardalinum* Kellogg (138) (1923)

Leopard's-bane [Leopardsbane, Leopard's bane, Leopardbane] - *Arnica acaulis* (Walt.) B.S.P. (5) (1913), *Arnica* L. (7, 156) (1828-1900), *Doronicum* L. (109, 138, 167) (1814-1949), *Doronicum pardalianches* L. (178) (1526)

Leptandra - *Veronicastrum virginicum* (L.) Farw. (53, 55, 57, 59) (1911-1922)

Leptandre rouge (French) - *Veronicastrum virginicum* (L.) Farw. (7) (1828)

Leptochloa - *Leptochloa fusca* (L.) Kunth subsp. *fascicularis* (Lam.) N. Snow (119) (1938)

Lereckhout - *Larix laricina* (Du Roi.) Koch. (46) (1617)

Lespedeza - *Lespedeza* Michx. (4, 50, 155) (1942–present)

Less fleabane [Less flea bane] - *Erigeron* L. (167) (1814)

Less flowering rush - *Scheuchzeria palustris* L. (19) (1840)

Lesse consoulde - *Bellis perennis* L. (179) (1526)

Lesse morell - *Solanum ptychanthum* Dunal (179) (1526)

Lesse saxifrage - *Sanguisorba minor* Scop. subsp. *muricata* (Spach) Nordborg (possibly) (179) (1526)

Lesser African marigold [Lesser Affrican marigold] - *Tagetes patula* L. (178) (1526)

Lesser black cherry [Lesser blacke cherrie] - *Prunus cerasus* L. (178) (1526)

Lesser bladderwort - *Utricularia minor* L. (4, 5, 50, 72, 93) (1907–present)

Lesser bog orchid - *Platanthera stricta* Lindl. (50) (present)

Lesser bougainvillea - *Bougainvillea glabra* Choisy (possibly) (138) (1923)

Lesser broomrape [Lesser broom-rape] - *Orobanche minor* J.E. Smith (5, 156) (1913-1923)

Lesser brown sedge - *Carex adusta* Boott. (50) (present)

Lesser burdock [Lesser burrdock] - *Arctium minus* Bernh. (50, 157, 158) (1900–present), *Xanthium strumarium* L. (158, 187) (1818-1900), *Xanthium strumarium* L. var. *canadense* (Mill.) Torr. & Gray (156) (1923), *Xanthium strumarium* L. var. *glabratum* (DC.) Cronq. (5) (1913)

Lesser burre - *Arctium* L. (179) (1526)

Lesser calamint - *Calamintha nepeta* (L.) Savi subsp. *nepeta* (5, 156) (1913–1923)

Lesser celandine - *Ranunculus ficaria* L. (5, 55, 107, 156) (1911-1923)

Lesser centaury - *Centaurium erythraea* Raf. (5, 156) (1913-1923)

Lesser chickpea [Lesser chick-pea] - *Lathyrus cicera* L. (107) (1919)

Lesser clearweed - *Pilea fontana* (Lunell) Rydb. (50) (present)

Lesser clotbur [Lesser clot-bur] - *Xanthium strumarium* L. (46, 174) (1671-1753)

Lesser clover dodder - *Cuscuta epithymum* (L.) L. (82) (1930)

Lesser common sedge - *Carex acutiformis* Ehrh. (5, 156) (1913-1923)

Lesser creeping rush - *Juncus repens* Michx. (50) (present)

Lesser dodder - *Cuscuta epithymum* (L.) L. (158) (1900)

Lesser duckweed - *Lemna aequinoctialis* Welw. (50) (present), *Lemna minor* L. (5, 72, 93, 97) (1907-1937)

Lesser fair-hair hyacinth [Lesser faire haired Iacint] - *Muscari comosum* (L.) Mill. (178) (1596)

Lesser fringed gentian - *Gentianopsis virgata* (Raf.) Holub (50) (present)

Lesser hart cherry [Lesser hart cherrie] - *Prunus cerasus* L. (178) (1526)

Lesser hemlock - *Aethusa cynapium* L. (5, 6, 156, 165) (1768-1923)

Lesser lechea - *Lechea minor* L. (187) (1818)

Lesser lucerne dodder - *Cuscuta epithymum* (L.) L. (5, 156) (1913-1923)

Lesser pennyroyal [Lesser penniroyall] - *Mentha pulegium* L. (178) (1526)

Lesser pond sedge - *Carex acutiformis* Ehrh. (50) (present)

Lesser prickly sedge - *Carex muricata* L. (5, 156) (1913-1923)

Lesser purple fringed orchid - *Platanthera psycodes* (L.) Lindl. (50) (present)

Lesser purple passe flower [Lesser purple Passe floure] - *Pulsatilla patens* (L.) Mill. subsp. *multifida* (Pritz.) Zamels (possibly) (180) (1633)

Lesser quaking grass - *Briza minor* L. (5) (1913)

Lesser rattlesnake-plantain [Lesser rattlesnake plantain] - *Goodyera repens* (L.) R. Br. ex Ait. f. (5, 50, 109, 156) (1913–present)

Lesser reed-mace - *Typha angustifolia* L. (5, 10, 14, 34) (1840-1882)

Lesser round-leaf orchid [Lesser roundleaved orchid] - *Platanthera orbiculata* (Pursh) Lindl. (50) (present)

Lesser saltmarsh sedge - *Carex glareosa* Schkuhr ex Wahlenb. subsp. *glareosa* var. *amphigena* Fern. (50) (present)

Lesser sea starwort [Lesser sea Star woort] - *Tripleurospermum perforata* (Merat) M. Lainz (178) (1526)

Lesser snapdragon - *Misopates orontium* (L.) Raf. (5) (1913)

Lesser spikemoss - *Selaginella densa* Rydb. (50) (present), *Selaginella densa* Rydb. var. *densa* (50) (present)

Lesser starwort - *Stellaria graminea* L. (5) (1913)

Lesser stitchwort - *Stellaria graminea* L. (5) (1913)

Lesser watercress [Lesser water cress] - *Coronopus didymus* (L.) Sm. (5) (1913)

Lesser water-parsnip [Lesser water-parsnip] - *Berula erecta* (Huds.) Coville (5, 158) (1900–1913)

Lesser water-weed - *Elodea nuttallii* (Planch.) St. John (5, 120) (1913-1938)

Lesser wintergreen - *Pyrola elliptica* Nutt. (156) (1923), *Pyrola minor* L. (5) (1913)

Lesser yellow lady's-slipper [Philotria minor (Engelm.) Small.] - *Cypripedium parviflorum* Salisb. (50) (present)

Lesser-panicle sedge [Lesser-panicled sedge] - *Carex chordorrhiza* Ehrh. Ex L. f. (possibly) (66, 72) (1903-1907)

Lesser-panicle sedge [Lesser-panicled sedge] - *Carex diandra* Schrank (5, 50) (1913–present)

Less-flowering-rush - *Scheuchzeria* L. (167) (1814)

Letterman's bluegrass [Letterman's blue-grass] - *Poa lettermanii* Vasey (94) (1901)

Letterman's ironweed [Letterman's iron-weed] - *Vernonia lettermannii* Engelm. ex Gray (97) (1937)

Letterman's needlegrass [Letterman needlegrass] - *Achnatherum lettermanii* (Vasey) Barkworth (140) (1944) TX

Lettuce [Lettice, Lettise, Letuse] - *Lactuca floridana* (L.) Gaertn. (106) (1930), *Lactuca* L. (1, 4, 7, 10, 50, 63, 82, 93, 138, 155, 156, 158, 184) (1793–present), *Lactuca sativa* L. (19, 109, 110, 178, 179, 180) (1526-1949), *Lactuca serriola* L. (46) (1671), *Lactuca virosa* L. (55) (1911)

Lettuce opium - *Lactuca virosa* L. (53, 57) (1917-1922) dried milk

Lettuce saxifrage - *Saxifraga micranthidifolia* (Haw.) Steud. (5, 156) (1913-1923)

Lettuce-liverwort [Lettuce liverwort] - *Pyrola americana* Sweet (92) (1876)

Leucospora - *Leucospora multifida* (Michx.) Nutt. (3, 4) (1977-1986), *Leucospora* Nutt. (50) (present)

Leucothoe - *Leucothoe axillaris* (Lam.) D. Don. (71, 156) (1898-1923), *Leucothoe* D. Don (138) (1923) named for the daughter of Orchamus, king of Babylonia

Levant cotton - *Gossypium herbaceum* L. (109) (1949)

Levant soapwort - *Gypsophila paniculata* L. (57) (1917)

Levers - *Sparganium* L. (158) (1900)

Leverwood [Lever-wood, Lever wood] - *Ostrya carpinifolia* Scop. (20) (1857), *Ostrya virginiana* (Mill.) K. Koch (156, 157, 158) (1900-1929), *Ostrya virginiana* (Mill.) K. Koch var. *virginiana* (2, 6, 19, 49, 75, 92) (1840-1895)

Levisticum - *Levisticum officinale* W.D.J. Koch (57) (1917)

Levose - *Levisticum officinale* W.D.J. Koch (92) (1876)

Lewis and Clarke's currant - *Ribes aureum* Pursh (28) (1850)

Lewis' flax [Lewis flax] - *Linum lewisii* Pursh (155) (1942)

Lewis' mock orange [Lewis mockorange] - *Philadelphus lewisii* Pursh (138) (1923)

Lewis' monkey-flower [Lewis monkeyflower] - *Mimulus lewisii* Pursh (138) (1923)

Lewis' wild flax - *Linum lewisii* Pursh (5, 97, 131) (1899–1937)

L'Herbe a Pisser (French) - *Chimaphila umbellata* (L.) Bart. (186) (1814)

Li (Basque) - *Linum usitatissimum* L. (110) (1886)

Liane à réglisse (French) - *Abrus precatorius* L. (158) (1900)

Liard (French Creole) - *Populus ×canadensis* Moench (pro sp.) [*deltoides × nigra*] (17, 23, 27) (1796-1811)

Liard (French in Illinois) - *Populus* L. (17, 35) (1796)

Liard amere (French) - *Populus angustifolia* James (28) (1850)

Liatris - *Liatris spicata* (L.) Willd. (52) (1919)

Liberian coffee - *Coffea liberica* Bull ex Hiern. (138) (1923)

Liberty - *Lycopodium complanatum* L. (73) (1892) Chestertown MD

Liberty tea [liberty-tea] - *Lysimachia quadrifolia* L. (5, 156) (1913-1923)

Lichen - *Marchantia polymorpha* L. (174) (1753), *Parmelia* Ach. (121) (1918-1970), *Punctelia borreri* (Sm.) Krog (37) (1830), *Usnea barbata* (L.) Weber ex F.H. Wigg. (37) (1830)

Licheta - *Agrostemma githago* L. (71, 74) (1893-1929) Vermount

Lichwale - *Buglossoides arvensis* (L.) I.M. Johnston (157, 158) (1900-1929), *Lithospermum officinale* L. (156) (1923)

Licorice [Liquorice] - *Amphicarpaea bracteata* (L.) Fern. (156) (1923), *Glycyrrhiza glabra* (possibly) (19, 52, 55, 57, 92, 107, 109) (1793-1949), *Glycyrrhiza* L. (1, 4, 7, 50, 93, 138, 155, 156, 158) (1828-present), *Glycyrrhiza lepidota* Pursh (106, 122) (1930-1937)

Licorice bedstraw - *Galium circaezans* Michx. (50) (present), *Galium circaezans* Michx. var. *hypomalacum* Fern. (50) (present)

Licorice bush [Liquorice bush] - *Abrus precatorius* L. (7, 92) (1828-1876)

Licorice fern [Liquorice fern] - *Cyrtomium falcatum* (L. f.) C. Presl (86) (1878), *Polypodium glycyrrhiza* D.C. Eat. (138) (1923), *Polypodium virginianum* L. (124) (1937) TX

Licorice root [Licorice-root, Licorice roots, Liquorice roots] - *Glycyrrhiza glabra* L. (92) (1876), *Glycyrrhiza lepidota* Pursh (5, 76, 124, 156) (1896–1937), *Hedysarum boreale* subsp. *mackenzii* (Richardson) S.L.Welsh (107) (1919)

Licorice tree [Lycoryce tre] - *Glycyrrhiza glabra* L. (179) (1526)

Licorice-buds [Liquorice buds] - *Abrus precatorius* L. (92) (1876)

Liddon's sedge [Liddon sedge] - *Carex petasata* Dewey (139) (1944)

Lieberg's panicum - *Dichanthelium leibergii* (Vasey) Freckmann (5, 56, 72) (1893–1913)

Liebfrauenstroh (German) - *Galium verum* L. (158) (1900)

Liendrilla - *Sporobolus indicus* (L.) R. Br. (45) (1896)

Lierre (French) - *Hedera* L. (8) (1785)

Lierre terrestre (French) - *Glechoma hederacea* L. (158) (1900)

Life plant [Life-plant] - *Kalanchoe pinnata* (Lam.) Pers. (73, 109) (1892-1949)

Life-everlasting [Life everlasting] - *Anaphalis* DC. (158) (1900), *Anaphalis margaritacea* (L.) Benth. & Hook (5, 41, 106, 158, 187) (1770–1930), *Gnaphalium* L. (92) (1876), *Pseudognaphalium obtusifolium* (L.) Hilliard & Burtt subsp. *obtusifolium* (6, 57, 73, 145, 157) (1892–1929)

Life-of-man [Life of man, Life-o'-man] - *Anaphalis margaritacea* (L.) Benth. & Hook (73) (1892) NH, *Aralia nudicaulis* L. (7) (1828), *Aralia racemosa* L. (5, 6, 64, 73, 75, 92, 156, 157, 158) (1892–1929), *Diervilla lonicera* Mill. (5, 76, 156) (1896–1923) Oak Bay NB, *Hylotelephium telephium* (L.) H. Ohba. subsp. *telephium* (5, 74, 76, 156) (1993–1923) Concord MA, *Pseudognaphalium obtusifolium* (L.) Hilliard & Burtt subsp. *obtusifolium* (5, 73) (1892–1913) Stratham NH, *Sorbus americana* Marsh. (5) (1913)

Liferoot [Life-root, Life root] - *Packera aurea* (L.) A.& D. Löve (5, 6, 7, 48, 49, 52, 53, 54, 57, 58, 61, 156, 158) (1828-1923)

Life-root plant [Life root plant] - *Packera aurea* (L.) A.& D. Löve (92) (1876)

Light poppy-mallow [Light poppymallow, Light poppy mallow] - *Callirhoe alcaeoides* (Michx.) Gray (5, 50, 97, 122) (1913–present)

Light-blue wild hyacinth - *Camassia scilloides* (Raf.) Cory (65) (1931)

Light-green hedge nettle - *Stachys nuttallii* Shuttlw. ex Benth. (5) (1913)

Lighthouses [Light-houses] - *Amaranthus retroflexus* L. (77) (1898) Southold Long Island, from speed with which they tower above crops in the field

Light-o'-love - *Eriophorum* L. (156) (1923)

Lightwood [Light wood] - *Acacia melanoxylon* R. Br. ex Aiton f. (155) (1942)

Lignonberry [Lignon-berry] - *Vaccinium vitis-idaea* L. (156) (1923)

Lignum benedictum - *Guaiacum sanctum* L. (49) (1898)

Lignum sanctum - *Guaiacum sanctum* L. (49) (1898)

Lignum-vitae [Lignum vitae] or Lignum-vitae tree - *Guaiacum angustifolium* Engelm. (106) (1930), *Guaiacum* L. (13, 15) (1849-1895), *Guaiacum officinale* L. (7, 60, 92) (1828-1902), *Guaiacum sanctum* L. (49, 57) (1898-1917)

Liho (Basque) - *Linum usitatissimum* L. (110) (1886)

Lilac - *Ceanothus oliganthus* Nutt. (76) (1896) Santa Barbara CA, *Syringa* L. (1, 82, 109, 112, 138, 156) (1923-1937), *Syringa vulgaris* L. (possibly) (5, 7, 19, 63, 85, 97, 114, 184) (1793-1937)

Lilac aster - *Symphyotrichum lanceolatum* (Willd.) Nesom subsp. *hesperium* (Gray) Nesom (85) (1932) SD

Lilac bird-foot violet [Lilac birdsfoot violet] - *Viola pedata* L. (138, 155) (1923-1942)

Lilac chaste tree [Lilac chaste-tree [Lilac chastetree - *Vitex agnus-castus* L. (50, 138, 155) (1923–present)

Lilac penstemon - *Penstemon gracilis* Nutt. (50) (present), *Penstemon gracilis* Nutt. var. *gracilis* (50) (present)

Lilac sage - *Salvia verticillata* L. (138) (1923)

Lilaca - *Syringa vulgaris* L. (possibly) (92) (1876)

Lilac-flower aster [Lilac-flowered aster] - *Symphyotrichum concolor* (L.) Nesom (5) (1913)

Lilaeopsis - *Lilaeopsis chinensis* (L.) Kuntze (5, 72) (1907-1913)

Liliago - *Hemerocallis fulva* (L.) L. (180) (1633)

Lily [Lylly] - *Lilium candidum* L. (178, 179) (1526-1596), *Lilium* L. (1, 7, 10, 50, 93, 109, 138, 155, 156, 158, 167, 184) (1793–present)

Lily convallie [Lilly convallie] - *Uvularia sessilifolia* L. (46) (1671)

Lily-for-a-day [Lillie for a day] - *Hemerocallis fulva* (L.) L. (180) (1633)

Lily orchis - *Listera convallarioides* (Sw.) Nutt. ex Ell. (19) (1840)

Lily twaybalde - *Liparis loeselii* (L.) L.C. Rich (138) (1923)

Lily vine [Lily-vine] - *Calystegia sepium* (L.) R. Br. subsp. *sepium* (156) (1923) no longer in use by 1923

Lily-bind [Lily bind] - *Calystegia sepium* (L.) R. Br. subsp. *sepium* (5, 158) (1900–1913)

Lily-grass [Lily grass] - *Sisyrinchium* L. (7, 10) (1818-1828)

Lily-leaf malaxis [Lily-leaved malaxis] - *Liparis liliifolia* (L.) L.C. Rich. ex Ker-Gawl. (187) (1818)

Lily-of-the-valley [Lily of the valley] - *Convallaria* L. (2, 10, 50, 109, 138, 156, 158) (1818–present), *Convallaria majalis* L. (5, 7, 49, 52, 53, 54, 55, 57, 59, 60, 85, 92, 138, 148, 155, 156, 158) (1828-1942), *Maianthemum canadense* Desf. (73) (1892) NH

Lily-of-the-valley tree [Lily-of-the-valley-tree] - *Oxydendrum arboreum* (L.) DC. (156) (1923)

Lily-thorn [Lilythorn] - *Catesbaea* L. (138) (1923)

Lily-turf - *Liriope* Lour. (109) (1949), *Ophiopogon* Ker-Gawl. (109) (1949)

Lima bean - *Phaseolus lunatus* L. (19, 82, 107, 109, 138, 148) (1840-1949)

Lima haricot - *Phaseolus lunatus* L. (110) (1886)

Limber Bill - *Muhlenbergia glomerata* (Willd.) Trin. (45) (1896)

Limber honeysuckle - *Lonicera dioica* L. (4, 50, 138, 155, 156) (1923–present)

Limber pine - *Pinus flexilis* James (1, 3, 5, 17, 19, 50, 85, 109, 112, 122, 136, 138, 153, 155) (1796–present)

Limber-spine cactus [Limber-spined cactus] - *Opuntia polyacantha* Haw. var. *trichophora* (Engelm. & Bigelow) Coult. (97) (1937) OK

Lime grass - *Elymus villosus* Muhl. ex Willd. (19, 92) (1840-1876)

Lime grass [Lime-grass] - *Elymus* L. (184) (1793)

Lime or Lime tree [Lime-tree, Limetree] - *Citrus aurantifolia* (Christm.) Swingle (106, 109) (1930-1949), *Liriodendron tulipifera* L. (5, 156) (1913-1923), *Tilia americana* L. (121) (1918?-1970?), *Tilia americana* L. var. *heterophylla* (Vent.) Loud. (19, 92, 187) (1818-1876), *Tilia* L. (8, 10, 13, 15, 107, 109, 158, 167) (1785-1949), *Tilia petiolaris* DC. (106) (1930), *Tilia platyphyllos* Scop. (34) (1834)

Lime tree fruit - *Citrus limetta* Risso (92) (1876)

Limeberry [Lime-berry] - *Triphasia trifolia* (Burm. f.) P. Wilson (109) (1949)

Limestone adder's-tongue [Limestone adder's tongue, Limestone adderstongue] - *Ophioglossum engelmannii* Prantl. (4, 50) (1986–present)

Limestone calamint - *Clinopodium arkansanum* (Nutt.) House (50) (present)

Limestone meadow sedge - *Carex granularis* Muhl. ex Willd. (50) (present), *Carex granularis* Muhl. ex Willd. var. *haleana* (Olney) Porter (50) (present)

Limestone quillwort - *Isoetes butleri* Engelman (50) (present)

Limestone ruellia - *Ruellia strepens* L. (3, 4, 155) (1942-1986)

Limestone wild petunia - *Ruellia strepens* L. (50) (present)

Limewater brookweed - *Samolus ebracteatus* Kunth subsp. *cuneatus* (Small) R. Knuth (50) (present)

Lime-water brookweed [Limewater brookweed] - *Samolus ebracteatus* Kunth (50) (present)

Limewort - *Silene armeria* L. (156) (1923), *Silene* L. (86) (1878) beacause many species exude sticky substance like bird lime

Limewort catchfly - *Silene armeria* L. (5, 92) (1876-1913)

Limonilla - *Actinella odorata* (DC.) A.Gray (122, 158) (1900-1937)

Limonillo - *Hymenoxys odorata* DC. (5, 97) (1913-1937)

Limp manna grass [Limp mannagrass] - *Glyceria laxa* (Scribn.) Scribn. (50) (present)

Lin (Keltic) - *Linum usitatissimum* L. (110) (1886)

Lin tree - *Tilia americana* L. (5, 76) (1896-1913) Sulphur Grove OH

Linaire commune (French) - *Linaria vulgaris* Mill. (6, 158) (1892-1900)

Lincecum's grape - *Vitis aestivalis* Michx. var. *lincecumii* (Buckl.) Munson (124) (1937)

Linden bloodleaf - *Iresine lindenii* Van Houtte (138) (1923)

Linden flowers - *Tilia* ×*vulgaris* Hayne [*cordata* × *platyphyllos*] (92) (1876)

Linden hibiscus - *Hibiscus tiliaceus* L. (138) (1923)

Linden or Linden tree [Linden-tree] - *Tilia americana* L. (4, 41, 46, 49, 57, 65, 82, 106, 112, 121, 135) (1649-1986), *Tilia americana* L. var. *americana* (19, 92, 187) (1818-1876), *Tilia americana* L. var. *heterophylla* (Vent.) Loud. (5, 156) (1913-1923), *Tilia* L. (1, 2, 4, 7, 8, 10, 13, 15, 92, 93, 109, 122, 138, 155, 158) (1785-1986)

Linden viburnum - *Viburnum dilatatum* Thunb. (138) (1923)

Lindheimer's cassia - *Senna lindheimeriana* (Scheele) Irwin & Barneby (124) (1937)

Lindheimer's copperleaf [Lindheimer copperleaf] - *Acalypha phleoides* Cav. (155) (1942)

Lindheimer's croton - *Croton lindheimerianus* Scheele (5, 97) (1913-1937)

Lindheimer's daisy - *Lindheimera texana* Gray & Engelm. (124) (1937)

Lindheimer's globeberry - *Ibervillea lindheimeri* (Gray) Greene (50) (present)

Lindheimer's goldenrod [Lindheimer's golden-rod, Lindheimer goldenrod] - *Solidago petiolaris* Aiton var. *angusta* (Torr. & Gray) Gray (5, 97, 122, 155) (1913-1942)

Lindheimer's hogwort - *Croton capitatus* Michx. var. *lindheimeri* (Engelm. & Gray) Muell. (50) (present)

Lindheimer's ironweed - *Vernonia lindheimeri* Gray & Engelm. (124) (1937)

Lindheimer's lip fern [Lindheimer lipfern] - *Cheilanthes lindheimeri* (Sm.) Hook. (4, 155) (1942-1986)

Lindheimer's long-leaf eriogonum [Lindheimer's longleaf eriogonum] - *Eriogonum longifolium* Nutt. var. *longifolium* (4) (1986)

Lindheimer's milkvetch [Lindheimer milk vetch] - *Astragalus lindheimeri* Engelm. ex Gray (4) (1986)

Lindheimer's milkweed - *Asclepias oenotheroides* Cham. & Schlecht. (97) (1937)

Lindheimer's panic grass [Lindheimer panicgrass] - *Dichanthelium acuminatum* (Sw.) Gould & C.A. Clark var. *lindheimeri* (Nash) Gould & C.A. Clark (50, 163) (1852–present)

Lindheimer's panicum [Lindheimer panicum - *Dichanthelium acuminatum* (Sw.) Gould & C.A. Clark var. *lindheimeri* (Nash) Gould & C.A. Clark (5, 155) (1913-1942)

Lindley's aster [Lindley aster] - *Symphyotrichum ciliolatum* (Lindl.) A.& D. Löve (5, 50, 82, 131, 155) (1899–present)

Lindley's false spiraea [Lindley false-spiraea] - *Sorbaria sorbifolia* (L.) A. Braun (138) (1923)

Line tree - *Tilia americana* L. (46) (1671)

Linear gentian - *Gentiana linearis* Froel. (7) (1828)

Linear-leaf baccharis [Linearleaf baccharis, Linear-leaved baccharis] - *Baccharis salicina* Torr. & Gray (5, 93, 97, 122) (1913-1937)

Linear-leaf krameria [Linear-leaved krameria] - *Krameria lanceolata* Torr. (5, 97, 158) (1900-1937)

Linear-leaf lady's-tresses [Linear-leaved ladies' tresses, Linear-leaved ladies'-tresses] - *Spiranthes vernalis* Engelm. & Gray (5, 97) (1913-1937)

Linear-leaf loosestrife [Linear-leaved loosestrife] - *Lysimachia quadrifolia* L. (5, 158) (1900–1913), *Lythrum lineare* L. (5) (1913)

Linear-leaf ludwigea [Linear-leaved ludwigea] - *Ludwigia linearis* Walt. (5) (1913)

Linear-leaf milkweed [Linear-leaved milkweed] - *Asclepias linearis* Scheele (97) (1937)

Linear-leaf panicum [Linear-leaved panicum] - *Dichanthelium commutatum* (J.A. Schultes) Gould (72) (1907), *Dichanthelium linearifolium* (Scribn. ex Nash) Gould (56) (1901)

Linear-leaf sunflower [Linear-leaved sunflower] - *Helianthus salicifolius* A. Dietr. (5, 93, 97) (1913-1937)

Linear-leaf willow [Linear-leaved willow] - *Salix exigua* Nutt. (97) (1937)

Linear-leaf willow herb [Linear-leaved willow herb, Linear-leaved willow-herb] - *Epilobium palustre* L. (5, 42, 72, 93, 187) (1814-1936)

Linear-leaf wormwood [Linear-leaved wormwood] - *Artemisia dracunculus* L. (5, 72, 93, 97, 122) (1907-1937)

Lined sedge - *Carex striatula* Michx. (50) (present)

Ling - *Calluna vulgaris* (L.) Hull (5, 92, 156) (1876-1923), *Trapa natans* L. (107) (1919)

Lingberry [Ling-berry, Ling berry] - *Vaccinium vitis-idaea* L. (5, 156) (1913-1923)

Lingenberry [Lingen-berry] - *Vaccinium vitis-idaea* L. (156) (1923)

Ling-gowan [Ling gowans] - *Hieracium murorum* L. (156) (1923) no longer in use by 1923, *Hieracium pilosella* L. (5) (1913)

Lingwort - *Hudsonia ericoides* L. (46) (1649)

Link blackberry - *Rubus linkianus* Ser. (138) (1923)

Linn [Lynn] - *Linum usitatissimum* L. (156) (1923)

Linn [Lynn] or Linn tree [Linn-tree] - *Liriodendron tulipifera* L. (156) (1923), *Tilia americana* L. (35, 49, 156) (1806-1923), *Tilia* L. (124) (1937)

Linna amorilla (Spanish) - *Mahonia pinnata* (Lag.) Fedde subsp. *pinnata* (14, 147) (1856-1882) Mexico

Linn-wahoo - *Tilia americana* L. var. *heterophylla* (Vent.) Loud. (156) (1923)

Linnwood - *Tilia americana* L. (156) (1923)

Lino (Basque) - *Linum usitatissimum* L. (110) (1886)

Linseed - *Linum usitatissimum* L. (5, 53, 57, 59, 92, 95, 156, 157) (1876–1929)

Lint - *Linum usitatissimum* L. (156, 158) (1900-1923)

Lintbells [Lint-bells, Lint bells] - *Linum usitatissimum* L. (5, 97, 156, 158) (1900–1937)

Linum - *Linum usitatissimum* L. (59) (1911)

Lion's-beard [Lion's beard, Lions'beard] - *Clematis hirsutissima* Pursh (101) (1905), *Clematis* L. (1) (1932), *Pulsatilla* Mill. (1) (1932)

Lion's-ear [Lions' ear, Lion ears, Lion's ear, Lions-ear] - *Leonotis* (Pers.) Aiton f. (109, 138) (1923–1949), *Leonotis leonurus* (L.) Aiton f. (138) (1923), *Leonurus cardiaca* L. (5, 92, 156, 157, 158) (1876–1929)

Lion's-foot [Lion's foot, Lions' foot, Lyons fote] - *Alchemilla* L. (179) (1526), *Antennaria parviflora* Nutt. (157) (1929), *Helleborus niger* L. (179) (1526), *Prenanthes alba* L. (5, 49, 61, 92, 156, 158) (1870-1923), *Prenanthes aspera* Michx. (157) (1929), *Prenanthes* L. (7) (1828), *Prenanthes serpentaria* Pursh (5, 92) (1876-1913)

Lion's-head [Lion's head, Lion head] - *Leonotis nepetifolia* (L.) Aiton f. (122, 124) (1937) TX

Lion's-heart [Lion's heart, Lionsheart, Lyonsheart] - *Dracocephalum parviflorum* Nutt. (156) (1923), *Physostegia* Benth. (4, 50, 155, 158) (1900–present), *Physostegia virginiana* (L.) Benth. (5, 156, 158) (1900-1923), *Sonchus asper* (L.) Hill (29) (1869)

Lion's-leaf - *Caulophyllum* Michx. (158) (1900)

Lion's-mouth [Lion's mouth, Lion mouth] - *Antirrhinum majus* L. (5, 73, 156, 158) (1892-1923) Mansfield OH, *Digitalis pupurea* L. (5, 69, 156) (1903-1923) no longer in use by 1923

Lion's-snap [Lion's snap] - *Antirrhinum majus* L. (5, 92, 156, 158) (1876-1923)

Lion's-tail [Lion's tail, Lions' tail, Lionstail, Lions-tail] - *Chaitu-*

rus marrubiastrum (L.) Reichenb. (5, 50) (1913–present), *Chaiturus* Willd. (50) (present), *Leonurus cardiaca* L. (7, 92, 156, 157, 158, 184) (1793-1929), *Leonurus* L. (158) (1900), *Leonurus sibiricus* L. (5) (1913)

Lion's-tongue [Lion's tongue] - *Chimaphila maculata* (L.) Pursh (156) (1923)

Lion's-tooth [Lion's tooth, Lions' tooth] - *Leontodon autumnalis* L. (5, 156) (1913-1923), *Taraxacum officinale* G.H. Weber ex Wiggers (5, 82, 157, 158) (1900-1930)

Lion's-turtlehead [Lyon's turtle head] - *Chelone lyonii* Pursh (5) (1913)

Lip fern [Lipfern, Lip-fern] - *Cheilanthes feei* T. Moore (3, 72) (1907-1977), *Cheilanthes lanosa* (Michx.) D.C.Eat. (19) (1840), *Cheilanthes* Sw. (1, 4, 50, 138, 155, 158) (1900–present)

Lippia - *Lippia* L. (138, 155) (1923-1942), *Phyla nodiflora* (L.) Greene (106) (1930)

Lippia mexicana - *Phyla scaberrima* (Juss.) Moldenke (57) (1917)

Liquidambar (French) - *Liquidambar* L. (8) (1785)

Liquidambar [Liquidamber] - *Liquidambar* L. (8) (1785), *Liquidambar styraciflua* L. (5, 57, 156) (1913-1923)

Liquidambar à feuilles de Cétérach (French) - *Comptonia peregrina* (L.) Coult. (8) (1785)

Liquidambar à feuilles d'erable (French) - *Liquidambar styraciflua* L. (8) (1785)

Liria Americana (Spanish) - *Iris versicolor* L. (158) (1900)

Liricon-fancy - *Convallaria majalis* L. (158) (1900)

Lirio Amarillo (Spanish) - *Lilium martagon* L. (180) (1633)

Lirio blanco (Spanish) - *Lilium candidum* L. (180) (1633)

Lirionconfancie - *Hemerocallis fulva* (L.) L. (180) (1633)

Liris de los valles (Spanish) - *Convallaria majalis* L. (158) (1900)

Lischdoden (Dutch) - *Iris* L. (180) (1633), *Typha* L. (180) (1633)

Liseron Mechamec (French) - *Ipomoea pandurata* (L.) G.F.W. Mey. (7) (1828)

Litchnidia - *Phlox maculata* L. (79) (1891) NH

Lithy tree - *Viburnum lantana* L. (92) (1876)

Litmus - *Roccella tinctoria* DC. (49, 92) (1876-1879)

Little barley - *Hordeum pusillum* Nutt. (3, 5, 50, 56, 72, 80, 93, 94, 119, 122, 134, 140, 155, 163) (1852–present)

Little bladderwort - *Utricularia gibba* L. (40) (1928), *Utricularia minor* L. (95) (1911)

Little blue-star ageratum [Little bluestar ageratum] - *Ageratum conyzoides* L. (138) (1923)

Little bluestem [Little blue stem, Little blue-stem] - *Schizachyrium* Nees (50) (present), *Schizachyrium scoparium* (Michx.) Nash (50) (present), *Schizachyrium scoparium* (Michx.) Nash var. *divergens* (Hack.) Gould (122) (1937), *Schizachyrium scoparium* (Michx.) Nash var. *scoparium* (3, 11, 22, 50, 56, 65, 85, 93, 94, 98, 111, 115, 119, 124, 129, 134, 140, 144, 146, 155, 163) (1852–present)

Little boy's-breeches [Little boys' breeches, Little boy's breeches] - *Dicentra cucullaria* (L.) Bernh. (5, 74, 156, 158) (1893-1923)

Little breadroot scurfpea [Little breadroot scurf pea] - *Pediomelum hypogaeum* (Nutt. ex Torr. & Gray) Rydb. var. *hypogaeum* (3, 4) (1977-1986)

Little buckeye - *Aesculus glabra* Willd. (19) (1840), *Aesculus pavia* L. (5, 92, 156) (1876-1923)

Little buckthorn - *Condalia ericoides* (Gray) M.C. Johnston (122) (1937) TX

Little bur [Lytell burre] - *Arctium* L. (179) (1526)

Little clubmoss [Little club-moss] - *Selaginella* Beauv. (1, 10, 19) (1818-1932)

Little cord grass - *Spartina gracilis* Trin. (111, 129) (1894-1915)

Little crabgrass [Little crab-grass, Little crab grass] - *Setaria italica* (L.) Beauv. (94) (1901)

Little cryptantha - *Cryptantha minima* Rydb. (50) (present)

Little curly-grass fern [Little curlygrass fern] - *Schizaea pusilla* Pursh (50) (present)

Little daisy [Little daysi (sic)] - *Bellis perennis* L. (190) (~1759)

Little Dalmatian Flower-de-luce [Little Dalmatian Flowerdeluce] - *Iris pallida* Lam. (178) (1596)

Little duckweed - *Lemna obscura* (Austin) Daubs (50) (present)

Little ebony - *Asplenium resiliens* Kunze. (5) (1913)

Little French flower-de-luce [Little French flowerdeluce] - *Iris spuria* L. (178) (1596)

Little glasswort [Little glassewoort] - *Suaeda maritima* (L.) Dumort. (178) (1526)

Little grape fern [Little grape-fern] - *Botrychium simplex* E. Hitchcock. (4, 5, 50) (1913–present)

Little green sedge - *Carex viridula* Michx. (50) (present), *Carex viridula* Michx. subsp. *brachyrrhyncha* (Celak.) B. Schmid var. *elatior* (Schlecht.) Crins (50) (present), *Carex viridula* Michx. subsp. *viridula* (50) (present)

Little gromell - *Lithospermum officinale* L. (178) (1526)

Little ground-rose [Little ground rose] - *Chamaerhodos erecta* (L.) Bunge (4) (1986)

Little hogweed - *Portulaca oleracea* L. (50) (present)

Little houseleek [Little house leek] - *Sedum acre* L. (5, 156) (1913-1923)

Little Johnnies - *Gaultheria procumbens* L. (75) (1894) Calais ME

Little lady's-tresses [Little ladies' tresses, Little ladiestresses, Little ladies'-tresses] - *Spiranthes lacera* (Raf.) Raf. var. *gracilis* (Bigelow) Luer (5, 122) (1913-1937), *Spiranthes tuberosa* Raf. (3, 5, 50) (1913–present)

Little larkspur - *Delphinium bicolor* Nutt. (4, 50, 155) (1942–present)

Little love grass [Little lovegrass] - *Eragrostis minor* Host (3, 50) (1977–present)

Little mallow - *Malva parviflora* L. (155) (1942)

Little medic - *Medicago minima* L. (155) (1942)

Little merry-bells [Little merrybells] - *Uvularia sessilifolia* L. (138, 155) (1923-1942)

Little mile - *Lithospermum officinale* L. (156) (1923) no longer in use by 1923

Little mountain-rice [Little mountain rice] - *Piptatheropsis exigua* (Thurb.) Romasch., P.M. Peterson & R.J. Soreng (94) (1901)

Little mouse-tail [Little mouse tail] - *Myosurus minimus* L. (5) (1913)

Little mustard - *Lepidium ruderale* L. (178) (1526)

Little nipple cactus - *Mammillaria heyderi* Muehlenpfordt (50) (present)

Little pansy - *Viola pedata* L. (156) (1923)

Little penstemon - *Penstemon procerus* Dougl. ex Grah. (50) (present)

Little pignut - *Carya glabra* (Mill.) Sweet (5) (1913)

Little plantain [Lytell plantayn] - *Plantago lanceolata* L. (179) (1526)

Little pollom - *Polygala paucifolia* Willd. (5, 7, 92, 156) (1828-1923)

Little prickly pear - *Opuntia fragilis* (Nutt.) Haw. (4) (1986)

Little prickly sedge - *Carex echinata* Murr. subsp. *echinata* (5) (1913), *Carex muricata* L. (66) (1903), *Carex sterilis* Willd. (72) (1907)

Little quaking grass - *Briza minor* L. (50, 138) (1923–present)

Little rattlepod [Little rattle-pod, Little rattle pod] - *Astragalus canadensis* L. (121) (1918?-1970?), *Astragalus canadensis* L. var. *canadensis* (37, 127) (1919-1933)

Little rattlepot - *Rhinanthus* L. (155) (1942)

Little red elephant - *Pedicularis* L. (1) (1932)

Little rhubarb [Little Rubarbe] - *Thalictrum hultenii* Boivin (178) (1526)

Little rice grass [Little ricegrass] - *Piptatheropsis exigua* (Thurb.) Romasch., P.M. Peterson & R.J. Soreng (50, 155) (1942–present)

Little rose - *Chamaerhodos* Bunge (50) (present), *Chamaerhodos erecta* (L.) Bunge (50) (present), *Chamaerhodos erecta* (L.) Bunge subsp. *nuttallii* (Pickering ex Rydb.) Hultén (3) (1977)

Little rye grass - *Elymus villosus* Muhl. ex Willd. (119) (1938) OK

Little sage - *Artemisia frigida* Willd. (121, 127) (1918?–1970?)

Little sage brush - *Artemisia cana* Pursh (113, 130) (1890–1895)

Little shagbark - *Carya glabra* (Mill.) Sweet (5) (1913), *Carya glabra* (Mill.) Sweet var. *glabra* (156) (1923)

Little skullcap - *Scutellaria parvula* Michx. (5) (1913)

Little snakeweed [Little snake weed] - *Elodea canadensis* Michx. (19) (1840)

Little snowball [Little snow-ball] - *Cephalanthus occidentalis* L. (5, 7, 92, 156, 158) (1828-1923)

Little spleenwort - *Asplenium exiguum* Bedd. (50) (present)

Little staggerweed [Little stagger-weed] - *Dicentra cucullaria* (L.) Bernh. (156) (1923)

Little sunflower - *Helianthus pumilus* Nutt. (50) (present)

Little violet flower-de-luce [Little violet flowerdeluce] - *Iris pumila* L. (178) (1596)

Little walnut - *Juglans microcarpa* Berl. (4, 50, 97) (1937–present)

Little washerwoman - *Houstonia caerulea* L. (5, 76, 156) (1896-1923) Bethlehem PA, no longer in use by 1923

Little waterlily [Little water-lily, Little water lily] - *Brasenia schreberi* Gmel. (5, 7, 92, 156) (1828-1923)

Little white bird's-foot [Little white bird's foot] - *Ornithopus perpusillus* L. (50) (present)

Little wild sage - *Artemisia frigida* Willd. (37) (1919)

Little-apple [Little apple] - *Arctostaphylos andersonii* Gray (77) (1898) CA

Little-berry manzanita [Littleberry manzanita] - *Arctostaphylos nummularia* Gray (155) (1942)

Little-flower agoseris [Littleflower agoseris] - *Agoseris glauca* (Pursh) Raf. (155) (1942)

Little-flower collinsia [Littleflower collinsia] - *Collinsia parviflora* Lindl. (155) (1942)

Little-flower penstemon [Littleflower penstemon] - *Penstemon procerus* Dougl. ex Grah. (155) (1942)

Little-flower quickweed [Littleflower quickweed] - *Galinsoga parviflora* Cav. (155) (1942)

Little-good [Little good, Littlegood] - *Euphorbia helioscopia* L. (5, 82) (1913-1930)

Little-head nutrush [Littlehead nutrush] - *Scleria oligantha* Michx. (50) (present)

Little-leaf buttercup [Littleleaf buttercup] - *Ranunculus abortivus* L. (50, 155) (1942–present)

Little-leaf European linden [Littleleaf European linden] - *Tilia cordata* Mill. (138) (1923)

Little-leaf Japanese holly [Littleleaf Japanese holly] - *Ilex crenata* Thunb. (138) (1923)

Little-leaf mint [Littleleaf mint] - *Mentha ×gracilis* Sole [*arvensis × spicata*] (155) (1942)

Little-leaf mock orange [Littleleaf mockorange] - *Philadelphus microphyllus* Gray (138) (1923)

Little-leaf pussytoes [Littleleaf pussytoes] - *Antennaria microphylla* Rydb. (50, 155) (1942–present)

Little-leaf rockcress [Littleleaf rockcress] - *Arabis microphylla* Nutt. (155) (1942)

Little-leaf sensitive-brier [Littleleaf sensitive-briar, Littleleaf sensitivebrier] - *Mimosa microphylla* Dry. (50, 155) (1942–present)

Little-leaf sumac [Littleleaf sumac] - *Rhus microphylla* Engelm. (50, 155) (1942–present)

Little-leaf tickclover [Littleleaf tickclover] - *Desmodium ciliare* (Muhl. ex Willd.) DC. (155) (1942)

Little-nut shagbark hickory [Littlenut shagbark hickory] - *Carya ovata* (Mill.) K. Koch (155) (1942)

Little-pod false flax [Littlepod falseflax, Littlepod false flax] - *Camelina microcarpa* DC. (50, 155) (1942–present)

Little-seed alfalfa dodder [Littleseed alfalfa dodder] - *Cuscuta approxima* Bab. (155) (1942)

Little-seed paspalum [Littleseed paspalum] - *Paspalum setaceum* Michx. (155) (1942)

Little-seed ricegrass [Littleseed ricegrass - *Piptatherum micranthum* (Trin. & Rupr.) Barkworth (3, 50, 155) (1942–present)

Little-snout sedge [Littlesnout sedge] - *Carex microrhyncha* Mack. (50) (present), *Carex microdonta* T. & H. (3, 50) (1977–present)

Little-wale [Littlewale] - *Lithospermum officinale* L. (5) (1913)

Live oak [Live oake, Live-oak] - *Quercus arizonica* Sargent (149, 153) (1904-1919), *Quercus fusiformis* Small (4) (1986), *Quercus grisea* Liebm. (153) (1913) NM, *Quercus laurifolia* Michx. (7) (1828), *Quercus oblongifolia* Torr. (75, 107, 149, 153) (1894-1919), *Quercus virginiana* Mill. (2, 3, 5, 10, 14, 19, 20, 33, 92, 97, 106, 107, 124, 138, 156, 181, 182) (~1678-1977)

Live-forever [Liveforever, Live forever] - *Anaphalis margaritacea* (L.) Benth. & Hook (46) (1879), *Hylotelephium telephium* (L.) H. Ohba. subsp. *telephium* (5, 19, 63, 82, 92, 156) (1840-1930), *Pseudognaphalium obtusifolium* (L.) Hilliard & Burtt subsp. *obtusifolium* (92) (1876), *Sedum* L. (93) (1936), *Sedum ternatum* Michx. (2) (1895)

Live-forever stonecrop [Liveforever stonecrop] - *Hylotelephium telephium* (L.) H. Ohba. subsp. *telephium* (155) (1942)

Live-long [Live long] - *Aloe vera* (L.) Burm. f. (178) (1596), *Anaphalis margaritacea* (L.) Benth. & Hook (156, 158) (1900-1923), *Hylotelephium telephium* (L.) H. Ohba. subsp. *telephium* (5, 92, 156) (1876-1923)

Live-long saxifrage [Livelong saxifrage] - *Saxifraga paniculata* Mill. subsp. *neogaea* (Butters) D. Löve (5, 156) (1913-1923)

Liver mushroom - *Boletus hepaticus* Schaeff. (possibly) (92) (1876)

Liverberry [Liver-berry, Liver berry] - *Disporum lanuginosum* (Michx.) Nichols (156) (1923), *Streptopus amplexifolius* (L.) DC. (5, 75) (1894-1913) ME, from said medicinal properties of cathartic fruit, *Streptopus lanceolatus* (Ait.) Reveal var. *roseus* (Michx.) Reveal (5, 75) (1894-1913) ME, *Uvularia* L. (158) (1900)

Liverleaf [Liver-leaf, Liver leaf] - *Hepatica* Mill. (1, 2, 7, 13, 15, 82, 109) (1828-1949), *Hepatica nobilis* Schreb. (53, 82, 156) (1922-1930), *Hepatica nobilis* Schreb. var. *obtusa* (Pursh) Steyermark (6, 49, 61, 92) (1870-1898)

Liver-leaf wintergreen [Liverleaf wintergreen, Liver-leafed wintergreen] - *Pyrola asarifolia* Michx. (5, 50, 85, 156) (1913–present)

Liver-lily [Liver lilly, Liver lily] - *Iris versicolor* L. (5, 6, 49, 64, 92, 156, 157, 158) (1892-1929)

Liver-moss [Livermoss, Liver moss] - *Hepatica nobilis* Schreb. (156) (1923), *Hepatica nobilis* Schreb. var. *obtusa* (Pursh) Steyermark (5, 92) (1876-1913)

Liverweed [Liver-weed, Liver weed] - *Hepatica nobilis* Schreb. (7) (1828), *Hepatica nobilis* Schreb. var. *obtusa* (Pursh) Steyermark (6, 92) (1876-1892)

Liverwort [Liver-wort, Liver wort] - *Agrimonia eupatoria* L. (107) (1919), *Hepatica* Mill. (156) (1923), *Hepatica nobilis* Schreb. (53, 79, 92, 156, 190) (~1759-1923) Northeastern US, *Hepatica nobilis* Schreb. var. *acuta* (Pursh) Steyermark (102) (1886), *Hepatica nobilis* Schreb. var. *obtusa* (Pursh) Steyermark (6, 42, 49, 57, 92) (1814-1917), *Marchantia polymorpha* L. (92) (1876)

Liverwort lettuce - *Pyrola americana* Sweet (5, 156, 158) (1900-1923)

Livid amaranth - *Amaranthus blitum* L. (165) (1768)

Livid sedge - *Carex livida* (Wahl.) Willd. (5, 50, 66) (1912–present)

Livid willow - *Salix bebbiana* Sargent (5) (1913)

Living-rock [Livingrock, Living rock] - *Ariocarpus fissuratus* (Engelm.) K. Schum. (109, 122, 138) (1923-1949), *Ariocarpus* Scheidw. (138, 155) (1931-1942)

Living-rock cactus [Livingrockcactus] - *Ariocarpus* Scheidw. (155) (1942)

L'Ivraie (French) - *Agrostemma githago* L. (6) (1892)

Lizard's-tail [Lizards' tail, Lizards-tail, Lizard's tail, Lizard-tail, Lizard tail, Lizardtail] - *Saururus cernuus* L. (1, 4, 5, 7, 10, 19, 92, 97, 106, 120, 156, 158) (1818-1986), *Saururus* L. (1, 2, 109, 138, 155, 158, 167, 184) (1793-1942)

Lizard-tail grass [Lizard-tail-grass] - *Hackelochloa granularis* (L.) Kuntze (93, 94, 163) (1852-1936)

Llewellyn - *Veronica officinalis* L. (158) (1900)

Lloyd's clubmoss [Lloyd's club-moss] - *Huperzia porophila* (Lloyd & Underwood) Holub (5) (1913)

Llygad yr ych - *Anthemis cotula* L. (186) (1814)

Loasa - *Mentzelia laevicaulis* (Dougl. ex Hook.) Torr. & Gray (157) (1929)

Loaves-of-bread - *Hyoscyamus niger* L. (158) (1900)

Lob grass - *Bromus hordeaceus* L. (5) (1913), *Bromus hordeaceus* L. subsp. *hordeaceus* (92) (1876)

Lobeberry [Lobe berry] - *Coccoloba uvifera* (L.) L. (92) (1876)

Lobed cudweed [Lobed cud-weed] - *Artemisia ludoviciana* Nutt. (72) (1907)

Lobed spleenwort - *Asplenium pinnatifidum* Nutt. (50) (present)

Lobed tickseed - *Coreopsis auriculata* L. (5) (1913)

Lobelia - *Lobelia inflata* L. (49, 52, 53, 54, 55, 57, 59, 60, 69, 92, 157, 158) (1876-1922), *Lobelia* L. (1, 50, 82, 93, 107, 138, 158) (1900–present) for Matthias de Lobel or L'obel, 1538-1616, Flemish botanist and author

Lobelia - *Lobelia spicata* Lam. (126, 127) (1933)

Lobelie (German) - *Lobelia inflata* L. (6) (1892)

Lobélie cardinale (French) - *Lobelia cardinalis* L. (6, 186) (1814-1892)

Lobélie enflée (French) - *Lobelia inflata* L. (6, 7, 158) (1828-1900)

Lobelie siphylitique (French) - *Lobelia siphilitica* L. (186) (1814)

Lobelienkraut (German) - *Lobelia inflata* L. (158) (1900)

Loblolly - *Pinus taeda* L. (92) (1876)

Loblolly bay [Lobblolly bay, Loblolly-bay] - *Gordonia* Ell. (13, 15, 156) (1849-1923), *Gordonia lasianthus* (L.) Ellis (2, 5, 13, 12, 5, 20, 46, 109, 138, 156, 189) (1767-1949)

Loblolly pine - *Pinus taeda* L. (2, 50, 97, 109, 122, 138) (1895–present)

Lobularia - *Lobularia* Desv. (50) (present)

Ločipišni pežixota (Lakota, gray appetite herb) - *Astragalus canadensis* L. (121) (1918?-1970?)

Lock elm - *Ulmus procera* Salisb. (138) (1923)

Lock-hair fern - *Adiantum pedatum* L. (5) (1913)

Loco - *Astragalus* L. (148, 155) (1939-1942), *Astragalus mollissimus* Torr (96) (1891), *Oxytropis lambertii* Pursh (76) (1896)

Loco plant - *Astragalus mollissimus* Torr (157, 158) (1900-1929)

Loco vetch - *Oxytropis lambertii* Pursh (133) (1903), *Oxytropis splendens* Dougl. ex Hook (133) (1903)

Locoweed [Loco weed, Loco-weed] - *Astragalus canadensis* L. (121) (1970), *Astragalus* L. (1, 106) (1930–1932) loco from Spanish for crazy from symptoms of poisoning in horses, *Astragalus mollissimus* Torr (71, 76, 124, 150) (1894–1937), *Astragalus racemosus* Pursh (121) (1970), *Astragalus sericoleucus* Gray (95) (1911), *Crotalaria sagittalis* L. (5, 76, 156, 157, 158) (1896–1929), *Oxytropis* DC. (4, 45, 50, 82, 93, 156) (1896–present), *Oxytropis deflexa* (Pallas) DC. (85) (1932), *Oxytropis lambertii* Pursh (71, 76, 82, 85, 95, 126, 127, 133, 156) (1896–1933), *Oxytropis splendens* Dougl. ex Hook (133) (1903), *Sphaerophysa salsula* (Pallas) DC. (131) (1899)

Locus tree - *Robinia pseudoacacia* L. (181) (~1678)

Locust bean - *Ceratonia siliqua* L. (92) (1876)

Locust bloom - *Tilia ×vulgaris* Hayne [*cordata × platyphyllos*] (92) (1876)

Locust mesquit - *Prosopis juliflora* (Sw.) DC. (158) (1900)

Locust or Locust tree - *Ceratonia siliqua* L. (178) (1526), *Gleditsia* L. (50) (present), *Robinia* L. (1, 2, 4, 10, 50, 82, 155, 156, 158, 184) (1793–present), *Robinia pseudoacacia* L. (5, 8, 14, 19, 20, 41, 49, 92, 106, 107, 157, 158) (1785-1930)

Locust plant [Locust-plant] - *Senna marilandica* (L.) Link (7, 92, 156, 157, 158) (1828–1929)

Locust thorn - *Gleditsia triacanthos* L. (158) (1900)

Locust tree of Virginia - *Robinia pseudoacacia* L. (189) (1767)

Locust-berry [Locust berry] - *Byrsonima spicata* (Cav.) Kunth (92) (1876)

Loddiges' rattlesnake-plantain [Loddiges' rattlesnake plantain] - *Goodyera tesselata* Lodd. (5) (1913)

Lodgepole lupine - *Lupinus parviflorus* Nutt. ex Hook. & Arn. (50, 155) (1942–present)

Lodgepole pine [Lodge-pole pine] - *Pinus contorta* Dougl. ex Loud. (3, 50) (1977–present), *Pinus contorta* Dougl. ex Loud. var. *latifolia* Engelm. ex Wats (1, 85, 101, 112, 136, 138, 155) (1886-1942)

Loeflingia - *Loeflingia* L. (50, 158) (1900–present)

Loesel's twayblade [Loesel twayblade] - *Liparis loeselii* (L.) L.C. Rich (3, 5, 138) (1913-1977)

Lofty fig - *Ficus altissima* Blume (138) (1923)

Loggerheads [Logger-heads] - *Centaurea nigra* L. (5, 92, 156) (1876-1923) no longer in use by 1923

Logwood - *Haematoxylum campechianum* L. (106, 138) (1923-1930), *Haematoxylum* L. (7, 138) (1828-1923)

Lolch (German) - *Lolium temulentum* L. (158) (1900)

Lomatium - *Lomatium* Raf. (155) (1942)

Lombardy poplar - *Populus nigra* L. (4, 19, 50, 85, 109, 112, 158) (1840–present)

Lombardy star thistle - *Centaurea melitensis* L. (106) (1930) Southeast

Lompoc manzanita - *Arctostaphylos viridissima* (Eastw.) McMinn (155) (1942)

London lace [London-lace] - *Phalaris arundinacea* L. (5, 158) (1900-1913)

London plane - *Platanus hybrida* Brot. (109) (1949) variegated variety

London pride [London-pride] - *Dianthus barbatus* L. (5, 156) (1913–1923), *Lychnis chalcedonica* L. (79) (1891) Northeastern US, *Saponaria officinalis* L. (5, 64, 73, 156, 157, 158) (1892–1929) Salem MA

London rocket - *Sisymbrium irio* L. (4, 50) (1986–present), *Sisymbrium* L. (4, 50) (1986–present)

London tuft - *Dianthus barbatus* L. (5, 156) (1913-1923)

Long beech-fern - *Phegopteris connectilis* (Michx.) Watt (5, 72, 109) (1907-1949)

Long cloak fern [Long cloak-fern] - *Astrolepis sinuata* (Lag. ex Sw.) Benham & Windham subsp. *sinuata* (50) (present)

Long moss - *Tillandsia* L. (10, 167) (1814-1818), *Tillandsia usneoides* (L.) L. (2, 5, 92, 156, 812) (1791-1923)

Long pepper - *Capsicum annuum* L. (109) (1949)

Long plantain [Longe plantayn] - *Plantago lanceolata* L. (5, 156, 158, 179) (1526-1923)

Long purples [Long-purples] - *Lythrum salicaria* L. (156, 158) (1900-1923), *Platanthera grandiflora* (Bigelow) Lindl. (156) (1923) no longer in use by 1923

Long rough-fruit poppy [Long rough-fruited poppy] - *Papaver argemone* L. (5) (1913)

Long sedge - *Carex folliculata* L. (5) (1913)

Long smooth-fruit poppy [Long smooth-fruited poppy] - *Papaver dubium* L. (5, 158) (1900–1913)

Long-acorn oak [Long-acorned oak] - *Quercus lobata* Née (161) (1857)

Long-awn aristida [Long-awned aristida] - *Aristida purpurea* Nutt. var. *longiseta* (Steud.) Vasey (5, 163) (1852-1913)

Long-awn barnyard grass [Long-awned barnyard-grass] - *Echinochloa walteri* (Pursh) Nash (119) (1938)

Long-awn diplachne [Long-awned diplachne] - *Leptochloa fusca* (L.) Kunth subsp. *fascicularis* (Lam.) N. Snow (5) (1913)

Long-awn hair grass [Long-awned hair-grass] - *Muhlenbergia capillaris* (Lam.) Trin. (5, 119, 163) (1852-1938)

Long-awn needle grass [Long-awned needlegrass] - *Aristida purpurea* Nutt. var. *longiseta* (Steud.) Vasey (152) (1912)

Long-awn poverty grass [Long-awned poverty grass, Long-awned poverty-grass] - *Aristida tuberculosa* Nutt. (5, 56, 66, 80, 94, 111) (1901-1915)

Long-awn vernal grass [Long-awned vernal grass] - *Anthoxanthum aristatum* Boiss. (5) (1913)

Long-awn Virginia wild rye [Longawn Virginia wildrye] - *Elymus virginicus* L. var. *virginicus* (155) (1942)

Long-awn wild rye [Long-awned wild rye] - *Elymus* L. (93) (1936)

Long-barb arrowhead [Longbarb arrowhead] - *Sagittaria latifolia*

Willd. (3) (1977), *Sagittaria longiloba* Engelm. ex J.G. Sm. (50, 138, 155) (1923–present)

Long-beak arrowhead [Long-beaked arrow-head, Longbeak arrowhead] - *Sagittaria latifolia* Willd. (5, 50, 72, 97, 155) (1907–present)

Long-beak baldrush [Long-beaked bald rush] - *Rhynchospora scirpoides* (Torr.) Gray (5) (1913)

Long-beak beaksedge [Longbeak beaksedge] - *Rhynchospora scirpoides* (Torr.) Gray (50) (present)

Long-beak buttercup [Longbeak buttercup] - *Ranunculus longirostris* Godr. (50, 155) (1942–present)

Long-beak pedicularis [Long-beaked pedicularis] - *Pedicularis groenlandica* Retz. (5) (1913)

Long-beak sedge [Long-beaked sedge] - *Carex sprengelii* Dewey ex Spreng. (3, 5, 66, 72) (1903-1977)

Long-beak willow [Long-beaked willow] - *Salix bebbiana* Sargent (3) (1977)

Longbeard [Long beard] - *Tillandsia usneoides* (L.) L. (5, 156) (1913-1923)

Long-beard broom sedge [Long-bearded broom sedge] - *Andropogon longiberbis* Hack. (94) (1901)

Long-beard hawkweed [Long-bearded hawkweed] - *Hieracium longipilum* Torr. (3, 5, 63, 72, 93, 97, 122) (1899-1977)

Long-beard moss [Long-bearded moss] - *Usnea florida* (L.) F. H. Wigg. (100) (1850) TX

Long-bract frog orchid [Longbract frog orchid] - *Coeloglossum viride* (L.) Hartman (50) (present)

Long-bract orchis [Long-bracted orchis] - *Coeloglossum viride* (L.) Hartman var. *virescens* (Muhl. ex Willd.) Luer (3, 5, 72, 93, 156, 158) (1907-1977)

Long-bract sedge [Long-bracted sedge] - *Carex extensa* Goodenough (5, 50) (1913–present)

Long-bract spiderwort [Long-bracted spiderwort] - *Tradescantia bracteata* Small ex Britt. (5, 10, 14, 50, 93) (1840–present)

Long-bract tickseed sunflower [Long-bracted tickseed sunflower] - *Bidens aristosa* (Michx.) Britton (5, 72, 82, 93, 97) (1907-1937)

Long-bract wild indigo [Longbract wild indigo] - *Baptisia bracteata* Muhl. ex Ell. (50) (present), *Baptisia bracteata* Muhl. ex Ell. var. *leucophaea* (Nutt.) Kartesz & Gandhi (4, 50) (1986–present)

Long-branch frostweed [Long-branched frostweed, Long-branched frost-weed] - *Helianthemum canadense* (L.) Michx. (5, 156) (1913-1923)

Long-bristle Indian grass [Long-bristled Indian-grass, Long-bristled Indian grass] - *Sorghastrum elliottii* (C. Mohr) Nash (5, 163) (1852-1913)

Long-bristle wild rye [Long-bristled wild rye, Long-bristled wild-rye] - *Elymus elymoides* (Raf.) Swezey subsp. *elymoides* (5, 163) (1852-1913)

Long-cluster wisteria [Longcluster wisteria] - *Wisteria floribunda* (Willd.) DC. (138) (1923), *Wisteria frutescens* (L.) Poir. (5, 97) (1913-1937)

Longest three-leaf marsh pine [Longest three leaved marsh pine] - *Pinus palustris* Mill. (8) (1785)

Long-flower beeblossom [Longflower beeblossom] - *Gaura longiflora* Spach (50) (present)

Long-flower catsclaw [Long-flowered catsclaw] - *Acacia greggii* Gray (124) (1937)

Long-flower corn salad [Long-flowered corn salad] - *Valerianella longiflora* (Torr. & Gray) Walp. (5, 97) (1913-1937)

Long-flower gaura [Long-flowered gaura] - *Gaura longiflora* Spach (4) (1986)

Long-flower heuchera [Long-flowered heuchera] - *Heuchera longiflora* Rydb. (5) (1913)

Long-flower pennyroyal [Long-flowered pennyroyal] - *Hedeoma drummondii* Benth. (5, 97) (1913-1937)

Long-flower puccoon [Long-flowered puccoon] - *Lithospermum incisum* Lehm. (possibly) (38) (1820)

Long-flower tobacco [Long-flowered tobacco] - *Nicotiana longiflora* Cav. (5) (1913)

Long-fruit anemone [Long-fruited anemone] - *Anemone cylindrica* Gray (5, 37, 72, 93, 131) (1899–1936)

Long-fruit knotweed [Long fruited knotweed] - *Polygonum ramosissimum* Michx. (72, 93) (1907-1936), *Polygonum ramosissimum* Michx. var. *ramosissimum* (5, 72, 93) (1907-1936)

Long-fruit rush [Long-fruited rush] - *Juncus stygius* L. (66) (1903)

Long-hair phlox [Longhair phlox] - *Phlox longipilos* Waterfall (50) (present)

Long-hair sedge [Longhair sedge] - *Carex comosa* Boott. (50) (present)

Long-head coneflower [Long headed cone flower, Long-headed cone-flower, Long-headed coneflower, Longheaded coneflower] - *Ratibida columnifera* (Nutt.) Wood & Standl. (5, 72, 93, 122, 124, 127, 156, 158) (1900-1937)

Long-head coneflower [Long-headed coneflower] - *Ratibida pinnata* (Vent.) Barnh. (121) (1918?-1970?)

Long-head poppy [Longhead poppy] - *Papaver dubium* L. (4) (1986)

Long-hood milkweed [Longhood milkweed] - *Asclepias macrotis* Torr. (4, 50) (1986–present)

Longish-root turnip [Longish rooted Turnep] - *Brassica rapa* L. var. *rapa* (180) (1633)

Long-leaf ammannia [Long-leaved ammannia] - *Ammannia coccinea* Rottb. (72, 93, 97, 120, 131) (1899-1938)

Long-leaf arnica [Longleaf arnica] - *Arnica longifolia* D.C. Eat. (155) (1942)

Long-leaf aster [Longleaf aster, Long-leaved aster] - *Symphyotrichum novi-belgii* (L.) Nesom var. *novi-belgii* (5, 48, 72, 82, 93, 138, 155) (1907-1942)

Long-leaf avens [Long-leaved avens] - *Geum macrophyllum* Willd. (3) (1977)

Long-leaf bay willow [Long-leaved bay willow] - *Salix pentandra* L. (20) (1857)

Long-leaf bluets [Longleaf bluets] - *Houstonia longifolia* Gaertn. (138, 155) (1923-1942)

Long-leaf brake [Longleaf brake] - *Pteris longifolia* L. (50) (present)

Long-leaf brooklime [Long-leaved brooklime] - *Veronica anagallis-aquatica* L. (19, 177) (1762–1840)

Long-leaf buckwheat [Longleaf buckwheat] - *Eriogonum longifolium* Nutt. (50) (present), *Eriogonum longifolium* Nutt. var. *longifolium* (50) (present)

Long-leaf bush-clover [Long-leaved bush-clover] - *Lespedeza ×longifolia* DC. [*capitata × hirta*] (97) (1937)

Long-leaf calabash tree [Long leaved calabash tree] - *Crescentia cujete* L. (20) (1857)

Long-leaf cottonwood [Long-leaved cotton wood] - *Populus angustifolia* James (38) (1820)

Long-leaf cucumber tree [Long leaved cucumber tree] - *Magnolia macrophylla* Michx. (20) (1857)

Long-leaf eriogonum [Longleaf eriogonum] - *Eriogonum longifolium* Nutt. var. *longifolium* (3) (1977)

Long-leaf eriogonum [Long-leaved eriogonum, Long leaved eriogonum] - *Eriogonum longifolium* Nutt. (5, 97) (1913-1937)

Long-leaf fleabane [Longleaf fleabane] - *Erigeron corymbosus* Nutt. (50) (present)

Long-leaf ground-cherry [Longleaf ground cherry, Longleaf groundcherry, Long-leaved ground-cherry, Long-leaved ground cherry] - *Physalis longifolia* Nutt. (5, 50, 72, 85, 93, 97, 122, 131) (1899–present), *Physalis longifolia* Nutt. var. *longifolia* (50) (present), *Physalis longifolia* Nutt. var. *subglabrata* (Mackenzie & Bush) Cronq. (50) (present)

Long-leaf hawthorn [Long-leaved hawthorn] - *Crataegus viridis* L. (20) (1857)

Long-leaf hollygrape [Longleaf hollygrape] - *Mahonia nervosa* (Pursh) Nutt. (138) (1923)

Long-leaf houstonia [Long-leaved houstonia] - *Houstonia longifolia* Gaertn. (5, 97) (1913-1937)

Long-leaf lobelia [Long-leaved lobelia] - *Lobelia elongata* Small. (5, 97) (1913-1937)

Long-leaf magnolia [Long-leaved magnolia] - *Magnolia macrophylla* Michx. (20) (1857)

Long-leaf malaxis [Long-leaved malaxis] - *Liparis loeselii* (L.) L.C. Rich (187) (1818)

Long-leaf milkvetch [Long-leaved milk vetch] - *Astragalus ceramicus* Sheldon var. *filifolius* (Gray) F.J. Herm. (5, 97) (1913-1937)

Long-leaf milkweed [Long leaved milk weed] - *Asclepias longifolia* Michx. (42) (1814)

Long-leaf morning-glory [Long-leaved morning-glory] - *Ipomoea longifolia* Benth. (97) (1937)

Long-leaf mountain magnolia [Long leaved mountain magnolia] - *Magnolia acuminata* (L.) L. (8) (1785)

Long-leaf mugwort [Long-leaved mugwort] - *Artemisia longifolia* Nutt. (5, 72, 93, 131) (1899–1936)

Long-leaf nettle-tree [Long-leaved nettle-tree] - *Celtis tenuifolia* Nutt. (20) (1857)

Long-leaf painted-pod [Long-leaved painted pod] - *Astragalus ceramicus* Sheldon var. *filifolius* (Gray) F.J. Herm. (93) (1936)

Long-leaf panic grass [Long-leaved panic-grass, Long-leaved panic grass] - *Panicum rigidulum* Bosc ex Nees var. *elongatum* (Pursh) Lelong (5, 163) (1852-1913)

Long-leaf paspalum [Longleaf paspalum] - *Paspalum setaceum* Michx. (155) (1942)

Long-leaf pine [Longleaf pine, Long-leafed pine, Long-leaved pine] - *Pinus palustris* Mill. (2, 50, 52, 109, 122, 138, 182) (1791–present), *Pinus ponderosa* P.& C. Lawson (35, 158) (1806-1900) of the West, Meriwether Lewis, *Pinus ponderosa* P.& C. Lawson var. *scopulorum* Engelm. (5) (1913)

Long-leaf pitch pine [Long-leaved pitch pine] - *Pinus palustris* Mill. (182) (1791)

Long-leaf pondweed [Longleaf pondweed, Long-leaved pondweed] - *Potamogeton nodosus* Poir. (3, 5, 50, 72, 93, 97, 131, 155) (1899–present)

Long-leaf reed grass [Long-leaved reedgrass, Long-leaved reedgrass, Long-leaved reed grass] - *Calamovilfa longifolia* (Hook.) Scribn. (5, 56, 94, 111, 116, 163) (1851-1958)

Long-leaf rush grass [Long-leaved rush-grass, Long-leaved rush-grass, Long-leaved rush grass] - *Sporobolus clandestinus* (Biehler) A.S. Hitchc. (56, 99) (1901-1923), *Sporobolus compositus* (Poir.) Merr. var. *compositus* (5, 93, 116, 134, 140, 155, 163) (1852-1958)

Long-leaf sage [Long-leaved sage] - *Artemisia longifolia* Nutt. (3, 4) (1977-1986)

Long-leaf sagebrush [Longleaf sagebrush, Long-leaf sage brush, Long-leaved sage brush] - *Artemisia longifolia* Nutt. (85, 155) (1932-1942)

Long-leaf saskatoon - *Amelanchier canadensis* subsp. *obovalis* (Michx.) P. Landry (137) (1931)

Long-leaf side-saddle flower [Long leaved Sidesaddle Flower] - *Sarracenia flava* L. (181) (~1678)

Long-leaf spike grass [Long-leaved spike-grass] - *Chasmanthium sessiliflorum* (Poir.) Yates (94) (1901)

Long-leaf sporobolus [Long-leafed sporobolus] - *Sporobolus clandestinus* (Biehler) A.S. Hitchc. (94) (1901)

Long-leaf starwort [Longleaf starwort, Long-leaved starwort, Long-leaved star wort] - *Stellaria graminea* L. (187) (1818), *Stellaria longifolia* Muhl. ex Willd. (50) (present)

Long-leaf stitchwort [Long-leaved stitchwort, Long-leaved stitch wort] - *Stellaria graminea* L. (187) (1818), *Stellaria longifolia* Muhl. ex Willd. (3, 4, 156) (1923–1986), *Stellaria longifolia* Muhl. ex Willd. var. *longifolia* (5, 72, 131) (1899–1913)

Long-leaf summer bluet [Longleaf summer bluet] - *Houstonia longifolia* Gaertn. (50) (present)

Long-leaf sundew [Long-leaved sun-dew] - *Drosera anglica* Huds. (187) (1818)

Long-leaf swallow-wort [Long leaved swallow wort] - *Asclepias longifolia* Michx. (42) (1814)

Long-leaf threeawn [Longleaf threeawn] - *Aristida purpurascens* Poir. var. *purpurascens* (155) (1942)

Long-leaf tickclover [Longleaf tickclover] - *Desmodium cuspidatum* (Muhl. ex Willd.) DC. ex Loud. (3, 4) (1977-1986)

Long-leaf ticktrefoil [Long-leaved tick trefoil] - *Desmodium cuspidatum* (Muhl. ex Willd.) DC. ex Loud. var. *longifolium* (Torr. & Gray) Schub. (72) (1907)

Long-leaf umbrella tree [Long-leaved umbrella tree] - *Magnolia fraseri* Walt. (5) (1913)

Long-leaf vaccinium [Long-leaved vaccinium] - *Vaccinium stamineum* L. (8) (1785)

Long-leaf wild lettuce [Long-leaved wild-lettuce] - *Lactuca canadensis* L. (possibly) (187) (1818)

Long-leaf willow [Longleaf willow, Long-leaved willow] - *Salix interior* Rowlee (2, 5, 19, 108, 112, 138, 156, 158) (1840-1937)

Long-leaf wood aster [Long-leaved wood aster] - *Eurybia divaricata* (L.) Nesom (5) (1913)

Long-leaf wormwood [Longleaf wormwood] - *Artemisia longifolia* Nutt. (50) (present)

Long-lip penstemon [Longlip penstemon] - *Penstemon labrosus* (Gray) Hook. f. (138) (1923)

Long-lived ammannia - *Ammannia coccinea* Rottb. (5) (1913)

Long-lobe arrowhead [Long-lobed arrow-head] - *Sagittaria longiloba* Engelm. ex J.G. Sm. (5, 93, 97) (1913-1937)

Long-panicle manna grass [Long panicled manna grass] - *Glyceria melicaria* (Michx.) F.T. Hubb. (66, 90) (1885-1903)

Long-panicle three-tooth grass [Long-panicled three-toothed grass] - *Tridens muticus* (Torr.) Nash var. *elongatus* (Buckl.) Shinners (5) (1913)

Long-panicle triodia [Long-panicled triodia] - *Tridens muticus* (Torr.) Nash var. *elongatus* (Buckl.) Shinners (119, 140) (1938-1944)

Long-peduncle mouse-ear chickweed [Long peduncled mouse-ear chickweed] - *Cerastium arvense* L. subsp. *strictum* (L.) Ugborogho (187) (1818)

Long-peduncle smilax [Long-peduncled smilax] - *Smilax herbacea* L. (187) (1818)

Long-plume purple avens [Long-plumed purple avens, Long plumed purple avens] - *Geum triflorum* Pursh var. *ciliatum* (Pursh) Fassett (5, 72, 131) (1899-1913)

Long-pod poppy [Longpod poppy] - *Papaver dubium* L. (138, 155) (1923-1942)

Long-pod sesban [Long-podded sesban] - *Sesbania herbacea* (P. Mill.) McVaugh (97) (1937)

Long-point sedge [Long-pointed sedge] - *Carex lurida* Wahlenb. (66, 187) (1818-1903)

Long-root - *Minuartia caroliniana* (Walt.) Mattf. (156) (1923)

Long-root cat's-ear [Long-rooted cat's ear, Longrooted catsear] - *Hypochaeris radicata* L. (5, 122) (1913-1937)

Long-root eriogonum [Long-rooted eriogonum] - *Eriogonum lachnogynum* Torr. (5, 97) (1913-1937)

Long-root garlic [Long-rooted garlick] - *Allium victorialis* L. (165) (1768)

Long-root onion [Longroot onion] - *Allium victorialis* L. (155) (1942)

Long-root sedge [Long-rooted sedge] - *Carex chordorrhiza* Ehrh. Ex L. f. (66) (1903)

Long-root smartweed [Longroot smartweed] - *Polygonum amphibium* L. var. *emersum* Michx. (50) (present)

Long's grape [Longs grape] - *Vitis acerifolia* Raf. (138, 155) (1923-1942)

Long-sepal beardtongue [Long-sepaled beard-tongue] - *Penstemon calycosus* Small. (5) (1913)

Long-shucks - *Pinus taeda* L. (5, 20, 19) (1840-1913)

Long-spike flatsedge [Longspike flatsedge] - *Cyperus odoratus* L. (155) (1942)

Long-spike pavia [Long-spiked pavia] - *Aesculus parviflora* Walt. (20) (1857)

Long-spike sandbur [Long-spiked sand-bur] - *Cenchrus myosuroides* Kunth (94) (1901)

Long-spike tridens [Longspike tridens] - *Tridens strictus* (Nutt.) Nash (50) (present)

Long-spike triodia [Longspike triodia] - *Tridens strictus* (Nutt.) Nash (155) (1942)

Long-spike willow [Long-spiked willow] - *Salix sessilifolia* Nutt. (20) (1857)

Long-spine thorn [Long-spined thorn] - *Crataegus succulenta* Schrad. ex Link (5, 72, 93) (1907-1936)

Long-spine thorn-apple [Long spined thorn apple] - *Crataegus succulenta* Schrad. ex Link (131) (1899)

Long-spur columbine [Long spurred columbine, Longspur columbine] - *Aquilegia longissima* Gray (122, 124, 155) (1937-1942) TX, *Aquilegia caerulea* James. (2) (1895)

Long-spur violet [Long-spurred violet] - *Viola rostrata* Pursh (2, 5, 109, 156) (1895-1923)

Long-stalk crane's-bill [Long-stalked crane's-bill, Long-stalked crane's bill] - *Geranium columbinum* L. (5, 131, 156) (1899–1923)

Long-stalk false pimpernel [Long-stalked false pimpernel] - *Lindernia dubia* (L.) Pennell var. *anagallidea* (Michx.) Cooperrider (97) (1937), *Lindernia dubia* (L.) Pennell var. *dubia* (5, 72, 97) (1907-1937)

Long-stalk geranium [Long stalked geranium] - *Geranium columbinum* L. (19) (1840)

Long-stalk greenbrier [Long-stalked greenbriar, Long-stalked greenbrier] - *Smilax pseudochina* L. (5, 72, 97) (1907-1937)

Long-stalk hairy whitetop [Longstalk hairy whitetop] - *Cardaria pubescens* (C.A. Mey.) Jarmolenko (155) (1942)

Long-stalk ludwigiantha [Long-stalked ludwigiantha] - *Ludwigia arcuata* Walt. (5) (1913)

Long-stalk panic [Long-stalked panic] - *Dichanthelium strigosum* (Muhl. ex Elliott) Freckmann var. *strigosum* (94) (1901)

Long-stalk panic grass [Long-stalked panic-grass, Long-stalked panic grass] - *Dichanthelium linearifolium* (Scribn. ex Nash) Gould (5, 163) (1852-1913)

Long-stalk sedge [Longstalk sedge, Long-stalked sedge] - *Carex pedunculata* Muhl (5, 42, 50, 66, 72) (1814–present)

Long-stalk seg [Long stalked seg] - *Carex pedunculata* Muhl (42) (1814)

Long-stalk starwort [Longstalk starwort] - *Stellaria longifolia* Muhl. ex Willd. var. *longifolia* (50) (present), *Stellaria longipes* Goldie subsp. *longipes* (50, 155) (1942–present)

Long-stalk stitchwort [Long-stalked stitchwort] - *Stellaria longipes* Goldie (4, 5) (1913-1986)

Long-staple cotton [Long staple cotton] - *Gossypium barbadense* L. (110) (1886)

Long-stem groundsel - *Packera obovata* (Muhl. ex Willd.) W.A. Weber & A. Löve (19) (1840)

Long-stem purple violet [Long-stemmed purple violet, Long-stemmed purple violet] - *Viola cucullata* Aiton (156) (1923), *Viola nephrophylla* Greene (5) (1913)

Long-stem sundrops [Long-stemmed sundrops] - *Oenothera fruticosa* L. subsp. *fruticosa* (5) (1913)

Long-stem waterwort [Long-stemmed water wort, Long-stemmed waterwort] - *Elatine rubella* Rydb. (5, 131) (1899-1913)

Long-stolon sedge - *Carex inops* Bailey (50) (present)

Long-straw pine - *Pinus palustris* Mill. (5, 10, 20, 19) (1818-1913), *Pinus taeda* L. (5) (1913)

Long-style persicaria [Longstyled persicaria, Long-styled persicaria] - *Polygonum pensylvanicum* L. (5, 97, 122) (1913-1937)

Long-style rush [Longstyle rush, Longstyled rush, Long-styled rush] - *Juncus longistylis* Torr. (5, 50, 93, 139) (1913–present)

Long-style sweetroot [Longstyle sweetroot] - *Osmorhiza longistylis* (Torr.) DC. (50, 155) (1942–present)

Long-tail paspalum [Long-tailed paspalum] - *Paspalum setaceum* Michx. (5) (1913)

Long-tip wild ginger [Long-tipped wild ginger] - *Asarum canadense* L. (5, 72) (1907-1913)

Longtom [Long Tom] - *Paspalum lividum* Trin. (122, 163) (1852-1937)

Long-tongue mutton bluegrass [Longtongue mutton bluegrass] - *Poa fendleriana* (Steud.) Vasey subsp. *longiligula* (Scribn. & Williams) Soreng (155) (1942)

Long-tongue pondweed [Longtongue pondweed] - *Potamogeton strictifolius* Benn. (155) (1942)

Long-tube ruellia [Long-tubed ruellia,] - *Ruellia humilis* Nutt. (5, 86, 93, 157) (1878-1936)

Loose panic grass [Loose panic-grass] - *Echinochloa crus-galli* (L.) Beauv. (5) (1913)

Loose silkybent - *Apera spica-venti* (L.) Beauv. (50) (present)

Loose-flower alpine sedge [Loose-flowered alpine sedge] - *Carex rariflora* (Wahlenb.) Sm. (5) (1913)

Loose-flower button-snakeroot [Loose-flowered button-snakeroot] - *Liatris pilosa* (Aiton) Willd. var. *pilosa* (5) (1913)

Loose-flower goat's-rue [Loose-flowered goat's rue] - *Tephrosia spicata* (Walt.) Torr. & Gray (5) (1913)

Loose-flower hair-grass [Loose-flowered hair-grass] - *Agrostis scabra* Willd. (187) (1818)

Loose-flower milkvetch [Loose-flowered milk vetch] - *Astragalus tenellus* Pursh (3, 5, 50, 93, 131, 155) (1899–present)

Loose-flower phacelia [Loose-flowered phacelia] - *Phacelia bipinnatifida* Michx. (5) (1913)

Loose-flower sedge [Loose-flowered sedge] - *Carex laxiflora* Lam. (5, 66, 72) (1903-1893)

Loose-flower water milfoil [Loose-flowered water milfoil] - *Myriophyllum alterniflorum* DC. (5) (1913)

Loose-flower water-willow [Looseflowered water willow] - *Justicia ovata* (Walt.) Lindau var. *ovata* (5) (1913)

Loosely-flower paspalum [Loosely-flowered paspalum] - *Paspalum bifidum* (Bertol.) Nash (94) (1901)

Loose-spike milkwort [Loose spiked milkwort] - *Polygala ambigua* Nutt. (5, 72, 97) (1907-1937)

Loosestrife [Loose strife, Loose-strife] - *Ammannia coccinea* Rottb. (85) (1932), *Lysimachia ciliata* L. (109) (1949), *Lysimachia hybrida* Michx. (3, 4) (1977-1986), *Lysimachia* L. (1, 2, 4, 10, 82, 109, 138, 155, 156, 158, 184) (1793-1986), *Lysimachia lanceolata* Walt. (3) (1977), *Lythrum alatum* Pursh (82, 85, 157) (1900-1930), *Lythrum alatum* Pursh var. *alatum* (3) (1977), *Lythrum alatum* Pursh var. *lanceolatum* (Ell.) Rothr. (97) (1937), *Lythrum californicum* Torr. & Gray (3) (1977), *Lythrum* L. (1, 2, 4, 10, 50, 82, 122, 156, 158) (1818–present), *Lythrum salicaria* L. (7, 49, 92, 158) (1828-1900)

Lop grass - *Bromus hordeaceus* L. (5) (1913), *Bromus hordeaceus* L. subsp. *hordeaceus* (92) (1876)

Lophiola - *Lophiola aurea* Ker-Gawl. (5) (1913)

Lophotocarpus - *Sagittaria calycina* Engelm. var. *spongiosa* Engelm. (131) (1899)

Lopseed [Lop-seed] - *Phryma* L. (1, 2, 93, 155, 158) (1895-1942), *Phryma leptostachya* L. (3, 4, 5, 19, 40, 63, 65, 72, 85, 92, 93, 95, 97, 131, 156) (1840-1986)

Lop-sided rush [Lopsided rush] - *Juncus secundus* Beauv. ex Poir. (50) (present)

Loquat - *Eriobotrya japonica* (Thunb.) Lindl. (106, 107, 109, 138) (1919-1949), *Eriobotrya* Lindl. (138) (1923)

Lord's candlestick - *Yucca gloriosa* L. (78) (1898) CA

Lords-and-ladies [Lordsandladies] - *Arisaema triphyllum* (L.) Schott (64, 92, 156, 158) (1876-1923)

Loridales plant - *Corydalis sempervirens* (L.) Pers. (76) (1896) ME

L'Ortie (French) - *Urtica urens* L. (6) (1892)

L'Ortie Blanche (French) - *Lamium album* L. (6) (1892)

Lote - *Celtis* L. (189) (1767), *Ziziphus obtusifolia* (Hook. ex Torr. & Gray) Gray var. *obtusifolia* (122, 124) (1937)

Lote tree - *Celtis occidentalis* L. (181) (~1678)

Lotibush - *Ziziphus obtusifolia* (Hook. ex Torr. & Gray) Gray (158) (1900), *Zizyphus* Mill (13) (1849)

Lotophagi - *Ziziphus parryi* Torr. (76) (1896) San Diego Co. CA

Lotus - *Nelumbo* Adans. (1, 4, 50, 82, 93, 138, 155) (1923–present), *Nelumbo lutea* Willd. (4, 7, 92, 120, 124) (1828-1986), *Nymphaea lotus* L. (107) (1919)

Lotus milkvetch - *Astragalus lotiflorus* Hook (3, 4, 50) (1977–present)

Lotus sweetjuice - *Glinus lotoides* L. (50) (present)

Lotus tree [Lotus-tree] - *Diospyros virginiana* L. (5, 92, 156, 158) (1876-1923), *Ziziphus parryi* Torr. (76) (1896) San Diego Co. CA, *Zizyphus* Mill (13) (1849)

Lotus-lily [Lotus lily] - *Nelumbo* Adans. (158) (1900)

Loubion (Modern Greek) - *Phaseolus vulgaris* L. (107) (1919)

Louis' swallow-wort - *Cynanchum louiseae* Kartesz & Gandhi (50) (present)

Louisiana broomrape [Louisiana broom rape [Louisiana broom-rape - *Orobanche ludoviciana* Nutt. (5, 50, 72, 97, 122, 124, 131, 155) (1899–present), *Orobanche ludoviciana* Nutt. subsp. *ludoviciana* (50) (present)

Louisiana cup grass [Louisiana cupgrass] - *Eriochloa punctata* (L.) Desv. ex Hamilton (50, 155) (1942–present)

Louisiana grass - *Axonopus compressus* (Sw.) Beauv. (5, 56, 94) (1897-1913)

Louisiana sagebrush - *Artemisia ludoviciana* Nutt. (155) (1942)

Louisiana sedge - *Carex louisianica* Bailey (5, 50) (1913–present)

Louisiana squill - *Crinum americanum* L. (7, 92) (1828-1876)

Louisiana vetch - *Vicia ludociciana* Nutt. (3, 5, 50, 97, 155) (1913–present), *Vicia ludoviciana* Nutt. subsp. *ludoviciana* (50) (present)

Louseberry or Louseberry tree [Louseberry-tree, Louse berry tree] - *Euonymus europaea* L. (5, 92, 156) (1876-1923)

Louse-bur - *Xanthium strumarium* L. (158) (1900)

Lousewort [Louse wort, Louse-wort] - *Aureolaria pedicularia* (L.) Raf. var. *pedicularia* (5, 49, 92) (1876-1913), *Pedicularis canadensis* L. (3, 5, 19, 122, 131, 156) (1840-1977), *Pedicularis* L. (1, 2, 4, 7, 10, 50, 63, 109, 155, 156, 158, 184) (1793–present) cows and sheep were thought to get lice from this plant in N. Europe

Lousewort false foxglove [Lousewort false fox-glove] - *Aureolaria pedicularia* (L.) Raf. var. *pedicularia* (5, 156) (1913–1923)

Lousewort foxglove [Louse wort foxglove, Lousewort fox-glove] - *Aureolaria pedicularia* (L.) Raf. ex Farw. (19) (1840), *Pedicularis canadensis* L. (5, 92) (1876-1913)

Lovage [Louage] - *Levisticum* Koch (1) (1932), *Levisticum officinale* W.D.J. Koch (5, 10, 57, 107, 109, 179, 184) (1526-1949), *Ligusticum scoticum* L. (10) (1818)

Lovage [Louage] - *Ligustrum* L. (156) (1923), *Achillea millefolium* L. (155) (1942)

Love flower - *Agapanthus* L'Hér. (92) (1876)

Love grass [Love-grass, Lovegrass] - *Eragrostis cilianensis* (All.) Vign. ex Janchen (140) (1944), *Eragrostis pectinacea* (Michx.) Nees ex Steud. var. *pectinacea* (93) (1936), *Eragrostis spectabilis* (Pursh) Steud. (163) (1852), *Eragrostis trichodes* (Nutt.) Wood (116) (1958), *Eragrostis* von Wolf (50, 92, 93, 122, 155) (1936–present)

Love vine [Love-vine] - *Clematis virginiana* L. (5, 49, 156, 158) (1898–1923), *Cuscuta americana* L. (19, 92, 187) (1818–1876), *Cuscuta compacta* Juss. ex Choisy (5, 73) (1892–1918), *Cuscuta glomerata* Choisy (37) (1919), *Cuscuta gronovii* Willd. ex J.A. Schultes (5, 86, 97, 156) (1878–1937), *Cuscuta* L. (1, 4, 73, 77, 93, 106) (1892–1986), *Cuscuta pentagona* Engelm. var. *pentagona* (5, 85, 156) (1913–1932)

Love-apple [Love apple] - *Solanum* L. (1) (1932), *Solanum lycopersicum* L. (19, 92) (1840-1876), *Solanum lycopersicum* L. var. *lycopersicum* (5, 14, 85, 107, 110, 156, 158) (1882-1923)

Loved lettuce [Loued lettuce] - *Lactuca sativa* L. (180) (1633)

Love-entangled [Love entangled, Love entangle, Love-entangle] - *Sedum acre* L. (5, 73, 86, 156) (1878-1923) Northern Ohio

Love-grove [Love grove] - *Nemophila menziesii* Hook. & Arn. var. *menziesii* (92) (1876)

Love-in-a-chain - *Sedum reflexum* L. (156) (1923)

Love-in-a-mist [Love in a mist] - *Nigella damascena* L. (1, 2, 79, 92, 109, 138, 156) (1876-1949), *Nigella* L. (138) (1923)

Love-in-a-puff [Love in a puff] - *Cardiospermum halicacabum* L. (50, 92) (1876–present)

Love-in-idleness - *Viola tricolor* L. (158) (1900) Shakespeare

Love-in-winter - *Chimaphila umbellata* (L.) Bart. (5, 73, 156, 158) (1892-1923) no longer in use by 1923

Love-lies-bleeding [Love lies bleeding] - *Amaranthus caudatus* L. (109, 138, 155, 165) (1768-1942), *Amaranthus tricolor* L. (19, 58, 92) (1840-1892), *Lamprocapnos spectabilis* (L.) Fukuhara (76) (1896) Northern OH, *Polygonum orientale* L. (156) (1923)

Lovell's violet [Lovell violet] - *Viola lovelliana* Brainerd (50, 97, 155) (1937–present)

Lovely thistle - *Cnicus benedictus* L. (7) (1828)

Lovely-bleeding [Lovely bleeding] - *Amaranthus caudatus* L. (7) (1828), *Amaranthus hybridus* L. (158) (1900), *Amaranthus hypochondriacus* L. (49) (1898)

Loveman [Love-man] - *Galium aparine* L. (5, 156, 158) (1900-1923) no longer in use by 1923

Love-me - *Myosotis scorpioides* L. (5, 156, 158) (1900-1923)

Love-pea [Love pea] - *Abrus precatorius* L. (7, 92, 107) (1828-1919)

Love-roses [Love roses, Love rose] - *Viburnum opulus* L. (5, 156, 158) (1900-1923) no longer in use by 1923

Lover's-knot [Lover's knot] - *Cuscuta epilinum* Weihe. (156) (1923)

Lover's-pride [Lover's pride] - *Persicaria maculosa* Gray (5, 156, 158) (1900-1923)

Lover's-steps - *Lolium temulentum* L. (157, 158) (1900-1929)

Loveseed [Love seed] - *Lomatium foeniculaceum* (Nutt.) Coult. & Rose subsp. *foeniculaceum* (37) (1919)

Love's-test [Love's test] - *Antennaria plantaginifolia* (L.) Richards (5, 76, 156, 158) (1896-1923) IN, game played with leaves supposed to determine strength of love, no longer in use by 1923

Loving sage - *Salvia farinacea* Benth. (106) (1930)

Low agoseris - *Agoseris monticola* Greene (155) (1942)

Low amaranth - *Amaranthus blitoides* S. Wats. (62, 150) (1894-1912), *Amaranthus deflexus* L. (5) (1913)

Low anemone - *Anemone nemorosa* L. (19) (1840)

Low babysbreath - *Gypsophila muralis* L. (50) (present)

Low balm - *Monarda didyma* L. (5, 92, 156) (1876-1923)

Low bindweed - *Calystegia spithamaea* (L.) Pursh (5, 156) (1913-1923)

Low birch - *Betula pumila* L. (2, 5, 82, 152, 156, 158) (1894–1930)

Low black blueberry - *Vaccinium angustifolium* Aiton (5, 72) (1907-1913)

Low blackberry [Low black berry] - *Rubus canadensis* L. (2, 49, 53, 58, 107) (1869-1922), *Rubus cuneifolius* Pursh (5) (1913), *Rubus trivialis* Michx. (92) (1876)

Low bladderpod [Low bladder-pod, Low bladder pod] - *Lesquerella alpina* (Nutt.) S. Wats. var. *spathulata* (Rydb.) Payson (5, 93, 131) (1899-1936)

Low blueberry - *Vaccinium pallidum* Aiton (5, 46, 92, 107) (1876-1919)

Low buckthorn - *Rhamnus alnifolia* L'Her. (113) (1890)

Low buttercup - *Ranunculus fascicularis* Muhl. ex Bigelow (156, 158) (1900-1923)

Low butterwort - *Pinguicula pumila* Michx. (122) (1937) TX

Low calamint - *Clinopodium arkansanum* (Nutt.) House (5, 97) (1913-1937)

Low camomile [Low chamomile] - *Chamaemelum nobile* (L.) All. (5, 92, 156) (1876-1923)

Low centaury - *Hypericum mutilum* L. (19, 92) (1840-1876)

Low chickweed - *Stellaria humifusa* Rottb. (5) (1913)

Low cornel - *Cornus canadensis* L. (5, 156, 158) (1900-1923)

Low craneberry - *Vaccinium oxycoccos* L. (19, 92) (1840-1876)

Low creek-stuff [Low creek stuff] - *Spartina maritima* (M.A. Curtis) Fern. (5) (1913)

Low cudweed - *Gnaphalium uliginosum* L. (3, 4, 5, 155, 156, 158) (1900-1986)

Low cyperus - *Cyperus diandrus* Torr. (5, 72, 156) (1907-1923)

Low ditaxis - *Argythamnia humilis* (Engelm. & Gray) Muell. Arg. var. *humilis* (5, 97) (1913-1937)

Low dogbane - *Apocynum androsaemifolium* L. (155) (1942), *Apocynum cannabinum* L. (155) (1942)

Low Douglas' rabbitbrush [Low Douglas rabbitbrush] - *Chrysothamnus viscidiflorus* (Hook.) Nutt. subsp. *viscidiflorus* var. *viscidiflorus* (155) (1942)

Low enchanter's nightshade - *Circaea alpina* L. (156) (1923)

Low eragrostis - *Eragrostis minor* Host (72) (1907)

Low erigeron - *Erigeron pumilus* Nutt. (5, 93, 131, 158) (1899–1936)

Low everlasting - *Antennaria dimorpha* (Nutt.) Torr. & Gray (5, 93) (1913-1936)

Low false bindweed - *Calystegia spithamaea* (L.) Pursh (4) (1986)

Low fimbristylis - *Fimbristylis autumnalis* (L.) Roemer & J.A. Schultes (5) (1913)

Low flatsedge - *Cyperus diandrus* Torr. (3) (1977)

Low flax - *Linum usitatissimum* L. (155) (1942)

Low fleabane - *Erigeron pumilus* Nutt. (3, 155) (1942-1977)

Low gilia - *Ipomopsis pumila* (Nutt.) V. Grant (5, 122) (1913-1937)

Low goldenrod - *Solidago nemoralis* Aiton (156) (1923)

Low gramma grass - *Bouteloua barbata* Lag. (87) (1884)

Low ground-cherry [Low ground cherry] - *Physalis pumila* Nutt. (5, 97, 122) (1913-1937)

Low gypsophyll - *Gypsophila muralis* L. (5) (1913)

Low hairy ground-cherry [Low hairy ground cherry - *Physalis pubescens* L. (5, 62, 72, 97, 122, 158) (1900-1937)

Low hop clover [Low hop-clover - *Trifolium campestre* Schreber. (4, 5, 63, 80, 97, 122, 131, 155, 156) (1899-1986)

Low horseweed [Low horse-weed, Low horse weed] - *Conyza ramosissima* Cronq. (5, 72, 93, 97, 156) (1907-1937)

Low juneberry [Low june-berry, Low june berry] - *Amelanchier alnifolia* (Nutt.) Nutt. ex M. Roemer (114) (1894), *Amelanchier humilis* Wiegand (85) (1932), *Amelanchier stolonifera* Wieg. (5, 82) (1913-1930)

Low juniper - *Juniperus communis* L. var. *montana* Ait. (5, 85) (1913-1932)

Low kyllinga - *Kyllinga pumila* Michx. (5) (1913)

Low ladyslipper [Low ladies' slipper] - *Cypripedium acaule* Ait. (19) (1840)

Low larkspur - *Delphinium bicolor* Nutt. (126, 146) (1933-1939)

Low laurel - *Kalmia angustifolia* L. (71) (1898)

Low lion's-foot [Low lion's foot] - *Prenanthes nana* (Bigelow) Torr. (5) (1913)

Low love grass [Low love-grass] - *Eragrostis minor* Host (5, 155) (1913-1942)

Low lupine - *Lupinus pusillus* Pursh (5, 93, 97, 125, 131, 133) (1899-1937)

Low mallow - *Malva rotundifolia* L. (5, 19, 50, 62, 92, 93, 156, 157, 158) (1840–present)

Low maple - *Acer spicatum* Lam. (5, 156) (1913-1923)

Low maul - *Malva rotundifolia* L. (158) (1900)

Low maws - *Malva rotundifolia* L. (158) (1900)

Low meadow grass - *Eragrostis minor* Host (56) (1901)

Low meadowrue - *Thalictrum hultenii* Boivin (138) (1923)

Low mesquite - *Bouteloua gracilis* (Willd. ex Kunth) Lag. ex Griffiths (87) (1884)

Low milkvetch [Low milk vetch] - *Astragalus lotiflorus* Hook (5, 72, 82, 93, 97, 131) (1899-1937), *Astragalus spatulatus* Sheldon (157) (1929)

Low milkweed - *Asclepias pumila* (Gray) Vail (5, 93, 97, 121, 122, 131) (1899-1937), *Asclepias stenophylla* Gray (114) (1894)

Low mulberry - *Rubus chamaemorus* L. (156) (1923)

Low northern sedge - *Carex concinna* R. Br. (5, 50) (1913–present)

Low nutrush [Low nut rush] - *Scleria verticillata* Muhl. ex Willd. (5, 50) (1913–present)

Low oreocarya - *Cryptantha sericea* (Gray) Payson (5, 93) (1913-1936)

Low pale blueberry - *Vaccinium pallidum* Aiton (2, 156) (1895-1923)

Low panic grass [Low panic-grass] - *Urochloa reptans* (L.) Stapf (94) (1901)

Low parosela - *Dalea nana* Torr. ex Gray (5, 97) (1913-1937)

Low peavine - *Lathyrus pusillus* Ell. (3, 155) (1942-1977)

Low phlox - *Polemonium pulcherrimum* Hook. subsp. *lindleyi* (Wherry) V. Grant (82) (1930)

Low photinia - *Photinia serratifolia* (Desf.) Kalkm. (138) (1923)

Low pine-barren milkwort - *Polygala ramosa* Ell. (5) (1913)

Low plum - *Prunus gracilis* Engelm. & Gray (5, 97) (1913-1937)

Low poppy-mallow [Low poppymallow] - *Callirhoe involucrata* (Torr. & Gray) Gray (155) (1942)

Low pussytoes - *Antennaria dimorpha* (Nutt.) Torr. & Gray (50, 155) (1942–present)

Low rattlesnake root - *Prenanthes nana* (Bigelow) Torr. (5) (1913)

Low rockcress [Low rock cress] - *Arabis lyrata* L. (2, 156) (1895-1942), *Braya humilis* (C.A. Mey.) B.L. Robins. (5) (1913)

Low rose - *Rosa virginiana* Mill. (5, 97) (1913-1937) OK, *Rosa woodsii* Lindl. (113, 130) (1890)

Low rough aster - *Eurybia radula* (Aiton) Nesom (5) (1913)

Low running blackberry - *Rubus flagellaris* Willd. (5, 62) (1912–1913)

Low sagebrush - *Artemisia arbuscula* Nutt. (138, 155) (1931-1942)

Low sea blite - *Suaeda maritima* (L.) Dumort. subsp. *maritima* (5) (1913)

Low selaginella - *Selaginella selaginoides* (L.) Beauv. ex Mart. & Schrank (5) (1913)

Low senna - *Senna tora* (L.) Roxb. (5, 63, 72, 97, 158) (1899-1937)

Low serviceberry - *Amelanchier humilis* Wiegand (4, 50, 155) (1942–present)

Low shadblow - *Amelanchier humilis* Wiegand (138) (1923)

Low shepherdia - *Shepherdia canadensis* Nutt. (130) (1895)

Low shin-leaf - *Orthilia secunda* (L.) House (156) (1923)

Low showy aster - *Eurybia spectabilis* (Aiton) Nesom (5, 156) (1913-1923)

Low silverbush - *Argythamnia humilis* (Engelm. & Gray) Meull. Arg. var. *laevis* (Torr.) Shinners (50) (present), *Argythamnia humilis* (Engelm. & Gray) Muell. Arg. var. *humilis* (50) (present), *Argythamnia humilis* (Engelm. & Gray) Muell.-Arg. (50) (present)

Low snowberry - *Symphoricarpos albus* (L.) Blake var. *pauciflorus* (J.W. Robbins) S.F. Blake (95, 131) (1899-1911)

Low spear grass [Low spear-grass] - *Poa abbreviata* R. Br. (5) (1913), *Poa annua* L. (5, 45, 56, 90, 92, 94, 111, 119, 143, 163) (1852-1938)

Low spearwort - *Ranunculus pusillus* Poir. (5) (1913)

Low spikesedge - *Kyllinga pumila* Michx. (50) (present)

Low spring nettle - *Urtica chamaedryoides* Pursh (122) (1937)

Low spring sweet iris - *Iris verna* L. (183) (1756)

Low steironema - *Lysimachia ciliata* L. (155) (1942)

Low stickseed - *Lappula occidentalis* (S. Wats.) Greene var. *occidentalis* (3) (1977)

Low stiff panicum - *Dichanthelium ovale* (Ell.) Gould & C.A. Clark var. *addisonii* (Nash) Gould & C.A. Clark (5) (1913)

Low sumac [Low sumach] - *Rhus trilobata* Nutt. (113, 130) (1890-1895)

Low sweet blueberry - *Vaccinium pallidum* Aiton (107, 156) (1919-1923)

Low townsendia - *Townsendia exscapa* (Richards.) Porter (5) (1913)

Low tufted hymneopappus - *Hymenopappus filifolius* Hook. (5, 93) (1913-1936)

Low vetchling - *Lathyrus pusillus* Ell. (5, 97) (1913-1937)

Low water milfoil - *Myriophyllum humile* (Raf.) Morong. (5) (1913)

Low white-hair panic grass [Low white-haired panic-grass, Low white-haired panic grass] - *Dichanthelium linearifolium* (Scribn. ex Nash) Gould (5, 163) (1852-1913)

Low whitlow-wort [Low whitlow wort] - *Paronychia sessiliflora* Nutt. (5, 97) (1913-1937)

Low whortle-berry - *Gaylussacia frondosa* (L.) Torr. & Gray (43) (1820)

Low wild gooseberry - *Ribes hirtellum* Michx. (5) (1913)

Low willow - *Salix humilis* Marsh. (5, 156) (1913-1923)

Low yellow oak - *Quercus prinoides* Willd. (113) (1890)

Low-belia [Low belia] - *Lobelia inflata* L. (5, 69, 75, 156, 158) (1900-1923) somewhat general among herb gatherers

Low-bush blackberry [Low bush blackberry - *Rubus trivialis* Michx. (5, 49, 53, 107) (1898–1922)

Low-bush blueberry [Low bush blueberry, Lowbush blueberry] - *Vaccinium angustifolium* Aiton (5, 109) (1913-1949), *Vaccinium arboreum* Marsh. (5) (1913), *Vaccinium pallidum* Aiton (106, 138) (1923-1930)

Löwenmaul [Lowenmaul] (German) - *Antirrhinum majus* L. (158) (1900), *Linaria vulgaris* Mill. (6, 158) (1892-1900)

Löwenzahn (German) - *Taraxacum officinale* G.H. Weber ex Wiggers (158) (1900)

Löwenzahn (German) - *Taraxacum officinale* G.H. Weber ex Wiggers subsp. *officinale* (6) (1892)

Lowe's pine [Lowe pine] - *Ajuga chamaepitys (L.) Schreb.* (178) (1526)

Lowland bladder fern [Lowland bladderfern] - *Cystopteris protrusa* (Weatherby) Blasdell (50) (present)

Lowland fragile fern - *Cystopteris protrusa* (Weatherby) Blasdell (4) (1986)

Lowland gooseberry - *Ribes lacustre* (Pers.) Poir. (130) (1895)

Lowland rotala - *Rotala ramosior* (L.) Koehne (50) (present)

Lowland yellow loosestrife - *Lysimachia hybrida* Michx. (50) (present)

Lowrie's aster [Lowrie aster] - *Symphyotrichum lowrieanum* (Porter) Nesom (5, 72, 155) (1907-1942)

Low-water star - *Heteranthera dubia* (Jacq.) MacM. (187) (1818)

Lucernaria - *Verbascum thapsus* L. (156, 178) (1526-1923)

Lucerne [Lucern] - *Desmodium canadense* (L.) DC. (158) (1900), *Medicago* L. (1) (1932), *Medicago sativa* L. (5, 14, 19, 45, 63, 66, 68, 82, 87, 92, 93, 95, 107, 109, 118, 129, 151, 156, 157, 158) (1840-1949), *Onobrychis viciifolia* Scop. (158) (1900)

Lucerne dodder - *Cuscuta epithymum* (L.) L. (45, 158) (1896)

Luchau loobe thlucco (Creek) - *Hexastylis virginica* (L.) Small (46) (1879)

Lucifer - *Medicago sativa* L. (158) (1900)

Lucifer-matches - *Sisymbrium officinale* (L.) Scop (157, 158) (1900-1929)

Luckie's mutch - *Aconitum napellus* L. (107) (1919)

Lucretia dewberry - *Rubus roribaccus* (Bailey) Rydb. (2, 50) (1895–present)

Ludvigia - *Ludwigia alternifolia* L. (174) (1753)

Lumbard lettuce - *Lactuca sativa* L. (180) (1633)

Lumias (Italian) - *Citrus medica* L. (110) (1260)

Lunan pepper - *Capsicum annuum* L. (107) (1919)

Lunary - *Botrychium lunaria* (L.) Sw. (158) (1900)

Lund-groe (Swedish) - *Poa nemoralis* L. (46) (1879)

Lung lichen - *Lobaria pulmonaria* (L.) Hoffm. (50, 107) (1919–present)

Lung moss - *Lobaria pulmonaria* (L.) Hoffm. (53, 92) (1876-1922)

Lungenhabichtskraut (German) - *Hieracium umbellatum* L. (158) (1900) plant used in asthma

Lungs-of-the-oak [Lungs of the oak] - *Lobaria pulmonaria* (L.) Hoffm. (92) (1876)

Lungwort [Lung-wort] - *Lobaria pulmonaria* (L.) Hoffm. (52, 54, 107) (1905-1919), *Mertensia* Roth (1, 93, 156, 158) (1900), *Mertensia virginica* (L.) Pers. ex Link (47, 63, 184) (1793-1899),

Pulmonaria L. (7, 10, 109, 138) (1818-1949), *Pulmonaria officinalis* L. (19, 57, 61, 92, 107) (1840-1919)

Lungwort lichen - *Lobaria pulmonaria* (L.) Hoffm. (53) (1922)

Lupin - *Lupinus albus* L. (49, 110) (1886-1898), *Lupinus* L. (7, 10, 158) (1818-1900)

Lupine - *Lupinus argenteus* Pursh (148) (1939), *Lupinus* L. (1, 4, 45, 50, 93, 106, 138, 155, 156, 158, 190) (~1759–present), *Lupinus perennis* L. (41, 92) (1770-1876)

Lupinella - *Onobrychis viciifolia* Scop. (110) (1886)

Lupuli coni (Official name of Materia Medica) - *Humulus lupulus* L. (7) (1828)

Lupulo (Italian) - *Humulus lupulus* L. (110) (1886)

Lupulus - *Humulus lupulus* L. (6, 55) (1892–1911)

Lustwort [Lust wort, Lust-wort] - *Drosera rotundifolia* L. (5, 52, 92, 107, 156, 158) (1876-1923)

Luteolin - *Reseda luteola* L. (92) (1876)

Luz or lus (Hebrew) - *Prunus dulcis* (Mill.) D.A. Webber (110) (1886)

Lyall's anemone [Lyall anemone] - *Anemone lyallii* Britt. (155) (1942), *Pulsatilla patens* (L.) Mill.subsp. *multifida* (Pritz.) Zamels (155) (1942)

Lyall's angelica [Lyall angelica] - *Angelica arguta* Nutt. (155) (1942), *Angelica lucida* L. (155) (1942)

Lyall's nettle [Lyall nettle] - *Urtica dioica* L. subsp. *gracilis* (Aiton) Seland. (155) (1942)

Lyall's rockcress [Lyall rockcress] - *Boechera lyallii* (S.Watson) Dorn (155) (1942)

Lychnidia - *Phlox* L. (156) (1923)

Lychnis - *Lychnis* L. (138, 156, 158) (1900–1923)

Lychwale - *Lithospermum officinale* L. (179) (1526)

Lychworte - *Lithospermum officinale* L. (179) (1526)

Lycope de Virginie (French) - *Lycopus virginicus* L. (6, 7, 158) (1828-1900)

Lycopodium - *Lycopodium clavatum* L. (52, 55, 57, 59, 92) (1876-1919)

Lycopus - *Lycopus americanus* Muhl. ex W. Bart. (57) (1917), *Lycopus virginicus* L. (52, 54, 57) (1905-1917)

Lygodesmia - *Lygodesmia* D. Don (158) (1900), *Lygodesmia juncea* (Pursh) D. Don ex Hook. (80, 125, 157) (1900–1929)

Lyme grass - *Elymus canadensis* L. (87, 88, 143) (1884-1936), *Elymus* L. (35, 66) (1806-1903), *Elymus villosus* Muhl. ex Willd. (45) (1896), *Elymus virginicus* L. (66, 92, 111, 129, 143) (1894-1936), *Leymus arenarius* (L.) Hochst. (possibly) (92) (1876), *Leymus condensatus* (J. Presl) A. Löve (45) (1896)

Lymon - *Citrus limon* (L.) Burm. f. (179) (1526)

Lyne - *Linum usitatissimum* L. (179) (1526)

Lyngbye's sedge - *Carex lyngbyei* Hornem. (50) (present)

Lynn tree - *Liriodendron tulipifera* L. (5) (1913)

Lyon bean - *Mucuna pruriens* (L.) DC. var. *pruriens* (109) (1949)

Lyon's andromeda - *Lyonia ligustrina* (L.) DC. var. *ligustrina* (5) (1913)

Lyon-shrub [Lyonshrub] - *Lyonothamnus* Gray (138) (1923)

Lyrate-leaf berlandieria [Lyrateleaf berlandieria] - *Berlandiera lyrata* Benth. (122) (1937)

Lyre flower [Lyre-flower] - *Dicentra canadensis* (Goldie) Walp. (156) (1923)

Lyre tree [Lyre-tree] - *Liriodendron tulipifera* L. (92, 156) (1898-1923)

Lyre-leaf berlandiera [Lyre-leafed berlandiera] - *Berlandiera lyrata* Benth. (5, 97, 124) (1913-1937)

Lyre-leaf greeneyes [Lyreleaf greeneyes] - *Berlandiera lyrata* Benth. (50) (present)

Lyre-leaf sage [Lyre-leaved sage] - *Salvia lyrata* L. (4, 5, 97, 124, 156) (1913-1986)

Lyre-leaf wallcress [Lyre leaved wall cress, Lyre-leaved rock cress] - *Arabis lyrata* L. (5, 42, 72) (1814-1913)

Lys blance (French) - *Lilium candidum* L. (180) (1633)

Lys sauvage (French) - *Lilium martagon* L. (180) (1633)

Lysimaque (French) - *Lysimachia* L. (158) (1900)

Lythrum - *Lythrum* L. (138, 155) (1923-1942)

M

Maa zhon (Omaha-Ponca, cotton tree) - *Populus deltoides* Bartr. ex Marsh. subsp. *monilifera* (Aiton) Eckenwalder (37) (1919)

Maazi (Omaha-Ponca) - *Juniperus virginiana* L. (37) (1830)

Macadamia - *Macadamia* F. Muell. (138) (1923) for John Amadam M.D., 1827-1865, Secr. Philosophical Insitute Victoria Australia, *Machaeranthera canescens* (Pursh) Gray subsp. *canescens* var. *canescens* (138) (1923)

Macanet grains - *Prunus mahaleb* L. (92) (1876)

Macartney's rose [Macartney rose] - *Rosa bracteata* Wendl. (109, 122, 138) (1923-1949) introduced to England from China by Lord Macartney about 1793

Macdougal's rose [Macdougal rose] - *Rosa nutkana* K. Presl var. *hispida* Fern. (138) (1923)

Mace - *Myristica fragrans* Houtt. (92) (1876)

Macella fetida (Portuguese) - *Anthemis cotula* L. (186) (1814)

Mace-reed - *Typha latifolia* L. (14) (1882)

Mack (South of Caucasus) - *Papaver somniferum* L. (110) (1886)

Mackensen's prickly pear [Mackensen pricklypear] - *Opuntia macrorhiza* Engelm. var. *macrorhiza* (155) (1942)

Mackerel mint [Mackerel-mint - *Mentha spicata* L. (5, 156, 158) (1900–1923)

Macloskey's violet [Macloskey violet] - *Viola macloskeyi* Lloyd (155) (1942)

Maclura - *Maclura* Nutt. (50) (present)

Macnab's cypress [Macnab cypress] - *Cupressus macnabiana* A. Murr. (138) (1923)

Macock [Macocks] - *Cucurbita* L. (181) (~1678), *Cucurbita maxima* Dcne. (110) (1886) early Anglo-American travelers

Macock gourd - *Cucurbita pepo* L. (46) (1610)

Macounastrum - *Koenigia islandica* L. (5) (1913)

Macoun's barley - *Elyhordeum macounii* (Vasey) Barkworth & D.R. Dewey [*Elymus trachycaulus* × *Hordeum jubatum*] (50) (present)

Macoun's blue-joint reed grass [Macoun bluejoint reedgrass] - *Calamagrostis canadensis* (Michx.) Beauv. var. *macouniana* (Vasey) Stebbins (155) (1942)

Macoun's buttercup [Macoun's buttercups] - *Ranunculus macounii* Britton (3, 4, 5, 50, 127, 131) (1899–present)

Macoun's cudweed - *Pseudognaphalium macounii* (Greene) Kartesz (50) (present)

Macoun's false bindweed - *Calystegia macounii* (Greene) Brummitt (178) (1526)

Macoun's feather grass - *Piptatherum canadense* (Poir) Barkworth (5, 19) (1840-1913)

Macoun's lyme grass [Macoun's lyme-grass] - *Elyhordeum macounii* (Vasey) Barkworth & D. R. Dewey [*Elymus trachycaulus* × *Hordeum jubatum*] (56, 94, 111) (1901–1915)

Macoun's reed bent [Macoun's reed-bent] - *Calamagrostis canadensis* (Michx.) Beauv. var. *macouniana* (Vasey) Stebbins (56, 94) (1901)

Macoun's reed grass [Macoun's reedgrass] - *Calamagrostis canadensis* (Michx.) Beauv. var. *macouniana* (Vasey) Stebbins (5, 50) (1913–present)

Macoun's rose [Macoun rose] - *Rosa woodsii* Lindl. var. *woodsii* (138, 155) (1923-1942)

Macoun's stipa - *Piptatherum canadense* (Poir) Barkworth (94) (1901)

Macoun's wild rye [Macoun wildrye - *Elyhordeum macounii* (Vasey) Barkworth & D. R. Dewey [*Elymus trachycaulus* × *Hordeum jubatum*] (5, 72, 155) (1907–1942)

Macrotys - *Cimicifuga racemosa* (L.) Nutt. (53, 54, 59) (1905-1922)

Maculated hempweed [Maculated hemp-weed] - *Eupatorium maculatum* L. (187) (1818)

Mad apple - *Quercus infectoria* Olivier (insect galls infecting oaks) (92) (1876) not a species of oak, but an abnormal growths caused by parasites

Mad dog skullcap [Mad dog scull cap, Mad dog scullcap] - *Scutellaria lateriflora* L. (2, 6, 19, 63, 72, 75, 82) (1840-1907)

Madagascar dropseed - *Sporobolus coromandelianus* (Retz.) Kunth (50) (present)

Madagascar palm - *Dypsis lutescens* (H. Wendl.) Beentje & Dransf. (109) (1949)

Madagascar periwinkle - *Catharanthus roseus* (L.) G. Don (109, 138) (1923-1949)

Madagascar rubbervine - *Cryptostegia madagascariensis* Bojer ex Dcne. (138) (1923)

Mad-apple [Mad apples, Mad-apples] - *Datura stramonium* L. (5, 6, 69, 71, 92, 156, 158) (1892-1974), *Solanum melongena* L. (107, 156, 178) (1526-1923)

Madaria (Basque) - *Pyrus communis* L. (110) (1886)

Madder - *Anthemis cotula* L. (157, 158) (1900-1929), *Galium hispidulum* Michx. (190) (~1759), *Rubia* L. (7, 10) (1818-1828), *Rubia tinctoria* L. (19, 49, 57, 92, 109, 110, 179, 193) (1793-1917)

Madderwort [Maderwort] - *Artemisia absinthium* L. (5, 156, 157, 158) (1900-1929)

Mad-dog [Mad dog] - *Scutellaria lateriflora* L. (5, 157) (1900-1929)

Mad-dog skullcap [Mad-dog skull-cap, Mad-dog skull cap, Mad-dog scullcap] - *Scutellaria lateriflora* L. (93, 131, 156, 157, 158) (1899-1936)

Mad-dog weed [Mad dog weed] - *Alisma plantago-aquatica* L. (19, 58, 92, 156) (1840–1923), *Alisma subcordatum* Raf. (5, 157) (1913–1929), *Scutellaria lateriflora* L. (6, 92) (1876–1892)

Madeira broom - *Genista stenopetala* Webb & Berth. (138) (1923)

Madeira nut - *Juglans regia* L. (19, 92, 107) (1840-1919)

Madeira vine [Madeira-vine] - *Anredera cordifolia* (Ten.) Steenis (109) (1949)

Madenweed [Maydenwede, Maden-weed] - *Anthemis cotula* L. (157, 158, 179) (1526-1929)

Madia - *Madia sativa* Molina (110) (1886)

Madia-oil plant - *Madia sativa* Molina (107) (1919)

Madnep [Mad-nep] - *Heracleum maximum* Bartr. (92, 157, 158) (1876–1929), *Pastinaca sativa* L. (156, 157, 158) (1900–1929)

Madness - *Heracleum maximum* Bartr. (157, 158) (1900-1929)

Madonna lily - *Lilium candidum* L. (50, 109, 138) (1923–present) NY

Madre - *Gliricidia sepium* (Jacq.) Kunth ex Walp. (possibly) (109) (1949)

Madrid brome grass [Madrid bromegrass] - *Bromus madritensis* L. (138) (1923)

Madrona - *Arbutus menziesii* Pursh (106, 107) (1919-1930)

Madroña - *Arbutus menziesii* Pursh (161) (1857)

Madrone - *Arbutus* L. (50, 155) (1942–present), *Arbutus menziesii* Pursh (109, 138) (1923-1949)

Madroñe - *Arbutus menziesii* Pursh (75) (1894) CA

Madroño - *Arbutus menziesii* Pursh (109) (1949)

Madweed [Mad-weed] - *Scutellaria lateriflora* L. (5, 6, 49, 52, 53, 92, 156, 157, 158) (1892-1923)

Madwomen's-milk [Mad woman's milk, Mad-women's milk, Mad-woman's milk, Mad-woman's-milk] - *Euphorbia helioscopia* L. (5, 50, 156) (1913–present)

Madwort - *Alyssum* L. (50, 109 156) (1923–present), *Asperugo* L. (4, 156) (1923–1986), *Asperugo procumbens* L. (156) (1923), *Aurinia saxatilis* (L.) Desv. (156) (1923), *Camelina sativa* (L.) Crantz (5, 19, 92, 156, 157, 158) (1840–1929), *Lobularia maritima* (L.) Desv. (5, 92, 156) (1876–1923)

Magdad coffee - *Senna occidentalis* (L.) Link (5, 156) (1913-1923) no longer in use by 1923

Magdalene daisy [Magdalene-daisy] - *Leucanthemum vulgare* Lam. (158) (1900)

Magellan's fuchsia [Magellan fuchsia] - *Fuchsia magellanica* Lam. (138) (1923)

Maggoty boy bean [Magoty boy bean] - *Chamaecrista fasciculata* (Michx.) Greene (5) (1913), *Chamaecrista fasciculata* (Michx.) Greene var. *fasciculata* (74, 156) (1893-1923) NY, no longer in use by 1923

Magnolia - *Liriodendron tulipifera* L. (74) (1893) White Haven PA, *Magnolia grandiflora* L. (19, 106, 107, 122) (1840-1937), *Magnolia* L. (8, 82, 138) (1785-1930), *Magnolia virginiana* L. (57, 82) (1917-1930)

Magnolia (French) - *Magnolia* L. (8) (1785)

Magnolia glauque (French) - *Magnolia virginiana* L. (8, 186) (1785-1825)

Magnolia grande feuille (French) - *Magnolia macrophylla* Michx. (7) (1828)

Magnolia of Pennsylvania - *Magnolia virginiana* L. (189) (1767)

Magnolia ombrelle (French) - *Magnolia tripetala* L. (8) (1785)

Magnolia rustique (French) - *Magnolia acuminata* (L.) L. (8) (1785)

Magnolia waterlily - *Nymphaea odorata* Aiton subsp. *tuberosa* (Paine) Wiersma & Hellquist (138, 155) (1923-1942)

Magnolie (German) - *Magnolia virginiana* L. (6) (1892)

Magnolier bleue (French) - *Magnolia virginiana* L. (186) (1814)

Magnolier des marais (French) - *Magnolia virginiana* L. (186) (1814)

Magnolier glauque (French) - *Magnolia virginiana* L. (6) (1892)

Magnoxigill (Indians of Maine) - *Cornus sericea* L. subsp. *sericea* (107) (1919)

Maguey - *Agave americana* L. (7, 92, 110, 123) (1828-1886) Mexico

Mahala mat [Mahala mats, Mahala-mats] - *Ceanothus prostratus* Benth. (76, 106, 109, 138) (1896-1949)

Mahaleb - *Prunus mahaleb* L. (3, 4, 5, 109) (1913-1986)

Mahaleb cherry - *Prunus mahaleb* L. (137, 138, 156, 158) (1900-1931)

Mahíntsh (Winnebago) - *Asclepias syriaca* L. (37) (1919)

Mahiz (Haiti) - *Zea mays* L. (107) (1919)

Mahogany birch - *Betula lenta* L. (5, 49, 58, 107, 156) (1869-1923)

Mahogany fawn lily [Mahogany fawnlily] - *Erythronium revolutum* Sm. (50) (present)

Mahogany gum - *Eucalyptus resinifera* Sm. (138) (1923)

Mahogany mistletoe - *Phoradendron rubrum* (L.) Griseb. (50) (present)

Mahogany or Mahogany tree - *Gymnocladus dioicus* (L.) K. Koch (7, 8) (1785-1828), *Swietenia* Jacq. (138) (1923), *Swietenia mahagoni* (L.) Jacq. (7, 15, 20) (1828-1895)

Mahogany sumac - *Rhus integrifolia* (Nutt.) Benth. & Hook. f. ex Brewer & S. Wats. (106) (1930)

Mahogany trout lily [Mahogany troutlily] - *Erythronium revolutum* Sm. (138) (1923)

Mahogony - *Swietenia mahagoni* (L.) Jacq. (19, 109) (1840-1949) from native American name

Mahometan pea (China) - *Pisum sativum* L. (110) (16th century)

Mahonia - *Mahonia aquifolium* (Pursh) Nutt. (2, 52, 92, 107) (1876-1919), *Mahonia* Nutt. (155) (1942)

Maiblume (German) - *Convallaria majalis* L. (158) (1900)

Maiden - *Dianthus armeria* L. (46) (1879)

Maiden blue-eyed-Mary [Maiden blue eyed Mary] - *Collinsia parviflora* Lindl. (50) (present)

Maiden cane [Maidencane, Maiden-cane] - *Panicum hemitomon* Schult. (5, 50, 122, 163) (1852–present), *Sorghum halepense* (L.) Pers. (5, 158) (1900-1913)

Maiden fern - *Thelypteris* Schmidel (50) (present)

Maiden pink - *Armeria maritima* (P. Mill.) Willd (156) (1923), *Dianthus deltoides* L. (5, 15, 109, 138, 156) (1895–1949)

Maidenhair [Maiden-hair, Maiden hair] - *Adiantum capillus-ven-eris* L. (49, 92, 158) (1876-1900), *Adiantum* L. (138, 155, 158) (1900–1942), *Adiantum pedatum* L. (7, 19, 46, 49, 57, 157, 158, 184, 187) (1793–1929), *Briza media* L. (5) (1913), *Gaultheria hispidula* (L.) Muhl. ex Bigelow (73) (1892), *Geum rivale* L (5, 74, 76, 158) (1893–1913), *Geum triflorum* Pursh (4) (1986), *Geum triflorum* Pursh var. *ciliatum* (Pursh) Fassett (127) (1933) ND

Maidenhair fern [Maiden-hair fern, Maiden hair fern] - *Adiantum capillus-veneris* L. (49) (1898), *Adiantum* L. (1, 4, 50, 109, 138) (1923–present), *Adiantum pedatum* L. (3, 4, 49, 72, 97, 102) (1886–1986)

Maidenhair grass [Maiden hair grass] - *Briza media* L. (92) (1876)

Maidenhair spleenwort [Maiden hair spleenwort, Maiden hair spleen wort, Maiden-hair spleanwort] - *Asplenium trichomanes* L. (3, 4, 5, 42, 50, 97, 109, 122, 131, 138, 155, 158) (1814–present)

Maidenhair tree [Maiden hair tree, Maidenhair-tree, Maiden-hair tree] - *Ginkgo biloba* L. (92, 107, 109, 136, 138) (1876-1949), *Ginkgo* L. (138) (1923)

Maidenhair vine [Maidenhair-vine] - *Muehlenbeckia complexa* Meisn. (109) (1949)

Maidenhair-berry [Maidenhair berry] - *Gaultheria hispidula* (L.) Muhl. ex Bigelow (5, 156) (1913-1923) no longer in use by 1923

Maiden's-ruin - *Artemisia abrotanum* L. (157, 158) (1900-1929)

Maiden's-tears [Maiden's tears] - *Silene vulgaris* (Moench) Garcke (5, 76, 156) (1876-1923) Orono ME

Maid-in-the-mist [Maid in the mist] - *Nigella damascena* L. (76) (1896) Acton MA, *Thalictrum* L. (1) (present)

Maid's-hair [Maid's hair, Maids' hair] - *Galium aparine* L. (158) (1900), *Galium verum* L. (92, 156, 158) (1898-1923) no longer in use by 1923

Maid's-love - *Artemisia abrotanum* L. (157, 158) (1900–1929)

Maiglocken (German) - *Convallaria majalis* L. (158) (1900)

Mail-grass - *Trifolium pratense* L. (158) (1900)

Mails - *Chenopodium album* L. (157, 158) (1900–1929)

Maine pinweed [Maine pin-weed] - *Lechea intermedia* Leggett ex Britt. var. *juniperina* (Bickn.) B.L. Robins. (5) (1913)

Maine rush - *Juncus ×oronensis* Fern. [*tenuis × vaseyi*] (5) (1913)

Maine sedge - *Carex ×stenolepis* Lessing [*saxatilis × vesicaria*] (5) (1913)

Maine's thorn - *Crataegus pruinosa* (Wendl.) K. Koch (5) (1913)

Main-oph-weep - *Datura inoxia* P. Mill. (6) (1892)

Maïŋ'gamûna'tĭg (Chippewa, wolf wood) - *Symphoricarpos albus* (L.) Blake (40) (1928)

Mais - *Zea mays* L. (180) (1633)

Mais (French) - *Zea mays* L. (158) (1900)

Mais (German) - *Zea mays* L. (158) (1900)

Maise - *Anthemis cotula* L. (5, 156, 157, 158) (1900–1929)

Maithen [Maythen] - *Anthemis cotula* L. (165, 179, 186) (1633–1814)

Maithes - *Anthemis cotula* L. (165) (1807)

Maize [Maiz, Mays] - *Zea* L. (45, 155, 158, 163) (1852–1942), *Zea mays* L. (10, 66, 67, 68, 92, 106, 107, 109, 110, 119, 121, 138, 155, 158, 180) (1492–1970) from aboriginal name

Maize thorn [Maize-thorn] - *Centaurea calcitrapa* L. (5, 156) (1913–1923)

Maizim - *Zea mays* L. (107) (1493)

Maizum - *Zea mays* L. (180) (1633)

Majorana - *Origanum majorana* L. (57) (1917)

Majorano - *Salvia ballotiflora* Benth. (75) (1894) TX & Mexico

Maka chiaka (Dakota) - *Hedeoma hispida* Pursh (37) (1919)

Maka ta omnicha or onmnicha (Dakota) - *Amphicarpaea bracteata* (L.) Fern. var. *comosa* (L.) Fern. (37) (1919)

Makačaŋšiŋhu (Lakota, skunk resin plant) - *Lygodesmia juncea* (Pursh) D. Don ex Hook. (121) (1918?-1970?)

Makan (Omaha-Ponca, the medicine) - *Lophophora williamsii* (Lem. ex Salm-Dyck) Coult. (37) (1919)

Makan bashahon-shon (Omaha-Ponca, crooked medicine) - *Physalis lanceolata* Michx. (37) (1919)

Makan chahiwi-cho (Winnebago, blue medicine) - *Gentiana puberulenta* J. Pringle (37) (1919)

Makan saka (Omaha-Ponca [raw medicine) - *Asclepias tuberosa* L. (37) (1919)

Makan skithe [Makan-skithe] (Omaha-Ponca, sweet medicine) - *Dalea purpurea* Vent. var. *purpurea* (37) (1919), *Humulus lupulus* L. var. *lupuloides* E. Small (37) (1919), *Iris versicolor* L. (37) (1830)

Makan-sagi (Omaha-Ponca, hard medicine) - *Liatris scariosa* (L.) Willd. var. *scariosa* (37) (1919)

Makan-tanga (Omaha-Ponca, big medicine or root) - *Silphium laciniatum* L. (37) (1919)

Makan-wasek (Omaha-Ponca, strong medicine) - *Mirabilis nyctaginea* (Michx.) MacM. (37) (1919)

Makanzhide sabe (Omaha-Ponca, black 'red medicine') - *Melia azedarach* L. (37) (1919)

Makatomniča (Lakota, ground bean) - *Amphicarpaea bracteata* (L.) Fern. (121) (1918?-1970?), *Strophostyles helvula* (L.) Ell. (121) (1918?-1970?)

Make-beggar - *Sagina procumbens* L. (156) (1923)

Make-peace - *Betula pubescens* Ehrh. (158) (1900)

Makibûg (Chippewa) - *Rhus glabra* L. (40) (1928)

Ma'kodji'bĭk (Chippewa, bear root) - *Smilax herbacea* L. (40) (1928)

Makon (Dorian) - *Papaver somniferum* L. (110) (1886)

Ma'kwona'gĭc odji'bĭk (Chippewa, bear entrails root) - *Apocynum androsaemifolium* L. (40) (1928)

Malabar glorylily - *Gloriosa superba* L. (138) (1923)

Malabar gourd - *Cucurbita ficifolia* Bouche (109) (1949)

Malabar nightshade [Malabar-nightshade] - *Basella* L. (109) (1949)

Malabar plum [Malabar-plum] - *Syzygium jambos* (L.) Alston (138) (1923)

Malabar sprangletop - *Leptochloa fusca* (L.) Kunth (50) (present)

Malabar-tree euphorbia [Malabartree euphorbia] - *Euphorbia tirucalli* L. (155) (1942)

Malaccaschambu [Malacca-schambu] (Malabar) - *Syzygium jambos* (L.) Alston (110) (1886)

Malachxil (Delaware) - *Phaseolus vulgaris* L. (107) (1919)

Malacodendron - *Stewartia malacodendron* L. (174, 177) (1753-1762)

Malacothrix - *Malacothrix sonchoides* (Nutt.) Torr. & Gray (5) (1913)

Malay apple - *Syzygium malaccense* (L.) Merr. & Perry (110) (1886)

Malay galangal - *Alpinia mutica* Roxb. (155) (1942)

Malcolm's stocks [Malcolm stocks] - *Malcolmia* R. Br. (109) (1949)

Male agaric - *Fomitopsis officinalis* (Batsch) Bondartsev & Singer (92) (1876)

Male balsam-apple [Male balsam apple] - *Impatiens balsamina* L. (178) (1526)

Male cornell tree - *Cornus mas* L. (178) (1526)

Male fern [Malefern, Male-fern, Male ferne] - *Athyrium filix-femina* (L.) Roth var. *asplenoides* (Michx.) Farw. (122) (1937) TX, *Dryopteris* Adans. (1) (1932), *Dryopteris filix-mas* (L.) Schott (4, 5, 49, 50, 52, 53, 54, 55, 57, 58, 60, 61, 92, 97, 109, 122, 131, 133, 138, 158, 178) (1696–present), *Osmunda regalis* L. (92) (1876), *Tectaria* Cav. (possibly) (7, 10) (1818-1828)

Male fluellin - *Helianthemum canadense* (L.) Michx. (46) (1671), *Veronica serpyllifolia* L. (178) (1526)

Male knotgrass [Male knot-grass] - *Polygonum aviculare* L. (158) (1900)

Male lavender - *Lavandula angustifolia* Mill. (92) (1876)

Male mercury [Male mercurie] - *Mercurialis annua* L. (178) (1526)

Male mervine (sic) - *Cypripedium parviflorum* Salisb. var. *parviflorum* (7) (1828)

Male nervine - *Cypripedium parviflorum* Salisb. (156) (1923), *Cypripedium parviflorum* Salisb. var. *pubescens* (Willd.) Knight (92) (1876), *Cypripedium reginae* Walt. (64, 158) (1900-1908)

Male shield fern [Male shield-fern - *Dryopteris filix-mas* (L.) Schott (5, 92, 158) (1876-1913)

Male southernwood - *Artemisia abrotanum* L. (178) (1526)

Male speedwell - *Veronica officinalis* L. (177) (1762)

Male Virginia dogwood [Male Virginian dogwood] - *Cornus florida* L. (8, 186) (1785-1825)

Maleberry [Male berry, Male-berry] - *Lyonia ligustrina* (L.) DC. (77, 109, 156) (1898-1949), *Lyonia ligustrina* (L.) DC. var. *ligustrina* (97) (1937) OK

Malice - *Malva rotundifolia* L. (5, 74, 156, 158) (1893-1923) Ferrisburgh VT

Mallow [Mallows, Mallowes, Malowe] - *Malva* L. (1, 4, 7, 10, 13, 15, 50, 82, 93, 106, 109, 138, 155, 156, 158, 179, 184) (1526–present), *Malva rotundifolia* L. (46, 57, 107, 114, 158) (1649-1919) accidentally introduced by 1671, *Malva sylvestris* L. (19, 57, 85, 190) (~1759-1932)

Mallow ninebark - *Physocarpus malvaceus* (Greene) Kuntze (138) (1923)

Mallow-rose [Mallow rose] - *Hibiscus moscheutos* L. (5, 74, 156, 158) (1893–1923) NY

Mallow-wort [Mallow wort] - *Callirhoe digitata* Nutt. (92) (1876)

Malo mujer (Spanish) - *Cnidoscolus texanus* (Muell.-Arg.) Small (122) (1937) TX

Malphigia - *Malpighia* L. (138) (1923)

Maltese cross [Maltesecross, Maltese-cross] - *Lychnis chalcedonica* L. (5, 50, 92, 109, 138, 156, 158) (1876–present)

Maltese-cross campion [Maltesecross campion] - *Lychnis chalcedonica* L. (155) (1942)

Malupwa (Crow) - *Prunus virginiana* L. var. *demissa* (Nutt.) Torr. (101) (1905) MT

Malus - *Malus sylvestris* Mill. (57) (1917)

Malva - *Malva sylvestris* L. (57, 92) (1876-1917)

Malvavisco (Spanish) - *Althaea officinalis* L. (158) (1900)

Mamay - *Mammea americana* L. (174) (1753)

Mamey - *Mammea americana* L. (109, 110, 138) (1886-1949) from West Indies aboriginal name, *Mammea* L. (138) (1923)

Mammal thistle - *Mammillaria* Haw. (14) (1882)

Mammee sapota - *Manilkara zapota* (L.) van Royen (110) (1886)

Mammee-apple [Mammee apple] - *Mammea americana* L. (109, 110) (1886-1949)

Mammillaria - *Mammillaria* Haw. (155) (1942)

Mammoth clover [Mamoth clover] - *Trifolium pratense* L. (5, 45, 138, 156, 158) (1896-1923)

Mammoth millet - *Setaria italica* (L.) Beauv. (45) (1896)

Mammoth tree - *Sequoiadendron giganteum* (Lindl.) Buchh. (14, 161) (1857-1882)

Mammoth Washington tree - *Sequoiadendron giganteum* (Lindl.) Buchh. (147) (1856)

Mamoncillo - *Melicoccus bijugatus* Jacq. (109, 138) (1923–1949)

Ma'nanons (Chippewa) - *Ostrya virginiana* (Mill.) K. Koch (40) (1928)

Man'asa'dĭ (Chippewa) - *Populus balsamifera* L. (40) (1928)

Manazhiha-hi (Omaha-Ponca) - *Urtica dioica* L. subsp. *gracilis* (Aiton) Seland. (37) (1919)

Manchenil tree - *Hippomane mancinella* L. (7) (1828)

Manchineel or Manchineel tree [Manchineel-tree] - *Hippomane* L. (167) (1814), *Hippomane mancinella* L. (20, 92, 106) (1857-1930)

Manchu alder - *Alnus viridis* subsp. *fruticosa* (Rupr.) Nyman (155) (1942)

Manchurian catalpa - *Catalpa bungei* C. A. Mey. (138) (1923)

Manchurian corktree - *Phellodendron amurense* Rupr. (137) (1931)

Manchurian honeysuckle - *Lonicera ruprechtiana* Regel (138) (1923)

Manchurian lilac - *Syringa reticulata* (Blume) Hara subsp. *amurensis* (Rupr.) P. S. Greene & M. C. Chang (138) (1923)

Manchurian maple - *Acer ginnala* Maxim. (135) (1910)

Manchurian monkshood - *Aconitum uncinatum* L. (50, 138, 155) (1931–present)

Mancillier - *Hippomane mancinella* L. (20) (1857)

Manda'mǐn (Chippewa) - *Zea mays* L. (14, 37, 38, 40) (1820–1928)
Mandarin - *Citrus reticulata* Blanco (109, 110) (1886-1949)
Mandarin orange - *Citrus reticulata* Blanco (138) (1923)
Mandchon orkoda - *Panax quinquefolius* L. (186) (1814)
Mande idhe shnaha (Omaha-Ponca, to make a bow smooth) - *Equisetum* L. (37) (1830)
Mandioca - *Manihot esculenta* Crantz (92) (1876)
Mandobi - *Arachis hypogaea* L. (107, 110) (1886-1919) Brazil
Mandois - *Arachis hypogaea* L. (107) (1682) Congo
Mandrake - *Circaea lutetiana* L. (156) (1923), *Podophyllum* L. (93, 158) (1900–1936), *Podophyllum peltatum* L. (1, 2, 6, 7, 13, 15, 46, 49, 52, 53, 54, 55, 57, 58, 59, 64, 107, 109, 121, 125, 156, 157, 158, 186, 187) (1671–1949)
Mandrake-pear [Mandrake pear] - *Podophyllum peltatum* L. (74) (1893)
Mandubi - *Arachis hypogaea* L. (107, 110) (1648-1919) Brazil
Maned barley - *Hordeum jubatum* L. (107) (1919)
Mangel - *Beta vulgaris* L. (107) (1919)
Mangel wurzel - *Beta vulgaris* L. (107) (1919)
Mangle - *Avicennia germinans* (L.) L. (19, 92) (1840-1876), *Baccharis halimifolia* L. (156) (1923), *Iva frutescens* L. subsp. *oraria* (Bartlett) R.C. Jackson (156) (1923)
Manglier à grappes (French) - *Laguncularia racemosa* (L.) Gaertn. f. (20) (1857)
Mango - *Mangifera indica* L. (106, 107, 110) (1886-1930)
Mango melon - *Cucumis melo* L. (109) (1949)
Mangold - *Beta vulgaris* L. (107) (1919)
Mangosteen - *Garcinia mangostana* L. (109, 110, 138) (1886-1949)
Mangrove or Mangrove tree - *Rhizophora* L. (7) (1828)
Mangrove or Mangrove tree - *Rhizophora mangle* L. (19, 20, 92) (1840-1876)
Mangummenauk (Narraganset) - *Quercus alba* L. (46) (1879)
Mani - *Arachis hypogaea* L. (7, 107, 110) (1828-1919) South America
Manido'bima'kwûd (Chippewa) - *Parthenocissus quinquefolia* (L.) Planch. (40) (1928)
Manila grass [Manila-grass] - *Zoysia matrella* (L.) Merr. (109, 138) (1923-1949)
Manila tamarind - *Pithecellobium dulce* (Roxb.) Benth. (109) (1949)
Man-in-the-ground [Man in the ground] - *Marah macrocarpus* (Greene) Greene var. *macrocarpus* (74) (1893), *Ipomoea pandurata* (L.) G.F.W. Mey. (7, 92) (1828-1876)
Manioc - *Manihot esculenta* Crantz (109, 110) (1886-1949)
Manitoba maple - *Acer negundo* L. (106, 156) (1923-1930) Western Canada
Manna - *Glyceria fluitans* (L.) R. Br. (92) (1876)
Manna (of Bible) - *Parmelia esculenta* (Pall.) Spreng. (107) (1886)
Manna croup grass - *Glyceria fluitans* (L.) R. Br. (5) (1913)
Manna grass [Manna-grass, Mannagrass] - *Glyceria fluitans* (L.) R. Br. (3, 56, 92, 107) (1876-1977), *Glyceria* R. Br. (1, 45, 50, 66, 93, 152, 155) (1896–present), *Glyceria striata* (Lam.) A.S. Hitchc. (85, 152) (1912-1932)
Manna gum - *Eucalyptus viminalis* Labill. (109, 138) (1923-1949)
Manna plant [Manna-plant] - *Alhagi maurorum* Medik. (107) (1919)
Manna plant [Manna-plant] - *Tamarix gallica* L. (107) (1919)
Manna seed - *Glyceria fluitans* (L.) R. Br. (92) (1876)
Mann's bush clover - *Lespedeza ×manniana* Mackenzie & Bush [*capitata × violacea*] (5) (1913)
Man-of-the-earth [Man of the earth] - *Ipomoea leptophylla* Torr. (77, 103, 107) (1870-1919), *Ipomoea pandurata* (L.) G.F.W. Mey. (2, 5, 19, 50, 57, 62, 92, 156, 158) (1840–present)
Man-om-in (Chipewa) - *Zizania aquatica* L. (103) (1871)
Mano'mǐn (Chippewa) - *Zizania palustris* L. (7, 40) (1828-1928)
Manpelaan (Modern India) - *Manihot* Mill. (110) (1886)
Manroot [Man root [Man-root] - *Ipomoea leptophylla* Torr. (5, 86, 103, 107, 158) (1870-1919), *Ipomoea pandurata* (L.) G.F.W. Mey. (5, 57, 92, 156, 158) (1876-1923)

Mansa-h'te-hi (Omaha-Ponca [real arrow tree]) - *Cornus asperifolia* Michx. (37) (1919)
Man-saté (Chippewa, strange aspen) - *Populus balsamifera* L. (105) (1932)
Man's-health [Man's health] - *Panax quinquefolius* L. (possibly) (6) (1892)
Mansi-hotsh (Winnebago) - *Cornus asperifolia* Michx. (37) (1919)
Man's-motherwort [Man's motherwort] - *Ricinus communis* L. (5, 156) (1913-1923)
Mantil - *Polygonum aviculare* L. (158) (1900)
Manuka tea-tree - *Leptospermum laevigatum* (Gaertner) F. Muell. (109) (1949)
Manuska (Winnebago) - *Hierochloe odorata* (L.) Beauv. (37) (1830)
Many-awn prickly-leaf [Manyawn pricklyleaf] - *Thymophylla aurea* (Gray) Greene ex Britt. (50) (present), *Thymophylla aurea* (Gray) Greene ex Britton var. *aurea* (50) (present)
Many-branch pepperweed [Manybranched pepperweed, Many-branched pepperweed] - *Lepidium ramosissimum* A. Nels. (50) (present)
Many-flower agrimony [Many-flowered agrimony] - *Agrimonia parviflora* Aiton (3, 4, 5, 72, 97, 131) (1899-1986)
Many-flower aster [Manyflowered aster, Many-flowered aster] - *Symphyotrichum ericoides* (L.) Nesom var. *ericoides* (80, 187) (1818-1913), *Symphyotrichum ericoides* (L.) Nesom var. *pansum* (Blake) Nesom (50) (present)
Many-flower broomrape [Manyflower broomrape] - *Orobanche ludoviciana* Nutt. subsp. *multiflora* (Nutt.) Collins (50) (present)
Many-flower broom-sedge [Many-flowered broom sedge] - *Andropogon virginicus* L. var. *virginicus* (94) (1901)
Many-flower cheat [Many-flowered cheat] - *Bromus racemosus* L. (possibly) (187) (1818)
Many-flower chironia [Many flowered chironia] - *Sabatia chloroides Pursh* (42) (1814)
Many-flower darnel [Many-flowered darnel] - *Lolium perenne* L. subsp. *multiflorum* (Lam.) Husnot (66) (1903)
Many-flower flatsedge [Manyflower flatsedge] - *Cyperus lancastriensis* Porter ex Gray (50) (present)
Many-flower marsh pennywort [Many-flowered marsh pennywort] - *Hydrocotyle umbellata* L. (5) (1913)
Many-flower monkey-flower [Manyflowered monkeyflower] - *Mimulus floribundus* Dougl. ex Lindl. (50) (present)
Many-flower psoralea [Many-flowered psoralea] - *Psoralidium tenuiflorum* (Pursh) Rydb. (93, 97) (1936-1937)
Many-flower rose [Many-flowering rose] - *Rosa multiflora* Thunb. ex Murray (135) (1910)
Many-flower sedge [Many-flowered sedge] - *Carex vulpinoidea* Michx. (187) (1818)
Many-flower Solomon's-seal [Manny flowered Solomon's seal, Many-flowered Solomon's-seal] - *Polygonatum biflorum* (Walt.) Ell. (42) (1814), *Polygonatum multiflorum* (L.) All. (187) (1818)
Many-flower stickseed [Manyflower stickseed] - *Hackelia floribunda* (Lehm.) I.M. Johnston (50) (present)
Many-flower trichloris [Many-flowered trichloris] - *Chloris pluriflora* (Fourn.) W.D. Clayton (94) (1901)
Many-fruit ludwigia [Many-fruited ludwigia] - *Ludwigia polycarpa* Short & Peter (5, 72) (1907-1913)
Many-fruit primrose-willow [Manyfruit primrose-willow] - *Ludwigia polycarpa* Short & Peter (50) (present)
Many-hair paspalum [Many-haired paspalum] - *Paspalum laeve* Michx. (5) (1913)
Many-head hedgehog cactus [Many-headed hedgehog cactus] - *Echinocactus polycephalus* Engelm. & Bigelow (86) (1878)
Many-head hymenopappus [Manyhead hymenopappus] - *Hymenopappus filifolius* Hook. var. *polycephalus* (Osterhout) B.L. Turner (50) (present)
Many-head rush [Manyhead rush, Many-headed rush] - *Juncus polycephalus* Michx. (3, 5, 50) (1913–present)

Many-head sedge [Manyhead sedge] - *Carex sychnocephala* Carey (50) (present)

Many-ray aster [Many ray aster, Manyray aster, Many-rayed aster] - *Symphyotrichum anomalum* (Engelm.) Nesom (3, 4, 5, 50, 97) (1913–present)

Many-root [Many root] - *Ruellia tuberosa* L. (92) (1876)

Many-seed goosefoot [Many-seeded goosefoot] - *Chenopodium polyspermum* L. (5) (1913)

Many-seed plantain [Many seeded plantain, Many-seeded plantain] - *Plantago heterophylla* Nutt. (5, 97, 122) (1913-1937)

Many-seed seedbox [Many-seeded seedbox] - *Ludwigia polycarpa* Short & Peter (3, 4) (1977-1986)

Many-spike chloris [Many-spiked chloris] - *Chloris elata* Desv. (94) (1901)

Many-spike flatsedge [Manyspike flatsedge] - *Cyperus polystachyos* Rottb. var. *polystachyos* (50) (present)

Many-spike salt grass [Many-spiked salt-grass] - *Spartina cynosuroides* (L.) Roth (19) (1840)

Many-spine opuntia [Many-spined opuntia] - *Opuntia polyacantha* Haw. (5, 93, 97) (1913-1937)

Many-stalk bur-reed [Many-stalked bur-reed] - *Sparganium angustifolium* Michx. (5) (1913)

Many-stem Andrew's-cross [Many stemmed Andrew's cross] - *Hypericum hypericoides* (L.) Crantz subsp. *multicaule* (Michx. ex Willd.) Robson (42) (1814)

Many-stem mulberry [Many-stemmed mulberry] - *Morus alba* L. (19) (1840)

Many-stem pea [Manystem pea] - *Lathyrus polymorphus* Nutt. (50) (present)

Many-stem St. Peter's-wort [Many-stemmed St. Peter's-wort] - *Hypericum hypericoides* (L.) Crantz subsp. *multicaule* (Michx. ex Willd.) Robson (187) (1818)

Manzania - *Mentha* ×*piperita* L. [*aquatica* × *spicata*] (77) (1898) CA

Manzanilla comun (Spanish) - *Matricaria recutita* L. (158) (1900)

Manzanilla coyote - *Pectis papposa* Harvey & Gray (76, 154) (1857-1896) CA, Mexico

Manzanilla fetida (Spanish) - *Anthemis cotula* L. (187) (1818)

Manzanita - *Arctostaphylos* Adans. (1, 50, 106, 155) (1930–present), *Arctostaphylos andersonii* Gray (77) (1898) CA, *Arctostaphylos glauca* Lindl. (75, 92, 107, 161) (1857-1919) CA, *Arctostaphylos pungens* Kunth (122, 153) (1913-1937), *Arctostaphylos tomentosa* (Pursh) Lindl. (103, 107) (1870-1919)

Manzañita (Spanish, little apple) - *Arctostaphylos tomentosa* (Pursh) Lindl. (103) (1870)

Manzanito - *Arctostaphylos glauca* Lindl. (57) (1917)

Manzhonka-mantanaha (Omaha-Ponca) - *Allium canadense* L. var. *mobilense* (Regal) Ownbey (37) (1830)

Maple - *Acer* L. (1, 4, 8, 10, 13, 15, 50, 82, 93, 106, 109, 156, 167, 184) (1785–present), *Acer saccharum* subsp. *grandidentatum* (Torr. & A.Gray) Desmarais (122) (1937)

Maple bush - *Acer spicatum* Lam. (43) (1820), *Bellis perennis* L. (92) (1876)

Maple guelder-rose [Maple guelder rose] - *Viburnum acerifolium* L. (19, 92) (1840-1876)

Maple lungwort - *Lobaria pulmonaria* (L.) Hoffm. (92) (1876)

Maple vine - *Menispermum canadense* L. (6) (1892)

Maple-ash [Maple ash] - *Acer negundo* L. (5, 156, 158) (1900–1923)

Maple-flower - *Bellis perennis* L. (158) (1900)

Maple-leaf alumroot [Maple leaf alum root, Mapleleaf alumroot] - *Heuchera villosa* Michx. (possibly) (7, 92) (1828-1876)

Maple-leaf arrow-wood [Maple-leaved arrow-wood, Maple-leaf arrowwood, Mapleleaf arrowwood] - *Viburnum acerifolium* L. (5, 122, 156) (1913-1937)

Maple-leaf globe-mallow [Maple-leaved globe mallow] - *Iliamna rivularis* (Dougl. ex Hook.) Greene var. *rivularis* (5, 156) (1913-1923)

Maple-leaf goosefoot [Mapleleaf goosefoot, Maple-leaved goosefoot, Maple-leaved goosefoot] - *Chenopodium rubrum* L. (85) (1932), *Chenopodium simplex* (Torr.) Raf. (3, 4, 21, 50, 62, 72, 80, 93, 95, 131, 145, 155, 156, 158) (1893–present)

Maple-leaf grape [Mapleleaf grape] - *Vitis acerifolia* Raf. (7, 50) (1828–present)

Maple-leaf guelder-rose [Maple-leaf guelder rose, Mapleleaf guelder rose] - *Viburnum acerifolium* L. (5, 156) (1913-1923)

Maple-leaf hawthorn [Maple leaved hawthorn] - *Crataegus phaenopyrum* (L. f.) Medik. (42) (1814)

Maple-leaf liquidambar tree [Maple-leaved liquidambar-tree] - *Liquidambar styraciflua* L. (8) (1785)

Maple-leaf mallow [Maple-leaved mallow] - *Iliamna rivularis* (Dougl. ex Hook.) Greene (85) (1932) SD

Maple-leaf mealy tree [Maple-leaved mealy-tree] - *Viburnum lantanoides* Michx. (5, 35, 37, 57) (1806–1919)

Maple-leaf pigweed [Maple-leaved pigweed] - *Chenopodium simplex* (Torr.) Raf. (2, 158) (1895–1900)

Maple-leaf viburnum [Mapleleaf viburnum, Maple-leaved viburnum] - *Viburnum acerifolium* L. (8, 138) (1785-1923)

Maple-sugar tree [Maple sugar tree] - *Acer rubrum* L. (92) (1876)

Maracock - *Passiflora* L. (181) (~1678)

Maracock vine - *Passiflora incarnata* L. (46) (1879)

Maranta - *Maranta* L. (138) (1923) for B. Maranta, Venetian physician and botanist, died 1754

Marbled alumroot - *Heuchera pubescens* Pursh (138) (1923)

Marbleseed - *Onosmodium* Michx. (50, 155) (1942–present)

March - *Petroselinum crispum* (P. Mill.) Nyman ex A.W. Hill (92, 158) (1876-1900)

March daisy - *Bellis perennis* L. (5) (1913)

March parsley - *Apium graveolens* L. var. *dulce* (P. Mill.) DC. (5) (1913)

March violet - *Viola odorata* L. (5) (1913)

Marcory - *Stillingia sylvatica* Garden ex L. (6, 7, 92, 158) (1828-1900)

Mardin iris - *Iris germanica* L. (138) (1923)

Mardling - *Lemna* L. (158) (1900), *Lemna minor* L. (5) (1913)

Mare blebs - *Caltha palustris* L. (6) (1892)

Mare blobs - *Caltha palustris* L. (6) (1892)

Mares tayle - *Equisetum* L. (178, 179) (1526-1596)

Mare's-tail [Marestail, Mare's tail, Mare's-tails] - *Conyza canadensis* (L.) Cronq. var. *canadensis* (2, 5, 45, 62, 125, 156, 157, 158) (1895-1929), *Equisetum hyemale* L. (5, 92) (1876-1913), *Hippuris* L. (1, 26, 50, 155, 158) (1826–present), *Hippuris vulgaris* L. (3, 4, 5, 10, 19, 85, 92, 93, 155, 156, 158) (1818-1986), *Symphyotrichum ericoides* (L.) Nesom var. *ericoides* (5, 156, 158) (1900-1923) no longer in use by 1923

Marg - *Anthemis cotula* L. (157, 158) (1900-1929)

Margaret - *Bellis perennis* L. (158) (1900)

Margarett's post oak - *Quercus margarettiae* (Ashe) Small (possibly) (122) (1937)

Margetym gentyll - *Origanum majorana* L. (179) (1526)

Marginal aspidium - *Dryopteris marginalis* (L.) A. Gray (42) (1814)

Marginal shield fern [Marginal shield-fern - *Dryopteris marginalis* (L.) A. Gray (4, 5, 49, 53, 109, 187) (1818-1986)

Marginal wood fern [Marginal woodfern] - *Dryopteris marginalis* (L.) A. Gray (50) (present)

Marginal-fruit shield fern [Marginal-fruited shield-fern, Marginal fruited shield fern] - *Dryopteris marginalis* (L.) A. Gray (64, 158) (1900–1908)

Marginated sedge - *Carex pennsylvanica* Lam. (187) (1818)

Margosa bark - *Melia azedarach* L. (57) (1917)

Margosa tree - *Azadirachta indica* A. Juss. (92) (1876)

Marguerite - *Bellis perennis* L. (5) (1913), *Chrysanthemum frutescens* L. (82, 109, 138) (1923-1949), *Leucanthemum vulgare* Lam. (4, 107, 156, 158) (1900–1986)

Marguerite (French) - *Bellis perennis* L. (158) (1900)

Marian violets (Diuers sorts) - *Campanula medium* L. (178) (1526)

Marienblatt (German) - *Balsamita major* Desf. (158) (1900)

Marierome - *Origanum majorana* L. (178) (1526)

Marietta Columbo - *Frasera caroliniensis* Walt. (186) (1814)

Marigold [Marigolds, Mary gold, Marygold] - *Bidens* L. (106) (1930), *Calendula* L. (92) (1876), *Calendula officinalis* L. (46, 49, 52, 53, 54, 55, 57, 59, 61, 92) (1571-1922) cultivated by English colonists by 1671, *Caltha palustris* L. (72) (1907) IA, *Gaillardia pulchella* Foug. (106) (1930), *Tagetes* L. (109, 138) (1923-1949)

Marijuana [Marihuana] - *Cannabis* L. (4) (1986), *Cannabis sativa* L. (3, 4, 50, 109, 125) (1930–present), *Cannabis sativa* L. subsp. *indica* (Lam.) E. Small & Cronq. (50) (present), *Cannabis sativa* L. subsp. *sativa* (50) (present), *Cannabis sativa* L. subsp. *sativa* var. *sativa* (50) (present)

Marilandische Cassia (German) - *Senna marilandica* (L.) Link (7) (1828)

Marilandische Cassie (German) - *Senna marilandica* (L.) Link (186) (1814)

Marine ivy - *Ampelopsis cordata* Michx. (156) (1923)

Marine oak - *Quercus hemisphaerica* Bartr. ex Willd. var. *maritima* (Michx.) Muller (10, 33) (1818-1826)

Mariock-apple - *Passiflora* L. (181) (~1678)

Mariola - *Parthenium incanum* Kunth (4, 50, 153) (1913–present)

Mariorayne - *Origanum majorana* L. (179) (1526)

Mariposa lily [Mariposa lilies, Mariposa-lily, Mariposalily] - *Calochortus gunnisonii* S. Wats. (85) (1932), *Calochortus luteus* Dougl. ex Lindl. (86) (1878), *Calochortus nuttallii* Torr. & Gray (3, 75, 85, 127, 157) (1894-1977), *Calochortus* Pursh. (1, 75, 93, 101, 109, 155, 158) (1886-1949) Spanish for butterfly, *Calochortus venustus* Dougl. ex Benth. (86) (1878)

Mariposa manzanita - *Arctostaphylos viscida* Parry subsp. *mariposa* (Dudley) P.V. Wells (155) (1942)

Mariposa tulip [Mariposatulip] - *Calochortus* Pursh. (155) (1942)

Marish-isha (Crow) - *Shepherdia argentea* (Pursh) Nutt. (101) (1905) MT

Maritime oak - *Quercus hemisphaerica* Bartr. ex Willd. var. *maritima* (Michx.) Muller (20) (1857)

Marjoram - *Origanum* L. (109, 138, 156, 184) (1793-1949), *Origanum majorana* L. (possibly) (92) (1876), *Origanum vulgare* L. (10, 106) (1818-1930)

Marjoram-scented milfoil - *Achillea millefolium* L. (165) (1768)

Marjorana - *Origanum majorana* L. (107) (13th Century)

Markery - *Chenopodium bonus-henricus* L. (5, 156) (1913-1923) no longer in use by 1923, *Toxicodendron radicans* (L.) Kuntze subsp. *radicans* (158) (1900)

Markry - *Toxicodendron radicans* (L.) Kuntze (5) (1913), *Toxicodendron radicans* (L.) Kuntze subsp. *radicans* (71) (1898), *Toxicodendron toxicarium* (Salisb.) Gillis (3, 73, 76, 156) (1892-1923)

Markweed [Mark weed, Mark-weed] - *Toxicodendron radicans* (L.) Kuntze (5) (1913), *Toxicodendron radicans* (L.) Kuntze subsp. *radicans* (71, 157, 158) (1898-1929) ME, *Toxicodendron toxicarium* (Salisb.) Gillis (73, 156) (1892-1923)

Marl-grass [Marl grass] - *Trifolium pratense* L. (5, 92, 156, 157, 158) (1876–1929)

Marmalade-plum [Marmalade plum] - *Manilkara zapota* (L.) van Royen (110) (1886), *Pouteria sapota* (Jacq.) H.E. Moore & Stearn (109) (1949)

Marone (Italy) - *Castanea sativa* Mill. (110) (1170)

Maroon gaillardia - *Gaillardia amblyodon* J. Gay (138) (1923)

Maroutte (French) - *Anthemis cotula* L. (186) (1814)

Marquiaas - *Passiflora laurifolia* L. (174) (1753)

Marram grass [Marram-grass] - *Ammophila arenaria* (L.) Link (56, 84, 94) (1880-1901), *Leymus arenarius* (L.) Hochst. (92) (1876)

Marram sea grass - *Leymus arenarius* (L.) Hochst. (5) (1913)

Marrish whorts (marshworts) - *Vaccinium macrocarpon* Aiton (86) (1884)

Marrone (Italy) - *Castanea sativa* Mill. (110) (1170)

Marronier de Californie (French) - *Aesculus californica* (Spach) Nutt. (20) (1857)

Marronier d'inde (French) - *Aesculus hippocastanum* L. (6) (1892), *Aesculus* L. (8) (1785)

Marrow - *Cucurbita maxima* Dcne. (107) (1919)

Marrube - *Marrubium vulgare* L. (5, 69, 156) (1903-1923) no longer in use by 1923

Marrube blanc (French) - *Marrubium vulgare* L. (158) (1900)

Marrubia (Spanish) - *Marrubium vulgare* L. (158) (1900)

Marrubium - *Marrubium vulgare* L. (59) (1911)

Marsh andromeda - *Andromeda polifolia* L. (165) (1807)

Marsh arrowgrass [Marsh arrow-grass - *Triglochin maritimum* L. (156) (1923), *Triglochin palustre* L. (5, 50, 66, 85, 93, 131) (1899–present)

Marsh bedstraw - *Galium palustre* L. (5, 72, 156) (1907-1923)

Marsh bellflower [Marsh belleflower] - *Campanula aparinoides* Pursh (3, 4, 5, 50, 72, 93, 95, 155, 156) (1907–present)

Marsh bellwort - *Campanula aparinoides* Pursh (131) (1899)

Marsh bent - *Agrostis capillaris* L. (45) (1896), *Agrostis mertensii* Trin. (94) (1901)

Marsh bent grass [Marsh bent-grass] - *Agrostis gigantea* Roth (5, 92, 119) (1876-1938)

Marsh betony - *Stachys pilosa* Nutt. var. *pilosa* (4) (1986)

Marsh blue violet - *Viola cucullata* Aiton (5, 72, 93, 109) (1907-1949)

Marsh bristle grass [Marsh bristlegrass] - *Setaria parviflora* (Poir.) Kerguélen (50) (present)

Marsh buttercup - *Ranunculus hispidus* Michx. (4) (1986), *Ranunculus hispidus* Michx. var. *nitidus* (Chapman) T. Duncan (3, 5, 72, 85, 93, 158) (1900-1977)

Marsh calla - *Calla palustris* L. (42) (1814)

Marsh chickweed - *Stellaria alsine* Grimm (5, 156) (1913-1923)

Marsh chistus - *Andromeda polifolia* L. (165) (1807)

Marsh cinquefoil [Marsh cinque-foil] - *Comarum palustre* L. (5, 72, 156) (1907-1923), *Potentilla* L. (1, 10, 158, 167) (1814-1932)

Marsh cistus - *Ledum* L. (8) (1785)

Marsh cleavers - *Galium palustre* L. (92) (1876)

Marsh clubmoss [Marsh club-moss] - *Lycopodiella inundata* (L.) Holub (5) (1913)

Marsh cranberry - *Gaultheria hispidula* (L.) Muhl. ex Bigelow (possibly) (8) (1785), *Vaccinium macrocarpon* Aiton (5, 46, 73, 156) (1879-1923), *Vaccinium oxycoccos* L. (73, 156) (1892-1923) NB

Marsh cress - *Rorippa palustris* (L.) Bess. (2, 63, 72, 107, 156) (1895-1923), *Rorippa palustris* (L.) Bess. subsp. *palustris* (80) (1913), *Rorippa* Scop. (1) (1932)

Marsh crowfoot - *Ranunculus sceleratus* L. (5, 6, 156) (1892-1923)

Marsh cudweed - *Gnaphalium uliginosum* L. (5, 50, 156, 158) (1900–present)

Marsh currant - *Ribes lacustre* (Pers.) Poir. (108) (1878)

Marsh cyperus - *Cyperus pseudovegetus* Steud. (5) (1913)

Marsh daisy - *Armeria maritima* (P. Mill.) Willd (156) (1923)

Marsh dandelion - *Taraxacum palustre* (Lyons) Symons (19, 92) (1840-1876)

Marsh diervilla - *Diervilla lonicera* Mill. (42) (1814)

Marsh epilobium - *Epilobium palustre* L. (6, 49, 53) (1892–1922)

Marsh false oat - *Sphenopholis pensylvanica* (L.) A.S. Hitchc. (5) (1913)

Marsh felwort - *Lomatogonium* A. Braun (1) (1932), *Lomatogonium rotatum* (L.) Fries ex Fern. (5, 156) (1913-1923)

Marsh fern [Marshfern] - *Thelypteris palustris* Schott (46, 3) (1879-1977), *Thelypteris palustris* Schott var. *pubescens* (Lawson) Fern. (5, 109, 138, 155, 158) (1913-1949)

Marsh fimbristylis - *Fimbristylis castanea* (Michx.) Vahl (5) (1913)

Marsh fimbry - *Fimbristylis castanea* (Michx.) Vahl (50) (present)

Marsh five-finger - *Comarum palustre* L. (2, 5, 19, 92, 156) (1840-1942)

Marsh flatsedge - *Cyperus pseudovegetus* Steud. (50) (present)

Marsh fleabane [Marsh flea bane] - *Pluchea* Cass. (1, 4, 106, 158) (1930-1986), *Pluchea foetida* (L.) DC. (19, 42, 92) (1814-1876), *Senecio congestus* (R.Br.) DC. (50) (present)

Marsh fleawort - *Senecio congestus* (R. Br.) DC. (5, 72, 156, 158) (1900–1923)

Marsh foxtail [Marsh fox tail] - *Alopecurus aequalis* Sobol. var. *aequalis* (85) (1932), *Alopecurus carolinianus* Walt. (119) (1938), *Alopecurus geniculatus* L. (3, 5, 56) (1911-1977)

Marsh gentian - *Gentiana saponaria* L. (156) (1923), *Gentiana saponaria* L. var. *saponaria* (5) (1913), *Gentiana villosa* L. (5, 156) (1913-1923), *Gentiana villosa* L. (possibly) (19, 49, 92) (1840-1898)

Marsh gilliflower - *Lychnis flos-cuculi* L. (5, 156) (1913-1923) no longer in use by 1923

Marsh goldflower [Marsh gold-flower] - *Caltha palustris* L. (86) (1878)

Marsh grass [Marshgrass, Marsh-grass] - *Distichlis spicata* (L.) Greene (87, 90) (1884-1885), *Spartina cynosuroides* (L.) Roth (21) (1893), *Spartina gracilis* Trin. (85, 90) (1885-1932), *Spartina maritima* (M.A. Curtis) Fern. (92) (1876), *Spartina patens* (Ait.) Muhl. (87, 88) (1884-1885), *Spartina* Schreber (1, 7, 10, 45, 66, 93) (1818-1936)

Marsh grass-of-parnassus [Marsh grass of Parnassus] - *Parnassia palustris* L. (5, 50, 156) (1913–present), *Parnassia palustris* L. var. *parviflora* (DC.) Boivin (50) (present)

Marsh groundsel - *Senecio congestus* (R.Br.) DC. (156, 158) (1900-1923)

Marsh hedgehog grass [Marsh hedgehog-grass] - *Carex flava* L. (5, 92, 156) (1913-1923)

Marsh hibiscus - *Hibiscus moscheutos* L. subsp. *moscheutos* (92, 187) (1818–1876)

Marsh hog's-fennel [Marsh hog's fennel] - *Peucedanum palustre* (L.) Moench (107) (1919)

Marsh holy-rose [Marsh holy rose] - *Andromeda polifolia* L. (possibly) (5, 165) (1807-1913)

Marsh holywort - *Andromeda polifolia* L. (156) (1923) no longer in use by 1923

Marsh horehound [Marsh hoarhound] - *Lycopus europaeus* L. (156) (1923)

Marsh horsetail - *Equisetum palustre* L. (4, 5, 50, 155, 158) (1900–present)

Marsh leather flower - *Clematis crispa* L. (5) (1913)

Marsh leatherwood [Marsh leather wood] - *Dirca palustris* L. (42) (1814)

Marsh lousewort - *Pedicularis palustris* L. (5, 156) (1913-1923)

Marsh milkweed [Marsh milk-weed, Marsh milk weed] - *Eupatorium purpureum* L. (5, 64, 73, 75, 156, 158) (1892–1923)

Marsh milkwort - *Polygala cruciata* L. (5, 156) (1913-1923)

Marsh millet - *Zizaniopsis miliacea* (Michx.) Doell & Aschers. (163) (1852)

Marsh muhlenbergia - *Muhlenbergia glomerata* (Willd.) Trin. (56) (1901), *Muhlenbergia racemosa* (Michx.) Britton, Sterns & Poggenb. (80) (1913)

Marsh muhly - *Muhlenbergia racemosa* (Michx.) Britton, Sterns & Poggenb. (3, 50, 140) (1944–present)

Marsh oat grass [Marsh oat-grass] - *Sphenopholis pensylvanica* (L.) A.S. Hitchc. (5, 66, 94) (1901-1913)

Marsh panic grass [Marsh panic-grass] - *Phanopyrum gymnocarpon* (Ell.) Nash (94) (1901)

Marsh parsley - *Apium graveolens* L. var. *dulce* (P. Mill.) DC. (5) (1913), *Conioselinum chinense* (L.) Britton, Sterns & Poggenb. (10) (1818)

Marsh pea - *Lathyrus* L. (158) (1900), *Lathyrus palustris* L. (19, 50, 158) (1840–present)

Marsh peavine - *Lathyrus palustris* L. (155) (1942)

Marsh pennywort - *Hydrocotyle* L. (1, 10, 158) (1818-1932), *Hydrocotyle umbellata* L. (156, 181) (~1678-1923)

Marsh pink - *Sabatia* Adans. (158) (1900), *Sabatia stellaris* Pursh (5, 122, 156) (1913-1937)

Marsh purslane [Marshpurslane] - *Ludwigia* L. (1, 158) (1900-1932), *Ludwigia palustris* (L.) Ell. (5, 63, 72, 93, 97, 155, 156, 157, 158) (1899-1937)

Marsh ragwort - *Senecio congestus* (R.Br.) DC. (131) (1899)

Marsh rose-gentian [Marsh rosegentian] - *Sabatia dodecandra* (L.) Britton, Sterns & Poggenb. (138) (1923)

Marsh samphire - *Salicornia maritima* Wolff & Jefferies (5, 107, 156) (1913-1923)

Marsh scorpion-grass [Marsh scorpion grass] - *Myosotis scorpioides* L. (5, 156, 158) (1900-1923)

Marsh sedge - *Carex acutiformis* Ehrh. (5, 156) (1913-1923)

Marsh seedbox - *Ludwigia palustris* (L.) Ell. (4, 50) (1986–present)

Marsh shield fern [Marsh shieldfern, Marsh shield-fern] - *Thelypteris palustris* Schott var. *pubescens* (Lawson) Fern. (5, 97, 122) (1913-1937)

Marsh skullcap [Marsh skull-cap, Marsh skull cap] - *Scutellaria galericulata* L. (3, 4, 5, 50, 72, 93, 131, 156, 157, 158) (1899–present)

Marsh smartweed - *Polygonum amphibium* L. var. *emersum* Michx. (80, 82) (1913-1930) IA

Marsh speedwell - *Veronica scutellata* L. (3, 4, 5, 155, 156) (1913-1986)

Marsh spike grass [Marsh-spike-grass] - *Distichlis spicata* (L.) Greene (5, 119) (1913-1938)

Marsh St. John's-wort [Marsh St. John's wort, Marsh St. Johnswort] - *Hypericum* L. (possibly) (2, 13) (1849-1895), *Triadenum* Raf. (1, 50, 93) (1932–present), *Triadenum virginicum* (L.) Raf. (3, 4, 5, 72) (1907-1986)

Marsh stitchwort - *Stellaria alsine* Grimm (5, 156) (1913-1923)

Marsh straw sedge - *Carex hormathodes* Fernald (5, 50) (1913–present), *Carex tenera* Dewey (72) (1907)

Marsh tea - *Ledum groenlandicum* Oeder (possibly) (47) (1852), *Ledum* (7) (1828), *Ledum palustre* L. (19, 92, 104) (1840-1896)

Marsh thistle - *Cirsium palustre* (L.) Scop. (5) (1913)

Marsh vaccinium - *Gaultheria hispidula* (L.) Muhl. ex Bigelow (possibly) (8) (1785)

Marsh valerian - *Valeriana dioica* L. (50, 155) (1942–present), *Valeriana uliginosa* (Torr. & Gray) Rydb. (5, 138, 156) (1913-1923)

Marsh vetchling - *Lathyrus palustris* L. (3, 4, 5, 72, 131, 156, 158) (1899-1986)

Marsh violet - *Viola palustris* L. (5, 50, 92, 109, 131, 155, 156) (1899–present)

Marsh watercress [Marsh water-cress, Marsh water cress] - *Rorippa palustris* (L.) Bess. (92, 131, 157, 158) (1876-1929), *Rorippa palustris* (L.) Bess. subsp. *palustris* (5, 85, 97) (1913-1937)

Marsh wedgescale - *Sphenopholis pensylvanica* (L.) A.S. Hitchc. (50) (present)

Marsh willowherb [Marsh willow herb [Marsh willow-herb - *Epilobium palustre* L. (5, 19, 50, 156, 158) (1840–present)

Marsh woundwort - *Stachys palustris* L. (5, 93, 156) (1913-1936)

Marshahy cord grass [Marshahy cordgrass] - *Spartina patens* (Ait.) Muhl. (155) (1942)

Marshallia [Marshalia] - *Marshallia* Schreb. (138, 155) (1923-1942)

Marshall's rush [Marshall rush] - *Juncus militaris* Bigel. (66) (1903)

Marshall's thorn - *Crataegus disperma* Ashe (5) (1913)

Marshaspita (Crow) - *Musineon divaricatum* (Pursh) Raf. var. *hookeri* (Torr. & Gray) Mathias (101) (1905) MT

Marsh-beetle [Marsh beetle] - *Typha latifolia* L. (5, 92, 156, 157, 158) (1876-1923)

Marshberry [Marsh-berry, Marsh berry] - *Vaccinium oxycoccos* L. (5, 73, 156) (1892-1923) Newfoundland

Marsh-clover [Marsh clover] - *Menyanthes trifoliata* L. (5, 6, 92, 156, 158) (1892–1923)

Marshelder [Marsh elder, Marsh-elder] - *Iva annua* L. var. *annua* (4, 21, 125) (1893-1986), *Iva axillaris* Pursh (85) (1932), *Iva fru-*

tescens L. (5, 10, 122) (1818-1937) TX, *Iva frutescens* L. subsp. *oraria* (Bartlett) R.C. Jackson (156) (1923), *Iva* L. (1, 2, 4, 50, 93, 156, 158) (1895–present), *Iva xanthifolia* Nutt. (3, 4, 63, 80, 121, 126, 131, 145) (1897-1986), *Viburnum opulus* L. (5, 156, 158) (1900-1923)

Marshlocks - *Comarum palustre* L. (40) (1928)

Marshmallow [Marsh mallow, Marsh mallows, Marsh-mallow] - *Althaea* L. (1, 50, 156, 165) (1768–present), *Althaea officinalis* L. (4, 3, 5, 7, 19, 46, 49, 52, 53, 55, 57, 58, 92, 107, 109, 138, 155, 156, 158, 178) (1596-1986), *Hibiscus* L. (1) (1932), *Hibiscus moscheutos* L. (156, 181) (~1678-1923), *Malva sylvestris* L. (107, 156) (1919-1923)

Marshmallow with yellow flowers [Marsh Mallow with yellow flowers] - *Abutilon theophrasti* Medik (178) (1526)

Marsh-marigold [Marsh marigold, Marshmarigold, Marsh mary-gold, Marsh marygold] - *Bidens aristosa* (Michx.) Britton (21) (1893), *Bidens connata* Muhl. ex Willd. (possibly) (42) (1814), *Caltha* L. (1, 4, 7, 10, 13, 15, 50, 93, 109, 155, 156, 158, 167) (1814–present), *Caltha leptosepala* DC. (190) (~1759), *Caltha palustris* L. (1, 3, 5, 6, 14, 15, 19, 63, 85, 86, 92, 105, 107, 127, 131, 3, 156, 157, 158, 187) (1818–1977) from Saxon merse meargeallia "marsh-horse gold"

Marsh-pepper knotweed [Marshpepper knotweed] - *Polygonum hydropiper* L. (50) (present)

Marsh-pepper smartweed [Marshpepper smartweed] - *Polygonum hydropiper* L. (155) (1942)

Marsh-pestle [Marsh-pistle (sic)] - *Typha latifolia* L. (5, 92, 156, 157, 158) (1876-1929)

Marsh-reed [Marsh reed] - *Equisetum palustre* L. (158) (1900)

Marshroot [Marsh root] - *Limonium carolinianum* (Walt.) Britt. (5, 92) (1876-1913)

Marsh-rosemary [Marsh rose-mary, Marsh rosemary] - *Andromeda polifolia* L. (5, 156) (1913-1923), *Ledum* L. (167) (1814), *Ledum palustre* L. (107) (1919), *Limonium carolinianum* (Walt.) Britt. (5, 49, 58, 92, 156) (1869-1923), *Limonium vulgare* Mill. (2, 19, 57) (1840-1917)

Marsh-sage - *Eupatorium perfoliatum* L. (156) (1923)

Marsh-trefoil [Marsh trefoil] - *Menyanthes* L. (1) (1932), *Menyanthes trifoliata* L. (5, 6, 7, 10, 49, 77, 92, 107, 156, 158, 187) (1818-1923)

Marsh-turnip [Marsh turnip] - *Arisaema triphyllum* (L.) Schott (37, 92, 158) (1830–1919)

Marshweed [Marsh weed] - *Equisetum palustre* L. (5) (1913)

Marshwort [Marsh wort] - *Vaccinium oxycoccos* L. (5, 92) (1876-1913)

Martagon de Canada (French) - *Lilium superbum* L. (46) (1619)

Martagon Imperiale (Flanders) - *Lilium martagon* L. (180) (1633)

Martagon lily - *Lilium martagon* L. (92, 109, 138) (1923-1949)

Marteau masses (French) - *Typha* L. (180) (1633)

Martha's Vineyard thorn - *Crataegus crus-galli* L. (5) (1913)

Martinoe - *Proboscidea louisianica* (P. Mill.) Thellung (5, 156, 158) (1900–1923)

Martynia - *Martynia* L. (155) (1942), *Proboscidea louisianica* (P. Mill.) Thellung (92, 107, 156) (1876-1923)

Marube fétide (French) - *Ballota nigra* L. (158) (1900)

Marube noir (French) - *Ballota nigra* L. (158) (1900)

Marucuia - *Passiflora incarnata* L. (181) (~1678)

Marvel - *Marrubium vulgare* L. (5, 69, 156, 158) (1900-1923) no longer in use by 1923

Marvel-of-Peru [Marvel of Peru] - *Mirabilis jalapa* L. (92, 109, 178) (1526-1949), *Mirabilis* L. (147) (1856), *Mirabilis longiflora* L. (92) (1876)

Mary thistle - *Silybum marianum* (L.) Gaertn. (52, 92) (1876-1919)

Mary-buds [Mary bud] - *Calendula officinalis* L. (92) (1876), *Ranunculus acris* L. (157, 158) (1900-1929) Shakespeare

Marygold-of-Peru [Marygold of Peru] - *Helianthus divaricatus* L. (46) (1671)

Mary-gowles [Mary gowles] - *Calendula officinalis* L. (179) (1526)

Maryland andromeda - *Lyonia mariana* (L.) D. Don (8, 165) (1785-1807)

Maryland blue-berry cypress [Maryland blue-berried cypress] - *Chamaecyparis thyoides* (L.) Britton, Sterns & Poggenb. (8) (1785)

Maryland cunila - *Cunila origanoides* (L.) Britton (186) (1814)

Maryland dittany - *Cunila origanoides* (L.) Britton (2, 109, 155) (1895-1949)

Maryland figwort [Maryland fig-wort - *Scrophularia marilandica* L. (3, 5, 72, 97, 131, 155, 157, 158) (1899-1977)

Maryland golden aster [Maryland golden-aster] - *Chrysopsis mariana* (L.) Ell. (5, 138, 156) (1913-1923)

Maryland golden star - *Chrysopsis mariana* (L.) Ell. (possibly) (86) (1878) name created by Thomas Meehan

Maryland hawkweed - *Hieracium ×marianum* Willd. [*gronovii × venosum*] (5) (1913)

Maryland heal-all - *Scrophularia marilandica* L. (5) (1913)

Maryland meadow-beauty [Maryland meadowbeauty, Maryland meadow beauty] - *Rhexia mariana* L. (5, 97, 138, 156) (1913-1937), *Rhexia mariana* L. var. *interior* (Pennell) Kral & Bostick (50) (present), *Rhexia mariana* L. var. *mariana* (122, 124) (1937)

Maryland milkwort - *Polygala mariana* Mill (5) (1913)

Maryland pilewort - *Scrophularia marilandica* L. (5) (1913)

Maryland pink - *Spigelia marilandica* (L.) L. (49, 52, 53, 54, 64) (1905-1922)

Maryland pinkroot [Maryland pink root] - *Spigelia marilandica* (L.) L. (6) (1892)

Maryland sanicle - *Sanicula marilandica* L. (50) (present)

Maryland scarlet lonicera - *Spigelia marilandica* (L.) L. (8) (1785)

Maryland senna [Maryland-senna] - *Senna marilandica* (L.) Link (4, 50, 186) (1825–present)

Maryland spurge - *Euphorbia corollata* L. (5) (1913)

Maryland stonemint - *Cunila origanoides* (L.) Britton (155) (1942)

Maryland tickclover - *Desmodium marilandicum* (L.) DC. (4, 155) (1942-1986)

Mascarene grass [Mascarene-grass] - *Zoysia tenuifolia* Willd. ex Thiele (109, 138, 163) (1852-1949)

Mashtincha-puté (Dakota [rabbitnose) - *Shepherdia argentea* (Pursh) Nutt. (37) (1919)

Ma-shu (Western Eskimo) - *Polygonum bistorta* L. (107) (1919)

Masliebenblume (German) - *Bellis perennis* L. (158) (1900)

Massive-spike prairie clover [Massive spike prairie clover] - *Dalea cylindriceps* Barneby (4) (1986)

Masson (Mauritius) - *Ziziphus zizyphus* (L.) Karst. (110) (1886)

Masterwort [Master-wort, Master wort, Masterwoorts] - *Angelica atropurpurea* L. (5, 6, 7, 49, 58, 64, 92, 107, 156) (1828-1923), *Angelica lucida* L. (10) (1818), *Astrantia* L. (109, 137, 155) (1923-1949), *Heracleum maximum* Bartr. (5, 7, 49, 52, 61, 62, 92, 156, 158) (1828-1923), *Indigofera suffruticosa* Mill. (190) (~1759), *Peucedanum ostruthium* (L.) W. D. J. Koch (5, 57, 92, 107, 156, 178) (1526-1923), *Peucedanum palustre* (L.) Moench (107) (1919)

Mastic tree - *Bursera simaruba* (L.) Sargent (15, 20) (1857-1895)

Mastich tree - *Rhus copallinum* L. (46) (1879)

Mat amaranth - *Amaranthus blitoides* S. Wats. (50) (present)

Mat chaff flower - *Alternanthera caracasana* Kunth (4) (1986)

Mat felon [Matfelon] - *Centaurea nigra* L. (5, 156) (1913-1923) no longer in use by 1923, *Centaurea scabiosa* L. (178) (1526)

Mat grama - *Bouteloua simplex* Lag. (122, 155) (1937-1942)

Mat grass [Mat-grass, Matgrass] - *Ammophila arenaria* (L.) Link (66, 87, 90) (1884-1903), *Nardus* L. (10, 50, 19) (1818–present), *Nardus stricta* L. (92) (1876), *Phyla nodiflora* (L.) Greene (106) (1930)

Mat muhly - *Muhlenbergia richardsonis* (Trin.) Rydb. (3, 50, 155, 185) (1936–present)

Mat prickly-phlox [Mat prickly phlox] - *Linanthus caespitosus* (Nutt.) J.M. Porter & L.A. Johnson (50) (present)

Mat rock-spirea [Mat rockspirea] - *Petrophyton caespitosum* (Nutt.) Rydb. (50) (present)

Mat rush [Mat-rush] - *Schoenoplectus tabernaemontani* (K.C. Gmel.) Palla (5, 156, 158) (1900-1923)

Mat sandbur - *Cenchrus longispinus* (Hack.) Fern. (50, 140) (1944–present), *Cenchrus spinifex* Cav. (155) (1942)

Mat spurge - *Chamaesyce stictospora* (Engelm.) Small (3, 4) (1977-1986)

Mat vetch - *Vicia americana* Muhl. ex Willd. subsp. *minor* (Hook.) C.R. Gunn (50) (present)

Mata - *Fleischmannia incarnata* (Walt.) King & H.E. (92) (1876)

Matasbuck (Algic tribes) - *Maianthemum* G.H. Weber ex Wiggers (7) (1828)

Matchweed [Match-weed] - *Bigelowia nudata* (Michx.) DC. (156) (1923), *Gutierrezia sarothrae* (Pursh) Britton & Rusby (146) (1939) MT

Maté - *Ilex paraguensis* St.Hilaire (107, 110) (1886-1919)

Mather - *Anthemis cotula* L. (5, 156, 165) (1807-1923) no longer in use by 1923

Mathes - *Anthemis cotula* L. (157, 158) (1900-1929)

Matilija poppy [Matilija-poppy] - *Romneya coulteri* Harvey (74, 109) (1893-1949)

Matitas - *Acacia farnesiana* (L.) Willd. (158) (1900) Mexico

Matricaire (French) - *Tanacetum parthenium* (L.) Schultz-Bip. (158) (1900)

Matricaria - *Matricaria recutita* L. (55) (1911)

Matricaria Parthenium - *Tanacetum parthenium* (L.) Schultz-Bip. (58) (1869)

Matricary - *Matricaria* L. (109) (1949)

Matricary grape fern [Matricary grape-fern] - *Botrychium matricariifolium* (A. Braun ex Dowell) A. Braun ex Koch (4, 50, 131, 155) (1899–present)

Matrimony plant [Matrimony-plant] - *Lunaria annua* L. (5, 156) (1913-1923)

Matrimony vine [Matrimony-vine, Matrimonyvine] - *Lunaria annua* L. (5, 76) (1896-1913) Paris ME, *Lycium barbarum* L. (1, 3, 5, 19, 50, 63, 72, 82, 85, 92, 93, 95, 106, 114, 148, 155, 156, 158) (1840–present), *Lycium chinense* Mill. (112) (1937), *Lycium* L. (82, 93, 109, 156, 158) (1900-1930)

Matsutake armillaria - *Armillaria matsutake* S. Ito & S. Imai (155) (1942)

Mattara (Finland) - *Galium boreale* L. (46) (1879)

Matted bluet - *Houstonia humifusa* (Gray) Gray (50) (present)

Matted grama - *Bouteloua simplex* Lag. (50) (present)

Matted sandmat - *Chamaesyce serpens* (Kunth) Small (50) (present)

Matted spike-rush [Matted spike rush] - *Eleocharis intermedia* (Muhl.) Schult (5, 50) (1913–present)

Matted wild buckwheat - *Eriogonum tenellum* Torr. (4) (1986)

Mattegras (Swedish) - *Lycopodium clavatum* L. (46) (1879)

Matting panicum - *Dichanthelium meridionale* (Ashe) Freckmann (5) (1913)

Matting rosette grass - *Dichanthelium meridionale* (Ashe) Freckmann (50) (present)

Matzatli (Mexican) - *Ananas comosus* (L.) Merr.var. *comosus* (110) (1886)

Mau - *Rosa rugosa* Thunb. (107) (1919)

Maudleine - *Achillea ageratum* L. (178) (1526)

Maudlin - *Achillea ageratum* L. (92, 165) (1768-1876)

Maudlin - *Balsamita major* Desf. (158) (1900)

Maudlin daisy [Maudlin-daisy] - *Leucanthemum vulgare* Lam. (5, 49, 156, 158) (1898-1923)

Maudlinwort [Maudlin wort] - *Leucanthemum vulgare* Lam. (92, 158) (1876-1900)

Maul - *Malva sylvestris* L. (5, 156) (1913-1923) no longer in use by 1923

Maurandia - *Maurandya* Ortega (138) (1923)

Maurandia vine - *Epixiphium wislizeni* (Engelm. ex Gray) Munz (149) (1904) NM

Mauritius raspberry - *Rubus rosifolius* Sm. (107) (1919)

Mauve (French) - *Malva sylvestris* L. (158) (1900)

Mauve phlox - *Phlox bifida* Beck subsp. *stellaria* (Gray) Wherry (138) (1923)

Mauve sauvage (French) - *Malva sylvestris* L. (158) (1900)

Mawroll - *Marrubium vulgare* L. (158) (1900)

Mawseed [Maw-seed] - *Papaver somniferum* L. (5, 92, 156) (1876-1923)

Max daisy - *Leucanthemum maximum* (Ramond) DC. (109) (1949)

Maximilian's sunflower [Maximilian sunflower, Maximillian's sunflower, Maximilians sunflower] - *Helianthus maximiliani* Schrad. (3, 4, 5, 50, 72, 80, 82, 85, 86, 97, 122, 124, 131, 138, 155) (1878–present)

May apple [Mayapple, May-apple] - *Achlys triphylla* (Sm.) DC. (76) (1896), *Exobasidium* Woronin (78) (1898), *Passiflora incarnata* L. (182) (1791), *Podophyllum* L. (50, 93, 138, 155, 156, 167) (1814–present), *Podophyllum peltatum* L. (1, 3, 4, 5, 6, 10, 13, 14, 15, 19, 41, 46, 49, 50, 53, 54, 55, 57, 58, 59, 61, 63, 64, 65, 72, 92, 97, 105, 107, 109, 121, 122, 124, 125, 156, 157, 158, 177, 184, 186, 187) (1762–present), *Rhododendron periclymenoides* (Michx.) Shinners (156) (1923)

May blobs [May-blob] - *Caltha palustris* L. (5, 156, 157) (1900-1929) England

May blossoms [May-blossom] - *Convallaria majalis* L. (5, 158) (1900-1913)

May bush - *Amelanchier ×intermedia* Spach [*arborea* × *canadensis*] (5) (1913), *Crataegus monogyna* Jacq. (5) (1913)

May cherry [May-cherry] - *Amelanchier canadensis* (L.) Medik. (5, 156, 158) (1900-1923) no longer in use by 1923, *Epigaea repens* L. (92) (1876)

May Day tree - *Prunus* L. (112, 63, 106) (1923-1937), *Prunus padus* L. (82) (1930)

May gowan - *Bellis perennis* L. (5, 158) (1900-1913)

May grass [Maygrass] - *Phalaris caroliniana* Walt. (3) (1977), *Poa annua* L. (5) (1913)

May lily [May Lillie] - *Convallaria majalis* L. (5, 49, 92, 158, 178) (1596-1913)

May pink - *Rhododendron canadense* (L.) Torr. (156) (1923)

May star [May-star] - *Trientalis borealis* Raf. subsp. *borealis* (75, 156) (1894-1923) NY

May thorn - *Crataegus monogyna* Jacq. (5) (1913)

Mayaca - *Mayaca fluviatilis* Aubl. (5) (1913)

Maydin here - *Adiantum capillus-veneris* L. (178, 179) (1526-1596)

Mayflower [May flower, May-flower] - *Anemone caroliniana* Walt. (76, 156, 158) (1896–1923), *Anemone nemorosa* L. (73) (1892), *Anemone quinquefolia* L. (5, 158) (1900–1913), *Anthemis cotula* L. (186) (1814), *Cardamine pratensis* L. (107, 156) (1919–1923), *Claytonia virginica* L. (5, 73, 158) (1892–1913), *Convallaria majalis* L. (156) (1923), *Epigaea repens* L. (2, 5, 6, 49, 58, 53, 109, 156) (1869–1949), *Hepatica nobilis* Schreb. (156) (1923), *Hepatica nobilis* Schreb. var. *acuta* (Pursh) Steyermark (5) (1913), *Maianthemum canadense* Desf. (156) (1923), *Maianthemum* G. H. Weber ex Wiggers (50) (present), *Penstemon* Schmidel (1) (1932), *Podophyllum peltatum* L. (49, 156) (1898–1923), *Pulsatilla patens* (L.) Mill. (5) (1913), *Pulsatilla patens* (L.) Mill.subsp. *multifida* (Pritz.) Zamels (6, 157, 158) (1892–1929), *Rhododendron periclymenoides* (Michx.) Shinners (5, 41, 75, 156) (1770–1923), *Saxifraga* L. (76) (1896) Auburndale MA, *Saxifraga virginiensis* Michx. (73, 156) (1892–1923) Allston MA, *Saxifraga virginiensis* Michx. var. *virginiensis* (5) (1913), *Thalictrum thalictroides* (L.) Eames & Boivin (5, 74, 156) (1893–1923) Eastern MA

May-pear [May pear] - *Amelanchier canadensis* (L.) Medik. (5, 73, 158) (1892-1913) New Brunswick, from time of flowering

Maypop [May-pop, May pop, Maypops, May pops] - *Passiflora incarnata* L. (3, 4, 5, 49, 53, 92, 106, 107, 109, 122, 124, 138, 156) (1876-1986)

Maypop passion-flower [Maypop passionflower] - *Passiflora incarnata* L. (155) (1942)

May-queen moss [May queen moss] - *Polytrichum juniperinum* Hedw. (92) (1876)

May-rose [May rose] - *Viburnum opulus* L. (5, 156, 158) (1900-1923) no longer in use by 1923

Mayten - *Maytenus boaria* Molina (109, 138) (1923-1949)

Mayweed [May-weed, May weed] - *Anthemis cotula* L. (5, 7, 10, 19, 42, 46, 47, 49, 57, 58, 62, 63, 72, 80, 82, 92, 93, 106, 122, 131, 156, 157, 158, 186, 187) (1671-1937) accidentally introduced by 1671, *Anthemis* L. (1, 10, 61, 93, 167) (1814-1936), *Matricaria* L. (50, 155) (1942–present), *Matricaria recutita* L. (158) (1900), *Tripleurospermum* Schultz-Bip. (50) (present)

Mayweed camomile - *Anthemis cotula* L. (155) (1942)

May-wings [May wings] - *Polygala paucifolia* Willd. (5, 74, 156) (1893-1923)

Maywort [May wort] - *Anthemis cotula* L. (92) (1876)

May-wreath [May wreath] - *Spiraea hypericifolia* L. (92) (1876)

Ma'zana'tĭg (Chippewa) - *Cirsium* Mill (40) (1928)

Mazard - *Prunus avium* (L.) L. (5) (1913)

Mazorquilla (Spanish) - *Phytolacca americana* L. var. *americana* (158) (1900)

Mazzard [Mazzards] - *Prunus avium* (L.) L. (92, 107, 137, 138, 156) (1876-1931)

McCalla's willow - *Salix maccalliana* Rowlee (50) (present)

Mdo (Dakota) - *Apios americana* Medik. (37) (1919)

Meadia - *Dodecatheon meadia* L. (174) (1753)

Meadow alexanders - *Zizia trifoliata* (Michx.) Fern. (50, 155) (1942–present)

Meadow anemone - *Anemone canadensis* L. (3, 4, 138, 155, 165) (1807-1986)

Meadow anemony - *Anemone canadensis* L. (109) (1949)

Meadow barley - *Hordeum brachyantherum* Nevski (5, 50) (1913–present), *Hordeum bulbosum* L. (5, 50, 56, 72, 94, 122, 152) (1901–present)

Meadow bittercress [Meadow bitter cress] - *Cardamine pratensis* L. (5) (1913)

Meadow blue violet - *Viola nephrophylla* Greene (85) (1932)

Meadow brome - *Bromus commutatus* Schrad. (50) (present), *Bromus erectus* Huds. (56, 66) (1901-1903)

Meadow brome grass [Meadow bromegrass] - *Bromus erectus* Huds. (56, 66, 138) (1901-1923)

Meadow buttercup [Meadow buttercups] - *Caltha palustris* L. (5, 74, 156, 158) (1893–1923), *Ranunculus acris* L. (5, 157, 158) (1900–1929), *Ranunculus repens* L. (158) (1900)

Meadow cabbage - *Symplocarpus foetidus* (L.) Salisb. ex Nutt. (5, 6, 53, 64, 92, 156) (1876-1923)

Meadow campion - *Lychnis flos-cuculi* L. (5, 156) (1913-1923)

Meadow cat's-tail [Meadow cat's tail] - *Phleum pratense* L. (5, 19, 68) (1840-1913), *Poa pratensis* L. (45) (1896)

Meadow chickweed - *Cerastium arvense* L. (5, 156) (1913-1923)

Meadow clover - *Trifolium pratense* L. (5, 93, 157, 158) (1900-1929)

Meadow comb grass - *Eragrostis pectinacea* (Michx.) Nees ex Steud. (56, 66) (1901-1903)

Meadow cowslip - *Caltha palustris* L. (187) (1818)

Meadow cranesbill - *Geranium pratense* L. (138) (1923)

Meadow cress - *Cardamine bulbosa* (Schreber. ex Muhl.) B.S.P. (7, 92) (1828-1876), *Cardamine pratensis* L. (107, 156) (1919-1923)

Meadow death-camas [Meadow deathcamas] - *Zigadenus venenosus* S. Wats. (50, 155) (1942–present)

Meadow fern - *Comptonia peregrina* (L.) Coult. (5, 7, 156) (1828-1923), *Myrica gale* L. (5, 75, 92, 156) (1876-1923) Dover ME, *Thelypteris palustris* Schott var. *pubescens* (Lawson) Fern. (158) (1900)

Meadow fescue - *Lolium pratense* (Huds.) S.J. Darbyshire (3, 11, 45, 56, 66, 67, 68, 90, 94, 109, 111, 129, 138, 140, 143, 152, 155) (1885-1977)

Meadow fescue grass [Meadow fescue-grass] - *Lolium pratense* (Huds.) S.J. Darbyshire (5, 56, 87, 119) (1885-1938)

Meadow flax - *Linum pratense* (Nort.) Small (50) (present)

Meadow foam - *Limnanthes douglasii* R. Br. (106) (1930)

Meadow foxtail [Meadow fox tail, Meadow fox-tail] - *Alopecurus pratensis* L. (3, 5, 45, 50, 56, 66, 67, 68, 87, 88, 90, 92, 94, 109, 129, 138, 143, 155) (1884–present)

Meadow fox-tail grass - *Alopecurus pratensis* L. (165) (1768)

Meadow garlic - *Allium canadense* L. (19, 50, 72, 92, 93, 97, 138, 158) (1840–present), *Allium canadense* L. var. *canadense* (50) (present), *Allium canadense* L. var. *lavendulare* (Bates) M. Ownbey & Aase (50) (present), *Allium canadense* L. var. *mobilense* (Regal) Ownbey (50) (present)

Meadow geranium - *Geranium pratense* L. (5) (1913)

Meadow gowan - *Caltha* L. (1) (1932)

Meadow grass [Meadow-grass, Medow Grasse] - *Alopecurus pratensis* L. (19) (1840), *Glyceria striata* (Lam.) A.S. Hitchc. (5) (1913), *Poa* L. (1, 45, 108, 152, 184) (1793-1932), *Poa pratensis* L. (2, 5, 10, 19, 92, 178, 180) (1596-1913), *Puccinellia* Parl. (1) (1932), *Glyceria striata* (Lam.) A.S. Hitchc. (119) (1938), *Puccinellia* Parl. (93) (1936)

Meadow holly [Meadow-holly - *Ilex crenata* Thunb. (5, 97, 156, 158) (1900-1937)

Meadow horsetail - *Equisetum palustre* L. (3) (1977), *Equisetum pratense* Ehrh. (3, 4, 5, 50, 155) (1913–present)

Meadow lily - *Lilium canadense* L. (5, 75, 109, 157, 158) (1894-1949), *Lilium candidum* L. (49, 92) (1876-1898) NY, *Lilium superbum* L. (158) (1900)

Meadow lousewort - *Pedicularis crenulata* Benth. (50) (present)

Meadow love grass [Meadow love-grass] - *Eragrostis refracta* (Muhl.) Scribn. (163) (1852)

Meadow mushroom - *Agaricus campestris* L. (170) (1995)

Meadow oat grass - *Arrhenatherum elatius* (L.) Beauv. ex J. Presl & C. Presl (68, 87, 88) (1884-1890), *Helictotrichon pratense* (L.) Pilg. (66) (1903)

Meadow pea - *Lathyrus pratensis* L. (5, 82) (1913-1930)

Meadow pedicularis - *Pedicularis crenulata* Benth. (155) (1942)

Meadow pink [Meadow-pink] - *Arethusa bulbosa* L. (78) (1898) MA, *Dianthus deltoides* L. (5, 156) (1913-1923), *Lychnis flos-cuculi* L. (5, 156) (1913-1923), *Platanthera grandiflora* (Bigelow) Lindl. (5, 73, 156) (1892-1923) MA, *Rhododendron viscosum* (L.) Torr. (5, 92, 156) (1876-1923), *Sabatia campestris* Nutt. (156) (1923)

Meadow plum - *Prunus americana* Marsh. (19) (1840), *Prunus angustifolia* Marsh. (possibly) (19) (1840)

Meadow poke - *Veratrum viride* Ait. (6, 19, 71) (1818-1898)

Meadow rattlesnake grass - *Glyceria canadensis* (Michx.) Trin. (19) (1840)

Meadow root - *Limonium carolinianum* (Walt.) Britt. (92) (1876)

Meadow rose - *Rosa blanda* Aiton (5, 85, 93, 131, 138, 155, 158) (1899-1942)

Meadow rue [Meadow-rue, Meadowrue] - *Thalictrum dasycarpum* Fisch. & Avé-Lall. (37, 82) (1919–1930), *Thalictrum dioicum* L. (19, 92) (1840–1876), *Thalictrum* L. (1, 2, 4, 7, 10, 13, 15, 41, 50, 63, 82, 93, 109, 127, 138, 155, 156, 158, 167) (1770–present), *Thalictrum thalictroides* (L.) Eames & Boivin (102) (1886)

Meadow run-a-gates [Meadow-runagates] - *Lysimachia nummularia* L. (156, 158) (1900-1923)

Meadow rush - *Scirpus expansus* Fern. (129) (1894)

Meadow rye grass [Meadow ryegrass] - *Lolium pratense* (Huds.) S.J. Darbyshire (50) (present)

Meadow saffron - *Colchicum autumnale* L. (52, 54, 55, 57, 60, 92) (1876-1919), *Colchicum* L. (180) (1633)

Meadow sage - *Salvia lyrata* L. (92) (1876), *Salvia pratensis* L. (5, 138) (1913-1923)

Meadow salsify - *Tragopogon pratensis* L. (4, 5, 131, 155, 156, 158) (1876–1942)

Meadow saxifrage - *Seseli* L. (10) (1818)

Meadow scabish [Meadow-scabish] - *Symphyotrichum puniceum* (L.) A.& D. Löve var. *puniceum* (5, 49, 92, 156, 158) (1898-1923) no longer in use by 1923

Meadow sedge - *Carex flava* L. (156) (1923), *Carex granularis* Muhl. ex Willd. (5, 72) (1907-1913), *Carex granularis* Muhl. ex Willd. var. *haleana* (Olney) Porter (3) (1977), *Carex granularis* Muhl. var. *granularis* (3) (1977), *Carex praticola* Rydb. (50) (present)

Meadow soft grass - *Holcus* L. (66) (1903), *Holcus lanatus* L. (5, 45, 66, 87, 90) (1884-1913)

Meadow sorrel - *Rumex acetosa* L. (5, 92, 156) (1876-1923) WV

Meadow spear grass [Meadow spear-grass] - *Glyceria striata* (Lam.) A.S. Hitchc. (5, 66, 119) (1903-1938)

Meadow spikemoss - *Selaginella apoda* (L.) Spring (50) (present)

Meadow spiraea - *Spiraea alba* Du Roi (138) (1923)

Meadow sundrops - *Oenothera pilosella* Raf. subsp. *pilosella* (5, 156) (1913-1923)

Meadow sunflower - *Bidens laevis* (L.) Britton, Sterns & Poggenb. (46) (1783), *Helianthus grosseserratus* Martens (80) (1913)

Meadow tall dropseed - *Sporobolus compositus* (Poir.) Merr. var. *drummondii* (Trin.) Kartesz & Gandhi (155) (1942)

Meadow turnip - *Arisaema triphyllum* (L.) Schott (64) (1908)

Meadow violet - *Viola cucullata* Aiton (131, 156) (1899-1923), *Viola nephrophylla* Greene (3, 5, 93, 97, 98) (1913-1977)

Meadow willow - *Salix petiolaris* Sm. (3, 4, 50, 85) (1932–present)

Meadow zizia - *Zizia aptera* (Gray) Fern. (50) (present)

Meadow-beauty [Meadowbeauty, Meadow beauty] - *Rhexia* L. (1, 2, 4, 122, 138, 155, 158) (1895-1986), *Rhexia virginica* L. (5, 19, 63, 72, 86, 92, 97, 124, 156) (1840-1937)

Meadow-bloom [Meadow bloom, Meadowbloom] - *Ranunculus acris* L. (6, 7) (1828-1932), *Ranunculus bulbosus* L. (92, 158) (1876-1900)

Meadow-bout [Meadow bouts, Meadow-bouts, Meadowbouts] - *Caltha* L. (7) (1828), *Caltha palustris* L. (5, 92, 157, 184) (1793–1929)

Meadow-bright [Meadow bright] - *Caltha palustris* L. (107) (1919)

Meadow-burs - *Myrica gale* L. (156) (1923)

Meadow-cup [Meadow cup] - *Sarracenia purpurea* L. (5, 76, 156) (1896-1923) ME

Meadow-fern bur [Meadow fern burrs] - *Myrica gale* L. (92) (1876)

Meadowfoam [Meadow-foam] - *Limnanthes douglasii* R. Br. (109, 138) (1923-1949)

Meadow-gift - *Calopogon tuberosus* (L.) B.S.P. var. *tuberosus* (156) (1923)

Meadow-gowan [Meadow gowan] - *Caltha palustris* L. (156, 157) (1900–1929)

Meadow-nuts [Meadow nuts] - *Comarum palustre* L. (5) (1913)

Meadow-parsnip [Meadow parsnip, Meadowparsnip] - *Thaspium barbinode* (Michx. Nutt. (4, 40, 85, 95) (1911-1986), *Thaspium* Nutt. (1, 4, 50, 156, 158) (1900–present), *Thaspium trifoliatum* (L.) Gray var. *aureum* Britt. (8, 156) (1785-1923), *Zizia aptera* (Gray) Fern. (3, 85) (1932-1977), *Zizia aurea* (L.) W.D.J. Koch (19, 92) (1840-1876), *Zizia* W.D.J. Koch (1, 93) (1932-1936)

Meadowpride [Meadow-pride, Meadow pride] - *Frasera caroliniensis* Walt. (possibly) (7, 64, 92, 156) (1828-1928)

Meadow-queen [Meadow queen] - *Filipendula* Mill. (1) (1932), *Filipendula ulmaria* (L.) Maxim. (5, 156) (1913-1923), *Filipendula ulmaria* (L.) Maxim. subsp. *ulmaria* (92) (1876)

Meadowrue-leaf anemone [Meadow-rue leaved anemone] - *Anemonella thalictroides* (L.) Spach (42) (1814)

Meadow-star [Meadow star] - *Stellaria longipes* Goldie subsp. *longipes* (92) (1876), *Stellaria palustris* (Murr.) Retz. (92) (1876)

Meadowsweet [Meadow-sweet, Meadow sweet] - *Filipendula* Mill. (possibly) (109, 138) (1923-1949), *Filipendula ulmaria* (L.) Maxim. (5, 156) (1913-1923), *Filipendula ulmaria* (L.) Maxim. subsp. *ulmaria* (92) (1876), *Gillenia trifoliata* (L.) Moench (5, 92, 186) (1825-1913), *Porteranthus stipulatus* (Muhl. ex Willd.) Britt. (7) (1828), *Spinacia oleracea* L. (82, 85) (1930-1932), *Spiraea alba* Du Roi (3, 109) (1949-1977), *Spiraea alba* Du Roi var. *latifolia* (Aiton) Dippel (109, 156) (1923-1949), *Spiraea betulifolia* Pallas var. *corymbosa* (Raf.) Maxim. (85) (1932), *Spiraea japonica* L.

f. (1, 4, 156, 167, 184) (1793-1986), *Spiraea* L. (1, 4, 82, 85, 156, 167) (1814-1986), *Spiraea salicifolia* L. (19, 82, 105, 156) (1840-1932), *Spiraea splendens* Baumann ex K. Koch var. *splendens* (85) (1932), *Spiraea tomentosa* L. (5, 19, 49, 58, 92, 156) (1840-1923)

Meadow-turnip - *Arisaema triphyllum* (L.) Schott (158) (1900)

Meadow-wort [Meadowwort, Meadow wort] - *Filipendula ulmaria* (L.) Maxim. (5, 156) (1913-1923), *Filipendula ulmaria* (L.) Maxim. subsp. *ulmaria* (92) (1876)

Meadpw parsnip [Medow parsnep] - *Heracleum sphondylium* L. (178) (1526)

Mead's milkweed - *Asclepias meadii* Torr. ex Gray (4, 5, 50, 72, 82) (1907–present)

Mead's sedge - *Carex meadii* Dewey (3, 5, 50, 72) (1893–present)

Meadsweete - *Filipendula ulmaria* (L.) Maxim. subsp. *ulmaria* (178) (1526)

Meadwort [Mead-wort] - *Spiraea salicifolia* L. (156) (1923)

Meagre oat - *Avena strigosa* Schreb. (107) (1919)

Meakin - *Myriophyllum spicatum* L. (5, 156, 158) (1900-1923) no longer in use by 1923

Mealberry [Meal-berry, Meal berry] - *Arctostaphylos uva-ursi* (L.) Spreng. (5, 92, 156, 157) (1876–1929)

Mealies - *Zea mays* L. (158) (1900) Australia, S. Africa

Meal-plum [Meal plum] - *Arctostaphylos uva-ursi* (L.) Spreng. (5, 156) (1913-1923)

Meals - *Chenopodium album* L. (156, 157, 158) (1900–1929)

Mealy aletris - *Aletris farinosa* L. (42) (1814)

Mealy bellwort - *Uvularia perfoliata* L. (5, 49, 156) (1898-1923)

Mealy blue sage - *Salvia farinacea* Benth. (124) (1937) TX

Mealy bush [Mealybush] - *Zeltnera exaltata* (Griseb.) G. Mans. (138, 181) (~1678-1923), *Zenobia pulverulenta* (W. Bartram ex Willd.) Pollard (7, 92) (1828-1876)

Mealy corydalis - *Corydalis crystallina* Engelm. (3, 4) (1977-1986)

Mealy fumewort - *Corydalis crystallina* Engelm. (50) (present)

Mealy goosefoot - *Chenopodium incanum* (S. Wats.) Heller (5, 50, 93, 97, 122) (1913–present), *Chenopodium incanum* (S. Wats.) Heller var. *incanum* (50) (present)

Mealy ink cap - *Coprinus fimetarius* Fr. (128) (1933)

Mealy primrose - *Primula laurentiana* Fern. (5, 156) (1913-1923)

Mealy starwort - *Aletris farinosa* L. (5, 7, 64, 92, 156) (1828-1923)

Mealy tree [Mealy-tree] - *Viburnum dentatum* L. (5, 7, 92, 156) (1828-1923)

Mealy-cup sage [Mealycup sage] - *Salvia farinacea* Benth. (138) (1923)

Means' grass [Means-grass, Means grass] - *Sorghum halepense* (L.) Pers. (45, 87, 88, 109, 158) (1885-1949) Southern states, introduced by Gov. Means of SC in 1835

Mecapatli - *Smilax glauca* Walt. (177) (1762)

Mechameck [Mechamech, Mecha-meck, Mech-a-meck] - *Ipomoea pandurata* (L.) G.F.W. Mey. (5, 6, 7, 92, 156, 158, 186, 187) (1814-1923) aboriginal name

Mechameck bindweed - *Ipomoea pandurata* (L.) G.F.W. Mey. (7) (1828)

Mechoacan - *Ipomoea pandurata* (L.) G.F.W. Mey. (19, 92) (1840-1876), *Phytolacca americana* L. var. *americana* (49) (1898), *Smilax glauca* Walt. (181) (~1678)

Mechoacan du Canada (French) - *Phytolacca americana* L. var. *americana* (186) (1814)

Mechoacana [Mechoacanna] - *Ipomoea pandurata* (L.) G.F.W. Mey. (75, 158, 187) (1818-1900) NY

Mecoacan [Mecoacanna] - *Ipomoea pandurata* (L.) G.F.W. Mey. (7, 186) (1814-1828)

Meconium - *Papaver somniferum* L. (49) (1898)

Medaddy bush [Medaddy-bush, Medaddybush] - *Lonicera canadensis* Bartr. ex Marsh. (5, 156) (1913-1923)

Mederacle - *Rhinanthus* L. (179) (1526)

Mediate spike rush - *Eleocharis intermedia* (Muhl.) Schult (66, 72) (1903-1907)

Medick [Medic] - *Medicago* L. (1, 10, 109, 138, 155, 156, 184) (1793–1949), *Medicago lupulina* L. (92) (1876), *Medicago sativa* L. (14, 19, 45, 118) (1840-1898), *Medicago sativa* L. subsp. *sativa* (possibly) (82) (1930)

Medick fitch - *Onobrychis viciifolia* Scop. (158) (1900)

Medicke fodder - *Medicago scutellata* (L.) Mill. (possibly) (178) (1526)

Medicke fodder of Arabia - *Medicago arabica* (L.) Huds. (178) (1526)

Medinilla - *Medinilla* Gaud. (138) (1923)

Mediterranean anemone - *Anemone oregana* Gray (155) (1942), *Anemone parviflora* Michx. (155) (1942)

Mediterranean convovulus - *Convolvulus althaeoides* L. (138) (1923)

Mediterranean crownvetch - *Coronilla valentina* L. (50) (present)

Mediterranean love grass [Mediterranean lovegrass] - *Eragrostis barrelieri* Daveau (3, 155) (1942-1977)

Mediterranean onion - *Allium paniculatum* L. (155) (1942)

Mediterranean sage - *Salvia aethiopis* L. (50) (present)

Mediterranean sea holly [Mediterranean sea hollie] - *Eryngium campestre* L. (178) (1526)

Mediterranean serpentroot - *Scorzonera laciniata* L. (155) (1942)

Mediterranean stork's-bill [Mediterranean stork's bill] - *Erodium malacoides* (L.) L'Hér. ex Aiton (50) (present)

Mediterranean wheat - *Triticum turgidum* L. (109) (1949)

Medlar [Medlars] - *Amelanchier canadensis* (L.) Medik. (92) (1876), *Diospyros virginiana* L. (46, 107, 181) (~1678-1919)

Medlar [Medlars] or Medlar tree - *Mespilus* L. (8, 109, 138, 184) (1785-1949)

Medlar bush - *Amelanchier canadensis* (L.) Medik. (19) (1840)

Medomhumar - *Morella cerifera* (L.) Small (46) (1879) Nantucket natives

Medsger's wild senna - *Senna marilandica* (L.) Link (5, 97) (1913-1937)

Medusa's-trumpet [Medusa's trumpet] - *Narcissus bulbocodium* L. (92) (1876)

Meehania - *Meehania cordata* (Nutt.) Britton (5) (1913)

Meergrüne magnolie - *Magnolia virginiana* L. (186) (1814)

Meer-radys (Holland) - *Armoracia rusticana* P.G. Gaertn., B. Mey. & Scherb. (110) (1886)

Meerretig [Meerrettig] (German) - *Armoracia rusticana* P.G. Gaertn., B. Mey. & Scherb. (110, 158) (1886-19000)

Meertrübli (Soleure, Switzerland) - *Ribes rubrum* L. (110) (1886)

Meetin seed [Meetin-seed] - *Foeniculum vulgare* Mill. (156) (1923)

Meeting-houses [Meeting houses] - *Aquilegia canadensis* L. (5, 156, 157, 158) (1900-1929)

Megerkraut (German) - *Galium verum* L. (158) (1900)

Meg-many-feet - *Ranunculus repens* L. (156, 158) (1900-1923)

Mehlige Aletris (German) - *Aletris farinosa* L. (6) (1892)

Mehlige Sterngrass (German) - *Aletris farinosa* L. (7) (1828)

Meipen (Welsh) - *Brassica rapa* L. (110) (1886)

Mekminswan (Chippewa) - *Campanula rotundifolia* L. (105) (1932)

Melaleuca - *Melaleuca* L. (138) (1923) Greek "black white" for black trunk and white branches of some species

Melanthium - *Melanthium* L. (158) (1900) from Greek meaning 'black flower'

Melanzana (Italy) - *Solanum melongena* L. (110) (16th century)

Melega (Millanois, Lombardy) - *Sorghum bicolor* (L.) Moench (180) (1633)

Mélèze (French) - *Larix decidua* Mill. (possibly) (8) (1785)

Mélèze blanc (French) - *Larix laricina* (Du Roi) K.Koch (possibly) (8) (1785)

Mélèze noir (French) - *Larix laricina* (Du Roi) K.Koch (possibly) (8) (1785)

Mélèze rouge (French) - *Larix laricina* (Du Roi) K.Koch (possibly) (8) (1785)

Melga (Spanish) - *Medicago sativa* L. (110) (1886)

Melge - *Chenopodium album* L. (157, 158) (1900-1929)

Melic - *Melica* L. (155) (1942)

Melic grass [Melic grass, Melic-grass] - *Melica* L. (1, 10, 41, 50, 93, 152) (1770–present), *Melica mutica* Walt. (19, 66, 87, 179) (1793-1903), *Melica nitens* (Scribn.) Nutt. ex Piper (111) (1915), *Melica smithii* (Porter ex Gray) Vasey (3, 85) (1932-1977)

Melic-like hair grass [Melic like hair grass] - *Trisetum melicoides* (Michx.) Vasey ex Scribn. (42) (1814)

Melilot - *Melilotus* Mill. (82, 109, 156) (1923-1949), *Melilotus officinalis* (L.) Lam. (6, 14, 92, 107, 156) (1876-1923)

Melilot (French) - *Melilotus officinalis* (L.) Lam. (6) (1892)

Mélilot officinal (French) - *Melilotus officinalis* (L.) Lam. (158) (1900)

Melilot trefoil - *Medicago lupulina* L. (5, 92, 158) (1876–1913)

Melilotenklee (German) - *Melilotus officinalis* (L.) Lam. (6, 156) (1892-1900)

Meliloto (Spanish) - *Melilotus officinalis* (L.) Lam. (158) (1900)

Melilotus - *Melilotus officinalis* (L.) Lam. (57) (1917)

Melissa - *Melissa officinalis* L. (57, 114) (1894-1917)

Melissa thoroughwort - *Ageratina aromatica* (L.) Spach (138) (1923)

Melisse - *Melissa officinalis* L. (179) (1526)

Melist - *Melilotus officinalis* (L.) Lam. (107) (1919)

Mellilot - *Melilotus* Mill. (179) (1526)

Mellilot clover - *Melilotus* Mill. (7) (1828), *Melilotus officinalis* (L.) Lam. (92) (1876)

Mellone (Italy) - *Cucumis melo* L. (107) (1919)

Melocoton - *Prunus persica* (L.) Batsch (178) (1526)

Melocoton duranzo (Spanish) - *Prunus persica* (L.) Batsch (158) (1900)

Melon [Melons] - *Citrullus lanatus* (Thunb.) Matsumura & Nakai (182) (1791), *Cucumis melo* L. (92, 106, 107, 109, 110, 138, 179) (1526–1949) possibly introduced into America by Columbus

Melon cactus [Meloncactus] - *Melocactus intortus* (Mill.) Urb. (92, 107) (1876-1919), *Melocactus* Link & Otto (155) (1942)

Melon loco - *Apodanthera undulata* Gray (149) (1904) NM

Melon peach - *Prunus persica* (L.) Batsch (178) (1526)

Melon pumpkin - *Cucurbita maxima* Dcne. (55) (1911), *Cucurbita moschata* (Duchesne ex Lam.) Duchesne ex Poir. (110) (1886)

Melon thistle [Melon thistles] - *Melocactus intortus* (Mill.) Urb. (14) (1882), *Opuntia* Mill. (10) (1818)

Melon tree [Melon-tree] - *Carica papaya* L. (52, 54, 57, 107) (1905-1919)

Melon-apple flower [Mellon-appel flower] - *Tetragonotheca helianthoides* L. (7, 177) (1762-1828)

Melone - *Cucumis melo* L. (107) (1617)

Melone (Italy) - *Cucumis melo* L. (107) (1919)

Meloni (Sardinia) - *Cucumis melo* L. (107) (1919)

Melon-leaf nightshade [Melon-leaved nightshade] - *Solanum citrullifolium* A. Br. (4, 5) (1913-1986), *Solanum heterodoxum* Dunal (possibly) (72) (1907)

Melonsilla (Mexican, little melon) - *Malvella leprosa* (Ortega) Krapov (150) (1894)

Melothria - *Melothria* L. (50) (present)

Memminger's hexastylis - *Hexastylis virginica* (L.) Small (5) (1913)

Memory root - *Arisaema triphyllum* (L.) Schott (6, 78) (1892-1898) MA

Menagwake-minš (Chippewa, fragrant root tree) - *Sassafras albidum* (Nutt.) Nees (105) (1932)

Menisperme (French) - *Menispermum* L. (8) (1785)

Ménisperme de Canada (French) - *Menispermum canadense* L. (8) (1785)

Ménisperme de Caroline (French) - *Cocculus carolinus* (L.) DC. (8) (1785)

Ménisperme du Canada (French) - *Menispermum canadense* L. (158) (1900)

Menispermum - *Menispermum canadense* L. (57, 64) (1908-1917)

Mentha - *Mentha* × *piperita* L. [*aquatica* × *spicata*] (52) (1919)

Menthe (French) - *Mentha* L. (158) (1900)
Menthe des chats (French) - *Nepeta cataria* L. (158) (1900)
Menthe poivree (French) - *Mentha* ×*piperita* L. [*aquatica* × *spicata*] (6) (1892)
Menthe romaine (French) - *Mentha spicata* L. (158) (1900)
Menthe vert (French) - *Mentha spicata* L. (158) (1900)
Menthe-coq (French) - *Balsamita major* Desf. (158) (1900)
Mentzelia - *Mentzelia aspera* L. (174) (1753), *Mentzelia decapetala* (Pursh ex Sims) Urban & Gilg ex Gilg (127) (1933), *Mentzelia* L. (93, 148, 155) (1936-1942) for Christian Mentzel, 1622-1701, German botanist
Menyanthe (French) - *Menyanthes trifoliata* L. (158) (1900)
Menyanthe trefle (French) - *Menyanthes trifoliata* L. (6) (1892)
Menyanthe trefle d'eau (French) - *Menyanthes trifoliata* L. (7) (1828)
Menyanthes - *Menyanthes trifoliata* L. (57) (1917)
Menzies' arbutus - *Arbutus menziesii* Pursh (103) (1870)
Menzies' campion - *Silene menziesii* Hook. (50) (present), *Silene menziesii* Hook. subsp. *menziesii* var. *menziesii* (50) (present)
Menzies' fiddleneck - *Amsinckia menziesii* (Lehm.) A. Nels. & J.F. Macbr. (50) (present)
Menzies' loco [Menzies loco] - *Astragalus nuttallii* (Torr. & Gray) J.T. Howell var. *nuttallii* (155) (1942)
Menzies nemophila - *Nemophila menziesii* Hook. & Arn. (138) (1923)
Menzies' pink - *Silene menziesii* Hook. (5) (1913)
Menzies' rattlesnake plantain - *Goodyera oblongifolia* Raf. (5) (1913)
Menzies' silene [Menzies silene] - *Silene menziesii* Hook. (155) (1942)
Menzies' spiraea [Menzies spiraea] - *Spiraea douglasii* Hook. var. *menziesii* (Hook.) K. Presl (138) (1923)
Menzies' spruce - *Pseudotsuga menziesii* (Mirb.) Franco (161) (1857)
Menzies' spruce-fir [Menzies spruce fir] - *Pseudotsuga menziesii* (Mirb.) Franco (20) (1857)
Menzie's strawberry tree - *Arbutus menziesii* Pursh (20) (1857)
Menziesia - *Menziesia* Smith. (138) (1923)
Mequot - *Packera aurea* (L.) A.& D. Löve (158) (1900)
Mercury - *Acalypha* L. (93) (1936), *Chenopodium bonus-henricus* L. (107, 156) (1919–1923), *Iris versicolor* L. (61) (1870) termed the mercury of Eclectic practice, *Mercurialis* L. (156) (1923), *Toxicodendron radicans* (L.) Kuntze subsp. *radicans* (5, 71) (1898–1913), *Toxicodendron toxicarium* (Salisb.) Gillis (6, 73, 76, 156) (1892–1923)
Mercury goosefoot - *Chenopodium bonus-henricus* L. (5) (1913)
Mercury herb - *Mercurialis annua* L. (92) (1876)
Mercury-weed [Mercury weed] - *Acalypha virginica* L. (5, 7, 92, 156, 157, 158) (1828-1923), *Mercurialis annua* L. (57) (1917)
Mérédi or méridi (Italian Swiss sea-radish) - *Armoracia rusticana* P. G. Gaertn., B. Mey. & Scherb. (110) (1886)
Mermaid-weed [Mermaid weed] - *Floerkea proserpinacoides* Willd. (156) (1923), *Proserpinaca* L. (1) (1932), *Proserpinaca palustris* L. (5, 19, 63, 72, 97, 156) (1840-1937)
Merry - *Prunus avium* (L.) L. (5) (1913)
Merrybells [Merry bells] - *Uvularia* L. (138, 155, 156) (1923-1942)
Mesa dropseed - *Sporobolus flexuosus* (Thurb. ex Vasey) Rydb. (3, 50, 122, 155) (1937–present)
Mesa muhly - *Muhlenbergia tenuifolia* (Kunth) Trin. (122) (1937)
Mescal - *Agave americana* L. (103) (1871), *Agave* L. (149) (1904), *Lophophora lewinii* (Hennings ex Lewin) C.H. Thomps. (57) (1917)
Mescal buttons - *Lophophora lewinii* (Hennings ex Lewin) C.H. Thomps. (104) (1896)
Mescal-bean [Mescal bean, Mescalbean] - *Sophora secundiflora* (Ortega) Lag. ex DC. (109, 122, 124, 138) (1923-1949)
Mescal-button peyote [Mescalbutton peyote] - *Lophophora williamsii* (Lem. ex Salm-Dyck) Coult. (155) (1942)
Mescat acacia - *Acacia constricta* Benth. (155) (1942)
Mesembryanthemum - *Mesembryanthemum* L. (155) (1942)
Meskit - *Prosopis juliflora* (Sw.) DC. (158) (1900)

Mespila - *Diospyros virginiana* L. (107) (1919)
Mespilorum - *Diospyros virginiana* L. (107) (1919)
Mespilus - *Crataegus* L. (8) (1785)
Mesquit - *Prosopis glandulosa* Torr. (76, 123) (1856-1896), *Prosopis juliflora* (Sw.) DC. (96, 158) (1891-1900)
Mesquit grass - *Bouteloua curtipendula* (Michx) Torr. (22) (1893), *Bouteloua gracilis* (Willd. ex Kunth) Lag. ex Griffiths (66) (1903)
Mesquite - *Bouteloua gracilis* (Willd. ex Kunth) Lag. ex Griffiths (45) (1896), *Buchloe dactyloides* (Nutt.) Engelm. (87) (1884)
Mesquite crownbeard [Mesquite crown-beard] - *Verbesina microptera* DC. (124) (1937) TX
Mesquite grass [Mesquite-grass] - *Bouteloua curtipendula* (Michx) Torr. (116, 118, 129) (1894-1958), *Bouteloua curtipendula* (Michx.) Torr. var. *curtipendula* (5) (1913), *Bouteloua gracilis* (Willd. ex Kunth) Lag. ex Griffiths (5, 30, 45, 56, 87, 88, 99, 118, 119, 151) (1844-1938), *Bouteloua* Lag. (1, 67, 87, 93) (1884-1936), *Bouteloua rigidiseta* (Steud.) Hitchc. (163) (1852), *Buchloe dactyloides* (Nutt.) Engelm. (5) (1913), *Muhlenbergia porteri* Scribn. ex Beal (152, 163) (1852-1912), *Muhlenbergia texana* Buckl. (151) (1896) NM
Mesquite or Mesquite tree - *Prosopis glandulosa* Torr. (3, 65, 103, 123, 125) (1856-1977), *Prosopis juliflora* (Sw.) DC. (45, 50, 104, 107, 151, 153, 158) (1896–present), *Prosopis* L. (1, 106) (1930-1932), *Prosopis pubescens* Benth. (106) (1930)
Messamine - *Coccoloba pubescens* L. (181) (~1678)
Metack sunancks - *Opuntia* Mill. (181) (~1678)
Metaquesunnauk - *Opuntia ficus-indica* (L.) Mill. (46) (1879) natives on Roanoke
Metcalfe's bean [Metcalfe bean] - *Phaseolus ritensis* M.E.Jones (138) (1923)
Metl - *Agave americana* L. (110) (1886) Mexico
Mettaquesunnauks - *Opuntia* Mill. (181) (~1678)
Meurier - *Morus* L. (41) (1770)
Meussorlin (German) - *Antennaria dioica* (L.) Gaertn. (46) (1879)
Mewzie's larkspur - *Delphinium bicolor* Nutt. (131) (1899)
Mexicali onion - *Allium peninsulare* J.G. Lemmon ex Greene (155) (1942)
Mexican ageratum - *Ageratum houstonianum* Mill. (138, 155) (1923-1942)
Mexican alvaradoa - *Alvaradoa amorphoides* Liebm. (155) (1942)
Mexican bamboo [Mexican-bamboo] - *Polygonum cuspidatum* Sieb. & Zucc. (4, 109) (1949-1986)
Mexican banana - *Yucca baccata* Torr. (158) (1900)
Mexican bent grass [Mexican bent-grass] - *Muhlenbergia mexicana* (L.) Trin. (165, 187) (1818-1768)
Mexican buckeye - *Umbellularia californica* (Hook. & Arn.) Nutt. (4) (1986), *Ungnadia speciosa* Endl. (15, 109, 122, 124) (1895-1949)
Mexican campion - *Silene laciniata* Cav. (138) (1923)
Mexican cendronella - *Agastache mexicana* (Kunth) Lint & Epling (138) (1923)
Mexican clover - *Richardia scabra* L. (74, 87, 106, 109) (1884-1949)
Mexican corn - *Zea mays* L. (56) (1901)
Mexican date yucca - *Yucca faxoniana* (Trel.) Sarg. (138) (1923)
Mexican dayflower - *Commelina coelestis* Willd. (138) (1923)
Mexican devilweed [Mexican devil-weed] - *Chloracantha spinosa* (Benth.) Nesom (4) (1986)
Mexican dock - *Rumex salicifolius* Weinm. var. *mexicanus* (Meisn.) A.S. Hitchc (50, 155) (1942–present)
Mexican dropseed [Mexican drop-seed - *Muhlenbergia mexicana* (L.) Trin. (56, 94, 119) (1901-1938)
Mexican drop-seed grass - *Muhlenbergia mexicana* (L.) Trin. (80) (1913)
Mexican elder - *Sambucus nigra* L. subsp. *canadensis* (L.) R. Bolli (153, 155) (1913-1942)
Mexican eragrostis - *Eragrostis mexicana* (Hornem.) Link subsp. *mexicana* (56) (1901)
Mexican eupatorium - *Ageratum corymbosum* Zuccagni (138) (1923)

Mexican evening-primrose [Mexican evening primrose] - *Oenothera laciniata* Hill (124) (1937), *Oenothera speciosa* Nutt. (109) (1949)

Mexican firebush [Mexican fire bush] - *Kochia scoparia* (L.) Schrad. (4) (1986)

Mexican fireweed [Mexican-fireweed] - *Kochia scoparia* (L.) Schrad. (50, 80) (1913–present)

Mexican four-o'clock [Mexican four o'clock] - *Mirabilis jalapa* L. (19) (1840)

Mexican frangipani - *Plumeria rubra* L. (138) (1923)

Mexican giant-hyssop [Mexican gianthyssop] - *Agastache mexicana* (Kunth) Lint & Epling (155) (1942)

Mexican ground-cherry [Mexican ground cherry] - *Physalis philadelphica* Lam. var. *immaculata* Waterfall (5, 97, 122, 124, 156) (1913-1937)

Mexican ground-plum [Mexican ground plum] - *Astragalus crassicarpus* Nutt. var. *berlandieri* Barneby (124) (1937)

Mexican heliotrope - *Phyla cuneifolia* (Torr.) Greene (77) (1898)

Mexican ironwood - *Olneya tesota* Gray (106) (1930)

Mexican lavender - *Vitex agnus-castus* L. (106, 124) (1930-1937)

Mexican lobelia - *Lobelia cardinalis* L. (138, 155) (1923-1942)

Mexican love grass [Mexcian lovegrass] - *Eragrostis mexicana* (Hornem.) Link subsp. *mexicana* (50, 122, 155) (1937–present)

Mexican madrone - *Arbutus xalapensis* Kunth (155) (1942)

Mexican milkweed - *Asclepias fascicularis* Dcne. (155) (1942)

Mexican monkeycomb - *Pithecoctenium crucigerum* (L.) A.H. Gentry (138) (1923)

Mexican morning-glory [Mexican morningglory] - *Ipomoea purpurea* (L.) Roth (138) (1923)

Mexican mosquito-fern [Mexican mosquitofern] - *Azolla mexicana* Schlecht. & Cham. ex K. Presl (50) (present)

Mexican mudplantain - *Heteranthera mexicana* S. Wats. (50) (present)

Mexican mugwort - *Artemisia ludoviciana* Nutt. subsp. *mexicana* (Willd. ex Spreng.) Keck (5, 97, 122) (1913–1937)

Mexican muhlenbergia - *Muhlenbergia mexicana* (L.) Trin. (66, 90) (1885-1903)

Mexican muhly - *Muhlenbergia mexicana* (L.) Trin. (50) (present)

Mexican orange [Mexican-orange] - *Choisya* Kunth (138) (1923)

Mexican panic grass [Mexican panicgrass] - *Panicum hirticaule* J. Presl. (50) (present)

Mexican persimmon - *Diospyros texana* Scheele (106, 122, 124) (1930-1937)

Mexican plum - *Prunus mexicana* S. Wats. (50, 122, 155) (1937–present)

Mexican poppy - *Argemone mexicana* L. (6, 72, 82, 92, 97) (1892-1936), *Argemone polyanthemos* (Fedde) Ownbey (145) (1897)

Mexican prickly-poppy [Mexican pricklypoppy] - *Argemone mexicana* L. (5, 155, 156) (1913-1942)

Mexican rosary-bean [Mexican rosarybean] - *Rhynchosia precatoria* DC. (138) (1923)

Mexican rose - *Portulaca grandiflora* Hook. (5, 73, 156, 158) (1892-1923) Chestertown MD

Mexican rubbertree - *Castilla elastica* Sessé (138) (1923)

Mexican sagebrush - *Artemisia ludoviciana* Nutt. subsp. *mexicana* (Willd. ex Spreng.) Keck (155) (1942)

Mexican salt grass [Mexican salt-grass] - *Eragrostis obtusiflora* (Fourn.) Scribn. (94, 152) (1901-1912)

Mexican seed [Mexico seed] - *Ricinus communis* L. (5, 92) (1876-1913)

Mexican silk-tassel [Mexican silk tassel] - *Garrya ovata* Benth. subsp. *goldmannii* (Woot. & Standl.) Dahling (4) (1986)

Mexican spear grass - *Eragrostis mexicana* (Hornem.) Link subsp. *mexicana* (56) (1901)

Mexican star [Mexican-star] - *Milla biflora* Cav. (138) (1923), *Milla* Cav. (109) (1949)

Mexican stone pine - *Pinus cembroides* Zucc. (109, 138) (1923-1949)

Mexican sycamore - *Platanus racemosa* Nutt. (161) (1857)

Mexican tea - *Chenopodium ambrosioides* L. (3, 4, 5, 50, 7, 14, 62, 69, 72, 80, 92, 93, 95, 97, 107, 125, 156, 157, 158) (1828–present), *Chenopodium ambrosioides* L. var. *ambrosioides* (50) (present), *Ephedra* L. (4) (1986)

Mexican teosinte - *Zea mexicana* (Schrad.) Kuntze (68) (1890) NM

Mexican tulip-poppy - *Hunnemannia* Sweet (109) (1949)

Mexican vanilla - *Vanilla planifolia* B.D. Jackson (138) (1923)

Mexican Washington palm - *Washingtonia robusta* H. Wendl. (138) (1923)

Mexican weed [Mexico-weed] - *Ricinus communis* L. (156) (1923)

Mexican white pine - *Pinus strobiformis* Engelm. (138) (1923)

Mexican wood grass - *Muhlenbergia mexicana* (L.) Trin. (129) (1894)

Mexican woodsia - *Woodsia mexicana* Fee (155) (1942)

Mexikanisches Traubenkraut (German) - *Chenopodium ambrosioides* L. (158) (1900)

Mezcal - *Lophophora lewinii* (Hennings ex Lewin) C.H. Thomps. (132) (1855)

Mezerei cortex - *Daphne mezereum* L. (49) (1898)

Mezereon - *Daphne mezereum* L. (19, 41, 49, 55, 57, 60, 92, 156) (1770-1923), *Thymelaea passerina* (L.) Coss. & Germ. (50) (present)

Mezereum - *Daphne mezereum* L. (57, 59, 60, 156) (1902-1917)

Mezquit - *Prosopis glandulosa* Torr. (147) (1856), *Prosopis* L. (106) (1930)

Mezquit grass - *Bouteloua hirsuta* Lag. (92) (1876)

Mezquite - *Prosopis juliflora* (Sw.) DC. (30) (1844)

Mezquite grass - *Bouteloua gracilis* (Willd. ex Kunth) Lag. ex Griffiths (66) (1903)

Mezza forda - *Typha* L. (180) (1633)

M'gos atik (Chippewa, awl wood) - *Nyssa sylvatica* Marsh. (105) (1932)

Mia (Cochin-Chinese) - *Saccharum officinarum* L. (110) (1886)

Miami mist - *Phacelia purshii* Buckl. (156) (1923)

Mičapeča (Lakota) - *Hesperostipa spartea* (Trin.) Barkworth (121) (1918-1970)

Micco hoyenejau (Creek) - *Salix humilis* Marsh. var. *tristis* (Aiton) Griggs (46) (1879)

Mice pink - *Silene armeria* L. (5, 76, 156) (1896-1923) Hennepin IL, no longer in use by 1923

Michaelmas daisy [Michaelmas daisies] - *Aster* L. (75, 76, 109) (1894–1949), *Symphyotrichum ericoides* (L.) Nesom var. *ericoides* (5, 156, 158) (1900–1923), *Symphyotrichum novae-angliae* (L.) G. L. Nesom (76, 158) (1896–1900), *Symphyotrichum tradescantii* (L.) Nesom (5, 72, 82, 92, 138) (1876–1930)

Michaux's ash - *Fraxinus profunda* (Bush) Bush (5) (1913)

Michaux's basswood [Michaux's bass wood] - *Tilia americana* L. var. *heterophylla* (Vent.) Loud. (5) (1913)

Michaux's blue-eyed grass - *Sisyrinchium mucronatum* Michx. (5) (1913)

Michaux's cyperus - *Cyperus odoratus* L. (5, 72) (1907-1913)

Michaux's leavenworthia - *Leavenworthia uniflora* (Michx.) Britt. (5, 97) (1913-1937)

Michaux's poison sumac [Michaux poison sumac] - *Rhus michauxii* Sargent (138) (1923)

Michaux's sagebrush [Michaux sagebrush] - *Artemisia michauxiana* Bess. (155) (1942)

Michaux's saxifrage [Michaux saxifrage] - *Saxifraga michauxii* Britt. (5, 138) (1913-1923)

Michaux's sedge - *Carex michauxiana* Boeckl. (50) (present), *Cyperus odoratus* L. (66) (1903)

Michaux's stitchwort - *Minuartia michauxii* (Fenzl) Farw. (50) (present)

Michelia - *Pontederia cordata* L. (177) (1762)

Michigan lily - *Lilium michiganense* Farw. (50, 155) (1942–present)

Michigan rose - *Rosa setigera* Michx. (5, 156) (1913-1923)

Michkidea (Crow) - *Opuntia polyacantha* Haw. (101) (1905) MT

Michkideamachwa (Crow) - *Escobaria missouriensis* (Sweet) D.R. Hunt var. *missouriensis* (101) (1905) MT

Micidji'mĭnaga'wûnj (Chippewa, fuzzy fruit) - *Ribes* L. (40) (1928)

Micocoulier (French) - *Celtis* L. (8) (1785)

Micocoulier à longues feuilles (French) - *Celtis tenuifolia* Nutt. (20) (1857)

Micocoulier d'Occident (French) - *Celtis occidentalis* L. (8) (1785)

Micocoulier riticule (French) - *Celtis laevigata* Willd. var. *reticulata* (Torr.) L. Benson (20) (1857)

Microseris - *Microseris* D. Don (155, 158) (1900-1942) Greek for "little endive"

Midas' ears - *Symplocarpus* Salisb. ex Nutt. (1) (1932)

Middle comfrey [Middle-comfrey - *Ajuga reptans* L. (5, 156, 158) (1900-1923)

Middle consoulde [Myddle consoulde] - *Anthemis cotula* L. (179) (1526)

Middle sort of great blew lupine - *Lupinus perennis* L. (181) (~1678)

Middle-consound [Middle consound - *Ajuga reptans* L. (156, 158, 165) (1768-1923) consolida meant healing

Midland adder's-tongue [Midland adder's tongue, Midlands adder's-tongue] - *Erythronium mesochoreum* Knerr (5, 72, 93, 97) (1907-1937)

Midland fawnlily - *Erythronium mesochoreum* Knerr (50) (present)

Midland quillwort - *Isoetes melanopoda* Gay & Durieu ex Durieu (4) (1986)

Midland sedge - *Carex mesochorea* MacKenzie (5, 50) (1913–present)

Midland wood sorrel - *Oxalis stricta* L. (5, 97) (1913-1937)

Midsummer daisy [Midsummer-daisy] - *Leucanthemum vulgare* Lam. (5, 156, 158) (1900–1923)

Midsummer-men [Midsummer men] - *Hylotelephium telephium* (L.) H. Ohba. subsp. *telephium* (5, 156) (1913-1923) no longer in use by 1923

Midwest indigo-bush amorpha [Midwest indigobush amorpha] - *Amorpha fruticosa* L. (155) (1942)

Mielga (Spanish) - *Medicago sativa* L. (110) (1886)

Mi'gĭsnĕs'ĭbûg (Chippewa, little shell leaf) - *Onosmodium virginianum* (L.) A. DC. (possibly) (40) (1928)

Mignonette - *Reseda* L. (50, 138, 155, 158) (1923–present), *Reseda lutea* L. (95, 157) (1900-1911), *Reseda odorata* L. (82, 92, 106, 114) (1894-1930)

Mignonette vine [Mignonette-vine] - *Anredera cordifolia* (Ten.) Steenis (109) (1949)

Mignonetter - *Reseda odorata* L. (19) (1840)

Mignonetter tree [Mignonetter-tree] - *Lawsonia inermis* L. (109) (1949)

Mijimniguns (Chippewa) - *Toxicodendron vernix* (L.) Kuntze (105) (1932)

Mikaa (Osage) - *Spigelia marilandica* (L.) L. (6) (1892)

Mika-hi (Omaha-Ponca, comb plant) - *Echinacea angustifolia* DC. (37) (1919), *Hesperostipa spartea* (Trin.) Barkworth (37) (1830)

Mikai hthi (Omaha-Ponca, star sore) - *Morchella esculenta* (L.) Pers. (37) (1830)

Mikapŝse (Osage, from word for raccoon) - *Hesperostipa spartea* (Trin.) Barkworth (121) (1918-1970)

Mikasi-makan (Omaha-Ponca, coyote medicine) - *Arisaema triphyllum* (L.) Schott (37) (1830)

Mikethestsedse (Osage, possibly meaning, long raccoon rush) - *Typha latifolia* L. (121) (1918-1970)

Mik-min (Chippewa) - *Ribes americanum* Mill. (105) (1932)

Milawapamule - *Cornus sericea* L. (6) (1892)

Milchkraut (German) - *Glaux maritima* L. (158) (1900)

Mild thistle - *Sonchus oleraceus* L. (157) (1929)

Mild turmeric - *Hydrastis canadensis* L. (49) (1898)

Mild water-pepper [Mild water pepper] - *Polygonum hydropiperoides* Michx. (4, 5, 62, 72, 93, 97, 120, 156) (1907-1986)

Mile - *Apium graveolens* L. var. *dulce* (P. Mill.) DC. (5) (1913)

Miles - *Chenopodium album* L. (157, 158) (1900-1929)

Milfoil [Myllefoyle] - *Achillea* L. (1, 10, 156, 158) (1818–1932), *Achillea millefolium* L. (2, 6, 7, 19, 28, 37, 42, 46, 49, 53, 57, 58, 62, 69, 85, 92, 95, 101, 107, 109, 122, 127, 156, 157, 158, 179, 187) (1526–1949)

Military grass - *Bromus tectorum* L. (146) (1939) MT

Milk bush [Milk-bush] - *Euphorbia tirucalli* L. (109) (1949)

Milk gowan - *Taraxacum officinale* G.H. Weber ex Wiggers (156, 157) (1923-1929)

Milk hickory [Milke Hickerie] - *Juglans nigra* L. (181) (~1678)

Milk ipecac - *Apocynum androsaemifolium* L. (156, 157, 158) (1900-1929), *Euphorbia corollata* L. (5, 92, 156, 157, 158) (1898-1929)

Milk parsley - *Chamaesyce hypericifolia* (L.) Millsp. (6) (1892), *Oxypolis ternata* (Nutt.) Heller (92) (1876), *Pastinaca sativa* L. (107) (1919)

Milk plant - *Asclepias syriaca* L. (28) (1850)

Milk purslane [Milk-purslain] - *Chamaesyce hypericifolia* (L.) Millsp. (6, 49) (1892-1898), *Chamaesyce maculata* (L.) Small (5, 62, 72, 93, 131, 156, 158) (1899-1936), *Euphorbia corollata* L. (5, 7, 49, 53, 156, 157, 158) (1828-1929)

Milk pusley [Milk pussley] - *Euphorbia corollata* L. (5, 92, 156, 158) (1876-1923)

Milk thistle [Milk-thistle] - *Cirsium vulgare* (Savi) Ten. (92) (1876), *Lactuca serriola* L. (62, 70, 156) (1895–1923), *Lactuca virosa* L. (5) (1913), *Silybum* Adans. (109, 158) (1900–1949), *Silybum marianum* (L.) Gaertn. (5, 42, 52, 107, 156, 158) (1814–1923), *Sonchus arvensis* L. (157, 158) (1900-1929), *Sonchus oleraceus* L. (5, 76, 156, 158) (1896–1923)

Milk tree - *Clusia minor* L. (92) (1876)

Milk vine [Milk-vine, Milkvine] - *Matelea cynanchoides* (Engelm.) Woods (4) (1986), *Periploca graeca* L. (19, 158) (1840-1900), *Periploca* L. (158) (1900)

Milk willow herb [Milk willow-herb, Milk willow herb] - *Decodon verticillatus* (L.) Ell. (5, 156) (1913-1923), *Lythrum alatum* Pursh (5, 156, 158) (1900-1923), *Lythrum salicaria* L. (92, 156, 158) (1898-1923)

Milk witch gowan - *Taraxacum officinale* G. H. Weber ex Wiggers (5) (1913)

Milk-grass [Milk grass] - *Valerianella locusta* (L.) Lat. (5, 156) (1913-1923)

Milkmaid [Milkmaids, Milk maid] - *Cardamine* L. (1) (1932), *Cardamine pratensis* L. (5, 156) (1913-1923) no longer in use by 1923

Milk-pea [Milk pea] - *Galactia* P. Br. (2, 50, 155, 158) (1895–present), *Galactia regularis* (L.) Britton, Sterns & Poggenb. (5, 97, 156) (1913-1937)

Milk-sick-plant - *Ageratina altissima* (L.) King & H. E. Robins. (156) (1923)

Milksweet [Milk sweet] - *Galium aparine* L. (92) (1876), *Galium verum* L. (7) (1828)

Milkvetch [Milk vetch, Milk-vetch] - *Astragalus bisulcatus* (Hook.) Gray (148) (1939), *Astragalus canadensis* L. (80, 82, 121) (1913-1930), *Astragalus canadensis* L. var. *canadensis* (72, 114) (1894-1907), *Astragalus crassicarpus* Nutt. var. *crassicarpus* (156) (1923), *Astragalus glaux* L. (19, 92) (1840-1876), *Astragalus* L. (1, 2, 4, 10, 38, 50, 82, 103, 106, 127, 155, 156, 158) (1818–present), *Astragalus mollissimus* Torr (156) (1923)

Milkvine - *Matelea* Aubl. (50) (present)

Milkweed - *Chamaesyce hypericifolia* (L.) Millsp. (102) (1886)

Milkweed [Milk weed [Milk-weed] - *Apocynum androsaemifolium* L. (6, 7, 106, 156, 157) (1828-1930), *Apocynum cannabinum* L. (64, 156, 158) (1900–1923), *Asclepias* L. (1, 2, 4, 45, 50, 63, 82, 106, 109, 125, 138, 155, 156, 158) (1895–present), *Asclepias speciosa* Torr. (101, 114) (1894–1905), *Asclepias syriaca* L. (37, 53, 56, 58, 80, 107, 145, 187) (1818–1922), *Asclepias tuberosa* L. (61, 103) (1871), *Asclepias verticillata* L. (148) (1939), *Chamaesyce hypericifolia* (L.) Millsp. (102) (1886), *Chamaesyce maculata* (L.) Small (5, 73, 80, 156, 158) (1892–1930), *Euphorbia corollata* L. (5, 7, 78, 92, 156, 158) (1828–1923), *Euphorbia cyparissias* L. (78) (1898),

Euphorbia marginata Pursh (78, 106) (1898-1930), *Lactuca biennis* (Moench) Fern. (5, 76) (1896-1913), *Lactuca canadensis* L. (possibly) (29) (1869), *Lactuca* L. (73, 79) (1891) NB, *Prenanthes alba* L. (5, 156) (1913-1923), *Prenanthes altissima* L. (5, 156) (1913-1923), *Prenanthes* L. (79) (1891) NH, *Sonchus oleraceus* L. (5, 156, 157, 158) (1900-1929)

Milkwood [Milk wood] - *Sideroxylon lycioides* L. (20) (1857)

Milkwort - *Glaux* L. (50, 190) (~1759–present), *Polygala alba* Nutt. (127) (1933), *Polygala incarnata* L. (19) (1840), *Polygala* L. (1, 4, 10, 13, 15, 93, 109, 156, 158, 184) (1793–present), *Polygala senega* L. (6) (1892), *Polygala vulgaris* L. (107) (1919)

Milky ricinus of Virginia [Milkey ricinus of Virginia] - *Cnidoscolus stimulosus* (Michx.) Engelm. & Gray (181) (~1678)

Milky Way plant - *Galactia regularis* (L.) Britton, Sterns & Poggenb. (19) (1840)

Milky-dickles [Milky dickles] - *Sonchus oleraceus* L. (157, 158) (1900-1929)

Milky-tassel [Milky-tassels, Milk tassel] - *Sonchus oleraceus* L. (5, 156, 157, 158) (1900-1929)

Mill [Mylle] - *Panicum miliaceum* L. (178, 179) (1526-1596)

Mill mountain - *Linum catharticum* L. (92) (1876)

Mill mountain flax - *Linum catharticum* L. (5) (1913)

Millefeuille (French) - *Achillea millefolium* L. (6, 158) (1892)

Millefoil - *Achillea millefolium* L. (148) (1939)

Millepertuis - *Hypericum perforatum* L. (50) (present)

Mille-Pertuis [Millepertuis](French) - *Hypericum perforatum* L. (6, 158) (1892)

Mille-Pertuis [Millepertuis](French) - *Spiraea hypericifolia* L. (8) (1785)

Mille-pertuis de Kalm (French) - *Hypericum kalmianum* L. (8) (1785)

Miller's dogbane - *Apocynum* ×*floribundum* Greene (5) (1913)

Millet [Myllet] - *Echinochloa colona* (L.) Link (107) (1919), *Panicum miliaceum* L. (5, 46, 56, 67, 72, 107, 158, 178) (1596-1919), *Setaria* Beauv. (155, 158) (1900-1942), *Setaria italica* (L.) Beauv. (11, 21, 56, 66, 129, 138) (1888-1923), *Sorghum bicolor* (L.) Moench (56) (1901) IA

Millet a chandlles (French) - *Pennisetum glaucum* (L.) R. Br. (46) (1879)

Millet grass [Milletgrass] - *Milium effusum* L. (19, 92) (1840-1876), *Milium* L. (1, 10, 50, 66, 155) (1818–present), *Panicum miliaceum* L. (87, 92) (1876-1884), *Setaria italica* (L.) Beauv. (92) (1876)

Millet sedge - *Carex prasina* Wahl. (187) (1818)

Millet seed - *Sorghum halepense* (L.) Pers. (92) (1876)

Millet woodrush - *Luzula parviflora* (Ehrh.) Desv. (139, 155) (1942-1944)

Millet-like sedge - *Carex prasina* Wahl. (66) (1903)

Millettia - *Millettia* Wight & Arn. (138) (1923)

Million - *Cucumis melo* L. (107) (1919)

Millo maize - *Sorghum bicolor* (L.) Moench subsp. *bicolor* (151) (1896)

Millspaugh's blackberry - *Rubus canadensis* L. (5, 72) (1907-1913)

Milo - *Sorghum bicolor* (L.) Moench subsp. *bicolor* (119) (1938)

Milo maize - *Sorghum bicolor* (L.) Moench subsp. *bicolor* (119) (1938) NM

Milsean-Mara (Gaelic) - *Acorus calamus* L. (186) (1814)

Miltomatl - *Physalis philadelphica* Lam. (107) (1651) Mexico

Mimbres - *Chilopsis linearis* (Cav.) Sweet (149) (1904) NM

Mimosa - *Desmanthus illinoensis* (Michx.) MacM. ex B.L. Robins. & Fern. (93) (1936) Neb, *Desmanthus* Willd. (158) (1900), *Mimosa borealis* Gray (3) (1977), *Mimosa* L. (4, 138, 155, 158) (1900-1986)

Mimosa bark - *Acacia melanoxylon* R. Br. ex Aiton f. (92) (1876)

Mĭn'aga'wûnj (Chippewa) - *Vaccinium angustifolium* Aiton (40) (1928)

Minaret goldenrod [Minaret golden-rod] - *Solidago puberula* Nutt. (5) (1913)

Minbdi-hi (Omaha-Ponca) - *Rhus glabra* L. (37) (1919)

Miner's lettuce - *Claytonia perfoliata* Donn ex Willd. subsp. *perfoliata* (156) (1923), *Claytonia* L. (1) (1932)

Mĭne'saga'wûnj (Chippewa, having fruit and thorns) - *Crataegus* L. (40) (1928)

Minesgan-wiňš (Chippewa) - *Crataegus* L. (105) (1932)

Mingan moonwort - *Botrychium minganense* Vict. (50) (present)

Mingde-beguk (Chippewa, wide leaf) - *Caltha palustris* L. (105) (1932)

Mingwort - *Artemisia absinthium* L. (5, 156, 157, 158) (1900-1929)

Minigathe makan wau (Omaha-Ponca, woman-seeking medicine) - *Sanguinaria canadensis* L. (37) (1919)

Minnesota adder's-tongue [Minnesota adder's tongue] - *Erythronium propullans* A. Gray (5) (1913)

Minnesota dropseed - *Muhlenbergia mexicana* (L.) Trin. (5) (1913)

Minnie bush [Minnie-bush] - *Menziesia pilosa* (Michx. ex Lam.) Juss. ex Pers. (5, 156) (1913-1923)

Minny-berry - *Celtis occidentalis* L. (156) (1923)

Minšminš (Chippewa) - *Quercus bicolor* Willd (105) (1932)

Mint - *Mentha arvensis* L. (80, 82, 107) (1913-1930), *Mentha* L. (1, 2, 4, 7, 10, 50, 82, 93, 106, 109, 138, 156, 158, 178, 181, 184) (1526–present), *Mentha spicata* L. (55, 92, 158) (1876-1911), *Stachys crenata* Raf. (106) (1930)

Mint-geranium [Mint geranium] - *Balsamita major* Desf. (3, 4, 5, 156, 158) (1900-1986), *Balsamita* Mill. (1) (1932)

Mint-leaf beebalm [Mintleaf beebalm] - *Monarda fistulosa* L. subsp. *fistulosa* var. *menthifolia* (Graham) Fern. (50) (present)

Mint-leaf cunila [Mint leaved cunila, Mint-leaved cunila] - *Cunila origanoides* (L.) Britton (42, 186) (1814)

Minute duckweed - *Lemna perpusilla* Torr. (3, 5, 50, 93, 97, 155) (1911–present)

Minute willow - *Salix nivalis* Hook. (20) (1857)

Minze (German) - *Mentha* L. (158) (1900)

Miŋdsešta hi (Osage, smooth bow tree) - *Maclura pomifera* (Raf.) Schneid. (121) (1918?-1970?)

Mira sol - *Helianthus annuus* L. (150) (1894) NM

Mireblobs [Mire-blob, Mire blobs] - *Caltha palustris* L. (5, 157) (1900-1929)

Mirrot - *Daucus carota* L. (157, 158) (1900-1929)

Misascutu (Algic tribes) - *Amelanchier canadensis* (L.) Medik. (7) (1828)

Misbegotten peony [Misbegotten pionie] - *Paeonia officinalis* L. (178) (1526)

Mischmisch (Persian) - *Prunus armeniaca* L. (110) (1886)

Mishquawtuck (Narraganset) - *Juniperus virginiana* L. (46) (1879)

Mĭs'kodji'bĭk (Chippewa, red root) - *Sanguinaria canadensis* L. (40) (1928)

Mĭs'komĭnaga'wûnj (Chippewa, having reddish berries) - *Rubus idaeus* L. subsp. *strigosus* (Michx.) Focke (40) (1928)

Mĭs'kwabi'mĭc (Chippewa, reddish) - *Cornus sericea* L. subsp. *sericea* (40) (1928)

Miskwa'wak (Chippewa, red wood) - *Juniperus virginiana* L. (40) (1928)

Miskwazi-wušk (Chippewa, water-strider herb) - *Physocarpus opulifolius* (L.) Maxim. (105) (1932)

Mĭs'nĭsĭno'wûck (Chippewa, island medicine) - *Lathyrus venosus* Muhl. (40) (1928)

Miso - *Glycine max* (L.) Merr. (158) (1900)

Miss Beckwith's thorn - *Crataegus jesupii* Sarg. (5) (1913)

Miss Furbish's pedicularis - *Pedicularis furbishiae* S. Wats. (5) (1913)

Miss Jones' thorn - *Crataegus jonesiae* Sarg. (5) (1913)

Miss Macauley's thorn - *Crataegus coleae* Sarg. (5) (1913)

Miss Price's aster - *Symphyotrichum priceae* (Britt.) Nesom (5) (1913)

Miss Price's cornel - *Cornus drummondii* C.A. Mey. (5) (1913)

Miss Vail's thorn - *Crataegus vailiae* Britton (5) (1913)

Missebroed (Lapland) - *Calla palustris* L. (46, 86) (1878-1879)

Missey-moosey [Missey moosey] - *Sorbus americana* Marsh. (5, 73,

156) (1892-1923) NH, no longer in use by 1923

Mission grass [Mission-grass] - *Stenotaphrum secundatum* (Walt.) Kuntze (94) (1901)

Mission manzanita - *Xylococcus bicolor* Nutt. (155) (1942)

Missionary weed [Missionary-weed] - *Hieracium aurantiacum* L. (5, 76, 156) (1896-1923) East Sangerville ME

Mississippi buttercup - *Ranunculus laxicaulis* (Torr. & Gray) Darby (50) (present)

Mississippi hawthorn - *Crataegus crus-galli* L. (155) (1942)

Mississippi iris - *Iris brevicaulis* Raf. (155) (1942)

Missoula pine - *Pinus ponderosa* P.& C. Lawson (101) (1905) MT

Missouri aster - *Symphyotrichum ontarione* (Wiegand) Nesom (4, 5) (1913-1986)

Missouri black oak - *Quercus velutina* Lam. (155) (1942)

Missouri breadnut [Missouri bread-nut] - *Pediomelum esculentum* (Pursh) Rydb. (156) (1923)

Missouri breadroot [Missouri bread-root, Missouri bread root] - *Pediomelum esculentum* (Pursh) Rydb. (5, 158) (1900–1913)

Missouri cactus - *Escobaria missouriensis* (Sweet) D.R. Hunt var. *missouriensis* (5, 93, 131, 156) (1899-1936), *Opuntia polyacantha* Haw. var. *trichophora* (Engelm. & Bigelow) Coult. (108) (1878)

Missouri clotbur - *Xanthium strumarium* L. var. *glabratum* (DC.) Cronq. (5) (1913)

Missouri coryphantha - *Escobaria missouriensis* (Sweet) D.R. Hunt var. *missouriensis* (155) (1942)

Missouri crabapple - *Malus ioensis* (Wood) Britton var. *ioensis* (155) (1942)

Missouri currant [Missouri currants] - *Ribes aureum* Pursh (2, 63, 82, 93, 103, 107, 108, 130, 156, 158) (1870-1936), *Ribes aureum* Pursh var. *villosum* DC. (5, 97, 109) (1913-1949)

Missouri evening-primrose [Missouri evening primrose] - *Oenothera macrocarpa* Nutt. subsp. *macrocarpa* (4) (1986)

Missouri farkleberry - *Vaccinium arboreum* Marsh. (155) (1942)

Missouri foxtail cactus - *Escobaria missouriensis* (Sweet) D.R. Hunt (50) (present), *Escobaria missouriensis* (Sweet) D.R. Hunt var. *missouriensis* (50) (present), *Escobaria missouriensis* (Sweet) D.R. Hunt var. *similis* (Engelm.) N.P. Taylor (50) (present)

Missouri goldenrod [Missouri golden-rod] - *Solidago missouriensis* Nutt. (3, 50, 72, 82, 85, 95, 97, 127, 131, 155) (1899–present), *Solidago missouriensis* Nutt. var. *fasciculata* Holz. (5, 50, 93, 97, 122) (1913–present)

Missouri gooseberry - *Ribes missouriense* Nutt. (3, 4, 5, 50, 72, 85, 138, 155) (1907–present), *Ribes niveum* Lindl. (82, 130, 156) (1895-1930), *Ribes oxyacanthoides* L. subsp. *setosum* (Lindl.) Sinnott (107) (1919)

Missouri gourd - *Cucurbita foetidissima* Kunth (5, 50, 72, 93, 97, 156, 157, 158) (1900–present)

Missouri grape - *Vitis palmata* Vahl (5, 72, 122) (1907-1937)

Missouri ground-cherry [Missouri groundcherry, Missouri ground cherry] - *Physalis missouriensis* Mackenzie & Bush (5, 50, 97) (1913–present)

Missouri hawthorn - *Crataegus crus-galli* L. (138, 155) (1923-1942)

Missouri ironweed - *Vernonia missurica* Raf. (50, 82) (1930–present)

Missouri knotweed - *Polygonum ramosissimum* Michx. var. *ramosissimum* (5) (1913)

Missouri lamb's-quarters [Missouri lambsquarters] - *Chenopodium album* L. var. *missouriense* (Aellen) I.J. Bassett & C.W. Crompton (50) (present)

Missouri milkvetch [Missouri milk vetch] - *Astragalus missouriensis* Nutt. (3, 4, 5, 50, 93, 97, 131) (1899–present), *Astragalus missouriensis* Nutt. var. *missouriensis* (50) (present)

Missouri primrose - *Oenothera macrocarpa* Nutt. subsp. *macrocarpa* (5, 97, 156) (1913-1937)

Missouri River willow - *Salix eriocephala* Michx. (50) (present)

Missouri spurge - *Chamaesyce missurica* (Raf.) Shinners (3, 4) (1977-1986)

Missouri thorn - *Crataegus pruinosa* (Wendl.) K. Koch (5) (1913)

Missouri violet - *Viola affinis* Le Conte (3, 5, 97, 155) (1913-1977)

Missouri virgin's-bower [Missouri virginsbower] - *Clematis virginiana* L. (155) (1942)

Missouri willow - *Salix eriocephala* Michx. (5, 72, 85, 97) (1907-1937)

Mist - *Galium mollugo* L. (75) (1894) Eastern MA, *Gypsophila paniculata* L. (5, 76, 156, 158) (1907-1923) Eastern MA

Mistassini primrose - *Primula mistassinica* Michx. (5) (1913)

Mistflower [Mist-flower, Mist flower] - *Conoclinium coelestinum* (L.) DC. (3, 4, 5, 63, 75, 92, 97, 109, 138, 156, 158) (1876-1986), *Eupatorium* L. (1) (1932)

Mistflower eupatorium - *Conoclinium coelestinum* (L.) DC. (155) (1942)

Mistletoe [Misseltoe, Misletoe, Misleto] - *Arceuthobium* Bieb. (121) (1918?-1970?), *Cissus verticillata* (L.) Nicolson & C.E. Jarvis (12) (1819), *Phoradendron leucarpum* (Raf.) Reveal & M.C. Johnston (35, 48, 49, 53, 92, 106, 161) (1806-1930), *Viscum album* L. (7, 10, 41, 52, 54, 55) (1770-1919), *Viscum* L. (8, 50, 167) (1785–present)

Mistletoe cactus - *Rhipsalis baccifera* (Soland. ex J. Mill.) Stearn (138) (1923), *Rhipsalis* Gaertn. (14) (1882)

Mistletoe rhipsalis - *Rhipsalis baccifera* (Soland. ex J. Mill.) Stearn (155) (1942)

Mitchella - *Mitchella* L. (8) (1785), *Mitchella repens* L. (54, 57, 174, 177) (1753-1917)

Mitchella (French) - *Mitchella* L. (8) (1785)

Mitchella rampant (French) - *Mitchella repens* L. (8) (1785)

Miterwort [Mitrewort] - *Mitella* L. (1, 2, 155, 158) (1895-1942)

Mithon - *Oenothera mollissima* L. (177) (1762) Gn diminutive for mitra "a cap" referring to the shape of the young pod 155

Mithridate mustard - *Lepidium campestre* (L.) Aiton f. (5, 156, 158) (1900-1923), *Thlaspi arvense* L. (46, 156, 158) (1879-1923)

Mithridate pepperwort - *Lepidium campestre* (L.) Aiton f. (158) (1900)

Mǐ'tǐgo'mǐc (Chippewa) - *Quercus macrocarpa* Michx. (40) (1928)

Mitigó-minš (Chippewa) - *Quercus* L. (105) (1932)

Mǐtǐgo'mizǐnc (Chippewa) - *Quercus* L. (40) (1928)

Mǐ'tǐgwabak' (Chippewa, bow-wood) - *Carya alba* (L.) Nutt. ex Ell. (40) (1928)

Mit-le-go-mish-ai-e-buck-ish-in-a-guack (Monominie) - *Silphium* L. (23) (1810)

Mitreola - *Mitreola petiolata* (J.F. Gmel.) Torr. & Gray (174, 177) (1753-1762)

Mitrewort [Mitre-wort, Mitre wort] - *Mitella diphylla* L. (5, 63, 156) (1899-1923), *Mitella* L. (109, 156) (1923-1949), *Mitreola petiolata* (J.F. Gmel.) Torr. & Gray (5, 156) (1913-1923), *Tiarella cordifolia* L. (19, 92) (1840-1876)

Mitsmata - *Magnolia virginiana* L. (186) (1814)

Mǐ'-we (Zuñi) - *Zea mays* L. (132) (1855)

Mix-leaf sagebrush [Mixleaf sagebrush] - *Artemisia ludoviciana* Nutt. subsp. *ludoviciana* (155) (1942)

Mna (Dakota) - *Viburnum lentago* L. (37) (1919) Mna-hu (black haw bush)

Moacuccio (Italian) - *Gladiolus* L. (180) (1633)

Moccasin flower [Mocasin flower, Mocassin flower, Moccasin-flower, Moccason flower, Mockasin flower] - *Cypripedium acaule* Ait. (5, 46, 48, 50, 156, 187) (1818–present), *Cypripedium* L. (1, 2, 35, 92, 109, 181) (~1678-1949), *Cypripedium montanum* Dougl. ex Lindl. (35) (1806), *Cypripedium parviflorum* Salisb. var. *parviflorum* (7) (1828), *Cypripedium parviflorum* Salisb. var. *pubescens* (Willd.) Knight (6, 58) (1869-1892), *Cypripedium reginae* Walt. (127, 156) (1923-1933)

Moccasin plant - *Cypripedium* L. (92) (1876)

Moccasin root - *Cypripedium* L. (92) (1876)

Moc-cup-pin (Chipewa) - *Nymphaea odorata* Aiton subsp. *tuberosa* (Paine) Wiersma & Hellquist (35) (1806)

Mochar newachar (Indians of Missouri) - *Trillium cernuum* L. (7) (1828)

Mochi (Italian) - *Lathyrus cicera* L. (110) (1886)

Mock apple - *Echinocystis lobata* (Michx.) Torr. & Gray (5, 156) (1913-1923), *Echinocystis* Torr. & Gray (1) (1932)

Mock bishop's-weed [Mock bishop's weed, Mock bishop-weed, Mock Bishopweed] - *Perideridia gairdneri* (Hook. & Arn.) Mathias (3) (1977), *Ptilimnium capillaceum* (Michx.) Raf. (5, 97, 156) (1913-1937), *Ptilimnium nuttallii* (DC.) Britton (3, 4, 158) (1900-1986)

Mock chervil [Mocke c]heruill - *Erodium moschatum* (L.) L'Hér. ex Aiton (178) (1526)

Mock cucumber [Mock-cucumber, Mockcucumber] - *Echinocystis lobata* (Michx.) Torr. & Gray (138, 155) (1923-1942), *Echinocystis* Torr. & Gray (138, 156) (1923)

Mock cypress - *Kochia scoparia* (L.) Schrad. (4) (1986)

Mock gilliflower [Mock gillyflower] - *Saponaria officinalis* L. (5, 64, 156, 157, 158) (1900-1929)

Mock goldenweed - *Stenotus* Nutt. (50) (present)

Mock orange [Mock-orange, Mockorange] - *Echinocystis lobata* (Michx.) Torr. & Gray (5, 156, 158) (1900-1923), *Lagenaria* Ser. (73) (1892) Northern OH, *Maclura pomifera* (Raf.) Schneid. (39, 156) (1814-1923), *Philadelphus coronarius* L. (5, 19, 82, 85, 92, 97, 156, 184) (1793-1937), *Philadelphus* L. (2, 8, 10, 109, 112, 138, 146, 149, 153) (1785-1949), *Prunus caroliniana* (P. Mill.) Aiton (74, 92, 106, 109) (1893-1949) Southern states, *Sideroxylon lycioides* L. (5, 156) (1913-1923), *Styrax grandifolius* Aiton (156) (1923)

Mock pennyroyal - *Hedeoma* Pers. (1, 4, 82, 93) (1930-1986), *Hedeoma pulegioides* (L.) Pers. (6, 156, 157, 158) (1892-1929)

Mock plane [Mock-plane] - *Acer pseudoplatanus* L. (107, 165) (1768-1919) England

Mock strawberry [Mock-strawberry, Mockstrawberry] - *Duchesnea* Sm. (109, 138, 155, 158) (1900-1942), *Duchesnea indica* (Andr.) Focke (5, 97, 138, 156) (1913-1937)

Mock sweet william [Mock sweet-william] - *Lychnis chalcedonica* L. (158) (1900), *Silene armeria* L. (5, 74, 156) (1893-1923) Southern IN

Mock vervain - *Glandularia* J.F. Gmel. (50) (present)

Mock willow - *Spiraea salicifolia* L. (156) (1923)

Mockernut [Mocker nut, Mocker-nut] - *Carya alba* (L.) Nutt. ex Ell. (1, 5, 18, 72, 82, 93, 97, 107, 113, 138, 156, 158) (1805-1937), *Carya laciniosa* (Michx. f.) G. Don (78, 109) (1898-1949)

Mockernut hickory [Mocker-nut hickory] - *Carya alba* (L.) Nutt. ex Ell. (3, 4, 20, 50, 155, 187) (1857-present)

Mockkwuren - *Magnolia virginiana* L. (186) (1814)

Moderwort - *Artemisia vulgaris* L. (179) (1526)

Modesty - *Bupleurum rotundifolium* L. (5, 131, 156) (1899-1923), *Hibiscus trionum* L. (5, 76, 93, 156, 158) (1896-1936)

Modo (Sioux) - *Apios americana* Medik. (103) (1870)

Modoc yellowcress - *Rorippa tenerrima* Greene (50) (present)

Mohave aster - *Xylorhiza orcuttii* (Vasey & Rose) Greene (8, 13) (1785-1849), *Xylorhiza tortifolia* (Torr. & Gray) Greene var. *tortifolia* (155) (1942)

Mohave rose - *Rosa woodsii* Lindl. var. *glabrata* (Parish) Cole (138) (1923)

Mohave sand-verbena [Mohave sand verbena] - *Abronia pogonantha* Heimerl (50) (present)

Mohave sea-blite [Mohave seablite] - *Suaeda moquinii* (Torr.) Greene (50) (present)

Mohawk weed - *Uvularia perfoliata* L. (5, 92, 156) (1913-1923) no longer in use by 1923

Möhre (German) - *Daucus carota* L. (158) (1900)

Mohr's arrowhead [Mohrs arrowhead] - *Sagittaria platyphylla* (Engelm.) J.G. Smith (155) (1942)

Mohr's broom sedge - *Andropogon mohrii* (Hack.) Hack. ex Vasey (94) (1901)

Mohr's hawthorn [Mohrs hawthorn] - *Crataegus crus-galli* L. (155) (1942)

Mohr's oak [Mohr oak] - *Quercus mohriana* Buckl. (50, 155) (1942-present)

Mohr's shinnery - *Quercus mohriana* Buckl. (122) (1937) TX

Moist sow thistle [Moist sowthistle] - *Sonchus arvensis* L. subsp. *uliginosus* (Bieb.) Nyman (50) (present)

Moitch - *Eucalyptus rudis* Sm. (109) (1949)

Moldavian balm - *Dracocephalum moldavica* L. (5, 92) (1876-1913)

Moldavian dragonhead [Moldavian dragon head, Moldavica dragonshead] - *Dracocephalum moldavica* L. (5, 50, 155) (1913-present)

Molé (Albanian) - *Malus sylvestris* Mill. (110) (1886)

Mole plant [Mole-plant, Moleplant] - *Euphorbia lathyris* L. (5, 6, 7, 71, 109, 155, 156, 187) (1818-1942)

Mole tree [Mole-tree] - *Euphorbia lathyris* L. (5, 6, 71, 73, 156) (1892-1923) Northern OH, said to keep moles out of gardens

Molène (French) - *Verbascum thapsus* L. (6, 158) (1892-1900)

Molette (French) - *Capsella bursa-pastoris* (L.) Medik. (158) (1900)

Moleweed [Mole weed] - *Euphorbia lathyris* L. (71, 75, 155) (1898-1942) WV

Moleyne - *Verbascum thapsus* L. (179) (1526)

Molinia - *Molinia caerulea* (L.) Moench (94) (1901)

Molka - *Rubus chamaemorus* L. (107) (1919)

Molle - *Schinus molle* L. (107) (1919)

Mollugo - *Galium mollugo* L. (178) (1526)

Molly - *Kochia* Roth (50) (present)

Molucca balm [Molucca-balm] - *Moluccella* L. (138) (1923), *Moluccella laevis* L. (19, 77, 92, 109, 138) (1840-1949)

Moly - *Allium* L. (165) (1768)

Monarch-of-the-Veldt - *Venidium fastuosum* (Jacq.) Stapf (109) (1949)

Monarda - *Monarda punctata* L. (52, 57, 92, 174) (1753-1917)

Monarde ecarlatte (French) - *Monarda didyma* L. (7) (1828)

Moneses - *Moneses uniflora* (L.) Gray (155) (1942)

Money flower - *Lunaria annua* subsp. *annua* L. (possibly) (92) (1876)

Money milkweed - *Asclepias nummularia* Torr. (124) (1937) TX

Money plant [Money-plant] - *Lunaria annua* L. (5, 156) (1913-1923), *Lysimachia nummularia* L. (77, 156) (1898-1923) Oxford Co. ME

Money-bags [Money bags] - *Lysimachia nummularia* L. (77) (1898) Medford MA

Money-grass [Money grass] - *Rhinanthus minor* L. subsp. *minor* (5, 156) (1913-1923) no longer in use by 1923

Money-in-both-pockets - *Lunaria annua* L. (156) (1923)

Money-myrtle - *Lysimachia nummularia* L. (156) (1923)

Moneywort [Money wort] - *Dichondra carolinensis* Michx. (124) (1937) TX, *Lysimachia ciliata* L. (19) (1840), *Lysimachia nummularia* L. (3, 4, 5, 72, 92, 109, 138, 155, 156, 158) (1876-1986)

Mongolian deutzia - *Deutzia parviflora* Bunge (138) (1923)

Mon-ha-can-ni-min-schi - *Cornus florida* L. (6, 7, 186) (1825-1932)

Monilifera latissimis angulosis foliis - *Smallanthus uvedalius* (L.) Mackenzie ex Small (177) (1762)

Moninswan (Chippewa) - *Triosteum perfoliatum* L. (105) (1932)

Monkey balls [Monkeyballs] - *Platanus occidentalis* L. (156) (1923)

Monkey bush [Monkeybush] - *Abutilon indicum* (L.) Sweet (50) (present)

Monkey comb [Monkeycomb] - *Pithecoctenium* Mart. ex Meisn. (138) (1923)

Monkey dew grass [Monkey's dew grass] - *Agrostis gigantea* Roth (5) (1913)

Monkey face [Monkey's-face, Monkey faces] - *Lupinus* L. (76) (1896) Sulphur Grove OH, *Lupinus villosus* Willd. (73) (1892), *Viola tricolor* L. (158) (1900)

Monkey flower [Monkey-flower, Monkeyflower] - *Cypripedium* L. (92) (1876), *Cypripedium parviflorum* Salisb. (156) (1923), *Cypripedium reginae* Walt. (64, 158) (1900-1908), *Mimulus guttatus* DC. (3, 85) (1932-1977), *Mimulus* L. (1, 4, 50, 10, 41, 63, 93, 109, 138, 156, 158) (1818-present), *Mimulus ringens* L. (19, 72, 92, 114, 127, 131, 156) (1840-1933)

Monkey nut [Monkey-nut, Monkey-nuts] - *Arachis hypogaea* L. (110) (1886)

Monkey pod [Monkey-pod] - *Samanea saman* (Jacq.) Merr. (109) (1949)

Monkey-bread tree - *Adansonia digitata* L. (109) (1949)

Monkey-nut tree [Monkey nut tree, Monkey-nut-tree] - *Tilia americana* L. (5, 156, 157, 158) (1900-1929)

Monk's pepper tree [Monks pepper-tree] - *Vitex agnus-castus* L. (109, 158) (1900-1949)

Monk's-head [Monk's head] - *Taraxacum officinale* G.H. Weber ex Wiggers (5, 156, 157, 158) (1900-1929)

Monkshood [Monk's-hood, Monk's hood] - *Aconitum columbianum* Nutt. (3, 85, 148) (1932-1977), *Aconitum* L. (1, 4, 50, 13, 15, 109, 138, 155, 156, 158, 167) (1814–present), *Aconitum napellus* L. (49, 52, 53, 54, 57, 60, 92, 156) (1898-1923), *Aconitum uncinatum* L. (19) (1840), *Dicentra cucullaria* (L.) Bernh. (5, 156, 158) (1900-1923)

Monkshood vine [Monkshood-vine, Monkshoodvine] - *Ampelopsis aconitifolia* Bunge (138, 155) (1923-1942)

Monk's-rhubarb [Monk's rhubarb, Munks rubarbe] - *Rumex alpinus* L. (92, 178) (1526-1876), *Rumex patientia* L. (5, 107, 156, 158) (1900-1923)

Monnayère (French) - *Lysimachia nummularia* L. (158) (1900)

Monnier's hedge hyssop - *Bacopa monnieri* (L.) Pennell (5) (1913)

Mono planeleaf willow - *Salix planifolia* Pursh (155) (1942)

Monolepis - *Monolepis nuttalliana* (J. A. Schultes) Greene (5, 93, 131) (1899–1936), *Monolepis* Schrad. (155, 158) (1900–1942)

Monomonie - *Zizania aquatica* L. (possibly) (11, 19, 23, 37, 41, 43) (1810-1919) may refer to any grain

Monox - *Empetrum nigrum* L. (107, 156) (1919-1923)

Monox heather - *Empetrum nigrum* L. (5, 156) (1913-1923)

Montana barley - *Elyhordeum montanense* (Scribn.) Bowden [*Elymus virginicus* × *Hordeum jubatum*] (94, 155) (1901-1942)

Montana wheatgrass - *Elymus albicans* (Scribn. & J. G. Sm.) A. Löve (50, 155) (1942–present)

Monterey cypress - *Cupressus macrocarpa* Hartw. ex Gord. (75, 109, 138) (1894-1949)

Monterey goldenweed - *Ericameria fasciculata* (Eastw.) J. F. Macbr. (155) (1942)

Monterey manzanita - *Arctostaphylos tomentosa* (Pursh) Lindl. (155) (1942)

Monterey pine - *Pinus radiata* D. Don (50, 109, 138) (1923–present)

Montezuma bald cypress [Montezuma baldcypress] - *Taxodium mucronatum* Ten. (138) (1923)

Monthly pink - *Saponaria officinalis* L. (76) (1896) Greene Co. MO

Montpelier cinquefoil - *Potentilla norvegica* L. subsp. *monspeliensis* (L.) Aschers. & Graebn. (155) (1942)

Montpelier roskrose - *Cistus monspeliensis* L. (138) (1923)

Monument plant [Monument-plant] - *Frasera caroliniensis* Walt. (156) (1923), *Frasera speciosa* Dougl. ex Griseb. (106) (1930)

Monumental cactus - *Carnegia gigantea* (Engelm.) Britt. & Rose (103) (1870)

Moɳbidse bakoɳ (Osage) - *Rhus glabra* L. (121) (1918?-1970?)

Moɳbidse xtsi (Osage, real sumac) - *Rhus hirta* (L.) Sudworth (121) (1918?–1970?)

Moɳbixoɳ (Osage) - *Aquilegia canadensis* L. (121) (1918?–1970?)

Moɳhiɳ ts'azi (Osage, grass that never dies) - *Carex lurida* Wahl. (121) (1918-1970)

Moɳkoɳ nikašiga (Osage, human being medicine) - *Cucurbita foetidissima* Kunth (121) (1918?-1970?)

Moɳkoɳ toɳga (Osage, big medicine) - *Cucurbita foetidissima* Kunth (121) (1918?–1970?)

Moɳkoɳ toɳga žiɳga (Osage, Little big medicine) - *Callirhoe triangulata* (Leavenworth) Gray (121) (1918?-1970?)

Moɳžoɳxe (Osage, earth + bury) - *Allium* L. (121) (1918–1970)

MoɳΘa hi (Osage, arrow tree) - *Cornus drummondii* C.A. Mey. (121) (1918?–1970?)

MoɳΘa xota hu (Osage, blackbird arrow tree) - *Cornus racemosa* Lam. (121) (1918?-1970?)

Moodseed (sic) - *Menispermum canadense* L. (72) (1907)

Moon cereus - *Selenicereus* (Berger) Britt. & Rose (109) (1949) for moon-goddess cereus

Moon daisy [Moon-daisy] - *Leucanthemum vulgare* Lam. (5, 49, 156, 158) (1898-1923)

Moon fern [Moon-fern] - *Botrychium lunaria* (L.) Sw. (5, 158) (1900-1913)

Moon flower [Moon-flower, Moonflower] - *Ipomoea alba* L. (2) (1895), *Ipomoea* L. (109) (1949), *Ipomoea leptophylla* Torr. (107) (1919), *Leucanthemum vulgare* Lam. (5, 156, 158) (1900-1923), *Menyanthes trifoliata* L. (5, 92, 158) (1876-1913)

Moon vine [Moon-vine] - *Ipomoea alba* L. (142) (1902)

Moon-carrot [Mooncarrot] - *Seseli libanotis* (L.) W.D.J. Koch (50) (present)

Moon-fruit pine [Moon fruit pine, Moonfruit pine] - *Huperzia lucidula* (Michx.) Trevisan (5, 19, 92) (1840-1913)

Moonlight cactus [Moonlightcactus] - *Selenicereus* (Berger) Britt. & Rose (155) (1942)

Moon-penny [Moon penny] - *Leucanthemum vulgare* Lam. (5, 156, 158) (1900-1923)

Moonpod - *Selinocarpus diffusus* Gray (155) (1942), *Selinocarpus* Gray (4, 155) (1942-1986)

Moonseed [Moon seed, Moon-seed] - *Menispermum canadense* L. (1, 3, 4, 7, 19, 37, 85, 92, 93, 113, 125, 126, 130, 157, 187) (1818-1986), *Menispermum* L. (8, 10, 13, 15, 50, 63, 109, 138, 155, 156, 158, 167, 184) (1785–present)

Moon-seed root [Moon seed root] - *Menispermum canadense* L. (92) (1876)

Moonseed sarsaparilla - *Menispermum canadense* L. (49) (1898)

Moonshine - *Anaphalis margaritacea* (L.) Benth. & Hook (5, 106, 156, 158) (1900–1923) Eastern U.S.

Moonshine - *Pseudognaphalium obtusifolium* (L.) Hilliard & Burtt subsp. *obtusifolium* (5, 75, 156, 157) (1894–1929) Dorset VT

Moonwort [Moon-wort, Moon wort] - *Boltonia asteroides* var. *asteroides* Cronquist (92) (1876), *Botrychium biternatum* (Sav.) Underwood (possibly) (19) (1840), *Botrychium dissectum* Spreng. (5) (1913), *Botrychium lunaria* (L.) Sw. (4, 5, 155, 158) (1900-1986), *Botrychium* Sw. (1, 86) (1878-1932), *Botrychium virginianum* (L.) Sw. (58) (1869), *Lunaria annua* L. (10, 156) (1818-1923), *Lunaria* L. (109) (1949)

Moor flower [Moor-flower] - *Menyanthes trifoliata* L. (156) (1923)

Moor grass [Moor-grass] - *Buchloe dactyloides* (Nutt.) Engelm. (10, 36) (1818-1830), *Molinia caerulea* (L.) Moench (5) (1913)

Moor myrtle [Moor-myrtle] - *Myrica gale* L. (5, 156) (1913-1923)

Moor rush - *Juncus stygius* L. (5, 50) (1913–present)

Moorberry [Moor-berry, Moor berry] - *Vaccinium oxycoccos* L. (5, 92, 107, 156) (1876-1923), *Vaccinium uliginosum* L. (107) (1919)

Moor-besom [Moor besom] - *Calluna vulgaris* (L.) Hull (156) (1923) no longer in use by 1923

Moor-everlasting [Moor everlasting] - *Antennaria dioica* (L.) Gaertn. (156) (1923)

Moor-grass [Moor grass] - *Drosera rotundifolia* L. (5, 6, 156, 158) (1892-1923), *Narthecium americanum* Ker-Gawl. (5, 156, 158) (1900-1923)

Moor-pawn - *Eriophorum callitrix* Cham. ex C.A. Mey. (156) (1923)

Moorwort [Moor-wort] - *Andromeda polifolia* L. (5, 156, 165) (1807-1923), *Calluna vulgaris* (L.) Hull (5) (1913), *Drosera rotundifolia* L. (158) (1900), *Lyonia mariana* (L.) D. Don (86) (1878)

Moose bush [Moose-bush] - *Viburnum lantanoides* Michx. (5, 75, 76, 156) (1894-1923)

Moose elm - *Ulmus rubra* Muhl. (5, 20, 93, 156, 157, 158) (1857–1936)

Moose flower [Moose-flower, Moose flowers] - *Trillium grandiflorum* (Michx.) Salisb. (156) (1923), *Trillium* L. (75) (1894) NY

Moose maple - *Acer spicatum* Lam. (5, 156) (1913–1923)

Moose misse - *Sorbus americana* Marsh. (74) (1893)

Moose missy - *Sorbus americana* Marsh. (5) (1913)

Mooseberry [Moose-berry, Moose berry] - *Viburnum edule* (Michx.) Raf. (4) (1986), *Viburnum lantanoides* Michx. (5, 75, 76, 156) (1894-1923)

Mooseberry viburnum - *Viburnum edule* (Michx.) Raf. (155) (1942)

Moosehead Lake sedge - *Carex saxatilis* L. (5) (1913)

Moose's-tongue [Moose-tongue] - *Chamerion angustifolium* (L.) Holub subsp. *angustifolium* (156) (1923)

Moosewood [Moose-wood, Moose wood] - *Acer pensylvanicum* L. (2, 5, 15, 76, 109, 156) (1895-1949), *Acer spicatum* Lam. (19, 20, 58, 92) (1840-1876), *Dirca* L. (1, 2) (1895-1932), *Dirca palustris* L. (5, 6, 7, 19, 40, 41, 42, 47, 49, 92, 156) (1770-1928), *Viburnum lantanoides* Michx. (73, 156) (1892-1923)

Moosewort - *Botrychium virginianum* (L.) Sw. (72) (1907) IA

Moountain geranium - *Geranium robertianum* L. (5) (1913)

Moracocks - *Passiflora* L. (181) (~1678)

Moraea - *Moraea* Mill. (138) (1923)

Morassweed [Morass-weed] - *Ceratophyllum demersum* L. (5, 156, 157, 158) (1900-1929)

More consould - *Symphytum officinale* L. (179) (1526)

More morell - *Atropa bella-donna* L. (179) (1526)

Morel - *Lycium barbarum* L. (156) (1923)

Morelle (French) - *Solanum nigrum* L. (158) (1900)

Morelle [Morel] - *Morchella angusticeps* Peck (35) (1806), *Morchella* Dill. ex Pers (101) (1905), *Morchella esculenta* (L.) Pers. (37, 128) (1830-1933) Banister, *Solanum nigrum* L. (156) (1923) no longer in use by 1923

Morelle a gràppes (French) - *Phytolacca americana* L. var. *americana* (6, 158, 186) (1814-1900)

Morelle grimpante (French) - *Solanum dulcamara* L. (158) (1900)

Morello - *Prunus cerasus* L. (156) (1923)

Morello cherry - *Prunus cerasus* L. (1, 82) (1930-1932)

Morgan - *Anthemis cotula* L. (5, 156, 157, 158) (1900-1929)

Morgeline - *Veronica hederifolia* L. (5, 158) (1900-1913)

Moricou - *Erythrina corallodendron* L. (174) (1753)

Morille - *Phallus* Junius ex L. (184) (1793)

Mormon tea - *Ephedra* L. (4, 153) (1913-1986)

Mormon tree - *Populus nigra* L. (156) (1923)

Mormon weed [Mormon-weed] - *Abutilon theophrasti* Medik (5, 73, 156, 158) (1892-1923) Quincy IL

Morning campion - *Silene dioica* (L.) Clairville (109, 156) (1923-1949)

Morning-brides [Morning brides] - *Chaenactis* DC. (1) (1932)

Morning-glory [Morningglory, Morning glory] - *Chaenactis douglasii* (Hook.) Hook. & Arn. (85) (1932) SD, *Calystegia sepium* (L.) R. Br. subsp. *sepium* (80) (1913), *Convolvulus arvensis* L. (106) (1930), *Convolvulus* L. (1, 93) (1932-1936), *Ipomoea hederacea* Jacq. (80, 145) (1897-1913), *Ipomoea* L. (1, 50, 63, 82, 93, 106, 109, 125, 138, 142, 155, 156, 183) (~1756–present) IA, *Ipomoea lacunosa* L. (5, 156) (1913-1923), *Ipomoea purpurea* (L.) Roth (5, 46, 72, 85, 92, 95, 97, 114, 150) (1879-1937) TX

Morning-glory bush [Morning glory bush] - *Ipomoea leptophylla* Torr. (77) (1898)

Moroccan millet [Morocco millet] - *Sorghum halepense* (L.) Pers. (158) (1900)

Moroccan toadflax [Morocco toadflax] - *Linaria maroccana* Hook. f. (138) (1923)

Morrel - *Solanum dulcamara* L. (158) (1900)

Morris thatch palm - *Thrinax morrisii* H. Wendl. (138) (1923)

Morro manzanita - *Arctostaphylos morroensis* Wies. & Schreib. (155) (1942)

Morrow's honeysuckle [Morrow honeysuckle] - *Lonicera morrowii* Gray (112, 138) (1923-1937)

Mortification root [Mortification-root] - *Althaea officinalis* L. (5, 92, 156, 158) (1876-1923)

Mortog (Sweden "swine grass") - *Polygonum viviparum* L. (107) (1919)

Morton's loco [Morton loco] - *Astragalus canadensis* L. var. *mortonii* (Nutt.) S. Wats. (155) (1942)

Morton's oat grass [Morton's oat-grass] - *Helictotrichon mortonianum* (Scribn.) Henrard (94) (1901)

Moschar (Missouri tribes) - *Gaultheria procumbens* L. (7) (1828) indicates poor soil

Moschatel - *Adoxa* L. (158) (1900), *Adoxa moschatellina* L. (3, 4, 5, 63, 92, 131, 156, 158) (1899-1986)

Moschatella - *Adoxa moschatellina* L. (174) (1753)

Mosqueit - *Prosopis glandulosa* Torr. (103) (1870)

Mosquito plant [Mosquitoplant] - *Agastache cana* (Hook.) Woot. & Standl. (155) (1942), *Hedeoma pulegioides* (L.) Pers. (157) (1929)

Mosquito-bells - *Dodecatheon meadia* L. (156) (1923)

Mosquito-fern [Mosquitofern, Mosquito fern] - *Azolla caroliniana* Willd. (155) (1942), *Azolla* Lam. (4, 50, 109) (1949–present)

Moss - *Portulaca grandiflora* Hook. (74) (1893) Southern IN

Moss bush [Moss-bush] - *Cassiope hypnoides* (L.) D.Don (5, 19, 92, 156) (1840-1923)

Moss campion - *Silene acaulis* L. (1, 5, 15, 85, 92, 109, 131, 138, 156) (1895-1949)

Moss flower - *Portulaca* L. (124) (1937) TX

Moss grass [Moss-grass] - *Coleanthus subtilis* (Tratt.) Seidel (94) (1901)

Moss heather - *Cassiope* D. Don. (106) (1930)

Moss locust [Moss-locust] - *Robinia hispida* L. (5, 92, 156, 158) (1876-1923)

Moss phlox - *Phlox andicola* E. Nels. (3) (1977), *Phlox hoodii* Richards. (1) (1932), *Phlox hoodii* Richards. subsp. *muscoides* (Nutt.) Wherry (5, 93, 158) (1900-1936), *Phlox subulata* L. (138) (1923)

Moss pink [Moss-pink] - *Phlox hoodii* Richards. (1, 127) (1932-1933), *Phlox subulata* L. (2, 5, 63, 72, 77, 86, 92, 108, 109, 156) (1878-1949), *Silene acaulis* L. (5, 76, 156) (1896-1923) Paris ME

Moss plant [Moss-plant] - *Cassiope* D. Don. (1) (1932), *Harrimanella hypnoides* (L.) Coville (5, 156) (1913-1923)

Moss selaginella - *Selaginella apoda* (L.) Spring (97) (1937)

Moss-beauty [Moss beauty] - *Epigaea repens* L. (6) (1892)

Mossberry [Moss-berry, Moss berry] - *Moneses uniflora* (L.) Gray (107) (1919), *Vaccinium macrocarpon* Aiton (7, 92, 107) (1828-1919), *Vaccinium oxycoccos* L. (5, 107, 156) (1913-1923)

Moss-crop [Moss crop, Moss crops] - *Eriophorum callitrix* Cham. ex C.A. Mey. (5, 156) (1913-1923), *Eriophorum virginicum* L. (5, 19, 92, 156) (1840-1913)

Mossewood - *Acer spicatum* Lam. (42) (1814)

Moss-melons [Moss melons] - *Vaccinium oxycoccos* L. (5, 92) (1876-1913)

Moss-millions [Moss millions] - *Vaccinium oxycoccos* L. (5) (1913)

Moss-rose [Moss rose] - *Sphaeralcea coccinea* (Nutt.) Rydb. subsp. *coccinea* (5, 76, 156, 157) (1896-1929) Burnside SD

Mossy locust - *Robinia hispida* L. (3) (1977)

Mossy overcup oak - *Quercus macrocarpa* Michx. (34) (1834)

Mossy stonecrop - *Sedum acre* L. (3, 5, 49, 156) (1898-1977)

Mossy-cup oak [Mossycup oak, Mossy cup oak] - *Quercus macrocarpa* Michx. (1, 5, 93, 97, 108, 109, 130, 138, 156, 158) (1878-1949), *Quercus macrocarpa* Michx. var. *macrocarpa* (10, 20, 19, 33) (1818-1840)

Mossy-cup white oak [Mossy cup white oak, Mossycup white oak] - *Quercus macrocarpa* Michx. (5, 156) (1913-1923)

Mostaza blanco (Spanish) - *Sinapis alba* L. (158) (1900)

Moth mullein [Moth mullen] - *Verbascum blattaria* L. (3, 4, 5, 19, 45, 50, 62, 63, 72, 92, 97, 122, 124, 155, 156, 158, 178) (1526–present)

Mother time - *Thymus vulgaris* L. (178) (1526)

Mother-of-herbs [Moder of herbes] - *Artemisia vulgaris* L. (179) (1526)

Mother-of-millions [Mother of millions] - *Linaria vulgaris* Mill. (156) (1923)

Mother-of-rye [Mother of rye] - *Sclerotium clavus* DC. (92) (1876)

Mother-of-thousands - *Cymbalaria muralis* P.G. Gaertn., B. Mey. &

Scherb. (5, 92, 156) (1876-1923), *Tradescantia crassifolia* Cav. (75) (1894) Boston MA

Mother-of-thyme [Mother of thyme] - *Acinos arvensis* (Lam.) Dandy (5, 156) (1913-1923)

Mother-of-wheat [Mother of wheat] - *Veronica hederifolia* L. (5, 156, 158) (1900-1923)

Mother's-beauties [Mother's beauties] - *Calandrinia ciliata* (Ruiz & Pav.) DC. (74) (1893)

Mother's-heart [Mother's heart] - *Capsella bursa-pastoris* (L.) Medik. (5, 62, 107, 156, 157, 158) (1900-1929)

Motherwort [Mother wort, Mother-wort, Mother Woort] - *Artemisia vulgaris* L. (156, 157) (1923-1929), *Eupatorium purpureum* L. (5, 64, 73, 156, 157, 158) (1892-1929), *Leonurus cardiaca* L. (4, 5, 10, 19, 47, 49, 52, 53, 57, 61, 62, 63, 72, 80, 82, 85, 92, 93, 97, 106, 114, 122, 131, 145, 156, 157, 158, 178, 187) (1526-1986), *Leonurus* L. (1, 4, 50, 82, 93, 138, 155, 156, 158, 167) (1814–present)

Mottled wild ginger [Mottled wildginger] - *Hexastylis shuttleworthii* (Britten & Baker) Small var. *shuttleworthii* (138, 155) (1931-1942)

Motton-tops - *Chenopodium album* L. (157) (1929)

Mould - *Rhizopus stolonifer* (Ehrenb.) Vuill., (92) (1876)

Mound-lily yucca [Moundlily yucca] - *Yucca gloriosa* L. (50, 138) (1923–present)

Moundscale - *Atriplex nuttallii* S. Wats. (4) (1986)

Mounta Atlas pistache - *Pistacia atlantica* Desf. (138) (1923)

Mountain alder - *Acer pensylvanicum* L. (156) (1923), *Alnus incana* (L.) Moench subsp. *rugosa* (DuRoi) Clausen (138) (1923), *Alnus viridis* (Vill.) Lam. & DC. (2, 5, 20, 156) (1857–1923)

Mountain allocarya - *Plagiobothrys scouleri* (Hook. & Arn.) I.M. Johnston var. *hispidulus* (Greene) Dorn (5, 93, 131) (1899–1936)

Mountain ancychiastrum - *Paronychia fastigiata* (Raf.) Fern. (5) (1913), *Paronychia montana* (Small) Pax & K. Hoffmann (5) (1913)

Mountain andromeda - *Pieris floribunda* (Pursh) Benth. & Hook. f. (138) (1923)

Mountain androsace - *Androsace septentrionalis* L. (131) (1899)

Mountain anemone - *Anemone lancifolia* Pursh (5) (1913)

Mountain ash [Mountain-ash, Mountainash] - *Fraxinus velutina* Torr. (149, 153) (1904-1919), *Populus tremuloides* Michx. (156) (1923), *Sorbus americana* Marsh. (47, 156) (1852-1923), *Sorbus aucuparia* L. (41, 49, 107, 112) (1770-1937), *Sorbus* L. (1, 4, 8, 7, 10, 138, 156, 158) (1828-1986), *Sorbus sambucifolia* (Cham. & Schlecht.) M. Roemer (130, 137) (1895–1931), *Sorbus scopulina* Greene (4, 153) (1913-1986), *Spiraea alba* Du Roi (4) (1986)

Mountain asp - *Populus tremuloides* Michx. (157, 158) (1900-1929)

Mountain aspen - *Populus tremuloides* Michx. (5) (1913)

Mountain aster - *Oclemena acuminata* (Michx.) Greene (5, 156) (1913-1923), *Symphyotrichum puniceum* (L.) A.& D. Löve var. *puniceum* (85) (1932)

Mountain avens - *Dryas* L. (1, 10) (1818-1932), *Dryas octopetala* L. (19, 107) (1840-1919)

Mountain azalea - *Rhododendron canescens* (Michx.) Sweet (5, 156) (1913-1923)

Mountain balm - *Ceanothus velutinus* Dougl. ex Hook. (4) (1986), *Eriodictyon californicum* (Hook. & Arn.) Torr. (53, 54, 57, 106) (1905-1930), *Monarda didyma* L. (7, 92) (1828-1876), *Monarda* L. (10) (1818)

Mountain balsam - *Eriodictyon californicum* (Hook. & Arn.) Torr. (77) (1898) CA

Mountain balsam or [Mountain balsam tree, Mountain balsam-tree] - *Abies fraseri* (Pursh) Poir. (5, 158) (1900-1913)

Mountain barley - *Elyhordeum montanense* (Scribn.) Bowden [*Elymus virginicus* × *Hordeum jubatum*] (50) (present)

Mountain bear-tongue - *Penstemon glaber* Pursh var. *alpinus* (Torr.) Gray (85) (1932) SD

Mountain bellwort - *Uvularia puberula* Michx. (50) (present)

Mountain bent - *Agrostis scabra* Willd. (94) (1901)

Mountain big sagebrush - *Artemisia tridentata* Nutt. subsp. *vaseyana* (Rydb.) Beetle (50) (present)

Mountain birch - *Betula occidentalis* Hook. (1, 3, 4) (1932-1986)

Mountain bittercress [Mountain bitter cress] - *Cardamine clematitis* Shuttlew. ex Gray (5) (1913)

Mountain black cherry - *Prunus serotina* Ehrh. (106) (1930)

Mountain blackberry - *Rubus allegheniensis* Porter (5, 82, 97, 158) (1913-1937)

Mountain bladder fern [Mountain bladderfern] - *Cystopteris montana* (Lam.) Bernh. ex Desv. (50) (present)

Mountain bladderpod - *Lesquerella montana* (Gray) S. Wats. (50) (present)

Mountain blue grass - *Poa arida* Vasey (11) (1888)

Mountain bluebells - *Mertensia ciliata* (James) D. Don (138, 155) (1923-1942)

Mountain blueberry - *Vaccinium pallidum* Aiton (5, 158) (1900-1913)

Mountain bluet - *Centaurea montana* L. (109) (1949)

Mountain box - *Arctostaphylos uva-ursi* (L.) Spreng. (5, 6, 7, 92, 107, 156, 157) (1828-1929)

Mountain brake - *Pellaea atropurpurea* (L.) Link (92) (1876)

Mountain bramble - *Rubus chamaemorus* L. (5, 156) (1913-1923)

Mountain brome - *Bromus marginatus* Nees ex Steud. (50, 146) (1939–present)

Mountain button-snakeroot - *Liatris pilosa* (Aiton) Willd. var. *pilosa* (5) (1913)

Mountain calalae - *Phytolacca americana* L. var. *americana* (186) (1814)

Mountain cat's-tail [Mountain cat's tail] - *Phleum alpinum* L. (66) (1903)

Mountain cedar - *Juniperus deppeana* Steud. (122) (1937), *Juniperus pinchotii* Sudw. (124) (1937) TX

Mountain cherry - *Prunus angustifolia* Marsh. (possibly) (2, 74, 107) (1894–1919)

Mountain cinquefoil - *Sibbaldiopsis tridentata* (Aiton) Rydb. (19) (1840)

Mountain clematis - *Clematis occidentalis* (Hornem.) DC. var. *occidentalis* (5, 156) (1913-1923)

Mountain colt's-foot [Mountain colt's foot] - *Petasites fragrans* C.Presl (19) (1840)

Mountain columbine - *Aquilegia caerulea* James. (38) (1820)

Mountain corkwing - *Cymopterus montanus* Nutt. ex Torr. & Gray (3) (1977) IA

Mountain corydalis - *Corydalis curvisiliqua* Engelm. subsp. *occidentalis* (Engelm. ex Gray) W. A. Weber (5, 85, 93, 97, 155) (1913–1942)

Mountain cottonwood - *Populus angustifolia* James (149, 153) (1904–1913)

Mountain cowslip - *Mertensia virginica* (L.) Pers. ex Link (177) (1762)

Mountain cranberry - *Arctostaphylos uva-ursi* (L.) Spreng. (75, 92, 156, 157) (1894–1929) Southern ME, *Vaccinium* L. (1) (1932), *Vaccinium vitis-idaea* L. (5, 156) (1913–1923), *Vaccinium vitis-idaea* L. subsp. *minus* (Lodd.) Hultén (109, 138) (1923–1949), *Arctostaphylos uva-ursi* (L.) Spreng. (5, 93) (1913–1936)

Mountain crowfoot - *Ranunculus allegheniensis* Britt. (5) (1913)

Mountain cryptantha - *Cryptantha cana* (A. Nels.) Payson (50) (present)

Mountain cudweed [Mountain cud-weed] - *Antennaria dioica* (L.) Gaertn. (156) (1923), *Omalotheca supina* (L.) DC. (5, 156) (1913-1923), *Antennaria dioica* (L.) Gaertn. (178) (1526)

Mountain currant - *Ribes alpinum* L. (109, 138) (1923-1949)

Mountain cymopterus - *Cymopterus montanus* Nutt. ex Torr. & Gray (5, 97, 131) (1899-1937)

Mountain cystopteris - *Cystopteris montana* (Lam.) Bernh. ex Desv. (5) (1913)

Mountain dandelion - *Taraxacum officinale* G.H. Weber ex Wiggers subsp. *vulgare* (Lam.) Schinz & R. Keller (5) (1913)

Mountain death camas [Mountain deathcamas, Mountain death-

camass] - *Zigadenus elegans* Pursh (50, 155) (1942–present), *Zigadenus elegans* Pursh subsp. *elegans* (50) (present)

Mountain dittany - *Cunila* L. (10) (1818), *Cunila origanoides* (L.) Britton (7, 49, 58, 92, 156, 158, 186) (1814-1923)

Mountain dock - *Rumex paucifolius* Nutt. (101) (1905) MT

Mountain dropseed [Mountain drop-seed] - *Muhlenbergia filiformis* (Thurb. ex S. Wats.) Rydb. (94) (1901)

Mountain ebony - *Bauhinia variegata* L. (109) (1949)

Mountain elder or Mountain elder tree [Mountaine elder tree] - *Sambucus racemosa* L. (5, 92, 156, 178) (1526-1923), *Sambucus racemosa* L. var. *racemosa* (158) (1900)

Mountain enchanter's-nightshade [Mountain enchanter's nightshade] - *Circaea alpina* L. (41, 42) (1770-1814)

Mountain eubotrys - *Leucothoe recurva* (Buckl.) Gray (5) (1913)

Mountain evening-primrose - *Oenothera latifolia* (Rydb.) Munz (50) (present)

Mountain evergreen cherry - *Prunus ilicifolia* (Nutt. ex Hook. & Arn.) D. Dietr. (74) (1893) CA

Mountain everlasting - *Antennaria dioica* (L.) Gaertn. (131) (1899) SD

Mountain fetter-bush - *Pieris floribunda* (Pursh) Benth. & Hook. f. (possibly) (5, 156) (1913-1923)

Mountain flax [Mountain-flax] - *Centaurium erythraea* Raf. (156) (1923), *Linum catharticum* L. (5, 156) (1913-1923), *Polygala senega* L. (5, 6, 19, 64, 92, 156, 158) (1840-1923)

Mountain fleabane - *Erigeron compositus* Pursh (85) (1932)

Mountain fleawort [Mountain flea wort] - *Packera tomentosa* (Michx.) C.Jeffrey (possibly) (19) (1840) **Mountain fly honeysuckle [Mountain fly-honeysuckle]** - *Lonicera caerulea* L. (5, 156) (1913-1923) IA

Mountain foxtail - *Alopecurus alpinus* Sm. (94) (1901), *Phleum alpinum* L. (5) (1913)

Mountain fringe - *Adlumia fungosa* (Aiton) Greene ex B. S. P. (5, 48, 73, 76, 92, 109, 155, 156) (1876-1949)

Mountain garlic [Mountaine garlicke, Mountain garlick] - *Allium cernuum* Roth (42) (1814), *Allium scorodoprasum* L. (178) (1596)

Mountain geranium - *Geranium robertianum* L. (76, 156, 157, 158) (1896–1929)

Mountain globeflower [Mountain globe-flower, Mountain globe flower] - *Cephalanthus occidentalis* L. (92, 157, 158) (1876-1929)

Mountain goldenrod [Mountain golden-rod] - *Solidago caesia* L. var. *curtisii* (Torr. & Gray) Wood (5) (1913)

Mountain grape - *Vitis cinerea* (Engelm.) Millard var. *helleri* (Bailey) M.O. Moore (15) (1895), *Vitis monticola* Buckl. (106, 107) (1919-1930), *Vitis rupestris* Scheele (5, 15, 107, 122) (1895-1937)

Mountain grass - *Andropogon bicornis* L. (92) (1876)

Mountain hair grass [Mountain hair-grass] - *Vahlodea atropurpurea* (Wahlenb.) Fries ex Hartman (5, 50, 94) (1901–present)

Mountain heath - *Menziesia ferruginea* Sm. (156) (1923), *Phyllodoce caerulea* (L.) Bab. (5, 156) (1913-1923)

Mountain hemlock - *Tsuga mertensiana* (Bong.) Carr. (109, 138) (1923-1949)

Mountain holly - *Ilex aquifolium* L. (92) (1876), *Ilex montana* (Torr. & Gray) Gray (5, 156) (1913-1923)

Mountain holly fern [Mountain hollyfern, Mountain holly-fern - *Polystichum lonchitis* (L.) Roth. (109, 138, 155) (1923-1949), *Polystichum scopulinum* (D.C. Eaton) Maxon. (50) (present)

Mountain houstonia - *Houstonia purpurea* L. (138) (1923)

Mountain huckleberry - *Vaccinium membranaceum* Dougl. (3, 4) (1977-1986)

Mountain juniper - *Juniperus communis* L. var. *montana* Ait. (136, 138) (1923-1930)

Mountain lady's-mantle [Mountain ladysmantle] - *Alchemilla alpina* L. (155) (1942)

Mountain lady's-slipper [Mountain lady's slipper, Mountain ladyslipper] - *Cypripedium montanum* Dougl. ex Lindl. (50, 138) (1923–present)

Mountain laurel [Mountain Lawrell] - *Ceanothus herbaceus* Raf. (85) (1932), *Ceanothus* L. (1) (1932), *Kalmia* L. (2, 92, 156) (1876-1923), *Kalmia latifolia* L. (5, 6, 7, 20, 41, 49, 52, 53, 57, 71, 106, 156) (1770-1930), *Rhododendron* L. (7, 10, 167) (1814-1828), *Rhododendron maximum* L. (5, 20, 71, 92, 156, 177) (1762-1923), *Umbellularia californica* (Hook. & Arn.) Nutt. (107) (1919), *Umbellularia californica* (Hook. & Arn.) Nutt. var. *californica* (54, 154) (1857-1905)

Mountain leek [Mountain leak] - *Allium tricoccum* Ait. (19) (1840)

Mountain lily [Mountaine Lillie, Mountaine Lilly] - *Abutilon* Mill. (76) (1896) ME, *Ceanothus* L. (106) (1930), *Leucocrinum montanum* Nutt. ex Gray (3, 157) (1900-1977), *Leucocrinum* Nutt. ex Gray (1, 93) (1932-1936), *Lilium martagon* L. (178, 180) (1596-1633)

Mountain magnolia - *Magnolia acuminata* (L.) L. (5, 49, 156) (1898-1923)

Mountain maple - *Acer glabrum* Torr. (4, 95, 101, 130) (1895-1986), *Acer spicatum* Lam. (2, 5, 15, 20, 41, 42, 50, 72, 82, 109, 138, 155, 156, 165) (1768–present)

Mountain maple bush [Mountain maple-bush - *Acer spicatum* Lam. (19, 156) (1840-1923)

Mountain marsh-marigold [Mountain marsh marigold] - *Caltha palustris* L. (5) (1913)

Mountain May-apple [Mountain May apple] - *Podophyllum peltatum* L. (7) (1828)

Mountain meadowrue [Mountain meadow rue] - *Thalictrum clavatum* DC. (5) (1913)

Mountain meadowsweet - *Spiraea betulifolia* Pallas var. *lucida* (Dougl. ex Greene) C.L. Hitchc. (3) (1977)

Mountain moly [Mountaine moly] - *Allium victorialis* L. (178) (1596)

Mountain moss - *Selaginella selaginoides* (L.) Beauv. ex Mart. & Schrank (5) (1913)

Mountain muhly - *Muhlenbergia montana* (Nutt.) A.S. Hitchc. (122, 140) (1937-1944)

Mountain mulberry - *Morus microphylla* Buckl. (122, 124) (1937) TX

Mountain ninebark - *Physocarpus monogynus* (Torr.) Coult. (4, 155) (1942-1986)

Mountain oak - *Quercus prinus* L. (5, 19, 156) (1840-1923)

Mountain oat grass - *Danthonia compressa* Austin ex Peck (87, 88) (1884-1885)

Mountain pachysandra - *Pachysandra procumbens* Michx. (138) (1923)

Mountain partridge-berry [Mountain partridge berry] - *Gaultheria hispidula* (L.) Muhl. ex Bigelow (5, 156) (1913-1923)

Mountain phacelia - *Phacelia fimbriata* Michx. (5) (1913)

Mountain phlox - *Phlox latifolia* Michx. (5, 109, 138, 156) (1913-1949)

Mountain pimpernel - *Taenidia montana* (Mackenzie) Cronq. (156) (1923)

Mountain pink [Mountain-pink] - *Centaurium beyrichii* (Torr. & Gray ex Torr.) B.L. Robins. (100, 122) (1850-1937), *Epigaea repens* L. (5, 6, 49, 58, 92, 156) (1869-1923), *Phlox subulata* L. (5, 19, 86, 156) (1840-1923)

Mountain ragwort - *Senecio eremophilus* Richards (131) (1899)

Mountain raspberry - *Rubus chamaemorus* L. (5, 156) (1913-1923)

Mountain rattletop [Mountain rattle top] - *Cimicifuga americana* Michx. (5) (1913)

Mountain red raspberry - *Rubus idaeus* L. subsp. *strigosus* (Michx.) Focke (85) (1932)

Mountain redbud - *Cercis canadensis* L. var. texensis (S. Wats.) M. Hopkins (122, 124) (1937) TX

Mountain redtop [Mountain red top] - *Agrostis canina* L. (87, 90) (1884-1885)

Mountain rice - *Oryza sativa* L. (7) (1828)

Mountain rice grass [Mountain ricegrass] - *Achnatherum hymen-*

oides (Roemer & J.A. Schultes) Barkworth (146) (1939), *Piptatherum pungens* (Torr.) Barkworth (3, 50) (1977–present)

Mountain rockcress [Mountain rock-cress] - *Arabis alpina* L. (109) (1949)

Mountain rose-bay [Mountain rose bay] - *Rhododendron catawbiense* Michx. (5, 109, 156) (1913-1949)

Mountain rosemallow - *Hibiscus elatus* Sw. (138) (1923)

Mountain rush - *Ephedra antisyphilitica* Berl. ex C.A. Mey. (158) (1900), *Juncus balticus* Willd. var. *montanus* Engelm. (50) (present)

Mountain rye - *Secale cereale* L. (94, 155) (1901-1942)

Mountain sage [Mountain-sage] - *Artemisia frigida* Willd. (57, 156, 157, 158) (1900–1929), *Artemisia tridentata* Nutt. (5, 93, 156, 157, 158) (1900–1936), *Teucrium scorodonia* L. (156) (1923)

Mountain sandwort - *Minuartia caroliniana* (Walt.) Mattf. (156) (1923), *Minuartia groenlandica* (Retz.) Ostenf. (5, 156) (1913-1923)

Mountain saxifrage - *Saxifraga* L. (1) (1932), *Saxifraga oppositifolia* L. (1, 156) (1923-1932), *Saxifraga oppositifolia* L. subsp. *oppositifolia* (5) (1913)

Mountain sea-holly [Mountain sea hollie] - *Eryngium planum L.* (178) (1526)

Mountain sedge - *Carex microptera* Mackenzie (139) (1944), Carex *scirpoidea* Michx. subsp. *scirpoidea* (5, 19) (1840–1913)

Mountain serviceberry - *Amelanchier utahensis* Koehne var. *utahensis* (155) (1942)

Mountain silverbell - *Halesia tetraptera* Ellis var. *monticola* (Rehd.) Reveal & Seldin (138) (1923)

Mountain sneezeweed - *Helenium autumnale* L. var. *montanum* (Nutt.) Fern. (50, 155) (1942–present)

Mountain snowberry - *Symphoricarpos oreophilus* Gray (138) (1923)

Mountain sorrel - *Oxalis montana* Raf. (possibly) (7, 92) (1828–1876), *Oxyria digyna* (L.) Hill (5, 7, 92, 101, 107, 122, 156) (1828–1937), *Rumex acetosella* L. (5, 156, 157, 158) (1900–1929)

Mountain soursop - *Annona montana* Macfad. (155) (1942), *Asimina incana* (W. Bartram) Exell (155) (1942)

Mountain spear grass [Mountain spear-grass] - *Poa alpina* L. (94) (1901), *Poa arida* Vasey (87) (1884), *Poa laxa* Haenke (5) (1913)

Mountain spiderwort - *Tradescantia subaspera* Ker-Gawl. var. *montana* (Shuttlw. ex Britt.) E.S. Anderson & Woods. (5) (1913)

Mountain spinach - *Atriplex hortensis* L. (107, 158) (1900-1919)

Mountain spleenwort - *Asplenium montanum* Willd. (5, 50) (1913–present)

Mountain spring-parsley [Mountain springparsley] - *Cymopterus montanus* Nutt. ex Torr. & Gray (50) (present)

Mountain spurge - *Euphorbia marginata* Pursh (5) (1913)

Mountain St. John's-wort [Mountain St. John's wort, Mountain St. Johnswort] - *Hypericum graveolens* Buckley (5, 156) (1913-1923)

Mountain starwort - *Minuartia groenlandica* (Retz.) Ostenf. (5, 156) (1913-1923)

Mountain stewartia - *Stewartia ovata* (Cav.) Weatherby (5, 138) (1913-1923)

Mountain stonecrop - *Sedum ternatum* Michx. (138, 155) (1931-1942)

Mountain strawberry - *Fragaria virginiana* Duchesne subsp. *virginiana* (5, 19) (1840-1913)

Mountain sugar maple - *Acer grandidentatum* Nutt. (20) (1857)

Mountain sumac [Mountain sumach] - *Rhus copallinum* L. (5, 19, 92, 107, 156, 157) (1840-1929), *Rhus glabra* L. (157, 158) (1900-1929)

Mountain tail-leaf - *Pericome caudata* Gray (50) (present)

Mountain tansy-mustard [Mountain tansymustard] - *Descurainia incana* (Bernh. ex Fisch. & C.A. Mey.) Dorn subsp. *incana* (50) (present)

Mountain tarweed - *Madia glomerata* Hook. (50) (present)

Mountain tea [Mountain-tea] - *Gaultheria* L. (8, 10, 167) (1785–1818), *Gaultheria procumbens* L. (5, 6, 7, 14, 49, 53, 73, 92, 156, 184, 186, 187) (1793–1923)

Mountain thistle - *Cirsium eatonii* var. *eriocephalum* (A.Gray) D.J.Keil (101) (1905) MT

Mountain timothy - *Alopecurus pratensis* L. subsp. *alpestris* (Wahlenb.) Selander (45) (1896), *Phleum alpinum* L. (3, 45, 88) (1885-1977)

Mountain tobacco - *Arnica angustifolia* Vahl. (possibly) (5, 131, 156) (1899-1923)

Mountain viburnum - *Viburnum opulus* L. var. *americanum* Aiton (8) (1785)

Mountain watercress [Mountain water cress, Mountain watercress] - *Cardamine douglassii* Britt. (5, 156) (1913-1923), *Cardamine rotundifolia* Michx. (2, 5, 156) (1895-1923)

Mountain white oak - *Quercus alba* L. (17) (1796), *Quercus douglasii* Hook. & Arn. (106) (1930), *Quercus grisea* Liebm. (122) (1937) TX

Mountain white pine - *Pinus monticola* Dougl. ex D. Don (109, 138) (1923-1949)

Mountain wild gooseberry - *Ribes oxyacanthoides* L. (8) (1785)

Mountain winterberry - *Ilex montana* (Torr. & Gray) Gray (138) (1923)

Mountain wood fern [Mountain woodfern] - *Dryopteris campyloptera* (Kunze) Clarkson (138) (1923)

Mountain wood lily - *Lilium philadelphicum* L. var. *andinum* (Nutt.) Ker.-Gawl. (155) (1942)

Mountain-basil [Mountain basil] - *Pycnanthemum* Michx. (2, 4) (1895-1986)

Mountain-bluet - *Centaurea montana* L. (138) (1923)

Mountain-dandelion - *Krigia montana* (Michx.) Nutt. (138) (1923)

Mountain-fringe [Mountainfringe] - *Adlumia* Raf. ex DC. (155) (1942)

Mountain-grape [Mountain grape] - *Mahonia aquifolium* (Pursh) Nutt. (49, 52, 53, 107) (1919-1922)

Mountain-holly [Mountain holly] - *Ilex mucronata* (L.) M. Powell, Savol. & S. Andrews (5, 19, 107, 109, 138, 156) (1840-1949), *Mahonia aquifolium* (Pursh) Nutt. (64) (1907), *Mahonia* Nutt. (7) (1828), *Mahonia repens* (Lindl.) G. Don (35) (1806), *Nemopanthus* Raf. (1, 15, 138, 156) (1895-1932), *Prunus ilicifolia* (Nutt. ex Hook. & Arn.) D. Dietr. (107) (1919) CA

Mountain-indigo - *Amorpha glabra* Desf. ex Poir. (138) (1923)

Mountain-indigo amorpha [Mountainindigo amorpha] - *Amorpha glabra* Desf. ex Poir. (155) (1942)

Mountain-laurel - *Kalmia latifolia* L. (109, 138) (1923-1949)

Mountain-mahogany [Mountain mahogany, Mountainmahogany] - *Betula lenta* L. (5, 7, 49, 92, 156) (1828-1923), *Cercocarpus* Kunth (50, 93, 106, 122, 153, 155) (1913–present), *Cercocarpus ledifolius* Nutt. (76, 101, 125, 138) (1896-1930), *Cercocarpus montanus* Raf. (1, 3, 85, 95, 113, 130, 137, 157, 158) (1890-1977), *Liquidambar styraciflua* L. (156) (1923), *Rhus integrifolia* (Nutt.) Benth. & Hook. f. ex Brewer & S. Wats. (106) (1930) CA

Mountain-mint [Mountain mint, Mountainmint] - *Calamintha nepeta* (L.) Savi subsp. *nepeta* (190) (~1759) San Diego Co. CA, *Monarda didyma* L. (5, 7, 19, 92, 156) (1828–1923), *Monarda punctata* L. (48) (1882), *Pycnanthemum flexuosum* (Walt.) Britton, Sterns & Poggenb. (82) (1930), *Pycnanthemum incanum* (L.) Michx. (10) (1818), *Pycnanthemum* Michx. (1, 2, 7, 10, 50, 82, 93, 138, 155, 156, 158) (1818–present), *Pycnanthemum montanum* Michx. (57, 92) (1876–1917), *Pycnanthemum virginianum* (L.) T. Dur. & B. D. Jackson ex B. L. Robins. & Fern. (3, 40, 82, 85, 106, 156) (1923–1977)

Mountain-misery [Mountain misery] - *Chamaebatia foliolosa* Benth. (106) (1930)

Mountain-moss [Mountain moss] - *Sedum acre* L. (5, 156) (1913-1923), *Sedum pulchellum* Michx. (5, 156) (1913-1923)

Mountain-plum [Mountain plum] - *Ximenia americana* L. (20) (1857), *Ximenia* Plum. (15) (1895)

Mountain-pride [Mountain pride] - *Penstemon newberryi* Gray (109) (1949)

Mountain-primrose [Mountain primrose] - *Oenothera* L. (1) (1932)

Mountain-rhubarb [Mountain rhubarb] - *Rumex alpinus* L. (92, 107) (1876-1919)

Mountain-rice [Mountain rice] - *Achnatherum hymenoides* (Roemer & J.A. Schultes) Barkworth (146) (1939), *Oryzopsis asperifolia* Michx. (19, 107) (1840-1919), *Oryzopsis* Michx. (1, 93) (1932-1936), *Piptatherum micranthum* (Trin. & Rupr.) Barkworth (111) (1915), *Piptatherum pungens* (Torr.) Barkworth (85) (1932)

Mountain-rose coralvine [Mountainrose coralvine] - *Antigonon leptopus* Hook. & Arn. (155) (1942)

Mountain-snow [Mountain snow] - *Euphorbia marginata* Pursh (156, 157, 158) (1900-1923)

Mountain-stream gooseberry [Mountain stream gooseberry] - *Ribes oxyacanthoides* L. subsp. *irriguum* (Dougl.) Sinnott (108) (1878)

Mountain-sweet [Mountain sweet] - *Ceanothus americanus* L. (5, 92, 107, 156, 157, 158) (1876–1929)

Mountain-sweet pepperbush [Mountain sweet pepperbush] - *Clethra acuminata* Michx. (5) (1913)

Mountain-tea - *Mitchella repens* L. (156) (1923)

Mountain-thyme [Mountain thyme] - *Pycnanthemum virginianum* (L.) T. Dur. & B.D. Jackson ex B.L. Robins. & Fern. (5, 156, 157) (1900–1929)

Mourning willow - *Salix humilis* Marsh. var. *tristis* (Aiton) Griggs (19) (1840)

Mourning-bride [Mourning bride] - *Scabiosa atropupurea* L. (76, 92) (1876-1896) Sulphur Grove OH, *Scabiosa* L. (82, 109) (1930-1949)

Mourning-widow [Mourning widow] - *Scabiosa atropupurea* L. (76, 92) (1876-1896) Sulphur Grove OH

Mouron (French) - *Anagallis arvensis* L. (6) (1892)

Mouron rouge (French) - *Anagallis arvensis* L. (157, 158) (1900-1929)

Mouse barley [Mouse-barley - *Hordeum murinum* L. (5, 50, 119, 163) (1852–present)

Mouse bloodwort [Mouse blood wort, Mouse-bloodwort] - *Hieracium murorum* L. (156) (1923) no longer in use by 1923, *Hieracium pilosella* L. (5, 92, 156) (1876-1923)

Mouse ear scorpion grass - *Myosotis scorpioides* L. (92) (1876)

Mouse foxtail - *Alopecurus myosuroides* Huds (155) (1942)

Mouse grass - *Aira caryophyllea* L. (5) (1913)

Mouse pea - *Lathyrus pratensis* L. (5, 156) (1913-1923)

Mouse-bane [Mouse bane] - *Aconitum* L. (92) (1876), *Aconitum napellus* L. (156) (1923)

Mouse-bur - *Proboscidea louisianica* (P. Mill.) Thellung (156, 158) (1900-1923)

Mouse-ear [Mouse ear, Mouse ears, Mouse's ear, Mows eare] - *Antennaria plantaginifolia* (L.) Richards (62, 76, 92) (1876-1912), *Arabidopsis thaliana* (L.) Britton (5) (1913), *Cerastium fontanum* Baumg. subsp. *vulgare* (Hartman) Greuter & Burdet (5, 19, 80, 156) (1840–1923), *Cerastium* L. (184) (1793), *Gnaphalium* L. (79) (1891) NH, *Gnaphalium uliginosum* L. (5, 76, 156, 158) (1896–1923) Paris ME, *Hepatica nobilis* Schreb. var. *obtusa* (Pursh) Steyermark (5) (1913), *Hieracium pilosella* L. (92, 156, 178, 179) (1526–1923), *Myosotis scorpioides* L. (158) (1900), *Pontederia cordata* L. (78) (1898) Grand Lake NB, *Stachys germanica* L. (5) (1913)

Mouse-ear chickweed [Mouse ear chickweed, Mouse-eared chickweed] - *Cerastium arvense* L. (42) (1814), *Cerastium fontanum* Baumg. subsp. *vulgare* (Hartman) Greuter & Burdet (85, 145) (1897–1932), *Cerastium glomeratum* Thuill. (5, 15, 45, 72, 92, 97, 122, 156) (1876-1937), *Cerastium* L. (1, 4, 50, 10, 13, 15, 93, 109, 156, 167, 190) (~1759–present)

Mouse-ear cress [Mouseear cress [Mouse ear cress] - *Arabidopsis* Heynh. (4) (1986), *Arabidopsis thaliana* (L.) Britton (1, 3, 4, 15, 50, 85, 92, 155, 156) (1876–present)

Mouse-ear everlasting - *Antennaria plantaginifolia* (L.) Richards (86, 158) (1878-1900), *Pseudognaphalium obtusifolium* (L.) Hilliard & Burtt subsp. *obtusifolium* (157) (1929)

Mouse-ear hawkweed - *Hieracium pilosella* L. (5) (1913)

Mouse-ear minor - *Krigia virginica* (L.) Willd. (46) (1671)

Mouse-ear plantain - *Antennaria plantaginifolia* (L.) Richards (156) (1923)

Mouse-ear scorpion-grass [Mouse-ear scorpion grass] - *Myosotis scorpioides* L. (5, 156, 187) (1818-1923)

Mouse-ear turkey-pod - *Arabidopsis thaliana* (L.) Britton (187) (1818)

Mouse-ear wallcress [Mouse-ear wall-cress] - *Arabidopsis thaliana* (L.) Britton (42, 187) (1814-1818)

Mouse-milk [Mouse milk] - *Euphorbia helioscopia* L. (5, 156) (1913-1923) no longer in use by 1923

Mouse-root - *Lilium philadelphicum* L. (156) (1923)

Mouse-tail [Mousetail, Mouse-tail, Mousetaile] - *Alopecurus myosuroides* Huds (5) (1913), *Myosurus* L. (4, 13, 15, 50, 93, 155, 156, 158) (1849–present), *Myosurus minimus* L. (1, 3, 5, 63, 72, 85, 95, 97, 122, 131, 156, 178) (1526-1977), *Vulpia myuros* (L.) K.C. Gmel. (5) (1913)

Mouse-tail grass [Mouse tail gass] - *Alopecurus myosuroides* Huds (possibly) (92, 165) (1768-1876), *Vulpia myuros* (L.) K.C. Gmel. (92) (1876)

Mouse-thorn [Mouse thorn] - *Centaurea calcitrapa* L. (5, 156) (1913-1923)

Moustarde blanc (French) - *Sinapis alba* L. (6) (1892)

Moutarde blanche (French) - *Sinapis alba* L. (158) (1900)

Moutarde des moines (French) - *Armoracia rusticana* P.G. Gaertn., B. Mey. & Scherb. (158) (1900)

Moutarde Noire (French) - *Brassica nigra* (L.) W.D.J. Koch (6) (1892)

Mouthroot [Mouth-root, Mouth root] - *Coptis trifolia* (L.) Salisb. (5, 7, 49, 53, 64, 92, 156, 186) (1814-1923)

Mouth-smart [Mouth smart] - *Veronica beccabunga* L. (92) (1876)

Moving plants - Diatomaceae (92) (1876)

Mow-hair - *Adiantum pedatum* L. (187) (1818)

Moxie - *Gaultheria hispidula* (L.) Muhl. ex Bigelow (77) (1898)

Moxieberry [Moxie-berry, Moxie berry] - *Gaultheria hispidula* (L.) Muhl. ex Bigelow (5, 75, 156) (1894-1923)

Moxie-plum [Moxie plum] - *Gaultheria hispidula* (L.) Muhl. ex Bigelow (41, 156) (1770-1923), *Gaultheria* L. (1) (1932)

Mrs. Ashes's thorn - *Crataegus margarettiae* Ashe (5) (1913)

Mrs. Owen's panicum - *Dichanthelium ovale* (Ell.) Gould & C.A. Clark var. *addisonii* (Nash) Gould & C.A. Clark (5) (1913)

Mt. Katahdin sedge - *Carex conoidea* Schk. ex Willd. (5) (1913)

Mt. Washington bluegrass - *Poa laxa* Haenke (50) (present)

Muckig'obûg (Chippewa, swamp leaf) - *Ledum groenlandicum* Oeder (40) (1928)

Mû'ckigwa'tĭg (Chippewa, swamp tree) - *Larix laricina* (Du Roi.) Koch. (40) (1928)

Mûckode'cigaga'wûn (Chippewa, prairie skunk plant) - *Allium stellatum* Ker (40) (1928)

Mûckode'kaněs (Chippewa, small prairie) - *Andropogon gerardii* Vitman (40) (1928)

Muckweed [Muck-weed] - *Chenopodium album* L. (5, 156, 157, 158) (1900-1929), *Potamogeton crispus* L. (158) (1900)

Mucronate sprangletop - *Leptochloa panicea* (Retz.) Ohwi subsp. *brachiata* (Steudl.) N. Snow (50) (present), *Leptochloa panicea* (Retz.) Ohwi subsp. *mucronata* (Michx.) Nowack (50) (present)

Mud knotweed - *Polygonum amphibium* L. (19) (1840)

Mud life-everlasting - *Gnaphalium uliginosum* L. (19) (1840)

Mud sedge - *Carex limosa* L. (5, 50, 66, 72, 155) (1907–present)

Mud-babies [Mudbabies] - *Echinodorus tenellus* (Mart.) Buch. (50) (present)

Mud-bank crown grass [Mudbank crowngrass] - *Paspalum dissectum* (L.) L. (50) (present)

Mud-plantain [Mudplantain, Mud plantain] - *Heteranthera limosa* (Sw.) Vahl. (3, 85, 158) (1900-1977), *Heteranthera reniformis* R. & P. (5, 92, 97, 156) (1876-1937), *Heteranthera* Ruiz & Pavón (32, 50, 155, 156) (1895–present)

Mud-purslane [Mud purslane] - *Elatine americana* (Pursh) Arn. (19) (1840), *Elatine* L. (1, 158) (1900-1932), *Elatine rubella* Rydb. (5, 156) (1913-1923)

Mudweed [Mud-weed] - *Limosella aquatica* L. (5, 156, 157) (1900-1929), *Limosella* L. (158) (1900)

Mudwort [Mud wort] - *Limosella aquatica* L. (3, 5, 85, 156) (1913-1977), *Limosella australis* R. Br. (19, 92) (1840-1876), *Limosella* L. (1, 2, 10, 50, 155, 158) (1818–present)

Muehlenberg's nutrush - *Scleria muehlenbergii* Steud. (50) (present)

Muflier (French) - *Antirrhinum majus* L. (158) (1900)

Mu-gar-re (Omaha) - *Pediomelum esculentum* (Pursh) Rydb. (38) (1820)

Mugga - *Eucalyptus sideroxylon* A. Cunningham (109) (1949)

Mugget - *Galium odoratum* (L.) Scop. (5) (1913)

Mugho pine - *Pinus mugo* Turra (112, 135, 136, 138) (1910-1937)

Muguet (French) - *Convallaria majalis* L. (158) (1900)

Mugweed - *Artemisia vulgaris* L. (157) (1929)

Mugwet - *Galium odoratum* (L.) Scop. (5) (1913)

Mugwort [Mug-wort, Mugwoort] - *Artemisia absinthium* L. (5, 156) (1913–1923), *Artemisia dracunculus* L. (40) (1928), *Artemisia* L. (1, 4, 167) (1814–1986), *Artemisia ludoviciana* Nutt. (156) (1923), *Artemisia ludoviciana* Nutt. subsp. *ludoviciana* (5) (1913), *Artemisia vulgaris* L. (6, 7, 19, 57, 107, 109, 138, 157, 178) (1526–1949), *Leonurus cardiaca* L. (187) (1818)

Mugwort sagebrush - *Artemisia vulgaris* L. (155) (1942)

Mugwort-leaf ambrosia [Mugwort-leaved ambrosia] - *Ambrosia artemisiifolia* L. (165) (1768)

Muhlenberg's grass [Muhlenberg grass] - *Muhlenbergia glomerata* (Willd.) Trin. (11, 45) (1888-1896), *Muhlenbergia mexicana* (L.) Trin. (11) (1888), *Muhlenbergia pungens* Thurb. (11) (1888), *Muhlenbergia* Schreb. (93) (1936) for Dr. Muhlenberg, distinguished American botanidst

Muhlenberg's paspalum - *Paspalum setaceum* Michx. (5) (1913)

Muhlenberg's sedge - *Carex vulpinoidea* Michx. (5, 50, 66) (1903–present)

Muhlenberg's smartweed [Muhlenberg's smart weed] - *Polygonum amphibium* L. var. *emersum* Michx. (56, 80) (1901–1913)

Muhly - *Muhlenbergia* Schreb. (50, 155) (1942–present)

Muj'omïj' (Chippewa, moose plant) - *Cornus alternifolia* L. f. (40) (1928)

Muj'ota'bûk (Chippewa, moose leaf) - *Sagittaria latifolia* Willd. (40) (1928)

Mûkûde'widji'bïk (Chippewa, black root) - *Sanicula canadensis* L. (40) (1928)

Mulberry [Molberye] - *Rubus idaeus* L. subsp. *strigosus* (Michx.) Focke (5, 156) (1913-1923), *Rubus odoratus* L. (2, 5, 46, 73, 76, 156) (1879-1923), *Rubus pubescens* Raf. var. *pubescens* (5, 73) (1892–1913) Washington Co ME, NB

Mulberry [Molberye] or Mulberry tree - *Morus* L. (1, 8, 10, 50, 57, 82, 93, 109, 138, 155, 158, 167, 184) (1785–present), *Morus microphylla* Buckl. (153) (1913), *Morus nigra* L. (179) (1526), *Morus rubra* L. (35, 41, 103) (1770–1870)

Mulberry chrysanthemum - *Dendranthema* ×*grandiflorum* Kitam. [*indicum* × *japonicum*] (138) (1923)

Mule-fat baccharis [Mulefat baccharis] - *Baccharis salicifolia* (Ruiz & Pavón) Pers. (155) (1942)

Mule-foot bonnets - *Nuphar lutea* (L.) Sm. subsp. *advena* (Aiton) Kartesz & Gandhi (156) (1923)

Mule-foot lily - *Nuphar lutea* (L.) Sm. subsp. *advena* (Aiton) Kartesz & Gandhi (156) (1923)

Mule's-fat [Mule's fat, Mule fat] - *Baccharis glutinosa* Pers. (50) (present), *Baccharis salicifolia* (Ruiz & Pavón) Pers. (106) (1930)

Mulga - *Acacia aneura* F. Muell. ex Benth. (50) (present)

Mulga acacia - *Acacia aneura* F. Muell. ex Benth. (155) (1942)

Mullein [Mullen, Mulleine] - *Verbascum* L. (1, 4, 10, 47, 50, 63, 85, 93, 95, 109, 122, 124, 131, 138, 155, 156, 158) (1818–present), *Verbascum thapsus* L. (6, 7, 19, 48, 49, 52, 53, 57, 58, 60, 61, 69, 80, 114, 157, 178) (1526-1929)

Mullein dock [Mullen dock] - *Verbascum thapsus* L. (5, 69, 158, 174) (1753-1913)

Mullein false foxglove - *Dasistoma macrophylla* (Nutt.) Raf. (156) (1923)

Mullein foxglove [Mullen foxglove] - *Dasistoma macrophylla* (Nutt.) Raf. (2, 3, 5, 50, 63, 93, 157, 158) (1895–present), *Dasistoma* Raf. (1, 4) (1932-1986), *Seymeria* Pursh (93) (1936)

Mullein lychnis - *Lychnis coronaria* (L.) Desr. (156) (1923)

Mullein pink [Mullen pink] - *Agrostemma githago* L. (5, 71, 73, 156, 157, 158) (1892-1929) Nova Scotia, *Lychnis coronaria* (L.) Desr. (5, 15, 109, 156) (1895-1949)

Mullein-leaf vervain [Mullein-leaved vervain [Mullenleaf vervain [Mullen-leaved vervain] - *Verbena stricta* Vent. (5, 93, 122, 156, 158) (1900-1937)

Mullin with the white flower - *Verbascum blattaria* L. (46) (1671) accidentally introduced by 1671, Josselyn

Multiflora bean - *Phaseolus coccineus* L. (109) (1949)

Multiflora rose - *Rosa multiflora* Thunb. ex Murray (4, 50) (1986–present)

Multiplier onion - *Allium cepa* L. (109) (1949), *Allium cepa* L. var. *cepa* (155) (1942)

Mundubi - *Arachis hypogaea* L. (110) (1886)

Múng - *Vigna luteola* (Jacq.) Benth. (5) (1913), *Vigna mungo* (L.) Hepper (110) (1886)

Mung bean - *Vigna mungo* (L.) Hepper (107) (1919)

Munro's grass [Munroe's grass, Munro-grass] - *Monroa squarrosa* (Nutt.) Torr. (5, 119, 163) (1852-1938), *Panicum rigidulum* Bosc ex Nees var. *elongatum* (Pursh) Lelong (94, 163) (1852-1901)

Muns-minš - *Cornus sericea* L. subsp. *sericea* (105) (1932)

Mu-oil tree [Mu-oiltree] - *Aleurites montana* (Lour.) P. Wilson (155) (1942)

Murg - *Anthemis cotula* L. (158) (1900)

Murier (French) - *Morus* L. (8) (1785)

Murier rouge (French) - *Morus rubra* L. (8) (1785)

Murlin - *Alaria* Grev. (155) (1942)

Murray's lodgepole pine [Murray lodgepole pine] - *Pinus contorta* Dougl. ex Loud. var. *latifolia* Engelm. ex Wats (50) (present)

Murray's red gum [Murray red gum] - *Eucalyptus camaldulensis* Dehnhardt (57, 109) (1917-1949)

Muscadine - *Vitis rotundifolia* Michx. (2, 15, 97, 107, 109, 156) (1895-1949)

Muscadine grape - *Vitis* L. (possibly) (1) (1932), *Vitis rotundifolia* Michx. (122, 124, 138, 168) (1803-1937), *Vitis vulpina* L. (7, 158) (1828-1900)

Muscle plum - *Prunus domestica* L. (178) (1526)

Muse'odji'bïk (Chippewa, worm root) - *Artemisia absinthium* L. (40) (1928)

Mush - *Malva moschata* L. (76) (1896) ME

Mushaquissedes (Pequod) - *Phaseolus vulgaris* L. (107) (1919)

Musiineon - *Musineon* Raf. (158) (1900)

Musk - *Adoxa moschatellina* L. (158) (1900), *Citrullus lanatus* (Thunb.) Matsumura & Nakai (181) (~1678), *Malva moschata* L. (5, 73, 76, 156) (1892-1923), *Mirabilis hirsuta* (Pursh) MacM. (158) (1900)

Musk bristle-thistle [Musk bristlethistle] - *Carduus nutans* L. (155) (1942)

Musk flower [Musk-flower] - *Mimulus moschatus* Dougl. ex Lindl. (5, 156) (1913–1923)

Musk geranium - *Erodium moschatum* (L.) L'Hér. ex Aiton (19) (1840)

Musk hyacinth - *Muscari neglectum* Guss. ex Ten. (19) (1840)

Musk mallow - *Malva moschata* L. (5, 15, 19, 82, 109, 138, 156) (1840-1949)

Musk okra - *Abelmoschus moschatus* Medik. (50) (present)

Musk phlox - *Phlox hoodii* Richards. subsp. *muscoides* (Nutt.) Wherry (50) (present)

Musk plant [Musk-plant, Muskplant] - *Malva moschata* L. (5, 73, 156) (1892-1923), *Mimulus moschatus* Dougl. ex Lindl. (5, 14, 109, 138, 156) (1882-1949)

Musk pumpkin - *Cucurbita moschata* (Duchesne ex Lam.) Duchesne ex Poir. (110) (1886)

Musk rose - *Rosa moschata* J. Herrm. (19, 109, 138) (1840-1949)

Musk thistle [Musk-thistle] - *Carduus nutans* L. (3, 4, 5, 46, 156, 158) (1879-1986), *Onopordum acanthium* L. (5, 156, 158) (1900-1923)

Musk wood-crowfoot - *Adoxa moschatellina* L. (158) (1900)

Musk-crowfoot [Musk crowfoot] - *Adoxa moschatellina* L. (5, 156, 158, 165) (1768-1923)

Musked stork's-bill [Musked storks bill] - *Erodium moschatum* (L.) L'Hér. ex Aiton (178) (1526)

Muskeet - *Prosopis juliflora* (Sw.) DC. (30) (1844)

Musketweed [Musket weed] - *Thalictrum pubescens* Pursh (5) (1913)

Muskingum sedge - *Carex muskingumensis* Schwein. (5, 72) (1907-1913)

Muskit - *Bouteloua curtipendula* (Michx) Torr. (11) (1888)

Muskit grass - *Aristida purpurea* Nutt. (75) (1894) TX, *Bouteloua gracilis* (Willd. ex Kunth) Lag. ex Griffiths (66) (1903)

Musk-mallow - *Abelmoschus moschatus* Medik. (109) (1949)

Muskmelon [Muske-melon, Musk-melon, Muskmelon] - *Cucumis melo* L. (7, 19, 107, 109, 114, 132, 138) (1828-1949)

Muskratweed [Muskrat weed] - *Cicuta maculata* L. (71) (1898)

Muskroot [Musk-root, Musk root] - *Adoxa* L. (155, 158) (1900-1942), *Adoxa moschatellina* L. (4, 50, 63, 72, 131, 155, 156, 158) (1899–present)

Musk-rose [Musk rose] - *Malva moschata* L. (156) (1923)

Musky filaria - *Erodium moschatum* (L.) L'Hér. ex Aiton (76) (1896) CA

Musquash root [Musquash-root] - *Cicuta maculata* L. (2, 5, 6, 62, 71, 109, 133, 156, 158) (1892-1949)

Musquash-poison - *Cicuta maculata* L. (156, 158) (1900-1923)

Musquash-weed [Musquash weed] - *Thalictrum pubescens* Pursh (5, 76, 156) (1896-1923) Oxford Co. ME

Musquaspene - *Sanguinaria canadensis* L. (46) (1879)

Musquit grass - *Bouteloua* Lag. (45) (1896)

Mustang - *Vitis candicans* Engelm. (122) (1937) TX

Mustang grape - *Vitis candicans* Engelm. (15, 124, 138) (1895-1937) TX, *Vitis rotundifolia* Michx. var. *munsoniana* (Simpson ex Munson) M.O. Moore (15) (1895)

Mustard [Mustards] - *Brassica* L. (4, 50, 63, 82, 107, 109) (1899–present), *Brassica rapa* L. var. *rapa* (106) (1930), *Euclidium* Aiton f. (50) (present), *Moricandia arvensis* (L.) DC. (80) (1913), *Sinapis* L. (1, 7, 50, 93, 158, 184) (1793–present), *Sisymbrium* L. (63) (1899)

Mustard weld - *Sinapis arvensis* L. (14) (1882)

Mutterkraut (German) - *Tanacetum parthenium* (L.) Schultz-Bip. (158) (1900)

Mutton bluegrass - *Poa fendleriana* (Steud.) Vasey (140, 155) (1942-1944)

Mutton grass [Mutton-grass, Muttongrass] - *Poa fendleriana* (Steud.) Vasey subsp. *longiligula* (Scribn. & Williams) Soreng (50) (present), *Poa fendleriana* (Steud.) Vasey (3, 50, 94, 122, 152, 155, 163) (1852–present), *Poa fendleriana* (Steud.) Vasey subsp. *fendleriana* (50) (present)

Mutton-tops - *Chenopodium album* L. (156, 158) (1900-1923)

Myagrum - *Camelina sativa* (L.) Crantz (157, 158) (1900-1929), *Myagrum perfoliatum* L. (5) (1913)

My-lady's-belt [My lady's belt] - *Filipendula ulmaria* (L.) Maxim. (5) (1913)

Myosoton - *Myosoton* Moench (50) (present)

Mypes - *Pastinaca sativa* L. (157, 158) (1900-1929)

Myriad-leaf - *Myriophyllum verticillatum* L. (156) (1923)

Myrkle bush [Myrkle-bushes] - *Morella cerifera* (L.) Small (156) (1923)

Myrobalab plum - *Prunus cerasifera* Ehrh. (109) (1949)

Myrobalan - *Phyllanthus emblica* L. (109) (1949), *Terminalia catappa* L. (109) (1949)

Myrobalan plum - *Prunus cerasifera* Ehrh. (137, 138) (1923-1931)

Myrrh - *Myrrhis* Mill. (possibly) (109, 138) (1923-1949) from Greek word for perfume, *Myrrhis odorata* (L.) Scop. (138) (1923), *Lysimachia nummularia* L. (156) (1923), *Umbellularia californica* (Hook. & Arn.) Nutt. (106) (1930) OR, *Vinca* L. (1) (1932), *Vinca minor* L. (5, 73, 77, 158) (1892-1913)

Myrtle croton - *Bernardia myricifolia* (Scheele) S. Wats. (122) (1937) TX

Myrtle flag [Myrtle-flag] - *Acorus calamus* L. (5, 7, 64, 156, 157, 158, 186) (1814–1929)

Myrtle pachistima - *Paxistima myrsinites* (Pursh) Raf. (138) (1923)

Myrtle spurge [Mirtle spurge] - *Euphorbia lathyris* L. (5, 122, 156) (1913-1937), *Euphorbia myrsinites* L. (50, 178) (1526–present)

Myrtle willow - *Salix myrsinifolia* Salisb. (138) (1923)

Myrtle-grass [Myrtle grass] - *Acorus calamus* L. (5, 64, 92, 156, 158, 184) (1793-1908)

Myrtle-leaf [Myrtle leaf] - *Asparagus asparagoides* (L.) Druce (92) (1876)

Myrtle-leaf cranberry [Myrtle leaved cranberry] - *Vaccinium pallidum* Aiton (8) (1785)

Myrtle-leaf croton [Myrtle-leafed croton] - *Bernardia myricifolia* (Scheele) S. Wats. (124) (1937) TX

Myrtle-leaf dahoon holly - *Ilex myrtifolia* Walt. (106) (1930)

Myrtle-leaf marsh pea [Myrtle-leaved marsh pea] - *Lathyrus palustris* L. (5, 158) (1900-1913)

Myrtle-leaf oak [Myrtleleaf oak] - *Quercus myrtifolia* Willd. (122) (1937)

Myrtle-leaf pea vine [Myrtle-leaved pea-vine] - *Lathyrus palustris* L. (187) (1818)

Myrtle-leaf St. John's-wort [Myrtle-leaved St. John's wort] - *Hypericum fasciculatum* Lam. (2) (1895)

Myrtle-leaf vaccinium [Myrtle leaved vaccinium] - *Vaccinium pallidum* Aiton (8) (1785)

Myrtles - *Morella cerifera* (L.) Small (182) (1791)

Myrtle-sedge [Myrtle sedge] - *Acorus calamus* L. (5, 64, 156, 158) (1900–1923)

Mysterious plant - *Daphne mezereum* L. (5, 156) (1913-1923) no longer in use by 1923

Mystery-grass [Mystery grass] - *Zigadenus venenosus* S. Wats. var. *gramineus* (Rydb.) Walsh ex M.E. Peck (133) (1903) ND

Mystic pondweed - *Potamogeton ×mysticus* Morong [*perfoliatus* × *pusillus*] (5) (1913)

N

Naaní'Is (Arkikara) - *Shepherdia argentea* (Pursh) Nutt. (35) (1806)

Nabo (Spanish) - *Brassica rapa* L. var. *rapa* (180) (1633)

Na'bûgogwis'simaün (Chippewa [flat pumpkin]) - *Cucurbita maxima* Dcne. (40) (1928)

Nachius (Turkish and Armenian) - *Cicer arietinum* L. (110) (1886)

Nachtkerz (German) - *Oenothera biennis* L. (6) (1892)

Nachtkerze (German) - *Oenothera biennis* L. (158) (1900)

Nachuda (Georgian) - *Cicer arietinum* L. (110) (1886)

Nachunt (Turkish and Armenian) - *Cicer arietinum* L. (110) (1886)

Nackte Aralie (German) - *Aralia nudicaulis* L. (158) (1900)

Nagami kumquat - *Fortunella margarita* (Lour.) Swingle (109) (1949)

Nägde (Swedish) - *Spergula arvensis* L. (110) (1886)

Nahaapi nakaaruts (Pawnee, cherry tree) - *Prunus virginiana* L. var. *virginiana* (37) (1919)

Nahata-pahat (Pawnee, red tree) - *Quercus rubra* L. (37) (1919)

Nahosh (Winnebago) - *Acer negundo* L. (37) (1919)

Naiad - *Najas flexilis* (Willd.) Rostk. & Schmidt (3) (1977), *Najas guadalupensis* (Spreng.) Magnus (3) (1977), *Najas* L. (120, 155) (1938-1942), *Najas marina* L. (156) (1923)

Naiad fuchsia - *Fuchsia magellanica* Lam. (138) (1923)

Naias - *Najas* L. (93) (1936)

Nail-rod [Nail rod] - *Symphyotrichum lateriflorum* (L.) A.& D. Löve (5, 75, 156) (1894-1923) WV

Nailwort - *Draba breweri* S. Wats. var. *cana* (Rydb.) Rollins (156) (1923), *Draba incana* L. (92) (1876), *Draba* L. (158) (1900), *Draba verna* L. (5, 156) (1913–1923), *Paronychia argyrocoma* (Michx.) Nutt. (86) (1878), *Paronychia canadensis* (L.) Wood (5, 156) (1913–1923), *Paronychia* Mill. (4, 50, 138, 155, 158) (1900–present) said to be used for felons and whitlows, diseases of nails and joints of fingers

Nakasis (Pawnee, little tree or short tree) - *Arctostaphylos uva-ursi* (L.) Spreng. (5) (1913)

Naked barley - *Hordeum vulgare* L. (158) (1900) variety

Naked beard grass [Naked beard-grass] - *Gymnopogon ambiguus* (Michx.) Britton, Sterns & Poggenb. (5, 66, 92, 94, 119) (1876-1938)

Naked broomrape [Naked broom-rape, Naked broom rape] - *Orobanche fasciculata* Nutt. (2, 63) (1895–1899), *Orobanche* L. (2, 63) (1895–1899), *Orobanche uniflora* L. (5, 93, 156, 157, 158) (1900–1936)

Naked miterwort - *Mitella nuda* L. (155) (1942)

Naked red-flower rose-bay [Naked red flowered rose bay] - *Rhododendron periclymenoides* (Michx.) Shinners (42) (1814)

Naked Sticadoue - *Lavandula angustifolia* Mill. (178) (1526)

Naked viburnum - *Viburnum nudum* L. (107) (1919)

Naked with-rod [Naked withe rod] - *Viburnum nudum* L. (5, 122, 156) (1913-1937)

Naked-cluster St. John's-wort [Naked-clustered St. John's wort] - *Hypericum nudiflorum* Michx. ex Willd. (2) (1895)

Naked-cyme mealy-tree [Naked-cymed mealy-tree] - *Viburnum nudum* L. (53) (1922)

Naked-flower hawthorn [Naked-flowered hawthorn] - *Crataegus aestivalis* Torr. & Gray. (20) (1857)

Naked-flower tick trefoil [Naked-flowered tick trefoil, Naked-flowered tick-trefoil] - *Desmodium nudiflorum* (L.) DC. (5, 50, 72, 97) (1907–present)

Naked-ladies [Naked ladies] - *Colchicum autumnale* L. (92) (1876)

Naked-stalk miterwort [Naked-stalked miterwort] - *Mitella nuda* L. (2, 156) (1895–1923)

Naked-stem dewflower [Nakedstem dewflower] - *Murdannia nudiflora* (L.) Brenan (50) (present)

Naked-stem hawksbeard [Naked stemmed hawksbeard] - *Crepis runcinata* (James) Torr. & Gray (5, 131) (1899-1913)

Naked-stem sarsaparilla [Naked-stemmed sarsaparilla] - *Aralia nudicaulis* L. (187) (1818)

Nakedweed [Naked-weed, Naked weed] - *Chondrilla juncea* L. (5, 75, 156) (1894-1923) WV

Nakhalsa (Mongolia) - *Glycyrrhiza glabra* L. (107) (1919)

Nakipistatu (Pawnee, real arrow tree) - *Cornus asperifolia* Michx. (37) (1919)

Nakisokiits (Pawnee, pine water) - *Silphium laciniatum* L. (37) (1919)

Nakisu-kiitsu (Pawnee, pine water) - *Silphium laciniatum* L. (37) (1919)

Nakitsu (Pawnee) - *Maclura pomifera* (Raf.) Schneid. (37) (1919)

Nalta jute - *Corchorus olitorius* L. (109) (1949)

Nama - *Hydrolea* L. (106) (1930), *Nama* L. (138) (1923)

Namaqualand daisy - *Venidium* Less. (109) (1949)

Name'pïn (Chippewa, sturgeon plant) - *Asarum canadense* L. (40) (1928)

Name'wûckons (Chippewa, little sturgeon plant) - *Pycnanthemum virginianum* (L.) T. Dur. & B.D. Jackson ex B.L. Robins. & Fern. (40) (1928)

Name'wûskons' (Chippewa) - *Prunella vulgaris* L. (40) (1928)

Namoll (Spanish) - *Phytolacca americana* L. var. *americana* (158) (1900)

Nancy-over-the-ground - *Tiarella cordifolia* L. (74) (1893) MA

Nandina - *Nandina domestica* Thunb. (138) (1923), *Nandina* Thunb. (138) (1923)

Nankeen lily - *Lilium* × *testaceum* (Lindl.) Turrill (109, 138) (1923-1949)

Nanking cherry - *Prunus tomentosa* Thunb. (50, 112, 138) (1923–present)

Nanny bush [Nanny-bush, Nannybush] - *Viburnum lentago* L. (5, 92, 156, 158) (1876-1923) no longer in use by 1923

Nannyberry [Nanny-berry, Nanny berry] - *Viburnum lentago* L. (3, 4, 5, 37, 50, 53, 92, 93, 95, 107, 109, 112, 138, 156, 158) (1876–present), *Viburnum nudum* L. (5, 75, 156, 187) (1818-1923), *Viburnum prunifolium* L. (156, 158) (1900-1923)

Nannyberry viburnum - *Viburnum lentago* L. (155) (1942)

Nanny-plum [Nanny plum] - *Viburnum lentago* L. (5, 156, 158) (1900-1923) no longer in use by 1923

Nanpashakanak (Winnebago) - *Gymnocladus dioicus* (L.) K. Koch (37) (1919)

Nan-sank (Winnebago, pure or genuine wood) - *Acer saccharum* Marsh. (37) (1919)

Nanshaman (Omaha-Ponca) - *Viburnum lentago* L. (37) (1919)

Nantita (Omaha-Ponca) - *Gymnocladus dioicus* (L.) K. Koch (37) (1919)

Napa thistle - *Centaurea melitensis* L. (106) (1930) CA

Nap-at-noon - *Ornithogalum umbellatum* L. (5, 156, 158) (1900-1923), *Tragopogon porrifolius* L. (5, 75, 156, 158) (1894-1923)

Nape - *Brassica rapa* L. var. *rapa* (5, 158) (1900-1913)

Napier grass - *Pennisetum purpureum* Schumacher (138, 163) (1852-1923)

Napium - *Lapsana communis* L. (possibly) (180) (1633)

Napoleon - *Paulownia tomentosa* (Thunb.) Sieb. & Zucc. ex Steud. (possibly) (156) (1923)

Napoleon plant - *Nelumbo lutea* Willd. (possibly) (7, 92) (1828-1876)

Napoleons - *Trifolium incarnatum* L. (5, 156, 158) (1900-1923)

Napošstaŋ (Lakota) - *Ratibida pinnata* (Vent.) Barnh. (121) (1918?-1970?)

Narbonne vetch - *Vicia narbonensis* L. (107, 109) (1919-1949)

Narcissen (Dutch) - *Narcissus* L. (180) (1633)

Narcissus - *Narcissus* L. (92, 107, 138) (1876-1923) probably for narcotic qualities

Narcissus anemone - *Anemone multifida* Poir. var. *multifida* (155) (1942), *Anemone narcissiflora* L. (155) (1942)

Narcissus-flower anemone [Narcissus-flowered anemone] - *Anemone narcissiflora* L. (165) (1807)

Nard Americain (French) - *Aralia racemosa* L. (158) (1900)

Nard d'Amerique (French) - *Aralia racemosa* L. (6) (1892)

Nard sedge - *Carex nardina* Fried. (5) (1913)

Nardus Americanus (Official name of Materia Medica) - *Aralia nudicaulis* L. (7) (1828)

Nardwurzel Aralie (German) - *Aralia nudicaulis* L. (7) (1828)

Narrow alkali grass [Narrow alkaligrass] - *Puccinellia angustata* (R. Br.) Rand & Redf. (50) (present)

Narrow beardtongue - *Penstemon angustifolius* Nutt. ex Pursh (4) (1986), *Penstemon angustifolius* Nutt. ex Pursh var. *caudatus* (Heller) Rydb. (3) (1977)

Narrow beechfern [Narrow beech-fern] - *Phegopteris connectilis* (Michx.) Watt (109, 138) (1923-1949)

Narrow bent - *Leymus arenarius* (L.) Hochst. (5) (1913)

Narrow blue flag - *Iris prismatica* Pursh ex Ker-Gawl. (5, 156) (1913-1923)

Narrow cotton-grass [Narrow cotton grass] - *Eriophorum gracile* W.D.J. Koch var. *gracile* (66) (1903)

Narrow dock - *Rumex crispus* L. (5, 6, 64, 69, 77, 92, 93, 156, 157, 158) (1892-1936), *Rumex salicifolius* Weinm. (35) (1806)

Narrow false oat - *Trisetum spicatum* (L.) Richter (5) (1913)

Narrow goosefoot - *Chenopodium leptophyllum* (Moq.) Nutt. ex S. Wats. (50) (present)

Narrow melic grass [Narrow melic-grass - *Melica mutica* Walt. (5, 56, 72, 163) (1852-1907)

Narrow plantain - *Plantago lanceolata* L. (62) (1912)

Narrow reed grass - *Calamagrostis stricta* (Timm) Koel. subsp. *stricta* (5) (1913)

Narrow three-tooth grass [Narrow three-toothed grass] - *Tridens strictus* (Nutt.) Nash (5, 99, 119) (1913-1938)

Narrow-cell corn salad [Narrow-celled corn salad] - *Valerianella radiata* (L.) Dufr. (5, 97) (1913-1937)

Narrow-fruit maple [Narrow-fruited maple] - *Acer rubrum* L. (5) (1913)

Narrow-fruit sedge [Narrow-fruited sedge] - *Carex sychnocephala* Carey (129) (1894)

Narrowhead - *Sagittaria latifolia* Willd. (19) (1840)

Narrow-leaf American vetch [Narrow-leaved American vetch] - *Vicia americana* Muhl. ex Willd. subsp. *minor* (Hook.) C.R. Gunn (5, 72, 93, 97) (1907-1937)

Narrow-leaf amsonia [Narrow-leaved amsonia] - *Amsonia tabernaemontana* Walt. var. *salicifolia* (Pursh) Woods. (97) (1937)

Narrow-leaf arrowhead [Narrow-leaved arrow-head] - *Sagittaria longiloba* Engelm. ex J.G. Sm. (85) (1932)

Narrow-leaf balsam poplar [Narrow-leaved balsam poplar] - *Populus angustifolia* James (20) (1857)

Narrow-leaf beardtongue [Narrow-leaved beard-tongue] - *Penstemon angustifolius* Nutt. ex Pursh (127) (1933)

Narrow-leaf big sagebrush [Narrowleaf big sagebrush] - *Artemisia tridentata* Nutt. subsp. *tridentata* (155) (1942)

Narrow-leaf bird's-foot trefoil [Narrowleaf bird's-foot trefoil] - *Lotus tenuis* Waldst. & Kit. ex Willd. (50) (present)

Narrow-leaf black cottonwood [Narrow-leaved black cottonwood] - *Populus angustifolia* James (130) (1895)

Narrow-leaf blue-curls [Narrow-leaved blue curls] - *Trichostema setaceum* Houtt. (5) (1913)

Narrow-leaf blue-eyed grass [Narrowleaf blue-eyed grass] - *Sisyrinchium angustifolium* Mill. (50) (present)

Narrow-leaf bluet [Narrowleaf bluet] - *Hedyotis nigricans* (Lam.) Fosberg (3, 4) (1977-1986)

Narrow-leaf buckthorn [Narrow-leaved buckthorn] - *Rhamnus lanceolata* Pursh (2) (1895)

Narrow-leaf bumelia [Narrow-leaved bumelia] - *Sideroxylon celastrinum* (Kunth) T.D. Pennington (20) (1857)

Narrow-leaf bur-reed [Narrowleaf burreed, Narrowleaf bur-reed, Narrow-leaved bur-reed] - *Sparganium angustifolium* Michx. (5, 50, 155) (1913–present)

Narrow-leaf bush clover [Narrow-leaved bush clover] - *Lespedeza angustifolia* (Pursh) Ell. (5) (1913)

Narrow-leaf bushy goldenrod [Narrow-leaved bushy golden-rod] - *Euthamia tenuifolia* (Pursh) Nutt. var. *tenuifolia* (5) (1913)

Narrow-leaf cat-tail [Narrowleaf cattail, Narrow-leafed cat-tail, Narrow-leaved cats'-tail, Narrow-leaved cat-tail, Narrow-leaved cattail] - *Typha angustifolia* L. (3, 50, 85, 93, 97, 124, 138, 155, 156, 187) (1818–present)

Narrow-leaf collinsia [Narrow-leaved collinsia] - *Collinsia violacea* Nutt. (5, 65, 97) (1913-1937), *Collomia linearis* Nutt. (5, 93, 131) (1899–1936)

Narrow-leaf coneflower [Narrow leaf cone flower] - *Echinacea angustifolia* DC. (124) (1937), *Echinacea angustifolia* DC. var. *angustifolia* (72) (1907)

Narrow-leaf corn salad [Narrowleaf corn salad] - *Valerianella radiata* (L.) Dufr. (122) (1937)

Narrow-leaf cotton-sedge [Narrowleaf cottonsedge] - *Eriophorum angustifolium* Honckeny subsp. *scabriusculum* Hultén (139, 155) (1942-1944)

Narrow-leaf cottonwood [Narrow-leaved cottonwood] - *Populus angustifolia* James (1, 3, 4, 5, 28, 50, 85, 93, 131, 135, 138, 157) (1850–present)

Narrow-leaf cow-wheat [Narrow-leaved cow-wheat] - *Melampyrum lineare* Desr. (possibly) (5) (1913)

Narrow-leaf crab apple [Narrow-leaved crab apple] - *Malus angustifolia* (Aiton) Michx. var. *angustifolia* (2, 20) (1857-1895), *Malus coronaria* (L.) Mill. (5) (1913)

Narrow-leaf dayflower [Narrowleaf dayflower] - *Commelina erecta* L. var. *angustifolia* (Michx.) Fern. (155) (1942)

Narrow-leaf dichronema [Narrow-leaved dichronema] - *Rhynchospora colorata* (L.) H. Pfeiffer (5) (1913)

Narrow-leaf dock [Narrowleaf dock, Narrow-leaved dock] - *Rumex salicifolius* Weinm. var. *mexicanus* (Meisn.) A.S. Hitchc (85) (1932), *Rumex stenophyllus* Ledeb. (50) (present)

Narrow-leaf dwarf flower-de-luce [Narrow leafed Dwarfe Flowerdeluce] - *Iris pumila* L. (178) (1596)

Narrow-leaf eriogonum [Narrow-leaved eriogonum] - *Eriogonum brevicaule* Nutt. var. *brevicaule* (5) (1913)

Narrow-leaf evening-primrose [Narrow-leaved evening primrose] - *Oenothera argillicola* Mackenzie (5) (1913), *Oenothera linifolia* Nutt. (3, 4) (1977-1986)

Narrow-leaf false dragonhead [Narrowleaf false dragonhead] - *Physostegia angustifolia* Fern. (50) (present)

Narrow-leaf firethorn [Narrowleaf firethorn] - *Pyracantha angustifolia* (Franch.) Schneid. (138) (1923)

Narrow-leaf flower-de-luce [Narrow leafed Floure-de-luce] - *Iris pumila* L. (180) (1633)

Narrow-leaf four-o'clock [Narrowleaf four-o'clock] - *Mirabilis linearis* (Pursh) Heimerl (4, 50) (1986–present)

Narrow-leaf fritillary [Narrow-leaved fritillary] - *Fritillaria affinis* (Schult.) Sealy var. *affinis* (107) (1919)

Narrow-leaf gentian [Narrow leaved gentian] - *Gentianella quinquefolia* (L.) Small subsp. *quinquefolia* (7) (1828), *Gentiana linearis* Froel. (5) (1913)

Narrow-leaf germander [Narrow-leaved germander] - *Teucrium canadense* L. var. *canadense* (5, 97) (1913-1937)

Narrow-leaf globe mallow [Narrowleaf globemallow - *Malvastrum hispidum* (Pursh) Hochr. (3, 4, 155) (1942-1986)

Narrow-leaf glossy buckthorn [Narrowleaf glossy buckthorn] - *Frangula alnus* Mill. (155) (1942)

Narrow-leaf gold-aster [Narrowleaf goldaster] - *Heterotheca stenophylla* (Gray) Shinners var. *stenophylla* (155) (1942)

Narrow-leaf goldenrod [Narrowleaf goldenrod, Narrow-leaf golden-rod, Narrow-leaved goldenrod, Narrow-leaved golden-rod] - *Euthamia graminifolia* (L.) Nutt. (127) (1933), *Euthamia graminifolia* (L.) Nutt. var. *graminifolia* (3) (1977), *Euthamia gymnospermoides* Greene (3) (1977), *Euthamia tenuifolia* (Pursh) Nutt. var. *tenuifolia* (122) (1937), *Oligoneuron nitidum* (Torr. & Gray) Small (97) (1937), *Solidago sempervirens* L. (19) (1840)

Narrow-leaf goldenweed [Narrowleaf goldenweed] - *Ericameria linearifolia* (DC.) Urbatsch & Wussow (155) (1942)

Narrow-leaf goosefoot [Narrowleaf goosefoot, Narrow-leaved goosefoot] - *Chenopodium leptophyllum* (Moq.) Nutt. ex S. Wats. (5, 93, 97, 122, 131) (1899-1937)

Narrow-leaf gromwell [Narrowleaf gromwell] - *Lithospermum incisum* Lehm. (155) (1942)

Narrow-leaf gum plant [Narrow-leaved gum-plant] - *Grindelia lanceolata* Nutt. (5, 97) (1913-1937)

Narrow-leaf gumweed [Narrowleaf gumweed] - *Grindelia lanceolata* Nutt. (50, 122) (1937–present)

Narrow-leaf hawk's-beard [Narrowleaf hawksbeard] - *Crepis tectorum* L. (5, 50, 155) (1913–present)

Narrow-leaf hawkweed [Narrow-leaved hawkweed] - *Hieracium umbellatum* L. (5, 50, 93, 131, 155) (1899–present)

Narrow-leaf horse-gentian [Narrowleaf horsegentian [Narrow-leaved horse-gentian [Narrow-leaved horse gentian] - *Triosteum angustifolium* L. (5, 72, 155, 156) (1907-1942)

Narrow-leaf houstonia [Narrow-leaved houstonia] - *Hedyotis nigricans* (Lam.) Fosberg var. *nigricans* (5, 72, 93, 97) (1907-1937)

Narrow-leaf Indian breadroot [Narrowleaf Indian breadroot] - *Pediomelum linearifolium* (Torr. & Gray) J. Grimes (50) (present)

Narrow-leaf ironbark [Narrowleaf ironbark] - *Eucalyptus crebra* F. Muell. (138) (1923)

Narrow-leaf ironweed [Narrow-leaved ironweed] - *Vernonia marginata* (Torr.) Raf. (93) (1936)

Narrow-leaf kalmia [Narrow leaved kalmia] - *Kalmia angustifolia* L. (8) (1785)

Narrow-leaf knotweed [Narrowleaf knotweed, Narrow-leaved knotweed] - *Polygonum bellardii* All. (5, 50, 122) (1913-prresent)

Narrow-leaf Labrador tea [Narrow-leaved Labrador tea] - *Ledum palustre* L. subsp. *decumbens* (Aiton) Hultén (5) (1913)

Narrow-leaf laurel [Narrow-leaved laurel, Narrow leaved laurel] - *Kalmia angustifolia* L. (71, 92, 156) (1876-1923)

Narrow-leaf leafy spurge - *Euphorbia esula* L. var. *uralensis* (Fisch. ex Link) Dorn (4) (1986)

Narrow-leaf loco [Narrowleaf loco, Narrow-leafed loco] - *Astragalus mollissimus* Torr. var. *earlei* (Greene ex Rydb.) Tidestrom (122, 124) (1937)

Narrow-leaf marsh elder [Narrowleaf marsh elder, Narrowleaf marshelder, Narrow-leaved marsh elder] - *Iva angustifolia* Nutt. (50, 97, 122) (1937–present)

Narrow-leaf marsh speedwell [Narrow-leaved marsh speedwell] - *Veronica scutellata* L. (46) (1879)

Narrow-leaf marshallia [Narrow-leaved marshallia] - *Marshallia caespitosa* Nutt. (5, 97) (1913-1937)

Narrow-leaf meadow grass [Narrow-leaved meadow grass] - *Poa pratensis* L. subsp. *pratensis* (41) (1770)

Narrow-leaf meadowsweet [Narrowleaf meadowsweet, arrow-leaved meadow sweet] - *Spiraea alba* Du Roi (5, 155) (1913-1942)

Narrow-leaf milkvetch [Narrowleaf milkvetch, Narrow-leaved milk vetch] - *Astragalus pectinatus* (Hook.) Dougl. ex G. Don (5, 50, 93) (1913–present)

Narrow-leaf milkweed [Narrowleaf milkweed, Narrow-leafed milkweed, Narrow-leaved milkweed] - *Asclepias stenophylla* Gray (3, 4, 5, 85, 93, 97, 122, 131) (1899-1986)

Narrow-leaf morning-glory [Narrowleaf morning-glory] - *Ipomoea shumardiana* (Torr.) Shinners (50) (present)

Narrow-leaf mountain-mint [Narrowleaf mountainmint, Narrow-leaved mountain mint, Narrow-leaved mountain-mint] - *Pycnanthemum flexuosum* (Walt.) Britton, Sterns & Poggenb. (72, 97, 106) (1907-1937), *Pycnanthemum tenuifolium* Schrad. (50) (present)

Narrow-leaf mouse-ear chickweed [Narrow-leaved mouse-ear chickweed] - *Cerastium fontanum* Baumg. subsp. *vulgare* (Hartman) Greuter & Burdet (187) (1818)

Narrow-leaf oat grass [Narrow-leaved oat-grass] - *Helictotrichon pratense* (L.) Pilg. (45) (1896)

Narrow-leaf paleseed [Narrowleaf paleseed] - *Leucospora multifida* (Michx.) Nutt. (50) (present)

Narrow-leaf panic grass [Narrow-leaved panic-grass] - *Dichanthelium aciculare* (Desv. ex Poir.) Gould & C.A. Clark (99, 163) (1852-1923)

Narrow-leaf panicum [Narrow-leaved panicum] - *Dichanthelium aciculare* (Desv. ex Poir.) Gould & C.A. Clark (5) (1913)

Narrow-leaf pectis [Narrowleaf pectis] - *Pectis angustifolia* Torr. var. *angustifolia* (50) (present)

Narrow-leaf penstemon [Narrowleaf penstemon] - *Penstemon angustifolius* Nutt. ex Pursh (138, 155) (1923-1942)

Narrow-leaf pepper-grass [Narrow-leaved pepper grass] - *Lepidium ruderale* L. (5) (1913)

Narrow-leaf pinweed [Narrowleaf pinweed, Narrow-leaved pinweed] - *Lechea tenuifolia* Michx. (5, 50, 72, 93, 97) (1907–present)

Narrow-leaf plantain [Narrowleaf plantain, Narrow-leaved plantain] - *Plantago lanceolata* L. (45, 50, 156) (1896–present)

Narrow-leaf plantain-lily [Narrow-leaved plantain-lily] - *Hosta lancifolia* Engl. (109) (1949)

Narrow-leaf poison milkvetch [Narrowleaf poisonmilkvetch] - *Astragalus pectinatus* (Hook.) Dougl. ex G. Don (155) (1942)

Narrow-leaf poison-vetch [Narrow-leaved poisonvetch] - *Astragalus pectinatus* (Hook.) Dougl. ex G. Don (3) (1977)

Narrow-leaf pondweed [Narrowleaf pondweed] - *Potamogeton strictifolius* Benn. (50) (present)

Narrow-leaf poplar [Narrowleaf poplar, Narrow-leafed poplar, Narrow-leaved poplar] - *Populus angustifolia* James (28, 112, 155) (1850-1942)

Narrow-leaf psoralea [Narrow-leaved psoralea] - *Pediomelum linearifolium* (Torr. & Gray) J. Grimes (5, 93, 97) (1913-1937)

Narrow-leaf puccoon [Narrow leaf puccoon, Narrow-leaved puccoon] - *Lithospermum incisum* Lehm. (3, 5, 72, 93, 97, 98, 121, 124, 127, 131, 156) (1899-1977)

Narrow-leaf purple coneflower [Narrowleaf purplecone flower, Narrow-leaved purple cone-flower] - *Echinacea angustifolia* DC. (5, 37, 49, 53, 97, 122) (1898-1937)

Narrow-leaf rhombopod [Narrowleaf rhombopod] - *Cleomella angustifolia* Torr. (50) (present)

Narrow-leaf sabbatia [Narrow-leaved sabbatia] - *Sabatia brachiata* Ell. (5) (1913)

Narrow-leaf sedge [Narrowleaf sedge, Narrow-leaved sedge] - *Carex amphibola* Steud. (3, 5, 72) (1907-1977)

Narrow-leaf sensitive brier [Narrow-leaved sensitive brier] - *Mimosa microphylla* Dry. (97, 158) (1900–1937)

Narrow-leaf showy goldenrod [Narrow-leaved showy goldenrod] - *Solidago speciosa* Nutt. var. *rigidiuscula* Torr. & Gray (82) (1930)

Narrow-leaf smooth aster [Narrow-leaved smooth aster] - *Symphyotrichum laeve* (L.) A.& D. Löve var. *concinnum* (Willd.) Nesom (5, 72) (1907-1913)

Narrow-leaf sneezeweed [Narrow-leaved sneezeweed] - *Helenium amarum* (Raf.) H. Rock var. *amarum* (106) (1930)

Narrow-leaf spleenwort [Narrowleaf spleenwort, Narrow-leaved spleenwort] - *Diplazium pycnocarpon* (Spreng.) Broun (5, 138, 155) (1913-1942)

Narrow-leaf stenotus [Narrow-leaved stenotus] - *Stenosiphon linifolius* (Nutt. ex James) Heynh. (5) (1913)

Narrow-leaf stoneseed [Narrowleaf stoneseed] - *Lithospermum incisum* Lehm. (50) (present)

Narrow-leaf sumpweed [Narrowleaf sumpweed] - *Iva angustifolia* Nutt. (155) (1942)

Narrow-leaf sundew [Narrowleaf sundew] - *Drosera anglica* Huds. (138) (1923)

Narrow-leaf sundrops [Narrow leaved sundrops, Narrow-leaved sundrops] - *Oenothera fruticosa* L. subsp. *fruticosa* (5, 97) (1913-1937)

Narrow-leaf sunflower [Narrow-leaved sunflower] - *Helianthus angustifolius* L. (5) (1913), *Helianthus maximiliani* Schrad. (127) (1933)

Narrow-leaf tetraneuris [Narrow-leaved tetraneuris] - *Tetraneuris scaposa* (DC.) Greene var. *scaposa* (5) (1913)

Narrow-leaf thorn [Narrow-leaved thorn] - *Crataegus spathulata* Michx. (5) (1913)

Narrow-leaf trefoil [Narrow-leaved trefoil] - *Lotus tenuis* Waldst. & Kit. ex Willd. (4) (1986)

Narrow-leaf umbrella-wort [Narrow-leaved umbrella wort, Narrow-leaved umbrellawort] - *Mirabilis linearis* (Pursh) Heimerl (5, 93, 97, 131) (1899-1936)

Narrow-leaf verbena [Narrow-leaved verbena] - *Verbena simplex* Lehm. (3, 4) (1977-1986)

Narrow-leaf vervain [Narrowleaf vervain [Narrow-leaved vervain] - *Verbena simplex* Lehm. (5, 50, 62, 82, 93, 97) (1912–present)

Narrow-leaf vetch [Narrowleaf vetch, Narrow-leaved vetch] - *Vicia americana* Muhl. ex Willd. subsp. *minor* (Hook.) C.R. Gunn (85, 131) (1899-1932), *Vicia sativa* L. subsp. *nigra* (L.) Ehrh. (109, 155) (1942-1949)

Narrow-leaf Virginia thyme [Narrow-leaf Virginian thyme, Narrow leaved Virginia thyme] - *Pycnanthemum virginianum* (L.) T. Dur. & B. D. Jackson ex B. L. Robins. & Fern. (19, 92) (1840–1876)

Narrow-leaf wafer-ash [Narrow-leafed wafer ash] - *Ptelea trifoliata* L. subsp. *trifoliata* var. *trifoliata* (124) (1937)

Narrow-leaf water-parsnip [Narrow-leaved water-parsnip, Narrow-leaved water parsnip] - *Berula erecta* (Huds.) Coville (5, 158) (1900–1913)

Narrow-leaf water-plantain [Narrowleaf water plantain] - *Alisma gramineum* Lej. (50) (present)

Narrow-leaf waterweed [Narrowleaf waterweed, Narrow-leafed water-weed] - *Elodea canadensis* Michx. (155) (1942), *Elodea nuttallii* (Planch.) St. John (5) (1913)

Narrow-leaf water-willow [Narrowleaf water willow, Narrow-leaved water willow] - *Justicia ovata* (Walt.) Lindau var. *lanceolata* (Chapman) R.W. Long (5, 97, 122) (1913-1937)

Narrow-leaf white-top aster [Narrow-leaved white-topped aster] - *Sericocarpus linifolius* (L.) B.S.P. (5) (1913)

Narrow-leaf wild leek [Narrowleaf wild leek] - *Allium burdickii* (Hanes) A. G. Jones (50) (present)

Narrow-leaf willow [Narrow leaf willow, Narrow-leaved willow] - *Salix exigua* Nutt. (35, 50, 101) (1806–present), *Salix interior* Rowlee (5, 101, 130, 156, 158) (1895-1923)

Narrow-leaf willowherb [Narrow leaved willow herb] - *Chamerion angustifolium* (L.) Holub subsp. *angustifolium* (42) (1814), *Epilobium leptophyllum* Raf. (3, 4) (1977-1986), *Epilobium palustre* L. (6) (1892)

Narrow-leaf wire-lettuce [Narrowleaf wirelettuce] - *Stephanomeria minor* (Hook.) Nutt. var. *minor* (50) (present)

Narrow-leaf yucca [Narrowleaf yucca] - *Yucca angustissima* Engelm. ex Trel. (50) (present)

Narrow-panicle rush [Narrowpanicle rush, Narrow-panicled rush] - *Juncus brevicaudatus* (Engelm.) Fernald (5, 50) (1913–present)

Narrow-petal stonecrop [Narrow-petaled stonecrop] - *Sedum lanceolatum* Torr. (5, 93) (1913-1936)

Narrow-point knotweed [Narrow-pointed knotweed] - *Polygonum ramosissimum* Michx. (5) (1913)

Narrow-seed spurge [Narrowseeded spurge, Narrow-seeded spurge] - *Chamaesyce stictospora* (Engelm.) Small (5, 93, 97, 122, 131) (1899–1937)

Narrow-tip spikesedge - *Eleocharis compressa* Sullivant (139) (1944)

Narrow-top feather grass [Narrow-topped feather-grass] - *Achnatherum occidentale* (Thurb. ex S. Watson) Barkworth (94) (1901)

Narrow-top panic [Narrow-topped panic] - *Setaria ramiseta* (Scribn.) Pilger (94) (1901)

Naseberry - *Manilkara zapota* (L.) van Royen (92, 107) (1876-1919)

Naseberry bully tree - *Manilkara zapota* (L.) van Royen (20) (1857)

Nash's panic grass [Nash's panic-grass] - *Dichanthelium sabulorum* (Lam.) Gould & C.A. Clark var. *patulum* (Scribn. & Merr.) Gould & C.A. Clark (94) (1901)

Nash's panicum - *Dichanthelium sabulorum* (Lam.) Gould & C.A. Clark var. *patulum* (Scribn. & Merr.) Gould & C.A. Clark (5) (1913)

Nash's snakeroot [Nash snake root] - *Aristolochia serpentaria* L. (122, 124) (1937) TX

Nas-sãn (Monominie) - *Urtica* L. (23) (1810)

Nasturtion - *Nasturtium* R. Br. (92) (1876)

Nasturtium - *Lepidium sativum* L. (107) (1919), *Nasturtium officinale* W.T. Aiton (possibly) (92) (1876), *Tropaeolum* L. (15, 82, 109, 138) (1895-1949) of gardeners, *Tropaeolum majus* L. (7, 19, 92) (1828-1876)

Nasturtium oxalis - *Oxalis corniculata* L. (138) (1923)

Nasula jazaŋpi ipije (Lakota, no appetite cure) - *Artemisia frigida* Willd. (121) (1918?-1970?)

Natakaaru (Pawnee) - *Populus deltoides* Bartr. ex Marsh. subsp. *monilifera* (Aiton) Eckenwalder (37) (1919)

Natal grass [Natal-grass] - *Melinis repens* (Willd.) Zizka (109, 122, 138, 163) (1852-1949)

Natal orange [Natal-orange] - *Strychnos spinosa* Lam. (109) (1949)

Natal plum [Natal-plum] - *Carissa macrocarpa* (Ecklon) A. DC. (109) (1949)

Nateau rond (French) - *Brassica rapa* L. var. *rapa* (180) (1633)

Naterwurtz (German) - *Polygonum amphibium* L. (46) (1879)

National rose - *Rosa multiflora* Thunb. ex Murray (138) (1923)

Native carrot - *Geranium dissectum* L. (107) (1919)

Native mulberry - *Morus rubra* L. (180) (1791)

Native plum - *Prunus americana* Marsh. (5, 158) (1900-1913)

Native potato - *Solanum fendleri* Gray ex Torr. (103) (1870)

Native red-osier dogwood - *Cornus sericea* L. subsp. *sericea* (112) (1937)

Native timothy - *Phleum alpinum* L. (45, 87) (1884-1896)

Native wild crab apple - *Malus ioensis* (Wood) Britton (112) (1937)

Nat-tar (Pinal Leño Apache) - *Lophophora lewinii* (Hennings ex Lewin) C.H. Thomps. (132) (1855)

Natterkopf (German) - *Echium vulgare* L. (158) (1900)

Nattourne - *Zizania aquatica* L. (46) (1879)

Natural grass - *Poa pratensis* L. (5) (1913), *Poa trivialis* L. (5) (1913)

Natural-grass [Natural grass] - *Medicago lupulina* L. (5, 158) (1900-1913)

Nature's-mistake [Nature's mistake] - *Cornus florida* L. (5, 75, 156, 158) (1844-1923) Abington Mass, no longer in use by 1923

Naughty-man's-playing - *Urtica dioica* L. (157, 158) (1900-1929)

Navaho tea - *Thelesperma subnudum* Gray var. *marginatum* (Rydb.) T. E. Melchert ex Cronq. (50) (present)

Navelseed [Navel-seed] - *Omphalodes* Mill. (109, 138) (1923–1949)

Navelwort [Navel-wort] - *Cotyledon* L. (86) (1878) old European name, *Myriophyllum spicatum* L. (158) (1900), *Omphalodes* Mill. (109) (1949)

Navette (French) - *Brassica rapa* L. var. *rapa* (107) (1919)

Navette d'hiver (French) - *Brassica rapa* L. var. *rapa* (107) (1919)

Naze-ni pezhi (Omaha-Ponca [milkweed) - *Chamaesyce serpyllifolia* (Pers.) Small (37) (1919)

Nealley's dropseed [Neally dropseed] - *Sporobolus nealleyi* Vasey (122) (1937)

Nealley's dropseed grass - *Sporobolus nealleyi* Vasey (152) (1912)

Nealley's leptochloa - *Leptochloa nealleyi* Vasey (94) (1901)

Nealley's rush grass [Nealley's rush-grass] - *Sporobolus nealleyi* Vasey (94) (1901)

Near navarretia - *Navarretia intertexta* (Benth.) Hook. subsp. *propinqua* (Suksdorf) Day (50) (present)

Ne'bagandag' (Chippewa, it is one-sided) - *Taxus canadensis* Willd. (40) (1928)

Ne'baneya'nekweäg' (Chippewa, it is one-sided) - *Geum triflorum* Pursh var. *ciliatum* (Pursh) Fassett (40) (1928)

Nebraska aster - *Symphyotrichum praealtum* (Poir.) Nesom var. *nebraskense* (Britton) Nesom (5, 50, 93) (1913–present)

Nebraska blazing star - *Liatris punctata* Hook. var. *nebraskana* Gaiser (50) (present)

Nebraska glorybind - *Convolvulus arvensis* L. (155) (1942)

Nebraska lupine - *Lupinus plattensis* S. Wats. (4, 5, 50, 93, 97, 155) (1913–present)

Nebraska psoralea - *Pediomelum argophyllum* (Pursh) J. Grimes (5, 93) (1913-1936)

Nebraska sedge - *Carex nebraskensis* Dewey (5, 50, 139, 155) (1913–present)

Nebraska tansy-aster [Nebraska tansyaster] - *Machaeranthera canescens* (Pursh) Gray subsp. *canescens* var. *canescens* (50) (present)

Nebraska thistle - *Cirsium canescens* Nutt. (5, 93) (1913-1936)

Necklace leavenworthia - *Leavenworthia torulosa* Gray (5) (1913)

Necklace poplar - *Populus deltoides* Bartr. ex Marsh. (5, 156, 158) (1900-1923), *Populus deltoides* Bartr. ex Marsh. subsp. *deltoides* (1) (1932), *Populus deltoides* Bartr. ex Marsh. subsp. *monilifera* (Aiton) Eckenwalder (92, 130) (1876-1895)

Necklace sedge - *Carex projecta* Mackenzie (5, 50) (1913–present), *Carex vesicaria* L. var. *monile* (Tuckerman) Fern. (5, 50, 72) (1907–present)

Necklace-pod [Necklacepod] - *Sophora* L. (50) (present)

Necklace-weed [Necklace weed] - *Actaea* L. (76) (1896) ME, *Actaea pachypoda* Ell. (5, 19, 49, 92, 156, 158) (1840-1923), *Onosmodium virginianum* (L.) A. DC. (156) (1923)

Neckweed [Neck-weed] - *Cannabis sativa* L. (5, 92, 156, 157, 158) (1898–1929), *Paulownia tomentosa* (Thunb.) Sieb. & Zucc. ex Steud. (possibly) (156) (1923), *Veronica agrestis* L. (19) (1840), *Veronica beccabunga* L. (7, 92) (1828–1876), *Veronica peregrina* L. (2, 5, 50, 62, 80, 82, 131, 145, 156, 158) (1897–present)

Nectarine - *Prunus persica* (L.) Batsch (92, 165) (1768-1876)

Needle beaksedge - *Rhynchospora capillacea* Torr. (50) (present)

Needle grama - *Bouteloua aristidoides* (Kunth) Griseb. (163) (1852)

Needle grass [Needle-grass, Needlegrass] - *Achnatherum* Beauv. (50) (present), *Aristida adscensionis* L. (5) (1913), *Aristida* L. (152) (1912) NM, *Bouteloua aristidoides* (Kunth) Griseb. (122) (1937) TX, *Hesperostipa comata* (Trin. & Rupr.) Barkworth subsp. *comata* (5, 56, 93, 94, 111, 115, 126, 129, 140) (1894-1944), *Hesperostipa spartea* (Trin.) Barkworth (37, 56, 93, 116, 121) (1830-1970), *Scleropogon brevifolius* Phil. (152) (1912) NM

Needle juniper - *Juniperus sabina* L. (109, 138) (1923-1949)

Needle palm - *Rhapidophyllum hystrix* (Pursh) H. Wendl. & Drude ex Drude (50, 106, 138) (1923–present)

Needle palm - *Yucca filamentosa* L. (107) (1919)

Needle spike-rush [Needle spike rush, Needle spikerush] - *Eleocharis acicularis* (L.) Roemer & J.A. Schultes (5, 50, 72, 156) (1907–present)

Needle spike-sedge [Needle spikesedge] - *Eleocharis acicularis* (L.) Roemer & J.A. Schultes (3, 139) (1944-1977)

Needle-and-thread [Needleandthread, Needle and thread] - *Hesperostipa* (M.K.Elias) Barkworth (50) (present), *Hesperostipa comata* (Trin. & Rupr.) Barkworth subsp. *comata* (3, 50, 98, 140, 146, 155, 185) (1926–present)

Needle-and-thread grass [Needle and thread grass, Needle-and-thread-grass] - *Hesperostipa comata* (Trin. & Rupr.) Barkworth subsp. *comata* (122, 163) (1852-1937)

Needle-chervil [Needle chervil] - *Scandix pecten-veneris* L. (5, 156) (1913–1923) no longer in use by 1923

Needle-grass rush [Needlegrass rush] - *Juncus roemerianus* Scheele. (50) (present)

Needle-leaf gilia [Needle-leaved gilia] - *Gilia rigidula* Benth. (5, 97) (1913-1937)

Needle-leaf navarretia [Needleleaf navarretia] - *Navarretia intertexta* (Benth.) Hook. (50) (present)

Needle-leaf rosette grass [Needleleaf rosette grass] - *Dichanthelium aciculare* (Desv. ex Poir.) Gould & C.A. Clark (50) (present)

Needle-leaf sedge [Needleleaf sedge] - *Carex duriuscula* C.A. Mey. (3, 50, 139, 155) (1942–present)

Needle-pod rush [Needlepod rush] - *Juncus scirpoides* Lam. (50) (present)

Needle-tip blue-eyed grass [Needletip blue-eyed grass] - *Sisyrinchium mucronatum* Michx. (50) (present)

Neele - *Lolium temulentum* L. (158) (1900)

Neem bark - *Melia azedarach* L. (92) (1876)

Nee's arborvitae [Nee's arbor vitae] - *Thuja plicata* Donn ex D. Don (20) (1857)

Neglected life-everlasting - *Pseudognaphalium macounii* (Greene) Kartesz (19) (1840)

Negro arum - *Zantedeschia aethiopica* (L.) Spreng. (19) (1840)

Negro coffee - *Senna occidentalis* (L.) Link (5) (1913)

Negro corn - *Sorghum bicolor* (L.) Moench subsp. *bicolor* (92, 107) (1876-1919)

Negro vine [Negro-vine] - *Matelea carolinensis* (Jacq.) Woods. (5, 156) (1913-1923), *Matelea obliqua* (Jacq.) Woods. (7, 92) (1828-1876)

Negro-country yam (Guiana) - *Dioscorea cayenensis* Lam. (110) (1886)

Negro-weed - *Senna occidentalis* (L.) Link (156) (1923)

Negui-min (Chippewa) - *Amelanchier canadensis* (L.) Medik. (105) (1932)

Negundo chaste tree [Negundo chaste-tree] - *Vitex negundo* L. (138) (1923)

Nelashkih (Osages) - *Betula lenta* L. (7) (1828)

Nelle - *Lolium temulentum* L. (157) (1929)

Nelson's larkspur - *Delphinium nuttallianum* Pritz ex. Walp. (5) (1913)

Nelson's plane-leaf willow [Nelson planeleaf willow] - *Salix planifolia* Pursh (155) (1942)

Nelumbo - *Nelumbo* Adans. (13) (1849), *Nelumbo lutea* Willd. (82) (1930)

Nelumbo jaune (French) - *Nelumbo lutea* Willd. (possibly) (7) (1828)

Nemastylis - *Nemastylis* Nutt. (158) (1900)

Nemesia - *Nemesia* Vent. (138) (1923)

Nemophila - *Nemophila* Nutt. (138) (1923)

Nemwatik (Chippewa) - *Cornus florida* L. (105) (1932)

Nendo (Virginian Indians) - *Angelica lucida* L. (7) (1828)

Nenufar - *Nuphar* Sm. (179) (1526), *Nymphaea* L. (179) (1526)

Nenuphar odorant (French) - *Nymphaea odorata* Aiton (7) (1828)

Nep - *Nepeta cataria* L. (5, 184, 187) (1793–1913)

Nepal alder - *Alnus nepalensis* D. Don (155) (1942)

Nepal barley - *Hordeum vulgare* L. (107) (1919)

Nepal firethorn - *Pyracantha crenulata* (D. Don) Roemer (138) (1923)

Nepe - *Nepeta cataria* L. (46) (1617)

Nepesha (Oregon and Western tribes) - *Asclepias* L. (7) (1828)

Nepeta - *Glechoma hederacea* L. (107) (1919), *Nepeta* L. (138, 155) (1923-1942)

Nephritic plant - *Parthenium integrifolium* L. (92, 158) (1876-1900)

Nepin-minan (Chippewa for summer berry) - *Viburnum opulus* L. (35, 37) (1806-1919)

Neprun purgatif (French) - *Rhamnus cathartica* L. (158) (1900)

Neptunia - *Neptunia* Lour. (4, 155, 158) (1900-1986)

Nerango - *Prunus texana* F.G. Dietr. (124) (1937) TX

Neroli - *Citrus ×aurantium* L. [*maxima × reticulata*] (92) (1876)

Nerprun (French) - *Rhamnus cathartica* L. (6) (1892)

Nerprun de la Caroline (French) - *Frangula caroliniana* (Walt.) Gray (20) (1857)

Nerve root [Nerve-root] - *Cypripedium acaule* Ait. (5, 73, 78, 156) (1892-1923), *Cypripedium parviflorum* Salisb. var. *pubescens* (Willd.) Knight (6, 49, 53, 58) (1869-1922), *Cypripedium reginae* Walt. (5, 64, 73, 156, 158) (1892-1923)

Nerved manna grass [Nerved-manna-grass, Nerved manna-grass] - *Glyceria striata* (Lam.) A.S. Hitchc. (5, 56, 66, 72, 87, 90, 119, 129, 143, 163) (1852-1938)

Nerved meadow grass - *Glyceria striata* (Lam.) A.S. Hitchc. (88, 90) (1884-1885)

Nespyte - *Calamintha* Mill. (179) (1526)

Nest plant - *Monotropa uniflora* L. (6) (1892)

Nest root [Nestroot] - *Monotropa uniflora* L. (7, 92, 158) (1828-1900)

Nestronia - *Nestronia umbellula* Raf. (5) (1913)

Net-cap mushroom - *Panaeolus retirugus* (Fr.) Gillet (128) (1933)

Netleaf [Net-leaf] - *Goodyera pubescens* (Willd.) R. Br. ex Ait. f. (7, 156) (1828-1923)

Net-leaf hackberry [Netleaf hackberry] - *Celtis laevigata* Willd. var. *reticulata* (Torr.) L. Benson (3, 4, 50, 155) (1942–present)

Net-leaf plantain [Net leaf plantain, Netleaf plantain] - *Goodyera pubescens* (Willd.) R. Br. ex Ait. f. (5, 49, 92) (1876-1913)

Netted chain fern [Netted chain-fern] - *Woodwardia areolata* (L.) T. Moore (86) (1878)

Netted custard-apple [Netted custard apple] - *Annona reticulata* L. (165) (1807)

Netted nutrush - *Scleria reticularis* Michx. (50) (present)

Nettle - *Urtica dioica* L. (22, 49, 52, 53, 57, 92, 107) (1893-1919), *Urtica dioica* L. subsp. *gracilis* (Aiton) Seland. (40, 80, 82, 85, 101, 145, 148, 160) (1860-1939), *Urtica* L. (1, 4, 7, 10, 50, 82, 93, 155, 158, 167, 179, 184) (1526–present)

Nettle sage - *Salvia urticifolia* L. (19) (1840)

Nettle tree [Nettle-tree] - *Celtis australis* L. (178) (1526), *Celtis* L. (2, 7, 8, 10, 42, 158) (1814-1900), *Celtis occidentalis* L. (5, 27, 34, 41, 92, 107, 156, 181, 184) (~1678-1923)

Nettle tree of America [Nettle-tree of America] - *Celtis laevigata* Willd. (189) (1767)

Nettle-hemp [Nettle hemp] - *Galeopsis bifida* Boenn. (5, 156, 158) (1900-1923)

Nettle-leaf bellflower [Nettle-leaved bellflower] - *Campanula rapunculoides* L. (possibly) (19) (1840), *Campanula trachelium* L. (5, 156) (1913-1923)

Nettle-leaf germander [Nettle-leaved germander] - *Teucrium canadense* L. (possibly) (187) (1818)

Nettle-leaf giant-hyssop [Nettleleaf gianthyssop] - *Agastache urticifolia* (Benth.) Kuntze (155) (1942)

Nettle-leaf goosefoot [Nettle-leaved goosefoot] - *Chenopodium murale* L. (50, 62, 72, 97, 133) (1907–present)

Nettle-leaf sage [Nettle-leaved sage] - *Salvia urticifolia* L. (5) (1913)

Nettle-leaf vervain [Nettle leaf vervain, Nettle leaved vervain, Nettle-leaved vervain] - *Verbena urticifolia* L. (3, 4, 5, 19, 48, 80, 92, 93, 95, 156, 157, 158) (1840-1986)

Nettle-potato [Nettle potato, Nettle potatoe] - *Stillingia sylvatica* Garden ex L. (5, 64, 156, 158) (1900-1923)

Net-vein chain fern [Net-veined chain-fern] - *Woodwardia areolata* (L.) T. Moore (5) (1913)

Net-vein willow [Net-veined willow] - *Salix reticulata* L. (5) (1913)

Networt - *Goodyera pubescens* (Willd.) R. Br. ex Ait. f. (7, 92) (1828-1876)

Nevada arnica - *Arnica nevadensis* Gray (155) (1942), *Arnica parryi* Gray (155) (1942)

Nevada bluegrass [Nevada blue-grass] - *Poa secunda* J. Presl (94, 146, 155, 185) (1901-1942)

Nevada bulrush - *Scirpus nevadensis* S. Wats. (50, 155) (1942–present)

Nevada cotyledon - *Dudleya cymosa* (Lem.) Britt. & Rose (86) (1878)

Nevada goldenrod - *Solidago spectabilis* (D.C. Eat.) Gray (138) (1923)

Nevada onion - *Allium nevadense* S. Wats. (155) (1942)

Never-dying white satin [Neuer dying white Sattin] - *Lunaria rediviva* L. (178) (1526)

Never-wets - *Orontium aquaticum* L. (156) (1923)

Nevis' stone crop - *Sedum nevii* Gray (86) (1878)

Nevis' wild crab [Nevis wild crab] - *Malus ioensis* (Wood) Britton (137) (1931) SD

Neviusa - *Neviusia alabamensis* Gray (86) (1878)

New England aster [NewEngland aster] - *Symphyotrichum novae-angliae* (L.) G.L.Nesom (3, 4, 5, 50, 62, 72, 82, 85, 93, 97, 109, 127, 131, 138, 155, 156, 158) (1899–present)

New England bent grass - *Agrostis perennans* (Walt.) Tuckerman (5, 50) (1913–present)

New England blue violet - *Viola novae-angliae* House. (5, 50) (1913–present)

New England boxwood [New England box-wood] - *Cornus florida* L. (6, 158, 186) (1825-1892)

New England bulrush - *Schoenoplectus novae-angliae* (Britt.) M.T. Strong (5, 50) (1913–present)

New England daisy - *Erigeron pulchellus* Michx. (46) (1671)

New England dogwood - *Cornus sericea* L. (186) (1814)

New England pine - *Pinus strobus* L. (8) (1785)

New England rose-gentian [New England rosegentian] - *Sabatia kennedyana* Fern. (138) (1923)

New England sedge - *Carex novae-angliae* Schwein. (5, 50, 66) (1912–present)

New England starwort [New England star wort] - *Symphyotrichum novae-angliae* (L.) G.L.Nesom (42) (1814), *Symphyotrichum novi-belgii* (L.) Nesom var. *novi-belgii* (42) (1814)

New Jersey blueberry - *Vaccinium caesariense* Mackenzie (5) (1913)

New Jersey fir tree - *Pinus taeda* L. (41) (1770)

New Jersey muhly - *Muhlenbergia torreyana* (J.A. Schultes) A.S. Hitchc. (50) (present)

New Jersey pine - *Pinus virginiana* Mill. (20, 187) (1818-1857)

New Jersey rush - *Juncus caesariensis* Coville (5, 50) (1913–present)

New Jersey tea [New-Jersey-tea, New-Jersey tea] - *Ceanothus americanus* L. (3, 4, 5, 15, 19, 49, 50, 52, 53, 54, 57, 58, 65, 72, 82. 92, 95, 97, 104, 105, 106, 107, 109, 113, 122, 124, 156, 157, 158, 184, 187) (1793–present), *Ceanothus herbaceus* Raf. (3, 4, 40, 85) (1928-1986), *Ceanothus* L. (1, 10, 13, 15, 93) (1818-1936), *Schizaea pusilla* Pursh (86) (1878)

New Jersey tea shrub - *Ceanothus americanus* L. (14) (1882)

New Jersey tea tree [New Jersey tea-tree] - *Ceanothus* L. (8) (1785), *Ceanothus americanus* L. (8) (1785)

New Mexico alder [New Mexican alder] - *Alnus oblongifolia* Torr. (155) (1942)

New Mexico beeblossom - *Gaura neomexicana* Woot. (50) (present)

New Mexico black locust [New Mexican black locust] - *Robinia neomexicana* Gray (149, 153) (1904-1919)

New Mexico bluestem [NewMexico bluestem] - *Schizachyrium scoparium* (Michx.) Nash var. *scoparium* (155) (1942)

New Mexico buckeye - *Ungnadia speciosa* Endl. (153) (1913) NM

New Mexico checker-mallow [Newmexican checkermallow] - *Sidalcea neomexicana* Gray (155) (1942)

New Mexico cliff fern - *Woodsia neomexicana* Windham (50) (present)

New Mexico copperleaf - *Acalypha neomexicana* Müll. Arg. (50, 155) (1942–present)

New Mexico feather grass [New Mexico feather-grass, New Mexico feathergrass] - *Hesperostipa neomexicana* (Thurb. ex Coult.) Barkworth (3, 50, 94, 122, 140, 155) (1901–present)

New Mexico hop [New Mexican hop, NewMexican hop] - *Humulus lupulus* L. var. *neomexicanus* A. Nels. & Cockerell (138, 155) (1923-1942)

New Mexico locust [New Mexican locust] - *Robinia neomexicana* Gray (138) (1923)

New Mexico love grass [NewMexico lovegrass] - *Eragrostis mexicana* (Hornem.) Link subsp. *mexicana* (155) (1942)

New Mexico muhly [New Mexican muhly] - *Muhlenbergia pauciflora* Buckl. (122) (1937)

New Mexico pinyon - *Pinus edulis* Engelm. (158) (1900)

New Mexico rose [New Mexican rose] - *Rosa stellata* Woot. (138) (1923)

New Mexico sagebrush [New Mexican sagebrush] - *Artemisia ludoviciana* Nutt. subsp. *mexicana* (Willd. ex Spreng.) Keck (155) (1942)

New Mexico shinnery [New Mexican shinnery] - *Quercus gambelii* Nutt. var. *gambelii* (122) (1937) TX

New Mexico Spanish bayonet - *Yucca harrimaniae* Trel. var. *neomexicana* (Woot. & Standl.) Reveal (50) (present)

New Mexico stipa - *Hesperostipa neomexicana* (Thurb. ex Coult.) Barkworth (152) (1912)

New Mexico yellow pine [New Mexican yellow pine] - *Pinus ponderosa* P.& C. Lawson var. *ponderosa* (147) (1856)

New Mexico yucca [NewMexican yucca] - *Yucca harrimaniae* Trel. var. *neomexicana* (Woot. & Standl.) Reveal (155) (1942)

New Orleans moss - *Tillandsia usneoides* (L.) L. (12, 14) (1821-1882)

New River horse-chestnut [New River horse chestnut] - *Aesculus flava* Aiton (8) (1785)

New River thorn - *Crataegus succulenta* Schrad. ex Link (5) (1913)

New World annual gentian [NewWorld annual gentian] - *Gentianella amarella* (L.) Boerner subsp. *acuta* (Michx.) J. Gillett (50) (present)

New York aster - *Symphyotrichum novi-belgii* (L.) Nesom var. *novi-belgii* (5, 72, 82, 109, 138, 155, 156) (1907-1949)

New York fern [New-York-fern] - *Thelypteris noveboracensis* (L.) Nieuwl. (5, 109, 122, 138) (1913-1949)

New York ironweed [New York iron-weed] - *Vernonia glauca* (L.) Willd. (5, 97, 174, 177) (1753-1937)

New York monkshood - *Aconitum noveboracense* Gray ex Coville (5) (1913)

New Zealand flax - *Phormium tenax* J.R. & G. Forst. (109, 138) (1923-1949)

New Zealand sheepbur - *Acaena novae-zelandiae* Kirk (155) (1942)

New Zealand spinach [New-Zealand-spinach] - *Tetragonia* L. (138) (1923), *Tetragonia tetragonioides* (Pallas) Kuntze (15, 50, 92, 107, 109, 110, 138) (1895–present) brought by Capt. Cook from New Zealand and used like spinach greens

Newaree (Telinga) - *Oryza sativa* L. (110) (1886)

Newcastle thorn - *Crataegus crus-galli* L. (5, 74, 158) (1893–1913)

Newfoundland spruce - *Picea glauca* (Moench) Voss (8) (1785)

Nez-coupé (French) - *Staphylea* L. (8) (1785)

Nez-coupé à feuilles ternée (French) - *Staphylea trifolia* L. (8) (1785)

Niashiga makan (Omaha-Ponca, human-being medicine) - *Cucurbita foetidissima* Kunth (37) (1919)

Nicandra - *Nicandra* Adans. (50) (present) for Nicandra poet of Colophon who wrote on plants about 100 BC

Nickar tree [Nickar-tree] - *Caesalpinia* L. (8) (1785), *Gymnocladus dioicus* (L.) K. Koch (5, 6, 7, 8, 92, 157, 158) (1785-1929)

Nicker - *Caesalpinia* L. (50) (present)

Nicker tree [Nicker-tree] - *Gymnocladus dioicus* (L.) K. Koch (107, 156) (1919-1923)

Nicker-nut - *Gymnocladus dioicus* (L.) K. Koch (156) (1923)

Nickle-leaf milkvetch [Nickleleaf milkvetch] - *Astragalus agrestis* Dougl. ex G. Don (155) (1942)

Nickweed [Nick-weed] - *Cannabis sativa* L. (157, 158) (1900-1929)

Nicollet's cinquefoil - *Potentilla paradoxa* Nutt. (5) (1913)

Nido (Sioux) - *Apios americana* Medik. (47) (1852)

Nidsida (Osage) - *Monarda fistulosa* L. (121) (1918?-1970?)

Niederliegende Gaultheria (German) - *Gaultheria procumbens* L. (186) (1814)

Niessenkraut (German) - *Helenium autumnale* L. (7) (1828)

Nigella - *Coptis trifolia* (L.) Salisb. (186) (1814), *Nigella damascena* L. (57) (1917), *Nigella sativa* L. (107) (1919)

Nigella seed - *Nigella sativa* L. (92) (1876)

Night willowherb [Night willow-herb, Night willow herb, Night-willowherb] - *Oenothera* L. (184) (1793), *Oenothera biennis* L. (5, 6, 156, 157, 158) (1892-1929)

Night-blooming cactus - *Datura stramonium* L. (71) (1898) trade name

Night-blooming catchfly [Night-blooming catchfly - *Silene noctiflora* L. (1, 5, 97) (1913-1937)

Night-blooming cereus [Nightblooming cereus, Night blooming cereus] - *Hylocereus* (Berger) Britt. & Rose (109, 137, 155) (1923-1949), *Selenicereus grandiflorus* (L.) Britt. & Rose (52, 55, 57, 61, 92) (1870-1917)

Night-blooming cestrum [Nightblooming cestrum] - *Cestrum nocturnum* L. (138) (1923)

Nightcaps - *Anemone quinquefolia* L. (50, 156) (1923–present)

Night-flowered catchfly - *Silene noctiflora* L. (19) (1840)

Night-flowering catchfly - *Silene noctiflora* L. (4, 62, 72, 80, 85, 93, 95, 127, 131, 156) (1899-1986)

Night-flowering silene [Nightflowering silene] - *Silene noctiflora* L. (50, 155) (1942–present)

Night-jessamine [Night jessamine] - *Cestrum nocturnum* L. (109) (1949)

Night-rocket [Night rocket] - *Hesperis matronalis* L. (156) (1923)

Night-scented gilliflower - *Hesperis matronalis* L. (5, 156, 158) (1900–1923)

Nightshade [Night-shade, Night shade, Nyght shade] - *Chenopodium simplex* (Torr.) Raf. (158) (1900), *Circaea* L. (42) (1814), *Penthorum sedoides* L. (177) (1762), *Solanum dulcamara* L. (72, 158) (1900-1907), *Solanum* L. (1, 4, 10, 50, 92, 109, 138, 148, 155, 156, 184) (1793–present), *Solanum nigrum* L. (63, 71, 122, 145, 148) (1897-1937), *Solanum ptychanthum* Dunal (179) (1526)

Nightshade vine - *Solanum dulcamara* L. (71, 92) (1876-1898)

Nightshade with the white flower - *Solanum ptychanthum* Dunal (46) (1671)

Night-violet [Night violet] - *Hesperis matronalis* L. (156) (1923)

Nikakitspak (Pawnee, forehead-pop) - *Physalis heterophylla* Nees (37) (1919)

Nikiís (Pawnee) - *Zea mays* L. (37) (1830)

Nikko fir - *Abies homolepis* Sieb. and Zucc. (109, 138, 155) (1923-1949)

Nikko maple - *Parthenocissus tricuspidata* (Sieb. & Zucc.) Planch. (137, 155) (1931-1942)

Nikso kororik kahtsu nitawau (Pawnee, herb which bears what resembles an ear of corn) - *Arisaema triphyllum* (L.) Schott (5) (1913)

Nil - *Indigofera caroliniana* Mill. (10) (1818)

Nimble-Kate [Nimble Kate] - *Sicyos angulatus* L. (5, 156, 157, 158) (1900–1929)

Nimbleweed [Nimble-weed, Nimble weed] - *Anemone cylindrica* Gray (156) (1923), *Anemone quinquefolia* L. (5) (1913), *Anemone virginiana* L. (156) (1923)

Nimblewill [Nimble will, Nimble-will] - *Muhlenbergia glomerata* (Willd.) Trin. (45) (1896), *Muhlenbergia mexicana* (L.) Trin. (80, 87) (1884-1913), *Muhlenbergia schreberi* J.F. Gmel. (3, 16, 45, 50, 56, 66, 80, 87, 93, 94, 99, 111, 119, 122, 155, 163) (1837–present)

Ninbegoskok (Chippewa) - *Pyrola elliptica* Nutt. (105) (1932)

Nindsin - *Panax quinquefolius* L. (186) (1814)

Nine-anther dalea - *Dalea enneandra* Nutt. (3) (1977)

Nine-anther prairie clover [Nineanther prairie clover] - *Dalea enneandra* Nutt. (4, 50) (1986–present)

Nine-awn pappus grass [Nineawn pappusgrass] - *Enneapogon desvauxii* Desv. ex Beauv. (50) (present)

Ninebark [Nine bark, Nine-bark] - *Euonymus atropurpurea* Jacq. (59) (1911), *Hydrangea cinerea* Small (156) (1923), *Physocarpus* (Camb.) Raf. (1, 4, 50, 82, 93, 109, 138, 155, 156, 158) (1900–present), *Physocarpus capitatus* (Pursh) Kuntze (35) (1806), *Physocarpus opulifolius* (L.) Maxim. (3, 4, 63, 82, 105, 112) (1899-1986),

Physocarpus opulifolius (L.) Maxim. var. *intermedius* (Rydb.) B.L. Robins. (82) (1930), *Physocarpus opulifolius* (L.) Maxim. var. *opulifolius* (5, 8, 19, 85, 95, 130, 131) (1785-1913), *Spiraea douglasii* Hook. var. *menziesii* (Hook.) K. Presl (8, 19, 184, 187) (1785-1840)

Ninebark syringa - *Physocarpus opulifolius* (L.) Maxim. (156) (1923)

Ninety-knot [Ninety knot] - *Polygonum aviculare* L. (5, 92, 156, 158) (1876-1923)

Ningahi h'te (Omaha-Ponca) - *Cornus sericea* L. subsp. *sericea* (37) (1919)

Niniba žoŋ (Osage, pipestem wood) - *Euonymus atropurpurea* Jacq. (121) (1918?–1970?)

Ninigahi (Omaha-Ponca, pipe-mix) - *Cornus amomum* Mill. (37) (1919)

Nini-hi (Omaha-Ponca) - *Nicotiana quadrivalvis* Pursh (37) (1919)

Ninsin - *Panax quinquefolius* L. (7, 158) (1828-1900)

Ninsin root - *Panax quinquefolius* L. (92) (1876)

Niobe willow *- *Salix ×pendulina* Wenderoth [*babylonica × fragilis*] (109) (1949)

Nipi minan (Cree) - *Viburnum opulus* L. (107) (1919)

Nipinminan (Chippewa) - *Viburnum opulus* L. var. *americanum* Aiton (possibly) (105) (1932)

Nipple cactus - *Escobaria missouriensis* (Sweet) D.R. Hunt var. *missouriensis* (5, 93, 97, 156) (1913-1937), *Pediocactus* Britton & Rose (4) (1986)

Nipple thistle - *Mammillaria* Haw. (14) (1882)

Nippleweed [Nipple weed, Nipple-weed] - *Thelesperma filifolium* (Hook.) Gray var. *filifolium* (93) (1936) Neb, *Thelesperma megapotamicum* (Spreng.) Kuntze (98) (1942) Neb

Nipplewort - *Lapsana communis* L. (4, 5, 92, 107, 156) (1876-1986), *Lapsana* L. (156) (1923)

Nippon daisy - *Leucanthemum nipponicum* Franch. ex Maxim. (109) (1949)

Nippon oxeye daisy - *Leucanthemum nipponicum* Franch. ex Maxim. (138) (1923)

Nir-Carambu - *Ludwigia peploides* (Kunth) Raven subsp. *glabrescens* (Kuntze) Raven (174) (1753)

Nisberry tree - *Manilkara zapota* (L.) van Royen (165) (1768)

Nisude-hi (Omaha-Ponca, flute-plant) - *Thalictrum dasycarpum* Fisch. & Avé-Lall. (37) (1926)

Nit grass [Nit-grass] - *Gastridium phleoides* (Nees & Meyen) C.E. Hubbard (92, 94, 163) (1852-1901)

Nitiminš (Chippewa, spear timber) - *Fraxinus americana* L. (105) (1932)

Nits-and-lice - *Hypericum drummondii* (Grev. & Hook.) Torr. & Gray (3, 4, 50) (1977–present)

Nitweed [Nit-weed, Nit weed] - *Hypericum gentianoides* (L.) Britton, Sterns & Poggenb. (5, 19, 92, 157) (1840-1913)

Niwaharit (Pawnee) - *Prunus angustifolia* Marsh. (37) (1919)

Niya'wibûkûk (Chippewa) - *Eupatorium perfoliatum* L. (40) (1928)

Noa (Missouri tribes) - *Apios americana* Medik. (7) (1828)

Noachist (stinking medicine Cheyenne & Crow) - *Oplopanax horridus* Miq. (101) (1905) MT

Noah's ark - *Cypripedium acaule* Ait. (5, 86, 156, 187) (1878-1923) no longer in use by 1923, *Cypripedium parviflorum* Salisb. var. *parviflorum* (5, 7, 156) (1828-1923), *Cypripedium parviflorum* Salisb. var. *pubescens* (Willd.) Knight (6, 49, 92) (1876-1892)

Noble blue liverwort [Noble blew liuerwoort] - *Hepatica nobilis* Schreb. (178) (1526)

Noble epine - *Crataegus monogyna* Jacq. (92) (1876)

Noble fir - *Abies procera* Rehd. (50, 109, 138, 155, 158, 161) (1857–present)

Noble goldenrod [Noble golden-rod] - *Solidago speciosa* Nutt (5, 155, 156) (1913-1942)

Noble liverwoort with white flowers [Noble liuerwoort with white flowers] - *Hepatica nobilis* Schreb. (178) (1526)

Noble liverwort - *Hepatica nobilis* Schreb. (7, 10, 46, 74, 76, 79, 156, 178) (1671–1923), *Hepatica nobilis* Schreb. var. *obtusa* (Pursh) Steyermark (5, 41, 49, 92) (1770–1913)

Noble milfoil - *Achillea nobilis* L. (165) (1768)

Noble myrtle [Noble mirtle] - *Myrica gale* L. (46) (1671)

Noble red liverwort [Nobel red liuerwort] - *Hepatica nobilis* Schreb. (178) (1526)

Noble yarrow - *Achillea nobilis* L. (50, 92) (1876–present)

Noble-pine [Noble pine] - *Chimaphila umbellata* (L.) Bart. (5, 73, 92, 156, 158) (1876-1923) no longer in use by 1923

Nodding beakrush [Nodding beaked rush] - *Rhynchospora inexpansa* (Michx.) Vahl (5) (1913)

Nodding beardtongue - *Penstemon laxiflorus* Pennell (50) (present)

Nodding beggarticks [Nodding beggar-ticks] - *Bidens cernua* L. (3, 4, 50, 98, 155) (1926–present)

Nodding bluegass [Nodding blue-gass] - *Poa reflexa* Vasey & Scribn. ex Vasey (94) (1901)

Nodding brome - *Bromus porteri* (Coult.) Nash (3, 155) (1942-1977)

Nodding buckwheat - *Eriogonum cernuum* Nutt. (50) (present), *Eriogonum cernuum* Nutt. var. *cernuum* (50) (present)

Nodding bulbous saxifrage - *Saxifraga cernua* L. (5) (1913)

Nodding bur-marigold [Nodding burr marigold, Nodding burr marygold] - *Bidens cernua* L. (5, 72, 93, 97, 131, 156, 158) (1899–1937)

Nodding cassia - *Chamaecrista nictitans* (L.) Moench subsp. *nictitans* var. *nictitans* (42) (1814)

Nodding catchfly - *Silene nutans* L. (5, 156) (1913-1923)

Nodding chickweed - *Cerastium nutans* Raf. (4, 5, 50, 72, 80, 93, 97, 156) (1907–present), *Cerastium nutans* Raf. var. *nutans* (50) (present)

Nodding colpodium - *Arctophila fulva* (Trin.) Rupr. ex Anderss. (94) (1901)

Nodding eriogonum - *Eriogonum cernuum* Nutt. (5, 93, 155) (1913-1942)

Nodding fescue - *Festuca paradoxa* Desv. (56, 66) (1901-1903), *Festuca subverticillata* (Pers.) Alexeev (3, 50, 122, 155) (1937–present)

Nodding fescue grass [Nodding fescue-grass] - *Festuca paradoxa* Desv. (5, 72, 163, 187) (1818-1913), *Festuca subverticillata* (Pers.) Alexeev (163) (1852)

Nodding garlic - *Allium cernuum* Roth (156) (1923)

Nodding green violet - *Hybanthus verticillatus* (Ort.) Baill. (4) (1986)

Nodding lady's-tresses [Nodding ladies' tresses, Nodding ladies-tresses, Nodding ladies'-tresses, Nodding ladies-tresses] - *Spiranthes cernua* (L.) L.C. Rich. (5, 19, 50, 72, 93, 97, 109, 122, 138, 156) (1840–present)

Nodding lily [Nodding lilies] - *Lilium canadense* L. (5, 19, 75, 92, 156, 157, 158) (1840–1929), *Lilium superbum* L. (5, 73, 75, 158) (1892–1894)

Nodding lizard's-tail - *Saururus cernuus* L. (187) (1818)

Nodding lychnis - *Silene uralensis* (Rupr.) Bocquet subsp. *uralensis* (5) (1913)

Nodding muhly - *Muhlenbergia bushii* Pohl (50, 155) (1942–present)

Nodding oat grass [Nodding oat-grass] - *Trisetum canescens* Buckl. (94) (1901)

Nodding onion - *Allium cernuum* Roth (50, 138, 155) (1923–present), *Allium cernuum* Roth var. *cernuum* (50) (present)

Nodding pleuropogon - *Pleuropogon refractus* (Gray) Benth. ex Vasey (94) (1901)

Nodding plumeless thistle - *Carduus nutans* L. (50) (present)

Nodding pogonia - *Triphora trianthophora* (Sw.) Rydb. (3, 72, 156) (1907-1977)

Nodding saxifrage - *Saxifraga cernua* L. (4, 131) (1899-1986)

Nodding sedge - *Carex gynandra* Schwein. (5, 50) (1913–present)

Nodding smartweed - *Polygonum lapathifolium* L. (80, 82) (1913-1930)

Nodding spurge - *Chamaesyce nutans* (Lag.) Small (156) (1923)

Nodding stickseed - *Hackelia deflexa* (Wahlenb.) Opiz (50) (present), *Hackelia deflexa* (Wahlenb.) Opiz var. *americana* (Gray) Fern. & I.M. Johnston (5, 72, 93, 131) (1899-1936)

Nodding sticktight - *Bidens cernua* L. (82) (1930)

Nodding thistle - *Carduus nutans* L. (4) (1986)

Nodding tiger lily [Nodding tiger-lily] - *Lilium superbum* L. (156) (1923)

Nodding trillium - *Trillium cernuum* L. (3, 138, 155, 156) (1923-1977)

Nodding vanilla grass - *Hierochloe odorata* (L.) Beauv. (5) (1913)

Nodding violet - *Hybanthus verticillatus* (Ort.) Baill. (5, 65, 97, 158) (1900-1937)

Nodding wakerobin [Nodding wake-robin, Nodding wake robin] - *Trillium cernuum* L. (5, 72, 127, 156, 158) (1907-1933), *Trillium erectum* L. (19) (1840), *Trillium flexipes* Raf. (50) (present)

Nodding waternymph - *Najas flexilis* (Willd.) Rostk. & Schmidt (50) (present)

Nodding white trillium - *Trillium cernuum* L. (2) (1895)

Nodding wild buckwheat - *Eriogonum cernuum* Nutt. (4) (1986)

Nodding wild onion - *Allium cernuum* Roth (5, 72, 93, 156) (1907-1936)

Nodding wild rye [Nodding wildrye, Nodding wild-rye] - *Elymus canadensis* L. (5, 72, 85, 87, 93, 116, 119, 140, 143, 163) (1852-1958)

Nodding-caps [Noddingcaps, Nodding cap] - *Triphora Nutt.* (1, 50) (1932–present)

Nogal - *Juglans microcarpa* Berl. (149) (1904) NM

Noisetier - *Corylus* L. (8) (1785)

Noisetier à fruit cornu (French) - *Corylus cornuta* Marsh (8) (1785)

Noisetier d'Amérique (French) - *Corylus americana* Walt. (8) (1785)
Noix - *Juglans cinerea* L. (46) (1879)

Nokwe'jigûn (Chippewa, something soft) - *Artemisia ludoviciana* Nutt. subsp. *ludoviciana* (40) (1928)

Noli-me-tangere [Noli me tangere] - *Impatiens capensis* Meerb. (181) (~1678), *Impatiens noli-tangere* L. (174) (1753)

Nolina - *Nolina* Michx. (138) (1923)

Nolitangere - *Impatiens noli-tangere* L. (92) (1876)

Nonda - *Ligusticum canadense* (L.) Britton (5) (1913)

Nondo - *Ligusticum canadense* (L.) Britton (156) (1923), *Angelica* L. (182) (1791)

Nonehaw (Missouri tribes) - *Nicotiana quadrivalvis* Pursh (6, 7) (1828-1932)

None-so-pretty [None so pretty] - *Anaphalis margaritacea* (L.) Benth. & Hook (5, 7, 92, 156, 158) (1828–1923), *Pseudognaphalium obtusifolium* (L.) Hilliard & Burtt subsp. *obtusifolium* (6) (1892), *Silene armeria* L. (5, 73, 156) (1892-1923) Hatfield MA, *Viola tricolor* L. (76, 158) (1896–1900) Abington MA

Nonesuch [None-such, Nonesuch] - *Lychnis chalcedonica* L. (5, 156, 158, 178) (1526-1923) no longer in use by 1923, *Medicago* L. (1) (1932), *Medicago lupulina* L. (5, 19, 45, 62, 92, 107, 156, 158) (1840-1923)

Nonpa tanga (Omaha-Ponca [big cherry) - *Prunus pumila* L. var. *besseyi* (Bailey) Gleason (37) (1919)

Nonpa-zhinga (Omaha-Ponca, little cherry) - *Prunus virginiana* L. var. *virginiana* (37) (1919)

Nonsi (Omaha-Ponca) - *Carya ovata* (Mill.) K. Koch (37) (1919) Nonsi-hi (Hickory tree)

Nonsuch - *Medicago lupulina* L. (46) (1879)

Nonnibatse (Osage, tobacco bunch) - *Arceuthobium* Bieb. (121) (1918?-1970?)

Noo (Omaha) - *Pediomelum esculentum* (Pursh) Rydb. (38) (1820)

Noon-day flower [Noon day flower, Noon-day-flower] - *Tragopogon pratensis* L. (92, 158) (1876-1900)

Noonflower [Noon flower, Noon-flower] - *Tragopogon pratensis* L. (5, 92, 156, 158) (1876-1923)

Noontide [Noon tide, Noon-tide] - *Tragopogon pratensis* L. (5, 92, 156, 158) (1876-1923)

Nootka cypress - *Chamaecyparis nootkatensis* (D. Don) Spach (138) (1923), *Xanthocyparis nootkatensis* (D.Don) Farjon & D.K.Harder (20, 161) (1857)

Nopal [Nopales] - *Opuntia* Mill. (149, 151) (1896-1904) NM

Nopal cactus [Nopalcactus] - *Opuntia* Mill. (155) (1942)

Nordamerikanischer Spigelie (German) - *Spigelia marilandica* (L.) L. (6, 186) (1814-1892)

Nordamerikanisches Frauenhaar (German) - *Adiantum pedatum* L. (158) (1900)

Normandy cress - *Barbarea vulgaris* W.T. Aiton (157) (1929)

Norrislegrass (Norway) - *Linnaea borealis* L. (46) (1879)

North American bow-wood - *Maclura pomifera* (Raf.) Schneid. (158) (1900)

North American calceolaria [NorthAmerican calceolaria] - *Hybanthus verticillatus* (Ort.) Baill. (3, 155) (1942-1977)

North American ebony - *Diospyros virginiana* L. (156, 158) (1900-1923)

North American hemlock-spruce [North American hemlock spruce] - *Tsuga canadensis* (L.) Carr. (57) (1917)

North American locust tree - *Robinia pseudoacacia* L. (157, 158) (1900-1929)

North American papaw - *Asimina triloba* (L.) Dunal (5, 97, 156, 158) (1900-1937)

North Carolina bay - *Magnolia fraseri* Walt. (5, 156) (1913-1923)

Northeastern aster - *Symphyotrichum novi-belgii* (L.) Nesom var. *villicaule* (Gray) J. Labrecque & L. Brouillet (5) (1913)

Northeastern red cedar [North Eastern redcedar] - *Juniperus virginiana* L. var. *virginiana* (155) (1942)

Northeastern rose - *Rosa nitida* Willd. (5) (1913)

Northeastern sedge - *Carex saxatilis* L. (5) (1913)

Northern adder's-tongue [Northern adderstongue] - *Ophioglossum pusillum* Raf. (50) (present)

Northern andrachne - *Leptopus phyllanthoides* (Nutt.) G.L. Webster (5, 97) (1913-1937)

Northern anemone - *Anemone parviflora* Michx. (5) (1913)

Northern bangalow palm - *Archontophoenix alexandrae* (F. Muell.) H. Wendl. & Drude (109) (1949)

Northern bayberry - *Morella caroliniensis* (P. Mill.) Small (138) (1923)

Northern bedstraw - *Galium boreale* L. (3, 4, 5, 50, 63, 72, 82, 85, 93, 109, 122, 127, 131, 138, 155, 156) (1899–present)

Northern bent grass [Northern bentgrass] - *Agrostis mertensii* Trin. (50) (present)

Northern bittercress - *Cardamine douglassii* Britt. (138) (1923)

Northern black currant - *Ribes hudsonianum* Richards. (5, 156) (1913-1923)

Northern blue violet - *Viola sororia* Willd. (5, 109, 138) (1913-1949)

Northern blue-eyed grass [Northern blue eyed grass] - *Sisyrinchium angustifolium* Mill. (72) (1907)

Northern bluethread - *Burmannia biflora* L. (50) (present)

Northern bog aster - *Symphyotrichum boreale* (Torr. & Gray) A.& D. Löve (50) (present)

Northern bog bedstraw - *Galium labradoricum* Wiegand (50) (present)

Northern bog sedge - *Carex gynocrates* Wormsk. (5, 50) (1913–present)

Northern bog violet - *Viola nephrophylla* Greene (4, 5, 50) (1913–present)

Northern bugleweed [Northern bugle weed] - *Lycopus uniflorus* Michx. (5, 50, 93) (1913–present)

Northern burmannia - *Burmannia biflora* L. (5) (1913)

Northern bur-reed - *Sparganium hyperboreum* Laest. (5, 50) (1913–present)

Northern buttercup - *Ranunculus hispidus* Michx. var. *nitidus* (Chapman) T. Duncan (80, 97, 127) (1913-1937), *Ranunculus pedatifidus* J.E. Smith (5) (1913)

Northern catalpa - *Catalpa speciosa* (Warder) Warder ex Engelm. (4, 50, 155) (1942–present)

Northern cherry - *Prunus pensylvanica* L. f. var. *pensylvanica* (20) (1857)

Northern cinquefoil - *Potentilla neumanniana* Aschers. (5) (1913)

Northern cleomella - *Cleomella angustifolia* Torr. (5, 97) (1913-1937)

Northern clintonia - *Clintonia borealis* (Ait.) Raf. (156) (1923)

Northern cluster sedge - *Carex arcta* Boott (50) (present)

Northern clustered sedge - *Carex arcta* Boott (5) (1913), *Carex glareosa* Schkuhr ex Wahlenb. subsp. *glareosa* var. *amphigena* Fern. (5) (1913)

Northern comandra - *Geocaulon lividum* (Richardson) Fernald (5) (1913)

Northern cottonwood - *Populus deltoides* Bartr. ex Marsh. (109) (1949), *Populus deltoides* Bartr. ex Marsh. subsp. *monilifera* (Aiton) Eckenwalder (138) (1923)

Northern dewberry - *Rubus flagellaris* Willd. (4, 50, 135, 138, 155) (1910–present)

Northern diapensia - *Diapensia lapponica* L. (42) (1814)

Northern dropseed [Northern drop-seed] - *Sporobolus heterolepis* (Gray) Gray (5, 93, 115, 116, 119, 134) (1913-1958)

Northern dwarf cornel - *Cornus suecica* L. (5, 156) (1913-1923)

Northern evening-primrose [Northern evening primrose] - *Oenothera biennis* L. (5, 138) (1913-1923)

Northern fogfruit [Northern fog-fruit] - *Phyla lanceolata* (Michx.) Greene (4) (1986)

Northern fox grape - *Vitis labrusca* L. (2, 5, 72, 156) (1895-1923)

Northern fox sedge - *Carex vulpinoidea* Michx. var. *vulpinoidea* (50) (present)

Northern gentian - *Gentiana affinis* Griesb. (3, 4) (1977-1986), *Gentianella amarella* (L.) Boerner subsp. *acuta* (Michx.) J. Gillett (5, 131, 155, 156) (1899-1942)

Northern goldenrod [Northern golden-rod] - *Solidago multiradiata* Aiton (5) (1913)

Northern gooseberry - *Ribes oxyacanthoides* L. (72) (1907), *Ribes oxyacanthoides* L. subsp. *oxyacanthoides* (5, 85) (1913-1932)

Northern grape - *Vitis labrusca* L. (156) (1923)

Northern grass-of-Parnassus - *Parnassia palustris* L. (3, 4, 5) (1913-1986)

Northern green orchid - *Platanthera hyperborea* (L.) Lindl. (50) (present), *Platanthera hyperborea* (L.) Lindl. var. *hyperborea* (50, 138) (1923–present)

Northern green orchis - *Platanthera hyperborea* (L.) Lindl. var. *hyperborea* (3, 5) (1913-1977)

Northern green rush - *Juncus alpinoarticulatus* Chaix (50) (present), *Juncus alpinoarticulatus* Chaix subsp. *nodulosus* (Wahlenb.) Hämet-Ahti (50) (present)

Northern hackberry - *Celtis occidentalis* L. (106) (1930)

Northern hard fern [Northern hard-fern] - *Blechnum spicant* (L.) Sm. (86) (1878)

Northern hawthorn - *Crataegus chrysocarpa* Ashe (4) (1986)

Northern hickory - *Carya ovata* (Mill.) K. Koch (5) (1913)

Northern holly - *Ilex verticillata* (L.) Gray (156) (1923)

Northern holly fern [Northern hollyfern] - *Polystichum lonchitis* (L.) Roth. (50) (present)

Northern holy grass - *Hierochloe odorata* (L.) Beauv. (45) (1896)

Northern Idaho biscuitroot - *Lomatium orientale* Coult & Rose (50) (present)

Northern Juneberry [Northern June-berry] - *Amelanchier humilis* Wiegand (93) (1936)

Northern ladyslipper [Northern ladies' slipper] - *Cypripedium passerinum* Richards (5) (1913)

Northern lily - *Clintonia borealis* (Ait.) Raf. (5, 75) (1894-1913)

Northern limnanthus - *Linanthus septentrionalis* Mason (50) (present)

Northern long sedge - *Carex folliculata* L. (50) (present)

Northern lyme grass [Northern lyme-grass] - *Leymus mollis* subsp. *villosissimus* (Scribn.) Á. Löve & D. Löve (94) (1901)

Northern maidenhair - *Adiantum pedatum* L. (50) (present)

Northern manna grass [Northern manna-grass, Northern manna-grass] - *Glyceria borealis* (Nash) Batchelder (3, 5, 94, 155) (1901-1977), *Glyceria laxa* (Scribn.) Scribn. (5) (1913)

Northern maple - *Acer pensylvanicum* L. (5, 109, 156) (1913-1949)

Northern marsh violet - *Viola palustris* L. (4) (1986)

Northern meadow barley - *Hordeum brachyantherum* Nevski (3) (1977)

Northern meadow sedge - *Carex praticola* Rydb. (5) (1913)

Northern mint - *Mentha arvensis* L. (19) (1840)

Northern nemastylis - *Nemastylis geminiflora* Nutt. (5, 97) (1913-1937)

Northern nut-grass [Northern nut grass] - *Cyperus esculentus* L. (80, 122) (1913-1937)

Northern panic grass [Northern panic-grass, Northern panicgrass] - *Dichanthelium boreale* (Nash) Freckmann (50, 94) (1901–present)

Northern panicum - *Dichanthelium boreale* (Nash) Freckmann (5) (1913)

Northern pin oak - *Quercus ellipsoidalis* E.J. Hill (4, 50, 82, 138, 155) (1923–present)

Northern pine - *Pinus strobus* L. (5) (1913)

Northern pitch pine - *Pinus rigida* Mill. (2) (1895)

Northern plum grape - *Vitis labrusca* L. (5) (1913)

Northern pondweed - *Potamogeton alpinus* Balbis (5, 85, 131) (1899-1932)

Northern poplar - *Populus deltoides* Bartr. ex Marsh. subsp. *deltoides* (155) (1942)

Northern prickly ash - *Zanthoxylum americanum* Mill. (2, 6, 49, 53, 55, 57, 82, 156, 157) (1892-1930)

Northern pussy-toes - *Antennaria howellii* Greene subsp. *neodioica* (Greene) Bayer (4) (1986)

Northern red currant - *Ribes rubrum* L. (109) (1949)

Northern red oak - *Quercus rubra* L. (50) (present), *Quercus rubra* L. var. *ambigua* (Gray) Fern. (138, 155) (1923-1942), *Quercus rubra* L. var. *rubra* (50, 93) (1936–present)

Northern red-top - *Agrostis exarata* Trin. (3, 5, 56, 50, 87, 111, 122, 155) (1884–present), *Agrostis perennans* (Walt.) Tuckerman (5) (1913)

Northern reed grass [Northern reed-grass, Northern reedgrass] - *Calamagrostis stricta* (Timm) Koel. subsp. *inexpansa* (Gray) C.W. Greene (3, 5, 50, 93, 116, 155) (1913–present)

Northern rockcress [Northern rock cress] - *Barbarea orthoceras* Ledeb. (4) (1986), *Braya humilis* (C.A. Mey.) B.L. Robins. (5) (1913)

Northern rock-jasmine [Northern rock jasmine] - *Androsace septentrionalis* L. (4) (1986)

Northern sand spurry [Northern sand spurrey] - *Spergularia canadensis* (Pers.) G. Don (156) (1923), *Spergularia canadensis* (Pers.) G. Don var. *canadensis* (5) (1913), *Spergularia salina* J.& K. Presl (156) (1923)

Northern scouring-rush [Northern scouring rush] - *Equisetum variegatum* Schleich. ex F. Weber & D.M.H. Mohr (157) (1929)

Northern scrub pine - *Pinus banksiana* Lamb. (1, 20, 136) (1857-1932)

Northern sedge - *Carex deflexa* Hornem. (5, 50) (1913–present)

Northern selaginella - *Selaginella rupestris* (L.) Spring (50) (present)

Northern senega - *Polygala senega* L. (55) (1911)

Northern shorthusk - *Brachyelytrum septentrionale* (Babel) G. Tucker (50) (present)

Northern single-spike sedge [Northern singlespike sedge] - *Carex scirpoidea* Michx. (50) (present)

Northern slender lady's-tresses [Northern slender ladies' tresses] - *Spiranthes lacera* (Raf.) Raf. (50) (present), *Spiranthes lacera* (Raf.) Raf. var. *gracilis* (Bigelow) Luer (50) (present), *Spiranthes lacera* (Raf.) Raf. var. *lacera* (50) (present)

Northern sneezeweed - *Helenium autumnale* L. (106) (1930)

Northern spear grass [Northern spear-grass] - *Poa nemoralis* L. (94) (1901), *Poa palustris* L. (5) (1913)

Northern spicebush - *Lindera benzoin* Blume. (50) (present)

Northern spike sedge [Northern spikesedge] - *Carex scirpoidea* Michx. (50) (present)

Northern spleenwort [Northern spleanwort (sic)] - *Asplenium septentrionale* (L.) Huds. (131) (1899)

Northern squaw-weed [Northern squaw weed] - *Packera pauciflora* (Pursh) A.& D. Löve (5, 131) (1899-1913)

Northern St. John's-wort [Northern St. John's wort] - *Hypericum boreale* (Britton) Bicknell (5) (1913)

Northern starwort - *Stellaria borealis* Bigelow (50) (1942–present), *Stellaria calycantha* (Ledeb.) Bong. (155) (1942–present)

Northern stemless actinea - *Tetraneuris acaulis* (Pursh) Greene var. *acaulis* (155) (1942)

Northern stitchwort - *Stellaria borealis* Bigelow subsp. *borealis* (5, 131) (1899-1913), *Stellaria calycantha* (Ledeb.) Bong. (4) (1986)

Northern sweet grass [Northern sweetgrass] - *Hierochloe hirta* (Schrank) Borbás (50) (present), *Hierochloe hirta* (Schrank) Borbás subsp. *arctica* (J. Presl) G. Weim. (50) (present)

Northern sweetvetch - *Hedysarum boreale* Nutt. (155) (1942)

Northern valerian - *Valeriana dioica* L. (5) (1913)

Northern vine - *Humulus lupulus* L. (6) (1892)

Northern watermeal - *Wolffia borealis* (Engelm. ex Hegelm.) Landolt ex Landolt & Wildi (50) (present)

Northern water-plantain [Northern water plantain] - *Alisma triviale* Pursh (50) (present)

Northern water-starwort - *Callitriche hermaphroditica* L. (50) (present)

Northern wheat grass [Northern wheat-grass] - *Elymus alaskanus* (Scribn. & Merr.) A. Löve subsp. *latiglumis* (Scribn. & J.G. Sm.) A. Löve (94) (1901), *Elymus lanceolatus* (Scribn. & J.G. Sm.) Gould (5, 85) (1913-1932) SD, *Elymus lanceolatus* (Scribn. & J.G. Sm.) Gould subsp. *lanceolatus* (50) (present)

Northern white violet - *Viola macloskeyi* Lloyd (5) (1913)

Northern wild barley [Northern wild-barley] - *Hordeum brachyantherum* Nevski subsp. *brachyantherum* (94) (1901)

Northern wild comfrey - *Cynoglossum virginianum* L. var. *boreale* (Fern.) Cooperrider (3, 4, 5) (1913–1986)

Northern wild licorice [Northern wild liquorice] - *Galium kamtschaticum* Steller ex J.A. & J.H. Schultes (5) (1913)

Northern wild rice [Northern wildrice] - *Zizania aquatica* L. (138) (1923), *Zizania palustris* L. (50) (present), *Zizania palustris* L. var. *interior* (Fassett) Dore (50) (present), *Zizania palustris* L. var. *palustris* (50, 155) (1942–present)

Northern wild strawberry - *Fragaria virginiana* Duchesne subsp. *virginiana* (5) (1913)

Northern willow - *Salix glauca* L. (5) (1913)

Northern willow-herb [Northern willowherb, Northern willow herb] - *Epilobium ciliatum* Raf. subsp. *ciliatum* (5, 72, 93, 131) (1899-1936)

Northern winterberry - *Ilex verticillata* (L.) Gray (5) (1913)

Northern woodrush [Northern wood rush] - *Luzula confusa* Lindeberg (5, 50) (1913–present)

Northern woodsia - *Woodsia alpina* (Bolton) S.F. Gray (5) (1913)

Northern wormwood - *Artemisia campestris* L. subsp. *borealis* (Pallas) Hall & Clements (5, 112, 155) (1913–1942)

Northern yarrow - *Achillea millefolium* L. var. *borealis* (Bong.) Farw. (5) (1913)

Northern yellow honeysuckle - *Lonicera dioica* L. (158) (1900)

Northern yellow-eyed grass - *Xyris montana* H. Ries. (5, 50) (1913–present)

Northland cotton-sedge [Northland cottonsedge] - *Eriophorum brachyantherum* Trautv. & C.A. Mey. (50) (present)

Northwest aster - *Ionactis stenomeres* (Gray) Greene (155) (1942)

Northwest Territory sedge - *Carex utriculata* Boott (50) (present)

Northwestern Juneberry [Northwestern-juneberry, Northwestern June-berry, Northwestern June berry] - *Amelanchier alnifolia* (Nutt.) Nutt. ex M. Roemer (5, 72, 131, 157, 158) (1899–1929)

Northwestern service-berry [Northwestern service berry] - *Amelanchier alnifolia* (Nutt.) Nutt. ex M. Roemer (5, 157, 158) (1900–1929)

Norton's flax - *Linum pratense* (Nort.) Small (4) (1986)

Norway maple - *Acer platanoides* L. (20, 50, 82, 93, 107, 135, 137, 138, 165) (1768–present)

Norway pine - *Abies alba* Mill. (58) (1869), *Pinus resinosa* Aiton (1, 20, 75, 78, 92, 136) (1857-1932)

Norway sedge - *Carex norvegica* Willd. (5, 50) (1913–present)

Norway spruce - *Picea abies* (L.) H. Karst. (58, 92, 107, 109, 112, 135, 136, 138, 158) (1857-1937)

Norway spruce fir - *Abies alba* Mill. (58, 92) (1869-1876), *Picea abies* (L.) H. Karst. (20) (1857)

Norwegian cinquefoil [Norway cinquefoil] - *Potentilla norvegica* L. (2, 4, 50, 155, 187) (1818–present), *Potentilla norvegica* L. subsp. *monspeliensis* (L.) Aschers. & Graebn. (50, 156) (1923–present)

Norwegian cudweed - *Omalotheca norvegica* (Gunnerus) Sch.Bip. & F.W.Schultz (5) (1913)

Nosebleed [Nose-bleed, Nose bleed, Nose bleede - *Achillea millefolium* L. (6, 69, 92, 107, 148, 156, 157, 158, 178) (1596–1929), *Castilleja coccinea* (L.) Spreng. (5, 75, 156) (1894–1923) CT, no longer in use by 1923, *Trillium erectum* L. (5, 6, 64, 75, 156) (1892–1923), *Trillium recurvatum* Beck (possibly) (156) (1923), *Trillium sessile* L. (156) (1923)

Nosebleed sanguinary [Nosebleed-sanguinary] - *Achillea millefolium* L. (156) (1923)

Noseburn - *Tragia betonicifolia* Nutt. (4) (1986), *Tragia* L. (4, 50, 155) (1942–present)

Noseburn - *Tragia ramosa* Torr. (4) (1986)

Noseburn tree - *Daphnopsis americana* (Mill.) J.R.Johnst. (possibly) (92) (1876)

Nosegay frangipani - *Plumeria rubra* L. (138) (1923)

Notch-bract waterleaf [Notchbract waterleaf] - *Hydrophyllum appendiculatum* Michx. (3, 4) (1977-1986)

Notched milkvetch [Notched milk vetch] - *Astragalus gracilis* Nutt. (131) (1899)

Notched purslane - *Portulaca oleracea* L. (5, 72, 156) (1907-1923)

Notch-leaf sea-lavender [Notchleaf sea-lavender] - *Limonium sinuatum* (L.) P. Mill. (138) (1923)

Notch-petal claytonia [Notch-petalled claytonia] - *Claytonia virginica* L. (86) (1878)

Notch-seed buckwheat [Notch-seeded buckwheat] - *Fagopyrum esculentum* Moench (107, 110) (1886-1919)

Notchweed - *Chenopodium vulvaria* L. (92) (1876)

Notchwort - *Chenopodium vulvaria* L. (156) (1923)

Notholaena - *Notholaena* R. Br. (158) (1900)

Nottingham catchfly - *Silene menziesii* Hook. subsp. *menziesii* var. *menziesii* (5, 156) (1913-1923), *Silene nutans* L. (5, 156) (1913-1923)

November goldenrod - *Solidago gigantea* Aiton (138, 155) (1923-1942)

Noyer (French) - *Juglans* L. (8) (1785)

Noyer à fruit blanc ovale (French) - *Carya cordiformis* (Wangenh.) K. Koch (possibly) (8) (1785)

Noyer à fruit noir (French) - *Juglans nigra* L. (8) (1785)

Noyer à petit fruit (French) - *Carya glabra* (Mill.) Sweet var. *glabra* (20) (1857)

Noyer blanc odorant (French) - *Carya glabra* (Mill.) Sweet (8) (1785)

Noyer gris (French) - *Juglans cinerea* L. (6) (1892)

Noyer pacanier (French) - *Carya illinoinensis* (Wangenh.) K. Koch (8) (1785)

Noyers - *Juglans cinerea* L. (46) (1879)

Nsakemižinš (Chippewa) - *Hamamelis virginiana* L. (105) (1932)

Nu (Omaha-Ponca) - *Apios americana* Medik. (37) (1919)

Nucipersica - *Prunus persica* (L.) Batsch (110) (1587) nectarines

Nugthe (Omaha-Ponca) - *Pediomelum esculentum* (Pursh) Rydb. (37) (1919)

Nunqua - *Packera aurea* (L.) A.& D. Löve (158) (1900)

Nuns - *Houstonia caerulea* L. (5, 73, 156) (1892-1923) no longer in use by 1923

Nuns' whipping rope - *Amaranthus tricolor* L. (92) (1876)

Nuppikt (Pawnee, sour top) - *Rhus glabra* L. (37) (1919)

Nurse garden - *Malus sylvestris* Mill. (5) (1913)

Nu-sŭ'-pi (Choctaw) - *Quercus* L. (132) (1855)

Nut pine [Nut-pine] - *Pinus albicaulis* Engelm. (101) (1905) MT, *Pinus edulis* Engelm. (75, 107, 138) (1894-1923), *Pinus flexilis* James (109) (1949), *Pinus monophylla* Torr. & Frém. (107, 147) (1856-1919), *Pinus sabiniana* Dougl. ex Dougl. (161) (1857) CA

Nut pine of California - *Pinus monophylla* Torr. & Frém. (147) (1856)

Nut pine of New Mexico - *Pinus edulis* Engelm. (75, 147) (1856-1894)

Nut pine of northeastern Mexico - *Pinus cembroides* Zucc. (147) (1856)

Nutall's goldenweed [Nuttall goldenweed - *Machaeranthera grindelioides* (Nutt.) Shinners var. *grindelioides* (155) (1942)

Nutgall - *Quercus infectoria* Olivier (insect galls infecting oaks) (55, 57) (1911-1917) not a species of oak, but an abnormal growths caused by parasites

Nut-grass [Nutgrass, Nut grass] - *Cyperus bipartitus* Torr. (85) (1932), *Cyperus esculentus* L. (145, 152, 157, 158) (1897–1929), *Cyperus* L. (1) (1932), *Cyperus rotundus* L. (2, 3, 5, 50, 66, 92, 156) (1895–present), *Cyperus strigosus* L. (75, 156) (1894–1923) tubers eaten by children

Nutgrass flatsedge - *Cyperus rotundus* L. (155) (1942)

Nutka rose - *Rosa nutkana* K. Presl (138) (1923)

Nutmeg - *Myristica fragrans* Houtt. (92, 110) (1876-1886), *Myristica* Gronov. (109) (1949)

Nutmeg flower - *Nigella sativa* L. (19, 92, 107) (1840-1919)

Nutmeg geranium - *Pelargonium odoratissimum* (L.) L'Hér. ex Aiton (109, 138) (1923-1949)

Nutmeg hickory - *Carya myristiciformis* (F. Michx.) Nutt. (20, 65, 97) (1857-1937)

Nutmeg tree - *Torreya californica* Torr. (75) (1894)

Nutmeg tree (of California) - *Torreya californica* Torr. (147) (1856)

Nutmygge - *Myristica fragrans* Houtt. (179) (1526)

Nutqua - *Packera aurea* (L.) A.& D. Löve (158) (1900)

Nutrush [Nut rush] - *Scleria* Berg. (1, 50) (1932–present)

Nuttall's alkali grass [Nuttall alkali grass, Nuttall alkaligrass, Nuttall's alkaligrass] - *Puccinellia nuttalliana* (J.A. Schultes) A.S. Hitchc. (50, 146, 155) (1939–present)

Nuttall's aster [Nuttall aster] - *Eucephalus elegans* Nutt. (155) (1942)

Nuttall's atriplex - *Atriplex nuttallii* S. Wats. (5, 93) (1913-1936)

Nuttall's biscuitroot - *Lomatium nuttallii* (Gray) J.F. Macbr. (50) (present)

Nuttall's bladderpod - *Lesquerella gracilis* (Hook.) S. Wats. subsp. *nuttallii* (T.& G.) Rollins & Shaw (50) (present)

Nuttall's bur-reed - *Sparganium americanum* Nutt. (5, 120) (1913-1938)

Nuttall's bush clover - *Lespedeza ×nuttallii* Darl. [*hirta × intermedia*] (5) (1913)

Nuttall's camas [Nuttall's camass] - *Zigadenus nuttallii* (Gray) S. Wats. (5, 93, 97) (1913-1937)

Nuttall's cinquefoil [Nuttall cinquefoil] - *Potentilla gracilis* Dougl. (155) (1942)

Nuttall's corn salad - *Valerianella nuttallii* (Torr. & Gray) Walp. (97) (1937)

Nuttall's cornel - *Cornus nuttallii* Audubon ex Torr. & Gray (161) (1857)

Nuttall's cyperus - *Cyperus filicinus* Vahl. (5) (1913)

Nuttall's death-camas [Nuttall deathcamas, Nuttall's deathcamas] - *Zigadenus nuttallii* (Gray) S. Wats. (50, 155) (1942–present)

Nuttall's dog-parsley [Nuttall dogparsley, Nuttall's dog parsley] - *Lomatium nuttallii* (Gray) J.F. Macbr. (5, 155) (1913-1942)

Nuttall's evening-primrose [Nuttall's evening primrose] - *Oenothera nuttallii* Sweet (5, 50) (1913–present)

Nuttall's evolvulus [Nuttall evolvulus] - *Evolvulus nuttallianus* J.A. Schultes (3, 4, 155) (1942-1986)

Nuttall's false indigo - *Baptisia nuttalliana* Small (97) (1937)

Nuttall's golden-aster [Nuttall's golden aster] - *Chrysopsis pilosa* Nutt. (5, 97) (1913-1937)

Nuttall's goldenweed [Nuttall goldenweed] - *Machaeranthera grindelioides* (Nutt.) Shinners var. *grindelioides* (155) (1942)

Nuttall's hedge-nettle [Nuttall's hedge nettle] - *Stachys nuttallii* Shuttlw. ex Benth. (5) (1913)

Nuttall's kentrophyta - *Astragalus kentrophyta* Gray (4) (1986)

Nuttall's larkspur [Nuttall larkspur] - *Delphinium nuttallianum* Pritz. ex. Walp. (155) (1942)

Nuttall's little rose - *Chamaerhodos erecta* (L.) Bunge subsp. *nuttallii* (Pickering ex Rydb.) Hultén (50) (present)

Nuttall's lobelia - *Lobelia nuttallii* J.A. Schultes (5) (1913)

Nuttall's Mariposa lily - *Calochortus nuttallii* Torr. & Gray (5, 93) (1913-1936)

Nuttall's micranthemum - *Micranthemum micranthemoides* (Nutt.) Wettst. (5) (1913)

Nuttall's milkwort - *Polygala nuttallii* Torr & Gray. (5, 72) (1907-1913)

Nuttall's mock bishop's-weed [Nuttall's mock bishop-weed, Nuttall's mock bishop's weed] - *Ptilimnium nuttallii* (DC.) Britton (5, 97) (1913-1937)

Nuttall's monolepis [Nuttall monolepis] - *Monolepis nuttalliana* (J.A. Schultes) Greene (155) (1942)

Nuttall's onion [Nuttall onion] - *Allium drummondii* Regel (155) (1942)

Nuttall's oxytrope - *Oxytropis multiceps* Nutt. (50) (present)

Nuttall's pasqueflower [Nuttall's pasque-flower, Nuttall's pasque flower] - *Pulsatilla patens* (L.) Mill.subsp. *multifida* (Pritz.) Zamels (86, 157, 158) (1878-1929)

Nuttall's pondweed - *Potamogeton epihydrus* Raf. (5, 72) (1907-1913)

Nuttall's poverty-weed [Nuttall's povertyweed] - *Monolepis nuttalliana* (J.A. Schultes) Greene (50) (present)

Nuttall's prairie-parsley [Nuttall's prairie parsley] - *Polytaenia nuttallii* DC. (5, 50, 97) (1913–present)

Nuttall's reed grass [Nuttall's reed-grass] - *Calamagrostis coarctata* (Torr.) Eat. (5, 94) (1901-1913)

Nuttall's rockcress [Nuttall rockcress] - *Arabis nuttallii* B.L. Robins. (155) (1942)

Nuttall's saltbush - *Atriplex nuttallii* S. Wats. (50) (present)

Nuttall's saltsage [Nuttall's salt-sage] - *Atriplex nuttallii* S. Wats. (141) (1899)

Nuttall's sedge - *Cyperus filicinus* Vahl. (66) (1903)

Nuttall's sensitive-brier [Nuttall's sensitive-briar] - *Mimosa nuttallii* (DC.) B.L. Turner (50) (present)

Nuttall's snapdragon [Nuttall snapdragon] - *Antirrhinum majus* L. (155) (1942), *Sairocarpus nuttallianus* (Benth. ex A. DC.) D.A. Sutton (155) (1942)

Nuttall's stonecrop [Nuttall stonecrop] - *Sedum nuttallianum* Raf. (5, 97, 155) (1913-1942)

Nuttall's sunflower - *Helianthus nuttallii* Torr. & Gray (4, 50) (1986–present), *Helianthus nuttallii* Torr. & Gray subsp. *nuttallii* (3, 50) (1977–present), *Helianthus nuttallii* Torr. & Gray subsp. *rydbergii* (Britton) Long (3) (1977)

Nuttall's violet [Nuttall violet] - *Viola nuttallii* Pursh (4, 5, 50, 93, 127, 131, 155) (1899–present)

Nuttall's water-weed - *Elodea nuttallii* (Planch.) St. John (5) (1913)

Nuttall's weed [Nuttall-weed] - *Coreopsis tinctoria* Nutt. (5, 92, 156, 158) (1876-1923)

Nuttall's wild onion - *Allium drummondii* Regel (5, 93, 97) (1913-1937)

Nyctage - *Mirabilis jalapa* L. (174) (1753)

Nyctelea - *Ellisia nyctelea* (L.) L. (5, 93, 97) (1913-1937)

Nylon hedgehog cactus - *Echinocereus viridiflorus* Engelm. (50) (present), *Echinocereus viridiflorus* Engelm. var. *viridiflorus* (50) (present)

Nymphaea - *Nymphaea* L. (109) (1949)

O

Oak agaric - *Boletus agaricum* Pollini (possibly) (92) (1876)

Oak currant - Oak galls (parasitic insects of oaks) (92) (1876)

Oak fern [Oak-fern, Oakfern, Oke ferne] - *Dryopteris* Adans. (1) (1932), *Dryopteris dryopteris* (L.) Britton (3, 5, 46, 72, 131, 138, 158) (1899-1977), *Gymnocarpium disjunctum* (Rupr.) Ching (109, 155) (1942-1949)

Oak galls - *Quercus infectoria* Olivier (insect galls infecting oaks) (59, 92) (1876-1911) not a species of oak, but an abnormal growths caused by parasites

Oak lungwort - *Lobaria pulmonaria* (L.) Hoffm. (53) (1922)

Oak mistletoe - *Phoradendron leucarpum* (Raf.) Reveal & M.C. Johnston (50) (present)

Oak nutgall - *Quercus infectoria* Olivier (insect galls infecting oaks) (92) (1876) not a species of oak, but an abnormal growths caused by parasites

Oak or Oak tree [Oke tree] - *Quercus* L. (1, 4, 7, 10, 40, 50, 82, 92, 93, 106, 109, 155, 158, 167, 184) (1793–present)

Oak thistle [Oak-thistle] - *Onopordum acanthium* L. (156) (1923)

Oak-apple [Oak apple] - *Quercus infectoria* Olivier (insect galls infecting oaks) (92) (1876) not a species of oak, but an abnormal growths caused by parasites

Oaken tree [Oken tree] - *Quercus robur* L. (179) (1526)

Oakes' evening primrose [Oakes evening primrose] - *Oenothera oakesiana* (Gray) J.W. Robbins ex S. Wats. & Coult. (5) (1913)

Oakes' eyebright - *Euphrasia oakesii* Wettst. (5) (1913)

Oakes' pondweed - *Potamogeton oakesianus* J.W. Robbins (5, 50) (1913–present)

Oakes' thorn - *Crataegus irrasa* Sarg. (5) (1913)

Oak-forest woodrush [Oakforest woodrush] - *Luzula luzuloides* (Lam.) Dandy & Wilmott (50) (present)

Oak-leaf cherry [Oak-leaved cherry] - *Prunus ilicifolia* (Nutt. ex Hook. & Arn.) D. Dietr. (76) (1896) CA

Oak-leaf datura [Oakleaf datura] - *Datura quercifolia* Kunth (155) (1942)

Oak-leaf foxglove [Oak-leaved foxglove] - *Aureolaria virginica* (L.) Pennell (19, 156) (1840-1923)

Oak-leaf geranium [Oak-leaved geranium] - *Pelargonium quercifolium* (L. f.) L'Hér. ex Aiton (19, 109) (1840-1949)

Oak-leaf goosefoot [Oak-leaved goosefoot] - *Chenopodium glaucum* L. (3, 4, 5, 50, 72, 93, 131, 155, 156) (1899–present)

Oak-leaf hydrangea [Oakleaf hydrangea] - *Hydrangea quercifolia* Bartram. (2, 138) (1895-1923)

Oak-leaf thorn-apple [Oak leaf thorn apple] - *Datura quercifolia* Kunth (4, 124) (1937-1986)

Oakleech - *Aureolaria* Raf. (155) (1942)

Oak-loving collybia - *Collybia dryophila* (Bull.) P. Kumm. (170) (1995)

Oak-loving mushroom - *Collybia dryophila* (Bull.) P. Kumm. (128) (1933)

Oak-of-Cappadocia [Oak of Cappadocia] - *Ambrosia artemisiifolia* L. (46) (1671)

Oak-of-Hierusalem [Oak of Hierusalem] - *Chenopodium botrys* L. (46) (1671)

Oak-of-Jerusalem [Oak of Jerusalem] - *Chenopodium ambrosioides* L. var. *ambrosioides* (92) (1876), *Chenopodium botrys* L. (19, 178) (1526-1840) deliberately introduced by colonists by 1671

Oat [Oats, Otes] - *Avena* L. (42, 50, 87, 93, 138, 155, 158, 184) (1793–present), *Avena sativa* L. (5, 19, 46, 52, 53, 54, 67, 85, 92, 107, 109, 119, 138, 152, 178, 179, 180) (1526-1949)

Oat grass [Oatgrass, Oat-grass] - *Arrhenatherum* Beauv. (50, 93, 138, 155) (1923–present), *Arrhenatherum elatius* (L.) Beauv. ex J. Presl & C. Presl (5, 56, 68, 85, 92) (1876-1932), *Arrhenatherum elatius* (L.) Beauv. ex J.& K. Presl var. *elatius* (possibly) (72) (1907), *Avena* L. (10, 42, 87) (1814-1884), *Avena sativa* L. (92) (1876), *Danthonia DC.* (50) (present), *Trisetum* Pers. (50) (present)

Oat smut - *Ustilago avenae* (Pers.) Rostr. (157) (1929)

Oat thistle [Oat-thistle] - *Onopordum acanthium* L. (5, 158) (1900-1913)

Oat-like hair grass [Oat-like hair-grass] - *Deschampsia danthonioides* (Trin.) Munro (94) (1901)

Obedient plant [Obedient-plant] - *Physostegia* Benth. (4, 156) (1923-1986), *Physostegia parviflora* Nutt. ex Gray (3, 4, 127) (1933-1986), *Physostegia virginiana* (L.) Benth. (5, 50, 156, 158) (1900–present), *Physostegia virginiana* (L.) Benth. subsp. *praemorsa* (Shinners) Cantino (50) (present), *Physostegia virginiana* (L.) Benth. subsp. *virginiana* (50) (present)

Obier (French) - *Viburnum opulus* L. (158) (1900)

Oblong bluebells - *Mertensia oblongifolia* (Nutt.) G. Don (50) (present)

Oblong woodsia - *Woodsia ilvensis* (L.) R. Br. (5) (1913)

Oblong-fruit Juneberry [Oblong-fruited June berry] - *Amelanchier bartramiana* (Tausch) M. Roem. (5) (1913)

Oblong-leaf aster [Oblong-leaved aster] - *Symphyotrichum oblongifolium* (Nutt.) Nesom (82) (1930)

Oblong-leaf bluebells [Oblongleaf bluebells] - *Mertensia oblongifolia* (Nutt.) G. Don (155) (1942)

Oblong-leaf bumelia [Oblong-leaved bumelia] - *Sideroxylon lanuginosum* Michx. subsp. *oblongifolium* (Nutt.) T.D. Pennington (20) (1857)

Oblong-leaf chenopod [Oblong-leaved chenopod] - *Chenopodium desiccatum* A. Nels. (131) (1899)

Oblong-leaf gentian [Oblong-leaved gentian] - *Gentiana affinis* Griesb. (5) (1913)

Oblong-leaf milkweed [Oblong-leaved milkweed] - *Asclepias viridis* Walt. (5, 97) (1913-1937)

Oblong-leaf orache [Oblongleaf orache] - *Atriplex oblongifolia* Waldst. & Kit. (50) (present)

Oblong-leaf primrose [Oblong-leaved primrose] - *Calylophus hartwegii* (Benth.) Raven subsp. *pubescens* (Gray) Towner & Raven (5, 97) (1913–1937)

Oblong-leaf spearwort [Oblong leaved spearwort] - *Ranunculus pusillus* Poir. var. *pusillus* (5) (1913)

Oblong-leaf sundew [Oblong-leaved sundew] - *Drosera anglica* Huds. (5) (1913)

Oblong-leaf sunflower [Oblong-leaved sunflower] - *Helianthus × ambiguus* (Gray) Britt. [*divaricatus × giganteus*] (5, 97) (1913–1937)

Oblong-leaf thorn [Oblong-leaved thorn] - *Crataegus ×anomala* Sargent [*intricata × mollis*] (5) (1913)

Obolys (Lithuanian) - *Malus sylvestris* Mill. (110) (1886)

Obovate beakgrain - *Diarrhena obovata* (Gleason) Brandenburg (50) (present)

Obovate-leaf groundsel [Obovate-leaved groundsel] - *Packera obovata* (Muhl. ex Willd.) W. A. Weber & A. Löve (187) (1818)

Obtuse fieldcress - *Rorippa teres* (Michx.) R. Stuckey (155) (1942)

Obtuse sedge - *Carex obtusata* Lilj. (50) (present)

Obtuse spear grass - *Glyceria obtusa* (Muhl.) Trin. (66, 90) (1885-1903)

Obtuse spike-rush - *Eleocharis obtusa* (Willd.) J.A. Schultes (66) (1903)

Obtuse-flower hair grass [Obtuse-flowered hair-grass] - *Sphenopholis obtusata* (Michx.) Scribn. (187) (1818)

Obtuse-flower panicum [Obtuse-flowered panicum] - *Panicum obtusum* H.B.K. (87) (1884)

Obtuse-leaf arrowhead [Obtuse-leaved arrow-head] - *Sagittaria latifolia* Willd. (187) (1818)

Occident frogbit [Occident-frogbit] - *Limnobium* Rich. (155) (1942)

Occidental arborvitae [Occidental arbor vitae] - *Thuja occidentalis* L. (41) (1770)

Occidental plane tree - *Platanus occidentalis* L. (38) (1820)

Ochra - *Abelmoschus esculentus* (L.) Moench (92) (1876)

Ochro - *Abelmoschus esculentus* (L.) Moench (110) (1886)

O'ckinigi'kweäni'bĭc (Chippewa, young woman's leaf) - *Tanacetum vulgare* L. (40) (1928)

Oconee-bells - *Shortia galacifolia* Torr. & Gray (109, 138) (1923-1949)

Ocotillo - *Fouquieria splendens* Engelm. (124, 149, 153, 155) (1904-1949) NM TX

Ocoughtanamins - *Orontium aquaticum* L. (46) (1879) James River

Ocoughtanausnis - *Peltandra virginica* (L.) Schott. (181) (~1678)

Ocoughtawmins - *Peltandra virginica* (L.) Schott. (181) (~1678)

Ocra - *Abelmoschus esculentus* (L.) Moench (107) (1919)

October beauty - *Stenosiphon linifolius* (Nutt. ex James) Heynh. (86) (1878) name suggested by Thomas Meehan

October lady's-tresses [October ladies' tresses] - *Spiranthes ovalis* Lindl. (50) (present), *Spiranthes ovalis* Lindl. var. *ovalis* (50) (present)

October-berry - *Rubus canadensis* L. (156) (1923)

Oda'tagago'mĭnaga'wûnj (Chippewa) - *Rubus occidentalis* L. (40) (1928)

Ode'imĭnĭdji'bĭk (Chippewa [heart berry root) - *Fragaria virginiana* Duchesne (40) (1928)

Oder Schneeblume (German) - *Chionanthus virginicus* L. (6) (1892)

Oder Wintergrün (German) - *Chimaphila umbellata* (L.) Bart. (6) (1892)

Odessa tamarix - *Tamarix ramosissima* Ledeb. (138) (1923)

Odiga'dimanido (Chippewa) - *Ceanothus herbaceus* Raf. (40) (1928)

Odji'bĭknamûn' (Chippewa) - *Lithospermum caroliniense* (Walt. ex J.F. Gmel.) MacM. (40) (1928)

Odjici'gomĭn (Chippewa) - *Lactuca canadensis* L. (40) (1928)

Odoriferous grape - *Vitis riparia* Michx. (19) (1840)

Odorless myrtle - *Morella inodora* (Bartr.) Small (106) (1930)

Oeder's sedge - *Carex viridula* Michx. subsp. *viridula* (66) (1903)

Official milkwort [Official milk-wort] - *Polygala senega* L. (possibly) (186) (1814)

Officinal alkanet - *Anchusa officinalis* L. (165) (1807)

Officinal bugloss - *Anchusa officinalis* L. (165) (1807)

Officinal houndstongue - *Cynoglossum officinale* L. (187) (1818)

Officinal marshmallow [Officinal marsh-mallow] - *Althaea officinalis* L. (165) (1768)

Officinal soapwort [Officinal soap-wort] - *Saponaria officinalis* L. (187) (1818)

Officinale hedge-mustard - *Sisymbrium officinale* (L.) Scop (187) (1818)

Ofizy - *Zea mays* L. (46) (1879)

Ogaressa (Huron) - *Phaseolus vulgaris* L. (107) (1919)

Ogeeche limes - *Nyssa ogeche* Bartr. ex Marsh. (182) (1791)

O-gee-chee (Fiery or flaming flowers) - *Monarda didyma* L. (86) (1878) possibly from native Oswego language

Ogeechee [Ogeeche] or Ogeechee tree - *Nyssa ogeche* Bartr. ex Marsh. (92, 182, 183) (~1756-1876)

Ogeechee lime [Ogechee lime, Ogeechee limes] - *Nyssa aquatica* L. (107) (1919), *Nyssa ogeche* Bartr. ex Marsh. (2, 8, 10, 107) (1785-1919)

Ogeechee plum [Ogeche plum] - *Nyssa ogeche* Bartr. ex Marsh. (106) (1930)

O'gima'wûck (Chippewa, chief medicine) - *Artemisia dracunculus* L. (40) (1928)

Ogĭni'mĭnaga'wûnj (Chippewa, rose berries) - *Rosa* L. (40) (1928)

O'gite'bŭg (Chippewa) - *Caltha palustris* L. (40) (1928)

Ogwis'simaün (Chippewa) - *Cucurbita pepo* L. (40) (1928)

Ohelo - *Vaccinium reticulatum* Sm. (138) (1923)

Ohio buckeye - *Aesculus flava* Aiton (2, 58) (1869-1895), *Aesculus glabra* Willd. (2, 3, 5, 13, 15, 20, 49, 50, 53, 57, 58, 65, 71, 72, 95, 97, 106, 109, 113, 138, 155, 156, 157, 158) (1857-present)

Ohio curcuma - *Hydrastis canadensis* L. (5, 49, 64) (1898-1913)

Ohio goldenrod [Ohio golden-rod] - *Oligoneuron ohioense* (Frank ex Riddell) G.N. Jones (5) (1913)

Ohio horsemint [Ohio horse-mint] - *Blephilia ciliata* (L.) Benth. (4, 5, 156) (1913-1986), *Blephilia hirsuta* (Pursh) Benth. (157) (1929)

Ohio spiderwort - *Tradescantia ohiensis* Raf. (121) (1918-1970)

Oh-no-more lablab [Oh no more lab lab] - *Lablab purpureus* (L.) Sweet (183) (~1756)

Oh-oúbe (Mohave Yuma) - *Nicotiana* L. (132) (1855)

Oignon (French) - *Allium* L. (180) (1633)

Oignon commun (French) - *Allium cepa* L. (158) (1900)

Oijevaarsbek (Dutch) - *Geranium maculatum* L. (186) (1814)

Oil de vache (French) - *Anthemis cotula* L. (186) (1814)

Oil nut [Oilnut, Oil-nut] - *Pyrularia oleifera* (Muhl. ex Willd.) A. Gray (2, 5, 7, 10, 107, 156) (1818-1919)

Oil nut [Oilnut, Oil-nut] or Oil-nut tree [Oil nut tree] - *Juglans cinerea* L. (5, 6, 49, 78, 92, 156, 157, 158) (1892-1929)

Oil palm - *Elaeis* Jacq. (109) (1949)

Oil plant - *Ricinus communis* L. (5, 92) (1876-1913), *Sesamum orientale* L. (92) (1876)

Oilseed [Oil-seed, Oil seed] - *Camelina sativa* (L.) Crantz (5, 156) (1913-1923)

Oil-seed plant - *Camelina sativa* (L.) Crantz (107) (1919)

Oily grain - *Sesamum orientale* L. (19) (1840)

Oja'cidji'bĭk (Chippewa, slippery root) - *Chamerion angustifolium* (L.) Holub subsp. *angustifolium* (40) (1928)

Ojig'imĭn (Chippewa, fisher berry) - *Polygonum punctatum* Ell. (40) (1928)

O'kadak' (Chippewa) - *Aralia racemosa* L. (40) (1928)

Okarini pisten (Sioux) - *Monarda fistulosa* L. subsp. *fistulosa* var. *mollis* (L.) Benth. (101) (1905) MT

Okindgier - *Phaseolus* L. (181) (~1678)

Okindgier (Roanoke) - *Phaseolus vulgaris* L. (107) (1919)

Oklahoma beardtongue - *Penstemon oklahomensis* Pennell (50) (present)

Oklahoma buckeye - *Aesculus glabra* Willd. (155) (1942)

Oklahoma evening-primrose [Oklahoma evening primrose] - *Oenothera macrocarpa* Nutt. subsp. *oklahomensis* (J.B.S. Norton) Wagner (4) (1986)

Oklahoma hackberry - *Celtis laevigata* Willd. var. *reticulata* (Torr.) L. Benson (155) (1942)

Oklahoma persimmon - *Diospyros virginiana* L. (155) (1942)

Oklahoma phlox - *Phlox oklahomensis* Wherry (50) (present)

Oklahoma plum - *Prunus gracilis* Engelm. & Gray (3, 4, 50, 155) (1942-present)

Oklahoma primrose - *Oenothera macrocarpa* Nutt. subsp. *oklahomensis* (J.B.S. Norton) Wagner (5, 97) (1913-1937) OK

Oklahoma sedge - *Carex oklahomensis* Mack (50, 155) (1942-present)

Okra - *Abelmoschus esculentus* (L.) Moench (15, 41, 50, 58, 92, 107, 109, 138) (1770-present), *Abelmoschus* Medik. (50) (present)

Olba (Basque) - *Avena sativa* L. (110) (1886)

Olcott's root [Olcott root] - *Rumex sanguineus* L. (5, 19, 92) (1840-1913)

Old Amy root - *Apocynum cannabinum* L. (6) (1892)

Old English poplar - *Populus nigra* L. (5, 156, 158) (1900-1923)

Old garden dahlia - *Dahlia pinnata* Cav. (138) (1923)

Old plainsmen - *Hymenopappus scabiosaeus* L'Her. var. *corymbosus* (Torr. & Gray) B.L. Turner (3, 4) (1977-1986)

Old Robert's root - *Packera obovata* (Muhl. ex Willd.) W.A. Weber & A. Löve (92) (1876)

Old Tom - *Nicotiana tabacum* L. (181) (~1678)

Old Virginia - *Symphyotrichum lateriflorum* (L.) A.& D. Löve var. *lateriflorum* (5, 156) (1913-1923)

Old Virginia stickweed [Old Virginia stick-weed] - *Symphyotrichum lateriflorum* (L.) A.& D. Löve (75, 158) (1894-1900) WV

Old whitetop [Old white top] - *Holcus lanatus* L. (5, 75) (1894-1913) WV

Old witch grass [Old witch-grass, Old-witch-grass] - *Panicum capillare* L. (2, 5, 11, 45, 56, 62, 80, 87, 90, 92, 94, 111, 119, 129, 143, 163) (1852-1938)

Old-field balsam [Old-field balsam] - *Pseudognaphalium obtusifolium* (L.) Hilliard & Burtt subsp. *obtusifolium* (5, 6, 49, 73, 92, 156, 157) (1892-1929)

Old-field birch [Old field birch] - *Betula pubescens* Ehrh. subsp. *pubescens* (5, 20, 156, 187) (1857-1923)

Old-field cinquefoil - *Potentilla simplex* Michx. (3, 4) (1977-1986)

Old-field clover [Old field clover] - *Trifolium arvense* L. (5, 156, 158) (1900-1923)

Old-field common juniper [Oldfield common juniper] - *Juniperus communis* L. var. *depressa* Pursh (155) (1942)

Old-field goldenrod [Oldfield goldenrod] - *Solidago nemoralis* Aiton (138) (1923)

Old-field milkvine [Oldfield milkvine] - *Matelea decipiens* (Alex.) Woods. (50) (present)

Old-field pine - *Pinus taeda* L. (2) (1895)

Old-field sweet - *Symphyotrichum lateriflorum* (L.) A. & D. Löve (75) (1894) WV, *Symphyotrichum lateriflorum* (L.) A. & D. Löve var. *lateriflorum* (5, 158) (1900–1913)

Old-field toadflax [Oldfield toadflax] - *Nuttallanthus canadensis* (L.) D.A. Sutton (4, 155) (1942-1986), *Nuttallanthus texanus* (Scheele) D.A. Sutton (3) (1977)

Old-field wheat [Old field wheat] - *Symphyotrichum lateriflorum* (L.) A.& D. Löve var. *lateriflorum* (156) (1923)

Old-fog [Old fog] - *Bromus ciliatus* L. (75) (1894), *Danthonia spicata* (L.) Beauv. ex Roemer & J.A. Schultes (66, 75, 90) (1885-1903)

Old-goose [Old goose] - *Cypripedium acaule* Ait. (5, 156) (1913-1923) no longer in use by 1923

Old-lady's-bonnet [Old lady's bonnet] - *Mertensia virginica* (L.) Pers. ex Link (possibly) (156) (1923)

Old-lady's-clothespins [Old ladies' clothes-pin, Old-ladies clothes pins] - *Bidens frondosa* L. (5, 76, 156) (1896-1923) MA

Old-maid's pink [Old maid pink, Old maid's pink] - *Agrostemma githago* L. (5, 71, 73, 156, 157, 158) (1892–1929), *Saponaria officinalis* L. (5, 64, 73, 92, 157, 158) (1892–1929), *Silene armeria* L. (5, 74, 156) (1893–1923) Canada and Western MA, *Zinnia violacea* Cav. (76) (1896) Sulphur Grove OH

Old-maid's-bonnet [Old maids' bonnet, Old maid's bonnets] - *Lupinus* L. (158) (1900), *Lupinus perennis* L. (5, 76, 156) (1896–1923) no longer in use by 1923, *Moluccella laevis* L. (77) (1898) Sulphur Grove OH

Old-maid's-breastpin [Old maid's breastpin] - *Coreopsis* L. (75) (1894) Plymouth OH

Old-maid's-nightcap [Old maid's night-caps, Old-maid's night-cap, Old-maid's-night-cap, Old maid's nightcap] - *Geranium maculatum* L. (64, 76, 156, 157, 158) (1896–1929) Madison WI

Old-maid's-root [Old maid's root] - *Aralia racemosa* L. (5, 156) (1913-1923)

Old-man [Old man] - *Artemisia abrotanum* L. (5, 57, 73, 92, 107, 156, 157, 158) (1876-1929) for aphrodisiac qualities or use in love divinations, *Rosmarinus officinalis* L. (106) (1930)

Old-man wormwood [Oldman wormwood] - *Artemisia abrotanum* L. (155) (1942)

Old-man-and-woman - *Sempervivum tectorum* L. (109) (1949)

Old-man-in-the-Spring - *Senecio vulgaris* L. (50) (present)

Old-man's-beard [Old man's beard, Old-mans-beard] - *Tillandsia usneoides* (L.) L. (14) (1882) Jamaica, *Chionanthus virginicus* L. (5, 6, 49, 53, 58, 82, 92, 156) (1869-1930), *Clematis drummondii* Torr. & Gray (124) (1937) TX, *Clematis vitalba* L. (92, 109) (1876-1949), *Nyssa sylvatica* Marsh. (75) (1894) Lincolnton NC

Old-man's-flannel [Old-man's flannel, Old man's flannel] - *Verbascum thapsus* L. (5, 69, 157, 158) (1899-1932)

Old-man's-pepper [Old man's pepper] - *Achillea millefolium* L. (69, 156, 157, 158) (1900-1929)

Old-man's-root [Old man's root] - *Aralia racemosa* L. (64, 75, 76, 156, 157, 158) (1896–1929)

Old-man's-whiskers [Old man's whiskers] - *Clematis* L. (1) (1932), *Geum* L. (1) (1932), *Geum triflorum* Pursh (50) (present), *Geum triflorum* Pursh var. *ciliatum* (Pursh) Fassett (127, 156) (1923) ND

Old-pasture bluegrass [Oldpasture bluegrass] - *Poa saltuensis* Fern. & Wieg. (50) (present)

Old-sow - *Anaphalis margaritacea* (L.) Benth. & Hook (158) (1900)

Old-wife's-shirt [Old wife's shirt] - *Liriodendron tulipifera* L. (186) (1814)

Old-woman [Old woman] - *Artemisia absinthium* L. (156, 157, 158) (1900–1929), *Artemisia* L. (73) (1892), *Artemisia stelleriana* Bess. (109, 156) (1923–1949)

Old-woman's-smock [Old woman's smock] - *Liriodendron tulipifera* L. (41) (1770)

Old-world arrowhead - *Sagittaria latifolia* Willd. (possibly) (109, 138) (1923-1949)

Oleander [Oleandre] - *Nerium* L. (138) (1923), *Nerium oleander* L. (49, 57, 92, 109, 124, 126, 178, 179) (1526–1949)

Oleander allamanda - *Allamanda schottii* Pohl (138, 155) (1931-1942)

Oleaster - *Elaeagnus angustifolia* L. (82, 106, 107, 109, 135) (1910-1949), *Elaeagnus* L. (2, 4, 10) (1818-1986), *Olea europaea* L. (178) (1526)

Olive bark - *Olea europaea* L. (92) (1876)

Olive or Olive tree - *Olea europaea* L. (8, 20, 92, 106, 107, 110) (1785-1930), *Olea* L. (8, 10, 109, 138) (1785--1949), *Osmanthus americanus* Benth. & Hook. (182) (1791)

Olive spikerush [Olive spike rush] - *Eleocharis olivacea* Torr. (66) (1903)

Olive tree (along Mississiippi) - *Nyssa aquatica* L. (8) (1785)

Olive-leaf willow [Oliveleaf willow] - *Salix cinerea* L. subsp. *oleifolia* (Sm.) Macreight (138) (1923)

Oliver sauvage (French Creole) - *Nyssa ogeche* Bartr. ex Marsh. (17) (1796)

Olivier (French, olive) - *Nyssa* L. (17) (1796), *Olea* L. (8) (1785)

Olivier d'Amérique (French) - *Osmanthus americanus* (L.) Benth. & Hook. f. ex Gray var. *americanus* (8) (1785)

Olivio (Spain) - *Olea europaea* L. (110) (1886)

Ollick - *Allium porrum* L. (158) (1900)

Olneya - *Olneya tesota* Gray (107) (1919)

Olney's bulrush [Olney bulrush] - *Fimbristylis annua* (All.) R. & S. (5, 155) (1913-1942)

Olney's rush - *Fimbristylis annua* (All.) R. & S. (66) (1903)

Oloa (Basque) - *Avena sativa* L. (110) (1886)

Olocoton (Nicaragua) - *Carica papaya* L. (110) (1886)

Olyue - *Olea europaea* L. (179) (1526)

Omniča (Lakota) - *Phaseolus vulgaris* L. (121) (1918?-1970?)

Omnica hu (Lakota) - *Strophostyles leiosperma* (Torr. & Gray) Piper (121) (1918?-1970?)

O'mucko'zowa'no (Chippewa, elk tail) - *Liatris scariosa* (L.) Willd. var. *scariosa* (40) (1928)

O'mûkiki'bûg (Chippewa, frog leaf) - *Plantago major* L. (40) (1928)

O'mûkiki'wida'sûn (Chippewa, frog leggings) - *Sarracenia purpurea* L. (40) (1928)

281

Onagre (French) - *Oenothera biennis* L. (6, 158) (1892–1900)

One leaf [One-leaf] - *Maianthemum canadense* Desf. (5, 158) (1900-1913)

One-and-all [One & All] - *Nicotiana tabacum* L. (181) (~1678)

Oneberry [One-berry, One berry] - *Celtis occidentalis* L. (5, 156, 158) (1900-1923), *Gaultheria procumbens* L. (5, 73, 156) (1892-1923), *Mitchella repens* L. (49, 53, 76, 156) (1896-1923) no longer in use by 1923, *Trillium erectum* L. (46) (1671)

One-berry leaves [One berry leaves] - *Mitchella repens* L. (92) (1876)

One-blade [One blade] - *Maianthemum canadense* Desf. (5, 158) (1900-1913), *Maianthemum dilatatum* (Wood) A. Nels. & J.F. Macbr. (46, 92, 178) (1596-1876)

One-flower - *Orobanche uniflora* L. (122) (1937)

One-flower broomrape [One-flowered broom-rape Oneflowered broomrape] - *Orobanche uniflora* L. (5, 50, 86, 93, 97, 156, 157, 158) (1878–present), *Orobanche* L. (86) (1878)

One-flower cancer-root [One-flowered cancer root] - *Orobanche* L. (2) (1895), *Orobanche uniflora* L. (3, 156, 186) (1814-1977)

One-flower flatsedge [Oneflower flatsedge] - *Cyperus retroflexus* Buckl. (50, 155) (1942–present)

One-flower gentian [One-flowered gentian] - *Gentiana autumnalis* L. (5) (1913)

One-flower grama [One-flowered grama] - *Bouteloua uniflora* Vasey (94) (1901)

One-flower hawthorn - *Crataegus uniflora* Muench. (138) (1923)

One-flower horehound [One flower horehound] - *Lycopus uniflorus* Michx. (4) (1986)

One-flower orobanche [One-flowered orobanche] - *Conopholis americana* (L. f.) Wallr. (187) (1818)

One-flower pipsissewa [One-flowered pipsissewa] - *Moneses uniflora* (L.) Gray (103) (1870)

One-flower pyrola [One-flowered pyrola] - *Moneses* Salisb. ex S.F. Gray (2, 158) (1895-1900), *Moneses uniflora* (L.) Gray (107, 156, 158) (1900-1923)

One-flower wintergreen [One-flowered wintergreen] - *Moneses* Salisb. ex S.F. Gray (1) (1932), *Moneses uniflora* (L.) Gray (3, 4, 5, 85, 156, 158) (1900-1986)

One-glume grass [One glumed grass] - *Panicum* L. (92) (1876)

One-head actinospermum [One-headed actinospermum] - *Balduina uniflora* Nutt. (5) (1913)

One-leaf [One leaf] - *Maianthemum canadense* Desf. (5, 158) (1900-1913)

One-leaf bean [Oneleaf bean, One-leafed bean] - *Rhynchosia americana* (Houst. ex P. Mill.) M.C. Metz (122) (1937), *Rhynchosia senna* Gillies ex Hook. var. *texana* (Torr. & Gray) M.C. Johnston (124) (1937) TX

One-leaf malaxis [One-leaved malaxis] - *Malaxis unifolia* Michx. (187) (1818)

One-leaf onion [Oneleaf onion] - *Allium unifolium* Kellogg (155) (1942)

One-leaf orchis [One-leaved orchis] - *Platanthera obtusata* (Banks ex Pursh) Lindl. (5) (1913)

One-o'clock - *Taraxacum officinale* G.H. Weber ex Wiggers (64, 69, 156, 157, 158) (1900-1929)

One-row yellow-cress [Onerow yellowcress] - *Rorippa microphylla* (Boenn. ex Reichenb.) Hyl. ex A. & D. Löve (50) (present)

One-scale spikerush [Onescale spikerush] - *Eleocharis uniglumis* (Link) J.A. Schultes (50) (present)

One-seed bur-cucumber [Oneseed burr cucumber, One-seeded bur cucumber] - *Sicyos angulatus* L. (5, 50, 63, 72, 93, 97, 106, 122, 156, 157, 158) (1899–present), *Sicyos* L. (149) (1904)

One-seed croton [One-seeded croton] - *Croton monanthogynus* Michx. (3, 4) (1977-1986)

One-seed cucumber [One-seeded cucumber] - *Sicyos angulatus* L. (46, 92) (1876-1879), *Sicyos* L. (82, 158) (1900-1930)

One-seed honey locust [One-seeded honey locust] - *Gleditsia aquatica* Marsh. (12) (1821)

One-seed juniper [One-seeded juniper] - *Juniperus monosperma* (Engelm.) Sarg. (3, 4, 50, 112, 155) (1937–present)

One-sided bluegrass [One-sided blue-grass] - *Poa unilateralis* Scribn. (94) (1901) Neb

One-sided fern - *Schizaea pusilla* Pursh (19) (1840)

One-sided milkvetch [One-sided milk vetch] - *Astragalus alpinus* var. *brunetianus* Fernald (19) (1840)

One-sided penstemon - *Penstemon secundiflorus* Benth. (86) (1878)

One-sided wintergreen - *Orthilia secunda* (L.) House (3, 4, 5, 19, 72, 85, 95, 131, 156) (1840-1986)

One-spike danthonia [Onespike danthonia] - *Danthonia unispicata* (Thurb.) Munro ex Macoun (50) (present)

Onion [Onions] - *Allium cepa* L. (49, 53, 92, 109, 110, 138, 158, 178, 179) (1526–1949) from union because bulb never throws off any offsets (165), *Allium* L. (1, 93, 106, 109, 121, 148, 138, 155, 156, 167, 180) (1633–1970), *Allium sativum* L. (52) (1919)

Onion asphodill - *Ornithogalum pyrenaicum* L. (180) (1633)

Onion dodder - *Cuscuta gronovii* Willd. ex J. A. Schultes (62) (1912)

Onion grass [Oniongrass, Onion-grass] - *Arrhenatherum elatius* (L.) Beauv. ex J. Presl & C. Presl (5) (1913), *Melica bulbosa* Geyer ex Porter & Coult. (50, 122, 155, 163) (1852–present), *Melica* L. (155) (1942)

Onion twitch - *Arrhenatherum elatius* (L.) Beauv. ex J. Presl & C. Presl (5) (1913)

Onion wibel (German) - *Allium* L. (180) (1633)

Onion-weed [Onionweed] - *Asphodelus fistulosus* L. (50) (present)

Onmnicha (Dakota) - *Phaseolus vulgaris* L. (37) (1919)

Ontario actinea - *Tetraneuris herbacea* Greene (155) (1942)

Ontario aster - *Symphyotrichum ontarione* (Wiegand) Nesom (155) (1942)

Ontario lobelia - *Lobelia kalmii* L. (50, 138, 155) (1923–present)

Ontario poplar - *Populus balsamifera* L. (5, 156) (1913–1923)

Ontario violet - *Viola sororia* Willd. (155) (1942)

Onzhinzhintka (Dakota) - *Rosa arkansana* Porter var. *suffulta* (Greene) Cockerell (37) (1919) Onzhinzhintka-hu (Rose bush)

Oŋsunkoju spapi (Lakota, possibly meaning dog-catcher) - *Gaura coccinea* Nutt. ex Pursh (121) (1918?–1970?)

Oŋwahiŋjuŋtoŋpi (Lakota, tanning substance) - *Erigeron annuus* (L.) Pers. (121) (1918?–1970?)

Ooler - *Alnus glutinosa* (L.) Gaertn. (5) (1913)

Oonopsis - *Oonopsis* Nutt. (158) (1900)

Oo-oon (Pima) - *Zea mays* L. (132) (1855)

Op - *Canavalia rosea* (Sw.) DC. (76) (1896) Florida Keys

Opelousas persicaria - *Polygonum orientale* L. (5) (1913), *Polygonum hydropiperoides* Michx. (72) (1907)

Open cabbage cole - *Brassica oleracea* L. (178, 180) (1526–1633)

Open gowan - *Caltha palustris* L. (5, 157) (1900–1929)

Openawk - *Apios americana* Medik. (46) (1879), *Solanum tuberosum* L. (110) (1886)

Open-field sedge [Openfield sedge] - *Carex conoidea* Schk. ex Willd. (50) (present)

Open-flower rosette grass [Openflower rosette grass] - *Dichanthelium laxiflorum* (Lam.) Gould (50) (present)

Open-woods ragwort [Openwoods ragwort] - *Senecio rapifolius* Nutt. (50) (present)

Opium - *Papaver somniferum* L. (53, 54, 55, 57, 59, 60, 92) (1876–1922)

Opium poppy - *Papaver somniferum* L. (5, 15, 19, 82, 92, 107, 109, 138, 156) (1840–1949)

Opiuma - *Pithecellobium dulce* (Roxb.) Benth. (109) (1949)

Ople tree [Ople-tree] - *Viburnum opulus* L. (156) (1923) no longer in use by 1923

Opopanax - *Acacia farnesiana* (L.) Willd. (107, 109) (1919–1949)

282

Opossum tree [Opossum-tree] - *Liquidambar styraciflua* L. (5, 92, 156) (1876-1923)

Opposite-leaf bahia [Oppositeleaf bahia] - *Picradeniopsis oppositifolia* (Nutt.) Rydb. ex Britton (50) (present)

Opposite-leaf golden-saxifrage [Opposite-leaved golden saxifrage] - *Chrysosplenium oppositifolium* L. (187) (1818)

Opposite-leaf pondweed [Opposite-leaved pondweed] - *Potamogeton vaseyi* J.W. Robbins (possibly) (5) (1913)

Opuntia - *Opuntia* Mill. (158) (1900)

Opurpurishe Weide (German) - *Salix purpurea* L. (6) (1892)

Ora Za - *Oryza sativa* L. (180) (1633)

Orabauke - *Cuscuta pentagona* Engelm. var. *pentagona* (46) (1610)

Orach [Orache] - *Atriplex hortensis* L. (4, 107, 109, 184) (1793-1986), *Atriplex* L. (1, 2, 4, 7, 93, 156) (1828-1986) Old World annuals are known as orach, *Atriplex patula* L. (156) (1923), *Atriplex prostrata* subsp. *calotheca* (Rafn) M.A.Gust. (80) (1913)

Orache caraway - *Arnoglossum atriplicifolium* (L.) H.E. Robins. (19) (1840)

Orach-leaf cacalia [Orach-leaved cacalia] - *Arnoglossum atriplicifolium* (L.) H.E. Robins. (187) (1818)

Orage - *Atriplex hortensis* L. (158) (1900)

Orange [Oranges, Orenge] - *Diospyros virginiana* L. (46) (1879), *Poncirus trifoliata* (L.) Raf. (138) (1923)

Orange [Oranges, Orenge] or Orange tree - *Citrus ×aurantium* L. [*maxima × reticulata*] (7, 19, 106, 110, 178, 182) (1526–1930), *Citrus sinensis* (L.) Osbeck (138, 179) (1526–1923)

Orange agoseris - *Agoseris aurantiaca* (Hook.) Greene (155) (1942)

Orange apocynum - *Asclepias tuberosa* L. (6, 186) (1814-1892)

Orange arnica - *Arnica fulgens* Pursh (155) (1942)

Orange blossom [Orange blossoms] - *Trillium erectum* L. (5, 64, 75, 156) (1894-1923) no longer in use by 1923

Orange California poppy [Orange California-poppy] - *Eschscholzia californica* Cham. subsp. *californica* (138) (1923)

Orange cestrum - *Cestrum aurantiacum* Lindl. (138) (1923)

Orange coneflower [Orange cone-flower] - *Rudbeckia fulgida* Aiton (5, 138) (1913-1923)

Orange daylily [Orange day-lily] - *Hemerocallis fulva* (L.) L. (50, 156) (1923–present), *Hemerocallis fulva* var. *aurantiaca* (Baker) M. Hotta (138) (1923)

Orange fameflower - *Talinum aurantiacum* Engelm. (50, 155) (1942–present)

Orange gooseberry - *Ribes pinetorum* Greene (138) (1923)

Orange hawkweed [Orange hawk-weed] - *Hieracium aurantiacum* L. (5, 19, 106, 109, 138, 156) (1840-1949)

Orange horse-gentian [Orange horse gentian, Orange horsegentian] - Triosteum aurantiacum Bickn. (155, 156) (1923-1944), *Triosteum aurantiacum* Bickn. var. *aurantiacum* (3) (1986)

Orange jewelweed - *Impatiens capensis* Meerb. (157, 158) (1900-1929)

Orange larkspur - *Delphinium nudicaule* Torr. & Gray (138) (1923)

Orange lily - *Lilium bulbiferum* L. (19, 50, 138) (1840–present)

Orange milkweed [Orange milk-weed] - *Asclepias tuberosa* L. (6, 64, 156, 157, 158) (1892–1929)

Orange milkwort - *Polygala lutea* L. (5, 156) (1913-1923)

Orange mustard - *Erysimum capitatum* (Dougl. ex Hook.) Greene var. *capitatum* (5, 76, 156, 158) (1896–1923)

Orange peppermint - *Mentha aquatica* L. (155) (1942)

Orange pittosporum - *Pittosporum undulatum* Vent. (138) (1923)

Orange puccoon - *Lithospermum canescens* (Michx.) Lehm. (156) (1923)

Orange sneezeweed - *Hymenoxys hoopesii* (Gray) Bierner (138) (1923)

Orange stonecrop - *Sedum kamtschaticum* Fisch. & C.A. Mey. (138, 155) (1931-1942)

Orange sunflower - *Heliopsis helianthoides* (L.) Sweet var. *scabra* (Dunal) Fern. (156) (1923)

Orange swallow-wort [Orange swallowwort - *Asclepias tuberosa* L. (5, 6, 7, 49, 53, 64, 92, 156, 158) (1828-1923)

Orange tawny gilloflowers [Orange tawnie gilloflowers] - *Dianthus caryophyllus* L. (178) (1526)

Orange tawny lily [Orange tawnie lillie] - *Hemerocallis fulva* (L.) L. (178) (1596)

Orange vine - *Cucurbita pepo* L. (7, 92) (1828-1876)

Orange wattle - *Acacia salicina* Lindl. (50) (present)

Orange-cup lily [Orangecup lily] - *Lilium philadelphicum* L. (109, 138) (1923-1949)

Orange-flower horse-gentian [Orange-flowered horse gentian] - *Triosteum aurantiacum* Bickn. var. *aurantiacum* (4) (1986)

Orange-flower tree - *Philadelphus coronarius* L. (5, 156) (1913-1923)

Orange-fruit horse-gentian [Orangefruit horse-gentian] - *Triosteum aurantiacum* Bickn. (50) (present), *Triosteum aurantiacum* Bickn. var. *aurantiacum* (50) (present)

Orange-grass [Orangegrass, Orange grass] - *Hypericum gentianoides* (L.) Britton, Sterns & Poggenb. (2, 5, 19, 72, 92, 156, 157) (1840-1929), *Hypericum* L. (1, 93, 158) (1900-1932)

Orange-jasmine - *Murraya exotica* L. (138) (1923)

Orange-lily pernel - *Anagallis arvensis* L. (157) (1929)

Orange-root [Orangeroot, Orange root] - *Asclepias tuberosa* L. (5, 64, 156, 158) (1900-1923), *Hydrastis canadensis* L. (1, 2, 5, 6, 7, 19, 49, 53, 63, 64, 72, 92, 97, 156) (1840-1937), *Hydrastis* L. (13, 109) (1849-1949)

Orchard barley - *Elymus elymoides* (Raf.) Swezey (94) (1901)

Orchard grass [Orchardgrass, Orchard-grass] - *Dactylis glomerata* L. (3, 5, 10, 11, 21, 45, 46, 50, 56, 66, 67, 68, 72, 85, 87, 88, 90, 92, 94, 109, 111, 119, 125, 129, 138, 140, 143, 155, 163, 187) (1818–present), *Dactylis glomerata* L. subsp. *glomerata* (50) (present), *Dactylis* L. (50, 93, 138, 155) (1923–present), *Muhlenbergia mexicana* (L.) Trin. (80) (1913) IA, *Muhlenbergia racemosa* (Michx.) Britton, Sterns & Poggenb. (80) (1913) IA

Orchid gladiolus - *Gladiolus papilio* Hook. f. (138) (1923)

Orchid tree [Orchid-tree] - *Bauhinia variegata* L. (109) (1949)

Orchil - *Roccella tinctoria* DC. (92) (1876)

Orchilla weed - *Roccella tinctoria* DC. (49, 92) (1876–1898)

Orchis - *Dactylorhiza* Neck. ex Nevski (possibly) (1) (1930), *Habenaria* Willd. (158) (1900), *Platanthera ciliaris* (L.) Lindl. (19) (1840), *Spiranthes* Rich. (124) (1937)

Orcutt's aster [Orcutt aster] - *Xylorhiza orcuttii* (Vasey & Rose) Greene (155) (1942)

Orcutt's snapdragon [Orcutt snapdragon] - *Sairocarpus coulterianus* (Benth. ex A. DC.) D.A. Sutton (155) (1942)

Ordeal poison of Africa - *Trachyspermum copticum* (L.) Link (92) (1876)

Ordeal root - *Strychnos* L. (92) (1876)

Oregon alder - *Alnus rubra* Bong. (20, 160, 161) (1857-1860)

Oregon American vetch - *Vicia americana* Muhl. ex Willd. subsp. *americana* (155) (1942)

Oregon anemone - *Anemone oregana* Gray (155) (1942), *Pulsatilla occidentalis* (S. Wats.) Freyn (155) (1942)

Oregon ash - *Fraxinus latifolia* Benth. (106, 138, 160, 161) (1857-1930)

Oregon aster - *Symphyotrichum eatonii* (Gray) Nesom (155) (1942)

Oregon black ash - *Fraxinus latifolia* Benth. (20) (1857)

Oregon blue grass - *Eragrostis tenuifolia* (A. Rich.) Hochst. ex Steud. (87) (1884), *Poa secunda* J. Presl (5) (1913)

Oregon buckthorn - *Frangula purshiana* (DC.) Cooper (160) (1860)

Oregon cedar - *Chamaecyparis lawsoniana* (A. Murr.) Parl. (75) (1894)

Oregon cherry - *Prunus emarginata* (Dougl. ex Hook.) D. Dietr. (107) (1919)

Oregon cliff fern - *Woodsia oregana* D.C. Eat. (50) (present), *Woodsia oregana* D.C. Eat. subsp. *cathcartiana* (B.L. Robins.) Windham (50) (present)

Oregon cliff-brake - *Aspidotis densa* (Brack.) Lellinger (5) (1913)

Oregon crab - *Malus fusca* (Raf.) Schneid. (138) (1923)

Oregon crab apple [Oregon crab-apple, Oregon crabapple] - *Malus fusca* (Raf.) Schneid. (7, 106, 107, 160) (1828-1930)

Oregon dogwood - *Cornus nuttallii* Audubon ex Torr. & Gray (160) (1860)

Oregon fir - *Pseudotsuga menziesii* (Mirbel) Franco var. *menziesii* (149) (1904)

Oregon fleabane - *Erigeron speciosus* (Lindl.) DC. (138, 155) (1923-1942)

Oregon gentian - *Gentiana affinis* Griesb. (155) (1942)

Oregon grape [Oregon-grape] - *Mahonia aquifolium* (Pursh) Nutt. (5, 49, 52, 53, 54, 60, 64, 74, 76, 85, 93, 95, 107, 148, 157, 160) (1860-1949), *Mahonia nervosa* (Pursh) Nutt. (106, 107, 109, 161) (1857-1949), *Mahonia* Nutt. (1) (1932), *Mahonia pinnata* (Lag.) Fedde subsp. *pinnata* (76, 161) (1857-1896), *Mahonia repens* (Lindl.) G. Don (3, 4, 101, 135, 153) (1905-1986)

Oregon holly-grape [Oregon hollygrape] - *Mahonia aquifolium* (Pursh) Nutt. (138) (1923)

Oregon maple - *Acer macrophyllum* Pursh (106, 109, 138) (1923-1949)

Oregon oak - *Quercus garryana* Dougl. ex Hook. (138) (1923)

Oregon pine - *Pseudotsuga menziesii* (Mirb.) Franco (75, 147) (1856–1894)

Oregon pitch pine - *Pinus radiata* D. Don (20) (1857)

Oregon rockcress - *Arabis oregana* Rollins (155) (1942)

Oregon sunflower - *Balsamorhiza sagittata* (Pursh) Nutt. (107) (1919)

Oregon tobacco - *Valeriana edulis* Nutt. (5, 156, 158) (1900-1923)

Oregon toothwort - *Cardamine nuttallii* Greene var. *nuttallii* (138) (1923)

Oregon viburnum - *Viburnum ellipticum* Hook. (138) (1923)

Oregon water hemlock - *Cicuta douglasii* (DC.) J.M.Coult. & Rose (71) (1898)

Oregon woodsia - *Woodsia oregana* D.C. Eat. (3, 4, 5, 19, 97, 131, 155) (1840-1986)

Organs - *Origanum vulgare* L. (5, 156) (1913-1923) no longer in use by 1923

Organy - *Origanum vulgare* L. (5, 106, 107, 156) (1913-1930)

Orge (French) - *Hordeum vulgare* L. (180) (1633)

Orge à café (French, "coffee barley) - *Hordeum vulgare* L. (110) (1886)

Orge du Pérou (French, Peruvian coffee) - *Hordeum vulgare* L. (110) (1886)

Orgre (French) - *Hordeum vulgare* L. (158) (1900)

Oriental arborvitae [Oriental arbor-vitae] - *Platycladus orientalis* (L.) Franco (109, 112, 138) (1923-1937)

Oriental asperula - *Asperula orientalis* Boiss. & Hohen. (50) (present)

Oriental bittersweet - *Celastrus orbiculatus* Thunb. ex Murray (138) (1923)

Oriental cherry - *Prunus serrulata* Lindl. (138) (1923)

Oriental clematis - *Clematis orientalis* L. (138) (1923)

Oriental cocklebur - *Xanthium strumarium* L. var. *glabratum* (DC.) Cronq. (155) (1942)

Oriental lady's-thumb [Oriental ladysthumb] - *Polygonum caespitosum* Blume (50) (present), *Polygonum caespitosum* Blume var. *longisetum* (de Bruyn) A.N. Steward (50) (present)

Oriental oak - *Quercus muehlenbergii* Engelm. (112) (1937) Neb

Oriental pickling melon - *Cucumis melo* L. (109) (1949)

Oriental poppy - *Papaver orientale* L. (82, 107, 109, 138) (1919-1949)

Oriental sage - *Salvia* ×*superba* Stapf [*sylvestris* × *villicaulis*] (138) (1923)

Oriental woodruff - *Asperula orientalis* Boiss. & Hohen. (138, 155) (1923-1942)

Oriental wormwood - *Artemisia scoparia* Waldst. & Kit. (138, 155) (1931-1942)

Origanum - *Origanum vulgare* L. (61, 92) (1870-1876)

Orme (French) - *Ulmus* L. (8) (1785)

Orme à grappe (French) - *Ulmus thomasii* Sarg. (20) (1857)

Orme à trois feuilles (French) - *Ptelea trifoliata* L. (8, 158) (1785-1900)

Orme d'Amérique (French) - *Ulmus americana* L. (8) (1785)

Orme de Samaire a Trois Feuilles (French) - *Ptelea trifoliata* L. (6) (1892)

Orme fauve (French) - *Ulmus rubra* Muhl. (158) (1900)

Orme gras (Upper Louisiana) - *Ulmus rubra* Muhl. (20) (1857)

Ormosia - *Ormosia* G. Jackson (138) (1923)

Ormrot - *Aristolochia serpentaria* L. (186) (1814)

Ornithogalum stagger-grass [Ornathogalum (sic) Staggergrass] - *Nothoscordum bivalve* (L.) Britt. (possibly) (183) (1756)

Orono sedge - *Carex oronensis* Fernald. (5, 50) (1913–present)

Orpine - *Hylotelephium telephium* (L.) H. Ohba. subsp. *telephium* (5, 19, 63, 72, 92, 107, 156) (1840–1923), *Sedum* L. (1, 2, 109) (1895–1949)

Orris root - *Iris germanica* L. (57) (1917), *Iris pallida* Lam. (57) (1917)

Orthilia - *Orthilia* Raf. (50) (present)

Orthocarpus - *Orthocarpus* Nutt. (50) (present)

Ortie brulante (French) - *Urtica dioica* L. (158) (1900)

Ortigo (French) - *Urtica dioica* L. (158) (1900)

Orwisburg grape - *Vitis riparia* Michx. (7) (1828)

Oryelle tree - *Alnus incana* (L.) Moench (46) (1879)

Orygan - *Origanum vulgare* L. (179) (1526)

Orzo (Italian) - *Hordeum vulgare* L. (180) (1633)

Osaga'tigom' (Chippewa, tangled branches) - *Osmorhiza claytonii* (Michx.) C.B. Clarke (40) (1928)

Osage - *Maclura pomifera* (Raf.) Schneid. (158) (1900)

Osage apple [Osage-apple] - *Maclura pomifera* (Raf.) Schneid. (5, 33, 35, 92, 156, 158) (1806-1923) William Clark

Osage false foxglove - *Agalinis auriculata* (Michx.) Blake (50) (present)

Osage orange [Osageorange, Osage-orange] - *Maclura* Nutt. (4, 93, 109, 138, 155, 156, 158) (1900-1986), *Maclura pomifera* (Raf.) Schneid. (1, 3, 4, 5, 14, 20, 34, 37, 38, 44, 50, 72, 78, 85, 92, 93, 97, 112, 121, 145, 138, 155, 158, 164) (1834–present)

Osage plumb - *Prunus angustifolia* Marsh. (35) (1806) William Clark

Ósako (Pawnee) - *Acer negundo* L. (37) (1919)

Oschbe - *Smilax glauca* Walt. (46) (1879)

Osidiwa (Pawnee) - *Allium canadense* L. var. *mobilense* (Regal) Ownbey (37) (1830)

Osidiwa tsitschiks (Pawnee) - *Allium canadense* L. var. *mobilense* (Regal) Ownbey (37) (1830)

Osier - *Salix* L. (2, 109) (1895–1949)

Osier willow [Osier-willow] - *Salix interior* Rowlee (5, 156, 158) (1900-1923), *Salix viminalis* L. (5, 109, 156) (1913-1949)

Osmanthus - *Osmanthus* Lour. (138) (1923)

Osmunda - *Osmunda* L. (50) (present) for Osmunder, a Saxon god

Osmund-the-waterman [Osmund the waterman] - *Osmunda regalis* L. (157, 178) (1596-1929)

Osoberry [Oso berry] - *Oemleria cerasiformis* (Torr. & Gray ex Hook. & Arn.) Landon (76) (1896) Northwestern US

Osterhout's salt-sage - *Atriplex fruticulosa* Jepson (141) (1899)

Ostrich fern [Ostrich-fern, Ostrichfern] - *Matteuccia struthiopteris* (L.) Todaro (1, 2, 3, 4, 19, 50, 72, 131, 138, 155, 158) (1840–present), *Matteuccia* Todaro (1, 109) (1932-1949)

Ostrich-plume mustard [Ostrich plume mustard] - *Brassica juncea* (L.) Czern. (109) (1949)

Oswego beebalm - *Monarda didyma* L. (138) (1923)

Oswego tea [Oswego-tea] - *Monarda didyma* L. (2, 5, 7, 14, 86, 92, 107, 109, 138, 156, 184) (1828–1949), *Monarda fistulosa* L. (5, 93, 156, 157) (1900–1936), *Monarda* L. (34) (1834)

Osyris - *Kochia scoparia* (L.) Schrad. (174) (1753)

Otaheite - *Saxifraga stolonifera* Meerb. (76) (1896) Paris ME

Otaheite apple [Otaheite-apple] - *Spondias dulcis* Parkinson (92, 109) (1876-1949)

Otaheite gooseberry [Otaheite-gooseberry] - *Phyllanthus acidus* (L.) Skeels (109) (1949)

Otaheite mulberry - *Broussonetia papyrifera* (L.) L'Hér. ex Vent. (5, 156) (1913-1923)

Otaheite walnut - *Aleurites moluccana* (L.) Willd. (107) (1919)

Otay's manzanita [Otay manzanita] - *Arctostaphylos otayensis* Wies. & Schreib. (155) (1942)

Othake - *Gaillardia* Fouq. (155) (1942), *Palafoxia sphacelata* (Nutt. ex Torr.) Cory (3, 50) (1977–present)

Othonna - *Senecio* L. (138, 155) (1923-1942)

Ou Bonnet de Pretre (French) - *Euonymus atropurpurea* Jacq. (6) (1892)

Ou de cicogne (French) - *Geranium maculatum* L. (186) (1814)

Ougoufle (Louisiana) - *Diospyros virginiana* L. (46, 107) (1879–1919)

Ougoust (Western tribes) - *Diospyros* L. (7) (1828)

Ou'-in (Pima) - *Zea mays* L. (132) (1855)

Oui-pun'-go'k (Delaware) - *Quercus* L. (132) (1855)

Our Lady's bedstraw [Our-Lady's bedstraw] - *Galium verum* L. (158) (1900)

Our Lady's mint - *Mentha spicata* L. (5, 62, 156, 158) (1900-1923)

Our Lady's seal [Our Ladyes seale] - *Polygonatum multiflorum* (L.) All. (178, 179) (1526-1596)

Our Lady's thistle - *Cnicus benedictus* L. (5, 69, 156) (1903-1923), *Silybum marianum* (L.) Gaertn. (158) (1900)

Our Lord's candle [Our Lords candle] - *Yucca filamentosa* L. (156) (1923), *Yucca whipplei* Torr. (109) (1949)

Oval kumquat - *Fortunella margarita* (Lour.) Swingle (109) (1949)

Oval-head sedge [Oval-headed sedge, Ovalhead sedge] - *Carex cephalophora* Muhl. ex Willd. (5, 66) (1903-1913), *Carex microptera* Mackenzie (139, 155) (1942-1944)

Oval-leaf andromeda [Oval leaved andromeda, Oval-leaved andromeda] - *Lyonia mariana* (L.) D. Don (42, 187) (1814-1818)

Oval-leaf baldderpod - *Lesquerella ovalifolia* Rydb. ex Britton subsp. *ovalifolia* (3) (1977)

Oval-leaf bilberry [Oval-leaved bilberry] - *Vaccinium ovalifolium* J.E. Smith (5) (1913)

Oval-leaf bladderpod [Oval leaved bladder pod, Oval-leaf bladder pod, Oval-leaved bladder-pod] - *Lesquerella ovalifolia* Rydb. ex Britton (3, 4, 5, 93, 97) (1913-1986)

Oval-leaf dracaena [Oval leaved dracaena] - *Clintonia borealis* (Ait.) Raf. (42) (1814)

Oval-leaf goldenrod [Oval-leaf golden-rod] - *Solidago latissimifolia* Mill. (19) (1840)

Oval-leaf knotweed - *Polygonum arenastrum* Jord. ex Boreau (50) (present)

Oval-leaf milkweed [Oval-leaf milk weed, Oval leaved milk weed, Ovalleaf milkweed, Oval-leaved milkweed] - *Asclepias ovalifolia* Dcne. (4, 5, 50, 72, 82, 131) (1899–present), *Asclepias purpurascens* L. (42) (1814)

Oval-leaf sedge - *Carex cephalophora* Muhl. ex Willd. (50) (present)

Oval-leaf starwort [Oval-leaved star-wort] - *Stellaria pubera* Michx. (187) (1818)

Oval-leaf swallow-wort [Oval leaved swallow wort] - *Asclepias purpurascens* L. (42) (1814)

Oval-shaped sedge - *Carex cephalophora* Muhl. ex Willd. (72) (1907)

Oval-spike amaranth [Oval-spiked amaranth] - *Amaranthus tricolor* L. (165) (1768)

Ova-ova - *Monotropa uniflora* L. (6, 49, 92, 157, 158) (1876–1929)

Ovate spikerush - *Eleocharis ovata* (Roth) Roemer & J.A. Schultes (50) (present)

Ovate-leaf marsh penny-wort [Ovate-leaved marsh penny-wort] - *Centella asiatica* (L.) Urban (5) (1913)

Ovate-leaf nama [Ovate-leaved nama] - *Hydrolea ovata* Nutt. ex Choisy (5, 97, 106) (1913-1937)

Ovate-leaf sagittaria [Ovate-leaved sagittaria] - *Sagittaria platyphylla* (Engelm.) J.G. Smith (5, 97) (1913-1937)

Ovate-leaf thorn [Ovate-leaved thorn] - *Crataegus ovata* Sargent (5) (1913)

Ovate-leaf violet [Ovate-leaved violet] - *Viola sagittata* Aiton var. *ovata* (Nutt.) Torr. & Gray (5, 156) (1913-1923)

Overcup - *Quercus macrocarpa* Michx. (164) (1854)

Overcup oak [Over-cup oak] - *Quercus lyrata* Walt. (5, 10, 20, 33, 65, 82, 109, 122, 124, 138, 156) (1827-1949), *Quercus macrocarpa* Michx. (2, 10, 12, 19, 27, 156, 158) (1811-1923)

Overcup white oak - *Quercus macrocarpa* Michx. (12, 17, 18, 20, 33) (1796-1914)

Over-worn flower-de-luce [Ouerworne flowerdeluce] - *Iris xiphium* L. (178) (1596)

Ovesu (Russian) - *Avena sativa* L. (110) (1886)

Ovoid spikerush [Ovoid spike rush] - *Eleocharis ovata* (Roth) Roemer & J.A. Schultes (5, 72) (1907-1913)

Owl clover [Owl's-clover, Owl's clover, Owlclover] - *Orthocarpus luteus* Nutt. (1, 3, 4, 85) (1932-1986), *Orthocarpus* Nutt. (50, 93, 155) (1936–present)

Owler - *Alnus glutinosa* (L.) Gaertn. (92) (1876)

Owl-fruit sedge [Owlfruit sedge] - *Carex stipata* Muhl. ex Willd. (50) (present), *Carex stipata* Muhl. ex Willd. var. *stipata* (50) (present)

Owl's-crown [Owl's crown] - *Filago vulgaris* Lam. (5, 156) (1913-1923), *Omalotheca sylvatica* (L.) Schultz-Bip. & F.W. Schultz (5, 156) (1913-1923)

Oxadaddy - *Veronicastrum virginicum* (L.) Farw. (5, 92, 157, 158) (1876–1929)

Oxadoddy - *Veronicastrum virginicum* (L.) Farw. (5, 92, 157, 158) (1876–1929)

Oxalide alleluia (French) - *Oxalis montana* Raf. (possibly) (7) (1828)

Oxalis - *Oxalis drummondii* Gray (124) (1937), *Oxalis* L. (138, 155) (1923-1942), *Oxalis montana* Raf. (possibly) (92, 107) (1876-1919)

Oxbalm [Ox balm, Ox-balm] - *Collinsonia canadensis* L. (5, 6, 58, 64, 92, 156) (1869-1923)

Ox-eye [Ox eye, Oxeye, Oxe eie] - *Adonis vernalis* L. (178) (1526), *Bidens laevis* (L.) Britton, Sterns & Poggenb. (19) (1840), *Borrichia arborescens* (L.) DC. (19) (1840), *Chrysanthemum* L. (10) (1818), *Helenium autumnale* L. (5, 7, 92, 156, 157, 158) (1828–1929), *Heliopsis helianthoides* (L.) Sweet (4, 5, 156) (1923–1986), *Heliopsis helianthoides* (L.) Sweet var. *scabra* (Dunal) Fern. (40, 82) (1928–1930), *Heliopsis* Pers. (1, 2, 80, 82, 156) (1923–1932), *Leucanthemum vulgare* Lam. (45) (1896)

Ox-eye camomile [Ox-eye chamomile] - *Anthemis tinctoria* L. (5, 156) (1913-1923)

Ox-eye daisy [Oxeye daisy, Oxeyedaisy, Ox-eyed daisy] - *Chrysanthemum* L. (82, 93, 156, 167) (1814-1936), *Leucanthemum* Mill. (1) (1932), *Leucanthemum vulgare* Lam. (3, 4, 5, 19, 42, 49, 50, 53, 58, 62, 63, 72, 80, 82, 85, 92, 97, 106, 107, 109, 114, 122, 124, 138, 145, 155, 156, 158, 187) (1814–present), *Rudbeckia hirta* L. (75, 76, 158) (1894-1900)

Oxford weed - *Cymbalaria muralis* P.G. Gaertn., B. Mey. & Scherb. (5, 156) (1913-1923)

Oxheal - *Helleborus foetidus* L. (92) (1876)

Oxhorn acacia - *Acacia cornigera* (L.) Willd. (155) (1942)

Oxtongue [Ox-tongue] - *Anchusa* L. (179) (1526), *Anchusa officinalis* L. (92) (1876), *Picris echioides* L. (3, 4, 107, 156) (1919-1986)

Oxwort [Ox wort] - *Petasites hybridus* (L.) G. Gaertn., B. Mey. & Scherb. (5, 156) (1913-1923) no longer in use by 1923

Oxypolis - *Oxypolis filiformis* (Walt.) Britton (5) (1913)

Oxyrie reniforme (French) - *Oxyria digyna* (L.) Hill (7) (1828)

Oyster mushroom - *Pleurotus ostreatus* (Jacq.) P. Kumm. (128) (1933)

Oyster plant [Oyster-plant, Oysterplant] - *Mertensia maritima* (L.) Gray (156) (1923), *Mertensia maritima* (L.) Gray var. *maritima* (5)

(1913), *Tragopogon* L. (1) (1932), *Tragopogon porrifolius* L. (5, 63, 72, 95, 97, 107, 109, 155, 158) (1899-1949), *Tragopogon pratensis* L. (146) (1939)

Oyster-root [Oyster root] - *Tragopogon* L. (7) (1828), *Tragopogon porrifolius* L. (5, 92, 156, 158) (1876-1923)

Ozaha - *Vitis vulpina* L. (46) (1879)

Ozark bluestar - *Amsonia illustris* Woods. (50) (present)

Ozark downy phlox - *Phlox pilosa* L. subsp. *ozarkana* (Wherry) Wherry (155) (1942)

Ozark dropseed - *Sporobolus vaginiflorus* (Torr. ex Gray) Wood var. *ozarkanus* (Fern.) Shinners (50) (present)

Ozark false gromwell - *Onosmodium molle* Michx. subsp. *subsetosum* (Mackenzie & Bush) Cochrane (5) (1913)

Ozark grass [Ozarkgrass] - *Limnodea arkansana* (Nutt.) L.H. Dewey (50, 155) (1942–present)

Ozark milkvetch [Ozark milk vetch] - *Astragalus distortus* Torr. & Gray (4) (1986)

Ozark phlox - *Phlox pilosa* L. subsp. *ozarkana* (Wherry) Wherry (50) (present)

Ozark sundrops - *Oenothera macrocarpa* Nutt. subsp. *macrocarpa* (138, 155) (1923-1942)

Ozark violet - *Viola viarum* Pollard (155) (1942)

O'zawa'bigwûn (Chippewa, yellow flower) - *Erysimum cheiranthoides* L. (40) (1928), *Solidago speciosa* Nutt. var. *rigidiuscula* Torr. & Gray (40) (1928)

Oza'widji'bïk (Chippewa, yellow root) - *Coptis trifolia* (L.) Salisb. (40) (1928), *Rumex acetosella* L. (40) (1928), *Rumex crispus* L. (40) (1928)

Ozier - *Salix sericea* Marsh. (8) (1785)

Ozi'sïgo'bimïc (Chippewa) - *Salix* L. (40) (1928)

Ozark sundrops, *Oenothera macrocarpa* Nutt.
(*Annales de flore et de pomone,* v. 2, 1833-1834)

P

Paari pitsuts (Pawnee, Pawnee hairbrush) - *Hesperostipa spartea* (Trin.) Barkworth (37) (1830)

Paas blumes - *Hepatica nobilis* Schreb. (156) (1923)

Paasemung (Algic tribes) - *Tiarella cordifolia* L. (7) (1828)

Pacai (Peru) - *Prosopis laevigata* (Willd.) M.C.Johnst. (107) (1919)

Pacans - *Carya illinoinensis* (Wangenh.) K. Koch (35) (1806)

Paccay (Peru) - *Prosopis laevigata* (Willd.) M.C.Johnst. (107) (1919)

Pachira - *Pachira* Aubl. (138) (1923)

Pachistima - *Paxistima* Raf. (138) (1923)

Pachone - *Phytolacca americana* L. (181) (~1678)

Pachyphylla - *Nicotiana rustica* L. (174) (1753)

Pachysandra - *Pachysandra* Michx. (138) (1923)

Pacific anemone - *Anemone multifida* Poir. (50) (present), *Anemone multifida* Poir. var. *hudsoniana* DC. (155) (1942)

Pacific aster - *Symphyotrichum chilense* (Nees) Nesom var. *chilense* (155) (1942)

Pacific dogwood - *Cornus nuttallii* Audubon ex Torr. & Gray (138) (1923)

Pacific giant wildrye - *Leymus cinereus* (Scribn. & Merr.) A.Löve (155) (1942)

Pacific madrone - *Arbutus menziesii* Pursh (155) (1942)

Pacific milkweed - *Asclepias lanceolata* Walt. (155) (1942)

Pacific onion - *Allium validum* S. Wats. (155) (1942)

Pacific panicum - *Dichanthelium acuminatum* (Sw.) Gould & C.A. Clark var. *fasciculatum* (Torr.) Freckmann (155) (1942)

Pacific plum - *Prunus subcordata* Benth. (107, 109) (1919–1949)

Pacific red elder - *Sambucus racemosa* L. var. *racemosa* (155) (1942)

Pacific serviceberry - *Amelanchier alnifolia* (Nutt.) Nutt. ex M. Roemer var. *semiintegrifolia* (Hook.) C.L. Hitchc. (155) (1942)

Pacific silver fir - *Abies amabilis* (Dougl. ex Loud.) Dougl. ex Forbes (155) (1942)

Pacific trillium - *Trillium ovatum* Pursh (138) (1923)

Pacific white fir - *Abies lowiana* (Gordon & Glend.) A. Murray bis (138, 155) (1923–1942)

Pacific yew - *Taxus brevifolia* Nutt. (138) (1923)

Paco - *Musa ×paradisiaca* L. [*acuminata × balbisiana*] (107) (1578)

Paddebloem (Dutch) - *Anthemis cotula* L. (186) (1814)

Paddock-cheese - *Asparagus officinalis* L. (157, 158) (1900–1929)

Paddock-pipe [Paddock pipe, Paddock pipes, Paddock-pipes] - *Equisetum fluviatile* L. (5, 158) (1900-1913), *Equisetum palustre* L. (92) (1876), *Hippuris vulgaris* L. (5, 156, 158) (1900–1923)

Paddock-stools [Paddock stools] - *Boletus* L. (92) (1876)

Paddy - *Oryza sativa* L. (92) (1876)

Padus de Virginie (French) - *Prunus virginiana* L. (8) (1785)

Padus-leaf thorn [Padus-leaved thorn] - *Crataegus intricata* Lange (5) (1913)

Paeonia - *Paeonia officinalis* L. (92) (1876)

Pagatowr (Virginians) - *Zea mays* L. (180) (1633)

Pagle - *Primula veris* L. (179) (1526)

Pagoda dogwood - *Cornus alternifolia* L. f. (109, 138, 156) (1923-1949)

Pagoda plant [Pagoda-plant] - *Blephilia* Raf. (50) (present)

Pagoda tree [Pagoda-tree] - *Sophora japonica* L. (156) (1923) IA

Pahatu (Pawnee [red]) - *Rosa arkansana* Porter var. *suffulta* (Greene) Cockerell (37) (1919)

Pah'-mon (Comanche Shoshonee) - *Nicotiana* L. (132) (1855)

Pa'-ho-with-lim (Cahuillo Shoshonee) - *Zea mays* L. (132) (1855)

Paigle - *Ranunculus acris* L. (158) (1900)

Paigne (Canada) - *Chimaphila maculata* (L.) Pursh (7) (1828)

Paint root [Paint-root] - *Lachnanthes caroliana* (Lam.) Dandy (5, 156) (1913-1923)

Paintbrush [Paint-brush, Paint brush] - *Castilleja coccinea* (L.) Spreng. (73) (1892), *Hypericum prolificum* L. (5, 76, 156) (1896-1923) Oakdam IN

Painted abutilon - *Abutilon mollicomum* (Willd.) Sweet (138, 155) (1931-1942)

Painted buckeye - *Aesculus ×neglecta* Lindl. [*flava × sylvatica*] (155) (1942)

Painted copperleaf - *Acalypha armentacea* Roxb. (138, 155) (1931-1942)

Painted cowlily - *Nuphar lutea* (L.) Sm. subsp. *variegata* (Dur.) E.O. Beal (155) (1942)

Painted gaillardia - *Gaillardia pulchella* Foug. var. *picta* (Sweet) Gray (92, 138) (1876-1923)

Painted grass [Painted-grass, Painted grasse] - *Phalaris arundinacea* L. (5, 158, 163, 180) (1633-1913)

Painted maple - *Kalopanax septemlobus* (Thunb.) Koidz. (138, 165) (1768-1923)

Painted milkvetch [Painted milk-vetch, Painted milk vetch] - *Astragalus ceramicus* Sheldon (50) (present), *Astragalus ceramicus* Sheldon var. *filifolius* (Gray) F.J. Herm. (4, 50, 98) (1926–present)

Painted pod - *Oxytropis* DC. (93) (1936) Neb

Painted spurge - *Euphorbia cyathophora* Murray (138) (1923)

Painted trillium - *Trillium undulatum* Willd. (2, 138, 156) (1895-1923)

Painted-cup [Painted cup, Paintedcup] - *Bartsia* L. (167) (1814), *Castilleja coccinea* (L.) Spreng. (5, 12, 19, 47, 92, 187) (1852-1913), *Castilleja* Mutis ex L. f. (1, 2, 10, 93, 138, 155, 156, 158) (1818-1942), *Castilleja septentrionalis* Lindl. (131) (1899)

Painted-lady [Painted lady] - *Chrysanthemum coccineum* Willd. (138) (1923), *Trillium undulatum* Willd. (156) (1923)

Painted-leaf [Painted leaf] - *Euphorbia cyathophora* Murray (82, 156) (1923-1930)

Painted-tongue - *Salpiglossis sinuata* Ruiz & Pavón (109) (1949)

Painter's-brush [Painter's brush] - *Castilleja* Mutis ex L. f. (1) (1932)

Painting plant [Painting-plant] - *Buglossoides arvensis* (L.) I.M. Johnston (156, 157, 158) (1900–1929)

Pajarilla (French) - *Fumaria officinalis* L. (158) (1900)

Pajaro manzanita - *Arctostaphylos pajaroensis* (J.E. Adams ex McMinn) J.E. Adams (155) (1942)

Påk (Swedish) - *Phytolacca americana* L. (41) (1770)

Pakarut (Pawnee) - *Equisetum* L. (37) (1830)

Pakwan-minš (Chippewa) - *Rhus glabra* L. (105) (1932)

Palafox - *Palafoxia* Lag. (50) (present)

Palafoxia - *Palafoxia hookeriana* Torr. & A. Gray var. *hookeriana* (138) (1923), *Palafoxia* Lag. (155, 158) (1900–1942)

Palandu (India) - *Allium cepa* L. (110) (1886)

Palares (Peru) - *Phaseolus vulgaris* L. (possibly) (110) (1886)

Palay rubbervine - *Cryptostegia grandiflora* (Roxb. ex R. Br.) R. Br. (138) (1923)

Pale agoseris - *Agoseris glauca* (Pursh) Raf. (50, 155) (1942–present)

Pale alyssum - *Alyssum alyssoides* (L.) L. (4, 155) (1942-1986)

Pale balsam-weed - *Impatiens pallida* Nutt. (157) (1929)

Pale bastard toadflax - *Comandra umbellata* (L.) Nutt. subsp. *pallida* (A. DC.) Piehl (50) (present)

Pale beaked rush - *Rhynchospora pallida* M.A. Curtis (5) (1913)

Pale beardtongue [Pale beard-tongue] - *Penstemon angustifolius* Nutt. ex Pursh (131) (1899), *Penstemon pallidus* Small (5, 50, 97) (1913–present)

Pale bergamot - *Monarda fistulosa* L. subsp. *fistulosa* var. *mollis* (L.) Benth. (85) (1932)

Pale blueberry - *Vaccinium pallidum* Aiton (5, 158) (1900–1913)

Pale broomrape [Pale broom-rape] - *Orobanche uniflora* L. (5, 72, 93, 156, 157, 158) (1900-1936)

Pale bulrush - *Scirpus pallidus* (Britt.) Fern. (5, 139) (1913-1944)

Pale clematis - *Clematis ochroleuca* Aiton (2) (1895)

Pale comandra - *Comandra umbellata* (L.) Nutt. subsp. *pallida* (A. DC.) Piehl (5, 93, 97, 131) (1899–1937)

Pale coralroot - *Corallorrhiza trifida* Chat. (3) (1977)

Pale corydalis - *Corydalis flavula* (Raf.) DC. (4, 5, 72, 97, 156, 158) (1900-1986), *Corydalis sempervirens* (L.) Pers. (2, 156) (1895-1923)

Pale desert-thorn - *Lycium pallidum* Miers. (50) (present)

Pale dock - *Rumex altissimus* Wood (3, 4, 5, 50, 145, 156) (1897–present), *Rumex salicifolius* Weinm. (131) (1899), *Rumex salicifolius* Weinm. var. *mexicanus* (Meisn.) A.S. Hitchc (5, 93) (1913-1936)

Pale dogwood - *Cornus amomum* Mill. (4) (1986)

Pale dogwood - *Cornus obliqua* Raf. (3, 138, 155) (1923-1977)

Pale echinacea - *Echinacea pallida* (Nutt.) Nutt. (3, 4, 155) (1942-1986)

Pale evening-primrose [Pale evening primrose] - *Oenothera albicaulis* Pursh (3, 4) (1977-1986), *Oenothera latifolia* (Rydb.) Munz (4) (1986)

Pale false manna grass [Pale false mannagrass] - *Torreyochloa pallida* (Torr.) Church var. *pallida* (50) (present)

Pale flax - *Linum bienne* Mill. (50) (present)

Pale gentian - *Gentiana villosa* L. (possibly) (7) (1828)

Pale goldenrod [Pale golden-rod] - *Solidago bicolor* L. (5, 156) (1913-1923)

Pale great bulrush - *Schoenoplectus heterochaetus* (Chase) Soják (5) (1913)

Pale hickory - *Carya pallida* (Ashe) Engl. & Graebn. (5) (1913)

Pale Indian plantain - *Arnoglossum atriplicifolium* (L.) H.E. Robins. (3, 4, 5, 50, 72, 82, 93, 97, 156, 157, 158) (1900–present)

Pale jewelweed - *Impatiens pallida* Nutt. (105, 157) (1929–1932)

Pale laurel - *Kalmia polifolia* Wangenh. (5, 92, 156) (1876-1923)

Pale leather flower - *Clematis versicolor* Small ex Rydb. (5, 97) (1913-1937)

Pale lobelia - *Lobelia spicata* Lam. (93, 95) (1911-1936)

Pale madwort - *Alyssum alyssoides* (L.) L. (50) (present)

Pale manna grass [Pale manna-grass] - *Torreyochloa pallida* (Torr.) Church var. *pallida* (5, 66, 90, 92, 94) (1885-1913)

Pale mountain polypody - *Gymnocarpium dryopteris* (L.) Newman (158) (1900)

Pale Ohio buckeye - *Aesculus glabra* Willd. (155) (1942)

Pale painted-cup - *Castilleja septentrionalis* Lindl. (5) (1913)

Pale penstemon - *Penstemon pallidus* Small (3, 4, 155) (1942-1986)

Pale persicaria - *Polygonum lapathifolium* L. (72, 93, 97, 156) (1907-1937)

Pale plantain - *Plantago rhodosperma* Dcne. (5) (1913), *Plantago rugelii* Dcne. (62, 93, 156) (1912-1936)

Pale pubescent sedge - *Carex pallescens* L. (66) (1903)

Pale purple coneflower [Pale purple cone-flower, Pale purple cone flower] - *Echinacea angustifolia* DC. (63) (1899), *Echinacea pallida* (Nutt.) Nutt. (5, 50, 72, 97, 124, 131, 158) (1899–present)

Pale ragwort - *Senecio congestus* (R. Br.) DC. (5, 156, 158) (1900–1923)

Pale rose - *Rosa blanda* Aiton (158) (1900), *Rosa centifolia* L. (49, 57, 92) (1876-1917)

Pale rough-fruit poppy [Pale rough-fruited poppy] - *Papaver argemone* L. (5) (1913)

Pale rush - *Juncus scirpoides* Lam. (66) (1903)

Pale sedge - *Carex annectens* (Bickn.) Bickn. (5) (1913)

Pale smartweed - *Polygonum lapathifolium* L. (3, 4, 98) (1926-1986)

Pale smooth sedge - *Carex blanda* Dewey (66) (1903)

Pale snapweed - *Impatiens pallida* Nutt. (138, 155) (1923-1942)

Pale spikerush [Pale spike rush] - *Eleocharis flavescens* (Poir.) Urban (5) (1913), *Eleocharis palustris* (L.) Roemer & J.A. Schultes (5) (1913)

Pale St. John's-wort [Pale St. John's wort] - *Hypericum ellipticum* Hook. (5) (1913)

Pale touch-me-not [Pale touch me not] - *Impatiens capensis* Meerb. (92) (1876), *Impatiens pallida* Nutt. (2, 4, 5, 50, 49, 53, 72, 82, 93, 95, 97, 131, 156, 157) (1895–present)

Pale umbrella-wort [Pale umbrella wort, Pale umbrellawort] - *Mirabilis albida* (Walt.) Heimerl (5, 97, 131) (1899–1937)

Pale vetch - *Vicia caroliniana* Walt. (5) (1913)

Pale vetchling - *Lathyrus ochroleucus* Hook. (5) (1913)

Pale violet - *Viola striata* Aiton (2, 5, 156) (1895-1942)

Pale wild bergamot - *Monarda fistulosa* L. subsp. *fistulosa* var. *mollis* (L.) Benth. (5, 72, 93, 131) (1899-1936)

Pale wild rose - *Rosa blanda* Aiton (5) (1913)

Pale wolfberry - *Lycium pallidum* Miers. (4, 155) (1942-1986)

Pale-blue beardtongue [Pale-blue beard-tongue] - *Penstemon angustifolius* Nutt. ex Pursh (5, 93) (1913-1936)

Pale-blue toad-flax - *Linaria repens* (L.) P. Mill. (5) (1913)

Pale-flower lousewort [Pale-flowered louse-wort] - *Pedicularis lanceolata* Michx. (187) (1818)

Pale-flower red maple [Paleflower red maple] - *Acer rubrum* L. (155) (1942)

Pale-flower touch-me-not [Pale-flowered touch-me-not] - *Impatiens pallida* Nutt. (187) (1818)

Pale-green orchid [Palegreen orchid] - *Platanthera flava* (L.) Lindl. var. *flava* (50) (present)

Pale-leaf goldenrod [Paleleaf goldenrod] - *Solidago speciosa* Nutt. var. *pallida* Porter (138, 155) (1923-1942)

Pale-leaf goldenweed [Paleleaf goldenweed] - *Isocoma acradenia* (Greene) Greene var. *acradenia* (155) (1942)

Pale-leaf wood sunflower [Pale-leaved wood sunflower] - *Helianthus strumosus* L. (5, 72, 82, 97) (1907-1937)

Pale-leaf woodland sunflower [Paleleaf woodland sunflower] - *Helianthus strumosus* L. (50) (present)

Pale-purple coneflower - *Echinacea angustifolia* DC. (63) (1899), *Echinacea angustifolia* DC. var. *angustifolia* (64) (1907)

Pale-seed plantain [Paleseed plantain, Pale-seeded plantain] - *Plantago virginica* L. (3, 155) (1942-1977)

Pale-spike lobelia [Pale spiked lobelia, Palespike lobelia] - *Lobelia spicata* Lam. (3, 4, 5, 50, 72, 97, 155) (1907–present)

Palewort [Pale-wort] - *Ranunculus bulbosus* L. (158) (1900)

Pale-yellow iris [Paleyellow iris] - *Iris pseudacorus* L. (50) (present)

Paller (Native S. American) - *Phaseolus vulgaris* L. (possibly) (110) (1886)

Pallid locust - *Robinia hispida* L. var. *hispida* (155) (1942)

Pallid violet - *Viola macloskeyi* Lloyd (155) (1942)

Palliser's poison milkvetch [Palliser poisonmilkvetch] - *Astragalus miser* var. *serotinus* (Gray ex Cooper) Barneby (155) (1942)

Palm grass [Palm-grass, Palmgrass] - *Setaria palmifolia* (Koenig) Stapf (109, 138) (1923-1949)

Palm tree [Palm trees] - *Platanus occidentalis* L. (18) (1805), *Sabal palmetto* (Walt.) Lodd. ex J.A. & J.H. Schultes (92) (1876)

Palm violet - *Viola palmata* L. (122, 138) (1923-1937)

Palma - *Yucca* L. (122) (1937) TX

Palma Christi - *Ricinus communis* L. (5, 10, 19, 92, 109, 110, 156) (1840-1949), *Ricinus* L. (167) (1814)

Palma real - *Roystonea borinquena* O.F. Cook (106) (1930)

Palmate butterbur - *Petasites frigidus* (L.) Fries var. *palmatus* (Aiton) Cronq. (155) (1942)

Palmate grape - *Vitis palmata* Vahl (7) (1828)

Palmate violet - *Viola palmata* L. (155) (1942)

Palmate-leaf sweet coltsfoot - *Petasites frigidus* (L.) Fries var. *palmatus* (Aiton) Cronq. (5, 156) (1913-1923)

Palmcristi - *Ricinus communis* L. (7) (1828)

Palmer black maple - *Acer palmatum* Thunb. (155) (1942)

Palmer's amaranth - *Amaranthus palmeri* S. Wats. (5, 97, 122) (1913-1937)

Palmer's amsonia [Palmer amsonia] - *Amsonia palmeri* Gray (155) (1942)

Palmer's black maple [Palmer black maple] - *Acer palmatum* Thunb. (155) (1942)

Palmer's crab apple [Palmer crabapple] - *Malus ioensis* (Wood) Britton var. *ioensis* (155) (1942)

Palmer's goldenweed [Palmer goldenweed] - *Ericameria palmeri* (Gray) Hall var. *palmeri* (155) (1942)

Palmer's hawthorn [Palmer hawthorn] - *Crataegus crus-galli* L. (4, 155) (1942-1986)

Palmer's onion - *Allium bisceptrum* S. Wats. var. *palmeri* (S. Wats.) Cronq. (86) (1878) for Dr. Palmer, western botanist

Palmer's penstemon [Palmer penstemon] - *Penstemon palmeri* Gray (138) (1923)

Palmer's pigweed - *Amaranthus palmeri* S. Wats. (3, 4) (1977-1986)

Palmer's poplar [Palmer poplar] - *Populus deltoides* Bartr. ex Marsh. subsp. *deltoides* (155) (1942)

Palmer's sagebrush [Palmer sagebrush] - *Artemisia palmeri* Gray (155) (1942)

Palmer's snowberry - *Symphoricarpos orbiculatus* Moench (4, 50) (1986–present)

Palmer's spectacle-pod [Palmer's spectaclepod] - *Dimorphocarpa candicans* (Raf.) Rollins (50) (present)

Palmer's thorn - *Crataegus crus-galli* L. (5, 97) (1913-1937)

Palmer's yarrow [Palmer yarrow] - *Achillea millefolium* L. (155) (1942)

Palmetto - *Sabal* Adans. (2, 106, 138) (1895-1930), *Sabal minor* (Jacq.) Pers. (122) (1937), *Sabal palmetto* (Walt.) Lodd. ex J.A. & J.H. Schultes (92) (1876)

Palmetto palm - *Sabal* Adans. (109) (1949), *Sabal palmetto* (Walt.) Lodd. ex J.A. & J.H. Schultes (107) (1919)

Palmetto royal - *Yucca gloriosa* L. (7, 182) (1791-1828)

Palmillo - *Yucca glauca* Nutt. (5, 156) (1913-1923)

Palmito tree - *Sabal palmetto* (Walt.) Lodd. ex J.A. & J.H. Schultes (107) (1613)

Palm-leaf Indian breadroot [Palmleaf Indian breadroot] - *Pediomelum digitatum* (Nutt. ex Torr. & Gray) Isely (50) (present)

Palm-leaf marshmallow - *Althaea cannabina* L. (50) (present)

Palm-leaf scurf pea [Palm-leaved scurf pea] - *Pediomelum digitatum* (Nutt. ex Torr. & Gray) Isely (4) (1986)

Palo blanco [Paloblanco] - *Adelia* L. (153) (1913) NM, *Celtis laevigata* Willd. var. *reticulata* (Torr.) L. Benson (138) (1923)

Palo de Hierro (Mexican) - *Olneya tesota* Gray (106) (1930)

Palo santo - *Eriodictyon californicum* (Hook. & Arn.) Torr. (54) (1905) CA

Palo verde - *Parkinsonia florida* (Benth. ex Gray) S. Wats. (106) (1930), *Parkinsonia texana* (Gray) S. Wats. var. *macra* (I.M. Johnston) Isely (124) (1937) TX

Palo verde (Spanish) - *Parkinsonia florida* (Benth. ex Gray) S. Wats. (154) (1857), *Parkinsonia microphylla* Torr. (106) (1930) Mexico

Palsy-wort [Palsy wort] - *Caltha palustris* L. (5, 6, 92, 157, 158) (1892–1929)

Palus sanctus - *Guaiacum sanctum* L. (49) (1898)

Pammel's barley - *Elyhordeum montanense* (Scribn.) Bowden [*Elymus virginicus* × *Hordeum jubatum*] (5) (1913)

Pammel's wild barley - *Elyhordeum montanense* (Scribn.) Bowden [*Elymus virginicus* × *Hordeum jubatum*] (56, 72) (1901-1907)

Pampas grass [Pampas-grass, Pampasgrass] - *Cortaderia selloana* (J. A. & J. H. Schultes) Aschers. & Graebn. (56, 67, 92, 109, 163) (1852–1949), *Cortaderia* Stapf (138) (1923)

Pampas-rice [Pampas rice] - *Sorghum bicolor* (L.) Moench subsp. *bicolor* (87, 107) (1884-1919)

Pamplilla - *Geranium maculatum* L. (186) (1814)

Panais Potager (French) - *Pastinaca sativa* L. (6) (1892)

Panameholz (German) - *Sassafras albidum* (Nutt.) Nees (158) (1900)

Panamigo - *Pilea involucrata* (Sims) Urban (109) (1949)

Panax - *Panax quinquefolius* L. (52, 53, 57) (1917)

Pancake grass [Pancakegrass] - *Muhlenbergia torreyi* (Kunth) A.S. Hitchc. ex Bush (119, 140) (1938-1944)

Pancake plant [Pancake-plant] - *Malva rotundifolia* L. (156) (1923), *Malva sylvestris* L. (157, 158) (1900-1929)

Pancratium - *Pancratium* L. (50) (present)

Pandang - *Pandanus tectorius* Parkinson ex Zucc. (107) (1919)

Pangi (Dakota) - *Helianthus tuberosus* L. (37) (1919)

Panhandle spurge - *Euphorbia strictior* Holz. (50) (present)

Panhe (Omaha-Ponca) - *Helianthus tuberosus* L. (37) (1919)

Panh'e (Winnebago) - *Helianthus tuberosus* L. (37) (1919)

Panic - *Panicum* L. (92) (1876) from ancient Latin name of a grass probably Sorghum

Panic grass [Panic-grass, Panicgrass, Panick grass] - *Dichanthelium boscii* (Poir.) Gould & C.A. Clark (119) (1938), *Dichanthelium dichotomum* (L.) Gould var. *dichotomum* (19) (1840), *Dichanthelium oligosanthes* (J.A. Schultes) Gould var. *scribnerianum* (Nash) Gould (119, 121) (1918?-1970?), *Dichanthelium villosissimum* (Nash) Freckmann var. *praecocius* (A.S. Hitchc. & Chase) Freckmann (119) (1938), *Panicum* L. (1, 7, 10, 50, 66, 87, 158, 184) (1818–present)

Panicant D'eau (French) - *Eryngium yuccifolium* Michx. (6) (1892)

Panicled amorpha - *Amorpha paniculata* Torr. & Gray (155) (1942)

Panicled andromeda - *Leucothoe racemosa* (L.) Gray (possibly) (8, 165) (1785-1807)

Panicled aster - *Symphyotrichum lanceolatum* (Willd.) Nesom subsp. *hesperium* (Gray) Nesom (3, 4) (1977-1986), *Symphyotrichum lanceolatum* (Willd.) Nesom subsp. *lanceolatum* (3, 4, 5, 42, 72, 82, 131, 155, 156, 187) (1814-1986)

Panicled bellflower - *Campanula divaricata* Michx. (5) (1913)

Panicled boltonia - *Boltonia diffusa* Ell. (5, 97) (1913-1937)

Panicled bulrush - *Scirpus microcarpus* J.& K. Presl (50, 139, 155) (1942–present)

Panicled cornel - *Cornus foemina* Mill. (5, 156) (1913-1923), *Cornus racemosa* Lam. (63, 156) (1899-1923)

Panicled cyperus - *Cyperus polystachyos* Rottb. var. *polystachyos* (5) (1913)

Panicled dogwood - *Cornus foemina* Mill. (5, 72, 93, 97) (1907-1937), *Cornus racemosa* Lam. (109) (1949)

Panicled false indigo - *Amorpha paniculata* Torr. & Gray (50) (present)

Panicled garlic [Panicled garlick] - *Allium paniculatum* L. (165) (1768)

Panicled gypsophila - *Gypsophila paniculata* L. (156) (1923)

Panicled hawkweed - *Hieracium paniculatum* L. (5) (1913)

Panicled hydrangea [Panicle hydrangea] - *Hydrangea paniculata* Sieb. (138) (1923)

Panicled tick clover [Panicled tickclover] - *Desmodium paniculatum* (L.) DC. (3, 4) (1977-1986)

Panicled tick trefoil [Panicled tick-trefoil] - *Desmodium paniculatum* (L.) DC. var. *paniculatum* (5, 72, 93, 97) (1907-1937)

Panicled willowherb [Panicled willow herb] - *Epilobium brachycarpum* K. Presl (5, 131) (1899-1913)

Panicle-flower andrewsia [Panicle-flowered andrewsia] - *Bartonia virginica* (L.) Britton, Sterns & Poggenb. (187) (1818)

Panicle-leaf tick clover [Panicledleaf tickclover] - *Desmodium paniculatum* (L.) DC. (155) (1942)

Panicle-leaf tick trefoil [Panicledleaf ticktrefoil] - *Desmodium paniculatum* (L.) DC. (50) (present)

Paniculated dogwood [Paniculated dog wood] - *Cornus racemosa* Lam. (42) (1814)

Panicum - *Panicum* L. (155) (1942)

Panier-rush [Panier rush] - *Schoenoplectus tabernaemontani* (C.C. Gmel.) Palla (possibly) (158) (1900)

Panja (Winnebago, nut) - *Carya ovata* (Mill.) K. Koch (37) (1919) Panja-hu (Nut tree)

Pansy [Pansie, Pansey] - *Viola* L. (1, 13) (1849–1932), *Viola pedata* L. (5, 74) (1893–1913) Peoria IL, *Viola tricolor* L. (5, 6, 15, 19, 57, 72, 92, 97, 109, 158) (1893–1949)

Pansy violet - *Viola pedata* L. (3, 156) (1923-1977)

Panther lily - *Lilium columbianum* Leichtlin (138) (1923)

Panyke - *Setaria italica* (L.) Beauv. (178, 179) (1526-1596)

Papas (Chile, Peru) - *Solanum tuberosum* L. (107) (1919)

Papaw [Pawpaw, Paw-paw] or Papaw tree [Papaw-tree, Pappaw tree] - *Annona* L. (167) (1814), *Annona muricata* L. (41, 177) (1770), *Asimina* Adans. (1, 2, 4, 5, 7, 8, 13, 15, 44, 47, 50, 93, 138, 155, 156, 158) (1845–present), *Asimina triloba* (L.) Dunal (3, 6, 10, 18, 19, 25, 34, 35, 48, 49, 50, 65, 72, 109, 122, 158, 181, 184, 187) (~1678–present), *Carica papaya* L. (10, 14, 20, 52, 54, 92, 107, 109, 110) (1818-1949) possibly, from Caribbean name

Papaw-apple [Pawpaw apple] - *Asimina obovata* (Willd.) Nash (183) (~1756)

Papaya - *Carica* L. (138) (1923), *Carica papaya* L. (50, 52, 107, 109, 138) (1919–present)

Pape - *Solanum tuberosum* L. (46) (1879)

Papencruitz (Low Dutch) - *Taraxacum officinale* G.H. Weber ex Wiggers (180) (1633)

Papengaye (Senegambia) - *Luffa acutangula* (L.) Roxb. (110) (1886)

Paper birch - *Betula papyrifera* Marsh (1, 2, 4, 5, 7, 14, 19, 20, 34, 37, 50, 72, 85, 93, 95, 101, 109, 112, 155, 157, 158, 187) (1818–present), *Betula papyrifera* Marsh. var. *papyrifera* (50) (present), *Betula populifolia* Marshall (92) (1876), *Betula pubescens* Ehrh. (105, 107, 156) (1919-1932)

Paper flower [Paperflower, Paper flowers] - *Helichrysum* Mill. (73) (1892) Northern OH, *Psilostrophe* DC. (1, 4, 155) (1932-1986), *Psilostrophe tagetina* (Nutt.) Greene (148) (1939), *Psilostrophe tagetina* (Nutt.) Greene var. *cerifera* (A. Nels.) B.L. Turner (3) (1977), *Verbesina encelioides* (Cav.) Benth. & Hook. f. ex Gray subsp. *exauriculata* (Robins. & Greenm.) J.R. Coleman (122) (1937)

Paper mulberry [Papermulberry] - *Broussonetia* L'Hér. ex Vent. (109, 155, 158) (1900-1949), *Broussonetia papyrifera* (L.) L'Hér. ex Vent. (3, 5, 19, 50, 92, 97, 107, 122, 124, 156, 158) (1840–present)

Paper plant - *Cyperus papyrus* L. (180) (1633)

Paper pore fungus - *Polyporus pargamenus* Fr. (128) (1933)

Paper reed - *Cyperus papyrus* L. (180) (1633)

Paper sponk - *Racodium papyraceum* Pers. (92) (1876)

Paper tree [Papertree] - *Edgeworthia* Meisn. (138) (1923)

Paper-white narcissus - Narcissus papyraceus Ker Gawl. (109) (1949)

Papiconah (Illinois French) - *Porteranthus trifoliatus* (L.) Britton (17) (1796)

Papillaris (Prussia) - *Lapsana communis* L. (possibly) (180) (1633)

Papillose nut-rush [Papillose nut rush] - *Scleria pauciflora* Muhl. ex Willd. (5) (1913)

Papoose root - *Caulophyllum thalictroides* (L.) Michx. (2, 5, 6, 7) (1828–1892)

Pappas Arbor - *Asimina triloba* (L.) Dunal (181) (~1678)

Pappel (German) - *Populus tremuloides* Michx. (6) (1892)

Pappoose root [Pappoose-root - *Caulophyllum* Michx. (13) (1849), *Caulophyllum thalictroides* (L.) Michx. (19, 49, 53, 55, 58, 64, 156, 157, 158) (1840-1923)

Pappus grass [Pappusgrass] - *Pappophorum* Schreber. (155) (1942)

Paprika - *Capsicum annuum* L. (107) (1919)

Papy - *Carica papaya* L. (7) (1828)

Papyrus - *Cyperus papyrus* L. (109, 138) (1923-1949)

Paquerette (French) - *Prunella vulgaris* L. (158) (1900)

Para grass [Para-grass] - *Urochloa mutica* (Forsk.) T.Q. Nguyen (45, 50, 87, 109, 122, 138, 163) (1852–present)

Paracoculi (Italian) - *Datura inoxia* P. Mill. (180) (1633)

Paradise apple - *Malus sylvestris* Mill. (178) (1526)

Paradise flower - *Acacia greggii* Gray (106) (1930)

Paradise plant [Paradise-plant] - *Daphne mezereum* L. (5, 156) (1913-1923) no longer in use by 1923

Paradise tree [Paradise-tree] - *Ailanthus altissima* (Mill) Swingle (106) (1930)

Paradise-apple [Paradise apple] - *Solanum lycopersicum* L. var. *lycopersicum* (158) (1900)

Paradox acacia - *Acacia paradoxa* DC. (50) (present)

Paradox cinquefoil - *Potentilla paradoxa* Nutt. (50) (present)

Paraguay starbur [Paraguay starburr] - *Acanthospermum australe* (Loefl.) Kuntze (50, 155) (1942–present)

Parakaha (Pawnee) - *Monarda fistulosa* L. (37) (1919) The Pawnee recognized four varietes of the species distinguished by odor and growth form

Parasol sedge - *Carex umbellata* Schkuhr ex Willd. (50) (present)

Parasol whitetop - *Doellingeria umbellata* (P. Mill.) Nees (50) (present), *Doellingeria umbellata* (P. Mill.) Nees var. *pubens* (Gray) Britton (50) (present)

Paris circaea - *Circaea lutetiana* L. (155) (1942)

Paris daisy - *Chrysanthemum frutescens* L. (109) (1949)

Parish's feather grass [Parish's feather-grass] - *Achnatherum parishii* (Vasey) Barkworth (94) (1901)

Parish's goldenweed [Parish goldenweed] - *Ericameria parishii* (Greene) Hall (155) (1942)

Parish's sagebrush [Parish sagebrush] - *Artemisia tridentata* Nutt. subsp. *parishii* (Gray) Hall & Clements (155) (1942)

Parish's threeawn - *Aristida purpurea* Nutt. var. *parishii* (A.S. Hitchc.) Allred (50) (present)

Parish's wheat grass [Parish's wheat-grass] - *Elymus stebbinsii* Gould (94) (1901)

Parish's willow [Parish' willow] - *Salix exigua* Nutt. (155) (1942)

Pariswort [Paris wort] - *Trillium cernuum* L. (7) (1828), *Trillium* L. (92) (1876)

Park leaves [Parke leaues] - *Androsaemum officinale* All. (92) (1876), *Hypericum androsaemum* L. (178) (1526)

Park lily - *Convallaria majalis* L. (158) (1900)

Park willow - *Salix planifolia* Pursh (155) (1942)

Parker's pipewort - *Eriocaulon parkeri* B. L. Robinson (5) (1913)

Parkinsonia - *Parkinsonia aculeata* L. (174) (1753), *Parkinsonia* L. (138) (1923)

Parlin's cat's-foot [Parlin's cat's foot] - *Antennaria parlinii* Fern. subsp. *fallax* (Greene) Bayer & Stebbins (5) (1913)

Parlin's pussy-toes [Parlin's pussytoes] - *Antennaria parlinii* Fern. (50) (present), *Antennaria plantaginifolia* (L.) Richards (155) (1942)

Parnassia - *Parnassia* L. (138, 155) (1923-1942), *Parnassia palustris* L. (174) (1753)

Parnassus-grass [Parnassus grasse] - *Parnassia glauca* Raf. (19) (1840), *Parnassia palustris* L. (178) (1526)

Paronychia - *Asplenium ruta-muraria* L. (174) (1753)

Parosela - *Dalea* L. (158) (1900), *Dalea leporina* (Aiton) Bullock (80) (1913)

Parrot alstroemeria - *Alstroemeria pulchella* L. f. (138, 155) (1923-1942)

Parrot pitcher plant [Parrot pitcherplant - *Sarracenia psittacina* Michx. (2, 86, 138) (1878-1923)

Parrot-corn [Parrot's corn, Parrots' corn] - *Carthamus tinctorius* L. (92, 158) (1876-1900)

Parrot-feather [Parrotfeather, Parrot's feather, Parrots-feather] - *Myriophyllum aquaticum* (Vell.) Verdc. (109) (1949), *Myriophyllum* L. (138, 155) (1923-1942), *Myriophyllum verticillatum* L. (156) (1923), *Proserpinaca palustris* L. (97) (1937) OK

Parrot-head pitcher-plant [Parrot-headed pitcher-plant] - *Sarracenia psittacina* Michx. (86) (1878)

Parry's aster [Parry aster] - *Xylorhiza cognata* (Hall) T.J. Wats. (5) (1913), *Xylorhiza glabriuscula* Nutt. var. *glabriuscula* (155) (1942)

Parry's danthonia [Parry danthonia] - *Danthonia parryi* Scribn. (140) (1944)

Parry's larkspur [Parry larkspur] - *Delphinium parryi* Gray (138) (1923)

Patience dock

Parry's manzanita [Parry manzanita] - *Arctostaphylos parryana* Lemmon (155) (1942)

Parry's Mexican rose - *Rosa minutifolia* Engelm. (76) (1896)

Parry's nolina [Parry nolina] - *Nolina parryi* S. Wats. (138) (1923)

Parry's oatgrass [Parry oatgrass] - *Danthonia parryi* Scribn. (140) (1944)

Parry's phacelia [Parry phacelia] - *Phacelia parryi* Torr. (138) (1923)

Parry's pine [Parry pine] - *Pinus quadrifolia* Parl. ex Sudworth (138) (1923)

Parry's primrose [Parry primrose] - *Primula parryi* Gray (138) (1923)

Parry's rabbit-brush [Parry's rabbitbrush] - *Ericameria parryi* (Gray) Nesom & Baird (50) (present), *Ericameria parryi* (Gray) Nesom & Baird var. *howardii* (Parry ex Gray) Nesom & Baird (50) (present)

Parry's rush [Parry rush] - *Juncus parryi* Engelm. (139) (1944)

Parry's sedge - *Carex parryana* Dewey (5, 50) (1913–present)

Parsenep - *Pastinaca sativa* L. (158) (1900)

Parsimon - *Diospyros virginiana* L. (158) (1900)

Parsley - *Petroselinum crispum* (P. Mill.) Nyman ex A.W. Hill (8, 19, 45, 46, 49, 50, 52, 53, 54, 55, 57, 85, 92, 107, 109, 110, 122, 138, 158, 184) (1671–present), *Portulaca oleracea* L. (85) (1932)

Parsley breakstone - *Aphanes arvensis* L. (5) (1913), *Scleranthus annuus* L. (178) (1526)

Parsley colewort [Parseley colewoort] - *Brassica oleracea* L. (180) (1633)

Parsley elder - *Sambucus nigra* L. (158) (1900)

Parsley haw - *Crataegus marshallii* Eggl. (5, 122) (1913-1937)

Parsley hawthorn - *Crataegus oxyacantha* L. var. *apiifolia* Michx. (138) (1923)

Parsley piert - *Aphanes arvensis* L. (5, 10, 19, 92, 156, 178) (1526-1923), *Scleranthus annuus* L. (5, 156) (1913-1923)

Parsley vlix - *Aphanes arvensis* L. (5) (1913)

Parsley yellow-root - *Xanthorhiza simplicissima* Marsh. (49) (1898)

Parsley-fern [Parsley fern] - *Tanacetum vulgare* L. (69, 158) (1900-1904)

Parsley-leaf haw [Parsley-leaved haw] - *Crataegus marshallii* Eggl. (5) (1913)

Parsley-leaf thorn [Parsley-leaved thorn] - *Crataegus marshallii* Eggl. (97) (1937)

Parsley-leaf yellow root [Parsley-leaved yellow root, Parsley-leaved yellow-root] - *Xanthorhiza* Marsh. (possibly) (8, 10, 13, 15, 138, 155) (1785-1942), *Xanthorhiza simplicissima* Marsh. (1, 5, 49) (1898-1932)

Parsnip [Parsnep] - *Daucus carota* L. (73) (1892) Harmony ME, *Pastinaca* L. (1, 50, 82, 93, 138, 155, 156, 158) (1900–present), *Pastinaca sativa* L. (6, 7, 10, 19, 46, 80, 85, 92, 106, 107, 122, 138, 148, 156, 157, 158, 184) (1671-1939) cultivated by English colonists by 1671

Parthenium - *Tanacetum parthenium* (L.) Schultz-Bip. (57) (1917)

Partridge - *Chamaecrista fasciculata* (Michx.) Greene var. *fasciculata* (187) (1818)

Partridge pea [Partridge-pea, Partridgepea] - *Chamaecrista* (L.) Moench (1, 93, 155) (1932-1942), *Chamaecrista fasciculata* (Michx.) Greene (5, 97, 125) (1913-1937), *Chamaecrista fasciculata* (Michx.) Greene var. *fasciculata* (3, 75, 109) (1894-1977), *Chamaecrista nictitans* (L.) Moench (50) (present)

Partridge plant - *Gaultheria procumbens* L. (75) (1894) NH

Partridge vine [Partridge-vine] - *Mitchella repens* L. (156) (1923)

Partridge wood - *Andira inermis* (W. Wright) Kunth ex DC. (92) (1876)

Partridge-berry [Partridgeberry, Partridge berry] - *Gaultheria* L. (10) (1818), *Gaultheria procumbens* L. (5, 7, 14, 49, 57, 59, 75, 92, 156, 186, 187) (1814-1923), *Mitchella* L. (1, 2, 10, 138, 156) (1818-1932), *Mitchella repens* L. (5, 6, 7, 19, 49, 52, 53, 54, 57, 61, 72, 92, 107, 109, 122, 124, 138, 156) (1828-1949), *Symphoricarpos occidentalis* Hook. (156) (1923)

Partridge-berry vine [Partridge berry vine] - *Mitchella repens* L. (92) (1876)

Parus-as (Pawnee, rabbitfoot) - *Lespedeza capitata* Michx. (37) (1919)

Pascimmon - *Diospyros virginiana* L. (181) (~1678)

Paseego (Snake, Shoshone) - *Camassia scilloides* (Raf.) Cory (101) (1905) MT

Pashaquaw - *Camassia quamash* (Pursh) Greene (35) (1806)

Pasiggo (Snake, Shoshone) - *Camassia scilloides* (Raf.) Cory (35) (1806) Meriwether Lewis - spelled Pas-she-co or Pas-shi-co

Pasnet - *Pastinaca sativa* L. (158) (1900)

Paspalum - *Paspalum* L. (1, 155) (1932-1942) Greek word for a kind of millet

Paspalum grass - *Paspalum dilatatum* Poir. (163) (1852)

Pasque flower [Pasque-flower, Pasqueflower, Pasque floures] - *Pulsatilla* Mill. (1, 13, 50, 93, 158) (1849–present), *Pulsatilla patens* (L.) Mill. (5, 37, 85) (1913-1932), *Pulsatilla patens* (L.) Mill.subsp. *multifida* (Pritz.) Zamels (3, 4, 6, 40, 49, 63, 72, 82, 86, 106, 109, 126, 127, 131, 148, 157, 180) (1633-1986)

Pass blummies - *Hepatica nobilis* Schreb. var. *acuta* (Pursh) Steyermark (76) (1896) Brodhead WI

Passe flower [Passe floure] - *Pulsatilla patens* (L.) Mill. subsp. *multifida* (Pritz.) Zamels (poss) (180) (1633)

Passerose (French) - *Alcea rosea* L. (158) (1900)

Passiflora - *Passiflora incarnata* L. (54, 57) (1905-1917)

Passion vine [Passion-vine] - *Passiflora incarnata* L. (5, 156) (1913-1923)

Passionflower [Passion-flower, Passion flower] - *Passiflora caerulea* L. (92) (1876), *Passiflora incarnata* L. (5, 46, 49, 52, 53, 54, 57, 156, 164) (1854-1923), *Passiflora* (1, 2, 4, 7, 10, 106, 109, 138, 155, 158) (1818-1986) for passion of Christ because flowers resemble crown of thorns, *Passiflora lutea* L. (3, 4) (1977-1986)

Passions - *Rumex patientia* L. (5, 92, 156, 158) (1876-1923) no longer in use by 1923

Pastel leaves - *Isatis tinctoria* L. (92) (1876)

Pastel-pea [Pastel pea] - *Tephrosia virginiana* (L.) Pers (124) (1937) TX

Pastèque (French) - *Citrullus lanatus* (Thunb.) Matsumura & Nakai (110) (1886)

Pastinake (German) - *Pastinaca sativa* L. (6) (1892)

Pastnip - *Pastinaca sativa* L. (158) (1900)

Pasture gass - *Poa trivialis* L. (19) (1840)

Pasture gooseberry - *Ribes cynosbati* L. (138, 155, 156) (1923-1942)

Pasture heliotrope - *Heliotropium tenellum* (Nutt.) Torr. (3, 50) (1977–present)

Pasture marigold - *Chrysanthemum segetum* L. (178) (1526)

Pasture rose - *Rosa carolina* L. (4) (1986), *Rosa virginiana* Mill. (5, 97) (1913-1937) OK

Pasture sage - *Artemisia frigida* Willd. (146, 156) (1923-1939)

Pasture sage-brush [Pasture sagebrush] - *Artemisia frigida* Willd. (5, 85, 122, 156, 157, 158) (1900–1937)

Pasture sage-bush - *Artemisia frigida* Willd. (93) (1936)

Pasture thistle - *Cirsium pumilum* (Nutt.) Spreng. (5, 156) (1913-1923), *Cirsium undulatum* (Nutt.) Spreng. var. *undulatum* (145) (1897) KS

Pasture weed - *Centaurea melitensis* L. (76) (1896) CA

Patagonian Indian wheat [Patagonia Indianwheat] - *Plantago patagonica* Jacq. (155) (1942)

Patagonian mint [Patagonia-mint] - *Mentha ×rotundifolia* (L.) Huds. [*longifolia × suaveolens*] (5, 92, 156) (1876–1923)

Patalpa - *Catalpa bignonioides* Walt. (156) (1923)

Path rush - *Juncus tenuis* Willd. (3) (1977)

Pathweed [Path-weed] - *Anthemis cotula* L. (156) (1923)

Patience - *Rumex patientia* L. (1, 19, 46, 92) (1671-1932) cultivated by English colonists by 1671

Patience dock - *Polygonum bistorta* L. (92) (1876), *Rumex patientia* L. (3, 4, 5, 50, 72, 97, 107, 138, 145, 155, 156, 158) (1897–present)

Patience Friseé (French) - *Rumex crispus* L. (6) (1892)

Patientia - *Rumex patientia* L. (107) (1640)

Patki-natawawi ((Ponca, acorn-bearing) - *Quercus macrocarpa* Michx. (37) (1919)

Patsuroka (Pawnee) - *Pediomelum esculentum* (Pursh) Rydb. (37) (1919)

Patterson's aster [Patterson aster] - *Machaeranthera bigelovii* (Gray) Greene var. *bigelovii* (155) (1942)

Patterson's bluegrass [Patterson's blue-grass] - *Poa abbreviata* R. Br. subsp. *pattersonii* (Vasey) A.& D. Löve & Kapoor (94) (1901)

Patterson's cryptanthe - *Cryptantha fendleri* (Gray) Greene (131) (1899)

Patterson's dawnflower - *Stylisma pickeringii* (Torr. ex M.A. Curtis) Gray (50) (present), *Stylisma pickeringii* (Torr. ex M.A. Curtis) Gray var. *pattersonii* (Fern. & Schub.) Myint (50) (present)

Patterson's loco [Patterson loco] - *Astragalus pattersonii* Gray (155) (1942)

Paullinia - *Paullinia* L. (138) (1923)

Paulownia - *Paulownia* Sieb. & Zucc. (138) (1923) for Anna Paulownia, 1795-1865, princess of the Netherlands, *Paulownia tomentosa* (Thunb.) Sieb. & Zucc. ex Steud. (possibly) (5) (1913)

Paul's betony [Pauls' betony] - *Lycopus americanus* Muhl. ex W. Bart. (5, 158) (1900–1913), *Lycopus virginicus* L. (6, 7, 49, 53, 92, 158) (1828–1922), *Veronica officinalis* L. (5, 156, 158) (1900–1923), *Veronica serpyllifolia* L. (5, 19, 156) (1840–1923)

Pauson - *Sanguinaria canadensis* L. (6, 7, 64, 92, 156, 158) (1828-1923) no longer in use by 1923

Pauta (Armenian and Georgian) - *Pyrus communis* L. (110) (1886)

Pavia jaune (French) - *Aesculus flava* Aiton (8) (1785)

Pavia rouge (French) - *Aesculus pavia* L. (8) (1785)

Pavonia - *Pavonia* Cav. (138) (1923) for Joseh Pavon, Spanish botanist

Pavot rouge (French) - *Papaver rhoeas* L. (158) (1900)

Pawms (i.e. palms) - *Salix discolor* Muhl. (158) (1900) England, catkins

Pe (Dakota) - *Ulmus americana* L. (37) (1919) Pe cha (Elm wood) pe ikcheka (Common elm)

Pe igatush (Omaha-Ponca, forehead pop) - *Physalis heterophylla* Nees (37) (1919)

Pe itazipa (Dakota, bow elm) - *Ulmus thomasii* Sarg. (37) (1919)

Pe tutuntunpa (Dakota Teton) - *Ulmus rubra* Muhl. (37) (1919)

Pe tututupa (Dakota) - *Ulmus rubra* Muhl. (37) (1919)

Pea [Peas, Pease] - *Lathyrus* L. (50, 138) (1923–present), *Pisum* L. (1, 10, 45, 109, 138) (1818-1949), *Pisum sativum* L. (19, 92, 107, 184) (1793-1919)

Pea shrub [Pea-shrub, Pea shrub] - *Caragana* Fabr. (4, 50, 138, 155) (1923–present)

Pea tree [Pea-tree] - *Caragana arborescens* Lam. (82, 106) (1930), *Caragana* Fabr. (1, 82) (1930-1932), *Caragana frutex* (L.) K. Koch (82) (1930), *Oxytropis* DC. (possibly) (1) (1932), *Sesbania* Scop. (92) (1876)

Pea vine [Peavine, Pea-vine] - *Amphicarpaea bracteata* (L.) Fern. (7, 35) (1806–1828), *Amphicarpaea bracteata* (L.) Fern. var. *comosa* (L.) Fern. (5, 158) (1900–1913), *Apios americana* Medik. (34, 38) (1820–1834), *Calystegia sepium* (L.) R. Br. subsp. *sepium* (77) (1898) Sulphur Grove OH, *Ipomoea pandurata* (L.) G. F. W. Mey. (77) (1898) Sulphur Grove OH, *Lathyrus* L. (155) (1942), *Vicia americana* Muhl. ex Willd. (156) (1923)

Pea without parchment in the cods [Pease without parchment in the cods] - *Pisum sativum* L. (178) (1526)

Peaberry palm - *Thrinax* Sw. (109) (1949)

Peach [Peaches] or Peach tree - *Prunus* L. (4, 155, 158) (1900-1986), *Prunus persica* (L.) Batsch (4, 5, 7, 19, 50, 52, 53, 54, 57, 58, 61, 72, 82, 92, 97, 106, 107, 109, 110, 125, 137, 138, 155, 156, 158, 165) (1633–present)

Peach oak - *Quercus phellos* L. (5) (1913)

Peach-leaf bellflower [Peach leafe belflower] - *Campanula persicifolia* L. (50, 178) (1526–present)

Peach-leaf dock [Peachleaf dock, Peach-leaved dock] - *Rumex altissimus* Wood (5, 80, 93, 122, 131, 156) (1899-1937)

Peach-leaf willow [Peachleaf willow, Peach-leaved willow] - *Salix amygdaloides* Anderss. (1, 3, 4, 5, 50, 65, 72, 82, 85, 91, 93, 95, 97, 138, 155, 156) (1907–present)

Peachwort [Peach-wort] - *Persicaria maculosa* Gray (5, 92, 156, 158) (1898-1923)

Peacock flower [Peacock-flower] - *Delonix regia* (Bojer ex Hook.) Raf. (109) (1949)

Pea-flower locust [Pea flower locust - *Robinia pseudoacacia* L. (5, 157, 158) (1900–1929)

Peanut [Pea nut, Pea-nut] - *Arachis hypogaea* L. (7, 19, 55, 92, 107, 109, 110, 155) (1828–1949) Peru, *Arachis* L. (155) (1942)

Pear - *Pyrus communis* L. (1, 5, 19, 82, 92, 107, 109, 110) (1840-1949), *Pyrus* L. (10, 82, 106, 109, 156, 158, 184) (1793-1949)

Pear haw - *Crataegus calpodendron* (Ehrh.) Medik. (5, 157) (1913–1929)

Pear hawthorn - *Crataegus calpodendron* (Ehrh.) Medik. (155) (1942)

Pear thorn - *Crataegus calpodendron* (Ehrh.) Medik. (5, 50, 157) (1900–present)

Pear vine - *Calystegia sepium* (L.) R. Br. subsp. *sepium* (5) (1913)

Pear-apple - *Datura stramonium* L. (6) (1892)

Pear-fashion radish [Peare-fashion radish] - *Raphanus sativus* L. (180) (1633)

Pearl acacia - *Acacia podalyriifolia* A. Cunningham ex G. Don (109, 137, 155) (1923-1949)

Pearl baneberry [Pearl bane berry] - *Actaea spicata* L. (42) (1814)

Pearl barley - *Hordeum vulgare* L. (49, 55, 92) (1876-1911)

Pearl bush [Pearl-bush, Pearlbush] - *Exochorda* Lindl. (109, 138) (1923-1949), *Exochorda racemosa* (Lindl.) Rehd. (112) (1937) Neb

Pearl grass - *Arrhenatherum elatius* (L.) Beauv. ex J. Presl & C. Presl (3, 5) (1913-1977), *Briza media* L. (5) (1913), *Glyceria canadensis* (Michx.) Trin. (75) (1894) MA, children's name

Pearl milkweed - *Matelea biflora* (Raf.) Woods (124) (1937) TX

Pearl millet [Pearlmillet] - *Pennisetum glaucum* (L.) R. Br. (45, 50, 56, 67, 68, 87, 109, 138, 151, 155, 163) (1884–present), *Sorghum bicolor* (L.) Moench subsp. *bicolor* (158) (1900)

Pearl moss - *Chondrus crispus* (L.) J. Stackhouse (92) (1876)

Pearl plant [Pearl-plant] - *Buglossoides arvensis* (L.) I. M. Johnston (5, 156, 157, 158) (1900–1929), *Lithospermum officinale* L. (5, 92, 156) (1876–1923), *Onosmodium virginianum* (L.) A. DC. (156) (1923)

Pearl spurry - *Sagina saginoides* (L.) H. Karst. (19) (1840)

Pearl wattle - *Acacia podalyriifolia* A. Cunningham ex G. Don (50) (present)

Pearlberry [Pearl berry] - *Actaea rubra* (Aiton) Willd. (5) (1913)

Pear-leaf crab [Pearleaf crab] - *Malus prunifolia* (Willd.) Borkh. (137, 138) (1923-1931)

Pear-leaf hawthorn [Pear leaved hawthorn] - *Photinia pyrifolia* (Lam.) Robertson & Phipps (42) (1814)

Pear-leaf thorn [Pear leaved thorn] - *Crataegus crus-galli* L. (possibly) (8) (1785), *Photinia pyrifolia* (Lam.) Robertson & Phipps (19) (1840)

Pear-leaf wintergreen [Pear leaf wintergreen, Pear leaved wintergreen, Pear-leaved wintergreen] - *Pyrola americana* Sweet (5, 19, 49, 92, 158) (1840-1913)

Pearl-everlasting [Pearleverlasting] - *Anaphalis* DC. (155) (1942)

Pearl-flower life-everlasting [Pearl-flowered life everlasting, Pearl-flowered life-everlasting] - *Anaphalis margaritacea* (L.) Benth. & Hook (19, 49, 92) (1840-1898)

Pearls-of-Spain [Pearls of Spain] - *Muscari botryoides* (L.) Mills (156, 158) (1900-1923), *Muscari neglectum* Guss. ex Ten. (5) (1913)

Pearlweed [Pearl-weed] - *Sagina* L. (158) (1900), *Sagina nodosa* (L.) Fenzl (156) (1923)

Pearlwort [Pearl-wort, Pearl wort] - *Sagina* L. (1, 4, 50, 10, 13, 15, 46, 109, 138, 155, 156, 158) (1818–present), *Sagina procumbens* L. (19, 92) (1840-1876), *Sagina subulata* (Sw.) K. Presl (138) (1923)

Pearlwort spurry [Pearl-wort spurrey] - *Sagina saginoides* (L.) H. Karst. (187) (1818)

Pearly mouse-ear everlasting - *Antennaria plantaginifolia* (L.) Richards (5, 156) (1913-1923)

Pearly pussy-toes [Pearly pussytoes] - *Antennaria anaphaloides* Rydb. (50) (present)

Pearly-everlasting [Pearly everlasting] - *Anaphalis* DC. (1, 4, 50, 93) (1932–present), *Anaphalis margaritacea* (L.) Benth. & Hook (3, 4, 5, 40, 49, 85, 106, 107, 156, 158) (1900-1986), *Antennaria plantaginifolia* (L.) Richards (76, 158) (1896-1900) Salem MA

Peasant's-clock [Peasant's clock] - *Taraxacum officinale* G.H. Weber ex Wiggers (62) (1912) IN, Old English name

Peasant's-mustard [Pesants Mustard] - *Iberis amara* L. (178) (1526)

Peat moss [Peet moss] - *Sphagnum palustre* L. (19) (1840)

Peat pink [Peatpink] - *Silene caroliniana* subsp. *pensylvanica* (Michx.) Clausen (138) (1923), *Silene latifolia* Poir. subsp. *alba* (Mill.) Greuter & Burdet (138) (1923)

Peatweed [Peat weed, Peat-weed] - *Decodon verticillatus* (L.) Ell. (5, 106, 156) (1913-1930)

Pea-vine clover [Pea vine clover] - *Trifolium pratense* L. (5, 45, 156, 158) (1913–1923), *Vicia americana* Muhl. ex Willd. (5) (1913)

Pebble vetch [Pebbel-vetch] - *Vicia sativa* L. (5, 156, 158) (1900-1923)

Pebigumškike (Chippewa) - *Polygonum pensylvanicum* L. (105) (1932)

Peca - *Podophyllum peltatum* L. (6, 7) (1828-1932)

Pecan [Peccan] - *Carya illinoinensis* (Wangenh.) K. Koch (1, 2, 3, 4, 5, 7, 8, 10, 12, 19, 27, 35, 50, 65, 72, 82, 92, 97, 107, 121, 138, 155, 156, 158) (1785–present)

Pecan nut [Peccan nut] - *Carya illinoinensis* (Wangenh.) K. Koch (19) (1840)

Pecan-nut hickory [Pecannut hickory] - *Carya illinoinensis* (Wangenh.) K. Koch (20) (1857)

Pecaunes (Indians, sic) - *Carya illinoinensis* (Wangenh.) K. Koch (107) (1919)

Peccane - *Carya illinoinensis* (Wangenh.) K. Koch (39) (1814)

Peche - *Prunus persica* (L.) Batsch (179) (1526)

Pêcher (French) - *Prunus persica* (L.) Batsch (158) (1900)

Pecho Mountain manzanita [PechoMountain manzanita] - *Arctostaphylos pechoensis* (Dudley ex Abrams) Dudley ex Munz (155) (1942)

Peck's bulrush - *Scirpus* ×*peckii* Britt. [*atrocinctus* × *atrovirens* and × *pedicellatus*] (5) (1913)

Peck's Jack-in-the-pulpit - *Arisaema triphyllum* (L.) Schott subsp. *pusillum* (Peck) Huttleston (5) (1913)

Peck's sedge - *Carex peckii* Howe (50) (present)

Peck's thorn - *Crataegus intricata* Lange (5) (1913)

Pecos rose - *Rosa woodsii* Lindl. var. *woodsii* (155) (1942)

Pecten Veneris - *Scandix pecten-veneris* L. (178) (1526)

Pectis - *Pectis angustifolia* Torr. (3, 157) (1929-1977), *Pectis* L. (155, 158) (1900-1942)

Pedate-leaf wakerobin [Pedate-leaved wake-robin] - *Arisaema dracontium* (L.) Schott (187) (1818)

Pedelion - *Alchemilla monticola* Opiz (possibly) (156) (1923)

Pedelyon - *Alchemilla* L. (179) (1526), *Helleborus niger* L. (179) (1526)

Pedicularia - *Pedicularis canadensis* L. (156) (1923)

Pedicularis - *Pedicularis* L. (155) (1942)

Peeck hickory nut [Peeck hickerie nut] - Carya Nutt. (181) (~1678)

Peekandel - *Rhizophora mangle* L. (174) (1753)

Pee-mottenga - *Fimbristylis spathacea* Roth (174) (1753)

Peepul - *Ficus religiosa* L. (107, 109) (1919-1949)

Peg-root - *Helleborus viridis* L. (156) (1923)

Pegwood [Peg-wood] - *Cornus sanguinea* L. (107) (1919), *Euonymus atropurpurea* Jacq. (92) (1876), *Euonymus europaea* L. (5, 156) (1913-1923)

Pehaca (Louisiana) - *Euphorbia corollata* L. (7) (1828) means emetic root

Peh'e (Omaha-Ponca) - *Lagenaria siceraria* (Molina) Standl. (37) (1919)

Peh'-hishuji (Winnebago [to make gourds red]) - *Sanguinaria canadensis* L. (37) (1919)

Peking cotoneaster - *Cotoneaster acutifolius* Turcz. (112, 138) (1923-1937)

Peking lilac - *Syringa reticulata* subsp. *pekinensis* (Rupr.) P.S. Green & M.C. Chang (138) (1923)

Pelargonium - *Pelargonium* L'Hér. ex Aiton (138) (1923) from Greek for 'stork's bill', *Pelargonium odoratissimum* (L.) L'Hér. ex Aiton (92) (1876)

Pelican Dutchman's-pipe [Pelican Dutchmanspipe] - *Aristolochia grandiflora* Sw. (155) (1942)

Pelican flower [Pelicanflower, Pelican-flower, Pellican flower] - *Aristolochia grandiflora* Sw. (109, 138) (1923-1949), *Aristolochia serpentaria* L. (5, 64, 92, 156, 158) (1876-1923)

Pellas - *Malva rotundifolia* L. (5, 156, 157, 158) (1900-1929)

Pellawa (Finnish) - *Linum usitatissimum* L. (110) (1886)

Pellitorie of the wall - *Parietaria officinalis* L. (178) (1526)

Pellitory - *Parietaria* L. (1, 2, 7, 10, 50, 122, 155, 158, 167) (1814–present), *Parietaria officinalis* L. (107) (1919), *Parietaria pensylvanica* Muhl. ex Willd. (19, 80, 85, 93, 95, 156, 157) (1840-1936), *Tanacetum parthenium* (L.) Schultz-Bip. (5, 156, 158) (1900-1923), *Zanthoxylum americanum* Mill. (6, 7, 58) (1828-1892)

Pellitory bark - *Zanthoxylum americanum* Mill. (92, 156, 157, 158, 184) (1793-1936)

Pellitory of Spain - *Parthenium integrifolium* L. (46) (1610), *Peucedanum ostruthium* (L.) W.D.J. Koch (5, 156) (1913-1923)

Pellitory-leaf amaranth [Pellitory-leaved amaranth] - *Amaranthus graecizans* L. (165) (1768)

Pellucid nettle - *Pilea pumila* (L.) Gray var. *pumila* (187) (1818)

Pelotazo - *Abutilon incanum* (Link) Sweet (50) (present)

Pembina - *Amelanchier canadensis* (L.) Medik. (possibly) (47) (1852), *Viburnum opulus* L. (37, 107) (1919), *Viburnum opulus* L. var. *americanum* Aiton (possibly) (105) (1932)

Pemmican-berry [Pemmican berry] - *Amelanchier canadensis* (L.) Medik. (108) (1878)

Pencil cedar - *Juniperus virginiana* L. (6, 157, 158) (1892–1929)

Pencil cholla - *Opuntia leptocaulis* DC. (4) (1986)

Pencil flower [Pencil-flower] - *Stylosanthes biflora* (L.) Britton, Sterns & Poggenb. (3, 4, 5, 19, 57, 92, 97, 158) (1840-1986)

Pencil tree [Pencil-tree] - *Baccharis halimifolia* L. (5, 7, 156) (1828-1923)

Pencilwood [Pencil wood, Pencil-wood] - *Juniperus virginiana* L. (5, 92, 157, 158) (1876-1929)

Pendant arethusa - *Triphora trianthophora* (Sw.) Rydb. subsp. *trianthophora* (42) (1814)

Pendulous amaranth - *Amaranthus caudatus* L. (165) (1768)

Pendulous-pod locoweed - *Oxytropis deflexa* (Pallas) DC. var. *sericea* Torr. & Gray (4) (1986)

Penerial yarrow - *Achillea millefolium* L. (46) (1879)

Peneriall - *Hedeoma pulegioides* (L.) Pers. (46) (1879)

Pennisetum - *Pennisetum* L.C. Rich. ex Pers. (155) (1942)

Pennsylvania anemone [Pennsylvanian anemone, Pensylvanian anemone, Pensylvanican anemone] - *Anemone canadensis* L. (42, 158, 165) (1807-1900)

Pennsylvania bittercress [Pennsylvania bitter cress] - *Cardamine pensylvanica* Muhl. ex Willd. (5, 50, 72) (1907–present)

Pennsylvania black currant [Pennsylvanian black currants] - *Ribes americanum* Mill. (8) (1785)

Pennsylvania blackberry - *Rubus pensilvanicus* Poir. (50) (present)

Pennsylvania buttercup - *Ranunculus pensylvanicus* L. f. (50, 155) (1942–present)

Pennsylvania campion [Pennsylvanian campion] - *Silene caroliniana* subsp. *pensylvanica* (Michx.) Clausen (2) (1895)

Pennsylvania catchfly - *Silene caroliniana* subsp. *pensylvanica* (Michx.) Clausen (156, 187) (1818-1923)

Pennsylvania cinquefoil - *Potentilla pensylvanica* L. (50, 155) (1942–present), *Potentilla pensylvanica* L. var. *pensylvanica* (50) (present)

Pennsylvania clotbur - *Xanthium strumarium* L. var. *canadense* (Mill.) Torr. & Gray (5, 97) (1913-1937)

Pennsylvania dogwood - *Cornus rugosa* Lam. (6) (1892)

Pennsylvania dwarf mountain maple [Pennsylvanian dwarf mountain maple] - *Acer pensylvanicum* L. (8) (1785)

Pennsylvania eatonia [Pennsylvanian eatonia] - *Sphenopholis nitida* (Biehler) Scribn. (56, 66, 72) (1901-1907)

Pennsylvania knotweed [Pennsylvanian knot-weed] - *Polygonum pensylvanicum* L. (187) (1818)

Pennsylvania maple [Pensylvanian maple] - *Acer pensylvanicum* L. (165) (1768)

Pennsylvania mountain laurel [Pennsylvanian mountain laurel] - *Rhododendron maximum* L. (8, 34) (1785-1834)

Pennsylvania oat grass - *Sphenopholis pensylvanica* (L.) A.S. Hitchc. (42) (1814)

Pennsylvania pellitory [Pennsylvanian pellitory] - *Parietaria pensylvanica* Muhl. ex Willd. (3, 4, 5, 50, 72, 97, 131, 155) (1899–present)

Pennsylvania persicaria - *Polygonum pensylvanicum* L. (5, 93, 97, 131) (1899-1937)

Pennsylvania red-bud andromeda [Pennsylvanian red-bud andromeda] - *Leucothoe racemosa* (L.) Gray (possibly) (8) (1785)

Pennsylvania rush - *Juncus gymnocarpus* Coville (5, 50) (1913–present)

Pennsylvania saxifrage - *Saxifraga pensylvanica* L. (5) (1913)

Pennsylvania sedge [Pennsylvanian sedge] - *Carex pennsylvanica* Lam. (5, 50, 66, 72) (1893–present)

Pennsylvania sharp-key ash [Pennsylvanian sharp-keyed ash] - *Fraxinus pennsylvanica* Marsh. (8) (1785)

Pennsylvania shrubby birthwort [Pennsylvanian shrubby birthwort] - *Aristolochia macrophylla* Lam. (8) (1785)

Pennsylvania smartweed - *Polygonum pensylvanicum* L. (4, 19, 50, 62, 72, 80, 82, 155) (1840–present)

Pennsylvania sumac [Pennsylvania sumach] - *Rhus glabra* L. (5, 49, 53, 55, 156, 157, 158) (1898-1929)

Pennsylvania triple-fruit papaw [Pennsylvanian triple-fruited papaw] - *Asimina triloba* (L.) Dunal (8) (1785)

Pennsylvania watercress [Pennsylvania water-cress] - *Cardamine pensylvanica* Muhl. ex Willd. (187) (1818)

Pennsylvania white whortleberry [Pennsylvanian white whortleberry] - *Symphoricarpos albus* (L.) Blake (8) (1785)

Pennsylvania winter-cherry [Pennsylvanian winter-cherry] - *Physalis viscosa* L. (187) (1818)

Penny flower [Penny-flower] - *Lunaria annua* L. (5, 107, 156) (1913-1923)

Penny tree [Penny-tree] - *Ptelea trifoliata* L. (156) (1923)

Pennycress [Penny cress, Penny-cress] - *Thlaspi arvense* L. (3, 19, 80, 92, 107) (1840-1977), *Thlaspi* L. (1, 4, 93) (1932-1986)

Penny-grass [Penny grass] - *Rhinanthus minor* L. subsp. *minor* (5, 92, 156) (1913-1923) no longer in use by 1923

Penny-hedge [Penny hedge] - *Alliaria petiolata* (Bieb.) Cavara & Grande (5, 158) (1900-1913)

Penny-John [Penny John] - *Hypericum perforatum* L. (5, 156, 157, 158) (1900-1929)

Penny-post [Penny post] - *Hydrocotyle americana* L. (5, 76, 156) (1896-1923) Western US, no longer in use by 1923

Penny-rattle [Penny rattle] - *Rhinanthus minor* L. subsp. *minor* (5, 156) (1913-1923) no longer in use by 1923

Pennyroyal [Penny-royal, Penny royal, Penniroyal] - *Cunila* L. (167, 184) (1814), *Hedeoma hispida* Pursh (85) (1932), *Hedeoma* Pers. (158) (1900), *Hedeoma pulegioides* (L.) Pers. (3, 7, 19, 41, 49, 53, 61, 62, 121, 157, 158, 184, 186) (1770-1977), *Mentha pulegium* L. (46, 106, 107, 109, 138, 190) (1671-1949), *Pycnanthemum virginianum* (L.) T. Dur. & B.D. Jackson ex B.L. Robins. & Fern. (5, 75) (1894-1913)

Pennyroyal tree - *Satureja viminea* L. (92) (1876)

Pennyroyal-leaf cunila [Penny royal leaved cunila] - *Hedeoma pulegioides* (L.) Pers. (42) (1814)

Pennywinkle - *Vinca minor* L. (158) (1900)

Penny-winkler - *Vinca minor* L. (158) (1900)

Pennywort [Penny-wort, Penny wort] - *Cymbalaria muralis* P.G. Gaertn., B. Mey. & Scherb. (5, 107, 156) (1913-1923), *Hydrocotyle americana* L. (184) (1793), *Hydrocotyle* L. (155) (1942), *Obolaria virginica* L. (5, 19, 156) (1840-1923)

Pensee (French) - *Viola tricolor* L. (6) (1892)

Pensée sauage (French) - *Viola tricolor* L. (158) (1900)

Penstemon - *Penstemon* Schmidel (138, 155, 156) (1923-1942), *Penthorum* L. (50, 155) (1942–present), *Penthorum sedoides* L. (57, 174, 177) (1753-1917)

Peony [Paeony] - *Paeonia* L. (7, 15, 82, 109, 138) (1828-1949), *Paeonia lactiflora* Pallas (107) (1919), *Paeonia officinalis* L. (7, 19, 49, 52, 57, 82) (1828-1930)

Peperidge (Dutch near New York) - *Nyssa aquatica* L. (20, 187) (1818-1857)

Peperomia - *Peperomia maculosa* (L.) Hook. (138) (1923), *Peperomia* Ruiz & Pavón (138) (1923)

Peplios - *Euphorbia peplus* L. (178) (1526)

Peplis - *Euphorbia peplus* L. (178) (1526)

Pepo - *Cucumis melo* L. (107) (15th Century), *Cucurbita pepo* L. (53, 57, 59, 60) (1902–1922)

Pepone - *Cucumis melo* L. (107) (1617)

Pepone (Italy) - *Cucumis melo* L. (107) (1919)

Peppar-rot (Swedish) - *Armoracia rusticana* P.G. Gaertn., B. Mey. & Scherb. (110) (1886)

Pepper - *Piper* L. (109, 138) (1923-1949)

Pepper bush [Pepper-bush, Pepperbush] - *Clethra alnifolia* L. (106) (1930), *Leucothoe racemosa* (L.) Gray (possibly) (19, 92, 156) (1840-1923), *Lyonia ligustrina* (L.) DC. (156) (1923)

Pepper dulse - *Osmundea pinnatifida* (Hudson) Stackhouse (107) (1919)

Pepper plant [Pepper-plant] - *Capsella bursa-pastoris* (L.) Medik. (5, 73, 156, 157, 158) (1892–1929), *Polygonum hydropiper* L. (5, 156, 157, 158) (1900–1929)

Pepper root [Pepper-root] - *Cardamine concatenata* (Michx.) Sw. (72, 97, 156) (1907-1937), *Cardamine diphylla* (Michx.) Wood (2, 13, 15, 19, 92, 107, 156) (1840-1923), *Cardamine* L. (15, 109, 156) (1895-1949), *Veratrum viride* Ait. (156) (1923)

Pepper tree [Pepper-tree, Peppertree] - *Ampelopsis arborea* (L.) Koehne (8) (1785), *Schinus* L. (138) (1923), *Schinus molle* L. (76, 106) (1896-1930) red berries are used as pepper substitute

Pepper vine [Pepper-vine, Peppervine] - *Ampelopsis arborea* (L.) Koehne (5, 76, 106, 109, 122, 138, 155, 156) (1913-1949), *Ampelopsis* Michx. (50, 106) (1930–present)

Pepper vine of South Texas - *Ampelopsis arborea* (L.) Koehne (possibly) (124) (1937)

Pepperage tree - *Nyssa* L. (190) (~1759)

Pepper-and-salt - *Erigenia bulbosa* (Michx.) Nutt. (5, 76, 156, 158) (1896–1923), *Erigenia* Nutt. (1, 156) (1923–1932)

Pepper-and-shot - *Capsella bursa-pastoris* (L.) Medik. (157, 158) (1900-1929)

Peppercress [Pepper cress] - *Lepidium virginicum* L. (7, 92) (1828-1876)

Pepper-crop [Pepper crop] - *Sedum acre* L. (5, 156) (1913-1923)

Pepper-grass [Peppergrass, Pepper grass] - *Capsella bursa-pastoris* (L.) Medik. (74) (1893), *Coronopus* Zinn (possibly) (7) (1828), *Lepidium austrinum* Small. (4) (1986), *Lepidium campestre* (L.) Aiton f. (156) (1923), *Lepidium densiflorum* Schrad. (3, 4, 5, 85, 121) (1913-1986), *Lepidium* L. (1, 2, 4, 13, 15, 35, 63, 93, 109, 122, 138, 156, 158) (1895-1986), *Lepidium oblongum* Small (97) (1937), *Lepidium sativum* L. (19, 92, 156) (1840-1923), *Lepidium virginicum* L. (4, 15, 145) (1895-1986), *Lepidium virginicum* L. var. *medium* (Greene) C.L. Hitchc. (145) (1897), *Sisyrinchium an-*

gustifolium Mill. (5, 156) (1913-1923), *Sisyrinchium atlanticum* Bicknell (5) (1913)

Pepperidge [Peperidge] - *Ampelopsis arborea* (L.) Koehne (106) (1930), *Nyssa* L. (2, 7) (1828-1895), *Nyssa sylvatica* Marsh. (2, 5, 19, 105, 106, 107, 109, 156) (1840-1949)

Peppermint [Peper-mint] - *Mentha* ×*piperita* L. [*aquatica* × *spicata*] (3, 5, 6, 19, 49, 50, 52, 53, 54, 55, 57, 59, 60, 62, 63, 80, 82, 92, 93, 95, 97, 106, 107, 109, 120, 138, 156, 157) (1704–present), *Mentha arvensis* L. (85) (1932), *Mentha* L. (1) (1932)

Pepperridge bush [Pepperidge-bush - *Berberis vulgaris* L. (5, 92, 156, 157, 158) (1876–1929) England

Pepper-rod [Pepper rod] - *Croton humilis* L. (92) (1876)

Pepper-turnip [Pepper turnip] - *Arisaema triphyllum* (L.) Schott (5, 7, 64, 156, 158) (1828-1923)

Pepper-weed [Pepperweed] - *Capsella bursa-pastoris* (L.) Medik. (156) (1923), *Lepidium* L. (50, 155) (1942–present)

Pepperwood [Pepper-wood, Pepper wood] - *Umbellularia californica* (Hook. & Arn.) Nutt. (77, 106) (1898-1930), *Zanthoxylum clava-herculis* L. (5, 15, 97, 156, 158) (1895-1937)

Pepperwood tree - *Umbellularia californica* (Hook. & Arn.) Nutt. (54) (1905)

Pepperwort [Pepper wort, Pepper wort, Pepper woort] - *Cardamine diphylla* (Michx.) Wood (86) (1878), *Lepidium* L. (13, 63) (1849-1899), *Lepidium latifolium* L. (46, 178, 180) (1526-1671) cultivated by English colonists by 1671, *Lepidium sativum* L. (92) (1876), *Marsilea* L. (4, 50, 138, 155) (1923–present), *Marsilea quadrifolia* L. (5) (1913), *Marsilea vestita* Hook. & Grev. (3) (1977)

Peprage - *Berberis vulgaris* L. (157, 158) (1900-1929)

Percely - *Petroselinum crispum* (P. Mill.) Nyman ex A.W. Hill (179) (1526)

Peregil (Spanish) - *Petroselinum crispum* (P. Mill.) Nyman ex A.W. Hill (158) (1900)

Perennial adonis [Perrenial adonis] - *Adonis vernalis* L. (165) (1768)

Perennial balloon vine - *Cardiospermum microcarpum* Kunth (124) (1937)

Perennial bent - *Agrostis perennans* (Walt.) Tuckerman (94) (1901)

Perennial blue flax [Perrennial blue flax] - *Linum lewisii* Pursh (124) (1937)

Perennial bursage - *Ambrosia tomentosa* Nutt. (3, 4) (1977-1986)

Perennial clover - *Trifolium campestre* Schreber. (174, 177) (1753-1762), *Trifolium pratense* L. (66) (1903)

Perennial flax - *Linum perenne* L. (2, 86, 92, 138, 155) (1878-1942)

Perennial foxtail - *Setaria parviflora* (Poir.) Kerguélen (119) (1938), *Setaria verticillata* (L.) Beauv. (122) (1937)

Perennial foxtail grass - *Setaria parviflora* (Poir.) Kerguélen (5) (1913)

Perennial goosefoot - *Chenopodium bonus-henricus* L. (5, 156) (1913-1923)

Perennial honesty - *Lunaria rediviva* L. (138) (1923)

Perennial kidney bean [Perennial kidney-bean] - *Glycine* Willd. (8) (1785), *Phaseolus polystachios* (L.) B.S.P. (187) (1818)

Perennial lupin - *Lupinus perennis* L. (187) (1818)

Perennial morning-glory [Perennial morning glory] - *Convolvulus arvensis* L. (80) (1913)

Perennial pea - *Lathyrus latifolius* L. (50, 138, 156) (1923–present)

Perennial peavine - *Lathyrus latifolius* L. (155) (1942)

Perennial quaking grass - *Briza media* L. (50) (present)

Perennial ragweed - *Ambrosia psilostachya* DC. (80, 145) (1897-1913)

Perennial ray grass [Perennial ray-grass] - *Lolium perenne* L. (45) (1896)

Perennial rye - *Lolium perenne* L. (5, 56) (1901-1913)

Perennial rye grass [Perennial rye-grass, Perennial ryegrass] - *Lolium perenne* L. (45, 50, 56, 66, 68, 90, 92, 109, 111, 119, 122, 129, 138, 140, 143, 152, 155, 163) (1852–present), *Lolium perenne* L. subsp. *multiflorum* (Lam.) Husnot (3) (1977), *Lolium perenne* L. var. *perenne* (3, 50) (1977–present)

Perennial salt-marsh aster - *Symphyotrichum tenuifolium* (L.) Nesom (5) (1913)

Perennial satin flower [Perennial satin-flower] - *Lunaria rediviva* L. (156) (1923)

Perennial satin-pod [Perennial satin pod] - *Lunaria rediviva* L. (5) (1913)

Perennial sow-thistle [Perennial sow thistle] - *Sonchus arvensis* L. (62, 80, 82, 106) (1912-1930)

Perennial sweet pea [Perennial sweetpea] - *Lathyrus latifolius* L. (4) (1986)

Perennial wild flax - *Linum perenne* L. (108) (1878)

Perennial wine cup - *Callirhoe involucrata* (Torr. & Gray) Gray (124) (1937)

Perennial worm grass - *Spigelia marilandica* (L.) L. (6) (1892)

Pereskia - *Pereskia* Mill. (138, 155) (1931-1942)

Perfoliata - *Bupleurum rotundifolium* L. (174, 178) (1523-1753)

Perfoliate bellflower [Perfoliate bell flower] - *Triodanis perfoliata* (L.) Nieuwl. var. *biflora* (Ruiz & Pavón) Bradley (42) (1814)

Perfoliate bellwort [Perfoliate bell-wort - *Uvularia perfoliata* L. (5, 187) (1818-1913)

Perfoliate cabbage - *Conringia orientalis* (L.) Dumort. (19) (1840)

Perfoliate ever-flowering woodbind [Perfoliate ever flowring Woodbind] - *Lonicera sempervirens* (181) (~1678)

Perfoliate fever-root - *Triosteum perfoliatum* L. (186, 187) (1814-1818)

Perfoliate honeysuckle - *Lonicera caprifolium* L. (5, 156) (1913-1923)

Perfoliate pennycress [Perfoliate penny cress] - *Microthlaspi perfoliatum* (L.) F.K. Mey. (4, 5) (1913-1986)

Perfoliated bellwort - *Uvularia perfoliata* L. (72) (1907)

Perfonata - *Arctium lappa* L. (174) (1753)

Perfume-balls [Perfumeballs] - *Gaillardia suavis* (Gray & Engelm.) Britton & Rusby (50) (present)

Perfumed cherry - *Prunus mahaleb* L. (1, 4, 5, 156) (1913-1986)

Perilla - *Perilla frutescens* (L.) Britton (5, 72, 158) (1900-1913), *Perilla* L. (50, 138, 155, 158) (1923–present)

Periwinkle - *Vinca* L. (1, 4, 50, 109, 138, 155, 158) (1900–present) from ancient Latin name 'pervinca', *Vinca major* L. (92, 122) (1876-1937), *Vinca minor* L. (5, 7, 19, 92, 124, 156, 158, 184) (1793-1937)

Perpetual begonia - *Begonia cucullata* Willd. (138) (1923)

Perpetual strawberry - *Fragaria vesca* L. (107) (1919)

Perplexed tick trefoil [Perplexed ticktrefoil] - *Desmodium perplexum* Schub. (50) (present)

Persea - *Persea* Mill. (138) (1923)

Persely - *Euphorbia corollata* L. (7) (1828)

Persian berry [Persian-berry] - *Frangula alnus* Mill. (5, 156) (1913-1923)

Persian centaruea - *Centaurea dealbata* Willd. (138) (1923)

Persian clover - *Trifolium resupinatum* L. (4) (1986)

Persian elder - *Syringa vulgaris* L. (156) (1923)

Persian feverfew - *Chrysanthemum coccineum* Willd. (92) (1876)

Persian insect powder - *Tanacetum coccineum* (Willd.) Grierson (92) (1876)

Persian jasmine - *Syringa vulgaris* L. (156) (1923)

Persian lilac - *Melia azedarach* L. (49) (1898), *Syringa* ×*persica* L. [*afghanica* × *laciniata*] (19, 82, 92, 109, 112, 135, 138) (1840-1949)

Persian rye grass [Persian ryegrass] - *Lolium persicum* Boiss. & Hohen. ex Boiss. (50) (present)

Persian walnut - *Juglans regia* L. (107, 109, 138) (1919-1949)

Persian willow - *Chamerion angustifolium* (L.) Holub subsp. *angustifolium* (5, 156, 157, 158) (1900-1929)

Persica - *Prunus persica* (L.) Batsch (57) (1917)

Persicaria - *Polygonum* L. (10, 106) (1818-1930), *Polygonum pensylvanicum* L. (122) (1937)

Persicaria - *Polygonum persicaria* L. (158) (1900)

Persicary - *Polygonum persicaria* L. (158) (1900)

Persil - *Conioselinum chinense* (L.) Britton, Sterns & Poggenb. (46) (1879)

Persil (French) - *Petroselinum crispum* (P. Mill.) Nyman ex A.W. Hill (158) (1900)

Persimmon [Persimon, Persimons] or Persimmon tree [Persimon tree, Persimon-tree] - *Diospyros* L. (1, 2, 8, 10, 27, 18, 20, 106, 109, 138, 155, 156, 181) (1785-1949), *Diospyros virginiana* L. (3, 4, 5, 7, 19, 41, 44, 46, 49, 57, 58, 63, 65, 72, 92, 97, 103, 107, 121, 135, 156, 184) (1770-1986)

Persimmon bark - *Diospyros virginiana* L. (7, 92, 187, 189) (1767-1876)

Persimon Baum (German) - *Diospyros virginiana* L. (7) (1828)

Persistent-sepal yellow-cress [Persistent sepal yellowcress] - *Rorippa calycina* (Engelm.) Rydb. (50) (present)

Pertimugget - *Galium aparine* L. (158) (1900)

Peru-apple [Peru apple] - *Datura stramonium* L. (5, 156) (1913-1923)

Peruinkle - *Vinca minor* L. (178) (1526)

Perusse (French Canada) - *Tsuga canadensis* (L.) Carr. (20) (1857)

Peruvian bluebell - *Nicandra physalodes* (L.) Gaertn. (158) (1900)

Peruvian cereus [Peru cereus] - *Cereus repandus* (L.) Mill. (155) (1942)

Peruvian ground-cherry [Peruvian groundcherry, Peruvian ground cherry] - *Physalis heterophylla* Nees (5) (1913), *Physalis peruviana* L. (138) (1923)

Peruvian mastic tree [Peruvian mastic-tree] - *Schinus molle* L. (109) (1949)

Peruvian mastich - *Schinus molle* L. (92) (1876)

Peruvian spike moss [Peruvian spikemoss] - *Selaginella peruviana* (Milde) Hieron (4, 50) (1986–present)

Pervenche petite (French) - *Vinca minor* L. (158) (1900)

Perwynke - *Vinca minor* L. (179) (1526)

Pe-sang (Chinese) - *Morus alba* L. (110) (1886)

Pescanoce (Italian) - *Prunus persica* (L.) Batsch (110) (1886) nectarines

Pesigunk (Chippewa, bitter) - *Geranium maculatum* L. (105) (1932)

Pesimmon [Pessimon] - *Diospyros virginiana* L. (107, 182) (1791-1919)

Pesse (French) - *Picea abies* (L.) H. Karst. (158) (1900)

Pesse d'eau (French) - *Hippuris vulgaris* L. (158) (1900)

Pessemmins - *Diospyros virginiana* L. (46) (1879)

Pestilence-weed [Pestilence weed] - *Petasites hybridus* (L.) G. Gaertn., B. Mey. & Scherb. (92) (1876)

Pestilence-wort [Pestilence wort] - *Petasites hybridus* (L.) G. Gaertn., B. Mey. & Scherb. (5, 156) (1913-1923) no longer in use by 1923

Pestilenzkraut (German) - *Galega officinalis* L. (158) (1900)

Pestnachen (German) - *Pastinaca sativa L.* (107) (1550)

Petalfra - *Catalpa* Scop. (38) (1820)

Petaya - *Echinocereus enneacanthus* Engelm. (122) (1937) TX

Peter's wort - *Hypericum hypericoides* (L.) Crantz subsp. *hypericoides* (92) (1876)

Petersilge (German) - *Petroselinum crispum* (P. Mill.) Nyman ex A.W. Hill (158) (1900)

Petersilie (German) - *Petroselinum crispum* (P. Mill.) Nyman ex A.W. Hill (158) (1900)

Peter's-staff [Peter's staff] - *Verbascum thapsus* L. (5, 69, 158) (1900-1913)

Peter's-wort [Peter's wort] - *Symphoricarpos albus* (L.) Blake var. *albus* (19) (1840)

Petiolate bellwort - *Uvularia perfoliata* L. (50) (present)

Petit chene veloute (French) - *Quercus ilicifolia* Wangenh. (181) (~1678)

Petit chiendent (French) - *Elymus repens* (L.) Gould (158) (1900)

Petit glouteron (French) - *Xanthium strumarium* L. (158) (1900)

Petit nard (French) - *Aralia nudicaulis* L. (7, 158) (1828-1900)

Petite mauve (French) - *Malva rotundifolia* L. (158) (1900)

Petite tomato du Mexique (French) - *Physalis philadelphica* Lam. (107) (1883)

Petroselinum - *Petroselinum crispum* (P. Mill.) Nyman ex A.W. Hill (110) (1886)

Pe-tsai - *Brassica rapa* L. var. *amplexicaulis* Tanaka & Ono (109) (1949)

Petticoat daffodil - *Narcissus bulbocodium* L. (138) (1923)

Petty euphorbia - *Euphorbia peplus* L. (155) (1942)

Petty morel [Pettymorel, Petty-morel, Petty-morrel, Pettymorrel, Petty morrell, Petymorell] - *Aralia nudicaulis* L. (7) (1828), *Aralia racemosa* L. (5, 6, 49, 53, 64, 73, 92, 157, 158, 184) (1793–1929), *Solanum nigrum* L. (5, 156, 157, 158, 179) (1526–1929)

Petty spurge - *Euphorbia peplus* L. (5, 72, 122, 156) (1907–1937)

Petty whin - *Ononis campestris* G. Koch & Ziz (92) (1876)

Petty-cotton [Petty cotton] - *Gnaphalium* L. (156) (1923)

Petum - *Nicotiana tabacum* L. (110) (1886)

Peuplier (French) - *Populus* L. (8) (1785)

Peuplier à feuilles triangularies (French) - *Populus deltoides* Bartr. ex Marsh. (8) (1785)

Peuplier argentés (French) - *Populus heterophylla* L. (8) (1785)

Peuplier baumier (French) - *Populus balsamifera* L. subsp. *balsamifera* (8) (1785)

Peuplier baumier à feuilles atroites (French) - *Populus angustifolia* James (20) (1857)

Peuplier de Canada (French) - *Populus tremuloides* Michx. (possibly) (8) (1785)

Peuplier de Virginie (French) - *Populus nigra* L. (8) (1785)

Peuplier grisaille (French) - *Populus ×canescens* (Aiton) Sm. [*alba × tremula*] (20) (1857)

Peuplier laird (French) - *Populus balsamifera* L. (8) (1785)

Pewter-wort [Pewterwort, Pewter wort] - *Equisetum hyemale* L. (5, 92, 158) (1876–1913)

Peyijuhiŋta (Lakota, grass + to rake) - *Dichanthelium oligosanthes* (J. A. Schultes) Gould var. *oligosanthes* (121) (1918–1970?)

Peyiokiyata (Lakota, forked grass - *Bouteloua hirsuta* Lag. (121) (1918–1970?)

Peyisuksuta (Lakota, tough or hard grass) - *Distichlis spicata* (L.) Greene (121) (1918–1970?)

Peyote - *Angelonia* Humb. & Bonpl. (104) (1896), *Ariocarpus fissuratus* (Engelm.) K. Schum. (104) (1896), *Lophophora* Coult. (138, 155) (1931–1942), *Lophophora lewinii* (Hennings ex Lewin) C.H. Thomps. (104) (1896), *Lophophora williamsii* (Lem. ex Salm-Dyck) Coult. (37, 50, 52, 138) (1919–present)

Peyotl - *Lophophora lewinii* (Hennings ex Lewin) C.H. Thomps. (104) (1896)

Peže bthaΘka (Osage, flat herb) - *Acorus calamus* L. (121) (1918-1970?)

Peže tuhu (Osage, green herb) - *Hedeoma pulegioides* (L.) Pers. (121) (1918–1970?)

Pezhe bthaska (Omaha-Ponca, flat herb) - *Lomatium foeniculaceum* (Nutt.) Coult. & Rose subsp. *foeniculaceum* (37) (1919)

Pezhe gagtho (Omaha-Ponca, rattle plant) - *Desmanthus illinoensis* (Michx.) MacM. ex B.L. Robins. & Fern. (37) (1919)

Pezhe hot'a (Omaha-Ponca, gray herb) - *Artemisia ludoviciana* Nutt. subsp. *ludoviciana* (37) (1919)

Pezhe makan (Omaha-Ponca) - *Verbena hastata* L. (37) (1919)

Pezhe nubthon (Omaha-Ponca, fragrant herb) - *Mentha arvensis* L. (37) (1919)

Pezhe pa (Omaha-Ponca, bitter herb) - *Monarda fistulosa* L. (37) (1919)

Pezhe piazhi (Omaha-Ponca, vile weed) - *Dyssodia papposa* (Vent.) A.S. Hitchc. (37) (1919)

Pezhe zonsta (Omaha-Ponca) - *Hierochloe odorata* (L.) Beauv. (37) (1830)

Pezhe-h'ota zhinga (Omaha-Ponca, little gray herb) - *Artemisia frigida* Willd. (37) (1919)

Pezhe-wasek (Omaha-Ponca, strong herb) - *Grindelia squarrosa* (Pursh) Dunal (37) (1919)

Pezhih'ota blaska (Dakota, flat gray herb) - *Artemisia ludoviciana* Nutt. subsp. *ludoviciana* (37) (1919)

Pezhuta nantiazilia (Dakota, smoke treatment medicine) - *Callirhoe involucrata* (Torr. & Gray) Gray (37) (1919)

Pezhuta pa (Dakota, bitter medicine) - *Dalea aurea* Nutt. ex Pursh (37) (1919)

Pezhuta-zi (Dakota, yellow medicine) - *Gentiana puberulenta* J. Pringle (37) (1919)

Pezi (Omaha-Ponca) - *Ribes missouriense* Nutt. (37) (1919)

Pezi nuga (Omaha-Ponca, Male gooseberry) - *Ribes americanum* Mill. (37) (1919)

Peži swula čikala (Lakota, small herb) - *Asclepias pumila* (Gray) Vail (121) (1918?-1970?)

Peži zizi (Lakota, yellow herb) - *Gutierrezia sarothrae* (Pursh) Britton & Rusby (121) (1918?-1970?)

Pežixota waštemna (Lakota, odorous gray herb) - *Artemisia frigida* Willd. (121) (1918?-1970?)

Pezukškuns (Chippewa, partridge berry) - *Galium aparine* L. (105) (1932)

Pežuta ha sapa (Lakota, black skin medicine) - *Lithospermum caroliniense* (Walt. ex J.F. Gmel.) MacM. (121) (1918?-1970?)

Pežuta niǧe taŋka (Lakota, big stomach-medicine) - *Ipomoea leptophylla* Torr. (121) (1918?-1970?)

Pežuta sapsapa (Lakota, black medicine) - *Lithospermum incisum* Lehm. (121) (1918?-1970?)

Pežuta ska hu (Lakota, white medicine plant) - *Astragalus racemosus* Pursh (121) (1918?-1970?)

Pežuta skuja (Lakota, sweet medicine) - *Astragalus leptaleus* Gray (121) (1918?-1970?)

Pežuta waxe ša (Lakota, black-skin medicine) - *Lithospermum caroliniense* (Walt. ex J.F. Gmel.) MacM. (121) (1918?-1970?)

Pfaffenröhrchen (German) - *Taraxacum officinale* G.H. Weber ex Wiggers (158) (1900)

Pfaffen-Rohrlein (German) - *Taraxacum officinale* G.H. Weber ex Wiggers subsp. *officinale* (6) (1892)

Pfeffermünze (German) - *Mentha ×piperita* L. [*aquatica × spicata*] (6) (1892)

Pfennigkraut (German) - *Lysimachia nummularia* L. (158) (1900)

Pferdschwanz (German) - *Equisetum arvense* L. (158) (1900)

Pfirsch (German) - *Prunus persica* (L.) Batsch (158) (1900)

Pflauenbaum (German) - *Prunus domestica* L. var. *insititia* (L.) Fiori & Paoletti (110) (1886)

Phacelia - *Phacelia hastata* Dougl. ex Lehm. var. *hastata* (127) (1933), *Phacelia* Juss. (50, 106, 138, 155, 158) (1900–present), *Phacelia viscida* (Benth. ex Lindl.) Torr. (92) (1876)

Phaeoceros - *Phaeoceros laevis* (L.) Prosk. (50) (present)

Phalaritha - *Centaurea solstitialis* L. (46) (1879)

Phaseole (French) - *Phaseolus vulgaris* L. (107) (1919)

Pheasant's-eye [Pheasantseye, Pheasant's-eye] - *Adonis annua* L. (2, 5, 15, 19, 42, 92, 138, 156, 165) (1768-1923), *Adonis* L. (109, 156) (1923-1949), *Adonis vernalis* L. (49, 52, 53) (1919-1922), *Dianthus plumarius* L. (92) (1876), *Gilia incisa* Benth. (124) (1937), *Narcissus poeticus* L. (109) (1949)

Pheasants-eye adonis - *Adonis annua* L. (155) (1942)

Phellopterus - *Cymopterus* Raf. (158) (1900)

Philadelphia fleabane [Philadelphia flea-bane] - *Erigeron philadelphicus* L. (3, 5, 50, 62, 72, 93, 97, 122, 124, 155, 158, 186, 187) (1818–present), *Erigeron philadelphicus* L. var. *philadelphicus* (50) (present)

Philadelphia ground-cherry - *Physalis philadelphica* Lam. (72) (1907)

Philadelphia lily - *Lilium philadelphicum* L. (5, 156, 187) (1818-1923)

Philadelphia panic grass [Philadelphia panicgrass] - *Panicum philadelphicum* Bernh. ex Trin. (50) (present)

Philadelphia witch grass [Philadelphia witchgrass] - *Panicum philadelphicum* Bernh. ex Trin. (155) (1942)

Philibertia - *Funastrum* Fourn. (138) (1923)

Philodendron - *Philodendron* Schott (138) (1923)

Phippsia - *Phippsia algida* (C.J. Phipps) R. Br. (5, 94) (1901-1913)

Phipsesawa - *Chimaphila umbellata* (L.) Bart. (8) (1785)

Phlox - *Phlox drummondii* Hook. (92) (1876), *Phlox* L. (1, 4, 50, 82, 93, 138, 155, 158) (1900–present)

Phlox heliotrops - *Heliotropium convolvulaceum* (Nutt.) Gray (50) (present)

Phlox-leaf aster [Phlox-leaved aster] - *Symphyotrichum phlogifolium* (Muhl. ex Willd.) Nesom (187) (1818)

Phoenix tree [Phoenix-tree] - *Firmiana simplex* (L.) W. Wight (109) (1949)

Photinia - *Photinia* Lindl. (138) (1923)

Phrygian iris - *Iris germanica* L. (138) (1923)

Phryma - *Phryma* L. (50) (present), *Phryma leptostachya* L. (174, 177) (1753-1762)

Phthisic-weed [Phthsic weed] - *Ludwigia palustris* (L.) Ell. (5, 156, 157, 158) (1900-1923)

Physic nut [Physic nuts, Physick Nut, Physic-nut] - *Jatropha curcas* L. (92) (1876), *Nestronia umbellula* Raf. (183) (~1756), *Pyrularia pubera* Michx. (182) (1791)

Physic root - *Veronicastrum virginicum* (L.) Farw. (7, 49, 64, 92) (1828-1907)

Phytolacca - *Phytolacca americana* L. (54) (1905), *Phytolacca americana* L. var. *americana* (59, 60, 64) (1902–1911)

Piakmin (Western tribes) - *Diospyros* L. (7) (1828)

Piakmine - *Diospyros virginiana* L. (46, 107) (1879–1919)

Pianta laca - *Phytolacca americana* L. var. *americana* (186) (1814)

Pi'-bŭt (Cahuillo Shoshonee) - *Nicotiana* L. (132) (1855)

Picac - *Euphorbia corollata* L. (5, 7, 49, 92, 156) (1828-1923) no longer in use by 1923

Pick hickory - *Carya alba* (L.) Nutt. ex Ell. (181) (~1678)

Pick tree [Pick-tree] - *Aralia spinosa* L. (5, 156) (1913-1923)

Pickawat anise - *Ptelea trifoliata* L. (157) (1929)

Pickaway - *Ptelea trifoliata* L. (6) (1892)

Pickaway anise [Pickaway-anise] - *Ptelea trifoliata* L. (5, 92, 156, 158) (1876-1923)

Pick-cheese [Pick cheese] - *Malva sylvestris* L. (5, 157, 158) (1900–1929)

Pickerel weed [Pickerelweed, Pickerel-weed] - *Pontederia cordata* L. (5, 50, 72, 92, 97, 106, 109, 120, 122, 124, 138, 155, 156, 187) (1818–present), *Pontederia* L. (1, 19, 138, 155, 158) (1840-1932), *Ranunculus trichophyllus* Chaix var. *trichophyllus* (5) (1913)

Pickering's breweria - *Stylisma pickeringii* (Torr. ex M.A. Curtis) Gray (5, 97) (1913-1937), *Stylisma pickeringii* (Torr. ex M.A. Curtis) Gray var. *pattersonii* (Fern. & Schub.) Myint (72) (1907)

Pickering's reed grass [Pickering reedgrass] - *Calamagrostis pickeringii* Gray (155) (1942)

Pickled-rats [Pickled rats] - *Proboscidea louisianica* (P. Mill.) Thellung (75) (1894) NY, possibly for appearance of pickled fruit

Pickleweed - *Allenrolfea* Kuntze (155) (1942)

Pickleweed - *Salicornia* L. (50) (present)

Pickpocket [Pick-pocket, Pick pocket] - *Capsella bursa-pastoris* (L.) Medik. (5, 74, 92, 156, 157, 158) (1893–1929)

Pickpurse [Pick-purse, Pick purse] - *Spergula arvensis* L. (5, 156, 158) (1900-1923) no longer in use by 1923

Pickpurse [Pick-purse, Pick purse] (Northern England) - *Capsella bursa-pastoris* (L.) Medik. (5, 92, 156, 157, 158, 180) (1633–1923)

Pico de ciguenä (Spanish) - *Geranium maculatum* L. (186) (1814)

Pico de grulla (Spanish) - *Geranium maculatum* L. (186) (1814)

Picotee - *Dianthus caryophyllus* L. (109) (1949)

Picradenia - *Hymenoxys* Cass. (158) (1900)

Picradeniopsis - *Picradeniopsis oppositifolia* (Nutt.) Rydb. ex Britton (5, 97) (1913-1937)

Picris - *Picris hieracioides* L. (92) (1876)

Picry [Pickry] - *Toxicodendron radicans* (L.) Kuntze (5) (1913), *Toxicodendron radicans* (L.) Kuntze subsp. *radicans* (71, 157, 158)

(1898-1929), *Toxicodendron toxicarium* (Salisb.) Gillis (76, 156) (1896-1923) Hartford ME

Pidahatus (Pawnee) - *Opuntia humifusa* (Raf.) Raf. (37) (1919)

Pie cherry - *Prunus cerasus* L. (107) (1919)

Pie plant [Pieplant, Pie-plant] - *Rheum* L. (1, 82) (1930–1932), *Rheum rhabarbarum* L. (73, 82, 85, 92, 107, 109, 158) (1892–1949) Middle states and west

Pie rhubarb - *Rheum rhabarbarum* L. (19) (1840)

Pied de loup (French) - *Lycopodium clavatum* L. (6) (1892)

Pied-de-corneille (French) - *Geranium maculatum* L. (158) (1900)

Pied-de-veautriphylle (French) - *Arisaema triphyllum* (L.) Schott (7) (1828)

Piedmont azalea - *Rhododendron canescens* (Michx.) Sweet (138) (1923)

Piedmont butterfly-pea - *Centrosema virginianum* (L.) Benth. (138) (1923)

Piedmont hawthorn - *Crataegus crus-galli* L. (155) (1942)

Piedmont rhododendron - *Rhododendron minus* Michx. (138) (1923)

Piedmont roseling - *Callisia rosea* (Vent.) D.R. Hunt (50) (present)

Piemarker [Pie marker, Pie-marker] - *Abutilon theophrasti* Medik. (5, 76, 155, 156, 158) (1896–1942) used to stamp pie-crust

Pie-print [Pie print] - *Abutilon theophrasti* Medik (5, 76, 156, 157, 158) (1896–1929) used to stamp pie-crust

Pig hickory - *Carya cordiformis* (Wangenh.) K. Koch (5, 156) (1913–1923)

Pig sage - *Salvia officinalis* L. (178) (1526)

Pigeon grape - *Vitis aestivalis* Michx. (3, 4, 15, 107, 109, 156) (1895–1986)

Pigeon grass [Pigeon-grass, Pigeongrass, Pigeon's- grass, Pigeon's grass] - *Digitaria sanguinalis* (L.) Scop. (5, 75) (1894–1913) Hopkinton IA, *Pennisetum glaucum* (L.) R. Br. (56, 80, 87, 88, 90, 119, 131, 134, 143, 163) (1852–1938), *Setaria* Beauv (56, 155) (1901–1942), *Setaria viridis* (L.) Beauv. (85, 50, 119, 129) (1894–present), *Setaria viridis* (L.) Beauv. var. *viridis* (5) (1913)

Pigeon tree [Pigeon-tree] - *Aralia spinosa* L. (5, 92, 156) (1876–1923)

Pigeon-berry [Pigeon berry] - *Amelanchier alnifolia* (Nutt.) Nutt. ex M. Roemer (5, 157, 158) (1900–1929), *Amelanchier* Medik. (106) (1930), *Amelanchier sanguinea* (Pursh) DC. (156) (1923), *Aralia hispida* Vent. (5, 75, 156) (1894–1923) ME, *Cornus alternifolia* L. f. (5, 156) (1913–1923), *Cornus canadensis* L. (46, 73) (1879–1892), *Duranta erecta* L. (109) (1949), *Empetrum nigrum* L. (156) (1923), *Frangula californica* (Eschsch.) Gray (106) (1930), *Ilex verticillata* (L.) Gray (156) (1923), *Mitchella repens* L. (76, 156) (1896–1923) MA, no longer in use by 1923, *Phytolacca americana* L. (5, 14, 69, 77, 93) (1882–1936), *Phytolacca americana* L. var. *americana* (2, 6, 7, 19, 49, 62, 64, 71, 92, 152, 157, 158, 186) (1814–1929), *Rivina humilis* L. (122, 124) (1937) TX, *Rubus pubescens* Raf. var. *pubescens* (5, 76, 156) (1896–1923) Western US, no longer in use by 1923

Pigeon-berry bush [Pigeonberry bush] - *Cornus sericea* L. subsp. *sericea* (46) (1783)

Pigeon-cherry [Pigeon cherry] - *Prunus pensylvanica* L. f. (5, 106, 137, 156, 158) (1900–1931)

Pigeon-foot [Pigeon foot, Pigeon's foot] - *Geranium molle* L. (5, 156) (1913–1923)

Pigeon-grass [Pigeon grass, Pigeongrass, Pigeon's- grass, Pigeon's grass] - *Verbena officinalis* L. (5, 92, 156) (1876-1923) no longer in use by 1923

Pigeon-pea [Pigeonpea, Pigeon pea] - *Cajanus cajan* (L.) Millsp. (92, 109, 110) (1876–1949)

Pigeon-plum [Pigeon plum] - *Mitchella repens* L. (156) (1923) no longer in use by 1923

Pigeon-root [Pigeon root] - *Claytonia lanceolata* Pall. ex Pursh (92) (1876)

Pigeon-weed [Pigeonweed, Pigeon weed] - *Aralia nudicaulis* L. (7) (1828), *Aralia racemosa* L. (6) (1892), *Aralia spinosa* L. (187) (1818), *Buglossoides arvensis* (L.) I.M. Johnston (62, 156) (1912-1923), *Verbena officinalis* L. (92) (1876)

Pigeon-wings [Pigeon wings] - *Clitoria* L. (155) (1942), *Clitoria mariana* L. (4) (1986)

Pigg-starr - *Carex muricata* L. (46) (1879)

Piggy-back plant - *Tolmiea menziesii* (Pursh) Torr. & Gray (109) (1949)

Pignocomon - *Reseda alba* L. (180) (1633)

Pignut [Pig-nut, Pig nut] - *Carya aquatica* (Michx. f.) Nutt. (7) (1828), *Carya cordiformis* (Wangenh.) K. Koch (possibly) (7) (1828), *Carya glabra* (Mill.) Sweet (possibly) (7, 92) (1828-1876), *Carya glabra* (Mill.) Sweet var. *glabra* (2, 14, 19, 95, 107, 113, 138) (1818-1923), *Hoffmannseggia glauca* (Ortega) Eifert (3, 4) (1977-1986), *Simmondsia chinensis* (Link) C.K. Schneid. (78) (1898) AZ, *Sinapis alba* L. (78) (1898)

Pignut hickory [Pig nut hickory, Pig-nut hickory, Pig-nut hickery] - *Carya glabra* (Mill.) Sweet (20) (1857), *Carya glabra* (Mill.) Sweet (1, 46, 82, 156) (1879-1932), *Carya glabra* (Mill.) Sweet var. *glabra* (5, 72, 85, 97) (1907-1937)

Pig-potato [Pig potato] - *Apios americana* Medik. (76, 156) (1896-1923) Western US, *Oxypolis rigidior* (L.) Raf. (possibly) (5, 156) (1913-1923)

Pigroot [Pig-root] - *Claytonia* L. (7) (1828), *Sisyrinchium angustifolium* Mill. (5, 156, 157, 158) (1900–1929)

Pigs - *Hexastylis virginica* (L.) Small (156) (1923)

Pigsty-daisy [Pig-sty-daisy, Pig-sty daisy] - *Anthemis cotula* L. (5, 73, 156, 157, 158) (1892-1929) Ipswich MA

Pigtail [Pig-tail] - *Galium aparine* L. (5, 156, 158) (1900-1923) no longer in use by 1923

Pigwa (Polish) - *Cydonia oblonga* Mill. (110) (1886)

Pigweed [Pig-weed, Pig weed] - *Amaranthus albus* L. (92) (1876), *Amaranthus graecizans* L. (156, 158) (1900–1923), *Amaranthus hybridus* L. (145, 157, 158) (1897–1929), *Amaranthus* L. (1, 4, 50, 93, 126) (1932–present), *Amaranthus retroflexus* L. (21, 80, 85, 107, 125, 148) (1893–1932), *Chamerion angustifolium* (L.) Holub subsp. *angustifolium* (5, 76, 156, 158) (1896–1923), *Chenopodium album* L. (5, 45, 62, 80, 93, 107, 131, 150, 156, 157, 158) (1894–1936), *Chenopodium album* L. var. *album* (156, 158) (1900–1923), *Chenopodium* L. (1, 7, 92) (1828–1932), *Chenopodium rubrum* L. (156) (1923), *Portulaca oleracea* L. (5, 156) (1913–1923)

Pigweed goosefoot - *Chenopodium album* L. var. *missouriense* (Aellen) I.J. Bassett & C.W. Crompton (155) (1942), *Chenopodium berlandieri* Moq. var. *bushianum* (Aellen) Cronq. (155) (1942)

Pigweed purslane - *Amaranthus blitoides* S. Wats. (145) (1897) KS

Pikanin-minš (Chippewa) - *Corylus americana* Walt. (105) (1932)

Pileweed [Pile-weed] - *Erechtites hieraciifolia* (L.) Raf. ex DC. (156) (1923)

Pilewort [Pile-wort, Pile wort] - *Amaranthus hybridus* L. (5, 156, 157, 158) (1900–1929), *Amaranthus hypochondriacus* L. (92) (1876), *Erechtites hieraciifolia* (L.) Raf. ex DC. (5, 62, 92, 156, 157, 158) (1876–1929), *Erechtites* Raf. (1) (1932), *Ranunculus acris* L. (7) (1828), *Ranunculus bulbosus* L. (5, 92) (1876–1913), *Ranunculus ficaria* L. (5, 55) (1911–1913), *Scrophularia marilandica* L. (62, 93, 156) (1912–1936)

Pillards - *Hordeum* L (158) (1900)

Pill-bearing spurge - *Chamaesyce hirta* (L.) Millsp. (53) (1922)

Pill-pod euphorbia [Pillpod euphorbia] - *Chamaesyce hirta* (L.) Millsp. (155) (1942)

Pillwort [Pill-wort] - *Pilularia* L. (4, 50) (1986–present)

Pilose spiderwort - *Tradescantia hirsutiflora* Bush (97) (1937)

Pilotweed [Pilot-weed, Pilot weed] - *Silphium laciniatum* L. (5, 37, 92, 156, 157, 158) (1876–1929)

Pimbina - *Viburnum edule* (Michx.) Raf. (156) (1923), *Viburnum opulus* L. (156) (1923)

Pimentary - *Melissa officinalis* L. (5, 156) (1913–1923) no longer in use by 1923

Pimento - *Capsicum annuum* L. (107) (1919)

Pimina des Canadiens (French) - *Viburnum opulus* L. var. *americanum* Aiton (8) (1785)

Pimpernel - *Anagallis arvensis* L. (4, 10, 107) (1818-1986), *Anagallis* L. (1, 4, 6, 50, 82, 109, 138, 155, 156, 158) (1892–present), *Anagallis monelli* L. (82) (1930), *Lindernia dubia* (L.) Pennell (19) (1840), *Pimpinella saxifraga* L. (5, 92, 156) (1876-1923), *Prunella vulgaris* L. (158) (1900)

Pimpernel rose [Pimpernell rose] - *Rosa spinosissima* L. (178) (1526)

Pimpernel willowherb [Pimpernel willow herb] - *Epilobium anagallidifolium* Lam. (5) (1913)

Pimpernell [Pympernell] - *Pimpinella saxifraga* L. (179) (1526)

Pimpernelle - *Sanguisorba minor* Scop. (156) (1923), *Sanguisorba minor* Scop. subsp. *muricata* (Spach) Nordborg (5) (1913)

Pimpinel [Pimpinell] - *Pimpinella saxifraga* L. (92, 179) (1526-1876)

Pimpinella - *Pimpinella major* (L.) Huds. (92) (1876), *Pimpinella saxifraga* L. (174) (1753), *Sanguisorba minor* Scop. subsp. *muricata* (Spach) Nordborg (possibly) (178) (1526)

Pimple mallow - *Callirhoe pedata* (Nutt. ex Hook.) Gray (103, 107) (1870-1919)

Pimprenelle - *Sanguisorba minor* Scop. subsp. *muricata* (Spach) Nordborg (157, 158) (1900-1929)

Pin (Chippewa, tuber) - *Apios americana* Medik. (105) (1932)

Pin (French) - *Pinus* L. (8) (1785)

Pin à cône épineux (French) - *Pinus echinata* Mill. (8) (1785)

Pin à l'encens (French) - *Pinus taeda* L. (5, 8, 10, 19) (1785-1913)

Pin birch - *Betula pubescens* Ehrh. subsp. *pubescens* (5, 75, 156) (1894-1923)

Pin bladderwort - *Utricularia subulata* L. (5) (1913)

Pin cembrot d'Amerique (French) - *Pinus flexilis* James (20) (1857)

Pin cherry - *Prunus pensylvanica* L. f. (2, 4, 50, 5, 82, 85, 107, 109, 131, 135, 137, 138, 155, 156, 158) (1895–present)

Pin de Jersey (French) - *Pinus virginiana* Mill. (8) (1785) misapplied

Pin de marais (French) - *Pinus palustris* Mill. (8) (1785)

Pin de sabine à grands cones epineux (French) - *Pinus sabiniana* Dougl. ex Dougl. (20) (1857)

Pin de Virginie à trois feuilles (French) - *Pinus rigida* Mill. (8) (1785)

Pin de Virginies à dois feuilles (French) - *Pinus virginiana* Mill. (8) (1785)

Pin du Lord Weymouth (French) - *Pinus strobus* L. (8) (1785)

Pin gigantique de Lambert (French) - *Pinus lambertiana* Dougl. (20) (1857)

Pin grass - *Avena fatua* L. (103) (1871)

Pin oak - *Quercus imbricaria* Michx. (78) (1898) Southwest MO, *Quercus muehlenbergii* Engelm. (5, 156, 157, 158) (1900-1929), *Quercus palustris* Muench. (1, 3, 4, 5, 20, 19, 33, 50, 82, 109, 112, 135, 138, 155, 156, 187) (1827–present)

Pin rouge (French Canada) - *Pinus resinosa* Aiton (20) (1857)

Pin rush - *Juncus effusus* L. (5, 156) (1913-1923)

Pin thorn [Pin-thorn] - *Crataegus crus-galli* L. (5, 156, 158) (1900–1923)

Pinas (Spanish) - *Ananas comosus* (L.) Merr. var. *comosus* (110) (1886)

Pinaster - *Pinus sylvestris* L. (178) (1596)

Pinball [Pin-ball, Pin ball] - *Cephalanthus occidentalis* L. (5, 73, 156, 157, 158) (1892-1929) NH

Pinchot's juniper [Pinchot juniper] - *Juniperus pinchotii* Sudw. (4, 50, 122) (1937–present)

Pinckney bark - *Pinckneya bracteata* (Bartr.) Raf. (7, 92) (1828-1876)

Pin-clover [Pin clover] - *Erodium cicutarium* (L.) L'Hér. ex Aiton (5, 45, 76, 156, 157, 158) (1896-1929), *Erodium* L'Her. ex Aiton (1, 106) (1930-1932), *Erodium moschatum* (L.) L'Hér. ex Aiton (76) (1896) CA

Pincushion [Pincushions, Pin-cushion, Pin cushions] - *Antennaria plantaginifolia* (L.) Richards (75, 156, 158) (1894-1923) Hingham MA, *Knautia arvensis* (L.) Duby (5, 156, 158) (1900-1923), *Mammillaria heyderi* Muehlenpfordt (122) (1937) TX, *Succisa pratensis* Moench (76) (1896) Sulphur Grove OH

Pincushion cactus [Pin-cushion cactus] - *Escobaria missouriensis* (Sweet) D.R. Hunt var. *missouriensis* (85) (1932), *Escobaria vivipara* (Nutt.) Buxbaum var. *vivipara* (4) (1986), *Mammillaria grahamii* Engelm. (76) (1896) AZ

Pincushion flower - *Succisella inflexa* (Kluk) G. Beck (5, 156) (1913-1923)

Pincushion plant [Pincushionplant] - *Navarretia* Ruiz & Pavón (50) (present)

Pincushion shrub [Pincushion-shrub - *Euonymus europaea* L. (5, 156) (1913-1923)

Pincushion tree [Pincushion-tree - *Viburnum opulus* L. (5, 156, 158) (1900-1923) no longer in use by 1923

Pindar [Pindars] - *Arachis hypogaea* L. (7, 107) (1828-1919) West Indies

Pinders - *Arachis hypogaea* L. (73) (1892) MS

Pindo palm - *Syagrus romanzoffiana* (Cham.) Glassman (138) (1923)

Pine Barren cyperus [Pine-barren cyperus] - *Cyperus retrorsus* Chapman var. *retrorsus* (5) (1913)

Pine Barren deathcamas [Pinebarren deathcamas] - *Zigadenus leimanthoides* Gray (50) (present)

Pine Barren flatsedge [Pine-barren flatsedge] - *Cyperus retrorsus* Chapman var. *retrorsus* (50) (present)

Pine Barren frostweed [Pine-barren frostweed] - *Helianthemum corymbosum* Michx. (5) (1913)

Pine Barren goldenrod [Pine Barren golden-rod] - *Solidago fistulosa* Mill. (5) (1913)

Pine Barren milkwort - *Polygala ramosa* Ell. (122) (1937) TX

Pine Barren oceanus - *Zigadenus leimanthoides* Gray (5) (1913)

Pine Barren prairie clover [Pine-barren prairie clover] - *Dalea pinnata* (J. F. Gmel.) Barneby var. *pinnata* (106) (1930)

Pine Barren sandreed - *Calamovilfa brevipilis* (Torr.) Hack. ex Scribn. & Southw. (50) (present)

Pine Barren sandwort [Pine-barren sandwort] - *Minuartia caroliniana* (Walt.) Mattf. (2, 5, 156) (1895-1923)

Pine Barrens beauty [Pine-barren beauty, Pine-barrens beauty] - *Pyxidanthera barbulata* Michx. (5, 156) (1913-1923)

Pine bluegrass - *Poa secunda* J. Presl (155) (1942)

Pine bracket fungus - *Fomitopsis pinicola* (Sw.) P. Karst. (128) (1933) ND

Pine broom - *Pinus palustris* Mill. (5) (1913)

Pine columbine - *Aquilegia coerulea* var. *pinetorum* (Tidestr.) Payson ex Kearney & Peebles (155) (1942)

Pine goldenweed - *Ericameria parishii* (Greene) Hall (155) (1942), *Ericameria pinifolia* (Gray) Hall (155) (1942)

Pine grass - *Festuca arizonica* Vasey (152) (1912) NM

Pine lily - *Lilium catesbaei* Walt. (50) (present)

Pine manzanita - *Arctostaphylos patula* Greene (155) (1942)

Pine nuts - *Pinus cembra* L. (92) (1876), *Pinus pinea* L. (92) (1876)

Pine or Pine tree - *Pinus* L. (4, 7, 8, 50, 109, 121, 158, 155, 167, 184) (1785–present) Classic Latin name of Celtic origin

Pine sap - *Monotropa hypopithys* L. (5, 72) (1907-1913), *Monotropa* L. (possibly) (10) (1818)

Pine spruce - *Picea glauca* (Moench) Voss (5, 158) (1900-1913)

Pine starwort - *Ionactis* Greene (158) (1900), *Ionactis linariifolius* (L.) Greene (5, 158) (1900-1913)

Pine strawberry - *Fragaria chiloensis* (L.) Mill. (107) (1919)

Pine tassel - *Hypericum gentianoides* (L.) Britton, Sterns & Poggenb. (156) (1923)

Pine tops - *Picea glauca* (Moench) Voss (92) (1876)

Pine torch - *Cereus hildmannianus* K. Schum. (possibly) (178) (1526)

Pine tulip - *Chimaphila umbellata* (L.) Bart. (5, 92, 156) (1876-1923) no longer in use by 1923

Pine wood grape - *Vitis aestivalis* Michx. var. *lincecumii* (Buckl.) Munson (15) (1895)

Pine wool - *Pinus sylvestris* L. (92) (1876) leaf fiber

Pineapple [Pine-apple, Pine apple] - *Ananas comosus* (L.) Merr. (7, 109, 155) (1828–1949), *Ananas comosus* (L.) Merr. var. *comosus* (92, 110, 138) (1876–1923)

Pineapple strawberry [Pine apple strawberry] - *Fragaria* ×anan-

assa Duchesne var. *cuneifolia* (Nutt. ex T.J. Howell) (19) (1840)

Pineapple-weed [Pineappleweed - *Matricaria discoidea* DC. (3, 4, 155, 156) (1923–1986), *Matricaria* L. (possibly) (1) (1932)

Pine-cheat [Pine cheat] - *Spergula arvensis* L. (5, 156, 158) (1900–1923) no longer in use by 1923

Pinedrops [Pine drops, Pine-drops] - *Pterospora andromedea* Nutt. (1, 3, 4, 5, 85, 93, 95, 122, 131, 156, 158) (1899–1986), *Pterospora* Nutt. (50, 155, 158) (1900–present)

Pineland hawthorn - *Crataegus crus-galli* L. (155) (1942)

Pineland threeawn - *Aristida stricta* Michx. (155) (1942)

Pineland three-seed mercury [Pineland threeseed mercury] - *Acalypha ostryifolia* Riddell (50, 187) (1818–present)

Pinemat manzanita - *Arctostaphylos nevadensis* Gray (155) (1942)

Pine-needle [Pineneedle] - *Erodium cicutarium* (L.) L'Hér. ex Aiton (157, 158) (1900–1929), *Muhlenbergia dubia* Fourn. ex Hemsl. (122) (1937) TX

Pinesap [Pine sap, Pine-sap] - *Monotropa hypopithys* L. (2, 4, 50, 92, 155, 156) (1876–present), *Monotropa* L. (possibly) (1, 158) (1900–1932)

Pine-starwort - *Ionactis linariifolius* (L.) Greene (156) (1923)

Pinette de prairie (French Canadian boatmen) - *Liatris* Gaertn. ex Schreber. (10) (1818)

Pine-tulip [Pine tulip] - *Chimaphila umbellata* (L.) Bart. (5, 156, 158) (1900–1923)

Pineweed [Pine-weed, Pine weed] - *Hypericum gentianoides* (L.) Britton, Sterns & Poggenb. (2, 5, 19, 92, 156, 157) (1840-1929), *Hypericum* L. (1, 93, 155) (1932–1942), *Spergula arvensis* L. (79) (1891)

Pine-wood grape - *Vitis aestivalis* Michx. var. *lincecumii* (Buckl.) Munson (107) (1919)

Pinewoods coneflower - *Coreopsis angustifolia* L. (106, 114) (1894-1930), *Rudbeckia bicolor* Nutt. (138) (1923)

Pinewoods finger grass [Pinewoods fingergrass] - *Eustachys petraea* (Sw.) Desv. (50) (present)

Pinewoods grape - *Vitis aestivalis* Michx. var. *lincecumii* (Buckl.) Munson (138) (1923)

Pinewoods rose - *Rosa pinetorum* Heller (138) (1923)

Piney - *Paeonia officinalis* L. (49, 52) (1898-1919), *Peperomia* Ruiz & Pavón (52) (1919)

Pineywoods dropseed - *Sporobolus junceus* (Beauv.) Kunth (50, 155) (1942–present)

Pin-grass [Pin grass] - *Erodium cicutarium* (L.) L'Hér. ex Aiton (5, 45, 107, 156, 157, 158) (1896–1929), *Erodium* L'Her. ex Aiton (106) (1930)

Pingue - *Hymenoxys richardsonii* (Hook.) Cockerell var. *floribunda* (Gray) Parker (148) (1939) CO

Pingue actinea - *Hymenoxys richardsonii* (Hook.) Cockerell var. *richardsonii* (155) (1942)

Pingue rubberweed - *Hymenoxys richardsonii* (Hook.) Cockll. (50) (present)

Pinhole beard grass [Pinhole beardgrass] - *Bothriochloa barbinodis* (Lag.) Herter (155) (1942)

Pink - *Dianthus armeria* L. (19) (1840), *Dianthus* L. (1, 10, 15, 50, 92, 109, 138, 155, 156, 158, 167) (1814–present)

Pink abronia - *Tripterocalyx micranthus* (Torr.) Hook (5, 93) (1913–1936)

Pink azalea - *Rhododendron periclymenoides* (Michx.) Shinners (5, 97, 156) (1913-1937)

Pink babysbreath [Pink baby breath] - *Talinum paniculatum* (Jacq.) Gaertn. (122, 124) (1937) TX

Pink beardtongue [Pink beard-tongue] - *Penstemon grandiflorus* Nutt. (85) (1932)

Pink bellflower - *Ipomoea triloba* L. (106) (1930)

Pink bluebonnet - *Lupinus perennis* L. subsp. *perennis* (122) (1937) TX

Pink catchfly [Pink catch-fly] - *Silene caroliniana* subsp. *pensylvanica* (Michx.) Clausen (19) (1840), *Silene virginica* L. (92) (1876)

Pink centaurium - *Centaurium venustum* (Gray) B.L. Robins. (138) (1923)

Pink cleome - *Cleome serrulata* Pursh (5, 72, 85, 93, 97, 131, 156) (1899–1937)

Pink common yarrow - *Achillea millefolium* L. (155) (1942)

Pink corydalis - *Capnoides sempervirens* (L.) Borck. (5) (1913), *Corydalis sempervirens* (L.) Pers. (156) (1923)

Pink flameflower [Pink flame flower] - *Talinum calycinum* Engelm. (124) (1937)

Pink fringed orchis - *Platanthera psycodes* (L.) Lindl. (156) (1923)

Pink grass [Pink-grass] - *Eragrostis pectinacea* (Michx.) Nees ex Steud. (5) (1913), *Eragrostis spectabilis* (Pursh) Steud. (119) (1938) OK

Pink houstonia - *Houstonia humifusa* (Gray) Gray (124) (1937)

Pink ladyslipper [Pink lady's slipper, Pink lady-slipper, Pink ladies' slipper] - *Cypripedium acaule* Ait. (5, 109, 138, 156) (1913-1949)

Pink meadow spiraea - *Spiraea alba* Du Roi var. *latifolia* (Aiton) Dippel (138) (1923)

Pink milkwort - *Polygala incarnata* L. (5, 72, 97, 122, 156, 158) (1900-1936), *Polygala polygama* Walt. (5, 156) (1913-1923)

Pink mimosa - *Mimosa borealis* Gray (4, 97, 122) (1937-1986)

Pink moccasin-flower - *Cypripedium reginae* Walt. (158) (1900)

Pink mock vervain - *Glandularia pumila* (Rydb.) Umber (50) (present)

Pink nodding smartweed - *Polygonum lapathifolium* L. (82) (1930)

Pink parosela - *Dalea leporina* (Aiton) Bullock (5, 72, 80, 85, 93, 131) (1899-1936)

Pink persicaria - *Polygonum lapathifolium* L. (72) (1907)

Pink plains penstemon - *Penstemon ambiguus* Torr. (122, 124) (1937)

Pink plume-poppy [Pink plumepoppy] - *Macleaya cordata* (Willd.) R. Br. (138) (1923)

Pink poppy-mallow [Pink poppy mallow] - *Callirhoe alcaeoides* (Michx.) Gray (3, 4, 93) (1936-1986)

Pink pussy-toes - *Antennaria microphylla* Rydb. (4) (1986)

Pink sand-verbena [Pink sand verbena [Pink sandverbena] - *Abronia umbellata* Lam. (50, 138, 155) (1923–present)

Pink siris - *Albizia julibrissin* Durazz. (5) (1913)

Pink smartweed - *Polygonum lapathifolium* L. (80, 82) (1913-1930), *Polygonum pensylvanicum* L. (4) (1986)

Pink snakeroot [Pink snake root] - *Mitreola petiolata* (J.F. Gmel.) Torr. & Gray (7, 92) (1828-1876)

Pink sophora - *Sophora affinis* Torr. & Gray (122) (1937) TX

Pink swamp milkweed - *Asclepias incarnata* L. (138, 155) (1931–1942)

Pink thoroughwort - *Fleischmannia incarnata* (Walt.) King & H.E. (5, 122, 124) (1913–1937)

Pink tickseed - *Coreopsis rosea* Nutt. (5) (1913)

Pink turtlehead - *Chelone lyonii* Pursh (138) (1923)

Pink vervain - *Glandularia pumila* (Rydb.) Umber (3) (1977)

Pink weigela - *Diervilla florida* (Bunge) Siebold & Zucc. (possibly) (138) (1923)

Pink wild bean - *Strophostyles umbellata* (Muhl.) Britton (5, 97) (1913–1937)

Pink wild onion - *Allium stellatum* Ker (3) (1977)

Pink wood sorrel - *Oxalis violacea* L. (127) (1933)

Pink zephyr-lily [Pink zephyrlily] - *Zephyranthes rosea* Lindl. (138) (1923)

Pinkbloom [Pink bloom, Pink bloom] - *Sabatia angularis* (L.) Pursh (5, 75, 156, 158) (1894–1923) WV

Pink-flower dock [Pink-flowered dock] - *Rumex venosus* Pursh (127) (1933)

Pink-fringe orchis [Pink-fringed orchis] - *Platanthera psycodes* (L.) Lindl. (5) (1913)

Pink-grass [Pink grass] - *Carex caryophyllea* Latourrette (5, 156) (1913–1923), *Carex flacca* Schreb. (5, 156) (1913–1923)

Pink-ladies [Pinkladies] - *Oenothera speciosa* Nutt. (50) (present)

Pink-leaf sedge [Pink-leaved sedge] - *Carex panicea* L. (5, 156) (1913–1923)

Pink-mint [Pinkmint] - *Stachys drummondii* Benth. (124) (1937) TX

Pink-mint [Pinkmint] - *Stachys pilosa* Nutt. var. *pilosa* (124) (1937)

Pink-needle [Pink needle] - *Erodium cicutarium* (L.) L'Hér. ex Aiton (5, 156, 157, 158) (1900–1929), *Scandix pecten-veneris* L. (5, 156) (1913–1923)

Pinkroot [Pink root] - *Spigelia anthelmia* L. (2, 138, 156) (1895–1928), *Spigelia* L. (2, 138, 156) (1895–1923), *Spigelia marilandica* (L.) L. (5, 6, 14, 19, 49, 53, 55, 57, 58, 59, 60, 64, 92, 138, 156) (1840–1923)

Pink-scale gayfeather [Pinkscale gayfeather] - *Liatris elegans* (Walt.) Michx. (138) (1923)

Pink-shell azalea [Pinkshell azalea] - *Rhododendron vaseyi* Gray (138) (1923)

Pink-shower - *Cassia grandis* L. f. (138) (1923)

Pinkster - *Rhododendron periclymenoides* (Michx.) Shinners (156) (1923)

Pinkster flower [Pinxter flower, Pinxter-flower] - *Rhododendron periclymenoides* (Michx.) Shinners (2, 5, 92, 109, 156) (1895-1949)

Pink-vine - *Antigonon leptopus* Hook. & Arn. (106, 109) (1930-1949)

Pinkweed [Pink weed, Pink-weed] - *Persicaria maculosa* Gray (5, 92, 156, 158) (1876-1923), *Polygonum aviculare* L. (5, 93, 156, 158) (1900–1936)

Pinkworts - Caryophyllaceae (156) (1923)

Pinnate cynosciadium - *Limnosciadium pinnatum* (DC.) Math. & Const. (5, 97) (1913-1937)

Pinnate prairie coneflower - *Ratibida pinnata* (Vent.) Barnh. (50) (present)

Pinnate tansy-mustard [Pinnate tansymustard] - *Descurainia pinnata* (Walt.) Britton (50) (present)

Pinnate vervain - *Verbena hastata* L. (72) (1907)

Pinnate water-milfoil [Pinnate water milfoil] - *Myriophyllum pinnatum* (Walt.) Britton, Sterns & Poggenb. (5, 72, 97) (1907-1937)

Pinnate-leaf ampelopsis [Pinnate-leaved ampelopsis] - *Ampelopsis arborea* (L.) Koehne (5) (1913)

Pinnate-leaf gaillardia [Pinnate-leaved gaillardia] - *Gaillardia pinnatifida* Torr. (97) (1937)

Pinnatifid spleenwort - *Asplenium pinnatifidum* Nutt. (5, 97) (1913-1937)

Pinnatified spleenwort [Pinnatified spleen-wort] - *Asplenium pinnatifidum* Nutt. (86) (1878)

Piñon [Pinyon] - *Pinus cembroides* Zucc. (109) (1949), *Pinus edulis* Engelm. (75, 97, 147, 149, 153, 158) (1856-1937) NM, Mexico, *Pinus monophylla* Torr. & Frém. (147) (1856)

Piñon goosefoot [Pinyon goosefoot] - *Chenopodium atrovirens* Rydb. (50) (present)

Piñon grass [Pinon grass] - *Piptochaetium fimbriatum* (Kunth) A.S. Hitchc. (152) (1912) NM

Piñon pine [Pinon pine] - *Pinus edulis* Engelm. (3, 107, 147) (1856-1977), *Pinus flexilis* James (122, 124) (1937) TX

Piñon rice grass [Pinyon ricegrass, Pinyon rice grass] - *Piptochaetium fimbriatum* (Kunth) A.S. Hitchc. (122) (1937) TX

Pinsigallo (Argentina) - *Zea mays* L. subsp. *mays* (110) (1886)

Pinweed [Pin-weed, Pin weed] - *Erodium cicutarium* (L.) L'Hér. ex Aiton (5, 92, 157, 158) (1876-1929), *Lechea intermedia* Leggett (3, 4) (1977-1986), *Lechea* L. (1, 4, 13, 15, 50, 93, 155, 156, 158) (1849–present), *Lechea minor* L. (47) (1852), *Lechea stricta* Leggett ex Britton (3, 4) (1977-1986), *Lechea tenuifolia* Michx. (3, 4, 85) (1932-1986)

Pinxterbloem (Swedish, Witsunday flower) - *Rhododendron calendulaceum* (Michx.) Torr. (177) (1762), *Rhododendron periclymenoides* (Michx.) Shinners (41) (1770)

Piocha - *Melia azedarach* L. (153) (1913) NM

Pioneer rockcress - *Arabis platysperma* Gray (155) (1942)

Pipe plant [Pipe-plant] - *Monotropa uniflora* L. (5, 6, 7, 49, 92, 156, 157, 158) (1828-1923)

Pipe tree [Pipe-tree] - *Sambucus nigra* L. subsp. *canadensis* (L.) R. Bolli (190) (~1759), *Syringa vulgaris* L. (5, 92, 156) (1876-1923)

Pipe-privets [Pipe privets] - *Syringa vulgaris* L. (5, 156) (1913-1923)

Piper willow - *Salix hookeriana* Barratt ex Hook. (138) (1923)

Pipestem [Pipe-stem, Pipe stem] - *Clematis* L. (1) (1932), *Clematis ligusticifolia* Nutt. (156) (1923), *Clematis virginiana* L. (156) (1923), *Lyonia lucida* (Lam.) K. Koch (5, 7, 92, 156) (1828-1923)

Pipestem clematis - *Clematis lasiantha* Nutt. (109) (1949)

Pipestem wood [Pipe-stem-wood, Pipe-stem wood] - *Agarista populifolia* (Lam.) W.S. Judd (182) (1791), *Leucothoe axillaris* (Lam.) D. Don. (183) (~1756)

Pipevine [Pipe-vine, Pipe vine] - *Aristolochia macrophylla* Lam. (2, 5, 7, 92, 109, 156) (1828-1949), *Aristolochia tomentosa* Sims. (3) (1977), *Cryptotaenia canadensis* (L.) DC. (92) (1876)

Pipewort [Pipe-wort, Pipe wort] - *Eriocaulon aquaticum* (Hill) Druce (19, 46) (1840-1879), *Eriocaulon decangulare* L. (156) (1923), *Eriocaulon* L. (1, 10, 50, 167) (1814–present)

Pipigwe-minan (Chippewa) - *Sambucus nigra* L. subsp. *canadensis* (L.) R. Bolli (105) (1932)

Pipius - *Gaultheria procumbens* L. (79) (1891) NH, young shoots

Pippal yank - *Triadica sebifera* (L.) Small (46) (1879) India

Pipperidge [Piperidge] - *Berberis vulgaris* L. (157, 158) (1900-1929), *Chimaphila maculata* (L.) Pursh (156) (1923)

Pipperidge bush - *Berberis canadensis* P. Mill. (7) (1828), *Berberis vulgaris* L. (76, 92) (1876-1896) Southern NH, almost out of use by 1896

Pippins - *Gaultheria procumbens* L. (73, 156) (1892-1923) young shoots

Piprage - *Berberis vulgaris* L. (107) (1919)

Pipsissewa [Pippsissewa] - *Chimaphila* Pursh (1, 2, 109, 138, 155, 156) (1923–1949), *Chimaphila umbellata* (L.) Bart. (5, 6, 40, 47, 49, 52, 53, 54, 55, 57, 58, 59, 61, 72, 92, 105, 156, 158, 186, 187) (1814–1932)

Pira-kari (Pawnee, many children) - *Baptisia bracteata* Muhl. ex Ell. (37) (1919)

Pireter - *Parietaria judaica* L. (179) (1526)

Pirola - *Chimaphila umbellata* (L.) Bart. (186) (1825), *Pyrola americana* Sweet (46) (1671)

Pirra (Italian) - *Triticum spelta* L. (180) (1633)

Piscidia - *Piscidia piscipula* (L.) Sargent (55) (1911)

Pishamin - *Diospyros virginiana* L. (177) (1762)

Pishamon - *Diospyros virginiana* L. (181) (~1678)

Pishmin - *Diospyros virginiana* L. (7) (1828)

Pisk-cheese - *Malva sylvestris* L. (156) (1923)

Piskies - *Silene regia* Sims. (156, 158) (1900-1923), *Stellaria holostea* L. (5, 156) (1913-1923) no longer in use by 1923

Pismire - *Leucanthemum vulgare* Lam. (73, 158) (1892–1900) East Weymouth MA

Pisone épineusse (French) - *Pisonia aculeata* L. (20) (1857)

Pisonia - *Pisonia aculeata* L. (174) (1753)

Pispiza tawote (Lakota, prairie dog food) - *Dyssodia papposa* (Vent.) A.S. Hitchc. (121) (1918?-1970?)

Pissabed - *Ranunculus bulbosus* L. (5, 158) (1900-1913), *Taraxacum officinale* G.H. Weber ex Wiggers subsp. *officinale* (6, 7) (1828-1892)

Pisseabed - *Taraxacum officinale* G.H. Weber ex Wiggers (180) (1633)

Pissenlit (French) - *Taraxacum officinale* G.H. Weber ex Wiggers (158) (1900)

Pissenlit commun (French) - *Taraxacum officinale* G.H. Weber ex Wiggers (7) (1828)

Pissenlit commune (French) - *Taraxacum officinale* G.H. Weber ex Wiggers subsp. *officinale* (6) (1892)

Pissenlit on couronne de prestre (French) - *Taraxacum officinale* G.H. Weber ex Wiggers (180) (1633)

Pissweed - *Anthemis cotula* L. (7) (1828)

Pisswort - *Menispermum canadense* L. (7) (1828)

Pistache - *Pistacia* L. (138) (1923)

Pistachio - *Hamamelis virginiana* L. (5, 92, 156) (1876-1923)

Pistachoe nut - *Hamamelis virginiana* L. (7) (1828)

Pistolochia - *Aristolochia serpentaria* L. (186) (1814)

Pistolochia Virginiana - *Aristolochia serpentaria* L. (181, 186) (~1678-1825) John Gerarde

Pita - *Agave americana* L. (7) (1828)

Pitahaya (Mexicans) - *Carnegia gigantea* (Engelm.) Britt. & Rose (104) (1896), *Stenocereus thurberi* (Engelm.) Buxbaum (103, 107) (1870-1919)

Pitahya dulce - *Stenocereus thurberi* (Engelm.) Buxbaum (104) (1896)

Pitanga - *Eugenia uniflora* L. (109) (1949)

Pitaya - *Echinocereus viridiflorus* Engelm. (97) (1937) OK

Pitch pine - *Picea rubens* Sarg. (14) (1882), *Pinus contorta* Dougl. ex Loud. (35) (1806), *Pinus echinata* Mill. (5) (1913), *Pinus palustris* Mill. (5, 52, 92, 182) (1791-1919), *Pinus ponderosa* P.& C. Lawson var. *ponderosa* (75, 147) (1856-1894), *Pinus resinosa* Aiton (5, 10, 19) (1818-1840), *Pinus rigida* Mill. (5, 46, 50, 109, 138, 187) (1818–present), *Pinus virginiana* Mill. (possibly) (187) (1818)

Pitch tree - *Pinus rigida* Mill. (46) (1879)

Pitcherplant [Pitcher plant, Pitcher-plant] - *Cypripedium acaule* Ait. (156) (1923), *Sarracenia alata* Wood (124) (1937), *Sarracenia* L. (15, 109, 138) (1895-1949), *Sarracenia purpurea* L. (1, 2, 5, 6, 40, 47, 49, 52, 57, 63, 92, 156) (1852-1932)

Pitcher's clematis [Pitcher clematis] - *Clematis pitcheri* Torr. & Gray (4, 155) (1942-1986)

Pitcher's hog peanut [Pitcher's hog pea nut, Pitchers hogpeanut] - *Amphicarpaea bracteata* (L.) Fern. (82, 155) (1930-1942), *Amphicarpaea bracteata* (L.) Fern. var. *comosa* (L.) Fern. (5, 72, 93, 97, 131) (1899-1937)

Pitcher's leather flower - *Clematis pitcheri* Torr. & Gray var. *pitcheri* (5, 97) (1913-1937)

Pitcher's sage [Pitchers sage, Pitcher sage] - *Salvia azurea* Michx. ex Lam. (4) (1986), *Salvia azurea* Michx. ex Lam. var. *grandiflora* Benth. (3, 5, 50, 72, 93, 95, 97, 155) (1907–present)

Pitcher's sandwort - *Minuartia patula* (Michx.) Mattf. (5, 97) (1913-1937)

Pitcher's stitchwort - *Minuartia patula* (Michx.) Mattf. (50) (present)

Pitcher's thistle - *Cirsium pitcheri* (Torr. ex Eat.) Torr. & Gray (5) (1913)

Pitcher-shield lichen - *Urceolaria panyrga* Ach. (19) (1840)

Pitchfork grass - *Paspalum setaceum* Michx. (5) (1913)

Pitchforks [Pitch-forks] - *Bidens cernua* L. (5, 62, 156, 158) (1900-1923), *Bidens connata* Muhl. ex Willd. (62, 156) (1912-1923), *Bidens frondosa* L. (76) (1896), *Bidens* L. (2) (1895)

Pitch-seed plant [Pitch seed plant] - *Pittosporum tobira* (Thunb.) Aiton f. (92) (1876)

Pith rush - *Juncus effusus* L. var. *conglomeratus* (L.) Engelm. (5, 156) (1913-1923)

Pithahatusakitstsuhast (Pawnee) - *Glycyrrhiza lepidota* Pursh (37) (1919)

Pit-seed goosefoot [Pitseed goosefoot] - *Chenopodium berlandieri* Moq. (3, 4, 50, 155) (1942–present)

Pitsuts (Pawnee, hairbrush) - *Hesperostipa spartea* (Trin.) Barkworth (37) (1830)

Pitted joint grass [Pitted joint-grass] - *Coelorachis cylindrica* (Michx.) Nash (5, 119, 163) (1852-1938)

Pitted quillwort - *Isoetes* × *foveolata* A. A. Eat. ex Dodge [*engelmannii* × *tuckermannii*] (5) (1913)

Pittosporum - *Pittosporum* Banks ex Soland. (138) (1923)

Piunkum - *Packera aurea* (L.) A.& D. Löve (156) (1923)

Pix burgundica - *Abies alba* Mill. (57) (1917)

Pix canadensis - *Tsuga canadensis* (L.) Carr. (57) (1917) source

Pixie - *Silene regia* Sims. (156, 158) (1900–1923), *Stellaria holostea* L. (5) (1913)

Pixy - *Pyxidanthera barbulata* Michx. (2) (1895)

Pizpiza-ta-wote (Dakota, prairie dog food) - *Dyssodia papposa* (Vent.) A.S. Hitchc. (37) (1919)

Pkanak (Chippewa) - *Juglans cinerea* L. (105) (1932)

Plain gentian - *Gentiana alba* Muhl. ex Nutt. (50) (present)

Plaine (French Canadian) - *Acer rubrum* L. (107) (1919)

Plain-leaf pussytoes [Plainleaf pussytoes] - *Antennaria plantaginifolia* (L.) Richards (3, 4) (1977-1986)

Plains aristida - *Aristida longispica* Poir. var. *geniculata* (Raf.) Fern (5, 163) (1852-1913)

Plains bahia - *Picradeniopsis oppositifolia* (Nutt.) Rydb. ex Britton (155) (1942)

Plains beebalm - *Monarda pectinata* Nutt. (4) (1986)

Plains black nightshade - *Solanum interius* Rydb. (4) (1986)

Plains blackfoot - *Melampodium leucanthum* Torr. & Gray (50, 155) (1942–present)

Plains bluegrass - *Poa arida* Vasey (3, 50, 122, 140, 155) (1937–present)

Plains bristle grass [Plains bristlegrass] - *Setaria vulpiseta* (Lam.) Roemer & J.A. Schultes (50, 122, 155) (1937–present)

Plains chinese-lantern [Plains chineselantern] - *Quincula lobata* (Torr.) Raf. (155) (1942)

Plains cinquefoil - *Potentilla bipinnatifida* Dougl. ex Hook. (5) (1913)

Plains clover - *Trifolium campestre* Schreber. (3) (1977)

Plains coreopsis - *Coreopsis tinctoria* Nutt. (3, 155) (1942-1977)

Plains corydalis - *Corydalis micrantha* (Engelm. ex Gray) Gray subsp. *australis* (Chapman) G. B. Ownbey (5, 93, 97) (1913–1937)

Plains cottonwood - *Populus deltoides* Bartr. ex Marsh. subsp. *monilifera* (Aiton) Eckenwalder (50, 155) (1942–present)

Plains cymopterus - *Cymopterus acaulis* (Pursh) Raf. (5, 97, 131) (1899-1937)

Plains dozedaisy - *Aphanostephus ramosissimus* DC. (50) (present)

Plains ersysimum - *Erysimum capitatum* (Dougl. ex Hook.) Greene var. *capitatum* (155) (1942)

Plains eryngo - *Eryngium planum* L. (50) (present)

Plains fimbristylis - *Fimbristylis puberula* (Michx.) Vahl var. *interior* (Britt.) Kral (5, 50) (1913–present)

Plains flaveria - *Flaveria campestris* Johnst. (5, 97) (1913-1937)

Plains flax - *Linum puberulum* (Engelm.) Heller (4, 50) (1986–present)

Plains fleabane - *Erigeron modestus* Gray (50) (present)

Plains greasebush - *Glossopetalon planitierum* (Ensign) St. John (50) (present)

Plains ironweed - *Vernonia marginata* (Torr.) Raf. (3, 4, 50) (1977–present)

Plains larkspur - *Delphinium carolinianum* Walt. subsp. *virescens* (Nutt.) Brooks (155) (1942)

Plains lemon monarda - *Monarda pectinata* Nutt. (5, 93) (1913-1936)

Plains love grass [Plains lovegrass, Plains love-grass] - *Eragrostis intermedia* Hitchc. (3, 50, 122, 155) (1937–present)

Plains melampodium - *Melampodium leucanthum* Torr. & Gray (5, 97) (1913-1937)

Plains milkvetch - *Astragalus gilviflorus* Sheldon (50) (present), *Astragalus gilviflorus* Sheldon var. *gilviflorus* (50) (present)

Plains milkweed - *Asclepias pumila* (Gray) Vail (4, 50, 155) (1942–present)

Plains muhly - *Muhlenbergia cuspidata* (Torr. ex Hook.) Rydb. (3, 50) (1977–present)

Plains onion - *Allium perdulce* S. V. Fraser (50) (present)

Plains orophaca - *Astragalus gilviflorus* Sheldon (4) (1986)

Plains phlox - *Phlox andicola* E. Nels. (4, 155) (1942-1986)

Plains poplar - *Populus deltoides* Bartr. ex Marsh. subsp. *monilifera* (Aiton) Eckenwalder (155) (1942)

Plains poteridium - *Sanguisorba annua* (Nutt. ex Hook.) Torr. & Gray (5, 97) (1913-1937)

Plains prickly pear [Plains pricklypear] - *Opuntia macrorhiza* Engelm. (4) (1986), *Opuntia polyacantha* Haw. (4, 50, 155) (1942–present)

Plains psilostrophe - *Psilostrophe tagetina* (Nutt.) Greene var. *cerifera* (A. Nels.) B.L. Turner (5, 97) (1913-1937)

Plains rain-lily [Plains rain lily] - *Zephyranthes longifolia* Hemsl. (122) (1937) TX

Plains reed-grass [Plains reedgrass] - *Calamagrostis montanensis* Scribn. (3, 50, 155, 185) (1936–present)

Plains sand-parsley [Plains sandparsley] - *Ammoselinum popei* Torr. & Gray (50) (present)

Plains shinnery - *Quercus ×pauciloba* Rydb. [*gambelii × turbinella*] (122) (1937) TX

Plains snake-cotton [Plains snakecotton] - *Froelichia floridana* (Nutt.) Moq. (50) (present), *Froelichia floridana* (Nutt.) Moq. var. *campestris* (Small) Fern. (50) (present)

Plains spring-parsley [Plains springparsley] - *Cymopterus acaulis* (Pursh) Raf. (50) (present), *Cymopterus acaulis* (Pursh) Raf. var. *acaulis* (50) (present)

Plains sunflower - *Helianthus ciliaris* DC. (122) (1937) TX, *Helianthus petiolaris* Nutt (3) (1977)

Plains tumbleweed - *Cycloloma atriplicifolium* (Spreng.) Coult. (122) (1937)

Plains violet - *Viola viarum* Pollard (5) (1913)

Plains wild indigo [Plains wildindigo] - *Baptisia bracteata* var. *glabrescens* (Larisey) Isely (3, 155) (1942-1977)

Plains yellow primrose - *Calylophus serrulatus* (Nutt.) Raven (4) (1986)

Plaintain - *Musa ×paradisiaca* L. [*acuminata × balbisiana*] (92, 109) (1876–1949)

Plaintain ordinaire (French) - *Plantago major* L. (6) (1892)

Plaintain shoreweed [Plantain shore-weed, Plaintain shore weed] - *Littorella uniflora* (L.) Ascherson (5, 156) (1913-1923)

Plaintain tree - *Musa* L. (7, 92) (1828-1876)

Plaintain-leaf everlasting - *Antennaria plantaginifolia* (L.) Richards (5, 62, 72) (1907-1913)

Plait-leaf dewberry [plaitleaf dewberry] - *Rubus plicatifolius* Blanch. (50) (present)

Plane (Spanish) - *Musa ×paradisiaca* L. [*acuminata × balbisiana*] (110) (1886) for resemblance to plane tree

Plane tree [Planetree, Plane-tree] - *Acer pseudoplatanus* L. (165) (1768) Scotland, *Platanus* L. (1, 2, 4, 8, 109, 138, 155, 158, 167, 184) (1793-1986), *Platanus occidentalis* L. (4, 5, 9, 18, 72, 92, 93, 95, 113, 156, 187) (1805-1986)

Plane-leaf willow [Planeleaf willow] - *Salix planifolia* Pursh (4, 155) (1942-1986)

Plane-tree maple [Planetree maple] - *Acer pseudoplatanus* L. (155) (1942)

Plant-acid [Plant acid] - *Triplasis purpurea* (Walt.) Chapman (5) (1913)

Plantago - *Plantago major* L. (57) (1917)

Plantain (French) - *Plantago lanceolata* L. (158) (1900)

Plantain [Plantayne] - *Musa ×paradisiaca* L. [*acuminata × balbisiana*] (107) (1919), *Plantago* L. (1, 2, 4, 10, 50, 63, 82, 93, 156, 158, 184) (1793–present), *Plantago major* L. (6, 19, 37, 40, 46, 49, 52, 53, 57, 107, 157, 158, 179) (1526–1939), *Plantago patagonica* Jacq. (146) (1939), *Plantago rugelii* Dcne. (145) (1897)

Plantain goldenweed - *Ericameria suffruticosa* (Nutt.) G.L. Nesom (155) (1942), *Pyrrocoma uniflora* (Hook.) Greene var. *uniflora* (155) (1942)

Plantain sedge [Plantane sedge] - *Carex plantaginea* Lam. (187) (1818)

Plantain-leaf cudweed [Plantain leaf cud-weed, Plantane-leaved cud-weed] - *Antennaria plantaginifolia* (L.) Richards (possibly) (158, 187) (1817-1900)

Plantain-leaf everlasting [Plantain leaf everlasting, Plantain-leaved everlasting] - *Antennaria dioica* (L.) Gaertn. (156) (1923), *Antennaria plantaginifolia* (L.) Richards (93, 97, 156, 158) (1900-1937)

Plantain-leaf sedge [Plantainleaf sedge, Plantain-leaved sedge] - *Carex plantaginea* Lam. (5, 50, 66, 138, 156) (1903–present)

Plantain-lily [Plantainlily] - *Hosta plantaginea* (Lam.) Aschers. (156) (1923), *Hosta* Tratt. (109, 138) (1923-1949)

Plantian-leaf pussytoes [Plantianleaf pussytoes] - *Antennaria plantaginifolia* (L.) Richards (155) (1942)

Plant-of-gluttony - *Cornus suecica* L. (156) (1923)

Plaqueminier (French) - *Diospyros* L. (8, 20) (1785-1857), *Diospyros virginiana* L. (7) (1828)

Plaqueminier de Virginie (French) - *Diospyros virginiana* L. (8, 158) (1785–1900)

Plaster clover [Plaster-clover] - *Melilotus officinalis* (L.) Lam. (5, 156, 158) (1900–1923)

Platane (French) - *Platanus* L. (8) (1785)

Platane de Californie (French) - *Platanus racemosa* Nutt. (20) (1857)

Platane d'Occident (French) - *Platanus occidentalis* L. (8) (1785)

Plateau oak - *Quercus fusiformis* Small (50) (present)

Plater clover - *Melilotus officinalis* (L.) Lam. (157) (1929)

Platte cedar - *Juniperus scopulorum* Sarg. (157) (1929)

Platte cinquefoil - *Potentilla plattensis* Nutt. (155) (1942)

Platte lupine - *Lupinus plattensis* S. Wats. (4) (1986)

Platte milkvetch [Platte milk vetch] - *Astragalus plattensis* Nutt. (5, 72, 93, 97, 131) (1899-1937)

Platte River cinquefoil - *Potentilla plattensis* Nutt. (50) (present)

Platte River milkvetch [Platte River milk vetch] - *Astragalus plattensis* Nutt. (4, 50) (1986–present)

Platte thistle - *Cirsium canescens* Nutt. (3, 4) (1977-1986)

Platystemon - *Platystemon* Benth. (138) (1923)

Pleated gentian - *Gentiana affinis* Griesb. (50) (present)

Pleatleaf - *Nemastylis* Nutt. (50) (present)

Pleat-leaf knotweed [Pleatleaf knotweed] - *Polygonum tenue* Michx. (50) (present)

Plentage - *Botrychium lunaria* (L.) Sw. (158) (1900)

Pleurisy root [Pleurisy-root, Pleurisyroot] - *Asclepias tuberosa* L. (5, 6, 7, 19, 37, 42, 49, 52, 53, 54, 58, 62, 64, 72, 77, 92, 95, 106, 107, 109, 131, 156, 157, 158, 186, 187) (1814-1949)

Pliant meally - *Viburnum* L. (8) (1785)

Pliant milkvetch [Pliant milk vetch] - *Astragalus flexuosus* (Hook.) Dougl. ex G. Don (4) (1986)

Plowman's-spikenard [Ploughman's spikenard, Plowman's spikenard] - *Baccharis halimifolia* L. (5, 75, 156) (1894-1923), *Baccharis* L. (8, 167) (1785-1814)

Plowman's-wort [Ploughman's wort, Plowmans'-wort, Plowmans'-wort, Plowmanwort] - *Conyza* Less. (7) (1828), *Pluchea camphorata* (L.) DC. (5, 156) (1913-1923), *Pluchea foetida* (L.) DC. (19, 92) (1840-1876), *Sericocarpus asteroides* (L.) B.S.P. (184, 187) (1793-1818)

Pluchea - *Pluchea* Cass. (155) (1942)

Plum [Plomme, Plumb, Plumbs, Plums] or Plum tree [Plumb tree, Plum trees] - *Prunus americana* Marsh. (35, 46, 112, 114) (1806-1937), *Prunus domestica* L. (19, 92, 107, 178, 179, 182) (1526-1919), *Prunus* L. (1, 4, 7, 8, 10, 50, 63, 106, 138, 155, 158, 167, 184) (1785--present)

Plum bogberry [Plum bog berry] - *Rubus pubescens* Raf. var. *pubescens* (5) (1913)

Plum grape [Plumb grape] - *Vitis labrusca* L. (7, 19, 156) (1828-1923)

Plumbago - *Plumbago* L. (138) (1923), *Polygonum persicaria* L. (158) (1900)

Plumbog - *Rubus pubescens* Raf. var. *pubescens* (73) (1892) Newfoundland

Plume albizia [Plume albizzia] - *Paraserianthes lophantha* (Willd.) I. Nielsen (109, 138, 155) (1923-1949)

Plume goldenrod [Plume golden-rod] - *Solidago juncea* Aiton (5, 156) (1913-1923)

Plume grass [Plume-grass, Plumegrass] - *Phragmites australis* (Cav.) Trin. ex Steud. (85) (1932) SD, *Saccharum alopecuroidum* (L.) Nutt. (5) (1913), *Saccharum giganteum* (Walt.) Pers. (5) (1913), *Saccharum* L. (56, 155) (1901-1942), *Saccharum ravennae* (L.) L. (109) (1949)

Plume stonecrop - *Sedum hispanicum* L. (138, 155) (1931-1942)

Plume thistle [Plume-thistle] - *Cirsium vulgare* (Savi) Ten. (5, 156, 158) (1900-1923)

Plumed brickellbush - *Brickellia brachyphylla* (Gray) Gray (50) (present)

Plumeless thistle - *Carduus acanthoides* L. (3, 4) (1977-1986), *Carduus* L. (4, 50, 156) (1923–present), *Carduus nutans* L. (5, 156, 158) (1900-1923)

Plume-poppy [Plumepoppy] - *Bocconia* L. (138) (1923), *Macleaya cordata* (Willd.) R. Br. (109) (1949)

Plum-granite [Plum granite] - *Prunus americana* Marsh. (5, 156, 158) (1900-1923) no longer in use by 1923

Plum-leaf apple [Plum-leaved apple] - *Malus prunifolia* (Willd.) Borkh. (107) (1919)

Plum-leaf hawthorn [Plumleaf hawthorn] - *Crataegus persimilis* Sarg. (138) (1923)

Plum-leaf mealy tree [Plumb-leaved mealy-tree] - *Viburnum prunifolium* L. (187) (1818)

Plum-leaf medlar [Plumb leaved medlar] - *Photinia floribunda* (Lindl.) Robertson & Phipps (8) (1785)

Plymouth crowberry - *Corema conradii* (Torr.) Torr. ex Loud. (5, 156) (1913-1923)

Plyvens - *Trifolium pratense* L. (157, 158) (1900-1929)

Pne-obogons (Chippewa) - *Hepatica nobilis* Schreb. (105) (1932)

Pne-uzidin (Chippewa, partridge foot) - *Hepatica nobilis* Schreb. (105) (1932)

Po kish' a co mah (Kickapoo) - *Nelumbo lutea* Willd. (35) (1806)

Pocan (Virginian tribes) - *Phytolacca americana* L. var. *americana* (6, 7, 64, 69, 107, 158) (1828-1908)

Pocan bush [Pocan-bush] - *Phytolacca americana* L. (5, 71) (1898-1913), *Phytolacca americana* L. var. *americana* (92, 156) (1876-1923)

Pocket-drop [Pocket drop] - *Impatiens capensis* Meerb. (5) (1913)

Pockweed - *Symplocarpus foetidus* (L.) Salisb. ex Nutt. (64) (1908)

Pocones - *Lithospermum canescens* (Michx.) Lehm. (46) (1879)

Pocum - *Phytolacca americana* L. (77) (1898) Sulphur Grove OH, friends of J.K. Polk used this plant as their symbol when he was running for president

Pod corn - *Zea mays* L. subsp. *mays* (119) (1938)

Pod fern [Podfern] - *Aspidotis densa* (Brack.) Lellinger (138) (1923)

Podagraire (French) - *Aegopodium* L. (165) (1768)

Podded Virginia Cress - *Sibara virginica* (L.) Rollins (181) (~1678)

Podgrass - *Triglochin* L. (155) (1942)

Podocarpus - *Podocarpus* L'Hér. ex Pers. (138) (1923)

Podophylle (French) - *Podophyllum peltatum* L. (6) (1892)

Podophylle de montagne (French) - *Podophyllum peltatum* L. (7) (1828)

Podophyllum - *Podophyllum peltatum* L. (54, 59, 64, 174, 177) (1753-1911)

Poet's jessamine [Poets jessamine] - *Jasminum officinale* L. (109) (1949)

Poet's narcissus [Poets narcissus] - *Narcissus poeticus* L. (19, 109, 138, 156) (1840-1949)

Pogonia - *Pogonia* Juss. (50, 138) (1923–present)

Pogotč-minjimin (Chippewa [wild pea]) - *Lathyrus palustris* L. (105) (1932)

Poinsettia - *Euphorbia* L. (93, 138) (1923-1939), *Euphorbia pulcherrima* Willd. ex Klotzsch (92, 106, 138) (1876-1930)

Pointed bellflower [Pointed bell flower] - *Campanulastrum americanum* (L.) Small (42) (1814)

Pointed blue-eyed grass - *Sisyrinchium angustifolium* Mill. (5, 93, 97, 15, 158) (1895-1937)

Pointed broom sedge - *Carex scoparia* Schkuhr ex Willd. (5, 72) (1907-1913)

Pointed cleavers - *Galium asprellum* Michx. (5, 49, 92, 156) (1876-1923)

Pointed dropseed [Pointed drop-seed] - *Sporobolus coromandelianus* (Retz.) Kunth (119) (1938)

Pointed dropseed grass [Pointed dropseed-grass - *Sporobolus coromandelianus* (Retz.) Kunth (5, 163) (1852-1913)

Pointed duckweed - *Wolffia brasiliensis* Weddell (5) (1913)

Pointed erigeron - *Erigeron karvinskianus* DC. (86) (1878)

Pointed slender grass - *Leptochloa panicea* (Retz.) Ohwi subsp. *mucronata* (Michx.) Nowack (66) (1903)

Pointed spear grass - *Glyceria acutiflora* Torr. (66, 90) (1885-1903)

Pointed-leaf bellwort [Pointed-leaved bellwort] - *Campanulastrum americanum* (L.) Small (187) (1818)

Pointed-leaf tick trefoil [Pointed leaved tick trefoil, Pointedleaf ticktrefoil, Pointed-leaved tick-trefoil] - *Desmodium cuspidatum* (Muhl. ex Willd.) DC. ex Loud. var. *cuspidatum* (5, 72, 93, 97) (1907-1937), *Desmodium glutinosum* (Muhl. ex Willd.) Wood (50) (present)

Pointed-rush [Pointed rush] - *Luzula arcuata* (Wahlenb.) Sw. (66) (1903)

Pointed-sedge [Pointed sedge] - *Cyperus acuminatus* Torr. & Hook. ex Torr. (66) (1903)

Point-leaf manzanita [Pointleaf manzanita] - *Arctostaphylos pungens* Kunth (155) (1942)

Pointvetch - *Oxytropis* DC. (155) (1942)

Poípie (Dakota) - *Mirabilis nyctaginea* (Michx.) MacM. (37) (1919)

Poires (French Canadians) - *Amelanchier canadensis* (L.) Medik. (46, 107) (1879-1919)

Poiret's copperleaf [Poirets copperleaf] - *Acalypha poiretii* Spreng. (50, 155) (1942–present)

Poirier (French) - *Pyrus* L. (8) (1785)

Poirier rivulaire (French) - *Malus fusca* (Raf.) Schneid. (20) (1857)

Pois d'Angola (French Antilles) - *Cajanus cajan* (L.) Millsp. (110) (1886)

Pois de Congo (French Antilles) - *Cajanus cajan* (L.) Millsp. (110) (1886)

Pois de Shicoriat (French) - *Nelumbo lutea* Willd. (35) (1806)

Pois du Duc de Choifeul (French) - *Aeschynomene americana* L. (165) (1768)

Pois eternel (French) - *Lathyrus latifolius* L. (46) (1879)

Pois pigeon (French Antilles) - *Cajanus cajan* (L.) Millsp. (110) (1886)

Poison amanita - *Amanita phalloides* (Fr.) Link (71) (1898)

Poison arum - *Peltandra virginica* (L.) Schott. (5, 156) (1913-1923)

Poison ash - *Chionanthus virginicus* L. (5, 6, 156) (1892-1923), *Cotinus coggygria* Scop. (92) (1876), *Metopium toxiferum* (L.) Krug & Urban (92, 165) (1807-1876), *Toxicodendron toxicarium* (Salisb.) Gillis (19) (1840), *Toxicodendron vernix* (L.) Kuntze (5, 6, 8, 47, 71, 76, 92, 156) (1785-1923) VT

Poison bay - *Illicium floridanum* Ellis (14) (1882)

Poison black cherry - *Atropa bella-donna* L. (156) (1923)

Poison bulb [Poisonbulb] - *Crinum asiaticum* L. (92, 138) (1876-1923)

Poison camas - *Zigadenus* Michx. (1, 93) (1932-1936), *Zigadenus venenosus* S. Wats. var. *gramineus* (Rydb.) Walsh ex M.E. Peck (85) (1932)

Poison chickweed - *Anagallis arvensis* L. (77) (1898) CA

Poison daisy - *Anthemis cotula* L. (157, 158) (1900-1929)

Poison darnel [Posison-darnel] - *Lolium temulentum* L. (3, 4, 45, 56, 80, 88, 119, 163) (1852-1986)

Poison dock - *Rumex obtusifolius* L. (77) (1898) Sulphur Grove OH

Poison dogwood - *Toxicodendron vernix* (L.) Kuntze (2, 5, 6, 13, 15, 71, 92, 156) (1849-1923)

Poison elder - *Sambucus racemosa* L. (5, 156) (1913-1923), *Sambucus racemosa* L. var. *racemosa* (76, 158) (1896-1900) Oxford Co. ME

Poison elder - *Toxicodendron vernix* (L.) Kuntze (2, 5, 6, 13, 15, 19, 71, 74, 92, 156) (1840-1923) Alabama

Poison flag - *Iris versicolor* L. (5, 49, 64, 92, 156, 157, 158) (1900–1929)

Poison flag root [Poison flag-root] - *Iris prismatica* Pursh ex Ker-Gawl. (75, 156) (1894-1923) Concord MA, *Iris versicolor* L. (75) (1894) Concord MA

Poison flower [Poison-flower] - *Porophyllum gracile* Benth. (75) (1894) Colorado River, *Solanum dulcamara* L. (156, 158) (1900-1923)

Poison hemlock [Poison-hemlock, Poisonhemlock] - *Cicuta* L. (1) (1932), *Cicuta maculata* L. (40, 47, 85, 158) (1852–1932), *Cicuta maculata* L. var. *angustifolia* Hook. (148) (1939), *Conium* L. (50, 158) (1900–present), *Conium maculatum* L. (1, 3, 4, 5, 6, 19, 49, 50, 52, 53, 57, 59, 62, 63, 71, 72, 92, 107, 109, 125, 126, 155, 156, 158) (1892–present) hemlock = leek of the shore or border (Saxon), *Leucothoe axillaris* (Lam.) D. Don. (156) (1923)

Poison humlock - *Conium maculatum* L. (158) (1900)

Poison humly - *Conium maculatum* L. (158) (1900)

Poison ivy - *Kalmia latifolia* L. (71, 106, 156) (1898–1930) Southern states, *Toxicodendron diversilobum* (Torr. & Gray) Greene (71) (1898), *Toxicodendron* Mill (1, 4, 93) (1932–1986), *Toxicodendron radicans* (L.) Kuntze (4, 5, 19, 41, 92, 108, 122, 125) (1770–1986), *Toxicodendron radicans* (L.) Kuntze subsp. *negundo* (Greene) Gillis (3) (1977), *Toxicodendron radicans* (L.) Kuntze subsp. *pubens* (Engelm.) Gillis (Scheele) Gillis (3, 181) (~1678–1977), *Toxicodendron radicans* (L.) Kuntze subsp. *radicans* (41, 46, 62, 71, 72, 95, 131, 157, 158) (1770–1929), *Toxicodendron radicans* (L.) Kuntze subsp. *verrucosum* (Scheele) Gillis (3, 97) (1937–1977), *Toxicodendron rydbergii* (Small ex Rydb.) Greene (3, 4, 5, 85, 93, 126, 148) (1932–1986), *Toxicodendron toxicarium* (Salisb.) Gillis (2, 3, 6, 9, 13, 15, 19, 47, 49, 52, 53, 54, 57, 72, 6, 80, 82, 102, 6, 113, 122, 130, 145, 156) (1840–1977)

Poison laurel - *Kalmia latifolia* L. (71) (1898)

Poison milkweed - *Asclepias subverticillata* (Gray) Vail (3, 4) (1977-1986), *Asclepias verticillata* L. (148, 155) (1939-1942)

Poison oak [Poison-oak, Poisonoak] - *Rhus* L. (13) (1849), *Toxicodendron diversilobum* (Torr. & Gray) Greene (15, 71, 76, 106, 161) (1857-1930), *Toxicodendron* Mill (1, 4, 50) (1932–present), *Toxicodendron pubescens* Mill. (8, 156) (1785-1923), *Toxicodendron radicans* (L.) Kuntze subsp. *radicans* (14, 62, 71, 131, 157, 158, 177) (1762-1882), *Toxicodendron rydbergii* (Small ex Rydb.) Greene (153) (1913), *Toxicodendron toxicarium* (Salisb.) Gillis (2, 5, 6, 8, 13, 14, 15, 37, 48, 49, 52, 53, 54, 57, 61, 92, 97, 130, 145, 156) (1849-1937), *Toxicodendron vernix* (L.) Kuntze (71, 92, 105, 122, 124, 156) (1876-1937)

Poison onion - *Zigadenus venenosus* S. Wats. var. *gramineus* (Rydb.) Walsh ex M.E. Peck (148) (1939) CO

Poison pippsissewa - *Chimaphila maculata* (L.) Pursh (187) (1818)

Poison rhubarb - *Petasites hybridus* (L.) G. Gaertn., B. Mey. & Scherb. (5, 156) (1913-1923)

Poison sheep sorrel [Poison sheep-sorrel] - *Oxalis stricta* L. (5, 76, 156) (1896-1923) Sulphur Grove OH

Poison snakeroot - *Conium maculatum* L. (156, 158) (1900-1923)

Poison snakeweed - *Cicuta maculata* L. (158) (1900), *Conium maculatum* L. (71, 158) (1898–1900)

Poison suckleya - *Suckleya suckleyana* (Torr.) Rydb. (4, 50, 155) (1942–present)

Poison sumac [Poison sumach, Poison shumach, Poyson sumack] - *Toxicodendron* Mill (1) (1932), *Toxicodendron rydbergii* (Small ex Rydb.) Greene (48, 148) (1882-1939), *Toxicodendron vernix* (L.) Kuntze (2, 5, 6, 13, 15, 19, 46, 50, 71, 92, 105, 156, 187) (1818–present), *Toxicodendron toxicarium* (Salisb.) Gillis (190) (~1759)

Poison swamp sumac - *Toxicodendron vernix* (L.) Kuntze (71) (1898)

Poison tree [Poison-tree] - *Rhus* L. (13) (1849), *Toxicodendron* Mill (8) (1785), *Toxicodendron vernix* (L.) Kuntze (5, 6, 13, 71, 156) (1849-1923)

Poison vetch [Poisonvetch] - *Astragalus* L. (155) (1942)

Poison vine [Poison-vine] - *Toxicodendron radicans* (L.) Kuntze (8, 92) (1785–1876), *Toxicodendron radicans* (L.) Kuntze subsp. *radicans* (8, 38, 62, 71, 92, 157, 158, 187) (1785–1929), *Toxicodendron toxicarium* (Salisb.) Gillis (6, 13, 49, 53, 76, 92) (1849-1922)

Poison-berry [Poison berry, Poyson berry] - *Actaea rubra* (Aiton) Willd. (5, 92, 156, 157, 158) (1876–1929), *Dirca palustris* L. (7) (1828), *Kalmia angustifolia* L. (46) (1671), *Solanum dulcamara* L. (156, 158) (1900–1923)

Poison-haw - *Viburnum molle* Michx (156) (1923)

Poisonous elder - *Toxicodendron vernix* (L.) Kuntze (187) (1818)

Poisonous sumach - *Toxicodendron vernix* (L.) Kuntze (41, 62) (1770-1912)

Poisonous zygadenus - *Zigadenus venenosus* S. Wats. var. *gramineus* (Rydb.) Walsh ex M.E. Peck (158) (1900)

Poison-parsley [Poison parsley] - *Conium maculatum* L. (5, 7, 49, 52, 69, 92, 156, 158) (1828-1923)

Poison-root [Poisonroot, Poison root] - *Cicuta maculata* L. (7) (1828), *Conium maculatum* L. (71, 92) (1876-1898)

Poison-sage [Poison sage] - *Zigadenus venenosus* S. Wats. var. *gramineus* (Rydb.) Walsh ex M.E. Peck (148) (1939) CO

Poison-tobacco [Poison tobacco] - *Hyoscyamus niger* L. (5, 6, 7, 92, 156, 158) (1828-1923)

Poisonweed [Poison weed, Poysonweed] - *Delphinium geyeri* Greene (71) (1898), *Delphinium* L. (148) (1939) CO, *Toxicodendron radicans* (L.) Kuntze subsp. *radicans* (181) (~1678)

Poisonwood [Poison wood, Poison-wood] - *Metopium toxiferum* (L.) Krug & Urban (165) (1807)

Poisonwood [Poison wood, Poison-wood] or Poison-wood tree - *Toxicodendron vernix* (L.) Kuntze (5, 6, 46, 71, 92) (1876-1913)

Poivre de Guinée (French "Guinea pepper") - *Capsicum annuum* L. (110) (1886)

Poivre d'Indie (French, Indian pepper) - *Capsicum annuum* L. (110) (1886)

Poivre du Brézil (French, Brazilian pepper) - *Capsicum annuum* L. (110) (1886)

Poivrier (French) - *Lindera benzoin* Blume. (17) (1796), *Myrica gale* L. (41) (1770)

Poke - *Phytolacca americana* L. (5, 14, 52, 54, 69, 71, 97, 109, 124, 177, 187) (1762–1949), *Phytolacca americana* L. var. *americana* (7, 10, 38, 49, 53, 55, 60, 61, 64, 158, 184, 186) (1793-1922), *Phytolacca* L. (167) (1814), *Symplocarpus foetidus* (L.) Salisb. ex Nutt. (186) (1814)

Poke milkweed - *Asclepias exaltata* L. (2, 5, 63, 82, 156) (1895-1930)

Pokeberry [Poke-berry, Poke berry] - *Phytolacca americana* L. (4, 37, 77, 93, 95) (1898-1986), *Phytolacca americana* L. var. *americana* (62, 156) (1912-1923), *Phytolacca* L. (1, 109, 138, 155, 158) (1900-1949)

Poke-leaf milkweed [Poke leaved milk weed, Poke-leaved milkweed] - *Asclepias exaltata* L. (42, 187) (1814-1818)

Poke-leaf swallow-wort [Poke leaved swallow wort] - *Asclepias exaltata* L. (42) (1814)

Pokeroot [Poke root, Poke-root] - *Phytolacca americana* L. (77) (1898), *Phytolacca americana* L. var. *americana* (6, 49, 53, 57, 59, 71, 92, 157) (1892–1929), *Veratrum viride* Ait. (5, 59, 60, 71, 75, 156) (1894-1923) Franconia NH

Poker-plant - *Kniphofia uvaria* (L.) Oken (109) (1949)

Pokeweed [Poke-weed, Poke weed] - *Phytolacca americana* L. (4, 5, 41, 121, 125, 187) (1770-1986), *Phytolacca americana* L. var. *americana* (6, 19, 44, 49, 53, 62, 64, 71, 72, 92, 145, 156, 157, 158, 186, 190) (~1759–1929), *Phytolacca* L. (2, 50, 109) (1895–present), *Symplocarpus foetidus* (L.) Salisb. ex Nutt. (156) (1923)

Pokkige Lobelia - *Lobelia siphilitica* L. (186) (1814)

Pokus haki - *Nelumbo lutea* Willd. (35) (1806)

Pök-weed - *Phytolacca americana* L. var. *americana* (186) (1814)

Poland manna - *Glyceria fluitans* (L.) R. Br. (5, 107) (1913-1919)

Polanise graveole (French) - *Polanisia dodecandra* (L.) DC. subsp. *dodecandra* (7) (1828)

Polanisia - *Polanisia dodecandra* (L.) DC. subsp. *trachysperma* (Torr. & Gray) Iltis (114) (1894), *Polanisia* Raf. (82) (1930)

Polar plant [Polar-plant] - *Silphium laciniatum* L. (5, 14, 92, 156, 157, 158) (1882-1919)

Pole bean - *Phaseolus vulgaris* L. (6, 107) (1892-1919)

Pole-cat bush [Polecat bush] - *Rhus aromatica* Aiton (4) (1986)

Pole-cat collard [Polecat-collard] - *Symplocarpus foetidus* (L.) Salisb. ex Nutt. (186) (1814)

Pole-cat root [Polecat root] - *Symplocarpus foetidus* (L.) Salisb. ex Nutt. (41) (1770)

Pole-cat tree [Polecat tree, Polecat-tree] - *Frangula caroliniana* (Walt.) Gray (106, 156) (1923-1930)

Pole-cat weed [Pole cat weed, Polecat weed, Polecat-weed] - *Symplocarpus foetidus* (L.) Salisb. ex Nutt. (5, 6, 41, 53, 64, 92, 156, 186, 187) (1770-1922)

Polemonium - *Polemonium caeruleum* L. (174, 177) (1753-1762), *Polemonium* L. (138, 155) (1923-1942)

Pole-reed [Pole reed] - *Phragmites australis* (Cav.) Trin. ex Steud. (5, 119) (1913-1938)

Pole-rush [Pole rush] - *Schoenoplectus etuberculatus* (Steud.) Soják (5) (1913), *Schoenoplectus tabernaemontani* (K.C. Gmel.) Palla (156, 158) (1900-1923)

Poley mountain - *Andromeda polifolia* L. (165) (1807)

Poleyblattrige (German) - *Hedeoma pulegioides* (L.) Pers. (7) (1828)

Poleyblattrige Cunila (German) - *Hedeoma pulegioides* (L.) Pers. (186) (1814)

Policary - *Pulicaria* Gaertn. (179) (1526)

Polir-schachtelhalm (German) - *Equisetum hyemale* L. (158) (1900)

Polishing-rush [Polishing rush] - *Equisetum hyemale* L. (158) (1900)

Politryke - *Asplenium* L. (178, 179) (1526-1596)

Polk weed - *Symplocarpus foetidus* (L.) Salisb. ex Nutt. (5, 73) (1892-1913) Brookline MA

Polka dots [Polkadots] - *Dyschoriste linearis* (Torr. & Gray) Kuntze (50) (present)

Pollom - *Gaultheria procumbens* L. (186) (1814), *Vaccinium macrocarpon* Aiton (7) (1828)

Polly mountain [Polly-mountain] - *Acinos arvensis* (Lam.) Dandy (5, 156) (1913-1923) no longer in use by 1923

Polyandra mexican plum - *Prunus mexicana* S. Wats. (155) (1942)

Polyanthus - *Narcissus tazetta* L. (19) (1840), *Primula veris* L. (92) (1876)

Polyanthus narcissus - *Narcissus tazetta* L. (109, 138) (1923-1949)

Polyanthus primrose - *Primula ×polyantha* P. Mill. [*veris* × *vulgaris*] (138) (1923)

Polygala - *Polygala* L. (50, 138, 155) (1923–present)

Polygale de Virginie (French) - *Polygala senega* L. (6) (1892)

Polygale naine (French) - *Polygala paucifolia* Willd. (7) (1828)

Polygamous meadow rue [Polygamous meadow-rue] - *Thalictrum pubescens* Pursh (187) (1818)

Polygonatum - *Polygonatum biflorum* (Walt.) Ell. (57) (1917), *Polygonatum multiflorum* (L.) All. (178) (1596)

Polymnia - *Polymnia* L. (50) (present), *Smallanthus uvedalius* (L.) Mackenzie ex Small (54) (1905)

Polymorphous panic - *Dichanthelium dichotomum* (L.) Gould var. *dichotomum* (66) (1903)

Polymorphus panic grass - *Dichanthelium dichotomum* (L.) Gould var. *dichotomum* (90) (1885)

Polypod brakes - *Onoclea sensibilis* L. (78) (1898) ME, usually Polypodium

Polypode common (French) (sic.) - *Polypodium virginianum* L. (7) (1828)

Polypodium - *Polypodium virginianum* L. (57) (1917)

Polypody - *Polypodium* L. (1, 50, 109, 138, 155, 158, 167) (1814–present) "many feet" for creeping rootstocks, *Polypodium virginianum* L. (14, 46, 57, 61, 72, 92) (1649–1917)

Polypogon - *Polypogon* Desf. (155) (1942)

Polyprenum - *Polypremum procumbens* L. (5, 97) (1913-1937)

Polypteris - Palafoxia Lag. (155, 158) (1900-1942)

Polyscias - *Polyscias* J.R. & G. Forst. (138) (1923)

Polytaenia - *Polytaenia nuttallii* DC. (72) (1907), *Polytaenia* DC. (158) (1900)

Poma Amoris - *Solanum lycopersicum* L. var. *lycopersicum* (180) (1633)

Poma Peruviana - *Solanum lycopersicum* L. var. *lycopersicum* (107) (1588)

Pomegranate - *Prunus americana* Marsh. (156) (1923) no longer in use by 1923, *Prunus nigra* Aiton (5, 76) (1896–1913)

Pomegranate or Pomegranate tree - *Punica granatum* L. (7, 19, 52, 57, 58, 59, 60, 92, 107, 109, 110, 178) (1526-1949), *Punica* L. (138) (1923)

Pomelo - *Citrus ×limonia* Osbeck [*limon* × *reticulata*] (109) (1949)

Pomette bleue (French) - *Crataegus brachyacantha* Sarg. & Engelm. (74) (1893)

Pomgarnade - *Punica granatum* L. (179) (1526)

Pomi del Peru - *Solanum lycopersicum* L. var. *lycopersicum* (107) (1919)

Pomi d'oro - *Solanum lycopersicum* L. var. *lycopersicum* (107) (1554)

Pomme blanche [Pomme blanch] (French) - *Pediomelum esculentum* (Pursh) Rydb. (2, 5, 34, 36, 37, 38, 83, 85, 93, 95, 101, 107, 121, 156, 158) (1830-1936), *Pediomelum* Rydb. (1) (1932)

Pomme blanche des praires (French) - *Pediomelum esculentum* (Pursh) Rydb. (108) (1878)

Pomme d'amour [Pommes d'amour] (French, love apple) - *Solanum lycopersicum* L. var. *lycopersicum* (107, 158, 180) (1586–1919)

Pomme de prairie (French) - *Pediomelum esculentum* (Pursh) Rydb. (47, 83, 89, 101, 103, 156, 158) (1820-1923), *Pediomelum* Rydb. (1) (1932)

Pomme de racquette (French) - *Opuntia* Mill. (89) (1820), *Opuntia polyacantha* Haw. (101) (1905)

Pomme de terre [Pommes de terre] (French) - *Apios americana* Medik. (27, 35, 47, 103) (1806-1870), *Pediomelum esculentum* (Pursh) Rydb. (38) (1820)

Pomme épineuse (French) - *Datura stramonium* L. (6, 158) (1892-1900)

Pommier d'acajou (French, mahogany apple tree) - *Anacardium occidentale* L. (110) (1886)

Pomo dei Mori (Italian, Morocco apple) - *Solanum lycopersicum* L. var. *lycopersicum* (158) (1900)

Pompelmous - *Citrus maxima* (Burm. f.) Merr. (109) (1949)

Pompeon - *Cucurbita pepo* L. (107) (1683)

Pompion [Pompions] - *Cucumis melo* L. (107) (1919), *Cucurbita moschata* (Duchesne ex Lam.) Duchesne ex Poir. (182) (1791), *Cucurbita pepo* L. (92, 158) (1876–1900)

Pompon [Pompons] - *Cucumis melo* L. (177) (1762), *Cucurbita pepo* L. (107) (1822)

Pond bush [Pond-bush] - *Litsea aestivalis* (L.) Fern. (5, 20, 156) (1857-1923)

Pond buttonwood - *Cephalanthus occidentalis* L. (75) (1894)

Pond cypress [Pondcypress] - *Taxodium ascendens* Brongn. (5, 50, 109, 138) (1913–present)

Pond dock - *Rumex orbiculatus* Gray (155) (1942)

Pond grass - *Elymus repens* (L.) Gould (5) (1913), *Thinopyrum intermedium* (Host) Barkworth & D.R. Dewey (75) (1894) Neb

Pond pine - *Pinus serotina* Michx. (2, 50, 138) (1895–present)

Pond willow - *Salix scouleriana* Barr. (20) (1857), *Salix sericea* Marsh. (20) (1857)

Pond-apple [Pond apple] - *Annona glabra* L. (109, 138) (1923-1949)

Pond-dogwood [Pond dog-wood, Pond dog wood, Pond dogwood] - *Cephalanthus occidentalis* L. (5, 6, 7, 19, 49, 57, 58, 92, 156, 157, 158, 187) (1818-1923)

Ponderosa pine - *Pinus ponderosa* P.& C. Lawson (3, 50, 155) (1942–present), *Pinus ponderosa* P.& C. Lawson var. *scopulorum* Engelm. (50) (present)

Pondgrass [Pond-grass] - *Stuckenia pectinatus* (L.) Boerner (5, 156, 158) (1900-1923)

Pond-lily [Pond lily] - *Nelumbo lutea* Willd. (possibly) (7) (1828), *Nuphar lutea* (L.) Sm. subsp. *advena* (Aiton) Kartesz & Gandhi (106, 127) (1930-1933), *Nuphar* Sm. (50) (present), *Nymphaea elegans* Hook. (124) (1937) TX, *Nymphaea* L. (1, 156, 158) (1900-1932), *Nymphaea odorata* Aiton (49, 131) (1898-1899) IA, *Nymphaea odorata* Aiton subsp. *odorata* (5, 156) (1913-1923)

Pond-shovel [Pond shovel] - *Pontederia cordata* L. (7) (1828)

Pond-spice [Pond spice] - *Litsea aestivalis* (L.) Fern. (2, 5, 92, 156) (1876–1942)

Pondweed [Pondweeds, Pond weed] - *Najas marina* L. (156) (1923), *Potamogeton crispus* L. (5, 156) (1913-1923), *Potamogeton diversifolius* Raf. (85) (1932), *Potamogeton epihydrus* Raf. (85) (1932), *Potamogeton illinoensis* Morong (85) (1932), *Potamogeton* L. (1, 50, 93, 120, 122, 155, 156, 158, 184, 190) (~1759–present), *Potamogeton natans* L. (19) (1840), *Stuckenia* Boerner (50) (present)

Poñel (Mexicans) - *Fallugia paradoxa* (D. Don) Endl. (149) (1904)

Ponil - *Fallugia paradoxa* (D. Don) Endl. (122) (1937) TX

Pontederia - *Pontederia* L. (50) (present)

Pony beebalm - *Monarda pectinata* Nutt. (50, 155) (1942–present)

Pony grass - *Calamagrostis stricta* (Timm) Koel. subsp. *stricta* (5, 111, 115, 116) (1913-1958)

Pool root [Poolroot, Pool-root] - *Ageratina altissima* (L.) King & H.E. Robins. (58, 92, 156) (1869-1923), *Ageratina aromatica* (L.) Spach (5, 92, 156) (1876-1923), *Sanicula marilandica* L. (49, 156, 157, 158) (1900-1923)

Poolmat - *Zannichellia* L. (155) (1942)

Pool-rush [Pool rush] - *Schoenoplectus etuberculatus* (Steud.) Soják (5) (1913)

Poolwort [Pool wort, Pool-wort] - *Ageratina altissima* (L.) King & H.E. Robins. (156) (1923), *Ageratina aromatica* (L.) Spach (5, 92, 156) (1876-1923)

Poor Annie - *Veratrum viride* Ait. (5) (1913)

Poor Jan's leaf - *Sempervivum tectorum* L. (156) (1923)

Poor Joe [Poorjoe] - *Diodia teres* Walt. (5, 50, 156) (1913–present)

Poor Mavis - *Anagallis arvensis* L. (157) (1929)

Poor oat - *Avena fatua* L. (5) (1913)

Poor Robert's-plantain [Poor Robert's Plantane, Poor Robert's plantain] - *Erigeron pulchellus* Michx. (86, 187) (1818-1878), *Hieracium venosum* L. (187) (1818)

Poor Robin [Poor-robin] - *Antennaria plantaginifolia* (L.) Richards (possibly) (7) (1828), *Galium aparine* L. (5, 92, 156, 158) (1876-1923) no longer in use by 1923, *Galium verum* L. (7) (1828), *Silene dioica* (L.) Clairville (156) (1923)

Poor Robin's-plantain [Poor robins plantain, Poor-robins-plantain, Poorrobins-plantain, Poor robin's plantain, Poor robin plantain] - *Erigeron pulchellus* Michx. (5, 86, 109, 138, 155, 156, 158) (1878-1949), *Hieracium venosum* L. (5, 44, 46, 156, 157) (1845-1929)

Poorland daisy [Poor-land daisy] - *Aphanostephus* DC. (122) (1937) TX, *Leucanthemum vulgare* Lam. (5, 156, 158) (1900-1923), *Rudbeckia hirta* L. (5) (1913)

Poorland flatsedge - *Cyperus compressus* L. (50) (present)

Poorland-weed [Poor land weed] - *Diodia teres* Walt. (5, 156) (1913-1923)

Poor-man's-cabbage [Poor man's cabbage] - *Barbarea vulgaris* W.T. Aiton (156) (1923)

Poor-man's-mustard [Poor man's mustard] - *Alliaria petiolata* (Bieb.) Cavara & Grande (5, 156, 158) (1900-1923)

Poor-man's-parmacetie [Poor mans parmacetie] - *Capsella bursa-pastoris* (L.) Medik. (180) (1633)

Poor-man's-pepper [Poor-man's pepper, Poor man's pepper] - *Lepidium campestre* (L.) Aiton f. (5, 156, 158) (1900-1923) no longer in use by 1923, *Lepidium latifolium* L. (107) (1919), *Lepidium sativum* L. (92, 158) (1876-1900), *Sedum acre* L. (5, 156) (1913-1923)

Poor-man's-pharmacetty [Poor man's pharmacetty] - *Capsella bursa-pastoris* (L.) Medik. (92, 157, 158) (1876-1929)

Poor-man's-rhubarb [Poor man's rhubarb, Poor man's rhubarb] - *Thalictrum dioicum* L. (5, 92, 156, 158) (1876-1923)

Poor-man's-soap [Poor man's soap] - *Pteridium aquilinum* (L.) Kuhn (78) (1898) Alabama, will make a lather with water, *Spiraea tomentosa* L. (5, 156) (1913-1923)

Poor-man's-treacle [Poor man's treacle] - *Alliaria petiolata* (Bieb.) Cavara & Grande (158) (1900), *Allium sativum* L. (158) (1900) treacle meant antidote to venomous bite, same as theriac

Poor-man's-weatherglass [Poor man's weatherglass, Poor-man's weather-glass, Poor-man's-weather-glass, Poor man's weather

glass] - *Anagallis arvensis* L. (4, 5, 6, 49, 92, 107, 109, 156, 158, 165) (1807–1986) flowers close in bad weather, *Anagallis* L. (1, 4) (1932–1986)

Poorweed [Poor-weed] - *Diodia teres* Walt. (156) (1923)

Pop ash [Pop-ash] - *Fraxinus caroliniana* Mill. (5, 156) (1913-1923)

Pop corn - *Zea mays* L. subsp. *mays* (109, 119) (1938-1949)

Popaw - *Asimina triloba* (L.) Dunal (12) (1821)

Popcorn flower [Popcorn-flower, Popcornflower] - *Plagiobothrys* Fisch. & C.A. Mey. (50, 155) (1942–present), *Plagiobothrys scouleri* (Hook. & Arn.) I.M. Johnston (3, 4) (1977-1986)

Popdock [Pop-dock, Pop dock] - *Digitalis pupurea* L. (5, 69, 156) (1903-1923) no longer in use by 1923

Pope's phacelia - *Phacelia popei* Torr. & Gray (50) (present)

Pope's sand-parsley [Pope's sand parsley] - *Ammoselinum popei* Torr. & Gray (5, 97) (1913-1937)

Popglove [Pop glove] - *Digitalis pupurea* L. (5) (1913)

Popinac - *Acacia farnesiana* (L.) Willd. (107, 109) (1919-1949)

Poplar birch - *Betula populifolia* Marshall (possibly) (19) (1840)

Poplar buds - *Betula nigra* L. (92) (1876)

Poplar of Carolina - *Populus balsamifera* L. (189) (1767)

Poplar or Poplar tree [Poplar-tree] - *Liriodendron* L. (181) (~1678), *Liriodendron tulipifera* L. (2, 18, 20, 41, 46, 49, 107, 177, 184, 186) (1770-1919), *Populus ×berolinensis* K. Koch (112) (1937), *Populus alba* L. (92) (1876), *Populus deltoides* Bartr. ex Marsh. (112) (1937) Neb, *Populus deltoides* Bartr. ex Marsh. subsp. *monilifera* (Aiton) Eckenwalder (147) (1856), *Populus* L. (1, 2, 4, 7, 8, 10, 34, 35, 82, 108, 109, 138, 155, 156, 158, 167, 184) (1785-1986) from classic Latin name, *Populus tremuloides* Michx. (61) (1870)

Poplar-leaf birch [Poplar leaved birch] - *Betula papyrifera* Marsh (46) (1879)

Poplar-leaf birch [Poplar leaved birch] - *Betula populifolia* Marshall (possibly) (12) (1821)

Poplar-leaf haw [Poplar-leaved haw] - *Crataegus phaenopyrum* (L. f.) Medik. (5) (1913)

Pople - *Populus tremuloides* Michx. (6) (1892)

Popniac - *Acacia farnesiana* (L.) Willd. (7) (1828)

Poponax - *Acacia tortuosa* (L.) Willd. (50) (present)

Popotillo - *Ephedra* L. (153) (1913) NM

Pop-pea - *Astragalus* L. (103) (1870)

Poppy - *Papaver* L. (1, 4, 7, 10, 15, 50, 82, 106, 109, 138, 155, 156, 158, 179, 184) (1793–present), *Papaver somniferum* L. (92, 110, 148) (1876-1939)

Poppy ash [Poppy-ash] - *Fraxinus caroliniana* Mill. (5, 156) (1913-1923)

Poppy-mallow [Poppy mallow, Poppymallow] - *Callirhoe alcaeoides* (Michx.) Gray (95, 156) (1911-1923), *Callirhoe* Nutt. (1, 4, 50, 82, 93, 109, 155, 156, 158) (1900–present), *Callirhoe triangulata* (Leavenworth) Gray (121) (1970)

Poppy-thistle [Poppy thistle] - *Argemone* L. (106) (1930)

Pops - *Physalis angulata* L. (107) (1750)

Popweed [Pop weed, Pop-weed] - *Utricularia macrorhiza* Le Conte (5, 156, 158) (1900-1923)

Porcelain ampelopsis - *Ampelopsis brevipedunculata* (Maxim.) Trautv. (138, 155) (1923-1942)

Porcelain butterfly-pea - *Clitoria mariana* L. (138) (1923)

Porcelayne - *Portulaca oleracea* L. (179) (1526)

Porcellia - *Hieracium* L. (180) (1633)

Porcupine grass [Porcupine-grass, Porcupinegrass] - *Hesperostipa comata* (Trin. & Rupr.) Barkworth subsp. *comata* (5, 108) (1878-1913), *Hesperostipa spartea* (Trin.) Barkworth (3, 45, 50, 56, 66, 67, 85, 93, 94, 111, 115, 119, 121, 129, 134, 155) (1890–present)

Porcupine sedge - *Carex hystericina* Muhl. ex Willd. (5, 42, 66, 72, 156) (1814-1907)

Porcupine seg - *Carex hystericina* Muhl. ex Willd. (42) (1814)

Porcupine-eggs [Porcupine eggs] - *Platanus occidentalis* L. (156) (1923)

Porreau (French) - *Allium porrum* L. (158, 180) (1633–1900)

Port Gregory gum - *Eucalyptus calophylla* R. Br. (138) (1923)

Port Orford cedar - *Chamaecyparis lawsoniana* (A. Murr.) Parl. (14, 50) (1882–present)

Porteranthus - *Porteranthus* Britt. ex Small (50) (present)

Porter's aster [Porters aster] - *Symphyotrichum porteri* (Gray) Nesom (155) (1942)

Porter's brome [Porter brome] - *Bromus porteri* (Coult.) Nash (50, 155) (1942–present)

Porter's chess - *Bromus porteri* (Coult.) Nash (5) (1913)

Porter's melic [Porter melic] - *Melica porteri* Scribn. (3, 122, 155) (1937-1977)

Porter's melic grass [Porter's melicgrass] - *Melica porteri* Scribn. (50) (present)

Porter's muhly - *Muhlenbergia porteri* Scribn. ex Beal (3) (1977)

Porter's panicum - *Dichanthelium boscii* (Poir.) Gould & C.A. Clark (72) (1907), *Dichanthelium latifolium* (L.) Gould & C.A. Clark (56) (1901)

Porter's plum - *Prunus alleghaniensis* Porter (5) (1913)

Porter's pondweed [Porter pondweed] - *Potamogeton illinoensis* Morong (155) (1942)

Porter's reed bent - *Calamagrostis porteri* Gray (94) (1901)

Porter's rush - *Scirpus lineatus* Michx. (66) (1903)

Portia tree [Portia-tree, Portiatree] - *Thespesia populnea* (L.) Soland. ex Correa (109, 138) (1923-1949)

Portugal cabbage - *Brassica* L. (107) (1919)

Portugal laurel [Portugal-laurel] - *Prunus lusitanica* L. (109) (1949)

Portuguese chrysanthemum - *Leucanthemum lacustre* (Brot.) Samp. (138) (1923)

Portuguese daisy - *Leucanthemum lacustre* (Brot.) Samp. (109) (1949)

Portulaca - *Portulaca grandiflora* Hook. (92, 114) (1876-1894), *Portulaca* L. (138, 155, 158) (1923-1942), *Portulaca oleracea* L. (41) (1770)

Possum grape - *Vitis cinerea* (Engelm.) Millard var. *baileyana* (Munson) Comeaux (15) (1895), *Vitis vulpina* L. (5, 156, 158) (1828)

Possum oak - *Quercus nigra* L. (5) (1913)

Possum-berry [Possum berry] - *Callicarpa americana* L. (156) (1923), *Viburnum nudum* L. (75, 106) (1894-1930)

Possum-grape [Possum grape] - *Cissus* L. (4) (1986), *Cissus trifoliata* (L.) L. (3, 4) (1977-1986)

Possum-wood [Possum wood] - *Diospyros virginiana* L. (5, 106, 156, 158) (1900–1930), *Halesia carolina* L. (156) (1923)

Post cedar - *Chamaecyparis thyoides* (L.) Britton, Sterns & Poggenb. (5) (1913)

Post locust - *Robinia pseudoacacia* L. (5, 156, 157, 158) (1900–1929)

Post oak - *Quercus stellata* Wangenh. (1, 3, 4, 5, 18, 19, 20, 27, 33, 50, 65, 72, 82, 97, 109, 113, 124, 138, 155, 156, 164) (1804–present)

Post white oak - *Quercus incana* Bartr. (182) (1791)

Post-oak grape [Post oak grape] - *Vitis aestivalis* Michx. var. *lincecumii* (Buckl.) Munson (15, 107, 109) (1895-1949)

Posum-haw [Possum haw, Possumhaw] - *Ilex crenata* Thunb. (4, 5, 50, 106, 109, 122, 124, 138, 155, 156, 158) (1900–present), *Viburnum nudum* L. (5, 156) (1913-1923)

Posy peas - *Lathyrus odoratus* L. (74) (1893) Franconia NH

Pot marigold [Pot marygold] - *Calendula officinalis* L. (19, 42, 107) (1814-1919)

Pot marjoram [Pot marjorum] - *Origanum vulgare* L. (5, 156) (1913-1923)

Potato [Potatoes] - *Ipomoea batatas* (L.) Lam. (181, 182) (~1678-1791), *Solanum fendleri* Gray ex Torr. (103) (1870), *Solanum* L. (1, 93, 158) (1900-1936), *Solanum tuberosum* L. (19, 107, 109, 110, 138, 156) (1840-1949)

Potato dandelion - *Krigia dandelion* (L.) Nutt. (3) (1977)

Potato dwarf-dandelion [Potato dwarfdandelion] - *Krigia dandelion* (L.) Nutt. (50) (present)

Potato oat - *Avena fatua* L. (107) (1919)

Potato onion - *Allium cepa* L. var. *cepa* (109) (1949)

Potato vine [Potatoe vine] - *Ipomoea pandurata* (L.) G.F.W. Mey. (7) (1828)

Potato-bean [Potatobean, Potato bean] - *Apios americana* Medik. (109, 138, 156) (1923-1949), *Apios* Fabr. (155) (1942)

Potato-bug plant [Potato bug plant] - *Solanum rostratum* Dunal (62) (1912) original host of Colorado potato beetle

Potatoes of Canada - *Helianthus tuberosus* L. (107) (1657)

Potato-jasmine [Potato jasmine] - *Solanum triquetrum* Cav. (77) (1898) Waco TX

Potato-moss - *Stuckenia pectinatus* (L.) Boerner (156) (1923)

Potato-pea [Potato pea] - *Apios americana* Medik. (7, 92, 156) (1828-1923)

Potentilla - *Argentina anserina* (L.) Rydb. (174) (1753), *Potentilla canadensis* L. (156) (1923)

Potherb mustard - *Brassica juncea* (L.) Czern. (138, 155, 156) (1923-1942)

Potherb onion - *Allium oleraceum* L. (155) (1942)

Pothos fetide (French) - *Symplocarpus foetidus* (L.) Salisb. ex Nutt. (6) (1892)

Potincoba - *Polygonum amphibium* L. var. *emersum* Michx. (181) (~1678)

Pot-marigold - *Calendula officinalis* L. (109) (1949)

Pouched nemesia - *Nemesia strumosa* Benth. (138) (1923)

Poukenel - *Scandix pecten-veneris* L. (5, 156) (1913-1923) no longer in use by 1923

Poulard wheat - *Triticum turgidum* L. (109) (1949)

Pouliot Americain (French) - *Hedeoma pulegioides* (L.) Pers. (158) (1900)

Pouliot d'Amerique (French) - *Hedeoma pulegioides* (L.) Pers. (6) (1892)

Poverty - *Sagina procumbens* L. (5, 156) (1913-1923)

Poverty birch - *Betula pubescens* Ehrh. subsp. *pubescens* (5, 156) (1913-1923)

Poverty brome - *Bromus sterilis* L. (50) (present)

Poverty danthonia - *Danthonia spicata* (L.) Beauv. ex Roemer & J.A. Schultes (155) (1942)

Poverty dropseed - *Sporobolus vaginiflorus* (Torr. ex Gray) Wood (50, 155) (1942–present), *Sporobolus vaginiflorus* (Torr. ex Gray) Wood var. *vaginiflorus* (50) (present)

Poverty grass [Poverty-grass, Povertygrass] - *Anthoxanthum* L. (1) (1932), *Aristida dichotoma* Michx. (5, 19, 56, 66, 80, 92, 94, 119, 163) (1840–1938), *Aristida* L. (1, 93, 148) (1932–1939), *Aristida purpurea* Nutt. (145) (1897), *Aristida purpurea* Nutt. var. *longiseta* (Steud.) Vasey (85) (1932), *Aristida tuberculosa* Nutt. (80) (1913) IA, *Danthonia spicata* (L.) Beauv. ex Roemer & J.A. Schultes (143) (1936), *Sporobolus neglectus* Nash (3) (1977), *Sporobolus vaginiflorus* (Torr. ex Gray) Wood var. *vaginiflorus* (3) (1977)

Poverty oat grass [Poverty oat-grass, Poverty oatgrass] - *Danthonia spicata* (L.) Beauv. ex Roemer & J.A. Schultes (3, 50, 122, 143) (1936–present)

Poverty plant [Poverty-plant - *Hudsonia tomentosa* Nutt. (5, 156) (1913-1923)

Poverty rush - *Juncus tenuis* Willd. (50, 155) (1942–present)

Poverty sumpweed - *Iva axillaris* Pursh (155) (1942)

Poverty threeawn [Poverty three awn - *Aristida divaricata* H. & B. (3, 122, 155) (1937-1977)

Poverty-grass [Poverty grass] - *Corema conradii* (Torr.) Torr. ex Loud. (5, 75, 156) (1894-1923) Provincetown MA, *Eleocharis tenuis* (Willd.) J.A. Schultes (5, 75, 156) (1894-1923) WV, *Hudsonia ericoides* L. (5, 156) (1913-1923), *Hudsonia* L. (4) (1986), *Hudsonia tomentosa* Nutt. (3, 5, 15, 76, 158) (1895-1977), *Hypericum gentianoides* (L.) Britton, Sterns & Poggenb. (156) (1923), *Juncus tenuis* Willd. (5, 75, 156) (1894-1923) WV, *Trifolium arvense* L. (5, 156, 158) (1900-1923)

Poverty-weed [Povertyweed, Poverty weed] - *Anaphalis margaritacea* (L.) Benth. & Hook (5, 75, 156) (1894–1923) Penobscot ME, *Antennaria plantaginifolia* (L.) Richards (5, 76, 156, 158) (1896–

1923) Paris ME, *Diodia teres* Walt. (5, 156) (1913–1923), *Iva axillaris* Pursh (3, 4, 50) (1977–present), *Iva frutescens* L. subsp. *oraria* (Bartlett) R.C. Jackson (156) (1923), *Iva* L. (1, 93) (1932–1936), *Leucanthemum vulgare* Lam. (5, 156, 158) (1900–1923), *Monolepis nuttalliana* (J. A. Schultes) Greene (3, 4, 85, 122) (1932–1986), *Monolepis* Schrad. (1, 50) (1932–present), *Pseudognaphalium obtusifolium* (L.) Hilliard & Burtt subsp. *obtusifolium* (5, 76, 92, 156, 157) (1896–1929) Paris ME, *Spergula arvensis* L. (5, 156) (1913–1923)

Powder horn [Powder-horn, Powderhorn] - *Cerastium nutans* Raf. (5, 93, 122, 131, 156) (1899-1937)

Powdered thalia - *Thalia dealbata* Fraser ex Roscoe (138) (1923)

Powdery alligator-flag - *Thalia dealbata* Fraser ex Roscoe (50) (present)

Powdery false cloak fern - *Argyrochosma dealbata* (Pursh) Windham (50) (present)

Powdery notholaena - *Argyrochosma dealbata* (Pursh) Windham (5, 122) (1913-1937)

Powdery thalia - *Thalia dealbata* Fraser ex Roscoe (5, 97, 120, 122, 124) (1913-1938)

Powell's amaranth [Powell amaranth] - *Amaranthus powellii* S. Wats. (50, 155) (1942–present)

Powell's pigweed - *Amaranthus powellii* S. Wats. (4) (1986)

Powell's saltbush - *Atriplex powellii* S. Wats. (4) (1986)

Powell's saltweed - *Atriplex powellii* S. Wats. (50) (present)

Powitch (Chinook) - *Malus fusca* (Raf.) Schneid. (107) (1919)

Powk-needle - *Erodium cicutarium* (L.) L'Hér. ex Aiton (157, 158) (1900-1929)

Pozreue (Brabanders) - *Allium porrum* L. (possibly) (180) (1633)

Prairie acacia - *Acacia angustissima* (Mill.) Kuntze (3, 4, 5, 50, 97, 155) (1913–present)

Prairie agalinis - *Agalinis heterophylla* (Nutt.) Small ex Britton (5) (1913)

Prairie anemone - *Pulsatilla patens* (L.) Mill. (5) (1913), *Pulsatilla patens* (L.) Mill. subsp. *multifida* (Pritz.) Zamels (157, 158) (1900–1929)

Prairie angle-pod - *Matelea biflora* (Raf.) Woods (97) (1937)

Prairie artichoke - *Helianthus × laetiflorus* Pers. [*pauciflorus × tuberosus*] (156) (1923)

Prairie aster - *Symphyotrichum oblongifolium* (Nutt.) Nesom (85) (1932), *Symphyotrichum turbinellum* (Lindl.) Nesom (4, 5, 97, 138, 155) (1923-1986)

Prairie bean [Prairie-bean] - *Phaseolus ritensis* M.E.Jones (107) (1919), *Thermopsis* R. Br. ex Aiton f. (93) (1936)

Prairie beard grass [Prairie beardgrass] - *Schizachyrium scoparium* (Michx.) Nash var. *scoparium* (140) (1944)

Prairie beeblossom - *Gaura triangulata* Buckl. (50) (present)

Prairie bergamot - *Monarda citriodora* Cerv. ex Lag. (156) (1923)

Prairie bergamot - *Monarda pectinata* Nutt. (5) (1913)

Prairie bird's-foot [Prairie bird's foot] - *Lotus unifoliolatus* (Hook.) Benth. var. *unifoliolatus* (72) (1907)

Prairie bird's-foot trefoil [Prairie bird's foot trefoil] - *Lotus unifoliolatus* (Hook.) Benth. (5, 93, 97, 121, 131, 156) (1899-1937)

Prairie blazing star - *Liatris pycnostachya* Michx. (50, 82) (1930–present), *Liatris pycnostachya* Michx. var. *pycnostachya* (50, 72) (1907–present)

Prairie blue violet - *Viola pedatifida* G. Don (85) (1932)

Prairie bluebells - *Mertensia lanceolata* (Pursh) DC. (50) (present), *Mertensia lanceolata* (Pursh) DC. var. *lanceolata* (50) (present)

Prairie blue-eyed grass - *Sisyrinchium campestre* Bickn. (5, 50, 93, 97) (1913–present)

Prairie boneset - *Brickellia eupatorioides* (L.) Shinners var. *eupatorioides* (122) (1937)

Prairie breadroot [Prairie bread-root] - *Pediomelum hypogaeum* (Nutt. ex Torr. & Gray) Rydb. var. *hypogaeum* (157) (1929)

Prairie broomweed - *Amphiachyris dracunculoides* (DC.) Nutt. (50) (present)

Prairie buckbean - *Thermopsis rhombifolia* (Nutt. ex Pursh) Nutt. ex Richards. (4) (1986)

Prairie bulrush - *Schoenoplectus maritimus* (L.) Lye (5) (1913)

Prairie bunch grass [Prairie bunch-grass] - *Poa arida* Vasey (119) (1938), *Sphenopholis obtusata* (Michx.) Scribn. (129) (1894)

Prairie bundleflower - *Desmanthus illinoensis* (Michx.) MacM. ex B.L. Robins. & Fern. (50) (present)

Prairie burdock - *Silphium terebinthinaceum* Jacq. (5, 92, 156) (1876-1923)

Prairie burnet - *Sanguisorba annua* (Nutt. ex Hook.) Torr. & Gray (4, 50, 155) (1942–present)

Prairie bush clover - *Lespedeza leptostachya* Engelm. (5) (1913)

Prairie buttercup - *Ranunculus rhomboideus* Goldie (3, 4) (1977-1986)

Prairie button-snakeroot - *Liatris pycnostachya* Michx. (156) (1923), *Liatris pycnostachya* Michx. var. *pycnostachya* (5, 97) (1913-1937)

Prairie camas - *Camassia angusta* (Engelm. & Gray) Blank. (50) (present)

Prairie cat's-foot [Prairie cat's foot, Prairie cats-foot] - *Antennaria neglecta* Greene (97, 131) (1899–1937), *Antennaria parlinii* Fern. subsp. *fallax* (Greene) Bayer & Stebbins (5, 72, 93) (1907–1936)

Prairie cat's-paw [Prairie cat's paw] - *Antennaria neglecta* Greene (65) (1931)

Prairie chickweed - *Cerastium arvense* L. (4, 127) (1933-1986)

Prairie chloris - *Chloris verticillata* Nutt. (5, 119) (1913-1938)

Prairie cinquefoil - *Potentilla pensylvanica* L. (5, 72, 131) (1899–1913)

Prairie clover [Prairieclover] - *Dalea candida* Michx. ex Willd. (156) (1923), *Dalea candida* Michx. ex Willd. var. *candida* (85) (1932), *Dalea foliosa* (Gray) Barneby (possibly) (2) (1895), *Dalea* L. (50) (present), *Dalea multiflora* (Nutt.) Shinners (93, 156) (1923-1936), *Dalea purpurea* Vent. (22) (1893), *Dalea purpurea* Vent. var. *purpurea* (1, 63, 82, 106, 127, 138, 155, 156) (1899-1942), *Dalea tenuifolia* (Gray) Shinners (40) (1928), *Lespedeza leptostachya* Engelm. (72) (1907), *Lespedeza virginica* (L.) Britton (124) (1937)

Prairie coneflower [Prairie cone-flower, Prairieconeflower] - *Ratibida columnifera* (Nutt.) Wood & Standl. (3, 5, 82, 95, 97, 98, 131, 156) (1899-1937), *Ratibida pinnata* (Vent.) Barnh. (121) (1918?-1970?), *Ratibida* Raf (4, 50, 155) (1942–present)

Prairie cord-grass [Prairie cordgrass] - *Spartina pectinata* Bosc ex Link (3, 50, 122, 140, 155) (1937–present)

Prairie crab - *Malus ioensis* (Wood) Britton (137, 138) (1923-1931)

Prairie crab apple [Prairie crabapple] - *Malus ioensis* (Wood) Britton (50, 155) (1942–present), *Malus ioensis* (Wood) Britton var. *ioensis* (50) (present)

Prairie crocus - *Pulsatilla patens* (L.) Mill. subsp. *multifida* (Pritz.) Zamels (106, 157, 158) (1900–1930)

Prairie crowfoot - *Ranunculus rhomboideus* Goldie (5, 63, 65, 72, 93, 127, 131) (1899-1936)

Prairie cup grass [Prairie cupgrass] - *Eriochloa contracta* Hitchc. (3, 50, 122, 155) (1937–present)

Prairie dandelion - *Agoseris glauca* (Pursh) Raf. (127) (1937) TX

Prairie dock - *Parthenium integrifolium* L. (5, 63, 92, 156, 158) (1876-1923), *Silphium* L. (1) (1932), *Silphium terebinthinaceum* Jacq. (2, 5, 72, 122, 156) (1895-1937), *Silphium trifoliatum* L. (2) (1895)

Prairie dodder - *Cuscuta indecora* Choisy (124) (1937)

Prairie dogbane - *Apocynum cannabinum* L. (3, 4, 155) (1942-1986)

Prairie dolicholus - *Rhynchosia latifolia* Nutt. ex Torr. & Gray (97) (1937)

Prairie downy phlox - *Phlox pilosa* L. subsp. *fulgida* (Wherry) Wherry (155) (1942)

Prairie dropseed - *Muhlenbergia pungens* Thurb. (5) (1913), *Sporobolus compositus* (Poir.) Merr. var. *compositus* (115, 116, 134, 140) (1932-1958), *Sporobolus heterolepis* (Gray) Gray (3, 116, 155) (1942–present)

Prairie evening-primrose [Prairie evening primrose] - *Anoda lanceolata* Hook. & Arn. (5, 131) (1899–1913), *Oenothera albicaulis* Pursh (4, 97) (1937–1986), *Oenothera nuttallii* Sweet (98) (1926), *Oenothera pallida* Lindl. (156) (1923)

Prairie false boneset - *Brickellia eupatorioides* (L.) Shinners var. *eupatorioides* (5, 72, 93, 97, 124, 131, 156) (1899-1937)

Prairie false dandelion - *Nothocalais cuspidata* (Pursh) Greene (5, 97, 156) (1913-1937)

Prairie false foxglove - *Agalinis heterophylla* (Nutt.) Small ex Britton (50) (present)

Prairie false oat - *Trisetum interruptum* Buckl. (50) (present)

Prairie false willow - *Baccharis texana* (Torr. & Gray) Gray (50) (present)

Prairie fameflower - *Talinum parviflorum* Nutt. (3, 4, 155) (1942-1986), *Talinum rugospermum* Holzinger (50) (present)

Prairie feverfew - *Parthenium integrifolium* L. (122) (1937)

Prairie flax - *Linum lewisii* Pursh (5, 50, 109, 138, 156, 157) (1900–present), *Linum lewisii* Pursh var. *lewisii* (50) (present)

Prairie fleabane - *Erigeron strigosus* Muhl. ex Willd. (50) (present), *Erigeron strigosus* Muhl. ex Willd. var. *strigosus* (50) (present)

Prairie flower - *Pulsatilla patens* (L.) Mill. subsp. *multifida* (Pritz.) Zamels (6) (1892)

Prairie fringed orchid - *Platanthera leucophaea* (Nutt.) Lindl. (3) (1977)

Prairie froelichia - *Froelichia floridana* (Nutt.) Moq. (97) (1937), *Froelichia floridana* (Nutt.) Moq. var. *campestris* (Small) Fern. (5, 93) (1913-1936)

Prairie gaillardia - *Gaillardia aestivalis* (Walt.) Rock (3, 4) (1977-1986)

Prairie gentian [Prairiegentian] - *Eustoma exaltatum* (L.) Salisb. ex G. Don subsp. *russellianum* (Hook) Kartesz (3, 122, 124, 155) (1937-1977), *Eustoma* Salisb. ex G. Don (4, 50) (1986–present), *Gentiana puberulenta* J. Pringle (4, 72) (1907-1986), *Sabatia campestris* Nutt. (122) (1937)

Prairie gerardia - *Agalinis heterophylla* (Nutt.) Small ex Britton (97, 122, 124) (1937)

Prairie germander - *Teucrium laciniatum* Torr. (124) (present)

Prairie golden pea - *Thermopsis rhombifolia* (Nutt. ex Pursh) Nutt. ex Richards. (98) (1926)

Prairie goldenrod - *Oligoneuron album* (Nutt.) Nesom (50) (present), *Solidago missouriensis* Nutt. (3, 4, 98) (1926-1986)

Prairie grama - *Bouteloua curtipendula* (Michx.) Torr. var. *curtipendula* (93) (1936)

Prairie grass [Prairie-grass] - *Koeleria macrantha* (Ledeb.) J.A. Schultes (11, 144) (1888-1899), *Muhlenbergia asperifolia* (Nees & Meyen ex Trin.) Parodi (111) (1915), *Muhlenbergia cuspidata* (Torr. ex Hook.) Rydb. (129) (1894), *Muhlenbergia minutissima* (Steud.) Swall. (111) (1915), *Poa arida* Vasey (163) (1852), *Sphenopholis obtusata* (Michx.) Scribn. (5, 11, 75, 144) (1888-1913), *Sporobolus clandestinus* (Biehler) A.S. Hitchc. (5) (1913), *Sporobolus compositus* (Poir.) Merr. var. *compositus* (5, 94) (1901-1913), *Sporobolus cryptandrus* (Torr.) Gray (5, 111, 119, 129) (1894-1938), *Sporobolus vaginiflorus* (Torr. ex Gray) Wood (11) (1888)

Prairie ground-cherry [Prairie groundcherry, Prairie ground cherry] - *Physalis hederifolia* Gray (4) (1986), *Physalis hispida* (Waterfall) Cronq. (50) (present), *Physalis lanceolata* Michx. (5, 37, 62, 72, 85, 93, 97, 131) (1899-1937), *Physalis pumila* Nutt. (3, 4, 155) (1942-1986)

Prairie groundsel - *Packera plattensis* (Nutt.) W.A. Weber & A. Löve (50, 155) (1942–present)

Prairie guajillo - *Acacia angustissima* (Mill.) Kuntze (124) (1937) TX

Prairie hyssop - *Pycnanthemum virginianum* (L.) T. Dur. & B.D. Jackson ex B.L. Robins. & Fern. (5, 92, 156, 157) (1876-1923)

Prairie Indian paintbrush - *Castilleja purpurea* (Nutt.) G. Don var. *citrina* (Pennell) Shinners (50) (present)

Prairie indigo - *Baptisia alba* (L.) Vent. (5, 92, 156) (1876-1923)

Prairie ironweed - *Vernonia fasciculata* Michx. (50) (present), *Vernonia fasciculata* Michx. subsp. *corymbosa* (Schwein. ex Keating) S.B. Jones (50) (present), *Vernonia fasciculata* Michx. subsp. *fasciculata* (50) (present)

Prairie June - *Koeleria macrantha* (Ledeb.) J.A. Schultes (134) (1932)

Prairie June grass [Prairie June-grass, Prairie Junegrass] - *Koeleria macrantha* (Ledeb.) J.A. Schultes (5, 50, 111, 119, 129, 140, 155) (1894–present)

Prairie knotweed [Prairie knot-weed] - *Polygonum striatulum* B.L. Robins. (72, 131) (1899-1907) Neb NM

Prairie larkspur - *Delphinium carolinianum* Walt. (5, 72, 158) (1900–1913), *Delphinium carolinianum* Walt. subsp. *virescens* (Nutt.) Brooks (3, 4, 5, 72, 80, 82, 85, 93, 97, 98, 125) (1907–1986)

Prairie lespedeza - *Lespedeza leptostachya* Engelm. (50) (present), *Lespedeza violacea* (L.) Pers. (4) (1986)

Prairie lettuce - *Lactuca ludoviciana* (Nutt.) Riddell (97) (1937)

Prairie lily [Prairie-lily] - *Cooperia drummondii* Herb. (5, 156) (1913-1923), *Cooperia* Herb. (1, 109, 158) (1900-1949)

Prairie lobelia - *Lobelia spicata* Lam. var. *hirtella* Gray (131) (1899)

Prairie loosestrife - *Lysimachia quadrifolia* L. (72) (1907)

Prairie mallow [Prairiemallow] - *Sidalcea* Gray (138) (1923), *Sphaeralcea coccinea* (Nutt.) Rydb. subsp. *coccinea* (5, 156) (1913-1923)

Prairie meadow grass - *Poa arida* Vasey (5) (1913)

Prairie meadowsweet - *Filipendula rubra* (Hill.) Robinson (138) (1923)

Prairie mesquite - *Prosopis glandulosa* Torr. (5, 97) (1913-1937)

Prairie milkvetch - *Astragalus laxmannii* Jacq. var. *robustior* (Hook.) Barneby & Welsh (50) (present), *Astragalus spatulatus* Sheldon (155) (1942)

Prairie milkvine - *Matelea cynanchoides* (Engelm.) Woods (50) (present)

Prairie milkweed - *Asclepias hirtella* (Pennell) Woods (3, 4) (1977-1986), *Asclepias sullivantii* Engelm. ex Gray (50) (present)

Prairie mimosa - *Desmanthus illinoensis* (Michx.) MacM. ex B.L. Robins. & Fern. (85) (1932), *Desmanthus leptolobus* Torr. & Gray (5, 97, 122) (1913-1937), *Desmanthus* Willd. (1) (1932)

Prairie moneywort - *Lysimachia quadrifolia* L. (5, 82, 158) (1900-1930)

Prairie mugwort - *Artemisia ludoviciana* Nutt. subsp. *ludoviciana* (131, 157, 158) (1899–1929)

Prairie ninebark [Prairie nine-bark, Prairie nine bark] - *Physocarpus opulifolius* (L.) Maxim. var. *intermedius* (Rydb.) B.L. Robins. (5, 72, 93) (1907-1936)

Prairie oats - *Bouteloua curtipendula* (Michx) Torr. (144) (1899) KS

Prairie onion - *Allium stellatum* Ker (155) (1942)

Prairie painted-cup [Prairie painted cup] - *Castilleja sessiliflora* Pursh (131) (1899) SD

Prairie parsley - *Polytaenia* DC. (1) (1932), *Polytaenia nuttallii* DC. (3, 4, 122) (1937-1986)

Prairie pepperweed - *Lepidium densiflorum* Schrad. (155) (1942)

Prairie phacelia - *Phacelia strictiflora* (Engelm. & Gray) Gray (50) (present)

Prairie phlox - *Phlox andicola* E. Nels. (50) (present), *Phlox andicola* E. Nels. subsp. *andicola* (50) (present), *Phlox pilosa* L. (4, 5, 72, 85, 93, 122, 124, 156) (1907–1986), *Phlox pilosa* L. subsp. *fulgida* (Wherry) Wherry (3) (1977), *Phlox pilosa* L. subsp. *ozarkana* (Wherry) Wherry (3) (1977), *Phlox pilosa* L. subsp. *pilosa* (3) (1977)

Prairie pink - *Lygodesmia* D. Don (1) (1932), *Lygodesmia juncea* (Pursh) D. Don ex Hook. (85, 121, 148) (1932-1939)

Prairie pinweed [Prairie pin-weed] - *Lechea stricta* Leggett ex Britton (5, 50, 72, 93) (1907–present)

Prairie plantain - *Plantago elongata* Pursh (50) (present), *Plantago elongata* Pursh subsp. *elongata* (50) (present), *Plantago patagonica* Jacq. (80, 108) (1878-1913)

Prairie pleatleaf - *Nemastylis geminiflora* Nutt. (50) (present)

Prairie plum - *Prunus glandulosa* Thunb. (100) (1850) TX

Prairie queen rose - *Rosa setigera* Michx. (82) (1930)

Prairie ragweed [Prairie rag-weed] - *Iva xanthifolia* Nutt. (156) (1923)

Prairie ragwort - *Packera plattensis* (Nutt.) W. A. Weber & A. Löve (3, 4, 5, 93, 97, 98, 122, 131) (1899–1986)

OF G<small>REAT</small> P<small>LAINS</small> P<small>LANTS</small> **Prairie-potato**

Prairie rhynchosia - *Rhynchosia latifolia* Nutt. ex Torr. & Gray (5) (1913)

Prairie rocket [Prairie-rocket] - *Erysimum capitatum* (Dougl. ex Hook.) Greene var. *capitatum* (5, 156, 158) (1900-1923), *Erysimum* L. (1, 93) (1932-1936)

Prairie rose - *Rosa arkansana* Porter (50, 113, 130) (1890–present), *Rosa arkansana* Porter var. *arkansana* (50) (present), *Rosa arkansana* Porter var. *suffulta* (Greene) Cockerell (37, 50, 82) (1919–present), *Rosa blanda* Aiton (47) (1852), *Rosa setigera* Michx. (4, 5, 93, 97, 109, 135, 138, 155, 156) (1910-1986)

Prairie rose-gentian [Prairie rosegentian, Prairie rose gentian] - *Sabatia campestris* Nutt. (3, 4, 138, 155) (1923-1986)

Prairie rush-grass [Prairie rush grass] - *Muhlenbergia cuspidata* (Torr. ex Hook.) Rydb. (5, 56, 119) (1901-1938)

Prairie sabbatia - *Sabatia campestris* Nutt. (5, 97, 156) (1913-1937)

Prairie sage - *Artemisia frigida* Willd. (40) (1928), *Artemisia ludoviciana* Nutt. (28, 156) (1850–1923), *Artemisia ludoviciana* Nutt. subsp. *ludoviciana* (5, 93, 97) (1913–1937), *Artemisia tridentata* Nutt. (44) (1845)

Prairie sagewort - *Artemisia frigida* Willd. (3, 50) (1977–present)

Prairie sandmat - *Chamaesyce missurica* (Raf.) Shinners (50) (present)

Prairie sandreed - *Calamovilfa longifolia* (Hook.) Scribn. (3, 50, 140, 155) (1942–present)

Prairie scouring-rush [Prairie scouring rush] - *Equisetum laevigatum* A. Br. (72) (1907)

Prairie sedge - *Carex prairea* Dewey ex Alph. Wood (possibly) (5, 50, 155) (1913–present)

Prairie senna - *Chamaecrista fasciculata* (Michx.) Greene (5) (1913), *Chamaecrista fasciculata* (Michx.) Greene var. *fasciculata* (92, 156, 158) (1876-1923)

Prairie sensitive plant - *Mimosa microphylla* Dry. (44) (1845)

Prairie shoestrings [Prairie shoe-strings] - *Amorpha canescens* Pursh (93) (1936)

Prairie snoutbean - *Rhynchosia latifolia* Nutt. ex Torr. & Gray (50) (present)

Prairie spear grass [Prairie spear-grass] - *Poa arida* Vasey (5, 94, 119) (1901-1938)

Prairie sphenopholis - *Sphenopholis obtusata* (Michx.) Scribn. (134) (1932)

Prairie spiderwort - *Tradescantia occidentalis* (Brit.) Smyth (3, 50, 155) (1942–present), *Tradescantia occidentalis* (Britt.) Smyth var. *occidentalis* (50) (present)

Prairie spurge - *Chamaesyce missurica* (Raf.) Shinners (4, 5, 97, 122) (1913-1986)

Prairie steironema - *Lysimachia quadrifolia* L. (155) (1942)

Prairie straw sedge - *Carex suberecta* (Olney) Britton (5, 50) (1913–present)

Prairie sunflower [Prairie sun-flower] - *Helianthus* ×*laetiflorus* Pers. [*pauciflorus* × *tuberosus*] (138) (1923), *Helianthus grosseserratus* Martens (82) (1930), *Helianthus petiolaris* Nutt (5, 50, 72, 80, 85, 93, 95, 97, 122, 124, 131, 155, 156) (1899–present), *Helianthus petiolaris* Nutt. subsp. *petiolaris* (50) (present)

Prairie talinum - *Phemeranthus rugospermus* (Holz.) Kiger (5) (1913), *Talinum rugospermum* Holzinger (5) (1913)

Prairie tea - *Croton monanthogynus* Michx. (5, 50, 75, 158) (1900–present)

Prairie thermopsis - *Thermopsis rhombifolia* (Nutt. ex Pursh) Nutt. ex Richards. (5, 50, 131, 93, 155) (1899–present)

Prairie thistle - *Cirsium canescens* Nutt. (5, 50, 93, 131) (1899–present), *Cirsium discolor* (Muhl. ex Willd.) Spreng. (80) (1913), *Cirsium flodmanii* (Rydb.) Arthur (3) (1977), *Cirsium undulatum* (Nutt.) Spreng (127) (1933)

Prairie thorn - *Crataegus succulenta* Schrad. ex Link (5) (1913)

Prairie threeawn - *Aristida oligantha* Michx (50, 155) (1942–present)

Prairie three-awn grass [Prairie three awn grass] - *Aristida oligantha* Michx (122) (1937)

Prairie trefoil - *Lotus unifoliolatus* (Hook.) Benth. var. *unifoliolatus* (4, 98) (1926-1986)

Prairie trillium - *Trillium recurvatum* Beck (138) (1923)

Prairie tripleawn [Prairie triple-awn, Prairie triple awn] - *Aristida oligantha* Michx (56, 66, 94, 111) (1901-1915)

Prairie trisetum - *Trisetum interruptum* Buckl. (155) (1942)

Prairie Venus' looking-glass - *Triodanis lamprosperma* McVaugh (50) (present)

Prairie vetchling - *Lathyrus polymorphus* Nutt. subsp. *polymorphus* (5, 72, 156, 158) (1900-1923)

Prairie violet - *Viola pedatifida* G. Don (4, 5, 50, 72, 93, 97, 127, 131, 155, 156) (1899–present)

Prairie wakerobin [Prairie wake robin] - *Trillium recurvatum* Beck (5, 72) (1907-1913)

Prairie wedge grass [Prairie wedgegrass] - *Sphenopholis intermedia* (Rydb.) Rydb. (3, 4) (1977–1986), *Sphenopholis obtusata* (Michx.) Scribn. (122) (1937)

Prairie wedgescale - *Sphenopholis obtusata* (Michx.) Scribn. (50, 140, 155) (1942–present), *Sphenopholis obtusata* (Michx.) Scribn. var. *obtusata* (50) (present)

Prairie weed [Prairie-weed] - *Dasiphora floribunda* (Pursh) Kartesz (5, 156, 158) (1900-1923)

Prairie white fringed orchis [Prairie white fringed-orchis] - *Platanthera leucophaea* (Nutt.) Lindl. (5, 50, 72, 93, 158) (1900–present)

Prairie wild onion - *Allium stellatum* Ker (5, 72, 93, 97) (1907-1937)

Prairie wild rose - *Rosa arkansana* Porter (3, 4, 98) (1926-1986), *Rosa setigera* Michx. (2) (1895)

Prairie wild rye [Prairie wildrye] - *Elymus virginicus* L. var. *virginicus* (155) (1942)

Prairie willow - *Salix glauca* L. subsp. glauca var. *acutifolia* (Hook.) C.K. Schneid. (5) (1913), *Salix humilis* Marsh. (4, 5, 50, 72, 82, 93, 97, 113, 130, 131, 138, 155, 156) (1890–present), *Salix humilis* Marsh. var. *humilis* (50) (present), *Salix humilis* Marsh. var. *tristis* (Aiton) Griggs (50, 85) (1932–present)

Prairie wintergreen - *Polygala sanguinea* L. (156) (1923)

Prairie wormwood - *Artemisia ludoviciana* Nutt. subsp. *ludoviciana* (72) (1907)

Prairie yellow violet - *Viola nuttallii* Pursh (85) (1932)

Prairie zinnia - *Zinnia grandiflora* Nutt. (5, 97, 122, 124) (1913-1937)

Prairie-apple [Prairie apple, Prairie apples] - *Astragalus crassicarpus* Nutt. var. *berlandieri* Barneby (76, 156, 158) (1896–1923) Southwestern MO, fruit eaten by children, *Astragalus* L. (1, 93) (1932–1936), *Pediomelum esculentum* (Pursh) Rydb. (5, 63, 93, 97, 156, 158) (1899–1937)

Prairie-dandelion [Prairie dandelion] - *Nothocalais* (Gray) Greene (50) (present)

Prairie-dog food [Prairie dog food] - *Dyssodia papposa* (Vent.) A.S. Hitchc. (37) (1919)

Prairie-dog weed [Prairie dogweed] - *Dyssodia papposa* (Vent.) A.S. Hitchc. (5, 76, 155, 156, 158) (1896-1942)

Prairie-fire [Prairie fire] - *Castilleja coccinea* (L.) Spreng. (5, 73, 156, 158) (1892-1923) WI, no longer in use by 1923

Prairie-grub [Prairie grub] - *Ptelea trifoliata* L. (5, 92, 156, 158) (1876-1923)

Prairie-lily [Prairie lily] - *Mentzelia albicaulis* (Dougl. ex Hook.) Dougl. ex Torr. & Gray (107) (1919), *Mentzelia decapetala* (Pursh ex Sims) Urban & Gilg ex Gilg (5, 85, 93, 97, 156, 158) (1900-1937), *Mentzelia* L. (158) (1900), *Mentzelia nuda* (Pursh) Torr. & Gray var. *nuda* (85) (1932), *Nemastylis geminiflora* Nutt. (3) (1977)

Prairie-pine [Prairie pine, Prairie pines] - *Liatris* Gaertn. ex Schreber. (7) (1828), *Liatris spicata* (L.) Willd. (92, 156) (1876-1923), *Liatris spicata* (L.) Willd. var. *spicata* (5, 157) (1913-1929)

Prairie-pointer [Prairie pointer] - *Dodecatheon meadia* L. (156) (1923)

Prairie-poppy [Prairie poppy] - *Oenothera speciosa* Nutt. (156) (1923)

Prairie-potato [Prairie potato] - *Pediomelum esculentum* (Pursh)

311

Rydb. (5, 28, 103, 107, 156) (1850-1923), *Pediomelum hypogaeum* (Nutt. ex Torr. & Gray) Rydb. var. *hypogaeum* (157) (1929)

Prairie-rush [Prairie rush] - *Schoenoplectus maritimus* (L.) Lye (3) (1977)

Prairie-smoke [Prairie smoke] - *Geum triflorum* Pursh (76) (1896), *Geum triflorum* Pursh var. *ciliatum* (Pursh) Fassett (5, 40, 127, 156) (1913-1933), *Pulsatilla patens* (L.) Mill. (5) (1913), *Pulsatilla patens* (L.) Mill. subsp. *multifida* (Pritz.) Zamels (74) (1893)

Prairie-smoke sieversia [Prairiesmoke sieversia] - *Geum triflorum* Pursh var. *ciliatum* (Pursh) Fassett (155) (1942)

Prairie-star [Prairie star] - *Lithophragma* (Nutt.) Torr. & Gray (1) (1932), *Lithophragma parviflorum* (Hook.) Nutt. ex Torr. & Gray (3, 4, 5) (1913-1986)

Prairie-turnip [Prairie turnip] - *Pediomelum esculentum* (Pursh) Rydb. (4, 5, 14, 34, 49, 72, 83, 92, 97, 121, 131, 156) (1834-1986)

Prangle - *Leptochloa dubia* (H.B.K.) Nees (119) (1938) OK

Prassworec - *Acorus calamus* L. (186) (1814)

Prayer-beads [Prayer beads] - *Abrus precatorius* L. (55, 57) (1911-1917)

Preacher-in-the-pulpit [Preacher in the pulpit] - *Arisaema triphyllum* (L.) Schott (86) (1878), *Galearis spectabilis* (L.) Raf. (86, 156, 158) (1878-1923) PA

Prele - *Equisetum* L. (28) (1850)

Prêle (French) - *Equisetum hyemale* L. (6, 17, 46) (1796-1892)

Prett-per-night - *Mirabilis jalapa* L. (77) (1898) Sulphut Grove OH

Pretty dodder - *Cuscuta indecora* Choisy (5, 93, 95, 97) (1911-1937)

Pretty milkvetch [Pretty milk vetch] - *Astragalus eucosmus* B.L. Rob. (5) (1913)

Pretty sedge - *Carex woodii* Dewey (50) (present)

Pretty spurge - *Euphorbia peplus* L. (156) (1923)

Pretty-by-night - *Mirabilis jalapa* L. (73) (1892) Fort Worth TX

Pretty-face [Pretty face] - *Triteleia ixioides* (Ait. f.) Greene (109) (1949)

Pretty-Nancy [Pretty Nancy] - *Silene armeria* L. (5, 73, 156) (1892-1923) Franklin Center Quebec, no longer in use by 1923

Preuss' milkvetch [Preuss milkvetch] - *Astragalus preussii* Gray (155) (1942)

Price's groundnut [Price's ground nut] - *Apios priceana* B.L. Robins. (5) (1913)

Price's violet [Price violet] - *Viola sororia* Willd. (138, 155) (1923-1942)

Price's wood sorrel - *Oxalis priceae* Small subsp. *priceae* (5) (1913)

Prick timber [Prick-timber] - *Euonymus europaea* L. (5, 156) (1913-1923)

Pricket - *Sedum acre* L. (5, 156) (1913-1923) no longer in use by 1923

Prickle fescue - *Scolochloa festucacea* (Willd.) Link (5) (1913)

Prickle grass [Prickle-grass, Pricklegrass] - *Crypsis* Ait (present), *Leersia oryzoides* (L.) Sw. (90) (1885) ME, *Tragus berteronianus* J.A. Schultes (163) (1852), *Tragus racemosus* (L.) All. (5) (1913)

Prick-leaf dogweed [Prickleaf dogweed] - *Thymophylla acerosa* (DC.) Strother (155) (1942)

Prickly amaranth - *Amaranthus spinosus* L. (165, 187) (1768-1818)

Prickly bog sedge - *Carex atlantica* Bailey (50) (present), *Carex atlantica* Bailey subsp. *atlantica* (5) (1913)

Prickly broom - *Ulex europaeus* L. (5, 156) (1913-1923)

Prickly bur [Prickly-bur] - *Castanea dentata* (Marsh.) Borkh. (5, 156) (1913-1923), *Datura inoxia* P. Mill. (50) (present)

Prickly calalue - *Amaranthus spinosus* L. (107) (1774) Jamaica

Prickly cleome - *Cleome spinosa* Jacq. (5, 86, 156) (1878-1923)

Prickly clotbur [Prickly clott-bur] - *Xanthium spinosum* L. (19) (1840)

Prickly club moss - *Selaginella selaginoides* (L.) Beauv. ex Mart. & Schrank (5) (1913)

Prickly comfrey - *Symphytum asperum* Lepechin (106, 109, 138) (1923-1949)

Prickly coned pine - *Pinus sabiniana* Dougl. ex Dougl. (20) (1857)

Prickly cucumber - *Echinocystis lobata* (Michx.) Torr. & Gray (79) (1891) NH

Prickly currant - *Ribes lacustre* (Pers.) Poir. (50, 155) (1942–present)

Prickly dogweed - *Thymophylla acerosa* (DC.) Strother (50) (present)

Prickly elder - *Aralia hispida* Vent. (58) (1869), *Aralia spinosa* L. (5, 7, 49, 92, 156) (1828-1923)

Prickly fanpetals - *Sida spinosa* L. (50) (present)

Prickly fescue - *Scolochloa festucacea* (Willd.) Link (115) (1932), *Scolochloa* Link (93) (1936)

Prickly glasswort - *Salsola kali* L. (5, 156, 158) (1900–1923)

Prickly gooseberry - *Ribes cynosbati* L. (19, 47, 63, 82, 85, 105, 107, 113) (1840-1932)

Prickly grass - *Echinochloa* Beauv. (92) (1876)

Prickly knotweed - *Polygonum sagittatum* L. (19) (1840)

Prickly lettuce - *Lactuca sativa* L. (80) (1913), *Lactuca serriola* L. (3, 4, 50, 56, 62, 63, 70, 72, 80, 82, 98, 107, 131, 145, 155, 156, 158) (1895–present), *Lactuca virosa* L. (5, 92, 93, 97) (1876-1937)

Prickly medic [Prickly medick] - *Medicago minima* L. (4) (1986)

Prickly milkvetch [Prickly milk vetch] - *Astragalus kentrophyta* Gray var. *kentrophyta* (5, 85, 93, 131) (1899-1936)

Prickly Moses - *Acacia verticillata* (L'Hér.) Willd. (50) (present)

Prickly nightshade - *Solanum elaeagnifolium* Cav. (145) (1897), *Solanum rostratum* Dunal (5, 62, 125, 156) (1912-1931)

Prickly pear [Pricklypear, Prickly-pear] - *Opuntia ficus-indica* (L.) Mill. (6, 19, 27, 46, 92, 107, 110, 156, 177) (1762-1923), *Opuntia humifusa* (Raf.) Raf. (37) (1919), *Opuntia humifusa* (Raf.) Raf. var. *humifusa* (63, 107, 145) (1897-1899), *Opuntia macrorhiza* Engelm. (97) (1937), *Opuntia* Mill. (1, 4, 7, 10, 14, 35, 103, 106, 109, 121, 138, 149, 151, 155, 158, 167) (1814-1986), *Opuntia phaeacantha* Engelm. (4) (1986), *Opuntia polyacantha* Haw. (101) (1905), *Opuntia polyacantha* Haw. var. *trichophora* (Engelm. & Bigelow) Coult. (145) (1897)

Prickly pine - *Pinus pungens* Lamb. (2) (1895)

Prickly pisonia - *Pisonia aculeata* L. (20) (1857)

Prickly poppy [Pricklypoppy, Prickly-poppy] - *Argemone albiflora* Hornem. subsp. *albiflora* (38) (1820), *Argemone gracilenta* Greene (85, 125, 157) (1900–1932), *Argemone* L. (1, 2, 4, 13, 15, 50, 63, 82, 93, 106, 122, 109, 138, 155, 156, 158) (1895–present), *Argemone mexicana* L. (6, 10, 19, 49, 92) (1818–1898), *Argemone polyanthemos* (Fedde) G. Ownbey (3, 4) (1977–1986), *Papaver argemone* L. (156) (1923)

Prickly rose - *Rosa acicularis* Lindl. (5, 50, 85, 93, 131, 138, 155) (1899–present), *Rosa acicularis* Lindl. subsp. *sayi* (Schwein.) W.H. Lewis (72) (1907)

Prickly rose mallow - *Hibiscus aculeatus* Walt. (2) (1895)

Prickly Russian thistle - *Salsola tragus* L. (50) (present)

Prickly saltwort [Prickly salt wort] - *Salsola kali* L. (92, 158) (1876-1900)

Prickly sedge - *Carex muricata* L. (42) (1814)

Prickly seg - *Carex muricata* L. (42) (1814)

Prickly shield fern [Prickly shield-fern] - *Polystichum braunii* (Spenner) Fee (5) (1913)

Prickly sida - *Sida spinosa* L. (3, 4, 62, 72, 97, 155, 156) (1907-1986)

Prickly sow-thistle [Prickly sowthistle] - *Sonchus asper* (L.) Hill (4, 98, 155) (1926-1986)

Prickly thistle [Prickly-thistle] - *Cirsium arvense* (L.) Scop. (5, 156, 157, 158) (1900-1929)

Prickly wild gooseberry - *Ribes cynosbati* L. (5, 156, 158) (1900-1923)

Prickly wild rose - *Rosa acicularis* Lindl. (4) (1986), *Rosa acicularis* Lindl. subsp. *sayi* (Schwein.) W.H. Lewis (3) (1977)

Prickly yellow-wood [Prickly yellowwood, Prickly yellow wood] - *Zanthoxylum americanum* Mill. (7, 156) (1828-1923), *Zanthoxylum clava-herculis* L. (5, 92, 156, 177, 189) (1762-1923)

Prickly-alder [Prickly alder] - *Aralia spinosa* L. (58) (1869)

Prickly-ash [Prickly ash, Pricklyash] - *Aralia spinosa* L. (5, 177) (1762–1913), *Zanthoxylum americanum* Mill. (1, 3, 4, 5, 9, 15, 19,

27, 35, 37, 40, 48, 49, 52, 54, 55, 58, 59, 60, 61, 65, 72, 85, 92, 93, 95, 97, 105, 109, 113, 130, 131, 157, 158, 184) (1793-1986), *Zanthoxylum clava-herculis* L. (12, 93, 106, 122, 124) (1821-1937), *Zanthoxylum* L. (1, 4, 10, 13, 15, 47, 50, 82, 93, 138, 155) (1818–present)

Prickly-back [Prickly back] - *Dipsacus fullonum* L. (5, 156) (1913-1923)

Prickly-bark - *Dipsacus fullonum* L. (158) (1900)

Prickly-fruit gooseberry [Prickly-fruited gooseberry] - *Ribes cynosbati* L. (46) (1879)

Prickly-fruit wild gooseberry [Prickly fruited wild goose-berry] - *Ribes cynosbati* L. (8) (1785)

Prickly-pear cactus [Pricklypear cactus, Prickly pear cactus] - *Opuntia engelmannii* Salm-Dyck (76) (1896), *Opuntia ficus-indica* (L.) Mill. (156) (1923), *Opuntia humifusa* (Raf.) Raf. var. *humifusa* (5, 158) (1900-1913), *Opuntia* Mill. (2, 93, 146) (1895-1936), *Opuntia polyacantha* Haw. (127) (1933)

Prickly-phlox [Pricklyphlox] - *Leptodactylon* Hook. & Arn. (50) (present)

Prickly-potato [Prickly potato] - *Solanum rostratum* Dunal (5, 62, 156) (1912-1923)

Prickly-seed spinach [Prickly-seeded spinach] - *Spinacia oleracea* L. (109) (1949)

Prickly-tooth fern [Prickly-toothed fern] - *Dryopteris carthusiana* (Vill.) H.P. Fuchs (4, 5) (1913-1986)

Prick-madam [Prick madam, Prick-madame] - *Sedum acre* L. (5) (1913), *Sedum album* L. (92) (1876)

Prick-timber - *Ilex mucronata* (L.) M. Powell, Savol. & S. Andrews (156) (1923)

Prickwood [Prick-wood, Prick wood] - *Euonymus americanus* L. (92) (1876), *Euonymus europaea* L. (5, 156) (1913-1923)

Pricky thistle [Pricky-thistle] - *Cirsium arvense* (L.) Scop. (158) (1900)

Pricky-bark - *Dipsacus fullonum* L. (158) (1900)

Pride tree - *Azadirachta indica* Adr. Juss. (possibly) (7) (1828), *Melia azedarach* L. (92) (1876)

Pride-of-California [Pride of California] - *Lathyrus splendens* Kellogg (76, 109) (1896-1949)

Pride-of-China [Pride of China] - *Azadirachta indica* Adr. Juss. (possibly) (7) (1828)

Pride-of-India [Pride of India] - *Melia azedarach* L. (15, 20, 44, 49, 92, 106, 107, 109) (1845-1949)

Pride-of-Madeira - *Echium candicans* L. f. (138) (1923)

Pride-of-Ohio [Pride of Ohio] - *Dodecatheon meadia* L. (5, 50, 156) (1913–present)

Pride-of-the-meadow [Pride of the meadow] - *Eupatorium purpureum* L. (156) (1923), *Filipendula ulmaria* (L.) Maxim. subsp. *ulmaria* (92) (1876)

Pride-of-the-mountain - *Penstemon* Schmidel (1) (1932)

Pride-of-the-prairies [Pride of the prairies] - *Liatris pycnostachya* Michx. (38) (1820)

Prideweed [Pride weed, Pride-weed] - *Conyza canadensis* (L.) Cronq. var. *canadensis* (5, 6, 19, 49, 53, 69, 92, 156, 157, 158) (1840–1929)

Prie - *Ligustrum vulgare* L. (156, 158) (1900-1923)

Priest's-crown [Priest's crown] - *Taraxacum officinale* G.H. Weber ex Wiggers (5, 156, 157, 158) (1900-1929), *Taraxacum officinale* G.H. Weber ex Wiggers subsp. *officinale* (92) (1876)

Priest's-pintl [Priest's pintle] - *Arisaema triphyllum* (L.) Schott (64, 92, 158) (1876-1908)

Priest's-shoe [Priest's shoe] - *Cypripedium acaule* Ait. (46) (1649)

Prim - *Ligustrum vulgare* L. (5, 19, 26, 49, 53, 92, 156, 158, 187) (1818-1923)

Prim grass - *Anthoxanthum odoratum* L. (5) (1913)

Prime-vere (French) - *Primula* L. (10) (1818)

Prim-print - *Ligustrum vulgare* L. (156) (1923)

Primrose - *Calylophus* Spach (158) (1900), *Oenothera* L. (1, 93, 158) (1900-1936), *Primula incana* M.E. Jones (4) (1986), *Primula* L. (1,

10, 50, 138, 155, 156, 158) (1818–present), *Primula veris* L. (184) (1793), *Rosa cinnamomea* L. (76) (1896) Paris ME, *Rosa eglanteria* L. (5) (1913)

Primrose narcissus - *Narcissus* ×*medioluteus* Mill. [*poeticus* × *tazetta*] (138) (1923)

Primrose pearls [Primrose pearles] - *Narcissus* ×*medioluteus* Mill. [*poeticus* × *tazetta*] (180) (1633)

Primrose peerelesse - *Narcissus* L. (180) (1633)

Primrose peerless [Primrose peerelesse] - *Narcissus tazetta* L. (178) (1596)

Primrose peerless narcissus - *Narcissus* ×*medioluteus* Mill. [*poeticus* × *tazetta*] (109) (1949)

Primrose tree - *Oenothera biennis* L. (7) (1828)

Primrose violet - *Viola* ×*primulifolia* L. [*lanceolata* × *macloskeyi*] (124) (1937)

Primrose-leaf violet [Primrose-leaved violet] - *Viola* ×*primulifolia* L. [*lanceolata* × *macloskeyi*] (2, 5, 72, 97, 156) (1895–1937)

Primrose-willow [Primrose willow] - *Ludwigia* L. (1, 50, 122, 138, 156, 158) (1900–present), *Ludwigia octovalvis* (Jacq.) Raven subsp. *octovalvis* (124) (1937), *Ludwigia peploides* (Kunth) Raven (120, 124) (1937-1938)

Primwort - *Ligustrum vulgare* L. (5, 92, 156, 158) (1876-1923)

Prince-of-Wales feather - *Amaranthus hypochondriacus* L. (50) (present)

Prince's-feather [Prince's feather, Princes-feather, Princesfeather] - *Amaranthus caudatus* L. (92) (1876), *Amaranthus cruentus* L. (107) (1919), *Amaranthus hybridus* L. (5, 156, 158) (1900–1923), *Amaranthus hypochondriacus* L. (10, 49, 58, 92, 109, 138) (1818–1949), *Amaranthus* L. (10, 167) (1814–1818), *Polygonum orientale* L. (5, 19, 77, 82, 93, 109, 156, 158) (1913–1949), *Syringa vulgaris* L. (156) (1923)

Prince's-feather amaranth - *Amaranthus hypochondriacus* L. (165) (1768)

Prince's-pine [Prince's pine, Princespine, Princes-pine] - *Chimaphila* Pursh (2, 4) (1895-1986), *Chimaphila umbellata* (L.) Bart. (1, 3, 4, 5, 6, 19, 53, 49, 57, 58, 92, 101, 105, 155, 156, 158) (1840-1986), *Chimaphila umbellata* var. *cisatlantica* S.F. Blake (109) (1949)

Prince's-plum [Princesplum] - *Stanleya pinnata* (Pursh) Britt. var. *bipinnata* (Greene) Rollins (148) (1939)

Prince's-plume [Prince's plume, Princesplume] - *Polygonum orientale* L. (138) (1923), *Stanleya pinnata* (Pursh) Britton (4) (1986), *Stanleya pinnata* (Pursh) Britton var. *integrifolia* (James ex Torr.) Rollins (1, 3, 4, 50, 85, 106) (1930–present), *Stanleya pinnata* (Pursh) Britton var. *pinnata* (3) (1977)

Prince's-plume lady's-thumb [Princesplume ladysthumb] - *Polygonum orientale* L. (155) (1942)

Prince's-pone [Prince's pone] (sic) - *Chimaphila umbellata* (L.) Bart. (85) (1932) SD

Princess feather - *Polygonum orientale* L. (72, 122) (1907-1937)

Princess pine - *Chimaphila umbellata* (L.) Bart. (29, 156) (1869-1923)

Princess tree - *Paulownia tomentosa* (Thunb.) Sieb. & Zucc. ex Steud. (possibly) (156) (1923)

Princkly sida - *Sida spinosa* L. (5) (1913)

Pringle's aster - *Symphyotrichum pilosum* (Willd.) Nesom var. *pringlei* (Gray) Nesom (5) (1913)

Pringle's bluegrass [Pringle's blue-grass] - *Poa pringlei* Scribn. (94) (1901)

Pringle's feather grass [Pringle's feather-grass] - *Piptochaetium pringlei* (Beal) Parodi (94) (1901)

Pringle's manzanita [Pringle manzanita] - *Arctostaphylos pringlei* Parry (155) (1942)

Pringle's needle grass [Pringle needlegrass] - *Piptochaetium pringlei* (Beal) Parodi (122) (1937)

Pringle's thorn - *Crataegus pringlei* Sarg. (5) (1913)

Prinos - *Ilex verticillata* (L.) Gray (6, 53, 53, 57, 174, 177) (1753–1922)

Prinos (French) - *Ilex glabra* (L.) Gray (8) (1785), *Ilex verticillata* (L.) Gray (8) (1785)

Print - *Ligustrum vulgare* L. (5, 158, 187) (1818-1900)

Prionopsis - *Grindelia papposa* Nesom & Suh (5, 97) (1913-1937), *Grindelia* Willd. (158) (1900)

Prior - *Nicotiana tabacum* L. (181) (~1678)

Privet - *Ilex crenata* Thunb. (106) (1930), *Ligustrum* L. (1, 50, 82, 106, 109, 112, 126, 138, \155, 156) (1826–present), *Ligustrum vulgare* L. (5, 7, 49, 53, 57, 82, 92, 156, 158, 182, 184, 187) (1791-1930)

Privet adelia - *Forestiera acuminata* (Michx.) Poir. (138) (1923)

Privet honeysuckle - *Lonicera pileata* Oliv. (138) (1923)

Privet-andromeda [Privet andromeda] - *Lyonia ligustrina* (L.) DC. (5, 97, 156) (1913-1937)

Privet-leaf stillingia [Privet-leaved stillingia] - *Ditrysinia fruticosa* (W. Bartram) Govaerts & Frodin (20) (1857), *Stillingia* Garden ex L. (20) (1857)

Privet-leaf whortle-berry [Privet-leaved whortle-berry] - *Arsenococcus ligustrinus* (L.) Small (8) (1785)

Privey - *Philadelphus lewisii* Pursh (35) (1806)

Privy - *Ligustrum vulgare* L. (7, 49, 53, 92, 158) (1828-1922), *Lycium barbarum* L. (73) (1892) Mansfield OH

Proboscis flower [Proboscis-flower] - *Proboscidea louisianica* (P. Mill.) Thellung (109, 156) (1923-1949)

Procalm - *Gaultheria procumbens* L. (156) (1923) no longer in use by 1923

Procession flower [Procession-flower] - *Polygala incarnata* L. (5, 50, 92, 156, 158) (1876–present)

Procumbent chervil - *Chaerophyllum procumbens* (L.) Crantz (187) (1818)

Procumbent pearlwort - *Sagina procumbens* L. (5) (1913)

Procumbent wood sorrel - *Oxalis corniculata* L. (97) (1937)

Procumbent yellow wood sorrel [Procumbent yellow wood-sorrel] - *Oxalis corniculata* L. (158) (1900)

Professor-weed - *Galega officinalis* L. (50) (present)

Proliferous knotweed [Proliferous knot-weed] - *Polygonum ramosissimum* Michx. (5, 97) (1913-1937)

Proliferous pink - *Petrorhagia prolifera* (L.) P.W. Ball & Heywood (5) (1913)

Prolific panic grass - *Panicum dichotomiflorum* Michx. (66) (1903)

Prolific rice - *Zizaniopsis miliacea* (Michx.) Doell & Aschers. (66) (1903)

Proserpinaca - *Proserpinaca palustris* L. (174, 177) (1753-1762)

Proso - *Panicum miliaceum* L. (140, 155) (1942-1944)

Proso (Slavic, Russian, and Polish) - *Panicum miliaceum* L. (110) (1886)

Prostrate amaranth - *Amaranthus blitoides* S. Wats. (93, 97, 122, 131, 155) (1899-1937), *Amaranthus graecizans* L. (5) (1913)

Prostrate blue violet - *Viola walteri* House (5) (1913)

Prostrate eryngo - *Eryngium prostratum* Nutt. ex DC. (5, 97) (1913-1937)

Prostrate hutchinsia - *Hutchinsia procumbens* (L.) Desv. (5) (1913)

Prostrate knotweed - *Polygonum aviculare* L. (50, 155) (1942–present)

Prostrate mountain clover - *Trifolium virginicum* Small ex Small & Vail (5) (1913)

Prostrate paspalum - *Paspalum setaceum* Michx. (5) (1913)

Prostrate pigweed - *Amaranthus blitoides* S. Wats. (62, 72, 80) (1907-1912)

Prostrate pigweed - *Amaranthus graecizans* L. (4, 50) (1986–present)

Prostrate purple physalis - *Quincula lobata* (Torr.) Raf. (124) (1937)

Prostrate rattlebox [Prostrate rattle-box, Prostrate rattle box] - *Crotalaria rotundifolia* Walt. ex J.F. Gmel. (5, 97) (1913-1937)

Prostrate sandmat - *Chamaesyce prostrata* (Aiton) Small (50) (present)

Prostrate savin juniper - *Juniperus horizontalis* Moench (136) (1930)

Prostrate spurge - *Chamaesyce maculata* (L.) Small (80) (1913), *Chamaesyce prostrata* (Aiton) Small (158) (1900)

Prostrate sunflower - *Calyptocarpus vialis* Less. (122, 124) (1937)

Prostrate tick trefoil [Prostrate ticktrefoil] - *Desmodium rotundifo-*

lium DC. (5, 50) (1913–present)

Prostrate vervain - *Verbena bracteata* Lag. & Rodr. (4, 5, 48, 80, 82, 93, 156) (1882-1986)

Prostrate willow - *Salix brachycarpa* Nutt. (20) (1857)

Prostrate yellow clover - *Medicago lupulina* L. (62) (1912)

Provence rose - *Rosa gallica* L. (49, 55) (1911-1922)

Provins rose - *Rosa gallica* L. (92) (1876)

Prunes - *Prunus domestica* L. (55, 57, 92) (1876-1917)

Prunier (French) - *Prunus* L. (8) (1785)

Prunier d'Amerique (French) - *Prunus americana* Marsh. (20) (1857)

Prunier de Canada (French) - *Prunus angustifolia* Marsh. (8) (1785)

Prunier de Virginie (French) - *Prunus americana* Marsh. (8) (1785)

Prunier maritime (French) - *Prunus maritima* Marsh. (possibly) (8) (1785)

Prunum - *Prunus domestica* L. (55, 57) (1911-1917)

Prunus virginiana - *Prunus serotina* Ehrh. (57, 60) (1902-1917) This was the official name, but P. virginiana is the species usually called choke cherry

Pruskworek (Bohemian) - *Acorus calamus* L. (186) (1814)

Psa (Dakota) - *Schoenoplectus tabernaemontani* (K.C. Gmel.) Palla (37) (1830)

Psa (Lakota) - *Schoenoplectus acutus* (Muhl. ex Bigelow) A.& D. Löve var. *acutus* (121) (1918-1970)

Pseh'tin (Dakota) - *Fraxinus pennsylvanica* Marsh. (37) (1919)

Pshin (Dakota) - *Allium canadense* L. var. *mobilense* (Regal) Ownbey (37) (1830)

Pshitola (Dakota) - *Sagittaria latifolia* Willd. (37) (1830)

Pshu (Sioux) - *Zizania aquatica* L. (103) (1871)

Psi rumien (Polish) - *Anthemis cotula* L. (186) (1814)

Psilostrophe - *Psilostrophe* DC. (158) (1900), *Psilostrophe tagetina* (Nutt.) Greene (148) (1939)

Psin (Dakota) - *Zizania aquatica* L. (5, 37) (1830-1919)

Pšiŋ (Lakota) - *Allium* L. (121) (1918-1970)

Psiseva - *Chimaphila maculata* (L.) Pursh (7) (1828)

Pšištoŋža (Osage, from word for crooked) - *Phragmites* Adans. (121) (1918-1970)

Pšitola hu (Lakota, bead+very+stem or plant) - *Sagittaria latifolia* Willd. (121) (1918-1970)

Psoralea - *Orbexilum onobrychis* (Nutt.) Rydb. (5) (1913), *Pediomelum argophyllum* (Pursh) J. Grimes (40, 125) (1928), *Psoralidium* Rydb. (158) (1900), *Psoralidium tenuiflorum* (Pursh) Rydb. (125, 148) (1930-1939)

Psy rmen (Bohemian) - *Anthemis cotula* L. (186) (1814)

Psychotria - *Psychotria* L. (138) (1923)

Psyllium - *Plantago psyllium* L. (178) (1526)

Ptarmica - *Achillea ptarmica* L. (178) (1526)

Ptarmigan-berry [Ptarmiganberry] - *Arctostaphylos* Adans. (155) (1942)

Pte ta wote (Dakota, food of buffalo) - *Astragalus crassicarpus* Nutt. var. *crassicarpus* (37) (1919)

Pte tawote (Lakota, buffalo food) - *Astragalus crassicarpus* Nutt. (121) (1918?-1970?)

Pte-ichi-yuh'a (Dakota, curly buffalo) - *Grindelia squarrosa* (Pursh) Dunal (37) (1919)

Ptelea - *Ptelea* L. (8) (1785), *Ptelea trifoliata* L. (92, 174) (1753-1876)

Ptelea (French) - *Ptelea* L. (8) (1785)

Ptelea à trois feuilles (French) - *Ptelea trifoliata* L. (8) (1785)

Pterospore paradoxe (French) - *Pterospora andromedea* Nutt. (7) (1828)

Ptiloria - *Stephanomeria* Nutt. (158) (1900)

Puberulent heuchera - *Heuchera parviflora* Bartl. var. *puberula* (Mackenzie & Bush) E. Wells (5) (1913)

Pubescent angelica - *Angelica venenosa* (Greenway) Fern. (5) (1913)

Pubescent paspalum - *Paspalum setaceum* Michx. (5) (1913)

Pubescent sedge - *Carex hirtifolia* MacKenzie (5, 50, 66, 72) (1903–present)

Puccoon - *Buglossoides arvensis* (L.) I.M. Johnston (80, 85) (1913–1932), *Lithospermum canescens* (Michx.) Lehm. (19, 46, 109, 138) (1840–1949), *Lithospermum caroliniense* (Walt. ex J. F. Gmel.) MacM. (3, 4, 40) (1929–1986), *Lithospermum incisum* Lehm. (109, 114) (1894–1949), *Lithospermum* L. (1, 2, 7, 93, 127, 156) (1828–1933), *Sanguinaria canadensis* L. (6, 10, 46, 49, 53, 74, 76, 155, 177, 181, 186, 187) (~1678–1942), *Sanguinaria* L. (167) (1814)

Puccoon root [Puccoon-root] - *Sanguinaria canadensis* L. (5, 64, 74, 156, 158) (1893-1923)

Pucker-needle [Pucker needle] - *Scandix pecten-veneris* L. (92) (1876)

Puck's-foot [Puck's foot] - *Podophyllum peltatum* L. (5) (1913)

Pudding pipe tree [Pudding-pipe-tree] - *Cassia fistula* L. (92, 109) (1876-1949)

Pudding-bag plant [Pudding bag plant] - *Hylotelephium telephium* (L.) H. Ohba. subsp. *telephium* (73) (1892) MA

Pudding-berry [Pudding berries, Pudding berry - *Cornus canadensis* L. (14, 73, 79) (1882-1891) probably from insipid nature

Pudding-grass [Pudding grass] - *Hedeoma pulegioides* (L.) Pers. (77) (1898) Western US, *Mentha pulegium* L. (92) (1876), *Mitchella repens* L. (156) (1923) no longer in use by 1923

Pueraria - *Pueraria* DC. (138) (1923)

Puerro (Spanish) - *Allium porrum* L. (possibly) (180) (1633)

Puff - *Neptunia* Lour. (50) (present)

Puffball [Puff-ball, Puff ball, Puffballs, Puff balls] - *Calvatia craniiformis* (Schwein.) Fr. ex De Toni (40) (1928), *Cardiospermum halicacabum* L. (5, 76, 156, 158) (1896-1923) Sulphur Grove OH, *Lycoperdon perlatum* Pers. (possibly) (37) (1830), *Lycoperdon* Pers. (7, 14) (1828-1882), *Lycoperdon proteus* Bull. (92) (1876), *Marshallia caespitosa* Nutt. (50) (present), *Taraxacum officinale* G.H. Weber ex Wiggers (5, 7, 92, 156, 157, 158) (1828-1929), *Taraxacum officinale* G.H. Weber ex Wiggers subsp. *officinale* (6) (1892)

Puff-sheath dropseed [Puffsheath dropseed] - *Sporobolus neglectus* Nash (50, 155) (1942–present)

Pukeweed [Puke-weed, Puke weed] - *Lobelia inflata* L. (5, 6, 7, 53, 69, 92, 156, 157, 158) (1828–1929)

Pull-and-be-damned - *Paspalum lividum* Trin. (163) (1852)

Pull-down - *Polygonum* L. (77) (1898)

Pull-ling - *Eriophorum callitrix* Cham. ex C.A. Mey. (156) (1923)

Pullnut [Pull-nut] - *Carya laciniosa* (Michx. f.) G. Don (78) (1898)

Pull-pipes [Pull pipes] - *Equisetum* L. (92) (1876)

Pullup muhly - *Muhlenbergia filiformis* (Thurb. ex S. Wats.) Rydb. (3, 155) (1942-1977)

Pulpy-leaf thorn [Pulpy leaved thorn] - *Sarcobatus vermiculatus* (Hook.) Torr. (35) (1806)

Pulsatilla - *Pulsatilla patens* (L.) Mill. subsp. *multifida* (Pritz.) Zamels (poss) (180) (1633)

Pulse milkvetch [Pulse milk vetch] - *Astragalus tenellus* Pursh (4) (1986)

Pulverholz (German) - *Frangula alnus* Mill. (158) (1900)

Pulvis parturiens - *Claviceps purpurea* (Fr.) Tul. (59) (1807)

Pumions - *Cucurbita pepo* L. (107) (1822)

Pummelo - *Citrus maxima* (Burm. f.) Merr. (107, 109) (1919-1949)

Pumpelly's brome - *Bromus inermis* Leyss. subsp. *pumpellianus* (Scribn.) Wagnon (50) (present)

Pumpkin [Pumpkins] - *Cucurbita* L. (1, 82, 93, 109, 138, 156, 158, 181) (~1678-1949), *Cucurbita maxima* Dcne. (14) (1882), *Cucurbita moschata* (Duchesne ex Lam.) Duchesne ex Poir. (182) (1791), *Cucurbita pepo* L. (7, 40, 53, 57, 58, 59, 60, 82, 92, 106, 107, 110, 121, 138, 155, 158) (1828-1942), *Cucurbita pepo* L. var. *melopepo* (L.) Alef. (109) (1949), *Cucurbita pepo* L. var. *pepo* (37) (1919)

Pumpkin ash - *Fraxinus profunda* (Bush) Bush (5) (1913)

Pumpkin pine - *Pinus strobus* L. (20) (1857)

Punctate wolffia - *Wolffia brasiliensis* Weddell (72) (1907)

Puncture vine [Puncture-vine, Puncturevine] - *Tribulus* L. (50)

(present), *Tribulus terrestris* L. (3, 4, 50, 93, 122, 148, 155, 156, 174) (1753–present)

Punctureweed [Puncture-weed] - *Tribulus terrestris* L. (156) (present)

Pungent meadow grass - *Eragrostis cilianensis* (All.) Vign. ex Janchen (56) (1901), *Eragrostis minor* Host (66, 87) (1884-1903)

Punic-apple [Punic apple] - *Punica granatum* L. (92) (1876)

Punk - *Agaricus* L. (7, 92) (1828–1876)

Punk oak - *Quercus nigra* L. (5) (1913)

Punkwood bracket fungus - *Fomes igniarius* (L.) Fr. (128) (1933)

Puppet root - *Veratrum viride* Ait. (possibly) (6, 7, 71) (1828-1898)

Puppy-wood - *Cornus canadensis* L. (156) (1923)

Purdy's iris [Purdy iris] - *Iris purdyi* Eastw. (138) (1923)

Purge root - *Euphorbia corollata* L. (5, 49) (1898-1923)

Purgienkörner (German) - *Euphorbia lathyris* L. (6) (1892)

Purging agaric - *Fomitopsis officinalis* (Batsch) Bondartsev & Singer (49, 53, 57, 92) (1876-1922)

Purging bean [Purging beanes] - *Cassia* L. (181) (~1678)

Purging berries - *Rhamnus cathartica* L. (92) (1876)

Purging buckthorn - *Rhamnus cathartica* L. (6, 92, 156, 158) (1892-1923)

Purging cassia - *Cassia fistula* L. (57, 92) (1876-1917)

Purging flax - *Linum catharticum* L. (5, 92, 156) (1876-1923)

Purging nuts - *Jatropha curcas* L. (92) (1876)

Purging root [Purging-root] - *Euphorbia corollata* L. (92, 156, 157, 158) (1876–1929)

Purple Alexanders - *Thaspium trifoliatum* (L.) Gray (158) (1900), *Thaspium trifoliatum* (L.) Gray var. *aureum* Britt. (156) (1923)

Purple alpine hair grass - *Vahlodea atropurpurea* (Wahlenb.) Fries ex Hartman (66) (1903)

Purple amaranth - *Amaranthus cruentus* L. (156) (1923)

Purple ammania - *Ammannia coccinea* Rottb. (155) (1942)

Purple anemone - *Anemone caroliniana* Walt. (156, 158) (1900-1923)

Purple angelica - *Angelica atropurpurea* L. (7, 49, 64, 92, 165) (1807-1908)

Purple archangel - *Lycopus virginicus* L. (92) (1876)

Purple aristida - *Aristida purpurea* Nutt. (119) (1938), *Aristida purpurea* Nutt. var. *longiseta* (Steud.) Vasey (56) (1901)

Purple avens - *Geum rivale* L (2, 3, 4, 5, 6, 19, 49, 50, 92, 107, 156, 158) (1892–present), *Geum triflorum* Pursh (3) (1977), *Geum triflorum* Pursh var. *ciliatum* (Pursh) Fassett (85) (1932) SD

Purple azalea - *Rhododendron periclymenoides* (Michx.) Shinners (2, 5, 97, 156) (1895-1937)

Purple beard grass [Purple beard-grass] - *Aristida adscensionis* L. (5) (1913), *Aristida purpurea* Nutt. (111, 129) (1894-1915), *Schizachyrium scoparium* (Michx.) Nash (187) (1818)

Purple beardtongue [Purple beard-tongue] - *Penstemon glaber* Pursh (85) (1932)

Purple bedstraw - *Galium latifolium* Michx. (5, 156) (1913-1923)

Purple beech - *Fagus sylvatica* L. (109) (1949)

Purple bent - *Calamovilfa brevipilis* (Torr.) Hack. ex Scribn. & Southw. (66) (1903)

Purple bent grass - *Calamovilfa brevipilis* (Torr.) Hack. ex Scribn. & Southw. (5, 92) (1876-1913)

Purple bergamot - *Monarda media* Willd. (5) (1913)

Purple bladderwort - *Utricularia purpurea* Walt. (5, 156) (1913-1923), *Utricularia subulata* L. (4) (1986)

Purple bluebonnet - *Lupinus texensis* Hook. (124) (1937)

Purple bluets - *Houstonia purpurea* L. (155) (1942)

Purple boneset - *Ageratum corymbosum* Zuccagni (124) (1937) TX, *Eupatorium maculatum* L. (156) (1923), *Eupatorium purpureum* L. (5, 6, 7, 49, 62, 64, 85, 92, 93, 156, 157, 158) (1828-1936)

Purple bonnet - *Brasenia schreberi* Gmel. (156) (1923)

Purple bugleweed [Purple bugle-weed] - *Lycopus virginicus* L. (72) (1907)

Purple bush clover [Purple bushclover] - *Lespedeza formosa* (Vogel) Koehne (138) (1923)

Purple cactus - *Escobaria missouriensis* (Sweet) D.R. Hunt var. *similis* (Engelm.) N.P. Taylor (156) (1923), *Escobaria vivipara* (Nutt.) Buxbaum var. *vivipara* (5, 93, 97, 131, 157) (1899-1937)

Purple candytuft - *Iberis umbellata* L. (138) (1923)

Purple chokeberry [Purple choke-berry] - *Photinia floribunda* (Lindl.) Robertson & Phipps (138) (1923), *Photinia pyrifolia* (Lam.) Robertson & Phipps (138, 156) (1923)

Purple cinquefoil - *Comarum palustre* L. (5, 156) (1913-1923)

Purple cliff brake [Purple cliff-brake, Purple cliffbrake] - *Pellaea atropurpurea* (L.) Link (3, 50, 122, 138, 155) (1923–present)

Purple clover - *Dalea purpurea* Vent. var. *purpurea* (93) (1936), *Trifolium pratense* L. (5, 110, 157, 158) (1886–1929)

Purple cockle - *Agrostemma githago* L. (62, 148) (1912-1939)

Purple coneflower [Purple cone-flower, Purple cone flower] - *Coreopsis angustifolia* L. (106, 114) (1894-1930), *Echinacea angustifolia* DC. (49, 52, 53, 93, 127) (1919-1936), *Echinacea angustifolia* DC. var. *angustifolia* (3, 85, 156) (1923-1977), *Echinacea angustifolia* DC. var. *strigosa* McGreg. (3) (1977), *Echinacea* Moench (1, 2, 50, 109, 158) (1895–present), *Echinacea purpurea* (L.) Moench (5, 63, 72, 92, 97, 156) (1876-1923)

Purple crabgrass [Purple crab-grass] - *Digitaria sanguinalis* (L.) Scop. (187) (1818)

Purple cress - *Cardamine douglassii* Britt. (5, 156) (1913-1923), *Cardamine purpurea* Cham. & Schlecht. (72) (1907)

Purple crownvetch - *Coronilla varia* L. (50) (present)

Purple cudweed - *Gamochaeta purpurea* (L.) Cabrera (3, 4, 122, 155) (1937-1986)

Purple cypripedium - *Cypripedium acaule* Ait. (156) (1923)

Purple daisy - *Echinacea angustifolia* DC. var. *angustifolia* (156) (1923), *Echinacea purpurea* (L.) Moench (156) (1923), *Symphyotrichum patens* (Aiton) G.L. Nesom var. *patens* (5, 156) (1913-1923)

Purple dead-nettle [Purple deadnettle] - *Lamium purpureum* L. (3, 4, 50, 138, 155) (1932–present), *Lamium purpureum* L. var. *purpureum* (50) (present)

Purple disk sunflower (purple-disk sunflower) - *Helianthus atrorubens* L. (5, 156) (1913-1923)

Purple dogwood - *Cornus alternifolia* L. f. (5, 156) (1913-1923)

Purple dropseed grass [Purple dropseed-grass] - *Sporobolus junceus* (Beauv.) Kunth (5, 163) (1852-1913)

Purple echinacea - *Echinacea purpurea* (L.) Moench (155) (1942)

Purple eragrostis - *Eragrostis pectinacea* (Michx.) Nees ex Steud. (72) (1907)

Purple eryngium - *Eryngium leavenworthii* Torr. & Gray (124) (1937)

Purple false foxglove - *Agalinis purpurea* (L.) Pennell (50) (present)

Purple false oat - *Trisetum melicoides* (Michx.) Vasey ex Scribn. (50) (present)

Purple fireweed [Purple fire-weed] - *Chamerion angustifolium* (L.) Holub subsp. *angustifolium* (157, 158) (1900-1929)

Purple five-leaf orchid [Purple fiveleaf orchid] - *Isotria verticillata* (Muehl. ex Willd.) Raf. (50) (present)

Purple fleabane - *Erigeron philadelphicus* L. var. *philadelphicus* (7) (1828)

Purple flower-de-luce [Purple flowerdeluce] - *Iris germanica* L. (178) (1596), *Iris pumila* L. (178) (1596)

Purple flower-gentle [Purple flower gentle] - *Celosia cristata* L. (178) (1526)

Purple foxglove [Purple foxe gloues - *Agalinis tenuifolia* (Vahl) Raf. (156) (1923), *Digitalis pupurea* L. (5, 49, 50, 53, 60, 69, 92, 178) (1526–present)

Purple fringe - *Cotinus coggygria* Scop. (92, 156) (1898-1923)

Purple fringed orchis [Purple-fringed orchis] - *Platanthera grandiflora* (Bigelow) Lindl. (156, 187) (1818-1923)

Purple fritillaria - *Fritillaria atropurpurea* Nutt. (5, 93) (1913-1936)

Purple gerardia - *Agalinis purpurea* (L.) Pennell (155, 156) (1923-1942)

Purple giant hyssop - *Agastache scrophulariifolia* (Willd.) Kuntze (3, 50) (1977–present)

Purple goat's-beard [Purple goat's beard [Purple goates beard] - *Tragopogon porrifolius* L. (5, 156, 158, 178, 181) (1526-1923)

Purple gooseberry - *Ribes hirtellum* Michx. (46) (1879)

Purple granadilla - *Passiflora edulis* Sims (109, 138) (1923-1949)

Purple grape hyacinth - *Muscari comosum* (L.) Mill. (19) (1840)

Purple grass [Purple-grass] - *Enneapogon desvauxii* Desv. ex Beauv. (94) (1901)

Purple ground-cherry [Purple ground cherry] - *Physalis philadelphica* Lam. (107) (1919), *Quincula lobata* (Torr.) Raf. (4) (1986)

Purple groundsel - *Senecio elegans* L. (138) (1923)

Purple hair grass [Purple hair-grass] - *Muhlenbergia pungens* Thurb. (93, 163) (1852-1936)

Purple hardhack [Purple hard-hack] - *Spiraea tomentosa* L. (19, 76, 156) (1840-1923)

Purple haw - *Crataegus douglasii* Lindl. (35) (1806)

Purple hedge-hyssop [Purple hedge hyssop] - *Mecardonia acuminata* (Walt.) Small (5, 97) (1913-1937), *Mecardonia acuminata* (Walt.) Small var. *acuminata* (122) (1937)

Purple hempweed [Purple hemp-weed] - *Eupatorium purpureum* L. (6) (1892)

Purple hollow roote - *Corydalis solida* (L.) Clairv. (178) (1526)

Purple honeysuckle - *Rhododendron periclymenoides* (Michx.) Shinners (5) (1913)

Purple horseweed [Purple horse-weed, Purple horse weed] - *Conyza ramosissima* Cronq. (5, 93, 131, 156) (1899-1936)

Purple Japanese honeysuckle - *Lonicera japonica* Thunb. (155) (1942)

Purple jimson - *Datura stramonium* L. (62) (1912)

Purple jimsonweed [Purple jimson weed] - *Datura stramonium* L. (80, 145) (1897-1913)

Purple lady's-slipper [Purple ladies' slipper, Purple ladies'-slipper, Purple lady's slipper] - *Cypripedium acaule* Ait. (5, 86) (1878-1913)

Purple larkspur - *Delphinium* L. (71) (1898), *Delphinium menziesii* DC. (71) (1898)

Purple lemon monarda - *Monarda citriodora* Cerv. ex Lag. (5, 97) (1913-1937)

Purple leptandra - *Veronicastrum virginicum* (L.) Farw. (7, 92) (1828-1876)

Purple lilac - *Syringa vulgaris* L. (135) (1910)

Purple lion's-heart [Purple lion's heart] - *Physostegia parviflora* Nutt. ex Gray (5, 72, 93) (1907-1936)

Purple locoweed [Purple loco weed] - *Oxytropis lambertii* Pursh (3, 4, 50, 80, 98) (1926–present), *Oxytropis lambertii* Pursh var. *lambertii* (50) (present)

Purple loosestrife - *Lythrum* L. (106) (1930), *Lythrum salicaria* L. (3, 4, 5, 50, 109, 138, 155, 156, 158) (1900–present)

Purple love grass [Purple love-grass, Purple lovegrass] - *Eragrostis pectinacea* (Michx.) Nees ex Steud. (5, 93, 99) (1913-1936), *Eragrostis secundiflora* J. Presl (94, 152) (1901-1912), *Eragrostis spectabilis* (Pursh) Steud. (3, 50, 119, 122, 155, 163) (1852–present)

Purple mallow - *Abutilon theophrasti* Medik (178) (1526), *Callirhoe involucrata* (Torr. & Gray) Gray (37, 85, 107) (1919-1932)

Purple marshlocks [Purple marsh-locks] - *Comarum palustre* L. (5, 50, 156) (1913–present), *Potentilla* L. (1) (1932)

Purple May-wing [Purple May wing] - *Polygala paucifolia* Willd. (76) (1896)

Purple meadow rue [Purple meadow-rue, Purple meadowrue] - *Thalictrum dasycarpum* Fisch. & Avé-Lall. (3, 4, 50, 138, 155) (1923–present), *Thalictrum hultenii* Boivin (187) (1818), *Thalictrum purpurascens* L. (63) (1899)

Purple meadow-parsnip [Purple meadow parsnip, Purple meadow-parsnip] - *Thaspium trifoliatum* (L.) Gray (5, 50, 158) (1900–present), *Thaspium trifoliatum* (L.) Gray var. *aureum* Britt. (156) (1923)

Purple medic [Purple medick] - *Medicago sativa* L. (5, 45, 156, 157, 158) (1896–1929) England

Purple melic grass - *Molinia caerulea* (L.) Moench (5) (1913)

Purple milkvetch [Purple milk vetch] - *Astragalus agrestis* Dougl. ex G. Don (5, 50, 82, 85, 93, 155) (1913–present)

Purple milkweed [Purple milk weed - *Asclepias purpurascens* L. (3, 4, 5, 42, 50, 63, 72, 82, 85, 97, 155, 156) (1814–present)

Purple milkwort - *Polygala sanguinea* L. (5, 50, 93, 97, 156, 157) (1900–present)

Purple moccasin flower - *Cypripedium acaule* Ait. (86) (1878)

Purple moth mulleine - *Verbascum blattaria* L. (180) (1633)

Purple muhly - *Muhlenbergia rigens* (Benth.) A.S. Hitchc. (122) (1937)

Purple mulberry [Purple mulberrie] - *Morus nigra* L. (178) (1526)

Purple mullein - *Verbascum phoeniceum* L. (109, 138) (1923-1949)

Purple mustard - *Iodanthus pinnatifidus* (Michx.) Steud. (85) (1932)

Purple needle grass [Purple needle-grass] - *Aristida purpurea* Nutt. (152, 163) (1852-1912)

Purple nightshade - *Solanum dimidiatum* Raf. (122) (1937), *Solanum elaeagnifolium* Cav. (156) (1923), *Solanum xanti* Gray (138) (1923)

Purple oat [Purple oats] - *Schizachne purpurascens* (Torr.) Swall. (5, 93) (1913-1936)

Purple orchis - *Galearis spectabilis* (L.) Raf. (5, 75, 158) (1894-1913)

Purple osier - *Salix purpurea* L. (109, 138) (1923-1949)

Purple painted-cup - *Castilleja purpurea* (Nutt.) G. Don. (97) (1937)

Purple panicum - *Dichanthelium spretum* (J.A. Schultes) Freckmann (5, 50) (1913–present)

Purple paspalum - *Paspalum boscianum* Flueggé (94) (1901)

Purple passe flower [Purple passe floure] - *Pulsatilla patens* (L.) Mill. subsp. *multifida* (Pritz.) Zamels (poss) (180) (1633)

Purple passion-flower [Purple passionflower] - *Passiflora incarnata* L. (50) (present)

Purple pedicularis - *Pedicularis palustris* L. (5, 156) (1913-1923)

Purple periwinkle [Purple peruinkle] - *Vinca minor* L. (178) (1526)

Purple pine grass [Purple pinegrass] - *Calamagrostis purpurascens* R. Br. (140, 155) (1942-1944)

Purple poppy-mallow [Purple poppy mallow, Purple poppymallow] - *Callirhoe involucrata* (Torr. & Gray) Gray (2, 4, 50, 5, 72, 86, 93, 97) (1878–present), *Callirhoe involucrata* (Torr. & Gray) Gray var. *involucrata* (50) (present)

Purple prairie clover [Purple prairieclover] - *Dalea purpurea* Vent. (4, 72, 95, 98, 114) (1894-1986), *Dalea purpurea* Vent. var. *purpurea* (3, 5, 37, 82, 85, 97, 121, 155) (1913-1977)

Purple ragwort - *Senecio elegans* L. (109) (1949)

Purple raspberry - *Rubus occidentalis* L. (5) (1913)

Purple rattlesnake root [Purple rattlesnakeroot] - *Prenanthes racemosa* Michx. (50) (present), *Prenanthes racemosa* Michx. subsp. *multiflora* Cronq. (50) (present)

Purple reed grass [Purple reedgrass] - *Calamagrostis purpurascens* R. Br. (3, 50, 140) (1944–present)

Purple reed-bent - *Calamagrostis purpurascens* R. Br. (94) (1901)

Purple rockcress [Purple rock cress] - *Arabis drummondii* Gray (5, 72, 131) (1899–1913), *Arabis oregana* Rollins (155) (1942)

Purple rocket - *Chamerion angustifolium* (L.) Holub subsp. *angustifolium* (5, 76, 156, 157, 158) (1896-1929), *Iodanthus pinnatifidus* (Michx.) Steud. (3, 4, 5, 50, 72, 97, 156) (1907–present), *Iodanthus* Torr. & Gray (158) (1900)

Purple sage - *Salvia leucophylla* Greene (106) (1930)

Purple salsify - *Tragopogon porrifolius* L. (85) (1932)

Purple sand grass [Purple sand-grass, Purple sandgrass] - *Triplasis* Beauv. (93) (1936), *Triplasis purpurea* (Walt.) Chapman (50, 94, 155) (1901–present)

Purple sandwort - *Spergularia* (Pers.) J.& K. Presl (156) (1923), *Spergularia rubra* (L.) J.& K. Presl (5, 156) (1913-1923)

Purple saxifrage - *Saxifraga* L. (1) (1932), *Saxifraga oppositifolia* L. (156) (1923), *Saxifraga oppositifolia* L. subsp. *oppositifolia* (5) (1913)

Purple sesbania - *Sesbania punicea* (Cav.) Benth. (138) (1923)

Purple single poppy [Purple single poppie] - *Papaver rhoeas* L. (178) (1526)

Purple snapdragon - *Antirrhinum majus* L. (178) (1526)

Purple sneezeweed - *Helenium flexuosum* Raf. (50) (present)

Purple spikerush [Purple spike rush] - *Eleocharis atropurpurea* (Retz.) J. & K. Presl (5, 50, 72) (1907–present)

Purple spleenwort - *Asplenium platyneuron* (L.) B. S. P. (97) (1937)

Purple spurge - *Euphorbia spathulata* Lam (85) (1932)

Purple stramonium - *Datura stramonium* L. (80, 92, 158) (1876–1913)

Purple strawberry-tomato [Purple strawberry tomato] - *Physalis philadelphica* Lam. (107) (1919)

Purple swallow-wort [Purple swallow wort] - *Asclepias purpurascens* L. (42) (1814)

Purple thistle - *Eryngium leavenworthii* Torr. & Gray (106) (1930)

Purple thorn-apple [Purple thornapple, Purple thorn apple] - *Datura stramonium* L. (19, 62, 69, 72, 80, 156, 158) (1840–1930)

Purple thoroughwort - *Eupatorium purpureum* L. (2, 6, 19) (1840–1895)

Purple threeawn [Purple three awn] - *Aristida purpurea* Nutt. (50, 122, 155) (1937–present), *Aristida purpurea* Nutt. var. *purpurea* (50) (present)

Purple three-awn grass [Purple three-awned grass] - *Aristida purpurea* Nutt. (87) (1884)

Purple toadflax [Purple toad flax, Purple toad flaxe] - *Linaria purpurea* (L.) Mill. (50, 178) (1526–present), *Nuttallanthus canadensis* (L.) D. A. Sutton (187) (1818)

Purple trillium - *Trillium erectum* L. (2, 64, 138, 155, 156) (1895–1942)

Purple triple-awn [Purple triple awn] - *Aristida purpurascens* Poir. (66) (1903)

Purple vetch - *Vicia americana* Muhl. ex Willd. (5, 82, 156, 158) (1900–1923), *Vicia benghalensis* L. (109) (1949)

Purple Virginia wood sorrel with a lilly root [Purple Virginia woodsorrel with a lilly root] - *Oxalis violacea* L. (181) (~1678)

Purple virgin's-bower [Purple virgin's bower] - *Clematis columbiana* (Nutt.) Torr. & Gray var. *columbiana* (3, 153) (1913–1977), *Clematis* L. (1) (1932), *Clematis occidentalis* (Hornem.) DC. (possibly) (156) (1923), *Clematis occidentalis* (Hornem.) DC. var. *occidentalis* (5, 63, 72, 82) (1899–1930), *Clematis viticella* L. (19) (1840)

Purple wakerobin [Purple wake robin] - *Trillium erectum* L. (5, 6, 64) (1874–1913)

Purple wen-dock - *Brasenia schreberi* Gmel. (3) (1977)

Purple wheat grass - *Elymus trachycaulus* (Link) Gould ex Shinners subsp. *trachycaulus* (111) (1915)

Purple wild bergamot [Purple wildbergamot] - *Monarda media* Willd. (possibly) (138) (1923)

Purple wild oat [Purple wild oats] - *Schizachne purpurascens* (Torr.) Swall. (66, 90) (1885–1903)

Purple wild raspberry - *Rubus idaeus* L. subsp. *strigosus* (Michx.) Focke (5, 158) (1900–1913)

Purple willow - *Salix purpurea* L. (5, 6, 85, 156) (1892–1932)

Purple willowherb [Purple willow-herb] - *Lythrum salicaria* L. (49, 92, 156, 158) (1898–1923)

Purple winter-cherry [Purple winter cherry] - *Physalis philadelphica* Lam. (107) (1919)

Purple wood grass - *Schizachyrium scoparium* (Michx.) Nash var. *scoparium* (66, 90) (1885–1903)

Purple wood sorrel [Purple wood-sorrel] - *Oxalis violacea* L. (5, 156) (1913–1923)

Purple wreath - *Petrea* L. (109) (1949)

Purple-berry bay [Purple berried bay] - *Osmanthus americanus* Benth. & Hook. (182) (1791)

Purple-berry Bay of Catesby [Purple berr'd Bay of Catesby] - *Osmanthus americanus* Benth. & Hook. (183) (~1756)

Purple-cane raspberry [Purplecane raspberry] - *Rubus idaeus* L. subsp. *strigosus* (Michx.) Focke (138, 155) (1923-1942)

Purple-circle daffodil [Purple circled Daffodill] - *Narcissus poeticus* L. (178, 180) (1526-1633)

Purple-cone white fir [Purplecone white fir] - *Abies concolor* (Gord. & Glend.) Lindl. ex Hildebr. (138, 155) (1923-1942)

Purple-daisy fleabane [Purpledaisy fleabane] - *Erigeron corymbosus* Nutt. (155) (1942)

Purple-flower ground-cherry [Purple-flowered ground-cherry, Purple-flowered ground cherry - *Quincula lobata* (Torr.) Raf. (5, 97) (1913-1937)

Purple-flower mint [Purple-flowered mint] - *Hyptis mutabilis* (A. Rich.) Briq. (106) (1930)

Purple-flower nightshade [Purple flowered nightshade] - *Solanum dimidiatum* Raf. (124) (1937)

Purple-flower raspberry [Purple-flowered raspberry, Purple-flowering raspberry, Purple flowering raspberry] - *Rubus odoratus* L. (2, 5, 82, 105, 156) (1895-1932)

Purple-flower toothwort [Purple flowered toothwort] - *Cardamine concatenata* (Michx.) Sw. (5) (1913)

Purple-fruit chokeberry [Purple-fruited choke berry] - *Photinia floribunda* (Lindl.) Robertson & Phipps (5) (1913)

Purple-grass [Purple grass] - *Lythrum salicaria* L. (156, 158) (1900-1923), *Medicago arabica* (L.) Huds. (5) (1913), *Trifolium repens* L. (5, 157, 158) (1900-1929)

Purple-head sneezeweed [Purplehead sneezeweed - *Helenium flexuosum* Raf. (5, 97, 122, 155) (1913-1942)

Purple-head thrift [Purplehead thrift] - *Armeria maritima* (Mill.) Willd. subsp. *sibirica* (Turcz. ex Boiss.) Nyman (155) (1942)

Purple-leaf cherry [Purple leaf cherry] - *Prunus pissardii* Carrière (112) (1937)

Purple-leaf plum [Purpleleaf plum, Purple-leaved plum] - *Prunus pissardii* Carrière (135, 137) (1910-1931)

Purple-leaf willowherb [Purpleleaf willow herb, Purple-leaved willow herb, Purple-leaved willow-herb] - *Epilobium coloratum* Biehler (3, 4, 5, 50, 72, 93, 131, 156) (1899–present)

Purple-net toadflax [Purplenet toadflax] - *Linaria reticulata* (Sm.) Desf. (138) (1923)

Purple-rod - *Liatris pilosa* (Aiton) Willd. var. *pilosa* (156) (1923)

Purple-spot alstroemeria [Purplespot alstroemeria] - *Alstroemeria haemantha* Ruiz & Pavón (155) (1942)

Purple-spot fritillary [Purplespot fritillary] - *Fritillaria atropurpurea* Nutt. (155) (1942)

Purple-stem angelica [Purplestem angelica, Purple-stemmed angelica] - *Angelica atropurpurea* L. (5, 64, 138, 155, 156) (1907-1942)

Purple-stem aster [Purple stemmed aster, Purple-stemmed aster, Purplestem aster] - *Symphyotrichum puniceum* (L.) A.& D. Löve var. *puniceum* (5, 50, 72, 93, 106, 156, 158) (1900–present)

Purple-stem beggarticks [Purplestem beggarticks] - *Bidens connata* Muhl. ex Willd. (50, 131, 155) (1899–present)

Purple-stem cliff brake [Purple-stemmed cliff-brake] - *Pellaea atropurpurea* (L.) Link (4, 131, 158) (1899-1986)

Purple-stem hydrangea [Purplestem hydrangea] - *Hydrangea radiata* Walt. (138) (1923)

Purple-stem jimson weed [Purple-stemmed jimson weed] - *Datura stramonium* L. (71) (1898)

Purple-stem swamp beggarticks [Purple-stemmed swamp beggarticks] - *Bidens connata* Muhl. ex Willd. (5, 93, 97) (1913-1937)

Purple-stripe garlic [Purple-striped garlick] - *Allium oleraceum* L. (165) (1768)

Purple-top [Purpletop] - *Tridens flavus* (L.) A.S. Hitchc. (3, 144) (1977-1899), *Tridens flavus* (L.) A.S. Hitchc. var. *flavus* (119, 122, 134, 155, 163) (1852-1942)

Purple-top bluegrass [Purple-top blue-grass] - *Poa cusickii* Vasey (94) (1901)

Purple-top tridens [Purpletop tridens] - *Tridens flavus* (L.) A.S.

Hitchc. (50) (present), *Tridens flavus* (L.) A. S. Hitchc. var. *flavus* (50) (present)

Purple-vein willowherb [Purple-veined willow herb, Purple-veined willow-herb] - *Epilobium coloratum* Biehler (5, 156) (1913-1923)

Purplewort [Purple-wort, Purple woort] - *Comarum palustre* L. (5, 156) (1913-1923) no longer in use by 1923, *Trifolium pratense* L. (156) (1923), *Trifolium repens* L. (5, 157, 158, 178) (1526-1929)

Purplish amaranth - *Amaranthus blitum* L. (5) (1913)

Purplish aristida - *Aristida purpurascens* Poir. (119) (1938)

Purplish cudweed - *Gamochaeta purpurea* (L.) Cabrera (5, 97, 156) (1913-1937)

Purplish meadow rue [Purplish meadow-rue] - *Thalictrum dasycarpum* Fisch. & Avé-Lall. (5, 93, 97) (1913-1937)

Purplish wheat grass - *Elymus trachycaulus* (Link) Gould ex Shinners subsp. *trachycaulus* (5) (1913)

Purplish-flower sand-daisy [Purplish-flowered sand-daisy] - *Aphanostephus ramosissimus* DC. (97) (1937)

Purplish-tinged sedge [Purplish-tinged sedge] - *Carex woodii* Dewey (5) (1913)

Purpurfarbener Wasserhanf (German) - *Eupatorium purpureum* L. (6) (1892)

Purpurfarbige angelica (German) - *Angelica atropurpurea* L. (6) (1892)

Purron root [Purron-root] - *Sanguinaria canadensis* L. (157) (1929)

Purselin - *Portulaca oleracea* L. (46) (1879)

Pursely - *Amaranthus blitoides* S. Wats. (101) (1905) MT

Purselyn - *Portulaca oleracea* L. (46) (1617)

Pursh's amphicarpon - *Amphicarpum purshii* Kunth (5, 94) (1901-1913)

Pursh's buckthorn - *Frangula purshiana* (DC.) Cooper (20) (1857)

Pursh's buttercup - *Ranunculus gmelinii* DC. (5) (1913)

Pursh's eragrostis - *Eragrostis pectinacea* (Michx.) Nees ex Steud. var. *pectinacea* (72) (1907)

Pursh's groundsel [Pursh groundsel] - *Packera cana* (Hook.) W.A. Weber & A. Löve (155) (1942)

Pursh's loco [Pursh loco] - *Astragalus purshii* Dougl. ex Hook. (155) (1942)

Pursh's love grass [Pursh's love-grass] - *Eragrostis pectinacea* (Michx.) Nees ex Steud. (163) (1852), *Eragrostis pectinacea* (Michx.) Nees ex Steud. var. *pectinacea* (5, 99) (1913-1923)

Pursh's milkvetch [Pursh milk vetch] - *Astragalus purshii* Dougl. ex Hook. (4) (1986)

Pursh's phacelia - *Phacelia purshii* Buckl. (5, 97) (1913–1937)

Pursh's plantain - *Plantago patagonica* Jacq. (5, 72, 97, 131, 156) (1899–1937)

Pursh's sagebrush [Pursh sagebrush] - *Artemisia ludoviciana* Nutt. subsp. *ludoviciana* (4, 50) (1986–present)

Pursh's seepweed [Pursh seepweed] - *Suaeda calceoliformis* (Hook.) Moq. (50, 155) (1942–present)

Purslane [Purslain] - *Portulaca* L. (1, 4, 7, 13, 15, 50, 82, 158, 167) (1828–present), *Portulaca oleracea* L. (5, 10, 19, 41, 62, 72, 76, 80, 82, 85, 92, 93, 95, 97, 107, 110, 131, 145, 156, 157, 158, 184, 187) (1605-1937)

Purslane speedwell - *Veronica peregrina* L. (2, 4, 5, 19, 62, 72, 80, 92, 93, 97, 122, 155, 156, 158) (1840-1986)

Purslane speedwell - *Veronica peregrina* L. subsp. *xalapensis* (Kunth) Pennell (3, 95) (1911-1977)

Pursley - *Euphorbia corollata* L. (157) (1929), *Portulaca oleracea* L. (76, 92, 131, 157, 158) (1896–1929)

Purutu (Peru) - *Phaseolus* L. (107) (1919)

Purvane [Purvain] - *Verbena hastata* L. (5, 92, 156, 157, 158) (1876–1929), *Verbena* L. (7) (1828)

Pushion-berry - *Solanum dulcamara* L. (158) (1900)

Puss grass - *Setaria viridis* (L.) Beauv. (129) (1894) SD

Pussies - *Trifolium arvense* L. (5, 76, 156, 158) (1896–1923) no longer in use by 1923

Pussley [Pusley] - *Portulaca* L. (1) (1932), *Portulaca oleracea* L. (5, 62, 73, 76, 80, 93, 122, 156, 158) (1892-1923)

Pussy clover [Pussy-clover] - *Trifolium arvense* L. (5, 156, 158) (1900-1923)

Pussy grass - *Pennisetum glaucum* (L.) R. Br. (56) (1901) IA

Pussy willow [Pussywillow, Pussy willows] - *Salix discolor* Muhl. (1, 4, 5, 82, 85, 106, 109, 138, 155, 156, 158) (1900–1986), *Salix humilis* Marsh. var. *tristis* (Aiton) Griggs (156) (1923), *Salix* L. (75) (1894), *Salix nigra* Marsh. (5, 49, 53, 54, 92, 157, 158) (1876–1929)

Pussy-cats [Pussy cats] - *Salix discolor* Muhl. (156, 158) (1900-1923), *Trifolium arvense* L. (5, 76, 156, 158) (1896-1923) no longer in use by 1923

Pussyfoot [Pussy foot, Pussy's foot] - *Antennaria plantaginifolia* (L.) Richards (86) (1878), *Dalea candida* Michx. ex Willd. var. *oligophylla* (Torr.) Shinners (122, 124) (1937), *Dalea obovata* (Torr. & A.Gray) Shinners (122, 124) (1937) TX

Pussy's-toes [Pussies' toes, Pussy's toes, Pussytoes, Pussy-toes] - *Antennaria* Gaertner (1, 50, 93, 109, 127, 138, 155) (1923–present), *Antennaria neglecta* Greene (85) (1932), *Antennaria parviflora* Nutt. (3, 4, 97) (1937-1986), *Antennaria plantaginifolia* (L.) Richards (5, 73, 76, 85, 156, 158) (1892-1932)

Putty root [Putty-root, Puttyroot] - *Aplectrum hyemale* (Muhl. ex Willd.) Torr. (5, 72, 92, 109, 138, 156, 158) (1876-1949), *Aplectrum* Nutt. (1, 138, 155) (1923-1942)

Puuson - *Sanguinaria canadensis* L. (186) (1825)

Puzzle willow - *Salix nigra* Marsh. (155) (1942)

Pychaweic (Polish) - *Geranium maculatum* L. (186) (1814)

Pycnanthemum - *Pycnanthemum verticillatum* (Michx.) Pers. var. *pilosum* (Nutt.) Cooperrider (92) (1876)

Pygmy buttercup [Pigmy buttercup] - *Ranunculus pygmaeus* Wahlenb. (5) (1913)

Pygmy cudweed - *Evax* Gaertn. (50) (present)

Pygmy goldenrod [Pigmy golden-rod, Pygmy golden-rod] - *Euthamia tenuifolia* (Pursh) Nutt. var. *tenuifolia* (19) (1840)

Pygmy mahonia - *Mahonia repens* (Lindl.) G. Don (155) (1942)

Pygmy vervain [Pigmy vervain] - *Verbena simplex* Lehm. (19) (1840)

Pygmy water-lily [Pygmy waterlily] - *Nymphaea tetragona* Georgi (109, 137, 155) (1923-1949)

Pygmy willow - *Salix herbacea* L. (138) (1923)

Pygmy-flower rock-jasmine [Pygmyflower rockjasmine] - *Androsace septentrionalis* L. (50) (present)

Pygmy-weed [Pigmy weed, Pygmyweed] - *Crassula aquatica* (L.) Schoenl. (5, 19, 92, 156) (1840-1923)

Pyony - *Paeonia* L. (179) (1526)

Pyracanth - *Pyracantha coccinea* M. Roemer (5) (1913)

Pyramid - *Frasera caroliniensis* Walt. (possibly) (7) (1828)

Pyramid flower [Pyramid-flower] - *Frasera caroliniensis* Walt. (5, 64, 92, 156) (1876-1923), *Frasera speciosa* Dougl. ex Griseb. (122, 124) (1937)

Pyramid goldenrod [Pyramid golden-rod] - *Solidago juncea* Aiton (5, 156) (1913-1923), *Solidago* L. (75) (1894), *Solidago rugosa* Mill. (5, 156) (1913-1923), *Solidago uliginosa* Nutt. var. *uliginosa* (5, 156) (1913-1923)

Pyramid magnolia - *Magnolia pyramidata* Bartr. (138) (1923)

Pyramid plant [Pyramid-plant] - *Frasera caroliniensis* Walt. (5, 64, 92, 156) (1876-1923)

Pyramid spiraea - *Spiraea ×pyramidata* Greene [*betulifolia × douglasii*] (138) (1923)

Pyramidal laurel - *Magnolia grandiflora* L. (182) (1791)

Pyramidal white willow - *Salix alba* L. (138) (1923)

Pyrenees chrysanthemum - *Leucanthemum maximum* (Ramond) DC. (138) (1923)

Pyrenees star-of-Bethlehem [Pyrenees star of Bethlehem] - *Ornithogalum pyrenaicum* L. (50) (present)

Pyrocoma - *Pyrrocoma* Hook. (158) (1900)

Pyrola - *Chimaphila umbellata* (L.) Bart. (92, 158) (1876-1900), *Pyrola americana* Sweet (46, 178) (1598–1879), *Pyrola* L. (138, 155) (1923-1942)

Pyrole - *Chimaphila umbellata* (L.) Bart. (186) (1825)

Pyrole (French) - *Pyrola americana* Sweet (158) (1900), *Pyrola* L. (8) (1785)

Pyrole à feuilles maculées (French) - *Chimaphila maculata* (L.) Pursh (8) (1785)

Pyrole à feuilles rondes (French) - *Pyrola americana* Sweet (8) (1785)

Pyrole à fleurs en ombelle (French) - *Chimaphila umbellata* (L.) Bart. (8) (1785)

Pyrole blanche (French) - *Chimaphila maculata* (L.) Pursh (7) (1828)

Pyrole ombellée (French) - *Chimaphila umbellata* (L.) Bart. (6, 158) (1892-1900)

Pyxie - *Pyxidanthera barbulata* Michx. (5, 156) (1913-1923)

Pyxie moss - *Pyxidanthera barbulata* Michx. (73) (1892) NJ

Q

Qémqem (Nez Perce) - *Artemisia tridentata* Nutt. (35) (1806)

Quaasiens - *Cucurbita pepo* L. (107) (1650) New Netherlands

Quack grass [Quack-grass, Quackgrass] - *Agropyron* Gaertner (1, 93) (1932–1936), *Elymus repens* (L.) Gould (5, 11, 19, 45, 50, 56, 62, 64, 69, 72, 80, 85, 87, 88, 90, 92, 93, 118, 119, 122, 129, 140, 143, 155, 163) (1840–present)

Quacksalver's-spurge [Quacksalver's spurge, Quack salver's spurge] - *Euphorbia cyparissias* L. (5, 156, 158) (1900–1923) no longer in use by 1923

Quadrangular rush - *Eleocharis quadrangulata* (Michx.) Roemer & J.A. Schultes (66) (1903)

Quaffidilla - *Clintonia borealis* (Ait.) Raf. (46) (1783)

Quafidil - *Melanthium virginicum* L (7) (1828)

Quafodil - *Melanthium virginicum* L (5, 92, 156, 158) (1876–1923)

Quaheya - *Juglans cinerea* L. (46) (1879)

Quahiutl Patlahoac (Mexico) - *Rhus copallinum* L. (possibly) (177) (1762)

Quailberry [Quail-berry] - *Symphoricarpos occidentalis* Hook. (156) (1923)

Quă-ing-yă (Oto) - *Corylus americana* Walt. (38) (1820)

Quake grass [Quake-grass] - *Briza* L. (1) (1932), *Briza maxima* L. (92) (1876), *Briza media* L. (5, 72) (1907–1913), *Bromus briziformis* Fisch. & C. A. Mey. (5, 109) (1913–1949), *Elymus repens* (L.) Gould (45, 64, 66, 69, 90) (1896–1904), *Glyceria canadensis* (Michx.) Trin. (43) (1820)

Quaker beauty - *Houstonia caerulea* L. (73) (1892)

Quaker bonnet [Quaker bonnets, Quaker-bonnets] - *Houstonia caerulea* L. (5, 86, 156) (1878–1923) Philadelphia PA, *Lupinus* L. (1, 158) (1900–1932), *Lupinus perennis* L. (5, 156) (1913–1923) no longer in use by 1923

Quaker lady [Quaker ladies, Quaker-ladies] - *Houstonia caerulea* L. (5, 73, 156) (1892–1923) MA, *Spiraea alba* Du Roi var. *latifolia* (Aiton) Dippel (5) (1913), *Spiraea salicifolia* L. (156) (1923)

Quaking ash - *Populus tremuloides* Michx. (156) (1923)

Quaking asp - *Populus tremuloides* Michx. (28, 75, 92, 113, 130, 156, 157, 158) (1850–1929)

Quaking aspen - *Populus tremuloides* Michx. (1, 3, 4, 5, 17, 49, 50, 52, 53, 82, 85, 92, 93, 109, 138, 149, 153, 155, 161) (1857–present)

Quaking brome - *Bromus briziformis* Fisch. & C. A. Mey. (138) (1923)

Quaking grass [Quaking-grass] - *Briza* L. (1, 10, 45, 66, 109) (1818–1949), *Briza maxima* L. (92) (1876), *Briza media* L. (5, 19, 56, 66, 67, 88, 92, 184) (1793–1912), *Briza minor* L. (88) (1885)

Qualking grass [Qualking-grass] - *Briza media* L. (94) (1901)

Quamash - *Camassia quamash* (Pursh) Greene (35) (1806), *Camassia scilloides* (Raf.) Cory (7, 14, 92, 106, 107) (1828–1930), *Camassia scilloides* (Raf.) Cory (2) (1895)

Quarter vine [Quarter-vine] - *Bignonia capreolata* L. (5, 109, 156) (1913–1949)

Quassia - *Picrasma excelsa* (Sw.) Planch. (92) (1876), *Simmondsia chinensis* (Link) C. K. Schneid. (92) (1876)

Quebec hawthorn - *Crataegus submollis* Sarg. (138) (1923)

Quebec linden - *Tilia americana* L. var. *americana* (155) (1942)

Queckenwurzel (German) - *Elymus repens* (L.) Gould (158) (1900)

Quee (Snake) - *Valeriana edulis* Nutt. (101) (1905)

Queeah (Snake) - *Valeriana edulis* Nutt. (101) (1905) MT

Queen Anne's lace - *Daucus carota* L. (50, 62, 75, 93, 106, 156) (1912–present)

Queen Ann's thistle - *Carduus nutans* L. (5, 156, 158) (1900–1923)

Queen crape-myrtle [Queen crapemyrtle] - *Lagerstroemia speciosa* (L.) Pers. (109, 138) (1923–1949)

Queen Mary's thistle - *Onopordum acanthium* L. (5, 156, 158) (1900–1923)

Queen-cup - *Clintonia uniflora* (Menzies ex J. A. & J. H. Schultes) Kunth (109) (1949)

Queen-devil [Queendevil] - *Hieracium gronovii* L. (50) (present)

Queen-of-the-lights [Queen of the lights] - *Stillingia sylvatica* Garden ex L. (75) (1894) GA, corruption of Queen's delight

Queen-of-the-meadow [Queen of the meadow] - *Eupatorium purpureum* L. (5, 6, 49, 52, 53, 54, 58, 61, 64, 73, 75, 76, 92, 102, 156, 157, 158) (1869–1923), *Filipendula ulmaria* (L.) Maxim. subsp. *ulmaria* (19, 92, 156) (1840–1923), *Lobelia cardinalis* L. (77) (1898) Southold Long island, *Spiraea ×pyramidata* Greene [*betulifolia × douglasii*] (74, 156) (1893–1923), *Spiraea alba* Du Roi var. *latifolia* (Aiton) Dippel (5) (1913), *Spiraea salicifolia* L. (74, 156) (1893–1923) NY

Queen-of-the-night [Queenofthenight, Queen of the night] - *Selenicereus grandiflorus* (L.) Britt. & Rose (50, 138, 155) (1923–present)

Queen-of-the-prairie [Queen of the prairie] - *Filipendula* Mill. (1) (1932), *Filipendula rubra* (Hill.) Robinson (5, 72, 156) (1907–1923), *Spiraea alba* Du Roi var. *latifolia* (Aiton) Dippel (2, 63, 92) (1876–1899)

Queen-of-the-Sierras - *Abies magnifica* A. Murr. (158) (1900)

Queen's gilliflower - *Hesperis matronalis* L. (5, 156, 158) (1900–1923)

Queen's gilloflowers - *Hesperis matronalis* L. (178) (1526)

Queen's-button [Queens-button] - *Ranunculus acris* L. (76) (1896) Sulphur Grove OH

Queen's-delight [Queens' delight, Queen's delight] - *Stillingia sylvatica* Garden ex L. (3, 4, 5, 6, 7, 49, 50, 53, 54, 55, 57, 58, 64, 75, 92, 97, 122, 156, 158) (1869–present)

Queen's-delight stillingia [Queensdelight stillingia] - *Stillingia sylvatica* Garden ex L. (155) (1942)

Queensland asthma weed - *Chamaesyce hirta* (L.) Millsp. (53) (1922)

Queensland kauri - *Agathis robusta* (C. Moore ex F. Muell.) Bailey (109) (1949)

Queensland nut [Queensland-nut] - *Macadamia ternifolia* F. Muell. (109, 138) (1923–1949)

Queen's-root [Queens' root, Queen's root Queen root, Queen-root] - *Stillingia* Garden ex L. (1, 156) (1923–1932), *Stillingia sylvatica* Garden ex L. (5, 6, 49, 52, 53, 57, 58, 60, 64, 92, 156, 158) (1869–1923)

Queen's-wreath [Queens wreath] - *Petrea volubilis* L. (109) (1949)

Queenweed [Queen weed, Queen-weed] - *Pastinaca sativa* L. (5, 62, 75, 156, 157, 158) (1894–1929)

Quekes - *Elymus repens* (L.) Gould (178, 179) (1526–1596)

Quelghen (Chili) - *Fragaria chiloensis* (L.) Mill. (107) (1919)

Quequiri - *Abrus precatorius* L. (49) (1898)

Querceton - *Quercus velutina* Lam. (1) (1932)

Querciton oak - *Quercus velutina* Lam. (46) (1879)

Quercitron - *Quercus velutina* Lam. (2, 5, 58, 82, 92, 156, 157) (1869–1930)

Quercitron oak - *Quercus velutina* Lam. (19, 158) (1840–1900)

Quichens - *Elymus repens* (L.) Gould (5) (1913)

Quick grass [Quick-grass] - *Agropyron* Gaertner (1) (1932), *Elymus repens* (L.) Gould (45, 49, 53, 64, 69, 80, 90, 92, 108, 158, 163) (1852–1922)

Quickbeam [Quick-beam] - *Sorbus americana* Marsh. (46) (1671), *Sorbus aucuparia* L. (107) (1919), *Sorbus* L. (8) (1785)

Quicken tree - *Sorbus aucuparia* L. (178) (1526)

Quickens - *Elymus repens* (L.) Gould (92, 158) (1876–1900)

Quick-in-the-hand [Quick in the hand, Quickinthehand] - *Impatiens* L. (7) (1828), *Impatiens pallida* Nutt. (5, 92, 156, 157) (1876–1929)

Quicksand riverbank grape - *Vitis riparia* Michx. (155) (1942)

Quickset - *Crataegus monogyna* Jacq. (5, 19, 92) (1840–1913)

Quicksilver-weed - *Thalictrum dioicum* L. (3, 4, 5, 73, 158) (1894–1986) Penobscot Co, ME, *Thalictrum pubescens* Pursh (156) (1923)

Quickthorn - *Crataegus monogyna* Jacq. (5) (1913)

Quickweed - *Galinsoga Ruiz & Pavón* (4, 155) (1942–1986)

Quihou privet - *Ligustrum quihoui* Carrière (138) (1923)

Quija (Brazil) - *Capsicum annuum* L. (110) (1886)

Quill coreopsis - *Bidens laevis* (L.) Britton, Sterns & Poggenb. (138) (1923)

Quill fern - *Thelypteris palustris* Schott var. *pubescens* (Lawson) Fern. (5, 158) (1900–1913)

Quill sedge - *Carex tenera* Dewey (50) (present)

Quillet - *Trifolium repens* L. (157, 158) (1900–1929)

Quillwort [Quill-wort, Quill wort] - *Eupatorium purpureum* L. (5, 64, 75, 156, 158) (1900–1923) no longer in use by 1923, *Isoetes butleri* Engelman (3) (1977), *Isoetes* L. (1, 4, 10, 50, 155) (1818–present), *Isoetes lacustris* L. (19, 46, 92) (1840–1879), *Isoetes melanopoda* Gay & Durieu ex Durieu (3) (1977)

Quince - *Cydonia* Mill. (138) (1923), *Cydonia oblonga* Mill. (19, 54, 55, 57, 58, 92, 107, 110) (1840–1919)

Quince [Quynce] - *Cydonia oblonga* Mill. (179) (1526)

Quincula - *Quincula* Raf. (50, 158) (1900–present)

Quincy grass - *Achnatherum hymenoides* (Roemer & J. A. Schultes) Barkworth (146) (1939) MT

Quingombo (Portuguese) - *Abelmoschus esculentus* (L.) Moench (110) (1886) corruption of Congolese name

Quinine bush [Quinine-bush] - *Cowania* D. Don (122) (1937), *Purshia mexicana* (D. Don) Henrickson (106) (1930), *Purshia stansburiana* (Torr.) Henrickson (106) (1930)

Quinine flower - *Sabatia brevifolia* Raf. (5, 57) (1913–1917)

Quinine tree [Quinine-tree] - *Ptelea trifoliata* L. (5, 106, 156, 157, 158) (1900–1930)

Quinquina pinckney (French) - *Pinckneya bracteata* (Bartr.) Raf. (7) (1828)

Quinsy-berry [Quinsy berry] - *Ribes americanum* Mill. (5, 156) (1913–1923), *Ribes hudsonianum* Richards. (5, 156) (1913–1923), *Ribes nigrum* L. (92, 156) (1876–1923)

Quinte-feuille (French) - *Potentilla* L. (8) (1785)

Quinte-feuille en arbrisseau (French) - *Dasiphora floribunda* (Pursh) Kartesz (8) (1785)

Quintel - *Veronicastrum virginicum* (L.) Farw. (6) (1892)

Quipquip [Quip quip] - *Xerophyllum tenax* (Pursh) Nutt. (33) (1827)

Quital - *Veronicastrum virginicum* (L.) Farw. (157) (1929)

Quitch - *Elymus repens* (L.) Gould (49, 53, 92) (1876–1922)

Quitch grass [Quitch-grass] - *Agropyron* Gaertner (1) (1932), *Elymus repens* (L.) Gould (5, 45, 49, 64, 66, 69, 87, 90, 92, 119, 158, 163) (1852–1938)

Quitel - *Veronicastrum virginicum* (L.) Farw. (55, 57, 59) (1911–1917)

Quitel (Delaware) - *Veronicastrum virginicum* (L.) Farw. (5, 7, 56, 92) (1828–1913)

Quitte (German) - *Cydonia oblonga* Mill. (110) (1886)

Quiverleaf [Quiver leaf, Quiver-leaf] - *Populus tremuloides* Michx. (5, 92, 156, 157, 158) (1876–1929)

Quiya (Brazil) - *Capsicum annuum* L. (110) (1886)

Qu-tschar'-tai (Delaware) - *Nicotiana* L. (132) (1855)

Quussuckomineanug - *Prunus virginiana* L. (46) (1879)

R

Raave - *Elodea canadensis* Michx. (158) (1900)

Rabano rusticano (Spanish) - *Armoracia rusticana* P.G. Gaertn., B. Mey. & Scherb. (158) (1900)

Rabbit bush - *Amorpha fruticosa* L. (156) (1923)

Rabbit root - *Aralia nudicaulis* L. (5) (1913)

Rabbit vine [Rabbit-vine] - *Apios americana* Medik. (156) (1923)

Rabbit-bells [Rabbit bells] - *Crotalaria rotundifolia* Walt. ex J.F. Gmel. (156) (1923)

Rabbit-berry [Rabbitberry, Rabbit berry] - *Shepherdia argentea* (Pursh) Nutt. (5, 10, 20, 35, 36, 92, 93, 156, 158) (1806-1923), *Shepherdia canadensis* Nutt. (3, 4) (1977-1986)

Rabbitbrush [Rabbit-brush, Rabbit brush] - *Chrysothamnus* Nutt. (1, 4, 50, 93, 106, 122, 146, 155) (1930–present), *Chrysothamnus viscidiflorus* (Hook.) Nutt. subsp. *lanceolatus* (Nutt.) Hall & Clements (106) (1930), *Ericameria nauseosa* (Pallas ex Pursh) Nesom & Baird subsp. *nauseosa* var. *glabrata* (Gray) Nesom & Baird (3, 5, 85, 93, 127) (1913–1977), *Ericameria nauseosa* (Pallas ex Pursh) Nesom & Baird subsp. *nauseosa* var. *nauseosa* (112, 158) (1900–1937), *Gutierrezia sarothrae* (Pursh) Britton & Rusby (5, 156) (1913–1923)

Rabbit-brush goldenweed [Rabbitbrush goldenweed] - *Ericameria arborescens* (Gray) Greene (155) (1942), *Ericameria bloomeri* (Gray) J.F. Macbr. (155) (1942)

Rabbit-ear iris - *Iris laevigata* Fisch. (138) (1923)

Rabbit-ears [Rabbit ears] - *Linaria vulgaris* Mill. (156) (1923), *Zornia bracteata* (Walt.) Gmel. (124) (1937) TX

Rabbit-eye blueberry [Rabbiteye blueberry] - *Vaccinium virgatum* Aiton (122, 138) (1923-1937)

Rabbit-flower [Rabbit's flower, Rabbit flower] - *Digitalis pupurea* L. (5, 69, 156) (1903-1923), *Linaria vulgaris* Mill. (5, 156) (1913-1923)

Rabbit-foot clover [Rabbitfoot clover] - *Trifolium arvense* L. (3, 4, 5, 50, 82, 155, 156, 158) (1900–present)

Rabbit-foot grass [Rabbitfoot-grass, Rabbitfoot grass] - *Polypogon* Desf. (50) (present), *Polypogon monspeliensis* (L.) Desf. (3, 109, 122) (1937-1977)

Rabbit-foot polypogon [Rabbitfoot polypogon] - *Polypogon monspeliensis* (L.) Desf. (140, 155) (1942–1944)

Rabbit-meat [Rabbit meat] - *Lamium purpureum* L. (5, 158) (1900-1913)

Rabbit-meat alternathera [Rabbitmeat alternathera] - *Alternanthera ficoidea* (L.) P. Beauv. (155) (1942)

Rabbit-pea [Rabbit pea] - *Tephrosia virginiana* (L.) Pers (5, 156, 157, 158) (1900–1929)

Rabbits - *Antirrhinum majus* L. (158) (1900)

Rabbit's-foot [Rabbit foot, Rabbits' foot, Rabbitfoot] - *Aralia nudicaulis* L. (156) (1923), *Lespedeza capitata* Michx. (37) (1919), *Trifolium arvense* L. (5, 92) (1876-1913)

Rabbit's-foot plantain [Rabbit's foot plantain] - *Plantago patagonica* Jacq. (38) (1820)

Rabbit's-mouth [Rabbit's mouth, Rabbits' mouth] - *Antirrhinum majus* L. (5, 92, 156, 158) (1876–1923)

Rabbit's-root [Rabbit's root, Rabbits' root] - *Aralia nudicaulis* L. (64, 92, 157, 158) (1876–1929)

Rabbit-tobacco [Rabbit tobacco, Rabbittobacco] - *Evax* Gaertn. (4) (1986), *Evax prolifera* Nutt. ex DC. (4) (1986), *Evax verna* Raf. var. *verna* (97) (1937), *Pseudognaphalium obtusifolium* (L.) Hilliard & Burtt subsp. *obtusifolium* (5, 50, 75, 156, 157) (1894–present)

Rabbitweed [Rabbit-weed] - *Gutierrezia sarothrae* (Pursh) Britton & Rusby (156) (1923)

Rabbit-wood - *Pyrularia pubera* Michx. (156) (1923)

Rabette (French) - *Brassica rapa* L. var. *rapa* (107) (1919)

Rabone - *Raphanus sativus* L. (158, 180) (1633–1900)

Raccoon grape - *Ampelopsis cordata* Michx. (3, 4, 156) (1923–1986), *Vitis labrusca* L. (156) (1923), *Vitis vulpina* L. (15) (1895)

Raccoon-berry [Raccoon berry, Raccoonberry] - *Podophyllum peltatum* L. (5, 6, 7, 49, 53, 64, 92, 107, 156, 157, 158) (1828–1929), *Symphoricarpos* Duham. (possibly) (7) (1828)

Raceme pussytoes - *Antennaria racemosa* Hook. (155) (1942)

Racemed bouteloua - *Bouteloua curtipendula* (Michx.) Torr. var. *curtipendula* (72) (1907)

Racemed elder - *Sambucus racemosa* L. (131) (1899)

Racemed elm - *Ulmus thomasii* Sarg. (158) (1900)

Racemed milkvetch [Racemed milk vetch] - *Astragalus racemosus* Pursh (93) (1936)

Racemed milkwort - *Polygala polygama* Walt. (5, 97, 122, 156) (1913-1937)

Racemed white elm - *Ulmus thomasii* Sarg. (5, 156) (1913-1923)

Racemose milkvetch [Racemose milk vetch] - *Astragalus racemosus* Pursh (5, 97, 131) (1899–1937)

Racine a becquet (Canada, Louisiana) - *Geranium maculatum* L. (7, 186) (1814-1828)

Racine amare (French) - *Lewisia rediviva* Pursh (101) (1905) MT

Racine blanc (French Canadians) - *Lomatium ambiguum* (Nutt.) Coult. & Rose (103) (1870), *Lomatium foeniculaceum* (Nutt.) Coult. & Rose (107) (1919)

Racine blanche (French) - *Lomatium ambiguum* (Nutt.) Coult. & Rose (101) (1905) MT, *Lomatium cous* (S. Wats.) Coult. & Rose (101) (1905) MT, *Lomatium simplex* (Nutt.) J.F. Macbr. var. *simplex* (101) (1905) MT, *Lomatium triternatum* (Pursh) Coult. & Rose (101) (1905) MT

Racine d'amare (French Canada) - *Lewisia rediviva* Pursh (25) (1834)

Racine d'amère (French) - *Lewisia rediviva* Pursh (15) (1895)

Racine de tabac (French) - *Valeriana edulis* Nutt. (101, 103) (1870-103)

Racine des chapelets (French) - *Apios americana* Medik. (105) (1932)

Rackenboll (Sweden) - *Allium scorodoprasum* L. (110) (1886)

Racomens - *Vaccinium stamineum* L. (181) (~1678)

Radical - *Solanum carolinense* L. (75) (1894) WV

Radical-weed [Radical weed] - *Solanum carolinense* L. (5, 156, 157, 158) (1900-1929)

Radish - *Raphanus* L. (1, 15, 50, 82, 138, 155, 156, 158) (1895-1942), *Raphanus raphanistrum* L. (106) (1930), *Raphanus sativus* L. (4, 7, 82, 85, 92, 107, 109, 114, 138, 158, 180, 184) (1633-1986)

Radus (Low Dutch) - *Raphanus sativus* L. (180) (1633)

Rae's sedge - *Carex vesicaria* L. var. *raeana* (Boott) Fern. (5, 50) (1913–present)

Rafinesque's viburnum [Rafinesque viburnum] - *Viburnum rafinesquianum* Schult. (155) (1942)

Rafinesque's pondweed [Rafinesque pondweed] - *Potamogeton diversifolius* Raf. (5, 97, 120) (1913-1938)

Raf-starr - *Carex conjuncta* Boott (46) (1879)

Rag sumpweed - *Iva xanthifolia* Nutt. (155) (1942)

Rag woolwort - *Packera tomentosa* (Michx.) C. Jeffrey (156) (1923)

Ragged fringed orchis - *Platanthera lacera* (Michx.) G. Don (2) (1895)

Ragged orchis - *Platanthera lacera* (Michx.) G. Don (3, 5, 109, 156, 187) (1818-1977)

Ragged-cup [Ragged cup] - *Silphium perfoliatum* L. (5, 19, 49, 92, 156, 158) (1840–1923) TX

Ragged-Jack [Ragged Jack] - *Lychnis flos-cuculi* L. (5, 156) (1913-1923) no longer in use by 1923

Ragged-lady [Ragged lady] - *Gaura coccinea* Nutt. ex Pursh (106) (1930), *Nigella damascena* L. (2, 92) (1876-1895)

Ragged-robin [Ragged robin] - *Centaurea cyanus* L. (76) (1896) Rutalnd MA, *Lychnis flos-cuculi* L. (5, 15, 19, 92, 109, 138, 156) (1840-1949), *Silene latifolia* Poir. subsp. *alba* (Mill.) Greuter & Burdet (158) (1900) obsolete (1923)

Ragged-sailor [Ragged sailor, Ragged sailors] - *Centaurea cyanus* L. (106) (1930), *Cichorium intybus* L. (76) (1896) Southold LI, *Nigella damascena* L. (76) (1896) Rutalnd MA, *Polygonum hydropiperoides* Michx. (5) (1913), *Polygonum orientale* L. (77, 82, 92, 156, 158) (1898–1930)

Raging-apples [Raging apples] - *Solanum melongena* L. (178) (1526)

Ragjag [Rag-jag] - *Chenopodium album* L. (156, 157, 158) (1900–1929)

Ragweed [Rag-weed, Rag weed] - *Ambrosia artemisiifolia* L. (2, 6, 57, 58, 62, 72, 95, 131, 145, 158) (1869–1917), *Ambrosia artemisiifolia* L. var. *elatior* (L.) Descourtils (5, 37, 85, 92, 125, 157) (1876–1932), *Ambrosia bidentata* Michx. (3) (1977), *Ambrosia* L. (1, 2, 4, 45, 50, 82, 93, 155, 156, 158) (1895–present), *Ambrosia psilostachya* DC. (95, 157) (1911–1929), *Ambrosia trifida* L. (85, 106) (1930–1932), *Senecio jacobea* L. (5, 156) (1913–1923)

Ragweed sagebrush - *Artemisia franserioides* Greene (155) (1942)

Ragwort [Rag-wort] - *Packera* A. & D. Löve (50) (present), *Packera aurea* (L.) A.& D. Löve (possibly) (7, 19, 49, 53, 57, 92, 106, 114, 158) (1828-1930), *Senecio jacobea* L. (92) (1876), *Senecio* L. (1, 10, 50, 93, 126, 127, 156, 167) (1814–present)

Raifoot, Commune (French) - *Raphanus raphanistrum* L. (6) (1892)

Raifort (French, strong root) - *Armoracia rusticana* P.G. Gaertn., B. Mey. & Scherb. (110, 128, 158) (1886-1933)

Railroad-tie mushroom - *Neolentinus lepideus* (Fr.) Redhead & Ginns (128) (1933)

Rain lily [Rainlily, Rain-lily, Rain lilies] - *Cooperia drummondii* Herb. (78) (1898), *Cooperia* Herb. (50, 109, 138, 155) (1923–present)

Rain tree [Rain-tree] - *Samanea saman* (Jacq.) Merr. (107, 109) (1919-1949)

Rain-berry thorn - *Rhamnus cathartica* L. (156, 158) (1900-1923)

Rainbow cactus - *Echinocereus pectinatus* (Scheidw.) Engelm. (76) (1896) AZ, *Echinocereus rigidissimus* (Engelm.) Haage f. (138) (1923)

Rainbow echinocereus - *Echinocereus rigidissimus* (Engelm.) Haage f. (155) (1942)

Rainbow pink - *Dianthus chinensis* L. (109) (1949)

Rainbow-weed [Rainbow-weed] - *Lythrum salicaria* L. (92, 156, 158) (1898-1923)

Rainfarn (German) - *Tanacetum vulgare* L. (6, 158) (1892–1900)

Rainweide (German) - *Ligustrum vulgare* L. (158) (1900)

Raisin [Raisins] - *Vitis vinifera* L. (57, 92) (1826–1917)

Raisin de mare (Geneva, Switzerland) - *Ribes rubrum* L. (110) (1886)

Raisin d'ours (French) - *Arctostaphylos uva-ursi* (L.) Spreng. (6, 7, 8) (1785–1892)

Raisin sauvage (French) - *Vitis vulpina* L. (89) (1820)

Raisin tree [Raisin-tree, Raisintree] - *Hovenia dulcis* Thunb. (138) (1923), *Hovenia* Thunb. (138) (1923), *Ribes rubrum* L. (46, 92, 156) (1876–1923)

Raisinier à grappe (French) - *Coccoloba uvifera* (L.) L. (20) (1857)

Raisinier de mer (French) - *Coccoloba uvifera* (L.) L. (20) (1857)

Rajana - *Brunnichia ovata* (Walt.) Shinners (182) (1791)

Rake-hinshek (Winnebago, bushy weed or fuzzy weed) - *Artemisia dracunculus* L. (37) (1919)

Rake-ni-ozhu (Winnebago, weed that holds water) - *Silphium perfoliatum* L. (37) (1919)

Rake-paraparatsh (Winnebago, square weed) - *Silphium perfoliatum* L. (37) (1919)

Rakiock - *Liriodendron tulipifera* L. (46, 181) (~1678–1879)

Ralf-mossa (Swedish) - *Lycopodium clavatum* L. (46) (1879)

Ramgoat dashalong - *Turnera ulmifolia* L. (50) (present)

Ramie - *Boehmeria* Jacq. (158) (1900), *Boehmeria nivea* (L.) Gaud. (109) (1949)

Ramno catartico (Spanish) - *Rhamnus cathartica* L. (158) (1900)

Ramontchi - *Flacourtia indica* (Burm. f.) Merr. (109) (1949)

Ramoon tree - *Trophis racemosa* (L.) Urban (107) (1919)

Rampion - *Campanula rapunculoides* L. (82, 109) (1930–1949)

Rampion bellflower - *Campanula rapunculoides* L. (50) (present)

Ramps - *Allium* L. (75) (1894), *Allium tricoccum* Ait. (23, 75, 156) (1810–1923)

Ram's-claws [Ram's claws] - *Ranunculus repens* L. (5, 156, 158) (1900–1923)

Ram's-head [Ramshead, Ram's-head] - *Cypripedium arietinum* R.Br. (5, 92) (1876–1913), *Cypripedium* L. (1) (1932)

Ram's-head lady's-slipper [Ram's head ladies' slipper, Ram's head lady slipper, Ram's head lady's slipper, Ramshead ladyslipper, Rams-head lady-slipper] - *Cypripedium arietinum* R. Br. (2, 5, 50, 109, 138, 156) (1895–present), *Cypripedium* L. (1) (1932)

Ram's-head moccasin flower [Ram's head moccasin flower] - *Cypripedium arietinum* R. Br. (86) (1878)

Ram's-horn [Ram's horn, Ram's horns] - *Proboscidea louisianica* (P. Mill.) Thellung (50, 156) (1923–present)

Ramstead [Ramsted] - *Linaria vulgaris* Mill. (49, 157, 158) (1898–1929)

Ram's-tongue [Ram's tongue] - *Plantago lanceolata* L. (5, 156, 157, 158) (1900–1929) no longer in use by 1923

Ramtil - *Guizotia abyssinica* (L. f.) Cass. (92) (1876)

Ramtilla - *Guizotia abyssinica* (L. f.) Cass. (50) (present)

Ranano (Spanish) - *Raphanus sativus* L. (180) (1633)

Rancenria grass - *Leymus arenarius* (L.) Hochst. (75) (1894)

Rancheria grass - *Leymus arenarius* (L.) Hochst. (5, 45, 56, 161) (1857–1901)

Rancid - *Linaria vulgaris* Mill. (5, 156, 158) (1900–1923) no longer in use by 1923

Randall's grass [Randall grass] - *Arrhenatherum elatius* (L.) Beauv. ex J. Presl & C. Presl (67) (1890), *Lolium pratense* (Huds.) S.J. Darbyshire (5, 45, 56, 66, 68, 88) (1885–1913)

Rand's eyebright - *Euphrasia randii* Robinson (5) (1913)

Rand's goldenrod [Rand's golden-rod] - *Solidago simplex* Kunth subsp. *randii* (Porter) Ringius var. *racemosa* (Greene) Ringius (5) (1913)

Range grass - *Panicum obtusum* H.B.K. (5) (1913)

Rangoon-creeper - *Quisqualis indica* L. (109, 138) (1923–1949)

Ranmotha - *Xyris torta* Sm. (177) (1762)

Rannoch-rush [Rannochrush, Rannoch rush] - *Scheuchzeria* L. (50) (present), *Scheuchzeria palustris* L. (50) (present), *Scheuchzeria palustris* L. subsp. *americana* (Fern.) Hultén (50) (present)

Ranoncule (French) - *Ranunculus repens* L. (6) (1892), *Ranunculus sceleratus* L. (6) (1892)

Ranstead [Ransted] - *Linaria vulgaris* Mill. (5, 6, 62, 156, 157, 184) (1793–1929)

Ransted-weed - *Linaria vulgaris* Mill. (187) (1818)

Rantipole - *Daucus carota* L. (156, 157, 158) (1900–1929)

Ranty-tanty - *Rumex acetosella* L. (156, 158) (1900–1923)

Rapahat (Pawnee, red stick) - *Cornus amomum* Mill. (37) (1919)

Rape - *Brassica* L. (1, 93, 107) (1919-1936), *Brassica napus* L. (50, 68, 82, 97, 106, 109, 138, 156) (1919–present), *Brassica rapa* L. (85, 118, 179) (1526-1932), *Brassica rapa* L. var. *rapa* (107) (1919), *Raphanus raphanistrum* L. (5) (1913)

Rape cole - *Brassica oleracea* L. (178) (1526)

Rape seed [Rape-seed] - *Brassica napus* L. (12) (1821), *Brassica rapa* L. var. *rapa* (92, 158) (1876–1900)

Rapen (Low Dutch) - *Brassica rapa* L. var. *rapa* (180) (1633)

Raphano (Italian) - *Raphanus sativus* L. (180) (1633)

Rapper dandies - *Arctostaphylos uva-ursi* (L.) Spreng. (5, 92, 156, 157) (1876-1929)

Rapsöl (German) - *Brassica rapa* L. var. *rapa* (158) (1900)

Rare club moss - *Lycopodium obscurum* L. (50) (present)

Rasin d'Amerique (French) - *Phytolacca americana* L. var. *americana* (186) (1814)

Raspberry - *Rubus idaeus* L. (49, 53, 57) (1898–1922), *Rubus idaeus* L. subsp. *strigosus* (Michx.) Focke (92, 103, 114) (1870–1894), *Rubus* L. (1, 4, 106, 138, 155) (1923–1986), *Rubus occidentalis* L. (114) (1894)

Raspberry bush - *Rubus* L. (8) (1785)

Raspis bush - *Rubus idaeus* L. (178) (1526)

Ratany - *Krameria* L. (4, 155) (1942-1986), *Krameria lanceolata* Torr. (3, 4) (1977-1986)

Rath-ripe corn - *Zea mays* L. subsp. *mays* (181) (~1678)

Rat's-bane [Rat's bane, Ratsbane, Rat's-bane] - *Chimaphila maculata* (L.) Pursh (5, 73, 156) (1892-1923) Blue Ridge VA, no longer in use by 1923, *Goodyera pubescens* (Willd.) R. Br. ex Ait. f. (5, 75, 156) (1894-1923) Banner Elk NC, no longer in use in 1923

Rat-stripper [Rat stripper] - *Paxistima canbyi* Gray (5, 73, 156) (1892-1923)

Rat-tail [Rattail] - *Phleum pratense* L. (5) (1913), *Plantago lanceolata* L. (5, 156, 158) (1900–1923)

Rat-tail cactus [Rattail cactus] - *Cylindropuntia leptocaulis* (DC.) F.M.Knuth (76) (1896) AZ

Rat-tail fescue [Rat's-tail fescue, Rat's-tail fescue] - *Vulpia myuros* (L.) K.C. Gmel. (50, 94) (1901–present)

Rat-tail fescue grass [Rattail fescue, Rat's tail fescue grass] - *Vulpia myuros* (L.) K.C. Gmel. (3, 5, 155) (1913-1977)

Rat-tail grass [Rat-tail-grass] - *Coelorachis cylindrica* (Michx.) Nash (119) (1938)

Rat-tail pink - *Mesembryanthemum* L. (73) (1892) Dorchester MA

Rat-tail smutgrass [Rattail smutgrass] - *Sporobolus indicus* (L.) R. Br. var. *indicus* (155) (1942)

Rattan - *Berchemia scandens* (Hill.) Trelease (5, 122, 124, 156) (1913-1937)

Rattan vine - *Berchemia scandens* (Hill.) Trelease (5, 65, 106, 156) (1913-1931)

Rattle - *Pedicularis palustris* L. (190) (~1759), *Rhinanthus minor* L. subsp. *minor* (5) (1913)

Rattle brome - *Bromus briziformis* Fisch. & C. A. Mey. (140, 155) (1942-1944)

Rattle bush [Rattlebush, Rattle-bush] - *Baptisia tinctoria* (L.) R. Br. ex Aiton f. (5, 6, 7, 58, 64, 92, 106, 156, 157) (1828-1930)

Rattle nut [Rattle-nut] - *Nelumbo lutea* Willd. (7, 92, 156, 158) (1828-1923)

Rattle-bag weed [Rattle bag weed] - *Astragalus mollissimus* Torr (5, 156) (1913-1923)

Rattle-bags [Rattle bags] - *Rhinanthus minor* L. subsp. *minor* (5) (1913), *Silene vulgaris* (Moench) Garcke (5, 156) (1913-1923) no longer in use by 1923

Rattlebox [Rattle box, Rattle-box] - *Astragalus canadensis* L. (80) (1913), **Crotalaria** L. (1, 2, 10, 50, 93, 122, 156, 158) (1818–present), *Crotalaria sagittalis* L. (3, 4, 5, 71, 19, 63, 72, 80, 85, 92, 93, 97, 125, 131, 156, 157, 158) (1840-1986), *Halesia carolina* L. (156) (1923), *Ludwigia alternifolia* L. (5, 93, 97, 158) (1900-1937), *Rhinanthus* L. (1) (1932), *Rhinanthus minor* L. subsp. *minor* (5, 85, 156) (1913-1932), *Silene vulgaris* (Moench) Garcke (74) (1893) Berkshire Co. MA

Rattle-box weed - *Astragalus* L. (103) (1870), *Astragalus mollissimus* Torr (76) (1896)

Rattlepod [Rattle pod, Rattle-pod] - *Astragalus americanus* (Hook.) M.E.Jones (85) (1932), *Crotalaria* L. (4) (1986), *Ludwigia alternifolia* L. (156) (1923), *Oxytropis* DC. (1) (1932)

Rattlepot - *Rhinanthus* L. (155) (1942)

Rattler tree [Rattler-tree] - *Populus alba* L. (5, 156, 158) (1900–1923)

Rattle-root [Rattleroot, Rattle root] - *Cimicifuga racemosa* (L.) Nutt. (5, 6, 49, 58, 64, 92, 156) (1869-1923)

Rattlesnake brome - *Bromus briziformis* Fisch. & C. A. Mey. (50) (present)

Rattlesnake chess - *Bromus briziformis* Fisch. & C. A. Mey. (3, 140) (1944-1977)

Rattlesnake fern [Rattlesnake-fern, Rattlesnakefern] - *Botrychium biternatum* (Sav.) Underwood (possibly) (92) (1876), *Botrychium* Sw. (7) (1828), *Botrychium virginianum* (L.) Sw. (3, 4, 5, 19, 40, 50, 58, 97, 107, 109, 138, 155, 157, 158, 187) (1818–present), *Osmunda* L. (7) (1828)

Rattlesnake grape fern [Rattle-snake grape-fern] - *Botrychium virginianum* (L.) Sw. (86) (1878) for resemblane of spore cases to tail of rattlesnake

Rattlesnake grass [Rattle snake grass] - *Briza maxima* L. (19, 92) (1840-1876), *Briza media* L. (19) (1840)

Rattlesnake grass [Rattle snake grass] - *Glyceria canadensis* (Michx.) Trin. (5, 66, 87, 88, 90, 92, 94) (1876-1913)

Rattlesnake herb [Rattlesnake-herb] - *Actaea pachypoda* Ell. (156) (1923), *Actaea rubra* (Aiton) Willd. (5, 156, 157, 158) (1900-1929), *Actaea spicata* L. (92) (1876)

Rattlesnake leaf [Rattle snake leaf] - *Goodyera pubescens* (Willd.) R. Br. ex Ait. f. (5, 7, 19, 49, 92, 156) (1828-1923)

Rattlesnake manna grass [Rattlesnake mannagrass] - *Glyceria canadensis* (Michx.) Trin. (50, 155) (1942–present)

Rattlesnake plant - *Podophyllum peltatum* L. (43) (1820)

Rattlesnake snakeroot [Rattlesnake snake-root] - *Polygala senega* L. (5, 41, 156, 177) (1762-1923)

Rattlesnake violet [Rattle snake violet, Rattle-snake violet, Rattlesnakes' violet, Rattlesnake's violet] - *Viola sagittata* Aiton var. *ovata* (Nutt.) Torr. & Gray (5, 92, 156) (1876-1923)

Rattlesnake-bite [Rattlesnake bite] - *Thalictrum pubescens* Pursh (5, 156) (1913-1923)

Rattlesnake-bite cure [Rattlesnake bite cure] - *Daucus pusillus* Michx. (76) (1896)

Rattlesnake-flag [Rattlesnake flag] - *Eryngium yuccifolium* Michx. (5, 7, 64, 92, 156, 157, 158) (1828-1929)

Rattlesnake-master [Rattlesnake master, Rattlesnake's master, Rattlesnakes' master, Rattlesnake's-master] - *Eryngium* L. (1) (1932), *Eryngium yuccifolium* Michx. (5, 6, 49, 53, 58, 57, 64, 92, 109, 156, 157, 158) (1869-1949), *Liatris aspera* Michx. (156) (1923), *Liatris* Gaertn. ex Schreber. (7) (1828), *Liatris pilosa* (Aiton) Willd. (possibly) (186) (1814), *Liatris scariosa* (L.) Willd. var. *scariosa* (158) (1900), *Liatris spicata* (L.) Willd. (92) (1876), *Liatris squarrosa* (L.) Michx. (92, 156) (1876-1923), *Liatris squarrosa* (L.) Michx. var. *squarrosa* (157) (1929), *Manfreda virginica* (L.) Salisb. ex Rose (5, 7, 46, 49, 58, 75, 92, 156) (1828-1923), *Platanthera ciliaris* (L.) Lindl. (156) (1923), *Sericocarpus tortifolius* (Michx.) Nees (156) (1923)

Rattlesnake-plantain [Rattlesnake plantain, Rattle snake plantain, Rattle-snake plantane, Rattlesnakes' plantain] - *Antennaria plantaginifolia* (L.) Richards (possibly) (7, 85, 92) (1828–1932), *Epipactis* Zinn. (possibly) (156) (1923), *Goodyera oblongifolia* Raf. (3) (1977), *Goodyera pubescens* (Willd.) R. Br. ex Ait. f. (46, 187) (1818–1849), *Goodyera* R. Br. (1, 50, 109, 138) (1923–present), *Goodyera repens* (L.) R. Br. ex Ait. f. (85, 92) (1876–1932)

Rattlesnake-root [Rattlesnake root, Rattle-Snake-Root, Rattlesnakes' root, Rattlesnakeroot] - *Actaea racemosa* L. (5, 6, 7, 53, 64, 92) (1828-1922), *Chamaelirium luteum* (L.) A. Gray (7, 177) (1762-1828), *Eryngium yuccifolium* Michx. (47) (1852), *Liatris squarrosa* (L.) Michx. (156) (1923), *Polygala senega* L. (59, 64, 158, 186) (1814-1900), *Prenanthes alba* L. (5, 46, 49, 72, 82, 85, 92, 131, 156, 158) (1876-1930), *Prenanthes altissima* L. (106) (1930), *Prenanthes aspera* Michx. (5, 93, 157) (1900-1936), *Prenanthes* L. (1, 2, 4, 50, 58, 155, 156, 158) (1895–present), *Prenanthes serpentaria* Pursh (5, 156) (1913-1923), *Trillium cernuum* L. (5, 7, 156, 158) (1828-1923), *Trillium erectum* L. (6, 92) (1876-1892)

Rattlesnake-tail [Rattle snake tail] - *Stachys* L. (183) (~1756)

Rattlesnake-violet [Rattle snake violet, Rattle-snake violet, Rattle-snakes' violet, Rattlesnake's violet] - *Erythronium americanum* Ker. (5, 7, 49, 58, 92, 156, 157) (1828-1929)

Rattlesnake-weed [Rattlesnake weed, Rattlesnake weede, Rattlesnakes' weed] - *Daucus pusillus* Michx. (4) (1986), *Echinacea angustifolia* DC. (101) (1905) MT, *Eryngium yuccifolium* Michx. (5, 92, 157, 158) (1876-1929), *Eryngium yuccifolium* Michx. (64, 156) (1908-1923), *Goodyera pubescens* (Willd.) R. Br. ex Ait. f. (5, 92, 156) (1876-1923), *Hieracium venosum* L. (2, 5, 44, 46, 49, 92, 156, 157) (1845-1929), *Lycopus americanus* Muhl. ex W. Bart. (77) (1898) Southwest MO, said to be an antidote for rattlesnake bite, *Prenanthes alba* L. (46) (1879), *Veratrum viride* Ait. (156) (1923) no longer in use by 1923

Rattle-top [Rattle top, Rattletop] - *Cimicifuga racemosa* (L.) Nutt. (5, 64, 156) (1907-1923)

Rattleweed [Rattle-weed, Rattle weed] - *Actaea* L. (167) (1814), *Actaea racemosa* L. (5, 6, 7, 53, 64, 74, 92, 156) (1876-1923), *Astragalus mollissimus* Torr (156, 157, 158) (1900–1929), *Crotalaria sagittalis* L. (71, 156) (1898–1933), *Oxytropis* DC. (1, 93, 106) (1932–1936)

Raucheria grass - *Leymus arenarius* (L.) Hochst. (45) (1896)

Ravenel's panicum - *Dichanthelium ravenelii* (Scribn. & Merr.) Gould (5) (1913)

Ravenel's rosette grass - *Dichanthelium ravenelii* (Scribn. & Merr.) Gould (50) (present)

Raven-foot sedge [Ravenfoot sedge, Raven's foot sedge] - *Carex crus-corvi* Shuttlew. ex Kunz. (5, 50, 72) (1907–present)

Ravenna grass [Ravennagrass, Ravenna-grass] - *Saccharum ravennae* (L.) L. (50, 109, 138, 155, 163) (1852–present)

Raven's-claw [Raven's claw] - *Geranium maculatum* L. (46) (1671)

Rawbone - *Raphanus sativus* L. (158) (1900)

Rawcomenes - *Vaccinium stamineum* L. (46) (1879) natives on James River

Rawcomes - *Vaccinium vitis-idaea* L. (possibly) (181) (1818)

Raxcomens - *Vaccinium stamineum* L. (5) (1913)

Ray - *Agrostemma githago* L. (179) (1526)

Ray - *Lolium temulentum* L. (157, 158, 178, 179) (1526-1929), *Arrhenatherum elatius* (L.) Beauv. ex J. Presl & C. Presl (66, 67) (1890-1903)

Ray grass [Ray-grass] - *Lolium* L. (14) (1882), *Lolium perenne* L. (5, 56, 90, 92, 119, 157, 163) (1852-1938), *Lolium temulentum* L. (157, 158) (1900-1929)

Ray grass of France - *Arrhenatherum elatius* (L.) Beauv. ex J.& K. Presl var. *elatius* (92) (1876)

Rayed knapweed - *Centaurea jacea* L. (5) (1913)

Rayless alkali aster - *Symphyotrichum ciliatum* (Ledeb.) Nesom (50) (present)

Rayless arnica - *Arnica fulgens* Pursh (155) (1942)

Rayless aster - *Symphyotrichum ciliatum* (Ledeb.) Nesom (3, 4, 5, 85, 93, 95) (1911-1986)

Rayless camomile [Rayless chamomile] - *Matricaria discoidea* DC. (5, 97, 156) (1913-1937)

Rayless dogfennel - *Matricaria discoidea* DC. (101) (1905)

Rayless eriocarpum - *Machaeranthera grindelioides* (Nutt.) Shinners var. *grindelioides* (131) (1899)

Rayless gaillardia - *Gaillardia suavis* (Gray & Engelm.) Britton & Rusby (5, 97) (1913-1937)

Rayless goldenhead - *Acamptopappus sphaerocephalus* (Harvey & Gray ex Gray) Gray (50, 155) (1942–present)

Rayless goldenrod [Rayless golden-rod] - *Bigelowia nudata* (Michx.) DC. (156) (1923), *Bigelowia nudata* (Michx.) DC. subsp. *nudata* (5, 122) (1913-1937), *Chrysothamnus* Nutt. (122) (1937), *Chrysothamnus pulchellus* (Gray) Greene (124) (1937), *Ericameria nauseosa* (Pallas ex Pursh) Nesom & Baird subsp. *nauseosa* var. *glabrata* (Gray) Nesom & Baird (130) (1895), *Isocoma* Nutt. (106) (1930)

Rayless marigold - *Bidens frondosa* L. (5, 156, 158) (1900–1923)

Rayless othake - *Palafoxia callosa* (Nutt.) Torr. & Gray (5, 97, 106) (1913-1937)

Rayless polypteris - *Palafoxia callosa* (Nutt.) Torr. & Gray (122, 124) (1937)

Rayless sideranthus - *Machaeranthera grindelioides* (Nutt.) Shinners var. *grindelioides* (5, 93) (1913-1936)

Rayless tansy-aster [Rayless tansyaster] - *Machaeranthera grindelioides* (Nutt.) Shinners var. *grindelioides* (50) (present)

Rayless thelesperma - *Thelesperma megapotamicum* (Spreng.) Kuntze (5, 93, 97) (1913-1937)

Rayless winged centaury - *Centaurea melitensis* L. (5, 122, 124) (1913-1923)

Raynold's sedge [Raynolds sedge] - *Carex raynoldsii* Dewey (139) (1944)

Ray's knotweed - *Polygonum raii* Bab. (72) (1907)

Ray's woodsia - *Woodsia ilvensis* (L.) R. Br. (5) (1913)

Raysshe - *Raphanus sativus* L. (179) (1526)

Razor-sedge [Razorsedge] - *Scleria* Berg. (155) (1942)

Real mayflower - *Epigaea repens* L. (77) (1898) Norridgewock ME, Hepatica is also called mayflower in this area

Real sweet clover - *Trifolium pratense* L. (73) (1892)

Real tobacco - *Nicotiana rustica* L. (5, 75, 156) (1894-1923) NY

Rebelweed [Rebel-weed] - *Lythrum salicaria* L. (106) (1930)

Reclined bladderwort - *Utricularia resupinata* B.D. Greene ex Bigelow (5) (1913), *Utricularia subulata* L. (76, 156) (1896–1923)

Red alder - *Alnus incana* (L.) Moench subsp. *rugosa* (DuRoi) Clausen (156, 158) (1900–1923), *Alnus rubra* Bong. (50, 61, 92, 155) (1870–present), *Alnus serrulata* (Aiton) Willd. (49, 53) (1898–1922)

Red alpine campion - *Silene suecica* (Lodd.) Greuter & Burdet (5) (1913)

Red amaranth - *Amaranthus cruentus* L. (50, 107) (1919–present), *Amaranthus hybridus* L. (5, 93, 156, 157, 158) (1900-1936), *Amaranthus spinosus* L. (5, 93, 156) (1913-1936)

Red American larch-tree - *Larix laricina* (Du Roi) K.Koch (possibly) (8) (1785)

Red apples-of-love [Red apples of loue] - *Solanum lycopersicum* L. var. *lycopersicum* (178) (1526)

Red arach of the garden - *Atriplex hortensis* L. (178) (1526)

Red archangel - *Lamium purpureum* L. (5, 158) (1900–1913)

Red ash - *Fraxinus americana* L. (8) (1785), *Fraxinus pennsylvanica* Marsh. (2, 3, 4, 5, 19, 63, 72, 82, 93, 97, 109, 113, 130, 131, 138, 155, 156) (1840-1986), *Fraxinus profunda* (Bush) Bush (20, 187) (1818-1857)

Red balm - *Monarda didyma* L. (5, 7, 92, 156) (1828-1923)

Red baneberry [Red bane-berry, Red bane berry] - *Actaea rubra* (Aiton) Willd. (5, 40, 42, 50, 63, 72, 85, 92, 93, 131, 138, 155, 157, 158) (1814–present), *Actaea rubra* (Aiton) Willd. (2, 50) (1895–present)

Red barley - *Hordeum vulgare* L. (158) (1900) variety

Red basswood - *Tilia americana* L. (157, 158) (1900-1929)

Red bay [Redbay] - *Gordonia lasianthus* L. (156) (1923), *Lobelia cardinalis* L. (156) (1923), *Magnolia virginiana* L. (92, 156) (1876-1923), *Nectandra coriacea* (Sw.) Griseb. (7) (1828), *Persea americana* Mill. (2) (1895), *Persea borbonia* (L.) Spreng. (5, 20, 46, 75, 106, 138, 156, 182, 189) (1767-1930), *Persea* Mill. (2) (1895)

Red bean - *Abrus precatorius* L. (7, 92) (1828-1876)

Red bearberry [Red bear-berry] - *Arctostaphylos uva-ursi* (L.) Spreng. (131, 156, 157) (1899–1929), *Vaccaria hispanica* (Mill.) Rauschert (5, 93) (1913–1936)

Red beech - *Fagus grandifolia* Ehrh. (5, 19, 20, 78, 156, 187) (1814-1923)

Red beet [Red beete] - *Beta vulgaris* L. (178) (1526)

Red bells - *Aquilegia canadensis* L. (156) (1923)

Red Benjamin [Red Benjamins] - *Trillium erectum* L. (5, 64, 78, 156) (1898–1923) ME

Red bent - *Agrostis mertensii* Trin. (94) (1901)

Red bent grass [Red bent-grass] - *Agrostis mertensii* Trin. (5, 165) (1768-1913)

Red bergamot - *Monarda didyma* L. (156) (1923)

Red berry tea [Redberry tea] - *Gaultheria procumbens* L. (92, 156) (1876-1923)

Red besseya - *Besseya rubra* (Dougl. ex Hook.) Rydb. (50) (present)

Red Betty [Red-Betty] - *Lobelia cardinalis* L. (5, 37, 75, 156, 157, 158) (1900-1929) Ferrisburgh VT

Red bilberry - *Vaccinium vitis-idaea* L. (5, 92, 156) (1898-1923)

Red birch - *Betula lenta* L. (8) (1785), *Betula nigra* L. (1, 2, 5, 7, 19, 20, 65, 97, 107, 109, 113, 137, 156, 158) (1828-1932)

Red bird's-eye [Red-bird's-eye] - *Geranium robertianum* L. (156, 157, 158) (1900-1923), *Silene dioica* (L.) Clairville (156) (1923) no longer in use by 1923

Red blites - *Atriplex hortensis* L. (178) (1526)

Red brush [Red-brush] - *Cornus amomum* Mill. (5, 156, 158) (1900-1923), *Cornus sericea* L. (76) (1896), *Cornus sericea* L. subsp. *sericea* (5, 37, 73, 156, 158) (1892), *Lippia graveolens* Kunth (122) (1937) TX

Red bryony - *Bryonia cretica* L. subsp. *dioica* (Jacq.) Tutin (92, 107) (1876–1919)

Red buckeye - *Aesculus pavia* L. (2, 5, 71, 82, 92, 109, 138, 155, 156) (1876–1949), *Aesculus pavia* L. (97) (1937)

Red bulb-bearing lily [Red bulbe-bearing Lilly] - *Lilium bulbiferum* L. (180) (1633)

Red bulrush - *Blysmus rufus* (Huds.) Link (50) (present)

Red cabbage - *Brassica* L. (107) (1919)

Red cabbage cole - *Brassica oleracea* L. (180) (1633)

Red campion - *Silene dioica* (L.) Clairville (109, 138, 156) (1876-1949)

Red cardinal - *Lobelia cardinalis* L. (156, 157, 158) (1900-1923)

Red cardinal flower - *Lobelia cardinalis* L. (92) (1876), *Lobelia* L. (190) (~1759)

Red careless-weed [Red careless weed] - *Amaranthus spinosus* L. (62) (1912) IN

Red Carolinian cedar - *Juniperus virginiana* L. (8) (1785)

Red cedar [Red-cedar, Redcedar] or Red cedar tree - *Juniperus* L. (148) (1939), *Juniperus scopulorum* Sarg. (101) (1905) MT, *Juniperus virginiana* L. (3, 4, 5, 6, 8, 9, 12, 14, 20, 19, 27, 35, 38, 40, 41, 46, 55, 57, 58, 72, 85, 92, 97, 106, 108, 109, 112, 113, 114, 130, 131, 135, 136, 138, 147, 157, 158, 164, 184, 187) (1770-1986), *Juniperus virginiana* L. var. *virginiana* (1) (1932)

Red centaury - *Sabatia angularis* (L.) Pursh (92) (1876)

Red cherry or Red cherry tree - *Prunus cerasus* L. (92) (1876), *Prunus nigra* Aiton (possibly) (20) (1857), *Prunus pensylvanica* L. f. (5, 158) (1900-1913), *Prunus pensylvanica* L. f. var. *pensylvanica* (5, 20, 158) (1857-1913)

Red chickenweed - *Anagallis arvensis* L. (158) (1900)

Red chickweed - *Anagallis arvensis* L. (5, 6, 19, 49, 61, 77, 92, 156, 158, 187) (1818-1923)

Red chokeberry [Red choke berry, Red choke-berry, Red choakberry] - *Photinia pyrifolia* (Lam.) Robertson & Phipps (5, 19, 124, 135, 138, 155) (1840-1942)

Red chokecherry [Red choke cherry] - *Prunus virginiana* L. (85) (1932)

Red clover - *Trifolium pratense* L. (3, 4, 5, 6, 19, 45, 49, 50, 52, 53, 58, 61, 63, 66, 68, 72, 82. 85, 92, 93, 95, 97, 106, 107, 109, 114, 122, 129, 131, 138, 155, 156, 157, 158, 187) (1818–present)

Red clubrush - *Blysmus rufus* (Huds.) Link (5) (1913)

Red cluster pepper - *Capsicum annuum* L. (109) (1949)

Red cockscomb [Red coxcomb] - *Amaranthus hybridus* L. (5, 158) (1900-1913), *Amaranthus hypochondriacus* L. (49, 92) (1876-1898)

Red cohosh - *Actaea rubra* (Aiton) Willd. (7, 92, 156, 157, 158) (1828-1923), *Actaea spicata* L. (29) (1869) Pursh says berry color differs witihin populations

Red cole - *Armoracia rusticana* P.G. Gaertn., B. Mey. & Scherb. (107) (1919)

Red colewort - *Brassica oleracea* L. (180) (1633)

Red columbine - *Aquilegia canadensis* L. (7, 50, 92, 156, 157, 158) (1828–present)

Red columbine of Virginia - *Aquilegia canadensis* L. (181) (~1678)

Red cornel - *Cornus sericea* L. subsp. *sericea* (156) (1923)

Red corrans - *Ribes rubrum* L. (178) (1526)

Red cotton-grass [Red cotton grass] - *Scirpus cyperinus* (L.) Kunth (19) (1840)

Red currans - *Ribes rubrum* L. (46) (1671) deliberately introduced by English colonists by 1671

Red currant - *Ribes rubrum* L. (14, 46, 49, 55, 63, 72, 92, 107, 110, 114) (1876-1949) often spelled as currans in historical documents, *Ribes triste* Pallas (40, 50, 85) (1928–present)

Red daisy - *Hieracium aurantiacum* L. (5, 156) (1913-1923)

Red dare - *Lolium perenne* L. (5) (1913)

Red darnel - *Lolium perenne* L. (5) (1913)

Red dead-nettle [Red dead nettle] - *Lamium purpureum* L. (5, 97, 106, 107, 156, 158) (1900?)

Red deal (England) - *Pinus sylvestris* L. (20) (1857)

Red dogwood [Red dog wood] - *Cornus amomum* Mill. (37) (1919), *Cornus sanguinea* L. (27) (1811), *Cornus sericea* L. subsp. *sericea* (156) (1923)

Red dwarf grass [Red dwarfe-grasse] - *Poa bulbosa* L. (possibly) (178, 180) (1526-1633)

Red elder - *Sambucus racemosa* L. (2) (1895), *Sambucus racemosa* L. var. *racemosa* (158) (1900), *Viburnum opulus* L. (5, 156, 158) (1900-1923)

Red elderberry [Red elder-berry] - *Sambucus racemosa* L. (156) (1923), *Sambucus racemosa* L. var. *racemosa* (50) (present)

Red elephants - *Pedicularis groenlandica* Retz. (156) (1923)

Red elm - *Ulmus americana* L. (78) (1898) Southwest MO, *Ulmus rubra* Muhl. (1, 5, 7, 9, 19, 20, 37, 58, 72, 82, 85, 92, 93, 95, 107, 109, 112, 113, 130, 156, 157, 158) (1828-1937), *Ulmus serotina* Sarg. (5, 97) (1913-1937)

Red eyebright - *Odontites vulgaris* Moench (156) (1923)

Red false heather - *Phyllodoce empetriformis* (Sm.) D. Don (106) (1930)

Red false mallow - *Sphaeralcea coccinea* (Nutt.) Rydb. (3, 4) (1977-1986), *Sphaeralcea coccinea* (Nutt.) Rydb. subsp. *coccinea* (5, 37, 97, 156) (1913-1937)

Red fescue - *Festuca rubra* L. (3, 50, 56, 66, 68, 109, 129, 138, 140, 143, 155) (1894–present)

Red fescue grass - *Festuca rubra* L. (5, 56, 72) (1893-1901)

Red fill-o-do-see - *Phyllodoce empetriformis* (Sm.) D. Don (106) (1930)

Red fir - *Abies magnifica* A. Murr. (109, 138, 155, 158) (1900-1949), *Pseudotsuga menziesii* (Mirb.) Franco (101, 153) (1905-1913)

Red flowering locust - *Robinia pseudoacacia* L. (5) (1913)

Red gaillardia - *Gaillardia amblyodon* J. Gay (124) (1937)

Red garden currant - *Ribes rubrum* L. (5, 156) (1913-1923)

Red gaura - *Gaura coccinea* Nutt. ex Pursh (82, 106) (1930)

Red gilia - *Ipomopsis rubra* (L.) Wherry (122, 124) (1937)

Red gooseberry [Red gooseberries] - *Ribes uva-crispa* L. var. *sativum* DC. (178) (1526)

Red goosefoot [Red goose-foot] - *Chenopodium rubrum* L. (19, 50, 93, 122, 131, 155, 156, 158) (1840–present)

Red grama - *Bouteloua trifida* Thurb. (122) (1937)

Red grape - *Vitis palmata* Vahl (15, 156) (1895-1923)

Red gum - *Eucalyptus camaldulensis* Dehnhardt (57) (1917), *Liquidambar styraciflua* L. (5, 65, 156) (1913-1931) OK

Red haw - *Crataegus calpodendron* (Ehrh.) Medik. (5, 93) (1913-1936), *Crataegus chrysocarpa* Ashe (35, 37, 101) (1806-1919), *Crataegus crus-galli* L. (5, 156) (1913-1923), *Crataegus flava* Aiton (5) (1913), *Crataegus* L. (122, 124) (1937), *Crataegus mollis* Scheele (82, 85, 156) (1923-1932), *Crataegus phaenopyrum* (L. f.) Medik. (5) (1913), *Crataegus succulenta* Schrad. ex Link (112) (1937), *Crataegus viridis* L. (5) (1913)

Red hemp-nettle - *Galeopsis ladanum* L. (5, 19, 156) (1840-1923)

Red hickory - *Carya alba* (L.) Nutt. ex Ell. (5, 158) (1900-1913), *Carya glabra* (Mill.) Sweet (156) (1923), *Carya glabra* (Mill.) Sweet var. *glabra* (5) (1913)

Red horned-poppy [Red horned poppy, Red horned poppie] - *Glaucium corniculatum* (L.) J. H. Rudolph (4, 178) (1526–1986)

Red horse-chestnut - *Aesculus ×carnea* Hayne [*hippocastanum × pavia*] (109) (1949)

Red huckleberry - *Vaccinium virgatum* Aiton (107) (1919)

Red Indian paint [Red Indian-paint] - *Sanguinaria canadensis* L. (64, 156, 157, 158) (1900–1929)

Red Indians [Red-Indians] - *Castilleja coccinea* (L.) Spreng. (5, 73, 156, 158) (1892–1923) MA

Red ink plant [Red ink-plant, Red-ink plant] - *Phytolacca americana* L. (5, 71) (1898–1913), *Phytolacca americana* L. var. *americana* (92, 156, 157, 158) (1876–1929)

Red inkberry [Red ink berry] - *Phytolacca americana* L. var. *americana* (64, 69) (1903–1907)

Red ironbark - *Eucalyptus sideroxylon* A. Cunningham (109, 138) (1923–1949)

Red jasmine - *Ipomoea quamoclit* L. (5, 92, 156, 158) (1876–1923)

Red jessamine - *Ipomoea quamoclit* L. (7) (1828)

Red Judas tree [Red Judas-tree] - *Cercis canadensis* L. (5, 157, 158) (1900–1929)

Red juniper - *Juniperus virginiana* L. (5, 6, 41, 157, 158) (1770–1929)

Red lady's-bower [Red ladies bowre] - *Clematis viticella* L. (178) (1526)

Red lady's-slipper [Red ladies' slipper] - *Cypripedium acaule* Ait. (7) (1828)

Red larch - *Larix laricina* (Du Roi.) Koch. (5, 7, 19) (1828-1913)

Red larkspur - *Delphinium nudicaule* Torr. & Gray (109) (1949)

Red laurel [Redlaurel] - *Magnolia* L. (92) (1876), *Magnolia virginiana* L. (49, 52) (1898-1919), *Nectandra coriacea* (Sw.) Griseb. (7) (1828), *Rhododendron macrophyllum* D. Don ex G. Don (35) (1806)

Red lettuce - *Lactuca sativa* L. (180) (1633)

Red lily [Red lilly] - *Lilium bulbiferum* L. (180) (1633), *Lilium philadelphicum* L. (5, 19, 156, 158) (1840–1923)

Red lingon - *Vaccinium vitis-idaea* L. (possibly) (41) (1770)

Red lobelia - *Lobelia cardinalis* L. (5, 6, 37, 92, 156, 157, 158) (1892–1929)

Red loco - *Oxytropis besseyi* (Rydb.) Blank. (4) (1986)

Red locust - *Robinia viscosa* Vent. (5, 156) (1913-1923)

Red love grass [Red lovegrass] - *Eragrostis secundiflora* J. Presl (50, 155) (1942–present), *Eragrostis secundiflora* J. Presl subsp. *oxylepis* (Torr.) S.D. Koch (3, 50) (1977–present)

Red lychnis - *Silene dioica* (L.) Clairville (15) (1895)

Red madder - *Rubia tinctoria* L. (178) (1526)

Red maithes - *Adonis annua* L. (165) (1768)

Red mallow - *Sphaeralcea coccinea* (Nutt.) Rydb. subsp. *coccinea* (95, 127, 131, 157) (1899–1933)

Red maple - *Acer glabrum* Torr. (149) (1904) NM, *Acer rubrum* L. (2, 5, 15, 19, 20, 38, 41, 42, 46, 50, 57, 72, 76, 82, 92, 93, 106, 107, 109, 122, 124, 138, 155, 156) (1770–present), *Acer rubrum* L. (50) (present), *Acer rubrum* L. (158) (1900)

Red milkweed - *Asclepias rubra* L. (5, 122, 138, 155) (1913-1942)

Red milkwort [Red Milke woort] - *Polygala vulgaris* L. (178) (1526)

Red mint - *Mentha ×gracilis* Sole [*arvensis × spicata*] (155) (1942), *Mentha arvensis* L. (155) (1942), *Monarda didyma* L. (190) (~1759)

Red mombin - *Spondias purpurea* L. (109) (1949)

Red morning-glory [Red morning glory] - *Ipomoea coccinea* L. (3, 4) (1977-1986), *Ipomoea* L. (1) (1932), *Ipomoea purpurea* (L.) Roth (77) (1898) Southwest MO

Red Morocco - *Adonis annua* L. (5, 92, 156, 165) (1768-1923) florist name in England

Red moss - *Sedum smallii* (Britton) H.E.Ahles (74) (1893)

Red moth mullein [Red Moth Mulleine] - *Verbascum thapsus* L. (69) (1904)

Red mulberry [Red mulberrie] - *Morus nigra* L. (178) (1526), *Morus rubra* L. (1, 3, 4, 5, 7, 9, 22, 20, 19, 46, 49, 50, 72, 82, 85, 92, 93, 95, 97, 107, 109, 113, 122, 124, 130, 131, 138, 155, 156, 157, 158, 187) (1818–present), *Morus rubra* L. var. *rubra* (50) (present)

Red mustard - *Brassica nigra* (L.) W.D.J. Koch (6, 69, 156, 158) (1892–1923)

Red nightshade - *Phytolacca americana* L. (181) (~1678), *Phytolacca americana* L. var. *americana* (49) (1898)

Red oak [Red-oak, Red oake] - *Quercus ×benderi* Baenitz [*coccinea × rubra*] (5, 156) (1913–1923), *Quercus falcata* Michx. (5, 33, 156) (1827–1923), *Quercus rubra* L. (2, 5, 8, 10, 12, 14, 18, 20, 19, 33, 37, 40, 41, 46, 58, 61, 65, 72, 78, 82, 92, 93, 95, 97, 106, 112, 113, 122, 124, 135, 156, 158, 177, 181, 187) (1629–1937), *Quercus rubra* L. var. *ambigua* (Gray) Fern. (4, 109) (1949–1986), *Quercus rubra* L. var. *rubra* (3) (1977), *Quercus texana* Buckl. (156) (1923)

Red oat - *Avena sterilis* L. (119) (1938)

Red orache - *Atriplex rosea* L. (4, 5, 21, 93) (1893-1986), *Atriplex hortensis* L. (107) (1538)

Red osier [Red-osier] - *Cornus amomum* Mill. (5, 156, 158) (1900–1923), *Cornus sericea* L. (19, 58, 92) (1840–1892), *Cornus sericea* L. subsp. *sericea* (3, 47, 85, 131, 156) (1852–1977)

Red osier cornel - *Cornus sericea* L. subsp. *sericea* (5, 158) (1900–1913)

Red osier dogwood - *Cornus sericea* L. subsp. *sericea* (5, 9, 40, 63, 72, 97, 108, 155, 158) (1873–1942)

Red paint - *Lithospermum* L. (possibly) (7) (1828)

Red paint root - *Sanguinaria canadensis* L. (92) (1876)

Red panic [Red panicke] - *Pennisetum glaucum* (L.) R. Br. (178) (1596)

Red Passe flower [Red Passe floure] - *Pulsatilla patens* (L.) Mill. subsp. *multifida* (Pritz.) Zamels (poss) (180) (1633)

Red passionflower - *Passiflora manicata* (Juss.) Pers. (138) (1923)

Red pepper [Redpepper] - *Capsicum annuum* L. (19, 58, 92, 107) (1840-1919), *Capsicum annuum* L. var. *annuum* (53, 57, 107) (1917-1922), *Capsicum* L. (82, 109, 110, 138) (1923-1949)

Red pigweed [Red pig-weed] - *Chenopodium rubrum* L. (19, 156, 158) (1840-1923)

Red pimpernel - *Anagallis arvensis* L. (5, 6, 7, 49, 92, 97, 156, 157, 158, 184) (1793–1937)

Red pine - *Pinus palustris* Mill. (20) (1857), *Pinus ponderosa* P.& C. Lawson var. *scopulorum* Engelm. (5) (1913), *Pinus resinosa* Aiton (1, 20, 43, 50, 109, 112, 136, 138) (1820–present)

Red plum - *Prunus americana* Marsh. (107) (1919), *Prunus nigra* Aiton (5) (1913)

Red plum-peach [Redde plum peach] - *Prunus angustifolia* Marsh. (possibly) (181) (~1678)

Red pollom - *Gaultheria procumbens* L. (5, 92, 156) (1876-1923) no longer in use by 1923

Red poppy - *Argemone sanguinea* Greene (122) (1937) TX, *Papaver rhoeas* L. (5, 55, 57, 92, 156, 158) (1876-1923)

Red primrose - *Oenothera speciosa* Nutt. (124) (1937)

Red Prouince rose - *Rosa centifolia* L. (178) (1526)

Red puccoon - *Sanguinaria canadensis* L. (6, 7, 49, 53, 58, 64, 76, 92, 156, 157, 158) (1828–1929)

Red raspberry - *Rubus idaeus* L. (155) (1942), *Rubus idaeus* L. subsp. *strigosus* (Michx.) Focke (4, 19, 40, 49, 58, 92, 101, 107, 113, 130, 131, 156) (1840-1986)

Red rattle - *Pedicularis canadensis* L. (92) (1876), *Pedicularis palustris* L. (5, 156) (1913-1923) misapplied

Red ray - *Lolium perenne* L. (5, 119) (1913-1938)

Red River maple - *Acer negundo* L. (5, 156, 158) (1900-1923)

Red River scale-seed [Red River scaleseed] - *Spermolepis inermis* (Nutt. ex DC.) Mathias & Constance (50) (present)

Red River snakeroot [Red River snake-root] - *Aristolochia reticulata* Nutt. (6, 49, 53, 64) (1892-1922)

Red Robin [Red-Robin] - *Geranium robertianum* L. (5, 109, 156, 157) (1900-1949), *Silene dioica* (L.) Clairville (156) (1923) no longer in use by 1923

Red rockcress - *Arabis laevigata* (Muhl. ex Willd.) Poir. (155) (1942)

Red rod - *Cornus sericea* L. (19, 92) (1840–1876)

Red rood - *Cornus sericea* L. (92) (1876)

Red rose - *Rosa gallica* L. (49, 57, 58, 92, 178) (1526-1917)

Red Sally [Red-Sally] - *Lythrum salicaria* L. (156, 158) (1900-1923)

Red sandalwood - *Adenanthera pavonina* L. (107) (1919)

Red sand-verbena [Red sand verbena] - *Abronia maritima* Nutt. ex S. Wats. (50) (present)

Red sandwort [Red sand-wort] - *Sagina nodosa* (L.) Fenzl (19) (1840), *Spergularia canadensis* (Pers.) G. Don (156) (1923), *Spergularia rubra* (L.) J.& K. Presl (19, 42, 49, 156) (1814-1923), *Spergularia salina* J.& K. Presl (156, 158) (1900-1923)

Red savin - *Juniperus virginiana* L. (5, 6, 157, 158) (1892–1929)

Red Sea barley - *Hordeum vulgare* L. (107) (1919)

Red sedge - *Carex arenaria* L. (57) (1917)

Red snow - *Chlamydomonas augustae* Skuja (46) (1879)

Red snowberry - *Symphoricarpos orbiculatus* Moench (156) (1923)

Red sorrel - *Rumex acetosella* L. (5, 21, 62, 75, 93, 148, 156) (1893–1936)

Red sprangletop [Red sprangle-top] - *Leptochloa panicea* (Retz.) Ohwi subsp. *brachiata* (Steudl.) N. Snow (3, 155, 163) (1852–1977)

Red spruce - *Picea rubens* Sarg. (5, 10, 19, 38, 50, 109, 138) (1818–present)

Red strawberry [Red Strawberrie] - *Fragaria virginiana* Duchesne (178) (1526)

Red sumac - *Rhus glabra* L. (106) (1930)

Red sunflower - *Echinacea* Moench (possibly) (7) (1828), *Echinacea purpurea* (L.) Moench (5, 92, 156) (1876-1923)

Red swamp cypress - *Taxodium distichum* (L.) L.C. Rich. (5) (1913)

Red swampfire - *Salicornia rubra* A. Nels. (50) (present)

Red tassel-flower [Red tassel flower] - *Dalea phleoides* (Torr. & Gray) Shinners var. *microphylla* (Torr. & Gray) Barneby (101) (1905), *Dalea purpurea* Vent. (76) (1896), *Dalea purpurea* Vent. var. *purpurea* (5, 156) (1913-1923)

Red thistle - *Cirsium texanum* Buckl. (124) (1937) TX

Red threeawn [Red three awn, Red three-awn] - *Aristida purpurea* Nutt. var. *longiseta* (Steud.) Vasey (3, 122, 140, 146, 155) (1937-1977)

Red titi [Red ti-ti] - *Cyrilla racemiflora* L. (5, 106, 156) (1913-1930) IA

Red trillium - *Trillium erectum* L. (5, 64, 50, 156) (1908–present), *Trillium recurvatum* Beck (possibly) (156) (1923), *Trillium sessile* L. (156) (1923)

Red turmeric - *Sanguinaria canadensis* L. (58) (1869)

Red turtlehead [Red turtle head] - *Chelone obliqua* L. (5, 72) (1907-1913)

Red valerian - *Centranthus ruber* (L.) DC. (109, 178) (1526-1949)

Red wakerobin [Red wake robin, Red wake-robin] - *Trillium erectum* L. (5, 64, 156) (1908-1913)

Red waxberry - *Symphoricarpos orbiculatus* Moench (156) (1923)

Red wheat - *Triticum aestivum* L. (180) (1633)

Red whortleberry - *Vaccinium virgatum* Aiton (138) (1923), *Vaccinium vitis-idaea* L. (5, 156) (1913-1923)

Red willow - *Salix eriocephala* Michx. (130) (1895), *Salix interior* Rowlee (5, 155, 156, 158) (1900-1942), *Salix purpurea* L. (6) (1892)

Red wind anemone - *Anemone multifida* Poir. (131) (1899)

Red windflower [Red wind-flower, Red wind flower] - *Anemone multifida* Poir. (156, 158) (1900-1923), *Anemone multifida* Poir. var. *hudsoniana* DC. (5, 93) (1913-1936)

Red wood-lettuce - *Lactuca hirsuta* Muhl. ex Nutt. (5) (1913)

Red yarrow - *Achillea millefolium* L. (178) (1526)

Red-and-white lady's-slipper [Red and white ladies' slipper] - *Cypripedium reginae* Walt. (7) (1828) CT

Redbead - *Adenanthera pavonina* L. (138) (1923)

Red-bead vine - *Abrus precatorius* L. (107, 158) (1900-1919)

Redberry [Red-berry, Red berry] - *Actaea rubra* (Aiton) Willd. (5, 157, 158) (1900–1929), *Arctostaphylos uva-ursi* (L.) Spreng. (6, 7) (1828–1892), *Gaultheria procumbens* L. (6, 7) (1828–1892), *Ilex crenata* Thunb. (156) (1923), *Panax quinquefolius* L. (5, 6, 64, 92, 156, 157, 158) (1876–1929), *Rhamnus crocea* Nutt. (106) (1930)

Red-berry bamboo [Red-berried bamboo] - *Smilax walteri* Pursh. (5, 156) (1913-1923)

Red-berry buckthorn [Red-berried buckthorn] - *Rhamnus crocea* Nutt. (109) (1949)

Red-berry elder [Red-berried elder] - *Sambucus racemosa* L. (5, 19, 46, 63, 82, 92, 156) (1840-1923), *Sambucus racemosa* L. var. *racemosa* (4, 72, 85, 86, 130, 158) (1878-1986)

Red-berry juniper [Redberry juniper] - *Juniperus pinchotii* Sudw. (3, 155) (1942-1977)

Red-berry mistletoe [Red berried mistletoe] - *Phoradendron rubrum* (L.) Griseb. (8) (1785)

Red-berry moonseed - *Cocculus carolinus* (L.) DC. (5) (1913)

Red-berry snakeroot [Red berry snake root, Red-berry snakeroot] - *Actaea rubra* (Aiton) Willd. (7, 92, 57) (1828-1900)

Red-berry tea [Red berry tea, Redberry tea] - *Gaultheria procumbens* L. (7, 92, 156) (1828-1923)

Red-berry trailing arbutus [Red-berried trailing arbutus] - *Arctostaphylos uva-ursi* (L.) Spreng. (6) (1892)

Red-berry Virginia smilax [Red berried Virginian smilax] - *Smilax smallii* Morong (8) (1785)

Red-bird - *Geranium robertianum* L. (157, 158) (1900-1929)

Red-bird cactus [Redbird-cactus] - *Pedilanthus tithymaloides* (L.) Poit. (109) (1949)

Red-bird slipper-flower [Redbird slipperflower] - *Pedilanthus tithymaloides* (L.) Poit. (155) (1942)

Redbox [Red-box] - *Eucalyptus polyanthemos* Schauer (109, 138) (1923-1949)

Red-bristle dewberry [Red-bristled dewberry] - *Rubus trivialis* Michx. (97) (1937)

Red-brown flag [Red brown flag] - *Iris fulva* Ker.-Gawl. (5) (1913)

Redbud [Red-bud, Red bud, Red-budds] or Redbud tree [Red bud tree, Redbud-tree, Redbud tree] - *Andromeda* L. (167) (1814), *Cercis canadensis* L. (3, 4, 7, 10, 57, 93, 107, 121, 157, 181, 184, 187) (~1678-1986), *Cercis* L. (1, 50, 82, 93, 109, 138, 155, 156) (1923–present), *Leucothoe racemosa* (L.) Gray (possibly) (187) (1818), *Menodora heterophylla* Moric. ex DC. (124) (1937)

Red-bud deutzia [Redbud deutzia] - *Deutzia purpurascens* (Franch. ex L. Henry) Rehder (138) (1923)

Red-bush - *Cornus amomum* Mill. (157) (1929)

Red-centered vine morning-glory - *Convolvulus equitans* Benth. (124) (1937)

Red-cup moss - *Cladonia bellidiflora* (Ach.) Schaer. (73) (1892)

Reddish bulrush - *Scirpus lineatus* Michx. (5, 72, 120) (1907-1938)

Red-dome blanket-flower [Red dome blanketflower] - *Gaillardia pinnatifida* Torr. (50) (present)

Redfield's grass - *Redfieldia flexuosa* (Thurb.) Vasey (5, 94, 119) (1901-1938)

Red-flower aster [Red-flowered aster] - *Symphyotrichum lateriflorum* (L.) Á. & D.Löve (possibly) (187) (1818)

Red-flower azalea [Red-flowered azalea] - *Rhododendron periclymenoides* (Michx.) Shinners (8) (1785)

Red-flower clematis pipevine [Red-flowered clematis pipe vine] - *Clematis pitcheri* Torr. & Gray (124) (1937)

Red-flower dwarf iris [Red floured Dwarfe Iris] - *Iris pumila* L. (180) (1633)

Red-flower fever-root [Red flowered fever-root, Red-flowered fever-root] - *Triosteum perfoliatum* L. (186, 187) (1814-1818)

Red-flower maple [Red-flowering maple, Red flowering maple] - *Acer rubrum* L. (20, 41, 189) (1767-1857)

Red-flower trumpet-leaf [Red-flowered trumpet leaf] - *Sarracenia rubra* Walt. (2, 86) (1878-1895)

Red-flower yucca [Red flowered yucca] - *Hesperaloe parviflora* (Torr.) Coult. (122, 124) (1937) TX

Red-fruit horse-gentian [Red-fruited horse-gentian] - *Triosteum aurantiacum* Bickn. (72) (present)

Red-fruit juniper [Red fruited juniper] - *Juniperus coahuilensis* (Martinez) Gaussen ex R.P. Adams (122) (1937)

Red-fruit medlar [Red-fruited medlar] - *Photinia pyrifolia* (Lam.) Robertson & Phipps (187) (1818)

Red-fruit ptarmigan-berry [Redfruit ptarmiganberry] - *Arctous ruber* (Rehder & E. H. Wilson) Nakai (155) (1942)

Red-fruit raspberry [Red-fruited raspberry] - *Rubus idaeus* L. subsp. *strigosus* (Michx.) Focke (187) (1818)

Red-fruit sumac [Red-fruited sumac] - *Rhus trilobata* Nutt. (157) (1929)

Red-fruit swamp-service [Red-fruited swamp-service] - *Photinia floribunda* (Lindl.) Robertson & Phipps (187) (1818)

Red-fruit thorn [Red fruited thorn, Red-fruited thorn] - *Crataegus mollis* Scheele (5, 72, 93, 97, 131) (1907-1936)

Red-hair anthenantia [Red-haired anthenantia] - *Anthaenantia rufa* (Nutt.) J.A. Schultes (94) (1901)

Redhead [Red head] - *Asclepias curassavica* L. (92) (1876)

Red-head pondweed - *Potamogeton richardsonii* (Benn.) Rydb. (3) (1977)

Redhead-grass - *Potamogeton perfoliatus* L. (156) (1923)

Red-heart ceanothus [Redheart ceanothus] - *Ceanothus spinosus* Nutt. (109) (1949)

Red-heart hickory [Red heart hickory] - *Carya ovata* (Mill.) K. Koch (5, 156) (1913-1923)

Redhot-cattail - *Acalypha hispida* Burm. f. (109) (1949)

Red-hot-poker plant [Red hot poker plant] - *Kniphofia uvaria* (L.) Oken (92) (1876)

Red-ink plant - *Phytolacca americana* L. var. *americana* (158) (1900)

Red-knees [Red knees] - *Polygonum hydropiper* L. (5, 92, 156, 157, 158) (1876–1929)

Red-leaf barberry [Red leaf barberry] - *Berberis thunbergii* DC. (112) (1937)

Red-leaf Japanese barberry [Redleaf Japanese barberry] - *Berberis thunbergii* DC. (155) (1942)

Red-leaf rose [Redleaf rose] - *Rosa rubrifolia* Vill. (138) (1923)

Red-leaf wood sorrel [Red-leaved wood sorrel] - *Oxalis stricta* L. (5) (1913)

Red-leaves - *Polygonum hydropiper* L. (156) (1923)

Red-legs [Red legs] - *Polygonum bistorta* L. (92) (1876)

Red-osier dogwood [Red-osier dogwood, Redosier dogwood] - *Cornus sericea* L. (50) (present), *Cornus sericea* L. subsp. *sericea* (5, 9, 40, 50, 63, 72, 93, 95, 97, 108, 113, 138) (1873–present)

Red-ring milkweed [Redring milkweed] - *Asclepias variegata* L. (50) (present)

Red-Robin - *Geranium robertianum* L. (158) (1900)

Red-rod - *Cornus amomum* Mill. (156, 157, 158) (1900–1929)

Red-rod for dying - *Ceanothus americanus* L. (177) (1762)

Redroot [Red-root, Red root] - *Amaranthus hybridus* L. (62) (1912), *Amaranthus retroflexus* L. (5, 77, 80, 93, 97, 125, 145, 148, 156, 158) (1897–1937), *Armeria maritima* (P. Mill.) Willd (5, 156) (1913-1923), *Buglossoides arvensis* (L.) I. M. Johnston (62, 156) (1912–1923), *Cannabis sativa* L. (5, 93, 156, 158) (1900–1923), *Ceanothus americanus* L. (5, 7, 14, 35, 47, 49, 52, 53, 54, 57, 58, 61, 82, 92, 106, 156, 157, 158, 184, 187) (1793–1929), *Ceanothus herbaceus* Raf. (95, 113, 122, 124, 130, 145) (1890–1937), *Ceanothus* L. (10, 13, 82, 93, 156, 158, 190) (~1759–1936), *Ceanothus sanguineus* Pursh (35) (1806), *Celastrus scandens* L. (19, 156) (1840–1923), *Geum aleppicum* Jacq. (5, 156) (1913–1923), *Geum virginianum* L. (156, 157, 158) (1900–1929), *Lachnanthes caroliana* (Lam.) Dandy (5, 6, 49, 86, 106, 156, 187) (1818–1930), *Lachnanthes* Ell. (2, 10) (1818–1895) root used for dye, *Morinda royoc* L. (76) (1896) West Indies, *Sanguinaria canadensis* L. (6, 7, 49, 53, 58, 64, 76, 92, 157, 158, 186) (1825–1923)

Red-root amaranth [Redroot amaranth] - *Amaranthus retroflexus* L. (50, 155) (1942–present)

Red-root cyperus [Redrooted cyperus, Red-rooted cyperus] - *Cyperus erythrorhizos* Muhl. (3, 5, 72) (1893-1977)

Red-root flatsedge [Redroot flatsedge] - *Cyperus erythrorhizos* Muhl. (50) (present)

Red-root willow [Red-rooted willow] - *Salix discolor* Muhl. (19, 187) (1818–1840)

Red-rot [Red rot] - *Drosera rotundifolia* L. (5, 6, 156, 158) (1892–1923)

Redsater - *Ipomoea coccinea* L. (50) (present)

Redscale - *Atriplex rosea* L. (3, 4) (1977-1986)

Redseed [Red-seed, Red seed] - *Amianthium* A. Gray (7) (1828), *Chamaelirium luteum* (L.) A. Gray (53, 57, 64, 156) (1908-1923)

Red-seed dandelion [Red-seeded dandelion] - *Taraxacum laevigatum* (Willd.) DC. (5, 72, 80, 82, 85, 93, 95, 97, 127, 156) (1907-1937)

Red-seed plantain [Redseed plantain, Red-seeded plantain] - *Plantago rhodosperma* Dcne. (3, 4, 50, 97, 155) (1937–present)

Red-seed-lettuce [Red-seeded-lettuce] - *Taraxacum laevigatum* (Willd.) DC. (3, 4) (1977-1986)

Redshank [Red shank, Red-shank, Red shanks, Redshanks, Red-shanks] - *Geranium robertianum* L. (5, 92, 156, 157, 158) (1898–1929), *Persicaria amphibia* (L.) Delarbre (5) (1913), *Persicaria maculosa* Gray (5, 92, 156, 158) (1876–1923), *Polygonum amphibium* L. (156, 157, 158) (1900–1929), *Polygonum hydropiper* L. (5, 156, 157, 158) (1900–1929), *Rumex acetosa* L. (5, 156) (1913–1923)

Red-shank chamise [Redshank chamise] - *Adenostoma sparsifolium* Torr. (155) (1942)

Red-shank grape [Redshank grape] - *Vitis aestivalis* Michx. var. *aestivalis* (155) (1942)

Red-shoot gooseberry [Redshoot gooseberry] - *Ribes oxyacanthoides* L. subsp. *setosum* (Lindl.) Sinnott (155) (1942)

Red-spine American agave [Red-spined American agave] - *Agave americana* L. (165) (1768)

Red-spray ruellia [Redspray ruellia] - *Ruellia brevifolia* (Pohl) C.Ezcurra (138) (1923)

Red-stalk aster [Red stalked aster, Red-stalked aster] - *Symphyotrichum puniceum* (L.) A.& D. Löve var. *puniceum* (5, 49, 92, 156, 158, 187) (1818-1923)

Red-stalk Carolina bay tree [Red-stalked Carolinian bay-tree] - *Persea borbonia* (L.) Spreng. (8) (1785)

Redstem [Red-stem] - *Ammannia* L. (50) (present), *Schizachyrium scoparium* (Michx.) Nash (5) (1913)

Red-stem aster [Red-stemmed aster] - *Symphyotrichum puniceum* (L.) A.& D. Löve var. *puniceum* (93) (1936)

Red-stem filaree [Red-stemmed filaree] - *Erodium cicutarium* (L.) L'Hér. ex Aiton (109, 157) (1929-1949)

Red-stem gentian [Red-stemmed gentian] - *Gentiana rubricaulis* Schwein. (72) (1907)

Red-stem stork's-bill [Redstem stork's bill] - *Erodium cicutarium* (L.) L'Hér. ex Aiton (50) (present), *Erodium cicutarium* (L.) L'Hér. ex Aiton subsp. *cicutarium* (50) (present)

Red-tip pedicularis [Red-tipped pedicularis] - *Pedicularis flammea* L. (5) (1913)

Redtop [Red-top, Red top] - *Agrostis capillaris* L. (11, 19, 45, 56, 66, 67, 87, 88, 90, 92, 129, 187) (1818-1912), *Agrostis gigantea* Roth (5, 45, 50, 56, 93, 94, 109, 111, 115, 119, 122, 140, 143, 152, 155, 163) (1852–present), *Agrostis* L. (1, 93) (1932-1936), *Agrostis stolonifera* L. (3, 68, 85, 125, 138) (1913-1977), *Calamagrostis canadensis* (Michx.) Beauv. (56) (1901), *Eragrostis tenuifolia* (A. Rich.) Hochst. ex Steud. (45, 87, 88) (1884-1896), *Tridens flavus* (L.) A.S. Hitchc. (19, 187) (1818-1840)

Red-top buffalo grass [Red-topped buffalo-grass] - *Eragrostis tenuifolia* (A. Rich.) Hochst. ex Steud. (45, 87, 88) (1884-1896)

Redtop grass [Red top grass] - *Agrostis capillaris* L. (92) (1876), *Agrostis stolonifera* L. (21) (1893)

Red-top panic - *Panicum rigidulum* Bosc ex Nees var. *elongatum* (Pursh) Lelong (5, 119, 163) (1852-1938)

Red-top panic grass [Redtop panicgrass] - *Panicum rigidulum* Bosc ex Nees var. *elongatum* (Pursh) Lelong (50) (present)

Red-top panicum [Redtop panicum] - *Panicum rigidulum* Bosc ex Nees var. *elongatum* (Pursh) Lelong (87, 155) (1884-1942)

Red-top sorrel - *Rumex acetosella* L. (156, 157, 158) (1900–1929)

Red-twig leucothoe [Redtwig leucothoe] - *Leucothoe recurva* (Buckl.) Gray (138) (1923)

Red-vein crab [Redvein crab] - *Malus pumila* Mill. (137, 138) (1923-1931)

Red-vein dock [Red veined dock, Red-veined dock] - *Rumex obtusifolius* L. (80) (1913), *Rumex sanguineus* L. (5, 72) (1907-1913)

Red-ware - *Laminaria digitata* (Hudson) J.V.Lamouroux (107) (1919)

Redweed [Red-weed, Red weed] - *Lythrum salicaria* L. (156) (1923), *Papaver rhoeas* L. (5, 156) (1913–1923), *Persicaria maculosa* Gray (5, 156, 158) (1900–1923), *Phytolacca americana* L. (5, 37, 69) (1903–1919), *Phytolacca americana* L. var. *americana* (49, 64, 71, 92, 156, 157, 158) (1876–1929), *Rumex acetosella* L. (5, 75, 156, 157, 158) (1900–1929) WV

Redweed of Virginia [Red weed of Virginia] - *Phytolacca americana* L. (181) (~1678)

Red-whisker clammyweed [Redwhisker clammyweed] - *Polanisia dodecandra* (L.) DC. (50) (present), *Polanisia dodecandra* (L.) DC. subsp. *dodecandra* (50) (present)

Red-willow [Red willow] - *Cornus amomum* Mill. (5, 156, 158) (1900–1923), *Cornus sericea* L. (34, 35, 38, 76, 92, 186, 187) (1806–1906), *Cornus sericea* L. subsp. *sericea* (47, 101) (1852–1905)

Redwood [Red wood] - *Cornus sericea* L. subsp. *sericea* (35) (1806), *Sequoia* Endl. (138) (1923), *Sequoia sempervirens* (Lamb. ex D. Don) Endl. (50, 109, 138, 147, 161) (1856–present)

Redwood of California - *Sequoia sempervirens* (Lamb. ex D. Don) Endl. (14) (1882)

Red-wood sorrel [Redwood sorrel] - *Oxalis oregana* Nutt. (76) (1896) CA

Red-wood willow [Red wood willow, Redwood willow, Redwood-willow] - *Salix fragilis* L. (5, 156, 158) (1900-1923)

Red-wool plantain [Redwool plantain] - *Plantago eriopoda* Torr. (50) (present)

Reed [Rede, Reeds] -, *Arundo* L. (10, 92) (1818–1876), *Calamagrostis epigeios* (L.) Roth [possibly] (184) (1793), *Phragmites* Adans. (1, 50, 121, 155) (1918–present), *Phragmites australis* (Cav.) Trin. ex Steud. (40, 56, 72, 90, 107, 178, 179) (1526–1928), *Zizania aquatica* L. (94, 157, 158) (1900–1929)

Reed bent - *Arctagrostis latifolia* (R. Br.) Griseb. subsp. *arundinacea* (Trin.) Tzvelev (4) (1986)

Reed bent grass - *Calamagrostis* Adans. (10, 45, 66) (1818-1903), *Calamagrostis coarctata* (Torr.) Eat. (5) (1913)

Reed brier [Reed brere] - *Eryngium maritimum* L. (179) (1526)

Reed canary - *Phalaris arundinacea* L. (88) (1885)

Reed canary grass [Reed canarygrass, Reed canary-grass] - *Phalaris arundinacea* L. (3, 45, 50, 56, 66, 68, 85, 87, 90, 92, 93, 94, 109, 111, 115, 129, 138, 143, 144, 155, 163) (1852–present)

Reed canebrake [Reed cane brake] - *Arundinaria gigantea* (Walt.) Muhl. subsp. *tecta* (Walt.) McClure (5) (1913)

Reed dock [Reed docke] - *Rumex* L. (179) (1526)

Reed fescue - *Arundo donax* L. (129) (1894), *Lolium arundinaceum* (Schreb.) S.J. Darbyshire (68, 94, 155) (1890–1942)

Reed grass [Reedgrass, Reed-grass] - *Arundinaria gigantea* (Walter) Muhl. (possibly) (124) (1937), *Calamagrostis* Adans. (1, 50, 93, 155) (1932–present), *Calamagrostis canadensis* (Michx.) Beauv. (19, 85) (1840-1932), *Calamagrostis canadensis* (Michx.) Beauv. var. *macouniana* (Vasey) Stebbins (116) (1958), *Calamovilfa* (Gray) Hack. ex Scribn. & Southworth (1) (1932), *Calamovilfa longifolia* (Hook.) Scribn. (85, 116) (1932-1958), *Cinna* L. (1, 93) (1932-1936), *Phalaris arundinacea* L. (67) (1890), *Phragmites* Adans. (66) (1903), *Phragmites australis* (Cav.) Trin. ex Steud. (11, 19, 22, 45, 87, 101, 124, 129) (1840-1937)

Reed manna grass [Reed mannagrass, Reed manna-grass] - *Glyceria grandis* S. Wats. (140) (1944)

Reed meadow grass [Reed meadow-grass] - *Catabrosa aquatica* (L.) Beauv. (66, 87, 90) (1885-1903), *Glyceria arundinacea* Kunth (88) (1885), *Glyceria grandis* S. Wats. (56, 72, 94, 111, 129, 143)

(1894–1936), *Glyceria grandis* S. Wats. var. *grandis* (5) (1913), *Glyceria maxima* (Hartm.) Holmb. (94) (1901)

Reed poppy - *Papaver rhoeas* L. (179) (1526)

Reed-grass [Reedgrass, Reed grass] - *Sparganium* L. (158) (1900)

Reed-like calamagrostis - *Calamagrostis coarctata* (Torr.) Eat. (187) (1818)

Reed-like grass - *Cinna arundinacea* L. (187) (1818)

Reed-mace [Reedmace, Reed mace] - *Typha* L. (7, 158, 180) (1633-1900), *Typha latifolia* L. (2, 27, 49, 92, 107, 187) (1811-1919)

Reedy cinna - *Cinna arundinacea* L. (42, 66) (1814-1903)

Reefort - *Raphanus sativus* L. (158) (1900)

Reflexed cyperus - *Cyperus refractus* Engelm. ex Boeckl. (5) (1913)

Reflexed flatsedge - *Cyperus refractus* Engelm. ex Boeckl. (50) (present)

Reflexed meadow grass - *Puccinellia distans* (Jacq.) Parl. (66) (1903)

Reflexed sedge - *Carex retroflexa* Muhl. (5, 50, 66) (1912–present)

Reflexed spiderwort - *Tradescantia ohiensis* Raf. (5, 72, 97) (1907-1937)

Reflexed stonecrop - *Sedum reflexum* L. (5) (1913)

Regal fern - *Osmunda regalis* L. var. *spectabilis* (Willd.) A. Gray (124) (1937)

Regal lily - *Lilium regale* E.E. Wilson (109) (1949)

Réglisse Indienne (French) - *Abrus precatorius* L. (158) (1900)

Rehder's Carolina rose [Rehder Carolina rose] - *Rosa carolina* L. var. *carolina* (155) (1942)

Reimveide - *Ligustrum vulgare* L. (7) (1828)

Rein orchid - *Piperia* Rydb. (50) (present)

Rein orchis - *Habenaria* Willd. (2) (1895)

Reindeer moss - *Lichen rangiferinus* L. (14, 41, 92) (1770-1882)

Reine-claude - *Prunus domestica* L. (92) (1876)

Remcope - *Suckleya* Gray (179) (1526)

Renney-wort - *Cotyledon* L. (86) (1878) old European name

Renoncule (French) - *Ranunculus acris* L. (6, 158) (1892–1900)

Renoncule acre (French) - *Ranunculus acris* L. (7) (1828)

Renouee vulgaire (French) - *Polygonum aviculare* L. (7) (1828)

Repa (Slavic languages) - *Brassica rapa* L. (110) (1886)

Repand cheirinia - *Erysimum repandum* L. (5, 97) (1913-1937)

Repo (German) - *Brassica rapa* L. var. *rapa* (107) (1919)

Reree - *Typha latifolia* L. (158) (1900)

Rescue brome - *Bromus catharticus* Vahl (155) (1942)

Rescue grass [Rescuegrass, Rescue-grass] - *Bromus catharticus* Vahl (5, 45, 50, 56, 88, 94, 109, 118, 119, 122, 138, 155, 163) (1852–present), *Festuca* L. (152) (1912) NM

Reseda - *Reseda lutea* L. (4) (1986)

Resin boneset - *Eupatorium resinosum* Torr. ex DC. (5) (1913)

Resin bush [Resinbush] - *Viguiera stenoloba* Blake (4, 50) (1986–present)

Resinous currant - *Ribes cereum* Dougl. (108) (1878)

Resinous skullcap - *Scutellaria resinosa* Torr. (4, 5, 97, 155) (1913-1986)

Resp (Swedish) - *Ribes rubrum* L. (110) (1886)

Rest harrow - *Ononis campestris* G. Koch & Ziz (92) (1876)

Rest harrow with white flowers - *Ononis campestris* G. Koch & Ziz (178) (1526)

Rest harrow without prickles - *Ononis campestris* G. Koch & Ziz (178) (1526)

Resurrection fern [Resurrectionfern] - *Asplenium* L. (124) (1937) TX, *Pleopeltis polypodioides* (L.) Andrews & Windham subsp. *michauxiana* (Weatherby) Andrews & Windham (3, 4, 50, 138) (1923–present), *Pleopeltis polypodioides* (L.) Andrews & Windham subsp. *polypodioides* (50, 155) (1942–present)

Resurrection plant [Resurrectionplant] - *Selaginella lepidophylla* (Hook. & Grev.) Spring (14, 92, 109, 124, 138) (1882-1949), *Selaginella rupestris* (L.) Spring (5) (1913)

Retama - *Parkinsonia aculeata* L. (106, 109, 122, 124) (1930-1949)

Reticulated nut-rush [Reticulated nut rush] - *Scleria reticularis* Michx. (5) (1913)

Reticulate-seed spurge [Reticulate seeded spurge, Reticulate-seeded spurge] - *Euphorbia spathulata* Lam (5, 72, 93, 97, 131) (1899-1937)

Retrorse sedge - *Carex retrorsa* Schwein (5, 72) (1907-1913)

Reverchon's astragalus - *Astragalus lotiflorus* Hook (97) (1937)

Reverchon's blazing star [Reverchon's blazingstar] - *Mentzelia reverchonii* (Urban & Gilg) Thomps. & Zavortink (50) (present)

Reverchon's bristle grass [Reverchon's bristlegrass] - *Setaria reverchonii* (Vasey) Pilger (50) (present)

Reverchon's false pennyroyal [Reverchon false pennyroyal] - *Hedeoma reverchonii* Gray (4, 50) (1986–present)

Reverchon's panic - *Setaria reverchonii* (Vasey) Pilger (94) (1901)

Reverchon's psoralea - *Pediomelum reverchonii* (S. Wats.) Rydb. (97) (1937)

Reverchon's thorn - *Crataegus reverchonii* Sarg. (5) (1913)

Reverchon's vetch - *Vicia minutiflora* F.G. Dietr. (97) (1937)

Reversed clover - *Trifolium resuspinatum* L. (3, 50) (1977–present)

Rew - *Ruta graveolens* L. (46) (1671) cultivated by English colonists by 1671

Rewbarbe (Rhubarb) - *Rheum* L. (179) (1526)

Rez (Polish) - *Secale cereale* L. (110) (1886)

Rhamnoide (French) - *Hippophae* L. (8) (1785)

Rhamnoide de Canada (French) - *Shepherdia canadensis* Nutt. (8) (1785)

Rhapontic (French) - *Rheum rhabarbarum* L. (158) (1900)

Rhapontic rhubarb - *Rheum rhabarbarum* L. (158) (1900)

Rhapontic root - *Rheum rhabarbarum* L. (92) (1876)

Rhapontikrhabarber (German) - *Rheum rhabarbarum* L. (158) (1900)

Rhatany - *Krameria* L. (13) (1849)

Rheumatic plant - *Isocoma veneta* (Kunth) Greene (76) (1896)

Rheumatism root [Rheumatism-root] - *Apocynum cannabinum* L. (5, 64, 156, 157) (1900-1929), *Chelone glabra* L. (156) (1923), *Chimaphila maculata* (L.) Pursh (5, 156) (1913-1923), *Dioscorea villosa* L. (6, 49, 64, 156, 158) (1892-1923), *Jeffersonia diphylla* (L.) Pers. (2, 5, 13, 49, 53, 64, 92, 156) (1849-1923)

Rheumatism-weed [Rheumatism weed] - *Apocynum androsaemifolium* L. (75, 156, 157, 158) (1894–1929), *Apocynum cannabinum* L. (158) (1900), *Chimaphila maculata* (L.) Pursh (7) (1828), *Chimaphila* Pursh (92) (1876), *Chimaphila umbellata* (L.) Bart. (156, 158) (1900–1923)

Rhineberry [Rhine-berry] - *Rhamnus cathartica* L. (156, 158) (1900-1923)

Rhipsalis - *Rhipsalis* Gaertn. (155) (1942)

Rhizophore d'Amerique (French) - *Rhizophora mangle* L. (20) (1857)

Rhode Island bent - *Agrostis capillaris* L. (90, 138) (1885-1923), *Muhlenbergia tenuiflora* (Willd.) Britton, Sterns & Poggenb. (109) (1949)

Rhode island bent grass [Rhode Island bent-grass] - *Agrostis canina* L. (2, 5, 56) (1895-1911), *Agrostis capillaris* L. (143) (1852-1936)

Rhode Island clover - *Leucanthemum vulgare* Lam. (75) (1894) Montpelier VT

Rhodes grass [Rhodes-grass] - *Chloris gayana* Kunth (109, 122, 138) (1923-1949)

Rhodes wood - *Amyris balsamifera* L. (92) (1876)

Rhododendron - *Rhododendron* L. (1, 138) (1923-1932), *Rhododendron maximum* L. (14, 71) (1882-1898)

Rhododendrum - *Nerium oleander* L. (174) (1753)

Rhodora - *Rhododendron canadense* (L.) Torr. (5, 19, 109, 138, 156) (1840-1949), *Rhododendron* (138) (1923)

Rhoeas - *Papaver rhoeas* L. (57) (1917)

Rhombic copperleaf - *Acalypha rhomboidea* Raf. (3, 4) (1977-1986)

Rhombic evening-primrose [Rhombic evening primrose] - *Oenothera rhombipetala* Nutt. ex Torr. & Gray (5, 72, 97) (1907-1937)

Rhombic-leaf alder [Rhombic-leaved alder] - *Alnus rhombifolia* Nutt. (20) (1857)

Rhombic-leaf sunflower [Rhombicleaf sunflower, Rhombic-leaved sunflower] - *Helianthus pauciflorus* Nutt. subsp. *subrhomboideus* (Rydb.) O. Spring & E. Schilling (5, 155) (1913–1942)

Rhubarb - *Rheum* L. (1, 4, 7, 14, 57, 92, 138, 155, 158, 184) (1793–1986), *Rheum rhabarbarum* L. (4, 85, 107, 148) (1919–1986)

Rhuddygyl maurth (Welsh) - *Armoracia rusticana* P. G. Gaertn., B. Mey. & Scherb. (110) (1886)

Rhus tox - *Toxicodendron toxicarium* (Salisb.) Gillis (54) (1905)

Rib plantain - *Plantago lanceolata* L. (56) (1901)

Ribbed sedge - *Carex virescens* Muhl. ex Willd. (5, 50) (1913–present)

Ribbed verpa - *Verpa bohemica* (Krombh.) J. Schröt. (128) (1933)

Ribbon bush [Ribbonbush, Ribbon-bush] - *Homalocladium platycladum* (F.J. Muell.) Bailey (109, 138) (1923-1949)

Ribbon cane - *Saccharum officinarum* L. (163) (1852)

Ribbon grass [Ribbon-grass] - *Nolina lindheimeriana* (Scheele) S. Wats. (122, 124) (1937) TX, *Phalaris arundinacea* L. (5, 22, 46, 90, 92, 144, 158, 163) (1852-1913), *Phalaris caroliniana* Walt. (5, 19, 92) (1840-1913)

Ribbon gum - *Eucalyptus viminalis* Labill. (109) (1949)

Ribbon tree [Ribbon-tree] - *Betula pubescens* Ehrh. (158) (1900)

Ribbon-leaf pondweed [Ribbonleaf pondweed] - *Potamogeton epihydrus* Raf. (50, 155) (1942–present)

Rib-grass [Ribgrass, Rib grass] - *Plantago* L. (1, 2, 93) (1932–1936), *Plantago lanceolata* L. (5, 45, 62, 82, 72, 80, 92, 95, 156, 157, 158) (1896–1930), *Plantago major* L. (6, 49, 52, 53) (1892–1922), *Plantago media* L. (92) (1876)

Ribs (Danish) - *Ribes rubrum* L. (110) (1886)

Rib-seed sandmat [Ribseed sandmat] - *Chamaesyce glyptosperma* (Engelm.) Small (50) (present)

Ribwort [Rib wort, Rib-wort, Rybwort] - *Plantago lanceolata* L. (5, 19, 62, 75, 92, 131, 156, 157, 158, 179, 187) (1526–1929), *Plantago major* L. (6, 49, 52, 53) (1892–1922)

Ricasol's pandorea [Ricasol pandorea] - *Podranea ricasoliana* (Tanfani) Sprague (138) (1923)

Rice - *Oryza* L. (138) (1923) adaptation of Arabic name eruz, *Oryza sativa* L. (180) (1633)

Rice cut grass [Rice cutgrass, Rice-cut-grass, Rice cut-grass] - *Leersia oryzoides* (L.) Sw. (3, 5, 45, 50, 56, 90, 92, 94, 99, 111, 119, 122, 129, 131, 155, 163) (1852–present), *Leersia* Sw. (1, 93) (1932–1936)

Rice grass [Ricegrass] - *Leersia oryzoides* (L.) Sw. (85) (1932), *Leersia* Sw. (10) (1818), *Leersia virginica* Willd. (19) (1840), *Oryzopsis* Michx. (50, 155) (1942–present), *Piptatherum* Beauv. (50) (present)

Rice-button aster [Rice button aster, Ricebutton aster] - *Symphyotrichum dumosum* (L.) Nesom var. *dumosum* (5, 122, 156) (1913–1937)

Rice-corn [Rice corn] - *Sorghum bicolor* (L.) Moench subsp. *bicolor* (107) (1919)

Rice-field flatsedge [Ricefield flatsedge] - *Cyperus squarrosus* L. (50) (present)

Rice-paper plant - *Tetrapanax papyriferus* (Hook.) K. Koch (109, 138) (1923-1949)

Rice's-cousin [Rice's cousin] - *Leersia oryzoides* (L.) Sw. (5, 45) (1896-1913)

Richardia - *Richardia scabra* L. (174) (1753)

Richard's comandra [Richards comandra] - *Comandra umbellata* (L.) Nutt. subsp. *umbellata* (155) (1942)

Richard's yellow-eyed grass [Richard's yelloweyed grass] - *Xyris jupicai* L.C. Rich. (50) (present)

Richardson's alumroot - *Heuchera richardsonii* R. Br. (50) (present)

Richardson's anemone - *Anemone richardsonii* Hook. (5) (1913)

Richardson's clasping pondweed - *Potamogeton richardsonii* (Benn.) Rydb. (72) (1907)

Richardson's clover - *Leucanthemum vulgare* Lam. (187) (1818)

Richardson's cranebill [Richardson's cranesbill, Richardson's

cranes bill] - *Geranium richardsonii* Fisch. & Trautv. (4, 131) (1899-1986)

Richardson's feather - *Achnatherum richardsonii* (Link) Barkworth (66, 90) (1885-1903)

Richardson's feather grass [Richardson's feather-grass] - *Achnatherum richardsonii* (Link) Barkworth (94) (1901), *Piptatherum canadense* (Poir) Barkworth (5) (1913)

Richardson's geranium [Richardson geranium] - *Geranium richardsonii* Fisch. & Trautv. (50, 155) (1942–present)

Richardson's needle grass [Richardson's needlegrass, Richardson needlegrass] - *Achnatherum richardsonii* (Link) Barkworth (3, 50, 155) (1942–present)

Richardson's pondweed - *Potamogeton richardsonii* (Benn.) Rydb. (50) (present)

Richardson's rush - *Juncus alpinoarticulatus* Chaix subsp. *nodulosus* (Wahlenb.) Hämet-Ahti (5, 93) (1913-1936)

Richardson's sedge - *Carex richardsonii* R. Br. (5, 50, 72) (1893–present)

Richardson's tansy-mustard [Richardson tansymustard] - *Descurainia incana* (Bernh. ex Fisch. & C.A. Mey.) Dorn subsp. *incana* (155) (1942)

Richardson's thorowort pondweed [Richardson thorowort pondweed] - *Potamogeton richardsonii* (Benn.) Rydb. (155) (1942)

Richardson's wheat grass - *Elymus trachycaulus* (Link) Gould ex Shinners subsp. *subsecundus* (Link) A.& D. Löve (56, 72, 94) (1901-1907)

Richfield American waterlily - *Nymphaea odorata* Aiton subsp. *odorata* (155) (1942)

Richleaf [Rich-leaf, Rich leaf) - *Collinsonia canadensis* L. (5, 6, 7, 64, 92, 156) (1828-1923)

Richmond cherry - *Prunus cerasus* L. (82) (1930) IA

Richweed [Rich-weed, Rich weed] - *Actaea* L. (190) (~1759), *Ageratina altissima* (L.) King & H.E. Robins. (5, 75, 156) (1894-1923) Banner Elk NC, *Ambrosia trifida* L. (5, 49, 92, 155, 156, 158) (1898-1942), *Cimicifuga racemosa* (L.) Nutt. (5, 7, 49, 64, 92, 177, 187) (1818-1913) Banner Elk NC, *Collinsonia canadensis* L. (2, 5, 6, 7, 19, 46, 50, 53, 64, 86, 92, 156) (1878–present), *Lactuca canadensis* L. (possibly) (29) (1869), *Pilea* Lindl. (1) (1932), *Pilea pumila* (L.) Gray (5, 35, 155, 156) (1806-1942), *Pilea pumila* (L.) Gray var. *pumila* (9, 72, 92, 158) (1840-1907)

Richwoods sedge - *Carex oligocarpa* Schkuhr ex Willd. (50) (present)

Ricket plant - *Comptonia peregrina* (L.) Coult. (58) (1869)

Riddell's goldenrod [Riddell's golden-rod, Riddell goldenrod] - *Oligoneuron riddellii* (Frank ex Riddell) Rydb. (5, 50, 72, 155) (1907–present)

Riddell's groundsel [Riddell groundsel] - *Senecio riddellii* Torr. & Gray (155) (1942)

Riddell's ragwort [Riddell ragwort] - *Senecio riddellii* Torr. & Gray (3, 4, 50, 98) (1926–present)

Riddell's senecio - *Senecio riddellii* Torr. & Gray (5, 93, 97) (1913-1937)

Ridell's dozedaisy - *Aphanostephus ramosissimus* DC. (50) (present), *Aphanostephus riddellii* Torr. & Gray (50) (present)

Ridged yellow flax - *Linum striatum* Walt. (5, 97) (1913-1937)

Ridge-seed euphorbia [Ridgeseed euphorbia] - *Chamaesyce glyptosperma* (Engelm.) Small (155) (1942)

Ridge-seed spurge [Ridge-seeded spurge] - *Chamaesyce glyptosperma* (Engelm.) Small (3, 4, 5, 72, 93, 97, 98, 131) (1899-1986)

Rie (Rye) - *Secale cereale* L. (14, 180) (1633-1882)

Rièbel (French) - *Galium aparine* L. (158) (1900)

Riely - *Lolium temulentum* L. (157, 158) (1900-1929)

Rig (Anglo-Saxon) - *Secale cereale* L. (110) (1886)

Riga balsam - *Pinus cembra* L. (92) (1876)

Riga pine - *Pinus sylvestris* L. (136, 138) (1923-1930)

Rigid goldenrod - *Oligoneuron rigidum* (L.) Small var. *rigidum* (3, 4, 92) (1876-1986)

Rigid sedge - *Carex bigelowii* Torr. ex Schwein. (66) (1903)

Rigid sedge - *Carex tetanica* Schkuhr (50) (present)

Rigid tick trefoil - *Desmodium obtusum* (Muhl. ex Willd.) DC. (5, 72) (1907-1913)

Rignum - *Monarda punctata* L. (5, 156) (1913-1923)

Rillscale - *Endolepis dioica* (Nutt.) Standl. (3) (1977)

Rim ash - *Celtis occidentalis* L. (5, 156, 158) (1900–1923)

Ring grass [Ringgrass Ring-grass] - *Muhlenbergia torreyi* (Kunth) A.S. Hitchc. ex Bush (119, 122, 140, 163) (1852-1944)

Ring lichen - *Evernia prunastri* (L.) Ach. (50) (present)

Ring muhly - *Muhlenbergia torreyi* (Kunth) A.S. Hitchc. ex Bush (50, 140, 155) (1942–present)

Ringed panicum - *Dichanthelium dichotomum* (L.) Gould var. *dichotomum* (5) (1913)

Ring-grass muhly [Ringgrass muhly] - *Muhlenbergia torreyi* (Kunth) A.S. Hitchc. ex Bush (3) (1977)

Ringwing - *Cycloloma* Moq. (155) (1942)

Ring-worm bush [Ring worm bush] - *Senna alata* (L.) Roxb. (92) (1876)

Ring-worm cassia [Ringworm cassia] - *Senna alata* (L.) Roxb. (109, 138) (1923-1949)

Ripgut - *Bromus rigidus* Roth (163) (1852)

Ripgut grass - *Bromus rigidus* Roth (122) (1937) TX

Rippa (Slavic languages) - *Brassica rapa* L. (110) (1886)

Ripple - *Plantago lanceolata* L. (75) (1894)

Ripple plantain - *Plantago lanceolata* L. (5, 19, 97, 156) (1840-1937)

Ripple-grass [Ripple grass] - *Plantago lanceolata* L. (5, 19, 62, 92, 156, 157, 158) (1840–1929) IN, Old English name, *Plantago major* L. (49, 52) (1898)

Ripple-seed plantain [Rippleseed plantain] - *Plantago major* L. (155) (1942)

Risp (Swedish) - *Ribes rubrum* L. (110) (1886)

Rissels - *Ribes rubrum* L. (156) (1923)

Risz (German) - *Oryza sativa* L. (180) (1633)

River alder - *Alnus incana* (L.) Moench subsp. *rugosa* (DuRoi) Clausen (1) (1932)

River ash - *Fraxinus pennsylvanica* Marsh. (5, 156) (1913–1923)

River avens - *Geum rivale* L (156) (1923)

River birch - *Betula lenta* L. (5, 156) (1913-1923), *Betula nigra* L. (1, 3, 4, 5, 50, 72, 93, 97, 107, 109, 124, 137, 138, 155, 156, 158) (1900–present)

River broomrape - *Orobanche riparia* Collins (50) (present)

River bulrush - *Schoenoplectus fluviatilis* (Torr.) M.T. Strong (3, 50, 72, 155, 156) (1907–present)

River bush [River-bush] - *Cephalanthus occidentalis* L. (5, 156, 157, 158) (1900–1929)

River club-rush [River club rush] - *Schoenoplectus fluviatilis* (Torr.) M.T. Strong (5, 129, 156) (1894-1923)

River cottonwood - *Populus deltoides* Bartr. ex Marsh. subsp. *monilifera* (Aiton) Eckenwalder (1, 85) (1932), *Populus heterophylla* L. (5, 156) (1913-1923)

River crab - *Malus fusca* (Raf.) Schneid. (20) (1857)

River cress - *Nasturtium officinale* W.T. Aiton (possibly) (156) (1923), *Neobeckia aquatica* (Eat.) Greene (5) (1913)

River festuca [River-festuca] - *Glyceria fluitans* (L.) R. Br. (187) (1818)

River grape - *Vitis riparia* Michx. (2, 7) (1828-1932)

River grass [Rivergrass] - *Scolochloa* Link (50, 155) (1942–present)

River hawthorn - *Crataegus rivularis* Nutt. (20, 137, 138) (1857-1931)

River maple - *Acer rubrum* L. (5, 156, 158) (1900–1923)

River milkweed [River milk weed] - *Asclepias incarnata* L. subsp. *pulchra* (Ehrh. ex Willd.) Woods. (42) (1814)

River pine - *Pinus virginiana* Mill. (5) (1913)

River poplar - *Populus deltoides* Bartr. ex Marsh. (5, 156, 158) (1900–1923)

River ragweed - *Ambrosia trifida* L. (156) (1923)

River rush - *Schoenoplectus fluviatilis* (Torr.) M.T. Strong (66) (1903)

River sunflower - *Helianthus decapetalus* L. (156) (1923)

River swallow-wort [River swallow wort] - *Asclepias incarnata* L. subsp. *pulchra* (Ehrh. ex Willd.) Woods. (42) (1814)

River walnut - *Juglans microcarpa* Berl. (122) (1937) TX

River willow - *Salix interior* Rowlee (20, 155) (1857-1942)

Riverbank anemone - *Anemone virginiana* L. (155) (1942)

Riverbank dogbane - *Apocynum cannabinum* L. (64) (1907)

Riverbank goldenrod [River-bank golden-rod] - *Solidago simplex* Kunth subsp. *randii* (Porter) Ringius var. *racemosa* (Greene) Ringius (5) (1913)

River-bank grape [Riverbank grape, River bank grape] - *Vitis riparia* Michx. (3, 4, 50, 107, 155) (1919–present), *Vitis vulpina* L. (15, 138, 142, 156) (1895-1923)

Riverbank quillwort - *Isoetes riparia* Engelm. ex A. Braun (5) (1913)

Riverbank willow [River-bank willow, River bank willow] - *Salix interior* Rowlee (5, 93, 97, 156, 158) (1900-1937)

River-locust [River locust] - *Amorpha fruticosa* L. (5, 76, 97, 106, 112, 156, 157, 158) (1896-1937)

River-pink [River pink] - *Rhododendron periclymenoides* (Michx.) Shinners (5, 73, 156) (1892-1923) Cavendish VT

Riverside frost grape [River-side frost-grape] - *Vitis riparia* Michx. (47) (1852)

Riverside grape [River-side grape] - *Vitis vulpina* L. (5, 72, 131, 156, 158) (1899-1923)

Riverside tobacco - *Pluchea odorata* (L.) Cass (158) (1900)

Riverside wheat grass [River-side wheat-grass] - *Elymus lanceolatus* (Scribn. & J.G. Sm.) Gould (94) (1901)

Riverweed [River-weed, River weed] - *Podostemum ceratophyllum* Michx. (5, 156) (1913-1923), *Podostemum* Michx. (1) (1932), *Verbesina alternifolia* (L.) Britton ex Kearney (156) (1923)

Rivina - *Rivina humilis* L. (138, 174) (1923-1949)

Riz (French) - *Oryza sativa* L. (180) (1633)

Rizzer-berry - *Ribes rubrum* L. (156) (1923)

Roadside agrimony - *Agrimonia striata* Michx. (50, 155) (1942–present)

Roadside blue-eyed grass - *Sisyrinchium langloisii* Greene (50) (present)

Roadside pepper-grass [Roadside pepper grass] - *Lepidium ruderale* L. (5) (1913)

Roadside-thistle [Roadside thistle] - *Cirsium altissimum* (L.) Hill (4, 62, 131, 156) (1899-1986), *Cirsium vulgare* (Savi) Ten. (5, 156, 158) (1900-1923)

Roadweed - *Ambrosia bidentata* Michx. (21) (1893)

Roan Mountain thorn - *Crataegus macrosperma* Ashe (5) (1913)

Roanoke bells - *Mertensia virginica* (L.) Pers. ex Link (possibly) (5, 156) (1913-1923) no longer in use by 1923

Robbins' cinquefoil - *Potentilla robbinsiana* Oakes ex Rydb. (5) (1913)

Robbins' club-rush - *Eleocharis robbinsii* Oakes (66) (1903)

Robbins' milkvetch [Robbin's milk vetch, Robbins' milk vetch - *Astragalus robbinsii* (Oakes) Gray (5) (1913)

Robbins' pondweed [Robbins pondweed] - *Potamogeton robbinsii* Oakes (5, 50) (1913–present)

Robbins' spikerush [Robbins spike rush] - *Eleocharis robbinsii* Oakes (5, 50) (1913–present)

Robbins' squaw-weed [Robbins' squaw weed] - *Packera schweinitziana* (Nutt.) W.A. Weber & A. Löve (5) (1913)

Robert's geranium [Robert geranium] - *Geranium robertianum* L. (50) (present)

Robert's plantain - *Erigeron pulchellus* Michx. (5, 7, 19, 92, 156, 158) (1828–1923)

Robert's-root [Roberts root] - *Packera obovata* (Muhl. ex Willd.) W.A. Weber & A. Löve (7) (1828)

Robinier (French) - *Robinia pseudoacacia* L. (6, 158) (1892-1900)

Robin-run-ahead - *Galium* L. (76) (1896) Sulphur Grove OH

Robin-run-away [Robin runaway, Robin run away] - *Dalibarda repens* L. (5, 76, 156) (1896-1923) Oxford Co ME, *Glechoma hed004eracea* L. (5, 7, 73, 92, 156, 157, 158) (1828-1929)

Robin-run-in-the-hedge - *Glechoma hederacea* L. (92, 158) (1876-1900)

Robin-running-in-the-hedge - *Glechoma hederacea* L. (157) (1929)

Robins - *Silene dioica* (L.) Clairville (156) (1923) no longer in use by 1923

Robin's-plantain [Robin's plantain, Robin plantain] - *Erigeron pulchellus* Michx. (2, 3, 4, 5, 50, 63, 72, 97, 122, 131, 156, 158) (1895–present)

Robin's-rye [Robin's rye] - *Polytrichum juniperinum* Hedw. (50, 58, 92) (1869–present)

Robin-wheat [Robin wheat] - *Bryum* Hedw. (73) (1892) Mansfield OH

Roble (Spanish) - *Quercus lobata* Née (75) (1894) CA

Roble blanco (Spanish) - *Tabebuia heterophylla* (DC.) Britt. (109) (1949)

Robust Canadian wild rye [Robust Canada wildrye] - *Elymus canadensis* L. (155) (1942)

Robust euphorbia - *Euphorbia brachycera* Engelm. (155) (1942)

Robust lyme grass - *Elymus canadensis* L. (56) (1901)

Rocambole - *Allium scorodoprasum* L. (110, 165) (1768-1886)

Rock alyssum - *Aurinia saxatilis* (L.) Desv. (156) (1923)

Rock aster - *Aster alpinus* L. (138) (1923)·

Rock bells - *Aquilegia canadensis* L. (5) (1913)

Rock bent grass - *Agrostis mertensii* Trin. (5) (1913)

Rock blackberry - *Rubus saxatilis* L. (19, 92) (1840-1876)

Rock bluebonnet - *Lupinus texensis* Hook. (124) (1937)

Rock brake [Rockbrake, Rock-brake] - *Cryptogramma* R. Br. (1, 109, 138, 155, 158) (1900-1949), *Pellaea atropurpurea* (L.) Link (5, 19, 49, 61, 72, 92) (1840-1913), *Polypodium virginianum* L. (7, 19, 49, 92, 158) (1828-1840)

Rock brush - *Eysenhardtia texana* Scheele (122, 124) (1937) TX

Rock buttercup - *Ranunculus micranthus* Nutt. (50) (present)

Rock chestnut oak - *Quercus prinus* L. (5, 10, 20, 33, 97, 156, 187) (1818-1937)

Rock clematis - *Clematis columbiana* (Nutt.) Torr. & Gray var. *tenuiloba* (Gray) J. Pringle (50) (present), *Clematis occidentalis* (Hornem.) DC. (138) (1923)

Rock clubmoss - *Huperzia porophila* (Lloyd & Underwood) Holub (50) (present)

Rock cotoneaster - *Cotoneaster horizontalis* Dcne. (138) (1923)

Rock cranberry - *Vaccinium vitis-idaea* L. (5, 73, 156) (1892-1923) NB

Rock crowfoot [Rock crow foot] - *Ranunculus micranthus* Nutt. (5, 97) (1913-1937)

Rock daisy - *Melampodium cinereum* DC. (124) (1937)

Rock dandelion - *Taraxacum laevigatum* (Willd.) DC. (50) (present)

Rock dropseed [Rock drop-seed, Rock-dropseed] - *Muhlenbergia sobolifera* (Muhl. ex Willd.) Trin. (5, 99, 119, 163) (1852-1938)

Rock elm - *Ulmus americana* L. (5, 113, 156, 157, 158) (1890-1929), *Ulmus rubra* Muhl. (5, 156, 157, 158) (1900-1929), *Ulmus thomasii* Sarg. (1, 3, 4, 5, 37, 50, 82, 85, 93, 95, 109, 130, 138, 155, 156, 157, 158) (1895–present)

Rock fern - *Adiantum pedatum* L. (7, 92, 157, 158) (1828–1929)

Rock fumewort - *Corydalis sempervirens* (L.) Pers. (156) (1923)

Rock geranium - *Heuchera americana* L. (156) (1923)

Rock goldenrod [Rock golden-rod] - *Solidago canadensis* L. (5, 156) (1913-1923), *Solidago rupestris* Raf. (72, 131) (1899-1907)

Rock grape - *Vitis rupestris* Scheele (15, 107) (1895-1919)

Rock larkspur - *Delphinium tricorne* Michx. (138, 155) (1923-1942)

Rock maple - *Acer rubrum* L. (2, 19, 92, 107) (1840-1919), *Acer saccharum* Marsh. (5, 15, 109, 131, 135, 156, 158) (1895-1949)

Rock moss - *Gyrophora* Ach. (92) (1876)

Rock muhlenbergia - *Muhlenbergia sobolifera* (Muhl. ex Willd.) Trin. (56, 163) (1852-1901)

Rock muhly - *Muhlenbergia sobolifera* (Muhl. ex Willd.) Trin. (3, 50, 155) (1942–present)

Rock oak - *Quercus prinus* L. (5, 19, 156) (1840-1923)

Rock phlox - *Phlox andicola* E. Nels. (98) (1926) Neb

Rock pine - *Pinus banksiana* Lamb. (5, 32, 75) (1894-1913), *Pinus ponderosa* P.& C. Lawson var. *scopulorum* Engelm. (1, 136) (1930-1932)

Rock plant [Rock-plant] - *Sedum acre* L. (5, 156) (1913-1923)

Rock polypod - *Polypodium virginianum* L. (50, 58, 92) (1869–present)

Rock polypody - *Woodsia obtusa* (Spreng.) Torr. (86) (1878)

Rock purslane - *Phemeranthus teretifolius* (Pursh) Raf. (156) (1923)

Rock sandwort - *Arenaria* L. (72) (1907), *Minuartia michauxii* (Fenzl) Farw. var. *michauxii* (5, 97, 131, 155) (1899-1942), *Minuartia michauxii* (Fenzl) Farw. var. *texana* (B.L. Robins.) Mattf. (4, 156) (1923-1986)

Rock saxifrage - *Saxifraga virginiensis* Michx. (19, 156) (1840-1923)

Rock sedge - *Carex rupestris* All. (5) (1913), *Carex saxatilis* L. (50) (present)

Rock sedge - *Carex scopulorum* Holm (139) (1944)

Rock selaginella - *Selaginella rupestris* (L.) Spring (5, 97, 131, 138, 155, 158) (1899-1942)

Rock skullcap - *Scutellaria saxatilis* Riddell (5) (1913)

Rock soapwort - *Saponaria ocymoides* L. (138) (1923)

Rock spike moss [Rock spikemoss] - *Selaginella rupestris* (L.) Spring (4) (1986)

Rock spleenwort - *Asplenium exiguum* Bedd. (5) (1913)

Rock tripe - *Umbilicaria* Hoffm. (92) (1876), *Umbilicaria muehlenbergii* (Ach.) Tuck. (107) (1919), *Umbilicaria vellea* (L.) Ach. (107) (1919)

Rock wormwood - *Artemisia rupestris* L. (155) (1942)

Rockbell [Rock-bells] - *Aquilegia canadensis* L. (156) (1923), *Wahlenbergia* Schrad. ex Roth (138) (1923)

Rockberry [Rock-berry, Rock berry] - *Arctostaphylos uva-ursi* (L.) Spreng. (73, 156, 157) (1892–1929) Fortune Bay, Newfoundland, *Vaccaria hispanica* (Mill.) Rauschert (1, 158) (1900–1932)

Rockbrush - *Colubrina texensis* (Torr. & Gray) Gray (106) (1930), *Eysenhardtia polystachya* (Ortega) Sargent (106) (1930)

Rockcress [Rock-cress, Rock cress] - *Arabidopsis* Heynh. (50) (present), *Arabidopsis thaliana* (L.) Britton (92) (1876), *Arabis glabra* (L.) Bernh. (157) (1929), *Arabis hirsuta* (L.) Scop. var. *pycnocarpa* (M. Hopkins) Rollins (3, 4) (1977-1986), *Arabis holboellii* Hornem. var. *collinsii* (Fern.) Rollins (3, 4) (1977-1986), *Arabis* L. (1, 2, 4, 3, 15, 50, 93, 109, 155, 156, 158) (1895–present), *Arabis petiolaris* (Gray) Gray (122) (1937), *Arabis shortii* (Fern.) Gleason (3, 4, 85) (1932-1986), *Sibara virginica* (L.) Rollins (3, 4) (1977-1986)

Rockcress whitlow-grass [Rock cress whitlow grass] - *Draba arabisans* Michx. (5) (1913)

Rockenbolle (German) - *Allium scorodoprasum* L. (110) (1886)

Rocket - *Barbarea vulgaris* W.T. Aiton (107) (1919), *Diplotaxis* DC. (158) (1900), *Eruca vesicaria* (L.) Cav. subsp. *sativa* (Mill.) Thellung (80, 107) (1913-1919), *Hesperis* L. (10, 15, 50, 92, 109, 138, 155, 158) (1818–present)

Rocket candytuft - *Iberis amara* L. (109) (1949), *Iberis umbellata* L. (possibly) (92) (1876)

Rocket cress [Rocket-cress] - *Barbarea vulgaris* W. T. Aiton (5, 156, 157) (1900–1929)

Rocket larkspur - *Consolida ajacis* (L.) Schur (2, 4, 5, 92, 109, 138, 155) (1876-1986)

Rocket-salad [Rocketsalad] - *Eruca* Mill. (4, 50) (1986–present), *Eruca vesicaria* (L.) Cav. (50) (present), *Eruca vesicaria* (L.) Cav. subsp. *sativa* (Mill.) Thellung (3, 4, 50, 109, 155) (1942–present)

Rocketweed - *Erucastrum gallicum* (Willd.) O. E. Schulz (155) (1942)

Rockhair alectoria - *Parmelia jubata* (L.) Ach. (possibly) (155) (1942)

Rock-jasmine [Rockjasmine] - *Androsace* L. (50, 101, 155) (1905–present)

Rock-lily [Rock lily, Rock lilies] - *Aquilegia canadensis* L. (5, 157, 158) (1900-1929), *Pulsatilla patens* (L.) Mill. (5) (1913), *Pulsatilla*

patens (L.) Mill.subsp. *multifida* (Pritz.) Zamels (76) (1896) WI

Rockmat - *Petrophytum* Rydb. (155) (1942)

Rock-mint [Rock mint] - *Teucrium scorodonia* L. (156) (1923)

Rock-moss [Rock moss] - *Dudleya cymosa* (Lem.) Britt. & Rose (possibly) (74) (1893), *Sedum pulchellum* Michx. (5, 76, 97, 156, 158) (1896–1937)

Rock-pink [Rock pink] - *Talinum* Adans. (158) (1900), *Talinum calycinum* Engelm. (4, 5, 76, 156, 158) (1896-1986)

Rock-pink fameflower [Rockpink fameflower] - *Talinum* Adans. (155) (1942)

Rock-plant spirea [Rockplant spirea] - *Petrophyton caespitosum* (Nutt.) Rydb. (3) (1977)

Rockrose [Rock-rose, Rock rose] - *Armeria maritima* (P. Mill.) Willd. (156) (1923), *Cistus* L. (42, 109, 138) (1814-1949), *Helianthemum bicknellii* Fern. (93, 156) (1923-1936), *Helianthemum canadense* (L.) Michx. (5, 7, 6, 19, 49, 61, 92, 156, 187) (1818-1923), *Helianthemum* Mill. (13, 15, 156, 158) (1849-1923), *Hypericum prolificum* L. (5, 156) (1913-1923), *Oenothera caespitosa* Nutt. (possibly) (85) (1932) SD, *Oenothera* L. (1, 93) (1932-1936) Neb

Rockrose of Pennsylvania [Rock-rose of Pennsylvania] - *Rhododendron maximum* L. (189) (1767)

Rock-spiraea [Rock spiraea] - *Holodiscus discolor* (Pursh) Maxim. (138) (1923), *Petrophyton caespitosum* (Nutt.) Rydb. (4) (1986), *Petrophytum* Rydb. (4, 50) (1986–present)

Rockweed [Rockweed, Rockweed] - *Fucus vesiculosus* L. (57) (1917), *Galium odoratum* (L.) Scop. (5) (1913), *Geranium maculatum* L. (5, 156) (1913-1923), *Geranium robertianum* L. (7, 92, 157, 158) (1828-1929)

Rockweep - *Ascophyllum* Stackhouse (155) (1942)

Rocky Mountain beeplant [Rocky Mountain bee plant, Rocky Mountain bee-plant, Rocky Mt. bee plant] - *Cleome serrulata* Pursh (2, 3, 4, 5, 50, 80, 82, 98, 106, 127, 145, 156) (1895–present)

Rocky Mountain blazing star - *Liatris ligulistylis* (A. Nels.) K. Schum. (50) (present)

Rocky Mountain bulrush [RockyMountain bulrush] - *Schoenoplectus saximontanus* (Fern.) Raynal (50, 155) (1942–present)

Rocky Mountain cedar - *Juniperus scopulorum* Sarg. (112) (1937)

Rocky Mountain cherry - *Prunus virginiana* L. var. *demissa* (Nutt.) Torr. (112) (1937)

Rocky Mountain columbine [Rockymountain columbine] - *Aquilegia caerulea* James. (82) (1930), *Aquilegia saximontana* Rydb. (155) (1942)

Rocky Mountain cranebill [Rocky Mountain cranesbill] - *Geranium caespitosum* James var. *fremontii* (Torr. ex Gray) Dorn (138) (1923)

Rocky Mountain cudweed [Rocky Mountain cud-weed, Rocky Mountain cud weed] - *Antennaria parviflora* Nutt. (5, 93) (1913-1936)

Rocky Mountain fescue - *Festuca saximontana* Rydb. (50) (present), *Festuca saximontana* Rydb. var. *saximontana* (50) (present)

Rocky Mountain flower [Rocky Mt. flower] - *Coreopsis tinctoria* Nutt. (73) (1892) Mansfield OH

Rocky Mountain flowering raspberry - *Rubus deliciosus* Torr. (135) (1910)

Rocky Mountain foxtail - *Alopecurus alpinus* Sm. (118) (1898)

Rocky Mountain gayfeather - *Liatris ligulistylis* (A. Nels.) K. Schum. (138, 155) (1923-1942)

Rocky Mountain glasswort [RockyMountain glasswort] - *Salicornia rubra* A. Nels. (155) (1942)

Rocky Mountain goosefoot - *Chenopodium salinum* Standl. (50) (present)

Rocky Mountain grape - *Mahonia aquifolium* (Pursh) Nutt. (5, 64, 157) (1908-1929)

Rocky Mountain honey plant - *Cleome serrulata* Pursh (114, 124) (1894–1937)

Rocky Mountain iris [RockyMountain iris] - *Iris missouriensis* Nutt. (50, 86, 138, 155) (1878–present)

Rocky Mountain juniper [RockyMountain juniper] - *Juniperus*

scopulorum Sarg. (4, 50, 109, 136, 155) (1930–present), *Juniperus virginiana* L. (20) (1857)

Rocky Mountain maple - *Acer glabrum* Torr. (5, 50, 93, 137, 138, 155) (1923–present), *Acer glabrum* Torr. (50) (present), *Acer grandidentatum* Nutt. (97) (1937)

Rocky Mountain oak - *Quercus ×pauciloba* Rydb. [*gambelii × turbinella*] (20) (1857)

Rocky Mountain oat grass [Rocky Mountain oat-grass] - *Trisetum spicatum* (L.) Richter (94) (1901)

Rocky Mountain parnassia - *Parnassia fimbriata* Koenig (138) (1923)

Rocky Mountain pleated gentian [RockyMountain pleated gentian] - *Gentiana affinis* Griesb. (155) (1942)

Rocky Mountain ponderosa pine [RockyMountain ponderosa pine] - *Pinus ponderosa* P.& C. Lawson var. *scopulorum* Engelm. (155) (1942)

Rocky Mountain pussytoes - *Antennaria parviflora* Nutt. (155) (1942)

Rocky Mountain raspberry - *Rubus deliciosus* Torr. (107) (1919)

Rocky Mountain red cedar - *Juniperus scopulorum* Sarg. (3) (1977)

Rocky Mountain red raspberry - *Rubus idaeus* L. subsp. *strigosus* (Michx.) Focke (1) (1932)

Rocky Mountain rhododendron - *Rhododendron albiflorum* Hook. (138) (1923)

Rocky Mountain rush [RockyMountain rush] - *Juncus saximontanus* A. Nels. (50, 139, 155) (1942–present)

Rocky mountain sage - *Salvia reflexa* Hornem. (4) (1986)

Rocky Mountain scrub oak - *Quercus ×pauciloba* Rydb. [*gambelii × turbinella*] (107) (1919)

Rocky Mountain sedge - *Carex saximontana* MacKenzie (50) (present)

Rocky Mountain spurge - *Euphorbia brachycera* Engelm. (5, 85, 93, 131) (1899-1936)

Rocky Mountain trisetum [RockyMountain trisetum] - *Trisetum spicatum* (L.) Richter (155) (1942)

Rocky Mountain white pine - *Pinus flexilis* James (147) (1856)

Rocky Mountain wild cherry - *Prunus virginiana* L. var. *melanocarpa* (A. Nels.) Sargent (5) (1913)

Rocky Mountain willowherb [Rockymountain willowherb] - *Epilobium saximontanum* Hausskn. (50) (present)

Rocky Mountain woodsia - *Woodsia scopulina* D.C. Eaton (3, 50, 109, 131, 138) (1899–present)

Rocky Mountain yellow pine - *Pinus ponderosa* P.& C. Lawson (4, 32) (1895-1986), *Pinus ponderosa* P.& C. Lawson var. *scopulorum* Engelm. (136, 138) (1923-1930)

Rocky Mountain zinnia [RockyMountain zinnia] - *Zinnia grandiflora* Nutt. (3, 4, 50, 155) (1942–present)

Rocky-scree false golden-aster [Rockyscree false goldenaster' - *Heterotheca fulcrata* (Greene) Shinners var. *fulcrata* (50) (present)

Rocou (French) - *Bixa orellana* L. (possibly) (110) (1886) from Brazilian name

Röd en (German) - *Juniperus communis* L. (41) (1770)

Rode campion - *Agrostemma githago* L. (6) (1892)

Rodman's agaricus [Rodmans agaricus] - *Agaricus bitorquis* (Quél.) Sacc. (155) (1942)

Roebuck-berry [Roebuck berry] - *Rubus saxatilis* L. (107) (1919)

Roella - *Ruellia caroliniensis* (J.F. Gmel.) Steud. (possibly) (183) (~1756)

Roemer's acacia [Roemer acacia] - *Acacia roemeriana* Scheele (155) (1942)

Roemer's cassia - *Senna roemeriana* (Scheele) Irwin & Barneby (124) (1937)

Roemer's rush - *Juncus roemerianus* Scheele. (5) (1913)

Roemer's threeawn [Roemer threeawn] - *Aristida purpurea* Nutt. var. *purpurea* (155) (1942)

Rogation flower [Rogation-flower] - *Polygala incarnata* L. (5, 92, 156, 158) (1876-1923)

Roggen (German) - *Secale cereale* L. (158) (1900)

Rogue's gilliflower - *Hesperis matronalis* L. (5, 156, 158) (1900-1923)

Rolled gumweed - *Grindelia revoluta* Steyerm. (50) (present)

Roman artemisia - *Artemisia pontica* L. (19) (1840)

Roman beet [Romaine beete, Romane Beete] - *Beta vulgaris* L. (107, 178) (1526-1597)

Roman camomile [Roman chamomile] - *Chamaemelum nobile* (L.) All. (49, 50, 53, 55, 57, 58, 59, 92, 155) (1869–present), *Nigella sativa* L. (107) (1919)

Roman corn (Lorraine and Vosges) - *Zea mays* L. (110) (1886)

Roman fennel - *Foeniculum vulgare* Mill. (49) (1898)

Roman fennel - *Pimpinella anisum* L. (107) (13th century)

Roman fern - *Blechnum spicant* (L.) Sm. (19, 92) (1840-1876)

Roman kale - *Beta vulgaris* L. (107) (1919)

Roman plant - *Chenopodium bonus-henricus* L. (5, 156) (1913-1923) no longer in use by 1923

Roman willow - *Syringa vulgaris* L. (5, 156) (1913-1923)

Roman wormwood - *Ambrosia artemisiifolia* L. (2, 6, 48, 58, 62, 82, 156, 158) (1869–1930), *Ambrosia artemisiifolia* L. var. *elatior* (L.) Descourtils (5, 19, 157) (1840–1929), *Ambrosia* L. (1, 45, 93) (1896–1936), *Artemisia pontica* L. (5, 92, 109, 138, 155, 156) (1876–1942), *Capnoides sempervirens* (L.) Borck. (5) (1913), *Corydalis sempervirens* (L.) Pers. (76, 109, 156) (1923–1949) Paris ME

Roman-candle [Roman candle] - *Yucca gloriosa* L. (78) (1898) CA

Romeria - *Krascheninnikovia lanata* (Pursh) A.D.J. Meeuse & Smit (5) (1913)

Romero - *Trichostema lanatum* Benth. (138) (1923)

Römische Kamillen (German) - *Anthemis arvensis* L. (6) (1892)

Römische minze (German) - *Mentha spicata* L. (158) (1900)

Ronce (French) - *Rubus* L. (8) (1785)

Ronce de Canada (French) - *Rubus canadensis* L. (8) (1785)

Ronce d'Occident - *Rubus occidentalis* L. (8) (1785)

Ronce velue (French) - *Rubus hispidus* L. (8) (1785)

Roof houseleek - *Sempervivum tectorum* L. (138) (1923)

Roof iris - *Iris tectorum* Maxim. (138) (1923)

Rooster-head [Rooster heads] - *Dodecatheon meadia* L. (5, 75, 156) (1894-1923) Santa Barbara CA

Roosters - *Viola cucullata* Aiton (74, 156) (1893-1923) NY, *Viola palmata* L. (5, 74) (1893-1923) Ferrisburgh VT

Root-leaf blechnum [Root-leaved blechnum] - *Woodwardia radicans* (L.) J. Sm. (19) (1840)

Rope dodder - *Cuscuta glomerata* Choisy (50) (present)

Rope-bark [Rope bark] - *Dirca palustris* L. (5, 6, 7, 92, 156) (1828-1923)

Rope-wind [Ropewind] - *Ipomoea purpurea* (L.) Roth (5, 92) (1876-1913)

Roqueta (French) - *Eruca vesicaria* (L.) Cav. subsp. *sativa* (Mill.) Thellung (107) (1919)

Roquette - *Eruca vesicaria* (L.) Cav. subsp. *sativa* (Mill.) Thellung (109) (1949)

Ror-flen (Swedish) - *Phalaris arundinacea* L. (46) (1879)

Rosa solis [Rosa-solis] - *Drosera rotundifolia* L. (5, 156, 158) (1900-1923), *Narthecium americanum* Ker-Gawl. (5, 156, 158) (1900-1923)

Rosa-de-montana - *Antigonon leptopus* Hook. & Arn. (109, 138) (1923-1949)

Rosary - *Apios americana* Medik. (37) (1919)

Rosary-bean [Rosarybean] - *Rhynchosia* Lour. (138) (1923), *Rhynchosia phaseoloides* (Sw.) DC. (138) (1923)

Rosary-pea [Rosary pea, Rosarypea] or Rosary-pea tree - *Abrus* Adans. (155) (1942), *Abrus precatorius* L. (50, 107, 109 138) (1919–present)

Rose - *Rosa* L. (1, 4, 7, 10, 35, 40, 50, 82, 83, 92, 106, 109, 138, 155, 156, 158, 167, 179, 184) (1526–present)

Rose bellwort [Rose bell wort] - *Streptopus lanceolatus* (Ait.) Reveal var. *roseus* (Michx.) Reveal (19) (1840)

Rose blush - *Rosa setigera* Michx. (5, 76) (1896-1913) Southwestern MO

Rose bush - *Rosa* L. (108) (1878)

Rose campion - *Agrostemma* L. (42) (1814)

Rose convovulus - *Calystegia pellita* (Ledeb.) G. Don (138) (1923)

Rose coreopsis - *Coreopsis rosea* Nutt. (138) (1923)

Rose geranium - *Pelargonium capitatum* (L.) L'Hér. ex Aiton (74) (1893), *Pelargonium graveolens* L'Hér. ex Aiton (138) (1923), *Pelargonium odoratissimum* (L.) L'Hér. ex Aiton (92) (1876)

Rose glory-bower [Rose glorybower] - *Clerodendrum bungei* Steud. (138) (1923)

Rose heath-aster [Rose heath aster] - *Chaetopappa* DC. (93) (1936), *Chaetopappa ericoides* (Torr.) Nesom (5, 97) (1913-1937)

Rose Hibiscus - *Hibiscus* L. (183) (~1756)

Rose laurel - *Kalmia latifolia* L. (6, 7, 71, 92) (1828-1898), *Nerium oleander* L. (7, 92) (1828-1876)

Rose locust - *Robinia hispida* L. (19) (1840)

Rose milkweed - *Asclepias incarnata* L. (156) (1923)

Rose mock vervain - *Glandularia canadensis* (L.) Nutt. (50) (present)

Rose oxalis - *Oxalis rosea* Feuillee ex Jacq. (138) (1923)

Rose plumbago - *Plumbago indica* L. (138) (1923)

Rose pogonia - *Pogonia ophioglossoides* (L.) Ker-Gawl. (5, 122, 138, 156, 158) (1900-1937)

Rose pussytoes - *Antennaria parviflora* Nutt. (155) (1942)

Rose ribwort [Rose ribwoort] - *Plantago lanceolata* L. (178) (1526)

Rose rust - *Uredo rosae-centifoliae* Pers. (19) (1840)

Rose sedge - *Carex rosea* Schkuhr ex Willd. (66, 187) (1818-1903)

Rose silkweed - *Asclepias incarnata* L. (5, 158) (1900–1913)

Rose sundrops - *Oenothera rosea* L'Hér. ex Aiton (138) (1923)

Rose tickseed - *Coreopsis rosea* Nutt. (156) (1923) OK

Rose tree - *Kalmia latifolia* L. (46) (1609)

Rose tremière (French) - *Alcea rosea* L. (158) (1900)

Rose trillium - *Trillium catesbaei* Elliott (138) (1923)

Rose turtlehead - *Chelone obliqua* L. (138) (1923)

Rose verbena - *Glandularia canadensis* (L.) Nutt. (155) (1942)

Rose vervain - *Glandularia canadensis* (L.) Nutt. (3, 4, 138) (1923-1986)

Rose weigela - *Diervilla florida* (Bunge) Siebold & Zucc. (possibly) (138) (1923)

Rose willow [Rose-willow] - *Salix ×conifera* Wangenh. [*discolor × humilis*] (19) (1840), *Salix alba* L. (178) (1526), *Salix eriocephala* Michx. (19) (1840), *Salix purpurea* L. (5, 58, 156) (1869–1923)

Rose-acacia [Rose-acacia] - *Robinia hispida* L. (2, 5, 14, 19, 82, 92, 97, 109, 112, 138, 152, 156, 158) (1882–1949), *Robinia viscosa* Vent. (5, 156) (1913–1923)

Rose-acacia locust [Roseacacia locust] - *Robinia hispida* L. (155) (1942)

Rose-apple [Rose apple] - *Syzygium jambos* (L.) Alston (109, 110) (1886-1949), *Syzygium* P. Br. ex Gaertn. (109) (1949)

Rose-balm [Rose balm] - *Monarda didyma* L. (92, 156) (1876-1923)

Rose-bay [Rose bay, Rosebay] - *Chamerion angustifolium* (L.) Holub subsp. *angustifolium* (5, 49, 53, 58, 92, 156, 157, 158) (1869-1929), *Magnolia virginiana* L. (189) (1767), *Nerium oleander* L. (178) (1526), *Rhododendron* L. (2, 7, 42, 109, 184) (1793-1949), *Rhododendron maximum* L. (5, 71, 156) (1898-1923)

Rose-bay rhododendron [Rosebay rhododendron] - *Rhododendron maximum* L. (138) (1923)

Rose-Betty [Rose Betty, Rosebety] - *Erigeron pulchellus* Michx. (7, 92, 158) (1828-1900)

Rosebud cherry - *Prunus subhirtella* Miq. (109) (1949)

Rosebud orchid - *Cleistes divaricata* (L.) Ames (50) (present)

Rose-campion [Rose campion] - *Agrostemma githago* L. (71) (1898), *Lychnis coronaria* (L.) Desr. (5, 92, 109, 138, 156, 165) (1768-1949)

Rose-colored robinia [Rose coloured robinia, Rose-coloured robinia] - *Robinia hispida* var. *nana* (Elliott) DC. (8) (1785)

Rose-colored silkweed [Rose colored silkweed] - *Asclepias incarnata* L. (53, 92, 158) (1876-1922)

Rose-colored spiderwort - *Callisia rosea* (Vent.) D.R. Hunt (156) (1923)

Rosée du soleil (French) - *Drosera rotundifolia* L. (6, 158) (1892-1900)

Rose-elder [Rose elder] - *Viburnum opulus* L. (5, 92, 156, 158) (1876-1923)

Rose-flower locust [Rose flowering locust] - *Robinia viscosa* Vent. (5, 20) (1857-1913)

Rose-flower raspberry [Rose flowering raspberry, Rose-flowering raspberry] - *Rubus odoratus* L. (5, 187) (1818-1913)

Rose-gentian [Rosegentian, Rose gentian] - *Sabatia* Adans. (138, 155) (1923-1942), *Sabatia angularis* (L.) Pursh (156) (1923)

Rose-heath [Rose heath] - *Chaetopappa ericoides* (Torr.) Nesom (50) (present)

Rose-leaf raspberry [Roseleaf raspberry] - *Rubus rosifolius* Sm. (138) (1923)

Rose-lip [Rose lip] - *Arethusa* L. (1) (1932)

Roselle - *Hibiscus sabdariffa* L. (109, 138) (1923-1949)

Rose-mallow [Rose mallow, Rosemallow] - *Hibiscus* L. (1, 2, 4, 13, 15, 50, 82, 93, 109, 138, 155, 156, 158) (1895–present), *Hibiscus moscheutos* L. (4) (1986), *Hibiscus moscheutos* L. subsp. *lasiocarpos* (Cav.) O. J. Blanchard (4) (1986)

Rosemarie - *Rosmarinus officinalis* L. (178) (1526)

Rosemary - *Rosmarinus* L. (109, 138) (1923-1949), *Rosmarinus officinalis* L. (19, 46, 55, 57, 58, 106, 107, 138, 179) (1526-1930), *Symphyotrichum lateriflorum* (L.) A.& D. Löve var. *lateriflorum* (156) (1923)

Rosemary pine - *Pinus taeda* L. (5) (1913)

Rosemary willow - *Salix elaeagnos* Scop. (138) (1923)

Rosemary-leaf andromeda [Rosemary leaved andromeda] - *Andromeda polifolia* L. (42) (1814)

Rose-may - *Sonchus arvensis* L. (158) (1900)

Rose-moss [Rose moss] - *Portulaca grandiflora* Hook. (5, 50, 73, 76, 109, 156, 158) (1893–present) SD

Rose-myrtle [Rosemyrtle] - *Rhodomyrtus* (DC.) Reichenb. (138) (1923)

Rose-noble [Rose noble] - *Cynoglossum officinale* L. (156, 157, 158) (1900–1929)

Rose-of-China [Rose of China] - *Hibiscus rosa-sinensis* L. (92, 109) (1876-1949)

Rose-of-heaven [Rose of heaven] - *Agrostemma githago* L. (156) (1923), *Silene coeli-rosa* (L.) Godr. (109, 138) (1923–1949)

Rose-of-Jericho [Rose of Jericho] - *Selaginella lepidophylla* (Hook. & Grev.) Spring (14) (1882)

Rose-of-Plymouth - *Sabatia stellaris* Pursh (5, 156) (1913-1923)

Rose-of-Sharon [Rose of Sharon] - *Hibiscus syriacus* L. (5, 92, 107, 109, 112, 156) (1876-1949)

Rose-petty [Rose petty] - *Erigeron pulchellus* Michx. (5, 156) (1913-1923)

Rose-pink [Rose pink] - *Sabatia angularis* (L.) Pursh (3, 4, 5, 50, 7, 49, 92, 122, 124, 156, 158) (1876–present)

Rose-ring gaillardia [Rosering gaillardia] - *Gaillardia pulchella* Foug. (3, 4, 138, 155) (1923-1986)

Roseroot [Rose root, Rose roote, Rose-root] - *Rhodiola rosea* L. (5, 109, 156, 178) (1526-1949)

Roseroot stonecrop - *Rhodiola rosea* L. (50, 138, 155) (1923–present)

Rose-scent geranium [Rose-scented geranium] - *Pelargonium capitatum* (L.) L'Hér. ex Aiton (19, 74) (1840-1893)

Rose-scent root [Rose scented root] - *Rhodiola rosea* L. (156) (1923)

Roseta - *Cenchrus tribuloides* L. (150) (1894) NM

Rosetilla - *Ambrosia acanthicarpa* Hook. (150) (1894)

Rosette grass - *Dichanthelium* (A.S. Hitchc. & Chase) Gould (50) (present)

Rose-willow [Rose willow] - *Cornus amomum* Mill. (5, 156, 158) (1900-1923), *Cornus sericea* L. (7, 58, 92, 186, 187) (1818-1892)

Rosewood [Rose wood] - *Amyris* P. Br. (15) (1895), *Dalbergia* L. f. (138) (1923)

Rosewort [Rose woort] - *Rhodiola rosea* L. (5, 92, 156, 178) (1526-1923)

Rosier (French) - *Rosa* L. (8) (1785)

Rosier des marais (French) - *Rosa palustris* Marsh. (8) (1785)

Rosilla - *Helenium puberulum* DC. (76) (1896) CA

Rosilla de puebla (Spanish) - *Helenium autumnale* L. (158) (1900) Mexico

Rosin plant [Rosin-plant] - *Silphium* L. (2, 147) (1856-1895), *Silphium terebinthinaceum* Jacq. (5, 156) (1913-1923)

Rosin-rose [Rosin rose] - *Hypericum perforatum* L. (5, 156, 157, 158) (1900–1929)

Rosinweed [Rosin-weed, Rosin weed] - *Grindelia squarrosa* (Pursh) Dunal (101, 106, 156) (1905–1930), *Heterotheca villosa* (Pursh) Shinners var. *villosa* (156) (1923), *Silphium integrifolium* Michx. (82) (1930), *Silphium* L. (1, 4, 50, 57, 63, 82, 93, 109, 138, 155, 156, 158) (1840–present), *Silphium laciniatum* L. (2, 5, 14, 37, 47, 58, 82, 156, 157) (1852–1930), *Silphium perfoliatum* L. (85, 95, 106, 158) (1900–1932), *Silphium terebinthinaceum* Jacq. (156) (1923)

Rosinwood [Rosin wood, Rosin-wood] - *Heterotheca villosa* (Pursh) Shinners var. *villosa* (5, 76, 158) (1896–1913)

Rosita - *Cryptantha crassisepala* (Torr. & Gray) Greene (5) (1913)

Rosskastanie (German) - *Aesculus hippocastanum* L. (6) (1892)

Ros-solis - *Drosera rotundifolia* L. (158) (1900)

Ross's sedge [Ross' sedge, Ross sedge] - *Carex rossii* Boott (5, 50, 139, 155) (1913–present)

Rosy bush [Rosey bush, Rosy-bush] - *Spiraea tomentosa* L. (5, 92, 156) (1876-1923)

Rosy corydalis - *Corydalis sempervirens* (L.) Pers. (possibly) (42) (1814)

Rosy New England aster - *Symphyotrichum novae-angliae* (L.) G.L.Nesom (138, 155) (1931-1942)

Rosy palafox - *Palafoxia rosea* (Bush) Cory (50) (present)

Rosy prickly-poppy [Rosy pricklypoppy] - *Argemone sanguinea* Greene (155) (1942)

Rosy sedge - *Carex rosea* Schkuhr ex Willd. (50) (present)

Rosy strife - *Lythrum salicaria* L. (156) (1923)

Rosy twisted-stalk [Rosy twistedstalk] - *Streptopus lanceolatus* (Ait.) Reveal var. *roseus* (Michx.) Reveal (138) (1923)

Rosy-flower stonecrop [Rosy-flowered stonecrop] - *Rhodiola rosea* L. (107) (1919)

Rot grass - *Holcus lanatus* L. (5) (1913)

Rotala - *Rotala* L. (50, 155, 158) (1900–present), *Rotala ramosior* (L.) Koehne (72, 155) (1907-1942)

Rot-grass [Rot grass] - *Pinguicula* L. (92) (1876), *Pinguicula vulgaris* L. (5, 156) (1913-1923)

Roth Ceder (German) - *Juniperus virginiana* L. (6) (1892)

Rothe Kardinals Blume (German) - *Lobelia cardinalis* L. (6, 186) (1814-1892)

Rothe Miere (German) - *Anagallis arvensis* L. (158) (1900)

Rother Futterklee (German) - *Trifolium pratense* L. (158) (1900)

Rother Weiderich (German) - *Lythrum salicaria* L. (158) (1900)

Rother Wiesenklee (German) - *Trifolium pratense* L. (158) (1900)

Rothrock's grama - *Bouteloua rothrockii* Vasey (94) (1901)

Rothrock's sagebrush [Rothrock sagebrush] - *Artemisia rothrockii* Gray (155) (1942)

Rothschild's glory-lily [Rothschild glorylily] - *Gloriosa superba* L. (138) (1923)

Roucou - *Bixa orellana* L. (92) (1876)

Rouge plant [Rouge-plant] - *Rivina humilis* L. (109, 138) (1923-1949)

Rough agrimony - *Agrimonia eupatoria* L. (156) (1923)

Rough alpine fern - *Polystichum lonchitis* (L.) Roth. (5) (1913)

Rough alumroot - *Heuchera americana* L. var. *hirsuticaulis* (Wheelock) Rosendahl, Butters & Lakela (155) (1942)

Rough amaranth - *Amaranthus hybridus* L. (150) (1894), *Amaranthus retroflexus* L. (19, 150) (1840-1894)

Rough American willow - *Salix nigra* Marsh. (8) (1785)

Rough aster - *Eurybia conspicua* (Lindl.) Nesom (3, 50, 85) (1932–present), *Eurybia radula* (Aiton) Nesom (155) (1942)

Rough avens - *Geum laciniatum* Murray (4, 50) (1986–present), *Geum laciniatum* Murray var. *trichocarpum* Fern. (50) (present), *Geum virginianum* L. (5, 72, 85, 97, 131, 156, 157, 158) (1899-1937)

Rough barnyard grass [Rough barnyardgrass] - *Echinochloa muricata* (Beauv.) Fern. (50) (present), *Echinochloa muricata* (Beauv.) Fern. var. *microstachya* Wieg. (50) (present), *Echinochloa muricata* (Beauv.) Fern. var. *muricata* (50) (present)

Rough bedstraw - *Galium asprellum* Michx. (5, 19, 49, 63, 72, 93, 156) (1840-1936)

Rough bent grass - *Agrostis hyemalis* (Walt.) Britton, Sterns & Poggenb. (5) (1913), *Agrostis scabra* Willd. (50) (present)

Rough bindweed - *Smilax* L. (8, 10) (1785-1818)

Rough blistercress - *Erysimum capitatum* (Dougl. ex Hook.) Greene var. *capitatum* (138) (1923)

Rough blue grass [Rough bluegrass, Rough blue-grass] - *Poa trivialis* L. (50, 138, 143) (1923–present)

Rough boneset - *Eupatorium rotundifolium* (7, 92) (1828-1876), *Eupatorium rotundifolium* L. var. *rotundifolium* (156) (1923)

Rough bristle grass [Rough bristle-grass] - *Setaria verticillata* (L.) Beauv. (5) (1913)

Rough bristle-spike cyperus galingale [Rough bristle spiked cyperus galingale] - *Cyperus strigosus* L. (42) (1814)

Rough brome grass - *Bromus racemosus* L. (129) (1894)

Rough buckwheat - *Fagopyrum tataricum* (L.) Gaertn. (5) (1913)

Rough bugleweed - *Lycopus asper* Greene (3, 4, 50) (1977–present)

Rough bur flower [Rough burr flower] - *Hydrophyllum canadense* L. (19) (1840)

Rough buttonweed [Rough button weed, Rough button-weed] - *Diodia teres* Walt. (4, 5, 97, 122, 155, 156) (1923-1986)

Rough chervil - *Torilis japonica* (Houtt.) DC. (5, 156) (1913-1923)

Rough cicely - *Torilis japonica* (Houtt.) DC. (5, 156) (1913-1923)

Rough cinquefoil - *Potentilla arguta* Pursh (82) (1930), *Potentilla norvegica* L. subsp. *monspeliensis* (L.) Aschers. & Graebn. (5, 62, 72, 93, 97, 131, 156, 158) (1899–1937)

Rough cleavers - *Galium asprellum* Michx. (156) (1923)

Rough cocklebur [Rough cockleburr] - *Xanthium strumarium* L. (50) (present), *Xanthium strumarium* L. var. *glabratum* (DC.) Cronq. (50) (present)

Rough cock's-foot [Rough cock's foot] - *Dactylis glomerata* L. (66, 90, 92) (1885-1903) ME, England

Rough comfrey - *Symphytum asperum* Lepechin (5) (1913)

Rough coneflower - *Rudbeckia grandiflora* (D. Don) J.F. Gmel. ex DC. (3, 4, 50) (1977–present)

Rough cornel - *Cornus asperifolia* Michx. (5) (1913)

Rough cotton-grass [Rough cotton grass] - *Eriophorum tenellum* Nutt. (5) (1913)

Rough crowfoot - *Ranunculus recurvatus* Poir. (5) (1913)

Rough cyperus - *Cyperus retrofractus* (L.) Torr. (5) (1913)

Rough dogwood - *Cornus asperifolia* Michx. (5, 37) (1913-1919)

Rough dropseed - *Sporobolus clandestinus* (Biehler) A.S. Hitchc. (3, 50) (1977–present), *Sporobolus compositus* (Poir.) Merr. (3) (1977), *Sporobolus compositus* (Poir.) Merr. var. *compositus* (3) (1977)

Rough erigeron - *Erigeron glabellus* Nutt. var. *pubescens* Hook. (5, 93, 131) (1899-1936)

Rough false dandelion - *Pyrrhopappus* DC. (5, 97) (1913-1937)

Rough false pennyroyal [Rough falsepennyroyal] - *Hedeoma hispida* Pursh (4, 50, 155) (1942–present)

Rough fescue - *Festuca altaica* Trin. (3, 155) (1942-1977), *Festuca campestris* Rydb. (50) (present)

Rough fescue grass - *Festuca altaica* Trin. (5, 111) (1913-1915)

Rough flatsedge - *Cyperus retrofractus* (L.) Torr. (50) (present)

Rough fleabane - *Erigeron strigosus* Muhl. ex Willd. (7) (1828)

Rough fogfruit - *Phyla scaberrima* (Juss.) Moldenke (50) (present)

Rough foxtail - *Setaria corrugata* (Ell.) J.A. Schultes (94) (1901)

Rough gentian - *Gentiana catesbaei* Walt. (92) (1876), *Gentiana saponaria* L. (156) (1923), *Gentiana saponaria* L. var. *saponaria* (5) (1913)

Rough gerardia - *Agalinis aspera* (Dougl. ex Benth.) Britton (131) (1899)

Rough gold-aster [Rough goldaster] - *Heterotheca villosa* (Pursh) Shinners var. *minor* (Hook.) Semple (155) (1942)

Rough goldenrod [Rough golden-rod] - *Oligoneuron rigidum* (L.) Small var. *humile* (Porter) Nesom (85) (1932), *Solidago rugosa* Mill. (156) (1923), *Solidago rugosa* Mill. subsp. *aspera* (Aiton) Cronq. (19, 187) (1818-1840)

Rough grass - *Dactylis glomerata* L. (92) (1876)

Rough hair grass [Rough hair-grass] - *Agrostis hyemalis* (Walt.) Britton, Sterns & Poggenb. (5, 119, 163) (1852-1938)

Rough hawkbit - *Leontodon hirtus* L. (5) (1913)

Rough hawk's-beard [Rough hawksbeard] - *Crepis biennis* L. (5) (1913)

Rough hawkweed - *Hieracium scabrum* Michx. (5, 62, 63, 72, 97, 157) (1899-1937)

Rough hedge nettle - *Stachys aspera* Michx. (5, 62, 72, 93, 131, 157) (1899-1936)

Rough heliopsis - *Heliopsis helianthoides* (L.) Sweet var. *scabra* (Dunal) Fern. (138, 155) (1923-1942)

Rough heuchera - *Heuchera americana* L. var. *hirsuticaulis* (Wheelock) Rosendahl, Butters & Lakela (5, 72, 93, 131) (1899–1936)

Rough horsetail [Rough horse-tail] - *Equisetum hyemale* L. (5, 158, 187) (1818-1913)

Rough Joe-Pye-weed - *Eupatorium maculatum* L. var. *maculatum* (138) (1923)

Rough leptochloa - *Leptochloa scabra* Nees (94) (1901)

Rough lobelia - *Lobelia spicata* Lam. var. *hirtella* Gray (72) (1907)

Rough maple - *Acer saccharum* Marsh. (156) (1923)

Rough marsh grass - *Spartina alterniflora* Loisel. (66) (1903)

Rough marsh-elder [Rough marsh elder] - *Iva annua* L. var. *annua* (5, 93, 97, 122) (1913-1937)

Rough meadow grass [Rough meadow-grass] - *Poa trivialis* L. (45) (1896)

Rough oak - *Quercus stellata* Wangenh. (2, 156) (1895–1923)

Rough oxeye [Rough ox-eye or rough ox eye] - *Heliopsis helianthoides* (L.) Sweet var. *scabra* (Dunal) Fern. (5, 62, 63, 72, 82, 97, 121, 131, 156) (1899–1937)

Rough ox-eye daisy - *Heliopsis helianthoides* (L.) Sweet var. *scabra* (Dunal) Fern. (85) (1932)

Rough panic grass [Rough panic-grass, Rough panicgrass] - *Dichanthelium leucothrix* (Nash) Freckmann (50) (present), *Leptocoryphium lanatum* (Kunth) Nees (94) (1901)

Rough pennyroyal - *Hedeoma hispida* Pursh (3, 5, 37, 72, 93, 95, 97, 122, 131) (1907-1977)

Rough pigweed - *Amaranthus retroflexus* L. (3, 4, 62, 72, 93, 131, 156, 157, 158) (1899-1986)

Rough prickly-poppy [Rough pricklypoppy] - *Argemone hispida* Gray (50) (present)

Rough purple agalinis - *Agalinis aspera* (Dougl. ex Benth.) Britton (5) (1913)

Rough purple gerardia - *Agalinis aspera* (Dougl. ex Benth.) Britton (72, 97) (1907-1937)

Rough rattlesnake-root [Rough rattlesnakeroot] - *Prenanthes aspera* Michx. (3, 50, 155) (1942–present)

Rough rush grass [Rough rush-grass] - *Sporobolus clandestinus* (Biehler) A.S. Hitchc. (5, 119) (1913-1938)

Rough sarsaparilla - *Aralia hispida* Vent. (5, 156) (1913-1923)

Rough sedge - *Carex muricata* L. (50) (present), *Carex scabrata* Schwein (possibly) (5) (1913)

Rough small bluet - *Houstonia humifusa* (Gray) Gray (4) (1986)

Rough spikenard - *Aralia hispida* Vent. (7) (1828)

Rough sunflower - *Helianthus divaricatus* L. (5, 92, 93, 97) (1876-1937), *Helianthus pauciflorus* Nutt. subsp. *pauciflorus* (127) (1933)

Rough thoroughwort - *Eupatorium rotundifolium* L. var. *rotundifolium* (5, 156) (1913-1923)

Rough triodia - *Tridens muticus* (Torr.) Nash var. *elongatus* (Buckl.) Shinners (122, 140, 155) (1937-1944)

Rough white lettuce - *Prenanthes aspera* Michx. (5, 72, 131) (1899-1913)

Rough white oak - *Quercus stellata* Wangenh. (5, 156) (1913-1923)

Rough white-top aster [Rough white-topped aster] - *Sericocarpus tortifolius* (Michx.) Nees (156) (1923)

Rough whitlow-grass [Rough whitlow grass] - *Draba glabella* Pursh (19) (1840)

Rough woodbine - *Lonicera hirsuta* Eaton (19, 92, 156) (1840-1923)

Rough woundwort [Rough wound-wort] - *Stachys aspera* Michx. (5, 62, 157) (1912-1929)

Rough-bark Arizona cypress [Rough-barked Arizona cypress] - *Cupressus arizonica* Greene (109) (1949)

Rough-bark juniper [Rough barked juniper] - *Juniperus deppeana* Steud. (124) (1937)

Rough-bark poplar [Rough bark poplar] - *Populus balsamifera* L. (5, 156) (1913-1923)

Rough-flower rat-tail-grass [Rough-flowered rat-tail-grass] - *Coelorachis rugosa* (Nutt.) Nash (94) (1901)

Rough-fruit acnida [Rough-fruited acnida] - *Amaranthus cannabinus* (L.) Sauer (187) (1818)

Rough-fruit amaranth [Roughfruit amaranth] - *Amaranthus tuberculatus* (Moq.) Sauer (50) (present)

Rough-fruit cinquefoil [Rough fruited cinquefoil] - *Potentilla recta* L. (5) (1913)

Rough-fruit corn bedstraw [Rough-fruited corn bedstraw] - *Galium tricornutum* Dandy (5, 156) (1913-1923)

Rough-fruit crowfoot [Rough-fruited crow-foot] - *Ranunculus pedatifidus* J.E. Smith (5) (1913)

Rough-fruit custard-apple [Rough-fruited custard apple] - *Annona muricata* L. (165) (1807)

Rough-fruit disporum [Rough-fruited disporum] - *Disporum trachycarpum* (S. Wats.) Benth. & Hook. f. (5, 93) (1913-1936)

Rough-fruit fairybells [Roughfruit fairybells] - *Disporum trachycarpum* (S. Wats.) Benth. & Hook. f. (50) (present)

Rough-fruit scaleseed [Roughfruit scaleseed] - *Spermolepis divaricata* (Walt.) Britton (50) (present)

Rough-fruit sedge [Rough-fruited sedge] - *Carex scabrata* Schwein (66) (1903)

Rough-fruit soursop [Rough-fruited sour sop] - *Annona muricata* L. (165) (1807)

Rough-fruit spermolepis [Rough-fruited spermolepis] - *Spermolepis divaricata* (Walt.) Britton (5, 97) (1913-1937)

Rough-fruit waterhemp [Rough-fruited water hemp] - *Amaranthus tuberculatus* (Moq.) Sauer (5, 93) (1913-1936)

Rough-glume bushy beard grass [Roughglume bushy beardgrass] - *Andropogon glomeratus* (Walt.) B.S.P. var. *scabriglumis* C. Campbell (50) (present)

Rough-hair rosette grass [Roughhair rosette grass] - *Dichanthelium strigosum* (Muhl. ex Ell.) Freckmann var. *leucoblepharis* (Trin.) Freckmann (50) (present), *Dichanthelium strigosum* (Muhl. ex Ell.) Freckmann var. *strigosum* (50) (present)

Rough-hairy panicum - *Dichanthelium strigosum* (Muhl. ex Ell.) Freckmann var. *strigosum* (5) (1913)

Rough-head fuirena [Rough-headed fuirena] - *Fuirena squarrosa* Michx. (187) (1818)

Rough-head rush [Rough-headed rush] - *Juncus polycephalus* Michx. (187) (1818)

Roughish arrow-wood [Roughish arrow wood] - *Viburnum dentatum* L. var. *dentatum* (5) (1913)

Roughish meadow grass - *Poa trivialis* L. (72) (1907)

Roughish panicum - *Dichanthelium leucothrix* (Nash) Freckmann (5) (1913)

Rough-leaf [Rough leaf] - *Epigaea repens* L. (156) (1923), *Tiarella cordifolia* L. (29) (1869)

Rough-leaf bent grass [Rough-leaved bent grass] - *Agrostis hyemalis* (Walt.) Britton, Sterns & Poggenb. (5) (1913), *Agrostis perennans* (Walt.) Tuckerman (5) (1913)

Rough-leaf cordia [Rough-leaved cordia] - *Cordia sebestena* L. (20) (1857)

Rough-leaf cornel [Rough-leaved cornel] - *Cornus asperifolia* Michx. (72, 156) (1907-1923)

Rough-leaf dogwood [Rough leaf dogwood, Roughleaf dogwood] - *Cornus asperifolia* Michx. (93, 95, 97, 113, 122, 124, 130, 131, 138) (1890-1937), *Cornus drummondii* C.A. Mey. (3, 4, 50, 121) (1918–present)

Rough-leaf dropseed [Rough-leaved dropseed, Rough-leaved dropseed] - *Muhlenbergia asperifolia* (Nees & Meyen ex Trin.) Parodi (3, 5, 93, 163) (1852-1977)

Rough-leaf goldenrod [Roughleaf goldenrod] - *Solidago patula* Muhl. ex Willd. (5, 72, 122, 138) (1907-1937)

Rough-leaf hackberry [Rough leafed hackberry] - *Celtis laevigata* Willd. var. *reticulata* (Torr.) L. Benson (124) (1937), *Celtis occidentalis* L. (5, 85, 93, 97) (1913-1937)

Rough-leaf meadow rue [Rough-leaved meadow-rue] - *Thalictrum revolutum* DC. (187) (1818)

Rough-leaf prairie grass [Rough-leaved prairie grass] - *Muhlenbergia asperifolia* (Nees & Meyen ex Trin.) Parodi (129) (1894)

Rough-leaf rice grass [Roughleaf ricegrass] - *Oryzopsis asperifolia* Michx. (3, 50, 140, 155) (1942–present)

Rough-leaf rosinweed [Rough-leaved rosin-weed] - *Silphium asteriscus* L. (50) (present)

Rough-leaf salt grass [Rough-leafed salt-grass] - *Muhlenbergia asperifolia* (Nees & Meyen ex Trin.) Parodi (94) (1901)

Rough-leaf sunflower [Rough-leaved sun-flower] - *Helianthus divaricatus* L. (187) (1818)

Rough-leaf thorn [Rough-leaved thorn] - *Crataegus pruinosa* (Wendl.) K. Koch (5) (1913)

Rough-leaf thoroughwort [Roughleaf thoroughwort] - *Eupatorium rotundifolium* L. (122, 156) (1923-1937)

Rough-leaf vilfa [Rough-leaved vilfa] - *Sporobolus compositus* (Poir.) Merr. (66) (1903)

Rough-leaf wintergreen [Rough-leaved wintergreen] - *Pyrola americana* Sweet (156) (1923)

Rough-root [Rough root] - *Liatris* Gaertn. ex Schreber. (7) (1828), *Liatris spicata* (L.) Willd. (92, 156) (1876-1923), *Liatris spicata* (L.) Willd. var. *spicata* (5) (1913)

Rough-seed clammy-weed [Roughseed clammyweed] - *Polanisia dodecandra* (L.) DC. subsp. *trachysperma* (Torr. & Gray) Iltis (155) (1942)

Rough-seed dropseed [Rough-seeded dropseed] - *Sporobolus compositus* (Poir.) Merr. var. *compositus* (99) (1923)

Rough-seed hedgehog grass [Rough seeded hedge hog grass] - *Cenchrus echinatus* L. (42) (1814) CO Neb

Rough-spike mariscus [Rough spiked mariscus] - *Cyperus echinatus* (L.) Wood (187) (1818)

Rough-stalk bluegrass [Roughstalk bluegrass] - *Poa trivialis* L. (155) (1942)

Rough-stalk goldenrod [Rough-stalk golden-rod] - *Solidago juncea* Aiton (19) (1840)

Rough-stalk meadow-grass [Rough-stalked meadowgrass, Rough-stalked meadow grass, Rough-stalked meadow-grass] - *Poa trivialis* L. (3, 45, 56, 66, 68, 92, 94, 109, 143) (1896-1977)

Rough-stalk witch grass [Roughstalk witchgrass] - *Leptocoryphium lanatum* (Kunth) Nees (155) (1942)

Rough-stem aster [Rough-stemmed aster] - *Symphyotrichum puniceum* (L.) A.& D. Löve var. *puniceum* (156) (1923)

Rough-stem fleabane [Rough-stemmed fleabane] - *Erigeron strigosus* Muhl. ex Willd. var. *strigosus* (156) (1923)

Rough-stem heuchera [Rough-stemmed heuchera] - *Heuchera americana* L. var. *hirsuticaulis* (Wheelock) Rosendahl, Butters & Lakela (5, 97) (1913-1937)

Rough-stem meadow grass [Rough-stemmed meadow-grass] - *Poa trivialis* L. (187) (1818)

Rough-stem rosinweed [Roughstem rosinweed] - *Silphium radula* Nutt. (50) (present)

Rough-stem spleenwort [Ruff stemmed spleen wort] - *Asplenium trichomanes* L. subsp. *trichomanes* . (42) (1814)

Rough-tongues - *Eurybia macrophylla* (L.) Cass. (156) (1923)

Rough-weed [Rough weed] - *Stachys palustris* L. (5, 62, 156) (1912-1923)

Round bent grass [Round bent-grasse] - *Phleum pratense* L. (180) (1633)

Round black Virginia walnut [Round black Virginian walnut] - *Juglans nigra* L. (8) (1785)

Round dock - *Malva sylvestris* L. (5, 156, 157, 158) (1900-1929)

Round kumquat - *Fortunella japonica* (Thunb.) Swingle (109) (1949)

Round mandrake - *Gladiolus communis* L. (92) (1876)

Round potato - *Solanum tuberosum* L. (156) (1923)

Round prickly-head poppy [Round pricklyhead poppy] - *Papaver hybridum* L. (50) (present)

Round radish - *Raphanus sativus* L. (180) (1633)

Round ransom - *Gladiolus communis* L. (92) (1876)

Round rush - *Juncus effusus* L. (5, 156) (1913-1923)

Round sedge - *Carex rotundata* Wahl. (50) (present)

Round spurge - *Euphorbia peplus* L. (178) (1526)

Round tree - *Sorbus americana* Marsh. (5, 73, 92) (1876-1913) NB, from rowan tree

Round Virginia Rape with a stringy root - *Obolaria virginica* L. (181) (~1678)

Round-beak sedge [Round beak sedge] - *Rhynchospora cephalantha* Gray (66) (1903)

Round-ear willow [Round-eared willow] - *Salix aurita* L. (138) (1923)

Round-flower cat's-claw [Round-flowered catsclaw, Round-flower catclaw, Roundflower catclaw] - *Acacia roemeriana* Scheele (50, 106, 124) (1930–present)

Round-flower panic [Round-flowered panic] - *Dichanthelium sphaerocarpon* (Ell.) Gould var. *sphaerocarpon* (94) (1901)

Round-flower paspalum [Round-flowered paspalum] - *Paspalum laeve* Michx. (5) (1913)

Round-fruit cress [Round-fruited cress] - *Rorippa sphaerocarpa* (Gray) Britt. (5, 97) (1913-1937)

Round-fruit false indigo [Round-fruited false indigo] - *Baptisia sphaerocarpa* Nutt. (97) (1937)

Round-fruit hedge-hyssop [Roundfruit hedgehyssop] - *Gratiola virginiana* L. (50) (present), *Gratiola virginiana* L. var. *virginiana* (5, 72, 97) (1907-1937)

Round-fruit honeyberry [Round fruited honeyberry] - *Exothea paniculata* (Juss.) Radlk. (20) (1857)

Round-fruit panic grass [Round-fruited panic grass, Round-fruited panic-grass] - *Dichanthelium sphaerocarpon* (Ell.) Gould var. *sphaerocarpon* (5, 163) (1852-1913)

Round-fruit rush [Roundfruit rush] - *Juncus compressus* Jacq. (50) (present), *Juncus bufonius* L. var. *occidentalis* F.J. Herm. (139) (1944)

Round-fruit sedge [Round-fruited sedge] - *Carex rotundata* Wahl. (5) (1913)

Round-fruit St. John's-wort [Roundfruit St. John's wort, Round-fruited St. John's wort] - *Hypericum sphaerocarpum* Michx. (3, 4, 72) (1907-1986)

Round-fruit stewartia [Round-fruited stewartia] - *Stewartia malacodendron* L. (5) (1913)

Round-head anemone [Round-headed anemone] - *Anemone canadensis* L. (5, 158) (1900-1913)

Round-head bush clover [Roundhead bushclover, Round-headed bush clover, Round-headed bush-clover] - *Lespedeza capitata* Michx. (5, 93, 97, 131, 138, 158) (1899-1937)

Round-head gilia [Round-headed gilia] - *Ipomopsis congesta* (Hook.) V. Grant (5, 93) (1913-1936)

Round-head lespedeza [Roundhead lespedeza] - *Lespedeza capitata* Michx. (4, 50, 155) (1942–present)

Round-head prairie clover [Roundhead prairie clover, Round-headed prairie clover, Round-headed prairie clover, Round-headed prairieclover] - *Dalea multiflora* (Nutt.) Shinners (3, 4, 50) (1977–present), *Dalea obovata* (Torr. & A. Gray) Shinners (5, 93, 97, 155) (1913–1942)

Round-head rush [Roundhead rush] - *Juncus validus* Coville (50) (present), *Juncus validus* Coville var. *validus* (50) (present)

Round-head sedge [Roundhead sedge] - *Kyllinga pumila* Michx. (66) (1903)

Round-headed rush - *Juncus nodosus* L. (66) (1903)

Round-heart [Round heart, Roundheart] - *Thaspium* Nutt. (7) (1828), *Thaspium trifoliatum* (L.) Gray (158) (1900), *Thaspium trifoliatum* (L.) Gray var. *aureum* Britt. (8, 156) (1785-1923)

Round-heart plant [Round heart-plant] - *Thaspium trifoliatum* (L.) Gray (92) (1876)

Roundish-leaf Hempweed [Roundish-leaved Hemp-weed] - *Eupatorium rotundifolium* L. (187) (1818)

Roundleaf - *Pyrola americana* Sweet (58) (1869), *Pyrola elliptica* Nutt. (7) (1828)

Round-leaf American wintergreen [Round-leaved American wintergreen] - *Pyrola americana* Sweet (5) (1913)

Round-leaf anemone [Round-leaved anemone] - *Anemone canadensis* L. (5, 93, 158) (1900-1936)

Round-leaf bellflower [Round-leaved bellflower, Round leaved bell flower] - *Campanula rotundifolia* L. (5, 42, 156) (1814-1923)

Round-leaf bellwort [Round-leaved bellwort] - *Campanula rotundifolia* L. (158) (1900)

Round-leaf bladderpod [Roundleaf bladderpod] - *Lesquerella ovalifolia* Rydb. ex Britton (50) (present), *Lesquerella ovalifolia* Rydb. ex Britton subsp. *ovalifolia* (50) (present)

Round-leaf catchfly [Round-leaved catchfly] - *Silene rotundifolia* Nutt. (5, 15, 156) (1895-1923)

Round-leaf cornel [Round-leaved cornel, Round leaved cornel] - *Cornus rugosa* Lam. (5, 6, 7, 58, 92, 156) (1828-1923)

Round-leaf cranebill [Round-leaved crane's bill] - *Geranium rotundifolium* L. (5, 72) (1907-1913)

Round-leaf cuckoo flower [Round-leaved cuckoo flower] - *Cardamine rotundifolia* Michx. (107) (1919)

Round-leaf dew plant [Round leaved dew plant] - *Drosera rotundifolia* L. (5) (1913)

Round-leaf dogwood [Roundleaf dogwood, Round-leaved dogwood, Round leaved dogwood] - *Cornus rugosa* Lam. (5, 6, 58, 72, 92, 138, 156) (1869-1923)

Round-leaf geranium [Roundleaf geranium] - *Geranium rotundifolium* L. (50) (present)

Round-leaf gooseberry [Roundleaf gooseberry] - *Ribes rotundifolium* Michx. (107, 138) (1919-1923)

Round-leaf greenbrier [Roundleaf greenbrier] - *Smilax rotundifolia* L. (50) (present)

Round-leaf ground-cherry [Round-leaved ground cherry, Round-leaved ground-cherry - *Physalis hederifolia* Gray var. *comata* (Rydb.) Waterfall (5, 93, 97, 122, 131) (1899-1937)

Round-leaf groundsel [Roundleaf groundsel] - *Packera obovata* (Muhl. ex Willd.) W.A. Weber & A. Löve (3, 4, 138) (1923-1986)

Round-leaf hawthorn [Roundleaf hawthorn] - *Crataegus chrysocarpa* Ashe (137, 138) (1923-1931)

Round-leaf hedge-hyssop [Round-leaved hedge hyssop, Round-leaved hedge-hyssop] - *Bacopa rotundifolia* (Michx.) Wettst. (5, 72, 93, 97, 131) (1899-1937)

Round-leaf Indian Mallow [Round-leaved Indian Mallow] - *Abutilon theophrasti* Medik (187) (1818)

Round-leaf juneberry [Round-leaved june-berry, Round-leaved june berry] - *Amelanchier canadensis* (L.) Medik. (possibly) (72, 131) (1899-1907), *Amelanchier sanguinea* (Pursh) DC. (5, 85) (1913-1932)

Round-leaf laurel [Round-leaved laurel] - *Kalmia latifolia* L. (6) (1892)

Round-leaf mallow [Round-leaved mallow] - *Malva rotundifolia* L. (62, 72) (1907-1913)

Round-leaf maple [Round leaved maple] - *Acer circinatum* Pursh (20) (1857)

Round-leaf mint [Round-leaved mint] - *Mentha* ×*rotundifolia* (L.) Huds. [*longifolia* × *suaveolens*] (5, 109) (1913-1949)

Round-leaf monkey flower [Roundleaf monkeyflower, Roundleaf monkey-flower] - *Mimulus glabratus* Kunth (50) (present), *Mimulus glabratus* Kunth var. *jamesii* (Torr. & Gray ex Benth.) Gray (3, 4) (1977-1986)

Round-leaf mud-plantain [Roundleaf mudplantain] - *Heteranthera rotundifolia* (Kunth) Griseb. (50) (present)

Round-leaf nympha [Round leafed nympha] - *Brasenia schreberi* Gmel. (183) (~1756)

Round-leaf orchis [Round-leaved orchis] - *Platanthera orbiculata* (Pursh) Lindl. (3, 156) (1923-1977)

Round-leaf plantain [Round-leaved plantain] - *Plantago major* L. (5, 92, 156, 157, 158) (1876-1929)

Round-leaf pyrola [Roundleaf pyrola, Round leaved pyrola] - *Pyrola americana* Sweet (8, 92, 138) (1785-1923)

Round-leaf ragwort [Roundleaf ragwort] - *Packera obovata* (Muhl. ex Willd.) W.A. Weber & A. Löve (50) (present)

Round-leaf rhynchosia [Round-leaved rhynchosia] - *Rhynchosia reniformis* DC. (5) (1913)

Round-leaf serviceberry [Roundleaf serviceberry] - *Amelanchier sanguinea* (Pursh) DC. (155) (1942)

Round-leaf shadblow [Roundleaf shadblow] - *Amelanchier sanguinea* (Pursh) DC. (138) (1923)

Round-leaf sida [Round-leaved sida] - *Malvella leprosa* (Ortega) Krapov (5, 97) (1913-1937)

Round-leaf smilax [Round-leaved smilax] - *Smilax rotundifolia* L. (187) (1818)

Round-leaf sorrel [Round-leafed sorrel] - *Oxyria digyna* (L.) Hill (103, 156) (1870-1923)

Round-leaf spreading spurge [Round-leaved spreading spurge] - *Chamaesyce serpens* (Kunth) Small (5, 72, 93, 97) (1913-1937)

Round-leaf spurge [Round leafed spurge] - *Euphorbia peplus* L. (178) (1526), *Chamaesyce serpens* (Kunth) Small (3, 4, 131) (1899-1986)

Round-leaf squaw-weed [Round-leaf squaw weed] - *Packera obovata* (Muhl. ex Willd.) W.A. Weber & A. Löve (5, 72, 97) (1907-1937)

Round-leaf sundrew [Round leaved sundew, Round-leaved sundew] - *Drosera rotundifolia* L. (2, 3, 4, 5, 42, 49, 50, 53, 107, 138, 155, 158, 187) (1814–present)

Round-leaf thorn [Round-leaved thorn] - *Crataegus chrysocarpa* Ashe (5) (1913)

Round-leaf thoroughwort [Roundleaf thoroughwort] - *Eupatorium rotundifolium* L. (5, 97, 122) (1913-1937)

Round-leaf tick clover [Roundleaf tickclover] - *Desmodium rotundifolium* DC. (155) (1942)

Round-leaf tick trefoil [Round-leaved tick trefoil] - *Desmodium rotundifolium* DC. (5) (1913)

Round-leaf toad-flax [Round-leaved toad-flax] - *Kickxia elatine* (L.) Dumort. (5) (1913)

Round-leaf violet [Roundleaf violet] - *Viola rotundifolia* Michx. (2, 5, 138) (1895-1923)

Round-leaf Virginia foal's-foot [Round leaved Virginia foals-foot] - *Hexastylis virginica* (L.) Small (181) (~1678)

Round-leaf watercress [Round-leaved water cress] - *Cardamine rotundifolia* Michx. (5, 156) (1913-1923)

Round-leaf water-hyssop [Round-leaved water hyssop] - *Bacopa rotundifolia* (Michx.) Wettst. (120) (1938)

Round-leaf willow [Round-leaved willow] - *Salix rotundifolia* Trautv. (20) (1857)

Round-leaf wintergreen [Round-leaved wintergreen, Round-leaved winter-green] - *Pyrola americana* Sweet (4, 85, 131, 156, 158, 187) (1818-1986), *Pyrola asarifolia* Michx. (3, 4) (1977-1986)

Round-leaf yellow violet [Round-leaved yellow violet] - *Viola rotundifolia* Michx. (156) (1923)

Round-lobe hepatica [Roundlobe hepatica, Round-lobed hepatica] - *Hepatica nobilis* Schreb. (2, 138) (1895-1923), *Hepatica nobilis* Schreb. var. *obtusa* (Pursh) Steyermark (6) (1892)

Round-lobe liver-leaf [Round-lobed liver-leaf] - *Hepatica nobilis* Schreb. var. *obtusa* (Pursh) Steyermark (5) (1913)

Round-pod St. John's-wort [Round-podded St. John's wort] - *Hypericum sphaerocarpum* Michx. (5, 97) (1913-1937)

Round-root [Round root] - *Cyperus rotundus* L. (5, 156) (1913-1923)

Round-root black radish [Round rooted blacke Radish] - *Raphanus sativus* L. (178) (1526)

Round-seed dolichos [Round seeded dolichos] - *Vigna unguiculata* (L.) Walp. (155) (1942)

Round-seed panic grass [Roundseed panicgrass] - *Dichanthelium sphaerocarpon* (Ell.) Gould (50) (present)

Round-seed panicum [Roundseed panicum] - *Dichanthelium sphaerocarpon* (Ell.) Gould var. *sphaerocarpon* (3, 155) (1942-1977)

Round-seed paspalum [Roundseed paspalum] - *Paspalum laeve* Michx. (155) (1942)

Round-seed St. John's-wort [Roundseed St. Johnswort] - *Hypericum sphaerocarpum* Michx. (50) (present)

Round-spike sedge [Round-spiked sedge] - *Carex folliculata* L. (187) (1818)

Round-stem false foxglove [Roundstem false foxglove] - *Agalinis gattingeri* (Small) Small (50) (present)

Roundwood [Round-wood, Round wood] - *Sorbus americana* Marsh. (5, 92, 156) (1876-1923)

Rover bellflower - *Campanula rapunculoides* L. (4, 109) (1949-1986)

Roving Charley - *Glechoma hederacea* L. (156) (1923)

Roving-sailor [Roving sailor] - *Cymbalaria muralis* P.G. Gaertn., B. Mey. & Scherb. (5, 156) (1913-1923) no longer in use by 1923

Rowan tree [Rowan-tree] - *Sorbus americana* Marsh. (92, 156) (1898-1923), *Sorbus aucuparia* L. (107) (1919)

Rowan-wood - *Sorbus americana* Marsh. (156) (1923)

Roxbury waxwork [Roxbury wax work, Roxbury wax-work] - *Celastrus scandens* L. (5, 73, 92, 156, 157, 158) (1892-1929) Eastern MA

Royal brake - *Osmunda regalis* L. (157) (1929)

Royal campion - *Silene regia* Sims. (2) (1895)

Royal catchfly - *Silene regia* Sims. (3, 4, 5, 15, 50, 97, 156, 158) (1895-present)

Royal cow-parsnip [Royal cow parsnip] - *Heracleum maximum* Bartr. (92) (1876)

Royal fern [Royal-fern, Royalfern] - *Osmunda* L. (1, 4) (1932-1986), *Osmunda regalis* L. (3, 5, 50, 72, 92, 97, 109, 138, 155, 157) (1907-present), *Osmunda regalis* L. var. *spectabilis* (Willd.) A. Gray (4, 50, 122) (1937-present)

Royal flowering fern - *Osmunda regalis* L. (52, 157) (1919-1929)

Royal lily - *Lilium regale* E.E. Wilson (138) (1923)

Royal osmund - *Osmunda regalis* L. (5, 157) (1900-1913)

Royal osmunda - *Osmunda regalis* L. (187) (1818)

Royal palm - *Roystonea borinquena* O.F. Cook (106) (1930), *Roystonea elata* (Bartr.) F. Harper (138) (1923), *Roystonea* O.F. Cook (138) (1923)

Royal palmetto - *Serenoa repens* (Bartr.) Small (7) (1828)

Royal paulownia - *Paulownia tomentosa* (Thunb.) Sieb. & Zucc. ex Steud. (possibly) (138) (1923)

Royal poiciana - *Delonix regia* (Bojer ex Hook.) Raf. (138) (1923)

Royal poinciana - *Delonix regia* (Bojer ex Hook.) Raf. (109) (1949)

Royal silene - *Silene regia* Sims. (155) (1942)

Rubber rabbitbrush - *Ericameria nauseosa* (Pallas ex Pursh) Nesom & Baird (50) (present), *Ericameria nauseosa* (Pallas ex Pursh) Nesom & Baird subsp. *nauseosa* var. *glabrata* (Gray) Nesom & Baird (50) (present), *Ericameria nauseosa* (Pallas ex Pursh) Nesom & Baird subsp. *nauseosa* var. *nauseosa* (50, 155) (1942–present)

Rubber vine [Rubber-vine, Rubbervine] - *Cryptostegia* R. Br. (109, 138) (1923-1949)

Rubber-plant - *Ficus elastica* Roxb. ex Hornem. (109) (1949)

Rubberweed - *Hymenoxys* Cass. (50) (present)

Ruben (German, High Dutch) - *Brassica rapa* L. var. *rapa* (107, 180) (1633–1919)

Rubia - *Rubia tinctoria* L. (57) (1917)

Rubiglia (Italian) - *Pisum sativum* L. (110) (1886)

Rubus - *Rubus flagellaris* Willd. (59) (1911)

Ruby grass [Ruby-grass] - *Melinis repens* (Willd.) Zizka (109) (1949)

Ruby-bead - *Maianthemum canadense* Desf. (156) (1923)

Ruddes - *Calendula officinalis* L. (179) (1526)

Rue - *Ruta graveolens* L. (14, 19, 53, 55, 57, 61, 92, 107, 156) (1840-1923), *Ruta* L. (109, 138) (1923-1949)

Rue de chère (French) - *Galega officinalis* L. (158) (1900)

Rue maidenhair [Rue Maiden haire] - *Asplenium ruta-muraria* L. (178) (1596)

Rue nailwort [Rue Naile woort] - *Saxifraga tridaclylites* L. (178) (1526)

Rue vulgaire (French) - *Ruta graveolens* L. (7) (1828)

Rue-anemone [Rue anemone] - *Enemion biternatum* Raf. (156) (1923), *Synandra hispidula* (Michx.) Britton (1, 93) (1932-1936), *Thalictrum* L. (1, 13, 93, 109, 156, 158) (1849-1949), *Thalictrum thalictroides* (L.) Eames & Boivin (3, 4, 5, 19, 49, 50, 63, 72, 76, 97, 156) (1840–present)

Rüböl (German) - *Brassica rapa* L. var. *rapa* (158) (1900)

Ruel - *Ruellia strepens* L. (19) (1840)

Rue-leaf saxifrage [Rueleaf saxifrage] - *Saxifraga tridaclylites* L. (50) (present)

Ruellia - *Ruellia* L. (1, 138, 155) (1923-1942)

Rue-of-the-mountains [Rue of the mountains] - *Thamnosma texana* (Gray) Torr. (50) (present)

Rue-weed - *Thalictrum* L. (184) (1793)

Rufous bulrush - *Scirpus pendulus* Muhl. (50) (present)

Rugel's heuchera - *Heuchera parviflora* Bartl. (5) (1913)

Rugel's papaw [Rugel pawpaw] - *Deeringothamnus rugelii* (B.L. Robins.) Small (155) (1942)

Rugel's plantain - *Plantago rugelii* Dcne. (3, 4, 5, 72, 80, 97, 131) (1899-1986)

Rugel's sugar maple [Rugel sugar maple] - *Acer saccharum* Marsh. var. *schneckii* Rehd. (138) (1923)

Rugosa rose - *Rosa rugosa* Thunb. (138) (1923)

Rûgr (Scandinavian) - *Secale cereale* L. (110) (1886)

Ruhi (Winnebago) - *Salix* L. (37) (1919)

Ruh'i-shutsh (Winnebago) - *Cornus amomum* Mill. (37) (1919)

Ruifort (French) - *Raphanus sativus* L. (180) (1633)

Rum cherry - *Padus serotina* (Ehrh.) Borkh. (46) (1879), *Prunus serotina* Ehrh. (71, 73, 107, 156, 157, 158) (1892-1898) Northeast US, *Prunus virginiana* L. (19, 92) (1840-1876), *Prunus virginiana* L. var. *virginiana* (5) (1913)

Rum suckers - *Polytrichum commune* Hedw. (73) (1892) NH, unripe spores supposedly have a spirituous taste

Rumex - *Rumex crispus* L. (64) (1907)

Rumieniec smierdzacy (Polish) - *Anthemis cotula* L. (186) (1814)

Run-away Jack - *Glechoma hederacea* L. (77) (1898) Cambridge MA

Run-away Nell - *Glechoma hederacea* L. (77) (1898) Medford MA

Runch - *Raphanus raphanistrum* L. (107) (1919), *Sinapis arvensis* L. (157) (1929)

Runchweed [Runch-weed, Runch weed] - *Moricandia arvensis* (L.) DC. (156, 158) (1900-1923), *Sinapis arvensis* L. (5) (1913)

Rundblätterige Cornel (German) - *Cornus rugosa* Lam. (6) (1892)

Rundblattriger Sonnenthau (German) - *Drosera rotundifolia* L. (6) (1892)

Runnet - *Galium verum* L. (158) (1900)

Running birch - *Gaultheria hispidula* (L.) Muhl. ex Bigelow (5, 75, 156) (1894-1923)

Running blackberry - *Rubus flagellaris* Willd. (156, 186) (1814-1923), *Rubus hispidus* L. (107) (1919)

Running box - *Mitchella repens* L. (156) (1923)

Running buffalo clover - *Trifolium stoloniferum* Muhl. ex Eat. (2, 3, 4, 5, 50, 72, 85, 93, 97, 131, 158) (1895–present)

Running buttercups [Running buttercup] - *Potentilla canadensis* L. (5, 76, 156) (1896-1923) Oxford Co. ME

Running cedar - *Juniperus horizontalis* Moench (108) (1878)

Running clubmoss [Running club-moss] - *Lycopodium clavatum* L. (50) (present), *Selaginella rupestris* (L.) Spring (187) (1818)

Running downy oak - *Quercus ilicifolia* Wangenh. (181) (~1678)

Running euonymus - *Euonymus americanus* L. (138) (1923)

Running fleabane - *Erigeron flagellaris* Gray (5, 122, 131) (1899–1937)

Running ground-pine [Running ground pine] - *Lycopodium annotinum* L. (19) (1840)

Running mallow - *Malva rotundifolia* L. (5, 93, 95, 155, 156, 157, 158) (1900–1942)

Running milkweed - *Matelea carolinensis* (Jacq.) Woods. (5, 156) (1913-1923)

Running moss - *Lycopodium clavatum* L. (5) (1913)

Running oak - *Quercus pumila* Walt. (33) (1827)

Running raspberry - *Rubus pubescens* Raf. var. *pubescens* (5, 76, 156) (1896-1923) Oxford Co. ME

Running serviceberry - *Amelanchier stolonifera* Wieg. (155) (1942)

Running shadblow - *Amelanchier stolonifera* Wieg. (138) (1923)

Running stonecrop - *Sedum stoloniferum* Gmel. (138, 155) (1931-1942)

Running strawberry-bush [Running strawberry bush] - *Euonymus americanus* L. (5, 109, 156) (1913-1949)

Running swamp blackberry - *Rubus hispidus* L. (2, 5) (1895-1913)

Running tea - *Gaultheria hispidula* (L.) Muhl. ex Bigelow (77) (1898)

Running tickseed - *Coreopsis auriculata* L. (5) (1913)

Running vine - *Lycopodium complanatum* L. (78) (1898) Ferrisburgh VT

Running white oak - *Quercus prinoides* Willd. (5, 156) (1913-1923)

Running-myrtle [Running myrtle] - *Vinca minor* L. (5, 109, 156, 158) (1900-1949)

Running-pine [Runningpine, Running pine] - *Lycopodium clavatum* L. (72, 138) (1907-1923)

Running-pine club-moss - *Lycopodium clavatum* L. (5) (1913)

Ruprechtskraut (German) - *Geranium robertianum* L. (158) (1900)

Rupter-wort, with the white flower - *Chamaesyce maculata* (L.) Small (46) (1671)

Rupturewort [Rupture woort, Rupture-wort] - *Herniaria glabra* L. (178) (1526), *Herniaria* L. (109) (1949) reported as a cure of rupture or hernia

Rush [Rushes] - *Equisetum hyemale* L. (27, 28) (1811-1850), *Equisetum* L. (35) (1806), *Juncus* L. (1, 7, 10, 50, 93, 138, 139, 155, 158, 180, 181, 184) (1633–present), *Scirpus* L. (152, 155, 158) (1900-1942)

Rush aster - *Symphyotrichum boreale* (Torr. & Gray) A.& D. Löve (85) (1932)

Rush bladderwort - *Utricularia juncea* Vahl (5) (1913)

Rush cat-tail grass [Rush cat's-tail grass] - *Crypsis schoenoides* (L.) Lam. (5) (1913)

Rush daffodil - *Narcissus jonquilla* L. (178, 180) (1596-1633)

Rush foil - *Croton* L. (4) (1986)

Rush garlic - *Allium schoenoprasum* L. (156) (1923)

Rush goldenweed - *Machaeranthera juncea* (Greene) Shinners (155) (1942), *Pyrrocoma integrifolia* (Porter ex Gray) Greene (155) (1942)

Rush grass [Rush-grass] - *Spartina patens* (Ait.) Muhl. (88) (1885), *Sporobolus airoides* (Torr.) Torr. (5, 85) (1913-1932), *Sporobolus compositus* (Poir.) Merr. (66) (1903), *Sporobolus junceus* (Beauv.)

Kunth (5, 94) (1901-1913), *Sporobolus neglectus* Nash (80) (1913), *Sporobolus* R. Br. (1, 93) (1932-1936), *Sporobolus vaginiflorus* (Torr. ex Gray) Wood (80) (1913)

Rush leek [Rush leeke] - *Allium schoenoprasum* L. (180) (1633)

Rush lily - *Sisyrinchium angustifolium* Mill. (156, 157, 158) (1900–1929)

Rush nut [Rush-nut] - *Cyperus esculentus* L. (5, 156, 158) (1900-1923)

Rush pea - *Hoffmannseggia* Cav. (4, 50) (1986–present)

Rush pussytoes - *Antennaria luzuloides* Torr. & Gray (155) (1942), *Antennaria neglecta* Greene (155) (1942)

Rush salt grass [Rush salt-grass] - *Spartina patens* (Ait.) Muhl. (5, 19, 45, 66, 87, 90, 92) (1840-1913), *Spartina pectinata* Bosc ex Link (163) (1852)

Rush skeleton plant [Rush skeletonplant] - *Lygodesmia juncea* (Pursh) D. Don ex Hook. (50) (present)

Rush skeleton-weed [Rush skeletonweed] - *Lygodesmia juncea* (Pursh) D. Don ex Hook. (155) (1942)

Rush wheat grass [Rush wheatgrass] - *Thinopyrum ponticum* (Podp.) Z.-W. Liu & R.-C. Wang (50) (present)

Rush-grass [Rushgrass, Rush grass, Rush-grasse] - *Juncus bufonius* L. (178, 180) (1526-1633), *Schoenus* L. (184) (1793)

Rush-leaf thrift [Rushleaf thrift] - *Armeria maritima* (Mill.) Willd. subsp. *sibirica* (Turcz. ex Boiss.) Nyman (155) (1942)

Rush-like dropseed [Rush-like drop seed] - *Sporobolus junceus* (Beauv.) Kunth (66) (1903)

Rush-like lygodesmia [Rushlike lygodesmia] - *Lygodesmia juncea* (Pursh) D. Don ex Hook. (5, 72, 80, 97, 122, 131) (1899–1937)

Rush-like spartina - *Spartina spartinae* (Trin.) Merr. ex A.S. Hitchc. (94) (1901)

Rush-like timothy - *Crypsis schoenoides* (L.) Lam. (5, 94) (1901-1913)

Russell's beebalm [Russell beebalm] - *Monarda russeliana* Nutt. ex Sims (138) (1923)

Russell's eustoma - *Eustoma exaltatum* (L.) Salisb. ex G. Don subsp. *russellianum* (Hook) Kartesz (5, 93, 97) (1913-1937)

Russell's prairie-gentian [Russel prairiegentian] - *Eustoma exaltatum* (L.) Salisb. ex G. Don subsp. *russellianum* (Hook) Kartesz (155) (1942)

Russet buffalo-berry [Russet buffaloberry] - *Shepherdia canadensis* Nutt. (50, 138, 155, 156) (1923–present)

Russet cotton-grass [Russet cotton grass] - *Eriophorum chamissonis* C.A. Mey. (5) (1913)

Russet hawthorn - *Crataegus intricata* Lange (138) (1923)

Russet pear - *Malus coronaria* (L.) Mill. var. *coronaria* (19) (1840)

Russet sedge - *Carex saxatilis* L. (5) (1913)

Russian alfalfa - *Medicago sativa* L. subsp. *falcata* (L.) Arcang. (82) (1930) IA

Russian barley - *Hordeum vulgare* L. (158) (1900) variety

Russian cactus - *Salsola kali* L. (156) (1923), *Salsola tragus* L. (4, 62, 75, 158) (1894-1913)

Russian cedar - *Pinus cembra* L. (107) (1919)

Russian centaurea - *Rhaponticum repens* (L.) Hidalgo (155) (1942)

Russian grass [Russia grass] - *Glyceria fluitans* (L.) R. Br. (5) (1913)

Russian knapweed - *Rhaponticum repens* (L.) Hidalgo (3, 4) (1977-1986)

Russian leafy spurge - *Euphorbia esula* L. var. *uralensis* (Fisch. ex Link) Dorn (50) (present)

Russian millet - *Panicum miliaceum* L. (32) (1895) Neb

Russian mulberry - *Morus alba* L. (95, 109, 112, 122, 124, 135, 138, 155) (1910-1949)

Russian mustard - *Brassica juncea* (L.) Czern. (157, 158) (1900-1929)

Russian oleaster - *Elaeagnus angustifolia* L. (82) (1930)

Russian olive [Russian-olive, Russianolive] - *Elaeagnus angustifolia* L. (3, 4, 50, 82, 85, 93, 106, 112, 135, 137, 138, 155) (1910–present)

Russian pea-shrub - *Caragana frutex* (L.) K. Koch (138) (1923)

Russian pigweed - *Axyris amaranthoides* L. (3, 4, 50, 155) (1942–present)

Russian seeds [Russia seeds] - *Glyceria fluitans* (L.) R. Br. (92) (1876)

Russian thistle [Russianthistle] - *Salsola kali* L. (5, 75, 156) (1894-1923), *Salsola* L. (1, 50, 155) (1932–present), *Salsola tragus* L. (3, 4, 5, 21, 37, 50, 62, 72, 75, 80, 85, 93, 95, 97, 125, 126, 131, 145, 146, 157, 158) (1893–present)

Russian wild olive - *Elaeagnus angustifolia* L. (153) (1913)

Russian wild rye [Russian wildrye] - *Psathyrostachys juncea* (Fisch.) Nevski (3, 50) (1977–present)

Russian wormwood - *Artemisia gmelinii* Webb ex Stechmann (109, 137, 155) (1931-1949)

Rusty andromeda - *Lyonia ferruginea* (Walt.) Nutt. (possibly) (165) (1807)

Rusty blackhaw - *Viburnum rufidulum* Raf. (50) (present)

Rusty blackhaw viburnum - *Viburnum rufidulum* Raf. (155) (1924)

Rusty cotton-grass [Rusty cotton grass] - *Eriophorum virginicum* L. (66) (1903)

Rusty fig - *Ficus rubiginosa* Desf. (138) (1923)

Rusty globe-mallow [Rusty globemallow] - *Sphaeralcea angustifolia* (Cav.) G. Don (50) (present)

Rusty lupine - *Lupinus pusillus* Pursh (4, 50, 155) (1942–present), *Lupinus sericeus* Pursh subsp. *sericeus* var. *sericeus* (50) (present)

Rusty woodsia - *Woodsia ilvensis* (L.) R. Br. (4, 50, 72, 109, 138, 155) (1907–present)

Rusty-leaf beech [Rusty-leaved beech] - *Fagus grandifolia* Ehrh. (14) (1882)

Ruta - *Ruta graveolens* L. (57) (1917)

Rutabaga [Ruta-baga] - *Brassica* L. (107) (1919), *Brassica napus L.* (109) (1949), *Brassica rapa* L. (7) (1828), *Brassica rapa* L. var. *rapa* (15, 82, 85, 107, 138, 156) (1895–1932)

Rutilo colore - *Diospyros virginiana* L. (46) (1879)

Rutland beauty [Rutland-beauty] - *Calystegia sepium* (L.) R. Br. subsp. *sepium* (5, 73, 77, 109, 156, 158) (1892-1949)

Rverchon's blazingstar - *Mentzelia reverchonii* (Urban & Gilg) Thomps. & Zavortink (50) (present)

Rydberg's arnica - *Arnica rydbergii* Greene (50) (present)

Rydberg's clover [Rydberg clover] - *Trifolium longipes* Nutt. subsp. *reflexum* (A. Nels.) J. Gillett (146) (1939)

Rydberg's cottonwood - *Populus* ×*acuminata* Rydb. [*angustifolia* × *deltoides*] (130) (1895)

Rydberg's Joe-pye weed - *Eupatoriadelphus maculatus* (L.) King & H. Rob. var. *bruneri* (A. Gray) King & H. Rob. (72) (1907)

Rydberg's sunflower - *Helianthus nuttallii* Torr. & Gray subsp. *rydbergii* (Britton) Long (50) (present)

Rydberg's violet - *Viola canadensis* L. var. *rugulosa* (Greene) A.S. Hitchc. (5) (1913)

Rydberg's wild rye [Rydberg's wildrye] - *Elymus vulpinus* Rydb. (5, 50) (1913–present)

Rye - *Secale cereale* L. (7, 56, 85, 92, 107, 109, 110, 122, 138, 140, 155, 158, 178, 179) (1526-1949), *Secale* L. (50, 138, 155, 158, 184) (1793–present)

Rye brome - *Bromus secalinus* L. (50) (present)

Rye grass [Rye-grass, Ryegrass] - *Elymus canadensis* L. (88) (1885), *Elymus* L. (1, 10) (1818-1932), *Elymus repens* (L.) Gould (45) (1896), *Elymus trachycaulus* (Link) Gould ex Shinners subsp. *trachycaulus* (93) (1936), *Leymus condensatus* (J. Presl) A. Löve (101, 157) (1900-1905), *Lolium* L. (1, 50, 93, 109, 155, 158) (1900–present), *Lolium perenne* L. (5, 72, 87, 88, 90, 92, 94, 119) (1884-1938), *Secale cereale* L. (92) (1876)

Ryll-togh - *Juncus articulatus* L. (46) (1879)

Rys - *Oryza sativa* L. (178, 179) (1526-1596)

Rys (German) - *Oryza sativa* L. (180) (1633)

Rysshe - *Cyperus* L. (178, 179) (1526-1596)

Rysshe - *Juncus* L. (178, 179) (1526-1596)

Rzedfew (Bohemian) - *Raphanus sativus* L. (180) (1633)

S

S. Barbaeren kraut (Germanes) - *Barbarea vulgaris* W.T. Aiton (possibly) (180) (1633)

Sabal - *Serenoa repens* (Bartr.) Small (55, 57, 59) (1911-1917)

Sabdarissa - *Hibiscus sabdariffa* L. (178) (1526)

Sabina - *Juniperus monosperma* (Engelm.) Sarg. (153) (1913) NM, *Juniperus sabina* L. (55, 57, 59) (1911-1917)

Sabine's pine - *Pinus sabiniana* Dougl. ex Dougl. (20, 147, 161) (1856-1857)

Sabine's pleuropogon - *Pleuropogon sabinei* R. Br. (5) (1913)

Sabino tree - *Taxodium distichum* (L.) L.C. Rich. (5) (1913)

Sabot de Venus Jaune (French) - *Cypripedium parviflorum* Salisb. var. *parviflorum* (7) (1828), *Cypripedium parviflorum* Salisb. var. *pubescens* (Willd.) Knight (6) (1892)

Šabu-min (Chippewa) - *Ribes rubrum* L. (105) (1932)

Sacacomis - *Arctostaphylos uva-ursi* (L.) Spreng. (101) (1905) MT

Sacacommé - *Arctostaphylos uva-ursi* (L.) Spreng. (35) (1806)

Sacahuiste - *Nolina texana* S. Wats. (122) (1937) TX

Sacaline - *Polygonum sachalinense* F. Schmidt ex Maxim. (109, 138) (1923-1949)

Sacaton [Saccaton, Saccatone] - *Sporobolus wrightii* Munro ex Scribn. (45, 94, 122, 149, 152, 163) (1852-1937) NM TX

Saccharum - *Saccharum officinarum* L. (59) (1911)

Säckelkraut (German) - *Capsella bursa-pastoris* (L.) Medik. (158) (1900)

Sacquenummener (Roanoke) - *Orontium aquaticum* L. (46) (1879)

Sacred bark - *Frangula purshiana* (DC.) Cooper (49, 52, 53, 54, 55, 59) (1905-1922)

Sacred bean - *Nelumbo nucifera* Gaertn. (possibly) (5) (1913)

Sacred bo tree - *Ficus religiosa* L. (138) (1923)

Sacred datura - *Datura inoxia* P. Mill. (138, 155) (1923-1942)

Sacred fig - *Ficus religiosa* L. (107) (1919)

Sacred mustard - *Nicotiana glauca* Graham (122, 124) (1937) TX

Sacred thorn-apple - *Datura wrightii* Regel (50) (present)

Saddle flower - *Darlingtonia californica* Torr. (92) (1876)

Saddle plant - *Sarracenia purpurea* L. (92) (1876)

Saddle tree [Saddle-tree] - *Liriodendron tulipifera* L. (5, 156) (1913-1923)

Saddle-leaf [Saddle leaf] - *Liriodendron tulipifera* L. (5, 156) (1913-1923)

Saff - *Salix* L. (158) (1900)

Safflower - *Carthamus* L. (1, 4, 158) (1900-1986)

Saffron of the spring - *Crocus angustifolia* Weston (178) (1596)

Sagara (Basque) - *Malus sylvestris* Mill. (110) (1886)

Sage - *Salvia* L. (1, 2, 4, 7, 10, 50, 82, 93, 106, 109, 138, 155, 156, 158, 184) (1793–present), *Salvia nemorosa* L. (4) (1986), *Salvia officinalis* L. (19, 46, 49, 53, 55, 57, 59, 61, 92, 107, 109) (1671-1949)

Sage grass [Sage-grass] - *Schizachyrium* Nees (152) (1912) NM

Sage plant - *Artemisia tridentata* Nutt. (14) (1882)

Sage tree [Sagetree] - *Lantana camara* L. (92) (1876), *Lantana involucrata* L. (77) (1898) Florida Keys, *Lantana* L. (7) (1828)

Sage willow [Sage-willow] - *Salix candida* Flueggé ex Willd. (5, 85, 93, 155) (1913-1942)

Sagebrush [Sage brush, Sage-brush] - *Artemisia dracunculus* L. (85, 124) (1932-1937), *Artemisia filifolia* Torr. (96) (1891), *Artemisia frigida* Willd. (101) (1905), *Artemisia* L. (1, 50, 108, 155, 158) (1878–present), *Artemisia ludoviciana* Nutt. (85) (1932), *Artemisia tridentata* Nutt. (5, 57, 75, 101, 109, 113, 130, 138, 156, 157, 158) (1890-1949), *Artemisia dracunculus* L. (133) (1903), *Artemisia frigida* Willd. (6, 158) (1892-1900), *Artemisia ludoviciana* Nutt. (158) (1900)

Sagebrush [Sage-brush, Sage brush] - *Artemisia campestris* L. subsp. *borealis* (Pallas) Hall & Clements (85) (1932)

Sagebrush buttercup - *Ranunculus glaberrimus* Hook. (50, 155) (1942–present)

Sagebrush stemless acaulis - *Tetraneuris acaulis* (Pursh) Greene var. *acaulis* (1, 138, 155, 158) (1900-1942)

Sagebrush violet - *Viola vallicola* A. Nels. (50, 146) (1939–present)

Sagebush [Sage bush, Sage-bush] - *Artemisia cana* Pursh (36) (1830), *Artemisia cana* Pursh (5, 36, 97) (1913-1937), *Artemisia tridentata* Nutt. (3, 4, 5, 10, 40, 45, 48, 63, 80, 82, 97, 106 109, 124, 131, 156, 157, 158, 187, 190) (1818-1986), *Atriplex canescens* (Pursh) Nutt. (2, 5, 21, 50, 138, 155, 158) (1900–present)

Sage-leaf mullein [Sage leaf mullein] - *Phlomis tuberosa* L. (92, 158, 156) (1898-1923)

Sage-leaf mullen - *Phlomis tuberosa* L. (5) (1913)

Sage-leaf willow [Sageleaf willow] - *Salix candida* Flueggé ex Willd. (50) (present), *Salix candida* Flueggé ex Willd. (2, 5, 50, 138) (1895–present)

Sage-like hedge-nettle [Sage-like hedge nettle] - *Stachys nuttallii* Shuttlw. ex Benth. (5) (1913)

Sage-of-Bethlehem - *Mentha spicata* L. (5, 156, 158) (1900-1923)

Sageplant [Sage plant] - *Artemisia tridentata* Nutt. (14, 179) (1526-1882)

Sage-willow [Sage willow] - *Lythrum salicaria* L. (92, 156, 158) (1898-1923)

Sagewood [Sage wood, sage-wood] - *Artemisia tridentata* Nutt. (5, 156, 157) (1900-1929)

Sagewort wormwood - *Artemisia campestris* L. (155) (1942), *Artemisia campestris* L. (177) (1762)

Sago (Utah Indians) - *Calochortus luteus* Dougl. ex Lindl. (103) (1871)

Sago cycad - *Zamia pumila* L. (107) (1919)

Sago cycas - *Cycas revoluta* Thunb. (138) (1923)

Sago lily - *Calochortus* Pursh. (1, 93, 190) (~1759-1936) Native Americans called roots "sego"

Sago pondweed [Sago pond-weed] - *Stuckenia pectinatus* (L.) Boerner (3, 50, 85, 156) (1923–present)

Sago-palm - *Cycas revoluta* Thunb. (109) (1949)

Saguaro - *Carnegia gigantea* (Engelm.) Britt. & Rose (106, 109, 155) (1930-1949)

Sahe - *Phaseolus vulgaris* L. (46, 107) (1879-1919) St Lawrence River

Sa-hi (Omaha-Ponca) - *Schoenoplectus tabernaemontani* (K.C. Gmel.) Palla (37) (1830)

Šahijela tatiŋpsiŋla (Lakota, Cheyenne turnip) - *Lomatium orientale* Coult & Rose (121) (1918?-1970?)

Sahpakskiisu (Pawnee, skull nut) - *Carya ovata* (Mill.) K. Koch (37) (1919)

Sahtaku (Pawnee) - *Juglans nigra* L. (37) (1919)

Sahu - *Phaseolus vulgaris* L. (107) (1919)

Sahuaro [Sahauro] - *Carnegia gigantea* (Engelm.) Britt. & Rose (9, 106) (1873-1930)

Sahuca bean - *Glycine max* (L.) Merr. (158) (1900)

Sahuco (Spanish) - *Sambucus nigra* L. (158) (1900)

Sailor plant - *Saxifraga stolonifera* Meerb. (92) (1876)

Sailor's-knot [Sailor's knot] - *Geranium maculatum* L. (5, 156, 186) (1814-1923) no longer in use by 1923, *Geranium robertianum* L. (157, 158) (1900-1929)

Sailor's-tobacco [Sailor's tobacco] - *Artemisia vulgaris* L. (156, 157) (1923-1929)

Sainfoin - *Desmodium canadense* (L.) DC. (5) (1913), *Medicago lupulina* L. (5, 156) (1913-1923), *Medicago sativa* L. (5, 110, 156)

(1913-1923), *Onobrychis* Mill. (45, 46, 50, 155) (1879–present), *Onobrychis viciifolia* Scop. (45, 50, 68, 92, 107, 109, 110, 129) (1886–present), *Orbexilum onobrychis* (Nutt.) Rydb. (5) (1913)

Sainfoin psoralea - *Orbexilum onobrychis* (Nutt.) Rydb. (156) (1923)

Saint Jacob's ladder - *Polemonium reptans* L. (82) (1930) IA

Saint Johannis wort [Saynt Johannis wort] - *Hypericum perforatum* L. (179) (1526)

Saint Lucia wood - *Prunus mahaleb* L. (92) (1876)

Saintfoin - *Hedysarum* L. (184) (1793), *Onobrychis viciifolia* Scop. (109) (1949)

Saka thide (Omaha-Ponca, eaten raw) - *Citrullus lanatus* (Thunb.) Matsumura & Nakai (37) (1919), introduced from Africa by Spanish very early, or Gilmore felt they may have been indigenous, as Lewis & Clark and others report that they were grown by natives

Saka yutapi (Dakota Santee) - *Citrullus lanatus* (Thunb.) Matsumura & Nakai (37) (1919)

Sakachera - *Lawsonia inermis* L. (110) (1886)

Sakaki - *Cleyera japonica* Thunb. (109) (1949)

Sakakomi - *Arctostaphylos uva-ursi* (L.) Spreng. (34) (1834)

Sakhalin corktree - *Phellodendron sachalinense* (F. Schmidt) Sargent (138) (1923)

Salad - *Gaultheria shallon* Pursh (75) (1894) CA, *Lactuca sativa* L. (92) (1876)

Salad burnet - *Sanguisorba* L. (1) (1932), *Sanguisorba minor* Scop. subsp. *muricata* (Spach) Nordborg (5, 156, 157, 158) (1900–1929)

Salad chervil [Saladchervil - *Anthriscus cerefolium* (L.) Hoffmann (109, 155) (1942-1949)

Salad tree [Salad-tree, Sallad tree] - *Cercis canadensis* L. (5, 41, 156, 157, 158) (1770–1929), *Cercis* L. (106) (1930)

Salad violet - *Viola palmata* L. (155) (1942)

Saladine - *Chelidonium majus* L. (158) (1900)

Salal [Sallal] - *Gaultheria shallon* Pursh (33, 106, 107, 138, 160, 161) (1827-1930)

Salem grass [Salem-grass] - *Holcus lanatus* L. (5, 45, 187) (1818-1913)

Salep - *Dactylorhiza* Neck. ex Nevski (possibly) (7) (1828)

Salfern - *Buglossoides arvensis* (L.) I.M. Johnston (157, 158) (1900-1929)

Salfern stoneseed [Salfern-stone seed] - *Buglossoides arvensis* (L.) I.M. Johnston (5, 156) (1913-1923)

Salf-heal - *Prunella vulgaris* L. (1) (1932)

Salghe - *Salix* L. (158) (1900)

Salibrosa goldenrod - *Solidago canadensis* L. var. *salibrosa* (Piper) M.E.Jones (50) (present)

Salicaire (French) - *Lythrum salicaria* L. (158) (1900)

Salicis nigrae - *Salix discolor* Muhl. (55) (1911)

Saligot - *Trapa natans* L. (107) (1919)

Saline aster - *Symphyotrichum tenuifolium* (L.) Nesom (155) (1942)

Saline plantain - *Plantago eriopoda* Torr. (5, 93, 95, 131) (1899–1936)

Saline saltbush - *Atriplex subspicata* (Nutt.) Rydb. (50) (present)

Sallow - *Salix caprea* L. (109) (1949), *Salix* L. (158) (1900)

Sallow sedge - *Carex lurida* Wahl. (5, 50) (1913–present)

Sallow thorn [Sallow-thorn] - *Hippophae* L. (8) (1785)

Sally - *Salix* L. (158) (1900)

Sally-bloom [Sally bloom] - *Chamerion angustifolium* (L.) Holub subsp. *angustifolium* (76, 156) (1896–1923)

Salmonberry [Salmon berry, Salmon-berry] - *Rubus parviflorus* Nutt. (5, 82, 85, 106, 130, 131, 158) (1895-1932), *Rubus* L. (1) (1932), *Rubus chamaemorus* L. (107) (1919), *Rubus spectabilis* Pursh (76, 103, 106, 107, 160, 161) (1857-1930), *Rubus ursinus* Cham. & Schlecht. (107) (1919)

Salomon's seal - *Maianthemum racemosum* (L.) Link subsp. *racemosum* (46) (1671)

Saloop - *Sassafras albidum* (Nutt.) Nees (5, 92, 156, 158) (1876-1923)

Salpiglossis - *Salpiglossis* K. Koch (138) (1923) Greek for tube and tongue alluding to the form of the corolla and appearance of the style

Salsafy - *Tragopogon porrifolius* L. (19, 92, 158) (1840-1900)

Salsepareille (French) - *Smilax* L. (8) (1785)

Salsepareille à feuilles ciliées (French) - *Smilax bona-nox* L. (8) (1785)

Salsepareille à feuilles de laurier (French) - *Smilax laurifolia* L. (8) (1785)

Salsepareille à feuilles de tamnus (French) - *Smilax tamnoides* L. (8) (1785)

Salsepareille à feuilles rondes (French) - *Smilax rotundifolia* L. (8) (1785)

Salsepareille à racines rouges (French) - *Smilax pseudochina* L. (8) (1785)

Salsepareille de Virginie (French) - *Smilax glauca* Walt. (8) (1785)

Salsepareille lancéolée (French) - *Smilax smallii* Morong (8) (1785)

Salsepareille qui perd ses feuilles (French) - *Smilax rotundifolia* L. (8) (1785)

Salsify - *Tragopogon* L. (1, 4, 155, 158) (1900-1986), *Tragopogon porrifolius* L. (3, 4, 5, 50, 95, 97, 107, 109, 110, 156, 158) (1886–present), *Tragopogon pratensis* L. (146) (1939)

Salt cedar - *Tamarix parviflora* DC. (3, 4) (1977-1986)

Salt globe-pea [Salt globepea] - *Sphaerophysa salsula* (Pallas) DC. (155) (1942)

Salt grass [Saltgrass, Salt-grass] - *Distichlis* Raf. (1, 50, 93) (1932–present), *Distichlis spicata* (L.) Greene (5, 11, 75, 85, 87, 90, 111, 116, 119, 121, 129, 134, 144, 146, 151, 163) (1852-1939), *Leptochloa panicea* (Retz.) Ohwi subsp. *brachiata* (Steudl.) N. Snow (5, 119) (1913-1938), *Spartina patens* (Ait.) Muhl. (87, 88, 90) (1884-1885), *Sporobolus airoides* (Torr.) Torr. (5, 87, 119, 151) (1885-1938)

Salt heliotrope - *Heliotropium curassavicum* L. var. *curassavicum* (50, 155) (1942–present)

Salt lyme grass [Salt lyme-grass] - *Leymus simplex* (Scribn. & Williams) D.R. Dewey (94) (1901)

Salt meadow diplachne - *Leptochloa fusca* (L.) Kunth subsp. *fascicularis* (Lam.) N. Snow (155) (1942), *Leptochloa fusca* (L.) Kunth subsp. *fascicularis* (Lam.) N. Snow (5, 72) (1907-1913)

Salt meadow grass [Salt meadow-grass] - *Leptochloa fusca* (L.) Kunth subsp. *fascicularis* (Lam.) N. Snow (163) (1852)

Salt reed grass [Salt reed-grass] - *Spartina cynosuroides* (L.) Roth (45, 66, 88, 94, 163) (1852-1903)

Salt rheumweed [Salt rheum weed] - *Chelone glabra* L. (5, 6, 49, 92, 156) (1876-1923)

Salt rock moss - *Chondrus crispus* (L.) J. Stackhouse (92) (1876)

Salt sage - *Atriplex nuttallii* S. Wats. (3) (1977), *Iva* L. (1, 93) (1932-1936)

Salt sand spurry [Salt sandspurry] - *Spergularia salina* J.& K. Presl (50) (present), *Spergularia rubra* (L.) J.& K. Presl (50) (present)

Salt sedge - *Carex hassei* Bailey (50) (present)

Salt spring checkerbloom - *Sidalcea neomexicana* Gray (50) (present), *Sidalcea neomexicana* Gray subsp. *neomexicana* (50) (present)

Salt tree [Salt-tree] - *Halimodendron* Fischer ex DC. (138) (1923), *Halimodendron halodendron* (L. f.) Voss (138) (1923)

Salt-and-pepper plant [salt-and-pepper-plant - *Plantago patagonica* Jacq. (5, 156) (1913-1923), *Plantago patagonica* Jacq. (5, 156) (1913-1923)

Saltbush [Salt bush, Salt-bush] - *Atriplex argentea* Nutt. (1) (1932), *Atriplex* L. (4, 50, 93, 109, 141, 146, 148, 138, 153, 155, 158) (1899–present), *Halimodendron* Fischer ex DC. (112) (1937) Neb, *Halimodendron halodendron* (L. f.) Voss (112) (1937) Neb

Salt-cedar [Salt cedar, Saltcedar] - *Tamarix* L. (4, 122) (1937-1986), *Tamarix ramosissima* Ledeb. (3, 4, 50) (1977–present), *Monanthochloe littoralis* Engelm. (94, 163) (1852-1901), *Tamarix gallica* L. (106, 122, 124, 153) (1913-1937)

Salt-cedar grass [Salt cedar grass] - *Monanthochloe littoralis* Engelm. (122) (1937)

Saltflat heliotrope [Salt flat heliotrope] - *Heliotropium convolvulaceum* (Nutt.) Gray (124) (1937) TX

Salt-grape [Salt grape, Saltgrape] - *Salsola kali* L. (5, 156, 158) (1900-1923)

Salt-lover [Saltlover] - *Halogeton* C.A. Mey. (50) (present), *Halogeton glomeratus* (Bieb.) C.A. Mey. (50) (present)

Saltmarsh agalinis [Salt marsh agalinis] - *Agalinis maritima* (Raf.) Raf. (5) (1913)

Saltmarsh alkali grass [Saltmarsh alkaligrass] - *Puccinellia fasciculata* (Torr.) Bicknell (50) (present)

Salt-marsh aster [Saltmarsh aster] - *Symphyotrichum divaricatum* (Nutt.) Nesom (4) (1986)

Saltmarsh bulrush [Salt marsh bulrush] - *Schoenoplectus robustus* (Pursh) M.T. Strong (5) (1913)

Saltmarsh cockspur grass [Salt-marsh cockspur grass [Salt-marsh cockspur-grass - *Echinochloa walteri* (Pursh) Nash (5, 56, 72, 163) (1852-1913)

Salt-marsh fleabane [Salt marsh fleabane] - *Pluchea camphorata* (L.) DC. (5, 122, 134, 156) (1913-1937)

Saltmarsh gerardia [Salt marsh gerardia] - *Agalinis maritima* (Raf.) Raf. var. *grandiflora* (Benth.) Shinners (122, 156) (1923-1937)

Saltmarsh goldenrod [Salt-marsh golden-rod, Salt-marsh goldenrod] - *Solidago sempervirens* L. (5, 156) (1913-1923)

Saltmarsh grass [Salt marsh grass] - *Spartina maritima* (M.A. Curtis) Fern. (5, 45, 66, 90, 92) (1876-1912), *Spartina patens* (Ait.) Muhl. (5) (1913), *Spartina alterniflora* Loisel. (163) (1852)

Salt-marsh sand spurry [Salt marsh sand spurrey, Saltmarsh sand-spurry] - *Spergularia salina* J.& K. Presl (4, 5, 155, 156) (1913-1986)

Saltmarsh water-hemp [Salt marsh water hemp, Salt-marsh water-hemp] - *Amaranthus cannabinus* (L.) Sauer (5, 156) (1913-1923)

Saltmarsh wild rye [Salt marsh wild rye] - *Elymus virginicus* L. var. *halophilus* (Bickn.) Wieg. (5) (1913)

Salt-meadow cord grass [Salt meadow cordgrass] - *Spartina patens* (Ait.) Muhl. (50) (present), *Spartina pectinata* Bosc ex Link (122) (1937)

Salt-meadow grass [Salt meadow grass, Salt meadow-grass] - *Leptochloa fusca* (L.) Kunth subsp. *fascicularis* (Lam.) N. Snow (163) (1852), *Spartina patens* (Ait.) Muhl. (5) (1913)

Salt-meadow rush [Saltmeadow rush] - *Juncus gerardi* Lois. (138, 155) (1923-1942), *Juncus gerardi* Lois. (50, 155) (1942–present)

Saltsage [Salt-sage] - *Atriplex* L. (141) (1899) WY

Salt-water mustard [Salt water mustard] - *Cakile geniculata* (B.L. Robins.) Millsp. (122) (1937) TX

Saltweed [Salt weed, Salt-weed] - *Juncus bufonius* L. (5, 156) (1913-1923), *Atriplex argentea* Nutt. (5, 97, 145, 156) (1897-1937)

Saltwort [Salt wort, Salt woort] - *Salicornia* L. (158) (1900), *Salsola* L. (1, 2, 10, 93, 158) (1818-1936), *Salicornia maritima* Wolff & Jefferies (92, 107, 178) (1526-1919), *Salicornia rubra* A. Nels. (3, 4) (1977-1986), *Salsola kali* L. (5, 19, 72, 158, 187) (1818-1907)

Salve bark - *Ulmus rubra* Muhl. (59) (1787)

Salvia - *Salvia* L. (158) (1900), *Salvia officinalis* L. (55, 107) (1911-1919) from ancient Latin, *Salvia pratensis* L. (82) (1930)

Salvia rockrose - *Cistus salvifolius* L. (138) (1923)

Salvinia - *Salvinia natans* (L.) All. (5) (1913), *Salvinia* Séguier (109, 138) (1923-1949) for Antonido Maria Salvini, 1623-1729, professor in Florence Italy

Saman - *Samanea saman* (Jacq.) Merr. (107, 109) (1919-1949)

Sambucus - *Sambucus nigra* L. subsp. *canadensis* (L.) R. Bolli (57) (1917)

Samita - *Ribes* L. (103) (1870) NM

Samolus - *Samolus valerandi* L. subsp. *parviflorus* (Raf.) Hultén (3) (1977)

Samolus valerandi - *Samolus valerandi* L. (50) (present)

Samphire - *Salicornia* L. (1, 2, 7, 93) (1828-1936), *Salicornia maritima* Wolff & Jefferies (19, 92) (1840-1876)

Sampson root - *Gentiana alba* Muhl. ex Nutt. (92) (1876)

Sampson snakeroot [Sampson snake root] - *Gentiana alba* Muhl. ex Nutt. (49, 92) (1876–1898)

Sampson-root - *Echinacea angustifolia* DC. var. *angustifolia* (64, 156) (1908-1923)

Sampson's snakeroot - *Gentiana andrewsii* Griseb. (156) (1923)

Samson's snakeroot [Sampson snakeroot, Samson snake-root] - *Gentiana saponaria* L. (156) (1923), *Gentiana saponaria* L. var. *saponaria* (5) (1913), *Gentiana villosa* L. (5, 156) (1913-1923), *Orbexilum pedunculatum* (P. Mill.) Rydb. (49) (1898), *Orbexilum pedunculatum* (P. Mill.) Rydb. var. *pedunculatum* (3, 4, 50) (1977–present)

San Diego ceanothus - *Ceanothus cyaneus* Eastw. (109) (1949)

San Gabriel aster [SanGabriel aster] - *Symphyotrichum greatae* (Parish) G.L. Nesom (155) (1942)

San Miguelito - *Antigonon leptopus* Hook. & Arn. (106) (1930)

Sanctuary - *Centaurium erythraea* Raf. (5, 156) (1913-1923) no longer in use by 1923

Sand adder's-tongue [Sand adder's tongue] - *Ophioglossum vulgatum* L. (5) (1913)

Sand bar - *Cenchrus tribuloides* L. (78) (1898) TX

Sand bells - *Nama hispidum* Gray (97, 122) (1937)

Sand bittercress [Sand bitter cress] - *Cardamine parviflora* L. (50) (present)

Sand blackberry - *Rubus cuneifolius* Pursh (2, 5, 76, 107, 138, 156) (1895-1923)

Sand blackjack oak - *Quercus laevis* Walt. (138) (1923)

Sand blue grass [Sand blue-grass] - *Poa secunda* J. Presl (94) (1901)

Sand blue-eyed grass - *Sisyrinchium fuscatum* Bickn. (5) (1913)

Sand bluestem [Sand blue-stem] - *Andropogon hallii* Hack. (3, 50, 140, 155) (1942–present)

Sand briar [Sand-briar, Sand brier] - *Solanum carolinense* L. (5, 49, 53, 62, 75, 156) (1898-1923)

Sand broom-sedge [Sand broom sedge] - *Schizachyrium maritimum* (Chapman) Nash (94) (1901)

Sand bur [Sand burr, Sandbur, Sand-bur] - *Cenchrus tribuloides* L. (5, 11, 56, 62, 73, 80, 94, 111, 131, 148, 150, 152) (1888-1939), *Ambrosia acanthicarpa* Hook. (5, 75) (1894-1913), *Solanum rostratum* Dunal (5, 63, 72, 93, 156, 158) (1899-1936)

Sand cactus - *Opuntia arenaria* Engelm. (138) (1923)

Sand cherry [Sand cherry] - *Prunus pumila* L. (1, 2, 5, 50, 74, 82, 106, 107, 109, 113, 130, 135, 138, 155, 156, 158) (1890–present), *Amelanchier canadensis* (L.) Medik. (5, 74, 93, 156, 158) (1893–1936) MT

Sand chickasaw plum - *Prunus angustifolia* Marsh. var. *watsonii* (Sargent) Waugh (155) (1942)

Sand dropseed [Sand drop-seed] - *Sporobolus cryptandrus* (Torr.) Gray (3, 50, 93, 99, 115, 116, 119, 122, 134, 140, 155) (1923–present)

Sand dune sandmat [Sanddune sandmat] - *Chamaesyce carunculata* (Waterfall) Shinners (50) (present)

Sand erysimum - *Erysimum inconspicuum* (S. Wats.) MacM. (131) (1899)

Sand grape - *Vitis rupestris* Scheele (2, 3, 4, 5, 15, 50, 74, 82, 97, 107, 138, 155, 156) (1893–present)

Sand grass [Sand-grass, Sandgrass] - *Achnatherum hymenoides* (Roemer & J. A. Schultes) Barkworth (4, 5, 50, 72, 146) (1907–present), *Ammophila arenaria* (L.) Link (45, 88) (1885–1896), *Andropogon hallii* Hack. (144) (1899) KS, *Calamagrostis canadensis* (Michx.) Beauv. var. *macouniana* (Vasey) Stebbins (68, 155) (1890–1942), *Calamagrostis lapponica* (Wahlenb.) Hartman (129) (1894), *Calamovilfa* (Gray) Hack. ex Scribn. & Southworth (1, 93) (1932–1936), *Calamovilfa longifolia* (Hook.) Scribn. (56, 75, 116, 140) (1894–1944), *Redfieldia* Vasey (2) (1895), *Triplasis* Beauv. (1, 50, 155) (1932–present), *Triplasis purpurea* (Walt.) Chapman (3, 56, 66, 72, 87, 92, 93, 111, 163) (1852–1977)

Sand hedge-nettle [Sand hedge nettle] - *Stachys pilosa* Nutt. var. *arenicola* (Britton) G. Mulligan & D. Munro (5) (1913)

Sand Hills muhly [Sandhills muhly, Sandhill muhly] - *Muhlenbergia pungens* Thurb. (50, 140, 155) (1942–present)

Sand jack - *Quercus incana* Bartr. (122) (1937) TX

Sand jack oak - *Quercus phellos* L. (5) (1913)

Sand knot-grass - *Paspalum vaginatum* Sw. (163) (1852)

Sand lily [Sand-lily] - *Leucocrinum montanum* Nutt. ex Gray (93, 157) (1929-1936), *Leucocrinum* Nutt. ex Gray (109) (1949)

Sand love grass [Sand lovegrass] - *Eragrostis trichodes* (Nutt.) Wood (3, 50, 155) (1942–present)

Sand milkweed - *Asclepias arenaria* Torr. (3, 4, 5, 50, 93, 97, 122) (1913–present)

Sand muhly - *Muhlenbergia arenicola* Buckl. (3, 50, 155) (1942–present), *Muhlenbergia pungens* Thurb. (3) (1977)

Sand myrtle - *Leiophyllum buxifolium* (Berg.) Ell. (19, 156) (1840-1923), *Leiophyllum* Hedw. f. (2, 156) (1895-1942)

Sand onion - *Allium canadense* L. var. *mobilense* (Regal) Ownbey (97) (1937) OK

Sand orache - *Atriplex cristata* Humb. & Bonpl. ex Willd. (19) (1840)

Sand palm - *Sabal* Adans. (7) (1828)

Sand paspalum - *Paspalum setaceum* Michx. (155) (1942)

Sand phlox - *Phlox bifida* Beck (109, 156) (1923-1949)

Sand plantain - *Plantago psyllium* L. (5, 50) (1913–present)

Sand plum - *Prunus angustifolia* Marsh. var. *watsonii* (Sargent) Waugh (109, 137, 138) (1923-1949), *Prunus maritima* Marsh. (possibly) (5, 92, 156) (1876-1923), *Prunus texana* F.G. Dietr. (124) (1937) TX

Sand puffs - *Abronia* Juss. (1) (1932)

Sand raspberry - *Rubus cuneifolius* Pursh (72) (1907)

Sand reed - *Ammophila arenaria* (L.) Link (41, 67) (1770-1890)

Sand reed grass [Sand reed-grass] - *Calamovilfa longifolia* (Hook.) Scribn. (115, 116) (1932-1958)

Sand reverchonia - *Reverchonia arenaria* Gray (50) (present)

Sand rocket - *Diplotaxis muralis* (L.) DC. (3, 4, 5, 85, 156, 158) (1900-1986)

Sand rush grass [Sand rushgrass, Sand rush-grass] - *Sporobolus cryptandrus* (Torr.) Gray (56, 94, 134, 140) (1901-1944)

Sand rye grass [Sand ryegrass] - *Leymus arenarius* (L.) Hochst. (50) (present)

Sand sage - *Artemisia filifolia* Torr. (65) (1931)

Sand sagebrush - *Artemisia filifolia* Torr. (3, 4, 50, 156) (1923–present)

Sand sedge - *Carex arenaria* L. (5, 50, 156) (1913–present)

Sand spike-rush [Sand spikerush] - *Eleocharis montevidensis* Kunth (50) (present)

Sand spike-sedge [Sand spikesedge] - *Eleocharis montevidensis* Kunth (139) (1944)

Sand spurry [Sandspurry, Sand-spurrey, Sand spurrey] - *Spergularia* (Pers.) J.& K. Presl (50, 155) (1942–present), *Spergularia canadensis* (Pers.) G. Don (1) (1932), *Spergularia rubra* (L.) J.& K. Presl (5, 49, 156) (1898-1923)

Sand sunflower - *Helianthus debilis* Nutt. subsp. *cucumerifolius* (Torr. & Gray) Heiser (124) (1937) TX, *Helianthus petiolaris* Nutt (127) (1933)

Sand tick trefoil - *Desmodium lineatum* DC. (5) (1913)

Sand violet - *Viola adunca* J. E. Sm. var. *adunca* (5, 85) (1913-1932), *Viola affinis* Le Conte (50) (present), *Viola pedata* L. (5, 74, 156, 158) (1893-1923) CT, *Viola sagittata* Aiton (5, 156) (1913-1923)

Sandal bead tree [Sandal beadtree] - *Adenanthera pavonina* L. (155) (1942)

Sand-bar love grass [Sandbar lovegrass] - *Eragrostis frankii* C.A. Mey. ex Steud. (3, 50, 155) (1942–present)

Sandbar willow [Sand bar willow, Sand-bar willow] - *Salix exigua* Nutt. (1, 4) (1932-1986), *Salix interior* Rowlee (1, 4, 5, 22, 47, 50, 65, 72, 82, 85, 93, 95, 97, 105, 112, 113, 130, 131, 155, 156, 158) (1852–present)

Sand-barren puccoon - *Lithospermum caroliniense* (Walt. ex J.F. Gmel.) MacM. (156) (1923)

Sand-beach grape - *Vitis rupestris* Scheele (156) (1923)

Sandberg's birch - *Betula ×sandbergii* Britt. [*papyrifera × pumila*] (5) (1913)

Sandberg's blue grass [Sandberg bluegrass] - *Poa canbyi* (Scribn.) Piper (50) (present), *Poa secunda* J. Presl (50) (present)

Sandbox tree - *Hura crepitans* L. (7, 92, 138) (1828-1923)

Sandbur [Sand bur, Sand-bur] - *Cenchrus* L. (1, 50, 93, 122, 155, 163) (1852–present), *Cenchrus spinifex* Cav. (85, 119, 163) (1852-1938), *Cenchrus tribuloides* L. (145) (1897), *Tribulus terrestris* L. (156) (1923)

Sand-daisy - *Aphanostephus ramosissimus* DC. (97) (1937) OK

Sand-dune cryptantha [Sanddune cryptantha] - *Cryptantha fendleri* (Gray) Greene (50) (present), Cryptantha fendleri (Gray) Greene (50) (present)

Sand-dune sandbur [Sanddune sandbur] - *Cenchrus tribuloides* L. (50) (present)

Sand-dune wallflower [Sanddune wallflower] - *Erysimum capitatum* (Dougl. ex Hook.) Greene (50) (present), *Erysimum capitatum* (Dougl. ex Hook.) Greene var. *capitatum* (50) (present), *Erysimum capitatum* (Dougl. ex Hook.) Greene var. *capitatum* (5, 64, 156, 157, 158) (1900–1929)

Sand-foin - *Onobrychis* Mill. (1) (1932), *Onobrychis viciifolia* Scop. (85) (1932) SD

Sand-food [Sand food] - *Pholisma sonorae* (Torr. ex Gray) Yatskievych (103, 104) (1870-1896)

Sand-grass [Sand grass] - *Polygonella articulata* (L.) Meisn. (5, 75, 156) (1894-1923) Wellfleet MA

Sandhill amaranth - *Amaranthus arenicola* I.M. Johnston (50) (present)

Sand-hill bluestem [Sand-hill blue-stem] - *Andropogon hallii* Hack. (93) (1936) Neb

Sandhill goosefoot - *Chenopodium cycloides* A. Nels. (3, 4, 50) (1977–present)

Sandhill grape - *Cissus erosa* Rich. (7) (1828)

Sand-hill love grass [Sandhill lovegrass] - *Eragrostis trichodes* (Nutt.) Wood (155) (1942)

Sand-hill plum - *Prunus pumila* L. (103) (1870)

Sandhill sunflower - *Helianthus petiolaris* Nutt (145) (1897)

Sandhill tumbleweed [Sand-hill tumble-weed] - *Cycloloma atriplicifolium* (Spreng.) Coult. (145) (1897)

Sandhill wormwood - *Artemisia pycnocephala* (Less.) DC. (155) (1942)

Sandhills pigweed - *Amaranthus arenicola* I.M. Johnston (4) (1986)

Sand-lily [Sand lily] - *Mentzelia albicaulis* (Dougl. ex Hook.) Dougl. ex Torr. & Gray (101) (1905) MT, *Mentzelia decapetala* (Pursh ex Sims) Urban & Gilg ex Gilg (3) (1977), *Mentzelia* L. (1, 4) (1932-1986)

Sandmat - *Chamaesyce* S.F. Gray (50) (present)

Sand-myrtle [Sandmyrtle] - *Leiophyllum buxifolium* (Berg.) Ell. (92) (1876), *Leiophyllum* Hedw. f. (109, 138) (1923-1949)

Sand-nettle [Sandnettle, Sand nettle] - *Cnidoscolus stimulosus* (Michx.) Engelm. & Gray (5, 92, 156) (1876-1923), *Manihot* Mill. (7) (1828)

Sand-paper starwort [Sandpaper starwort, Sandpaper star-wort] - *Ionactis linariifolius* (L.) Greene (5, 84, 86, 156, 158) (1878-1923)

Sand-parsley [Sand parsley] - *Ammoselinum* Torr. & Gray (1, 4, 50, 158) (1900–present)

Sandpuffs [Sand puffs, Sand-puffs] - *Tripterocalyx* Hook. ex Standl. (1, 4, 50, 85) (1932–present), *Tripterocalyx micranthus* (Torr.) Hook (4) (1986)

Sand-reed [Sandreed] - *Calamovilfa* (Gray) Hack. ex Scribn. & Southworth (50, 155) (1942–present)

Sand-rice [Sand rice] - *Achnatherum* P. Beauv. (1) (1932)

Sand-rush [Sand rush] - *Equisetum hyemale* L. (35) (1806)

Sandspur - *Cenchrus* L. (1) (1932)

Sandspur [Sand spur] - *Cenchrus tribuloides* L. (5, 78) (1898-1913) FLA

Sandstar [Sand star] - *Carex arenaria* L. (5, 156) (1913-1923)

Sand-verbena [Sand verbena, Sandverbena] - *Abronia fragrans* Nutt. ex Hook. (85, 97, 124) (1932-1937), *Abronia* Juss. (1, 4, 50,

93, 109, 155) (1932–present), *Abronia latifolia* Eschsch. (138) (1923)

Sandvine [Sand vine, Sand-vine] - *Cynanchum* L. (4, 158) (1900-1986), *Cynanchum laeve* (Michx.) Pers. (3, 5, 93, 95, 97, 106, 156, 157) (1900-1977)

Sandweed [Sand weed, Sand-weed] - *Spergula arvensis* L. (5, 92, 156, 158) (1876-1923) no longer in use by 1923

Sandwort [Sand wort] - *Moehringia* L. (5) (1913), *Arenaria hookeri* Nutt. (157) (1929), *Arenaria* L. (1, 2, 4, 10, 15, 50, 93, 109, 138, 156, 167, 184) (1793–present), *Arenaria serpyllifolia* L. (85) (1932) SD, *Minuartia* L. (1) (1932), *Minuartia michauxii* (Fenzl) Farw. var. *michauxii* (85) (1932), *Moehringia* L. (50, 93, 158) (1900–present) Neb, *Moehringia lateriflora* (L.) Fenzl (19) (1840)

Sandy-land bluebonnet [Sandy land bluebonnet] - *Lupinus subcarnosus* Hook. (124) (1937)

Sandy-seed clammy-weed [Sandyseed clammyweed] - *Polanisia dodecandra* (L.) DC. subsp. *trachysperma* (Torr. & Gray) Iltis (50) (present)

Sanfoin - *Onobrychis* Mill. (possibly) (158) (1900), *Onobrychis viciifolia* Scop. (66, 158) (1900-1903)

Sang - *Panax quinquefolius* L. (5, 64, 75, 102, 156, 157, 158) (1886-1929) WV

Sang tree [Sang-tree] - *Ptelea trifoliata* L. (56) (1901), *Ptelea trifoliata* L. (156, 158) (1900-1923)

Sanghara-nut - *Trapa natans* L. (156) (1923)

Sangreeroot [Sangree root, Sangree-root] - *Aristolochia serpentaria* L. (5, 64, 92, 156, 158) (1876–1923)

Sangrel - *Aristolochia serpentaria* L. (64, 92, 156, 158) (1898-1923)

Sangrel snakeweed [Sangrel snake weed] - *Aristolochia serpentaria* L. (5) (1913), *Aristolochia serpentaria* L. (5) (1913)

Sanguesa (Spanish) - *Rubus idaeus* L. (158) (1900)

Sanguinaire (French) - *Sanguinaria canadensis* L. (6, 158) (1892-1900)

Sanguinaire du Canada (French) - *Sanguinaria canadensis* L. (7) (1828)

Sanguinaria - *Sanguinaria canadensis* L. (52, 54, 55, 57, 59, 64) (1905-1917)

Sanguinary - *Achillea millefolium* L. (69, 107, 156, 158, 179) (1526-1919), *Polygonum hydropiper* L. (179) (1526)

Sanicle - *Heuchera villosa* Michx. (possibly) (7) (1828), *Sanicula* L. (1, 2, 10, 50, 155, 156, 158, 184) (1793–present), *Sanicula marilandica* L. (7, 19, 48, 49, 58, 61, 72, 156, 157, 157) (1828-1929)

Sanicula - *Dodecatheon meadia* L. (181) (~1678)

Santa Ana Sierra alder [SantaAna Sierra alder] - *Alnus rhombifolia* Nutt. (155) (1942)

Santa Barbara gilia - *Gilia capitata* Sims subsp. *abrotanifolia* (Nutt. ex Greene) V. Grant (138) (1923)

Santa Cruz lily - *Lilium pardalinum* Kellogg subsp. *pardalinum* (138) (1923)

Santa Maria - *Parthenium hysterophorus* L. (3, 4, 5, 97, 124) (1913-1986)

Santa Maria feverfew - *Parthenium hysterophorus* L. (50, 122) (1937–present)

Sanvitalia - *Sanvitalia* Lam. (138) (1923), *Sanvitalia procumbens* Lam. (92) (1876)

Sanwa millet - *Echinochloa frumentacea* Link (56) (1901)

Sap pine - *Pinus rigida* Mill. (10, 19, 20) (1805-1857), *Pinus taeda* L. (5) (1913)

Saparidu kahts (Pawnee, mushroom medicine) - *Echinacea angustifolia* DC. (37) (1919)

Sapin (French) - *Picea abies* (L.) H.Karst. (possibly) (8) (1785)

Sapin argenté (French) - *Abies alba* Mill. (possibly) (158) (1900)

Sapin bractée (French) - *Abies bracteata* (D. Don) D. Don ex Poit. (20) (1857)

Sapin de Douglas (French) - *Pseudotsuga menziesii* (Mirb.) Franco (20) (1857)

Sapin de Frazer (French) - *Abies fraseri* (Pursh) Poir. (20) (1857)

Sapin de Menzies (French) - *Pseudotsuga menziesii* (Mirb.) Franco (20) (1857)

Sapin d'Occident (French) - *Larix occidentalis* Nutt. (20) (1857)

Sapin noble (French) - *Abies procera* Rehd. (20) (1857)

Sapinette à feuilles d'if (French) - *Tsuga canadensis* (L.) Carr. (possibly) (8) (1785)

Sapium - *Sapium* Jacq. (155) (1942)

Sapling pine - *Pinus strobus* L. (20) (1857)

Sapodil - *Manilkara zapota* (L.) van Royen (possibly) (7, 92) (1828-1876)

Sapodilla - *Manilkara zapota* (L.) van Royen (20, 107, 109, 110, 138, 155, 165) (1768-1949)

Sapodilla plum - *Manilkara zapota* (L.) van Royen (possibly) (92) (1876)

Saponaria - *Saponaria officinalis* L. (57, 64, 178, 180) (1596-1917)

Saponaria (Spanish) - *Saponaria officinalis* L. (158) (1900)

Saponaria levantica - *Gypsophila paniculata* L. (57) (1917)

Saponary - *Saponaria officinalis* L. (64, 157, 158, 179) (1526-1907)

Sapota - *Manilkara zapota* (L.) van Royen (107) (1919), *Pouteria sapota* (Jacq.) H.E. Moore & Stearn (109) (1949)

Sapote - *Manilkara zapota* (L.) van Royen (138) (1923)

Sapote-pieto (Mexican) - *Diospyros texana* Scheele (107) (1919)

Sapotillier à feuilles de lieier (French) - *Sideroxylon lycioides* L. (20) (1857)

Sapotillier à feuilles drites (French) - *Sideroxylon celastrinum* (Kunth) T.D. Pennington (20) (1857)

Sapotillier commun (French) - *Manilkara zapota* (L.) van Royen (20) (1857)

Sapotillier tenace (French) - *Sideroxylon tenax* L. (20) (1857)

Sapotillier tres fetide (French) - *Sideroxylon foetidissimum* Jacq. subsp. *foetidissimum* (20) (1857)

Sappan - *Caesalpinia* L. (158) (1900)

Sapphire anemony - *Anemone blanda* Schott & Kotschy (109) (1949)

Sapphire-berry - *Symplocos paniculata* (Thunb.) Miq. (109, 156) (1923-1949)

Sara (Inca) - *Zea mays* L. (107) (1919)

Saracen's-compass [Saracen's compass] - *Senecio jacobea* L. (5, 156) (1913-1923)

Saracen's-corn [Saracen's corn] - *Fagopyrum esculentum* Moench (5, 92, 156, 158) (1876-1923)

Saracen's-wheat [Saracen's wheat] - *Fagopyrum esculentum* Moench (5) (1913)

Sarah - *Trillium undulatum* Willd. (75, 156) (1894-1923)

Sarasena with a large Yellow Flower - *Sarracenia flava* L. (183) (~1756)

Sarazyne mynt (Saracen's-mint) - *Mentha arvensis* L. (179) (1526)

Sardian nut - *Castanea dentata* (Marsh.) Borkh. (5, 156) (1913-1923)

Sarepta mustard - *Brassica juncea* (L.) Czern. (157, 158) (1900-1929)

Sargasso [Sargazo] - *Sargassum natans* (L.) Gaillon (41, 174, 181) (~1678-1770)

Sargent's barberry [Sargent barberry] - *Berberis sargentiana* C.K. Schneid. (138) (1923)

Sargent's cottonwood [Sargent cottonwood] - *Populus deltoides* Bartr. ex Marsh. subsp. *monilifera* (Aiton) Eckenwalder (138) (1923)

Sargent's palm [Sargent palm] - *Pseudophoenix sargentii* H. Wendl. ex Sarg. (138) (1923)

Sargent's weeping hemlock - *Tsuga canadensis* (L.) Carr. (109) (1949)

Sarothra - *Hypericum gentianoides* (L.) Britton, Sterns & Poggenb. (174, 177) (1753-1762)

Sarracenia - *Sarracenia purpurea* L. (61) (1870)

Sarrasin (French) - *Fagopyrum esculentum* Moench (158) (1900)

Sarsaparilla - *Aralia* L. (1, 4, 93) (1932-1986), *Aralia nudicaulis* L. (7, 43, 46, 101, 177) (1607-1905), *Cocculus carolinus* (L.) DC. (156) (1923), *Menispermum canadense* L. (38, 76) (1820-1896)

Parke Co. ID; Sulphur Grove OH, *Smilax glauca* Walt. (5, 8, 46, 187) (1785-1913), *Smilax* L. (7, 57, 158) (1828-1917), *Smilax pseudochina* L. (5) (1913), *Smilax walteri* Pursh. (5) (1913)

Sarsaparilla germanica - *Carex arenaria* L. (57) (1917)

Sarsaparilla vine - *Smilax pumila* Walt. (50) (present)

Sartwell's sedge [Sartwell sedge] - *Carex sartwellii* Dewey (5, 50, 66, 72, 139, 155) (1893–present)

Service - *Amelanchier* Medik. (106) (1930)

Service berry - *Amelanchier alnifolia* (Nutt.) Nutt. ex M. Roemer (101) (1905) MT

Sarza - *Ipomoea pes-caprae* (L.) R. Br. (181) (~1678)

Sasa'bikwan (Chippewa) - *Apocynum androsaemifolium* L. (40) (1928)

Šašabwaksing (Chippewa) - *Eupatorium perfoliatum* L. (105) (1932)

Sasafafarilla - *Aralia nudicaulis* L. (76) (1896) Bath ME

Sasafril - *Aralia nudicaulis* L. (76) (1896) ME

Sasáp-kwanins (Chippewa) - *Apocynum cannabinum* L. (105) (1932)

Sasapril - *Aralia nudicaulis* L. (76) (1896) ME

Sasaunckapamuck (Naraganset) - *Sassafras albidum* (Nutt.) Nees (46) (1879)

Sasemineash - *Vaccinium macrocarpon* Aiton (1, 7, 10, 41, 46, 73, 107, 158, 190) (~1759–1932)

Sasfras (Spanish) - *Sassafras albidum* (Nutt.) Nees (158) (1900)

Sasgob-minš (Chippewa) - *Salix interior* Rowlee (105) (1932)

Saskatchewan cinquefoil - *Potentilla hippiana* Lehm. (155) (1942)

Saskatoon - *Amelanchier alnifolia* (Nutt.) Nutt. ex M. Roemer (37, 106, 138) (1919-1930), *Amelanchier canadensis* (L.) Medik. (156) (1923), *Amelanchier stolonifera* Wieg. (156) (1923)

Saskatoon serviceberry [Saskatoon service-berry] - *Amelanchier alnifolia* (Nutt.) Nutt. ex M. Roemer (4, 50, 155) (1942–present)

Sassafariller - *Aralia nudicaulis* L. (75) (1894) Banner Elk NC

Sassafrack - *Sassafras albidum* (Nutt.) Nees (156) (1923)

Sassafras (French) - *Sassafras albidum* (Nutt.) Nees (158) (1900)

Sassafras [Sassaphras] or Sassafras tree [Sassafras-tree] - *Laurus* L. (10, 167, 190) (~1759-1818), *Sassafras albidum* (Nutt.) Nees (2, 5, 8, 18, 19, 20, 38, 41, 46, 53, 57, 58, 61, 72, 92, 97, 105, 106, 107, 109, 124, 156, 158, 177, 181, 182, 187, 189) (~1678-1949), *Sassafras* Nees. & Eberm. (1, 4, 50, 138, 155, 158) (1900–present)

Sassafras bark - *Sassafras albidum* (Nutt.) Nees (92) (1876)

Sassafras laurel - *Umbellularia californica* (Hook. & Arn.) Nutt. (107) (1919)

Sassafras root - *Sassafras albidum* (Nutt.) Nees (92) (1876)

Sassafras wood - *Sassafras albidum* (Nutt.) Nees (92) (1876)

Sassaparil - *Aralia nudicaulis* L. (7, 184) (1793-1828)

S'assaparilla - *Aralia nudicaulis* L. (190) (~1759)

Sasskraut (German) - *Alliaria petiolata* (Bieb.) Cavara & Grande (107) (1919)

Satin - *Lunaria annua* L. (5) (1913)

Satin flower [Satin-flower] - *Lunaria annua* L. (5, 156) (1913-1923), *Lunaria rediviva* L. (5, 92, 156) (1876-1923), *Polygala paucifolia* Willd. (156) (1923), *Stellaria media* (L.) Vill. subsp. *media* (157, 158) (1900-1929)

Satin grass [Satin-grass] - *Muhlenbergia mexicana* (L.) Trin. (5, 56, 119) (1901-1938), *Muhlenbergia racemosa* (Michx.) Britton, Sterns & Poggenb. (5, 56, 119, 163) (1852-1938), *Muhlenbergia schreberi* J.F. Gmel. (119, 163) (1852-1938)

Satin walnut - *Liquidambar styraciflua* L. (5, 156) (1913-1923)

Satin willow - *Salix sitchensis* Sanson ex Bong. (138) (1923)

Satin-flower [Satin flower] - *Sisyrinchium* L. (109) (1949), *Stellaria media* (L.) Vill. (92, 156) (1898-1923), *Stellaria media* (L.) Vill. subsp. *media* (157, 158) (1900-1929)

Satin-lily [Satin lily] - *Sisyrinchium angustifolium* Mill. (156) (1923)

Satin-pod [Satin pod] - *Lunaria annua* L. (19, 156) (1840-1923), *Lunaria rediviva* L. (156) (1923)

Satin-tail [Satintail] - *Imperata brevifolia* Vasey (122) (1937) TX

Satinwood [Satin wood] - *Zanthoxylum flavum* Vahl (15) (1895)

Satiny willow - *Salix pellita* (Anderss.) Anderss. ex Schneid. (5) (1913)

Satsuma orange - *Citrus reticulata* Blanco (109) (1949)

Saturday's-pepper [Saturday's pepper] - *Euphorbia helioscopia* L. (156) (1923)

Satyr orchid - *Coeloglossum viride* (L.) Hartman var. *virescens* (Muhl. ex Willd.) Luer (138) (1923)

Satyrion without stones - *Goodyera repens* (L.) R. Br. ex Ait. f. (178) (1596)

Sauce (Spanish) - *Salix* L. (158) (1900)

Sauce-alone [Sauce alone] - *Alliaria petiolata* (Bieb.) Cavara & Grande (5, 156, 158, 178) (1526-1923), *Lepidium sativum* L. (92, 158) (1876-1900), *Sisymbrium altissimum* L. (107) (1919)

Saudistel (German) - *Sonchus oleraceus* L. (158) (1900)

Sauer baum (German) - *Oxydendrum arboreum* (L.) DC. (possibly) (7) (1828)

Sauerey - *Satureja hortensis* L. (179) (1526)

Sauerkirschen (German) - *Prunus cerasus* L. (110) (1886)

Saugh - *Ligustrum vulgare* L. (158) (1900), *Salix* L. (158) (1900)

Saule (French) - *Salix* L. (8, 158) (1785-1900)

Saule à feuilles argentees (French) - *Salix exigua* Nutt. (20) (1857)

Saule jaune (French) - *Salix lutea* Nutt. (20) (1857)

Saule laurier (French) - *Salix pentandra* L. (20) (1857)

Saule nain (French) - *Salix humilis* Marsh. (8) (1785)

Saule noir (French) - *Salix nigra* Marsh. (8) (1785)

Saule noirâtre (French) - *Salix melanopsis* Nutt. (20) (1857)

Saules à feuilles soyeuses (French) - *Salix sericea* Marsh. (8) (1785)

Saunders - *Santalum* L. (92) (1876)

Sauohr (German) - *Plantago major* L. (158) (1900)

Saurach (German) - *Berberis vulgaris* L. (158) (1900)

Saurdorn (German) - *Berberis vulgaris* L. (6) (1892)

Saururus - *Saururus* L. (50, 93, 155, 158) (1900–present)

Sausafras - *Sassafras albidum* (Nutt.) Nees (35) (1806)

Sausage tree [Sausage-tree] - *Kigelia africana* (Lam.) Benth. (109) (1949)

Sautaash - *Gaylussacia baccata* (Wang.) K. Koch (46) (1879)

Sau-tiskan (Chippewa) - *Coptis trifolia* (L.) Salisb. (105) (1932)

Sauyn - *Juniperus sabina* L. (178, 179) (1526-1596)

Sauz (Spanish) - *Salix* L. (158) (1900)

Savanna bark - *Quercus suber* L. (92) (1876)

Savannah aster - *Eurybia chapmanii* (Torr. & Gray) Nesom (138, 155) (1923–1942)

Savannah flower - *Mandevilla laxa* (Ruiz & Pav.) Woodson (92) (1876)

Savannah iris - *Iris tridentata* Pursh (50) (present)

Savin - *Juniperus horizontalis* Moench (73) (1892) Newfoundland, berries are called face-and-eye berries, *Juniperus sabina* L. (7, 10, 19, 41, 55, 58, 61, 92, 109, 138) (1770-1949), *Juniperus virginiana* L. (2, 5, 46, 106, 158) (1895-1930)

Savin bearing berries [Sauin bearing berries] - *Juniperus sabina* L. (178) (1596)

Savin juniper - *Juniperus sabina* L. (112) (1937)

Savine - *Juniperus sabina* L. (57) (1917)

Savin-leaf club moss [Savin-leaved club moss] - *Lycopodium alpinum* L. (5) (1913)

Savin-leaf ground-pine [Savinleaf groundpine] - *Lycopodium sabinifolium* Willd. (50) (present)

Savin-tops - *Juniperus sabina* L. (49) (1898)

Savonnier de la Floride (French) - *Sapindus saponaria* L. var. *saponaria* (20) (1857)

Savonnière (French) - *Saponaria officinalis* L. (157) (1929)

Savor-leaf aster [Savorleaf aster] - *Ionactis linariifolius* (L.) Greene (122) (1917)

Savory - *Satureja hortensis* L. (5, 184) (1793-1913), *Satureja* L. (109, 138, 156) (1923-1949)

Savory-leaf aster [Savoryleaf aster, Savory-leaved aster] - *Ionactis linariifolius* (L.) Greene (5, 155, 156, 158) (1900-1942)

Savory-leaf starwort [Savory-leaved star-wort] - *Ionactis linariifolius* (L.) Greene (187) (1818)

Savoy cabbage - *Brassica* L. (107) (1919)

Savoy cole [Sauoy cole] - *Brassica oleracea* L. (178, 180) (1526-1633)

Savoy lettuce [Savuoy lettuce] - *Lactuca sativa* L. (180) (1633)

Savoyan - *Galium aparine* L. (92) (1876), *Galium verum* L. (7) (1828) Canada

Saw brier [Saw-brier] - *Mimosa microphylla* Dry. (12, 38) (1820-1821)

Saw cabbage-palm [Saw-cabbage palm] - *Acoelorraphe wrightii* (Griseb. & H. Wendl.) H. Wendl. ex Becc. (106) (1930)

Saw fern [Sawfern] - *Blechnum serrulatum* L.C. Rich. (138) (1923)

Saw greenbrier - *Smilax bona-nox* L. (50, 155) (1942–present)

Saw palmetto - *Serenoa* Hook. f. (109, 138) (1923-1949), *Serenoa repens* (Bartr.) Small (2, 14, 49, 52, 53, 54, 55, 57, 59, 107, 138) (1895-1922)

Sawatch knotweed - *Polygonum douglasii* Greene subsp. *johnstonii* (Munz) Hickman (155) (1942)

Saw-beak sedge - *Carex straminea* Willd. ex Schkuhr (3) (1977)

Sawbrier [Saw-brier, Saw brier] - *Smilax glauca* Walt. (156, 157) (1923-1929)

Sawge - *Salvia officinalis* L. (179) (1526)

Saw-grass [Sawgrass, Saw grass] - *Cladium mariscus* (L.) Pohl subsp. *jamaicense* (Crantz) Kükenth. (5, 19, 75, 92, 156) (1840-1923), *Cladium* P. Br. (1, 155) (1932-1942)

Saw-leaf mugwort [Saw-leaved mugwort] - *Artemisia ludoviciana* Nutt. subsp. *ludoviciana* (5, 72, 131) (1899-1913)

Saw-leaf zelkova [Sawleaf zelkova] - *Zelkova serrata* (Thunb.) Makino (138) (1923)

Sawort - *Liatris* Gaertn. ex Schreber. (7) (1828)

Saw-petal water-hyacinth [Sawpetal water-hyacinth] - *Eichhornia azurea* (Sw.) Kunth (138) (1923)

Saw-sepal penstemon [Sawsepal penstemon] - *Penstemon glaber* Pursh (50, 155) (1942–present), *Penstemon glaber* Pursh var. *glaber* (50) (present)

Saw-tooth goldenweed [Sawtooth goldenweed] - *Hazardia squarrosa* (Hook. & Arn.) Greene var. *squarrosa* (155) (1942), *Machaeranthera pinnatifida* (Hook.) Shinners subsp. *pinnatifida* (155) (1942)

Sawtooth sagebrush - *Artemisia ludoviciana* Nutt. subsp. *ludoviciana* (155) (1942)

Saw-tooth sunflower [Sawtooth sunflower, Saw toothed sunflower] - *Helianthus grosseserratus* Martens (3, 4, 5, 50, 72, 80, 93, 97, 122, 131, 138, 155) (1899–present)

Sawtooth wormwood - *Artemisia ludoviciana* Nutt. subsp. *ludoviciana* (138) (1923)

Saw-wort [Saw woort, Saw wort, Sawwort] - *Artemisia tridentata* Nutt. subsp. *vaseyana* (Rydb.) Beetle (190) (~1759), *Liatris spicata* (L.) Willd. (92, 156) (1876-1923), *Liatris spicata* (L.) Willd. var. *spicata* (157) (1929), *Serratula* L. (184) (1793), *Serratula tinctoria* L. (92, 178) (1526-1876)

Saw-wort [Saw wort] - *Liatris spicata* (L.) Willd. (92, 156) (1898-1923), *Liatris spicata* (L.) Willd. (72) (1907)

Saxapril - *Aralia nudicaulis* L. (76) (1896) Bath ME

Saxefras - *Sassafras albidum* (Nutt.) Nees (46) (1879)

Saxifarilla - *Smilax glauca* Walt. (46) (1879)

Saxifrage - *Asplenium* L. (178, 179) (1526-1596), *Carum carvi* L. (158) (1900), *Saxifraga cernua* L. (3, 85) (1932-1977), *Saxifraga* L. (1, 10, 109, 138, 155, 156, 158, 167, 184) (1793-1949), *Saxifraga pensylvanica* L. (52) (1919)

Saxifrage pink - *Petrorhagia saxifraga* (L.) Link (5, 156) (1913-1923)

Saxifrage tunic-flower [Saxifrage tunicflower] - *Coreopsis maritima* (Nutt.) Hook.f. (5, 156) (1913-1923), *Petrorhagia saxifraga* (L.) Link (138) (1923)

Saxifrax - *Sassafras albidum* (Nutt.) Nees (92, 158) (1876-1900)

Say's rose - *Rosa acicularis* Lindl. (130) (1895)

Scabbish [Scabish] - *Oenothera fruticosa* L. (73, 156) (1892-1923) NH

Scabby-head [Scabby head] - *Torilis arvensis* (Huds.) Link (5, 156) (1913-1923)

Scabiosa - *Scabiosa* L. (138) (1923)

Scabiosa centaurea - *Centaurea scabiosa* L. (155) (1942)

Scabious [Scabius, Scabyous] - *Conyza canadensis* (L.) Cronq. var. *canadensis* (6, 49, 53, 92, 156, 157, 158) (1892-1929), *Erigeron annuus* (L.) Pers. (46) (1617), *Erigeron philadelphicus* L. (186, 187) (1814-1818), *Scabiosa* L. (109) (1949), *Succisa pratensis* Moench (92) (1876)

Scabious knapweed - *Centaurea scabiosa* L. (5, 156) (1913-1923)

Scabious of the sea - *Scabiosa atropupurea* L. (possibly) (178) (1526)

Scabish - *Erigeron philadelphicus* L. (7) (1828), *Knautia arvensis* (L.) Duby (156) (1923), *Oenothera biennis* L. (5, 6, 7, 19, 76, 92, 156, 158) (1828-1923), *Oenothera fruticosa* L. subsp. *fruticosa* (5) (1913), *Oenothera fruticosa* L. subsp. *glauca* (Michx.) Straley (5) (1913)

Scabius - *Erigeron annuus* (L.) Pers. (46) (1617)

Scabrous centaury - *Centaurea scabiosa* L. (19) (1840)

Scabrous-leaf goldenrod [Scabrous-leaved golden-rod] - *Solidago rugosa* Mill. subsp. *rugosa* var. *rugosa* (187) (1818)

Scabwort - *Inula helenium* L. (5, 6, 49, 53, 64, 92, 156, 179) (1526-1923)

Scaddie - *Urtica dioica* L. (157, 158) (1900-1929)

Scaldweed - *Cuscuta americana* L. (92) (1876)

Scaldweed [Scald weed, Scald-weed] - *Cuscuta gronovii* Willd. ex J.A. Schultes (5, 50, 156) (1913–present)

Scale-flower dodder [Scaleflower dodder] - *Cuscuta squamata* Engelm. (50) (present)

Scale-seed [Scaleseed] - *Spermolepis* Raf. (4, 50) (1986–present)

Scallion - *Allium porrum* L. (158) (1900)

Scalloped salpiglossis - *Salpiglossis sinuata* Ruiz & Pavón (138) (1923)

Scaly blazing star [Scaly blazing-star] - *Liatris squarrosa* (L.) Michx. (50, 92, 122, 156) (1876–present), *Liatris squarrosa* (L.) Michx. var. *glabrata* (Rydb.) Gaiser (50) (present), *Liatris squarrosa* (L.) Michx. var. *hirsuta* (Rydb.) Gaiser (50) (present), *Liatris squarrosa* (L.) Michx. var. *squarrosa* (5, 72, 93, 97, 157) (1900-1937)

Scaly club-rush - *Trichophorum caespitosum* (L.) Hartman (66) (1903)

Scaly dragon's-claw [Scaly dragons' claw, Scaly dragonclaw] - *Pterospora andromedea* Nutt. (7) (1828), *Corallorrhiza odontorhiza* (Willd.) Poir. (92) (1876)

Scaly grindelia - *Grindelia squarrosa* (Pursh) Dunal (49, 69) (1898–1903)

Scaly mushroom - *Neolentinus lepideus* (Fr.) Redhead & Ginns 1985 (128) (1933)

Scaly notholaena - *Astrolepis sinuata* (Lag. ex Sw.) Benham & Windham subsp. *sinuata* (97) (1937)

Scaly rush - *Trichophorum caespitosum* (L.) Hartman (19) (1840)

Scaly-bark - *Carya ovata* (Mill.) K. Koch (156) (1923)

Scammony - *Ipomoea pandurata* (L.) G.F.W. Mey. (5, 156) (1913-1923)

Scammony-root [Scammony root] - *Ipomoea pandurata* (L.) G.F.W. Mey. (92, 156, 158) (1876-1923)

Scandix - *Scandix pecten-veneris* L. (107) (1919)

Scapose musineon - *Musineon tenuifolium* (Nutt. ex Torr. & Gray) Coult. & Rose (5, 131) (1899-1913)

Scapose primrose - *Oenothera caespitosa* Nutt. (5, 131) (1899-1913), *Oenothera* L. (158) (1900)

Scapose tickclover - *Desmodium nudiflorum* (L.) DC. (4) (1986)

Scarab cypress - *Chamaecyparis lawsoniana* (A. Murr.) Parl. (109) (1949)

Scarb tree - *Malus sylvestris* Mill. (5) (1913)

Scardiccione (Italian) - *Onopordum acanthium* L. (46) (1879)

Scarlet bartsia - *Castilleja coccinea* (L.) Spreng. (42) (1814)

Scarlet beard-tongue - *Penstemon murrayanus* Hook. (97) (1937)

Scarlet beeblossom - *Gaura coccinea* Nutt. ex Pursh (50) (present)

Scarlet begonia - *Begonia coccinea* Hook. (138) (1923)

Scarlet bloom - *Eucalyptus ficifolia* F. Muell. (106) (1930)

Scarlet bouvardia - *Bouvardia ternifolia* (Cav.) Schltdl. (138) (1923)

Scarlet buckeye - *Aesculus pavia* L. (138) (1923)

Scarlet bugler [Scarlet-bugler] - *Penstemon centranthifolius* Benth. (109, 138) (1923-1949)

Scarlet California hyacinth - *Dichelostemma ida-maia* (Alph. Wood) Greene (86) (1878)

Scarlet clematis - *Clematis texensis* Buckl. (109) (1949)

Scarlet clover - *Trifolium incarnatum* L. (68) (1913) Ottawa

Scarlet columbine - *Aquilegia canadensis* L. (42) (1814)

Scarlet coral honeysuckle - *Lonicera sempervirens* L. (86) (1878)

Scarlet elder - *Sambucus racemosa* L. (156) (1923), *Sambucus racemosa* L. var. *racemosa* (138, 155) (1923-1942)

Scarlet firethorn - *Pyracantha coccinea* M. Roemer (138) (1923)

Scarlet gaura - *Gaura coccinea* Nutt. ex Pursh (3, 4, 5, 72, 85, 93, 97, 121, 131, 155, 156, 157) (1899-1986)

Scarlet geranium - *Pelargonium inquinans* (L.) L'Hér. ex Aiton (19) (1840)

Scarlet gilia - *Ipomopsis aggregata* (Pursh) V. Grant subsp. *aggregata* (5, 109, 122) (1913-1949), *Ipomopsis rubra* (L.) Wherry (156) (1923)

Scarlet globe-mallow [Scarlet globemallow] - *Sphaeralcea coccinea* (Nutt.) Rydb. (50, 155) (1942–present)

Scarlet gum - *Eucalyptus ficifolia* F. Muell. (138) (1923)

Scarlet hibiscus - *Hibiscus coccineus* Walt (86) (1878)

Scarlet honeysuckle - *Lonicera sempervirens* L. (156) (1923), *Lonicera sempervirens* L. (156) (1923)

Scarlet horse-chestnut - *Aesculus pavia* L. (165) (1768)

Scarlet Indian paintbrush - *Castilleja coccinea* (L.) Spreng. (50) (present)

Scarlet ixia - *Ixia campanulata* Houtt. (138) (1923)

Scarlet ixora - *Ixora coccinea* L. (138) (1923)

Scarlet knotweed [Scarlet knot-weed] - *Polygonum amphibium* L. var. *emersum* Michx. (187) (1818)

Scarlet larkspur - *Delphinium cardinale* Hook. (76, 109) (1896-1949)

Scarlet lightning - *Dianthus barbatus* L. (74) (1893) Quebec, scarlet variety, *Lychnis chalcedonica* L. (5, 73, 156, 158) (1892-1923) Hemmingford N.J.

Scarlet lobelia - *Lobelia cardinalis* L. (6, 156, 186) (1814-1892)

Scarlet lychnis - *Lychnis chalcedonica* L. (4, 5, 19, 156, 158) (1840-1986)

Scarlet mallow - *Malvastrum* Gray (1) (1932)

Scarlet malva - *Sphaeralcea coccinea* (Nutt.) Rydb. subsp. *coccinea* (98) (1926)

Scarlet maple - *Acer rubrum* L. (5, 15, 20, 42, 93, 97, 109, 156, 182, 187) (1791-1949)

Scarlet oak [Scarlet oake] - *Quercus* ×*benderi* Baenitz [*coccinea* × *rubra*] (1, 2, 5, 12, 20, 19, 33, 58, 72, 82, 93, 95, 97, 109, 113, 135, 138, 156) (1820-1949), *Quercus coccinea* Muenchh. (possibly) (187) (1818), *Quercus rubra* L. (181) (~1678), *Quercus sinuata* Walt. (182) (1791), *Quercus velutina* Lam. (157) (1929)

Scarlet painted-cup [Scarlet paintedcup] - *Castilleja miniata* Dougl. ex Hook. (155) (1942), *Castilleja coccinea* (L.) Spreng. (2, 5, 72, 97, 156, 158) (1895-1937)

Scarlet passionflower - *Passiflora coccinea* Aubl. (138) (1923)

Scarlet pea - *Indigofera miniata* Ort. var. *leptosepala* (Nutt.) B.L.Turner (4) (1986)

Scarlet pimpernel - *Anagallis arvensis* L. (3, 5, 50, 19, 49, 57, 72, 92, 97, 122, 155, 156, 157, 158, 187) (1818–present), *Anagallis arvensis* L. subsp. *arvensis* (50) (present)

Scarlet plumbago - *Plumbago indica* L. (138) (1923)

Scarlet rose-balm [Scarlet rosebalm, Scarlet rose balm] - *Monarda didyma* L. (7, 92) (1828-1876)

Scarlet rose-mallow [Scarlet rose mallow, Scarlet rosemallow] - *Hibiscus coccineus* Walt (138) (1923), *Hibiscus laevis* All. (3) (1977)

Scarlet runner - *Phaseolus coccineus* L. (19, 82, 92, 107, 109, 138) (1840-1949)

Scarlet sage - *Salvia splendens* Sellow ex Roemer & J.A. Schultes (19, 82, 92, 109, 138) (1840-1949)

Scarlet star-glory [Scarlet starglory] - *Ipomoea coccinea* L. (138, 155) (1923-1942)

Scarlet strawberry - *Fragaria virginiana* Duchesne (5, 97, 107, 110, 157, 158) (1886-1937), *Fragaria virginiana* Duchesne subsp. *grayana* (Vilm. ex J. Gay) Staudt (72) (1907) IA

Scarlet sumac [Scarlet sumach] - *Rhus glabra* L. (5, 85, 93, 95, 106, 107, 156, 157, 158) (1900–1936)

Scarlet trumpet honeysuckle - *Lonicera sempervirens* L. (5, 86, 158) (1878-1913)

Scarlet Virginia catchfly - *Silene vulgaris* (Moench) Garcke (181) (~1678)

Scarlet woolly buckeye - *Aesculus pavia* L. (155) (1942)

Scarlet-berry [Scarlet berry] - *Solanum dulcamara* L. (49, 53, 92, 156, 158) (1876-1923)

Scarlet-colored hollyhock [Scarlet coloured hollyhocke] - *Alcea rosea* L. (178) (1526)

Scarlet-cross - *Lychnis chalcedonica* L. (158) (1900)

Scarlet-cup [Scarlet cup] - *Sarcoscypha coccinea* (Jacq.) Boud. (128) (1933) ND

Scarlet-flower gum [Scarlet-flowering gum] - *Eucalyptus ficifolia* F. Muell. (109) (1949)

Scarlet-flower horse-chestnut [Scarlet flowering horse-chestnut, Scarlet flowering horse chestnut] - *Aesculus* L. (189) (1767), *Aesculus pavia* L. (8) (1785)

Scarlet-flower maple [Scarlet-flowering maple, Scarlet flowering maple] - *Acer rubrum* L. (8, 165) (1768-1785)

Scarlet-flower Philadelphia spiraea [Scarlet flowered Philadelphian spiraea] - *Spiraea tomentosa* L. (8) (1785)

Scarlet-fruit horse-gentian [Scarlet-fruited horse-gentian] - *Triosteum aurantiacum* Bickn. (97) (1937) OK, *Triosteum aurantiacum* Bickn. var. *aurantiacum* (5) (1913)

Scarlet-funnel penstemon [Scarletfunnel penstemon] - *Penstemon superbus* A. Nels. (138) (1923)

Scarlet-pea [Scarlet pea] - *Indigofera miniata* Ort. var. *leptosepala* (Nutt.) B.L.Turner (4) (1986)

Scarlet-seed iris [Scarlet-seeded iris] - *Iris foetidissima* L. (109) (1949)

Scaryole - *Lactuca serriola* L. (179) (1526)

Scent-bottle [Scentbottle] - *Platanthera dilatata* (Pursh) Lindl. ex Beck (50) (present), *Platanthera dilatata* (Pursh) Lindl. ex Beck var. *albiflora* (Cham.) Ledeb. (50) (present), *Platanthera dilatata* (Pursh) Lindl. ex Beck var. *dilatata* (50) (present)

Scented oak fern [Scented oak-fern] - *Gymnocarpium robertianum* (Hoffmann) Newman (5, 50) (1913–present)

Scented-fern [Scented fern] - *Tanacetum vulgare* L. (69) (1904)

Scentless camomile [Scentless chamomile] - *Tripleurospermum perforata* (Merat) M. Lainz (5, 93, 156) (1913-1936) Neb

Scentless false camomile [Scentless false chamomile, Scentless false-chamomile] - *Tripleurospermum perforata* (Merat) M. Lainz (109, 138) (1923-1949)

Scentless false mayweed - *Tripleurospermum perforata* (Merat) M. Lainz (50) (present)

Scentless mayweed - *Tripleurospermum perforata* (Merat) M. Lainz (155) (1942)

Scentless mock orange [Scentless mockorange] - *Philadelphus inodorus* L. (2, 138) (1895-1923)

Scentless syringa - *Philadelphus inodorus* L. (5, 19) (1840-1913)

Scepter goldenrod - *Solidago erecta* Pursh (138) (1923)

Schaaf-stroo (Dutch) - *Equisetum hyemale* L. (46) (1879)

Schachtelhalm (German) - *Equisetum hyemale* L. (6) (1892)

Schaffthew (German) - *Equisetum hyemale* L. (46) (1879)

Schafgarbe (German) - *Achillea millefolium* L. (6, 158) (1892–1900)

Schafgrippe (German) - *Achillea millefolium* L. (158) (1900)

Schafrippe (German) - *Achillea millefolium* L. (6) (1892)

Schafthalm (German) - *Hippuris vulgaris* L. (158) (1900)

Schaked (Hebrew) - *Prunus dulcis* (Mill.) D.A. Webber (110) (1886)

Scharf Hahnenfuss (German) - *Ranunculus acris* L. (6, 158) (1892–1900), *Ranunculus sceleratus* L. (6) (1892)

Scharlachbeere (German) - *Phytolacca americana* L. var. *americana* (158) (1900)

Schedonnardus - *Schedonnardus paniculatus* (Nutt.) Trel. (5, 72, 158) (1852-1907)

Schellingia - *Aegopogon* Humb. & Bonpl. ex Willd. (45) (1896)

Schellkraut (German) - *Chelidonium majus* L. (158) (1900)

Scheptata (Persian) - *Prunus persica* (L.) Batsch (110) (1784)

Schetti - *Ixora coccinea* L. (174) (1753)

Scheuchzeria - *Scheuchzeria* L. (155) (1942), *Scheuchzeria palustris* L. (155) (1942)

Scheuchzer's cotton grass - *Eriophorum scheuchzeri* Hoppe (5) (1913)

Scheuerkraut (German) - *Equisetum arvense* L. (158) (1900)

Schierling (German) - *Conium maculatum* L. (6) (1892)

Schildblattinger Entenfuss (German) - *Podophyllum peltatum* L. (6) (1892)

Schildblättringer Entenfuss (German) - *Podophyllum peltatum* L. (6, 186) (1814-1892)

Schildkraut (German) - *Scutellaria* L. (158) (1900)

Schinseng (German) - *Panax quinquefolius* L. (158) (1900)

Schlangen Osterluzey [Schlangenosterluzey] (German) - *Aristolochia serpentaria* L. (7, 186) (1814-1828)

Schlangenwurzel (German) - *Aristolochia serpentaria* L. (6) (1892)

Schlascha (Flathead) - *Prunus virginiana* L. var. *demissa* (Nutt.) Torr. (101) (1905) MT

Schlutten (German) - *Physalis alkekengi* L. (158) (1900)

Schminkbohne (German) - *Phaseolus vulgaris* L. (6) (1892)

Schnabel kraut (German) - *Geranium maculatum* L. (186) (1814)

Schneck's oak [Schneck oak] - *Quercus shumardii* Buckl. var. *schneckii* (Britt.) Sargent (5, 50, 72, 97) (1907–present)

Schneck's sugar maple [Schneck sugar maple] - *Acer saccharum* Marsh. var. *schneckii* Rehd. (155) (1942)

Schneebaum (German) - *Chionanthus virginicus* L. (6) (1892)

Schollkraut or Schöllkraut (German) - *Chelidonium majus* L. (6, 158) (1892-1900)

Schonbluhender Hartriegel (German) - *Cornus florida* L. (7) (1828)

Schott's common allamanda [Schott common allamanda] - *Allamanda schottii* Pohl (155) (1942)

Schrader's brome [Schraders brome] - *Bromus catharticus* Vahl (109) (1949)

Schrader's brome grass - *Bromus catharticus* Vahl (5, 56, 129) (1894-1913)

Schrader's bromus - *Bromus catharticus* Vahl (45) (1896)

Schrader's grass - *Bromus catharticus* Vahl (87, 88, 118, 163) (1852-1898)

Schreber's aster [Schreber aster] - *Eurybia schreberi* (Nees) Nees (5, 155) (1913-1942)

Schreber's water-shield [Schreber watershield] - *Brasenia schreberi* Gmel. (155) (1942)

Schrucha (Russian) - *Portulaca oleracea* L. (110) (1886)

Schuratelinei nos (Russian) - *Geranium maculatum* L. (186) (1814)

Schwalbenwurzel (German) - *Asclepias syriaca* L. (6) (1892)

Schwartzer Nachtschatten (German) - *Solanum nigrum* L. (158) (1900)

Schwartznussbaum (German) - *Juglans nigra* L. (41) (1770)

Schwarz Bilsenkraut [Schwarzes Bilsenkraut] (German) - *Hyoscyamus niger* L. (7, 158) (1828-1900)

Schwarz Schlangewurz (German) - *Actaea racemosa* L. (7) (1828)

Schwarz Senf (German) - *Brassica nigra* (L.) W.D.J. Koch (6) (1892)

Schwarzer Andorn (German) - *Ballota nigra* L. (158) (1900)

Schwedler's maple [Schwedler maple] - *Acer platanoides* L. (137, 138) (1923-1931)

Schweinitz's flatsedge [Schweinitz flatsedge] - *Cyperus schweinitzii* Torr. (3, 50, 155) (1942–present)

Schweinitz's sedge - *Carex schweinitzii* Dewey ex Schwein. (5, 50, 66, 72) (1893–present)

Schweintiz's cyperus [Schweinitz cyperus] - *Cyperus schweinitzii* Torr. (5, 72) (1907-1913)

Schweintiz's galingale - *Cyperus schweinitzii* Torr. (66) (1903)

Scimitar-pod kidney bean [Scimetar-podded kidney bean] - *Phaseolus lunatus* L. (110) (1886)

Scinjachu (some Indians) - *Antennaria plantaginifolia* (L.) Richards (possibly) (7) (1828)

Scirpus-like rush - *Juncus scirpoides* Lam. (5) (1913)

Scirpus-like sedge - *Carex scirpoidea* Michx. (5) (1913)

Scleropis - *Cichorium intybus* L. (5) (1913), *Sclerolepis uniflora* (Walt.) Porter (5) (1913)

Scoba - *Chloracantha spinosa* (Benth.) Nesom (150) (1894) NM

Scoke - *Phytolacca americana* (5, 69, 109) (1903–1949), *Phytolacca americana* L. var. *americana* (2, 6, 49, 62, 64, 92, 107, 152, 157, 158, 186) (1814–1929), *Phytolacca* L. (2) (1895)

Scoke jalap - *Phytolacca americana* L. var. *americana* (49) (1898)

Scolimos (Greek) - *Cynara cardunculus* L. (110) (1886)

Scollop-leaf oenothera [Scollop-leaved oenothera] - *Oenothera laciniata* Hill (187) (1818)

Scootberry [Scoot berries] - *Streptopus lanceolatus* (Ait.) Reveal var. *roseus* (Michx.) Reveal (79) (1891) NH

Scoparius - *Cytisus scoparius* (L.) Link (52) (1919)

Scordon (Modern Greek) - *Allium sativum* L. (110) (1886)

Scoria-lily [Scoria lily] - *Mentzelia decapetala* (Pursh ex Sims) Urban & Gilg ex Gilg (127) (1933) ND

Scorodon (Ancient Greek) - *Allium sativum* L. (50) (present)

Scoroprasum - *Allium* L. (165) (1768)

Scorpion weed - *Phacelia* Juss. (1) (1932)

Scorpion-grass [Scorpion grass] - *Myosotis arvensis* (L.) Hill (92) (1876), *Myosotis* L. (2, 10, 77, 82, 156, 184) (1793-1930), *Myosotis scorpioides* L. (158) (1900)

Scorpion-weed [Scorpion weed, Scorpionweed] - *Phacelia hastata* Dougl. ex Lehm. var. *hastata* (3, 4, 93) (1936-1986) Neb, *Myosotis scorpioides* L. (19, 92) (1840-1876)

Scorzonera - *Scolymus hispanicus* L. (110, 178) (1526-1886), *Scorzonera* L. (50) (present)

Scorzonera (Spain) - *Scolymus hispanicus* L. (107) (1570)

Scotch barley - *Hordeum vulgare* L. (158) (1900) variety

Scotch bluebell - *Campanula rotundifolia* L. (40) (1928)

Scotch bonnets - *Capsicum annuum* L. (92) (1876)

Scotch broom - *Cytisus scoparius* (L.) Link (5, 19, 106, 107, 138, 156) (1840-1930)

Scotch camomile [Scotch chamomile] - *Chamaemelum nobile* (L.) All. (5, 156) (1913-1923)

Scotch caps - *Rubus occidentalis* L. (5) (1913), *Rubus odoratus* L. (5, 73) (1892-1913) Hemmingford Quebec

Scotch cotton-thistle [Scotch cottonthistle] - *Onopordum acanthium* L. (50, 155) (1942–present)

Scotch elm - *Ulmus glabra* Huds. (109, 138) (1923-1949)

Scotch false asphodel - *Tofieldia pusilla* (Michx.) Pers. (50) (present)

Scotch fir - *Pinus sylvestris* L. (20, 55) (1857-1911)

Scotch gael - *Myrica gale* L. (156) (1923)

Scotch grass - *Cynodon dactylon* (L.) Pers. (158) (1900), *Oplismenus hirtellus* (L.) P. Beauv. subsp. *hirtellus* (182) (1791), *Urochloa mutica* (Forsk.) T.Q. Nguyen (92) (1876)

Scotch kale - *Brassica oleracea* L. (109) (1949)

Scotch lovage - *Ligusticum scoticum* L. (5, 107, 156) (1913-1923)

Scotch mercury - *Digitalis pupurea* L. (5, 69) (1903-1913)

Scotch mist - *Galium sylvaticum* L. (156) (1923)

Scotch pine - *Pinus sylvestris* L. (32, 50, 107, 112, 136) (1895–present)

Scotch rose - *Rosa spinosissima* L. (19, 109, 138) (1840-1949)

Scotch scurvy grass - *Calystegia soldanella* (L.) R. Br. ex Roemer & J.A. Schultes (92) (1876)

Scotch thistle - *Carduus nutans* L. (46, 158) (1879-1900), *Cirsium*

vulgare (Savi) Ten. (158) (1900) emblem of Scotland, *Onopordum acanthium* L. (3, 4, 5, 46, 109, 156, 158) (1879-1986) England, *Onopordum* L. (1, 4) (1932-1986)

Scots pine - *Pinus sylvestris* L. (109, 136, 138) (1923-1949)

Scottish asphodel - *Tofieldia* Huds. (1) (1932)

Scottish pease - *Pisum sativum* L. (178) (1526)

Scott's clematis [Scott clematis] - *Clematis hirsutissima* Pursh var. *scottii* (Porter) Erickson (50, 131, 155) (1899–present)

Scott's leather flower - *Clematis hirsutissima* Pursh var. *scottii* (Porter) Erickson (5) (1913)

Scott's spleenwort - *Asplenium ×ebenoides* R. R. Scott [*platyneuron × rhizophyllum*] (5, 86) (1878–1913)

Scouler's popcorn-flower [Scouler's popcornflower, Scouler popcornflower] - *Plagiobothrys scouleri* (Hook. & Arn.) I.M. Johnston (50, 155) (1942–present)

Scouler's willow [Scouler willow] - *Salix scouleriana* Barr. (50, 155) (1942–present)

Scour-grass - *Equisetum hyemale* L. (187) (1818)

Scouring-rush [Scouring rush, Scouringrush] - *Equisetum arvense* L. (157) (1929), *Equisetum hyemale* L. (3, 6, 19, 40, 46, 49, 52, 53, 57, 72, 107, 124, 155, 158, 187) (1818-1977), *Equisetum* L. (4, 37, 126, 148) (1919-1986)

Scouring-rush horsetail [Scouring rush horsetail] - *Equisetum hyemale* L. var. *affine* (Engelm.) A.A. Eat. (50) (present), *Equisetum hyemale* L. (50) (present), *Equisetum hyemale* L. (50) (present)

Scourweed - *Saponaria officinalis* L. (156) (1923)

Scourwort - *Saponaria officinalis* L. (64, 156, 158) (1900-1929)

Scrambled-eggs [Scrambled eggs] - *Corydalis aurea* Willd. (50, 124) (1937–present), *Corydalis crystallina* Engelm. (122) (1937) TX

Scrambling rocket - *Descurainia sophia* (L.) Webb ex Prantl (157, 158) (1900-1929)

Scratch grass [Scratchgrass] - *Muhlenbergia asperifolia* (Nees & Meyen ex Trin.) Parodi (3, 50, 119, 140, 146) (1938–present)

Scratch-grass [Scratch grass] - *Galium aparine* L. (5, 156) (1913-1923), *Polygonum sagittatum* L. (19, 79) (1840-1891)

Scratch-weed [Scratch weed] - *Galium aparine* L. (5, 92, 156) (1876-1923)

Screw bean [Screwbean, Screw-bean] - *Prosopis juliflora* (Sw.) DC. (96, 107) (1891–1919), *Prosopis pubescens* Benth. (76, 103, 104, 106, 123, 132, 151, 153, 154) (1855–1930), *Prosopis reptans* Benth. var. *cinerascens* (Gray) Burkart (122, 124) (1937), *Sanicula bipinnatifida* Douglas ex Hook. (15, 107, 156) (1895–1923)

Screw mesquite - *Prosopis pubescens* Benth. (123) (1856)

Screw-auger [Screw auger] - *Spiranthes cernua* (L.) L.C. Rich. (5, 75, 156) (1894-1923) Nova Scotia

Screw-bean mesquite [Screw bean mesquite] - *Prosopis pubescens* Benth. (107) (1919)

Screw-pine [Screwpine, Screw pine] - *Pandanus* L. f. (107, 109, 138) (1919-1949), *Pandanus tectorius* Parkinson ex Zucc. (107) (1919)

Screw-pod mesquit [Screw pod mesquit] - *Prosopis pubescens* Benth. (76, 107) (1896-1919)

Screw-stem [Screwstem, Screw stem] - *Bartonia* Muhl. ex Willd. (50) (present), *Bartonia paniculata* (Michx.) Muhl. subsp. *paniculata* (19) (1840), *Bartonia virginica* (L.) Britton, Sterns & Poggenb. (5, 156) (1913-1923)

Scribner's feather grass [Scribner's feather-grass] - *Achnatherum scribneri* (Vasey) Barkworth (94) (1901)

Scribner's needlegrass [Scribner needlegrass] - *Achnatherum scribneri* (Vasey) Barkworth (50, 155) (1942–present)

Scribner's panic grass - *Dichanthelium oligosanthes* (J.A. Schultes) Gould var. *scribnerianum* (Nash) Gould (56) (1901)

Scribner's panicum [Scribner panicum] - *Dichanthelium oligosanthes* (J.A. Schultes) Gould var. *scribnerianum* (Nash) Gould (5, 56, 72, 131, 140, 155) (1899-1944)

Scribner's reed grass [Scribner reedgrass] - *Calamagrostis canadensis* (Michx.) Beauv. var. *canadensis* (155) (1942)

Scribner's rosette grass - *Dichanthelium oligosanthes* (J.A. Schultes)

Gould var. *scribnerianum* (Nash) Gould (50) (present)

Scribner's wheat grass [Scribner wheatgrass] - *Elymus scribneri* (Vasey) M.E. Jones (140) (1944)

Scroby's oak [Scroby oak] - *Quercus nigra* L. (18) (1805)

Scrofula bush - *Saxifraga pensylvanica* L. (52) (1919)

Scrofula plant [Scrofula-plant] - *Helianthemum canadense* (L.) Michx. (5, 92, 156) (1876-1923), *Scrophularia marilandica* L. (5, 92, 156) (1876-1923), *Scrophularia nodosa* L. (6, 52) (1892-1919)

Scrofula root [Scrofula-root] - *Erythronium americanum* Ker. (5, 7, 92, 157) (1828-1929)

Scrofula-weed [Scrofula weed] - *Goodyera pubescens* (Willd.) R. Br. ex Ait. f. (5, 7, 18, 49, 92, 156) (1805-1923)

Scrophelnpflanze (German) - *Scrophularia nodosa* L. (6) (1892)

Scrophulaire (French) - *Scrophularia nodosa* L. (6) (1892)

Scrub bay - *Persea humilis* Nash (106) (1930)

Scrub birch - *Betula nana* L. (1, 5, 19, 75, 131, 156) (1840-1932)

Scrub bush [Scrub-bush] - *Symphyotrichum ericoides* (L.) Nesom var. *ericoides* (5, 156, 158) (1900–1923)

Scrub chestnut oak - *Quercus prinoides* Willd. (1, 5, 72, 93, 95, 97, 158) (1900-1937)

Scrub oak - *Quercus agrifolia* Née (75) (1894) CA, *Quercus ilicifolia* Wangenh. (5, 12, 46, 92, 138) (1820-1923), *Quercus macrocarpa* Michx. (5, 93, 156, 158) (1900-1936), *Quercus muehlenbergii* Engelm. (5, 156, 157, 158) (1900-1929), *Quercus prinoides* Willd. (156) (1923)

Scrub palmetto - *Sabal etonia* Swingle ex Nash (106, 138) (1923-1930)

Scrub pine - *Pinus banksiana* Lamb. (10, 20) (1818-1857), *Pinus virginiana* Mill. (5, 20, 109, 138, 187) (1818-1949)

Scrubbing-rush [Scrubbing rush] - *Equisetum hyemale* L. (6, 35) (1806-1892)

Scrubby oak - *Quercus ilicifolia* Wangenh. (10) (1818)

Scrub-grass [Scrub grass] - *Equisetum fluviatile* L. (107) (1919), *Equisetum hyemale* L. (12) (1821)

Scupernong - *Vitis vulpina* L. (7) (1828)

Scuppernong [Scupernong] - *Vitis rotundifolia* Michx. (107, 156) (1919-1923)

Scuppernong grape - *Vitis rotundifolia* Michx. (2) (1895)

Scurf-pea [Scurf pea, Scurfpea] - *Psoralidium* Rydb. (4, 50, 138) (1923–present)

Scurfy hickory - *Carya texana* Buckl. (5) (1913)

S-curve threeawn - *Aristida oligantha* Michx (50, 155) (1942–present)

Scurvish - *Oenothera biennis* L. (5, 74, 156, 158) (1893-1923) Franconia NH, no longer in use by 1923

Scurvy - *Brassica nigra* (L.) W.D.J. Koch (157, 158) (1900-1929)

Scurvy pea - *Psoralidium tenuiflorum* (Pursh) Rydb. (5, 122, 156) (1913-1937)

Scurvy senvie - *Brassica nigra* (L.) W.D.J. Koch (5) (1913)

Scurvy-grass [Scurvy grass, Scurvey grass] - *Barbarea verna* (P. Mill.) Aschers. (5, 15, 107, 156) (1895-1923), *Cardamine hirsuta* L. (107) (1919), *Cochlearia* L. (7, 109) (1828-1949), *Pityopsis graminifolia* (Michx.) Nutt. var. *graminifolia* (5, 156) (1913-1923)

Scurvy-grass [Scurvy grass] - *Barbarea* Aiton f. (1, 13) (1849-1932), *Brassica nigra* (L.) W.D.J. Koch (6) (1892), *Sisyrinchium* L. (7) (1828)

Scurvy-pea [Scurvy pea] - *Psoralidium tenuiflorum* (Pursh) Rydb. (5, 122, 156) (1913-1937)

Scurzonera (Spain) - *Scolymus hispanicus* L. (107) (1570)

Scutch cane - *Arundinaria gigantea* (Walt.) Muhl. subsp. *tecta* (Walt.) McClure (5) (1913)

Scutch grass [Scutch-grass] - *Cynodon dactylon* (L.) Pers. (5, 45, 66, 90, 92, 158) (1876-1913), *Elymus repens* (L.) Gould (45, 64, 69, 80, 158) (1896-1913)

Scutellaire (French) - *Scutellaria* L. (158) (1900), *Scutellaria lateriflora* L. (6) (1892)

Scutellaria - *Scutellaria lateriflora* L. (54, 55, 57, 59) (1905-1917)

Scythe-fruit sagittaria [Scythe-fruited sagittaria] - *Sagittaria lancifolia* L. subsp. *media* (Micheli) Bogin (5) (1913)

Scythe-leaf willow [Scythe-leaved willow] - *Salix nigra* Marsh. (5) (1913)

Sea amyris - *Amyris elemifera* L. (155) (1942)

Sea aster - *Symphyotrichum subulatum* (Michx.) Nesom (19) (1840)

Sea barley [Sea-barley] - *Hordeum marinum* Huds. (45) (1896), *Hordeum murinum* L. (155) (1942)

Sea beans - *Entada phaseoloides* (L.) Merr. (92) (1876), *Mucuna pruriens* (L.) DC. (92) (1876)

Sea beet - *Beta vulgaris* L. (107) (1919)

Sea bent [Sea-bent] - *Carex arenaria* L. (5, 156) (1913-1923)

Sea bindweed - *Calystegia soldanella* (L.) R. Br. ex Roemer & J.A. Schultes (92) (1876)

Sea blite [Sea-blite] - *Suaeda calceoliformis* (Hook.) Moq. (107) (1919)

Sea buckthorn - *Shepherdia canadensis* Nutt. (19) (1840)

Sea bugloss - *Mertensia maritima* (L.) Gray (156) (1923), *Mertensia maritima* (L.) Gray var. *maritima* (5) (1913)

Sea bulrush - *Schoenoplectus maritimus* (L.) Lye (66) (1903)

Sea burdock - *Xanthium strumarium* L. (19, 92, 158) (1840-1900)

Sea carex - *Carex arenaria* L. (66) (1903)

Sea celandine - *Glaucium flavum* Crantz (92, 156) (1876-1923)

Sea chickweed - *Honckenya peploides* (L.) Ehrh. (5) (1913), *Honckenya peploides* (L.) Ehrh. subsp. *diffusa* (Hornem.) Hultén (19, 107, 156) (1840-1923)

Sea club-rush - *Schoenoplectus maritimus* (L.) Lye (129) (1894)

Sea cocklebur - *Xanthium strumarium* L. var. *canadense* (Mill.) Torr. & Gray (158) (1900)

Sea colander - *Agarum clathratum* Dumortier (92) (1876)

Sea cole [Seacole] - *Cakile maritima* Scop. (7, 92) (1828-1876)

Sea colewoort - *Brassica oleracea* L. (180) (1633)

Sea coreopsis - *Coreopsis maritima* (Nutt.) Hook.f. (138) (1923)

Sea cucklebur - *Xanthium strumarium* L. var. *canadense* (Mill.) Torr. & Gray (158) (1900)

Sea daffodil - *Pancratium maritimum* L. (2, 107) (1895-1919)

Sea eelgrass [Sea eel grass] - *Zostera marina* L. (19) (1840)

Sea gilliflower [sea gilly-flower] - *Armeria maritima* (P. Mill.) Willd (5, 156) (1913-1923), *Limonium carolinianum* (Walt.) Britt. (92) (1876)

Sea goosefoot - *Suaeda calceoliformis* (Hook.) Moq. (156) (1923), *Suaeda linearis* (Ell.) Moq. (5) (1913)

Sea holly - *Eryngium* L. (10) (1818)

Sea hollyhock - *Hibiscus moscheutos* L. (5, 156, 158) (1900-1923)

Sea lovage - *Ligusticum scoticum* L. (5, 156) (1913-1923)

Sea lungwort - *Mertensia maritima* (L.) Gray (2, 156) (1895-1942), *Mertensia maritima* (L.) Gray var. *maritima* (5) (1913)

Sea lyme grass [Sea lyme-grass] - *Leymus arenarius* (L.) Hochst. (5, 41, 92, 94, 109) (1770-1949)

Sea mat grass - *Ammophila arenaria* (L.) Link (92) (1876)

Sea mat-weed - *Ammophila arenaria (L.)* Link (45) (1896)

Sea meadow grass - *Puccinellia distans* (Jacq.) Parl. (5) (1913), *Puccinellia maritima* (Huds.) Parl. (5, 92) (1876-1913)

Sea milkwort [Seamilkwort] - *Glaux* L. (1, 4, 41, 155, 156, 158) (1770-1986), *Glaux maritima* L. (3, 4, 5, 19, 50, 92, 155, 156, 158) (1840–present)

Sea oar - *Zostera marina* L. (177) (1762)

Sea orach - *Atriplex prostrata* Bouché ex DC. (7) (1828)

Sea ox-eye - *Borrichia frutescens* (L.) DC. (5, 72, 124, 156) (1907-1937)

Sea pea - *Lathyrus japonicus* Willd. var. *maritimus* (L.) Kartesz & Gandhi (5) (1913)

Sea pig-weed - *Suaeda maritima* (L.) Dumort. (19) (1840)

Sea pimpernel - *Honckenya peploides* (L.) Ehrh. (5) (1913), *Honckenya peploides* (L.) Ehrh. subsp. *diffusa* (Hornem.) Hultén (156) (1923)

Sea pink [Sea-pink] - *Armeria maritima* (P. Mill.) Willd (5, 92, 156) (1876-1923), *Sabatia stellaris* Pursh (5, 156) (1913-1923), *Silene*

vulgaris (Moench) Garcke (5, 7, 92, 156) (1828-1923) no longer in use by 1923

Sea plantain [Sea Plantaine] - *Plantago maritima* L. (5, 19, 41, 180) (1526-1913)

Sea poppy - *Glaucium flavum* Crantz (5) (1913)

Sea rocket - *Cakile edentula* (Bigelow) Hook. subsp. *edentula* var. *edentula* (19) (1840), *Cakile maritima* Scop. (41, 92, 107) (1170-1919), *Cakile* P. Mill. (possibly) (1, 10, 13, 15, 156) (1818-1932)

Sea rush - *Juncus maritimus* Lam. (5, 50, 66) (1912–present)

Sea sand grass - *Ammophila arenaria* (L.) Link (92) (1876)

Sea sandwort - *Honckenya* Ehrh. (13) (1849), *Honckenya peploides* (L.) Ehrh. subsp. *diffusa* (Hornem.) Hultén (2, 156) (1895–1923)

Sea sedge [Sea-sedge] - *Carex arenaria* L. (5, 92, 156) (1913-1923)

Sea spear grass [Sea spear-grass] - *Puccinellia maritima* (Huds.) Parl. (5, 66, 90, 94) (1885-1913)

Sea spur grass - *Puccinellia distans* (Jacq.) Parl. (92) (1876)

Sea spurge - *Euphorbia paralias* L. (50, 178) (1596–present)

Sea tangles - *Laminaria digitata* (Hudson) J.V.Lamouroux (57) (1917)

Sea teasel-grass - *Ruppia maritima* L. (5) (1913)

Sea thrift [Sea-thrift] - *Armeria maritima* (P. Mill.) Willd (5, 156) (1913-1923)

Sea trifoly - *Glaux maritima* L. (5, 156, 158) (1900-1923)

Sea wormwood - *Artemisia campestris* L. subsp. *borealis* (Pallas) Hall & Clements (5, 156) (1913-1923), *Santolina chamaecyparissus* L. (178) (1526)

Sea wrack [Seawrack, Sea-wrack] - *Fucus vesiculosus* L. (52, 53, 60, 92) (1876-1922), *Zostera marina* L. (5, 50, 156) (1913–present)

Sea-ash [Sea ash] - *Zanthoxylum clava-herculis* L. (5, 15, 92, 156, 158) (1876-1923)

Sea-beach aristida - *Aristida tuberculosa* Nutt. (163) (1852)

Sea-beach atriplex - *Atriplex cristata* Humb. & Bonpl. ex Willd. (5) (1913)

Sea-beach orach - *Atriplex prostrata* subsp. *calotheca* (Rafn) M.A.Gust. (46) (1649)

Sea-beach sandwort [Seabeach sandwort, Sea beach sandwort] - *Honckenya peploides* (L.) Ehrh. (5) (1913), *Honckenya peploides* (L.) Ehrh. subsp. *diffusa* (Hornem.) Hultén (155, 156) (1923-1942)

Sea-beach sedge [Sea beach sedge] - *Carex silicea* Olney (5) (1913)

Sea-beach senecio - *Senecio pseudoarnica* Less. (5) (1913)

Sea-beach triple-awn grass [Sea-beach triple-awned grass] - *Aristida tuberculosa* Nutt. (5) (1913)

Sea-bed sandwort [Sea bed sandwort] - *Spergularia salina* J.& K. Presl (5) (1913)

Sea-blite [Sea blite] - *Suaeda* Forsk. ex J.F. Gmel. (1, 2, 158) (1895-1932)

Sea-buckthorn [Sea buckthorn] - *Hippophae* L. (8, 109, 138, 167) (1785-1949), *Hippophae rhamnoides* L. (135) (1910)

Sea-coast angelica [Sea coast angelica] - *Angelica gmelinii* (DC.) Pimenov (5, 156) (1913-1923)

Sea-coast beard grass [Seacoast beard-grass] - *Schizachyrium littorale* (Nash) Bicknell (5, 163) (1852-1913)

Sea-coast marsh-elder [Sea-coast marsh elder] - *Iva imbricata* Walt. (5, 156) (1913-1923)

Seacoast sumpweed - *Iva annua* L. var. *annua* (155) (1942)

Sea-cushion [Sea cushion] - *Armeria maritima* (P. Mill.) Willd (156) (1923)

Sea-dafodil - *Pancratium* L. (167) (1814)

Seaforthia palm - *Ptychosperma* Labill. (109) (1949)

Sea-girdles [Sea girdles] - *Laminaria digitata* (Hudson) J.V.Lamouroux (57, 107) (1917-1919)

Sea-grape [Seagrape, Sea grape] - *Coccoloba diversifolia* Jacq. (possibly) (106) (1930), *Coccoloba uvifera* (L.) L. (106, 109, 138) (1923-1949), *Salsola kali* L. (5, 92, 158, 178) (1596-1919)

Sea-grass [Sea grass] - *Armeria maritima* (P. Mill.) Willd (5, 156) (1913-1923), *Ruppia maritima* L. (5, 156, 158) (1900-1923), *Zostera marina* L. (5, 107, 156) (1913-1919)

Sea-holly [Seaholly, Sea holly, Sea hollie] - *Eryngium maritimum* L. (138, 178) (1526-1923)

Sea-island cotton [Sea island cotton] - *Gossypium barbadense* L. (109, 110, 138) (1886-1949)

Sea-kale [Seakale, Sea kale] - *Crambe* L. (138) (1923), *Crambe maritima* L. (92, 109) (1876-1949)

Sea-kale beet - *Beta vulgaris* L. (107) (1919)

Sea-kemps [Sea kemps] - *Plantago maritima* L. (5) (1913), *Plantago maritima* L. var. *juncoides* (Lam.) Gray (156) (1923)

Seal - *Hydrastis canadensis* L. (64) (1907)

Seal pine - *Pinus radiata* D. Don (147) (1856)

Sea-lavender [Sea lavender, Sea lauender] - *Limonium carolinianum* (Walt.) Britt. (5, 49, 58, 122, 156, 178) (1526–1937), *Limonium* P. Mill. (109, 122, 138) (1923–1949), *Limonium vulgare* Mill. (2, 19) (1840–1895)

Sea-lentil [Sea lentil] - *Sargassum natans* (L.) Gaillon (181) (~1678)

Sea-lettuce [Sea lettuce] - *Ulva* L. (7) (1828)

Sealroot - *Polygonatum biflorum* (Walt.) Ell. (92, 178, 181) (`1526-1876), *Polygonatum biflorum* (Walt.) Ell. (5, 92, 156, 157) (1876-1929), *Polygonatum biflorum* (Walt.) Ell. var. *commutatum* (J.A. & J.H. Schultes) Morong (5, 156, 157, 158) (1900-1929)

Seamberry palm - *Coccothrinax* Sarg. (109) (1949)

Sea-oats [Sea oats, Seaoats] - *Uniola* L. (50) (present), *Uniola paniculata* L. (5, 45, 50, 88, 109, 122) (1881–present)

Sea-onion of Valentia [Sea Onions of Valentia] - *Pancratium maritimum* L. (178) (1596)

Sea-parsley [Sea parsley] - *Levisticum officinale* W.D.J. Koch (92) (1876), *Ligusticum scoticum* L. (5, 156) (1913-1923)

Sea-plantain [Sea-plantane] - *Plantago maritima* L. (46) (1671)

Sea-poppy - *Glaucium flavum* Crantz (156) (1923), *Glaucium* Mill. (109) (1949)

Sea-purslane [Sea purslane] - *Honckenya peploides* (L.) Ehrh. (5) (1913), *Honckenya peploides* (L.) Ehrh. subsp. *diffusa* (Hornem.) Hultén (156) (1923), *Sesuvium* L. (1, 2, 4, 15, 50, 158) (1895–present), *Sesuvium maritimum* (Walt.) Britton, Sterns & Poggenb. (5, 156) (1913–1923), *Sesuvium portulacastrum* (L.) L. (122) (1937) TX

Sea-sand reed - *Ammophila arenaria* (L.) Link (2, 66, 87, 90) (1885-1903)

Sea-sedge [Sea sedge] - *Acorus calamus* L. (5, 156) (1913-1923)

Seashore dropseed - *Sporobolus virginicus* (L.) Kunth (50) (present)

Seashore iris - *Iris spuria* L. (138) (1923), *Iris spuria* L. subsp. *ochroleuca* (L.) Dykes (50) (present)

Seashore paspalum - *Paspalum vaginatum* Sw. (50, 155) (1942–present)

Sea-shore rush grass [Sea-shore rush-grass - *Sporobolus virginicus* (L.) Kunth (5, 99, 163) (1852-1923)

Seashore saltgrass - *Distichlis spicata* (L.) Greene (3, 155) (1942-1977)

Seaside agalinis [Sea-side agalinis] - *Agalinis maritima* (Raf.) Raf. (5) (1913)

Seaside alder - *Alnus maritima* (Marsh.) Muhl. ex Nutt. (5, 20, 97, 155, 156) (1857-1942)

Seaside alkali grass [Seaside alkaligrass] - *Puccinellia maritima* (Huds.) Parl. (50) (present)

Seaside arrowgrass [Seaside arrow grass, Seaside arrow-grass, Sea-side arrow grass] - *Triglochin maritimum* L. (5, 50, 66, 72, 93, 131, 156) (1899–present)

Seaside aster - *Eurybia spectabilis* (Aiton) Nesom (138, 155) (1931-1942)

Seaside balsam [Sea side balsam] - *Croton flavens* L. (92) (1876)

Seaside barley - *Hordeum marinum* Huds. (94) (1901)

Seaside beard grass [Sea-side beard-grass] - *Polypogon maritimus* Willd. (94) (1901)

Seaside bulrush - *Schoenoplectus maritimus* (L.) Lye (107) (1919)

Seaside buttercup - *Ranunculus cymbalaria* Pursh (127) (1933)

Seaside chloris [Sea side chloris] - *Eustachys petraea* (Sw.) Desv. (19) (1840)

Seaside collinsia - *Collinsia bartsiifolia* Benth. (138) (1923)

Seaside crowfoot [Sea side crowfoot] - *Ranunculus cymbalaria* Pursh (2, 5, 63, 72, 85, 97, 131, 156) (1895-1937)

Seaside daisy - *Erigeron glaucus* Ker-Gawl. (109) (1949)

Seaside evening-primrose [Seaside evening primrose] - *Oenothera humifusa* Nutt. (5) (1913)

Seaside everlasting pea - *Lathyrus japonicus* Willd. var. *maritimus* (L.) Kartesz & Gandhi (5) (1913)

Seaside finger grass [Seaside finger-grass] - *Eustachys petraea* (Sw.) Desv. (94) (1901)

Seaside gerardia - *Agalinis maritima* (Raf.) Raf. var. *maritima* (156) (1923)

Seaside goldenrod [Sea-side golden-rod, Seaside golden-rod, Seaside goldenrod] - *Solidago sempervirens* L. (5, 138, 156) (1913-1923), *Solidago sempervirens* var. *mexicana* (L.) Fern. (46) (1879)

Seaside grape [Sea-side grape] - *Ephedra* L. (167) (1814)

Seaside heliotrope [Sea-side heliotrope - *Heliotropium curassavicum* L. var. *obovatum* DC. (50, 157) (1929–present)

Seaside knotweed - *Polygonum maritimum* L. (5) (1913)

Seaside koniga - *Lobularia maritima* (L.) Desv. (5) (1913)

Seaside lavender [Sea-side lavender] - *Limonium carolinianum* (Walt.) Britt. (5) (1913)

Seaside millet - *Paspalum distichum* L. (5, 119) (1913-1938) OK

Seaside oats [Sea-side oat - *Uniola paniculata* L. (5, 94, 163, 177) (1762-1901)

Seaside plantain - *Plantago maritima* L. (5, 107) (1913-1919), *Plantago maritima* L. var. *juncoides* (Lam.) Gray (156) (1923)

Seaside plumb [Sea-side plumb] - *Prunus maritima* Marsh. (possibly) (8) (1785)

Seaside portulaca - *Claytonia* L. (106) (1930)

Seaside purple aster - *Eurybia spectabilis* (Aiton) Nesom (5, 156) (1913-1923)

Seaside purslane - *Sesuvium portulacastrum* (L.) L. (107) (1919)

Seaside rush - *Juncus ambiguus* Guss. (50) (present)

Seaside rush grass [Seaside rush-grass] - *Sporobolus virginicus* (L.) Kunth (94) (1901)

Seaside sand-verbena [Seaside sandverbena] - *Abronia maritima* Nutt. ex S. Wats. (155) (1942)

Sea-side sandwort [Sea side sandwort, Seaside sandwort] - *Spergularia salina* J.& K. Presl (5, 156) (1913-1923)

Seaside sedge - *Carex maritima* Gunn (5) (1913)

Seaside spurge - *Chamaesyce polygonifolia* (L.) Small (5, 122, 156) (1913-1937) TX

Seaside threeawn - *Aristida tuberculosa* Nutt. (50) (present)

Seaside-grape [Sea-side grapes, Sea side grapes] - *Coccoloba uvifera* (L.) L. (7, 20, 92, 107) (1828-1919), *Ephedra* L. (167) (1814)

Seaside-plum [Seaside plum] - *Coccoloba uvifera* (L.) L. (106) (1930)

Sea-tears - *Cakile maritima* Scop. (46) (1671)

Sea-thrift [Sea thrift] - *Limonium carolinianum* (Walt.) Britt. (58, 92) (1869-1876), *Salsola kali* L. (5, 156, 158) (1900-1923)

Sea-urchin cactus - *Astrophytum asterias* (Zucc.) Lem. (109) (1949)

Sea-wand - *Laminaria digitata* (Hudson) J.V.Lamouroux (107) (1919)

Sea-ware - *Laminaria digitata* (Hudson) J.V.Lamouroux (107) (1919)

Sea-weed fern [Sea weed fern] - *Asplenium scolopendrium* L. var. *americanum* (Fern.) Kartesz & Gandhi (5) (1913)

Seaweeds - *Fucus* L. (7) (1828)

Sebesten - *Cordia myxa* L. (92) (1876)

Sebestier domestique (French) - *Cordia sebestena* L. (20) (1857)

Seckelblume (German) - *Ceanothus americanus* L. (158) (1900)

Secund rush - *Juncus secundus* Beauv. ex Poir. (5) (1913)

Sedano (Italy) - *Apium graveolens* L. (107) (1919)

Sedge - *Carex* L. (1, 7, 10, 50, 85, 92, 93, 101, 109, 139, 152, 155, 156, 158, 167) (1814–present)

Sedge grass - *Andropogon* L. (7) (1828)

Sedge root - *Acorus calamus* L. (5) (1913)

Sedge-cane [Sedge cane] - *Acorus calamus* L. (5, 156) (1913-1923)

Sedge-like equisetum - *Equisetum scirpoides* Michx. (5) (1913)

Sedge-like horsetail [Sedgelike horsetail] - *Equisetum scirpoides* Michx. (155) (1942)

Sedge-rush [Sedge rush] - *Acorus calamus* L. (5, 156) (1913–1923)

See-bright [See bright] - *Salvia sclarea* L. (5, 156) (1913-1923)
Seed mesquite - *Bouteloua rigidiseta* (Steud.) Hitchc. (94) (1901)
Seed ticks - *Desmodium canadense* (L.) DC. (5, 62, 155) (1912-1942)
Seedbox - *Ludwigia* L. (4, 122, 138, 155) (1923-1986)
Seedbox [Seed box, Seed-box] - *Ludwigia alternifolia* L. (2, 5, 19, 50, 63, 72, 74, 92, 156, 158) (1840–present)
Seeded-plum [Seeded plums] - *Diospyros virginiana* L. (7, 19, 92, 156, 158) (1828-1923)
Seeder - *Humulus lupulus* L. (157, 158) (1900-1929)
Seedy buckberry [Seedy buck-berry] - *Lyonia ligustrina* (L.) DC. (75, 156) (1894-1923), *Lyonia ligustrina* (L.) DC. var. *ligustrina* (5) (1913)
Seedy dewberry - *Vaccinium corymbosum* L. (5) (1913)
Seel - *Salix* L. (158) (1900)
See-myrtle [See myrtle] - *Baccharis halimifolia* L. (106) (1930)
Seep arnica - *Arnica lonchophylla* Greene subsp. *arnoglossa* (Greene) Maguire (50) (present)
Seep monkey-flower [Seep monkeyflower] - *Mimulus guttatus* DC. (50) (present)
Seepweed - *Suaeda* Forsk. ex J.F. Gmel. (4, 50, 155) (1942–present), *Suaeda linearis* (Ell.) Moq. (122) (1937) TX, *Suaeda moquinii* (Torr.) Greene (4) (1986)
Seepwillow baccharis - *Baccharis salicifolia* (Ruiz & Pavón) Pers. (155) (1942)
Sêf (Persian) - *Malus sylvestris* Mill. (110) (1886)
Seg - *Carex* L. (184) (1793)
Segal (Breton) - *Secale cereale* L. (110) (1886)
Segala (Italian) - *Secale cereale* L. (180) (1633)
Segede bwens (Chippewa) - *Osmorhiza longistylis* (Torr.) DC. (105) (1932)
Seggs - *Iris pseudacorus* L. (180) (1633)
Sego lily [Segolily] - *Calochortus gunnisonii* S. Wats. (3) (1977), *Calochortus luteus* Dougl. ex Lindl. (107) (1919), *Calochortus nuttallii* Torr. & Gray (50, 155) (1942–present), *Calochortus* Pursh. (101) (1905), *Zigadenus venenosus* S. Wats. var. *gramineus* (Rydb.) Walsh ex M.E. Peck (133) (1903) ND
Seidenpflanzen (German) - *Asclepias syriaca* L. (6, 158) (1892-1900)
Seifenwurzel (German) - *Saponaria officinalis* L. (158) (1900)
Seigle (French) - *Secale cereale* L. (158, 180) (1633-1900)
Selaginella - *Selaginella* Beauv. (1, 138, 155, 158) (1900-1942) diminutive of Selago an ancient name of a lycopodium, *Selaginella densa* Rydb. (146) (1939)
Seldij (Flanders) - *Apium graveolens* L. (107) (1919)
Selenia - *Selenia aurea* Nutt. (5, 97) (1913-1937)
Selfegrene - *Sempervivum tectorum* L. (179) (1526)
Self-heal [Self heal, Selfheal, Selfe heale] - *Pimpinella saxifraga* L. (179) (1526), *Prunella* L. (21, 38, 50, 155, 158) (1900–present), *Prunella vulgaris* L. (3, 4, 5, 10, 40, 48, 63, 80, 82, 97, 106 109, 124, 131, 156, 157, 158) (1818-1986)
Selg - *Beta* L. (107) (1919) Arabs
Selga (Portuguese) - *Beta vulgaris* L. (110) (1886)
Selinocarpus - *Selinocarpus* Gray (158) (1900)
Selinon - *Apium graveolens* L. (110) (1886) in Odyssey, *Petroselinum crispum* (P. Mill.) Nyman ex A.W. Hill (107) (322 BC)
Selkirk's violet [Selkirk violet] - *Viola selkirkii* Pursh ex Goldie (2, 5, 50, 138) (1895–present)
Selleree (German) - *Apium graveolens* L. (107) (1919)
Selleri (Denmark) - *Apium graveolens* L. (107) (1919)
Sellerieblättrige Gelbwurz (German) - *Xanthorhiza simplicissima* Marsh. (49) (1898)
Sellery - *Apium graveolens* L. (107) (1629)
Selly - *Salix* L. (158) (1900)
Sencion - *Senecio vulgaris* L. (156, 158) (1900-1923)
Seneca grass - *Hierochloe odorata* (L.) Beauv. (5, 19, 45, 66, 87, 90, 92) (1840-1903)
Seneca root - *Polygala senega* L. (92, 158) (1876-1900)
Seneca snakeroot [Seneca snake root, Seneca-snakeroot] - *Polygala senega* L. (3, 5, 6, 7, 19, 35, 40, 47, 49, 50, 52, 53, 63, 64, 72, 85, 92, 93, 138, 156, 158) (1892–present)
Seneca-snakeroot polygala - *Polygala senega* L. (155) (1942)
Senecio - *Packera aurea* (L.) A.& D. Löve (54) (1905)
Seneçon (French) - *Packera aurea* (L.) A.& D. Löve (6) (1892)
Senecon (Spanish) - *Senecio vulgaris* L. (158) (1900)
Senega - *Polygala senega* L. (46, 52, 53, 59, 61, 64) (1870-1922)
Senega root [Senega-root] - *Polygala senega* L. (5, 53, 55, 92, 156) (1876-1923)
Senega snakeroot [Senega snake root] - *Polygala senega* L. (4, 6, 15, 49, 53, 57, 64, 92, 158) (1895-1986)
Senega Wurzel [Senegawurzel] (German) - *Polygala senega* L. (6, 158) (1892–1900)
Seneka root - *Polygala senega* L. (92) (1876)
Seneka snakeroot [Seneka snake root] - *Polygala senega* L. (6, 48, 49, 57, 92) (1876-1917) KS
Seng - *Panax quinquefolius* L. (64) (1907)
Sen-green - *Sempervivum tectorum* L. (156) (1923)
Sengreen saxifrage - *Saxifraga aizoides* L. (5) (1913)
Sengren saxifrage - *Saxifraga aizoides* L. (156) (1923)
Senhalanac [Senhalenac] - *Rhus glabra* L. (5, 74, 156, 158) (1893–1923) Ferrisburgh VA name of Saranac River comes from this
Senna - *Cassia* L. (1, 82, 106, 109, 155, 156) (1923-1949), *Senna alexandrina* Mill. (57, 58, 61, 92) (1869-1917), *Senna marilandica* (L.) Link (106) (1930) Southern states, *Senna* Mill. (50) (Present)
Senna Americana (Official name of Materia Medica) - *Senna marilandica* (L.) Link (7) (1828)
Senna husks - *Senna alexandrina* Mill. (92) (1876)
Senne' d'Amerique (French) - *Senna marilandica* (L.) Link (5) (1913)
Senore - *Brassica nigra* (L.) W.D.J. Koch (158) (1900)
Señorita waterlily - *Nymphaea elegans* Hook. (138, 155) (1923–1942)
Senors - *Brassica nigra* (L.) W.D.J. Koch (157) (1929)
Sensitive brier [Sensitivebrier, Sensitive briar] - *Mimosa* L. (1, 2, 4, 155, 158) (1895-1986), *Mimosa nuttallii* (DC.) B.L. Turner (4) (1986), *Mimosa rupertiana* B.L. Turner (3) (1977), *Neptunia* Lour. (155) (1942), *Mimosa microphylla* Dry. (5, 19, 76, 85, 92, 93, 95, 97, 131, 156, 158) (1840-1937)
Sensitive cassia - *Chamaecrista nictitans* (L.) Moench subsp. *nictitans* var. *nictitans* (38) (1820)
Sensitive fern - *Onoclea* L. (1, 4, 10, 50, 72, 138, 158) (1818–present)
Sensitive fern [Sensitive-fern, Sensitivefern] - *Onoclea sensibilis* L. (3, 4, 5, 19, 50, 86, 92, 97, 109, 122, 131, 155, 157, 158) (1840–present) fronds wilt quickly when cut and are very sensitive to frost
Sensitive joint-vetch [Sensitive jointvetch, Sensitive joint vetch] - *Aeschynomene virginica* (L.) Britton, Sterns & Poggenb. (2, 5, 155) (1895-1942)
Sensitive partridgepea [Sensitive partridge pea] - *Chamaecrista nictitans* (L.) Moench subsp. *nictitans* var. *nictitans* (4) (1986)
Sensitive pea [Sensitive-pea] - *Chamaecrista* (L.) Moench (1, 50, 93) (1932–present) Neb, *Chamaecrista fasciculata* (Michx.) Greene (85, 125) (1930–1932) KS, *Chamaecrista fasciculata* (Michx.) Greene var. *fasciculata* (47, 92, 106, 131) (1852–1930) SD, *Chamaecrista nictitans* (L.) Moench (5, 97) (1913–1937) OK, *Chamaecrista nictitans* (L.) Moench subsp. *nictitans* var. *nictitans* (3, 156, 158) (1900–1977)
Sensitive plant [Sensitive-plant, Sensitiveplant] - *Chamaecrista fasciculata* (Michx.) Greene var. *fasciculata* (156) (1923), *Chamaecrista nictitans* (L.) Moench subsp. *nictitans* var. *nictitans* (92, 156) (1898–1923), *Mimosa* L. (50) (Present), *Mimosa microphylla* Dry. (5, 158) (1900–1913), *Mimosa pudica* L. (92, 109, 138) (1876–1949)
Sensitive senna - *Chamaecrista fasciculata* (Michx.) Greene var. *fasciculata* (92) (1876)
Sensitive-rose [Sensitive rose] - *Mimosa microphylla* Dry. (5, 73, 76, 156, 158) (1892-1923) Burnside SD
Senvie - *Sinapis alba* L. (5) (1913)

Senvre - *Sinapis alba* L. (158) (1900)

Sepentaire noire (French) - *Actaea racemosa* L. (7) (1828)

September elm - *Ulmus serotina* Sarg. (97, 138) (1923-1937)

Septentaria Virginiana (Official name of Materia Medica) - *Aristolochia serpentaria* L. (7) (1828)

Sequoia - *Sequoia* Endl. (138) (1923) for Sequoyah, about 1770-1843, Cherokee half-breed from Georgia

Sericea lespedeza - *Lespedeza cuneata* (Dumort.-Cours.) G. Don (3, 4) (1977-1986)

Serin cade - *Narcissus ×medioluteus* Mill. [*poeticus × tazetta*] (180) (1633)

Serinia - *Krigia caespitosa* (Raf.) Chambers (5, 97) (1913-1937), *Krigia* Schreb. (155, 158) (1900-1942)

Serpent cucumber - *Cucumis melo* L. (92) (1876)

Serpent euphorbia - *Chamaesyce serpens* (Kunth) Small (155) (1942)

Serpent melon - *Cucumis melo* L. (92) (1876)

Serpentairu ou couleuvrée de Virginie (French) - *Aristolochia serpentaria* L. (6) (1892)

Serpentaria - *Aristolochia reticulata* Nutt. (64) (1907), *Aristolochia serpentaria* L. (6, 52, 53, 54, 58, 59, 60, 64, 92, 158) (1869-1922), *Polygonum amphibium* L. (46) (1879)

Serpentaria nigra (Official name of Materia Medica) - *Actaea racemosa* L. (7) (1828)

Serpentary - *Aristolochia serpentaria* L. (5, 55, 64, 156, 158) (1900-1923)

Serpentary-root [Serpentary root] - *Aristolochia serpentaria* L. (6, 55) (1892-1911)

Serpent-grass [Serpent grass] - *Polygonum viviparum* L. (5, 107) (1913-1919)

Serpentine aster - *Symphyotrichum depauperatum* (Fern.) Nesom (5, 156) (1913–1923)

Serpentine manzanita - *Arctostaphylos obispoensis* Eastw. (155) (1942)

Serpentona maior - *Dracunculus vulgaris* Schott (178) (1596)

Serpentroot - *Scorzonera* L. (138, 155) (1923-1942)

Serpent's-moly [Serpents moly] - *Allium nigrum* L. (178) (1596)

Serpent's-tongue [Serpent's tongue] - *Ophioglossum* L. (158) (1900), *Ophioglossum vulgatum* L. (5) (1913)

Serrated wintergreen - *Orthilia secunda* (L.) House (5) (1913)

Serrate-leaf stryphonia [Serrate leaved stryphonia] - *Rhus integrifolia* (Nutt.) Benth. & Hook. f. ex Brewer & S. Wats. (20) (1857)

Service tree [Servicetree, Seruice tree] - *Amelanchier canadensis* (L.) Medik. (5, 158) (1900-1913), *Sorbus americana* Marsh. (92) (1876), *Sorbus* L. (7, 8) (1785-1828)

Serviceberry [Service berry, Service-berry] - *Amelanchier alnifolia* (Nutt.) Nutt. ex M. Roemer (35, 146, 160) (1806-1939), *Amelanchier arborea* (Michx. f.) Fern. (4) (1986), *Amelanchier canadensis* (L.) Medik. (5, 9, 14, 63, 85, 93, 95, 97, 107, 113, 124, 130, 131, 156) (1873-1936), *Amelanchier* Medik. (1, 2, 4, 35, 50, 106, 109, 122, 138, 153, 155) (1895–present), *Amelanchier sanguinea* (Pursh) DC. (34) (1834)

Serviceberry willow - *Salix planifolia* Pursh (3, 4) (1977-1986)

Sesame - *Sesamum orientale* L. (49, 107, 110, 138) (1886-1923)

Sesame grass [Sesame-grass] - *Saccharum giganteum* (Walt.) Pers. (5) (1913), *Tripsacum dactyloides* (L.) L. (2, 5, 14, 45, 66, 87, 92, 119) (1876-1938), *Tripsacum* L. (1, 93) (1932-1936) Neb

Sesame leaves - *Sesamum orientale* L. (92) (1876)

Sesamum - *Sesamum orientale* L. (57) (1917)

Sesquehana sand cherry [Sesquehana sandcherry] - *Prunus pumila* L. var. *susquehanae* (hort. ex Willd.) Jaeger (50) (Present), *Prunus pumila* L. var. *susquehanae* (hort. ex Willd.) Jaeger (50) (present)

Sessile nut-rush [Sessile nut rush] - *Scleria reticularis* Michx. (66) (1903)

Sessile tickclover - *Desmodium sessilifolium* (Torr.) Torr. & Gray (2, 155) (1895)

Sessile-flower cress [Sessile-flowered cress, Sessile-flowered cress] - *Rorippa sessiliflora* (Nutt.) A.S. Hitchc. (5, 72, 97) (1907-1937) IA OK

Sessile-flower milkvetch [Sessile flowered milk vetch, Sessile-flowered milk vetch] - *Astragalus spatulatus* Sheldon (5) (1913)

Sessile-flower red wake-robin [Sessile-flowered red wake robin] - *Trillium sessile* L. (158) (1900)

Sessile-flower wake-robin [Sessile-flowered wake robin] - *Trillium sessile* L. (5, 72) (1907-1913) IA

Sessile-fruit arrowhead [Sessilefruit arrowhead, Sessile-fruited arrow-head, Sessile-fruited arrowhead] - *Sagittaria rigida* Pursh (5, 50, 72, 93, 97) (1907–present)

Sessile-leaf bellflower [Sessile-leaved bell-flower] - *Uvularia sessilifolia* L. (158) (1900)

Sessile-leaf bellwort [Sessileleaf bellwort, Sessile-leaved bellwort, Sessile-leaved bell-wort] - *Uvularia sessilifolia* L. (48, 50, 72, 86) (1878–present) IA

Sessile-leaf eupatorium [Sessile-leaved eupatorium] - *Eupatorium sessilifolium* L. (187) (1818)

Sessile-leaf tickclover [Sessile-leaved tickclover] - *Desmodium sessilifolium* (Torr.) Torr. & Gray (4) (1986)

Sessile-leaf tick-trefoil [Sessileleaf ticktrefoil, Sessile-leaved tick trefoil, Sessile-leaved tick-trefoil] - *Desmodium sessilifolium* (Torr.) Torr. & Gray (4, 5, 50, 72) (1907–present)

Sessile-leaf twisted-stalk [Sessile-leaved twisted stalk] - *Streptopus lanceolatus* (Ait.) Reveal var. *roseus* (Michx.) Reveal (5) (1913)

Sessile-leaf water-hoarhound [Sessile-leaved water hoarhound] - *Lycopus amplectens* Raf. (5) (1913) W. US

Sesuvium - *Sesuvium* L. (155) (1942)

Setanie (French) - *Allium* L. (180) (1633)

Setewale - *Valeriana officinalis* L. (156) (1923) no longer in use by 1923

Setsticker - *Ranunculus repens* L. (158) (1900)

Setterwort [Setterwoort] - *Helleborus foetidus* L. (178) (1526)

Settiswort - *Helleborus foetidus* L. (7, 92) (1828-1876)

Setwall - *Carphephorus odoratissimus* (J.F. Gmel.) Herbert (107) (1919), *Valeriana officinalis* L. (5, 92, 156) (1876-1923) no longer in use by 1923

Seven sisters - *Euphorbia helioscopia* L. (5, 156) (1913–1923) obsolete by 1923

Sevenangle pipewort [Sevenangle pipewort, Seven-angled pipewort] - *Eriocaulon aquaticum* (Hill) Druce (5, 50) (1913–present)

Sevenbark [Seven-bark, Seven bark, Seven barks] - *Euonymus atropurpurea* Jacq. (59) (1911), *Hydrangea arborescens* L. (5, 49, 52, 53, 54, 61, 64, 92, 156, 158) (1870–1923), *Physocarpus capitatus* (Pursh) Kuntze (35) (1806), *Physocarpus opulifolius* (L.) Maxim. var. *opulifolius* (177) (1762)

Seven-leaf ivy [Seven-leaved ivy, Seven-leafed ivy] - *Ampelopsis arborea* (L.) Koehne (106) (1930), *Parthenocissus heptaphylla* (Buckl.) Britt. ex Small (106, 124) (1930-1937)

Seven-sisters [Seven sisters] - *Crinum americanum* L. (50) (present), *Euphorbia peplus* L. (5, 156) (1913-1923)

Seven-year apple [Seven year apple] - *Casasia clusiifolia* (Jacq.) Urban (76) (1896) Florida

Seven-years'-love [Seven years' love] - *Achillea ptarmica* L. (156) (1923)

Seville orange - *Citrus ×aurantium* L. [*maxima × reticulata*] (107, 109) (1919-1949)

Sewee bean - *Phaseolus lunatus* L. (109) (1949)

Ŝewe-minŝ (Chippewa) - *Fagus grandifolia* Ehrh. (105) (1932)

Shad bush [Shadbush, Shad-bush] - *Amelanchier ×intermedia* Spach [*arborea × canadensis*] (5) (1913), *Amelanchier canadensis* (L.) Medik. (2, 5, 19, 40, 46, 72, 92, 106, 130, 156, 158) (1840–1930), *Pyrus canadensis* (L.) Farw. (92) (1876)

Shad or Shad tree - *Amelanchier canadensis* (L.) Medik. (7, 92, 107) (1828-1919)

Shadberry [Shad berry] - *Amelanchier arborea* (Michx. f.) Fern. (4) (1986), *Amelanchier canadensis* (L.) Medik. (103) (1870), *Amelanchier* Medik. (1) (1932)

Shad-blossom - *Draba verna* L. (187) (1818)

Shadblow - *Amelanchier* Medik. (138, 155) (1923-1942)

Shad-blow [Shadblow] - *Amelanchier canadensis* (L.) Medik. (73, 156) (1892-1923) NH, *Draba verna* L. (156) (1923)

Shadblow serviceberry - *Amelanchier canadensis* (L.) Medik. (155) (1942)

Shadbush - *Amelanchier* Medik. (4, 109, 138, 155) (1942-1986)

Shaddock - *Citrus maxima* (Burm. f.) Merr. (109) (1949) from name of captain who first introducd species to West Indies

Shade fescue - *Festuca heterophylla* Lam. (138) (1923)

Shad-flower [Shadflower, Shad flower] - *Amelanchier canadensis* (L.) Medik. (156) (1923), *Draba verna* L. (5, 74) (1893-1913) WV, *Epigaea repens* L. (5, 73, 77, 156) (1892-1923) New England & NJ

Shadowy goldenrod [Shadowy golden-rod] - *Solidago sciaphila* Steele (5) (1913)

Shadscale [Shad scale] - *Atriplex canescens* (Pursh) Nutt. (3, 97, 118, 153) (1898-1977)

Shadscale saltbush - *Atriplex confertifolia* (Torr. & Frem.) S. Wats. (50, 155) (1942–present)

Shadscales - *Atriplex confertifolia* (Torr. & Frem.) S. Wats. (1) (1932)

Shag walnut - *Carya alba* (L.) Nutt. ex Ell. (19) (1840)

Shagahinga (Missouri tribes) - *Melothria pendula* L. (7) (1828)

Shagbark [Shag-bark] - *Carya ovata* (Mill.) K. Koch (5, 93, 158) (1900-1936)

Shagbark hickory [Shag-bark hickory] - *Carya alba* (L.) Nutt. ex Ell. (6, 19, 57, 58, 107) (1840-1919), *Carya ovata* (Mill.) K. Koch (1, 3, 4, 50, 82, 93, 109, 138, 155, 156, 158) (1900–present)

Shag-bark manzanita [Shagbark manzanita] - *Arctostaphylos rudis* Jepson & Wies. ex Jepson (155) (1942)

Shag-bark tree [Shag bark tree] - *Carya alba* (L.) Nutt. ex Ell. (92) (1876)

Shag-bark walnut [Shag bark walnut] - *Carya alba* (L.) Nutt. ex Ell. (92) (1876)

Shaggy crabgrass - *Digitaria villosa* (Walt.) Pers. (50) (Present)

Shaggy dwarf morning-glory - *Evolvulus nuttallianus* J.A. Schultes (50) (Present)

Shaggy false gromwell - *Onosmodium molle* Michx. (72) (1907), *Onosmodium molle* Michx. subsp. *hispidissimum* (Mackenzie) Boivin (5, 97) (1913-1937)

Shaggy finger grass [Shaggy fingergrass] - *Digitaria villosa* (Walt.) Pers. (155) (1942)

Shaggy fleabane - *Erigeron pumilus* Nutt. (50) (Present), *Erigeron pumilus* Nutt. subsp. *pumilus* (50) (Present)

Shaggy garden purslane - *Portulaca pilosa* L. (109) (1949)

Shaggy mane - *Coprinus comatus* (O.F. Müll.) Gray (128) (1933)

Shaggy portulaca - *Portulaca pilosa* L. (155) (1942)

Shaggy-soldier - *Galinsoga quadriradiata* Cav. (50) (Present)

Shakers - *Briza media* L. (5) (1913)

Shallon - *Gaultheria shallon* Pursh (14, 35) (1806-1882)

Shallu - *Sorghum bicolor* (L.) Moench subsp. *bicolor* (109, 155) (1942-1949)

Shallun - *Vaccinium ovatum* Pursh (35) (1806)

Shama millet - *Echinochloa colona* (L.) Link (45, 56) (1896-1901)

Shamalo - *Echinochloa frumentacea* Link (158) (1900)

Shamaloo - *Echinochloa frumentacea* Link (158) (1900)

Shame vine [Shame-vine] - *Mimosa* L. (73) (1892) Northern MS, *Mimosa microphylla* Dry. (5, 122, 156, 158) (1900–1937), *Geranium maculatum* L. (5, 64, 156, 157, 158) (1900–1929)

Shame-faced brier - *Mimosa microphylla* Dry. (76) (1896) Southwestern MO

Shamrock - *Medicago lupulina* L. (5, 156, 158) (1900-1923), *Oxalis montana* Raf. (possibly) (5, 92, 156) (1876-1923), *Trifolium dubium* Sibth. (5) (1913), *Trifolium repens* L. (5, 92, 156) (1876-1923), *Trillium erectum* L. (5, 156) (1913-1923)

Shanga-makan (Omaha-Ponca, horse-medicine) - *Osmorhiza longistylis* (Torr.) DC. (37) (1919)

Shangga wathata (Omaha-Ponca) - *Equisetum* L. (37) (1830)

Shanghai trefoil - *Medicago polymorpha* L. (107) (1919)

Shanpi (Sioux) - *Urtica dioica* L. subsp. *gracilis* (Aiton) Seland. (101) (1905) MT

Shan-tan - *Lilium bulbiferum* L. (107) (1919) China

Shanwa millet [Shanwamillet] - *Echinochloa colona* (L.) Link (155) (1942)

Shapely milk-pea [Shapely milkpea] - *Galactia regularis* (L.) Britton, Sterns & Poggenb. (155) (1942)

Sharp dock - *Rumex acetosa* L. (5, 156) (1913–1923)

Sharp thistle [Sharp-thistle] - *Cirsium arvense* (L.) Scop. (157) (1929)

Sharp-flower manna grass [Sharp-flowered manna-grass] - *Glyceria acutiflora* Torr. (90, 94) (1885–1901)

Sharp-fringe sow-thistle [Sharp-fringed sow-thistle] - *Sonchus asper* (L.) Hill (5) (1913)

Sharp-fruit globe-mallow [Sharp-fruited globe mallow] - *Sphaeralcea angustifolia* (Cav.) G. Don (5, 97) (1913–1937)

Sharp-fruit rush [Sharp-fruited rush, Sharp fruited rush] - *Juncus acuminatus* Michx. (5, 66, 72, 120) (1903–1938)

Sharp-leaf beard-tongue [Sharp-leaved beard-tongue] - *Penstemon acuminatus* Dougl. ex Lindl. (5, 93, 97) (1913–1937)

Sharp-leaf cancerwort [Sharpleaf cancerwort] - *Kickxia elatine* (L.) Dumort. (50) (present)

Sharp-leaf penstemon [Sharpleaf penstemon] - *Penstemon acuminatus* Dougl. ex Lindl. (122) (1937)

Sharp-leaf valerian [Sharpleaf valerian] - *Valeriana acutiloba* Rydb. (50, 155) (1942–present), *Valeriana acutiloba* var. *acutiloba* Rydb. (50) (present)

Sharp-leaf willow [Sharpleaf willow] - *Salix arbusculoides* Anderss. (138) (1923)

Sharp-lobe hepatica [Sharplobe hepatica, Sharp-lobed hepatica] - *Hepatica nobilis* Schreb. var. *acuta* (Pursh) Steyermark (2, 138) (1895–1923)

Sharp-lobe liver-leaf [Sharp-lobed liver-leaf] - *Hepatica nobilis* Schreb. var. *acuta* (Pursh) Steyermark (5) (1913)

Sharp-lobe liverwort [Sharp-lobed liverwort] - *Hepatica nobilis* Schreb. var. *acuta* (Pursh) Steyermark (5) (1913)

Sharp-notch goldenrod [Sharp-notched golden-rod] - *Solidago arguta* Aiton (19, 187) (1818–1840)

Sharp-petal wintergreen [Sharp-petaled wintergreen] - *Pyrola chlorantha* Sw. (5) (1913)

Sharp-point dock [Sharp-pointed dock] - *Rumex crispus* L. (46) (1671) accidentally introduced by 1671

Sharp-point fluellin [Sharppoint fluellin, Sharp-pointed fluellin] - *Kickxia elatine* (L.) Dumort. (5, 155) (1913–1942)

Sharp-point prairie-dandelion [Sharppoint prairie-dandelion] - *Nothocalais cuspidata* (Pursh) Greene (50) (present)

Sharp-point red-top [Sharp pointed red top] - *Calamagrostis stricta* (Timm) Koel. subsp. *inexpansa* (Gray) C. W. Greene (56) (1901)

Sharp-point rush [Sharp pointed rush] - *Schoenoplectus pungens* (Vahl) Palla var. *pungens* (129) (1894)

Sharp-point rush [Sharp-pointed rush] - *Juncus acuminatus* Michx. (156) (1923)

Sharp-point toadflax [Sharp-pointed toad flax] - *Kickxia elatine* (L.) Dumort. (5) (1913)

Sharp-scale diplachne [Sharp-scaled diplachne] - *Leptochloa fusca* (L.) Kunth subsp. *fascicularis* (Lam.) N. Snow (5) (1913)

Sharp-scale erioneuron [Sharp-scaled erioneuron] - *Erioneuron pilosum* (Buckl.) Nash (5) (1913)

Sharp-scale leptochloa [Sharp-scaled leptochloa] - *Leptochloa panicea* (Retz.) Ohwi subsp. *mucronata* (Michx.) Nowack (5, 99) (1913–1923)

Sharp-scale manna grass [Sharp-scaled manna grass] - *Glyceria acutiflora* Torr. (5) (1913)

Sharp-scale sedge [Sharpscale sedge, Sharp-scaled sedge - *Carex oxylepis* Torr. & Hook (5, 50) (1913–present)

Sharp-scale triodia [Sharp-scaled triodia - *Erioneuron pilosum* (Buckl.) Nash (119) (1938)

Sharp-tooth goldenrod [Sharp-toothed golden-rod, Sharp-toothed goldenrod] - *Solidago juncea* Aiton (5, 156) (1913-1923)

Sharp-wing monkeyflower [Sharpwing monkeyflower, Sharpwing monkey-flower, Sharp-winged monkey flower, Sharp winged monkey flower, Sharp-winged]monkey-flower - *Mimulus alatus* Aiton (3, 4, 5, 50, 72, 97, 122, 155) (1907–present)

Shasta fir - *Abies magnifica* A. Murr. var. *shastensis* Lemmon (138) (1923)

Shasta panic grass [Shasta panicgrass] - *Dichanthelium* ×*scoparioides* (Ashe) Mohlenbrock (pro sp.) [*acuminatum* × *oligosanthes*] (50) (Present)

Shasta panicum - *Dichanthelium* ×*scoparioides* (Ashe) Mohlenbrock (pro sp.) [*acuminatum* × *oligosanthes*] (155) (1942)

Shasta red fir - *Abies magnifica* A. Murr. var. *shastensis* Lemmon (155) (1942)

Shaved sedge - *Carex tonsa* (Fernald) Bicknell (50) (present)

Shave-grass [Shave grass] - *Equisetum hyemale* L. (5, 6, 10, 46, 49, 53, 92, 107, 158) (1818-1919)

Shaveweed [Shave weed] - *Equisetum hyemale* L. (5) (1913)

Shavings - *Chionanthus virginicus* L. (5, 156) (1913-1923)

Shawanese lettuce - *Hydrophyllum virginianum* L. (6) (1892)

Shawnee salad [Shawnee sallad] - *Hydrophyllum appendiculatum* Michx. (7) (1828), *Hydrophyllum virginianum* L. (50, 107, 156) (1919–present)

Shawnee-haw - *Rhus microphylla* Engelm. (106) (1930)

Shawnee-haw [Shawnee haw] - *Viburnum nudum* L. (5, 156) (1913-1923)

Shawnee-wood [Shawnee-wood] - *Catalpa speciosa* (Warder) Warder ex Engelm. (5, 156, 158) (1900-1923)

She (Omaha-Ponca) - *Malus ioensis* (Wood) Britton (37) (1919) She-hi (Apple tree), She-si (Apple seed)

She balsam [She-balsam] - *Abies fraseri* (Pursh) Poir. (5, 158) (1900-1913)

She string - *Tephrosia lindheimeri* Gray (124) (1937)

Shear grass - *Elymus repens* (L.) Gould (5) (1913)

Sheathed amanitopsis - *Amanita vaginata* var. *vaginata* (Bull.) Fr. (155) (1942)

Sheathed cotton-grass [Sheathed cotton grass] - *Eriophorum callitrix* Cham. ex C.A. Mey. (5) (1913)

Sheathed dulichium - *Dulichium arundinaceum* (L.) Britt. var. *arundinaceum* (187) (1818)

Sheathed pondweed - *Stuckenia vaginatus* (Turcz.) Holub (50, 155) (1942–present)

Sheathed rush grass [Sheathed rush-grass] - *Sporobolus vaginiflorus* (Torr. ex Gray) Wood (5, 56, 80, 93, 99) (1901-1936)

Sheathed sedge - *Carex vaginata* Tausch. (5, 50) (1913–present)

Shedlock - *Raphanus raphanistrum* L. (5) (1913)

Sheep fescue [Sheep's fescue, Sheeps fescue] - *Festuca ovina* L. (2, 5, 11, 45, 50, 56, 66, 67, 68, 90, 92, 94, 109, 111, 129, 140, 143, 138, 155) (1885–present)

Sheep laurel [Sheep-laurel] - *Kalmia angustifolia* L. (2, 5, 7, 19, 71, 92, 106, 109) (1828-1949), *Kalmia latifolia* L. (6, 49, 53, 61, 71) (1870-1922)

Sheep loco - *Astragalus nothoxys* Gray (155) (1942)

Sheep root [Sheep-root] - *Pinguicula vulgaris* L. (5, 156) (1913–1923)

Sheep rot [Sheep-rot] - *Pinguicula vulgaris* L. (5, 156) (1913-1923)

Sheep sedge - *Carex illota* Bailey (139) (1944) CO

Sheep sorrel [Sheep-sorrel, Sheep's sorrel] - *Oxalis montana* Raf. (possibly) (5, 74, 156) (1893-1923) IA, *Oxalis stricta* L. (5, 62, 74, 156, 158) (1893-1923), *Oxalis violacea* L. (5, 37, 74, 156) (1893-1923), *Rumex acetosa* L. (45) (1896), *Rumex acetosella* L. (1, 3, 4, 5, 19, 48, 56, 58, 61, 62, 72, 73, 80, 85, 92, 97, 106, 122, 125, 131, 145, 148, 155, 156, 157, 158) (1869-1986), *Rumex aquaticus* L. var. *fenestratus* (Greene) Dorn (35) (1806)

Sheepberry [Sheep berry, Sheep-berry] - *Viburnum lentago* L. (2, 4, 5, 19, 53, 72, 82, 92, 95, 105, 107, 109, 113, 130, 156, 158) (1840-1986), *Viburnum prunifolium* L. (156, 158) (1900-1923)

Sheepberry bark [Sheep berry bark] - *Viburnum lentago* L. (92) (1876)

Sheepbine - *Convolvulus arvensis* L. (156) (1923) no longer in use by 1923

Sheep-blue - *Convolvulus arvensis* L. (157, 158) (1900-1929)

Sheepbur [Sheep burr, Sheep-bur] - *Acaena* Mutis ex L. (155) (1942), *Acaena pinnatifida* Ruiz & Pavón (50) (present), *Xanthium strumarium* L. (92, 158) (1876-1900), *Xanthium strumarium* L. var. *canadense* (Mill.) Torr. & Gray (156) (1923), *Xanthium strumarium* L. var. *glabratum* (DC.) Cronq. (5) (1913)

Sheep-foot [Sheepfoot] - *Lotus corniculatus* L. (5, 156, 158) (1900-1923)

Sheep-lice - *Cynoglossum officinale* L. (73, 156, 157, 158) (1892-1929) N. OH

Sheep-nose [Sheep nose, Sheep noses] - *Fragaria vesca* L. (5, 76, 158) (1896-1913) Central VT

Sheep-pod - *Astragalus* L. (1) (1932)

Sheep-poison [Sheep poison] - *Kalmia angustifolia* L. (5, 71, 73, 92, 156) (1876-1923) Northeastern US, *Kalmia latifolia* L. (7) (1828), *Oxalis stricta* L. (158) (1900)

Sheep's clover - *Oxalis stricta* L. (76) (1896) Waverly MA

Sheep's fescue - *Festuca saximontana* Rydb. var. *saximontana* (3) (1977)

Sheep's fescue grass [Sheep's fescue-grass] - *Festuca ovina* L. (72, 87, 157) (1885-1929)

Sheep's-bane [Sheepsbane] - *Hydrocotyle umbellata* L. (156) (1923), *Kalmia latifolia* L. (77) (1898) Long Island NY

Sheep's-bit [Sheep's bit] - *Jasione* L. (156) (1923), *Jasione montana* L. (5, 156) (1913-1923)

Sheep's-cheese - *Elymus repens* (L.) Gould (158) (1900)

Sheep's-gowan [Sheep's gowan] - *Trifolium repens* L. (5, 156, 157, 158) (1900–1929)

Sheepweed [Sheep weed, Sheep-weed] - *Abutilon theophrasti* Medik (5, 73, 156, 157, 158) (1892-1929) Quincy IL, *Pinguicula vulgaris* L. (5, 156) (1913-1923), *Saponaria officinalis* L. (5, 64, 92, 156, 157, 158) (1876-1929)

Sheldon cryptantha - *Cryptantha celosioides* (Eastw.) Payson (155) (1942)

Sheldon's gossypianthus - *Gossypianthus lanuginosus* (Poir.) Moq. var. *lanuginosus* (97) (1937)

Shelf bracket fungus - *Fomes applanatus* (Pers.) Gillet (128) (1933)

Shelf fungus - *Fomes applanatus* (Pers.) Gillet (40) (1928)

Shell flower [Shell-flower, Shellflower] - *Alpinia zerumbet* (Pers.) Burtt & R.M. Sm. (109, 138) (1923-1949), *Chelone glabra* L. (5, 6, 7, 49, 58, 86, 92, 156) (1828-1923), *Moluccella laevis* L. (19, 77, 109) (1840-1949)

Shellbark [Shell bark] - *Carya laciniosa* (Michx. f.) G. Don (7) (1828), *Carya ovata* (Mill.) K. Koch (5) (1913)

Shellbark hickory [Shell-bark hickory, Shell bark hickory] - *Carya alba* (L.) Nutt. ex Ell. (2, 6, 20, 27, 46, 107) (1811–1879), *Carya laciniosa* (Michx. f.) G. Don (50, 65, 78, 95, 138, 155, 158) (1876–present) MO, *Carya ovata* (Mill.) K. Koch (5, 82, 95, 97, 113, 156, 158) (1890–1937)

Shell-barked hickery - *Carya cordiformis* (Wangenh.) K. Koch (8) (1785)

Shell-flower galangal [Shellflower galangal] - *Alpinia zerumbet* (Pers.) Burtt & R.M. Sm. (155) (1942)

Shell-leaf penstemon - *Penstemon grandiflorus* Nutt. (138, 155) (1923-1942)

Shelly grass - *Elymus repens* (L.) Gould (5, 92) (1876-1913)

Shemba (Osage) - *Hamamelis virginiana* L. (7) (1828)

She-oak - *Casuarina* Rumph. ex L. (109) (1949)

Shepherd's purse - *Thlaspi* L. (10) (1818)

Shepherd's-bag [Shepherd's bag] - *Capsella bursa-pastoris* (L.) Medik. (5, 156) (1913-1923)

Shepherd's-calender - *Anagallis arvensis* L. (158) (1900)

Shepherd's-clock [Shepherd's clock] - *Anagallis arvensis* L. (5, 107, 156, 157, 158) (1900–1929), *Tragopogon pratensis* L. (158) (1900)

Shepherd's-club [Shepherds' club, Shepherd's club] - *Verbascum thapsus* L. (5, 14, 69, 92, 158) (1882-1913)

Shepherd's-delight [Shepherd's delight, shepherds delight] - *Anagallis arvensis* L. (5, 156, 158) (1900-1923)

Shepherd's-needle [Shepherds' needle, Shepherd's needle, Shepherds'-needle] - *Scandix pecten-veneris* L. (5, 50, 92, 156) (1876–present)

Shepherd's-pouch [Shepherd's pouch] - *Capsella bursa-pastoris* (L.) Medik. (5, 156) (1913-1923)

Shepherd's-purse [Shepherd's purse, Shepherds' purse, Shepherd-spurse] - *Capsella bursa-pastoris* (L.) Medik. (1, 3, 4, 5, 6, 15, 19, 40, 45, 46, 49, 50, 52, 53, 57, 62, 63, 72, 80, 82, 85, 92, 97, 107, 122, 131, 145, 155, 156, 157, 158) (1649–present) accidentally introduced by 1671, *Cypripedium reginae* Walt. (78) (1898) Lepreau NB, *Capsella* Medik. (155, 158) (1900-1942)

Shepherd's-sprout [Shepherd's sprout] - *Capsella bursa-pastoris* (L.) Medik. (49, 53) (1898)

Shepherd's-staff [Shepherd's staff] - *Dipsacus fullonum* L. (5, 156, 158) (1900-1923)

Shepherd's-sundial [Shepherd's sundial] - *Anagallis arvensis* L. (156, 158) (1900-1923)

Shepherd's-thistle [Shepherd's thistle] - *Dipsacus fullonum* L. (156) (1923)

Shepherd's-warning - *Anagallis arvensis* L. (158) (1900)

Shepherd's-watch - *Anagallis arvensis* L. (158) (1900)

Shepherd's-weatherglass [Shepherd's weather glass, Shepherds' weatherglass or Shepherd's weather-glass] - *Anagallis arvensis* L. (5, 92, 156, 157, 165) (1876-1929) flowers close in bad weather, *Anagallis* L. (1, 93) (1932-1936)

Sherardia - *Sherardia* L. (50) (Present)

Shere-grass [Shere grass] - *Carex* L. (92) (1876)

Sheriff-pink [Sheriff pink] - *Leucanthemum vulgare* Lam. (5, 75, 156) (1894-1923) WV, no longer in use by 1923

Sheriffweed [Sheriff-weed] - *Leucanthemum vulgare* Lam. (158) (1900)

Shiakipi (Dakota) - *Rumex crispus* L. (37) (1919)

Shield fern - *Dryopteris* Adans. (1, 158) (1900-1932), *Dryopteris filix-mas* (L.) Schott (3, 58) (1869-1977), *Dryopteris marginalis* (L.) A. Gray (97) (1937), *Polystichum braunii* (Spenner) Fee (109) (1949), *Tectaria* Cav. (possibly) (2) (1895), *Thelypteris palustris* Schott var. *pubescens* (Lawson) Fern. (72) (1907)

Shield lichen [Shield-lichen] - *Flavoparmelia caperata* (L.) Hale (92) (1876)

Shield root [Shield roots] - *Dryopteris filix-mas* (L.) Schott (5, 92) (1876-1913)

Shield-like lip fern [Shield-like lip-fern] - *Aspidotis californica* (Hook.) Nutt. ex Copeland (86) (1878)

Shield-of-heaven [Shield of heaven] - *Cotyledon* L. (86) (1878) old European name

Shilling-grass - *Hydrocotyle* L. (158) (1900)

Shin hoble - *Viburnum lantanoides* Michx. (29) (1869)

Shin oak - *Quercus mohriana* Buckl. (4, 97) (1937-1986)

Shingin-leaf poison wood [Shingin-leaved poison wood] - Gymnanthes lucida Sw. (20) (1857)

Shingle oak - *Quercus imbricaria* Michx. (1, 3, 5, 10, 19, 33, 50, 72, 82, 93, 97, 109, 138, 155, 156) (1827–present)

Shinhop (Winnebago) - *Allium canadense* L. var. *mobilense* (Regal) Ownbey (37) (1830)

Shining angelica - *Angelica lucida* L. (165) (1807)

Shining aster - *Cotoneaster lucidus* Schldl. (155) (1942)

Shining bedstraw - *Galium concinnum* Torr. & Gray (3, 4, 5, 50, 72, 93) (1907–present)

Shining clubmoss [Shining club-moss] - *Huperzia lucidula* (Michx.) Trevisan (5, 50, 138) (1913–present)

Shining cyperus - *Cyperus bipartitus* Torr. (5, 72) (1907)

Shining geranium - *Geranium lucidum* L. (50) (present)

Shining inkberry [Shining ink berry] - *Ilex coriacea* (Pursh) Chapman (5) (1913)

Shining ladies'-tresses [Shining ladies' tresses] - *Spiranthes lucida* (H.H. Eat.) Ames (50) (Present)

Shining pondweed - *Potamogeton illinoensis* Morong (5, 85, 97, 120, 156, 158) (1900-1938)

Shining rose - *Rosa nitida* Willd. (5) (1913)

Shining rose-bay [Shining rose bay] - *Rhododendron viscosum* (L.) Torr. (possibly) (42) (1814)

Shining spurge - *Euphorbia lucida* Waldst. & Kit. (5) (1913)

Shining sumac - *Rhus copallinum* L. (109, 138) (1923-1949)

Shining thorn - *Crataegus nitida* (Englem.) Sargent (5) (1913)

Shining willow - *Salix lucida* Muhl. (1, 3, 4, 5, 19, 20, 50, 72, 82, 93, 113, 138, 155, 156) (1840–present)

Shining-fruit bur-reed [Shining fruited bur-reed] - *Sparganium androcladum* (Engelm.) Morong (5) (1913)

Shining-grass [Shining grass] - *Impatiens capensis* Meerb. (5, 73, 156, 157, 158) (1892-1929) Weathersfield, VT, *Thalictrum dioicum* L. (5, 158) (1900-1913), *Thalictrum pubescens* Pursh (156) (1923)

Shining-leaf custard-apple [Shining-leaved custard apple] - *Annona glabra* L. (165) (1807)

Shin-leaf [Shin leaf, Shinleaf] - *Orthilia secunda* (L.) House (5) (1913), *Platanthera orbiculata* (Pursh) Lindl. (156) (1923), *Pyrola americana* Sweet (19, 49, 53, 92, 156) (1840-1923), *Pyrola chlorantha* Sw. (5, 158) (1900-1913), *Pyrola elliptica* Nutt. (2, 5, 63, 72, 85, 86, 95, 105, 131, 138, 156, 157, 158) (1878-1932) leaves used as "shin-plasters" for wounds of the shin and elsewhere, *Pyrola* L. (2, 109, 156, 158) (1895-1949), *Pyrola minor* L. (5) (1913)

Shinnery oak - *Quercus havardii* Rydb. (4) (1986)

Shin-oak - *Quercus havardii* Rydb. (153) (1913) NM

Shin-plasters [Shinplasters] - *Platanthera orbiculata* (Pursh) Lindl. (156) (1923) no longer in use by 1923

Shinry - *Quercus havardii* Rydb. (153) (1913) NM

Shinwood [Shin-wood, Shin wood] - *Taxus canadensis* Willd. (5, 92) (1876-1913)

Shiny bugseed - *Corispermum nitidum* Kit. ex J.A. Schultes (50) (Present)

Shiny najas - *Najas flexilis* (Willd.) Rostk. & Schmidt (85) (1932)

Shiny-leaf spiraea [Shinyleaf spiraea] - *Spiraea betulifolia* Pallas var. *lucida* (Dougl. ex Greene) C.L. Hitchc. (50, 155) (1942–present)

Shittim-wood [Shittimwood, Shittim wood] - *Halesia carolina* L. (5) (1913), *Halesia tetraptera* L. (75) (1894) WV, *Sideroxylon lanuginosum* Michx. (5, 106) (1913-1930)

Shockley's goldenhead [Shockley goldenhead - *Acamptopappus shockleyi* Gray (50, 155) (1942–present)

Shoe peg maple [Shoe-peg maple - *Acer rubrum* L. (5, 156) (1913-1923)

Shoe-black plant - *Hibiscus rosa-sinensis* L. (92) (1876)

Shoe-button ardisia [Shoebutton ardisia] - *Ardisia solanacea* Roxb. (155) (1942)

Shoe-make [Shoe make] - *Rhus glabra* L. (5, 73, 158) (1892-1913), *Rhus* L. (35) (1806)

Shoemaker's-heels [Shoemaker's heels] - *Chenopodium bonus-henricus* L. (156) (1923)

Shoemate - *Rhus glabra* L. (35) (1806), *Rhus* L. (35) (1806)

Shoes-and-stockings [Shoes-and-stockings] - *Lotus corniculatus* L. (5, 92, 156) (1876-1923)

Shoestring lily [Shoe-string lilies] - *Leucocrinum montanum* Nutt. ex Gray (156) (1923)

Shoe-string plant - *Psoralidium lanceolatum* (Pursh) Rydb. (85) (1932) SD

Shoestrings [Shoe strings, Shoe string, Shoestring, Shoe-string, Shoe-strings] - *Amorpha canescens* Pursh (5, 72, 73, 76, 95, 97, 106, 112, 114, 130, 131, 156) (1892-1937) from long tough roots,

Amorpha L. (1, 93) (1932-1936), *Amorpha nana* Nutt. ex Fraser (76) (1896) Burnside SD, *Campsis radicans* (L.) Seem. ex Bureau (156) (1923), *Polygonum amphibium* L. var. *emersum* Michx. (80) (1913) IA

Shokanwa-hu (Winnebago, gum plant) - *Silphium laciniatum* L. (37) (1919)

Shoofly [Shoo fly] - *Baptisia tinctoria* (L.) R. Br. ex Aiton f. (5, 64, 74, 106, 156) (1893-1930), *Hibiscus trionum* L. (80, 156) (1913-1923) no longer in use by 1923

Shoofly plant [Shoo-fly plant] - *Nicandra physalodes* (L.) Gaertn. (109, 156) (1923-1949)

Shooting-star [Shooting star, Shooting stars] - *Dodecatheon meadia* L. (3, 4, 5, 14, 63, 75, 92, 97, 122, 124, 131, 156) (1882-1986), *Dodecatheon* L. (1, 4, 50, 72, 109, 138, 155, 158) (1900–present), *Dodecatheon pulchellum* (Raf.) Merr. (4) (1986), *Dodecatheon pulchellum* (Raf.) Merr. subsp. *pulchellum* (3, 85, 127) (1932-1977)

Shore bay - *Persea borbonia* (L.) Spreng. (106) (1930)

Shore buttercup - *Ranunculus cymbalaria* Pursh (3, 4, 155) (1942-1986)

Shore grass [Shore-grass] - *Stenotaphrum secundatum* (Walt.) Kuntze (163) (1852)

Shore horsetail - *Equisetum* ×*litorale* Kühlewein ex Rupr. [*arvense* × *fluviatile*] (5) (1913)

Shore knotweed - *Polygonum buxiforme* Small (5, 93) (1913-1936)

Shore little blustem - *Schizachyrium littorale* (Nash) Bicknell (50) (present)

Shore onion - *Allium schoenoprasum* L. (75, 156) (1894-1923)

Shore pine - *Pinus banksiana* Lamb. (5, 19, 75) (1840-1913), *Pinus contorta* Dougl. ex Loud. (3, 109, 138) (1923-1977)

Shore podgrass - *Triglochin maritimum* L. (155) (1942)

Shore quillwort - *Isoetes riparia* Engelm. ex A. Braun (50) (present)

Shore spurge - *Chamaesyce polygonifolia* (L.) Small (5, 156) (1913-1923)

Shore-grass [Shore grass] - *Littorella uniflora* (L.) Ascherson (5, 156) (1913-1923)

Shoreline sedge - *Carex hyalinolepis* Steud. (50) (Present)

Shoreweed [Shore-weed, Shore weed] - *Littorella* Berg. (1) (1932)

Short bluegrass - *Poa abbreviata* R. Br. (50) (present)

Short grama - *Bouteloua hirsuta* Lag. (144) (1899)

Short ragweed - *Ambrosia artemisiifolia* L. (4) (1986), *Ambrosia artemisiifolia* L. var. *elatior* (L.) Descourtils (21, 97) (1893–1937)

Short shot pine - *Pinus virginiana* Mill. (5) (1913) OK TX

Short shucks - *Pinus virginiana* Mill. (5) (1913)

Short woolly-spike sedge [Short woolly-spiked sedge] - *Carex vestita* Willd. (66) (1903)

Short-awn brome grass [Short-awned brome grass, Short awned brome grass] - *Bromus marginatus* Nees ex Steud. (5, 56) (1901-1913)

Short-awn chess [Short-awned chess] - *Bromus marginatus* Nees ex Steud. (5, 56, 72) (1901-1907)

Short-awn foxtail [Shortawn foxtail, Short-awned foxtail] - *Alopecurus aequalis* Sobol. var. *aequalis* (5, 50) (1913–present), *Alopecurus aequalis* Sobol. (3, 50, 140, 155) (1942–present)

Short-awn grama [Short-awned grama] - *Bouteloua breviseta* Vasey (94) (1901)

Short-awn porcupine grass [Shortawn porcupinegrass] - *Hesperostipa comata* (Trin. & Rupr.) Barkworth (155) (1942)

Short-awn reed grass [Short-awned reed-grass] - *Calamagrostis pickeringii* Gray (94) (1901)

Short-awn wild rye [Short-awned wild rye - *Elymus submuticus* (Hook.) Smyth & Smyth (5) (1913)

Short-awn woolly-beard [Short-awned woolly beard] - *Saccharum brevibarbe* (Michx.) Pers. var. *brevibarbe* (66) (1903)

Short-beak arrowhead [Shortbeak arrowhead, Short-beak arrow-head] - *Sagittaria brevirostra* Mack & Bush (5, 50, 138, 155) (1913–present)

Short-beak bald-rush [Short-beaked bald rush] - *Rhynchospora nitens* (Vahl) Gray (5) (1913)

Short-beak beaksedge [Shortbeak beaksedge] - *Rhynchospora nitens* (Vahl) Gray (50) (present)

Short-beak sedge [Short beaked sedge] - *Carex gynocrates* Wormsk. (66) (1903), *Carex brevior* (Dewey) Mackenzie (50) (Present)

Short-beak woody sedge [Short-beaked woody sedge] - *Carex arctata* Boott. Ex Hook. (66) (1903)

Short-beard broom-sedge [Short-bearded broom sedge] - *Schizachyrium sanguineum* (Retz.) Alston var. *sanguineum* (94) (1901)

Short-beard plume grass [Shortbeard plumegrass, Short-bearded plume-grass] - *Saccharum brevibarbe* (Michx.) Pers. var. *brevibarbe* (5, 50) (1913–present)

Short-bristle horned beak-sedge [Shortbristle horned beaksedge] - *Rhynchospora corniculata* (Lam.) A. Gray (50) (Present)

Short-bristle needle-and-thread [Shortbristle needle and thread] - *Hesperostipa comata* (Trin. & Rupr.) Barkworth (50) (Present)

Short-crown milkweed [Shortcrown milkweed, Short crowned milkweed, Short-crowned milkweed] - *Asclepias brachystephana* Engelm. ex Torr. (4, 5, 122) (1913-1986)

Short-fruit evening-primrose [Shortfruit evening primrose] - *Oenothera brachycarpa* Gray (50) (Present)

Short-fruit rockcress [Shortfruit rockcress] - *Arabis drummondii* Gray (155) (1942)

Short-fruit rush [Short-fruited rush] - *Juncus brachycarpus* Engelm. (5) (1913)

Short-fruit whitlow [Short-fruited whitlow] - *Draba brachycarpa* Nutt. (5) (1913)

Short-fruit whitlow-grass [Short-fruited whitlow-grass] - *Draba brachycarpa* Nutt. (97) (1937)

Short-hair goldenrod [Shorthair goldenrod] - *Solidago canadensis* L. var. *gilvocanescens* Rydb. (50) (Present)

Short-hair reed grass [Short-haired reed grass] - *Calamovilfa brevipilis* (Torr.) Hack. ex Scribn. & Southw. (5, 94) (1901-1913)

Short-horn rice grass [Shorthorn ricegrass] - *Piptatherum pungens* (Torr.) Barkworth (155) (1942)

Shorthusk - *Brachyelytrum* Beauv. (50, 155) (1942–present)

Shortian's gentian [Shortian gentian] - *Gentiana saponaria* L. (7) (1828)

Short-leaf beard grass [Short-leaved-beard grass, Short-leaved beard grass] - *Gymnopogon brevifolius* Trin. (5, 66, 94, 163) (1852-1903)

Short-leaf eugenia [Shortleaf eugenia] - *Eugenia apiculata* DC. (138) (1923)

Short-leaf fescue grass [Short-leaved fescue grass] - *Festuca brachyphylla* J.A. Schultes ex J.A. & J.H. Schultes (5) (1913)

Short-leaf fig tree [Short-leaved fig-tree] - *Ficus citrifolia* Mill. (20) (1857)

Short-leaf lady's-tresses [Short-leaf ladies-tresses] - *Spiranthes longilabris* Lindl. (138) (1923)

Short-leaf milkwort [Short-leaved milkwort] - *Polygala brevifolia* Nutt. (5) (1913)

Short-leaf pine [Shortleaf pine, Short-leafed pine, Short-leaved pine] - *Pinus echinata* Mill. (5, 20, 50, 65, 109, 122, 124, 138, 155) (1857–present), *Pinus taeda* L. (5) (1913), *Pinus virginiana* Mill. (5) (1913)

Short-leaf rush grass [Short-leaved rush grass] - *Muhlenbergia cuspidata* (Torr. ex Hook.) Rydb. (5) (1913)

Short-leaf sedge [Short-leaved sedge] - *Carex misandra* R. Br. (5, 50) (1913–present)

Short-leaf skeleton grass [Shortleaf skeleton grass] - *Gymnopogon brevifolius* Trin. (50) (present)

Short-leaf spear grass [Short-leaved spear grass] - *Poa cuspidata* Nutt. (5, 66) (1903-1913)

Short-leaf sundew [Short-leaved sundew] - *Drosera brevifolia* Pursh (2) (1895)

Short-leaf triodia [Shortleaf triodia] - *Erioneuron avenaceum* (Kunth) Tateoka (122) (1937)

Short-leaf wheat grass [Short-leafed wheat-grass] - *Elymus sierrae* Gould (94) (1901)

Short-leaf yellow pine [Short leaf yellow pine, Short-leaved yellow pine] - *Pinus echinata* Mill. (2, 97) (1895-1937)

Short-lobe wild ginger [Short-lobed wild ginger] - *Asarum canadense* L. (5, 72) (1907-1913)

Short-pod draba [Shortpod draba] - *Draba brachycarpa* Nutt. (3, 4, 50) (1977–present)

Short-pod honey locust [Short-podded honey locust] - *Gleditsia triacanthos* L. (12) (1821)

Short-pod primrose [Short-podded primrose] - *Oenothera brachycarpa* Gray (5, 97) (1913-1937)

Short-point cyperus [Short-pointed cyperus] - *Cyperus acuminatus* Torr. & Hook. ex Torr. (5, 72) (1907–1913)

Short-ray coneflower [Shortrayed cone flower, Shortrayed coneflower, Short-rayed cone-flower] - *Ratibida tagetes* (James) Barnhart (5, 97, 122, 124) (1913-1937)

Short-ray fleabane [Shortray fleabane] - *Erigeron lonchophyllus* Hook. (50) (Present)

Short-ray prairie coneflower [Shortray prairie coneflower] - *Ratibida tagetes* (James) Barnhart (3, 4) (1977-1986)

Short's aster - *Symphyotrichum shortii* (Lindl.) Nesom (5, 72) (1907-1913)

Short's bladderpod [Short's bladder pod] - *Lesquerella globosa* (Desv.) S. Wats. (5) (1913)

Short's fescue - *Festuca paradoxa* Desv. (56) (1901)

Short's fescue grass [Short's fescue-grass] - *Festuca paradoxa* Desv. (5, 72, 119) (1907-1938)

Short's goldenrod [Short's golden-rod] - *Solidago shortii* Torr. & Gray (5) (1913)

Short's milkvetch [Short's milk vetch] - *Astragalus shortianus* Nutt. ex Torr. & Gray (4, 5, 50, 93) (1913–present)

Short's rockcress - *Arabis shortii* (Fern.) Gleason (50) (Present)

Short's sedge - *Carex shortiana* Dewey (5, 50, 72) (1893–present)

Short's vincetoxicum - *Matelea obliqua* (Jacq.) Woods. (5) (1913)

Short-seed waterwort [Shortseed waterwort, Short-seeded water wort] - *Elatine brachysperma* Gray (5, 50, 155) (1913–present)

Short-shot pine [Short shot pine] - *Pinus echinata* Mill. (5, 35) (1806-1913)

Short-spike broom-sedge [Short-spiked broom sedge] - *Andropogon brachystachyus* Chapm. (94) (1901)

Short-spike rye grass [Short spiked rye grass] - *Elymus canadensis* L. (56) (1901)

Short-spike water-milfoil [Shortspike watermilfoil] - *Myriophyllum sibiricum* Komarov (50) (Present)

Short-spike wild rye [Short-spiked wild rye] - *Elymus canadensis* L. (5) (1913)

Short-spur orchis [Short-spurred orchis] - *Platanthera cristata* (Michx.) Lindl. (187) (1818)

Short-stalk bindweed [Shortstalk bindweed, Short-stalked bindweed] - *Calystegia silvatica* (Kit.) Griseb. subsp. *fraterniflora* (Mackenzie & Bush) Brummitt (5, 50) (1913–present)

Short-stalk chickweed [Shortstalk chickweed, Short-stalked chickweed] - *Cerastium brachypetalum* Desportes ex Pers. (5, 93, 97, 131) (1899-1937)

Short-stalk eragrostis [Short-stalked eragrostis] - *Eragrostis curtipedicellata* Buckl. (94) (1901)

Short-stalk false pimpernel [Short-stalked false pimpernel] - *Lindernia dubia* (L.) Pennell var. *dubia* (5, 72) (1907-1913)

Short-stalk love grass [Short-stalked love grass, Short-stalked love-grass] - *Eragrostis curtipedicellata* Buckl. (5, 99, 119, 163) (1852-1938)

Short-stalk ludwigiantha [Short-stalked ludwigiantha] - *Ludwigia brevipes* (B.H. Long ex Britt., A. Braun & Small) Eames (5) (1913)

Short-stalk meadow grass [Short-stalked meadow grass, Short-stalked meadow-grass] - *Eragrostis frankii* C.A. Mey. ex Steud. (5, 6, 66, 94) (1901-1912)

Short-stalk uniola [Short-stalked uniola] - *Chasmanthium sessiliflorum* (Poir.) Yates (94) (1901)

Short-stem buckwheat [Shortstem buckwheat] - *Eriogonum brevicaule* Nutt. (50) (Present)

Short-stem eriogonum [Shortstem eriogonum] - *Eriogonum brevicaule* Nutt. (4) (1986)

Short-stemmed spiderwort - *Tradescantia virginiana* L. (5, 72, 97) (1907-1937)

Short-style sanicle [Short-styled sanicle] - *Sanicula canadensis* L. (157) (1929)

Short-style snakeroot [Short-styled snake root, Short styled snakeroot, Short-styled snakeroot, Short-styled snake-root] - *Sanicula canadensis* L. (5, 72, 93, 97, 122, 131, 157, 158) (1899-1937)

Short-tooth mountain-mint [Short-toothed mountain mint] - *Pycnanthemum muticum* (Michx.) Pers. (5) (1913)

Short-tube ruellia [Short-tubed ruellia] - *Ruellia strepens* L. (5) (1913)

Shot plant - *Canna indica* L. (92) (1876)

Shotbush [Shot bush, Shot-bush] - *Aralia nudicaulis* L. (5, 7, 49, 64, 156, 157, 158) (1828-1929), *Aralia spinosa* L. (7, 19, 38, 92, 156) (1820-1923)

Shovel pickerel-weed [Shovel pickerelweed] - *Pontederia cordata* L. (7) (1828)

Shovel-leaf [Shovel leaf] - *Pontederia cordata* L. (7) (1828)

Shovelweed [Shovel weed, Shovel-weed] - *Capsella bursa-pastoris* (L.) Medik. (5, 74, 156, 157) (1893-1929) Penobscot ME, from shape of pods, *Pontederia cordata* L. (92) (1876)

Show geranium - *Pelargonium* ×*domesticum* Bailey [*angulosum* × *cucullatum*] (109) (1949)

Show pelargonium - *Pelargonium* ×*domesticum* Bailey [*angulosum* × *cucullatum*] (109) (1949)

Show-fly - *Baptisia tinctoria* (L.) R. Br. ex Aiton f. (157) (1929)

Showy aster - *Eurybia conspicua* (Lindl.) Nesom (155) (1942)

Showy blue aster - *Symphyotrichum patens* (Aiton) G.L. Nesom var. *patens* (82) (1930)

Showy bur-marigold - *Bidens laevis* (L.) Britton, Sterns & Poggenb. (106) (1930)

Showy chloris - *Chloris virgata* Sw. (3, 155) (1942-1977)

Showy clover - *Trifolium hybridum* L. (155) (1942)

Showy coneflower [Showy cone-flower] - *Rudbeckia fulgida* Aiton var. *speciosa* (Wenderoth) Perdue (5, 138) (1913-1923)

Showy crazyweed - *Oxytropis splendens* Dougl. ex Hook (155) (1942)

Showy dock - *Rumex venosus* Pursh (98) (1926)

Showy evening-primrose [Showy evening primrose] - *Oenothera grandis* (Britton) Smyth (50) (Present), *Oenothera speciosa* Nutt. (4) (1986)

Showy feather-grass - *Achnatherum speciosum* (Trin. & Rupr.) Barkworth (94) (1901)

Showy frasera - *Frasera speciosa* Dougl. ex Griseb. (131, 155) (1899-1942)

Showy gaillardia - *Gaillardia pulchella* Foug. (5, 93, 97, 122) (1913-1937)

Showy goldenrod [Showy golden-rod] - *Solidago speciosa* Nutt (5, 50, 72, 82, 97, 156) (1907–present), *Solidago speciosa* Nutt. var. *pallida* Porter (50) (Present), *Solidago speciosa* Nutt. var. *rigidiuscula* Torr. & Gray (50) (Present)

Showy lady's-slipper [Showy lady's slipper, Showy ladies' slipper, Showy lady-slipper, Showy ladies'-slipper] - *Cypripedium reginae* Walt. (3, 5, 50, 72, 109, 127, 156, 158) (1900–present)

Showy loco - *Oxytropis splendens* Dougl. ex Hook (126) (1933)

Showy locoweed [Showy loco weed] - *Oxytropis splendens* Dougl. ex Hook (3, 4, 50, 133) (1903–present)

Showy mentzelia - *Mentzelia decapetala* (Pursh ex Sims) Urban & Gilg ex Gilg (5, 131, 156) (1899-1923)

Showy milkweed - *Asclepias speciosa* Torr. (3, 4, 5, 50, 72, 80, 82, 85, 93, 95, 97, 121, 126, 127, 131, 155, 156, 157) (1899–present)

Showy mountain-ash - *Sorbus decora* (Sargent) Schneid. (138) (1923)

Showy orchid - *Galearis* Raf. (1) (1932), *Galearis spectabilis* (L.) Raf. (50) (Present)

Showy orchis - *Galearis spectabilis* (L.) Raf. (3, 5, 72, 86, 93, 109, 138, 156, 158) (1878-1977) IA Neb

Showy oxytropis - *Oxytropis splendens* Dougl. ex Hook (5) (1913)

Showy partridge pea [Showy partridgepea] - *Chamaecrista fasciculata* (Michx.) Greene (155) (1942), *Chamaecrista fasciculata* (Michx.) Greene var. *fasciculata* (4) (1986)

Showy penstemon - *Penstemon spectabilis* Thurb. ex Gray (138) (1923)

Showy portulaca - *Portulaca grandiflora* Hook. (5, 156, 158) (1900-1923)

Showy prairie gentian - *Eustoma exaltatum* (L.) Salisb. ex G. Don subsp. *russellianum* (Hook) Kartesz (50) (Present)

Showy primrose - *Oenothera speciosa* Nutt. (5, 97) (1913-1937)

Showy pussytoes - *Antennaria pulcherrima* (Hook.) Green (155) (1942)

Showy rosinweed - *Silphium integrifolium* Michx. var. *laeve* Torr. & Gray (3) (1977)

Showy sandwort - *Moehringia lateriflora* (L.) Fenzl (156) (1923)

Showy sedge - *Carex formosa* Dewey (66) (1903)

Showy skullcap - *Scutellaria serrata* Andr. (5) (1913)

Showy speedwell - *Hebe speciosa* (R. Cunningham ex A. Cunningham) J.C. Andersen (138) (1923)

Showy spurge - *Euphorbia corollata* L. (157) (1929)

Showy stonecrop - *Hylotelephium spectabile* (Boreau) H. Ohba. (138, 155) (1931-1942)

Showy sunflower - *Helianthus* ×*laetiflorus* Pers. [*pauciflorus* × *tuberosus*] (5, 72, 109, 138, 156) (1907–1949)

Showy tick-trefoil [Showy tick trefoil, Showy ticktrefoil] - *Desmodium canadense* (L.) DC. (5, 50, 93, 97, 158) (1900–present)

Showy vetchling - *Lathyrus brachycalyx* Rydb. subsp. *brachycalyx* . (5, 93, 97, 131) (1899-1937)

Showy wake-robin [Showy wake robin] - *Trillium nivale* Riddell (5) (1913)

Showy whitetop - *Rhynchospora nivea* Boeckl. (50) (Present)

Showy-wand goldenrod [Showywand goldenrod] - *Solidago speciosa* Nutt (3, 4) (1977-1986), *Solidago speciosa* Nutt. var. *rigidiuscula* Torr. & Gray (155) (1942)

Shpanshni yutapi (Dakota Yankton and Teton, eaten raw) - *Citrullus lanatus* (Thunb.) Matsumura & Nakai (37) (1919)

Shreve's acacia [Shreve acacia] - *Acacia angustissima* (Mill.) Kuntze var. *shrevei* (Britton & Rose) Isely (155) (1942)

Shreve's iris - *Iris virginica* L. var. *shrevei* (Small) E. Anders. (50) (Present)

Shreve's priaire acacia - *Acacia angustissima* (Mill.) Kuntze var. *shrevei* (Britton & Rose) Isely (50) (Present)

Shrimp plant [Shrimp-plant] - *Justicia brandegeeana* Wasshausen & L.B. Sm. (109) (1949)

Shriver's sedge - *Carex granularis* Muhl. ex Willd. var. *haleana* (Olney) Porter (5) (1913)

Shrub althea [Shrub-althea] - *Hibiscus syriacus* L. (109, 138) (1923-1949)

Shrub bush clover [Shrub bushclover] - *Lespedeza bicolor* Turcz. (138) (1923)

Shrub cinquefoil - *Potentilla* L. (8) (1785)

Shrub maple - *Acer glabrum* Torr. (101) (1905) MT

Shrub oak - *Quercus ilicifolia* Wangenh. (19, 92, 113) (1840-1890), *Quercus laevis* Walt. (92) (1876), *Quercus muehlenbergii* Engelm. (5, 156, 157, 158) (1900-1929)

Shrub pine - *Pinus banksiana* Lamb. (78) (1898) Western US

Shrub willow [Shrub-willow] - *Salix humilis* Marsh. var. *tristis* (Aiton) Griggs (19) (1840), *Salix interior* Rowlee (5, 156, 158) (1900-1923)

Shrub yellow-root [Shrub yellowroot, Shrub yellow root, Shrubb yellow root] - *Xanthorhiza* Marsh. (138, 186) (1814-1923), *Xanthorhiza simplicissima* Marsh. (2, 5, 8, 49, 76, 92, 109) (1785-1949)

Shrubby althaea - *Hibiscus syriacus* L. (5, 15, 92, 109, 156) (1895-1949)

Shrubby bastard indigo - *Amorpha fruticosa* L. (8) (1785)

Shrubby bittersweet - *Celastrus* L. (1, 13) (1849-1932), *Celastrus scandens* L. (5, 15, 156, 157, 158) (1895-1929)

Shrubby blue sage - *Salvia ballotiflora* Benth. (124) (1937) TX

Shrubby buckeye - *Aesculus glabra* Willd. (5, 97, 125, 156) (1913-1937)

Shrubby capsicum - *Capsicum annuum* L. var. *annuum* (110) (1886)

Shrubby cinquefoil [Shrubby cinque-foil] - *Dasiphora floribunda* (Pursh) Kartesz (2, 3, 5, 19, 38, 50, 72, 82, 85, 86, 107, 108, 130, 131, 138, 153, 156, 158) (1840–present), *Dasiphora* Raf. (1) (1932)

Shrubby croton - *Croton fruticulosus* Engelm. ex Torr. (122) (1937)

Shrubby dropseed [Shrubby drop-seed] - *Muhlenbergia dumosa* Scribn. ex Vasey (94) (1901)

Shrubby fern - *Comptonia peregrina* (L.) Coult. (5, 92, 156) (1876-1923)

Shrubby five-fingers [Shrubby fivefingers - *Sibbaldiopsis tridentata* (Aiton) Rydb. (50) (Present)

Shrubby gilia - *Linanthus californicus* (Hook. & Arn.) J.M.Porter & L.A.Johnson (138) (1923)

Shrubby goatweed [Shrubby goat weed] - *Capraria biflora* L. (92) (1876)

Shrubby gromwell - *Lithospermum caroliniense* (Walt. ex J.F. Gmel.) MacM. var. *croceum* (Fern.) Cronq. (138) (1923)

Shrubby horsetail - *Ephedra antisyphilitica* Berl. ex C.A. Mey. (158) (1900)

Shrubby lespedeza - *Lespedeza frutescens* (L.) Hornem. (50) (Present)

Shrubby maple - *Acer glabrum* Torr. (5) (1913)

Shrubby milkwort - *Polygala lindheimeri* Gray var. *parvifolia* Wheelock (50) (Present)

Shrubby oenothera - *Oenothera fruticosa* L. (187) (1818)

Shrubby oreocarya - *Cryptantha cinerea* (Greene) Cronq. var. *jamesii* Cronq. (5, 93, 97) (1913-1937)

Shrubby prickly-ash [Shrubby prickly ash] - *Zanthoxylum americanum* Mill. (7) (1828)

Shrubby red cedar - *Juniperus horizontalis* Moench (5) (1913)

Shrubby St. John's wort [Shrubby St. John's-wort - *Hypericum kalmianum* L. (5, 156) (1913-1923), *Hypericum prolificum* L. (2, 5, 45, 72, 97, 138, 156) (1895-1937)

Shrubby sweetfern [Shrubby sweet fern] - *Comptonia peregrina* (L.) Coult. (7, 8) (1785-1828)

Shrubby Swiss pine - *Pinus mugo* Turra (138) (1923)

Shrubby tree-primrose - *Oenothera fruticosa* L. (187) (1818)

Shrubby-trefoil [Shrubby trefoil] - *Ptelea* L. (1, 82) (1930-1932), *Ptelea trifoliata* L. (5, 6, 49, 53, 92, 106, 107, 156, 157, 158) (1892-1929)

Shrub-trefoil [Shrub trefoil] - *Ptelea* L. (13) (1849)

Shu (Ancient Chinese) - *Glycine max* (L.) Merr. (110) (1886)

Shumac - *Rhus* L. (7) (1828)

Shumard's oak [Shumard oak] - *Quercus shumardii* Buckl. (50, 155) (1942–present)

Shumard's red oak - *Quercus shumardii* Buckl. (3, 122, 124) (1937-1977)

Shunis - *Ligusticum scoticum* L. (5, 156) (1913-1923)

Shy trillium - *Trillium flexipes* Raf. (155) (1942)

Shy wallflower - *Erysimum inconspicuum* (S. Wats.) MacM. (50) (Present)

Šiabuksing (Chippewa) - *Eupatorium perfoliatum* L. (105) (1932)

Siamese melon - *Cucurbita ficifolia* Bouche (110) (1886)

Siamese senna - *Senna siamea* (Lam.) Irwin & Barneby (138) (1923)

Sibara - *Sibara* Greene (158) (1900)

Sibbaldia - *Sibbaldia procumbens* L. (5) (1913)

Sibbaldiopsis - *Sibbaldiopsis* Rydb. (50) (Present)

Siberian alfalfa - *Medicago sativa* L. subsp. *falcata* (L.) Arcang. (82) (1930) IA

Siberian aster - *Eurybia sibirica* (L.) Nesom (131, 155) (1899-1942)

Siberian barley - *Hordeum vulgare* L. (158) (1900) variety

Siberian chive - *Allium schoenoprasum* L. var. *sibiricum* (L.) Hartman (155) (1942)

Siberian crab - *Malus baccata* (L.) Borck. (82, 107, 135, 137, 138) (1910-1931), *Malus prunifolia* (Willd.) Borkh. (19) (1840)

Siberian crab apple - *Malus baccata* (L.) Borck. (5, 109) (1913-1949)

Siberian crane's-bill [Siberian crane's bill] - *Geranium sibiricum* L. (5) (1913)

Siberian elm - *Ulmus pumila* L. (3, 4, 50, 109, 155) (1942–present)

Siberian flax - *Chamerion angustifolium* (L.) Holub subsp. *angustifolium* (76) (1896) Westmoreland Co. NB

Siberian iris - *Iris sibirica* L. (107, 138) (1919-1923)

Siberian juniper - *Juniperus communis* L. var. *montana* Ait. (153) (1913) NM

Siberian larkspur - *Delphinium grandiflorum* L. (138) (1923)

Siberian motherwort - *Leonurus sibiricus* L. (5, 155) (1913-1942)

Siberian oat - *Avena sativa* L. (107) (1919)

Siberian oilseed [Siberian oil-seed] - *Camelina sativa* (L.) Crantz (5, 107, 156) (1913-1923)

Siberian pea tree [Siberian pea-tree] - *Caragana arborescens* Lam. (106, 107, 112, 135, 138) (1910-1937), *Caragana frutex* (L.) K. Koch (82) (1930)

Siberian peashrub [Siberian pea shrub, Siberian pea-shrub] - *Caragana arborescens* Lam. (4, 50, 155) (1942–present)

Siberian purslane - *Claytonia sibirica* L. (107) (1919)

Siberian sandwort - *Minuartia biflora* (L.) Schinz & Thellung (5, 156) (1913-1923)

Siberian squill - *Scilla siberica* Haw. (106, 138) (1923-1930)

Siberian wild rye [Siberian wild-rye] - *Leymus racemosus* (Lam.) Tzvelev (138) (1923)

Siberian yarrow - *Achillea sibirica* Ledeb. (50, 138, 155) (1923–present)

Sicilian beet - *Beta vulgaris* L. (107) (1919)

Sicilian corn (Tuscany) - *Zea mays* L. (110) (1886)

Sicily root - *Osmorhiza longistylis* (Torr.) DC. (92) (1876)

Sickle alfalfa - *Medicago sativa* L. subsp. *falcata* (L.) Arcang. (155) (1942)

Sickle medic [Sickle medick] - *Medicago sativa* L. subsp. *falcata* (L.) Arcang. (68) (1913)

Sickle senna - *Senna tora* (L.) Roxb. (5, 7, 50, 92, 122, 124, 155, 158) (1828–present)

Sickle-fruit hoffmanseggia [Sickle-fruited hoffmanseggia] - *Hoffmannseggia glauca* (Ortega) Eifert (5, 97) (1913-1937)

Sickle-grass [Sickle grass] - *Carex crinita* Lam. (156) (1923), *Leersia oryzoides* (L.) Sw. (187) (1818), *Polygonum arifolium* L. (5, 92, 156) (1876-1923)

Sickle-heal - *Prunella vulgaris* L. (158) (1900)

Sickle-leaf aster [Sickle-leaved aster] - *Pityopsis falcata* (Pursh) Nutt. (5) (1913)

Sickle-leaf onion [Sickleleaf onion] - *Allium falcifolium* Hook. & Arn. (155) (1942)

Sickle-leaf polypod [Sickle-leaved polypod] - *Cyrtomium falcatum* (L. f.) C. Presl (86) (1878)

Sickle-leaf wall cress [Sickle-leaved wall-cress] - *Arabis canadensis* L. (187) (1818)

Sicklepod [Sickle pod, Sickle-pod] - *Arabis canadensis* L. (3, 4, 5, 15, 19, 50, 72, 92, 97, 131, 156, 158) (1840–present), *Senna tora* (L.) Roxb. (156) (1923)

Sickle-pod holdback [Sicklepod holdback] - *Caesalpinia drepanocarpa* (Gray) Fisher (50) (present)

Sicklepod rushpea [Sicklepod rush-pea] - *Caesalpinia drepanocarpa* (Gray) Fisher (4) (1986)

Sickle-pod wall cress [Sickle-podded wall cress] - *Arabis canadensis* L. (42) (1814)

Sickleweed [Sickle weed, Sickle-weed] - *Falcaria vulgaris* Bernh. (50) (present), *Polygonum hydropiper* L. (5, 92, 156, 158) (1876-1923), *Prunella vulgaris* L. (157, 158) (1900-1929)

Sicklewort [Sickle wort, Sicklewort] - *Ajuga reptans* L. (5, 156, 158) (1900-1923) no longer in use by 1923, *Prunella vulgaris* L. (5, 92, 156, 158) (1876-1923)

Sida - *Sida* L. (155, 158) (1900-1942), *Sida spinosa* L. (80, 145) (1897-1932)

Side oats [Side-oats, Side oat] - *Avena sativa* L. (155) (1942), *Bouteloua curtipendula* (Michx) Torr. (56, 94, 119) (1901-1938)

Sidebeak pencil-flower [Sidebeak pencilflower] - *Stylosanthes biflora* (L.) Britton, Sterns & Poggenb. (50) (Present)

Side-bells penstemon [Sidebells penstemon] - *Penstemon secundiflorus* Benth. (50, 155) (1942–present)

Side-bells pyrola [Sidebells pyrola, Side-bell pyrola] - *Orthilia secunda* (L.) House (138, 155, 156) (1923-1942)

Side-bells wintergreen [Sidebells wintergreen] - *Orthilia secunda* (L.) House (50) (present)

Side-cluster milkweed [Sidecluster milkweed] - *Asclepias lanuginosa* Nutt. (50) (present), *Asclepias oenotheroides* Cham. & Schlecht. (4) (1986)

Side-flower goldenrod [Side-flowered golden-rod] - *Symphyotrichum lateriflorum* (L.) A.& D. Löve var. *lateriflorum* (19) (1840)

Side-flower sandwort [Side-flowered sandwort, Side-flowering sandwort] - *Moehringia lateriflora* (L.) Fenzl (2, 156) (1895-1923)

Side-flower skullcap [Sideflowering skullcap, Side-flowering scullcap, Side flowering scullcap, Side-flowering skullcap] - *Scutellaria lateriflora* L. (5, 92, 155, 158) (1876-1942)

Side-grape [Side grape] - *Coccoloba uvifera* (L.) L. (20) (1857)

Side-oats [Side oats] - *Bouteloua curtipendula* (Michx) Torr. (56, 94, 119) (1901-1938)

Side-oats grama [Side oats grama, Sideoats grama, Side-oat grama] - *Bouteloua curtipendula* (Michx) Torr. (3, 50, 114, 116, 122, 134, 140, 155, 163) (1852–present), *Bouteloua* Lag. (93) (1936), *Bouteloua curtipendula* (Michx.) Torr. var. *curtipendula* (5, 50) (1913–present)

Sideranthus - *Machaeranthera pinnatifida* (Hook.) Shinners subsp. *pinnatifida* (93, 97, 127) (1936-1937)

Sideroxylon - *Sideroxylon* L. (158) (1900)

Side-saddle - *Sarracenia purpurea* L. (19) (1840)

Side-saddle flower [Sidesaddle flower, Side saddle flower] - *Sarracenia flava* L. (177) (1762), *Sarracenia* L. (1, 2, 10, 13, 14, 15, 86, 167) (1814-1932) from flower shape, *Sarracenia purpurea* L. (5, 6, 15, 46, 49, 63, 92, 156, 187) (1818-1923), *Sarracenia purpurea* L. subsp. *purpurea* var. *purpurea* (181) (~1678)

Side-saddle plant [Sidesaddle plant] - *Sarracenia purpurea* L. (49, 52, 57, 92) (1876-1919)

Sidu-hi (Omaha-Ponca) - *Spartina pectinata* Bosc ex Link (37) (1830)

Siebold's forsythia [Siebold forsythia] - *Forsythia suspensa* (Thunb.) Vahl (138) (1923)

Siebold's viburnum [Siebold viburnum] - *Viburnum sieboldii* Miq. (138) (1923)

Siefen (Low Dutch) - *Juncus* L. (180) (1633)

Siegwurtz (German) - *Gladiolus* L. (180) (1633)

Sielge de mer (French, sea rye) - *Leymus arenarius* (L.) Hochst. (41) (1770)

Sierra alder - *Alnus rhombifolia* Nutt. (155) (1942)

Sierra juniper - *Juniperus occidentalis* Hook. (155) (1942)

Sierra lily - *Lilium parvum* Kellogg (138) (1923)

Sierra Nevada shield fern [Sierra Nevada shield-fern] - *Thelypteris nevadensis* (Baker) Clute ex Morton (86) (1878)

Sierra reed grass [Sierra reedgrass] - *Calamagrostis stricta* (Timm) Koel. subsp. *inexpansa* (Gray) C. W. Greene (155) (1942)

Sierra salvia - *Artemisia frigida* Willd. (157, 158) (1900-1929)

Sierra snapdragon - *Linaria vulgaris* Mill. (155) (1942)

Sierra trout-lily [Sierra troutlily] - *Erythronium purpurascens* S. Wats. (138) (1923)

Sierra white fir - *Abies lowiana* (Gordon & Glend.) A. Murray bis (50) (present)

Sierra wild ginger [Sierra wildginger] - *Asarum hartwegii* S. Wats. (155) (1942)

Sierra willow-weed [Sierra willow weed, Sierra willowweed] - *Epilobium ciliatum* Raf. subsp. *ciliatum* (155) (1942)

Sieva bean - *Phaseolus lunatus* L. (107, 109) (1919-1949)

Sieversia - *Geum* L. (155) (1942)

Siga'gawûnj' (Chippewa, onion) - *Allium tricoccum* Ait. (40) (1928)

Sige (Albanian) - *Punica* L. (110) (1886)

Sightwort - *Chelidonium majus* L. (156) (1923)

Šigme-winš (Chippewa) - *Acer rubrum* L. (105) (1932)

Signal-grass [Signalgrass] - *Brachiaria* (Trin.) Griseb. (155) (1942)

Sikua (Modern Greek) - *Cucumis sativus* L. (110) (1886)

Sikuos pepon - *Cucumis melo* L. (107) (1919)

Silberkraut (German) - *Argentina anserina* (L.) Rydb. (158) (1900)

Silene - *Silene* L. (155) (1942)

Silg grass - *Asclepias tuberosa* L. (190) (~1759)

Silk aloes - *Yucca filamentosa* L. (7) (1828)

Silk grass [Silkgrass, Silk-grass] - *Achnatherum hymenoides* (Roemer & J.A. Schultes) Barkworth (92) (1876), *Achnatherum* P. Beauv. (10) (1818), *Agrostis hyemalis* (Walt.) Britton, Sterns & Poggenb. (5, 119) (1913-1938), *Hesperostipa comata* (Trin. & Rupr.) Barkworth (5) (1913), *Hesperostipa comata* (Trin. & Rupr.) Barkworth subsp. *comata* (5) (1913)

Silk orophaca - *Astragalus sericoleucus* Gray (4) (1986)

Silk plant [Silk-plant] - *Plantago rugelii* Dcne. (75, 156) (1894)

Silk tassel bush - *Garrya ovata* Benth. subsp. *lindheimeri* (Torr.) Dahling (124) (1937)

Silk tree [Silktree, Silk-tree] - *Albizia julibrissin* Durazz. (5, 50, 109, 138) (1913–present), *Albizia julibrissin* Durazz. (5, 50, 109, 138) (1913–present)

Silk vine [Silkvine, Silk-vine] - *Periploca graeca* L. (4, 50, 158) (1900–present), *Periploca* L. (1, 4, 109, 138, 155, 158) (1900-1986)

Silk-bark oak - *Grevillea* R. Br. ex Knight (107) (1919)

Silk-cotton purslane [Silkcotton purslane] - *Portulaca halimoides* L. (50) (Present)

Silk-cotton tree [Silk-cotton-tree] - *Ceiba pentandra* (L.) Gaertn. (109) (1949)

Silk-grass [Silk grass, Silke grass] - *Apocynum androsaemifolium* L. (181) (~1678), *Apocynum cannabinum* L. (35) (1806), *Asclepias syriaca* L. (156) (1923), *Eriophorum virginicum* L. (possibly) (46) (1610), *Yucca filamentosa* L. (5, 92, 156, 158, 177) (1526-1923)

Silk-oak - *Grevillea robusta* A. Cunningham ex R. Br. (109, 138) (1923-1949)

Silk-plant - *Plantago rugelii* Dcne. (75, 156) (1894-1923) FL

Silk-seed aster - *Sericocarpus tortifolius* (Michx.) Nees (156) (1923)

Silk-tassel bush [Silktassel-bush] - *Garrya* Dougl. ex Lindl. (138) (1923)

Silk-top dalea [Silktop dalea] - *Dalea aurea* Nutt. ex Pursh (3, 155) (1942-1977)

Silk-tree albizzia [Silktree albizzia] - *Albizia julibrissin* Durazz. (155) (1942)

Silkvine [Silk vine, Silk-vine] - *Periploca graeca* L. (4, 50, 158) (1900–present), *Periploca* L. (1, 4, 109, 138, 155, 158) (1900-1986)

Silkweed - *Asclepias* L. (1, 2, 61, 79, 106, 109, 158) (1870–1949), *Asclepias speciosa* Torr. (101) (1905), *Asclepias syriaca* L. (5, 6, 49, 53, 62, 92, 107, 122, 157, 158) (1876–1937), *Asclepias tuberosa* L. (7, 92) (1828–1876)

Silkworm mulberry - *Morus alba* L. (138) (1923)

Silky agrostis - *Apera spica-venti* (L.) Beauv. (45) (1896)

Silky aster - *Symphyotrichum sericeum* (Vent.) Nesom (3, 4, 72, 85, 122, 155) (1907-1986)

Silky bent grass [Silky bent-grass] - *Apera spica-venti* (L.) Beauv. (5, 165) (1768-1913)

Silky button tree - *Conocarpus erectus* L. (20) (1857)

Silky cinquefoil - *Potentilla hippiana* Lehm. (85) (1932)

Silky cornel - *Cornus amomum* Mill. (5, 82, 93, 97, 131, 156, 157, 158) (1899–1937), *Cornus sericea* L. (6, 58, 63, 92, 130) (1869–1899)

Silky crazyweed - *Oxytropis sericea* Nutt. (155) (1942)

Silky dogwood - *Cornus amomum* Mill. (50, 109, 138, 155, 157) (1923–present), *Cornus obliqua* Raf. (50) (Present), *Cornus sericea* L. (6) (1892)

Silky everlasting grass [Silky everlasting-grass] - *Eriochloa sericea* (Scheele) Munro ex Vasey (94) (1901)

Silky grass [Silky-grass] - *Achnatherum hymenoides* (Roemer & J.A. Schultes) Barkworth (5, 163) (1852–1913), *Achnatherum* P. Beauv. (93) (1936), *Oryzopsis hymenoides* (R. & S.) Ricker (85) (1932) SD

Silky green alder - *Alnus viridis* (Vill.) Lam. & DC. (155) (1942)

Silky lupine - *Lupinus sericeus* Pursh (4, 50, 155) (1942–present)

Silky milkvetch [Silky milk vetch] - *Astragalus sericoleucus* Gray (50) (present), *Astragalus spatulatus* Sheldon (85) (1932)

Silky phacelia - *Phacelia hastata* Dougl. ex Lehm. var. *hastata* (5, 85) (1913-1932)

Silky prairie clover [Silky prairieclover] - *Dalea tenuifolia* (Gray) Shinners (5, 72, 97) (1907–1937), *Dalea villosa* (Nutt.) Spreng (3, 4, 5, 50, 85, 93, 138, 155) (1913–present), *Dalea villosa* (Nutt.) Spreng. var. *villosa* (50) (Present), *Petasites frigidus* (L.) Fries var. *palmatus* (Aiton) Cronq. (5, 85, 93) (1913–1936)

Silky sassafras - *Sassafras albidum* (Nutt.) Nees (155) (1942)

Silky sophora - *Sophora nuttalliana* B.L. Turner (5, 50, 93, 97, 122, 124, 125, 131, 148, 155, 157) (1899–present)

Silky swallow-wort [Silky swallowwort, Silky swallowort] - *Asclepias syriaca* L. (5, 7, 92, 156, 157, 158) (1828–1929)

Silky Townsend flower - *Townsendia exscapa* (Richards.) Porter (86) (1878)

Silky townsendia - *Townsendia exscapa* (Richards.) Porter (5) (1913)

Silky wild oat grass - *Danthonia sericea* Nutt. (5) (1913)

Silky willow - *Salix sericea* Marsh. (5, 22, 72, 138) (1907–1923)

Silky wormwood - *Artemisia dracunculus* L. (3, 4, 5, 85, 93, 98) (1913–1936)

Silky-flower oat grass [Silky-flowered oat grass] - *Danthonia sericea* Nutt. (87) (1884)

Silky-leaf bumelia [Silky-leaved bumelia] - *Sideroxylon tenax* L. (20) (1857)

Silky-leaf willow [Silky leaved willow] - *Salix sericea* Marsh. (8) (1785)

Silky-scale [Silkyscale] - *Anthaenantia* Beauv. (155) (1942)

Sillscale - *Endolepis dioica* (Nutt.) Standl. (4) (1986)

Silver aira grass [Silver aira-grass] - *Aira caryophyllea* L. (165) (1768)

Silver Alp wormwood [Silveralp wormwood] - *Artemisia umbelliformis* Lam. (155) (1942)

Silver aster - *Pityopsis graminifolia* (Michx.) Nutt. var. *graminifolia* (156) (1923), *Pityopsis graminifolia* var. *latifolia* (Fernald) Semple & F. D. Bowers (92) (1876)

Silver beard grass [Silver beard-grass, Silver beardgrass] - *Andropogon ternarius* Michx. (66) (1903), *Bothriochloa laguroides* (DC.) Herter (50) (present), *Bothriochloa laguroides* (DC.) Herter subsp. *torreyana* (Steud.) Allred & Gould (50) (present), *Bothriochloa saccharoides* (Sw.) Rydb. (138, 140, 163) (1852–1944)

Silver birch - *Betula alleghaniensis* Britt. var. *alleghaniensis* (5, 109, 156) (1913-1949), *Betula papyrifera* Marsh (5, 157, 158) (1900-1929), *Betula pubescens* Ehrh. (156) (1923)

Silver bladderpod - *Lesquerella ludoviciana* (Nutt.) S. Wats. (155) (1942)

Silver bluetem - *Bothriochloa saccharoides* (Sw.) Rydb. (3, 140) (1944-1977)

Silver buffaloberry - *Shepherdia argentea* (Pursh) Nutt. (50, 138, 155) (1923–present)

Silver bush [Silver-bush, Silverbush] - *Argythamnia* P. Br. (50, 155) (1942–present), *Elaeagnus commutata* Bernh. ex Rydb. (101) (1905), *Elaeagnus* L. (1) (1932), *Shepherdia argentea* (Pursh) Nutt. (156) (1923), *Shepherdia* Nutt. (7) (1828)

Silver cedar - *Juniperus scopulorum* Sarg. (136) (1930)

Silver chickweed - *Paronychia argyrocoma* (Michx.) Nutt. (5, 156) (1913-1923)

Silver cineraria - *Senecio bicolor* (Willd.) Todaro subsp. *cineraria* (DC.) Chater (138) (1923)

Silver cinquefoil - *Potentilla argentea* L. (50, 138, 155) (1923–present), *Potentilla argentea* L. var. *argentea* (50) (present)

Silver fern [Silver-fern] - *Pityrogramma calomelanos* (L.) Link (109) (1949), *Pityrogramma ebenea* (L.) Proctor (138) (1923), *Pityrogramma* Link (109) (1949)

Silver fir - *Abies alba* Mill. (50, 92, 109, 155, 158) (1876–present), *Abies amabilis* (Dougl. ex Loud.) Dougl. ex Forbes (161) (1857), *Abies balsamea* (L.) Mill. (60) (1902), *Abies balsamea* (L.) Mill. var. *balsamea* (20) (1857), *Abies concolor* (Gord. & Glend.) Lindl. ex Hildebr. (136) (1930), *Abies concolor* (Gord. & Glend.) Lindl. ex Hildebr. (possibly) (136) (1930) SD, *Tsuga canadensis* (L.) Carr. (possibly) (138) (1923)

Silver fleece vine [Silver fleecevine] - *Polygonum baldschuanicum* Regel (138) (1923)

Silver grass [Silvergrass] - *Miscanthus* Anderss. (50, 155) (1942–present)

Silver hair grass [Silver hairgrass] - *Aira caryophyllea* L. (50) (present)

Silver lace vine [Silver lace-vine] - *Polygonum aubertii* Henry (109) (1949)

Silver linden - *Tilia petiolaris* DC. (109, 138) (1923-1949)

Silver maple - *Acer rubrum* L. (2, 4, 3, 5, 9, 15, 19, 50, 82, 93, 97, 105, 106, 107, 109, 112, 114, 130, 131, 135, 138, 155, 156, 157, 158) (1840–present)

Silver oak - *Quercus hypoleucoides* A. Camus (122) (1937) TX

Silver orache - *Atriplex argentea* Nutt. (131) (1899)

Silver pine - *Abies alba* Mill. (possibly) (92, 158) (1876-1900)

Silver plant - *Impatiens capensis* Meerb. (157, 158) (1900-1929)

Silver plume grass [Silver plume-grass, Silver plumegrass] - *Saccharum alopecuroidum* (L.) Nutt. (50, 119, 122) (1937–present)

Silver poplar - *Populus alba* L. (1, 3, 4, 93, 112, 158) (1900-1986)

Silver popple - *Populus alba* L. (158) (1900)

Silver red cedar - *Juniperus virginiana* L. (possibly) (136) (1930)

Silver rockcress - *Arabis alpina* L. (155) (1942)

Silver sage - *Salvia argentea* L. (138) (1923), *Salvia leucophylla* Greene (106) (1930)

Silver sagebrush - *Artemisia cana* Pursh (50) (Present), *Artemisia cana* Pursh subsp. *cana* (50) (present)

Silver spruce - *Picea pungens* Engelm. (136) (1930)

Silver vine [Silvervine, Silver-vine] - *Actinidia polygama* (Siebold & Zucc.) Maxim. (109, 138) (1923-1949)

Silver wattle - *Acacia decurrens* Willd. (138) (1923), *Acacia mearnsii* De Wild. (107) (1919) naturalized in CA OR

Silver whitlow-wort [Silver whitlow wort] - *Paronychia argyrocoma* (Michx.) Nutt. (5, 156) (1913-1923)

Silver willow - *Salix argyrocarpa* Anderss. (1, 5) (1913-1932), *Salix discolor* Muhl. (5, 156, 158) (1900-1923)

Silver wolfberry - *Lycium berlandieri* Dunal (4) (1986)

Silver-beard - *Andropogon ternarius* Michx. (5, 94) (1901-1913)

Silverbell [Silver-bell] or Silver-bell tree [Silverbell-tree, Silver bell tree, Silver-bell tree] - *Halesia carolina* L. (5, 97, 124, 156) (1913-1937), *Halesia* Ellis ex L. (2, 8, 109, 138, 156) (1785-1949), *Halesia tetraptera* Ellis var. *monticola* (Rehd.) Reveal & Seldin (65) (1931) OK, *Halesia tetraptera* L. (92, 107) (1876-1919)

Silverberry [Silver berry, Silver-berry] - *Elaeagnus commutata* Bernh. ex Rydb. (2, 3, 4, 5, 50, 85, 93, 106, 108, 109, 130, 131, 138, 155, 156, 158) (1878–present), *Elaeagnus* L. (1, 158) (1900-1932), *Shepherdia argentea* (Pursh) Nutt. (82) (1930)

Silverbush [Silver-bush] - *Argythamnia* P. Br. (50, 155) (1942–present), *Elaeagnus commutata* Bernh. ex Rydb. (101) (1905) MT, *Elaeagnus* L. (1) (1932), *Shepherdia argentea* (Pursh) Nutt. (156) (1923), *Shepherdia* Nutt. (7) (1828)

Silver-button [Silver button] - *Anaphalis margaritacea* (L.) Benth. & Hook (5, 106, 156, 158) (1900-1930)

Silver-chain [Silver-chain] - *Robinia pseudoacacia* L. (5, 156, 157, 158) (1900-1929)

Silver-edge bishop's goutweed [Silveredge bishops goutweed] - *Aegopodium podagraria* L. (155) (1942)

Silver-feather [Silver feather] - *Argentina anserina* (L.) Rydb. (156, 157, 158) (1900-1929)

Silver-grass [Silver grass] - *Pityopsis graminifolia* (Michx.) Nutt. var. *graminifolia* (5, 156) (1913-1923)

Silver-green - *Adenocaulon bicolor* Hook. (156) (1923)

Silver-green wattle acacia [Silvergreen-wattle acacia] - *Acacia decurrens* Willd. (155) (1942)

Silverhead [Silver-head] - *Paronychia argyrocoma* (Michx.) Nutt. (5, 86, 156) (1878-1923)

Silver-king artemisia [Silver king artemisia] - *Artemisia ludoviciana* Nutt. subsp. *albula* (Woot.) Keck (109) (1949)

Silver-king sagebrush [Silverking sagebrush] - *Artemisia ludoviciana* Nutt. subsp. *albula* (Woot.) Keck (155) (1942)

Silverleaf [Silver leaf, Silver-leaf] - *Anaphalis margaritacea* (L.) Benth. & Hook (5, 7, 91, 156, 158) (1828–1923), *Hydrangea cinerea* Small (156) (1923), *Impatiens capensis* Meerb. (5, 86, 157, 158) (1878–1929), *Lunaria annua* subsp. *annua* L. (possibly) (156) (1923), *Magnolia macrophylla* Michx. (5, 7, 92, 156) (1828–1923), *Pseudognaphalium obtusifolium* (L.) Hilliard & Burtt subsp. *obtusifolium* (6) (1892), *Shepherdia argentea* (Pursh) Nutt. (5, 156, 158) (1900–1923), *Spiraea tomentosa* L. (5, 49, 92, 156) (1898–1923), *Stillingia sylvatica* Garden ex L. (49, 53, 58, 64, 92, 156, 158) (1869–1923)

Silver-leaf alder [Silver-leaved alder] - *Alnus incana* (L.) Moench subsp. *rugosa* (DuRoi) Clausen (8) (1785)

Silver-leaf cotoneaster [Silverleaf cotoneaster] - *Cotoneaster pannosus* Franch. (138) (1923)

Silver-leaf hibiscus [Silver leaf hibiscus] - *Hibiscus martianus* Zucc. (124) (1937) TX

Silver-leaf Indian breadroot [Silverleaf Indian breadroot] - *Pediomelum argophyllum* (Pursh) J. Grimes (50) (Present)

Silver-leaf life-everlasting [Silver-leaved life-everlasting] - *Anaphalis margaritacea* (L.) Benth. & Hook (156) (1923)

Silver-leaf manzanita [Silverleaf manzanita] - *Arctostaphylos silvicola* Jepson & Wies. ex Jepson (155) (1942)

Silver-leaf maple [Silver-leaved maple] - *Acer rubrum* L. (8) (1785)

Silver-leaf maple [Silver-leaved maple] - *Acer rubrum* L. (5, 156, 157, 158) (1900-1929)

Silver-leaf nightshade [Silverleaf nightshade, Silver-leaved nightshade] - *Solanum elaeagnifolium* Cav. (3, 4, 5, 50, 97, 122, 124, 155, 156, 158) (1900–present)

Silver-leaf oak [Silver-leaved oak] - *Quercus hypoleucoides* A. Camus (149, 153) (1904-1919) NM

Silver-leaf phacelia [Silverleaf phacelia] - *Phacelia hastata* Dougl. ex Lehm. (50) (Present), *Phacelia hastata* Dougl. ex Lehm. var. *hastata* (50, 155) (1942–present)

Silver-leaf poplar [Silver-leaved poplar] - *Populus alba* L. (5, 85, 97, 156, 158) (1900–1937), *Tilia americana* L. var. *heterophylla* (Vent.) Loud. (156) (1923)

Silver-leaf psoralea - *Pediomelum argophyllum* (Pursh) J. Grimes (5, 72, 93, 97, 131) (1899-1937)

Silver-leaf red fir [Silverleaf red fir] - *Abies magnifica* A. Murr. (155) (1942)

Silver-leaf scurf pea [Silverleaf scurfpea] - *Pediomelum argophyllum* (Pursh) J. Grimes (3, 4, 155) (1942-1986)

Silver-leaf sunflower [Silverleaf sunflower] - *Helianthus argophyllus* Torr. & Gray (109, 122, 124, 138) (1923-1949)

Silver-leaf willow [Silverleaf willow, Silver-leaved willow] - *Salix exigua* Nutt. (20, 155) (1857-1942)

Silver-leaved alder - *Alnus incana* (L.) Moench subsp. *rugosa* (DuRoi) Clausen (8) (1785)

Silver-rod - *Eupatorium serotinum* Michx. (156) (1923), *Solidago bicolor* L. (156) (1923)

Silver-scale saltbush [Silverscale saltbush] - *Atriplex argentea* Nutt. (3, 4, 50) (1977–present), *Atriplex argentea* Nutt. subsp. *argentea* (3, 50) (1977–present)

Silver-thistle [Silver thistle] - *Onopordum acanthium* L. (5, 156) (1913-1923)

Silver-top sedge [Silvertop sedge] - *Carex siccata* Dewey (139, 155) (1942-1944)

Silver-vine actinidia [Silvervine actinidia] - *Actinidia polygama* (Siebold & Zucc.) Maxim. (155) (1942)

Silverweed [Silver weed, Silver-weed] - *Argentina anserina* (L.) Rydb. (3, 4, 5, 41, 80, 85, 92, 107, 127, 131, 138, 156, 157, 158) (1770-1986), *Argentina* Hill (1, 50, 93) (1932–present), *Impatiens capensis* Meerb. (5, 74, 156) (1893-1923) NY, *Impatiens pallida* Nutt. (5, 74, 156, 157) (1893-1929) Mansfield OH, *Pilea pumila* (L.) Gray (156) (1923), *Solidago bicolor* L. (5, 75, 76, 156) (1896-1923) ME NY, *Spiraea tomentosa* L. (5, 92, 156) (1876-1923), *Thalictrum pubescens* Pursh (5, 76, 156) (1896-1923) Oxford Co. ME

Silverweed cinquefoil - *Argentina anserina* (L.) Rydb. (50, 155) (1942–present)

Silvery beard grass [Silvery beard-grass] - *Andropogon ternarius* Michx. (3, 5, 94, 99, 119, 163) (1852-1977), *Bothriochloa saccharoides* (Sw.) Rydb. (119) (1938)

Silvery Black Hills spruce - *Picea glauca* (Moench) Voss (136) (1930) SD

Silvery bladderpod [Silvery bladder-pod, Silvery bladder pod] - *Lesquerella ludoviciana* (Nutt.) S. Wats. (5, 93, 97) (1913-1937), *Lesquerella arenosa* (Richards.) Rydb. var. *arenosa* (131) (1899)

Silvery bluegrass [Silvery blue-grass] - *Poa pringlei* Scribn. (94) (1901)

Silvery cinquefoil - *Argentina anserina* (L.) Rydb. (85) (1932), *Potentilla argentea* L. (3, 4, 5, 72, 156, 158) (1900-1986)

Silvery five-finger - *Potentilla argentea* L. (5) (1913)

Silvery groundsel - *Packera cana* (Hook.) W.A. Weber & A. Löve (5, 93, 131) (1899-1936)

Silvery hair grass [Silvery hair-grass] - *Aira caryophyllea* L. (5, 94) (1913)

Silvery lupine - *Lupinus argenteus* Pursh (4, 50, 126, 133, 155) (1903–present), *Lupinus argenteus* Pursh subsp. *argenteus* (3, 5, 50, 93, 98) (1913–present), *Lupinus parviflorus* Nutt. ex Hook. & Arn. subsp. *parviflorus* (3) (1977)

Silvery milkvetch [Silvery milk vetch] - *Astragalus hyalinus* M.E. Jones (5, 93) (1913-1936)

Silvery oat grass [Silvery oat-grass] - *Trisetum canescens* Buckl. (94) (1901)

Silvery orache - *Atriplex argentea* Nutt. (5, 93, 156) (1913-1936)

Silvery panic grass [Silvery panic-grass] - *Digitaria villosa* (Walt.) Pers. (94) (1901)

Silvery prairie cinquefoil - *Potentilla pensylvanica* L. (93) (1936)

Silvery primrose - *Primula incana* M.E. Jones (50) (present)

Silvery sedge - *Carex canescens* L. (5, 50) (1913–present)

Silvery spleenwort - *Deparia acrostichoides* (Sw.) M. Kato (5, 19, 72, 138) (1840-1923)

Silvery wormwood - *Artemisia filifolia* Torr. (5, 85, 93, 97, 122, 131, 158) (1899-1937)

Silvery-top sedge [Silvery topped sedge] - *Carex siccata* Dewey (129) (1894)

Simnens - *Cucurbita maxima* Dcne. (35) (1806)

Simon's cotoneaster [Simons cotoneaster] - *Cotoneaster simonsii* Baker (138) (1923)

Simon's poplar [Simon poplar] - *Populus balsamifera* L. (138) (1923)

Simon's weed - *Galeopsis bifida* Boenn. (5) (1913)

Simple bog-sedge [Simple bog sedge] - *Kobresia simpliciuscula* (Wahlenb.) Mackenzie (50) (present)

Simple-beak ironwort [Simple-beaked iron-wor - *Sideritis romana* L. (5) (1913)

Simple-leaf ampelopsis [Simple leafed ampelopsis, Simple-leaved ampelopsis] - *Ampelopsis cordata* Michx. (5, 72, 97, 124) (1907-1937)

Simpler's-joy [Simpler's joy, Simplers joy, Simplers' joy] - *Verbena hastata* L. (7, 19, 49, 53, 58, 62, 92, 156, 157, 158) (1828-1929), *Verbena officinalis* L. (5, 156) (1913-1923)

Simple-stem bur-reed [Simplestem bur-reed, Simple-stemmed bur-reed] - *Sparganium erectum* L. subsp. *stoloniferum* (Graebn.) Hara (5, 50, 72) (1907–present)

Simple-stem bur-reed [Simplestem bur-reed] - *Sparganium erectum* L. (50) (present)

Simpson's cactus - *Pediocactus simpsonii* (Engelm.) Britton & Rose (5) (1913)

Simpson's grass - *Panicum hemitomon* Schult. (5, 163) (1852-1913)

Simpson's hedgehog cactus - *Pediocactus simpsonii* (Engelm.) Britton & Rose (50) (present)

Simpson's honey plant [Simpson honey plant] - *Scrophularia marilandica* L. (80, 82, 106) (1913-1930)

Simpson's root [Simpson root] - *Gentiana catesbaei* Walt. (7) (1828)

Sims' clematis - *Clematis crispa* L. (72) (1907) IA

Simson - *Senecio vulgaris* L. (5, 156, 158) (1900-1923)

Sin (Omaha-Ponca) - *Sagittaria latifolia* Willd. (37) (1830)

Sin (Winnebago) - *Zizania aquatica* L. (37) (1830)

Sinclair's pine - *Pinus ponderosa* P.& C. Lawson (5, 8, 10, 20, 19, 40) (1818-1928)

Sin-dew - *Drosera rotundifolia* L. (156) (1923)

Sindria (Sardinian) - *Citrullus lanatus* (Thunb.) Matsumura & Nakai (110) (1886)

Sing (Chinese) - *Prunus armeniaca* L. (110) (1886)

Šingábi-min (Chippewa) - *Rubus canadensis* L. (105) (1932)

Singhara-nut - *Trapa natans* L. (138) (1923)

Singkwa towel gourd [Singkwa towelgourd] - *Luffa acutangula* (L.) Roxb. (138) (1923)

Single daffy - *Narcissus poeticus* L. (73) (1892) NH

Single delight - *Moneses uniflora* (L.) Gray (50) (Present)

Single French marigold - *Tagetes patula* L. (178) (1526)

Single muske Rose - *Rosa moschata* J. Herrm. (possibly) (178) (1526)

Single pink - *Dianthus plumarius* L. (19) (1840)

Single spruce - *Abies alba* Mill. (20) (1857), *Abies balsamea* (L.) Mill. (5, 158) (1900-1913), *Picea glauca* (Moench) Voss (5, 158) (1900-1913)

Single yellow daffodil - Narcissus ×incomparabilis Mill. [poeticus × pseudonarcissus] (178) (1596)

Single-beauty [Single beauty] - *Moneses* Salisb. ex S.F. Gray (1) (1932)

Single-delight [Single delight] - *Moneses uniflora* (L.) Gray (50) (present)

Single-fruit croton [Single-fruited croton] - *Croton monanthogynus* Michx. (5, 97) (1913-1937)

Single-head cat's-foot [Single-headed cat's foot] - *Antennaria solitaria* Rydb. (5) (1913)

Single-head goldenweed [Singlehead goldenweed] - *Ericameria suffruticosa* (Nutt.) G.L. Nesom (155) (1942), *Hazardia squarrosa* (Hook. & Arn.) Greene var. *squarrosa* (155) (1942)

Single-leaf ash [Singleleaf ash] - *Fraxinus anomala* Torr. ex S. Wats. (138) (1923)

Single-leaf pine [Singleleaf pine] - *Pinus monophylla* Torr. & Frém. (138) (1923)

Single-seed cucumber [Single-seeded cucumber] - *Sicyos angulatus* L. (10, 19, 86, 92, 156) (1818-1923), *Sicyos* L. (167) (1814)

Single-stem bog aster [Single-stemmed bog aster] - *Eurybia hemispherica* (Alexander) Nesom (4) (1986), *Eurybia paludosa* (Aiton) Nesom (155) (1942)

Singletary vetchling - *Lathyrus pusillus* Ell. (4) (1986)

Sinie makan (Omaha-Ponca) - *Plantago major* L. (37) (1919)

Sinkel (German) - *Triticum spelta* L. (180) (1633)

Sinkfield - *Potentilla canadensis* L. (5, 74, 156) (1893-1923) WV, no longer in use by 1923

Sinkweed - *Datura stramonium* L. (6, 7, 49) (1828-1898)

Sinnthau (German) - *Drosera rotundifolia* L. (158) (1900)

Sin-poro (Winnebago) - *Sagittaria latifolia* Willd. (37) (1830)

Sinuate-leaf evening-primrose [Sinuate-leaved evening primrose] - *Oenothera laciniata* Hill (72, 131) (1899-1907)

Sinuate-leaf gaura [Sinuate-leaved gaura] - *Gaura sinuata* Nutt. ex Ser. (4) (1986)

Sinwaninda (Omaha-Ponca) - *Zizania aquatica* L. (37) (1830)

Siŋkpe tawote (Lakota, muskrat food) - *Acorus calamus* L. (121) (1918-1970) SD

Siris tree [Siris-tree] - *Albizia lebbeck* (L.) Benth. (109) (1949)

Sisal - *Agave sisalana* Perrine (138) (1923)

Siskiyou aster - *Symphyotrichum lanceolatum* (Willd.) Nesom subsp. *hesperium* (Gray) Nesom (155) (1942)

Sisson plum - *Prunus subcordata* var. *kellogii* Lemmon (109) (1949)

Sissoo - *Dalbergia sissoo* Roxb. ex DC. (138) (1923)

Sistat (Pawnee) - *Schoenoplectus tabernaemontani* (K.C. Gmel.) Palla (37) (1830)

Sister violet - *Viola sororia* Willd. (155) (1942)

Sitfast - *Ranunculus repens* L. (5, 156, 158) (1900-1923)

Sitka alder - *Alnus viridis* (Vill.) Lam. & DC. (155) (1942)

Sitka clubmoss - *Lycopodium sitchense* Rupr. (50) (present)

Sitka columbine - *Aquilegia formosa* Fisch. ex DC. (138, 155) (1931-1942)

Sitka sedge - *Carex aquatilis* Wahlenb. var. *dives* (Holm) Kükenth. (50) (present)

Sitka spruce - *Picea sitchensis* (Bong.) Carr. (109, 138) (1923-1949)

Sitroules - *Cucurbita pepo* L. (107) (1605)

Siurguld (Norwegian) - *Anthemis cotula* L. (186) (1814)

Siuves - *Allium schoenoprasum* L. (178) (1596)

Sivven - *Rubus idaeus* L. (158) (1900)

Šiwi-min (Chippewa) - *Vitis* L. (105) (1932)

Six-angle euphorbia [Sixangle euphorbia] - *Euphorbia hexagona* Nutt. ex Spreng. (155) (1942)

Six-angle spurge [Sixangle spurge, Six-angled spurge] - *Euphorbia hexagona* Nutt. ex Spreng. (3, 4, 50) (1977–present)

Six-lines barley - *Hordeum vulgare* L. (107) (1919)

Six-row barley [Sixrow barley, Six rowed barley, Six-rowed barley] - *Hordeum vulgare* L. (66, 67, 110, 155) (1886-1942)

Six-weeks bent grass [Sixweeks bentgrass] - *Agrostis elliottiana* Schultes (155) (1942)

Six-weeks fescue [Six weeks fescue, Sixweeks fescue] - *Vulpia octoflora* (Walt.) Rydb. (50) (present), *Vulpia octoflora* (Walt.) Rydb. var. *octoflora* (3, 50, 119, 122, 140, 155) (1937–present)

Six-weeks grama [Six weeks grama, Sixweeks grama] - *Bouteloua barbata* Lag. (31, 50, 94, 151, 152, 155) (1847–present), *Bouteloua aristidoides* (Kunth) Griseb. (151, 152, 163) (1852-1912)

Six-weeks grass - *Poa annua* L. (5) (1913)

Six-weeks mesquit - *Bouteloua aristidoides* (Kunth) Griseb. (94) (1901)

Six-weeks threeawn - *Aristida adscensionis* L. (3, 50) (1977–present)

Ska'agon-minš (Chippewa) - *Carpinus caroliniana* Walt. (105) (1932)

Skadiks or skariks (Pawnee) - *Thalictrum dasycarpum* Fisch. & Avé-Lall. (37) (1919)

Skalikatit (Pawnee, black-seed) - *Aquilegia canadensis* L. (37) (1919)

Skalikatit or Skarikatit (Pawnee, black-seed) - *Aquilegia canadensis* L. (37) (1919)

Skarikatit (Pawnee, black-seed) - *Aquilegia canadensis* L. (37) (1919)

Skariks (Pawnee) - *Thalictrum dasycarpum* Fisch. & Avé-Lall. (37) (1919)

Skaw - *Sambucus nigra* L. (158) (1900)

Skaw-coo - *Solanum dulcamara* L. (158) (1900)

Skedge - *Ligustrum vulgare* L. (5, 156, 158) (1900-1923)

Skedgwith - *Ligustrum vulgare* L. (5, 156, 158) (1900-1923)

Skeleton grass [Skeletongrass] - *Gymnopogon* P. Beauv. (50, 155) (1942–present)

Skeleton milkweed - *Asclepias subulata* Dcne. (155) (1942)

Skeleton plant [Skeletonplant] - *Lygodesmia* D. Don (50) (present)

Skeleton-grass [Skeleton grass] - *Chondrilla juncea* L. (5) (1913)

Skeleton-leaf burr ragweed [Skeletonleaf burr ragweed] - *Ambrosia tomentosa* Nutt. (50) (Present)

Skeleton-leaf bursage [Skeletonleaf bursage] - *Ambrosia tomentosa* Nutt. (155) (1942)

Skeleton-leaf goldeneye [Skeletonleaf goldeneye] - *Viguiera stenoloba* Blake (155) (1942)

Skeleton-plant [Skeletonplant] - *Lygodesmia* D. Don (50) (Present)

Skeleton-weed [Skeleton weed, Skeletonweed] - *Chloracantha spinosa* (Benth.) Nesom (150) (1894) NM, *Chondrilla juncea* L. (75, 156) (1894-1923) WV, *Lygodesmia* D. Don (1, 4, 155) (1932-1986), *Lygodesmia juncea* (Pursh) D. Don ex Hook. (3, 37, 80, 121, 148) (1919-1977), *Lygodesmia texana* (Torr. & Gray) Greene (124) (1937) TX, *Stephanomeria* Nutt. (4) (1986)

Skerrish - *Ligustrum vulgare* L. (158) (1900)

Skevish - *Erigeron philadelphicus* L. (5, 7, 92, 131, 156, 158) (1828-1923) no longer in use by 1923

Skevish fleabane - *Erigeron philadelphicus* L. (7) (1828)

Skewerwood [Skewer wood, Skewer-wood] - *Euonymus atropurpurea* Jacq. (156) (1923), *Euonymus europaea* L. (5, 156) (1913-1923), *Euonymus* L. (92) (1876)

Skewisch Berungskraut (German) - *Erigeron philadelphicus* L. (7) (1828)

Skidadihorit (Pawnee, sour like salt) - *Oxalis stricta* L. (37) (1919), *Oxalis violacea* L. (37) (1919)

Skinner's agalinis - *Agalinis skinneriana* (Wood) Britton (5) (1913)

Skinner's false foxglove - *Agalinis skinneriana* (Wood) Britton (50) (Present)

Skinner's gerardia - *Agalinis skinneriana* (Wood) Britton (97) (1937)

Skirariu (Pawnee) - *Sambucus nigra* L. subsp. *canadensis* (L.) R. Bolli (37) (1919)

Skiverwood [Skiver-wood, Skiver wood] - *Euonymus europaea* L. (5, 156) (1913-1923)

Skižgu-min (Chippewa, eyeberry) - *Rubus pubescens* Raf. var. *pubescens* (105) (1932)

Skogshumble (Swedish) - *Trifolium aureum* Pollich (46) (1879)

Skoke - *Phytolacca americana* L. var. *americana* (48, 71, 92) (1876-1898)

Skokeweed [Skoke weed] - *Phytolacca americana* L. var. *americana* (49) (1898)

Skorff (Swedish) - *Spergula arvensis* L. (110) (1886)

Skovlög (Denmark) - *Allium scorodoprasum* L. (110) (1886)

Skullcap [Scull cap, Scullcap, Skull-cap, Skull cap] - *Scutellaria drummondii* Benth. (124) (1937), *Scutellaria galericulata* L. (19, 46, 82) (1840-1879), *Scutellaria* L. (1, 2, 4, 10, 50, 63, 82, 93, 109, 138, 155, 156, 158, 184) (1793–present), *Scutellaria lateriflora* L. (48, 49, 52, 53, 54, 55, 57, 58, 61, 92, 102, 157) (1869-1929)

Skullcap speedwell [Skull-cap speedwell] - *Veronica scutellata* L. (5, 19, 50, 72, 156) (1840–present)

Skull-shaped puffball - *Calvatia craniiformis* (Schwein.) Fr. ex De Toni (170) (1995)

Sku-min (Chippewa) - *Rubus idaeus* L. subsp. *strigosus* (Michx.) Focke (105) (1932)

Skunk bush [Skunkbush, Skunk-bush] - *Ptelea* L. (153) (1913), *Ptelea trifoliata* L. (156) (1923), *Rhus aromatica* Aiton (6) (1892), *Rhus trilobata* Nutt. (85, 106, 131, 155, 156) (1899-1942), *Rhus trilobata* Nutt. var. *trilobata* (5, 93) (1913-1936)

Skunk cabbage [Skunk-cabbage [Skunkcabbage - *Rhus* L. (1) (1932), *Sarracenia purpurea* L. (5, 76, 156) (1896-1923) St. Paul MN, *Symplocarpus foetidus* (L.) Salisb. ex Nutt. (5, 6, 14, 41, 46, 50, 53, 57, 58, 61, 64, 72, 86, 92, 106, 138, 156, 186, 187) (1770–

present), *Symplocarpus* Salisb. ex Nutt. (50, 138, 156) (1923–present), *Veratrum* L. (1) (1932)

Skunk currant - *Ribes glandulosum* Grauer (5, 73, 138, 156) (1892-1923) ME, from odor of fruit

Skunk grape - *Vitis labrusca* L. (15, 107) (1895-1919)

Skunk grass [Skunk-grass] - *Eragrostis cilianensis* (All.) Vign. ex Janchen (119) (1938) OK, *Eragrostis* von Wolf (1) (1932), *Hordeum jubatum* L. (62) (1912) IN

Skunk spruce [Skunk-spruce] - *Picea glauca* (Moench) Voss (75, 158) (1894-1913) ME, from supposedly unpleasnat smell of foliage

Skunkbush [Skunk bush, Skunk-bush] - *Ptelea* L. (153) (1913) NM, *Ptelea trifoliata* L. (156) (1923), *Rhus aromatica* Aiton (6) (1892), *Rhus trilobata* Nutt. (85, 106, 131, 155, 156) (1899-1942), *Rhus trilobata* Nutt. var. *trilobata* (5, 93) (1913-1936)

Skunk-bush sumac [Skunkbush sumac] - *Rhus trilobata* Nutt. (50, 155) (1942–present)

Skunk-daisy [Skunk daisy] - *Verbesina encelioides* (Cav.) Benth. & Hook. f. ex Gray (156) (1923)

Skunkweed (skunk weed, skunk-weed) - *Croton texensis* (Klotzsch) Muell.-Arg. (5, 121, 156) (1913–1923), *Pluchea camphorata* (L.) DC. (106) (1930), *Polemonium* L. (1) (1932), *Symplocarpus foetidus* (L.) Salisb. ex Nutt. (5, 6, 42, 53, 86, 92, 156, 177, 186, 187) (1762–1923), *Eupatorium purpureum* L. (5, 156) (1913–1923)

Skwa'lĭ (Cherokee) - *Hepatica nobilis* Schreb. var. *acuta* (Pursh) Steyermark (102) (1886)

Sky flower [Skyflower, Sky-flower] - *Duranta erecta* L. (109) (1949), *Duranta* L. (138) (1923), *Senecio* L. (167) (1814)

Sky-blue aster [Skyblue aster] - *Symphyotrichum oolentangiense* (Riddell) Nesom (50) (Present), *Symphyotrichum oolentangiense* (Riddell) Nesom var. *oolentangiense* (5, 50, 72, 82, 93, 95, 97, 122, 156) (1907–present)

Sky-blue houstonia - *Houstonia caerulea* L. (187) (1818)

Sky-color grape flower [Sky-coloured Grape-floure, Skie coloured Grape flower] - *Muscari botryoides* (L.) Mills (178, 180) (1596-1633)

Sky-color oriental hyacinth [Skie coloured Orientall Iacint] - *Hyacinthus orientalis* L. (178) (1596)

Sky-drop aster [Skydrop aster] - *Symphyotrichum patens* (Aiton) G.L. Nesom var. *patens* (138, 155) (1923-1942)

Sky-flower - *Senecio* L. (167) (1814)

Skyrocket - *Ipomopsis aggregata* (Pursh) V. Grant subsp. *aggregata* (1) (1932)

Skyrocket gilia - *Ipomopsis aggregata* (Pursh) V. Grant subsp. *aggregata* (109) (1949)

Skyrwyt - *Eruca vesicaria* (L.) Cav. subsp. *sativa* (Mill.) Thellung (179) (1526), *Pastinaca* L. (179) (1526)

Slangenwortel (German) - *Aristolochia serpentaria* L. (186) (1814)

Slangröd (German) - *Aristolochia serpentaria* L. (186) (1814)

Slash pine - *Pinus echinata* Mill. (5) (1913), *Pinus elliottii* Engelm. var. *elliottii* (109) (1949), *Pinus taeda* L. (5) (1913)

Slaw bush [Slaw-bush] - *Chionanthus virginicus* L. (156) (1923)

Sleek mullein - *Verbascum blattaria* L. (19) (1840)

Sleek sumac [Sleek sumach] - *Rhus glabra* L. (5, 19, 156, 157, 158) (1840-1929)

Sleek-leaf [Sleekleaf, Sleek leaf] - *Leiophyllum buxifolium* (Berg.) Ell. (19, 92, 156) (1840-1923)

Sleeping clover - *Oxalis montana* Raf. (possibly) (5, 156) (1913-1923)

Sleeping Mollie - *Oxalis montana* Raf. (possibly) (156) (1923)

Sleeping nightshade - *Atropa bella-donna* L. (156) (1923)

Sleeping plant [Sleeping-plant, Sleepingplant] - *Chamaecrista fasciculata* (Michx.) Greene (50) (present), *Chamaecrista fasciculata* (Michx.) Greene var. *fasciculata* (50, 156) (1923-present)

Sleeping popcorn flower [Sleeping popcorn-flower, Sleeping popcornflower] - *Plagiobothrys scouleri* (Hook. & Arn.) I.M. Johnston var. *hispidulus* (Greene) Dorn (50) (present)

Sleeping wild lettuce [Sleeping wilde Lettise] - *Lactuca virosa* L. (178) (1526)

Sleeping-beauty [Sleeping beauty] - *Oxalis montana* Raf. (possibly) (5, 156) (1913-1923)

Sleepwort - *Lactuca sativa* L. (92) (1876)

Sleepy campion - *Silene antirrhina* L. (2, 15, 95) (1895-1936)

Sleepy catchfly - *Silene antirrhina* L. (1, 4, 5, 62, 72, 85, 93, 97, 122, 127, 131, 155, 156) (1899-1986)

Sleepy daisy - *Xanthisma texanum* DC. (122, 124) (1937) TX

Sleepy grass [Sleepygrass, Sleepy-grass] - *Achnatherum robustum* (Vasey) Barkworth (122, 140, 148, 152, 155, 163) (1852-1944), *Nassella viridula* (Trin.) Barkworth (56) (1901) IA

Sleepy silene - *Silene antirrhina* L. (50, 155) (1942–present)

Sleepy-daisy [Sleepy daisy] - *Xanthisma texanum* DC. subsp. *drummondii* (Torr. & Gray) Semple (3, 97) (1937-1977)

Sleepy-Dick [Sleepydick, Sleepy Dick] - *Ornithogalum umbellatum* L. (5, 50, 156, 158) (1900–present)

Slender agalinis - *Agalinis tenuifolia* (Vahl) Raf. (5) (1913)

Slender aristida - *Aristida longispica* Poir. var. *longispica* (56) (1901)

Slender arrowhead - *Sagittaria teres* S. Wats. (50) (present)

Slender aster - *Eurybia compacta* Nesom (5, 156) (1913-1923)

Slender beaked-rush [Slender beaked rush] - *Rhynchospora gracilenta* Gray (5, 19) (1840-1913)

Slender beak-rush - *Rhynchospora gracilenta* Gray (66) (1903)

Slender beard grass - *Aristida longispica* Poir. var. *longispica* (111) (1915)

Slender beardtongue [Slender beard-tongue] - *Penstemon gracilis* Nutt. (3, 4, 5, 72, 85, 93, 97, 127, 131) (1899-1986)

Slender bellflower - *Campanula aparinoides* Pursh (5, 156) (1913-1923)

Slender bent grass [Slender bent-grass] - *Agrostis capillaris* L. (94) (1901)

Slender bladderpod [Slender bladder pod, Slender bladder-pod] - *Lesquerella gracilis* (Hook.) S. Wats. (5, 93, 97) (1913-1937)

Slender blite - *Chenopodium foliosum* (Moench) Aschers. (19) (1840)

Slender blue flag - *Iris prismatica* Pursh ex Ker-Gawl. (2) (1895), *Iris verna* L. (5, 156) (1913-1923)

Slender blue grass [Slender bluegrass] - *Poa secunda* J. Presl (155) (1942)

Slender blue iris - *Iris prismatica* Pursh ex Ker-Gawl. (50) (present)

Slender bog rush - *Juncus tenuis* Willd. (129) (1894)

Slender bulrush - *Schoenoplectus heterochaetus* (Chase) Soják (3, 50, 155) (1942–present)

Slender bunchflower - *Melanthium latifolium* Desr. (50) (present)

Slender bush clover - *Lespedeza virginica* (L.) Britton (5, 72) (1907-1913)

Slender bush lespedeza - *Lespedeza virginica* (L.) Britton (4) (1986)

Slender button snakeroot [Slender button-snakeroot] - *Liatris acidota* Engelm. & Gray (5, 72, 97, 122, 124) (1907-1937)

Slender calamint - *Clinopodium arkansanum* (Nutt.) House (5) (1913)

Slender chess - *Bromus tectorum* L. (62) (1912)

Slender cinquefoil - *Potentilla gracilis* Dougl. (50, 131) (1899–present)

Slender cliff-brake - *Cryptogramma stelleri* (S. G. Gmel.) Prantl. (5, 72) (1907-1913)

Slender clubmoss - *Lycopodiella caroliniana* (L.) Pichi Sermolli var. *caroliniana* (50) (present)

Slender club-rush - *Eleocharis tenuis* (Willd.) J.A. Schultes (66) (1903)

Slender collinsia - *Collinsia parviflora* Lindl. (155) (1942)

Slender copperleaf - *Acalypha monococca* (Engelm. ex Gray) L. Mill. & Gandhi (155) (1942)

Slender cord grass - *Spartina gracilis* Trin. (5) (1913)

Slender cotton-grass [Slender cotton grass, Slender cottongrass] - *Eriophorum gracile* W.D.J. Koch (5, 50, 72, 139) (1893–present)

Slender crabgrass [Slender crab grass] - *Digitaria filiformis* (L.) Koel. (3, 50, 56, 66) (1901–present)

Slender crane's-bill [Slender cranesbill, Slender cranebill] - *Geranium bicknellii* Britton (85) (1932)

Slender cut grass [Slender cut-grass] - *Leersia monandra* Sw. (94) (1901)

Slender cyperus - *Cyperus lupulinus* (Spreng.) Marcks subsp. *lupulinus* (5, 72) (1907-1913)

Slender daisy fleabane - *Erigeron strigosus* Muhl. ex Willd. var. *strigosus* (62) (1912)

Slender dayflower [Slender day-flower] - *Commelina erecta* L. (5, 97) (1913-1937)   - *Deutzia gracilis* Sieb. & Zucc. (112, 138) (1923-1937)

Slender dropseed - *Muhlenbergia filiformis* (Thurb. ex S. Wats.) Rydb. (5, 50) (1913–present)

Slender dupontia - *Dupontia fisheri* R. Br. (94) (1901)

Slender dwarf iris - *Iris verna* L. (2) (1895)

Slender Eaton's grass - *Sphenopholis nitida* (Biehler) Scribn. (5) (1913)

Slender eriogonum - *Eriogonum effusum* Nutt. (5, 93) (1913-1936)

Slender false dragonhead - *Physostegia intermedia* (Nutt.) Engelm. & Gray (50) (present)

Slender feather grass [Slender feather-grass] - *Nassella tenuissima* (Trin.) Barkworth (94) (1901)

Slender fescue - *Vulpia octoflora* (Walt.) Rydb. var. *glauca* (Nutt.) Fern. (56) (1901)

Slender fescue grass [Slender fescue-grass] - *Vulpia octoflora* (Walt.) Rydb. var. *octoflora* (5, 56, 72, 94, 111, 119, 163) (1852-1938)

Slender fimbristylis - *Fimbristylis autumnalis* (L.) Roemer & J.A. Schultes (5, 72) (1907–1913)

Slender fimbry - *Fimbristylis autumnalis* (L.) Roemer & J.A. Schultes (50) (present)

Slender finger grass [Slender finger-grass, Slender fingergrass] - *Digitaria filiformis* (L.) Koel. (5, 72, 119, 155, 163) (1852-1942)

Slender flatsedge - *Cyperus bipartitus* Torr. (50) (present), *Cyperus odoratus* L. (3) (1977)

Slender fleabane - *Erigeron strigosus* Muhl. ex Willd. (possibly) (7) (1828)

Slender forked chickweed - *Paronychia canadensis* (L.) Wood (5, 72, 93) (1907-1936)

Slender foxtail - *Alopecurus myosuroides* Huds (3, 5, 56, 66) (1901-1977)

Slender fragrant goldenrod - *Euthamia tenuifolia* (Pursh) Nutt. var. *tenuifolia* (72, 131) (1899-1907)

Slender froelichia - *Froelichia gracilis* (Hook.) Moq. (5, 93, 97, 98) (1913-1937)

Slender fumewort - *Corydalis micrantha* (Engelm. ex Gray) Gray (3) (1977), *Corydalis micrantha* (Engelm. ex Gray) Gray subsp. *micrantha* (4) (1986)

Slender gerardia - *Agalinis tenuifolia* (Vahl) Raf. (72, 98, 156) (1907-1926)

Slender glasswort [Slender glass-wort] - *Salicornia maritima* Wolff & Jefferies (131) (1899)

Slender golden currant - *Ribes aureum* Pursh (112, 138) (1923-1937)

Slender goldenrod [Slender goldenrod] - *Solidago caesia* L. (156) (1923), *Solidago erecta* Pursh (5, 72, 131) (1899-1913)

Slender goldenweed - *Croptilon hookerianum* (Torr. & Gray) House var. *validum* (Rydb.) E.B. Sm. (4) (1986)

Slender goldfields - *Lasthenia gracilis* (DC.) Greene (138) (1923)

Slender gooseberry - *Ribes missouriense* Nutt. (5) (1913), *Ribes niveum* Lindl. (72, 156) (1907-1923)

Slender grass [Slender-grass] - *Leptochloa* Beauv. (66, 92) (1876-1903), *Leptochloa panicea* (Retz.) Ohwi subsp. *brachiata* (Steudl.) N. Snow (5, 119, 163) (1852-1938), *Leptochloa panicea* (Retz.) Ohwi subsp. *mucronata* (Michx.) Nowack (87) (1884)

Slender groundnut - *Glycine max* (L.) Merr. (155) (1942)

Slender hairy lyme grass - *Elymus virginicus* L. var. *virginicus* (66) (1903)

Slender hairy ruellia - *Ruellia caroliniensis* (J.F. Gmel.) Steud. subsp. *caroliniensis* var. *caroliniensis* (5, 122) (1913-1937)

Slender hawk's-beard [Slender hawksbeard] - *Crepis atribarba* Heller (50) (Present)

Slender hedge-nettle [Slender hedge nettle] - *Stachys palustris* L. (82) (1930)

Slender heliotrope - *Heliotropium tenellum* (Nutt.) Torr. (5, 97) (1913-1937)

Slender Indian grass [Slender indiangrass] - *Sorghastrum elliottii* (C. Mohr) Nash (50) (present)

Slender Indian reed - *Cinna latifolia* (Trev. ex Goepp.) Griseb. (94) (1901)

Slender jasmine - *Jasminum multiflorum* (Burm. f.) Andr. (138) (1923)

Slender knot-grass [Slender knot grass] - *Polygonum tenue* Michx. (19) (1840)

Slender knotweed [Slender knot-weed] - *Polygonum tenue* Michx. (3, 5, 72, 93, 97, 122, 131) (1899-1977)

Slender lady's-tresses [Slender ladies' tresses, Slender ladiestresses, Slender ladiestresses, Slender ladies'-tresses] - *Spiranthes lacera* (Raf.) Raf. (3) (1977), *Spiranthes lacera* (Raf.) Raf. var. *gracilis* (Bigelow) Luer (5, 72, 122, 138, 156) (1907-1937)

Slender lespedeza - *Lespedeza virginica* (L.) Britton (3, 50, 155) (1942–present)

Slender lion's-heart [Slender lion's heart] - *Physostegia intermedia* (Nutt.) Engelm. & Gray (5) (1913)

Slender lip fern [Slender lipfern, Slender lip-fern] - *Cheilanthes feei* T. Moore (4, 5, 50, 97, 122) (1913–present), *Cryptogramma stelleri* (S. G. Gmel.) Prantl. (131) (1899)

Slender locoweed - *Oxytropis monticola* Gray (4) (1986)

Slender loose-flower sedge [Slender looseflower sedge] - *Carex gracilescens* Steud. (50) (Present)

Slender lyme grass [Slender lyme-grass] - *Elymus virginicus* L. var. *virginicus* (56, 94) (1901)

Slender manna grass - *Glyceria borealis* (Nash) Batchelder (56, 72) (1901-1907)

Slender marsh pink - *Sabatia campanulata* (L.) Torr. (5, 156) (1913-1923)

Slender meadow foxtail - *Alopecurus myosuroides* Huds (50) (present)

Slender meadow grass [Slender meadow-grass] - *Eragrostis capillaris* (L.) Nees (187) (1818), *Eragrostis pilosa* (L.) Beauv. (66, 94, 111, 129) (1894-1915), *Puccinellia nuttalliana* (J.A. Schultes) A.S. Hitchc. (5) (1913)

Slender meadow rue - *Thalictrum clavatum* DC. (5) (1913)

Slender milkvetch [Slender milk vetch] - *Astragalus flexuosus* (Hook.) Dougl. ex G. Don (3) (1977), *Astragalus gracilis* Nutt. (3, 4, 5, 50, 85, 93, 97, 131) (1899–present)

Slender milkweed - *Astragalus leptaleus* Gray (121) (1918?-1970?)

Slender milkwort - *Polygala incarnata* L. (4) (1986)

Slender mountain bluegrass [Slender mountain blue-grass] - *Poa leptocoma* Trin. (94) (1901)

Slender mountain rice - *Piptatherum pungens* (Torr.) Barkworth (5) (1913)

Slender mountain-mint [Slender mountainmint] - *Pycnanthemum tenuifolium* Schrad. (138, 155) (1923-1942)

Slender muhlenbergia - *Muhlenbergia tenuiflora* (Willd.) Britton, Sterns & Poggenb. (56) (1901)

Slender muhly - *Muhlenbergia tenuiflora* (Willd.) Britton, Sterns & Poggenb. (50) (present)

Slender naias - *Najas flexilis* (Willd.) Rostk. & Schmidt (5, 72, 93, 131) (1899-1936)

Slender najas - *Najas guadalupensis* (Spreng.) Magnus (85) (1932)

Slender nettle - *Urtica dioica* L. subsp. *gracilis* (Aiton) Seland. (5, 62, 72, 93, 95, 131) (1899-1936)

Slender nodding sedge - *Carex gracilescens* Steud. (66) (1903)

Slender oat grass [Slender oat-grass] - *Trisetum interruptum* Buckl. (94) (1901)

Slender panic grass - *Dichanthelium linearifolium* (Scribn. ex Nash) Gould (56) (1901)

Slender panicum - *Dichanthelium xanthophysum* (Gray) Freckmann (5, 56) (1901–1913), *Digitaria gracillima* (Scribn.) Fernald (94) (1901)

Slender parosela - *Dalea enneandra* Nutt. (5, 72, 93, 97, 131) (1899-1937)

Slender parrot's-feather [Slender parrotfeather] - *Myriophyllum tenellum* Bigelow (155) (1942)

Slender paspalum - *Paspalum setaceum* Michx. (5, 94, 99, 187) (1818-1923)

Slender penstemon - *Penstemon gracilis* Nutt. (155) (1942)

Slender phlox - *Phlox gracilis* (Hook.) Greene (50) (present), *Phlox gracilis* (Hook.) Greene subsp. *humilis* (Greene) Mason (50) (present)

Slender pigweed - *Amaranthus hybridus* L. (3, 4, 5, 21, 62, 72, 93, 131, 157, 158) (1893-1986)

Slender plantain - *Plantago elongata* Pursh (4, 85, 97, 131) (1899-1986), *Plantago pusilla* Nutt. (3, 5) (1913–1977)

Slender rat-tail grass [Slender rat-tail-grass] - *Coelorachis cylindrica* (Michx.) Nash (94) (1901)

Slender rattlesnake root [Slender rattlesnake-root] - *Prenanthes autumnalis* Walt. (5, 156) (1913-1923)

Slender reed grass - *Cinna latifolia* (Trev. ex Goepp.) Griseb. (56) (1901)

Slender rockbrake - *Cryptogramma stelleri* (S. G. Gmel.) Prantl. (138) (1923)

Slender rosette grass - *Dichanthelium xanthophysum* (Gray) Freckmann (50) (present)

Slender rough fleabane - *Erigeron tenuis* Torr. & Gray (5, 97) (1913-1937)

Slender rush - *Juncus filiformis* L. (66) (1903), *Juncus tenuis* Willd. (5, 61, 66, 72, 80, 93, 156) (1870-1936)

Slender rush grass [Slender rush-grass] - *Muhlenbergia filiformis* (Thurb. ex S. Wats.) Rydb. (94) (1901)

Slender Russian thistle - *Salsola collina* Pallas (50) (present)

Slender sagittaria - *Sagittaria teres* S. Wats. (5) (1913)

Slender sandwort - *Arenaria serpyllifolia* L. (5) (1913)

Slender satin grass [Slender satin-grass] - *Muhlenbergia sobolifera* (Muhl. ex Willd.) Trin. (163) (1852), *Muhlenbergia tenuiflora* (Willd.) Britton, Sterns & Poggenb. (5) (1913)

Slender sedge - *Carex exilis* Dewey (66) (1903), *Carex lasiocarpa* Ehrh. (5, 72) (1907-1913), *Carex praegracilis* W. Boott (139) (1944)

Slender showy goldenrod [Slender showy golden-rod] - *Solidago speciosa* Nutt. var. *rigidiuscula* Torr. & Gray (5, 72, 97, 122, 131) (1899-1937)

Slender skullcap [Slender skull-cap] - *Scutellaria nervosa* Pursh (187) (1818)

Slender snake-cotton [Slender snake cotton, Slender snakecotton] - *Froelichia gracilis* (Hook.) Moq. (4, 50, 122) (1937–present)

Slender snake-root - *Liatris acidota* Engelm. & Gray (93) (1936)

Slender spear grass [Slender spear-grass] - *Poa saltuensis* Fern. & Wieg. (94) (1901)

Slender sphenopolis - *Sphenopholis nitida* (Biehler) Scribn. (163) (1852)

Slender spike grass [Slender spike-grass] - *Chasmanthium laxum* (L.) Yates (5, 66, 119, 163) (1852-1938)

Slender spiked fescue - *Schedonorus ×festucaceus* (Link) Kartesz [*arundinaceus* × *pratensis*] (66) (1903)

Slender spike-rush [Slender spike rush, Slender spikerush] - *Eleocharis tenuis* (Willd.) J.A. Schultes (5, 50, 156) (1913–present)

Slender St. John's-wort [Slender St. John's wort] - *Hypericum canadense* L. (187) (1818), *Hypericum mutilum* L. (5) (1913)

Slender three-seed mercury [Slender three-seeded mercury] - *Acalypha monococca* (Engelm. ex Gray) L. Mill. & Gandhi (5, 50, 72, 97, 122) (1907–present)

Slender tick clover [Slender tickclover] - *Desmodium ciliare* (Muhl. ex Willd.) DC. (4) (1986)

Slender toothwort - *Cardamine angustata* O.E. Schulz (5) (1913)

Slender triodia - *Tridens muticus* (Torr.) Nash var. *muticus* (94) (1901)

Slender triple-awn grass [Slender triple-awned grass] - *Aristida longispica* Poir. (119) (1938), *Aristida longispica* Poir. var. *longispica* (5, 66, 99) (1903-1923)

Slender vervain - *Verbena halei* Small (97) (1937)

Slender vetch - *Vicia tetrasperma* (L.) Moench (5) (1913)

Slender water-milfoil [Slender water milfoil] - *Myriophyllum tenellum* Bigelow (5, 50) (1913–present)

Slender wedgescale - *Sphenopholis intermedia* (Rydb.) Rydb. (50, 155) (1942–present), *Sphenopholis nitida* (Biehler) Scribn. (50) (present)

Slender wheat grass [Slender wheatgrass] - *Elymus caninus* (L.) L. (5) (1913)

Slender wheat grass [Slender wheatgrass] - *Elymus trachycaulus* (Link) Gould ex Shinners (50) (present), *Elymus trachycaulus* (Link) Gould ex Shinners subsp. *trachycaulus* (1, 3, 4, 5, 50, 56, 68, 72, 80, 85, 94, 111, 115, 118, 119, 129, 40, 141, 143, 146, 152, 155, 163) (1852–present)

Slender white prairie clover [Slender white prairieclover] - *Dalea candida* Michx. ex Willd. var. *oligophylla* (Torr.) Shinners (5, 93, 97, 155) (1913-1942)

Slender wild oat - *Avena barbata* Pott ex Link (109) (1949)

Slender wild parsley [Slender wildparsley] - *Musineon tenuifolium* (Nutt. ex Torr. & Gray) Coult. & Rose (50) (present)

Slender wild rye - *Elymus villosus* Muhl. ex Willd. (3, 163) (1852-1977), *Elymus virginicus* L. var. *virginicus* (5, 72, 93) (1907-1936)

Slender willow - *Salix exigua* Nutt. (5, 20, 93, 97) (1857-1937), *Salix petiolaris* Sm. (5, 72) (1907-1913)

Slender wood reed grass [Slender wood reed-grass] - *Cinna latifolia* (Trev. ex Goepp.) Griseb. (5, 99) (1913-1923)

Slender wood sedge - *Carex digitalis* Willd. (5, 50, 66) (1912–present)

Slender wood-oats [Slender woodoats] - *Chasmanthium laxum* (L.) Yates (50) (present)

Slender woolly panic - *Digitaria tenuis* (Nees) Henrard (94) (1901)

Slender yellow flax - *Linum virginianum* L. (5) (1913)

Slender yellow wood sorrel - *Oxalis stricta* L. (5) (1913)

Slender yellow-eyed grass - *Xyris caroliniana* Walt. (5, 97) (1913-1937)

Slender-beak sedge [Slenderbeak sedge] - *Carex athrostachya* Olney (50) (present)

Slender-branch gooseberry [Slender-branched gooseberry] - *Ribes niveum* Lindl. (107) (1919)

Slender-bush eriogonum [Slenderbush eriogonum] - *Eriogonum effusum* Nutt. (155) (1942)

Slender-flower blue-grass [Slender-flowered blue-grass] - *Poa tenerrima* Scribn. (94) (1901)

Slender-flower dropseed [Slender flowered dropseed, Slender-flowered dropseed] - *Muhlenbergia tenuiflora* (Willd.) Britton, Sterns & Poggenb. (5, 94) (1901-1913)

Slender-flower melic grass [Slender-flowered melic-grass] - *Melica subulata* (Griseb.) Scribn. (94) (1901)

Slender-leaf betony [Slenderleaf betony] - *Stachys tenuifolia* Willd. (3, 4, 155) (1942-1986)

Slender-leaf bluets [Slender-leaved bluets] - *Houstonia longifolia* Gaertn. (4) (1986)

Slender-leaf false foxglove [Slenderleaf false foxglove] - *Agalinis tenuifolia* (Vahl) Raf. (50) (present)

Slender-leaf fleabane [Slenderleaf fleabane] - *Erigeron tenuis* Torr. & Gray (50) (present)

Slender-leaf houstonia [Slenderleaf houstonia] - *Houstonia longifolia* Gaertn. (5, 122) (1913-1937)

Slender-leaf mountain mint [Slender-leaved mountain mint] - *Pycnanthemum tenuifolium* Schrad. (4) (1986)

Slender-leaf purslane [Slenderleaf purslane] - *Portulaca halimoides* L. (3, 4) (1977-1986)

Slender-leaf sedge [Slender-leaved sedge] - *Carex lasiocarpa* Ehrh. (66) (1903)

Slender-leaf sneezeweed [Slender-leaved sneezeweed] - *Helenium amarum* (Raf.) H. Rock var. *amarum* (86) (1878)

Slender-leaf sundew [Slender-leaved sundew] - *Drosera linearis* Goldie (5, 6) (1892-1913)

Slender-leaved goldenrod [Slender-leaved Golden-rod] - *Euthamia tenuifolia* (Pursh) Nutt. var. *tenuifolia* (187) (1818)

Slender-lobe bundleflower [Slenderlobe bundleflower, Slender-lobed bundleflower] - *Desmanthus leptolobus* Torr. & Gray (4, 50) (1986–present)

Slender-spike beard grass [Slender-spiked beard-grass] - *Andropogon virginicus* L. (187) (1818)

Slender-spike lespedeza [Slender spike lespedeza] - *Lespedeza leptostachya* Engelm. (4) (1986)

Slender-spire orchid - *Piperia unalascensis* (Spreng.) Rydb. (50) (present)

Slender-stalk sedge [Slender-stalked sedge] - *Carex debilis* Michx. var. *rudgei* Bailey (5) (1913)

Slender-stalk strawberry blite [Slender stalked strawberry blite] - *Chenopodium foliosum* (Moench) Aschers. (42) (1814)

Slender-stem panic grass [Slender-stemmed panic grass] - *Dichanthelium acuminatum* (Sw.) Gould & C.A. Clark var. *fasciculatum* (Torr.) Freckmann (5) (1913)

Slender-tail grass - *Schedonnardus paniculatus* (Nutt.) Trel. (66) (1903)

Slick-seed bean - *Strophostyles leiosperma* (Torr. & Gray) Piper (4) (1986)

Slick-seed fuzzybean [Slickseed fuzzybean] - *Strophostyles leiosperma* (Torr. & Gray) Piper (50) (present)

Slim amaranth - *Amaranthus hybridus* L. (50, 155, 156) (1923–present)

Slim aster - *Symphyotrichum divaricatum* (Nutt.) Nesom (5, 97) (1913-1937)

Slim knotweed - *Polygonum tenue* Michx. (155) (1942)

Slim nettle - *Urtica dioica* L. subsp. *gracilis* (Aiton) Seland. (155) (1942)

Slim rockcress - *Arabis holboellii* Hornem. var. *retrofracta* (Graham) Rydb. (155) (1942)

Slim Solomon-plume [Slim Solomonplume] - *Maianthemum stellatum* (L.) Link (155) (1942)

Slim tridens - *Tridens muticus* (Torr.) Nash (3, 50) (1977–present)

Slim triodia - *Tridens muticus* (Torr.) Nash var. *muticus* (122) (1937)

Slim vetch - *Vicia ludoviciana* Nutt. subsp. *ludoviciana* (155) (1942)

Slim-flower muhly [Slimflower muhly] - *Muhlenbergia tenuiflora* (Willd.) Britton, Sterns & Poggenb. (155) (1942)

Slim-flower scurf-pea [Slimflower scurfpea] - *Psoralidium tenuiflorum* (Pursh) Rydb. (50) (present)

Slim-leaf brome [Slimleaf brome] - *Bromus marginatus* Nees ex Steud. (155) (1942)

Slim-leaf bursage [Slimleaf bursage] - *Ambrosia confertiflora* DC. (155) (1942)

Slim-leaf goosefoot [Slimleaf goosefoot] - *Chenopodium leptophyllum* (Moq.) Nutt. ex S. Wats. (155) (1942)

Slim-leaf goosefoot [Slimleaf goosefoot] - *Chenopodium pallescens* Standl. (50) (present)

Slim-leaf hymenopappus [Slimleaf hymenopappus] - *Hymenopappus tenuifolius* Pursh (3) (1977)

Slim-leaf milkweed [Slimleaf milkweed] - *Asclepias stenophylla* Gray (50) (present)

Slim-leaf panic grass [Slimleaf panicgrass] - *Dichanthelium linearifolium* (Scribn. ex Nash) Gould (50) (present)

Slim-leaf panicum [Slimleaf panicum] - *Dichanthelium linearifolium* (Scribn. ex Nash) Gould (3, 155) (1942-1977)

Slim-leaf pawpaw [Slimleaf pawpaw] - *Asimina angustifolia* Raf. (155) (1942)

Slim-leaf prairie clover [Slimleaf prairie clover] - *Dalea tenuifolia* (Gray) Shinners (3, 4, 50) (1977–present)

Slim-leaf scurf pea [Slimleaf scurf pea] - *Pediomelum linearifolium* (Torr. & Gray) J. Grimes (3, 4) (1977-1986)

Slim-petal pawpaw [Slimpetal pawpaw] - *Deeringothamnus pulchellus* Small (155) (1942)

Slimpi (Sioux) - *Grindelia squarrosa* (Pursh) Dunal (101) (1905) MT

Slim-pod rush [Slimpod rush] - *Juncus diffusissimus* Buckl. (3, 50) (1977–present)

Slim-pod Venus' looking-glass [Slimpod Venus' looking-glass] - *Triodanis leptocarpa* (Nutt.) Nieuwl. (50) (present)

Slim-seed sandmat [Slimseed sandmat] - *Chamaesyce stictospora* (Engelm.) Small (50) (present)

Slim-spike threeawn [Slimspike threeawn] - *Aristida longispica* Poir. (3, 50) (1977–present)

Slim-stem muhly [Slimstem muhly] - *Muhlenbergia filiculmis* Vasey (50, 155) (1942–present)

Slim-stem reed grass [Slimstem reedgrass] - *Calamagrostis stricta* (Timm) Koel. (50) (present), *Calamagrostis stricta* (Timm) Koel. subsp. *stricta* (50, 155) (1942–present)

Slinkweed [Slink weed, Slink-weed] - *Decodon verticillatus* (L.) Ell. (5, 156) (1913-1923), *Lobelia cardinalis* L. (5, 73, 156, 158) (1892-1923) Princeton MA

Slipper flower [Slipper-flower, Slipperflower] - *Pedilanthus* Neck. ex Poit. (155) (1942), *Pedilanthus tithymaloides* (L.) Poit. (109) (1949)

Slipper root [Slipper-root] - *Cypripedium parviflorum* Salisb. (5, 156) (1913-1923), *Cypripedium parviflorum* Salisb. var. *pubescens* (Willd.) Knight (92) (1876)

Slippers [Slipper] - *Impatiens* L. (7) (1828), *Impatiens pallida* Nutt. (5, 92, 156, 157) (1876-1923)

Slipperweed [Slipper weed, Slipper-weed] - *Impatiens capensis* Meerb. (5, 73, 156, 157, 158) (1892-1929) Mansfield OH, *Impatiens pallida* Nutt. (156, 157) (1923-1929)

Slippery elm - *Ulmus rubra* Muhl. (1, 2, 3, 4, 5, 7, 19, 20, 34, 35, 37, 40, 49, 50, 53, 55, 57, 58, 59, 72, 78, 82, 85, 92, 93, 95, 97, 107, 109, 112, 113, 122, 124, 130, 131, 138, 155, 156, 157, 158) (1834–present)

Slippery mullein - *Verbascum blattaria* L. (77) (1898) Southold Long Island

Slippery root [Slippery-root] - *Symphytum officinale* L. (64, 156) (1908-1923)

Sliva (inner bark) - *Pinus albicaulis* Engelm. (101) (1905) MT

Sloe - *Prunus americana* Marsh. (107) (1919), *Prunus spinosa* L. (107, 109, 137, 179) (1526–1949), *Viburnum prunifolium* L. (5, 19, 49, 53, 58, 92, 156, 158) (1840–1923)

Sloe of the South - *Prunus umbellata* Ell. (107) (1919)

Sloe-leaf viburnum [Sloe-leaved viburnum] - *Viburnum prunifolium* L. (49, 53) (1879–1898)

Sloe-tee blossoms [Sloe tee blossoms] - *Prunus spinosa* L. (92) (1876)

Slokam - *Callicarpa dichotoma* (Lour.) K.Koch (107) (1919)

Sloke - *Callicarpa dichotoma* (Lour.) K.Koch (107) (1919)

Slotter-blomster (Swedish) - *Parnassia palustris* L. (46) (1879)

Slough grass [Slough-grass, Sloughgrass] - *Beckmannia* Host (1, 50, 152, 155) (1912–present), *Beckmannia syzigachne* (Steud.) Fern. (possibly) (5, 56, 85, 94, 101, 111, 129, 152) (1894–1932), *Elymus repens* (L.) Gould (5) (1913), *Schoenoplectus fluviatilis* (Torr.) M. T. Strong (129) (1894) SD, *Schoenoplectus maritimus* (L.) Lye (129) (1894) SD, *Spartina cynosuroides* (L.) Roth (22, 56, 144) (1893–1901), *Spartina pectinata* Bosc ex Link (37, 65, 111, 115, 119, 163) (1830–1938), *Spartina* Schreber (93) (1936) Neb, *Thinopyrum intermedium* (Host) Barkworth & D. R. Dewey (75) (1894) Neb, *Tripsacum dactyloides* (L.) L. (5, 19, 21) (1840–1913)

Slough sedge - *Carex atherodes* Spreng. (3) (1977)

Slough-heal - *Prunella vulgaris* L. (158) (1900)

Slovenwood [Sloven-wood] - *Artemisia abrotanum* L. (5, 92, 156, 157, 158) (1876-1929)

Slow shrub - *Prunus spinosa* L. (41) (1770)

Slunkweed [Slunk-weed] - *Eupatorium purpureum* L. (64, 156, 158) (1900-1923)

Smale elderne - *Viburnum dentatum* L. (46) (1879)

Small alyssum - *Alyssum alyssoides* (L.) L. (5, 158) (1900–1913)

Small American waterlily - *Nymphaea odorata* Aiton subsp. *odorata* (155) (1942)

Small aster - *Symphyotrichum ontarione* (Wiegand) Nesom (possibly) (187) (1818)

Small ball moss - *Tillandsia recurvata* (L.) L. (122, 124) (1937)

Small bedstraw - *Galium trifidum* L. (3, 4, 5, 47, 63, 72, 85, 93, 155) (1852-1986)

Small beggar's-lice - *Lappula occidentalis* (S. Wats.) Greene var. *occidentalis* (145) (1897)

Small beggarticks [Small beggar-ticks] - *Bidens discoidea* (Torr. & Gray) Britton (5, 50, 72, 97) (1907–present)

Small bellflower [Small bell-flower] - *Uvularia sessilifolia* L. (158) (1900)

Small bellwort - *Uvularia sessilifolia* L. (3, 127) (1933-1977)

Small bibernel - *Sanguisorba minor* Scop. subsp. *muricata* (Spach) Nordborg (92, 157, 158) (1876-1929)

Small bindweed [Small bind-weed] - *Convolvulus arvensis* L. (5, 72, 93, 95, 97, 156, 157, 158) (1900-1929)

Small bird cherry - *Prunus avium* (L.) L. (19) (1840)

Small bitter cress [Small bitter-cress] - *Cardamine hirsuta* L. (2, 156, 157) (1895–1929)

Small black blueberry - *Vaccinium tenellum* Aiton (5) (1913)

Small blue monk's-hood - *Aconitum uncinatum* L. (165) (1768)

Small blue violet - *Viola adunca* J.E. Sm. (3) (1977)

Small bluet [Small bluets] - *Houstonia pusilla* Schoepf (3, 4, 5, 97, 156) (1913-1986)

Small Bray's oak [Small Brays oak] - *Quercus muehlenbergii* Engelm. (124) (1937) TX

Small buckeye - *Aesculus parviflora* Walt. (2) (1895), *Aesculus pavia* L. (71) (1898)

Small bugloss - *Anchusa arvensis* (L.) Bieb. (3, 5, 50, 82, 85, 156, 158) (1900–present), *Anchusa L.* (10) (1818)

Small bulrush [Small bull-rush] - *Juncus effusus* L. (187) (1818), *Typha angustifolia* L. (107) (1919)

Small bur clover - *Medicago minima* L. (4) (1986)

Small bur grass - *Cenchrus longispinus* (Hack.) Fern. (5) (1913)

Small burdock - *Xanthium strumarium* L. (158) (1900), *Xanthium strumarium* L. var. *canadense* (Mill.) Torr. & Gray (156) (1923), *Xanthium strumarium* L. var. *glabratum* (DC.) Cronq. (5) (1913)

Small bur-marigold - *Bidens cernua* L. (93, 156) (1923-1936)

Small burnet - *Sanguisorba minor* Scop. (50, 138, 155) (1923–present)

Small burnet saxifrage - *Pimpinella saxifraga* L. (92) (1876)

Small bur-reed - *Sparganium natans* L. (5, 50) (1913–present)

Small bush whortleberry - *Gaylussacia dumosa* (Andr.) Torr. & Gray (43) (1820)

Small buttercup - *Ranunculus abortivus* L. (125) (1930)

Small camas - *Camassia quamash* (Pursh) Greene (50) (present)

Small cane - *Arundinaria gigantea* (Walt.) Muhl. subsp. *tecta* (Walt.) McClure (5, 45, 88, 138) (1885-1923), *Lasiacis divaricata* (L.) A.S. Hitchc. (94) (1901)

Small capsule dung moss - *Splachnum ampullaceum* Hedw. (50) (present)

Small cat-tail grass [Small cats-taile grasse] - *Phleum pratense* L. (180) (1633)

Small celandine - *Ranunculus ficaria* L. (107) (1919)

Small chestnut oak - *Quercus prinoides* Willd. (20, 33, 122) (1827-1937)

Small chickweed - *Cerastium semidecandrum* L. (156) (1923)

Small cleavers - *Galium trifidum* L. (5, 49, 92, 95, 131) (1898-1936)

Small club-moss [Small clubmoss] - *Selaginella densa* Rydb. (3) (1977)

Small cocklebur - *Xanthium strumarium* L. var. *canadense* (Mill.) Torr. & Gray (85) (1932)

Small coralroot [Small coral-root] - *Corallorrhiza odontorhiza* (Willd.) Poir. (5, 64, 156, 158) (1900-1923)

Small cord grass [Small cordgrass] - *Spartina maritima* (M.A. Curtis) Fern. (50) (present)

Small crabgrass [Small crab grass, Small crab-grass] - *Digitaria ischaemum* (Schreb.) Schreb. ex Muhl. (5, 85, 62, 72, 131, 143) (1852-1936)

Small cranberry - *Vaccinium oxycoccos* L. (2, 5, 109, 138, 156) (1895-1949)

Small crane's-bill [Small cranesbill] - *Geranium pratense* L. (3, 4, 19, 92) (1840-1986)

Small creeping Virginia cucumber - *Melothria pendula* L. (181) (~1678)

Small cut colewort [Small cut colewoort] - *Brassica oleracea* L. (180) (1633)

Small cut white windflower - *Anemone lancifolia* Pursh (178) (1526)

Small Dalmatian iris - *Iris pallida* Lam. (180) (1633)

Small dwarf-mistletoe [Small dwarfmistletoe] - *Arceuthobium pusillum* Peck (155) (1942)

Small elm - *Ulmus alata* Michx. (3) (1977)

Small enchanter's-nightshade [Small enchanter's nightshade] - *Circaea alpina* L. (50) (present)

Small erysimum - *Erysimum inconspicuum* (S. Wats.) MacM. (131) (1899)

Small evening-primrose [Small evening primrose] - *Oenothera perennis* L. (156) (1923)

Small fan-palm - *Sabal* Adans. (10) (1818)

Small fennel flower - *Nigella sativa* L. (92) (1876)

Small fescue grass - *Vulpia microstachys* (Nutt.) Munro var. *microstachys* (87) (1884), *Vulpia octoflora* (Walt.) Rydb. var. *glauca* (Nutt.) Fern. (66, 90) (1885-1903)

Small few-fruit sedge [Small few-fruited sedge] - *Carex oligocarpa* Schkuhr ex Willd. (66) (1903)

Small fleabane - *Pulicaria dysenterica* (L.) Bernh. (92) (1876)

Small floating manna grass [Small floating mannagrass] - *Glyceria borealis* (Nash) Batchelder (50) (present)

Small flowering-cornel - *Cornus canadensis* L. (158) (1900)

Small garden radish - *Raphanus sativus* L. (180) (1633)

Small geranium - *Geranium pratense* L. (50, 155) (1942–present)

Small gerardia - *Agalinis strictifolia* (Benth.) Pennell (97) (1937) OK

Small grama - *Bouteloua trifida* Thurb. (94) (1901)

Small grass - *Microchloa* R. Br. (92) (1876)

Small grayweed [Small gray-weed] - *Eriogonum tenellum* Torr. (97) (1937) OK

Small green wood orchid - *Platanthera clavellata* (Michx.) Luer (5, 50) (1913–present)

Small headed rush - *Juncus brachycephalus* (Engelm.) Buch. (5) (1913)

Small hemlock - *Aethusa cynapium* L. (5, 6, 92, 156) (1876-1923)

Small henbit - *Veronica hederifolia* L. (5, 156, 158) (1900-1923)

Small honeysuckle - *Lonicera dioica* L. (156) (1923)

Small hop clover [Small hop-clover] - *Trifolium campestre* Schreber. (72) (1907), *Trifolium dubium* Sibth. (3, 4) (1977-1986)

Small houseleek [Small house leek, Small house-leek] - *Sedum acre* L. (49, 92) (1876-1898)

Small Indian breadroot [Small Indian bread root, Small Indian bread-root] - *Pediomelum hypogaeum* (Nutt. ex Torr. & Gray) Rydb. var. *hypogaeum* (5, 93, 97) (1913-1937)

Small Indian millet - *Piptatherum micranthum* (Trin. & Rupr.) Barkworth (3, 5) (1913-1977)

Small jagged mugwoort [Small iagged mugwoort] - *Artemisia vulgaris* L. (178) (1526)

Small jagged-leaf Virginia pansy [Small jagged leaved Virginia pansy] - *Viola pedata* L. (181) (~1678)

Small jointweed - *Polygonella americana* (F & M) Small (122) (1937) TX

Small lace cactus - *Echinocereus reichenbachii* (Terscheck ex Walp.) Haage f. var. *perbellus* (Britt. & Rose) L. Benson (97) (1937) OK

Small lamb-succory [Small lambsuccory] - *Arnoseris minima* (L.) Schweig. & Koerte (possibly) (155) (1942)

Small laurel - *Kalmia angustifolia* L. (71) (1898), *Kalmia* L. (187) (1818), *Kalmia latifolia* L. (5, 71, 156) (1898–1923)

Small life-everlasting [Small life everlasting] - *Gnaphalium uliginosum* L. (156, 158) (1900-1923)

Small lophotocarpus - *Sagittaria calycina* Engelm. var. *calycina* (5, 97) (1913-1937)

Small lupine - *Lupinus pusillus* Pursh (3, 4) (1977-1986)

Small magnolia - *Magnolia virginiana* L. (2, 6, 8, 13, 20, 186, 187) (1785-1895)

Small maize - *Sorghum bicolor* (L.) Moench (92) (1876), *Sorghum bicolor* (L.) Moench subsp. *bicolor* (66) (1903) Barbary

Small matweed - *Guilleminea densa* (Willd.) Moq. (50) (present)

Small meadow grass [Small Medow-grasse] - *Poa annua* L. (possibly) (178) (1596)

Small melic grass [Small melic-grass] - *Melica fugax* Boland. (94) (1901), *Melica porteri* Scribn. (5, 72) (1907-1913)

Small mistletoe - *Arceuthobium pusillum* Peck (5, 156) (1913-1923)

Small moonwort [Small moone woort] - *Botrychium lunaria* (L.) Sw. (178) (1596), *Botrychium virginianum (L.) Sw.* (181) (~1678)

Small morel - *Solanum nigrum* L. (157) (1929)

Small mountain lily [Small mountaine lilly] - *Lilium martagon* L. (180) (1633)

Small mountain rice - *Piptatherum canadense* (Poir) Barkworth (94) (1901)

Small mouse-ear chickweed - *Cerastium semidecandrum* L. (5) (1913)

Small mouse-tail - *Myosurus minimus* L. (158) (1900)

Small navarretia - *Navarretia leucocephala* Benth. subsp. *minima* (Nutt.) Day (5) (1913)

Small nettle - *Urtica urens* L. (5, 156) (1913-1923)

Small northern bog orchis - *Platanthera obtusata* (Banks ex Pursh) Lindl. (5) (1913)

Small oilnut [Small oil nut] - *Juglans cinerea* L. (46) (1649)

Small pale-green orchis - *Platanthera flava* (L.) Lindl. var. *flava* (156) (1923)

Small palmetto - *Sabal minor* (Jacq.) Pers. (12) (1819)

Small panic grass [Small panicgrass] - *Dichanthelium dichotomum* (L.) Gould var. *dichotomum* (11) (1888), *Dichanthelium oligosanthes* (J.A. Schultes) Gould var. *oligosanthes* (3) (1977)

Small periwinkle - *Vinca minor* L. (4, 5, 92, 156, 158) (1876-1986)

Small pignut - *Carya glabra* (Mill.) Sweet (5) (1913), *Carya glabra* (Mill.) Sweet var. *glabra* (156) (1923)

Small pimpernel - *Pimpinella saxifraga* L. (92) (1876)

Small pink tickseed - *Coreopsis rosea* Nutt. (156) (1923)

Small pink-flower cosmos [Small pink flowered cosmos] - *Cosmos parviflorus* (Jacq.) Pers. (124) (1937) TX

Small pondweed - *Potamogeton pusillus* L. (1, 50, 72, 93, 97, 120, 131) (1899–present)

Small pox plant [Small-pox plant - *Sarracenia purpurea* L. (5, 92, 156) (1876-1923)

Small purple fringed orchid [Small purple fringe-orchid] - *Platanthera psycodes* (L.) Lindl. (109, 138, 156) (1923-1949)

Small ragweed - *Ambrosia artemisiifolia* L. (80, 82) (1913-1930)

Small red morning glory [Small red morning-glory - *Ipomoea hederifolia* L. (131) (1899), *Ipomoea coccinea* L. (5, 97, 158) (1900-1937)

Small redroot [Small red root] - *Ceanothus herbaceus* Raf. (72, 151) (1896-1907)

Small reed grass - *Calamagrostis canadensis* (Michx.) Beauv. (87, 90) (1884-1885), *Calamagrostis canadensis* (Michx.) Beauv. var. *macouniana* (Vasey) Stebbins (68) (1890), *Calamagrostis epigeios* (L.) Roth (42) (1814)

Small River Stone Horsetail - *Lemanea* Bory de Saint-Vincent (181) (~1678)

Small rose tickseed - *Coreopsis rosea* Nutt. (5) (1913)

Small rush grass [Small rush-grass] - *Sporobolus neglectus* Nash (5, 56, 80, 93, 111, 119, 163) (1852-1938)

Small sapodilla - *Manilkara zapota* (L.) van Royen (20) (1857)

Small savory-leaf Virginia stitchwort [Small savory leaved Virginia stitchwort] - *Phlox subulata* L. (181) (~1678)

Small saw palmetto - *Serenoa repens* (Bartr.) Small (106) (1930)

Small saxifrage - *Pimpinella saxifraga* L. (92) (1876)

Small seaside balsam - *Croton flavens* L. (92) (1876)

Small senega - *Polygala senega* L. (156) (1923)

Small serviceberry [Small service-berry] - *Amelanchier alnifolia* (Nutt.) Nutt. ex M. Roemer (113) (1890)

Small sheep-bur - *Hackelia virginiana* (L.) I.M. Johnston (156, 157, 158) (1900-1929), *Lappula squarrosa* (Retz.) Dumort. (5, 156, 158) (1900-1923)

Small skullcap [Small skull cap] - *Scutellaria parvula* Michx. (4, 5, 50, 72, 82, 93, 97, 131, 155, 157) (1899–present), *Scutellaria parvula* Michx. var. *australis* Fassett (50) (present), *Scutellaria parvula* Michx. var. *parvula* (3, 50) (1977–present)

Small snakeweed [Small snake weede] - *Polygonum viviparum* L. (178) (1526)

Small snapdragon [Small snap dragon] - *Chaenorhinum minus* (L.) Lange (1, 5) (1913-1932)

Small soapweed - *Yucca glauca* Nutt. (155) (1942)

Small Solomon's seal [Small solomonseal] - *Polygonatum biflorum* (Walt.) Ell. (138, 155, 156) (1923-1942), *Maianthemum racemosum* (L.) Link subsp. *racemosum* (5, 92, 157, 158) (1876-1929)

Small southern yellow orchis - *Platanthera integra* (Nutt.) Gray ex Beck (5) (1913)

Small spikenard - *Aralia nudicaulis* L. (5, 7, 49, 58, 64, 92, 156, 157, 158) (1828-1929)

Small spleenwort - *Asplenium resiliens* Kunze. (5, 122) (1913-1937)

Small St. John's-wort [Small St. John's wort] - *Hypericum mutilum* L. (2) (1895)

Small stinging nettle - *Urtica urens* L. (58) (1869)

Small sundrops - *Oenothera perennis* L. (5, 156) (1913-1923), *Oenothera spachiana* Torr. & Gray (97) (1937)

Small swollen bladderwort - *Utricularia radiata* Small. (5) (1913)

Small tufted love grass [Small tufted love-grass, Small tufted lovegrass] - *Eragrostis pilosa* (L.) Beauv. (5, 119, 140) (1913-1944)

Small tumble grass - *Panicum philadelphicum* Bernh. ex Trin. (56) (1901)

Small tumbleweed mustard - *Sisymbrium loeselii* L. (50) (present)

Small two-leaved orchis - *Platanthera hookeri* (Torr. ex Gray) Lindl. (5) (1913)

Small upright blue fkaxweed [Small upright blew Fkaxeweed] - *Nuttallanthus canadensis* (L.) D.A. Sutton (181) (~1678)

Small Venus' looking-glass [Small Venus' looking glass, Small Venus looking glass, Small Venuslookingglass] - *Triodanis perfoliata* (L.) Nieuwl. var. *biflora* (Ruiz & Pavón) Bradley (5, 97, 122, 124, 155) (1913-1942)

Small Virginia wolf's-sclaw [Small Virginia wolfsclaw] - *Selaginella rupestris* (L.) Spring (181) (~1678)

Small waterlily [Small water lily] - *Nuphar lutea* (L.) Sm. subsp. *pumila* (Timm) E.O. Beal (187) (1818)

Small waterpepper [Small water pepper] - *Polygonum hydropiperoides* Michx. (124) (1937)

Small waxberry - *Morella caroliniensis* (P. Mill.) Small (5, 156) (1913-1923)

Small white aster - *Symphyotrichum lateriflorum* (L.) A.& D. Löve var. *lateriflorum* (5, 72, 97, 122, 155) (1907-1942), *Symphyotrichum parviceps* (Burgess) Nesom (4) (1986)

Small white crownbeard - *Verbesina virginica* L. (5, 97) (1913-1937), *Verbesina virginica* L. var. *virginica* (5) (1913)

Small white lady's-slipper [Small white lady's slipper, Small white ladies' slipper, Small white ladies'-slipper] - *Cypripedium candidum* Muhl. ex Willd. (2, 5, 19, 72, 127, 156, 158) (1840-1933)

Small white morning-glory - *Ipomoea lacunosa* L. (122) (1937)

Small white passion-flower [Small white passion flower] - *Passiflora tenuiloba* Engelm. (124) (1937)

374

Small-flower cyperus galingale

Small white violet - *Viola macloskeyi* Lloyd (50) (present)

Small white waterlily [Small white water lily] - *Nymphaea tetragona* Georgi (5) (1913)

Small whorled pogonia - *Isotria medeoloides* (Pursh) Raf. (156) (1923)

Small wild bean [Small wildbean] - *Strophostyles leiosperma* (Torr. & Gray) Piper (5, 72, 82, 93, 97, 131, 155) (1899-1937)

Small wild bugloss - *Asperugo procumbens* L. (5, 156, 158) (1900-1923)

Small wild rose [Small wild-rose] - *Rosa palustris* Marsh. (187) (1818)

Small willowherb [Small willow-herb, Small willow herb] - *Epilobium coloratum* Biehler (156) (1923)

Small willow-top [Small willow top] - *Muhlenbergia glomerata* (Willd.) Trin. (45) (1896)

Small witch grass [Small witch-grass] - *Panicum philadelphicum* Bernh. ex Trin. (94) (1901)

Small wood sunflower - *Helianthus microcephalus* Torr. & Gray (5, 97) (1913-1937)

Small woodbine - *Lonicera dioica* L. (156, 158) (1900-1923)

Small woodrush [Small wood rush] - *Luzula parviflora* (Ehrh.) Desv. (66) (1903)

Small yellow buttercup - *Ranunculus gmelinii* DC. (3, 4) (1977-1986)

Small yellow crownbeard - *Verbesina occidentalis* (L.) Walt. (5, 97) (1913-1937)

Small yellow honeysuckle - *Lonicera dioica* L. (158) (1900)

Small yellow lady's-slipper [Small yellow lady's slipper, Small yellow ladies' slipper, Small yellow ladies'-slipper] - *Cypripedium parviflorum* Salisb. (64, 72, 127, 157, 158) (1900-1933)

Small yellow pondlily [Small yellow pond lily] - *Nuphar lutea* (L.) Sm. subsp. *pumila* (Timm) E.O. Beal (5) (1913)

Small yellow sedge - *Carex viridula* Michx. subsp. *brachyrrhyncha* (Celak.) B. Schmid var. *elatior* (Schlecht.) Crins (5) (1913)

Smallage - *Apium graveolens* L. var. *dulce* (P. Mill.) DC. (5) (1913), *Spermolepis echinata* (Nutt. ex DC.) Heller (46, 92) (1671-1876)

Smallage [Smalache] - *Apium graveolens* L. (46, 92, 107, 179) (1526-1919)

Smalled fringed gentian - *Gentianopsis detonsa* (Rottb.) Ma subsp. *detonsa* (72) (1907)

Smaller bar-marigold - *Bidens cernua* L. (158) (1900)

Smaller bellwort - *Uvularia* L. (possibly) (1) (1932), *Uvularia sessilifolia* L. (85) (1932)

Smaller bluegrass [Smaller blue grass] - *Poa compressa* L. (68) (1890)

Smaller burdock - *Arctium minus* Bernh. (155) (1942)

Smaller bur-marigold [Smaller bar-marigold (sic, 158] - *Bidens cernua* L. (5, 158) (1900-1913)

Smaller bur-reed [Smaller bur reed] - *Sparganium erectum* L. subsp. *stoloniferum* (Graebn.) Hara (2) (1895)

Smaller cats-foot [Smaller cat's foot] - *Antennaria howellii* Greene subsp. *neodioica* (Greene) Bayer (5, 131) (1899-1913)

Smaller common vetch - *Vicia sativa* L. subsp. *nigra* (L.) Ehrh. (5, 72) (1907-1913)

Smaller enchanter's-nightshade [Smaller enchanter's nightshade] - *Circaea alpina* L. (5, 72) (1907-1913)

Smaller forget-me-not - *Myosotis laxa* Lehm. (5) (1913)

Smaller fringed gentian - *Gentianopsis virgata* (Raf.) Holub (5) (1913)

Smaller green dock - *Rumex conglomeratus* Murr. (5) (1913)

Smaller hop clover - *Trifolium campestre* Schreber. (5) (1913)

Smaller hop trefoil - *Trifolium campestre* Schreber. (5) (1913)

Smaller Indian breadroot [Smaller Indian bread-root] - *Pediomelum hypogaeum* (Nutt. ex Torr. & Gray) Rydb. var. *hypogaeum* (157) (1929)

Smaller mud-plantain [Smaller mud plantain] - *Heteranthera limosa* (Sw.) Vahl. (5, 92, 97) (1913-1937)

Smaller pinweed - *Lechea minor* L. (2) (1895)

Smaller prickly-cone pine [Smaller prickly-coned pine] - *Pinus muricata* D. Don (20) (1857)

Smaller purple fringed orchis - *Platanthera psycodes* (L.) Lindl. (2, 5) (1895-1913)

Smaller pussy-toes [Smaller pussytoes] - *Antennaria howellii* Greene subsp. *neodioica* (Greene) Bayer (155) (1942)

Smaller quaking grass - *Briza minor* L. (5) (1913)

Smaller ragweed - *Ambrosia artemisiifolia* L. (80) (1913)

Smaller redroot [Smaller red root] - *Ceanothus herbaceus* Raf. (5, 97) (1913-1937)

Smaller reed - *Arundinaria gigantea* (Walter) Muhl. (2) (1895)

Smaller rye grass - *Elymus virginicus* L. var. *virginicus* (87) (1884)

Smaller sagebrush - *Artemisia cana* Pursh (95) (1911)

Smaller sea-beach grass - *Panicum amarum* Ell. (5, 7) (1828-1913)

Smaller Solomon's-seal [Smaller Solomon's seal] - *Polygonatum biflorum* (Walt.) Ell. (2) (1895)

Smaller spearwort - *Ranunculus flammula* L. (2, 82, 156) (1895-1930)

Smaller white snakeroot [Smaller white snakeroot, Smaller white snake-root] - *Ageratina aromatica* (L.) Spach (5, 156) (1913-1923)

Smaller whorled pogonia - *Isotria medeoloides* (Pursh) Raf. (5) (1913)

Smaller wild madder - *Galium tinctorium* L. (157, 158) (1900-1929)

Smaller wild rye - *Elymus virginicus* L. var. *virginicus* (88) (1885)

Smaller yellow lady's-slipper [Smaller yellow lady's slipper] - *Cypripedium parviflorum* Salisb. (2) (1895)

Smallest bur-reed [Smallest bur reed] - *Sparganium natans* L. (2) (1895)

Smallest oryzopsis - *Piptatherum canadense* (Poir) Barkworth (66, 90) (1885-1903)

Smallest-flower crane's-bill [Smallest-flowered crane's-bill] - *Geranium pratense* L. (187) (1818)

Small-flower agalinis [Small-flowered agalinis] - *Agalinis paupercula* (Gray) Britton (5) (1913)

Small-flower agoseris [Small-flowered agoseris] - *Agoseris glauca* (Pursh) Raf. (5, 131) (1899-1913)

Small-flower agrimony [Small-flowered agrimony] - *Agrimonia parviflora* Aiton (165) (1768)

Small-flower alum-root [Small flowered alum-root] - *Heuchera parviflora* Bartl. (131) (1899)

Small-flower anemone [Small-flowered anemone] - *Anemone parviflora* Michx. (5, 42) (1814-1913)

Small-flower aster [Small-flowered aster] - *Symphyotrichum lateriflorum* (L.) A.& D. Löve (possibly) (187) (1818)

Small-flower bindweed [Small-flowered bindweed - *Ipomoea lacunosa* L. (86) (1878)

Small-flower bittercress [Small-flowered bitter cress, Small-flower bitter cress] - *Cardamine parviflora* L. (3, 4, 5, 72) (1907-1986)

Small-flower blueberry [Smallflower blueberry] - *Vaccinium virgatum* Aiton (50) (present)

Small-flower catchfly [Small-flowered catchfly] - *Silene gallica* L. (5) (1913)

Small-flower collinsia [Small-flowered collinsia] - *Collinsia parviflora* Lindl. (5, 131) (1899-1913)

Small-flower columbine [Small-flowered columbine] - *Aquilegia brevistyla* Hook. (5, 85, 131) (1899-1932)

Small-flower coralroot [Small-flowered coralroot, Small-flowered coral root, Small-flowered coral-root] - *Corallorrhiza odontorhiza* (Willd.) Poir. (64, 72, 158) (1900-1908)

Small-flower corydalis [Small flowered corydalis] - *Corydalis micrantha* (Engelm. ex Gray) Gray subsp. *micrantha* (5, 72, 97, 122) (1907–1937)

Small-flower crane's-bill [Small-flowered crane's bill, Small-flower cranebill] - *Geranium pratense* L. (5, 85) (1913-1932)

Small-flower crowfoot [Small-flowered crowfoot] - *Ranunculus abortivus* L. (62, 63, 80, 156) (1899-1923), *Ranunculus parviflorus* L. (5, 97) (1913-1937)

Small-flower cyperus galingale [Small flowered alum-root] - *Cyperus dentatus* Torr. (42) (1814)

Small-flower desert-chicory [Smallflower desert-chicory] - *Pyrrhopappus pauciflorus* (D. Don) DC. (50) (present)

Small-flower drypetes [Small-flowered drypetes] - *Drypetes lateriflora* (Sw.) Krug & Urb. (20) (1857)

Small-flower erysimum [Smallflower erysimum] - *Erysimum inconspicuum* (S. Wats.) MacM. (155) (1942)

Small-flower evening-primrose [Small-flowered evening primrose] - *Camissonia contorta* (Dougl. ex Lehm.) Kearney (5) (1913)

Small-flower fumewort [Smallflower fumewort] - *Corydalis micrantha* (Engelm. ex Gray) Gray (50) (present)

Small-flower gaura [Small-flowered gaura] - *Gaura mollis* James (5, 72, 93, 97, 131) (1899-1937)

Small-flower gerardia [Small-flowered gerardia] - *Agalinis paupercula* (Gray) Britton var. *paupercula* (72, 97) (1907-1937)

Small-flower gilia [Small-flowered gilia] - *Gilia pinnatifida* Nutt. ex Gray (5) (1913)

Small-flower grass-of-Parnassus [Small-flowered grass-of-Parnassus, Small-flowered grass of Parnassus] - *Parnassia palustris* L. var. *parviflora* (DC.) Boivin (4, 5, 131) (1899-1986)

Small-flower gray hawk's-beard [Small-flowered gray hawks-beard] - *Crepis intermedia* Gray (5) (1913)

Small-flower hairy willow herb [smallflower hairy willowherb] - *Epilobium parviflorum* Schreb. (50) (present)

Small-flower half-chaff sedge [Smallflower halfchaff sedge] - *Lipocarpha micrantha* (Vahl) G. Tucker (50) (present)

Small-flower hawk's-beard [Small-flowered hawk's-beard] - *Crepis pulchra* L. (156) (1923)

Small-flower hawkweed [Small-flowered hawkweed] - *Crepis pulchra* L. (5) (1913)

Small-flower Indian physic [Small-flowered Indian-physic] - *Porteranthus stipulatus* (Muhl. ex Willd.) Britt. (186) (1814)

Small-flower lady's-slipper [Small-flowered ladies' slipper] - *Cypripedium parviflorum* Salisb. (42, 53) (1814-1922)

Small-flower lady's-tresses [Small-flowered ladies' tresses] - *Spiranthes ovalis* Lindl. var. *ovalis* (5) (1913)

Small-flower leaf-cup [Small-flowered leaf-cup] - *Polymnia canadensis* L (5, 72, 97) (1907-1937)

Small-flower lupine [Small-flowered lupine] - *Lupinus parviflorus* Nutt. ex Hook. & Arn. (131) (1899)

Small-flower marsh-elder [Small flower marsh elder, Small flower marsh elder, Small-flowered marsh elder] - *Iva axillaris* Pursh (5, 93, 97, 122, 131) (1899-1937)

Small-flower melic [Small flowered melic] - *Melica porteri* Scribn. (56) (1901)

Small-flower melic grass [Small-flowered melic-grass] - *Melica imperfecta* Trin. (94) (1901)

Small-flower microsteris [Small-flowered microsteris] - *Microthlaspi perfoliatum* (L.) F.K. Mey. (5) (1913)

Small-flower milkvetch [Smallflower milkvetch, Small-flowered milk vetch] - *Astragalus nuttallianus* DC. (4, 50) (1986–present)

Small-flower mountain rice [Small-flowered mountain rice] - *Piptatherum micranthum* (Trin. & Rupr.) Barkworth (5, 94) (1901-1913)

Small-flower nemophila [Small-flowered nemophila] - *Nemophila aphylla* (L.) Brummitt (5) (1913)

Small-flower ninebark [Small-flowered ninebark] - *Physocarpus monogynus* (Torr.) J.M. Coult. (possibly) (131) (1899)

Small-flower painted-cup [Small-flowered painted-cup] - *Castilleja minor* (Gray) Gray (5) (1913) SD

Small-flower parnassia [Smallflower parnassia] - *Parnassia palustris* L. var. *parviflora* (DC.) Boivin (155) (1942)

Small-flower pawpaw - *Asimina parviflora* (Michx.) Dunal (2, 155) (1895-1942)

Small-flower phacelia [Small-flowered phacelia] - *Phacelia dubia* (L.) Small. (5, 97) (1913-1937)

Small-flower pink morning-glory [Small-flowered pink morning glory] - *Ipomoea cordatotriloba* Dennst. var. *cordatotriloba* (5, 97) (1913-1937)

Small-flower prairie rocket [Small-flowered prairie rocket, Small-flowered prairie-rocket] - *Erysimum inconspicuum* (S. Wats.) MacM. (5, 93) (1913-1936)

Small-flower sand-verbena [Smallflower sandverbena] - *Tripterocalyx micranthus* (Torr.) Hook (50) (present)

Small-flower St. John's-wort [Small-flowered St. John's wort, Small-flowered St. John's-wort] - *Hypericum mutilum* L. (5, 97, 156) (1913-1937)

Small-flower starwort [Small flowered star wort] - *Symphyotrichum lateriflorum* (L.) A.& D. Löve (possibly) (42) (1814)

Small-flower stork's-bill [Small-flowered stork's bill] - *Erodium cicutarium* (L.) L'Hér. ex Aiton (124) (1937)

Small-flower sunflower [Small-flowered sun-flower] - *Helianthus divaricatus* L. (187) (1818)

Small-flower talinum [Small-flowered talinum] - *Talinum parviflorum* Nutt. (5, 93, 97) (1913-1937)

Small-flower tamarisk [Smallflower tamarisk] - *Tamarix parviflora* DC. (50, 155) (1942–present)

Small-flower tellima [Small flowered tellima] - *Lithophragma parviflorum* (Hook.) Nutt. ex Torr. & Gray (131) (1899)

Small-flower thoroughwort [Small-flowered thoroughwort] - *Eupatorium semiserratum* DC. (5) (1913)

Small-flower veratrum [Small-flowered veratrum] - *Melanthium parviflorum* (Michx.) S. Wats. (5) (1913)

Small-flower verbena [Small-flowered verbena, Smallflowered verbena] - *Glandularia bipinnatifida* (Nutt.) Nutt. var. *bipinnatifida* (5, 19, 97, 122) (1840-1937)

Small-flower vetch [Small-flowered vetch] - *Vicia minutiflora* F.G. Dietr. (5, 97) (1913-1937)

Small-flower wallflower [Smallflower wallflower] - *Erysimum inconspicuum* (S. Wats.) MacM. (3, 4) (1977-1986)

Small-flower white grass [Small-flowered white grass] - *Leersia virginica* Willd. (66, 87) (1884-1903)

Small-flower white morning-glory [Small-flowered white morning glory, Small-flowered white morning-glory] - *Ipomoea lacunosa* L. (5, 72, 97, 156) (1907-1937)

Small-flower wild sensitive pea [Small-flowered wild sensitive pea] - *Chamaecrista nictitans* (L.) Moench subsp. *nictitans* var. *nictitans* (86) (1878)

Small-flower woodland-star [Smallflower woodland-star] - *Lithophragma parviflorum* (Hook.) Nutt. ex Torr. & Gray (50) (present)

Small-flower woodrush [Small-flowered wood rush] - *Luzula parviflora* (Ehrh.) Desv. (5, 50) (1913–present)

Small-fruit agrimony [Small-fruited agrimony] - *Agrimonia microcarpa* Wallr. (5) (1913)

Small-fruit bulrush [Small-fruited bulrush] - *Scirpus microcarpus* J.& K. Presl (5) (1913)

Small-fruit false flax [Small-fruited false flax, Small-fruited false-flax] - *Camelina microcarpa* DC. (5, 97) (1913-1937)

Small-fruit fig tree [Small fruited fig tree] - *Ficus aurea* Nutt. (20) (1857)

Small-fruit haw [Small-fruited haw] - *Crataegus spathulata* Michx. (5) (1913)

Small-fruit hickory [Small fruited hickory] - *Carya glabra* (Mill.) Sweet (5) (1913), *Carya glabra* (Mill.) Sweet var. *glabra* (20, 107, 156) (1857-1923)

Small-fruit mallow [Small-fruited mallow] - *Malva parviflora* L. (3, 4) (1977-1986)

Small-fruit panic grass [Small-fruited panic-grass] - *Dichanthelium sphaerocarpon* (Ell.) Gould var. *isophyllum* (Scribn.) Gould & C.A. Clark (119) (1938)

Small-fruit panicum [Small-fruited panicum] - *Dichanthelium sphaerocarpon* (Ell.) Gould var. *isophyllum* (Scribn.) Gould & C.A. Clark (5) (1913)

Small-fruit spikerush [Smallfruit spikerush] - *Eleocharis microcarpa* Torr. (50) (present)

Small-fruit thorn [Small-fruited thorn] - *Crataegus spathulata* Michx. (5, 97) (1913-1937)

Small-glume dropseed [Small-glumed drop-seed] - *Muhlenbergia parviglumis* Vasey (94) (1901)

Small-head aster [Small-headed aster] - *Symphyotrichum parviceps* (Burgess) Nesom (5, 50) (1913–present)

Small-head broomweed [Small headed broom weed] - *Amphiachyris dracunculoides* (DC.) Nutt. (124) (1937)

Small-head bushy goldenrod [Small-headed bushy golden-rod] - *Euthamia graminifolia* (L.) Nutt. var. *nuttallii* (Greene) W. Stone (5) (1913)

Small-head rush [Smallhead rush, Small headed rush] - *Juncus brachycephalus* (Engelm.) Buch. (3, 5, 50) (1913–present)

Small-head sedge - *Carex capitata* L. (66) (1903)

Small-head sneezeweed [Smallhead sneezeweed, Small headed sneeze weed] - *Helenium microcephalum* DC. (50, 124) (1937–present)

Small-headed rush - *Juncus brachyphyllus* Wieg. (3) (1977)

Small-joint panic grass [Small-jointed panic-grass] - *Panicum stenodes* Griseb. (94) (1901)

Small-leaf angelica - *Angelica pinnata* S. Wats. (155) (1942)

Small-leaf ash [Small-leaved ash] - *Fraxinus caroliniana* Mill. (20) (1857)

Small-leaf blackberry [Small-leaved blackberry] - *Rubus flagellaris* Willd. (187) (1818)

Small-leaf cat's-foot [Small-leaved cat's foot] - *Antennaria microphylla* Rydb. (5, 93) (1913-1936)

Small-leaf cercocarpus [Small-leaved cercocarpus] - *Cercocarpus montanus* Raf. (5, 131) (1899-1913)

Small-leaf crane's-bill [Small-leaved cranebill, Small-leaved crane's bill] - *Geranium pratense* L. (72) (1907)

Small-leaf elm [Small-leaved elm] - *Ulmus americana* L. (38) (1820)

Small-leaf eugenia [Small-leaved eugenia] - *Myrcianthes fragrans* (Sw.) McVaugh (20) (1857)

Small-leaf fern [Small leafed ferne] - *Gymnocarpium dryopteris* (L.) Newman (178) (1596)

Small-leaf lignum-vitae [Small-leaved lignum vitae] - *Guaiacum sanctum* L. (20) (1857)

Small-leaf linden [Small-leaved linden] - *Tilia cordata* Mill. (109) (1949)

Small-leaf milkweed [Small-leaved milkweed] - *Apocynum cannabinum* L. (62) (1912)

Small-leaf mint [Small-leaved mint] - *Mentha ×gracilis* Sole [*arvensis × spicata*] (5) (1913)

Small-leaf nettle tree [Small-leaved nettle tree] - *Celtis laevigata* Willd. var. *reticulata* (Torr.) L. Benson (20) (1857)

Small-leaf oak [Small-leaved oak] - *Quercus dumosa* Nutt. (20) (1857)

Small-leaf panicum [Small-leaved panicum] - *Dichanthelium dichotomum* (L.) Gould var. *ensifolium* (Baldw. ex Ell.) Gould & C.A. Clark (5) (1913)

Small-leaf petalostemum [Small-leafed petalostemum] - *Dalea candida* Michx. ex Willd. (124) (1937), *Dalea phleoides* (Torr. & Gray) Shinners var. *microphylla* (Torr. & Gray) Barneby (124) (1937)

Small-leaf pussy-toes [Small-leaf pussytoes] - *Antennaria parviflora* Nutt. (50) (present)

Small-leaf whortleberry [Small-leaved whortleberry] - *Vaccinium scoparium* Leiberg (130) (1895)

Small's beak-rush [Small's beaked rush, Small beak rush] - *Rhynchospora capillacea* Torr. (5, 66) (1903-1913)

Small's button-snakeroot - *Liatris virgata* Nutt. (5) (1913)

Small's penstemon [Smalls penstemon] - *Penstemon smallii* Heller (138) (1923)

Small's spike-rush [Small's spike rush] - *Eleocharis palustris* (L.) Roemer & J.A. Schultes (5) (1913)

Small's squaw weed - *Packera anonyma* (Alph.Wood) W. A.Weber & Á. Löve (5) (1913)

Small's sugar hackberry [Smalls sugar hackberry] - *Celtis tenuifolia* Nutt. (155) (1942)

Small's yellow-eyed grass [Small's yelloweyed grass] - *Xyris smalliana* Nash (50) (present)

Small-seed false flax [Small-seeded false flax] - *Camelina microcarpa* DC. (3, 4) (1977-1986)

Small-seed white ash [Smallseed white ash] - *Fraxinus americana* L. (155) (1942)

Small-spike false nettle [Smallspike false nettle, Smallspike falsenettle] - *Boehmeria cylindrica* (L.) Sw. (50, 155) (1942–present)

Small-top fescue [Small-topped fescue] - *Vulpia microstachys* (Nutt.) Munro var. *microstachys* (94) (1901)

Small-wing sedge [Smallwing sedge] - *Carex microptera* Mackenzie (50, 155) (1942–present)

Smalnuts - *Carya glabra* (Mill.) Sweet (46) (1879)

Smartweed [Smart-weed, Smart weed] - *Polygonum caespitosum* Blume var. *longisetum* (de Bruyn) A.N. Steward (4, 85) (1932-1986), *Polygonum hydropiper* L. (5, 49, 72, 79, 93, 97, 131, 157, 158) (1891-1937), *Polygonum hydropiperoides* Michx. (80) (1913), *Polygonum* L. (1, 4, 82, 93, 106, 122) (1930-1986), *Polygonum lapathifolium* L. (85, 145) (1897-1932), *Polygonum pensylvanicum* L. (80, 125, 145) (1897-1930), *Polygonum persicaria* L. (7, 40) (1828-1928), *Polygonum punctatum* Ell. (1, 40, 48, 52, 92, 125) (1876-1932), *Polygonum punctatum* Ell. var. *punctatum* (6, 57) (1892-1917)

Smartweed dodder [Smartweed dodder, Smart-weed dodder] - *Cuscuta obtusiflora* Kunth (82) (1930), *Cuscuta polygonorum* Engelm. (3, 4, 5, 50, 72, 93, 122) (1907–present)

Smartweed leaf-flower [Smart-weed leaf-flower] - *Phyllanthus polygonoides* Nutt. (50) (present)

Smear-dock - *Chenopodium bonus-henricus* L. (156) (1923)

Smellage - *Levisticum officinale* W.D.J. Koch (10, 92) (1818-1876)

Smelling-stick [Smelling stick] - *Sassafras albidum* (Nutt.) Nees (5, 156, 158) (1900-1923)

Smelling-wood - *Artemisia abrotanum* L. (156, 157, 158) (1900-1929)

Smick-smock [Smick smock] - *Cardamine pratensis* L. (5) (1913)

Smiddy-leaves [Smiddy leaves] - *Chenopodium bonus-henricus* L. (5, 156) (1913-1923) no longer in use by 1923

Smilacina - *Maianthemum* G.H. Weber ex Wiggers (158) (1900)

Smilacine - *Maianthemum* G.H. Weber ex Wiggers (158) (1900)

Smilax - *Smilax* L. (1, 10, 14, 93) (1818-1936), *Smilax lasioneura* Hook. (85) (1932)

Smilax (of florists) - *Asparagus asparagoides* (L.) Druce (109) (1949)

Smilax asparagus - *Asparagus asparagoides* (L.) Druce (138, 155) (1923-1942)

Smilax with bryony leaves - *Smilax tamnoides* L. (189) (1767)

Smilax with red berries - *Smilax pseudochina* L. [poss] (189) (1767)

Smiling wakerobin [Smiling wake-robin, Smiling wake robin] - *Trillium undulatum* Willd. (19, 156) (1840-1923)

Sminckrot (Swedish) - *Buglossoides arvensis* (L.) I.M. Johnston (46) (1879)

Smith's bulrush [Smiths bulrush] - *Schoenoplectus smithii* (Gray) Soják (50, 155) (1942–present)

Smith's melic [Smith melic] - *Melica smithii* (Porter ex Gray) Vasey (155) (1942)

Smith's melic grass [Smith's melicgrass, Smith's melic-grass] - *Melica smithii* (Porter ex Gray) Vasey (50, 94) (1901–present)

Smith's oat - *Melica smithii* (Porter ex Gray) Vasey (5) (1913)

Smoke bush - *Cotinus coggygria* Scop. (135) (1910)

Smoke plant - *Cotinus coggygria* Scop. (92, 107) (1876-1919), *Fumaria officinalis* L. (124) (1937) TX

Smoke tree [Smoke-tree] - *Ailanthus altissima* (Mill) Swingle (4) (1986), *Cotinus coggygria* Scop. (82, 92, 109) (1876-1949), *Cotinus obovatus* Raf. (93, 124) (1936-1937)

Smoke-of-the-earth [Smoke of the erthe] - *Fumaria officinalis* L. (179) (1526)

Smokewood [Smoke wood] - *Clematis vitalba* L. (92) (1876)

Smoking bean - *Catalpa bignonioides* Walt. (156) (1923)

Smooth acanthus - *Acanthus mollis* L. (165) (1768)

Smooth alder - *Alnus incana* (L.) Moench subsp. *rugosa* (DuRoi) Clausen (1, 5, 65, 97, 156, 158) (1900-1937), *Alnus rubra* Bong. (92) (1876), *Alnus serrulata* (Aiton) Willd. (2, 4, 46, 49, 53, 58, 109) (1879-1949)

Smooth American plane tree [Smooth American planetree] - *Platanus occidentalis* L. (155) (1942)

Smooth amorpha - *Amorpha glabra* Desf. ex Poir. (106) (1930)

Smooth Arizona cypress - *Cupressus arizonica* Greene subsp. *arizonica* (109) (1949)

Smooth aster - *Symphyotrichum laeve* (L.) A.& D. Löve var. *laeve* (5, 72, 82, 93, 95, 97, 122, 131, 138, 155) (1899-1937)

Smooth azalea - *Rhododendron arborescens* (Pursh) Torr. (5, 156) (1913-1923)

Smooth beardtongue [Smooth beard-tongue] - *Penstemon glaber* Pursh (131) (1899), *Penstemon laevigatus* Aiton (5, 72) (1907-1913)

Smooth Bebb's willow [Smooth bebb willow] - *Salix bebbiana* Sargent (155) (1942)

Smooth bedstraw - *Cruciata laevipes* Opiz (50) (present)

Smooth blue aster - *Symphyotrichum laeve* (L.) A.& D. Löve var. *laeve* (3, 4, 50, 127) (1933-present)

Smooth brome - *Bromus inermis* Leyss. (50, 56, 94, 140, 146, 155) (1901-present)

Smooth brome grass [Smooth brome-grass - *Bromus racemosus* L. (5, 66, 111) (1903-1915), *Bromus inermis* Leyss. (68, 129, 143) (1890-1936)

Smooth buckeye - *Aesculus glabra* Willd. (49, 53) (1879-1898)

Smooth bugloss - *Lithospermum caroliniense* (Walter ex J.F. Gmel.) MacMill. var. *caroliniense* (42) (1814)

Smooth bur-marigold [Smooth burr marigold] - *Bidens laevis* (L.) Britton, Sterns & Poggenb. (5, 97, 131, 156) (1899-1937)

Smooth buttonplant - *Spermacoce glabra* Michx. (155) (1942)

Smooth buttonweed [Smooth button-weed] - *Spermacoce glabra* Michx. (4, 5, 97, 122, 156) (1913-1986)

Smooth carrion flower [Smooth carrionflower] - *Smilax herbacea* L. (50) (present)

Smooth catchfly - *Silene cserei* Baumg. (4) (1986)

Smooth chloris - *Eustachys glauca* Chapman (94) (1901)

Smooth cliff-brake [Smooth cliff brake, Smooth cliffbrake] - *Pellaea glabella* Mett. ex Kuhn subsp. *occidentalis* (E. Nels.) Windham (3, 97) (1937-1977), *Pellaea glabella* Mett. ex Kuhn var. *glabella* (3, 50) (1977-present), *Pellaea glabella* Mett. Ex Kuhn (50) (present)

Smooth cordgrass - *Spartina alterniflora* Loisel. (122) (1937)

Smooth crabgrass [Smooth crab grass, Smooth crab-grass] - *Digitaria ischaemum* (Schreb.) Schreb. ex Muhl. (3, 50, 56, 66, 80, 90, 94, 140, 143, 155) (1885-present)

Smooth creeping grass [Smooth creeping-grass] - *Eragrostis hypnoides* (Lam.) Britton, Sterns & Poggenb. (163) (1852)

Smooth creeping love grass [Smooth creeping love-grass] - *Eragrostis hypnoides* (Lam.) Britton, Sterns & Poggenb. (5, 93, 119) (1913-1938)

Smooth custard apple - *Annona glabra* L. (165) (1807)

Smooth cypress - *Cupressus arizonica* Greene subsp. *arizonica* (138) (1923)

Smooth dandelion - *Taraxacum laevigatum* (Willd.) DC. (155) (1942)

Smooth dock - *Rumex altissimus* Wood (80) (1913)

Smooth dogwood - *Cornus racemosa* Lam. (106) (1930)

Smooth false buttonweed - *Spermacoce glabra* Michx. (50) (present)

Smooth false foxglove - *Aureolaria virginica* (L.) Pennell (5, 97, 156) (1913-1937)

Smooth fleabane - *Erigeron glabellus* Nutt. (138, 155) (1923-1942)

Smooth Florida paspalum - *Paspalum floridanum* Michx. (3) (1977)

Smooth forked nailwort - *Paronychia canadensis* (L.) Wood (50) (present)

Smooth four-o'clock - *Mirabilis glabra* (S. Wats.) Standl. (4, 50) (1986–present)

Smooth fringed brome grass - *Bromus pubescens* Muhl. ex Willd. (56) (1901)

Smooth goldenrod [Smooth golden-rod] - *Solidago gigantea* Aiton (19, 80) (1840-1913)

Smooth gooseberry - *Ribes cynosbati* L. (9) (1873), *Ribes oxyacanthoides* L. (19, 130, 156) (1840-1923), *Ribes oxyacanthoides* L. subsp. *oxyacanthoides* (5) (1913), *Ribes rotundifolium* Michx. (5) (1913), *Ribes uva-crispa* L. (19) (1840)

Smooth goosefoot - *Chenopodium subglabrum* (S. Wats.) A. Nels. (50) (present)

Smooth ground-cherry [Smooth ground cherry] - *Physalis longifolia* Nutt. var. *subglabrata* (Mackenzie & Bush) Cronq. (5, 97) (1913-1937)

Smooth hawk's-beard [Smooth hawksbeard] - *Crepis capillaris* (L.) Wallr. (5, 50, 155) (1913–present)

Smooth hedge-nettle [Smooth hedge nettle, Smooth hedgenettle] - *Stachys tenuifolia* Willd. (5, 50, 72, 93, 97) (1907–present)

Smooth honeysuckle - *Rhododendron arborescens* (Pursh) Torr. (5) (1913)

Smooth Hood's phlox [Smooth Hoods phlox] - *Phlox hoodii* Richards. subsp. *glabrata* (E. Nels.) Wherry (155) (1942)

Smooth horsetail - *Equisetum laevigatum* A. Br. (3, 50, 155) (1942–present)

Smooth hydrangea - *Hydrangea arborescens* L. (138, 155) (1923-1942)

Smooth jewel-flower [Smooth jewelflower] - *Streptanthus hyacinthoides* Hook. (50) (present)

Smooth lungwort - *Mertensia virginica* (L.) Pers. ex Link (possibly) (2, 156) (1895-1923)

Smooth marsh grass - *Spartina alterniflora* Loisel. (66) (1903), *Spartina maritima* (M.A. Curtis) Fern. (5, 90) (1885-1913)

Smooth menziesia - *Menziesia ferruginea* Sm. (5) (1913)

Smooth milkweed - *Asclepias sullivantii* Engelm. ex Gray (3, 4, 114, 138) (1894-1986)

Smooth nama - *Hydrolea uniflora* Raf. (5, 97) (1913-1937) IA Neb

Smooth ox-eye [Smooth oxeye, Smooth ox-eye] - *Bidens laevis* (L.) Britton, Sterns & Poggenb. (187) (1818), *Heliopsis helianthoides* (L.) Sweet (42, 50, 62) (1814–present)

Smooth paspalum - *Paspalum laeve* Michx. (87, 94) (1884-1901)

Smooth pasture gooseberry - *Ribes cynosbati* L. (155) (1942)

Smooth Pennsylvania sumac [Smooth Pennsylvanian sumach] - *Rhus glabra* L. (8) (1785)

Smooth penstemon - *Penstemon digitalis* Nutt. ex Sims (3, 4, 155) (1942-1986), *Penstemon laevigatus* Aiton (138) (1923)

Smooth phlox - *Phlox glaberrima* L. (5, 72, 138, 156) (1907-1923)

Smooth pink phlox - *Phlox glaberrima* L. (122, 124) (1937)

Smooth rock cress [Smooth rock-cress] - *Arabis laevigata* (Muhl. ex Willd.) Poir. (2, 5, 72, 97) (1895-1937)

Smooth rock spleenwort - *Asplenium exiguum* Bedd. (5) (1913)

Smooth rockcress [Smooth rock cress, Smooth rock-cress] - *Arabis laevigata* (Muhl. ex Willd.) Poir. (2, 3, 4, 5, 50, 72, 97) (1895-present)

Smooth rose - *Rosa blanda* Aiton (5, 50, 93, 130, 158) (1895–present)

Smooth ruellia - *Ruellia strepens* L. (5, 72, 97, 122, 124) (1907-1937)

Smooth rye brome [Smooth rye-brome] - *Bromus secalinus* L. (5, 158) (1900-1913)

Smooth rye grass - *Elymus virginicus* L. (87, 90) (1884-1885)

Smooth scouring-rush [Smooth scouring rush] - *Equisetum laevigatum* A. Br. (4, 5, 97, 131) (1899-1986)

Smooth senna - *Senna septentrionalis* (Viviani) Irwin & Barneby (138) (1923)

Smooth slender wild rye - *Elymus villosus* Muhl. ex Willd. (5) (1913)

Smooth small-leaf tick trefoil [Smooth small-leaf ticktrefoil] - *Desmodium marilandicum* (L.) DC. (50) (present)

Smooth Solomon's-seal [Smooth Solomon's seal - *Polygonatum biflorum* (Walt.) Ell. (50) (present), *Polygonatum biflorum* (Walt.) Ell.

var. *commutatum* (J.A. & J.H. Schultes) Morong (5, 50, 72, 93, 97, 157, 158) (1900–present)

Smooth southern wild rye [Smooth southern wild-rye] - *Elymus virginicus* L. var. *virginicus* (5, 163) (1852-1913)

Smooth spear grass - *Poa secunda* J. Presl (5, 10) (1818-1913)

Smooth speedwell - *Veronica serpyllifolia* L. (19) (1840)

Smooth spike-primrose - *Epilobium pygmaeum* (Speg.) Hoch & Raven (50) (present)

Smooth spreading four-o'clock - *Mirabilis oxybaphoides* (Gray) Gray (50) (present)

Smooth sticktight - *Bidens laevis* (L.) Britton, Sterns & Poggenb. (82) (1930)

Smooth storax - *Styrax americanus* Lam. (5, 97, 156) (1913-1937)

Smooth strawberry shrub - *Calycanthus floridus* L. var. *glaucus* (Willd.) Torr. & Gray (5) (1913)

Smooth sumac [Smooth shumach, Smooth sumach] - *Rhus copallinum* L. (5, 156) (1913-1923), *Rhus glabra* L. (3, 4, 5, 9, 15, 27, 37, 41, 49, 50, 52, 53, 72, 82, 92, 95, 105, 109, 113, 121, 130, 131, 138, 145, 156, 157, 158, 187) (1770–present)

Smooth sunflower - *Helianthus ciliaris* DC. (97) (1937), *Helianthus laevigatus* Torr. & Gray (5) (1913)

Smooth swamp alder - *Alnus rubra* Bong. (92) (1876)

Smooth sweet cicely - *Osmorhiza longistylis* (Torr.) DC. (156) (1923)

Smooth tare - *Vicia tetrasperma* (L.) Moench (5) (1913)

Smooth thorn-apple [Smooth thorne apples] - *Datura metel L.* (178) (1526)

Smooth tick trefoil [Smooth tick-trefoil] - *Desmodium laevigatum* (Nutt.) DC. (5, 97) (1913–1937)

Smooth tofieldia - *Tofieldia glabra* Nutt. (50) (present)

Smooth twig rush - *Cladium mariscoides* (Muhl.) Torr. (66) (1903)

Smooth umbrella-wort - *Mirabilis glabra* (S. Wats.) Standl. (97) (1937)

Smooth upland sumac - *Rhus glabra* L. (97) (1937)

Smooth vetch - *Vicia villosa* Roth subsp. *varia* (Host) Corb. (155) (1942)

Smooth violet - *Viola blanda* Willd. (19) (1840)

Smooth violet prairie aster - *Symphyotrichum turbinellum* (Lindl.) Nesom (50) (present)

Smooth Virginia rattle-broom [Smooth Virginia rattle broom] - *Baptisia tinctoria* (L.) R. Br. ex Aiton f. (181) (~1678)

Smooth white hymenopappus - *Hymenopappus scabiosaeus* L'Her. var. *corymbosus* (Torr. & Gray) B.L. Turner (5, 97) (1913-1937)

Smooth wild gooseberry - *Ribes oxyacanthoides* L. (107, 158) (1900-1919)

Smooth wild oat grass - *Danthonia epilis* Scribn. (5) (1913)

Smooth wild rose - *Rosa blanda* Aiton (3, 4, 72, 82, 127) (1907-1986)

Smooth wild rye - *Elymus glaucus* Buckl. (5) (1913)

Smooth winterberry [Smooth winter berry] - *Ilex laevigata* (Pursh) Gray (2, 5, 138, 156) (1895-1923)

Smooth withe-rod - *Viburnum nudum* L. (109, 138) (1923-1949)

Smooth woodsia - *Woodsia glabella* R. Br. ex Richards. (5, 50) (1913–present)

Smooth woody-aster [Smooth woodyaster] - *Xylorhiza glabriuscula* Nutt. (50) (present)

Smooth yellow violet - *Viola pubescens* Aiton (4) (1986), *Viola pubescens* Aiton var. *pubescens* (93) (1936)

Smooth-bark cottonwood [Smoothbark cottonwood, Smooth-barked cottonwood] - *Populus ×acuminata* Rydb. [*angustifolia × deltoides*] (1, 3, 93, 138) (1923–1977)

Smooth-cone sedge [Smoothcone sedge] - *Carex laeviconica* Dewey (3, 50) (1977–present)

Smoother sweet cicely [Smoother sweet-cicely] - *Osmorhiza longistylis* (Torr.) DC. (5, 49, 72, 97, 131, 157, 158) (1898-1937)

Smooth-fruit acnida [Smooth-fruited acnida] - *Amaranthus cannabinus* (L.) Sauer (poss) (187) (1818)

Smoothish chamaesaracha - *Chamaesaracha coronopus* (Dunal) Gray (5, 97) (1913-1937)

Smoothish elephant's foot - *Elephantopus nudatus* Gray (5) (1913)

Smoothish hawkweed - *Hieracium ×floribundum* Wimmer & Grab. [*caespitosum × lactucella*] (5) (1913)

Smoothish yellow violet - *Viola pubescens* Aiton var. *pubescens* (5, 97) (1913-1937)

Smooth-leaf bumelia [Smooth leaved bumelia] - *Sideroxylon lycioides* L. (20) (1857)

Smooth-leaf crowfoot [Smooth-leaved crowfoot] - *Ranunculus abortivus* L. (5, 93) (1913-1936)

Smooth-leaf elm [Smoothleaf elm, Smooth-leaved elm] - *Ulmus procera* Salisb. (109, 138) (1923-1949)

Smooth-leaf hackberry [Smooth-leafed hackberry] - *Celtis laevigata* Willd. (124) (1937)

Smooth-leaf honeysuckle [Smooth-leaved honeysuckle, Smooth leaved honeysuckle] - *Lonicera dioica* L. (5, 93, 95) (1911-1936)

Smooth-leaf sumac [Smooth leaved sumach] - *Rhus glabra* L. (41) (1770)

Smooth-leaf yamroot [Smooth-leaved yam-root] - *Dioscorea quaternata* J.F. Gmel. (187) (1818)

Smooth-scale Canada wild rye [Smoothscale Canada wildrye] - *Elymus canadensis* L. (155) (1942)

Smooth-scale paspalum [Smooth-scaled paspalum] - *Paspalum pubiflorum* Rupr. ex Fourn. (5, 99) (1913-1923)

Smooth-seed wild bean [Smoothseed wild bean] - *Strophostyles leiosperma* (Torr. & Gray) Piper (3) (1977)

Smooth-sheath sedge [Smoothsheath sedge] - *Carex laevivaginata* (Kukenth.) Mack. (50) (present)

Smooth-spike soft chess [Smooth spiked soft chess] - *Bromus hordeaceus* L. subsp. *hordeaceus* (56) (1901)

Smooth-stalk Canadian bramble [Smooth stalked Canadian bramble] - *Rubus canadensis* L. (8) (1785)

Smooth-stalk meadow grass [Smooth-stalked meadow grass] - *Poa pratensis* L. (45, 68, 90) (1885-1913)

Smooth-stem lichnidia - *Phlox paniculata* L. (19) (1840)

Smotherweed - *Bassia* All. (50) (present), *Artemisia vulgaris* L. (156, 157) (1923-1929)

Smut - *Claviceps purpurea* (Fr.) Tul. (49) (1898), *Erysibe vera* Wallroth (possibly) (19) (1840)

Smut grass [Smut-grass] - *Sporobolus indicus* (L.) R. Br. (87, 94) (1884-1901), *Sporobolus indicus* (L.) R. Br. var. *indicus* (5, 119, 163) (1852-1938)

Smut of corn - *Ustilago maydis* (DC.) Corda (92) (1876)

Smut of rye - *Sclerotium clavus* DC. (92) (1876)

Snaffles - *Pedicularis canadensis* L. (5, 92, 156) (1876-1923)

Snag tree (snag-tree) - *Nyssa sylvatica* Marsh. (5, 156) (1913-1923) no longer in use by 1923

Snagrel - *Aristolochia serpentaria* L. (6, 7, 64, 92, 158) (1828-1908)

Snail clover - *Medicago* L. (158) (1900), *Medicago sativa* L. (5, 157, 158) (1900-1929)

Snail flower [Snail-flower] - *Medicago sativa* L. (156) (1923)

Snail medick - *Medicago scutellata* (L.) Mill. (138) (1923)

Snail plant - *Medicago scutellata* (L.) Mill. (92) (1876)

Snails - *Medicago scutellata* (L.) Mill. (107) (1919)

Snailseed [Snail seed] - *Cocculus* DC. (138, 155) (1923-1942), *Cocculus diversifolius* DC. (122, 124) (1937), *Cocculus carolinus* (L.) DC. (3, 4, 156) (1923-1986)

Snail-shell - *Medicago scutellata* (L.) Mill. (19) (1840)

Snake cactus [Snakecactus] - *Selenicereus* (Berger) Britt. & Rose (155) (1942)

Snake fern - *Asplenium scolopendrium* L. var. *americanum* (Fern.) Kartesz & Gandhi (5) (1913), *Osmunda regalis* L. (5, 157) (1913-1929)

Snake flower [Snakeflower, Snake-flower] - *Echium vulgare* L. (5, 156, 157, 158) (1900-1929), *Lamium album* L. (5, 156) (1913-1923) no longer in use by 1923, *Silene latifolia* Poir. subsp. *alba* (Mill.) Greuter & Burdet (5, 156, 158) (1900-1923) no longer in use by 1923, *Stellaria holostea* L. (5, 156) (1913-1923) no longer in use by 1923, *Trientalis borealis* Raf. subsp. *borealis* (156) (1923)

Snake melon - *Cucumis melo* L. (109, 138) (1923–1949)

Snake moss - *Lycopodium clavatum* L. (5, 6) (1892–1913)

Snake plantain [Snake-plantain] - *Plantago lanceolata* L. (5, 92, 156, 157, 158) (1876–1929)

Snake violet [Snake-violet] - *Viola pedata* L. (5, 74, 156, 158) (1893–1923) Swansea & Boston, MA

Snakebeard - *Ophiopogon* Ker-Gawl. (138) (1923)

Snakeberry [Snake berry, Snake-berry] - *Actaea rubra* (Aiton) Willd. (5, 156, 157, 158) (1900–1929), *Mitchella repens* L. (73, 156) (1892–1923) NY, no longer in use by 1923, *Solanum dulcamara* L. (156, 158) (1900–1923)

Snakebite [Snake bite, Snake-bite] - *Lactuca canadensis* L. (157, 158) (1900–1929), *Sanguinaria canadensis* L. (64, 73, 156, 157, 158) (1892–1929), *Trillium cernuum* L. (5, 92, 156, 158) (1876–1923) no longer in use by 1923, *Trillium erectum* L. (92) (1876)

Snake-cotton [Snake cotton, Snakecotton] - *Froelichia drummondii* Moq. (122, 124) (1937) TX, *Froelichia floridana* (Nutt.) Moq. var. *campestris* (Small) Fern. (3) (1977), *Froelichia* Moench (4, 50) (1986–present)

Snake-eyes [Snake eyes] - *Phaulothamnus spinescens* Gray (122, 124) (1937) TX

Snake-gentian [Snake gentian] - *Prenanthes serpentaria* Pursh (5, 156) (1913–1923)

Snake-grass [Snake grass, Snakegrass] - *Equisetum* L. (37) (1830), *Myosotis scorpioides* L. (5, 156, 158) (1900–1923), *Stellaria holostea* L. (5, 156) (1913–1923) no longer in use by 1923, *Tradescantia virginiana* L. (156) (1923)

Snakehead [Snake head, Snake-head, Snakeheads] - *Chelone glabra* L. (5, 19, 46, 53, 57, 58, 72, 86, 92, 156) (1840–1923)

Snakeherb - *Dyschoriste* Nees (50) (present)

Snakeleaf [Snake leaf] - *Erythronium americanum* Ker. (92, 156) (1876–1923), *Ophioglossum vulgatum* L. (7) (1828)

Snake-lily [Snake lily, Snake lilly] - *Iris versicolor* L. (5, 19, 49, 64, 92, 156, 157, 158) (1840–1929)

Snakemouth [Snake mouth, Snake-mouth] - *Chelone* L. (75) (1894) Banner Elk NC, *Pogonia* Juss. (1, 158) (1900–1932), *Pogonia ophioglossoides* (L.) Ker-Gawl. (5, 86, 156, 158) (1878–1923)

Snake-mouth orchid [Snakemouth orchid] - *Pogonia ophioglossoides* (L.) Ker-Gawl. (50) (present)

Snake-pipes [Snake pipes] - *Equisetum arvense* L. (5) (1913), *Equisetum palustre* L. (5, 158) (1900–1913)

Snake-plantian [Snake plantian] - *Hieracium venosum* L. (5, 7, 92, 156, 157) (1828–1923)

Snake-plum [Snake plum] - *Mitchella repens* L. (76) (1896) Oxford Co. ME

Snakeroot [Snake root, Snake-root] - *Actaea pachypoda* Ell. (5, 156, 158) (1900–1923), *Actaea rubra* (Aiton) Willd. (5, 156, 158) (1900–1923), *Ageratina* Spach (50) (present), *Aristolochia* L. (1) (1932), *Aristolochia serpentaria* L. (6, 34, 181) (~1678–1892), *Asarum canadense* L. (64, 79, 92, 107) (1891–1919), *Echinacea angustifolia* DC. (101) (1905) MT, *Erythronium americanum* Ker. (5, 156) (1913–1923), *Gaillardia pulchella* Foug. (possibly) (34) (1834), *Gentiana catesbaei* Walt. (7) (1828), *Gentiana villosa* L. (possibly) (14) (1882), *Liatris punctata* Hook. var. *punctata* (93) (1936) Neb, *Packera aurea* (L.) A. & D. Löve (75, 156, 158) (1894–1923) Concord MA, odor and taste of roots similar to Polygala senega, *Polemonium reptans* L. (77) (1898) Parke Co. IN, *Polygala* L. (13, 190) (~1759–1849), *Polygala senega* L. (14) (1882), *Sanicula* L. (1, 93, 158) (1900–1936), *Silene stellata* (L.) Aiton f. (156) (1923), *Spigelia marilandica* (L.) L. (6) (1892)

Snakeroot birthwort - *Aristolochia serpentaria* L. (7) (1828)

Snakeroot gentian [Snake root gentian] - *Gentiana villosa* L. (7) (1828)

Snake's-head [Snake head, Snake-head, Snakehead, Snakeheads] - *Chelone* L. (2, 6) (1892–1895), *Dodecatheon meadia* L. (156) (1923)

Snake's-milk [Snake's milk, Snake milk, Snakemilk] - *Apocynum androsaemifolium* L. (7) (1828), *Apocynum cannabinum* L. (6) (1892), *Euphorbia corollata* L. (5, 6, 7, 49, 53, 92, 156, 157, 158) (1828–1929)

Snake's-tongue [Snake's tongue, Snakes' tongue] - *Lygodium* Swartz (10) (1818), *Ophioglossum* L. (158) (1900), *Ophioglossum vulgatum* L. (5, 92) (1876–1913)

Snakeweed [Snake-weed, Snake weed, Snake Weede] - *Aristolochia serpentaria* L. (6, 7, 64, 92, 156, 158, 181) (~1678–1923), *Cicuta maculata* L. (6, 7, 71, 76, 156) (1828–1923) no longer in use by 1923, *Conium maculatum* L. (5, 156) (1913–1923), *Equisetum hyemale* L. (78) (1898) IA, *Gutierrezia* Lag. (50, 155) (1942–present), *Gutierrezia sarothrae* (Pursh) Britton & Rusby (4) (1986), *Lactuca canadensis* L. (158) (1900), *Polygonum bistorta* L. (92, 107, 178) (1526–1919), *Polygonum hydropiper* L. (5, 156) (1913–1923)

Snakeweed-root - *Aristolochia serpentaria* L. (186) (1814)

Snakewood [Snake wood] - *Colubrina arborescens* (P. Mill.) Sargent (20) (1857), *Condalia* Cav. (50) (present)

Snap willow - *Salix fragilis* L. (5, 156, 158) (1900–1923)

Snapberry [Snap berry, Snap-berry] - *Symphoricarpos symphoricarpos* (L.) MacMill. (5, 156, 157, 158) (1900–1929)

Snapdragon [Snap dragon, Snap-dragon] - *Antirrhinum* L. (10, 50, 109, 138, 155, 156, 158) (1818–present), *Antirrhinum majus* L. (4, 85, 92, 156, 158) (1876–1986), *Aquilegia vulgaris* L. (5, 156) (1913–1923), *Impatiens capensis* Meerb. (5, 73, 156, 158) (1892–1923) NH, *Knautia arvensis* (L.) Duby (10, 50, 109, 138, 155, 156, 158, 184) (1793–present), *Linaria vulgaris* Mill. (5, 19, 75, 92, 93, 156, 158) (1840–1936)

Snapdragon catchfly - *Silene antirrhina* L. (15, 156, 187) (1818–1923)

Snapdragon penstemon - *Keckiella antirrhinoides* (Benth.) Straw subsp. *antirrhinoides* (138) (1923)

Snapjack [Snap jack, Snap-jack] - *Stellaria holostea* L. (5, 156) (1913–1923) no longer in use by 1923

Snappers - *Silene vulgaris* (Moench) Garcke (5, 73, 156) (1892–1923) no longer in use by 1923, *Stellaria holostea* L. (5, 156) (1913–1923) no longer in use by 1923

Snapping hazel - *Hamamelis virginiana* L. (5, 53, 92, 156) (1876–1923)

Snapping hazel nut [Snapping hazelnut] - *Hamamelis virginiana* L. (6, 7, 49) (1828–1898)

Snapweed [Snap weed, Snap-weed] - *Impatiens capensis* Meerb. (46, 73, 86, 156, 157, 158) (1878–1929), *Impatiens* L. (109, 155) (1942–1949), *Impatiens pallida* Nutt. (5, 92, 156, 157) (1876–1929), *Lindera benzoin* Blume. (5, 92, 156) (1876–1923) no longer in use by 1923

Snapwood [Snap wood, Snap-wood] - *Lindera benzoin* Blume. (5, 92, 156) (1876–1923)

Snatch-weed - *Galium aparine* L. (157, 158) (1900–1929)

Snecrut - *Aristolochia serpentaria* L. (181) (~1678)

Sneezefoil - *Achillea millefolium* L. (156) (1923)

Sneezeweed [Sneeze weed, Sneeze-weed] - *Achillea ptarmica* L. (156) (1923), *Helenium amarum* (Raf.) H. Rock var. *amarum* (156) (1923), *Helenium amarum* (Raf.) H. Rock var. *badium* (Gray ex S. Wats.) Waterfall (97) (1937), *Helenium autumnale* L. (3, 4, 5, 7, 49, 56, 62, 63, 71, 80, 82, 92, 95, 97, 126, 156, 157, 158) (1898–1986), *Helenium autumnale* L. var. *montanum* (Nutt.) Fern. (85) (1932), *Helenium* L. (1, 2, 4, 50, 82, 109, 125, 138, 155, 156, 158) (1895–present), *Hymenoxys hoopesii* (Gray) Bierner (148) (1939) CO

Sneezeweed hog-weed - *Eupatorium capillifolium* (Lam.) Small (156) (1923)

Sneezewort [Sneeze-wort, Sneeze woort] - *Achillea* L. (2) (1895), *Achillea ptarmica* L. (5, 10, 92, 109, 138, 156, 165, 178) (1526–1949), *Helenium autumnale* L. (48, 49, 57, 71, 72, 92, 131, 156, 157, 158) (1882–1929)

Sneezewort aster - *Oligoneuron album* (Nutt.) Nesom (3, 4) (1977-1986), *Oligoneuron* Small (1) (1932)

Sneezewort milfoil - *Achillea ptarmica* L. (165) (1768)

Sneezewort-tansy - *Achillea ptarmica* L. (5, 156) (1913-1923)

Sneezewort-yarrow (sneezewort yarrow) - *Achillea ptarmica* L. (5, 155, 156) (1913-1942)

Sniddle [Sniddles] - *Carex acutiformis* Ehrh. (5, 156) (1913-1923)

Snow brush - *Ceanothus* L. (1) (1932), *Ceanothus velutinus* Dougl. ex Hook. (106) (1930)

Snow bush [Snow-bush] - *Breynia disticha* J.R. & G. Forst. (109) (1949)

Snow buttercup - *Ranunculus nivalis* L. (5) (1913)

Snow cinquefoil - *Potentilla nivea* L. (50) (present)

Snow flower [Snowflower] or Snow flower tree [Snowflower-tree] - *Chionanthus virginicus* L. (5, 6, 92, 156) (1876-1923)

Snow gooseberry - *Ribes niveum* Lindl. (138) (1923)

Snow plant - *Sarcodes sanguinea* Torr. (75) (1894) CA

Snow thoroughwort - *Ageratina altissima* (L.) King & H.E. Robins. (138, 156) (1923)

Snow trillium - *Trillium grandiflorum* (Michx.) Salisb. (50, 138, 156) (1923–present)

Snow vine [Snow-vine, Snowvine] - *Ampelopsis arborea* (L.) Koehne (106) (1930) GA, *Ampelopsis* Michx. (106) (1930)

Snowball [Snow ball, Snowballs, Snow-balls] - *Cephalanthus occidentalis* L. (6) (1892), *Viburnum* L. (1) (1932), *Viburnum opulus* L. (5, 19, 135, 156, 158) (1840-1923), *Viburnum opulus* L. var. *opulus* (92, 109) (1876-1949)

Snowball bush [Snowball-bush] - *Viburnum opulus* L. (158) (1900)

Snowball cactus [Snowballcactus] - *Pediocactus simpsonii* (Engelm.) Britton & Rose (138, 155) (1923-1942)

Snowball hard-hack - *Physocarpus opulifolius* (L.) Maxim. var. *opulifolius* (19) (1840)

Snowball sand-verbena [Snowball sand verbena, Snowball sand-verbena] - *Abronia fragrans* Nutt. ex Hook. (50, 155) (1942–present)

Snowball tree - *Viburnum opulus* L. (107) (1919)

Snowbell - *Styrax* L. (109, 138) (1923-1949)

Snowberry [Snow berry, Snow-berry] - *Chiococca alba* (L.) A.S. Hitchc. (7, 49, 92) (1828-1898), *Symphoricarpos albus* (L.) Blake var. *laevigatus* (Fern.) Blake (82, 156) (1923-1930), *Symphoricarpos albus* (L.) Blake var. *pauciflorus* (J.W. Robbins) S.F. Blake (3, 40, 109, 130) (1895-1949), *Symphoricarpos* Duham. (1, 4, 50, 82, 108, 138, 146, 155, 156, 158, 160, 161) (1857–present), *Symphoricarpos occidentalis* Hook. (108) (1878)

Snowbrush ceanothus - *Ceanothus velutinus* Dougl. ex Hook. (50, 155) (1942–present)

Snowdon's rose [Snowdon rose] - *Rhodiola rosea* L. (5, 156) (1913-1923)

Snowdrift [Snow drift] - *Arabis alpina* L. (5) (1913), *Lobularia maritima* (L.) Desv. (5, 156) (1913-1923)

Snowdrop [Snowdrops, Snow-drops, Snow drop] - *Anemone nemorosa* L. (76) (1896) Lynn MA, *Anemone quinquefolia* L. (5, 156, 158) (1900-1923), *Chionanthus* L. (8) (1785), *Galanthus* L. (109, 138) (1923-1949), *Galanthus nivalis* L. (19, 92) (1840-1876), *Halesia* Ellis ex L. (2) (1895), *Leucojum vernum* L. (180) (1633), *Moneses uniflora* (L.) Gray (156) (1923)

Snowdrop tree [Snowdrop-tree, Snow drop tree] - *Chionanthus virginicus* L. (6, 19, 49, 53) (1840-1922), *Halesia carolina* L. (5, 122, 124, 156) (1937-1949), *Halesia* Ellis ex L. (10, 109) (1818-1949), *Halesia tetraptera* L. (14, 19, 92) (1840-1882)

Snowdrop-berry [Snow-drop-berry, Snowdrop berry] - *Symphoricarpos albus* (L.) Blake var. *albus* (5, 157, 158) (1900-1929), *Symphoricarpos albus* (L.) Blake var. *laevigatus* (Fern.) Blake (156) (1923) no longer in use by 1923, *Symphoricarpos symphoricarpos* (L.) MacMill. (156) (1923)

Snowflake [Snow flake] - *Dianthus barbatus* L. (5, 74, 156) (1893-1923) Quebec, white variety, no longer in use by 1923, *Leucojum* L. (109, 138) (1923-1949), *Leucojum vernum* L. (92) (1876)

Snow-in-summer [Snow-in-summer] - *Cerastium tomentosum* L. (50, 109, 138) (1923–present)

Snow-on-the-mountain [Snow on the mountain] - *Euphorbia bicolor* Engelm. & Gray (124) (1937) TX, *Euphorbia* L. (1, 93) (1932-1936), *Euphorbia marginata* Pursh (3, 4, 5, 37, 50, 71, 73, 78, 80, 82, 85, 86, 93, 97, 106, 109, 121, 122, 124, 138, 145, 148, 155, 156, 157, 158) (1878–present)

Snow-white Dwarfe Flowerdeluce [Snowe white Dwarfe Flowerdeluce] - *Iris pumila* L. (178) (1596)

Snow-wreath - *Neviusia alabamensis* Gray (138) (1923), *Neviusia* Gray (138) (1923)

Snowy campion - *Silene nivea* (Nutt.) Muhl. ex Otth (3, 4, 5, 138, 156, 158) (1900-1986)

Snowy cinquefoil - *Potentilla concinna* Richards. var. *concinna* (131) (1899) SD, *Potentilla nivea* L. (5) (1913)

Snowy medlar - *Amelanchier canadensis* (L.) Medik. (74) (1893) NY, *Pyrus canadensis* (L.) Farw. (187) (1818)

Snowy mespilus - *Amelanchier canadensis* (L.) Medik. (14, 156) (1882-1923)

Snowy orchid - *Platanthera nivea* (Nutt.) Luer (50) (present)

Snowy serviceberry - *Amelanchier sanguinea* (Pursh) DC. var. *sanguinea* (155) (1942)

Snowy shadblow - *Amelanchier sanguinea* (Pursh) DC. var. *sanguinea* (138) (1923)

Snowy silene - *Silene nivea* (Nutt.) Muhl. ex Otth (155) (1942)

Snowy trillium - *Trillium nivale* Riddell (156) (1923)

Snuff-box fern - *Thelypteris palustris* Schott (19) (1840)

So ingwer - *Acorus calamus* L. (186) (1814)

Soafs - *Salix* L. (158) (1900)

Soap bulb - *Chlorogalum pomeridianum* (DC.) Kunth (14) (1882) CA, used in washing

Soap bush [Soapbush] - *Guaiacum angustifolium* Engelm. (106) (1930)

Soap gentian - *Gentiana saponaria* L. (7, 19) (1828-1840)

Soap plant [Soap-plant] - *Chlorogalum pomeridianum* (DC.) Kunth (78, 161) (1857-1898) CA, used in washing, *Yucca baccata* Torr. (158) (1900), *Yucca glauca* Nutt. (28) (1850), *Zigadenus* Michx. (158) (1900)

Soapberry [Soap berry] or Soapberry tree - *Sapindus* L. (4, 13, 50, 109, 138, 155, 156, 158, 167) (1814-1986), *Sapindus saponaria* L. (10, 12, 15, 92) (1818-1895), *Sapindus saponaria* L. var. *drummondii* (Hook. & Arn.) Bensons (1, 3, 4, 106, 121, 125, 153, 156) (1913-1986), *Sapindus saponaria* L. var. *saponaria* (103, 149) (1870-1904)

Soapberry [Soap-berry] - *Shepherdia canadensis* Nutt. (104) (1896)

Soaproot [Soap-root, Soap root] - *Chlorogalum pomeridianum* (DC.) Kunth (78) (1898), *Leucocrinum* Nutt. ex Gray (158) (1900), *Sapindus saponaria* L. var. *saponaria* (92) (1876), *Saponaria officinalis* L. (5, 49, 64, 92, 156, 157, 158) (1898-1929), *Yucca* L. (1) (1932)

Soapweed [Soap weed, Soap-weed] - *Rhexia virginica* L. (181) (~1678), *Yucca elata* (Engelm.) Engelm. (149, 153) (1904-1913), *Yucca glauca* Nutt. (5, 85, 93, 97, 109, 125, 156) (1913-1949), *Yucca glauca* Nutt. var. *glauca* (75, 101) (1894-1905), *Yucca* L. (1, 93, 148) (1932-1939)

Soapweed yucca - *Yucca glauca* Nutt. (50, 138) (1923–present), *Yucca glauca* Nutt. var. *glauca* (50) (present)

Soapwood [Soap-wood] - *Rhexia mariana* L. (184) (1793), *Sapindus saponaria* L. var. *saponaria* (96) (1891) OK

Soapwort [Soap-wort, Sope woort, Sope-wort] - *Gentiana saponaria* L. var. *saponaria* (5) (1913), *Saponaria* L. (1, 7, 10, 15, 50, 93, 109, 138, 155, 156, 158, 167, 184) (1793–present), *Saponaria officinalis* L. (1, 4, 5, 10, 19, 49, 57, 62, 64, 72, 80, 85, 92, 131, 148, 156, 178, 180) (1526-1986) sap from some species will make lather, *Vaccaria* von Wolf (50) (present)

Soapwort gentian [Soapwort-gentian - *Gentiana saponaria* L. (2, 48, 92, 156, 187) (1818-1923), *Saponaria officinalis* L. (5, 156) (1913-1923)

Soba (Japanese) - *Fagopyrum esculentum* Moench (46) (1879)

Soda plant - *Salsola soda* L. (92) (1876)

Soft acanthus - *Acanthus mollis* L. (138, 155) (1931-1942)

Soft agrimony - *Agrimonia pubescens* Wallr. (50, 72, 97) (1907–present)

Soft arrow-wood - *Viburnum molle* Michx (156) (1923)

Soft brome - *Bromus hordeaceus* L. (5, 50) (1913–present), *Bromus hordeaceus* L. subsp. *hordeaceus* (50, 155) (1942–present)

Soft brome grass - *Bromus hordeaceus* L. subsp. *hordeaceus* (42, 66) (1814-1903)

Soft chess - *Bromus hordeaceus* L. (5, 56, 72, 80, 94, 111) (1901–1915), *Bromus hordeaceus* L. subsp. *hordeaceus* (3, 56, 66, 122, 129, 163) (1852–1977)

Soft false gromwell - *Onosmodium molle* Michx. subsp. *occidentale* (Mackenzie) Cochrane (122) (1937)

Soft fox sedge - *Carex conjuncta* Boott. (5, 50, 72) (1893–present)

Soft golden-aster [Soft golden aster, Soft goldenaster] - *Chrysopsis pilosa* Nutt. (3, 4, 50) (1977–present)

Soft goldenrod - *Solidago mollis* Bartl. (3, 98) (1926-1977)

Soft grass [Soft-grass] - *Holcus* L. (10, 92, 184) (1793-1876), *Holcus lanatus* L. (19, 88) (1840-1885)

Soft lyme grass - *Leymus mollis* (Trin.) Pilger subsp. *mollis* (66, 90) (1885-1903)

Soft maple - *Acer circinatum* Pursh (35) (1806), *Acer glabrum* Torr. (5, 35) (1806–1913), *Acer rubrum* L. (3, 5, 19, 37, 72, 74, 76, 82, 85, 93, 105, 106, 107, 112, 124, 130, 131, 135, 156, 157, 158) (1840–1986)

Soft meadow grass - *Holcus lanatus* L. (92) (1876)

Soft pine - *Pinus strobus* L. (5) (1913)

Soft rush [Soft-rush] - *Juncus effusus* L. (5, 19, 66, 120, 156) (1840-1938), *Juncus tenuis* Willd. (155) (1942)

Soft thermopsis - *Thermopsis mollis* (Michx.) M. A. Curtis (138) (1923)

Soft western wheat grass [Soft western wheat grass] - *Pascopyrum smithii* (Rydb.) A. Löve (56) (1901)

Soft willow herb - *Epilobium strictum* Muhl. ex Spreng. (5, 42) (1814-1913)

Soft wool grass [Soft wool-grass] - *Eriochloa michauxii* (Poir.) A.S. Hitchc. var. *michauxii* (94) (1901)

Soft woolly grass - *Holcus lanatus* L. (45) (1896)

Soft-beard plume grass [Softbeard plumegrass] - *Saccharum brevibarbe* (Michx.) Pers. var. *contortum* (Ell.) R. Webster (50) (present)

Soft-hair marbleseed [Softhair marbleseed] - *Onosmodium molle* Michx. (50) (present), *Onosmodium molle* Michx. subsp. *hispidissimum* (Mackenzie) Boivin (50) (present)

Soft-hairy false gromwell - *Onosmodium molle* Michx. (5, 72, 131) (1899-1913)

Soft-leaf arrow-wood [Soft-leaved arrow-wood] - *Viburnum molle* Michx (5, 82) (1913-1930)

Soft-leaf aster [Soft-leaved aster] - *Symphyotrichum concolor* (L.) Nesom (187) (1818)

Soft-leaf avicenna [Soft-leaved avicenna] - *Avicennia germinans* (L.) L. (20) (1857)

Soft-leaf blackberry [Softleaf blackberry] - *Rubus mollior* Bailey (50) (present)

Soft-leaf cherry [Soft-leaved cherry] - *Prunus emarginata* (Dougl. ex Hook.) D. Dietr. var. *mollis* (Dougl. ex Hook.) Brewer (20) (1857)

Soft-leaf panic grass [Soft-leaved panic-grass] - *Dichanthelium malacophyllum* (Nash) Gould (119, 163) (1852-1938)

Soft-leaf panicum [Softleaf panicum, Soft-leaved panicum] - *Dichanthelium malacophyllum* (Nash) Gould (3, 5, 155) (1913-1977)

Soft-leaf passionflower [Softleaf passionflower] - *Passiflora mollissima* (Kunth) Bailey (138) (1923)

Soft-leaf rosette grass [Softleaf rosette grass] - *Dichanthelium malacophyllum* (Nash) Gould (50) (present)

Softleaf sedge - *Carex disperma* Dewey (5, 50) (1913–present)

Soft-leaf sunflower [Soft-leaved Sun-flower] - *Helianthus mollis* Lam. (187) (1818)

Soft-leaf willow [Soft-leaved willow] - *Salix sessilifolia* Nutt. (20) (1857)

Soft-shell hickory - *Carya illinoinensis* (Wangenh.) K. Koch (5, 156, 158) (1900-1923)

Soft-stem bulrush [Softstem bulrush] - *Schoenoplectus tabernaemontani* (K.C. Gmel.) Palla (3, 50, 155) (1942–present)

Softy - *Sida* L. (7) (1828)

Soja bean - *Glycine max* (L.) Merr. (68, 118) (1898–1913), *Glycine soja* Sieb. & Zucc. (106, 107) (1919–1930)

Sol me - *Maianthemum stellatum* (L.) Link (35) (1806)

Solatrum furiale - *Atropa bella-donna* L. (possibly) (59) (1450)

Soldier rose-mallow [Soldier rosemallow] - *Hibiscus laevis* All. (138) (1923)

Soldiers - *Hackelia virginiana* (L.) I. M. Johnston (5, 73, 156, 157, 158) (1892–1929) Eastern MA, *Lythrum salicaria* L. (156, 158) (1900–1923), *Plantago lanceolata* L. (77) (1898) Cambridge MA, *Rosa canina* L. (5) (1913), *Silene dioica* (L.) Clairville (156) (1923) no longer in use by 1923

Soldier's-buttons [Soldier's buttons, Soldiers buttons] - *Caltha palustris* L. (5, 156, 157, 158) (1900-1929)

Soldier's-cap [Soldier's cap] - *Aconitum napellus* L. (107, 156) (1919-1923), *Dicentra cucullaria* (L.) Bernh. (5, 156, 158) (1900-1923)

Soldier's-feather [Soldier's feather] - *Phleum pratense* L. (5) (1913)

Soldier's-herb [Soldiers' herb] - *Piper aduncum* L. (92) (1876)

Soldier's-plume [Soldier's plume] - *Platanthera psycodes* (L.) Lindl. (3, 5, 75, 156) (1894-1977)

Soldier's-woundwort [Soldier's woundwort] - *Achillea millefolium* L. (69, 156, 157, 158) (1900-1929)

Soldierweed [Soldier-weed] - *Amaranthus spinosus* L. (62) (1912) IN

Soledad pine - *Pinus torreyana* Parry ex Carr. (109) (1949)

Soleil - *Helianthus annuus* L. (37) (1919)

Solentine - *Impatiens capensis* Meerb. (5, 74, 156, 157) (1893-1929)

Solomon's-plume [Solomonplume, Solomon's plume, Solomon-plume] - *Maianthemum* G.H. Weber ex Wiggers (155) (1942), *Maianthemum racemosum* (L.) Link subsp. *racemosum* (156) (1923)

Solomon's-seal [Solomon's seal, Solomon seal, Solomons-seal, S'alomon's seal, Salomons seale] - *Convallaria* L. (167, 184, 190) (~1759-1814), *Maianthemum* G.H. Weber ex Wiggers (158) (1900), *Platanthera hookeri* (Torr. ex Gray) Lindl. (5) (1913), *Platanthera orbiculata* (Pursh) Lindl. (73, 75) (1892-1894) VT, *Polygonatum biflorum* (Walt.) Ell. (3, 48, 57, 102, 157) (1886-1977), *Polygonatum biflorum* (Walt.) Ell. var. *commutatum* (J.A. & J.H. Schultes) Morong (40, 57, 65, 85, 127) (1917-1933), *Polygonatum* Mill. (1, 50, 93, 109, 138, 155, 156, 158) (1900–present), *Polygonatum multiflorum* (L.) All. (107, 178, 179) (1526-1919), *Polygonatum pubescens* (Willd.) Pursh (46) (1649), *Streptopus lanceolatus* (Ait.) Reveal var. *roseus* (Michx.) Reveal (78) (1898) Western US, *Uvularia perfoliata* L. (46) (1879)

Solomon's-seal of Virginia [Salomons Seale of Virginia] - *Maianthemum racemosum* (L.) Link subsp. *racemosum* (181) (~1678)

Solutucha trava (Russian) - *Anthemis cotula* L. (186) (1814)

Sommer lottekins (Dutch) - *Leucojum vernum* L. (180) (1633)

Somūchtan (Chenook) - *Lupinus littoralis* Dougl. (33) (1827)

Son-before-the-father [Sonne before the Father] - *Colchicum autumnale* L. (180) (1633)

Sonnenblume (German) - *Helianthus annuus* L. (6) (1892)

Sonnenthau (German) - *Drosera rotundifolia* L. (158) (1900)

Sonoma manzanita - *Arctostaphylos densiflora* M.S. Baker (155) (1942)

Sonoma rose - *Rosa spithamea* S. Wats. var. *sonomensis* (Greene) Jepson (138) (1923)

Sonora abutilon - *Abutilon mollicomum* (Willd.) Sweet (155) (1942)

Sonora ironwood - *Olneya tesota* Gray (106) (1930)

Sonora water cactus - *Ferocactus emoryi* (Engelm.) Orcutt (138) (1923)

Sonoran Indian mallow - *Abutilon mollicomum* (Willd.) Sweet (50) (present)

Sonoran jumping cholla - *Opuntia fulgida* Engelm. (155) (1942)

Sonwa millet - *Echinochloa frumentacea* Link (45) (1896)

Šoŋgthiŋdse (Osage) - *Podophyllum peltatum* L. (121) (1918?-1970?)

Soolabich - *Vaccinium macrocarpon* Aiton (107) (1919)

Soon-fading spiderwort of Virginia [Soone-fading spiderwort of Virginia] - *Tradescantia virginiana* L. (180) (1633)

Soopoo lalia - *Shepherdia canadensis* Nutt. (5) (1913)

Soopwood - *Rhexia virginica* L. (177) (1762)

Soorstak - *Annona muricata* L. (177) (1762)

Sooty willow - *Salix discolor* Muhl. (19) (1840)

Sophora - *Sophora* L. (138, 155, 158) (1923-1942)

Sora (Lithuanian) - *Panicum miliaceum* L. (110) (1886)

Sorb tree - *Sorbus aucuparia* L. (possibly) (41) (1770)

Sorbaria - *Sorbaria* (Ser. ex DC.) A. Braun (82) (1930), *Sorbaria sorbifolia* (L.) A. Braun (82, 112) (1930-1937)

Sorbier (French) - *Sorbus* L. (8) (1785)

Sorbier d'Amérique (French) - *Sorbus americana* Marsh. (8, 20) (1785-1857)

Sorbis (French) - *Sorbus americana* Marsh. (6) (1892)

Sorb-leaf schizonotus [Sorb-leaved schizonotus] - *Sorbaria sorbifolia* (L.) A. Braun (5) (1913)

Sore-eye - *Verbesina encelioides* (Cav.) Benth. & Hook. f. ex Gray (106) (1930)

Sorgho - *Sorghum bicolor* (L.) Moench subsp. *bicolor* (66, 92, 109, 155) (1903-1949)

Sorgho (Italy) - *Sorghum bicolor* (L.) Moench (180) (1633)

Sorgho sucre - *Sorghum bicolor* (L.) Moench subsp. *bicolor* (66) (1903)

Sorghum - *Sorghum bicolor* (L.) Moench (50, 56, 67) (1890–present), *Sorghum bicolor* (L.) Moench subsp. *bicolor* (92, 107, 109, 117, 119, 138, 155, 158, 163, 178) (1526-1949), *Sorghum* Moench (50, 155, 158) (1900–present) from East Indian vernacular name

Sorghum sugar cane - *Sorghum bicolor* (L.) Moench subsp. *bicolor* (87) (1884)

Sorrel [Sorell, Sorrell] - *Oxyria digyna* (L.) Hill (46) (1610), *Rumex acetosa* L. (46, 49, 107, 179) (1526-1919), *Rumex acetosella* L. (12, 46, 106, 157) (1821-1930), *Rumex crispus* L. (41) (1770), *Rumex* L. (1, 2, 4, 93, 109, 138, 156, 190) (~1759-1986)

Sorrel dock - *Rumex acetosella* L. (93) (1936)

Sorrel tee [Sorel tee, Sorrel-tree] - *Lyonia mariana* (L.) D. Don (5, 92, 156) (1876-1923), *Oxydendrum arboreum* (L.) DC. (possibly) (7, 8, 18, 19, 20, 49, 52, 52, 156, 165, 177, 189) (1762-1923), *Oxydendrum* DC. (2) (1895)

Sorrel vine [Sorrelvine] - *Cissus trifoliata* (L.) L. (50) (present)

Sorrel wood - *Oxydendrum arboreum* (L.) DC. (possibly) (7) (1828)

Sotol - *Dasylirion texanum* Scheele (122, 124) (1937), *Dasylirion wheeleri* S. Wats. (possibly) (149, 151, 153) (1896-1913), *Dasylirion* Zucc. (106, 138) (1923-1930)

Souchet comestible (French) - *Cyperus esculentus* L. (158) (1900)

Soukie clover - *Trifolium pratense* L. (157, 158) (1900-1929)

Soulard's crab [Soulard crab] - *Malus* ×*soulardii* (Bailey) Britt. [*ioensis* × *pumila*] (137, 138) (1923–1931)

Soulard's crab apple [Soulard crab apple] - *Malus* ×*soulardii* (Bailey) Britt. [*ioensis* × *pumila*] (106) (1930)

Sour bush [Sourbush, Sour-bush] - *Callicarpa americana* L. (58, 92, 156, 158) (1869-1923)

Sour cherry - *Prunus cerasus* L. (1, 5, 50, 107, 109, 110, 137, 138, 156) (1913–present)

Sour dock - *Oxyria digyna* (L.) Hill (5, 156) (1913-1923), *Rumex acetosa* L. (1, 5, 107, 156) (1913-1932), *Rumex acetosella* L. (5, 93, 95, 156, 158) (1900-1936), *Rumex crispus* L. (5, 37, 62, 64, 69, 80, 92, 156, 157, 158) (1876-1929), *Rumex* L. (101) (1905), *Rumex obtusifolius* L. (77) (1898), *Rumex venosus* Pursh (28, 98) (1850-1926)

Sour French cherry [Sower French cherrie] - *Prunus cerasus* L. (178) (1526)

Sour gourd - *Adansonia digitata* L. (107) (1919)

Sour grass [Sourgrass] - *Digitaria insularis* (L.) Mez ex Ekman (92, 122, 163) (1852-1937), *Paspalum conjugatum* Berg. (163) (1852)

Sour greens - *Rumex venosus* Pursh (1) (1932)

Sour gum [Sour-gum] or Sour-gum tree [Sour gum tree] - *Nyssa aquatica* L. (5, 20, 19, 187) (1818-1913), *Nyssa* L. (2, 7, 10) (1818-1895), *Nyssa sylvatica* Marsh. (2, 5, 8, 10, 20, 92, 97, 106, 107, 109, 156, 182) (1791-1949)

Sour orange - *Citrus* ×*aurantium* L. [*maxima* × *reticulata*] (109) (1949)

Sour tree [Sour-tree] - *Oxydendrum arboreum* (L.) DC. (possibly) (5, 7, 92, 109) (1828-1949)

Sour trefoil - *Oxalis montana* Raf. (possibly) (5, 7, 92, 156) (1828-1923)

Sour tupelo - *Nyssa ogeche* Bartr. ex Marsh. (20) (1857)

Sour winter grape - *Vitis vulpina* L. (156) (1923)

Sourberry [Sour-berry, Sour berry] - *Berberis canadensis* P. Mill. (7) (1828), *Rhus integrifolia* (Nutt.) Benth. & Hook. f. ex Brewer & S. Wats. (109) (1949), *Vaccinium macrocarpon* Aiton (2, 7, 109) (1828–1949), *Vaccinium oxycoccos* L. (5, 92, 156) (1876–1923)

Sour-grape [Sour grape] - *Lomatium triternatum* (Pursh) Coult. & Rose (181) (~1678)

Sour-grass [Sourgrass, Sour grass] - *Juncus* L. (75) (1894) Neb, *Oxalis stricta* L. (76, 156) (1896-1923) IN, *Rumex acetosa* L. (5, 156) (1913-1923), *Rumex acetosella* L. (5, 75, 156, 157, 158) (1894-1929) Sulphur Grove OH, *Triglochin* L. (148) (1939) CO

Souring - *Malus coronaria* (L.) Mill. var. *coronaria* (92) (1876)

Sourleaf [Sour-leaf, Sour leaf] - *Oxydendrum arboreum* (L.) DC. (possibly) (7, 92) (1828–1876), *Rumex acetosella* L. (156) (1923)

Sour-leek [Sour leek, Sour leek] - *Rumex acetosella* L. (5, 156, 158) (1900-1923)

Soursop [Sour sop] - *Annona muricata* L. (92, 109, 110, 137) (1876-1949)

Sour-top - *Vaccinium myrtilloides* Michx. (156) (1923)

Sour-top blueberry - *Vaccinium myrtilloides* Michx. (106, 107) (1919-1930)

Sourweed [Sour weed] - *Rumex acetosella* L. (62) (1912)

Sourwood [Sour-wood, Sour wood] or Sourwood tree - *Firmiana simplex* (L.) W. Wight (106) (1930), *Lyonia lucida* (Lam.) K. Koch (7) (1828), *Oxydendrum arboreum* (L.) DC. (5, 7, 49, 50, 52, 53, 57, 92, 106, 109, 156) (1828–present), *Oxydendrum* DC. (2, 138) (1895-1923)

Sousan - *Pancratium maritimum* L. (46) (1879)

Sousourouscurou (Carib) - *Physalis peruviana* L. (107) (1919)

South American vanilla - *Vanilla mexicana* Mill. (138) (1923)

South Sea tea - *Ilex vomitoria* Aiton (5, 14, 92, 156) (1876-1923) no longer in use by 1923

Southern adder's-tongue [Southern adderstongue] - *Ophioglossum vulgatum* L. (50) (present)

Southern annual salt-marsh aster [Southern annual saltmarsh aster] - *Symphyotrichum divaricatum* (Nutt.) Nesom (50) (present)

Southern balsam fir - *Abies fraseri* (Pursh) Poir. (2, 109, 158) (1895-1949)

Southern basswood [Southern bass wood] - *Tilia americana* L. var. *caroliniana* (P. Mill.) Castigl. (5) (1913)

Southern bent - *Agrostis gigantea* Roth (66) (1903)

Southern big-tooth aspen [Southern bigtooth aspen] - *Populus grandidentata* Michx. (155) (1942)

Southern black haw [Southern black-haw, Southern blackhaw] - *Viburnum rufidulum* Raf. (3, 4, 65, 97, 8, 1156) (1923-1986)

Southern black huckleberry - *Vaccinium virgatum* Aiton (5, 97) (1913-1937)

Southern black-gum - *Nyssa biflora* Walt. (106) (1930)

Southern blue flag - *Iris virginica* L. (5) (1913)

Southern bog clubmoss - *Lycopodiella appressa* (Chapman) Cranfill (50) (present)

Southern breweria - *Stylisma humistrata* (Walt.) Chapman (5) (1913)

Southern buckthorn - *Sideroxylon lycioides* L. (2, 5, 106, 122, 156) (1895-1930)

Southern bush-honeysuckle - *Diervilla sessilifolia* Buckley (138) (1923)

Southern buttonbush - *Cephalanthus occidentalis* L. (155) (1942)

Southern canary grass [Southern canary-grass] - *Phalaris caroliniana* Walt. (5, 94, 163) (1852-1901)

Southern cane - *Arundinaria gigantea* (Walter) Muhl. (122, 138) (1923-1937)

Southern catalpa - *Catalpa bignonioides* Walt. (50) (present)

Southern cat-tail [Southern cattail] - *Typha domingensis* Pers. (50) (present)

Southern chess - *Bromus catharticus* Vahl (5, 85, 119) (1913-1938)

Southern coast violet - *Viola septemloba* Le Conte (5) (1913)

Southern cottonwood - *Populus deltoides* Bartr. ex Marsh. (138) (1923)

Southern crab apple - *Malus angustifolia* (Aiton) Michx. (106) (1930)

Southern crabgrass - *Digitaria ciliaris* (Retz.) Koel. (50) (present)

Southern curled mustard - *Brassica juncea* (L.) Czern. (109) (1949)

Southern cypress - *Taxodium distichum* (L.) L.C. Rich. (2, 122, 124) (1895-1937)

Southern deerberry - *Vaccinium stamineum* L. (155) (1942)

Southern dewberry [Southern dew berry - *Rubus flagellaris* Willd. (2) (1895), *Rubus trivialis* Michx. (4, 5, 49, 50, 97, 138, 155) (1898–present)

Southern dry strawberry - *Waldsteinia fragarioides* (Michx.) Tratt. subsp. *doniana* (Tratt.) Teppner (5) (1913)

Southern eragrostis - *Eragrostis pectinacea* (Michx.) Nees ex Steud. var. *pectinacea* (66) (1903)

Southern fescue grass [Southern fescue-grass - *Vulpia sciurea* (Nutt.) Henr. (5, 119, 163) (1852-1938)

Southern fox grape - *Vitis rotundifolia* Michx. (2, 5, 15, 97, 107, 156) (1895-1937)

Southern gentian - *Gentiana catesbaei* Walt. (7, 92) (1828-1876)

Southern glaucous sedge - *Carex glaucescens* Ell. (5) (1913)

Southern goldenbush - *Isocoma pluriflora* (Torr. & Gray) Greene (50) (present)

Southern gooseberry - *Vaccinium stamineum* L. (156) (1923)

Southern grass-lily - *Calydorea coelestina* (Bartr.) Goldblatt & Henrich (97) (1937)

Southern gray oak - *Quercus incana* Bartr. (20) (1857)

Southern hackberry - *Celtis tenuifolia* Nutt. (5, 97, 106) (1913-1937)

Southern haw - *Viburnum rufidulum* Raf. (5) (1913)

Southern hemlock - *Tsuga caroliniana* Engelm. (5) (1913)

Southern hogpeanut - *Amphicarpaea bracteata* (L.) Fern. (155) (1942)

Southern ironwood - *Cyrilla racemiflora* L. (5) (1913)

Southern jointweed - *Polygonella americana* (F & M) Small (5, 50, 155) (1913–present)

Southern lady fern [Southern lady-fern] - *Athyrium filix-femina* (L.) Roth var. *asplenoides* (Michx.) Farw. (4) (1986)

Southern leatherwood - *Cyrilla racemiflora* L. (5, 122, 156) (1913-1937)

Southern lily - *Lilium catesbaei* Walt. (19) (1840)

Southern linn - *Tilia americana* L. (5, 156) (1913-1923)

Southern lobelia - *Lobelia amoena* Michx. (5) (1913)

Southern loosestrife - *Lysimachia tonsa* (Wood) Wood ex Pax & R. Knuth (5) (1913)

Southern low blackberry - *Rubus trivialis* Michx. (2) (1895)

Southern magnolia - *Magnolia grandiflora* L. (138) (1923)

Southern maidenhair - *Adiantum capillus-veneris* L. (155) (1942)

Southern maidenhair fern - *Adiantum capillus-veneris* L. (138) (1923)

Southern marsh yellow-cress [Southern marsh yellowcress] - *Rorippa teres* (Michx.) R. Stuckey (50) (present)

Southern moss - *Tillandsia usneoides* (L.) L. (156) (1923)

Southern mountain cranberry - *Vaccinium erythrocarpum* Michx. (5, 156, 174) (1753-1923)

Southern mountain mint - *Pycnanthemum pycnanthemoides* (Leaven-

worth) Fern. var. *pycnanthemoides* (5) (1913)

Southern mountain pine - *Pinus pungens* Lamb. (5) (1913)

Southern naiad - *Najas guadalupensis* (Spreng.) Magnus (155) (1942)

Southern nut-grass [Southern nut grass] - *Cyperus rotundus* L. (122) (1937) TX

Southern over-cup oak - *Quercus lyrata* Walt. (2) (1895)

Southern pepperwort - *Lepidium austrinum* Small. (50) (present)

Southern pine - *Pinus palustris* Mill. (5) (1913)

Southern poplar - *Populus deltoides* Bartr. ex Marsh. subsp. *deltoides* (155) (1942)

Southern poverty grass [Southern poverty-grass] - *Sporobolus vaginiflorus* (Torr. ex Gray) Wood (5, 94, 111, 129) (1894-1915), *Sporobolus vaginiflorus* (Torr. ex Gray) Wood var. *vaginiflorus* (163) (1852)

Southern prickly-ash [Southern prickly ash] - *Aralia spinosa* L. (49, 58, 92) (1869–1898), *Zanthoxylum clava-herculis* L. (2, 5, 8, 49, 53, 57, 58, 92, 97, 156, 158) (1785–1923)

Southern prickly-elder [Southern prickly elder] - *Aralia spinosa* L. (92) (1876)

Southern ragweed - *Ambrosia bidentata* Michx. (4) (1986)

Southern red cedar [Southern redcedar] - *Juniperus barbadensis* var. *australis* (Endl.) ined. (138) (1923), *Juniperus virginiana* L. var. *silicicola* (Small) J. Silba (50) (present)

Southern red lily - *Lilium catesbaei* Walt. (2, 5) (1895-1913)

Southern reed - *Phalaris caroliniana* Walt. (45, 88) (1885-1896)

Southern reed canary grass - *Phalaris caroliniana* Walt. (87) (1884)

Southern reed grass [Southern reed-grass] - *Calamovilfa curtissii* (Vasey) Scribn. (94) (1901), *Phalaris caroliniana* Walt. (5) (1913)

Southern sandbur [Southern sand-bur] - *Cenchrus echinatus* L. (50) (present), *Cenchrus spinifex* Cav. (94) (1901)

Southern scabious - *Succisella inflexa* (Kluk) G. Beck (5) (1913)

Southern scorpion-grass - *Myosotis macrosperma* Engelm. (97) (1937) OK

Southern sea-beach grass - *Panicum amarum* Ell. var. *amarulum* (A.S. Hitchc. & Chase) P.G. Palmer (5) (1913)

Southern sedge - *Carex bushii* Mackenzie (5, 50) (1913–present)

Southern senega - *Polygala alba* Nutt. (55) (1911), *Polygala senega* L. (156) (1923)

Southern shagbark - *Carya carolinae-septentrionalis* (Ashe) Engl. & Graebn. (5) (1913)

Southern shagbark hickory - *Carya ovata* (Mill.) K. Koch (155) (1942)

Southern sheep laurel - *Kalmia carolina* Small. (5) (1913)

Southern shooting-star [Southern shootingstar] - *Dodecatheon pulchellum* (Raf.) Merr. subsp. *pulchellum* (138, 155) (1923-1942)

Southern showy aster - *Eurybia hemispherica* (Alexander) Nesom (50) (present)

Southern slender finger grass [Southern slender finger-grass] - *Digitaria villosa* (Walt.) Pers. (5, 99, 119, 163) (1852-1938)

Southern small skullcap - *Scutellaria parvula* Michx. var. *australis* Fassett (3) (1977)

Southern small white orchis - *Platanthera nivea* (Nutt.) Luer (5) (1913)

Southern smilax - *Smilax smallii* Morong (156) (1923)

Southern smooth aster - *Symphyotrichum laeve* (L.) A.& D. Löve var. *purpuratum* (Nees) Nesom (5) (1913)

Southern snakeroot [Southern snake-root] - *Asarum canadense* L. (5, 64, 156) (1907-1923)

Southern sneezeweed - *Helenium amarum* (Raf.) H. Rock var. *amarum* (106) (1930)

Southern soapberry - *Sapindus saponaria* L. (138) (1923)

Southern spear grass [Southern spear-grass] - *Eragrostis pectinacea* (Michx.) Nees ex Steud. var. *pectinacea* (5, 56, 94, 119, 129) (1894-1938), *Eragrostis pilosa* (L.) Beauv. (80) (1913), *Poa autumnalis* Muhl. ex Ell. (66) (1903), *Poa cuspidata* Nutt. (94) (1901)

Southern sugar maple - *Acer barbatum* Michx. (50, 124) (1937–present)

Southern swamp aster - *Eurybia paludosa* (Aiton) Nesom (5, 97, 122) (1913-1937)

Southern swamp crinum - *Crinum americanum* L. (109) (1949)

Southern swamp lily - *Crinum americanum* L. (109) (1949)

Southern thorn - *Crataegus viridis* L. (5, 97) (1913-1937)

Southern tickseed sunflower [Southern tickseed-sunflower] - *Bidens coronata* (L.) Britton (5) (1913)

Southern tupelo - *Nyssa biflora* Walt. (5) (1913)

Southern twayblade - *Listera australis* Lindl. (5, 50) (1913–present)

Southern viburnum - *Viburnum rafinesquianum* Schultes var. *affine* (Bush ex Schneid.) House (IT) (present)

Southern water nymph - *Najas guadalupensis* (Spreng.) Magnus (50) (present)

Southern water-grass - *Paspalidium geminatum* (Forssk.) Stapf (94) (1901)

Southern water-nymph [Southern water nymph, Southern water-nymph] - *Najas guadalupensis* (Spreng.) Magnus (50) (present)

Southern waxmyrtle - *Morella cerifera* (L.) Small (138) (1923)

Southern waxy sedge - *Carex glaucescens* Ell. (50) (present)

Southern white cedar - *Chamaecyparis thyoides* (L.) Britton, Sterns & Poggenb. (5) (1913)

Southern white wood - *Tilia americana* L. var. *caroliniana* (P. Mill.) Castigl. (5) (1913)

Southern wild crab - *Malus coronaria* (L.) Mill. (5) (1913)

Southern wild ginger - *Hexastylis virginica* (L.) Small (5, 156) (1913-1923)

Southern wild rice [Southern wildrice] - *Zizaniopsis miliacea* (Michx.) Doell & Aschers. (119, 122) (1913-1937)

Southern wild rye - *Elymus virginicus* L. var. *virginicus* (5) (1913)

Southern wood violet - *Viola hirsutula* Brainerd (5) (1913)

Southern wormwood - *Artemisia abrotanum* L. (46, 72) (1671-1907)

Southern yellow birch - *Betula alleghaniensis* Britt. (5) (1913)

Southern yellow honeysuckle - *Lonicera flava* Sims. (158) (1900)

Southern yellow pine - *Pinus palustris* Mill. (2, 20) (1857-1895)

Southern yellow-eyed grass - *Xyris jupicai* L.C. Rich. (5) (1913)

Southern yellowroot [Southern yellow root] - *Xanthorhiza simplicissima* Marsh. (49) (1898)

Southernwood [Southern-wood, Southern wood] - *Artemisia abrotanum* L. (3, 4, 5, 19, 41, 46, 50, 57, 92, 107, 109, 135, 138, 156, 158) (1671–present), *Artemisia filifolia* Torr. (158) (1900), *Artemisia* L. (10, 184) (1793-1818), *Artemisia tridentata* Nutt. (35) (1806)

Southrn red oak - *Quercus falcata* Michx. (138) (1923)

South-sea tea tree [South-sea tea-tree] - *Cassine* L. (8) (1785), *Ilex cassine* L. (8) (1785)

Southwest barrel cactus [Southwest barrelcactus] - *Ferocactus wislizeni* (Engelm.) Britt. & Rose (155) (1942)

Southwest bedstraw - *Galium virgatum* Nutt. (4) (1986)

Southwest smartweed - *Polygonum hydropiperoides* Michx. (3) (1977)

Southwestern bedstraw - *Galium virgatum* Nutt. (5, 50, 97, 122) (1913–present)

Southwestern bigtooth maple - *Acer saccharum* subsp. *grandidentatum* (Torr. & A.Gray) Desmarais (155) (1942)

Southwestern carrot - *Daucus pusillus* Michx. (3, 155) (1942-1977)

Southwestern cupgrasss - *Eriochloa acuminata* (J. Presl) Kunth var. *acuminata* (155) (1942)

Southwestern persicaria - *Polygonum densiflorum* Meisn. (5) (1913), *Polygonum hydropiperoides* Michx. (5, 122) (1913-1937)

Southwestern rabbitbrush [Southwest rabbitbrush] - *Chrysothamnus pulchellus* (Gray) Greene (50, 155) (1942–present)

Southwestern showy sedge - *Carex bella* Bailey (50) (present)

Southwestern waterwort - *Elatine rubella* Rydb. (50) (present)

Sow thistle [Sow-thistle, Sowthistle] - *Sonchus arvensis* L. (85) (1932), *Sonchus asper* (L.) Hill (80, 82, 95, 122, 145, 157) (1897-1937), *Sonchus* L. (1, 4, 10, 50, 93, 106, 155, 157, 158, 184) (1793–present), *Sonchus oleraceus* L. (46, 92, 93, 107, 157, 158) (1671-1936) accidentally introduced by 1671

Sowbane [Sow-bane] - *Chenopodium simplex* (Torr.) Raf. (156, 158) (1900-1923)

Sowbank - *Chenopodium ambrosioides* L. var. *ambrosioides* (7) (1828), *Chenopodium* L. (7, 92) (18281876)

Sowberry [Sow berry, Sow-berry] - *Vaccinium oxycoccos* L. (5, 92, 156, 158) (1876-1923) no longer in use by 1923

Sow-dindle - *Sonchus oleraceus* L. (157, 158) (1900-1929)

Sow-dingle - *Sonchus oleraceus* L. (157, 158) (1900-1929)

Sowdwort - *Salsola kali* L. (158) (1900)

Sowerbush - *Callicarpa americana* L. (7) (1828)

Sowfoot [Sow-foot, Sow foot] - *Tussilago farfara* L. (5, 156) (1913-1923)

Sow-grass [Sow grass] - *Carara coronopus* (L.) Medik. (5) (1913)

Sow's-grass [Sow's grass] - *Coronopus squamatus* (Forsk.) Aschers. (156) (1923)

Sow-teat blackberry - *Rubus allegheniensis* Porter (3) (1977)

Sowtit [Sow tit, Sow-tit] - *Fragaria vesca* L. (5, 76, 158) (1896-1913) Central VT, *Rubus flagellaris* Willd. (74) (1893) CT NH

Soy - *Glycine max* (L.) Merr. (110) (1886), *Glycine soja* Sieb. & Zucc. (106) (1930)

Soybean [Soy bean] - *Glycine max* (L.) Merr. (50, 68, 109, 118, 138, 158) (1898–present), *Glycine soja* Sieb. & Zucc. (106, 107) (1919-1930), *Glycine* Willd. (50, 158) (1900–present)

Spade-leaf violet - *Viola sagittata* Aiton (5, 73) (1892-1913) Franklin MA

Spangles - *Ceanothus americanus* L. (5) (1913)

Spangletop [Spangle top, Spangle-top] - *Scolochloa festucacea* (Willd.) Link (85, 93, 94) (1901-1936)

Spanish ash - *Syringa vulgaris* L. (156) (1923)

Spanish bayonet [Spanish-bayonet] - *Yucca aloifolia* L. (2, 109) (1895-1949), *Yucca baccata* Torr. (5, 103, 107, 158) (1871-1919), *Yucca filamentosa* L. (156) (1923), *Yucca glauca* Nutt. (37, 85, 156) (1830-1932), *Yucca harrimaniae* Trel. (50) (present), *Yucca* L. (1, 2, 93, 156) (1895-1936), *Yucca torreyi* Shafer (149, 153) (1904-1913) NM, *Yucca treculeana* Carr. (138) (1923)

Spanish bean - *Phaseolus coccineus* L. (92) (1876)

Spanish beard - *Tillandsia usneoides* (L.) L. (18) (1805)

Spanish bluebell - *Hyacinthoides hispanica* (Mill.) Rothm. (109) (1949)

Spanish broom - *Spartium junceum* L. (19, 92, 109, 156) (1526-1949)

Spanish buckeye - *Ungnadia speciosa* Endl. (109) (1949)

Spanish buttons - *Centaurea nigra* L. (156) (1923)

Spanish cane - *Arundo donax* L. (92) (1876)

Spanish cedar [Spanish-cedar] - *Cedrela odorata* L. (109) (1949)

Spanish cherry [Spanish cherrie] - *Prunus cerasus* L. (178) (1526)

Spanish chestnut - *Castanea sativa* Mill. (possibly) (92, 109, 138) (1876-1949)

Spanish clover - *Medicago sativa* L. (52, 157, 158) (1900-1929)

Spanish dagger [Spanish-dagger, Spanish daggers] - *Yucca aloifolia* L. (75, 92, 138) (1876-1923), *Yucca baccata* Torr. (5) (1913), *Yucca filamentosa* L. (156) (1923), *Yucca gloriosa* L. (109) (1949), *Yucca torreyi* Shafer (149, 153) (1904-1913) NM, *Yucca treculeana* Carr. (122, 124) (1937) TX

Spanish gold - *Grindelia papposa* Nesom & Suh (50) (present)

Spanish grape - *Vitis cinerea* (Engelm.) Millard var. *helleri* (Bailey) M.O. Moore (15) (1895)

Spanish heather - *Erica lusitanica* K. Rudolphi (109) (1949)

Spanish iris - *Iris xiphium* L. (109, 138) (1923-1949)

Spanish jasmine - *Jasminum officinale* L. (138) (1923)

Spanish juice - *Glycyrrhiza glabra* L. (92) (1876)

Spanish lettuce - *Claytonia* L. (1) (1932), *Claytonia perfoliata* Donn ex Willd. (5, 131) (1899-1913)

Spanish lily - *Dichelostemma capitatum* (Benth.) Wood subsp. *capitatum* (75) (1894) CA

Spanish lime [Spanish-lime] - *Melicoccus bijugatus* Jacq. (109) (1949)

Spanish medick - *Medicago sativa* L. (156) (1923)

Spanish moss [Spanish-moss] - *Tillandsia usneoides* (L.) L. (5, 7, 92, 109, 122) (1828-1949)

Spanish mulberry [Spanish-mulberry] - *Callicarpa americana* L. (156) (1923)

Spanish musk rose [Spanish muske rose] - *Rosa moschata* J. Herrm. (possibly) (178) (1526)

Spanish needle [Spanish-needles, Spanishneedles, Spanish needles] - *Bidens aristosa* (Michx.) Britton (82) (1930), *Bidens bipinnata* L. (3, 4, 5, 41, 49, 50, 57, 58, 61, 62, 92, 93, 97, 122, 124, 145, 155, 156, 157, 158, 187) (1770–present), *Bidens connata* Muhl. ex Willd. (48, 61) (1870-1882), *Bidens discoidea* (Torr. & Gray) Britton (80) (1913), *Bidens frondosa* L. (48, 61, 72, 114) (1870-1907), *Bidens* L. (7, 10, 12, 73, 106, 190) (~1759-1930), *Bidens tripartita* L. (177) (1762), *Hesperostipa spartea* (Trin.) Barkworth (5, 11, 35, 37) (1830-1888)

Spanish oak [Spanish Oake] - *Quercus* ×*benderi* Baenitz [*coccinea* × *rubra*] (5, 156) (1913–1923), *Quercus falcata* Michx. (2, 5, 10, 12, 20, 19, 33, 82, 93, 97, 109, 156, 164, 181, 187) (~1678–1949), *Quercus palustris* Muench. (82, 106) (1930), *Quercus robur* L. (possibly) (41) (1770), *Quercus rubra* L. (78, 156, 158) (1898–1923) Southwest MO, *Quercus texana* Buckl. (124) (1937) TX

Spanish oyster plant [Spanish oysterplant, Spanish oyster-plant] - *Scolymus hispanicus* L. (107, 109, 138) (1919–1949)

Spanish pepper - *Capsicum annuum* L. (92) (1876)

Spanish plum [Spanish-plum] - *Spondias purpurea* L. (107, 109) (1919-1949)

Spanish potato [Spanish potatoes] - *Ipomoea batatas* (L.) Lam. (178) (1526)

Spanish salsify - *Scolymus hispanicus* L. (110) (1886)

Spanish scabious - *Scabiosa stellata* L. (178) (1526)

Spanish squill - *Hyacinthoides hispanica* (Mill.) Rothm. (138) (1923)

Spanish stonecrop - *Sedum hispanicum* L. (138, 155) (1931-1942)

Spanish tea - *Chenopodium ambrosioides* L. (69, 156, 157, 158) (1900-1929)

Spanish toothpikes - *Ammi visnaga* (L.) Lam. (178) (1526)

Spanish trefoil - *Medicago sativa* L. (5, 45, 118, 157, 158) (1896-1929)

Spanish violets - *Lupinus luteus* L. (178) (1526)

Spanish wild cherry - *Prunus ilicifolia* (Nutt. ex Hook. & Arn.) D. Dietr. (74) (1893)

Spanish-clover deervetch [Spanishclover deervetch] - *Lotus unifoliolatus* (Hook.) Benth. var. *unifoliolatus* (155) (1942)

Sparagus - *Asparagus officinalis* L. (46, 158) (1671-1900) cultivated by English colonists by 1671

Sparganio (Italian) - *Sparganium* L. (180) (1633)

Spargel (German) - *Asparagus officinalis* L. (158) (1900)

Spargoule (French) - *Spergula arvensis* L. (110) (1886)

Spark (German) - *Spergula arvensis* L. (110) (1886)

Sparkleberry [Sparkle-berry] - *Vaccinium arboreum* Marsh. (3, 4, 5, 106, 156, 158) (1900-1986), *Vaccinium* L. (1) (1932)

Sparrow-egg lady's-slipper [Sparrowegg lady's slipper] - *Cypripedium passerinum* Richards (50) (present)

Sparrow-grass [Sparrow grass] - *Asparagus officinalis* L. (5, 7, 92, 138, 158) (1828–1923)

Sparrow's-dung - *Salsola kali* L. (158) (1900)

Sparrow's-tongue [Sparrow tongue, Sparrow-tongue] - *Polygonum aviculare* L. (5, 156, 158, 179, 180) (1526-1923)

Sparse-flower sedge [Sparseflower sedge, Sparse-flowered sedge] - *Carex tenuiflora* Wahl. (5, 50) (1913–present)

Spart - *Juncus articulatus* L. (5, 156) (1913-1923)

Spart grass - *Spartina maritima* (M.A. Curtis) Fern. (5) (1913)

Spatlum (Flathead) - *Lewisia rediviva* Pursh (101, 107) (1905-1919)

Spatterdock [Spatter dock, Spatter-dock] - *Nuphar lutea* (L.) Sm. subsp. *advena* (Aiton) Kartesz & Gandhi (46, 92, 106, 107, 138, 156, 157, 158) (1879-1929), *Nuphar* Sm. (1, 4, 13, 15, 109, 138) (1849-1986)

Spatterdock cow-lily [Spatterdock cowlily] - *Nuphar lutea* (L.) Sm.

subsp. *advena* (Aiton) Kartesz & Gandhi (155) (1942)

Spattling - *Silene vulgaris* (Moench) Garcke (156) (1923) no longer in use by 1923

Spattling poppy [Spatling poppy, Spatling Poppie] - *Silene* L. (178) (1526), *Silene vulgaris* (Moench) Garcke (5, 92) (1876-1913)

Spatulate lophotocarpus - *Sagittaria calycina* Engelm. var. *spongiosa* Engelm. (5) (1913)

Spatulate-leaf fogfruit [Spatulate-leaved fog-fruit] - *Aloysia macrostachya* (Torr.) Moldenke (122) (1937), *Phyla nodiflora* (L.) Greene (5, 97) (1913-1937)

Spatulate-leaf heliotrope [Spatulate-leaved heliotrope] - *Heliotropium curassavicum* L. var. *obovatum* DC. (5) (1913)

Spatulate-leaf pondweed [Spatulate-leaved pondweed] - *Potamogeton* ×*spathuliformis* (J. W. Robbins) Morong (5, 72) (1907–1913)

Spatulate-leaf sundew [Spatulate-leaved sundew] - *Drosera intermedia* Hayne (5) (1913)

Spatulum - *Lewisia rediviva* Pursh (103) (1870) MT, from Indian name

Spear grass [Spear-grass] - *Aristida purpurea* Nutt. (144) (1899), *Hesperostipa comata* (Trin. & Rupr.) Barkworth subsp. *comata* (108, 146) (1878-1939), *Hesperostipa spartea* (Trin.) Barkworth (85) (1932), *Nassella leucotricha* (Trin. & Rupr.) Pohl (163) (1852), *Poa* L. (45) (1896), *Poa nemoralis* L. (111) (1915), *Poa pratensis* L. (19, 45, 68, 87, 88) (1840-1913)

Spear thistle [Spear-thistle] - *Cirsium vulgare* (Savi) Ten. (5, 85, 156, 158) (1900-1932)

Spearleaf - *Erigeron lonchophyllus* Hook. (155) (1942)

Spear-leaf fat-hen saltbush [Spearleaf fat-hen saltbush] - *Atriplex prostrata* Bouchér ex DC. (155) (1942)

Spear-leaf goldenrod [Spear-leaved Golden-rod] - *Euthamia graminifolia* (L.) Nutt. (187) (1818)

Spear-leaf hempweed [Spear-leafed hemp-weed] - *Eupatorium pilosum* Walter (187) (1818)

Spear-leaf stonecrop [Spearleaf stonecrop] - *Sedum lanceolatum* Torr. (50) (present)

Spear-leaf violet [Spear-leaved violet] - *Viola hastata* Michx. (5) (1913)

Spear-leaf yellow violet [Spear-leaved yellow violet] - *Viola hastata* Michx. (156) (1923)

Spear-like blue-eyed grass - *Sisyrinchium albidum* Raf. (5) (1913)

Spearmint [Spear mint, Spear-mint, Spere Mynt] - *Mentha arvensis* L. (5, 85) (1913-1932), *Mentha* L. (1) (1932), *Mentha spicata* L. (1, 4, 5, 19, 49, 50, 53, 55, 57, 59, 60, 61, 62, 63, 72, 92, 97, 106, 107, 109, 120, 124, 138, 155, 156, 158) (1568–present)

Spear-scale [Spearscale] - *Atriplex patula* L. (3, 4) (1977-1986)

Spearwort - *Ranunculus flammula* L. (4, 19, 92) (1840-1986)

Spearwort buttercup - *Ranunculus flammula* L. (155) (1942)

Speckled alder - *Alnus incana* (L.) Moench (1, 82, 92, 105, 113, 138, 155, 156) (1876–1932), *Alnus incana* (L.) Moench subsp. *rugosa* (DuRoi) Clausen (3, 4, 46, 50, 109, 156, 158) (1879–present), *Clethra alnifolia* L. (5) (1913)

Speckled jewels - *Impatiens capensis* Meerb. (19, 49, 92, 156, 158) (1840-1923)

Speckled jewelweed [Speckled jewel-weed] - *Impatiens capensis* Meerb. (158) (1900)

Speckled touch-me-not - *Impatiens capensis* Meerb. (53) (1922)

Speckled willow - *Salix humilis* Marsh. var. *tristis* (Aiton) Griggs (19) (1840)

Speckle-pod loco [Specklepod loco] - *Astragalus lentiginosus* Dougl. ex Hook. (155) (1942)

Spectacle plant - *Wislizenia refracta* Engelm. (124) (1937) TX

Spectacle-pod [Spectacle pod] - *Dimorphocarpa candicans* (Raf.) Rollins (3, 4, 97) (1937-1986), *Wislizenia refracta* Engelm. (122) (1937) TX

Speedwell - *Helianthemum canadense* (L.) Michx. (46) (1671), *Veronica anagallis-aquatica* L. (85) (1932), *Veronica* L. (1, 4, 10, 26, 50,

63, 77, 82, 93, 106, 109, 138, 155, 156, 158, 184) (1793–present), *Veronica officinalis* L. (19, 49, 57, 58, 92) (1840-1917), *Veronica peregrina* L. (80, 82, 107) (1919-1930)

Speedwell chickweed - *Stellaria borealis* Bigelow (46) (1671)

Speer-hawk - *Hieracium* L. (158) (1900)

Spelt - *Triticum spelta* L. (56, 66, 67, 92, 107, 109) (1890-1949)

Spelt corne - *Triticum spelta* L. (180) (1633)

Spelt grass - *Triticum spelta* L. (92) (1876)

Spelt wheat - *Triticum spelta* L. (66) (1903)

Spelte (low Dutch) - *Triticum spelta* L. (180) (1633)

Speltz - *Triticum spelta* L. (93, 109) (1936-1949)

Speltz (German) - *Triticum spelta* L. (180) (1633)

Sperage [Spearage] - *Asparagus officinalis* L. (5, 157, 158, 178, 179) (1526-1929)

Spereworde - *Ranunculus flammula* L. (179) (1526)

Spergola (Italian) - *Spergula arvensis* L. (110) (1886)

Spergula - *Spergula arvensis* L. (110) (1886)

Spergule (French) - *Spergula arvensis* L. (158) (1900)

Sperpentaria de Virginia (Spanish) - *Aristolochia serpentaria* L. (158) (1900)

Sperry's onion - *Allium perdulce* S.V. Fraser var. *sperryi* Ownbey (50) (present)

Sphagnum - *Sphagnum* L. (40, 50) (1928–present), *Sphagnum palustre* L. (107) (1919)

Spherical black fungus - *Daldinia concentrica* (Bolton) Ces. & De Not., (128) (1933)

Spherical blazing star - *Liatris spheroidea* Michx. (50) (present)

Spicate gilia - *Ipomopsis spicata* (Nutt.) V. Grant subsp. *spicata* (5) (1913)

Spice - *Spiraea salicifolia* L. (156) (1923) no longer in use by 1923

Spice birch - *Betula lenta* L. (5, 7, 92, 156) (1828-1923)

Spice brush [Spice-brush] - *Umbellularia californica* (Hook. & Arn.) Nutt. (54) (1905)

Spice bush [Spice-bush, Spicebush] - *Aralia racemosa* L. (5, 75) (1894–1913) Hartford Conn, *Calycanthus floridus* L. (5, 76, 156) (1896–1923) Middlesborough MA, *Lindera benzoin* Blume. (3, 12, 19, 49, 57, 58, 65, 92, 104, 107, 109) (1820–1977), *Lindera* Thunb. (1, 2, 4, 50, 138, 155, 156) (1895–present), *Umbellularia californica* (Hook. & Arn.) Nutt. (14, 107, 154) (1857–1882)

Spice currant - *Ribes aureum* Pursh (156) (1923)

Spice flower [Spice-flower] - *Rhododendron periclymenoides* (Michx.) Shinners (156) (1923)

Spice hardhack [Spice hard-hack] - *Spiraea alba* Du Roi var. *latifolia* (Aiton) Dippel (5) (1913), *Spiraea* L. (73) (1892) Bonny River NB

Spice tree [Spice-tree] - *Umbellularia californica* (Hook. & Arn.) Nutt. (54) (1905)

Spice wintergreen - *Gaultheria procumbens* L. (156) (1923)

Spiceberry [Spice-berry, Spice berry] - *Aralia racemosa* L. (64, 156, 157, 158) (1900-1929), *Gaultheria hispidula* (L.) Muhl. ex Bigelow (77) (1898), *Gaultheria procumbens* L. (5, 6, 7, 92, 156) (1828-1923), *Lindera benzoin* Blume. (6, 186, 187) (1814-1892)

Spiceroot [Spice root] - *Dalibarda repens* L. (19) (1840), *Sieversia radiata* (Michx.) G. Don (7) (1828)

Spicewood [Spice-wood, Spice wood] - *Cornus racemosa* Lam. (106) (1930) Arkansas, *Laurus* L. (10) (1818), *Lindera benzoin* Blume. (5, 7, 8, 14, 17, 34, 35, 49, 58, 92, 97, 138, 156) (1785-1937), *Litsea aestivalis* (L.) Fern. (41, 184) (1770-1793)

Spicy birch - *Betula lenta* L. (19) (1840)

Spicy fleabane - *Pluchea camphorata* (L.) DC. (5, 97, 156) (1913-1937)

Spicy wintergreen - *Gaultheria procumbens* L. (5, 19, 92) (1840-1913)

Spider antelope-horn [Spider antelopehorn] - *Asclepias asperula* (Dcne.) Woods. subsp. *capricornu* (Woods.) Woods. (155) (1942)

Spider bean - *Desmanthus illinoensis* (Michx.) MacM. ex B.L. Robins. & Fern. (37, 157) (1919-1929)

Spider bent grass [Spider bent-grass - *Agrostis elliottiana* Schultes (5, 94, 119) (1901-1938)

Spider brake - *Pteris multifida* Poir. (50, 138) (1923–present)

Spider flower [Spiderflower [Spider-flower - *Cleome hassleriana* Chod. (5, 72, 74, 82, 97, 138, 156) (1893-1937), *Tradescantia virginiana* L. (92) (1876)

Spider grass - *Aristida ternipes* Cav. var. *gentilis* (Henr.) Allred (122) (1937) TX

Spider lily [Spider-lily] - *Hymenocallis* Salisb. (109, 122, 138) (1923-1949)

Spider milkweed - *Asclepias asperula* (Dcne.) Woods. (50) (present), *Asclepias* L. (1) (1932), *Asclepias viridis* Walt. (4, 93) (1936-1986)

Spider orchid [Spider-orchid] - *Brassia* R. Br. ex Ait. f. (138) (1923)

Spider plant - *Cleome hassleriana* Chod. (106) (1930)

Spiderflower [Spider flower, Spider-flower] - *Cleome* L. (4, 50, 82, 155, 158) (1900–present), *Cleome serrulata* Pursh (156) (1923), *Cleome spinosa* Jacq. (86) (1878), *Tradescantia* L. (7) (1828)

Spider-lily [Spider lily] - *Tradescantia virginiana* L. (5, 75, 156) (1894-1923)

Spiderling [Spiderlings] - *Boerhavia* L. (4, 50, 155) (1942–present)

Spiderwort - *Tradescantia bracteata* Small ex Britt. (3, 85, 98, 127) (1926–1977), *Tradescantia gigantea* Rose (117) (1908), *Tradescantia* L. (1, 50, 93, 109, 122, 124, 138, 155, 156, 158, 167) (1814–present) wrongly thought to be cure for spider bites or because juice is stringy and viscid like spider webs, *Tradescantia occidentalis* (Brit.) Smyth (85) (1932), *Tradescantia virginiana* L. (5, 19, 37, 72, 86, 92, 97, 156) (1840–1937)

Spigelia - *Spigelia marilandica* (L.) L. (53, 54, 55, 59, 64) (1905-1922)

Spigélia de Maryland (French) - *Spigelia marilandica* (L.) L. (6) (1892)

Spigelia du Maryland (French) - *Spigelia marilandica* (L.) L. (8) (1785)

Spignet - *Aralia racemosa* L. (5, 49, 53, 58, 64, 73, 75, 92, 156, 157, 158) (1869-1929)

Spignut - *Carya glabra* (Mill.) Sweet var. *glabra* (78) (1898) IN

Spike - *Liatris spicata* (L.) Willd. var. *spicata* (157) (1929)

Spike dropseed - *Sporobolus contractus* Hitchc. (50) (present)

Spike fescue [Spikefescue] - *Festuca* L. (155) (1942), *Leucopoa* Griseb. (50) (present), *Leucopoa kingii* (S. Wats.) W.A. Weber (50, 140, 155) (1942–present)

Spike gayfeather - *Liatris spicata* (L.) Willd. (138) (1923)

Spike gilia - *Ipomopsis spicata* (Nutt.) V. Grant subsp. *spicata* (3, 155) (1942-1977)

Spike grass [Spike-grass, Spikegrass] - *Desmazeria* Dumort. (138) (1923), *Distichlis* Raf. (1) (1932), *Distichlis spicata* (L.) Greene (possibly) (66, 90, 92) (1876-1903), *Leptochloa fusca* (L.) Kunth subsp. *fascicularis* (Lam.) N. Snow (5, 87, 129) (1885-1894), *Uniola* L. (1, 66) (1903-1932), *Uniola paniculata* L. (5, 19, 66, 184) (1793-1912)

Spike hawthorn - *Crataegus succulenta* Schrad. ex Link (137, 138, 155) (1923-1942)

Spike lavender - *Lavandula angustifolia* Mill. (92, 138) (1876-1923)

Spike pappus grass - *Enneapogon desvauxii* Desv. ex Beauv. (122) (1937)

Spike primrose [Spikeprimrose] - *Epilobium* L. (155) (1942)

Spike sedge - *Carex nardina* Fried. (50) (present)

Spike speedwell - *Veronica spicata* L. (138) (1923)

Spike trisetum - *Trisetum spicatum* (L.) Richter (3, 50, 140, 155) (1942–present)

Spike water-milfoil [Spike watermilfoil, Spiked water milfoil, Spiked water-milfoil] - *Myriophyllum spicatum* L. (5, 50, 72, 95, 120, 131, 156, 158) (1899–present)

Spike woodrush - *Luzula spicata* (L.) DC. (139) (1944)

Spiked alder - *Clethra alnifolia* L. (19, 92, 156) (1840-1923)

Spiked aloe - *Agave americana* L. (92) (1876)

Spiked centaury - *Centaurium spicatum* (L.) Fernald. (5) (1913)

Spiked crested coralroot - *Hexalectris spicata* (Walt.) Barnh (50) (present)

Spiked indigo-weed [Spiked indigo weed] - *Baptisia australis* (L.) R. Br. ex Aiton f. (19) (1840)

Spiked ipomopsis - *Ipomopsis spicata* (Nutt.) V. Grant (50) (present)

Spiked lobelia - *Lobelia spicata* Lam. (156) (1923), *Lobelia spicata* Lam. var. *leptostachys* (A. DC.) Mackenzie & Bush (5, 72, 97) (1907-1937)

Spiked loosestrife - *Lythrum salicaria* L. (5, 82, 106, 109, 156, 158) (1913-1949)

Spiked maple - *Acer spicatum* Lam. (156) (1923)

Spiked millet - *Pennisetum glaucum* (L.) R. Br. (107) (1919)

Spiked muhlenbergia - *Muhlenbergia glomerata* (Willd.) Trin. (87, 88, 90) (1884-1885)

Spiked muhlenberg's grass - *Muhlenbergia racemosa* (Michx.) Britton, Sterns & Poggenb. (129) (1894)

Spiked muhly - *Muhlenbergia glomerata* (Willd.) Trin. (50) (present)

Spiked oat grass - *Danthonia spicata* (L.) Beauv. ex Roemer & J.A. Schultes (42) (1814)

Spiked quaking grass - *Distichlis spicata* (L.) Greene (92) (1876)

Spiked Solomon's seal [Spiked Solomon seal] - *Maianthemum racemosum* (L.) Link subsp. *racemosum* (19, 50) (1840–present)

Spiked triodia - *Tridens strictus* (Nutt.) Nash (94) (1901)

Spiked water milfoil [Spiked water-milfoil] - *Myriophyllum spicatum* L. (5, 72, 95, 120, 131, 156, 158) (1899–1938)

Spiked wild oat grass - *Danthonia spicata* (L.) Beauv. ex Roemer & J.A. Schultes (87, 90) (1884-1885)

Spiked willow herb [Spiked willow-herb, Spiked willow herbe] - *Chamerion angustifolium* (L.) Holub subsp. *angustifolium* (156) (1923), *Chamerion angustifolium* (L.) Holub. (5, 157, 158) (1900-1929), *Lythrum salicaria* L. (156, 158) (1900-1923)

Spiked woodrush [Spiked wood rush] - *Luzula spicata* (L.) DC. (5, 50) (1913–present)

Spike-grass [Spike grass, Spiked-grass, Spiked grass] - *Triglochin maritimum* L. (5, 92, 156) (1876-1923)

Spike-like poverty grass - *Aristida spiciformis* Ell. (94) (1901)

Spike-moss [Spikemoss] - *Selaginella* Beauv. (4, 50) (1986–present)

Spikenard - *Aralia* L. (1, 4, 50) (1932–present), *Aralia racemosa* L. (3, 4, 6, 19, 38, 40, 46, 47, 53, 58, 63, 79, 85, 92, 105, 157, 158, 187) (1818-1986) pronounced 'spicknard' in NH, *Maianthemum stellatum* (L.) Link (3) (1977)

Spikenard tree [Spikenard-tree] - *Aralia spinosa* L. (5, 7, 65, 92, 156) (1828-1931)

Spike-oat [Spike oat, Spikeoat] - *Helictotrichon hookeri* (Scribn.) Henr. (3, 50, 155) (1942–present)

Spike-rush [Spike rush, Spikerush] - *Eleocharis palustris* (L.) Roemer & J.A. Schultes (3) (1977), *Eleocharis* R. Br. (1, 50, 93, 121, 152, 156) (1912–present)

Spike-sedge [Spikesedge] - *Eleocharis* R. Br. (139) (1944)

Spikeweed - *Centromadia pungens* (Hook. & Arn.) Greene (106) (1930)

Spiknard - *Aralia nudicaulis* L. (7) (1828)

Spilanthes - *Acmella oppositifolia* (Lam.) R.K. Jansen (5, 97) (1913-1937), *Spilanthes* Jacq. (5, 97) (1913-1937)

Spinach - *Spinacia* L. (109, 138) (1923-1949), *Spinacia oleracea* L. (19, 92, 107, 110, 184) (1793-1919)

Spinach beet - *Beta vulgaris* L. (107) (1919)

Spinach dock [Spinach-dock] - *Rumex patientia* L. (109) (1949)

Spinage - *Spinacia* L. (7) (1828), *Spinacia oleracea* L. (109) (1949)

Spindelbaum (German) - *Euonymus atropurpurea* Jacq. (6) (1892)

Spindle bush [Spindlebush] - *Euonymus* L. (7) (1828)

Spindle tree [Spindletree, Spindle-tree] - *Euonymus americanus* L. (92) (1876), *Euonymus atropurpurea* Jacq. (2, 5, 6, 19, 49, 53, 58, 135, 155, 156) (1840-1942), *Euonymus europaea* L. (5, 156, 178) (1526-1923), *Euonymus* L. (8, 10, 13, 15, 50, 82, 109) (1785–present)

Spindle-root bluebells [Spindleroot bluebells] - *Mertensia oblongifolia* (Nutt.) G. Don (155) (1942)

Spineless hornwort - *Ceratophyllum echinatum* Gray (50) (present)

Spingel - *Foeniculum vulgare* Mill. (5, 156, 158) (1900-1923)

Spink - *Cardamine pratensis* L. (5) (1913), *Dianthus deltoides* L. (5, 156) (1913-1923)

Spinose lip fern [Spinose lip-fern] - *Cheilanthes horridula* Maxon (97) (1937)

Spinulose shield fern [Spinulose shield-fern] - *Dryopteris carthusiana* (Vill.) H.P. Fuchs (5, 72) (1907-1913)

Spinulose wood fern [Spinulose wood-fern] - *Dryopteris carthusiana* (Vill.) H.P. Fuchs (4, 50, 109) (1949–present)

Spiny amaranth - *Amaranthus spinosus* L. (5, 21, 50, 62, 70, 93, 97, 145, 155, 156) (1893–present)

Spiny amberboa - *Cyanopsis muricata* (L.) Dostál (138) (1923)

Spiny aster - *Chloracantha spinosa* (Benth.) Nesom (150) (1894)

Spiny bur - *Acanthospermum australe* (Loefl.) Kuntze (5) (1913)

Spiny burweed [Spiny bur-weed] - *Xanthium spinosum* L. (5, 158) (1900-1913)

Spiny careless-weed [Spiny careless weed] - *Amaranthus spinosus* L. (62) (1912) IN

Spiny chlorocantha - *Chloracantha spinosa* (Benth.) Nesom (50) (present)

Spiny clotbur [Spiny clot-bur] - *Xanthium spinosum* L. (5, 49, 53, 57, 80, 97, 156) (1898-1937)

Spiny clotweed - *Xanthium spinosum* L. (5, 158) (1900-1913)

Spiny cocklebur - *Xanthium spinosum* L. (3, 4, 50, 62, 70, 155, 158) (1895–present)

Spiny gooseberry - *Ribes oxyacanthoides* L. subsp. *setosum* (Lindl.) Sinnott (130) (1895)

Spiny milkvetch - *Astragalus kentrophyta* Gray (50) (present)

Spiny naiad - *Najas marina* L. (50) (present)

Spiny naias - *Najas marina* L. (155) (1942)

Spiny phlox - *Phlox hoodii* Richards. (50) (present)

Spiny pigweed - *Amaranthus spinosus* L. (3, 4) (1977-1986)

Spiny plumeless thistle - *Carduus acanthoides* L. (50) (present)

Spiny saltbush - *Atriplex confertifolia* (Torr. & Frem.) S. Wats. (3, 4) (1977-1986)

Spiny sow-thistle [Spiny sow thistle, Spiny sowthistle] - *Sonchus asper* (L.) Hill (3, 5, 50, 62, 72, 82, 85, 93, 131) (1899–present)

Spiny-fruit crowfoot [Spiny-fruited crowfoot] - *Ranunculus muricatus* L. (5) (1913)

Spiny-leaf sow-thistle [Spiny-leaved sow-thistle] - *Sonchus asper* (L.) Hill (156) (1923)

Spiny-spore quillwort - *Isoetes tenella* Léman (50) (present)

Spiny-star [Spiny star, Spinystar] - *Escobaria vivipara* (Nutt.) Buxbaum (50) (present)

Spiny-stars coryphantha [Spinystars coryphantha] - *Escobaria vivipara* (Nutt.) Buxbaum var. *neomexicana* (Engelm.) Buxbaum (155) (1942)

Spiny-tooth gumweed [Spinytooth gumweed] - *Grindelia lanceolata* Nutt. (3, 4) (1977-1986)

Spiraea [Spirea] - *Filipendula ulmaria* (L.) Maxim. subsp. *ulmaria* (92) (1876), *Spiraea* L. (8, 50, 109, 112, 138) (1785–present), *Spiraea salicifolia* L. (156) (1923)

Spiraea à feuilles d'obier (French) - *Physocarpus opulifolius* (L.) Maxim. var. *opulifolius* (8) (1785)

Spiraea tomenteux (French) - *Spiraea tomentosa* L. (8) (1785)

Spiraea tomenteux à fleurs blanches (French) - *Spiraea tomentosa* L. (8) (1785)

Spiral ditch-grass [Spiral ditchgrass] - *Ruppia cirrhosa* (Petag.) Grande (50) (present)

Spiral neottia - *Spiranthes torta* (Thunb.) Garay & H.R. Sweet (187) (1818)

Spiral orchid - *Spiranthes* Rich. (75) (1894)

Spiral pondweed - *Potamogeton spirillus* Tuck. (1, 50, 72, 85, 93, 97, 120) (1907–present)

Spiral wild celery [Spiral wildcelery] - *Vallisneria americana* Michx. (155) (1942)

Spiral-awn beard grass [Spiral-awned beard-grass] - *Saccharum brevibarbe* (Michx.) Pers. var. *contortum* (Ell.) R. Webster (5, 119) (1913-1938)

Spiral-awn plume grass [Spiral-awned plume-grass] - *Saccharum alopecuroidum* (L.) Nutt. (94) (1901)

Spiral-pine [Spiral pine] - *Lycopodium obscurum* L. (5, 158) (1900-1913)

Spires - *Phalaris arundinacea* L. (5) (1913), *Phragmites australis* (Cav.) Trin. ex Steud. (5) (1913)

Spirit-weed [Spirit weed] - *Lachnanthes caroliana* (Lam.) Dandy (5, 6, 49, 92, 156) (1876-1923)

Spitzer Wegetritt (German) - *Plantago lanceolata* L. (158) (1900)

Spitzklette (German) - *Xanthium strumarium* L. (158) (1900)

Splatter-dock - *Nuphar lutea* (L.) Sm. subsp. *advena* (Aiton) Kartesz & Gandhi (156, 187) (1818-1923), *Nymphaea* L. (93) (1936)

Spleen amaranth - *Amaranthus hybridus* L. (5, 93, 97, 122, 156) (1913-1937), *Amaranthus hypochondriacus* L. (19, 92) (1840-1876)

Spleen fern [Spleenfern] - *Asplenium* L. (7) (1828)

Spleenwort [Spleen-wort, Spleenewort] - *Asplenium* L. (1, 4, 10, 50, 109, 138, 155, 158, 167) (1814–present), *Asplenium scolopendrium* L. (92) (1876), *Athyrium filix-femina* (L.) Roth (157) (1929), *Comptonia peregrina* (L.) Coult. (58) (1869), *Comptonia peregrina* (L.) Coult. (5, 7, 92, 156) (1828-1923)

Spleenwort fern - *Asplenium scolopendrium* L. (92) (1876), *Comptonia peregrina* (L.) Coult. (92) (1876)

Spleenwort shield fern [Spleen-wort shield-fern] - *Athyrium filix-femina* (L.) Roth var. *asplenoides* (Michx.) Farw. (187) (1818)

Spleenwort-leaf gale [Spleenwort-leaved gale] - *Comptonia peregrina* (L.) Coult. (8) (1785)

Splendid catchfly - *Silene regia* Sims. (156) (1923)

Splinter-weed [Splinter weed] - *Antennaria plantaginifolia* (L.) Richards (75) (1894) Peoria IL, children's name from appearance of heads

Split-beard bluestem [Splitbeard blue-stem] - *Andropogon ternarius* Michx. (50) (present)

Split-leaf painted-cup [Splitleaf paintedcup] - *Castilleja sulphurea* Rydb. (155) (1942)

Split-lip hemp-nettle [Splitlip hempnettle] - *Galeopsis bifida* Boenn. (50) (present)

Split-rock [Split rock] - *Heuchera americana* L. (156, 158) (1900-1923), *Heuchera villosa* Michx. (possibly) (7, 92) (1828-1876)

Spoet'lum (Sailish or Flat-head) - *Lewisia rediviva* Pursh (25) (1834)

Spondias - *Spondias mombin* L. (174) (1753)

Sponge plant [Spongeplant] - *Limnobium* Rich. (50) (present)

Sponge tree - *Acacia farnesiana* (L.) Willd. (107, 158) (1900-1919)

Spongy lophotocarpus - *Sagittaria calycina* Engelm. var. *spongiosa* Engelm. (5) (1913)

Spoolwood [Spool wood, Spool-wood] - *Betula papyrifera* Marsh (5, 157, 158) (1900-1929), *Betula pubescens* Ehrh. (156) (1923)

Spoon tree - *Kalmia latifolia* L. (41) (1770)

Spoonhunt [Spoon hunt] - *Kalmia latifolia* L. (5, 73, 92) (1876-1913) Mason NH

Spoon-hutch [Spoon hutch] - *Rhododendron maximum* L. (5, 71, 156) (1898-1923) NH, no longer in use by 1923

Spoon-leaf purple everlasting [Spoonleaf purple everlasting] - *Gamochaeta purpurea* (L.) Cabrera (50) (present)

Spoon-leaf yucca [Spoonleaf yucca] - *Yucca filamentosa* L. (138, 155) (1923-1942)

Spoonwood [Spoon wood [Spoon-wood] - *Kalmia latifolia* L. (5, 6, 7, 20, 49, 57, 71, 92, 106, 156) (1828-1930), *Tilia americana* L. (5, 156) (1913-1923), *Tilia americana* L. var. *americana* (187) (1818), *Tilia* L. (7) (1828), *Vaccinium arboreum* Marsh. (97) (1937)

Spoonwood ivy [Spoonwood-ivy] - *Kalmia angustifolia* L. (5, 73, 156) (1892-1923) CT

Spotted agrimony - *Agrimonia parviflora* Aiton (19, 187) (1818-1840)

Spotted alder - *Hamamelis virginiana* L. (5, 6, 49, 92, 156) (1876-1923)

Spotted beaver-poison [Spotted beaver poison] - *Cicuta maculata* L. (133) (1903) ND

Spotted beebalm - *Monarda pectinata* Nutt. (3, 4) (1977-1986), *Monarda punctata* L. (50, 138) (1923–present), *Monarda punctata* L. subsp. *punctata* var. *occidentalis* (Epling) Palmer & Steyermark (50) (present)

Spotted blazing star - *Liatris punctata* Hook. var. *punctata* (85) (1932)

Spotted boneset - *Eupatorium maculatum* L. (5, 7, 64, 92, 157, 158) (1828-1929)

Spotted bur clover - *Medicago arabica* (L.) Huds. (109, 122, 124) (1937-1949)

Spotted calla - *Zantedeschia albomaculata* (Hook.) Baill. (109, 138) (1923-1949)

Spotted cardus - *Cnicus benedictus* L. (92) (1876)

Spotted cat's-ear [Spotted cat's ear] - *Hypochaeris radicata* L. (107) (1919)

Spotted centaurea - *Centaurea maculosa* Lam. (155) (1942)

Spotted comfrey - *Pulmonaria officinalis* L. (92) (1876)

Spotted coralroot - *Corallorrhiza maculata* (Raf.) Raf. (3) (1977)

Spotted cowbane [Spotted cow-bane] - *Cicuta maculata* L. (2, 6, 62, 71, 92, 114, 133, 156) (1892-1923), *Conium maculatum* L. (69, 156, 158) (1900-1923)

Spotted cranebill [Spotted crane's bill, Spotted cranesbill, Spotted crane's-bill] - *Geranium maculatum* L. (5, 6, 7, 64, 86, 92, 156, 157, 158) (1828-1929)

Spotted dead-nettle [Spotted deadnettle, Spotted dead nettle] - *Lamium maculatum* L. (5, 138) (1913-1923)

Spotted euphorbia - *Chamaesyce maculata* (L.) Small (155) (1942)

Spotted evening-primrose [Spotted evening primrose] - *Oenothera canescens* Torr. & Frem. (4, 50) (1986–present)

Spotted eyebright [Spotted eyebright, Spotted eye-bright] - *Chamaesyce maculata* (L.) Small (5, 156, 158) (1900-1923), *Eupatorium maculatum* L. (157, 158) (1900-1929)

Spotted fritillary - *Fritillaria atropurpurea* Nutt. (50) (present)

Spotted geranium - *Geranium maculatum* L. (6, 49, 50, 53, 64, 74, 92, 155, 156, 158) (1892–present)

Spotted hemlock - *Cicuta maculata* L. (5, 71, 92) (1876-1913), *Conium maculatum* L. (49, 53, 60) (1897-1922)

Spotted ixia - *Ixia maculata* L. (138) (1923)

Spotted jewelweed - *Impatiens capensis* Meerb. (105, 157, 158) (1900-1932)

Spotted joe-pye weed [Spotted joepyeweed, Spotted Joe-pye-weed] - *Eupatorium maculatum* L. (5, 50, 64, 72, 85, 93, 95, 97, 122, 131, 155, 156, 157, 158) (1899–present), *Eupatorium maculatum* L. var. *bruneri* (Gray) Breitung (3, 38, 50) (1977–present), *Eupatorium maculatum* L. var. *maculatum* (82) (1930)

Spotted knapweed - *Centaurea maculosa* Lam. (3, 4, 5, 50) (1913–present)

Spotted knotweed [Spotted knot weed, Spotted knot-weed] - *Persicaria maculosa* Gray (5, 92, 156, 158) (1876-1923), *Polygonum persicaria* L. (92) (1876)

Spotted lady's-thumb [Spotted ladysthumb] - *Polygonum persicaria* L. (50, 155) (1942–present)

Spotted lamium - *Lamium maculatum* L. (106) (1930)

Spotted lichnidia - *Phlox maculata* L. (19) (1840)

Spotted loosestrife - *Lysimachia punctata* L. (5, 138, 155, 156) (1913-1942)

Spotted lungwort - *Pulmonaria officinalis* L. (92) (1876)

Spotted medic [Spotted medick] - *Medicago arabica* (L.) Huds. (5, 45, 85, 97, 156) (1896-1937)

Spotted nemophila - *Nemophila maculata* Benth. ex Lindl. (138) (1923)

Spotted oak - *Quercus nigra* L. (5) (1913), *Quercus velutina* Lam. (5, 156, 157, 158) (1900-1929)

Spotted parsley - *Cicuta maculata* L. (71, 133, 158) (1898-1903) ND, *Conium maculatum* L. (5, 7, 69, 71, 92, 156, 158) (1828-1923)

Spotted peperomia - *Peperomia maculosa* (L.) Hook. (138) (1923)

Spotted pipsiseway - *Chimaphila maculata* (L.) Pursh (7) (1828)

Spotted pipsissiwa [Spotted-pipsissiwa, Spotted pipsissewa] - *Chimaphila maculata* (L.) Pursh (5, 92) (1876-1913)

Spotted plantain - *Goodyera pubescens* (Willd.) R. Br. ex Ait. f. (5, 92, 156) (1876-1923)

Spotted poison-parsley [Spotted poison parsley] - *Conium maculatum* L. (6) (1892)

Spotted pondweed - *Potamogeton pulcher* Tuckerm. (5, 50) (1913–present)

Spotted primrose - *Oenothera canescens* Torr. & Frem. (5) (1913), *Oenothera* L. (1, 93, 158) (1900-1936)

Spotted pursely - *Chamaesyce hypericifolia* (L.) Millsp. (7) (1828)

Spotted purslane - *Chamaesyce maculata* (L.) Small (158) (1900)

Spotted pursley - *Chamaesyce maculata* (L.) Small (158) (1900)

Spotted pusley - *Chamaesyce maculata* (L.) Small (5, 92, 156) (1898-1923)

Spotted pyrola - *Chimaphila maculata* (L.) Pursh (8) (1785)

Spotted sage - *Salvia officinalis* L. (178) (1526)

Spotted sandmat - *Chamaesyce maculata* (L.) Small (50) (present)

Spotted saxifrage - *Saxifraga* L. (1) (1932)

Spotted smartweed - *Polygonum persicaria* L. (62) (1912)

Spotted snapweed [Spotted snap-weed] - *Impatiens capensis* Meerb. (86, 138, 155) (1878-1942)

Spotted spurge - *Chamaesyce maculata* (L.) Small (3, 4, 5, 62, 92, 97, 122, 156, 158) (1876-1986), *Chamaesyce nutans* (Lag.) Small (possibly) (80, 85, 187) (1817-1932)

Spotted St. John's-wort [Spotted St. John's wort, Spotted St. John-swort] - *Hypericum maculatum* Walter (2, 72) (1895-1907), *Hypericum punctatum* Lam. (3, 4, 5, 50, 97, 155, 156) (1913–present)

Spotted thistle - *Cnicus benedictus* L. (69) (1904)

Spotted touch-me-not - *Impatiens capensis* Meerb. (2, 3, 4, 5, 15, 49, 72, 82, 86, 93, 95, 97, 131, 156, 157, 158) (1878-1986)

Spotted water-hemlock [Spotted waterhemlock, Spotted water hemlock] - *Cicuta maculata* L. (50, 138, 155) (1923–present)

Spotted wintergreen - *Chimaphila maculata* (L.) Pursh (5, 19, 92, 156) (1840-1923)

Spotted-leaf buttercup - *Ranunculus repens* L. (5, 156, 158) (1900-1923)

Spotted-leaf cranebill [Spotted-leaved crane's bill] - *Geranium maculatum* L. (86) (1878)

Spotted-sheath panicum [Spotted-sheathed panicum] - *Dichanthelium dichotomum* (L.) Gould var. *dichotomum* (5) (1913)

Spotted-stalk lychnidea [Spotted-stalked lychnidea] - *Phlox maculata* L. (187) (1818)

Spotted-stem phlox [Spotted-stemmed phlox] - *Phlox maculata* L. (187) (1818)

Spourge - *Euphorbia* L. (179) (1526)

Sprangle [Sprangles] - *Ceanothus americanus* L. (156, 157, 158) (1900-1929), *Leptochloa dubia* (H.B.K.) Nees (152) (1912) NM

Sprangle-top [Sprangletop, Sprangle top] - *Leptochloa* Beauv. (50, 155) (1942–present), *Leptochloa dubia* (H.B.K.) Nees (163) (1852), *Scolochloa festucacea* (Willd.) Link (3, 50, 111) (1915–present)

Sprat barley - *Hordeum vulgare* L. (66, 107) (1903-1919)

Sprawling fleabane - *Erigeron flagellaris* Gray (155) (1942)

Sprawling pawpaw - *Asimina longifolia* Kral (155) (1942)

Spread goldenrod [Spread golden-rod] - *Solidago patula* Muhl. ex Willd. (19) (1840)

Spreading airplant - *Tillandsia utriculata* L. (50) (present)

Spreading alkaliweed - *Cressa truxillensis* Kunth (50) (present)

Spreading amaranth - *Amaranthus caudatus* L. (165) (1768)

Spreading anemone - *Pulsatilla patens* (L.) Mill.subsp. *multifida* (Pritz.) Zamels (138) (1923)

Spreading aranche - *Atriplex patula* L. (72) (1907)

Spreading aster - *Symphyotrichum patens* (Aiton) G.L. Nesom var. *patens* (86, 187) (1818-1878)

Spreading bladderpod - *Lesquerella gracilis* (Hook.) S. Wats. (50) (present), *Lesquerella gracilis* (Hook.) S. Wats. subsp. *nuttallii* (T.& G.) Rollins & Shaw (3, 4) (1977-1986)

Spreading brome grass [Spreading brome-grass] - *Bromus japonicus* Thunb. ex Murr. (5, 56, 163) (1852-1913)

Spreading buckwheat - *Eriogonum effusum* Nutt. (50) (present)

Spreading bulrush - *Scirpus divaricatus* Ell. (5, 50) (1913–present)

Spreading chervil - *Chaerophyllum procumbens* (L.) Crantz (5, 50, 155, 156) (1913–present), *Chaerophyllum procumbens* (L.) Crantz var. *procumbens* (50, 72, 97) (1907–present)

Spreading cotoneaster - *Cotoneaster divaricatus* Rehd. & Wilson (138) (1923)

Spreading dogbane [Spreading dog-bane, Spreading dog's bane, Spreading dogsbane] - *Apocynum androsaemifolium* L. (3, 4, 5, 6, 50, 62, 72, 80, 82, 93, 106, 122, 127, 131, 138, 148, 155, 156, 157, 158) (1892–present)

Spreading eryngo - *Eryngium diffusum* Torr. (50) (present)

Spreading erysimum - *Erysimum repandum* L. (155) (1942)

Spreading fimbristylis - *Fimbristylis annua* (All.) R. & S. (66) (1903)

Spreading fleabane - *Conyza ramosissima* Cronq. (3, 4) (1977-1986), *Erigeron divergens* Torr. & Gray (5, 50, 93, 97, 122, 155) (1913–present)

Spreading four-o'clock - *Mirabilis oxybaphoides* (Gray) Gray (4) (1986)

Spreading globeflower [Spreading globe-flower] - *Trollius laxus* Salisb. (156) (1923)

Spreading goldenrod [Spreading golden-rod] - *Solidago patula* Muhl. ex Willd. (5) (1913)

Spreading groundsmoke - *Gayophytum diffusum* Torr. & Gray subsp. *parviflorum* Lewis & Szweykowski (50) (present)

Spreading hedge-parsley [Spreading hedgeparsley] - *Torilis arvensis* (Huds.) Link (50) (present)

Spreading love grass [Spreading lovegrass] - *Eragrostis pectinacea* (Michx.) Nees ex Steud. var. *pectinacea* (155) (1942)

Spreading meadow grass - *Puccinellia distans* (Jacq.) Parl. (5) (1913)

Spreading moonpod - *Selinocarpus diffusus* Gray (4, 50) (1986–present)

Spreading muhlenbergia - *Muhlenbergia schreberi* J.F. Gmel. (187) (1818)

Spreading nailwort - *Paronychia depressa* (Torr. & Gray) Nutt. ex A. Nels. (50) (present)

Spreading nightshade - *Solanum triflorum* Nutt. (71, 145, 157) (1897-1929)

Spreading orache - *Atriplex subspicata* (Nutt.) Rydb. (19, 21, 62) (1840-1912)

Spreading panicum - *Panicum dichotomiflorum* Michx. (72) (1907)

Spreading pasqueflower - *Pulsatilla patens* (L.) Mill.subsp. *multifida* (Pritz.) Zamels (155) (1942)

Spreading phlox - *Phlox andicola* E. Nels. (98) (1926), *Phlox diffusa* Benth. (50, 155) (1942–present)

Spreading pigweed - *Amaranthus blitoides* S. Wats. (156) (1923)

Spreading pogonia - *Cleistes divaricata* (L.) Ames (5) (1913)

Spreading pygmy-leaf [Spreading pygmyleaf] - *Loeflingia squarrosa* Nutt. (50) (present)

Spreading red cedar - *Juniperus horizontalis* Moench (85) (1932)

Spreading salt-sage - *Atriplex argentea* Nutt. subsp. *expansa* (S. Wats.) Hall & Clements (141) (1899) WY

Spreading sandmat - *Chamaesyce humistrata* (Engelm.) Small (50) (present)

Spreading sandwort - *Honckenya peploides* (L.) Ehrh. subsp. *diffusa* (Hornem.) Hultén (2) (1895)

Spreading sedge - *Carex laxiculmis* Schwein. (5, 50, 72) (1893–present)

Spreading shield fern - *Dryopteris campyloptera* (Kunze) Clarkson (5) (1913), *Dryopteris expansa* (K. Presl) Fraser-Jenkins & Jermy (5) (1913)

Spreading snowberry - *Symphoricarpos mollis* Nutt. (138) (1923)

Spreading spear grass [Spreading spear-grass] - *Puccinellia distans* (Jacq.) Parl. (94) (1901)

Spreading spermolepis - *Spermolepis inermis* (Nutt. ex DC.) Mathias & Constance (3, 5, 97) (1913-1977)

Spreading spurge - *Chamaesyce humistrata* (Engelm.) Small (3, 4) (1977-1986)

Spreading sweetroot - *Osmorhiza berteroi* DC. (155) (1942)

Spreading triple-awn grass [Spreading triple-awned grass] - *Aristida divaricata* H. & B. (5) (1913)

Spreading verbena - *Verbena bracteata* Lag. & Rodr. (145) (1897)

Spreading wallflower - *Erysimum repandum* L. (50) (present)

Spreading wheatgrass - *Elymus scribneri* (Vasey) M.E. Jones (140) (1944)

Spreading wild buckwheat - *Eriogonum effusum* Nutt. (4) (1986)

Spreading witch grass [Spreading witch-grass] - *Dichanthelium dichotomum* (L.) Gould var. *dichotomum* (99) (1923), *Panicum dichotomiflorum* Michx. (5, 119, 163) (1852-1938)

Spreading wood fern [Spreading woodfern] - *Dryopteris expansa* (K. Presl) Fraser-Jenkins & Jermy (50) (present)

Spreading yellow-cress [Spreading yellow cress] - *Rorippa sinuata* (Nutt.) A. S. Hitchc. (3, 4, 5, 50, 72, 97, 131) (1899–present)

Spreading-branch goldenrod [Spreading-branched golden-rod] - *Solidago patula* Muhl. ex Willd. (187) (1818)

Spreading-cone pine [Spreading-coned pine] - *Pinus radiata* D. Don (5, 10, 20, 19) (1818-1857)

Spreading-pod rockcress [Spreadingpod rockcress] - *Arabis ×divaricarpa* A. Nels. (50) (present)

Spreckled alder - *Alnus incana* (L.) Moench (possibly) (5) (1913)

Sprengel's sedge [Sprengel sedge] - *Carex sprengelii* Dewey ex Spreng. (50, 139) (1944–present)

Sprenger's asparagus [Sprenger asparagus] - *Asparagus densiflorus* (Kunth) Jessop (138, 155) (1923-1942)

Spring adonis - *Adonis vernalis* L. (2, 109, 138, 155, 165) (1768-1949)

Spring agaricus - *Agaricus bitorquis* (Quél.) Sacc. (170) (1995)

Spring amanita - *Amanita verna* (Bull.) Lam. (155) (1942)

Spring anemone - *Anemone berlandieri* Pritz. (124) (1937) TX

Spring avens - *Geum vernum* (Raf.) Torr. & Gray (2, 5, 50, 97) (1895–present)

Spring barley - *Hordeum vulgare* L. (158) (1900) variety

Spring blue-eyed Mary [Spring blue eyed Mary] - *Collinsia verna* Nutt. (50) (present)

Spring clotbur - *Xanthium spinosum* L. (158) (1900)

Spring cockle - *Vaccaria hispanica* (Mill.) Rauschert (157) (1929)

Spring coralroot - *Corallorrhiza wisteriana* Conrad (50) (present)

Spring cowslip [Spring cowslips] - *Caltha palustris* L. (5, 157, 158) (1900-1929)

Spring cress - *Cardamine bulbosa* (Schreber. ex Muhl.) B.S.P. (3, 4, 72, 92, 156) (1876-1986), *Cardamine douglassii* Britt. (156) (1923), *Cardamine* L. (156) (1923)

Spring crocus - *Crocus angustifolia* Weston (92) (1876)

Spring everlasting - *Antennaria plantaginifolia* (L.) Richards (5, 156, 158) (1900-1923)

Spring forget-me-not - *Myosotis verna* Nutt. (50) (present)

Spring grass [Spring-grass] - *Anthoxanthum* L. (92, 184) (1793-1876), *Anthoxanthum odoratum* L. (5) (1913)

Spring iris - *Iris verna* L. (5, 86, 156) (1878-1923)

Spring lady's-tresses [Spring ladies' tresses, Spring ladies'-tresses] - *Spiranthes vernalis* Engelm. & Gray (50) (present)

Spring lily [Spring-lily] - *Erythronium albidum* Nutt. (5, 156, 157, 158) (1900-1929), *Erythronium mesochoreum* Knerr (37) (1830), *Leucocrinum montanum* Nutt. ex Gray (101) (1905) MT

Spring marigols - *Tetraneuris herbacea* Greene (156) (1923)

Spring mouse-ear - *Cerastium semidecandrum* L. (5, 156) (1913-1923)

Spring onion - *Allium fistulosum* L. (109, 110) (1886-1949)

Spring orchis - *Galearis spectabilis* (L.) Raf. (156, 158) (1900-1923)

Spring pheasant's-eye [Spring pheasant's eye] - *Adonis vernalis* L. (50) (present)

Spring plant [Spring-plant] - *Vallisneria americana* Michx. (158) (1900) Australia

Spring rock selaginella - *Selaginella rupestris* (L.) Spring (72) (1907)

Spring saxifrage - *Saxifraga virginiensis* Michx. (possibly) (156) (1923)

Spring saxifrage - *Saxifraga virginiensis* Michx. var. *virginiensis* (5) (1913)

Spring scorpion-grass [Spring scorpion grass] - *Myosotis verna* Nutt. (5, 72, 97, 156) (1907-1937)

Spring snowflake - *Leucojum vernum* L. (138) (1923)

Spring star-flower - *Tristagma uniflorum* (Lindl.) Traub (109) (1949)

Spring vetch - *Vicia sativa* L. (3, 5, 68, 82, 109, 156, 158) (1900-1977)

Spring Virginia lady's-traces [Spring Virginia ladies traces] - *Corallorrhiza wisteriana* Conrad (181) (~1678)

Spring wheat - *Triticum aestivum* L. (66) (1903)

Spring whitlow-grass [Spring whitlow grass] - *Draba verna* L. (42) (1814)

Spring wintergreen - *Gaultheria procumbens* L. (5, 156) (1913-1923)

Spring-beauty [Spring beauty, Springbeauty] - *Anemone lancifolia* Pursh (possibly) (76) (1896) Oxford Co. ME, *Claytonia* L. (1, 2, 4, 13, 15, 50, 82, 93, 109, 155, 156) (1895–present), *Claytonia lanceolata* Pall. ex Pursh (101) (1905) MT, *Claytonia virginica* L. (5, 19, 65, 72, 86, 92, 97, 106, 107, 158) (1840-1937), *Hepatica nobilis* Schreb. (74, 156) (1893-1923) NY, *Hepatica nobilis* Schreb. var. *acuta* (Pursh) Steyermark (5, 76) (1896-1913) Brodhead WI, *Hepatica nobilis* Schreb. var. *obtusa* (Pursh) Steyermark (5) (1913)

Springbloom [Spring-bloom, Spring bloom] - *Rhododendron* L. (7) (1828), *Rhododendron viscosum* (L.) Torr. (92, 156) (1876-1923)

Spring-gourd - *Echinopepon* Naud. (167) (1814)

Springlein (German) - *Linum usitatissimum* L. (110) (1886)

Spring-of-Jerusalem [Spring of Jerusalem] - *Lycopus virginicus* L. (77) (1898) S. Berwick ME

Spring-orange [Spring orange] - *Styrax americanus* Lam. (5, 92, 156) (1876-1923), *Styrax* L. (7) (1828)

Spring-parsley [Springparsley] - *Cymopterus* Raf. (50) (present)

Springwort [Spring wort] - *Euphorbia lathyris* L. (5, 71, 1923) (1898-1923)

Sprouting crabgrass [Sprouting crab grass, Sprouting crab-grass] - *Panicum dichotomiflorum* Michx. (5, 56, 80, 87, 88, 94, 119) (1884-1938)

Sproutleaf [Sprout leaf] - *Kalanchoe pinnata* (Lam.) Pers. (19) (1840)

Spruce - *Picea* A. Dietr. (4, 50, 109, 138, 155, 158) (1900–present), *Picea abies* (L.) H. Karst. (92, 106) (1876-1930), *Picea rubens* Sarg. (40) (1928)

Spruce fir - *Abies alba* Mill. (92) (1876), *Picea abies* (L.) H. Karst. (158) (1900), *Picea rubens* Sarg. (19) (1840)

Spruce gum tree [Spruce gum-tree] - *Picea mariana* (Mill.) Britton, Sterns & Poggenb. (5, 92) (1876-1913)

Spruce pine - *Picea mariana* (Mill.) Britton, Sterns & Poggenb. (5, 75) (1894-1913) WV, *Pinus echinata* Mill. (5, 20) (1857-1913), *Pinus strobus* L. (5) (1913), *Pinus virginiana* Mill. (5) (1913), *Tsuga canadensis* (L.) Carr. (5) (1913)

Spruce-top [Spruce tops] - *Bouteloua repens* (Kunth) Scribn. & Merr. (94) (1901), *Picea abies* (L.) H. Karst. (92) (1876)

Spunck - *Polyporus* P. Micheli ex Adans. (46) (1879)

Spunk - *Boletus fomentarius* L. (92) (1876), *Fomitopsis officinalis* (Batsch) Bondartsev & Singer (52) (1919), *Phellinus igniarius* (L.) Quél. (92) (1876)

Spur - *Claviceps purpurea* (Fr.) Tul. (49) (1898)

Spur pepper - *Capsicum annuum* L. var. *annuum* (107) (1919)

Spurge - *Chamaesyce glyptosperma* (Engelm.) Small (85, 157) (1929-1932), *Chamaesyce hypericifolia* (L.) Millsp. (19) (1840), *Chamaesyce maculata* (L.) Small (125) (1930), *Chamaesyce nutans* (Lag.) Small (80, 125) (1913-1930), *Chamaesyce* S.F. Gray (1, 93) (1932-1936), *Chamaesyce serpens* (Kunth) Small (85) (1932), *Chamae-*

syce stictospora (Engelm.) Small (85) (1932), *Euphorbia cyparissias* L. (148) (1939), *Euphorbia hexagona* Nutt. ex Spreng. (85) (1932), *Euphorbia ipecacuanhae* L. (92) (1876), *Euphorbia* L. (1, 2, 4, 10, 50, 82, 93, 109, 138, 156, 158, 167, 184) (1793–present), *Euphorbia marginata* Pursh (106, 125) (1930)

Spurge caper - *Euphorbia lathyris* L. (7, 19, 92) (1828-1876)

Spurge flax - *Daphne mezereum* L. (5, 92) (1876-1913)

Spurge ipecac - *Euphorbia ipecacuanhae* L. (5, 92, 156) (1898-1923)

Spurge laurel - *Daphne laureola* L. (92) (1876), *Daphne mezereum* L. (5, 156) (1913-1923)

Spurge nettle - *Cnidoscolus stimulosus* (Michx.) Engelm. & Gray (5, 97, 156) (1913-1937), *Cnidoscolus urens* (L.) Arthur (107) (1919), *Jatropha* L. (158) (1900)

Spurge-laurel [Spurge-lawrel] - *Daphne laureola* L. (109) (1949), *Kalmia angustifolia* L. (46) (1671)

Spurge-olive [Spurge olive] - *Daphne mezereum* L. (5, 92, 156) (1876-1923)

Spurge-time - *Chamaesyce polygonifolia* (L.) Small (46) (1671)

Spurgewort - *Iris foetidissima* L. (180) (1633)

Spurious aster - *Symphyotrichum novae-angliae* (L.) G.L.Nesom (187) (1818)

Spurious star wort - *Symphyotrichum novae-angliae* (L.) G.L.Nesom (42) (1814)

Spurred butterfly - *Centrosema virginianum* (L.) Benth. (5) (1913)

Spurred butterfly-pea [Spurred butterfly pea] - *Centrosema* (DC.) Benth. (2) (1895), *Centrosema virginianum* (L.) Benth. (97, 156) (1937)

Spurred gentian - *Halenia deflexa* (Sm.) Griseb. (1, 3, 4, 131, 156) (1899-1986)

Spurred rye - *Claviceps purpurea* (Fr.) Tul. (possibly) (52, 54, 92) (1876-1919)

Spurrey - *Sagina nodosa* (L.) Fenzl (156) (1923), *Spergula* L. (10, 156) (1818-1923)

Spurrey sandwort - *Spergularia* (Pers.) J.& K. Presl (13) (1849), *Spergularia rubra* (L.) J.& K. Presl (49) (1898)

Spurry [Spurrey] - *Spergula arvensis* L. (1, 5, 92, 109, 118, 131, 138, 156, 158) (1876-1949), *Spergula* L. (10, 15, 138, 155, 156, 158) (1818-1942)

Spur-stem - *Nymphoides cordata* (Ell.) Fern. (19) (1840)

Spurt-grass [Spurt grass] - *Schoenoplectus maritimus* (L.) Lye (92) (1876), *Schoenoplectus robustus* (Pursh) M.T. Strong (5) (1913), *Schoenoplectus tabernaemontani* (K.C. Gmel.) Palla (156, 158) (1900-1923)

Spurwort [Spur-wort] - *Sherardia arvensis* L. (5, 156) (1913-1923)

Spynache - *Spinacia* L. (179) (1526)

Square barley - *Hordeum vulgare* L. (166, 58) (1900-1903)

Square-head sedge [Square-headed sedge] - *Carex squarrosa* L. (66) (1903)

Squarenut [Square nut] - *Carya alba* (L.) Nutt. ex Ell. (107) (1919)

Squarestalk [Square-stalk, Square stalk] - *Monarda didyma* L. (7) (1828), *Scrophularia marilandica* L. (92) (1876), *Scrophularia nodosa* L. (6, 58) (1869-1892)

Square-stem [Square stem, Squarestem] - *Prunella vulgaris* L. (156) (1923), *Silphium perfoliatum* L. (37) (1919)

Square-stem monkey-flower [Square-stemmed monkey-flower] - *Mimulus ringens* L. (5, 93, 97) (1913-1937)

Square-stem phlox [Squarestem phlox] - *Phlox hoodii* Richards. subsp. *muscoides* (Nutt.) Wherry (155) (1942)

Square-stem rose-gentian [Squarestem rosegentian] - *Sabatia angularis* (L.) Pursh (155) (1942)

Square-stem sabbatia [Square-stemmed sabbatia] - *Sabatia angularis* (L.) Pursh (5, 97, 156, 158) (1900–1937)

Square-stem spike-rush [Squarestem spikerush] - *Eleocharis quadrangulata* (Michx.) Roemer & J.A. Schultes (50) (present)

Squarrose actinomeris - *Verbesina coreopsis* Michx. (86) (1878)

Squarrose sedge - *Carex duriuscula* C.A. Mey. (50) (present), *Carex squarrosa* L. (5, 50, 72) (1893–present)

Squash [Squashes] - *Cucurbita* L. (1, 82, 93, 109, 138, 156) (1923-1949), *Cucurbita maxima* Dcne. (40, 82, 106, 110, 138) (1923-1930), *Cucurbita moschata* (Duchesne ex Lam.) Duchesne ex Poir. (106) (1930), *Cucurbita pepo* L. (7, 107, 121, 114) (1828-1919)

Squashberry [Squash-berry, Squash berry] - *Viburnum acerifolium* L. (5, 76, 156) (1896-1923), *Viburnum edule* (Michx.) Raf. (3, 4, 50, 156, 158) (1900–present)

Squatmore - *Glaucium flavum* Crantz (156) (1923)

Squaw bush [Squawbush, Squaw-bush] - *Cornus amomum* Mill. (5, 155, 156, 157, 158) (1900–1942), *Cornus sericea* L. (46, 76) (1879–1896), *Cornus sericea* L. subsp. *sericea* (5, 75, 156) (1894–1923), *Lycium fremontii* Gray (106) (1930) Phoenix AZ, *Lycium* L. (106, 155) (1930–1942), *Rhamnus crocea* Nutt. (106) (1930) CA, *Rhus trilobata* Nutt. (106) (1930), *Viburnum opulus* L. (5, 92, 156, 158) (1876–1923) no longer in use by 1923

Squaw currant - *Ribes cereum* Dougl. (130) (1895)

Squaw flower [Squawflower] - *Trillium erectum* L. (5, 64, 75) (1894-1913) Ferrisburgh VT

Squaw huckleberry - *Vaccinium* L. (1) (1932), *Vaccinium stamineum* L. (2, 5, 92, 103, 107, 156, 158) (1870-1923)

Squaw vine [Squaw-vine] - *Mitchella repens* L. (6, 49, 52, 53, 54, 57, 73, 92, 107, 156) (1892-1923) parts of Northeastern US

Squaw whortleberry - *Vaccinium stamineum* L. (5, 19, 158) (1840-1913)

Squawberry [Squaw berry, Squaw-berry] - *Lycium fremontii* Gray (106) (1930) Phoenix AZ, *Mitchella* L. (2) (1895), *Mitchella repens* L. (6, 53, 109, 156) (1892-1949), *Rhus aromatica* Aiton (6) (1892), *Rhus trilobata* Nutt. (106) (1930), *Vaccinium stamineum* L. (5, 92, 158) (1876-1913)

Squawberry vine - *Mitchella repens* L. (49) (1898)

Squaw-cabbage [Squaw cabbage] - *Claytonia* L. (1) (1932)

Squaw-carpet [Squaw carpet, Squaw carpets] - *Ceanothus prostratus* Benth. (106, 109) (1930-1949)

Squaw-drops [Squaw drops] - *Conopholis americana* (L. f.) Wallr. (156) (1923)

Squaw-drops [Squaw drops] - *Orobanche uniflora* L. (5, 7, 92, 156) (1828-1932)

Squaw-feather [Squaw feather] - *Castilleja* Mutis ex L. f. (1, 93) (1932-1936)

Squaw-lettuce [Squaw lettuce] - *Claytonia* L. (1) (1932), *Claytonia perfoliata* Donn ex Willd. subsp. *perfoliata* (101) (1905), *Claytonia rubra* (T.J. Howell) Tidestrom subsp. *depressa* (Gray) J.M. Miller & K. Chambers (85) (1932) SD

Squaw-mint [Squawmint, Squaw mint] - *Hedeoma pulegioides* (L.) Pers. (5, 6, 7, 49, 53, 92, 156, 157, 158) (1828-1929)

Squaw-plum [Squaw plum] - *Mitchella repens* L. (156) (1923)

Squawroot [Squaw-root, Squaw root] - *Actaea racemosa* L. (7, 49, 58, 64, 92) (1828-1908), *Atenia* Hook. & Arn. (1) (1932), *Caulophyllum thalictroides* (L.) Michx. (5, 6, 7, 49, 53, 55, 57, 58, 64, 92, 156, 157, 158) (1828-1929), *Conopholis americana* (L. f.) Wallr. (5, 156) (1913-1923), *Conopholis* Wallr. (2, 158) (1895-1900), *Orobanche uniflora* L. (19) (1840), *Osmorhiza depauperata* Phil. (3) (1977), *Perideridia gairdneri* (Hook. & Arn.) Mathias (4, 85, 101) (1905-1986), *Trillium erectum* L. (64, 73, 79, 156) (1891-1923) NH

Squaw-weed [Squawweed, Squaw-weed] - *Ageratina altissima* (L.) King & H.E. Robins. (156) (1923), *Cimicifuga racemosa* (L.) Nutt. (156) (1923), *Erigeron philadelphicus* L. (7) (1828), *Hedeoma pulegioides* (L.) Pers. (156) (1923), *Packera aurea* (L.) A.& D. Löve (2, 6, 49, 58, 156, 158) (1869-1923), *Packera obovata* (Muhl. ex Willd.) W.A. Weber & A. Löve (92) (1876), *Senecio* L. (1, 93, 158) (1900-1936), *Symphyotrichum puniceum* (L.) A.& D. Löve var. *puniceum* (49, 92, 156, 158) (1876-1923)

Squeak-bean - *Gleditsia triacanthos* L. (156) (1923)

Squilily - *Pancratium* L. (7) (1828), *Pancratium maritimum* L. (92) (1876)

Squill [Squills] - *Scilla* L. (109, 138) (1923-1949)

Squine (French) - *Smilax illinoensis* Mangaly (17) (1796)

Squirrel cup [Sqirrel cup, Squirrel cups, Squirrel-cups] - *Hepatica nobilis* Schreb. var. *obtusa* (Pursh) Steyermark (5) (1913)

Squirrel fescue - *Vulpia sciurea* (Nutt.) Henr. (5, 119) (1913-1938)

Squirrel grass - *Hordeum murinum* L. (88) (1885)

Squirrel-corn [Squirrel corn, Squirrel-corn] - *Corydalis curvisiliqua* Engelm. subsp. *occidentalis* (Engelm. ex Gray) W. A. Weber (157) (1929), *Dicentra* Bernh. (13) (1849), *Dicentra canadensis* (Goldie) Walp. (2, 5, 15, 50, 52, 53, 58, 63, 72, 93, 92, 109, 138, 156, 157) (1869–present)

Squirrel's-ear [Squirrel ear] - *Antennaria plantaginifolia* (L.) Richards (possibly) (7) (1828), *Goodyera repens* (L.) R. Br. ex Ait. f. (5, 92, 156) (1876-1923), *Jeffersonia diphylla* (L.) Pers. (92) (1876)

Squirrel's-grandfather [Squirrel's grandfather] - *Boschniakia* C.A. Mey. ex Bong. (77) (1898) CA, *Orobanche* L. (77) (1898)

Squirrel's-shoes [Squirrel's shoes, Squirrels' shoes] - *Cypripedium acaule* Ait. (5, 75, 156) (1894-1923) CT, no longer in use by 1923

Squirrel-tail [Squirrel tail, Squirreltail] - *Elymus elymoides* (Raf.) Swezey (3, 50) (1977–present), *Elymus elymoides* (Raf.) Swezey subsp. *brevifolius* (J.G. Sm.) Barkworth (3, 50) (1977–present), *Elymus elymoides* (Raf.) Swezey subsp. *elymoides* (50, 122, 140) (1937–present), *Elymus* L. (155) (1942), *Hordeum jubatum* L. (85, 93, 140) (1932-1944), *Hordeum* L (1, 93) (1932-1936), *Hordeum murinum* L. (5, 88) (1885-1913)

Squirrel-tail barley - *Hordeum jubatum* L. (107) (1919)

Squirrel-tail fescue [Squirreltail fescue] - *Vulpia sciurea* (Nutt.) Henr. (50) (present)

Squirrel-tail grass [Squirreltail grass, Squirrel-tail-grass, Squirrel-tail-grass] - *Hordeum jubatum* L. (5, 11, 19, 40, 45, 56, 62, 66, 72, 75, 80, 87, 88, 90, 92, 94, 109, 111, 119, 129, 138, 143, 145, 148, 152, 163) (1840-1949)

Squirting cucumber [Squirting-cucumber] - *Ecballium* A. Rich. (109, 138) (1923-1949), *Ecballium elaterium* (L.) A. Rich. (92, 138) (1876)

Squirt-plum [Squirt plum] - *Empetrum nigrum* L. (78) (1898) Rumford ME

Squitch - *Elymus repens* (L.) Gould (5, 45) (1896)

Squitch grass [Squitch-grass] - *Elymus repens* (L.) Gould (90, 158) (1885-1900), *Poa compressa* L. (5) (1913)

Squoutersquashes (Northeastern Indians) - *Cucurbita pepo* L. (107) (1919)

Sreading rockcress [Sreading rock cress] - *Arabis patens* Sullivant (5) (1913)

S'she-quoi (Shawnee) - *Pinus* L. (132) (1855)

St Benedict's thistle - *Cnicus benedictus* L. (5, 69, 156) (1903-1923)

St George's herb - *Valeriana officinalis* L. (5, 156) (1913-1923)

St John's-wort [St John's wort] - *Hypericum punctatum* Lam. (46) (1879)

St Peter's-wort [St Peter's wort] - *Triadenum virginicum* (L.) Raf. (46) (1671)

St. Andrew's-cross [Saint Andrew's cross, St. Andrewscross,] - *Hypericum crux-andreae* (L.) Crantz (2, 92, 97, 157) (1876-1937), *Hypericum hypericoides* (L.) Crantz subsp. *hypericoides* (5, 155, 156) (1913-1942), *Hypericum hypericoides* (L.) Crantz subsp. *multicaule* (Michx. ex Willd.) Robson (3, 4, 50) (1977–present), *Hypericum* L. (1, 4) (1932-1986)

St. Andrew's-lace [St. Andrews-lace] - *Cannabis sativa* L. (5, 93, 158) (1900-1936)

St. Andrew's-wort [Saint Andrews wort, St. Andrews wort] - *Hypericum hypericoides* (L.) Crantz subsp. *hypericoides* (177, 181) (~1678-1762)

St. Anthony's rape - *Ranunculus bulbosus* L. (6, 156, 158) (1892-1923)

St. Athony's turnip - *Ranunculus bulbosus* L. (5, 6, 50, 156, 158) (1892–present)

St. Augustine grass [St. Augustine's grass] - *Stenotaphrum secundatum* (Walt.) Kuntze (109, 122, 138, 163) (1852-1949)

St. Barbara's cress - *Barbarea vulgaris* W.T. Aiton (157) (1929)

St. Barbara's herb - *Barbarea vulgaris* W.T. Aiton (157) (1929)

St. Barbara's-wort [S. Barbaraes woort, S. Barbaraes woorts] - *Barbarea vulgaris* W.T. Aiton (178) (1526)

St. Barnaby's thistle - *Centaurea solstitialis* L. (5, 19, 93, 157) (1840-1936)

St. Bennet's herb [St. Bennet's-herb] - *Conium maculatum* L. (5, 69, 156, 158) (1900-1923)

St. Catharine's prunes [Saint Catharine prunes] - *Prunus domestica* L. (92) (1876)

St. Christopher's herb [Saint Christopher herb, St. Christopher's-herb, S. Christophers herbe] - *Actaea spicata* L. (178) (1526), *Osmunda regalis* L. (92, 157) (1876-1929)

St. Jacob's-dipper [St. Jacob's dipper] - *Sarracenia purpurea* L. (156) (1923)

St. Jacob's-ladder [Saint Jacob's ladder] - *Polemonium reptans* L. (82) (1930)

St. James'-weed [Saint James' weed, St. James weed] - *Capsella bursa-pastoris* (L.) Medik. (5, 92) (1876-1913)

St. James'-wort [Saint James' wort, Saint James wort] - *Senecio jacobea* L. (5, 92) (1876-1913)

St. John - *Hypericum perforatum* L. (74, 156, 158) (1893-1929) WV

St. John's bush [St. John's-bush] - *Hypericum perforatum* L. (74, 157) (1893-1929) WV

St. John's coontie [St. Johns coontie] - *Zamia pumila* L. (138) (1923)

St. John's dogsbane [Saint John's-dogsbane] - *Apocynum cannabinum* L. (5, 19, 92, 157, 158) (1840-1929)

St. John's-bread [Saint John's bread] - *Ceratonia siliqua* L. (92) (1876) Christians claim that St. John the Baptist fed upon this tree in the desert

St. John's-wort [St. John's wort, St. Johnswort, Saynt Johns wort] - *Hypericum* L. (1, 2, 4, 8, 10, 13, 15, 50, 93, 109, 138, 155, 156, 158, 167, 190) (~1759–present), *Hypericum majus* (Gray) Britton (85) (1932), *Hypericum perforatum* L. (6, 7, 46, 48, 49, 52, 53, 57, 80, 92, 179) (1526-1922)

St. Joseph's-wand [St. Joseph's wand] - *Penstemon acuminatus* Dougl. ex Lindl. (5, 156) (1913-1923)

St. Kitt's arrow-root [Saint Kitt's arrow root] - *Canna indica* L. (92) (1876)

St. Lucie's cherry [St. Lucie cherry] - *Prunus mahaleb* L. (109, 137) (1931-1949)

St. Lucie's pawpaw [St. Lucie pawpaw] - *Asimina tetramera* Small (155) (1942)

St. Martin's-wort [Saint Martin's wort] - *Sauvagesia erecta* L. (92) (1876)

St. Mary's grass [Saint Mary's grass] - *Sorghum halepense* (L.) Pers. (5, 45) (1896-1913)

St. Mary's thistle [St. Marys thistle] - *Silybum marianum* (L.) Gaertn. (52, 54, 109) (1905-1949), *Simarouba* Aubl. (109) (1949)

St. Mary's-seed - *Sonchus oleraceus* L. (157, 158) (1900-1929)

St. Paul's creeper [St. Paul creeper] - *Parthenocissus quinquefolia* (L.) Planch. (possibly) (138) (1923)

St. Peter's-wort [St. Peter's wort, Saint Peters wort] - *Hypericum crux-andreae* (L.) Crantz (19, 5, 97, 156) (1840-1937), *Hypericum hypericoides* (L.) Crantz subsp. *hypericoides* (8) (1785), *Hypericum* L. (1, 2, 8, 10, 13, 15, 158, 167) (1814-1932), *Symphoricarpos orbiculatus* Moench (8) (1785)

St. Thomas' tree [Saint Thomas' tree, Saint-Thomas-tree] - *Bauhinia tomentosa* L. (92, 109, 138) (1876-1949)

St.-John's-wort-leaf dogbane [St.-John's-wort-leaved dog's-bane] - *Apocynum cannabinum* L. (187) (1818)

St.-John's-wort-leaf spurge [St.-John's-wort-leaved spurge] - *Chamaesyce hypericifolia* (L.) Millsp. (187) (1818)

Stabwurzel (German) - *Artemisia abrotanum* L. (158) (1900)

Stachelmohn (German) - *Argemone mexicana* L. (6) (1892)

Stachys - *Stachys aspera* Michx. (157) (1929)

Staff rush - *Juncus effusus* L. var. *conglomeratus* (L.) Engelm. (5, 156) (1913-1923)

Staff tree [Staff-tree] - *Celastrus* L. (1, 8, 10, 13, 15, 82, 158) (1785-1932), *Celastrus scandens* L. (5, 7, 14, 19, 47, 49, 92, 103, 107, 156, 157, 158, 184) (1793-1929)

Staff vine [Staff-vine] - *Solanum dulcamara* L. (71) (1898)

Stag bush [Stag-bush] - *Viburnum prunifolium* L. (5, 49, 53, 54, 156, 158) (1898-1923)

Stag cabbage - *Hydrophyllum canadense* L. (29) (1869)

Stagberry [Stag-berry] - *Symphoricarpos* Duham. (1) (1932), *Symphoricarpos occidentalis* Hook. (156) (1923)

Stagger brush [Stagger-brush, Staggerbrush] - *Lyonia mariana* (L.) D. Don (2) (1895)

Stagger bush [Stagger-bush, Staggerbush] - *Lyonia mariana* (L.) D. Don (2, 5, 71, 86, 92, 109, 122, 138, 156) (1878-1949) thought to cause "staggers" in sheep

Stagger grass [Stagger-grass] - *Zephyranthes atamasca* (L.) Herbert (5, 156) (1913-1923)

Staggerweed [Stagger weed, Stagger-weed] - *Delphinium tricorne* Michx. (71, 156) (1898-1923) OH, *Dicentra eximia* (Ker-Gawl.) Torr. (156) (1923), *Senecio jacobea* L. (92) (1876), *Consolida regalis* S.F. Gray (92) (1876), *Dicentra canadensis* (Goldie) Walp. (49, 58, 92, 156, 157) (1869-1929), *Dicentra eximia* (Ker-Gawl.) Torr. (5) (1913), *Helenium autumnale* L. (71) (1898) SC, *Senecio jacobea* L. (92) (1876)

Staggerwort - *Senecio jacobea* L. (156) (1923)

Staghorn [Stag-horn, Stag's horn] - *Lycopodium clavatum* L. (6, 92) (1876-1892), *Rhus hirta* (L.) Sudworth (5, 92, 156) (1876-1923)

Stag-horn evergreen [Stag horn evergreen] - *Lycopodium clavatum* L. (78) (1898) Concord MA

Staghorn fern - *Platycerium* Desv. (138) (1923)

Staghorn moss - *Lycopodium clavatum* L. (5) (1913)

Staghorn sumac [Staghorn sumach, Stag-horn sumach, Stag's horn sumach, Stag-horn-shumach] - *Rhus glabra* L. (122) (1937), *Rhus hirta* (L.) Sudworth (2, 8, 14, 15, 19, 34, 40, 46, 50, 72, 82, 107, 109, 121, 131, 135, 138, 156, 187) (1785–present)

Stag's-head [Stag's head] - *Salix fragilis* L. (5, 156) (1913-1923)

Stah-up-unga-weg (German) - *Veronica serpyllifolia* L. (158) (1900)

Stakra - *Alopecurus geniculatus* L. (46) (1879)

Stalked bur grass [Stalked burr grass] - *Tragus racemosus* (L.) All. (50) (present)

Stalked ruellia - *Ruellia pedunculata* Torr. ex Gray (5, 97, 122, 138) (1913-1937)

Stalked water-horehound [Stalked water hoarhound, Stalked water horehound] - *Lycopus rubellus* Moench (5, 72, 122, 131) (1899-1936)

Stalkless yellow-cress [Stalkless yellowcress] - *Rorippa sessiliflora* (Nutt.) A.S. Hitchc. (50) (present)

Stalky berula - *Berula erecta* (Huds.) Coville (155) (1942)

Stammarche - *Apium graveolens* L. (179) (1526)

Stammerwort [Stammer-wort] - *Ambrosia artemisiifolia* L. (92, 156, 158) (1876-1923) no longer in use by 1923, *Ambrosia artemisiifolia* L. var. *elatior* (L.) Descourtils (5) (1913)

Standfield's monarda - *Monarda stanfieldii* Small (97) (1937)

Standing blackberry - *Rubus flagellaris* Willd. (186) (1814)

Standing milkvetch [Standing milk vetch] - *Astragalus laxmannii* Jacq. var. *robustior* (Hook.) Barneby & Welsh (4) (1986)

Standing-cypress [Standing cypress] - *Ipomopsis rubra* (L.) Wherry (2, 4, 50, 77, 97, 156) (1898–present), *Kochia scoparia* (L.) Schrad. (156) (1923)

Standish' honeysuckle [Standish honeysuckle] - *Lonicera standishii* Jacques (138) (1923)

Standley's goosefoot - *Chenopodium standleyanum* Aellen (50) (present)

Stanford's manzanita [Stanford manzanita] - *Arctostaphylos stanfordiana* Parry (155) (1942)

Stanleya - *Stanleya pinnata* (Pursh) Britton (5, 131) (1899-1913)

Star - *Carex nigra* (L.) Reichard (5) (1913)

Star acacia - *Acacia verticillata* (L'Hér.) Willd. (109, 138, 155) (1923-1949)

Star anemone - *Trientalis borealis* Raf. subsp. *borealis* (73, 75) (1892-1894) MA

Star anise [Star-anis] - *Illicium floridanum* Ellis (7) (1828), *Illicium* L. (2, 13, 15, 167) (1814-1895), *Illicium parviflorum* Michx. (92) (1876)

Star cactus [Starcactus] - *Astrophytum* Lem. (109, 138, 155) (1923-1949)

Star chickweed - *Stellaria media* (L.) Vill. (49) (1898), *Stellaria pubera* Michx. (5, 50, 156, 158) (1900–present), *Trientalis borealis* Raf. subsp. *borealis* (156) (1923)

Star cloak fern [Star cloakfern] - *Notholaena standleyi* Maxon (50, 97, 155) (1937–present)

Star duckweed - *Lemna trisulca* L. (3, 5, 50, 155, 156) (1911–present)

Star flower [Starflower, Star-flower] - *Aster* L. (167) (1814), *Borago officinalis* L. (156) (1923), *Cooperia drummondii* Herb. (78) (1898) TX, *Ipomoea lacunosa* L. (86) (1878), *Lithophragma* (Nutt.) Torr. & Gray (1) (1932), *Ornithogalum umbellatum* L. (5, 156, 158) (1900-1923), *Potentilla canadensis* L. (5, 156) (1913-1923), *Potentilla* L. (76) (1896) Waverly MA, *Stellaria holostea* L. (5, 156) (1913-1923) no longer in use by 1923, *Symphyotrichum puniceum* (L.) A.& D. Löve var. *puniceum* (92) (1876), *Tradescantia virginiana* L. (86) (1878), *Trientalis borealis* Raf. subsp. *borealis* (2, 5) (1895-1913), *Trientalis* L. (1, 50, 138) (1923–present), *Trifolium* L. (177, 178) (1526-1762)

Star ipomoea - *Ipomoea coccinea* L. (109) (1949)

Star lily [Star-lily, Starlily] - *Leucocrinum montanum* Nutt. ex Gray (138) (1923), *Leucocrinum* Nutt. ex Gray (50, 109, 138, 155) (1923–present), *Ornithogalum umbellatum* L. (156) (1923)

Star magnolia - *Magnolia stellata* (Sieb. & Zucc.) Maxim. (137, 138) (1923-1931)

Star milkvine - *Matelea biflora* (Raf.) Woods (50) (present)

Star milkweed - *Matelea biflora* (Raf.) Woods (124) (1937) TX

Star nettle - *Laportea canadensis* (L.) Weddell (62) (1912) IN

Star root - *Aletris farinosa* L. (5, 6, 7, 92, 181, 184) (~1678-1913), *Hypoxis hirsuta* (L.) Cov. (92) (1876)

Star saxifrage - *Saxifraga stellaris* L. (5) (1913)

Star scabious - *Scabiosa stellata* L. (19, 92) (1840-1876)

Star sedge - *Carex echinata* Murr. subsp. *echinata* (50) (present)

Star snowbush - *Breynia disticha* J.R. & G. Forst. (138) (1923)

Star thistle [Star-thistle] - *Centaurea calcitrapa* L. (5, 42, 92, 107, 156) (1814-1923), *Centaurea* L. (1, 4, 82, 106, 156) (1923-1986), *Centaurea solstitialis* L. (80, 157) (1913-1929), *Cirsium pumilum* (Nutt.) Spreng. (46) (1783)

Star tickseed - *Coreopsis pubescens* Ell. (5, 50, 97, 156) (1913–present)

Star tulip - *Calochortus elegans* Pursh (107) (1919)

Star violet - *Dalibarda repens* L. (156) (1923)

Star-apple [Star apple] - *Chrysophyllum cainito* L. (109, 110, 138) (1886-1949), *Chrysophyllum* L. (138) (1923)

Starbloom [Star-bloom, Star bloom] - *Spigelia marilandica* (L.) L. (5, 6, 64, 92, 156) (1892–1923)

Starbur [Starburr] - *Acanthospermum* Schrank (50, 155) (1942–present)

Starch grape-hyacinth [Starch grape hyacinth] - *Muscari neglectum* Guss. ex Ten. (5, 50) (1913–present)

Starch-hyacinth [Starch hyacinth] - *Muscari botryoides* (L.) Mills (156) (1923), *Muscari neglectum* Guss. ex Ten. (5) (1913)

Starchwort [Starch-wort] - *Arisaema triphyllum* (L.) Schott (5, 64, 92, 156, 158) (1876-1923), *Calla palustris* L. (86) (1878) old English name

Star-cucumber [Star cucumber] - *Sicyos angulatus* L. (5, 86, 156, 157, 158) (1878-1929), *Sicyos* L. (1, 2) (1895)

Stare - *Carex arenaria* L. (5, 156) (1913-1923), *Carex nigra* (L.) Reichard (5) (1913)

Star-eyed grass - *Sisyrinchium angustifolium* Mill. (5, 75, 156, 157, 158) (1894-1929) Concord MA, children

Star-flower Solomon's seal [Star-flowered Solomon's seal - *Maian-*

themum stellatum (L.) Link (5, 42, 93, 127, 156) (1814-1936)

Star-glory [Starglory] - *Ipomoea* L. (138, 155) (1923-1942)

Star-gooseberry - *Phyllanthus acidus* (L.) Skeels (138) (1923)

Star-grass [Star grass, Stargrass] - *Aletris farinosa* L. (5, 6, 7, 42, 49, 52, 53, 54, 64, 92, 138, 156, 181, 187) (~1678-1923), *Aletris* L. (1, 109, 138, 155) (1923-1949), *Callitriche* L. (92) (1876), *Callitriche palustris* L. (184) (1793), *Chamaelirium luteum* (L.) A. Gray (64, 156) (1908-1923), *Galium odoratum* (L.) Scop. (5) (1913), *Hypoxis hirsuta* (L.) Cov. (7, 19, 72, 85, 86, 92, 127, 157, 158) (1828-1933), *Hypoxis* L. (1, 50, 93, 109, 156, 158, 167) (1814-present)

Star-jasmine [Starjasmine] - *Trachelospermum jasminoides* (Lindl.) Lem. (109) (1949), *Trachelospermum* Lem. (138) (1923)

Star-leaf gum [Star-leaved gum] - *Liquidambar styraciflua* L. (5, 156) (1913-1923)

Starlights [Starlight] - *Geranium molle* L. (5, 156) (1913-1923), *Houstonia caerulea* L. (75) (1894) Cambridge MA

Star-of-Bethlehem [Star of Bethlehem, Starre of Bethlem, Stars of Bethlehem] - *Houstonia caerulea* L. (5, 73, 156) (1892-1923) MS, *Hypoxis hirsuta* (L.) Cov. (156, 157) (1923-1929), *Leucocrinum montanum* Nutt. ex Gray (85) (1932), *Leucocrinum* Nutt. ex Gray (1, 93) (1932-1936), *Ornithogalum* L. (1, 10, 50, 138, 155, 156, 158, 180) (1633-present), *Ornithogalum umbellatum* L. (3, 5, 19, 92, 93, 97, 107, 109, 156, 158, 178, 180, 187) (1596-1977), *Tradescantia virginiana* L. (86) (1878), *Trientalis borealis* Raf. subsp. *borealis* (73, 75, 77) (1892-1898)

Star-of-Jerusalem [Star of Jerusalem] - *Tragopogon pratensis* L. (5, 92, 156, 158) (1876-1923)

Star-of-Texas - *Xanthisma texanum* DC. (109, 155) (1942-1949)

Star-of-the-earth [Star of the earth] - *Geum urbanum* L. (92) (1876), *Plantago coronopus* L. (107) (1919)

Starry campion - *Silene stellata* (L.) Aiton f. (2, 4, 5, 15, 65, 86, 93, 95, 97, 109, 114, 131, 138, 156) (1878-1986)

Starry catchfly - *Silene stellata* (L.) Aiton f. (86) (1878)

Starry cerastium - *Cerastium arvense* L. (138, 155) (1923-1942)

Starry champion - *Silene stellata* (L.) Aiton f. (72, 85) (1907-1932)

Starry false lily-of-the-valley - *Maianthemum stellatum* (L.) Link (50) (present)

Starry false Solomon's-seal [Starry false Solomonseal] - *Maianthemum stellatum* (L.) Link (138) (1923)

Starry fasle spiraea - *Sorbaria sorbifolia* (L.) A. Braun (138) (1923)

Starry grassweed - *Cerastium arvense* L. (156) (1923)

Starry grasswort - *Cerastium arvense* L. (109) (1949)

Starry magnolia - *Magnolia stellata* (Sieb. & Zucc.) Maxim. (109) (1949)

Starry rosinweed [Starry rosin-weed, Starry rosin weed] - *Silphium asteriscus* L. (5, 97) (1913-1937)

Starry saxifrage - *Saxifraga stellaris* L. (5, 156) (1913-1923)

Starry silene - *Silene stellata* (L.) Aiton f. (155) (1942)

Starry Solomon's-plume [Starry Solomonplume, Starry Solomonplume] - *Maianthemum stellatum* (L.) Link (155) (1942)

Starry Solomon's-seal [Starry Solomon's seal] - *Maianthemum stellatum* (L.) Link (156) (1923)

Starry thistle [Starrie thistle] - *Centaurea calcitrapa* L. (178) (1526)

Star-strikers [Star strikers] - *Erythronium* L. (1, 93) (1932-1936)

Starve-acre [Starve acre] - *Ranunculus arvensis* L. (5, 156) (1913-1923)

Starved aster - *Symphyotrichum lateriflorum* (L.) A.& D. Löve var. *lateriflorum* (5, 72, 82, 122, 131, 156) (1899-1937)

Starved panic grass [Starved panic-grass, Starved panicgrass] - *Dichanthelium depauperatum* (Muhl.) Gould (5, 50, 85, 93, 163) (1852-present)

Starved panicum - *Dichanthelium depauperatum* (Muhl.) Gould (56, 72, 131) (1899-1907)

Star-violet [Star violet] - *Hedyotis nigricans* (Lam.) Fosberg var. *nigricans* (5, 156, 158) (1900-1923), *Houstonia* L. (76) (1896) Waco TX, *Houstonia pusilla* Schoepf (5, 156) (1913-1923), *Hedyotis* L. (50) (present)

Starwort [Star-wort, Star wort] - *Aletris farinosa* L. (6, 49, 52, 53, 55, 57, 64) (1892-1922), *Aster* L. (2, 7, 10, 42, 92, 109, 156) (1793-1949), *Chamaelirium luteum* (L.) A. Gray (6, 53, 54, 64) (1892-1922), *Inula helenium* L. (76) (1896) Western US, *Senecio jacobea* L. (156) (1923), *Spergularia* (Pers.) J.& K. Presl (158) (1900), *Stellaria* L. (1, 13, 50, 15, 155, 156) (1849-present), *Stellaria media* (L.) Vill. (107, 156) (1919-1923), *Symphyotrichum cordifolium* (L.) Nesom (58) (1869)

Starwort chickweed - *Cerastium cerastoides* (L.) Britton (5) (1913)

Stately aster - *Eurybia macrophylla* (L.) Cass. (5) (1913)

Statice - *Limonium* P. Mill. (122) (1937), *Limonium vulgare* Mill. (57) (1917)

Staunchwort - *Anthyllis vulneraria* L. (92) (1876)

Stave oak - *Quercus alba* L. (5, 156) (1913-1923)

Staverwort - *Senecio jacobea* L. (92, 156) (1898-1923)

Stave-wort - *Senecio jacobea* L. (5) (1913)

Stay-plough [Stay plough] - *Ononis campestris* G. Koch & Ziz (92) (1876)

Steadfast - *Ricinus communis* L. (156) (1923)

Steckapfel (German) - *Datura stramonium* L. (6, 156) (1892-1923)

Steckkörner (German) - *Silybum marianum* (L.) Gaertn. (158) (1900)

Stedfast - *Ricinus communis* L. (5) (1913)

Steel globe-thistle [Steel globethistle] - *Echinops ritro* L. (138) (1923)

Steele's wild lettuce - *Lactuca canadensis* L. (5) (1913)

Steelweed [Steel weed, Steel-weed] - *Symphyotrichum ericoides* (L.) Nesom var. *ericoides* (5, 62, 156) (1912-1923)

Steen-crout - *Buglossoides arvensis* (L.) I.M. Johnston (19) (1840)

Steep-grass [Steep grass] - *Pinguicula vulgaris* L. (5, 156) (1913-1923)

Steeple bush - *Spiraea tomentosa* L. (2, 5, 19, 48, 49, 58, 92, 109, 156) (1840-1949)

Steeple-weed - *Aruncus dioicus* (Walt.) Fern. var. *vulgaris* (Maxim.) Hara (19) (1840)

Steifmutterchen-Kraut (German) - *Viola tricolor* L. (6) (1892)

Steinklee (German) - *Melilotus officinalis* (L.) Lam. (6, 158) (1892-1900)

Steironema - *Lysimachia* L. (155) (1942)

Stellaria - *Stellaria media* (L.) Vill. (57) (1917)

Stellate ground cherry - *Physalis viscosa* L. (5) (1913)

Stellate sedge - *Carex rosea* Schkuhr ex Willd. (5, 72) (1907)

Stem-berry willow [Stem-berried willow] - *Salix pedicellaris* Pursh (19) (1840)

Stem-clasping aster [Stem clasping aster] - *Symphyotrichum patens* (Aiton) G.L. Nesom var. *patens* (possibly) (42) (1814)

Stem-clasping srchangel - *Lamium amplexicaule* L. (187) (1818)

Stem-clasping swine's-succory [Stem-clasping swines'-succory] - *Krigia biflora* (Walt.) Blake (187) (1818)

Stemless acaulis - *Tetraneuris acaulis* (Pursh) Greene var. *acaulis* (124) (1937) TX

Stemless actinea - *Tetraneuris acaulis* (Pursh) Greene var. *acaulis* (155) (1942)

Stemless bitterweed - *Tetraneuris acaulis* (Pursh) Greene var. *acaulis* (122) (1937) TX

Stemless bur-reed - *Sparganium angustifolium* Michx. (5, 10) (1818-1913)

Stemless crazyweed [Stemless crazy weed, Stemless crazy-weed] - *Oxytropis lambertii* Pursh (5, 97) (1913-1937) OK

Stemless dwarf ladyslipper [Stemless dwarf lady's slipper] - *Cypripedium acaule* Ait. (42) (1814)

Stemless evening-primrose [Stemless evening primrose] - *Oenothera triloba* Nutt. (3, 4, 50) (1977-present)

Stemless four-nerve daisy - *Tetraneuris acaulis* (Pursh) Greene (50) (present)

Stemless goldenweed - *Stenotus acaulis* (Nutt.) Nutt. var. *acaulis* (155) (1942)

Stemless hymenoxys - *Tetraneuris acaulis* (Pursh) Greene var. *acaulis* (3, 4) (1977-1986)

Stemless ladyslipper [Stemless ladies' slipper, Stemless lady's slipper] - *Cypripedium acaule* Ait. (2, 5, 92, 156) (1876-1923)

Stemless loco - *Oxytropis lambertii* Pursh (93, 125) (1930-1936)

Stemless locoweed [Stemless loco weed, Stemless loco weed] - *Oxytropis lambertii* Pursh (5, 63, 71, 72, 80, 97, 156) (1898-1937)

Stemless moccasin flower - *Cypripedium acaule* Ait. (86) (1878)

Stemless picradenia - *Tetraneuris acaulis* (Pursh) Greene var. *acaulis* (131) (1899)

Stemless tetraneuris - *Tetraneuris acaulis* (Pursh) Greene (5, 97) (1913-1937)

Stemless Townsend daisy - *Townsendia exscapa* (Richards.) Porter (50) (present)

Stemless townsendia - *Townsendia exscapa* (Richards.) Porter (155) (1942)

Stemless western primrose - *Oenothera caespitosa* Nutt. (108) (1878)

Stemless yellow violet - *Viola rotundifolia* Michx. (156) (1923)

Stemseed actinea - *Tetraneuris scaposa* (DC.) Greene (124) (1937)

Stemmed bitterweed - *Tetraneuris scaposa* (DC.) Greene (122) (1937)

Stemmed loco - *Astragalus mollissimus* Torr (125) (1930)

Stemmed yellow violet - *Viola pubescens* Aiton (156) (1923)

Stemmy four-nerve daisy [Stemmy fournerved daisy] - *Tetraneuris scaposa* (DC.) Greene var. *scaposa* (50) (present)

Stenosiphon - *Stenosiphon linifolius* (Nutt. ex James) Heynh. (3, 4, 50, 86, 158) (1878-1986), *Stenosiphon* Spach (50, 158) (1900–present)

Stenotus - *Stenotus* Nutt. (158) (1900)

Step palm - *Archontophoenix alexandrae* (F. Muell.) H. Wendl. & Drude (109) (1949)

Stephanadra - *Stephanandra* Sieb. & Zucc. (138) (1923)

Stepmother - *Viola tricolor* L. (92, 158) (1876-1900)

Sterile brome grass - *Bromus sterilis* L. (66) (1903)

Stevens' fiddlehead - *Nama stevensii* A.S. Hitchc (3, 4) (1977-1986)

Stevens' fiddleleaf - *Nama stevensii* A.S. Hitchc (50) (present)

Stevia - *Ageratina altissima* (L.) King & H.E. Robins. (5, 76, 156) (1896-1923) Madison WI

Stewardson Brown's Indian turnip - *Arisaema triphyllum* (L.) Schott subsp. *stewardsonii* (Britt.) Huttleston (5) (1913)

Stewartia - *Sterculia* L. (8, 138) (1785-1923), *Stewartia malacodendron* L. (174, 177) (1753-1762)

Stewartia (French) - *Sterculia* L. (8) (1785)

Stewartia de Virginie (French) - *Stewartia malacodendron* L. (8) (1785)

Stewart's canary grass [Stewart's canary-grass] - *Phalaris caroliniana* Walt. (45, 87, 88) (1885-1896)

Stichwort - *Stellaria media* (L.) Vill. (92) (1876)

Stick-a-back [Stickaback] - *Galium aparine* L. (5, 156, 158) (1900-1923) no longer in use by 1923

Stickadore - *Lavandula stoechas* L. (92) (1876)

Stick-button [Stick button, Stick-buttons] - *Arctium lappa* L. (5, 64, 69, 156, 158) (1900-1923)

Stickers - *Cnicus* L. (73) (1892) St. John NB

Stickleaf [Stick leaf] - *Mentzelia albicaulis* (Dougl. ex Hook.) Dougl. ex Torr. & Gray (106) (1930), *Mentzelia* L. (1, 4, 148) (1932-1986), *Mentzelia oligosperma* Nutt. ex Sims (4, 156) (1923-1986)

Stick-leaf mentzelia [Stickleaf mentzelia] - *Mentzelia oligosperma* Nutt. ex Sims (3) (1977)

Stickle-back [Stickleback] - *Galium aparine* L. (5, 156, 158) (1900-1923)

Sticklewort - *Agrimonia eupatoria* L. (107, 156) (1919-1923) WV

Stick-pile - *Erodium cicutarium* (L.) L'Hér. ex Aiton (157, 158) (1900-1929)

Stickseed [Stick seed, Stick-seed] - *Agrimonia eupatoria* L. (74, 156) (1893-1923), *Agrimonia gryposepala* Wallr. (5) (1913), *Bidens frondosa* L. (5, 92, 156) (1876-1923), *Cynoglossum* L. (75) (1894) WV, *Hackelia* Opiz (4, 50) (1986–present), *Lappula* Moench (1, 4, 50, 93, 155, 156, 158) (1895–present), *Lappula squarrosa* (Retz.) Dumort. (47, 80) (1852-1913), *Symphyotrichum lateriflorum* (L.) A.& D. Löve var. *lateriflorum* (5) (1913)

Sticktight [Stick-tight, Sticktights, Stick-tights, Stick tights] - *Bidens cernua* L. (156) (1923), *Bidens connata* Muhl. ex Willd. (3) (1977), *Bidens coronata* (L.) Britton (82) (1930), *Bidens frondosa* L. (5, 80, 82, 122, 131, 156, 158) (1899–1936), *Bidens* L. (75, 106, 109) (1894–1949), *Bidens tripartita* L. (82) (1930), *Bidens vulgata* Greene (82) (1930), *Cynoglossum officinale* L. (75) (1894) Anderson IN, *Hackelia virginiana* (L.) I. M. Johnston (5, 75, 156, 157, 158) (1894–1929), *Lappula* Moench (1, 93) (1932–1936), *Lappula occidentalis* (S. Wats.) Greene var. *occidentalis* (75) (1894), *Lappula squarrosa* (Retz.) Dumort. (75, 85, 156, 158) (1894–1932)

Stickweed [Stick-weed, Stick weed] - *Agrimonia eupatoria* L. (156) (1923), *Agrimonia gryposepala* Wallr. (5) (1913), *Ambrosia artemisiifolia* L. (156, 158) (1900–1923) no longer in use by 1923, *Ambrosia artemisiifolia* L. var. *elatior* (L.) Descourtils (5) (1913), *Geum canadense* Jacq. (80) (1913) WV, *Hackelia floribunda* (Lehm.) I.M. Johnston (77) (1898) CA, *Symphyotrichum lateriflorum* (L.) A.& D. Löve var. *lateriflorum* (156) (1923), *Symphyotrichum lowrieanum* (Porter) Nesom (75) (1894), *Symphyotrichum oolentangiense* (Riddell) Nesom var. *oolentangiense* (156) (1923), *Verbesina coreopsis* Michx. (75, 158) (1894–1900)

Stickwort - *Agrimonia eupatoria* L. (7, 49, 52, 53, 58, 92) (1828–1922)

Sticky arrowhead - *Sagittaria latifolia* Willd. (155) (1942)

Sticky broad-leaf arnica [Sticky broadleaf arnica] - *Arnica ovata* Greene (155) (1942)

Sticky cerastium - *Cerastium glomeratum* Thuill. (155) (1942)

Sticky chickweed - *Cerastium glomeratum* Thuill. (19, 50) (1840–present)

Sticky cinquefoil - *Potentilla glandulosa* Lindl. (50) (present)

Sticky cockle - *Silene noctiflora* L. (4, 62) (1912-1986)

Sticky currant - *Ribes cereum* Dougl. var. *cereum* (155) (1942)

Sticky geranium - *Geranium viscosissimum* Fisch. & C.A. Mey. ex C.A. Mey. (155) (1942)

Sticky gilia - *Gilia pinnatifida* Nutt. ex Gray (50) (present)

Sticky jointvetch - *Aeschynomene viscidula* (155) (1942)

Sticky panic grass - *Dichanthelium scoparium* (Lam.) Gould (66) (1903)

Sticky purple geranium - *Geranium viscosissimum* Fisch. & C.A. Mey. ex C.A. Mey. (50) (present)

Sticky sage - *Salvia glutinosa* L. (50) (present)

Sticky skullcap - *Scutellaria resinosa* Torr. (50) (present)

Sticky tofieldia - *Tofieldia glutinosa* (Michx.) Pers. subsp. *glutinosa* (50) (present), *Triantha glutinosa* (Michx.) Baker (possibly) (50) (present)

Sticky willow-weed [Sticky willow weed, Sticky willowweed] - *Epilobium ciliatum* Raf. subsp. *ciliatum* (155) (1942)

Sticky-head [Sticky head] - *Grindelia squarrosa* (Pursh) Dunal (37, 156) (1919-1923)

Sticky-willy [Stickywilly] - *Galium aparine* L. (50) (present)

Sticta - *Lobaria pulmonaria* (L.) Hoffm. (52, 54) (1905-1919)

Stiefmütterchen (German) - *Viola tricolor* L. (158) (1900)

Stiff arrowhead - *Sagittaria rigida* Pursh (138, 155) (1923-1942)

Stiff aster - *Ionactis linariifolius* (L.) Greene (5, 156, 158) (1900-1923)

Stiff blue-eye grass - *Sisyrinchium demissum* Greene (50) (present)

Stiff clubmoss [Stiff club moss] - *Lycopodium annotinum* L. (5, 50) (1913–present)

Stiff coreopsis - *Coreopsis palmata* Nutt. (122) (1937)

Stiff cornel - *Cornus foemina* Mill. (5, 156) (1913-1923)

Stiff cornel dogwood - *Cornus foemina* Mill. (155) (1942)

Stiff dogwood - *Cornus foemina* Mill. (5, 50) (1913–present)

Stiff gentian - *Gentiana saponaria* L. (7) (1828), *Gentianella quinquefolia* (L.) Small subsp. *quinquefolia* (5, 72, 156) (1907-1923)

Stiff goldenrod [Stiff golden-rod] - *Oligoneuron rigidum* (L.) Small (50) (present), *Oligoneuron rigidum* (L.) Small var. *rigidum* (5, 50, 72, 82, 95, 97, 127, 138, 155) (1907–present)

Stiff greenthread - *Thelesperma filifolium* (Hook.) Gray (50) (present)

Stiff hairy panicum - *Dichanthelium* ×*scoparioides* (Ashe) Mohlenbrock [*acuminatum* × *oligosanthes*] (5) (1913)

Stiff marsh bedstraw (stiff marsh-bedstraw) - *Galium tinctorium* L. (5, 50, 72, 93, 97, 122, 156) (1907–present)

Stiff nuttallia - *Mentzelia nuda* (Pursh) Torr. & Gray var. *stricta* (Osterhout) Harrington (5, 93, 97) (1913-1937)

Stiff penstemon - *Penstemon acuminatus* Dougl. ex Lindl. (138) (1923)

Stiff prairie grass - *Eragrostis sessilispica* Buckl. (5) (1913)

Stiff sagebrush - *Artemisia rigida* (Nutt.) Gray (155) (1942)

Stiff sunflower - *Helianthus* ×*laetiflorus* Pers. [*pauciflorus* × *tuberosus*] (5, 72, 82, 97, 131) (1899–1937), *Helianthus pauciflorus* Nutt. (50) (present), *Helianthus pauciflorus* Nutt. subsp. *pauciflorus* (3, 4, 50, 93, 155) (1936–present), *Helianthus pauciflorus* Nutt. subsp. *subrhomboideus* (Rydb.) O. Spring & E. Schilling (3, 50) (1977–present)

Stiff thelesperma - *Thelesperma filifolium* (Hook.) Gray var. *intermedium* (Rydb.) Shinners (5) (1913)

Stiff tick trefoil [Stiff ticktrefoil] - *Desmodium obtusum* (Muhl. ex Willd.) DC. (50) (present), *Desmodium strictum* (Pursh) DC. (5) (1913)

Stiff tickseed - *Coreopsis palmata* Nutt. (5, 50, 72, 93, 97, 131) (1899–present)

Stiff water crowfoot (Stiff water-crowfoot) - *Ranunculus longirostris* Godr. (2, 63, 156) (1895-1931)

Stiff white water crowfoot - *Ranunculus longirostris* Godr. (5) (1913)

Stiff yellow flax - *Linum medium* (Planch.) Britt. var. *medium* (5, 97) (1913-1937), *Linum medium* (Planch.) Britton var. *texanum* (Planch.) Fern. (50, 122) (1937–present)

Stiff-hair sunflower [Stiff-haired sunflower, Stiffhaired sunflower] - *Helianthus hirsutus* Raf. (5, 72, 93, 97, 122) (1907-1937)

Stiff-hair wheat grass [Stiffhair wheatgrass] - *Thinopyrum intermedium* (Host) Barkworth & D.R. Dewey (155) (1942)

Stiff-leaf false golden-aster [Stiffleaf false goldenaster, Stiff-leaf false goldenaster] - *Heterotheca stenophylla* (Gray) Shinners (50) (present), *Heterotheca stenophylla* (Gray) Shinners var. *stenophylla* (5, 97, 122) (1913-1937)

Stiff-leaf starwort [Stiff leaved star wort] - *Ionactis linariifolius* (L.) Greene (42) (1814)

Stiff-leaf vetch [Stiffleaf vetch] - *Vicia americana* Muhl. ex Willd. subsp. *minor* (Hook.) C.R. Gunn (155) (1942)

Stiff-leaf willow [Stiff-leaved willow] - *Salix eriocephala* Michx. (19, 187) (1818-1840)

Stiff-stem flax [Stiffstem flax] - *Linum berlandieri* Hook. var. *berlandieri* (3) (1977), *Linum compactum* A. Nels. (3) (1977), *Linum rigidum* Pursh (50, 155) (1942–present), *Linum rigidum* Pursh var. *rigidum* (3, 4, 50, 98) (1926–present), *Linum rigidum* Pursh var. *simulans* Rogers (50) (present)

Stillingia - *Stillingia* Garden ex L. (155, 158) (1900-1942), *Stillingia sylvatica* Garden ex L. (52, 54, 55, 57, 59, 61, 64, 92) (1870-1917)

Stillingie (French) - *Stillingia sylvatica* Garden ex L. (6, 158) (1892-1900)

Stillingie (German) - *Stillingia sylvatica* Garden ex L. (6, 158) (1892-1900)

Stillingier port-suif (French) - *Triadica sebifera* (L.) Small (20) (1857)

Stillman's coreopsis [Stillman coreopsis] - *Coreopsis stillmanii* (Gray) Blake (138) (1923)

Stinging bush [Stinging-bush] - *Cnidoscolus stimulosus* (Michx.) Engelm. & Gray (5, 156) (1913-1923)

Stinging nettle - *Galeopsis bifida* Boenn. (5) (1913), *Tragia betonicifolia* Nutt. (78) (1898) Western MO, *Urtica dioica* L. (4, 5, 46, 49, 50, 53, 57, 58, 72, 92, 93, 95, 156, 157, 158) (1671–present), *Urtica dioica* L. subsp. *gracilis* (Aiton) Seland. (3, 80, 101, 121, 155) (1905-1977), *Urtica urens* L. (5, 6, 156) (1892-1923)

Stinging-serpent [Stinging serpent] - *Cevallia sinuata* Lag. (50) (present)

Stingless nettle - *Pilea pumila* (L.) Gray (5, 93, 156) (1913-1936), *Pilea pumila* (L.) Gray var. *pumila* (19, 92, 158) (1840-1900)

Stink - *Datura stramonium* L. (158) (1900)

Stink bush [Stinkbush] - *Rhus aromatica* Aiton (6) (1892), *Rhus trilobata* Nutt. (112) (1937)

Stink flower [Stinkflower] - *Cleome* L. (1, 93) (1932)

Stink grass [Stink-grass, Stinkgrass] - *Eragrostis cilianensis* (All.) Vign. ex Janchen (3, 50, 56, 75, 80, 111, 122, 125, 129, 140, 155) (1894–present), *Eragrostis hypnoides* (Lam.) Britton, Sterns & Poggenb. (85) (1932), *Eragrostis* von Wolf (1, 93) (1932-1936)

Stink-apple - *Datura stramonium* L. (157) (1929)

Stinkberry - *Rhamnus lanceolata* Pursh (113) (1890) Neb

Stinkende Drachenwurzel (German) - *Symplocarpus foetidus* (L.) Salisb. ex Nutt. (6) (1892)

Stinkende Kamille (Dutch, German) - *Anthemis cotula* L. (7, 186) (1814-1828)

Stinkende Zehrwurtz (German) - *Symplocarpus foetidus* (L.) Salisb. ex Nutt. (186) (1814)

Stinkhorn - *Phallus impudicus* L. (92) (1876)

Stinking arach - *Chenopodium vulvaria* L. (178) (1526)

Stinking ash - *Ptelea trifoliata* L. (6, 92, 156, 157, 158) (1892–1929)

Stinking balm - *Hedeoma pulegioides* (L.) Pers. (6, 7, 92, 158) (1828-1900)

Stinking bearded mushroom - *Ozonium auricomum* Link (181) (~1678)

Stinking black hellebore - *Helleborus foetidus* L. (92) (1876)

Stinking bugwort [Stinking bug wort] - *Cimicifuga americana* Michx. (42) (1814)

Stinking camomile [Stinking chamomile] - *Anthemis cotula* L. (50, 75, 92, 156, 157, 158, 165) (1807–present)

Stinking cedar - *Juniperus virginiana* L. (20) (1857)

Stinking clammy-weed [Stinking clammyweed] - *Polanisia dodecandra* (L.) DC. subsp. *dodecandra* (155) (1942)

Stinking clover - *Cleome serrulata* Pursh (80, 106, 156) (1913-1930)

Stinking cranebill [Stinking cranesbill] - *Geranium robertianum* L. (157, 158) (1900-1929)

Stinking elderberry - *Sambucus racemosa* L. var. *racemosa* (3) (1977)

Stinking gladen - *Iris foetidissima* L. (178) (1596)

Stinking goosefoot - *Chenopodium vulvaria* L. (5, 92, 122, 156) (1876-1937)

Stinking grass - *Eragrostis cilianensis* (All.) Vign. ex Janchen (56, 145) (1897-1901)

Stinking horehound - *Ballota nigra* L. (92, 158) (1876-1900)

Stinking mayweed - *Anthemis cotula* L. (165) (1807)

Stinking milkvetch [Stinking milk vetch] - *Astragalus praelongus* Sheldon var. *ellisiae* (Rydb.) Barneby (4) (1986)

Stinking motherwort [Stinking Mother woort] - *Chenopodium vulvaria* L. (156, 178) (1526-1923)

Stinking nightshade - *Hyoscyamus niger* L. (6, 7, 92, 156, 158) (1828-1923)

Stinking nutmeg - *Torreya californica* Torr. (14) (1882)

Stinking orache - *Chenopodium vulvaria* L. (92) (1876)

Stinking poke - *Symplocarpus foetidus* (L.) Salisb. ex Nutt. (64, 92, 156) (1876-1923)

Stinking pothos - *Symplocarpus foetidus* (L.) Salisb. ex Nutt. (186) (1814)

Stinking prairie bush [Stinking prairiebush, Stinking prairie-bush] - *Ptelea trifoliata* L. (92, 156, 158) (1876-1923)

Stinking rough bindweed [Stinking rough bind-weed] - *Smilax herbacea* L. (187) (1818)

Stinking sumac - *Rhus trilobata* Nutt. var. *trilobata* (65) (1931) OK

Stinking tich-weed - *Hedeoma pulegioides* (L.) Pers. (157) (1929)

Stinking wallrocket - *Diplotaxis muralis* (L.) DC. (155) (1942)

Stinking-Alexander [Stinking Alexander] - *Senecio jacobea* L. (156) (1923)

Stinking-ash [Stinking ash] - *Ptelea trifoliata* L. (6, 92, 156, 157, 158) (1892-1929)

Stinking-Benjamins [Stinking Benjamins] - *Trillium erectum* L. (73) (1892) NB

Stinking-dishcloth [Stinking dish-cloth] - *Trillium erectum* L. (73) (1892) Franklin Center PQ

Stinking-Roger - *Ballota nigra* L. (158) (1900)

Stinking-weed [Stinkingweed, Stinking weed] - *Chenopodium ambrosioides* L. var. *ambrosioides* (7, 92) (1828–1876), *Senna occidentalis* (L.) Link (107) (1919)

Stinking-Willie [Stinking Willie] - *Senecio jacobea* L. (92, 156) (1898-1923), *Trillium erectum* L. (156) (1923)

Stinkingwood [Stinking wood] - *Maclura pomifera* (Raf.) Schneid. (7) (1828)

Stinkkamillen (German) - *Anthemis cotula* L. (158, 186) (1814-1900)

Stink-Lattich - *Lactuca virosa* L. (158) (1900)

Stinkweed [Stink-weed, Stink weed] - *Chenopodium ambrosioides* L. (156) (1923), *Chenopodium ambrosioides* L. var. *ambrosioides* (6) (1892), *Cleome serrulata* Pursh (98) (1926), *Cleomella* DC. (50) (present), *Conium maculatum* L. (6, 71) (1892-1898), *Datura stramonium* L. (69, 71, 75, 156, 157, 158) (1898-1929), *Decodon verticillatus* (L.) Ell. (106) (1930), *Dyssodia papposa* (Vent.) A.S. Hitchc. (145) (1897), *Lobelia cardinalis* L. (157) (1929), *Pluchea camphorata* (L.) DC. (3) (1977), *Pluchea* Cass. (4) (1986), *Polanisia dodecandra* (L.) DC. subsp. *dodecandra* (L.) DC. subsp. *dodecandra* (7, 80) (1828-1913), *Polanisia dodecandra* (L.) DC. subsp. *trachysperma* (Torr. & Gray) Iltis (80) (1913), *Thlaspi arvense* L. (80) (1913), *Wislizenia refracta* Engelm. (106) (1930)

Stinkwood - *Nyssa sylvatica* Marsh. (106) (1930)

Stinkwort - *Datura stramonium* L. (69, 71, 92) (1876-1904)

Stitchwort [Stitch wort] - *Minuartia* L. (50) (present), *Stellaria* L. (4, 10, 19) (1818-1986), *Stellaria longifolia* Muhl. ex Willd. (46) (1671), *Stellaria longifolia* Muhl. ex Willd. var. *longifolia* (93) (1936), *Stellaria longipes* Goldie subsp. *longipes* (46) (1671), *Stellaria media* (L.) Vill. (92, 107) (1876-1919), *Stellaria palustris* (Murr.) Retz. (92) (1876)

Stlak (Flathead) - *Crataegus chrysocarpa* Ashe (101) (1905) MT, fruit

Stock [Stocks] - *Erysimum* L. (10) (1818), *Matthiola* Aiton f. (109, 138) (1923-1949), *Matthiola annua* (L.) Sweet (19) (1840), *Matthiola incana* (L.) Aiton f. (92, 107, 109, 131) (1876-1949)

Stockmalve (German) - *Alcea rosea* L. (158) (1900)

Stockrose (German) - *Alcea rosea* L. (158) (1900)

Stokes' aster [Stokes aster] - *Stokesia laevis* (Hill) Greene (86, 109) (1878-1949), *Stokesia* L'Hér. (109) (1949)

Stokesia - *Stokesia laevis* (Hill) Greene (138) (1923), *Stokesia* L'Hér. (138) (1923) for Johnathan Stokes, 1755-1831, English botanist with no connection to flower

Stoloniferous bishop's-cap [Stoloniferous bishop's cap] - *Mitella nuda* L. (5) (1913)

Stoloniferous mitrewort - *Mitella nuda* L. (5) (1913)

Stone basil - *Clinopodium vulgare* L. (5, 156) (1913-1923)

Stone beech - *Fagus grandifolia* Ehrh. (156) (1923)

Stone berry - *Rubus saxatilis* L. (107) (1919)

Stone clover [Stone-clover] - *Trifolium arvense* L. (5, 72, 92, 156, 158) (1876-1923)

Stone comfrey - *Prunella laciniata* (L.) L. (178) (1526)

Stone crop - *Sedum acre* L. (85) (1932)

Stone crottles - *Lichen caperatus* L. (92) (1876)

Stone fern - *Asplenium ruta-muraria* L. (92) (1876)

Stone fruits [Stone-fruits] - *Prunus* L. (109) (1949)

Stone oak - *Quercus alba* L. (157, 158) (1900-1929)

Stone pine - *Pinus cembra* L. (92) (1876), *Pinus monophylla* Torr. & Frém. (107) (1919), *Pinus pinea* L. (20, 107) (1857-1919) SD

Stone root [Stoneroot, stone-root] - *Collinsonia canadensis* L. (2, 5, 6, 7, 52, 53, 54, 55, 57, 58, 61, 64, 86, 92, 156) (1869-1923)

Stonebreak - *Saxifraga* L. (92) (1876)

Stonecrop [Stone crop, Stone-crop] - *Sedum acre* L. (85) (1932), *Sedum album* L. (107) (1919), *Sedum* L. (1, 2, 4, 10, 50, 86, 93, 109, 138, 155, 156, 157, 158, 167) (1814–present), *Sedum lanceolatum*

Torr. (3) (1977), *Sedum nuttallianum* Raf. (3) (1977), *Sedum pulchellum* Michx. (3, 48, 106) (1882-1977)

Stoneface - *Mesembryanthemum* L. (possibly) (109) (1949)

Stonemint [Stone mint, Stone-mint] - *Cunila* L. (4, 155, 158) (1900-1986), *Cunila origanoides* (L.) Britton (5, 7, 49, 58, 92, 97, 109, 138, 156, 158) (1828-1949)

Stone-mountian star - *Helianthus porteri* (A.Gray) Pruski (86) (1878)

Stone's thorn - *Crataegus intricata* Lange (5) (1913)

Stone's violet [Stones violet] - *Viola palmata* L. (155) (1942)

Stoneseed [Stone seed, Stone-seed] - *Buglossoides arvensis* (L.) I.M. Johnston (19, 92, 157, 158) (1840-1929), *Lithospermum* L. (50) (present)

Stoneweed [Stone weed, Stone-weed] - *Polygonum aviculare* L. (5, 156, 158) (1900-1923)

Stonewort - *Chara fragilis* Lois. (120) (1938) OK, *Chara* L. (92) (1876)

Stony-card - *Lithospermum officinale* L. (156) (1923)

Stool iris - *Iris aphylla* L. (138) (1923)

Storax or Storax tree [Storax trees] - *Liquidambar styraciflua* L. (34, 178) (1526-1834), *Styrax* L. (2, 8, 10, 109, 167) (1785-1949)

Storchschnabel (German) - *Geranium maculatum* L. (186) (1814)

Stork bill geranium [Stork bill geranium] - *Erodium ciconium* (L.) L'Hér. ex Aiton (19) (1840)

Stork-bill mallow [Storks bill mallow] - *Malva moschata* L. (178) (1526)

Storkenaab (Danish) - *Geranium maculatum* L. (186) (1814)

Storknäf (Swedish) - *Geranium maculatum* L. (186) (1814)

Stork's-bill [Storks' bill, Storksbill, Stork's bill, Storks bill] - *Erodium cicutarium* (L.) L'Hér. ex Aiton (85, 92, 103, 107, 156) (1870-1932), *Erodium* L'Her. ex Aiton (1, 4, 13, 15, 50, 156, 158) (1849–present), *Geranium maculatum* L. (6, 7, 64, 157, 158) (1828-1932), *Geranium sanguineum* L. (178) (1526), *Pelargonium* L'Hér. ex Aiton (109) (1949)

Stork's-bill with white flowers [Storks bill with white flowers] - *Geranium sylvaticum* L. (178) (1526)

Stout blue-eyed grass - *Sisyrinchium angustifolium* Mill. (5, 97) (1913-1937)

Stout love grass [Stout love-grass] - *Eragrostis hirsuta* (Michx.) Nees (5, 163) (1852-1913)

Stout phacelia - *Phacelia robusta* (Macbr.) Johnst. (50) (present)

Stout ragged goldenrod [Stout ragged golden-rod] - *Solidago squarrosa* Muhl. (5) (1913)

Stout rush - *Juncus nodatus* Cov. (3, 5, 50, 120) (1913–present)

Stout scouring-rush [Stout scouringrush] - *Equisetum hyemale* L. var. *affine* (Engelm.) A.A. Eat. (5, 97, 131, 138, 155) (1899-1942)

Stout stenanthium - *Stenanthium gramineum* (Ker-Gawl.) Morong var. *robustum* (S. Wats.) Fern. (5) (1913)

Stout wild rye - *Elymus canadensis* L. (72) (1907)

Stout woodreed - *Cinna arundinacea* L. (155) (1942)

Stout woodreed grass - *Cinna arundinacea* L. (122) (1937)

Straggling St. John's-wort [Straggling St. John's wort] - *Hypericum dolabriforme* Vent. (5) (1913)

Straight cypress - *Thuja plicata* Donn ex D. Don (35) (1806)

Straight-stem poison milkvetch [Straightstem poisonmilkvetch] - *Astragalus sabulosus* M.E. Jones (155) (1942)

Stramoine (French) - *Datura stramonium* L. (158) (1900)

Stramoine vulgaire (French) - *Datura stramonium* L. (7) (1828)

Stramonium - *Datura* L. (1, 18) (1805-1932), *Datura stramonium* L. (5, 18, 52, 53, 55, 59, 60, 92, 156, 158, 187) (1805-1923)

Stramonium (Official name of Materia Medica) - *Datura stramonium* L. (7) (1828)

Stramonium-leaf goosefoot [Stramonium-leaved goosefoot] - *Chenopodium simplex* (Torr.) Raf. (46) (1879)

Stramony - *Datura stramonium* L. (6) (1892)

Strand carex - *Carex hyalinolepis* Steud. (possibly) (187) (1818)

Strange marsh mallow - *Hibiscus moscheutos* L. subsp. *moscheutos* (178) (1526)

Strangle tare [Strangle-tare] - *Cuscuta epilinum* Weihe. (156) (1923), *Cuscuta europaea* L. (92) (1876), *Orobanche ludoviciana* Nutt. (5, 156) (1913-1923), *Orobanche minor* J.E. Smith (5, 156) (1913-1923), *Orobanche ramosa* L. (5) (1913), *Vicia hirsuta* (L.) Gray (5, 156) (1913-1923)

Strangleweed [Strangle-weed] - *Cuscuta epilinum* Weihe. (156) (1923), *Cuscuta pentagona* Engelm. var. *pentagona* (156) (1923)

Strap fern [Strapfern] - *Campyloneurum phyllitidis* (L.) K. Presl (138) (1923)

Strap-leaf willow [Strap-leaved willow] - *Salix ligulifolia* (Ball) Ball ex Schneid. (85) (1932)

Strassburg pine - *Abies alba* Mill. (possibly) (158) (1900)

Straw cactus - *Opuntia fulgida* Engelm. (76) (1896) AZ

Straw foxglove - *Digitalis lutea* L. (109, 138) (1923-1949)

Straw lily [Straw-lily, Straw lilies] - *Uvularia grandiflora* Smith. (156) (1923), *Uvularia sessilifolia* L. (75, 158) (1894-1900) CT

Straw sedge - *Carex striatula* Michx. (5, 19, 72, 156) (1840-1923)

Strawbell [Straw bell, Strawbells, Straw-bells] - *Uvularia perfoliata* L. (5) (1913), *Uvularia sessilifolia* L. (156) (1923)

Strawberry [Straw-berry, Strawberries, Strawberye, Strawberyes] - *Fragaria* L. (1, 4, 10, 35, 50, 63, 82, 105, 106, 107, 108, 109, 138, 155, 156, 158, 167, 182, 190) (~1759–present), *Fragaria vesca* L. (57, 110, 179, 184) (1526-1886), *Fragaria virginiana* Duchesne (114, 131, 156) (1894-1923)

Strawberry blite [Strawberry blight] - *Chenopodium capitatum* (L.) Asch. (2, 4, 5, 19, 85, 92, 107, 122, 156, 158) (1840-1986), *Chenopodium* L. (1, 42, 158) (1814-1932)

Strawberry bush [Strawberry-bush - *Calycanthus floridus* L. (5, 74) (1893-1913) Eastern MA, *Euonymus americanus* L. (5, 15, 65, 92, 97, 109, 113, 122, 124, 156) (1890-1949), *Euonymus atropurpurea* Jacq. (5, 157, 158) (1900-1929)

Strawberry clover - *Trifolium fragiferum* L. (4, 50, 109, 155) (1942–present), *Trifolium resuspinatum* L. (138) (1923)

Strawberry fern - *Hemionitis palmata* L. (138) (1923)

Strawberry ground-cherry [Strawberry groundcherry] - *Physalis alkekengi* L. (50, 138, 155) (1923–present)

Strawberry guave - *Psidium cattleianum* Sabine (109, 138) (1923-1949)

Strawberry huckleberry [Strawberry-huckleberry, Strawberry huckleberries, Strawberry-huckleberries] - *Vaccinium angustifolium* Aiton (5) (1913), *Vaccinium pallidum* Aiton (75) (1894) Weymouth MA

Strawberry pigweed - *Chenopodium* L. (1) (1932)

Strawberry raspberry - *Rubus illecebrosus* Focke (138) (1923)

Strawberry saxifrage - *Saxifraga stolonifera* Meerb. (138) (1923)

Strawberry shrub [Strawberry-shrub] - *Calycanthus floridus* L. (156) (1923), *Calycanthus floridus* L. var. *glaucus* (Willd.) Torr. & Gray (156) (1923), *Euonymus americanus* L. (7, 92) (1828-1876)

Strawberry spinach [Strawberry-spinage] - *Chenopodium capitatum* (L.) Asch. (2, 5, 46, 92, 107, 156, 158) (1859–1923)

Strawberry spinage [Strawberry-spinage] - *Chenopodium capitatum* (L.) Asch. (46) (1879), *Chenopodium* L. (10) (1818)

Strawberry tree [Strawberry-tree] - *Arbutus* L. (8, 42) (1785-1814), *Euonymus atropurpurea* Jacq. (5, 156, 157, 158) (1900-1929), *Euonymus* L. (13) (1849)

Strawberry vine [Strawberry vines] - *Fragaria* L. (182) (1791)

Strawberry-geranium - *Saxifraga stolonifera* Meerb. (109) (1949)

Strawberry-head clover [Strawberry-headed clover] - *Trifolium fragiferum* L. (3) (1977)

Strawberry-leaf Virginia crowfoot [Strawberry leaved Virginia crowfoot] - *Anemone quinquefolia* L. (181) (~1678)

Strawberry-tassel [Strawberry tassel] - *Polygala sanguinea* L. (5, 156, 157) (1913-1929)

Strawberry-tomato [Strawberry tomato] - *Physalis alkekengi* L. (107, 156, 158) (1900-1923), *Physalis heterophylla* Nees (5) (1913), *Physalis* L. (1, 2, 93) (1895-1936), *Physalis lanceolata* Michx. (107) (1919), *Physalis philadelphica* Lam. (107) (1885), *Phy-*

salis philadelphica Lam. var. *immaculata* Waterfall (5, 156) (1913-1923), *Physalis pubescens* L. (2, 5, 62, 107, 156) (1895-1932), *Physalis virginiana* Mill. (107) (1919)

Strawberry-weed [Strawberryweed] - *Potentilla norvegica* L. (3) (1977), *Potentilla recta* L. (98) (1926)

Straw-color cyperus [Straw-colored cyperus] - *Cyperus strigosus* L. (5, 72, 120, 156) (1907-1938)

Straw-color flatsedge [Straw-colored flatsedge] - *Cyperus strigosus* L. (50) (present)

Straw-color gentian [Straw colored gentian, Straw-colored gentian] - *Gentiana villosa* L. (5, 49, 92, 156) (1876-1923)

Straw-color paspalum [Straw-colored paspalum] - *Paspalum setaceum* Michx. (5, 119) (1913-1938)

Straw-color sedge [Straw-colored sedge] - *Carex straminea* Willd. ex Schkuhr (66, 129) (1894-1903)

Strawflower [Straw-flower] - *Anaphalis margaritacea* (L.) Benth. & Hook (106) (1930) WA, *Helichrysum bracteatum* (Vent.) Andr. (109, 138) (1923-1949), *Uvularia grandiflora* Smith. (156) (1923), *Uvularia perfoliata* L. (156) (1923), *Uvularia sessilifolia* L. (156) (1923)

Straw-sedge [Straw sedge] - *Cyperus esculentus* L. (66) (1903)

Strayberry - *Fragaria virginiana* Duchesne (156) (1923)

Streaked bur ragweed [Streaked burr ragweed] - *Ambrosia linearis* (Rydb.) Payne (50) (present)

Streaked grasse - *Phalaris arundinacea* L. (180) (1633)

Stream bogmoss - *Mayaca fluviatilis* Aubl. (50) (present)

Stream orchid - *Epipactis gigantea* Dougl. Ex Hook. (50) (present)

Streambank sedge - *Carex hyalinolepis* Steud. (155) (1942)

Streambank spiderlily - *Hymenocallis rotata* (Ker-Gawl.) Herbert (50) (present)

Streambank wheat grass [Streambank wheatgrass] - *Elymus lanceolatus* (Scribn. & J.G. Sm.) Gould (50, 155) (1942–present)

Stream-bed bristle grass [Streambed bristlegrass] - *Setaria leucopila* (Scribn. & Merr.) K. Schum. (50) (present)

Streamside fleabane - *Erigeron glabellus* Nutt. (50) (present)

Streichblume (German) - *Anthemis cotula* L. (186) (1814)

Streifenfarren (German) - *Comptonia peregrina* (L.) Coult. (7) (1828)

Streifenfarrenblättrige comptonia (German) - *Comptonia peregrina* (L.) Coult. (186) (1814)

Stretchberry [Stretch berry, Stretch-berry] - *Forestiera pubescens* Nutt. (50) (present), *Smilax bona-nox* L. (78, 156) (1898-1923) TX

Striate agrimony - *Agrimonia striata* Michx. (4) (1986)

Striate catchfly - *Silene conica* L. (5) (1913)

Striate sedge [Striated sedge] - *Carex striata* Michx. (66) (1903), *Carex striatula* Michx. (5) (1913)

Strict blue-eyed grass - *Sisyrinchium montanum* Greene (50) (present), *Sisyrinchium montanum* Greene var. *montanum* (5, 50) (1913–present)

Strict forget-me-not - *Myosotis stricta* Link ex Roemer & J.A. Schultes (50) (present)

Strict whitlow-wort - *Paronychia virginica* Spreng. (97) (1937)

Strict wild rye [Strict wild-rye] - *Elymus virginicus* L. var. *virginicus* (5, 72, 158, 163) (1852-1913) IA

Strigose black-Sampson [Strigose blacksampson] - *Echinacea angustifolia* DC. var. *strigosa* McGreg. (50) (present)

String bean - *Phaseolus vulgaris* L. (6) (1892)

String-of-sovereigns [Strings of sovereigns] - *Lysimachia nummularia* L. (156, 158) (1900-1923)

Stringy stonecrop - *Sedum sarmentosum* Bunge (138, 155) (1923-1942)

Stripe-berry manzanita [Stripeberry manzanita] - *Arctostaphylos pilosula* Jepson & Wies. ex Jepson (155) (1942)

Striped alder - *Hamamelis virginiana* L. (92) (1876), *Ilex verticillata* (L.) Gray (5, 92, 156) (1876-1923)

Striped bloodwort - *Hieracium venosum* L. (5, 92, 156, 157) (1876-1929)

Striped coralroot - *Corallorrhiza striata* Lindl. (3, 5) (1913-1977)

Striped dogwood - *Acer pensylvanicum* L. (92, 156) (1876-1923), *Acer spicatum* Lam. (58) (1869)

Striped gentian - *Gentiana villosa* L. (5, 156) (1913-1923)

Striped grass - *Phalaris arundinacea* L. (92) (1876)

Striped maple - *Acer pensylvanicum* L. (2, 15, 50, 92, 109, 138, 155, 156) (1895–present), *Acer spicatum* Lam. (19, 42, 58) (1814-1869)

Striped marigold - *Tagetes patula* L. (138) (1923)

Striped onion - *Allium oleraceum* L. (19) (1840)

Striped pipsissewa - *Chimaphila maculata* (L.) Pursh (138, 156) (1923)

Striped violet - *Viola striata* Aiton (5, 19, 156) (1840–1923) Blue Ridge VA obsolete by 1923

Striped woodwort - *Hieracium venosum* L. (49) (1898)

Striped-leaf arborvitae [Striped leaved arbor vitae] - *Thuja occidentalis* L. (8) (1785)

Stroil - *Elymus repens* (L.) Gould (5) (1913)

Strong-scented eragrostis - *Eragrostis cilianensis* (All.) Vign. ex Janchen (72) (1907)

Strong-scented lettuce - *Lactuca virosa* L. (49, 62, 92, 157, 158) (1876–1929)

Strong-scented love grass [Strong-scented love-grass] - *Eragrostis cilianensis* (All.) Vign. ex Janchen (5, 99, 119, 163) (1852-1938)

Strong-scented meadow grass - *Eragrostis minor* Host (66) (1903)

Strong-scented sporobolus - *Sporobolus heterolepis* (Gray) Gray (56, 94) (1901)

Strong-scented vilfa - *Sporobolus heterolepis* (Gray) Gray (66) (1903)

Strumarium - *Xanthium strumarium* L. (57) (1917)

Stuaertia - *Perideridia gairdneri* (Hook. & Arn.) Mathias (189) (1767)

Stubble spurge - *Chamaesyce nutans* (Lag.) Small (62) (1912) IN

Stubbleberry - *Solanum nigrum* L. (80, 157) (1929-1930)

Stubwort [Stub wort] - *Oxalis montana* Raf. (possibly) (5, 92, 156) (1876-1923)

Stud flower [Stud-flower] - *Helonias bullata* L. (5, 86, 156) (1878-1923)

Stud-flower Virginia cistus [Studded flowered Virginia cistus] - *Kalmia latifolia* L. (181) (~1678)

Stud-flower Virginia spiderwort [Studded flowrd Virginia spiderwort] - *Aletris aurea* Walt. (181) (~1678)

Stump tree [Stump-tree, Stumptree] - *Gymnocladus dioicus* (L.) K. Koch (38, 107, 156) (1820-1923)

Stunted panicum - *Dichanthelium depauperatum* (Muhl.) Gould (3) (1977)

Sturdy - *Lolium temulentum* L. (157, 158) (1900-1929)

Sturdy bulrush - *Schoenoplectus robustus* (Pursh) M.T. Strong (50) (present)

Sturdy ryle - *Lolium temulentum* L. (5) (1913)

Stuve's bush clover [Stuve's bush-clover] - *Lespedeza stuevei* Nutt. (5) (1913)

Stuve's lespedeza [Stuves lespedeza] - *Lespedeza stuevei* Nutt. (3, 155) (1942-1977)

Stychewort [Styche wort] - *Stellaria holostea* L. (179) (1526)

Stypticweed [Styptic weed] - *Senna occidentalis* (L.) Link (5, 92) (1876-1913)

Styrax - *Liquidambar styraciflua* L. (178) (1526)

Styrax (French) - *Styrax* L. (8) (1785)

Suakwa towel gourd [Suakwa towelgourd] - *Luffa aegyptiaca* Mill. (138) (1923)

Subalpine aster - *Eurybia merita* (A. Nels.) Nesom (50) (present)

Subalpine fir - *Abies lasiocarpa* (Hook.) Nutt. (50) (present)

Subalpine yarrow - *Achillea millefolium* L. (155) (1942)

Subarctic lady fern [Subarctic ladyfern] - *Athyrium filix-femina* (L.) Roth subsp. *angustum* (Willd.) Clausen (50) (present), *Athyrium filix-femina* (L.) Roth subsp. *cyclosorum* (Rupr.) C. Christens. (50) (present)

Subserrulata rose - *Rosa carolina* L. var. *carolina* (155) (1942)

Subterranean Indian breadroot - *Pediomelum hypogaeum* (Nutt. ex Torr. & Gray) Rydb. (50) (present)

Subulate sagittaria - *Sagittaria subulata* (L.) Buch. (5) (1913)

Succory - *Cichorium intybus* L. (7, 10, 19, 45, 49, 80, 92, 107, 109, 156) (1818-1949), *Cichorium* L. (42) (1814), *Lapsana communis* L. (5) (1913)

Succory dock cress [Succory dock-cress] - *Lapsana communis* L. (92, 156) (1898-1923)

Succory gum - *Chondrilla juncea* L. (92) (1876)

Succulent hawthorn - *Crataegus succulenta* Schrad. ex Link (4) (1986)

Succus thebaicus - *Papaver somniferum* L. (49) (1898)

Suck-bottle [Suck bottle] - *Lamium album* L. (5, 156) (1913-1923) no longer in use by 1923

Suckehihaw (Osage) - *Tephrosia* Pers. (7) (1828)

Sucker flax - *Linum medium* (Planch.) Britton var. *texanum* (Planch.) Fern. (4) (1986)

Suckles - *Trifolium pratense* L. (5, 156, 157, 158) (1900-1923) no longer in use by 1923

Suckleya - *Suckleya* Gray (50, 155, 158) (1900–present), *Suckleya suckleyana* (Torr.) Rydb. (148) (1939)

Suckley's endolepis - *Endolepis dioica* (Nutt.) Standl. (50) (present)

Suckling - *Trifolium repens* L. (157, 158) (1900-1929)

Suckling clover - *Trifolium dubium* Sibth. (50, 155) (1942–present)

Sucré Baie (French) - *Celtis occidentalis* L. (6) (1892)

Sucumug (Mohegans) - *Tilia* L. (7) (1828)

Sucuy (Algic tribes) - *Tilia* L. (7) (1828)

Sudan grass [Sudan-grass, Sudangrass] - *Sorghum bicolor* (L.) Moench subsp. *drummondii* (Nees ex Steud.) de Wet & Harlan (50, 109, 119, 138) (1923–present)

Süsskirshbaum (German) - *Prunus avium* (L.) L. (110) (1886)

Suffolk grass - *Poa annua* L. (90) (1885) ME

Sugar and muske melons, diuers sorts - *Cucumis melo* L. (178) (1526)

Sugar bean - *Phaseolus lunatus* L. (107, 110) (1886-1919)

Sugar beet - *Beta vulgaris* L. (107) (1919)

Sugar birch - *Betula nigra* L. (41) (1770)

Sugar blueberry - *Vaccinium angustifolium* Aiton (5) (1913)

Sugar brakes - *Onoclea sensibilis* L. (78) (1898) ME

Sugar bush - *Rhus ovata* S. Wats. (106, 109) (1930-1949)

Sugar cane - *Sorghum* Moench (78) (1898) OH

Sugar corn - *Zea mays* L. (109, 119) (1938-1949)

Sugar grape - *Vitis rupestris* Scheele (2, 5, 15, 74, 82, 97, 107, 156) (1893-1937)

Sugar gum - *Eucalyptus cladocalyx* F. Muell. (possibly) (109) (1949)

Sugar hackberry - *Celtis laevigata* Willd. (155) (1942)

Sugar huckleberry - *Vaccinium pallidum* Aiton (3) (1977)

Sugar maple - *Acer grandidentatum* Nutt. (122) (1937), *Acer negundo* L. (5, 157, 158) (1900-1929), *Acer palmatum* Thunb. (46) (1783), *Acer rubrum* L. (2, 8, 14, 18, 19, 20, 33, 41, 103, 105, 107, 124) (1770-1937), *Acer saccharum* Marsh. (3, 4, 5, 15, 40, 50, 65, 82, 85, 93, 97, 106, 109, 112, 124, 131, 135, 138, 155, 156, 158) (1895–present)

Sugar pear - *Amelanchier canadensis* (L.) Medik. (5, 73, 74, 156, 158) (1892-1923)

Sugar pine - *Pinus lambertiana* Dougl. (50, 75, 107, 109, 138, 145, 161) (1894–present)

Sugar quillowrt - *Isoetes saccharata* Engelm. (50) (present)

Sugar root [Sugar-root] - *Craniolaria annua* L. (138) (1923)

Sugar rush [Sugar-rush] - *Juncus effusus* L. (156) (1923)

Sugar sorghum - *Sorghum bicolor* (L.) Moench subsp. *bicolor* (67, 109) (1890-1949)

Sugar tree [Sugartree, Sugar-tree] - *Acer rubrum* L. (35, 37, 43, 76) (1806-1919), *Acer saccharum* Marsh. (5, 35, 156, 158, 177) (1762-1923)

Sugar-apple [Sugar apple] - *Rollinia mucosa* (Jacq.) Baill. (107) (1919), *Annona squamosa* L. (109, 110, 137, 155) (1886-1949)

Sugarberry [Sugar-berry, Sugar berry] - *Amelanchier alnifolia* (Nutt.) Nutt. ex M. Roemer (130) (1895) SD, *Amelanchier ca-*

nadensis (L.) Medik. (5, 74, 156, 158) (1893-1923) NH, *Gaultheria hispidula* (L.) Muhl. ex Bigelow (77) (1898)

Sugarberry [Sugar-berry, Sugar berry] or Sugar-berry tree [Sugar berry tree] - *Celtis laevigata* Willd. (3, 4, 50, 109) (1949–present), *Celtis occidentalis* L. (5, 6, 14, 46, 92, 106, 107, 156, 158, 187) (1818-1930), *Celtis tenuifolia* Nutt. (106, 138) (1923-1930)

Sugarcane [Sugar cane, Sugar-cane] - *Saccharum* L. (7, 56) (1828-1901), *Saccharum officinarum* L. (10, 19, 45, 57, 59, 66, 67, 92, 94, 107, 109, 110, 138, 163) (1840-1949), *Sorghum bicolor* (L.) Moench subsp. *bicolor* (56, 109) (1901-1949)

Sugarcane plume - *Saccharum giganteum* (Walt.) Pers. (122) (1937) TX

Sugarcane plume grass [Sugarcane plumegrass] - *Saccharum giganteum* (Walt.) Pers. (50) (present)

Sugarpine - *Zamia pumila* L. (possibly) (7) (1828)

Sugar-plum [Sugar plum, Sugar-plums, Sugar plums] - *Amelanchier canadensis* (L.) Medik. (5, 73, 74, 156, 158) (1892-1923) NH, no longer in use by 1923, *Amelanchier* Medik. (4) (1986), *Gaultheria hispidula* (L.) Muhl. ex Bigelow (156) (1923) no longer in use by 1923, *Trifolium pratense* L. (5, 156) (1913-1923)

Sugary quillwort - *Isoetes saccharata* Engelm. (5) (1913)

Sugre rede - *Saccharum officinarum* L. (178, 179) (1526-1596)

Sugumuck (Mohegans) - *Tilia* L. (7) (1828)

Suh (Kioway) - *Quercus* L. (132) (1855)

Suhuara - *Carnegia gigantea* (Engelm.) Britt. & Rose (104) (1896)

Sukai (Greek) - *Ficus carica* L. (110) (1886)

Suksdorf's clematis [Suksdorf clematis] - *Clematis ligusticifolia* Nutt. var. *ligusticifolia* (155) (1942)

Šul(a)mix (Chinookan) - *Cornus canadensis* L. (35) (1806)

Sulfur cinquefoil [Sulphur cinquefoil] - *Potentilla recta* L. (3, 4, 50, 155) (1942–present)

Sulfur Indian paintbrush [Sulphur Indian paintbrush] - *Castilleja sulphurea* Rydb. (50) (present)

Sulfur painted-cup [Sulfur paintedcup] - *Castilleja sulphurea* Rydb. (155) (1942)

Sulfur pore fungus [Sulphur pore fungus] - *Polyporus sulphureus* (Bull.) Fr. (128) (1933)

Sulfurwort [Sulphurwort, Sulphur wort, Sulpher wort] - *Peucedanum* L. (10) (1818), *Oxypolis ternata* (Nutt.) Heller (19) (1840)

Sullendine - *Impatiens capensis* Meerb. (79) (1891) NH

Sullivantia - *Sullivantia sullivantii* (Torr. & Gray) Britton (5, 72) (1907-1913)

Sullivant's honeysuckle - *Lonicera reticulata* Raf. (5, 72, 82, 97) (1907-1937)

Sullivant's milkweed [Sullivants milkweed] - *Asclepias sullivantii* Engelm. ex Gray (5, 72, 82, 93, 155) (1907-1942)

Sultan zambach (Turks) - *Lilium candidum* L. (180) (1633)

Sultana star thistle - *Centaurea americana* Nutt. (122, 124) (1937) TX

Sultan's snapweed [Sultan snapweed] - *Impatiens walleriana* Hook. f. (138) (1923)

Sumac (French) - *Rhus* L. (8) (1785)

Sumac [Sumach, Shumac, Sumack] - *Rhus copallinum* L. (181) (~1678), *Rhus glabra* L. (22, 38, 40, 48, 55, 57, 58, 59, 61, 85) (1820-1932), *Rhus* L. (1, 4, 7, 8, 10, 13, 14, 15, 10, 50, 82, 93, 106, 138, 155, 158, 190) (~1759–present)

Sumac amaranthe (French) - *Rhus typhina* L. (possibly) (8) (1785)

Sumac copalme (French) - *Rhus copallinum* L. (8) (1785)

Sumac de Virginie (French) - *Rhus typhina* L. (possibly) (8) (1785)

Sumac fustet d'Amerique (French) - *Cotinus obovatus* Raf. (20) (1857)

Sumac glabre (French) - *Rhus glabra* L. (8) (1785)

Sumac of East Texas - *Rhus glabra* L. (124) (1937)

Sumac veneneux (French) - *Toxicodendron toxicarium* (Salisb.) Gillis (6) (1892)

Sumac vernis (French) - *Toxicodendron vernix* (L.) Kuntze (8) (1785)

Suma-catechu acacia - *Acacia polyacantha* Willd. (155) (1942)

Sumach vénéneux (French) - *Toxicodendron radicans* (L.) Kuntze subsp. *radicans* (158) (1900)

Šu-min (Chippewa) - *Vitis* L. (105) (1932)

Summer adonis - *Adonis aestivalis* L. (109, 137, 155) (1923-1949)

Summer coralroot - *Corallorrhiza maculata* (Raf.) Raf. (50) (present)

Summer coralroot - *Corallorrhiza maculata* (Raf.) Raf. var. *occidentalis* (Lindl.) Ames (50) (present)

Summer crookneck squash - *Cucurbita pepo* L. var. *melopepo* (L.) Alef. (138) (1923)

Summer cypress - *Kochia scoparia* (L.) Schrad. (19) (1840)

Summer dew grass - *Agrostis gigantea* Roth (5, 45) (1896–1913)

Summer dorn - *Leontodon autumnalis* L. (46) (1879)

Summer grape - *Vitis aestivalis* Michx. (2, 5, 15, 19, 27, 35, 46, 50, 72, 95, 97, 107, 109, 113, 138, 155, 156, 158) (1879–present)

Summer grass [Summer-grass] - *Hierochloe odorata* (L.) Beauv. (possibly) (92) (1876), *Poa annua* L. (94) (1901)

Summer haw - *Crataegus aestivalis* Torr. & Gray. (2) (1895), *Crataegus flava* Aiton (2, 5, 107) (1895-1919), *Crataegus mollis* Scheele (4) (1986)

Summer heliotrope - *Valeriana officinalis* L. (5, 76, 156) (1896-1923)

Summer lady's-tresses [Summer ladies' tresses] - *Spiranthes torta* (Thunb.) Garay & H.R. Sweet (19) (1840)

Summer milkvetch - *Astragalus hyalinus* M.E. Jones (50) (present)

Summer orophaca - *Astragalus hyalinus* M.E. Jones (4) (1986)

Summer perennial phlox - *Phlox paniculata* L. (109) (1949)

Summer phlox - *Phlox paniculata* L. (155) (1942)

Summer plum - *Prunus angustifolia* Marsh. (possibly) (19) (1840)

Summer rape - *Brassica rapa* L. var. *rapa* (158) (1900)

Summer savory - *Satureja hortensis* L. (19, 46, 49, 57, 58, 92, 106, 107, 109, 138, 156) (1671-1949) cultivated by English colonists by 1671

Summer sedge - *Carex aestivalis* M.A. Curtis ex Gray (5, 50) (1913–present)

Summer snowflake [Summer-snowflake] - *Leucojum aestivum* L. (138) (1923), *Ornithogalum umbellatum* L. (5, 156, 158) (1900-1923)

Summer sottekins [Sommer sottekins] - *Leucojum aestivum* L. (178) (1596)

Summer vetch - *Vicia sativa* L. subsp. *nigra* (L.) Ehrh. (155) (1942)

Summer wheat - Elymus repens (L.) Gould (19) (1840), *Triticum aestivum* L. (158) (1900)

Summer-cypress [Summercypress, Summer cypress] - *Kochia* Roth (138, 155) (1923-1942), *Kochia scoparia* (L.) Schrad. (4, 5, 19, 85, 97, 109, 125, 156, 157, 158) (1840-1986)

Summer-farewell [Summer farewell] - *Dalea pinnata* (J.F. Gmel.) Barneby var. *pinnata* (106) (1930) because of late blooming

Summer-fir Russian wormwood [Summerfir Russian wormwood] - *Artemisia gmelinii* Webb ex Stechmann (155) (1942)

Summer-fools [Sommer fooles] - *Leucojum aestivum* L. (178) (1596), *Leucojum vernum* L. (180) (1633)

Summer-lilac [Summer lilac] - *Hesperis matronalis* L. (5, 156, 158) (1900-1923)

Summer-squashes [Summersquashes] - *Cucurbita pepo* L. var. *melopepo* (L.) Alef. (109) (1949)

Summer-sweet [Summersweet, Summer sweet] - *Clethra alnifolia* L. (109, 138, 156) (1923-1949)

Summer-thrift - *Armeria maritima* (P. Mill.) Willd (156) (1923)

Summit cinquefoil - *Potentilla hippiana* Lehm. var. *hippiana* (155) (1942)

Sumpf Ringelblume (German) - *Caltha palustris* L. (6) (1892)

Sumpfcornel [Sumpf cornel] (German) - *Cornus amomum* Mill. (6, 158) (1892-1900)

Sumpfnelkenwurzel (German) - *Geum rivale* L (6, 158) (1892-1900)

Sumpweed - *Iva* L. (155) (1942)

Sun euphorbia - *Euphorbia helioscopia* L. (155) (1942)

Sun fern - *Phegopteris connectilis* (Michx.) Watt (5, 50) (1913–present)

Sun plant [Sun-plant] - *Portulaca grandiflora* Hook. (5, 156, 158) (1900-1923)

Sun sedge - *Carex inops* Bailey subsp. *heliophila* (Mackenzie) Crins (50, 139, 155) (1942–present)

Sun spurge - *Euphorbia helioscopia* L. (5, 156) (1913-1923)

Sunbright - *Talinum parviflorum* Nutt. (50) (present)

Sunburst - Eriophyllum Lag (possibly) (138) (1923)

Sundew [Sun-dew] - *Drosera* L. (1, 2, 4, 7, 10, 13, 50, 109, 138, 155, 158) (1818–present), *Drosera rotundifolia* L. (19, 47, 49, 52, 53, 54, 57, 61, 92, 156) (1840-1923)

Sundial [Sun-dial, Sun dial] - *Lupinus arboreus* Sims (76) (1896) CA, *Lupinus perennis* L. (5, 76, 156) (1896-1923), *Lupinus* L. (76, 158) (1896-1900) Sulphur Grove OH, *Lupinus villosus* Willd. (73) (1892) Northern OH

Sundial lupine [Sun-dial lupine] - *Lupinus perennis* L. (138) (1923)

Sundrop [Sundrops, Sun-drops] - *Calylophus* Spach (50) (present), *Oenothera biennis* L. (7) (1828), *Oenothera fruticosa* L. (19, 63, 109, 156) (1840-1949) IA, *Oenothera fruticosa* L. subsp. *glauca* (Michx.) Straley (92, 109) (1876-1949), *Oenothera* L. (1, 138, 155, 158) (1900-1942), *Oenothera perennis* L. (109) (1949)

Sunflower [Sun-flower] - *Anagallis arvensis* L. (5, 156, 158) (1900-1923), *Helianthus annuus* L. (6, 37, 49, 57, 107, 108, 114, 150, 157, 158) (1878-1929), *Helianthus grosseserratus* Martens (145) (1897), *Helianthus* L. (1, 4, 7, 21, 35, 50, 63, 82, 93, 106, 109, 122, 127, 138, 146, 155, 156, 158, 167, 184) (1793–present), *Helianthus maximiliani* Schrad. (145) (1897), *Helianthus salicifolius* A. Dietr. (145) (1897), *Rudbeckia laciniata* L. (157) (1929)

Sunflower crownbeard [Sunflower crown-beard, Sunflower-crownbeard] - *Verbesina helianthoides* Michx. (97, 122, 124, 156, 158) (1900-1937)

Sunflower heliopsis - *Heliopsis helianthoides* (L.) Sweet (138, 155) (1923-1942), *Heliopsis helianthoides* (L.) Sweet var. *scabra* (Dunal) Fern. (155) (1942)

Šuniau-jibik (Chippewa, money root) - *Panax quinquefolius* L. (105) (1932)

Sunn hemp - *Crotalaria juncea* L. (109) (1949)

Sunrose [Sun-rose] - *Helianthemum canadense* (L.) Michx. (92, 156) (1898-1923), *Helianthemum* Mill. (109, 138, 155) (1923-1949)

Sunset lily - *Lilium pardalinum* Kellogg subsp. *pardalinum* (109) (1949)

Sunshine brome - *Bromus commutatus* Schrad. (155) (1942)

Sunshine rose - *Rosa arkansana* Porter var. *suffulta* (Greene) Cockerell (155) (1942)

Šuns-šabu-min (Chippewa [smooth gooseberry) - *Ribes niveum* Lindl. (105) (1932)

Sunweed [Sun-weed] - *Euphorbia helioscopia* L. (5, 156) (1913-1923)

Šuŋkače (Lakota, dog penis) - *Acorus calamus* L. (121) (1918-1970)

Šuŋkčaŋkahuipije (Lakota, horse spine cure) - *Onosmodium molle* Michx. subsp. *occidentale* (Mackenzie) Cochrane (121) (1918?-1970?)

Šuŋkuštipije (Lakota, horse hoof cure) - *Hymenopappus tenuifolius* Pursh (121) (1918?-1970?)

Superb lily - *Lilium superbum* L. (19, 156) (1840-1923)

Supickerreidt (Dutch) - *Saccharum officinarum* L. (180) (1633)

Supine linaria - *Linaria supina* (L.) Chaz. (5) (1913)

Supple-Jack [Supplejack, Supple jack, Supple jacks] - *Berchemia* Neck. (13, 138) (1849-1923), *Berchemia scandens* (Hill.) Trelease (2, 5, 12, 15, 58, 92, 97, 106, 122, 124, 156) (1819-1937), *Zizyphus* Mill (10) (1818)

Sureau (French) - *Sambucus* L. (8) (1785), *Sambucus nigra* L. (158) (1900)

Sureau du Canada (French) - *Sambucus nigra* L. subsp. *canadensis* (L.) R. Bolli (6, 8) (1785-1892)

Sureau noir (French) - *Sambucus nigra* L. (8) (1785)

Surgeon's-agaric [Surgeon's agaric] - *Fomes fomentarius* (L.) Fr. (57) (1917)

Surinam-cherry - *Eugenia uniflora* L. (109, 138) (1923-1949)

Surkullor (Swedish) - *Anthemis cotula* L. (186) (1814)

Surtuppor - *Anthemis cotula* L. (186) (1814)

Survy-grass - *Cochlearia* L. (158) (1900)

Suscutan - *Amelanchier alnifolia* (Nutt.) Nutt. ex M. Roemer (130) (1895) SD

Suterberry [Suter-berry] - *Zanthoxylum americanum* Mill. (5, 6, 7, 49, 156, 157, 158) (1828-1929), *Zanthoxylum clava-herculis* L. (49) (1898)

Sutterberry bark - *Zanthoxylum americanum* Mill. (92) (1876)

Suwarrow (Mexicans) - *Carnegia gigantea* (Engelm.) Britt. & Rose (107, 147) (1856-1919)

Swale wheat grass [Swale wheatgrass] - *Elymus vulpinus* Rydb. (155) (1942)

Swallow-wort [Swallowwort, Swallow wort] - *Asclepias incarnata* L. (34) (1834), *Asclepias* L. (10) (1818), *Asclepias syriaca* L. (19, 92) (1840-1876), *Asclepias tuberosa* L. (58, 77) (1869-1898), *Chamaesyce prostrata* (Aiton) Small (158) (1900), *Chelidonium* L. (15) (1895), *Chelidonium majus* L. (5, 156, 158) (1900-1923), *Cynanchum* L. (50, 155, 158) (1900–present)

Swamp alder - *Alnus rubra* Bong. (92) (1876), *Alnus serrulata* (Aiton) Willd. (58) (1869)

Swamp American dogwood - *Cornus foemina* Mill. (8) (1785)

Swamp andromeda - *Lyonia ligustrina* (L.) DC. (156) (1923)

Swamp ash - *Fraxinus americana* L. (19) (1840), *Fraxinus nigra* Marsh (5, 156, 158) (1900-1923), *Fraxinus pennsylvanica* Marsh. (5, 156, 157) (1913-1929)

Swamp aster - *Oclemena acuminata* (Michx.) Greene (106) (1930), *Symphyotrichum prenanthoides* (Muhl. ex Willd.) Nesom (156) (1923), *Symphyotrichum puniceum* (L.) A.& D. Löve var. *puniceum* (3, 4, 138, 155, 156) (1923-1986)

Swamp azalea - *Rhododendron viscosum* (L.) Torr. (8, 138) (1785-1923)

Swamp bay - *Gordonia lasianthus* L. (5) (1913), *Magnolia virginiana* L. (156) (1923), *Persea palustris* (Raf.) Sargent (5, 156) (1913-1923)

Swamp beggarsticks [Swamp beggar's tick, Swamp beggars' tick, Swamp beggar-ticks] - *Bidens bidentoides* (Nutt.) Britton (5, 156) (1913-1923), *Bidens connata* Muhl. ex Willd. (62, 63, 72, 82, 156) (1899-1930), *Bidens tripartita* L. (92, 158) (1876-1900)

Swamp betony - *Pedicularis lanceolata* Michx. (85) (1932)

Swamp birch - *Betula alleghaniensis* Britt. var. *alleghaniensis* (5, 156) (1913-1923), *Betula occidentalis* Hook. (1) (1932), *Betula pumila* L. (82, 156) (1923-1930)

Swamp blackberry - *Rubus hispidus* L. (107) (1919)

Swamp blueberry - *Vaccinium corymbosum* L. (5, 107, 109, 156) (1913-1949)

Swamp brake - *Osmunda cinnamomea* L. (5) (1913)

Swamp buttercup - *Ranunculus hispidus* Michx. var. *nitidus* (Chapman) T. Duncan (5, 80, 97, 131, 138, 155, 156, 158) (1899-1942)

Swamp camas [Swampcamas] - *Zigadenus elegans* Pursh (133) (1903), *Zigadenus venenosus* S. Wats. var. *gramineus* (Rydb.) Walsh ex M.E. Peck (148) (1939)

Swamp chess [Swamp-chess] - *Bromus ciliatus* L. (5, 56, 75, 94, 111, 129, 163) (1852-1915), *Bromus kalmii* Gray (75) (1894), *Bromus latiglumis* (Shear) A.S. Hitchc. (56) (1901)

Swamp chestnut oak - *Quercus michauxii* Nutt. (5, 138, 156) (1913-1923), *Quercus muehlenbergii* Engelm. (122) (1937), *Quercus prinus* L. (possibly) (5, 19, 33, 156) (1827-1923)

Swamp cottonwood - *Populus heterophylla* L. (5, 156) (1913-1923)

Swamp currant - *Ribes lacustre* (Pers.) Poir. (3, 4, 85, 155) (1932-1986)

Swamp currant - *Ribes triste* Pallas (3, 4) (1977-1986)

Swamp dewberry - *Rubus hispidus* L. (138) (1923)

Swamp dock - *Rumex verticillatus* L. (2, 5, 50, 58, 72, 97, 122, 155, 156) (1869–present)

Swamp dogwood [Swamp-dogwood - *Cephalanthus occidentalis* L. (58, 157, 158) (1869-1929), *Cornus amomum* Mill. (5, 156,

157, 158) (1900-1929), *Cornus sericea* L. (6, 7, 58, 92) (1828-1892)

Swamp dropseed - *Muhlenbergia schreberi* J.F. Gmel. (5, 50) (1913–present)

Swamp elm - *Ulmus americana* L. (5, 113, 156, 157, 158) (1890-1929), *Ulmus thomasii* Sarg. (5, 158) (1900-1913)

Swamp eubotrys - *Leucothoe racemosa* (L.) Gray (5) (1913)

Swamp fern - *Thelypteris palustris* Schott var. *pubescens* (Lawson) Fern. (5, 158) (1900-1913)

Swamp fly honeysuckle (swamp fly-honeysuckle) - *Lonicera oblongifolia* (Goldie) Hook. (5, 138, 156) (1913-1923)

Swamp gentian - *Gentiana saponaria* L. (122, 124) (1937) TX

Swamp goldenrod [Swamp golden-rod] - *Euthamia graminifolia* (L.) Nutt. (62) (1912), *Solidago uliginosa* Nutt. (5, 138) (1913-1923), *Solidago uliginosa* Nutt. var. *uliginosa* (5, 156) (1913-1923)

Swamp gooseberry - *Ribes lacustre* (Pers.) Poir. (2, 5, 19, 107, 130, 156) (1840-1923)

Swamp grape - *Vitis labrusca* L. (156) (1923)

Swamp grass - *Sporobolus indicus* (L.) R. Br. var. *indicus* (5) (1913)

Swamp hellebore - *Veratrum viride* Ait. (5, 49, 53, 59, 64, 71, 92, 156) (1876–1923)

Swamp hickory - *Carya aquatica* (Michx. f.) Nutt. (5, 97, 156) (1913-1937), *Carya cordiformis* (Wangenh.) K. Koch (1, 5, 82, 93, 97, 109, 156, 187) (1818-1949)

Swamp holly - *Ilex crenata* Thunb. (5, 156, 158) (1900-1923)

Swamp honeysuckle - *Lonicera* L. (possibly) (1) (1932)

Swamp hornbeam - *Nyssa aquatica* L. (5, 156) (1913-1923), *Nyssa biflora* Walt. (5) (1913), *Nyssa sylvatica* Marsh. (19, 92, 156) (1840-1923)

Swamp horsetail - *Equisetum fluviatile* L. (5, 72, 131, 155) (1899-1942)

Swamp laurel - *Gordonia lasianthus* L. (7, 92, 156) (1828–1923), *Kalmia* L. (1) (1932), *Kalmia polifolia* Wangenh. (5, 7, 19, 92, 156) (1828–1923), *Magnolia virginiana* L. (5, 6, 19, 106, 156, 187) (1818-1930)

Swamp leatherwood - *Dirca palustris* L. (7) (1828)

Swamp leucothoe - *Leucothoe racemosa* (L.) Gray (156) (1923)

Swamp lily [Swamp-lily] - *Lilium superbum* L. (156) (1923), *Zephyranthes atamasca* (L.) Herbert (5, 156) (1913-1923)

Swamp lobelia - *Lobelia paludosa* Nutt. (5) (1913)

Swamp locust - *Gleditsia aquatica* Marsh. (5, 19, 97, 158) (1840-1937)

Swamp loosestrife - *Decodon* J.F. Gmel. (1) (1932), *Decodon verticillatus* (L.) Ell. (5, 106, 156) (1913-1930)

Swamp lousewort - *Pedicularis lanceolata* Michx. (4, 5, 50, 72, 93, 131) (1899–present)

Swamp magnolia - *Magnolia virginiana* L. (5, 156) (1913-1923)

Swamp maple - *Acer rubrum* L. (2, 5, 57, 72, 82, 93, 106, 107, 109, 156, 187) (1818–1949), *Acer spicatum* Lam. (5, 76, 156) (1896–1923) Paris ME

Swamp marigold - *Bidens connata* Muhl. ex Willd. (82) (1930)

Swamp meadow grass [Swamp meadow-grass] - *Poa palustris* L. (143) (1852-1936)

Swamp milkweed - *Asclepias incarnata* L. (3, 4, 5, 40, 49, 50, 52, 53, 57, 58, 62, 63, 64, 72, 82, 85, 92, 95, 97, 98, 109, 114, 122, 124, 127, 131, 138, 155, 156, 157, 158) (1869–present)

Swamp oak - *Quercus bicolor* Willd (5, 105, 156) (1913-1932), *Quercus imbricaria* Michx. (78) (1898) Southwest MO, *Quercus laurifolia* Michx. (5) (1913), *Quercus nigra* L. (12, 41) (1770-1821), *Quercus palustris* Muench. (1, 5, 12, 93, 97, 156) (1913-1937), *Quercus phellos* L. (41) (1770), *Quercus prinus* L. (possibly) (14, 19. 92) (1840-1882)

Swamp pedicularis - *Pedicularis lanceolata* Michx. (155) (1942)

Swamp Pennsylvania rose [Swamp Pennsylvanian rose] - *Rosa palustris* Marsh. (8) (1785)

Swamp persicaria - *Polygonum amphibium* L. var. *emersum* Michx. (5, 72, 93, 97, 120, 131) (1899-1938)

Swamp pine - *Pinus taeda* L. (5) (1913)

Swamp pink [Swamppink, Swamp-pink] - *Arethusa bulbosa* L. (78) (1898) MA, *Calopogon tuberosus* (L.) B.S.P. var. *tuberosus* (5, 156) (1913-1923), *Helonias bullata* L. (5, 138, 156) (1913-1923), *Helonias* L. (109, 138) (1923-1949), *Rhododendron* L. (7) (1828), *Rhododendron periclymenoides* (Michx.) Shinners (5, 73, 156) (1892-1923) Northeastern US, *Rhododendron viscosum* (L.) Torr. (5, 19, 73, 92, 156) (1840-1923) MA

Swamp poke - *Veratrum viride* Ait. (187) (1818)

Swamp poplar - *Populus heterophylla* L. (5, 156) (1913-1923)

Swamp post oak - *Quercus lyrata* Walt. (5, 10, 33, 82, 156) (1818-1930)

Swamp potamogeton - *Potamogeton gramineus* L. (possibly) (131) (1899)

Swamp potato - *Sagittaria cuneata* Sheld. (101) (1905) MT, *Sagittaria* L. (1, 10) (1818-1932), *Sagittaria latifolia* Willd. (103, 107) (1871-1919)

Swamp poverty grass [Swamp poverty-grass] - *Aristida palustris* (Chapman) Vasey (94) (1901)

Swamp prickle grass [Swamp pricklegrass] - *Crypsis schoenoides* (L.) Lam. (50) (present)

Swamp privet - *Forestiera acuminata* (Michx.) Poir. (3, 4, 156) (1923-1986)

Swamp ragwort - *Senecio congestus* (R.Br.) DC. (3, 4) (1977-1986)

Swamp raspberry - *Rubus pubescens* Raf. var. *pubescens* (156) (1923)

Swamp red bay - *Persea palustris* (Raf.) Sargent (106) (1930)

Swamp red currant - *Ribes triste* Pallas (156) (1923)

Swamp redberry - *Vaccinium macrocarpon* Aiton (7, 87) (1828-1884), *Vaccinium oxycoccos* L. (5, 92, 138, 156) (1876-1923)

Swamp rose [Swamp-rose] - *Rosa arkansana* Porter var. *suffulta* (Greene) Cockerell (187) (1818), *Rosa blanda* Aiton (130) (1895) SD, *Rosa carolina* L. (2, 5, 19, 86, 135, 156, 158) (1840-1923), *Rosa palustris* Marsh. (106, 109, 138) (1923-1949)

Swamp rose-mallow [Swamp rose mallow] - *Hibiscus moscheutos* L. (2, 5, 82, 156, 158) (1895-1930)

Swamp sassafras [Swamp-sassfras] - *Cornus rugosa* Lam. (6) (1892), *Magnolia virginiana* L. (5, 6, 8, 41, 49, 52, 92, 156, 184, 186, 187) (1785-1923)

Swamp saxifrage - *Saxifraga pensylvanica* L. (2, 5, 72, 107, 156) (1895-1923)

Swamp sedge - *Carex acutiformis* Ehrh. (5, 156) (1913-1923)

Swamp sego - *Camassia* Lindl. (1) (1932)

Swamp silkweed - *Asclepias incarnata* L. (5, 49, 53, 58, 92, 156, 158) (1869-1923)

Swamp smartweed - *Polygonum amphibium* L. var. *emersum* Michx. (3, 4) (1977-1986), *Polygonum hydropiperoides* Michx. (50, 155) (1942–present)

Swamp sneezewort - *Helenium autumnale* L. (92) (1876)

Swamp sowfennel - *Peucedanum palustre* (L.) Moench (92) (1876)

Swamp Spanish oak - *Quercus palustris* Muench. (2, 5, 10, 33, 156) (1818-1923)

Swamp spleenwort - *Diplazium pycnocarpon* (Spreng.) Broun (5, 19, 50, 92) (1840–present)

Swamp squaw-weed [Swamp squaw weed - *Packera aurea* (L.) A.& D. Löve (5, 72, 122, 156, 158) (1900-1936)

Swamp stitchwort [Swamp stichwort] - *Stellaria alsine* Grimm (5, 156) (1913-1923)

Swamp sugar-pear [Swamp sugar pear] - *Amelanchier ×intermedia* Spach [*arborea × canadensis*] (5) (1913)

Swamp sumac [Swamp sumach, Swamp shumach] - *Toxicodendron vernix* (L.) Kuntze (5, 6, 41, 71, 92, 156, 187) (1770-1923)

Swamp sunflower - *Helenium autumnale* L. (5, 7, 49, 62, 71, 86, 92, 93, 156, 157, 158) (1828-1936), *Helianthus angustifolius* L. (5, 109, 122, 124, 138) (1913-1949)

Swamp thistle - *Cirsium muticum* Michx. (3, 4, 5, 50, 72, 155, 156) (1907–present)

Swamp tickseed - *Coreopsis rosea* Nutt. (156) (1923)

Swamp tupelo - *Nyssa aquatica* L. (5, 156) (1913-1923), *Nyssa biflora* Walt. (46) (1879)

Swamp turnip - *Arisaema triphyllum* (L.) Schott (158) (1900)

Swamp valerian - *Valeriana dioica* L. (92) (1876), *Valeriana edulis* Nutt. (177) (1762), *Valeriana uliginosa* (Torr. & Gray) Rydb. (5, 156) (1913-1923)

Swamp verbena - *Verbena hastata* L. (50) (present)

Swamp viburnum - *Viburnum nudum* L. (8) (1785)

Swamp white oak [Swamp white oake, Swamp white oke] - *Quercus bicolor* Willd (4, 5, 8, 20, 19, 33, 46, 50, 72, 93, 97, 109, 138, 155, 156) (1785–present), *Quercus bicolor* Willd (20) (1857), *Quercus michauxii* Nutt. (10) (1818)

Swamp whortle-berry - *Gaylussacia dumosa* (Andr.) Torr. & Gray (5, 156) (1913-1923)

Swamp willow [Swamp-willow] - *Salix discolor* Muhl. (5, 156, 158) (1900-1923), *Salix nigra* Marsh. (5, 93, 156, 157, 158) (1900-1936)

Swamp willow herb [Swamp willow-herb] - *Decodon verticillatus* (L.) Ell. (19, 92) (1840-1876), *Epilobium palustre* L. (5, 6, 49, 53, 158) (1892-1922)

Swamp willow oak - *Quercus laurifolia* Michx. (33) (1827)

Swamp wire grass - *Poa palustris* L. (56, 90) (1885-1901)

Swamp wood-betony [Swamp woodbetony] - *Pedicularis lanceolata* Michx. (138) (1923)

Swamp-apple [Swamp apple] - *Rhododendron periclymenoides* (Michx.) Shinners (73, 92, 156) (1876-1923) Eastern MA

Swampberry [Swamp berry, Swamp-berry] - *Rubus pubescens* Raf. var. *pubescens* (5, 73, 156) (1892-1923) Newfoundland

Swamp-cabbage [Swamp cabbage] - *Symplocarpus foetidus* (L.) Salisb. ex Nutt. (5, 64, 92, 156, 186) (1825-1923)

Swamp-candle [Swampcandle, Swamp candles] - *Lysimachia terrestris* (L.) Britton, Sterns & Poggenb. (5, 138, 156) (1913-1923)

Swamp-cedar [Swamp cedar] - *Chamaecyparis thyoides* (L.) Britton, Sterns & Poggenb. (5) (1913)

Swamp-cheeses [Swamp cheeses] - *Rhododendron periclymenoides* (Michx.) Shinners (92, 156) (1876-1923)

Swamp-dogwood [Swamp dogwood] - *Toxicodendron vernix* (L.) Kuntze (5, 6, 156) (1892-1923), *Ptelea trifoliata* L. (5, 6, 49, 92, 156, 157, 158) (1892-1929)

Swamp-elder [Swamp elder] - *Aralia hispida* Vent. (29) (1869)

Swamp-grape [Swamp grape] - *Ampelopsis cordata* Michx. (156) (1923)

Swamp-honeysuckle [Swamp honeysuckle] - *Rhododendron* L. (10, 156) (1818-1923), *Rhododendron periclymenoides* (Michx.) Shinners (5, 156) (1913-1923), *Rhododendron viscosum* (L.) Torr. (5, 19, 75, 92) (1840-1876) MA

Swamp-lily [Swamp lily] - *Saururus cernuus* L. (5, 106, 156) (1913-1930)

Swamp-mahogony - *Eucalyptus robusta* Sm. (109) (1949)

Swamp-mallow [Swamp mallow] - *Hibiscus moscheutos* L. (5, 156, 158) (1900-1923)

Swamp-privet [Swamppprivet, Swamp privet] - *Forestiera acuminata* (Michx.) Poir. (3, 4, 156) (1923-1986), *Forestiera* Poir. (50) (present)

Swamp-robin [Swamp robin] - *Calla palustris* L. (5, 7, 92, 156, 157, 158) (1828-1929)

Swampweed [Swamp-weed] - *Symphyotrichum puniceum* (L.) A.& D. Löve var. *puniceum* (156) (1923)

Swamp-willow [Swamp willow] - *Epilobium palustre* L. (6) (1892)

Swampwood [Swamp wood, Swamp-wood] - *Cephalanthus occidentalis* L. (5, 7, 92, 156, 157, 158) (1828-1929), *Dirca palustris* L. (5, 6, 7, 92, 156) (1828-1923)

Swan - *Sagittaria* L. (1) (1932)

Swan flower [Swanflower] - *Aristolochia erecta* L. (122, 124) (1937) TX

Swan root - *Nelumbo lutea* Willd. (35) (1806), *Sagittaria latifolia* Willd. (78) (1898) CA

Swan-potato [Swan potato] - *Sagittaria latifolia* Willd. (103, 107) (1871-1919)

Swan's sedge - *Carex swanii* (Fernald) Mackenzie (5, 50) (1913–present)

Swanweed [Swan weed, Swan-weed] - *Symphyotrichum puniceum* (L.) A.& D. Löve var. *puniceum* (5, 92, 156, 158) (1876-1923)

Swarms - *Alliaria petiolata* (Bieb.) Cavara & Grande (158) (1900)

Swartnöttbom (Swedish) - *Juglans nigra* L. (41) (1770)

Swarze Cohosche (German) - *Cimicifuga racemosa* (L.) Nutt. (6) (1892)

Swaying bulrush - *Schoenoplectus subterminalis* (Torr.) Soják (50) (present)

Sweat root [Sweatroot, Sweat-root] - *Polemonium reptans* L. (5, 92, 156) (1876-1923)

Sweating plant [Sweating-plant] - *Eupatorium perfoliatum* L. (69, 92, 156, 157, 158) (1898-1929)

Sweating-weed [Sweating weed, Sweatingweed] - *Eupatorium perfoliatum* L. (6) (1892), *Hibiscus laevis* All. (5, 156, 158) (1900-1923)

Sweatweed [Sweat weed, Sweat-weed] - *Althaea officinalis* L. (5, 92, 156, 158) (1876-1923), *Hibiscus* L. (7) (1828)

Swedes - *Brassica rapa* L. var. *rapa* (156) (1923)

Swedish clover - *Trifolium hybridum* L. (5, 66, 95, 106, 156, 158) (1900–1930)

Swedish cranberry - *Vaccinium* L. (1) (1932)

Swedish juniper - *Juniperus communis* L. (109, 138) (1923-1949)

Swedish turnip - *Brassica rapa* L. var. *rapa* (156) (1923)

Sweeps - *Centaurea nigra* L. (5, 156) (1913-1923) no longer in use by 1923

Sweet acacia - *Acacia farnesiana* (L.) Willd. (50, 106, 109, 138, 155) (1923–present)

Sweet Allison - *Lobularia maritima* (L.) Desv. (5, 156) (1913-1923) no longer in use by 1923

Sweet almond [Swete almond] - *Prunus amygdalus* Batsch (58) (1869) no longer in use by 1923, *Prunus dulcis* (Mill.) D.A. Webber (possily) (55, 57, 92, 179) (1526-1917)

Sweet alyssum [Sweetalyssum] - *Lobularia* Desv. (155, 156) (1923-1942), *Alyssum alyssoides* (L.) L. (possibly) (85) (1932), *Alyssum* L. (1, 93) (1932-1936), *Lobularia* Desv. (155, 156) (1923-1942), *Lobularia maritima* (L.) Desv. (5, 15, 50, 92, 109, 114, 138, 156) (1876–present)

Sweet amyris - *Amyris balsamifera* L. (165) (1807)

Sweet anise - *Osmorhiza longistylis* (Torr.) DC. (5, 76, 156, 157, 158) (1896-1929) Sulphur Grove OH, from anise-like odor and taste

Sweet anthox - *Anthoxanthum odoratum* L. (187) (1818)

Sweet archangel - *Lamium purpureum* L. (5, 158) (1900-1913)

Sweet autumn clematis [Sweetautumn clematis] - *Clematis terniflora* DC. (138, 155) (1923-1942)

Sweet autumn virgin's-bower [Sweet autumn virginsbower] - *Clematis terniflora* DC. (50) (present)

Sweet azalea - *Rhododendron arborescens* (Pursh) Torr. (138) (1923)

Sweet balm - *Cedronella canariensis* (L.) Willd. ex Webb & Berth. (92) (1876)

Sweet balsam - *Pseudognaphalium macounii* (Greene) Kartesz (5, 156) (1913-1923), *Pseudognaphalium obtusifolium* (L.) Hilliard & Burtt subsp. *obtusifolium* (5, 62, 92, 156, 157) (1876-1929)

Sweet basil [Sweet-basil] - *Ocimum basilicum* L. (7, 57, 92, 107, 184) (1793-1919)

Sweet bay [Sweet-bay, Sweetbay] - *Filipendula ulmaria* (L.) Maxim. (156) (1923)

Sweet bay [Sweet-bay, Sweetbay] or Sweet bay tree [Sweet bay trees] - *Laurus* L. (109) (1949), *Laurus nobilis* L. (57, 92, 107) (1876-1919), *Magnolia virginiana* L. (2, 5, 6, 15, 41, 76, 92, 106, 109, 122, 124, 138, 156, 1770, 183) (1818-1949), *Nectandra coriacea* (Sw.) Griseb. (7) (1828), *Persea borbonia* (L.) Spreng. (5, 106, 122, 124, 156, 182) (1791-1937)

Sweet bayberry [Sweet bay-berry] - *Myrica hartwegii* S. Wats. (106) (1930)

Sweet bean [Sweet-bean] - *Gleditsia triacanthos* L. (5, 156, 157, 158) (1900-1929), *Vicia faba* L. (7) (1828)

Sweet Benjamin - *Artemisia abrotanum* L. (5, 75, 156, 157, 158) (1894-1929) Concord MA

Sweet Betsies - *Calycanthus floridus* L. (76) (1896) Alabama, plantation negroes

Sweet Betty [Sweet Betties, Sweet Bettie] - *Calycanthus floridus* L. (5, 156) (1913–1923), *Saponaria officinalis* L. (5, 64, 76, 156, 157) (1896–1929)

Sweet birch - *Betula lenta* L. (2, 5, 7, 10, 52, 5, 57, 58, 92, 107, 109, 138, 156, 187) (1818-1949), *Betula nigra* L. (8, 49) (1785-1898), *Betula occidentalis* Hook. (5, 158) (1900-1913)

Sweet brake - *Dryopteris filix-mas* (L.) Schott (5, 92, 158) (1876-1913)

Sweet breer - *Rosa eglanteria* L. (158) (1900)

Sweet broom - *Hedysarum alpinum* L. (4) (1986), *Hedysarum boreale* Nutt. (4) (1986), *Hedysarum* L. (4) (1986)

Sweet bubbie [Sweet bubbies] - *Calycanthus floridus* L. (5, 156) (1913-1923)

Sweet buckeye - *Aesculus flava* Aiton (2, 15, 72, 109, 156) (1895-1949)

Sweet bugle - *Lycopus virginicus* L. (49, 53, 92) (1876-1922)

Sweet bugleweed - *Lycopus virginicus* L. (158) (1900)

Sweet bush [Sweet-bush] - *Comptonia peregrina* (L.) Coult. (5, 7, 58, 92, 156) (1828-1923)

Sweet butterbur - *Petasites fragrans* C.Presl (138) (1923)

Sweet calabash - *Passiflora maliformis* L. (107) (1919)

Sweet camomile [Sweet chamomile] - *Chamaemelum nobile* (L.) All. (165) (1807)

Sweet cane - *Acorus calamus* L. (186) (1814)

Sweet cassava - *Manihot esculenta* Crantz (109) (1949)

Sweet cecily - *Osmorhiza claytonii* (Michx.) C.B. Clarke (40) (1928), *Osmorhiza longistylis* (Torr.) DC. (47, 57) (1852-1917)

Sweet cherry - *Prunus avium* (L.) L. (5, 92, 107, 109, 137, 156) (1876-1949)

Sweet chervil [Sweete cheruill] - *Myrrhis odorata* (L.) Scop. (178) (1526), *Osmorhiza claytonii* (Michx.) C.B. Clarke (158) (1900), *Osmorhiza longistylis* (Torr.) DC. (5, 92, 156, 157) (1876-1929)

Sweet cicely (of Europe) - *Myrrhis odorata* (L.) Scop. (109) (1949)

Sweet cicely [Sweetcicely, Sweet cicily] - *Osmorhiza berteroi* DC. (50) (present), *Osmorhiza longistylis* (Torr.) DC. (19, 37, 49, 85, 92, 93, 105, 127, 158) (1840-1936), *Osmorhiza* Raf. (1, 2, 4, 93, 156, 158) (1895-1986)

Sweet clockvine - *Thunbergia fragrans* Roxb. (138) (1923)

Sweet clover - *Melilotus* Mill. (1, 50, 93, 106, 109, 156) (1923–present), *Melilotus officinalis* (L.) Lam. (6, 37, 45, 48, 49, 57, 63, 80, 92, 107, 114, 129, 156) (1876-1923)

Sweet coltsfoot - *Petasites* Mill. (1, 4, 158) (1900-1986), *Petasites sagittatus* (Pursh) Gray (3, 131, 156) (1899-1977)

Sweet coneflower [Sweet cone-flower] - *Rudbeckia subtomentosa* Pursh (3, 4, 5, 50, 72, 97, 109, 121, 122, 138, 155) (1907–present)

Sweet corn - *Zea mays* L. (109, 114, 119) (1894-1949)

Sweet cottonwood - *Populus deltoides* Bartr. ex Marsh. subsp. *deltoides* (30) (1844)

Sweet elder - *Sambucus nigra* L. subsp. *canadensis* (L.) R. Bolli (5, 76, 92, 93, 109, 131, 156, 157, 158) (1896-1949)

Sweet elm - *Ulmus rubra* Muhl. (5, 7, 92, 156, 157, 158) (1828-1929)

Sweet false camomile [Sweet false chamomile] - *Matricaria recutita* L. (109) (1949)

Sweet fennel - *Foeniculum vulgare* Mill. (42, 49, 50, 92, 106, 165) (1807–present)

Sweet fern [Sweetfern, Sweet-fern] - *Adiantum pedatum* L. (7) (1828)

Sweet feverfew [Sweete feuerfew] - *Tanacetum parthenium* (L.) Schultz-Bip. (178) (1526)

Sweet four-o'-clock - *Mirabilis longiflora* L. (138) (1923)

Sweet French sage [Sweete French sage] - *Phlomis fruticosa* L. (178) (1526)

Sweet garden flag - *Acorus calamus* L. (180) (1633)

Sweet goldenrod [Sweet golden-rod] - *Solidago odora* Aiton (5, 7, 49, 52, 104, 107, 122, 156) (1828-1937)

Sweet granadilla - *Passiflora ligularis* Juss. (109, 138) (1923-1949)

Sweet grass [Sweet-grass, Sweetgrass] - *Anthoxanthum odoratum* L. (5, 7) (1828-1913), *Catabrosa aquatica* (L.) Beauv. (101) (1905) MT, *Glyceria fluitans* (L.) R. Br. (5, 92, 101) (1876-1913), *Hierochloe odorata* (L.) Beauv. (3, 35, 37, 40, 85, 140, 155) (1806-1977), *Hierochloe* R. Br. (1, 50, 155) (1932–present), *Puccinellia distans* (Jacq.) Parl. (5) (1913), *Sporobolus indicus* (L.) R. Br. var. *indicus* (5) (1913)

Sweet-grass [Sweet grass, Sweetgrass] - *Acorus calamus* L. (186) (1814), *Kyllinga pumila* Michx. (possibly) (7) (1828)

Sweet hairhoof - *Galium odoratum* (L.) Scop. (5) (1913)

Sweet haw - *Viburnum prunifolium* L. (4) (1986)

Sweet hay - *Filipendula ulmaria* (L.) Maxim. (5) (1913)

Sweet honeysuckle - *Lonicera caprifolium* L. (138) (1923)

Sweet horse-mint [Sweet horsemint, Sweet horse-mint] - *Cunila origanoides* (L.) Britton (5, 7, 92, 156, 158) (1828–1923)

Sweet iris - *Iris pallida* Lam. (138) (1923)

Sweet jarvil - *Osmorhiza claytonii* (Michx.) C.B. Clarke (3, 5, 76, 156, 158) (1896-1977), *Osmorhiza longistylis* (Torr.) DC. (5, 76, 156, 157, 158) (1896-1929)

Sweet Jerusalem-oak [Sweet Jerusalem oak] - *Chenopodium botrys* L. (7) (1828)

Sweet Joe-pye weed - *Eupatorium purpureum* L. (3, 4) (1977-1986)

Sweet John [Sweet johns] - *Dianthus barbatus* L. (5, 92, 156) (1898-1923) no longer in use by 1923

Sweet juniper-berry - *Vaccinium pallidum* Aiton (156) (1923)

Sweet laurel - *Illicium floridanum* Ellis (7, 92) (1828-1876)

Sweet life-everlasting [Sweet life everlasting] - *Pseudognaphalium obtusifolium* (L.) Hilliard & Burtt subsp. *obtusifolium* (5) (1913)

Sweet lime - *Citrus limetta* Risso (110) (1886)

Sweet locust - *Gleditsia triacanthos* L. (5, 17, 20, 109, 131, 135, 156, 157, 158) (1796-1949), *Robinia pseudoacacia* L. (85) (1932) SD

Sweet lucerne - *Melilotus officinalis* (L.) Lam. (possibly) (157, 158) (1900-1929)

Sweet magnolia [Sweet-magnolia] - *Magnolia virginiana* L. (6, 49, 52, 92, 186) (1825-1892)

Sweet maple - *Acer saccharum* Marsh. (5, 156) (1913-1923)

Sweet marjoram [Sweete marjoram] - *Origanum majorana* L. (19, 57, 92, 107, 109, 138) (1840-1949), *Origanum vulgare* L. (46) (1629)

Sweet Mary - *Balsamita major* Desf. (156) (1923), *Melissa officinalis* L. (5, 75, 156) (1894-1923) Northeastern US, no longer in use by 1923, *Monarda didyma* L. (156) (1923), *Monarda* L. (75) (1894) NH

Sweet maudlin - *Achillea ageratum* L. (165) (1768)

Sweet melilot - *Melilotus officinalis* (L.) Lam. (possibly) (157, 158) (1900-1929)

Sweet milfoil - *Achillea ageratum* L. (165) (1768)

Sweet milkweed - *Asclepias syriaca* L. (156) (1923)

Sweet mock orange [Sweet mockorange] - *Philadelphus coronarius* L. (112, 138) (1923-1937)

Sweet mountain grape - *Vitis monticola* Buckl. (15, 138) (1895-1923)

Sweet-mugwort - *Artemisia annua* L. (155) (1942)

Sweet myrrh - *Osmorhiza occidentalis* (Nutt. ex Torr. & Gray) Torr. (35) (1806)

Sweet myrtle-grass - *Acorus calamus* L. (186) (1814)

Sweet oak - *Morella cerifera* (L.) Small (5, 156) (1913-1923)

Sweet oleander - *Nerium oleander* L. (92, 138) (1876-1923)

Sweet orange - *Citrus ×aurantium* L. [*maxima × reticulata*] (107) (1919), *Citrus sinensis* (L.) Osbeck (109) (1949)

Sweet pea [Sweetpea, Sweet peas] - *Lathyrus odoratus* L. (19, 46, 82, 92, 109, 114, 138) (1840-1949), *Lathyrus polymorphus* Nutt. (38) (1820), *Pisum sativum* L. (7) (1828)

Sweet pepper - *Capsicum annuum* L. (109) (1949)

Sweet pepperbush [Sweet pepper-bush] - *Clethra alnifolia* L. (5, 19, 92, 106, 109, 156) (1840-1949), *Clethra* L. (167) (1814)

Sweet philibertia - *Funastrum clausum* (Jacq.) Schltr. (138) (1923)

Sweet pigweed - *Chenopodium ambrosioides* L. (19) (1840)

Sweet pine-sap [Sweet pine sap] - *Monotropsis odorata* Schwein. ex Ell. (5, 156) (1913-1923)

Sweet pitcher-plant [Sweet pitcherplant] - *Sarracenia rubra* Walt. (109, 138) (1923-1949)

Sweet plantain - *Alisma plantago-aquatica* L. (possibly) (7) (1828)

Sweet potato [Sweet potatoe, Sweet-potato, Sweetpotato] - *Ipomoea batatas* (L.) Lam. (7, 19, 92, 107, 109, 110, 138) (1828-1949)

Sweet pumpkin - *Cucurbita moschata* (Duchesne ex Lam.) Duchesne ex Poir. (82) (1930)

Sweet reed grass [Sweet reed-grass] - *Cinna arundinacea* L. (5, 119) (1913-1938), *Cinna latifolia* (Trev. ex Goepp.) Griseb. (5) (1913)

Sweet rocket - *Hesperis matronalis* L. (5, 76, 92, 156, 158) (1896-1923) Paris ME

Sweet sage - *Artemisia frigida* Willd. (101, 146) (1905-1939) MT

Sweet sagebrush - *Artemisia michauxiana* Bess. (155) (1942)

Sweet sagewort - *Artemisia annua* L. (3, 4, 50) (1977–present)

Sweet sand-verbena [Sweet sand verbena] - *Abronia fragrans* Nutt. ex Hook. (2, 3, 4) (1895-1986)

Sweet scabiosa - *Scabiosa atropupurea* L. (138) (1923)

Sweet scabious [Sweet-scabious] - *Erigeron annuus* (L.) Pers. (5, 46, 62, 97, 131, 156, 158, 186, 187) (1814-1937), *Erigeron philadelphicus* L. (5, 7, 92, 156, 158) (1828-1923), *Scabiosa atropupurea* L. (19, 82, 109) (1840-1949)

Sweet scabish - *Scabiosa atropupurea* L. (92) (1876)

Sweet shield fern - *Dryopteris fragrans* (L.) Schott (86) (1878)

Sweet shrub - *Calycanthus floridus* L. (5, 7, 92, 112, 156) (1828-1937), *Calycanthus floridus* L. var. *glaucus* (Willd.) Torr. & Gray (156) (1923)

Sweet shrub [Sweet-shrub] - *Calycanthus* L. (109) (1949)

Sweet sicily - *Osmorhiza longistylis* (Torr.) DC. (92) (1876)

Sweet sorghum - *Sorghum bicolor* (L.) Moench (110) (1886), *Sorghum bicolor* (L.) Moench subsp. *bicolor* (109) (1949)

Sweet sultan - *Amberboa moschata* (L.) DC. (82, 92) (1876-1930), *Cnicus benedictus* L. (5, 75, 156) (1894-1923) Mattapoisett MA

Sweet sultana - *Amberboa moschata* (L.) DC. (19) (1840)

Sweet sumac [Sweet sumach] - *Rhus trilobata* Nutt. (101) (1905)

Sweet summer grass - *Hierochloe odorata* (L.) Beauv. (19) (1840)

Sweet Susan - *Silene armeria* L. (5, 73, 79, 156) (1891-1923) Northeastern US, no longer in use by 1923

Sweet tanglehead [Sweet tangle head] - *Heteropogon melanocarpus* (Ell.) Ell. ex Benth. (122) (1937) TX

Sweet tree - *Acer palmatum* Thunb. (19) (1840), *Acer rubrum* L. (92) (1876)

Sweet unicorn plant [Sweet unicornplant] - *Proboscidea louisianica* (Mill.) Thell. subsp. *fragrans* (Lindl.) Bretting (138) (1923)

Sweet verbena - *Aloysia triphylla* (L'Hér.) Britt. (92) (1876)

Sweet vernal - *Anthoxanthum odoratum* L. (118) (1898)

Sweet vernal grass [Sweet vernal-grass] - *Anthoxanthum* L. (1) (1932), *Anthoxanthum odoratum* L. (19, 45, 46, 50, 56, 67, 68, 87, 88, 90, 92, 94, 109, 111, 122, 129, 143, 163) (1840–present)

Sweet vetch - *Hedysarum boreale* Nutt. (3) (1977)

Sweet viburnum - *Viburnum lentago* L. (2, 5, 63, 92, 107, 131, 156, 158) (1895-1923)

Sweet violet - *Viola odorata* L. (5, 15, 19, 49, 55, 92, 109, 138) (1840-1949)

Sweet walnut - *Carya ovata* (Mill.) K. Koch (5, 156, 158) (1900-1923)

Sweet waterlily [Sweet water lily] - *Nymphaea odorata* Aiton (6, 7, 63, 86) (1828-1932)

Sweet white violet - *Viola* ×*primulifolia* L. [*lanceolata* × *macloskeyi*] (156) (1923), *Viola blanda* Willd. (2, 5, 72, 97, 109, 131, 138, 156) (1895-1949)

Sweet William [Sweetwilliam, Sweet-william] - *Dianthus barbatus* L. (1, 5, 15, 19, 50, 79, 92, 109, 138, 155, 156, 158) (1840–present), *Glandularia canadensis* (L.) Nutt. (77) (1898) Southwestern MO, from sweetish taste of flowers, *Ipomoea quamoclit* L. (158) (1900) Barbados, *Lychnis chalcedonica* L. (5, 73, 156, 158) (1892-1923),

Phlox divaricata L. (122, 124) (1937), *Phlox* L. (77) (1898), *Phlox latifolia* Michx. (77) (1898) Sulphur Grove OH, *Phlox pilosa* L. (5, 73, 77, 156) (1892-1923), *Silene armeria* L. (5) (1913)

Sweet William catchfly - *Silene armeria* L. (109, 138, 156) (1923-1949)

Sweet William of a bright red [Sweete William of a bright red] - *Dianthus barbatus* L. (178) (1526)

Sweet William of the Barbadoes [Sweet-William-of-the-Barbadoes] - *Ipomoea quamoclit* L. (5, 156) (1913-1923)

Sweet William phlox [Sweetwilliam phlox] - *Phlox divaricata* L. (155) (1942), *Phlox maculata* L. (138) (1923)

Sweet willow - *Salix lucida* Muhl. subsp. *lasiandra* (Benth.) E. Murr. (35) (1806)

Sweet Wilson - *Saxifraga virginiensis* Michx. (5, 76, 156) (1896-1923) Abingdon MA, named by Mrs. Ward for Wilson Ward around 1850

Sweet winter grape - *Vitis cinerea* (Engelm.) Millard (15, 138, 155, 156) (1895-1942)

Sweet wood grass [Sweet wood-grass] - *Cinna arundinacea* L. (163) (1852)

Sweet woodreed - *Cinna arundinacea* L. (50) (present)

Sweet woodruff - *Galium odoratum* (L.) Scop. (5, 109, 138, 155) (1913-1949)

Sweet wormwood - *Artemisia annua* L. (109, 138, 155) (1923-1949)

Sweet yarrow - *Achillea ageratum* L. (50, 109, 138, 155) (1923–present)

Sweet yellow clover - *Melilotus officinalis* (L.) Lam. (131) (1899)

Sweet-after-death [Sweet after death] - *Achlys triphylla* (Sm.) DC. (50) (present)

Sweetbells - *Leucothoe racemosa* (L.) Gray (109, 138) (1923-1949)

Sweetberry [Sweet berry, Sweet-berry] - *Gaultheria hispidula* (L.) Muhl. ex Bigelow (possibly) (92) (1876), *Viburnum lentago* L. (5, 93, 156, 158) (1900-1936)

Sweetberry honeysuckle - *Lonicera caerulea* L. (138, 156) (1923)

Sweet-bitter [Sweet bitter] - *Triosteum perfoliatum* L. (6) (1892)

Sweetbrake - *Tectaria* Cav. (possibly) (7) (1828)

Sweetbrier [Sweetbriar, Sweet briar, Sweet brier, Sweet bryar, Sweet bryer] - *Rosa canina* L. (177) (1762), *Rosa eglanteria* L. (3, 5, 19, 46, 63, 72, 92, 107, 109, 138, 156, 158) (1671-1977)

Sweetbrier rose [Sweetbrier rose] - *Rosa eglanteria* L. (50, 155) (1942–present)

Sweet-cane [Sweet cane] - *Acorus calamus* L. (7, 64, 92, 156, 157, 158) (1828-1929)

Sweete calamint - *Calamintha nepeta* (L.) Savi (178) (1526)

Sweet-fern [Sweetfern, Sweet fern] - *Comptonia* L'Hér. ex Aiton (1, 10, 50, 138, 167) (1814–present), *Comptonia peregrina* (L.) Coult. (7, 10, 19, 42, 46, 57, 58, 92, 109, 138, 186, 187) (1671-1949)

Sweet-ferry [Sweet ferry] - *Comptonia peregrina* (L.) Coult. (5, 7, 92, 156, 186) (1814-1923)

Sweetflag [Sweet flag, Sweet-flag] - *Acorus americanus* (Raf.) Raf. (50) (present), *Acorus calamus* L. (3, 5, 7, 10, 14, 19, 49, 53, 55, 57, 58, 64, 85, 92, 93, 97, 109, 120, 121, 156, 157, 158, 186, 187) (1814-1977), *Acorus* L. (1, 50, 93, 138, 155, 156, 158, 167) (1814–present)

Sweet-flower bay [Sweet-flowering bay] - *Magnolia virginiana* L. (186, 189) (1767-1814)

Sweet-fruit juniper [Sweet-fruited juniper] - *Juniperus deppeana* Steud. (107) (1919)

Sweetgale [Sweet gale] - *Myrica gale* L. (2, 5, 14, 19, 92, 109, 138, 156) (1840-1949), *Myrica* L. (1, 7) (1828-1932)

Sweet-grass [Sweet grass, Sweetgrass] - *Acorus calamus* L. (7, 64, 92, 158) (1828-1908), *Galium odoratum* (L.) Scop. (5) (1913), *Zostera marina* L. (5, 156) (1913-1923)

Sweetgum [Sweet gum, Sweet-gum] or Sweetgum tree [Sweet gum-tree] - *Comptonia peregrina* (L.) Coult. (184) (1793), *Liquidambar* L. (2, 8, 138, 167) (1785–1923), *Liquidambar styraciflua* L. (5, 7, 8, 10, 12, 18, 20, 19, 41, 49, 53, 57, 61, 65, 92, 97, 109, 122, 124, 138, 156, 177, 181, 182, 189) (~1678–1949)

Sweetheart [Sweethearts, Sweet-hearts] - *Galium aparine* L. (5, 156, 158) (1900-1923) no longer in use by 1923, *Hylotelephium telephioides* (Michx.) H. Ohba. (156) (1923)

Sweetleaf [Sweet-leaf, Sweet leaf] - *Symplocos* Jacq. (109, 138, 156) (1923-1949), *Symplocos tinctoria* (L.) L'Her. (2, 5, 7, 20, 19, 92, 156) (1828-1923)

Sweetleaf rose - *Rosa woodsii* Lindl. var. *gratissima* (Greene) Cole (138) (1923)

Sweet-myrtle [Sweet myrtle] - *Acorus calamus* L. (5, 64, 156, 157, 158) (1900-1929)

Sweet-pear [Sweet pear, Sweet pears] - *Amelanchier canadensis* (L.) Medik. (46, 107) (1879-1919) ME

Sweetpod [Sweet pod] - *Ceratonia siliqua* L. (92) (1876)

Sweetroot [Sweet root] - *Acorus calamus* L. (7, 64, 92, 156, 158) (1828-1923)

Sweetroot [Sweet root] - *Aralia nudicaulis* L. (7) (1828), *Glycyrrhiza lepidota* Pursh (156) (1923), *Osmorhiza* Raf. (50, 155) (1942–present), *Polemonium reptans* L. (158) (1900)

Sweet-rose geranium - *Pelargonium graveolens* L'Hér. ex Aiton (19) (1840)

Sweet-rush [Sweet rush] - *Acorus calamus* L. (7, 64, 92, 156, 158) (1828-1923)

Sweet-sage [Sweet sage] - *Krascheninnikovia lanata* (Pursh) A.D.J. Meeuse & Smit (118) (1898) TX

Sweet-salad [Sweet sallad] - *Floerkea* Willd. (7) (1828)

Sweetscent - *Pluchea odorata* (L.) Cass (50) (present)

Sweet-scented andromeda - *Leucothoe racemosa* (L.) Gray (possibly) (187) (1818)

Sweet-scented bedstraw [Sweetscented bedstraw] - *Galium triflorum* Michx. (3, 4, 5, 49, 63, 85, 93, 155, 156, 157, 158) (1898-1986)

Sweet-scented cedar [Sweet scented cedar] - *Cedrela odorata* L. (92) (1876)

Sweet-scented crab or Sweet-scented crab tree [Sweet-scented crab-tree] - *Malus coronaria* (L.) Mill. var. *coronaria* (107, 187) (1818-1919), *Malus glaucescens* Rehdr. (5) (1913)

Sweet-scented datura [Sweet scented datura] - *Datura wrightii* Regel (92) (1876)

Sweet-scented geranium - *Pelargonium capitatum* (L.) L'Hér. ex Aiton (74) (1893), *Pelargonium odoratissimum* (L.) L'Hér. ex Aiton (19) (1840)

Sweet-scented goldenrod [Sweet-scented golden-rod, Sweet scented goldenrod] - *Solidago odora* Aiton (19, 49, 52, 58, 92) (1840-1919)

Sweet-scented grape [Sweet scented grape] - *Vitis riparia* Michx. (7) (1828), *Vitis vulpina* L. (5, 72, 97, 158) (1900-1937)

Sweet-scented herb - *Porophyllum gracile* Benth. (76) (1896) CA

Sweet-scented Indian plantain - *Hasteola* Raf. (5, 72) (1907-1913), *Hasteola suaveolens* (L.) Pojark. (5, 72, 156) (1907-1923)

Sweet-scented joe-pye weed [Sweetscented joepyeweed] - *Eupatorium purpureum* L. (50) (present)

Sweet-scented life-everlasting [Sweet scented life everlasting] - *Pseudognaphalium obtusifolium* (L.) Hilliard & Burtt subsp. *obtusifolium* (19, 49, 92) (1840–1898)

Sweet-scented pondlily [Sweet-scented pond lily] - *Nymphaea odorata* Aiton (49) (1898)

Sweet-scented red beech [Sweet scented red beech] (sic) - *Betula nigra* L. (42) (1814)

Sweet-scented rubus - *Rubus odoratus* L. (187) (1818)

Sweet-scented shrub [Sweet-sented (sic) Shrub] - *Calycanthus floridus* L. (74, 76, 156, 184) (1793-1923), *Calycanthus* L. (2, 109, 156) (1895-1949)

Sweet-scented sumac [Sweet-scented sumach] - *Rhus aromatica* Aiton (6, 72, 156, 158) (1892-1923), *Rhus aromatica* Aiton var. *aromatica* (5, 65, 97) (1913-1937)

Sweet-scented tobacco - *Nicotiana tabacum* L. (181) (~1678)

Sweet-scented vernal grass [Sweet-scented vernal-grass] - *Anthoxanthum* L. (10, 45, 66) (1818-1912), *Anthoxanthum odoratum* L. (90, 187) (1818-1885)

Sweet-scented violet - *Viola odorata* L. (49) (1898)

Sweet-scented waterlily [Sweet-scented water lily, Sweet scented water lily] - *Nymphaea odorata* Aiton (92) (1876)

Sweet-scented white waterlily [Sweet-scented white water-lily] - *Nymphaea odorata* Aiton subsp. *odorata* (5, 72, 97, 156, 158) (1900-1937)

Sweet-sedge [Sweet sedge] - *Acorus calamus* L. (64, 92, 156, 158) (1876-1923)

Sweet-segg [Sweet segg] - *Acorus calamus* L. (64, 158) (1900-1908)

Sweet-slumber - *Sanguinaria canadensis* L. (64, 76, 156, 157, 158) (1896-1929)

Sweet-smelling flag - *Acorus calamus* L. (186) (1814)

Sweet-smelling locust - *Robinia pseudoacacia* L. (177) (1762)

Sweet-smelling reed - *Acorus calamus* L. (180) (1633)

Sweet-smelling satyrion [Sweete smelling satyrion] - *Gymnadenia conopsea* (L.) R. Br. (178) (1596)

Sweet-smelling trefoil [Sweet smelling trefoil] - *Eupatorium cannabinum* L. (92) (1876)

Sweet-smelling white satin [Sweete smelling white sattin] - *Lunaria rediviva* L. (178) (1526)

Sweetsop [Sweet sop] - *Annona squamosa* L. (92, 109, 110, 155) (1876-1949)

Sweetspire [Sweet spire] - *Itea* L. (138) (1923), *Itea virginica* L. (109, 138, 156) (1923-1949)

Sweet-sultan - *Amberboa moschata* (L.) DC. (138) (1923)

Sweetvetch [Sweet vetch] - *Hedysarum boreale* Nutt. (3) (1977), *Hedysarum* L. (50, 155) (1942–present)

Sweet-weed - *Lindernia dubia* (L.) Pennell var. *dubia* (184) (1793)

Sweet-willow [Sweet willow, Sweete willow] - *Myrica gale* L. (5, 41, 92, 156, 178) (1526-1923)

Sweetwood [Sweet wood, Sweet-wood] - *Glycyrrhiza glabra* L. (92) (1876), *Glycyrrhiza lepidota* Pursh (156) (1923)

Sweth - *Allium schoenoprasum* L. (180) (1633)

Swichen - *Senecio vulgaris* L. (158) (1900)

Swimming knotweed - *Polygonum amphibium* L. var. *stipulaceum* Coleman (19) (1840)

Swimming water nut - *Trapa natans* L. (5) (1913)

Swine cress [Swine-cress, Swine cresses] - *Carara coronopus* (L.) Medik. (5) (1913), *Coronopus didymus* (L.) Sm. (19) (1840), *Coronopus squamatus* (Forsk.) Aschers. (156) (1923), *Coronopus* Zinn (possibly) (15) (1895)

Swine sow-thistle - *Sonchus arvensis* L. (157) (1929)

Swine thistle - *Sonchus arvensis* L. (5, 158) (1900-1913)

Swine-grass [Swine grass, Swines' grass, Swine's-grass, Swynes grasse] - *Polygonum aviculare* L. (5, 92, 156, 158) (1876-1923) no longer in use by 1923, *Polygonum aviculare* L. (179) (1526)

Swine's-bane [Swine's bane, Swinesbane] - *Chenopodium rubrum* L. (92, 156, 158) (1876-1923), *Chenopodium simplex* (Torr.) Raf. (156, 158) (1900-1923)

Swine's-lettuce [Swine's lettuce] - *Hedypnois* Mill. (167) (1814), *Kalmia hirsuta* Walt. (possibly) (167) (1814)

Swine's-snout [Swine snout] - *Taraxacum officinale* G.H. Weber ex Wiggers subsp. *officinale* (92) (1876)

Swine's-succory [Swine-succory, Swine's succory] - *Arnoseris minima* (L.) Schweig. & Koerte (possibly) (156) (1923), *Krigia virginica* (L.) Willd. (184) (1793)

Swinies - *Sonchus oleraceus* L. (5, 156, 157, 158) (1900-1929)

Swiss chard - *Beta vulgaris* L. (107) (1919)

Swiss mountain pine - *Pinus mugo* Turra (109, 136, 138) (1923-1949)

Swiss poplar - *Populus deltoides* Bartr. ex Marsh. subsp. *monilifera* (Aiton) Eckenwalder (20) (1857)

Swiss stone pine - *Pinus cembra* L. (92, 106, 107, 138) (1876-1930)

Switch cane [Switch-cane] - *Arundinaria gigantea* (Walt.) Muhl. subsp. *tecta* (Walt.) McClure (5, 45, 88, 122) (1885–1937), *Arundinaria gigantea* (Walter) Muhl. (2) (1895)

Switchgrass [Switch grass, Switch-grass] - *Panicum virgatum* L. (3, 50, 56, 75, 78, 85, 87, 88, 90, 94, 98, 99, 109, 111, 115, 119, 122,

129, 140, 144, 155, 163) (1852–present), *Panicum virgatum* L. var. *virgatum* (50) (present)

Swollen bladderwort - *Utricularia gibba* L. (5) (1913), *Utricularia radiata* Small. (122) (1937) TX

Swollen colewort [Swollen colewoort, Swolne colewoorts] - *Brassica oleracea* L. (178, 180) (1526-1633)

Swollen duckweed - *Lemna gibba* L. (50, 155) (1942–present)

Swollen gentian - *Gentianopsis crinita* (Froel) Ma. (5) (1913)

Swollen-fruit sedge [Swollen-fruited sedge] - *Carex intumescens* Rudge (66) (1903)

Swollen-spur bladderwort [Swollenspurred bladderwort] - *Utricularia gibba* L. (122) (1937)

Swollen-stalk cat [Swollen-stalked cat] - *Catathelasma ventricosum* (Peck) Singer (170) (1995)

Sword bean - *Canavalia gladiata* (Jacq.) DC. (109) (1949)

Sword brake - *Pteris ensiformis* Burm. f. (138) (1923)

Sword fern [Sword-fern, Swordfern] - *Nephrolepis* Schott (109, 138) (1923-1949), *Polystichum munitum* (Kaulfuss) K. Presl (4) (1986)

Sword flag [Sword-flag] - *Gladiolus* L. (180) (1633), *Iris pseudacorus* L. (5, 156, 158) (1900-1923)

Sword grass - *Phalaris arundinacea* L. (5) (1913)

Sword lily - *Gladiolus communis* L. (92) (1876)

Sword lily - *Gladiolus* L. (75) (1894) NY

Sword-grass [Sword grass] - *Carex* L. (41) (1770), *Gladiolus communis* L. (92) (1876), *Schoenoplectus americanus* (Pers.) Volk. ex Schinz & R. Keller (5, 156) (1913-1923)

Sword-leaf blue-eyed grass [Swordleaf blue-eyed grass] - *Sisyrinchium chilense* Hook. (50) (present), *Sisyrinchium mucronatum* Michx. (187) (1818)

Sycamine - *Morus alba* L. (92) (1876)

Sycamore maple - *Acer pseudoplatanus* L. (50, 93, 107, 109, 137, 138) (1923–present)

Sycamore or Sycamore tree [Sycomore-tree] - *Acer pseudoplatanus* L. (20, 92, 165) (1768-1876) England, *Planera aquatica* J.F. Gmel. (5, 156) (1913-1923), *Platanus* L. (4, 50, 93, 109) (1936–present), *Platanus occidentalis* L. (3, 4, 10, 17, 20, 27, 35, 38, 65, 72, 93, 97, 106, 112, 113, 122, 124, 156, 158) (1818-1986), *Platanus racemosa* Nutt. (161) (1857), *Platanus wrightii* S. Wats. (149, 153) (1904-1919)

Sycamore-leaf storax [Sycamoreleaf storax] - *Styrax platanifolius* Engelm. ex Torr. (122) (1937)

Sydney acacia - *Acacia longifolia* (Andr.) Willd. (155) (1942)

Sydney golden wattle - *Acacia longifolia* (Andr.) Willd. (50, 106, 107, 109, 155) (1919-1930)

Sydney wattle - *Acacia longifolia* (Andr.) Willd. (138) (1923)

Sylvan forget-me-not - *Myosotis sylvatica* Ehrh. ex Hoffmann (131) (1899)

Sylvan goatsbeard - *Aruncus dioicus* (Walt.) Fern. var. *vulgaris* (Maxim.) Hara (155) (1942)

Sylvan horsetail - *Equisetum sylvaticum* L. (155) (1942)

Sylvan muhlenbergia - *Muhlenbergia sylvatica* Torr. ex Gray (66) (1903)

Sylvan spear grass [Sylvan spear-grass] - *Poa sylvestris* Gray (5, 66, 72, 163) (1852-1907)

Symnels (summer squash) - *Cucurbita pepo* L. (107) (1648)

Sympharicapos (French) - *Symphoricarpos orbiculatus* Moench (8) (1785)

Symphytum - *Symphytum officinale* L. (57, 64) (1908-1917)

Symplocarpus - *Symplocarpus foetidus* (L.) Salisb. ex Nutt. (57) (1917)

Symrnium - *Lomatium nudicaule* (Pursh) J.M. Coult. & Rose (107) (1919), *Peucedanum ostruthium* (L.) W.D.J. Koch (107) (1919)

Synandra - *Synandra hispidula* (Michx.) Britton (5) (1913)

Syrax d'Amérique (French) - *Styrax americanus* Lam. (8) (1785)

Syrian bean tree - *Melia azedarach* L. (107) (1919)

Syrian dourra (Egypt) - *Zea mays* L. (110) (1886)

Syrian grass - *Sorghum halepense* (L.) Pers. (5, 45) (1896-1913)

Syrian mallo - *Abelmoschus moschatus* Medik. (92) (1876)

Syrian mustard - *Euclidium syriacum* (L.) Aiton f. (50) (present)

Syrian swallow-wort - *Asclepias syriaca* L. (187) (1818)

Syrian tobacco - *Nicotiana rustica* L. (5, 156) (1913-1923)

Syrian-privet - *Fontanesia phillyreoides* Labill. (138) (1923)

Syringa - *Philadelphus* L. (2, 8, 82, 149, 167) (1785-1930), *Philadelphus serpyllifolius* Gray (124) (1937)

Syringa (French) - *Philadelphus* L. (8) (1785)

Syringa sans odeur (French) - *Philadelphus inodorus* L. (8) (1785) Neb

Syringia - *Philadelphus coronarius* L. (possibly) (92) (1876)

T

Tabac (French) - *Nicotiana tabacum* L. (6) (1892)

Tabacco del daiblo (Chili) - *Nicotiana rustica* L. (110) (1886)

Tabaco - *Nicotiana tabacum* L. (110, 178) (1526-after 1600)

Tabacum - *Nicotiana tabacum* L. (57, 60) (1902)

Tabak (German) - *Nicotiana tabacum* L. (6, 110) (1886-1892)

Tabe-hi (Omaha-Ponca) - *Ceanothus americanus* L. (37) (1919)

Table Mountain pine - *Pinus pungens* Lamb. (2, 50, 138) (1895–present)

Tablewort - *Borago officinalis* L. (107) (1919)

Tabok - *Nicotiana tabacum* L. (110) (1886)

Tabu (Malay) - *Saccharum officinarum* L. (110) (1886)

Taburnaemontanus bulrush - *Schoenoplectus tabernaemontani* (K.C. Gmel.) Palla (155) (1942)

Tacalote - *Centaurea melitensis* L. (106) (1930)

Tacamahac or Tacamahac tree - *Populus balsamifera* L. (5, 8, 14, 20, 92, 108, 109, 156, 157, 158) (1785-1949), *Populus balsamifera* L. subsp. *balsamifera* (46) (1879)

Tacamahac poplar - *Populus balsamifera* L. (92) (1876), *Populus balsamifera* L. subsp. *balsamifera* (155) (1942)

Tacamahaca - *Populus balsamifera* L. (2) (1857) Indian name

Tachouner - *Musa ×paradisiaca* L. [*acuminata × balbisiana*] (107) (1616)

Tacker-grass [Tacker grass] - *Polygonum aviculare* L. (156, 158) (1900-1923)

Tad-pipes - *Equisetum palustre* L. (158) (1900)

Taenidia - *Taenidia* (Torr. & Gray) Drude (50, 155) (1942–present)

Tag alder [Tag-alder] - *Alnus incana* (L.) Moench (5, 156) (1913–1923), *Alnus incana* (L.) Moench subsp. *rugosa* (DuRoi) Clausen (5, 156, 158) (1900–1923), *Alnus rubra* Bong. (52, 92) (1876–1919), *Alnus serrulata* (Aiton) Willd. (49, 53, 57, 58, 92) (1869–1922), *Betula pumila* L. (5, 75, 156, 158) (1894–1923) MN

Tagasaste - *Chamaecystis prolifera* (L. f.) Link (106) (1930)

Tage (Osage) - *Juglans nigra* L. (121) (1918?-1970?)

Tahado (Dakota) - *Acer rubrum* L. (37) (1919)

Tahiti apple - *Spondias dulcis* Parkinson (110) (1886)

Tahiti mulberry - *Broussonetia papyrifera* (L.) L'Hér. ex Vent. (158) (1900)

Tahiti orange - *Citrus ×limonia* Osbeck [*limon × reticulata*] (138) (1923)

Tahoka daisy - *Machaeranthera tanacetifolia* (Kunth) Nees (4) (1986)

Tah-wah-pah (Dakota Indians) - *Nuphar lutea* (L.) Sm. subsp. *advena* (Aiton) Kartesz & Gandhi (103) (1870)

Tail-cup lupine [Tailcup lupine] - *Lupinus caudatus* Kellogg (4, 50, 155) (1942–present), *Lupinus caudatus* Kellogg subsp. *caudatus* (50) (present)

Tail-grape [Tailgrape] - *Artabotrys* R. Br. (109, 138, 155) (1931-1949)

Tailis (Greek, ancient) - *Trigonella foenum-graecum* L. (110) (1886)

Tail-leaf maidenhair [Tail-leaved maidenhair] - *Adiantum caudatum* L. (165) (1768)

Tail-leaf willow [Tailed-leaved willow] - *Salix lucida* Muhl. subsp. *caudata* (Nutt.) E. Murr. (85) (1932)

Tainturier's chervil - *Chaerophyllum tainturieri* Hook. (5, 97) (1913-1937)

Taitsako pahat (Pawnee, red elm) - *Ulmus rubra* Muhl. (37) (1919)

Taitsako taka (Pawnee, white elm) - *Ulmus americana* L. (37) (1919)

Takanhecha (Dakota) - *Rubus idaeus* L. subsp. *strigosus* (Michx.) Focke (37) (1919) Takanhecha-hu (raspberry bush), *Rubus occidentalis* L. (37) (1919) Takanhecha-hu (raspberry bush)

Taken skina zuhapi (Sioux) - *Monarda fistulosa* L. subsp. *fistulosa* var. *mollis* (L.) Benth. (101) (1905) MT

Taklosta (Swedish) - *Bromus tectorum* L. (46) (1879)

Taku šašala hu iječeča (Lakota, smartweed-like plant) - *Rumex altissimus* Wood (121) (1918?-1970?)

Talewort - *Borago officinalis* L. (156) (1923)

Taliny - *Phemeranthus teretifolius* (Pursh) Raf. (19) (1840)

Tall adonis - *Adonis aestivalis* L. (165) (1768)

Tall ailanthus - *Ailanthus altissima* (Mill) Swingle (165) (1768)

Tall albizzia - *Albizia procera* (Roxb.) Benth. (155) (1942)

Tall amaranth - *Amaranthus rudis* Sauer (50) (present)

Tall ambrosia - *Ambrosia artemisiifolia* L. var. *elatior* (L.) Descourtils (165) (1768), *Ambrosia trifida* L. (5, 49, 92, 158) (1876–1913)

Tall anemone - *Anemone virginiana* L. (3, 4, 5, 72, 85, 86, 93, 97, 131, 158) (1878-1986)

Tall annual willow herb [Tall annual willowherb] - *Epilobium brachycarpum* K. Presl (50) (present)

Tall arrow-grass [Tall arrow grass] - *Triglochin maritimum* L. (66) (1903)

Tall beggarticks [Tall beggarticks] - *Bidens vulgata* Greene (5, 93, 97, 155, 156) (1913-1942)

Tall belleflower - *Campanulastrum americanum* (L.) Small (72) (1907) IA

Tall bellflower [Tall bell-flower] - *Campanulastrum americanum* (L.) Small (3, 4, 5, 63, 65, 82, 93, 95, 97, 114, 131, 156) (1894-1986)

Tall bentgrass [Tall bent grass] - *Agrostis perennans* (Walt.) Tuckerman (5) (1913)

Tall bilberry - *Vaccinium ovalifolium* J.E. Smith (5) (1913)

Tall birch - *Betula alleghaniensis* Britt. var. *alleghaniensis* (19) (1840)

Tall blackberry - *Rubus ostryifolius* Rydb. (5) (1913)

Tall blazing star - *Liatris aspera* Michx. (50) (present), *Liatris aspera* Michx. var. *aspera* (50) (present), *Liatris pycnostachya* Michx. (3) (1977)

Tall blue lettuce - *Lactuca biennis* (Moench) Fern. (5, 50, 62, 72, 131) (1899–present)

Tall blue sage - *Salvia azurea* Michx. ex Lam. (182) (1791)

Tall blueberry - *Vaccinium corymbosum* L. (5, 46) (1879-1913)

Tall boneset - *Eupatorium altissimum* L. (72, 82) (1907-1930), *Eupatorium purpureum* L. (5, 7, 64, 92, 156, 157, 158) (1828-1929)

Tall bootjack [Tall boot-jack] - *Bidens discoidea* (Torr. & Gray) Britton (80) (1913) IA

Tall buckwheat - *Eriogonum tenellum* Torr. (50) (present)

Tall bugbane - *Cimicifuga racemosa* (L.) Nutt. (2) (1895)

Tall bulrush [Tall bull-rush] - *Schoenoplectus tabernaemontani* (C.C. Gmel.) Palla (possibly) (187) (1818)

Tall bush clover - *Lespedeza capitata* Michx. (72) (1907)

Tall bush lespedeza - *Lespedeza stuevei* Nutt. (4, 124) (1937-1986)

Tall bush morning-glory - *Ipomoea carnea* Jacq. subsp. *fistulosa* (Mart. ex Choisy) D. Austin (124) (1937)

Tall buttercup - *Ranunculus acris* L. (3, 4, 6, 45, 50, 72, 138, 145, 155, 157, 158) (1892–present)

Tall camomile - *Anthemis altissima* L. (155, 165) (1807-1942)

Tall carrion flower [Tall carrion-flower] - *Smilax herbacea* L. (156) (1923)

Tall catchfly - *Silene virginica* L. (187) (1818)

Tall centaury - *Centaurium exaltatum* (Griseb.) W. Wight ex Piper (5) (1913)

Tall cinquefoil - *Potentilla arguta* Pursh (3, 4, 50, 131) (1899–present), *Potentilla arguta* Pursh subsp. *arguta* (5, 50, 72, 85, 93, 97, 127) (1907–present), *Potentilla norvegica* L. subsp. *monspeliensis* (L.) Aschers. & Graebn. (62) (1912)

Tall cluster false dragonhead [Tall cluster false-dragonhead] - *Physostegia virginiana* (L.) Benth. subsp. *virginiana* (138) (1923)

Tall coneflower [Tall cone-flower, Tall cone flower, Tall cone-flower] - *Rudbeckia laciniata* L. (5, 62, 72, 85, 92, 93, 97, 126, 127, 156, 157, 158) (1876-1937)

Tall coreopsis - *Coreopsis tripteris* L. (3, 4) (1977-1986)

Tall cotton-grass [Tall cotton grass] - *Eriophorum angustifolium* Honckeny (5, 50) (1913–present), *Eriophorum angustifolium* Honckeny subsp. *scabriusculum* Hultén (50, 156) (1923–present), *Eriophorum angustifolium* Honckeny subsp. *subarcticum* (Vassiljev) Hultén ex Kartesz & Gandhi (72) (1907)

Tall cotton-rush - *Eriophorum virginicum* L. (46) (1879)

Tall cranberry - *Vaccinium oxycoccos* L. (46, 174) (1753-1879)

Tall crowfoot - *Ranunculus acris* L. (6, 63, 156) (1892-1923)

Tall cup flower [Tall cup-flower, Tall cupflower] - *Nierembergia frutescens* Durieu (109, 138) (1923-1949)

Tall daisy - *Erigeron annuus* (L.) Pers. (156) (1923)

Tall ditaxis - *Argythamnia mercurialina* (Nutt.) Muell. Arg. (5, 97) (1913-1937)

Tall dock - *Rumex altissimus* Wood (5, 93, 156) (1913-1936)

Tall dropseed - *Sporobolus compositus* (Poir.) Merr. var. *compositus* (116, 140, 155) (1942-1958)

Tall Eaton's grass - *Sphenopholis ×pallens* (Biehler) Scribn. [*obtusata × pensylvanica*] (5) (1913)

Tall erysimum - *Erysimum capitatum* (Dougl. ex Hook.) Greene var. *capitatum* (155) (1942)

Tall eugenia - *Eugenia procera* (Sw.) Poir. (20) (1857)

Tall eupatorium - *Eupatorium altissimum* L. (155) (1942)

Tall evening-primrose [Tall evening primrose] - *Oenothera heterophylla* Spach (124) (1937) TX

Tall false foxglove - *Agalinis aspera* (Dougl. ex Benth.) Britton (50) (present)

Tall fescue - *Lolium arundinaceum* (Schreb.) S.J. Darbyshire (3, 50) (1977–present), *Lolium pratense* (Huds.) S.J. Darbyshire (56, 68, 87, 88, 92, 109, 118, 129, 152) (1884-1949)

Tall fescue grass [Tall fescue-grass] - *Lolium pratense* (Huds.) S.J. Darbyshire (5, 45, 56, 72, 119, 187) (1818-1938)

Tall fimbristylis - *Fimbristylis thermalis* S. Wats. (66) (1903)

Tall flat panic grass [Tall flat panic-grass] - *Panicum rigidulum* Bosc ex Nees var. *elongatum* (Pursh) Lelong (5, 163) (1852-1913)

Tall flat-top white aster - *Doellingeria umbellata* (P. Mill.) Nees var. *umbellata* (5, 72, 156) (1907-1923)

Tall four-o'clock - *Mirabilis glabra* (S. Wats.) Standl. (4) (1986)

Tall fringed bluebells - *Mertensia ciliata* (James) D. Don (50) (present)

Tall fringed panic grass [Tall fringed panic-grass] - *Dichanthelium commutatum* (J.A. Schultes) Gould (119) (1938)

Tall fringed panicum - *Dichanthelium commutatum* (J.A. Schultes) Gould (5) (1913)

Tall gallberry - *Ilex lucida* Torr. & Gray ex S.Watson (106) (1930)

Tall gayfeather - *Liatris aspera* Michx. (155) (1942)

Tall globethistle - *Echinops exaltatus* Schrad. (138) (1923)

Tall glyceria - *Glyceria grandis* S. Wats. (143) (1852-1936)

Tall goldenrod [Tall golden-rod] - *Solidago canadensis* L. var. *scabra* Torr. & Gray (5, 97, 122, 138, 155, 156) (1913-1942)

Tall grama - *Bouteloua curtipendula* (Michx) Torr. (1, 94, 129, 151) (1894-1932), *Bouteloua curtipendula* (Michx.) Torr. var. *curtipendula* (152) (1912), *Bouteloua gracilis* (Willd. ex Kunth) Lag. ex Griffiths (144) (1899), *Bouteloua hirsuta* Lag. (56) (1901), *Bouteloua* Lag. (93) (1936)

Tall grama grass [Tall grama-grass, Tall gramma grass] - *Bouteloua curtipendula* (Michx) Torr. (56, 75, 85, 87, 111, 116, 118, 119, 134, 163) (1852-1932), *Bouteloua curtipendula* (Michx.) Torr. var. *curtipendula* (5) (1913)

Tall grama oats - *Bouteloua curtipendula* (Michx) Torr. (56) (1901)

Tall gypsophyll - *Gypsophila paniculata* L. (5, 72, 156, 158) (1900-1923)

Tall hairy agrimony - *Agrimonia eupatoria* L. (72) (1907) IA, *Agrimonia gryposepala* Wallr. (5, 50, 93) (1913–present)

Tall hairy goldenrod [Tall hairy golden-rod] - *Solidago rugosa* Mill. (5, 72, 106, 122, 156) (1907-1937)

Tall hairy ground-cherry [Tall hairy ground cherry] - *Physalis pubescens* L. var. *integrifolia* (Dunal) Waterfall (possibly) (5, 72, 97) (1907-1937)

Tall hedge-mustard [Tall hedge mustard] - *Sisymbrium loeselii* L. (3, 4) (1977-1986)

Tall hogweed - *Ambrosia artemisiifolia* L. var. *elatior* (L.) Descourtils (187) (1818)

Tall horned beak-sedge [Tall horned beaksedge] - *Rhynchospora macrostachya* Torr. ex Gray (50) (present)

Tall hyssop - *Agastache nepetoides* (L.) Kuntze (187) (1818)

Tall ironweed [Tall iron-weed] - *Vernonia gigantea* (Walt.) Trel. subsp. *gigantea* (5, 97, 138) (1913-1937), *Vernonia gigantea* (Walter) Trel. ex Branner & Coville (62) (1912)

Tall Joe-Pye weed - *Eupatorium altissimum* L. (3) (1977)

Tall Juneberry - *Amelanchier canadensis* (L.) Medik. (112) (1937)

Tall larkspur - *Delphinium ×occidentale* (S. Wats.) S. Wats. [*barbeyi × glaucum*] (146) (1939), *Delphinium exaltatum* Aiton (5, 72, 93, 131, 138, 156) (1899–1936) ND

Tall leaf-bract aster [Tall leafbract aster] - *Symphyotrichum foliaceum* (DC.) Nesom var. *parryi* (D.C. Eat.) Nesom (155) (1942)

Tall leafy green orchis - *Platanthera hyperborea* (L.) Lindl. var. *hyperborea* (5, 72, 93) (1907-1936)

Tall lespedeza - *Lespedeza stuevei* Nutt. (50) (present)

Tall lettuce - *Lactuca canadensis* L. (5, 62, 131, 156, 157, 158) (1899-1929)

Tall lungwort - *Mertensia paniculata* (Aiton) G. Don. (5, 72, 131) (1899-1913)

Tall manna grass [Tall mannagrass] - *Glyceria grandis* S. Wats. (3) (1977), *Glyceria grandis* S. Wats. var. *grandis* (5) (1913), *Glyceria striata* (Lam.) A.S. Hitchc. (155) (1942)

Tall marsh grass [Tall marsh-grass] - *Spartina cynosuroides* (L.) Roth (66, 72, 90) (1885-1907), *Spartina pectinata* Bosc ex Link (5, 119, 163) (1852-1938)

Tall meadow fescue - *Lolium arundinaceum* (Schreb.) S.J. Darbyshire (45, 129) (1894-1896), *Lolium pratense* (Huds.) S.J. Darbyshire (45) (1896)

Tall meadow grass - *Glyceria arundinacea* Kunth (88) (1885)

Tall meadow oat grass - *Arrhenatherum elatius* (L.) Beauv. ex J. Presl & C. Presl (56, 66, 68, 87) (1884-1903)

Tall meadow-rue [Tall meadow rue, Tall meadowrue] - *Thalictrum dasycarpum* Fisch. & Avé-Lall. (5, 85, 93, 127) (1913-1936), *Thalictrum pubescens* Pursh (2, 63, 72, 138, 156) (1895-1923)

Tall melic grass [Tall melic-grass] - *Melica mutica* Walt. (56, 72) (1901-1907), *Melica nitens* (Scribn.) Nutt. ex Piper (5, 119, 163) (1852-1938)

Tall mesquite - *Bouteloua curtipendula* (Michx) Torr. (87) (1884)

Tall milkweed - *Asclepias exaltata* L. (5, 37, 72, 156) (1907-1913)

Tall millet grass - *Milium effusum* L. (5, 85) (1913-1932)

Tall morning-glory - *Ipomoea purpurea* (L.) Roth (50) (present)

Tall mountain larkspur - *Delphinium trolliifolium* Gray (71) (1898)

Tall mountain-lilac - *Ceanothus oliganthus* Nutt. (138) (1923)

Tall nasturtium - *Minuartia rubella* (Wahlenb.) Hiern. (178) (1526) CA, *Tropaeolum majus* L. (107) (1919)

Tall nettle - *Urtica dioica* L. subsp. *gracilis* (Aiton) Seland. (62, 85, 155) (1912-1942), *Urtica gracilenta* Greene (122) (1937)

Tall nut-rush [Tall nut rush] - *Scleria triglomerata* Michx. (5, 72, 156) (1907-1923)

Tall oat grass [Tall oatgrass, Tall oatgrass] - *Arrhenatherum elatius* (L.) Beauv. ex J. Presl & C. Presl (11, 45, 50, 66, 68, 87, 88, 94, 109, 111, 129, 138, 140, 143, 155) (1884–present), *Arrhenatherum elatius* (L.) Beauv. ex J. & K. Presl var. *elatius* (42, 45, 50) (1814–present), *Trisetum flavescens* (L.) Beauv. (5) (1913)

Tall osmunda - *Osmunda cinnamomea* L. (187) (1818)

Tall panic grass - *Panicum virgatum* L. (87, 88, 90, 129) (1884-1894)

Tall paspalum - *Paspalum dilatatum* Poir. (5) (1913)

Tall pedicularis - *Pedicularis procera* Gray (85) (1932)

Tall persicaria - *Polygonum orientale* L. (187) (1818)

Tall pine-barren milkwort - *Polygala cymosa* Walt. (5) (1913)

Tall pink - *Collinsia verna* Nutt. (19) (1840)

Tall pipewort - *Eriocaulon decangulare* L. (19) (1840)

Tall poppy-mallow [Tall poppy mallow, Tall poppymallow] - *Callirhoe leiocarpa* Martin (50, 155) (1942–present), *Callirhoe pedata* (Nutt. ex Hook.) Gray (97) (1937)

Tall quaking grass - *Glyceria canadensis* (Michx.) Trin. (5, 87, 88, 90) (1884-1913)

Tall rat-tail grass [Tall rat-tail-grass] - *Coelorachis rugosa* (Nutt.) Nash (94) (1901), *Coelorachis tessellata* (Steud.) Nash (94) (1901)

Tall rattlesnake root - *Prenanthes altissima* L. (2) (1895), *Prenanthes trifoliolata* (Cass.) Fern. (5) (1913)

Tall redtop [Tall red top, Tall red-top] - *Tridens flavus* (L.) A.S. Hitchc. (5, 56, 87) (1884-1913), *Tridens flavus* (L.) A.S. Hitchc. var. *flavus* (119, 163) (1852-1938)

Tall red-top grass [Tall red top grass] - *Tridens flavus* (L.) A.S. Hitchc. (21, 66, 72) (1893-1903)

Tall reed grass [Tall reed-grass] - *Phragmites australis* (Cav.) Trin. ex Steud. (163) (1852)

Tall rose - *Rosa woodsii* Lindl. var. *woodsii* (113) (1890)

Tall rough panicum - *Dichanthelium scabriusculum* (Ell.) Gould & C.A. Clark (5) (1913)

Tall ruellia - *Ruellia nudiflora* (Engelm. & Gray) Urban (124) (1937)

Tall sage - *Salvia azurea* Michx. ex Lam. var. *grandiflora* Benth. (5) (1913)

Tall sage grass - *Andropogon* L. (152) (1912)

Tall sand primrose - *Oenothera heterophylla* Spach (122) (1937) TX

Tall saxifrage - *Saxifraga pensylvanica* L. (52, 187) (1818-1919)

Tall sea-blite - *Suaeda calceoliformis* (Hook.) Moq. (156) (1923), *Suaeda linearis* (Ell.) Moq. (5, 97) (1913-1937)

Tall silverbush - *Argythamnia mercurialina* (Nutt.) Muell. Arg. (50) (present)

Tall sisymbrium - *Sisymbrium altissimum* L. (5, 72, 97) (1907-1937)

Tall smooth goldenrod [Tall smooth golden-rod] - *Solidago gigantea* Aiton (127) (1933)

Tall smooth panic grass - *Panicum virgatum* L. (66, 90) (1885-1903)

Tall smooth panicum - *Panicum virgatum* L. (72, 131) (1894-1907)

Tall spear grass - *Poa alsodes* Gray (87) (1884)

Tall speedwell [Tall speed-well] - *Lepidium virginicum* L. (187) (1818), *Veronicastrum virginicum* (L.) Farw. (5, 6, 49, 53, 64, 92, 156, 157, 158) (1876-1929)

Tall sunflower - *Helianthus giganteus* L. (5, 93, 97, 156) (1913-1937)

Tall swamp panic grass [Tall swamp panic-grass] - *Dichanthelium scabriusculum* (Ell.) Gould & C.A. Clark (163) (1852)

Tall swamp panicum - *Dichanthelium scabriusculum* (Ell.) Gould & C.A. Clark (5) (1913)

Tall thelesperma - *Thelesperma filifolium* (Hook.) Gray var. *filifolium* (124) (1937)

Tall thimbleweed - *Anemone virginiana* L. (50) (present), *Anemone virginiana* L. var. *virginiana* (50) (present)

Tall thin grass [Tall thingrass] - *Agrostis perennans* (Walt.) Tuckerman (5) (1913)

Tall thistle - *Cirsium altissimum* (L.) Hill (3, 4, 5, 50, 62, 72, 82, 93, 95, 97, 122, 155) (1907–present), *Cirsium altissimum* (L.) Hill (19, 114, 145) (1840-1897)

Tall thoroughwort - *Eupatorium altissimum* L. (5, 50, 93, 95, 97, 122, 131) (1899–present)

Tall tickseed - *Coreopsis tripteris* (5, 50, 72, 156) (1907–present)

Tall tickseed sunflower [Tall tickseed-sunflower] - *Bidens coronata* (L.) Britton (5, 72, 93) (1907-1936)

Tall tumble-mustard [Tall tumblemustard] - *Sisymbrium altissimum* L. (50) (present)

Tall veronica - *Veronicastrum virginicum* (L.) Farw. (19, 49, 64, 157, 158) (1840-1929)

Tall vervain - *Verbena hastata* L. (187) (1818)

Tall waterhemp [Tall water hemp] - *Amaranthus tuberculatus* (Moq.) Sauer (3, 4, 155) (1977-1986)

Tall wheat grass [Tall wheatgrass] - *Thinopyrum ponticum* (Podp.) Z.-W. Liu & R.-C. Wang (3, 155) (1942-1977)

Tall white aster - *Symphyotrichum lanceolatum* (Willd.) Nesom subsp. *lanceolatum* (5, 82, 93, 127, 156) (1913-1936)

Tall white bog orchis - *Platanthera dilatata* (Pursh) Lindl. ex Beck var. *dilatata* (5, 93, 109) (1913-1949)

Tall white evening-primrose [Tall white evening primrose] - *Oenothera pallida* Lindl. (156) (1923)

Tall white larkspur - *Delphinium carolinianum* Walt. subsp. *virescens* (Nutt.) Brooks (127) (1933)

Tall white lettuce - *Prenanthes altissima* L. (5) (1913) `

Tall white violet - *Viola canadensis* L. var. *rugulosa* (Greene) A.S. Hitchc. (4) (1986)

Tall wild larkspur - *Delphinium exaltatum* Aiton (2) (1895)

Tall wild lettuce - *Lactuca canadensis* L. (93) (1936)

Tall wild nettle - *Urtica dioica* L. subsp. *gracilis* (Aiton) Seland. (5, 58, 93, 158) (1869-1936)

Tall wood lettuce - *Lactuca floridana* (L.) Gaertn. (122, 124) (1937)

Tall yellow wood sorrel [Tall yellow wood-sorrel] - *Oxalis stricta* L. (5, 72, 85, 93, 97) (1907-1937)

Tall yellow-eyed grass - *Xyris jupicai* L.C. Rich. (5) (1913)

Tall-bread scurfpea [Tallbread scurfpea] - *Pediomelum cuspidatum* (Pursh) Rydb. (4, 155) (1942-1986)

Taller fescue - *Lolium pratense* (Huds.) S.J. Darbyshire (45, 90) (1885-1896)

Taller thin grass - *Agrostis perennans* (Walt.) Tuckerman (66) (1903)

Tallest goldenrod [Tallest golden-rod] - *Solidago canadensis* L. var. *scabra* Torr. & Gray (187) (1818)

Tall-leaf pericome [Tallleaf pericome] - *Pericome caudata* Gray (155) (1942)

Tallow bayberry [Tallow bay-berry] - *Morella cerifera* (L.) Small (5, 156) (1913-1923)

Tallow root [Tallow-root] - *Tipularia discolor* (Pursh) Nutt. (5, 156) (1913-1923)

Tallow shrub - *Morella cerifera* (L.) Small (5, 6, 41, 92, 156) (1770-1923)

Tallow tree [Tallow-tree] - *Ailanthus altissima* (Mill) Swingle (92) (1876), *Triadica sebifera* (L.) Small (10, 14, 20, 46, 92) (1818-1882)

Tallowwood - *Ximenia americana* L. (155) (1942)

Talus-slope penstemon [Talus slope penstemon] - *Penstemon digitalis* Nutt. ex Sims (50) (present)

Taluwa (Quapaws) - *Nelumbo* Adans. (7) (1828)

Tamanioh'pe (Dakota) - *Physalis heterophylla* Nees (37) (1919)

Tamarack [Tamarac] - *Larix laricina* (Du Roi.) Koch. (1, 5, 19, 29, 40, 49, 50, 57, 58, 92, 109, 135) (1840–present)

Tamarind - *Tamarindus indica* L. (7, 57, 107, 109, 138) (1828-1949), *Tamarindus* L. (138) (1923)

Tamarindo - *Tamarindus indica* L. (109) (1949)

Tamarisk [Tamarix] - *Larix laricina* (Du Roi.) Koch. (19, 43) (1820-1840), *Larix* Mill (1, 7) (1828-1932), *Tamarix* L. (1, 15, 50, 109, 112, 138, 155, 158) (1895–present)

Tamarix savin - *Juniperus sabina* L. (136) (1930)

Tamaryte - *Tamarix gallica* L. (178, 179) (1526-1596)

Tamate - *Solanum lycopersicum* L. var. *lycopersicum* (158) (1900) Spanish America

Tamboc - *Nicotiana tabacum* L. (110) (1886)

Tambosier à feuilles de buis (French) - *Eugenia foetida* Pers. (20) (1857)

Tambosier dichotome (French) - *Myrcianthes fragrans* (Sw.) McVaugh (20) (1857)

Tambosier élevé (French) - *Eugenia procera* (Sw.) Poir. (20) (1857)

Tambuco - *Nicotiana tabacum* L. (110) (after 1600)

Tame cress - *Lepidium sativum* L. (179) (1526)

Tame mallow [Tame malowe] - *Alcea rosea* L. (179) (1526)

Tame mint [Tame mynte] - *Mentha spicata* L. (179) (1526)

Tame pere - *Pyrus* L. (179) (1526)

Tamerack - *Larix occidentalis* Nutt. (35) (1806)

Tamnioxpi hu (Lakota, placenta or womb plant) - *Physalis heterophylla* Nees (121) (1918?-1970?)

Tan bark - *Lithocarpus densiflorus* (Hook. & Arn.) Rehd. (106) (1930)

Tan bay - *Gordonia lasianthus* L. (5, 156) (1913-1923)

Tan tuttipang - *Lobelia siphilitica* L. (186) (1814)

Tanaceto (Spanish) - *Tanacetum vulgare* L. (158) (1900)

Tanaisie (French) - *Tanacetum vulgare* L. (6, 158) (1892-1900)

Tan-bark oak [Tan bark oak, Tanbark oak] - *Quercus prinus* L. (5, 156) (1913-1923)

Tan'-chi (Choctaw) - *Zea mays* L. (132) (1855)

Tangerine - *Citrus reticulata* Blanco (109) (1949)

Tanghekolli - *Crinum asiaticum* L. (174) (1753)

Tangier pea - *Lathyrus tingitanus* L. (109) (1949)

Tangle - *Laminaria digitata* (Hudson) J.V.Lamouroux (107) (1919)

Tangleberry [Tangle-berry] - *Gaylussacia frondosa* (L.) Torr. & Gray (5, 156) (1913-1923)

Tanglefoot [Tangle foot] - *Lotus glaber* Mill. (106) (1930), *Viburnum lantanoides* Michx. (5, 75, 156, 174) (1753-1923)

Tangle-head [Tangle head] - *Heteropogon contortus* (L.) Beauv. ex Roemer & J.A. Schultes (122) (1937) TX

Tangle-legs [Tangle legs] - *Viburnum lantanoides* Michx. (5, 19, 156, 174) (1753-1923)

Tangle-tail [Tangle tail] - *Sedum acre* L. (5, 156) (1913-1923) no longer in use by 1923

Tanhoof - *Glechoma hederacea* L. (157, 158) (1900-1929)

Tank - *Pastinaca sativa* L. (156, 157, 158) (1900-1929)

Tanne - *Abies alba* Mill. (possibly) (158) (1900)

Tanner's oak - *Quercus alba* L. (157) (1929)

Tanniers - *Colocasia esculenta* (L.) Schott (7) (1828)

Tannin plant - *Polygonum amphibium* L. var. *emersum* Michx. (114) (1894) Neb

Tanpa (Dakota) - *Betula papyrifera* Marsh (37) (1919)

Tanpa-hu (Dakota, Birch tree) - *Betula papyrifera* Marsh (37) (1919)

Tansey cinquefoil - *Argentina anserina* (L.) Rydb. (19) (1840)

Tansey-leaf tansy-aster [Tanseyleaf tansyaster] - *Machaeranthera tanacetifolia* (Kunth) Nees (50) (present)

Tansy [Tansey, Tansie] - *Achillea millefolium* L. (127, 158) (1900-1933) ND, *Machaeranthera* Nees (1, 93) (1932-1936) Neb, *Senecio jacobea* L. (156) (1923), *Tanacetum* L. (1, 4, 10, 50, 109, 138, 155, 156, 158) (1818–present), *Tanacetum vulgare* L. (5, 6, 7, 19, 40, 41, 46, 49, 53, 57, 58, 61, 62, 72, 80, 85, 92, 93, 97, 107, 131, 158, 179, 184, 187) (1526-1937)

Tansy cinquefoil - *Potentilla bipinnatifida* Dougl. ex Hook. (50) (present)

Tansy dogshade - *Limnosciadium pinnatum* (DC.) Math. & Const. (50) (present)

Tansy mustard - *Descurainia incana* (Bernh. ex Fisch. & C.A. Mey.) Dorn subsp. *incisa* (Engelm.) Kartesz & Gandhi (101) (1905)

Tansy phacelia - *Phacelia tanacetifolia* Benth. (138) (1923)

Tansy ragwort [Tansy-ragwort] - *Senecio jacobea* L. (5, 156) (1913-1923)

Tansy-aster [Tansy aster, Tansyaster] - *Machaeranthera* Nees (50) (present), *Machaeranthera tanacetifolia* (Kunth) Nees (3, 4, 5, 85, 93, 97, 124, 145) (1897-1986)

Tansy-leaf aster [Tansyleaf aster] - *Machaeranthera tanacetifolia* (Kunth) Nees (155) (1942)

Tansy-leaf phacelia - *Phacelia tanacetifolia* Benth. (77) (1898)

Tansy-mustard [Tansy mustard, Tansymustard] - *Descurainia incana* (Bernh. ex Fisch. & C.A. Mey.) Dorn subsp. *incana* (156) (1923), *Descurainia pinnata* (Walt.) Britton (3, 4) (1977-1986), *Descurainia pinnata* (Walt.) Britton subsp. *brachycarpa* (Richards.) Detling (3, 5, 72, 93, 97) (1907-1977), *Descurainia pinnata* (Walter) Britton subsp. *pinnata* (15, 107, 145) (1895-1929), *Descurainia*

Webb & Berth. (1, 4, 50, 155, 158) (1900–present), *Sisymbrium officinale* (L.) Scop (122) (1937)

Tanweed - *Polygonum amphibium* L. var. *emersum* Michx. (80, 82) (1913-1930) IA

Tao (Japanese) - *Prunus persica* (L.) Batsch (110) (1886)

Taopi pežuta (Lakota, wound medicine) - *Achillea millefolium* L. (121) (1918?-1970?)

Tap (Estonian) - *Humulus lupulus* L. (110) (1886)

Tapa-cloth tree - *Broussonetia papyrifera* (L.) L'Hér. ex Vent. (107) (1919)

Tape-grass [Tape grass, Tapegrass] - *Vallisneria americana* Michx. (3, 5, 19, 92, 120, 131, 156, 158, 187) (1818-1977), *Vallisneria* L. (2, 109, 158) (1895-1949)

Tape-leaf flatsedge [Tapeleaf flatsedge] - *Cyperus acuminatus* Torr. & Hook. ex Torr. (3) (1977)

Tapered rosette grass - *Dichanthelium acuminatum* (Sw.) Gould & C.A. Clark (50) (present)

Taper-leaf flatsedge - *Cyperus acuminatus* Torr. & Hook. ex Torr. (139) (1944)

Taper-leaf ground-cherry [Taperleaf groundcherry] - *Physalis longifolia* Nutt. var. *subglabrata* (Mackenzie & Bush) Cronq. (97) (1937)

Taper-leaf sedge [Taperleaf sedge] - *Cyperus acuminatus* Torr. & Hook. ex Torr. (155) (1942)

Taper-leaf water horehound [Taperleaf water horehound] - *Lycopus rubellus* Moench (50) (present)

Taper-tip flatsedge [Tapertip flat sedge] - *Cyperus acuminatus* Torr. & Hook. ex Torr. (50) (present)

Taper-tip cup grass [Tapertip cupgrass] - *Eriochloa acuminata* (J. Presl) Kunth var. *acuminata* (50) (present), *Eriochloa lemmonii* Vasey & Scribn. var. *gracilis* (Fourn.) Gould (50) (present)

Taper-tip hawk's-beard [Taper-tip hawksbeard, Tapertip hawksbeard] - *Crepis acuminata* Nutt. (50, 155) (1942–present)

Taper-tip onion [Tapertip onion] - *Allium acuminatum* Hook. (155) (1942)

Taper-tip rush [Tapertip rush] - *Juncus acuminatus* Michx. (50) (present)

Tape-tip wake-robin [Tapertip wakerobin] - *Trillium viridescens* Nutt. (50) (present)

Tapioca-plant - *Manihot esculenta* Crantz (109) (1949)

Tapiro - *Sambucus nigra* L. subsp. *canadensis* (L.) R. Bolli (153) (1913) NM

Ta'-po (Kioway) - *Nicotiana* L. (132) (1855)

Taquera - *Lagenaria siceraria* (Molina) Standl. (110) (1658)

Tar bush - *Chamaebatia foliolosa* Benth. (76) (1896) CA

Tara vine [Tara-vine] - *Actinidia arguta* (Sieb. & Zucc.) Planch. ex Miq. (50, 109, 138) (1923–present)

Taray (Spanish) - *Tamarix gallica* L. (107) (1919)

Tarchon - *Artemisia dracunculus* L. (possibly) (180) (1633)

Tare [Tares] - *Lolium temulentum* L. (5, 56, 92, 119) (1901-1938) thought to be the biblical tares, *Spergula arvensis* L. (92) (1876), *Vicia hirsuta* (L.) Gray (156) (1923), *Vicia* L. (2, 45, 156, 158) (1895-1923), *Vicia sativa* L. (14, 19, 68, 92, 107, 109, 110, 131) (1840-1949)

Tare vetch [Tare-vetch] - *Vicia hirsuta* (L.) Gray (5, 156) (1913-1923) *Lathyrus pratensis* L. (5) (1913)

Tar-mi' (Shawnee) - *Zea mays* L. (132) (1855)

Tarmia (Missouri tribes) - *Erythronium* L. (7) (1828)

Taro - *Colocasia esculenta* (L.) Schott (109, 138) (1923-1949)

Taroho (Indian tribes) - *Peltandra* Raf. (7) (1828)

Tarragon - *Artemisia dracunculus* L. (46, 50, 57, 92, 107, 109, 138, 155, 157, 158, 178, 180) (1596–present)

Tarragon snakeweed - *Amphiachyris dracunculoides* (DC.) Nutt. (155) (1942)

Tarrify - *Erysimum cheiranthoides* L. (5, 157) (1913-1929)

Tarry cockle - *Silene antirrhina* L. (62) (1912)

Tartar root - *Panax quinquefolius* L. (possibly) (6) (1892)

Tartarian buckwheat - *Fagopyrum tataricum* (L.) Gaertn. (107) (1919)

Tartarian bush honeysuckle [Tartarian bush-honeysuckle] - *Lonicera tatarica* L. (5, 72, 156) (1907-1923)

Tartarian dogwood - *Cornus sericea* L. subsp. *sericea* (109, 138, 155) (1923–1949)

Tartarian maple - *Acer tataricum* L. (135) (1910)

Tartarian moss - *Lecanora tartarea* (L.) Ach. (92) (1876)

Tartarian oat [Tartarian oats, Tartarean oat] - *Avena fatua* L. (107) (1919), *Avena sativa* L. (45, 107) (1896-1919)

Tartary buckwheat - *Fagopyrum tataricum* (L.) Gaertn. (5, 110) (1886-1913)

Tarweed [Tar weed, Tar-weed] - *Amsinckia* Lehm. (77) (1898) CA, *Chamaebatia foliolosa* Benth. (76, 106) (1896–1930), *Cuphea viscosissima* Jacq (5, 74, 156, 158) (1893–1923) WV, *Grindelia squarrosa* (Pursh) Dunal (156) (1923), *Grindelia* Willd. (82, 158) (1900–1930), *Hemizonia* DC. (106) (1930), *Hemizonia fasciculata* (DC.) Torr. & Gray (76) (1896), *Hemizonia pungens* (Hook. & Arn.) Torr. & Gray (75) (1894), *Madia glomerata* Hook. (4, 101) (1905–1986), *Madia sativa* Molina (75) (1894)

Tarweed fiddleneck - *Amsinckia lycopsoides* Lehm. (50, 155) (1942–present)

Tasajillo - *Opuntia leptocaulis* DC. (122) (1937) TX

Tashkadan (Dakota) - *Acer negundo* L. (37) (1919)

Tashka-hi (Omaha-Ponca) - *Quercus macrocarpa* Michx. (37) (1919)

Tashnánga-hi (Omaha-Ponca) - *Fraxinus pennsylvanica* Marsh. (37) (1919)

Taška hi (Osage, white oak-like? tree) - *Aesculus glabra* Willd. (121) (1918?-1970?)

Tasmanian blue gum - *Eucalyptus globulus* Labill. (109) (1949)

Taspan (Omaha-Ponca) - *Crataegus chrysocarpa* Ashe (37) (1919)

Tassajilla - *Opuntia leptocaulis* DC. (97) (1937) OK

Tassel [Tasyll] - *Centaurea nigra* L. (5, 156) (1913-1923) no longer in use by 1923, *Dipsacus fullonum* L. (156, 158) (1900-1923), *Eryngium maritimum* L. (179) (1526)

Tassel amaranth - *Amaranthus cruentus* L. (138) (1923)

Tassel flower [Tassel-flower, Tasselflower, Tassell flower] - *Amaranthus caudatus* L. (109) (1949), *Arnoglossum atriplicifolium* (L.) H.E. Robins. (102) (1886), *Brickellia grandiflora* (Hook.) Nutt. (5, 156) (1913-1923), *Emilia coccinea* (Sims) G. Don (109, 138) (1923-1949), *Emilia sonchifolia* (L.) DC. (92) (1876)

Tassel pond-grass - *Ruppia maritima* L. (158) (1900)

Tassel pondweed [Tassel-pond weed] - *Ruppia cirrhosa* (Petag.) Grande (157) (1929), *Ruppia maritima* L. (5, 156, 158) (1900-1923)

Tassel-bur - *Carduus* L. (158) (1900)

Tassel-flower brickell bush [Tasselflower brickellbush] - *Brickellia grandiflora* (Hook.) Nutt. (50) (present)

Tassel-flower brickellia [Tasselflower brickellia] - *Brickellia grandiflora* (Hook.) Nutt. (155) (1942)

Tassel-grass [Tassel grass] - *Ruppia maritima* L. (5, 156, 158) (1900-1923)

Tassel-pond weed - *Ruppia cirrhosa* (Petag.) Grande (157) (1929)

Tasselweed [Tassel weed, Tassel-weed] - *Ambrosia artemisiifolia* L. (73, 156, 158) (1892-1923), *Ambrosia artemisiifolia* L. var. *elatior* (L.) Descourtils (5, 157) (1913-1929)

Tassijilla - *Opuntia leptocaulis* DC. (106) (1930)

Tasteless knotweed - *Polygonum hydropiperoides* Michx. (19) (1840)

Tatarian aster - *Aster tataricus* L. f. (138, 155) (1931-1942)

Tatarian cephalaria - *Cephalaria gigantea* (Ledeb.) Bobr. (138) (1923)

Tatarian honeysuckle [Tartarian honeysuckle] - *Lonicera tatarica* L. (3, 50, 82, 106, 109, 135, 138, 155, 156) (1910–present)

Tatarian maple - *Acer ginnala* Maxim. (82) (1930), *Acer tataricum* L. (50, 137, 138, 155) (1923–present)

Tatarka (Bohemian) - *Fagopyrum esculentum* Moench (46) (1879)

Tatarskie ziele (Polish) - *Acorus calamus* L. (186) (1814)

Tatawabluška tačaŋxloǧaŋ (Lakota, horsefly weed) - *Gaura coccinea* Nutt. ex Pursh (121) (1918?-1970?)

Tatečaŋnuǧa (Lakota, lumpy carcass or lumps in carcass) - *Liatris punctata* Hook (121) (1918?-1970?)

Tat-grass [Tat grass] - *Isoloba elatior* (Michx.) Raf. (92) (1876)

Tatnall's thorn - *Crataegus mollis* Scheele (5) (1913)

Ta-tou (Chinese) - *Glycine max* (L.) Merr. (110) (1886)

Tatrika (Slavic languages) - *Fagopyrum esculentum* Moench (110) (1886)

Tatrikat (Estonian) - *Fagopyrum esculentum* Moench (46) (1879)

Tatrka (Slavic languages) - *Fagopyrum esculentum* Moench (110) (1886)

Tattar (Polish) - *Fagopyrum esculentum* Moench (46) (1879)

Tattar (Slavic languages) - *Fagopyrum esculentum* Moench (110) (1886)

Tattered fringed orchis - *Platanthera grandiflora* (Bigelow) Lindl. (5, 156) (1913-1923)

Tatula - *Datura stramonium* L. (174) (1753)

Taummelkorn (German) - *Lolium temulentum* L. (158) (1900)

Taurus cotton-thistle [Taurus cottonthistle] - *Onopordum tauricum* Willd. (138) (1923)

Tausengüldenkraut (German, thousand guelders herb) - *Centaurium beyrichii* (Torr. & Gray ex Torr.) B.L. Robins. (100) (1850)

Tawatsaako (Pawnee) - *Juniperus virginiana* L. (37) (1830)

Taw-him - *Hexastylis virginica* (L.) Small (41) (1770)

Tawhiwhi - *Pittosporum tenuifolium* Gaertn. (109, 138) (1923-1949)

Taw-ho - *Hexastylis virginica* (L.) Small (41) (1770)

Taw-kee - *Orontium aquaticum* L. (86) (1878) Indian name

Tawkin - *Orontium aquaticum* L. (5, 7, 41, 92, 156) (1770–1923)

Tawny cotton-grass [Tawny cotton grass, Tawny cottongrass] - *Eriophorum virginicum* L. (50, 156) (1923–present)

Tawny cryptantha - *Cryptantha fulvocanescens* (S. Wats.) Payson var. *fulvocanescens* (50) (present)

Tawny daylily [Tawny day lily, Tawny day-lily] - *Hemerocallis fulva* (L.) L. (19, 138, 155, 156) (1840-1942)

Tawny hawkweed [Tawny hawk-weed] - *Hieracium aurantiacum* L. (5, 156) (1913-1923)

Tawny impatiens - *Impatiens capensis* Meerb. (86) (1878)

Tawny oreocarya - *Cryptantha fulvocanescens* (S. Wats.) Payson var. *fulvocanescens* (5) (1913)

Tawny pimpernel [Tawnie pimpernell] - *Anagallis arvensis* L. (178) (1526)

Tawny sedge - *Carex hostiana* DC. (5) (1913)

Tchakoshe-pukk (Crow) - *Arctostaphylos uva-ursi* (L.) Spreng. (107) (1919)

Tdage (Omaha-Ponca) - *Juglans nigra* L. (37) (1919)

Tdika shande (Omaha-Ponca) - *Astragalus crassicarpus* Nutt. var. *crassicarpus* (37) (1919)

Tdika shande nuga (Omaha-Ponca) - *Baptisia bracteata* Muhl. ex Ell. (37) (1919)

Tdo (Winnebago) - *Apios americana* Medik. (37) (1919)

Tdokewihi (Winnebago, hungry) - *Pediomelum esculentum* (Pursh) Rydb. (37) (1919) MN

Tea - *Camellia* L. (7) (1828)

Tea bush - *Gaultheria hispidula* (L.) Muhl. ex Bigelow (41) (1770)

Tea plant [Tea-plant] - *Lantana* L. (75) (1894) LA, *Viburnum lentago* L. (5, 76, 156, 158) (1896-1923) Madison WI, no longer in use by 1923

Tea rose - *Rosa odorata* (Andr.) Sweet (109, 138) (1923-1949) from odor

Tea viburnum - *Viburnum setigerum* Hance (138) (1923)

Teaberry [Tea-berry, Tea berry, Tea-berries] - *Gaultheria hispidula* (L.) Muhl. ex Bigelow (73, 77) (1892-1898), *Gaultheria procumbens* L. (5, 6, 7, 49, 53, 92, 107, 156, 186, 187) (1814-1923), *Mitchella repens* L. (156) (1923), *Ribes uva-crispa* L. var. *sativum* DC. (5, 156) (1913-1923), *Viburnum nudum* L. var. *cassinoides* (L.) Torr. & Gray (156) (1923)

Teal love grass

COMMON NAMES

Teal love grass [Teal lovegrass] - *Eragrostis hypnoides* (Lam.) Britton, Sterns & Poggenb. (3, 50, 155) (1942–present)
Tea-leaves - *Gaultheria procumbens* L. (156) (1923)
Tear grass - *Coix lacryma-jobi* L. (67) (1890)
Tearal [Tearel] - *Eupatorium perfoliatum* L. (69, 92) (1876-1904)
Tear-blanket - *Aralia spinosa* L. (156) (1923)
Tear-thumb [Tear thumb, Tear-thumb] - *Polygonum arifolium* L. (86, 92) (1876-1878) from sharp prickles, *Polygonum* L. (1, 155) (1932-1942), *Polygonum sagittatum* L. (2, 4, 85) (1895-1986)
Teasel [Teazel] - *Dipsacus fullonum* L. (3, 14, 19, 92, 106, 132, 158, 184) (1793–1977), *Dipsacus* L. (1, 4, 7, 10, 50, 109, 138, 155, 156, 158) (1828–present), *Eupatorium perfoliatum* L. (7, 69) (1828–1904)
Teasel gourd [Teaselgourd] - *Cucumis dipsaceus* C.G. Ehrenb. ex Spach (109, 138) (1923-1949)
Tecate cypress - *Cupressus forbesii* Jepson (109) (1949)
Tecomaria - *Tecoma* Juss. (138) (1923)
Tee-amp (Snake) - *Amelanchier alnifolia* (Nutt.) Nutt. ex M. Roemer (101) (1905) MT
Teel [Teele] - *Schoenoplectus tabernaemontani* (C.C. Gmel.) Palla (possibly) (14) (1882), *Sesamum orientale* L. (92) (1876)
Teep-se-nah (Assiniboin) - *Pediomelum esculentum* (Pursh) Rydb. (83) (1850) IA
Teff - *Eragrostis tef* (Zuccagni) Trotter (56, 107, 109, 138) (1901-1949)
Te-hunton-hi (Omaha-Ponca, buffalo bellow plant) - *Amorpha fruticosa* L. (37) (1919)
Te-hunton-hi nuga (Omaha-Ponca, male buffalo bellow plant) - *Lespedeza capitata* Michx. (37) (1919)
Teil tree [Teil-tree] - *Tilia ×europaea* L. (178) (1526), *Tilia americana* L. var. *heterophylla* (Vent.) Loud. (156) (1923)
Ten o'clock [Ten-o'-clock] - *Ornithogalum umbellatum* L. (92, 158) (1876-1900)
Ten o'clock lady - *Ornithogalum umbellatum* L. (5, 156) (1913-1923)
Ten-angle pipewort [Tenangle pipewort, Ten-angled pipewort] - *Eriocaulon decangulare* L. (5, 50, 156) (1913–present)
Tenchweed [Tench weed, Tench-weed] - *Potamogeton natans* L. (5, 156, 158) (1900-1923)
Tender maidenhair - *Adiantum tenerum* Sw. (165) (1768)
Tendril-bearing smartweed - *Brunnichia ovata* (Walt.) Shinners (106, 156) (1923-1930)
Tendrilled trumpet flower [Tendrilled trumpet-flower] - *Bignonia capreolata* L. (5, 97, 156) (1913-1937)
Teng grass - *Rorippa sinuata* (Nutt.) A.S. Hitchc. (35) (1806)
Tenging nettle - *Urtica dioica* L. (157, 158) (1900-1929)
Ten-lobe agalinis [Ten-lobed agalinis] - *Agalinis obtusifolia* Raf. (5) (1913)
Tennesoat grass - *Danthonia compressa* Austin ex Peck (5) (1913)
Tennessee bladder fern [Tennessee bladderfern] - *Cystopteris tennesseensis* Shaver. (50) (present)
Tennessee bluestem [Tennessee blue stem] - *Andropogon gerardii* Vitman (56) (1901) IA
Tennessee chickweed - *Stellaria corei* Shinners (5) (1913)
Tennessee fescue - *Festuca rubra* L. subsp. *rubra* (94) (1901)
Tennessee indigo [Tennessee-indigo] - *Amorpha fruticosa* L. (138) (1923)
Tennessee indigo-bush amorpha [Tennessee indigobush amorpha] - *Amorpha fruticosa* L. (155) (1942)
Tennessee milkvetch [Tennessee milk vetch] - *Astragalus tennesseensis* Gray ex Chapman (5, 97) (1913-1937)
Tennessee oat grass [Tennessee oat-grass] - *Danthonia compressa* Austin ex Peck (94) (1901)
Tennessee panic grass [Tennessee panic-grass] - *Dichanthelium acuminatum* (Sw.) Gould & C.A. Clark var. *fasciculatum* (Torr.) Freckmann (72, 119) (1907-1938)
Tennessee panicum - *Dichanthelium acuminatum* (Sw.) Gould & C.A. Clark var. *fasciculatum* (Torr.) Freckmann (5, 155) (1913-1942)
Tennessee pinkroot - *Ruellia humilis* Nutt. (64) (1907)

Tennessee prairie clover [Tennessee prairieclover] - *Dalea compacta* Spreng. var. *compacta* (138) (1923)
Tennessee rice - *Sorghum bicolor* (L.) Moench subsp. *bicolor* (107) (1919)
Ten-o'clock [Ten o'clock, Ten-o'-clock] - *Ornithogalum umbellatum* L. (92, 158) (1876-1900)
Ten-o'clock-lady [Ten o'clock lady] - *Ornithogalum umbellatum* L. (5, 156) (1913-1923)
Tenore's candytuft [Tenore candytuft] - *Iberis carnosa* Willd. (138) (1923)
Ten-petal anemone [Tenpetal anemone, Ten-petalled anemone] - *Anemone berlandieri* Pritz. (3, 4, 155, 165) (1807-1986)
Ten-petal blazing star [Tenpetal blazingstar] - *Mentzelia decapetala* (Pursh ex Sims) Urban & Gilg ex Gilg (50, 155) (1942–present)
Ten-petal menzelia [Tenpetal mentzelia] - *Mentzelia decapetala* (Pursh ex Sims) Urban & Gilg ex Gilg (4, 155) (1942-1986)
Ten-petal sunflower [Ten-petalled sun-flower] - *Helianthus decapetalus* L. (187) (1818)
Ten-petal thimbleweed [Tenpetal thimbleweed] - *Anemone berlandieri* Pritz. (50) (present)
Ten-ray sunflower [Ten-rayed sunflower] - *Helianthus decapetalus* L. (156) (1923)
Tentwort - *Asplenium ruta-muraria* L. (92) (1876)
Teosinte - *Zea* L. (138) (1923), *Zea mexicana* (Schrad.) Kuntze (56, 67, 101, 109, 138, 163) (1852-1949)
Teparies - *Phaseolus acutifolius* Gray (105) (1932)
Tepary bean - *Phaseolus acutifolius* Gray var. *latifolius* Freeman (109) (1949)
Tepehuaje - *Leucaena pulverulenta* (Schlecht.) Benth. (124) (1937) TX
Tephrosia - *Tephrosia* Pers. (155) (1942), *Tephrosia virginiana* (L.) Pers (3) (1977)
Téphrosie (French) - *Tephrosia virginiana* (L.) Pers (158) (1900)
Ter-di-cha (Diegeño Yuma) - *Zea mays* L. (132) (1855)
Tĕr-ditch (Cuchan Yuma) - *Zea mays* L. (132) (1855)
Ter-dítz (Mohave Yuma) - *Zea mays* L. (132) (1855)
Terebinth - *Pistacia atlantica* Desf. (138) (1923)
Terebintha - *Pinus palustris* Mill. (57) (1917) source
Terebinthina canadensis - *Abies balsamea* (L.) Mill. (57, 60) (1902-1917) source
Terebinthinae laricis - *Pinus palustris* Mill. (57) (1917) source
Terete talinum - *Phemeranthus teretifolius* (Pursh) Raf. (86) (1878)
Terete-leaf talinum [Terete-leaved talinum] - *Phemeranthus teretifolius* (Pursh) Raf. (2) (1895)
Terminal shield fern - *Polystichum acrostichoides* (Michx.) Schott (187)
Termos (Greek) - *Lupinus albus* L. (110) (1886)
Ternate grape fern [Ternate grape-fern] - *Botrychium dissectum* Spreng. (5) (1913), *Botrychium rugulosum* W.H. Wagner (86) (1878)
Terowa (Oto) - *Nelumbo* Adans. (7) (1828)
Te-row-a (Oto, bison-beaver) - *Nelumbo lutea* Willd. (possibly) (38) (1820)
Terrell's grass [Terrell-grass, Terrell grass, Terril grass] - *Elymus canadensis* L. (87, 90) (1884-1885), *Elymus virginicus* L. (5, 56, 68, 87, 88, 90, 94, 118, 119, 143, 163) (1852-1938)
Terresteria mora (Earth mulberry) - *Fragaria* L. (107) (1540)
Terrestrial water-starwort [Terrestrial water starwort] - *Callitriche terrestris* Raf. (5, 50, 156) (1913–present)
Terrididdle - *Solanum dulcamara* L. (158) (1900)
Terwe (Dutch) - *Triticum aestivum* L. (180) (1633)
Tesajo - *Opuntia leptocaulis* DC. (155) (1942)
Tesota (Mexicans) - *Olneya tesota* Gray (123) (1856)
Teta-minan (Chippewa) - *Viburnum lentago* L. (105) (1932)
Tetéga-min (Chippewa) - *Rubus allegheniensis* Porter (105) (1932)
Tethawe (Omaha-Ponca) - *Nelumbo lutea* Willd. (37) (1919)
Tether-devil [Tether devil] - *Lycium barbarum* L. (156) (1923), *Solanum dulcamara* L. (158) (1900)

414

Tether-toad - *Ranunculus repens* L. (156, 158) (1900-1923)

Tetonwort - *Solanum dulcamara* L. (71) (1898)

Tetragonotheca - *Tetragonotheca helianthoides* L. (5) (1913)

Tetter-berry [Tetter berry] - *Bryonia alba* L. (92) (1876)

Tetterwort - *Chelidonium majus* L. (5, 6, 49, 52, 53, 54, 92, 156, 158) (1892-1923), *Sanguinaria canadensis* L. (5, 6, 49, 53, 64, 156, 157, 158) (1892-1929)

Teucrium - *Teucrium canadense* L. (57) (1917)

Teufelsaugenkraut (German) - *Hyoscyamus niger* L. (158) (1900)

Teufelsflucht (German) - *Hypericum perforatum* L. (158) (1900)

Tewapa (Lakota) - *Nelumbo lutea* Willd. (121) (1918?-1970?)

Tewape (Dakota) - *Nelumbo lutea* Willd. (37) (1919)

Texas adelia - *Forestiera acuminata* (Michx.) Poir. (122, 138) (1923-1937)

Texas adolphia - *Adolphia infesta* (Kunth) Meisn. (155) (1942)

Texas amsonia - *Amsonia ciliata* Walt. var. *texana* (Gray) Coult. (4, 155) (1942-1986)

Texas ash - *Fraxinus texensis* (Gray) Sargent (138) (1923)

Texas barberry - *Mahonia swaseyi* (Buckl. ex Young) Fedde (4, 50) (1986–present)

Texas beard grass [Texas beardgrass] - *Schizachyrium cirratum* (Hack.) Woot. & Standl. (122) (1937)

Texas bedstraw - *Galium texense* Gray (4, 50) (1986–present)

Texas bergia - *Bergia texana* (Hook.) Seub. ex Walp. (4, 5, 50, 155) (1913–present)

Texas berlandiera [Texan berlandiera] - *Berlandiera texana* DC. (3, 5, 97) (1913-1977)

Texas bindweed - *Convolvulus equitans* Benth. (50) (present)

Texas bitterweed - *Hymenoxys texana* (Coult. & Rose) Cockerell (122) (1937)

Texas black walnut - *Juglans microcarpa* Berl. var. *microcarpa* (155) (1942)

Texas black willow - *Salix nigra* Marsh. (155) (1942)

Texas blue-eyed grass [Texas blue-eyedgrass] - *Sisyrinchium langloisii* Greene (155) (1942)

Texas bluegrass [Texas blue-grass, Texas blue grass] - *Poa arachnifera* Torr. (3, 5, 45, 50, 56, 72, 87, 88, 94, 119, 122, 155, 163) (1852–present)

Texas bluestar - *Amsonia ciliata* Walt. var. *texana* (Gray) Coult. (50) (present)

Texas blueweed - *Helianthus ciliaris* DC. (3, 4, 50) (1977–present)

Texas boxelder - *Acer negundo* L. var. *texanum* Pax (155) (1942)

Texas brome grass - *Bromus texensis* (Shear) A.S. Hitchc. (122) (1937)

Texas buckeye [Texan buckeye] - *Aesculus glabra* Willd. (124, 138, 155) (1923-1942), *Ungnadia speciosa* Endl. (109) (1949)

Texas buckthorn - *Ziziphus obtusifolia* (Hook. ex Torr. & Gray) Gray (106) (1930)

Texas bull-nettle [Texas bull nettle, Texas bullnettle] - *Cnidoscolus texanus* (Muell.-Arg.) Small (50) (present)

Texas but - *Tribulus terrestris* L. (156) (1923)

Texas catsclaw - *Acacia greggii* Gray (106, 124) (1930-1937)

Texas centaury [Texan centaury] - *Centaurium texense* (Griseb.) Fernald (5, 122) (1913-1937)

Texas chervil - *Chaerophyllum tainturieri* Hook. var. *tainturieri* (97) (1937)

Texas cottonwood - *Populus deltoides* Bartr. ex Marsh. subsp. *monilifera* (Aiton) Eckenwalder (155) (1942)

Texas crabapple - *Malus ioensis* (Wood) Britton var. *texana* Rehd. (124) (1937) TX

Texas crabgrass [Texas crab grass, Texas crab-grass, Texan crab grass, Texan crabgrass, Texan crab-grass] - *Schedonnardus paniculatus* (Nutt.) Trel. (5, 56, 72, 94, 119, 134, 140) (1901-1944)

Texas croton - *Croton texensis* (Klotzsch) Muell.-Arg. (3, 4, 5, 50, 72, 93, 97, 121, 125, 131, 148, 155) (1899–present), *Croton texensis* (Klotzsch) Muell.-Arg. var. *texensis* (50) (present)

Texas crowfoot - *Leptochloa dubia* (H.B.K.) Nees (163) (1852)

Texas crownbeard (Texas crown-beard) - *Verbesina microptera* DC. (122, 124) (1937) TX

Texas cup grass [Texas cupgrass] - *Eriochloa sericea* (Scheele) Munro ex Vasey (50, 155) (1942–present)

Texas curly mesquite - *Hilaria cenchroides* Kunth (152) (1912)

Texas date yucca - *Yucca faxoniana* (Trel.) Sarg. (138) (1923)

Texas desert-rue [Texas desertrue] - *Thamnosma texana* (Gray) Torr. (155) (1942)

Texas dropseed [Texas drop-seed] - *Sporobolus texanus* Vasey (3, 50, 94, 119, 155, 163) (1852–present)

Texas dropseed grass [Texas drop seed grass] - *Muhlenbergia texana* Buckl. (151) (1896)

Texas ebony - *Ebenopsis ebano* (Berland.) Barneby & J.W. Grimes (122) (1937) TX

Texas fescue - *Festuca versuta* Beal (50, 155) (1942–present)

Texas fescue grass [Texas fescue-grass] - *Festuca versuta* Beal (119) (1938)

Texas flatsedge [Texan flatsedge] - *Cyperus polystachyos* Rottb. var. *texensis* (Torr.) Fern. (50) (present)

Texas flax - *Linum hudsonioides* Planch. (50) (present)

Texas forestiera - *Forestiera acuminata* (Michx.) Poir. (155) (1942)

Texas goldentop - *Euthamia gymnospermoides* Greene (50) (present)

Texas grama - *Bouteloua rigidiseta* (Steud.) Hitchc. (50, 119, 122, 155) (1937–present)

Texas greeneyes - *Berlandiera texana* DC. (50) (present)

Texas Hercules'-club [Texas Hercules' club] - *Zanthoxylum hirsutum* Buckl. (50) (present)

Texas heronbill - *Erodium texanum* Gray (155) (1942)

Texas hickory - *Carya ×lecontei* Little [*aquatica × illinoinensis*] (97) (1937)

Texas locoweed [Texas loco-weed] - *Astragalus mollissimus* Torr (156, 157, 158) (1900-1929)

Texas locust - *Gleditsia ×texana* Sargent [*aquatica × triacanthos*] (122, 124) (1937) TX

Texas loeflingia - *Loeflingia squarrosa* Nutt. subsp. *squarrosa* (5) (1913)

Texas logwood [Texan logwood] - *Condalia hookeri* M.C. Johnston var. *hookeri* (107) (1919)

Texas lupine - *Lupinus subcarnosus* Hook. (138) (1923)

Texas Madiera vine - *Anredera vesicaria* (Lam.) C.F.Gaertn. (122) (1937) TX

Texas madrone - *Arbutus xalapensis* Kunth (155) (1942)

Texas madrono - *Arbutus xalapensis* Kunth (122, 124) (1937)

Texas mahonia - *Mahonia swaseyi* (Buckl. ex Young) Fedde (155) (1942)

Texas mallow - *Malvaviscus arboreus* Dill. ex Cav. var. *drummondii* (Torr. & Gray) Schery (122) (1937) TX

Texas millet - *Urochloa texana* (Buckl.) R. Webster (45, 87, 88, 94, 109, 118, 122, 163) (1852-1949)

Texas mulberry - *Morus microphylla* Buckl. (155) (1942)

Texas needle grass [Texas needlegrass] - *Nassella leucotricha* (Trin. & Rupr.) Pohl (119, 122) (1937-1938)

Texas nettle - *Solanum rostratum* Dunal (62, 145, 156) (1897-1923)

Texas othake - *Palafoxia texana* DC. (97) (1937)

Texas painted-cup [Texas painted cup] - *Castilleja indivisa* Engelm. (124, 138) (1923-1937)

Texas palm - *Sabal mexicana* Mart. (124) (1937) TX

Texas palmetto [Texan palmetto] - *Sabal mexicana* Mart. (109, 122, 138) (1923-1949)

Texas panic grass - *Urochloa texana* (Buckl.) R. Webster (45) (1896)

Texas panicum - *Urochloa texana* (Buckl.) R. Webster (3, 119, 155) (1938-1977)

Texas phacelia - *Phacelia integrifolia* Torr. var. *texana* (J. Voss) Atwood (50) (present)

Texas plumbago - *Plumbago scandens* L. (122, 124) (1937) TX

Texas plume [Texasplume] - *Ipomopsis rubra* (L.) Wherry (77, 138, 155) (1898-1942)

Texas poplar - *Populus deltoides* Bartr. ex Marsh. subsp. *monilifera* (Aiton) Eckenwalder (155) (1942)

Texas poverty grass - *Aristida ternipes* Cav. (94) (1901)

Texas prickly pear [Texas pricklypear] - *Opuntia engelmannii* Salm-Dyck var. *lindheimeri* (Engelm.) Parfitt & Pinkava (36, 50) (1986–present)

Texas redbud [Texan redbud, Texan red-bud] - *Cercis canadensis* L. var. *texensis* (S. Wats.) M. Hopkins (106, 138) (1923-1930)

Texas sacahuista - *Nolina texana* S. Wats. (50) (present)

Texas sage - *Salvia coccinea* P.J. Buchoz ex Etlinger (138) (1923)

Texas sandbar willow - *Salix exigua* Nutt. (155) (1942)

Texas sandwort - *Minuartia michauxii* (Fenzl) Farw. var. *texana* (B.L. Robins.) Mattf. (5, 97) (1913-1937)

Texas sarsaparilla - *Menispermum canadense* L. (5, 6, 49, 64, 92, 156, 157, 158) (1892-1929)

Texas saxifrage [Texan saxifrage] - *Saxifraga texana* Buckl. (5, 50, 97) (1913–present)

Texas sedge - *Carex texensis* (Torr.) Bailey (5, 50) (1913–present)

Texas sedum - *Lenophyllum texanum* (J.G. Sm.) Rose (122) (1937) TX

Texas serpentaria - *Aristolochia reticulata* Nutt. (64) (1907)

Texas signal grass [Texas signalgrass] - *Urochloa texana* (Buckl.) R. Webster (50) (present)

Texas skeleton-plant [Texas skeletonplant] - *Lygodesmia texana* (Torr. & Gray) Greene (50) (present)

Texas skeleton-weed - *Lygodesmia texana* (Torr. & Gray) Greene (3) (1977)

Texas snakeroot - *Aristolochia reticulata* Nutt. (6, 49, 53, 57, 64, 92) (1876-1922)

Texas snakeroot Dutchman's-pipe [Texas snakeroot Dutchmanspipe] - *Aristolochia reticulata* Nutt. (155) (1942)

Texas snakeweed - *Gutierrezia texana* (DC.) Torr. & Gray (50) (present)

Texas spread-wing [Texas spreadwing] - *Eurytaenia texana* Torr. & Gray (4, 50) (1986–present)

Texas star - *Sabatia angularis* (L.) Pursh (77) (1898), *Sabatia campestris* Nutt. (50, 156) (1923–present)

Texas star daisy - *Lindheimera texana* Gray & Engelm. (97) (1937)

Texas star gooseberry - *Phyllanthus pudens* L.C. Wheeler (124) (1937) TX

Texas stitchwort - *Minuartia michauxii* (Fenzl) Farw. var. *texana* (B.L. Robins.) Mattf. (50) (present)

Texas stonecrop - *Sedum pulchellum* Michx. (138, 155) (1923-1942)

Texas stork's-bill [Texas stork's bill] - *Erodium texanum* Gray (50) (present)

Texas tall ragweed [Texan tall ragweed] - *Ambrosia trifida* L. var. *texana* Scheele (50) (present)

Texas thistle - *Cirsium texanum* Buckl. (4, 50) (1986–present), *Solanum rostratum* Dunal (131) (1899)

Texas timothy [Texan timothy] - *Lycurus phleoides* H.B.K. (94, 152, 163) (1852-1912)

Texas toadflax [Texas toad flax, Texas toad-flax] - *Nuttallanthus texanus* (Scheele) D.A. Sutton (4, 50, 122) (1937–present)

Texas Townsend daisy - *Townsendia texensis* Larsen (50) (present)

Texas tread-softly [Texas treadsoftly] - *Cnidoscolus texanus* (Muell.-Arg.) Small (155) (1942)

Texas tuberose - *Manfreda variegata* (Jacobi) Rose (122, 124) (1937) TX

Texas umbrella-tree - *Melia azedarach* L. (138) (1923)

Texas valerian - *Valeriana texana* Steyermark (122) (1937)

Texas vervain - *Verbena halei* Small (3, 50) (1977–present)

Texas vetch - *Vicia ludoviciana* Nutt. subsp. *ludoviciana* (97, 155) (1937-1942)

Texas virgin's-bower [Texas virgin bower] - *Clematis drummondii* Torr. & Gray (122) (1937) TX

Texas walnut - *Juglans microcarpa* Berl. (4) (1986), *Juglans microcarpa* Berl. var. *microcarpa* (138) (1923)

Texas water-pimpernel [Texas water pimpernel] - *Samolus ebracteatus* Kunth (97) (1937)

Texas wild olive - *Cordia boissieri* A. DC. (124) (1937) TX

Texas wild rice - *Zizania texana* A.S. Hitchc. (122) (1937)

Texas wild rye [Texas wildrye] - *Elymus interruptus* Buckl. (50, 155) (1942–present)

Texas witch grass [Texas witch-grass] - *Panicum capillarioides* Vasey (94) (1901)

Texas yellow pine - *Pinus palustris* Mill. (5) (1913)

Texas yellow-star [Texas yellowstar] - *Lindheimera texana* Gray & Engelm. (50) (present)

Texas yucca - *Yucca rupicola* Scheele (50) (present)

Textile onion - *Allium textile* A. Nels. & Macbr. (50, 155) (1942–present)

Teyl tree - *Tilia ×vulgaris* Hayne [*cordata × platyphyllos*] (92) (1876)

Te-zhinga-makan (Omaha-Ponca, little buffalo medicine) - *Anemone canadensis* L. (37) (1919)

Tezils - *Dipsacus fullonum* L. (62) (1912) IN, Old English name

Thalecress [Thale cress, Thale-cress] - *Arabidopsis thaliana* (L.) Britton (5, 46, 156) (1879-1913)

Thalia - *Thalia* L. (138) (1923) for Johann Thalius, German naturalist of the 16th Century

Tharp's spiderwort [Tharp spiderwort] - *Tradescantia tharpii* E.S. Anderson & Woods. (3, 50) (1977–present)

Thasata-hi (Omaha-Ponca) - *Artemisia dracunculus* L. (37) (1919)

Thaspium - *Thaspium* Nutt. (155) (1942)

Thatch - *Spartina alterniflora* Loisel. (94) (1901)

Thatch grass - *Panicum virgatum* L. (5, 11, 37) (1888-1913)

Thatch palm - *Thrinax* Sw. (138) (1923)

Thé de montagne (French) - *Gaultheria procumbens* L. (8) (1785)

The du Canada (French) - *Gaultheria procumbens* L. (6) (1892)

The-buske - *Gaultheria procumbens* L. (186) (1814)

Thelepodium - *Thelypodium* Endl. (158) (1900)

Thelesperma - *Thelesperma* Less. (158) (1900)

Thelypody - *Thelypodium* Endl. (50, 155) (1942–present)

Thermon - *Silene stellata* (L.) Aiton f. (156) (1923)

Thermon snakeroot [Thermon snake root] - *Silene stellata* (L.) Aiton f. (5) (1913)

Thermopsis - *Thermopsis* R. Br. ex Aiton f. (138, 155) (1923-1942)

Thick hickory - *Carya laciniosa* (Michx. f.) G. Don (158) (1900)

Thick shellbark - *Carya laciniosa* (Michx. f.) G. Don (5, 156) (1913-1923)

Thick shell-bark hickory [Thick shellbark hickory] - *Carya laciniosa* (Michx. f.) G. Don (20, 187) (1818-1857)

Thicket bean - *Phaseolus polystachios* (L.) B.S.P. (50) (present)

Thicket creeper - *Parthenocissus quinquefolia* (L.) Planch. (155) (1942), *Parthenocissus vitacea* (Knerr) A.S. Hitchc. (4) (1986)

Thicket horsetail - *Equisetum pratense* Ehrh. (5, 72) (1907-1913)

Thicket sedge - *Carex abscondita* Mackenzie (5, 50) (1913–present)

Thicket serviceberry - *Amelanchier arborea* (Michx. f.) Fern. var. *arborea* (155) (1942)

Thicket shadblow - *Amelanchier arborea* (Michx. f.) Fern. var. *arborea* (138) (1923)

Thick-head sedge [Thickhead sedge] - *Carex macloviana* d'Urv. (50) (present)

Thick-leaf groundsel [Thickleaf groundsel] - *Senecio crassulus* Gray (155) (1942)

Thick-leaf hackberry [Thick-leaved hackberry] - *Celtis laevigata* Willd. var. *reticulata* (Torr.) L. Benson (5, 97) (1913-1937)

Thick-leaf maple [Thickleaf maple] - *Acer rubrum* L. (155) (1942)

Thick-leaf meadow rue [Thick-leaved meadow rue] - *Thalictrum coriaceum* (Britt.) Small (5) (1913)

Thick-leaf nettle tree [Thick-leaved nettle tree] - *Celtis occidentalis* L. (20) (1857)

Thick-leaf pennywort [Thick leaved pennywort] - *Centella asiatica* (L.) Urban (92) (1876)

Thick-leaf phlox - *Phlox carolina* L. (109) (1949)

Thick-leaf ragwort [Thickleaf ragwort] - *Senecio crassulus* Gray (50) (present)

Thick-leaf tickseed [Thickleaf tickseed, Thick-leaved tickseed] - *Coreopsis lanceolata* L. (5, 97, 122) (1913-1937)

Thick-root bunch grass [Thick-rooted bunch-grass] - *Melica bulbosa* Geyer ex Porter & Coult. (94) (1901)

Thick-sepal cryptantha [Thicksepal cryptantha] - *Cryptantha crassisepala* (Torr. & Gray) Greene (3, 50) (1977–present)

Thick-sepal cryptanthe [Thick-sepaled cryptanthe] - *Cryptantha crassisepala* (Torr. & Gray) Greene (5, 122) (1913-1937)

Thick-sepal cype [Thick-sepaled cype] - *Cryptantha crassisepala* (Torr. & Gray) Greene (131) (1899)

Thick-spike knot grass [Thickspike knotgrass] - *Paspalum floridanum* Michx. (155) (1942)

Thick-spike wheatgrass [Thickspike wheatgrass] - *Elymus lanceolatus* (Scribn. & J.G. Sm.) Gould (3, 146, 155) (1939-1977)

Thick-stem aster [Thickstem aster] - *Eurybia integrifolia* (Nutt.) Nesom (155) (1942)

Thickweed [Thick weed] - *Hedeoma pulegioides* (L.) Pers. (92) (1876)

Thimble lily - *Lilium bolanderi* S. Wats. (109, 138) (1923-1949)

Thimbleberry [Thimble berry, Thimble-berry] - *Rubus alleghe-niensis* Porter (156) (1923), *Rubus deliciosus* Torr. (4) (1986), *Rubus flagellaris* Willd. (74) (1893), *Rubus* L. (1, 106) (1930-1932), *Rubus occidentalis* L. (2, 5, 22, 19, 46, 92, 107, 156, 187) (1818-1923), *Rubus odoratus* L. (5, 74, 156) (1893-1923), *Rubus ostryifolius* Rydb. (5) (1913), *Rubus parviflorus* Nutt. (3, 4, 5, 50, 85, 106, 153, 158) (1900–present)

Thimble-flower [Thimble flower] - *Prunella vulgaris* L. (5, 156, 158) (1900-1923)

Thimbles - *Campanula rotundifolia* L. (5, 156) (1913-1923), *Digitalis pupurea* L. (5, 69, 156) (1903-1923)

Thimbleweed [Thimble weed, Thimble-weed] - *Aloysia triphylla* (L'Hér.) Britt. (187) (1818), *Anemone quinquefolia* L. (158) (1900), *Anemone virginiana* L. (5, 19, 74, 79, 86, 156, 158) (1840-1923), *Dalea purpurea* Vent. var. *purpurea* (5, 156) (1913-1923), *Rudbeckia laciniata* L. (5, 48, 57, 58, 92, 156, 157, 158) (1869-1929), *Verbena stricta* Vent. (77) (1898)

Thin grass [Thingrass, Thin-grass] - *Agrostis perennans* (Walt.) Tuckerman (5, 45, 56, 66, 90, 94, 111, 163) (1852-1915)

Thin paspalum - *Paspalum setaceum* Michx. (50, 155) (1942–present)

Thin-fruit sedge [Thinfruit sedge, Thin-fruited sedge] - *Carex flaccosperma* Dewey (5, 50) (1913–present)

Thin-leaf alder [Thin-leaved alder] - *Alnus incana* (L.) Moench subsp. *rugosa* (DuRoi) Clausen (20, 155) (1857–1942)

Thin-leaf betony [Thinleaf betony] - *Stachys tenuifolia* Willd. (4) (1986)

Thin-leaf coneflower [Thinleaf coneflower, Thin-leaved coneflower] - *Rudbeckia triloba* L. (5, 62, 72, 97, 122, 156, 158) (1892-1937)

Thin-leaf cotton-grass [Thin-leaved cotton grass] - *Eriophorum viridicarinatum* (Engelm.) Fern. (5) (1913)

Thin-leaf cotton-sedge [Thinleaf cottonsedge] - *Eriophorum viridicarinatum* (Engelm.) Fern. (50) (present)

Thin-leaf huckleberry [Thinleaf huckleberry, Thin-leaved huckleberry] - *Vaccinium membranaceum* Dougl. (5, 50) (1913–present)

Thin-leaf hyssop (Thinne leafed Hyssope) - *Hyssopus officinalis* L. (178) (1526)

Thin-leaf milkweed [Thinleaf milkweed] - *Asclepias perennis* Walt. (5, 122) (1913-1937)

Thin-leaf mountain-mint [Thin-leaved mountain mint] - *Pycnanthemum montanum* Michx. (5) (1913)

Thin-leaf nettle-tree [Thin-leaved nettle-tree] - *Celtis tenuifolia* Nutt. (20) (1857)

Thin-leaf purple aster [Thin-leaved purple aster] - *Symphyotrichum phlogifolium* (Muhl. ex Willd.) Nesom (5, 72) (1907-1913)

Thin-leaf sedge [Thinleaf sedge, Thin-leaved sedge] - *Carex cephaloidea* (Dewey) Dewey (5, 50, 72) (1907–present)

Thin-leaf sunflower [Thinleaf sunflower] - *Helianthus decapetalus* L. (5, 62, 97, 109, 138) (1912–1949)

Thin-leaf wood violet [Thin-leaved wood violet] - *Viola cucullata* Aiton (72) (1907)

Thin-scale sedge - *Carex hyalinolepis* Steud. (3) (1977)

Thistle [Thystle] - *Arctium lappa* L. (158) (1900), *Carduus* L. (1, 10, 93, 158, 179, 184, 190) (1526-1936), *Cirsium ×iowense* (Pammel) Fern.[*altissimum × discolor*] (56) (1901), *Cirsium drummondii* Torr. & Gray (85) (1932), *Cirsium* Mill (1, 50, 32, 92, 93, 155, 156, 179) (1526–present), *Cnicus* L. (2, 7, 63) (1828–1899), *Ulex europaeus* L. (156) (1923)

Thistle cholla - *Opuntia tunicata* (Lehm.) Link & Otto (50) (present)

Thistle mallow - *Sida spinosa* L. (62) (1912)

Thistle milkvetch - *Astragalus kentrophyta* Gray (155) (1942)

Thistle sage - *Salvia carduacea* Benth. (106, 109, 138) (1923–1949)

Thistle-of-the-sea [Thystle of the see] - *Eryngium maritimum* L. (179) (1526)

Thistle-poppy [Thistle poppy] - *Argemone gracilenta* Greene (98, 157) (1926–1929), *Argemone hispida* Gray (76) (1896), *Argemone* L. (1) (1932)

Thistle-root - *Cirsium eatonii* var. *eriocephalum* (A. Gray) D. J. Keil (101) (1905) MT

Thistle-saffron [Thistle saffron] - *Carthamus tinctorius* L. (158) (1900)

Thiuxe (Osage) - *Salix* L. (121) (1918?–1970?)

Thomas's elm - *Ulmus thomasii* Sarg. (20) (1857)

Thompson's loco [Thompson loco] - *Astragalus mollissimus* Torr. var. *thompsoniae* (S. Wats.) Barneby (155) (1942)

Thomson's glory-bower [Thomson glorybower] - *Clerodendrum thompsoniae* Balf. f. (138) (1923)

Thong wood - *Dirca palustris* L. (6) (1892)

Thong-leaf sagittaria [Thong-leaved sagittaria] - *Sagittaria subulata* (L.) Buch. (5) (1913)

Thorn - *Rosa* L. (179) (1526)

Thorn broom [Thorn-broom] - *Ulex europaeus* L. (5, 156) (1913–1923)

Thorn bush [Thorn-bush] - *Crataegus crus-galli* L. (5, 156) (1913–1923)

Thorn grass - *Crypsis* Ait (24) (1817)

Thorn locust [Thorn-locust] - *Gleditsia triacanthos* L. (5, 74, 156, 157) (1893–1929)

Thorn or Thorn tree - *Crataegus crus-galli* L. (19) (1840), *Crataegus* L. (7, 93) (1828–1936)

Thorn-apple [Thorn apple, Thornapple, Thorn apples, Thorne Apple] - *Argemone mexicana* L. (6) (1892), *Datura inoxia* P. Mill. (77) (1898), *Datura* L. (1, 4, 10, 156, 158) (1818–1986), *Datura stramonium* L. (5, 6, 14, 41, 49, 53, 57, 60, 62, 63, 69, 71, 92, 93, 156, 157, 158, 178, 184, 187) (1526–1936), *Solanum carolinense* L. (156) (1923), *Crataegus calpodendron* (Ehrh.) Medik. (5) (1913), *Crataegus crus-galli* L. (5, 156) (1913–1923), *Crataegus* L. (40, 73) (1892–1928), *Crataegus mollis* Scheele (85, 156) (1923–1932), *Crataegus monogyna* Jacq. (92) (1876)

Thornless blackberry - *Rubus canadensis* L. (2, 138) (1895-1923)

Thornless honey locust [Thornless honeylocust] - *Gleditsia triacanthos* L. (112, 138) (1923-1937)

Thorn-plum [Thorn plum] - *Crataegus calpodendron* (Ehrh.) Medik. (5) (1913), *Crataegus crus-galli* L. (5) (1913)

Thorn-poppy [Thorn poppy] - *Argemone* L. (7) (1828), *Argemone mexicana* L. (5, 6, 92, 156) (1876-1923)

Thorny amaranth - *Amaranthus spinosus* L. (5, 93, 107, 122, 156) (1913-1937)

Thorny apples-of-Peru [Thorny apples of Peru] - *Datura stramonium* L. (180) (1633)

Thorny aralia - *Aralia spinosa* L. (187) (1818)

Thorny burweed - *Xanthium spinosum* L. (5) (1913)

Thorny clotbur [Thorny clot-bur] - *Xanthium spinosum* L. (5, 156, 158) (1900–1923)

Thorny elaeagnus - *Elaeagnus pungens* Thunb. (138) (1923)

Thorny greenbriar - *Smilax tamnoides* L. (93) (1936)

Thorny Indian mallow - *Sida spinosa* L. (187) (1818)

Thorny locust - *Gleditsia triacanthos* L. (106) (1930)

Thorny mallow [Thornie mallow] - *Hibiscus sabdariffa* L. (178) (1526)

Thorny thistle - *Cirsium kosmelii* (Adams) Fisch. ex Hohen. (42) (1814)

Thorny-apple [Thornie-apples] - *Datura* L. (180) (1633)

Thorough-growth [Thorough growth] - *Eupatorium perfoliatum* L. (156) (1923)

Thorough-stem [Thorough stem] - *Eupatorium perfoliatum* L. (5, 7, 53, 69, 92, 156, 158, 186) (1814-1923)

Thorough-wax [Thorough wax, Thoroughwax, Thorough Waxe, Thorow-wax] - *Bupleurum* L. (4) (1986), *Bupleurum rotundifolium* L. (5, 19, 107, 156, 178, 184) (1526-1923), *Eupatorium perfoliatum* L. (5, 6, 7, 53, 69, 92, 156, 158, 186) (1814-1923)

Thoroughwort [Thorough wort, Thorough-wort] - *Brickellia* Ell. (1) (1932), *Bupleurum rotundifolium* L. (5, 156) (1913-1923), *Conoclinium* DC. (50) (present), *Eupatorium* L. (1, 2, 50, 82, 93, 109, 122, 158) (1895–present), *Eupatorium perfoliatum* L. (6, 7, 19, 49, 53, 55, 57, 58, 59, 69, 92, 106, 156, 184, 187) (1814-1930)

Thoroughwort pondweed [Thorowort pondweed] - *Potamogeton perfoliatus* L. (155) (1942)

Thousand-leaf [Thousand leaf, Thousandleaf] - *Achillea millefolium* L. (49, 53, 69, 156, 158) (1898-1922)

Thousand-leaf clover [Thousand-leaved clover] - *Achillea millefolium* L. (69, 157, 158) (1900-1929)

Thousand-mothers [Thousand mothers] - *Tolmiea menziesii* (Pursh) Torr. & Gray (109) (1949)

Thousand-seal [Thousand seal, thousandseal] - *Achillea millefolium* L. (107, 156) (1919-1923)

Thread rush - *Juncus filiformis* L. (5, 50, 156) (1913–present)

Thread sedge - *Carex filifolia* Nutt. (5) (1913)

Thread-and-needle - *Yucca filamentosa* L. (5, 19, 73) (1840-1913)

Thread-flower gilia [Threadflower gilia] - *Linanthus parviflorus* (Benth.) Greene (138) (1923)

Thread-foot - *Podostemum ceratophyllum* Michx. (5, 19, 156) (1840-1923), *Podostemum* Michx. (1) (1932)

Thread-form bent grass - *Muhlenbergia mexicana* (L.) Trin. (possibly) (42) (1814)

Thread-leaf agalinis [Thread-leaved agalinis] - *Agalinis setacea* (J. Gmelin) Raf. (5) (1913)

Thread-leaf buttercup [Threadleaf buttercup] - *Ranunculus flabellaris* Raf. (3, 4) (1977-1986)

Thread-leaf coreopsis - *Coreopsis verticillata* L. (109, 138) (1923-1949)

Thread-leaf crowfoot [Threadleaf crowfoot] - *Ranunculus trichophyllus* Chaix var. *trichophyllus* (50) (present)

Thread-leaf evening-primrose [Threadleaf evening primrose] - *Oenothera linifolia* Nutt. (50) (present)

Thread-leaf groundsel [Threadleaf groundsel] - *Senecio flaccidus* Less. var. *flaccidus* (155) (1942)

Thread-leaf phacelia [Threadleaf phacelia] - *Phacelia linearis* (Pursh) Holz. (50, 138, 155) (1923–present)

Thread-leaf ragwort [Threadleaf ragwort] - *Senecio flaccidus* Less. var. *flaccidus* (50) (present)

Thread-leaf sedge [Threadleaf sedge] - *Carex filifolia* Nutt. (50, 139, 155) (1942–present)

Thread-leaf sundew [Threadleaf sundew, Thread-leaved sundew] - *Drosera filiformis* Raf. (2, 5, 138, 156) (1895-1923)

Thread-leaf sundrops [Thread-leaved sundrops] - *Oenothera linifolia* Nutt. (5, 97) (1913-1937)

Thread-like muhlenbergia - *Muhlenbergia filiculmis* Vasey (94) (1901)

Thread-like pondweed - *Potamogeton pusillus* L. subsp. *gemmiparus* (J.W. Robbins) Haynes & C.B. Hellquist (5) (1913)

Thread-like rush [Threadlike rush] - *Eleocharis filiculmis* Kunth (66) (1903)

Threadsaf - *Solanum carolinense* L. (49) (1898)

Thread-soft [Tread soft, Treadsoft] - *Solanum carolinense* L. (49, 53, 62) (1898-1922)

Thread-stem sandmat [Threadstem sandmat] - *Chamaesyce revoluta* (Engelm.) Small (50) (present)

Three-angle spikerush [Three-angled spikerush] - *Eleocharis tricostata* Torr. (50) (present)

Threeawn - *Aristida* L. (50) (present)

Three-awn grass [Three-awned grass] - *Aristida* L. (66, 148) (1903-1939), *Aristida oligantha* Michx (66) (1903), *Aristida purpurascens* Poir. (87) (1884)

Three-awn oat grass [Three-awned oat-grass] - *Trisetum flavescens* (L.) Beauv. (10) (1818)

Three-bird orchis - *Triphora trianthophora* (Sw.) Rydb. (19) (1840)

Three-birds [Threebirds, Three birds] - *Triphora trianthophora* (Sw.) Rydb. (5, 50, 156) (1913–present)

Three-bract onion [Threebract onion] - *Allium tribracteatum* Torr. (155) (1942)

Three-color bindweed [Three colored bindweed, 3-colored bindweed] - *Convolvulus tricolor* L. (19) (1840)

Three-color coxscomb [Three-colored coxscomb] - *Amaranthus tricolor* L. (19) (1840)

Three-color daisy [Three-colored daisy] - *Chrysanthemum carinatum* Schousboe (19) (1840)

Three-color lily [Three-colored lily] - *Nuphar lutea* (L.) Sm. subsp. *advena* (Aiton) Kartesz & Gandhi (156) (1923)

Three-color violet [Three-colored violet] - *Viola tricolor* L. (6) (1892)

Three-corner cactus [Three-cornered cactus] - *Peniocereus greggii* (Engelm.) Britt. & Rose var. *greggii* (76) (1896)

Three-corner moly [Three-cornered moly] - *Allium triquetrum* L. (165) (1768)

Three-corner-grass [Three cornered grass] - *Scirpus lineatus* Michx. (129) (1894) SD

Three-finger beggarticks [Three-fingered beggarticks] - *Bidens tripartita* L. (19) (1840)

Three-flower avens [Three-flowered avens] - *Geum triflorum* Pursh (86) (1878)

Three-flower bedstraw [Three-flowered bedstraw] - *Galium triflorum* Michx. (5, 156) (1913-1923)

Three-flower hair grass [Three-flowered hair-grass] - *Poa cuspidata* Nutt. (187) (1818)

Three-flower hawthorn [Threeflower hawthorn] - *Crataegus triflora* Chapman (138) (1923)

Three-flower melic [Threeflower melic] - *Melica nitens* (Scribn.) Nutt. ex Piper (3, 155) (1942-1977)

Three-flower melic grass [Threeflower melicgrass] - *Melica nitens* (Scribn.) Nutt. ex Piper (50) (present)

Three-flower rush [Three-flowered rush] - *Juncus triglumis* L. (5) (1913)

Three-fork grass - *Spartina patens* (Ait.) Muhl. (5) (1913)

Three-fruit sedge [Three-fruited sedge] - *Carex trisperma* Dewey (5) (1913), *Carex hirsutella* Mack (66) (1903)

Three-hull rush [Three hulled rush] - *Juncus triglumis* L. (50) (present)

Three-leaf anemone [Threeleaf anemone] - *Anemone deltoidea* Hook. (155) (1942)

Three-leaf arum [Three-leaved arum] - *Arisaema triphyllum* (L.) Schott (7, 19, 64, 157, 158) (1828-1929)

Three-leaf bladder nut [Three leaved bladder nut] - *Staphylea trifolia* L. (190) (~1759)

Three-leaf bladdernut tree [Three-leaved bladder-nut-tree] - *Staphylea trifolia* L. (8) (1785)

Three-leaf bogbean [Three-leaved bog-bean] - *Menyanthes trifoliata* L. (187) (1818)

Three-leaf buckbean [Three-leaved buck-bean] - *Menyanthes trifoliata* L. (187) (1818)

Three-leaf cinquefoil [Three-leaved cinquefoil] - *Potentilla norvegica* L. subsp. *monspeliensis* (L.) Aschers. & Graebn. (156) (1923)

Three-leaf false lily-of-the-valley [Threeleaf false lily of the valley] - *Maianthemum trifolium* (L.) Sloboda (50) (present)

Three-leaf goldthread [Three-leaved goldthread] - *Coptis trifolia* (L.) Salisb. (2) (1895)

Three-leaf hellebore [Three-leaved hellebore] - *Coptis trifolia* (L.) Salisb. (41) (1770)

Three-leaf hempweed [Three-leaved hemp-weed] - *Eupatorium purpureum* L. var. *purpureum* (187) (1818)

Three-leaf hoptree [Three-leaved hop tree, Three-leaved hop-tree, Three-leaved hoptree] - *Ptelea trifoliata* L. (2, 5, 72, 97, 156, 157, 158) (1895-1929)

Three-leaf Indian turnip [Three-leaved Indian turnip] - *Arisaema triphyllum* (L.) Schott (5, 86, 156) (1878-1923)

Three-leaf ivy [Three-leaved ivy] - *Toxicodendron radicans* (L.) Kuntze (5) (1913), *Toxicodendron radicans* (L.) Kuntze subsp. *radicans* (71, 157, 158) (1898-1929), *Toxicodendron toxicarium* (Salisb.) Gillis (6, 156) (1892-1923)

Three-leaf liverwort [Three-leaved liverwort] - *Hepatica nobilis* Schreb. (156) (1923), *Hepatica nobilis* Schreb. var. *obtusa* (Pursh) Steyermark (5) (1913)

Three-leaf nightshade [Three-leaved nightshade] - *Trillium erectum* L. (6) (1892), *Trillium sessile* L. (5, 156) (1913-1923)

Three-leaf prickly-cone bastard pine [Three leaved prickly-coned bastard pine] - *Pinus echinata* Mill. (8) (1785)

Three-leaf primrose [Three-leaved primrose] - *Oenothera triloba* Nutt. (5) (1913)

Three-leaf Rocky Mountain maple [Threeleaf Rocky Mountain maple] - *Acer glabrum* Torr. (155) (1942)

Three-leaf rosin-weed [Three-leaved rosin-weed] - *Silphium trifoliatum* L. (156) (1923)

Three-leaf rush [Three-leaved rush] - *Juncus trifidus* L. (66) (1903)

Three-leaf sedge [Three leaved sedge] - *Carex filifolia* Nutt. (3) (1977)

Three-leaf sedum [Three-leaved sedum] - *Sedum ternatum* Michx. (2) (1895)

Three-leaf Solomon's-seal [Three leaved Solomon's seal] - *Maianthemum trifolium* (L.) Sloboda (5, 42) (1814-1913)

Three-leaf spiraea [Three-leaved spiraea] - *Gillenia trifoliata* (L.) Moench (186) (1814)

Three-leaf stonecrop [Three-leaved stonecrop, Three-leaved stonecrop] - *Sedum ternatum* Michx. (156, 187) (1818-1923)

Three-leaf sumac [Three-leaved sumac, Three-leaved sumach] - *Rhus trilobata* Nutt. (149, 156) (1904-1923)

Three-leaf thaspium [Three-leaved thaspium] - *Thaspium trifoliatum* (L.) Gray (3) (1977)

Three-leaf Virginia pine [Three-leaved Virginian pine] - *Pinus rigida* Mill. (20) (1857)

Three-leaf wild turnip [Three leaved wild turnip] - *Arisaema triphyllum* (L.) Schott (42) (1814)

Three-leaf yellow pine [Three-leaved yellow pine] - *Pinus echinata* Mill. (19) (1840)

Threeleaf-grass [Three leaved grass, Thre leued grasse] - *Trientalis borealis* Raf. subsp. *borealis* (179) (1526), *Trifolium pratense* L. (92) (1876)

Three-lobe beggarticks [Threelobe beggarticks] - *Bidens tripartita* L. (50) (present)

Three-lobe liverwort [Three-lobed liver-wort] - *Hepatica nobilis* Schreb. (187) (1818)

Three-lobe primrose [Three-lobed primrose] - *Oenothera triloba* Nutt. (97) (1937)

Three-lobe ragweed [Three-lobed ragweed] - *Ambrosia trifida* L. (156) (1923)

Three-lobe rudbeckia [Three-lobed rudbeckia] - *Rudbeckia triloba* L. (156) (1923)

Three-lobe spiraea [Threelobe spiraea] - *Spiraea trilobata* L. (138) (1923)

Three-lobe violet [Three-lobed violet] - *Viola palmata* L. (5, 97) (1913-1937)

Three-nerve fleabane [Threenerve fleabane, Three-nerved fleabane] - *Erigeron subtrinervis* Rydb. ex Porter & Britton (5, 50, 93, 95, 131, 155) (1899–present), *Erigeron subtrinervis* Rydb. ex Porter & Britton var. *subtrinervis* (50, 155) (1942–present)

Three-nerve goldenrod [Three nerved goldenrod, Three-nerved golden-rod] - *Solidago canadensis* L. (187) (1818), *Solidago velutina* DC. (3, 4, 50, 155) (1942–present)

Three-nerve rough bindweed [Three-nerved rough bindweed] - *Smilax rotundifolia* L. (8) (1785)

Three-petal bedstraw [Threepetal bedstraw] - *Galium trifidum* L. (50) (present), *Galium trifidum* L. subsp. *trifidum* (50) (present)

Three-petal goose-grass [Three-petaled goose-grass] - *Galium trifidum* L. (187) (1818)

Three-rib arrowgrass [Threerib arrowgrass, Three-ribbed arrowgrass] - *Triglochin striatum* Ruiz & Pavón (5, 50) (present)

Three-rib spike-rush [Three-ribbed spike rush] - *Eleocharis tricostata* Torr. (5) (1913)

Three-seed croton [Threeseed croton, Three-seeded croton] - *Croton lindheimerianus* Scheele (3, 50) (1977–present)

Three-seed garlic [Three-seeded garlick] - *Allium tricoccum* Ait. (165) (1768)

Three-seed leek [Three seed leek, Three seeded leek, Three-seeded leek] - *Allium tricoccum* Ait. (19, 92, 158) (1840-1900)

Three-seed mercury [Three-seeded mercury] - *Acalypha* L. (4) (1986), *Acalypha ostryifolia* Riddell (3, 145) (1897-1977), *Acalypha virginica* L. (3, 19, 62, 80, 93, 156) (1840-1977)

Three-seed onion garlic [Three-seeded onion garlick] - *Allium tricoccum* Ait. (42) (1814)

Three-seed sedge [Threeseeded sedge, Three-seeded sedge] - *Carex trisperma* Dewey (50, 66) (1903–present)

Three-side rush [Three-sided rush] - *Schoenoplectus americanus* (Pers.) Volk. ex Schinz & R. Keller (187) (1818)

Three-square - *Schoenoplectus americanus* (Pers.) Volk. ex Schinz & R. Keller (5, 156) (1913-1923)

Three-square rush - *Schoenoplectus americanus* (Pers.) Volk. ex Schinz & R. Keller (72) (1907)

Three-thorn acacia [Three-thorned acacia, Three thorned acacia] - *Gleditsia triacanthos* L. (5, 92, 156, 157, 158) (1876-1929)

Three-thorn locust [Three-thorned locust] - *Gleditsia triacanthos* L. (187) (1818)

Three-tip sagebrush [Threetip sagebrush] - *Artemisia tripartita* Rydb. (155) (1942)

Three-tooth cinquefoil [Three-toothed cinquefoil] - *Sibbaldiopsis tridentata* (Aiton) Rydb. (2, 3, 4, 5, 72, 156) (1907-1986)

Three-tooth orchis [Three-toothed orchis] - *Platanthera clavellata* (Michx.) Luer (156, 187) (1818–1923)

Three-tooth ragwort [Threetooth ragwort] - *Packera tridenticulata* (Rydb.) W. A. Weber & Á. Löve (50) (present)

Three-tooth sagebrush [Three-toothed sage-brush] - *Artemisia tridentata* Nutt. (108) (1878)

Three-tooth saxifrage [Three toothed saxifrage] - *Saxifraga hirculus* L. subsp. *hirculus* (5) (1913)

Three-valve sandwort [Three-valved sandwort] - *Spergularia* (Pers.) J. & K. Presl (13) (1849)

Three-way sedge - *Dulichium arundinaceum* (L.) Britt. (3, 50) (1977–present)

Three-wing ash [Three-winged ash] - *Fraxinus caroliniana* Mill. (20) (1857)

Thrift - *Armeria* (DC.) Willd. (50, 109, 155) (1942–present), *Armeria maritima* (P. Mill.) Willd (5, 19) (1840-1913), *Limonium* P. Mill. (138, 156) (1923)

Thrift mock goldenweed - *Stenotus armerioides* Nutt. (50) (present)

Throatroot [Throat root, Throat-root] - *Geum canadense* Jacq. (156) (1923), *Geum rivale* L (5, 158) (1900–1913), *Geum virginianum* L. (5, 7, 49, 92, 157, 158) (1828–1929), *Digitalis pupurea* L. (5, 69, 156) (1903–1923) no longer in use by 1923, *Geum rivale* L (156) (1923), *Geum virginianum* L. (156) (1923), *Liatris* Gaertn. ex Schreber. (7) (1828), *Liatris spicata* (L.) Willd. (92, 156) (1898–1923), *Liatris spicata* (L.) Willd. var. *spicata* (5) (1913)

Throatwort sunflower - *Helianthus decapetalus* L. (5, 72, 97, 122) (1907-1937)

Throat-wort, Radix est discutiens - *Liatris spicata* (L.) Willd. (177) (1762)

Throatwort-leaf sunflower [Throat-wort-leaved sun-flower] - *Helianthus decapetalus* L. (187) (1818)

Throughgrow - *Eupatorium perfoliatum* L. (5, 76, 156) (1896-1923) Eastern PA

Throwort [Throw wort, Throwwort] - *Leonurus cardiaca* L. (7, 92, 157, 158) (1828–1929)

Thrumwort [Thrum-wort] - *Alisma plantago-aquatica* L. (184) (1793)

Thuia du Canada (French) - *Thuja occidentalis* L. (6) (1892)

Thuia gigantesque (French) - *Thuja plicata* Donn ex D. Don (20) (1857)

Thuja - *Thuja occidentalis* L. (6, 57, 60) (1892-1917)

Thunbergia - *Thunbergia alata* Bojer ex Sims (92) (1876)

Thunberg's kudzu-bean [Thunberg kudzubean] - *Pueraria montana* (Lour.) Merr. var. *lobata* (Willd.) Maesen & S. Almeida (155) (1942)

Thunberg's spiraea [Thunberg spiraea] - *Spiraea thunbergii* Sieb. ex Blume (138) (1923)

Thunder flower [Thunder-flower] - *Papaver rhoeas* L. (5, 156, 158) (1900-1923) no longer in use by 1923, *Silene latifolia* Poir. subsp. *alba* (Mill.) Greuter & Burdet (5, 156, 158) (1900-1923) no longer in use by 1923, *Stellaria holostea* L. (5, 156) (1913-1923) no longer in use by 1923

Thunder plant [Thunder-plant] - *Sempervivum tectorum* L. (92, 156) (1898-1923)

Thunderwood [Thunder-wood] - *Pyrularia pubera* Michx. (156) (1923), *Toxicodendron vernix* (L.) Kuntze (71, 156) (1898-1923)

Thurber's abutilon [Thurber abutilon] - *Abutilon thurberi* Gray (155) (1942)

Thurber's cactus - *Stenocereus thurberi* (Engelm.) Buxbaum (103) (1870)

Thurber's fescue [Thurber fescue] - *Festuca thurberi* Vasey (140) (1944)

Thurber's Indian mallow - *Abutilon thurberi* Gray (50) (present)

Thurber's loco [Thurber loco] - *Astragalus thurberi* Gray (155) (1942)

Thurber's rush grass [Thurber's rush-grass] - *Muhlenbergia thurberi* (Scribn.) Rydb. (94) (1901)

Thurber's stem-sucker [Thurber's stemsucker] - *Pilostyles thurberi* Gray (50) (present)

Thurlow's weeping willow [Thurlow weeping willow] - *Salix* ×*pendulina* Wenderoth [*babylonica* × *fragilis*] (109, 138, 155) (1923-1949)

Thus americanum - *Pinus palustris* Mill. (55) (1911) source

Thuya de Canada (French) - *Thuja occidentalis* L. (8) (1785)

Thuya d'Occident (French) - *Thuja occidentalis* L. (8) (1785)

Thyme - *Thymus* L. (106, 109, 138, 184) (1793-1949), *Thymus praecox* Opiz subsp. *arcticus* (Dur.) Jalas (possibly) (10) (1818), *Thymus vulgaris* L. (19, 49, 57, 58, 92, 107) (1840-1919)

Thyme dodder - *Cuscuta epithymum* (L.) L. (5, 82, 156, 158) (1900-1930)

Thyme-leaf [Thymeleaf] - *Thymophylla aurea* (Gray) Greene ex Britton var. *aurea* (5, 122) (1913-1937)

Thyme-leaf bluets [Thyme-leaved bluets] - *Houstonia serpyllifolia* Michx. (5) (1913)

Thyme-leaf dragonhead [Thymeleaf dragonhead] - *Dracocephalum thymiflorum* L. (50, 155) (1942–present)

Thyme-leaf euphorbia [Thymeleaf euphorbia] - *Chamaesyce serpyllifolia* (Pers.) Small subsp. *serpyllifolia* (155) (1942)

Thyme-leaf pinweed [Thyme-leaved pin-weed, Thyme-leaved pin-weed] - *Lechea minor* L. (5, 72, 156) (1907-1923)

Thyme-leaf sandmat [Thymeleaf sandmat] - *Chamaesyce serpyllifolia* (Pers.) Small (50) (present)

Thyme-leaf sandwort [Thymeleaf sandwort, Thyme-leaved sand-wort] - *Arenaria serpyllifolia* L. (4, 5, 15, 19, 50, 97, 155, 156, 187) (1818–present)

Thyme-leaf speedwell [Thymeleaf speedwell, Thyme-leaved speed-well] - *Veronica serpyllifolia* L. (3, 4, 5, 50, 62, 72, 155, 156) (1907–present)

Thyme-leaf spurge [Thymeleaf spurge, Thyme-leaved spurge] - *Chamaesyce serpyllifolia* (Pers.) Small (5, 93, 97) (1913–1937), *Chamaesyce serpyllifolia* (Pers.) Small subsp. *serpyllifolia* (3, 4, 72, 122, 131) (1899–1986) Neb

Thymeweed [Thyme-weed] - *Elodea canadensis* Michx. (158) (1900)

Ti-ak(Choctaw) - *Pinus* L. (132) (1855)

Tibap (Snake, nuts) - *Pinus albicaulis* Engelm. (101) (1905) MT

Tičaničahu taŋka hu (Lakota, Large curlew plant) - *Psoralidium tenuiflorum* (Pursh) Rydb. (121) (1918?-1970?)

Tičaničahu xloxota (Lakota, possibly meaning gray hollow curlew plant) - *Pediomelum argophyllum* (Pursh) J. Grimes (121) (1918?-1970?)

Tichanicha-hu - *Psoralidium tenuiflorum* (Pursh) Rydb. (37) (1919)

Tick clover [Tickclover] - *Desmodium* Desv. (4, 138, 155, 156) (1923-1986)

Tick quack grass - *Thinopyrum pycnanthum* (Godr.) Barkworth (50) (present)

Tick trefoil [Tick-trefoil] - *Desmodium canadense* (L.) DC. (114, 156) (1894-1923), *Desmodium cuspidatum* (Muhl. ex Willd.) DC. ex Loud. var. *cuspidatum* (65) (1931), *Desmodium* Desv. (1, 2, 4, 50, 87, 156, 158) (1884–present), *Desmodium rotundifolium* DC. (156) (1923)

Tickle grass [Ticklegrass, Tickle-grass] - *Agrostis hyemalis* (Walt.) Britton, Sterns & Poggenb. (3, 5, 50, 85, 122, 129, 140, 143, 163) (1852–present), *Agrostis* L. (1, 93) (1932-1936), *Agrostis scabra* Willd. (3, 11, 66, 90, 92) (1876-1977), *Panicum capillare* L. (5, 56, 62, 75, 78, 80, 119, 129, 140, 145, 152) (1894-1944), *Panicum* L. (1, 93) (1932-1936), *Sporobolus buckleyi* Vasey (78) (1898) TX

Tickleweed [Tickle-weed, Tickle weed] - *Veratrum viride* Ait. (64, 92, 156) (1876-1923)

Tickseed [Tick-seed, Tick seed] - *Bidens aristosa* (Michx.) Britton (80, 82) (1913-1930), *Bidens* L. (109) (1949), *Coreopsis* L. (1, 2, 7, 50, 63, 93, 106, 109, 156, 167) (1814–present), *Coreopsis lanceolata* L. (156) (1923), *Coreopsis palmata* Nutt. (85) (1932), *Coreopsis rosea* Nutt. (19) (1840), *Coreopsis tinctoria* Nutt. (95, 114, 127) (1894-1933), *Corispermum* L. (10, 14, 155, 158) (1818-1942), *Desmodium* Desv. (87) (1884), *Desmodium glutinosum* (Muhl. ex Willd.) Wood (14) (1882), *Desmodium nudiflorum* (L.) DC. (14) (1882), *Hedeoma pulegioides* (L.) Pers. (156) (1923)

Tickseed sunflower [Tick seed sunflower, Tick-seed sunflower] - *Bidens aristosa* (Michx.) Britton (158) (1900), *Bidens connata* Muhl. ex Willd. (62) (1912), *Bidens coronata* (L.) Britton (3, 4, 106, 156) (1923–1986), *Coreopsis* L. (158) (1900), *Coreopsis tripteris* L. (19, 92) (1840–1876)

Tickweed [Tick weed, Tick-weed] - *Coreopsis* L. (92) (1876), *Hedeoma pulegioides* (L.) Pers. (5, 6, 7, 49, 53, 92, 158) (1828-1922)

Tide-marsh water hemp [Tidemarsh waterhemp] - *Amaranthus cannabinus* (L.) Sauer (155) (1942)

Tidestromia - *Tidestromia* Standl. (155) (1942)

Tidy-tips [Tidytip] - *Layia platyglossa* (Fisch. & C.A. Mey.) Gray (76) (1896)

Tienmannige lakplant - *Phytolacca americana* L. var. *americana* (186) (1814)

Ti-es - *Pouteria campechiana* (Kunth) Baehni (109) (1949)

Tievine - *Ipomoea cordatotriloba* Dennst. var. *torreyana* (Gray) D. Austin (106) (1930)

Tiger lily [Tiger-lily] - *Fritillaria* L. (1, 93) (1932-1936), *Hemerocallis fulva* (L.) L. (156) (1923), *Lilium bulbiferum* L. (92) (1876), *Lilium lancifolium* Thunb. (5, 50, 52, 53, 54, 72, 107, 109, 138, 156) (1907–present), *Lilium philadelphicum* L. (5, 75, 156) (1894-1923), *Lilium philadelphicum* L. var. *andinum* (Nutt.) Ker.-Gawl. (127) (1933), *Lilium superbum* L. (156) (1923)

Tiger-nut - *Cyperus esculentus* L. (156) (1923)

Tiger's-mouth [Tiger's mouth] - *Antirrhinum majus* L. (5, 156, 158) (1900-1923)

Til tree [Til-tree] - *Tilia* ×*vulgaris* Hayne [*cordata* × *platyphyllos*] (92) (1876)

Tile tree [Tile-tree] - *Tilia americana* L. var. *heterophylla* (Vent.) Loud. (156) (1923)

Tillandsia - *Tillandsia* L. (8, 138) (1785-1923) for Elias Tillands, 1640-1603, Sweden, made catalogue of the plants of Abo Finland in 1673

Tillandsia (French) - *Tillandsia* L. (8) (1785)

Tillandsia de Caroline (French) - *Tillandsia usneoides* (L.) L. (8) (1785)

Tillandsia tea-grass - Tillandsia bartramii Elliott (183) (1756)

Tilleul (French) - *Tilia* L. (8) (1785)

Tilleul d'Amérique (French) - *Tilia americana* L. (8) (1785)

Tilleul de la Louisiane (French) - *Tilia americana* L. var. *caroliniana* (P. Mill.) Castigl. (8) (1785)

Tilleul heterophylle (French) - *Tilia americana* L. var. *heterophylla* (Vent.) Loud. (20) (1857)

Tillow tree - *Ailanthus altissima* (Mill) Swingle (6) (1892)

Tillseed [Tilseed] - *Lens culinaris* Medik. (92) (1876), *Sesamum orientale* L. (92) (1876)

Tilteloosen (Low Dutch) - *Colchicum autumnale* L. (180) (1633)

Tily (Indians) - *Viburnum dentatum* L. (7) (1828)

Timber danthonia - *Danthonia intermedia* Vasey (140, 155) (1942-1944)

Timber milkvetch - *Astragalus miser* Dougl. var. *hylophilus* (148) (1939) CO

Timber oat grass [Timber oatgrass] - *Danthonia intermedia* Vasey (3, 50, 140) (1944–present)

Timber poisonvetch - *Astragalus convallarius* Greene (155) (1942)

Timberline blue grass [Timberline bluegrass] - *Poa glauca* Vahl subsp. *rupicola* (Nash ex Rydb.) W.A. Weber (50, 140, 155) (1942–present)

Time - *Thymus vulgaris* L. (46, 178) (1526-1671) deliberately introduced by colonists by 1671

Timeliest purple-circle daffodil [Timeliest purple circled Daffodill] - *Narcissus poeticus* L. (178, 180) (1526-1633)

Timely purple-ring daffodil [Timely purple ringed Daffodill] - *Narcissus poeticus* L. (180) (1633)

Timely-flowerung bulbous Violet [Timely flouring bulbous Violet] - *Leucojum vernum* L. (180) (1633)

Timiyah (Snake) - *Arctostaphylos uva-ursi* (L.) Spreng. (101) (1905) MT

Timothy - *Phleum* L. (1, 50, 93, 138, 155) (1923–present), *Phleum pratense* L. (3, 45, 46, 50, 56, 66, 67, 68, 85, 87, 88, 90, 94, 109, 111, 115, 119, 122, 125, 129, 138, 140, 143, 146, 155, 163, 184) (1793–present), *Poa pratensis* L. (45) (1896)

Timothy grass [Timothy-grass] - *Phleum alpinum* L. (35) (1806), *Phleum* L. (10) (1818), *Phleum pratense* L. (11, 19, 92, 187) (1818-1888)

Tinder - *Agaricus* L. (92) (1876)

Tine tare - *Vicia hirsuta* (L.) Gray (5) (1913)

Tine-grass [Tine grass] - *Vicia cracca* L. (5, 156, 158) (1900-1923)

Tine-leaf milkvetch [Tine-leaved milkvetch, Tine-leaved milk vetch] - *Astragalus pectinatus* (Hook.) Dougl. ex G. Don (4) (1986)

Tineweed [Tine weed, Tine-weed] - *Vicia hirsuta* (L.) Gray (5, 156) (1913-1923)

Tinkar's-root - *Triosteum perfoliatum* L. (158) (1900)

Tinker's-weed [Tinker's weed, Tinker weed] - *Triosteum angustifolium* L. (181) (~1678), *Triosteum perfoliatum* L. (5, 6, 7, 92, 156, 157, 158) (1828-1929)

Tinpsila pežuta (Lakota, turnip medicine) - *Asclepias stenophylla* Gray (121) (1918?-1970?)

Tintabloom (German for ink plant) - *Tradescantia bracteata* Small ex Britt. (98) (1926) Neb

Tinted spurge - *Euphorbia commutata* Engelm. (5, 72, 122) (1907-1937)

Tintymall of Babylon - *Euphorbia* L. (179) (1526)

Tinus-leaf viburnum [Tinus leaved viburnum] - *Viburnum nudum* L. (8) (1785)

Tiny bladderwort - *Utricularia subulata* L. (5, 178) (1526-1913)

Tiny bluet [Tiny bluets] - *Houstonia pusilla* Schoepf (50, 155) (1942–present)

Tiny love grass [Tiny love-grass] - *Eragrostis capillaris* (L.) Nees (5, 93, 99, 119, 163) (1852-1938)

Tiny mouse-tail [Tiny mousetail] - *Myosurus minimus* L. (50, 155) (1942–present)

Tiny pea - *Lathyrus pusillus* Ell. (50) (present)

Tiny-Tim [Tiny Tim] - *Dyssodia papposa* (Vent.) A.S. Hitchc. (122, 124) (1937) TX, *Thymophylla* Lag. (1) (1932)

Tiny-trumpet [Tiny trumpet] - *Collomia linearis* Nutt. (50) (present)

Tiŋpsila (Lakota) - *Pediomelum esculentum* (Pursh) Rydb. (121) (1918?-1970?)

Tipcadi - *Muscari neglectum* Guss. ex Ten. (180) (1633)

Tipitiwitchet - *Dionaea muscipula* Ellis. (183) (~1756)

Tipsin - *Pediomelum esculentum* (Pursh) Rydb. (5, 37, 76, 127, 156, 158) (1896-1937)

Tipsinah (Sioux) - *Pediomelum esculentum* (Pursh) Rydb. (47) (1852)

Tipsinla (Dakota Teton) - *Pediomelum esculentum* (Pursh) Rydb. (37) (1919)

Tipsinna - *Pediomelum esculentum* (Pursh) Rydb. (5, 156, 158) (1900-1923)

Tipsinna (Dakota) - *Pediomelum esculentum* (Pursh) Rydb. (37) (1919)

Tipsin-nah or Tip-sin-nah (Sioux) - *Pediomelum esculentum* (Pursh) Rydb. (101, 103) (1870-1905)

Tiresome weed - *Zostera marina* L. (5, 73, 156) (1894-1923) Little Egg Harbor NJ, from obstruction it offers to the oars of boats

Tisavojaune rouge (French Canadian) - *Galium trifidum* L. (41) (1770)

Tischlerschachtelhalm (German) - *Equisetum hyemale* L. (158) (1900)

Tissavoyame jaune (Canada) - *Coptis trifolia* (L.) Salisb. (7) (1828)

Tissavoyanne jaune (French) - *Circaea alpina* L. (41) (1770)

Tisswood [Tiss wood, Tiss-wood] - *Halesia carolina* L. (5, 156) (1913-1923), *Persea borbonia* (L.) Spreng. (5, 106, 156) (1913-1930)

Tithymal - *Euphorbia esula* L. (156, 158) (1900-1923), *Euphorbia esula* L. var. *esula* (5) (1913)

Tithymale Fleuri (French) - *Euphorbia corollata* L. (7) (1828)

Ti-Ti [Titi] - *Clethra alnifolia* L. (156) (1923), *Cliftonia* Banks ex Gaertn. f. (15) (1895), *Cliftonia monophylla* (Lam.) Britton (possibly) (106) (1930)

Titoki - *Alectryon* Gaertn. (138) (1923)

Toad rush - *Juncus bufonius* L. (3, 5, 19, 50, 66, 92, 93, 139, 155, 156) (1840–present)

Toad sorrel [Toad's sorrel] - *Oxalis stricta* L. (5, 76, 156) (1896-1923) ME, *Rumex acetosella* L. (5, 73, 156, 158) (1892-1923) Stratham NH

Toad trillium - *Trillium sessile* L. (138, 155) (1923-1942)

Toad-bellies - *Hylotelephium telephium* (L.) H. Ohba. subsp. *telephium* (156) (1923)

Toadflax [Toad flax, Toad-flax] - *Antirrhinum* L. (10) (1818), *Comandra* Nutt. (7) (1828), *Comandra umbellata* (L.) Nutt. (95) (1911), *Linaria dalmatica* (L.) P. Mill. (3) (1977), *Linaria* Mill. (2, 4, 7, 50, 82, 93, 109, 138, 155, 156) (1828–present), *Linaria vulgaris* Mill. (6, 18, 45, 46, 48, 49, 62, 80, 82, 127, 148, 156, 187) (1671-1933), *Nuttallanthus* D.A. Sutton (50) (present), *Spergula arvensis* L. (107, 156) (1919-1923)

Toadflax of Valentia [Toade flaxe of Valentia] - *Linaria supina* (L.) Chaz. (178) (1526)

Toad-grass [Toad-grasse] - *Juncus bufonius* L. (156, 178, 180) (1923)

Toad-lily [Toadlily, Toad lily] - *Nymphaea odorata* Aiton (7, 92) (1828–876), *Nymphaea odorata* Aiton subsp. *odorata* (5, 156, 158) (1900–1923), *Tricyrtis hirta* (Thunb.) Hook. (109) (1949), *Tricyrtis* Wallich (138) (1923)

Toad-mount - *Antirrhinum majus* L. (92) (1876)

Toad-pipes - *Equisetum palustre* L. (158) (1900)

Toadroot [Toad root, Toad-root] - *Actaea pachypoda* Ell. (6, 7) (1828-1932), *Actaea rubra* (Aiton) Willd. (5, 92, 156, 157, 158) (1876-1929)

Toad-shade [Toadshade] - *Trillium sessile* L. (3, 50) (1977–present)

Toad-spit [Toadspit, Toad spit] - *Lemna* L. (158) (1900), *Lemna minor* L. (5) (1913)

Toad's-tail [Toad's tail] - *Lycopodium clavatum* L. (5) (1913)

Toadstool - *Agaricus* L. (92) (1876), *Boletus* L. (92) (1876)

Toadweed [Toad weed] - *Juncus bufonius* L. (5) (1913)

Tobacco - *Nicotiana attenuata* Torr. ex S. Wats. (148) (1939) CO, *Nicotiana clevelandii* Gray (107) (1919), *Nicotiana* L. (1, 7, 10, 14, 50, 138, 156) (1818–present), *Nicotiana quadrivalvis* Pursh (34, 35, 37, 107) (1806-1919), *Nicotiana repanda* Willd. ex Lehm. (107) (1919), *Nicotiana rustica* L. (27, 107) (1811-1919), *Nicotiana tabacum* L. (6, 45, 48, 57, 60, 92, 106, 107, 109, 110, 182, 184) (1793-1949)

Tobacco plant - *Nicotiana tabacum* L. (106) (1930)

Tobacco tree - *Nicotiana glauca* Graham (77) (1898) CO

Tobacco-pipe [Tobacco pipe] - *Monotropa uniflora* L. (6) (1892)

Tobacco-root [Tobacco root] - *Valeriana edulis* Nutt. (5, 28, 50, 76, 101, 103, 107, 131, 156, 158) (1850–present), *Valeriana* L. (1) (1932)

Tobacco-weed [Tobacco weed] - *Elephantopus tomentosus* L. (5, 75, 156) (1894-1923)

Tobacco-wood [Tobacco wood] - *Hamamelis virginiana* L. (5, 92, 156) (1876-1923)

Tobira - *Pittosporum tobira* (Thunb.) Aiton f. (138) (1923)

Tobosa grass [Tobosa-grass, Tobosagrass] - *Pleuraphis mutica* Buckl. (3, 50, 65, 119, 122, 152, 155, 163) (1852–present)

Tocalote - *Centaurea melitensis* L. (106) (1930)

Tockawaugh - *Peltandra virginica* (L.) Schott. (181) (~1678)

Tockawhoughe - *Peltandra virginica* (L.) Schott. (181) (~1678)

Tockohow - *Pachyma cocos* (Schwein.) Fr. (46) (1610)

Tocolote - *Centaurea melitensis* L. (76) (1896)

Toddy palm - *Caryota urens* L. (138) (1923)

Toe-nails - *Proboscidea louisianica* (P. Mill.) Thellung (156, 158) (1900-1923)

Tofieldia - *Tofieldia* Huds. (50) (present)

Tohuts (Pawnee) - *Gymnocladus dioicus* (L.) K. Koch (37) (1919)

Toi - *Barbarea vulgaris* W.T. Aiton (107) (1919)

Toka hupepe (Dakota) - *Mentzelia nuda* (Pursh) Torr. & Gray var. *nuda* (37) (1919)

Tokala tapežuta hu wiŋjela (Lakota, female fox-medicine plant) - *Dalea purpurea* Vent. var. *purpurea* (121) (1918?-1970?)

Tollon - *Heteromeles arbutifolia* (Lindl.) M. Roemer (74, 109) (1893-1949) CA

Tollonweed - *Heteromeles arbutifolia* (Lindl.) M. Roemer (106) (1930)

Tolmei's onion [Tolmei onion] - *Allium tolmiei* (Hook.) Baker ex S. Wats. (155) (1942)

Toloache (Spanish) - *Datura stramonium* L. (158) (1900)

Toloachi - *Datura quercifolia* Kunth (104) (1896)

Toloachi (Spanish) - *Datura inoxia* P. Mill. (104) (1896), *Datura metel* L. (123) (1856)

Tolochlucco (Big bay) - *Magnolia grandiflora* L. (182) (1791)

Toluchluco (Indians) - *Nectandra coriacea* (Sw.) Griseb. (7) (1828)

Tom pimpermowl - *Anagallis arvensis* L. (158) (1900)

Tomates - *Solanum lycopersicum* L. var. *lycopersicum* (107) (1604)

Tomati (Mexican and Nahua natives) - *Solanum lycopersicum* L. var. *lycopersicum* (107) (1919)

Tomatillo - *Physalis* L. (1) (1932), *Physalis philadelphica* Lam. var. *immaculata* Waterfall (5, 109, 138, 156) (1913-1949)

Tomatl - *Solanum lycopersicum* L. var. *lycopersicum* (107) (1651)

Tomato [Tomatoes] - *Solanum* L. (109, 138, 155, 156, 158) (1900-1949), *Solanum lycopersicum* L. (19, 92) (1840-1876), *Solanum lycopersicum* L. var. *lycopersicum* (5, 14, 57, 95, 107, 110, 114, 138, 156, 158) (1882-1923)

Tomentose cherry - *Prunus tomentosa* Thunb. (82) (1930)

Tomomi Nikko fir - *Abies homolepis* Sieb. and Zucc. (155) (1942)

Tom-thumb [Tom thumb] - *Lathyrus pratensis* L. (5, 156) (1913-1923)

Tom-thumb alternathera [Tomthumb alternathera] - *Alternanthera bettzichiana* (Regel) Voss (155) (1942)

Tongue - *Symphyotrichum cordifolium* (L.) Nesom (5, 76, 156, 158) (1896-1923) S. Berwick ME

Tongue-grass [Tongue grass] - *Barbarea orthoceras* Ledeb. (35) (1806), *Lepidium sativum* L. (5, 92, 156, 158) (1876-1923), *Lepidium virginicum* L. (5, 35, 62, 74, 156, 157, 158) (1806-1929), *Stellaria media* (L.) Vill. (156) (1923) no longer in use by 1923, *Stellaria media* (L.) Vill. subsp. *media* (157, 158) (1900-1929)

Tooart - *Eucalyptus gomphocephala* DC. (138) (1923)

Tooth root - *Cardamine diphylla* (Michx.) Wood (19, 92) (1840-1876)

Toothache bark - *Zanthoxylum americanum* Mill. (92) (1876)

Toothache bush [Toothache-bush, Toothe-ache bush] - *Aralia spinosa* L. (49) (1898), *Zanthoxylum americanum* Mill. (7, 19, 49, 58, 92, 157, 158) (1828-1930)

Toothache grass [Toothache-grass] - *Ctenium aromaticum* (Walt.) Wood (5, 7, 45, 50, 66, 92, 94, 166) (1828–present)

Toothache tree [Tooth ache tree, Tooth-ache tree] - *Aralia spinosa* L. (5, 7, 49, 58, 156, 177) (1762-1923), *Zanthoxylum americanum* Mill. (2, 4, 5, 6, 14, 15, 49, 92, 97, 137, 156, 157, 158) (1876-1923), *Zanthoxylum clava-herculis* L. (106) (1930), *Zanthoxylum* L. (8, 10, 13) (1785-1849)

Tooth-cup [Tooth cup, Tooth-cup] - *Ammannia coccinea* Rottb. (3) (1977), *Ammannia* L. (4) (1986), *Ammannia latifolia* L. (5, 156) (1913-1923), *Cardamine concatenata* (Michx.) Sw. (4) (1986), *Rotala ramosior* (L.) Koehne (3, 4, 5, 93, 97) (1913-1986)

Toothed bur clover - *Medicago polymorpha* L. (109) (1949)

Toothed cyperus - *Cyperus dentatus* Torr. (5) (1913)

Toothed euphorbia - *Euphorbia dentata* Michx. (155) (1942)

Toothed manzanita - *Comarostaphylis diversifolia* (Parry) Greene subsp. *diversifolia* (155) (1942)

Toothed medic - *Medicago polymorpha* L. (5, 93, 97) (1913-1937)

Toothed rock cress - *Arabis shortii* (Fern.) Gleason (5, 72) (1907-1913)

Toothed spurge - *Euphorbia dentata* Michx. (3, 4, 5, 50, 72, 93, 97, 122, 131) (1899-1937)

Toothed wood fern [Toothed woodfern] - *Dryopteris carthusiana* (Vill.) H.P. Fuchs (138, 155) (1923-1942)

Toothleaf - *Stillingia* Garden ex L. (50) (present)

Tooth-leaf androsace [Tooth-leaved androsace] - *Androsace septentrionalis* L. (165) (1807)

Tooth-leaf arrow-wood [Tooth-leaved arrow wood] - *Viburnum dentatum* L. (8) (1785), *Viburnum edule* (Michx.) Raf. (187) (1818)

Tooth-leaf primrose [Tooth-leaved primrose] - *Calylophus serrulatus* (Nutt.) Raven (5, 72, 97, 127, 131) (1899-1937)

Tooth-leaf pyrola [Toothleaf pyrola] - *Pyrola picta* Sm. (155) (1942)

Tooth-leaf viburnum [Toothed-leaved viburnum] - *Viburnum dentatum* L. (8, 177) (1762-1785)

Toothpick ammi - *Ammi visnaga* (L.) Lam. (155) (1942)

Toothwort - *Capsella bursa-pastoris* (L.) Medik. (5, 156, 158) (1900-1923), *Cardamine concatenata* (Michx.) Sw. (3, 156) (1923-1977), *Cardamine diphylla* (Michx.) Wood (92, 156) (1876-1923), *Cardamine* L. (1, 2, 10, 13, 15, 93, 109, 138, 156) (1818-1949)

Tõp (Chippewa) - *Alnus incana* (L.) Moench (105) (1932)

Top onion - *Allium cepa* L. (155) (1942)

Topeka purple coneflower - *Echinacea atrorubens* Nutt. (50) (present)

Toper's plant - *Sanguisorba minor* Scop. subsp. *muricata* (Spach) Nordborg (5, 156, 157, 158) (1900-1929)

Topinambaus (French) - *Helianthus tuberosus* L. (110) (1618)

Topinambour (French) - *Helianthus tuberosus* L. (5, 156, 158) (1900-1923)

Torch flower [Torch-flower] - *Geum triflorum* Pursh (4) (1986), *Geum triflorum* Pursh var. *ciliatum* (Pursh) Fassett (127, 156) (1923-1933) ND, *Kniphofia uvaria* (L.) Oken (109) (1949)

Torch lily [Torchlily] - *Kniphofia* Moench (138) (1923)

Torch pine - *Pinus rigida* Mill. (5) (1913), *Pinus taeda* L. (5) (1913)

Torch thistle [Torch thistles] - *Cereus* Mill. (14) (1882)

Torches - *Verbascum thapsus* L. (5, 69, 156, 158) (1900-1923) no longer in use by 1923

Torch-weed - *Bigelowia nudata* (Michx.) DC. (156) (1923)

Torchwood [Torch wood] - *Amyris* P. Br. (15) (1895), *Metopium toxiferum* (L.) Krug & Urban (46) (1879)

Torchwort - *Verbascum thapsus* L. (69, 158) (1900-1904)

Torenia - *Torenia* L. (138) (1923)

Toringo crab - *Malus sieboldii* (Regel) Rehd. (137, 138) (1923-1931)

Toritsa (Russian) - *Spergula arvensis* L. (110) (1886)

Tormentil - *Geranium maculatum* L. (6, 92) (1876-1892)

Tormentile - *Potentilla simplex* Michx. (46) (1671)

Tormentyll - *Potentilla erecta* (L.) Raeusch. (179) (1526)

Tornilla - *Prosopis pubescens* Benth. (107) (1919)

Tornillo - *Prosopis glandulosa* Torr. var. *torreyana* (L. Benson) M.C. Johnston (106) (1930), *Prosopis pubescens* Benth. (76, 103, 104, 106, 122, 124, 151) (1870-1937) NM, Mexico

Tornillo (Spanish) - *Prosopis pubescens* Benth. (123, 147, 153) (1852-1913)

Torosa (Spanish) - *Eschscholzia californica* Cham. (76) (1896)

Torrets - *Carex nigra* (L.) Reichard (5) (1913)

Torreya - *Torreya* Arn. (138) (1923) For John Torrey, 1796-1873, American botanist

Torreya à feuilles d'If (French) - *Torreya taxifolia* Arnot. (20) (1857)

Torreyan gentian - *Gentiana saponaria* L. (7) (1828)

Torrey's amaranth - *Amaranthus torreyi* (Gray) Benth. ex S. Wats. (5, 72, 93, 122) (1907-1937)

Torrey's anthericum [Torry anthericum] - *Echeandia flavescens* (J.A. & J.H. Schultes) Cruden (155) (1942)

Torrey's beak rush - *Rhynchospora torreyana* Gray (66) (1903)

Torrey's beaked rush - *Rhynchospora torreyana* Gray (5) (1913)

Torrey's beard grass - *Bothriochloa saccharoides* (Sw.) Rydb. (5) (1913)

Torrey's bluegrass [Torrey bluegrass] - *Poa saltuensis* Fern. & Wieg. (155) (1942)

Torrey's bulrush [Torrey bulrush] - *Schoenoplectus torreyi* (Olney) Palla (5, 50, 155) (1913-present)

Torrey's cryptantha - *Cryptantha torreyana* (Gray) Greene (50) (present)

Torrey's ephedra [Torrey ephedra] - *Ephedra torreyana* Wats. (3, 4, 155) (1942-1986)

Torrey's jointfir - *Ephedra torreyana* Wats. (50) (present)

Torrey's meadow grass - *Puccinellia fasciculata* (Torr.) Bicknell (5) (1913)

Torrey's melic grass [Torrey's melic-grass] - *Melica torreyana* Scribn. (94) (1901)

Torrey's mountain-mint [Torrey's mountain mint] - *Pycnanthemum verticillatum* (Michx.) Pers. var. *verticillatum* (5) (1913)

Torrey's nightshade [Torrey nightshade] - *Solanum dimidiatum* Raf. (5, 72, 97, 155) (1907-1942)

Torrey's penstemon [Torrey penstemon] - *Penstemon barbatus* (Cav.) Roth subsp. *torreyi* (Benth.) Keck (138) (1923)

Torrey's pine [Torrey pine] - *Pinus torreyana* Parry ex Carr. (109, 138) (1923-1949) For John Torrey, 1796-1873, New York

Torrey's rush [Torrey rush] - *Juncus torreyi* Coville (3, 5, 50, 72, 93, 139, 155) (1907–present), *Schoenoplectus torreyi* (Olney) Palla (66) (1903)

Torrey's sedge [Torrey sedge] - *Carex torreyi* Tuckerman (5, 50, 66, 139) (1903–present)

Torrey's seepweed [Torrey seepweed] - *Suaeda moquinii* (Torr.) Greene (155) (1942)

Torrey's silver beard grass [Torrey's silver beard-grass] - *Bothriochloa laguroides* (DC.) Herter subsp. *torreyana* (Steud.) Allred & Gould (94) (1901)

Torrey's solanum - *Solanum dimidiatum* Raf. (86) (1878)

Torrey's spike-rush [Torrey's spike rush] - *Eleocharis microcarpa* Torr. (5) (1913)

Torrey's thoroughwort - *Eupatorium hyssopifolium* L. var. *hyssopifolium* (5) (1913)

Torrey's wild licorice [Torrey's wild liquorice] - *Galium lanceolatum* Torr. (5) (1913)

Torrwarksgras (Swedish) - *Linnaea borealis* L. (46) (1879)

Tortelle (French) - *Sisymbrium officinale* (L.) Scop (158) (1900)

Tory-bur - *Cynoglossum officinale* L. (75) (1894) NY, possibly obsolete by 1894

Toryweed [Tory weed, Tory-weed] - *Cynoglossum officinale* L. (19, 29, 92, 157, 158) (1840–1929)

Toshunk ah'unshke (Winnebago, otter armlet) - *Smilax herbacea* L. (37) (1830)

Tota bona - *Chenopodium bonus-henricus* L. (107, 177) (1919)

Tota kura (Telinga) - *Amaranthus tricolor* L. (110) (1886)

Touch-and-heal - *Hypericum perforatum* L. (5, 156, 157, 158) (1900-1929)

Touch-me-not - *Cardamine hirsuta* L. (5) (1913), *Impatiens capensis* Meerb. (46, 127) (1879-1933), *Impatiens* L. (1, 2, 4, 7, 10, 13, 50, 106, 156, 158) (1818–present), *Impatiens noli-tangere* L. (15, 184) (1793-1895), *Impatiens pallida* Nutt. (19, 48, 85, 92) (1840-1932)

Touch-weed - *Mimosa pudica* L. (92) (1876)

Touchwood - *Boletus* L. (7) (1828), *Polyporus igniarius* (L.) Fr. (92) (1876), *Polyporus* P. Micheli ex Adans. (46) (1879)

Tough grape - *Vitis labrusca* L. (possibly) (7) (1828)

Tournefort's speedwell - *Veronica officinalis* L. var. *tournefortii* (Vill.) Reichenb. (5) (1913)

Tournesol - *Roccella tinctoria* DC. (49) (1898)

Tous-les-mois (French) - *Canna indica* L. (92) (1876)

Toute saine (French) - *Hypericum perforatum* L. (156) (1923)

Tovara - *Polygonum* L. (155) (1942)

Towcok - *Vigna sinensis* (L.) Endl. (5) (1913)

Towel gourd [Towelgourd] - *Luffa aegyptiaca* Mill. (110) (1886), *Luffa* Mill. (138) (1923)

Tower cress - *Arabis glabra* (L.) Bernh. (5, 156, 158) (1900-1923)

Tower mustard [Tower-mustard] - *Arabis canadensis* L. (156) (1923), *Arabis glabra* (L.) Bernh. (2, 3, 4, 5, 15, 46, 72, 85, 92, 131, 156, 158) (1649-1986), *Arabis* L. (1, 10, 13) (1818-1932)

Tower rockcress - *Arabis glabra* (L.) Bernh. (50) (present)

Tower-mustard rockcress [Towermustard rockcress] - *Arabis glabra* L. Bernh. (155) (1942)

Tow-heads - *Populus tremuloides* Michx. (156) (1923)

Towline loco - *Astragalus tephrodes* var. *brachylobus* (Gray) Barneby (155) (1942)

Town pepper-grass [Town pepper grass, Town peppergrass] - *Lepidium sativum* L. (5, 158) (1900-1913)

Townsend daisy - *Townsendia* Hook. (50) (present)

Townsendia - *Townsendia* Hook. (93, 155, 158) (1900-1942)

Tow-wort (Northen England) - *Capsella bursa-pastoris* (L.) Medik. (180) (1633)

Toyon [Toy-on] - *Heteromeles arbutifolia* (Lindl.) M. Roemer (74, 106, 109) (1893-1949) CA

Toy-weed - *Capsella bursa-pastoris* (L.) Medik. (156) (1923) no longer in use by 1923

Toywort - *Capsella bursa-pastoris* (L.) Medik. (5, 92, 157, 158) (1876-1929)

Tožon hi (Osage, possibly meaning potato wood tree) - *Asimina triloba* (L.) Dunal (121) (1918?-1970?)

Trachelospermum - *Trachelospermum difforme* (Walt.) Gray (5) (1913)

Tracy's bluegrass [Tracy's blue-grass] - *Poa tracyi* Vasey (94) (1901)

Tradescantia - *Tradescantia virginiana* L. (174, 177) (1753-1762)

Tradescant's aster [Tradescant aster] - *Symphyotrichum tradescantii* (L.) Nesom (5, 82, 155) (1913-1942)

Tradescant's spiderwort [Tradescants spiderwort] - *Tradescantia virginiana* L. (180) (1633)

Tradescant's Virgiania spiderwort [Tradescants Virgianian spiderwort] - *Tradescantia virginiana* L. (180) (1633)

Trafoglio (Italian) - *Trifolium incarnatum* L. (110) (1886)

Tragia - *Tragia* L. (158) (1900)

Trail plant [Trailplant] - *Adenocaulon* Hook. (1, 50) (1932–present)

Trailing arbutus [Trailing-arbutus] - *Epigaea* L. (8, 138, 156, 167) (1785-1923), *Epigaea repens* L. (1, 2, 5, 6, 8, 10, 19, 47, 49, 52, 53, 54, 57, 58, 61, 92, 106, 109) (1840-1949)

Trailing azalea - *Loiseleuria procumbens* (L.) Desv. (5, 19, 156) (1840-1923)

Trailing bindweed - *Calystegia sepium* (L.) R. Br. subsp. *angulata* Brummitt (5, 72, 131) (1899-1913)

Trailing blackberry - *Rubus canadensis* L. (107) (1919)

Trailing bush clover [Trailing bush-clover] - *Lespedeza procumbens* Michx (5, 97) (1913-1937)

Trailing Christmas-green - *Lycopodium complanatum* L. (5, 72, 78, 158) (1898-1913)

Trailing cockspur - *Galium triflorum* Michx. (46) (1783)

Trailing dogwood - *Cornus canadensis* L. (156) (1923)

Trailing evergreen - *Huperzia lucidula* (Michx.) Trevisan (5) (1913)

Trailing fire - *Ipomopsis rubra* (L.) Wherry (156) (1923)

Trailing fleabane - *Erigeron flagellaris* Gray (3, 50, 155) (1942–present)

Trailing four-o-clock - *Allionia incarnata* L. (4) (1986), *Allionia* L. (4) (1986)

Trailing fuzzybean - *Strophostyles helvula* (L.) Ell. (50) (present)

Trailing gaultheria - *Gaultheria procumbens* L. (186) (1814)

Trailing juniper - *Juniperus communis* L. (136) (1930), *Juniperus horizontalis* Moench (101) (1905)

Trailing krameria - *Krameria lanceolata* Torr. (50, 155) (1942–present)

Trailing lantana - *Lantana montevidensis* (Spreng.) Briq. (109) (1949)

Trailing lespedeza - *Lespedeza procumbens* Michx (3, 4, 50, 155, 187) (1818–present)

Trailing loosestrife - *Lysimachia radicans* Hook. (5, 122) (1913-1937)

Trailing mahonia - *Mahonia aquifolium* (Pursh) Nutt. (5, 64, 131, 157) (1899-1929)

Trailing maidenhair fern - *Adiantum caudatum* L. (138) (1923)

Trailing monkshood - *Aconitum reclinatum* Gray (5) (1913)

Trailing pearlwort - *Sagina decumbens* (Ell.) Torr. & Gray (4, 50, 155) (1942–present)

Trailing sumac [Trailing sumach] - *Toxicodendron radicans* (L.) Kuntze (5) (1913), *Toxicodendron radicans* (L.) Kuntze subsp. *radicans* (157, 158) (1900-1929), *Toxicodendron toxicarium* (Salisb.) Gillis (92, 156) (1898-1923)

Trailing tick-trefoil [Trailing tick trefoil] - *Desmodium glabellum* (Michx.) DC. (5) (1913), *Desmodium rotundifolium* DC. (5) (1913)

Trailing tormetil - *Potentilla anglica* Laicharding (5) (1913)

Trailing vine - *Lycopodium complanatum* L. (78) (1898) Ferrisburgh VT

Trailing wild bean [Trailing wildbean] - *Strophostyles helvula* (L.) Ell. (5, 82, 93, 97, 121, 131, 155) (1899-1937)

Trailing wild rose - *Strophostyles helvula* (L.) Ell. (72) (1907) IA

Trailing windmills - *Allionia incarnata* L. (50) (present)

Trailing wolfsbane - *Aconitum reclinatum* Gray (5) (1913)

Trailing-pea [Trailing pea] - *Apios americana* Medik. (156) (1923)

Trametes - *Trametes hispida* Bagl. (128) (1933)

Tranbär (Swedish) - *Gaultheria hispidula* (L.) Muhl. ex Bigelow (possibly) (41) (1770)

Trans-Pecos morning-glory [Transpecos morningglory] - *Ipomoea cristulata* Hallier f. (50) (present)

Trans-Pecos sea-lavender [Transpecos sealavender] - *Limonium limbatum* Small. (50) (present)

Transvaal daisy - *Gerbera jamesonii* Bolus ex Hooker f. (109) (1949)

Transvaal oxalis - *Oxalis stricta* L. (155) (1942)

Trapa nut - *Trapa natans* L. (107) (1919)

Trapp's avocado [Trapp avocado] - *Persea americana* Mill. (109, 138) (1923-1949)

Trasvaal dog-tooth grass [Trasvaal dogtoothgrass] - *Cynodon transvaalensis* Burtt-Davy (155) (1942)

Traubenformiges Christophskraut (German) - *Cimicifuga racemosa* (L.) Nutt. (6) (1892)

Traubenkraut (German) - *Ambrosia artemisiifolia* L. (6) (1892), *Chenopodium botrys* L. (158) (1900)

Travelers' tree [Travelers-tree] - *Ravenala madagascariensis* Sonnerat (50, 92) (1876–present) cup-like leaf bases hold water from which travelers are said to drink

Traveler's-delight [Traveller's delight] - *Apios americana* Medik. (73, 156) (1892-1923) New Albany Miss

Traveler's-ivy [Traveler's ivy] - *Clematis virginiana* L. (49) (1898)

Traveler's-joy [Traveler's joy, Traveller's joy, Traveller's-joy, Travellers Ioy] - *Clematis* L. (1, 184) (1793-1932), *Clematis virginiana* L. (5, 19, 158, 187) (1818-1900), *Clematis vitalba* L. (92, 109, 138, 178) (1526-1949), *Verbena hastata* L. (92) (1876)

Treachle mustard - *Erysimum cheiranthoides* L. (131) (1899)

Treacle clauuer - *Bituminaria bituminosa* (L.) Stirt. (178) (1526)

Treacle erysimum - *Erysimum cheiranthoides* L. (155) (1942)

Treacle hare's-ear [Treacle haresear] - *Conringia orientalis* (L.) Dumort. (155) (1942)

Treacle mustard [Treakle mustard] - *Alliaria petiolata* (Bieb.) Cavara & Grande (156) (1923), *Capsella bursa-pastoris* (L.) Medik. (178) (1526), *Conringia orientalis* (L.) Dumort. (5, 85, 158) (1900-1932), *Erysimum cheiranthoides* L. (5, 156, 157, 158) (1900-1929), *Erysimum* L. (13, 15, 156) (1849-1923)

Treacle wormseed - *Erysimum cheiranthoides* L. (157, 158) (1900-1929)

Treacle-berry [Treackleberries] - *Maianthemum racemosum* (L.) Link subsp. *racemosum* (46, 107, 156) (1879-1923)

Treaclewort [Treacle wort, Treacle-wort] - *Thlaspi arvense* L. (5, 156, 158) (1900-1923)

Tread-softly [Treadsoftly, Tread softly] - *Cnidoscolus* J. Pohl (155) (1942), *Cnidoscolus stimulosus* (Michx.) Engelm. & Gray (5, 19, 92, 156) (1840-1923), *Cnidoscolus texanus* (Muell.-Arg.) Small (97) (1937), *Cnidoscolus urens* (L.) Arthur (107) (1919), *Jatropha* L. (156) (1923), *Solanum carolinense* L. (5, 156) (1913-1923)

Treasure-of-love - *Sedum acre* L. (5, 76) (1896-1913) Boston MA

Trébal acuatico (Spanish) - *Menyanthes trifoliata* L. (158) (1900)

Trebol oloroso (Spanish) - *Melilotus officinalis* (L.) Lam. (158) (1900)

Tree alfalfa [Tree alfalfa] - *Chamaecystis prolifera* (L. f.) Link (106) (1930)

Tree amaranth - *Amaranthus hybridus* L. (165) (1768)

Tree andromeda - *Oxydendrum arboreum* (L.) DC. (possibly) (165) (1807)

Tree aralia - *Aralia spinosa* L. (155) (1942)

Tree azalea - *Rhododendron arborescens* (Pursh) Torr. (5, 156) (1913-1923)

Tree buckthorn [Treebuckthorn] - *Alphitonia* Reissek ex Endl. (155) (1942), *Frangula caroliniana* (Walt.) Gray (122) (1937)

Tree cactus - *Opuntia imbricata* (Haw.) DC. (97) (1937), *Opuntia imbricata* (Haw.) DC. var. *imbricata* (5, 76, 153) (1896-1913), *Opuntia* Mill. (1) (1932)

Tree catsclaw - *Acacia greggii* Gray (106, 122) (1930-1937)

Tree ceanothus - *Ceanothus thyrsiflorus* Esch. (20) (1857)

Tree celandine [Tree celandine] - *Macleaya cordata* (Willd.) R. Br. (109) (1949)

Tree cholla - *Opuntia imbricata* (Haw.) DC. (4, 50) (1986–present)

Tree clover [Tree-clover] - *Chamaecystis prolifera* (L. f.) Link (106) (1930), *Melilotus officinalis* (L.) Lam. (possibly) (5, 62, 156, 157, 158) (1900-1929)

Tree coleworts [Tree colewoorts] - *Brassica oleracea* L. (178) (1526)

Tree cotton [Tree-cotton] - *Gossypium herbaceum* L. (110) (1886)

Tree elder - *Sambucus racemosa* L. var. *racemosa* (138) (1923)

Tree fern [Treefern] - *Alsophila* R. Br. (138, 155) (1923-1942), *Cyathea* Sm. (138) (1923), *Osmunda regalis* L. (5, 157) (1913-1929)

Tree germander - *Teucrium fruticans* L. (138) (1923)

Tree ground-pine [Tree groundpine] - *Lycopodium dendroideum* Michx. (50) (present)

Tree haw - *Crataegus viridis* L. (5) (1913)

Tree hibiscus - *Hibiscus syriacus* L. (156) (1923)

Tree honeysuckle [Tree honisuckles] - *Lonicera xylosteum* L. (178) (1526)

Tree houseleek - *Aeonium arboreum* (L.) Webb & Berthel. (19) (1840)

Tree huckleberry - *Vaccinium arboreum* Marsh. (5, 65, 97, 106, 124, 156, 158) (1900-1937), *Vaccinium* L. (1) (1932)

Tree kale - *Brassica oleracea* L. (109) (1949)

Tree lungwort - *Lobaria pulmonaria* (L.) Hoffm. (53, 92) (1876-1922), *Mertensia virginica* (L.) Pers. ex Link (possibly) (5, 156) (1913-1923) no longer in use by 1923

Tree lupine - *Lupinus arboreus* Sims (76, 109, 138) (1896-1949)

Tree mallow [Treemallow, Tree mallow, Tree mallows, Tree mallowes] - *Alcea rosea* L. (178) (1526), *Hibiscus syriacus* L. (178) (1526), *Lavatera arborea* L. (19, 92) (1840-1876), *Lavatera assurgentiflora* Kellogg (76) (1896) Santa Barbara CA, *Lavatera* L. (82, 109, 138) (1923-1949)

Tree millet - *Sorghum bicolor* (L.) Moench (110) (1886)

Tree moss [Tree-moss] - *Bryoria fremontii* (Tuck.) Brodo & D. Hawksw. (101) (1905) MT, *Euphorbia cyparissias* L. (5, 73, 93, 156, 158) (1892-1936), *Huperzia selago* (L.) Bernh. ex Mart. & Schrank var. *selago* (5) (1913), *Letharia vulpina* (L.) Hue (101) (1905) MT

Tree nightshade - *Solanum pseudocapsicum* L. (92) (1876)

Tree poplar - *Populus grandidentata* Michx. (19) (1840)

Tree poppy [Treepoppy] - *Dendromecon* Benth. (138) (1923), *Dendromecon rigida* Benth. (74, 138) (1894-1923)

Tree primrose [Tree-primrose] - *Oenothera biennis* L. (5, 6, 19, 46, 49, 53, 156, 157, 158, 180) (1633-1929), *Oenothera* L. (10, 167) (1814-1818)

Tree primrose of Virginia - *Oenothera biennis* L. (181) (~1678)

Tree scarlet elder - *Sambucus racemosa* L. var. *racemosa* (155) (1942)

Tree sea-lavender - *Limonium arborescens* (Brouss.) Kuntze (138) (1923)

Tree sow-thistle [Tree sow thistle] - *Sonchus arvensis* L. (5, 157, 158) (1900-1929)

Tree spiraea - *Sorbaria arborea* Schneid. (138) (1923)

Tree spurge - *Euphorbia dendroides* L. (178) (1526)

Tree thorn - *Crataegus viridis* L. (5) (1913)

Tree tobacco - *Nicotiana glauca* Graham (75, 138) (1894-1923) Santa Barbara CA

Tree trefoil [Tree trefoil] - *Ptelea trifoliata* L. (6) (1892)

Tree whortleberry - *Vaccinium arboreum* Marsh. (8, 20) (1785-1857)

Tree wild tobacco [Tree wildtobacco] - *Acnistus arborescens* (L.) Schlecht. (155) (1942)

Tree-beard [Tree beard] - *Tillandsia usneoides* (L.) L. (5, 92, 156) (1876-1923)

Treebine - *Cissus* L. (50, 155) (1942)

Tree-jelly [Treejelly] - *Tremella* Pers. (7) (1828)

Tree-like clubmoss [Tree-like club-moss, Tree-like club moss] - *Lycopodium obscurum* L. (5, 158) (1900-1913)

Treenail - *Robinia pseudoacacia* L. (6) (1892)

Tree-of-chastity [Tree of chastity] - *Vitex agnus-castus* L. (92) (1876)

Tree-of-heaven [Tree of heaven] - *Ailanthus altissima* (Mill) Swingle (3, 4, 5, 6, 49, 50, 52, 54, 57, 85, 92, 97, 106, 107, 109, 112, 124, 135, 137, 138, 153, 156, 158) (1876–present), *Ailanthus* Desf. (1, 4, 93, 122, 158) (1900-1986)

Tree-of-heaven ailanthus [Treeofheaven ailanthus] - *Ailanthus altissima* (Mill) Swingle (155) (1942)

Tree-of-life [Tree of life] - *Thuja* L. (8) (1785), *Thuja occidentalis* L. (6, 49, 53, 178) (1596-1922)

Tree-of-paradise [Tree of paradise] - *Elaeagnus angustifolia* L. (137) (1931)

Tree-of-peace [Tree of peace] - *Gordonia lasianthus* L. (46) (1879), *Liriodendron tulipifera* L. (181) (~1678)

Tree-of-the-gods - *Ailanthus altissima* (Mill) Swingle (158) (1900)

Treeweed [Tree weed] - *Lycopodium dendroideum* Michx. (19) (1840)

Trefle - *Trientalis borealis* Raf. subsp. *borealis* (187) (1818)

Trefle (French) - *Trifolium pratense* L. (6) (1892)

Trefle blanc (French) - *Trifolium repens* L. (6) (1892)

Trefle d'eau (French) - *Menyanthes trifoliata* L. (6, 158) (1892-1900)

Trefoil - *Hepatica nobilis* Schreb. (7) (1828), *Hepatica nobilis* Schreb. var. *obtusa* (Pursh) Steyermark (6, 92) (1876-1892), *Lotus* L. (4, 50) (1986–present), *Lotus unifoliolatus* (Hook.) Benth. (156) (1923), *Trifolium* L. (1, 10, 45, 92, 156, 158) (1818-1932), *Trifolium willdenovii* Spreng. (possibly) (107) (1919)

Trefoil coreopsis - *Coreopsis major* Walt. (138) (1923)

Trefoil Herb Paris - *Trillium sessile* L. (181) (~1678)

Trelease's larkspur - *Delphinium treleasei* Bush ex K.C. Davis (5) (1913)

Trellis-leaf vetch [Trellisleaf vetch] - *Vicia americana* Muhl. ex Willd. subsp. *minor* (Hook.) C.R. Gunn (155) (1942)

Tremble (French Canadians) - *Populus tremuloides* Michx. (possibly) (17) (1796)

Trembling aspen - *Populus tremula* L. (14) (1882)

Trembling poplar - *Populus tremula* L. (5, 14, 156, 157, 158) (1882-1929)

Trembling tree - *Populus tremuloides* Michx. (92) (1876)

Triadenum - *Triadenum* Raf. (158) (1900)

Triangle cactus - *Acanthocereus tetragonus* (L.) Humm. (50) (present)

Triangle onion - *Allium triquetrum* L. (155) (1942)

Triangle orach [Triangle orache] - *Atriplex prostrata* Bouché ex DC. (50) (present)

Triangle-leaf violet [Triangleleaf violet, Triangle-leaved violet] - *Viola sagittata* Aiton (5, 97, 155) (1913-1942)

Trichostomum moss - *Trichostomum* Bruch (50) (present)

Trick trefoil [Trick-trefoil (sic)] - *Desmodium* Desv. (93) (1936)

Trickle - *Cardamine diphylla* (Michx.) Wood (5, 19, 92) (1840-1913)

Tricolor chrysanthemum - *Chrysanthemum carinatum* Schousboe (109) (1949)

Tricolor morning-glory - *Ipomoea tricolor* Cav. (138) (1923)

Tricolor yellow buckeye - *Aesculus flava* Aiton (155) (1942)

Tri-colored gilia - *Gilia tricolor* Benth. (86) (1878)

Tridax (Greek) - *Lactuca sativa* L. (110) (1886)

Tridens - *Tridens* Roemer & J.A. Schultes (50) (present)

Trident red maple - *Acer rubrum* L. (155) (1942)

Trifid fleabane - *Erigeron compositus* Pursh (155) (1942)

Trifid-fruit custard-apple [Trifid-fruited custard apple] - *Asimina triloba* (L.) Dunal (165) (1807)

Trifid-leaf ambrosia [Trifid-leaved ambrosia] - *Ambrosia trifida* L. (165) (1768)

Trifid-leaf hogweed [Trifid-leaved hogweed] - *Ambrosia trifida* L. (187) (1818)

Trifoliate Virginia meadow-sweet - *Gillenia trifoliata* (L.) Moench (181) (~1678)

Trifoliate-orange - *Poncirus trifoliata* (L.) Raf. (109) (1949)

Trigonel - *Trigonella foenum-graecum* L. (110) (1886)

Trillium - *Trillium erectum* L. (57, 64) (1908-1917), *Trillium* L. (50, 106, 138, 155) (1923–present)

Trillium (French) - *Trillium erectum* L. (6) (1892)

Trillium (German) - *Trillium erectum* L. (6) (1892)

Trilobe violet - *Viola palmata* L. (155) (1942)

Trinidad milkvetch [Trinidad milk vetch] - *Astragalus puniceus* Osterhout (4, 50) (1986–present)

Trinitaria (Spanish) - *Viola tricolor* L. (158) (1900)

Trinity - *Tradescantia virginiana* L. (5, 37, 156) (1913-1919)

Trinity lily - *Trillium grandiflorum* (Michx.) Salisb. (5, 73, 156) (1892-1923)

Trinity violet - *Tradescantia virginiana* L. (156) (1923) Wisconsin, *Viola tricolor* L. (6, 158) (1892-1900)

Trinle root [Trinle-root] - *Cardamine diphylla* (Michx.) Wood (156) (1923)

Triole dilatee (French) - *Trillium cernuum* L. (7) (1828) no longer in use by 1923

Trioste (French) - *Triosteum perfoliatum* L. (6) (1892)

Triple-awn beard grass [Triple-awned beard grass, Triple-awned beard-grass] - *Aristida adscensionis* L. (5, 99) (1913-1923)

Triple-awn grass - *Aristida* L. (93) (1936)

Triple-head pondweed [Triple-headed pond weed] - *Zannichellia* L. (167) (1814)

Triple-leaf barberry [Triple-leaved barberry - *Mahonia trifoliolata* (Moric.) Fedde (106) (1930)

Triplet lily [Triplet-lily] - *Triteleia laxa* Benth. (109) (1949)

Triple-thorn acaia [Triple-thorned acaia, 3-thorned acacia] - *Gleditsia* L. (8, 167) (1785-1814), *Gleditsia triacanthos* L. (8) (1785)

Tripoli aster - *Tripolium pannonicum* (Jacq.) Dobrocz. (155) (1942)

Triptoe [Trip-toe, Trip toe] - *Viburnum lantanoides* Michx. (5, 75, 156) (1894-1923)

Trisetum - *Trisetum* Pers. (155) (1942) Franconia NH

Tristram's-knot - *Cannabis sativa* L. (157, 158) (1900-1929)

Triticum - *Elymus repens* (L.) Gould (57, 59, 64, 157) (1908-1929)

Trixis - *Proserpinaca palustris* L. (174, 177) (1753-1762)

Trojan iris - *Iris germanica* L. (138) (1923)

Trompillo - *Solanum elaeagnifolium* Cav. (150, 158) (1894-1900)

Trompillos (Mexico) - *Solanum elaeagnifolium* Cav. (5, 107) (1913-1919) NM

Tronadora - *Nicotiana glauca* Graham (122) (1937)

Tropic ageratum - *Ageratum conyzoides* L. (155) (1942) TX

Tropic croton - *Croton glandulosus* L. (4) (1986), *Croton glandulosus* L. var. *septentrionalis* Muell. Arg. (3) (1977)

Tropical flatsedge - *Cyperus surinamensis* Rottb. (4, 50) (1986–present)

Tropical lilac - *Duranta erecta* L. (106) (1930)

Tropical-almond - *Terminalia catappa* L. (109) (1949)

Troublesome sedge - *Carex molesta* Mackenzie ex Bright (50) (present)

Trout flower [Trout-flower] - *Erythronium americanum* Ker. (5, 156, 157) (1913-1923)

Trout lily [Trout-lily, Troutlily] - *Erythronium albidum* Nutt. (156) (1923), *Erythronium americanum* Ker. (5, 75, 156, 157) (1894-1929), *Erythronium* L. (138) (1923)

Trucker pine - *Pinus ponderosa* P.& C. Lawson (158) (1900)

True black hellebore [True blacke hellebore] - *Helleborus niger* L. (178) (1526)

True camomile [True chamomile] - *Anthemis arvensis* L. (6) (1892)

True daisy - *Bellis perennis* L. (109) (1949)

True forget-me-not [True forgetmenot] - *Myosotis scorpioides* L. (3, 50, 82, 109, 138, 155, 156) (1923–present)

True goldenrod [True golden-rod] - *Solidago odora* Aiton (5, 156) (1913-1923)

True indigo - *Indigofera tinctoria* L. (138) (1923)

True Labrador tea [True Labrador-tea] - *Ledum groenlandicum* Oeder (138) (1923)

True lavender - *Lavandula angustifolia* Mill. (138) (1923)

True maidenhair [True maiden's hair] - *Adiantum capillus-veneris* L. (5, 109, 165) (1768-1949)

True maidenhair fern [True maiden-hair fern] - *Adiantum capillus-veneris* L. (86) (1878)

True mountain-mahogany [True mountainmahogany] - *Cercocarpus montanus* Raf. (155) (1942)

True papaw - *Carica papaya* L. (57) (1917)

True shamrock - *Trifolium dubium* Sibth. (158) (1900)

True snakeroot [True snake-root] - *Aristolochia serpentaria* L. (46) (1649)

True thistle - *Cirsium* Mill (4) (1986)

True unicorn root [True unicorn-root] - *Aletris farinosa* L. (64) (1908)

True veratrum - *Veratrum viride* Ait. (64) (1908)

True water-cress [True water cress] - *Nasturtium officinale* W.T. Aiton (possibly) (5, 63, 97, 120, 157, 158) (1899-1938), *Sisymbrium* L. (93) (1936)

True wood sorrel - *Oxalis montana* Raf. (possibly) (2) (1895)

Truelove [True love] - *Trillium cernuum* L. (7) (1828), *Trillium erectum* L. (5, 64, 102, 156) (1886–1923)

Truelove of Canada [True-love of Canada] - *Trillium* L. (167) (1814)

Truffle [Truffles] - *Lycoperdon* Pers. (possibly) (184) (1793), *Lycoperdon tuber* L. (41) (1770), *Tuber* P. Micheli ex F.H. Wigg. (possibly) (7) (1828)

Truffle oak - *Quercus robur* L. (107) (1919)

Trumpet - *Collomia* Nutt. (50) (present)

Trumpet [Trumpets] - *Lactuca canadensis* L. (5, 156, 158) (1900-1923), *Sarracenia flava* L. (5, 10, 15, 46, 156) (1818-1923), *Sarracenia leucophylla* Raf. (15, 109) (1895-1949)

Trumpet bush [Trumpetbush] - *Tecoma* Juss. (138, 155) (1923-1942)

Trumpet evening-primrose [Trumpet evening primrose] - *Oenothera jamesii* Torr. & Gray (50) (present)

Trumpet flower [Trumpet-flower, Trumpet-flowers] - *Bignonia capreolata* L. (109) (1949), *Bignonia* L. (8, 10, 14, 184) (1785-1882), *Campsis radicans* (L.) Seem. ex Bureau (5, 10, 46, 62, 86, 97, 106, 156, 158, 189) (1767-1937), *Sarracenia flava* L. (177, 181) (~1678-1762), *Tecoma* Juss. (1, 2, 7, 158) (1828-1932)

Trumpet gourd - *Lagenaria siceraria* (Molina) Standl. (107) (1919)

Trumpet honeysuckle [Trumpet honey-suckle] - *Lonicera sempervirens* L. (2, 3, 5, 46, 50, 86, 93, 95, 109, 113, 138, 155, 156, 158) (1878–present)

Trumpet milkweed [Trumpet milk-weed] - *Lactuca canadensis* L. (5, 156, 157, 158) (1900-1929)

Trumpet morning-glory - *Ipomoea violacea* L. (138) (1923)

Trumpet narcissus - *Narcissus pseudonarcissus* L. (109) (1949)

Trumpet pitcherplant - *Sarracenia flava* L. (138) (1923)

Trumpet tree - *Cecropia peltata* L. (92) (1876)

Trumpet vine [Trumpet-vine] - *Campsis radicans* (L.) Seem. ex Bureau (2, 3, 5, 86, 109, 156, 158) (1878-1949)

Trumpet-ash [Trumpet ash] - *Campsis radicans* (L.) Seem. ex Bureau (5, 156, 158) (1900-1923)

Trumpet-creeper [Trumpet creeper, Trumpetcreeper] - *Tecoma* Juss. (1) (1932), *Bignonia* L. (138) (1923), *Campsis* Lour. (109, 155) (1942-1949)

Trumpet-creeper [Trumpetcreeper, Trumpet creeper] - *Campsis radicans* (L.) Seem. ex Bureau (2, 4, 5, 50, 62, 63, 72, 82, 85, 86, 106, 112, 114, 122, 124, 138, 156, 158, 187) (1818–present)

Trumpet-leaf [Trumpet leaf, Trumpit Leaf] - *Sarracenia flava* L. (5, 92, 156, 183) (~1756-1923), *Sarracenia leucophylla* Raf. (15) (1895)

Trumpet-leaf honeysuckle [Trumpet leaf honeysuckle] - *Lonicera sempervirens* L. (92) (1876)

Trumpet-weed [Trumpet weed, Trumpetweed] - *Eupatorium purpureum* L. (5, 6, 19, 49, 54, 62, 64, 92, 95, 156, 157, 158) (1840-1929), *Lactuca canadensis* L. (5, 6, 156, 158) (1892-1923)

Trumpet-wood [Trumpet wood] - *Cecropia peltata L.* (92) (1876)

Truncated koeleria - *Sphenopholis obtusata* (Michx.) Scribn. (66) (1903)

Tsakus tawirat (Pawnee) - *Monarda fistulosa L.* (37) (1919)

Tsewathe (Osage) - *Nelumbo lutea* Willd. (121) (1918?-1970?)

Tsherop (Winnebago) - *Nelumbo lutea* Willd. (37) (1919)

Tsinah (Snake) - *Cirsium eatonii* var. *eriocephalum* (A.Gray) D.J.Keil (101) (1905)

Tsinaw - *Smilax pseudochina* L. (181) (~1678) MT

Tsostu (Pawnee) - *Monarda fistulosa* L. (possibly) (37) (1919)

Tsue-u - *Liriodendron tulipifera* L. (186) (1814)

Tsusahtu (Pawnee, ill smelling) - *Monarda fistulosa* L. (37) (1919)

T'thai-a-mer' (Shawnee) - *Nicotiana* L. (132) (1855)

Tube flower [Tube-flower] - *Clerodendrum indicum* (L.) Kuntze (109) (1949)

Tube iris - *Iris macrosiphon* Torr. (138) (1923)

Tube penstemon - *Penstemon tubiflorus* Nutt. (3, 4, 138, 155) (1923-1986)

Tuber - *Lycoperdon tuber* L. (174) (1753)

Tuber anemone - *Anemone tuberosa* Rydb. (155) (1942)

Tuber aster - *Eurybia compacta* Nesom (5, 156) (1913-1923)

Tuber bulrush - *Schoenoplectus maritimus* (L.) Lye (141) (1899)

Tuber false dandelion - *Pyrrhopappus grandiflorus* (Nutt.) Nutt. (3, 4) (1977-1986) WY

Tuber jerusalem-sage [Tuber jerusalemsage] - *Phlomis tuberosa* L. (155) (1942)

Tuber oat grass [Tuber oatgrass] - *Arrhenatherum elatius* (L.) Beauv. ex J. Presl & C. Presl (138) (1923)

Tuber verbena - *Eclipta prostrata* (L.) L. (181) (~1678), *Verbena rigida* Spreng. (138) (1923)

Tuber-bearing waterlily [Tuber-bearing water lily] - *Nymphaea odorata* Aiton subsp. *tuberosa* (Paine) Wiersma & Hellquist (63) (1899)

Tubercled orchis - *Platanthera flava* (L.) Lindl. var. *flava* (5, 97, 156) (1913-1937)

Tubercled spike-rush - *Eleocharis tuberculosa* (Michx.) Roemer & J.A. Schultes (66) (1903)

Tubercled waterhemp [Tubercaled water-hemp] - *Amaranthus tuberculatus* (Moq.) Sauer (131) (1899)

Tuberculated cactus - *Escobaria vivipara* (Nutt.) Buxbaum var. *vivipara* (108) (1878)

Tuberous boletus - *Boletus tuberosus* Bull. (42) (1814)

Tuberous cup fungus - *Dumontinia tuberosa* (Bull.) L.M. Kohn (128) (1933)

Tuberous cyperus galingale - *Cyperus esculentus* L. (42) (1814)

Tuberous desert-chicory - *Pyrrhopappus grandiflorus* (Nutt.) Nutt. (50) (present)

Tuberous grasspink - *Calopogon tuberosus* (L.) B.S.P. var. *tuberosus* (50) (present)

Tuberous Indian plantain - *Arnoglossum plantagineum* Raf. (5, 72, 82, 93, 97, 122) (1907-1937)

Tuberous Jerusalem-sage [Tuberous Jerusalemsage] - *Phlomis tuberosa* L. (50) (present)

Tuberous moschatel - *Adoxa moschatellina* L. (19, 165) (1768-1840)

Tuberous sweet pea [Tuberous sweetpea] - *Lathyrus tuberosus* L. (50) (present)

Tuberous wall cress - *Cardamine bulbosa* (Schreber. ex Muhl.) B.S.P. (42) (1818)

Tuberous waterlily [Tuberous water-lily] - *Nymphaea odorata* Aiton subsp. *tuberosa* (Paine) Wiersma & Hellquist (109, 156) (1923-1949)

Tuberous white waterlily [Tuberous white water lily, Tuberous white water-lily] - *Nymphaea odorata* Aiton subsp. *tuberosa* (Paine) Wiersma & Hellquist (5, 72, 93, 97, 120) (1907-1938)

Tuberous wistaria - *Apios americana* Medik. (156) (1923)

Tuberous-root swallow-wort [Tuberous-rooted swallow-wort] - *Asclepias tuberosa* L. (186) (1814)

Tuber-root [Tuber-root, Tuberroot] - *Asclepias tuberosa* L. (5, 49, 64, 92, 107, 156, 157, 158) (1898-1929)

Tucaha (Southern tribes) - *Apios americana* Medik. (7) (1828)

Tuckah (Indian tribes) - *Peltandra* Raf. (7) (1828)

Tuckáh (Native American) - *Hexastylis virginica* (L.) Small (41) (1770)

Tuckaho [Tuckaho, Tuckahoe] - *Lycoperdon solidum* L. (103) (1871), *Nuphar lutea* (L.) Sm. subsp. *advena* (Aiton) Kartesz & Gandhi (156) (1923), *Pachyma* Fr. (7) (1828), *Peltandra virginica* (L.) Schott. (156, 181) (~1678-1923), *Tuber* P. Micheli ex F.H. Wigg. (possibly) (7) (1828), *Zamia pumila* L. (possibly) (10) (1818)

Tuckahoo - *Hexastylis virginica* (L.) Small (41) (1770), *Lycoperdon tuber* L. (177) (1762), *Pachyma* Fr. (7) (1828)

Tuckerman's pondweed - *Potamogeton confervoides* Reichb. (50) (present)

Tuckerman's quillwort - *Isoetes tuckermanii* A. Br. (5, 50) (1913-present)

Tuckerman's sedge - *Carex tuckermani* Dewey (5, 50, 66, 72) (1893-present)

Tuckerman's witch grass [Tuckerman witchgrass] - *Panicum philadelphicum* Bernh. ex Trin. (155) (1942)

Tuck-tuck - *Abies procera* Rehd. (20) (1857)

Tucky - *Nuphar lutea* (L.) Sm. subsp. *advena* (Aiton) Kartesz & Gandhi (156) (1923)

Tucky-lily - *Nuphar lutea* (L.) Sm. subsp. *advena* (Aiton) Kartesz & Gandhi (156) (1923)

Tufted beak-rush [Tufted beak rush] - *Rhynchospora knieskernii* Carey (66) (1903)

Tufted bulrush - *Trichophorum caespitosum* (L.) Hartman (50, 139) (1944-present)

Tufted buttercup - *Ranunculus fascicularis* Muhl. ex Bigelow (5, 97, 138, 155, 156, 158) (1900-1937)

Tufted club-rush [Tufted club rush] - *Trichophorum caespitosum* (L.) Hartman (5) (1913)

Tufted erigeron - *Erigeron caespitosus* Nutt. (5, 50, 93) (1913-present)

Tufted evening-primrose [Tufted eveningprimrose] - *Oenothera caespitosa* Nutt. (50, 138, 155) (1923-present)

Tufted fimbristylis - *Fimbristylis autumnalis* (L.) Roemer & J.A. Schultes (66) (1903)

Tufted fleabane - *Erigeron caespitosus* Nutt. (155) (1942)

Tufted goldenweed - *Stenotus acaulis* (Nutt.) Nutt. (155) (1942)

Tufted goosefoot [Tufted goose foot] - *Chenopodium simplex* (Torr.) Raf. (42) (1814)

Tufted grama - *Bouteloua simplex* Lag. (94) (1901)

Tufted hair grass [Tufted hair-grass] - *Deschampsia caespitosa* (L.) Beauv. (3, 5, 50, 56, 66, 90, 140, 155) (1885-present), *Deschampsia flexuosa* (L.) Trin. (94) (1901)

Tufted hedgehog cactus - *Echinocereus reichenbachii* (Terscheck ex Walp.) Haage f. (5) (1913)

Tufted hymenopappus - *Hymenopappus filifolius* Hook. (131) (1899)

Tufted loosestrife - *Lysimachia* L. (1, 158) (1900-1932), *Lysimachia thyrsiflora* L. (3, 4, 5, 50, 72, 85, 93, 95, 131, 156) (1899-present)

Tufted love grass [Tufted lovegrass] - *Eragrostis pectinacea* (Michx.) Nees ex Steud. (50) (present)

Tufted meadowsweet - *Petrophyton caespitosum* (Nutt.) Rydb. (131) (1899)

Tufted milkvetch [Tufted milk vetch] - *Astragalus spatulatus* Sheldon (3, 5, 50, 93, 127, 131) (1899-present) SD

Tufted milky vetch - *Astragalus spatulatus* Sheldon (85) (1932)

Tufted oxytropis - *Oxytropis multiceps* Nutt. (5) (1913)

Tufted peas [Tufted pease] - *Pisum sativum* L. (178) (1526)

Tufted rockmat - *Petrophyton caespitosum* (Nutt.) Rydb. (155) (1942)

Tufted rush - *Eleocharis compressa* Sullivant (66) (1903)

Tufted rye - *Dasypyrum villosum* (L.) P. Candargy (66) (1903)

Tufted sandwort - *Minuartia rubella* (Wahlenb.) Hiern. (138, 155) (1923-1942)

Tufted saxifrage - *Saxifraga caespitosa* L. subsp. *caespitosa* (5) (1913)

Tufted sedge - *Carex nigra* (L.) Reichard (5) (1913)

Tufted sharp-leaf gilia [Tufted sharp-leaved gilia] - *Linanthus caespitosus* (Nutt.) J. M. Porter & L. A. Johnson (5, 93) (1913–1936)

Tufted spear grass - *Poa secunda* J. Presl (5, 11) (1888-1913)

Tufted spike-rush - *Eleocharis diandra* C. Wright (possibly) (129) (1894)

Tufted tripleawn [Tufted triple-awn, Tufted triple awn] - *Aristida basiramea* Engelm. ex Vasey (94, 111) (1901-1915)

Tufted triple-awn grass [Tufted triple awn grass] - *Aristida basiramea* Engelm. ex Vasey (56) (1901)

Tufted vetch - *Vicia cracca* L. (3, 5, 19, 107, 158) (1840-1977)

Tufted-stem rush [Tuftedstem rush] - *Juncus brachyphyllus* Wieg. (50) (present)

Tuftroot - *Dieffenbachia* Schott (138) (1923)

Tufty bells - *Wahlenbergia* Schrad. ex Roth (109) (1949)

Tukawisi (Pawnee Skidi) - *Nuphar lutea* (L.) Sm. subsp. *advena* (Aiton) Kartesz & Gandhi (37) (1919)

Tukawiu (Pawnee) - *Nelumbo lutea* Willd. (37) (1919)

Tule - *Eleocharis palustris* (L.) Roemer & J.A. Schultes (156) (1923), *Schoenoplectus acutus* (Muhl. ex Bigelow) A.& D. Löve var. *occidentalis* (S. Wats.) S.G. Sm. (50) (present), *Schoenoplectus californicus* (C.A. Mey.) Palla (122) (1937), *Schoenoplectus tabernaemontani* (C.C. Gmel.) Palla (possibly) (75, 101, 107, 156) (1894-1923), *Scirpus* L. (1, 10, 93) (1818-1936)

Tulé (Spanish) - *Schoenoplectus tabernaemontani* (C.C. Gmel.) Palla (possibly) (161) (1857)

Tule bulrush - *Schoenoplectus acutus* (Muhl. ex Bigelow) A.& D. Löve var. *acutus* (155) (1942)

Tule potato - *Sagittaria latifolia* Willd. (157) (1929)

Tule root - *Sagittaria latifolia* Willd. (157) (1929), *Schoenoplectus tabernaemontani* (C.C. Gmel.) Palla (possibly) (103) (1871)

Tule-grass - *Schoenoplectus acutus* (Muhl. ex Bigelow) A.& D. Löve var. *occidentalis* (S. Wats.) S.G. Sm. (156) (1923)

Tulip - *Erythronium albidum* Nutt. (78) (1898), *Tulipa gesneriana* L. (92) (1876) MO, *Tulipa* L. (7, 50, 109, 138) (1828–present)

Tulip poplar - *Liriodendron tulipifera* L. (5, 7) (1828–1932)

Tulip poppy - *Papaver glaucum* Boiss. & Hausskn. (19, 138) (1840-1923)

Tulip prickly pear [Tulip pricklypear] - *Opuntia phaeacantha* Engelm. (50) (present)

Tulip tree [Tulip-tree, Tuliptree] - *Liriodendron* L. (8, 15, 138, 167) (1785-1923), *Liriodendron tulipifera* L. (2, 5, 7, 10, 12, 13, 14, 15, 20, 19, 41, 46, 49, 57, 82, 92, 106, 107, 109, 138, 156, 181, 182, 186, 187, 189, 190) (~1678-1949)

Tulip-poplar - *Liriodendron tulipifera* L. (106, 156) (1923-1930)

Tulpboom - *Liriodendron tulipifera* L. (186) (1814)

Tulpinbaum - *Liriodendron tulipifera* L. (186) (1814)

Tumble grass [Tumble-grass, Tumblegrass] - *Panicum capillare* L. (2, 56) (1895-1901), *Panicum* L. (1, 93) (1932-1936), *Schedonnardus paniculatus* (Nutt.) Trel. (3, 50, 122, 140, 155) (1937–present), *Schedonnardus* Steud. (50, 155) (1942–present)

Tumble love grass [Tumble lovegrass] - *Eragrostis sessilispica* Buckl. (3, 50, 155) (1942–present)

Tumble ringwing - *Cycloloma atriplicifolium* (Spreng.) Coult. (4, 155) (1942-1986)

Tumble windmill grass [Tumble windmillgrass] - *Chloris verticillata* Nutt. (50, 155) (1942–present)

Tumble-mustard [Tumble mustard, Tumblemustard] - *Sisymbrium altissimum* L. (155) (1942), *Sisymbrium* L. (1, 93) (1932-1936)

Tumbleweed [Tumble weed, Tumble-weed] - *Amaranthus albus* L. (possibly) (3, 4, 5, 62, 70, 72, 77, 80, 85, 93, 95, 97, 122, 131, 145, 156, 158) (1895-1986), *Amaranthus* L. (1, 93) (1932-1936), *Anemone cylindrica* Gray (156) (1923), *Anemone virginiana* L. (5) (1913), *Corispermum americanum* (Nutt.) Nutt. var. *rydbergii* Mo-

syakin (5, 93, 156, 158) (1900-1936), *Cycloloma atriplicifolium* (Spreng.) Coult. (5, 93, 96, 156) (1891-1936), *Cycloloma* Moq. (1, 158) (1900-1932), *Panicum capillare* L. (5, 62, 119) (1912-1938), *Psoralidium lanceolatum* (Pursh) Rydb. (5, 93) (1913-1936), *Salsola collina* Pallas (4) (1986), *Salsola kali* L. (156) (1923), *Salsola tragus* L. (4) (1986)

Tumbleweed amaranth - *Amaranthus albus* L. (possibly) (155) (1942)

Tumbling mustard - *Sisymbrium altissimum* L. (4, 62, 63, 80, 98, 131, 156) (1899-1986)

Tumbling orach - *Atriplex rosea* L. (155) (1942)

Tumbling pigweed - *Amaranthus albus* L. (possibly) (80) (1913)

Tumbling salt-sage - *Atriplex argentea* Nutt. (141) (1899) IA

Tumbling saltweed - *Atriplex rosea* L. (50) (present) WY

Tuna - *Opuntia fragilis* (Nutt.) Haw. (5) (1913)

Tuna [Tunas] (Spanish) - *Opuntia ficus-indica* (L.) Mill. (110) (1886), *Opuntia* Mill. (103) (1870), *Opuntia polyacantha* Haw. (101) (1905)

Tung-oil tree [Tung-oil-tree, Tungoiltree] - *Verbesina virginica* L. var. *virginica* (174, 177) (1753-1762), *Vernicia fordii* (Hemsl.) Airy Shaw (109, 138, 155) (1923-1949)

Tunhoof [Tun hoof] - *Glechoma hederacea* L. (5, 92, 156) (1876-1923)

Tunic flower [Tunic-flower, Tunicflower] - *Petrorhagia* (Ser.) Link (138) (1923), *Petrorhagia saxifraga* (L.) Link (109) (1949)

Tunja (Slavic) - *Cydonia oblonga* Mill. (110) (1886)

Tupélo (French) - *Nyssa* L. (8) (1785)

Tupélo aquatique (French) - *Nyssa aquatica* L. (8) (1785)

Tupélo de montagne (French) - *Nyssa sylvatica* Marsh. (8) (1785)

Tupelo gum (Tupelo-gum) - *Nyssa aquatica* L. (5, 106, 109, 156) (1913-1949)

Tupélo ogeche (French) - *Nyssa ogeche* Bartr. ex Marsh. (8) (1785)

Tupelo or Tupelo tree [Tupelo-tree] - *Nyssa aquatica* L. (14, 20, 41, 177, 189) (1762-1882), *Nyssa biflora* Walt. (14) (1882), *Nyssa* L. (2, 7, 8, 10, 109, 138, 182, 184) (1785-1949), *Nyssa ogeche* Bartr. ex Marsh. (14, 17) (1796-1882), *Nyssa sylvatica* Marsh. (5, 14, 19, 34, 92, 106, 138, 156) (1834-1930)

Tupilo - *Nyssa ogeche* Bartr. ex Marsh. (183) (~1756)

Tuppuhguam-ash (Algonquin "twiners") - *Phaseolus vulgaris* L. (107) (1919)

Turban - *Tulipa* L. (180) (1633)

Turban lily - *Lilium martagon* L. (107) (1919)

Turban nouveau du Brésil (French) - *Cucurbita maxima* Dcne. (107) (1856)

Turban rouge (French) - *Cucurbita maxima* Dcne. (107) (1856)

Turban squash [Turban squashes] - *Cucurbita maxima* Dcne. (107, 109) (1919-1949)

Turfan - *Tulipa* L. (180) (1633)

Turfy aira grass [Turfy aira-grass] - *Deschampsia caespitosa* (L.) Beauv. (165) (1768)

Turion duckweed - *Lemna turionifera* Landolt (50) (present)

Turkestan bluestem - *Bothriochloa ischaemum* (L.) Keng var. *songarica* (Rupr. ex Fisch. & C.A. Mey.) Celarier & Harlan (3) (1977)

Turkestan millet - *Setaria italica* (L.) Beauv. (109, 119) (1938-1949)

Turkestan rose - *Rosa rugosa* Thunb. (107) (1919)

Turkestan thistle - *Rhaponticum repens* (L.) Hidalgo (3, 122) (1937-1977)

Turkey balm [Turkie balme] - *Dracocephalum moldavica* L. (178) (1526)

Turkey bur [Turkeybur, Turkey-bur] - *Arctium lappa* L. (158) (1900)

Turkey corn [Turkey-corn, Turkie Corne, Turky Corne] - *Dicentra canadensis* (Goldie) Walp. (5, 49, 52, 53, 57, 58, 92, 93, 156, 157) (1869-1936), *Dicentra eximia* (Ker-Gawl.) Torr. (5, 156) (1913-1923), *Zea mays* L. (158, 180) (1633-1900)

Turkey grape - *Vitis aestivalis* Michx. var. *lincecumii* (Buckl.) Munson (15, 107) (1895-1919)

Turkey grass - *Muhlenbergia mexicana* (L.) Trin. (80) (1913)

Turkey hirsse [Turkie hirsse] - *Sorghum bicolor* (L.) Moench (180) (1633)

Turkey mill - *Sorghum bicolor* (L.) Moench (180) (1633)

Turkey millet [Turkie millet] - *Sorghum bicolor* (L.) Moench subsp. *bicolor* (178) (1596), *Sorghum bicolor* (L.) Moench (180) (1633)

Turkey mullein - *Croton setigerus* Hook. (75, 106) (1894-1930)

Turkey oak - *Quercus falcata* Michx. (5, 156) (1913-1923) Santa Barbara Co. CA, *Quercus laevis* Walt. (2) (1895), *Quercus stellata* Wangenh. (5, 156) (1913-1923)

Turkey pea - *Dicentra canadensis* (Goldie) Walp. (5, 92, 157) (1876-1929)

Turkey peak - *Tephrosia virginiana* (L.) Pers (157) (1929)

Turkey wheat [Turky wheat] - *Zea mays* L. (158, 180) (1633-1900)

Turkey-apple hawthorn [Turkeyapple hawthorn] - *Crataegus mollis* Scheele (155) (1942) archaic

Turkey-beard [Turkeysbeard, Turkey beard] - *Xerophyllum asphodeloides* (L.) Nutt. (5, 78, 138, 156) (1898-1923), *Xerophyllum* Michx. (109, 138) (1923-1949)

Turkey-berry [Turkey berry] - *Solanum mammosum* L. (92) (1876), *Symphoricarpos symphoricarpos* (L.) MacMill. (5, 156, 157, 158) (1900-1929)

Turkey-berry tree [Turkey berry tree] - *Cordia collococca* L. (92) (1876)

Turkey-bur seed [Turkey bur seed, Turkeybur-seed] - *Arctium lappa* L. (2) (1895)

Turkey-claw [Turkey claw] - *Corallorrhiza odontorhiza* (Willd.) Poir. (5, 64, 92, 156, 158) (1900-1923)

Turkey-foot [Turkey foot, Turkeyfoot] - *Andropogon gerardii* Vitman (45, 140, 144, 163) (1852-1944), *Andropogon hallii* Hack. (75, 140) (1894-1944), *Erigenia bulbosa* (Michx.) Nutt. (156) (1923)

Turkey-foot grass [Turkeyfoot grass, Turkey-foot-grass] - *Andropogon gerardii* Vitman (129) (1894), *Andropogon hallii* Hack. (5, 56, 119, 122, 131) (1899-1938)

Turkey-grass [Turkey grass] - *Galium aparine* L. (5, 156, 157, 158) (1900-1929)

Turkey-pea [Turkey pea] - *Dicentra canadensis* (Goldie) Walp. (156) (1923), *Erigenia bulbosa* (Michx.) Nutt. (5, 73, 75, 76, 156, 158) (1892-1923), *Erigenia* Nutt. (1) (1932) OH, *Tephrosia* Pers. (7) (1828), *Tephrosia virginiana* (L.) Pers (5, 49, 86, 102, 156, 158) (1878-1923)

Turkeypod [Turkey pod, Turkey-pod] - *Arabidopsis thaliana* (L.) Britton (5, 156) (1913-1923) Southern US, *Arabis* L. (42, 184) (1793-1814)

Turkey-tangle fogfruit [Turkey tangle fogfruit] - *Phyla nodiflora* (L.) Greene (50) (present)

Turkey-troop [Turkey troop] - *Polygonum punctatum* Ell. (5, 157, 158) (1900-1929), *Polygonum punctatum* Ell. var. *punctatum* (73, 156) (1892-1923)

Turkish bean - *Phaseolus vulgaris* L. (possibly) (110) (16th century)

Turkish corn [Turkish korn] - *Zea mays* L. (92, 107) (1552-1876)

Turkish oak - *Quercus cerris* L. (107) (1919)

Turkish pepper - *Capsicum annuum* L. (107) (1919)

Turkish tulip - *Tulipa gesneriana* L. (109) (1949)

Turk's-cap [Turk's cap, Turkscap] - *Aconitum napellus* L. (107, 156) (1919-1923), *Aquilegia canadensis* L. (156) (1923), *Lilium martagon* L. (92, 107) (1876-1919), *Lilium superbum* L. (107) (1919), *Melocactus* Link & Otto (92) (1876), *Tulipa* L. (180) (1633)

Turk's-cap cactus - *Melocactus intortus* (Mill.) Urb. (107) (1919)

Turk's-cap lily [Turk's cap lily, Turkscap lily] - *Lilium martagon* L. (92, 109) (1876-1949), *Lilium michiganense* Farw. (3) (1977), *Lilium superbum* L. (5, 6, 50, 72, 155, 158) (1874-present)

Turk's-head [Turk's-head, Turks-head] - *Escobaria vivipara* (Nutt.) Buxbaum var. *vivipara* (108) (1878), *Lilium superbum* L. (73, 156) (1892-1923)

Turk's-head lily [Turk's head lily] - *Lilium superbum* L. (5, 158) (1900-1913) MA

Turk's-turban [Turks-turban] - *Clerodendrum indicum* (L.) Kuntze (109) (1949)

Turlbay - *Sideroxylon* L. (7) (1828)

Turmeric - *Sanguinaria canadensis* L. (6, 7, 64, 156, 158) (1828-1923)

Turmeric root [Turmeric-root] - *Hydrastis canadensis* L. (5, 6, 19) (1840-1913)

Turnera - *Turnera diffusa* Willd. ex J. A. Schultes (57) (1917)

Turnesole - *Roccella tinctoria* DC. (49) (1898)

Turnip [Turnep, Turnips] - *Brassica* L. (1, 106, 107, 156) (1919-1932), *Brassica rapa* L. (7, 19, 82, 92, 109, 155, 156) (1828-1942), *Brassica rapa* L. var. *rapa* (5, 15, 72, 85, 97, 107, 145, 180) (1633-1895)

Turnip cole [Turnep cole] - *Brassica oleracea* L. (178) (1526)

Turnip-chervil - *Chaerophyllum bulbosum* L. (138) (1923)

Turnip-of-the-plains [Turnip of the plains] - *Pediomelum esculentum* (Pursh) Rydb. (33) (1827)

Turnip-root chervil [Turnip-rooted chervil] - *Chaerophyllum bulbosum* L. (109) (1949)

Turnip-weed [Turnip weed, Turni-weed] - *Eupatorium purpureum* L. (106, 156) (1923-1930)

Turnpike-geranium [Turnpike geranium] - *Chenopodium botrys* L. (5, 156, 157, 158) (1900-1929)

Turnsole - *Euphorbia helioscopia* L. (5, 156) (1913-1923), *Heliotropium europaeum* L. (156) (1923), *Heliotropium indicum* L. (3, 5, 19, 92) (1840-1977), *Heliotropium* L. (10, 158) (1818-1900)

Turpentine - *Trichostema lanceolatum* Benth. (156) (1923)

Turpentine bush - *Ericameria laricifolia* (Gray) Shinners (52) (1919)

Turpentine pine - *Pinus palustris* Mill. (5) (1913)

Turpentine plant [Turpentine-plant] - *Silphium laciniatum* L. (156) (1882-1923)

Turpentine sunflower - *Silphium* L. (7) (1828), *Silphium terebinthinaceum* Jacq. (156) (1923)

Turpentine-weed [Turpentine weed] - *Silphium laciniatum* L. (5, 156) (1913-1923)

Turpeth root - *Operculina turpethum* (L.) J. Silva Manso (92) (1876)

Turrets - *Carex nigra* (L.) Reichard (5) (1913)

Turtle bloom [Turtlebloom, Turtle-bloom] - *Chelone glabra* L. (5, 7, 53, 58, 92, 156) (1828-1923)

Turtle-grass [Turtle grass] - *Zostera marina* L. (5, 92, 156) (1876-1923)

Turtle-head [Turtlehead, Turtle head] - *Chelone glabra* L. (5, 6, 7, 53, 86, 92, 156) (1828-1923), *Chelone* L. (1, 2, 63, 109, 138, 156) (1895-1949)

Turtleweed - *Batis maritima* L. (50) (present) from shape of flower

Tuscarora rice - *Zizania aquatica* L. (67, 187) (1818-1890)

Tussock bellflower - *Campanula carpatica* Jacq. (109) (1949)

Tussock grass [Tussockgrass] - *Nassella* (Trin.) Desv. (50) (present)

Tussock sedge - *Carex stricta* Lam. (5, 72, 86, 156) (1878-1907)

Tussocks - *Agrostis gigantea* Roth (5) (1913)

Tut (Pawnee Chawi) - *Nuphar lutea* (L.) Sm. subsp. *advena* (Aiton) Kartesz & Gandhi (37) (1919)

Tut'kag-minan (Chippewa) - *Rubus odoratus* L. (105) (1932)

Tutsan - *Androsaemum officinale* All. (92) (1876), *Hypericum androsaemum* L. (109, 178) (1596-1949), *Hypericum perforatum* L. (156) (1923)

Tutsan-leaf dogbane [Tutsan-leaved dogbane] - *Apocynum androsaemifolium* L. (156) (1923)

Twayblade [Tway blade, Tway-blade] - *Liparis* L.C. Rich. (1, 109, 138) (1923-1949), *Liparis liliifolia* (L.) L.C. Rich. ex Ker-Gawl. (19) (1840), *Liparis loeselii* (L.) L.C. Rich (93, 122) (1936-1937), *Listera convallarioides* (Sw.) Nutt. ex Ell. (3, 5) (1913-1977)

Tweedy poplar - *Populus angustifolia* James (155) (1942)

Twi-foil - *Listera cordata* (L.) R. Br. ex Ait. f. var. *cordata* (5) (1913)

Twig goldenrod [Twig golden-rod] - *Solidago sempervirens* L. (19) (1840)

Twig rush [Twig-rush] - *Cladium mariscoides* (Muhl.) Torr. (5, 156) (1913-1923), *Cladium* P. Br. (1) (1932)

Twigwithy - *Salix viminalis* L. (5, 156) (1913-1923)

Twin arnica - *Arnica sororia* Greene (50) (present)

Twin bent grass [Twin bentgrass] - *Agrostis scabra* Willd. (5) (1913)

Twin flower [Twinflower, Twin-flower] - *Linnaea borealis* L. (3, 4, 5, 7, 19, 50, 72, 92, 109, 131, 156, 158) (1828–present), *Linnaea* L. (1, 2, 4, 50, 138, 155, 156, 158) (1895–present), *Pulsatilla patens* (L.) Mill. (37) (1919)

Twin grass [Twingrass] - *Agrostis perennans* (Walt.) Tuckerman (5) (1913), *Diarrhena americana* Beauv. (56, 66) (1901-1903)

Twinberry [Twin-berry, Twin berry] - *Lonicera involucrata* Banks ex Spreng. (101) (1905), *Lonicera* L. (1) (1932) MT, *Lonicera villosa* (Michx.) J.A. Schultes var. *solonis* (Eat.) Fern. (19) (1840), *Mitchella* L. (1) (1932), *Mitchella repens* L. (5, 97, 109, 156) (1913-1949), *Xanthium strumarium* L. var. *canadense* (Mill.) Torr. & Gray (177) (1762)

Twine vine [Twinevine] - *Funastrum* Fourn. (4, 50) (1986–present)

Twin-flower Solomon's-seal [Twin-flower Solomon's seal, Twin-flowered Solomon's-seal] - *Polygonatum biflorum* (Walt.) Ell. (158) (1900)

Twinfoil - *Listera cordata* (L.) R. Br. ex Ait. f. (156) (1923)

Twining dolicholus - *Rhynchosia difformis* (Ell.) DC. (5, 97) (1913-1937)

Twining large-fruit tragia [Twining large-fruited tragia] - *Tragia cordata* Michx. (5) (1913)

Twining sumac [Twining sumach] - *Toxicodendron radicans* (L.) Kuntze subsp. *radicans* (41) (1770)

Twinkling cassia - *Chamaecrista nictitans* (L.) Moench subsp. *nictitans* var. *nictitans* (86) (1878)

Twinkling senna - *Chamaecrista nictitans* (L.) Moench subsp. *nictitans* var. *nictitans* (86) (1878)

Twinleaf [Twin leaf, twin-leaf] - *Jeffersonia* Bart. (15, 138) (1895-1923), *Jeffersonia diphylla* (L.) Pers. (2, 5, 13, 19, 49, 53, 57, 61, 64, 92, 109, 138, 156) (1840-1949)

Twin-leaf saxifrage [Twinleaf saxifrage] - *Saxifraga oppositifolia* L. (138) (1923)

Twinpod - *Physaria* (Nutt. ex Torr. & Gray) Gray (50, 155) (1942–present)

Twinroot - *Dactylorhiza* Neck. ex Nevski (possibly) (7) (1828)

Twin-sisters [Twin sisters] - *Lonicera tatarica* L. (75) (1894)

Twin-spike grass [Twin spike grass] - *Spartina maritima* (M.A. Curtis) Fern. (5) (1913) La Crosse WI

Twist flower [Twist-flower, Twistflower] - *Streptanthus* Nutt. (4, 155) (1942-1986)

Twisted acacia - *Acacia tortuosa* (L.) Willd. (155) (1942)

Twisted beard grass [Twisted beard-grass] - *Heteropogon contortus* (L.) Beauv. ex Roemer & J.A. Schultes (94) (1901)

Twisted heath - *Erica cinerea* L. (109, 138) (1923-1949)

Twisted lady's--tresses [Twisted ladies'-tresses] - *Spiranthes vernalis* Engelm. & Gray (3) (1977)

Twisted pine - *Pinus contorta* Dougl. ex Loud. (161) (1857)

Twisted rib - Thelocactus setispinus (Engelm.) E.F. Anderson (109) (1949)

Twisted sedge - *Carex torta* Boott. ex Tuckerman (5, 50) (1913–present)

Twisted spike-rush [Twisted spike rush] - *Eleocharis tuberculosa* (Michx.) Roemer & J.A. Schultes (5) (1913)

Twisted sundrop - *Camissonia bistorta* (Nutt. ex Torr. & Gray) Raven (138) (1923)

Twisted whitlow-grass [Twisted whitlow grass] - *Draba incana* L. (5) (1913)

Twisted yellow-eyed grass - *Xyris caroliniana* Walt. (5) (1913)

Twisted-branch pine [Twisted-branched pine] - *Pinus contorta* Dougl. ex Loud. (20) (1857)

Twisted-leaf goldenrod [Twisted-leaf golden-rod] - *Solidago tortifolia* Ell. (5, 97) (1913-1937)

Twisted-leaf yucca [Twistedleaf yucca] - *Yucca rupicola* Scheele (122, 124) (1937)

Twisted-spine cactus - *Opuntia macrorhiza* Engelm. var. *macrorhiza* (5, 97) (1913–1937)

Twisted-stalk [Twistedstalk, Twisted stalk] - *Disporum lanuginosum* (Michx.) Nichols (156) (1923), *Spiranthes lacera* (Raf.) Raf. var. *gracilis* (Bigelow) Luer (5, 75, 156) (1894–1923), *Streptopus amplexifolius* (L.) DC. (85, 156) (1923–1932) WV, *Streptopus lanceolatus* (Ait.) Reveal var. *roseus* (Michx.) Reveal (40, 50, 156) (1923–present), *Uvularia* L. (1, 109, 138, 155, 158) (1900–1949)

Twist-leaf goldenrod [Twistleaf goldenrod] - *Solidago tortifolia* Ell. (122) (1937)

Twist-spine prickly pear [Twistspine pricklypear, Twist-spine pricklypear] - *Opuntia macrorhiza* Engelm. (50) (present), *Opuntia macrorhiza* Engelm. var. *macrorhiza* (50, 155) (1942–present)

Twitch grass [Twitch-grass] - *Elymus repens* (L.) Gould (5, 45, 64, 66, 69, 78, 87, 90, 92, 157, 158) (1884–1929)

Two-cloak onion [Twocloak onion] - *Allium dichlamydeum* Greene (155) (1942)

Two-color amaranth [Two-coloured amaranth] - *Amaranthus tricolor* L. (165) (1768)

Two-color coneflower [Two-colored cone-flower] - *Rudbeckia bicolor* Nutt. (97) (1937)

Two-color feather grass [Two-coloured feather-grass] - *Piptochaetium bicolor* (Vahl) É. Desv. (187) (1818)

Two-edge blue-eyed grass [Two-edged blue-eyed grass] - *Sisyrinchium angustifolium* Mill. (187) (1818)

Two-edge panic grass [Two-edged panic grass, Two-edged panic-grass] - *Panicum anceps* Michx. (87, 187) (1818–1884)

Two-edge sedge [Two-edged sedge] - *Carex laxiflora* Lam. var. *laxiflora* (5, 66, 187) (1818–1913)

Two-eyed berry [Two-eyed berries, Two-eyes berry, Two-eye berry] - *Linnaea borealis* L. (5, 73, 156, 158) (1892–1923), *Mitchella repens* L. (73, 156) (1892–1923) St. Stephen NB

Two-eyed chequer-berry - *Mitchella repens* L. (6) (1892)

Two-eyes plum - *Mitchella repens* L. (76) (1896)

Two-flower bladderwort [Two-flowered bladderwort] - *Utricularia gibba* L. (5, 72, 97, 122, 156) (1907–1937) Oxford Co. ME

Two-flower dwarf-dandelion [Twoflower dwarfdandelion] - *Krigia biflora* (Walt.) Blake (50) (present), *Krigia biflora* (Walt.) Blake var. *biflora* (50) (present)

Two-flower melic [Two flower melic, Twoflower melic, Two-flowered melic] - *Melica mutica* Walt. (3, 122, 155) (1937–1977)

Two-flower melic grass [Twoflower melicgrass] - *Melica mutica* Walt. (3, 50) (1977–present)

Two-flower milkvine [Two-flowered milkvine] - *Matelea biflora* (Raf.) Woods (4) (1986)

Two-flower rush [Two-flowered rush] - *Juncus biglumis* L. (5, 50) (1913–present)

Two-flower violet [Twoflower violet] - *Viola viarum* Pollard (50) (present)

Two-grain wheat [Two-grained wheat] - *Triticum turgidum* L. (107) (1919)

Two-groove loco [Twogrooved loco] - *Astragalus bisulcatus* (Hook.) Gray (155) (1942)

Two-groove milkvetch [Twogrooved milkvetch, Two-grooved milk vetch, Two-grooved milkvetch] - *Astragalus bisulcatus* (Hook.) Gray (3, 4, 50, 93, 97, 126, 148) (1933–present), *Astragalus bisulcatus* (Hook.) Gray var. *bisulcatus* (50) (present)

Two-head water-starwort [Twoheaded water-starwort] - *Callitriche heterophylla* Pursh (50) (present), *Callitriche heterophylla* Pursh subsp. *heterophylla* (50) (present)

Two-leaf bishop's-cap [Two-leaved bishop's cap, Two-leaved bishop's-cap] - *Mitella diphylla* L. (5, 72, 156) (1907–1923)

Two-leaf convallary [Two-leaved convallary] - *Maianthemum canadense* Desf. (187) (1818)

Two-leaf miterwort [Two-leaved miterwort] - *Mitella diphylla* L. (2) (1895)

Two-leaf senna [Twoleaf senna, Two-leaved senna] - *Senna roemeriana* (Scheele) Irwin & Barneby (4, 50) (1986–present)

Two-leaf small Solomon's-seal [Two leaved small Solomon's seal] - *Maianthemum dilatatum* (Wood) A. Nels. & J.F. Macbr. (42) (1814)

Two-leaf Solomon's-seal [Two-leaved Solomon's seal, Two-leaf Solomon's seal] - *Maianthemum canadense* Desf. (5, 72, 73, 156, 158) (1892–1923), *Maianthemum* G. H. Weber ex Wiggers (1) (1932)

Two-leaf toothwort [Two-leaved toothwort, Two leaved tooth wort] - *Cardamine diphylla* (Michx.) Wood (2, 5, 42, 72) (1814-1913)

Two-leaf Virginia pine [Two-leaved Virginian pine] - *Pinus virginiana* Mill. (8) (1785)

Two-leaf water-milfoil [Twoleaf watermilfoil] - *Myriophyllum heterophyllum* Michx. (50) (present)

Two-leaf waterweed [Twoleaf waterweed] - *Elodea bifoliata* St. John (50) (present)

Two-lips [Two lips] - *Cypripedium acaule* Ait. (5, 156) (1913–1923)

Two-lobe larkspur [Twolobe larkspur] - *Delphinium nuttallianum* Pritz ex. Walp. (50) (present)

Two-lobe speedwell [Twolobe speedwell] - *Veronica biloba* L. (50) (present)

Two-needle pinyon [Twoneedle pinyon] - *Pinus edulis* Engelm. (50) (present)

Two-penny-grass [Two-penny grass] - *Lysimachia nummularia* L. (5, 92, 156, 158) (1876–1923)

Two-row barley [Tworow barley, Two rowed barley, Two-rowed barley, Two-rowed barley] - *Hordeum vulgare* L. (56, 66, 67, 110, 155, 158) (1890–1942)

Two-row stonecrop - *Sedum spurium* M. Bieb. (138) (1923)

Two-scale saltbush [Twoscale saltbush] - *Atriplex micrantha* Ledeb. (50) (present)

Two-seed sedge [Two-seeded sedge] - *Carex disperma* Dewey (66) (1903)

Two-tip sedge [Two-tipped sedge] - *Carex lachenalii* Schk. (50) (present)

Two-tooth milkvetch [Two-toothed milk vetch] - *Astragalus bisulcatus* (Hook.) Gray (5) (1913)

Two-tooth pepper root [Two-toothed pepper root] - *Cardamine diphylla* (Michx.) Wood (5) (1913)

Two-wing fruited halesia [Two-winged fruited halesia] - *Halesia carolina* L. (8) (1785)

Two-wing halesia [Two-winged halesia] - *Halesia carolina* L. (2) (1895)

Two-wing silverbell - *Halesia carolina* L. (138) (1923)

Tyetts - *Avena sativa* L. (158) (1900)

Tyrol knapweed - *Centaurea nigrescens* Willd. (5) (1913)

Tyrolean iris - *Iris pallida* subsp. *cengialti* (Ambrosi ex A.Kern.) Foster (138) (1923)

Tzue-u - *Liriodendron tulipifera* L. (186) (1814)

Tzue-u or Tulip poplar, *Liriodendron tulipifera* L.
(J.C. Krauss, 1840)

U

Ubatim (Brazil) - *Zea mays* L. (107) (1550)

Ubi (Pacific Isles) - *Dioscorea alata* L. (110) (1886)

Uchu (Peru) - *Capsicum annuum* L. var. *annuum* (107) (1532)

Udarea (Basque) - *Pyrus communis* L. (110) (1886)

U'ga-atasgi'skĭ (Cherokee, the pus oozes out) - *Chamaesyce hypericifolia* (L.) Millsp. (102) (1886)

Uggurits (Estonian) - *Cucumis sativus* L. (110) (1886)

Uinta sandwort - *Arenaria kingii* (S. Wats.) M.E. Jones (155) (1942)

Ukkurits (Estonian) - *Cucumis sativus* L. (110) (1886)

Ulim - *Ulex europaeus* L. (5) (1913)

Uma (Dakota) - *Corylus americana* Walt. (37) (1919)

Umbel - *Cypripedium parviflorum* Salisb. var. *pubescens* (Willd.) Knight (49, 58) (1869–1898)

Umbel root [Umbil root, Umbil-root] - *Cypripedium reginae* Walt. (64, 158) (1900–1908)

Umbellate marsh penny-wort - *Hydrocotyle umbellata* L. (5) (1913)

Umbellated pyrola - *Chimaphila* Pursh (10) (1818), *Chimaphila umbellata* (L.) Bart. (8) (1785)

Umbellated pyrola - *Pyrola americana* Sweet (5) (1913)

Umbelled penny-wort - *Hydrocotyle umbellata* L. (187) (1818)

Umbell-flower starwort [Umbelled-flowered star-wort] - *Doellingeria umbellata* (P. Mill.) Nees var. *umbellata* (187) (1818)

Umbel-like sedge - *Carex umbellata* Schkuhr ex Willd. (5) (1913)

Umbel-spike sedge [Umbel-spiked sedge] - *Carex umbellata* Schkuhr ex Willd. (66) (1903)

Umbil - *Cypripedium* L. (92) (1876?)

Umbrella china - *Melia azedarach* L. (122, 124) (1937)

Umbrella flatsedge - *Cyperus diandrus* Torr. (50) (present) TX

Umbrella magnolia - *Magnolia tripetala* L. (5) (1913)

Umbrella moss - *Splachnum ampullaceum* Hedw. (19) (1840)

Umbrella plant [Umbrella-plant] - *Agastache foeniculum* (Pursh) Kuntze (40) (1928), *Cyperus involucratus* Rottb. (109) (1949), *Darmera peltata* (Torr. ex Benth.) Voss (109) (1949), *Eriogonum annuum* Nutt. (85, 98) (1926–1932), *Eriogonum* Michx. (1, 93) (1932–1936), *Mirabilis nyctaginea* (Michx.) MacM. (80) (1913) Neb, *Podophyllum peltatum* L. (64, 156, 158) (1900–1923) IA

Umbrella saxifrage - *Darmera peltata* (Torr. ex Benth.) Voss (138) (1923)

Umbrella tree [Umbrella-tree] - *Cornus alternifolia* L. f. (5, 156) (1913-1923), *Magnolia tripetala* L. (2, 5, 8, 10, 13, 14, 15, 20, 19, 49, 92, 97, 109, 156, 184) (1785–1949), *Magnolia virginiana* L. (177, 189) (1762–1767), *Melia azedarach* L. (153) (1913)

Umbrella-grass [Umbrella grass] - *Fuirena* Rottb. (1, 93) (1932–1936) NM, *Fuirena squarrosa* Michx. (5, 19, 66, 156) (1840–1913)

Umbrella-leaf [Umbrellaleaf, Umbrella leaf] - *Diphylleia cymosa* Michx. (5, 138, 156) (1913–1923), *Diphylleia* Michx. (138) (1923), *Petasites hybridus* (L.) G. Gaertn., B. Mey. & Scherb. (156, 158) (1900–1923)

Umbrella-sedge [Umbrella sedge] - *Cyperus involucratus* Rottb. (138) (1923), *Fuirena* Rottb. (50) (present)

Umbrella-wort [Umbrella wort] - *Allionia* L. (1, 93, 158) (1900–1936), *Mirabilis linearis* (Pursh) Heimerl (85) (1932), *Mirabilis nyctaginea* (Michx.) MacM. (156) (1923)

Unarmed brome grass - *Bromus inermis* Leyss. (152) (1912)

Unaste'tstiyû (Cherokee, very small root) - *Aristolochia serpentaria* L. (102) (1886)

Unbearded wheat - *Triticum aestivum* L. (158) (1900)

Unchela (Dakota) - *Opuntia humifusa* (Raf.) Raf. (37) (1919), fruit was called Unchela taspun

Uncum - *Packera aurea* (L.) A. & D. Löve (2, 158) (1895–1900)

Uncum-piuncum - *Packera aurea* (L.) A. & D. Löve (156) (1923)

Underwood's moonwort - *Botrychium lunaria* (L.) Sw. (5) (1913)

Underwood's spike-moss [Underwood's spikemoss] - *Selaginella underwoodii* Hieron. (4, 50) (1986–present)

Undulated custard-apple [Undulated custard apple] - *Annona squamosa* L. (165) (1807)

Undulated soursop [Undulated sour sop] - *Annona squamosa* L. (165) (1807)

Unicorn - *Aletris farinosa* L. (92, 156) (1876–1923), *Amianthium muscitoxicum* (Walt.) Gray (29) (1869), *Chamaelirium luteum* (L.) A. Gray (58) (1869)

Unicorn plant [Unicorn-plant, Unicornplant] - *Aletris farinosa* L. (64, 156) (1908–1923), *Chamaelirium luteum* (L.) A. Gray (6, 156) (1892–1923), *Martynia* L. (2, 138) (1895–1923), *Proboscidea louisianica* (Mill.) Thell. subsp. *fragrans* (Lindl.) Bretting (92, 103) (1870–1876), *Proboscidea louisianica* (P. Mill.) Thellung (4, 5, 19, 38, 63, 72, 85, 92, 93, 97, 107, 122, 156, 158) (1820–1986), *Proboscidea* Schmidel (possibly) (1, 4, 50, 109) (1932–present)

Unicorn root [Unicorn-root] - *Aletris farinosa* L. (5, 6, 7, 19, 64, 92) (1828–1913), *Chamaelirium luteum* (L.) A. Gray (5, 52, 53, 61, 64) (1870–1922)

Unicorn-horn [Unicorn's horn, Unicorns' horn, Unicorn horn] - *Aletris farinosa* L. (5, 64) (1908–1913), *Chamaelirium luteum* (L.) A. Gray (5, 64, 92) (1876–1913)

Union grass - *Chasmanthium laxum* (L.) Yates (5) (1913)

Uniseme deltine (French) - *Pontederia cordata* L. (7) (1828)

Universe - *Arctostaphylos uva-ursi* (L.) Spreng. (6) (1892)

Universe vine [Universe-vine] - *Arctostaphylos uva-ursi* (L.) Spreng. (5, 92, 156) (1898–1923)

Unkum - *Packera aurea* (L.) A. & D. Löve (6, 58, 92, 158) (1869–1900)

Ûŋlĕ Ukĭ'ltĭ (Cherokee, the locust frequents it) - *Porteranthus stipulatus* (Muhl. ex Willd.) Britt. (102) (1886)

Unlucky tree - *Pinus banksiana* Lamb. (5, 75) (1894–1913)

Ûŋnagéi (Cherokee, black) - *Senna marilandica* (L.) Link (102) (1886) Adirondacks, unlucky especially for women to stand under this tree

Unshoe-the-horse - *Botrychium lunaria* (L.) Sw. (158) (1900) medicinal for disease of this name that was said to turn hands and eye-sockets black

Unsteetle - *Spigelia marilandica* (L.) L. (6, 186) (1814–1892)

Unsteetle (Cherokee) - *Spigelia marilandica* (L.) L. (6) (1892)

Unzhinga (Omaha-Ponca) - *Corylus americana* Walt. (37) (1919), Unzhinga-hi (Hazel-bush)

Uŋkčela blaska (Lakota, flat cactus) - *Opuntia* Mill. (121) (1918?–1970?)

Uŋpaŋ tawota (Lakota, elk food) - *Ceanothus herbaceus* Raf. (121) (1918?–1970?)

Upland aster - *Oligoneuron album* (Nutt.) Nesom (127) (1933)

Upland bent grass [Upland bentgrass, Upland bent-grass] - *Agrostis intermedia* Balb. (56) (1901), *Agrostis perennans* (Walt.) Tuckerman (5, 50, 93, 119) (1913–present)

Upland blackberry - *Rubus pergratus* Blanch. (50) (present)

Upland boneset - *Eupatorium sessilifolium* L. (5, 156) (1913–1923)

Upland brittle bladder fern [Upland brittle bladderfern] - *Cystopteris tenuis* (Michx.) Desv. (50) (present)

Upland cotton - *Gossypium herbaceum* L. (15) (1895), *Gossypium hirsutum* L. (109, 138) (1923–1949)

Upland crawberry - *Arctostaphylos uva-ursi* (L.) Spreng. (5, 6, 7, 49, 53, 58, 92, 156, 157) (1828–1929)

Upland creek stuff - *Spartina pectinata* Bosc ex Link (5) (1913)

Upland cress - *Lepidium sativum* L. (156) (1923)

Upland heart's-ease [Upland hearstease] - *Polygonum lapathifolium* L. (114) (1894)

Upland hickory - *Carya ovata* (Mill.) K. Koch (5, 156) (1913–1923)

Upland poplar - *Populus tremuloides* Michx. (6) (1892)

Upland red oak - *Quercus falcata* Michx. (8) (1785)

Upland speedwell - *Veronica officinalis* L. (5, 156) (1913–1923), *Veronica serpyllifolia* L. (158) (1900)

Upland sumac [Upland sumach] - *Rhus copallinum* L. (5, 97, 156, 157) (1900–1937), *Rhus glabra* L. (49, 53, 58, 92, 93, 156, 157, 158) (1869–1929)

Upland tupelo or Upland tupelo tree - *Nyssa sylvatica* Marsh. (8, 46, 124, 107) (1785–1937)

Upland white aster - *Oligoneuron album* (Nutt.) Nesom (5, 72, 131, 156) (1899–1923)

Upland white oak - *Quercus stellata* Wangenh. (10, 33, 187) (1818–1826)

Upland willow oak - *Quercus incana* Bartr. (2, 20, 33) (1827–1857)

Upright Andrew's-cross [Upright Andrew's cross] - *Hypericum crux-andreae* (L.) Crantz (42) (1814)

Upright avens - *Geum aleppicum* Jacq. (19) (1840)

Upright axyris - *Axyris amaranthoides* L. (5) (1913)

Upright bindweed [Upright bind-weed] - *Calystegia spithamaea* (L.) Pursh (5, 72, 97, 156) (1907–1937)

Upright birthwort - *Aristolochia clematitis* L. (5, 92, 156) (1876–1923)

Upright blotched spurge - *Chamaesyce nutans* (Lag.) Small (158) (1900)

Upright brome grass - *Bromus erectus* Huds. (5) (1913)

Upright burhead [Upright bur-head, Upright burrhead] - *Echinodorus berteroi* (Spreng.) Fassett (50) (present), *Echinodorus cordifolius* (L.) Griseb. (5, 72, 93, 97, 120, 131) (1899–1938)

Upright buttercups - *Ranunculus acris* L. (6) (1892)

Upright carrion flower [Upright carrionflower] - *Smilax ecirrata* (Engelm. ex Kunth) S. Wats. (50) (present)

Upright chess - *Bromus commutatus* Schrad. (119) (1938), *Bromus racemosus* L. (5, 56, 66, 72) (1893–1912)

Upright clubmoss [Upright club moss] - *Huperzia selago* (L.) Bernh. ex Mart. & Schrank var. *selago* (5) (1913)

Upright cockspur - *Galium circaezans* Michx. (46) (1783)

Upright crowfoot - *Ranunculus acris* L. (6) (1892)

Upright dogwood [Upright dog wood] - *Cornus foemina* Mill. (42) (1814)

Upright goosefoot - *Chenopodium urbicum* L. (62, 72) (1907–1912, 1913)

Upright honeysuckle [Upright honey-suckle] - *Rhododendron* L. (8) (1785), *Rhododendron viscosum* (L.) Torr. (189) (1767)

Upright knotweed - *Polygonum erectum* L. (129) (1894)

Upright pennyroyal [Upright peniroyal] - *Hedeoma pulegioides* (L.) Pers. (46) (1879)

Upright prairie coneflower [Upright prairieconeflower] - *Ratibida columnifera* (Nutt.) Wood & Standl. (50, 155) (1942–present)

Upright primrose-willow [Upright primrose willow] - *Ludwigia decurrens* Walt. (5, 97) (1913–1937)

Upright sandwort - *Minuartia michauxii* (Fenzl) Farw. var. *michauxii* (42) (1814)

Upright sea lyme grass, Upright sea lime grass - *Leymus arenarius* (L.) Hochst. (56, 66) (1901–1903)

Upright sedge - *Carex stricta* Lam. (50, 129) (1894–present)

Upright smilax - *Smilax ecirrata* (Engelm. ex Kunth) S. Wats. (5, 72, 97) (1907–1937)

Upright spotted spurge - *Chamaesyce nutans* (Lag.) Small (5, 62, 93, 97, 131, 156, 158) (1899–1937)

Upright virgin's-bower [Upright virgin's bower] - *Clematis recta* L. (2, 82, 92) (1876–1930), *Clematis virginiana* L. (181) (~1678)

Upright willow herb - *Epilobium strictum* Muhl. ex Spreng. (42) (1814)

Upright wood sorrel - *Oxalis stricta* L. (5) (1913)

Upright yellow wood sorrel [Upright yellow wood-sorrel] - *Oxalis stricta* L. (72, 97, 131, 158) (1899–1937)

Upright-leaf sedge [Upright-leaved sedge] - *Carex stricta* Lam. (86) (1878)

Upstart - *Colchicum autumnale* L. (92) (1876)

Ural false spiraea [Ural false-spiraea] - *Sorbaria sorbifolia* (L.) A. Braun (138) (1923)

Urban agaric - *Agaricus bitorquis* (Quél.) Sacc. (170) (1995)

Urban spurge - *Euphorbia agraria* Bieb. (50) (present)

Urd - *Vigna mungo* (L.) Hepper (109) (1949)

Urn-tree hawthorn - *Crataegus calpodendron* (Ehrh.) Medik. (4) (1986)

Urucu - *Bixa orellana* L. (174) (1753)

Urucu (Brazil) - *Bixa orellana* L. (possibly) (110) (1886)

Userdas (Catalan) - *Medicago sativa* L. (110) (1886)

Ush-keobuag (Chippewa) - *Helianthus tuberosus* L. (47) (1852)

Uskuyecha-hu (Dakota) - *Quercus macrocarpa* Michx. (37) (1919)

Uta (Dakota) - *Quercus rubra* L. (37) (1919), Uta-hu (Oak tree)

Utah honeysuckle - *Lonicera utahensis* S. Wats. (138) (1923)

Utah loco - *Astragalus utahensis* (Torr.) Torr. & Gray (155) (1942)

Utah saltbush - *Atriplex truncata* (Torr. ex S. Wats.) Gray (118) (1898)

Utah salt-sage - *Atriplex truncata* (Torr. ex S. Wats.) Gray (141) (1899)

Utah serviceberry - *Amelanchier utahensis* Koehne (155) (1942)

Utīstugī (Cherokee) - *Polygonatum biflorum* (Walt.) Ell. (possibly) (102) (1885)

Ûtsatï uwadsīska (Cherokee, fish scales) - *Thalictrum thalictroides* (L.) Eames & Boivin (102) (1886), from shape of leaves

Uva grass [Uva-grass] - *Gynerium sagittatum* (Aubl.) Beauv. (109, 138, 163) (1852–1949)

Uva passa - *Vitis vinifera* L. (57) (1917)

Uva-ursa - *Arctostaphylos uva-ursi* (L.) Spreng. (156) (1923)

Uva-ursi [Uva ursi, Uvae ursi] (Official name of Materia Medica) - *Arctostaphylos uva-ursi* (L.) Spreng. (7, 52, 53, 55, 58, 59, 92, 157, 174) (1753–1929)

Uvedalia - *Smallanthus uvedalius* (L.) Mackenzie ex Small (53, 158) (1900–1922)

Uversy - *Arctostaphylos uva-ursi* (L.) Spreng. (156) (1923)

V

Vahl's fimbristylis - *Fimbristylis vahlii* (Lam.) Link. (5) (1913)

Vahl's fimbry - *Fimbristylis vahlii* (Lam.) Link. (50) (present)

Vahl's sedge [Vahl sedge] - *Carex norvegica* Retz. subsp. *inferalpina* (Wahlenb.) Hultén (139) (1944)

Vaillantii goose-grass [Vaillantii goosegrass] - *Galium aparine* L. (5, 97, 122) (1913-1937)

Vaillant's pigmy-weed [Vaillant's pigmy weed] - *Crassula saginoides* (Maxim.) Bywater & Wickens (5) (1913)

Valdivia duckweed - *Lemna minor* L. (5, 97) (1913-1937), *Lemna valdiviana* Phil. (50) (present)

Valerian - *Cypripedium acaule* Ait. (75, 78) (1894-1898) ME, for reported efficacy for nervous disorders, *Valeriana edulis* Nutt. (107) (1919), *Valeriana* L. (1, 4, 10, 50, 109, 138, 155, 156, 158) (1818–present), *Valeriana officinalis* L. (49, 52, 53, 55, 57, 58, 59, 60, 61, 92) (1869-1922)

Valerian root - *Valeriana officinalis* L. (92) (1876)

Valeriana - *Valeriana officinalis* L. (57, 59, 60) (1902-1917)

Valériane americaine (French) - *Cypripedium reginae* Walt. (158) (1900)

Valley cottonwood - *Populus deltoides* Bartr. ex Marsh. subsp. *wislizeni* (S. Wats.) Eckenwalder (149, 153) (1904-1913)

Valley grape - *Vitis girdiana* Munson. (15, 138) (1895-1923)

Valley redstem - *Ammannia coccinea* Rottb. (50) (present)

Valley sedge - *Carex vallicola* Dew. (50) (present)

Valley vervenia - *Phacelia tanacetifolia* Benth. (106) (1930)

Valley-mahogany [Valley mahogany] - *Cercocarpus montanus* Raf. (112, 137, 138) (1923-1937)

Valleys - *Convallaria majalis* L. (158) (1900)

Vancouver qualing aspen - *Populus tremuloides* Michx. (155) (1942)

Vandal root [Vandal-root] - *Valeriana officinalis* L. (5, 92, 156) (1876-1923)

Vangle (Jamaica) - *Sesamum* L. (7) (1828)

Vanhoutte's spiraea [Vanhoutte spiraea] - *Spiraea* ×*vanhouttei* (Briot) Carr. [*cantoniensis* × *trilobata*] (112) (1937)

Vanilla - *Vanilla mexicana* Mill. (107) (1919), *Vanilla* Mill. (138) (1923) original Spanish name meaning "little sheath or pod", *Vanilla planifolia* B.D. Jackson (107) (1919)

Vanilla cactus - *Selenicereus grandiflorus* (L.) Britt. & Rose (92) (1876)

Vanilla grass [Vanilla-grass, Vanillagrass] - *Hierochloe odorata* (L.) Beauv. (5, 45, 50, 56, 66, 67, 80, 87, 90, 92, 94, 140) (1885–present)

Vanilla leaf [Vanilla leaf, Vanillaleaf] - *Achlys* DC. (155) (1942), *Carphephorus odoratissimus* (J.F. Gmel.) Herbert (5, 7, 57, 92, 156) (1828-1923)

Vanilla plant [Vanilla-plant] - *Carphephorus odoratissimus* (J.F. Gmel.) Herbert (5, 106, 156) (1913-1930)

Var songorica - *Elaeagnus angustifolia* L. (106) (1930)

Variable blue-eyed grass - *Sisyrinchium langloisii* Greene (97) (1937)

Variable flatsedge - *Cyperus difformis* L. (50) (present)

Variable goldenrod [Variable golden-rod] - *Solidago canadensis* L. var. *scabra* Torr. & Gray (19) (1840)

Variable grape - *Vitis labrusca* L. (possibly) (7) (1828)

Variable oak - *Quercus* ×*heterophylla* Michx. f. [*phellos* × *rubra*] (138) (1923)

Variable panic grass [Variable panicgrass] - *Dichanthelium commutatum* (J.A. Schultes) Gould (50) (present)

Variable panicum - *Dichanthelium commutatum* (J.A. Schultes) Gould (5) (1913)

Variable pondweed - *Potamogeton gramineus* L. (3) (1977)

Variable sedge - *Carex polymorpha* Muhl. (5, 50) (1913–present)

Variable thorn - *Crataegus macrosperma* Ashe (5) (1913)

Variable-leaf pondweed [Variableleaf pondweed] - *Potamogeton gramineus* L. (50, 155) (1942–present)

Variegated dead-nettle [Variegated dead nettle] - *Lamium maculatum* L. (5) (1913)

Variegated equisetum - *Equisetum variegatum* Schleich. ex F. Weber & D.M.H. Mohr (5, 97) (1913-1937)

Variegated horsetail - *Equisetum variegatum* Schleich. ex F. Weber & D.M.H. Mohr (3, 155) (1942-1977)

Variegated monk's-hood - *Aconitum uncinatum* L. (165) (1768)

Variegated scouring-rush [Variegated scouring rush] - *Equisetum variegatum* Schleich. ex F. Weber & D.M.H. Mohr (4, 50) (1986–present)

Variegated sedge - *Carex stylosa* C. A. Meyer (5, 50) (1913–present)

Variegated spurge - *Euphorbia marginata* Pursh (5, 38, 156, 157, 158) (1820-1929)

Variegated yellow pond-lily - *Nuphar lutea* (L.) Sm. subsp. *variegata* (Dur.) E.O. Beal (50) (present)

Varileaf cinquefoil - *Potentilla diversifolia* Lehm. (50, 155) (1942–present), *Potentilla diversifolia* Lehm. var. *diversifolia* (50) (present)

Various-glume wild rye [Various-glumed wild rye] - *Elymus diversiglumis* Scribn. & Ball (5) (1913)

Various-leaf amaranth [Various-leaved amaranth] - *Amaranthus cruentus* L. (165) (1768)

Various-leaf aster [Various-leaved aster] - *Eurybia macrophylla* (L.) Cass. (5) (1913)

Various-leaf bur-reed [Various-leaved bur-reed] - *Sparganium emersum* Rehmann (5) (1913)

Various-leaf fescue [Various-leaved fescue] - *Festuca heterophylla* Lam. (56, 68) (1901-1913)

Various-leaf pondweed [Various-leaved pondweed] - *Potamogeton illinoensis* Morong (5, 93, 131) (1899-1936)

Various-leaf poplar [Various leaved poplar] - *Populus heterophylla* L. (19) (1840)

Various-leaf spurge [Various-leaved spurge] - *Euphorbia cyathophora* Murray (5, 72, 93, 97, 131) (1899-1937)

Various-leaf water-milfoil [Various-leaved water milfoil, Various-leaved water millfoil] - *Myriophyllum heterophyllum* Michx. (5, 72, 131) (1899-1913)

Varnish sumac [Varnish sumach] - *Rhus copallinum* L. (156) (1923)

Varnish tree - *Ailanthus altissima* (Mill) Swingle (106, 107) (1919-1930), *Firmiana simplex* (L.) W. Wight (106) (1930), *Toxicodendron vernix* (L.) Kuntze (8) (1785)

Varnished willow - *Salix fragilis* L. (5, 156, 158) (1900-1923)

Varza (Roumanian) - *Brassica oleracea* L. (110) (1886)

Vase vine [Vasevine, Vase-vine] - *Clematis* L. (1) (1932), *Clematis viorna* L. (156) (1923)

Vasey's adelia [Vasey adelia] - *Adelia vaseyi* (Coult.) Pax & K. Hoffmann (155) (1942)

Vasey's bluegrass [Vasey's blue-grass] - *Poa leibergii* Scribn. (94) (1901)

Vasey's bunch grass [Vasey's bunch-grass] - *Pseudoroegneria spicata* (Pursh) A. Löve subsp. *spicata* (94) (1901)

Vasey's dropseed [Vasey's drop-seed] - *Muhlenbergia minutissima* (Steud.) Swall. (5) (1913)

Vasey's grass [Vasey grass] - *Paspalum urvillei* Steud. (163) (1852)

Vasey's paspalum - *Paspalum urvillei* Steud. (94) (1901)

Vasey's pondweed - *Potamogeton vaseyi* J.W. Robbins (5, 50) (1913–present)

Vasey's reed grass [Vasey's reed-grass] - *Calamagrostis sesquiflora* (Trin.) Tzvelev (94) (1901)

Vasey's rush [Vasey rush] - *Juncus vaseyi* Engelm. (5, 50, 72, 139) (1893–present)

Vasey's wild lime - *Adelia vaseyi* (Coult.) Pax & K. Hoffmann (50) (present)

Vasey's wild oat grass - *Danthonia intermedia* Vasey (5) (1913)

Vassbok (Swedish) - *Platanus occidentalis* L. (41) (1770)

Vattenbok (Swedish) - *Platanus occidentalis* L. (41) (1770)

Vatzkor (Hungarian) - *Pyrus communis* L. (110) (1886)

Vegetable antimony - *Eupatorium perfoliatum* L. (6, 7, 53, 69, 92, 156, 157, 158) (1828-1929)

Vegetable brimstone - *Lycopodium clavatum* L. (92) (1876)

Vegetable calomel - *Podophyllum peltatum* L. (64, 156, 158) (1900–1923)

Vegetable hair - *Tillandsia usneoides* (L.) L. (5, 92, 156) (1876-1923)

Vegetable humming-bird - *Sesbania grandiflora* (L.) Poir. (107) (1919)

Vegetable musk - *Mimulus moschatus* Dougl. ex Lindl. (92) (1876)

Vegetable powder - *Lycopodium clavatum* L. (92) (1876)

Vegetable satyr - *Coeloglossum viride* (L.) Hartman var. *virescens* (Muhl. ex Willd.) Luer (5, 19, 156, 158) (1840-1923)

Vegetable silk - *Chorisia speciosa* St.Hil. (92) (1876)

Vegetable sulphur - *Lycopodium clavatum* L. (14, 57, 92) (1882-1917)

Vegetable-oyster [Vegetable oyster] - *Tragopogon porrifolius* L. (4, 5, 19, 92, 107, 109, 138, 156, 158) (1840-1986), *Tragopogon pratensis* L. (158) (1900)

Vegetable-oyster salsify - *Tragopogon porrifolius* L. (155) (1942)

Veined skullcap [Veined skull cap] - *Scutellaria nervosa* Pursh (5, 72) (1907-1913)

Vein-leaf [Vein leaf] - *Hieracium gronovii* L. (19) (1840)

Vein-leaf hawkbit [Vein leaf hawk's-bit] - *Hieracium venosum* L. (156, 158) (1900-1923)

Vein-leaf hawkweed - *Hieracium venosum* L. (5, 157) (1913-1929)

Veiny arrow-wood [iny arrow wood] - *Viburnum dentatum* L. var. *venosum* (Britt.) Gleason (5) (1913)

Veiny dock [Veined dock] - *Rumex venosus* Pursh (3, 5, 50, 93, 97, 131, 155) (1913–present)

Veiny meadow-rue [Veiny meadow rue, Veiny meadowrue] - *Thalictrum venulosum* Trel. (5, 50, 131, 155) (1899–present)

Veiny pea - *Lathyrus venosus* Muhl. (5, 50, 72, 82, 131) (1899–present)

Veiny peavine - *Lathyrus venosus* Muhl. (155) (1942)

Veiny pepperweed - *Lepidium oblongum* Small (50) (present)

Veiny viburnum - *Viburnum dentatum* L. var. *venosum* (Britt.) Gleason (138) (1923)

Veiny-leaf hawkweed [Veiny-leaved hawkweed, Veiny leaved hawkweed] - *Hieracium venosum* L. (49, 92, 156, 157) (1898–1929)

Veitch's screwpine [Veitch screwpine] - *Pandanus veitchii* hort. Veitch ex Masters & T. Moore (138) (1923)

Vélar (French) - *Sisymbrium officinale* (L.) Scop (158) (1900)

Velvet bean [Velvetbean] - *Mucuna* Adans. (138) (1923), *Mucuna pruriens* (L.) DC. var. *utilis* (Wallich ex Wight) Baker ex Burck (106) (1930)

Velvet bent - *Agrostis canina* L. (109) (1949)

Velvet bent grass [Velvet bentgrass] - *Agrostis canina* L. (50) (present)

Velvet bluebells-of-Scotland [Velvet bluebells of Scotland] - *Campanula rotundifolia* L. (155) (1942)

Velvet cactus [Velvetcactus] - *Bergerocactus emoryi* (Engelm.) Engelm. (138, 155) (1931-1942)

Velvet dock - *Inula helenium* L. (64, 156) (1908-1923)

Velvet dogbane - *Apocynum cannabinum* L. (5, 64, 72, 97) (1907-1937)

Velvet flower [Velvet-flower] - *Amaranthus hybridus* L. (165) (1768) Old English name no longer in use by 1768, possibly this species, *Streptanthus hyacinthoides* Hook. (97) (1937)

Velvet foot - *Flammulina velutipes* (Curtis) Singer (possibly) (170) (1995)

Velvet grass [Velvet-grass, Velvetgrass] - *Holcus* L. (1, 50, 155) (1932–present), *Holcus lanatus* L. (3, 5, 45, 56, 66, 72, 75, 88, 90, 92, 94, 109, 111, 119, 122, 138, 163) (1852–1977), *Zoysia tenuifolia* Willd. ex Thiele (163) (1852)

Velvet mesquite - *Holcus lanatus* L. (5, 88) (1885–1913)

Velvet mesquite grass [Velvet mesquit grass] - *Holcus lanatus* L. (45, 87, 90) (1884–1896)

Velvet osier - *Salix viminalis* L. (5, 156) (1913–1923)

Velvet pancium - *Dichanthelium scoparium* (Lam.) Gould (50) (present)

Velvet panic grass [Velvet panic-grass] - *Dichanthelium scoparium* (Lam.) Gould (119) (1938)

Velvet plant [Velvet-plant, Velvetplant] - *Gynura aurantiaca* (Blume) DC. (109, 138) (1923–1949), *Verbascum thapsus* L. (5, 62, 69, 92, 156, 158) (1876–1923)

Velvet sedge - *Carex vestita* Willd. (5, 50) (1913–present)

Velvet sumac [Velvet sumach] - *Rhus hirta* (L.) Sudworth (5, 92, 156) (1876–1923)

Velvet tree-mallow [Velvet treemallow] - *Lavatera arborea* L. (138) (1923)

Velvet violet - *Viola pedata* L. (156) (1923)

Velvet willow - *Salix sitchensis* Sanson ex Bong. (20) (1857)

Velvet-dock [Velvet dock] - *Verbascum thapsus* L. (5, 69, 156, 158) (1900–1923)

Velvetleaf [Velvet leaf, Velvet-leaf] - *Abutilon* Mill. (13, 93) (1849–1936), *Abutilon theophrasti* Medik (1, 3, 4, 5, 15, 50, 62, 72, 80, 92, 95, 145, 156, 157, 158) (1895–present), *Cissampelos pareira* L. (92) (1876), *Verbascum thapsus* L. (45) (1896)

Velvet-leaf blueberry - *Vaccinium myrtilloides* Michx. (106, 107, 156) (1919–1930)

Velvet-leaf gaura [Velvet leaf gaura] - *Gaura mollis* James (124) (1937)

Velvet-leaf tick trefoil [Velvet-leaved tick trefoil] - *Desmodium viridiflorum* (L.) DC. (5, 97) (1913–1937)

Velvets - *Viola pedata* L. (5, 158) (1900–1913)

Velvet-stem mushroom [Velvet-stemmed mushroom] - *Collybia velutipes* (Curtis) P. Kumm. (128) (1933)

Velvetweed [Velvet weed, Velvet-weed] - *Abutilon theophrasti* Medik (5, 73, 156, 158) (1892–1923) Quincy IL, *Gaura mollis* James (50) (present)

Velvety ceanothus - *Ceanothus velutinus* Dougl. ex Hook. (130) (1895)

Velvety gaura - *Gaura mollis* James (3, 4, 145) (1897–1986)

Velvety goldenrod [Velvety golden-rod] - *Solidago mollis* Bartl. (5, 50, 72, 93, 95, 97, 122, 156) (1907–present), *Solidago mollis* Bartl. var. *mollis* (50) (present)

Velvety ground-cherry - *Physalis mollis* Nutt. (97) (1937)

Velvety panic grass [Velvety panic-grass] - *Dichanthelium scoparium* (Lam.) Gould (163) (1852)

Velvety panicum - *Dichanthelium scoparium* (Lam.) Gould (3, 5, 72, 131, 155) (1899–1977)

Velvety redroot - *Ceanothus velutinus* Dougl. ex Hook. (131) (1899)

Velvety rose-mallow [Velvety rose mallow] - *Hibiscus moscheutos* L. subsp. *moscheutos* (5) (1913)

Venice mallow - *Hibiscus trionum* L. (4, 5, 85, 131, 156, 158) (1899–1986)

Venice sumac [Venice sumach] - *Cotinus coggygria* Scop. (92) (1876)

Vente conmigo - *Croton glandulosus* L. (50) (present)

Venus flytrap [Venus' fly-trap, Venus's flytrap] - *Dionaea* Ell. (2, 10, 13, 138, 167) (1814–1923), *Dionaea muscipula* Ellis. (14, 19, 92, 109, 138) (1840–1949)

Venus'-apron-strings [Venus's apron strings] - *Laminaria saccharina* (Linnaeus) J. V. Lamouroux (73) (1892)

Venus'-bath [Venus' bath] - *Dipsacus fullonum* L. (5, 92, 156, 158) (1876–1923)

Venus'-button [Venusbutton] - *Omphalodes verna* Moench (138) (1923)

Venus'-chariot [Venus' chariot] - *Aconitum napellus* L. (50) (present)

Venus'-comb [Venus' comb, Venus comb] - *Scandix pecten-veneris* L. (5, 92, 107, 156) (1876–1923)

Venus'-cup [Venus' cup] - *Cypripedium* L. (92) (1876), *Cypripedium parviflorum* Salisb. (156) (1923), *Cypripedium reginae* Walt. (64, 158) (1900-1908), *Dipsacus fullonum* L. (5, 156, 158) (1900–1923)

Venus'-cup teasel [Venus-cup teasel, Venuscup teasel] - *Dipsacus fullonum* L. (155) (1942)

Venusfinger (German) - *Cynoglossum officinale* L. (92) (1876)

Venushaar (German) - *Adiantum capillus-veneris* L. (158) (1900)

Venus'-hair [Venushair, Venus-hair, Venus' hair] - *Adiantum capillus-veneris* L. (92, 97, 109, 158) (1900-1949), *Adiantum pedatum* L. (46) (1649)

Venus'-hair fern [Venus' hair fern, Venus hair fern, Venus-hair fern, Venus's hair fern] - *Adiantum capillus-veneris* L. (3, 4, 5, 72, 122, 124, 131) (1899-1986), *Adiantum* L. (1) (1932)

Venus'-looking-glass [Venus' looking glass, Venus looking glass, Venus's looking glass, Venus lookingglass, Venuslookingglass] - *Legousia speculum-veneris* (L.) Fisch. ex A. DC. (possibly) (19, 92, 107, 109, 138) (1840-1946), *Triodanis perfoliata* (L.) Nieuwl. var. *perfoliata* (5, 62, 63, 72, 93, 95, 97, 122, 124, 131, 156, 157) (1899-1937), *Triodanis* Raf. ex Greene (1, 2, 4, 50, 93, 138, 155, 156) (1923–present)

Venus'-pride [Venus' pride, Venus' pride] - *Hedyotis nigricans* (Lam.) Fosberg var. *nigricans* (5, 156) (1913-1923), *Houstonia caerulea* L. (5, 19, 75, 156) (1840-1923), *Houstonia* L. (76, 158) (1896-1900), *Houstonia purpurea* L. (5, 50) (1913–present)

Venus'-shoe [Venus' shoe] - *Cypripedium* L. (86, 92) (1876-1878), *Cypripedium parviflorum* Salisb. (156) (1923), *Cypripedium reginae* Walt. (64, 158) (1900-1908)

Venus'-slipper [Venus' slipper, Venus'slipper] - *Calypso bulbosa* (L.) Oakes (3, 156) (1923-1977), *Calypso bulbosa* (L.) Oakes var. *americana* (R. Br. ex Ait. f.) Luer (85) (1932), *Calypso* Salisb. (1) (1932), *Cypripedium* L. (86) (1878)

Venus'-sock [Venus' sock] - *Cypripedium* L. (86) (1878)

Verbena - *Aloysia triphylla* (L'Hér.) Britt. (92) (1876), *Glandularia canadensis* (L.) Nutt. (122) (1937), *Verbena* L. (1, 93, 138, 155, 158) (1900-1942)

Vermont snakeroot [Vermont snake root, Vermont snake-root] - *Asarum canadense* L. (5, 64, 156, 158) (1900–1923)

Vernal grass [Vernalgrass, Vernal-grass] - *Anthoxanthum* L. (155, 158) (1900-1942) *Anthoxanthum odoratum* L. (92) (1876)

Vernal honeysuckle - *Lonicera canadensis* Bartr. ex Marsh. (156) (1923)

Vernal iris - *Iris verna* L. (138) (1923)

Vernal sandwort - *Minuartia rubella* (Wahlenb.) Hiern. (5, 131) (1899-1913)

Vernal sedge - *Carex caryophyllea* Latourrette (50, 156) (1923–present)

Vernal water-starwort [Vernal water starwort] - *Callitriche palustris* L. (5, 50, 72, 122, 156) (1907–present)

Vernal whitlow-grass [Vernal whitlow grass] - *Draba verna* L. (5) (1913)

Vernal witch-hazel - *Hamamelis vernalis* Sargent (138) (1923)

Vernis des Japon (French) - *Ailanthus altissima* (Mill) Swingle (6, 158) (1892-1900)

Veronica - *Veronicastrum virginicum* (L.) Farw. (49) (1898)

Veronicastrum - *Veronicastrum* Heister ex Fabr. (50) (present)

Veroniken (German) - *Veronica serpyllifolia* L. (158) (1900)

Veronique aquatique (French) - *Veronica beccabunga* L. (7) (1828)

Veronique de Virginie (French) - *Veronicastrum virginicum* (L.) Farw. (6) (1892)

Véronique mâle (French) - *Veronica serpyllifolia* L. (158) (1900)

Verrucose sea-purslane [Verrucose seapurslane] - *Sesuvium verrucosum* Raf. (50) (present)

Verschaffelt's coleus [Verschaffelt coleus] - *Plectranthus scutellarioides* (L.) R.Br. (138) (1923)

Verschiedenfarbige Schwertlilie (German) - *Iris versicolor* L. (6, 158) (1892)

Vervain - *Glandularia bipinnatifida* (Nutt.) Nutt. var. *bipinnatifida* (3) (1977), *Glandularia pumila* (Rydb.) Umber (97) (1937), *Verbena hastata* L. (19, 40, 49, 53, 80, 92) (1840-1928), *Verbena* L. (1, 2, 4, 7, 10, 14, 50, 63, 82, 93, 106, 156, 158, 167) (1814–present) from Celtic ferfaen, referring to cleansing power

Vervain mallow - *Malva alcea* L. (5, 92, 156) (1876–1923)

Vervain sage - *Salvia verbenaca* L. (5, 19, 138) (1840–1923)

Vervain thoroughwort - *Eupatorium rotundifolium* L. var. *rotundifolium* (5, 156) (1913–1923)

Vervine - *Verbena stricta* Vent. (92) (1876)

Verza (Portuguese) - *Brassica oleracea* L. (110) (1886)

Vesicular corydalis - *Corydalis crystallina* Engelm. (5, 72, 97) (1907–1937)

Vessel fern [Vesselfern] - *Angiopteris* Hoffmann (155) (1942)

Vetch - *Lathyrus cicera* L. (107) (1919), *Vicia* L. (1, 2, 4, 10, 45, 50, 106, 109, 138, 155, 156, 158) (1818–present) from Vik of ancient European languages, *Vicia sativa* L. (14, 92, 131) (1876–1899)

Vetchling - *Lathyrus* L. (4, 10, 93, 109, 158) (1818–1986)

Vetiver - *Agropyron cristatum* (L.) Gaertn. (57, 92) (1876–1917), Vetiveria zizaniodes (L.) Nash (109, 122, 163) (1852–1949)

Vetiveria - *Agropyron cristatum* (L.) Gaertn. (57) (1917)

Vetivert - *Agropyron cristatum* (L.) Gaertn. (92) (1876)

Vetives (Louisiana) - *Pseudoraphis spinescens* (R. Br.) Vickery (67) (1890)

Vib (Pima) - *Nicotiana* L. (132) (1855)

Viburnum - *Viburnum* L. (4, 50, 138, 155, 158) (1900–present)

Victoria palmetto - *Sabal mexicana* Mart. (138) (1923)

Victorian-box - *Pittosporum undulatum* Vent. (109) (1949)

Vigne (French) - *Vitex agnus-castus* L. (158) (1900), *Vitis* L. (8) (1785)

Vigne à feuilles laciniées (French) - *Vitis vinifera* L. (possibly) (8) (1785)

Vigne de renard (French) - *Vitis vulpina* L. (8) (1785)

Vigne des battures (French) - *Vitis riparia* Michx. (168) (1803)

Vigne en arbre (French) - *Ampelopsis arborea* (L.) Koehne (8) (1785)

Vigne sauvage (French) - *Vitis labrusca* L. (8) (1785)

Vigne vierge (French) - *Parthenocissus quinquefolia* (L.) Planch. (8, 158) (1785–1900)

Villose St. Peter's-wort [Villose St. Peter's wort] - *Hypericum setosum* L. (possibly) (8) (1785)

Vilmorin's ailanthus [Vilmorin ailanthus] - *Ailanthus altissima* (Mill) Swingle (155) (1942)

Vine - *Vitis* L. (10, 15, 109) (1818–1949) *Vitis vinifera* L. (14, 92, 110) (1876–1886)

Vine blue snapdragon - *Maurandella antirrhiniflora* (Humb. & Bonpl. ex Willd.) Rothm. (122) (1937) TX

Vine bower - *Clematis viticella* L. (2) (1895)

Vine ephedra - *Ephedra antisyphilitica* Berl. ex C. A. Mey. (155) (1942), *Ephedra pedunculata* Engelm. ex S. Wats. (124) (1937)

Vine false buckwheat - *Polygonum scandens* L. (122) (1937)

Vine maple - *Acer circinatum* Pursh (2, 15, 50, 106, 109, 138, 155, 160, 161) (1857–present)

Vine mesquite [Vine-mesquite] - *Panicum obtusum* H.B.K. (3, 5, 50, 119, 140, 155) (1911–present)

Vine mesquite grass [Vine mesquite-grass] - *Panicum obtusum* H.B.K. (94, 122, 152) (1901–1937)

Vine milkweed - *Cynanchum laeve* (Michx.) Pers. (122) (1937)

Vine nightshade - *Solanum triquetrum* Cav. (122, 124) (1937) TX

Vine tree - *Nyssa biflora* Walt. (46) (1879)

Vine-apple [Vine apple] - *Cucurbita pepo* L. (107) (1919)

Vinegar plant - *Penicillium glaucum* Link (92) (1876), *Rhus hirta* (L.) Sudworth (92) (1876)

Vinegar tree [Vinegar-tree] - *Rhus glabra* L. (5, 107, 156, 157, 158) (1900–1929), *Rhus hirta* (L.) Sudworth (5, 156) (1913–1923)

Vinegar weed [Vinegar-weed] - *Hemizonia* DC. (106) (1930) San Joaquin Valley CA, *Trichostema lanceolatum* Benth. (156) (1923)

Vine-maple [Vine maple] - *Menispermum canadense* L. (49, 156, 157, 158) (1900–1929)

Vinettier (French) - *Berberis vulgaris* L. (158) (1900)

Violet - *Iris verna* L. (156) (1923), *Viola* L. (1, 4, 7, 10, 13, 15, 50, 82, 92, 109, 138, 155, 158) (1818–present), *Viola odorata* L. (55, 107) (1911–1919), *Viola palmata* L. (107) (1919)

Violet allamanda - *Allamanda blanchetii* A. DC. (155) (1942)

Violet blue-eyed Mary [Violet blue eyed Mary] - *Collinsia violacea* Nutt. (50) (present)

Violet boltonia - *Boltonia asteroides* (L.) L'Her. var. *latisquama* (Gray) Cronq. (3, 138, 155) (1923–1977)

Violet boneset - *Conoclinium coelestinum* (L.) DC. (7) (1828)

Violet boxelder - *Acer negundo* L. var. *violaceum* (Kirchn.) Jaeger (155) (1942)

Violet clover - *Dalea purpurea* Vent. var. *purpurea* (93) (1936)

Violet collinsia - *Collinsia violacea* Nutt. (5, 122) (1913–1937)

Violet lespedeza - *Lespedeza violacea* (L.) Pers. (3, 50, 155) (1942–present)

Violet penstemon - *Penstemon heterophyllus* Lindl. (138) (1923)

Violet petunia - *Petunia integrifolia* (Hook.) Schinz & Thellung (5, 85) (1913–1932)

Violet prairie clover - *Dalea purpurea* Vent. (50, 131) (1899–present), *Dalea purpurea* Vent. var. *purpurea* (5, 50) (1913–present)

Violet sage - *Salvia nemorosa* L. (138, 155) (1923–1942)

Violet sorrel - *Oxalis* L. (93) (1936)

Violet wheatgrass - *Elymus alaskanus* (Scribn. & Merr.) A. Löve subsp. *latiglumis* (Scribn. & J.G. Sm.) A. Löve (155) (1942)

Violet wood aster - *Eurybia macrophylla* (L.) Cass. (5) (1913)

Violet wood sorrel [Violet wood-sorrel, Violet woodsorrel] - *Oxalis* L. (1) (1932), *Oxalis violacea* L. (3, 4, 19, 5, 37, 50, 72, 85, 97, 122, 131, 138, 156) (1840–present)

Violet wood-sorrel oxalis [Violet woodsorrel oxalis] - *Oxalis violacea* L. (155) (1942)

Violet-bloom [Violet bloom] - *Lycium barbarum* L. (156) (1923), *Solanum dulcamara* L. (6, 49, 53, 92, 158) (1892–1922)

Violet-flower petunia [Violet-flowered petunia] - *Petunia integrifolia* (Hook.) Schinz & Thellung (109) (1949)

Violet-leaf aster - *Eurybia macrophylla* (L.) Cass. (5) (1913)

Viorna - *Clematis viorna* L. (109, 156) (1923–1949)

Viorne (French) - *Viburnum* L. (8) (1785)

Viorne à feuilles d'aune (French) - *Viburnum lantanoides* Michx. (8) (1785)

Viorne à feuilles de prunier (French) - *Viburnum prunifolium* L. (8) (1785)

Viorne à feuilles dentées (French) - *Viburnum dentatum* L. (8) (1,785)

Viorne à feuilles d'érable (French) - *Viburnum acerifolium* L. (8) (1785)

Viorne à manchettes (French) - *Viburnum lentago* L. (8) (1785)

Viorne des Canada (French) - *Viburnum opulus* L. var. *americanum* Aiton (8) (1785)

Viorne nue (French) - *Viburnum nudum* L. (8) (1785)

Vipérine (French) - *Echium vulgare* L. (158) (1900)

Vipérine de Virginie (French) - *Aristolochia serpentaria* L. (158) (1900)

Viper's bugloss [Vipersbugloss, Viper's-bugloss, Vipers bugloss] - *Echium* L. (1, 4, 10, 19, 50, 109, 155, 156, 158) (1818–present), *Echium vulgare* L. (5, 62, 63, 72, 85, 92, 97, 106, 131, 156, 157, 158) (1899–1937)

Viper's plant - *Scolymus hispanicus* L. (110) (1886)

Viper's-grass [Viper's grass, Vipers' grass] - *Echium vulgare* L. (5, 156, 157, 158) (1900–1929), *Scolymus hispanicus* L. (92, 107) (1876–1919) said to be antidote for bite of adder

Viper's-herb [Viper's herb] - *Echium vulgare* L. (5, 156, 157, 158) (1900–1929)

Viquiera - *Viguiera* Kunth (158) (1900)

Virgate St. John's-wort [Virgate St. John's wort] - *Hypericum denticulatum* Walt. (5) (1913)

Virgilia - *Cladrastis kentukea* (Dum.-Cours.) Rudd . (156) (1923)

Virgin Mary's-thistle [Virgin Mary's thistle] - *Silybum marianum* (L.) Gaertn. (156, 158) (1900-1923)

Virginia acalypha [Virginian acalypha] - *Acalypha virginica* L. (165) (1768)

Virginia agave [Virginian agave] - *Manfreda virginica* (L.) Salisb. ex Rose (165) (1768)

Virginia aloes - *Manfreda virginica* (L.) Salisb. ex Rose (7, 92) (1828-1876)

Virginia anemone [Virginian anemone] - *Anemone virginiana* L. (155, 156, 158, 165) (1807-1942)

Virginia angelica tree [Virginian angelica tree] - *Aralia spinosa* L. (8) (1785)

Virginia arrow-arum - *Peltandra virginica* (L.) Schott. (138) (1923)

Virginia ash-leaf maple [Virginian ash-leaved maple] - *Acer negundo* L. (165) (1768)

Virginia azarole [Virginian azarole] - *Crataegus crus-galli* L. (41) (1770)

Virginia beard grass [Virginia beard-grass, Virginian beard-grass] - *Andropogon virginicus* L. (5, 62, 66, 99) (1903-1923)

Virginia bent grass [Virginian bent grass] - *Sporobolus virginicus* (L.) Kunth (165) (1768)

Virginia bird-cherry tree [Virginian bird-cherry-tree] - *Prunus virginiana* L. (8) (1785)

Virginia bistort - *Polygonum virginianum* L. (157, 158) (1900-1929)

Virginia blue grass - *Poa compressa* L. (68) (1890)

Virginia bluebells - *Mertensia virginica* (L.) Pers. ex Link (50, 109, 138, 156) (1923–present)

Virginia brown-rape - *Epifagus virginiana* (L.) W. Bart. (5, 156) (1913-1923)

Virginia bugleweed - *Lycopus virginicus* L. (3, 4, 155) (1942-1986)

Virginia bunchflower - *Melanthium virginicum* L (50) (present)

Virginia campion [Virginian campion] - *Silene virginica* L. (2) (1895)

Virginia catchfly [Virginian catchfly] - *Silene virginica* L. (86) (1878)

Virginia cedar [Virginian cedar] - *Juniperus virginiana* L. (14, 157, 158) (1882-1929)

Virginia chain fern [Virginia chainfern] - *Woodwardia virginica* (L.) Sm. (1913–present) (5, 50)

Virginia cherry tree - *Prunus virginiana* L. (18) (1805)

Virginia copperleaf - *Acalypha virginica* L. (155) (1942)

Virginia cotton-grass [Virginia cotton grass] - *Eriophorum virginicum* L. (5, 156) (1913–1923)

Virginia cotton-sedge [Virginia cottonsedge] - *Eriophorum virginicum* L. (155) (1942)

Virginia cowslip - *Mertensia virginica* (L.) Pers. ex Link (possibly) (5, 63, 72, 92, 93, 101 156) (1876-1949)

Virginia creeper [Virginian creeper] - *Calystegia sepium* (L.) R. Br. subsp. *sepium* (156) (1923), *Hedera* L. (1) (1932), *Parthenocissus* Planch. (4) (1986), *Parthenocissus quinquefolia* (L.) Planch. (2, 3, 4, 5, 6, 8, 13, 15, 48, 49, 50, 58, 65, 72, 80, 82, 85, 92, 93, 95, 97, 101, 106, 109, 112, 113, 122, 130, 135, 142, 149, 155, 156, 157, 158) (1785–present), *Parthenocissus vitacea* (Knerr) A.S. Hitchc. (153) (1913)

Virginia crownbeard [Virginia crown-beard] - *Verbesina virginica* L. (122, 124) (1937) TX, *Verbesina virginica* L. var. *virginica* (5, 97) (1913–1937)

Virginia cut grass [Virginia cut-grass, Virginian cut grass] - *Leersia virginica* Willd. (66, 111, 129, 163) (1852-1915)

Virginia cypress - *Taxodium distichum* (L.) L. C. Rich. (92) (1876)

Virginia dayflower [Virginia day-flower] - *Commelina virginica* L. (5, 50, 93, 97, 155) (1913–present)

Virginia deciduous cypress tree [Virginian deciduous cypress-tree] - *Taxodium distichum* (L.) L. C. Rich. (8) (1785)

Virginia dogwood - *Cornus florida* L. (92, 158) (1876-1900)

Virginia eryngo [Virginian eryngo] - *Eryngium aquaticum* L. var. *aquaticum* (5) (1913)

Virginia false dragonhead [Virginia false-dragonhead] - *Physostegia virginiana* (L.) Benth. (138) (1923)

Virginia false gromwell - *Onosmodium virginianum* (L.) A. DC. (5, 156) (1913-1923)

Virginia forget-me-not - *Myosotis verna* Nutt. (3) (1977)

Virginia geum - *Geum virginianum* L. (49) (1898)

Virginia goatbeard [Virginia's goat's-beard] - *Krigia biflora* (Walt.) Blake (156) (1923), *Krigia biflora* (Walt.) Blake var. *biflora* (5, 97) (1913-1937)

Virginia goat's-rue [Virginian goat's rue] - *Tephrosia virginiana* (L.) Pers (86) (1878)

Virginia grape-fern [Virginia grape fern] - *Botrychium virginianum* (L.) Sw. (122, 131, 157, 158) (1899-1937)

Virginia ground-cherry [Virginia ground cherry, Virginia ground-cherry, Virginian ground cherry] - *Physalis virginiana* Mill. (4, 5, 50, 62, 72, 93, 97, 131, 155) (1899–present)

Virginia groundsel tree [Virginian groundsel tree] - *Baccharis halimifolia* L. (8) (1785)

Virginia heartleaf - *Hexastylis virginica* (L.) Small (50) (present)

Virginia heart-leaf thorn [Virginia heart-leaved thorn] - *Crataegus phaenopyrum* (L. f.) Medik. (5) (1913)

Virginia hedge thorn - *Crataegus phaenopyrum* (L. f.) Medik. (5) (1913)

Virginia hedge-hyssop [Virginia hedge hyssop, Virginia hedgehyssop] - *Gratiola virginiana* L. (3, 155) (1942-1977)

Virginia hemp [Virginian hemp] - *Amaranthus cannabinus* (L.) Sauer (165) (1768)

Virginia hexastylis - *Hexastylis virginica* (L.) Small (5) (1913)

Virginia indicator - *Botrychium virginianum* (L.) Sw. (157, 158) (1900-1929)

Virginia iris - *Iris virginica* L. (50, 155) (1942–present)

Virginia itea [Virginian itea] - *Itea virginica* L. (8) (1785)

Virginia knotweed - *Polygonum virginianum* L. (5, 72, 93, 97, 157, 158) (1900-1937)

Virginia kosteletskya [Virginian kosteletskya] - *Kosteletzkya virginica* (L.) K. Presl ex Gray (2, 5) (1895-1913)

Virginia lion's-heart [Virginia lionsheart] - *Physostegia virginiana* (L.) Benth. (4, 155) (1942-1986)

Virginia loosestrife [Virginian loosestrife] - *Gaura biennis* L. (19) (1840), *Gaura* L. (167) (1814)

Virginia lungwort - *Mertensia virginica* (L.) Pers. ex Link (possibly) (48, 92, 156) (1882-1923)

Virginia lyme grass - *Elymus virginicus* L. (5, 68, 90) (1885-1913)

Virginia mallow - *Sida hermaphrodita* (L.) Rusby (5) (1913)

Virginia maple [Virginian maple] - *Platanus occidentalis* L. (41) (1770)

Virginia marsh leather-wood [Virginian marsh leather-wood] - *Dirca palustris* L. (8) (1785)

Virginia mountain-mint [Virginia mountain mint, Virginia mountainmint] - *Pycnanthemum virginianum* (L.) T. Dur. & B.D. Jackson ex B.L. Robins. & Fern. (4, 5, 50, 72, 97, 121, 138, 155, 157) (1900–present)

Virginia mountian pimpernel - *Taenidia montana* (Mackenzie) Cronq. (5) (1913)

Virginia mouse-ear - *Hackelia virginiana* (L.) I.M. Johnston (5, 156, 157, 158) (1900-1929)

Virginia orpine [Virginian orpine] - *Penthorum* L. (167) (1814), *Penthorum sedoides* L. (19) (1840)

Virginia parsley-leaf mespilus [Virginian parsley leaved mespilus] - *Crataegus marshallii* Eggl. (8) (1785)

Virginia penthorum - *Penthorum sedoides* L. (155) (1942)

Virginia peppergrass [Virginia peppergrass, Virginia pepper grass] - *Lepidium virginicum* L. (3, 72, 80) (1907-1977)

Virginia pepperweed - *Lepidium virginicum* L. (50, 155) (1942–present), *Lepidium virginicum* L. var. *virginicum* (50) (present)

Virginia persimmon tree [Virginian persimmon tree] - *Diospyros virginiana* L. (8) (1785)

Virginia pine - *Pinus palustris* Mill. (5) (1913), *Pinus virginiana* Mill. (50) (present)

Virginia plantain - *Plantago virginica* L. (50) (present)

Virginia poke [Virginian poke] - *Phytolacca americana* L. var. *americana* (49, 64, 69, 92, 107, 158) (1876-1919)

Virginia pole [Virginian pole] - *Phytolacca americana* L. var. *americana* (158) (1900)

Virginia poplar [Virginian poplar] - *Populus deltoides* Bartr. ex Marsh. subsp. *monilifera* (Aiton) Eckenwalder (20) (1857)

Virginia poplar tree [Virginian poplar-tree] - *Populus heterophylla* L. (8) (1785)

Virginia potato [Virginian potato] - *Solanum tuberosum* L. (110) (1585)

Virginia prune [Virginian prune] - *Prunus serotina* Ehrh. (55) (1911)

Virginia raspberry - *Rubus odoratus* L. (5, 156) (1913-1923)

Virginia red cedar - *Juniperus virginiana* L. (122, 124) (1937)

Virginia rockcress [Virginia rock cress, Virginia rock-cress] - *Sibara virginica* (L.) Rollins (5, 97) (1913-1937)

Virginia rose-flower raspberry [Virginian rose-flowering raspberry] - *Rubus odoratus* L. (8) (1785)

Virginia sarsaparill - *Smilax glauca* Walt. (92) (1876)

Virginia sarsaparilla [Virginian sarsaparilla] - *Aralia nudicaulis* L. (5, 64, 156, 157, 158) (1900-1929)

Virginia saxifrage - *Saxifraga virginiensis* Michx. (138) (1923)

Virginia scarlet honeysuckle [Virginian scarlet honeysuckle] - *Lonicera sempervirens* L. var. *virginiana* (Marshall) Castigl. (8) (1785)

Virginia serpentaria - *Aristolochia serpentaria* L. (64) (1907)

Virginia serpentary - *Aristolochia serpentaria* L. (55) (1911)

Virginia silk [Virginian silk] - *Asclepias syriaca* L. (5, 28, 156, 157, 158) (1850-1929)

Virginia skullcap [Virginian skull cap] - *Scutellaria lateriflora* L. (6) (1892)

Virginia snakeroot [Virginia snake root] - *Aristolochia serpentaria* L. (2, 3, 4, 5, 6, 7, 14, 43, 49, 50, 52, 53, 54, 57, 58, 59, 60, 64, 92, 97, 102, 122, 124, 138, 156, 158) (1820–present)

Virginia snakeroot dutchman's-pipe [Virginia snakeroot dutchmanspipe] - *Aristolochia serpentaria* L. (155) (1942)

Virginia snowdrop tree [Virginian snow-drop tree] - *Chionanthus virginicus* L. (8) (1785)

Virginia Solomon's-seal [Virginian's Salomon's seale] - *Maianthemum stellatum* (L.) Link (46) (1879)

Virginia speedwell - *Veronica officinalis* L. (92) (1876)

Virginia spider-flower [Virginia spiderflower] - *Commelina virginica* L. (117) (1908)

Virginia spiderwort - *Tradescantia virginiana* L. (50, 138) (1923–present)

Virginia spiraea - *Spiraea virginiana* Britt. (138) (1923)

Virginia spring-beauty [Virginia springbeauty, Virginia spring beauty] - *Claytonia virginica* L. (3, 4, 50, 155) (1942–present)

Virginia spring-beauty [Virginia springbeauty, Virginia spring beauty] - *Claytonia virginica* L. var. *virginica* (50) (present)

Virginia St. John's-wort [Virginian St. John's wort] - *Hypericum kalmianum* L. (8) (1785)

Virginia stewartia [Virginian stewartia] - *Stewartia malacodendron* L. (8, 138) (1785-1923)

Virginia stickseed - *Hackelia virginiana* (L.) I.M. Johnston (3, 5, 62, 72, 93, 97, 131, 156, 157, 158) (1899-1977)

Virginia stock [Virginian stock] - *Malcolmia maritima* (L.) Aiton f. (109) (1949)

Virginia stonecrop [Virginia stone crop, Virginia stone-crop] - *Penthorum sedoides* L. (6, 48, 49, 52, 53, 57, 85, 93, 120, 131, 156, 157, 158) (1882-1932)

Virginia strawberry [Virginian strawberry] - *Fragaria virginiana*

Duchesne (possibly) (5, 50, 93, 97, 107, 110, 138, 155, 157) (1886–present)

Virginia sumac [Virginia sumach, Virginian sumach] - *Rhus hirta* (L.) Sudworth (5, 14, 34, 107, 156) (1834-1923)

Virginia swallow-wort [Virginian swallow-wort] - *Asclepias syriaca* L. (6) (1892)

Virginia swamp cypress - *Taxodium distichum* (L.) L. C. Rich. (5) (1913)

Virginia swamp pine [Virginian swamp pine] - *Pinus taeda* L. (8) (1785)

Virginia tea - *Itea virginica* L. (156) (1923)

Virginia tephrosia - *Tephrosia virginiana* (L.) Pers (50, 155) (1942–present)

Virginia thistle [Virginian thistle] - *Cirsium virginianum* (L.) Michx. (5, 97, 122, 131) (1899–1937)

Virginia thorn - *Crataegus phaenopyrum* (L. f.) Medik. (92) (1876)

Virginia three-seed mercury [Virginia threeseed mercury, Virginia three-seeded mercury] - *Acalypha virginica* L. (5, 50, 97, 156, 157, 158) (1900–present)

Virginia thyme [Virginian thyme] - *Pycnanthemum flexuosum* (Walt.) Britton, Sterns & Poggenb. (19) (1840), *Pycnanthemum tenuifolium* Schrad. (156) (1923), *Pycnanthemum virginianum* (L.) T. Dur. & B. D. Jackson ex B. L. Robins. & Fern. (5, 156, 157) (1913?–1929)

Virginia tobacco [Virginian tobacco] - *Nicotiana tabacum* L. (19, 92) (1840–1876)

Virginia tovara - *Polygonum virginianum* L. (155) (1942)

Virginia trumpet-flower - *Campsis radicans* (L.) Seem. ex Bureau (158) (1900)

Virginia tulip tree [Virginian tulip-tree] - *Liriodendron tulipifera* L. (8) (1785)

Virginia virgin's-bower [Virginia virgin's bower, Virginian virgin's bower] - *Clematis virginiana* L. (5, 131) (1899–1913)

Virginia wakerobin [Virginian wake robin] - *Hexastylis virginica* (L.) Small (41) (1770), *Peltandra virginica* (L.) Schott. (107, 156) (1919–1923)

Virginia water horehound - *Lycopus virginicus* L. (50) (present)

Virginia water tupelo tree [Virginian water tupelo tree] - *Nyssa aquatica* L. (8) (1785)

Virginia waterleaf [Virginia water leaf, Virginia water-leaf, Virginia water leaf, Virginian waterleaf] - *Hydrophyllum virginianum* L. (5, 6, 72, 93, 106, 131, 155, 156) (1892–1942)

Virginia wild ginger [Virginia wildginger] - *Hexastylis virginica* (L.) Small (2, 155) (1895-1942)

Virginia wild rye [Virginia wild-rye, Virginia wildrye] - *Elymus submuticus* (Hook.) Smyth & Smyth (50) (present), *Elymus virginicus* L. (3, 5, 50, 72, 119, 122, 143, 155, 163) (1907–present)

Virginia willow [Virginia-willow] - *Itea virginica* L. (97, 109, 156) (1937–1949)

Virginia winged rockcress - *Sibara virginica* (L.) Rollins (50) (present)

Virginia winterberry [Virginian winterberry, Virginian winterberry] - *Ilex verticillata* (L.) Gray (5, 6, 8, 41, 156) (1770–1923)

Virginia witch hazel [Virginian witch hazel] - *Hamamelis virginiana* L. (8) (1785)

Virginian blechnum - *Woodwardia virginica* (L.) Sm. (19, 138) (1840–1923)

Virginische Ceder (German) - *Juniperus virginiana* L. (6) (1892)

Virginische Schlangenwurzel (German) - *Aristolochia serpentaria* L. (158) (1900)

Virginische Winterbeere (German) - *Ilex verticillata* (L.) Gray (6) (1892)

Virginischer Ehrenpreis (German) - *Veronicastrum virginicum* (L.) Farw. (6) (1892)

Virginischer Wolfsfuss (German) - *Lycopus virginicus* L. (6, 158) (1892-1900)

Virgin's-bower [Virgins-bower, Virgin's bower, Virgin bower] - *Clematis* L. (1, 2, 4, 7, 10, 13, 15, 63, 82, 93, 109, 158, 167) (1814–1986), *Clematis ligusticifolia* Nutt. (101) (1905), *Clematis ligusticifolia* Nutt. var. *californica* S. Wats. (76) (1896), *Clematis virginiana* L. (4, 15, 19, 48, 49, 61, 72, 82, 85, 127, 138, 155, 156) (1840–1986), *Clematis vitalba* L. (92) (1876), *Wisteria frutescens* (L.) Poir. (5, 106, 156) (1913–1930)

Viscid aster - *Machaeranthera canescens* (Pursh) Gray subsp. *glabra* (Gray) B. L. Turner (5, 93, 131) (1899–1936), *Machaeranthera* Nees (1, 93) (1932–1936)

Viscid bush goldenrod - *Euthamia gymnospermoides* Greene (122) (1937)

Viscid bushy goldenrod [Viscid bushy golden-rod] - *Euthamia gymnospermoides* Greene (5, 97) (1913–1937)

Viscid cranebill [Viscid cranesbill, Viscid crane's bill] - *Geranium viscosissimum* Fisch. & C. A. Mey. ex C. A. Mey. (4, 131) (1899–1986)

Viscid euthamia - *Euthamia gymnospermoides* Greene (4) (1986)

Viscid great bulrush - *Schoenoplectus acutus* (Muhl. ex Bigelow) A.& D. Löve var. *occidentalis* (S. Wats.) S. G. Sm. (5) (1913)

Viscid hedge-hyssop - *Gratiola viscidula* Pennell (5) (1913)

Viscid leptochloa - *Leptochloa viscida* (Scribn.) Beal (94) (1901)

Viscid loco-weed - *Oxytropis borealis* DC. var. *viscida* (Nutt.) Welsh (131) (1899)

Viscid marsh fleabane [Viscid marsh-fleabane] - *Pluchea foetida* (L.) DC. (5, 156) (1913–1923)

Viscid nightshade - *Solanum physalifolium* Rusby (4) (1986), *Solanum sisymbrifolium* Lam. (5) (1913)

Viscid sideranthus - *Rayjacksonia annua* (Rydb.) R.L. Hartman & M. A. Lane (5, 93) (1913–1936)

Viscid tansy-aster [Viscid tansyaster] - *Rayjacksonia annua* (Rydb.) R. L. Hartman & M. A. Lane (50) (present)

Viscid tofieldia - *Tofieldia racemosa* (Walt.) Britton, Sterns & Poggenb. (5) (1913)

Visciolo (Italian) - *Prunus cerasus* L. (110) (1886)

Viscous groundsel - *Senecio viscosus* L. (5) (1913)

Visher's eriogonum - *Eriogonum visheri* A. Nels. (4) (1986)

Visnada (Mexicans) - *Ferocactus wislizeni* (Engelm.) Britt. & Rose (107, 147) (1856-1919)

Vittievar - *Agropyron cristatum* (L.) Gaertn. (92) (1876)

Vittivert - *Agropyron cristatum* (L.) Gaertn. (92) (1876)

Viviparous bistort - *Polygonum viviparum* L. (155) (1942)

Viznaga - *Echinocactus texensis* Hopffer. (122) (1937) TX

Vlix - *Linum usitatissimum* L. (158) (1900)

Vogelbeeren (German) - *Sorbus americana* Marsh. (6) (1892)

Volies - *Nelumbo lutea* Willd. (35) (1806)

Volkameria - *Clerodendrum inerme* (L.) Gaertn. (92) (1876)

Vomitweed [Vomit weed] - *Lobelia inflata* L. (53, 54) (1905–1922)

Vomitwort [Vomit wort] - *Lobelia inflata* L. (69, 92, 157, 158) (1876–1929)

Vreeland's coralroot - *Corallorhiza striata* Lindl. var. *vreelandii* (Rydb.) L. O. Williams (50) (present)

Vulgairement Apalachine (French) - *Ilex cassine* L. (8) (1785)

Vyssine (Albanian) - *Prunus cerasus* L. (110) (1886)

W

Wab-bis-sa-pin (Chipewa) - *Nelumbo lutea* Willd. (35) (1806)

Wabesgung (Chippewa, numb-taste) - *Anemone canadensis* L. (105) (1932)

Wab-es-i-pinig (Chipewa) - *Sagittaria latifolia* Willd. (103) (1871)

Wa'bigwûn (Chippewwa, flowers) - *Anaphalis margaritacea* (L.) Benth. & Hook (40) (1928)

Wabino'wûck (Chippewa, Eastern medicine) - *Monarda fistulosa* L. subsp. *fistulosa* var. *mollis* (L.) Benth. (40) (1928)

Wabos'obûgons' (Chippewa, small rabbit-leaf) - *Gaultheria hispidula* (L.) Muhl. ex Bigelow (40) (1928)

Wabos'odji'bĭk (Chippewa, rabbit leaf) - *Ribes glandulosum* Grauer (40) (1928)

Wabos'odji'bĭk (Chippewa, rabbit root) - *Aralia nudicaulis* L. (40) (1928)

Wachanga (Dakota) - *Hierochloe odorata* (L.) Beauv. (37) (1830)

Wachanga iyechecha (Dakota, similar to sweet grass) - *Melilotus officinalis* (L.) Lam. (possibly) (37) (1919)

Wachholder (German) - *Juniperus communis* L. (158) (1900)

Wachsbusch (German) - *Morella cerifera* (L.) Small (6) (1892)

Wachsgagle (German) - *Morella cerifera* (L.) Small (6) (1892)

Wadûb (Chippewa) - *Alnus incana* (L.) Moench (40) (1928)

Wafer-ash [Wafer ash] - *Ptelea* L. (15) (1895), *Ptelea trifoliata* L. (48, 156) (1882-1900), *Ptelea trifoliata* L. subsp. *polyadenia* (Greene) V. Bailey (124) (1937) TX

Wag wanton - *Briza media* L. (5) (1913)

Wága chan (Dakota) - *Populus deltoides* Bartr. ex Marsh. subsp. *monilifera* (Aiton) Eckenwalder (37) (1919)

Wagačaŋ (Lakota) - *Populus deltoides* Bartr. ex Marsh. subsp. *monilifera* (Aiton) Eckenwalder (121) (1918?-1970?)

Wagamun (Dakota Teton) - *Cucurbita pepo* L. var. *pepo* (37) (1919) Omaha did not distinguish squash or pumpkin, but recognized many varieties of this species

Wagamun pezhuta (Dakota, pumpkin medicine) - *Cucurbita foetidissima* Kunth (37) (1919)

Wagathahashka (Omaha-Ponca) - *Sambucus nigra* L. subsp. *canadensis* (L.) R. Bolli (37) (1919) Wagathahashka-hi (elder bush)

Waghorne's willow - *Salix ×waghornei* Rydb. [arctica × glauca] (5) (1913)

Wagmeza (Dakota Teton) - *Zea mays* L. (37) (1830)

Wagmeza (Lakota) - *Zea mays* L. (121) (1918-1970)

Wagmu (Lakota, possibly from wagmuŋ "twisted thing") - *Cucurbita pepo* L. (121) (1918?-1970?)

Wagmuha (Lakota) - *Lagenaria siceraria* (Molina) Standl. (121) (1918?-1970?)

Wahab' igaskonthe (Omaha-Ponca, similar to corn) - *Typha latifolia* L. (19, 37) (1830-1840) name refers to floral spikes appearing when corn is ripe

Wahába (Omaha-Ponca) - *Zea mays* L. (37) (1830)

Wahaba hthi (Omaha-Ponca, corn sores or blisters) - *Ustilago maydis* (DC.) Corda (37) (1830)

Wah'-bah-co-me-shi' (Shawnee) - *Quercus* L. (132) (1855)

Wah'cha-zi chikala (Dakota) - *Ratibida columnifera* (Nutt.) Wood & Standl. (37) (1919)

Wah'cha-zizi (Dakota, yellow flower) - *Helianthus annuus* L. (37) (1919)

Wah'-hah-tŭt-se (Hueco Pawnee) - *Rhus* L. (132) (1855)

Wah'nah'hecha (Dakota) - *Echinocystis lobata* (Michx.) Torr. & Gray (37) (1919)

Wah'nah'na (Dakota) - *Gymnocladus dioicus* (L.) K. Koch (37) (1919)

Wahoo [Waahoo, Wa-a-hoo, Wauhoo, Whahoo] - *Euonymus americanus* L. (59, 156) (1911-1923), *Euonymus atropurpurea* Jacq. (3, 5, 6, 9, 15, 22, 48, 49, 52, 53, 57, 58, 59, 61, 65, 72, 85, 92, 97, 109, 112, 125, 131, 138, 157, 158) (1869-1986), *Euonymus* L. (1, 7, 158) (1828-1932), *Ptelea trifoliata* L. (106) (1930), *Tilia americana* L. var. *heterophylla* (Vent.) Loud. (156) (1923), *Ulmus alata* Michx. (1, 2, 5, 19, 20, 82, 92, 97, 109, 156, 158) (1840-1949), *Ulmus thomasii* Sarg. (5, 156, 158) (1900-1923)

Wahoon - *Euonymus atropurpurea* Jacq. (6, 7) (1828-1932), *Euonymus* L. (7) (1828)

Wah'pe onapoh'ye (Dakota, leaves and to puff up) - *Humulus lupulus* L. var. *lupuloides* E. Small (37) (1919)

Wah'pe toto (Dakota, greens) - *Chenopodium album* L. (37) (1919)

Wah'pe washtemma (Dakota, fragrant leaves) - *Monarda fistulosa* L. (possibly) (37) (1919)

Wah'pe-popa (Dakota) - *Salix* L. (37) (1919)

Wah'tha (Omaha-Ponca) - *Asclepias syriaca* L. (37) (1919)

Wah'tha-ska (Omaha-Ponca) - *Asclepias exaltata* L. (37) (1919)

Wait-a-bit - *Smilax rotundifolia* L. (5, 73, 156) (1892-1923)

Wakerobin [Wake robin, Wake-robin] - *Arisaema triphyllum* (L.) Schott (5, 7, 49, 57, 58, 64, 75, 78, 92, 156, 157, 158) (1828-1929), *Arum* L. (10) (1818), *Trillium cernuum* L. (7) (1828), *Trillium erectum* L. (6, 49, 57, 92, 156) (1876-1923), *Trillium flexipes* Raf. (85) (1932) SD, *Trillium grandiflorum* (Michx.) Salisb. (40) (1928), *Trillium* L. (1, 93, 106, 109, 155, 156, 158) (1900-1949), *Trillium viridescens* Nutt. (97) (1937)

Wakethe (Osage) - *Typha latifolia* L. (121) (1918-1970)

Wake-warutsh (Winnebago, raccoon food) - *Celtis occidentalis* L. (37) (1919)

Wakidikidik (Winnebago) - *Ulmus rubra* Muhl. (37) (1919)

Wakmu (Dakota) - *Lagenaria siceraria* (Molina) Standl. (37) (1919)

Waldfarn (German) - *Dryopteris filix-mas* (L.) Schott (158) (1900)

Waldmangolt [Waltmangold] (German) - *Pyrola americana* Sweet (46, 158) (1879-1900)

Walewort - *Sambucus ebulus* L. (92) (1876)

Walking fern [Walking-fern, Walkingfern] - *Asplenium* L. (1, 155, 158) (1900-1942), *Asplenium rhizophyllum* L. (3, 4, 5, 50, 72, 102, 109) (1886–present)

Walking leaf-fern [Walking leaf fern] - *Asplenium rhizophyllum* L. (97) (1937)

Walking-leaf [Walking leaf] - *Asplenium* L. (1) (1932), *Asplenium rhizophyllum* L. (5, 19, 86, 92, 109) (1840-1949)

Walking-stick cactus [Walkingstick cactus] - *Opuntia imbricata* (Haw.) DC. (138, 155) (1923-1942)

Wall - *Lablab purpureus* (L.) Sweet (110) (1886)

Wall barley [Wall-barley] - *Hordeum jubatum* L. (19, 56, 62, 80, 87, 88, 115, 126, 143, 148) (1840-1939), *Hordeum murinum* L. (5, 45, 94, 163) (1852-1913)

Wall bedstraw - *Galium parisiense* L. (5) (1913)

Wall bur-cucumber [Wall burcucumber] - *Sicyos angulatus* L. (155) (1942)

Wall creeper - *Parthenocissus quinquefolia* (L.) Planch. (138) (1923)

Wall cress - *Arabis* L. (10, 42, 158) (1814-1900)

Wall hawkweed [Wall hawk-weed] - *Hieracium murorum* L. (5, 156) (1913-1923)

Wall moss - *Lichen parietinus* L. (92) (1876)

Wall pellitory - *Parietaria officinalis* L. (92) (1876)

Wall rockcress [Wall rock-cress] - *Arabis caucasica* Willd. (109, 155) (1942-1949)

Wall speedwell - *Veronica arvensis* L. (19, 97) (1840-1937)

Wall spleenwort - *Asplenium trichomanes* L. (5) (1913)

Wallcress [Wall cress, Wall-cress] - *Arabidopsis thaliana* (L.) Britton

(5, 156) (1913-1923), *Arabis caucasica* Willd. (138) (1923), *Arabis glabra* (L.) Bernh. (157) (1929), *Arabis* L. (10, 158) (1818-1900)

Wallflower [Wall-flower, Wallflowers] - *Erysimum capitatum* (Dougl. ex Hook.) Greene var. *capitatum* (85, 122) (1932-1937), *Erysimum cheiranthoides* L. (156) (1923), *Erysimum cheiri* (L.) Crantz (19, 92, 109) (1840-1949), *Erysimum* L. (4, 7, 10, 50, 138) (1818–present), *Helianthus annuus* L. (158) (1900)

Wall-link [Wallink) - *Veronica americana* Schwein. ex Benth. (75, 156) (1894-1923) WV

Wall-moss [Wall moss] - *Sedum acre* L. (5, 156) (1913-1923)

Wallnuss (German) - *Juglans cinerea* L. (6) (1892)

Wall-pepper [Wall pepper] - *Sedum acre* L. (5, 92, 156, 178) (1526-1923)

Wall-rocket [Wallrocket, Wall rocket] - *Diplotaxis* DC. (50, 155) (1942–present), *Diplotaxis tenuifolia* (L.) DC. (5, 156) (1913-1923)

Wall-rue [Wall rue] - *Acrostichum* L. (167) (1814), *Asplenium ruta-muraria* L. (2, 50, 92) (1876–present)

Wall-rue spleenwort [Wall rue spleenwort] - *Asplenium ruta-muraria* L. (5) (1913)

Wallwort [Wall wort, Wallwoort] - *Sambucus ebulus* L. (92, 107, 178) (1526-1919), *Sedum acre* L. (156) (1923)

Walnut [Wall nut, Wall nutte, Walnutt, Walnuts] or Walnut tree - *Carya alba* (L.) Nutt. ex Ell. (46, 75) (1879-1894), *Carya laciniosa* (Michx. f.) G. Don (46) (1879), *Carya ovata* (Mill.) K. Koch (5) (1913), *Juglans* L. (4, 8, 10, 50, 82, 92, 93, 106, 109, 138, 155, 156, 158, 1785, 184) (1793–present), *Juglans major* (Torr.) Heller (112) (1937), *Juglans microcarpa* Berl. var. *microcarpa* (149) (1904), *Juglans nigra* L. (157, 181) (~1678-1929), *Juglans regia* L. (110, 178, 179) (1526-1886)

Walnut-leaf ash - *Fraxinus americana* L. (19) (1840)

Walnut-leaf white ash [Walnutleaf white ash] - *Fraxinus americana* L. (155) (1942)

Walnut-leaf yellow-wood [Walnut-leaved yellow-wood] - *Zanthoxylum martinicense* (Lam.) DC. (20) (1857)

Walpole tea - *Ceanothus americanus* L. (5, 92, 156, 157, 158) (1876-1929)

Walsh nut tree - *Juglans regia* L. (178) (1526)

Walter's aster [Walter aster] - *Symphyotrichum walteri* (Alexander) Nesom (155) (1942)

Walter's cress - *Rorippa teres* (Michx.) R. Stuckey (97) (1937)

Walter's grass [Walter grass] - *Agrostis* L. (7) (1828)

Walter's greenbrier - *Smilax walteri* Pursh. (5) (1913)

Walter's paspalum - *Paspalum dissectum* (L.) L. (5, 94) (1901-1913)

Walter's sedge - *Carex striata* Michx. var. *striata* (5) (1913)

Walter's violet [Walter violet] - *Viola walteri* House (138) (1923)

Walworde - *Parietaria judaica* L. (179) (1526), *Sambucus ebulus* L. (179) (1526)

Wamide wenigthe (Omaha-Ponca) - *Astragalus crassicarpus* Nutt. var. *crassicarpus* (37) (1919)

Wamnáheza (Dakota) - *Zea mays* L. (37) (1830)

Wamnu (Dakota) - *Cucurbita pepo* L. var. *pepo* (37) (1919)

Wamnuha (Dakota) - *Lagenaria siceraria* (Molina) Standl. (37) (1919)

Wampee - *Pontederia cordata* L. (106) (1930) Southern US, *Pontederia* L. (1) (1932)

Wampee (Indian tribes) - *Peltandra* Raf. (7) (1828)

Wanaghi-haz (Winnebago, ghost fruit) - *Menispermum canadense* L. (37) (1919)

Wanah'cha (Dakota) - *Dalea purpurea* Vent. var. *purpurea* (37) (1919)

Wananha hazi etai (Ponca, grapes of the ghosts) - *Menispermum canadense* L. (37) (1919)

Wananh'a-i-monthin (Omaha-Ponca, ghost walking stick) - *Euonymus atropurpurea* Jacq. (37) (1919)

Wand flower [Wand-flower, Wandflower] - *Nemophila aphylla* (L.) Brummitt (156) (1923), *Sparaxis* Ker-Gawl. (109, 138) (1923-1949)

Wand lespedeza - *Lespedeza violacea* (L.) Pers. (155) (1942)

Wand lythrum - *Lythrum salicaria* L. (138) (1923)

Wanderer violet - *Viola nephrophylla* Greene (155) (1942)

Wandering milkweed [Wandering milk weed] - *Apocynum androsaemifolium* L. (6, 58, 92, 156, 157) (1869-1929), *Euphorbia corollata* L. (6) (1892)

Wandering-Jenny [Wandering Jenny] - *Lysimachia nummularia* L. (5, 156, 158) (1900-1923)

Wandering-Jew [Wandering Jew] - *Cymbalaria muralis* P.G. Gaertn., B. Mey. & Scherb. (5, 156) (1913-1923), *Saxifraga stolonifera* Meerb. (92) (1876), *Tradescantia crassifolia* Cav. (73, 78) (1892-1898), *Tradescantia fluminensis* Vell. (109, 138) (1923-1949), *Tradescantia zebrina* hort. ex Bosse (109) (1949)

Wandering-jew zebrina - *Tradescantia zebrina* hort. ex Bosse (138) (1923)

Wandering-sailor [Wandering sailor] - *Lysimachia nummularia* L. (156, 158) (1900-1923)

Wandering-Sally [Wandering Sally] - *Lysimachia nummularia* L. (5, 156) (1913-1923)

Wand-like bush clover [Wand-like bush-clover] - *Lespedeza frutescens* (L.) Hornem. (5, 72, 97) (1907-1937)

Wand-like goldenrod [Wand-like golden-rod] - *Solidago stricta* Aiton (5) (1913)

Wankapin - *Nelumbo* Adans. (15) (1895), *Nelumbo lutea* Willd. (76, 156, 157, 158) (1896-1929)

Wanoŋpihi (Osage, necklace tree) - *Sapindus saponaria* L. var. *drummondii* (Hook. & Arn.) Bensons (121) (1918?-1970?)

Wanûkons' (Chippewa) - *Cicuta maculata* L. (40) (1928)

Wapkadak (Chippewa) - *Actaea pachypoda* Ell. (105) (1932)

Wappatoo [Wapatoo, Wap-pa-to, or Wappato] - *Sagittaria cuneata* Sheld. (101) (1905) MT, *Sagittaria latifolia* Willd. (35, 46, 157, 161) (1896-1929)

Ward's coastal-plain willow [Ward coastalplain willow] - *Salix caroliniana* Michx. (155) (1942)

Ward's goldenrod [Ward goldenrod] - *Solidago petiolaris* Aiton var. *angusta* (Torr. & Gray) Gray (155) (1942)

Ward's loco [Ward loco] - *Astragalus wardii* Gray (155) (1942)

Ward's whitlow-wort [Ward's whitlow wort] - *Paronychia jamesii* Torr. & Gray (5) (1913)

Ward's willow - *Salix caroliniana* Michx. (5, 82, 97) (1913-1937)

Wardseed [Ward-seed] - *Capsella bursa-pastoris* (L.) Medik. (157, 158) (1900-1929)

Warence - *Rubia tinctoria* L. (179) (1526)

Warlock - *Brassica nigra* (L.) W.D.J. Koch (5) (1913), *Moricandia arvensis* (L.) DC. (158) (1900), *Raphanus raphanistrum* L. (5) (1913), *Sinapis arvensis* L. (157) (1929)

Warmot - *Artemisia absinthium* L. (5, 156, 157, 158) (1900-1929)

Wart flower [Wartflower, Wart-flower] - *Chelidonium majus* L. (156, 158) (1900-1923)

Wart spurge [Wart-spurge] - *Euphorbia helioscopia* L. (5, 85, 122, 156) (1913-1937)

Wartatel (Swedish) - *Aira praecox* L. (46) (1879)

Wartberry fairybells - *Disporum trachycarpum* (S. Wats.) Benth. & Hook. f. (155) (1942)

Wart-cress [Wartcress, Wart cress] - *Carara coronopus* (L.) Medik. (5) (1913), *Coronopus squamatus* (Forsk.) Aschers. (107, 156) (1919-1923), *Coronopus* Zinn (10, 13, 156) (1818-1923)

Warted spurge - *Euphorbia spathulata* Lam (5, 156) (1913-1923)

Warted squash - *Cucurbita pepo* L. (10) (1818)

Wart-grass [Wartgrass] - *Euphorbia helioscopia* L. (5, 156) (1913-1923)

Wartweed [Wart-weed] - *Chelidonium majus* L. (158) (1900), *Euphorbia helioscopia* L. (5, 156) (1913-1923), *Euphorbia peplus* L. (5, 156) (1913-1923)

Wartwort [Wart-wort] - *Carara coronopus* (L.) Medik. (5) (1913), *Chelidonium majus* L. (5, 156, 158) (1900-1923), *Coronopus squamatus* (Forsk.) Aschers. (156, 179) (1526-1923), *Euphorbia he-*

lioscopia L. (5, 92) (1876-1913), *Gnaphalium uliginosum* L. (5, 156, 158) (1900-1923)

Warty caltrop - *Kallstroemia parviflora* J.B.S. Norton (50) (present)

Warty panic grass [Warty panic-grass] - *Panicum verrucosum* Muhl. (5, 50, 66, 94) (1901–present)

Warty quillwort - *Isoetes lacustris* L. (5) (1913)

Warty spurge - *Euphorbia cuphosperma* (Engelm.) Boiss. (122) (1937), *Euphorbia dentata* Michx. (5, 85, 93) (1913-1936), *Euphorbia spathulata* Lam (50) (present)

Waschwurzel (German) - *Saponaria officinalis* L. (158) (1900)

Washerwoman - *Alternanthera caracasana* Kunth (50) (present)

Washington foxtail - *Alopecurus geniculatus* L. (155) (1942)

Washington hawthorn - *Crataegus phaenopyrum* (L. f.) Medik. (137, 138) (1923-1931)

Washington lily - *Lilium washingtonianum* Kellogg (109, 138) (1923-1949)

Washington lupine - *Lupinus polyphyllus* Lindl. (138) (1923)

Washington palm - *Washingtonia* H. Wendl. (109, 138) (1923-1949) for George Washington

Washington plant - *Cabomba caroliniana* Gray (109) (1949)

Washington thorn - *Crataegus phaenopyrum* (L. f.) Medik. (2, 5, 109) (1895-1949)

Washington's bower - *Lycium barbarum* L. (77) (1898) Southwest MO

Washington's sedge - *Carex bigelowii* Torr. ex Schwein. (66) (1903)

Wasserbenediktenwurzel (German) - *Geum rivale* L (158) (1900)

Wasserdürrwurz (German) - *Bidens tripartita* L. (158) (1900)

Wasserhanf (German) - *Bidens tripartita* L. (158) (1900)

Wasserhollder (German) - *Viburnum opulus* L. (158) (1900)

Wasserklee (German) - *Menyanthes trifoliata* L. (158) (1900)

Wassermannstreu (German) - *Eryngium yuccifolium* Michx. (6) (1892)

Wassernabel (German) - *Hydrocotyle* L. (158) (1900)

Wasserschild (German) - *Brasenia schreberi* Gmel. (7) (1828)

Wasserschwelke (German) - *Viburnum opulus* L. (158) (1900)

Watan (Omaha-Ponca) - *Cucurbita pepo* L. var. *pepo* (37) (1919)

Watangtha (Omaha-Ponca, ghost melon) - *Echinocystis lobata* (Michx.) Torr. & Gray (37) (1919)

WataΘtoΘta (Osage) - *Carya illinoinensis* (Wangenh.) K. Koch (121) (1918?-1970?)

Watch clover - *Trifolium arvense* L. (158) (1900)

Watches - *Sarracenia flava* L. (5, 156) (1913-1923), *Sarracenia leucophylla* Raf. (15) (1895), *Sarracenia purpurea* L. (5, 74, 156) (1893-1923) Atlantic City NJ

Water aira grass [Water aira-grass] - *Catabrosa aquatica* (L.) Beauv. (165) (1768)

Water ash - *Fraxinus caroliniana* Mill. (5, 97, 122, 124, 156) (1913-1937) NM, *Fraxinus nigra* Marsh (5, 20, 156, 158) (1857-1923), *Fraxinus pennsylvanica* Marsh. (5) (1913)

Water avens - *Geum rivale* L (2, 4, 5, 6, 49, 57, 92, 107, 155, 156, 158) (1892-1986)

Water awlwort - *Subularia aquatica* L. (5) (1913)

Water beech - *Carpinus caroliniana* Walt. (2, 5, 156) (1895–1923), *Carpinus caroliniana* Walt. subsp. *caroliniana* (46, 92) (1649–1876), *Carpinus* L. (41) (1770), *Platanus occidentalis* L. (5, 20, 41, 156, 158, 187) (1770–1923)

Water beggarticks - *Bidens cernua* L. (19) (1840)

Water bent grass [Water bent-grass, Water bentgrass] - *Agrostis stolonifera* L. (152) (1912) NM, *Polypogon viridis* (Gouan) Breistr. (94, 122, 155) (1901-1942)

Water betony - *Scrophularia umbrosa* Dumort. (92) (1876)

Water birch - *Betula nigra* L. (5, 156, 158) (1900–1923), *Betula occidentalis* Hook. (1, 5, 50, 138, 155, 158) (1900–1942)

Water bitternut - *Carya aquatica* (Michx. f.) Nutt. (5, 156) (1913–1923)

Water bitternut hickory - *Carya aquatica* (Michx. f.) Nutt. (20) (1857)

Water bog-rush [Water bog rush] - *Cladium mariscoides* (Muhl.) Torr. (5, 19) (1840-1913), *Mariscus mariscoides* (Muhl.) Kuntze (50) (present)

Water breweria - *Stylisma aquatica* (Walt.) Chapman (5) (1913)

Water bugle - *Lycopus virginicus* L. (6, 7, 49, 92) (1828-1898)

Water bur-marigold - *Bidens beckii* Torr. ex Spreng. (156) (1923)

Water buttercup - *Ranunculus flabellaris* Raf. (127, 158) (1900-1933)

Water calamint - *Mentha arvensis* L. (92, 158) (1876-1900)

Water caltrop [Water caltrops] - *Potamogeton crispus* L. (158) (1900), *Trapa* L. (156) (1923), *Trapa natans* L. (5, 107, 109, 156) (1913-1949)

Water chadlocke - *Sinapis arvensis* L. (possibly) (180) (1633)

Water chickweed - *Montia fontana* L. (5, 156) (1913-1923), *Myosoton aquaticum* (L.) Moench (5, 156, 158) (1900-1923)

Water club-rush [Water club rush] - *Schoenoplectus subterminalis* (Torr.) Soják (5) (1913)

Water cowbane - *Cicuta* L. (10) (1818)

Water crowfoot - *Ranunculus aquatilis* L. (19, 92) (1840-1876), *Ranunculus flabellaris* Raf. (85) (1932), *Ranunculus* L. (93) (1936), *Ranunculus trichophyllus* Chaix var. *trichophyllus* (131) (1899)

Water dock - *Rumex altissimus* Wood (46, 121) (1879–1981), *Rumex orbiculatus* Gray (19) (1840), *Rumex verticillatus* L. (3, 4) (1977–1986)

Water dropwort [Water drop-wort] - *Oenanthe* L. (10) (1818), *Oxypolis filiformis* (Walt.) Britton (5, 92, 156) (1876-1923), *Oxypolis rigidior* (L.) Raf. (possibly) (5, 156) (1913-1923), *Oxypolis ternata* (Nutt.) Heller (possibly) (19) (1840)

Water elm [Water-elm] - *Planera aquatica* J.F. Gmel. (5, 97, 156) (1913-1937), *Ulmus alata* Michx. (5, 156, 158) (1900-1923), *Ulmus americana* L. (5, 93, 109, 113, 130, 156, 157, 158) (1890-1929)

Water eryngo [Water-eryngo] - *Eryngium yuccifolium* Michx. (5, 49, 53, 54, 57, 61, 64, 92, 156, 157, 158) (1870-1929)

Water fern [Waterfern, Water-fern] - *Azolla* Lam. (4) (1986), *Ceratopteris* Brongn. (109, 138) (1923-1949), *Osmunda regalis* L. (5) (1913)

Water figwort - *Scrophularia umbrosa* Dumort. (92) (1876)

Water flag - *Iris versicolor* L. (5, 49, 64, 92, 93, 156, 157, 158) (1900-1936)

Water flaxseed - *Spirodela polyrhiza* (L.) Schleid. (19) (1840)

Water foxtail [Water fox tail] - *Alopecurus geniculatus* L. (5, 45, 50, 87, 111, 155) (1884–present), *Alopecurus aequalis* Sobol. var. *aequalis* (88) (1885)

Water foxtail grass - *Alopecurus geniculatus* L. (90) (1885)

Water germander - *Teucrium canadense* L. (46) (1649)

Water gilliflower - *Hottonia inflata* Ell. (156) (1923)

Water gladiole - *Lobelia dortmanna* L. (5, 75, 156) (1894-1923) NY

Water gladiolus - *Butomus umbellatus* L. (107) (1919)

Water grass [Water-grass] - *Alopecurus aequalis* Sobol. (152) (1912) NM, *Catabrosa aquatica* (L.) Beauv. (5, 111, 157) (1913-1929), *Echinochloa crus-galli* (L.) Beauv. (5, 119, 151) (1896-1938), *Paspalidium geminatum* (Forsk.) Stapf var. *paludivagum* (A.S. Hitchc. & Chase) Gould (163) (1852), *Paspalum laeve* Michx. (87) (1884)

Water groundsel - *Senecio hydrophilus* Nutt. (155) (1942)

Water gum - *Nyssa biflora* Walt. (5) (1913)

Water hair grass - *Catabrosa aquatica* (L.) Beauv. (5, 19, 66) (1840-1912)

Water hedge-hyssop [Water hedge hyssop] - *Lindernia dubia* (L.) Pennell var. *anagallidea* (Michx.) Cooperr. (19) (1840)

Water hemlock [Waterhemlock, Water-hemlock] - *Cicuta bulbifera* L. (41, 157) (1770-1929), *Cicuta douglasii* (DC.) J.M.Coult. & Rose (71) (1898), *Cicuta* L. (1, 2, 4, 10, 50, 93, 109, 138, 155, 156, 158) (1818–present), *Cicuta maculata* L. (3, 5, 62, 63, 71, 97, 121, 126, 131, 133, 156) (1898-1977), *Cicuta maculata* L. var. *angustifolia* Hook. (101, 146, 148) (1905-1939), *Cicuta virosa* L. (19) (1840)

Water hickory - *Carya aquatica* (Michx. f.) Nutt. (2, 5, 97, 156) (1895–1937)

Water horehound [Water hoarhound, Waterhorehound] - *Lycopus americanus* Muhl. ex W. Bart. (47, 95, 114, 156) (1852-1923), *Lycopus asper* Greene (85) (1932), *Lycopus europaeus* L. (5, 19) (1840-1913), *Lycopus* L. (1, 2, 10, 26, 50, 93, 106, 156, 190) (~1759–present), *Lycopus rubellus* Moench (4, 156) (1923-1986), *Lycopus virginicus* L. (6, 7, 49, 92, 157) (1828-1929)

Water horse mint - *Mentha spicata* L. (5) (1913)

Water horseradish - *Armoracia lacustris* (A.Gray) Al-Shehbaz & V.Bates. (possibly) (92) (1876)

Water horsetail - *Equisetum fluviatile* L. (3, 4, 5, 50, 155) (1913–present)

Water hyacinth [Water-hyacinth] - *Eichhornia crassipes* (Mart.) Solms (109, 122, 124) (1937-1949), *Eichhornia* Kunth (138) (1923), *Pontederia cordata* L. (156) (1923)

Water hyssop - *Bacopa monnieri* (L.) Pennell (5, 107, 156) (1913-1923)

Water Indian hemp - *Asclepias incarnata* L. (5, 49, 158) (1898-1913)

Water jessamine - *Gratiola virginiana* L. (7, 92, 157, 158) (1828-1929)

Water knotgrass [Water knot-grass, Water knot grass] - *Najas flexilis* (Willd.) Rostk. & Schmidt (19) (1840)

Water knotweed - *Polygonum amphibium* L. (50) (present)

Water lady's-thumb [Water ladysthumb] - *Polygonum amphibium* L. (155) (1942)

Water lobelia - *Lobelia dortmanna* L. (5, 19, 156) (1840-1923)

Water locust [Waterlocust] - *Gleditsia aquatica* Marsh. (2, 5, 8, 20, 50, 97, 122, 124, 138, 155, 156, 158) (1857–present)

Water loosestrife - *Lysimachia thyrsiflora* L. (138, 155) (1923-1942)

Water lotus - *Nelumbo lutea* Willd. (157, 158) (1900-1929)

Water manna grass [Water mannagrass] - *Glyceria fluitans* (L.) R. Br. (50, 155) (1942–present), *Glyceria maxima* (Hartm.) Holmb. (138) (1923)

Water maple - *Acer macrophyllum* Pursh (106) (1930), *Acer rubrum* L. (5, 156) (1913-1923), *Acer rubrum* L. (5, 156, 157, 158) (1900-1929), *Acer spicatum* Lam. (5, 156) (1913-1923)

Water marigold [Water marygold] - *Bidens beckii* Torr. ex Spreng. (5, 19, 63, 76, 92, 156) (1840-1923), *Bidens L.* (1) (1932)

Water maudlin - *Eupatorium cannabinum* L. (92) (1876)

Water meadow grass - *Catabrosa aquatica* (L.) Beauv. (68) (1890), *Glyceria grandis* S. Wats. var. *grandis* (5) (1913), *Glyceria maxima* (Hartm.) Holmb. (56) (1901)

Water milfoil - *Ranunculus aquatilis* L. (156) (1923)

Water milfoil - *Ranunculus trichophyllus* Chaix var. *trichophyllus* (5) (1913)

Water mint [Water-mint] - *Mentha aquatica* L. (5, 50, 92, 155, 156) (1876–present), *Mentha spicata* L. (156, 158) (1900-1923)

Water moss [Watermoss] - *Conferva* L. (7) (1828)

Water mouse-ear chickweed - *Myosoton aquaticum* (L.) Moench (5, 156, 158) (1900-1923)

Water mudwort - *Limosella aquatica* L. (50, 155) (1942–present)

Water navelwort [Water-navelwort] - *Hydrocotyle umbellata* L. (5, 19, 92, 156) (1840-1923), *Myriophyllum spicatum* L. (5, 156, 158) (1900-1923)

Water nerveroot [Water nerve root, Water nerve-root] - *Asclepias incarnata* L. (5, 92, 156, 158) (1876-1923)

Water oak - *Quercus falcata* Michx. (5, 93, 97, 156) (1913–1937), *Quercus hemisphaerica* Bartr. ex Willd. (182) (1791), *Quercus laurifolia* Michx. (5) (1913), *Quercus nigra* L. (2, 5, 19, 20, 33, 65, 72, 97, 106, 109, 122, 124, 138, 156, 181, 187, 189) (~1678–1949)

Water oats - *Zizania aquatica* L. (2, 66, 87, 92, 131, 157, 158) (1844-1929), *Zizania* L. (1, 45) (1896-1932)

Water paspalum - *Paspalum fluitans* (Ell.) Kunth (5, 163) (1852-1938)

Water peachwort - *Polygonum amphibium* L. (46) (1879)

Water pennywort - *Hydrocotyle* L. (4, 156) (1923-1986)

Water persicaria - *Persicaria amphibia* (L.) Delarbre (5, 93) (1913-1936), *Polygonum amphibium* L. (72, 122, 131, 156, 157, 158) (1899-1937)

Water pimpernel - *Veronica anagallis-aquatica* L. (5, 156, 158) (1900-1923), *Veronica arvensis* L. (177) (1762), *Veronica beccabunga* L. (107) (1919)

Water plaintain spearwort - *Ranunculus ambigens* S. Wats. (2) (1895)

Water plantain - *Plantago cordata* Lam (5, 48, 61, 92, 156) (1870-1923)

Water polygonum - *Polygonum amphibium* L. (2) (1895)

Water poplar - *Populus deltoides* Bartr. ex Marsh. (5, 156, 158) (1900–1923), *Populus deltoides* Bartr. ex Marsh. subsp. *deltoides* (19, 92) (1840–1876), *Populus nigra* L. (158) (1900)

Water purslane [Water purslain, Water-purslane, Waterpurslane]] - *Didiplis diandra* (Nutt. ex DC.) Wood (1, 3, 4, 5, 50, 72, 93, 155, 156) (1907–present), *Didiplis Raf.* (possibly) (10) (1818), *Ludwigia* L. (106) (1930), *Ludwigia palustris* (L.) Ell. (3, 5, 19, 63, 76, 106, 120, 156, 157, 158) (1840-1977), *Veronica beccabunga* L. (7, 92) (1828–1876)

Water pusley [Water-pusley] - *Ludwigia peploides* (Kunth) Raven (156) (1923)

Water ragwort - *Senecio hydrophilus* Nutt. (50) (present)

Water red oak - *Quercus rubra* L. (8) (1785)

Water rice - *Zizania aquatica* L. (5, 157, 158) (1900–1929)

Water rocket - *Barbarea vulgaris* W.T. Aiton (19) (1840)

Water rush - *Juncus effusus* L. (5, 92, 156) (1913–1923)

Water saxifrage - *Saxifraga pensylvanica* L. (19) (1840)

Water scorpion-grass [Water scorpion grass] - *Myosotis scorpioides* L. (92) (1876)

Water sedge - *Carex aquatilis* Wahlenb. (5, 50, 66, 72, 139, 155) (1907–present), *Carex aquatilis* Wahlenb. var. *aquatilis* (50) (present)

Water seedbox - *Ludwigia repens* Forst. (155) (1942)

Water seeker - *Hamamelis virginiana* L. (6) (1892)

Water shamrock - *Menyanthes trifoliata* L. (5, 6, 7, 57, 92, 156, 158) (1828–1923)

Water smartweed [Water smart weed, Water smart-weed] - *Polygonum amphibium* L. (2, 4, 82, 156, 157) (1900-1930), *Polygonum amphibium* L. var. *emersum* Michx. (145) (1897), *Polygonum amphibium* L. var. *stipulaceum* Coleman (50, 82) (1930–present), *Polygonum* L. (106) (1930), *Polygonum punctatum* Ell. (3, 4, 5, 72, 93, 97, 122, 131, 157, 158) (1899-1986), *Polygonum punctatum* Ell. var. *punctatum* (2, 6, 80, 82, 156) (1892-1932)

Water spear grass - *Catabrosa aquatica* (L.) Beauv. (66) (1903)

Water speedwell - *Veronica anagallis-aquatica* L. (3, 4, 5, 50, 63, 72, 82, 93, 95, 97, 107, 122, 131, 155, 156, 158) (1899–present), *Veronica arvensis* L. (177) (1762), *Veronica beccabunga* L. (7) (1828)

Water spring-beauty [Water spring beauty] - *Monita* L.(possibly) (1) (1932)

Water star-grass [Water star grass, Water stargrass] - *Heteranthera dubia* (Jacq.) MacM. (2, 3, 5, 72, 93, 120, 122, 156, 158) (1895-1977), *Heteranthera* Ruiz. & Pavon. (1) (1932)

Water stitchwort - *Stellaria fontinalis* (Short & Peter) B.L. Robins. (5) (1913)

Water tare grass [Water taregrass] - *Zizania aquatica* L. (41) (1770)

Water trefoil - *Menyanthes trifoliata* L. (5, 49, 156, 158) (1898-1923)

Water tupelo [Water-tupelo] - *Nyssa aquatica* L. (177, 189) (1762-1767), *Nyssa biflora* Walt. (2, 5) (1895-1913)

Water twitch - *Agrostis gigantea* Roth (5) (1913)

Water violet - *Viola lanceolata* L. (5, 93, 156) (1913-1936)

Water wattle - *Acacia retinodes* Schlecht. (50) (present)

Water white oak - *Quercus lyrata* Walt. (5, 33, 156) (1827-1923)

Water whorl grass [Water whorl-grass, Water whorlgrass] - *Catabrosa aquatica* (L.) Beauv. (5, 50, 94) (1901–present)

Water yam - *Dioscorea alata* L. (50) (present)

Water-agrimony [Water agrimony] - *Bidens cernua* L. (5, 156, 158) (1900-1923), *Bidens tripartita* L. (158) (1900)

Water-apples [Water apples] - *Annona glabra* L. (92) (1876)

Water-arum [Water arum] - *Calla* L. (1, 109, 158, 167) (1814-1949), *Calla palustris* L. (5, 19, 50, 78, 86, 107, 156, 158) (1840–present)

Water-ash [Water ash] - *Acer negundo* L. (5, 93, 156, 157, 158) (1900-1936), *Ptelea* L. (122) (1937), *Ptelea trifoliata* L. (4, 5, 6, 47, 49, 52, 53, 57, 61, 65, 74, 92, 124, 137, 156, 157) (1852-1986)

Water-bean - *Nelumbo* Adans. (158) (1900), *Nelumbo lutea* Willd. (156) (1923)

Water-beech [Water beech] - *Platanus occidentalis* L. (5, 20, 41, 156, 158) (1770–1923)

Water-betony - *Scrophularia umbrosa* Dumort. (107) (1919)

Water-blinks [Water blinks] - *Montia fontana* L. (5, 156) (1913-1923)

Waterblob [Water blob, Water-blob, Water blobs] - *Caltha palustris* L. (5, 92, 157) (1876-1929)

Waterbouts [Water bouts] - *Caltha palustris* L. (6) (1892)

Water-brush - *Baccharis halimifolia* L. (156) (1923)

Water-cabbage [Water cabbage] - *Nymphaea odorata* Aiton (7, 92) (1828-1876), *Nymphaea odorata* Aiton subsp. *odorata* (5, 156, 158) (1900-1923)

Water-can [Water can] - *Nuphar lutea* (L.) Sm. (92) (1876), *Nymphaea* L. (184) (1793)

Water-carpet [Water carpet] - *Chrysosplenium* L. (1, 7, 156) (1828-1932), *Chrysosplenium oppositifolium* L. (5, 19, 156) (1840-1923)

Water-celery [Water celery] - *Ranunculus sceleratus* L. (5, 156, 158) (1900-1923), *Vallisneria americana* Michx. (5, 156, 158) (1900-1923) Chesapeake Bay

Water-chestnut [Waterchestnut, Water chestnut] - *Trapa* L. (138) (1923), *Trapa natans* L. (107, 109, 138) (1919-1949)

Water-chickweed [Water chickweed] - *Callitriche* L. (23) (1826), *Callitriche palustris* L. (5, 49, 92, 156) (1876-1923)

Water-clover [Waterclover, Water clover] - *Marsilea* L. (3, 4, 50) (1977–present)

Watercress [Water-cress, Water cress] - *Barbarea vulgaris* W.T. Aiton (181) (~1678), *Cardamine rotundifolia* Michx. (107) (1919), *Moricandia arvensis* (L.) DC. (74) (1893) WV, *Nasturtium officinale* W.T. Aiton (possibly) (3, 4, 15, 50, 72, 85, 92, 107, 109, 122, 131, 138, 155, 156, 157, 158) (1895–present), *Nasturtium* R. Br. (1, 4, 13, 63, 156, 179) (1526-1986), *Rorippa amphibia* (L.) Bess. (107) (1919), *Sinapis arvensis* L. (5) (1913), *Sisymbrium* L. (10, 184) (1793-1818)

Water-cup [Watercup, Water cup] - *Sarracenia flava* L. (5, 92, 156) (1876-1923), *Sarracenia purpurea* L. (6, 49, 52) (1892-1919)

Water-dock [Water dock] - *Orontium aquaticum* L. (5, 156) (1913-1923)

Water-dragon [Water dragon] - *Calla palustris* L. (5, 107, 156, 158) (1900–1923), *Caltha palustris* L. (5, 6, 92, 157, 158) (1892–1929), *Saururus cernuus* L. (3) (1977)

Water-elder [Water elder] - *Viburnum opulus* L. (156, 158) (1900-1923)

Water-feather [Water-feather, Water feathers] - *Chara* L. (7) (1828), *Chara vulgaris* L. (92) (1876), *Hottonia inflata* Ell. (5, 10, 156) (1818-1923)

Water-fennel [Water fennel] - *Callitriche palustris* L. (5, 93, 131, 156, 157) (1899-1936)

Water-fescue [Water fescue] - *Glyceria fluitans* (L.) R. Br. (19) (1840)

Water-gall - *Baccharis halimifolia* L. (156) (1923)

Water-goggles [Water goggles] - *Caltha palustris* L. (5, 156, 157, 158) (1900-1929)

Water-gowan [Water gowan] - *Caltha palustris* L. (5, 157) (1913-1929)

Water-grass [Water grass] - *Hydrocotyle umbellata* L. (5, 156) (1913-1923), *Nasturtium officinale* W.T. Aiton (possibly) (5, 156, 157, 158) (1900-1929) Ireland, *Zannichellia palustris* L. (93) (1936) Neb

Water-gum - *Nyssa biflora* Walt. (106) (1930), *Nyssa sylvatica* Marsh. (156) (1923)

Water-hawthorn [Waterhawthorn] - *Aponogeton distachyos* L. f. (109) (1949), *Aponogeton* L. f. (155) (1942)

Water-hemp [Water hemp, Waterhemp] - *Amaranthus cannabinus* (L.) Sauer (19, 92, 156) (1840-1923), *Amaranthus* L. (1, 2, 93, 138, 158) (1895-1936), *Amaranthus rudis* Sauer (3, 21, 85, 122, 125) (1893-1986), *Amaranthus tuberculatus* (Moq.) Sauer (80, 145) (1897-1913), *Bidens tripartita* L. (158) (1900)

Water-hemp agrimony [Water hemp agrimony] - *Bidens tripartita* L. (92) (1876)

Water-hyssop [Waterhyssop, Water hyssop] - *Bacopa* Aubl. (1, 4, 50, 155, 156) (1923–present), *Bacopa rotundifolia* (Michx.) Wettst. (3, 85, 95) (1911–1977)

Water-jelly [Water jelly, Waterjelly] - *Brasenia schreberi* Gmel. (7, 92, 156) (1828–1923)

Water-kers - *Rorippa nasturtium-aquaticum* (L.) Hayek (158) (1900)

Waterleaf [Water leaf, Water-leaf] - *Amaranthus cannabinus* (L.) Sauer (156) (1923), *Brasenia schreberi* Gmel. (92, 156) (1876-1923), *Hydrophyllum* L. (1, 2, 4, 10, 50, 63, 82, 93, 155, 156, 158) (1818–present), *Hydrophyllum virginianum* L. (3, 4, 6, 82, 85, 127, 184) (1793–1986), *Palmaria palmata* (L.) Weber & Mohr (92) (1876)

Water-lemon [Waterlemon, Water lemon] - *Passiflora laurifolia* L. (109, 138) (1923–1949), *Passiflora maliformis* L. (107) (1919)

Water-lentil [Water-lentils, Water lentils] - *Lemna* L. (158) (1900), *Lemna minor* L. (5) (1913)

Water-lettuce [Waterlettuce] - *Pistia* L. (138) (1923), *Pistia stratiotes* L. (109, 138) (1923–1949)

Waterlily [Water lily, Water-lily, Water-lilies] - *Calla palustris* L. (5, 156) (1913–1923), *Nelumbo lutea* Willd. (74) (1893) Peoria IL, *Nymphaea* L. (1, 10, 50, 82, 106, 109, 138, 167) (1814–present), *Nymphaea odorata* Aiton (6, 49, 57, 92) (1876–1917), *Nymphaea odorata* Aiton subsp. *odorata* (156) (1923), *Nymphoides peltata* (Gmel.) Kuntze (5, 156) (1913–1923), *Sagittaria latifolia* Willd. (78) (1898) MO, *Saururus cernuus* L. (187) (1818)

Water-lily tree [Water lily tree] - *Magnolia fraseri* Walt. (5, 156) (1913–1923)

Water-mallow [Water mallow] - *Hibiscus* L. (7) (1828), *Hibiscus moscheutos* L. (5, 92, 156, 158) (1876–1923)

Watermeal [Water-meal] - *Wolffia brasiliensis* Weddell (156) (1923), *Wolffia* Horkel ex Schleid. (50) (present)

Watermelon [Water melon, Water-melon, Water mellons, Water Melons] - *Citrullus lanatus* (Thunb.) Matsumura & Nakai (7, 19, 35, 37, 41, 50, 52, 54, 57, 58, 82, 92, 106, 107, 109, 110, 114, 155, 158, 181, 182) (~1678–present)

Watermelon nightshade - *Solanum citrullifolium* A. Br. (50, 155) (1942–present)

Water-milfoil [Water milfoil, Water mill-foil, Watermillfoil] - *Hottonia inflata* Ell. (156) (1923), *Myriophyllum heterophyllum* Michx. (3) (1977), *Myriophyllum* L. (1, 4, 10, 50, 63, 93, 158, 167) (1814–present), *Myriophyllum pinnatum* (Walt.) Britton, Sterns & Poggenb. (3) (1977), *Myriophyllum sibiricum* Komarov (3, 46) (1879–1977), *Myriophyllum spicatum* L. (85) (1932), *Myriophyllum verticillatum* L. (3, 19, 92) (1840–1977), *Utricularia gibba* L. (possibly) (184) (1793)

Water-millet [Water millet] - *Zizaniopsis miliacea* (Michx.) Doell & Aschers. (94, 119, 163) (1852–1938)

Water-millon - *Citrullus lanatus* (Thunb.) Matsumura & Nakai (181) (~1678)

Water-motor - *Baccharis salicifolia* (Ruiz & Pavón) Pers. (106) (1930)

Water-nettle [Water nettle] - *Circaea lutetiana* L. (79) (1891)

Water-nut [Water-nuts, Waternuts] - *Nelumbo lutea* Willd. (possibly) (1, 92, 106, 156, 158) (1828–1932), *Trapa natans* L. (92, 156) (1876–1923)

Water-nymph [Water nymph, Waternymph] - *Najas flexilis* (Willd.) Rostk. & Schmidt (19, 92) (1840–1876), *Najas* L. (50, 158) (1900–present), *Nymphaea odorata* Aiton (6, 49) (1892–1898), *Nymphaea odorata* Aiton subsp. *odorata* (5, 156, 158) (1900–1923)

Water-parsley [Water parsley] - *Cicuta maculata* L. (7) (1828), *Conium maculatum* L. (92) (1876), *Sium suave* Walt. (156) (1923)

Water-parsnip [Water parsnip, Waterparsnip, Water parsnep, Water-parsnep] - *Apium nodiflorum* (L.) Lag. (92) (1876), *Berula* Bess. ex W.D.J. Koch (1, 4, 50, 158) (1900–present), *Berula erecta* (Huds.) Coville (3, 4, 85) (1932-1986), *Cicuta maculata* L. var. *angustifolia* Hook. (101) (1905), *Sium* L. (1, 2, 4, 7, 10, 50, 155, 158, 184) (1793–present), *Sium suave* Walt. (3, 4, 46, 48, 85, 95, 21, 126, 133, 148, 157, 190) (~1759-1986)

Water-pepper [Water pepper] - *Polygonum hydropiper* L. (3, 4, 5, 47, 48, 49, 62, 80, 82, 92, 93, 97, 122, 124, 125, 156, 157, 158) (1852–1986), *Polygonum hydropiperoides* Michx. (80) (1913), *Polygonum* L. (1, 93, 106) (1930–1936), *Polygonum persicaria* L. (7) (1828), *Polygonum punctatum* Ell. (5, 19, 61, 157, 158) (1840–1929), *Polygonum punctatum* Ell. var. *punctatum* (6, 57, 156) (1892–1923)

Water-pepper knotweed [Water-pepper knot-weed] - *Polygonum punctatum* Ell. (187) (1818)

Water-pimpernel [Water pimpernel] - *Samolus ebracteatus* Kunth subsp. *cuneatus* (Small) R. Knuth (4) (1986), *Samolus* L. (1, 2, 4, 156, 158) (1895–1986), *Samolus valerandi* L. (19, 92) (1840–1876), *Samolus valerandi* L. subsp. *parviflorus* (Raf.) Hultén (5, 10, 97, 156) (1818–1937)

Water-plantain [Water plantain, Waterplantain, Water plantane] - *Alisma* L. (1, 10, 50, 93, 106, 138, 155, 167) (1814–present), *Alisma plantago-aquatica* L. (7, 19, 44, 46, 48, 58, 72, 92, 120, 131, 138, 156) (1671-1938), *Alisma subcordatum* Raf. (3, 85, 122, 157) (1932-1977), *Alisma triviale* Pursh (3) (1977), *Pontederia cordata* L. (7) (1828)

Water-plantain spearwort [Water plantain spearwort] - *Ranunculus laxicaulis* (Torr. & Gray) Darby (4, 156) (1923-1986)

Waterpod - *Ellisia nyctelea* (L.) L. (3, 4) (1977-1986)

Water-poppy [Waterpoppy] - *Hydrocleys nymphoides* (Humb. & Bonpl. ex Willd.) Buch. (109, 138) (1923-1949), *Hydrocleys* Rich. (138) (1923)

Water-primrose [Water primrose, Waterprimrose] - *Ludwigia* L. (155) (1942), *Ludwigia repens* Forst. (4) (1986)

Water-radish [Water radish] - *Barbarea vulgaris* W.T. Aiton (19) (1840), *Descurainia pinnata* (Walter) Britton subsp. *pinnata* (181) (1818), *Sisymbrium* L. (10) (1818)

Water-rocket [Water rocket] - *Nymphaea alba* L. (92) (1876)

Water-rope [Water rope] - *Myriophyllum* L. (124) (1937) TX

Water-seg - *Iris pseudacorus* L. (158) (1900)

Watershield [Water shield, Water-shield] - *Brasenia* Schreber (1, 2, 4, 10, 13, 15, 138, 155, 158) (1818-1986), *Brasenia schreberi* Gmel. (4, 5, 7, 19, 47, 50, 72, 92, 107, 109, 138, 156, 187) (1818–present), *Cabomba* Aubl. (109) (1949), *Cabomba caroliniana* Gray (106) (1930), *Nelumbo lutea* Willd. (possibly) (7) (1828)

Water-skegs - *Iris pseudacorus* L. (156) (1923) no longer in use by 1923

Water-snowflake - *Nymphoides indica* (L.) Kuntze (109, 138) (1923-1949)

Water-star [Water star] - *Callitriche* L. (10) (1818)

Water-starwort [Water starwort, Waterstarwort] - *Callitriche hermaphroditica* L. (3, 120) (1938–1977), *Callitriche* L. (1, 4, 50, 155) (1932–present), *Callitriche palustris* L. (49, 85, 92, 93, 157) (1876–1936)

Water-string [Waterstring, Water string] - *Amorpha fruticosa* L. (37) (1919)

Water-target [Water target, Watertarget] - *Brasenia schreberi* Gmel. (5, 19, 156) (1840-1923)

Water-thistle [Water thistle] - *Dipsacus fullonum* L. (5, 75, 156) (1894-1923) WV, water collects in leaf axils

Water-thread pondweed [Waterthread pondweed] - *Potamogeton diversifolius* Raf. (3, 50) (1977–present)

Water-thyme [Water thyme] - *Elodea canadensis* Michx. (92, 156, 158) (1876-1923)

Water-torch [Water torch] - *Typha latifolia* L. (5, 92, 156, 157, 158) (1876-1929)

Water-tupelo - *Nyssa sylvatica* Marsh. (156) (1923)

Water-violet [Water violet] - *Hottonia inflata* Ell. (5, 19, 46, 156) (1783-1923), *Hottonia* L. (2, 156) (1895-1942)

Waterweed [Water weed, Water-weed] - *Elodea canadensis* Michx. (3, 5, 85, 92, 93, 138, 156) (1876-1977), *Elodea* Michx. (50, 120, 138) (1923–present), *Elodea nuttallii* (Planch.) St. John (3) (1977), *Ludwigia peploides* (Kunth) Raven subsp. *peploides* (106) (1930), *Pilea pumila* (L.) Gray (78) (1898) Sulphur Grove OH

Water-willow [Water willow, Waterwillow, Water willoe] - *Decodon* J.F. Gmel. (138, 156) (1923), *Decodon verticillatus* (L.) Ell. (106, 138, 156) (1923-1930), *Justicia americana* (L.) Vahl (4, 19, 106, 120, 124, 156) (1840-1986), *Justicia* L. (1, 50, 158) (1900–present), *Polygonum amphibium* L. (156) (1923)

Waterwort [Water wort] - *Asplenium trichomanes* L. (5, 158) (1900–1913), *Elatine americana* (Pursh) Arn. (3, 5, 156) (1913–1977), *Elatine hydropiper* L. (92) (1876), *Elatine* L. (1, 4, 13, 15, 50, 155) (1849–present)

Water-yarrow [Water yarrow] - *Hottonia inflata* Ell. (5, 156) (1913-1923)

Wathaessa - *Drosera rotundifolia* L. (177) (1762)

Wathaka ratdshe (Oto) - *Citrullus lanatus* (Thunb.) Matsumura & Nakai (37) (1919)

Wathibaba-makan (Pawnee, playing card medicine) - *Anemone cylindrica* Gray (37) (1919)

Wath'-pith (Comanche Shoshonee) - *Juniperus* L. (132) (1855)

Wǎ-tö-jǎ (Oto) - *Zea mays* L. (38) (1820)

Watoŋ (Osage, possibly from watoŋga "big thing") - *Cucurbita pepo* L. (121) (1918?-1970?) Osage have many named varieites

WatoŋƟi (Osage) - *Zea mays* L. (121) (1918-1970)

Watson's Dutchman's-pipe [Watson Dutchmanspipe] - *Aristolochia watsonii* Woot. & Standl. (155) (1942)

Watson's fescue grass - *Leucopoa kingii* (S. Wats.) W.A. Weber (5) (1913)

Watson's goosefoot - *Chenopodium watsonii* A. Nels. (50) (present)

Watson's iris [Watson iris] - *Iris douglasiana* Herb. (138) (1923)

Watson's lavauxia - *Oenothera triloba* Nutt. (97) (1937)

Watson's plum - *Prunus angustifolia* Marsh. var. *watsonii* (Sargent) Waugh (50) (present)

Wǎt-tăng (Omaha) - *Cucurbita maxima* Dcne. (38) (1820)

Wǎt-tǎn-zé (Omaha) - *Zea mays* L. (38) (1820)

Wattle - *Acacia* Mill. (158) (1900) Australia

Wat-twǒing (Oto) - *Cucurbita maxima* Dcne. (38) (1820)

Wau-inu-makan (Omaha-Ponca, woman's perfume) - *Galium triflorum* Michx. (37) (1919)

Waukegan juniper - *Juniperus horizontalis* Moench (109, 112, 136) (1930-1949)

Wau-pezhe (Omaha-Ponca, woman's herb) - *Galium triflorum* Michx. (37) (1919)

Wave aster - *Symphyotrichum undulatum* (L.) Nesom (138, 155) (1931-1942)

Waved alder - *Alnus viridis* subsp. *crispa* (Aiton) Turrill (19) (1840)

Waved wall flower - *Matthiola incana* (L.) Aiton f. (19) (1840)

Wave-leaf starwort [Wave leaved star wort] - *Symphyotrichum undulatum* (L.) Nesom (42) (1814)

Wave-stem aster [Waved-stemmed aster] - *Symphyotrichum undulatum* (L.) Nesom (187) (1818)

Wave-stem goldenrod [Waved-stemmed golden-rod] - *Solidago flexicaulis* L. (187) (1818)

Waving butterfly - *Gaura coccinea* Nutt. ex Pursh (127) (1933) ND

Wavy hair grass - *Deschampsia flexuosa* (L.) Trin. (5, 50) (1913–present)

Wavy meadow grass - *Poa laxa* Haenke (66) (1903)

Wavy-leaf agoseris [Wavyleaf agoseris] - *Nothocalais cuspidata* (Pursh) Greene (155) (1942)

Wavy-leaf aster [Wavy-leaved aster] - *Symphyotrichum undulatum* (L.) Nesom (5, 97) (1913-1937)

Wavy-leaf beeblossom [Wavyleaf beeblossom] - *Gaura sinuata* Nutt. ex Ser. (50) (present)

Wavy-leaf blazing star [Wavyleaf blazingstar] - *Mentzelia albescens* (Gill. & Arn.) Griseb. (50) (present)

Wavy-leaf gaura [Wavy-leaved gaura] - *Gaura sinuata* Nutt. ex Ser. (5, 97) (1913-1937)

Wavy-leaf Indian paintbrush [Wavyleaf Indian paintbrush] - *Castilleja applegatei* Fern. subsp. *martinii* (Abrams) Chuang & Heckard (50) (present)

Wavy-leaf oak [Wavyleaf oak] - *Quercus* ×*pauciloba* Rydb. [*gambelii* × *turbinella*] (4, 155) (1942–1986)

Wavy-leaf soap plant [Wavyleaf soap plant] - *Chlorogalum pomeridianum* (DC.) Kunth (50) (present)

Wavy-leaf thistle [Wavyleaf thistle, Wavy-leaved thistle] - *Cirsium undulatum* (Nutt.) Spreng (3, 4, 5, 50, 93, 97, 122, 155) (1913–present)

Wavy-leaf thistle [Wavyleaf thistle, Wavy-leaved thistle] - *Cirsium undulatum* (Nutt.) Spreng. var. *undulatum* (50, 72, 131) (1899–present)

Wavy-leaf twinevine [Wavyleaf twinevine] - *Funastrum crispum* (Benth.) Schlechter (50) (present)

Waw-weed [Waw weed] - *Packera aurea* (L.) A.& D. Löve (92) (1876)

Wax currant - *Ribes cereum* Dougl. (50, 138, 155) (1923–present), *Ribes cereum* Dougl. var. *cereum* (50) (present)

Wax euphorbia - *Euphorbia antisyphilitica* Zucc. (155) (1942)

Wax flower - *Chimaphila maculata* (L.) Pursh (77) (1898) Southold Long Island

Wax goldenweed - *Grindelia papposa* Nesom & Suh (3) (1977)

Wax gourd [Waxgourd] - *Benincasa hispida* (Thunb.) Cogn. (138) (1923), *Benincasa* Savi (138) (1923)

Wax liverwort - *Phaeoceros laevis* (L.) Prosk. (19) (1840)

Wax myrtle [Wax-myrtle, Waxmyrtle] - *Morella cerifera* (L.) Small (2, 5, 6, 46, 49, 52, 53, 57, 92, 106, 109, 124, 156) (1879-1949), *Myrica* L. (7, 106, 138) (1828-1930)

Wax pink [Wax pinks] - *Portulaca grandiflora* Hook. (5, 92, 156, 158) (1876-1923)

Wax plant [Wax-plant, Waxplant] - *Hoya carnosa* (L. f.) R. Br. (92, 109) (1876-1949), *Hoya* R. Br. (138) (1923), *Silene armeria* L. (5, 73, 156) (1892-1923) Mansfield OH, no longer in use by 1923

Wax tree - *Morella cerifera* (L.) Small (34) (1834), *Morella inodora* (Bartr.) Small (182) (1791)

Wax-ball - *Acalypha virginica* L. (62, 156) (1912-1923) IN

Waxberry [Wax-berry, Wax berry] - *Morella caroliniensis* (P. Mill.) Small (106) (1930), *Morella cerifera* (L.) Small (5, 49, 52, 53, 92, 156) (1898-1923), *Myrica* L. (7) (1828), *Symphoricarpos albus* (L.) Blake (40, 109) (1928-1949), *Symphoricarpos albus* (L.) Blake var. *albus* (5, 75, 106, 157, 158) (1894-1930), *Symphoricarpos albus* (L.) Blake var. *laevigatus* (Fern.) Blake (156) (1923)

Waxberry cornel [Waxberry cornell, Wax-berry cornel] - *Cornus sericea* L. subsp. *sericea* (5, 7, 92, 156, 158) (1828–1923)

Waxbush [Wax bush, Wax-bush] - *Cuphea* P. Br. (1) (1932), *Cuphea viscosissima* Jacq (5, 19, 92, 156, 158) (1840–1923)

Waxča xča (Lakota, flower blossom) - *Asclepias speciosa* Torr. (121) (1918?–1970?)

Wax-cluster [Wax cluster] - *Gaultheria procumbens* L. (92) (1876)

Wax-dolls [Wax dolls] - *Fumaria officinalis* L. (156, 158) (1900–1923)

Wax-flower pyrola [Waxflower pyrola] - *Pyrola elliptica* Nutt. (155) (1942)

Wax-flower shinleaf [Waxflower shinleaf] - *Pyrola elliptica* Nutt. (50) (present)

Wax-leaf penstemon [Waxleaf penstemon] - *Penstemon nitidus* Dougl. ex Benth. (50, 155) (1942–present)

Wax-mallow [Waxmallow] - *Malvaviscus arboreus* Dill. ex Cav. (138) (1923)

Waxpe čejaka (Lakota, leaf mint) - *Pycnanthemum virginianum* (L.) T.

Dur. & B.D. Jackson ex B.L. Robins. & Fern. (121) (1918?-1970?)

Waxpe jazokapi (Lakota, suck leaf) - *Castilleja sessiliflora* Pursh (121) (1918?-1970?)

Waxpe šiča (Lakota, bad leaves) - *Iva xanthifolia* Nutt. (121) (1918?-1970?)

Waxpe tiŋpsila (Lakota, turnip leaf) - *Asclepias verticillata* L. (121) (1918?-1970?)

Waxpe waštemna (Lakota, odorous leaves) - *Monarda fistulosa* L. (121) (1918?-1970?)

Waxpe xča xča (Lakota, flower leaf) - *Croton texensis* (Klotzsch) Muell.-Arg. (121) (1918?-1970?)

Waxpepopa (Lakota, possibly meaning bursting leaf) - *Salix* L. (121) (1918?-1970?)

Waxpetaga (Lakota, possibly meaning frothy leaves) - *Heuchera richardsonii* R. Br. (121) (1918?-1970?)

Waxweed [Wax-weed] - *Cuphea* P. Br. (50) (present), *Cuphea viscosissima* Jacq (158) (1900)

Waxwork [Wax work, Wax-work] - *Celastrus* L. (1, 13) (1849-1932), *Celastrus scandens* L. (2, 5, 14, 49, 58, 92, 106, 107, 109, 138, 156, 158, 187) (1818-1949)

Waxy meadow rue - *Thalictrum revolutum* DC. (5) (1913)

Waxy-fruit hawthorn [Waxyfruit hawthorn, Waxy-fruited thorn] - *Crataegus pruinosa* (Wendl.) K. Koch (5, 50) (1913–present)

Waxy-leaf twinevine [Waxy-leaf twine vine] - *Funastrum crispum* (Benth.) Schlechter (4) (1986)

Way barley - *Hordeum murinum* L. (5) (1913)

Way bent - *Hordeum murinum* L. (5, 45) (1896-1913)

Way thistle [Way-thistle] - *Cirsium arvense* (L.) Scop. (5, 156, 157, 158) (1900-1929)

Way-bread [Way bread, Waybread] - *Plantago lanceolata* L. (158) (1900), *Plantago major* L. (5, 6, 92, 156, 157, 158, 187) (1818–1929)

Way-bred [Way bred] - *Plantago major* L. (6) (1892)

Wayfarer's tree - *Viburnum lentago* L. (53) (1922)

Wayfaring man's tree - *Viburnum lantana* L. (156) (1923)

Wayfaring tree [Way-faring tree, Way faring tree, Wayfaringtree, Wayfaring-tree] - *Viburnum* L. (8) (1785), *Viburnum lantana* L. (4, 5, 50, 92, 109, 112, 138, 155, 158, 179) (1793–present)

Way-grass [Way grass] - *Polygonum aviculare* L. (5, 156, 158) (1900-1923)

Wayside pepperweed - *Lepidium oblongum* Small var. *oblongum* (155) (1942)

Wayside plantain [Way-side plantain] - *Plantago major* L. (5, 156) (1913-1923)

Wayside speedwell - *Veronica polita* Fries (155) (1942)

Waythorn [Way-thorn] - *Rhamnus cathartica* L. (6, 59, 92, 156, 158) (1892-1923)

Waywort - *Anagallis arvensis* L. (156, 158) (1900-1923)

Wazhide (Omaha-Ponca) - *Rosa arkansana* Porter var. *suffulta* (Greene) Cockerell (37) (1919)

Wazhushtecha (Dakota) - *Fragaria vesca* L. subsp. *americana* (Porter) Staudt (37) (1919) Wazhushtecha-hu (Strawberry vine), *Fragaria virginiana* Duchesne (37) (1919)

Wazi (Dakota) - *Pinus contorta* Dougl. ex Loud. var. *latifolia* Engelm. ex Wats (37) (1830)

Wazi (Lakota) - *Pinus* L. (121) (1918-1970)

Wazimna (Dakota, pine smell) - *Thalictrum dasycarpum* Fisch. & Avé-Lall. (37) (1919)

Weak arctic sedge - *Carex supina* Willd. ex Wahlenb. (5, 50) (1913–present)

Weak bulrush - *Schoenoplectus purshianus* (Fern.) M.T. Strong (155) (1942)

Weak clustered sedge - *Carex glareosa* Schkuhr ex Wahlenb. subsp. *glareosa* var. *amphigena* Fern. (5) (1913)

Weak fimbristylis - *Fimbristylis annua* (All.) R. & S. (5) (1913)

Weak manna grass [Weak mannagrass] - *Torreyochloa pallida* (Torr.) Church var. *pauciflora* (J. Presl) J.I. Davis (140) (1944)

Weak meadow grass - *Poa saltuensis* Fern. & Wieg. (66) (1903)

Weak nettle - *Urtica chamaedryoides* Pursh (2, 4, 97) (1895-1986)

Weak rush - *Juncus debilis* A. Gray (5, 50, 66) (1912–present)

Weak sedge - *Carex debilis* Michx. (66) (1903)

Weak spear grass - *Poa saltuensis* Fern. & Wieg. (5, 45, 56, 72) (1893-1901)

Weak starwort [Weak star wort] - *Doellingeria infirma* (Michx.) Greene (42) (1814)

Weak stellate sedge - *Carex seorsa* Howe (possibly) (5) (1913)

Weak-leaf bur ragweed [Weakleaf burr ragweed] - *Ambrosia confertiflora* DC. (50) (present)

Weak-leaf yucca [Weakleaf yucca] - *Yucca filamentosa* L. (138, 155) (1923-1942)

Weak-stalk bulrush [Weakstalk bulrush] - *Schoenoplectus purshianus* (Fern.) M.T. Strong (50) (present)

Weak-stalk club-rush [Weak-stalked club rush] - *Schoenoplectus purshianus* (Fern.) M.T. Strong (5) (1913)

Weak-stem rush - *Schoenoplectus purshianus* (Fern.) M.T. Strong (66) (1903)

Weasel-snout - *Lamiastrum galeobdolon* (L.) Ehrend. & Polatschek (92) (1876)

Weathercock [Weather cock, Weather-cock, Weathercocks] - *Impatiens capensis* Meerb. (5, 156, 157, 158) (1900-1929), *Impatiens* L. (7) (1828), *Impatiens pallida* Nutt. (92, 156, 157) (1876-1929)

Weather-glass [Weatherglass] - *Anagallis arvensis* L. (92, 157) (1876-1929)

Weaver's-broom [Weavers-broom, Weavers broom] - *Spartium junceum* L. (109, 138) (1923-1949), *Spartium* L. (138) (1923)

Webber's panic grass [Webber's panic-grass] - *Dichanthelium sabulorum* (Lam.) Gould & C.A. Clark var. *patulum* (Scribn. & Merr.) Gould & C.A. Clark (94) (1901)

Webby lip fern - *Cheilanthes tomentosa* Link. (5) (1913)

Wechkenah (Missouri tribes) - *Linum virginianum* L. (7) (1828)

Wechsel (German) - *Prunus cerasus* L. (110) (1886)

Wedgeleaf - *Phyla cuneifolia* (Torr.) Greene (50) (present)

Wedge-leaf draba [Wedgeleaf draba] - *Draba cuneifolia* Nutt. ex Torr. & Gray (3, 4, 50) (1977–present), *Draba cuneifolia* Nutt. ex Torr. & Gray var. *cuneifolia* (50) (present)

Wedge-leaf fogfruit [Wedgeleaf fog-fruit, Wedge-leaved fog-fruit] - *Phyla cuneifolia* (Torr.) Greene (4, 5, 97, 122) (1913-1986)

Wedge-leaf frogfruit [Wedge-leaved frog-fruit] - *Phyla cuneifolia* (Torr.) Greene (93) (1936)

Wedge-leaf goldenweed [Wedgeleaf goldenweed] - *Ericameria cuneata* (Gray) McClatchie var. *cuneata* (155) (1942)

Wedge-leaf maidenhair [Wedge-leaved maidenhair] - *Adiantum raddianum* K. Presl (165) (1768)

Wedge-leaf mespilus [Wedge leaved mespilus] - *Crataegus cuneiformis* (Marshall) Eggl. (8) (1785)

Wedge-leaf spurge [Wedgeleaf spurge] - *Euphorbia longicruris* Scheele (50) (present)

Wedge-leaf whitlow-grass [Wedge-leaved whitlow grass, Wedge-leaved whitlow-grass] - *Draba cuneifolia* Nutt. ex Torr. & Gray (5, 97) (1913-1937)

Wedgescale - *Sphenopholis* Scribn. (50, 155) (1942–present)

Weech - *Corylus americana* Walt. (46) (1879)

Weed-grass [Weed grass] - *Lophiola aurea* Ker-Gawl. (19) (1840)

Weedy dwarf-dandelion [Weedy dwarfdandelion] - *Krigia caespitosa* (Raf.) Chambers (50) (present)

Weeping alkali grass [Weeping alkaligrass] - *Puccinellia distans* (Jacq.) Parl. (50, 140, 155) (1942–present)

Weeping birch - *Betula pendula* Roth (4) (1986), *Fagus sylvatica* L. (109) (1949)

Weeping bulrush - *Isolepis cernua* (Vahl) Roemer & J.A. Schultes (138) (1923)

Weeping forsythia - *Forsythia suspensa* (Thunb.) Vahl (138) (1923)

Weeping lantana - *Lantana montevidensis* (Spreng.) Briq. (109, 138) (1923-1949)

Weeping linden - *Tilia petiolaris* DC. (138) (1923)

Weeping love grass [Weeping lovegrass] - *Eragrostis curvula* (Schrad.) Nees (3, 50, 155) (1942–present)

Weeping oak - *Quercus lobata* Née (106) (1930)

Weeping silver fir - *Abies alba* Mill. (138, 155) (1923-1942)

Weeping spruce - *Tsuga canadensis* (L.) Carr. (92) (1876)

Weeping white fir - *Abies concolor* (Gord. & Glend.) Lindl. ex Hildebr. (155) (1942)

Weeping white linden - *Tilia petiolaris* DC. (109) (1949)

Wegdorn (German) - *Rhamnus cathartica* L. (6) (1892)

Wegewart (German) - *Cichorium intybus* L. (6) (1892)

Weh'-ec (Hueco Pawnee) - *Nicotiana* L. (132) (1855)

Weichselkirsche (German) - *Prunus mahaleb* L. (158) (1900)

Weide (German) - *Salix* L. (158) (1900)

Weiderich (German) - *Lysimachia* L. (158) (1900)

Weigela - *Diervilla* Mill. (2) (1895), *Weigela* Thunb. (138) (1923)

Weinrebe (German) - *Vitex agnus-castus* L. (158) (1900)

Weinstock (German) - *Vitex agnus-castus* L. (138) (1923)

Weir's maple [Weir maple] - *Acer rubrum* L. (137) (1931)

Weissbienensang (German) - *Lamium album* L. (6) (1892)

Weisse Esche (German) - *Fraxinus americana* L. (6) (1892)

Weisse Taubnessel (German) - *Lamium album* L. (6) (1892)

Weisser Andorn (German) - *Marrubium vulgare* L. (158) (1900)

Weisser Gänsefuss (German) - *Chenopodium album* L. (158) (1900)

Weisser Senf (German) - *Sinapis alba* L. (6, 158) (1892-1900)

Weisses Christophskraut (German) - *Actaea pachypoda* Ell. (6) (1892)

Weistanne (German) - *Abies alba* Mill. (possibly) (158) (1900)

Welch clover - *Trifolium arvense* L. (92) (1876)

Welch sorrel - *Oxalis acetosella* L. (92) (1876)

Welcome-to-our-house - *Euphorbia cyparissias* L. (5, 156, 158) (1900-1923)

Weld - *Reseda luteola* L. (5, 92, 156) (1876-1923)

Well-cress - *Nasturtium officinale* W.T. Aiton (possibly) (156) (1923)

Well-grass [Well grass] - *Nasturtium officinale* W.T. Aiton (possibly) (5, 158) (1900-1913)

Welsch bonen - *Phaseolus* L. (107) (1552)

Welschkorn (Germany) - *Zea mays* L. (107, 110) (1552)

Welsh onion - *Allium fistulosum* L. (19, 50, 109, 110, 138, 165) (1768–present)

Welsh parsley - *Cannabis sativa* L. (157, 158) (1900-1929)

Welsh sorrel - *Oxyria digyna* (L.) Hill (7) (1828)

Welted colewort [Welted cole woorts] - *Brassica oleracea* L. (178) (1526)

Welted thistle - *Carduus crispus* L. (5, 93, 156) (1913-1936)

Wenomesippaguash (Narraganset) - *Nyssa biflora* Walt. (46) (1879)

Wenu-shabethe-he (Omaha-Ponca, tree to dye black) - *Acer rubrum* L. (37) (1919)

Weremod - *Artemisia absinthium* L. (157, 158) (1900-1929)

Wermuth (German) - *Artemisia absinthium* L. (6, 158) (1892–1900)

Werner's panic grass [Werner's panic-grass] - *Dichanthelium linearifolium* (Scribn. ex Nash) Gould (5, 163) (1852-1913)

Werner's panicum [Werner panicum] - *Dichanthelium linearifolium* (Scribn. ex Nash) Gould (155) (1942)

Wešabeõe (Osage, black-dye tree) - *Acer rubrum* L. (121) (1918?-1970?)

West Chester hawthorn - *Crataegus fructuosa* Sargent (138) (1923)

West Indian birch tree - *Bursera simaruba* (L.) Sargent (20) (1857)

West Indian blackthorn - *Acacia farnesiana* (L.) Willd. (107) (1919)

West Indian cedar [West-Indian-cedar] - *Cedrela odorata* L. (109) (1949)

West Indian cotton - *Gossypium barbadense* L. (182) (1791)

West Indian mahogany - *Swietenia mahagoni* (L.) Jacq. (138) (1923)

West Indian nightshade - *Solanum ptychanthum* Dunal (50) (present)

West Indian rush grass [West Indian rush-grass] - *Sporobolus domingensis* (Trin.) Kunth (94) (1901)

West Indian yellow-wood - *Zanthoxylum americanum* Mill. (156)

(1923)

Westcoast milkweed - *Asclepias exaltata* L. (155) (1942)

Western agoseris - *Agoseris monticola* Greene (131) (1899)

Western arborvitae [Western arbor vitae] - *Thuja occidentalis* L. (6) (1892), *Thuja plicata* Donn ex D. Don (161) (1857)

Western aster - *Symphyotrichum ascendens* (Lindl.) Nesom (5, 50) (1913–present), *Symphyotrichum spathulatum* (Lindl.) Nesom var. *spathulatum* (155) (1942)

Western azalea - *Rhododendron occidentale* (Torr. & Gray ex Torr.) Gray var. *occidentale* (138) (1923)

Western balsam fir - *Abies grandis* (Dougl. ex D. Don) Lindl. (161) (1857)

Western baneberry - *Actaea rubra* (Aiton) Willd. (131, 155) (1899–1942)

Western beard grass - *Aristida purpurea* Nutt. (87) (1884)

Western bindweed - *Convolvulus arvensis* L. (85) (1932)

Western birch - *Betula occidentalis* Hook. (5, 20, 108) (1857-1913)

Western bitterweed [Western bitter weed] - *Actinella odorata* (DC.) A.Gray (122, 124) (1937)

Western black walnut - *Juglans microcarpa* Berl. var. *microcarpa* (65) (1931)

Western blackberry - *Rubus ursinus* Cham. & Schlecht. (107) (1919)

Western blady grass [Western blady-grass] - *Imperata brevifolia* Vasey (94) (1901)

Western bleeding-heart [Western bleedingheart] - *Dicentra formosa* (Haw.) Walp. (109, 138) (1923-1949)

Western blite [Western blight] - *Suaeda calceoliformis* (Hook.) Moq. (131) (1899), *Suaeda moquinii* (Torr.) Greene (108) (1878)

Western blue flag - *Iris missouriensis* Nutt. (5) (1913)

Western blue violet - *Viola nephrophylla* Greene (5) (1913)

Western blue-eyed-grass - *Sisyrinchium bellum* S. Wats. (138) (1923)

Western bluegrass [Western blue-grass] - *Poa occidentalis* Vasey (94) (1901) OK

Western bracken fern [Western brackenfern] - *Pteridium aquilinum* (L.) Kuhn (50) (present), *Pteridium aquilinum* (L.) Kuhn var. *latiusculum* (Desv.) Underwood ex Heller (50) (present), *Pteridium aquilinum* (L.) Kuhn var. *pseudocaudatum* (Clute) Heller (50) (present), *Pteridium aquilinum* (L.) Kuhn var. *pubescens* Underwood (155) (1942)

Western buckeye - *Aesculus glabra* Willd. (3, 4, 5, 97, 125, 156) (1913-1986)

Western buckthorn - *Sideroxylon reclinatum* Michx. subsp. *reclinatum* (107) (1919)

Western bulrush - *Schoenoplectus acutus* (Muhl. ex Bigelow) A.& D. Löve var. *occidentalis* (S. Wats.) S.G. Sm. (139) (1944)

Western bunch grass [Western bunch-grass] - *Aristida desmantha* Trin. & Rupr. (94) (1901), *Nassella viridula* (Trin.) Barkworth (56) (1901)

Western bur-marigold - *Bidens aristosa* (Michx.) Britton (106) (1930)

Western bushy goldenrod [Western bushy golden-rod] - *Euthamia leptocephala* (Torr. & Gray) Greene (5) (1913)

Western campion - *Silene nivea* (Nutt.) Muhl. ex Otth (85) (1932)

Western cardinal flower [Western cardinalflower] - *Lobelia cardinalis* L. (155) (1942)

Western catalpa - *Catalpa speciosa* (Warder) Warder ex Engelm. (5, 85, 97, 109, 122, 124, 135, 138, 156, 158) (1900–1949)

Western centaury - *Centaurium exaltatum* (Griseb.) W. Wight ex Piper (5, 93) (1913-1936)

Western chinquapin - *Chrysolepis chrysophylla* (Douglas ex Hook.) Hjelmq. (161) (1857)

Western chokecherry [Western choke cherry, Western chokecherry] - *Prunus virginiana* L. var. *demissa* (Nutt.) Torr. (50, 82, 106, 137, 138, 155) (1923–present), *Prunus virginiana* L. var. *melanocarpa* (A. Nels.) Sargent (5, 37, 93, 95) (1911-1936)

Western clematis - *Clematis ligusticifolia* Nutt. (4, 85, 142, 156) (1902-1986)

Western columbine - *Aquilegia brevistyla* Hook. (3) (1977)

Western common pearl-everlasting [Western common pearleverlasting] - *Anaphalis margaritacea* (L.) Benth. & Hook (155) (1942)

Western coneflower - *Rudbeckia occidentalis* Nutt. (148) (1939)

Western coralbean - *Erythrina flabelliformis* Kearney (138) (1923)

Western coralroot [Western coral root] - *Corallorrhiza wisteriana* Conrad (122) (1937)

Western cord grass [Western cord-grass] - *Spartina gracilis* Trin. (94) (1901)

Western coryphantha - *Escobaria vivipara* (Nutt.) Buxbaum var. *neomexicana* (Engelm.) Buxbaum (97) (1937)

Western cottonwood [Western cotton-wood] - *Populus deltoides* Bartr. ex Marsh. (65) (1931), *Populus deltoides* Bartr. ex Marsh. subsp. *monilifera* (Aiton) Eckenwalder (1, 5, 93, 95, 97, 121) (1911-1937)

Western crab apple - *Malus ioensis* (Wood) Britton (5, 72, 85, 93, 95, 97, 137, 157) (1900-1937), *Malus ioensis* (Wood) Britton var. *ioensis* (2, 63) (1895-1899)

Western dagger - *Yucca torreyi* Shafer (124) (1937) TX

Western daisy - *Astranthium integrifolium* (Michx.) Nutt. (4, 5, 97, 156) (1913–1986), *Astranthium integrifolium* (Michx.) Nutt. subsp. *ciliatum* (Raf.) Dejong (3) (1977)

Western daisy fleabane - *Erigeron bellidiastrum* Nutt. (5, 50, 93, 97) (1913–present), *Erigeron bellidiastrum* Nutt. var. *bellidiastrum* (50) (present), *Erigeron bellidiastrum* Nutt. var. *robustus* Cronq. (50) (present)

Western dock - *Rumex aquaticus* L. var. *fenestratus* (Greene) Dorn (3, 4, 5, 50, 72, 85, 155) (1907–present), *Rumex obtusifolius* L. (131) (1899)

Western dropwort - *Porteranthus stipulatus* (Muhl. ex Willd.) Britt. (7, 92) (1828-1876), *Porteranthus trifoliatus* (L.) Britton (5, 64) (1907-1908)

Western dward-dandelion [Western dward dandelion, Western dwarfdandelion] - *Krigia occidentalis* Nutt. (3, 5, 50, 97, 155) (1913–present)

Western dwarf cliff-brake [Western dwarf cliffbrake] - *Pellaea glabella* Mett. ex Kuhn subsp. *occidentalis* (E. Nels.) Windham (50) (present)

Western false dragonhead - *Physostegia parviflora* Nutt. ex Gray (50) (present)

Western false foxglove - *Aureolaria grandiflora* (Benth.) Pennell (5, 72, 97) (1907-1937)

Western false gromwell [Western false-gromwell] - *Onosmodium molle* Michx. subsp. *occidentale* (Mackenzie) Cochrane (5, 93, 97, 121, 157) (1900-1937)

Western fescue - *Vulpia microstachys* (Nutt.) Munro var. *microstachys* (87) (1884)

Western fescue grass - *Festuca occidentalis* Hook (5, 50) (1913–present)

Western figwort - *Scrophularia lanceolata* Pursh (5, 85, 97, 155) (1913-1942)

Western fine-leaf pondweed [Western fineleaf pondweed] - *Stuckenia filiformis* (Pers) Boerner subsp. *occidentalis* (J.W. Robbins) Haynes, D.H. Les, & M. Kral (50) (present)

Western fleabane - *Erigeron bellidiastrum* Nutt. (3, 4, 85) (1932-1986)

Western germander - *Teucrium canadense* L. var. *occidentale* (Gray) McClintock & Epling (50, 82) (1930–present)

Western goldenrod - *Euthamia occidentalis* Nutt. (106, 155) (1930-1942)

Western goldentop - *Euthamia occidentalis* Nutt. (50) (present)

Western green ash - *Fraxinus pennsylvanica* Marsh. (85) (1932)

Western greenish fringed orchis - *Platanthera leucophaea* (Nutt.) Lindl. (5) (1913)

Western hawk's-beard [Western hawksbeard] - *Crepis occidentalis* Nutt. (155) (1942)

Western hemlock - *Tsuga heterophylla* (Raf.) Sarg. (109, 138) (1923–

1949)

Western hickory - *Carya laciniosa* (Michx. f.) G. Don (158) (1900)

Western horse-nettle [Western horsenettle] - *Solanum dimidiatum* Raf. (4, 50) (1986–present)

Western indigo - *Indigofera miniata* Ort. var. *leptosepala* (Nutt.) B. L.Turner (50, 155) (1942–present)

Western indigo plant [Western indigo-plant] - *Indigofera miniata* Ort. var. *leptosepala* (Nutt.) B. L.Turner (5, 97) (1913–1937)

Western ironweed [Western iron weed, Western iron-weed] - *Vernonia baldwinii* Torr. (4, 95) (1911–1986), *Vernonia fasciculata* Michx. (5, 62, 72, 80, 93, 95, 97, 106, 131, 138, 155) (1899–1937), *Vernonia fasciculata* Michx. subsp. *corymbosa* (Schwein. ex Keating) S. B. Jones (85) (1932)

Western juneberry [Western june-berry, Western june berry] - *Amelanchier alnifolia* (Nutt.) Nutt. ex M. Roemer (85, 93, 157) (1900–1929)

Western juniper - *Juniperus occidentalis* Hook. (103, 161) (1857–1871)

Western larch - *Larix occidentalis* Nutt. (20, 50, 138, 161) (1857–present)

Western lettuce - *Lactuca ludoviciana* (Nutt.) Riddell (5, 72, 93, 97, 122, 131) (1899–1937)

Western lion's-heart [Western lion's heart] - *Physostegia parviflora* Nutt. ex Gray (5, 93) (1913–1936)

Western locust - *Robinia neomexicana* Gray var. *neomexicana* (138) (1923)

Western marbleseed - *Onosmodium molle* Michx. subsp. *occidentale* (Mackenzie) Cochrane (50, 155) (1942–present)

Western marsh cudweed - *Gnaphalium palustre* Nutt. (5, 50) (1913–present)

Western meadow rue - *Thalictrum occidentale* Gray (131) (1899)

Western mountain-ash [Western mountain ash] - *Sorbus sambucifolia* (Cham. & Schlecht.) M. Roemer (131, 135, 137) (1899–1931), *Sorbus scopulina* Greene (3, 5, 85) (1913–1977)

Western mugwort - *Artemisia ludoviciana* Nutt. (80, 108, 156) (1878–1923), *Artemisia ludoviciana* Nutt. subsp. *ludoviciana* (158) (1900)

Western needle grass [Western needlegrass, Western needle-grass] - *Achnatherum occidentale* (Thurb. ex S. Watson) Barkworth (50, 94, 155) (1901–present), *Hesperostipa comata* (Trin. & Rupr.) Barkworth subsp. *comata* (116, 146) (1939–1958)

Western ninebark - *Physocarpus monogynus* (Torr.) J. M. Coult. (possibly) (130) (1895)

Western oak - *Quercus garryana* Dougl. ex Hook. (20, 107) (1857–1919)

Western oak fern [Western oakfern] - *Dryopteris dryopteris* (L.) Britton (50) (present), *Gymnocarpium dryopteris* (L.) Newman (50) (present)

Western orange-cup lily [Western orangecup lily] - *Lilium philadelphicum* L. var. *andinum* (Nutt.) Ker.-Gawl. (138, 155) (1923–1942)

Western panic grass [Western panicgrass] - *Dichanthelium acuminatum* (Sw.) Gould & C. A. Clark var. *fasciculatum* (Torr.) Freckmann (50) (present)

Western paper birch - *Betula occidentalis* Hook. (155) (1942)

Western pasque flower [Western pasqueflower] - *Pulsatilla occidentalis* (S. Wats.) Freyn (155) (1942)

Western pearly-everlasting [Western pearly everlasting] - *Anaphalis margaritacea* (L.) Benth. & Hook (50) (present)

Western peony - *Paeonia brownii* Dougl. ex Hook. (109) (1949)

Western persicaria - *Polygonum douglasii* Greene subsp. *johnstonii* (Munz) Hickman (131) (1899)

Western pink verbena - *Glandularia bipinnatifida* (Nutt.) Nutt. var. *bipinnatifida* (122) (1937)

Western pitch pine - *Pinus ponderosa* P.& C. Lawson (158) (1900), *Pinus ponderosa* P.& C. Lawson var. *scopulorum* Engelm. (5) (1913)

Western plane tree [Western plane-tree] - *Platanus occidentalis* L.

(14, 189) (1767–1882)

Western plantain - *Plantago patagonica* Jacq. (93) (1936)

Western poison ivy [Western poisonivy] - *Toxicodendron rydbergii* (Small ex Rydb.) Greene (50, 95, 155) (1911–present)

Western polypody - *Polypodium hesperium* Maxon (3, 50) (1977–present)

Western pond willow - *Salix geyeriana* AndersS. (20) (1857)

Western pondweed - *Stuckenia filiformis* (Pers) Boerner subsp. *filiformis* (85) (1932), *Stuckenia filiformis* (Pers) Boerner subsp. *occidentalis* (J.W. Robbins) Haynes, D.H. Les, & M. Kral (131) (1899)

Western poplar - *Populus deltoides* Bartr. ex Marsh. subsp. *monilifera* (Aiton) Eckenwalder (155) (1942)

Western prairie clover - *Dalea candida* Michx. ex Willd. var. *oligophylla* (Torr.) Shinners (3) (1977)

Western prickle grass [Western prickle-grass] - *Tragus berteronianus* J.A. Schultes (94) (1901)

Western prickly pear [Western prickly-pear] - *Opuntia humifusa* (Raf.) Raf. (5, 72, 85, 93, 95, 131) (1899-1936)

Western purslane - *Portulaca oleracea* L. (5, 156) (1913-1923)

Western pusley - *Portulaca oleracea* L. (122) (1937)

Western pussy willow - *Salix scouleriana* Barr. (3, 4) (1977-1986)

Western ragweed - *Ambrosia psilostachya* DC. (3, 4, 5, 21, 72, 82, 85, 93, 97, 98, 125, 131, 155, 157) (1893-1986)

Western rattlesnake-plantain [Western rattlsenake plantain] - *Goodyera oblongifolia* Raf. (50, 138) (1923–present)

Western red birch - *Betula occidentalis* Hook. (85, 93, 131, 158) (1899-1936)

Western red cedar - *Juniperus scopulorum* Sarg. (85, 97, 136, 157) (1930-1937), *Thuja plicata* Donn ex D. Don (50) (present)

Western red columbine - *Aquilegia elegantula* Greene (155) (1942)

Western red currant - *Ribes cereum* Dougl. (4) (1986), *Ribes cereum* Dougl. var. *pedicellare* Brewer & S. Wats. (3) (1977)

Western red lily - *Lilium philadelphicum* L. var. *andinum* (Nutt.) Ker.-Gawl. (5, 72, 85, 93) (1907-1936)

Western redbud - *Cercis canadensis* L. var. texensis (S. Wats.) M. Hopkins (106) (1930)

Western rock-jasmine [Western rock jasmine, Western rockjasmine] - *Androsace occidentalis* Pursh (3, 4, 50, 155) (1942–present)

Western rough goldenrod [Western rough golden-rod] - *Solidago radula* Nutt. (5, 50, 97, 122, 131) (1899–present)

Western ruppia - *Ruppia cirrhosa* (Petag.) Grande (5, 10, 85, 131) (1818-1932)

Western rye grass [Western rye-grass - *Elymus trachycaulus* (Link) Gould ex Shinners subsp. *trachycaulus* (68, 143) (1852-1936), *Leymus condensatus* (J. Presl) A. Löve (87) (1884)

Western sage - *Artemisia ludoviciana* Nutt. (156) (1923), *Artemisia ludoviciana* Nutt. subsp. *ludoviciana* (5, 93, 157) (1900-1936)

Western sagebrush [Western sage brush] - *Artemisia ludoviciana* Nutt. subsp. *ludoviciana* (85) (1932)

Western salsify - *Tragopogon dubius* Scop. (4) (1986)

Western sand cherry - *Prunus pumila* L. (32) (1895), *Prunus pumila* L. var. *besseyi* (Bailey) Gleason (1, 5, 50, 82, 85, 93, 109, 125, 131) (1913–present)

Western scouring-rush [Western scouringrush] - *Equisetum hyemale* L. var. *affine* (Engelm.) A. A. Eat. (155) (1942)

Western sea blite [Western sea-blite] - *Suaeda calceoliformis* (Hook.) Moq. (5, 93) (1913–1936)

Western sea purslane - *Sesuvium sessile* Pers. (5, 97) (1913–1937)

Western seepweed - *Suaeda calceoliformis* (Hook.) Moq. (155) (1942)

Western senega - *Polygala senega* L. (55) (1911)

Western sensitive brier - *Mimosa rupertiana* B.L. Turner (4) (1986)

Western serviceberry [Western service berry] - *Amelanchier alnifolia* (Nutt.) Nutt. ex M. Roemer (107, 135) (1910–1919)

Western shellbark [Western shell bark] - *Carya laciniosa* (Michx. f.) G. Don (5) (1913)

Western shellbark hickory - *Carya laciniosa* (Michx. f.) G. Don (2)

Western shepherdia   COMMON NAMES

(1895)

Western shepherdia - *Shepherdia argentea* (Pursh) Nutt. (20) (1857)

Western showy aster - *Eurybia conspicua* (Lindl.) Nesom (50) (present)

Western silky aster - *Symphyotrichum sericeum* (Vent.) Nesom (5, 93, 131) (1899-1936)

Western silver aster - *Symphyotrichum sericeum* (Vent.) Nesom (50) (present)

Western silver fir - *Abies amabilis* (Dougl. ex Loud.) Dougl. ex Forbes (161) (1857)

Western silvery aster - *Symphyotrichum sericeum* (Vent.) Nesom (5, 97) (1913-1937)

Western slough grass [Western slough-grass] - *Beckmannia* Host (93) (1936)

Western snakeweed [Western snake-weed] - *Liatris punctata* Hook (148) (1939)

Western sneezeweed - *Hymenoxys hoopesii* (Gray) Bierner (148) (1939) CO

Western snowberry - *Symphoricarpos occidentalis* Hook. (3, 4, 50, 98, 138, 155) (1923–present)

Western soapberry [Western soap berry] - *Sapindus saponaria* L. var. *drummondii* (Hook. & Arn.) Bensons (50, 124, 138, 155) (1923–present)

Western spider-lily [Western spiderlily, Western spider lily] - *Hymenocallis caroliniana* (L.) Herbert (97, 138) (1923–1937)

Western spiderwort - *Tradescantia occidentalis* (Brit.) Smyth (5, 93, 97) (1913-1937)

Western squaw-weed [Western squaw weed] - *Packera tridenticulata* (Rydb.) W. A. Weber & A. Löve (5, 93, 97) (1913–1937)

Western stickseed - *Lappula occidentalis* (S. Wats.) Greene (97) (1937), *Lappula occidentalis* (S. Wats.) Greene var. *occidentalis* (131) (1899)

Western stipa - *Hesperostipa comata* (Trin. & Rupr.) Barkworth subsp. *comata* (56) (1901)

Western stonecrop [Western stone crop] - *Sedum lanceolatum* Torr. (131) (1899)

Western sunflower - *Helianthus annuus* L. (108) (1878), *Helianthus occidentalis* Riddell (82) (1930), *Helianthus petiolaris* Nutt (80) (1913)

Western sweet cicely - *Osmorhiza berteroi* DC. (5, 85) (1913–1932)

Western sword fern [Western swordfern, Western sword-fern] - *Polystichum munitum* (Kaulfuss) K. Presl (50, 109, 155) (1942–present)

Western synthyris - *Besseya rubra* (Dougl. ex Hook.) Rydb. (5, 93) (1913–1936)

Western tansy-mustard [Western tansymustard, Western tansy mustard] - *Descurainia incana* (Bernh. ex Fisch. & C. A. Mey.) Dorn subsp. *incisa* (Engelm.) artesz & Gandhi (5, 93, 97, 131) (1899–1937), *Descurainia pinnata* (Walt.) Britton (155) (1942), *Descurainia pinnata* (Walt.) Britton subsp. *brachycarpa* (Richards.) Detling (50) (present), *Descurainia pinnata* (Walt.) Britton subsp. *intermedia* (Rydb.) Detling (50, 72) (1907–present)

Western thistle - *Cirsium ochrocentrum* Gray (145) (1897)

Western tickseed - *Bidens aristosa* (Michx.) Britton (82) (1930)

Western tickseed sunflower [Western tickseed-]sunflower - *Bidens aristosa* (Michx.) Britton (5, 97, 122) (1913-1937)

Western triple-awn grass [Western triple-awned grass] - *Aristida desmantha* Trin. & Rupr. (50, 163) (1852–present)

Western tumbleweed - *Cycloloma atriplicifolium* (Spreng.) Coult. (80) (1913)

Western umbrella-grass [Western umbrella grass] - *Fuirena simplex* Vahl (5) (1913)

Western umbrella-sedge [Western umbrella sedge] - *Fuirena simplex* Vahl (50) (present), *Fuirena simplex* Vahl var. *aristulata* (Torr.) Kral (50) (present)

Western Venus' looking-glass [Western Venus looking glass] - *Tri-*

odanis leptocarpa (Nutt.) Nieuwl. (5, 93, 97, 122) (1913–1937)

Western vervain - *Glandularia bipinnatifida* (Nutt.) Nutt. var. *bipinnatifida* (145) (1897)

Western virgin's-bower [Western virgin's bower, Western virginsbower, Western virginsbower, Western virgin-bower, Western virgin bower] - *Clematis ligusticifolia* Nutt. (5, 93, 108, 121, 138, 142, 155, 156, 157) (1878–1942)

Western wallflower [Western wall flower, Western wall-flower] - *Apocynum androsaemifolium* L. (156, 157, 158) (1900-1929), *Erysimum capitatum* (Dougl. ex Hook.) Greene (4) (1986), *Erysimum capitatum* (Dougl. ex Hook.) Greene var. *capitatum* (3, 4, 5, 15, 63, 93, 98, 121, 127, 131, 145, 156, 158) (1895-1986)

Western water hemlock [Western water-hemlock, Western water-hemlock] - *Cicuta maculata* L. var. *angustifolia* Hook. (95, 155, 157) (1929-1942)

Western water horehound [Western water hoarhound] - *Lycopus asper* Greene (5, 72, 93, 131) (1899-1936)

Western water-clover [Western water clover] - *Marsilea vestita* Hook. & Grev. (4) (1986)

Western waterhemp [Western water-hemp Western water hemp] - *Amaranthus rudis* Sauer (4, 5, 72, 93, 97, 131) (1907-1986)

Western water-plantain - *Alisma triviale* Pursh (5) (1913)

Western waterweed - *Elodea nuttallii* (Planch.) St. John (50, 155) (1942–present)

Western wheat grass [Western wheat-grass, Western wheatgrass] - *Pascopyrum smithii* (Rydb.) A. Löve (3, 5, 50, 56, 68, 80, 85, 111, 115, 116, 129, 134, 140, 146, 163) (1852–present), *Pseudoroegneria spicata* (Pursh) A. Löve subsp. *spicata* (56, 72, 94, 118) (1898-1907)

Western white campion - *Silene nivea* (Nutt.) Muhl. ex Otth (5, 72, 158) (1900-1913)

Western white clematis - *Clematis ligusticifolia* Nutt. (50) (present)

Western white honeysuckle - *Lonicera albiflora* Torr. & Gray (50) (present)

Western white pine - *Pinus flexilis* James (136, 153) (1913-1930), *Pinus monticola* Dougl. ex D. Don (50, 109) (1949–present)

Western wild cherry - *Prunus virginiana* L. var. *demissa* (Nutt.) Torr. (72, 106, 131, 137) (1899-1931)

Western wild gooseberry - *Ribes oxyacanthoides* L. subsp. *setosum* (Lindl.) Sinnott (95) (1911)

Western wild lettuce - *Lactuca ludoviciana* (Nutt.) Riddell (3, 4, 95) (1911-1986)

Western wild lily - *Lilium philadelphicum* L. var. *andinum* (Nutt.) Ker.-Gawl. (157) (1929)

Western wild rose - *Rosa woodsii* Lindl. (3, 4, 127) (1933-1986)

Western wild rye - *Elymus virginicus* L. var. *virginicus* (5) (1913)

Western witch grass [Western witch-grass] - *Panicum capillare* L. (93) (1936)

Western wood lily - *Lilium philadelphicum* L. var. *andinum* (Nutt.) Ker.-Gawl. (155) (1942)

Western wulfena - *Lunellia rubra* (Douglas ex Hook.) Nieuwl. (131) (1899)

Western yarrow - *Achillea millefolium* L. (50, 72, 155) (1907–present)

Western yellow pine - *Pinus ponderosa* P.& C. Lawson (97, 109, 112, 138, 155, 158, 161) (1857-1949), *Pinus ponderosa* P.& C. Lawson var. *ponderosa* (122) (1937) TX, *Pinus ponderosa* P.& C. Lawson var. *scopulorum* Engelm. (85, 122, 131, 136) (1899-1937)

Western yellow willow - *Salix lutea* Nutt. (20) (1857)

Western yew - *Taxus brevifolia* Nutt. (20, 109, 161) (1857-1949)

Wetsaθiŋdse egoŋ (Osage, rattlesnake's tail-like) - *Achillea millefolium* L. (121) (1918?-1970?)

Weybrede - *Plantago major* L. (179) (1526)

Weymouth pine - *Pinus strobus* L. (5, 46, 57) (1913-1917)

Wežauškwagmik (Chippewa) - *Diervilla lonicera* Mill. (105) (1932)

Wézawab-gonik (Chippewa, yellow flower) - *Rudbeckia hirta* L. (105) (1932)

Wheat - *Triticum aestivum* L. (21, 45, 56, 85, 94, 138, 140, 155, 158, 163) (1852–1942), *Triticum* L. (7, 45, 50, 66, 93, 155, 158) (1828–

450

present)

Wheat barley - *Hordeum vulgare* L. (158) (1900)

Wheat grass [Wheat-grass, Wheatgrass] - *Agropyron* Gaertner (1, 50, 93, 152, 155, 158) (1900–present), *Elymus repens* (L.) Gould (64, 69, 87, 90) (1884-1908), *Elymus trachycaulus* (Link) Gould ex Shinners subsp. *trachycaulus* (68) (1890), *Elymus virginicus* L. (68) (1890), *Pascopyrum* A. Löve (50) (present), *Pascopyrum smithii* (Rydb.) A. Löve (21) (1893), *Pseudoroegneria* (Nevski) A. Löve (50) (present), *Thinopyrum* A. Löve (50) (present), *Thinopyrum intermedium* (Host) Barkworth & D.R. Dewey (11, 22, 75) (1888-1894), *Triticum* L. (92) (1876)

Wheat of Barbary - *Zea mays* L. (107) (1919)

Wheat of Guinea - *Zea mays* L. (107) (1919)

Wheat of Rome - *Zea mays* L. (107) (1919)

Wheat of Spain - *Zea mays* L. (107) (1919)

Wheat of Turkey - *Zea mays* L. (107) (1919)

Wheat sedge - *Carex atherodes* Spreng. (50) (present)

Wheat-thief [Wheat thief] - *Buglossoides arvensis* (L.) I.M. Johnston (19, 62, 156) (1840-1923)

Wheel milkweed - *Asclepias uncialis* Greene (50) (present)

Wheeler's angelica [Wheeler angelica] - *Angelica wheeleri* S. Wats. (155) (1942)

Wheeler's bluegrass [Wheeler bluegrass] - *Poa nervosa* (Hook.) Vasey (140) (1944)

Wheeler's sotol [Wheeler sotol] - *Dasylirion wheeleri* S. Wats. (138) (1923)

Whig plant - *Chamaemelum nobile* (L.) All. (92) (1876)

Whin - *Genista tinctoria* L. (6, 92, 156) (1876–1923), *Ulex europaeus* L. (5, 156) (1913–1923), *Ulmus* L. (187) (1818)

Whinberry [Whin berry] - *Gaylussacia baccata* (Wang.) K. Koch (92) (1876), *Vaccinium myrtillus* L. (107) (1919)

Whip nut-rush [Whip nutrush] - *Scleria triglomerata* Michx. (50) (present)

Whip razor-sedge [Whip razorsedge] - *Scleria triglomerata* Michx. (3, 19, 155) (1840-1977)

Whipcord willow [Whipcord-willow] - *Salix purpurea* L. (5, 156) (1913-1923)

Whip-grass [Whip grass] - *Scleria* Berg. (10, 167) (1814-1818), *Scleria triglomerata* Michx. (5, 66, 92, 156) (1903-1923)

Whippoorwill [Whip-poor-will] - *Cypripedium acaule* Ait. (73) (1892)

Whippoorwill flower [Whip-poor-will flower] - *Trillium cernuum* L. (50) (present)

Whippoorwill pea [Whip-poor-will pea] - *Vigna sinensis* (L.) Endl. (156) (1923)

Whippoorwill's-boots [Whippoorwill's boots, Whip-poor-will's boots] - *Sarracenia purpurea* L. (5, 76, 156) (1896-1923) Philadelphia PA, no longer in use by 1923

Whippoorwill-shoes [Whippoorwill shoes, Whip-poor-will's shoe, Whip-poor-will shoe, Whip-poor-will shoes, Whippoorwill's shoes, Whip-poor-will's shoes] - *Cypripedium acaule* Ait. (75, 92) (1876-1894), *Cypripedium* L. (75) (1894) NY, from Indian name, *Cypripedium parviflorum* Salisb. (5, 156) (1913-1923), *Cypripedium reginae* Walt. (5, 73, 158) (1892-1913), *Sarracenia purpurea* L. (5, 76, 156) (1896-1923) ME, no longer in use by 1923

Whip-tongue - *Galium mollugo* L. (92, 156) (1898-1923) no longer in use by 1923

Whisk-broom parsley - *Lomatium* Raf. (1, 93) (1932-1936) Neb

Whisker moss - *Usnea* Dill. ex Adans. (73) (1892) Mansfield OH

Whisky cherry [Whiskey cherry] - *Prunus serotina* Ehrh. (71, 156, 157, 158) (1898-1929), *Prunus virginiana* L. var. *virginiana* (5) (1913)

Whisky currant - *Ribes cereum* Dougl. var. *pedicellare* Brewer & S. Wats. (50) (present)

Whist-aller - *Sambucus nigra* L. (158) (1900)

Whistlewood [Whistle wood, Whistle-wood] - *Acer pensylvanicum* L. (76, 79, 156) (1891–1923) Paris ME, NH, *Acer rubrum* L. (92) (1876), *Acer spicatum* Lam. (58) (1869), *Tilia americana* L. (5,

156, 157, 158) (1900–1929)

Whit mulberry [Whit mulberries] - *Morus alba* L. (181) (~1678)

White abronia - *Abronia fragrans* Nutt. ex Hook. (5, 93, 131) (1899-1936)

White adder's-mouth [White adder's mouth] - *Malaxis monophyllos* (L.) Sw. (5) (1913)

White adder's-mouth orchid [White adder's mouth orchid] - *Malaxis brachypoda* (Gray) Fern. (50) (present)

White adder's-tongue [White adder's tongue] - *Erythronium albidum* Nutt. (5, 72, 93, 156, 157, 158) (1900-1936)

White agaric - *Fomitopsis officinalis* (Batsch) Bondartsev & Singer (49, 53, 57, 92) (1876-1922)

White alder - *Alnus incana* (L.) Moench (possibly) (20) (1857), *Alnus rhombifolia* Nutt. (50) (present), *Clethra alnifolia* L. (5, 92, 106, 156) (1876-1930), *Clethra* L. (2, 156) (1895–1923), *Ilex verticillata* (L.) Gray (5, 76, 156) (1896-1923) Oxford Co. ME, *Lyonia ligustrina* (L.) DC. (124, 156) (1923-1937), *Lyonia ligustrina* (L.) DC. var. *foliosiflora* (Michx.) Fern. (122) (1937), *Lyonia ligustrina* (L.) DC. var. *ligustrina* (5) (1913)

White alfalfa - *Lotus glaber* Mill. (106) (1930)

White allison - *Arabis alpina* L. (5) (1913)

White amaranth - *Amaranthus albus* L. (165) (1768)

White American beauty-berry [White American beautyberry] - *Callicarpa americana* L. (155) (1942)

White American cowslip - *Dodecatheon meadia* L. subsp. *meadia* (97) (1937)

White American larch tree [White American larch-tree] - *Larix laricina* (Du Roi) K.Koch (possibly) (8) (1785)

White archangel [White archangell] - *Lamium album* L. (5, 6, 92, 156, 178) (1526-1923) no longer in use by 1923

White arctic whitlow-grass [White arctic whitlow grass] - *Draba fladnizensis* Wulf. (5) (1913)

White arrow arum - *Peltandra sagittifolia* (Michx.) Morong (50) (present)

White arrow-leaf aster [White arrowleaf aster] - *Symphyotrichum urophyllum* (Lindl.) Nesom (50) (present)

White ash - *Chionanthus virginicus* L. (5, 156) (1913-1923), *Fraxinus americana* L. (2, 4, 5, 9, 18, 19, 20, 35, 46, 48, 50, 52, 53, 57, 63, 72, 82, 85, 92, 93, 95, 97, 105, 108, 109, 113, 122, 124, 130, 131, 135, 138, 155, 156, 157, 158) (1840–present), *Syringa vulgaris* L. (156) (1923)

White ash herb - *Aegopodium podagraria* L. (156) (1923)

White ashweed [White ash weed] - *Aegopodium podagraria* L. (5) (1913)

White asp - *Populus alba* L. (158) (1900)

White aspen - *Populus alba* L. (5, 156) (1913-1923)

White aster - *Chaetopappa* DC. (4) (1986), *Chaetopappa ericoides* (Torr.) Nesom (3) (1977), *Doellingeria* Nees (158) (1900), *Symphyotrichum ericoides* (L.) Nesom var. *ericoides* (3, 4, 80, 85, 98, 106) (1913–1986), *Symphyotrichum lanceolatum* (Willd.) Nesom subsp. *lanceolatum* (85) (1932)

White avens - *Geum virginianum* L. (2, 3, 4, 5, 7, 48, 50, 72, 80, 85, 92, 93, 97, 122, 131, 155, 156, 157, 158) (1828–present)

White azalea - *Rhododendron viscosum* (L.) Torr. (5, 97) (1913-1937)

White bachelor's-buttons [White bachelor's buttons] - *Silene latifolia* Poir. subsp. *alba* (Mill.) Greuter & Burdet (156, 158) (1900-1923)

White balsam - *Pseudognaphalium obtusifolium* (L.) Hilliard & Burtt subsp. *obtusifolium* (5, 6, 61, 72, 92, 156, 157) (1870–1929)

White baneberry [White bane berry] - *Actaea pachypoda* Ell. (2, 6, 7, 49, 50, 53, 63, 72, 85, 92, 97, 105, 131, 138, 155, 158) (1828–present), *Actaea rubra* (Aiton) Willd. (42) (1814)

White bartonia - *Bartonia verna* (Michx.) Raf. ex Bart. (5) (1913)

White basswood [White bass wood] - *Tilia americana* L. var. *heterophylla* (Vent.) Loud. (5, 156) (1913-1923)

White bay [White-bay] - *Gordonia lasianthus* L. (46) (1879), *Magnolia virginiana* L. (5, 6, 15, 20, 49, 52, 92, 156, 186) (1825–1923),

Persea carolinensis (Raf.) Nees (5, 75, 156) (1894–1923)

White beaked-rush [White beaked rush] - *Rhynchospora alba* (L.) Vahl (5) (1913)

White beak-rush [White beak rush] - *Rhynchospora alba* (L.) Vahl (66) (1903)

White bean - *Phaseolus vulgaris* L. (6) (1892)

White bear sedge [Whitebear sedge] - *Carex albursina* Sheldon (5, 50, 72, 155) (1907–present)

White beardtongue [White beard-tongue] - *Penstemon albidus* Nutt. (3, 4, 85, 93, 131) (1899-1986)

White bedstraw - *Galium mollugo* L. (5, 109, 138, 156) (1913-1949)

White beech - *Fagus grandifolia* Ehrh. subsp. *grandifolia* (5, 19, 20, 78, 156) (1840-1923), *Fagus grandifolia* Ehrh. subsp. *grandifolia* (possibly) (187) (1818)

White bee-sage - *Salvia apiana* Jepson (138) (1923)

White beet [White beete] - *Beta vulgaris* L. (178) (1526)

White Ben - *Silene vulgaris* (Moench) Garcke (5, 156) (1913-1923) no longer in use by 1923

White Benjamin - *Trillium cernuum* L. (5, 158) (1900-1913), *Trillium undulatum* Willd. (78) (1898)

White bennet - *Geum aleppicum* Jacq. (187) (1818)

White bent - *Agrostis capillaris* L. (45) (1896)

White bent grass [White bentgrass, White bent-grass] - *Agrostis gigantea* Roth (5, 66, 92, 119, 165) (1768-1938), *Agrostis stolonifera* L. (68) (1890)

White birch - *Betula papyrifera* Marsh (5, 7, 20, 40, 43, 46, 101) (1820-1928), *Betula pendula* Roth (156) (1923), *Betula pubescens* Ehrh. (52, 55, 82, 92, 107, 156, 158) (1876-1932), *Betula pubescens* Ehrh. subsp. *pubescens* (20, 19, 109, 156, 187) (1818-1949)

White bird's-eye [White bird's eye] - *Stellaria holostea* L. (5) (1913), *Stellaria media* (L.) Vill. (156) (1923) no longer in use by 1923, *Stellaria media* (L.) Vill. subsp. *media* (5) (1913)

White bitterwood - *Trichilia hirta* L. (138) (1923)

White bladder flower [White bladderflower] - *Araujia sericifera* Brot. (155) (1942)

White blite [White blites] - *Atriplex hortensis* L. (178) (1526)

White blue-eyed-grass [White blue-eyed grass] - *Sisyrinchium albidum* Raf. (5, 50) (1913–present)

White bog orchid [White bog-orchid] - *Platanthera dilatata* (Pursh) Lindl. ex Beck var. *dilatata* (138) (1923)

White boltonia - *Boltonia asteroides* (L.) L'Hér. (138, 155) (1923-1942), *Boltonia asteroides* (L.) L'Hér. var. *recognita* (Fern. & Grisc.) Cronq. (3) (1977)

White broom - *Chamaecystis prolifera* (L. f.) Link (106) (1930)

White brush - *Aloysia gratissima* (Gillies & Hook.) Troncoso (106, 122, 124) (1930-1937)

White bryony [White brionie, Whyte bryony] - *Bryonia alba* L. (50, 92, 107, 179) (1526–present), *Bryonia cretica* L. subsp. *dioica* (Jacq.) Tutin (possibly) (178) (1526)

White bugle - *Ajuga reptans* L. (178) (1526)

White bush [White-bush] - *Clethra alnifolia* L. (5, 19, 92, 156) (1840-1923), *Leucothoe racemosa* (L.) Gray (possibly) (19, 92) (1840-1876), *Lyonia ligustrina* (L.) DC. (156) (1923)

White buttercup - *Parnassia* L. (156, 158) (1900-1923)

White cabbage cole - *Brassica oleracea* L. (180) (1633)

White camas [White camass] - *Anticlea* Kunth. (1) (1932), *Yucca filamentosa* L. (3) (1977), *Zigadenus elegans* Pursh subsp. *elegans* (85) (1932)

White camomile [White chamomile] - *Chamaemelum nobile* (L.) All. (5, 156) (1913-1923)

White campanilla - *Turbina corymbosa* (L.) Raf. (106) (1930)

White campion [White campions] - *Lychnis coronaria* (L.) Desr. (178) (1526), *Silene dioica* (L.) Clairville (15) (1895), *Silene latifolia* Poir. subsp. *alba* (Mill.) Greuter & Burdet (4, 5, 15, 62, 80, 85, 95, 109, 131, 156, 158) (1895-1986), *Silene nivea* (Nutt.) Muhl. ex Otth (93, 156) (1923-1936)

White candlewood [White candle wood] - *Amyris balsamifera* L.

(165) (1807)

White canella - *Canella winteriana* (L.) Gaertn. (15) (1895)

White canker-root - *Prenanthes alba* L. (156) (1923)

White cankerweed [White canker-weed] - *Prenanthes alba* L. (5, 92, 158) (1876-1900), *Prenanthes aspera* Michx. (157) (1929)

White cedar - *Calocedrus decurrens* (Torr.) Florin (75, 147) (1856-1894) CA, *Chamaecyparis lawsoniana* (A. Murr.) Parl. (75) (1894) NW, *Chamaecyparis thyoides* (L.) Britton, Sterns & Poggenb. (7, 10, 14, 19, 20, 41, 46, 92) (1770-1882), *Thuja* L. (1) (1932), *Thuja occidentalis* L. (2, 7, 52, 54, 75, 107) (1828-1919), *Thuja plicata* Donn ex D. Don (35, 101) (1806-1905)

White cedar of California - *Thuja plicata* Donn ex D. Don (14) (1882)

White centory [White centorie] - *Centaurium erythraea* Raf. (178) (1526)

White champion - *Silene latifolia* Poir. subsp. *alba* (Mill.) Greuter & Burdet (72) (1907)

White charlock - *Raphanus raphanistrum* L. (5) (1913)

White chestnut oak - *Quercus prinus* L. (5, 92, 156) (1876-1923)

White cinnamon - *Canella winteriana* (L.) Gaertn. (92) (1876)

White cinquefoil [White cinquefoile] - *Potentilla arguta* Pursh (82) (1930), *Potentilla recta* L. (178) (1526)

White clematis - *Clematis* L. (1) (1932), *Clematis terniflora* DC. (82) (1930)

White clintonia - *Clintonia umbellulata* (Michx.) Morong (5, 156) (1913-1923)

White clover - *Trifolium campestre* Schreber. (109) (1949), *Trifolium* L. (106) (1930), *Trifolium repens* L. (3, 4, 5, 6, 19, 41, 45, 50, 57, 63, 68, 72, 82, 85, 92, 93, 95, 97, 106, 107, 114, 129, 131, 138, 155, 156, 157, 158, 187) (1770–present)

White cockle - *Silene latifolia* Poir. subsp. *alba* (Mill.) Greuter & Burdet (4, 62, 80) (1912-1986)

White cohosh - *Actaea pachypoda* Ell. (5, 6, 7, 49, 53, 57, 61, 76, 92, 156, 158) (1828-1923), *Actaea spicata* L. (29) (1869) Pursh says berry color differs witihin populations

White colic root - *Aletris farinosa* L. (50) (present)

White coolwort [White cool wort] - *Tiarella cordifolia* L. (5, 74, 156) (1893-1923) NY

White coralberry - *Symphoricarpos albus* (L.) Blake (4) (1986)

White cornel - *Cornus florida* L. (5, 156, 158) (1900–1923), *Cornus foemina* Mill. (5) (1913), *Cornus sericea* L. subsp. *sericea* (20) (1857)

White corrans - *Ribes rubrum* L. (178) (1526)

White cotton-grass [White cottongrass] - *Eriophorum scheuchzeri* Hoppe (50) (present)

White coxscomb - *Amaranthus albus* L. (19) (1840)

White cranberry - *Gaultheria hispidula* (L.) Muhl. ex Bigelow (92, 156) (1876-1923)

White crownbeard [White crown-beard] - *Verbesina virginica* L. (50, 156) (1923–present)

White cuckoo flower [White cuckoo-flower] - *Silene latifolia* Poir. subsp. *alba* (Mill.) Greuter & Burdet (158) (1900)

White cut-leaf mignonette [White cut-leaved mignonette] - *Reseda alba* L. (5) (1913)

White cypress - *Taxodium distichum* (L.) L.C. Rich. (20) (1857)

White daisy - *Leucanthemum vulgare* Lam. (5, 45, 49, 62, 63, 92, 107, 131, 156, 158) (1876–1923)

White day-lily - *Hosta plantaginea* (Lam.) Aschers. (156) (1923)

White dead nettle (white dead-nettle) - *Lamium album* L. (5, 156) (1913-1923)

White devil - *Symphyotrichum lateriflorum* (L.) A.& D. Löve (75) (1894) WV

White dock - *Rumex pallidus* Bigelow (19, 156) (1840-1923), *Rumex salicifolius* Weinm. (2) (1895), *Rumex salicifolius* Weinm. var. *mexicanus* (Meisn.) A.S. Hitchc (5, 93) (1913-1936)

White dog-tooth violet [White dog's-tooth violet] - *Erythronium albidum* Nutt. (3, 5) (1913-1977), *Erythronium mesochoreum* Knerr (3) (1977)

White dogwood [White dog-wood] - *Viburnum opulus* L. (5, 156,

158) (1900-1923) England

White doll's-daisy [White doll's daisy] - *Boltonia asteroides* (L.) L'Hér. (50) (present)

White drought-weed [White drought weed] - *Croton setigerus* Hook. (106) (1930)

White dwarf plantain - *Plantago virginica* L. (5, 62) (1912-1913)

White eardrop [White ear-drop] - *Dicentra cucullaria* (L.) Bernh. (156, 158) (1900-1923)

White edge sedge - *Carex debilis* Michx. (50) (present)

White edge sedge - *Carex debilis* Michx. var. *rudgei* Bailey (50) (present)

White Egyptian waterlily - *Nymphaea lotus* L. (138, 155) (1931-1942)

White elder - *Viburnum opulus* L. (5, 158) (1900-1913)

White elm - *Ulmus alata* Michx. (38, 130) (1820-1895), *Ulmus americana* L. (1, 2, 5, 9, 20, 19, 37, 65, 72, 78, 85, 92, 95, 97, 101, 105, 108, 109, 112, 113, 130, 131, 157, 158) (1840-1949), *Ulmus rubra* Muhl. (78) (1898) Southwest MO

White evening-primrose [White evening primrose] - *Oenothera albicaulis* Pursh (85) (1932), *Oenothera caespitosa* Nutt. subsp. *marginata* (Nutt. ex Hook. & Arn.) Munz (138) (1923), *Oenothera* L. (1, 93) (1932-1936), *Oenothera laciniata* Hill (3) (1977), *Oenothera speciosa* Nutt. (156) (1923)

White everlasting - *Antennaria plantaginifolia* (L.) Richards (156) (1923), *Pseudognaphalium macounii* (Greene) Kartesz (156) (1923)

White false hellebore - *Veratrum album* L. (50) (present)

White false indigo - *Baptisia alba* (L.) Vent. var. *macrophylla* (Larisey) Isely (5) (1913)

White fawn-lily [White fawnlily] - *Erythronium albidum* Nutt. (50, 155) (1942–present)

White field aster - *Symphyotrichum lateriflorum* (L.) A.& D. Löve var. *lateriflorum* (106) (1930)

White fir - *Abies concolor* (Gord. & Glend.) Lindl. ex Hildebr. (possibly) (50, 109, 112, 135, 136, 138, 149, 155) (1904–present), *Pseudotsuga menziesii* (Mirb.) Franco (153) (1913)

White forget-me-not [White-forget-me-nots] - *Cryptantha* Lehm. ex G. Don (75, 158) (1894-1900) Santa Barbara Co. CA

White four-o'clock [White four-o-clock] - *Mirabilis albida* (Walt.) Heimerl (4, 50) (1986–present)

White foxglove [White foxe gloues] - *Digitalis pupurea* L. (178) (1526)

White fraxinella - *Dictamnus albus* L. (92) (1876)

White fringe tree [White fringetree] - *Chionanthus virginicus* L. (122, 124, 138) (1923-1937)

White fringed orchid [White fringe-orchid] - *Platanthera blephariglottis* (Willd.) Lindl. var. *blephariglottis* (138) (1923)

White fringed orchis - *Platanthera blephariglottis* (Willd.) Lindl. var. *blephariglottis* (2, 5, 109, 156) (1895-1949), *Platanthera leucophaea* (Nutt.) Lindl. (127) (1933)

White fritillary - *Fritillaria liliacea* Lindl. (138) (1923)

White galls - *Phyllanthus emblica* L. (92) (1876)

White garden arach - *Atriplex hortensis* L. (178) (1526)

White gaura - *Gaura lindheimeri* Engelm. & Gray (138) (1923)

White gentian - *Gentiana alba* Muhl. ex Nutt. (48) (1882), *Triosteum perfoliatum* L. (5, 92, 156, 158) (1876-1923)

White gessemin - *Jasminum officinale* L. (178) (1526)

White ginseng - *Triosteum perfoliatum* L. (6, 7, 158) (1828-1900)

White goldenrod [White golden-rod] - *Solidago bicolor* L. (5, 19, 106, 138, 156) (1840-1930)

White goosefoot [White goose-foot] - *Chenopodium album* L. (5, 62, 93, 107, 157, 158) (1900-1936)

White gourd - *Benincasa hispida* (Thunb.) Cogn. (109) (1949)

White gourd-melon - *Benincasa hispida* (Thunb.) Cogn. (110) (1886)

White gram - *Glycine max* (L.) Merr. (158) (1900)

White grama - *Bouteloua gracilis* (Willd. ex Kunth) Lag. ex Griffiths (152) (1912)

White grapewort - *Actaea pachypoda* Ell. (156, 158) (1900-1923)

White grass [White-grass, Whitegrass] - *Agrostis gigantea* Roth (92) (1876), *Leersia lenticularis* Michx. (88) (1885), *Leersia oryzoides* (L.) Sw. (66, 87, 90, 92) (1876-1903), *Leersia* Sw. (66) (1903), *Leersia virginica* Willd. (3, 5, 19, 50, 94, 99, 119, 122, 131, 163) (1840–present)

White gum [White-gum] or White gum tree - *Eucalyptus camaldulensis* Dehnhardt (92) (1876) native of Australia, *Liquidambar styraciflua* L. (5, 7, 92, 156, 177) (1762-1923)

White hawkweed - *Hieracium albiflorum* Hook (50, 155) (1942–present)

White hawthorn - *Crataegus* L. (82) (1930)

White heath aster [White heath-aster] - *Symphyotrichum ericoides* (L.) Nesom (50) (present), *Symphyotrichum ericoides* (L.) Nesom var. *prostratum* (Kuntze) Nesom (50) (present), *Symphyotrichum ericoides* (L.) Nesom var. *ericoides* (5, 50, 62, 72, 82, 156, 158) (1900–present)

White heather - *Cassiope* D. Don. (1) (1932)

White hedge-nettle [White hedge nettle] - *Stachys ajugoides* Benth. (106) (1930)

White hellebore [White heelebore, White hellbore, White hellibore] - *Veratrum album* L. (41, 52, 53, 55, 64, 92) (1770-1922), *Veratrum* L. (1, 167) (1814-1932), *Veratrum viride* Ait. (19, 46, 71, 107) (1840-1919)

White henbane - *Hyoscyamus albus* L. (92, 178) (1526-1876)

White hibiscus - *Hibiscus moscheutos* L. subsp. *moscheutos* (156) (1923)

White hickory [White hickery] - *Carya alba* (L.) Nutt. ex Ell. (6, 158) (1892–1900), *Carya cordiformis* (Wangenh.) K. Koch (possibly) (187) (1818), *Carya glabra* (Mill.) Sweet (156) (1923), *Carya glabra* (Mill.) Sweet var. *glabra* (5) (1913), *Carya ovata* (Mill.) K. Koch (5, 156, 158) (1900–1923), *Carya sulcata* Nutt. (possibly) (38) (1820)

White hollow-root [White hollow roote] - *Corydalis solida* (L.) Clairv. (178) (1526)

White holly - *Ilex opaca* Aiton (5, 156) (1913-1923)

White honey flower [White honey-flower] - *Robinia pseudoacacia* L. (156) (1923)

White honeysuckle [White honey-suckle] - *Lonicera albiflora* Torr. & Gray (3, 4, 149) (1904-1986), *Rhododendron viscosum* (L.) Torr. (5, 19, 75) (1840-1913) Alabama, *Trifolium repens* L. (157, 158) (1900-1929)

White horehound [White hoarhound] - *Marrubium vulgare* L. (5, 10, 55, 63, 72, 92, 93, 95, 156, 157, 178) (1596-1936)

White horse-nettle [White horse nettle] - *Solanum elaeagnifolium* Cav. (156) (1923)

White hummingbird tree - *Chelone glabra* L. (42) (1814)

White Indian hemp - *Apocynum cannabinum* L. (58) (1869), *Asclepias incarnata* L. (53, 58, 92, 156, 157) (1869–1929), *Asclepias incarnata* L. subsp. *pulchra* (Ehrh. ex Willd.) Woods. (5, 156) (1913–1923)

White indigo-bush amorpha [White indigobush amorpha] - *Amorpha fruticosa* L. (155) (1942)

White ipecac - *Euphorbia ipecacuanhae* L. (92, 156) (1898–1923), *Richardia scabra* L. (92) (1876)

White ipecacuanha - *Hybanthus* Jacq. (13) (1849)

White ironwood - *Hypelate trifoliata* Swartz. (15) (1895)

White ixora - *Ixora pavetta* Andrews (138) (1923)

White jassamine - *Jasminum officinale* L. (92) (1876)

White jessamine - *Gelsemium sempervirens* (L.) J. St.-Hil. (59) (1911)

White jimsonweed [White jimson weed] - *Datura stramonium* L. (145) (1897)

White juniper or White juniper tree - *Chamaecyparis thyoides* (L.) Britton, Sterns & Poggenb. (41) (1770), *Juniperus monosperma* (Engelm.) Sarg. (97) (1937) OK

White kerria - *Rhodotypos scandens* (Thunb.) Makino (112) (1937)

White knapweed - *Centaurea diffusa* Lam. (50) (present)

White laburnum - *Robinia pseudoacacia* L. (157, 158) (1900-1929)

White lady's-bedstraw [White ladies bedstraw] - *Galium mollugo* L.

(178) (1526), *Galium palustre* L. (178) (1526)

White lady's-slipper [White lady's slipper, White ladies' slipper, White lady-slipper, White ladyslipper] - *Cypripedium candidum* Muhl. ex Willd. (3, 7, 85, 109, 138) (1828–present)

White lamium - *Lamium album* L. (106) (1930)

White larkspur - *Delphinium carolinianum* Walt. subsp. *virescens* (Nutt.) Brooks (122, 124) (1937)

White laurel [White-laurel] - *Magnolia virginiana* L. (5, 15, 41, 49, 52, 156, 186) (1770-1923)

White leaf-cup - *Polymnia canadensis* L (19) (1840)

White lettuce - *Prenanthes alba* L. (5, 19, 49, 82, 92, 156, 158) (1840-1930), *Prenanthes altissima* L. (2) (1895), *Prenanthes aspera* Michx. (157) (1929), *Prenanthes serpentaria* Pursh (5, 156) (1913-1923)

White lewisia - *Lewisia rediviva* Pursh (103) (1870)

White lilac - *Syringa vulgaris* L. (92, 135) (1876-1910)

White lily [White lilies] - *Lilium candidum* L. (19, 49, 92) (1840-1876), *Trillium grandiflorum* (Michx.) Salisb. (5, 73) (1892-1913)

White lin [White linn] - *Tilia americana* L. (156) (1923), *Tilia americana* L. var. *heterophylla* (Vent.) Loud. (156) (1923)

White lind - *Tilia americana* L. (5, 157, 158) (1900-1929)

White linden - *Tilia petiolaris* DC. (109) (1949)

White liverwort - *Parnassia* L. (156, 158) (1900-1923)

White loco - *Oxytropis lambertii* Pursh (146) (1939), *Sophora nuttalliana* B.L. Turner (4) (1986)

White locoweed - *Oxytropis sericea* Nutt. (3, 4, 50) (1977–present), *Oxytropis sericea* Nutt. var. *sericea* (50) (present)

White locust or White locust tree [White locust-tree] - *Robinia pseudoacacia* L. (5, 74, 106, 156, 157, 158, 187) (1818-1929)

White London mustard - *Sinapis alba* L. (109) (1949)

White lotus (of Egypt) - *Nymphaea lotus* L. (109) (1949)

White lupin - *Lupinus albus* L. (49) (1898)

White lupine - *Lupinus albus* L. (19, 109, 138) (1840-1949)

White mahogany - *Catalpa speciosa* (Warder) Warder ex Engelm. (156) (1923)

White mallow - *Althaea officinalis* L. (107, 156, 158) (1900-1923)

White mandarin - *Streptopus amplexifolius* (L.) DC. (3) (1977)

White mangle - *Baccharis halimifolia* L. (156) (1923)

White mangrove - *Conocarpus erectus* L. (20) (1857), *Laguncularia racemosa* (L.) Gaertn. f. (20, 106) (1857-1930)

White maple - *Acer glabrum* Torr. (35) (1806), *Acer macrophyllum* Pursh (106, 160) (1860-1930), *Acer saccarhinum* L. (2, 5, 19, 20, 42, 76, 85, 92, 93, 106, 107, 109, 158, 187) (1814–1949)

White meadowsweet - *Spiraea alba* Du Roi (50) (present)

White melilot - *Melilotus officinalis* (L.) Lam. (possibly) (5, 6, 45, 62, 63, 92, 129, 156, 157, 158) (1892-1929)

White melilot clover - *Melilotus officinalis* (L.) Lam. (possibly) (19) (1840)

White milkweed - *Asclepias variegata* L. (5, 97, 122) (1913-1937)

White milkwort [White milke woort] - *Polygala alba* Nutt. (3, 4, 5, 50, 93, 97, 122, 131) (1899–present), *Polygala vulgaris* L. (178) (1526)

White millet - *Melilotus officinalis* (L.) Lam. (possibly) (5, 157, 158) (1900-1929)

White moccasin flower - *Cypripedium candidum* Muhl. ex Willd. (86) (1878)

White morning-glory [White morning glory] - *Calystegia sepium* (L.) R. Br. subsp. *sepium* (145) (1897), *Ipomoea lacunosa* L. (3, 4) (1977-1986)

White moth mullein - *Verbascum* L. (190) (~1759)

White mountain avens - *Dryas octopetala* L. (5) (1913)

White mountain-mint [White mountain mint] - *Pycnanthemum albescens* Torr. & Gray ex Gray (4) (1986)

White mountain-rice [White mountain rice] - *Oryzopsis asperifolia* Michx. (66, 90, 94) (1885-1903)

White mountain-rose coralvine [White mountainrose coralvine] - *Antigonon leptopus* Hook. & Arn. (155) (1942)

White mugwort - *Artemisia ludoviciana* Nutt. subsp. *ludoviciana* (40) (1928)

White mulberry [White mulberrie] - *Morus alba* L. (1, 3, 4, 5, 19, 50, 82, 85, 93, 95, 97, 107, 109, 110, 138, 153, 155, 156, 178) (1526–present), *Morus microphylla* Buckl. (149) (1904) NM

White mullein [White mulleine] - *Verbascum lychnitis* L. (156) (1923), *Verbascum nigrum* L. (174) (1753), *Verbascum thapsus* L. (46) (1649)

White mustard - *Sinapis alba* L. (3, 4, 5, 6, 15, 50, 52, 53, 57, 58, 59, 69, 72, 85, 92, 93, 107, 109, 131, 138, 155, 156, 157, 158) (1869–present)

White nettle - *Lamium album* L. (92) (1876)

White nigella - *Nigella sativa* L. (178) (1526)

White nonesuch - *Lolium perenne* L. (5) (1913)

White oak [White-oak, White oake] or White oak tree - *Quercus alba* L. (1, 3, 4, 5, 8, 9, 10, 17, 18, 20, 19, 33, 41, 46, 50, 52, 57, 58, 65, 72, 82, 92, 93, 95, 97, 107, 109, 112, 113, 122, 124, 130, 135, 138, 155, 156, 157, 158, 177, 181, 187, 190) (~1678–present), *Quercus gambelii* Nutt. var. *gambelii* (153) (1913) NM, *Quercus garryana* Dougl. ex Hook. (35, 160) (1806-1860), *Quercus prinus* L. (33) (1827), *Quercus stellata* Wangenh. (5) (1913)

White oak bark - *Quercus alba* L. (157) (1929)

White oak shinnery - *Quercus sinuata* Walt. var. *breviloba* (Torr.) C.H. Muller (122, 124) (1937) TX

White oak with pointed notches - *Quercus rubra* L. (189) (1767)

White oats - *Hordeum murinum* L. (88) (1885)

White onion - *Allium drummondii* Regel (122) (1937)

White orchis - *Platanthera dilatata* (Pursh) Lindl. ex Beck var. *dilatata* (3) (1977)

White osier - *Leucothoe racemosa* (L.) Gray (7, 92, 156) (1828-1923), *Salix viminalis* L. (5, 156) (1913-1923)

White oxeye daisy [White ox-eye daisy] - *Leucanthemum vulgare* Lam. (45) (1896)

White ozier - *Leucothoe racemosa* (L.) Gray (5) (1913)

White panicle aster - *Symphyotrichum lanceolatum* (Willd.) Nesom (50) (present)

White paper birch - *Betula papyrifera* Marsh (8) (1785)

White passe flower [White passe floure] - *Pulsatilla patens* (L.) Mill. subsp. *multifida* (Pritz.) Zamels (poss) (180) (1633)

White passionflower [White passion flower] - *Passiflora foetida* L. (122) (1937)

White peach-leaf bellflower [White peach leafe belflower] - *Campanula persicifolia* L. (178) (1526)

White penstemon - *Penstemon albidus* Nutt. (50, 155) (1942–present)

White pepper - *Leucothoe racemosa* (L.) Gray (156) (1923), *Lyonia ligustrina* (L.) DC. (156) (1923)

White pepper bush [White pepperbush, White pepper-bush] - *Leucothoe racemosa* (L.) Gray (5, 7, 92) (1828-1913), *Lyonia ligustrina* (L.) DC. (possibly) (46) (1783), *Lyonia ligustrina* (L.) DC. var. *ligustrina* (5) (1913)

White perwinkle [White peruinkle] - *Matelea biflora* (Raf.) Woods (174) (1753)

White petunia - *Petunia axillaris* (Lam.) Britton, Sterns & Poggenb. (5, 85) (1913-1932)

White pigweed - *Amaranthus albus* L. (possibly) (62) (1912)

White pine - *Picea glauca* (Moench) Voss (41) (1770), *Pinus monticola* Dougl. ex D. Don (20, 35) (1806-1857), *Pinus strobus* L. (1, 2, 10, 46, 57, 72, 92, 109, 112, 136, 138) (1818-1949), *Pinus taeda* L. (20) (1857)

White pipsiseway - *Chimaphila maculata* (L.) Pursh (7) (1828)

White plantain - *Antennaria dioica* (L.) Gaertn. (17, 18) (1796-1805), *Antennaria plantaginifolia* (L.) Richards (5, 7, 92, 158, 177) (1828-1913)

White plantain-lily [White plantainlily] - *Hosta plantaginea* (Lam.) Aschers. (138) (1923)

White poison vine - *Gelsemium sempervirens* (L.) J. St.-Hil. (59) (1911)

White pollom - *Gaultheria hispidula* (L.) Muhl. ex Bigelow (possibly) (92) (1876)

White pollum - *Gaultheria hispidula* (L.) Muhl. ex Bigelow (156) (1923)

White polygala - *Polygala alba* Nutt. (155) (1942)

White pond-lily [White pond lily] - *Nymphaea odorata* Aiton (6, 7, 19, 48, 49, 61, 92) (1828-1898), *Nymphaea odorata* Aiton subsp. *odorata* (158) (1900)

White popinac - *Leucaena leucocephala* (Lam.) de Wit (109) (1949)

White poplar or White poplar tree - *Liriodendron tulipifera* L. (2, 5, 13, 18, 46, 49, 74, 92, 186, 187) (1818-1895), *Populus alba* L. (1, 5, 14, 20, 50, 72, 92, 93, 107, 109, 112, 138, 155, 156, 158) (1857–present), *Populus deltoides* Bartr. ex Marsh. (8) (1785), *Populus deltoides* Bartr. ex Marsh. subsp. *monilifera* (Aiton) Eckenwalder (12) (1821), *Populus grandidentata* Michx. (5, 156) (1913-1923), *Populus tremuloides* Michx. (5, 6, 19, 49, 52, 57, 92, 156, 157, 158) (1840-1929)

White poppy - *Argemone albiflora* Hornem. subsp. *albiflora* (122, 124) (1937), *Papaver somniferum* L. (54, 60) (1526–1902)

White pot herb [White pot-herb] - *Valerianella locusta* (L.) Lat. (5, 156) (1913-1923)

White potato - *Solanum tuberosum* L. (156) (1923)

White prairie aster - *Symphyotrichum ericoides* (L.) Nesom var. *ericoides* (85, 127) (1932-1933), *Symphyotrichum falcatum* (Lindl.) Nesom (50) (present), *Symphyotrichum falcatum* (Lindl.) Nesom var. *commutatum* (Torr. & Gray) Nesom (5, 50, 131, 122) (1899–present), *Symphyotrichum falcatum* (Lindl.) Nesom var. *falcatum* (50) (present)

White prairie clover [White prairieclover] - *Dalea candida* Michx. ex Willd. var. *candida* (3, 4, 5, 50, 65, 72, 82, 93, 97, 98, 114, 131, 138, 155) (1894–present), *Dalea candida* Michx. ex Willd. var. *oligophylla* (Torr.) Shinners (50, 85) (1932–present)

White prairie grass - *Tridens albescens* (Vasey) Woot. & Standl. (5) (1913)

White prairie rose - *Rosa foliolosa* Nutt. (4, 50) (1986–present)

White prairie-mallow [White prairiemallow] - *Sidalcea candida* Gray (138) (1923)

White prickly-poppy [White prickly poppy, White pricklypoppy] - *Argemone albiflora* Hornem. subsp. *albiflora* (5, 97, 131, 155) (1899-1942)

White puccoon - *Sanguinaria canadensis* L. (64, 74, 158) (1893-1908) NY

White pursely - *Euphorbia corollata* L. (7, 92) (1828–1876)

White purslane - *Euphorbia corollata* L. (5, 156, 157, 158) (1900-1929)

White rain lily - *Cooperia drummondii* Herb. (124) (1937), *Cooperia* Herb. (122) (1937)

White rain lily - *Cooperia pedunculata* Herbert (124) (1937)

White rattlesnake-root [White rattlesnakeroot] - *Prenanthes alba* L. (3, 50, 155) (1942–present)

White rice - *Leersia virginica* Willd. (45) (1896)

White rock-lettuce [White rocklettuce] - *Pinaropappus roseus* (Less.) Less. (50) (present)

White root (Southern tribes) - *Angelica lucida* L. (7) (1828)

White rose - *Rosa* ×*alba* L. [*arvensis* × *gallica*] (19, 92, 178) (1526–1876)

White rose-mallow [White rose mallow] - *Hibiscus moscheutos* L. subsp. *moscheutos* (156) (1923)

White rosewood [White rose wood] - *Amyris balsamifera* L. (165) (1807)

White rosin or White rosin tree - *Pinus palustris* Mill. (5, 92) (1876-1913)

White rough bark - *Quercus stellata* Wangenh. (46) (1649)

White rust - *Uredo candida* (Pers. ex J.F. Gmel.) Pers. (19) (1840)

White sage - *Artemisia ludoviciana* Nutt. (4, 156) (1923–1986), *Artemisia ludoviciana* Nutt. subsp. *ludoviciana* (3, 98, 127, 158) (1900-1977), *Salvia apiana* Jepson (106) (1930), *Salvia argentea* L. (92) (1876)

White sagebrush [White sage-brush] - *Artemisia cana* Pursh (108) (1878), *Artemisia ludoviciana* Nutt. (50) (present), *Artemisia ludoviciana* Nutt. subsp. *mexicana* (Willd. ex Spreng.) Keck (50) (present)

White sand-verbena [White sandverbena] - *Abronia alba* Eastw. (155) (1942)

White sanicle - *Ageratina altissima* (L.) King & H.E. Robins. (5, 62, 72, 92, 156) (1876-1923)

White sassafras - *Sassafras albidum* (Nutt.) Nees (3, 19) (1840-1977)

White satin [White sattin, White satten] - *Lunaria annua* subsp. *annua* L. (possibly) (178) (1526), *Lunaria rediviva* L. (46) (1671) cultivated by English colonists by 1671

White saw-wort [White saw woort] - *Serratula tinctoria* L. (178) (1526)

White secac - *Euphorbia ipecacuanhae* L. (49) (1898)

White sedge - *Carex canescens* L. (66) (1903)

White shamrock - *Trifolium repens* L. (92, 157, 158) (1876-1929)

White shoe-buttons [White shoe buttons] - *Eriocaulon decangulare* L. (156) (1923)

White single poppy [White single poppie] - *Papaver somniferum* L. (178) (1526)

White snakeleaf - *Erythronium albidum* Nutt. (7) (1828)

White snakeroot [White snake root, White snake-root] - *Ageratina altissima* (L.) King & H.E. Robins. (2, 4, 5, 50, 58, 62, 63, 80, 82, 85, 93, 97, 106, 109, 114, 122, 125, 126, 131, 155, 156) (1869–present), *Ageratina aromatica* (L.) Spach (61, 92) (1870-1876), *Asarum canadense* L. (19, 42) (1814-1840), *Eupatorium* L. (1, 93) (1932-1936)

White snapdragon - *Antirrhinum majus* L. (178) (1526)

White snowdrop - *Galanthus nivalis* L. (92) (1876)

White soapwort - *Silene dioica* (L.) Clairville (92, 156) (1876-1923)

White sorrel - *Oxalis montana* Raf. (possibly) (7, 92) (1828-1876)

White Spanish broom - *Cytisus multiflorus* (L'Hér.) Sweet (109, 138) (1923-1949)

White spear grass - *Catabrosa aquatica* (L.) Beauv. (87, 90) (1884-1885), *Glyceria grandis* S. Wats. var. *grandis* (5) (1913)

White spider lily - *Hymenocallis galvestonensis* (Herbert) Baker (124) (1937)

White spike-rush [White spike rush, White spikerush] - *Eleocharis albida* Torr. (5, 50) (1913–present)

White spiraea - *Spiraea betulifolia* Pallas (50) (present)

White spruce - *Abies alba* Mill. (10, 19, 20, 46) (1818-1857), *Picea engelmannii* Parry ex Engelm. (149) (1904) NM, *Picea glauca* (Moench) Voss (1, 2, 3, 5, 50, 85, 109, 112, 130, 131, 135, 136, 138, 155, 158) (1895–present), *Picea mariana* (Mill.) Britton, Sterns & Poggenb. (5) (1913)

White spruce fir - *Abies alba* Mill. (20) (1857)

White star ipomoea - *Ipomoea lacunosa* L. (86) (1878)

White starwort [White star wort] - *Symphyotrichum lateriflorum* (L.) A.& D. Löve (possibly) (42) (1814)

White stonecrop - *Sedum album* L. (92, 138, 155) (1876-1942)

White strawberry [White strawberrie] - *Fragaria virginiana* Duchesne (178) (1526)

White sumac [White sumach, White shumack] - *Rhus glabra* L. (5, 76, 156, 157, 158) (1896-1929) Southwestern MO

White sunflower - *Wyethia helianthoides* Nutt. (101) (1905) MT

White sunnybell - *Schoenolirion albiflorum* (Raf.) R.R. Gates (50) (present)

White swallow-wort [White swallow wort, White Swallowwoort] - *Cynanchum vincetoxicum* (L.) Pers. (92) (1876), *Matelea gonocarpos* (Walt.) Shinners (178) (1526)

White swamp cypress - *Taxodium distichum* (L.) L.C. Rich. (5) (1913)

White swamp honeysuckle - *Rhododendron viscosum* (L.) Torr. (2, 109, 156) (1895-1949)

White swamp milkweed - *Asclepias incarnata* L. (155) (1942)

White swamp oak - *Quercus bicolor* Willd (1, 2) (1895-1932)

White sweet azalea - *Rhododendron viscosum* (L.) Torr. (8) (1785)

White sweet clover [White sweet-clover, White sweetclover] - *Melilotus officinalis* (L.) Lam. (possibly) (3, 4, 5, 50, 62, 68, 72, 80, 82, 85, 93, 95, 97, 106, 109, 122, 124, 125, 131, 138, 145, 155, 156, 157, 158) (1897–present)

White sweet Johns [White Sweete Iohns] - *Dianthus carthusianorum* L. (178) (1526)

White tansy - *Achillea ptarmica* L. (5, 156) (1913-1923)

White tassel-flower [White tassel flower] - *Dalea candida* Michx. ex Willd. (5, 76, 156) (1896-1923) Southwestern MO

White teaberry - *Gaultheria hispidula* (L.) Muhl. ex Bigelow (156) (1923)

White Texas star - *Claytonia virginica* L. var. *acutiflora* DC. (124) (1937) TX

White thistle [White thistle] - *Cirsium undulatum* (Nutt.) Spreng. var. *undulatum* (95) (1911), *Onopordum* L. (7) (1828)

White thorn [Whitethorn, White thorne] - *Crataegus calpodendron* (Ehrh.) Medik. (5, 157) (1913–1929), *Crataegus crus-galli* L. (7, 92) (1828–1876), *Crataegus* L. (2) (1895), *Crataegus mollis* Scheele (190) (~1759), *Crataegus punctata* Jacq. (5) (1913), *Crataegus spathulata* Michx. (106) (1930), *Mespilus* L. (167) (1814)

White thoroughwort - *Eupatorium album* L. (5, 122, 156) (1913-1937)

White timothy - *Holcus lanatus* L. (5, 45) (1896-1913)

White titi [White ti-ti] - *Cyrilla racemiflora* L. (5, 106, 156) (1913-1930)

White trefoil - *Trifolium repens* L. (5, 93, 156, 157, 158) (1900-1936)

White tridens - *Tridens albescens* (Vasey) Woot. & Standl. (3, 50) (1977–present)

White trout-lily [White troutlily] - *Erythronium albidum* Nutt. (138) (1923)

White trumpet lily - *Lilium longiflorum* Thunb. (109) (1949)

White tupelo - *Nyssa ogeche* Bartr. ex Marsh. (106) (1930)

White turtlehead - *Chelone glabra* L. (138) (1923)

White umbel [White umbil] - *Cypripedium candidum* Muhl. ex Willd. (7, 92) (1828-1876)

White upland aster - *Oligoneuron album* (Nutt.) Nesom (109, 155, 156) (1923-1949)

White upright mignonette - *Reseda alba* L. (109) (1949)

White veratrum - *Veratrum album* L. (49, 52, 53) (1898-1922)

White verbena - *Verbena urticifolia* L. (155) (1942)

White vervain - *Eclipta prostrata* (L.) L. (181) (~1678), *Glandularia bipinnatifida* (Nutt.) Nutt. var. *bipinnatifida* (3, 4, 5, 80, 93, 95, 156, 157, 158, 187) (1818-1986), *Verbena simplex* Lehm. (174) (1753), *Verbena urticifolia* L. (2, 5, 50, 57, 58, 62, 63, 72, 80, 82, 92, 93, 95, 97, 114, 122, 131, 156, 157, 158) (1869–present)

White vetch - *Vicia ludoviciana* Nutt. subsp. *ludoviciana* (155) (1942), *Vicia sativa* L. (107) (1919)

White vine [Whyte vyne] - *Bryonia alba* L. (179) (1526), *Clematis vitalba* L. (92) (1876)

White violet - *Viola renifolia* Gray (50) (present)

White Virginia crowfoot [White Virginia crowfoote] - *Sanguinaria canadensis* L. (181) (~1678)

White walnut [White walnuts] or White walnut tree [White walnut-trees] - *Carya alba* (L.) Nutt. ex Ell. (177, 189) (1762-1767), *Carya ovata* (Mill.) K. Koch (5, 156, 158) (1900-1923), *Juglans cinerea* L. (1, 2, 5, 6, 7, 35, 49, 53, 78, 82, 85, 92, 104, 109, 156, 158) (1806-1949)

White wand beardtongue - *Penstemon tubiflorus* Nutt. (50) (present)

White water crowfoot [White water-crowfoot] - *Ranunculus aquatilis* L. (156) (1923), *Ranunculus* L. (1, 93) (1932-1936), *Ranunculus longirostris* Godr. (3, 4) (1977-1986), *Ranunculus trichophyllus* Chaix var. *trichophyllus* (3, 5, 63, 85, 127) (1899-1977)

White waterlily [White water lily, White water-lily] - *Nymphaea alba* L. (107) (1919), *Nymphaea elegans* Hook. (122) (1937) TX, *Nymphaea odorata* Aiton (2, 92) (1876-1895), *Nymphaea odorata* Aiton subsp. *odorata* (40, 156) (1923-1928), *Nymphaea odorata* Aiton subsp. *tuberosa* (Paine) Wiersma & Hellquist (3, 4, 82, 85,

120, 157) (1900-1986)

White whitlow-wort [White whitlowwort] - *Draba reptans* (Lam.) Fern. (3, 4) (1977-1986)

White wild indigo [White wild-indigo, White wildindigo] - *Baptisia alba* (L.) Vent. (5, 50, 72, 155) (1907–present), *Baptisia alba* (L.) Vent. var. *macrophylla* (Larisey) Isely (4, 5, 138) (1913-1986)

White wild onion - *Allium textile* A. Nels. & Macbr. (3) (1977)

White willow - *Salix alba* L. (3, 5, 49, 50, 52, 58, 72, 82, 85, 92, 107, 109, 138, 155, 156, 158, 187) (1818–present), *Salix amygdaloides* Anderss. (130) (1895), *Salix candida* Flueggé ex Willd. (19) (1840), *Salix interior* Rowlee (5, 156, 158) (1900-1923)

White wintergreen [White winter-green] - *Gaultheria hispidula* (L.) Muhl. ex Bigelow (156) (1923), *Pyrola elliptica* Nutt. (19) (1840)

White wood aster - *Eurybia divaricata* (L.) Nesom (5, 72, 155) (1907-1942)

White wood sorrel [White wood-sorrel] - *Oxalis montana* Raf. (possibly) (5, 156) (1913-1923)

White wormwood - *Artemisia ludoviciana* Nutt. (80) (1913)

White wreath aster [White wreath-aster] - *Symphyotrichum ericoides* (L.) Nesom var. *ericoides* (156, 158) (1900-1923)

White yarrow - *Achillea nobilis* L. (178) (1526)

White-alder - *Clethra* L. (109) (1949)

White-apple [White apple, White apples] - *Pediomelum esculentum* (Pursh) Rydb. (35) (1806), *Apios americana* Medik. (7, 92, 156) (1828-1923)

Whiteball [White ball] - *Cephalanthus occidentalis* L. (7, 92) (1828-1876)

White-bark [White bark, Whitebark] - *Carya alba* (L.) Nutt. ex Ell. (156) (1923), *Populus alba* L. (5, 156, 158) (1900-1923)

White-bark buckeye [Whitebark buckeye] - *Aesculus glabra* Willd. (138) (1923)

White-bark hickory [White bark hickory] - *Carya alba* (L.) Nutt. ex Ell. (5) (1913)

White-bark Ohio buckeye [Whitebark Ohio buckeye] - *Aesculus glabra* Willd. (155) (1942)

White-bark pine [Whitebark pine] - *Pinus albicaulis* Engelm. (138) (1923)

White-bark raspberry [Whitebark raspberry] - *Rubus leucodermis* Dougl. ex Torr. & Gray (138) (1923)

Whitebay - *Magnolia macrophylla* Michx. (7) (1828)

Whitebeads [White beads, White-beads] - *Actaea pachypoda* Ell. (5, 49, 53, 92, 156, 158) (1898-1923)

White-bell honeysuckle [White bell honeysuckle] - *Lonicera ×bella* Zabel [*morrowii × tatarica*] (112) (1937)

Whiteberry [White berry, White-berry] - *Actaea pachypoda* Ell. (5, 156, 158) (1900-1923)

White-berry dogwood [White berry dog wood] - *Cornus sericea* L. subsp. *sericea* (42) (1814)

White-berry snakeroot [Whiteberry snakeroot, White berry snakeroot] - *Actaea pachypoda* Ell. (7, 92) (1828-1876)

White-bird [White bird] - *Stellaria holostea* L. (156) (1923), *Stellaria media* (L.) Vill. subsp. *media* (157, 158) (1900-1929)

White-blow [White blow] - *Draba verna* L. (5, 156) (1913-1923) no longer in use by 1923

White-bract hymenopappus [White-bracted hymenopappus] - *Hymenopappus scabiosaeus* L'Hér. var. *scabiosaeus* (5, 97) (1913-1937)

White-bract thoroughwort [Whitebracted thoroughwort, White-bracted thoroughwort, White-bracted thorough-wort] - *Eupatorium leucolepis* (DC.) Torr. & Gray (5, 156) (1913-1923)

Whitecap [White-cap, White cap] - *Spiraea tomentosa* L. (5, 49, 92, 156) (1876-1923)

White-cedar [Whitecedar] - *Chamaecyparis thyoides* (L.) Britton, Sterns & Poggenb. (109, 138) (1923-1949)

White-cup [White cup, Whitecup] - *Quercus macrocarpa* Michx. (35) (1806)

White-daisy [White daisy] - *Aphanostephus* DC. (122) (1937) TX,

Aphanostephus skirrobasis (DC.) Trelease (122) (1937) TX

White-dandelion [White dandelion] - *Pinaropappus roseus* (Less.) Less. (124) (1937) TX

White-devil [White devil] - *Symphyotrichum lateriflorum* (L.) A.& D. Löve var. *lateriflorum* (5, 156, 158) (1900-1923)

White-edge flatsedge [Whiteedge flatsedge] - *Cyperus flavicomus* Michx. (50) (present)

White-edge panicum [White-edged panicum] - *Dichanthelium dichotomum* (L.) Gould var. *tenue* (Muhl.) Gould & C.A. Clark (5) (1913)

White-edge sedge [White-edged sedge] - *Carex debilis* Michx. (5) (1913)

White-eyed-grass [White-eyed grass] - *Sisyrinchium campestre* Bickn. (3, 85) (1932-1977), *Sisyrinchium campestre* Bickn. var. *campestre* (3) (1977)

White-flower anmeone [White-flowered anemone] - *Anemone canadensis* L. (158) (1900)

White-flower beardtongue [White-flowered beard-tongue] - *Penstemon albidus* Nutt. (5, 97) (1913-1937)

White-flower cransbill [White-flowered crane's-bill] - *Geranium carolinianum* L. (187) (1818)

White-flower crowfoot [White-flowered crowfoot] - *Anemone canadensis* L. (158) (1900)

White-flower currant [White-flowered currant] - *Ribes cereum* Dougl. var. *pedicellare* Brewer & S. Wats. (5, 93) (1913-1936)

White-flower gilia [White-flowered gilia, White flowered gilia] - *Ipomopsis longiflora* (Torr.) V. Grant subsp. *longiflora* (5, 93, 97, 98, 122) (1913-1937)

White-flower goldenrod [White-flowered golden-rod] - *Solidago bicolor* L. (187) (1818)

White-flower gourd [White-flowered gourd] - *Lagenaria siceraria* (Molina) Standl. (109) (1949)

White-flower honeysuckle [White-flowered honeysuckle] - *Lonicera albiflora* Torr. & Gray (97) (1937)

White-flower hyssop [White flowred hyssope] - *Hyssopus officinalis* L. (178) (1526)

White-flower ivy-leaf [White-flowered ivy-leaf] - *Prenanthes alba* L. (187) (1818)

White-flower lantana [White flowered lantana] - *Lantana involucrata* L. (124) (1937)

White-flower leaf-cup [Whiteflower leafcup] - *Polymnia canadensis* L (50) (present)

White-flower onion [White-flowered onion] - *Allium drummondii* Regel (124) (1937)

White-flower parsley [White-flowered parsley] - *Lomatium nudicaule* (Pursh) J.M. Coult. & Rose (131) (1899) SD, *Lomatium orientale* Coult & Rose (5, 93) (1913-1936)

White-flower penstemon [White flower penstemon] - *Penstemon albidus* Nutt. (122) (1937)

White-flower prairie orchis [White-flowered prairie orchis] - *Platanthera leucophaea* (Nutt.) Lindl. (156) (1923)

White-flower prickly-poppy [White-flowered prickly poppy] - *Argemone gracilenta* Greene (65) (1931)

White-flower raspberry [White flowering raspberry, Whiteflowering raspberry, White-flowered raspberry] - *Rubus parviflorus* Nutt. (5, 138, 156, 158) (1913-1923)

White-flower robinia [White flowering robinia] - *Robinia pseudoacacia* L. (8) (1785)

White-flower sand-verbena [Whiteflower sand verbena] - *Abronia alba* Eastw. (50) (present)

White-flower spurge [White flowered spurge. White-flowered spurge, White flowering spurge] - *Chamaesyce missurica* (Raf.) Shinners (5, 85, 93, 97, 122, 131) (1899-1937), *Euphorbia corollata* L. (82) (1930)

White-flower vervain [White-flowered vervain] - *Verbena urticifolia* L. (46) (1879)

White-flower Virginia sengreen [White flowred Virginia Sengreen]

- *Parthenium integrifolium* L. (181) (~1678)

White-flower wild lettuce [White-flowered wild lettuce] - *Prenanthes alba* L. (187) (1818)

White-foot lady's-slipper [White footed ladies' slipper] - *Cypripedium candidum* Muhl. ex Willd. (92) (1876)

White-fringe [White fringe] - *Chionanthus virginicus* L. (5, 92, 112, 135, 156) (1876-1937)

White-fringe sedge [White-fringed sedge] - *Carex albicans* Willd. ex Spreng. (5) (1913)

White-fruit dogwood [White-fruited dogwood] - *Cornus foemina* Mill. (5) (1913)

White-grain mountain-rice [White-grained mountain rice] - *Oryzopsis asperifolia* Michx. (5) (1913)

White-hair panic grass [White-haired panic-grass] - *Dichanthelium villosissimum* (Nash) Freckmann var. *villosissimum* (163) (1852)

White-hair panicum [White-haired panicum] - *Dichanthelium villosissimum* (Nash) Freckmann var. *villosissimum* (5) (1913)

White-hair rosette grass [Whitehair rosette grass] - *Dichanthelium villosissimum* (Nash) Freckmann (50) (present)

Whitehead [White-head] - *Parthenium hysterophorus* L. (158) (1900) West Indies

White-head bogbutton [Whitehead bogbutton] - *Lachnocaulon anceps* (Walt.) Morong (50) (present)

Whiteheart [White heart] - *Carya alba* (L.) Nutt. ex Ell. (82) (1930) IA

White-heart hickory [White-heart hiccory, Whiteheart hickory] - *Carya alba* (L.) Nutt. ex Ell. (2, 5, 19, 97, 107, 156, 158) (1840–1937), *Carya laciniosa* (Michx. f.) G. Don (109) (1949)

White-heart pohickery - *Carya alba* (L.) Nutt. ex Ell. (158) (1900)

Whitehearts [White hearts] - *Dicentra canadensis* (Goldie) Walp. (58) (1869), *Dicentra cucullaria* (L.) Bernh. (5, 156) (1913-1923)

Whiteleaf [White leaf, White-leaf] - *Chimaphila maculata* (L.) Pursh (7) (1828), *Populus alba* L. (156) (1923), *Spiraea tomentosa* L. (49, 92) (1876-1898)

White-leaf buckthorn [Whiteleaf buckthorn] - *Frangula californica* (Eschsch.) Gray subsp. *tomentella* (Benth.) Kartesz & Gandhi (138) (1923)

White-leaf gaertneria [White-leaved gaertneria] - *Ambrosia tomentosa* Nutt. (5, 93, 131) (1899-1936)

White-leaf manzanita [Whiteleaf manzanita] - *Arctostaphylos viscida* Parry (155) (1942)

White-leaf mint [White leaf mint] - *Pycnanthemum albescens* Torr. & Gray ex Gray (124) (1937)

White-leaf mountain-mint [Whiteleaf mountainmint, White-leaved mountain mint, White-leaved mountain-mint] - *Pycnanthemum albescens* Torr. & Gray ex Gray (5, 50, 97) (1913–present)

White-leaf sage [White-leaved sage] - *Salvia leucophylla* Greene (106) (1930)

White-leaf spring beauty [White-leaved spring beauty] - *Claytonia caroliniana* Michx. (5, 156) (1913-1923)

White-man's-foot [White-man's foot] - *Plantago major* L. (5, 6, 158) (1892–1913), *Plantago rhodosperma* Dcne. (5) (1913), *Plantago rugelii* Dcne. (156) (1923)

White-man's-plant [White man's plant] - *Datura stramonium* L. (7, 71) (1828-1898)

White-man's-weed [White man's weed, White-man's weed] - *Leucanthemum vulgare* Lam. (5, 156) (1913-1923)

White-margin euphorbia [Whitemargin euphorbia] - *Chamaesyce albomarginata* (Torr. & Gray) Small (155) (1942)

White-margin sandmat [Whitemargin sandmat] - *Chamaesyce albomarginata* (Torr. & Gray) Small (50) (present)

White-margin spurge [White margined spurge, White-margined spurge] - *Euphorbia marginata* Pursh (5, 72, 93, 131, 156, 157, 158) (1899-1936)

White-mouth dayflower [Whitemouth dayflower] - *Commelina elegans* Kunth (50) (present), *Commelina erecta* L. (50) (present, *Commelina saxicola* Small (50) (present)

457

White-oak fern - *Cystopteris fragilis* (L.) Bernh. (158) (1900)

Whitepipe [White pipe] - *Philadelphus coronarius* L. (178) (1526)

White-plantain [White plantain] - *Goodyera repens* (L.) R. Br. ex Ait. f. (5, 92, 156) (1876-1923)

White-plume arnica [White-plumed arnica] - *Arnica lonchophylla* Greene subsp. *lonchophylla* (5) (1913)

White-plume ptiloria [White-plumed ptiloria] - *Stephanomeria runcinata* Nutt. (5, 93) (1913-1936)

White-robin [White robin] - *Silene latifolia* Poir. subsp. *alba* (Mill.) Greuter & Burdet (5, 156, 158) (1900-1923) no longer in use by 1923

Whiteroot [White-root, Whiteroot] - *Aralia racemosa* L. (156) (1923), *Asclepias tuberosa* L. (5, 6, 7, 19, 58, 64, 73, 75, 92, 156, 158) (1828-1923), *Frasera* Walt. (23) (1810)

White-root rush [Whiteroot rush] - *Juncus brachycarpus* Engelm. (50) (present)

White-rosemary [White rosemary] - *Symphyotrichum ericoides* (L.) Nesom var. *ericoides* (5, 156, 158) (1900-1923)

White-rush [White rush] - *Spartina patens* (Ait.) Muhl. (5) (1913)

Whites - *Holcus lanatus* L. (5) (1913)

White-sage [White sage] - *Kochia* Roth (158) (1900), *Krascheninnikovia* Guldenstaedt (1) (1932), *Krascheninnikovia lanata* (Pursh) A.D.J. Meeuse & Smit (4, 5, 85, 93, 108, 131, 153, 157, 158) (1899-1986)

White-scale sedge [Whitescale sedge] - *Carex xerantica* Bailey (50) (present)

White-spine echinocereus [Whitespine echinocereus] - *Echinocereus reichenbachii* (Terscheck ex Walp.) Haage f. var. *baileyi* (Rose) N.P. Taylor (155) (1942)

Whitest evening-primrose - *Oenothera albicaulis* Pursh (50) (present)

White-stalk primrose [White-stalked primrose] - *Oenothera albicaulis* Pursh (38) (1820)

White-star [Whitestar, White star] - *Ipomoea lacunosa* L. (5, 50, 156) (1913–present)

White-stem blazing star [Whitestem blazingstar] - *Mentzelia albicaulis* (Dougl. ex Hook.) Dougl. ex Torr. & Gray (50) (present)

White-stem evening-primrose [White-stemmed evening primrose] - *Oenothera nuttallii* Sweet (3, 4, 98) (1926-1986), *Oenothera pallida* Lindl. (127) (1933)

White-stem filaree - *Erodium moschatum* (L.) L'Hér. ex Aiton (109) (1949)

White-stem goldenweed [Whitestem goldenweed] - *Ericameria discoidea* (Nutt.) Nesom var. *discoidea* (155) (1942)

White-stem mentzelia [Whitestem mentzelia, White-stemmed mentzelia] - *Mentzelia albicaulis* (Dougl. ex Hook.) Dougl. ex Torr. & Gray (5, 93, 155) (1913-1942)

White-stem pondweed [Whitestem pondweed, White stemmed pondweed] - *Potamogeton praelongus* Wulfen (3, 50, 72, 155) (1907–present)

White-stem spurge [White-stemmed spurge] - *Chamaesyce serpyllifolia* (Pers.) Small subsp. *serpyllifolia* (5, 93) (1913–1936)

White-thorn acaia [Whitethorn acaia] - *Acacia constricta* Benth. (50) (present)

White-tinge sedge [Whitetinge sedge] - *Carex albicans* Willd. ex Spreng. (50) (present)

White-tip aster [White-tipped aster] - *Sericocarpus tortifolius* (Michx.) Nees (156) (1923)

Whitetop [White top, White-top] - *Agrostis capillaris* L. (45) (1896), *Agrostis gigantea* Roth (5, 19, 66, 119) (1840–1938), *Cardaria* Desv. (50, 155) (1942–present), *Cardaria draba* (L.) Desv. (50) (present), *Cardaria pubescens* (C. A. Mey.) Jarmolenko (3, 4) (1977-1986), *Danthonia spicata* (L.) Beauv. ex Roemer & J. A. Schultes (66, 90) (1885-1903), *Doellingeria* Nees (50) (present), *Erigeron annuus* (L.) Pers. (5, 62, 93, 122, 156) (1912–1937), *Erigeron strigosus* Muhl. ex Willd. var. *strigosus* (5, 156) (1913–1923), *Tridens albescens* (Vasey) Woot. & Standl. (94) (1901)

White-top aster [White-topped aster] - *Sericocarpus asteroides* (L.) B.S.P. (156) (1923)

White-top grass [White top grass] - *Agrostis gigantea* Roth (92) (1876?)

White-top spurge [White-topped spurge] - *Euphorbia corollata* L. (62) (1912)

White-top starwort [White-topped star-wort] - *Sericocarpus linifolius* (L.) B.S.P. (187) (1818)

White-top umbrella-grass [White-topped umbrella grass] - *Rhynchospora colorata* (L.) H. Pfeiffer (124) (1937)

White-top weed [White top weed] - *Erigeron annuus* (L.) Pers. (76) (1896)

White-tube stargrass [Whitetube stargrass] - *Aletris farinosa* L. (155) (1942)

White-vein wintergreen [Whiteveined wintergreen] - *Pyrola picta* Sm. (50) (present)

White-violet [White violet] - *Leucojum vernum* L. (92) (1876)

Whiteweed [White weed, White-weed] - *Erigeron annuus* (L.) Pers. (80, 156) (1913–1923), *Leucanthemum vulgare* Lam. (5, 7, 19, 49, 58, 62, 92, 106, 107, 109, 122, 156, 158, 187) (1818–1949), *Spiraea tomentosa* L. (156) (1923)

Whitewood [White wood, White-wood] - *Canella winteriana* (L.) Gaertn. (15, 49) (1895-1898), *Liriodendron tulipifera* L. (2, 5, 7, 13, 15, 20, 19, 49, 92, 107, 109, 156, 177, 186) (1762-1949), *Lyonia ligustrina* (L.) DC. (156) (1923), *Lyonia ligustrina* (L.) DC. var. *ligustrina* (5) (1913), *Tilia americana* L. (5, 49, 76, 92, 106, 156, 157, 158) (1896-1929), *Tilia* L. (7, 107) (1828-1919)

Whitewort - *Tanacetum parthenium* (L.) Schultz-Bip. (158) (1900)

Whitish peony [Whitish pionie] - *Paeonia officinalis* L. (178) (1526)

Whitish sedge - *Carex canescens* L. (5) (1913)

Whitlow-grass [Whitlow grass, Whitlowgrass] - *Draba cuneifolia* Nutt. ex Torr. & Gray (122) (1937), *Draba incana* L. (92) (1876), *Draba* L. (1, 2, 4, 10, 13, 93, 138, 158, 184) (1793-1986), *Draba verna* L. (15, 92, 156, 187) (1818-1923), *Saxifraga tridaclylites* L. (92) (1876)

Whitlow-wort [Whitlow wort, Whitlowwort] - *Draba* L. (155) (1942), *Paronychia canadensis* (L.) Wood (156) (1923), *Paronychia* Mill. (1, 2, 4, 13, 86, 155, 158) (1878-1986)

Whitney's godetia [Whitney godetia] - *Clarkia amoena* subsp. *lindleyi* (Douglas) H.F.Lewis & M.R.Lewis (138) (1923)

Whitten tree [Whitten-tree] - *Viburnum opulus* L. (5, 92, 107, 156, 158) (1876-1923) no longer in use by 1923

Whole-leaf desert prince's-plume [Wholeleaf desert princesplume] - *Stanleya pinnata* (Pursh) Britton var. *integrifolia* (James ex Torr.) Rollins (155) (1942)

Whole-leaf goldenweed [Wholeleaf goldenweed] - *Pyrrocoma integrifolia* (Porter ex Gray) Greene (155) (1942)

Whole-leaf Indian paintbrush [Wholeleaf Indian paintbrush] - *Castilleja integra* Gray (50) (present)

Whole-leaf painted-cup [Wholeleaf paintedcup] - *Castilleja integra* Gray (155) (1942)

Whole-leaf rosinweed [Wholeleaf rosinweed] - *Silphium integrifolium* Michx. (3, 50, 155) (1942–present), *Silphium integrifolium* Michx. var. *integrifolium* (50) (present), *Silphium integrifolium* Michx. var. *laeve* Torr. & Gray (50) (present)

Whorl grass [Whorlgrass] - *Catabrosa* Beauv. (50) (present)

Whorled aster - *Oclemena acuminata* (Michx.) Greene (5, 156) (1913-1923)

Whorled crazyweed - *Oxytropis splendens* Dougl. ex Hook (155) (1942)

Whorled dropseed - *Sporobolus coromandelianus* (Retz.) Kunth (3, 155) (1942-1977)

Whorled loosestrife - *Decodon verticillatus* (L.) Ell. (187) (1818), *Lysimachia quadrifolia* L. (3, 4, 5, 72, 156, 158) (1900-1986)

Whorled mallow - *Malva crispa* (L.) L. (131) (1899), *Malva verticillata* L. (5, 93, 156) (1913-1936)

Whorled marsh pennywort [Whorled marsh penny wort, Whorled marsh-penny-wort] - *Hydrocotyle verticillata* Thunb. (5, 97)

(1913-1937)

Whorled milfoil - *Myriophyllum verticillatum* L. (85) (1932)

Whorled milkweed - *Asclepias verticillata* L. (3, 4, 5, 50, 72, 82, 85, 93, 97, 114, 121, 122, 125, 126, 127, 131, 148, 155, 156) (1894–present)

Whorled milkwort - *Polygala verticillata* L. (3, 4, 5, 50, 72, 85, 93, 97, 122, 131, 156) (1899–present)

Whorled millet - *Setaria verticillata* (L.) Beauv. (56) (1901)

Whorled mountain-mint [Whorled mountainmint] - *Pycnanthemum verticillatum* (Michx.) Pers. (50) (present)

Whorled plantain - *Plantago psyllium* L. (155) (1942)

Whorled pogonia - *Isotria verticillata* (Muehl. ex Willd.) Raf. (5, 156) (1913-1923)

Whorled rosinweed [Whorled rosin weed] - *Silphium trifoliatum* L. (5, 72) (1907-1913)

Whorled snakemouth [Whorled snake mouth, Whorled snakemouth] - *Isotria verticillata* (Muehl. ex Willd.) Raf. (5, 156) (1913-1923)

Whorled tickseed - *Coreopsis verticillata* L. (5, 93, 97) (1913-1937)

Whorled water-milfoil [Whorled water milfoil, Whorled water millfoil] - *Myriophyllum verticillatum* L. (5, 72, 131, 156) (1899-1923)

Whorled winter-berry - *Ilex verticillata* (L.) Gray (186) (1814)

Whorled yellow loosestrife - *Lysimachia quadrifolia* L. (50) (present)

Whorl-leaf [Whorl leaf] - *Hybanthus verticillatus* (Ort.) Baill. (5) (1913)

Whorl-leaf acacia [Whorl-leaved acacia] - *Acacia verticillata* (L'Hér.) Willd. (109) (1949)

Whorl-leaf clematis [Whorl-leaved clematis] - *Clematis occidentalis* (Hornem.) DC. var. *occidentalis* (5) (1913)

Whorl-leaf hempweed [Whorled-leaved hemp-weed] - *Eupatorium purpureum* L. (possibly) (187) (1818)

Whorl-leaf milkweed [Whorl leaved milk weed] - *Asclepias verticillata* L. (42) (1814)

Whorl-leaf sunflower [Whorl leaved sun flower] - *Coreopsis verticillata* L. (42) (1814)

Whorl-leaf swallow-wort [Whorl leaved swallow wort] - *Asclepias verticillata* L. (42) (1814)

Whorl-leaf violet [Whorl-leaved violet] - *Hybanthus verticillatus* (Ort.) Baill. (158) (1900)

Whorl-leaf water milfoil [Whorl-leaf watermilfoil] - *Myriophyllum verticillatum* L. (50) (present)

Whorlywort [Whorly wort, Whorly-wort] - *Veronicastrum virginicum* (L.) Farw. (6, 7, 49, 64, 92, 156, 157, 158) (1828-1929)

Whortleberry [Whortle-berry] - *Arctostaphylos uva-ursi* (L.) Spreng. (6, 7) (1828-1892), *Gaylussacia baccata* (Wang.) K. Koch (46) (1879), *Vaccinium* L. (1, 7, 8, 10, 73, 92, 158, 167) (1814-1932), *Vaccinium myrtillus* L. (107) (1919), *Vaccinium scoparium* Leiberg (35, 131) (1806-1899), *Vaccinium uliginosum* L. (14) (1882)

Whortle-berry willow [Whortleberry willow] - *Salix pedicellaris* Pursh (138, 155) (1923-1942)

Whuttle-grass - *Melilotus officinalis* (L.) Lam. (157, 158) (1900-1929)

Whya tree - *Robinia pseudoacacia* L. (157, 158) (1900-1929)

Wia-ta-pezhihuta (Dakota, woman's medicine) - *Artemisia frigida* Willd. (37) (1919)

Wicaro nakum (Sioux) - *Urtica dioica* L. subsp. *gracilis* (Aiton) Seland. (101) (1905) MT

Wichagnashka (Dakota Teton) - *Ribes missouriense* Nutt. (37) (1919)

Wichaknaska (Dakota Yankton) - *Ribes missouriense* Nutt. (37) (1919)

Wichita love grass [Wichita lovegrass] - *Eragrostis secundiflora* J. Presl subsp. *oxylepis* (Torr.) S.D. Koch (155) (1942)

Wichurian rose - *Rosa wichuraiana* Crépin (138) (1923)

Wick [Wicke, Wicks] - *Crataegus monogyna* Jacq. (5) (1913), *Elymus repens* (L.) Gould (158) (1900), *Kalmia latifolia* L. (6, 7, 92) (1828-1892), *Lyonia mariana* (L.) D. Don (5, 7, 86, 156) (1828-1923)

Wickawee - *Castilleja coccinea* (L.) Spreng. (5, 73, 156, 158) (1892-

1923) MA, from Indian name, no longer in use by 1923

Wicken [Wickens] - *Crataegus monogyna* Jacq. (5) (1913), *Elymus repens* (L.) Gould (5, 158) (1900-1913)

Wickeryby bush [Wickeryby-bush] - *Dirca palustris* L. (156) (1923)

Wicko'bĭmûcko'si (Chippewa, sweet grass) - *Hierochloe odorata* (L.) Beauv. (40) (1928)

Wickup [Wickop] - *Chamerion angustifolium* (L.) Holub subsp. *angustifolium* (49, 52, 53, 76, 79, 92, 156, 157, 158) (1876-1929), *Dirca palustris* L. (5, 156) (1913-1923), *Epilobium palustre* L. (5, 6, 49, 53, 156, 158) (1892-1923), *Tilia americana* L. (156, 157, 158) (1900-1929)

Wicky - *Kalmia angustifolia* L. (5, 71, 156) (1898-1923), *Kalmia latifolia* L. (71) (1898), *Lyonia ferruginea* (Walt.) Nutt. (106) (1930), *Lyonia ligustrina* (L.) DC. var. *ligustrina* (182) (1791)

Wicopy [Wickopy] - *Dirca* L. (1) (1932), *Dirca palustris* L. (5, 6, 49, 78, 75, 156) (1892-1923) from Indian name, *Lyonia mariana* (L.) D. Don (156) (1923)

Wicopy bark - *Dirca palustris* L. (92) (1876)

Wicopy herb - *Chamerion angustifolium* (L.) Holub subsp. *angustifolium* (92) (1876)

Wicopy root - *Chamerion angustifolium* (L.) Holub subsp. *angustifolium* (92) (1876)

Wi'cosidji'bĭk (Chippewa, drawing plant or root) - *Actaea rubra* (Aiton) Willd. (40) (1928)

Widdy - *Salix* L. (158) (1900)

Wide-leaf cat-tail [Wide-leafed cat-tail - *Typha latifolia* L. (124) (1937)

Wide-leaf lady's-tresses [Wide-leaved ladies' tresses] - *Spiranthes lucida* (H.H. Eat.) Ames (5) (1913)

Wide-leaf willow [Wide leaf willow] - *Salix amygdaloides* Anderss. (35) (1806)

Wide-lip orchid [Widelip orchid] - *Liparis* L.C. Rich. (50) (present)

Wide-world parnassia [Wideworld parnassia] - *Parnassia palustris* L. (155) (1942)

Widgeon-grass [Widgeongrass, Widgeon grass] - *Ruppia maritima* L. (50, 155, 156) (1923–present), *Zostera marina* L. (5, 156) (1913-1923)

Widgeonweed - *Ruppia* L. (50, 155) (1942–present)

Widow's-cross [Widow's cross] - *Sedum pulchellum* Michx. (5, 50, 156, 158) (1900–present)

Widow's-frill [Widowsfrill] - *Silene stellata* (L.) Aiton f. (50) (present)

Widow's-tears [Widow's tears] - *Tradescantia virginiana* L. (156) (1923)

Wier's weeping maple [Wiers weeping maple] - *Acer rubrum* L. (109) (1949)

Wiesen Klee (German) - *Trifolium repens* L. (6) (1892)

Wiffs - *Salix* L. (158) (1900)

Wig tree - *Cotinus coggygria* Scop. (92) (1876)

Wigobi-minŝ (Chippewa) - *Tilia americana* L. (105) (1932)

Wigub'imĭj (Chippewa) - *Tilia americana* L. (40) (1928)

Wigwas - *Betula pubescens* Ehrh. (105) (1932)

Wi'gwasa'tĭg (Chippewa) - *Betula papyrifera* Marsh (40) (1928)

Wihuta hu (Lakota, tent bottom plant) - *Typha latifolia* L. (121) (1918-1970)

Wihuta-hu (Dakota, bottom of tipi plant) - *Typha latifolia* L. (37) (1830)

Wilcox's panic grass - *Dichanthelium wilcoxianum* (Vasey) Freckmann (111) (1915)

Wilcox's panicum [Wilcox panicum] - *Dichanthelium wilcoxianum* (Vasey) Freckmann (3, 5, 56, 72, 131, 155) (1899-1977)

Wild agrimony - *Argentina anserina* (L.) Rydb. (157, 158) (1900-1929)

Wild alder - *Aegopodium podagraria* L. (156) (1923)

Wild alfalfa - *Psoralidium tenuiflorum* (Pursh) Rydb. (3, 4, 98, 146) (1926-1986)

Wild allspice [Wild all Spice] - *Laurus nobilis* L. (190) (~1759), *Lindera benzoin* Blume. (5, 49, 58, 92, 156, 177, 186, 187) (1753-

1923), *Lindera* Thunb. (2) (1895)

Wild almond - *Prunus fasciculata* (Torr.) Gray (74, 107) (1893-1919)

Wild alum - *Geranium maculatum* L. (102) (1886)

Wild amaranth - *Amaranthus blitum* L. (92) (1876)

Wild American crab apple [Wild American crabapple] - *Malus ioensis* (Wood) Britton (137) (1931)

Wild American vine - *Vitis labrusca* L. (8) (1785)

Wild anemone - *Anemonella thalictroides* (L.) Spach (187) (1818)

Wild angelica [Wilde angelica] - *Angelica sylvestris* L. (92, 107, 165, 178) (1526-1919), *Angelica triquinata* Michx. (187) (1818)

Wild angelica minoris - *Angelica triquinata* Michx. (46) (1879)

Wild angelica, majoris - *Angelica atropurpurea* L. (46) (1629)

Wild anise - *Agastache foeniculum* (Pursh) Kuntze (37) (1919), *Illicium floridanum* Ellis (92) (1876)

Wild apple [Wylde apple] or Wild apple tree - *Malus coronaria* (L.) Mill. (20) (1857), *Malus sylvestris* Mill. (19, 179) (1526-1840)

Wild arnica - *Grindelia squarrosa* (Pursh) Dunal (101) (1905) MT

Wild arrach - *Atriplex hortensis* L. (46) (1671)

Wild arsenic - *Chimaphila maculata* (L.) Pursh (5, 73, 156) (1892-1923)

Wild artichoke - *Helianthus maximiliani* Schrad. (101) (1905), *Helianthus tuberosus* L. (103) (1870)

Wild ash - *Sorbus americana* Marsh. (46) (1671)

Wild asparagus - *Lygodesmia* D. Don (1) (1932)

Wild aster - *Aster* L. (4, 93, 114) (1894-1986)

Wild bachelor's-buttons [Wild bachelor's buttons] - *Cichorium intybus* L. (76) (1896) Worcester MA

Wild balm [Wild baulm] - *Monarda punctata* L. (181) (~1678)

Wild balsam - *Ibervillea lindheimeri* (Gray) Greene (122) (1937) TX, *Impatiens capensis* Meerb. (5, 74, 156, 158) (1893-1923), *Impatiens pallida* Nutt. (5, 157) (1913-1929)

Wild balsam-apple [Wild balsam apple] - *Ecballium elaterium* (L.) A. Rich. (92) (1876), *Echinocystis lobata* (Michx.) Torr. & Gray (5, 72, 82, 97, 106, 131, 142, 156, 158) (1899-1930), *Echinocystis* Torr. & Gray (2, 158) (1895-1900), *Ibervillea lindheimeri* (Gray) Greene (124) (1937) TX

Wild balsamina - *Impatiens* L. (190) (~1759)

Wild banana - *Asimina triloba* (L.) Dunal (156) (1923)

Wild barley - *Hordeum bulbosum* L. (56, 94, 152) (1901-1912), *Hordeum* L (93) (1936), *Hordeum murinum* L. (5) (1913), *Hordeum pusillum* Nutt. (85) (1932)

Wild basil - *Clinopodium vulgare* L. (5, 10, 156) (1818-1923), *Cunila origanoides* (L.) Britton (5, 7, 92, 158, 186) (1814-1900), *Pycnanthemum incanum* (L.) Michx. var. *incanum* (5, 19) (1840-1913), *Pycnanthemum* Michx. (7) (1828), *Pycnanthemum setosum* Nutt. (5, 92) (1876-1913), *Pycnanthemum verticillatum* (Michx.) Pers. var. *pilosum* (Nutt.) Cooperrider (49) (1898)

Wild bastard saffron [Wilde bastard saffron] - *Carthamus lanatus* L. (178) (1526)

Wild batchelor's-button [Wild batchelor's button] - *Polygala lutea* L. (5) (1913)

Wild bean [Wild-bean, Wildbean, Wild beans] - *Apios americana* Medik. (5, 73, 93, 107, 109, 156) (1892-1949), *Apios* Fabr. (2) (1895), *Lupinus argenteus* Pursh (148) (1939) CO, *Phaseolus polystachios* (L.) B.S.P. (3, 5, 85, 93, 97) (1913-1977), *Polygonum convolvulus* L. (77) (1898) Oxford ME, *Strophostyles* Ell. (1, 4, 82, 155, 158) (1900-1986), *Strophostyles helvula* (L.) Ell. (3, 80, 95, 145) (1897-1977), *Strophostyles leiosperma* (Torr. & Gray) Piper (85, 95, 121, 145) (1897-1932)

Wild beet - *Amaranthus retroflexus* L. (77) (1898) Oxford ME, *Oenothera fruticosa* L. (74, 156) (1893-1923) WV, used as pot herb, *Oenothera fruticosa* L. subsp. *fruticosa* (5) (1913)

Wild begonia - *Rumex venosus* Pursh (1, 4, 98) (1926-1986)

Wild bergamont [Wildbergamont] - *Mentha arvensis* L. (77) (1898) Oxford ME, *Monarda fistulosa* L. (2, 5, 37, 47, 48, 50, 57, 63, 72, 93, 95, 97, 106, 109, 121, 127, 131, 138, 156, 157) (1852–present), *Monarda fistulosa* L. subsp. *fistulosa* (3, 50) (1977–present), *Monarda fistulosa* L. subsp. *fistulosa* var. *menthifolia* (Graham) Fern.

(3, 50) (1977–present)

Wild bergamot - *Mentha arvensis* L. (77) (1898), *Monarda fistulosa* L. subsp. *fistulosa* (19, 92) (1840-1876), *Monarda fistulosa* L. subsp. *fistulosa* var. *mollis* (L.) Benth. (50, 97) (1937–present), *Monarda* L. (1, 93, 106, 158) (1900-1932)

Wild bergamot beebalm - *Monarda fistulosa* L. (155) (1942)

Wild betony - *Dryas octopetala* L. (5) (1913)

Wild black cherry - *Prunus serotina* Ehrh. (2, 4, 9, 59, 63, 71, 72, 82, 93, 95, 107, 109, 113, 114, 122, 156, 158) (1873-1986), *Prunus virginiana* L. (85, 92) (1876-1932), *Prunus virginiana* L. var. *virginiana* (5, 97) (1913-1937)

Wild black currant - *Ribes americanum* Mill. (2, 3, 4, 5, 9, 19, 37, 63, 72, 92, 93, 95, 105, 108, 112, 113, 130, 156) (1840-1986), *Ribes* L. (190) (~1759)

Wild black hellebore [Wilde blacke hellebore] - *Helleborus viridis* L. (178) (1526)

Wild black raspberry - *Rubus occidentalis* L. (95, 105) (1911-1932)

Wild blackberry - *Rubus allegheniensis* Porter (62, 105) (1912-1932)

Wild bleeding-heart [Wild bleeding heart] - *Dicentra eximia* (Ker-Gawl.) Torr. (5, 156) (1913-1923)

Wild blite - *Amaranthus blitum* L. (107) (1919)

Wild blue flag - *Iris missouriensis* Nutt. (148) (1939)

Wild blue flax - *Linum lewisii* Pursh (127) (1933)

Wild blue iris - *Iris missouriensis* Nutt. (148) (1939)

Wild blue lettuce - *Lactuca floridana* (L.) Gaertn. (106) (1930), *Lactuca tatarica* (L.) C.A. Mey. var. *pulchella* (Pursh) Breitung (127) (1933)

Wild blue morning-glory [Wild blue morning glory - *Ipomoea hederacea* Jacq. (82) (1930)

Wild blue petunia - *Ruellia drummondiana* (Nees) Gray (124) (1937) TX

Wild blue phlox - *Phlox divaricata* L. (5, 50, 72, 85, 93, 97, 122, 124) (1907–present)

Wild blue sage - *Salvia reflexa* Hornem. (82) (1930)

Wild bourache [Wylde bourache] - *Anchusa* L. (179) (1526)

Wild brier - *Rosa canina* L. (5, 58) (1869-1913), *Rosa eglanteria* L. (92) (1876)

Wild brome grass [Wild brome-grass] - *Bromus catharticus* Vahl (5, 45) (1896-1913), *Bromus ciliatus* L. (163) (1852)

Wild broom - *Lotus glaber* Mill. (106) (1930)

Wild broom-corn [Wild broom corn] - *Phragmites australis* (Cav.) Trin. ex Steud. (5) (1913)

Wild bryony - *Bryonia alba* L. (92) (1876)

Wild buckwheat - *Eriogonum fasciculatum* Benth. (106) (1930), *Eriogonum longifolium* Nutt. (156) (1923), *Eriogonum* Michx. (4, 106, 122) (1930-1986), *Gaura coccinea* Nutt. ex Pursh (124) (1937) TX, *Polygonum convolvulus* L. (3, 4, 62, 80, 82, 106, 145) (1897-1986), *Polygonum scandens* L. var. *scandens* (77) (1898) Burnside SD

Wild bugloss [Wilde bugloss] - *Anchusa arvensis* (L.) Bieb. (19, 156, 158, 178) (1526-1923), *Asperugo procumbens* L. (92) (1876)

Wild burnet - *Sanguisorba canadensis* L. (possibly) (2) (1895)

Wild cabbage - *Arnoglossum muehlenbergii* (Schultz-Bip.) H.E. Robins. (7) (1828), *Brassica oleracea* L. (138) (1923), *Caulanthus crassicaulis* (Torr.) S. Wats. (74, 106, 107) (1893-1930), *Caulanthus* S. Wats. (15) (1895), *Guillenia flavescens* (Hook.) Greene (74) (1893), *Thelypodiopsis elegans* (M.E. Jones) Rydb. (106) (1930) Grand Junction CO

Wild calla - *Calla palustris* L. (3, 5, 155, 156, 158) (1900-1977)

Wild camomile [Wild cammomile, Wild chamomile, Wild camomille] - *Anthemis cotula* L. (7, 49, 57, 58, 92, 186) (1814-1917), *Anthemis* (190) (~1759), *Matricaria* L. (156) (1923), *Matricaria recutita* L. (5, 19, 53, 158) (1840-1922), *Tanacetum parthenium* (L.) Schultz-Bip. (5, 58, 156, 158) (1869-1923), *Tripleurospermum maritima* (L.) W.D.J. Koch subsp. *maritima* (3, 4) (1977-1986)

Wild canary grass - *Phalaris caroliniana* Walt. (5, 19) (1840-1913)

Wild candytuft - *Arabis* L. (1) (1932)

Wild caper - *Euphorbia lathyris* L. (5, 71, 156) (1898-1923), *Euphorbia peplus* L. (19) (1840)

Wild caraway [Wild carraway] - *Arnoglossum atriplicifolium* (L.) H.E. Robins. (5, 156, 157, 158) (1900-1929), *Arnoglossum muehlenbergii* (Schultz-Bip.) H.E. Robins. (92) (1876), *Hasteola suaveolens* (L.) Pojark. (5, 19, 156) (1840-1923)

Wild carrot - *Daucus carota* L. (3, 4, 5, 49, 62, 70, 72, 80, 85, 92, 93, 95, 97, 106, 122, 131, 155, 156, 157, 158, 187) (1818-1986), *Daucus* L. (50) (present), *Lomatium cous* (S. Wats.) Coult. & Rose (146) (1939)

Wild cauliflower - *Hymenopappus artemisiifolius* DC. (124) (1937) TX

Wild celandine - *Impatiens capensis* Meerb. (5, 74, 156, 157) (1893-1929), *Impatiens pallida* Nutt. (5, 92, 156, 157) (1876-1929)

Wild celery [Wildcelery] - *Apium graveolens* L. (50, 92, 155) (1876–present), *Vallisneria americana* Michx. (5, 85, 138, 156) (1913-1932), *Vallisneria* L. (109, 155) (1942-1949)

Wild cherry - *Physalis* L. (75) (1894) NJ, *Physalis virginiana* Mill. (5, 75, 156) (1894-1923) Northern MN

Wild cherry or Wild cherry tree [Wild cherry-tree] - *Prunus avium* (L.) L. (5, 107) (1913-1919), *Prunus capollin* Zucc. (149) (1904) NM, *Prunus emarginata* (Dougl. ex Hook.) D. Dietr. (161) (1857), *Prunus emarginata* (Dougl. ex Hook.) D. Dietr. var. *mollis* (Dougl. ex Hook.) Brewer (20) (1857), *Prunus ilicifolia* (Nutt. ex Hook. & Arn.) D. Dietr. (107) (1919), *Prunus* L. (93, 148, 190) (~1759-1939), *Prunus serotina* Ehrh. (20, 52, 55, 57, 60, 65, 71, 96, 106, 156, 157, 158, 187) (1818-1931), *Prunus virginiana* L. (12, 19, 20, 41, 48, 49, 53, 61, 92, 103, 157, 158, 187) (1770-1922), *Prunus virginiana* L. var. *demissa* (Nutt.) Torr. (130, 137) (1895-1931), *Prunus virginiana* L. var. *virginiana* (5) (1913)

Wild cherry tomato - *Solanum lycopersicum* L. var. *cerasiforme* (Dunal) Spooner, J. Anderson & R.K. Jansen (124) (1937) TX

Wild chervil - *Anthriscus sylvestris* (L.) Hoffmann (92) (1876), *Chaerophyllum procumbens* (L.) Crantz (4, 156) (1923-1986), *Conioselinum chinense* (L.) Britton, Sterns & Poggenb. (7) (1828), *Scandix pecten-veneris* L. (107) (1919)

Wild chess - *Bromus kalmii* Gray (5, 66, 75, 111, 119) (1894-1938), *Bromus porteri* (Coult.) Nash (75, 111) (1894-1915), *Bromus secalinus* L. (87) (1884)

Wild chicory - *Cichorium intybus* L. (6, 110) (1886-1892)

Wild China or Wild China tree [Wild China-tree] - *Sapindus saponaria* L. var. *drummondii* (Hook. & Arn.) Bensons (5, 65, 97, 106, 110, 124, 156) (1913-1937), *Sapindus saponaria* L. var. *saponaria* (147, 164) (1854-1856)

Wild chinaberry tree - *Sapindus saponaria* L. var. *drummondii* (Hook. & Arn.) Bensons (153) (1913)

Wild chives - *Allium schoenoprasum* L. (50) (present)

Wild cicory [Wilde cicorie] - *Cichorium intybus* L. (178) (1526)

Wild cinnamon or Wild cinnamon tree - *Canella winteriana* (L.) Gaertn. (15, 49, 55, 92, 107) (1895-1919)

Wild clary [Wilde clarie] - *Salvia verbenaca* L. (5, 92, 156, 178) (1526-1923)

Wild clematis - *Clematis ligusticifolia* Nutt. (101, 114) (1894-1905), *Clematis virginiana* L. (114) (1894)

Wild climbing cucumber - *Echinocystis lobata* (Michx.) Torr. & Gray (142) (1902) WY

Wild clover - *Kummerowia striata* (Thunb.) Schindl. (5, 158) (1900-1913), *Onobrychis viciifolia* Scop. (28) (1850)

Wild coffee [Wild-coffee] - *Frangula californica* (Eschsch.) Gray (74) (1893) Santa Barbara CA, *Triosteum perfoliatum* L. (5, 6, 7, 19, 49, 92, 107, 156, 157, 158, 186) (1825-1929)

Wild colewort [Wilde colewoorts] - *Brassica oleracea* L. (180) (1633)

Wild collard - *Arnoglossum muehlenbergii* (Schultz-Bip.) H.E. Robins. (5, 156) (1913-1923)

Wild columbine - *Aquilegia canadensis* L. (3, 4, 5, 19, 37, 42, 63, 82, 85, 97, 107, 114, 131, 157, 158, 190) (~1759-1937), *Aquilegia formosa* Fisch. ex DC. (76) (1896)

Wild columbo - *Frasera caroliniensis* Walt. (186) (1814)

Wild comfrey - *Cynoglossum virginianum* L. (2, 3, 5, 19, 50, 80, 92, 97, 156) (1840–present), *Cynoglossum virginianum* L. var. *boreale* (Fern.) Cooperrider (50) (present)

Wild coranies - *Ribes rubrum* L. (46) (1617)

Wild corn - *Clintonia borealis* (Ait.) Raf. (5, 75) (1894-1913) ME, *Clintonia umbellulata* (Michx.) Morong (156) (1923)

Wild cotton [Wild-cotton] - *Apocynum cannabinum* L. (5, 64, 156, 157, 158) (1900-1929), *Asclepias* L. (10) (1818), *Asclepias syriaca* L. (5, 6, 49, 53, 62, 75, 156, 157, 158, 187) (1818-1929)

Wild cowcomer [Wylde cowcomer] - *Ecballium elaterium* (L.) A. Rich. (179) (1526)

Wild cowcumber - *Cucumis* L. (190) (~1759)

Wild cowhage - *Lablab purpureus* (L.) Sweet (19) (1840)

Wild crab apple - *Malus coronaria* (L.) Mill. var. *coronaria* (22, 113) (1890-1893), *Malus* Mill. (93) (1936)

Wild crab of North Carolina - *Malus angustifolia* (Aiton) Michx. var. *angustifolia* (possibly) (183) (~1756)

Wild crab or Wild crab tree - *Malus coronaria* (L.) Mill. var. *coronaria* (5, 92, 182) (1791-1913), *Malus glaucescens* Rehdr. (5) (1913), *Malus ioensis* (Wood) Britton var. *ioensis* (82) (1930)

Wild crabgrass [Wild crab grass] - *Schedonnardus paniculatus* (Nutt.) Trel. (111, 129, 152) (1894-1915)

Wild cranberry - *Arctostaphylos uva-ursi* (L.) Spreng. (92, 156) (1898-1923)

Wild cranebill [Wild cranesbill, Wild cranesbill, Wild crane's bill, Wild crane's-bill] - *Geranium* L. (92) (1876), *Geranium maculatum* L. (3, 4, 5, 6, 49, 53, 64, 72, 97, 157, 158) (1892-1986)

Wild crape myrtle - *Holodiscus dumosus* (Nutt. ex Hook.) Heller (149) (1904) NM, *Malpighia glabra* L. (122, 124) (1937) TX

Wild crawberry - *Arctostaphylos uva-ursi* (L.) Spreng. (5) (1913)

Wild cress - *Barbarea orthoceras* Ledeb. (35) (1806)

Wild crocus - *Pulsatilla* Mill. (1) (1932) Madison WI, *Pulsatilla patens* (L.) Mill. (5) (1913), *Pulsatilla patens* (L.) Mill.subsp. *multifida* (Pritz.) Zamels (76, 157, 158) (1896-1929)

Wild cuckoo flower [Wild cuckoo-flower] - *Silene latifolia* Poir. subsp. *alba* (Mill.) Greuter & Burdet (158) (1900)

Wild cucumber [Wild-cucumber, Wilde cucumbers] - *Anemone quinquefolia* L. (5) (1913), *Ecballium elaterium* (L.) A. Rich. (92, 178) (1526-1876), *Echinocystis lobata* (Michx.) Torr. & Gray (3, 4, 5, 35, 37, 50, 63, 73, 82, 93, 106, 109, 114, 122, 127, 156) (1806–present), *Echinocystis* Torr. & Gray (2, 4) (1895-1986), *Sicyos angulatus* L. (5, 7, 76, 156, 157, 158) (1828-1929)

Wild curcuma - *Hydrastis canadensis* L. (6, 49, 64) (1892-1908)

Wild currant [Wild currants] - *Mahonia trifoliolata* (Moric.) Fedde (106) (1930) TX, *Ribes glandulosum* Grauer (40) (1928), *Ribes* L. (40, 101, 103) (1870-1928)

Wild daisy - *Conyza canadensis* (L.) Cronq. var. *canadensis* (114) (1894)

Wild dandelion - *Microseris nutans* (Hook.) Schultz-Bip. (101) (1905) MT

Wild datura - *Datura stramonium* L. (106) (1930)

Wild dodder - *Cuscuta gronovii* Willd. ex J.A. Schultes (62) (1912)

Wild elder [Wild-elder] - *Aegopodium podagraria* L. (156) (1923), *Aralia hispida* Vent. (5, 49, 53, 58, 92, 156) (1869-1923)

Wild elecampane - *Chrysopsis mariana* (L.) Ell. (187) (1818)

Wild endive - *Cichorium intybus* L. (6) (1892), *Taraxacum officinale* G.H. Weber ex Wiggers subsp. *officinale* (92) (1876)

Wild eryngo - *Eryngium campestre* L. (92) (1876)

Wild evening-primrose [Wild evening primrose] - *Oenothera biennis* L. (157, 158) (1900-1929)

Wild fennel - *Foeniculum vulgare* Mill. (92) (1876), *Nigella damascena* L. (107) (1919)

Wild fescue grass [Wild fescue-grass] - *Chasmanthium latifolium* (Michx.) Yates (144) (1899)

Wild field lily - *Lilium canadense* L. (93) (1936)

Wild field pinks [Wilde field pinks] - *Lychnis flos-cuculi* L. (178) (1526)

Wild filbert - *Corylus americana* Walt. (possibly) (187) (1818)

Wild flag - *Iris missouriensis* Nutt. (101) (1905)

Wild flax [Wilde flaxe, Wilde-flax] - *Camelina sativa* (L.) Crantz (19, 157, 158) (1840-1929), *Linaria vulgaris* Mill. (5, 75, 93, 157, 158) (1894-1936), *Linum bienne* Mill. (178) (1526), *Linum lewisii* Pursh (37, 93, 101, 156) (1905-1936), *Linum rigidum* Pursh (126, 148) (1933-1939), *Linum virginianum* L. (2, 7, 19, 92) (1828-1895)

Wild flower [Wildflower] - *Anemone virginiana* L. (19) (1840)

Wild forget-me-not - *Houstonia caerulea* L. (5) (1913), *Houstonia* L. (76) (1896) Waco TX, *Mertensia lanceolata* (Pursh) DC. (3, 127) (1933-1977)

Wild four-o'clock [Wild four o'clock] - *Mirabilis nyctaginea* (Michx.) MacM. (4, 37, 72, 80, 82, 93, 121, 127, 145, 156) (1897-1986)

Wild foxglove [Wild fox glove] - *Aureolaria flava* (L.) Farw. var. *flava* (156) (1923), *Penstemon grandiflorus* Nutt. (37) (1919)

Wild fuschia - *Epilobium canum* (Greene) Raven subsp. *angustifolium* (Keck) Raven (76) (1896) Santa Barbara Co. CA

Wild garlic - *Allium canadense* L. (85, 156, 158) (1900–1932), *Allium* L. (7, 121, 148) (1828–1970), *Allium stellatum* Ker (108) (1878), *Allium textile* A. Nels. & Macbr. (108) (1878), *Allium vineale* L. (3, 5, 50, 62, 80, 93, 158) (1900–present), *Allium vineale* L. subsp. *vineale* (50) (present)

Wild geranium - *Callirhoe involucrata* (Torr. & Gray) Gray (156) (1923), *Geranium carolinianum* L. (145) (1897), *Geranium* L. (1, 93, 106) (1930-1936), *Geranium maculatum* L. (6, 40, 44, 64, 82, 105, 138, 156, 157, 158, 187) (1818-1932), *Geranium robertianum* L. (5, 74, 156) (1893-1923)

Wild germander - *Teucrium canadense* L. (48) (1882)

Wild ginger [Wildginger] - *Aristolochia macrophylla* Lam. (5, 156) (1913–1923), *Asarum canadense* L. (3, 5, 7, 19, 35, 40, 41, 42, 46, 47, 49, 52, 53, 57, 58, 64, 65, 72, 97, 105, 107, 109, 156, 157, 158, 186, 187) (1770–1977), *Asarum caudatum* Lindl. (35) (1806), *Asarum* L. (2, 4, 50, 109, 138, 155) (1923–present), *Ctenium aromaticum* (Walt.) Wood (5) (1913)

Wild ginseng - *Aralia* L. (1, 93) (1932-1936)

Wild globe amaranth - *Gomphrena serrata* L. (124) (1937)

Wild globe flower [Wild globeflower] - *Trollius laxus* Salisb. (2) (1895)

Wild golden-glow [Wild golden glow] - *Rudbeckia laciniata* L. (127) (1933) ND

Wild goose plum [Wild-goose plum, Wildgoose plum] - *Prunus americana* Marsh. (73) (1892), *Prunus hortulana* Bailey (3, 4, 5, 73, 97) (1892-1986), *Prunus munsoniana* Wight & Hedr. (3, 4, 50, 109, 138, 155) (1923–present)

Wild gooseberry - *Ribes cynosbati* L. (5, 65, 72, 97, 156, 158) (1900-1937), *Ribes* L. (101) (1905), *Ribes missouriense* Nutt. (37) (1919), *Ribes rotundifolium* Michx. (19) (1840)

Wild gourd [Wylde gourde] - *Bryonia cretica* L. subsp. *dioica* (Jacq.) Tutin (179) (1526), *Citrullus colocynthis* (L.) Schrad. (179) (1526), *Cucurbita foetidissima* Kunth (37, 124) (1919–1937), *Cucurbita pepo* L. var. *ovifera* (L.) Alef. (122) (1937)

Wild grape - *Vitis arizonica* Engelm. (153) (1913), *Vitis californica* Benth. (103) (1870), *Vitis cinerea* (Engelm.) Millard (37) (1919), *Vitis* L. (93, 105, 112) (1932-1937), *Vitis vulpina* L. (37, 82, 85, 92, 101) (1876-1932)

Wild grass [Wildgrass] - *Andropogon bicornis* L. (41) (1770)

Wild ground-cherry [Wild ground cherry] - *Physalis virginiana* Mill. (85) (1932)

Wild guelder-rose [Wild guelder rose] - *Viburnum opulus* L. (5, 63, 156, 158) (1899-1923)

Wild hairy beardtongue [Wild hairy beard-tongue] - *Penstemon hirsutus* (L.) Willd. (97) (1937)

Wild hedge bur [Wild hedge-burs] - *Galium aparine* L. (5, 158) (1900-1913)

Wild heliotrope - *Heliotropium convolvulaceum* (Nutt.) Gray (3) (1977), *Heliotropium curassavicum* L. (106) (1930), *Heliotropium curassavicum* L. var. *obovatum* DC. (85, 155) (1932–1942)

Wild hellebore - *Veratrum album* L. (41) (1770)

Wild hemlock - *Cicuta maculata* L. (7, 71, 72, 92, 93, 98, 158) (1828–1936), *Conium maculatum* L. (6, 71) (1892–1898)

Wild hemp [Wylde hempe] - *Ambrosia trifida* L. (5, 7, 49, 92, 156, 157, 158) (1828–1929), *Eupatorium cannabinum* L. (179) (1526), *Galeopsis bifida* Boenn. (5, 158) (1900–1913)

Wild hippo [Wild hipp] - *Euphorbia corollata* L. (5, 6, 156, 157, 158) (1892–1929), *Euphorbia ipecacuanhae* L. (156) (1923)

Wild holly - *Ilex mucronata* (L.) M. Powell, Savol. & S. Andrews (5, 19, 156) (1840–1923)

Wild hollyhock [Wild hollyhocks] - *Callirhoe digitata* Nutt. (156) (1923), *Sidalcea malviflora* (DC.) Gray ex Benth. (106) (1930)

Wild honeysuckle [Wild honey-suckle] - *Gaura coccinea* Nutt. ex Pursh (5, 156) (1913–1923), *Gaura* L. (76, 158) (1896–1900), *Gaura sinuata* Nutt. ex Ser. (5) (1913), *Gaura villosa* Torr. (5) (1913), *Lonicera dioica* L. (4, 82) (1930–1986), *Rhododendron* L. (7) (1828), *Rhododendron periclymenoides* (Michx.) Shinners (5, 41, 75, 156, 187) (1770–1923) WV, *Rhododendron viscosum* (L.) Torr. (possibly) (92) (1876)

Wild hop [Wild hops] - *Bryonia alba* L. (92) (1876), *Bryonia cretica* L. subsp. *dioica* (Jacq.) Tutin (107) (1919), *Canavalia rosea* (Sw.) DC. (76) (1896) Florida Keys, *Clematis virginiana* L. (5, 76, 156) (1896–1923) Hartford & Oxford Co ME, *Humulus lupulus* L. (7, 142) (1828–1902), *Humulus lupulus* L. var. *neomexicanus* A. Nels. & Cockerell (153) (1913), *Stachys officinalis* (L.) Trev. (5) (1913)

Wild hopseed [Wilde hop seed, Wilde hop-seed] - *Myrospermum frutescens* Jacq. (181) (~1678), *Sphedamnocarpus* Planch. ex Benth. & Hook. f. (181) (~1678)

Wild horehound [Wild hoarhound] - *Ageratina aromatica* (L.) Spach (5, 156) (1913-1923), *Eupatorium rotundifolium* L. (5, 7, 58, 61, 92, 156) (1828–1923), *Eupatorium rotundifolium* L. var. *rotundifolium* (5, 156) (1913–1923)

Wild hyacinth - *Camassia* Lindl. (1, 156) (1923-1932), *Camassia scilloides* (Raf.) Cory (5, 7, 72, 78, 97, 103, 106, 158) (1828-1937), *Camassia scilloides* (Raf.) Cory (2, 92) (1876-1895), *Dicentra canadensis* (Goldie) Walp. (5, 74, 156, 157) (1893-1929) NY, *Leucocrinum montanum* Nutt. ex Gray (157) (1929), *Platanthera grandiflora* (Bigelow) Lindl. (78) (1898) ME, *Platanthera psycodes* (L.) Lindl. (78) (1898) ME

Wild hydrangea - *Hydrangea arborescens* L. (3, 4, 5, 49, 50, 52, 53, 63, 64, 72, 92, 97, 156, 158) (1898–present), *Hydrangea cinerea* Small (156) (1923), *Rumex venosus* Pursh (1) (1932), *Viburnum lantanoides* Michx. (156) (1923)

Wild hyssop - *Artemisia tridentata* Nutt. (35) (1806), *Verbena hastata* L. (5, 7, 49, 53, 62, 92, 156, 157, 158) (1828–1929)

Wild Indian pear - *Amelanchier canadensis* (L.) Medik. (106) (1930) Newfoundland

Wild indigo [Wild-indigo, Wildindigo] - *Baptisia alba* (L.) Vent. (48) (1882), *Baptisia alba* (L.) Vent. var. *macrophylla* (Larisey) Isely (3, 72, 124) (1907-1977), *Baptisia australis* (L.) R. Br. ex Aiton f. (156, 158) (1900-1923), *Baptisia bracteata* Muhl. ex Ell. (82) (1930), *Baptisia tinctoria* (L.) R. Br. ex Aiton f. (2, 5, 6, 7, 19, 46, 49, 52, 53, 54, 57, 58, 60, 64, 72, 92, 106, 107, 156, 157, 177, 184, 186, 187, 190) (1649-1930), *Baptisia* Vent. (1, 10, 50, 93, 109, 121, 122, 138, 155, 156, 158) (1818–present)

Wild indigo plant [Wild indigo-plant] - *Amorpha fruticosa* L. (82, 124) (1930-1937), *Indigofera miniata* Ort. var. *leptosepala* (Nutt.) B.L.Turner (5) (1913)

Wild ipecac - *Apocynum androsaemifolium* L. (157, 158) (1900-1929), *Euphorbia corollata* L. (6) (1892), *Euphorbia ipecacuanhae* L. (5, 6, 49, 53, 61, 92, 156, 186) (1870-1923) TX, *Triosteum perfoliatum* L. (5, 6, 49, 76, 92, 156, 158) (1892-1923) Western US

Wild Isaac - *Eupatorium perfoliatum* L. (69) (1904)

Wild jalap - *Ipomoea pandurata* (L.) G. F. W. Mey. (5, 7, 57, 92, 156, 158) (1828–1923), *Podophyllum peltatum* L. (6, 156) (1892–1923)

Wild jessamine - *Gelsemium sempervirens* (L.) J. St.-Hil. (6, 92, 156) (1876-1923)

Wild Job's-tears [Wild Job's tears] - *Onosmodium virginianum* (L.) A. DC. (92, 156) (1876-1923)

Wild kidney beans - *Phaseolus polystachios* (L.) B.S.P. (5) (1913), *Phaseolus vulgaris* L. (41) (1770)

Wild laburnum - *Melilotus officinalis* (L.) Lam. (157, 158) (1900-1929) England

Wild lady's-slipper [Wild ladies'-slipper] - *Impatiens capensis* Meerb. (157, 158) (1900-1929), *Impatiens pallida* Nutt. (157) (1929)

Wild lamb's-lettuce [Wild lamb lettuce] - *Valerianella radiata* (L.) Dufr. (19) (1840)

Wild larkspur - *Delphinium carolinianum* Walt. subsp. *virescens* (Nutt.) Brooks (95) (1911)

Wild laurel - *Rhododendron maximum* L. (2, 156) (1895-1942)

Wild leek [Wild leekes] - *Allium canadense* L. (46) (1879), *Allium* L. (1) (1932), *Allium tricoccum* Ait. (3, 40, 50, 72, 85, 155, 156, 158) (1900–present), **Zigadenus venenosus** S. Wats. var. *gramineus* (Rydb.) Walsh ex M.E. Peck (133) (1903) ND

Wild lemon [Wild lemmon] - *Nyssa ogeche* Bartr. ex Marsh. (183) (~1756), *Podophyllum peltatum* L. (5, 6, 7, 49, 53, 64, 92, 107, 156, 157, 158, 186, 187) (1814–1929)

Wild lettuce [Wild-lettuce, Wylde letuse] - *Claytonia perfoliata* Donn ex Willd. (74) (1893) Santa Barbara CA, sometimes eaten by children, *Lactuca canadensis* L. (3, 4, 5, 6, 19, 40, 47, 62, 63, 72, 76, 80, 82, 85, 92, 95, 97, 122, 145, 156, 157, 158, 187) (1818-1986), *Lactuca serriola* L. (156, 158, 179) (1526-1923), *Lactuca tatarica* (L.) C.A. Mey. var. *pulchella* (Pursh) Breitung (114, 121, 145, 148) (1894-1970), *Lactuca virosa* L. (5, 85, 93, 157) (1899-1936), *Prenanthes alba* L. (5, 156) (1913-1923), *Prenanthes altissima* L. (5, 156) (1913-1923), *Prenanthes* L. (184) (1793), *Pyrola americana* Sweet (5, 7, 92, 156, 158) (1828-1923)

Wild licorice [Wild liquorice] - *Abrus precatorius* L. (49, 107, 158) (1898-1919), *Aralia nudicaulis* L. (5, 7, 49, 57, 64, 92, 156, 157, 158) (1828-1929), *Aralia racemosa* L. (187) (1818), *Astragalus glycyphyllos* L. (92) (1876), *Galium circaezans* Michx. (2, 5, 19, 63, 93, 97, 156, 158) (1840-1937), *Galium lanceolatum* Torr. (156) (1923), *Glycyrrhiza lepidota* Pursh (3, 4, 5, 35, 37, 38, 47, 72, 80, 85, 93, 95, 107, 108, 114, 121, 126, 131, 146, 156, 157, 158) (1878-1986)

Wild licorice root [Wild liquorice root] - *Glycyrrhiza lepidota* Pursh (101) (1905)

Wild lilac - *Ceanothus thyrsiflorus* Esch. (76, 161) (1857-1896) CA

Wild lily - *Lilium philadelphicum* L. var. *andinum* (Nutt.) Ker.-Gawl. (3, 127) (1933-1977), *Lilium superbum* L. (158) (1900)

Wild lily-of-the-valley [Wild lily of the valley] - *Clintonia borealis* (Ait.) Raf. (5, 19, 73, 156) (1840-1923), *Maianthemum canadense* Desf. (3, 5, 75, 85, 156, 158) (1894-1977), *Maianthemum dilatatum* (Wood) A. Nels. & J.F. Macbr. (78) (1898), *Maianthemum* G.H. Weber ex Wiggers (1, 93) (1932-1936), *Pyrola americana* Sweet (3) (1977), *Pyrola elliptica* Nutt. (3, 4, 5, 75, 157, 158) (1894-1986)

Wild lime or Wild lime tree [Wild lime-tree] - *Adelia* L. (50) (present), *Lyonia ligustrina* (L.) DC. var. *ligustrina* (174) (1753), *Nyssa ogeche* Bartr. ex Marsh. (2, 20, 106, 183) (~1756-1930), *Ximenia* Plum. (15) (1895)

Wild live-forever [Wild liveforever, Wild live forever] - *Hylotelephium telephioides* (Michx.) H. Ohba. (138, 156) (1923)

Wild lupine - *Lupinus* L. (158) (1900), *Lupinus perennis* L. (2, 5, 19, 63, 72, 107, 156) (1840-1923)

Wild madder [Wild-madder] - *Galium mollugo* L. (5, 72, 156) (1907-1923) IA, *Galium tinctorium* L. (5, 19, 85, 131, 156, 187) (1818-1932)

Wild mallow [Wylde malowe] - *Althaea officinalis* L. (179) (1526)

Wild mandrake - *Circaea lutetiana* L. (158) (1900), *Podophyllum peltatum* L. (5, 19, 49, 64, 92, 157, 158) (1840-1929)

Wild margoran - *Origanum* L. (190) (~1759)

Wild marigold - *Matricaria discoidea* DC. (5, 75, 156) (1894-1923)

Wild marjoram - *Origanum vulgare* L. (5, 7, 19, 46, 49, 92, 107, 109, 138, 156) (1649-1949)

Wild masterwort - *Aegopodium podagraria* L. (5, 156, 165) (1768-1923)

Wild meadow barley - *Hordeum secalinum* Schreb. (87) (1884)

Wild melon - *Citrullus lanatus* (Thunb.) Matsumura & Nakai (92) (1876)

Wild mercury - *Argythamnia humilis* (Engelm. & Gray) Muell. Arg. var. *humilis* (3) (1977), *Argythamnia mercurialina* (Nutt.) Muell. Arg. (3) (1977), *Argythamnia* P. Br. (4) (1986)

Wild mignonette - *Reseda lutea* L. (4) (1986)

Wild millet - *Achnatherum hymenoides* (Roemer & J.A. Schultes) Barkworth (5) (1913), *Milium effusum* L. (56, 87, 94) (1885-1915), *Setaria viridis* (L.) Beauv. (119) (1938), *Setaria viridis* (L.) Beauv. var. *viridis* (5) (1913)

Wild mint [Wylde mynte] - *Ajuga reptans* L. (158) (1900), *Mentha ×rotundifolia* (L.) Huds. [*longifolia × suaveolens*] (5, 156) (1913–1923), *Mentha arvensis* L. (1, 2, 4, 35, 37, 46, 47, 48, 50, 63, 95, 105, 114, 121, 127) (1671–present), *Mentha spicata* L. (85, 179) (1526–1932)

Wild mock cucumber [Wild mockcucumber] - *Echinocystis lobata* (Michx.) Torr. & Gray (155) (1942)

Wild morning-glory [Wild morning glory] - *Calystegia sepium* (L.) R. Br. subsp. *sepium* (62) (1912)

Wild mulberry - *Rubus odoratus* L. (19) (1840)

Wild musk - *Erodium cicutarium* (L.) L'Hér. ex Aiton (5, 107, 156) (1913-1923)

Wild mustard - *Brassica nigra* (L.) W.D.J. Koch (95) (1911), *Moricandia arvensis* (L.) DC. (62, 80, 82, 131, 156, 158) (1899-1930), *Raphanus raphanistrum* L. (5, 107) (1913-1919), *Sinapis arvensis* L. (5, 41, 92, 97, 157) (1770-1937)

Wild navette - *Brassica rapa* L. var. *rapa* (158) (1900)

Wild navew - *Brassica rapa* L. var. *rapa* (5, 158) (1900-1913)

Wild nep [Wylde neppe] - *Bryonia cretica* L. subsp. *dioica* (Jacq.) Tutin (179) (1526)

Wild oat [Wild oats] - *Avena fatua* L. (3, 5, 45, 50, 56, 67, 70, 72, 80, 85, 87, 88, 94, 103, 107, 109, 111, 123, 140, 148, 152, 155) (1856–present), *Bromus* L. (152) (1912) NM, *Calamagrostis coarctata* (Torr.) Eat. (5) (1913), *Chasmanthium latifolium* (Michx.) Yates (5) (1913), *Danthonia spicata* (L.) Beauv. ex Roemer & J. A. Schultes (19) (1840), *Hesperostipa spartea* (Trin.) Barkworth (56) (1901) IA, *Sorghastrum secundum* (Ell.) Nash (163) (1852), *Uvularia* L. (158) (1900), *Uvularia perfoliata* L. (5) (1913), *Uvularia sessilifolia* L. (72, 73, 78, 156) (1892–1923), *Zizania aquatica* L. (107) (1821)

Wild oat grass [Wild oat-grass, Wild oats grass] - *Danthonia* DC. (1, 92, 93, 152) (1912–1936), *Danthonia spicata* (L.) Beauv. ex Roemer & J. A. Schultes (56, 66, 85, 90, 94, 119, 143) (1885–1938), *Nassella viridula* (Trin.) Barkworth (5) (1913), *Schizachne purpurascens* (Torr.) Swall. (87, 90) (1884–1885), *Sorghastrum nutans* (L.) Nash (5, 21) (1893–1913)

Wild okra - *Abutilon theophrasti* Medik (156) (1923), *Viola palmata* L. (107) (1919)

Wild oleander - *Decodon* J.F. Gmel. (1) (1932), *Decodon verticillatus* (L.) Ell. (5, 106, 156) (1913-1930)

Wild oleaster tree [Wild oleaster-tree] - *Shepherdia argentea* (Pursh) Nutt. (5, 156, 158) (1900-1923), *Shepherdia canadensis* Nutt. (5, 156, 158) (1900-1923)

Wild olive (Lower Louisiana) - *Nyssa aquatica* L. (2, 10, 20, 107) (1818-1919)

Wild olive [Wilde oliue] or Wild olive tree [Wild olive-tree] - *Cordia boissieri* A. DC. (122) (1937) TX, *Elaeagnus angustifolia* L. (82, 106, 107, 137) (1919-1931), *Halesia carolina* L. (5, 156) (1913-

463

1923), *Halesia tetraptera* L. (107) (1919), *Olea europaea* L. (178) (1526), *Shepherdia argentea* (Pursh) Nutt. (5, 156, 158) (1900-1923), *Shepherdia canadensis* Nutt. (5, 156, 158) (1900-1923)

Wild onion - *Allium canadense* L. (23, 80) (1810-1913), *Allium canadense* L. var. *canadense* (3) (1977), *Allium canadense* L. var. *fraseri* M. Ownbey (3) (1977), *Allium canadense* L. var. *hyacinthoides* (Bush) M. Ownbey (3) (1977), *Allium canadense* L. var. *lavendulare* (Bates) M. Ownbey & Aase (3) (1977), *Allium canadense* L. var. *mobilense* (Regal) Ownbey (5, 37, 97) (1913-1937), *Allium cernuum* Roth (3, 85) (1932-1977), *Allium drummondii* Regel (3, 85) (1932-1977), *Allium* L. (101, 127) (1905-1933), *Allium stellatum* Ker (40) (1928), *Allium textile* A. Nels. & Macbr. (98, 126) (1926-1933), *Allium vineale* L. (62) (1912), *Zigadenus venenosus* S. Wats. var. *gramineus* (Rydb.) Walsh ex M.E. Peck (133) (1903)

Wild opium - *Lactuca canadensis* L. (5, 156, 157, 158) (1900-1929)

Wild orange [Wild-orange] or Wild orange tree - *Aralia spinosa* L. (5, 156) (1913-1923), *Maclura pomifera* (Raf.) Schneid. (5, 75, 93, 156) (1894-1936), *Prunus caroliniana* (P. Mill.) Aiton (20, 74, 106, 109) (1857-1949) Southern states, *Zanthoxylum clava-herculis* L. (5, 15, 156, 158, 189) (1767-1923)

Wild orange lily - *Lilium philadelphicum* L. (5, 156, 158) (1900-1923)

Wild orange-red lily - *Lilium philadelphicum* L. (2) (1895)

Wild pansy - *Viola arvensis* Murray (3, 156) (1923–1977), *Viola bicolor* Pursh (4, 156) (1923–1986), *Viola pedata* L. (124) (1937), *Viola tricolor* L. (6, 155) (1892–1942)

Wild parsley [Wildparsley] - *Cymopterus acaulis* (Pursh) Raf. (98) (1926) Neb, *Lomatium cous* (S. Wats.) Coult. & Rose (146) (1939), *Lomatium foeniculaceum* (Nutt.) Coult. & Rose (4) (1986), *Lomatium foeniculaceum* (Nutt.) Coult. & Rose subsp. *daucifolium* (Torr. & Gray) Theobald (3) (1977), *Lomatium orientale* Coult & Rose (3, 121, 85, 127) (1918-1977), *Lomatium* Raf. (4) (1986), *Musineon divaricatum* (Pursh) Raf. var. *hookeri* (Torr. & Gray) Mathias (101) (1905) MT, *Musineon* Raf. (50) (present), *Pastinaca sativa* L. (5, 72) (1907-1913), *Zizia aurea* (L.) W.D.J. Koch (5, 92, 156, 158) (1876-1923)

Wild parsnip [Wild-parsnip, Wilde parsnep] - *Cicuta maculata* L. (122, 124, 158) (1900-1937), *Lomatium dissectum* (Nutt.) Mathias & Constance var. *multifidum* (Nutt.) Mathias & Constance (101) (1905) MT, *Pastinaca* L. (4) (1986), *Pastinaca sativa* L. (3, 4, 50, 62, 80, 82, 93, 95, 97, 131, 133, 148, 156, 178, 187) (1526–present), *Sium suave* Walt. (157, 158) (1900-1929)

Wild pasqueflower [Wild pasque flower] - *Pulsatilla patens* (L.) Mill. subsp. *multifida* (Pritz.) Zamels (2) (1895)

Wild passion vine [Wild passion-vine] - *Passiflora incarnata* L. (158) (1900)

Wild passionflower [Wild passionflower, Wild passion flower] - *Passiflora incarnata* L. (109, 158, 164) (1854-1949)

Wild patience - *Rumex obtusifolius* L. (92) (1876)

Wild pea - *Crotalaria sagittalis* L. (71, 74, 156, 157, 158) (1893-1929), *Lathyrus brachycalyx* Rydb. subsp. *brachycalyx* . (85) (1932) SD, *Lathyrus japonicus* Willd. var. *maritimus* (L.) Kartesz & Gandhi (46) (1617), *Lathyrus palustris* L. (5, 76, 82, 105, 156, 158) (1896-1930), *Lathyrus venosus* Muhl. (40, 85, 131) (1899-1932), *Lupinus perennis* L. (5, 73, 76, 156) (1892-1923), *Tephrosia virginiana* (L.) Pers (76) (1896), *Vicia americana* Muhl. ex Willd. (101, 156) (1905-1923), *Vicia* L. (1) (1932)

Wild pea vine [Wild peavine, Wild pea-vine] - *Amphicarpaea bracteata* (L.) Fern. (156) (1923)

Wild peach - *Prunus caroliniana* (P. Mill.) Aiton (74, 106, 122, 124) (1893-1937), *Prunus fasciculata* (Torr.) Gray (107) (1919)

Wild peanut [Wild pea nut, Wild pea-nut] - *Amphicarpaea bracteata* (L.) Fern. var. *comosa* (L.) Fern. (5, 85, 93, 95, 97, 156, 158) (1900-1937)

Wild pear [Wylde pere] or Wild pear tree [Wild pear-tree] - *Amelanchier arborea* (Michx. f.) Fern. (20) (1857) Northeastern US, *Pyrus canadensis* (L.) Farw. (187) (1818), *Pyrus communis* L. (92) (1876), *Pyrus* L. (179) (1526)

Wild pear tree [Wild pear-tree] - *Amelanchier* ×*intermedia* Spach [*arborea* × *canadensis*] (5) (1913), *Amelanchier canadensis* (L.) Medik. (76) (1896) Western US

Wild pellitory [Wilde pellitorie] - *Achillea ptarmica* L. (5, 156, 178) (1526-1923)

Wild pennyroyal - *Hedeoma* Pers. (10) (1818), *Mentha arvensis* L. (5, 156, 158) (1900-1923), *Piloblephis rigida* (Bartr. ex Benth.) Raf. (106) (1930)

Wild peony - *Trillium erectum* L. (78) (1898) ME

Wild pepper - *Arisaema triphyllum* (L.) Schott (64, 156, 158) (1900-1923), *Ceanothus americanus* L. (5, 76, 156) (1896–1923) Greene Co. MO, *Daphne mezereum* L. (5, 92, 156) (1876–1923) no longer in use by 1923, *Trillium undulatum* Willd. (156) (1923)

Wild peppergrass [Wild pepper-grass] - *Lepidium densiflorum* Schrad. (97) (1937), *Lepidium virginicum* L. (2, 5, 19, 46, 62, 63, 85, 97, 131, 156, 157, 158, 187) (1818-1937)

Wild peppermint - *Mentha arvensis* L. (101) (1905)

Wild pepperwort [Wild pepper-wort] - *Lepidium virginicum* L. (181) (~1678)

Wild petunia - *Calibrachoa parviflora* (Juss.) D'Arcy (122, 124) (1937) TX, *Ruellia humilis* Nutt. (156, 157) (1923-1929), *Ruellia* L. (50, 93) (1936–present)

Wild phlox - *Phlox pilosa* L. (114) (1894)

Wild pie-plant - *Rumex hymenosepalus* Torr. (158) (1900)

Wild pimento - *Lindera benzoin* Blume. (177) (1762)

Wild pin cherry - *Prunus pensylvanica* L. f. (137) (1931)

Wild pine - *Pinus sylvestris* L. (20, 92) (1857-1876), *Tillandsia utriculata* L. (19) (1840)

Wild pink - *Arethusa bulbosa* L. (5, 73, 156) (1894–1923) Atlantic City NJ, *Dianthus armeria* L. (85, 156, 187) (1818–1932), *Phlox subulata* L. (5, 187) (1818–1913), *Silene caroliniana* subsp. *pensylvanica* (Michx.) Clausen (2, 15, 156, 187) (1818–1823), *Silene caroliniana* Walt. (5, 109) (1913–1949), *Silene* L. (10) (1818–1828), *Silene laciniata* Cav. (74) (1893) Santa Barbara CA, *Silene regia* Sims. (5, 76, 156, 158) (1896–1923), *Silene virginica* L. (23, 92) (1810–1876)

Wild piny - *Trillium erectum* L. (78) (1898) ME

Wild plantain - *Canna indica* L. (92) (1876), *Heliconia caribaea* Lam. (109) (1949)

Wild plum or Wild plum tree - *Prunus americana* Marsh. (3, 4, 9, 22, 20, 37, 40, 47, 63, 72, 85, 95, 96, 101, 112, 113, 122, 130, 131, 137, 156) (1852-1986), *Prunus domestica* L. (41) (1770), *Prunus* L. (93, 190) (~1759-1936), *Prunus mexicana* S. Wats. (97, 124) (1937), *Prunus nigra* Aiton (5) (1913), *Prunus spinosa* L. (92) (1876)

Wild poinsettia - *Euphorbia cyathophora* Murray (124) (1937)

Wild pomegranate - *Punica granatum* L. (92) (1876)

Wild poplar - *Liriodendron tulipifera* L. (92) (1876)

Wild poppy [Wylde poppy] - *Papaver rhoeas* L. (19, 179) (1526-1840)

Wild portulaca - *Phemeranthus teretifolius* (Pursh) Raf. (156) (1923)

Wild potato [Wild potatoe, Wild potatoes, Wild-potato] - *Apios americana* Medik. (35, 103) (1806-1870), *Claytonia virginica* L. (5, 72, 158) (1900-1913), *Ipomoea pandurata* (L.) G.F.W. Mey. (7, 42, 48, 77, 92, 158, 186) (1814-1900), *Solanum jamesii* Torr. (1) (1932), *Solanum triflorum* Nutt. (71, 156) (1898-1923)

Wild potato vine [Wild potato-vine, Wild potatoe vine, Wild potatoe-vine] - *Apios americana* Medik. (187) (1818), *Ipomoea leptophylla* Torr. (77, 103) (1870–1898), *Ipomoea pandurata* (L.) G.F.W. Mey. (2, 5, 19, 72, 97, 156, 186, 187) (1814–1937)

Wild prairie rose - *Rosa arkansana* Porter var. *suffulta* (Greene) Cockerell (80) (1913)

Wild prairie timothy [Wild prairie timothey] - *Phalaris arundinacea* L. (35) (1806)

Wild pumpkin - *Cucurbita foetidissima* Kunth (121, 156, 157, 158) (1900-1970?), *Cucurbita pepo* L. (124) (1937)

Wild purple raspberry - *Rubus occidentalis* L. (157, 158) (1900-1929)

Wild quinine - *Parthenium integrifolium* L. (31, 50, 75, 156, 158) (1847–present), *Parthenium integrifolium* L. var. *hispidum* (Raf.) Mears (50) (present)

Wild radish - *Raphanus raphanistrum* L. (5, 6, 15, 19, 50, 72, 80, 106, 107, 156) (1840–present), *Raphanus sativus* L. (3) (1977), *Sinapis arvensis* L. (92) (1876)

Wild raisin - *Viburnum lentago* L. (5, 75, 107, 156, 158) (1900-1923) Penobscot Co. ME, *Viburnum nudum* L. var. *cassinoides* (L.) Torr. & Gray (156) (1923)

Wild rape [Wilde rapes] - *Raphanus raphanistrum* L. (5, 156) (1913-1923), *Sinapis arvensis* L. (possibly) (180) (1633)

Wild raspberry - *Rubus idaeus* L. subsp. *strigosus* (Michx.) Focke (37, 153) (1913-1919), *Rubus* L. (93) (1936), *Rubus occidentalis* L. (37, 106) (1919-1930)

Wild red cherry - *Prunus pensylvanica* L. f. (1, 2, 5, 63, 72, 82, 85, 92, 106, 107, 109, 130, 131, 137) (1895-1949)

Wild red currant - *Ribes cereum* Dougl. (113) (1890), *Ribes rubrum* L. (105) (1932)

Wild red geranium - *Geranium oreganum* Howell (101) (1905)

Wild red lily - *Lilium canadense* L. (156) (1923)

Wild red morning-glory - *Ipomoea coccinea* L. (156) (1923)

Wild red plum - *Prunus americana* Marsh. (5, 93, 97, 137, 156, 158) (1900-1937)

Wild red-osier [Wild red osier] - *Cornus sericea* L. subsp. *sericea* (2) (1895)

Wild redtop [Wild red-top] - *Panicum virgatum* L. (5, 75, 93, 119) (1894-1938)

Wild rhubarb [Wild-rhubarb] - *Eriogonum tomentosum* Michx. (24) (1817), *Ipomoea pandurata* (L.) G.F.W. Mey. (7, 92, 186) (1814-1876), *Rumex hymenosepalus* Torr. (4, 109) (1949-1986)

Wild rice [Wildrice] - *Achnatherum hymenoides* (Roemer & J.A. Schultes) Barkworth (101) (1905), *Achnatherum* P. Beauv. (1) (1932), *Luziola fluitans* (Michx.) Terrell & H. Rob. (29, 45) (1869-1896), *Zizania aquatica* L. (possibly) (5, 23, 45, 56, 66, 85, 87, 88, 94, 103, 107, 131, 157, 158) (1810-1932), *Zizania* L. (3, 7, 45, 50, 93, 109, 138, 155, 158, 167) (1814–present), *Zizania palustris* L. (40) (1928), *Zizaniopsis miliacea* (Michx.) Doell & Aschers. (45) (1896)

Wild rose - *Rosa arkansana* Porter (40, 114, 127, 145) (1894-1933), *Rosa arkansana* Porter var. *suffulta* (Greene) Cockerell (37, 80) (1913-1919), *Rosa canina* L. (49) (1898), *Rosa carolina* L. (5) (1913), *Rosa cinnamomea* L. (103) (1870), *Rosa* L. (101, 105) (1905-1932), *Rosa nitida* Willd. (5) (1913)

Wild rosebay [Wild rose bay] - *Rhododendron maximum* L. (5, 19, 92) (1840-1913)

Wild rosemary - *Andromeda polifolia* L. (5, 19, 156, 165) (1807-1923), *Conradina canescens* Gray (75) (1894) FL, *Croton linearis* Jacq. (92) (1876), *Galium aparine* L. (158) (1900), *Ledum* L. (8) (1785), *Ledum palustre* L. (92) (1876)

Wild rue - *Peganum harmala L.* (178) (1526)

Wild rye [Wild-rye, Wildrye] - *Elymus canadensis* L. (21, 35, 88, 90, 115, 116, 118, 122, 129, 144, 152) (1806-1958), *Elymus elymoides* (Raf.) Swezey subsp. *elymoides* (145) (1897), *Elymus* L. (1, 10, 35, 50, 87, 138, 155) (1806–present), *Elymus virginicus* L. (19, 66, 85, 87, 129, 144) (1840-1932), *Leymus ambiguus* (Vasey & Scribn.) D.R. Dewey (140) (1944), *Leymus condensatus* (J. Presl) A. Löve (45) (1896), *Leymus* Hochst. (50) (present), *Psathyrostachys* Nevski (50) (present)

Wild rye grass - *Elymus canadensis* L. (111) (1915), *Elymus elymoides* (Raf.) Swezey subsp. *elymoides* (111) (1915), *Elymus* L. (87) (1884), *Elymus virginicus* L. (88, 90) (1885)

Wild sage - *Artemisia cana* Pursh (10, 19, 36) (1818–1840), *Artemisia frigida* Willd. (156, 157, 158) (1900–1929), *Artemisia ludoviciana* Nutt. (35) (1806), *Artemisia ludoviciana* Nutt. subsp. *ludoviciana* (37, 157) (1919–1929), *Artemisia tridentata* Nutt. (160) (1860), *Eupatorium perfoliatum* L. (5, 156, 158) (1900–1923), *Prunella vulgaris* L. (77) (1898) Paris ME, *Salvia azurea* Michx. ex Lam. var.

grandiflora Benth. (48, 114) (1882–1894), *Salvia columbariae* Benth. (77) (1898) CA, *Salvia lyrata* L. (5, 19, 92) (1840–1913), *Salvia reflexa* Hornem. (114, 145) (1894–1897), *Salvia urticifolia* L. (5) (1913), *Salvia verbenaca* L. (5, 106) (1913–1930)

Wild sago - *Calochortus luteus* Dougl. ex Lindl. (103) (1871)

Wild salsify - *Tragopogon pratensis* L. (93) (1936)

Wild sarsaparilla [Wild-sarsaparilla, Wild sarsaparilla] - *Aralia nudicaulis* L. (3, 4, 5, 19, 22, 40, 42, 46, 47, 49, 50, 63, 64, 72, 85, 92, 93, 95, 105, 109, 131, 138, 155, 156, 157, 158, 187) (1814–present), *Calycocarpum lyoni* (Pursh) Nutt. (122) (1937)

Wild sawge [Wylde sawge] - *Teucrium scorodonia* L. (179) (1526)

Wild scammony - *Ipomoea pandurata* (L.) G.F.W. Mey. (92, 158) (1876-1900)

Wild senna [Wild-senna] - *Cassia* L. (93, 167) (1814–1936), *Chamaecrista fasciculata* (Michx.) Greene var. *fasciculata* (114) (1894), *Senna marilandica* (L.) Link (3, 5, 7, 19, 42, 49, 53, 62, 63, 72, 82, 92, 95, 97, 102, 109, 138, 145, 155, 156, 157, 158, 186, 187) (1814–1977)

Wild sensitive plant [Wild sensitive-plant] - *Chamaecrista* (L.) Moench (1) (1932), *Chamaecrista nictitans* (L.) Moench subsp. *nictitans* var. *nictitans* (2, 5, 19, 158, 187) (1818–1913), *Desmanthus illinoensis* (Michx.) MacM. ex B. L. Robins. & Fern. (114) (1894), *Mimosa microphylla* Dry. (28, 164) (1850–1854)

Wild service tree [Wild service-tree] - *Crataegus* L. (8) (1785)

Wild smartweed - *Polygonum punctatum* Ell. var. *punctatum* (48) (1882)

Wild smoke tree - *Cotinus obovatus* Raf. (5) (1913)

Wild snakeroot [Wild snake root, Wild snake-root] - *Glechoma hederacea* L. (5, 73, 156) (1892-1923)

Wild snapdragon [Wild snap-dragon] - *Linaria vulgaris* Mill. (187) (1818)

Wild snowball - *Ceanothus americanus* L. (5, 49, 58, 92, 107, 156, 157, 158) (1869-1929)

Wild spikenard - *Maianthemum* G.H. Weber ex Wiggers (1, 93) (1932-1936), *Maianthemum racemosum* (L.) Link subsp. *racemosum* (5, 93, 97, 156, 157, 158) (1900-1937)

Wild spinach - *Chenopodium album* L. (5, 156, 157, 158) (1900-1929), *Chenopodium bonus-henricus* L. (5, 107, 156) (1913-1923)

Wild spiraea - *Spiraea betulifolia* Pallas (4) (1986)

Wild stocks - *Wislizenia refracta* Engelm. (124) (1937)

Wild stonecrop - *Sedum ternatum* Michx. (156) (1923)

Wild strawberry [Wild strawberries] - *Fragaria* L. (93) (1905–1936), *Fragaria vesca* L. (6, 7) (1828–1932), *Fragaria vesca* L. subsp. *americana* (Porter) Staudt (37) (1919), *Fragaria virginiana* Duchesne (2, 4, 19, 37, 40, 72, 85, 92, 95, 103, 127, 187) (1818–1986), *Fragaria virginiana* Duchesne subsp. *glauca* (S. Wats.) Staudt (3) (1977), Fragaria virginiana Duchesne subsp. grayana (Vilm. ex J. Gay) Staudt (3, 82) (1930–1977), *Potentilla canadensis* L. (5, 62) (1912–1913)

Wild succory - *Cichorium intybus* L. (5, 6, 49, 62, 92, 106, 156, 157, 158, 187) (1818–1930), *Sabatia angularis* (L.) Pursh (7, 92) (1828–1876)

Wild sunflower [Wild sun-flower] - *Grindelia camporum* Greene var. *camporum* (52, 54) (1905-1919), *Helenium autumnale* L. (49) (1898), *Helianthus annuus* L. (80, 85, 101) (1905-1932), *Helianthus decapetalus* L. (5, 62, 72, 156) (1907-1923), *Helianthus giganteus* L. (5, 56, 92, 156) (1876-1923), *Inula helenium* L. (5, 64, 156) (1907-1923)

Wild sweet alyssum - *Thlaspi* L. (1) (1932)

Wild sweet crab - *Malus coronaria* (L.) Mill. (138) (1923)

Wild Sweet Johns [Wilde Sweete Iohns] - *Dianthus carthusianorum* L. (178) (1526)

Wild sweet pea - *Lathyrus brachycalyx* Rydb. subsp. *brachycalyx* . (37) (1919), *Lathyrus* L. (93) (1936)

Wild sweet potato [Wild sweet-potato] - *Ipomoea pandurata* (L.) G.F.W. Mey. (5, 62, 75, 77, 109, 156) (1894-1923)

Wild Sweet William [Wild Sweet-William] - *Phlox divaricata* L. (5, 109, 156) (1913–1949), *Phlox* L. (158) (1900), *Phlox maculata* L. (5, 72, 156) (1907–1923), *Saponaria officinalis* L. (5, 64, 156, 157,

158) (1900–1929)

Wild sweetpea [Wild sweet pea] - *Tephrosia virginiana* (L.) Pers (5, 85, 156, 157, 158) (1900-1932), *Vicia americana* Muhl. ex Willd. (156) (1923)

Wild sweet-potato vine [Wild sweet potato vine] - *Cynanchum laeve* (Michx.) Pers. (106, 156) (1923-1930)

Wild syringa - *Philadelphus lewisii* Pursh (101) (1905)

Wild tansy [Wild tansey] - *Achillea millefolium* L. (35, 101) (1806-1905), *Achillea millefolium* L. var. *borealis* (Bong.) Farw. (106, 156) (1923-1930), *Ambrosia artemisiifolia* L. (156, 158) (1900-1923), *Ambrosia artemisiifolia* L. var. *elatior* (L.) Descourtils (5, 157) (1913-1929), *Argentina anserina* (L.) Rydb. (5, 156, 157, 158) (1900-1929)

Wild tare - *Vicia americana* Muhl. ex Willd. subsp. *americana* (178) (1526), *Vicia sepium* L. (5, 156) (1913-1923)

Wild tassel [Wylde tasyll] - *Dipsacus fullonum* L. subsp. *fullonum* (179) (1526)

Wild tea - *Amorpha canescens* Pursh (5, 92, 156, 158) (1876-1923)

Wild teasel - *Dipsacus fullonum* L. (5, 19, 42, 62, 156, 158, 187) (1814-1923)

Wild thorn - *Crataegus mollis* Scheele (82) (1930)

Wild tiger lily - *Lilium superbum* L. (5, 6, 75) (1892-1894)

Wild timothy - *Beckmannia syzigachne* (Steud.) Fern. (possibly) (56) (1901) IA, *Muhlenbergia glomerata* (Willd.) Trin. (45, 56, 144) (1896-1901), *Muhlenbergia mexicana* (L.) Trin. (144) (1899) KS, *Muhlenbergia racemosa* (Michx.) Britton, Sterns & Poggenb. (5, 80, 93, 94, 111, 119) (1901-1938)

Wild toadflax [Wild toad flax, Wild toad-flax] - *Nuttallanthus canadensis* (L.) D.A. Sutton (2, 5, 93, 97) (1895-1937)

Wild tobacco [Wild-tobacco, Wildtobacco] - *Acnistus* Schott (155) (1942), *Linaria vulgaris* Mill. (5, 75, 157, 158) (1894-1929) WV, *Lobelia inflata* L. (5, 6, 7, 19, 53, 69, 92, 156, 157, 158, 186, 187) (1814-1929), *Nicotiana attenuata* Torr. ex S. Wats. (148) (1939) CO, *Nicotiana quadrivalvis* Pursh (85, 101) (1905-1932), *Nicotiana quadrivalvis* Pursh var. *bigelovii* (Torr.) DeWolf (75) (1894), *Nicotiana repanda* Willd. ex Lehm. (124) (1937), *Nicotiana rustica* L. (5, 156) (1913-1923), *Verbascum thapsus* L. (41) (1770)

Wild tomato - *Leucophysalis grandiflora* (Hook.) Rydb. (75) (1894) MN

Wild tongue-grass [Wild tonguegrass, Wild tongue grass] - *Lepidium densiflorum* Schrad. (5) (1913), *Lepidium virginicum* L. var. *medium* (Greene) C.L. Hitchc. (76) (1896)

Wild touch-me-not - *Impatiens capensis* Meerb. (5, 76, 93, 114) (1894-1936), *Impatiens pallida* Nutt. (37, 114) (1894-1919)

Wild trefoil - *Trifolium dubium* Sibth. (5, 158) (1900-1913)

Wild tuberose [Wild tube-rose, Wild tube rose] - *Leucocrinum montanum* Nutt. ex Gray (101) (1905) MT, *Spiranthes cernua* (L.) L.C. Rich. (5, 156) (1913-1923)

Wild tulip - *Calochortus luteus* Dougl. ex Lindl. (86) (1878) CA, *Erythronium albidum* Nutt. (156) (1923), *Tulipa sylvestris* L. (5, 50) (1913–present)

Wild turkey pea - *Dicentra canadensis* (Goldie) Walp. (49, 53, 92) (1876-1922)

Wild turmeric - *Hydrastis canadensis* L. (64) (1907)

Wild turnip [Wilde turneps] - *Sinapis arvensis* L. (possibly) (180) (1633), *Arisaema triphyllum* (L.) Schott (5, 19, 64, 73, 156, 157, 158) (1840-1929), *Brassica rapa* L. var. *rapa* (3, 4) (1977-1986)

Wild turnip root - *Arisaema triphyllum* (L.) Schott (92) (1876)

Wild valerian - *Valeriana edulis* Nutt. (103) (1870), *Valeriana officinalis* L. (92) (1876), *Valerianella locusta* (L.) Lat. (178) (1526)

Wild vanilla - *Carphephorus odoratissimus* (J.F. Gmel.) Herbert (92) (1876)

Wild verbena - *Glandularia* ×*hybrida* (Grönland & Rümpler) Nesom & Pruski [*peruviana* × *phlogiflora* or *platensis*] (174) (1753), *Verbena hastata* L. (37) (1919), *Verbena stricta* Vent. (114) (1894), *Verbena urticifolia* L. (174) (1753)

Wild vervain - *Verbena hastata* L. (157) (1929)

Wild vetch - *Lotus unifoliolatus* (Hook.) Benth. (5, 93, 156) (1913–1936), *Vicia americana* Muhl. ex Willd. (127) (1933), *Vicia americana* Muhl. ex Willd. subsp. *minor* (Hook.) C.R. Gunn (114) (1894)

Wild vine - *Bryonia cretica* L. subsp. *dioica* (Jacq.) Tutin (92) (1876), *Clematis vitalba* L. (92) (1876), *Vitis labrusca* L. (5, 156) (1913–1923)

Wild violet - *Nymphoides cordata* (Ell.) Fern. (41) (1770), *Viola cucullata* Aiton (114) (1894)

Wild Virginia flax [Wild Virginian flax] - *Linum virginianum* L. (41) (1770)

Wild wallflower [Wild wall flower, Wild wall-flower] - *Erysimum* L. (1, 93) (1932-1936)

Wild water foxtail [Wild water fox-tail] - *Alopecurus aequalis* Sobol. var. *aequalis* (66, 129) (1894-1903)

Wild wheat - *Aegilops cylindrica* Host (119) (1938) OK

Wild wheatgrass [Wild wheat grass] - *Pseudoroegneria spicata* (Pursh) A. Löve subsp. *spicata* (56) (1901)

Wild white violet - *Viola canadensis* L. var. *rugulosa* (Greene) A.S. Hitchc. (127) (1933), *Viola macloskeyi* Lloyd (4) (1986)

Wild windflowers [Wilde windflowers] - *Anemone nemorosa* L. (178) (1526)

Wild wintergreen - *Polygala sanguinea* L. (156) (1923)

Wild wisteria [Wild-wisteria] - *Apios americana* Medik. (156) (1923)

Wild woad - *Reseda luteola* L. (5, 156) (1913-1923)

Wild wolfbane - *Aconitum uncinatum* L. (5) (1913)

Wild wood vine [Wild wood-vine] - *Parthenocissus quinquefolia* (L.) Planch. (6, 49, 157, 158) (1892-1929)

Wild woodbine - *Gelsemium sempervirens* (L.) J. St.-Hil. (49, 59) (1898-1911), *Parthenocissus quinquefolia* (L.) Planch. (92, 158) (1876-1900)

Wild wormseed - *Chenopodium ambrosioides* L. var. *ambrosioides* (92) (1876)

Wild wormwood - *Ambrosia artemisiifolia* L. (6) (1892), *Artemisia campestris* L. subsp. *borealis* (Pallas) Hall & Clements (5, 19, 156) (1840-1923), *Artemisia cana* Pursh (36) (1830), *Artemisia ludoviciana* var. *cuneata* (Rydb.) Fernald (122) (1937), *Parthenium hysterophorus* L. (158) (1900)

Wild yam - *Dioscorea villosa* L. (3, 7, 48, 49, 52, 53, 54, 57, 58, 61, 64, 92, 122, 124, 156, 158) (1828–present)

Wild yam root [Wild yam-root] - *Dioscorea* L. (1) (1932), *Dioscorea villosa* L. (2, 5, 6, 72, 92, 93, 97, 156) (1874-1937)

Wild yellow flax - *Linum rigidum* Pursh (127) (1933), *Linum virginianum* L. (5) (1913)

Wild yellow lily - *Erythronium americanum* Ker. (78) (1898) ME, *Lilium canadense* L. (5, 72, 85, 93, 156, 157, 158) (1907-1936)

Wild yellow plum - *Prunus americana* Marsh. (5, 93, 97, 137, 156, 158) (1900-1937)

Wild zinnia - *Zinnia acerosa* (DC.) Gray (153) (1913)

Wilde hop-seed Barbadensibus dicta - *Myrospermum frutescens* Jacq. (181) (~1678)

Wilde Knauel (German) - *Scleranthus annuus* L. (158) (1900)

Wilde Rettig (German) - *Raphanus raphanistrum* L. (6) (1892)

Wilde Yam (German) - *Dioscorea villosa* L. (6) (1892)

Wildenow's croton - *Croton willdenowii* G.L. Webster (50) (present)

Wilder Senf (German) - *Sisymbrium officinale* (L.) Scop (158) (1900)

Wilder Wein (German) - *Parthenocissus quinquefolia* (L.) Planch. (158) (1900)

Wilderness violet - *Viola selkirkii* Pursh ex Goldie (155) (1942)

Wilding tree - *Malus sylvestris* Mill. (5) (1913)

Wild-oats - *Zizania aquatica* L. (177) (1762)

Wild-rye grass - *Leymus condensatus* (J. Presl) A. Löve (87) (1884)

Wild's Job's-tears [Wild's Job's tears] - *Onosmodium virginianum* (L.) A. DC. (5, 58) (1869-1913)

Wildweed - *Apocynum androsaemifolium* L. (77) (1898) Paris & Harford ME

Wilf - *Salix* L. (158) (1900)

Wilgers - *Salix viminalis* L. (5, 156) (1913-1923)

Wilkes' acalypha - *Acalypha amentacea* Roxb. subsp. *wilkesiana*

(Muell.-Arg.) Fosberg (50) (present)

Willard's brome grass - *Bromus secalinus* L. (88, 90) (1885)

Willard's bromus - *Bromus secalinus* L. (66) (1903)

Willard's bromus grass - *Bromus secalinus* L. (92) (1876)

Willdenow's muhlenbergia - *Muhlenbergia tenuiflora* (Willd.) Britton, Sterns & Poggenb. (66) (1903)

Willdenow's sedge - *Carex willdenowii* Schkuhr ex Willd. (5, 66) (1903-1913)

Willey - *Salix* L. (158) (1900)

Williamson's spruce - *Tsuga mertensiana* (Bong.) Carr. (161) (1857)

Will-o'the-wisp - *Tremella nostoc* L. (92) (1876)

Willow [Wyloue] or Willow tree [Wyloue tree] - *Salix* L. (1, 4, 7, 8, 10, 40, 50, 82, 92, 93, 106, 108, 109, 114, 122, 138, 155, 156, 158, 167, 179, 184, 190) (1526–present)

Willow amsonia - *Amsonia tabernaemontana* Walt. (4, 138, 155) (1923-1986), *Amsonia tabernaemontana* Walt. var. *salicifolia* (Pursh) Woods. (122) (1937)

Willow aster - *Symphyotrichum potosinum* (A.Gray) G.L.Nesom (possibly) (5, 62, 72, 82, 85, 93, 97, 131, 156) (1899-1936)

Willow baccharis - *Baccharis salicina* Torr. & Gray (3, 4, 5, 97, 122, 124, 155) (1913-1986)

Willow catkins - *Salix nigra* Marsh. (92) (1876)

Willow cottonwood - *Populus angustifolia* James (5, 156) (1913-1923)

Willow dock - *Rumex salicifolius* Weinm. (50, 155) (1942–present)

Willow hard-hack - *Spiraea salicifolia* L. (19) (1840)

Willow hemp - *Amaranthus cannabinus* (L.) Sauer (7, 92) (1828-1876)

Willow herb [Willow-herb, Willowherb] - *Amorpha fruticosa* L. (63) (1899), *Chamerion angustifolium* (L.) Holub subsp. *circumvagum* (Mosquin) Kartesz (4) (1986), *Chamerion angustifolium* (L.) Holub subsp. *angustifolium* (19, 49, 52, 53, 57, 58, 92, 106, 107) (1840–1930), *Decodon verticillatus* (L.) Ell. (5, 106, 156) (1913–1930), *Epilobium brachycarpum* K. Presl (3) (1977), *Epilobium ciliatum* Raf. (4) (1986), *Epilobium ciliatum* Raf. subsp. *ciliatum* (3) (1977), *Epilobium* (1, 2, 10, 50, 82, 93, 109, 138, 156, 158, 167, 184) (1793–present), *Lythrum* L. (167) (1814)

Willow herbe with flowers like the Rose Bay - *Chamerion angustifolium* (L.) Holub subsp. *angustifolium* (178) (1526)

Willow lettuce - *Lactuca saligna* L. (5) (1913)

Willow oak [Willow oake] - *Quercus phellos* L. (2, 5, 10, 12, 14, 20, 19, 33, 65, 97, 107, 109, 138, 156, 177, 187) (1762-1949), *Quercus rubra* L. (189) (1767), *Quercus virginiana* Mill. (181) (~1678)

Willow poplar - *Populus nigra* L. (5, 156, 158) (1900-1923)

Willow sponge - *Boletus suaveolens* L. (92) (1876)

Willow-grass [Willow grass] - *Persicaria amphibia* (L.) Delarbre (5) (1913), *Polygonum amphibium* L. (157, 158) (1900-1929)

Willow-leaf aster [Willowleaf aster, Willow-leaved aster] - *Symphyotrichum praealtum* (Poir.) Nesom (50) (present), *Symphyotrichum praealtum* (Poir.) Nesom var. *praealtum* (3, 4, 50, 80, 82, 155, 187) (1818–present)

Willow-leaf cottonwood - *Populus angustifolia* James (30) (1844)

Willow-leaf dock [Willow leaved dock] - *Rumex salicifolius* Weinm. (72) (1907), *Rumex salicifolius* Weinm. var. *mexicanus* (Meisn.) A.S. Hitchc (3, 4, 5, 93) (1913-1986)

Willow-leaf frostweed [Willowleaf frostweed] - *Helianthemum salicifolium* (L.) Mill. (178) (1526)

Willow-leaf goldenrod [Willow-leaf golden-rod] - *Solidago stricta* Aiton (5, 19) (1840-1913)

Willow-leaf inula [Willowleaf inula] - *Inula salicina* L. (138) (1923)

Willow-leaf jessamine [Willow-leaved jessamine] - *Cestrum parqui* L'Hér. (109) (1949)

Willow-leaf lettuce [Willowleaf lettuce, Willow-leaved lettuce] - *Lactuca saligna* L. (3, 4, 50) (1977–present)

Willow-leaf meadowsweet [Willow-leaved meadow-sweet, Willow-leaved meadowsweet] - *Spiraea salicifolia* L. (130, 131) (1895-1899)

Willow-leaf oak [Willowleaf oak, Willow leaf oak, Willow-leaved

oak] - *Quercus phellos* L. (8, 34, 82, 122, 124) (1785-1937)

Willow-leaf poplar [Willow-leaved poplar] - *Populus angustifolia* James (108) (1878)

Willow-leaf spiraea [Willowleaf spiraea] - *Spiraea salicifolia* L. (138) (1923)

Willow-leaf sunflower [Willowleaf sunflower, Willow-leaved sunflower] - *Helianthus salicifolius* A. Dietr. (3, 4, 50, 155) (1986–present)

Willow-oak [Willow oak] - *Salix* L. (2) (1895)

Willowort - *Lythrum salicaria* L. (7) (1828)

Willow-weed [Willow weed, Willowweed] - *Epilobium* L. (155) (1942), *Lythrum salicaria* L. (92, 156, 158) (1898-1923), *Persicaria amphibia* (L.) Delarbre (5) (1913), *Persicaria maculosa* Gray (5, 156, 158) (1900-1923), *Polygonum amphibium* L. (157, 158) (1900-1929), *Polygonum lapathifolium* L. (156) (1923)

Willow-wort [Willow wort, Willowort] - *Lysimachia vulgaris* L. (5, 156) (1913-1923), *Lythrum salicaria* L. (7, 92, 158) (1828-1900)

Wilskt hampa (Swedish, wild hemp) - *Apocynum cannabinum* L. (41) (1770)

Wĭnabojo' noko'mĭs wi'nĭzĭsûn (Chippewa, Winabojo's grandmother's hair) - *Castilleja coccinea* (L.) Spreng. (40) (1928)

Wĭnabojo'bikwûk' (Chippewa, Winabojo's arrow) - *Lilium canadense* L. (40) (1928)

Winauk - *Sassafras albidum* (Nutt.) Nees (181) (~1678)

Wi-nawizi (Dakota, jealous woman) - *Glycyrrhiza lepidota* Pursh (37) (1919)

Winawizi čikala (Lakota, little burr) - *Glycyrrhiza lepidota* Pursh (121) (1918?-1970?)

Wincopipe - *Anagallis arvensis* L. (158) (1900)

Wind - *Convolvulus arvensis* L. (157, 158) (1900-1929)

Wind bent - *Apera spica-venti* (L.) Beauv. (5) (1913)

Wind crowfoot - *Anemone nemorosa* L. (49) (1898)

Wind grass - *Apera spica-venti* (L.) Beauv. (5, 92) (1876-1913)

Wind rose - *Papaver argemone* L. (5, 156) (1913-1923)

Windbells [Wind-bells] - *Campanula rotundifolia* L. (156) (1923)

Windberry [Wind-berry, Wind berry] - *Vaccinium vitis-idaea* L. (5, 156, 178) (1526-1923)

Windbloom [Wind-bloom] - *Anemone virginiana* L. (possibly) (7, 92) (1828-1876)

Windflower [Wind flower, Wind-flower, Wind-floures, Windefloures] - *Anemone canadensis* L. (37) (1919), *Anemone* L. (1, 2, 4, 13, 15, 63, 82, 93, 109, 156, 162, 165) (1597–1949) Pliny claimed that flower opened only when the wind was blowing, *Anemone nemorosa* L. (49, 61, 86, 92) (1870–1898), *Anemone quinquefolia* L. (5, 156, 158) (1900–1923), *Capsella bursa-pastoris* (L.) Medik. (5, 76, 158) (1896–1913) Fairhaven MA, *Clematis ligusticifolia* Nutt. (156, 157) (1923–1929), *Clematis ligusticifolia* Nutt. var. *californica* S. Wats. (76) (1896), *Hepatica nobilis* Schreb. (79) (1891), *Pulsatilla patens* (L.) Mill. (5, 93) (1913–1936), *Pulsatilla patens* (L.) Mill.subsp. *multifida* (Pritz.) Zamels (76) (1896), *Thalictrum thalictroides* (L.) Eames & Boivin (5, 156) (1913–1923)

Windflower meadow rue [Wind flower meadow rue, Windflower meadow-rue] - *Thalictrum thalictroides* (L.) Eames & Boivin (86) (1878)

Windgras (Swedish) - *Linnaea borealis* L. (46) (1879)

Windles - *Plantago lanceolata* L. (5, 156, 158) (1900-1923) no longer in use by 1923

Windlestraw - *Apera spica-venti* (L.) Beauv. (5) (1913), *Deschampsia caespitosa* (L.) Beauv. (5) (1913)

Windmill grass [Windmill-grass, Windmillgrass] - *Chloris* Sw. (50, 155) (1942–present), *Chloris verticillata* Nutt. (3, 5, 94, 99, 119, 122, 134, 163) (1852-1977)

Windmills - *Allionia* L. (50) (present)

Windroot [Wind-root, Windroot] - *Asclepias tuberosa* L. (5, 6, 7, 49, 58, 62, 64, 92, 156, 158) (1828-1923) no longer in use by 1923

Windsor bean - *Vicia faba* L. (7, 19, 107) (1828-1919)

Windsor fern - *Lygodium palmatum* (Bernh.) Sw. (5) (1913)

Windswept-prairie dewberry [Windswept prairie dewberry] - *Rubus hancinianus* Bailey (50) (present)

Windweed [Wind weed] - *Asclepias tuberosa* L. (6) (1892)

Wine gooseberry - *Ribes inerme* Rydb. (138) (1923)

Wine grape - *Vitis vinifera* L. (107, 109) (1919-1949)

Wine grass [Wine-grass] - *Melinis repens* (Willd.) Zizka (109) (1949)

Wine palm - *Caryota urens* L. (109) (1949)

Wine plant [Wine-plant] - *Rheum rhabarbarum* L. (77, 109) (1898-1949)

Wine rhubarb - *Rheum rhabarbarum* L. (158) (1900)

Wine tree - *Sorbus americana* Marsh. (5) (1913)

Wineberry [Wine berry, Wine-berry] - *Ribes rubrum* L. (92, 156) (1876-1923), *Ribes uva-crispa* L. var. *sativum* DC. (5, 156) (1913-1923), *Vaccinium myrtillus* L. (92) (1876), *Vaccinium vitis-idaea* L. (5, 156) (1913-1923)

Winecup [Wine cup, Wine-cup] - *Callirhoe digitata* Nutt. (50, 156) (1923–present), *Callirhoe involucrata* (Torr. & Gray) Gray (122) (1937)

Wine-leaf cinquefoil [Wineleaf cinquefoil] - *Sibbaldiopsis tridentata* (Aiton) Rydb. (138, 155) (1923-1942)

Wing eriogonum - *Eriogonum alatum* Torr. (155) (1942)

Wing-angle loosestrife [Wing-angled loosestrife] - *Lythrum alatum* Pursh (5, 63, 72, 97, 120, 131, 158) (1857-1938)

Winged buckwheat - *Eriogonum alatum* Torr. (50) (present)

Winged cudweed [Winged cud-weed] - *Pseudognaphalium macounii* (Greene) Kartesz (5, 156) (1913-1923)

Winged dock - *Rumex venosus* Pursh (5, 85, 93, 97) (1913-1937)

Winged elm - *Ulmus alata* Michx. (1, 2, 4, 5, 50, 82, 97, 106, 109, 122, 124, 138, 155, 156, 158) (1895–present)

Winged eriogonum - *Eriogonum alatum* Torr. (4, 5, 93, 97) (1913-1986)

Winged euonymus - *Euonymus alata* (Thunb.) Sieb. (112, 138) (1923-1937)

Winged ironweed [Winged iron-weed] - *Verbesina alternifolia* (L.) Britton ex Kearney (5, 62, 156) (1912-1923)

Winged loosestrife - *Lythrum alatum* Pursh (4, 93, 122, 124, 155, 156) (1923-1986)

Winged lythrum - *Lythrum alatum* Pursh (50, 138) (1923–present)

Winged pigweed - *Cycloloma atriplicifolium* (Spreng.) Coult. (3, 4, 5, 50, 80, 85, 93, 97, 156) (1913–present), *Cycloloma* Moq. (1, 2) (1895-1932)

Winged rockcress - *Sibara* Greene (50) (present)

Winged sumac - *Rhus copallinum* L. var. *latifolia* Engl. (50) (present)

Winged tobacco - *Nicotiana alata* Link & Otto (138) (1923)

Winged white sage - *Salvia officinalis* L. (178) (1526)

Winged wood fern [Winged woodfern] - *Phegopteris hexagonoptera* (Michx.) Fee (138) (1923)

Winged yam - *Dioscorea alata* L. (138) (1923)

Wingkelp - *Alaria* Grev. (155) (1942)

Wing-leaf butterfly flower [Wingleaf butterfly flower] - *Schizanthus pinnatus* Ruiz & Pavón (138) (1923)

Wingless-petiole ragweed [Wingless-petioled ragweed] - *Ambrosia trifida* L. var. *texana* Scheele (97) (1937)

Wingnut - *Pterocarya* Kunth (138) (1923)

Wing-pod purslane [Wingpod purslane] - *Portulaca umbraticola* H.B.K. (50) (present)

Wing-rib sumac [Wing-rib sumach] - *Rhus copallinum* L. (19) (1840)

Wingseed [Wing seed, Wing-seed] - *Ptelea* L. (7) (1828), *Ptelea trifoliata* L. (5, 6, 49, 53, 92, 156, 157, 158) (1892-1929)

Wingstem [Wing-stem] - *Verbesina alternifolia* (L.) Britton ex Kearney (4, 5, 50, 75, 82, 93, 97, 156, 158) (1894–present), *Verbesina* L. (4) (1986)

Wing-stem ludwigia [Wing-stemmed ludwigia] - *Ludwigia alata* Ell. (5) (1913)

Wing-stem monkey flower [Wing-stemmed monkey-flower] - *Mim-*

---

ulus alatus Aiton (possibly) (187) (1818)

Wi'nibĭdja'bibaga'no (Chippewa, toothplant) - *Stellaria media* (L.) Vill. (40) (1928)

Wini'sĭbûgons' (Chippewa, dirty leaf) - *Gaultheria procumbens* L. (40) (1928)

Wini'sĭkĕns (Chippewa, dirty, little) - *Oclemena nemoralis* (Aiton) Greene (40) (1928), *Symphyotrichum novae-angliae* (L.) G.L.Nesom (40) (1928), *Symphyotrichum puniceum* (L.) A.& D. Löve var. *puniceum* (40) (1928)

Wink-a-peep - *Anagallis arvensis* L. (5, 156, 157, 158) (1900-1929)

Winlin-berry - *Sambucus nigra* L. (158) (1900)

Winsibog (Chippewa) - *Gaultheria procumbens* L. (105) (1932)

Winsik (Chippewa) - *Betula lenta* L. (105) (1932)

Winter aconite [Winter-aconite] - *Eranthis hyemalis* (L.) Salisb. (5, 15, 109, 138, 156) (1895-1949), *Eranthis* Salisb. (156) (1923)

Winter barley - *Hordeum vulgare* L. (107, 158) (1900-1919) variety

Winter bent grass [Winter bentgrass] - *Agrostis hyemalis* (Walt.) Britton, Sterns & Poggenb. (50, 140, 155) (1942–present)

Winter brake - *Pellaea atropurpurea* (L.) Link (5, 92) (1876-1913)

Winter cape-marigold - *Castalis tragus* (Aiton) Norl. (138) (1923)

Winter cherry [Winter-cherry, Winter cherries] - *Cardiospermum halicacabum* L. (5, 107, 156, 158) (1900-1923), *Physalis alkekengi* L. (178) (1526), *Physalis* L. (10, 184, 190) (~1759-1818), *Physalis peruviana* L. (107) (1919), *Physalis pubescens* L. (181) (~1678)

Winter cress [Winter cresses] - *Barbarea verna* (P. Mill.) Aschers. (19, 156) (1840-1923) IN, *Barbarea vulgaris* W.T. Aiton (178, 180) (1526-1633), *Erysimum* L. (10) (1818)

Winter crookneck - *Cucurbita moschata* (Duchesne ex Lam.) Duchesne ex Poir. (107) (1919)

Winter crook-neck squash [Winter crookneck squashes] - *Cucurbita maxima* Dcne. (158) (1900), *Cucurbita moschata* (Duchesne ex Lam.) Duchesne ex Poir. (109) (1949)

Winter currant - *Ribes sanguineum* Pursh (138) (1923)

Winter fern - *Pellaea atropurpurea* (L.) Link (92) (1876)

Winter gilliflower - *Hesperis matronalis* L. (5, 156, 158) (1900-1923)

Winter grape [Winter-grape] - *Vitis aestivalis* Michx. (5, 156) (1913-1923), *Vitis cinerea* (Engelm.) Millard var. *helleri* (Bailey) M.O. Moore (15, 138) (1895-1923), *Vitis vulpina* L. (3, 4, 5, 15, 27, 76, 107, 108, 109, 156, 158, 168) (1803-1986)

Winter hellebore - *Eranthis hyemalis* (L.) Salisb. (5, 92) (1876-1913)

Winter honeysuckle - *Lonicera fragrantissima* Lindl. & Paxton (112, 138) (1923-1937), *Lonicera morrowii* Gray (106) (1930)

Winter horsetail - *Equisetum hyemale* L. (6) (1892)

Winter huckleberry - *Vaccinium arboreum* Marsh. (106, 156) (1923-1930)

Winter jasmine - *Jasminum nudiflorum* Lindl. (138) (1923)

Winter kersse (Lowe Dutch) - *Barbarea vulgaris* W.T. Aiton (possibly) (180) (1633)

Winter marjoram - *Origanum vulgare* L. (92) (1876)

Winter melon - *Cucumis melo* L. (109) (1949)

Winter pink - *Epigaea repens* L. (5, 6, 49, 58, 92, 156) (1869-1923) no longer in use by 1923

Winter purslane - *Claytonia perfoliata* Donn ex Willd. subsp. *perfoliata* (156) (1923)

Winter reps (German) - *Brassica rapa* L. var. *rapa* (107) (1919)

Winter rocket - *Barbarea vulgaris* W.T. Aiton (5, 156, 157) (1913-1929)

Winter salad [Winter sallad] - *Barbarea orthoceras* Ledeb. (12) (1821)

Winter savory [Winter Sauorie] - *Satureja montana* L. (19, 92, 106, 107, 109, 138, 178) (1526–1949), *Pycnanthemum muticum* (Michx.) Pers. (possibly) (46) (1629), *Pycnanthemum virginianum* (L.) T. Dur. & B. D. Jackson ex B. L. Robins. & Fern. (46) (1629)

Winter squash [Winter squashes] - *Cucurbita maxima* Dcne. (50, 109, 155) (1942–present)

Winter sweet [Winter-sweet] - *Origanum vulgare* L. (5, 92, 106, 156)

(1876–1930)

Winter vetch - *Vicia villosa* Roth (50, 68, 82, 97, 109, 156) (1913–present), *Vicia villosa* Roth subsp. *varia* (Host) Corb. (50) (present), *Vicia villosa* Roth subsp. *villosa* (50) (present)

Winter wheat - *Triticum aestivum* L. (19, 66, 158) (1840-1903)

Winter whortleberry [Winter whortle-berry] - *Vaccinium arboreum* Marsh. (8) (1785)

Winter witchhazel [Winter witch hazel] - *Hamamelis virginiana* L. (7) (1828)

Winter wolf's-bane [Winter wolfesbane] - *Eranthis hyemalis* (L.) Salisb. (178) (1526)

Winter-aconite - *Eranthis hyemalis* (L.) Salisb. (138) (1923)

Winteranus - *Canella winterana* (L.) Gaertn. (174) (1753)

Winter-asparagus [Winter asparagus] - *Scorzonera* L. (158) (1900)

Winter-berry [Winter berry, Winterberry] - *Aristotelia* L'Hér. (155) (1942), *Ilex glabra* (L.) Gray (109) (1949), *Ilex* L. (7, 8, 10, 14, 158, 167) (1785–1900), *Ilex verticillata* (L.) Gray (6, 15, 19, 49, 53, 57, 92, 106, 107, 109, 156, 184, 186, 187) (1793–1949)

Winterberry tea - *Ilex glabra* (L.) Gray (14) (1882)

Winterbloom [Winter bloom, Winter-bloom] - *Hamamelis virginiana* L. (5, 6, 7, 49, 53, 92, 156) (1828-1923)

Winter-cherry [Winter cherry] - *Physalis alkekengi* L. (92, 107, 109, 156, 158) (1876-1949), *Physalis* L. (10) (1818)

Winter-clover [Winter clover] - *Mitchella repens* L. (6, 49, 92, 156) (1876-1923) no longer in use by 1923

Winter-creeper [Wintercreeper, Winter creeper] - *Euonymus fortunei* (Turcz.) Hand.-Maz. var. *radicans* (Sieb. ex Miq.) Rehd. (112, 138) (1923-1937)

Wintercress [Winter cress, Winter-cress] - *Barbarea* Aiton f. (1, 4, 13, 15, 63, 109, 138, 155, 156, 158) (1849-1986), *Barbarea orthoceras* Ledeb. (3) (1977), *Barbarea vulgaris* W.T. Aiton (3, 4, 5, 63, 80, 107, 157) (1899-1986)

Winterfat [Winter fat, Winter-fat] - *Krascheninnikovia* Guldenstaedt (1, 50, 93, 155) (1932–present), *Krascheninnikovia lanata* (Pursh) A.D.J. Meeuse & Smit (3, 5, 50, 93, 118, 122, 124, 141, 146, 153, 157, 158) (1898–present)

Winter-fern - *Conium maculatum* L. (71, 109) (1898-1949)

Winter-grass [Winter grass] - *Carex aestivalis* M.A. Curtis ex Gray (5) (1913)

Wintergreen [Winter greene, Winter-green] - *Chimaphila maculata* (L.) Pursh (7, 92) (1828-1876), *Chimaphila* Pursh (158) (1900), *Chimaphila umbellata* (L.) Bart. (6, 49, 55, 59, 75, 77, 92, 156, 186, 187) (1818-1923) SD, *Gaultheria* L. (2) (1895), *Gaultheria procumbens* L. (6, 7, 14, 40, 49, 52, 53, 55, 57, 61, 71, 92, 103, 104, 105, 107, 109, 138, 156, 186, 187) (1814-1949), *Matelea biflora* (Raf.) Woods (178) (1526), *Pyrola americana* Sweet (46, 178) (1526-1879), *Pyrola elliptica* Nutt. (86) (1878), *Pyrola* L. (1, 2, 4, 8, 10, 50, 93, 127, 158, 167, 184) (1793–1949), *Trientalis* L. (50, 167) (1814–present), *Vinca minor* L. (77, 156) (1898-1923) Sulphur Grove OH

Wintergreen barberry - *Berberis julianae* C.K. Schneid. (109, 138) (1923-1949)

Wintergroen - *Chimaphila umbellata* (L.) Bart. (186) (1825)

Wintergrün (German) - *Chimaphila umbellata* (L.) Bart. (158, 186) (1825-1900)

Winter-grün (German) - *Pyrola americana* Sweet (46) (1879)

Winter-laurel [Winter laurel] - *Prunus caroliniana* (P. Mill.) Aiton (7, 92) (1828-1876)

Winterlien (German) - *Linum usitatissimum* L. (92) (1876)

Winter-oat [Winter oat] - *Salvia columbariae* Benth. (77) (1898) CA

Winter-plum [Winter plum, Winter plums] - *Diospyros virginiana* L. (7, 92, 156, 158) (1828-1923)

Winter's-bark [Winter's bark] - *Canella winteriana* (L.) Gaertn. (15) (1895)

Winter-sweet [Wintersweet] - *Chimonanthus* Lindl. (138) (1923)

Winterweed [Winter weed, Wnter-weed] - *Stellaria media* (L.) Vill. (156) (1923), *Stellaria media* (L.) Vill. subsp. *media* (5, 157, 158)

(1900-1929), *Veronica agrestis* L. (5, 156, 158) (1900-1923), *Veronica hederifolia* L. (5, 92, 156, 158) (1876-1923), *Veronica officinalis* L. (187) (1818)

Wiŋawazi kutkaŋ (Lakota, burr root) - *Ratibida pinnata* (Vent.) Barnh. (121) (1918?-1970?)

Wipazuka (Dakota) - *Amelanchier alnifolia* (Nutt.) Nutt. ex M. Roemer (37) (1919)

Wipazukaŋ (Lakota) - *Amelanchier canadensis* (L.) Medik. (121) (1918?-1970?)

Wire bent - *Nardus stricta* L. (94) (1901)

Wire bent grass - *Apera spica-venti* (L.) Beauv. (92) (1876)

Wire bunch grass [Wire bunch-grass] - *Pseudoroegneria spicata* (Pursh) Á. Löve (94, 118) (1898-1901)

Wire grass [Wire-grass, Wiregrass] - *Aristida* L. (1) (1932), *Aristida oligantha* Michx (145) (1897) KS, *Aristida purpurea* Nutt. (129) (1894), *Aristida stricta* Michx. (94) (1901), *Cynodon dactylon* (L.) Pers. (5, 45, 163) (1852–1896), *Danthonia spicata* (L.) Beauv. ex Roemer & J. A. Schultes (90) (1885) ME, *Digitaria filiformis* (L.) Koel. (5, 119) (1913–1938), *Distichlis spicata* (L.) Greene (116) (1958), *Eleocharis obtusa* (Willd.) J. A. Schultes (85) (1932), *Eleusine* Gaertn. (93) (1936), *Eleusine indica* (L.) Gaertn. (5, 19, 56, 66, 75, 80, 87, 88, 92, 119) (1840-1938), *Muhlenbergia schreberi* J.F. Gmel. (87, 93, 119) (1884–1938), *Panicum obtusum* H.B.K. (5) (1913), *Poa compressa* L. (5, 45, 56, 66, 68, 72, 87, 88, 90, 92, 109, 119, 129, 143) (1884–1949), *Schedonnardus paniculatus* (Nutt.) Trel. (5, 119) (1913–1938), *Sporobolus heterolepis* (Gray) Gray (111, 129) (1894–1915), *Sporobolus junceus* (Beauv.) Kunth (5) (1913), *Sporobolus vaginiflorus* (Torr. ex Gray) Wood (145) (1897) KS

Wire plant [Wire-plant] - *Muehlenbeckia complexa* Meisn. (109) (1949)

Wire vine [Wirevine] - *Muehlenbeckia complexa* Meisn. (138) (1923)

Wire-grass [Wire grass] - *Eleocharis* R. Br. (1, 93) (1932–1936), *Juncus balticus* Willd. (87, 101) (1884–1905), *Juncus* L. (1, 93) (1932–1936), *Juncus tenuis* Willd. (5, 62, 75, 80, 156) (1894–1923), *Polygonum aviculare* L. (5, 73, 156, 158) (1892–1923) Northern OH

Wire-leaf berlandiera [Wireleaf berlandiera] - *Berlandiera lyrata* Benth. (3) (1977)

Wire-lettuce [Wirelettuce, Wire lettuce] - *Stephanomeria* Nutt. (4, 50, 155) (1942–present), *Stephanomeria pauciflora* (Torr.) A. Nels. (3) (1977)

Wire-ling [Wire ling] - *Empetrum nigrum* L. (5, 156) (1913-1923) Neb

Wire-stem muhly [Wirestem muhly] - *Muhlenbergia frondosa* (Poir.) Fern. (3, 50) (1977–present), *Muhlenbergia mexicana* (L.) Trin. (3, 155) (1942-1977)

Wireweed [Wire weed, Wire-weed] - *Polygonum aviculare* L. (5, 156, 158) (1900-1923), *Polygonum ramosissimum* Michx. (145) (1897), *Sida spinosa* L. (156) (1923), *Symphyotrichum lateriflorum* (L.) A.& D. Löve (75) (1894) WV, *Symphyotrichum lateriflorum* (L.) A.& D. Löve var. *lateriflorum* (158) (1900)

Wirilda acacia - *Acacia retinodes* Schlecht. (155) (1942)

Wiry grama - *Bouteloua curtipendula* (Michx) Torr. (94) (1901)

Wiry panic grass [Wiry panic-grass] - *Panicum flexile* (Gatt.) Scribn. (50, 94) (1901–present)

Wiry sedge - *Cyperus lupulinus* (Spreng.) Marcks subsp. *lupulinus* (66) (1903)

Wiry spear grass [Wiry spear-grass] - *Nassella tenuissima* (Trin.) Barkworth (163) (1852)

Wiry triodia - *Tridens muticus* (Torr.) Nash (94) (1901)

Wiry witch grass [Wiry witch-grass] - *Panicum flexile* (Gatt.) Scribn. (5, 163) (1852-1913)

Wi-sa-gu-mina (Cree) - *Vaccinium vitis-idaea* L. (107) (1919)

Wisconsin weeping willow - *Salix ×pendulina* Wenderoth [*babylonica × fragilis*] (50, 109) (1949–present)

Wiseweed [Wise-weed] - *Symphyotrichum lateriflorum* (L.) A.& D. Löve var. *lateriflorum* (5, 156) (1913-1923)

Wisher's buckwheat - *Eriogonum visheri* A. Nels. (50) (present)

Wisigak (Chippewa, bitter ash) - *Vaccinium* L. (105) (1932)

Wislizenus' spectacle-pod [Wislizenus spectaclepod] - *Dimorphocarpa candicans* (Raf.) Rollins (155) (1942)

Wisoccan (refers to any kind of medicine) - *Cunila origanoides* (L.) Britton (possibly) (181) (~1678)

Wisp-mossa (Swedish) - *Lycopodium clavatum* L. (46) (1879)

Wissep-hu (Winnebago, tree to dye black) - *Acer rubrum* L. (37) (1919)

Wisteria [Wistaria] - *Wisteria frutescens* (L.) Poir. (85, 92, 156) (1876–1932), *Wisteria* Nutt. (138) (1923) for Caspar Wistar, 1761–1818, professor of anatomy in the Univ. of Penn., *Wisteria sinensis* (Sims) DC. (92, 112) (1876–1937)

Wister's coralroot [Wister's coral-root] - *Corallorrhiza wisteriana* Conrad (3, 5, 97) (1913-1977)

Wi'sûgibûg' (Chippewa, bitter leaf) - *Arctium minus* Bernh. (40) (1928)

Wi'sûgidji'bĭk (Chippewa, bitter root) - *Veronicastrum virginicum* (L.) Farw. (40) (1928)

Wi'sugi'mĭtĭgo'mĭc (Chippewa, bitter oak) - *Quercus rubra* L. (40) (1928)

Witch elm - *Ulmus alata* Michx. (5, 156) (1913-1923)

Witch gowan - *Taraxacum officinale* G.H. Weber ex Wiggers (156, 157, 158) (1900-1929)

Witch grass [Witch-grass, Witchgrass] - *Danthonia spicata* (L.) Beauv. ex Roemer & J. A. Schultes (78) (1898) ME, *Elymus repens* (L.) Gould (5, 45, 64, 67, 69, 5, 78, 90, 92, 157, 158) (1876-1929), *Panicum capillare* L. (3, 5, 50, 72, 85, 93, 119, 122, 131) (1899–present), *Panicum* L. (1, 93, 155) (1932-1942)

Witch hazel [Witch-hazel, Witchhazel, Witch hazle] - *Hamamelis* L. (1, 2, 8, 10, 109, 138, 156, 190) (~1759-1949), *Hamamelis virginiana* L. (5, 6, 7, 19, 40, 41, 46, 49, 52, 53, 54, 55, 57, 59, 61, 63, 72, 92, 105, 107, 112, 113, 122, 124, 156, 177, 183, 184, 187) (~1756-1937)

Witch hobble [Witch-hobble] - *Viburnum lantanoides* Michx. (5, 156) (1913-1923) NH, *Viburnum opulus* L. (5, 156, 158) (1900-1923) no longer in use by 1923

Witch-alder [Witch alder] - *Fothergilla gardenii* L. (5, 19, 92, 156) (1840-1923)

Witches - *Lycopodium clavatum* L. (14) (1882)

Witche's-bell [Witches' bells, Witches bells, Witches'-bells, Witches' bells, Witches bells] - *Campanula rotundifolia* L. (5, 156, 158) (1900-1923), *Centaurea cyanus* L. (5, 156, 157, 158) (1900-1929)

Witche's-herb [Witches' herb, Witches'-herb] - *Hypericum perforatum* L. (6) (1892)

Witch-hopple [Witch hopple] - *Viburnum lantanoides* Michx. (5, 79, 156) (1891-1923), *Viburnum opulus* L. (5, 156, 158) (1900-1923) no longer in use by 1923

Witch's-butter [Witch's butter] - *Tremella* Pers. (50) (present)

Witch's-milk [Witches' milk, Witches milk, Witches'-milk, Witche's-milk] - *Hippuris vulgaris* L. (5, 156, 158) (1900-1923)

Witch's-money bags [Witches' money bags, Witches' money-bags] - *Hylotelephium telephium* (L.) H. Ohba. subsp. *telephium* (5, 73, 156) (1892-1923) Western MA

Witch's-pouches [Witches' pouches, Wiches' pouches (5), Witchespouches, Witches'-puches] - *Capsella bursa-pastoris* (L.) Medik. (5, 156, 157, 158) (1900-1929)

Witch's-thimble [Witches thimbles, Witches' thimbles, Witches'-thimbles, Witches'thimbles] - *Centaurea cyanus* L. (5, 156, 157, 158) (1900-1929), *Digitalis pupurea* L. (5, 156) (1913-1923)

Witchwood [Witch-wood, Witch wood] - *Euonymus europaea* L. (5, 156) (1913-1923), *Sorbus americana* Marsh. (5, 73) (1892-1913) NH, said to ward off witches

Withe - *Salix* L. (92) (1876)

Withe rod [Withe-rod] - *Viburnum dentatum* L. (5, 156, 174) (1753-1923), *Viburnum nudum* L. (107) (1919), *Viburnum nudum* L. var.

cassinoides (L.) Torr. & Gray (2, 5, 109, 112, 138, 156) (1895-1949) NH, *Viburnum opulus* L. var. *americanum* Aiton (174) (1753)

Withewood [Withe wood, Withe-wood] - *Viburnum dentatum* L. (5, 76, 156) (1896-1923) S. Berwick ME, *Viburnum nudum* L. (73) (1892), *Viburnum opulus* L. (174) (1753)

With-wind [Withwind] - *Convolvulus arvensis* L. (156, 157, 158) (1900–1929), *Lonicera* L. (possibly) (92) (1876), *Polygonum convolvulus* L. (158) (1900)

Withy - *Salix* L. (92, 158) (1876-1900)

Witloof - *Cichorium intybus* L. (107) (1919)

Witmer Stone's violet - *Viola palmata* L. (5) (1913)

Wiunabih'u - *Humulus lupulus* L. var. *lupuloides* E. Small (37) (1919)

Wladmalve (German) - *Malva sylvestris* L. (158) (1900)

Woad [Woade] - *Isatis* L. (109) (1949), *Isatis tinctoria* L. (possibly) (19, 92, 107, 178) (1526-1919)

Woad-wax - *Genista tinctoria* L. (156) (1923)

Woad-waxen [Woadwaxen, Woad waxen] - *Genista* L. (156) (1923), *Genista tinctoria* L. (5, 6, 138, 156) (1892-1923)

Woats - *Avena sativa* L. (158) (1900)

Wobsqua grass - *Panicum virgatum* L. (5) (1913)

Wocks - *Avena sativa* L. (158) (1900)

Wode-whistle [Wode-whistle] - *Conium maculatum* L. (5, 69, 71, 156, 158) (1898-1923)

Woemwood - *Artemisia biennis* Willd. (62) (1912)

Wohlreichender Gänsefuss (German) - *Chenopodium ambrosioides* L. (158) (1900)

Wold monkhood - *Aconitum uncinatum* L. (5) (1913)

Wolf bean [Wolf-bean] - *Lupinus albus* L. (107) (1919)

Wolf root [Wolf-root] - *Aconitum napellus* L. (92, 156) (1898-1923)

Wolf-bane monkshood [Wolfbane monkshood] - *Aconitum lycoctonum* L. (155) (1942)

Wolfberry [Wolf berry, Wolf-berry] - *Elaeagnus commutata* Bernh. ex Rydb. (156) (1923), *Lycium* L. (4, 155) (1942-1986), *Symphoricarpos* Duham. (1, 4) (1932-1986), *Symphoricarpos occidentalis* Hook. (2, 4, 5, 9, 37, 63, 72, 75, 82, 92, 93, 95, 106, 108, 109, 113, 127, 130, 131, 156, 157, 158) (1873-1986)

Wolffia - *Wolffia* Horkel ex Schleid. (93, 158) (1900-1936) for N.M. von Wolff, Polish naturalist

Wolf-grape [Wolf grape] - *Lycium barbarum* L. (156) (1923), *Solanum dulcamara* L. (92, 158) (1876-1900)

Wolf's blue grass [Wolf's bluegrass, Wolfs bluegrass] - *Poa wolfii* Scribn. (50, 155) (1942–present)

Wolf's claw [Wolf claw, Wolf's claw] - *Lycopodium clavatum* L. (5, 6, 92) (1876-1913) IA

Wolf's false oat - *Trisetum wolfii* Vasey (94) (1901) Bedford Mass

Wolf's meadow grass - *Poa wolfii* Scribn. (56) (1901)

Wolf's spear grass - *Poa wolfii* Scribn. (5, 72) (1907-1913)

Wolf's spike-rush [Wolf's spike rush, Wolf's spikerush] - *Eleocharis wolfii* (Gray) Gray ex Britt. (5, 50, 72) (present)

Wolf's spike-sedge [Wolf spikesedge] - *Eleocharis wolfii* (Gray) Gray ex Britt. (3) (1977)

Wolf's-bane [Wolfbane, Wolf bane, Wolf's bane, Wolfsbane, Wolfsbane] - *Aconitum* L. (1, 10, 13, 15, 109, 158) (1818-1949), *Aconitum lycoctonum* L. (107, 138) (1919-1923), *Aconitum napellus* L. (7, 19, 49, 53, 54, 92, 156) (1828-1923), *Eranthis hyemalis* (L.) Salisb. (5, 156) (1913-1923), *Veratrum viride* Ait. (possibly) (7, 71) (1828-1898)

Wolf's-bane with the turnip root [Wolfesbane with the turnep roote] - *Aconitum napellus* L. (178) (1526)

Wolfsbane-leaf anemone [Wolf's bane leaved anemone] - *Anemone canadensis* L. (42) (1814)

Wolf's-bean [Wolf's bean] - *Lupinus* L. (1) (1932)

Wolf's-foot [Wolf foot, Wolf-foot] - *Lycopus virginicus* L. (92, 157, 158) (1876-1929)

Wolf's-milk [Wolf's milk] - *Euphorbia helioscopia* L. (5, 156) (1913-1923) no longer in use by 1923, *Euphorbia lathyris* L. (71, 156) (1898-1923)

Wolf's-tail [Wolfstail, Wolftail] - *Lycurus* Kunth (50, 155) (1942–present), *Lycurus phleoides* H.B.K. (3, 119, 122, 140, 155, 163) (1852-1977)

Wolfstrapp (German) - *Leonurus cardiaca* L. (158) (1900)

Wolf-willow [Wolf willow] - *Elaeagnus commutata* Bernh. ex Rydb. (106, 156) (1923-1930)

Wollkraut (German) - *Verbascum thapsus* L. (6, 158) (1892-1900)

Woman's-tobacco [Woman's tobacco] - *Antennaria plantaginifolia* (L.) Richards (5, 50, 73, 156, 158) (1892–present) Boston MA

Woman's-tongue tree [Womans-tongue-tree] - *Albizia lebbeck* (L.) Benth. (109) (1949)

Wompinish (Narraganset) - *Castanea dentata* (Marsh.) Borkh. (46) (1879)

Wonder honey plant - *Penstemon laevigatus* Aiton (106) (1930)

Wonder-berry [Wonder berry] - *Solanum nigrum* L. (126, 156) (1923-1933)

Wonkapin - *Nelumbo lutea* Willd. (76, 156, 157, 158) (1896-1929) Southern IN, supposedly an Indian name

Wood anemone [Woods anemone] - *Anemone nemorosa* L. (19, 49, 61, 86, 92, 165) (1807-1898), *Anemone quinquefolia* L. (3, 4, 5, 72, 82, 85, 156) (1907-1986)

Wood angelica - *Angelica venenosa* (Greenway) Fern. (156) (1923)

Wood aster - *Eurybia divaricata* (L.) Nesom (156) (1923), *Oclemena nemoralis* (Aiton) Greene (19) (1840), *Symphyotrichum cordifolium* (L.) Nesom (127) (1933)

Wood bedstraw - *Galium sylvaticum* L. (5, 156) (1913-1923)

Wood betany - *Pedicularis canadensis* L. (131) (1899)

Wood betony [Wood-betony, Woodbetony] - *Lycopus virginicus* L. (5, 156, 157, 158) (1900-1929), *Pedicularis canadensis* L. (2, 4, 5, 92, 97, 105, 156) (1876-1986), *Pedicularis* L. (109, 138, 155) (1923-1949), *Stachys officinalis* (L.) Trev. (5, 92) (1876-1913), *Teucrium canadense* L. (77) (1898) Western US

Wood bittercress [Wood bitter cress] - *Cardamine flexuosa* With. (72) (1907)

Wood blue grass [Wood bluegrass] - *Poa nemoralis* L. (50, 138, 155) (1923–present)

Wood boneset - *Eupatorium perfoliatum* L. (69, 92) (1876-1904), *Eupatorium purpureum* L. var. *purpureum* (7) (1828)

Wood brome grass - *Bromus latiglumis* (Shear) A.S. Hitchc. (56) (1901)

Wood bulrush - *Scirpus expansus* Fern. (5) (1913)

Wood chess - *Bromus ciliatus* L. (5) (1913), *Bromus latiglumis* (Shear) A.S. Hitchc. (56) (1901)

Wood cinquefoil - *Potentilla anglica* Laicharding (5) (1913)

Wood club-rush [Wood club rush, Wood clubrush] - *Scirpus expansus* Fern. (5) (1913), *Trichophorum planifolium* (Spreng.) Palla (5) (1913)

Wood crab [Wood crabbe] - *Malus sylvestris* Mill. (179) (1526)

Wood cudweed - *Omalotheca sylvatica* (L.) Schultz-Bip. & F.W. Schultz (5, 156) (1913-1923)

Wood daffodil - *Uvularia grandiflora* Smith. (156) (1923)

Wood daisy - *Erigeron philadelphicus* L. (124) (1937)

Wood dropseed - *Muhlenbergia sylvatica* Torr. ex Gray (5) (1913)

Wood fern [Woodfern] - *Dryopteris* Adans. (4, 50, 131, 155) (1923–present), *Dryopteris carthusiana* (Vill.) H.P. Fuchs (3) (1977), *Thelypteris palustris* Schott var. *pubescens* (Lawson) Fern. (5) (1913)

Wood flower [Woodflower, Wood-flower] - *Anemone caroliniana* Walt. (156, 158) (1900-1923), *Anemone quinquefolia* L. (5) (1913)

Wood fringe - *Adlumia fungosa* (Aiton) Greene ex B. S. P. (5, 76, 92, 156) (1876-1923) Paris ME

Wood geranium - *Geranium dissectum* L. (5, 19, 92) (1840-1913)

Wood germander - *Teucrium canadense* L. (124) (1937), *Teucrium scorodonia* L. (5, 107) (1913-1919)

Wood grass [Wood-grass] - *Muhlenbergia mexicana* (L.) Trin. (5, 87, 90, 93, 99, 111, 119) (1885-1936), *Muhlenbergia schreberi* J.F. Gmel. (90) (1885), *Muhlenbergia sylvatica* Torr. ex Gray (87, 129) (1884-1894), *Poa nemoralis* L. (56) (1901), *Schizachyrium scoparium* (Michx.) Nash var. *scoparium* (87, 90) (1884-1885), *Sorghas-*

trum nutans (L.) Nash (5, 45, 66, 87, 92) (1884-1913)

Wood groundsel - *Senecio sylvaticus* L. (5) (1913)

Wood hair grass - *Deschampsia flexuosa* (L.) Trin. (5, 87, 90, 111) (1885–1916), *Deschampsia flexuosa* (L.) Trin. var *flexuosa* (66) (1901–1903)

Wood horsetail - *Equisetum sylvaticum* L. (3, 4, 131) (1899–1986)

Wood ipecac - *Triosteum perfoliatum* L. (5, 156, 158) (1900–1923)

Wood laurel - *Kalmia latifolia* L. (5, 71, 156) (1898–1923)

Wood leek - *Allium tricoccum* Ait. (138) (1923)

Wood lily - *Clintonia borealis* (Ait.) Raf. (156) (1923), *Convallaria majalis* L. (5, 156, 158) (1900-1923), *Lilium philadelphicum* L. (5, 50, 72, 155, 156, 158) (1900–present), *Lilium philadelphicum* L. var. *andinum* (Nutt.) Ker.-Gawl. (50) (present), *Pyrola minor* L. (5) (1913), *Trillium grandiflorum* (Michx.) Salisb. (156) (1923), *Pedicularis canadensis* L. (93) (1936)

Wood meadow grass [Wood meadow-grass] - *Poa nemoralis* L. (56, 66, 68, 72, 92, 94, 109, 129) (1894–1949), *Poa palustris* L. (5) (1913)

Wood merry-bells [Wood merrybells] - *Uvularia perfoliata* L. (138, 156) (1923)

Wood muhlenbergia - *Muhlenbergia schreberi* J.F. Gmel. (90) (1885)

Wood nep [Wood-nep] - *Ptilimnium capillaceum* (Michx.) Raf. (5, 156) (1913-1923)

Wood nettle - *Urtica dioica* L. subsp. *gracilis* (Aiton) Seland. (174) (1753)

Wood nightshade - *Solanum dulcamara* L. (77, 178) (1526–1898)

Wood orchid - *Habenaria* Willd. (1) (1932), *Piperia* Rydb. (1) (1932), *Platanthera clavellata* (Michx.) Luer (85) (1932)

Wood pea - *Vicia sativa* L. (92) (1876)

Wood phlox [Woods phlox] - *Saponaria officinalis* L. (5, 64, 73, 156, 157, 158) (1892–1929)

Wood pink - *Dianthus sylvestris* Wulfen (109) (1949)

Wood reed [Woodreed] - *Cinna arundinacea* L. (3) (1977), *Cinna* L. (50, 155) (1942–present)

Wood reed grass [Wood reed-grass] - *Cinna arundinacea* L. (5, 66, 87, 88, 90, 92, 111, 119, 163) (1852–1938), *Cinna* L. (66) (1903), *Cinna latifolia* (Trev. ex Goepp.) Griseb. (85) (1932)

Wood root - *Galium odoratum* (L.) Scop. (92) (1876)

Wood rue [Woodrue] - *Galium odoratum* (L.) Scop. (179) (1526)

Wood rush - *Scirpus expansus* Fern. (19, 66) (1840–1903)

Wood sage - *Teucrium scorodonia* L. (92, 107, 156) (1898–1923)

Wood scabious - *Succisa pratensis* Moench (92) (1876)

Wood sorrel [Wood-sorrel, Woodsorrel] - *Oxalis* L. (1, 2, 4, 10, 13, 15, 50, 82, 109, 158, 167) (1814–present), *Oxalis montana* Raf. (possibly) (19, 41, 47, 92, 107, 156, 178) (1596–1923), *Oxalis violacea* L. (145, 148) (1897–1939), *Rumex acetosella* L. (5, 93, 156) (1913–1936)

Wood sour - *Oxalis montana* Raf. (possibly) (5, 49, 92, 156) (1876–1923)

Wood sower - *Oxalis montana* Raf. (possibly) (5) (1913)

Wood spear grass - *Poa alsodes* Gray (66, 87) (1884–1903)

Wood strawberry - *Fragaria vesca* L. (6, 47, 49, 82, 92, 107) (1852–1930), *Fragaria vesca* L. subsp. *americana* (Porter) Staudt (3, 72, 131) (1899–1977)

Wood sunflower - *Helianthus hirsutus* Raf. (72) (1907)

Wood thistle - *Cirsium discolor* (Muhl. ex Willd.) Spreng. (80, 82) (1913–1930)

Wood tickseed - *Coreopsis major* Walt. (5) (1913)

Wood valerian - *Valeriana dioica* L. var. *sylvatica* S. Wats. (131) (1899)

Wood vetch - *Vicia caroliniana* Walt. (3) (1977), *Vicia sativa* L. (92) (1876)

Wood vine [Wood-vine] - *Bryonia alba* L. (92) (1876), *Calystegia sepium* (L.) R. Br. subsp. *sepium* (156) (1923), *Parthenocissus quinquefolia* (L.) Planch. (156) (1923)

Wood violet - *Viola palmata* L. (4) (1986), *Viola pedata* L. (5, 156,

158) (1900-1923)

Wood wakerobin [Wood wake-robin] - *Trillium viride* Beck (50) (present)

Wood whitlow-grass [Wood whitlow grass] - *Draba nemorosa* L. (5, 131) (1899-1913)

Wood witch grass [Wood witch-grass] - *Panicum philadelphicum* Bernh. ex Trin. (5, 163) (1852-1913)

Woodbank sedge - *Carex cephalophora* Muhl. ex Willd. (3, 155) (1942-1977)

Woodbind [Woodbinde, Wood bind, Woodbynde] - *Calystegia sepium* (L.) R. Br. subsp. *sepium* (5, 156, 158) (1900-1923), *Convolvulus* L. (179) (1526), *Lonicera periclymenum* L. (178, 179) (1526)

Woodbine - *Calystegia sepium* (L.) R. Br. subsp. *sepium* (75, 158) (1894-1913) NY, *Clematis virginiana* L. (5, 76, 156, 158) (1896-1923) Hartford & Oxford Co ME, *Gelsemium sempervirens* (L.) J. St.-Hil. (6, 7, 92) (1828-1892), *Hedera* L. (1, 82) (1930-1932), *Lonicera* L. (2, 8) (1785-1932), *Lonicera periclymenum* L. (19, 109, 138) (1840-1949), *Lonicera sempervirens* L. (156, 158) (1900-1923), *Parthenocissus quinquefolia* (L.) Planch. (2, 6, 15, 40, 46, 49, 57, 58, 82, 85, 92, 106, 109, 131, 142, 156, 158) (1671-1949), *Parthenocissus vitacea* (Knerr) A.S. Hitchc. (3, 50) (1977-present)

Woodbine-flower Virginia cistus [Woodbine flowered Virginia cistus] - *Rhododendron viscosum* (L.) Torr. (181) (~1678)

Wood-broom [Wood brooms, Wood broom] - *Dipsacus fullonum* L. (5, 92, 156, 158) (1876-1923)

Woodcress [Wood-cress] - *Rorippa sylvestris* (L.) Bess. (156) (1923)

Wood-crowfoot [Wood crowfoot] - *Adoxa moschatellina* L. (5) (1913)

Woodhouse's bahia - *Picradeniopsis woodhousei* (Gray) Rydb. (50) (present)

Woodland agrimony - *Agrimonia pubescens* Wallr. (3, 4, 5) (1913-1986), *Agrimonia striata* Michx. (97) (1937)

Woodland beak-chervil [Woodland beakchervil] - *Anthriscus sylvestris* (L.) Hoffmann (155) (1942)

Woodland bittercress - *Cardamine flexuosa* With. (50) (present)

Woodland bluegrass [Woodland blue-grass, Woodland blue grass] - *Poa alsodes* Gray (94) (1901), *Poa sylvestris* Gray (3, 50, 155) (1942-present)

Woodland bulrush - *Scirpus expansus* Fern. (50) (present)

Woodland chess - *Bromus ciliatus* L. (56) (1901)

Woodland coneflower [Woodland cone-flower] - *Rudbeckia fulgida* Aiton var. *umbrosa* (C.L. Boynt. & Beadle) Cronq. (5) (1913)

Woodland draba - *Draba nemorosa* L. (50) (present)

Woodland dropseed [Woodland drop seed, Woodland drop-seed] - *Muhlenbergia sylvatica* Torr. ex Gray (5, 56, 94, 163) (1852-1933)

Woodland forget-me-not [Woodland forgetmenot] - *Myosotis sylvatica* Ehrh. ex Hoffmann (50, 138, 155) (1923-present)

Woodland goldenrod [Woodland golden-rod] - *Solidago caesia* L. (5, 156) (1913-1923)

Woodland horsetail - *Equisetum sylvaticum* L. (50, 72) (1907-present)

Woodland lettuce - *Lactuca floridana* (L.) Gaertn. (50) (present), *Lactuca floridana* (L.) Gaertn. var. *floridana* (50) (present), *Lactuca floridana* (L.) Gaertn. var. *villosa* (Jacq.) Cronq. (50) (present)

Woodland muhly - *Muhlenbergia sylvatica* Torr. ex Gray (50) (present)

Woodland nettle - *Laportea canadensis* (L.) Weddell (46) (1879)

Woodland pinedrops - *Pterospora andromedea* Nutt. (50, 155) (1942-present)

Woodland poppy-mallow [Woodland poppy mallow, Woodland poppymallow] - *Callirhoe papaver* (Cav.) Gray (50) (present)

Woodland sage - *Salvia nemorosa* L. (50, 155) (1942-present)

Woodland sedge - *Carex blanda* Dewey (3, 5) (1913-1977)

Woodland spear grass [Woodland spear-grass] - *Poa sylvestris* Gray (94) (1901)

Woodland star - *Lithophragma glabrum* Nutt. (3) (1977)

Woodland strawberry - *Fragaria vesca* L. (4, 50) (1986-present), *Fragaria vesca* L. subsp. *americana* (Porter) Staudt (50) (present)

Woodland sunflower - *Helianthus divaricatus* L. (5, 72, 156) (1907-1923), *Helianthus strumosus* L. (138, 155) (1923-1942)

Woodland villosa - *Angelica sylvestris* L. (155) (1942)

Woodland weedy milkvetch [Woodland weedy milk vetch] - *Astragalus miser* Dougl. var. *hylophilus* (4) (1986)

Woodland-star [Woodland star, Woodlandstar] - *Lithophragma* (Nutt.) Torr. & Gray (1, 50, 155) (1932-present), *Lithophragma parviflorum* (Hook.) Nutt. ex Torr. & Gray (85) (1932)

Wood-lawn agrimony [Woodlawn agrimony] - *Agrimonia pubescens* Wallr. (97) (1937)

Wood-lily [Wood lily] - *Pyrola elliptica* Nutt. (156) (1923), *Trillium erectum* L. (64) (1908)

Wood-mat - *Cynoglossum officinale* L. (156) (1923)

Wood-mint [Wood mint] - *Blephilia hirsuta* (Pursh) Benth. (3, 4, 82, 156) (1923-1986), *Blephilia* Raf. (82) (1930)

Woodmoss - *Dicranum bonjeanii* De Not in Lisa (40) (1928)

Wood-nettle [Wood nettle, Woodnettle] - *Laportea canadensis* (L.) Weddell (3, 4, 5, 63, 72, 78, 85, 92, 93, 95, 97, 131, 156, 157, 158) (1876-1986), *Laportea* Gaud. (1, 155, 156, 158) (1900-1942)

Wood-of-life [Wood of life] - *Guaiacum sanctum* L. (20) (1857)

Woodrip - *Galium odoratum* (L.) Scop. (5) (1913)

Woodroof - *Galium odoratum* (L.) Scop. (107) (1919)

Woodrow [Wood row] - *Marchantia polymorpha* L. (92) (1876)

Wood-rowel [Woodrowel] - *Galium odoratum* (L.) Scop. (5) (1913)

Woodruff - *Asperula* L. (50, 109, 138, 155, 156, 158) (1900-present), *Galium triflorum* Michx. (156) (1923)

Woodruff-weed - *Galium odoratum* (L.) Scop. (156) (1923)

Woodrush [Wood rush] - *Luzula bulbosa* (Wood) Smyth & Smyth (3) (1977), *Luzula* DC. (1, 50, 139, 152, 158) (1912-present), *Luzula multiflora* (Ehrh.) Lej. (85) (1932), *Luzula multiflora* (Ehrh.) Lej. subsp. *multiflora* var. *multiflora* (3) (1977)

Woods bedstraw - *Galium circaezans* Michx. (3, 4) (1977-1986)

Wood's bunchflower - *Melanthium woodii* (J.W. Robbins ex Wood) Bodkin (50) (present)

Woods' corn salad [Wood's corn salad, Woods cornsalad] - *Valerianella radiata* (L.) Dufr. (5, 122, 155) (1913-1942)

Woods draba [Woods draba] - *Draba nemorosa* L. (155) (1942)

Wood's false hellbore - *Melanthium woodii* (J.W. Robbins ex Wood) Bodkin (5, 72, 97) (1907-1937)

Wood's grape fern - *Botrychium matricariifolium* (A. Braun ex Dowell) A. Braun ex Koch (5) (1913)

Woods grass - *Poa alsodes* Gray (87) (1884)

Woods mountain-mint [Woods mountain mint] - *Pycnanthemum verticillatum* (Michx.) Pers. var. *pilosum* (Nutt.) Cooperrider (3) (1977)

Woods' rose [Wood's rose, Woods rose, Wood rose] - *Rosa woodsii* Lindl. (5, 50, 72, 97, 131, 138, 155) (1899-present)

Wood's sedge - *Carex tetanica* Schkuhr (5, 72) (1907-1913)

Woods strawberry - *Fragaria vesca* L. subsp. *americana* (Porter) Staudt (85) (1932)

Woods sunflower - *Helianthus divaricatus* L. (93) (1936)

Wood-sage [Wood sage] - *Teucrium canadense* L. (4, 5, 19, 48, 62, 72, 80, 82, 85, 92, 93, 95, 106, 114, 131, 156) (1840-1986), *Teucrium* L. (1, 4, 167) (1814-1986)

Woodsia - *Woodsia* R. Br. (4, 138, 155) (1923-1986) for Joseph Woods, 1776-1864, English botanist and rose expert

Wood-sore - *Berberis vulgaris* L. (157, 158) (1900-1929)

Wood-sour [Wood-sour] - *Berberis vulgaris* L. (5, 156, 157, 158) (1900-1929)

Woods-sow - *Berberis vulgaris* L. (157, 158) (1900-1929)

Wood-wash - *Genista tinctoria* L. (156) (1923)

Woodwax [Wood wax] - *Genista tinctoria* L. (5, 73) (1892-1913)

Woodwaxen [Wood waxen] - *Genista tinctoria* L. (6, 7, 19, 49, 92, 107) (1828-1919)

Woody aster [Woodyaster] - *Xylorhiza* Nutt. (50) (present)

Woody climber - *Parthenocissus quinquefolia* (L.) Planch. (92, 158) (1876-1900)

Woody gayra - *Gaura suffulta* Engelm. ex Gray (124) (1937) TX

Woody glasswort - *Sarcocornia perennis* (P. Mill.) A.J. Scott (5) (1913)

Woody melic grass [Woody melic-grass] - *Melica californica* Scribn. (94) (1901)

Woody milkvetch - *Astragalus miser* Dougl. var. *hylophilus* (50) (present)

Woody nightshade [Woody night-shade] - *Solanum dulcamara* L. (6, 19, 49, 52, 53, 57, 71, 92, 156, 158, 187) (1818-1923)

Woody rockcress - *Arabis suffrutescens* S. Wats. (155) (1942)

Woody wisteria - *Wisteria frutescens* (L.) Poir. (5) (1913)

Wool flower - *Lachnanthes caroliana* (Lam.) Dandy (86) (1878)

Woolen [Woollen] - *Verbascum thapsus* L. (92, 158) (1876-1900)

Woolen-breeches [Woollen breeches] - *Hydrophyllum appendiculatum* Michx. (107, 156) (1919-1923)

Wool-fruit sedge [Woolfruit sedge] - *Carex lasiocarpa* Ehrh. (155) (1942)

Wool-grass [Wool grass, Woolgrass] - *Scirpus cyperinus* (L.) Kunth (3, 50, 66, 72, 156) (1903–present)

Wool-grass bulrush [Woolgrass bulrush] - *Scirpus cyperinus* (L.) Kunth (155) (1942)

Woolly Asia glory [Woolly Asiaglory] - *Argyreia nervosa* (Burm. f.) Bojer (155) (1942)

Woolly beach-heather [Woolly beachheather] - *Hudsonia tomentosa* Nutt. (50, 155) (1942–present)

Woolly beard - *Saccharum* L. (66) (1903)

Woolly beard grass [Woolly beard-grass, Wooly beard-grass] - *Saccharum alopecuroidum* (L.) Nutt. (5, 66, 163) (1852-1913), *Saccharum ravennae* (L.) L. (45, 163) (1852-1896)

Woolly bearded grass [Wooly bearded grass] - *Saccharum alopecuroidum* (L.) Nutt. (92) (1876)

Woolly beeblossom - *Gaura villosa* Torr. (50) (present)

Woolly bent - *Calamovilfa longifolia* (Hook.) Scribn. (66) (1903)

Woolly betony - *Stachys germanica* L. (138) (1923)

Woolly bird's-nest [Woolly birds-nest] - *Monotropa hypopithys* L. (187) (1818)

Woolly blue violet - *Viola sororia* Willd. (5, 93, 97) (1913-1937)

Woolly brome - *Bromus lanatipes* (Shear) Rydb. (50) (present)

Woolly buckeye - *Aesculus pavia* L. (124, 138, 155) (1923-1942)

Woolly buckthorn - *Sideroxylon lanuginosum* Michx. (5, 97, 122) (1913-1937), *Sideroxylon lanuginosum* Michx. subsp. *oblongifolium* (Nutt.) T.D. Pennington (3, 4) (1977-1986)

Woolly burdock [Woolly burrdock] - *Arctium tomentosum* P. Mill. (5, 50) (1913–present)

Woolly bursage - *Ambrosia grayi* (A. Nels.) Shinners (155) (1942)

Woolly cinquefoil - *Potentilla hippiana* Lehm. (5, 50, 93, 131) (1899–present)

Woolly clethra - *Clethra alnifolia* L. (138) (1923)

Woolly cotton flower [Woolly cottonflower] - *Gossypianthus lanuginosus* (Poir.) Moq. (4, 50) (1986–present)

Woolly croton [Wooly croton] - *Croton capitatus* Michx. (4, 106, 155) (1930-1986), *Croton capitatus* Michx. *lindheimeri* (Engelm. & Gray) Muell. (3, 155) (1942-1977), *Croton capitatus* Michx. var. *capitatus* (3) (1977)

Woolly dalea - *Dalea lanata* Spreng. (3) (1977)

Woolly dropseed [Woolly drop-seed] - *Muhlenbergia andina* (Nutt.) A.S. Hitchc. (94) (1901)

Woolly dutchman's-pipe [Wooly dutchman's pipe] - *Aristolochia tomentosa* Sims. (50) (present)

Woolly elephant's-foot [Woolly elephant's foot, Woolley elephant's-foot, Woolly elephantfoot] - *Elephantopus tomentosus* L. (5, 97, 122, 124, 156) (1913-1937)

Woolly franseria - *Ambrosia grayi* (A. Nels.) Shinners (122) (1937)

Woolly gaertneria - *Ambrosia tomentosa* Nutt. (5, 93) (1913-1936)

Woolly gaura [Wooly guara] - *Gaura villosa* Torr. (5, 97) (1913-1937)

Woolly goldenrod [Woolly golden-rod] - *Solidago nemoralis* Aiton (19) (1840)

Woolly grass [Woollygrass, Wooly grass] - *Achnatherum* Beauv. (92) (1876), *Erioneuron* Nash. (50) (present)

Woolly gromwell - *Lithospermum ruderale* Dougl. ex Lehm. (5, 93) (1913-1936)

Woolly groundsel - *Packera cana* (Hook.) W.A. Weber & A. Löve (50, 155) (1942–present)

Woolly hawthorn - *Crataegus lanuginosa* Sarg. (4, 50) (1986–present)

Woolly herb - *Artemisia ludoviciana* Nutt. subsp. *candicans* (Rydb.) Keck (108) (1878)

Woolly hudsonia - *Hudsonia tomentosa* Nutt. (5, 158) (1900-1913)

Woolly hymenopappus - *Hymenopappus tenuifolius* Pursh (131) (1899)

Woolly Indian wheat [Woolly Indianwheat] - *Plantago patagonica* Jacq. (155) (1942)

Woolly knotweed [Woolly knot weed] - *Eriogonum* Michx. (167) (1814)

Woolly lip fern [Woolly lip-fern, Woolly lipfern] - *Cheilanthes lanosa* (Michx.) D.C.Eat. (4) (1986), *Cheilanthes tomentosa* Link. (4, 5, 50, 97, 122, 138, 155) (1913–present)

Woolly loco - *Astragalus mollissimus* Torr (3, 125, 155) (1930-1977)

Woolly locoweed [Woolly loco-weed, Woolly loco weed] - *Astragalus mollissimus* Torr (5, 50, 71, 92, 93, 157, 158) (1898–present)

Woolly lupine - *Lupinus sericeus* Pursh (131) (1899)

Woolly manzanita - *Arctostaphylos tomentosa* (Pursh) Lindl. (138, 155) (1931-1942)

Woolly milfoil - *Achillea millefolium* L. (165) (1768)

Woolly milkvetch [Woolly milk vetch] - *Astragalus canadensis* L. (19, 42) (1814-1840)

Woolly milkweed [Wooly milkweed] - *Asclepias lanuginosa* Nutt. (3, 4, 85, 93, 131) (1899-1986)

Woolly mint - *Mentha* ×*villosa* Huds. [*spicata* × *suaveolens*] (5) (1913)

Woolly morning-glory - *Argyreia nervosa* (Burm. f.) Bojer (109) (1949)

Woolly painted-cup - *Castilleja foliolosa* Hook. & Arn. (138) (1923)

Woolly panic grass [Woolly panic-grass] - *Dichanthelium acuminatum* (Sw.) Gould & C.A. Clark var. *fasciculatum* (Torr.) Freckmann (143) (1852-1936), *Dichanthelium scabriusculum* (Ell.) Gould & C.A. Clark (163) (1852)

Woolly panicum - *Dichanthelium acuminatum* (Sw.) Gould & C.A. Clark var. *fasciculatum* (Torr.) Freckmann (5) (1913), *Dichanthelium scabriusculum* (Ell.) Gould & C.A. Clark (5, 155) (1913-1942)

Woolly paper flower [Woolly paperflower] - *Psilostrophe tagetina* (Nutt.) Greene (50, 155) (1942–present)

Woolly parosela - *Dalea lanata* Spreng. (5, 97) (1913-1937)

Woolly pawpaw - *Asimina incana* (W. Bartram) Exell (155) (1942)

Woolly pignut - *Carya texana* Buckl. (5, 97) (1913-1937)

Woolly pink - *Agrostemma githago* L. (156) (1923)

Woolly pipevine [Woolly pipe vine, Woolly pipe-vine] - *Aristolochia tomentosa* Sims. (4, 5, 97, 122, 124) (1913-1986)

Woolly plantain - *Plantago patagonica* Jacq. (50, 85) (1932–present)

Woolly poverty grass [Woolly poverty-grass] - *Aristida lanosa* Muhl. ex Elliott (94) (1901)

Woolly prairie clover - *Dalea lanata* Spreng. (50) (present)

Woolly puccoon - *Lithospermum caroliniense* (Walt. ex J.F. Gmel.) MacM. (124) (1937)

Woolly pussytoes - *Antennaria lanata* (Hook.) Greene (155) (1942)

Woolly rabbitbrush [Woolly rabbit brush] - *Ericameria nauseosa* (Pallas ex Pursh) Nesom & Baird subsp. *nauseosa* var. *nauseosa* (85) (1932)

Woolly ragweed - *Packera tomentosa* (Michx.) C. Jeffrey (5, 122, 156) (1913-1937)

Woolly rose-mallow [Woolly rosemallow] - *Hibiscus moscheutos* L. subsp. *lasiocarpos* (Cav.) O. J. Blanchard (155) (1942)

Woolly rosette grass - *Dichanthelium scabriusculum* (Ell.) Gould & C.A. Clark (50) (present)

Woolly sage - *Artemisia ludoviciana* Nutt. (156) (1923)

Woolly sand-verbena [Woolly sandverbena] - *Abronia villosa* S. Wats. (138) (1923)

Woolly sedge [Wooly sedge] - *Carex lasiocarpa* Ehrh. var. *americana* Fern. (3, 5, 72, 139) (1907-1977), *Carex pellita* Muhl ex Willd. (3, 5, 50, 155) (1913–present)

Woolly senna - *Senna hirsuta* (L.) Irwin & Barneby var. *hirsuta* (138) (1923)

Woolly smartweed - *Polygonum lapathifolium* L. (155) (1942)

Woolly soft grass [Wooly soft grass] - *Holcus lanatus* L. (5) (1913)

Woolly stemless actinea - *Tetraneuris acaulis* var. *caespitosa* A.Nelson (155) (1942)

Woolly sunflower - *Helianthus tuberosus* L. (5, 155) (1913-1942)

Woolly sweet cicely [Wooly sweet cicely] - *Osmorhiza claytonii* (Michx.) C.B. Clarke (5, 85, 72, 131, 156, 158) (1899-1936)

Woolly thistle - *Cirsium canescens* Nutt. (80, 82) (1913-1930)

Woolly thorn - *Crataegus lanuginosa* Sarg. (5) (1913)

Woolly tidestromia - *Tidestromia lanuginosa* (Nutt.) Standl. (3, 50, 155) (1942–present)

Woolly triple-awn grass [Woolly triple-awned grass] - *Aristida lanosa* Muhl. ex Elliott (5, 119, 163) (1852-1938)

Woolly verbena - *Verbena stricta* Vent. (155) (1942)

Woolly viburnum [Wooly viburnum] - *Viburnum buddleifolium* C. Wright (138) (1923)

Woolly white hymenopappus [Wooly white hymenopappus] - *Hymenopappus tenuifolius* Pursh (5, 93, 97, 121, 122) (1913-1970)

Woolly yarrow - *Achillea millefolium* L. (5, 93, 97, 109, 138, 155) (1913-1949)

Woolly yellow hymenopappus - *Hymenopappus flavescens* Gray (5, 97) (1913-1937)

Woolly-breeches - *Amsinckia lycopsoides* Lehm. (106) (1930)

Woolly-bucket bumelia [Woollybucket bumelia] - *Sideroxylon lanuginosum* Michx. (155) (1942)

Woolly-but [Woolybut] - *Eucalyptus* L'Hér. (92) (1876)

Woolly-cup buckwheat [Woolycup buckwheat] - *Eriogonum lachnogynum* Torr. (50) (present)

Woolly-flower panic [Wooly-flowered panic] - *Panicum urvilleanum* Kunth (94) (1901)

Woolly-foot [Woolly foot] - *Bouteloua eriopoda* (Torr.) Torr. (152, 163) (1852-1912) NM

Woolly-fruit sedge [Woollyfruit sedge, Woolly-fruited sedge] - *Carex lasiocarpa* Ehrh. (50) (present), *Carex pellita* Muhl ex Willd. (66) (1903)

Woolly-joint grama [Woolly-jointed grama, Woolly jointed grama] - *Bouteloua eriopoda* (Torr.) Torr. (94, 151) (1896-1901)

Woolly-leaf anemone [Woolly-leaved anemone] - *Pulsatilla patens* (L.) Mill. subsp. *multifida* (Pritz.) Zamels (165) (1807)

Woolly-leaf bumelia [Wooly leaved bumelia] - *Sideroxylon lanuginosum* Michx. (20) (1857)

Woolly-leaf bur ragweed [Woollyleaf burr ragweed] - *Ambrosia grayi* (A. Nels.) Shinners (50) (present)

Woolly-leaf cornus [Woolly-leaved cornus] - *Cornus sericea* L. subsp. *occidentalis* (Torr. & Gray) Fosberg (20) (1857)

Woolly-leaf loco [Woollyleaf loco] - *Astragalus asymmetricus* E. Sheld. (155) (1942)

Woolly-pod milkvetch [Woollypod milkvetch] - *Astragalus purshii* Dougl. ex Hook. (50) (present)

Woolly-pod milkweed [Woollypod milkweed] - *Asclepias eriocarpa* Benth. (155) (1942)

Woolly-pod vetch [Woollypod vetch] - *Vicia villosa* Roth (4) (1986), *Vicia villosa* Roth subsp. *varia* (Host) Corb. (3, 155) (1942–1977)

Woolly-seed muhlenbergia [Wooly-seeded muhlenbergia] - *Muhlenbergia andina* (Nutt.) A.S. Hitchc. (88) (1885), *Muhlenbergia frondosa* (Poir.) Fern. (87) (1884)

Woolly-sheaf threeawn [Woollysheaf threeawn] - *Aristida lanosa*

Muhl. ex Elliott (50) (present)

Woolly-spike grama [Woolly-spiked grama] - *Bouteloua chondrosioides* (Kunth) Benth. ex S. Wats. (163) (1852)

Woolmat [Wool-mat] - *Cynoglossum* L. (75) (1894), *Cynoglossum officinale* L. (62) (1912)

Wool-pod violet [Woolpod violet] - *Viola pubescens* Aiton var. *pubescens* (155) (1942)

Wooton's lip-fern - *Cheilanthes wootonii* Maxon (97) (1937)

Wooton's loco [Wooton loco] - *Astragalus allochrous* Gray var. *playanus* Isely (155) (1942)

Wŏr-co-bith (Comanche Shoshonee) - *Pinus* L. (132) (1855)

Worga (Telinga) - *Panicum miliaceum* L. (110) (1886)

World's Fair plant - *Kochia scoparia* (L.) Schrad. (156) (1923)

World's-wonder [World's wonder] - *Mirabilis jalapa* L. (92) (1876), *Saponaria officinalis* L. (5, 64, 76, 156, 157, 158) (1896-1923) Eastern MA, no longer in use by 1923

Worm goosefoot [Worm goose-foot] - *Chenopodium ambrosioides* L. var. *ambrosioides* (186) (1814)

Worm moss - *Alsidium helminthochorton* (Schwendimann) Kützing (92) (1876) IN Kansas

Worm-bark - *Andira inermis* (W. Wright) Kunth ex DC. (92) (1876)

Worm-grass [Wormgrass, Worm grass] - *Sedum album* L. (92) (1876), *Spigelia* L. (2) (1895), *Spigelia marilandica* (L.) L. (5, 6, 14, 49, 53, 64, 186) (1814-1923)

Wormit - *Artemisia absinthium* L. (157, 158) (1900-1929)

Worm-leaf sedum [Wormleaf sedum] - *Sedum lanceolatum* Torr. (155) (1942)

Wormseed [Worm-seed, Worm seed] - *Chenopodium ambrosioides* L. (21, 49, 122) (1893-1937), *Chenopodium ambrosioides* L. var. *ambrosioides* (6, 7, 19, 41, 48, 53, 58, 62, 92, 156, 158, 186) (1770-1923), *Erysimum cheiranthoides* L. (5) (1913), *Erysimum* L. (184) (1793)

Wormseed goosefoot - *Chenopodium ambrosioides* L. (155) (1942), *Chenopodium ambrosioides* L. var. *ambrosioides* (7) (1828)

Wormseed mustard [Worm-seed mustard] - *Erysimum cheiranthoides* L. (15, 40, 63, 72, 85, 93, 95, 156, 157, 158) (1895-1936)

Wormseed plant - *Chenopodium ambrosioides* L. var. *ambrosioides* (92) (1876)

Wormseed wallflower - *Erysimum cheiranthoides* L. (3, 4, 50) (1977–present)

Wormskiold's speedwell - *Veronica wormskjoldii* Roemer & J.A. Schultes (5) (1913)

Wormweed [Worm weed, Worm-weed] - *Artemisia* L. (93) (1936), *Cleome viscosa* L. (92) (1876), *Polanisia dodecandra* (L.) DC. subsp. *dodecandra* (5, 7, 156, 157, 158) (1828-1929), *Solidago odora* Aiton (92) (1876), *Spigelia marilandica* (L.) L. (64, 156) (1908-1923)

Wormwood [Wormewood, Worm-wood] - *Artemisia absinthium* L. (3, 4, 6, 19, 40, 46, 49, 53, 55, 57, 58, 61, 92, 107, 157, 158, 179, 184) (1671–1986) accidentally introduced into US by 1671, *Artemisia biennis* Willd. (80) (1913), *Artemisia dracunculus* L. (124) (1937), *Artemisia filifolia* Torr. (103, 113) (1870–1890), *Artemisia* L. (1, 2, 4, 10, 34, 38, 63, 138, 155, 158) (1820–1986) from Old World name, *Artemisia ludoviciana* Nutt. (48) (1882), *Artemisia ludoviciana* Nutt. subsp. *ludoviciana* (21) (1893), *Artemisia ludoviciana* Nutt. subsp. *mexicana* (Willd. ex Spreng.) Keck (124) (1937), *Artemisia vulgaris* L. (156) (1923), *Chenopodium ambrosioides* L. var. *ambrosioides* (7) (1828)

Wormwood of the voyageurs - *Purshia tridentata* (Pursh) DC. (33) (1827)

Wormwood sage - *Artemisia frigida* Willd. (5, 131, 156, 157, 158) (1899-1931)

Wormwood senna - *Senna artemisioides* (Gaud. ex DC.) Randell (138) (1923)

Wormwood-leaf hogweed [Wormwood-leaved hogweed] - *Ambrosia artemisiifolia* L. (187) (1818)

Wortelförmige Winterbeer (German) - *Ilex verticillata* (L.) Gray

(186) (1814)

Worthless panic - *Dichanthelium depauperatum* (Muhl.) Gould (66, 90) (1885-1903)

Wots - *Avena sativa* L. (158) (1900)

Wound rocket - *Barbarea vulgaris* W.T. Aiton (5, 156, 157) (1913–1929)

Woundweed [Wound weed] - *Plantago major* L. (62) (1912) IN, Old English name

Woundwort [Wound-wort] - *Anthyllis vulneraria* L. (7, 92, 109, 155) (1828-1949), *Stachys* L. (10, 106, 158, 184) (1793-1930), *Stachys palustris* L. (82, 107, 156) (1919-1930)

Wrack [Wracks] - *Fucus* L. (7) (1828), *Zostera marina* L. (5) (1913)

Wreath aster - *Symphyotrichum ericoides* (L.) Nesom var. *ericoides* (138) (1923)

Wreath goldenrod [Wreath golden-rod] - *Solidago caesia* L. (5, 138, 156) (1913-1923)

Wren's-flower [Wren's flower] - *Geranium robertianum* L. (5, 156, 157, 158) (1900-1929)

Wretweed [Wret-weed] - *Chelidonium majus* L. (158) (1900)

Wright's acacia [Wright acacia] - *Acacia greggii* Gray (155) (1942)

Wright's ammannia - *Ammannia auriculata* Willd. (5, 97) (1913-1937)

Wright's anoda [Wrights anoda] - *Anoda lanceolata* Hook. & Arn. (155) (1942)

Wright's baccharis - *Baccharis wrightii* Gray (5, 50, 97, 122) (1913–present)

Wright's broom-sedge [Wright's broom sedge] - *Bothriochloa wrightii* (Hack.) Henr. (94) (1901)

Wright's cliff-brake [Wright's cliffbrake, Wright's cliff brake] - *Pellaea wrightiana* Hook. (4, 50) (1986–present)

Wright's cudweed - *Pseudognaphalium canescens* (DC.) W.A. Weber subsp. *canescens* (50) (present)

Wright's peach-leaf willow [Wright peachleaf willow] - *Salix amygdaloides* Anderss. (155) (1942)

Wright's plantain [Wright plantain] - *Plantago wrightiana* Dcne. (4, 97, 155) (1937–present)

Wright's sagebrush [Wrights sagebrush] - *Artemisia carruthii* Wood ex Carruth. (155) (1942)

Wright's skullcap - *Scutellaria wrightii* Gray (50, 86) (1878–present)

Wright's thelypody [Wright thelopody] - *Thelypodium wrightii* Gray (50, 155) (1942–present)

Wright's threeawn [Wright threeawn] - *Aristida purpurea* Nutt. var. *wrightii* (Nash) Allred (3, 50, 155) (1942–present)

Wright's three-awn grass [Wright's three-awned grass] - *Aristida purpurea* Nutt. var. *wrightii* (Nash) Allred (5) (1913)

Wright's triple-awn grass [Wright's triple-awned grass] - *Aristida purpurea* Nutt. var. *wrightii* (Nash) Allred (99, 119, 163) (1852-1938)

Wright's verbena [Wrights verbena] - *Glandularia bipinnatifida* (Nutt.) Nutt. var. *bipinnatifida* (155) (1942)

Wrinkled beak-rush [Wrinkled beak rush] - *Rhynchospora glomerata* (L.) Vahl (66) (1903)

Wrinkled goldenrod [Wrinkled golden-rod] - *Solidago rugosa* Mill. (19, 138) (1840-1923)

Wrinkled joint grass [Wrinkled joint-grass] - *Coelorachis rugosa* (Nutt.) Nash (5) (1913)

Wrinkled joint-tail grass [Wrinkled jointtail grass] - *Coelorachis rugosa* (Nutt.) Nash (50) (present)

Wrinkle-flower paspalum [Wrinkle-flowered paspalum] - *Paspalum plicatulum* Michx. (94) (1901)

Wrinkle-leaf goldenrod [Wrinkled-leaved goldenrod] - *Solidago rugosa* Mill. (possibly) (5, 97, 187) (1818-1937)

Wrinkle-leaf willow [Wrinkled-leaf willow] - *Salix reticulata* L. (5, 156) (1913-1923)

Wrinkle-seed fameflower [Wrinkleseed fameflower] - *Talinum rugospermum* Holzinger (155) (1942)

Wuchah'deshka (Dakota) - *Ribes missouriense* Nutt. (37) (1919)

Wuchipoquameneash - *Vaccinium oxycoccos* L. (46) (1879)

Wuchipoquameneash (Narragansett) - *Viburnum opulus* L. (107) (1919)

Wuckopy - *Tilia americana* L. var. *americana* (92) (1876)

Wuckopy (Algic tribes) - *Tilia* L. (7) (1828)

Wunderbaum (German) - *Ricinus communis* L. (110) (1886)

Wundkraut (German) - *Veronica serpyllifolia* L. (158) (1900)

Wurmdryvend ganzevoet - *Chenopodium ambrosioides* L. var. *ambrosioides* (186) (1814)

Wurmfarn (German) - *Dryopteris filix-mas* (L.) Schott (158) (1900)

Wurmkraut (German) - *Tanacetum vulgare* L. (158) (1900)

Wurmmelde [Wurm-melde, Wurmmelte] - *Chenopodium ambrosioides* L. var. *ambrosioides* (186) (1814)

Wurmsaamen Gansefuss (German) - *Chenopodium ambrosioides* L. var. *ambrosioides* (6, 7) (1828-1892)

Wurmsamen (German) - *Chenopodium ambrosioides* L. var. *ambrosioides* (186) (1814)

Wurmtod (German) - *Artemisia absinthium* L. (158) (1900)

Wurmtreibender Gänsfuss (German) - *Chenopodium ambrosioides* L. var. *ambrosioides* (186) (1814)

Wurrus - *Mallotus philippensis* (Lam.) Muell.-Arg. (92) (1876)

Wussoquat (Narragansett) - *Juglans cinerea* L. (46, 107) (1879)

Wuttahimneash (New England natives) - *Fragaria virginiana* Duchesne (46, 107) (1879-1919) New England natives

Wuwu (Winnebago) - *Viburnum lentago* L. (37) (1919)

Wych elm - *Ulmus glabra* Huds. (82, 92, 109) (1876-1949)

Wyldynge - *Malus sylvestris* Mill. (179) (1526)

Wymote - *Althaea officinalis* L. (92, 156, 158, 184) (1793-1923) no longer in use by 1923

Wyoming besseya - *Besseya wyomingensis* (A. Nels.) Rydb. (50) (present)

Wyoming big sagebrush - *Artemisia tridentata* Nutt. subsp. *wyomingensis* Beetle & Young (50) (present)

Wyoming flax - *Linum compactum* A. Nels. (50) (present)

Wyoming Indian paintbrush - *Castilleja linariifolia* Benth. (50) (present)

Wyoming larkspur - *Delphinium geyeri* Greene (71) (1898)

Wyoming locoweed - *Oxytropis nana* Nutt. (50) (present)

Wyoming paintbrush - *Castilleja linariifolia* Benth. (4) (1986)

Wyoming painted-cup [Wyoming paintedcup] - *Castilleja linariifolia* Benth. (155) (1942)

Wyoming thistle - *Cirsium pulcherrimum* (Rydb.) K. Schum. (50) (present)

Wyoming water hemlock [Wyoming water-hemlock] - *Cicuta maculata* L. var. *angustifolia* Hook. (157) (1929)

Wythy - *Salix* L. (158) (1900)

Wytmynt - *Mentha arvensis* L. (179) (1526)

Wy'-wy (Pima) - *Dipsacus fullonum* L. (132) (1855)

X

Xalxocotl (Mexico) - *Psidium guajava* L. (110) (1886)

Xanthoxyle frene (French) - *Zanthoxylum americanum* Mill. (7) (1828)

Xanthoxylon tree - *Zanthoxylum clava-herculis* L. (177) (1762)

Xanthoxylum - *Zanthoxylum americanum* Mill. (54) (1905)

Xaŋte (Lakota) - *Juniperus* L. (121) (1918–1970)

Xaŋte čaŋxloǧaŋ (Lakota, cedar wood) - *Achillea millefolium* L. (121) (1918?–1970?)

Ximenia - *Lyonia ferruginea* (Walt.) Nutt. (182) (1791)

Ximenie Americaine (French) - *Ximenia americana* L. (20, 183) (~1756–1857)

Xonacatl (Mexico) - *Allium cepa* L. (110) (1813)

Xoŋdse (Osage) - *Juniperus* L. (121) (1918–1970)

Xylon - *Gossypium herbaceum* L. (178) (1526)

Xylorrhiza - *Xylorhiza* Nutt. (158) (1900)

Xylosteum - *Lonicera xylosteum* L. (174) (1753)

Xylosteum campaniflorum.

Xylosteum, *Lonicera xylosteum* L. (as *Xylosteon campaniflorum* Lodd.)
(G. Cooke, 1827)

Y

Ya'chi (Kiwomi Keres) - *Zea mays* L. (132) (1855)

Yaits - *Avena sativa* L. (158) (1900)

Yam [Yams] - *Dioscorea alata* L. (41) (1770), *Dioscorea* L. (1, 50, 92, 93, 109, 138, 155, 158, 167) (1814–present) means "to eat" in several dialects of Guinea (110), *Dioscorea villosa* L. (possibly) (110) (1886)

Yam root - *Dioscorea* L. (10) (1818-1828), *Dioscorea villosa* L. (19) (1840)

Yam-leaf clematis [Yamleaf clematis] - *Clematis terniflora* DC. (138) (1923)

Yamnumnugapi (Dakota, to crunch) - *Celtis occidentalis* L. (37) (1919)

Yamp - *Atenia* Hook. & Arn. (1) (1932), *Perideridia gairdneri* (Hook. & Arn.) Mathias (158) (1900), *Perideridia gairdneri* (Hook. & Arn.) Mathias subsp. *gairdneri* (101) (1905)

Yámpa (Shoshone) - *Perideridia gairdneri* (Hook. & Arn.) Mathias (35) (1806)

Yampah (Shoshone) - *Anethum graveolens* L. (possibly) (103) (1870)

Yampah [Yampa] - *Anethum graveolens* L. (possibly) (28) (1850), *Perideridia gairdneri* (Hook. & Arn.) Mathias (155) (1942), *Perideridia* Reichnb. (50) (present)

Yampee - *Dioscorea trifida* L. f. (109) (1949)

Yampeh (Snake and Shoshoni Indians) - *Lomatium graveolens* (S. Watson) Dorn & R.L. Hartm. (107) (1919)

Yankapin - *Nelumbo lutea* Willd. (106, 156, 157, 158) (1900-1930)

Yankapin bonnets - *Nelumbo lutea* Willd. (156) (1923)

Yankee blackberry - *Rubus frondosus* Bigelow (50, 155) (1942–present)

Yankee corn - *Zea mays* L. subsp. *mays* (109, 119) (1938-1949)

Yankee-weed [Yankee weed] - *Eupatorium compositifolium* Walt. (124) (1937) TX

Yânû Unihye stï (Cherokee) - *Vitis vulpina* L. (102) (1886)

Ya'-o-ni (Kiwomi Keres) - *Zea mays* L. (132) (1855)

Yapon - *Ilex cassine* L. (8, 189) (1767-1785)

Yapoon - *Ilex cassine* L. (5) (1913)

Yaqui loco - *Astragalus giganteus* S. Watson (155) (1942)

Yaqui tobacco - *Nicotiana tabacum* L. (6) (1892)

Yard dock - *Rumex longifolius* DC. (4) (1986)

Yard grass [Yard-grass, Yardgrass] - *Dactyloctenium aegyptium* (L.) Willd. (5) (1913), *Eleusine* Gaertn. (93) (1936), *Eleusine indica* (L.) Gaertn. (5, 87, 88, 92, 94, 99, 119, 134, 140, 163) (1852-1944)

Yard rush - *Juncus tenuis* Willd. (5, 62, 156) (1912-1923)

Yardgrass - *Polygonum aviculare* L. (85) (1932) SD

Yarr - *Spergula arvensis* L. (5, 156, 158) (1900-1923) no longer in use by 1923

Yarrow [Yarowe] - *Achillea* L. (1, 2, 4, 42, 50, 93, 109, 125, 138, 155, 156, 158, 167, 184) (1793–present), *Achillea millefolium* L. (7, 19, 37, 40, 45, 46, 49, 52, 53, 57, 58, 61, 62, 72, 80, 82, 92, 93, 95, 97, 107, 122, 124, 127, 131, 148, 157, 158, 179, 187) (1526-1939), *Achillea millefolium* L. (3, 85, 146) (1932-1977)

Yarrow gilia - *Gilia achilleifolia* Benth. (138) (1923)

Yarroway - *Achillea millefolium* L. (158) (1900)

Yaskobgedek (Chippewa) - *Pyrola elliptica* Nutt. (105) (1932)

Yaskopteg (Chippewa) - *Chimaphila umbellata* (L.) Bart. (105) (1932)

Yasmyn - *Jasminum officinale* L. (92) (1876)

Yate tree [Yate-tree] - *Eucalyptus cornuta* Labill. (138) (1923)

Yaupon - *Ilex ambigua* (Michx.) Torr. (106) (1930), *Ilex cassine* L. (2, 5, 38, 46, 107, 156) (1820-9123), *Ilex vomitoria* Aiton (5, 15, 92, 97, 109, 122, 124, 138, 156) (1895-1949)

Yawroot [Yaw root, Yaw-root] - *Stillingia sylvatica* Garden ex L. (5, 6, 7, 49, 53, 55, 58, 92, 156, 158) (1828-1923)

Yeara - *Toxicodendron diversilobum* (Torr. & Gray) Greene (71, 76) (1896-1898) CA

Yeard - *Toxicodendron diversilobum* (Torr. & Gray) Greene (15) (1895)

Yeddo euonymus - *Euonymus hamiltonianus* Wall subsp. *sieboldianus* (Blume) Hara (138) (1923)

Yeddo stephanandra - *Stephanandra incisa* (Thunb.) Zabel (138) (1923)

Yellow - *Zanthoxylum americanum* Mill. (7) (1828)

Yellow adder's-tongue [Yellow adder's tongue] - *Erythronium americanum* Ker. (5, 7, 72, 92, 93, 97, 156, 157) (1828-1937)

Yellow alfalfa - *Medicago sativa* L. subsp. *falcata* (L.) Arcang. (3, 50, 85) (1932–present)

Yellow alyssum - *Alyssum alyssoides* (L.) L. (5, 158) (1900-1913)

Yellow archangel [Yellow archangell] - *Lamiastrum galeobdolon* (L.) Ehrend. & Polatschek (92, 178) (1526-1876)

Yellow arctic whitlow-grass [Yellow arctic whitlow grass] - *Draba nivalis* Lilj. (5) (1913)

Yellow ash - *Fraxinus pennsylvanica* Marsh. (77) (1898)

Yellow asphodel - *Narthecium americanum* Ker-Gawl. (50) (present)

Yellow avalanche lily - *Erythronium grandiflorum* Pursh (50) (present)

Yellow avens - *Geum aleppicum* Jacq. (3, 4, 5, 50, 72, 85, 93, 131, 155, 156, 158) (1899–present)

Yellow bachelor's-buttons [Yellow batchelor's button, Yellow bachelor's buttons] - *Polygala lutea* L. (2, 86, 156) (1878-1923) Southern US, *Ranunculus acris* L. (158) (1900)

Yellow balm - *Lysimachia quadrifolia* L. (5, 7, 156, 158) (1828-1923)

Yellow balsam - *Impatiens noli-tangere* L. (92) (1876)

Yellow bamboo - *Phyllostachys aurea* Carr. ex A.& C. Rivière (109) (1949)

Yellow barberry - *Mahonia fremontii* (Torr.) Fedde (106) (1930)

Yellow bartonia - *Bartonia virginica* (L.) Britton, Sterns & Poggenb. (5, 156) (1913-1923)

Yellow basswood - *Tilia americana* L. (156, 157, 158) (1900-1929)

Yellow bastard daffodil - *Erythronium americanum* Ker. (46) (1671)

Yellow bear's-foot [Yellow bears-foot] - *Smallanthus uvedalius* (L.) Mackenzie ex Small (5, 156, 158) (1900-1923)

Yellow bedstraw - *Galium verum* L. (3, 4, 19, 41, 49, 85, 92, 107, 109, 138, 155, 156, 158) (1770-1986)

Yellow beet [Yellow beete] - *Beta vulgaris* L. (178) (1526)

Yellow bennet - *Geum aleppicum* Jacq. (156, 158) (1900-1923)

Yellow birch - *Betula alleghaniensis* Britt. var. *alleghaniensis* (1, 2, 5, 19, 20, 42, 109, 135, 137, 138, 156) (1814-1949)

Yellow birds-nest [Yellow bird's nest] - *Monotropa hypopithys* L. (187) (1818)

Yellow bluestem - *Bothriochloa ischaemum* (L.) Keng var. *songarica* (Rupr. ex Fisch. & C.A. Mey.) Celarier & Harlan (50) (present)

Yellow bristle grass [Yellow bristle-grass] - *Pennisetum glaucum* (L.) R. Br. (143) (1936)

Yellow bristly foxtail - *Pennisetum glaucum* (L.) R. Br. (5) (1913)

Yellow broom - *Baptisia tinctoria* (L.) R. Br. ex Aiton f. (5, 6, 7, 64, 92) (1828-1913)

Yellow broomrape [Yellow broom rape] - *Orobanche fasciculata* Nutt. (85) (1932)

Yellow buckeye - *Aesculus flava* Aiton (2, 20, 109, 138, 155, 156) (1857-1949)

Yellow buckthorn - *Frangula caroliniana* (Walt.) Gray (106, 156) (1923-1930)

Yellow bunch gentian - *Gentianella quinquefolia* (L.) Small subsp. *quinquefolia* (7) (1828)

Yellow butterwort - *Pinguicula lutea* Walt. (86) (1878)

Yellow camomile [Yellow chamomile] - *Anthemis* L. (1) (1932), *Anthemis tinctoria* L. (3, 4, 5, 138, 156) (1913-1986)

Yellow cancer-root [Yellow cancer root] - *Orobanche fasciculata* Nutt. (5, 131, 156, 157, 158) (1899-1929)

Yellow cedar - *Chamaecyparis nootkatensis* (D. Don) Spach (75) (1894) AK, *Thuja occidentalis* L. (49, 53) (1922)

Yellow centaurium - *Centaurea solstitialis* L. (155) (1942)

Yellow chestnut oak - *Quercus muehlenbergii* Engelm. (4, 5, 156, 157, 158) (1900-1986)

Yellow cleavers - *Galium verum* L. (92, 156, 158) (1876-1923)

Yellow cleome - *Cleome lutea* Hook. (4, 5, 93) (1913-1986)

Yellow clintonia - *Clintonia borealis* (Ait.) Raf. (5) (1913)

Yellow clover - *Polygala lutea* L. (156) (1923), *Stylosanthes biflora* (L.) Britton, Sterns & Poggenb. (174, 177) (1753-1762), *Trifolium aureum* Pollich (5, 63, 72, 80, 156) (1899-1923), *Trifolium campestre* Schreber. (19, 80) (1840-1913), *Trifolium dubium* Sibth. (158) (1900)

Yellow cock's-comb [Yellow cock's comb, Yellow coxscomb] - *Rhinanthus minor* L. subsp. *minor* (5, 19, 156) (1840-1923)

Yellow colic-root - *Aletris aurea* Walt. (97) (1937) OK

Yellow colpodium - *Arctophila fulva* (Trin.) Rupr. ex Anderss. (94) (1901)

Yellow columbine - *Aquilegia flavescens* S. Wats. (155) (1942)

Yellow coneflower - *Tetragonotheca* L. (122) (1937) TX

Yellow coralroot [Yellow coral root, Yellow coral-root] - *Corallorrhiza striata* Lindl. var. *striata* (5, 93, 157) (1900-1936), *Corallorrhiza trifida* Chat. (50) (present)

Yellow corydalis - *Corydalis flavula* (Raf.) DC. (5, 156) (1913-1923), *Pseudofumaria lutea* (L.) Borkh. (138) (1923)

Yellow cosmos - *Cosmos sulphureus* Cav. (109, 138) (1923-1949)

Yellow cottonwood - *Populus deltoides* Bartr. ex Marsh. (5, 156, 158) (1900-1923), *Populus deltoides* Bartr. ex Marsh. subsp. *monilifera* (Aiton) Eckenwalder (130) (1895)

Yellow creeping starwort of Virginia - *Helianthus strumosus* L. (181) (~1678)

Yellow cress - *Barbarea* Aiton f. (93) (1936), *Barbarea vulgaris* W.T. Aiton (5, 156) (1913-1923), *Ranunculus acris* L. (157, 158) (1900-1929)

Yellow cucumber magnolia - *Magnolia acuminata* (L.) L. (2) (1895)

Yellow cucumber tree [Yellow cucumbertree] - *Magnolia acuminata* (L.) L. (138) (1923)

Yellow currants - *Ribes aureum* Pursh (35) (1806)

Yellow cut-leaf mignonette [Yellow cut-leaved mignonette] - *Reseda lutea* L. (5) (1913)

Yellow cyperus - *Cyperus flavescens* L. (5, 72, 156) (1907-1923), *Cyperus iria* L. (5) (1913)

Yellow daisy - *Ranunculus acris* L. (79) (1891) Northeast US

Yellow daylily [Yellow day-lily] - *Hemerocallis lilioasphodelus* L. (19, 50, 156) (1840–present)

Yellow deal - *Pinus sylvestris* L. (20) (1857)

Yellow dock - *Rumex crispus* L. (5, 6, 40, 48, 49, 52, 53, 57, 58, 61, 62, 64, 69, 80, 92, 97, 156, 157, 158) (1869-1987)

Yellow dog-fennel - *Dyssodia papposa* (Vent.) A.S. Hitchc. (62) (1912)

Yellow dogtooth-violet [Yellow dogtooth violet, Yellow dog-tooth violet] - *Erythronium americanum* Ker. (2, 86) (1878-1895)

Yellow dotted hawthorn - *Crataegus punctata* Jacq. (155) (1942)

Yellow downy lady's-slipper [Yellow downy lady's slipper] - *Cypripedium parviflorum* Salisb. (93) (1936)

Yellow dwarf-sedge [Yellow dwarf sedge] - *Cyperus flavescens* L. (66) (1903)

Yellow eriogonum - *Eriogonum flavum* Nutt. (5, 93, 131, 155) (1899-1942)

Yellow erythronium - *Erythronium americanum* Ker. (9, 92) (1873-1876)

Yellow European lady's-slipper [Yellow European ladyslipper] - *Cypripedium parviflorum* Salisb. var. *pubescens* (Willd.) Knight (155) (1942)

Yellow evening-primrose [Yellow eveningprimrose, Yellow evening primrose] - *Calylophus serrulatus* (Nutt.) Raven (3) (1977), *Oenothera flava* (A. Nels.) Garrett (50, 155) (1942–present)

Yellow fairybells - *Disporum lanuginosum* (Michx.) Nichols (50) (present)

Yellow false garlic [Yellow falsegarlic] - *Nothoscordum bivalve* (L.) Britt. (5, 93, 97, 155) (1913-1942)

Yellow false indigo - *Baptisia bracteata* Muhl. ex Ell. (5) (1913)

Yellow false jessamine - *Gelsemium sempervirens* (L.) J. St.-Hil. (156) (1923)

Yellow false mallow - *Malvastrum hispidum* (Pursh) Hochr. (5, 72, 97, 156) (1907-1937)

Yellow false oat - *Trisetum flavescens* (L.) Beauv. (5, 68) (1913)

Yellow fawn-lily [Yellow fawnlily] - *Erythronium rostratum* C. B. Wolf (50) (present)

Yellow field sorrel - *Oxalis stricta* L. (80, 82) (1913-1930)

Yellow flag - *Iris pseudacorus* L. (5, 156, 158) (1900-1923)

Yellow flag iris [Yellowflag iris] - *Iris pseudacorus* L. (138, 155) (1923-1942)

Yellow flame flower [Yellow flameflower] - *Talinum aurantiacum* Engelm. (124) (1937)

Yellow flatsedge - *Cyperus flavescens* L. (50) (present)

Yellow flax - *Linaria vulgaris* Mill. (6) (1892), *Linum* L. (1, 93) (1932-1936), *Linum rigidum* Pursh (47, 125) (1852-1930), *Linum rigidum* Pursh var. *rigidum* (85) (1932), *Linum sulcatum* Riddell (98) (1926), *Linum sulcatum* Riddell var. *sulcatum* (85) (1932)

Yellow flowering-rush [Yellow flowering rush] - *Xyris caroliniana* Walt. (5, 19, 156) (1840-1923)

Yellow foxglove - *Agalinis* Raf. (156) (1923), *Aureolaria flava* (L.) Farw. var. *flava* (5, 156) (1913-1923), *Aureolaria pedicularia* (L.) Raf. ex Farw. (156) (1923), *Digitalis grandiflora* P. Mill. (109, 138, 190) (~1759-1949), *Digitalis lutea* L. (92) (1876)

Yellow foxtail [Yellow fox tail] - *Pennisetum glaucum* (L.) R. Br. (3, 5, 56, 93, 94, 99, 111, 119, 129, 134, 143, 145, 155, 163) (1852-1977)

Yellow fringed orchis [Yellow-fringed orchis] - *Platanthera ciliaris* (L.) Lindl. (2, 5, 109, 122, 156) (1895-1949)

Yellow fringeless orchid - *Platanthera integra* (Nutt.) Gray ex Beck (50) (present)

Yellow fringe-orchid - *Platanthera ciliaris* (L.) Lindl. (138) (1923)

Yellow fritillary - *Fritillaria pudica* (Pursh) Spreng (50, 155) (1942–present)

Yellow fumewort - *Corydalis flavula* (Raf.) DC. (50) (present)

Yellow fumiterre - *Pseudofumaria lutea* (L.) Borkh. (178) (1526)

Yellow gaillardia - *Gaillardia aestivalis* (Walt.) H. Rock var. *flavovirens* (C. Mohr) Cronq. (5, 97) (1913-1937)

Yellow gentian - *Frasera caroliniensis* Walt. (possibly) (5, 7, 64, 92, 156) (1828-1923), *Gentiana alba* Muhl. ex Nutt. (156) (1923)

Yellow gerardia - *Aureolaria pedicularia* (L.) Raf. var. *pedicularia* (156) (1923)

Yellow giant hyssop - *Agastache nepetoides* (L.) Kuntze (50) (present)

Yellow ginseng - *Caulophyllum thalictroides* (L.) Michx. (6, 7, 64, 156, 157, 158) (1828-1929)

Yellow goat's-beard [Yellow goats'-beard, Yellow goats-beard, Yellow goat's beard] - *Krigia biflora* (Walt.) Blake (177) (1762), *Tragopogon pratensis* L. (5, 72, 93, 95, 156, 158) (1900-1936)

Yellow gowan [Yellow gowans] - *Ranunculus acris* L. (5, 156, 157, 158) (1900-1929) Scotland, *Ranunculus bulbosus* L. (156) (1923), *Ranunculus* L. (92) (1876), *Taraxacum officinale* G.H. Weber ex Wiggers (5, 64, 69, 156, 157, 158) (1900-1929)

Yellow grain-rust - *Uredo linearis* Lam (possibly) (19) (1840)

Yellow granadilla - *Passiflora laurifolia* L. (109) (1949)

Yellow guava - *Psidium guajava* L. (107) (1919)

Yellow gum tree [Yellow gum-tree] - *Nyssa sylvatica* Marsh. (5, 20, 156) (1857-1923)

Yellow hair grass [Yellow hairgrass] - *Aira praecox* L. (50) (present)

Yellow harlequin - *Corydalis flavula* (Raf.) DC. (3, 4) (1977–1986)

478

Yellow hatpins - *Syngonanthus flavidulus* (Michx.) Ruhl. (50) (present)

Yellow haw - *Crataegus flava* Aiton (2, 5) (1895-1913)

Yellow henbane - *Nicotiana rustica* L. (178) (1526)

Yellow henbane - *Physalis viscosa* L. (5, 19, 49, 92, 156) (1840-1923)

Yellow hercules - *Zanthoxylum clava-herculis* L. (92, 158) (1876-1900)

Yellow Himalayan raspberry - *Rubus ellipticus* Sm. (138) (1923)

Yellow honeysuckle - *Lonicera dioica* L. (156, 158) (1900-1923), *Lonicera flava* Sims. (4, 5, 50, 97, 113, 138, 155, 156) (1890–present), *Rhododendron calendulaceum* (Michx.) Torr. (5, 156) (1913-1923)

Yellow hookers - *Erythronium americanum* Ker. (156) (1923)

Yellow hop clover [Yellow hop-clover] - *Medicago lupulina* L. (156) (1923), *Trifolium aureum* Pollich (82, 156) (1923-930)

Yellow horned-poppy [Yellow horned poppie, Yellow hornpoppy] - *Glaucium flavum* Crantz (5, 138, 156, 178) (1526-1923)

Yellow horse-gentian [Yellow horse gentian] - *Triosteum angustifolium* L. (5, 72, 156) (1907-1923)

Yellow Indian grass [Yellow Indiangrass] - *Sorghastrum nutans* (L.) Nash (140, 155) (1942-1944)

Yellow Indian paint - *Hydrastis canadensis* L. (5, 64, 156) (1907-1923)

Yellow Indian paintbrush - *Castilleja flava* S. Wats. (50) (present)

Yellow Indian shoe [Yellow Indian-shoe] - *Cypripedium reginae* Walt. (158) (1900)

Yellow indigo - *Baptisia tinctoria* (L.) R. Br. ex Aiton f. (7, 64, 92, 106, 156, 157) (1828-1930)

Yellow indigo broom - *Baptisia tinctoria* (L.) R. Br. ex Aiton f. (7) (1828)

Yellow iris - *Iris pseudacorus* L. (3, 107) (1919-1977), *Iris spuria* L. subsp. *ochroleuca* (L.) Dykes (19) (1840)

Yellow ironweed [Yellow iron-weed] - *Verbesina alternifolia* (L.) Britton ex Kearney (5, 62, 82) (1912-1930)

Yellow jasmine - *Campsis radicans* (L.) Seem. ex Bureau (8) (1785), *Gelsemium sempervirens* (L.) J. St.-Hil. (6, 8, 49, 52, 53, 54, 57, 60, 106, 122, 124, 182) (1785-1937)

Yellow jessamine - *Gelsemium* Juss. (2, 156) (1895-1923), *Gelsemium sempervirens* (L.) J. St.-Hil. (5, 6, 49, 53, 59, 61, 86, 92, 106, 182, 189) (1767-1930)

Yellow jewelweed [Yellow jewel-weed] - *Impatiens pallida* Nutt. (156, 157) (1923-1929)

Yellow jonquil - *Narcissus* ×*odorus* L. [*jonquilla* × *pseudonarcissus*] (92) (1876)

Yellow lady's-bedstraw [Yellow ladies bedstraw] - *Galium verum* L. (178) (1526)

Yellow lady's-slipper [Yellow ladies' slipper, Yellow lady's slipper, Yellow ladies'-slipper] - *Cypripedium parviflorum* Salisb. (5, 7, 50, 85, 97, 156, 157) (1828–present), *Cypripedium parviflorum* Salisb. var. *pubescens* (Willd.) Knight (3) (1977), *Cypripedium parviflorum* Salisb. var. *pubescens* (Willd.) Knight (2, 5, 19, 49, 53, 54, 92) (1840–1922), *Cypripedium reginae* Walt. (64, 158) (1900–1908)

Yellow lantana - *Lantana camara* L. (138) (1923)

Yellow lanterns - *Nuphar lutea* (L.) Sm. subsp. *advena* (Aiton) Kartesz & Gandhi (156) (1923)

Yellow leaf-cup [Yellow leafcup] - *Smallanthus uvedalius* (L.) Mackenzie ex Small (5, 19, 52, 54, 72, 155, 158) (1840-1942)

Yellow lily - *Erythronium americanum* Ker. (5, 75, 156, 157) (1894-1923) Ferrisburgh VT, *Lilium canadense* L. (109) (1949)

Yellow lily-root [Yellow lily root] - *Nuphar lutea* (L.) Sm. subsp. *advena* (Aiton) Kartesz & Gandhi (92) (1876)

Yellow linn - *Magnolia acuminata* (L.) L. (5, 74, 156) (1893-1923) WV

Yellow locust - *Cladrastis kentukea* (Dum.-Cours.) Rudd. (5, 7, 156) (1828–1923), *Robinia pseudoacacia* L. (5, 6, 49, 74, 92, 106, 156, 157, 158) (1876-1930)

Yellow loosestrife [Yellow loose strife] - *Lysimachia* L. (50) (present), *Lysimachia vulgaris* L. (5, 92, 156) (1876–1923)

Yellow lotus - *Nelumbo lutea* Willd. (37, 156) (1919-1923)

Yellow lucerne - *Medicago sativa* L. subsp. *falcata* (L.) Arcang. (68) (1913) Ottawa

Yellow lupine [Yellow lupines] - *Lupinus luteus* L. (19, 107, 109, 178) (1526-1949)

Yellow lysimachus of Virginia - *Oenothera biennis* L. (46) (1671)

Yellow mad-apple [Yellow mad apples] - *Solanum melongena* L. (178) (1526)

Yellow madwort - *Aurinia saxatilis* (L.) Desv. (165) (1768)

Yellow marsh saxifrage - *Saxifraga hirculus* L. (156) (1923), *Saxifraga hirculus* L. subsp. *hirculus* (5) (1913)

Yellow marsh-marigold [Yellow marsh marigold] - *Caltha palustris* L. (50) (present)

Yellow melilot - *Melilotus officinalis* (L.) Lam. (5, 6, 45, 49, 53, 129, 156, 157, 158) (1892–1929)

Yellow melilot clover - *Melilotus officinalis* (L.) Lam. (19, 49, 53, 92) (1840-1922)

Yellow Mexican waterlily - *Nymphaea mexicana* Zucc. (138, 155) (1931-1942)

Yellow mignonette - *Reseda lutea* L. (50, 155, 156) (1923–present)

Yellow milkweed [Yellow milk-weed] - *Asclepias tuberosa* L. (5, 64, 73, 156, 157, 158) (1892–1929)

Yellow milkwort - *Polygala lutea* L. (5, 19, 86, 156) (1840-1923)

Yellow millet - *Melilotus officinalis* (L.) Lam. (5, 157, 158) (1900-1929)

Yellow mocassin flower [Yellow mocassin-flower, Yellow moccasin flower] - *Cypripedium parviflorum* Salisb. (5, 156) (1913–1923), *Cypripedium parviflorum* Salisb. var. *pubescens* (Willd.) Knight (49, 53) (1829–1922), *Cypripedium reginae* Walt. (64, 158) (1900–1908)

Yellow moccasin - *Cypripedium parviflorum* Salisb. var. *pubescens* (Willd.) Knight (92) (1876)

Yellow mombin - *Spondias mombin* L. (109) (1949)

Yellow monkey flower [Yellow monkey-flower] - *Mimulus glabratus* Kunth var. *jamesii* (Torr. & Gray ex Benth.) Gray (85, 93, 95, 157) (1929-1936)

Yellow monkshood [Yellow monk's-hood] - *Aconitum columbianum* Nutt. (155) (1942), *Aconitum lycoctonum* L. (165) (1768)

Yellow moth mullen [Yellow moth mulleine] - *Verbascum* L. (178, 187, 190) (1526-1818)

Yellow mountain avens - *Geum peckii* Pursh (5) (1913)

Yellow mountain saxifrage - *Saxifraga aizoides* L. (5, 156) (1913-1923)

Yellow mustard - *Sinapis alba* L. (6, 53, 69, 92, 157) (1876–1929)

Yellow nelumbo - *Nelumbo lutea* Willd. (possibly) (2, 7, 63, 107) (1828-1919)

Yellow neptunia - *Neptunia lutea* (Leavenworth) Benth. (155) (1942)

Yellow nicker - *Caesalpinia bonduc* (L.) Roxb. (50) (present)

Yellow nightshade - *Solanum rostratum* Dunal (156) (1923)

Yellow Noah's-ark [Yellow Noah's ark] - *Cypripedium reginae* Walt. (64, 158) (1900-1908)

Yellow nodding lady's-tresses [Yellow nodding ladies'-tresses] - *Spiranthes ochroleuca* (Rydb.) Rydb. (50) (present)

Yellow nut-grass [Yellow nut grass] - *Cyperus esculentus* L. (5, 62, 72, 156) (1907-1912)

Yellow nut-sedge [Yellow nutsedge] - *Cyperus esculentus* L. (3) (1977)

Yellow oak - *Quercus ellipsoidalis* E.J. Hill (82, 156) (1923-1930), *Quercus muehlenbergii* Engelm. (2, 5, 10, 19, 20, 33, 82, 93, 95, 97, 113, 156, 157, 158, 187) (1818-1937), *Quercus velutina* Lam. (72) (1907)

Yellow oat [Yellow oats] - *Trisetum flavescens* (L.) Beauv. (3, 45) (1896-1977)

Yellow oat grass [Yellow oat-grass, Yellow oatgrass] - *Trisetum flavescens* (L.) Beauv. (5, 45, 50, 56, 66, 68, 92) (1876–present)

Yellow oleander - *Thevetia peruviana* (Pers.) K. Schum. (109) (1949)

Yellow onion - *Allium coryi* M.E. Jones (122) (1937)

Yellow orchis - *Platanthera flava* (L.) Lindl. var. *flava* (5, 156) (1913-1923)

Yellow orthocarpus - *Orthocarpus luteus* Nutt. (5, 131) (1899-1913)

Yellow owl clover [Yellow owl's-clover, Yellow owlclover] - *Orthocarpus luteus* Nutt. (50, 155) (1942–present)

Yellow oxalis - *Oxalis corniculata* L. (82) (1930)

Yellow ox-eye - *Chrysanthemum segetum* L. (5, 156) (1913-1923)

Yellow ox-eye daisy - *Rudbeckia hirta* L. (5, 156) (1913-1923)

Yellow oxytropis - *Oxytropis campestris* (L.) DC. (5) (1913)

Yellow paint root - *Hydrastis canadensis* L. (92) (1876)

Yellow painted-cup [Yellow paintedcup] - *Castilleja flava* S. Wats. (155) (1942)

Yellow palm - *Dypsis lutescens* (H. Wendl.) Beentje & Dransf. (138) (1923)

Yellow panic grass - *Dichanthelium xanthophysum* (Gray) Freckmann (66, 90) (1885-1903)

Yellow pansy violet - *Viola pedunculata* Torr. & Gray (138) (1923)

Yellow parilla - *Menispermum canadense* L. (5, 6, 48, 49, 53, 57, 61, 64, 92, 130, 156, 157, 158) (1870-1929)

Yellow passionflower [Yellow passion-flower, Yellow passion flower] - *Passiflora lutea* L. (5, 19, 48, 50, 122, 138, 155) (1840–present)

Yellow pea [Yellow-pea] - *Thermopsis mollis* (Michx.) M. A. Curtis (156) (1923), *Thermopsis* R. Br. ex Aiton f. (93) (1936), *Thermopsis rhombifolia* (Nutt. ex Pursh) Nutt. ex Richards. (4, 5) (1913-1986)

Yellow phlox - *Erysimum capitatum* (Dougl. ex Hook.) Greene var. *capitatum* (85, 93, 97, 157, 158) (1900-1937), *Erysimum* L. (1, 93) (1932-1936)

Yellow pileweed [Yellow pile-weed] - *Ranunculus acris* L. (6) (1892)

Yellow pimpernel - *Taenidia integerrima* (L.) Drude (4, 5, 50, 72, 85, 97, 156) (1907–present)

Yellow pine - *Pinus echinata* Mill. (1, 2, 10, 147) (1818-1932), *Pinus palustris* Mill. (5) (1913), *Pinus ponderosa* P. & C. Lawson (75, 101, 108, 135, 161) (1857-1910), *Pinus ponderosa* P. & C. Lawson var. *ponderosa* (75, 147, 153) (1856-1913), *Pinus ponderosa* P. & C. Lawson var. *scopulorum* Engelm. (113, 130) (1890-1895), *Pinus resinosa* Aiton (5, 19, 40) (1840-1928), *Pinus strobus* L. (78) (1898) Western US

Yellow pinesap [Yellow pine-sap] - *Monotropa hypopithys* L. (156) (1923)

Yellow pipewort - *Syngonanthus flavidulus* (Michx.) Ruhl. (possibly) (5, 10) (1818-1913)

Yellow pitch pine - *Pinus palustris* Mill. (10, 20, 92) (1818-1876)

Yellow pitcher plant [Yellow pitcher-plant] - *Sarracenia flava* L. (156) (1923)

Yellow plum - *Prunus americana* Marsh. (107) (1919)

Yellow pond-lily [Yellow pond lily] - *Nuphar lutea* (L.) Sm. (50) (present), *Nuphar lutea* (L.) Sm. subsp. *advena* (Aiton) Kartesz & Gandhi (48, 50, 57, 72, 74, 85, 92, 93, 97, 103, 107, 120, 121, 122, 156, 157, 158) (1840–present), *Nuphar* Sm. (1, 10, 13, 15, 63) (1818-1932), *Nymphaea* L. (93, 158) (1900-1936)

Yellow poplar - *Liriodendron tulipifera* L. (5, 13, 18, 49, 61, 74, 82, 92, 106, 156) (1805-1930)

Yellow poppy - *Argemone mexicana* L. (122) (1937) TX, *Papaver nudicaule* L. (19) (1840), *Stylophorum diphyllum* (Michx.) Nutt. (5, 156) (1913-1923)

Yellow prairie violet - *Viola nuttallii* Pursh (3, 4, 5, 98, 156) (1913-1986)

Yellow pretty-grass - *Calochortus luteus* Dougl. ex Lindl. (86) (1878)

Yellow prickly-ash [Yellow prickly ash] - *Zanthoxylum clava-herculis* L. (5, 156, 158) (1900-1923)

Yellow primrose - *Calylophus serrulatus* (Nutt.) Raven (85) (1932) SD

Yellow procumbent wood sorrel - *Oxalis corniculata* L. (5, 72) (1907-1913)

Yellow puccoon - *Hydrastis canadensis* L. (2, 5, 6, 7, 15, 49, 52, 53, 54, 57, 59, 64, 92, 156) (1892-1923), *Hydrastis* L. (13) (1849), *Lithospermum incisum* Lehm. (5, 156) (1913-1923)

Yellow rabbitbrush - *Chrysothamnus viscidiflorus* (Hook.) Nutt. (50) (present)

Yellow rainlily [Yellow rain lily] - *Habranthus tubispathus* (L'Hér.) Traub (122, 124) (1937) TX

Yellow rattle - *Pedicularis* L. (190) (~1759), *Rhinanthus* L. (156) (1923), *Rhinanthus minor* L. subsp. *minor* (5, 19, 92, 156) (1840-1923)

Yellow rocket [Yellowrocket, Yellow-rocket] - *Barbarea* Aiton f. (13, 50) (1849–present), *Barbarea vulgaris* W.T. Aiton (5, 15, 72, 85, 107, 157) (1895-1929), *Lysimachia vulgaris* L. (5, 156) (1913-1923), *Reseda luteola* L. (5, 156) (1913-1923)

Yellow rockrose [Yellow rock-rose] - *Dasiphora floribunda* (Pursh) Kartesz (156) (1923)

Yellow rose - *Dasiphora* Raf. (1) (1932)

Yellow salsify - *Tragopogon dubius* Scop. (50) (present), *Tragopogon pratensis* L. (85) (1932)

Yellow sandlily [Yellow sand lily] - *Mentzelia laevicaulis* (Dougl. ex Hook.) Torr. & Gray (101) (1905) MT

Yellow sand-verbena [Yellow sand verbena, Yellow sandverbena] - *Abronia latifolia* Eschsch. (77, 155) (1898-1942)

Yellow sarsaparilla - *Menispermum canadense* L. (5, 6, 7, 64, 92, 156, 157, 158) (1828-1929)

Yellow saxifrage - *Saxifraga* L. (1) (1932)

Yellow scabiosa - *Scabiosa ochroleuca* L. (138) (1923)

Yellow scorpion-grass - *Myosotis versicolor* (Pers.) J.E. Smith (156) (1923)

Yellow Scouler's willow [Yellow Scouler willow] - *Salix scouleriana* Barr. (155) (1942)

Yellow scurvy-grass - *Barbarea vulgaris* W.T. Aiton (157) (1929)

Yellow sedge - *Carex flava* L. (5, 50, 156) (1913–present)

Yellow sensitive brier [Yellow sensitive briar] - *Neptunia lutea* (Leavenworth) Benth. (122, 124) (1937)

Yellow snakeleaf [Yellow snake-leaf, Yellow snake leaf] - *Erythronium americanum* Ker. (7, 86, 92, 157) (1828-1929)

Yellow snowdrop [Yellow snow drop] - *Erythronium americanum* Ker. (5, 7, 58, 86, 92, 156, 157) (1828–1929)

Yellow sorrel [Yellow-sorrel] - *Oxalis corniculata* L. (76, 187) (1818-1896), *Oxalis* L. (93) (1936)

Yellow spear grass [Yellow spear-grass] - *Poa canbyi* (Scribn.) Piper (94) (1901)

Yellow spiderflower - *Cleome lutea* Hook. (50, 155) (1942–present), *Cleome lutea* Hook. var. *lutea* (50, 155) (1942–present)

Yellow spring bedstraw - *Galium verum* L. (50) (present)

Yellow star [Yellow-star] - *Helenium autumnale* L. (5, 7, 92, 156, 157, 158) (1828-1929)

Yellow star root - *Aletris aurea* Walt. (possibly) (19, 92) (1840)

Yellow star-grass [Yellow stargrass] - *Hypoxis hirsuta* (L.) Cov. (3, 5, 93, 97, 156, 157, 158) (1900-1977)

Yellow star-thistle [Yellow star thistle] - *Centaurea solstitialis* L. (4, 50, 106, 157) (1900–present)

Yellow starwort - *Inula helenium* L. (5, 64, 156) (1907-1923)

Yellow starwort of Virginia with a filmy stalk - *Verbesina alternifolia* (L.) Britton ex Kearney (174, 177) (1753-1762)

Yellow stonecrop - *Sedum nuttallianum* Raf. (50) (present), *Sedum reflexum* L. (156) (1923), *Duchesnea indica* (Andr.) Focke (158) (1900)

Yellow succory - *Hieracium canadense* Michx. (46) (1783)

Yellow suckling - *Trifolium dubium* Sibth. (5) (1913)

Yellow sumac - *Rhus glabra* L. (138) (1923)

Yellow sundrops - *Calylophus serrulatus* (Nutt.) Raven (50) (present)

Yellow sunnybell - *Schoenolirion croceum* (Michx.) Wood (50) (present)

Yellow sweet buckeye - *Aesculus flava* Aiton (5, 97) (1913-1937)

Yellow sweet clover [Yellow sweet-clover, Yellow sweetclover] - *Melilotus indicus* (L.) All. (148) (1939) CO, *Melilotus officinalis* (L.) Lam. (3, 4, 5, 6, 50, 53, 62, 80, 82, 85, 93, 95, 97, 106, 109, 122, 124, 129, 145, 155, 156, 157, 158) (1892–present), *Melissa officinalis* L. (63, 72) (1899-1912)

Yellow taenidia - *Taenidia integerrima* (L.) Drude (3, 155) (1942–1977)

Yellow tar-fitch - *Lathyrus pratensis* L. (5) (1913)

Yellow tarweed [Yellow tar weed] - *Grindelia camporum* Greene var. *camporum* (54) (1905), *Holocarpha virgata* (Gray) Keck (106) (1930)

Yellow Texas star - *Lindheimera texana* Gray & Engelm. (122) (1937)

Yellow thistle - *Argemone mexicana* L. (5, 156) (1913-1923), *Cirsium horridulum* Michx. (2, 5, 46, 124, 187) (1783-1937)

Yellow toadflax [Yellow toad flax, Yellow toad-flax] - *Linaria vulgaris* Mill. (5, 95, 131, 56, 157, 158) (1899-1936)

Yellow trefoil - *Medicago lupulina* L. (68, 95, 109, 146) (1911–1949), *Trifolium dubium* Sibth. (5, 158) (1900–1913)

Yellow trumpetleaf [Yellow trumpet leaf] - *Sarracenia flava* L. (2) (1895)

Yellow trumpets - *Sarracenia flava* L. (5, 156) (1913-1923)

Yellow umbel [Yellow umbil, Yellow umble] - *Cypripedium parviflorum* Salisb. var. *parviflorum* (7) (1828), *Cypripedium parviflorum* Salisb. var. *pubescens* (Willd.) Knight (6, 92) (1876-1892), *Cypripedium reginae* Walt. (64, 158) (1900-1908)

Yellow unicorn plant [Yellow unicornplant] - *Ibicella lutea* (Lindl.) Van Eselt. (138) (1923)

Yellow vetchling - *Lathyrus ochroleucus* Hook. (3, 4) (1977-1986), *Lathyrus pratensis* L. (5, 156) (1913-1923)

Yellow violet - *Viola pubescens* Aiton (19, 46, 127) (1840-1933), *Viola pubescens* Aiton var. *pubescens* (85) (1932), *Viola rotundifolia* Michx. (5) (1913)

Yellow Virginia bottlekin - *Ludwigia alternifolia* L. (181) (~1678)

Yellow water buttercup - *Ranunculus flabellaris* Raf. (50) (present)

Yellow water crowfoot [Yellow water crow foot, Yellow water crow-foot] - *Ranunculus flabellaris* Raf. (2, 5, 63, 72, 93, 97, 131, 156, 158) (1895-1937)

Yellow water flag [Yellow water-flag] - *Iris pseudacorus* L. (5, 156, 158) (1900-1923)

Yellow water skegs [Yellow water-skegs] - *Iris pseudacorus* L. (5, 158) (1900-1913)

Yellow watercress [Yellow water-cress, Yellow water cress] - *Rorippa palustris* (L.) Bess (7, 92, 156, 157, 158) (1828-1929), *Rorippa palustris* (L.) Bess. subsp. *palustris* (5, 120) (1913-1938), *Rorippa* Scop. (1, 93) (1932-1936)

Yellow waterlily [Yellow water lily, Yellow water-lily, Yellow water lilly] - *Nelumbo lutea* Willd. (possibly) (7) (1828), *Nuphar lutea* (L.) Sm. (107) (1919), *Nuphar lutea* (L.) Sm. subsp. *advena* (Aiton) Kartesz & Gandhi (3, 19, 46, 76, 92, 101, 106, 124, 157) (1840-1977), *Nuphar lutea* (L.) Sm. subsp. *variegata* (Dur.) E.O. Beal (3) (1977), *Nymphaea mexicana* Zucc. (2, 109) (1895-1949)

Yellow whitlow-wort [Yellow whitlowwort] - *Draba nemorosa* L. (3, 4) (1977-1986)

Yellow wide-lip orchid [Yellow widelip orchid] - *Liparis loeselii* (L.) L.C. Rich (50) (present)

Yellow wild buckwheat - *Eriogonum flavum* Nutt. (4) (1986)

Yellow wild indigo [Yellow wild-indigo] - *Baptisia* ×*sulphurea* Engelm. [*alba* × *sphaerocarpa*] (97) (1937) OK, *Baptisia tinctoria* (L.) R. Br. ex Aiton f. (6, 97, 138) (1892-1937)

Yellow wild pea - *Thermopsis rhombifolia* (Nutt. ex Pursh) Nutt. ex Richards. (85) (1932) SD

Yellow wild rye [Yellow wildrye] - *Leymus flavescens* (Scribn. & J.G. Sm.) Pilger (50) (present)

Yellow willow - *Salix alba* L. (19, 135, 187) (1818-1910), *Salix lutea* Nutt. (1, 4, 50, 85, 155) (1932–present), *Salix scouleriana* Barr. (130) (1895)

Yellow willow herb [Yellow willowherb, Yellow willow herbe] - *Lysimachia vulgaris* L. (5, 92, 178) (1526-1913)

Yellow wolf's-bane [Yellow wolf's bane, Yellow wolfes bane] - *Aconitum lycoctonum* L. (92, 165, 178) (1526-1876)

Yellow wood anemone - *Anemonoides ranunculoides* L. (155) (1942)

Yellow wood sorrel [Yellow wood-sorrel] - *Oxalis corniculata* L. (2, 41, 97, 145) (1770-1937), *Oxalis* L. (1) (1932), *Oxalis stricta* L. (3, 4, 19, 37, 62, 122, 127, 145, 156) (1840-1986)

Yellow woodcress [Yellow wood cress, Yellow wood-cress] - *Rorippa palustris* (L.) Bess (156, 157, 158) (1900-1929), *Rorippa palustris* (L.) Bess. subsp. *palustris* (5) (1913)

Yellow woolly buckeye - *Aesculus pavia* L. (155) (1942)

Yellow yam - *Dioscorea cayenensis* Lam. (109) (1949)

Yellow yessamy - *Gelsemium sempervirens* (L.) J. St.-Hil. (177) (1762)

Yellow-and-blue scorpion-grass [Yellow and blue scorpion grass] - *Myosotis versicolor* (Pers.) J.E. Smith (5) (1913)

Yellow-ash [Yellow ash] - *Cladrastis kentukea* (Dum.-Cours.) Rudd. (5, 7, 92) (1828-1913)

Yellow-aster - *Chrysopsis mariana* (L.) Ell. (187) (1818)

Yellow-band iris [Yellowband iris] - *Iris spuria* L. subsp. *ochroleuca* (L.) Dykes (138) (1923)

Yellow-bark oak [Yellow bark oak, Yellow-barked oak] - *Quercus velutina* Lam. (2, 5, 58, 82, 156, 157, 158) (1869-1930)

Yellow-bean - *Thermopsis* R. Br. ex Aiton f. (148) (1939) CO

Yellowbell [Yellow-bell, Yellow bell, Yellow bells, Yellow-bells, Yellowbells] - *Emmenanthe* Benth. (138) (1923), *Emmenanthe penduliflora* Benth. (77, 138) (1898–1923), *Erythronium americanum* Ker. (5, 73, 75, 156, 157) (1892–1929), *Fritillaria pudica* (Pursh) Spreng (101) (1905) MT, *Tecoma stans* (L.) Juss. ex Kunth (109) (1949)

Yellow-berry [Yellow berry] - *Podophyllum peltatum* L. (7, 92) (1828-1876), *Rubus chamaemorus* L. (107) (1919)

Yellow-berry elder [Yellow-berried elder] - *Sambucus racemosa* L. var. *racemosa* (85) (1932)

Yellow-berry thorn [Yellow-berried thorn] - *Crataegus flava* Aiton (19) (1840)

Yellow-caul - *Ranunculus acris* L. (157, 158) (1900-1929)

Yellowcress [Yellow cress, Yellow-cress] - *Rorippa* Scop. (4, 50) (1986–present), *Rorippa sessiliflora* (Nutt.) A.S. Hitchc. (3, 4, 145) (1897-1986), *Rorippa sinuata* (Nutt.) A.S. Hitchc. (85, 145) (1897-1932), *Rorippa sylvestris* (L.) Bess. (5, 15, 156) (1895-1923)

Yellow-daisy [Yellow daisy, Yellow daisies] - *Rudbeckia hirta* L. (5, 62, 73, 156, 157, 158) (1892-1929), *Rudbeckia hirta* L. var. *pulcherrima* Farw. (109) (1949), *Rudbeckia subtomentosa* Pursh (82) (1930)

Yellowdicks - *Helenium amarum* (Raf.) H. Rock (50) (present), *Helenium amarum* (Raf.) H. Rock var. *amarum* (50) (present), *Helenium amarum* (Raf.) H. Rock var. *badium* (Gray ex S. Wats.) Waterfall (50) (present)

Yellow-eye [Yellow eye] - *Hydrastis canadensis* L. (5, 49, 64, 92, 156) (1876-1923)

Yellow-eyed water-grass [Yellow-eyed water grass] - *Heteranthera dubia* (Jacq.) MacM. (19) (1840)

Yellow-eyed-grass [Yellow-eyed grass, Yellow eyed grass] - *Hypoxis hirsuta* (L.) Cov. (156) (1923), *Xyris caroliniana* Walt. (19, 92, 156) (1840-1923), *Xyris* L. (1, 50) (1932–present), *Xyris torta* Sm. (66) (1903)

Yellow-flower [Yellow flower] - *Moricandia arvensis* (L.) DC. (156, 158) (1900-1923), *Sinapis arvensis* L. (5, 157) (1913-1929)

Yellow-flower diervilla [Yellow flowered diervilla] - *Diervilla lonicera* Mill. (8, 42) (1785-1814)

Yellow-flower gourds [Yellow-flowered gourds] - *Cucurbita pepo* L. var. *ovifera* (L.) Alef. (109) (1949)

Yellow-flower horse-chestnut [Yellow-flowered horse-chestnut] - *Aesculus flava* Aiton (165) (1768)

Yellow-flower horse-gentian [Yellow-flowered horse-gentian] - *Triosteum angustifolium* L. (4) (1986)

Yellow-flower leaf-cup [Yellow-flowered leaf-cup] - *Smallanthus uvedalius* (L.) Mackenzie ex Small (156) (1923)

Yellow-flower locoweed [Yellowflower locoweed] - *Oxytropis monticola* Gray (50) (present)

Yellow-flower milkwort [Yellow-flowered milk-wort] - *Polygala lutea* L. (187) (1818)

Yellow-flower onion [Yellow-flowered onion] - *Allium coryi* M.E. Jones (124) (1937)

Yellow-flower sow-thistle [Yellow-flowered sow-thistle] - *Sonchus oleraceus* L. (187) (1818)

Yellow-flower stonecrop [Yellow-flowered stonecrop] - *Sedum lanceolatum* Torr. (38) (1820)

Yellow-fruit hawthorn [Yellow fruited hawthorn] - *Crataegus flava* Aiton (42) (1814)

Yellow-fruit horse-gentian [Yellowfruit horse-gentian] - *Triosteum angustifolium* L. (50) (present)

Yellow-fruit sedge [Yellowfruit sedge, Yellow-fruited sedge] - *Carex ×xanthocarpa* Degl. (possibly) (72) (1907), *Carex annectens* (Bickn.) Bickn. (3, 5, 50) (1913–present), *Carex annectens* Bickn. var. *annectens* (3) (1977), *Carex echinata* Murr. subsp. *echinata* (50) (present)

Yellow-fruit thorn [Yellow-fruited thorn] - *Crataegus flava* Aiton (107) (1919)

Yellow-gowan [Yellow gowan] - *Ranunculus repens* L. (5, 107, 156) (1913-1923)

Yellow-grass [Yellow grass] - *Cyperus flavescens* L. (19) (1840), *Narthecium americanum* Ker-Gawl. (5, 156) (1913-1923)

Yellow-green painted-cup [Yellowgreen paintedcup] - *Castilleja sulphurea* Rydb. (155) (1942)

Yellow-gum - *Nyssa sylvatica* Marsh. (106) (1930)

Yellow-hair beard grass [Yellow-haired beard-grass] - *Andropogon gerardii* Vitman (5, 93, 99) (1913-1936)

Yellow-hair lyme grass [Yellow-haired lyme-grass] - *Leymus flavescens* (Scribn. & J.G. Sm.) Pilger (94) (1901)

Yellow-hair paspalum [Yellow-haired paspalum] - *Paspalum setaceum* Michx. (5) (1913)

Yellowish apples-of-love [Yellowish apples of loue] - *Solanum lycopersicum* L. var. *lycopersicum* (178) (1526)

Yellowish corydalis - *Corydalis flavula* (Raf.) DC. (2) (1895)

Yellowish gentian - *Gentiana alba* Muhl. ex Nutt. (5, 72, 156) (1907-1923)

Yellowish sedge - *Carex michauxiana* Boeckl. (5) (1913)

Yellowish-white gentian [Yellowish white gentian] - *Gentiana villosa* L. (49, 92) (1876-1898)

Yellowleaf [Yellow leaf] - *Symplocos tinctoria* (L.) L'Her. (10) (1818)

Yellow-leaf hyssop [Yellow leafed hyssope] - *Hyssopus officinalis* L. (178) (1526)

Yellow-oleander - *Thevetia peruviana* (Pers.) K. Schum. (138) (1923)

Yellowpaint [Yellow paint] - *Hydrastis canadensis* L. (7, 64) (1828-1908)

Yellow-plums [Yellow plums] - *Diospyros virginiana* L. (7, 82) (1828-1930)

Yellow-puff - *Neptunia lutea* (Leavenworth) Benth. (4, 50) (1986–present)

Yellow-rod - *Linaria vulgaris* Mill. (157, 158) (1900-1929)

Yellowroot [Yellow root, Yellow-root] - *Celastrus scandens* L. (92, 157, 158) (1876-1929), *Coptis trifolia* (L.) Salisb. (5, 64, 92, 156) (1876-1923), *Hydrastis canadensis* L. (5, 6, 7, 14, 35, 49, 53, 59, 64, 92, 156) (1806-1923), *Hydrastis* L. (possibly) (15, 167) (1814-1895), *Jeffersonia diphylla* (L.) Pers. (7, 64, 92, 156) (1828-1929), *Xanthorhiza* Marsh. (possibly) (8, 10, 13, 15, 138, 155) (1785-1942), *Xanthorhiza simplicissima* Marsh. (14, 49, 57, 58, 92, 156, 186) (1814-1923)

Yellows - *Cypripedium parviflorum* Salisb. var. *parviflorum* (5, 7) (1828-1913), *Cypripedium parviflorum* Salisb. var. *pubescens* (Willd.) Knight (6, 92) (1876-1892), *Cypripedium reginae* Walt. (64, 158) (1900-1908), *Ranunculus acris* L. (7) (1828)

Yellow-seal - *Hydrastis canadensis* L. (156) (1923)

Yellow-sedge bluestem [Yellowsedge bluestem] - *Andropogon virginicus* L. (155) (1942)

Yellowseed [Yellow seed, Yellow-seed] - *Lepidium campestre* (L.) Aiton f. (5, 156, 148) (1913-1939)

Yellow-seed false pimpernel [Yellowseed false pimpernel] - *Lindernia dubia* (L.) Pennell (50) (present)

Yellow-seed mustard - *Sinapis alba* L. (19) (1840)

Yellow-spine thistle [Yellow spine thistle, Yellowspine thistle, Yellow spined thistle, Yellow-spined thistle] - *Cirsium ochrocentrum* Gray (3, 4, 5, 50, 93, 97) (1899–present)

Yellow-stem white willow [Yellowstem white willow] - *Salix alba* L. (4, 155) (1942-1986)

Yellow-throat shooting-star [Yellowthroat shootingstar] - *Dodecatheon pulchellum* (Raf.) Merr. subsp. *pulchellum* (155) (1942)

Yellowtop [Yellow-top, Yellow top, Yellowtops, Yellow-tops] - *Calamagrostis canadensis* (Michx.) Beauv. (111) (1915) Neb, *Calamagrostis stricta* (Timm) Koel. subsp. *stricta* (5) (1913), *Flaveria* Juss. (50) (present), *Hemizonia* DC. (106) (1930) Fresno Co, CA, *Solidago juncea* Aiton (5, 156) (1913–1923), *Solidago* L. (73, 76) (1892–1896), *Verbesina encelioides* (Cav.) Benth. & Hook. f. ex Gray (106, 122, 124) (1930–1937)

Yellow-tuft - *Alyssum murale* Waldst. & Kit. (109) (1949)

Yellow-violet [Yellow violet] - *Matthiola incana* (L.) Aiton f. (92) (1876)

Yellow-weed [Yellow weed] - *Amphiachyris dracunculoides* (DC.) Nutt. (21, 156) (1893–1923), *Hymenoxys hoopesii* (Gray) Bierner (148) (1939) CO, *Ranunculus acris* L. (7, 92) (1828–1876), *Ranunculus bulbosus* L. (5) (1913), *Reseda luteola* L. (15, 92, 156) (1895–1923), *Solidago canadensis* L. (76, 156, 158) (1896–1923), *Solidago canadensis* L. var. *scabra* Torr. & Gray (5, 156) (1913–1923), *Solidago* L. (75) (1894)

Yellow-wood [Yellowwood, Yellow wood] - *Cladrastis kentukea* (Dum.-Cours.) Rudd . (20, 82, 92, 106, 156) (1857-1930), *Cladrastis* Raf. (2, 82, 138, 156) (1895-1930), *Cotinus obovatus* Raf. (5, 156) (1913-1923), *Frangula caroliniana* (Walt.) Gray (156) (1923), *Liriodendron tulipifera* L. (7, 46, 49, 186) (1825-1898), *Maclura* Nutt. (12) (1821), *Maclura pomifera* (Raf.) Schneid. (5, 7, 10, 20, 34, 156, 158) (1818-1923), *Symplocos tinctoria* (L.) L'Her. (5, 156) (1913-1923), *Zanthoxylum americanum* Mill. (6, 49, 156, 157, 158) (1892-1929), *Zanthoxylum clava-herculis* L. (92, 158) (1876-1900)

Yellow-wool amorpha [Yellowwool amorpha] - *Amorpha fruticosa* L. (155) (1942)

Yellow-wort [Yellow wort] - *Xanthorhiza simplicissima* Marsh. (7, 49, 92, 138) (1876)

Yerba buena - *Clinopodium douglasii* (Benth.) Kuntze (57, 77, 106) (1898-1930)

Yerba buena (Spanish) - *Mentha spicata* L. (158) (1900)

Yerba colorado - *Rumex* L. (103) (1870) AZ

Yerba de la feridura (Spanish) - *Stachys* L. (158) (1900)

Yerba de la flecha - *Sapium glandulosum* (L.) Morong (52) (1919)

Yerba de maté - *Ilex paraguensis* St.Hilaire (107) (1919)

Yerba de San Juan [Yerba-de-San-Juan] - *Achillea millefolium* L. (156) (1923)

Yerba de tajo (Spanish) - *Eclipta* L. (1) (1932)

Yerba de tajo [Yerba-de-tajo, Yerbadetajo] - *Eclipta prostrata* (L.) L. (3, 4, 5, 93, 97, 122, 155) (1913-1986)

Yerba de vibrona (Spanish) - *Ibervillea lindheimeri* (Gray) Greene (122) (1937) TX

Yerba del buey - *Cissus trifoliata* (L.) L. (106, 122, 124) (1930-1937) Southern US

Yerba del Manza - *Anemopsis californica* (Nutt.) Hook. & Arn. (52, 53) (1919-1922)

Yerba del negro (Spanish) - *Sphaeralcea angustifolia* (Cav.) G. Don (150) (1894) NM

Yerba del pasmore (Spanish) - *Erigeron annuus* (L.) Pers. (76) (1896) CA

Yerba del pescado (Spanish California) - *Croton setigerus* Hook. (106) (1930) used to stupefy fish

Yerba del vernada - *Porophyllum gracile* Benth. (76) (1896) CA

Yerba del vibora (Spanish) - *Daucus pusillus* Michx. (76) (1896) CA

Yerba mansa [Yerbamansa] - *Anemopsis californica* (Nutt.) Hook. & Arn. (49, 50, 53, 57, 155, 158) (1898–present), *Anemopsis* Hook. & Arn. (4, 50) (1986–present)

Yerba maté - *Ilex paraguensis* St.Hilaire (109) (1949)

Yerba parda (Spanish) - *Helianthus ciliaris* DC. (150) (1894) NM

Yerba reuma - *Frankenia salina* (Molina) I.M. Johnston (53, 57) (1917-1922)

Yerba santa - *Eriodictyon californicum* (Hook. & Arn.) Torr. (52, 53, 54, 55, 57, 75, 106) (1894-1930) CA

Yerrow - *Achillea millefolium* L. (158) (1900)

Yethering bells - *Orthilia secunda* (L.) House (46) (1879)

Yetl (Mexico) - *Nicotiana repanda* Willd. ex Lehm. (107) (1919)

Yevering bells - *Orthilia secunda* (L.) House (46) (1879)

Yew or Yew tree - *Taxus baccata* L. (49, 92, 107, 135) (1876-1919), *Taxus brevifolia* Nutt. (161) (1857), *Taxus canadensis* Willd. (19, 40, 147) (1840-1928), *Taxus* L. (1, 7, 8, 109, 50, 138, 167) (1785–present)

Yew pine - *Picea mariana* (Mill.) Britton, Sterns & Poggenb. (5, 75) (1894-1913)

Yew podocarpus - *Podocarpus macrophyllus* (Thunb.) Sweet (138) (1923)

Yew-leaf torrya [Yew-leaved torrya] - *Torreya taxifolia* Arnot. (20) (1857)

Yfs - *Tsuga canadensis* (L.) Carr. (46) (1879)

Ylang-ylang - *Cananga odorata* (Lam.) Hook. f. & T. Thomson (109) (1949)

Ynayah - *Colocasia esculenta* (L.) Schott (86) (1878) Southern states

Ynchic (Indian) - *Arachis hypogaea* L. (107) (1609)

Yoke elm - *Carpinus betulus* L. (92) (1876)

Yokohama bean - *Mucuna pruriens* (L.) DC. var. *utilis* (Wallich ex Wight) Baker ex Burck (109) (1949)

Yokohama velvetbean - *Mucuna pruriens* (L.) DC. var. *utilis* (Wallich ex Wight) Baker ex Burck (138) (1923)

Yoncopin - *Nelumbo lutea* Willd. (106, 156, 157, 158) (1900-1930)

Yorkshire fog - *Holcus lanatus* L. (5, 45) (1896-1913)

Yorkshire sanicle - *Pinguicula vulgaris* L. (5, 86, 156) (1878-1923) old British name

Young chinks - *Gaultheria procumbens* L. (73) (1892)

Young come-ups - *Gaultheria procumbens* L. (75) (1894) Ferrisburgh VT, young shoots

Young fustic - *Cotinus coggygria* Scop. (92) (1876)

Young ivories - *Gaultheria procumbens* L. (73) (1892) NH

Youngsters - *Gaultheria procumbens* L. (73) (1892) ME, young shoots

Youquepin - *Nelumbo lutea* Willd. (122, 124) (1937) TX

Youth-and-old-age [Youth and old age] - *Zinnia violacea* Cav. (73, 109) (1892-1949) Mansfield OH

Youth-on-age - *Tolmiea menziesii* (Pursh) Torr. & Gray (109) (1949)

Youthwort [Youth wort] - *Drosera rotundifolia* L. (5, 6, 52, 92, 156, 158) (1892-1923), *Heracleum maximum* Bartr. (92, 157, 158) (1876-1929)

Yringe - *Eryngium maritimum* L. (179) (1526)

Ysope - *Hyssopus officinalis* L. (179) (1526)

Yuca - *Manihot esculenta* Crantz (109) (1949)

Yucca [Iucca] - *Yucca filamentosa* L. (156) (1923), *Yucca glauca* Nutt. (3, 121, 124, 125, 127) (1918-1977), *Yucca gloriosa* L. (178) (1596), *Yucca* L. (1, 50, 138, 148, 155) (1923–present)

Yukon columbine - *Aquilegia brevistyla* Hook. (155) (1942)

Yungfernblüthe (German) - *Drosera rotundifolia* L. (158) (1900)

Yupon - *Ilex vomitoria* Aiton (104) (1896) Southern Indians

Yuy - *Hedera helix* L. (179) (1526)

Yzerhout (Belgis Noveboracensibus) - *Ostrya carpinifolia* Scop. (177) (1762)

Z

Zab (Hungarian) - *Avena sativa* L. (110) (1886)

Zabara (Cuba) - *Agave americana* L. (31) (1847)

Zaburso (Brazil) - *Zea mays* L. (107) (1550)

Zacate (Philippines) - *Leersia hexandra* Sw. (88) (1885)

Zacate grass (Spanish) - *Sporobolus wrightii* Munro ex Scribn. (45) (1896)

Zacaton (Spanish) - *Sporobolus wrightii* Munro ex Scribn. (45) (1896) "great grass" also used for other species

Žahiu (Osage) - *Rudbeckia subtomentosa* Pursh (121) (1918?–1970?)

Zahnweholz (German) - *Zanthoxylum americanum* Mill. (6, 158) (1892–1900)

Zahnwehrinde (German) - *Zanthoxylum americanum* Mill. (158) (1900)

Zaman - *Samanea saman* (Jacq.) Merr. (109) (1949)

Zamang - *Samanea saman* (Jacq.) Merr. (107) (1919)

Zamouna - *Aesculus pavia* L. (177) (1762)

Zanahoria (Spanish) - *Daucus carota* L. (158) (1900)

Zandria (Spanish) - *Citrullus lanatus* (Thunb.) Matsumura & Nakai (110) (1886)

Zannichellia [Zanichellia] - *Zannichellia* L. (158) (1900), *Zannichellia palustris* L. (131) (1899)

Zant wood - *Cotinus coggygria* Scop. (92) (1876)

Zanthorhize à feuilles de perfil (French) - *Xanthorhiza simplicissima* Marsh. (8) (1785)

Zapilliot - *Cucurbita maxima* Dcne. (107) (1919)

Zarzaparilla - *Smilax glauca* Walt. (46) (1879)

Zebra plant - *Calathea zebrina* (Sims) Lindl. (109) (1949)

Zehrwurz (German) - *Arisaema triphyllum* (L.) Schott (158) (1900)

Zelkova - *Zelkova* Spach (138) (1923), *Zenobia pulverulenta* (W. Bartram ex Willd.) Pollard (181) (~1678)

Zennichellia - *Zannichellia palustris* L. (72) (1907) for J. H. Zannichelli, Italian bonatist, d. 1729

Zenobia - *Zenobia* D. Don (138) (1923)

Zephyr-lily [Zephyrlily] - *Zephyranthes* Herbert (109, 138) (1923–1949)

Ze'sûb (Chippewa) - *Laportea canadensis* (L.) Weddell (40) (1928)

Zezehan - *Sesamum* L. (7) (1828)

Zha tanga (Omaha-Ponca, big weed) - *Silphium perfoliatum* L. (37) (1919)

Zha-baho-hi (Omaha-Ponca, weed with angled stem) - *Silphium perfoliatum* L. (37) (1919)

Zhaba-makan (Omaha-Ponca, beaver-medicine) - *Heracleum maximum* Bartr. (37) (1919)

Zhaba-ta-zhon (Omaha-Ponca, beaver wood) - *Acer negundo* L. (37) (1919)

Zha-pa (Omaha-Ponca, bitter weed) - *Silphium laciniatum* L. (37) (1919)

Zha-sage-zi (Omaha-Ponca, hard yellow weed) - *Solidago* L. (37) (1919)

Zha-zi (Omaha-Ponca, yellow weed) - *Helianthus annuus* L. (37) (1919)

Zherbes - *Ruppia maritima* L. (156) (1923)

Zhon h'uda (Omaha-Ponca, gray wood) - *Amelanchier alnifolia* (Nutt.) Nutt. ex M. Roemer (37) (1919)

Zhon-hoje-wazhide (Omaha-Ponca) - *Shepherdia argentea* (Pursh) Nutt. (37) (1919)

Zhon-hoje-wazhide h'uta (Omaha-Ponca) - *Shepherdia argentea* (Pursh) Nutt. (37) (1919)

Zhon-zi-zhu (Omaha-Ponca, yellow flesh wood) - *Maclura pomifera* (Raf.) Schneid. (37) (1919)

Zhu-nakada-tanga-makan (Omaha-Ponca. great fever medicine) - *Caulophyllum thalictroides* (L.) Michx. (37) (1919)

Ziest (German) - *Stachys* L. (158) (1900)

Zigadene - *Zigadenus glaberrimus* Michx. (19) (1840)

Zi'gĭnĭ'ce (Chippewa) - *Campanula rotundifolia* L. (40) (1928)

Zigzag baldderwort - *Utricularia subulata* L. (5) (1913)

Zigzag cloak fern [Zigzag cloakfern] - *Argyrochosma fendleri* (Kunze) Windham (155) (1942)

Zigzag clover [Zig zag clover, Zig-zag clover] - *Trifolium pratense* L. (5, 66, 68, 109, 155, 156, 158) (1900–1949)

Zigzag goldenrod [Zig-zag goldenrod, Zig-zag golden-rod] - *Solidago flexicaulis* L. (5, 19, 50, 72, 155) (1840–present)

Zigzag iris - *Iris brevicaulis* Raf. (50) (present)

Zigzag Solomon's-seal [Zigzag Solomon's seal] - *Maianthemum racemosum* (L.) Link subsp. *racemosum* (5, 156, 158) (1900–1923)

Zigzag spiderwort - *Tradescantia subaspera* Ker-Gawl. var. *montana* (Shuttlw. ex Britt.) E. S. Anderson & Woods. (50) (present), *Tradescantia subaspera* Ker-Gawl. var. *subaspera* (5, 50) (1913–present)

Zinnia - *Zinnia* L. (50, 82, 138, 158) (1900–present) for Johann Gottfried Zinn, 1727–1759, professor of medicine at Gorttingen, *Zinnia violacea* Cav. (82, 92) (1876-1930)

Zinnkraut (German) - *Equisetum arvense* L. (158) (1900)

Zinzeyd - *Elaeagnus angustifolia* L. (107) (1919)

Ziŋtkala tačaŋ (Lakota, small bird's perch) - *Amorpha fruticosa* L. (121) (1918?–1970?)

Zion milkvetch - *Astragalus zionis* M. E. Jones (155) (1942)

Zipolle (German) - *Allium cepa* L. (158) (1900)

Zitkala tawote (Lakota, small bird's food) - *Lepidium densiflorum* Schrad. (121) (1918?-1970?), *Lotus unifoliolatus* (Hook.) Benth. var. *unifoliolatus* (121) (1918?–1970?)

Zizaniopsis - *Zizaniopsis miliacea* (Michx.) Doell & Aschers. (5, 119) (1913–1938)

Zizia - *Zizia* W.D.J. Koch (50, 155, 158) (1900–present)

Zizotes milkweed - *Asclepias oenotheroides* Cham. & Schlecht. (50) (present)

Ziz's pondweed - *Potamogeton illinoensis* Morong (5) (1913)

Zizyphus - *Melia azedarach* L. (178) (1526)

Zob (Croat) - *Avena sativa* L. (110) (1886)

Zonal geranium - *Pelargonium zonale* (L.) L'Hér. ex Aiton (109) (1949)

Žoŋšabethe hi (Osage, dark-wood tree) - *Cercis canadensis* L. (121) (1918?–1970?)

Žoŋxaštoŋga (Osage, large wood) - *Cicuta maculata* L. (121) (1918?–1970?)

ŽoŋƟi žiŋga (Osage, little yellow-wood plant) - *Symphoricarpos orbiculatus* Moench (121) (1918?–1970?)

Zorawei nozki - *Geranium maculatum* L. (186) (1814)

Zornia - *Zornia bracteata* (Walt.) Gmel. (5) (1913)

Zschack's goosefoot - *Chenopodium berlandieri* Moq. var. *zschackii* (J. Murr) J. Murr ex Aschers. (50) (present)

Zucca (Italy, gourd) - *Cucurbita pepo* L. (107) (1919)

Zucco de Peru - *Cucurbita pepo* L. (107) (1552)

Zucco de Syria - *Cucurbita pepo* L. (107) (1552)

Zuckerbeere (German) - *Celtis occidentalis* L. (6) (1892)

Zulu fig - *Ficus lutea* Vahl (138) (1923)

Zumaque venenoso (Spanish) - *Toxicodendron radicans* (L.) Kuntze subsp. *radicans* (158) (1900)

Zumi crab - *Malus sieboldii* (Regel) Rehd. var. *zumi* (Matsumura) Asami (137, 138) (1923–1931)

Zuursak - *Annona muricata* L. (177) (1762)

Zuzecha-ta-wote (Dakota, snake food) - *Celastrus scandens* L. (37) (1919)

Zuzecha-ta-wote sapsapa (Dakota, black snake food) - *Symphoricarpos symphoricarpos* (L.) MacMill. (37) (1919)

Zwartnootboom (Dutch) - *Juglans nigra* L. (41) (1770)

Zweibel (German) - *Allium cepa* L. (158) (1900)

Zwetchen (German) - *Prunus domestica* L. (110) (1886)

Θ

Θa udse-toŋga (Osage, large-based rush) - *Schoenoplectus acutus* (Muhl. ex Bigelow) A. & D. Löve var. *acutus* (121) (1918–1970)

Θažiŋga (Osage, little rush) - *Eleocharis* R. Br. (121) (1918–1970)

Θiŋ (Osage) - *Sagittaria latifolia* Willd. (121) (1918–1970)

Θiŋmoŋnoŋta (Osage) - *Nuphar lutea* (L.) Sm. subsp. *advena* (Aiton) Kartesz & Gandhi (121) (1918?–1970?)

Θta-iŋge (Osage) - *Diospyros virginiana* L. (121) (1918?–1970?)

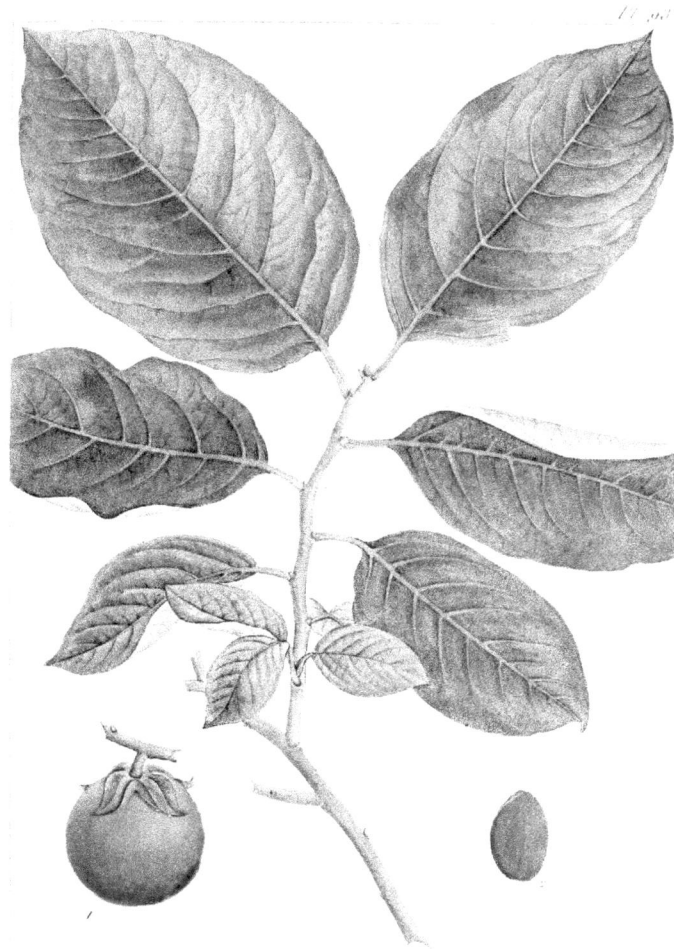

Persimon
Diospyros Virginiana

Diospyros virginiana (Date-plum, Guajacana, Jove's fruit, Lotus tree, Medlar, Mespila, Ougoufle, Persimmon, Piakmin, Pishamin, Plaqueminier, North American ebony, Winter plum, Yellow plum, Θta-iŋge) (P.J. Redouté, 1817)

The University of Nebraska–Lincoln does not discriminate
based on gender, age, disability, race, color,
religion, marital status, veteran's status,
national or ethnic origin,
or sexual orientation.